THE
PULPIT COMMENTARY

THE PULPIT COMMENTARY

Edited by
H. D. M. Spence *and* Joseph S. Exell

This large-type edition republished
from new plates by

WM. B. EERDMANS PUBLISHING COMPANY
Grand Rapids, Michigan

ISBN 0-8028-8071

Reprinted 1978

PHOTOLITHOPRINTED BY EERDMANS PRINTING COMPANY
GRAND RAPIDS, MICHIGAN, UNITED STATES OF AMERICA

THE
PULPIT COMMENTARY

Edited by

H. D. M. Spence

and

Joseph S. Exell

Volume 14

AMOS to MALACHI

Wm. B. Eerdmans Publishing Company, Grand Rapids, Michigan

AMOS

EXPOSITION BY

W. J. DEANE

HOMILETICS BY

EDGAR HENRY

HOMILIES BY VARIOUS AUTHORS

J. R. THOMSON   A. ROWLAND

D. THOMAS

THE BOOK OF AMOS

INTRODUCTION

§ I. Subject of the Book

At the time when Amos prophesied both Israel and Judah stood high in prosperity and wealth. The warlike Jeroboam II. had overcome the Syrians, and recovered the original territory of his kingdom from Hamath in the extreme north to the Dead Sea (2 Kings xiv. 25, 28). Uzziah King of Judah had subdued the restless Edomites and Philistines, reduced the Ammonites to subjection; and, while largely encouraging agriculture and the arts of peace, he raised a powerful army, and strongly fortified Jerusalem (2 Chron. xxvi.). Israel, secure from outward enemies and strong in inward resources, was very far from expecting ruin and destruction. Prosperity in both kingdoms had produced its too common fruits—pride, luxury, selfishness, oppression. In Zion and Samaria alike such sins were rife; but in the northern kingdom they were accentuated and increased by the calf-worship which was still practised there. To Bethel, the central seat of this idolatry, Amos was sent from Jerusalem. His mission was to rebuke this iniquity, and to announce to these careless sinners the approach of Divine judgment. It was probable that, in a kingdom where impostors abounded, a seer, coming from a foreign district and claiming to be commissioned by the Lord, might command respect; though the issue proved very different. Never since the man of God came out of Judah by the word of the Lord in the days of the first Jeroboam (1 Kings xiii.) had any southern prophet gone on such an errand. Now a second message was sent; and in this book the utterances of the prophet on this great occasion are gathered together and arranged in due order. Though his special mission was directed to Israel, Amos does not confine himself altogether to denunciations of this kingdom. His cry extended to Judah and to the hostile nations which surrounded the covenant people.

The book naturally divides itself into four parts—an introduction; addresses; visions; and Messianic prophecy.

The introduction (ch. i., ii.) consists of denunciations of the heathen kingdoms bordering on Israel, foretelling the destruction that shall befall them, viz. Damascus, Philistia, Tyre, Sidon, Edom, Ammon, Moab. Judah, too, is placed in the same category, because it also was alienated from God. The judgment on Israel is proclaimed here in general terms; the remainder of the book particularizes the denounced sins and confirms the awful sentence.

The second part (ch. iii.—vi.) contains three prophetic addresses, divided by the recurrence of the solemn refrain, "Hear ye." The first address con-victs Israel of ingratitude for God's past mercies; shows that the Lord must needs punish the nation, and that he has commissioned the prophet to announce the judgment. Israel has sinned by injustice and violence; its palaces and holy places shall be destroyed, and its people carried into captivity. The second address depicts the sins of oppression and idolatry; tells how God had visited the people with various chastisements, but they were still incorrigible; therefore he will inflict further punishment, to see if perchance they will repent. In his third address Amos laments the fate of Israel, exhorts earnestly to amendment, and then, with a double "Woe!" he shows how hopeless is their trust in their covenant relation to Jehovah, and how baseless their fancied security from danger; for ere long their land should be invaded, their cities should be destroyed, and they themselves should be carried into captivity. This last "woe" is to affect Judah also, even "them that are at ease in Zion" (ch. vi. 1).

The visions (ch. vii.—ix. 10) are closely connected with the preceding addresses, and carry on the warnings there enunciated, giving, as it were, the stages or gradations of punishment. The first two visions, of locusts and fire, correspond to the visitations mentioned in ch. iv. 6—11. These chastisements stop short of utter destruction, being alleviated at the inter-cession of the prophet. The third and fourth visions confirm the irrevocable character of the judgments threatened in the previous addresses. The plumb-line intimates that forgiveness is now not to be expected. Here Amos introduces an historical episode, detailing Amaziah's opposition to his prophecy and God's sentence upon him. He then proceeds to the fourth vision, which, under the figure of a basket of summer fruit, exhibits Israel as ripe for judgment; and he enforces this lesson by foretelling that their feasts should be turned to mourning, and that those who now despise the Word of God shall some day suffer a famine of the Word. The last vision displays the Lord destroying the temple and its worshippers, yea, the whole sinful nation. Yet it should not be utterly annihilated. "Sifted" shall the people be among the nations, yet shall not one good grain perish.

The prophecy ends with one promise—the only one in the book—that the fallen kingdom should be raised again, should be extended by the incoming of the heathen, should be glorified and enriched with Divine graces, and that its duration should be eternal—a promise which has its fulfilment, not in any temporary restoration of Israel to its own land, but in the foundation of the Christian Church and its final conquest of the world (see the reference to this prophecy by St. James in Acts xv. 16). Amos nowhere mentions the person of the Messiah, but his reference to the house of David includes and leads up to Christ.

§ II. Author.

Amos is the third of the minor prophets. His name is usually taken to signify "Carrier," but is better interpreted "Heavy" or "Burden," in allusion to the grievous message which he had to deliver. Jewish commentators suggest that he was so called because he stammered or was slow of speech, as St. Paul says of himself that his speech was considered contemptible. In old time he was by some confounded with Amoz, the father of Isaiah; but the final letter of the two names is different, being *samec* in the case of the prophet, and *tzadi* in that of the other. The name does not occur elsewhere in the Old Testament; but in St. Luke's genealogy of our Lord (iii. 25), we meet with an Amos, son of Naum and father of Mattathias. Amos was, as he himself tells, a native of Tekoah, a small town of Judah, situate on a hill about five miles south of Bethlehem, lying in a pastoral district. "A road," says Dr. Thomson, "leads from Hebron, through a rough and mostly deserted region, to Tekua, the ancient Tekoah. . . . The ruins of that city are some three miles south of the Pools of Solomon, and cover a broad swell of the mountain, which runs up to a great height towards the south-west" ('The Land and the Book,' pp. 304, 330). "Tekoa," says Mr. Porter, "is now, and has been for ages, an uninhabited waste. So complete has been the overthrow that I could not find even a fragment of a wall sufficient to shade me from the scorching sun. The ruins are scattered over the broad summit of one of the highest hills in the Judæan range. The view is magnificent and full of interest. On the west is seen the sweep of the range from Mizpah to Hebron; on the east, 'the wilderness of Judah' sinks down, white, rugged, bare, to the Dead Sea. In that wilderness David kept his sheep, and afterwards wandered a refugee from the court of Saul. On the north, a few miles off, I saw Bethlehem. To the right, in the bottom of a wild ravine, is the cave of Adullam. Further down, on the shores of the Dead Sea, are 'the cliffs of the wild goats,' from whose side springs the fountain of Engedi. And beyond the sea is the wall-like ridge of Moab, and to the south the ruddy-tinted mountains of Edom. A mournful and solitary silence broods over that wonderful panorama. In the touching words of the old Hebrew prophet, 'the earth mourneth and languisheth'" ('Travels in Palestine,' p. 20). From Tekoah came the wise woman who, suborned by Joab, made use of a parable to incline David's heart to his banished son Absalom (2 Sam. xiv.). It was also one of the places fortified by Rehoboam as a defence against invasion from the south (2 Chron. xi. 6). Thither Jonathan and Simon, the Maccabeans, fled to escape the attack of Bacchides (see 1 Macc. ix. 33, etc.). At this place Amos was born. At first a herdsman and a poor cultivator of sycamore trees (ch. vii. 14), he received the Divine call, and, untrained in the schools, no prophet nor prophet's son, was sent to prophesy against Israel. So, like an apostle, leaving all at his Master's word, travelling from Judah he came to Bethel, the temple and summer palace of the king, in order to raise his voice against the worship of the calf which prevailed there in profane union with the service of Jehovah. Here he was opposed by Amaziah, the idolatrous high priest, who complained of him to the king as a dangerous conspirator. He was accordingly banished from the northern kingdom, and compelled to return to Judah, where probably he composed the book in the form in which it has reached our hands. But he seems to have found opportunity to deliver his stern message in Samaria (ch. iii. 9 ; iv. 1) before his final expulsion at Bethel; for Amaziah complains that he had " conspired in the midst of the house of Israel," and that " the land was not able to bear his words " (ch. vii. 10).

Though of such humble extraction, Amos had an eye to the geographical peculiarities of his native land, so as to use with effect his knowledge of various localities; nor was he unacquainted with the history of his own and other countries. Tradition (ap. Pseudo-Epiph., c. xii., ' De Vit. Proph.') asserts that he was cruelly maltreated at Bethel, and returned to Tekoah only to die. His tomb there was still shown in St. Jerome's time.

§ III. Date.

Amos is said (ch. i. 1) to have prophesied " in the days of Uzziah King of Judah, and in the days of Jeroboam the son of Joash King of Israel." Uzziah's reign (according to data corrected by Assyrian monuments) lasted from B.C. 792 to 740, and Jeroboam's from B.C. 790 to 749. The time specified above probably refers to the period during which the two monarchs were contemporaneous, viz. from B.C. 790 to 749, a period of forty-one years. Another computation assigns Jeroboam's reign to B.C. 816—775; but there is still some uncertainty about the exact date. Hence we cannot determine the time of our prophecy with perfect satisfaction. It could not have been the commencement of Jeroboam's reign, as Amos intimates that this king had already overcome his enemies and regained his lost territory (ch. vi. 2, 13, compared with 2 Kings xiv. 25) ; nor could it have been the end, because he makes no mention of the Assyrians who about that time were beginning to threaten Palestine. The further specification in the text, " two years before the earthquake," is not determinate, as that event is not mentioned in the historical books. One that happened in Uzziah's day, as Jewish tradition said, in consequence of or coincident with his usurpation of the priest's office (Josephus, 'Ant.,' ix. 10), was well remembered some centuries afterwards (Zech. xiv. 5), and is perhaps alluded to elsewhere (e.g. Joel iii. 16; Isa. ii. 19); but we are unable to fix the date of the occurrence. Every detail in the prophecy confirms the authenticity of the statement in the introduction. Jeroboam is mentioned (ch. vii. 10), and the circumstances of his time, as we noted above, are accurately alluded to. The taking of Gath by Uzziah is inferred (ch. vi. 2 compared with 2 Chron. xxvi. 6).

The prophet uttered his warnings, not at intervals during all the period named, but at some definite time therein, and probably during a very short space. He must have been contemporaneous with, if not a little earlier than Hosea, and later than Joel, as he takes up this prophet's words in the commencement of his own prediction (comp. ch. i. 2 with Joel iii. 16), and quotes him in ch. ix. 13 (see Introduction to Joel).

§ IV. GENERAL CHARACTER.

Critics since Jerome have called Amos *imperitus sermone*, reasoning from his occasional use of homely images drawn from flock and herd and pastoral life, the matters with which his occupation was concerned (ch. ii. 13; iii. 4, 5, 8, 12; iv. 6—9; v. 11, 17; vi. 12; viii. 8; ix. 5). And certainly his style is not sublime or pitched in the highest strain of poetry, but it is notable for clearness and energy, and shows considerable literary skill both in the arrangement of rhythm and in the grouping of parallelisms. The imagery based on scenes amongst which he dwelt, far from being a defect in the work, adds a special charm; and one would be very loath to miss the vividness and naturalness which are thereby imparted to it. The changes in nature (ch. iv. 13), the dangers from wild beasts, the starry sky (ch. v. 8), flood, tempest, lightning, were observed by him in his watchings and wanderings, and left their reminiscence in his language. If at times, as some critics suppose, he uses the dialect of the people instead of the more refined terms of court and school, this would be in entire keeping with his simple life and character. We are not to suppose that inspiration overrides a man's habitual mode of expression, or compels an untrained peasant to adopt the language of a learned scribe. The book, at any rate, shows that we have received it such as its author wrote it, without adventitious ornamentation or amendment. If he speaks mostly in prose, surely visions such as he narrates, denunciations such as he utters, are thus more effectively presented. The very simplicity of his language makes it impressive. We see in him a confirmation of the theory with which Wordsworth has made us familiar, that the diction of uneducated people has in itself a certain poetic power which raises it to an equality with that of higher social station. Without anything of poetry in the words, what force is there in that sudden and unexpected summons, "Because I will do *this* [what?] unto thee, prepare to meet thy God, O Israel" (ch. iv. 12)! There is true pathos when, having shown how the luxurious spared nothing in ministering to their own selfishness, Amos ends with the accusing cry, " But they are not grieved for the affliction of Joseph." The strophic arrangement of some of the periods is very remarkable. The oft-recurring formula, " for three transgressions, and for four " (ch. i., ii.), the sorrowful burden, " Yet have ye not returned unto me, saith the Lord " (ch. iv.), are patent instances of this.

This uneducated prophet's accurate acquaintance with the Law of Moses denotes much more than a familiarity with the national traditions. His knowledge of the Pentateuch appears not only in general allusions to history, ritual, ceremony, but in the actual use of verbal forms and expressions which belong to the Mosaic writings. "Blasting and mildew" are the punishment of disobedience (ch. iv. 9 compared with Deut. xxviii. 22); "gall and wormwood" are the bitter fruits into which the sinners turned righteousness and judgment (ch. vi. 12 with Deut. xxix. 18); the sad refrain mentioned above (ch. iv. 6, 8, 9, 10, 11) is founded on Deut. iv. 29, 30. The oppressors "lie down on clothes laid to pledge" (ch. ii. 8 with Exod. xxii. 26), "turn aside the way of the meek, and turn aside the poor in the gate" (ch. ii. 7; ver. 12 with Exod. xxiii. 6; Deut. xvi. 19, etc.). Unnatural immorality "profanes God's holy Name" (ch. ii. 7 with Lev. xviii. 21; xx. 3). One hardly need multiply quotations to prove the prophet's knowledge of the history and ritual of the Mosaic books. He alludes to the Exodus, the overthrow of Sodom, the gigantic stature of the Amorites, the sacrifices of the Law, the Nazarite vow. His threats and promises are often couched in Mosaic language (comp. ch. iv. 6, 7 with Deut. xxviii. 23, 48, 57 and Lev. xxvi. 19, 20; ch. iv. 11 with Deut. xxix. 23; ch. v. 11 with Deut. xxviii. 30).

Thus Amos presupposes that his hearers were well acquainted with the Pentateuch, and had a firm belief in its history; otherwise much of the prophecy would have lost its force or have been unintelligible. Hosea and Jeremiah seem to have borrowed from or to have been acquainted with our prophet. Compare, for instance, ch. ii. 5 with Hos. viii. 14; ch. vii. 17 with Hos. ix. 3; ch. i. 4 with Jer. xlix. 27; ch. i. 15 with Jer. xlix. 3. Further parallelisms will be found noted in the Exposition.

We may conclude that in simple, unadorned eloquence, in structural regularity, in natural vigour, and in loftiness of thought, Amos reaches a well-grounded eminence; and, as Lowth decides ('De Poes. Hebr. Præl.,' xx. 1), the author of such writings was in no wise behind the very chiefest of the prophets.

§ V. Literature.

We need not enumerate the commentators who have written upon the whole of the minor prophets, patristic, mediæval, and modern, as the chief of them have already been mentioned in the Introduction to Hosea. Two recent Roman Catholic commentaries, however, may be specially noted, one by L'Abbé Trochon (Paris, 1883), containing the Latin Vulgate with a French translation, and a commentary considerably indebted to Keil; and the other by J. Knabenbauer (Paris, 1886), forming a part of the 'Cursus Scripturæ Sacræ,' edited by Jesuit Fathers. It consists of a commentary written in Latin, and containing useful answers to the rationalistic theories of the present day. Here, too, may be mentioned Archdeacon Farrar's 'The Minor Prophets,' in the 'Men of the Bible' series (1891). Among monographs on this prophet may be mentioned the following: Luther, 'Enarratio in Prophetam Amos;' Gerhard, 'Annotationes' (Jena, 1676); Harenberg, 'Amos Expositus' (Leyden, 1763); Dahl, 'Amos, neu übers. und erläut.' (Göttingen, 1795); Bishop Horsley, 'Critical Notes;' Baur, 'Der P. Amos erklärt' (1847); Bishop Ryan, 'Lectures' (1850); and works by Uhland,

Justi, Vater, Benefield, and Laurent. Of the above, the commentary of Baur, with a valuable introduction, is most generally useful. Articles by Wellhausen, in the 'Brit. Encyclop.,' xiii., and by Nöldeke, in Schenkel's 'Bibel-Lexicon,' will repay examination.

§ VI. Arrangement of the Book in Sections.

The book is best arranged in four parts.

Part I. (Ch. i., ii.) Approaching judgment : a prelude.
　§ 1. (Ch. i.—ii. 3.) Summons of the nations bordering on the Holy Land.
　§ 2. (Ch. ii. 4, 5.) Summons of Judah.
　§ 3. (Ch. ii. 6—16.) Summons and general denunciation of Israel.
Part II. (Ch. iii.—vi.) Three addresses particularizing the sins of Israel and announcing imminent punishment.
　§ 1. (Ch. iii.) First address.
　§ 2. (Ch. iv.) Second address.
　§ 3. (Ch. v., vi.) Third address.
Part III. (Ch. vii.—ix. 10.) Five visions, with explanations.
　§ 1. (Ch. vii. 1—3.) First vision : locusts.
　§ 2. (Ch. vii. 4—6.) Second vision : fire.
　§ 3. (Ch. vii. 7—9.) Third vision : plumb-line.
　§ 4. (Ch. vii. 10—17.) Historical parenthesis.
　§ 5. (Ch. viii. 1—14.) Fourth vision : basket of fruits.
　§ 6. (Ch. ix. 1—10.) Fifth vision : the Lord at the altar.
Part IV. (Ch. ix. 11—15.) Epilogue : establishment of the new kingdom.

THE BOOK OF AMOS

EXPOSITION

CHAPTER I.

Ver. 1—ch. ii. 16.—Part I. APPROACHING JUDGMENT.

Ver. 1—ch. ii. 3.—§ 1. *The nations bordering on the Holy Land are solemnly summoned to judgment.*

Vers. 1, 2.—Heading of the book, with short summary of its contents.

Ver. 1.—Heading. **The words.** So Jeremiah begins his prophecy (Jer. i. 1), and the writer of Ecclesiastes (i. 1). That the words are not those of Amos, but of Jehovah, is shown by the succeeding clause, "which he saw." **Herdmen.** The Hebrew word *noked* used here is found in 2 Kings iii. 4, applied to Mesha King of Moab, a great "sheepmaster;" hence some have considered that Amos was not a mere mercenary, but a rich possessor of flocks. His own words, however (ch. vii. 14, 15), decide his position as that of a poor labouring man. **Tekoah.** A small town of Judah (see above in the account of the author, Introduction, § II.). **He saw,** with inward intuition. Hence his "words" were inspired (comp. Isa. ii. 1; Hab. i. 1). Concerning Israel chiefly, mention of Judah being introduced only incidentally and as connected with the destinies of Israel. The Septuagint reads, by some mistake, "concerning Jerusalem." **In the days.** (For the date of the prophecy, see above, Introduction, § III.) **Earthquake.** No mention is made of this event in the historical books. It was remembered in after-years (see Zech. xiv. 5), and Amos alludes to it as a token of the judgment which he foretold, such catastrophes being regarded as signs of the majesty of God and his vengeance on sinners (comp. Exod. xix. 18; Ps. lxviii. 8; Micah i. 4; Hab. iii. 6, 10). Josephus ('Ant.,' ix. 10. 4) attributes this earthquake to God's displeasure at Uzziah's usurpation of the priest's office (2 Chron. xxvi. 16).

Ver. 2.—**And he said.** This is the commencement of "the words" of Amos (ver. 1); and herein the prophet gives a short summary of the judgment which he has to pronounce. The following clause is a repetition of Joel iii. 16; and Amos thus connects his prophecy with that of his predecessor, to show the unity of prophetic mission, and to warn the Jews that God's punishments are not directed exclusively on heathen nations. To the nations denounced by Joel, Amos adds others of Israel's enemies, viz. Syria, Ammon, and Moab. **Roar . . . voice.** The thunder is the voice of God, announcing his coming to judge. **From Zion.** Not from Dan and Bethel, the seats of idolatrous worship, but from Jerusalem, the abode of his presence. **The habitations;** better, *the pastures.* It is only natural that Amos, the shepherd, should use such terms to express the idea that the whole land, from Jerusalem on the south to Carmel on the north, should feel the vengeance of the Lord. **Shall mourn;** explained by the following term, **shall wither;** *i.e.* shall lose their verdure (comp. Jer. xii. 11; Hos. iv. 3). **The top of Carmel.** This is the Mount Carmel, which stretches boldly into the sea on the south of the Bay of Acre, and is remarkable for its extreme fertility, its rich pastures, its vines, olives, fruits, and flowers. Thomson, 'The Land and the Book,' writes thus about it: "The celebrated ridge, called in the Bible Mount Carmel, and by the Arabs Jebel Kurmul, or Mâr Elyâs, in honour of Elijah, is an extension of the hills of Samaria, in a north-westerly direction, for a distance of about eighteen miles, terminating in the bold promontory of Carmel, which descends almost literally into the sea. It is steep and lofty where it overhangs the Mediterranean above Haifa, and on that face which overlooks the Plain of Acre on the north, and that of Esdraelon towards the south-east. There is no special excellency in Carmel at the present day, whatever may be said of Sharon. Its name, Kurmul, or Kerm-el, signifies 'the vineyard of God;' but its vineyards have all disappeared. It was a glorious mountain, however, and a prominent landmark; according to Jeremiah (xlvi. 18), Carmel was a resort of herdsmen. Amos says, 'The habitations of the shepherds shall mourn, and the top of Carmel shall wither,' in the time of the threatened judgment, and this implies that its pastures were not ordinarily liable to wither. This may, in part, have been occasioned by the heavy dews which its lofty elevation, so near the sea, causes to distil nightly upon its thirsty head. I found it quite green and flowery in midsummer. It was a noble pasture-field, and, in reference to that characteristic, Micah utters his sweet prayer, 'Feed thy people with thy rod, the flock of thine heritage, which dwell solitarily in the wood, in the midst of Carmel; let them feed in Bashan and Gilead, as in the days of old.'"

Vers. 3—5.—Before announcing the judgment on Israel, Amos proclaims the punishment on neighbouring heathen nations for their injurious treatment of the chosen people, thus showing God's care for his elect, and leading them to fear vengeance for their own greater sins towards him. The order observed in denouncing these nations is not geographical, but is regulated by the nature of each people's relation to Israel, and the degree in which they have sinned against her. The denunciation begins with Syria, her hitherto most oppressive enemy, and the least akin.

Ver. 3.—**For three transgressions of Damascus, and for four.** This form of expression is repeated in each of the following strophes, and some critics have taken the terms literally, and have tried to identify that particular number of transgressions in each case; but this is trifling. The phrase and others similar to it are not uncommon, and are used to signify a great number, the last-mentioned being supposed to fill up the measure and make it overflow. Thus Job v. 19, "He shall deliver thee in six troubles, yea, in seven there shall no evil touch thee" (comp. Job xxxiii. 29; Prov. xxx. 15, 18, 21; Eccles. xi. 2). So Hom., 'Od.,' v. 306, Τρισμάκαρες Δαναοὶ καὶ τετράκις: and Virg., 'Æn.,' i. 94, "O terque quaterque beati;" comp. Hor., 'Carm.,' i. 31. 13. **Damascus** had been an active enemy of Israel since the time that Rezon

threw off his allegiance (1 Kings xi. 23, etc.), and seized Damascus, which had been tributary to David (2 Sam. viii. 5). The history of the wars carried on by Syria against the Jews may be read in the sacred books (see 1 Kings xv. 19, etc.; 2 Chron. xvi. 2, etc.; 1 Kings xx.; xxii.; 2 Kings vii.; ix. 14, etc.; x. 32, etc.; xii. 18; xiii. 5, 25; 2 Chron. xxiv. 23, etc.; 2 Kings xiv. 28). **I will not turn away** the punishment **thereof.** So in the following strophes. Literally, *I will not reverse it.* Amos does not expressly say *what;* but he means the sentence or judgment (comp. Numb. xxiii. 20, "I cannot reverse it," where the same word is used). The Latin Vulgate gives, *Non convertam eum,* i.e. *Damascum,* which Knabenbauer explains, "I will not avert its destruction, will not turn it aside from its downward course." The LXX. renders, Οὐκ ἀποστραφήσομαι αὐτόν, "I will not turn away from it," *i.e.,* as explained by Theodoret, "I will no longer disregard its sins." **Because they have threshed Gilead.** This is the culminating offence of the Syrians. The word rendered "threshing-instrument" (*charutz*) signifies a kind of corn-drag made of heavy planks fastened together and armed beneath with sharp stones or iron points. This machine, weighted with the driver who sat or stood upon it, was drawn by oxen over the corn (comp. Isa. xxviii. 27; xli. 15). A representation of it is given by Smith, 'Dict. of Bible,' i. 31, and Kitto, 'Cyclop.,' i. 86. Such an instrument, set with sharp flints in rows, was to be seen in the Indian and Colonial Exhibition of the year 1886, in the Cyprus department. Another kind of instrument (*moreg*) is thus described by Jerome: "Est autem genus plaustri, quod rotis subter ferreis atque dentatis volvitur, ut excussis frumentis stipulam in areis conterat, et in cibos jumentorum propter fœni sterilitatem paleas comminuat." Such an implement was used in the infliction of capital punishment by David (2 Sam. xii. 31; comp. Prov. xx. 26). *Gilead* is here put for all the country east of Jordan (Josh. xxii. 9). The cruel treatment referred to in the text occurred in the time of Hazael during the reign of Jehu (2 Kings x. 32, etc.; comp. xiii. 7). The Septuagint has, "Because with iron saws they sawed asunder women with child." This is doubtless a reminiscence of Elisha's words to Hazael (2 Kings viii. 12).

Ver. 4.—**Fire.** Material fire, though elsewhere the term is used metaphorically for war and its evils (comp. Numb. xxi. 28; Ps. lxxviii. 63; Jer. xlviii. 45). This passage of Amos, combined with ver. 14, is quoted by Jeremiah (xlix. 27), where he is pronouncing the doom of Damascus. **House of Hazael . . . palaces of Benhadad.** The two expressions are parallel, or they may signify the family of Hazael, and Damascus itself with its magnificent royal palaces. There were three kings of Syria named Benhadad. The first of the name made alliance with Asa, and fought successfully against Baasha (1 Kings xv. 20); Benhadad II. was the contemporary of Ahab, and carried on war for many years with the northern kingdom (1 Kings xx.). He was murdered either by Hazael or his servants (2 Kings viii. 15). Benhadad III., the son of Hazael, was a monarch of small ability, and Syria under his sway sank into insignificance (2 Kings xiii. 4, etc.; xiv. 27; xv. 17). All this happened before the time of Amos, who probably refers to all the kings of that name, Benhadad, "Son of the Sun," being the title of the dynasty.

Ver. 5.—**The bar** which secured the gate of the city (1 Kings iv. 13; Jer. li. 30; Nah. iii. 13). Breaking the bar is equivalent to laying the place open to the enemy. **From the plain of Aven**; Vulgate, *de campo idoli*; Hebrew, *bikath-Aven*; Septuagint, ἐκ πεδίου Ὤν; better, *from the valley of Aven*, or *vanity*, perhaps so called analogously with Hosea's naming *Bethel*, *Bethaven*, "House of God" and "House of vanity" (Hos. v. 8). Robinson ('Bibl. Res.,' 677) and Pusey refer the name to a valley between Lebanon and Antilibanus, a continuation of the Arabah, still called *Bukaa*, in the middle of which stood Baalbec, "the Temple of the sun of the valley," called Heliopolis by Greek and Roman writers (see 'Classical Museum,' iii. 136). The LXX. renders "On" in Gen. xli. 45 by "Heliopolis;" and On and Baal being both titles of the sun, and indeed synonymous, the introduction of "On" into this passage may be accounted for. **Him that holdeth the sceptre.** The king and princes, as ver. 8. **From the house of Eden**; Hebrew, *Beth-Eden*, "House of delight;" Vulgate, *de domo voluptatis*; Septuagint, ἐξ ἀνδρῶν Χαρράν, "out of the men of Charran." This last rendering arises from considering that the reference was to the Eden of Gen. ii., which the translators placed in the region of Haran. The place in the text Keil supposes to be the Paradisus of the Greeks, which Ptolemy (v. 15. 20) locates southeast of Laodicea. Schrader suggests a place on the banks of the middle Euphrates between Bâlis and Biredschich called *Bit-Adini* in inscriptions of Asurnasirhabal and Salmanassur II. But this seems to be a wrong locality (see 'Die Keilinschriften,' p. 327). The passage means that all the inhabitants of valley and city, king and peasant, shall be cut off. **Shall go into captivity.** The word implies that the land shall be "stripped" or "bared" of its inhabitants. Wholesale deportation had not hitherto been common in these regions. Kir has been identified with the country on the banks of the river Kar, which flows into the Araxes on the south-west of the Caspian Sea. It forms part of the territory known as Transcaucasia. From this region the Syrians originally emigrated (ch. ix. 7), and back to this land a large body were carried when Tiglath-Pileser, some fifty years later, killed Rezin and sacked Damascus, as related in 2 Kings xvi. 9. **Saith the Lord.** This is the solemn confirmation of the prophet's announcement, and recurs in vers. 8, 15 and ch. ii. 3.

Vers. 6—8.—The judgment on Philistia.

Ver. 6.—**Gaza** is here used as the representative of the five cities of the Philistines. Three others are mentioned in ver. 8, Gath being omitted as having long lost its importance, if not already destroyed (comp. 2 Chron. xxvi. 6; Jer. xxv. 20; Zeph. ii. 4, where see note; Zech. ix. 5, 6). Gaza, modern *Guzzeh*, was the most southern city of Philistia in the immediate neighbourhood of the desert. (For a description of the Plain of Philistia, see Sir C. Warren, 'Survey Memoirs,' volume on Jerusalem, p. 436.) **The whole captivity**; Hebrew, "an entire captivity," the whole people, so that neither age nor sex was spared. A similar complaint is made in Joel iii. 4, 6. What the LXX. mean by their rendering here and ver. 9, αἰχμαλωσίαν τοῦ Σαλωμών, it is very hard to say. Probably they punctuated the word translated "perfect" (*shelemah*) *shelomoh*, making "Solomon" stand for his people Israel. Cyril supposes that the reference is to cities which Solomon established among neighbouring nations; these had now been destroyed or seized. The event referred to may be the invasion of Judah by Philistines and Arabians in the time of Joram, mentioned in 2 Chron. xxi. 16, etc., and in which it is possible that a compact was made that the captive Judæans should be delivered to their bitterest enemies, the Edomites. One would rather have expected a reference to some evil inflicted on Israel (as in ver. 3) instead of an injury done to Judah.

Ver. 7.—**A fire.** Each guilty city is to have its own special punishment, though probably the calamity of each is common to all. Gaza was conquered by Sennacherib when he invaded Judæa in the time of Hezekiah, by Pharaoh-Necho (Jer. xlvii. 1), and by Alexander the Great, who spent more than two months in its siege (Josephus, 'Ant.,' xi. 8. 4; Arrian, ii. 27; see note on Zeph. ii. 4).

Ver. 8.—**Ashdod**, "the Waster," *hod. Esdud*, or *Shdood* (called Azotus in Acts viii. 40), and still a large village, lay about thirty-five miles north of Gaza, three miles from the sea. **Ashkelon** was situate between the two. "Askelon differs from the other celebrated cities of the Philistines, being seated on the sea, while Ekron, Gath, Jamnia, Ashdod, and Gaza are in the interior. It never could have had a harbour of any considerable size, however. . . . The topography of the place is peculiar. An abrupt ridge begins near the shore, runs up eastward, bends round to the south, then to the west, and finally north-west to the sea again, forming an irregular amphitheatre. On the top of this ridge ran the wall, which was defended at its salient angles by strong towers. The specimens which still exist show that it was very high and thick, built, however, of small stones, and bound together by broken columns of granite and marble. This clearly proves that it is patchwork, and not Askelon's original rampart. . . . The position is one of the fairest along this part of the Mediterranean coast; and when the interior of the amphitheatre was adorned with splendid temples and palaces, ascending, rank above rank, from the shore to the summit, the appearance from the sea must have been very imposing. Now the whole area is planted over with orchards of the various kinds of fruit which flourish in this region" (Thomson, 'The Land and the Book,' *Southern Palestine*, p. 171). In spite of its bad harbour, it carried on a lucrative foreign commerce, which was the chief cause of its power and importance (Ewald, ' Hist. of Israel,' i. 247, Eng. transl.). It was about fifty Roman miles from Jerusalem. In mediæval times there were two cities of the name, one on the coast (Jer. xlvii. 7), the same as Herod's Ascalon, and one inland. In its palmiest days the former could never have had a real harbour ('Survey Memoirs,' iii. pp. 245, 246). **Ekron,** hod. *Akir*, was twelve miles north-east of Ashdod, and some nine from the coast. Ashdod was taken by Uzziah (2 Chron. xxvi. 6), by the tartan, or commander-in-chief, of Sargon (Isa. xx. 1), and by Psammetichus King of Egypt (B.C. 635), when it sustained a siege of twenty-nine years (Herod., ii. 157). Sennacherib, in a cuneiform inscription, records how he treated the two other cities: "Zedekiah King of Ashkelon," he says, "who had not submitted himself to my yoke, himself, the gods of the house of his fathers, his wife, his sons, his daughters, and his brothers, the seed of the house of his fathers, I removed, and I sent him to Assyria. I set over the men of Ashkelon, Sarludari, the son of Rukipti, their former king, and I imposed upon him the payment of tribute, and the homage due to my majesty, and he became a vassal. . . . I marched against the city of Ekron, and put to death the priests and the chief men who

had committed the sin (of rebellion), and I hung up their bodies on stakes all round the city. The citizens who had done wrong and wickedness I counted as a spoil " (Professor Sayce, ' Fresh Light from the Monuments,' pp. 120, 121). **I will turn mine hand;** literally, *will bring back my hand;* visit again with punishment, or repeat the blow (Isa. i. 25; Jer. vi. 9; see note on Zech. xiii. 7). **The remnant.** All the Philistines who had as yet escaped destruction (comp. ch. ix. 12; Jer. vi. 9).

Vers. 9, 10.—The judgment on Tyre.

Ver. 9.—**They delivered up the whole captivity** (see note on ver. 6). The sin of Tyre, the great Phœnician merchant city, was committed in concert with the Philistines (comp. Ps. lxxxiii. 7), and was of the same character, except that she is not accused of carrying away the captives, but only of handing them over to the Edomites. It is probable that the Phœnicians had gotten into their hands, by purchase or some other means, Israelitish prisoners, whom they delivered over to the Edomites, **forgetting the brotherly covenant** made by their forefathers with David and Solomon (2 Sam. v. 11; 1 Kings v. 1, 7—11; ix. 11—14; 2 Chron. ii. 11). The cruel conduct of Tyre was quite unprovoked, as no Jewish king had made war against Phœnicia or its capital.

Ver. 10.—**A fire,** as ver. 7; see Ezekiel's prophecy against Tyre (xxvi.). She had long been tributary to Assyria, but, revolting, was punished by Sargon, and later was attacked by Nebuchadnezzar, who besieged it for thirteen years, with what success is not known. The Assyrian monuments afford no account of its capture by this monarch (comp. Isa. xxiii.; Jer. xlvii. 4; Arrian., ii. 16—24). (For its capture and destruction by Alexander the Great, see notes on Zech. ix. 2, 4.)

Vers. 11, 12.—The judgment on Edom.

Ver. 11.—**His brother.** The prophet proceeds to denounce the three nations cognate to Israel, of which the Edomites were the nearest and the most inimical. From the time of Esau until now they had been consistent in enmity, and it is this unbrotherly conduct rather than any specific outrages which Amos here condemns. Edom is accused of relentless persecution, inhumanity, savage fury, and persistent anger. (For the brotherhood of Edom, see Numb. xx. 14; Deut. ii. 4, 5, 8; xxiii. 7, etc. For his hostility to Israel, see Numb. xx. 18; 1 Kings xi. 14; 2 Kings viii. 20; 2 Chron. xx. 10; xxv. 11, 12; xxviii. 17.) The prophecy of Obadiah is directed against Edom (comp. also Ezek. xxv. 12; xxxv. 5, 15; Joel iii. 19). **Did cast off all pity;** literally, *corrupted his compassions;* i.e. did violence to his natural feelings. So Ezek. xxviii. 17, "Thou hast corrupted thy wisdom," perverted it from its proper end. The LXX. gives, ἐλυμήνατο μητέρα (μήτραν, Alex.) ἐπὶ γῆς, "did violence to the mother that bare them." On this Jerome remarks, "Pro misericordia Septuaginta vulvam transtulerunt, ducti ambiguitate verborum, quia *re-hem* et vulvam et misericordiam significat." Did tear, as a wild beast tears his prey. So in Job xvi. 9, where the same word is used, "He hath torn me in his wrath" (comp. Hos. vi. 1). And he kept his wrath for ever; more literally, *and its fury it* (Edom) *keeps for ever.* The quarrels of relations are proverbially bitter. Arist., 'Polit.,' vii. 7, Ὅθεν εἴρηται, χαλεποὶ γὰρ πόλεμοι ἀδελφῶν, καὶ ὅι τοι πέρα στέρξαντες, οἱ δὲ καὶ πέρα μισοῦσιν (p. 193, Bekk.).

Ver. 12.—Teman is the region of Idumæa, of which Bozrah is the capital. Both Jerome and Eusebius ('Onomast.') speak of a city so called not far from Petra; but in the Old Testament the name is applied to a district; and as the word in Hebrew means "south," it is probably the southern portion of the land of Edom. Bozrah (*hod. Busaireh*) was the old capital of Edom, situated on a hill south of the Dead Sea (see Gen. xxxvi. 33; Isa. xxxiv. 6). Jeremiah (xlix. 17) predicts the punishment of Edom, and Ezekiel (xxv. 12—14) does likewise. The monologue of Obadiah has been already referred to. The instrument of vengeance in the present case was Nebuchadnezzar, though it suffered much at the hands of other enemies, as the Nabathæans and Maccabees.

Vers. 13—15.—The judgment on Ammon.

Ver. 13.—Ammon was connected with Israel as being sprung from Lot, and together with Moab, which had the same origin, retained the stamp of its incestuous birth in habits, character, and worship (Gen. xix. 30, etc.). The Ammonites seem to have been a predatory and roving nation, though the abundance of ruins in the district shows that they possessed fixed abodes; but Rabbah was the only city of importance in their territory (2 Sam. xi. 1). Their hostility to Israel was first shown in their participation with Moab in the affair of Balaam (Deut. xxiii. 4). Other instances are seen in their treatment of Jabesh-Gilead (1 Sam. xi. 1—3) and of David's messengers, and in hiring the Syrians to make war on David (2 Sam. x. 1—6). We have no historical account of the atrocious outrage on the Gileadites mentioned in the text, but it is quite in character with the ferocity of their disposition, and was doubtless intended to depopulate the territory which they wished to acquire. This barbarity is spoken of in connection with Hazael (2 Kings viii. 12), in concert with whom probably the Ammonites acted (comp. 2 Kings xv. 16; Hos. xiii. 16). Another rendering would refer the clause to the removing of landmarks, and yet a third to the storming of lofty fortresses. But the Authorized Version is undoubtedly correct. That they might enlarge their border. The Ammonites laid claim to the territory which the Israelites had wrested from Sihon, lying between the Arnon and Jabbok, and made an attempt upon it in the time of Jephthah (Judg. xi.), and in later years seized on the possessions of Gad—a proceeding which brought upon them the denunciation of Jeremiah (xlix. 2—6).

Ver. 14.—Rabbah, "the Great," or *Rabbath-Ammon,* the capital of Ammon, was situated on the southern arm of the Jabbok, and was a place of remarkable strength (see Deut. iii. 11; 2 Sam. xi. 1; xii. 26, etc.; 1 Chron. xx. 1—3). "For picturesqueness of situation, I know of no ruins to compare with Ammon. The most striking feature is the citadel, which formerly contained not merely the garrison, but an upper town, and covered an extensive area. The lofty plateau on which it was situated is triangular in shape; two sides are formed by the valleys which diverge from the apex, where they are divided by a low neck, and thence separating, fall into the valley of the Jabbok, which forms the base of the triangle, and contained the lower town. Climbing up the citadel, we can trace the remains of the moat, and, crossing it, find ourselves in a maze of ruins. The massive walls—the lower parts of which still remain, and which, rising from the precipitous sides of the cliff, rendered any attempt at scaling impossible— were evidently Ammonite. As I leant over them and looked sheer down about three hundred feet into one wâdy, and four hundred feet into the other, I did not wonder at its having occurred to King David that the leader of a forlorn hope against these ramparts would meet with certain death, and consequently assigning the position to Uriah. . . . Joab afterwards took the lower city, which he called 'the city of waters,' indicating very probably that the Jabbok was dammed into a lake near the lower city, to which the conformation of the valley would lend itself" (Oliphant, 'Land of Gilead,' p. 259, etc.). There is a sketch of the citadel-hill in the 'Dictionary of the Bible,' ii. 985. The city was taken by Nebuchadnezzar (Jer. xxvii. 3, 6; xlix. 2, 3), either at the time of the destruction of Jerusalem, or in the course of his Egyptian campaign (Josephus, 'Ant.,' x. 9. 7). The expression, I will kindle a fire (not "send," as elsewhere), possibly implies, as Pusey suggests, a conflagration from within. The shouting is the battle-cry of the opposing host, which adds to the horror of the scene (Job xxxix. 25). **With a tempest.** The idea is that the walls should fall before the invaders, as if they were tents swept away in a whirl-wind.

Ver. 15.—**Their king**; Septuagint, οἱ βασιλεῖς αὐτῆς. So Keil, Trochon, and others consider that the King of the Ammonites is meant. The Vulgate, with Aquila, Symmachus, the Syriac, and Jerome, retains the word Melchous, or Melcham, which is the same as Molech, their god. This interpretation is favoured by passages in Jeremiah, of which one is evidently quoted from Amos,

"For Malcam shall go into captivity, his priests and his princes together" (Jer. xlix. 3); and the other (xlviii. 7) is similar, with the substitution of "Chemosh," the god of Moab, for "Malcam." That the localized deity should share the fortunes of his worshippers is quite in accordance with the ideas of the time (comp. Isa. xlvi. 1, 2). Probably Amos meant to include both notions—their "Malcam," whether king or god, should be carried into captivity, accompanied by the princes, all the chiefs, military and sacerdotal, so that no one should be left to head a future revolt.

HOMILETICS.

Ver. 1.—*A voice from the sheepcotes.* The Jewish nation is almost seven centuries old. A wayward nonage had passed into a maturity incorrigibly perverse. Alarmed by prophetic thunders, and riven by the lightning-bolts of judgment (ch. iv. 6—11), Israel clung to its iniquities in spite of all (ch. ii. 4; v. 11; Isa. i. 5). Yet God had not cast off his people whom he foreknew. There were other arrows in his quiver still, and he would shoot them against national obduracy with a stronger bow. Amos shall take up his controversy against Israel where Moses, and Samuel, and Elijah, and Elisha had laid it down. Famine and the sword and captivity shall maintain and strengthen his expostulation (ch. ii. 14—16). The argument shall at length prevail, and, the irreconcilables destroyed, a remnant shall enjoy his grace and choose his way (ch. ix. 11—15). In this prefatory word consider—

I. THE SEER. An idol-priest supplies the title (ch. vii. 12), but it is suitable and endures. A prophet sees, where other men are blind, the meaning of what is and the nature of what shall be. 1. *His name.* Amos signifies "Bearer," or "Burden," or "Heavy." And it was prophetically significant of the owner's work. His words were weighty (ch. vii. 10), the burden of them was weightier still (ch. vi. 1), and weightiest of all was the Divine authority with which they came (ver. 3). 2. *His extraction.* "From among the shepherds." These were probably small sheep-owners, who tended their own flocks (Keil, Lange, etc.). They were in the lower ranks of life, the rank from which God has called, and calls the majority of his servants (1 Cor. i. 27, 28). The poor man depends for all his well-being on spiritual good (Luke vi. 24). He therefore chooses it more readily (Mark xii. 37), advances in it more easily (Matt. xiii. 22), rejoices in it more entirely (Isa. xxix. 19), and is chosen to it rather than the rich (Jas. ii. 5). "Poverty is the sister of a sound mind," was a heathen maxim embodying a kindred truth. 3. *His calling.* "A herdsman and gatherer of sycamores." This occupation would be no mean preparation for his prophetic office. A true prophet must be tender of human life, even when he denounces death; and if from the love of man we may rise to the love of God (1 John iv. 20), why not from the love of plant and animal to the love of man?

> "He prayeth best, who loveth best
> All things both great and small;
> For the dear God who loveth us
> Hath made and loveth all."

4. *His home.* Tekoah, a city south of Bethlehem, in the land of Judah. Thence he went to Bethel, in the land of Israel, to prophesy. That he may not be "without honour," and corresponding influence, he goes from his own to a neighbouring country (Matt. xiii. 57). Then, like Elijah and John the Baptist, he goes to the pampered and dissolute town-dwellers, that with the healthy tastes and simple habits and strong pure life of a dweller in the fields, he might put their laxity and luxury to shame (ch. vi. 1—6).

II. THE VISION. The term does not occur in Amos, but the equivalent of it does, and it is common elsewhere in Scripture (Isa. i. 1; Hab. ii. 2).   1. *It was what "he saw."* Of the way in which God revealed truth to inspired men we know nothing.   It is above reason and outside revelation.   It was not with the bodily eye, nor in the natural sense, that the vision was seen; but the revelation was adequate, and the result was knowledge (Acts iv. 20).   Their cognizance of matters was at once sure and clear (1 John i. 1), and comparable in both respects to that of Christ himself (John iii. 11). 2. *It was "words."*   A word is the body of a thought.   A thought is the spirit of a word.   It is only by words, or something answering to words, that thoughts can be conveyed from man to man.   Analogy would suggest that the same method is employed by God.   If, as some hold, we think in words, the hypothesis would be greatly strengthened.   In any case, what Amos got was not simply thoughts, but words, and the words of Scripture are, in some real and important sense, " words which the Holy Ghost teacheth " (1 Cor. ii. 13; 2 Sam. xxiii. 2).

III. THE SPEAKING OF THE VISION.   Coming from his simple shepherd-life into a luxurious city, and with the burden of his heavy tidings on his heart, the prophet's speech is : 1. *Deeply serious.*   A grave character and a grave message make a prophetic utterance a solemn thing.   Amos had to tell of a cup of iniquity full, of a Divine patience exhausted, of a dispensation of forbearance expired, and of a national ruin ready to fall; and he tells it as one weighted down with the piteous tidings, which yet he cannot choose but speak (ch. iii. 1; iv. 1; v. 1; vi. 1). 2. *Blunt.*   Amos is outspoken and honest, names the condemned, and unequivocally denounces their impending doom.   He may not mince his tidings who is the messenger of death (Matt. iii. 10; Luke xiii. 3; Rom. i. 18).   Suppression would be murder, and even euphemy would be cruel.   Life and death hang on his lips, and all sentiment apart he must speak out.

> " The power to bind and loose to truth is given ;
> The mouth that speaks it is the mouth of Heaven."

3. *Characteristic.*   His style is bold and clear and tender, like his own nature (ch. iv. 4, 12, 13; ix. 5, 6; vi. 9, 10); and his imagery is racy of the mountains and fields in which his character was formed (ver. 2; ch. ii. 9, 13; iii. 4, 5; v. 19).   The word of God in one sense, it is in another, and no less really, the word of Amos.   The Divine Spirit supplies the breath and the fingering, and determines and directs the time, but the human instrument gives forth its own characteristic sound.

IV. THE WRITING OF THE VISION.   Scripture contains matters that were written at the Divine dictation, and first promulgated in their written form.   But it also contains much that was spoken first and written afterwards, for preservation.   Such is the Book of Amos.   The writing of it was: 1. *Some years after the speaking.*   He spoke years before an earthquake, after which he wrote his book.   This earthquake he had foretold in his oral prophecy (ch. viii. 8; ix. 5), and he thus puts on record the fulfilment of his own prediction.   " After fulfilling his mission, he probably returned to Judah, his native land, where his prophecies were most likely first committed to writing " (Keil). 2. *In a different form from the speaking.*   Amaziah (ch. vii. 10, 11) refers to, and gives a summary of " words " that are not recorded.   The book is a *résumé* of the essential contents of the oral prophecies (Keil, Lange).   Accordingly, it does not contain them in the very form, nor necessarily in the exact order, in which they were spoken. 3. *With a widened purpose.*   The oral prophecies were for those whom they directly concerned.   The written prophecies were for the sages and the ages that were to follow.   They were the flower of the prophecies that went before (Joel iii. 16, 18), and the bud of those that came after (Hos. viii. 14; ix. 3; Jer. xlix. 3, 13—27; xlvi. 6; xxv. 30; see Lange).   They also contain truths essentially important and requisite for the perfecting of the man of God in all ages (ch. iii. 3, 6, 7; v. 4—6, 14, 15; vii. 2, 3). 4. *Under the same Divine guidance.*   The contents of the book lie between the expressions, " thus saith the Lord " (ch. i. 3), and " saith the Lord thy God " (ch. ix. 15).   These formulæ cover both the oral and the written prophecy, each being the subject of a distinct inspiration for its own special purpose.   So Paul takes an inspired utterance of David, and, under inspiration, charges it with a new lesson (comp. Ps. xl. 6 with Heb. x. 5; also Isa. lx. 1 with Eph. v. 14).

V. THE SUBJECT OF THE VISION.   It is brief, but it covers much ground. 1. *The Jews.*   Judah and Israel are mentioned separately, having been distinct kingdoms for above a century (ch. ii. 4, 6). The entire Hebrew people are also grouped together as forming the family of Israel which God redeemed from Egypt (ch. iii. 1). It is as earthly kingdoms that destruction is denounced on both (ch. ii. 4, 6), but it is as one covenant people that they survive in a remnant, and are restored (ch. ix. 11—15). 2. *Their oppressors.* God had made the neighbouring nations "the rod of his anger" (ch. iii. 11; v. 27; Isa. x. 4) to smite Israel. They accomplished his purpose unconsciously, and impelled by evil motives of their own (vers. 3, 6, 9, 13; Isa. x. 7). Accordingly, their wars and oppressions, inflicted on Israel, were essentially wicked, and deserving punishment in turn. It is thus that the wrath of man, which he punishes at last, God makes meanwhile to praise him by the unwitting execution of his will. 3. *Those who resemble either.* God acts on the same principles in all ages. He afflicts the Church for the sins of its members. To the insincere his judgments mean punishment only (Rom. i. 18). To the sincere but faulty they mean discipline also (2 Cor. iv. 17). To the Church as a whole they mean separation between tares and wheat (Matt. xiii. 29, 30). To the outside wicked, through whom they often come, they mean more sin now, and a heavier punishment at last (Luke xviii. 7).

VI. THE TIME OF THE VISION. On this point we have information the most explicit. 1. *Generally it was in the days of Uzziah and Jeroboam.* During those reigns Judah and Israel were in the zenith of their career. It was, therefore, a vision of adversity when prosperity was at its height, of disastrous war when peace by conquest had been obtained with neighbouring powers, of both these as punishment when idolatry and corruption were at their worst. This proves its *genuineness,* as it could not have been suggested by the observed shadows of coming events. At the same time, it accounts for its comparative failure as a warning, the future predicted being so utterly unlike the present. 2. *Specially it was "before the earthquake."* "The presumption is natural that these words indicate not only the period but the motive of the composition" (Lange). The approach of the earthquake was the occasion of the oral prophecy, and the occurrence of it the occasion of the written one. That the latter should contain a record of the fulfilment of the former (ch. viii. 8; ix. 5) is proof that in addition to being *genuine* the vision is *authentic.*

Ver. 2.—*The thunder that both frights and smites.* These words are an echo of Joel iii. 16. We hence infer the continuity of the two prophetic messages. The one strikes the key-note, and the other takes up and continues the strain.

I. DIVINE INTERVENTION. This is to end a period of quiescence. It is: 1. *Intervention.* "Utters his voice." The silence of God is often treated as equivalent to inaction (Ps. xxviii. 1; l. 21). So his speech would mean his becoming active, whether for good or for evil. Here the breaking silence is for evil. God bears long with his open enemies, and longer still with his seeming friends. But inactivity does not show indifference nor inattention. It is simply forbearance, that will not strike till it must. Action delayed is no less certain, and will be no less vigorous for the delay. 2. *Angry intervention.* Shall "roar," like a lion ready to devour. Not till his anger burneth sore does God break the silence. But when he breaks it he does so emphatically. He thunders with his voice. His roar expresses wrath, and preludes a stroke; and is thus power and light in one (Job xxxvii. 5; xl. 9). 3. *Forcible intervention.* God's speech is followed by action. It is more; it is accompanied by action. It is more still; it is itself action. Creative power, preserving power, redeeming power, each goes forth in a word (Ps. xxxiii. 6, 9; Matt. ix. 2). Christ says, "Be clean," "Come forth;" and the sick are whole, and the dead live at his word. In speaking, God acts. The thunder of his voice is loaded with the electricity of his power. The vehicle of the Divine active energy is, in fact, a word.

II. GOD'S BASIS OF OPERATIONS. God intervenes in character, and along established lines. He operates: 1. *From Jerusalem.* This is God's own city, the metropolis of his earthly kingdom. Nothing could be more appropriate. Going forth to war, the king marches from his capital. There he has his magazine, his arsenal, and his headquarters. From thence he can bear down resistlessly on foes from whatever side, with all the resources of his kingdom. 2. *From Zion.* God's seat and citadel within his city. The place he loves and chooses and honours above all others (Ps. lxxxvii. 2; cxxxii. 13; xlviii. 12, 13). Here he has made his dwelling-place (Ps. lxviii. 16; cxxxii.

14). *The place out of which go forth salvation and destruction.* The place out of which the things that come are perfect after their kind. If they be blessings, there are no others so sweet; if curses, no others so stern. Zion is the beating heart of the spiritual world, which sends forth pure or poisoned blood to each greatest and least extremity. 3. *From the temple.* This is not mentioned, but it is necessarily implied. The glory of Jerusalem was Zion, and the glory of Zion (using the word in its broad sense) was God's house. This was his sanctuary. There he dwelt in symbolic presence. There he revealed himself in symbolic portraiture. There he operated in unparalleled energy. Thence accordingly we might expect his activity to issue (Ps. xx. 2). There, too, was his mercy-seat, from which judgment never came till every merciful expedient had been tried, but would come then with the fury of outraged goodness. Now, Jerusalem and Zion and God's house are each a type, and their common anti-type is the Church of Christ. And this is God's base of spiritual operations through all time (Isa. ii. 3; Luke xxiv. 47). He dwells in it (Acts vii. 38; Eph. i. 23), speaks by it (Eph. iii. 10), operates through it (Dan. ii. 44), and conquers in it (Dan. vii. 13, 22).

III. AFTER THE CAMPAIGN. God makes no fruitless expedition. The armies of his judgments leave desolation in their track. 1. *The pastures wither.* God's voice, as a figure for meteorological phenomena, is often spoken of as changing the surface of the earth (Ps. xxix. 3—9). Here it stands for many agencies, including these, and especially drought. Nature is one, and if any part suffers the other parts suffer with it (Jer. xxv. 36). Amos, as a herdsman, thinks naturally first of the calamity as it would affect the pastures by which he made his living. God's judgments strike each man in his special interest. It is as menacing this interest chiefly that they are feared. 2. *The head of Carmel is dried up.* Carmel was in the north, and the pastures in the prophet's mind were in the south. The enumeration, therefore, points to the withering as prevailing over the entire land. Carmel was one of the richest and best-watered spots in Palestine. When it was withered, all other places must have been scorched. God's judgments come seldom, and with tardy foot; but they are thorough, and make an end of their work (1 Sam. iii. 12: Isa. lx. 12). Nor was this a passing visitation. It remains in its leading characteristics till the present day. Carmel, as its name implies, was rich in vineyards. Now there is only scrub, and the *débris* of ruined walls. The "head" is dried up, that might once have been said to "drop down new wine."

Ver. 3—ch. ii. 3.—*A hexade of woes. The heathen in judgment: general features.* In these verses is denounced a series of six woes, on six of the oppressing nations, round about the land of Israel. Each woe has characteristics peculiar to itself, but there are points common to them all to which it will be well to make preliminary reference.

I. IN EVERY CASE JUDGMENT IS THE ACT OF GOD. "I will send;" "I will kindle" (vers. 4, 7, 10, 12). It is not fate, whose "winged shaft" is but a phantasy. It is not chance, which is but another name for inscrutable direction. It is not idols, the guess-work likenesses of imaginary things. It is not natural laws, which are simply forces put into things by their Maker. It is God—God in intelligence of device and energy of execution, who "creates evil" (Isa. xlv. 7)—the evil of calamitous events.

II. IN EVERY CASE GOD'S JUDGMENT IS THE COMPLEMENT OF MAN'S SIN. "Because they have threshed;" "Because they carried away." The connection between human sin and human suffering is original, constant, and necessary. They came together, dwell together, and will die together. And just as our common suffering is the abiding result of our common sinfulness, so special suffering connects itself somewhere with special sin. Its relation to the sin, whether as a punishment, a deterrent, or a chastisement, is often obscure. The particular sin, or even the particular sinner, can seldom be pointed to with certainty. There is a warning against judging harshly of the specially afflicted (Luke xiii. 4, 5). Yet the plain teaching of Scripture and experience and reason is that sin has "brought death into the world, and all our woe" (Rom. v. 12; Job iv. 7, 8).

III. IN EVERY CASE THE SIN SELECTED FOR PUNISHMENT IS THAT COMMITTED AGAINST GOD'S PEOPLE. In five cases out of the six the sin was committed directly against Israel, and in the sixth case it was committed against their ally. God loves the world as a whole, but he loves his people best (John iii. 16; xiv. 23). He gives to the wicked

" life and breath and all things," but he gives to his saints the wicked, and all they have (1 Cor. iii. 21, 22; Eph. i. 22). He avenges the ill done even to the sinner, but he avenges more sternly, because he personally feels, the ill done to his people (Zech. ii. 8, 9). Their persons are more sacred than those of others (Matt. x. 30), and their lives more precious in his sight (Ps. lxxii. 14; cxvi. 15). Accordingly, the worst form of murder is martyrdom (Luke xviii. 7, 8), and the worst form of theft is sacrilege (Mal. iii. 8).

IV. JUDGMENT IS PRECIPITATED BY PERSEVERANCE IN SIN. "For three transgressions and for four" is the invariable formula. The expression (see Prov. xxx. 15, 18, 21; Job v. 19; Eccles. xi. 2) means for many transgressions, culminating in a final one. Persistent sin means cumulative guilt. Drop is added to drop till at last the cup is full. The tendency toward sin God warns; the first sin he rebukes; the second he threatens; the third he menaces with uplifted hand; the fourth he smites. God bears long with the wicked, but they may sin once too often. Your past offences have escaped, your next one may endanger the Divine forbearance. "Sin no more, lest a worse thing come upon you."

V. IN EVERY CASE THE EXTREME OF GUILT INVOLVES THE EXTREME OF PUNISHMENT OR ENTIRE DESTRUCTION. This is inflicted by fire, the most destructive element in each case. God employed fire in many of his most startling miracles (Gen. xix. 24; Exod. ix. 23; Numb. xi. 1; xvi. 35; Lev. x. 2; 2 Kings i. 10, 12). In the language of figure it is the ideal destructive agent (Isa. iv. 4; ix. 5). In prophecy, too, fire is or symbolizes the agent that destroys the beast, the false prophet, and all the wicked (Dan. vii. 11; Rev. xix. 20; xx. 15). To the impenitent, fire will be a destroying, not a cleansing power. It points onward to the vengeance of eternal fire, which will be the fitting retribution of sin at last.

Vers. 3—5.—*The woe against Damascus.* The kingdom of Syria is here named from its capital. The crime charged against it had been foretold by Elisha to Hazael, and by him indignantly repudiated (2 Kings viii. 12, 13). But a man in one set of circumstances little knows what he would do under an entirely different set; especially a man beginning a sinful life, the magnitude of the crimes of which he may yet be capable. Accordingly, Hazael fulfilled one prophecy, and supplied the materials of another, by smiting Israel as the man of God had said (2 Kings x. 32, 33).

I. THE CRIMINAL. Damascus stands by metonymy for Syria, judging of whom by her representative we see that: 1. *Riches do not prevent rapacity.* Damascus was noted for wealth, the fertile neighbourhood being irrigated by numerous canals, and the city itself lying in the highway of commerce. Yet greed instigated the barbarous treatment described. The wars waged against Israel were wars of rapine and annexation. "The eye that loveth silver shall not be satisfied with silver." Rather does the lust of gain grow by what it feeds on. Whether it be culture, or power, or pleasure, or wealth, men tend to make a god of the thing they abound in. It was when Israel was richest that her oppression of the poor was most extreme. It was by her richest neighbours that she herself was most rapaciously despoiled. It is thus that the conditions leading men to sin are the guarantee of its punishment in kind. 2. *Beautiful surroundings do not humanize.* Writers speak in glowing terms of the unrivalled beauty of this ancient city. "Its white buildings, embedded in the deep green of its engirdling orchards, were like diamonds encircled by emeralds" (Pusey). Yet here, in scenes of ideal beauty, grew up the monsters of barbarity who took the women and children of Gilead, and, "casting them as into a sort of threshing-floor, savagely threshed them out like ears of corn with saw-armed wheels" (see 2 Kings xiii. 7). Physical scenery and moral character have no necessary connection. The fairest lands have often produced the coarsest and most cruel men. The determining element is the presence or absence of the gospel of Christ. It is not æsthetics, but Christianity, we must look to for the moral elevation of men. 3. *The possession of strength is a temptation to violence.* The beauty of Damascus was also its strength. The miles on miles of walled orchards in which it was set formed an admirable defence against an advancing enemy (see Pusey), and, thus entrenched, the legions of Syria were strong beyond their seeming. Now, just as the subtle choose diplomacy and the rich subsidy in the settlement of disputed matters, so do the strong choose force. It is the readiest and most effective weapon within their reach. How many wars, how much bloodshed and desolation and misery, are directly traceable to "the strong man glorying in his strength"!

II. THE CRIME. Gilead, meaning the whole land given to the two tribes and a half, is here put by metonymy for the inhabitants. The horrible and atrocious outrages on the people described by Amos suggest that : 1. *The obverse of ungodliness is inhumanity.* The relation to God is the fundamental one. If it be wrong, all others are awry. Morality has its basis in religion. There is no duty to men apart from a God and a revelation of his will. There is no good will toward men apart from his gracious influence (Titus iii. 3). The mere animal nature is selfish, and regardless of all life but its own. It will kill for the most trifling advantage, and sometimes in the lust of blood for no advantage at all. Heathen hearts are "hateful and hating one another," and a heathen home is "a habitation of cruelty." 2. *Bloodthirsty men make war even with the implements of peace.* There is a time coming when warlike weapons will be converted into farming implements (Isa. ii. 4; Micah iv. 3). This will be when the gospel shall universally prevail. Meanwhile a readier ear is leant to Joel (iii. 10) than to Micah, and the converse process goes on instead. The threshing-instrument was not made, but only pressed into service, for the occasion. Fallen man is at heart a savage, and, under excitation, his inner nature will break out through the artificial habits of peace. So little is there between work and war, between lawful industry and lawless murder, in the godless life. 3. *Ideal cruelty is utterly indiscriminate.* Elisha's prophecy to Hazael (2 Kings viii. 12), of which this horrid butchery was the fulfilment, mentions women and children as the chief victims of the outrage. There is a bloodhound instinct in wicked men which is aroused to fury by the taste of blood. The horrors of the French Revolution and of the Spanish Inquisition reveal it in the infidel and the fanatic respectively. It knows no distinction of age, or condition, or sex. It simply wants to "slay, and slay, and slay." It is a humiliating thought about our species, but it is a fact that must be faced by all who would humanize the race. The tie of blood is perhaps a natural one, and respected more or less by even heathen peoples, as it is by the very beasts that perish. But even this scarcely operates beyond the filial relation and the period of childhood. And then, as for friendship and philanthropy, they have no place in the sphere of mere nature. The question, "Is man utterly selfish?" is rather a nice one than practical. He has shown himself sufficiently selfish to make unsafe the life of any human being whom he could gain by killing.

III. THE SENTENCE. This is severe, detailed, and striking. 1. *It falls on the things in which the nation was pre-eminent.* "I will break also the bar of Damascus." The bar or bolt which secured the gate was an essential part of the city defence. To break it would be to throw open the city to the enemy. By this figure is meant the breaking of the national strength and means of resistance, and leaving the nation helpless before its enemies. Thus God declares himself omnipotent. Those who glory in their strength are broken, and those who trust in their riches are impoverished (Isa. ii. 11; xiii. 11; Ps. lii. 7). Punishment adjusted so is more effectual for its purpose, whether of mercy or of judgment, for it brings the criminal to his knees at once. The niceness of the adjustment is, moreover, a revelation of the Divine directing hand in the whole event, and so a lesson in itself. 2. *It strikes at the national sin.* The "vale of Aven," whose inhabitant was to be cut off, was remarkable as containing Baalbec, or Heliopolis, the seat and centre of the Syrian sun-worship. There were observed idolatrous orgies, in which men and women abandoned themselves to shameless profligacy; and there, where their "offence smells rank to Heaven," the hottest bolts of Heaven's vengeance fall. Others would be carried into captivity, but the inhabitants of Aven would be utterly cut off. The flies of God's judgment alight upon the sores of our idol sins. He strikes the covetous in his pocket, and the self-indulgent in his power of enjoyment. And so in every other case. The practice that provokes his judgment is the one on which its first and heaviest effects fall. 3. *It includes the royal house.* The king is in a sense the figure-head of the nation. His policy embodies the national sentiment, if it does not inspire it. Accordingly, national guilt culminates in him. It would be an anomaly if the people were to perish and he escape. Then the destruction that includes king and people is utter and irretrievable. There could be no restoration, no resurrection. When only ashes remain, the rekindling of the fire of national existence has become impossible. 4. *It denounces on all poetic justice.* "Shall go into captivity to Kir." "From Kir the forefathers of the Syrians had, of their own will, been brought by the good all-disposing providence of God. Now, softened as they were by luxury, they were to be transported back to the austere though healthy climate whence they had come" (Pusey). The family of Ne'er-do-well fall into the mud out of which they were raised at first, and find it has got deeper in the interval. The last state of the misuser of good, in the nature of the case, is worse than the first.

IV. THE EXECUTION. The woe fell half a century later, in the time of Tiglath-Pileser, who slew Rezin the king, and carried the Syrians away captive. *Thus the event was fifty years after the prediction.* Prophecy by the Spirit of God is as easy to the prophet a millennium before the event as an hour. But if it has not been forgotten in the mean time, it is the more impressive and striking, the longer the interval between the utterance and the fulfilment. *Then the evil prophesied was one previously unheard of, and antecedently most unlikely.* "The transportation of whole populations was not, so far as we know, any part of Eastern policy at the time of the prophet" (Pusey). There are unfulfilled predictions, loaded with the world's weal or ill, whose fulfilment is even more distant and more unlikely. But the "sure Word of prophecy" overrides both time and chance, and lifts remotest events above the horizon, and into the light of decisive certitude. For all we fear and hope this is the guarantee, "Hath he said it, and shall he not do it? Hath he spoken, and shall he not make it good?"

Vers. 6—8.—*The woe against Philistia.* Gaza was one of the capitals of Philistia, and is put for the country as a whole. Its wealth and strength and special activity against Israel fitted it to be the representative of all the other capitals which are afterwards (ver. 8) enumerated as sharing its punishment. The outrage charged against Gaza is probably that recorded in 2 Chron. xxi. 16 and Joel iii. 6, and which occurred in the time of Jehoram. The crime denounced was—

I. THE CROWNING ACT OF A LONG SERIES. Israel and Philistia were hereditary foes. In the history of their feud were many bloody acts, which culminated in this wholesale deportation. In the judgment provoked by it, however, these acts would all be punished. So the murders of the prophets, throughout a series of ages, remained unavenged till they culminated in the death of Christ, and then it and they were all avenged together (Luke xi. 49—51). Thus vicarious is much of human suffering. God visits the iniquities of the fathers upon the children generally (Exod. xx. 5), and specially on those like-minded with the fathers (Matt. xxiii. 34—36). The sufferings of each age are largely an inheritance from the ages before.

II. AN ACT OF WHOLESALE DESTRUCTION. "Because they carried away captives in full number." This cruelty was gratuitous, as many captives could have given their captors no offence; and it was senseless as well, for many would be utterly worthless as slaves. It indicated deep and indiscriminating hate of the entire people, and a fixed purpose to root out and utterly exterminate them. Such hatred, directed doubtless against Israel in their character as the people of God, is specially criminal, and calls for special punishment (see Matt. x. 40, 41).

III. AN ACT OF AGGRAVATED CRUELTY. Not satisfied with the suffering they could inflict themselves, they called in the help of Israel's bitterest foe. They sold the people to the Edomites, and so became responsible for the intolerable cruelties to which they were handed over. We are in God's sight as guilty of the crime we procure as of the crime we commit. The Church's mediæval device of condemning heretics, and handing them over to the civil power to be executed, was as vain as the washing of Pilate's hands. The blood shed at our instigation, and with our connivance or through our indifference, is blood that will be required of us in the great day (Ezek. iii. 18—20).

IV. A PUNISHMENT IN WHICH THE CAPITAL CITIES ARE SPECIALLY PROMINENT. Of the five capitals of Philistia, four are mentioned by name, and the fifth is included under the word "remnant." Capitals are centres of opinion, and are largely responsible for the moulding of the national sentiment. They are centres of power, and take the lead in determining the national policy. They were in this case centres of commerce, and so took a prominent part in the work of bartering Israel to the Edomites. Moreover Gaza, the one singled out and emphasized, was through its character and position the chief sinner in this business, and so is the chief sufferer. They were also the seats of as many different idols—Ashdod of Dagon, Ashkelon of Derceto, Ekron of Baalzebub, and Gaza of Marua—and therefore centres of national sin (see Pusey). Add to this that they were the national depôts and strongholds, and therefore the places which it would most weaken the nation to destroy.

V. A PUNISHMENT TO BE FRAMED AFTER THE FASHION OF THE CRIME. "The remnant of the Philistines shall perish." As they had spared none, so none of them would be spared. This is God's way often. That it may be adequate, and all may be able to recognize it, punishment often comes in the likeness of the crime. The rule, "Whoso sheddeth man's blood, by man shall his blood be shed," embodies the principle that like will be the punishment of like. It reappears in the gospel dictum, "With what measure ye mete, it shall be measured to you again." Not only will sin be punished, it will all be punished, and punished fully. When God's last word has been spoken, the criminal shall be even as his victim, and be God's enemy besides.

Vers. 9, 10.—*The woe against Tyre.* Tyre stands for Phœnicia, of which it was the capital. It was a renowned and very ancient city. Greatest, richest, proudest, and most luxurious, perhaps, of all the cities of its time, it passed through vicissitudes which were equally beyond the common lot. As with most ancient capitals, there were points at which its path and that of Israel crossed, involving that there should be corresponding points where they would recross, and on these the prophet has intently fixed his eye. Of the denunciation against it observe—

I. IT SINNED IN CHARACTER. The Phœnicians were a commercial people, and theirs was a commercial sin. "They delivered up the whole captivity to Edom." They did not make war, nor take prisoners, but they traded in them as slaves—bought them probably from the Syrians and sold them to the Ionians ("Grecians," Joel iii. 6). For this their woe is denounced; and thus early was branded with condemnation "the wild and guilty phantasy that man can hold a property in man." The image of God is not a thing to be trafficked in. "The law" is against men-stealers (1 Tim. i. 10) among other criminals. A man's liberty is precious to him next to life itself. Slavery is the intolerable theft of his manhood and moral agency, and is contrary to the entire spirit of the Bible.

II. IT SINNED AGAINST A COVENANT. This was no doubt the covenant between Hiram and Solomon (1 Kings v. 12). It was a covenant of peace, of which the trading in Hebrew captives was a flagrant violation. This circumstance made the detestable traffic doubly guilty. It was two sins in one—perjury added on to oppression. And all Christian sin is in this respect its counterpart. The believer is in covenant with God. He has said, "This God is my God for ever and ever," etc. Any after-sin is, therefore, a breach both of God's Law and his own vow. The believing sinner has broken through more restraints and violated more laws than the unbelieving, and so is double-dyed in guilt. The difficulty of bringing such to repentance again (Heb. vi. 4—6) is no doubt closely connected with this fact.

III. THE FORGOTTEN COVENANT WAS A BROTHERLY COVENANT. This circumstance aggravated the guilt of the violation. Ties are strong in proportion as they are amicable. The electric core of friendship in the cable of a mutual tie gives it a character all its own. The breaking of it means to both parties more of change and loss in proportion as this core is relatively large. The Phœnicio-Israelitish covenant was brotherly: 1. *In its origin.* It was the outcome of brotherly feeling and affection previously existing. "Hiram," we read, "was ever a lover of David" (1 Kings v. 1), and in token of it he had voluntarily sent materials and workmen, and had built him a house (2 Sam. v. 11). And the feeling was evidently transferred to Solomon. Hiram and he were on such cordial terms that he asked for, and Hiram readily sent him, skilful Sidonian woodmen to hew trees, and an accomplished Tyrian graver to act as foreman over his own workmen in carving, engraving, embroidery, and doing other cunning work for the temple (2 Chron. ii. 3—16). Solomon in turn gave Hiram wheat and oil in liberal measure for provisioning his house, and the outcome of these cordial relations was that "they two made a league together" (1 Kings v. 11, 12), the brotherly covenant referred to. The covenant was brotherly also: 2. *In its working.* It was renewed from time to time with various additions, and was long kept by both parties. Israel never made war against Tyre, nor broke the letter or spirit of their fraternal league. The heartless sin of Tyre was, therefore, not only a violation of the covenant provisions, but of the intimate and cordial relations which it both expressed and fostered. It was a sin against both vows and close relations, and put on thus an aspect of double criminality. 3. *The covenant had even a religious aspect.* Hiram grounds the good will and help, extended to Solomon, on the facts that the people he ruled and the house he was going to build were God's, as well as on the fact that he had a special gift of wisdom from above (2 Chron. ii. 11, 12). His covenant was thus made with Israel as God's people, and in testimony of his belief in Jehovah as the true God, and his desire to advance his glory. This fact adds much to the significance and solemnity of the covenant, and so of the breach of it. What is done in God's name and as an act of homage to him is done under the highest sanctions possible. The commonest act is glorified, the smallest act becomes great in the greatness of its underlying principle. And as is the doing so is the undoing. The higher the promiser has risen, the lower has the violator fallen. Tyre's sin implied and sealed a large amount of previous deterioration, and so the more emphatically sealed her doom.

Vers. 11, 12.—*The woe against Edom.* We have here an inspired description of an ideal hate. It is loaded with every quality, and emphasized by every circumstance, and stained by every act, which could conspire to establish for it an "unbeaten record" in the emulation of evil passions.

I. IT RESTS ON A BROTHER. Over and above the brotherhood arising out of their common humanity (Acts xvii. 26; Gen. ix. 5), Israel and Edom were bound by the nearer tie of descent from the twin sons of their common ancestor Isaac. And on the basis of this relation they are spoken of as brothers in a special sense (Deut. xxiii. 7). To the relation of brotherhood belongs the duty of love (1 John ii. 10), which must be distinctive in proportion as the relation is close (1 Pet. ii. 17). And the breach of this law of love is great in proportion to its normal strength. It is bad to hate an enemy, but it is worse to hate a friend, and worse still to hate a brother. It is against nature, for "no man hateth his own flesh" (Eph. v. 29). It is against our innate tendency to love them that love us. And it is against the popular sentiment which expects us to "love as brethren." Hatred of a brother is the grossest hate there is.

II. IT IS AGGRESSIVE. "He pursues his brother with the sword." It is hard for hatred to be still. It is a restless devil in the heart. It wants to inflict injury. It actually inflicts it the first opportunity. If opportunity does not come, it seeks it and makes it. In the presence of the hated one it can no more be quiescent than fire in contact with fuel. Edom's hatred of Israel did not fail thus to express its intensity. On every opportunity it broke out into offensive and cruel action (2 Chron. xxviii. 17; Ps. cxxxvii. 7; Ezek. xxv. 12). Rapine, outrage, and murder, and the incitement of others to these, are fitting credentials to an ideal hate.

III. IT IS MURDEROUS. "Tears in pieces." It inflicts not injury only, but deadly injury. It must have blood. And it not only kills, but murders. Unable to fight Israel in battle, Edom always played the part of "wrecker," and spoiled the dead, and murdered the wounded, after some stronger enemy had defeated them (Ps. cxxxvii. 7). Then it murdered with an excess of truculence and savage cruelty that were natural to weakness rather than to strength. Hatred is a passion "blood alone can quell." "Whosoever hateth his brother is a murderer;" a murderer in fact if opportunity offers, in any case a murderer in heart. Let hatred enter your heart, and from the moment it settles you wear the brand of Cain.

IV. IT IS PITILESS. "Did cast off all pity." No special occasion or act is mentioned, because the thing was habitual. A traditional and inordinate hate of Israel was fostered till it became a first principle of the Edomite's creed, and was gratified till it ate all his humanity out. Too weak to be a soldier, he became a murderous looter, and when the Assyrian or Philistine had vanquished Israel in battle, the Edomite came vulture-like on the scene to butcher the living, and pillage and mangle the dead (Obad. 10—14). There is a pity proper to the human heart on the platform of mere nature. Of the "flowers of Eden we still inherit" is a ruth that shrinks from murder in cold blood. Where the crime is committed, this feeling has previously been choked out. The power to do this, to harden and deaden his own nature, is one of man's most fatal gifts. He disregards the voice of pity till it becomes dumb. He fights against the movings of passion till at last they are felt no more.

V. IT IS INSATIABLE. "His anger endures for ever." The persistence of Edom's hate was matter of contemporary notoriety (Ezek. xxxv. 5), and it was precisely what one might expect. There is an infinity that belongs to the human soul, and which imparts itself to all its affections. Love is not exhausted by indulgence, but strengthened. It goes on and grows for ever, and so with hate. One who knew well has said—

> "Now hatred is by far the longest pleasure;
> Men love in haste, but they detest at leisure."
>
> (Byron.)

Hate is fed by indulgence as a fire is fed by fuel. Do not think your hatred will be appeased when you have got what you consider a just revenge. It will only then begin to burn with normal fierceness. Such feelings grow by what they feed on. The only way to banish them is to cut off the supplies. Starve a hungry hate, by giving it neither outlet nor audience, and it will soon atrophy and die.

VI. IT IS ALL ON ONE SIDE. Israel's relation to Edom as friendly, considerate, and disinterested, was laid down in explicit terms (Deut. xxiii. 7; ii. 4, 5), whilst the brotherhood of the two nations was emphasized (Numb. xx. 14; Deut. ii. 8). Cruel things were done in spite of this (1 Sam. xiv. 47; 2 Sam. viii. 14; 1 Kings xi. 15, 16), but they were done in defensive wars, and after Edom's enmity had proved itself incurable. It is a robust and thoroughly malignant hate that beats down and burns in spite of others' friendly attitude and feeling. Such hate belongs to a nature utterly inverted, and no longer human but devilish. And in proportion as it is such it becomes impossible of cure. The fire that burns without fuel, and in spite of water, has the elements of perpetuity in it. It is the beginning of the fire that shall never be quenched.

Vers. 13—15.—*The woe against Ammon: brutality in its element.* There is a climax in these woes as we advance. Each seems to outdo in horror the one before. This one in which Ammon figures has circumstances of wanton atrocity and senseless savagery in it unparalleled in any other.

I. UNNATURAL CONNECTIONS MAY BE EXPECTED TO BREED UNNATURAL MONSTERS. Ammon and Moab were the children of unnatural and shameful lust (Gen. xix. 30—38). Begotten in drunkenness, and conceived in a paroxysm of lewdness, their chance of inheriting a healthy physical, mental, or moral organization was very small. The almost inevitable moral twist with which they entered the world, their education by dissolute mothers would only strengthen and confirm. And the passionate and sensual nature he inherited, Ammon transmitted to the nation of which he became the father. An illustration of this inherited coarse corruption in the Ammonites was their gross and indecent treatment of David's servants, sent on a friendly errand (2 Sam. x. 4, 5). The other occasion, recorded in our text, is an example of savage and senseless atrocity unparalleled in the annals of human violence. As to the women, it was from their number that Solomon's harem was largely recruited (1 Kings xi. 1, 7), and they took to harlotry as easily as their ancestress herself (Numb. xxv. 1; xxxi. 16). Our besetting sins are likely to be those of our forefathers, and therefore against these we should be specially on our guard. They are likely also to beset our children after us, and should be all the more vigorously rooted out, lest we transmit to posterity the heritage of our sin and shame. That the thing can be done, let the virtuous simplicity of Ruth the Moabitess prove. Trained and moulded in a godly Hebrew family, she responds to religious influence, and exhibits a character that has been the admiration of all the ages.

II. OTHER THINGS BEING EQUAL, THAT IS THE GREATEST SIN FOR WHICH THERE IS THE LEAST OCCASION. "He who has committed injustice for a less advantage has done it under the impulse of a less temptation. . . . The more paltry it is in respect of profit, the more profane it may be in respect of principle" (Chalmers). In the case of Ammon there was the extreme of disproportion between the crime and the incentive to it. The object was to enlarge their border, an object (1) unnecessary, (2) under the circumstances unjust, (3) in itself supplying no occasion for the horrid outrage, and (4) to the attainment of which the atrocity was in no wise essential. The act was simply one of stolid barbarism, unsoftened by any extenuating circumstance, and unaccounted for by any consideration of need or fitness.

III. MURDER AS AN ACT OF REPRISAL IS STILL MURDER. David had put the inhabitants of Rabbah of the sons of Ammon to a death as dreadful as that inflicted on the women in Gilead (2 Sam. xii. 31). The present act of Ammon might look like a just retaliation. But, whatever may be thought of David's conduct, it is clear that sin does not justify more sin. Then David's siege and destruction of Rabbah was a natural and suitable act of defensive warfare against persistent attacks by Ammon in league with Syria. The aggressor in such a case is responsible for the bloodshed on both sides. Man has a natural right to kill in self-defence, and he whose action necessitates such bloodshed is the party on whose head the guilt of it must lie.

IV. GOD'S JUDGMENTS STRIKE THE DEVISERS OF WICKEDNESS AS WELL AS THE DOERS OF IT. "The king and his princes." These ancient kings were absolute monarchs. Every national act was an expression of their will. With them, therefore, the responsibility for it ultimately rested. It was done by their direction and under their superintendence, done often in part by their own hand, and so was in every case their own act. And the princes, as the king's advisers, were parties to it. Therefore kings and princes alike must suffer. To strike them was to strike the criminal on the head. Thus far and wide do the consequences of sin reach, devouring from every side. The committer of sin, the suggester of sin, the deviser of sin, the tempter to sin, the procurer of sin, the knowing occasion of sin, the person privy to sin, all are sinners, and as such are written down for the sword. Some are nearer the centre than others, but all are in the vortex, and all must be swallowed up together.

HOMILIES BY VARIOUS AUTHORS.

Ver. 1.—*Amos the herdsman.* There must be some special reason why this prophet puts upon record the employments in which he spent his earlier years, and from which he was called to assume the office of the Lord's messenger to Israel. On the barren hills to the south of Bethlehem, where there is no tillage, and where the population must always have been scanty, Amos tended flocks of sheep or of goats, and at certain seasons of the year gathered the fruit from the wild sycamore trees.

I. RURAL AND MENIAL OCCUPATIONS WERE NO BARRIER TO THE ENJOYMENT OF DIVINE FAVOUR OR TO ELECTION TO SPECIAL AND HONOURABLE SERVICE. This lesson, taught by the career of Amos, was taught again by the election of the apostles of the Lord Christ. The great of this world are often apt to regard men of lowly station with disdain, but God takes no heed of social and artificial distinctions.

II. THE SECLUSION OF A PASTORAL LIFE WAS A SUITABLE TRAINING FOR THE PROPHETIC VOCATION. As David, when guarding the sheepfolds and leading the flocks to water, enjoyed many opportunities for solitary meditation and for devout communion with God, so Amos in the lonely pastures of Tekoah must have listened to the voice that speaks especially to the quiet and the contemplative, the voice of inspiration and of grace.

III. THE RURAL SURROUNDINGS OF THE PROPHET AFFORDED HIM MUCH APPROPRIATE AND STRIKING IMAGERY. The rain and the harvest, the sheep and the lion, the bird and the snare, the fish and the hook, the cart and the sheaf, the earthquake, the fire, and the flood, etc., are all pressed into the service of this poetic prophecy. God taught his servant lessons which stood him in good stead in after-years.

IV. BY RAISING AMOS FROM THE HERDSMAN'S TO THE PROPHET'S LIFE GOD MAGNIFIED HIS OWN GRACE. The cultivated and the polished are liable to take credit to themselves for the efficiency of their ministry. But when the comparatively untaught and those who have enjoyed but few advantages are raised to a position in which they do a great work for God, "the excellency of the power is seen to be of God himself."—T.

Ver. 2.—*The voice of terror.* This imagery is evidently derived from the prophet's own experience. In the south-east of Palestine the lion was a frequent and formidable visitor, which every herdsman had reason to dread. The majestic roar of the king of beasts is here employed to denote the judgments of the Lord upon the disobedient and rebellious, especially of Israel.

I. OBSERVE WHENCE THE VOICE OF THREATENING PROCEEDS. 1. It is the voice of the Lord—that voice which assumes now the accents of compassion and mercy, and again the tones of wrath, but which is always authoritative. 2. It proceeds from the sacred city, which was the favoured abode of Jehovah.

II. AND WHITHER THE VOICE OF THREATENING PENETRATES. From the habitations of the shepherds in the south, to the flowery Carmel in the north, this roar makes itself heard. That is to say, it fills the land. Judah and Israel alike have by disobedience and rebellion incurred Divine displeasure, and against both alike the denunciations of the prophet go forth.

III. CONSIDER THE EFFECT WHICH THE VOICE OF THREATENING SHOULD PRODUCE. 1. Reverent attention. 2. Deep humiliation and contrition. 3. Repentance and prayer. 4. Such reformation as the heavenly summons imperatively demands.—T.

Vers. 3—5.—*The judgment on Damascus.* The beauty of Damascus has been the admiration of travellers and the praise of poets. It is a mournful reflection that a city so magnificently situated, and with associations so romantic, should so often have been the scene of human injustice, cruelty, and bloodshed. The " pearl girdled with emeralds "—as Damascus was gracefully designated—is beautiful without, but, as the text reminds us, has often contained a lawless and godless population.

I. THE OFFENCE OF DAMASCUS. 1. In itself this consisted of atrocious cruelty. The records inform us that war frequently prevailed between Syria and Israel. By Gilead in this passage we understand the land possessed by the Israelites on the east side of Jordan. The inhabitants of this pastoral territory were treated by the Syrians in a way fitted to awaken the indignation even of those who lived in times when savage cruelty was but the too common accompaniment of war. The unfortunate Israelites who were conquered in war seem to have been literally torn to pieces and mangled by the threshing-implements fitted with wheels and armed with teeth of iron. Thus was God's image defaced and God's Law defied. 2. The offence was aggravated by repetition. Thrice, nay, four times, had the Damascenes offended the Divine Ruler of men by their violence and inhumanity. The sin was thus shown to be no mere outbreak of passion, but a habit, evincing a corrupt and degraded nature.

II. THE PUNISHMENT OF DAMASCUS. 1. Observe upon whom it came. (1) Upon the king, the rulers and princes of the land. These were the leaders in the nefarious practices here censured. Their ambition and unfeeling selfishness accounted for the sin; and upon them came down the righteous penalty. The annals of many a nation may prove to the reflective student of history that a righteous retribution visits those royal houses which have been infamous for selfish ambition, for perfidy, for tyranny, for self-indulgence. The King of kings asserts his authority, and brings down the lofty from the throne. (2) The people of Syria shared in the disaster, which thus became national. They may have been misled by their rulers, but it seems rather to have been the case that there was sympathy between kings and subjects, and that the soldiers in the Syrian army delighted in the opportunity of venting their evil passions upon their prostrate foes. 2. Observe in what the punishment consisted. (1) Destruction (" a fire ") came upon the royal house. (2) The splendid and powerful city was laid open to the incursion of the enemy. The brazen " bar " which secured the city gate was broken. (3) The people were carried into captivity, the worst misfortune which could humiliate and distress a nation.—T.

Vers. 6—8.—*The judgment on Philistia.* The great religious truth which is conveyed in this prophetic warning addressed to Philistia is this—national retribution is inevitable.

I. NATIONAL RETRIBUTION IS NOT AVERTED BY WEALTH AND PROSPERITY. Philistia was a fertile plain, abounding in all material riches. The people not only possessed the produce of a fruitful soil; they were versed in the arts of life, being famous as artificers and craftsmen; and they enjoyed the fruits of commerce both by sea and land. There is danger lest a prosperous nation should trust in its riches. Yet history tells us that the wealthiest communities have been overtaken by the righteous judgments of God.

II. NATIONAL RETRIBUTION IS NOT AVERTED BY UNION AND CONFEDERACY. The five cities of the Philistines were leagued together ; each supported the other, and every one furnished a contingent to the national armies. Union is strength. But the united strength of the Philistines could not avail them in the day of the Lord. "Though hand join in hand, the wicked shall not be unpunished."

III. NATIONAL RETRIBUTION IS NOT AVERTED BY POWERFUL ALLIANCES. The Philistines on the west of Judah leagued with the Edomites on the east. And when the Philistines gained an advantage over the Jews, they delivered their foes into the hands of their allies of Mount Seir. But Edom was not able to deliver her confederate in the time of trial and of retribution.

IV. NATIONAL RETRIBUTION IS NOT AVERTED BY CRUELTY TO A FOE. Human policy sometimes urges that the complete destruction of an enemy by the sword or by captivity is the surest protection against revenge. But Divine government dominates human policy. The crafty and the cruel must submit to the decrees of the Judge of the whole earth.—T.

Vers. 9, 10.—*The violation of a brotherly covenant.* The reproach addressed to Tyre, on account of Tyre's league with Edom against the Israelites, is peculiarly severe. This is to be explained by the previous history of the two nations. Hiram, King of Tyre, had been a warm friend both of David and of Solomon. A close and intimate connection had thus been formed. And when Tyre made war upon the Jews and, like Philistia, gave Israel into the hands of Edom, the grievance was felt to be peculiarly distressing. In fact, it was recognized as such by the inspired prophet of Jehovah.

I. THE DEEPEST FOUNDATION FOR NATIONAL FRIENDSHIPS IS THEIR COMMON BROTHERHOOD IN THE FAMILY OF GOD. The Creator has made them of one blood, has appointed the bounds of their habitation, has given to each nation its own advantages, its own opportunities, its own responsibilities. Each has thus a service to render to the Lord and Father of all ; and consequently each has a claim to the respect and good will of neighbouring nations.

II. NATIONAL FRIENDSHIP IS RECOMMENDED AND PROMOTED BY MUTUAL INTEREST. The exchange of commodities which had taken place between Tyre and Jerusalem may be regarded as an example of the use which one country may be to another—a use in some way or other always to be reciprocated. In peace every nation may supply the lack of others; whilst in war both nations so engaged inflict loss and injury. No doubt, when excited by passion, nations lose sight of their welfare; yet it is well to cultivate in men's minds the conviction that unity and concord are of the highest material as well as moral advantage.

III. NATIONAL FRIENDSHIP MAY BE CEMENTED BY SOLEMN COVENANTS AND ALLIANCES. Human nature is such that it is contributive to many desirable ends that men should enter into solemn compact and should ratify covenants with one another. When nations enter into friendly alliance, it is always regarded as peculiarly base when one nation, without overpowering reason for doing so, turns against the other, and betrays or attacks it. Such seems to have been the action of Tyre.

IV. BROTHERLY COVENANTS BETWEEN NATIONS CANNOT BE VIOLATED WITH IMPUNITY. Tyre was one of the great cities of antiquity, especially famous for maritime and commercial prosperity. Proud and confident in its greatness, Tyre little anticipated the fate which Providence had in reserve for it. Yet the inspired prophet foresaw the ruin of Tyre, and connected that ruin with the perfidy for which the city was in this passage so justly blamed. The Lord who rules in the whole earth is a Judge righteous and supreme, whose sentences will surely be executed.—T.

Vers. 11, 12.—*A brother's faithlessness and injustice.* If Tyre was doubly blamable because, being an ally, she turned against Israel, much more deserving of censure was Edom, inasmuch as Edom was near akin to Israel, and yet was guilty of the conduct described in this passage.

I. KINDRED INVOLVES SACRED OBLIGATIONS TO MUTUAL REGARD AND SUCCOUR. Moses had addressed Edom as a brother, and Israel had forborne to attack Edom, even when tempted to do so by most unneighbourly, unbrotherly conduct. The proper response to such conduct would have been something very different from what is here recorded. Amongst all nations, and in every stage of society, common descent from one ancestor is accepted as a bond of brotherhood and a pledge of friendliness.

II. THERE ARE INSTANCES IN WHICH THESE OBLIGATIONS ARE UTTERLY DISREGARDED. Such was the case with the Edomites. We trace in their conduct towards their kinsmen of Israel several stages of iniquity. 1. Aggression. Edom "pursued his brother with the sword." 2. Pitiless anger. Edom "corrupted his compassions." 3. Implacability. Edom "kept his wrath for ever." Such treatment would have been unjustifiable from any nation towards another; but the relation and circumstances made it flagrantly and atrociously wicked in the instance under consideration.

III. VIOLATION OF OBLIGATIONS SO SACRED INCURS DIVINE DISPLEASURE AND MERITED PUNISHMENT. A nation sins and a nation suffers. Doubtless innocent persons endure in many cases the sufferings which the guilty deserve. This is a mystery of Divine providence. Yet it is evident that cities, tribes, nations, may be, and often have been, chastised, as a proof of the Divine rule, as a correction for human disobedience, and as an inducement to repentance.—T.

Vers. 13—15.—*Greed of territory.* The history of the Ammonites is full of indications of their natural qualities and of their conduct towards Israel. They were an unprincipled and cruel people, and were continually at war with their neighbours. Their settlement on the east of the Jordan brought them into constant conflict with the Jews, and from the Book of Deuteronomy down to that of Nehemiah references to Ammon occur from which we gather that they were an idolatrous, restless, pitiless, lustful, and treacherous tribe. The incident upon which Amos founds this prediction was an incursion which the Ammonites made into Gilead during the reign of King Uzziah.

I. GREED OF TERRITORY IS A NATIONAL SIN. How many a nation has been possessed with a selfish desire to "enlarge its border"! When population increases, emigration and colonization may become necessary, and may be for good. What is blamed is the desire for a neighbour's land, the extirpation or subjugation of friendly neighbours, in order to obtain room for expansion or increase of luxury or of power.

II. GREED OF TERRITORY LEADS TO NEFARIOUS CRUELTY. The instance here mentioned is no doubt an extreme one; it shows convincingly that Ammon had no sense of humanity, compassion, or decency. Alas! the annals of our race afford too many an instance of the cruelty to which ambition leads. The history of the Spaniards in America is a sufficient proof of the awful lengths to which conquerors will go when urged by greed of power or of gold. And settlers even from our own land have not seldom been guilty of most indefensible cruelty and oppression towards the natives of the territories they have acquired. For the protection of *aborigines* it has been necessary to awaken public opinion, to institute special laws. Men plead necessity or expediency in defence or in extenuation of conduct which is a reproach to any people.

III. GREED OF TERRITORY AND ITS FRUITS ARE NOT UNNOTICED BY HIM WHO RULES OVER ALL. "The earth is the Lord's." He has "given it to the children of men." But when he beholds sordid greed animate men to robbery, and not to robbery only but to inhumanity and vile cruelty, his indignation is aroused. Amos makes use of the fire, the tempest, the whirlwind, to set forth the retribution which must overtake the capital of Ammon, its king and princes. But the Lord reigneth over all lands. The violent shall not always prosper. The day shall come when their schemes shall be defeated, and they themselves be laid low in the dust.—T.

Ver. 1.—*The true teacher.* "The words of Amos, who was among the herdmen of Tekoa." In the little village of Tekoa, six miles south of Bethlehem, the young peasant Amos lived. He was a lad of humble birth and lowly occupation. Sometimes he trimmed the sycamore trees, and sometimes drove the cattle to and from their pasture. But he heard the voice of God everywhere, and saw his works in all the scenes around him; for he was devout, and feared the Lord exceedingly. Although he lived in Judah, his heart was stirred with the thought of the sins committed in the neighbouring kingdom of Israel, and of the judgments which would ultimately ensue. It was a time when Israel had every sign of prosperity. The warlike Jeroboam II. was on the throne, and his frequent victories gave his kingdom power, wealth, and security greater than it had before, or would ever have again. Amos, however, as a true "seer," saw under the surface of society. He was not to be diverted from sins and woes at home by dashing enterprises abroad. He knew that the poor were oppressed, that other classes were sinking into luxurious effeminacy, that the worship of Jehovah was ignored; and these and other evils he rightly traced to the idolatry which had its seat in Bethel. Inspired by God to denounce these sins, he visited the towns and villages of Israel, everywhere delivering his message, until he came to Bethel itself, and boldly denounced idolatry in its chosen seat. He was expelled the kingdom by force, in obedience to the order of Jeroboam, who was instigated by Amaziah the high priest. But (as Church history has often shown) the attempt to silence a voice from God made its echoes reverberate through all the ages. Secluded in his little native village, Amos recorded the words which God had given him as a message to his contemporaries, and hence they have come down to us for our instruction. The history of the man and the style of his teaching in themselves teach us important lessons. We are reminded first—

I. THAT GOD OFTEN CHOOSES HIS SERVANTS FROM AMONGST MEN OF LOW ESTATE. We often quote the words (1 Cor. i. 27, 28), "God hath chosen the foolish things of the world to confound the wise; and God hath chosen the weak things of the world to confound the things which are mighty; and base things of the world, and things which are despised, hath God chosen." But we glide over the surface of that assurance without noting, as we should do, its deep significance and profound truth. As a matter of history, however, it is true that the world is most indebted, not to its kings, but to its shepherds, fishermen, and tentmakers. In the stress of poverty and toil, not in the indulgences of luxury, the noblest characters have been formed. It is what a man *is*, and not what a man *has*, that fits him for the service of God. The Church has lost much moral power by ignoring that. No one can visit our places of worship without noticing that members of the artisan class are conspicuous by their absence. Their energy and activity are too often antagonistic to religion. And since they form the basis of society, and it is ultimately their work which makes our wealth, the outlook is sufficiently serious. Doubtless they are to blame, but the Church is to blame also. Abstention from places of worship is often due, in its initial stage, to absence of welcome; to the unexpressed desire, on the part of Christians, to treat certain of their fellow-men as a separate class, which is "to be done good to" with effusive benevolence. Once more let it be true that "the rich and the poor meet together, and the Lord is the Maker of them all," that "the poor have the gospel preached to them," and we shall see a marvellous change. Those who now, when intelligent, are too often cynically sceptical, or, when degraded, are too often sunk low in drunkenness, will become as of yore—amongst the noblest upholders of love, righteousness, and truth.

II. THAT GOD DESIRES HIS SERVANTS TO DO THEIR WORK NATURALLY. Amos drew almost all his illustrations from the natural objects and scenes with which he was familiar in his calling among the herdmen. Perfect naturalness is a source of moral power to any teacher, especially to a teacher of religious truth. Nothing is more offensive in him than pretence, unreality, and affectation. To ape the style of another man, to speak confidently on subjects which have not been personally studied, etc., brings nothing but contempt. Be real and genuine, and thoroughly yourself, wherever you are, but most of all in speaking for God. Amos the herdman would not put on the style of Solomon the king. He was as wise as David was when he put off the armour of Saul because it was untried and therefore unsuitable. The shepherd lad was mightiest with the shepherd's sling and stone.

III. THAT GOD MAKES HIS WORLD TO BE VOCAL WITH TEACHING. The prophecy of Amos is crowded with scenes which the herdman had witnessed. It is worthy of study, if only as a bold picture of the incidents of village life in the East in olden days. Let us trust ourselves to his guidance in imagination. We see the gin set for the bird, and the snare spread for the game. We hear the roar of the lion in the thicket when he has caught his prey, and stand by the fisherman with his hooks, as with skill and patience he plies his craft. We watch the man fleeing from the lion only to meet the bear, and the fugitive bandit hoping for refuge in the caverns of Mount Carmel. We follow Amos to the field. Here the ploughman and vinedresser are busy at work; and there the gardens, cursed with mildew and blasting, bear no fruit. Now we hear the chirp of the grasshopper in the meadow, and now the patter of the rain as it falls after the king's mowings.   In harvest-time, as we walk with Amos, we see the laden cart pressed down with the weight of the sheaves, and hear the thud of the flail as it falls on the threshing-floor, and watch the corn beaten out flung into the sieve, and note that while the chaff is scattered " not the least grain falls upon the earth."   Then in the evening, when the land is quiet, and the heavens are glorious with stars, we hear Amos speak of him who " made the Pleiades and Orion," who makes the day dark with night, and then, in all the splendour of the Oriental dawn, turns the shadow of death into morning.   What an example is he to us!   Let us re-echo the prayer of Keble—

> " Thou, who hast given me eyes to see
>   And love this sight so fair,
> Give me a heart to find out thee,
>   And see thee everywhere."

IV. THAT GOD WOULD HAVE HOLY THOUGHTS ASSOCIATED WITH ORDINARY THINGS. We all know the power of association.   Sometimes we hear a riddle or a joke which presents a text or hymn in a ludicrous aspect.   We never hear the text or the hymn afterwards without being reminded of the grotesque thought.   Hence such " jesting which is not convenient," and which is unhappily a staple ingredient of American humour, should be repressed by thoughtful men.   Our endeavour should be in the opposite direction.   Instead of making sacred things profane, let us rather make profane things sacred, so that the prophecy of Zechariah shall be fulfilled, " In that day there shall be upon the bells of the horses, Holiness unto the Lord; and the pots in the Lord's house shall be like the bowls before the altar."   All things belong to God.   He is present in the fields as well as in his house.   He is near us in our homes as well as in our temples; and the life we live as Christian men has sanctity, whether it be spent in the engagements of business or in the services of the sanctuary. Let us seek grace to follow in the footsteps of Amos, or rather in the footsteps of One infinitely greater than he; and then when we see the sower in the field, or the merchant in his business, when we gaze on the lilies in the garden, or on the tares amid the corn, we shall have sweet thoughts of those higher truths which our Lord has associated with them.   The voice from heaven still says, " What God hath cleansed, that call not thou common."—A. R.

Vers. 3, 6, 9, 11, 13; ch. ii. 1, 4, 6.—*Great sufferings following great sins.*   " For three transgressions of Damascus, and for four, I will not turn away the punishment," etc.   Amos, we are informed, was a native of Tekoah, a small region in the tribe of Judah, about twelve miles south-east of Jerusalem.   Nothing is known of his parents. He evidently belonged to the humbler class of life, and pursued the occupation of the humble shepherd and dresser of sycamore trees.   From his flock he was divinely called to the high office of prophet; and though himself of the tribe of Judah, his mission was to Israel.   He was sent to Bethel, into the kingdom of the ten tribes.   He commenced his ministry in the reign of Uzziah, between B.C. 772 and 746, and therefore laboured about the same time as Hosea.   In his time idolatry, with its concomitant evils and immoralities of every description, reigned with uncontrolled sway amongst the Israelites, and against these evils he hurls his denunciations.   The book has been divided into three or four parts: First, sentences pronounced against the Syrians, the Philistines, the Phoenicians, the Edomites, the Ammonites, the Moabites, the Jews, and the Israelites (ch. i. and ii.).   Second, special discourses delivered against Israel (ch. iii. to vi.).   Third, visions, partly of a consolatory and partly of a comminatory nature, in which reference is had both to the times that were to pass over the ten tribes previous to the coming of the Messiah, and finally to what was to take place under his reign (ch. vii. to ix.).   His style is marked by perspicuity, elegance, energy, and fulness.   His images are mostly original, and taken from the natural scenery with which he was familiar.   We may say that the whole passage, extending from ch. i. 13 to ch. ii. 8, illustrates the three following great truths: 1. The sins of all the people on the earth, whatever the peculiarities of their character or conduct, are under the cognizance of God. 2. That of all the sins of the people, that of persecution is peculiarly abhorrent to the Divine nature. **3.** That these sins expose to suffering not only the actual offenders, but others also. The first and second of these truths we will not here notice; but to the third we must now give a moment's attention. In all the passages to which we have referred at the head of this sketch punishment is the subject. We offer two remarks on this subject.

I. GREAT SINS ENTAIL GREAT SUFFERINGS. The calamities threatened to these different tribes of different lands are of the most terrible description. But they are all such as to match their crimes. **1.** The connection between great sins and great sufferings is *inevitable.* The moral Governor of the world has so arranged matters that every sin brings with it its own punishment, and it is only when the sin is destroyed the suffering ceases. Thank God, this sin can be destroyed through faith in the mediation of him who came to put away sin by faith in the sacrifice of himself. **2.** The connection between great sins and great sufferings is *universal.* All these sinful peoples had to realize it from their own bitter experience. It does not matter where, when, or how a man lives, his sins will find him out.

II. GREAT SINS OFTEN ENTAIL GREAT SUFFERINGS UPON PEOPLE WHO ARE NOT THE ACTUAL OFFENDERS. "The fire," which is here the instrument of God's retribution to us sinners, would not only scathe the persons and consume the property of the *actual* offenders, but others. The fact is patent in all history and in all experience, that men here suffer for the sins of others. We are so rooted together in the great field of life, that if the tares are pulled up the wheat will be injured if not destroyed. The cry of men in all ages has been, "Our fathers have sinned, and we have borne their iniquities." Two facts may reconcile our consciences to this. **1.** *That few, if any, suffer more than their consciences tell them they deserve.* **2.** *That there is to come a period when the whole will appear to be in accord with the justice and goodness of God.*—D. T.

Vers. 3, 6, 9, 11, 13; ch. ii. 1, 4, 6.—*The enormity of the sin of persecution.* "For three transgressions of Damascus, and for four," etc. "They are all charged in general," says an old expositor, "with three transgressions, yea, with four; that is, with many transgressions, as by 'one or two' we mean many; as, in Latin, a man that is very happy is said to be *terque quaterque beatus*—'three and four times happy;' or, 'with three and four,' that is, with seven transgressions—a number of perfection, intimating that they have *filled up the measure of their iniquities,* and are ripe for ruin; or, 'with three' (that is, a variety of sins), and with a *fourth* especially, which is specified concerning each of them, though the other three are not, as Prov. xxx. 15, 18, 21, 29. Where we read of 'three things, yea, four,' generally one seems to be more especially intended" (Henry). Now, the sin especially referred to here as the "fourth" is taken to be that of *persecution,* that is, the sin of inflicting suffering upon others because of their peculiar religious convictions and doings. Other sins innumerable, varied and heinous, they had committed, but this fourth seems to be the crowning of their evil. Persecution has been called the measure-filling sin of any people, the sin that will be taken into account on the last great day. "I was hungry, and ye gave me no meat," etc.

I. PERSECUTION IS A MOST ARROGANT CRIME. The religious persecutor acts upon the assumption that his ideas of religion are absolutely true, that his theological knowledge is the test by which all other opinions are to be tried. Such a man is represented by the apostle as one that "sitteth in the temple of God, showing himself that he is God" (2 Thess. ii. 4). Presumptuous mortal! The proud tyrant who has won his way through seas of blood to the throne, and claims authority over men's bodily movements, shows an arrogance before which servile spirits bow, but from which all thoughtful and noble men recoil with disgust and indignation. But his arrogance is shadowy and harmless compared with the arrogance of him who enters the temple of human conscience, and claims dominion over the moral workings of the soul. Yes, such arrogant men abound in all ages, and are by no means rare even in this age and land of what is called civil and religious liberty. The most arrogant title that mortal man can wear is " Vicar of Christ."

II. PERSECUTION IS A MOST ABSURD CRIME. Far wiser is the fool who would legislate for the winds or the waves, and, like Canute, give commands to the billows.

than he who attempts to legislate for human thoughts and moral convictions. Still more foolish to attempt to crush men's religious beliefs by inflicting civil disabilities or corporeal suffering. In sooth, the way to give life, power, and influence to religious errors is to persecute. And truth never seems to rise in greater power and majesty than under the bloody hand of cruel persecution. It has been well said that "the blood of the martyrs is the seed of the Church."

> "A blameless faith was all the crime the Christian martyr knew;
> And where the crimson current flowed upon that barren sand,
> Up sprang a tree, whose vigorous boughs soon overspread the land;
> O'er distant isles its shadow fell, nor knew its roots decay,
> E'en when the Roman Cæsar's throne and empire passed away."

III. PERSECUTION IS A MOST CRUEL CRIME. What ruthless inhumanities are in these verses charged against the various peoples mentioned—those of Damascus, Gaza, Tyrus, etc.! It has often been observed that no anger is so savage as the anger which springs up between relations of blood. A brotherly hate is the chief of hates; and it may be truly said that there is no animosity that burns with a more hellish heat than that connected with religion. Gibbon, referring to the cruelties inflicted upon the early Christians, says, "They died in torments, and their torments were embittered by insult and derision. Some were nailed on crosses, others sewn up in the skins of wild beasts and exposed to the fury of dogs; others, again, smeared over with combustible material, were used as torches to illuminate the darkness of the night. The gardens of Nero were destined for the melancholy spectacle, which was accompanied by a horse-race and honoured with the presence of the emperor, who mingled with the populace in the dress and attitude of a charioteer."—D. T.

EXPOSITION.

CHAPTER II.

Vers. 1—3.—Judgment on Moab.

Ver. 1.—Moab. The prophet now denounces the other nation connected by ties of blood with Israel (see on ch. i. 13). Moab's hostility had been shown in the hiring of Balaam to curse the Israelites, and in seducing them to idolatry (Numb. xxii.—xxv. 3). He was their oppressor in the time of the Judges (Judg. iii. 12); and David had to take most stringent measures against him (2 Sam. viii. 2). The Moabites joined in a league against Jehoshaphat (2 Chron. xx. 22), and later against Jehoiakim (2 Kings xxiv. 2), and, as we see by the inscription on the Moabite Stone, were always ready to profit by the disasters or weakness of the chosen people. "I erected this stone," says Mesha, "to Chemosh at Kirkha, a stone of salvation, for he saved me from all despoilers, and made me see my desire upon all mine enemies, even upon Omri, King of Israel." And then he goes on to recount his victories. He burned the bones of the King of Edom into lime. This profanation of the corpse of the King of Edom (see 2 Kings xxiii. 16; Jer. viii. 1, 2) is not mentioned in the historical books. Some of the older commentators, as Tirinus and Corn. a Lapide, think that the prophet wishes to show that the sympathy of God extends beyond the covenant people, and

that he punishes wrongs inflicted even on heathen nations. But as in the case of the other nations, Amos reproves only crimes committed against Israel or Judah, so the present outrage must have the same connection. The reference to the King of Moab's sacrifice of "his eldest son," even if we suppose (which is improbable) the son of the King of Edom to be meant, is plainly inapplicable (2 Kings iii. 27), as the offence regarded the king himself, and not his son, and the expression, "burned into lime," can hardly be thought to refer to a human sacrifice. The act mentioned probably occurred during the time that the Edomites joined Jehoram and Jehoshaphat in the league against Mesha, the King of Moab (2 Kings iii. 7, 9), the author of the inscription on the celebrated stone erected by him at Dibon. Unfortunately, the last lines of that inscription, describing the war against the Edomites, are lost. The paragraph that remains is this: "And Chemosh said to me, Go down, make war against Horonaim [*i.e.* the men of Edom], and take . . . Chemosh . . . in my days. Wherefore I made . . . year . . . and I . . ." The Jewish tradition, quoted by Jerome, tells that after this war the Moabites, in revenge for the assistance which the King of Edom had given to the Israelites, dug up and dishonoured his bones. Edom was then in vassalage to Israel, but regained its independence some ten years later (2 Kings viii. 20). The sacrilegious act was meant to redound to the disgrace of Israel.

Ver. 2.—**Kirioth**; *cities*, and so taken as an appellative by the Septuagint translators, τῶν πόλεων αὐτῆς: but it is doubtless a proper name of one of the chief Moabite towns (Jer. xlviii. 24, 41). Keil, after Burckhardt, identifies it with the decayed town of *Kereyat*, or *Korriat*; others, with Ar, or Kir, the old capital (Isa. xv. 1). The plural termination of the word, like Athenæ, Thebæ, etc., may denote a double city—upper and lower, or old and new. **Moab shall die.** The nation is personified. **With tumult**; caused by war (comp. Jer. xlviii. 45, and the prophecy of Balaam, Numb. xxiv. 17). Septuagint, ἐν ἀδυναμίᾳ, "in weakness." **With shouting.** Omitted by the Vulgate (see on ch. i. 14). **Trumpet** (ch. iii. 6; Jer. iv. 19). Trochon cites Virgil, 'Æneid,' ii. 313, "Exoritur clamorque virum clangorque tubarum," "Rises the shout of men and trumpets' blare."

Ver. 3.—**The judge**; *shophet*, probably here a synonym for "king" (comp. Micah v. 1). It implies the chief magistrate, like the Carthaginian *sufes*, which is the same word. There is no ground for deducing, as Hitzig and Ewald do, from the use of this form that Moab had no king at this time. The country was conquered by the Chaldeans, and thenceforward sank into insignificance (Jer. xlviii.; Ezek. xxv. 8—11).

Vers. 4, 5.—§ 2. *Judah is summoned to judgment, the prophet thus passing from alien nations, through the most favoured people, to Israel, the subject of his prophecy.*

Ver. 4.—**They have despised the Law of the Lord.** The other nations are denounced for their offences against God's people; Judah is sentenced for her offences against God himself. The former likewise had offended against the law of conscience, natural religion; the latter against the written Law, revealed religion. By thus denouncing Judah, Amos shows his perfect impartiality. The Law, *Torah*, is the general name for the whole body of precepts and commandments, *chuqqim*, moral and ceremonial. **Their lies**; Vulgate, *idola sua*, which is the sense, though not the translation, of the word. Idols are so called as being nonentities in themselves, and deceiving those who trust in them. "We know," says St. Paul (1 Cor. viii. 4), "that an idol is nothing in the world." The Septuagint gives, τὰ μάταια αὐτῶν ἃ ἐποίησαν, "their vain things which they made." **Their fathers have walked.** This is the usual expression for attachment to idolatrous practices. From this error the Israelites were never weaned till their return from the penal Captivity.

Ver. 5.—The destruction of Jerusalem by the Chaldeans is here briefly foretold (Jer. xvii. 27; Hos. viii. 14; 2 Kings xxv. 9, 10).

Vers. 6—16.—§ 3. *Summons and general denunciation of Israel for injustice, cruelty, incest, luxury, and idolatry.*

Ver. 6.—**They sold the righteous for silver.** The first charge against Israel is perversion of justice. The judges took bribes and condemned the righteous, *i.e.* the man whose cause was good. Pusey thinks that the literal selling of debtors by creditors, contrary to the Law (Exod. xxi. 7; Lev. xxv. 39; Neh. v. 5), is meant (comp. ch. viii. 6 and Matt. xviii. 25). **The needy for a pair of shoes.** For the very smallest bribe they betray the cause of the poor (cómp. Ezek. xiii. 19); though, as sandals were sometimes of very costly materials (Cant. vii. 1; Ezek. xvi. 10; Judith xvi. 9), the expression might mean that they sold justice to obtain an article of luxury. But the form of expression is opposed to this interpretation.

Ver. 7.—**That pant after the dust of the earth on the head of the poor.** This is the second charge—oppression of the poor. The obscure expression in the text is capable of two explanations. Hitzig, Pusey, Trochon, assume that its meaning is that in their avarice and cupidity the usurers or tyrannous rich men grudge even the dust which the poor man strews upon his head in token of his sorrow at being brought to so low a state. But this seems unnatural and farfetched, and scarcely in harmony with the simple style of Amos. The other explanation, supported by Kimchi, Schegg, Keil, and Knabenbauer, is preferable. These oppressors desire eagerly to see the poor crushed to the earth, or so miserable as to scatter dust on their heads (comp. 1 Sam. iv. 12; 2 Sam. i. 2; Job ii. 12). *The poor* (*dal*, not the same word as in ver. 6); *depressed*, as brought low in condition. The Septuagint joins this with the previous clause, "And the poor for sandals, the things that tread on the dust of the earth, and smote on the heads of the needy." The Vulgate gives, *Qui conterunt super pulverem terræ capita pauperum*, "Who bruise the heads of the poor on the dust of the earth." **Turn aside the way of the meek.** They thwart and hinder their path of life, and force them into crooked and evil ways. Or *way*, according to Kimchi, may mean "judicial process," as Prov. xvii. 23. This gives to the clause much the same meaning as ver. 6. *The meek* are those who are lowly and unassuming (see note on Zeph. ii. 3). And a man and his father will go in unto the same maid; LXX., Εἰσεπορεύοντο πρὸς τὴν αὐτὴν παιδίσκην. The Vulgate, which omits "the same," is closer to the Hebrew, *Et filius ac pater ejus ierunt ad puellam*, though the Greek doubtless gives the intended meaning. This sin, which was tantamount to incest, was virtually forbidden (Lev. xviii. 8, 15; xx. 11). Some (as Ewald, Maurer, Gandell) see here an allusion to the organized prostitution in idol-temples (Hos. iv. 14), but this seems unnecessary. To profane my holy Name (Lev. xxii. 32). Such crimes dishonoured the God who called them his people, so that to them could be applied what St. Paul says (Rom. ii. 24), "The Name of God is blasphemed among the Gentiles through you" (comp. Lev. xx. 3; Ezek. xxxvi. 20, 23). The word *lemuan*, "in order that," implies that they committed these sins, not through ignorance, but intentionally, to bring discredit upon the true faith and worship.

Ver. 8.—The prophet condemns the cruel luxury which, contrary to the Law, made the poor debtor's necessities minister to the rich man's pleasures. They lay themselves down upon; Vulgate, *accubuerunt*. Ewald translates, "they cast lots upon;" but the Authorized Version is supported by the highest authorities, and gives the most appropriate meaning. The Septuagint, with which the Syriac partly agrees, refers the clause to the immoralities practised in heathen worship, which the perpetrators desired to screen from observation, Τὰ ἱμάτια αὐτῶν δεσμεύοντες σχοινίοις παραπετάσματα ἐποίουν ἐχόμενα τοῦ θυσιαστηρίου, "Binding their clothes with cords, they made them curtains near the altar." This is far from the intention of the prophet's words. Upon clothes laid to pledge; or, *taken in pledge*. The "clothes" (*begadim*) are the large outer garments which formed poor men's dress by day and cover by night, and which, if pledged, were ordered to be returned by nightfall (Exod. xxii. 26, etc.; Deut. xxiv. 12, etc.). These the hard-hearted usurers kept as their own, and reclined luxuriously upon them at their feasts and carousals in their temples. By every altar. At the sacrificial feasts in the temples at Dan and Bethel. They drink the wine of the condemned; Septuagint, οἶνον ἐκ συκοφαντιῶν. Wine obtained by fines extorted from the oppressed. So it is better to translate, "of such as have been fined." In the house of their god. The true God, whom they worshipped there under the symbol of the calf.

Ver. 9.—God complains of Israel's ingratitude for the favour which he had shown them. And yet I. The personal pronoun has a prominent position, and is continually repeated, to contrast God's faithfulness and the people's unthankfulness. The Amorite (Josh. xxiv. 8, 18). The representative of the seven nations of Canaan who were dispossessed by the Israelites (Gen. xv. 16; Exod. xxiii. 27; xxxiv. 11). The hyperbolical description of this people is taken from Numb. xiii. 32, etc.; Deut. i. 28. Thus is shown Israel's inability to cope with such an enemy, and their entire dependence on the help of the Lord. Fruit . . . roots. Keil explains that the posterity of a nation is regarded as its fruit, and the kernel of the nation out of which it springs as the root, comparing Job xviii. 16; Ezek. xvii. 9; Hos. ix. 16. The expression is equivalent to our "root and branch" (Mal. iv. 1).

Ver. 10.—The deliverance from Egypt and the guidance through the desert, though chronologically first, are mentioned last, as the great and culminating example of the favour and protection of God. First God prepared the land for Israel, and then trained them for possessing it. From the many allusions in this section, we see how familiar Amos and his hearers were with the history and law of the Pentateuch. Led you forty years (Deut. ii. 7; viii. 2—4).

Ver. 11.—Having mentioned two temporal benefits conferred on Israel, the prophet now names two spiritual favours—the presence of holy speakers and holy doers. I raised up. The prophet and the Nazarite were alike miracles of grace. The former gave heavenly teaching, the latter exhibited holiness of life. It was the Lord who gave the prophet power and authority to proclaim his will; it was the Lord who inspired the vow of the Nazarite and enabled him to carry it out in practice. Prophets. To Israel belonged Samuel (1 Sam. i. 1), Ahijah of Shiloh (1 Kings xiv. 2, 4), Jehu, son of Hanani (1 Kings xvi. 7), Elijah and Elisha, Hosea and Jonah. Young men. In the height of their passions, lusty and strong. Nazarites. The law concerning the Nazarites is given in Numb. vi. The special restrictions by which they bound themselves (viz. abstention from strong drink, from the use of the razor, and from all ritual defilement) were the outward signs of inward purity and devotion to God. Their very name implied separation from the world and devotion to God. They were, in fact, the religious of the old Law, analogous to the monks of Christian times. The vow was either temporary or lifelong. Of perpetual Nazarites we have as instances Samson, Samuel, and John the Baptist. Is it not even thus? Is not the existence of prophets and Nazarites among you a proof that you are signally favoured by God, separate from other nations, and bound to be a holy people? Taking the general import of the passage and the signification of the word "Nazarite," the LXX. renders, εἰς ἁγιασμόν, "I took. . . . and of your young men for consecration."

Ver. 12.—**Ye gave the Nazarites wine to drink.** Far from profiting by their example, or acknowledging the grace of God displayed in their holy lives, ye tried to get rid of their testimony by seducing or forcing them to break their vow. **Prophesy not.** Israel was impatient of the continued efforts of the prophets to warn and to win; and, unmindful of the fact that the man of God had a message which he was bound to deliver (comp. Jer. xx. 9; 1 Cor. ix. 16), this ungrateful nation systematically tried to silence the voices which were a standing rebuke to them. Thus Amos himself was treated (ch. vii. 10, etc.). (For proof of this opposition, see 1 Kings xiii. 4; xviii. 10, etc.; xix. 2; xxii. 26, 27; 2 Kings vi. 31; 2 Chron. xxv. 15, 16; and comp. Isa. xxx. 10, etc.; Micah ii. 6; Matt. xxiii. 37.

Vers. 13—16 threaten severe punishment for the sins mentioned above.

Ver. 13.—**Behold, I am pressed under you;** Septuagint, κυλίω ὑποκάτω ὑμῶν, "I roll under you;" Vulgate, *stridebo subter vos*; Syriac, as Anglican; Hitzig, "I make it totter beneath you, as a cart tottereth;" Ewald, Keil, "I will press you down, as the cart presseth;" Baur, Pusey, "I straiten myself under you, as a cart is straitened;" Revised Version, "I will press you in your place, as a cart presseth." The translation of Keil, which is that of Gesenius, is most suitable,

meaning, "I will press you with the full force of war, as a loaded wain presses the earth over which it passes." The sense of the English Version is that God is burdened and wearied with their sins, as Isa. xliii. 24; Mal. ii. 17. The verb, being hiphil, is an objection to this explanation. The comparison of the wain is very natural in the mouth of the shepherd Amos.

Ver. 14.—In this and the two following verses Amos individualizes the "pressure" that awaits them, when every means of resistance and escape shall fail. **The flight shall perish from the swift.** The swift of foot shall have no time or way to flee (Jer. xxv. 35; xlvi. 6). Ewald, Pusey, Gandell, for "flight" render "place of flight, refuge," as Job xi. 20; Ps. cxli. 5; Septuagint, φυγή: Vulgate, *fuga*. **Shall not strengthen his force.** The strong man shall not be able to collect or put forth his strength to any good purpose (comp. Prov. xxiv. 5; Nah. ii. 1). **Neither shall . . . himself.** Some of the Greek manuscripts omit this clause. **Deliver himself** occurs three times —a kind of solemn refrain.

Ver. 15.—**Stand** (Jer. xlvi. 21; Nah. ii. 8). The skilled archer shall not stand firm. **That handleth the bow** (Jer. xlvi. 9).

Ver. 16.—**He that is courageous among the mighty;** literally, *the strong in his heart*; i.e. the bravest hero. The LXX. takes the words differently, Ὁ κραταιὸς οὐ μὴ εὑρήσει τὴν καρδίαν αὐτοῦ ἐν δυναστείαις, "The strong shall not find his heart (confidence) in powers." **Naked.** Casting away heavy garments and weapons and whatever might hinder flight (comp. Mark xiv. 52; John xxi. 7). Virgil, 'Georg.,' i. 299, "Nudus ara, sere nudus."

HOMILETICS.

Vers. 1—3.—*The woe against Moab.* Much that has been said of Ammon applies equally to Moab. The two nations had close relations and affinities, and in Scripture are generally mentioned together. Both were mildly treated by Israel (Deut. ii. 9, 19) as long as such treatment was possible. Yet were they at one in an implacable hatred of her, and a national policy of outrage towards her. A spring raid into Hebrew territory seems to have been an established Moabitish institution (2 Kings xiii. 20, literally, "were wont to come"). Again, Moab adopted the novel and unlikely expedient of employing a prophet of God to curse his own people (Numb. xxiii. 7). Of the comprehensive and thorough character of the national hatred, which these doings reveal, we have evidence in the passage before us.

I. THE NATIONAL HATES OF MOAB WERE DETERMINED BY ITS HATE OF ISRAEL. "It has burned the bones of the King of Edom." The particular occasion referred to here is not known. But the events that led up to it are briefly recorded. Moab was for some time tributary to Israel, and rebelled against it in the reign of Jehoram (2 Kings iii. 1, 4, 5). In the repressive war that followed, Jehoram was joined by the King of Judah and the King of Edom, then probably a tributary of Judah (2 Kings viii. 20). This war, the only one in which Edom and Moab came into conflict, exasperated Moab against it even more fiercely than against Israel itself (2 Kings iii. 26, 27). The horrible sacrifice of the King of Edom's son by the King of Moab, and the subsequent burning of the King of Edom's bones by the Moabites, were both expressions of this wild and savage resentment. Moab's hatred of Edom was hatred of her as Israel's ally, and therefore at bottom was hatred of Israel itself. So the ungodly hate things from the standpoint of their connection with religion. They hate believers for Christ's sake (Matt. x. 22), and the friends of believers for believers' sakes. The compensation for this is that for Christ's sake also Christians love each other and the ungodly as well, and God for his own sake loves them all.

II. MOAB'S WAS A HATE THAT EVEN DEATH COULD NOT APPEASE. This fact illustrates its insatiability. "The soul being after death beyond man's reach, the hatred vented upon his remains is a sort of impotent grasping at eternal vengeance. It wreaks on what it knows to be insensible the hatred with which it would pursue, if it could, the living being who is beyond it" (Pusey). The employment of the burnt bones as lime is a circumstance which, like the ripping of pregnant women by Ammon, reveals the savage debasement of the people, and that contemptuous disregard of the human body which is generated by a career of blood and lust. There is a sacredness about death. It introduces an unseen factor, marks off a territory into which we may not intrude. There is a sacredness, too, about the human body. It is for a temple of the Holy Ghost, and to be treated as holy (1 Cor. vi. 19, 20). Its members are to be members of Christ, and to be treated as consecrated things (1 Cor. vi. 15—18). The best guarantee against intemperance, uncleanness, violence, and every abuse of the body is respect for it as the home and instrument of God.

III. THE CIRCUMSTANCE THAT MAKES MOAB THE ENEMY OF EDOM MAKES GOD HER FRIEND. Edom's alliance with Israel had results in two directions. It embroiled her with Israel's enemies, and commended her to Israel's friends. And primarily it commended her to Israel's God. His favour to his people includes, to certain intents, their friends. Members of the families of Noah and Lot were spared for their fathers' sake. A mixed multitude of foreigners were fed miraculously in the desert, because they were servants to the Israelites. Even the Egyptians were favoured because they for a time had given Israel a home (Deut. xxiii. 7). So with Edom. He was a brother by blood (Deut. xxiii. 7), and had been an ally against Moab, and so his cause is championed by God in this exactly as the cause of Israel is in the other woes. So with more spiritual relations. The virgin-companions of the bride, the Church, are brought, as her companions, to the King (Ps. xlv. 14). The final judgment apart, service rendered to God's people will not go unrewarded (Matt. x. 40—42). No investment brings in surer return than help and kindness shown to the saints of God.

IV. MOAB'S DOOM WAS ONE THAT MATCHED ITS LIFE. "Shall die with tumult." The Moabites were "sons of tumult" (Numb. xxiv. 17; Jer. xlviii. 45), and as in tumult they lived, so in tumult they should die (see Pusey). This is providential, the punishment being made appropriate to the crime. It is also natural, violence provoking violence, and so fixing the character of its own punishment. Moab had probably lost its kings before the prophecy was fulfilled, but the judges and princes who had headed the nation in its violence fitly head it in its destruction also.

Vers. 4, 5.—*The woe against Judah.* In the form of this woe, as compared with those before, is nothing to indicate the difference of underlying principles which it involves. A woe on a Hebrew and a heathen have little in common but the inevitable connection between punishment and sin.

I. THE SINS FOR WHICH GOD VISITS RESPECTIVELY THOSE WHO KNOW HIM AND THOSE WHO KNOW HIM NOT ARE VERY DIFFERENT. The six woes against the heathen are fathered exclusively on their sins against Israel or its friends. This woe against Judah is denounced with exclusive reference to sins against God himself. This is exactly what we might expect. Each is judged out of his own law (Rom. ii. 12). The revelation of God and duty to him was the first great commandment of the Law given to the Jews (Matt. xxii. 37, 38), and for this God reckons with them—first, because it was at once the guiltiest sin, and the sin of which they were oftenest guilty. The law revealed to the heathen made known the existence and many perfections of God (Ps. xix. 1; Rom. i. 20), and threw a side-light on the way to worship him (Acts xvii. 29). But this was not their clearest revelation, and so their sin against it is not the sin that is emphasized. The law written on their heart (Rom. ii. 14, 15)—*i.e.* speaking in reason, conscience, and human feeling—was specially the law of duty to their fellow-creatures; and it is for their sin in this matter specially that God brings them into judgment. It is its blindness, and not its darkness, that is the condemnation of the world (John iii. 19). Where the white ray of revelation focusses, there the red ray of judgment shall fall and burn.

II. CONTEMPT OF LAW AND THE VIOLATION OF LAW INVOLVE EACH OTHER. "Despised the Law of Jehovah, and kept not his commandments." The Law is the abstract thing —God's revealed will as a whole. The commandments are the " particular precepts " (Keil) into which it is broken up. The first, being general, is fitly described as being "despised;" *i.e.* its drift disliked and its authority spurned. The second, being precepts enjoining particular duties, is said with propriety to be disobeyed. The order of enumeration is also the logical and natural order. Action is ever the outcome of sentiment, and its expression. What a man outwardly disobeys he has begun by inwardly despising. And so what he begins by despising he naturally goes on to disobey. It is in the heart that the eggs are hatched which, in a later stage, are the birds of evil-doing. It is, therefore, at the door of his heart that the wise man will mount guard (Prov. iv. 23).

III. ALL TRANSGRESSION IS THE OUTCOME OF IDOLATRY. Their lies led them astray. "By 'lies' here we are to understand idols. And the figure is most appropriate. Amos calls the idols 'lies,' not only as *res quæ fallunt*, but as fabrications and nonentities" (Keil; see 1 Cor. viii. 4). It is this lying character that makes them inevitably the occasion of sin. The first sin was brought about by a lie, in which the truth of God's threat was denied, and so its practical power destroyed. And every idol is just such a lie in embodied form. It is an abrogation of God's authority, a denying of his very existence; and it is a substitution for these of a god and a code congenial to our fallen nature. Under such circumstances violation of God's Law is a foregone conclusion.

IV. THE IDOLS OF THE CHILDREN ARE THE IDOLS OF THE FATHERS. Imitation is easier than invention. Hence Israel, when they first wanted an idol, adopted the calf of Egypt (Exod. xxxii. 4); and Jeroboam, also just left Egypt, set up calf-worship in Dan and Bethel (1 Kings xii. 28). Then, other things being equal, the persons men are most likely to imitate are their fathers, who are their teachers and guides and natural examples. Add to this that national tastes and habits and characters, formed in connection with a particular idol-worship, would be in special harmony with it, and would be transmitted with it from sire to son.

V. SIN INSIDE AND OUTSIDE THE SPIRITUAL CIRCLE IS DEALT WITH ON THE SAME PRINCIPLES. *The manner of the sin was the same* with Judah and the heathen. It was a transgression, or act of disobedience to a known law, as distinguished from a sinful disposition. It was a series of these acts, culminating in a final one of special enormity. "For three transgressions, and for four." *The manner of treatment was the same.* God threatened to strike. Then he lifted his hand for the stroke. Then he withheld it for a time. Then he declared the limit of forbearance was past, and nothing could now prevent the falling of the blow. *The mode of punishment was to be the same.* The agent would be devouring fire. This would fall on the capital. Sin in a visible spiritual relation, and however mixed up with acts of worship, is no whit less guilty. There is only one hell, and all sin alike deserves it, and, unrepented of, must bring to it.

Ver. 4.—*Heredity and the idol-taint.* "And their lies led them astray, after which their fathers walked." Idolatry was Israel's besetting sin. Within two months of their leaving Egypt they fell into it, and, in spite of Divine deterrent measures, they returned to it persistently for nine hundred years. They took to idol-worship, in fact, as "to the manner born." And that the sin was constitutional, and in the grain, is evident from the fact that there was no corresponding secession from idol-worship to the service of the true God (Jer. ii. 11). It was, moreover, the germinal sin. Deranging the primary relation to God, it led to the derangement of all other relations subordinate to this. From it, as a fruitful seed, sprang up in a luxuriant crop the hateful national vices, in which the heathen around were not merely imitated but outdone. And then, as was natural, all the national troubles, including the crowning one of captivity in Babylon, were brought on them by this and its resultant sins, and were designed to be at once its punishment and cure. How near the practice lay to the sources of national corruption and calamity this passage shows. We have here—

I. AN IDOL A LIE. This is a strong figure, and very apt (Jer. xvi. 19, 20; Rom. i. 25). 1. *It is a figment of the imagination.* "An idol is nothing in the world" (1 Cor. viii. 4). It is simply, as the very name implies, the creation of an errant fancy. If we think that to be something which is nothing, we deceive ourselves; and the idol which is the occasion of the deception is an illusion and a lie. There are idols in every human heart. Such are all its passions and lusts (Col. iii. 5; 1 John v. 21). And they are lies. They are conversant with unrealities only. They deceive by false shows and promises. They promise joys that are purely visionary. They afford joys that turn out greatly poorer than they seemed. They refuse to believe in evil consequences that are manifold and inevitable. Every man who has given them entertainment has deceived himself (Rom. vi. 21). 2. *It is the devil's figure-head.* This is Paul's reading of the natural history of an idol (1 Cor. x. 19, 20), and it was that of Moses (Lev. xvii. 7; Deut. xxxii. 17) and Ezra (2 Chron. xi. 15) and David (Ps. cvi. 37) before him. Thus the imaginary god is, after all, a real devil, and therefore doubly a lie; for he "is a liar, and the father of it." He suggests it, and designs it, and works through it, and embodies himself in it, and then crowns all by concealing the fact. The "kingdom of the beast" in prophecy is probably the great idolatrous confederation or false Church in which idolatry is wedded to empire (Dr. Wylie, 'Great Exodus'). So with the spiritual idols of our hearts. They are of the devil (1 John iii. 8), produced by his working (Acts v. 3) and charged with his evil nature (John viii. 44). To serve the flesh in the lusts of it is, in a very literal sense, to serve the devil. 3. *It disappoints all expectations from it.* "Ye are of nothing," says Isaiah, addressing idols, "and your work of nought" (Isa. xli. 24). So we say, "Out of nothing nothing comes." Idol impotence, declared in Scripture (Jer. xiv. 22), and proved by experiment (1 Kings xviii. 24, 29), is a corollary from the very nature of things. So with spiritual idols. Nothing comes out of them to the purpose. Covetousness and concupiscence and frivolity promise happiness, and it never comes, but is wasted by them beyond recovery. And then, instead of happiness, there comes a ruined estate, and shattered health, and blasted hopes, and an accusing conscience, and the first tooth of the worm that never dies.

II. AN IDOL A CORRUPTING LIE. "Caused them to err," or "led them astray." There is a whole philosophy of morals in this statement. 1. *Wrong belief leads to wrong action.* The modern byword that "religion is not a creed, but a life," is cant generally, and a blunder always. Religion is neither a creed nor a life; it is both. "If ye know these things, happy are ye if ye do them." You cannot do them otherwise; and in that case, to know them is useless. It is impossible to steer right with a wrong theory of navigation or with no theory. So a right life is impossible where there is a wrong creed or no creed. A creed is but a formula, of which the intelligent life is the filling up. Belief in idols, or in any ordinance of their worship, is a mistake, and acted on must lead astray. So, too, with the idols of sinful appetites. We expect happiness from serving them, and serve them with that view. What is this but committing sin on principle—wrong practice the inevitable outcome of wrong theory? 2. *Idolatry casts off God, and so all restraints on ill-doing.* Morality has its basis in religion. The standard of it is God's character. The ground of it is God's command. If there is no God there is no duty, as theists understand duty, and men may live as they list. This was what Israel did as soon as they became idolatrous (ver. 7). Idolatry was equivalent with them to a deed of idemnity for sinning. So with the worshippers of idol lusts. The idolatry that makes a god of ourselves makes us also a law to ourselves. 3. *An idol is evil even as a conception, and the worship of it makes the idolater like it.* "Who can bring a clean thing out of an unclean?" The idol invented by corrupt man is a corrupt creation. The gods of Greece and Rome were many of them simply the embodiments of human vices; and as they were models for men to study and imitate, the worship of them made the people like them. We are naturally assimilated to the likeness of the thing we serve, if we serve it truly. Let this warn us to take service only with a pure master.

III. AN IDOL AN HEREDITARY LIE. "After which their fathers walked." Reason suggests and history shows that the idols of the fathers are the idols of the children. 1. *All practices tend to become hereditary.* Children are imitative. They do what they see done. An act repeated becomes a habit, and the habit leading to persistence in the act, presses it on others' attention, and leads to its being imitated. It is thus that the social and religious customs of a community assume an aspect of heredity, and propagate themselves down the generations. 2. *Evil practices do so especially.* (Prov. xxii. 15.) Evil is congenial to human nature, and men will do the thing that is pleasant. Hence evil never dies, whilst good is dying out continually; and evil propagates itself, whilst good can be propagated only by a perpetual exercise of Divine influence. 3. *Family sins are the most surely hereditary of all.* Dispositions run in the blood. The drunkard, the thief, the libertine, each transmits his evil appetite or tendency to his children, and so practically ensures their falling into his sin. There is no reason to except a taste for idol-worship from the operation of this law. In the literal sense it is an appetency easily transmissible. In the spiritual sense it is more easily propagable still. If "the fathers have eaten the sour grapes" of idol-service in any form, "the children's teeth" are more than likely to be "set on edge." 4. *Idol-worship is self-worship in an insidious form, and therefore specially congenial to human nature.* Self is the idol easiest to enthrone. The injunction to love ourselves is not given in Scripture. It is safely and properly assumed, and made the model and measure of our love to others (Matt. xix. 19). Self-love is an affection native to the heart, and that in ideal strength. Now, an idol represented the maker's ideal of himself. It was, therefore, agreeable to his nature, and its service congenial, and so of easy transmission from generation to generation. All sin is really at bottom self-worship. We prefer ourselves to God; our will, our pleasure, our way, to his. We push him off the throne, and ourselves on it, and then do as we list. It is only grace that says, "Lord, what wilt *thou* have me to do?"

Vers. 6—8.—*The woe against Israel.* This is the last woe and the greatest. "The thunder-cloud of God's judgments having passed over all the nations round about, and even discharged the fire from heaven on Judah and Jerusalem, settles at last on Israel" (Pusey). Just as God's honour suffered specially by their sin, so does his heart suffer specially in their punishment. And so, whilst compendious justice may be meted out to heathen nations, the destruction of the chosen people cannot be denounced without regretful enlargement on the circumstances of the case.

I. COVETOUSNESS PUTS A CONTEMPTUOUS ESTIMATE ON HUMAN LIFE. "They sell the righteous for money, and the poor for a pair of shoes." This may be either a commercial or a judicial transaction, but in either case the principle involved is the same. An undue estimate of wrong involves an inadequate estimate of all else. Wealth becomes the one good, and gain the one pursuit. Human life is as nothing in comparison with personal aggrandizement to the extent of even a paltry sum. Officialism, to which the death of a human being is mainly a question of a burial or registration fee, is not an altogether unheard-of thing. This principle has a bearing, not only on murder and the perversion of justice, but on slavery, oppression, the opium and liquor traffics, and every method of making money at the expense of human life or health or well-being. The extent to which such things prevail, and the tens of thousands of human lives annually sacrificed for gain, is a startling commentary on the maxim that "the love of money is a root of all evil."

II. THE DOMINATING VICE OF A COMMUNITY MAKES ALL THE OTHER VICES ITS TRIBUTARIES. Israel's besetting sin as against their fellow-men was covetousness. 1. *This was inhuman.* It bore hardest on the poor. These, being helpless, were its easiest victims. Humanity was put out of the question, and the unspeakably greater suffering involved in making the same gain off the poor, as compared with the rich, was no deterrent whatever. Gain, though it be the very heart's blood of miserable fellow-creatures, was all they had an eye for or a heart to consider. 2. *It was ungodly.* It made special victims of the righteous. This course was partly utilitarian, no doubt. The righteous might be expected to submit to the maximum of wrong with the minimum of retaliation. But it was profane as well. The wicked hate good, and all in whom it is found. "If any man love the world, the love of the Father is not in

him." It was natural, therefore, that a worldly act should assume an ungodly character where opportunity arose. 3. *It was devilish.* "Who pant after the dust of the
earth on the head of the poor." It rejoiced in all the incidental evils which oppression
of the poor involved. When those it impoverished were levelled in the dust of misery
and degradation, this was the sort of thing it panted after. One side of a man's moral
nature cannot become vitiated without affecting the other sides. The vices have an
affinity for one another, and tend to come together in groups. If evil gets in the little
finger of one vice, the intrusion of the whole body is only a question of time.

III. WHEN MEN GET SATED WITH SIMPLE SINS, THEY RESORT TO COMPOUND SINS FOR
A NEW SENSATION. Sin does not satisfy any time, and the longer it is followed up it
satisfies the less. In the commission of it appetite increases, and relish diminishes
pari passu, and so the candle of actual enjoyment is being shortened at both ends.
One device in mitigation of this is to increase the dose, and another to multiply the
ingredients. Reduced to the latter expedient, Israel mixed: 1. *Carousal with uncleanness.* The two things often go together. They are the two chief indulgences craved
for by carnal appetite. The one, moreover, helps to produce the other. A Falstaff
who combines the drunkard with the libertine is the typical debauchee. 3. *Uncleanness with incest.* "A man and his father go to the same girl." This act was
equivalent to incest, which was a capital crime according to the Mosaic code (Lev.
xviii. 7, 15; xx. 11). It outdid the heathen themselves, among whom this crime was
not so much as named (1 Cor. v. 1). An apostate is always the vilest sinner (2 Pet.
ii. 21, 22). 3. *Robbery with all three.* "Stretch themselves upon pawned clothes."
This was robbery in two forms. They retained pawned clothes overnight, contrary to
the Law of Moses (Exod. xxii. 26, 27), and in further violation of it used them to sleep
on (Deut. xxiv. 12, 13). "And drink the wine of the amerced." Again a double
injustice. The fine was unjustly inflicted, and then dishonestly appropriated. 4.
Profanity with the entire troupe. "In order to profane my holy Name." Incest was
the guiltiest, but as a carnal indulgence it had no advantage over any other form of
uncleanness. It must, therefore, have been sought out because of its very horrors, and
with a view to the profanation of God's holy Name, making the "members the members of an harlot." "Before every altar," *i.e.* at Beersheba and Dan, where Jehovah
was worshipped after a fashion (see Keil), and therefore in determinate contempt of
God. "In the house of their God," not the idol-god probably, but the God of Israel.
"In the time of Jeroboam II. there was no heathenish idolatry in the kingdom of the
ten tribes, or at any rate it was not publicly maintained" (Keil). But the sin, though
less complicated, was scarcely less heinous than if idolatry had been a part of it. It
was done of set purpose to dishonour him, and in order to this the place selected for
the commission of it was his house, and the occasion the celebration of his worship.
What a horrible exhibition of extreme and multiplex depravity! "They condensed
sin. By a sort of economy in the toil of sinning they blended many sins in one . . .
and in all the express breach of God's commandments" (Pusey).

Vers. 9—11.—*The manifold mercies of the covenant people.* In striking contrast to
Israel's treatment of God stands out his treatment of them. Mercy rises above mercy,
tier on tier, in a mighty pyramid of blessing. Of these there was—

I. NATIONAL ADOPTION. This is not mentioned, but it is implied, as underlying all
the other favours. God's first step was to make them his people. He loved and
chose them (Deut. x. 15; vii. 7, 8). He separated them from the peoples, and took
them into covenant with himself (Exod. xxxiii. 16; Gen. xvii. 7, 19). That covenant
he sealed (Gen. xvii. 13), and all who observed the seal he styled his own people
(Isa. xliii. 1), lavishing on them in addition many a title of affection. This national
adoption is the fact that subtends the whole line of Israel's national favours.

II. NATIONAL DELIVERANCE. "Brought you up," etc. (ver. 10). This was a
stupendous providence; stupendous in its measures and stupendous in its results, and
therefore of immense moral significance and weight. The mighty forces of nature are
utilized. A haughty heathen nation is brought to its bended knees before the God of
the down-trodden Israel. A rabble becomes an army. Crouching slaves become the
fearless free. And, out of the chaos of despair and death emerges the young world of
a fresh national life. This astounding work was Jehovah's rod to conjure with in the

after-centuries. He makes it the fulcrum on which to rest the lever of resistless motive. His Law, in its moral (Exod. xx. 2), judicial (Deut. xxiv. 18—22; xv. 15), and ceremonial aspects (Deut. xvi. 12), is bespoken a ready and glad obedience in the word, "I am the Lord thy God, which brought thee out of the land of Egypt," etc.

III. NATIONAL PRESERVATION. "And led you forty years." The sustained but quiet miracles of the desert-pilgrimage were a worthy sequence to the prodigies of the Exodus. Divine energies were not exhausted in the thunder-bursts under which Egypt was made to reel. They were but the stormy prelude to the sunshine and soft showers and gentle wooing winds of a long spiritual husbandry. In the manna falling silently, and the mystic guiding pillar, and the Shechinah-glory lighting up the most holy place, Jehovah by a perpetual miracle kept himself before the nation's eye in all providential and saving relations. The resistless Deliverer was the jealous Protector, the bounteous Provider, and the solicitous and tender Friend.

IV. NATIONAL TRIUMPH. "I destroyed the Amorite," etc. The Hebrews had fierce and powerful enemies in all the neighbouring nations. These were generally their superiors in physical strength and courage and the warlike arts. Apart from miraculous help, it is doubtful whether Israel would not have been overmatched by almost any one of them (Exod. xvii. 11; 1 Sam. xvii. 42). Yet the giant races were subdued before them and wasted off the earth. When the grasshopper (Numb. xiii. 33) seizes on the lion's domain there are forces at work that invert the natural order of things. To make the minnows of unwarlike, timid, plodding Israel victorious over the tritons of Anak, the colossal warriors of Hebron (Josh. xi. 21), was a moral miracle, sufficient in itself to carry a nation's faith and a nation's gratitude till the end of time.

V. NATIONAL ENFEOFMENT. "To possess the land of the Amorite." An earthly inheritance was included in the earliest promise to Israel (Gen. xvii. 8). The tradition of this ideal provided home was never lost. In the stubble-fields and by the brick-kilns, where, "like dumb, driven cattle," they toiled throughout the years of their Egyptian bondage, the vision of it came as a ray of comfort lighting the darkest hours. When they marched from Egypt they consciously went to possess their own land, and the long detention in the desert was taken as a tedious but appropriate schooling to prepare them for the coming of age. Palestine, when at last they settled in it, was the very garden of the world, and a home so perfect of its kind as to be made an emblem of the eternal home above. God's standing monument, written over with the story of his goodness, was to every Israelite the teeming, smiling land in which he lived.

VI. NATIONAL EVANGELIZATION. "And I raised up of your sons," etc. The prophet was a characteristic national institution among the Jews. He was a man to whom God made revelations of his will (Numb. xii. 6), and through whom he communicated that will to the people (Heb. i. 1). Of this communication more or less was generally, although not invariably, committed to writing, and embodied in the Scriptures. The prophet did not regularly instruct the people; that was rather the business of the priest. But he did so often, and was besides God's mouthpiece for the communication of new truth, speaking it always according to the analogy of faith (Deut. xiii. 1—5). The permanent establishment thus of a Divine oracle in their midst, giving constant access to the fountain-head of truth, was a notable privilege to Israel. The institution of Nazarites was little less so in another direction. They were consecrated ones, separated from common men and common uses, and devoted in a special manner to God (Numb. vi. 1—21). Such consecration was the ideal human life (John xvii. 19). Therefore what the prophet did for truth in the abstract the Nazarite did for it in the concrete. The one revealed God's will, the other embodied it, or at least its great central principle. Their respective functions were complementary of each other, and between the two the Israelitish nation was "throughly furnished unto good works."

Ver. 12.—" *Children that are corrupters.*" "But ye made the dedicated drink wine; and ye commanded the prophets, saying, Ye shall not prophesy." Action and reaction have a natural connection and a normal relation to each other. In all departments of being they meet and answer, as face answers to face in a glass. The rebound is as the blow, the conviction as the argument, the response as the appeal. The mention of what God had done for Israel brings up the question—How had Israel been affected by it all? Had things occurred in the normal way? Had gratitude waited on blessing in due proportion, and improvement followed privilege? This verse is the disappointing answer. Israel's response to God's appeal, as contained in his gracious dealings, was not the gratitude and fealty due, but unaccountable and aggravated sin. God delivered them from bondage, and they oppressed each other; he defended them against unjust violence, and they wrought injustice. He guided them in their journeys, and they led one another astray. He plied them with evangelizing agencies, and they responded by committing sacrilege and procuring blasphemy. The last is the sin charged against them here.

I. THIS WAS PRIMARILY A SIN AGAINST GOD. The Nazarite and the prophet were both Divine institutions. The vow of the one and the message of the other were alike prescribed by God (Numb. vi. 1; xii. 6). It was his will that they should perform their characteristic acts. In doing so they were but his instruments, accomplishing his purpose toward the nation. Accordingly, Israel's action against them was really against him, against his servants, against his ordinance, against his authority. So with all action against God's people as such. As we deal by them will he regard us as dealing by himself. They are all God's prophets, understanding the mysteries of his kingdom, and "holding forth the Word of life." They are all his dedicated ones, separate from the world, and living, "not to themselves, but to him who died and rose again for them." And whether as the one thing or the other, they are his accredited representatives on earth (Matt. x. 40). Our treatment of them is virtually our treatment of him that sent them (Matt. xxv. 40). A kiss to them reaches the Master's lips; a blow to them touches the apple of his eye.

II. PROXIMATELY THIS WAS A SIN AGAINST MAN. It consisted in compelling the prophet and the Nazarite to disobey God. Now, disobedience is sin, even when committed under pressure. "We ought to obey God rather than men." Men have faced death rather than the guilt of disobedience to known law. And so long as there is any alternative, even death itself, there is no place for disobedience. Israel's was the sin of compelling others to sin. This was soul-murder, and therefore guilt of the darkest dye. Early persecutors sometimes compelled Christians to swallow poison, an infernal device to make them suicides as well as martyrs, and so destroy them soul and body both. So diabolically ingenious was the young persecutor, Saul of Tarsus, that he compelled believers to blaspheme (Acts xxvi. 11); and when recalling the sin of his unconverted life he makes that fact the bitterest count in his self-accusation. Kindred to this was Israel's sin. It was an attempt to compass not men's death alone, but their damnation—a crime to which killing the body is as nothing. And it is not so uncommon in Christian lands and Christian Churches. How many among us are tempters to drunkenness, tempters to uncleanness, tempters to falsehood, tempters to profanity! Well, every tempter is a murderer—a murderer not merely in the ordinary sense, but in the Satanic sense of destroying or trying to destroy an immortal soul.

III. ULTIMATELY IT WAS A SIN AGAINST THE SINNER'S OWN INTERESTS. All sin is unprofitable, but this was doubly so. The prophet brought God's message, not for their destruction, but for their salvation. When they shut his mouth they cut themselves off from their only chance of being saved. "Where no vision is the people perish;" and in deliberately cutting it off, Israel sealed its own destruction. Then the Nazarite was an embodied revelation, a typical representation of a consecrated life. A heedful eye might have read a spiritual lesson out of his separation. "The life of the Nazarites was a continual protest against the self-indulgence and worldliness of the people. . . . It was a life above nature and thought. . . . They were an evidence what all might do and be if they used the grace of God" (Pusey). But, in the compulsory violation of his vow, the rich page was blotched and its lesson blotted out. It presents the piteous sight of a people stopping the fount of life in order that they may die of thirst. Israel would neither listen to the Divine voice nor look at the Divine life. And the sight is not confined to Israel (2 Tim. iv. 3). There are Churches that will not tolerate faithful preaching. There is a preaching that minces the gospel testimony against sin. It is the case of Israel over again. The people sinfully silence the preacher, and the preacher sinfully submits to be silenced. A Church asleep, and the minister rocking the cradle, is a poor interpretation of the pastoral relation.

IV. ALTOGETHER IT WAS A SIN AGGRAVATED BY THE ENJOYMENT OF SPECIAL

MERCIES. All that God had done was a motive to obedience and an argument against sin. But all the arrows of influence fell pointless and broken from their hearts of stone. The more Divine mercies multiplied, the more did abominable wickedness increase. Sin, under such unlikely circumstances, argues special inveteracy, and involves corresponding aggravation of guilt (Rom. ii. 4). With every want supplied and every better feeling appealed to, it was sin not only without temptation, but in spite of strong deterrents, and was therefore hopeless as it was guilty. The love and goodness of God are the most potent persuasives to his service. Where these fail the case is desperate. What mercy cannot bend judgment will only break. If you sin against mercy you can sin eternally. There is no spiritual argument that can make you yield (2 Pet. iii. 15; Rom. ii. 4).

Vers. 13—16.—*The wrath of outraged goodness.* "A wounded spirit who can bear?" Even God will not bear it for evermore. A "base contempt of covenant mercies," exemplified here, may go too far. The limit of intelligent forbearance will be passed, and the pent-up vials of wrath restrained will be poured forth.

I. THE CRUSHER. "Behold, I will press you down as the cart presses that is filled with sheaves" (Keil). This is a strong figure. God, in his retributive action, is compared not only to a cart, but to a heavily loaded one, which crushes all it passes over. His stroke, when it falls, will be heavy in proportion as, in mercy, it has been long suspended. His love had long been spurned, and now at last it is turned into righteous hatred. Unspeakable goodness disregarded persistently will now give place to thick disasters. His power had been insanely dared, and Israel would now discover whether they had an arm like his. "On whomsoever it shall fall, it shall grind him to powder." How indignant love can be that has suffered persistent outrage! How stern goodness becomes when it finds itself thrown away on inappreciation and contempt! How overwhelming Omnipotence is, which nevertheless endures defiance from worms of the dust so long! How terrible God will be as a Foe where he will not be accepted as a Friend (Ps. xviii. 26; Prov. i. 24—28)!

II. THE CRUSHED. These are not the nation in general, but each class in particular —the strong, the courageous, the swift, the fighter, the runner, and the rider alike. None shall escape. God's wrath, like his love, is distinctive—rests not on masses, but on individuals. And, answering to this, the judgments which execute his wrath are elaborated in detail. They are no more necessary than reluctant, no more reluctant than sure, no more sure than thorough.

> "The mills of God grind slowly,
> But they grind exceeding small."

It is noticeable, too, that of those who fall in the sweep of God's sword, it is the best protected who are emphasized. Nothing is said of the weak and timid and slow. Their destruction might be taken for granted. But, lest any should cherish a hope of escape under any circumstances, the persons to whom such hope would be most natural are doomed by name. An occasion of remaining in sin is, with many wicked, the stealthy hope that somehow or other they will escape at last (Isa. xxviii. 15). Perhaps they have no definite expectation, no theory even, on the subject. They know the Word of God to be decisive, and feel the chances are against them. But they cajole the judgment into negligently making the wish the father to the thought, and go down to death the half-conscious victims of a make-believe. The gospel to such wants heralding with a Saviour's warning cry, "How can ye escape the damnation of hell?"

III. THE CRUSHING. A variety of figures combine to illustrate this. 1. *It cannot be resisted.* "The strong one will not fortify his strength," etc. There are no arms we can use against God. They are suited to a material, not a spiritual, foe. There is no strength to be put in competition with his. The bare thought of a struggle is the climax of all absurdity. "Let the potsherds strive with the potsherds of the earth." 2. *It cannot be faced.* "The courageous one among the heroes will flee away." Man has strength, and confidence in it, for a struggle with fellow-man. But his strength leaves him in God's presence (John vii. 44). He cannot even attempt resistance. "He falls at his feet like one dead." 3. *It cannot be escaped.* "The flight will be lost to the swift." To fly from Omnipresence is as inconceivable as to fight against Omnipotence. Darkness cannot hide, nor distance separate, from God. We live in his presence. We sin in his presence. We die in his presence. Even the destruction *from* his presence as gracious (2 Thess. i. 9) is destruction *in* his presence as filling heaven and earth. (1) *Judgment is the obverse of grace.* There are only the two ways of it. There is no compromise between obedience and disobedience (Matt. xii. 30). So there is no *via media* between salvation and destruction. The coin of Scripture truth comes to us with a *nimbus* on the one side and a death's head on the other. We may choose between the two, but one or other we must take (Mark xvi. 16). God will save if he may, but he will destroy if he must. (2) *Grace is the converse of judgment.* Judgment empties the strong of strength. Grace makes the weak to be strong in God. You may have either; and you must have one. Which shall it be?

HOMILIES BY VARIOUS AUTHORS.

Vers. 1—3.—*Moab's brutality avenged.* It is natural for the mind to lay hold upon and to retain in memory some one out of many characteristics of a nation, some one out of many incidents of a war. The one thing that is remembered is representative of many things that are forgotten. So is it with Amos's treatment of the sins of the surrounding nations. Several of these are characterized by some special quality. In the case before us in this passage an incident of malignant brutality is mentioned, not as standing alone, but evidently as a sample of the conduct of which the children of Lot had been guilty, and which was about to bring down upon them the wrath of Heaven.

I. IRREVERENCE AND INSULT OFFERED TO THE DEAD INDICATE A BASE AND ABANDONED DISPOSITION. We know nothing of the circumstance here referred to. The Moabites had made war upon the Edomites; had conquered them, had captured their king, and had slain him, and then consumed his bones with fire. This last action must be judged by the standard of the habits and feelings of the time. In some nations and at some periods cremation has been regarded as an honourable mode of disposing of dead bodies. In the time of the prophet, and among the Hebrews and their neighbours, it was held in detestation. No greater insult, no more horrible evidence of brutality, was possible. The dead are always considered, by civilized and religious communities, as entitled to tender and reverential treatment. Especially those who believe in a future life are bound to support their creed by treating a dead body as something better than a carcase. The instance of irreverence here recorded was aggravated by the fact that it was a king whose body was thus treated. War is in itself bad enough; but savage brutality renders war still worse.

II. DIVINE PROVIDENCE VISITS BRUTALITY WITH APPROPRIATE RETRIBUTION. 1. War, with all its accompanying horrors, is the doom of the savage slaughterers. They that take the sword perish by the sword. The measure they mete is measured to them again. 2. In this retribution the great suffer equally with the multitude. They who insult their neighbours' kings may suffer in the person of their own mighty ones. Fire devours the palaces as well as the cottages, and the judges and princes are cut off and slain along with the meanest of the subjects. The Lord is King and Judge, and he will not allow those nations always to prosper which violate his Law and defy his authority.—T.

Ver. 4.—*The privileged but faithless.* The preceding denunciations refer to the idolatrous nations by whom the chosen people were surrounded. But the impartiality of the prophet is apparent from his condemnation of his own kindred. Amos came from Tekoah, a city of Judah, and, instructed by the righteous Ruler of all, he did not spare his own tribe.

I. THE TRANSGRESSION OF JUDAH WAS AGGRAVATED BY THEIR POSSESSION AND THEIR NEGLECT OF THE DIVINE LAW. From the days of the desert wanderings the Jewish people had enjoyed the unspeakable privilege of possessing the laws of Moses, which were the laws of Jehovah. A treasure of incomparable value should have been highly esteemed and diligently used. That there were those to whom the Law was as "fine gold," as "honey and the honeycomb," cannot be questioned. But the people as a whole were insensible of their privileges, and neglected and abused them; indeed, they are charged with having despised them. The surrounding and heathen nations were not guilty of this heinous offence. Great is the sin of those who have the Word of God, but who treat it with neglect and disdain.

II. THE TRANSGRESSION OF JUDAH WAS AGGRAVATED BY THEIR FAILURE TO PROFIT BY THE LESSON OF WARNING OFFERED IN THE HISTORY OF THEIR FOREFATHERS. The chosen people were taught not only by words, but by facts; not only by the books of Moses, but by the history of their ancestors. How often had the Hebrew people forsaken their God! How grievously had they sinned! And how terribly had they been scourged for their folly! Yet the lesson, emphatic and impressive though it was, was overlooked and unlearnt.

III. THE TRANSGRESSION OF JUDAH WAS AGGRAVATED BY THEIR LAPSE INTO IDOLATRY. The "lies" spoken of by the prophet refer to the deceptive and hideous rites and practices of the heathen. Jehovah was the true God; the "gods of the nations" were but idols, the professions of whose worshippers and priests were delusive and vain. That those who had been trained to idolatry should persevere in it was intelligible; but that Judah should forsake the righteous, pure, and gracious God for the capricious and obscene and ridiculous divinities of the surrounding nations, was monstrous, and only to be accounted for by an awful abandonment to self and sin. The greater the height from which one falls, the deeper is his descent.

IV. THE AGGRAVATED TRANSGRESSION OF JUDAH MET WITH A SEVERE RETRIBUTION. Nebuzaradan and the army of the Chaldees fulfilled this prediction to the letter.—T.

Vers. 6—8.—*A nation's crimes.* The ministry of Amos was mainly to the northern kingdom. With this passage commences the long impeachment and warning which the prophet was inspired to address to Israel. The previous denunciations are pungent, but brief; now Amos puts forth all his strength of invective, reproach, and expostulation.

I. UNGODLINESS IS AT THE ROOT OF A NATION'S MORAL DEBASEMENT. Israel did not, indeed, abjure religion; but Israel abjured God. "The house of *their* god," says the prophet with a quiet irony, referring to the idol-temples which the people had taken to frequenting. The reverence of the supreme Lord of righteousness is the very root of national morality. Let a people worship such deities as were worshipped by Israel's neighbours, the Philistines, the Amorites, the Syrians, and it is well known to what fatal results such worship will surely lead. And let a nation abandon all worship, and live a life of sense, and it is certainly upon the high-road to moral ruin.

II. GREED AND OPPRESSION ARE AMONG THE FRUITS OF NATIONAL UNGODLINESS. In the state of society with which Amos was conversant, these immoral habits displayed themselves in the enslavement of the poor or in their deprivation of the ordinary comforts of life. There was no human law to prevent some of the base transactions mentioned, and all belief in a Divine Law was abandoned. History gives us many proofs of the pernicious effect of secularism and superstition upon human relations. Not only are all restraints, save those of civil law and physical force, spurned and ridiculed; there is no impulse and no motive to a higher than the selfish and animal life.

III. FLAGRANT LICENTIOUSNESS IS ANOTHER FRUIT OF A NATION'S IRRELIGION. The passions which lead to such atrocities as those here mentioned are, no doubt, deep seated in human nature. But religion assists men, not in repressing them wholly, but in controlling and guiding them. It is believed by many that Amos refers to some of the practices which were encouraged by the idolatries to which the Israelites were conforming. Certain it is that infidelity is often associated with the vilest principles of an immoral life, and tends to the letting loose of that wild beast—sensual appetite—which works dire devastation in society.

APPLICATION. These considerations should induce those who prize true religion for themselves to seek its maintenance at home against the assaults of infidelity, and to seek its propagation in lands where its absence is so morally deleterious.—T.

Vers. 9—11.—*A nation's privileges.* The transgressions of Israel were all the more reprehensible because of the peculiar favour which had been shown to the people who were descendants of the father of the faithful and the friend of God. Upon these special privileges the prophet here dwells and expatiates, with a view to bring home to the offenders the magnitude of their sin.

I. A NATION SHOULD TRACE THE HAND OF GOD IN THE DELIVERANCES WROUGHT ON ITS BEHALF. Israel was established in the land of the Canaanites, of whom the Amorites are in this passage taken as the representatives. These foes of the chosen nation are pictured majestic as the cedar and mighty as the oak. Yet Jehovah had smitten them in the lofty branches, and had extirpated them from the roots, and had planted in their stead the vine brought out of Egypt. It was not by Israel's sword or bow, but by the right hand of the Lord, that the Amorites had been vanquished. A devout mind will trace the presence and the action of Divine Providence in a nation's history. In great crises England has been succoured by the interposition of Omnipotence from the assaults of powerful and unpitying foes. The "good hand of our God" has been upon us to protect and to deliver.

II. A NATION SHOULD REMARK THE GUIDANCE OF THE ALL-WISE GOD APPARENT IN THE EVENTS OF ITS POLITICAL LIFE. "I led you:" such is the language in which Jehovah reminded the forgetful and unfaithful Hebrews of his treatment of his chosen. The epoch of wilderness-wandering was the critical epoch of Israel's life; it was then that the nation was consolidated and disciplined. A marvellous story it remains to this day, the story of the forty years in the Peninsula of Sinai. Fraught, too, with encouragement for all who trust God. What Christian nation has not reason to give thanks to "him who led his people through the wilderness: for his mercy endureth for ever"? The eye must be dull which cannot see, the heart must be cold which does not confess, the directing hand of the Eternal in the career of such a nation as our own.

III. A NATION SHOULD GRATEFULLY HONOUR GOD FOR RAISING UP WISE AND HOLY MEN AS NATIONAL TEACHERS AND EXAMPLES. The prophets and Nazarites of the Jews may represent men of sanctified genius and insight, and mental and moral force, whom Providence appoints to be the inspiration of the community towards all that is beautiful and good. A people's greatest strength and most valuable possession must be sought in its finest, purest, ablest *men*. God did much for Israel in the way of outward guidance and interposition; but all his mercies were transcended by the gift of heroes and saints, judges and seers, valiant, true-hearted kings, fearless prophets, faithful priests. Rich as our own country is in many other respects, its true wealth must be sought in its noblest, most unselfish sons. God give us grace to appreciate and to profit by his goodness in this respect!—T.

Ver. 13.—*Men's sins a Divine burden.* The figure of the text is one taken by Amos from his own experience as a husbandman. In the harvest-field the cart is piled high with sheaves to be taken to the garner or the threshing-floor. The wain groans—as poets put it—beneath the load. Even so, it is represented that the sins of Israel oppress Jehovah; he is distressed by their magnitude and their aggravations.

I. LIGHT IS CAST BY THIS LANGUAGE UPON THE CHARACTER OF GOD. 1. His *repugnance* to sin is here brought before us. The deities of the heathen do not seem to have been represented as hating sin, though they were pictured as resenting the neglect of their worshippers. It was otherwise with Jehovah, for he was not an invention of human ignorance and frailty. The Old Testament writers, with one consent, represent the Eternal as holy, and as hating sin as sin. 2. His *distress* at sin is conveyed in this declaration. This is no imperfection. Mere disapproval would have been an imperfection. But it is an encouraging view which we are justified in taking of the Divine character, as we read that God is pained by human iniquity. What an appeal to sinful man is this, "I am pressed under you"!

II. LIGHT IS CAST BY THIS LANGUAGE UPON THE NATURE OF HUMAN SIN. Men's transgressions are not unheeded by God, neither are they a matter of indifference to him. The Supreme Being is not oppressed by the vast care of the material universe. But *sin* is so heinous and awful that it affects his feelings—if we may use language so human. Shall man be careless with regard to that which is so felt by the infinite heart? Of all ills there can be none like this.

III. LIGHT IS CAST BY THIS LANGUAGE UPON THE PROSPECT OF REDEMPTION. This light may be dim, but it is an advance upon darkness. If man's sin is so distressing to God, there is reason to hope that Divine wisdom and grace will concur to provide means for its forgiveness and its cancelling. The feeling which is uttered in the figurative language of the text found full expression in the cross of Christ, in the gospel of salvation.—T.

Vers. 14—16.—*Judgment inevitable.* In the preceding verses there is observable an accumulation of human transgression and iniquity. And in these closing verses of the chapter the reader is equally struck with the rhetorical accumulation of figures intended to convey a deep impression of the inevitableness of retribution.

I. A PICTURE OF HUMAN GREATNESS. Man has his own standard of greatness. The prophet piles up epithets to represent man's power. In vivid colours and in rapid succession there rise before the imagination the figures of the "swift" runner who is wont to overtake his foe, the "strong" hero whose blow cleaves the helmet in twain, the "mighty" whose praise is upon all lips, the "bowman" whose arrow pierces the fugitive in the battle-field, the "swift on foot" who trusts for safety to his speed, the "horseman" whose charge has often broken the doughty ranks of the enemy, the "courageous," "the strong of his heart," whom no danger daunts.

II. A VISION OF INEVITABLE RETRIBUTION AND OF THE DISCOMFITURE OF THE ENEMIES OF GOD. Even such as those who have been described shall be powerless in the day of the Lord. Exemption from the operation of righteous law is not to be obtained by any human craft or might. The swift shall be overtaken, and the arm of the warrior shall fall powerless by his side. Justice must be vindicated; the Lord of right will never abandon his sovereign throne.—T.

Vers. 9—13.—*God and nations.* "Yet destroyed I the Amorite before them, whose height was like the height of the cedars, and he was strong as the oaks; yet I destroyed his fruit from above, and his roots from beneath," etc. These verses suggest a few remarks in relation to God and nations.

I. He reminds nations of the GREATNESS OF HIS KINDNESS TOWARDS THEM. In these verses he reminds Israel of two great merciful interpositions of his on their behalf. (1) The destruction of the Amorite—the original inhabitant of Canaan. Amorite here stands for all the old Canaanites. He drove out the Canaanites that Israel might possess and enjoy the goodly land in which they then lived (Exod. xxiii. 27). (2) Their emancipation from Egypt and their guidance into the Holy Land. "Also I brought you up from Egypt, and led you into the promised land." These two great acts of kindness are mentioned only as specimens of millions of others. The language in which these acts are represented suggest three great truths in relation to God's conduct toward the world. 1. *He often sacrifices one people in order to advance the interests of another.* The old Canaanites he sacrificed for the good of Israel. In the history of the world this is often done; one country ruined for the advantage of another. This is marvellous; it clashes with our primitive ideas of justice and Divine goodness. But we cease to murmur when we remember that there is a great explaining day, and that the peoples that have been ruined for the interests of others have never suffered more from the hands of God than they have justly deserved. 2. *That the mightiest human powers cannot obstruct him in his procedure.* The Amorites, the original inhabitants of Canaan, were a great people. It is said their "height was like the height of cedars," and they were "strong as oaks." They were in the great field of mankind not like the tender sapling or the stunted shrub; they were tall as the cedars and mighty as the oak (Numb. xiii. 32, 33). Then Egypt, too, from which he delivered them, was a mighty power. Pharaoh was the greatest despot of the old world. But what was all this human power before the march of Omnipotence? The mighty Canaanite and the powerful Egyptian were as mere stubble under his feet. God will not be hindered. 3. *That he fulfils his great purposes with nations by the agency of men.* He crushed the Canaanites and he crushed the Egyptians, not by hurling directly from his hand the thunderbolts. No; but by the agency of Joshua and Moses. God works with men by men. By men he blesses and by men he punishes. He allows man to be the devil of man, and he makes man the saviour of man.

II. He reminds nations of THE ABUSE OF THE MERCIES HE HAD CONFERRED ON THEM.

He specifies here two special mercies which he had bestowed upon Israel. 1. *A spiritual ministry.* "And I raised up of your sons for prophets." He gave them men whom he duly qualified to indoctrinate and inspire them with the highest truths of duty and of destiny. The greatest blessing which God bestows upon a people is a *true ministry.* 2. *Virtuous young men.* "Your young men for Nazarites." "These were young men who," to use the language of another, "bound themselves by a vow to God and his service, and, in pursuance of that, denied themselves many of the lawful delights of sense, as drinking wine and eating grapes. There were some of their young men that were in their prime for the enjoyment of the pleasures of this life, and yet voluntarily abridged themselves of them; these God raised up by the power of his grace to be *monuments of his grace,* to his glory, and to be his witnesses against the impieties of that degenerate age." Virtuous and high-minded young men are amongst the chief ornaments and brightest hopes of a people. But how did Israel treat these Divine mercies? "They commanded the prophets, saying, Prophesy not." They did not wish to hear their voices; they closed their ears to their ministry. To a great extent this is the case with our own country now. The great bulk of our people say to the pulpits of England, by their conduct, "Prophesy not;" we do not want your ministry. Sad state this—a state of sin and the precursor of ruin. How did Israel treat these virtuous young men? "They gave the Nazarites wine to drink." They caused them to break their vow. This they did, it may be, by seductive promises, or frightening threats, or abashing ridicule and reproach. A greater crime than the crime of a people endeavouring to make young men drunkards can scarcely be imagined, and this crime England is on all hands earnestly promoting. The multiplication in our midst of beer-houses and gin-palaces, all under the sanction of law, is an insult to Heaven, an outrage on decency, a curse to the country. It behoves every philanthropist to take his stand against this abomination, and to sweep from the earth such huge establishments of the devil as the Burton breweries and the infernal spirit-distilleries, whence streams of poison flow through every grade of social life. "Every inordinate cup is unbless'd, and the ingredient is a devil;" "O thou invisible spirit of wine, if thou hast no name to be known by, let us call thee devil!" (Shakespeare).—D. T.

EXPOSITION.

CHAPTER III.

Ver. 1—ch. vi. 14.—Part II. Three Addresses particularizing the Sins of Israel and announcing Imminent Judgment.

Vers. 1—15.—§ 1. *First address: the prophet begins by showing Israel's ingratitude for past mercies* (vers. 1, 2), *and his own commission to announce the coming judgment* (vers. 3—8). *They have drawn this upon themselves by iniquities which astonish even heathen nations; and they shall be punished by the overthrow of the kingdom and the destruction of their city* (vers. 9—15).

Ver. 1.—The peculiar favour which God has shown the Israelites enhances the guilt of their ingratitude and increases their punishment. **Hear this word.** Each address (ch. iv. 1; v. 1) begins with this solemn call. **O children of Israel.** The summons is addressed to the twelve tribes, as the following words prove; but the succeeding denunciation is confined to Israel,

Judah being only indirectly warned that she may expect a similar fate unless she turns in time. **I brought up from the land of Egypt.** This is mentioned as the crowning act of God's favour (ch. ii. 10).

Ver. 2.—**Have I known;** *i.e.* loved, acknowledged, chosen. So in Hos. xiii. 5 God says, "I knew thee in the wilderness;" and St. Paul (2 Tim. ii. 19), "The Lord knoweth them that are his" (comp. Nah. i. 7). The peculiar relation in which God allowed Israel to stand to him is much dwelt upon (see Deut. iv. 8, 20; xiv. 2; 2 Sam. vii. 23; 1 Chron. xvii. 21). **Therefore I will punish you;** literally, *visit upon you.* They must not presume upon their privileges: the retention of God's favour depended upon obedience to his Word (Exod. xix. 5): the nearer they were brought to God, the greater their guilt if they fell from him. Unlike the nations denounced in the former chapters, Israel had sinned against light and knowledge and love, therefore the sentence on her must be heavier (comp. Ezek. ix. 6; Luke xii. 47; 1 Pet. iv. 17).

Vers. 3—8.—Before announcing more particularly the coming judgment, Amos, by a series of little parables or comparisons, establishes his right to prophesy, and intimates the necessity laid upon him to deliver his message. He illustrates the truths that all effects have causes, and that from the cause you can infer the effect.

Ver. 3.—**Can two walk together except they be agreed?** or, *except they have agreed?* The "two" are God's judgment and the prophet's word. These do, not coincide by mere chance, no more than two persons pursue in company the same end without previous agreement. The prophet announces God's judgment because God has commissioned him; the prophet is of one mind with God, therefore the Lord is with him, and confirms his words. The application of the parables is seen in vers. 7, 8. The Septuagint, reading differently, has, "except they know one another."

Ver. 4.—**Will a lion roar**, etc.? The lion roars when he has his prey in sight, and is about to spring upon it. So God makes the prophet utter his voice because he is ready to execute vengeance. The second clause expresses the same fact in different terms. The young lion (*kephir*) is not a whelp, but one able to provide for itself. He growls over the prey which he has in his lair. So Israel lies helpless as the words of God's threatenings strike upon him.

Ver. 5.—The thought here is that the punishment is deserved as well as certain. A bird is not caught unless a trap is set for it. The trap which the sinner sets for himself is sin. **Can a bird fall in a snare** (*pach*) **upon the earth, where** *no gin* (*moqesh*) **is for him?** *i.e.* is set for him? The "gin" is a net with a stick for a spring, which flew up when touched, carrying part of the net with it, and thus the bird was enclosed and caught (see Kitto, 'Cyclop.,' *s.v.* "Fowling," ii. 36). The LXX. probably read *yoqesh*, as they translate, ἄνευ ἰξευτοῦ, "without a fowler." So the Vulgate, *absque aucupe.* The second clause should be, *Shall a snare* (*pach*) *spring up from the ground without taking anything?* The snare, or trap-stick, would not rise if it had not caught something. The sin is there, and the sinners shall surely not escape. When God appoints retributive punishments for the guilty, and announces the same by his prophets, they may be expected with absolute certainty.

Ver. 6.—The prophet must needs speak: shall not his denunciation arouse alarm among the people, as the trumpet suddenly heard in a city excites the terror of the inhabitants (comp. Ezek. xxxiii. 2—5)? **Shall there be evil in a city, and the Lord hath not done it?** The "evil" is affliction,

calamity, *malum pœnæ.* As states have no future, all temporal calamities in their case may rightly be regarded as the punishment of sin. Thus the ruin impending on Israel was sent by the Lord, whose agent was the enemy now approaching. All phenomena are ascribed in the Bible to Divine operation, no second causes being allowed to interfere with this appropriation (see Job i.; 1 Sam. xviii. 10; 1 Kings xxii. 19, etc.; Isa. xlv. 7). The verb "do" is often used absolutely, the context defining the result (see note on Hag. ii. 4).

Ver. 7.—This and the following verse apply the foregoing parables. All the evils announced come from the Lord; but he brings none of them on the people without first warning by his prophets (comp. John xiii. 19; xiv. 29). **His secret** (*sod*); unrevealed till then. Septuagint, παιδείαν, "instruction;" so the Arabic.

Ver. 8.—As the lion's roar forces every one to fear, so the Divine call of the prophet forces him to speak (Jer. xx. 9; Ezek. ii. 8; 1 Cor. ix. 16, etc.). St. Gregory, moralizing, takes the lion in a spiritual sense: "After the power of his Creator has been made known to him, the strength of his adversary ought not to be concealed from him, in order that he might submit himself the more humbly to his defender, the more accurately he had learned the wickedness of his enemy, and might more ardently seek his Creator, the more terrible he found the enemy to be whom he had to avoid. For it is certain that he who less understands the danger he has escaped, loves his deliverer less; and that he who considers the strength of his adversary to be feeble, regards the solace of his defender as worthless" ('Moral.,' xxxii. 14). Of course, this exposition does not regard the context.

Vers. 9—15.—Having vindicated his own commission, Amos proclaims what God purposes to do unto Israel. He is bidden to summon the heathen Ashdod and Egypt to bear witness to the iniquities of Samaria, which should bring about the overthrow of the kingdom, the destruction of the city with its altars and palaces, and the exile of the people.

Ver. 9.—**Ashdod** (ch. i. 8). God bids the prophets (publish ye) summon the inhabitants of the palaces of Philistia (of which Ashdod is the representative) and Egypt, because they had been the chief enemies of his people, and in their sight had mighty works been wrought for Israel; thus they could appreciate her iniquity and ingratitude. Some, translating *al* "upon," say that the prophets are bidden publish their message upon the flat roofs of the palaces, that it may be heard far and near (comp. 2 Sam. xvi. 22; Matt. x. 27). Keil thinks that not all the inhabitants of the town are summoned, but only those who live in the palaces, who alone "could pronounce a correct sentence as to the mode of life commonly adopted in the palaces of Samaria." But this seems an unnecessary refinement. The Septuagint reads, Ἀναγγείλατε χώραις ἐν Ἀσσυρίοις, "Proclaim ye to the regions among the Assryians," doubtless by some mistake of copyists. Assemble yourselves upon the mountains of Samaria. The city of Samaria was built on a hill which stands alone in the valley or basin, but it is surrounded by higher *mountains*, from whence, though at some distance, spectators could look down into its streets, and, as from the seats in an amphitheatre, behold the iniquities transacted there. Their implacable enemies, the Philistines, and those they were then courting, the Egyptians (Hos. vii. 11; xii. 1), are alike called to witness this spectacle. Tumult; the disorder, where might makes right. LXX., θαυμαστὰ πολλά, "many marvels," as if the sight were a surprise even to the heathen. The oppressed (*ashuqim*); better, *the oppressions*, i.e. of the weak at the hands of the powerful (comp. ch. ii. 6; iv. 1). It was to the eternal disgrace of Israel that there were doings in her cities which the very heathen would condemn.

Ver. 10.—**They know not how to do right.** The Samaritans have lost all sense of justice, the foundation of social life (Jer. v. 22). LXX., Οὐκ ἔγνω ἃ ἔσται ἐναντίον αὐτῆς, "She knew not what things shall be before her." **Store up violence;** *i.e.* the fruits of violence and robbery (ταλαιπωρίαν, "misery," Septuagint), what they had wrung from the poor by oppression and rapine.

Ver. 11.—**An adversary.** The Hebrew is forcible, the Lord speaking as though he saw the foe present: "an enemy and around the land." Ewald and Hitzig take *tsar* as an abstract noun, "distress;" the LXX. and Aquila, pointing it differently, read, Τύρος, but the continuation of the sentence is scarcely to be deemed a translation, κυκλόθεν ἡ γῆ σου ἐρημωθήσεται, "Thy land shall be made desolate round about thee." The adversary meant is Shalmaneser, who attacked Israel more than once and besieged Samaria; or his successor, Sargon, who claims to have reduced the city and removed the inhabitants (2 Kings xvii. and xviii. 9, etc.; see Introduction to Micah). **Thy strength.** All wherein thou trustedst shall be brought down to the ground (Obad. 3). Palaces, in which were stored the fruits of injustice and rapine (ver. 10).

Ver. 12.—The prophet shows that the chastisement is inevitable, and that only the smallest remnant, the most worthless among the inhabitants, and they with much difficulty, can escape. The illustration from a common incident in a shepherd's life is very natural in Amos. **Taketh;** better, *rescueth.* So below, shall be taken out; *shall be rescued.* The usual explanation is that a shepherd attacks the lion which has seized one of his sheep (comp. 1 Sam. xvii. 34, etc.), and rescues from it the most worthless parts—"a couple of shank-bones or a bit, or tip, of an ear." But as an attack on a lion would be an abnormal act of courage on the part of a shepherd, and the comparison is with things likely and usual, it is probable that the meaning is that the shepherd finds only these poor remnants after the lion has left his prey. So such a poor remnant shall be rescued from the ten tribes of Israel. **That dwell in Samaria in the corner of a bed; that sit at ease,** lounging in the cosiest corner of the divan, an image of indolent ease and careless security in the face of impending judgment. **And in Damascus in a couch;** LXX., καὶ ἐν Δαμασκῷ: Vulgate, *et in Damasci grabato.* The Syriac and Jewish Versions agree in considering the word "Damascus" to be a proper name. The other modern rendering takes it to mean the material which we call "damask," or something similar. Hence our Revised Version gives, "on the silken cushions of a bed;" and others, "on the damask of a couch." Dr. Pusey retains the old rendering, on the grounds that there is no evidence to prove that the manufactures for which Damascus was celebrated in aftertime existed at this period, its exports being then wine and white wool (Ezek. xxvii. 18), and that the Arabic word *dimaso* (which critics have cited as connected with the term "damask") has nothing to do with Damascus, and meant "raw," not manufactured, "silk." He translates, "in Damascus, a couch," and explains this to mean that Damascus, which Jeroboam II. had won for Israel (2 Kings xiv. 28), "was a canopied couch to them, in which they stayed themselves." This agrees with the ancient Jewish interpretation, which explains the clause to mean that the Israelites would some day depend for help on the Syrians represented by Damascus. A third exposition, favoured by the Latin Vulgate, makes the words to mean, "on a couch of Damascus;" *i.e.* a Syrian couch of a costly and luxurious nature. This comes to the same as the modern rendering given above and seems to be the easiest explanation of the expression. The difficulty depends chiefly on the punctuation of the word דמשק; or there may be some corruption in the text. What the LXX. meant by their rendering is proble-

matical, Κατέναντι τῆς φυλῆς καὶ ἐν Δαμασκῷ,
"The children of Israel who dwell in
Samaria in the presence of the tribe and in
Damascus."

Ver. 13. — **Hear ye**; Septuagint, Ἱερεῖς
ἀκούσατε, "Hear, O ye priests." The address
is to the heathen, already summoned (ver.
9) to witness the sins of Israel, and now
called to witness her punishment. In the
house; better, *against the house of Jacob*,
the tribes of Israel (ver. 1). **God of hosts.**
God of the powers of heaven and earth, and
therefore able to execute his threats. Septuagint, ὁ Παντοκράτωρ, "the Almighty."

Ver. 14.—**That in the day**, etc. This
verse is rightly joined to the preceding, as
it particularizes the threats which the
heathen are summoned to testify. **Visit
upon**; equivalent to "punish" (Zeph. i. 8).
Altars of Bethel. We read of one altar
being set up by Jeroboam I. (1 Kings xii.
29, 33), but doubtless others had been
added in the course of time. The denunciation of 1 Kings xiii. 2, 3 is here repeated.
The horns of the altar. These were certain
projections at the four angles of the altar,
perhaps in the form of an ox's horn, on
which the blood of the sin offering was
smeared, and which therefore were considered the holiest part of the altar (see
Exod. xxvii. 2; xxix. 12; Lev. xvi. 18).
The instruments of idolatry or impure worship should share the destruction of the
idolaters.

Ver. 15.—**The winter house.** The luxurious habits of kings and princes had led them
to have different houses for the various
seasons of the year, facing north or south
as the case might be (comp. Judg. iii. 20;
Jer. xxxvi. 22). Septuagint, τὸν οἶκον τὸν
περίπτερον, "the turreted house," which
Jerome explains, *Domum pinnatam, eo quod
ostiola habeat per fenestras, et quasi pinnas,
ad magnitudinem frigoris depellendam.*
Houses of ivory; panelled or inlaid with
ivory, such as Ahab had (1 Kings xxii. 39).
Solomon's throne was thus decorated (1
Kings x. 18; comp. Ps. xlv. 8). (For the
Assyrian practice of veneering in ivory, see
Rawlinson, 'Ancient Monarchies,' i. 463;
comp. also Homer, 'Od.,' iv. 73; Virgil,
'Æneid,' vi. 895.) **The great houses**; better,
many houses; Septuagint, ἕτεροι οἶκοι πολλοί,
"many other houses." Not only palaces,
but many private houses, shall be destroyed
(comp. Isa. v. 9, where the same words are
used).

HOMILETICS.

Vers. 1, 2.—*The judgment of apostates a foregone conclusion.* This chapter, like
ch. v. and vi., opens with a call to attention. God is going to speak, and his voice is
worth listening to. He is going to speak a word, moreover, the issues of which are
capital. To attend to his communication is as vitally important as dutiful.

I. GOD, WHO HAD ONLY SPOKEN ABOUT THE HEATHEN, SPEAKS TO ISRAEL. Syria and
Edom and Tyre may never have heard of the doom to which they were going down.
Their first intimation of the tempest of Divine wrath was likely the falling of the first
drops. Their chance of repentance and escape was in this way minimized. Left in
ignorance of the danger of advance, there was little likelihood of their turning back of
their own accord. But Israel hears from inspired lips that never lied the guilt of her
sin, and its inevitable end. This putting of "prophecy between his secret and its
execution" is a special favour on God's side, and a corresponding advantage on her
side, whilst, like all advantage, it involves a proportionate responsibility.

II. GOD'S SPECIAL REGARD FOR ISRAEL HAD EXPRESSED ITSELF IN PECULIAR FAVOURS.
1. *He had constituted them a family by themselves.* Other nations in their rise had
been left to circumstances and the play of natural affinities. Israel had been called
out of the peoples, constituted a nation by itself, furnished with a national organization
and policy, and set consciously to work out an exalted destiny. This was fitted to
awake a lofty national aspiration, and give direction and dignity to the national life.
The choosing of God's people out of the world is the beginning of his favours. 2. *He
had brought them out of Egypt.* This was an act of Divine power, an instance of
Divine championship, an expression of Divine distinguishing favour, and a beginning
of Divine help, which contained in it the promise of more to come. Conversion,
following on election (Acts xiii. 48), is another privilege of God's people, and another
spur to grateful service. 3. *He had taken them into intimate personal relations.*
"Known," etc. This is "practically equivalent to electing, including both the motive
and result of election" (Keil). God took special notice of them, set them in a gracious
relation to himself, acknowledged them to be his people, and brought to bear on them
the influences that are ever coming forth on those in covenant with him.

III. Judgment is inevitable where mercy has been received in vain. "Therefore will I visit," etc. (ver. 2). Mercy extended is made here the ground of judgment denounced. Each gift bestowed in the past is a count in the present indictment. 1. *It is inevitable as punishment.* Sin by God's professing people is specially heinous. It involves ingratitude to a special Benefactor, insensibility to his love, contempt of his gifts, and disregard of special claims on their allegiance. The guilt is in every aspect extreme, and so the punishment is sure. 2. *It is inevitable as testimony.* God's honour is closely identified with his people's conduct, which must therefore be closely looked after. Any sin in it must be rigidly punished if God would vindicate his purity and impartiality, hating sin as such, and wherever it appears. "It is necessary that God should vindicate his own honour by making it appear that he hates sin, and hates it most in those that are nearest him" (M. Henry). 3. *It is inevitable as discipline.* Judgments are corrective as well as punitive. In this aspect they are sure, and will be severe in proportion to the love and mercy despised. Whom God leaves without correction he bastardizes (Heb. xii. 8), but he expresses fatherly interest in the application of the rod. Judgment with Israel was just a change of corrective treatment. Mercy had failed, and now love would try another way, that nothing might be left undone to separate Israel from sin. This is why judgment begins at the house of God.

Vers. 3—8.—*No smoke without fire.* God cannot utter empty threats. His every declaration is *bona fides.* When he roars he is about to rend. Let, then, the doomed sinner tremble. For all his insensibility he is no better than a dead man.

I. Sin involves disconnection from a holy God. "Can two walk together," etc. ? This deep principle involves that: 1. *Israel, quarrelling with God, cannot reckon on his company.* For so far God had associated with them. In Egypt, in the wilderness, in Canaan, he had vouchsafed them close companionship. But their rebellious attitude against him, approaching as it was a climax of irreconcilableness, must make a continuance of intimate relations impossible. 2. *The prophet, walking as he did with God, must be regarded as in agreement with him, and so expressing his will.* Amos spoke as God's servant and mouthpiece. He looked at Israel's sin from God's standpoint. In reference to it he was as emphatically associated with God as he was dissociated from them. Underlying this formal association it must be believed there was real agreement. "He whom God hath sent speaketh the words of God."

II. When the thunder of God's threatenings is heard, the lightning of his judgments is imminent. That peril is sure and near is taught in a series of similes of a graphic kind. 1. *When God utters his war-cry it is evident that he is just about to strike his enemy.* (Ver. 4.) The lion roars when he has marked his prey, and is about to spring. God sees the sinful nation ripe for judgment. He sees that the time for sending it has come. His roar out of Zion (ch. i. 2) is, therefore, the prelude to striking his prey forthwith. "The threatenings of the Word and providence of God are not bugbears to frighten children and fools, but are certain inferences from the sin of man and certain presages of the judgments of God" (M. Henry). 2. *When God reaches forth his hand there is something to take, and within his reach.* (Ver. 5.) It is the lighting of the bird on the trap that snaps it. If there were no trap laid no bird would be caught. If there were no bird in the trap it would not rise from the ground. Israel is the bird, and God is the Fowler, and his judgment is the snare, and the lesson of all is that she is already in God's destroying grasp. 3. *When some are already alarmed it shows that danger to all is real and close.* (Ver. 6, "Is a trumpet blown," etc.?) The prophet, who knew what was coming, was alarmed, and those like-minded with him. The note of alarm was already ringing over the land. Signs of evil will not show themselves until the evil is comparatively at hand. So surely as the smoke rises the fire is kindling. 4. *When misfortune falls it is a proof that God has been at work.* "Does misfortune happen in the city," etc.? (ver. 6). "All things are of God," is an axiom that in one sense or other covers all events, whether good or bad. The qualification of it is that the sin of any of them is exclusively of man. God "creates evil" (Isa. xlv. 7)—the evil of suffering—whilst the evil of sin he allows us to create, that he may bring out of it greater good.

III. God warns his prophets of evil before it comes. (Ver. 7.) The prophet is a negotiator, hearing the truth from God, and handing it on to men. God does not destroy men unwarned, nor warn them but through his accredited messengers. The history of his judgments illustrates this. Through Noah he revealed the coming deluge, through Lot the destruction of Sodom, through Joseph the famine in Egypt, through Moses the Egyptian plagues, through Jonah the sentence on Nineveh, and through Christ and his apostles the destruction of Jerusalem. "Thus God has ever warned the world of coming judgments in order that it may not incur them" (Lange). "He foretelleth the evil to come that he may not be compelled to inflict it" (Pusey).

IV. GOD'S TRUE PROPHETS CANNOT BUT SPEAK HIS MESSAGE. (Ver. 8.) It is his will that they should prophesy. He tells them his purposes mainly with a view to this. To prophesy is their function and duty, and is made their business. They are moved at the sight of coming evil. They are in sympathy with the Divine compassion, giving a last chance to the doomed; and so, like the apostles, they "cannot but speak the things they have seen and heard" (1 Cor. ix. 16, 17; Acts iv. 19, 20). "Moses was not excused though slow of speech, nor Isaiah though of polluted lips, nor Jeremiah because he was a child. Ezekiel was bidden 'be not rebellious like that rebellious house;' and when Jeremiah would keep silence he saith, 'His Word was in mine heart as a burning fire, shut up in my bones, and I was weary with forbearing, and I could not stay'" (Pusey). Taken in connection, vers. 7 and 8 reveal a perfect arrangement for making known God's purpose in reference to sin. God anticipates action by a communication to his prophets, and the prophets execute orders, and hand the communication on.

Ver. 2.—*The inevitable punishment of Christian sin.* "You only have I known of all the families of the earth, therefore I will punish you for all your iniquities." These words are at once an accusation, a condemnation, and a sentence. What God had done for Israel in vain was a ground and the measure of what he now must do against them. Blessing abused is but the faggot feeding the fire of merited curse. They had given themselves up to wickedness, and the fire-tongue of a lofty privilege sits above every sin, revealing its demon-face.

I. THERE IS A GRACIOUS SENSE IN WHICH GOD KNOWS MEN. "I know my sheep;" "I never knew you." These sentences mean salvation and condemnation respectively. For God to know men is with them a question of life and death. This knowledge may be: 1. *National.* It was so with Israel. "You only have I known." This meant that God loved them (Deut. x. 15), chose them (Deut. vii. 6), formally acknowledged them as his people (Deut. xiv. 2), and gave them privileges—not necessarily saving in every case—of light (Ps. cxlvii. 19; Rom. iii. 2), and help (Ps. cxxxvi. 10—24), and fellowship (Exod. xx. 24; Numb. xiv. 14; Deut. iv. 7), and promise (Rom. ix. 4, 5), answering to this visible relation. This knowledge may also be: 2. *Personal.* Then it means, in addition to what has been mentioned, the forth-putting of Divine energy in them, making them new creatures in Christ, and so "partakers of the Divine nature" (Gal. vi. 15; 2 Pet. i. 4). God brings them into his family (Gal. iii. 26) by this spiritual birth (John i. 13), calls them sons (1 John iii. 1), makes them co-heirs with Christ (Rom. viii. 17), and gives them all family privileges and graces, chiefest of these the spirit of adoption, by which we cry, "Abba, Father" (Gal. iv. 6). Man, in fact, is by nature an alien and a stranger, and for God to know him is to substitute a gracious for his natural relation.

II. THIS KNOWLEDGE IS A SPECIAL, NOT A GENERAL, AFFECTION. "You only." There are gifts of God that are indiscriminate (Job xxv. 3; Matt. v. 45). Man gets them as man, and irrespective of personal character. But spiritual gifts are necessarily confined to the spiritual circle. It is evident as regards God's gracious knowledge of men. 1. *That it rests on a minority of the race.* Israel at best was little among the nations of the earth. In comparison with the Chaldean, Medo-Persian, Greek, or Roman empires, it was scarcely worthy of being named; and a dozen peoples bordered Palestine from time to time, any one of which, in the natural course, would have wiped it off the earth. Yet, passing by the many and the mighty, God says to single, feeble Israel, "You only have I known of all the families of the earth" (Deut. iv. 32—38). And this action is of a piece with other Divine action for similar purposes. The saints are now, and have always been, a "little flock." It is the few who go in at the "strait gate" of the kingdom. Even the nominally Christian peoples are less than a third of the population of the earth. If out of the number of these were taken the actual Christians, the true believers in Christ, the saintly company would assume smaller dimensions still. This state of matters will no doubt be reversed before the dispensation ends. Christ "in all things shall have the pre-eminence," and the minority which his followers compose will, during the millennial era, be converted into a vast majority (Isa. xi. 9). Meantime God looks on a small circle of transfigured souls, and says, "You only have I known." 2. *It does not follow human probabilities.* If any single nation was to be made the repository of revealed truth, and the teacher of the other nations, we should have expected one or other of the four universal empires to be chosen for the purpose, rather than a second or third rate power, located in a circumscribed and excentric spot. Then the typical Jew was, like his ancestor Jacob, a sordid fellow, deficient in the more heroic qualities, and, from the standpoint of the natural, decidedly inferior to his brother the Edomite, or almost any neighbour you would select. The greater readiness with which the Gentiles received the gospel, when it came to them, would seem, moreover, to indicate that they would have responded more worthily to the Divine Old Testament culture than Israel did, if it had pleased God to bring it to bear. It is the same with individuals. Not only does God pass by the rich and great for the humble poor (Jas. ii. 5; 1 Cor. i. 26—28), but he passes by the wise and prudent, and gives the light of his salvation to babes (Matt. xi. 25). It is not the great geniuses of society, but the commonplace average men, who form the circle of the saints. The reasons for this are adequate, but God keeps them to himself. Obvious to reason in many cases, they are not revealed, because in many others they would be above it, and God acts without reasons given, that "no flesh may glory in his presence."

III. It does not inevitably prevent sin in the object of it. The life of the Hebrews was as a whole above the moral level of the heathen life around them. But still it was far from pure. If we subtracted from Jewish history all that arises out of sin, and the punishment of it, comparatively little would remain. So little congenial to human nature is God's service, and so congenial the service of sin, that Israel was perpetually turning aside after the idols of the heathen, whilst in no instance did the heathen ever turn from their idols to God (Jer. ii. 11). And not only does outward religious privilege fail to put an end to the sinful life, it is to some extent the same with inward religious principle. The saint remains a sinner all his days. Grace, like the house of David, is getting stronger with him, and corruption, like the house of Saul, is getting weaker through life. But it is still with him as with the apostle, striving after perfection, yet burdened with a feeling of the surviving power of sin (Phil. iii. 12; Rom. vii. 24).

IV. It does make the punishment of sin on earth certain. "Therefore will I punish you." Sin inside the kingdom necessitates punishment, and will be visited with it promptly. 1. *Because it is guiltiest as against God.* More has been done to prevent it than in other cases. It is sin against light (Jas. iv. 17; Luke xii. 47, 48), against love (2 Cor. v. 14), against favours (Ps. ciii. 2), against restraining grace (1 John iii. 9). In proportion to the strength and number of deterrent influences against which sin is committed must be the strength of our sinful bent, and so the guilt of our wrong-doing. 2. *Because it is most hurtful as against his cause.* The sin of the wicked is natural. It is to be expected from one who consults lust, and serves the devil. It is done, moreover, from the standpoint of opposition to God, and responsibility for it is thus kept outside the spiritual circle. God and his cause are not dishonoured in the eyes of men by what is formally done against them. It is sin by the professedly righteous that brings righteousness into disrepute. Religion is charged with all the evil that is done in its name. The more closely identified wrong-doing is with the Christian name, the more hurtful is it to the Christian cause. Therefore Christian sin, in addition to the general reasons, involves punishment for reasons peculiar to itself. If God would have his Church a tree for the healing of the nations, he must lop off every unsound and rotten branch. 3. *Because it is most incompatible with the destiny of the person sinning.* The sin of the wicked need not necessarily be punished here. It will be amply visited on him throughout eternity. It is quite in the line of the man's life-course that he should suffer the vengeance of eternal fire. But the sin of the righteous presents a different aspect. Its commission is the contradiction of his gracious nature, and its future punishment would be the contradiction of his exalted destiny. It is vital to his well-being that the judgment, inevitable somewhere, should fall here (Ps. lxxxix. 30—33). Only thus can his happy immortality be safeguarded. The present destruction of his flesh conditions the saving of his spirit in the day of the Lord Jesus (1 Cor. v. 5).

Ver. 3.—*Communion and concord inseparable.* " Do two walk together unless they have agreed?" The special reference of this general question is not apparent. But the scope of the context suggests two points on either or both of which it would throw light. The one is the prophet's claim to be speaking the truth, the other is the people's claim to be doing the right. Between his words and their works there was utter incompatibility. Those must be wrong if these were right, and *vice versâ.* And the axiom quoted supplies a decisive test. Amos walked with God—there could be no denying that; took his side and sought his glory amidst prevailing defection and disobedience. Must it not be argued from this that he was at one with God, and so in all his utterances spoke agreeably to his will? Israel, on the other hand, had clearly not agreed with God, for they were red-handed in rebellion against him. Was not the inference from this resistless that they could not walk with him, here by faith or hereafter by sight? Consider here—

I. THE WALKING WITH GOD THAT IS THE IDEAL OF HUMAN LIFE. " Enoch walked with God." That is a short biography. But there is more in it, more important in its character and more adequately expressed than in many an octavo volume. " They shall walk with me in white " is a summary of the joy and glory of redeemed spirits on high. And life below is ideal in proportion as it approximates the life above. To walk with God implies: 1. *That we walk with the same purpose as God.* The *raison d'être* of things is God's glory first (Rom. xi. 36; Col. i. 16), the good of his people next (2 Cor. iv. 15; Rom. viii. 28), then the happiness of the race (1 Tim. iv. 10; Gal. vi. 10), and ultimately the well-being of the planet as a whole (Ps. xxxvi. 6; Rom. viii. 20, 21). The attainment of these objects in this order is God's purpose as revealed in Scripture. With this purpose it is the design and nature of religion to make man at one. By creating him in God's image he is endowed with a spiritual nature which exalts God (1 Cor. x. 31), loves the brethren (1 John iii. 4), consults the interests of others (Phil. ii. 4), and regards the life even of the beasts (Prov. ii. 10). In proportion as the godly endorse and homologate the Divine purpose thus are they in the image of Christ (John xii. 28; xiii. 1, etc.) and do they walk with God. 2. *That we walk like God.* " The Christian," says Joseph Cook, " is a man who has changed eyes with God." Subtle affinities have arisen involving a marvellous unity of thought and aim. The end of our walking is God's end, and naturally his way becomes our way. " The secret of the Lord is with them that fear him." In Christ, " the Image of the invisible God," it became an open secret to all who believe. He has left " us an example," and there are no relations in life to which it does not apply. We " follow his steps," and by consequence walk like God, being " imitators of him as dear children." 3. *That we walk in company with God.* The ungodly are far from God, and of set purpose keep their distance. But faith brings near and keeps near his side. The humble, contrite heart, which is the home of faith, is also the temple of God (Isa. lvii. 15). The love by which faith works is his welcome and feast (Rev. iii. 20). The believer lives in God's presence. He walks by faith, holding on as it were by the Divine hand. It is the promise and the thought of God's presence with him that makes the journey light (Isa. xliii. 2), whilst the reality of it is the guarantee of safety and ease. God with us, we have unfailing provision, unerring guidance, and an invincible escort. No marvel if they who thus travel " go from strength to strength."

II. THE AGREEMENT WITH GOD THAT IS THE CONDITION OF WALKING WITH HIM. Walking with God is not an occasional act, but a habit of life, and must arise out of an established relation. 1. *The parties must both be willing.* Men are naturally at enmity with God, and so averse to his company. They know not and desire not to know his ways, and the expression of this feeling is the " Depart from us!" in which they decline the establishment of spiritual relations (Job xxi. 14). The operation of grace, however, is one " to will and to do of God's good pleasure," and the result of it is " a willing people in the day of God's power." They choose God (Josh. xxiv. 15), desire his fellowship, and adopt the course that will best consist with its enjoyment. 2. *They must have arranged it.* "Unless they have agreed." Spiritual relations are not accidental relations, nor such as men may drift into unconsciously. There are understood objects to be intelligently adopted. There are explicit terms (Matt. xvi. 24) to be deliberately accepted. There is a distinct transaction in which God and his way are adopted, and made our life-King and life-programme respectively (Hos. xiv. 2). If it be a question of faith, we say, " Lord, I believe." If it be a question of penitence, we say, "I abhor myself, and repent." If it be a question of allegiance, we declare, "I will be for the Lord." If it be a question of fellowship, we vow, "I will walk before the Lord in the land of the living." Our walking with God is not only with consent, but by arrangement, duly and solemnly subscribed. 3. *They must be congenial spirits.* Like draws to like. Companionship with God bases itself in conformity to him. If there be no affinity there will be no association. If this fails, association will be broken off. Duty must be our choice, or it will never be begun ; and our joy, or it will never be continued. Walking with God implies a previous coming to him, and both are conditioned by a spiritual change creating us in the Divine image. Hearts have begun to beat in unison when hands are clasped for life.

III. THE BEARING OF THIS MAXIM ON THE CASE IN HAND. The two whose walking together is in question are Jehovah and the prophet, according to some ; Jehovah and the nation, according to others. But as it is a general maxim, it may be legitimately applied to both, and every other case on which it can throw light. 1. *The words of a teacher who walks with God will be on the whole agreeable to his will.* The authenticity of Amos's message was called in question by many. But he was on God's side in this controversy with Israel. He spoke as it were out of the arms of the Divine fellowship. The truth of his deliverance was therefore a foregone conclusion. With every religious teacher the same principle holds. Communion with God gives insight into truth attainable in no other way. It conditions that "unction from the Holy One" by which "we know all things." The best guarantee of orthodoxy is to be spiritually minded. "The anointing" by Christ in the work of grace, among other benefits, " teacheth of all things, and is truth" (1 John ii. 27). Let a man read the Bible, so to speak, over God's shoulder, and the thing he will read out of it will be truth. 2. *A life of rebellion cannot possibly be a walk with God.* The prophet foretold to Israel a final rupture of visible covenant relations. And the prophecy was along the lines of natural fitness. The parties were already alienated in heart and sympathy, and in the nature of things formal separation must follow. To walk with God whilst fighting with him was an unworkable arrangement. The men who try it are men whose religious life is failure. When hearts go apart their owners go after them ; and the soul, loveless to-day, will be godless to-morrow. Sinful man will have it so, and a holy God can have it no otherwise. Alienation leads to apostasy, and the apostate is *ipso facto* an outlaw. Are our affections given to Christ in self-surrender and love and happy trust ? It is the one condition of walking with him to any purpose of spiritual effect. Is the dedication made maintained in unswerving true allegiance ? See to that, for the beginning of estrangement is as the letting out of water, and what is deflection now will be defection in the next stage.

Ver. 6.—*Calamity one of the works of God.* It is not sin, but suffering, that is here meant. We are to regard temporal calamities as the warning voice of God, a manifestation of his character, and a corrective expression of his displeasure. God maintains his controversy with Israel. The verses before contain language of unimpeachable equity, ill-requited kindness, and injured honour. On every ground the threatened punishment was merited, and only in mercy had it been suspended so long. There is a natural atheism in the human heart, a constantly prevailing tendency to forget God. This tendency is most powerful in prosperity, and must often be counterworked by a dispensation of adversity. Not that Divine judgments, acting on human corruption, necessarily lead to repentance. But in God's hand they have often been overruled to this effect, and it is in this reclaiming and reforming capacity that they are alluded to in this text.

1. WE DISTINGUISH THE AGENCY OF JEHOVAH FROM CHANCE. "Chance" is a word much used, and little understood. When we say that an event has happened by

chance, we mean either that it had no cause, which is atheism, or that we do not know the cause, which is an abuse of language. Chance, in fact, is nothing but a term of human ignorance. Yet the use of the word implies either atheism, denying the Divine existence, or naturalism, denying his superintending agency; the two coming to the same thing, for we might as well have no God as no providence. The sentiment of our text is the refutation of both, and as such is but the echo of all Scripture. "All things are of God." Not creation only, but providence, which is as wonderful as a continuous creation. Not great events only, but the very least, without any one of which the whole machinery would be incapable of a single revolution. How beautifully yet powerfully is this brought out by Christ in his illustration from the sparrows (Matt. x. 29—31)! If a sparrow cannot fall to the ground without our Father, much less can a whole city. When evil is in a city, it is not a visitation of chance, but of the hand of God, under which it has come.

II. THE DIVINE AGENCY IS HERE DISTINGUISHED FROM THAT OF IDOLS. Something to worship is a necessity of human nature. Hence men, when they forsake the true God, set up a false one in his place. The existence and power of this idol they believe without proof, and even against presumption. Unconquerable incredulity in reference to the true God becomes irrational credulity in reference to the false ones. Thus atheism is more a question of the heart than of the head. Men do not like to retain God in their knowledge (Rom. i. 23, 28), and so discard him for gods of their own devising. This fact shows polytheism a form of atheism. And it was demonstrably so with the Jews. The obverse of apostasy with them was always idolatry; and this text affirms that Jehovah, whom they had forsaken, not any senseless idol which they had chosen, dominated history and sent good and evil to men (see Isa. xli. 21—24; Jer. x. 3—16). We think we are in no danger of making their mistake. But the world, in its ambition, avarice, or pleasure, may take away our hearts from God, and become their idol, climbing to his throne. And we give it credit often for what God does and alone can do, and to that extent misread the providential events in which God is dealing with us.

III. DIVINE AGENCY IS TO BE DISTINGUISHED FROM THE AGENCY OF SECOND CAUSES. The deification of nature is a common practice. Conventionally, nature is a kind of mystical personification of some unknown existence, and to which the omnipotence denied to God is freely attributed. If "nature" does a thing, it is assumed that God has no hand in it, and that it wants no explanation further. "Nature is that created realm of being or substance which has an acting, a going on or process from within itself, under and by its own laws" (Bushnell). But these laws are just "the actuating power of God." They are not powers in themselves, but only the rules according to which his power operates. We have various kinds of seasons which we trace to various causes in nature. But these are second causes, and under the sovereign control of the First Cause. "Can the heavens give showers? art not thou he, O Lord our God?... for thou hast made all these things" (Jer. xiv. 22). Air, earth, and sea, and all that they contain, are subject to him (Ps. civ. 4; cxlviii. 8). From the natural cause of this or that we must rise to him who makes it what and puts it where it is, and gives it a commission to work. "All things are of God."

> "This truth philosophy, though eagle-eyed
> In nature's tendencies, oft o'erlooks;
> And having found his instrument, forgets
> Or disregards, or, more presumptuous still,
> Denies the Power that wields it."

The same principle rules events in which men are agents. "Men are in God's hand" as well as matter. The King of Assyria was simply the rod with which God struck Israel (Isa. x. 5—16). *In attributing temporal evils to God's sovereign control of things, distinguish between sovereignty and caprice.* What God does he could assign the best of reasons for. He exercises his sovereignty in declining to do so. But he tells us that the great general cause of suffering is sin. Evil does not come on us as creatures, but as sinners. The infliction of it has not to do with sovereignty, but with equity. All good is from God, all evil from the sinner. All good is gratuitous, all evil is deserved. All evil is righteous retribution, all good is free and sovereign love. Nor is suffering destitute of a large benevolent element. On the contrary, it often serves a merciful purpose, and would always do so were it properly received. When the sun of prosperity fails to soften, God casts men into the furnace of trial, if perchance the stronger method may prevail. If there be evil in your city, then consider who sends it, on what account, and for what purpose; so, it may be, you will "turn to him that smiteth you," as he means you should. (From a sermon by Ralph Wardlaw, D.D., supplemented and condensed.)

Ver. 7.—*The hounds that bay before they bite.* The prophet speaks here as if he were announcing axiomatic truth. And it is nothing less. It might be argued from reason; it is historic fact; and it is a prominent Scripture doctrine.

I. JUDGMENT NEVER COMES WITHOUT WARNING. The Deluge, the destruction of Sodom, the plagues of Egypt, and the fall of Jerusalem, are cases in point. Sometimes judgment has taken people unawares (Matt. xxiv. 39), but this is because the warning has been disregarded (Gen. xix. 14; vi. 3). When there has been no warning the judgment has been provoked, not by a course of wickedness, but by a single flagrant transgression in connection with which warning was out of the question (Exod. xxxii. 27, 28; Numb. xxvi. 10; Acts xii. 23). The warning of coming judgment is: 1. *A disclosure of sin.* To allow men to sin unheeded, and to find it satisfactory, would be to amnesty evil-doing and practically to encourage it. To erect the gallows of impending judgment, on the other hand, brings into sight the fact of sin, and emphasizes its demerit. Next to execution, the sentence of death is a revelation to the criminal of the enormity of his crime. It is a mental association of guilt with penalty, and so a measuring of its moral proportions. It is also: 2. *A deterrent from sin.* Judgment executed without warning loses half its value. The fear of the rod is a wholesome restraint on the folly of the child; greater often than the actual blow, because it operates through a longer period. God's moral government in its relation to sin aims at cure rather than mere punishment, at prevention rather than either. His blows fall only after his threats have failed to move (Prov. i. 24, etc.; Jer. vi. 10, 11). Accordingly: 3. *To denounce judgment sometimes makes it unnecessary to inflict it.* A notable instance was that of Nineveh. If her repentance were more common, her escape would be more common also (Matt. xii. 41). God frights with the thunder of his threats, that he may not be compelled to smite with the lightning of his judgments. He makes a display of his resistless forces that the rebels may yield without going into action. "Turn ye, turn ye: why will ye die?" that is the message of his open preparations to destroy.

II. THIS WARNING REACHES MEN THROUGH THE PROPHETS. On his way to the establishment of personal relations, God always treats with men through mediators. Covenants are made with representatives, such as Adam, Noah, Abraham, and Christ. Justifying righteousness is negotiated typically through a priesthood, and antitypically through Jesus Christ. So saving knowledge is negotiated through the Holy Ghost, and by the instrumentality of inspired men. 1. *This was the only feasible way.* Not every man is fit to receive a revelation direct from God. To do so implies mental and moral conditions that are realized in but a small percentage of men. His revelation must reach many through a third party in any case. If the worse qualified must be spoken to through the better qualified, it is only carrying out the principle to speak to both through the best qualified of all, *i.e.* the prophet selected by God himself. The Scripture is God's revelation, and adequate to man's need (2 Tim. iii. 15—17). The attempt to substitute for it an "inner light," or any other device, is to substitute our own nonentity for God's reality. 2. *It tends to call faith into action.* God wants his Word believed. And he wants it believed in a certain way and on certain grounds. To believe what we see is not the faith he wants (John xx. 29), nor properly faith at all. "Blessed are they who have not seen, and yet have believed." Only such believing is intelligent or voluntary, and therefore possessed of moral qualities. If God revealed his will directly to each individual, bearing it in resistlessly on his consciousness, the moral discipline involved in faith would be lost to men. 3. *It secures a record of God's message for universal use.* A revelation given to men individually would be only for the individual, and for the time then being. It would neither be common property nor permanent property. And it is worth being made both. God's way is one in all ages. He is in the same mind about sin, and deals with it on the same principles always. The record of what he has done is the prophecy of what in similar circumstances he will do. The prophet wrote so much of his message as had permanent interest, and the aggregate of such inspired deliverances is the Scripture, which is "a light in a dark place until the day dawn." It is not a revelation for an individual merely. Having served its turn with one, it is no less available for others in endless succession.

III. GOD'S PROPHETS ARE FIRST OF ALL HIS SERVANTS. "His servants the prophets." The explanatory words, "his servants," widen greatly the sentiment of the clause. 1. *To prophesy under Divine direction is itself an act of service.* There is a wide sense in which all are God's servants who carry out any of his purposes. Thus Cyrus and Nebuchadnezzar (Isa. xlv. 1; Jer. xxv. 9) are styled respectively the "anointed" and the "servant" of God, because they were designated to and did a work for him. This was a purely external relation, but it was real. All the prophets, even the wicked Balaam, were God's servants in this sense. They represented his interest. They went his errand. They carried his message. They laboured to accomplish his purpose. Their exercise of the prophetic office was service. 2. *Official relations have their basis in personal relations.* Shepherds and sheep alike come into the fold by the Door, Jesus Christ (John x. 1—14). All come in to the effect of their own salvation first, and being in fall into rank as gatherers-in of others. First faith, and then works, is thus the spiritual order; faith establishing personal relations with Christ, and work, among other things, trying to get others to do likewise. Hence Church officers are to be chosen out of the number of Church members. The conditions of spiritual work are spiritual gifts, and the condition of spiritual gifts is to be in the spiritual connection (John xiv. 6; Eph. ii. 18).

Vers. 9—12.—*The prophet gets his heavy commission.* It is Jehovah that speaks. He addresses the prophets (Keil), or the heathen (Lange), or the heathen through the prophets. The passage is a summons to the nations to appear as witnesses of Israel's flagrant sin, and her dreadful punishment. There are many articles in her predicted woe. Not least of these is condemnation by the heathen, who for less heinous sins were to be themselves destroyed. When a professed follower of God apostatizes in such a fashion that even God's enemies cry shame, and endures a corresponding punishment in their sight, the cup of his iniquity and of his retribution are both full.

I. THE CRIME CHARGED. There are many counts in this grave indictment. 1. *The confusion of sordid money-seeking.* "See the great confusions in the midst thereof." The restlessness of greed, the fever of speculation, the wrangling of barter, and the tumult of audacious extortion are all included here. The mingling of excitement, disorder, and noise in a struggle for money, suggest a scene in which little is left to fancy with one who has been "on 'Change." 2. *The oppression of power without principle.* "And the oppressed in the heart thereof." From fraud to oppression is but a single step, and a short one. It is simply a question of power. The swindler would steal if he could. The thief would rob with violence if he dare. When dishonesty, moreover, prevails in private life, a system of public plunder is only a question of opportunity. 3. *Wrong-doing till the way to do right had been forgotten.* "They know not to do right." "In the nature of things every sin against light draws blood on the spiritual retina" (Joseph Cook). Men are both hardened and blinded by a course of sin. Evil actions repeated become habits, and evil habits indulged in work themselves into the very texture of the soul. The wrong of ill-doing soon ceases to be felt, which naturally leads to its ceasing to be seen (Jer. iv. 22; cf. Rom. xvi. 19). When we can sin without conscience, we are very near to sinning without consciousness. The way to preserve a good conscience, a conscience that knows evil and condemns it, is to respect its least dictate. "Sow an act, and you reap a habit; sow a habit, and you reap a character; sow a character, and you reap a destiny." 4. *Putting by plunder in store.* "Who store up violence and devastation in their palaces." Plunder has not even the poor excuse of need. It is practised gratuitously, as without limit. The poor were fleeced and impoverished, that the sordid rich might heap up enormous and superfluous stores. And by the terms there was stored up not only the spoil of violence, but violence itself. *Pari passu,* with the accumulation of ill-gotten gain was the heaping up of the sin of their unrighteous getting, whilst in heaping up sin they were necessarily treasuring up wrath (Rom. ii. 5).

II. THE WITNESSES SUMMONED. "Assemble upon the mountains," etc. A reference to the topography of Samaria brings out the graphic fitness of the language here. The city was built on a hill, surrounded and overlooked by mountains higher than itself, and from the tops of which the nations could look down into the very streets, and observe the daily doings of the inhabitants. As regards these we notice: 1. *Abandonment in sin is a sight for a man's worst enemy to see.* The certainty, severity, and nearness of avenging judgment makes sin, from even the low utilitarian standpoint, the greatest possible evil. The enemy, who rejoices in our ill, can find no such occasion of malignant joy as our giving ourselves up to sin. After the fact that it offends God, the strongest argument against sin is the fact, the obverse of the other, that it pleases the devil and wicked men. 2. *When men lose the sense of sin, God appeals to their sense of shame.* It is strange that the sense of shame should survive the sense of sin, but so it is. We fear men more than God. We are not ashamed to do what we would be very much ashamed to acknowledge. The poet's sarcasm is just, that in the matter of sin our care is "not to leave undone, but keep unknown." The bitterness of punishment is greatly aggravated by its being inflicted in the presence of an exulting enemy. Philistia and Egypt were, moreover, the enemies whose cognizance of their way and end Israel would most feel and fear (2 Sam. i. 20). To this last shred of feeling on which a motive could lay hold Jehovah here appeals. They would be a gazing-stock to their bitterest enemies. "Like the woman set in the midst amid one encircling sea of accusing, insulting faces, with none to pity, none to intercede, none to show mercy to them who had showed no mercy. Faint image of the shame of that day when not men's deeds only, but the secrets of all hearts, shall be revealed, and they shall begin 'to say to the mountains, Fall on us, and to the hills, Cover us'" (Pusey). 3. *The pupil in the art of ill-doing often outdoes the master.* It is assumed that even Egypt and Philistia would be shocked at the sight of the wrong-doing of apostate Israel, and so become witnesses against them. Yet Egypt had taught them "oppression," and Philistia had given them many a lesson in "violence and devastation." The art of wrong-doing advances with rapid strides as it is handed on. The son of the "smart" trader is a swindler, the son of the swindler is the burglar, the son of the burglar is the robber-assassin. The pupil of the religious liberal is the rationalist, and the pupil of the rationalist is the atheist. Begin by imitating wicked men, and you will end by outstripping them in sin.

III. THE SENTENCE PRONOUNCED. This is at once heavy in its nature and explicit in its details. We see here that: 1. *When God's judgments come against a man they surround him.* (Ver. 11, "An enemy, and that round about the land.") The impossibility of escaping when God attacks is axiomatic. Punishment is in such a way interwoven with sin that they cannot be dissociated. When we sin against God we sin against the nature of things. Physical, mental, and social law jump each with moral law, are broken in the breach of it, and so are each of them a channel to guide to us the full flood of retribution. "Though hand join in hand, yet shall not the wicked go unpunished." 2. *When God strikes a sinner he strikes him on the seat of his sin.* "And he shall bring down," etc. (ver. 11); "That dwell in Samaria," etc. (ver. 12). The strong had oppressed and pillaged the weak, and God's hand would fall on their strength. In the palaces the spoil of violence had been heaped up, and the palaces should be the special prey of the plunderer. The beds and couches which had ministered to their sinful indulgence would be carried away to the last stick. It is so always. The punishment of drunkenness, uncleanness, pride, theft, lying, comes in many ways, but in every case pre-eminently through the lust or appetite involved. This is according to natural laws, but is none the less the arrangement of God. He has put latent in every power a mystic spark, which, if the power be abused, becomes a retributive fire to burn the breaker of his Law. 3. *When sin is adequately punished the sinner's well-being is practically destroyed.* "Delivers out of the mouth of the lion two shin-bones and an ear-lappet," etc. (ver. 12). These are paltry leavings, not worth the rescue. And such, and so insignificant, would be the surviving good of Israel, when God's controversy was settled. Where the scythe of God's judgment has passed there is little left for the gleaner. The detected thief, the broken-down sensualist, the besotted drunkard, what is each but a human wreck? The kernel of life is wasted, and only a husk remains. No wallflower of good can ever grow to cover these wrecks of time.

Vers. 13—15.—*The residue of Israel's woe.* Those who had been called to witness the sin of Israel are now summoned to hear and report her sentence. In connection with this we see that—

I. EVEN HEATHENS CAN TESTIFY AGAINST APOSTATE ISRAEL IN THE JUDGMENT. To testify is not merely to convey intelligence; it contains in it the idea of protest, *i.e.* testifying against. 1. *The heathen had a natural sense of right and wrong.* Paul says they "show the work of the law written in their hearts," and "are a law unto themselves." A rule of duty is included in the constitution of their nature. They know right from wrong, and are governed by a sense of obligation. They could, therefore, judge the conduct of Israel. They could see and testify that it did not come up to even their own imperfect standard of right. 2. *They had been truer to their standard of right than Israel had.* Paul tells us that the heathen had not been true to their light (Rom. i. 21—28), and that the punishment of that was diminished light. But they had been truer, on the whole, than Israel had been to hers. Their morality was not so far below Israel's as their inferior light would lead us to expect. Hence the assumption that they would be shocked at Israel's manifold corruptions. Moral deterioration is measured, not so much by the absolute amount and kind of wrong-doing as by the extent to which it falls below the known standard of right. Other things being equal, he is relatively the best man who most closely follows his light (John iii. 19; Rom. ii. 14). 2. *They would learn something for themselves from this witness-bearing.* Discrimination would see that Israel's sin was not a result, but the contradiction, of the national religion; that it was an evil result of heathen influence, and involving the heathen more or less in its guilt; that Israel's God was a God that judgeth righteously, and taketh vengeance on evil-doers; and that judgment, beginning at God's chosen people, would not miss his open enemies. The very act of testifying against Israel, moreover, would involve such an exercise of the moral sense, in reference to their sin, as could not fail to be beneficial.

II. SIN IS PUNISHED BY BEING RETURNED ON THE SINNER'S HEAD. "When I visit Israel's transgression upon him." The sin not only leads to the punishment, but as it were re-embodies itself in it. 1. *The memory of it haunts him.* When sin is done it is not done with. Like the dead bird around the Ancient Mariner's neck, an avenging Providence ties the memory of it to our soul. Like the crime of Eugene Aram, it becomes an evil-haunting memory, to dog our steps for ever.

> ' And still no peace for the restless clay
>   Will wave or mould allow;
> The horrid thing pursues my soul—
>   It stands before me now."
>
>   (Hood.)

2. *The permanent evil consequences of it keep it before the memory.* The sins of youth are the sowing of which the sufferings of manhood and age are the harvest—a harvest too constantly and painfully reaped to allow the harvester to forget. The sins of one man are the fruitful source of the sins and sorrows of many, and find in each of these a mentor who makes it impossible to forget. In addition to the sinner and the sinned against, wrong-doing injures those whose well-being depends on either. It is thus a poison-tree that forks and branches in the bearing of its deadly fruit. While the evil consequences of his wrong-doing are around him, and propagating themselves in everwidening circles, the sinner apart from conscience cannot get his iniquities out of sight. 3. *Not seldom the punishment is a resurrection of the sin itself.* Laban's trick on Jacob was a repetition of Jacob's trick on Isaac (Gen. xxix. 23; xxvii. 15—27). The deaths of Haman and Jezebel were similarly adjusted punishments. So with the cutting off the thumbs and great toes of the arch-mutilator Adoni-bezek (Judg. i. 6, 7). In such cases the sin is palpably returned in retribution on the sinner's head.

III. IDOL-WORSHIP IS A SIMULATION OF THE WORSHIP OF GOD. "The altars of Bethel, and the horns of the altar." Both in the use of an altar and in the form of the altar used the idol-worship set up by Jeroboam was a plagiarism from the worship of Jehovah. 1. *Man cannot create in religion, but he can adapt.* He can form no idea of spiritual things apart from Divine revelation (1 Cor. ii. 9). At the same time, God's revelation of spiritual things is too pure for his taste. The result is that he compromises the matter by adopting ready-made ordinances, and loading them with his own corrupt spirit and meaning. 2. *Idolatrous worship seems less of an apostasy in proportion as it retains the forms of true worship.* The devil lets man down into idolatry as into other sin by easy stages. First he parts with the spirit of true worship, whilst retaining the form. Then he parts with the object of it, corrupting the form. Then he adopts a new object, and adapts to its worship the already corrupted form. And so with all sin, which is spiritual idolatry. Man does not first abandon the forms of godliness, and then the practice of it. He gives up the substance of it as a matter of taste, and tries to salve his conscience for this by adhering to its forms (2 Tim. iii. 5). 3. *This also makes it more plausible and insidious.* The worship set up in Dan and Bethel by Jeroboam was not idol-worship pure and simple. It was the worship of God by means of idols, and in forms which mimicked the worship at Jerusalem. Heresy at the outset always masquerades in the guise of truth. By adopting the sheep's clothing the wolf gets easy access to the fold. It is only after he has entered, and the danger of eviction is over, that his true character is assumed.

IV. ONE IDOL BREEDS MANY. "The altars of Bethel." There was but one sacrificial altar in connection with the worship of Jehovah, but when many gods were invented, many altars were provided to correspond to them. This multiplication of idols is accounted for by the fact that: 1. *Evil naturally spreads.* One sin leads to more. Covetousness leads to theft, drunkenness to uncleanness, all three often to murder, and almost every sin to deceit and lying. No man can set up one sinful idol and say he will have no more. It will bring others with it whether he will or no. It is the first swallow of the summer of evil-doing, and heralds a coming flock. 2. *Idolatry must become polytheism in the attempt to meet the spiritual wants of men.* God is an infinite Being, and so can meet our human necessity all round. But an idol is the creation of a finite mind, and so a finite thing. It is to meet one need of our nature, the need that was uppermost in the consciousness of the inventor. But a different need will be uppermost in another worshipper, and a different idol will be wanted to meet his case. Accordingly, in the mythology were many gods, who distributed among them the various functions necessary to complete the circle of human good. It was, in fact, an attempt, by multiplying deities indefinitely, to provide a substitute for the infinite God of revelation. 3. *A worship that is all error is more logical than one that is half truth.* Everything has its own proper form. You do not find an eagle in the form of a dove, nor an apple in the form of a plum, nor an evil principle in the form of a good one. If such a form is artificially put round it, the result is a palpable misfit. Polytheism is the nearest approach to logical idolatry, and in proportion as it is self-consistent is dangerous, and wins its way.

V. THE FIRST THING JUDGMENT DOES AGAINST THE IDOLATER IS TO DEPRIVE HIM OF HIS GODS. "The horns of the altar shall be cut off," etc. This would put an effectual stop to the idol-worship. We thus see that: 1. *God wants his judgments to be recognized.* He never punishes men *incognito.* When he puts forth his power he wants men to see that it is his (Exod. vii. 5; 1 Kings xx. 28; Ezek. vi. 7), and striking the very seat of sin inflicts a stroke at once significant and effectual, a revelation at once of the Divine hand and power. 2. *He wants them to be effective.* The moral effect of a judgment depends very much on our knowing whence it comes. If we recognize it as sent by God, it is tenfold more impressive. Now, to exercise the maximum of beneficial influence with the minimum of afflictive visitation is ever God's way (Lam. iii. 32, 33). He does not strike an aimless or a needless blow. Each stroke is meant to tell, and the medicine of affliction is stopped the moment the patient is cured. 3. *Idolatry is at the root of all other sin.* It is the complement of atheism, which is radically the heart departing from God. It is a sublimated self-worship, making an idol of our own mental creation. A god dethroned, and a self enthroned, is a state of things which "contains the promise and potency" of all evil. To strike at Israel's idolatry was to lay the axe to the root of the national evil. The idols abolished, and God restored to the national heart, its life would be again a consecrated one.

VI. MAN'S SELF-INDULGENCE, THE DEAREST IDOL HE HAS, WILL BE TAKEN FROM HIM ALONG WITH THE REST. (Ver. 15, "And I will smite," etc.) Luxuries long enjoyed become necessities of life, and no judgment would be thorough that left them untouched. Self-indulgence, if it were left, would soon invent a new idolatry for its own accommodation. It is only by making a clean sweep of the idols already in possession that God can get his place in the sinner's heart.

HOMILIES BY VARIOUS AUTHORS.

Vers. 1, 2.—*Sin against light and love.* This language of reproach and threatening was addressed to Israel and Judah. Yet all who occupy a parallel position of privilege, and who are guilty of similar insensibility, ingratitude, and apostasy, are subject to the condemnation and the penalty pronounced upon the favoured but sinful descendants of Israel.

I. UNPARALLELED FAVOURS ARE RECOUNTED. As a matter of history, Israel had been treated in a singular manner, with unique favour. However we may explain the fact, a fact it is which is here recalled to the memory of the too oblivious Hebrews. 1. Israel had been treated as the family of God. The heavenly Father had cared for, provided for, and protected his peculiar family, the children whom he had adopted. 2. Israel had been brought up from the land of Egypt. To the marvellous deliverance and interposition recorded by Moses, to the equally marvellous guidance and guardianship experienced in the wilderness of wandering, the sacred writers frequently refer. This is not surprising; for never was a more signal instance of Divine compassion than that afforded in the earlier passages of the national life of the chosen people. 3. Israel had been the object of the Divine knowledge. By this we understand (for the language is accommodated to our human weakness) that God had regarded and selected Israel in his inscrutable wisdom for a certain purpose, viz. in order by Israel to make himself known to mankind at large. A peculiar honour was conferred upon the Hebrew nation, not, however, for any excellence or worthiness in them, but for reasons larger and higher than any which were generally apprehended.

II. UNPARALLELED INIQUITIES ARE IMPUTED. Idolatry was charged upon those who had been distinguished as the recipients of the revelation of the Divine unity. Immorality of various kinds was rife amongst those who enjoyed the advantage of the purest moral code known amongst the nations of mankind. The just principle was applied, "To whom much is given of him will be much required." And the application of this principle made manifest the peculiar guilt of Israel. The Word of the Lord by his prophet was therefore righteously severe; other nations were guilty of equal enormities, but the privileges of Israel rendered their iniquities more reprehensible.

III. UNPARALLELED CHASTISEMENT IS THREATENED. *All* the iniquities of Israel were to be visited by Divine correction. In the remainder of his prophecies Amos enlarges upon this theme. Whether we consider the captivities and humiliations undergone by the favoured nation in the period immediately succeeding, or the history of subsequent centuries, we see the truth of this prediction. Much more apparent is it when we look at the national life of Israel as a whole; and, connecting the earlier apostasies with the rejection of the Messiah, recognize in the present dispersion of the tribes the fulfilment of a Divine purpose and the inculcation of a Divine lesson.—T.

Ver. 3.—*Harmonious followship.* These words have passed into a proverb, which fact is in itself a proof that they accord with human experience.

I. HARMONY OF SENTIMENT AND PURPOSE ALONE CAN ENSURE AGREEMENT IN LIFE. The spiritual is a key to the outward life. And this holds not only with regard to the individual, but with regard to society. Because people live together in a house, they are not necessarily a true family; because they meet together in an ecclesiastical building, they are not therefore a true congregation; because they occupy the same territory, they are not therefore a true nation. There must be inner accord in order that fellowship may be real.

II. WANT OF HARMONY OF HEART WILL SURELY MANIFEST ITSELF IN LIFE. This is the other side of the same law. The strifes of society are an indication of conflicting principles. Even Christ came to send, not peace, but a sword. Where there is no agreement, one will walk in this road and another in that. External uniformity is of little value. In fact, manifest discord may be of service in revealing the want of spiritual unity, and so leading to repentance.

III. IN THE RELATION BETWEEN GOD AND MAN AGREEMENT IS ONLY TO BE ATTAINED BY THE CONFORMITY OF MAN'S MIND AND WILL TO GOD'S. It is not to be expected, it is not to be desired, that God's purpose should bend to man's. The human ignorance must accept the Divine wisdom, and the human error and sin must embrace the Divine grace and holiness. Such is the teaching of revelation, of the Law, and of the gospel.

IV. WHERE THERE IS WANT OF HARMONY BETWEEN GOD AND MAN, IT IS FOR MAN TO SEEK THE RECONCILIATION AND UNITY WHICH ALONE CAN BRING ABOUT MAN'S WELFARE. If these blessings were not offered, there would be room to doubt their accessibility. But the revelation of God's counsels in Scripture assures us that our heavenly Father desires that his children should be at one with him.—T.

Ver. 6.—*Warning notes.* There is something in this interrogatory style that arrests the attention and excites inquiry. Combined as it is with bold figures of speech, it gives both vivacity and impressiveness to the prophecies of the herdsman of Tekoah.

I. THE PRESENCE OF CALAMITY. The phrase, "evil in a city," is certainly vague, but how much it may imply! How many forms of misery may be suggested by the expression!—*e.g.* famine, pestilence, war, riot, and faction, all are evils, and evils which do not always come singly to a community.

II. THE MORAL SIGNIFICANCE OF CALAMITY. The suggestion of the prophet is that "the Lord hath done it." We are not warranted in applying the test of our opinions to events permitted by Divine providence. It is foolish to profess ourselves able to interpret all the events, and especially all the calamities, that occur; to see God's "judgments" in all human distresses. Yet no devout mind can question that there is a very important sense in which, when evil happens to a city or a country, the Lord hath done it. The world is governed by moral laws; but the Governor is the supreme Creator of all things, the supreme Disposer of all events. Disobedience to his authority and ordinances entails suffering, privation, disaster. Men reap as they sow.

III. THE PROPHETIC WARNING OF COMING CALAMITY. The prophet was a watchman, as Ezekiel so vigorously shows us, whose office it is to recognize the approach of ill, and to give the people timely and faithful warning. The same office is still fulfilled by those who being dead yet speak, whose declarations concerning Divine government remain for the instruction of all generations. The Bible abounds with admonitions to which cities and nations will do well to give heed. And all ministers of religion are bound to explain to the people the principles of moral rule and law, of moral retribution, of repentance and reformation.

IV. THE PROPER EFFECT OF CALAMITY. The immediate result is that described in the text—fear, trembling, alarm. But the remote result, that chiefly to be desired, is the turning of men's hearts unto the Lord, and their consequent acceptance and forgiveness.—T.

Ver. 7.—*The revelation of secrets.* That there must be assumed to be some limitation to this broad statement is manifest. It is not intended to declare that God made his prophets acquainted with *all* his counsels and intentions, but rather that revelation and inspiration are realities, and that prophecy is a Divine ordinance.

I. THE ACTIONS OF GOD ARE THE RESULT OF DELIBERATE COUNSEL AND PURPOSE. This way of representing the conduct of Divine affairs is out of harmony with much current teaching of our time. We are often told that it is childish to conceive of God as personal, as thinking, feeling, and acting. But so far from such representations being derogatory to the Divine dignity, they do, in fact, enhance our conceptions of him. Reason and will are the lofty attributes of mind; and whilst the Eternal is not bound by the limitations which circumscribe our faculties, these faculties are the finite reflection of what is infinite in him. It is the glory of our Scriptures that they reveal to us a God who commands, not a blind awe, but an intelligent veneration, and elicits an appreciative and grateful love.

II. THE COUNSELS AND PURPOSES OF GOD ARE REVEALED TO THE SYMPATHETIC

MINDS OF HIS SERVANTS THE PROPHETS. The mode of this communication is concealed from us; it may have been but partially understood even by the prophets themselves. There is nothing unreasonable in the fellowship of mind between the Creator and created spirits. The human consciousness is above all vehicles surely the fittest medium for the intercourse between the Divine and the finite. God has his own servants employed in his household, his husbandry; and he chooses his own agents for the several works he has for them to do. Among his servants are the prophets—men selected and qualified to speak forth his mind and will to their fellow-men. Perhaps we are too restricted in the view we commonly take of the prophetic office. We know that there were schools of prophets among the Hebrews, and that there was an order of prophets in the primitive Church. There were cases in which by the agency of prophets new truth was revealed, but there were also cases in which prophets were inspired to apprehend and republish truth already familiar. Prophets in this second sense there certainly are among us to this day.

III. THE COUNSELS AND PURPOSES OF GOD COMMUNICATED BY THE PROPHETS DEMAND OUR REVERENTIAL ATTENTION AND CHEERFUL OBEDIENCE. When the Omniscient declares his mind, when the Omnipotent unfolds his purpose, by the agency he has chosen, the revelation is first made by the Spirit to the human minister, and then by the human minister to his fellow-men. The holiness of the Divine character and the righteousness of the Divine government are thus brought effectively before the minds of the intelligent and responsible sons of men. The secret is revealed, not simply to excite wonder, but to guide conduct. The appropriate attitude of those privileged with a revelation so precious is that expressed in the resolution, " All the words which the Lord hath spoken will we do."—T.

Ver. 10.—*The corruption of conscience.* The conception of Amos is remarkable for grandeur. He sees in prophetic vision the approaching siege of Samaria, the capital of the northern kingdom, and poetically summons the Egyptians and Philistines to gather themselves together upon the surrounding hills, and to witness the tumults within the city, the assaults from without, and the impending ruin. But the moral significance of history, in the prophet's mind, transcends the pictorial interest; and in this verse he gives utterance to a profound and awful truth with regard to human nature. Wrong-doing corrupts the conscience and interferes with a correct perception of right and goodness.

I. IT IS A LAW OF HUMAN NATURE THAT CONDUCT REACTS UPON CHARACTER. No doubt actions are the expression of the moral nature, the moral habits, of men. But, on the other hand, those who persevere in a certain course of conduct are by that very fact moulded and fashioned and even transformed. Thus it is that those who submit to circumstances and who yield to influences are affected even in their inmost moral nature by the experience they pass through.

II. PASSION AND INTEREST WARP THE MORAL JUDGMENT. Nations which, like Israel, are guilty of luxury and of idolatry, which pillage their neighbours' goods, and wage unlawful war, involving widespread calamity, thereby blunt their sensibilities to right and wrong. They habituate themselves to regard all questions in the light of their own ambition, or their own aggrandizement and enrichment. As a consequence they are tempted to call evil good, and good evil. Especially are they liable to form a false judgment upon their own conduct.

III. THUS WRONG-DOING HAS A TENDENCY TO PERPETUATE ITSELF. They who by reason of abandoning themselves to evil courses have silenced the voice of conscience, lose the moral power to do better. Because they " know not to do right," they continue to do wrong. They reap as they have sown. They advance upon the road of sin by the momentum derived from past iniquity.—T.

Vers. 13—15.—*Retribution upon the altar and the palace.* The language of the prophet in this passage is severe in its import and graphic in its style. He foresees the approach of the invaders, the powerlessness of Israel to resist their attack, the completeness with which their work is destined to be done. In two directions especially the blow of vengeance is seen to fall.

I. IDOLATRY IS PUNISHED BY THE DESTRUCTION OF IDOL TEMPLES AND ALTARS.

Departure from Jehovah was the radical offence of Israel. Beside the great altar set up at Bethel by Jeroboam, where the golden calves were worshipped, there seem to have been other sacred places, which were polluted by idol-service and idol-sacrifice. Heathenism was seen to encroach upon the territory consecrated to Jehovah. Altars were reared to deities, imaginary indeed, but endowed by popular superstition with characters altogether opposed to the pure and perfect character of the Eternal who had revealed himself to the ancestors of the Hebrew nation. It was most appropriate that retribution should fall upon the centres and the symbols of a worship so debasing as that which had been substituted for the service of Jehovah. The powerlessness of the so-called "gods" to protect their sanctuaries and their altars was made manifest; the defeat of Baal was the triumph of Jehovah.

II. Pride and luxury are punished by the destruction of the mansions and palaces of the great. Whether we regard these "summer houses" as simply the upper apartments, or as country villas erected in rural retreats, the prophetic lesson is the same. Their destruction, and the destruction of the sumptuous residences decorated with ornaments of ivory, was a retribution upon those who esteemed the splendour and luxuriousness of their abodes more dear than the practice of virtue, of benevolence, of piety. No lesson is more frequently repeated in Scripture than the lesson that the Judge of all the earth delights to abase the proud, whilst he exalts the lowly. When the princes of Israel beheld their sumptuous dwellings razed to the ground, and when they themselves passed into exile, how could they fail to recognize the hand of a righteous and indignant God?—T.

Vers. 2, 3.—*A specially blest people.* "You only have I known of all the families of the earth: therefore I will punish you for all your iniquities. Can two walk together, except they be agreed?" "You only have I known," says God, "of all the families of the earth." What does this mean? It does not mean that he was ignorant of all other people. God knows everything connected with each individual of all generations. Nor does it mean that he had not been kind to other people. "His tender mercies are over all the works of his hands." But by the expression, "I have known," he means, "I have bestowed on you privileges which I have bestowed on no other people" (see Rom. ix. 4, 5). Now, it is a fact that some men are far more highly favoured by Heaven than others. Some have more health, some more riches, some more intellect, some more friendships, some more means of spiritual improvement. We offer three remarks about specially favoured people.

I. They are oftentimes the greatest sinners. Who of all the people on the face of the earth were greater sinners than the Israelites? Yet they were specially favoured of Heaven. There was not a crime they did not commit; and they filled up the measure of their iniquity by crucifying the Son of God. England is a *specially favoured land*, but where is there more moral corruption? The fountain of moral iniquity is as deep, as full, as noxious, as active, here as in the darkest and most corrupt parts of the earth. It is true that civilization has so decorated it that its loathsomeness is to some extent concealed; but here it is. The corpse is painted, but it is still a putrid mass.

II. They are exposed to special punishment. "Therefore will I punish you for all your iniquities." Men are not to be envied simply because they are endowed with special favours. Those very endowments, unless they are faithfully used, only augment responsibility, deepen guilt, and ensure a more terrible retribution. Where much has been given, much will be required. "It will be more tolerable for Sodom and Gomorrah in the day of judgment," etc. "Therefore will I punish you." I who know all your sins, I who abhor all your sins, I who have power to punish you, will execute vengeance.

III. They should, like all people, place themselves in harmony with God. "Can two walk together, except they be agreed?" 1. *Agreement with God is essential to the well-being of all intelligent existences.* No spirit in the universe can be happy without thorough harmony with the will and mind of God. Heaven is happy because of this harmony; hell is miserable because of antagonism to the Divine mind. 2. *The condition of all sinners is that of hostility to the will of God.* Indeed, enmity to God is the essence of sin. What, then, is the conclusion? *Reconciliation.* "We beseech you on behalf of Christ, be ye reconciled unto God" (2 Cor. v. 20).—D. T.

Vers. 4—6.—*Retribution.* "Will a lion roar in the forest, when he hath no prey?" etc. These verses suggest certain remarks on retribution.

I. RETRIBUTION SPRINGS OUT OF THE NATURE OF THINGS. The lion roars in the forest for prey; the young lion cries in his den from an instinct of nature. They are hungry, and they roar; they crave for food, and they cry; this is natural. The lion is quiet till he sees his prey, but roars at the sight of it, and thereby inspires it with such terror that it is deprived of the power of escape. In like manner the young lion which has been weaned and is just beginning to hunt for prey, will lie silent in the den till it is brought near, when the smell of it will rouse him from his quiet. Poiset, in his travels, states that the lion has two different modes of hunting his prey. When not very hungry, he contents himself with watching behind a bush for the animal which is the object of his attack, till it approaches; when by a sudden leap he springs at it, and seldom misses his aim. But if he is famished he does not proceed so quietly; but, impatient and full of rage, he leaves his den and fills with his terrific roar the echoing forest. His voice inspires all beings with terror; no creature deems itself safe in its retreat; all flee they know not whither, and by this means some fall into his fangs. The naturalness of punishment, perhaps, is the point at which the prophet aims in the similitude. It is so with moral retribution. It arises from the constitution of things. Punishment grows out of vice. Misery follows iniquity. Every sin carries with it its own penalty. It does not require the Almighty to inflict any positive suffering on the sinner. He has only to leave him alone, and his sins will find him out.

II. RETRIBUTION IS NOT ACCIDENTAL, BUT ARRANGED. "Can a bird fall in a snare upon the earth, where no gin is for him? shall one take up a snare from the earth, and have taken nothing at all?" The bird is not taken in a snare by chance. The fowler has been there and made preparation for its entanglement and death. Every sinner is a bird that must be caught; the snare is laid in the constitution of things. Instruments were prepared by the providence of God for the capture of the Israelites, which would certainly do their work.

III. RETRIBUTION ALWAYS SOUNDS A TIMELY ALARM. "Shall a trumpet be blown in the city, and the people not be afraid?" Heaven does not punish without warnings. Nature warns, providence warns, conscience warns; there is no sinful soul in which the trumpet of alarm does not sound.

IV. RETRIBUTION, HOWEVER IT COMES, IS ALWAYS DIVINE. "Shall there be evil in a city, and the Lord hath not done it?" God is in all. He has established the connection between sin and suffering. He has planned and laid the snare. The everlasting destruction with which the sinner is punished comes from the presence of the Lord and the glory of his power.—D. T.

Vers. 7, 8.—*The irrepressibility of moral truth.* "Surely the Lord God will do nothing, but he revealeth his secret unto his servants the prophets," etc. These words mean that although punishment for the guilty Israelites was natural, arranged, and withal Divine, yet it would come according to a warning made to them through the prophets, and which these would feel compelled to deliver. The words suggest two remarks.

I. GOD HAS MADE A SPECIAL REVELATION TO HIS SERVANTS. "He revealeth his secret unto his servants the prophets." In all ages God has selected men to whom he has made communications of himself. In times past he spake unto the fathers by the prophets. In truth, he makes *special* revelations of himself to all true men. "Shall I hide from Abraham the thing that I do?" "The secrets of the Lord are with them that fear him, and he will show them his covenant." God has given to all men a general revelation. In nature without and within, in the material domain, and in the spiritual. But he makes a special revelation to some. The Bible is indeed a special revelation. 1. Special in its *occasion.* It is made on account of the abnormal moral condition into which man has fallen—made in consequence of human sin and its dire consequences. Had there been no sin, in all probability we should have had no written revelation. The great book of nature would have sufficed. 2. Special in its *doctrines.* The grand characteristic truth is this—that God so loved men as sinners that he gave his only begotten Son for their redemption. This is the epitome of the gospel.

II. That the right reception of this special revelation necessitates preaching. "The lion hath roared, who will not fear? the Lord God hath spoken, who can but prophesy?" The idea is that the men who have rightly taken the truth into them can no more conceal it than men can avoid terror at the roar of the lion. There are some truths which men may receive and feel no disposition to communicate, such as the truths of abstract science, which have no relation to the social heart. But gospel truths have such a relation to the tenderest and profoundest affections of the spirit, that their genuine recipients find them to be irrepressible. They feel like Jeremiah, that they have fire shut up in their bones; like the apostles before the Sanhedrin, "We cannot but speak the things that we have seen and heard;" like Paul, "Necessity is laid upon me to preach the gospel." "Who can but prophesy?" None but those who have not received the truth.—D. T.

Vers. 10, 11.—*Rectitude.* "For they know not to do right, saith the Lord, who store up violence and robbery in their palaces," etc. We derive from this passage three general remarks.

I. That there is an eternal law of "right" that should govern man in all his relations. Right, as a sentiment, is one of the deepest, most ineradicable, and operative *sentiments* in humanity. All men feel that there is such a thing as right. What the right is, is a subject on which there has been and is a variety of opinion. Right implies a standard, and men differ about the standard. Some say the law of your country is the standard; some say public sentiment is the standard; some say temporal expediency is the standard. All these are fearfully mistaken. Philosophy and the Bible teach that there is but one standard—that is the *will* of the Creator. That will he reveals in many ways—in nature, in history, in conscience, in Christ. Conformity to that will is *right.* 1. The law of right should govern man in his relations with *God.* That law says—Thank the kindest Being most, love the best Being most, reverence the greatest Being most. "Thou shalt love the Lord thy God," etc. 2. The law of right should govern man in his relation to *his fellow-men.* "Whatsoever ye would that men should do unto you, do ye even so unto them." This law of right is *immutable.* It admits of no modification. It is *universal.* It is binding alike on all moral beings in the universe. It is *benevolent.* It seeks the happiness of all. Earth will be Paradise again when the will of God is done here "as it is in heaven."

II. That a practical disregard of this law leads to fraud and violence. "For they know not to do right, saith the Lord, who store up violence and robbery in their palaces." The magnates of Samaria had no respect for the practice of right, hence they "stored up violence and robbery in their palaces." Fraud and violence are the *two great primary crimes in all social life.* By the former men are deceived, befooled, rifled of their rights, and disappointed of their hopes and expectations. Never was fraud stronger in England than to-day—fraud in literature, commerce, religion, legislation. By the latter, men are disabled, wounded, crushed, murdered. Can the history of the world furnish more terrible manifestations of violence than we have had in the wars of Christendom in this age? Why this fraud and violence? Why are these devils let loose to fill the world with lamentation and woe? The answer is in the text, "Men know not to do right." That is, they do not practise the right.

III. That fraud and violence must ultimately meet with condign punishment. "Therefore thus saith the Lord God; An adversary there shall be even round about the land; and he shall bring down thy strength from thee, and thy palaces shall be spoiled." How was this realized? "Against him came up Shalmaneser King of Assyria; and Hoshea became his servant, and gave him presents. . . . In the ninth year of Hoshea the King of Assyria took Samaria, and carried Israel away into Assyria, and placed them in Halah and in Habor by the river of Gozan, and in the cities of the Medes" (2 Kings xvii. 3—6; xviii. 9—11). The cheats and murderers of mankind will, as sure as there is justice in the world, meet with a terrible doom. "Go to now, ye rich men, weep and howl for your miseries that shall come upon you. Your riches are corrupted, and your garments are moth-eaten. Your gold and silver is cankered; and the rust of them shall be a witness against you, and shall eat your flesh as it were fire. Ye have heaped treasure together for the last days. Behold, the hire of the labourers who have reaped down your fields, which is of you kept back by fraud, crieth: and the cries of them which have reaped are entered into the ears of the Lord of sabaoth. Ye have lived in pleasure on the earth, and been wanton; ye have nourished your hearts, as in a day of slaughter. Ye have condemned and killed the just; and he doth not resist you" (Jas. v. 1—6). "Punishment is the recoil of crime; and the strength of the back-stroke is in proportion to the original blow."—D. T.

Vers. 13—15.—*National judgments.* "Hear ye, and testify in the house of Jacob, saith the Lord God, the God of hosts," etc. The same persons are here addressed who in the ninth verse were summoned from Philistia and Egypt. They were now to testify to the facts of the case, that it might be seen that the punishment inflicted upon the inhabitants was richly deserved. The subject of the words is *national judgment,* which we are here led to regard in three aspects.

I. IN RELATION TO THE TRUE PROPHETS. "Hear ye, and testify in the house of Jacob." We may perhaps regard the words also as spoken to the prophets. Hear, ye prophets. 1. The prophets were to *make themselves acquainted with the coming judgments.* They were to be watchmen who were to descry afar the coming danger. All true ministers of religion should by earnest study acquaint themselves with the terrible punishment that awaits the guilty world. 2. The prophets were to *announce the coming judgment.* "Hear ye, and testify." Their work is to sound the alarm, to blow the trumpet. "So thou, O son of man, I have set thee a watchman unto the house of Israel: therefore thou shalt hear the word at my mouth, and warn them from me" (Ezek. xxxiii. 7). One of the chief duties of a true minister is to "warn every man" (Col. i. 28).

II. IN RELATION TO ITS MORAL CAUSE. What was the cause of these threatened judgments? Here it is. "I shall visit the transgressions of Israel." Judgments do not come on men as a matter of necessity; they do not roll on man like the billows of ocean on the shore, by blind force; nor do they come because the Governor of the universe is malevolent, and has pleasure in the sufferings of his creatures. No; he is love. He "desireth not the death of a sinner." They come because of *sin.* The sins of a nation draw judgment after them as the moon draws after it the billows that beat upon the shore. Let no nation hope to escape judgments until it gets rid of sin. Judgments are but sins ripened into a harvest, subterranean fires breaking into volcanoes. Eternal love requires for the order and happiness of the universe that sins and sorrows, transgressions and troubles, should be inseparably linked together.

III. IN RELATION TO ITS TERRIBLE ISSUES. 1. There is the deprivation of *religious institutions.* "I will also visit the altars of Bethel: and the horns of the altar shall be cut off, and fall to the ground." "Signal vengeance was to be taken on the place whence all the evils which spread through the ten tribes originated. The 'horns' were four projecting points, in the shape of horns, at the corners of ancient altars. They may be seen in the representations of those dug up by Belzoni in Egypt. As they were ornamental, the action here described was designed to express the contempt in which the altar would be held by the Assyrians." Corrupt punishment for a nation's transgressions would involve the ruin of religious institutions. 2. There is a deprivation of all their *conveniences and luxuries.* "And I will smite the winter house with the summer house; and the houses of ivory shall perish, and the great houses shall have an end, saith the Lord." Eastern monarchs and princes, we are told, have summer as well as winter houses. The "ivory houses" do not mean houses composed of that material, but richly ornamented dwellings. These were to be destroyed. "The pomp or pleasantness of men's houses," says Matthew Henry, "will be so far from fortifying them against God's judgments, that it will make them the more grievous and vexatious, as their extravagance about them will be put to the score of their sins and follies. —D. T.

EXPOSITION.

CHAPTER IV.

Vers. 1—13.—§ 2. *Second address. The prophet reproves the voluptuous women of* Samaria, and foretells their captivity (vers. 1—3); *with bitter irony he describes the people's devotion to idolatry* (vers. 4, 5); *he shows how incorrigible they have proved them-*

selves under God's chastisements (vers. 6—11); *therefore they must expect further punishment, if so be that they will learn to fear the Lord* (vers. 12, 13).

Ver. 1.—The very women are leaders in dissoluteness and oppression. **Ye kine of Bashan.** Fat and well-liking, such as the rich pastures of Bashan produce. Some have supposed that by this term are meant the luxurious nobles of Samaria, who are called "cows" as being effeminate and licentious. This is possible; but such grandees would be called rather "bulls of Bashan," and the "masters" mentioned just below signify more naturally these women's husbands than the kings. Pusey notes that the genders in the sentence are interchanged. "Hear ye," "your Lord," "upon you," "they shall take you," being masculine; "that oppress," "that crush," "that say," "your posterity," "ye shall go out," "each before her," "ye shall cast," feminine. Evidently the prophet addresses his reproaches to the luxurious of both sexes, though he begins with the women. The land of Bashan extended from Hermon to the Jabbok, including Gaulonitis, Auronitis, Batanea, and Trachonitis. It was always famous for its pasturage, cattle, and oaks. The Vulgate takes the term as metaphorical, and has, *vaccæ pingues*. So Symmachus, βόες εὔτροφοι, which translation Jerome adopts. **Mountain of Samaria.** The hill of Shomer, on which Samaria was built (see note on ch. iii. 9). **Oppress the poor.** This they did in ministering, or getting their husbands to minister, to their luxury and debauchery. Apparently they urged their husbands to violence and fraud in order to obtain means to satisfy their extravagance. A bad woman is thoroughly unscrupulous (see the case of Ahab and Naboth, 1 Kings xxi. 7, etc.). **Their masters;** *their lords;* i.e. husbands (comp. Gen. xviii. 12; 1 Pet. iii. 6). **Bring, and let us drink.** They invite their husbands to supply the means of debauchery and to join in their revels.

Ver. 2.—**By his holiness.** God swears by his holiness, which cannot tolerate iniquity, and which they had profaned (ch. ii. 7; comp. ch. vi. 8). **That he will take you away.** "That one, or they, shall take you away;" the enemy, the instrument of God's vengeance, is meant. **With hooks;** *tsinnoth;* Septuagint, ἐν ὅπλοις: Vulgate, *in contis.* The translation, "with hooks," is correct, the idea being that the people shall be utterly helpless and taken for destruction, like fish caught with hooks (Jer. xvi. 16; Hab. i. 15). **Your posterity;** *acharith* (ch. ix. 1); better, *your residue,* those who have not been destroyed previously. The Septuagint and the Vulgate give quite a different notion to

the passage. The former (according to the Vatican manuscript) has, Καὶ τοὺς μεθ᾽ ὑμῶν εἰς λέβητας ὑποκαιομένους ἐμβαλοῦσιν ἔμπυροι λοιμοί, "And fiery destroyers shall cast those with you into boiling caldrons;" the latter, *Et levabunt vos in contis, et reliquias vestras in ollis ferventibus.* (For the explanation of these versions, which arise from mistakes in the meanings of ambiguous words, see Schegg and Knabenbauer.)

Ver. 3.—**At the breaches made in the city walls,** as cattle hurry through gaps in a fence. Thus they should go forth when Samaria was taken. **Every cow at that which is before her;** better, *each straight before her,* just where the opening offered itself (comp. Josh. vi. 5, 20). The LXX. inserts γυμναί, "naked." **And ye shall cast them into the palace;** Septuagint, Καὶ ἀποῤῥιφήσεσθε εἰς τὸ ὄρος τὸ Ῥομμάν (Ῥεμμάν, Alex.), "And ye shall be cast forth into the mountain Romman;" Vulgate, *et projiciemini in Armon.* The Syriac and Arabic Versions, and Aquila, render, "unto Mount Armon;" the Chaldee paraphrast, "far beyond the mountains of Armenia." The Hebrew expression *haharmonah* occurs nowhere else. Our version takes it in the sense of *armon,* "a palace," intending probably a palace or citadel of the enemy, which certainly ought to have been expressed. Kimchi renders, "Ye shall cast yourselves into the palace of the king." The passage is probably corrupt. If the verb is taken as passive, the unusual word must be considered to denote the place of banishment. Thus, "Ye shall be cast forth into Harmon." Whether Harmon means Armenia, as many ancient commentators thought, or not, cannot be determined. Various opinions may be seen in Keil, Schegg, Trochon, and others; but the simplest explanation is that of Orelli and Ewald, viz. that each fugitive shall fling away her idol Rimmona (the wife of the god Rimmon, 2 Kings v. 18), in order to be more free for flight (comp. Isa. ii. 20).

Ver. 4.—The prophet now turns to Israel, and ironically bids them exhibit their zeal for idolatry, and thus increase their guilt. **Bethel;** as the chief seat of idol-worship (ch. iii. 14). **At Gilgal;** rather, *to Gilgal,* "come ye" being repeated in thought. Gilgal was a strong position in the plain of Jordan, three miles east of Jericho, taking its name probably from the stone circles erected for purposes of worship in very early times. Joshua (v. 9) gave a new meaning to the old name. There is a large pool of water in this neighbourhood called Jiljulieh, about four miles from the Jordan, which is doubtless a corruption of the ancient name Gilgal. It seems to have been regarded as a holy place in Samuel's days or even before (see Judg. iii. 19; 1 Sam. vii. 16;

x. 8; xi. 14, etc.; xiii. 8, etc.); and later was appropriated to false worship, though we have no information as to the date of this declension. Gilgal and Bethel are associated together in idolatrous worship (ch. v. 5 and in Hos. iv. 15; ix. 15; xii. 11). Bring your sacrifices every morning. They were careful to maintain the outward semblance of the regular Levitical worship, even beyond the letter of the Law in some respects, though their service was all the time idolatry. As this and the following clause are still ironical, Amos is speaking, not of the daily prescribed sacrifice (olah, Numb. xxviii. 3), but of the offerings (zebach) of individual Israelites which were not required to be presented every day. Your tithes after three years; literally, on the three of days; lishlosheth yamim; Vulgate, tribus diebus; Septuagint, εἰς τὴν τριημερίαν, "every third day." Revised Version, "every three days." So Gesenius, Ewald, Keil, Schegg, Hitzig, Baur. The prophet bids them bring their tithes, not as the Law ordered, every year (Lev. xxvii. 30), or, as in the case of the second tithe, every three years (Deut. xiv. 28; xxvi. 12), but, by an ironical exaggeration, "every three days." Dr. Pusey defends the English Version on the ground of the idiomatic use of "days" for one circle of days, i.e. a year (Lev. xxv. 29; Judg. xvii. 10; 1 Sam. xxvii. 7). But this loses the irony which is so marked in the whole passage. Keil, "If ye would offer slain sacrifices every morning, and tithe every three days, ye would only thereby increase your apostasy from the living God."

Ver. 5.—Offer a sacrifice of thanksgiving with leaven; more definitely, offer by burning a thank offering of that which is leavened. This is an alteration of the prescribed ritual in two particulars. The Law forbade leaven in any meat offering consumed by fire (Lev. ii. 11; vii. 12); and if it allowed cakes of leavened bread to be offered on one occasion, these were not to be placed on the altar and burned, but one was to be assigned to the officiating priest, and the rest eaten at the sacrificial meal (Lev. vii. 13, 14). The ironical charge to the Israelites is that in their unlicensed zeal they should not only burn on the altar that which was leavened, but, with the idea of being more bountiful, they should also offer by fire that which was to be set apart for other uses. The Septuagint Version can only be explained by considering the translators to have had a different reading, καὶ ἀνέγνωσαν ἔξω νόμον, "and they read the Law without." Proclaim . . . publish. Make public proclamation that free-will offerings are to be made, or else, like the Pharisees (Matt. vi. 2), announce with ostentation that you are about to offer. The essence of such

offerings was that they should be voluntary, not of command or compulsion (Lev. xxii. 18, etc.; Deut. xii. 6). Septuagint, καὶ ἐπεκαλέσαντο ὁμολογίας, "and called for public professions" (as Deut. xii. 6, 17, 18). This liketh you; this ye love; Septuagint, "Proclaim ye that the children of Israel loved these things." Their whole heart was set on this will-worship.

Ver. 6.—In this and the five following verses God sets forth instances of the judgments which he had sent at various times to correct Israel; viz. famine, drought, blight, pestilence, earthquake; but all had been in vain. Five times recurs the sad refrain, "Yet have ye not returned unto me, saith the Lord." God's unwearied love had not conquered their rebellion. Cleanness of teeth; Septuagint, γομφιασμὸν ὀδόντων, "dulness of teeth;" Vulgate, stuporem dentium. It is not "toothache" that is meant, but famine, as is seen by the parallel term, want of bread; as Corn. à Lapide says, "Cum enim in fame et penuria dentes non habent quod mordeant et mandant, innocentes sunt et mundi." This is the first chastisement mentioned. It was threatened in the Law as a consequence of backsliding (see Lev. xxvi.; Deut. xxviii. 48, 57). The famines to which Amos alludes are not recorded. Plainly they were not fortuitous, but were providential inflictions, in accordance with previous warnings. Yet have ye not returned unto me. Pusey notes that the words imply, not that they returned not at all, but that they did after a fashion return, but not so as to reach God, their repentance being a half-repentance and their worship a half-worship, and therefore unacceptable.

Ver. 7.—The second punishment is drought, as predicted (Lev. xxvi. 19, etc.; Deut. xxviii. 23). When there were yet three months to the harvest, and when rain was most necessary to swell the grain. The season meant is in February and March, when what was called "the latter rain" fell. In the south of Palestine the harvest commenced at the end of April, but in the northern parts it was some weeks later, so that it might be said in round numbers that it took place three months after the latter rain. I caused it to rain upon one city. That they might not attribute this drought to the blind laws of nature, God caused it to be of a partial character, giving rain to one city while he withheld it from another. One piece. The portion of ground belonging to an individual is so called (Deut. xxxiii. 21; Ruth ii. 3; iv. 3).

Ver. 8.—This want of rain produced great dearth of water to drink, and persons had to go long distances to procure supplies. Wandered; literally trembled, staggered, as spent and exhausted by thirst. The word is used in Ps. lix. 15; cix. 10. The supply thus used was soon exhausted, and brought no permanent relief.

Ver. 9.—The third chastisement is occasioned by blight (Deut. xxviii. 22) and palmerworm (Deut. xxviii. 39, 42). Blasting; the scorching east wind spoken of by Isaiah (xxvii. 8) and Ezekiel (xvii. 10). Vulgate, *in vento urente;* Septuagint, ἐν πυρώσει, "with parching;" Aquila, Symmachus, and Theodotion, ἀνεμοφθορία. Mildew; a *blight*, under the influence of which the ears of corn turned yellow and became unfruitful. "Blasting and mildew" are mentioned together in Moses' curse (Deut. xxviii. 22) and in Solomon's dedication prayer (1 Kings viii. 37; comp. Hag. ii. 17). The LXX. has, ἐν ἰκτέρῳ, "with jaundice." When your gardens . . . increased. It is better to take this sentence as the English margin, "The multitude of your gardens . . . hath the palmerworm devoured." So the Vulgate, *Multitudinem hortorum tuorum . . . comedit eruca.* *Gardens* included orchards, herbaries, and pleasure-grounds. The palmerworm; *gazam;* Septuagint, κάμπη: Vulgate, *eruca.* The word occurs in Joel i. 4; ii. 25, and is taken by many commentators to mean some kind of locust; but it is more probable that the Greek and Latin translators are right in regarding it as "a caterpillar" (see Smith, 'Dict. of the Bible,' ii. 696, etc.; 'Bible Educator,' iv. 293). Amos seems to be referring to the visitation in Joel's time, if we take *gazam* ("biter") to be a kind of locust.

Ver. 10.—The fourth visitation is pestilence and the sword (Lev. xxvi. 25; Deut. xxviii. 60). After the manner of Egypt. In the manner in which Egypt is stricken (comp. Isa. x. 24, 26; Ezek. xx. 30). There is here no reference to the plague of Exod. ix. 3, etc., or xii. 29. The allusion is to the plague which was reckoned to be epidemic in Egypt, and to other loathsome diseases for which that country was notorious (see Deut. vii. 15; xxviii. 27, 60). Sir G. Wilkinson notes that the plague used to occur about every ten years ('Handbook,' p. 7). Your young men have I slain with the sword. Pestilence and war are allied scourges in Lev. xxvi. 25. A reference may here be made to the wars with the Syrians, wherein the Israelites suffered heavy losses (2 Kings vi. 25; viii. 12; xiii. 3, 7, 22). And have taken away your horses; rather, *together with your captive horses,* still under the regimen of "I have slain." The destruction of men and horses is mentioned in 2 Kings xiii. 7. The stink of your camps. These unburied carcases caused pestilence in the district. Septuagint, Καὶ ἀνήγαγον ἐν πυρὶ τὰς παρεμβολὰς ἐν τῇ ὀργῇ ὑμῶν, or, according to the Alexandrian manuscript, παρεμβολὰς

ὑμῶν ἐν τῇ ὀργῇ μου, "In my wrath against you I set fire to your camps."

Ver. 11.—The fifth visitation is the earthquake (Deut. xxix. 23). I have overthrown. This is the word used to describe the destruction of Sodom and Gomorrah (Gen. xix. 25; Jer. xx. 16), and it seems better to refer the occurrence mentioned to some such convulsions of nature which caused widespread destruction, than, as Keil and others, "to the utter confusion of the state by which Israel was brought to the verge of ruin." We do not know anything about the particular earthquake to which the prophet alludes. (For an exhaustive catalogue of the earthquakes in this country, see Pusey's notes on this verse.) As God overthrew. The substitution of the name of God for the personal pronoun, when the Lord himself is speaking, is not uncommon in Hebrew. Here it rather takes the form of a quotation from Genesis. Ye were as a firebrand plucked out of the burning (Zech. iii. 2, where see note)—a phrase which implies, not only a narrow escape, but an escape accompanied with loss. The "brand" not wholly consumed is yet blackened and diminished by the burning (comp. 2 Kings xiii. 5).

Ver. 12.—Therefore. Because all previous judgments have been in vain, therefore will I send upon them something more terrible still. Thus. God says not how; he leaves the nature of the coming chastisement in mysterious uncertainty, that the very suspense may work fear and repentance. Because I will do this (pointing back to the mysterious "thus" above) unto thee; because I am ready to bring on thee still heavier punishment. Prepare to meet thy God; Septuagint, Ἑτοιμάζου τοῦ ἐπικαλεῖσθαι τὸν Θεόν σου, "Prepare to call upon thy God." Make ready to meet thy God in judgment, turning to him with changed heart, if perchance he may forgive thee and withdraw his heavy hand. Another explanation, derived from Symmachus and adopted by à Lapide, Schegg, and others, "Præparare ut adverseris Deo tuo"—an ironical encouragement to them to withstand God—deprives the following verse of its suitability to the context. For the prophet would hardly invite them to this contest by expatiating upon God's almightiness.

Ver. 13.—The prophet enforces his threats by declaring God's power and omniscience. He that formeth the mountains; ἰδοὺ ἐγὼ στερεῶν βροντήν, "I am he that strengtheneth thunder" (Septuagint, reading differently). The mountains are mentioned as the most solid and everlasting of his works; the wind, as the subtlest and most immaterial of created things. Declareth unto man what is his thought; *i.e.* man's thought; reveals man to himself, shows that he knows man's thought before man puts it into words. This he does sometimes by the stings of conscience, sometimes by inspiring his prophets to declare men's secret motives and the real state of their heart (see Jer. xvii. 9, 10; and comp. 1 John iii. 20). Vulgate, *Annuntians homini eloquium suum*, where *eloquium* is equivalent to *cogitatio*. The LXX., with some change of letters, has, ἀπαγγέλλων εἰς ἀνθρώπους τὸν Χριστὸν αὐτοῦ, "proclaiming unto men his Christ"—a reading which supports the misinterpretation of "his thought" as meaning God's thought, Christ being regarded as the Λόγος of God. Many of the Fathers have seen here a prophecy of the Messiah. See Tirinus and Corn. à Lapide on this verse. That maketh the morning darkness. Keil, after Calvin, takes these words as asyndeton for "the morning dawn and darkness." So the Septuagint, ποιῶν ὄρθρον καὶ ὁμίχλην,

"making morning and gloom." This would be simply a further instance of God's creative power. The Vulgate gives, *faciens matutinam nebulam;* and it seems probable (comp. ch. v. 8; viii. 9) that the clause means that the Lord turns the dawn into darkness. This may refer to the action of clouds or an eclipse; or it may be said metaphorically of prosperity and adversity. Treadeth upon the high places of the earth. An anthropomorphic representation of the might and majesty of God, who governs all things, and has the loftiest in perfect subjection (comp. Deut. xxxii. 13; xxxiii. 29; Job ix. 8; Micah i. 3). The Lord, Jehovah, the eternal, self-existent, covenant God, is he who in these things manifests himself, and therefore his threats are not to be despised (ch. v. 8). In the prophet's view the laws and powers of nature have their scope in executing God's commands.

HOMILETICS.

Vers. 1—3.—*The woes of the women at ease.* By a contemptuous and striking figure, the women of Samaria are styled the "kine of Bashan." They were as kine, unmindful of the past, unheeding of the future, their attention limited to the present, and living in it only the life of sense. They were as Bashan's kine, wandering in richest pastures, overfed, indulged, and pampered, and therefore waxed voluptuous and wanton. In explanation of the special reference to them, observe—

I. THAT THE WOMEN OF A NATION ARE ALWAYS MORE OR LESS RESPONSIBLE FOR ITS SINS. This appears from the fact that: 1. *They reflect the national character.* Soft, and easily receptive of influence, whether good or bad, the female character is, to a greater extent than the male, a compound tincture of the prevailing qualities of the land and time. It is natural that, as reflecting the national sin, the women will be obnoxious to national punishment. 2. *They form the national character.* They have earliest, most constant, and most affectionate access to the young. They influence character at its softest and most pliant stage, and they approach it, moreover, on its softest side. Reflecting national character so truly, and impressing this so inevitably on the rising generation, it is through them chiefly that good or evil becomes hereditary in society.

> "O woman, nature made thee
> To temper man."

The "tempering" is oftener for good than ill, converting into porcelain the common clay, purifying and ennobling all she comes near.

> "Woman's empire, holier, more refined,
> Moulds, moves, and sways the fallen yet God-breathed mind."

But if she reigns as the devil's vicegerent, if the influences that go forth from her tend to the enthronement of corruption and wrong, she must be deposed as a matter of policy, and punished as a matter of justice (Isa. iii. 16—24; xxxii. 9—13).

II. A COURSE THAT INVOLVES EVIL IS AS GUILTY BEFORE GOD AS A COURSE THAT INFLICTS IT. The evil a woman does outside her family circle is largely indirect. Of the women of Israel it appears that: 1. *They were self-indulgent at the necessary expense of the poor.* "Which oppress the humble, which crush the needy." This would sometimes be done directly, but generally through the agency of the men. A luxurious mistress often makes a hard and oppressive master. Her extravagant demands must be met by an increased income, and that is only too likely to be sought in exactions from the dependent poor. Let it be in overcharged dues or in underpaid work, in every case the luxury that forces on the demand is responsible for the evils of the enforced supply. "Those at ease often know not that their luxuries are continually watered by the tears of the poor . . . but God counts wilful ignorance no excuse" (Pusey). Hood's stanza, addressed to men, is doubly pertinent to women.

> " O men with sisters dear !
> O men with mothers and wives !
> It is not linen you're wearing out,
> But human creatures' lives."

The self-indulgence of the women of Israel meant really the grinding of the poor, out of whose poverty "their lords" were' driven to wring the means of carrying on their shameful excesses. 2. *They encouraged their husbands in self-indulgence.* "Bring, and let us drink." This was a doubling of the evil. They not only did wrong, but tempted others to do it. They wasted much, and procured the wasting of more. They were at pains to increase the number of harpies who would gorge themselves on the hard earnings of the poor. 3. *This was not an isolated act, but a habit.* "Oppress" is equivalent to "are continually oppressing." Luxury had settled into a chronic social evil. The demand for fuel to feed the fire of indulgence was constant. It was a cancer eating out the well-being of society continually, and devouring, generation after generation, the inheritance of the poor. The evil of it smelled rank to Heaven, and the guilt of it clamoured for punishment.

III. GOD'S OUTRAGED PERFECTIONS ARE THE GUARANTEE OF THE SINNER'S PUNISHMENT. "The Lord Jehovah hath sworn by his holiness." The occasions of God's action are often supplied by men, but the grounds of it are in himself—in the perfections of his character and the purposes of his will. 1. *Holiness is God's characteristic quality.* There is a universal ascription of it to him in Scripture (Exod. xv. 11 ; Isa. vi. 1—3 ; lvii. 15 ; Hab. i. 13). Absolutely his "name is holy ;" relatively he is the "Holy One of Israel." This holiness is an infinite contrariety to all that is morally impure. It characterizes all his other perfections, and is, in this aspect, not so much a distinct attribute as the blending together of them all. Administratively, he swears by his holiness, and sits upon the throne of his holiness (Ps. lxxxix. 35 ; xlvii. 8) ; believers are the people of his holiness, and heaven the habitation of his holiness (Isa. lxiii. 18, 15) ; whilst a synonym for the consecrated life is "holiness to the Lord." 2. *God's holiness was the quality specially profaned.* (Ch. ii. 7.) It was to profane his holy Name that they had sinned. The perfection specially sinned against is naturally the one to be vindicated. "He pledges his own holiness that he will avenge their unholiness" (Pusey). Jealous of all his perfections, the one our conduct tends to obscure or hurt is the one God will most emphatically illustrate and glorify. 3. *Holiness is the quality that makes punishment of sin inevitable.* It is the recoil of God's infinitely pure nature from moral evil. It is the expression and sum of an essential and external antagonism to it. It is incompatible with impurity as light is with darkness, and its necessary and natural action toward it is destructive. Fundamentally it is because God is holy that he punishes, and must punish, sin.

IV. THE SINNER'S PUNISHMENT WHEN IT COMES WILL MATCH AND SQUARE WITH HIS SIN. (Vers. 2, 3.) Here the dovetailing of retribution with crime is very complete. There would be : 1. *Deportation from luxurious scenes.* "I will take you away." The indulgences become habitual would be violently interrupted. The luxurious and vicious tastes, developed into tremendous strength by long-continued sensuality, would be deprived of their gratification. Instead of the high living, become by long enjoyment a thing of course, and a necessity of their life, they would have the coarse and scanty fare of slaves. To visit with want and bondage, when habits of rule and luxury have become a second nature, is a judgment bitterly felt. 2. *This in a violent and painful manner.* "With hooks." The figure is drawn from fishing. The drawing out of the fish by means of a hook is always painful, and is rendered doubly so by its resistance. So with the soft and delicately nurtured women of Samaria in the hands of a rough and brutal soldiery. They would suffer as a fish transfixed by a barbed hook, and their former luxury would be in a sense its own avenger. 3. *This to the last one.* "And your last one with fish-hooks." Not one should escape. God's judgments are particular. He does not visit people in the mass, but individuals. Not a cow but would feel the cut of the drover's whip, and experience the famine-pangs of the scanty pasture. 4. *This in connection with their own lusts as auxiliaries.* The hook that draws out the fish has been baited for it, and voluntarily swallowed, though under a wrong inpression. In heathen luxury and dissolution the Hebrew women found a bait which they swallowed greedily. Now they should find that, with the bait, they had swallowed also a cruel hook, which would draw them away to suffer evils worse than they had themselves inflicted. "And be cast away to Harman" (Authorized Version, "into the palace"), *i.e.* probably Armenia (see Pusey). Here, being used to minister to heathenish luxury and lust, they would be victims in the matter in which they had been so long the victimizers of others. There is a nameless cruelty in debauchery, which only the victims of it know. This, with the added burden of heathen horrors, the delicate and pampered Israelitish women would now suffer. Their punishment would rise upon them in familiar shape, the resurrection of their own sin. 5. *The bovine stolidity of their prosperous days would make them helpless as driven cattle in the day of calamity.* "In the wall ye shall go out every one before her," *i.e.* "as a herd of cows go one after another through a gap in the fence" (Pusey). The level of intelligence goes down with the level of morality. The penalty of living the brutes' life of sense is a weakening of the heavenly gift of reason, by which we are distinguished from them.

Vers. 4, 5.—*Corruption and religiosity in unholy alliance.* Here the prophet turns from the women of Israel, and addresses the people at large. His language is that of strong irony. What he bids the people do is the thing he knows they have been doing and will go on doing, notwithstanding the imminence of the punishment he predicts. He means, by a sarcastic co-ordination of their acts of hollow worship with those of their sin-stained lives, to bring them to see themselves as God and others saw them.

I. MORAL CORRUPTION AND A ZEAL FOR RELIGIOUS FORMS MAY EXIST TOGETHER. (Ver. 4.) Here it would seem as if the multiplication of transgressions and of observances went *pari passu* together. 1. *The observance of religious forms involves nothing in the way of spirituality.* Taste is wanted, and feeling and judgment, but that is all. Enjoyment in the formal acts of worship may be an æstheticism which is altogether apart from spirituality. The sensuous delight in music, oratory, attitudinizing, millinery, upholstery, and other ecclesiastical impedimenta is just as abundant and as much at home in the theatre as in the church, and is the same non-spiritual thing wherever found. 2. *Worship may even be made so sensuous as to become the minister of luxury.* Other things being equal, the largest congregations gather where the adjuncts of worship are most elaborate and most gorgeous. Many confessedly attend the house of God exclusively for the music and singing, never waiting to hear the gospel preached, or consenting to do so only for appearance' sake. And the thing is perfectly intelligible. A musical and ornate service is decenter than a music-hall, and pleasanter than their own room, and makes an agreeable break in their idle Sunday afternoon. So far from such an observance involving or tending to produce spirituality of feeling, it leaves this out in the cold, and makes its appeal entirely to sense. It has no more bearing on the religious life than theatre-going, or club-going, or race-going, or any other mode of raising the sensational wind. 3. *External religious observance quiets the conscience, and so smooths the path of the self-indulgent.* Even after the sinful life has far advanced, his conscience gives the sinner trouble. Failing to prevent the sin, it suggests the performance of some compensatory work. To sin, and then do penance, is easier than to crucify the flesh and be separate from sin. And one of the commonest salves for an accusing conscience is diligence in the externals of religious observance. It looks and feels like worship, and it makes no demands on the religious faculty. Rather, by substituting an emotional exercise for one of the conscience and heart, it deadens the moral sense, and lulls the transgressor into a dangerous complacency.

II. MEN WHO REST IN FORMS ARE PRONE TO MULTIPLY THEM. This is a logical necessity. If the form be everything, then the more of it the better. Besides, the sensation produced by observing it gets stale after a time, and, in order to keep it at its first strength and freshness, there must be a continual increase of the dose. Israel illustrated this principle in two degrees. 1. *They were particular about ceremonial observances.* They offered the slain sacrifices, the praise offerings, the free offerings, and the tithes at their appointed times. In addition to the annual tithe they also gave a second tithe every three years (Deut. xiv. 28 ; xxvi. 12). This was keeping up to the very letter of the Law. A Pharisee in later times could not have given more circumstantial obedience to it than they did. When the *opus operatum* is made the whole of a religious ordinance, it is sure to be circumstantially observed ; and the rule is that the more completely the spirit is lost sight of, the more elaborately is the letter observed. To the exhaustive observance of ordinances by Israel, according to our text, there was one significant exception. This was the omission of the sin offering and the trespass offering. They had no consciousness of sin. They deported themselves as men who had praise to offer and gifts to bestow, but no sin to be atoned or to confess. To the formalist an adequate idea of sin is impossible, and in his worship the question is not raised. 2. *They went beyond the letter of Divine requirement.* In addition to the morning sacrifice required by the Law, they offered *slain sacrifices* (so the Hebrew) every day. Then, not content with burning unleavened cakes on the altar as a praise offering, they burned also the leavened cakes which were to be eaten at the sacrificial meal (see Keil, *in loc.*). As to the free offerings, they carried the provision for having them made beyond the command by having them cried. Thus, so far as forms went, the idol-loving, corrupt, rebellious people were almost exemplary worshippers—went further, indeed, than true worshippers had always felt called upon to go. "It is a characteristic of idolatry and schism to profess extraordinary zeal for God's worship, and go beyond the letter and spirit of his Law by arbitrary will-worship and self-idolizing fanaticism" (Lange). To compensate for the utter absence of the spirit, the letter is made to do double and vicarious duty.

III. Too MUCH ATTENTION TO THE EXTERNAL FORM OF AN ORDINANCE TENDS TO THE VIOLATION OF THE SPIRIT OF IT. On the one hand, the spirit gets lost sight of through inattention, and on the other hand, the inventive faculty introduces practices inconsistent with it. 1. *In their anxiety to offer more than was required Israel offered a thing that was forbidden.* To " kindle praise offerings of that which is leavened " was contrary to Levitical law. The leavened bread of the praise offering, which they burned along with the unleavened cakes and oil, was not to be burned, but eaten (Lev. ii. 11 ; vii. 12—14). The human mind cannot add to a Divine ordinance anything in character. The addendum will either obscure or traverse the religious rite to which it is attached. God's ordinances, like his oracles, can only be added to under a heavy penalty—the penalty of mistaken action arising out of erroneous thought. 2. *They destroyed the essentially spontaneous character of the free-will offerings by endeavouring to make them practically compulsory.* These offerings must be made of the offerer's free will (Lev. xxii. 19). Made under compulsion, moral or otherwise, they lost their spontaneous character, and might as well not have been made at all. And what but compulsion was it to " proclaim and publish," or literally to " call out " for them ? God's ordinance can be safely and rightly observed only in God's way. In such a matter human invention, if it interferes, is sure to err. Hence the so emphatic and frequent warnings in Scripture against " the commandments and ordinances of men." 3. *This amateur tinkering of Divine institutions is very agreeable to human nature.* " For so ye love it." Unspiritual men love the forms of religion if they serve as a means of escape from its realities. They love them more still if, by observing them, they can seem to accomplish a salvation by works. They love them most of all when they are partially of their own invention. Almost all human ordinances in religion are the expression of man's love of his own intellectual progeny.

IV. THE MULTIPLICATION OF ACTS OF WILL-WORSHIP IS ONLY THE MULTIPLICATION OF SIN. The close association of the words " transgression " and " sacrifice " would indicate that the sacrifice itself was sinful. 1. *It was not meant to please God, being an act of pure self-will.* That which will please God must be meant to please him. A formal religious act, if done for our own pleasure, and not as an act of service to God, is valueless (Col. ii. 20—23). Will-worship is self-worship. It is only an insidious way of " satisfying the flesh." It is a thing by which God is not honoured, but dethroned, and by which man is prejudiced with God and not commended (Isa. ii. 11). 2. *It was not fitted to please him, being observed in a manner contrary to his will.* God's ordinances had been altered. The alteration of form in every case had been a violation of the spirit. The ordinances were no longer God's, but something different from and inconsistent with the thing he had appointed. The observance of them was not service, but disobedience and rebellion. For the Nadabs and Abihus who offer strange fire before the Lord there is reserved the fire of his wrath and not the light of his favour. 3. *It was reeking with the wickedness with which it was deliberately mixed up.* "Multiply transgression; and bring your sacrifices." The "obedience" to himself which "is better than sacrifice" was entirely wanting. The "mercy" to men which he will have "and not sacrifice" had been desiderated in vain. With one hand they piled high the offering, and with the other piled higher still the trespass. And in so doing they piled the mountain of a moral impossibility between them and acceptance. The form of worship, in combination with the reality of sin, is a spiritual monstrosity which, as an offering to God, may not be so much as named. God will take no gift from a sin-stained hand (Isa. i. 15). "If we regard iniquity in our heart, the Lord will not hear us" (Ps. lxvi. 18). If we lift up unclean hands in worship, he will not accept (1 Tim. ii. 8). Let us "wash our hands in innocence" when we go to the "holy altar." With clouds of sin hovering over our sanctuary service no dews of Divine favour can ever fall.

Vers. 6—13.—*Judgment the Divine retort to human sin.* This is the sad history of God's vain contendings with an incorrigible nation. In ch. iii. is an account of the mercies by which he at first had tried to draw them. All that had failed utterly. They met privilege with inappreciation, friendship with rebuff, and favour with incredible disregard. Then he had changed his tactics. They would not be drawn, perhaps they might be driven. The experiment was worth the making, and the record of it is in these verses.

I. THE VARIED VISITATIONS OF JEHOVAH. "So then God had but one gift which he could bestow, one only out of the rich storehouse of his mercies, since all besides were abused—chastisement" (Pusey). This he sent: 1. *In diverse forms.* He reduced them by famine, which often acts as a moral depletive, by cutting off its supply from lust. He plagued them with pestilence—a visitation that strikes terror into the boldest hearts. He slew them with the sword of their enemies—a fate which has terrors peculiarly its own. He swallowed them up in earthquakes—the most portentous and awful of earthly phenomena. 2. *In increasing severity.* Famine is direful, but it is directed primarily against the means of life. Pestilence is ghastlier, for it is directed against the life itself. The sword is more terrible than either, for it takes the life with circumstances of cruelty, which are an added horror. The earthquake is the most terror-moving of all, for it summons the overwhelming forces of nature to our destruction. 3. *With differentiating circumstances in different cases.* There was nothing humdrum in the visitations, no pitching them on the dead level of hackneyism or prescription. (1) *The drought came three months before harvest.* This was a most unseasonable and fatal time. It was in February, just when the latter rain was due. The seed would be brairded, or just in the stage in which rain was the one thing absolutely essential to life and growth. Drought at this season "is utterly ruinous to the hopes of the farmer. A little earlier or a little later would not be so fatal, but drought three months before harvest is entirely destructive" ('The Land and the Book'). (2) *It came on one place and not on another.* Ordinarily the showers fall impartially. They water the fields of the just and the unjust alike (Matt. v. 45). They refresh the wilderness where no man is, as abundantly as the cultivated land, with its teeming population (Job xxxviii. 26). When they become eclectic, falling on one city or field and not on another, the feature reveals miraculous intervention. When, as probably in this case (see Prov. iii. 33), the watered fields or cities are those of the righteous, the adjustment is eloquent of the moral government of a God who hates sin (Isa. lxv. 13). On the artificially irrigated gardens, where drought would not readily tell, he sent blasting, mildew, and worms (ver. 9). In the repertory of nature he found an instrument of destruction suited to every possible case, and in the allocation of these was revealed his omnipotent and resourceful hand. The overthrow of "some" when others escaped (ver. 11) was a providence burdened with the same lesson. (3) *The cause and its effect are set close together for identification.* "The piece whereupon it rained not withered," etc. The nearer results are to their causes the easier it is to see the connection between them. God, both in the visitation and the record of it, pointedly associates the drought with the sin, and the withering with the drought, and thus puts his signature and endorsement on his disciplinary work. 4. *In minute correspondence to prophetic warnings.* They were plagued with pestilence " after the manner of Egypt " (ver. 10). This Moses had circumstantially announced would be the result of disobeying the Law revealed on Sinai (Deut. xxviii. 27, 60), whilst immunity from it was promised in connection with fealty and obedience (Deut. vii. 15). Then, with blood-curdling explicitness (vers. 6, 7, 10), famine, pestilence, the sword, and desolation (Lev. xxvi. 23—33), blasting, mildew, drought, and locusts (ver. 9; Deut. xxviii. 21—26, 38, 42), and, to crown all, destruction and ruin, as of Sodom and Gomorrah (Deut. xxix. 22 —28), are piled (ver. 11), Ossa on Pelion, in prophetic intimation to Israel to be " upon thee for a sign and for a wonder, and upon thy seed for ever " (Deut. xxviii. 46). In all this the work of identifying national judgments, as from a pledge-keeping and sin-avenging Jehovah, is made easy to all but the wilfully blind.

II. THEIR MEAGRE RESULTS. Judgments fell thick and wide in five varieties of terror-moving severity and appositeness, and five times the prophet, gleaning vainly after the scythes of God for a grain of good result, can but repeat the sadly reproachful refrain, " Yet ye have not returned unto me, saith the Lord." 1. *The sinner refuses to believe that his affliction is punishment.* He attributes it to accident, or bad management, or natural causes, or the malice of others, as the case may be. While unconscious of his sin, he is necessarily blind to the significance of his suffering, and until he sees this he cannot profit by it. If men would " hear the rod and who hath appointed it " they would have realized a primary condition of improvement under it. 2. *Suffering is not in itself purifying.* A bad man it often makes worse. He wants to " curse God and die." Even if the hardening stops short of this, he is frequently soured and embittered. Suffering, to be beneficial, must not go alone. It prepares for other measures. It makes men more amenable to moral influence, but if no such influence be brought to bear in connection with it, it is no more fitted of itself to purify the character than ploughing is to fertilize the desert sand. " Bray a fool in a mortar, yet will not his folly depart from him." 3. *The love of sin is stronger than the fear of suffering.* Courses, which all observation and experience declare to be ruinous to health and happiness, are entered on deliberately by millions. Even the physical evil consequences of the early steps in sinful indulgence, which are soon felt, do not arrest the evil-doer in his way. By the confirmed sinner hell itself is practically, if not consciously, preferred to reformation. Only what weakens the love of sin secures the successful application of suffering for its removal. The operation of one or other of these principles, or the concurrence of them all, no doubt accounted for Israel's persistent sinning even in the fire.

III. THE LAST RESORT TO WHICH GOD WILL NOW BETAKE HIMSELF. " Therefore thus will I do unto thee." The terror of these words is in nothing lessened by their vagueness. It is evident rather: 1. *That the thing menaced would in point of severity be an advance upon all that had yet been done.* Only thus would there be any use in adopting it. After expostulation the rod, and after the rod a sword—that is the logical order of corrective measures. " Sin no more, lest a worse thing come upon thee," was a foreshadowing of God's consistent policy. 2. *It would involve being brought face to face with God.* " Because I will . . . prepare " (ver. 12). The kind or occasion of the meeting with God is not explained. It is, therefore, to be taken to include all modes and occasions, whether in life, at death, or at the final judgment. And the thought of it is one of terror to the ungodly, under whatever circumstances. They can face his judgments; God is not in them, unless in figurative sense. They can face his prophets; God is not in them, unless in a spiritual sense. But to face God literally was, even to a pious Jew, like facing death (Exod. xxxiii. 20; Judg. xiii. 22); whilst to the impious it must have been the embodiment of all terror. It is from the " presence of the Lord " that the wicked in the judgment call upon the hills to hide them. That, of all things in the universe, is an ordeal they cannot face. 3. *It is left undefined that it may seem the more terrible.* We have here the eloquence of silence. The terror of the threat is enhanced by its vagueness. Familiarity breeds contempt. If a thing, however bad, is exactly defined, we can familiarize ourselves with the thought of it in time, and brace our courage up to meet it. " It doth not yet appear what we shall be," but our idea of it, meantime, has an element of enlargement in its very indefiniteness. God says vaguely "Thus," and stops short, that imagination may fill up the blank. His silence is charged with deeper meaning than any words could carry.

IV. ONE FINAL APPEAL BEFORE THE STROKE FALLS. "Prepare," etc. 1. *Look for a meeting with God.* It is inevitable. It is at hand. The fact must be faced. No good, but harm, can come out of the attempt to escape or blink it (2 Cor. v. 10; Ps. cxxxix. 7—12). 2. *Prepare for it.* This is a word of hope. Meeting with God is inevitable; but it need not necessarily be injurious. Preparation for it is possible, being enjoined, and would avail something if it were made. "God never in this life bids people or individuals prepare to meet him without a purpose of good to those who do prepare" (Pusey). 3. *Do this because of impending judgments.* "Because I will do this unto thee." We might suppose that if God was going to destroy, the preparation to meet him would be too late. But that does not follow. When Nineveh was wicked God expressed his purpose to destroy it, but when it became penitent he spared it. Hezekiah, prayerless in the particular matter, was bidden prepare to die; but Hezekiah, praying for more life, was spared fifteen years (Isa. xxxviii. 1, 5). What God will do to us, so far as it comes within our cognizance, is conditioned by what we will do to him. Until the judgment has actually fallen, the threat of it is a message of mercy. A sentence of destruction itself is a call to repentance, and so has woven into it a thread of hope. "Because I will do this unto thee, prepare."

Ver. 11.—*Burning, yet not turning.* From Moses to Amos was about seven hundred years. It is a long time with men and the works of men. But it is little in the two eternities through which the purposes of God extend. There were prophecies which it had taken all this period to mature; courses of treatment for the cure of sin pursued through all the interval, and whose last measure had not yet been taken. One of these finds record here. A new event looks out at us in the guise of an ancient prophecy (Deut. xxix. 22—24). What seven centuries before had been conceived in the womb of time is here "delivered upon the mellowing of occasion."

I. GOD'S JUDGMENTS A FIRE. "Plucked out of the burning." A commentary on this figure is the association by Isaiah of "the spirit of judgment" and "the spirit of burning" (Isa. iv. 4). Like a fire: 1. *Judgments are painful.* The sensation of burning is about the most painful we know. Too severe for capital punishment, too cruel even for prisoners of war, death by burning has been generally reserved for the martyred saints. This intensest form of physical pain is a fitting symbol of the effects of God's inflictions. What he sends is the greatest of its kind. If it be pleasure it is ideal—a pleasure at his right hand for evermore. If it be pain it is phenomenal—a torment whose smoke ascendeth up for ever and ever. 2. *They are consuming.* What fire feeds on it destroys. Where the flames have passed no organic matter remains. So with God's judgments. They are the mills of God which "grind exceeding small." That on which they must fall "they destroy and consume unto the end." They are nothing if not adequate to their purpose. 3. *They are purifying.* By burning out what is inflammable they leave what is incombustible behind, unmixed and pure. This idea of refining is often associated with the fires of judgment (Zech. xiii. 9; Mal. iii. 2, 3). They seize on the dross of evil, and burn it out of the mass. When their work is done there is only the fine gold of a pure nature in the crucible. 4. *They are irresistible.* Fuel, in contact with fire, can do nothing but burn. If the flame is to be quenched it must be done by some extra agency. To be as "tow" or "stubble" in the flames (Isa. i. 31; Neh. i. 10) is the strongest possible figure for helplessness under the avenging stroke of God. Men cannot prevent it, cannot avoid it, cannot arrest it, cannot in any degree reduce its force. When he works "who shall let it"? When his day burns as an oven, who shall withstand the fire (Isa. xliii. 13; Mal. iv. 1)?

II. SINNERS ARE THE BRANDS ON WHICH IT FEEDS. "Ye were as a firebrand." There are certain steps which lead up to burning, whether literal or figurative. The brand was: 1. *Withered.* It is not on the sappy growing branch that the fire seizes. Before, in the natural course, it reaches the flames, a preliminary process has been finished. Its leaf yellows and falls, its bark shrivels, its sap dries up. Then it is mere tinder, and fit for nothing but the fire. So sin withers and kills the branches of the tree of human character. It dries up the sap of spiritual life, and so turns sere the leaf of profession, and destroys the fruit of well-doing. In a little no function of life is possible, and all its uses are lost. To cut it down is all the husbandman can do, and to burn it follows in the natural course. 2. *Brought to the flames.* There are no prairie fires in God's domain. What is burned is first prepared, and then bound in bundles (Matt. xiii. 30) and then set fire to. There is no accident anywhere. The man by his ill-doing makes himself tinder, and God in his providence uses him for the only purpose he suits. 3. *Combustible.* Fire seeks out and feeds on what is most inflammable. There is an affinity between the two things that does not fail to bring them together. So with God's avenging fires and the fuel they consume. The vultures of his judgments spy out, and alight upon the carrion of the sinner's lusts. Every transgression of the written Law is a transgression also of the unwritten law of the nature of things, and brings punishment on and through the instrument of the sin.

III. The burning that scathes without consuming. "Plucked out of the burning." This language implies: 1. *A narrow escape.* The brand had been in the fire, and actually alight. A little while and it would have been inextinguishable. The fires of judgment had been around Israel, and around her close and long. If she had been in them but a little longer she could not have come out alive. The narrowness of her escape was a fact charged with the double influence of fear as to what might have been, and gratitude for what actually was. 2. *An escape with a certain amount of injury.* The brand that has been alight has suffered. Its fair surface has been scathed and charred. It can never be its original self again. Such a thing was Israel. "Once it had been green, fresh, fragrant, with leaf or flower; now scorched, charred, blackened, all but consumed. In itself it was fit for nothing but to be cast back into the fire whence it had been rescued. Man would so deal with it, a re-creation alone could restore it. Slight emblem of a soul whose freshness sin hath withered, then God's severe judgment has half consumed; in itself meet only for the everlasting fire, from which yet God withdraws it" (Pusey). 3. *An escape managed for an important purpose.* God tries all means before going to extremities. He threatens, menaces, sets fire to, and scorches, yet after all delays to consume. (1) *This gives the sinner a final opportunity of reconsidering his relation to sin.* It is possible that a last chance of reformation may be embraced for the very reason that it is the last one. The prospect of death is a new factor in the problem of a man's relation to the Prince of life, and is likely to modify the solution. (2) *It gives him a chance of viewing sin in the light of its effects.* The charred brand knows the taste of the fire. The ultimate like the immediate punishment of sin is burning (Mark ix. 43, 44). The plagued sinner has tasted the firstfruits of his terrible retribution. He can argue from it what the harvest will be. This is all in favour of his profiting under the dispensation.

IV. The nature that will consume before it will melt. Israel had not repented, and was not going to repent. Rescued from the flame in unspeakable mercy for a season, the brand would have to be thrust in again and burned. This unconquerable hardness was that: 1. *Of a nature that had strayed.* The hardest sinner is the apostate. He sins against light, against favours received, against experience enjoyed, against gracious influences felt. To have beaten down, and sinned in spite of all these deterrents, argues a hardness and determination that the stranger to gracious influences has not had an opportunity of acquiring. Paul tells us that those who have so sinned cannot be "renewed to repentance" (Heb. vi. 4—6). 2. *Of a nature that had been hardened by punishment.* There is a degree of induration in the back that has experienced the lash. The brand put into the fire and taken out again is hardened by the process. The criminal often leaves the prison more callous than he entered it. So with the subjects of Divine judgment. If they are not melted by it they are indurated. Hatred to God and love to the sin are intensified, rebelliousness is stirred up, self-will is put on its mettle, and so moral insensibility is increased by the process of resistance. 3. *Of a nature in which sin is supreme.* In most natures there is a struggle between good and evil. It is largely a question of circumstances, which will preponderate at any given time. Temptation is resisted sometimes, and sometimes yielded to, according to our mood and the manner in which it is brought to bear. This indicates a state of war between the law in the members and the law in the mind, victory inclining to Israel or to Amalek as the hands of conscience are upheld. But when a man sins invariably, under whatever pressure of temptation, and when there is no temptation at all—sins in spite of all conceivable deterrent circumstances—the case is different. He says to evil, "Be thou my good." His moral nature is inverted. He will not mould into a vessel of mercy now. He is "a vessel of wrath and fitted for destruction."

Ver. 12.—*The great preparation.* "Therefore thus will I do unto thee, O Israel," etc. Here an important duty fathers itself on a stupendous fact. An omnipotent God is in judgment with sinful Israel. His wrath has expressed itself in bolt after bolt of judgment already hurled. But these measures are far from embodying all his punitive resources. In the failure of these to bring repentance there are woes unnamed, because unutterable, still in store. If Israel, then, would have the heaviest artillery of retribution kept out of action, they had need bestir themselves in the matter of a duty the further neglect of which must precipitate disaster.

I. GOD AND MEN LIVING APART. The enjoyment of God's presence was paradise (Gen. iii. 8), and will be heaven (1 Thess. iv. 17); that privilege lost is death (Gen. iii. 24), and will be hell (Luke xvi. 26). 1. *The wicked neither have God's presence nor desire it.* "God drove out the man," when he became a sinner; and all men, as sinners, are "afar off." Purity and impurity are incompatible, and there can be no fellowship between them. Righteousness and unrighteousness are antagonistic, and cannot come together without coming into collision. Man's instinctive consciousness of this led him to anticipate expulsion from God's presence by trying to run away (Gen. iii. 8). The separation between God and the sinner is thus by consent, and in the nature of the case, and so inevitable during the *status quo.* 2. *The righteous enjoy it in the imperfect measure in which they desire it.* The need of Divine fellowship, universal with men, becomes conscious when they become spiritual (Ps. xlii. 2). As supply everywhere meets demand (Phil. iv. 19), and measures it, the drawing near of God is synchronous with the springing of desire for it (Matt. v. 6), as well as proportioned to its strength (Rev. xxi. 3). To each of us God comes when we desire him, and as we desire him. If the presence is intermittent or incognizable, it is because appreciation is inadequate, and the longing for it irregular or weak (Isa. lvii. 15; xliii. 22). 3. *To desire it perfectly and possess it fully is heaven.* "Heaven is endless longing accompanied with an endless fruition" (Maclaren). In it there is perfection of the faculties which commune with God. There is perfection of opportunity for their exercise. Accordingly, there is perfect attainment of the normal result. We are "with Christ," and "know even as also we are known."

II. CERTAIN OCCASIONS ON WHICH THEY NEVERTHELESS MEET. The wicked fear God (Rom. viii. 15) and hate him (Rom. viii. 7), would be miserable in his presence (Rev. vi. 16), and so do all they can to keep away from it (Job xxii. 17; xxi. 14). But: 1. *They meet him in the dispensations of providence.* He is their King. He rules their life. All the events in it are of his disposing. He is where he operates, and so in each operation of which they are the subjects they meet him. Especially does he come to them in his judgments, which they are provoking every day. Misfortune, sickness, death,—these in their order, for a widening circle, and at ever closer quarters, are occasions of meeting God which none would choose, yet none can shun. 2. *They meet him in the influences of his grace.* "No one's salvation is so desperate, no one is so stained with every kind of sin, but that God cometh to him by holy inspirations to bring back the wanderer to himself" (Jerome, in Pusey). The strivings of the Spirit are unnoticed often, and resisted often (Luke xix. 44; Acts vii. 51), and so are in the end withdrawn (Gen. vi. 3); but, so far as we know, they are universal. As truly as he met the Prophet Balaam in the way does God meet men in the exercise of constraining or restraining grace. 3. *They shall meet him in the judgment-day.* "Before him shall be gathered all nations." This meeting is sure, and will be unutterably momentous. All other meetings are preliminary and preparatory to it. It will gather up and declare and finally administer their cumulative results. The wicked shall be finally banished from God's presence, and the righteous be finally admitted to it; and so for each it shall be the great meeting and the last meeting.

III. THE PREPARATION NEEDED FOR SUCH ENCOUNTERS. Israel was evidently deficient in this; not expecting the meeting and not furnished for it. In making it we must : 1. *Prepare a character.* To meet God satisfactorily men must be like him. To see him on the one hand, or relish him on the other, or be capable in any sense of holding communion with him, a man must be pure (Matt. v. 8; 2 Cor. vi. 14). He must bring to the meeting a character in sympathy with God's, if he would bring a blessing away. 2. *Prepare a case.* Man before God is a criminal, guilty, condemned, and sentenced. He wants all this reversed, and he must be able to show reason before it can be done. And what are the elements essential to his case? Clearly the penalty he was under must have been exhaustively endured (1 Pet. ii. 24) ; the Law he is under must have been perfectly obeyed (Isa. xlii. 21); both these things must have been done with the approval and by the appointment of God (Heb. v. 4, 5); and the man must be intelligently resting his case on these facts. In other words, there must be Divine vicarious obedience and death, divinely recognized, and rested in by faith. Any appearance before God apart from these must end in confusion. 3. *Prepare an advocate.* Man cannot plead his own case. He has no *locus standi.* He can approach God only through a mediator (1 John ii. 1). This mediator, to be admissible, must have Divine recognition (Isa. xlii. 1; Heb. v. 4, 5); to be efficient, must have Divine power (Ps. lxxxix. 19; Matt. xxviii. 18); and to be available, must have Divine sovereign love for men (Eph. v. 2). These conditions meet, and meet only, and always met, in Jesus Christ. He is the one Advocate of every dispensation. Access into the antitypical holiest of all has been one thing and by one way always (Heb. ix. 8; x. 19—22). It is and was and shall be only spiritual and through the Son of God. 4. *Prepare at once.* To Israel a meeting in judgment had been long foreshadowed, and was now overdue. It might be any time, and must be soon. A surprise—and in like circumstances it is the same with all—was probable, and would be disastrous (Rev. iii. 3). To prepare immediately was, therefore, a duty as urgent as it was clear (Matt. xxiv. 44). It is ill beginning to dig a well when the house of life is already on fire.

IV. THE CONSIDERATIONS THAT MOVE US TO PREPARE. In the context these are written large. There is : 1. *An implied promise.* "It has hope in it to be bidden to prepare" (Pusey). The person so enjoined is not yet given up. The menaced doom is not yet inevitable. The way in which God shall be met, and so the result of the meeting, is still capable of being modified. Every call to action is an implicit promise of the result to which it naturally leads. There is also : 2. *An explicit threat.* "Thus will I do unto thee." There is a vagueness here that is far more terrible than the most explicit denunciation. A series of woes already sent has just been named. But there is a woe that is unutterable in reserve, and already on its way. This, because words are too weak to express it, is left to the imagination to picture. "Thus will I do unto thee," he says, and attempts to particularize no further, where the sentiment is too terrible for words. And so it is with the woe in store for all the impenitent wicked. It cannot be literally defined, and so is suggested by figures such as "the blackness of darkness" (Jude 13), "the worm that dieth not, and the fire that is not quenched" (Mark ix. 48). But, however figuratively represented, the woe is real, is prepared, is being kept in store, is incomparably great, and shall fall as God is true. 3. *Whether we are prepared or not, the meeting with God must come.* "We must all appear before the judgment-seat of Christ." There is a needs be in the case. The purpose of God must be fully carried out in issuing all the matters that go down unsettled to the grave. The righteousness of God must conclusively be vindicated in meting out to all rewards according to their works. The truth of the Divine Word, pledged in promise and in threat, must be established for ever in the answering of event to explicit prediction. The meeting may be a joy to us or a shame, as we choose to have it; but it must be a fact. 4. *A feeling of unreadiness is a necessary step to preparation.* The measure of a sinner's fancied readiness to face his Maker is the measure of his ignorance as to what real fitness implies. The man who has been brought to say, "I dare not face God," has made one step in advance. He is disillusionized. His eyes are open and his conscience awake. Self-deception and false security are at an end (Rev. iii. 17, 18). The first step toward grappling with the facts has been taken when once we have fairly faced them. Realize that you are sinners, and the grace of God that bringeth salvation will find appreciation and an open door.

Ver. 13.—*The God with whom we have to do.* God always acts in character. From the thing he is may be inferred the quality of the thing he will do. We see him here—

I. As REVEALED BY HIS NAMES. Each Divine name and title is a Divine revelation; sets forth some one of God's incomparable perfections. 1. *Jehovah.* "The Being;" "the Living One." In contradistinction to idols, having real existence. In contradistinction to created things, having eternal existence. In contradistinction to all outside himself, having necessary existence. Jehovah is the true God and alone claiming faith, the self-existent God and alone giving life, the eternal God and alone conferring immortality. 2. *God.* "The Adorable One." The Sum of all excellence. The Object of all worship. The Inspirer of all veneration. The Being who at once deserves and commands the heart's whole allegiance and devotion. 3. *Of hosts.* "God of the armies." The hosts are the heavenly bodies (Gen. ii. 1; Deut. iv. 19), the angels (Josh. v. 14, 15; 1 Kings xxii. 19; Ps. ciii. 21; cxlviii. 2), and men (Exod. xii. 41). All these he made, owns, keeps, controls, and uses. He is the universal Sovereign, and "doeth according to his will" everywhere, always, and without appeal. Such a Being it is no light thing to meet. Just as it is done will utter ruin or absolute safety result.

II. As REVEALED BY HIS WORKS. The worker puts something of himself into his work—the author into his book, the painter into his picture, the mechanic into his machine. And so with God (Ps. xix. 1). 1. *He produces physical phenomena.* Three kinds are enumerated: (1) solid matter, "the mountains;" (2) gaseous matter, "the wind;" (3) ethereal matter, "dawn, darkness." Matter in all forms is the creature of God. Its mutations are the doing of his power. Its elements are the instruments of his hand. He does to it and by it what his own moral excellence prompts. And thus it reveals him. We

> "View great Nature's open eye,
> And see within it trembling lie
> The portrait of the Deity."

2. *He reveals mental phenomena.* "Maketh known to man what is his [man's] thought." The power of introspection is peculiar to man of earthly creatures. He takes cognizance of what passes in his own mind; reads his thoughts, and analyzes the process of thinking. This is among the highest exercises of reason. It is a revelation of its marvellous powers, and so of the wisdom and power of him by whom the faculty was bestowed. If a man's thoughts are open to himself, much more are they to God. The mind can do all this; what cannot the Maker of it do (Jer. xvii. 9, 10)? 3. *He rules moral phenomena.* "Goeth over the high places of the earth." The "high places" are the exalted people. All these he rules. The highest do his bidding. From prince to peasant all are but clay in the Potter's hands. Who, then, shall strive with him? What can avail against his transcendent might? All natural forces, all creaturely existences, are but tools in his hand, and ministers that do his will. This is the God we must meet, and to meet whom we may well prepare.

HOMILIES BY VARIOUS AUTHORS.

Vers. 4, 5.—*Hypocrisy.* The rhetorical fervour of the prophet leads him in this passage to address himself to the guilty nobles of Israel in terms of bitter irony. That descendants of Abraham should have forsaken Jehovah, should have set up altars to a golden calf, or to deities of their heathen neighbours,—this cuts the prophet to the heart. But that, even whilst acting thus, they should retain some of their ancient observances, should profess any reverence for the precepts of the Law of God,— this is the most cruel wound. Hence this language of irony, the severity of which is apparent to every reader.

I. IT IS HYPOCRISY OUTWARDLY TO REVERENCE THE ORDINANCES OF GOD WHILST REALLY SERVING GOD'S ENEMIES. Sacrifices, tithes, leaven, offerings—all of which are mentioned in this passage—were prescribed in the Mosaic Law. The sin of the Israelites lay here. All the time that they were attending to these observances, they were worshipping idols, and breaking the first and second commandments of the ten. Virtually, all men who profess Christianity, and yet love the sinful practices and pleasures of the world, are guilty of this sin. It is hypocrisy, which is worse than an open defiance of the Divine authority.

II. HYPOCRISY SEEMS TO MEET A NEED OF DEPRAVED AND SINFUL NATURES. "This liketh you;" "So ye love to have it;"—such is the reflection of Amos upon this evil conduct. Men do not "like" to break off the associations of the past; they do not "like" to turn their back upon the principles they have formerly professed; they do not "like" to forfeit the apparent advantages of conformity to the requirements of religion. Yet, at the same time, they are not willing to forsake the pleasures of sin, to deny self, to take up the cross.

III. HYPOCRISY MAY DECEIVE SOCIETY, AND MAY EVEN DECEIVE THE HYPOCRITE, BUT IT CANNOT DECEIVE GOD. The conscious aim of the hypocritical is often to impress their companions with the belief of their goodness. But in many cases men actually persuade themselves of their own piety, whilst their life is in flagrant contradiction to the assumption. Let it never be forgotten that God "searcheth the heart, and trieth the reins of the children of men;" that his scrutinizing gaze cannot be averted, nor his righteous judgment avoided. Those who multiply insincere observances really "multiply transgression." And multiplied transgressions surely involve multiplied penalties.

APPLICATION. Bethel and Gilgal are not the only spots on earth where hypocrisy has been practised. The question of all importance for every professed worshipper to put to himself is this—Is there harmony between the language which I use in devotion and the thoughts and desires of my heart, the actions and habits of my life?—T.

Vers. 6—11.—*National calamities are Divine chastisements.* Graphic and morally impressive is the catalogue of Divine judgments which the inspired prophet here draws up and puts upon record for the admonition of future ages.

I. OF WHAT THESE CALAMITIES CONSIST. They are thus enumerated in the several verses. 1. Famine. 2. Drought. 3. Blight. 4. Pestilence. 5. War. 6. Destruction. Alas! from the beginnings of human history such have been the sad and weary experiences of the nations. Some of these ills appear to be beyond human control; others of them are more or less attributable to human ignorance, to human neglect, to unbridled lust and passion. The peculiarity of their treatment in the books of Scripture is not in their description, but in the connection shown to exist between them and the moral life and probation of man, and the righteous government of God.

II. FOR WHAT INTENT THESE CALAMITIES WERE INFLICTED. They are not here regarded simply as events; even the philosophical historian does not regard them thus. 1. They convince the observant and pious mind of the concern of God in human affairs, and of God's indignation with human sin. Certain philosophers imagined the great rulers of the universe to be indifferent to all the affairs of men. The Scriptures teach us that nothing escapes Divine observation, that nothing eludes Divine justice, God's censure, or approval. 2. They induce, in the case of the right-minded, repentance and reformation. When God's judgments are abroad, the inhabitants of the earth will learn righteousness. If events teach men that "the way of transgressors is hard," they may also teach them that "whom the Lord loveth he chasteneth, and scourgeth every child whom he receiveth." "Before I was afflicted," said the psalmist, "I went astray; but now have I kept thy Word."

III. IN WHAT SPIRIT THESE CALAMITIES ARE RECEIVED. 1. There can be no question that, in many instances, they are the occasion of hardening of the heart. As in the case of Pharaoh King of Egypt, afflictions may increase insensibility and rebelliousness. 2. There are cases in which chastisements of the kind here described produce national humiliation and repentance. Such was the case with Nineveh, even when Jonah preached and foretold the city's doom; the people repented even before the calamity came, and so averted it. And there were instances in the history of stiff-necked Israel where chastisement led to general abasement and repentance. 3. There are cases in which calamity fails to produce a general reformation, but is nevertheless the means of effecting in individuals a genuine repentance and a sincere conversion unto God.—T.

Ver. 6.—*Obduracy reproached.* There is a mingling of severity and pathos in this language of Jehovah addressed to Israel. The repetition of the reproach adds to its effectiveness and solemnity. As one calamity after another is described, and as all are represented as chastisements inflicted by Divine righteousness, the touching words are added, "Yet have ye not returned unto me, saith the Lord."

I. THE WANDERINGS IMPLIED. In order that there may be a return to God, there must first have been a departure from God. Such had certainly been the case with Israel. The people and their rulers had alike done wickedly in departing from their covenant God. They had mingled with the worship of Jehovah practices superstitious and idolatrous. They had broken the Divine laws of morality, and that in a flagrant and shameful manner.

II. THE SUMMONS AND INVITATION TO RETURN WHICH HAD BEEN ADDRESSED BY GOD TO ISRAEL. Dealing with sinful men, a benevolent God has not been content simply to reveal truth and to inculcate holiness. He has ever addressed the children of men as those who have disregarded the truth and disobeyed the Law. Revelation is full of declarations of Divine mercy and promises of Divine forgiveness.

III. THE CHASTISEMENTS WHICH WERE INTENDED TO PRODUCE REPENTANCE AND REFORMATION. Words proving insufficient, they were followed by acts. It is dangerous for us confidently to interpret the plans of Divine providence. Yet God most high is the supreme Ruler of the nations, and in his own Word his "dealings" with the nations are interpreted with unerring justice and truth. The several disasters recounted in this passage as having befallen Israel are declared to have been of the nature of chastisements designed to awaken reflection and to call to penitence and to newness of life. "The voice of the rod" is a voice sometimes effectual, and always morally authoritative.

IV. THE INATTENTION OF ISRAEL TO THE SUMMONS AND TO THE CHASTISEMENTS. It is amazing to learn that not only the messages of prophets and authorized heralds, but even the "judgments" of the righteous Ruler, failed to produce the intended effect. Yet so it was, and those who had been often reproved hardened their neck. In this Israel was an example of that obduracy which may be discovered in all ages and in all communities. The power of man to resist the appeals and the entreaties, the commands and the chastisements, of a righteous God, is one of the most surprising and awful facts of the moral universe.

V. THE PATHETIC REPROACH. He whose power could smite and destroy the rebellious speaks as if himself wounded and distressed by the perseverance in rebellion of those he governs. It seems as if Omniscience were astonished and appalled at human obstinacy and obduracy. Hence the expostulation, the reproach addressed to the impenitent and rebellious, "Yet have ye not returned unto me."—T.

Ver. 11.—*The brand snatched from the burning.* Amongst the methods employed by the Divine Ruler to bring Israel to repentance was some calamity, some "judgment," which overtook certain of the cities of the land. It may be doubtful whether we are to understand that those cities were, like Sodom, struck by lightning and partially consumed by fire from heaven; or were attacked and given to the flames by an invading, hostile force; or were overtaken by some disaster figuratively described in this pictorial language. In any case, the circumstances are naturally suggestive of reflections upon the methods and purposes of God's treatment of sinful men.

I. A STRIKING PICTURE OF PUNISHMENT FOR SIN. Like a city given to the flames, like a brand flung upon the blazing fire, is the man, the community, that, on account of disobedience and rebelliousness, is abandoned for a time and for a purpose to the ravages of affliction and calamity. How often has a sinful, proud, luxurious, oppressive nation been consigned to this baptism of fire! How often has the wilful and obdurate nature been made to endure the keen and purifying flames! The connection between sin and suffering does indeed abound in mysteries; yet it is a reality not to be denied.

II. A STRIKING PICTURE OF THE DANGER OF DESTRUCTION TO WHICH THE IMPENITENT AND SINFUL ARE EXPOSED. Fire may purify the gold from dross, but it may consume and utterly destroy the chaff. Some nations exposed to the flames of war and calamity have perished and disappeared. Some individual lives seem, at all events, to have vanished in the flames of Divine judgment. The peril is imminent and undeniable.

III. A STRIKING PICTURE OF DIVINE DELIVERANCE. As the brand is plucked, snatched from the burning, so that, although bearing the traces of fire upon it, it is not consumed, even so did it happen to Israel that Divine mercy saved, if not the community, yet many individuals, from destruction. Where, indeed, is the soul, saved from spiritual death, of which it may not be said, "Here is a brand plucked from the burning"? And there are instances of salvation in which the similitude is peculiarly appropriate. There are those whose sins have, by reason of enormity and repetition, deserved and received no ordinary punishment in this life. And amongst such there are not a few whom the pity, the wisdom, and the power of our Saviour-God have preserved from destruction, and who abide living witnesses to his delivering might and grace.

APPLICATION. Here is encouragement for those who labour for the conversion and salvation of the degraded and debased. Even such, though nigh unto burning, may be plucked by Divine mercy from the flames of judgment.—T.

Ver. 12.—"*Prepare to meet thy God.*" Forbearance has its limits, and probation is not for ever. Discipline itself is temporary, and, when the purposes of God concerning men are fulfilled, will come to an end. There is a time for preparation, and then after that comes the time for reckoning and for recompense.

I. THE PERSONS DIRECTED TO PREPARE FOR THIS MEETING. 1. Especially the disobedient, the threatened, the chastened. The previous verses make it evident that it was to these that the admonition was particularly addressed. The people of Israel, as a whole, had departed from God, and had been censured and chastened by God. It seems to have been in consequence of their impenitence and obduracy that they were addressed in the solemn language of the text. 2. Yet the appeal has surely reference to such as were learning the lessons so powerfully though so painfully inculcated by Divine providence. There were individuals disposed to profit by the awful dispensations that were befalling the nation, and by the faithful admonitions addressed by inspired prophets.

II. THE EVENT DESCRIBED AS A MEETING WITH GOD. 1. It is not to be supposed that there is ever a time when God is not in immediate contact with his creatures. We meet him at every turn, we meet him at every moment. His eye is ever upon us, his hand is ever over us. "Whither shall we flee from his presence?" To the pious soul this thought is grateful, congenial, welcome. To the irreligious soul this thought should be productive of sincere humiliation and penitence. 2. There are, however, occasions appointed by the providence of God upon which the sons of men are constrained, manifestly and unmistakably, to meet their God. Nations meet God in national crises, in solemn conjunctures of incident, of probation, of destiny. Individuals meet God in critical events in human life, in remarkable experiences of the inevitable incidence of the moral law of God. 3. All Scripture declares that there is a future judgment, when all the intelligent and accountable shall be summoned into the Divine presence and before the Divine tribunal. "After death the judgment;" "Then shall every man give account of himself to God." We are directed to keep this day of account before our view, and to live in prospect of it.

III. THE PREPARATION HERE ENJOINED. 1. In character it must be thorough and sincere. Nothing hypocritical or superficial can suffice. For the meeting anticipated is with him who is the Searcher of all hearts. 2. In nature it must consist of true repentance and true faith. A turning of the heart from evil, and a turning unto God,—these are essential. Unfeigned repentance and cordial faith are indispensable. 3. In manifestation it must be in conformity with Divine requirements. If thou wouldst meet God with holy confidence, then must thou "do justly, love mercy, and walk humbly with thy God."—T.

Ver. 13.—*The majesty of God.* This and several other passages in this book of prophecy prove to us that Amos was a man who lived much in communion with nature and nature's God. A herdsman and a gatherer of figs, he passed his earlier years, not in towns, in palaces, in libraries, in schools, in the temple, but beneath the open sky, and in the presence of the solemnity, the grandeur, the sublimity, of the works of the Eternal. He had climbed the mountains of Judæa, had gazed upon the rugged ranges that closed in the Dead Sea, had scanned the desert of the south, and had delighted himself in the blue waters of the Mediterranean. He had out-watched the stars and greeted the glorious dawn ; he had bowed his head before the tempest, and heard the voice of the Almighty in the thunder's crash. He had read the scroll which unfolds itself to every observant eye ; he had listened to the language best heard in solitude and seclusion. His meditations concerning God as known, not by the book of the law, but by the book of nature, relate to—

I. GOD'S CREATIVE POWER. This he doubtless recognized wherever he turned, by day and by night, in the peaceful plain and upon the awful hills. He here refers to two instances of the Maker's might, two proofs of his incomparable majesty. "He formeth the *mountains.*" The stability and the immensity of the mountains have ever possessed a charm and an inspiration for the sensitive and thoughtful student of nature. Little as Amos could have known of those processes by which the enduring hills have been fashioned, he was capable of appreciating their testimony to the Creator, and probably of recognizing their symbolism of Divine attributes. The *wind* is a phe-nomenon which has always impressed the observer of God's works. Its immense power and its inscrutable mystery, its tenderness as it breathes through the forests at eventide, its awfulness when it roars upon the mountains, when it lashes into fury the mighty waves of the sea, are suggestive of the manifold operations of the all-compre-hending Deity. And our Lord himself has reminded us of its symbolical significance as setting forth the wonderful, varied, and inexplicable manifestations of the presence and the working of the Divine Spirit.

II. GOD'S SPIRITUAL INSIGHT. When the prophet describes God as " declaring unto man what is his thought," the language has sometimes been taken to refer to the Divine thought revealed to man ; but it probably is to be interpreted of that omniscient energy by virtue of which the Eternal penetrates the spiritual nature of men and reads their thoughts afar off. That the creating Spirit is thus in perpetual and inti-mate contact with those created spirits into which he has breathed the breath of life, and which he has fashioned in his own likeness : this is reasonable enough. Yet the enunciation of this unquestionable truth should have two effects upon us. It should enhance our conception of God's majesty, and so call forth our adoration and our praise ; and it should make us concerned as to the moral quality of the thoughts of our minds, which the omniscient and holy God must surely estimate with justice, and by a standard infinitely lofty and pure.

III. GOD'S PROVIDENTIAL RULE. If we take literally the language, "That maketh the morning darkness, and treadeth upon the high places of the earth," then these clauses are additional acknowledgments of the Creator's power and wisdom as displayed in nature. But coming after the preceding clause, which refers to men's thoughts, they seem to invite another interpretation. God's presence is to be recognized in the order of the world, in the tokens of moral government, in the workings of retributive law—in a word, in the facts which are justly deemed providential.

IV. GOD'S GLORIOUS NAME. To the Hebrew mind there was a very close connection between the nature and attributes and the Name of the Divine Ruler and Lord. He was Jehovah, *i.e.* the Self-existing and Eternal, whose Being accounts for all being beside. He was the Lord of hosts, *i.e.* supreme over all powers, possessed of all might, ordering all natures and all processes according to his own wisdom. The angelic hosts of unseen ministers and warriors, the armies of Israel and of the nations, the innumerable forces that obey the Divine behests and bring to pass the Divine purposes,—all these are beneath the cognizance and the sway of the Eternal, all these are ever executing his authoritative commandments and establishing his universal and everlasting kingdom. In the presence of a Being so glorious, so mighty, so holy, what power attaches to the monition of Scripture, " Stand in awe, and sin not " !—T.

Ver. 12.—" *Prepare to meet thy God.*" The threats which precede this summons are very indefinite. Designedly so ; for the prophet wished to arouse a *general* fore-boding of retribution amongst the careless people, which would have its fulfilment in national disasters, but its final consummation in another world. Such indefiniteness also makes it possible to apply his words to men of every age and country. All responsible beings must at last meet their God, and may wisely be urged to "prepare."

From the time of man's fall the all-merciful Father has been calling men to return from their evil ways. Adam was encouraged to hope in his mercy. The antediluvians were faithfully warned through Noah, the preacher of righteousness. Israel was constantly being exhorted by the inspired prophets. John the Baptist had as the burden of his preaching this same word "prepare;" and it has come ringing down the centuries to make itself heard among us also.

I. THE JUDGMENT FORETOLD. It is clear that the reference is to a summons to the tribunal of God, the Judge of quick and dead. There is a sense in which we may meet God in the study of his wonderful works in nature; in the strange and sometimes startling events of his providence; in the pages of his Word; in earnest supplication at his footstool. But another special and more solemn occasion is alluded to in our text—even that day when the great white throne will be set, and every man will have to give an account of all the deeds done in the body, whether good or bad. 1. *That judgment is certain to come.* Even nature seems to point onward to some crisis in the future of our race. Conscience warns us that sin cannot always go unpunished, for the world is governed by a God of righteousness. Scripture constantly affirms that he has appointed a day in the which he will judge the world by that Man whom he has ordained. 2. *It is quite uncertain when it will come.* "Of that day and of that hour knoweth no man." It will come suddenly and unexpectedly, as a thief in the night. Death will end our time of probation, and no one knows where and when it may meet him. Therefore "prepare to meet thy God." 3. *When it comes the trial will be thorough and final.* All actions, together with their motives, are under the Divine cognizance. None will escape his notice. No false excuses will avail; and, on the other hand, no mere errors will be condemned as if they were wilful sins. The good will be severed from the evil, as our Lord teaches us in the parables of the drag-net and the tares of the field.

II. THE PREPARATION NEEDED. We should not be urged to "prepare" unless by nature we were unprepared. It is merciful of our Judge to give us warning, counsel, and opportunity. He willeth not the death of a sinner, but would rather that he should repent and live. Had it not been possible for us to make ready, had he wished us only to hurry onward to a certain doom, we should not have heard this exhortation. But he gives us forewarning in many ways, and at certain seasons with peculiar force; *e.g.* when death enters our family, or some accident befalls ourselves. 1. *We need self-examination.* "Know thyself" was the advice of a heathen philosopher; but it is worth heeding by us all. We want the illumination of God's Spirit and the instruction of God's Word to aid us. "The candle of the Lord" must throw its rays into the recesses of our hearts. 2. *We need confession and repentance.* "If we confess our sins, he is faithful and just to forgive us our sins, and to cleanse us from all unrighteousness." 3. *We need faith in the atonement of Jesus.* It is said of all sinners who safely pass the great tribunal and enter into the heavenly world, "They have washed their robes, and made them white in the blood of the Lamb."

III. THE REASONS URGED. These appear in the next verse. 1. *God is omnipotent.* "He formeth the mountains." The mightiest cannot resist him; the most subtle will not escape him. 2. *God is omniscient.* "He declareth unto man what is his thought." He is the Searcher of hearts (Ps. cxxxix. 2; Jer. xvii. 10). Nothing eludes his notice. There is warning in this thought for the wicked; and there is comfort for the righteous, because these may reflect that their unspoken prayers, and their secret self-denials, and their unfulfilled purposes, are all recognized by him. They are represented by our Lord (Matt. xxv. 37—40) as being surprised at reward coming for acts which they thought little of or had quite forgotten. "God is not unfaithful to forget your work of faith and labour of love."

Apply the words of the exhortation to the careless.—A. R.

Vers. 4, 5.—*Worship abounding with abounding sin.* "Come to Bethel, and transgress; at Gilgal multiply transgression; and bring your sacrifices every morning," etc. "The language of these verses," says Henderson, "is that of the keenest irony. The Israelites were addicted to the worship of the golden calf, and to that of idols, whereby they contracted guilt before Jehovah, and exposed themselves to his judgments; at the same time, they hypocritically professed to keep up the observance of certain feasts which had been appointed by Moses." The subject that the text teaches is —*abounding worship with abounding sin.* The sins of Israel, the frauds, violences, and nameless iniquities, are referred to in the preceding chapters. Crimes ran riot amongst them at this period; and yet how religious they seemed to be! "Amos has described how zealously the people of Israel went on pilgrimage to Bethel and Gilgal and Beersheba, those places of sacred associations; with what superabundant diligence they offered sacrifice and paid tithes; how they would rather do too much than too little, so that they even burnt upon the altar a portion of the leavened loaves of the praise offering, which were only intended for the sacrificial meals, although none but unleavened bread was allowed to be offered; and, lastly, how in their pure zeal for multiplying the works of piety, they so completely mistook their nature as to summon by a public proclamation to the presentation of free-will offerings, the very peculiarity of which consisted in the fact that they had no other prompting than the will of the offerer" (Delitzsch). We offer two remarks on this subject.

I. Abounding worship often IMPLIES ABOUNDING SIN. This is the case when the worship is: 1. *Selfish.* More than half the worship of England is purely selfish. Men crowd churches, attend to religious ceremonies, and contribute to religious institutions purely with the idea of avoiding hell and getting to a happier world than this. They do not serve God for naught. Selfishness, which is bad everywhere, is never worse than when engaged in religion. 2. *Formal.* When religion is attended to as a matter of form, when sentiments are expressed without conviction, services rendered without self-sacrifice, the insincerity is an insult to Omniscience. "God is a Spirit, and they that worship him must worship him in spirit and in truth." Abounding worship is no proof of abounding virtue and abounding godliness. Often, alas! the more worship in a community, the more corruption.

II. Abounding worship often SPRINGS FROM ABOUNDING SIN. It may spring from: 1. A desire to *conceal sin.* Sin is an ugly thing; it is hideous to the eye of conscience. Hence efforts on all hands to conceal. Nations endeavour to conceal the terrible abominations of infernal wars by employing the ministers of religion in connection with their fiendish work. The greatest villains have often sought to conceal their villanies by worship. 2. A desire to *compensate for evils.* Great brewers build churches and endow religious institutions in order to compensate in some measure for the enormous evil connected with their damning trade. 3. A desire to *appear good.* The more corrupt a man is, the stronger his desire to appear otherwise; the more devil in a man, the more anxious he is to look like an angel.

CONCLUSION. Do not judge the character of a nation by the number of its churches, the multitude of its worshippers, or the amount of its contributions, or efforts to proselytize men to its faith.—D. T.

Vers. 6—11.—*God's government of the world a chastising government.* "And I also have given you cleanness of teeth in all your cities, and want of bread in all your places," etc. In these verses the Almighty describes the various corrective measures which he had employed for effecting a moral reformation in the character of the Israelites. At the end of each chastising measure which he describes, he marks their obstinate impenitence with the expression, "Yet have ye not returned unto me." As if he had said, "The grand end of all my dealings is to bring you in sympathy, heart, and life back to me." The subject of the verses is this—God's government of the world is a *chastising* government; and three remarks are here suggested.

I. The chastisements employed are often OVERWHELMINGLY TERRIFIC. 1. He sometimes employs *blind nature.* Here is *famine.* "I also have given you cleanness of teeth in all your cities, and want of bread in all your places." The transgressors under the Law God had threatened with famine (Deut. xxviii. 48). The Divine government has often employed famine as a ruthless and resistless messenger to chasten mankind. In the days of Elisha the demon wielded his black sceptre for seven long years (2 Kings viii. 1). The second is *drought.* "I have withholden the rain from you, when there were yet three months to the harvest: and I caused it to rain upon one city, and caused it not to rain upon another city: one piece was rained upon, and the piece whereupon it rained not withered. So two or three cities wandered unto one city, to drink water; but they were not satisfied." Rain—indispensable to the life of the world—comes not by accident or blind necessity, but by the Divine will. "He watereth the hills from his chambers." To show that the rain is entirely at the disposal of the Almighty, it came upon one field and one city, and not upon another. Hence the inhabitants of the places where it rained not had to go great distances for water, and yet "were not satisfied." This is a terrible chastisement. The third is *blight*. "I have smitten you with blasting and mildew: when your gardens, and your vineyards, and your fig trees, and your olive trees increased, the palmerworm devoured them." A malignant atmosphere combined with devouring reptiles to destroy the produce of the land. The fourth is *pestilence and the sword*. "I have sent among you the pestilence after the manner of Egypt: your young men have I slain with the sword, and have taken away your horses; and I have made the stink of your camps to come up unto your nostrils." The allusion, perhaps, is to the pestilence with which God visited Egypt (Exod. ix.). The pestilence is God's destroying angel. Thus by blind nature God has often chastised mankind. He makes the stars in their courses fight against Sisera. Nature is a rod in his chastening hand; and what a rod it is! At his pleasure, by a touch, he can wake tempests that shall shake the globe, earthquakes that shall engulf cities, etc. Yes, whatever materialistic scientists may say, nature is nothing more than a rod in the hand of its Maker. The fifth is *fire*. "I have overthrown some of you, as God overthrew Sodom and Gomorrah, and ye were as a firebrand plucked out of the burning." 2. He sometimes employs *human wickedness*. The sword is mentioned here. "Your young men have I slain with the sword." War, unlike famine, drought, pestilence, and fire, is human, devilish. It is the work of free agents, under the influence of infernal evil. But God employs it; he does not originate it, he does not sanction it, he does not inspire it; but he permits it and controls it for purposes of chastisement. Thus all things are at the use of his chastising government—matter and mind, angels and fiends, heaven and hell.

II. The chastisements employed are ever DESIGNED FOR MORAL RESTORATION. After each judgment described we have the words, "Yet have ye not returned unto me, saith the Lord." "Yet have ye not returned unto me, saith the Lord." "Yet have ye not returned unto me, saith the Lord." This is the burden and design of the whole. Note: 1. Men are alienated from the Lord. They are estranged in thought, sympathy, and purpose. Like the prodigal, they are in a far country, away from their Father. 2. Their alienation is the cause of all their misery. Estrangement from God means distance, not only from virtue, but from freedom, light, progress, dignity, blessedness. Hence the benevolence of all these chastisements. They are to restore souls. "Lo! all these things worketh God oftentimes with man, to bring him back from the pit, that he may be enlightened with the light of the living" (Job. xxxiii. 29, 30). To every unconverted man God can say, "I have chastised you in this way and in that way, on this occasion and on that, but 'yet have ye not returned unto me, saith the Lord.'"

III. The chastisements employed often FAIL IN THEIR GRAND DESIGN. "Yet have ye not returned unto me, saith the Lord." This shows (1) the force of human depravity, and (2) the force of human freedom. Almighty goodness does not force us into goodness. Almighty love does not dragoon us into goodness. He treats us as free agents and responsible beings.—D. T.

Vers. 12, 13.—*Preparation for meeting God.* "Therefore thus will I do unto thee, O Israel: and because I will do this unto thee, prepare to meet thy God, O Israel," etc. "All the means that had been employed to reform the Israelites having proved ineffectual, are here summoned to prepare for the final judgment, which was to put an end to their national existence. To this judgment reference is emphatically made in the terms כֹּה, 'thus;' and זֹאת, 'this.' There is a brief resumption of the sentence delivered in vers. 2 and 3." We raise three observations from these words.

I. MAN MUST HAVE A CONSCIOUS MEETING WITH GOD. "Prepare to meet thy God." "I shall see God," says Job: "whom I shall see for myself, and not another." Yes, we shall all see God. All men ought ever and everywhere to see him, for he is the great Object in the horizon, nearer to them infinitely than aught besides. But they do not. Their spiritual eye is so closed that they see him not; they are utterly unconscious of his presence. But see him they *must* one day. All must be brought into conscious contact with him, and in his presence they will feel the greatest things in the universe melt into nothing. The atheist who denies his existence shall see God; the worldling who ignores his existence shall see God; the theologian who misrepresents his existence shall see God. We must all see God.

II. This conscious meeting with God requires on our part preparation. 1. To meet him, *reconciliation* is needed. Practically we are at enmity with him. How shall an enemy stand in his presence? Who does not feel uneasy and even distressed when he confronts a man he hates, although the man may have no disposition and no power whatever to injure him? How will the soul with enmity in its heart then confront him? "I beseech you then in Christ's stead, be ye reconciled to God." 2. To meet him, *moral purity* is necessary. How will a consciously corrupt soul feel in the presence of absolute holiness? How are the flames of hell kindled? By the rays of Divine holiness falling on corrupt spirits.

"Eternal Light, eternal Light,
How pure the soul must be,
When, placed within thy searching sight,
It shrinks not, but with calm delight
Can live and look on thee!"

III. The procedure of God is an argument for this preparation. 1. His procedure is *terribly judicial*. "Therefore thus will I do unto thee, O Israel: and because I will do this unto thee, prepare to meet thy God, O Israel." He was approaching the sinner in judgment, moving towards him judicially. He was coming towards the Israelites as an Avenger. And so he is ever coming towards wicked men. Prepare, therefore, to meet him. He is coming as a Judge—slowly it may be, but surely and terribly. 2. His procedure is *overwhelmingly grand*. "Lo, he that formeth the mountains, and createth the wind, and declareth unto man what is his thought, that maketh the morning darkness, and treadeth upon the high places of the earth, The Lord, The God of hosts, is his Name." This magnificent description of Jehovah is given in order to urge the call to preparation.

Conclusion. The one mighty, loud, unceasing voice of God to man through all nature, history, and special revelation is, "Prepare to meet thy God."—D. T.

EXPOSITION.

CHAPTER V.

Ver. 1—ch. vi. 14.—§ 3. *Third address: the prophet utters a lamentation over the fall of Israel.* (Vers. 1—3.) He calls her to repentance, while he shows wherein she has declined from the right way. To make this plain, he contrasts God's power and majesty with the people's iniquity, instances of which he gives (vers. 4—12). The only condition of safety is amendment (vers. 13—15); and as they refuse to reform, they shall have cause to lament (vers. 16, 17). This threat is enforced by the two emphatic "woes" that follow, the first of which demonstrates the baselessness of their trust in their covenant relation to God (vers. 18—27); the second denounces the careless lives of the chiefs, who, revelling in luxury, believed not in the coming judgment (ch. vi. 1—6). Therefore they shall go into captivity, and the kingdom shall be utterly overthrown (vers. 7—11), because they act iniquitously and are self-confident (vers. 12—14).

Ver. 1.—Hear ye this word. To show the certainty of the judgment and his own feeling about it, the prophet utters his prophecy in the form of a dirge (*kinah*, 2 Sam. i. 17; 2 Chron. xxxv. 25). Which I take up against you; or, *which I raise over you*, as if the end had come. O house of Israel; in the vocative. The Vulgate has, *Domus Israel cecidit*; so the LXX. But the present Hebrew text is most suitable, making the dirge begin at ver. 2. The ten tribes are addressed as in ver. 6.

Ver. 2.—The virgin of Israel; *i.e.* the virgin Israel; so called, not as having been pure and faithful to God, but as tenderly treated and guarded from enemies (comp. Isa. xxiii. 12; xlvii. 1; Jer. xiv. 17). Is fallen (comp. 2 Sam. i. 19); she shall no more rise. This is apparently a contradiction to the promise of restoration elsewhere expressed, but is to be explained either as referring exclusively to the ten tribes, very few of whom returned from exile, and to the kingdom of Israel, which was never re-established; or, as Pseudo-Rufinus says, "Ita debemus accipere, quod lugentis affectu cumulatius æstimavit illata discrimina, sicque funditus appellasse deletos, quos ex majore videret parte contritos." Forsaken upon her land; better, *she shall be dashed upon her own land;* her own soil shall witness her ruin—that soil which was "virgin," unconquered, and her own possession.

Ver. 3.—The vindication of the prophet's lament. The city that went out by a thousand. Septuagint and Vulgate, "from which went forth thousands," or, "a thousand;" *i.e.* which could send out a thousand warriors to the fight. In such a city only a tenth of the inhabitants shall remain; and this shall happen to small cities as well as great.

Ver. 4.—The more formal proof that Israel has merited her punishment here begins. In calling her to repentance the prophet contrasts God's requirements with her actual conduct. Seek ye me, and ye shall live. Two imperatives: "Seek me, and (so) live;" duty and its reward. "Seek me in the appointed way, and ye shall be saved from destruction" (comp. Gen. xlii. 18).

Ver. 5.—Bethel . . . Gilgal. The scenes of idolatrous worship, where was no true seeking of God (see note on ch. iv. 4). Beersheba. A spot about fifty miles south-south-west of Jerusalem, the site of which has never been lost, and is marked to this day by seven much-frequented wells. As being one of the holy places celebrated in the history of the patriarchs (Gen. xxi. 31, 33; xxvi. 23, etc.; xlvi. 1), it had become a shrine of idolatrous worship, to which the Israelites resorted, though it lay far out of their territory (comp. ch. viii. 14). Gilgal shall surely go into captivity. There is in the Hebrew a play on the words here and in the following clause (*Hag-gilgal galoh yigleh*), which commentators have paralleled with such expressions as, *Capua capietur, Cremona cremabitur, Paris périra,* "London is undone." Or, taking Joshua's explanation of the name, we may say, "Roll-town shall be rolled away." Bethel shall come to nought. As *Bethel,* "House of God," had become *Bethaven,* "House of vanity" (see Hos. iv. 15), as being the temple of an idol (comp. 1 Cor. viii. 4), so the prophet, with allusion to this, says that "Bethel shall become *aven*"—vanity, nothingness, itself. No mention is made of the fate of Beersheba, because Amos has in view only the ten tribes, and the destiny of places beyond their territory is not here the object of his prediction; and indeed, when Israel was ruined, Beersheba escaped unharmed.

Ver. 6.—Break out like fire. God is called "a consuming fire" (Deut. iv. 24; Heb. xii. 29; comp. Jer. iv. 4). And devour it; Septuagint, Ὅπως μὴ ἀναλάμψῃ ὡς πῦρ ὁ οἶκος Ἰωσήφ, καὶ καταφάγῃ αὐτόν, "Lest the house of Joseph blaze as fire, and he devour him;" Vulgate, *Ne forte comburatur ut ignis domus Joseph, et devorabit.* But it

is best to take the last member of the sentence thus: "and it (the fire) devour." The house of Joseph. Ephraim, *i.e.* the kingdom of Israel, of which Ephraim was the distinguishing tribe. In Bethel; or, *for Bethel.* The LXX., paraphrasing, has, τῷ οἴκῳ Ἰσραήλ, "for the house of Israel."

Ver. 7.—The prophet brings out the contrast between Israel's moral corruption and God's omnipotence. Ye who turn judgment to wormwood. As Jerome puts it, "Converterunt dulcedinem judicii in absinthii amaritudinem," "They turned the sweetness of judgment into the bitterness of absinth" (comp. ch. vi. 12). Who make judgment the occasion of the bitterest injustice. There is no syntactical connection between this verse and the last, but virtually we may append it to "seek the Lord." It would sound in people's ears as a reminiscence of Deut. xxix. 18, 20. The LXX. reads, ὁ ποιῶν εἰς ὕψος κρίμα, "that executeth judgment in the height," referring the sentence to the Lord, or else taking *laanah,* "wormwood," in a metaphorical sense, as elsewhere they translate it by ἀνάγκη, πικρία, ὀδύνη (Deut. xxix. 18; Prov. v. 4; Jer. ix. 15; xxiii. 15). The name "wormwood" is applied to all the plants of the genus that grew in Palestine the taste of which was proverbially bitter. And leave off righteousness in the earth; rather, *cast down righteousness to the earth* (as Isa. xxviii. 2), despise it and trample it underfoot (comp. Dan. viii. 12). This is Israel's practice; and yet God, as the next verse shows, is almighty, and has power to punish. *Righteousness* includes all transactions between man and man. The LXX. (still referring the subject to the Lord), καὶ δικαιοσύνην εἰς γῆν ἔθηκεν, "and he established righteousness on earth."

Ver. 8.—Striking instances are given of God's creative power and omnipotence. Seek him that maketh the seven stars. "Seek him" is not in the Hebrew. "He that maketh," etc., is in direct antithesis to "ye who turn," etc. (ver. 7). *The seven stars;* Hebrew, *kimah,* "the heap," the constellation of the Pleiades (Job ix. 9; xxxviii. 31). The Septuagint here has, ὁ ποιῶν πάντα, but in Job has πλειάς. The Vulgate gives, *facientem Arcturum.* Symmachus and Theodotion give πλειάδα in the present passage. The identification of this term is discussed in the 'Dictionary of the Bible,' ii. 891. The observation of this most remarkable cluster among the heavenly bodies would be natural to the pastoral life of Amos. And Orion; Hebrew, *kesil,* "foolish," a rebel, the name being applied to Nimrod, whose representation was found by the Easterns in this constellation. Some render *kesil,* "gate;" others connect it with the Arabic *sohail*, equivalent to Sirius, or Canopus. The Septuagint here has, καὶ μετασκευάζων, " and changing," which looks as if the translator was not familiar with the Hebrew word, and substituted something in its place. It reads Ὠρίωνος in Job xxxviii. 31. **Turneth the shadow of death into the morning.** "The shadow of death," the depth of darkness. This and the following clause do not simply state that the regular interchange of day and night is in God's hands, but rather notify that God is a moral Governor of the world. He saves men from the utmost dangers, from the darkness of sin and from the night of ignorance; and, on the other hand, he sends calamity on those that offend his Law (comp. ch. iv. 13). **Maketh the day dark with night;** literally, as the Septuagint, ἡμέραν εἰς νύκτα συσκοτάζων, "darkeneth day into night." That **calleth for the waters of the sea,** etc. As judgments are the prophet's theme, this expression cannot be an intimation of the working of the natural law by which the moisture taken up from the sea as cloud returns upon the earth as rain (comp. ch. ix. 6). Rather it is an allusion to the Flood and similar catastrophes, which are proofs of God's judicial government of the universe, when "he maketh the creature his weapon for the revenge of his enemies" (Wisd. v. 17). **The Lord is his Name.** Jehovah, the self-existent God, doeth all these marvellous things, and men presume to scout his Law and think to be unpunished (ch. iv. 13).

Ver. 9.—**That strengtheneth,** etc. Translate, *That causeth destruction to flash forth upon the strong, so that destruction cometh upon the fortress.* The idea is that God, as with a lightning-flash, smites the strongest man, and no fortress is a refuge from him. Septuagint, Ὁ διαιρῶν συντριμμὸν ἐπὶ ἰσχύν, "Who divideth destruction unto strength." The Vulgate, taking the Hebrew verb *balag* in the sense of lighting up the countenance, renders, *Qui subridet vastitatem super robustum,* which means that the Lord smiles while he brings desolation on the mighty—a figurative expression denoting his anger at man's pride, and the ease with which he punishes. We may add that Rosenmüller agrees with the Authorized Version in the first clause: "Who strengtheneth the weak against the strong, and giveth the plunderers power over the fortresses of the strong."

Vers. 10—12.—The prophet gives further instances of the people's corruption.

Ver. 10.—**Him that rebuketh in the gate** (Isa. xxix. 21). The gate of Eastern cities was the place of public resort (Prov. i. 21), either for business (Deut. xxv. 7), or the ad-

ministration of justice (2 Sam. xv. 2), or for gossip. So "he that rebuketh in the gate" may be a judge, or a chief, or a prophet (Jer. xvii. 19; xix. 2). It seems better to take the words thus than to join "in the gate" to "they hate," with the meaning that those who resort to the gate—kings, chiefs, judges—hate the prophet's reproof, for the following verses show that Amos is referring chiefly to judicial proceedings, and not to his own mission. **Uprightly;** literally, *perfectly;* Vulgate, *perfecte;* i.e. without reserve, keeping nothing back.

Ver. 11.—**Therefore.** Because ye refuse reproof, and oppress the poor. **Your treading is upon the poor ;** *ye trample upon.* The Hebrew word *boshes* is found nowhere else, and is variously explained. Septuagint, κατεκονδύλιζον, "smote with the fists;" so the Syriac; Vulgate, *diripiebatis,* with which the Chaldee agrees. Keil, Schegg, and most modern commentators explain the word, by a slight dialectical variation, as equivalent to *conculcare.* **Burdens of wheat ;** rather, *tribute,* exactions of wheat, or presents like enforced "benevolences." They exacted such gifts before they would do justice to the poor. Or it may refer to interest for money or victuals lent, which took the form of presents in order to evade the Law (Exod. xxii. 25; Lev. xxv. 37; Deut. xxiii. 19). Septuagint, δῶρα ἐκλεκτά: Vulgate, *prædam electam,* the Hebrew word *bar* meaning either "wheat" or "elect." **Hewn stone.** Houses thus built were a mark of luxury and wealth, sun-dried brick being the usual material employed (comp. Isa. ix. 10; Ezek. xii. 5, 7). **Ye shall not dwell in them.** This is the punishment of their evil doings, according to the threat in Deut. xxviii. 30, 39. The people shall be banished and the land desolated (Micah vi. 15; Zeph. i. 13).

Ver. 12.—Your punishment is richly deserved, for "I know how many are your transgressions and how mighty are your sins," especially, as it follows, your sins of oppression and injustice. They afflict the just. The construction is continuous: "afflicters of the just." *Hostes justi* (Vulgate); κατατατοῦντες δίκαιον, "trampling down the just" (Septuagint); comp. Wisd. ii. 12—15. **They take a bribe.** The translation of *kopher* as "bribe" is justified, perhaps, by 1 Sam. xii. 3; but the word is elsewhere used for "ransom," redemption-money paid to escape the consequences of crime (Prov. vi. 35), in direct opposition to the Law in Numb. xxxv. 31, which forbade any ransom to be taken for the life of a murderer. The Septuagint has, λαμβάνοντες ἀλλάγματα, "taking wares;" the Vulgate (with which the Syriac agrees), *accipientes munus.* **Turn aside the poor in the gate** from their right; or, *bow down the needy in the gate*, i.e. in the place of judgment (see note on ver. 10). Vulgate, *pauperes deprimentes in porta*; Septuagint, πένητας ἐν πύλαις ἐκκλίνοντες, "turning aside the poor in the gates." The crime specified is that of wresting judgment in the case of the poor, or not giving the poor man justice unless he could pay for it (comp. Exod. xxiii. 6; Deut. xvi. 19).

Ver. 13.—Even while he speaks, the prophet feels that his reproof is useless (comp. Jer. vii. 27, etc.; Hos. iv. 1, 17). In that time; *at such a time* as this, the man who acts wisely holds his peace, because it is a time of moral corruption and of personal danger. But the prophet cannot restrain his call (comp. Ezek. xxxiii. 3, etc.). In Micah ii. 3 the "evil time" is one of calamity.

Ver. 14.—He repeats his loving summons to repentance, as in vers. 4, 6, showing that their only hope of safety lay in amendment of life (comp. Zeph. ii. 3). Seek good, and not evil. Use that diligence and zeal in pursuing what is good which you have hitherto shown in the pursuit of evil. The Lord, the God of hosts, shall be with you, as ye have spoken; or, *as ye say.* The Israelites fancied that, owing to their covenant relation to God, he would be always with them and ready to help them under any circumstances. Their prosperity under Jeroboam II., as Calmet remarks, seemed an argument in their favour, proving that God blessed them, and that they had no cause for fear (comp. Jer. vii. 4, etc.; Micah iii. 11; Matt. iii. 9; John viii. 39). But really God's help and favour were conditioned by their obedience.

Ver. 15.—Reverse your former conduct, undo what ye have done (ver. 10). This verse emphasizes the preceding; hating and loving are more real and hearty than mere seeking. The LXX. makes this clause to be what the people said, Ὃν τρόπον εἴπατε, μεμισήκαμεν τὰ πονηρὰ, καὶ ἠγαπήσαμεν τὰ καλά, "As ye said, We have hated evil, and loved good." Establish judgment. Maintain justice in your tribunals (in contrast to ver. 7); then it may be that the Lord will have mercy on you or some of you. The remnant of Joseph; implying that only a few of them will be saved after this heavy chastisement, which points to the final ruin of their city and nation. The prophet speaks of the "remnant of Joseph" instead of Ephraim, to remind them of their forefather, who received the patriarchal blessing of Jacob, for whose sake this remnant should be spared (comp. Isa. vi. 13; x. 21, etc.; Joel ii. 32; Rom. xi. 4, etc.).

Vers. 16, 17.—The retribution for their incorrigible iniquity is here announced.

For "they that would not be reformed by that correction, wherein he dallied with them, shall feel a judgment worthy of God" (Wisd. xii. 26).

Ver. 16.—Therefore. The prophet returns to what was said in ver. 13 about the uselessness of reproof; vers. 14 and 15 being a kind of parenthetical exhortation which his love for his nation forced from him. "Jehovah, the God of hosts, the Lord," *Adonai*, saith what follows, these solemn titles being used to add solemnity, certainty, and weight to the announcement. Wailing; *misped*, "the death-wail." Streets; *broad places*; πλατείαις (Septuagint); *plateis* (Vulgate). Highways; the narrower *streets*; ὁδοῖς (Septuagint); *in cunctis quæ foris sunt* (Vulgate). Everywhere in town and country shall the wail be heard. Alas! alas! ho! ho! This is the death-wail (comp. Jer. xxii. 18), which should sound abroad when Samaria was besieged and taken. They shall call the husbandman to mourning. The husbandman shall be called from his labour in the fields to mourn for a calamity in his house. Pusey thinks the mourning is for his occupation gone, his tillage now only furnishing food for the enemy; but the context involves the notion of death. And such as are skilful of lamentation to wailing; literally, *proclaim wailing to such*, etc. These are the hired mourners, both male and female, who sang mournful songs at deaths (comp. 2 Chron. xxxv. 25; Jer. ix. 17; Matt. ix. 23).

Ver. 17.—Vineyards. The place of mirth and gladness, that, says St. Jerome, "ubi quondam fuit materia lætitiæ, sit origo lacrymarum" (Isa. xvi. 10). I will pass through thee. A terrible echo of the last plague of Egypt (Exod. xii. 12), when God will not "pass over" thee as he did then, but treat thee as Egypt, and "pass through" to smite and punish (Nah. i. 12).

Vers. 18—27.—The prophet enforces the threat by denouncing woe on those that trust to their covenant relation to God, expecting the day when he would punish the heathen for their sakes, and thinking that external, heartless worship was acceptable to him.

Ver. 18.—The day of the Lord. Any crisis in the nation's history is so called, when God interposes to punish and correct. To our minds it looks forward to the final judgment. It is often mentioned by the prophets (*e.g.* Isa. ii. 12; xiii. 6, 9; Joel ii. 1, 11; iii. 18; Zeph. i. 7, 14) as a time when the heathen should be judged, all the enemies of Israel defeated, and when Israel herself was exalted to the highest pitch of prosperity and dominion. Without any regard

to the moral condition affixed to the realization of these expectations (see Joel ii. 32),
the people " desired " the appearance of this
day, thus foolishly confirming themselves in
their sinful life and false security. Some
think scoffers are intended, but the context
shows that the persons signified are sincere
but mistaken believers in the safety of
Israel's covenant position. **To what end is
it for you? the day of the Lord is darkness;
Why would ye have the day of the Lord? It
is darkness.** Why do ye, such as ye are,
want this day to come? Ye know not what
ye ask. It will be the very contrary to
your expectations; it will be **darkness, and
not light,** tribulation and misery, not joy
and triumph for you (comp. Micah vii. 8).

Ver. 19.—Amos explains the dangers of
this judgment-day by illustrations drawn
from pastoral life, equivalent to the rushing
from Charybdis into Scylla. Every place
is full of danger—the open country, the
shelter of the house. Jerome applies the
passage to the fate of the kingdom in general:
" Fugientibus vobis a facie Nabuchodonosor
leonis occurrent Medi, Persæ, demum Antiochus Epiphanes, qui moretur in templo
et vos instar colubri mordeat, nequaquam
foris in Babylone, sed intra terminos terræ
sanctæ."

Ver. 20.—The character of **the day of the
Lord** is enforced with reiterated earnestness
(ver. 18) by an appeal to the conscience of
the hearers. Do you not feel in your inmost
hearts that in the case of such guilt as yours
the Lord can visit but to punish?

Ver. 21.—Outward, formal worship will
not avert the threatened danger or secure
the favour of God in the day of visitation.
Your feast days (chaggim)**; your feasts;** your
counterfeit worship, the worship of the true
God under an idol symbol (compare God's
repudiation of merely formal worship in
Isa. i. 11—15). **I will not smell;** οὐ μὴ
ὀσφρανθῶ θυσίας (Septuagint). No sweet
savour ascends to God from such sacrifices;
so the phrase is equivalent to " I will not
accept," " I will take no delight in " (comp.
Gen. viii. 21; Exod. xxix. 18; Lev. xxvi.
31). **Solemn assemblies;** πανηγύρεσιν (Septuagint); atsaroth; the convocations for the
keeping of the great festivals.

Ver. 22.—They maintained the formal
ritual of the Mosaic worship in their idolatry. The various offerings are here enumerated. **Burnt offerings;** ὁλοκαντώματα (Exod.
xxix. 38, 42; Numb. xxviii. 9—11). **Meat
offerings;** θυσίας (Septuagint); munera
(Vulgate); Exod. xxix. 40, 41; Lev. ii. 1.
Peace offerings of your fat beasts; σωτη-
ρίους ἐπιφανείας ὑμῶν, " **your grand peace
offerings** " (Septuagint); vota pinguium
vestrorum (Vulgate); Lev. iii. 1, etc.

Ver. 23.—**The noise of thy songs.** Their

psalms and hymns of praise were mere noise
in God's ear, and wearied him (Isa. i. 14;
xxiv. 8; Ezek. xxvi. 13). **Viols** (ch. vi. 5);
ὀργάνων (Septuagint). The nebel, usually
translated " psaltery," was a kind of harp.
Josephus (' Ant.,' vii. 12. 3) describes it as
having twelve strings, played by the fingers.
Music, both instrumental and vocal, was
used in the temple-worship (see 1 Chron.
xvi. 42; xxiii. 5; and xxv.).

Ver. 24.—**But let judgment run down as
waters;** let judgment roll on; Septuagint,
καὶ κυλισθήσεται ὡς ὕδωρ κρίμα, " and judgment shall roll along as water; " Et revela-
bitur quasi aqua judicium (Vulgate). This
verse has been explained in different ways.
Hitzig, Keil, with many ancient commentators, find in it a threat of chastisement, " the
flooding of the land with judgment and the
punitive righteousness of God." Pusey, Professor Gandell, and others consider it to be a
call to amendment. " He bids them let judgment, which had hitherto been perverted in
its course, roll on like a mighty tide of waters,
sweeping before it all hindrances," filling
the whole land with righteousness. Schegg
makes it to be a promise of the coming of
the day of the Lord, that is, the revelation
of Messiah. But such a promise in this
position is very forced and unnatural. The
second interpretation seems most suitable.
In the midst of the denunciation of men's
formal worship, the prophet announces their
duty in the present crisis, attention to which
could alone win God's favour. Judgment
and righteousness, long neglected and forgotten, should permeate the land like refreshing streams of water—a simile of special
signification to an inhabitant of an Eastern
country, where the neighbourhood of a
perennial stream was as delightful as it was
unusual. **Mighty** (ethan); ἄβατος, " impassable " (Septuagint); fortis (Vulgate). The
word may mean " strong," or " perennial."
" Whence the seventh month, just before the
early rain, was called the month Ethanim,
i.e. the month of the perennial streams, when
they alone flowed " (Pusey).

Ver. 25.—Ye have always been idolaters,
corrupters of pure worship. Your service in
the wilderness, when you were little exposed
to external influence, was no more true and
faithful than that which you offer now;
that was as unacceptable as this. **Have ye
offered unto me?** Did ye offer unto me? The
answer expected is " No; " i.e. you did not
so really, because your worship was mixed
with falsehood, and was not offered simply
and genuinely to me. It is certain, too, that
during the sojourn in the wilderness sacrificial worship fell greatly into desuetude,
as we know that the rite of circumcision
was suspended (Josh. v. 5—7), the Passover
was not duly celebrated, and Joshua urged

the people to put away the strange gods from among them (xxiv. 23). Moses, too, doubtless with a view to existing practices, warns them against worshipping the heavenly bodies (Deut. iv. 19), and offering sacrifice unto devils (*seirim*), "after whom they had gone a-whoring" (Lev. xvii. 7). The prophets, too, allude to the idolatry practised in the desert (see Ezek. xx. 7—26; Hos. ix. 10). But to argue (as some neologians do) from this passage of Amos that the Israelites during those forty years knew nothing of Jehovah, or that Amos himself denies that they offered him any worship, is absurd, seeing that the prophet presupposes the fact, and blames them for corrupting the Divine service and mingling the prescribed and enacted ritual with idolatrous accretions. Sacrifices; slain, bloody sacrifices. Offerings; bloodless sacrifices, meal offerings.

Ver. 26.—This verse has occasioned great perplexity to commentators. The connection with the context, the meaning of some of the terms, and whether the reference is to past, present, or future, are questions which have roused much controversy. We need not here recapitulate the various opinions which have been held. It will be sufficient to state what seems to be the simplest and most probable explanation of the passage. But we must not omit to mention first the explanation adopted by Ewald, Schrader, Farrar, König, and others, viz. that this verse refers to the punitive deportation which was to be the people's lot, when they should take their shrines and images with them into captivity. "So shall ye take (into exile) Sakkuth your king," etc. But the punishment is foretold in ver. 27; and this verse contrasts their idol-worship with the neglected worship of Jehovah (ver. 25). But ye have borne; *and ye bare; καὶ ἀνελάβετε* (Septuagint); *et portastis* (Vulgate). Ye offered me no pure worship in the wilderness, seeing that ye took false gods with you, and joined their worship with, or substuted it for, mine. The tabernacle of your Moloch; *τὴν σκηνὴν τοῦ Μολόχ* (Septuagint); *tabernaculum Moloch vestro* (Vulgate). The Hebrew word rendered "tabernacle" (*sikkuth*), which is found nowhere else, has been variously explained. Aquila gives *συσκιασμούς*: Theodotion, "vision," reading the whole sentence thus: *Καὶ ἤρατε τὴν ὅρασιν τοῦ βασιλέως ὑμῶν, ἀμαύρωσιν εἰδώλων ὑμῶν, ἄστρον τοῦ Θεοῦ ὑμῶν.* Many moderns render, "stake," "column," or "shrine." Others suppose it to be equivalent to *Sakkuth*, an Assyrian name for Molech (or Adar); but this is very uncertain (see 'Studien und Kritiken,' 1874, p. 387), and the parallelism requires the word to be an appellative and not a proper name. It most probably means "shrine," a portable

shrine, like those spoken of in Acts xix. 24 in connection with the worship of Diana. The Syriac and Arabic versions call it "tent," and thus the reproach stands forth emphatically that, instead of, or in conjunction with, the true tabernacle, they bore aloft, as if proud of their apostasy, the tabernacle of a false god. Such shrines were used by the Egyptians, according to Herodotus (ii. 63, where see Rawlinson's note) and Diod. Sic. (i. 97). Many such may be seen in the Egyptian room of the British Museum. Keil quotes Drumann, 'On the Rosetta Inscription,' p. 211, "These were small chapels, generally gilded and ornamented with flowers and in other ways, intended to hold a small idol when processions were made, and to be carried or driven about with it." Hence we must look to Egypt as the source of this idolatry. Moloch, though sanctioned by the LXX. and St. Stephen (Acts vii. 43), is a mistranslation. De Rossi, indeed, mentions that one Hebrew manuscript gives *Moloch*, but the received reading is *Malkekem*, which is confirmed by Symmachus and Theodotion, who have *τοῦ βασιλέως ὑμῶν*, and by the Syriac. The translation, therefore, should run, "Ye took up the shrine of your king," *i.e.* of him whom ye made your king in the place of Jehovah, meaning some stellar divinity. And Chiun your images; *καὶ τὸ ἄστρον τοῦ θεοῦ ὑμῶν 'Ραιφάν*, "and the star of your god Ræphan" (Septuagint); *et imaginem idolorum vestrorum;* literally, *the kiyyun of your images.* The parallelism again requires us to take this unknown word as an appellative; and according to its probable derivation, its meaning is "pedestal," or "framework," that on which the image stood. The Greek rendering is, as Keil thinks, owing to a false reading of the unpointed text, in old Hebrew *kaph* and *resh* being easily confounded, and *vau* and *pe*. Theodotion considered the word a common noun, translating it by *ἀμαύρωσιν*. It is probably a mere coincidence that in some Assyrian inscriptions the name *Kairan* occurs as that of a deity, who is identified with Saturn; that the Egyptians (from whom the Israelites must have derived the notion) ever acknowledged such a deity is quite unproved. St. Stephen merely quotes the *Textus Receptus* of his day, which was close enough to the original for his argument. The star of your god. These words are in loose apposition with the preceding, and are equivalent to "your star-god," or the star whom ye worship as god. Whether some particular star is meant, or whether the sun is the deity signified, cannot be determined, although the universal prevalence of the worship of sun-gods in Egypt makes the latter supposition very probable.

St. Stephen puts the sin in a general form : "God gave them up to serve the host of heaven" (Acts vii. 42 ; comp. Deut. iv. 19 ; xvii. 3). **Which ye made to yourselves.** This was the crime, self-will, desertion of the appointed way for devices of their own invention.

Ver. 27.—**Therefore.** The consequence of their continued alienation from God should be deportation to a foreign land, beyond Damascus, far away from the confines of the country once their own possession (2 Sam. viii. 6), thus dimly denoting Assyria, at that time not hostile, but known in the time of Tiglath-Pileser I. (see the accomplishment, 2 Kings xv. 29 ; xvii. 6). St. Stephen says (Acts vii. 43), "beyond Babylon ; " " Magis enim," observes Jerome, "intelligentiam quam verbum posuit ; " and he is probably blending other prophecies with that of Amos, *e.g.* Jer. xx. 4.

HOMILETICS.

Vers. 1—3.—*Israel's elegy.* It is poor work singing the things that might have been. It means sweet dreams dispelled, fair hopes blighted, and human lives in ruins. Yet such is the prophet's task in this passage—writing Israel's elegy among the graves of her dead millions. He had been denouncing nameless woes against the rebellious people. Here he changes his tone to that of a mournful spectator of accomplished ills. In imagination he throws himself forward out of the sinful present into the calamitous future, and in accommodation to the change of scene his denunciation becomes a dirge. It is a natural transition, and at the same time a new form of appeal. When ears become inattentive, the skilled musician will vary his tune. We have here—

I. A BROKEN IDEAL. The things that might have been with Israel were far enough from existing facts. The Israel of God's ideal was: 1. *A holy people.* (Exod. xix. 6; Deut. xxviii. 9.) Theoretically they were, as the word " holy " means (Deut. vii. 6), a people separated from men and sin and set apart to God. But the fair ideal of their national life remained an ideal and nothing more. The reality never reached it, never approached it. They connected themselves freely with heathen men and heathenish sin. They at times outdid the nations (ch. ii. 6—9) in avarice, injustice, spoiling the poor, abominable rites, and every nameless infamy. 2. *An unconquered people.* This is the force of the expression " virgin (of) Israel." God was to champion their cause, and to fight for them as his loyal people (Deut. i. 30, etc.). If, and so long as he did so, they would be invincible. But they never claimed his help on the appointed terms. His promise was doubted (Deut. i. 32) and its conditions disregarded, with the inevitable result that it failed of fulfilment in many a critical time. Israel, theoretically " the unconquered," was practically the often vanquished, the twice carried captive, the soon-to-be-destroyed. God's help comes surely, but comes only where there is attention to the conditions on which it is offered and given. 3. *A prosperous people.* Palestine, their national inheritance, was the very garden of the earth ; unique in the combination of the highest agricultural capacities, with the finest commercial situation. The prosperity of an industrious, peaceful nation in it was, so far as favourable circumstances went, a foregone conclusion. But war had devastated, and mildew blighted, and drought laid bare its fertile fields. God saw his gifts abused and made the ministers of sin, and he was driven to destroy these in their hands. When temporal good begins to be made the occasion of moral evil, our tenure of it will soon end. 4. *A happy people.* A people prosperous, strong, and pure, could not but be happy as well (Ps. cxliv. 15). And such was Israel in the Divine ideal (Deut. xxxiii. 29). But the actual misery experienced was as complete as the theoretical happiness revealed. Happiness is nowhere so impossible, misery nowhere so intense, as with a people who have fallen beneath themselves. In proportion as the former might have been, will the latter be.

II. AN ANTICIPATIVE DIRGE. Prescient of coming evil, the prophet's lamentation becomes a funeral song. 1. *A nation made shipwreck is a sight for tears.* It is the destruction of magnificent possibilities of good. It is the falling of a tremendous reality of evil. It is the ruin of most precious interests on a gigantic scale. If one soul lost is the occasion of grief to pure spirits and a travailing Saviour, what must the calamity be when multiplied a millionfold ? 2. *When the wicked fall the truest mourners are the righteous.* Not the heathen who had seduced them, not the remnant of apostate Israel that might escape, but the prophet of God, who had kept himself unspotted in the midst of national corruption, was the tearful mourner by the ruined nation's grave. The wicked are too selfish to care for any sorrows but their own. They are as the wolves, which would make a prey of the dead one's remains, rather than any mourning for his fall. God and the God-like alone truly mourn when the wicked perish. 3. *A prophetic sight of his own epitaph ought to stay the hand of the suicide.* Men supposed to be dead have lived to read their own obituary notice. It has enabled them to see themselves for once as others see them. And it ought to have a practical influence for good. Israel, reading beforehand the inscription on their own tomb, might have been warned away, if anything could have warned them, from the course in which they were rushing on. It showed them what was coming, and how it was being brought on, and how it looked, whether as a morality or a policy, in enlightened eyes. An adequate idea of sin must include its end and issues and place in history, and this it was in Israel's power to learn from Amos's prophetic wail.

III. An inspired commentary. An act of God is an expression of his way. The way of God is a revelation of his purpose. All three are along the lines of the just and fitting. Now: 1. *Adequate punishment means practical extermination.* Sin is an infinite crime, merits an infinite punishment, and failing this will receive a punishment exhaustive of the criminal's good. The proverbial question, " Wherefore doth a living man complain? " (Lam. iii. 39), is an understatement of the case. While a field, or a blessing, or a living man remained, Israel had not been punished as it deserved. When body and soul have been both destroyed, there will still be no more than justice done. If our sin have not its punishment in Christ, then that punishment must be utter destruction. 2. *When wrath smites many, mercy spares a remnant.* Nine-tenths were to be destroyed. The thousand should become a hundred, and the hundred ten. Neither the strength of the great nor the insignificance of the small should avail them for escape. With perfect impartiality, all should be made to suffer proportionally. Yet decimation was to stop short of utter extinction. A tenth part (see Isa. i. 9 ; vi. 13) should be spared. This less guilty remnant, taught and chastened by the judgments which swept away the bulk of the nation, might form the nucleus of a new and better Israel. When judgment has destroyed the " bread to the eater," mercy often steps in and saves a " seed to the sower." There is seldom a deluge without its ark and its Noah family, the conditions and materials of a fresh start for the reduced. 3. *Israel decimated is Israel still.* The remnant would retain the national name, and with it the covenant relation and privileges to which the name referred (Gen. xxxii. 28). Toward the Gentile Church, for its sin " cast down but not destroyed," the same gracious policy was announced (Isa. liv. 7—10). While a Mephibosheth remains the royal line of God's anointed is not extinct. Chastisement makes a chaos only to bring out of it the young world of a new life and a new hope (Ps. lxxxix. 30—33).

Vers. 4—6.— *The seeking that is life.* This passage contains at once a vindication of the coming destruction on Israel, and a last offer of escape. All past evil had been justly incurred by departure from God. All coming evil might yet be avoided by return to him. " Seek ye me " was the direction on their treatment of which the whole issue turned.

I. Even the foredoomed are not abandoned of God. The antediluvians were preached to for a century after their destruction was denounced. So Jerusalem got a Pentecost, and the ordinances of a Christian Church for forty years after Christ had pronounced her doom (Matt. xxiii. 37—39). 1. *God's threatenings are in a certain sense conditional on men's conduct.* They are addressed to men in their character or circumstances at the time they are uttered. If and when the character or circumstances cease to exist, the threatenings cease to apply. It was so in the case of Hezekiah (Isa. xxxviii. 1, 5), and also of Nineveh (Jonah iii. 4, 10). God in such cases does not change, but the circumstances do, and his modes of treatment change accordingly. 2. *They are designed to turn men, not to plunge them in despair.* All life is disciplinary. Each event and experience is fitted, and meant, to exercise a moral influence. Being, moreover, controlled by a holy God, the moral influence of each must be in the direction of right. It is so with blessings and the promise of them (Rom. ii.

4; Isa. i. 19). It is so also with judgments and the threat of them (Isa. xxvi. 9; Luke xiii. 3, 5). God takes pleasure in the soul's turning (Ezek. xviii. 23, 32), and all his dealings with it aim at and tend to this result. Therefore, until judgment actually falls, the threat of it is kept as a deterrent before the sinner's eyes. 3. *Individuals may turn after national repentance has become hopeless.* Language addressed to a nation is really meant for the individuals composing it; and as individuals they would be influenced by it. No general forsaking of sin was probable in Israel. Still, some might turn, as many did in Jerusalem, and were saved after the destruction of the city as a whole was foretold; and, so long as this was possible, the means fitted to turn would not be withdrawn. God's expostulations will go forth to glean in corners even when the prospects of a harvest are blighted.

II. THERE IS A SEEKING IN CONNECTION WITH WHICH IT IS LIFE TO FIND. To Israel here and to all men everywhere the great object of search is God, not mere good (Ps. xlii. 2); and God for himself, not for his gifts. 1. *This seeking implies previous non-possession.* God is neither the property of the wicked nor his possession. Sin made separation between them, and a severing of all previously existing ties. Man abandoned God, and God drove out man. Now he is "without God," is "enmity against God," bids God depart from him, says in his heart, "No God." It is only by the saint, and after seeking, that it can be said, "I have found him whom my soul loveth." "This God is our God for ever and ever." Grace it is that knits again the ties broken by sin, and restores man and God to a condition of mutual love and possession and indwelling. 2. *It is a quest with the whole heart and strength.* The essence of seeking God is to desire him. And to desire him really is to desire him heartily. Not to desire him with other things. Not to desire him more than other things. Not to desire him weakly. Not even to desire him strongly. But to desire him wholly, supremely, and intensely. Seeking God is heart-seeking, or it is nothing. Heart-seeking is truly such when it is seeking with the whole heart. Therefore only to such seeking is there a promise of finding (Jer. xxix. 13; xxiv. 7). God cannot be had till he is adequately wanted, and to be wanted adequately is to be wanted supremely. 3. *It is synonymous with finding.* In God's world everywhere supply meets and measures demand. Plant, animal, and man, each finds on earth, in climate, habitat, covering, and food, exactly the thing it needs. There is no want for which there is not full and fitting provision. So in the spiritual sphere. "Blessed are they that do hunger and thirst," etc. Over against every need of the soul is a Divine supply. That need become conscious, means help waiting; that need expressed, means help already on the way. Spiritual good is obtained on the simple condition of its being truly desired. 4. *To find God is to find all good which inheres in him.* God is himself the greatest Good; he is, moreover, the Sum, and therefore the Source, of all good. There is certain good which he unconditionally bestows on all, even the ungodly. But it is good of the lower kinds, and which ministers to the lower needs. All spiritual good, and all temporal good that has any spiritual aspect, God gives only with and in Jesus Christ (Rom. viii. 32; Matt. vi. 33). The planets attend the sun and follow where he leads. So on Christ, as God's unspeakable Gift, the other lesser gifts wait. We have them when we grasp him. 5. *This good, summed up in one word, is life.* Life is a general term for the highest good (Ps. xxx. 5; cxxxiii. 3). It is physical life, the prevention or withdrawal of destroying judgments. It is judicial life, or the reversal of the death-sentence on the soul, and the privilege for it of living. It is spiritual life, being quickened once for all out of the death in sin, being made alive and kept alive. It is everlasting life, the outblooming in eternity of the flower of soul-life planted on earth.

III. THIS IS NOT THE SEEKING TO WHICH MEN NATURALLY TURN. It was under pretence of greater convenience that Jeroboam's calves were set up in Dan and Bethel. But Beersheba was fifty miles south of Jerusalem, and Gilgal was on the other side of Jordan, and so most inconvenient of access. That Israel preferred them to Jerusalem was proof that they preferred idolatrous rites to the worship of God (see Pusey). 1. *Idols are man's own invention, and therefore the egoist's choice.* There is self-sufficiency verging on self-worship in all sin. Man puts his own opinion and will and work above God's. An idol is his own creation, and for that reason, if for no other, is preferred to God. It is a subtle form of self-worship, and so inevitably preferred to any other. 2. *They are credited with qualities congenial to his nature.*

A man impresses himself on his work, virtually puts himself into it. It reflects his genius and his moral character. The idol a man makes is thus substantially a repetition of himself, and therefore congenial to him all round. Made by his hand, it is after his heart, which the God of heaven is very far from being. 3. *The fall into idol-worship is broken by the retention in it of a flavouring of the worship of God.* Bethel and Beersheba, its shrines, were spots where the Divine presence had of old been richly manifested. Its rites mimicked, to some extent, the national worship of God. It was added on at first to Divine worship, not substituted for it. Satan lets men down into idolatry by easy stages. It begins in the sanctuary. It appears at first in the likeness of a better thing. Then, when men have become sufficiently familiar with it and degraded by it to bear the sight, it puts on its natural shape, and is idol-worship pure and simple.

IV. In the seeking of the natural heart success must mean disaster. By a play upon words, Gilgal, " the Great Rolling," is to be rolled away; and Bethel, styled elsewhere " Bethaven," shall become " aven," or vanity. •1. *An idol is a figment, and the worship of it can only result in deception and loss.* It is not a thing, but only the image of a thing. It is the image, moreover, not of a real, but of an imaginary thing. It is, therefore, " nothing," and " a thing of nought " (1 Cor. viii. 4), and out of nothing nothing can come. To worship it is delusion, to trust it inevitable disappointment. 2. *God's infinite power and his wrath are against them that forsake him.* The idolater pits idol impotence against Divine omnipotence, with the inevitable result of discomfiture and destruction. There are idols of the heart the service of which is no less ruinous. They group themselves under the heading " world," and the love of them is incompatible with the love of God, and so " Anathema " (1 John ii. 15; 1 Cor. xvi. 22).

Vers. 7—13.—*The contrast presaging the conflict.* Judgment is coming. Warning has been given. Duty, and the prevailing derelictions of it, have been pointed out. Here God's perfections and Israel's iniquities are set in juxtaposition, and the collocation is suggestive. Such incompatibility must lead to collision. It is by God's character and ours that our mutual relations and attitudes are shaped. We see here—

I. God revealing himself. (Vers. 8, 9.) God's work is an important revelation of himself. He has written all over it the glorious lineaments of his character. Each part of it reflects some feature, and in the whole we see his face. Here he shows himself: 1. *In the sphere of creation.* " He maketh the seven stars and Orion." This is a pregnant thought. Alcyone, one of the seven stars, or Pleiades, is the central orb of the heavens, round which the others move. It is as it were the heart of the material universe; and the Creator of it is by implication the Creator of all. In this fact speak the power and wisdom of the Great Uncaused, who is the Cause not only of all effects, but of all causes as well. 2. *In the sphere of providence.* " And turneth the shadow," etc. (vers. 8, 9). We have here three classes of operations. The first was illustrated in the miraculous light that shone around Paul at his conversion, is seen daily in the rise of the morning sun, and appears in the turning of the night of adversity into the day of prosperity. The second was seen in the three hours' miraculous darkness at the Crucifixion, is seen in the gathering shades of every night, and in the darkening down into adverse circumstances of many a life-day. The third was seen in the Deluge, is seen in every shower of rain, and will be seen in future widespread judgments on the wicked. Ver. 9, " Who causeth desolations to flash on the strong," etc. God's judgments are bold, as singling out the strong and the fortress; swift, as coming on them like the lightning's flash; sweeping, as involving them in utter destruction. 3. *In the sphere of redemption.* God scatters spiritual night. He illuminates the darkness of the soul. He makes men light in the Lord. He gives them the inheritance of the saints in light. He also judicially blinds, by leaving impenitent souls to the natural effects of wrong-doing; and he casts into outer darkness at last. In all these things we behold power—power here as goodness, power there as severity; but power everywhere as resistless and Divine.

II. Israel revealing herself. (Ver. 12.) This is a sad apocalypse. In many transgressions and great sins Israel's many-sided and deep corruption comes out. Particulars are: 1. *As unjust.* Injustice is a natural form for the sin, which is at bottom selfishness, to take. It was a specially prevalent form, moreover, among the Hebrew people. From Jacob down the sordid race has cheated the strong and imposed on the weak. Action is in a sense the fruit of character, and answers to the tree. God's grace is to convert the thorn into the fir tree, and the briar into the myrtle tree; but man's sin works the converse process, and changes the sweet "tree of righteousness" into bitter wormwood. Casting "righteousness down to earth" is another aspect of the same charge. Righteousness ought to rule. Its proper place is the throne of human life. But Israel had dethroned and cast it down to the earth, and set injustice, a usurper, in its place. 2. *As oppressive.* (Vers. 11, 12.) The oppression suffered by Israel had done nothing to produce detestation of the thing. What other nations had inflicted on them in this way, they were only too ready to inflict, with interest, on each other as they had opportunity. Humiliation does not always prepare for exaltation, nor poverty for wealth, nor the endurance of injustice for power. The freed slave will often make the very worst master, and the erewhile victim of wrong the most outrageous inflictor of it (Prov. xix. 10; xxx. 22, 23). 3. *As venal.* "Who take a bribe." They did injustice, not only in their private, but in their public, capacity. They not only plundered the public themselves, but made a profit by helping others to do the same. A dishonest man will make a corrupt magistrate. He will use for his own aggrandizement whatever power he gains. 4. *As impious.* (Vers. 10, 12.) As cowardice appeared in oppressing the poor, so did impiety in oppressing the righteous. Much of what the righteous suffer is due to the hatred of righteousness by the wicked. They hate the thing itself, they hate it as a standing rebuke to their own ways, and their antipathy invariably exhibits itself as it has occasion.

III. THEIR FUTURE RELATIONS CLEAR IN THE LIGHT OF BOTH. Given what God is and what Israel is, and the Divine course of treatment may easily be anticipated. 1. *God will disappoint their schemes of self-aggrandizement.* (Ver. 11.) Their labour and pains and sin would prove in the end to have been thrown away. Their ill-gotten gains would never be enjoyed. The vineyards and houses, in which they had invested them, would, after having been acquired at great pains, be lost again before they had even begun to be used. Gain gotten by injustice is seldom abiding, and never remunerative. The one condition of getting satisfaction out of earthly good is to acquire it according to the will of God. 2. *He will leave them unrebuked.* (Ver. 13.) The prophets and the wise would both be silent. This would be a great calamity. It would be followed by an increase of sin, involving in turn an aggravation of punishment. It would mean abandonment to fate; for when God ceases to strive, a man's doom is sealed. It is the Physician discontinuing his treatment because the hand of death is on the patient. The sinner sins conviction away, and then congratulates himself on the discovery of peace. But it is only God saying, "Ephraim is joined to his idols: let him alone." It is the one spiritual case that is utterly desperate.

Ver. 13.—"*A time to be silent.*" "Therefore the prudent shall keep silence in that time; for it is an evil time." These words describe an evil time, and specify one of its most evil features. It is a time of culminating wickedness, of imminent destruction, and, as related to both, of Divine non-intervention. "There is a time to keep silence" (Eccles. iii. 7) as well as "a time to speak." And that time, as pointed out by characteristic features, was at hand in this case. Israel, which in vain had been pled with and plagued, would then be severely left alone. Her victims would suffer in silence. Her prophets would cease to expostulate. God, in judgment, would cease to strive for her restraint or turning. In an awful and unnatural calm she would pass the moments before there broke on her the storm of doom. And the dawning of this "dies iræ" was almost come. As to the particular characteristic of this day, note that God's servants are silent—

I. WHEN THERE IS NOTHING THAT CAN BE SAID TO THE PURPOSE. This will often happen. Seasonable speech is a valuable thing. But men are not infallible, and occasions are often puzzling, and the right thing to say is hard to find. 1. *Silence is sometimes the resource of feeling too deep for words.* There are unspeakable things. "Speech is but broken light on the depth of the unspoken." The finest thoughts, the deepest feelings, are unuttered often because they cannot be expressed in words. As a noted Shakespearian character says—

> "Silence is the perfectest herald of joy:
> I were but little happy if I could say how much."

And the sentiment is not uncommon. "Does the wind write what it sings in those sounding leaves above our heads? Does the sea write the moaning of its surge? Nothing is fine that is written; the divinest in man's heart never issues forth. The instrument is flesh, the note is fire. What would you have? Between what one feels and what one expresses, there is the same space as between the soul and the twenty-four letters of the alphabet; that is to say, the Infinite. Can you on a rosewood flute give forth the harmony of the spheres?" (Raffaelle). 2. *Silence is often more impressive than any speech.*

> "The silence of pure innocence
> Persuades, when speaking fails."

So also do the silence of deep feeling and of strong passion, uttering "speech in their dumbness, language in their very gesture." Christ but looked on the recreant Peter after his miserable desertion and denial. Yet that silent look, as the denied One passed him in the hall, was eloquent of wounded love, and cut the denier more keenly than any words. No word was uttered on the cross where the dying thief was brought to faith. The God-like fortitude, the ineffable meekness of the Saviour, suffering silently the devilish malice of sin,—it was that broke his heart and won his free allegiance. In this dumbness was speech to the power of which articulate speech admits of no comparison. The gift of being "eloquently silent" is one that is not unworthy of more general cultivation. To Israel the sudden silence of the prophets, after centuries of expostulation, would tell its own startling tale. It would indicate discouragement and disgust, and duplicate to their minds the "let him alone" (Hos. iv. 17) of Divine desertion at a similar crisis. And this unequivocal proof that they are given up might bring the tardy repentance which all else had failed to stir. When communications are broken off, the dream of a lasting peace is over. The patient will believe that death is at hand when the physician turns away and refuses to prescribe. 3. *Silence is always better than haphazard speech.* When a man knows not what to say he should guard against saying he knows not what. "Silence, when nothing need be said, is the eloquence of discretion." Peter would have escaped some blunders and rebukes if he had followed this rule. But it was when "he wist not what to say" (Mark ix. 6) that he was given to saying most. Such speech is more likely to be inappropriate than silence, and being inappropriate there are many more ways in which it can work evil. Hence the numerous Scripture references to the tongue, the power of it, the difficulty of governing it, and the danger of it if unruly. Indeed, so liable are men to err and so specially liable to err in speech as compared with overt act, that the proper government of the tongue is made the highest religious act (Jas. iii. 2).

II. WHEN IT IS EVIDENT THAT SPEECH MUST BE UNAVAILING. There are many such cases. 1. *Sometimes men will refuse to listen.* The Jews did in the beginning of the gospel. Faithfully and firmly Stephen pressed the truth home; but they "stopped their ears, and ran upon him" (Acts vii. 57). Here was a case for silence. Speech, had it been possible, would have been unheeded. Those men, with murder in their hearts, and their fingers in their ears, would listen to no words. With Israel now things had come to a like pass. Their ears were stopped, and their hearts within them were set to do iniquity. For such a state of matters the appropriate measure is the silence which the prophet predicts. And all God's servants, in the exercise of their enlightened judgment, will do likewise in a like case. When men will not hear, they will refuse to waste on them unregarded speech. Bawling into an ear that is deaf or stopped is effort thrown away, and unworthy of common sense (Matt. x. 14; Mark vi. 11). 2. *Sometimes evil has gone so far that words can be of no avail.* God's Spirit will not always strive. With the antediluvians by Noah's preaching he strove above a century, but when iniquity reached a certain stage he ceased, and his *ultima ratio* was the Deluge. He strove with Saul for years, but when insensibility and hardness became confirmed, communications were broken off; and whether by dreams, or by Urim, or by prophets, God spoke no more (1 Sam. xxviii. 6). He strove with Israel during the ministry of our Lord, but they would not listen to his word, and at last he was silent, and the doomed people were left to die (Luke xix. 42). God ceases to speak when he is ready to strike. Expostulation would be an anachronism when execution is imminent. The point at which he will give up the persistent wrong-doer and withdraw all deterrent measures none can fix. But there is such a point, and, to each of the ungodly, the danger of passing it (Prov. i. 26). Every hour we continue in rebellion is cutting down our chance of being longer striven with. Those who speak for God to men are sometimes conscious that the time to be silent has come. The sinner seems to have reached a final fixity. In the nature of things he cannot be expected now to change. Paul at a certain stage concluded the Jew to be incorrigible, and turned deliberately to the Gentile (Acts xiii. 46). And like Paul, when it becomes clear that further dealing with men must be barren of result, the servant of Christ will transfer his strength from the hopeless to some hopeful form of effort.

III. WHEN IT IS JUST AS LIKELY TO DO HARM AS GOOD. This is no remote contingency. Such times are cropping up continually. Under certain circumstances speech : 1. *May do harm to men.* The truth of God and the sinful heart are uncongenial. Men love the darkness and hate the light. The truth forbidding all lust is actually through the corruption of our nature the occasion of stirring it up (Rom. vii. 7—9). This, of course, is no reason for withholding it or suppressing our testimony to it. But there are circumstances and moods in which this tendency attains its maximum of strength, and it will then be prudent to keep silence "even from good." It is as "fishers of men" that we speak the truth, and we must justify our claim to the title by presenting the truth in the time and way in which it is most likely to tell. If we "testify" at random, and uniformly, in all companies and on all occasions, we shall oftener harm than help the people whom we wish to serve. 2. *It may do harm to the truth.* There is such a thing as "casting pearls before swine" (Matt. vii. 6) to no better purpose than the prostitution of sacred things. The difference between truth profaned and necessarily inoperative, and the same truth listened to and the power of God, is often the difference between the untimely presentation of it and the timely. To force it on men when they are out of humour and will not give it a fair hearing is only to bring it into contempt—to lessen its dignity in the eyes of others, and diminish its chance of winning their acceptance. The truth is meant to sanctify and save, and we must be careful to do nothing that would place it at a disadvantage in the work. 3. *It may do harm to ourselves without any compensating advantage.* "He that reproveth a scorner getteth himself shame"—the shame of aggravating the case and bringing needless evil on himself. No Scottish Covenanter was called on to enter the camp and preach the gospel of good will and peace to the bloodthirsty troopers of Claverhouse or Dalziel. The thing would have been good in itself, and was deeply needed, but to attempt it meant not merely failure, but death. If there was no one else to do it, this work must be left undone. There is room for judgment and discretion in timing and planning the work of winning souls. The most acceptable service and the most useful we can give to God is our "reasonable service." We are not to "count our lives dear to us" in comparison with his work ; but it must appear that the work demands the sacrifice, and will benefit by it, before we are at liberty to give up the life which we hold in trust for God. Pearls are to be withheld from swine for this among other reasons, "lest they turn again and rend you." The characters of the "time to keep silence" deserve attention no less than those of the "time to speak," and he has mastered both who rightly divides the Word of life.

1. *Silence is sometimes a Divine form of appeal.* 2. *In that case it is probably the last appeal.* 3. *Disregarded, it is the lull before the storm.*

Vers. 14, 15.—*The nation with which God will dwell.* The opening words of this passage imply a history. Israel "not only did evil, but they sought it out and the occasions of it" (Pusey). They gave evil their special attention, never failing to do it when they had opportunity, and seeking opportunities when none presented themselves. In fact, they did it with an amount of method and pains which they are now called upon to direct into a new channel, and apply to the doing of good.

I. THE PRESENCE OF GOD WITH MEN IS THE CHIEFEST EXPRESSION OF HIS FAVOUR. It was the original, and remains the normal condition of human life. 1. *It is the restoration of acceptance.* Separation from God is penal. God "drove out the man," and we remain "afar off" because of sin committed. He will dwell with us again only when our sin is put away. The king will not consort with rebels as such. He will meet them only as subjects and friends. The condition of access to his presence is the equitable recovery of his forfeited favour. In the promise to dwell with Israel was the implied promise to restore them to his favour. 2. *It is the restoration of God-likeness.* "What communion hath light with darkness?" None. The two things are essentially antagonistic, and fellowship between them is impossible. Accordingly, Adam left God's presence and hid even before he was driven out of the garden. In losing the Divine likeness he had lost all relish or fitness for the Divine presence. The one could be recovered only with the other. Born from above, and made partakers of the Divine nature, we are in affinity with God, and come with relish to his presence. 3. *It is the restoration of happiness.* "In thy presence is fulness of joy." Sin means loss on the one side and infliction on the other. Its guilt separates from God, with the result that our being is incomplete. Its corruption introduces disorder among our own powers, and disease in each, and so unrest and misery become inevitable (Isa. xlviii. 22; lvii. 20). In reunion with God these two occasions of unhappiness are removed. By regeneration the old nature is crucified, and the new one is set by faith in union with God, where it has spiritual completeness, and so its ideal of a happy state. Hence the Christian's aspiration is summed up in one idea—to "be with Christ, which is far better."

II. Israel had a theoretical Divine presence with them which was not now in fact enjoyed. (Exod. xxix. 45, 46.) It is implied in God's offer to be with them under certain circumstances, that he was not with them then. 1. *He was not with them in worship.* God's presence at the Jewish national worship was pledged (Exod. xx. 24). But the worship must be his worship, conducted according to his appointment. This it now was not. Where not positively idolatrous or profane, the worship of Israel was utterly formal and hollow. In such worship the Divine presence is not desired and is not enjoyed (Isa. i. 13—15). The worship must be real, the heart contrite, in which God promises to be present. Israel failed of God's promised presence by failing to claim it on the appointed terms. 2. *He was not with them in war.* For centuries he had been (Judg. vi. 16), and victory attended their arms (Josh. xxiv. 12, 18; 1 Chron. xvii. 21). Nothing could withstand them. The nations of Canaan, in whose sight they had felt as grasshoppers, were subdued before them. And God had explicitly connected their victories with his presence and help (Exod. xvii. 11, 14; Ps. xliv. 1—3). But there came a time of which the psalmist had to say, "Thou hast cast off and put us to shame, and goest not forth with our armies" (Ps. xliv. 9). The conditions on which the Divine promise of help in the field was suspended were violated or ignored, and God left them to fight with the arm they preferred to his. 3. *He was not with them in their daily walk.* They did not seek him nor want him, nor were they fit to be near him. The graces to which his presence is congruous, the means by which his presence is secured, were all absent, and so they were a nation given up of God and forsaken (Isa. ii. 6; Jer. vii. 29). He no longer dwelt with them, nor met them, nor directed them, nor spoke to them. He became, as he does to all under like conditions, "a God afar off, and not a God near at hand;" and the journey of their national existence, begun in such goodly company, was left to be finished alone.

III. To make the theory of God's presence fact, the theory of Israel's separation must also be fact. God's withdrawal was the natural reply to Israel's forsaking. His resumption of relations would synchronize with their return to righteousness. 1. *Evil must be rejected.* This duty is laid down in three degrees. It is not to be sought, nor done, nor loved. It had been all three. It could cease to be the one only by ceasing to be the others also. The seeking implies that the love and the doing have gone before. The love guarantees that the doing and seeking shall follow in due course. The way to break off from evil is to be utterly separate. The least link of connection will develop into a mighty chain. 2. *Good must be chosen.* This is dutiful. Duty has a positive side still more important than its negative one. Mere avoidance of what is wrong would be a colourless thing. God's Law is not merely a system of restrictions, but a system of commands. There must be actual doing of what is right, with a knowledge that it is right, and because it is right. And this is no more dutiful than natural. The qualities that turn away from evil turn instinctively to good. Indeed, the two things are so antagonistic that the love of the one and the hatred of the other are only different aspects of the same feeling. And in this choosing of God, again, there are three phases or degrees answering to those in the avoidance of sin. It is to be *loved*, as the fairest and most amiable thing on earth. It is to be done, as the only thing that is fitting and right. It is to be sought, as a thing important and desirable in the highest possible degree. 3. *Justice must be done.* "Established in the gate." Unjust judgment was a prevalent and crying evil. The Jewish character was prone to it, and the experience of it at the hands of strangers only strengthened the tendency. Perversion of justice is one of the most constant elements in natural corruption everywhere. A corrupt man makes a dishonest trader, an unjust judge, and an oppressive master. Fair and upright dealing between man and man has no natural basis, unless in the fear of God. The fear of God. on the other hand, will naturally co-ordinate itself with regard for man. The man who "does justly and loves mercy" is one who "walks humbly with God."

IV. WHAT GOD DOES FOR ISRAEL HE DOES FOR THEM AS BEING "THE REMNANT OF JOSEPH." This form of expression is significant. 1. *The remnant.* This implies weeding out by previous judgment. Israel had sinned long, and in punishment had been almost decimated. This was necessary as a matter of justice. Until it had been done they could not be saved. Sinners, individually and collectively, must receive for the wrong they have done. God's original promises were made to Israel as a nation, and not to individuals, and the nation in his eye was the remnant left after his judgments had run their course. To this remnant hope of deliverance is here held out as a brand plucked from the fire; a thing on which, justice having been vindicated, mercy may now, and not till now, be shown. 2. *The remnant of Joseph.* This means Israel as the covenant people. Joseph was Israel's favourite, "the man that was separate from his brethren," and the recipient of the promise (Gen. xlviii. 4) given to Abraham (Gen. xvii. 8) and repeated to Isaac and Jacob. Accordingly, the "remnant of Joseph" is equivalent to the "remnant according to the election of grace" (Rom. xi. 5). God never forgets his covenant, never fails to give its promised blessings, never gives them to the covenant people, but as covenanted mercies. On the broad ground of creaturehood his general mercies are distributed, but special mercies are on the narrower basis of a spiritual relation. All wherein we are made to differ from others is the gift of a God in covenant, and the story of providence is at bottom the story of grace (Rom. viii. 32, 28).

Vers. 16, 17.—*The track of the destroyer.* Each name of God is a guarantor of his action. It expresses a character, or relation, or operation, in which he thereby reveals himself. The multiplication of his names and titles here is a cumulative argument for the sureness of the matter revealed. He who is God of hosts or the Omnipotent One, Lord or the Absolute One, and Jehovah or the Self-existent One, is the Being with whom to decide is to act, and to will is to accomplish. Of the deliverance so emphasized observe—

I. THE MORAL CERTAINTY THAT THE WARNING TO AN APOSTATE WILL BE VAIN. The possibility of a happy end, by the grace of God, to Israel's sin and troubles is held out in the previous verse. Yet here the falling of the judgments denounced is assumed to be inevitable. Paul declares that it is impossible to restore to repentance those who might fall away from a high degree of spiritual attainment. The apostate is a hopeless case: 1. *Because he loves sin more than other men.* They love it knowing nothing better, but he does so with experimental knowledge of the way of peace. He loves it under a less impulse than they, and in the face of stronger deterrents than they, and must therefore love it more than they. The fuel that kindles with the least fire, and burns in spite of most water, is clearly the most inflammable. 2. *Because he is harder than other men.* The strain is proportioned to the wrench. All sin hardens, and hardens in proportion as we are active and resolute in it. Sinning against more light, and more deterrent influence than others, the apostate's sin involves a more decided act of will, and so a more violently hardening effect. The more firmly the branding-iron is applied, the more deeply it scars. The more violently the moral sense is sinned against, the more the organ is indurated and injured. 3. *Because his day of grace will be shorter than that of other men.* The only chance of men's turning at all is God's striving with them. This he does with all men during a longer or shorter period. In the case of the antediluvians the striving was for a hundred and twenty years (Gen. vi. 3). In the case of Jerusalem it was three years (Matt. xxiii. 39). In the case of Saul, King of Israel, it was till within about seven years of his death (1 Sam. xviii. 12). In the case of many it is during the entire life (Matt. xx. 6—9). Thus each man has his day of grace, during which God strives with him to bring him to repentance. In the nature of the case the day of grace for the apostate must be far advanced. He has been more and longer striven with than other men, and so is presumably nearer the limit beyond which the process does not go.

II. A THREAT THE OBVERSE OF A CONDITIONAL PROMISE. "For I will pass through the midst of thee;" *i.e.* as elsewhere (Exod. xii. 12) in judgment. The language is a threat. God, so far from dwelling with them, as under other circumstances he was ready to do (ver. 14), would pass through them in wrath and destroying power. Underlying the announcement of this alternative is the fact: 1. *That compromise is impossible with God.* He will save or he will destroy. There is no half-way house between the good of his promise and the evil of his threat. He can yield nothing and abate nothing of either. He will come as a Friend to abide and bless unspeakably, or he will pass through as an invading Foe, making desolation in his track. 2. *That the incentive to repentance must be double-edged.* There are people who must be led, and others who must be driven. "The mercies of God" are the strongest motive power with some minds, whilst "the terrors of the Lord" are most potent with others. The Divine machinery of impulsion, to be perfect in itself and for its purpose, must include both. Hence men are plied with each in turn and often with both together (John iii. 36) in connection with the salvation which they ultimately embrace. Israel's case would not be abandoned as hopeless until both menace and promise had made their contribution to the work of its persuasion.

III. CREATION LANGUISHING WHEN THE CREATOR FROWNS. The connection between man and the creation is very close. The judgment on Israel would mean evil: 1. *In the fields.* They would not be fertile as heretofore. Their crops would fail to grow, or be blighted before they could be gathered (ch. iv. 7). Enemies would devastate the country and destroy the fruit of the ground. Rapacious officials would confiscate the earnings of honest industry. In each calamity, much more in all together, was enough to quench the joy of harvest, and cause the husbandman to mourn. 2. *In the vineyards.* The whole food of the people, the corn, the wine together, would be swept away. The grape-gathering was a proverbial occasion of joy (Isa. xvi. 10). But with no vintage to gather, or no chance to gather it for the lawful owner, the "vintage shouting" would cease, and for the usual singing in the vineyards would be substituted a universal wail. 3. *In the streets.* "God made the country, and man made the town." And the human depends on the Divine. Trade and commerce draw from agriculture their chief materials, and so when it fails they fail with it. When the husbandman has cause to weep there can be no dry eye in the community. The wail that begins in the fields, and spreads through the vineyards, will rise to a mighty roar when it reaches the streets, where the sufferers herd and lament together.

IV. THE LAMENTATION SYMPTOMATIC OF A GREAT DISASTER. 1. *This is universal.* In all "streets and vineyards," etc. The judgment affecting all classes in the community, all should mourn. 2. *It is in concert.* Men would call their fellows to lamentation. Not as individuals merely, but as a community, they sinned and suffer, and so as a community they should wail. 3. *It is worked up.* "And lamentation to those skilled in lamenting." The mourning would not be left to take any form that happened. It would be appointed and organized, and then observed according to programme. All this implies an intelligent and vivid idea of the significance of the occasion. God's judgments, however long despised, will make themselves to be understood and respected at last. In hell there is no misappreciation of the nature and strength of Divine retribution; and on earth appreciation comes infallibly with experience.

Vers. 18—20.—*The day of the Lord the night of the impenitent.* Divine judgments will be as sharp as they are sure. Sent in wrath, proportioned to guilt, falling on the vulnerable points, they are the least desirable of all imaginable things. The very thought of them should be sobering, and the sure prospect of them overwhelming. Now, the scoffer is the worst type of sinner, and will, in the nature of the case, be the greatest sufferer when judgment comes. He is at the same time the most utterly blinded character, and therefore likely to be taken most violently by surprise. How he shall be so, and to what extent, is made in these verses to appear.

I. "THE DAY OF THE LORD." This is a common expression in the prophets, and its meaning is well defined. It is applied: 1. *To the day of active Divine intervention on earth.* (Job i. 15 ; ii. 1 ; Isa. ii. 12 ; Jer. xlvi. 10 ; Obad. 15.) There are periods which God signalizes by special doings. Long quiescent, he becomes conspicuously active. He intervenes in human affairs with unusual emphasis. Judgments often menaced are sent. Sinners long borne with are punished. The godly, for a time imposed on, are delivered. Abuses, the growth of centuries, are dealt with on their merits, and swept away. Such a period is called "the day of the Lord" because it is the time of obvious and special Divine activity. God not only strikes, but shows his hand. 2. *To the day of final judgment.* All others foreshadow, lead up to, culminate and lose themselves in this. "The day of the Lord had already become the name for every day of judgment, leading on to the last day" (Pusey). This is the day of the Lord in a unique sense. It is unique as regards universality. It will see dealt with, not individuals merely, or nations even, but the entire race (Matt. xxv. 31). It is unique in the matter of thoroughness. There will be inquisition as to each person, and as to every act of each (2 Cor. v. 10). It is unique also in the matter of finality. Questions already dealt with by temporal judgments will be reopened to be settled once for all. Its sentence will be final, and its adjudication of rewards and punishments for all eternity (Matt. xxv. 46).

II. ITS SIGNIFICANCE TO THE WICKED. This is explicitly and minutely defined as: 1. *Evil.* "Darkness, and not light." It could not be otherwise. Sin means wrath, and wrath means infliction. Between a righteous God and all unrighteousness there must exist an infinite antagonism. Between his Law and such there is an essential incompatibility. Therefore his action towards them must be adverse, his judgment on them that of condemnation. It is a result of God's purity, of the majesty of law, of the needs of moral government, that "with the froward he shall show himself froward." 2. *Only evil.* "And no brightness in it." The dispensation of forbearance, the time for any measure or kind of good, is over. While any hope of reformation remained, judgment was mingled with mercy. But when this is hopeless, and the question is only one of punishing the reprobate, the exercise of goodness would be an anachronism, and only severity can be meted out. 3. *Evil playing into the hands of evil.* "As if a man fleeth before the lion, and the bear meets him." Divine punitive measures are various and complete. They surround us. They hem us in on every side. They form as it were a circle of fire round us. They are not to be evaded or escaped (Jer. xi. 11; Rom. ii. 3; Heb. ii. 3). In running away from one, we only run into the jaws of another. If it is not the lion's tooth, then in any case it will be the bear's claws. If health escape, property will suffer. If both escape, the good name will be tarnished. If all three escape, conscience will be wounded and happiness destroyed. If earthly evil consequences do not reach us, there are eternal fires kindled against which there will be no appeal. 4. *Evil in the arms of good.* "And rests his hand upon the wall, and the snake bite him." The wall, a ready support for the feeble or weary to lean on, may furnish in its chinks a hiding-place for the venomous snake. So with all human refuges in God's day of visitation. They will fail us. Their help will not be available, or it will not be sufficient, or it will involve some other evil as great as the one it will relieve. "The staff of bruised reed" (Isa. xxxvi. 6) is the fitting emblem of all fancied helps in the day of God's wrath. Even the likeliest will be found wanting in the very matter in which it promises most.

III. THEIR FOOLISH DESIRE FOR IT. "Woe to those who desire the day of Jehovah!" The sinner's desiring the day of vengeance on his sins may mean: 1. *Misapprehension.* Israel did not realize the enormity of their sin. They did not see that the threatened judgments were for themselves and on account of it. They trusted to their position as "Israel after the flesh" to secure them the immunity that only belonged to Israel after the Spirit. And so their idea of the day of God was a time when their enemies would be destroyed, and they themselves delivered and exalted. With all the wicked, the eye for the sins of others is so much keener than the eye for their own, that coming good is unconsciously allocated to themselves and coming evil to others, and so Divine judgments desired which can only destroy them when they come. 2. *Bravado.* The prophets who foretold the coming of God's day rebuked the people's sin on account of which it was to come. Put on their mettle by the rebuke, many would affect to ridicule the prophecy. Like others (Jer. xvii. 15 ; 2 Pet. iii. 3, 4), they would say, with an affectation of unbelief, "You are trying to frighten us with a bugbear. Let your talked-of judgment fall, and then we will believe it." The delay of God's judgment, which means that when it comes it shall be the more terrible, is often taken as meaning that it is not coming at all (Ezek. xii. 22, 27). 3. *Vindictiveness.* Some would deem themselves less criminal than others—their enemies, it may be, and oppressors. On these they would expect the heaviest strokes to fall, and to bring this about they would suffer more or less themselves. There are Samsons among sinners who would run the risk of perishing themselves in order to secure the destruction of others. To all three classes "the day of the Lord is darkness, and no brightness in it." Evil will come none the less surely because it is good that is expected, and it will come all the more sharply on those who to their other sin have added malice against men and mockery of God.

Vers. 21—23.—*The autograph of the unreal.* Wicked Israel, strange to say, was worshipping Israel still. Theirs was sanctimonious sinning. It was done more or less in a religious connection. It was accompanied, and attempted to be covered, by an unstinted dressing of pietistic cant. But it only smelled the more rank to Heaven. Unreal worship is no mitigation, but only an aggravation, of the guilt of unholy living.

I. INSINCERITY IS OFTEN SCRUPULOUS ABOUT ALL THE CIRCUMSTANTIALS OF WORSHIP. This is natural. It builds on the form as a substitute for the spirit, and on the observance of the ordinance thus as a substitute for a godly life. Going through religious forms costs nothing in the way of crucifying the flesh. Accordingly, the scrupulosity of Israel seemed to be great in proportion to their hypocrisy. 1. *They kept the feasts.* "Feasts" (ver. 21) means the annual feasts. There is no hint that these, or any of them, were neglected or overlooked. The routine of celebration went mechanically on. They were observed without purpose and without heart, but they were observed. 2. *They performed the acts of worship.* "The assemblies" (ver. 21) were probably the meetings for worship (Lev. xxiii. 36) appointed to be held at the feasts. These as a class, no exception to which is indicated, are spoken of as having been held. "Then 'songs,' no doubt of Zion, and inspired by God, were duly sung, and the accompaniment played on harps—instruments almost exclusively consecrated to the service of God" (Pusey). 3. *They offered the usual gifts.* The "burnt offering," the "meat offering," and the "peace offering," which are all voluntary offerings, were regularly made, so far as appears. They were made, moreover, with fatlings—beasts the best of their kind, and such as the Law prescribed. So far, therefore, as form went, their worship was scrupulously correct. And the same is generally true of hollow and unspiritual worship. Being purely formal, it will seem excellent in proportion as it is elaborate. The absence of the spirit is attempted to be compensated for by the exaltation of the letter. Worship can no more be appraised by its fulness, and fairness of outward form, than the dietary value of a fruit by its size and colour.

II. INSINCERITY IS CHARACTERISTIC NO LESS IN WHAT IT OMITS THAN IN WHAT IT OBSERVES. No mention is made of the "sin offering" or the "trespass offering." Yet these were both compulsory, whereas the three observed were optional. Hence it appears that : 1. *To the formalist that is least acceptable which is most Divine.* He has no true respect for God's authority. He is a self-pleaser first of all and most of all, and will find the ordinance most acceptable into the observance of which there enters most of his own will and least of God's. On this principle the *optional* in worship will be preferred to the *prescribed* (Isa. i. 12), and the *unauthorized* to either (Mark vii. 9). The illustration of this in the countless vagaries of the Romanist and Ritualist is easy to trace. Practical attention to the various details of worship by the unspiritual almost seems to be inversely as their Divine authority. 2. *To the formalist that is most distasteful which most closely connects him with his sin.* The sin offering was an acknowledgment, and involved a remembrance, of guilt. This is distasteful to the natural heart. Give a sinful man his way, and the last matter he will face will be his own sinfulness. Allow a formalist discretion in worship, and the ordinance that most articulately speaks of sin will be the one least observed. Singing will be preferred to praying, a form of prayer will be preferred to the directness of spontaneous utterance, and preaching, which most distinctly brings face to face with personal responsibility and duty, will be almost crowded out. Worship, in fact, in proportion as it becomes formal, becomes impersonal and indirect.

III. SUCH HOLLOW WORSHIP IS UTTERLY OFFENSIVE TO GOD. The degrees of Divine disapprobation run up a graduated scale. " 1 will not accept; " " I will not take pleasure in; " " I will not regard; " " I hate; " " I despise." In all such worship the moral element, the first element of acceptability, is altogether wanting. The thing is not meant for worship, and cannot be treated as such. It is not observed according to God's will, nor as God's appointment at all, but as our own invention or choice. It is not aimed at the God-glorifying, soul-saving objects prescribed in Scripture. Gone through without interest or heart, done for fashion, or freak, or gain, it honours neither God nor his command, whilst it calls into play no grace of the religious life whatever. It is a mere performance, not only destitute of moral value, but distasteful to God, and in gratuitous violation of his Law. Hence the vocabulary of condemnation is exhausted on it (Isa. i. 11—15) as the meanest and most hateful thing in the whole spiritual connection.

Ver. 24.—*Real calamity waiting upon unreal service.* "The meaning of this verse is not, ' Let justice and righteousness take the place of your sacrifices.' . . . The verse threatens the flooding of the land with judgment and the punitive righteousness of God " (Keil). Adopting this interpretation, we observe—

I. THAT WHICH IS REJECTED " IS NIGH UNTO CURSING." Hollow service has been sitting for its portrait, and the picture is striking. Now we have the Divine appraisement revealed in the action to be taken forthwith. Instead of approval there is condemnation. Instead of reward there is punishment. Instead of profit resulting there is loss on every issue. 1. *It deserves this.* Want of conformity to law is a sufficient ground of condemnation. Positive transgression of law is ground more decided still. Wilful mockery of the Lawgiver is most deeply criminal of all. All these elements pertained to Israel's sham observances, and, together, they constitute an indictment on which the criminal's conviction is inevitable. 2. *It requires it.* God's moral government must show itself strong and just, and in order to this, sin, and all sin, must be visited with his avenging stroke. Especially must this be done in the sphere of " things whereby God maketh himself known." The thing whose function it is to make him known must do so in the glorious character he bears.

II. THE JUDGMENTS THAT ENGULF ARE RIGHTEOUSNESS. This could be argued, and is here affirmed. 1. *They express righteousness.* They are deserved. They are all deserved. They are deserved in the proportions in which they come. If they did not come, the moral balance of things would be disturbed. If they came in less decided form, this balance would be only half adjusted. They are "righteous judgments" in the fullest and highest sense. 2. *They accomplish righteousness.* They are sent in the interests of it. They fall on the unrighteous. They are designed and fitted to lead to their reformation (Isa. xxvi. 9). Sometimes the righteous suffer from them also. In that case their tendency is on the one hand to promote the righteousness of the sufferer, and on the other to emphasize the evil of unrighteousness in any section of a community, and so prevent it. As a matter of fact, Divine judgments have often wrought righteousness both in individuals (2 Chron. xxxiii. 11—16) and communities (Isa. xliii. 21). Even in eternity they bulk largely, in the thought of the redeemed, among the helpful experiences of earth (Rev. vii. 14).

III. WHEN JUDGMENT IN RIGHTEOUSNESS COMES, IT COMES LIKE A FLOOD. There are two ideas here. The first is : 1. *Let judgment roll on like water.* In this : (1) It will be deep (Ps. xxxvi. 6), swallowing up all its victims. (2) It will be sudden, taking the evil-doers by surprise (Luke xvii. 20—31). (3) It will be irresistible, sweeping before it every opposing object (Ps. xc. 5). (4) It will be destroying, leaving no living thing in its track. (5) It will be ultimately fertilizing, leaving behind it the rich ooze of an abiding lesson. 2. *And righteousness like an inexhaustible stream.* Judgment is the act of which righteousness is the principle. God's righteousness, whether in himself or in his judgments, is like an inexhaustible stream. (1) *It is perennial.* The righteousness of God's judgments is a constant quantity. It never intermits. Each is righteous and all are righteousness. (3) *It is pure.* Righteousness in God is necessarily so. There is no foreign ingredient, no cloud of mixture in it whatever. It is righteous through and through. "There is," there can be, "no unrighteousness in him." (3) *It is cleansing.* It purifies all it touches; the person it is laved on, the city it passes through. (4) *It is irrigating.* It waters the fields of human life. It makes the graces, like the grass, to grow in the desert, and withering things revive. The righteousness of God, like water-streams, is rich in every element of blessing for time, and is a benefactor for eternity as well.

Vers. 25—27.—*Trusting in idols that cannot save.* In these words, God's case against Israel just announced is strengthened. Their services now were hollow and insincere; their sacrifices formal acts in which the heart had no part. This, in itself, was ground of punishment even to destruction. But it is only a portion of the iniquity chargeable against them. In the wilderness the course had been already entered on. Appointed ordinances had been neglected. Idolatrous ordinances had been introduced. As now they were going on, so they had long ago begun. There was a diuturnity in their wrong-doing which made the fall of destroying judgments a foregone conclusion. We see here—

I. ISRAEL'S PRESENT JUDGED IN THE LIGHT OF ITS PAST. What Israel in Amos's time was and should receive was affected by what Israel had been and done in the desert of sin. This is according to principles universally received. 1. *Every nation is held responsible for its own entire past.* The England of to-day not only owns responsibility for, but is striving nobly to make compensation for, errors of the England of three hundred years ago. The prophet-killing Israel of our Lord's time are declared responsible for all the martyr-blood shed from that of Abel down (Matt. xxiii. 35). The logic of this is unassailable. The national identity remains unbroken. The national policy remains unchanged. The national life maintains its continuity. And so among its heirlooms is the inherited responsibility for the sins of other days. 2. *A nation is further responsible for its past, in that the present takes its tone from it.* A certain proportion of almost every evil is hereditary. From the past generations we inherit evil qualities and learn evil ways. The father's vices reappear in the child. The present is the child of the past, begotten in its likeness, and liable as such for the evil it has taken up and perpetuates. 3. *The life of a nation, like that of an individual, can be judged of only as a whole.* If a nation from its birth to its death be one thing, so is a nation's life. Now, the glory of God's dealing is its perfect equity, arising out of its exhaustive induction of facts. He leaves nothing out of account, no smallest word, no slightest desire, no most trifling act. His verdict in each case is based on the entire life of the party in court. The method is fair. No other method would be fair. Each part is modified by its relation to all the others, and cannot be fairly judged unless in connection with them.

II. THAT PAST PERSISTENTLY UNFAITHFUL. The interrogative form of ver. 25 is equivalent to a strong negation. 1. *They had neglected sacrifice in the wilderness.* "Have ye offered me sacrifices and gifts in the desert forty years?" Typifying the atonement of Christ, through which men draw near to God, sacrifice was the fundamental exercise of Old Testament worship. This was not abandoned by the priests (Numb. xvi. 46), but it was, like circumcision (Josh. v. 5), neglected by the people, and superseded by sacrifices to idols (Deut. xxxii. 17; Ezek. xx. 16). In this neglect or perversion were included the voluntary gifts (offerings) as well as the prescribed sacrifices. Thus early adopted, and long persisted in, was Israel's rebellious way. Emphasizing the pronoun, God says in effect of the whole run of Jewish national history, "Ye either offered no sacrifice at all, or none to *me.*" 2. *They were at pains to make, and carry, idolatrous appliances with them.* "But ye have borne the tabernacle of your Moloch." Divinely appointed sacrifice they found too burdensome to be followed. Of Divine worship in each of its ordinances they said, "What a weariness is it!" But they thought it no trouble to make and carry about portable shrines and pedestals for use in the worship of heathen idols. A man will do for his idol what he will not do for God. Be it idol lust, or habit, or opinion, he loves it more, and is more like it, and so finds its service more congenial. The God of the legalist is not the God of Scripture, but a God of his own devising, and so he serves him laboriously in works of self-righteousness, whilst stubbornly declining the far easier call of the true God to simple faith in Jesus Christ. It was in following his affinities thus that Israel was ever found joined to his idols, and alien to the God of heaven. 3. *This idolatry they had derived from Egypt.* " It was no doubt to these Egyptian sun-gods that the star-god which the Israelites carried about with them belonged " (Keil). They were not seduced into idolatry merely by the nations among whom they passed. They did not wait for that. They tired of Jehovah's service, and sought out false gods for themselves. They were bent on having idols, come whence they would. Failing others, they adopted, in their blind and besotted perverseness, those of Egypt itself Their return to Jehovah for deliverance was desertion, and the lesson learned under idolatrous Egypt's savage oppression was to adopt the idol-worship that produced it. This is eloquent of the godlessness of the corrupt heart. Nothing can disgust it with idols, nothing can attach it to God. It hates him always, and embraces, or seeks, or makes occasions of abandoning his worship. 4. *Israel's worship of idols involved the serving of them.* " The booth of your king." Every man's god is his king. Worship is the highest act of service. When it is rendered, the other and lower acts necessarily follow ; when it is abandoned, they logically and actually cease. A new idol in the heart means a new sovereign over the life.

III. THE DIVINE PUNISHMENT TO BE ADJUSTED TO THE SIN. This it always 's, but in the present case the correspondence is specially obvious. 1. *They should go into captivity.* God often punishes sins against himself by human instrumentality, gene-rally that of the wicked (2 Sam. xxiv. 13 ; Ps. cix. 6). The severity of such punish-ment is guaranteed by the native cruelty of the human heart. As the conqueror and owner of the vanquished and enslaved, the wicked puts on his worst character, and his treatment becomes punishment corresponding to the worst sin of idolatry. 2. *Their captivity should be among idolaters.* The rod of God's anger in this case was to be the Assyrian (Isa. x. 5). In captivity with him, Israel would find out what kind of masters idolatry makes of its votaries. This would disenchant them, if anything could. The test of the god we worship is the practical one of the character of his service. When our idol lusts become our masters, we know them as they really are. The drunkard has attained to a knowledge of the drink-appetite that would be a wholesome revela-tion to those who are just beginning to indulge. 3. *They should die as slaves in the land out of which their progenitor had at first been called.* " I will carry you beyond Damascus." Stephen (Acts vii. 42, 43) quotes this " beyond Babylon." In either case the neighbourhood of Ur of the Chaldees would be referred to. This, which had been the cradle of the nation, would be its grave. There, where their godly ancestor had been a prince, the idolatrous nation would be slaves (Josh. xxiv. 14, 3) ; his faith, and the promises to it, having been lost together.

IV. GOD'S THREATS EMPHASIZED BY HIS NAME. This says what he is, and so indicates how he will act. 1. *He is Jehovah, the Self-existent One.* " He cannot but be, and he is, the Source of all being ; the unchangeable, infinite, eternal Essence." As Jehovah, he originates all things (ver. 8 ; ch. ix. 6 ; Jer. xxxiii. 2), controls all things (Ps. x. 16 ; xcix. 1), fills and possesses all things, and " nothing is too hard for him " (Jer. xxxii. 27). 2. *He is Lord of hosts.* " The Lord of the heavenly hosts, for whose worship they forsook God ; the Lord of the hosts on earth, whose ministry he employs to punish those who rebel against him. All creatures in heaven and earth are, as he says of the holy angels, ' ministers of his that do his pleasure ' " (Pusey). " Jehovah," the great First Cause, " God of hosts," the Controller of all second causes whatever, there is that in the Name of God which guarantees the execution, literal and exhaustive, of all his threats.

HOMILIES BY VARIOUS AUTHORS.

Ver. 4.—" *Seek the Lord.*" Man is by nature a seeker. He desires good, of one kind or another, and what he desires he makes the object of his quest, more or less diligent and persevering. Hence the restlessness, the energy, the effort, so distinctive of human life. Religion does not destroy or repress natural characteristics; it hallows and dignifies them. Religion gives to human search a just direction and noble aim.

I. THE REASONS IN MAN'S NATURE AND CIRCUMSTANCES WHICH SHOULD LEAD HIM TO SEEK THE LORD. 1. Man is so constituted that he cannot find a full satisfaction in any earthly and created good. He returns from every such endeavour with the complaint, "All is vanity." "Our heart," said St. Augustine—"our heart is restless till it rests in thee." 2. Especially do all human religions prove their insufficiency. Israel was learning this by bitter experience. "Seek not Bethel," etc., was the admonition of the prophet to those who had been in the habit of resorting to idol-shrines. The gods of the heathen were known to the Jews as "vanities."

II. THE REASONS TO BE FOUND IN GOD WHY HE SHOULD ENGAGE THE SEEKING POWERS OF MAN. 1. His own proper excellence is such that the soul that gains even a glimpse of it may well devote to the pursuit of Divine knowledge and favour all powers and all opportunities. 2. God alone is able to succour and to save those who set their affection and desire upon him. 3. God condescends to invite the children of men to seek him. By the mouth of the prophet he gives an express command and invitation. We may be assured that this language is sincere and trustworthy. 4. There is an express promise of incomparable preciousness addressed to such as are ready to respond to the heavenly call. "Ye shall live," is the authoritative assurance. By this we may understand that seekers after God shall be delivered from destruction, that they shall be made partakers of the Divine life, in all its spiritual energy and happiness.

III. THE METHODS IN WHICH GOD MAY BE SOUGHT AND FOUND. 1. Observe *where* he is to be found : *i.e.* in his holy Word; in his blessed Son, by whom in this Christian dispensation he has revealed himself unto us, and who has said, "No man cometh unto the Father, but by me." 2. Consider *how* he is to be found : *i.e.* by penitence, in humility, through faith, with prayer ; in a word, by the exercises special to the spiritual nature. 3. Notice *when* he is to be found : *i.e.* now. "Seek ye the Lord while he may be found, call ye upon him while he is near."—T.

Vers. 7—9.—*The Lord of the universe.* The herdsman of Tekoah was a true poet. His eyes were open to the beauty and to the splendour of nature ; and his heart felt the presence of the Unseen and Eternal in all the works of his hands, in all his providential arrangements. More than this, the moral character and rule of the Omnipotent were very present and very real to him ; he felt the force of the appeal made to the spiritual nature of man, and calling for a life of religious faith, of practical obedience. There is nothing strained or unnatural in the striking conjunction in this passage of poetic sensibility with ethical and religious exhortation.

I. A REPRESENTATION OF DIVINE GREATNESS AND GLORY. 1. Seen in the creation of the starry host. The Pleiades and Orion are mentioned as two of the most noticeable and most splendid of the constellations of the midnight sky. 2. In the alternations of day and night, in sunrise and sunset, in storm and in eclipse. 3. In the grandeur of the sea, in the torrents of rain, in the floods which pour their waters over the earth ; in a word, in all the processes of nature. 4. In the providential interpositions and the righteous rule of the Most High, who does according to his will among the inhabitants of the earth.

II. AN INFERENCE AS TO HUMAN CONDUCT. The poet-prophet is more than a mirror to reflect the visible splendour, the awful forces of the universe. To him nature has a voice of authority, appealing to the understanding and to the conscience of the sons of men. There is a summons to the unrighteous and the irreligious to forsake their ways and to choose a better path. This summons will take a different form according to the character, the moral development, of those addressed. 1. There is what may be called the *lower* view—a God so great will not suffer iniquity to triumph, or injustice and disobedience to go unpunished. All are in the hands of the Almighty ; and he whose power is so evidently revealed in the heavens above and on the earth beneath will not fail to assert his authority over all the creatures of his power. Although wickedness may prosper for a season, the law of righteousness shall be maintained and vindicated. 2. There is a *higher* view—not inconsistent with the other, but presenting itself to natures more morally cultivated and advanced. Great as God appears in nature, our conceptions of his excellence are enhanced when we reflect upon his glorious attributes and his righteous reign. The eternal law of righteousness administered by Omnipotence demands our lowly reverence, deserves our grateful obedience.—T.

Vers. 14, 15.—*The great alternative.* The coincidence between religion and morality is brought very strikingly before us in such passages as these. How different are such appeals as these, made by the prophet in the name of the Lord, from the requirements of merely formal religion! The highest conception of good is revealed, the noblest standard of right is exhibited; and all the sanctions furnished by the authority and the loving-kindness of the Eternal are brought to bear upon human nature to induce to consecration and obedience. I. MAN'S NATURE AND POSITION RENDER NECESSARY A MORAL CHOICE. 1. Man's emotional nature impels him to adopt an object of supreme love. Human affection may be diffused or it may be concentrated, it may be languid or it may be intense. But in any case it exists and acts as a principle of the moral life. 2. Man's voluntary and practical nature requires an object of supreme quest and endeavour. We seek what we love, we avoid what we hate. II. THE GREAT ALTERNATIVE WHICH PRESENTS ITSELF TO MAN IS THE CHOICE BETWEEN GOOD AND EVIL. This is a real and not a fictitious or conventional distinction. It would be as reasonable to deny the distinction between straight and crooked, between light and darkness, as that between moral good and moral evil. The distinction is vital and eternal, connected with the "nature of things," with the attributes and character of God, with the constitution of man. The choice between pleasure and pain, between worldly prosperity and adversity, is as nothing compared with this choice. The appeals of revelation, from the beginning to the end of the Bible, urge men to choose the good in preference to the evil. There are doubtless inducements to another choice; but this remains the choice enforced by reason, by conscience, by God. III. HOWEVER IT MAY BE REPRESENTED OTHERWISE, THE FACT IS THAT THE PRACTICAL PREFERENCE OF GOOD CONDUCES TO MAN'S WELFARE. The inducements offered to adopt a life of selfishness and of pleasure are many and powerful; there are "pleasures of sin for a season." The way of virtue and religion is a steep and rugged path. Yet it yields a deep and pure satisfaction not to be found in the ways, the broad and primrose paths, of sin. We are not called upon to balance pleasures. The voice of right, of God, is authoritative, and demands obedience without hesitation or calculation. Yet God promises such as listen to and obey his voice that he will "be with" them, that he will be "gracious unto" them, and that they shall "live."—T.

Vers. 21—23.—*Ceremonialism disdained.* Although the Jewish religion prescribed, as is evident especially from the Book of Leviticus, innumerable observances, elaborate ritual, frequent and costly sacrifices, still nowhere are there to be found more disclaimers, more denunciations, of a merely ritual and ceremonial piety than in the Scriptures of the Old Testament. This is but one of many declarations that the true and living God will not accept any tribute of the hands which may be offered in lieu of the homage of the heart. I. THE OUTWARD MANIFESTATIONS OF RELIGION WHICH GOD REJECTS. 1. Sacred assemblies are displeasing to him. He does, indeed, love the gates of Zion more than all the dwellings of Jacob; yet the prophet is inspired to declare that God hates and despises the gatherings of his own people. 2. Solemn festivals are equally distasteful. These, indeed, have been prescribed in the Law; they are commemorative of great mercies, great deliverances; their neglect or omission is viewed with displeasure. Yet here God is indignant that these feasts should be celebrated. 3. The same detestation is extended to the burnt offerings, meat offerings, and peace offerings, which the Hebrews were instructed on proper occasions to present to their Divine King. 4. More remarkable still, sacred songs and strains of music are as discord in the ear of God. The very psalms in which the Divine attributes are celebrated and the Divine gifts acknowledged are no longer acceptable to him who inhabiteth the praises of Israel. II. THE GROUNDS UPON WHICH GOD REJECTS THE OUTWARD MANIFESTATIONS OF

RELIGION. 1. Not because they are themselves an inappropriate tribute of religious emotion and religious consecration. 2. But because they are not expressive of sincere worship, gratitude, confidence, and love. "This people," saith the Searcher of hearts, "draweth nigh unto me with their lips, but their heart is far from me." And our Lord Christ has taught us that "God is a Spirit, and they that worship him must worship him in spirit and in truth." 3. And because ceremonial observances may be, and in the cases in question are, consistent with an idolatrous and wicked life. The very men who were punctilious in these ceremonies and sacrifices were tampering with the idolatry of surrounding peoples, and were acting with injustice and selfishness in the ordinary relationships of life. 4. Because, further, these manifestations are as a matter of fact substituted for those feelings and purposes which they are intended to promote. In fact, seeming religiousness hides the absence of real religion, so that this absence is sometimes unnoticed by the apparent but heartless and formal worshipper.—T.

Ver. 24.—*The river of righteousness.* Whilst the holy King and Judge rejects the mere service of the lip and of the hand, when unaccompanied by genuine piety, he desires above all things the prevalence of those practical principles of rectitude which are the secret, hidden power of an upright and acceptable life. In a very bold and beautiful metaphor the Divine wish and pleasure are declared. Let the hypocritical festivals, the unmeaning sacrifices, the hollow songs, be swept away, and let the river of righteousness roll through the land, and God shall be pleased, and his people shall be blessed.

I. ITS DIVINE SOURCE. The fountain of rectitude is not to be found in the arrangements of human society, in the laws of human device, in the expediency which aims at human pleasures. We are to look up to the hills, to the heavens, for its source. It wells from the eternal constitution of the moral universe, from the very nature, from the glorious government, of the Eternal.

II. ITS VAST VOLUME. There is no community of men, there is no social relationship, in which righteousness may not be exemplified. Even the heathen philosophers could say great things of justice.

"Nor morning star, nor evening star, so fair!"

Ardent religionists sometimes lose sight of this principle and its necessity, thinking justice too sublunary and commonplace to be deserving of their attention. Such a practice is not sanctioned by Scripture, which from beginning to end lays stress upon the faithful and honourable discharge of human duty, as between man and man, in all the varied relationships of life.

III. ITS MIGHTY CURRENT. There is a power in righteousness which only the morally blind can overlook, which commands the homage of the observant and the thoughtful. For whilst it is not the kind of power that the worldly cannot but see, and the vulgar cannot but admire, it is nevertheless power—enduring, effective, undoubted power. The state is strong in which justice is administered, in which a high standard of uprightness is maintained in social and public life; whilst injustice, insincerity, oppression, corruption, and deceit are detrimental to the true interests of any community.

IV. ITS PERENNIAL FLOW. A river differs from a cistern, a reservoir, in this—that it does not run dry, that it is not exhausted, that it flows on from age to age. And the righteousness that the eternal King desires to see prevail in human society is an ever-flowing stream. Not like the mountain-torrent, which is dried up in summer heat; but like the vast river, which is fed from the everlasting hills, and is replenished by many a tributary stream, is the course of Divine righteousness upon earth. Not in one nation, in one age, in one dispensation only, but in every time and place does this river of righteousness flow for the welfare of mankind.

V. ITS BENEFICENT RESULTS. From insincere religious observances no good can come; but from justice, from a proper discharge of duty, from right principles, we may look for every good. God is pleased that his attribute becomes his creature's law. And righteousness exalts nations and establishes thrones.—T.

Vers. 25, 26.—*A divided homage rejected.* The continuity of Israel's national life is here assumed. Amos addressed the same people that was brought by Moses out of Egypt, that was led by Joshua into Canaan. The same temptations were followed by the same falls; in fact, until after the Captivity, the chosen nation was ever liable to relapse into partial and temporary idolatry. This was especially the case with the northern kingdom, which had not the benefit of the temple services, sacrifices, and priesthood. The peculiarity of the case was the attempt to combine two systems of religion so inconsistent as the worship of Jehovah and the worship of the false deities of the neighbouring nations. Yet this attempt is substantially one which is renewed by some in every generation, even under this spiritual and Christian dispensation. Displeasing as was the conduct of Israel in the view of a holy and "jealous" God, equally offensive is every endeavour to serve two masters, to divide the allegiance and devotion of the heart.

I. THE FACT THAT MEN DO ATTEMPT TO DIVIDE THEIR HOMAGE AND WORSHIP. This is no doubt an evidence of human inconsistency and instability; but it is not to be denied that our nature frequently exhibits these qualities. On the one hand, education, the voice of conscience, the aspirations of better moments, the influence of pious friends, tend to retain the heart beneath the sway of true religion. On the other hand, the example of the pleasure-seeking and the worldly, the baser impulses of our nature, the suggestions of our spiritual adversary, all draw our hearts towards an inferior good, towards an ignoble choice. Hence many are found neither renouncing God nor rejecting the allurements of a sinful world.

II. THE GROUNDS UPON WHICH THE SUPREME REJECTS THE DIVIDED HOMAGE AND WORSHIP WHICH ARE SOMETIMES OFFERED. 1. God's just claim is to the whole nature and the whole life of his intelligent creatures. The Father of the spirits of all flesh cannot consent to share his rightful possession with any rival, any pretender, be he who he may. 2. The nature of man is such that he can only give religious reverence and service that shall be worthy of the name to one Lord. Christ has emphatically pronounced upon the case in his words, "Ye cannot serve God and mammon." 3. The moral degradation and disaster involved in the endeavour are palpable. There is inconsistency, nay, there is opposition, between the two services. A riven heart is a wretched heart. Hypocrisy is a sandy foundation upon which to build the character and life; upon this no secure and stable edifice can possibly be reared.

III. THE URGENCY OF THE ALTERNATIVE CONSEQUENTLY PRESENTED TO EVERY MORAL NATURE. It is the alternative which Joshua urged upon the Israelites: "Choose ye this day whom ye will serve." It is the alternative which Elijah urged upon a later generation: "How long halt ye between two opinions [between the two sides]? If Jehovah be God, serve him; but if Baal, then serve him."—T.

Ver. 4.—*Seeking the Lord.* "For thus saith the Lord unto the house of Israel, Seek ye me, and ye shall live." It is impossible to read this chapter without noticing the tenderness of the prophet, his compassion and pitifulness, his yearning wish to help and save. This feeling is the more remarkable because Amos belonged to the tribe of Judah, and felt thus towards the neighbouring and hostile kingdom of Israel. Such pity is ever a sign of Divine inspiration. Thus Isaiah (xxii. 4) says, "Look away from me; I will weep bitterly, labour not to comfort me, because of the spoiling of the daughter of my people," etc. Samuel, too, after Saul the king had proved himself so headstrong and wilful that nothing could save him, although he went down to his own house and, in accordance with Divine command, saw him no more, nevertheless mourned for Saul to the day of his death. And, loftiest of all, Christ Jesus stood on the Mount of Olives, and as he beheld the city which had rejected him, he wept over it, saying, "O Jerusalem," etc.! It was in this spirit that Amos wrote the passage before us, and thrice repeated the message in our text. Meditation on this subject gives us some thoughts: 1. *On the loss of God.* 2. *On the search for God* 3. *On life in God.*

I. THE LOSS OF GOD. The exhortation to "seek" him implies that he has been lost sight of by his creatures. This is brought about by various influences. 1. *By intellectual temptations.* These vary in different ages. In the time of Amos the study of God's works led to superstition, while in these days it leads many to scepticism. Then the stars were believed to affect human destiny (ver. 8); each season had its own deity; every element obeyed some unseen being. The polytheist would have joined heartily with the Jew in saying, "The fool hath said in his heart, There is no God." In our day, on the contrary, folly is supposed to lie in the other direction, namely, in the heart of him who believes in that which is beyond sensuous perception and purely intellectual research. Science, which has driven fairies from the woods, elves from the mountains, and nymphs from the sea, is now supposed to be almost prepared to drive God from his universe. Articles in our magazines, addresses in our halls, speak with such ill-disguised contempt of religious men that their language is, "The fool hath said in his heart, There *is* a God." But the world never wanted God more. Men are not satisfied with knowing, and some who see no evidence for a future heaven are bitterly asking—Is life worth living? Amidst the miseries of civilized society, and the wrangling of sects, many a one secretly says, "My heart and my flesh cry out for the living God!" In an age when men believed in gods who had no personal love or righteousness, they wanted to know the heavenly Father; and in this age, when scepticism has swept the world bare of some of its old creeds, we do well to hearken to the message of God, "Seek ye me, and ye shall live." 2. *By prevailing idolatries.* Show how places of sacred memory had become sources of idolatry and pollution (ver. 5). *Bethel,* where Jacob saw the heavenly ladder, and vowed that he and his would be the Lord's; *Gilgal,* where the people reconsecrated themselves on entering Canaan; *Beersheba,* where Abraham called on the Lord, and Isaac built his altar, and Israel offered sacrifice when going with his sons into Egypt; —were all transformed into idolatrous resorts. From this, point out how easily creeds, forms of worship, holy places and relics, nominal profession of Christianity, etc., may hide God, instead of bearing witness to him. Suggest also certain modern idolatries. 3. *By practical unrighteousness.* Amos addressed his hearers as "Ye who turn judgment to wormwood [that is, who, instead of rendering justice, commit bitter wrong], and leave off righteousness in the earth [or, rather, 'dethrone it from rule']." Trace these sins in some trades and professions, and in some social customs and ecclesiastical movements, of our own day. Yet, in spite of such sins, which will incur the penalties here foretold, the message comes to every sinner from him who is not willing that any should perish, "Seek ye me, and ye shall live."

II. THE SEARCH FOR GOD. Let us rightly estimate the privilege offered to us. God is great beyond our conceptions. "He maketh the seven stars and Orion," etc., yet says, "To that man will I look . . . who is of a humble and contrite heart." 1. *There is necessity for seeking him.* He will not force himself on our notice, nor blazen his name in the sky. Any man, if he chooses, is free to live as if God were not. It is "he who seeketh findeth." 2. *There are advantages in seeking him.* These are additional to the advantages of *finding* him. The most precious things (jewels, corn, knowledge, etc.) are not the most easily obtained. The self-discipline, the steadfast effort, the trials of faith and hope, etc., cultivate character. So, in seeking God, we find that the pains and difficulties resulting from doubts, indolence, sins, etc., are part of our Heaven-appointed discipline. If God were visible as the sun is visible, there would be no moral advantage in "seeking" him; but as he is visible only through faith and prayer, we rise heavenward in our very seeking after him. 3. *There is a right way of seeking him.* Hence ver. 5, "Seek not Bethel," etc. Some hoped to get help in other directions rather than in the path of penitential prayer. Multitudes now, instead of turning to him who is the Light of the world, pursue false lights, which, like the will-o'-the-wisp, will lead to destruction. Hear the words of Jesus Christ: "He that hath seen me hath seen the Father;" "I and the Father are one."

III. THE LIFE IN GOD. "And ye shall *live.*" This does not allude to national life. That was irrevocably doomed. But in the doomed nation any sinner turning to God would live. Nor is the allusion to natural life, but to that spiritual life which is referred to in the verse, "This is life eternal, that they might know thee," etc. This life in its nature and source is more fully revealed to us than to Amos himself. 1. *The source of this life* is found in God, revealed to us in Jesus Christ our Lord. No man can create life where it is not, nor restore it where it once was. Christ, by the raising of the dead, showed in a visible sphere what he alone can do in the invisible. "The wages of sin is death; but the gift of God is eternal life through Jesus Christ our Lord." 2. *The nature of this life.* It is Divine, and constitutes us "partakers of the Divine nature." Its germ is faith, its inspiration is love, its breath is prayer, its manifestation the likeness of Christ. 3. *The vigour of this life.* It will live amid the influences of an evil atmosphere, as a hale man walks unhurt through a tainted hospital. It will assert itself in streams of benediction to the world around, and it will finally prove itself victorious over death; for the Lord has said, "He that liveth and believeth in me shall never die;" text.—A. R.

Ver. 8.—*The message of the stars.* "Seek him that maketh the seven stars and Orion, and turneth the shadow of death into the morning, and maketh the day dark with night: that calleth for the waters of the sea, and poureth them out upon the face of the earth: The Lord is his Name." This recognition of God amidst the phenomena of nature is characteristic of Amos. He looked on the Pleiades and Orion, as they shone radiantly in the heavens, changeless in their relations, calm amidst human vicissitudes, and constant in diffusing their light upon a troubled world, and bade men seek him who created them. He speaks of night, that "shadow of death," and reminds his hearers that, though it be long and fearsome, the light of dawn comes at last, and God turns it into morning; and again, after the work of the day is done, and tired men want rest, God draws the curtains, and "makes the day dark with night." The last clause is more obscure. Sometimes the waters have been "poured out upon the earth" in destructive deluge, and this has occurred at the command of God; but we prefer the application of the prophet's words to that familiar and constant display of the Divine power by means of which the waters are secretly gathered up into the sky, that they may be poured out in showers of blessing upon the earth. Our text is true of nature; but it is also true of that of which nature is the symbol and shadow, as we shall endeavour to show. It reminds us—

I. THAT GOD OVERRULES THE OUTWARD CONDITIONS OF HUMAN LIFE. "Seek him that maketh the seven stars and Orion." The words are literally true. Philosophy teaches us to find an adequate cause for all effects, and science acknowledges that the First Cause eludes its search, and is beyond its sphere. Revelation declares, "God made the sun to rule by day, and the moon to rule by night: he made the stars also." More than this primal fact is, however, asserted here. Amos was speaking to those who saw in the stars more than material lights. His hearers believed in astrology, which has been prevalent in all ages, from the very dawn of history. This superstition, which has left its mark on the earliest records of our race, in the literature of the Egyptians, Chaldeans, Hindus, and Chinese, was not without effect on the people of Israel, as many passages in Scripture show. Indeed, it only received its deathblow when the Copernican system was finally established; for even Kepler would not deny that there was a connection between the movements of the stars and the fortunes of men. Now, two constellations so peculiar and brilliant as Pleiades and Orion naturally had special powers ascribed to them. Thus Rabbi Isaac Israel, in his remarks on Job xxxviii. 31, says, "Some of the stars have operations in the ripening of fruits, and such is the opening of the Pleiades; and some of the stars retard and delay the fruits from ripening, and this is the opening of Orion." In other words, the Pleiades were associated with the spring, when Nature was bursting into new life, when she was emitting the sweetest influences from every blade and flower, when ships which had been shut up through stress of weather could put out once more to sea. Hence the question, "Canst thou bind the sweet influence of Pleiades?"—Canst thou prevent the outpouring of vernal life? Whether you will or not, the change comes; for it is of God. Similarly, Orion was associated with autumn, when the earth was throwing off her beauty, and the voyages of the ancient times came to an end, and frost bound the streams as in fetters of iron. "Canst thou loose the bands of Orion?"—Canst thou check the storms, and break up the reign of frost? Now, says Amos, look beyond these constellations to him who made them; and when you rejoice in the spring, or dread the approaching winter, when you are glad over the pleasantness of life, or faint under its adversity;—think of him who is above and beyond all material forces and all visible influences. There is a spring and autumn known in human experience which have their sources beyond ourselves and beyond all visible agency; and our hearts find rest in the assurance of this. Compare the lot of two children in dissimilar circumstances—the one with every comfort and care, as if " born under a lucky star," and sharing " the sweet influences of Pleiades ; " the other in the drunken home, with curses temporal and moral on every side. These children do not choose their lot, they do not appear to deserve treatment so different; yet their circumstances are not the result of chance nor the decree of blind fate, but are to be ascribed to him " who made the seven stars and Orion," and, as the Judge of all the earth, he will do right. (Suggest other examples of seeming unfairness in men's circumstances.) This Divine revelation in Scripture affirms of God that he appoints the lot of each, and this with a view to the training of character, which far outweighs the pleasantness or the painfulness found in mere circumstances. Adversity will by-and-by appear to be but a small thing to him who amidst it proved himself faithful, and prosperity will seem in the retrospect of little worth to him who, through his thanklessness and prayerlessness, has failed to " lay hold on eternal life." Whatever influences surround us, we are, for our own sakes, called on to recognize God as overruling them. If we are prosperous, it is " the Lord who gives power to get wealth ; " if we are in adversity, we are not to blame our luck or our friends, but to seek the comfort and help of him " who maketh the seven stars and Orion."

II. That God overrules the inward experience of men. "He turneth the shadow of death into the morning," etc. The Hebrew word translated "shadow of death " almost always means more than natural night, however black that may be (see references in Job and Psalms). Admitting this figurative use of the word here, the reference of the prophet would seem to be to the changes from sorrowfulness to joyfulness, and from joyfulness to sorrowfulness, which we frequently experience. These are not dependent on circumstances. The wealthiest men have often said of their surroundings, "I have no pleasure in them ; " while the poor and persecuted have sometimes made their miserable abodes resound with praise. We may illustrate this from the life of our Lord. At one time " he rejoiced in spirit," at another time he was " exceeding sorrowful, even unto death ; " yet the Father's hand was recognized in both experiences. God inspires the children's songs, and he gives the cup of agony. What abundant reason we have to praise God for certain inward changes—the carelessness turned into serious and sad penitence, and this again into the joyfulness of pardon ! To many a weeping penitent, sitting in darkness, he has come and " turned the shadow of death into morning." Others have been in the darkness of doubt. They have cried, " Why hast thou forsaken me ? " They have felt around them for some hand to help in their dire extremity. At last the sense of Christ's love has come home to them, and though their questions are not all answered, they believe in him, and enter into rest, and soon they find that " he that believeth does not walk in darkness, but has the light of life." God turns for them the shadow of death into morning. Soon " the shadow feared of man " will come. Yet even the darkness of death shall be transformed into the brightness of heaven ; and in the place where " there is no need of the sun or moon to shine," because God himself is the Light thereof, we shall see how God has for evermore turned the shadow of death into morning.

III. That God transforms curses into blessings. God " calls for the waters of the sea." They secretly ascend to heaven, and then descend in refreshing showers. The transformation effected in that phenomenon is noteworthy. If we pour sea water on flowers, they will die ; but when it is called up into the heavens the pernicious salt is left behind, the water is purged from its destructiveness, and the curse is made a blessing. A transforming influence passes over all that comes to us, if it is caught up to heaven. Suppose prosperity comes to you. It may enervate and destroy your spiritual life, but if praise to God is associated with it, and habitual prayer that you may use this for God, you may become by your very prosperity a more generous, tender-hearted, and Christ-like man. If adversity is yours, and you take all your troubles before the Lord, they will be transfigured before you in the light of God's love and Christ's sufferings, and through your valley of Achor you will enter into deeper rest and nobler hope. If doubts or temptations try you, they will not curse, but bless you, if they arouse the earnest prayer, " Lord, help me ! " Christ was never more precious to Thomas than when, after his doubts, he exclaimed, " My Lord and my God ! " But his doubts would have ruined him had they kept him from the presence of the Lord. Let all your troubles and joys be wafted, by prayer and praise, into the heaven of God's presence, and they shall be poured down upon you in showers of spiritual blessings.

CONCLUSION. If you would know the comfort of the text, you will only find it in obedience to its first clause, "Seek him!" "Seek ye the Lord while he may be found," etc.; "Acquaint now thyself with him, and be at peace." Then, under the quiet light of the stars, or in the splendours of sunset and dawn, or watching the fall of the heaven-sent showers, you will have thoughts of him who rules over all, as of one who through Jesus Christ is your Father and your Friend.—A. R.

Vers. 8, 9.—*The glory of religion.* "Seek him that maketh the seven stars and Orion, and turneth the shadow of death into the morning," etc. The word reveals two things.

I. THE CONNECTION WHICH GOD HAS WITH HIS UNIVERSE. His connection is that: 1. Of a *Creator.* "He maketh the seven stars and Orion." These constellations are only given as specimens of all the things he has created in different parts of the universe. "In the beginning God created the heavens and the earth." 2. Of a *Governor.* "He turneth the shadow of death into the morning, and maketh the day dark with night: that calleth for the waters of the sea, and poureth them out upon the face of the earth." The truth taught is this—that he presides over the revolution of day and night, and the changes of the seasons, and the fortunes of men. All nature is under his control. "He maketh his sun to rise on the evil and on the good, and sendeth rain on the just and on the unjust." 3. Of a *Redeemer.* "That strengtheneth the spoiled against the strong, so that the spoiled shall come against the fortress." The reference is here undoubtedly to his redemptive work in human history.

II. THE CONNECTION WHICH MAN SHOULD HAVE WITH GOD. "Seek him." A phrase of frequent use in the Bible, denoting the duty of man to attain to the knowledge, the friendship, and the fellowship of the Eternal. And in this all true religion consists. The pursuit implies: 1. Faith in God's personal existence. A belief that he is. 2. A consciousness of moral distance from God. We do not seek what we possess. 3. A felt necessity of friendly connection with God. 4. An assurance that such a connection can be obtained.

CONCLUSION. What a grand thing is religion! It is not a thing of mere doctrine, or ritual, or sect, or party. It is a moral pursuit of "him that maketh the seven stars and Orion," etc.—D. T.

Ver. 14.—*Religion.* "Seek good, and not evil, that ye may live: and so the Lord, the God of hosts, shall be with you, as ye have spoken." From these words two things may be inferred concerning *religion.*

I. IT IMPLIES A SPECIFIC PURSUIT. "Seek good, and not evil." Good and evil are both in the world; they work in all human souls; they explain all history. 1. *They imply a standard of right.* By what do we determine the good and evil in human life? The revealed will of God. What accords with that will is good, what disagrees with it is evil. 2. *Their object is a human pursuit.* There are those who pursue evil; they follow it for worldly wealth, animal pleasure, secular aggrandizement. There are those who pursue good; and their grand question is, "Lord, what wilt thou have me to do?" 3. *The pursuit of good is the specific effort of religion.* Good in thought, spirit, aim, habit, as embodied in the life of Christ. To get good requires strenuous, persistent, devout, prayerful effort.

II. IT INVOLVES THE HIGHEST BENEDICTION. 1. The enjoyment of *true life.* "That ye may live." Without goodness you cannot really live: goodness is life. Everlasting goodness is everlasting life. "This is life eternal, to know thee," etc. (John xvii. 3). 2. The enjoyment of the *Divine friendship.* "So the Lord, the God of hosts, shall be with you." What a benediction is this! "The Lord God of hosts," the Almighty Creator, Proprietor, and Governor of the universe to be with us, to guide, guard, beautify existence! "I will walk among you," says he; "I will be your God, and ye shall be my people."—D. T.

Ver. 19.—*Selfishness in terror.* "As if a man did flee from a lion, and a bear met him; or went into the house, and leaned his hand on the wall, and a serpent bit him."

The Israelites rested their hope of deliverance from every kind of foreign danger upon their outward connection with the covenant made with their forefathers; hence many put their trust in the days spoken of in the context, when Jehovah would judge all the heathen, expecting that he would then in all probability raise Israel to might and dominion. All this was simple delusion, the delusion of selfishness; for when Jehovah would appear to punish the nations, Amos says they would be so panic-struck as to be confounded in their efforts to escape. Running from the lion, they would fall into the jaws of the bear; or fleeing into a house, they would be met by a serpent that would bite them. The passage illustrates *selfishness in terror*. Its characteristic is that in seeking protection from one danger it rushes into another. This is often seen—

I. IN COMMERCIAL LIFE. A selfish man in trade often finds himself running down the hill of insolvency, and ruthless bankruptcy appears before him as a lion ready to destroy him. What does he do? Where does he seek protection? Perhaps in absconscion. But he is apprehended, and he finds he has fled from "a lion" to "a bear," enters the house where the "serpent" of enraged justice fastens on him. Or perhaps he resorts to forgery. Here he is detected, and the same result is experienced. He has fled from the lion only to rush into the jaws of the bear.

II. IN SOCIAL LIFE. In few social circles are men not to be found who in some way or other commit a wrong against their members. Indeed, in family life it is so. Children do some injury to their parents, and parents to their children, husbands to their wives, and wives to their husbands. After the commission of the deed, selfish terror is awakened, and they fabricate falsehoods in order to escape the danger. The falsehood is detected, and then it is felt that the man has only fled from the lion to the bear. He has run for protection where he has found the "serpent."

III. IN RELIGIOUS LIFE. Men get convinced of sin, their consciences are roused, and hell appears before them as a ravenous lion, which they endeavour to escape; and they fly for protection to what? To selfish prayers, selfish sacrifices, selfish performances; but to attempt to escape from hell by selfish efforts is only running from the lion to the bear. "He that seeketh his life shall lose it."

CONCLUSION. This subject is capable of endless illustrations. It is an eternal truth that he who seeks protection from selfish fear only rushes from one danger into another. There is no protection for a soul but in self-renunciation, in the entire consecration of self to the worship and service of the great God.—D. T.

Vers. 21—24.— *The divinely abhorrent and the divinely demanded.* "I hate, I despise your feast days, and I will not smell in your solemn assemblies," etc. Notice—

I. THE DIVINELY ABHORRENT. What is that? Mere ceremonial religion; empty ritual. "I hate, I despise your feast days, and I will not smell in your solemn assemblies," etc. "The same aversion from the ceremonial observances of the insincere and rebellious Israelites which Jehovah here expresses he afterwards employed Isaiah to declare to the Jews (Isa. i. 10, etc.). The two passages are strikingly parallel, only the latter prophet amplifies what is set forth in a more condensed form by Amos. It is also to be observed that where Amos introduces the musical accompaniments of the sacrifices, Isaiah substitutes the prayers; both concluding with the Divine words, 'I will not hear.' 'Take thou away from me the noise of thy songs; for I will not hear the melody of thy viols.' The singing of their psalms was nothing more to God than a wearisome round which was to be brought to an end. Singing and playing on harps was a part of the worship of the temple (1 Chron. xvi. 41; xxiii. 5; xxv.). Nothing seems more abhorrent to the holy eye and heart of Omniscience than empty ceremony in religion. No sacrifices are acceptable to him, however costly, unless the offerer has presented himself. No psalmody is acceptable to his ear but the psalmody of self-oblivious devotion." "God is a Spirit: and they that worship him must worship him in spirit and in truth."

II. THE DIVINELY DEMANDED. "Let judgment run down as waters, and righteousness as a mighty stream." While no direction is given respecting the regulation of the sacrifices in order that they may be rendered acceptable, here is a special demand for morality in life, moral rectitude in conduct. Thus God once more expresses the idea that "to obey is better than sacrifice, and to hearken than the fat of rams." The way to worship God acceptably is not by ceremonial observances, not by religious contributions, not in singing psalms, but in doing the right and loving thing towards our fellow-men. The true practical expression of our love to God is that of a virtuous and generous conduct towards mankind. Stud your country with fine churches if you like, fill them with æsthetic worshippers and enthusiastic devotees. But all that is abhorrent to God unless you feel and act rightly towards your fellow-men in your daily life. We had rather see justice rolling on like mighty waters, and righteousness as a swelling and ever-flowing stream, than crowded churches. " Show me your faith ... by your works." Show me your worship by your morality ; show me your love to God by your devotion to your fellow-men. " If we love one another, God dwelleth in us." " If a man say, I love God, and hateth his brother, he is a liar : for if he loveth not his brother whom he hath seen, how can he love God whom he hath not seen ? "—D. T.

EXPOSITION.

CHAPTER VI.

Vers. 1—6.—With a second woe the prophet denounces the chiefs of the whole nation, who were quite satisfied with the present state of things, and, revelling in luxury, feared no coming judgment.

Ver. 1.—**Them** that are **at ease in Zion** ; living in fancied security and self-pleasing (Isa. xxxii. 9, 11 ; Zeph. i. 12). Judah is included in the denunciation, because she is equally guilty ; the whole covenant nation is sunk in the same dangerous apathy. Septuagint, τοῖς ἐξουθενοῦσι Σιών, " them that set at naught Zion." The same rendering is found in the Syriac, and can be supported by a small change in the Hebrew. It may have been intended thus to confine the announcement to Israel alone, in conformity with the prophet's chief scope. But he has introduced mention of Judah elsewhere, as ch. ii. 4 ; vi. 5 ; ix. 11, and his sense of his own people's careless ease may well lead him to include them in his warning. **Trust in the mountain of Samaria.** The city was deemed impregnable, and it kept the Assyrians at bay for three years before it was finally taken (2 Kings xviii. 9, etc. ; see notes on ch. iii. 9 and iv. 1). Another rendering, not so suitable, is, *the careless ones upon the mountain of Samaria.* The point, however, is the supposed impregnability of the city which occasioned a feeling of perfect security. Which are **named chief of the nations** ; rather, *to the notable men of the chief of nations* ; i.e. the principal men of Israel, which had the proud title of the chief of the nations because it was beloved and elected of God, and was designed to keep alive true religion, and to set an example to the rest of the world (Exod. xix. 5 ; Numb. i. 17 ; Deut. iv. 20 ; 2 Sam. vii. 23). Septuagint, ἀπετρύγησαν ἀρχὰς ἐθνῶν, " they plucked the chiefs of the nations," where the verb is a mistaken rendering. **To whom the house of Israel came** ; or, *come.* Resort for counsel and

judgment (2 Sam. xv. 4), and who ought therefore to be patterns of righteousness and equity. The rendering of the Vulgate, *ingredientes pompatice domum Israel,* " entering with pomp into the house of Israel " (which does not agree with the present Hebrew text), implies that these chieftains carried themselves haughtily in the congregation of Israel.

Ver. 2.—**Pass ye.** Go and compare your condition with that of other countries, from the furthest east to the north, to your own neighbours—has not God done more for you than for them ? Nothing is said about the destruction of the three capitals, nor is Samaria threatened with similar ruin. Rather the cities are contemplated as still flourishing and prosperous (though by this time they had suffered at their enemies' hands), and Israel is bidden to remember that she is more favoured than they. **Calneh,** one of the five great Babylonian cities, is probably the *Kul-unu* of the inscriptions, a town in Southern Babylonia, whose site is unknown. In Gen. x. 10 and Isa. x. 9 the LXX. call it *Chalanné* or *Chalané*; in the present passage they mistake the Hebrew, and render, διάβητε πάντες, " pass ye all by " (see Schrader, ' Die Keilinschriften,' p. 442). St. Jerome identifies it with Ctesiphon, on the east bank of the Tigris. Others (see Rawlinson, ' Herodotus,' i. p. 490, 2nd edit.) find in it Nopher or Nipur, the modern *Niffer,* some sixty miles south-east of Babylon. As one of the oldest cities in the world, ranking with Babel, Erech, and Accad, it was well known to the Israelites. **Hamath the great** ; Septuagint, 'Εματραββά. This was the principal city of Upper Syria, and a place of great importance. In after-years it was called Epiphania, after Antiochus Epiphanes (Gen. x. 18 ; Numb. xxxiv. 8 ; Isa. x. 9). It fell in Sargon's reign, B.C. 720 ; afterwards it lost its independence, and was incorporated in the Assyrian empire. **Gath of the Philistines.** One of their five chief cities, and at one time the principal (1 Chron. xviii.

1). The site is placed by Porter at *Tell-es-Sâfi*, an isolated hill, standing above the broad valley of Elah, and "presenting on the north and west a white precipice of many hundred feet." Dr. Thomson ('The Land and the Book,' p. 215, etc.) considers Gath to be the same city as Betogabra, Eleutheropolis, and the modern *Beit Jibrin*, which is some few miles south of *Tell Sâfi*. He thinks the site of Tell Sâfi is not adapted for the seat of a large city, and he saw few indications of ancient ruins there; whereas Beit Jibrin has in and around it the most wonderful remains of antiquity to be found in all Philistia. It had probably declined in importance at this time (see note on ch. i. 6), but its old reputation was still remembered. It was taken by Uzziah, but seems not to have remained long in his possession (2 Chron. xxvi. 6). In the year B.C. 711 Sargon reduced Ashdod and Gath, which he calls Gimtu Asdudim, *i.e.* Gath of the Ashdodites. Be they better? Have they received more earthly prosperity at God's hands than you? Is their territory greater than yours? No. How ungrateful, then, are you for all my favours (comp. Jer. ii. 5—11)! Schrader and Bickell regard the verse as an interpolation, grammatically, metrically, and chronologically inadmissible; but their arguments are not strong, and Amos makes no mention of the fate of these cities.

Ver. 3.—**Ye that put far away the evil day.** They assigned a distant date to the time of punishment and calamity; they would not look it in the face or contemplate it as approaching and ready to come upon them. Septuagint, Οἱ ἐρχόμενοι εἰς ἡμέραν κάκην, "Ye who are coming unto the evil day." The Alexandrian manuscript has οἱ εὐχόμενοι, "ye who pray for" (ch. v. 18), with which the Syriac seems to agree. The Vulgate (as Aquila, Symmachus, and Theodotion), taking the verb passively, renders, *qui separati estis in diem malum.* But it is best to translate it as above, in the sense of "repelling," "putting away with aversion," as in Isa. lxvi. 5. **And cause the seat of violence to come near.** They erected the throne (*shebheth*, "the sitting," or "enthroning") of violence in their midst, made themselves the subjects and slaves of wickedness and oppression. The LXX., mistaking *shebheth* for *shabbath*, translates, Οἱ ἐγγίζοντες καὶ ἐφαπτόμενοι σαββάτων ψευδῶν, "Ye who are drawing near and clinging to false sabbaths."

Ver. 4.—**That lie upon beds of ivory;** couches inlaid with ivory (see note on ch. iii. 15) at meals. The prophet substantiates his denunciation by describing their selfish luxury and debauchery. **Stretch themselves;** literally, *are poured out;* Septuagint, κατα-

σπαταλῶντες, "wantoning." **Out of the midst of the stall.** Calves put up to be fattened. They do this presumably not on festivals, when it would have been proper and excusable, but every day.

Ver. 5.—**That chant.** The word *parat* (ἅπαξ λεγόμενον) means rather "to prattle," "to sing idle songs," as the Revised Version translates it. The reading of the Septuagint varies between ἐπικρατοῦντες, "excelling," and ἐπικροτοῦντες, the latter of which words might mean "applauding." **Viol** (see note on ch. v. 23). **Invent to themselves instruments of music, like David.** As David devised stringed instruments and modes of singing to do honour to God and for the service of his sanctuary (see 1 Chron. xv. 16, etc.; xxiii. 5; 2 Chron. xxix. 26, 27; and the supernumerary psalm at the end of the Psalter in the Septuagint), so these debauchees invented new singing and playing to grace their luxurious feasts. The Septuagint rendering, which Jerome calls "sensus pulcherrimus," is not to be explained by the present Hebrew text, however true to fact it may be considered, Ὡς ἑστηκότα ἐλογίσαντο, καὶ οὐχ ὡς φεύγοντα, "Regarded them as abiding and not as fleeting things."

Ver. 6.—**Wine in bowls** (*mizraqim*); *sacrificial bowls;* used in libations of wine and in the sprinkling of blood (comp. Exod. xxxviii. 3; Numb. vii. 13, etc.; 1 Chron. xxviii. 17; 2 Chron. iv. 8, 22; Zech. ix. 15; xiv. 20). These vessels the luxurious and sacrilegious princes employed in their feasts, proving thus their impiety and their excess (comp. Dan. v. 2). Septuagint, οἱ πίνοντες τὸν διυλισμένον οἶνον, "who drink strained wine." **The chief ointments.** Such as were used in Divine service (Exod. xxx. 23, etc.), and nowhere else. If they had felt as they ought to feel in this time of rebuke and sorrow, they would, like mourners, have refrained from anointing themselves (Ruth iii. 3; 2 Sam. xiv. 2); but, on the contrary, **they are not grieved for the affliction of Joseph.** The coming ruin of the ten tribes affects them not; in their selfish voluptuousness they have no sympathy with calamity and suffering, and shut their eyes to coming evil. "The affliction of Joseph" is probably a proverbial expression derived from the narratives in Gen. xxxvii. 25, etc., and xl. 14, 23 (comp. Gen. xlii. 21).

Vers. 7—11.—Here follows the announcement of punishment for the crimes mentioned above: the people shall go into captivity; they shall be rejected of God, and given over to utter ruin.

Ver. 7.—**With the first.** They shall have a pre-eminence indeed, being the first to go into captivity. St. Jerome, "Vos qui primi estis divitiis, primi captivitatis sustinebitis jugum, secundum illud quod in Ezechiele scriptum est: 'a sanctuario meo incipite'" (Ezek. ix. 6). *With the first*; literally, *at the head*, with reference doubtless to ver. 1. The banquet (*mirzakh*); *the screech* of revellers. The word is used of the scream of mourners in Jer. xvi. 5; here of the cries and shouts of feasters at a banquet. Them that stretched themselves on couches, as ver. 4. The Septuagint, reading differently, has, "They shall depart into captivity from the dominion of princes, and the neighing of horses shall be taken away from Ephraim." From this passage of Amos St. Augustine takes occasion to show that the most untrained of the prophets possessed eloquence and literary skill (' De Doctr. Christ.,' iv. 7).

Ver. 8.—Hath sworn by himself (*nephesh*); *in anima sua* (Vulgate), "by his soul;" a concession to human language (comp. ch. iv. 2; Jer. li. 14; Heb. vi. 13, 17, 18). God thus shows that the threat proceeds from him, and is immutable. The excellency; *the pride* (ὕβριν, Septuagint; *superbiam*, Vulgate); that of which Jacob is proud (Hos. v. 5), as, for instance, his palaces, built by exaction, maintained in voluptuous luxury. Will deliver up to the enemy for destruction (Deut. xxxii. 30; Obad. 14).

Ver. 9.—If there remain ten men in one house. If these escape death in war, they shall die of famine and pestilence in the three years' siege of Samaria (2 Kings xvii. 5). If the prophet is still referring to the rich chieftains, ten would be only a poor remnant of the inhabitants of their palaces. The LXX. adds, very unnecessarily, Καὶ ὑπολειφθήσονται οἱ κατάλοιποι, "And those remaining shall be left behind."

Ver. 10.—The prophet gives an instance of the terror and misery in that common calamity. He depicts a scene where the nearest surviving kinsman comes into the house to perform the funeral rites for a dead man. And a man's uncle; better, *and when a man's kinsman*; the apodosis being at the end of the verse, "Then shall he say." *Dod* is sometimes rendered "beloved," but usually "father's brother," but it may mean any near relation upon whom, in default of father and brethren, would devolve the duty of burying the corpse. Septuagint, *οἱ οἰκεῖοι αὐτῶν*: *propinquus suus* (Vulgate). And he that burneth him; literally, *and his burner.* This is the same person as the kinsman, the burier; but for some reason, either from the number of deaths, or from the pestilence, or from the distance of the burying-place, which would be out of the city and inaccessible in the blockade, he cannot lay the body in the grave, and is forced to take

and burn it. Though the Jews generally buried dead bodies, cremation was sometimes used, both in honour or emergency (1 Sam. xxxi. 12) and in punishment (Lev. xx. 14; xxi. 9). The bones; *i.e.* the corpse, as in Exod. xiii. 19; Josh. xxiv. 32; and 2 Kings xiii. 21; Keil. The kinsman takes it up to bring it out of the house to burn it. Him that is by the sides of the house; *him that is in the innermost parts of the house; qui in penetralibus domus est* (Vulgate). This is the last living person, who had hidden himself in the most remote chambers; or it may be a messenger whom the kinsman had sent to search the house. He asks him—Is there yet any with thee? Is there any one left alive to succour, or dead to bury? And he shall say, No; Vulgate, *et respondebit, Finis est.* Then he (the kinsman) shall say, Hold thy tongue (*Has!*); Hush! He stays the man in the inner chamber from speaking; and why? For we may not make mention of the name of the Lord; Vulgate, *et non recorderis nominis Domini.* Some, as Pusey, Schegg, and Gandell, see here the voice of despair. It is too late to call upon God now; it is the time of vengeance. We rejected him in life; we may not cry to him in death. St. Jerome refers the prohibition to the hardness of heart and unbelief of the people, who even in all this misery will not confess the name of the Lord. Keil says, "It indicates a fear lest, by the invocation of the name of God, his eye should be drawn towards this last remaining one, and he also should fall a victim to the judgment of death." Others again think that the notion in the mind of the impious speaker is that Jehovah is the Author of all their calamities, and that he is impatient at the very mention of his name. The simplest explanation is the first, or a modification of it. The person addressed is about to pray or to call on God in his distress. "Be silent," says the speaker; "we can no longer appeal to Jehovah as the covenant God; by naming him we call to his remembrance how we have broken the covenant, violated our relation to him; therefore provoke him not further by making mention of his name."

Ver. 11.—The prophet confirms the judgment denounced in ver. 8. The Lord commandeth, and he will smite. The expression, thus taken, implies that God executes his commands through the ministers of his judgment; but it may well be rendered, "and men shall smite" (comp. ch. ix. 9). Breaches . . . clefts. The great palace requires a breach to bring it to the ground; the little hut is ruined by a small rent or cleft. All houses, great and small, shall be smitten. Possibly Israel and Judah are signified respectively by "the great house" and "the little house" (comp. ch. ix. 11);

and their treatment by the Assyrians may be thus symbolized.

Vers. 12—14.—The prophet shows the folly of these evil-doers who think in their own strength to defy judgment and to resist the enemy whom God is sending against them.

Ver. 12.—**Shall horses run upon the rock?** Can horses gallop safely over places covered with rocks and stones? **Will one plough there with oxen?** Do men plough the rock with their oxen? The answer, of course, is "No." Yet your conduct is equally foolish, your labour is equally lost. Some, dividing the words differently, translate, "Does one plough the sea with oxen?" which reminds one of the Latin proverb, "Litus arare bubus." Thus Ovid, 'Ep. Heroid,' v. 115—

"Quid facis Œnone? Quid arenæ semina mandas?
Non protecturis litora bubus aras."

For ye have turned; or, *that ye have turned.* **Judgment into gall** (see note on ch. v. 7). **Hemlock.** Some plant with an acrid juice. Ye turn the administration of justice, which is "the fruit of righteousness," into the bitterest injustice and wrong. It were "more easy," says Pusey, "to change the course of nature or the use of things of nature, than the course of God's providence or the laws of his just retribution."

Ver. 13.—**In a thing of nought;** *a nothing* —a thing which does not really exist, viz. your prosperity and power. **Horns;** symbols of strength (Deut. xxxiii. 17; 1 Kings xxii. 11); the idea being derived from the wild bull, the strongest animal of their fauna. Their boast was a consequence of the successful wars with the Syrians (2 Kings xiv. 25—28). The prophet proceeds to demolish their proud vaunt.

Ver. 14.—**I will raise up** (comp. 1 Kings xi. 14, 23; Hab. i. 6, where see note). **A nation.** The Assyrians. **From the entering in** of Hamath. A district in the upper part of Cœle-Syria, *hod. El-Bukaa,* the northern boundary of the kingdom of Israel (Numb. xxxiv. 8; see on ver. 2). **The river of the wilderness;** rather, *the torrent of the Arabah,* which is the curious depression in which the Jordan flows, and which continues, though now on a higher level, south of the Dead Sea, towards the Gulf of Akaba. The torrent is probably the *Wady es Safieh,* just south of the Dead Sea. The limits named define the territory which Jeroboam recovered (2 Kings xiv. 25). The LXX. gives, τοῦ χειμάρρου τῶν δυσμῶν, "the torrent of the west."

HOMILETICS.

Vers. 1—7.—*Wantonness the way to woe.* God's thoughts are not as ours. He sees things all round; we see but one side of them. He sees the inner reality of things; we see but their outward semblance. He sees the tendency and ultimate result of things; we but guess their probable tendency, knowing nothing of distant results whatever. Hence, in their estimates of life and of good, "the wisdom of men is foolishness with God." The passage before us is an illustration of this. The conditions of being desiderated by carnal wisdom are here declared utterly baneful, its calculations fallacious, and its canons of judgment false. We see here—

I. THE GREATNESS OF THE WICKED. This is no uncommon sight (Ps. xxxvii. 35), nor one whose lesson is hard to read (Ps. xcii. 7). 1. *Israel was first of the nations.* (Ver. 1.) In its palmy days, and even now, it would have compared favourably with the neighbouring heathen states (ver. 2). It had the power of unique knowledge. It had the greatness of a unique culture. It had the glory of a unique Divine connection (Exod. xix. 5; 2 Sam. vii. 23). With an equal numerical, financial, and territorial strength, it held, in virtue of these advantages, a pre-eminence above any other people. Its wealth and magnificence were the admiration of even Oriental sovereigns (1 Kings x.); its armies, under normal circumstances, could hold their own with any of the time (1 Sam. xv. 1—8); and the white wings of its commerce gleamed on every sea. In spite of national unfaithfulness and rebellion and wickedness, God's promise to Abraham to make of him "a great nation" had been, in the fullest sense, accomplished. 2. *These were the chiefs of Israel.* (Ver. 1.) They were magistrates, rulers, and judges of the people. They occupied the position of princes, and the house of Israel came to them for the regulation of its affairs. "They were the descendants of those tribe-princes who had once been honoured to conduct the affairs of the chosen family along with Moses and Aaron, and whose light shone forth from that better age as brilliant examples of what a truly theocratical character was" (Hengstenberg). This was a proud position, and it had brought the usual amount of arrogance with it.

II. THE SECURITY OF THE GREAT. "Woe to the secure!" Conscious strength makes men and nations feel secure. As to Israel: 1. *They were secure in religious privilege.* "In Zion." They presumed on their covenant relation. They ignored its sanctions, disregarded its responsibilities, and took it as a guarantee of immunity, even in sin. Religion is only good as a whole. To have its privileges without its spiritual character leads through carnal security to carnal indulgence, and so to a condition worse than to be destitute of both. 2. *They were secure in strategic strength.* "And to the careless upon the mountain of Samaria." Samaria was a strong place, a mountain-fortress, situated in a rich valley. It held out against Benhadad, King of Syria, defying assault, and escaping reduction even by famine (2 Kings vii.). To Shalmaneser, long afterwards, it only yielded after a three years' siege (2 Kings xvii. 5, 6). Man naturally looks for victory to "the big battalion." This is reasonable in the case of a human enemy, but mere fatuity if the enemy be God. 3. *They were secure in self-deception.* "Put far away the evil day." Security, beaten out of one retreat, betakes itself to another. Trust in our earthly resources will ultimately fail. Security in external religious advantages will some day be broken also by a rude awaking. But the Fabian policy still prevails, and proves an almost impregnable last resort. "It cannot be for a long while yet" is an argumentative device that seldom fails to reassure.

III. THE WANTONNESS OF THE SECURE. The idea of immunity is an encouragement to sin. Among Israel's sins were: 1. *Indolence.* "Stretch themselves upon their couches." This is the first temptation of wealth. Work has ceased to be necessary, and the easily acquired habit of idleness very soon develops indolence of disposition. Having nothing to do leads to doing nothing, and when a man does nothing for a while he wants to go on with it. 2. *Luxury.* "Lie upon beds of ivory;" "Eat lambs," etc. Luxury is a direct result of indolence. Having nothing else to occupy their attention, men concentrate it on themselves. They make it the business of their life to coddle themselves, with the inevitable result of becoming harder to please. As the appetite is pampered it becomes more dainty, and must be tempted with luxury after luxury, if any measure of relish would be retained. 3. *Effeminacy.* "Who trill to the sound of the harp" (ver. 5). The tendency of luxury is to unman. On the discontinuance of manly exercises follows closely the loss of manly qualities. Pampering the body weakens body and mind both, and prepares the way for occupations that will be in character. Effeminacy grows fastest when nursed in the lap of luxury. The Israel that was too fastidious to lie on anything but an ivory couch, or too dainty to touch coarser fare than "the fatted calf," was too enervated in a little while for any manlier pastime than trilling to a harp. 4. *Profanity.* "Drink wine out of sacrificial bowls." "The pleasures of sin" are only "for a season." They quickly wear out. Zest and relish fail, and satiety and disgust follow. Hence the tendency of indulgence to become more and more extravagant and eccentric. It is an attempt to stimulate failing powers of enjoyment by presenting new sensations. Then the natural heart is essential enmity against God. Accordingly, in the case of a thoroughly perverted nature, when a sinful indulgence has ceased to give pleasure as indulgence, it will continue to do so as sin. Israel had now fallen so low as this. Sensual indulgence began to pall, and it took a fresh lease of enjoyableness by becoming sacrilegious. 5. *Heartless egotism.* "And do not grieve for the hurt of Joseph." Sin is essentially selfish, and the sin of self-indulgence supremely so. The happiness, and even the lives, of others are as nothing in the balance against lust. Let who may suffer, let what may happen, the sensualist will indulge. To such a person philanthropy and patriotism are alike impossible. He will "not grieve for the hurt of Joseph" even when he is himself responsible for it. He could play comfortably "while Rome burns." 6. *Increasing violence.* "And bring near the seat of violence." As destruction becomes more imminent, the violence that provokes it becomes more extreme. This is sometimes due to the blindness that will not see; sometimes to the recklessness that does not care; sometimes to the malignity that, forecasting overthrow, would do all the evil possible before it comes. In any case it is aggravated and judgment-hastening sin.

IV. THE DOOM OF THE WANTON. Here, as elsewhere, punishment answers to crime, both as to degree and kind. 1. *Cherished indulgence should be interrupted.* "The shouting of tne revellers will depart" (ver. 7). This is about the first step in retributive punishment. The criminal's enjoyment comes to be centred in his sin, and to interrupt it is a sharp blow. The retributive measure to which lust is most of all amenable is to put a stop to indulgence. Deprive the oppressor of his power, the extortioner of his opportunity, the drunkard of his drink, and already the work of taking vengeance on him is well begun. 2. *Apposite hardship should be inflicted.* "Shall go captive." As captives they should endure oppression, not inflict it. For indulgence would be substituted privation in every form. They would make juster acquaintance with luxury by having the means of it wrung out of their own helplessness and misery. It is no doubt along these lines that eternal reward and punishment are arranged. Heaven will be the perfect exercise and enjoyment of all that is pure and spiritual in desire and taste. Hell, among other things, will be the cutting off for ever of sinful sources of enjoyment, for which the wicked had learned to live. 3. *Those who had been first among the nations should be first among the captives.* This is only fitting. The guilt of any evil movement culminates in its ringleaders, and "first in transgression, first in punishment," is a maxim of natural justice. Those who organize and officer a wicked movement are those on whom justice will lay the earliest and the heaviest hand.

Ver. 1.—*Sorrow dogging the secure.* Human life is proverbially uncertain. "We know not what shall be on the morrow," whether we ourselves shall be. "The unexpected" is always happening; and the lesson of this is—take nothing for granted that is still future. In the religious sphere the application of this principle would put an end to carnal security, and at this object our text aims. As to the security denounced here, notice—

I. THE SPHERE OF IT. "In Zion." This is often in Scripture a name for the Church on earth (Rom. ix. 33; see on ch. i. 2). The membership of this is mixed (Matt. xiii. 30, 41). There are cold and hot and lukewarm among them. Some love God, some hate him; some are *in equilibrio*, having neither declared for him nor against him. Of the last two classes many are at ease. The ideal of spiritual life is watchfulness, activity, and self-suspicion; but these qualities need not be looked for in unspiritual men. Their fitness is not seen, nor the motives to them felt. Though in the Church, they are not of it; and the characters of their life are not those proper to the sincere believer.

II. THE MEANING OF IT. There are principles at hand on which to account for it without difficulty. 1. *Preoccupation.* Spiritual things ought to get our first and best and continuous attention (Matt. vi. 33; xxvi. 41; Luke xiii. 24). But they do not. The careless "eat, and drink, and marry, and are given in marriage" (Luke xvii. 27), and so events come on them unawares. The householder relaxes his vigilance, and as a result his house is broken into (Matt. xxiv. 43). The wise virgins as well as the foolish sleep (Matt. xxv. 5), and the bridegroom comes on them unawares. The security is foolish in proportion to the interests involved, and criminal in proportion to the number and plainness of arousing circumstances. 2. *Blindness.* The natural man is blind in spiritual things (1 Cor. ii. 14). He does not see the beauty of spiritual qualities (Isa. liii. 2), nor the self-evidentness of spiritual principles, nor the inviolability of spiritual deliverances, nor the grounds of spiritual assurance, nor the evidences of approaching Divine action. He sees neither what has been, nor what is, nor what is coming. Accordingly, he is secure and at ease in the very teeth of danger. 3. *Presumption.* Men do not adequately realize sin as to either its guilt or danger. They live in it equably and calmly, as if it were the normal thing. They anticipate no evil and no disturbance. They reckon on being spiritual fixtures, and on the perpetual maintenance of the *status quo.* They do not mean to turn, nor take account of being disturbed; but assume that there will be "no changes" for evermore. Character is become stereotyped, conscience is silent, and the quiet of strong delusion is within them and around.

III. THE VARIETIES OF IT. The secure in Zion are not all secure in the same degree or sense. 1. *Some are secure in sin.* They expect to sin on and suffer no evil. Either they do not recognize the inseparable connection between the two, or they trust to the chapter of accidents for something to intervene and stay proceedings before evil actually falls (Isa. xxviii. 15). 2. *Some are secure in morality.* They trust in the arm of flesh. They persuade themselves that they are but little to blame. They view the coming judgments as provoked by, and meant for, others. They see nothing in their own life to provoke them; and they build on this as a ground of immunity from evil when the day of it shall come. And so they are secure; less guiltily, it may be, but no more reasonably than the secure in sin (Jer. xvii. 5 ; Rom. iii. 20). 3. *Some are secure in ordinances.* They locate spiritual power in Church forms. The sacraments, they say, contain and convey the grace they signify. Regeneration with them means a sprinkled face, and justification an elevated host, and sanctification an exhaustive observance of ordinances. Many are secure in the persuasion of these things. They put a hollow form of godliness for its spirit and power, and lull their souls to rest in its deep recesses.

IV. THE OCCASIONS OF IT. There is an incongruity about it that seems to call for explanation. In the case of Israel, and others like it, one cause was: 1. *Unvarying prosperity.* "Because they have no changes they forget God." People calculate on uniformity. As life has been, so they easily assume it will be. A smiling world is a dangerous tranquillizer. Even the godly experience this (Ps. cxix. 67), and the direct tendency of adversity is to prevent it (2 Cor. iv. 17, 18). An unbroken run of prosperity is most unfavourable to spiritual life and liveliness. 2. *Luxurious living.* (Ver. 4.) The course of religion in the soul is just the progress of a warfare between flesh and spirit (Rom. vii. 23). To this warfare there is one uniform issue—the triumph of the spiritual principle. But victory is not won without a struggle. The spiritual principle waxes strong only under culture. The flesh gets weak only by being crucified. If it be let alone it will grow strong, much more if it is indulged and fed. Hence "fulness of bread and abundance of idleness" (Ezek. xvi. 19) are a revealed occasion of spiritual declension; and God was lightly esteemed and forsaken when Jeshurun "waxed fat, and grew thick" (Deut. xxxii. 15). Luxury is leaving its mark on all the Churches in indolence and self-indulgence and a lowered spiritual tone. 3. *Companionship of the ungodly.* "He that walketh with wise men shall be wise," etc. Character propagates itself—begets character in its own likeness. Familiarity with sin breeds tolerance of it. A sinful example is a temptation to sin. So long as men not impeccable instinctively imitate each other, association with the wicked must, to a certain extent, corrupt. The corrupter any society is, the lower will be the spiritual tone of the Church in it. All Israel were not alike guilty, nor alike secure. Many were innocent, no doubt, of the special national sins; and there is no reason to suppose that they all were recklessly at ease in Zion. But it is certain that the security of many was due to the hardening influence of the sins become familiar to his mind. 4. *Sin.* This is not an occasion merely, but a cause, and the most fruitful cause of all. Sin both blinds and hardens. The more sin we commit the less do we see of its consequences, the less do we fear what we can see, and the further are we from an appreciative knowledge of God in those characters which lead inevitably to the punishment of it. The climax of security is more than likely to correspond to the extreme of wickedness. It was so with Israel. Never was she more corrupt, yet never was she more recklessly at ease, than when these words were spoken.

V. THE EVIL OF IT. "Woe to them," etc.! Wherever the security is the woe is denounced. 1. *With the godly it comes before a fall.* They stand by faith. That faith is not an act merely; it is a habit of soul. It is not maintained at normal strength without an effort. And the frame most favourable to its maintenance at par is evident from the injunction, "Be not high-minded, but fear" (Rom. xi. 20). In the perfect realization of our dependence on God is the condition of abiding faith, and in the maintenance of such faith is the condition of escaping a fall. From the moment Peter soared in his own imagination, his fall was a foregone conclusion (Matt. xxvi. 33, 34). 2. *With the ungodly it comes before destruction.* Carnal security is in proportion to blindness, and blindness is in proportion to corruption. When a sinner is most secure he most of all deserves his doom, and is least of all on his guard against it. Hence, as the height of imagined safety is the depth of real danger (1 Thess. v. 3). No surer sign of destruction near than the cry, "Peace, peace!"

Ver. 3.—*The procrastinator family.* The fear of suffering is universal and instinctive. All the lower animals exhibit it. So do men in different ways. It is not joyous, but grievous. Human life and happiness are shaped largely by this feeling. Men make their relations to it a chief concern. If it be past, they seek compensations for it. If it be present, they seek relief. If it be coming, they try to prevent it; or, failing that, to postpone it; or, failing both, to mitigate it. And as a certain proportion of the pain is altogether mental, and due to our thoughts about it, one of the commonest palliatives for it is the endeavour to ignore it altogether. Among her other follies and sins, the attempt to do so on the part of Israel is here announced.

I. THE EVIL DAY WHICH MEN WOULD PUT OFF. This will be: 1. *The day of actual evil.* To the wicked there are many such days, with almost as many individual characteristics. Such a day pre-eminently is: (1) *The day of death.* This is the king of terrors. To the wicked it means the end of all the good they know of, and the beginning of sufferings of every possible kind and a magnitude inconceivable. It is, therefore, the day of evil in a sense peculiar to itself. (2) *The day of visitation for sin.* Such days are sure and frequent. Israel had experienced many of them, and the reminiscence was not agreeable. They had brought, and might again bring, every calamity for body, mind, and estate short of utter destruction. They were evil days in a very emphatic sense, and as such were specially feared. 2. *The day of imagined evil.* Such days would be: (1) The day of submission to God, which is an evil day in the estimation of pride. (2) The day of forsaking sin, which is disagreeable to lust. (3) The day of coming into relation to spiritual things, against all which the carnal mind is enmity. For such things the "more convenient season" is convenient in proportion as it is or can be regarded as distant.

II. THE FOOLISH DEVICES BY WHICH MEN TRY TO ACCOMPLISH THE IMPOSSIBLE. A foolish thing is never attempted for a wise reason or in a wise way. As to the evil day: 1. *Some do not practically believe that it is coming at all.* They minimize their own guilt, which is the provoking cause. They magnify the considerations which bear in the direction of postponement. They ignore the sure Word of God, which denounces inevitable suffering on sin. The result is an amount of ignorance or scepticism about the matter sufficient to prevent its exercising any practical effect. It is believed in a vague and heedless way, but not so as to lead to appropriate, nor in fact to any, action. 2. *Some trust to the chapter of accidents.* They know the evil day is denounced. They know it is coming. They know that, if it comes, it will involve them in its calamities. But they hope events will take some happy turn, and something indefinite, but highly convenient, will occur, which will change the issue, and prevent the crisis from touching them (Isa. xxviii. 15). All sinners persist in the life of sin, yet hope, somehow or other, to escape hell. 3. *Some endeavour not to think about it at all.* They, of set purpose, divert their attention from the subject. They refuse to "consider their latter end." They busy themselves about other things. They insanely act as if the danger would be annihilated by being ignored. Into this snare of the devil many fall. They cannot see the nearness of the evil day who refuse to look at the matter. Blinder and more stupid than the ox or the ass is the people that will not consider (Isa. i. 3).

III. THE LAST STATE OF THE PROCRASTINATOR, WHICH IS WORSE THAN THE FIRST. What he gains is a heritage of woe (ver. 1). As to the coming of this, it is evident: 1. *He cannot prevent it.* God makes his own arrangements and keeps to them. We cannot resist his power. We cannot change his purpose. His word on any matter is the last word, and fixes it once for all. What he has spoken, and as he has spoken, must come to pass. 2. *He cannot postpone it.* The justice, goodness, and wisdom that combine in fixing an event enter also into the timing of it. All possible considerations are taken into account, and infinite power no more surely does the thing it means than at the time it means. It would be as wise to attempt and as easy to accomplish the defeat of God's purposes as their postponement. Our mental and active attitude are alike inoperative as to both. 3. *He disqualifies himself for facing it.* "Be ye also ready" is the Divine prescription in reference to the unrevealed date of the day of God. To be unready is to face it at tremendous disadvantage. To be inexpectant besides is to aggravate the disadvantage to the very utmost. Prepare and watch are equally essential conditions of meeting the day of God in safety. Wilful delusion about the event means woeful injury by it. Men ought to be prepared for what is sure to come, and when it comes be in expectation of it. "Be ye also ready;" "Watch therefore." By the confluence of these streams of action is made the river of a life "throughly furnished."

Ver. 6.—*The dry eye of the destroyer.* "But they are not grieved for the hurt of Joseph." Of the many aspects of Israel's sin, this is among the most repulsive. It is bad enough to sin against our brother, and by our wrong-doing to blight his life; but it makes the crime hideous to look, uncaring and callous, on the desolation we ourselves have wrought.

I. ONE MAN'S SUFFERING IS A FIT OCCASION OF ANOTHER MAN'S SORROW. Men are brothers (Acts xvii. 26), and owe a mutual regard for each other's concerns (Phil. ii. 4). Suffering is evil, and the proper relation toward those enduring it is sympathy (1 John iii. 17). God pities the afflicted, and compassion in him is the reason and measure of its dutifulness in us (Matt. ix. 36; Luke x. 33—37). We cannot disregard the sufferings of men without sinning against God and against our own humanity.

II. THE GREAT OBSTACLE TO SYMPATHY IS THE SELFISHNESS OF SIN. This leads to atheism on the one hand, and misanthropy on the other. The first man showed this tendency, the second that. Adam failed in regard for God, Cain in regard for his brother. But both transgressions arose out of the one sinful character of selfishness. Adam violated God's command because he preferred his own way; Cain destroyed Abel's life because he thought less of it than of his own wounded self-love. And all men, in proportion as they are sinful, are selfish, inconsiderate, and misanthropic. Love is of God, and rules where God dwells. Where God dwells not we have men "hateful and hating one another." Selfishness and disregard of others' happiness is the very mark and token of a corrupt nature.

III. SELFISHNESS IS WORST IN KIND WHEN MANIFESTED TOWARD OUR OWN KINDRED. In addition to the philanthropy which has its basis in the brotherhood of the race, is the stronger affection which arises out of nearer ties. "Our neighbour," "our own," "those of our own household," are, in an ascending scale, the prescribed and natural objects of our love and care (Matt. xix. 19; 1 Tim. v. 8). In proportion to the closeness of our relation to an individual is the normal strength of the tie between us, and so the guilt of disregarding it. The disregard of Israel for Israelites was selfishness of a peculiarly heartless kind. It was the sin of brother against brethren, and involved the violation of blood ties sacred by every law.

IV. THE GREATEST DEGREE OF SELFISHNESS IS THAT IN REGARD TO THE SUFFERINGS OF OTHERS, INFLICTED OR BROUGHT ABOUT BY OURSELVES. In Israel, the men who disregarded the judgments decimating the nation were the men whose wickedness had brought them on. They were indifferent, in fact, about sufferings of which they were themselves the authors. And they have their counterparts in the world still. The drunkard who ruins his own family, the libertine who ruins the family of his neighbour, are the only men in the community who "care for none of these things." The explanation is that special sin produces special hardness of heart, and the man whose wickedness involves society in misery is the man who, by the very fact, is constituted most incapable of feeling it.

Vers. 8—11.—*Wrath revealing itself in judgment.* The squaring of a sinner's account with God is of necessity a bitter experience. It is the last fact in a wide induction, and completes our knowledge of what sin really is. The best and only adequate view of this is reached when a man reads it in the light of its punishment. We are enabled to perform this office for Israel's crying and incredible wickedness here.

I. THE WORD THAT CANNOT BE BROKEN. Accommodating himself to our mode of conceiving things, God condescends to give assurance of his faithfulness in three degrees of assertion. The word that cannot be broken is: 1. *What God says.* "Thy Word is truth." God can neither err nor lie. He does when he promises (Numb. xxiii. 19). He does as much as he promises. He does exactly the thing he promises. The fact of his truth lies at the foundation of all religion and all knowledge. Because he is true, we not only believe his testimony absolutely, but we believe absolutely the testimony of our own consciousness as being his gift. 2. *What God swears.* In itself his word is as good as his oath. But to our apprehension there may be a difference.

For God to swear is an act of special condescension. It is making a great concession to our unbelief, and the limitation of our faculties, that God conforms to our human modes of making solemn affirmation, in order if possible to win our implicit credence for his words (Heb. vi. 17). His oath, added to his word in any matter, is for fulness of confirmation and assurance, and is a specially gracious act. 3. *What he swears by himself.* In default of a greater, God swears by himself (Heb. vi. 13). He is "the true God," and a "God of truth." An oath in his name has the highest sanction possible, and assumes its most solemn form. God's oath in his own name is as sure as his own existence—is, in fact, a putting of his existence in pledge for the word of his mouth.

II. THE ESSENTIAL ANTAGONISM BETWEEN DIVINE HOLINESS AND HUMAN SIN. This is extreme, utter, and necessary. 1. *God does not hate men, but their sin.* He is not said to do so here. The statements elsewhere, that he hates the wicked (Ps. v. 5; Rom. ix. 13), must be taken in connection with the clearly revealed fact that he also loves them (John iii. 16), and loved his people while they were of them. It cannot be that he loves the wicked and hates them in the same sense. His love has reference to their humanity, his hatred to their sinfulness (Rom. i. 18). He hates them as sinners, yet loves them as men; forgives them often, yet takes vengeance on their inventions (Ps. xcix. 8). 2. *God's hatred of sin extends to the occasions of it.* "I abhor the pride of Jacob." God's abhorrence of sin extends to everything that tends to produce it. Pride or loftiness, being in itself sinful, and a fruitful occasion of sin, he must hate. Excellence or greatness, whether imaginary or real, is, in so far as it leads to pride, included in the reach of the Divine abhorrence. Sin, like a cesspool, fouls all approaches to it. It is spiritual treason, and attaints its nearest of kin. 3. *It includes even the scenes of it.* "And I hate his palaces." The palaces were closely connected with the sin. They were built with the wages of unrighteousness, for luxurious gratification, and as a means to further exaction. Accordingly, as at once an expression of sin and an accessory of it, they were hateful in God's sight. God's attitude in the matter is the model for ours. If we are baptized into his Spirit we shall "hate even the garments spotted by the flesh." Not only is sin hateful, but all that leads to it, all that borders on it, all that has any connection with it. Even the remotest contact with it will be hateful to the spiritually minded.

III. THE SWEEPING JUDGMENTS THAT EXPRESS A HOLY WRATH. These are set forth in various forms and degrees of severity. 1. *The capital would be delivered up.* "And give up the city and the fulness thereof." Samaria, the capital, was the strength and pride of Israel. It was the impregnable metropolis, the great storehouse of national wealth, the seat of government, the home of luxury, the social, political, economical, and military centre of the kingdom. To destroy it was like taking the heart out of their kingdom at one fell stroke. Notwithstanding this, or rather perhaps because of this, it would be captured and pillaged. In sin it had set the example, and taken the lead, and in punishment its leading position would be retained. 2. *Not even one out of ten should escape.* (Ver. 9.) Such sweeping destruction as this was almost unheard of. Even Sodom and Gomorrah were not more utterly destroyed. This was due ultimately to the almost universal impenitence, and proximately to the length and stubbornness of the fighting. God would not allow the persistently impenitent to escape, and the Assyrian armies, his instruments, would not spare the obstinate defenders of Samaria, who had kept them three years at bay. 3. *The straggling survivors should be in abject fear of the almost universal fate.* (Ver. 10.) The solitary survivor is no nearer faith in God than those who have been destroyed. He does not cast himself on his mercy. He does not even in that dreadful hour seek his face. His stupid but thoroughly characteristic impulse is to hide away from his presence. Apart from Divine grace, sin committed drives away from God (Gen. iii. 8), and punishment approaching drives further still (Rev. vi. 16). In prosperity the wicked will not even fear God; in adversity, if they fear, they still refuse to trust him. 4. *The work of destruction would be carried out systematically and in detail.* (Ver. 11.) Neither palace nor cabin should escape. The great house would be broken into great pieces, and the small house into small pieces. God's judgments are nothing if not effective. The greatest cannot defy, nor can the smallest elude them. The destruction of each shall be elaborately and circumstantially complete.

IV. GOD THE AUTHOR OF THE PUNISHMENT HE PROCURES. "The Lord commandeth," etc. 1. *The sin of man is often a factor in the accomplishment of God's purpose.* It was so with the transportation of Joseph (Gen. xlv. 5, 8; l. 20), with the death of Christ (Acts ii. 23; iv. 28), and with the affliction of Israel by Assyria (Isa. x. 5—7). The actors are in each case impelled by their own evil motives, aim at their own evil ends, use their own evil means, and act altogether of their own free will; and yet, when they succeed, the result is found to serve some important collateral interest they think nothing of, and so to be part of the infinitely good purpose of God. It is thus that God accomplishes his will by the instrumentality of men, without infringing on their perfect freedom, or being implicated in the sin which, in unconscious furtherance of it, they commit. The Assyrian destroying Israel in an unjustifiable war was at once carrying out God's purpose and sinning against him. 2. *God destroys the chosen people, not as "Israel," but as "Jacob."* "Israel," the covenant name, is given them in connection with promises of covenant treatment. God blesses them as "Israel," and afflicts them as "Israel," and even decimates them as "Israel," all these being elements of a gracious discipline. But destruction is not so. It is the penalty of a covenant already broken, and God marks them out for this by the uncovenanted name of "Jacob."

Vers. 12—14.—*The doomed people who will not turn.* Sin brings often present gain, but it never pays in the end. When the balance is struck, the wrong-doer always finds it on the wrong side of the book. A sinner is one who sets himself against God, and in the nature of things ignorance cannot overreach knowledge, nor weakness overcome omnipotence. Israel had long been under instruction in this matter, and they would see it one day when the knowledge would be too late. Many Scripture maxims are illustrated here.

I. "BEHOLD, YE ARE OF NOTHING, AND YOUR WORK OF NOUGHT." (Ver. 13.) "In a thing of nought;" literally, a "non-thing," a phantasm, what has an appearance of being, and yet is not. 1. *Human strength is nothing.* It is nothing in comparison with God's. It is nothing apart from God's. Being derived wholly from God, it has no existence independent of him. It is, therefore, virtually and practically "a thing of nought;" incapable of being used for any purpose either against him or irrespective of him. 2. *Out of nothing nothing comes.* Human power being a nonentity, belief in it is delusion, trust in it is baseless, and expectation from it must be disappointed. Doubly, therefore, and trebly "cursed is he that maketh flesh his arm." 3. *Yet it is in this nonentity that men rejoice.* Sin is at bottom a deification of self. We believe in ourselves—in our own power and knowledge and excellence. We are satisfied with ourselves, expect great things from ourselves, and rejoice in ourselves (Ps. x. 6; lii. 7). Only by a work of grace are we disabused of our carnal confidence and won to a higher trust. It is as complementary of our "trusting in the Lord" that we "lean not to our own understanding."

II. "WHO CAN BRING A CLEAN THING OUT OF AN UNCLEAN? NOT ONE." (Ver. 12.) Israel joined oppression to unrighteousness, and out of this endeavoured to bring themselves lasting gain. This is likened to an attempt by the husbandman to cultivate the rock. It implies: 1. *Utter futility.* The husbandman does not attempt impracticable things. He knows there is no fertility in a bare rock—no soil for crop, no bed for seed, no furrow for plough; and so he cultivates the good soil, and leaves the rock alone. And no more than till the rock for a harvest need men seek safety by wrong-doing. They cannot find it so. It is not where they seek it. Good cannot come out of evil by natural generation, for it is not in it. 2. *Loss instead of gain.* An attempt to plough the rock, like every other offence against the nature of things, must be worse than futile. It means lost time, lost labour, and broken implements. So with the perversion of justice, and the corruption of the fruit of righteousness. It is evil, and can only lead to evil. It increases the sum total of the wickedness that provokes Divine wrath, and itself creates a new source of danger.

III. "THEREFORE LET NO MAN GLORY IN MEN." (Ver. 13.) It is the very essence of unreason. 1. *It is a crime.* It involves departure from God. The soul is capable of sustaining but one great attachment at a time. We cannot love both the Father and the world, or "serve God and mammon," or "make flesh our arm," without our heart departing from the Lord. And it is not only that the two trusts are one too many; they are incompatible and mutually destructive. To deify self, and defy Jehovah, are acts of the same moral quality. The blindness, and only the blindness, that is capable of the one is capable of the other. 2. *It is a blunder.* It is putting faith in the faithless. It is attributing power to the impotent. It is pitting the creature against the Creator, the vessel against the potter, the thing formed against him that formed it. Only disappointment can come out of this. A pierced hand is the natural and inevitable penalty of leaning on a broken reed. "Hast thou an arm like God," etc.?

IV. "O ASSYRIAN, THE ROD OF MINE ANGER." Israel's overthrow was decided on, and the instrument of it prepared. 1. *War the minister of God.* He does not command, nor authorize, nor sanction it. He forbids the lusts of ambition and greed and revenge that lead to it. He inculcates a love of others which, carried out, would make it impossible. The progress of his religion leads to the diminution of war, and its final establishment will co-ordinate itself with the turning of war into peace to the ends of the earth. Yet, as with other evil things, he permits it to happen, controls its operation, utilizes its results, and makes it a means of good, and the minister of his holy will. War has always been a prominent agency in the judgments that fall on nations. And a terrible agency it is, more ruthlessly destructive than any other. It expresses all the evil qualities of corrupt humanity, deserving the poet's scathing words—

> "O war, thou son of hell,
> Whom angry Heavens do make their minister."

And war, apart from its severity as a scourge, is well calculated to be disciplinary. As a revelation of human wickedness, it indirectly lays bare to us the plagues of our own heart. Linked hand in hand as it is, moreover, with deceit and treachery, it exhibits carnal human nature as "a thing of nought," and so is an effective antidote to confidence in the flesh. 2. *The heathen the rod in his hand.* God is not fastidious in the matter of instruments. He uses every man, however vile, for some purpose or other. Israel, moreover, was so enamoured of the heathen—of their gods and worship and ways—that to know them in the character of enemies and conquerors and masters would be a great advantage. It would be in these capacities that the worst effects of idolatry on the human character would show themselves, and closer acquaint-ance with them might help to disenchant the idol-loving Israel. 3. *Victory always on God's side.* God, for the time being, would be on the Assyrian's side. Without reference to the intrinsic merits of the struggle, as between parties almost equally wicked, he would help the heathen to overcome the apostates. Israel's victories over the nations were due, not to their own valour or strength, but to God's assisting arm (Ps. xliv. 2, 3). Left to themselves, they would be utterly beaten now. The difference between defeat and victory is the difference between the God-forsaken and the God-defended. 4. *God-sent affliction covers all the ground covered by the provoking sin.* "And it shall oppress you from the entrance Hamath"—the extreme northern boundary (Numb. xxxiv. 8)—"to the brook of the desert," the southern boundary, whether "the brook of the willows," Isa. xv. 7 (Pusey), or the present "El Ahsy" (Keil). This territory they had recovered under Jeroboam II., and lost soon to Tiglath-Pileser, defeat and loss retracing to the last inch the steps of conquest. Not only was "the whole scene of their triumphs one scene of affliction and woe" (Pusey), but the very thing, and the whole thing, which they had made an occasion of pride and carnal confidence, vainly deeming that they had conquered it in their own strength, is made an occasion of humiliation and distress. The only way to put us out of conceit with our idol is to destroy it all, and destroy it utterly.

Ver. 13.—*Joy in the unreal always precarious.* It is quite unaccountable. It is almost incredible. But it is unquestionably true. Men reject the staff, and lean upon the broken reed. Whatever is worthy of trust they doubt, whatever is utterly unreli-able they confide in. This was the way of Israel, and it is the way of humanity. They do not see the reality of things. They attribute to them qualities they do not possess, qualities sometimes the very opposite of the actual ones. Then they act on their theory of things, and rejoice in a figment, the creation of their own fancy, whilst repudiating or disregarding real and reliable objects of trust.

I. THE THINGS THAT ARE "THINGS OF NOUGHT." The arm of flesh, or human help, as against God's strength, is the "non-thing" or nonentity referred to primarily. But the expression is capable of wider application. Among the nonentities are: 1. *All things sinful*. This is an extreme case. Sin is an ephemera, offering only what fleets away. It is a negation, the privation of all good. It is a phantasm, having an appearance of good with no reality below it. It is a deception, having a lie at the bottom of it. It is a non-thing in a unique sense. 2. *All things material*. The positivist only believes in material phenomena, as those of which alone he has positive knowledge. But these are really the most uncertain phenomena there are. The bodily sense that notes them is more certain, and the thinking mind that has cognizance of the bodily sense is more certain than either, and the ultimate test of the existence of both. What we know most surely and directly is spirit. Observation may be incorrect, and lead us astray, but consciousness speaks only truth. If there are things which "are not as they seem," they are physical, as distinguished from psychical things. 3. *All things temporal*. These are evanescent in their nature. "The world passeth away." They are still more evanescent in their form: "The fashion of this world passeth away." They are doubly evanescent in their character as a means of happiness; for not alone the world, but the "lust thereof," passeth away. This evanescence means unreality. The thing that perishes in the using is conspicuously a thing of nought. Such a thing is human nature, and each of its temporal blessings and relations—in other words, human life. It is a vapour on the hill, a bubble on the stream, a ripple on the wave, a meteor in the sky, an unsubstantial thing that passes and leaves no trace. 4. *All things created*. God, the "I Am," is essential Existence. He alone hath immortality, exists of himself and from himself. The existence of creatures is derived, an existence from God and in him. It is not, therefore, real as God's is. We are phantoms, he is reality. We are shadows, he is substance. Creation as contrasted with the Creator is a "non-thing," a thing of nought.

II. THE CHARACTER THAT FINDS ITS JOY IN UNREALITY. This character is one with a wide geographical range. It might almost be said to belong to sinful man as such. As to its qualities, it is: 1. *Blind*. Such a man "cannot see afar off." He does not see things through and through. He does not see things as they are. He sees things through coloured glasses. He dwells in the superficies of things. He is deceived by appearances. He confounds the qualities of things. He cannot, in fact, be said to "know anything as he ought." The blindness of our heart is a universal infirmity. Sin blinds, and prejudice blinds, and infirmity blinds us all; and the most convincing proof of the fact is that we choose the worst and poorest in the universe, and often and long reject the true riches. 2. *Prejudiced*. The blindness that permits us to rejoice in the flesh must have prejudice behind it. It involves a wrong condition of heart. "The carnal mind is enmity against God" is a maxim which explains the rejection of him by the sinner. "They that are after the flesh do mind the things of the flesh" is one which explains his choice of sin. In the spiritual, as in other departments, things follow their affinities. 3. *Proud*. Well says the poet—

> "What the weak head with strangest bias rules
> Is pride, the never-failing vice of fools."

It misreads altogether the proportions of things. It has an overweening estimate of self. "Thinking of ourselves more highly than we ought to think," and "thinking God to be altogether such a one as ourselves," the transfer of trust from heaven to earth, is not alone natural, but inevitable.

III. THE JOY THAT FLAMES WITHOUT FUEL. That there should be such joy at all is an abnormal thing. *A priori* it is not what we should expect. And we are prepared to find something anomalous about a joy that could exist in such circumstances. This we do. 1. *It is a passing joy*. It cannot last. The meteor irradiating the sky, the thorns crackling under the pot, both blaze and both burn quickly out. The fire has too little to feed on. It is only a puff, and done with. So with joy in the earthly. It has an unsubstantial and unenduring basis. The thing it rests on perishes, and it cannot itself endure. 2. *It is an unreal joy*. It is not alone that it has reference to an ephemeral thing, but to an unsubstantial thing. It is a mere figment of the mind; an appearance rather than an existence; not a fire in the proper sense, but a phosphorescence. 3. *Its unreality is the parent of real woe.* To rejoice in a nonentity is a course on which disappointment clearly waits. It also involves distrust, and so incurs the wrath of God. No man can deceive himself with impunity. The line of action into which his false notion will lead him must end in calamity. Mistaken opinion associates itself with unfitting action, and this in turn with undesired results. He who follows the fen fire lands in the fen. 4. *Of all who rejoice in a thing of nought the most hopelessly deceived are the self-righteous.* With others the trust is something apart from religion, and adopted in preference to it. But with the self-righteous it masquerades in the name of religion itself. There is an idea, either that nothing is wrong, or that the man can help himself. In either case Divine help is despised. God's right is spurned. The one only way is refused. And on the moral impossibility of escaping if they neglect so great salvation, the self-deluded soul makes shipwreck. "Behold, all ye that kindle a fire," etc.

HOMILIES BY VARIOUS AUTHORS.

Ver. 1.—*Religious indifference and false security.* Amos was a native of the southern kingdom, but his ministry was mainly to Israel. His impartiality appears in the censures and reproaches which he addresses, as in this passage, to both Judah and Samaria. But the description applies to professing Christians to-day as accurately as if it had just then been written, and had been explicitly applied to such. How many who are called to devotion and diligence are "at ease," are "confident," or "secure"!

I. THE DISPOSITION AND HABIT HERE CONDEMNED. The following elements are to be recognized. 1. Self-satisfaction. 2. Self-indulgence. 3. Indifference. 4. Carelessness. 5. Negligence.

II. THE CIRCUMSTANCES WHICH AGGRAVATE THE SIN OF INDIFFERENCE AND SECURITY. In the case of those here addressed we observe: 1. That they resided in places which were themselves a reminder of the character of Jehovah and of his past "dealings" with the chosen people. 2. That they occupied positions fitted to inspire them with a sense of personal responsibility. They were the distinguished chiefs of the nations—the men to whom the people looked as their leaders, and in whom they might reasonably expect to find an example of piety, unselfishness, and zeal. 3. That they lived in times when the judgments of God were abroad, and when insensibility to duty and religion were all the more inexcusably culpable.

III. THE EVIL FOLLOWING UPON THE DISPOSITION AND HABIT HERE CONDEMNED. 1. Divine displeasure is prophetically declared against those who are at ease when they should be at work, against those who are secure and confident when they should be examining and judging themselves, and beginning a new and better life. 2. Moral deterioration cannot but follow upon such a state of mind as is here depicted. The slothful are the first to feel the ill effects of their sloth; the habit grows, and a religious, not to say an heroic, life becomes an impossibility. 3. National disaster and punishment are entailed by the indifference and unfaithfulness of those who are called to be a nation's guides and rulers.—T.

Ver. 3.—*Putting away the evil day.* By the "evil day" must be meant the day of account and reckoning which comes to all men and to all communities. As surely as there is a moral government and a moral Governor in the universe, so surely must all reasonable and intelligent natures be held responsible for their conduct and for their influence. Yet it is no unusual thing for men to follow the example of those who are censured in this verse.

I. THE THOUGHT OF A DAY OF ACCOUNT IS UNWELCOME TO THE UNFAITHFUL AND THE IRRELIGIOUS. Such persons need not be disbelievers in judgment, in accountability; they may accept the assurance of their own reason and conscience that an account must be rendered to the Judge of all. Yet, as the thought of a reckoning is one altogether repugnant to them, they persuade themselves that it may be indefinitely deferred. It must come, but it may not come yet; it may not come for a very long time; indeed, may be so remote that it need not be taken into consideration in arranging the plans of life. " Because sentence against an evil work is not executed speedily, therefore the heart of the sons of men is fully set in them to do evil."

II. THE DEFERRING OF THE THOUGHT OF THE DAY OF ACCOUNT WILL NOT DEFER THE DAY ITSELF. Moral law is never inoperative, is never suspended. Judgment lingereth not. The history alike of nations and of individuals proves that there is a Ruler on high, who is not remiss in carrying out his purposes. There is a reckoning in time; there will be a reckoning in eternity.

> "Though the mills of God grind slowly, yet they grind exceeding small ;
> Though with patience he stands waiting, he exactly judgeth all."

It is irrational and futile to imagine that by forgetting responsibility men can efface it. Such a supposition reminds of the action of the foolish ostrich who thrusts his head into a bush, and, because he loses sight of his pursuers, supposes that he has eluded them. There is no discharge in this war.

III. NEGLIGENCE CONCERNING RESPONSIBILITY MAY EVEN HASTEN THE APPROACH OF THE INEVITABLE DAY OF ACCOUNT. They who forget their accountability to God for their unfaithfulness are likely to be confirmed in their sinful courses ; and, as iniquity abounds, judgment approaches. Thus the dreaded retribution is hastened rather than postponed; and the evil day which men would fain put far from them is brought near, and the tempest, which they dread and would avoid and escape, breaks upon them in all its force and fury.—T.

Vers. 4—7.—*The sin of dissolute life.* A herdsman and gatherer of wild figs like Amos, brought into contact with the nobility and the courtiers of a wealthy and luxurious city like Samaria, was likely enough to be shocked and scandalized. The judgments he formed were naturally severe, but they were not unjust or passionate. His language remains a merited and everlasting rebuke to those in high station who live for their own gratification and indulgence.

I. A LUXURIOUS AND DISSOLUTE LIFE IS A SHAMEFUL MISUSE OF PRECIOUS OPPOR TUNITIES. It is sometimes judged that those who are " born in the purple," those who inherit great estates, great wealth, are to be excused if they form in youth, and retain in manhood, habits of expensive self-indulgence. But as all men are, above all, the children of God, endowed with a spiritual nature and entrusted with sacred opportunities, it is not to be for a moment admitted that the advantages of high station absolve them from the obligations involved in human nature and human life. A man has no right to pamper the body and exalt it to a lordship over the spirit; he has no right to gratify his tastes as though self-gratification were the great end of existence.

II. A LUXURIOUS AND DISSOLUTE LIFE IS MORALLY DEBASING AND DEGRADING. No one can live below the appointed level of humanity without paying the inevitable penalty, without incurring the inevitable deterioration. The light burns dim ; the fine gold turns to clay. The couch of indolence, the feast of gluttony, the voluptuous music, the brimming bowls of wine, the costly unguents,—these are dangerous indulgences. Men may give them fine names, and call them the bounties of Divine providence. And it is quite true that the evil is not in the instruments of self-indulgence, but in the bad uses to which they are put. But none can live merely for bodily, for æsthetic, for social, enjoyment, without injuring his own character, without losing self-respect and the esteem of those whose esteem is worth having.

III. A LUXURIOUS AND DISSOLUTE LIFE ON THE PART OF THE GREAT IS A BAD EXAMPLE TO THE COMMUNITY AT LARGE. Bad habits penetrate from the so-called upper to the so-called lower class. When the nobility and gentry are self-indulgent, the tradespeople who grow wealthy are likely to follow their example, and the poor are likely enough to grow envious and discontented. The Samaritan chiefs were reproached for misleading the people, and justly. The ignorant and the thoughtless are naturally influenced by an example of selfishness, and none can altogether escape receiving some measure of harm.

IV. A LUXURIOUS AND DISSOLUTE LIFE RENDERS THE GREAT INSENSIBLE TO THE AFFLICTIONS OF THE POOR AND OPPRESSED. The language of the prophet is very touching : the self-indulgent " are not grieved for the affliction of Joseph." Wrapped up in their own enjoyments, comforts, and luxuries, the great fail to sympathize with those whom we call " the masses." A self-denying and benevolent and public-spirited course of conduct would have precisely an opposite effect. There is no reason in the nature of things why nobles should not feel with and for the poor and unfortunate; as a matter of fact, they often do so. But those whose absorbing thought is of self have neither heart nor time to give to their less-favoured neighbours.

V. A LUXURIOUS AND DISSOLUTE LIFE OFTEN INVOLVES A SPEEDY AND FEARFUL RETRIBUTION. The table of the epicure is overthrown. The sybarite is dragged from his palace, and sent away into exile. Those who have been worthless members of their own state become banished mourners in a strange land. And the song of pleasure is exchanged for the wail of woe.—T.

Ver. 11.—" *The Lord commandeth.*" It was the office and function of a prophet to lose himself in becoming the vehicle of Divine communications, the organ of Divine decisions. His prefatory words were these: "Thus saith the Lord." He saw and felt the Lord's presence, not only in his own ministry, but in all the events that occurred in the range of his observation, whether affecting individuals or nations.

I. THERE IS AN ELEMENT OF AUTHORITY IN EVERY WORD OF THE LORD. Whether God addresses to men language of rebuke or reproach, of entreaty or of threatening, he speaks with authority. His invitation is that of a King; it is a command When our Lord Christ spoke in the course of his ministry, he spoke with authority. The Divine judgment is always correct, the Divine will is always obligatory.

II. ALL AGENCIES AND INSTRUMENTALITIES ARE OBEDIENT TO THE LORD'S BEHESTS. It is so with the forces of nature. "The stormy wind fulfilleth his word;" "His ministers are a flaming fire." It is so with the institutions of human society, with the purposes and the activities of men. The hand which is visible in a work may be that of a creature; the power that directs that hand may, nevertheless, be creative wisdom and creative might. God gives the word; it is executed by ten thousand ministers of his holy will. He maketh even the wrath of man to praise him.

III. THE POWER OF THE GREATEST AMONG MEN IS INCAPABLE OF RESISTING THE DIVINE COMMANDS. The " great house " and the " little house " alike are smitten when the Lord makes bare his arm. Israel and Judah, the prince and the husbandman, may know that nothing can protect them from the might of the Eternal when his decree of judgment has gone out against them. Well may the people that rebel against God tremble and fear, and remember that they are but men.—T.

Ver. 12.—*The vanity of the sinner's principles and hopes.* The perfect naturalness and genuineness of Amos must be apparent to every reader. The sources from which he drew his graphic imagery were his own life and experiences. As a husbandman employed upon the land, he was brought into contact both with the phenomena of nature and with the processes of agriculture; and from these sources his mind was supplied with the bold similitudes which occur in his prophecies. Wishing to depict the irrational and absurd suppositions and expectations of the sinful and rebellious, he compared them to husbandmen who should attempt to drive horses up a steep cliff, or to plough the hard, barren rock by oxen.

I. JUSTICE IS THE ETERNAL LAW OF THE MORAL UNIVERSE. Here is the true and Divine bond of human society; here is the principle which should govern earthly rulers, judges, and princes. The higher men's station, the greater men's power, the more important is it that justice should guide and inspire their conduct.

II. IN A CORRUPT STATE OF SOCIETY OPPRESSION AND VIOLENCE ARE SUBSTITUTED FOR JUSTICE. Amos complained that the kings and nobles of Israel were guilty of the basest and most degrading conduct; they exchanged the sweet and wholesome fruit of righteousness for the bitterness of gall and wormwood and the poison of hemlock, *i.e.* for bribery, for violence, for oppressiveness. History is full of such instances. The noble institutions of society are perverted into instruments of personal ambition, aggrandizement, and wrong. Cruel kings, luxurious nobles, corrupt judges, are morally disastrous to the state; their example spreads through all classes, and faith, honour, and purity decay and perish.

III. IT IS IMPOSSIBLE THAT TRUE PROSPERITY SHOULD PREVAIL WHERE THE FOUNTAIN

OF RIGHTEOUSNESS IS POISONED. The great men of Israel had come to confide in their own strength, in their military power, and, like so many in high estate, thought that physical force was sufficient to secure a nation's greatness. The prophet justly characterizes such a doctrine as " a thing of nought," a nonentity, an absurdity! As well may horses climb the scaur, as well may oxen plough the bare, hard rock, as a nation prosper which has renounced the Law of God, and is attempting to base its success upon physical force, military prestige, ostentatious luxury, judicial corruption. We in our own days need not look far for an exemplification of the folly of such confidence. " Be wise now therefore, O ye kings: be instructed, ye judges of the earth."—T.

Ver. 14.—*The hand of God seen in national retribution.* Coming when it did, this prophecy was an unmistakable proof of Divine foresight. Samaria was rejoicing and boasting because of a temporary victory obtained by her arms. The kingdom of Israel had taken horns, and by its own strength had pushed back the foe from the borders. This was the moment appointed for Amos to utter the faithful warning contained in this verse. Subsequent events proved the predictive authority from which this language proceeded. The advance of Assyria soon reminded the unbelieving and impenitent of the warning to which they had been indifferent. But we are chiefly concerned to trace the truths and to draw the lessons regarding Divine government upon earth, which this prediction so strikingly unfolds.

I. THE FACT THAT A NATION IS CHOSEN BY GOD FOR A SPECIAL PURPOSE DOES NOT EXEMPT THAT NATION FROM THE OPERATION OF THE LAWS OF THE DIVINE GOVERNMENT. It is sometimes represented that the descendants of Abraham, Isaac, and Jacob were treated by the Ruler of all with an especial favouritism. But such a view cannot be justified from the sacred records. Undoubtedly, this nation was selected for high purposes, and appointed to occupy a position of enlightenment and eminence; but this was in order that the Jews might fulfil the purposes of God's wisdom, might in the fulness of the time produce the Messiah, and might become a blessing to all the nations of the earth. But never was a nation subjected to more stringent discipline than the Hebrew theocracy endured. No transgression was unnoticed or unchastised. Such afflictions have indeed seldom been endured as Israel has known, both in ancient and in modern times.

II. GOD, WHO IS NOT CONFINED TO ANY SPECIAL AGENCIES, HAS OFTEN EMPLOYED ONE NATION AS THE SCOURGE BY WHICH ANOTHER NATION HAS BEEN CHASTISED. It may be asked why Assyria, an idolatrous nation, should be employed to punish the transgressions of Israel. To such a question we can give no answer; but we may point out that the moral qualities of the chastising instrument have no bearing upon the purposes of punishment. God raiseth up one and setteth down another. History is full of examples of this principle. Amidst very much that is mysterious, there is not a little that is plain. Only in the most general way is it permitted us to interpret the methods of the Divine government. But the authoritative language of this and other passages of Scripture assure us that he who doeth according to his will among the inhabitants of the earth is impressing his own great lessons and fulfilling his own great designs by the changes which occur among the nations. Even wars, conquests, and captivities are the means by which God's Law is vindicated and God's kingdom is advanced.

III. NATIONAL TRIBULATION MAY BE THE MEANS OF NATIONAL PURIFICATION AND PROGRESS. Punishment is not an end in itself; however deserved and just, it is inflicted with a view to the good of the community or individual punished, or the good of human society at large. We can to some extent trace, in the subsequent history of the Hebrew people, the beneficial results of the conquest and captivity here foretold. Idolatry, at all events, came to an end; more spiritual views of religion became general; the nation, or that portion of it which returned to the land of promise, was prepared for giving birth to the Messiah, and for furnishing the elements which were to constitute the primitive Church. Thus God brought the light of morning out of the darkness, and a spiritual spring from the long winter of affliction.—T.

Vers. 1—6.—*Woeful ease.* " Woe to them that are at ease in Zion, and trust in the mountain of Samaria, which are named chief of the nations, to whom the house of Israel came!" etc. "This chapter embraces the character and punishment of the whole

Hebrew nation. The inhabitants of the two capitals are directly addressed in the language of denunciation, and charged to take warning from the fate of other nations (vers. 1, 2). Their carnal security, injustice, self-indulgence, sensuality, and total disregard of the Divine threatenings are next described (vers. 3—6). After which the prophet announces the Captivity and the calamitous circumstances connected with the siege of Samaria, by which it was to be preceded (vers. 7—11). He then exposes the absurdity of their conduct, and threatens them with the irruption of an enemy that should pervade the whole country (vers. 12—14)" (Henderson). The words of our text (ver. 1) denounce a state of mind which most men desiderate—"ease." Amidst the harassing cares, turmoils, and agitating events of life, men on all hands are crying out for ease. Like mariners that have long battled with tempests, they long for a calm sea in which to drop anchor and be at rest. But here there is a fearful "woe" denounced against ease. What is this ease?

I. IT IS THE EASE OF PRIDE. These great nations, Judah and Israel, the one having its seat in Zion and the other in Samaria, because of their imaginary superiority as the chief of the nations, settled down in carnal security. Those that dwelt in Zion, or Jerusalem, felt themselves safe because of its historic grandeur, its temple, the dwelling-place of the Almighty, and its mountain fortifications. Those that dwelt in Samaria—the ten tribes—had the same false confidence in their safety. The mountains of Samaria, the seat both of the religion and government of a strong people, they relied upon, free from all apprehension of dangers. It was the ease of pride and overrated power.

II. IT IS THE EASE OF RUIN. "Pass ye unto Calneh [this was an ancient city built by Nimrod] and see; and from thence go ye to Hamath the great [one of the chief cities of Syria]: then go down to Gath of the Philistines [the great city in Philistia]." Remember these cities, "Be they better than these kingdoms?" Are you who live at Zion and Samaria greater people than they were, more strong and invincible? Yet they are gone. Calneh gone, Hamath gone, Gath gone. All are in ruins, long, long ago. Why, then, should you feel yourselves safe and be at ease in Zion and Samaria? Their example condemns your false security and predicts your ruin. The ease here denounced is like the ease of stolid indifference or the ease of a torpid conscience, terribly general, fearfully criminal, and awfully dangerous. It must sooner or later be broken. The hurricanes of retribution must sooner or later lash the sleeping ocean into foaming fury. Souls are everywhere sleeping on the bosom of volcanoes. Oh for some voice from the heavens above or the earth beneath, to startle the men of this generation!

CONCLUSION. Learn from this subject: 1. *That the mere feeling of security is no infallible proof of safety.* Men are prone to deceive themselves. "The heart is deceitful above all things, and desperately wicked." Some men, like the drunkard whose vessel is going down, feel themselves safe because they are unconscious of the danger. Some men feel themselves safe because of the confidence they have in objects that are utterly unable to sustain them. The only feeling of security that warrants safety is that which springs from a conscious trust in God. Such as have this can say, "God is our Refuge and Strength," etc. 2. *That great advantages may prove great curses.* It was a great advantage for Judah to have Zion, and Israel to have Samaria—great in many respects, national and religious. But these advantages, because they were overrated, trusted in, put in the place of God himself, proved to them most disastrous. So it ever is. Our civilization, our literature, our Churches, our Bibles, have proved curses to millions, and will perhaps to millions more. The Pharisee in the temple is an illustration of this. 3. *That retributions which have overtaken others should be a warning to us.* The prophet calls upon these men of Judah and Israel to remember Calneh, Hamath, Gath. "All these things," says Paul, "happened unto them for ensamples." Learn to read our fate in history. Ungodly nations, where are Egypt, Babylon, Greece, Rome? Ungodly Churches, where are the Churches of Asia Minor?—D. T.

Ver. 3.—*Man's evil day.* "Ye that put far away the evil day, and cause the seat of violence to come near." This is another denunciation addressed to the great men in Zion and Samaria. They are said "to keep the day of calamity afar off, and bring the seat of violence near" (Delitzsch). Three remarks are suggested by these words.

I. ALL MEN HAVE AN "EVIL DAY" IN THEIR FUTURE. Even the holiest men, men whose path through life has been most calm and prosperous, have to expect certain calamities that befall all.   There are trials common to all men, whatever their condition or character—afflictions, bereavements, infirmities; these await most men. There is one evil day, however, for us all.   Death is in many respects an "evil day." What mysterious sufferings it generally involves!   What privileges and pleasures it terminates!   What disruptions it produces!   Sinner, thy death will be an evil day; and it is before thee, and it is nearer now than ever.

II. SOME MEN ADJOURN IN THOUGHT THIS "EVIL DAY."   They "put far away the evil day."   Ungodly men put this evil day so far on in the course of time that they seldom discern it and never realize it.   It is a mere speck, seldom visible on the horizon of many years of unclouded sunshine.   Why do men adjourn in thought this evil day?   1. Not because they *have any doubt as to its advent.*   No day is more certain.   Sooner shall all the wheels of nature be stopped than the sun of this day fail to break on every eye.   "It is appointed to men once to die."   2. Not because they *lack reminders of its approach.*   Every physical pain, every tolling knell, every funeral procession, every graveyard—all remind us almost every moment that our evil day is coming.   Why, then, adjourn the thought?   The reason is found: 1. In the *strength of our material attachments.*   2. In our *dread of the mysterious.*   3. In our *lack of interest in the spiritual and material.*   4. In our *conscious want of preparation for the scenes of retribution.*

III. NONE WHO ADJOURN THIS "EVIL DAY" IN THOUGHT CAN DELAY IT IN FACT. "And cause the seat of violence to come near."   Perhaps what is meant here is that these men so ignored their coming calamities that by their conduct they hastened them on.   Ignoring the evil day, they pursued such a course of injustice, falsehood, dishonesty, sinful indulgence, and impiety as served to bring it nearer.   Thus the more they put it off in thought the nearer it drew, because they became more self-destructive in their conduct.   A general truth is suggested here, viz. *that a man who adjourns all thought of his end will pursue such a course of conduct as will hasten its approach.* Some men imagine that by thinking upon death they will hasten its advent; hence their dread of making wills.   But such is not the fact.   He who keeps the evil day in view, rightly regards it, prepares for it, will render such a practical obedience to the laws of health as to delay rather than hasten it.   "Teach us to number our days, that we may apply our hearts unto wisdom."—D. T.

Vers. 4—7.—*Carnal indulgence.*   "That lie upon beds of ivory, and stretch themselves upon their couches, and eat the lambs out of the flock, and the calves out of the midst of the stall," etc.   Here is a sketch of the way in which these leading men of the chief nations luxuriated in carnal pleasures and sensual indulgences.   Observe two things.

I. THE MORAL TORPOR OF CARNAL INDULGENCE.   Observe two things.   1. These people wrought *entirely for the senses.*   See how they *slept!*   They provided themselves with "beds of ivory."   They did not require rest for their weary limbs, otherwise beds of straw would have done.   They wanted to be grand, they loved glitter, hence "beds of ivory."   Here is the lust of the eye.   See how they *ate!*   "And stretch themselves upon their couches, and eat the lambs out of the flock, and the calves out of the midst of the stall."   They abounded in superfluities; they partook of the choicest dainties of nature, and that in a recumbent position.   Here is the lust of the palate.   See how they *sang!*   "That chant to the sound of the viol, and invent to themselves instruments of music, like David."   Musical sounds gratified their auricular sensibilities, and they chanted to the "viol."   Here is the lust of the ear.   See how they *drank!* They "drink wine in bowls."   Small vessels would not do; they must take long, deep draughts of the pleasing beverage.   Here again is the lust of the palate.   See how they *anointed themselves!*   "With the chief ointments."   They regaled their olfactory nerves with the choicest perfumes of nature.   Here is the lust of the smell.   See how *indifferent* they were to the suffering of the true Church of God!   "They are not grieved for the affliction of Joseph."   What a description this of a people that lived and wrought entirely for the senses!   They were practical materialists.   They had no spiritual vision, sensibilities, or experience.   Their imperishable souls were submerged in the deep flowing sea of mere animal pleasures.   Are there no such men now?   For what do our prosperous tradesmen and the upper ten thousand live? For the most part, we fear, for the senses. Grand furniture—"beds of ivory;" choicest viands—"lambs out of the flock, and calves out of the midst of the stall;" ravishing music—"chants to the sound of the viol;" delectable beverages—the choicest wines in "bowls;" the most delicious aromas—"the chief ointments." Has carnal indulgence been more rife in any land or age than this? Matter everywhere governs spirit; the body everywhere is the despot, men are "carnal, sold under sin." 2. These people wrought *without conscience.* In all this there is no effort of conscience recorded, no word uttered. There is, indeed, a reference to intellectual effort, for it is said "they invented to themselves instruments of music." Carnal indulgence has ever been and is now as much, if not more than ever, the great employer of man's inventive faculties. Luxury in England to-day is the great employer of human ingenuity. But there is no conscience here. When conscience is touched in such a state of things, and startled by the sense of its guilt, it exclaims, "O wretched man that I am! who shall deliver me from the body of this sin and death?"

II. THE RETRIBUTIVE RESULT OF CARNAL INDULGENCE. The threat in the text is: 1. The loss of *liberty.* "Therefore now shall they go captive with the first that go captive." Those who had taken the lead in revelry and all manner of wickedness were to be the first in the procession of captives. In such a position their disgrace would be more conspicuous. Luxury always leads to slavery: it is the eternal law of justice, that those who live to the flesh shall lose their freedom and be exiled into the region of tyranny. "Lust, when it hath conceived, bringeth forth sin; and sin, when it is full-grown, bringeth forth death" (Jas. i. 15). 2. The loss of *provisions.* "And the banquet of them that stretched themselves shall be removed." They shall have scarcity, perhaps starvation, instead of the profusion of dainties with which their tables have been spread. All this carnal indulgence and voluptuousness, this luxury in ease, and diet, and music, and aroma will not go on for ever. They are abnormal conditions of human nature; retribution will one day put an end to them.

> "O luxury,
> Bane of elated life, of affluent states,
> What ruin is not thine? . . . Behind thee gapes
> Th' unfathomable gulf where Ashur lies
> O'erwhelmed, forgotten; and high boasting Cham;
> And Elam's haughty pomp; and beauteous Greece;
> And the great queen of earth, imperial Rome."
>
> (Dyer.)
>
> D. T.

Ver. 8.—*National depravity.* "The Lord God hath sworn by himself, saith the Lord the God of hosts, I abhor the excellency of Jacob, and hate his palaces: therefore will I deliver up the city with all that is therein." In order to show the voluptuous debauchees referred to in the preceding verses the terrible judgments that would overtake them, Jehovah is here represented as making a solemn oath. Whether the city here refers to Samaria or Jerusalem, or both, is of little moment. The subject is national depravity, and we infer from the words—

I. THAT DEPRAVITY MAY EXIST IN A NATION WHERE THERE IS MUCH THAT IS MAGNIFICENT. Here is a reference to the "excellency"—or, as some render it, the splendour—"of Jacob;" and here is a reference to "palaces," the homes of princes. There was much that was magnificent amongst the Jewish people of old in their own land. Great cities and their palaces, and, above all, the temple at Jerusalem, beautiful in architecture and situation, with an organized priesthood and gorgeous ceremonies. Still, its depravity at this time was wide and deep and hideous. A nation may have much that is magnificent, and yet be deeply sunk in moral corruption. Witness ancient Greece and Rome; witness England to-day. The arts, sculpture, painting, architecture, music, have reached their perfection, and abound. On all hands our eyes are attracted by grand churches, splendid mansions, marts, banks, museums, colleges, and galleries of art. Albeit was depravity ever more rife in any age or country than this? Greed, ambition, selfishness, sensuality, fraud, falsehood, and self-indulgence,—these, the elements of depravity and the fountains of crime, abound in all directions.

It is true they do not appear in their naked deformity, as in barbaric lands. Our civilization not only spreads a veil over them, but paints and decorates them, and thus conceals their native hideousness. Still, though the devil robes himself in the garb of an angel, he is yet the devil. Poison is poison, however much you may flavour it.

II. That depravity under the most magnificent form is utterly abhorrent to the great God. "I abhor the excellency of Jacob, and hate his palaces." No veil can cover it from his eye; his glance pierces through all its decorations; to his view its ornamentations add to its ugliness. The same vices displayed in the hut of a savage chief, are more hideous to him when developed in the gorgeous palaces of Christian sovereigns. "I abhor the excellency [splendour] of Jacob." God has moral sensibility. He has not only a sensibility for the beautiful in form and the perfect in arrangement, but for the moral. He loves the true, the beautiful, and the good; he loathes the false, the selfish, and the corrupt. "Oh, do not this abominable thing, which I hate" (Jer. xliv. 4).

III. That depravity, which is ever abhorrent to God, must bring ruin on its subjects. "Therefore will I deliver up the city with all that is therein." Observe: 1. The *completeness* of the ruin. "All that is therein"—utter destruction. 2. The *certainty* of the ruin. "The Lord God hath sworn by himself."

Conclusion. What an argument does this subject furnish for national seriousness and investigation! The progress of civilization is not the true progress of humanity. A nation may advance in the arts, and go back in morals; may be robed in artistic beauty, and yet be loathsome in moral corruption. Heaven will not smile on a nation because it is externally grand, but only when it is internally good.—D. T.

Ver. 12.—*Trying the impossible.* "Shall horses run upon the rock? will one plough there with oxen?" The folly of expecting real prosperity by committing acts of injustice or pursuing courses of sin is here forcibly represented by comparing it to the absurdity of attempting to run horses upon a rock or to plough the rock with oxen. The strength of the representation is increased by its interrogative form. Our subject is—*Trying the impossible.* Men are constantly doing this. Let us furnish a few examples.

I. When they attempt to destroy an enemy by physical force. An individual has an enemy, a man who hates him with an inveterate antipathy. In order to overcome him, what does he do? He disables or perhaps kills him. Or a nation has an enemy, strong and malignant. How does it seek to overcome it? In the same way, by brute force—swords, cannons, bayonets, these are employed. Now, the attempt to destroy an enemy by brute force is as absurd as to make horses run on the peaks of craggy rocks, or to put oxen to plough them. To destroy the enemy's body is not to destroy either him or his enmity. Philosophy and the Bible teach that the body is not the man; it is his, not himself. All the men that have fallen in duels, campaigns, or private assassinations are living, thinking, acting still, and await their murderers in another state. No bullet or sword can touch the man.

II. When they attempt to make society morally good by mere secular instruction. There are men who imagine that by teaching children the arts of reading, writing, ciphering, and the rudiments of science they will improve the morality of the nation. When you remember that the moral character grows out of the heart and not out of the brain, out of the likings and dislikings, not out of the ideas or intelligence, all this seems as absurd as the attempt to make horses run on rocks. Secular knowledge cannot change the heart, cannot alter a man's likes or dislikes. It may strengthen them, but not alter them. Dishonesty, uneducated, may commit petty thefts; but educated, it will legally swindle a nation. Knowledge, alas! is all in vain.

III. When they attempt to get happiness from without. All mankind are in search of happiness. "Who will show us any good?"—this is the universal cry. The great bulk seek happiness from without, from what they can see, and taste, and hear, and handle. They look for happiness in the titillation of the nerves and the gratification of the senses. Now, were man nothing but body, this would do. This does for the brute and the bird. But man is spirit; and matter in no form or combination can satisfy spirit. A man's life, or happiness, consisteth not in the abundance of material things. True happiness springs from within, not from without; arises from holy loves, hopes, aspirations, and aims. In one word, love is the well of water that springs up unto everlasting life.

IV. WHEN THEY ATTEMPT TO SAVE SOULS BY MINISTERING TO THEIR SELFISHNESS. There are men in all Churches who give themselves to saving souls, as they say. Salvation is the burden of all their thought and talk. But how do they endeavour to accomplish their object? By everlasting appeals to the selfish fears and hopes of men. Tragic descriptions are given of hell in order to frighten men, and sensuous descriptions of heaven in order to attract them. But can this save the soul? Impossible. It will only aggravate its damnation. Salvation consists in the extinction of all that is selfish in human nature, and in the generating, fostering, and perfecting disinterested, self-oblivious love. " He that seeketh his life shall lose it: he that loseth his life shall find it." A preacher may increase his congregation by appealing to the selfishness of his hearers, but he does not add one to the family of the good. The man who tries to save souls by constant appeals to the selfishness of human nature acts more absurdly than he who attempts to gallop horses upon the sharp peaks of rugged rocks.

V. WHEN THEY ATTEMPT TO CONVERT HEATHENS ABROAD BEFORE CONVERTING THE HEATHENS AT HOME. London abounds with heathens. All the heathens of the heathen world have their representatives in London; besides, the great bulk of the resident population are heathens; they are without God and without hope in the world. The influence of London upon the most distant parts of the world is a thousand times as great as that of all the missionaries from England and America. Under such circumstances, to send a few lonely men to distant peoples, who are ignorant of our language, modes of thought, and habits, with the idea of converting the world, is more absurd than to put horses to run on the rock, and oxen to plough thereon. Are we not bound to go into all the world to spread the gospel? Yes, but is there a greater world than London? and should not our sailors, our merchants, our travellers, and emigrants be the missionaries to foreign lands? Whilst your missionaries carry teaspoonfuls of the gospel here and there, your London pours out floods of depravity on every zone.

CONCLUSION. Alas! how much human effort and sacrifice are lost for the want of practical wisdom and common sense! " Shall horses run upon the rock? will one plough there with oxen?" Yes, more successfully than we poor fools can accomplish some things that we labour to attain.—D. T.

Ver. 12.—*Man's perverting power.* " For ye have turned judgment into gall, and the fruit of righteousness into hemlock." The meaning of this is that they had turned the best things into bad use. Judgment and righteousness, the laws of right, they had made as nauseous and noxious as " gall" and " hemlock." Our subject is *man's perverting power.* Our blessed Maker in our constitution has endowed us with a force which no other creature under heaven seems to have, of turning things to wrong uses, and making those things which he intended to bless us the means of misery and ruin. You can see man exercising this power in many departments of action.

I. IN PHYSICAL OPERATIONS. What does he do with the iron which he discovers in the depths of the earth? Forges it into implements of human destruction. What does he do with the vineyards and the corn-fields? He turns them into inebriating liquids, and rolls them like rivers of poison through every district of society. What does he do with his own physical appetites? Instead of attending to them as means of relief, he makes their gratification the chief sources of his pleasure, and thus degrades his mental and moral nature. Everywhere you see man perverting nature—perverting the metals, the rivers, the fruits, and the chemical elements of the world.

II. IN CIVIC LIFE. The principle of human *government* is a Divine ordinance, intended to secure equal justice and protection. But how has man perverted it! He has turned it into an instrument to benefit the few at the expense of the many, an instrument of tyranny and oppression. The principle of *judicature*, intended to secure for all a just administration of law, man notoriously perverts. Men are appointed to occupy the throne of judgment who are not always, or generally, known as incorruptibly just and morally pure. Hence often in the name of justice iniquities are enacted. Man's perversion of the law is proverbial as a hideous enormity. The principle of *merchandise*, intended to band man together by the exchange of commodities in mutual obligation and fellowship, man has awfully perverted. He has made it the instrument of cupidity, monopoly, and nameless frauds. Thus, in every part of social life you see this perverting power in action—man turning "judgment into gall, and the fruits of righteousness into hemlock."

III. In the religious sphere. In spiritual matters and in scenes that should be the most sacred, its action is perhaps more flagrant and formidable than anywhere else. Without going into the great world of heathenism, or even to remote parts of Christendom, look into our own religious England, and what do you see? You see the gospel ministry, which is essentially self-denying, humble, devout, turned into an arrogant and plethoric priesthood. You see gospel ceremonies, intended to adumbrate spiritual truths, employed as mystic channels of saving grace. You see a system of universal philanthropy made an instrument of miserable sectarianism and intolerable bigotry.

Conclusion. Do not let man say he has no power. His moral power is something stupendous. He has power to turn the things of God to the use of Satan, heavenly blessings into hellish curses. This he is doing everywhere. "Ye have turned judgment into gall, and the fruit of righteousness into hemlock."—D. T.

Ver. 13.—*Human joy in the unsubstantial.* "Ye which rejoice in a thing of nought, which say, Have we not taken to us horns by our own strength?" "Horns" are signs and symbols of power; here they stand for the military resources with which they fancied that they could conquer every foe. "These delusions of God-forgetting pride the prophet casts down, by saying that Jehovah, the God of hosts, will raise up a nation against them, which will crush them down in the whole length and breadth of the kingdom. This nation was Assyria" (Delitzsch). What these ancient Hebrews did is an evil prevalent in all times and lands—rejoicing in the things of nought, taking pleasure in the unreal, the empty, and the fleeting.

I. To rejoice in worldly wealth is to "rejoice in a thing of nought." Rich men everywhere are always disposed to rejoice in their wealth. Houses, lands, and funded treasures, of these worldly men are ever boasting, in these they proudly exult. But what is earthly wealth? It is, in truth, so far as the possessor is concerned, "a thing of nought." It was not his a few years ago, and may not be his to-morrow. "Wilt thou set thine eyes upon that which is not? for riches certainly make themselves wings; they fly away as an eagle towards heaven" (Prov. xxiii. 5). Wealth, at best, is a most unsubstantial thing; it is a mere air-bubble rising on the stream of life, glittering for a moment, and then departing for ever. Great fortunes are but bubbles; they vanish before a ripple on the stream or a gust in the atmosphere. "Wealth," says old Adams, "is like a bird; it hops all day from man to man as the bird from tree to tree, and none can say where it will roost or rest at night."

> "Go, enter the mart where the merchantmen meet,
> Get rich, and retire to some rural retreat:
> Ere happiness comes, comes the season to die;
> Quickly, then will thy riches all vanish and fly.
> Go, sit with the mighty in purple and gold;
> Thy mansions be stately, thy treasures untold;
> But soon shalt thou dwell in the damp house of clay,
> While thy riches make wings to themselves and away."

II. To rejoice in personal beauty is to "rejoice in a thing of nought." Nature has endowed some with personal charms which it has denied to others—finely chiselled features, a radiant countenance, commanding brow, symmetrical form, majestic presence. He who is thus blest has many advantages; he commands admiration and exerts an influence upon human hearts. But is this beauty a thing to rejoice in? Those who possess it do rejoice in it; many pride themselves on their good looks and fine figures. But what is beauty? It is "a thing of nought." Why rejoice in that for which we can take no credit? Does the moss-rose deserve praise for unfolding more beauty and emitting more fragrance than the nettle? Who can make one hair white or black, or add one cubit to his stature? Why rejoice, too, in that which is so evanescent? Socrates called beauty "a short-lived tyranny;" and Theophrastus, "a silent cheat." One old divine says it is like an almanac—it "lasts for one year, as it were." Men are like the productions of the fields and the meadows. In the summer the variety is striking, some herbs and flowers appear in more stately form and attractive hues than others; but when old winter comes round, who sees the distinctions? Where are the plants of beauty? They are faded and gone. "All flesh is grass, and all the goodliness thereof as the flower of the field."

> "Beauty is but a vain and doubtful good,
> A shining gloss, that fadeth suddenly;
> A flower that dies, when first it 'gins to bud;
> A brittle glass, that's broken presently:
> A doubtful good, a gloss, a glass, a flower,
> Lost, faded, broken, dead within an hour.

> "And as good lost is seldom or never found,
> As fading gloss no rubbing will refresh,
> As flowers dead lie withered on the ground,
> As broken glass no cement can redress,
> So beauty, blemished once, for ever's lost,
> In spite of physic, painting, pain, and cost."
>
> (Shakespeare.)

III. To REJOICE IN ANCESTRAL DISTINCTION is to "rejoice in a thing of nought." There are those who are constantly exulting in their pedigree. Some who in this country can go back to the days of William the Conqueror, how delighted they are! But who were the men that William brought over with him, and between whom he divided this England of ours? Cobblers, tailors, smiths, plunderers, men of rapine and blood, most of them destitute alike of intellectual culture and morality. But even had we come from the loins of the intellectual and moral peers of the race, what cause in this is there for rejoicing? It is truly "a thing of nought." Our ancestry is independent of us; we are not responsible for it. It is not a matter either of blame or praise. Each man is complete in himself—an accountable unity, a moral cause. A prime minister has a number of earnest servile lackeys—they are printers, jewellers, clothmakers, tailors, and such-like; in the zenith of his power he rewards them by causing them to be titled "sir," "lord," "baron," etc. In this their children rejoice. But is it not "a thing of nought"? What is there in it? Nothing.

> "Knighthoods and honours borne
> Without desert, are titles but of scorn."
>
> (Shakespeare.)

IV. To REJOICE IN MORAL MERITORIOUSNESS is to "rejoice in a thing of nought." There are many who rejoice in their morality. Like the Pharisee in the temple, they thank God they are not as "other men." They consider they are "rich, and increased with goods, and have need of nothing," whereas they are "wretched, and miserable, and poor, and blind, and naked." Moral merit in a sinner is a baseless vision, a phantom of a proud heart. The man exulting in his own self-righteousness acts as foolishly as the man who endeavours to secure himself from the scorching rays of the sun under his own shadow. He seeks to bring his shadow between him and the sun, but cannot. If he runs, the shadow is before or behind him; if he falls down, the shadow falls with him, and leaves him in contact with the burning beam. No; our righteousness is "a thing of nought;" it is "filthy rags."

> "Beware of too sublime a sense
> Of your own worth and consequence.
> The man who deems himself so great,
> And his importance of such weight,
> That all around, in all that's done,
> Must move and act for him alone,
> Will learn in school of tribulation
> The folly of his expectation."
>
> (Cowper.)

CONCLUSION. Ah me! how many on all hands are rejoicing in "a thing of nought"! Wealth, beauty, ancestry, self-righteousness,—what are these? Fleeting shadows, dying echoes. They are clouds without water; to the eye they may for a minute or two appear in gorgeous forms, but before a breeze they melt into thin air and are lost. Rejoice in the *real*, the spiritual, the eternal, the Divine.—D. T.

Ver. 14.—*God chastising nations by nations.* "But, behold, I will raise up against you a nation, O house of Israel, saith the Lord the God of hosts; and they shall afflict you from the entering in of Hamath unto the river of the wilderness." What "nation" is here referred to as about to be raised up by God against Israel? Undoubtedly, Assyria. This Assyrian nation is here represented as overspreading the country "from the entering in of Hamath unto the river of the wilderness." Hamath was a point of entrance for an invading army into Israel from the north, which had just been subjugated by Jeroboam II. The boundaries are virtually the same as those mentioned (2 Kings xiv. 25) as restored to Israel by Jeroboam II., "from the entering of Hamath unto the sea of the plain," *i.e.* the Dead Sea, into which the river of the wilderness here mentioned flows. Do not glory in your recently acquired city, for it shall be the starting-point for the foe to afflict you. How sad the contrast to the feast of Solomon, attended by a congregation from the same Hamath, the most northern boundary of Israel, to the Nile, the river of Egypt, the most southern boundary! "Unto the river of the wilderness," *i.e.* to Kedron, or that part of it which empties itself into the northern bay of the Dead Sea below Jericho (2 Chron. xxviii. 15), which city was at the southern boundary of the ten tribes (Maurer). To the river Nile, which skirts the Arabian wilderness and separates Egypt from Canaan (Grotius). If this verse includes Judah as well as Israel, Grotius's view is correct, and it agrees with 1 Kings viii. 65, "Solomon held a feast, and all Israel . . . from the entering in of Hamath unto the river of Egypt" (Fausset). The subject suggested by the words is this—*God chastising nations by nations.* He now threatens to chastise the kingdoms of Judah and Israel by the Assyrian people. This is how the Almighty has acted from the beginning. He has chastised nations by nations. The history of the world is little else than a history of civil wars. Let us for a moment notice the how and the why of this.

I. THE HOW. How does the Almighty bring about wars? 1. Not by his *inspiration.* The God of peace does not breathe into any people greed, ambition, revenge. These principles, from which all war emanates, are repugnant to his nature. He denounces them. His grand aim in the world is to annihilate them, and in their place propagate disinterestedness, humility, and magnanimous love. 2. Not by his *authority.* All war is directly against his command; whilst everywhere he prohibits covetousness, pride, and revenge, he inculcates, in almost every page of inspiration and every form of utterance, love to our neighbours. The God of peace works everywhere in the world through peace, works by the peaceful influences of nature and the love of the gospel to produce "peace on earth, and good will towards men." How, then, can he be said to raise a nation to war? Simply by *permission.* He allows human nature freedom to work out the evil principles that are operating in it. The power of free action with which he endowed men at first he does not crush, he does not restrict; he treats it with respect, and leaves men free to do evil as well as good. He who permits the river at times to overflow its boundaries, and the subterranean fires to break forth, permits the passions of men to issue in war and bloodshed. Permission is not authorship.

II. THE WHY. Why does the Almighty chastise nations by nations? Why not employ the elements of nature or angelic intelligences? or why not do it by his own direct volition, without any instrumentality whatever? He may, for aught we know, chastise men in all these ways; but we can see reasons for his employing nations to chastise nations by wars. In acting thus: 1. Man has revealed to him in the most impressive way the *wickedness of the human heart.* It has been well said that war is the effect, the embodiment, and manifestation of every conceivable sin. In every war hell is revealed; its fires flash, its thunders roll, its fiends revel and shriek. For man to get rid of sin, he must be impressed with its enormity; and does not war make that impression? Does not every crimson chapter in its history reveal to the human heart the stupendous enormity of sin? 2. Man has revealed to him *the utter folly of putting confidence in his fellow-man.* War reveals falsehood, treachery, cunning, fraud, cruelty;

and who can trust these? Does not war say to every man, "Cursed is the man that trusteth in man, and maketh flesh his arm"? To-day a man may fondle you as a friend, to-morrow foam at you as a fiend. "Put not your trust in princes, nor in the son of man, in whom there is no hope." 3. Man has revealed to him the *supreme importance of cultivating the true friendship of his fellow-men.* What thoughtful men have not groaned and wept over the utter failure of all means to produce the results for which they were ostensibly commenced—to vindicate national honour, to establish peace? Such ends are never realized. What, then, is the lesson? Cultivate friendship with your fellow-men, the friendship of man with man, family with family, tribe with tribe, nation with nation. Wars are God's moral lessons to man in tragedy.— D. T.

EXPOSITION.

CHAPTER VII.

Ver. 1—ch. ix. 10.—Part III. FIVE VISIONS, WITH EXPLANATIONS, CONTINUING AND CONFIRMING THE PREVIOUS PROPHECY. The afflictions are climactic, increasing in intensity. The first two symbolize judgments which have been averted by the prophet's intercession; the third and fourth adumbrate judgments which are to fall inevitably; and the fifth proclaims the overthrow of the temple and the old theocracy.

Vers. 1—3.—§ 1. *The first vision, of locusts, represents Israel as a field eaten down to the ground, but shooting up afresh, and its utter destruction postponed at the prophet's prayer.*

Ver. 1.—**Thus hath the Lord God showed unto me.** By an inward illumination (comp. vers. 4, 7; and ch. viii. 1; Jer. xxiv. 1—3). **He formed grasshoppers;** rather, *locusts* (Nah. iii. 17). This points to the moral government of God, who uses nature to work his purposes, "wind and storm fulfilling his word." **In the beginning of the shooting up of the latter growth;** when the aftermath was beginning to grow under the influence of the latter rains. If the herbage was destroyed then, there would be no hope of recovery in the rest of the year. **After the king's mowings.** It is deduced from this expression that the first crop on certain grounds was taken for the king's use—a kind of royal perquisite, though there is no trace of such a custom found in Scripture, the passage in 1 Kings xviii. 5, where Ahab sends Obadiah to search for pasture, having plainly nothing to do with it; and in this case, as Keil remarks, the plague would seem to fall upon the people only, and the guilty king would have escaped. But to interpret the expression entirely in a spiritual sense, with no substantial basis, as "Jehovah's judgments," destroys the harmony of the vision, ignoring

its material aspect altogether. It is quite possible that the custom above mentioned did exist, though it was probably limited to certain lands, and did not apply to the whole pasturage of the country. It is here mentioned to define the time of the plague of locusts—the time, in fact, when its ravages would be most irremediable. The LXX., by a little change of letters, render, ἰδοὺ βροῦχος εἷς Γὼγ ὁ βασιλεύς, by which they imply that the locusts would be as innumerable as the army of Gog. The whole version is, "Behold, a swarm of locusts coming from the East; and behold, one caterpillar, King Gog." The vision is thought to refer to the first invasion by the Assyrians, when Pul was bribed by Menahem to withdraw.

Ver. 2.—**The grass of the land.** The term includes vegetables of all sorts, the food of man and beast (Gen. i. 11; see note on Zech. x. 1). **O Lord, . . . forgive.** The prophet is not concerned to obtain the fulfilment of his prophecy; his heartfelt sympathy for his people yearns for their pardon, as he knows that punishment and restoration depend upon moral conditions. **By whom shall Jacob arise?** better, *How shall Jacob stand?* literally, *as who?* If he is thus weakened, as the vision portends, how shall he endure the stroke? **Small;** weakened by internal commotions and foreign attack (2 Kings xv. 10—16, 19).

Ver. 3.—**Repented for this;** or, *concerning this* destruction. The punishment was conditioned by man's behaviour or other considerations. Here the prophet's intercession abates the full infliction of the penalty (compare analogous expressions, Deut. xxxii. 36; 1 Sam. xv. 11; 2 Sam. xxiv. 16; Jer. xviii. 8; xlii. 10; Jonah iii. 10, where see note). Amos may have had in memory the passage in Joel ii. 13. The LXX. here and in ver. 6 has, Μετανόησον, Κύριε, ἐπὶ τούτῳ· καὶ τοῦτο οὐκ ἔσται, λέγει Κύριος, "Repent, O Lord, for this; and this shall not be, saith the Lord." Hence some early commentators gathered that the prophet's intercession was rejected; but the words do not necessarily bear that sense (see St. Cyril Alex. and Theodoret, *in loc.*). **It shall not be.** This respite refers to the retreat of the Assyrians under Pul, the usurping monarch who assumed the name of Tiglath-Pileser II. (2 Kings xv. 17, etc.). Some commentators consider the judgment to be literally a plague of locusts; but this is not probable.

Vers. 4—6.—§ 2. *The second vision, devouring fire, represents a more severe judgment than the preceding one, involving greater consequences, but still one which was again modified by the prayers of the righteous prophet.*

Ver. 4.—Called to contend by fire; Septuagint, ἐκάλεσε τὴν δίκην ἐν πυρί, "called for judgment by fire;" Vulgate, *vocabat judicium ad ignem.* God called the people to try their cause with him by sending fire as a punishment among them (comp. Isa. lxvi. 16; Ezek. xxxviii. 22); and in the vision the fire is represented as so vehement that it devoured the great deep, drank up the very ocean itself (Gen. vii. 11; Isa. li. 10); or the subterranean fountains and springs, as Gen. xlix. 25. **And did eat up a part;** τὴν μερίδα κυρίου (Septuagint). This version takes *eth-hacheleq* as the "inheritance" or "portion" of the Lord, *i.e.* the land of Israel (Jer. xii. 10); but Canaan is nowhere called absolutely "the portion;" nor were the ten tribes specially so designated. Rather, *the portion* (not *a part*) is that part of the land and people which was marked out for judgment. The particular calamity alluded to is the second invasion of Tiglath-Pileser II., when he conquered Gilead and the northern part of the kingdom, and carried some of the people captive to Assyria (2 Kings xv. 29).

Vers. 5, 6.—The intercession is the same as in ver. 2, except that the prophet says **cease** instead of "forgive;" and in effect the tide of war was rolled back from Israel, and Samaria itself was spared for the time.

Vers. 7—9.—§ 3. *The third vision, the plumb-line, represents the Lord himself as coming to examine the conduct of Israel, and finally deciding on its entire ruin.*

Ver. 7.—Upon (rather, *over*) **a wall made by a plumb-line.** The word translated "plumb-line" (*anakh*) occurs only here. Septuagint, ἀδάμας: so the Syriac; Vulgate, *trulla cæmentarii;* Aquila, γάνωσις, "brightening," "splendour;" Theodotion, τηκόμενον. As the word in other dialects means tin or lead, it is usually taken here to mean the plumb-line which builders use to ascertain that their work is even and per-

pendicular (see a very different explanation in Knabenbauer, p. 314, etc.). The "wall" is the kingdom of Israel, once carefully built up, solidly constructed, accurately arranged. God had made it upright; how was it now?

Ver. 8.—Amos, what seest thou? A question asked to give occasion for the explanation of the symbol, as in Jer. i. 11, 13; xxiv. 3. **I will set a plumb-line in the midst of my people Israel.** As it was built by rule and measure, so it should be destroyed. The line was used not only for building, but also for pulling down (see 2 Kings xxi. 13; Isa. xxxiv. 11; Lam. ii. 8). And this should be done "in the midst" of the people, that all might be tried individually, and that all might acknowledge the justice of the sentence, which now denounced complete ruin. **Pass by;** so as to spare, or forgive (ch. viii. 2; Prov. xix. 11; Micah vii. 18). The judgment is irremediable, and the prophet intercedes no more. The final conquest by Shalmaneser is here typified.

Ver. 9.—The high places of Isaac. The shrines of idolatry all over the land. The *bamoth* are the altars erected on high places and now dedicated to idols (1 Kings iii. 2; 2 Kings xxiii. 8; Isa. xvi. 12; Hos. x. 8). Isaac here and in ver. 16 is used as a synonym for Israel, perhaps with some idea of contrasting the deeds of the people with the blameless life of the patriarch and his gentle piety (Pusey). Septuagint, βωμοὶ τοῦ γέλωτος, with reference to the meaning of the name Isaac, "altars of derision," whence Jerome's version, *excelsa idoli.* **The sanctuaries of Israel.** The idol-temples at Dan and Bethel (1 Kings xii. 29), at Gilgal (ch. iv. 4), and perhaps in other places, which had been sanctified by ancient patriarchal worship. Septuagint, αἱ τελεταὶ τοῦ Ἰσραήλ, "the rites of Israel;" Vulgate, *sanctificationes Israel.* **With the sword.** God is represented as standing like an armed warrior taking vengeance on the guilty family. Jeroboam II. had saved Israel from Syria, and was popular owing to his success in war (2 Kings xiv. 25—28); but his dynasty was overthrown, and this overthrow was the destruction of the Israelitish monarchy. The murder of his son Zachariah by Shallum (2 Kings xv. 10) led to those disastrous commotions which culminated in the conquest of Samaria by the Assyrians and the deportation of the people.

Vers. 10—17.—§ 4. *This bold prophecy, no longer conceived in general terms or referring to distant times, but distinct and personal, arouses the animosity of the priestly authorities at Bethel, who accuse Amos before the king, and warn him to leave the country without more words, or to fear the worst.*

Ver. 10.—**Amaziah the priest of Bethel.** Amaziah ("the Lord is strong"), the chief of the idol-priests at Bethel, a crafty and determined man, hearing this prophecy against the royal house, takes it up as a political matter, and makes a formal accusation against Amos with the view of silencing him. **Hath conspired against thee.** Probably some of the Israelites had been convinced by the prophet's words, and had joined themselves to him; hence Amaziah speaks of "a conspiracy" (1 Sam. xxii. 8, 13; 1 Kings xv. 27) against the king. Or very possibly the story was fabricated in order to accentuate the charge against Amos. **In the midst of the house of Israel.** In the very centre of the kingdom, where his treasonable speeches would have the greatest effect. The land, personified, cannot endure such language, which is calculated to disturb its peace, and is quite contrary to its ideas and hopes.

Ver. 11.—This is a partly correct account of what the prophet had said, but it differed in some important particulars. Amaziah carefully omits the fact that Amos had merely been the mouthpiece of God in all his announcements; he says falsely that a violent death had been predicted for Jeroboam himself; and, in stating that Amos had foretold the captivity of Israel, he says nothing of the sins which led to this doom, or of the hope held out to repentance, or of the prophet's intercession.

Ver. 12.—**Also Amaziah said.** Jeroboam appears to have taken no steps in consequence of this accusation, either deeming that the words of a visionary were unworthy of serious consideration, or, like Herod (Matt. xiv. 5), fearing the people, who had been impressed by the prophet's words and bold bearing. Therefore Amaziah endeavours by his own authority to make Amos leave the country, or else does not wait for the command of the king, who was probably at Samaria. **O thou seer!** Amaziah calls Amos *chozeh*, ὁ ὁρῶν (1 Chron. xxi. 9; xxv. 5), either with reference to the visions just given, or in derision of his claims—as we might say, "visionary." **Flee thee away;** fly for thine own good to escape punishment, patronizing and counselling him. **Go to the land of Judah;** where doubtless your announcement of the ruin of the rival kingdom will be acceptable. **Eat bread.** Amaziah speaks as if Amos was paid for his prophecies, made a gain of godliness. **Prophesy there.** "Vaticinare in terra Juda, ubi libenter audiuntur insani" (St. Jerome). The idolatrous priest has no conception of the in-

spiration under which the prophet speaks. He judges others by himself, attributing to Amos the sordid motives by which he himself was influenced.

Ver. 13.—**The king's chapel;** *i.e.* "a sanctuary" (Exod. xxv. 8; Lev. xix. 30) founded by the king (1 Kings xii. 28), not by God. So in truth it had only an earthly sanction, and the prophet of the Lord was out of place there. **The king's court;** literally, *house of the kingdom.* "National temple" (Kuenen); "a royal temple, the state church" (Pusey). Not the political, but the religious, capital, the chief seat of the religion appertaining to the nation. Amaziah speaks as a thorough Erastian; as if the human authority were everything, and the Lord, of himself, had no claims on the land.

Ver. 14.—The prophet, undaunted by Amaziah's threats, in simple language declares that he does not practise prophecying as a profession or to gain a livelihood, but in obedience to the voice of God. The exercise of the prophetical office was restricted neither to sex nor rank. There were many prophetesses in Israel, *e.g.* Deborah (Judg. iv.), Huldah (2 Kings xxii. 14), Noadiah (Neh. vi. 14); and besides a large number of nameless prophets there are twenty-three whose names are preserved in Holy Writ, omitting those whose writings have come down to us (Ladd, 'Doctrine of Scripture,' i. 117, etc.). **A prophet's son;** *i.e.* brought up in the schools of the prophets, the pupils of which were called "sons of the prophets" (see 1 Kings xx. 35; 2 Kings ii. 5). Amos was neither self-commissioned nor trained in any human institution. **A herdman** (*boger*); usually "a cow-herd;" here "a shepherd;" αἰπόλος (Septuagint). **A gatherer of sycomore fruit.** The phrase, *boles shiqmim,* may mean either one who plucks mulberry-figs for his own sustenance, or one who cultivates them for others. The latter is probably the meaning of the term here. The Septuagint rendering, κνίζων συκάμινα, "pricking sycamore fruit," and that of the Vulgate, *vellicans sycomoros,* indicate the artificial means for ripening the fruit, which was done by scraping, scratching, or puncturing it, as is sometimes done to the figs of commerce. As the tree bore many crops of fruit in the year, it would afford constant employment to the dresser (see 'Dict. of the Bible,' iii. p. 1394; 'Bible Educator,' iv. p. 343).

Ver. 15.—**As I followed;** literally, *from after, from behind,* as in the call of David (2 Sam. vii. 8; Ps. lxxviii. 70). The Divine call came to him suddenly and imperatively, and he must needs obey it. He, therefore, could not follow Amaziah's counsel.

Ver. 16.—Hear thou the word of the Lord. The punishment of him who tried to impede God's message. Drop not thy word. Be not continually pouring forth prophecy. The word is used similarly in Micah ii. 6, 11 and Ezek. xxi. 2. The idea, though not the term, is taken from Deut. xxxii. 2. Septuagint, μὴ ὀχλαγωγήσῃς, "raise no tumult," which rather expresses Amaziah's fear of the effect of the utterance than translates the word. St. Jerome's explanation is somewhat too subtle, "*Stillare prophetas idioma Scripturarum est, quod non totam Dei simul inferant iram, sed parvas stillas comminatione denuntient.*"

Ver. 17.—With this denunciation compare that of Jeremiah (xx. 3, etc.) against Pashur. As husband, as father, as citizen, Amaziah shall suffer grievously. Shall be an harlot in the city. Not play the harlot willingly, but suffer open violence when the city is taken (comp. Isa. xiii. 16; Lam. v. 11). And thy daughters. This would be abnormal cruelty, as the Assyrians usually spared the women of conquered towns. Shall be divided by line. Amaziah's own land was to be portioned out to strangers by the measuring-line (Zech. ii. 2). A polluted land; *an unclean land;* i.e. a Gentile country. Amaziah himself was to share his countrymen's captivity. The sins and idolatry of the people are often said to defile the land; *e.g.* Lev. xviii. 25; Numb. xxxv. 33; Jer. ii. 7. Shall surely go into captivity; or, *be led away captive.* Amos repeats the very words which formed part of his accusation (ver. 11), in order to show that God's purpose is unchanged, and that he, the prophet, must utter the same denunciation (see the accomplishment, 2 Kings xvii. 6).

HOMILETICS.

Vers. 1—3.—*The vision of devouring locusts.* The prophet is appropriately called a seer. He sees clear and he sees far. Not only has Amos foresight of what is coming; he has insight into what, in certain circumstances, would have come. He is taken as it were behind the scenes, and made a witness of the forging of Heaven's thunderbolts, to be laid up for use as occasion may require. In this case he is cognizant by spiritual intuition of the preparation of judicial measures which, as circumstances turn out, are never executed.

I. ALL HIS CREATURES ARE MINISTERS OF GOD TO DO HIS WILL. The angels are his "hosts"—ministers of his that do his pleasure. The Assyrian was the rod of his anger. He says, "I will command the serpent, and it shall bite them." He maketh the winds his messengers, the flaming fire his minister (Ps. civ. 4). All created things, in fact, are but different elements in a vast ministry, by which he executes his purpose. 1. *Judgments are generally brought about by second causes.* To this rule there is scarcely an exception. Sometimes it is famine, brought about by drought, or mildew, or locusts. Sometimes it is desolating war, brought about by jealousy, love of power, and greed. Sometimes it is pestilence, the result of causes all within the natural sphere. We know nothing of afflictive judgments coming apart from the interposition of the causes out of which they would naturally arise. 2. *Second causes are all in the hands of the First Cause.* They do not operate at random. Theirs is action "co-operant to an end." They are adjusted and controlled. They are combined in schemes of order and proportion, nicely fitted to the achievement of their ultimate results. The eye is of the blindest that cannot see how—

"Behind the dim unknown
Standeth God, within the shadow, keeping watch above his own."

(Lowell.)

3. *Natural causes are prepared and used for a moral end.* Manasseh's captivity leads to his conversion (2 Chron. xxxiii. 11—13). Israel's desert discipline cultivates a robustness of national character which was wanting at the Exodus (Isa. xliii. 21). So a long captivity in heathen Babylon puts an end to the ever-recurring national idolatry. When all God's measures were executed, he could look on the Hebrews and say, "This people have I formed for myself; they shall show forth my praise." And that is God's method in all cases. Scripture declares, and experience and observation argue—

"All discord, harmony not understood;
All partial evil, universal good."

(Pope.

II. God's agents strike in the nick of time. "He formed locusts in the beginning of the springing up of the second crop." In consequence of the timing of this judgment, it is: 1. *More thorough-going.* If the locusts had been sent earlier, there might have been time after they had gone for the second crop to grow. If they had come later, it might have been already saved. God will not beat the air. He will strike how and when and where the culprit shall feel his blow. 2. *It is more striking.* The element of time is the chief index to the miraculous character of many events. They follow immediately on the Divine word or act, and so reveal themselves to be Divine works. The catching of a netful of fishes, or the sudden calming of a storm, or the recovery of a woman from fever, were none of them necessarily miraculous events. It was their occurrence at the Saviour's word that revealed the Divine agency in them. The coming of the locusts at the prophet's word, and at the critical time, revealed God's hand in the event. 3. *It is more effectual.* A judgment is likely to serve its disciplinary purpose in proportion as it is real, appropriate, and manifestly of God. The difference between a timely judgment and an untimely one would be the difference between one blessed to its proper effect and one utterly futile.

III. They make an end of the work they take in hand. In all that God does we should expect thoroughness. 1. *There is the power.* All forces and agents are under his control. He can bring them to bear in any quantity and on any point. For him "nothing is too hard," and "all things are possible." When God lifts his hand he can "smite through." 2. *There is the need.* Divine judgments never come unneeded, nor till it is evident that nothing else will do. Each is wanted, and the whole of each. If anything less, or anything else, were sent it would be inadequate. The last atom of imagined strength must be destroyed. The last remnant of fancied resource must be swept away. Only when every conceivable prop has been knocked away will men be brought to their knees in absolute submission.

IV. The hand of judgment may be arrested by the touch of prayer. "Jehovah repented of this: It shall not take place, saith Jehovah." The pictured events never transpired. The adoption and abandonment of them as retributive measures occurred only in vision. Still, a parallel for this "plastic vision" may be found in God's actual doings, as in the case of the antediluvians, of Saul, of Hezekiah, of Jerusalem, and of Nineveh (Gen. vi. 6; 1 Sam. xv. 11; Isa. xxxviii. 1—5; 2 Sam. xxiv. 16; Jonah iii. 10). As to this: 1. *God does not change his mind, but his method.* His immutability arising out of his infinity is clearly revealed (Numb. xxiii. 19; 1 Sam. xv. 29; Ezek. xxiv. 14; Mal. iii. 6). As self-existent and independent he is above the causes of change, whilst as an absolute Being he is above the possibility of it. And the immutability of his Being is true of his purpose. His ends are unchallengeably right and his means resistlessly powerful. He may change his method, and often does. Up to a certain point is mercy. Then it is expostulation, denunciation, and judgment in quick succession. When one method fails to bring about desired results, another and another are resorted to by a God who will not fail. The variation of method is really the expression of an unalterable plan. 2. *This change of method is correlative to a change of circumstances.* It is the varying of the one that leads to the varying of the other. New circumstances justify and even call for a new line of action. Yet these circumstances are themselves part of his wider purpose, which therefore remains unchanged and unchangeable. 3. *Such a change of circumstances is often the introduction of the element of prayer.* This is a new factor in the problem, and puts another complexion on the case. Nineveh, sinning with a high hand, God said he would destroy. But Nineveh, praying in dust and ashes, was a different thing. God does not destroy penitent people. This, and not the sparing of them, would imply a change of purpose, and even of nature itself. Intercessory prayer, as here, modifies the circumstances in a different way; but the modification is real, and will be co-ordinated with a corresponding modification in God's way. 4. *The necessity of a case is a legitimate plea with God.* "How can Jacob stand? for it is small." So David prays, "Pity me, for I am weak." God's blessings are not only gifts, but mercies. He bestows them freely, and in pity for our need. The extremity of this need is, therefore, its strength as an appeal for God's help. "My God shall supply all your need, according to his riches in glory by Christ Jesus."

Ver. 2.—*The problem of stability.* The prayer of faith is free. The believing soul has the privilege of reasoning with God, and embraces it. It asks what it wills, and as it wills, and for whom it wills. There is room for originality in it, and scope for inventive resource; yet little risk of impropriety. The Spirit safeguards that in an effective "unction." Then grace is one thing ever, and there is a ground-plan of supplication which is practically the same with all the faithful. It has centrifugal energy, flowing from the individual outwards. Its rivers wind and wander and discharge themselves ultimately on the desolate places of ungodly lives; but they run first by the homes of the household of faith. And then it has a spiritual stream. It blesses temporal interests too, but leaves its fertilizing ooze most richly on the things of the religious life. Of the prophet's prayer here all this is characteristic. It reveals to us—

I. JACOB'S ACTUALITY. "Small." There is a natural Israel and a spiritual Israel also, the one at once the type and the germ of the other. The Christian Church is not distinct from, but a continuation and expansion of, the Jewish; and both together are the one visible Church of God. To this, an already existing community, many were added at Pentecost (Acts ii. 47). In the congregation of Israel to which the sweet psalmist sang (Ps. xxii. 22) Paul sees the one Church of God (Heb. ii. 12); and with Stephen (Acts vii. 38) the wandering host of the tribes (Exod. xvi. 2) was nothing else than the "Church in the wilderness." This Church, continuous from the beginning, and one in all ages, is the "good olive tree" (Rom. xi. 17—24), whose Jewish "branches" excised, and again to be "graffed in," are meantime displaced by the ingraffed Gentile shoots, which partake "of the root and fatness of the olive tree." In Amos's time it was a little flock, whose preservation was matter to him of anxiety and prayer. 1. *He is small in comparison with Esau.* The heathen around outnumbered Israel overwhelmingly. Left to itself in the struggle among them for existence, it would inevitably have been swallowed up. So with the spiritual Israel. Satan has had in his kingdom a majority of the race for so far. Faith-gate is a strait one, Purity-way is a narrow one (Matt. vii. 13, 14), and the saints who enter the one and follow the other are a little flock (Luke xii. 32). And no wonder. Unbelief is natural, living after the flesh is congenial (Exod. xxiii. 2), and an overwhelming preference for both is a foregone conclusion. Hence, not only has the Church been smaller than the world, but within the Church itself the wheat has apparently been less than the tares. Relatively to Esau, Jacob is, and has been, small indeed. 2. *He is small in comparison with what he might have been.* Smallness is sometimes a misfortune, but it was Israel's fault. It was a result of persistent national sin, drawing down the destroying judgments of Heaven. Their ranks had been thinned by war, or pestilence, or famine in just and necessary retribution for their incorrigible unfaithfulness. So the small number of the saints is the sin of all concerned. It means opportunities neglected, ordinances abused, and a Holy Spirit resisted. None of the agencies of a heavenly culture have been withheld (Isa. v. 1—4). Every unbeliever is such in despite of influences that ought to have brought him to faith (Acts vii. 51). Every spiritual weakling is one who has debilitated himself (Heb. v. 12; 1 Cor. iii. 1—3). Moreover, as workers for God the saints are not guiltless, for which of them has exercised his full influence for good? The difference between what the Church is and what she might have been is the measure of her delinquency before God. When the sun shines and the showers fall, something subjective is wrong with the crop that stunts. 3. *He is small in comparison with what he will yet be.* Israel is not yet full grown. The Gentiles are Abraham's seed (Gal. iii. 7), and their in-bringing is the increase of spiritual Israel. That increase is to attain world-wide proportions yet. The Church's limits shall be the ends of the earth (Ps. lxxii. 8), and its constituents the heathen nations (Ps. ii. 8; lxxii. 11). It shall be a centre to which all the peoples shall gravitate (Isa. ii. 2). It shall be a light illuminating and incorporating in its own radiance the entire globe (Hab. ii. 14). It is only a stone as yet, but it will be a mountain one day, and fill the whole earth (Dan. ii. 35, 44). In the faith of such a destiny the Church may well find strength to avail her, even in the day of small things.

II. JACOB'S IDEAL. "Stand." It is assumed here that he ought to stand; that standing is his appropriate and normal position. And so it is. In the ideal and purpose and promise, and as the handiwork of God, he is not to fall. He is: 1. *To stand against destruction*. Israel was not to perish. Low she might fall, small she might become, contemptible she might long remain; but in all, and through all, and after all, she was to live. The spiritual Israel has a perpetuity of existence also. The individual Christian "shall never perish" (John x. 28). The grace that is in him is a Divine thing, and indestructible (Gal. ii. 20). His life is a living Christ within, and he is immortal while Christ lives. This involves that the Church—God's kingdom—is an everlasting kingdom. If even a member cannot perish, much less the whole body. Redeemed by his Son, and dowered in permanence with his Spirit, the Church stands, let what may fall (Dan. ii. 44). A structure of God's building, on a foundation of God's laying, according to a plan of God's devising, it stands impregnable on its rock (Matt. xvi. 18), and the gates of hell cannot prevail against it. Its immovable stability is a question of Divine will and resource. There is the unchangeable purpose, the unconquerable power, the inviolable promise. The house is impregnable over which these three mount triple guard (John x. 28). In the soil of God's plan, in the rock-cleft of his might, in the showers and sunshine of his pledge, the fair Church-flower can neither fall nor fade, but must bloom while the ages run. 2. *To stand against temptation*. Israel was separate and to be pure. The Divine ideal was set before her not to mingle with the nations, nor serve their gods, nor learn their ways (Numb. xxiii. 9; Deut. vi. 14; xviii. 9). So with the Church as a whole, and individual members in particular. Temptation in some degree is inevitable. While within is the iron of a corrupt nature, and outside the loadstone of a corrupt surrounding, there will be the drawing toward sin. But while God is stronger than the devil, and his grace stronger than sin, there shall not be a lapsing into wickedness. The word of acceptance is peace-bringing. The change by regeneration is radical. The measure of grace conferred is sufficient (2 Cor. xii. 9). Therefore Israel, harnessed in armour of proof, shall defy the devil's darts, and stand in the evil day (Eph. vi. 13). The bride of Christ will abide in loyal love, and be to eye and heart at last his "undefiled," with no spot in her (Cant. vi. 9; iv. 7). She may grow languid almost to slothfulness, but even in her sleep her "heart waketh" (Cant. v. 2—6). Her love may at times burn low (Matt. xxiv. 12), but the fire remains alight, and glows at the slightest breath from heaven. In the end she is presented to Christ a glorious Church, without spot, or wrinkle, or any such thing (Eph. v. 27). 3. *To stand against misfortune*. From this there is no earthly immunity (Job v. 7). God's Israel will get a share, and a large share, of the shocks of calamity. There will even be special evils to which their character will expose them alone of men. But over against this stand the Divine helps which also are theirs alone. God is for them. They are the objects of a special providence. The Divine favour—their shield and buckler—is armour of proof. The darts of evil are turned aside, and fall pointless and broken to the ground. Nay, the evil, having been endured and survived, may be utilized. God constitutes it the appropriate and effective means of a heavenly culture (Heb. xii. 11; 2 Cor. iv. 17). It destroys nothing, not even a hair of their head; and it prunes the tree into richer and choicer fruit-bearing. It even increases future glory, adding the piquancy of contrast to its otherwise perfect bliss.

III. JACOB'S ATTAINMENT OF HIS IDEAL A CARE OF GOD. God concerns himself about all that concerns his people. The prophet assumes that one way or other Jacob is bound to be upheld, and that God in the last appeal will see it done. As to this ideal: 1. *God loves it*. It is set up by his own hand, and characterized by his own excellences, and it must be a thing after his own heart. All the graces that are acceptable with God shine in the saints, and the interests dear to his heart are those with which they are inseparably identified. Righteous himself, he loveth righteousness; unchangeable, he loveth steadfastness; and the things his heart loves his hand will guard. 2. *God appoints it*. Salvation from first to last is of his devising. He decides that salvation shall be, and what, and how. It is the purpose of his adorable grace, and therefore something along the lines of which he may be expected to work. He has predestinated the individual "to be conformed to the image of his Son," and the Church to "come to a perfect man." And we may safely reckon that his measures will work in these directions; helping the individual, that he is "changed into the same image from glory to glory;" and blessing the Church, that she gathers up and exemplifies in her many-sidedness the graces of Christ's faultless character. The Divine forceful action propels things in the direction of the Divine gracious appointment. 3. *God has already committed himself to it.* To Israel his word of promise was pledged, "I will never leave thee nor forsake thee." To us it is pledged with greater emphasis still, "They shall never perish;" "Whom he justified, them he also glorified," etc. None shall pluck the Christian out of Christ's hand, nor shall the gates of hell prevail against his Church. The circle of the promises towers a wall of fire around the saints. The result is pledged to them; so are the means. The inheritance is reserved for them, and they for the inheritance (1 Pet. i. 4, 5). Their faith will keep them, and God will keep their faith (1 Pet. i. 5). *Then God had already begun to help.* Israel had been upheld in many an evil. And there is continuity in the operations of God. He does not abandon a work once begun, nor allow after-disaster to neutralize accomplished good. He had done something for Israel; he has done something for us. Then he will do more, and he will do all. Having bestowed his grace, he swears by the gift that the circle of our good will be made complete. A part already of the work of God, invulnerable in his armour, and immortal in his life, they have "a strong consolation," surely, "who have fled for refuge," etc.

IV. THE WHOLE MATTER A FITTING SUBJECT OF PRAYER. The prophet comes between God and Israel as an intercessor. In his act we see that: 1. *Prayer is a universal means of grace.* "Men ought always to pray;" "In everything by prayer and supplication," etc. There is no blessing, temporal or spiritual, that is not the gift of God. There is no way of securing the least of these but by seeking it in prayer. The heart must throb continuously if the blood would be driven through the body; the breath must be regularly drawn if this blood would be purified and oxidized. So prayer, the throb of the new heart, the breath of the new creature, must go on if the new life is to be maintained. The interruption of it means the suspension of the most essential vital function. There is nothing we can count on getting without it (Ezek. xxxvi. 37; Jas. iv. 2). There is nothing legitimate we may despair of getting by it (John xiv. 13). In prayer the soul puts forth its tentacles round about, and lays hold of good on every side. 2. *Prayer is a universal instinct of grace.* All vital functions go on without an act of the will or the exercise of attention. And so with prayer in the new-created soul. It does not require a specific injunction. It does not wait on an effort of the will. It goes up as naturally as the hunger-cry of the young raven. The new man breathes, the new heart pulsates, the opened lips speak, and the action in each case is prayer. "Behold, he prayeth," is an infallible token of a converted man. 3. *Prayer is expansive like grace.* Sin is selfish. Seeking salvation, the sinner prays for himself only. He is conscious of need, but as yet knows nothing of supply. Only when he gets spiritual blessing himself does he know how valuable it would be to others, and begin to desire it for them. Selfishness gives way with sin. Philanthropy grows with the love of God. And prayer answers to and expresses the change. The prayer-circle widens as personal religion deepens. Its instinct is catholic. It goes out to the Church of the Firstborn. It seeks the coming of the kingdom. We pray for Israel when we are Israelites indeed. Request for the household of faith is God's will, the Church's weal, and the spontaneous offering of the gracious soul.

Vers. 4—6.—*The vision of consuming fire.* The prophet's vision goes on, and the situation in it becomes more critical. One woe is averted only for a worse to take its place. The Divine avenging hosts remain in battle-line. They return to the attack with renewed vigour. For the fusillade is substituted the booming of the great guns. Escaping as by the skin of their teeth from the wasting locust, incorrigible Israel are met in the prophet's eye by the devouring fire. In connection with this second scene in the panoramic vision notice—

I. GOD CONTENDING BY FIRE. Again and again is it so in Scripture. 1. *It is the most destuctive element in nature.* It destroys all comfort, inflicting intense pain. It destroys all life, no animal or vegetable organism being capable of enduring it. It destroys the very form of organic matter, reducing it to its original elements. It destroys with unparalleled rapidity and thoroughness almost anything it attacks.

2. *It is the element used and to be used by God in bringing about the greatest catastrophes.* It was in the fire-shower from heaven that Sodom was overwhelmed (Gen. xix. 24). Fire "very grievous" was mingled with the plague of hail which smote the land of Egypt (Exod. ix. 24). It was the fire of the Lord that burnt up complaining Israel at Taberah, and also Korah and his company in their gainsaying (Numb. xi. 1; xxvi. 10). By fire from heaven were Ahaziah's two captains and their fifties consumed before Elijah (2 Kings i. 10—12). It was by bringing down fire that James and John proposed to destroy the inhospitable Samaritans (Luke ix. 54). And it is in a lake burning with fire that the beast, the false prophet, and all the finally impenitent shall be overwhelmed at last. 3. *It is in Scripture a frequent emblem of active power.* God the Father in wrath (Deut. iv. 24; ix. 3), God the Son in judgment (2 Thess. i. 8), God the Holy Ghost in grace, are each so figured (Luke iii. 16). Indwelling sin is fire (1 Cor. vii. 9; 2 Cor. xi. 29); the busy mischief-making tongue is fire (Jas. iii. 6); God's Word is a fire (Jer. xxiii. 29); his ministers are "burning ones" (seraphim); spiritual life is fire (Luke xii. 49); affliction is fire (1 Cor. iii. 13; 1 Pet. iv. 12); and the misery of the finally lost is fire (Mark ix. 44). A God contending by fire is a God putting forth the extreme of destructive energy.

II. JUDGMENT DRINKING UP THE GREAT DEEP. As the fire is figurative, so probably is the "deep." It is the heathen world. God's judgment which includes this is: 1. *Discriminating.* "The deep." The sweltering, restless sea is a fit symbol of the wicked in their unrest of heart and rebellion against God (Isa. lvii. 20; Ps. xlvi. 3). These are the natural prey of the eagles of judgment. They deserve it, provoke it, and are its characteristic objects. The righteous may suffer sometimes with the wicked, but the ungodly cannot escape. 2. *Extensive.* "The great deep." Not merely "wells," which are individuals (2 Pet. ii. 7), nor "rivers," which are nations (Isa. viii. 7; Jer. xlvi. 7, 8), nor "seas," which are races (Ps. lxv. 7; Isa. xvii. 12), but "the great deep," or rebellious humanity in its entire extent, shall be contended with and destroyed. When the last word has been spoken God's argument against sin will be overwhelming; and all the ground covered by sin will have been covered also by judgment.

III. JUDGMENT EATING UP "THE PORTION" DOOMED. "Probably the definite portion foreappointed by God to captivity and desolation" (Pusey). 1. *God's acts are coextensive with his decrees.* His plan has reference to all events, and these in turn exactly embody his plan. He had devoted beforehand a definite number to judgment; and all these, and these only, would it eat up in the day of its falling. No tares escape, nor is any wheat burned. "The Lord knoweth them that are his." 2. *To be nominally God's people establishes no special relation to him.* Outward relations, if they have not inward relations to which they correspond, are nothing. Mere names and semblances leave unchanged the underlying realities which God regards, and to which his dealings are adjusted. A hollow profession is simply unbelief plus hypocrisy. 3. *God's judgments on his professing people are not for annihilation, but for weeding out.* The "portion" was not all Israel (Isa. x. 20—22; xxxvii. 31, 32). After it had been devoured, a remnant would remain. Judgments are the gardener's knife; they prune out the worthless branches, but leave the tree. Exposure to the wind is not for destruction of the wheat, but for the scattering of the chaff. In the track of the fire is to be found all that is fire-proof.

IV. THE LEGITIMATE MEASURE OF ASKING IN PRAYER. (Ver. 5.) It seems a forlorn hope to offer such prayer. Yet here it is done by a man under the guidance of God's Spirit. In imitation of him: 1. *We may ask anything that is innocent.* It may not be promised. No one else may have received it. It may be a thing utterly unlikely to be done. It may be what God is threatening not to do. Yet it is legitimate matter of prayer, and we need not despair of it. God cannot do less than he promises, but he may do more; and, as a matter of fact, he does much for which no explicit promise is to be found. 2. *We may ask any amount that can be enjoyed.* God's is no niggard heart or hand. He has exhaustless store. He loves to see us filled and thoroughly furnished. Hence he giveth liberally, satisfies with his mercy, gives all we can receive, and more than we can ask or think. Economy in asking where there is infinity to draw on is modesty run mad. 3. *We may ask it up till the last moment.* While, in the nature of things, answer is possible, request may be made. Who knows whether evil may not be averted until it has actually fallen? Besieged cities have been saved even after the garrison had thrown open the gates, and battles won after the ranks of the victors had begun to break. With God all things are possible, and by prayer he is always moved. Till the moment of death we may pray for life, for salvation till the moment of destruction. 4. *Having received, we may ask again and again.* "Men ought always to pray." Prayer has reference to returning wants, and is normally a habit of soul. As often as we hunger we eat, and, on the same principle, as often as we need we pray. Continued prayer is matter of necessity, a command of God, and an instinct of the soul. "In everything by prayer and supplication," etc. Half a century later the mercy of God's dealings appeared. After ravaging the greater portion of the land, the Assyrians unaccountably withdrew, and left the capital untouched. The connection between Amos's prayer and the unwonted slackness of Tiglath-Pileser belongs to that region into which sense cannot penetrate, but which is all patent to the eye of faith.

V. THE MERCIFUL ASPECT OF GOD'S THREATS. (Ver. 6.) The perseverance of the prophet's prayer is justified by the event. God's threat is not executed. Judgment is arrested on the way. Does God, then, change? No; but circumstances do, and with them his adjusted mode of action. The unexecuted threat is not unmeaning nor unnecessary. 1. *It forewarns of the coming evil.* When the black clouds rise we know the storm is brewing. So when God speaks we know he is going to act and how. A threat is a conditional prophecy. It tells us exactly what, in given circumstances, we may expect. Knowledge of the evil coming is a prerequisite to any measure of precaution. 2. *It thereby often turns from the path in which the evil lies.* All actions have their proper issues, and whatever changes the one changes the other. God's judgments are directed against us as transgressors in a certain way. If we cease so to transgress the reason for them is gone, and they will not be sent. The knowledge of these two facts operates as a powerful incentive to reformation, and so a means to the arrest of impending judgment. We face a different way when we adequately realize that we thereby face a different end. 3. *It displays God's character in a most attractive aspect.* He warns before he strikes. He warns that he may not need to strike at all. His threats are the merciful heralds of his judgments, offering terms of peace before the stern hour of intervention arrives. "Except ye repent, ye shall all likewise perish." A threat like that is only a promise in disguise. It speaks of a gracious heart which "wills not that any should perish, but that all should come to repentance."

Vers. 7—9.—*Righteousness to the plumb-line.* There has been reprieve after reprieve. The enemy of God's wrath has been met in the breach by intercessory prayer, and, for the time, turned back. Once and again the hounds of vengeance have been cried off. But respite is not escape. There is a certain limit beyond which the system of Divine reprieves cannot go. And that limit has now been reached. The locust has been disappointed of his meal. The fire has been beaten back from the tinder. But the criminal is obdurate, and now the plumb-line is applied to the bowing wall, and the word goes forth to overturn and destroy utterly. In this graphic delineation we notice—

I. THE WALL. This figure for Israel (ver. 8) suggests: 1. *Something built.* Other nations grow up as it may happen, shaped by the circumstances in which they arise. The nation of Israel was not a natural growth, but a Divine creation. "This people have I formed for myself." So with the Church. It is not a voluntary association. It is not a human institution. It is a vineyard of God's husbandry, a house of God's building (Matt. xvi. 18). Every stone in it is quarried and chiselled and laid by the Divine hand. 2. *Something strong.* A wall has substance, stability, resisting power, and is in Scripture emblematic of these things (Ezek. iv. 3; Isa. xxv. 4; Zech. ii. 5). In regard to these qualities Israel is a wall. God is "known within her palaces for a Refuge." Salvation is to her for walls and bulwarks. In these things is her strength; and fortified thus, she "shall not be moved" (Ps. xlvi. 5). 3. *Something upright.* "Made by a plumb-line." God "made man upright." And he made Israel upright. Whatever comes out of his hands comes out of them free of any moral twist. It is made according to righteousness. Formed into a nation by God, Israel had a constitution, laws, and administration theoretically faultless. The uprightness of this God-built wall was a main condition of its strength. In the perfection of the one was the perfection of the other. The loss of one would be the loss of both. The wall that leans is about to fall.

II. THE PLUMB-LINE. This is the regulating appliance, and the testing instrument with which the building must tally. 1. *It is righteousness.* Righteousness in the moral world answers to straightness in the world of matter. It is the moral rectilineal, or line of "oughtness"—the line along which moral beings ought to move. This is manifestly the plumb-line by which to adjust the wall Israel to the perpendicular. Exemplified in the character, this righteousness is uprightness. Exemplified in the conduct, it is justice. In either case it is the ideal of rightness. 2. *It is righteousness as it exists in God.* God is universal Perfection—"Light," "Love," "Truth," "the Holy One," "the righteous God," and all in ideal form. He is, in fact, the typical moral Being. Each grace exists in him in its highest form. His righteousness is unspotted righteousness, and the realized ideal of all that righteousness ought to be. 3. *It is this righteousness as it is revealed in Scripture.* Scripture is the rule of man, just as being the revelation of God. What he is is our Model. What he does is our Exemplar. What he is and does and requires is the burden of Scripture—a formulation of his whole will. "To the Law and to the testimony," etc. By the Law must Israel be tried, its true character revealed, and its fitting destiny settled. "Those that have sinned in the Law shall be judged by the Law." The Law is the unerring plumb-line, exposing every deviation from the moral perpendicular.

III. THE TESTING. "Behold, I will set," etc. (ver. 8). This is to apply the plumb-line to the wall, so as to reveal irregularity if it exists. 1. *This is no longer to be put off.* "I shall pass by it no more." The limit of Divine forbearance was now reached. No more passing by, no longer indulgence, no further forgiveness, no more postponement of the vengeance vowed. There is a last word of God to every man, and after it nothing can come but the blow. 2. *The wall is to be tried by the rule it was built by.* (Ver. 7.) "He destroys it by that same rule of right wherewith he had built it. By that law, that right, those providential leadings, that grace which we have received, by the same we are judged" (Pusey). God has only one standard, and he uses it always. Things ought to be as he made them, and he tries them to discover if they are so. The measure of divergence from original righteousness, whether in men or Churches, is the measure of guilt in the diverging party. Comparison with its own pure ideal would bring out Israel's corruption in the strongest light. 3. *The testing is to be one of the entire nation.* "The wall is not the emblem of Samaria, or of any one city. It is the strength and defence of the whole people" (Pusey). There was general deflection, and to discover this there will be a general plumbing. All the wall must be tested before it can be all destroyed.

IV. THE DEMOLITION. The wall is found to have bowed, and the word is given to pull it down. In this destruction would be involved : 1. *The idolatrous places.* "The sacrificial heights of Isaac," all the high places at Dan, Bethel, and Gilgal, where idol-worship was carried on. In the wasting of these would appear, on the one hand, the vanity of idol-worship, and, on the other, God's special wrath against it—matters which it was necessary to emphasize in the mind of idol-loving Israel. 2. *Idolatrous objects.* "The holy things of Israel" (ver. 9) are the objects and adjuncts of their idolatrous worship. Dan and Bethel, as rivals of Jerusalem, having been desolated, Baal, Ashtaroth, etc., as rivals of Jehovah, would be destroyed. Broken idols and levelled shrines would alone remain, a commentary on the impotence of the "lying vanities" to which blinded Israel persistently turned. 3. *The Hebrew monarchy.* "The house of Jeroboam" was the reigning family. It was the last dynasty of the Israelitish monarchy. In it and with it was to perish (Hos. i. 4), and did perish, "the kingdom of the house of Israel." The royal house was so identified with the national idol-worship as of necessity to be involved in whatever destruction this provoked. It was specially fitting, moreover, that the family of the arch-idolater should be the one to sink in the burning grave of the idolatry he set up.

Vers. 10—17.—*Machination foiled by fearless candour.* Amos had deserved well of Israel. He took a more practical interest in their welfare than any other man from the king down. He saw their sin, and lamented it ; their impending ruin, and would have averted it; their one way of escape, and pressed its adoption strenuously. Had they not been as blind as besotted, they would have revered him as a national benefactor. But the reformation he preached meant the abandonment of rooted habits and the harassing of vested interests in sin, neither of which would be so much as named. Accordingly, Amos anticipated the experience of all reformers since, in being assailed by a policy of falsehood, backed by force. We have here—

I. A MEDDLING PRIEST. "The priest of Bethel" was the chief idol-priest at the sanctuary of the golden calf there. His position and functions were in profane mimicry of those of the high priest at Jerusalem. In making this charge: 1. *He appeals to force.* The tyrant Jeroboam was the embodiment of irresponsible power in Israel. Idolatry is the religion of brute force. Its appeal to the strong arm as the only argument worth using is characteristic. Error eschews argument. The kingdom of darkness instinctively fears the light. What is an outrage on reason takes its shelter fitly behind a sword. "My kingdom is not of this world;" "The weapons of your warfare are not carnal." The true religion makes its appeal to truth. The religion that appeals to the sword is *primâ facie* false. 2. *He is prompted by jealousy.* He had a vested interest in the national idolatry. To abolish it would be to take the bread out of his mouth. Like the chief priests and scribes with Christ, and the Ephesian silversmiths with Paul, Amaziah was striking for his livelihood. "He went away sorrowful, for he had great possessions." Conflicting self-interest, actual or supposed, is a constant and effective obstacle in the way of the religious life. It is the preliminary necessity of leaving all in act or spirit that makes the followers of the Lord so few. 3. *He makes a lying accusation.* (Ver. 11.) Amos had not really made either statement. That applied to Jeroboam had been made about Jeroboam's house. That about Israel had been accompanied by a call to repentance, and a conditional promise of escape, which modified its character altogether. The charge, therefore, consists of a lie and a half-truth, and is an attempt to work on the king's personal fears, by construing into a conspiracy against his kingdom and life what Amos did to save both. For this now stale device persecutors in all ages have shown a characteristic predilection. Christ was calumniously accused of speaking against Cæsar (Luke xxiii. 2; John xix. 12; Matt. xxii. 21). Paul was falsely charged with "doing contrary to the decrees of Cæsar," and "stirring up sedition among the Jews" (Acts xvii. 7; xxiv. 5). And often since has the assertion of liberty of conscience been construed into rebellion against the civil power. Falsehood and violence are the traditional propaganda of the kingdom of darkness. 4. *He judges the prophet's morals by the standard of his own.* (Ver. 12.) His relation to his own office was utterly sordid. He held the office of priest for the "bit of bread" it secured him. And he assumes that Amos is like himself. It is thus that the saint "judges the world, yet himself is judged of no man." Forming an estimate of the righteous, the wicked leave conscience out of the computation, and so vitiate the finding. 5. *He condemns idolatry by the argument he uses in its defence.* (Ver. 13.) "The king's sanctuary," set up and consecrated by the king, maintained by his authority, and subordinated to his purposes. The national idolatry was a creature of the king. Its claim to be a religion was no stronger than his claim to be a god. For religious ordinances state authority is so inadequate as only to expose them to suspicion—the suspicion of adjustment to a state policy rather than to the Word and glory of God.

II. A FAITHFUL PROPHET. Like every true man, Amos was: 1. *Humble.* (Ver. 14.) He remembers and confesses his lowly origin. He asks no respect but such as might be due to his native condition. He treats the prophetic office as an entirely unmerited dignity. His exercise of it was disinterested. He was neither a professional prophet nor the son of one. His prophesying was an incident, and the trust of Divine grace. The man whom office spoils was unfit for it. The religion that is puffed up by employment in God's work was never intelligent, or of a high order. 2. *Loyal to his Divine commission.* (Ver. 15.) In a believing life God is all. His will is the supreme interest and exclusive rule. God has chosen the man, and that means unconditional consecration. God has commissioned him, and he makes the fact the basis of his whole life-programme. "I must work the works of him that sent me." That is a comprehensive life-maxim. In the spiritual circle nothing is held supremely important but that God's work be done. 3. *Zealous.* Amos made the salvation of Israel a personal concern and his life-effort. He could think, speak, be active about nothing else. "The land could not bear his words," so vehement were they and so persistent. The advocacy that will take no refusal, that must be either yielded to or silenced, is that which alone beseems the stupendous importance of the cause of God. "The zeal of thine house hath eaten me up." If this is not an all-absorbing passion, it is not after the one Example. 4. *Bold.* (Vers. 16, 17.) Prohibition is treated as a challenge. It only leads him to repeat and emphasize. There is no bravado in this, but only a supreme regard for the principle, "We ought to obey God rather than men." The King's messenger, on the King's business, must brook obstruction from none. The best soldier is the boldest. Perfect devotion to and faith in his Captain speaks in absolute fearlessness in his service. 5. *Explicit.* (Ver. 17.) The heathen oracles always "paltered in a double sense." After the event their deliverances could be reconciled with whatever happened. But the prophet, delivering God's message, is sure of his ground. He specifies details with confidence, for no jot or tittle of the Divine Word can fail. As in other cases, the fulfilment of this particular detail of the prophecy is not recorded (Isa. xxii. 17, 18; Jer. xxix. 22), nor could it be expected to be in the condensed account of the Scripture narrative. "Scripture hath no leisure to relate all which befalls those of the viler sort." Yet the broad fact of the Captivity and exile, accompanied by all the horrors of Oriental warfare, forms a constructive record of the events.

III. A HARROWING PICTURE. (Ver. 17.) These are the horrors born of idolatry. When Amaziah came to suffer them in his family he would know practically what his chosen idolatry was, and made of men. 1. *Family dishonour.* "Wife dishonoured," etc. A common atrocity (Isa. xiii. 16; Zech. xiv. 2), and to all concerned the most diabolically cruel conceivable. Between this crime and idolatry there are analogies, and probably affinities, in virtue of which the one is figuratively called by the name of the other (Jer. iii. 9; Ezek. xxiii. 37). The patron of the one is fitly punished by being made the victim of the other. The conduct of Turkish troops in recent wars, in respect to this matter, is a commentary on the assertion that Mohammedanism is a valuable protest against idolatry. 2. *Family impoverishment.* A Hebrew's property is inalienable. If he lost it by mismanagement, it reverted to his family at the jubilee. But the Assyrian would know nothing of jubilees. The chance of disgorgement was small when he had eaten up the inheritance. 3. *Family extermination.* We all like to perpetuate our name and family. The Hebrew had this feeling in almost unparalleled strength. To die childless was with him the sum of all disaster. What more appropriate than that it should wait on idolatry, "the sum of all sin"? 4. *Dishonoured death.* Dying in a strange country, both Jacob and Joseph made provision for being buried in their own land (Gen. xlvii. 30; l. 25; Heb. xi. 22). No Jew could die happy expecting burial in a heathen country. Exposure to such a fate would cap the climax of Amaziah's wretchedness. 5. *Exile for all Israel.* They had polluted their land, and were unworthy longer to remain in it. They had become assimilated to the heathen in their character and ways, and would be associated with them yet on closer terms. It was a holiday heathenism they were in love with, and they would be cured of their *penchant* by a sight of it in its working dress.

IV. A CLENCHING ARGUMENT. "The word of Jehovah." It was Amos who spoke it; but the word was God's. And it cannot be broken. The Divine truth is pledged to it. The Divine energy is lodged in it. The Divine purpose is couched in it. The thing it affirms is potentially a fact.

HOMILIES BY VARIOUS AUTHORS.

Ver. 2.—*Intercessory prayer.* In the language which the prophet employed in his appeal to God, he copied that of the great leader and lawgiver of his nation; and he was probably encouraged by remembering that Moses had not pleaded for Israel in vain.

I. THE PROMPTING TO INTERCESSORY PRAYER. Why should one man plead with God on another's behalf? It is evident that there is in human nature not only a principle of self-love, but also a principle of sympathy and benevolence. Amos interceded for the nation from which he sprang, in which he was interested, and which was endeared to him by sacred associations. He was well aware of his countrymen's offences, and of

God's just displeasure with them. He knew and had foretold that retribution should befall them. Yet he entreated mercy—a withholding of judgment, a little respite at the least. He identified himself with the sinful, and sought forbearance.

II. THE GROUND OF CONFIDENCE IN INTERCESSORY PRAYER. Amos could not ask for the withholding of punishment on the ground that punishment was undeserved; for he confessed that the people's sin had merited chastening. His reliance was not upon justice, but upon mercy. It was forgiveness he besought; and forgiveness presumes disobedience on the part of the subject and offence taken on the part of the ruler. In pleading for our fellow-men, as in pleading for ourselves, we have to rely upon the pity and loving-kindness of our God.

III. THE PLEA BY WHICH INTERCESSORY PRAYER IS URGED. "Who is Jacob?" is the language of the prophet. "Who is Jacob, that he should stand, that he should endure, if such a visitation befall him? He is feeble and impoverished." Thus, whilst the main reliance of him who intercedes must ever be upon the character and promises of the Eternal, he will naturally bring before God—as well known to the Omniscient—the weakness and helplessness of those whose interest he would promote. God is not as man. Men sometimes are found willing to favour the great, though they are indifferent to the woes of the obscure; whilst with God need, poverty, and helplessness are a commendation to compassion and assistance.

IV. THE SUCCESSFUL ISSUE OF INTERCESSORY PRAYER. The entreaty of the prophet was not in vain. The calamity—whether we understand it literally, as a plague of locusts, or figuratively, as the invasion by Pul—was averted and withdrawn. This is but one of many instances in Old and New Testament Scripture in which God represents himself as willing to listen to the pleading of the pious on behalf of their sinful fellow-men. It is one office of the Church of Christ to plead perpetually for mankind, uttering the plaintive and effectual intercession, "Spare them, good Lord!"—T.

Ver. 3.—*The repentance of Jehovah.* Whatever it was of which the Lord is here said to have repented, the meaning, the lesson, is the same. The plague of locusts, the incursion of the foe, was stayed, and it was stayed in consequence of the prophet's intercession, and because of the pity and loving-kindness of Jehovah.

I. NO CHANGE IS ASSERTED IN THE CHARACTER, THE GOVERNMENT, THE WILL, OF THE ETERNAL. In this sense the Lord is not a man that he should repent. Whilst all men are subject not only to vicissitudes of circumstances, but to variations in disposition, and even in principles of action, God is a stranger to all such mutability. "I," says he, "am the Lord that changeth not." Well for us is it that this is so; that we have not to do with a mutable, a capricious deity. Because he is the Lord that changeth not, therefore the sons of Jacob are not consumed.

II. BUT ALL THE THREATS OF THE DIVINE JUDGE ARE CONDITIONAL UPON HUMAN CONDUCT. The whole of revelation bears out this statement. What God commands he enforces with the promise of reward and with the threat of punishment. This is in accordance with his character and position as the Moral Governor of his universe. He does not, as an earthly tyrant might do, take pleasure in inflicting punishment upon any of his dependent creatures. On the contrary, he desireth not the death of a sinner. If the threatened respond to the appeal of Heaven, if they turn from their wickedness, they shall surely live, and not die. He repenteth him of the evil, and is favourable and forgiving towards the penitent.

III. THE DIVINE REPENTANCE DEMANDS THE ADORATION AND THE PRAISE OF THOSE WHO OWE TO IT THEIR SALVATION. There is not one child of Adam who is not indebted to the repentance of Jehovah for the sparing of life, for long-suffering, for the aversion of judgment. In fact, but for this, the original sentence against the sinner must have been fulfilled, and the race of mankind must have perished. Every successive interposition of Divine mercy has been the evidence of that relenting which exclaims, "How shall I give thee up?" And the advent and sacrifice of Immanuel, the mediatorial scheme, the redemption of mankind, the recovery of the lost, are all to be attributed to this same cause. The fountain of salvation must be discovered in the repentance of the Unchanging. It is a paradox; but it is a paradox honouring to God and life-giving to man.—T.

Vers. 7—9.—*The plumb-line of judgment.* The pictorial style of Amos here sets before us in an impressive and memorable way a great truth. Whether in a dream or in a prophetic ecstasy, the prophet beheld one with a plumb-line standing by a wall. He recognized in the wall the palaces, the temples, the city ramparts of Samaria; in the figure, a representation of the eternal Ruler of the nations; in the plumb-line, the emblem of just and orderly procedure. And a voice explained the vision as predictive of the destruction and ruin of the capital of Israel, in execution of the decree of Divine justice against the unfaithful, sinful, rebellious, and impenitent people.

I. THE SIN OF MAN MAY EXHAUST THE PATIENCE OF GOD. It must not, indeed, be supposed that the Divine nature is susceptible of capricious changes, such as men are liable to experience. But we have to consider God as the moral Governor of the nations of mankind. And we are taught that he is, as we say, in earnest in the laws which he promulgates, and in the promises and threats by which he accompanies them. He will not continue to threaten, and then falsify his own words, by withholding punishment from those who withhold repentance. With no weariness, with no irritability, but with a righteous judgment and a compassionate heart, he will execute his threats.

II. THE JUST RETRIBUTION OF GOD IS ACCORDING TO UNCHANGING AND INFLEXIBLE RULES OF RIGHTEOUSNESS. In human punishment there is often an element of caprice and an element of vindictiveness. From the Divine mind both are for ever absent. No sinner can complain, or ever will be able to complain, that he has been punished beyond his deserts. On the contrary, he will ever recognize that wisdom and righteousness have characterized all the appointments of the eternal King. The plumb-line is employed not only in construction but in destruction. And God who has made men's moral nature, and who rules over it and in it, will not violate his principles of righteousness in the administration of his government or in the execution of his sentences.

III. THE RIGHTEOUSNESS OF GOD IS A POWERFUL ENCOURAGEMENT TO REPENTANCE AND OBEDIENCE. It is a dissuasive from sin and impenitence, inasmuch as it is a guarantee that rebellion shall not go unpunished. It is an inducement to repentance, for it is part of God's unchanging purpose that the penitent and submissive shall receive pardon and acceptance. And it is not to be forgotten that God's purposes of mercy are as much distinguished by law as are his purposes of punishment. Mercy is in accordance with the "plumb-line" of Divine righteousness, and in his gospel God appears, as he is, just and "the Justifier of him who believeth in Jesus."—T.

Vers. 14, 15.—*The herdsman becomes a prophet.* The simple dignity of Amos's reply to Amaziah must strike every reader with admiration. The priest of Bethel treated him as a professional prophet, who had a calling which he was constrained to fulfil in some place or other. But Amos did not prophesy because he had been trained to the prophetic vocation; he prophesied because the Lord constrained him to do so. The Lord had made him very sensitive to the prevailing sins of his countrymen, had sent him with a message of warning to the court of Samaria, and had imparted to him supernatural qualifications for the fulfilment of this sacred ministry.

I. GOD IS NOT DEPENDENT UPON EDUCATION OR LEARNING FOR THE QUALIFICATION OF THE AGENTS HE SELECTS. Amos was not the first or the last unlettered, intellectually uncultivated man employed by Infinite Wisdom upon a high and sacred ministry of usefulness. There were in Palestine "schools of the prophets," but in these Amos was not trained. The spiritual power, which is the true "note" of a prophetic calling, is not confined to those who are reared in seats of learning, who have acquired the scholarship which is imparted by the intellectual discipline of school and university.

II. GOD CAN, HOWEVER, GIVE AN EDUCATION AND TRAINING OF HIS OWN, EFFECTIVE FOR THE PURPOSES OF A SPIRITUAL MINISTRY. It is a common mistake to suppose that those who have not been educated in the way which is familiar to us have not been educated at all. The Lord taught Amos in the solitude of the fields, the valleys, the hills of Judæa, as he tended the cattle, as he gathered the fruit of the sycomore. His education was, in a sense, very thorough. It gave him insight into the mighty works of the Creator, into his wonderful ways in dealing with the children of men, into the secrets of the human heart. His writings are a sufficient proof of his familiarity with the works and ways of God. His sublime descriptions of natural scenery, of the heavens and the earth, his minute acquaintance with the processes of growth and of husbandry, his knowledge of the human heart and all its conflicts,—these are evidences that his mind was not uninformed or untrained.

III. AN UNLETTERED BUT DIVINELY TAUGHT NATURE MAY BE A BLESSING TO MEN, AND MAY BRING GLORY TO GOD. The service which Amos rendered to Israel, to Judah, to the Church of God in subsequent ages, is a proof that God can use instruments, which seem to man's wisdom unsuitable, in order to effect his own purposes. The power of this prophet's ministry is unquestionable. To some extent his message was heeded; and that it was not more effective was not owing to any fault in him, but rather to the hardness of heart which distinguished those to whom he was sent. At the same time, there was so manifest an evidence of Divine power in the life and work of Amos as must have impressed all who knew him with the conviction that the power of God was upon him. A Divine election, Divine qualifications, may be as really present in the case of a minister of religion who has enjoyed every social and educational advantage, as in the case of him who is called from the plough to prophesy in the name of the Lord. But the impression upon the popular mind is in the former case far more deep, and naturally so. Thus God is honoured, whilst witness is borne to him before men, and the cause of righteousness is maintained and advanced.—T.

Ver. 15.—*Prophecy.* Amos was one of the "goodly fellowship of the prophets," who once witnessed for God on earth, and who now praise God in heaven. There was a long succession of prophets in Hebrew history, and especially during one epoch of that history. The Christian dispensation has also enjoyed the benefit of prophetic gifts and prophetic ministrations.

I. THE AUTHOR AND THE AUTHORITY OF PROPHECY. No true prophet ever spake the counsels of his own wisdom merely. The preface to a prophetic utterance is this: "Thus saith the Lord." "The Lord took me," says Amos, in his simple, graphic style, "as I was following the flock, and the Lord said unto me, Go, prophesy." 1. The prophet was called and appointed by the Lord of all truth and power. 2. The prophet was entrusted by the Lord with a special message. It was these facts that aggravated the guilt of those who were inattentive to the Divine message, who rejected and persecuted the Divine messengers.

II. THE MATTER AND SUBSTANCE OF PROPHECY. The function of the prophet was to utter forth the mind and will of the Eternal. Sometimes it is supposed that it was his special duty to declare things to come, to foretell. Doubtless the prophet was often directed to warn of evils about to descend upon the guilty and impenitent. But to foretell was not so much his distinctive office as to tell forth the commands and the counsels of the Lord.

III. THE PROPHET AS THE VEHICLE OF PROPHECY. Personality, loving intelligence and will, a truly human nature,—such was the condition to be fulfilled by the chosen vehicle of the Divine purposes. Men of temperaments as different as Elijah and Jeremiah were selected by him who can make use of every instrument for the fulfilment of his own purposes. One thing was necessary, that the prophet's whole nature should be penetrated by the Spirit of God, that he should give himself up entirely to become the minister and the messenger of Eternal Wisdom.

IV. THE METHODS OF PROPHECY. *Speech* was no doubt the chief means by which the prophet conveyed his message to his fellow-men; speech of every kind, bold and gentle, figurative and plain, commanding and persuasive. *Life* was no inconsiderable part of prophecy. There were cases in which the very actions and habits of the prophet were a testimony to men. *Symbols* were not infrequently employed in order to impart lessons which could be better taught thus than by the logical forms of speech. God made use of every method which human nature allowed and the conditions of the prophetic ministry suggested.

V. THE PURPORT OF PROPHECY. An agency so special and so highly qualified must have aimed at an end proportionably important and valuable. It may be noted that: 1. Prophecy was largely intended to lead sinful people to repentance and reformation. 2. To encourage the obedient and spiritual amidst difficulties and persecutions. 3. To introduce higher views of religion than those current at the time, and thus to prepare the way for the dispensation of the Messiah, for the religion of the Spirit, for the universal kingdom of truth and righteousness.—T.

Ver. 17.—*A polluted land.* If in Amos we have an example of a faithful prophet, in Amaziah we have an example of an unfaithful priest. One servant of the Lord seems in this narrative to be set against another; but, in fact, the priest was a nominal servant, whilst the prophet was sincere and devoted. The fate predicted for Amaziah was indeed terrible; but we discern in its appointment, not the malice of a human foe, but the justice of a Divine Ruler. Among the circumstances which enhanced the horror of this fate is mentioned the pollution of the heathen land in which the wicked priest should close his life.

I. A LAND MAY BE POLLUTED NOTWITHSTANDING ITS WEALTH, LUXURIOUSNESS, AND POLITICAL EMINENCE AND POWER. Some of the ancient monarchies of the world were no less remarkable for moral corruption than for grandeur, prosperity, and military strength. Such was the case with Assyria. And it is well to be upon our guard against the deceptiveness of external appearances. The semblance of national greatness may mislead us in our judgment. The surface may deceive; there may be much to outward view fascinating and commanding. Yet beneath the surface there may be injustice, oppression, selfishness, wretchedness, and disunion; the land may be polluted by vice and, if not by idolatry, yet by practical atheism.

II. A LAND MAY BE POLLUTED ALTHOUGH IT BE CHOSEN AS THE SCENE OF THE EXECUTION OF PURPOSES OF DIVINE JUDGMENT. It must not be supposed that, because certain nations were appointed by Divine providence to be the ministers of retribution upon Israel, those nations must have been morally admirable or even superior to that upon which their power was exercised for purposes of chastisement. The records of the Old Testament Scriptures are decisive upon this point. Idolatrous people were permitted to scourge Israel for idolatry. A polluted land was to be the means of cleansing those defiled by sin.

III. To CLEANSE A LAND FROM POLLUTION IS THE HIGHEST END WHICH THE PATRIOTIC AND RELIGIOUS CAN SET BEFORE THEM. Splendour, opulence, military power, are in the view of the enlightened as nothing compared with the righteousness which exalteth a nation.—T.

Vers. 1—6.—*Revelation and prayer.* "Thus hath the Lord God showed unto me," etc. This portion of the Book of Amos (ch. vii. and viii.) contains four symbolical visions respecting successive judgments that were to be inflicted on the kingdom of Israel. They were delivered at Bethel, and in all probability at the commencement of the prophet's ministry. Each of them, as it follows in the series, is more severe than the preceding. The first presented to the mental eye of the prophet a swarm of young locusts, which threatened to cut off all hope of the harvest (vers. 1—3); the second, a fire which effected a universal conflagration (vers. 4—6); the third, a plumb-line ready to be applied to mark out the edifices that were to be destroyed (vers. 7—9); and the fourth, a basket of ripe fruit, denoting the near and certain destruction of the kingdom (ch. viii. 1—3). The intervening eight verses which conclude the seventh chapter (vers. 10—17) contain an account of the interruption of Amos by Amaziah the priest of Bethel, whose punishment is specially predicted. In point of style, this portion differs from that of the rest of the book, being almost exclusively historical and dialogistic (Henderson). In the words we have two subjects of thought—*A Divine revelation leading to human prayer,* and *human prayer leading to a Divine revelation.*

I. A DIVINE REVELATION LEADING TO HUMAN PRAYER. 1. Here is a *Divine revelation.* What is the revelation? It is a vision of judgments made to the mind of the prophet. Both judgments are symbolically represented. (1) Destruction by grasshoppers at the beginning, or the "shooting up of the latter growth after the king's mowings."[1] The prophet saw the devouring grasshoppers eating up the grass of the

[1] As we write, glancing at the *Times,* we are struck with the following statements referring to such judgments: "Australian papers state that in the Riverina district the grasshoppers, or locusts, have been very troublesome recently, not only destroying crops, but filling up wells and water-holes, and even consuming textile fabrics, such as blinds and window-curtains, in the houses."

land. No agents are too insignificant for the employment of Jehovah. He can inflict terrible judgments by insects. Here was a prospect of famine set before the prophet. (2) Destruction by fire. ",Thus hath the Lord God showed unto me : and, behold, the Lord God called to contend by fire, and it devoured the great deep, and did eat up a part." Perhaps this represents a great drought, the sun's fire burning up all vegetation. It is said this fire " devoured the great deep." It drank up the pools, the lakes, the rivers. Thus in two symbolical forms is a Divine revelation made to the mind of Amos. Most terrible and alarming is the prospect of his country, thus divinely spread out before him. God makes revelations of his mind to his people. " Shall I hide from Abraham the thing that I do?" 2. Here is a *human prayer*. What is the prayer? Here it is : " O Lord God, forgive, I beseech thee : by whom shall Jacob arise? for he is small." And again, in ver. 5, " O Lord God, cease, I beseech thee : by whom shall Jacob arise? for he is small." " Forgive." This calamity is brought on by the sin of the nation. Forgive the sin; remove the moral cause of the judgment. " By whom shall Jacob arise?" Or, better, " How can Jacob stand? for he is small." Jacob's— the nation's—weakness is the plea of the prayer for forgiveness. The Israelites had been greatly reduced by internal commotions and hostile invasions, and were now on the point of being attacked by the Assyrians, but purchased their retreat by a payment of a thousand talents of silver (2 Kings xv. 19, 20). The nation was now so weakened that it was unable to stand before another invader. How can Jacob stand? The time has come when men may well ask this question in relation to the Church. How can it stand? The numbers are decreasing, viewed in relation to the growth of the population. By whom shall it arise? Not by statesmen, scientists, ritualists, priests. A new order of men is required to enable the Church to stand. Heaven raise them up!

II. HUMAN PRAYER LEADING TO A DIVINE REVELATION. The prophet prays, and the great God makes a new revelation—a revelation of mercy. " The Lord repented for this : It shall not be, saith the Lord." " The Lord repented for this : This also shall not be, saith the Lord God." " Repented," which means merely that he appeared to Amos as if he repented. The Immutable One changeth not. Though we are far enough from holding the absurdity that human prayer effects any alteration in the ordinances of nature or the purposes of the Almighty, we nevertheless hold with a tenacious faith the doctrine that a *man gets from God by prayer that which he would not get without it.* Indeed, in every department of life man gets from the Almighty, by a certain kind of activity, that which he would never obtain without the effort. A man has a field which he has never tilled, and on which Providence has bestowed no crop for many a long year. He tills it this year, and in autumn God crowns it with his goodness. Another man has no health; for many years he has neglected the conditions of physical vigour, and he is infirm and afflicted. This year he attends rigorously to the laws of his physical well-being. He takes the proper exercise, the right food, the pure air, and he feels his infirmities and his pains decrease, and new vigour pulsating through his veins. Another man has never enjoyed the light of Divine knowledge; his soul has been living in the region of indolence; he has neglected all the means of intelligence. He alters his course and sets to work ; he reads and thinks, studies God's holy book, and prays ; he feels his nature gradually brightening under the genial rays of truth. Thus everywhere God reveals to man his goodness in connection with his activity, which never comes without human effort. It is so in prayer. "The effectual fervent prayer of a righteous man availeth much." It puts the soul in that angle on which the Divine light falls, in that soil in which its intellectual and moral powers will grow. " Ask, and ye shall receive."

> " More things are wrought by prayer
> Than this world dreams of. Wherefore let thy voice
> Rise like a fountain for me night and day.
> For what are men better than sheep or goats,
> That nourish a blind life within the brain,
> If, knowing God, they lift not hands of prayer
> Both for themselves and those who call them friends?
> For so the whole round earth is every way
> Bound by gold chains about the feet of God."

(Tennyson.)

D. T.

Vers. 7—9.—*Man's moral character.* " Thus he showed me : and, behold, the Lord stood upon a wall made by a plumb-line, with a plumb-line in his hand," etc. " Behold, the Lord stood upon a wall made by a plumb-line," viz. perpendicular. " Amos." " The Lord knoweth them that are his" (2 Tim. ii. 19), as he saith to Moses, " I know thee by name " (Exod. xxxiii. 12, 17). " He calleth his own sheep by name " (John x. 3). " Behold, I will set a plumb-line in the midst of my people Israel." No longer are the symbols, as in the former two, stated generally ; this one is expressly applied to Israel. God's long-suffering is worn out by Israel's perversity ; so Amos ceases to intercede, as Abraham did in the case of Sodom. The plummet-line was used, not only in building, but in destroying houses (2 Kings xxi. 13 ; Isa. xxviii. 17 ; xxxiv. 11 ; Lam. ii. 8). It denotes that God's judgments are measured out by the exactest rules of justice. Here it is placed in the midst of Israel ; *i.e.* the judgment is not to be confined to an outer part of Israel, as by Tiglath-Pileser—it is to reach the very centre. This was fulfilled when Shalmaneser, after a three years' siege of Samaria, took it, in the ninth year of Hoshea the King of Israel, and carried away Israel captive finally to Assyria (2 Kings xvii. 3, 5, 6, 23). " I will not again pass by them any more." I will not forgive them any more (ch. viii. 2 ; Prov. xix. 11 ; Micah vii. 18). " And the high places," dedicated to idols, " of Isaac." They boasted of following the example of their fore-father Isaac, in erecting high places at Beersheba (ch. v. 5); but he and Abraham erected them before the temple was appointed at Jerusalem. But these Israelites did so after the temple had been fixed as the only place for sacrifices and worship. The mention of Isaac and Israel is in all probability intended simply to express the names which their posterity boasted in, as if they would ensure their safety ; but these shall not save them. Homiletically, we may use these words as suggesting certain things concerning man's moral character.

I. There is a kind of masonry in the formation of man's character. " Thus he showed me : and, behold, the Lord stood upon a wall made by a plumb-line, with a plumb-line in his hand. And the Lord said unto me, Amos, what seest thou ? And I said, A plumb-line." A plumb-line is an architectural instrument ; and the wall on which the Lord stood was being measured by a plumb-line. Moral masonry is suggested. Man's character may be compared to masonry in several respects. 1. It has *one foundation.* Walls are built, not upon two, but upon one foundation. So is every man's character. There is some one principle on which it is organized, some one fount to which you can trace all the streams of human activity. The principle is the paramount affection of the man. Whatever he loves most, governs him. If he loves pleasure most, his character is sensual ; if he loves money most, his character is worldly ; if he loves wisdom most, his character is philosophic ; if he loves God most, his character is Divine, etc. 2. It has a *variety of materials.* In a building there are earth, lime, stones, bricks, wood, iron, etc. These are brought together into a whole. Character is not formed of one set of actions, thoughts, impulses, volitions. All kinds of acts enter into it, mental, moral, muscular, personal, political, religious—all are materials in the building. 3. It is a *gradual advancement.* You cannot build a house in a day ; stone by stone it must advance : so the formation of character is a slow work. Men cannot become either devils or saints at once, cannot spring into these characters by a bound. It takes time to build up a Satan, and a longer time still to build up a seraph within us. Acts make habits ; habits make character.

II. There is a Divine standard by which to test man's character. Here is the great God standing on the wall with a " plumb-line " in his hand, with which to test his people Israel. What is the Divine " plumb-line " by which to test character ? Here it is : " Whatsoever ye would that men should do unto you, do ye even so unto them." Or, perhaps more intelligibly, the moral character of Christ : " If any man have not the spirit of Christ, he is none of his." That spirit is love for God and men. Without love we are "nothing." Here is a plumb-line. Are you *Christly ?* If not, your moral masonry is not architecturally sound or symmetric. He who now stood before Amos on the wall, with a " plumb-line in his hand," stands to-day amongst men with this moral test of character.

III. There is a terrible ruin for those whose characters will not bear the test of this plumb-line. " Behold, I will set a plumb-line in the midst of my people Israel : I will not again pass by them any more : and the high places of Isaac shall be desolate, and the sanctuaries of Israel shall be laid waste; and I will rise against the house of Jeroboam with the sword." See this test applied on the day of judgment, as represented in Matt. xxv. 31—46, "When the Son of man shall come in his glory," etc.—D. T.

Vers. 10—17.—*The conventional and the genuine priests of a people.* "Then Amaziah the priest of Bethel sent to Jeroboam King of Israel, saying, Amos hath conspired against thee in the midst of the house of Israel: the land is not able to bear all his words," etc. In these words we have types of two classes of priests who are ever found amongst the people.

I. THE CONVENTIONAL PRIEST OF A PEOPLE. Amaziah was the recognized, authorized, conventional priest of Bethel—the chief priest of the royal sanctuary of the calves at Bethel. He was the recognized religious teacher—a kind of archbishop. We find this man doing three things which such conventional priests have done in all ages, and are doing now. 1. He was *in close intimacy with the king.* He "sent to Jeroboam King of Israel." Conventional priests have always an eye upward, always towards kings and those in authority; they have generally proved ready to obey their behests, study their caprices, and wink at their abominations. In their prayers they will often insult the Omniscient by describing their royal masters, whatever their immoralities, as "our most religious," "our most gracious sovereign." As a rule, they are the mere creatures of kings. 2. He seeks to *expel an independent teacher from the dominion of the king.* He seeks to do this in two ways. (1) By appealing to the king. He does this in a spirit that has ever characterized his class—by bringing against Amos the groundless charge of treason. "Amos hath conspired against thee in the midst of the house of Israel: the land is not able to bear all his words." By a base slander he endeavours to influence the king against the true teacher. He does this: (2) By alarming the prophet. "Amaziah said unto Amos, O thou seer, go, flee thee away into the land of Judah, and there eat bread, and prophesy there: but prophesy not again any more at Bethel: for it is the king's chapel, and it is the king's court." It does not appear that the king took any notice of the message which this authorized religious teacher had sent him concerning Amos; hence, in order to carry out his malignant purpose, he addresses the prophet and says, "O thou seer, go, flee thee away." Not imagining that Amos could be actuated by any higher principle than that of selfishness, which reigned in his own heart, the priest advised him to consult his safety by fleeing across the frontier into the kingdom of Judah, where he might obtain his livelihood by the unrestrained exercise of his prophetical gifts. Here, then, we have, in this Amaziah, a type of many so-called authorized religious teachers of a country. Two feelings inspire them—a miserable *servility* towards their rulers, and a cruel *envy* towards their religious rivals. They want to sweep the land of all schismatics. Thank God, the days of the Amaziahs, through the advancement of popular intelligence, are drawing to a close!

II. HERE WE HAVE THE GENUINE PRIEST OF A PEOPLE. Amos seems to have been a prophet not nationally recognized as such. He was no professional prophet. Observe three things concerning the prophet. 1. He is *not ashamed of his humble origin.* "I was no prophet"—that is, "I am not a prophet by profession,"—"neither was I a prophet's son." By the son of a prophet he means a disciple or pupil. He had not studied in any prophetic college. On the contrary, "I am nothing but a poor labouring man"—"an herdsman, and a gatherer of sycomore fruit." No true prophet is ever ashamed of his origin, however humble. As a rule, the greatest teachers of the world have struggled up from the regions of poverty and obscurity. From the lower grades of social life the Almighty generally selects his most eminent servants; "not many mighty does he call." 2. He is *conscious of the Divinity of his mission.* "The Lord took me as I followed the flock, and the Lord said unto me, Go, prophesy unto my people Israel." Amos seems to have had no doubt at all as to the fact that the Lord called him. How he was called does not appear. When God calls a man to work, the man knows it. No argument will convince him to the contrary. The conventional teacher may say, "You are unauthorized, unrecognized, unordained; you have intruded yourself into the holy calling." But the true teacher knows when he is divinely called, and under this impression he carries on his work. "The Lord took me as I followed the flock." 3. In the name of Heaven he *denounces the conventional priest.* In return for this rebellion against Jehovah, Amos foretells for the priest the punishment which will fall upon him when the judgment shall come upon Israel, meeting his words, "Thou sayest, Thou shalt not prophesy," with the keen retort, "Thus saith Jehovah." The punishment is thus described in ver. 17, "Thy wife shall be an harlot in the city," *i.e.* at the taking of the city she will become a harlot through violation. His children also would be slain by the foe, and his landed possessions assigned to others, viz. to the fresh settlers in the land. He himself, viz. the priest, would die in an unclean land, that is to say, in the land of the Gentiles; in other words, would be carried away captive, and that with the whole nation, the carrying away of which is repeated by Amos in the words which the priest had reported to the king (ver. 11) as a sign that what he has prophesied will assuredly stand (Delitzsch).

CONCLUSION. To which class of teachers dost thou belong, my brother? That represented by Amaziah, who, though recognized by his king and country as the true teacher, was nevertheless destitute of loyalty to the one true God and the spirit of true philanthropy and honest manhood; or that represented by Amos, who although a poor labourer, unrecognized by his country as a true teacher, yet was called of God and manfully fulfilled his Divine mission? Heaven multiply in this country and throughout the world religious teachers of this Amos type!—D. T.

EXPOSITION.

CHAPTER VIII.

Vers. 1—14.—§ 5. *In the fourth vision, the basket of summer fruit, the Lord shows that the people is ripe for judgment.* Explaining this revelation, Amos denounces the oppression and greed of the chieftains (vers. 4—10), and warns them that those who despise the Word of God shall some day suffer from a famine of the Word (vers. 11—14).

Ver. 1.—**A basket of summer fruit;** Septuagint, ἄγγος ἰξευτοῦ, "a fowler's vessel;" Vulgate, *uncinus pomorum*, which Jerome explains, "Sicut uncino rami arborum detrahuntur ad poma carpenda, ita ego proximum captivitatis tempus attraxi." The word *chelub* is taken to mean "a basket of wickerwork;" it is used for "a cage" in Jer. v. 27, but is found nowhere else. The gathering of fruit was the last harvest of the year, and thus fitly typified the final punishment of Israel. This is set forth by the play on the word in the next verse.

Ver. 2.—**The end** (*kets*). This is very like the word for "fruit" (*kaits*). **Pass by** (see note on ch. vii. 8).

Ver. 3.—**The songs of the temple;** Septuagint, τὰ φατνώματα τοῦ ναοῦ, "the pannels of the temple;" Vulgate, *cardines templi*. These versions point to a different reading. It is better rendered, "the songs of the palace," referring to the songs of the revellers mentioned already (ch. vi. 5). These shall be changed into **howlings** of lamentation for the dead which lie around (comp. ver. 10). There shall be **many dead bodies.** The Hebrew is more forcible:

"Many the corpses; in every place he hath cast them forth. Hush!" The Lord is represented as casting dead bodies to the ground, so that death is everywhere; and the interjection "hush!" (comp. ch. vi. 10) is an admonition to bend beneath the hand of an avenging God (comp. Zeph. i. 7). Orelli takes it as an expression of the apathy that accompanies severe and irremediable suffering—suffering too deep for words. The Greek and Latin versions take this onomatopoetic word *has!* "hush!" as a substantive. Thus the Septuagint, ἐπιρρίψω σιωπήν, "I will cast upon them silence;" Vulgate, *projicietur silentium*—an expressive rendering, but one not supported by grammatical considerations.

Ver. 4.—The prophet, by admonishing the grandees of their iniquities, which they will not cast away, shows how ripe they are for judgment. **That swallow up;** better, *that pant after* (ch. ii. 6, 7), like a beast after its prey, eager to devour. **Even to make the poor of the land to fail;** *and cause the meek of the land to fail.* They grasp at the property of the unresisting poor, adding field to field, and impoverishing them in various ways, to root them out of the land.

Ver. 5.—**When?** expresses impatience and desire, as in the hymn—

"Thy joys *when* shall I see?"

The new moon. The first day of the month was a holiday, on which all trade was suspended. It is not mentioned in Exodus, Leviticus, or Deuteronomy; but its observance is enjoined in Numb. xxviii. 11, and various notices of this occur in later Scriptures; *e.g.* 1 Sam. xx. 5; 2 Kings iv. 23; Hos. ii. 11; Col. ii. 16. These greedy sinners kept the festivals, indeed, but they grudged the time given to them, and considered it as wasted. **The sabbath.** Compare the difficulties with which Nehemiah had to contend in upholding the sanctity of the sabbath (Neh. x. 31; xiii. 15—22). **May set forth;** literally, *open;* so Septuagint, καὶ ἀνοίξομεν θησαυρόν. The word expresses the opening of the granaries and storehouses. **The ephah,** by which corn was measured (see note on Micah vi. 10). This they made small, and so gave less than was paid for. **The shekel.** The weight by which money was weighed. This they made great, and thus gained too high a price for the quantity of corn. Coined money of determined value seems not to have been used before the return from Captivity, all payments of fixed amount previous to that period being made by weighing (comp. Gen. xxiii. 16; xxxiii. 19; xliii. 21; Exod. xxx. 13; Isa. xlvi. 6). **Falsifying the balances by deceit;** better, as in the Revised Version, *dealing falsely with balances of deceit.* To increase their gains they falsified their scales or used fraudulent weights (see Lev. xix. 36). Thus they cheated the poor probably in three ways—by small measure, exorbitant price, and light weight.

Ver. 6.—**Buy the poor for silver** (comp. ch. ii. 6). The probable meaning is that they so reduced the poor man by their exactions and injustice, that he was compelled to pay his debt by selling himself into slavery (Lev. xxv. 39; Deut. xv. 12). **For a pair of shoes.** For the smallest debt they would deal in this harsh manner. **The refuse;** literally, *that which fell through the sieve;* Septuagint, Ἀπὸ παντὸς γεννήματος ἐμπορευσόμεθα, "We will trade in every kind of produce;" Vulgate, *Quisquilias frumenti vendamus,* "Let us sell the refuse of corn."

Ver. 7.—Such crimes as these, which sap the very foundations of social life, shall meet with vengeance. **The Excellency of Jacob.** This is a title of God himself, as in Hos. v. 5; vii. 10, where it is rendered "pride." Thus the Lord is said to swear by his holiness (ch. iv. 2), by his soul (ch. vi. 8; comp. 1 Sam. xv. 29). So here he swears by himself, who is the Glory and Pride of Israel; as truly as he is this, he will punish. The Vulgate treats the sentence differently, *Juravit in superbium Jacob,* i.e. "The Lord hath sworn against the pride of Jacob," against the arrogancy with which they treat the poor, and trust in their riches, and deem themselves secure. So the Septuagint, Ὀμνύει Κύριος κατὰ τῆς ὑπερηφανίας Ἰακώβ. **I will never forget,** so as to leave unpunished. Literally, *if I forget,* equivalent to a most decided denial, as Heb. iv. 3, 5, etc. "Nec mirum est, si Deus jurare dicatur; quum dormientibus

dormiat et vigilantibus vigilet; hisque qui sibi thesaurizaverunt iram in die iræ, dicatur irasci" (St. Jerome).

Ver. 8.—**Shall not the land tremble for this?** "This" is the coming judgment, or the oath with which God announced it in the previous verse; and the prophet asks, "Shall not the land tremble as with an earthquake when the Lord comes to judgment?" The LXX., rendering ἐπὶ τούτοις, takes the reference to be to the "works" or sins of the people (ver. 7); but the thought in these two verses is the punishment of the transgressions, not the transgressors themselves. **And it shall rise up wholly as a flood** (ch. ix. 5). The LXX., pointing differently, renders, Καὶ ἀναβήσεται ὡς ποταμὸς συντέλεια, "And destruction shall come up as a river;" the Vulgate, *Et ascendet quasi fluvius universus;* it is best, however, to refer both clauses to the Nile: "Yea, it shall rise up wholly like the river"—the land shall heave and swell like the waters of the Nile at its annual rising. **And it shall be cast out and drowned, as by the flood of Egypt;** better, *it shall be tossed up and sink again, like the river of Egypt*—a picturesque comparison, which would allude to a phenomenon well known to the Israelites. It is as though the whole earth were turned into a sea, tossing and labouring under a tempestuous wind (comp. Isa. xxiv. 4).

Ver. 9.—**I will cause the sun to go down at noon.** This is probably to be taken metaphorically of a sudden calamity occurring in the very height of seeming prosperity, such as the fate of Israel in Pekah's time, and Pekah's own murder (2 Kings xv. 29, 30; see also 2 Kings xvii. 1—6). A like metaphor is common enough; *e.g.* Joel ii. 2; iii. 15; Micah iii. 6; Job v. 14; Isa. xiii. 10; Jer. xv. 9. Hind calculates that there were two solar eclipses visible in Palestine in Amos's time, viz. June 15, B.C. 763, and February 9, B.C. 784. Some have suggested that the prophet here predicts the latter in the year of Jeroboam's death; but this, it is discovered, would have been so partial as hardly to be noticeable at Samaria. And it is improbable that such natural phenomena, unconnected with God's moral government, should be the subject of the prophet's prediction (Pusey). Doubtless a sudden reverse is signified (comp. Matt. xxiv. 29, etc.), expressed in terms rendered particularly appropriate by some late and well-remembered eclipse. The Fathers note here how the earth was darkened at the Passion of our Lord.

Ver. 10.—**I will turn your feasts into mourning,** etc. (comp. ver. 3; ch. v. 16, 17; Lam. v. 15; Hos. ii. 11; Tobit ii. 6). **Sackcloth.** A token of mourning (1 Kings xx. 31; Isa. xv. 3; Joel i. 8, 13). **Baldness**

On shaving the head as a sign of mourning, see note on Micah i. 16; and comp. Job i. 20; Isa. iii. 24; Jer. xvi. 6; xlvii. 5; Ezek. vii. 18). **I will make it;** *Ponam eam* (Vulgate); *sc. terram.* But it is better to take it to refer to the whole state of things mentioned before. The mourning for an only son was proverbially severe, like that of the widow of Nain (Luke vii. 12, etc.; comp. Jer. vi. 26; Zech. xii. 10). **And the end thereof as a bitter day.** The calamity should not wear itself out; it should be bitter unto the end. Septuagint, Θήσομαι . . . τοὺς μέτ' αὐτοῦ ὡς ἡμέραν ὀδύνης, "I will make . . . those with him as a day of anguish."

Ver. 11.—This shall be the bitterness at the end; they had rejected the warnings of the prophets (ch. vii. 12, etc.); now the Word of God and the light of his teaching should fail them. **Famine.** When the light of God's revelation is withdrawn, their longing for the Word, however sore and great, shall remain unsatisfied, like that of Saul (1 Sam. xxviii. 6). They may grieve like the psalmist, "We see not our signs; there is no more any prophet; neither is there among us any that knoweth how long" (Ps. lxxiv. 9); but it will be in vain (see a similar punishment threatened, Lam. ii. 9; Ezek. vii. 26; Micah iii. 7).

Ver. 12.—**They shall wander;** literally, *they shall reel.* The verse implies the eagerness of their unsatisfied desire, which seeks everywhere for the revelation which for their sin is denied them. **From sea to sea.** This expression is taken, by Keil and others, to mean here "all the world over," as Ps. lxxii. 8; Micah vii. 12; Zech. ix. 10; but it is probably used by the prophet in a more restricted sense, as it would not be natural for him to refer in the first place to the seeking of the words of God beyond the limits of the Holy Land. Therefore "from sea to sea" means from the Sea of Galilee or the Dead Sea to the Mediterranean; and **from the north even to the east**—from the north round again to the east, the south not being mentioned, because there alone was the true worship of God to be found, and they refused to seek it there (Pusey). Of course, according to the wide scope taken by prophecy, which is not exhausted

by one fulfilment, we may see here the fate of the Jews to the present time hopelessly seeking Messiah and the Word of God, never finding that which they once recklessly rejected. By some error the LXX. render, Σαλευθήσονται ὕδατα ἀπὸ τῆς θαλάσσης, κ.τ.λ., unless they mean, "They shall be tossed as waters," etc.

Ver. 13.—This verse is parallel to the preceding. The thirst, spiritual and physical, shall affect **the fair virgins and young men**—those in all the freshness, beauty, and vigour of youth. **Shall faint;** literally, *shall be veiled,* covered, expressive of the feeling of faintness, when the sight grows dim and a mantle of darkness drops over one (Jonah iv. 8). If the strongest thus fail, much more will the rest succumb to the threatened calamity.

Ver. 14.—They who trusted in idols shall find no help in them. **They who swear by.** Those who reverence and worship, as Deut. vi. 13; x. 20. **The sin of Samaria.** The golden calf at Bethel (comp. Deut. ix. 21; Hos. viii. 5, 6). Septuagint, κατὰ τοῦ ἱλασμοῦ Σαμαρείας, "by the propitiation of Samaria." **Thy god, O Dan, liveth;** *i.e.* as thy god liveth, by the life of thy god. This was the other calf erected at Dan, near the source of the Jordan, in the extreme north (1 Kings xii. 29). **The manner of Beersheba liveth;** Septuagint, Ζῇ ὁ θεός σου βηρσαβεέ, "Thy god, O Beersheba, lives." Some commentators, ancient and modern, think that the actual road which led to Beersheba is here meant, and would translate, "As the way to Beersheba liveth," "By the life of the way to Beersheba," as Mohammedans swear by the pilgrimage to Mecca. But it is best to take the word rendered "manner" in the sense of "way," as ὁδὸς is used in Acts (ix. 2; xix. 9, 23) for mode of worship, or form of religion, the ritual, or use of the service there. (For Beersheba, see note on ch. v. 5.) From Dan to Beersheba is just a hundred and forty-four miles. **They shall fall,** etc. This was partially fulfilled by the destruction of the kingdom of Israel and the deportation of its inhabitants; and its truth to this day is demonstrated by the fate of the Jews who will not receive Jesus as the promised Messiah.

HOMILETICS.

Vers. 1—3.—*A nation ripe for ruin.* While immunity lasts iniquity will go on. Men only love it less than they fear suffering. In the actual presence of the penalty the hand of the transgressor is stayed. The murderer will not strike the death-blow under a policeman's eye. The blasphemer will not move a lip when the thunderbolt is crashing through his roof. But by so little does the one feeling master the other that if punishment be not both certain and at hand, the fear of it will fail to deter from sin. "My lord delayeth his coming." Let escape be out of the question, yet even the chance of respite will turn the scale in favour of doing the forbidden thing. Israel, sentenced and to be destroyed *some time*, sinned with a high hand. Israel, sentenced to be destroyed *soon*, yet sinned still. Perhaps Israel, sentenced to be destroyed at once, may be brought to bay. Here God tries the experiment.

I. THERE IS A TIME WHEN THE VINE OF SODOM RIPENS ITS FRUIT. Sin has its day. It disturbs the harmony of things, and when derangement reaches a climax a catastrophe comes, and arrests the process with a "thus far and no further." Israel's wicked course had reached this critical point. 1. *Idolatry, the archetypal sin against the first table, had practically superseded the worship of God.* It was the religion of the king and court and people. It was established and endowed by the state. Its rites were observed at Bethel and elsewhere, in profane mimicry of the Levitical worship at Jerusalem. The substitution of it for the worship of Jehovah was part of the royal policy. Short of this the national apostasy could go no further. Interference, if it would be in time to save anything, must take place at once. 2. *Oppression, the archetypal sin against the second table, had reduced society to dissolution.* The safeguards of property, liberty, and life were alike removed (ch. iii. 9, 10; v. 7, 12; vi. 3). The order of society had been converted into chaos. Incapable of using liberty without perverting it into licence, it was high time to deprive Israel of the grossly abused trust. As slaves they would be under a *regimé* of the strong arm, which was the only one that suited them in present circumstances. There are chains forging somewhere for the man who can neither consider others nor rule himself.

II. SUCH RIPENING FOREBODES AN EARLY GATHERING. (Ver. 2, "The end is come upon my people of Israel.") The sickle is put in as soon as the harvest is ripe. No practical husbandry could delay the operation longer. 1. *The crop has then reached the limits of its growth.* Like the corn ripe unto harvest, or the grape purple and mellow, the natural life of Israel had fully developed itself. Tastes were matured, habits acquired, and characters settled into crystalline form. Things generally had put on an aspect of finality, and the sickle of judgment that follows the ripening of character need no longer wait. Let the ripe sinner beware the scythe. The fruits of unrighteousness full grown are suggestive of the harvesters on their way. 2. *It is then ready to serve its natural purpose.* Green grapes are useless in the vat, and green faggots would only put out the fire. It is in the harvest, when both are mature, that the wheat and the tares alike are sent to their ultimate destination. One purpose, a high and noble one, Israel had at last proved their unfitness to serve; their exclusive fitness for another purpose had only now by the same events become apparent. Reward and punishment alike take typical form only when they have reference to lives and characters which have assumed an aspect of finality. The hard grain and the dry faggot are waiting respectively for the mill and for the fire. 3. *After this it will be in the way of the next crop.* When the reaper goes the ploughman comes. If the harvesting were neglected the ploughing must be postponed. Israel had failed utterly to accomplish its Divine mission, and, left longer alone, would only prevent its accomplishment by other agency. "Take the talent from him, and give it to him that hath ten talents." The unfruitful become in a little while cumberers of the ground, and a necessary measure of practical husbandry is then to cut them off. 4. *At this stage it will begin naturally to decay.* Overripe fruit will "go bad" at once. If not used or preserved when ripe, it will be lost altogether. National decline waits on the development of national corruption. Israel become utterly dissolute would go to pieces according to a natural law, even if the Assyrian never came. Indeed, it was in the degeneracy already apparent that the invader saw his opportunity and found the occasion of his coming. The disease that stops the career of the sensualist means God's judgment on one side, and the natural break-down of his constitution on the other.

III. THE DUNGHILL IS THE DESTINATION OF ALL TAINTED PRODUCE. (Ver. 3.) The incorrigible wrong-doer is involved at last in overwhelming calamity. God's judgments must fall, his mercy notwithstanding. Indeed, they are an aspect of it. "A God all mercy is a God unjust." He is leaving the lion to prey on the lamb. The most merciful course is that which offers most effective opposition to the wicked doings of wicked men. Israel's manners are past reforming, and past enduring. By their intolerable abuse of freedom they showed their fitness only to be slaves. And according to character and capacity they must be treated. What is bad for the table may be good for the dunghill. The life of many had become a curse, and it only remained to stop that, and make their death a warning. That is one crop which even the sluggard's garden cannot refuse to bear (Prov. xxiv. 30—32).

IV. THE OCCASION OF SUCH A HARVEST HOME TOO DEPLORABLE FOR WORDS. (Ver. 3, "Hush!") When judgment is overwhelming, silence is fitting. 1. *As opposed to songs.* These had resounded from the palace. They spoke of mirth and revelry. But they would be turned into yells ere long. In awestruck anticipation of the utterance of pain and horror, the prophet bids the revellers be silent. 2. *As opposed to lamentations.* You cannot always "give sorrow words." There is a grief that " speaks not "— the grief of the overwrought heart. "I was dumb, opening not the mouth, because this stroke was thine." Such grief would befit a time like this. Words, however strong, must be beneath the occasion. Let them then remain unspoken, and let the eloquence of silence meet the overwhelming severity of the visitation. 3. *As opposed to reproaches.* Israel had outlived the period of probation, and therefore of expostulation. Its " great transgression " was committed, its course unchangeably chosen, its doom sealed. The condemned and sentenced murderer is removed to his cell in silence. In sterner measures than abuse of words must his crime be expiated. His very life is to be exacted, and windy denunciation may well be spared. " Let him alone " is of all measures the most sternly significant. It is the preternatural hush of the elemental world, presaging the thunder-crash that shall make the very earth to reel.

Vers. 4—6.—*The covetous man's way.* Punishment, however stern, is proportioned rigidly to sin. They answer to each other as face to face. From the contemplation of Israel's deplorable fate we turn to the horrors of her crime. And they are dark beyond exaggerating. To idolatry, dethroning God and robbing him of his glory, is added covetousness defrauding and destroying men. Indeed, the one is but a department of the other. The worst type of mammon-worshipper, the covetous, is an idolater in a very real sense. And Israel's covetousness, detached as it was from all religious restraints, and operating in a purely heathen connection, was of the most aggravated and repulsive kind. Acting in character, observe that—

I. IT SELECTS AN EASY PREY. (Ver. 4, "the poor;" "the meek.") 1. *The poor cannot defend themselves.* Their poverty makes them helpless, and the weakness which ought to commend them to protection commends them to plunder. Covetousness, the meanest of the vices in any circumstances, goes down to the nadir of paltriness when it wrings its gold "from the hard hands" of the poor. 2. *The meek will not resist.* Their position and disposition are both against it. They would "rather suffer wrong." And they get enough of it to suffer. Weak on one hand, and unresisting on the other, they are a doubly tempting prey to the pitiless vulture's beak.

II. IT HAS MURDER IN ITS HEART. "Gape to destroy," as the beast of prey its victim at hand. There is a covetousness that puts its own paltriest gain above another's life. It will have men's money although their life should pay the forfeit. This is the very spirit of murder. To make money, at the necessary cost of human life, is to break the sixth commandment as well as the eighth.

III. IT HANKERS AFTER SUNDAY TRADING. (Ver. 5, "When is the new moon over," etc.?) These people retained the form of sabbath observance, but the reality had been altogether abandoned. They occupied its sacred hours with wishes that they were over. "Sabbath days and sabbath work are a burden to carnal hearts" (Henry). The hours drag heavily. Time-killing devices are exhausted. "Behold, what a weariness it is!" is the verdict on God's day, given weekly through all their years. "When shall I come and appear before God?" a question that the spiritually minded ask, is one which the carnally minded cannot even understand. They are making markets mentally in the very house of God, and, with the words of worship on their lips, "their heart goes after covetousness." From Sunday devising to Sunday transacting of business the step is but a small one—too small not to be taken when opportunity and temptation meet.

IV. IT PRACTISES UNFAIR DEALING. (Vers. 5, 6.) As they fear not God, neither do they regard man. When religion is abandoned, morality is undermined. Given greed present, and religious restraint absent, and dishonest dealing is inevitable. 1.

One device is the use of a false balance. "Make the ephah small, and the shekel great," *i.e.* give thirteen pounds to the stone, and charge twenty-one shillings to the pound. They perpetrate thus a double swindle, robbing "with both hands earnestly." Such fraud is too unscientific and direct for any but the coarser cheats. There are more delicate ways of fraudulent dealing, which the more refined rogues affect. Such a method is: 2. *Selling an adulterated or inferior article.* "The refuse of the corn we will sell" (ver. 6). This is probably the commonest form of commercial fraud. There are few who possess the strength of moral fibre to avoid it entirely. We might arrange it on a graduated scale. At one end is the man who bluntly sells one thing under the name of another. At the other end is the man who, in selling, insinuates the impression that the thing is of better quality than it really is. Between these two are dishonest artifices of all varieties and shades. All, however, originate in covetousness, eventuate in injustice, and deserve the generic name of fraud.

V. It traffics in human life, and that for a contemptible price. (Ver. 6.) The law, compelling the poor to sell themselves to their creditors to work for what they owed, was enforced in the case of the paltriest debts, and the needy might be brought into bondage for want of the price of even a pair of shoes. To work such hardship on such trifling occasion argues inhumanity too gross to be long endured. The worker has inverted the natural order, has lost out the sense of reverence, is blind to the dignity of human nature, and has conclusively shown that he is an eyesore, and his life a curse, to the society in which he lives. His selfishness puts the least interest of his own above the most essential interest of others. His greed of gain has so intensified that he is blind at last to all other considerations. He has fallen altogether beneath the human level, and when a man has done this, the chances are that he has lived his day. Well may we pray, "Incline my heart to thy testimonies, and not to covetousness."

Ver. 7.—*Confirming by an oath.* God's judgments sometimes take, and will continue to take, the wicked by surprise (Matt. xxiv. 36—39). But this need not be, and should not be, and can be only where blindness, or heedlessness, or incredulity make warning useless. God always warns before he strikes. Sometimes he warns by divers methods at once. Often he warns again and again. Invariably he warns with a solemnity that makes disbelief a crime and stupid. Here is a case in point.

I. The oath that cannot be broken. "God is not a man, that he should lie." To do so would be a natural impossibility, a contradiction of himself. For the same reason his truthfulness can have no degrees; his slightest word is absolutely inviolable. Yet to human apprehension an oath is peculiarly convincing, and, accommodating himself to men's weakness, God condescends, on peculiarly solemn occasions, not merely to say, but swear. Here he swears: 1. *By himself.* "The Pride of Jacob" is Jehovah himself. Elsewhere explicitly God swears by "himself" (Jer. li. 14), by his "great Name" (Jer. xliv. 26), by his "holiness" (ch. iv. 2), by his "*life*" (Ezek. xxxiii. 11). This is of necessity. Men "swear by the greater." God, "because he can swear by no greater, swears by himself" (Heb. vi. 17, 13). In this form of oath the greatest Being is invoked, and so the maximum of solemnity is reached, whether it is God who swears or man. 2. *By himself in his ideal relation to Israel.* "By the Pride of Jacob." Israel, alas! did not "glory in the Lord." They gloried in their idols. "These be thy gods, which brought thee out of the land of Egypt," they had said, in their blind fatuity, of the molten calf. God had been forgotten and his wonders ignored before they were many days accomplished, and in this forgetfulness they had persistently gone on. Yet was he none the less their Glory still, the Strength of Israel, their Light and Life, the Founder, Builder, Sustainer, of their kingdom, the one Source and Spring of all that made them great. This fundamental relation he emphasizes here in vowing vengeance on their sin. By this character, as their Life and Strength and Excellence, he swears he will now degrade and destroy them utterly. The nearer God's tie to the rebels, the grosser outrage is their rebellion, and the more embittered the after-relations. It is on the ruins of violated friendship that the most irreconcilable enmity arises. Not even the heathen is as hateful, or doomed to a fate as direful, as the apostate.

II. The record that cannot be erased. "I will not forget and for ever." To forget is to forgive, put out of sight, treat as non-existent. "I will remember their iniquities no more." *Sin unatoned for cannot be forgiven.* God must be just in his justifying, and justice demands satisfaction. From the provided satisfaction the unbelieving sinner has turned away, and so from the grace of his own salvation. *Neither can sin unforsaken.* The sinner is in actual conflict with God, and the rebel may not be forgiven with arms in his hands. *Neither can sin unrepented of.* Still loving sin, the impenitent is not in a moral condition to appreciate pardon, and the gift of God is not to be thrown away. By such a threefold cord was Israel bound to inevitable destruction.

III. The works that cannot be forgotten. There are sins more heinous, and for the authors of which it will be less tolerable in the judgment than for others (Matt. xi. 22). 1. *Such are the sins committed against the poor and needy.* "God hath chosen the poor of this world." Their poverty presents the minimum of resistance to his grace. Their hardships excite his special pity. Their helplessness commends them to his special protection. He gives them the most prominent place in his religion. He champions them against their enemies. He requires his people to do the same. He identifies himself with them in the judgment, and he deals with men then in terms of their relation to the duties they owe the needy (Matt. xxv. 35—45). While God is "the Avenger of all such," oppression of the poor shall not go unpunished. 2. *Such especially are the sins committed against the poor by those who bear his Name.* The element of beneficence bulked large in Judaism. Besides the general injunctions to regard the poor (Deut. xv. 7—11), there were special enactments allocating to them a poor tithe (Deut. xiv. 28, 29), the spontaneous produce of the soil (Lev. xxv. 5), the droppings from the sheaves, and the produce of the corners of the fields (Lev. xix. 9, 10; xxiii. 22), also sheaves accidentally dropped (Deut. xxiv. 19), as much from vineyard or field as the hungry wayfarer required to eat on the spot (Deut. xxiii. 24, 25), and periodical entertainments at the tables of the rich (Deut. xvi. 10, 11). Thus nothing could be more utterly antagonistic to the genius of the Jewish religion than to rob or oppress the poor. The Israelite guilty of it sinned against Scripture, against custom, against education, against every deterrent powerful with men and increasing guilt before God. Christianity, too, is essentially benevolent. To "love one another," and "do good unto all," is the very spirit and essence of the religion of Christ. Injustice or oppression under Christian auspices is sin in its most abominable and heinous form.

Vers. 8—10.—*Carried away as with a flood.* A man in earnest is always graphic. If he be also inspired he can afford to be explicit. In this passage Amos is both. The words were spoken before the convulsions they foretell, and written after some of them had occurred. But the descriptions of events, transpired between the speaking and the writing, have no flavour of an *ex post facto* deliverance. There is a bare record of the original verbal utterance without the attempt to write into any part of it details of what meantime had become history. Such an apologetic device, suicidal in any case, is a thing to which a man who is God's mouthpiece could not and needs not stoop.

I. The earth trembling when God swears. "For this" (ver. 8), *i.e.* the oath of God, and its purport. That oath means a catastrophe on the way in the shock of which the earth would tremble. The very utterance of it was a cause of trembling. "He uttered his voice, the earth melted." His word is a word of power. It operates in the physical forces, and shakes the whole frame of nature. In the poetic language of the psalmist, "the voice of the Lord breaketh the cedars," "shaketh the wilderness," "divideth the flames of fire." In the world of matter, as in the world of spirit, the great ultimate force is the word of God.

II. The creation suffering in the sufferings of men. Man sins, and the earth is smitten. It was so at first with the ground. It was so at the Deluge with the lower animals and plants. It is so here. The universe is one throughout, and all its parts are in closest connection and interdependence. "Not a leaf rotting on the highway but is an indissoluble part of solar and stellar worlds" (Carlyle). Our life, our animal spirits, our reason itself, have fundamental and probably undiscovered relations with the sun and moon and stars. Relations so intimate may be assumed to be mutual, and we need not be surprised if we find casualties meant primarily for either extending to both.

III. God's judgments, long menaced, take the incredulous by surprise at last. (Ver. 9.) The antediluvians were no better prepared for the Flood by their hundred and twenty years' warning. They absorbed themselves in their work and pleasure, and knew not till the Flood came (Matt. xxiv. 38). So with the Sodomites, warned by Lot (Gen. xix. 14); and the inhabitants of Jerusalem at its capture, warned by Christ (Matt. xxiv. 33). Warning is thrown away on unbelief, and its end is always a surprise. In this case the sun would set at noon. The end would come untimely. In the midst of days and prosperity Israel would be cut off. There would be no anticipation, no fear, no suspicion even, of such an event. So with the ungodly at last. The judgment will surprise them and look untimely, but only because their incredulity will be unconquerable.

IV. RETRIBUTION CLOSELY ADJUSTED TO THE CIRCUMSTANCES OF THE CRIMINAL. (Ver. 10.) *Sinners are smitten in their joys.* The covetous in their possessions, the luxurious in their luxuries, the revellers in their revelries. When sackcloth and ashes are substituted for " ivory couches," and baldness for hair fragrant with the chief ointments, when howls rend the throats till lately melodious in song, the stroke is identified as that of One who never " beats the air." The fly of judgment, selecting infallibly the sore spot of the sufferer, reveals its mission as from God himself. *The joys in which the sinner is smitten are, moreover, those most closely connected with his sins.* God's stroke is as obviously righteous as appropriate. Falling on the sins that provoke them, God's judgments are self-interpreting. Israel's luxurious appliances were simply plunder, the wages of iniquity, sometimes even the price of blood. Hence God singles them out for special attack, and will plague Israel rigorously in every pleasure that has its root in sin.

V. THE FINALITY OF GOD'S RETRIBUTIVE ACT. The rule is that judgment is more severe in proportion as it is long delayed. 1. *It makes an end.* The sun goes down, and ends the day of life. After that nothing can come but night—the night of death. Destruction for sinners of Israel, destruction for all such sinners while the world stands, is the Divine provision. When the last measure of retribution is executed, the last shred of the sinner's good has been torn away. 2. *That end unspeakably bitter.* The wine-cup of God's fury is necessarily a bitter draught. There is wounded dignity in it, and wasted mercy, and outraged love, and all ingredients which are gall and wormwood in the mouth. They are digging for themselves Marah-pools no branch can sweeten, who " heap up wrath against the day of wrath," etc. 3. *That bitterness the bitterness of utter desolation.* " And make it like mourning for an only one." That is bitter mourning indeed. The loss of an only one is total loss, including our all. It is irreparable loss, for the dead cannot come back. It is loss not physical merely, nor sentimental merely, but loss wringing the heart-strings, and leaving us with the very jewel of life torn from its setting. Such is the mourning in which unforgiven sin is expiated at last. It is heart-agony, unrelieved, unmitigated, and never to end. " Son, remember; " " There shall be wailing and gnashing of teeth; " " Their worm dieth not, and their fire is not quenched."

Ver. 9.—*A sunset at noon.* This language is at once prophetic and figurative. It predicts an event in the moral world under the figure of an analogous event in the physical world. The symbolical event is not an eclipse of the sun, which the language does not suit, but his going down at midday; and the event symbolized is clearly death in the midst of young life. Israel was rich and prosperous and young. To all outward seeming she was just in the meridian of her life. But her sun would never reach the west. Her end would be premature, sudden, and tragic. As if the sun dropped in an instant beneath the horizon from mid-sky, and the radiancy of noon gave place in that instant to the darkness of night; so Israel's day would darken suddenly, and the night of death fall in a sky all lit with the golden glow of noon.

I. THERE IS TO MEN A NATURAL TERM OF EXISTENCE, WHICH IS THEIR DAY. There is a natural life-term to all earthly creatures. This varies endlessly for each, between limits so far apart as a millennium and a day. There are cheloniæ that lengthen out their slow existence to centuries, and there are insects that sport out their little life in an afternoon. Intermediate between these widely distant limits is man with his three score years and ten (Ps. xc. 10). This period is his day. Beyond it few may hope, and none expect, to live. To reach it even there must be normal conditions of life within and around. This is not a long time at best. Let the utmost diligence be used, and the work that can be done in it is not much. Take from it the two childhoods, infancy and infirm age, and it becomes greatly shorter still. Not more than fifty active years enter into the longest life. On the most sanguine assumption these are the working hours of our day of life. What we do for God and men is done while they pass. They may not be so many, but they can scarcely be more, and if they are all given us we may thankfully reckon that we have lived our time.

II. THERE ARE EXCEPTIONAL CASES IN WHICH THIS PERIOD IS CUT SHORT. The normal life-term is not the actual one. The overwhelming majority never see it. When the septuagenarian has his birthday feast, the friends of his youth are not one in ten among the guests. From childhood till that hour they have been dropping off, and now nine-tenths and more are gone. 1. *A moiety of the race die in childhood.* Infant mortality is an obscure subject. Whether from the standpoint of equity or economy, there is much in it we cannot explain. Their death before they have transgressed brings up the solemn mystery of original sin, and the suffering of one for the sin of another (Rom. v. 14). Then their death before activity begins or consciousness dawns, and so apparently before they have been used, raises the almost equally perplexing question—Is there, so far as this life goes, a single human being made in vain? 2. *Many more die before or at maturity.* They are healthy till growth is almost complete. The body has acquired the strength and hardness needed for the burden of life's work. The mind has received the training which fits it to solve the problems of existence, and govern and use the body in accomplishing the highest purposes of both. Yet just now, when the tool has been formed and tempered and finished, it is broken before it has once been used at its best in the more serious work of life. Here we are face to face not only with an apparently purposeless creation, but also with what seems an unproductive training. 3. *Many also die with their work to all appearance unfinished, or only well begun.* Their capacity is growing; their field is widening; their influence is increasing. They are in the full swing of activity and usefulness. Yet at the very moment when the richest fruit of their life-work is beginning to form, they are cut down—cut down, too, where their death leaves a permanent blank, and no one is available to take up their work. Their mysterious character and solemn interest prepare a field for faith in the fact that—

III. THESE SUNSETS AT NOON ARE DIVINELY ORDERED. "I will cause," etc. To kill and to make alive are Divine prerogatives. Let the sun set where he will, the event is God's doing. And, in the light of Scripture and observation, a philosophy of such events is not altogether impossible to conceive. 1. *Take noon sunsets in sin.* These are often untimely and far from unaccountable. (1) *Sin is war against God;* and while he is omnipotent and righteous and the Disposer of life, it cannot conduce to length of days. The wickedness of men is a continual provocation of his just judgment, and therefore an inevitable shortener of life. (2) *Sin is also war against the species.* The wicked are hateful and hating one another. The essential selfishness of the corrupt heart is misanthropy in another aspect. Misanthropy, again, is murder in its earlier stage (1 John iii. 15), leading on to the other stages of it (Jas. iv. 1, 2); and a dispensation of universal murder must mean many a life cut short and many a sun untimely set. (3) *Sin does violence to our own nature.* The normal life of the body is a pure one; the direction of appetites only to their legitimate objects, and to these in the strictest moderation. This is obviously the royal road to health and length of days. Perversion of appetite on the one hand, and excessive indulgence of it on the other, do violence to the natural order. If the life is impure, in fact, and as it is impure, it is unnatural, and therefore likely to be short. There is no "fleshly lust" which does not "war against the life" (1 Pet. ii. 11) of soul and body both. Of course, the operation of second causes, such as the laws of reciprocity and health, is not something distinct from the Divine agency, but the instrumentality it employs. The laws of nature are simply God's executive, the hands and fingers which weave the threads of his purpose into the web of his work. 2. *Take noon sunsets in grace.* These also are not unknown. The good die young. Sometimes they die through the sin of others, sometimes in consequence of sin of their own. These, however, are the occasions only of their removal. The reason of it lies deep in the purposes of God. (1) *Some are taken away from the evil to come.* (Isa. lvii. 1.) The young Ahijah, "because in him was found some good thing toward the Lord God of Israel in the house of Jeroboam," was carried peacefully to his rest before the falling of the provoked disaster (1 Kings xiv. 10—14). The good King Josiah also, because he repudiated and mourned the sin of Judah, "was gathered to his grave in peace, that his eyes did not see all the evil which God brought upon Jerusalem" (2 Kings xxii. 19, 20). In many a family, on whose survivors the shock of a great calamity falls, the previous removal of some gentle spirit from their circle becomes intelligible as a merciful folding of the tender lamb before the crash of the nearing storm. (2) *Some are taken away because their work, although apparently only beginning, is really done.* Not every man's life-work can be identified, during its progress, by either his cotemporaries or himself. Sometimes it is incidental, aside from his line of effort, and altogether unconscious. A child lives to awake by its endearing ways a parent's sleeping heart. A youth lives by the tokens of early grace to bring brothers and sisters to look at the unseen, and the life for God. A man lives to carry some movement over its crisis, which, in its after-stages, will require a different hand. If we only knew "the end of the Lord" (Jas. v. 11), we should see that it is always attained before the means are discontinued; that he never breaks a tool till its work is done. (3) *Some can only do their work by dying.* The errand of Bathsheba's first child into the world was by its death to bring David to his knees and a right mind (2 Sam. xii. 13—23). And how many an early death in a careless family has been that family's salvation! Even the minister cut down in his early prime, with a life of usefulness opening out, as it seems, before him, may preach a sermon by his death more potent for good than all he could have said alive. Untimely death may even in certain cases anticipate the loss of influence for good. We know men of influence in the Church who in their erratic age are undoing the good they were honoured to do in their earlier years. Such men have only lived too long. If their sun had set at noon their life-work would have been far greater, humanly speaking, than it will now be. Looking as we do at the surface of things, and blind to their deeper relations and far-reaching issues, we are not in a position to criticize the providential arrangements of God. To believe that there is order in the seeming tangle, and ultimate and wider good behind the present partial evil, is the attitude of that enlightened faith which argues that Infinite Wisdom, omnipotent on the one hand and benevolent on the other, being at the helm of things, will steer in character.

Vers. 11—14.—*The scarcity that swallows the residue of good.* To waste is to want, in things temporal and spiritual alike. Abuse is inevitably followed by deprivation, and the prodigal is one who is purveying for himself a suit of rags. God caps our "will not" with his "shall not," and the rude hand of change soon spills the cup of good we have refused to taste. Under the operation of this law the nation of Israel would now come. They had wasted the Word of God, neglecting it, despising it, and at last forbidding it to be spoken. Now they should "want" it as a penal result. It would be taken from them in anger, and that at a time when even their inappreciation would long for it as for life itself. Observe here—

I. THE WORST OF ALL FAMINES. "Not a hungering for bread, nor a thirst for water, but to hear the words of Jehovah." This is a new form of disaster, and one that is specially severe. This follows from the fact that: 1. *It is in the spiritual sphere.* "Fear not them which kill the body." It is the least part of us. Whether it live or die, enjoy or suffer, is a question involving trivial interests, and these during a limited period. The soul is the man, and its well-being, next to God's glory, the great interest. For its injury there is no compensation, for its loss no parallel. When it suffers, the worst has happened. 2. *It is due to the loss of a necessary of spiritual life.* The deepest need of humanity is a communication from God. "This is life eternal, to know thee the only true God," etc. Hence the Word which God speaks is the Word of life. Apart from it spiritual life is impossible. (1) *It is the revelation of spiritual things.* God and his will and way; the soul, its duty and destiny,—are subjects on which it alone throws adequate light. The light of nature makes known the existence of God, and some features of his character. But its twilight, whilst touching here and there a mountain-top, leaves all the valleys in darkness. After trying four thousand years, "the world by wisdom knew not God," and did not because it could not. In all saving relations Christ is the Revelation of the Father (Heb. i. 1; John i. 18), and

Scripture alone reveals Christ (John v. 39), and the way of life through him. (2) *It is the vehicle of spiritual power.* "The power of God unto salvation" is Paul's synonym for the gospel. Spiritual energy, no doubt, inheres in the Holy Spirit, but he operates only through or with the truth. It carries the power by which life is given (1 Pet. i. 23), by which life-functions are discharged (Rom. x. 17), by which the life-principle is sustained (Jer. xv. 16), by which growth is promoted (1 Pet. ii. 2). In fine, the "engrafted Word," received with meekness, "is able to save our souls." The power that begins, that sustains, that develops, that matures religious life is a power linked inseparably to the Word. That any saving grace is attainable in the absence of it is a thing impossible of proof, and which all Scripture testimony bears against. (3) *It is the assurance of spiritual good.* "We are saved by hope," and it is through patience and comfort of the Scriptures that this heavenly candle is lighted in the soul (Rom. viii. 24; xv. 4). The Scriptures reveal the heavenly blessings in store, and thus supply the warp and woof out of which the web of comfort is woven. What we shall have, and that we shall have it, is the burden of the Word of promise, which, making the rich future sure, makes thus the present glad and strong. Poor indeed would man be if there were no such word to twine the heart's-ease when his brow is wrung in anguish and distress. To Israel, sinful but penitent, God elsewhere, allotting the bread of adversity, promises, "Thine eyes shall see thy teachers," etc. (Isa. xxx. 20, 21). This is calamity, but with compensation. "Man shall not live by bread alone, but by every word that cometh out of the mouth of God;" and with God, their Guide and Counsellor, no scarcity of bread could make them altogether wretched. But, *vice versâ*, the proposition will not hold. For the loss of the Word there is no offset possible. The impoverishment is central and radical, and all hedging is out of the question. 3. *This loss at a time when it would be most keenly felt.* "The Word of the Lord was precious in those days; there was no open vision." The mere fact of the sudden withdrawal of the Word would create an immediate demand for it. In this case the demand would rest on a practical necessity. "Crushed by oppressors, hearing only of gods more cruel than those who make them, how will they hunger and thirst for any tidings of One who cares for the weary and heavy laden?" (Maurice).

II. THE CIRCUMSTANCES THAT PROVOKE IT. The unique rigour of the penalty suggests some special circumstances in the provoking crime. One of these would be: 1. *Extreme heinousness.* "There is a sin unto death." It will never be forsaken. It precludes the idea of penitence. It involves the perversion, or rather inversion, of character, which "calls evil good, and good evil." There is nothing for it but the extreme penalty of being let alone. And even that will be inflicted. Saul had provoked it when "God answered him not, neither by dreams, nor by Urim, nor by prophets." Israel had provoked it when God said to his servant, "Thou shalt be dumb, and shalt not be to them a reprover" (Ezek. iii. 26; vii. 26). When a man sins on principle, he is not far off "a famine of hearing the words of the Lord." 2. *Failure of other judgments to turn.* "Why should ye be stricken any more? ye will revolt more and more." Other judgments had been for reformation and had failed; this would be for destruction—the only alternative left. When "cure" is out of the question, what else is to be done but "kill"? 3. *Chafing under and rejecting the Word itself.* Israel had heard more of the words of the Lord than they wished. They had made an effort to get rid of them, or some of them, by forbidding his prophets to speak his message. More of the Word to men in that mind would have been thrown away, and God never wastes his gifts. If we shut our eyes, he will take away the light. If we close our ears, "the voice of the charmer" will soon be silent. The men who will not have the words of the Lord shall be treated to a dispensation of silence.

III. THE PERSONS IT ASSAILS. When judgment falls upon a nation, the righteous often suffer with the wicked. Yet here there are persons against whom the shock is specially directed. They are: 1. *Those who put their trust in idols.* The idolater would naturally feel the extreme of dislike to the Word of God, and adopt the strongest measures against his prophets. He was therefore in that moral condition which needed, and that opposing attitude which provoked, the heaviest stroke. God will not give his "praise to graven images," and he will give the man who trusts in them an early opportunity of discovering whether they will suffice for his need. The more unreservedly he has chosen them, the more entirely will he be left to them. 2. *The young and buoyant among these.* (Ver. 13.) Youth and hope are hardest to overcome. There is a buoyancy in them, and a recuperative energy, that rises above calamity to which the old and broken would succumb. Yet even these would not avail. Physical suffering, breaking down even youth and vigour, mental suffering, overwhelming the most buoyant hopefulness, were among the enginery of the wrath of God.

IV. THE EFFECTS IT PRODUCES. These are distressing as the calamity producing them is stern (ver. 12). 1. *They seek the Word in vain.* It is sought as a last resource. In the extremity of trouble, and the failure of other help, men turn perforce to God. And then the quest is vain. It is made too late, and from a motive to which there is no promise given (Prov. i. 24—28). It is sought in an extremity, as the lesser evil of two; and in abject fear, in which there is no element of loyalty or love; and, thus sought, cannot in the nature of things be found. The time for God to give it has passed, because the time has passed in which men might have received it to any effect of spiritual good. 2. *They faint in the search.* "They shall reel from sea to sea." "The word [reel] is used of the reeling of drunkards, of the swaying to and fro of trees in the wind, of the quivering of the lips of one agitated, and then of the unsteady seeking of persons bewildered, looking for what they know not where to find" (Pusey) It is characteristic that search is made everywhere but in the South, where alone the true worship of God was, and where, if anywhere, his Word might have been found. Wrong seeking is wrong all round, and so is of necessity in vain. It is a loss of effort, which is "a grievous labour won." It wearies itself out in aimless blind exertion, made out of season, and vitiated by the very ills that drive men to make it. 3. *They fall and never rise.* God will "make an end." The time for it had come. Sin had reached a climax. Evil character had reached a final fixity. Calamity had ceased to improve. The tardy anxiety for a Divine communication meant simply that every other resource was exhausted. "Cut it down" is the one process of husbandry for which the tree is fitted. (1) *There is a famine of the Word on Israel still.* "Blindness in part has happened" to them, in that, "when Moses is read, the veil is on their heart." This practically amounts to the removal of the Word. It is a sealed book to them—sealed by their blindness to its spiritual sense. Not heathen ignorance is more effectually cut off from the knowledge of the truth than Jewish prejudice and hate. (2) *It rests on them for the same reason for which it came.* Persistently, blindly, bitterly, they rejected the truth of the gospel. They made it evident that they would not have it (Acts xiii. 46). And so sadly, reluctantly, but sternly, it was taken from them. "Lo, we turn to the Gentiles." When that Word was spoken, Israel was left to the darkness it loved. In that chosen darkness they still grope, and will till the latter-day glory dawns. (3) *It will give place one day to a period of plenty.* "God hath not cast off his people which he foreknew." There is a remnant to which the promise belongs, and with which it will be kept (Rom. ix. 27; xi. 5). "When it shall turn to the Lord, the veil shall be taken away." The period, extent, and occasion of this turning are not revealed, but it will be the crowning triumph of the "glorious grace" of God.

HOMILIES BY VARIOUS AUTHORS.

Ver. 1.—*Ripeness in iniquity.* The figure here employed by Amos comes very naturally from him who had been a gatherer of the fruit of the sycomore tree. But at the same time, it is somewhat of a shock to the reader of this prophecy to find such a similitude employed for such a purpose. Our associations with "a basket of summer fruit" are all agreeable; but here the ripeness is in iniquity, and is unto condemnation and destruction.

I. A PAST PROCESS OF MATURITY IN SIN IS IMPLIED. As the fruit has been ripened during months of growth unto maturity, so the nation of Israel has gradually and progressively come to such a condition as that lamented and censured by the prophet of the Lord. 1. Past privileges have been misused. No nation had been so favoured as the descendants of Jacob; the greater the privileges, the greater the guilt of neglect and abuse. 2. Past warnings have been despised. If the people could not, in the exercise of their own faculties, foresee the end of all their misdeeds, they had no excuse, for prophet after prophet had arisen to rebuke them for unfaithfulness, and to warn them of impending judgment. **3. Past invitations have been unheeded.** Often had the messengers of God mingled promises with threats, invitations with censure. But in vain. The voice of the charmer had been disregarded; the tenderness of Divine compassion had been despised. Hence the process of deterioration had gone on. And circumstances which should have ripened the national character into heroic virtue, into saintly piety, had only served to mature irreligiousness and rebellion. Thus the sun and the showers which ripen the corn and the wholesome fruit bring also every poisonous growth to perfection.

II. A SPEEDY PROSPECT OF CONSEQUENT DESTRUCTION IS REVEALED. The ripe fruit speaks not only of the sunshine of the bygone days, but of the consumption which awaits it. In this passage the figurative language of the prophet is to be interpreted as foreboding approaching ruin. "He that being often reproved hardeneth his neck, shall suddenly be destroyed, and that without remedy." **1.** Perseverance in irreligiousness issues in deterioration of character. The very years, the very privileges, which make the good man better, make the bad man worse. It was so with Israel as a nation. The operation of the same law may be traced in human society to-day. **2.** Perseverance in irreligiousness will, under the Divine government, involve chastisement and punishment. The captivity foretold was to be accompanied by the desolation of the capital and the cessation, or at least the interruption, of national life. "The end is come," saith God, "to my people Israel." The prosperity and superficial peace of the wicked must be brought to a disgraceful close.—T.

Ver. 2.—"*My people.*" The occurrence of this expression in such a connection as this is very amazing and very encouraging. Even when, by the mouth of his prophet, the Lord is uttering language of regretful denunciation, the prediction of sore chastisement, he still calls Israel his own! God's ways are indeed higher than our ways, and his thoughts than our thoughts.

I. THIS LANGUAGE IS A REMINISCENCE OF PAST ELECTION. God called Israel his people, because he had chosen them from among the nations of the earth, to be the depositary of his truth, the recipients of his Law, the instrument of his purposes among men. As early associations are strong amongst men, as we always retain a tender interest in those whom we have watched over, befriended, and benefited from their childhood, so the Lord represents himself as cherishing kindness for the people whom he had called as it were in their childhood, and nursed into maturity. He did not forget the days "when Israel was a child."

II. THIS LANGUAGE IS PROOF OF PRESENT KINDNESS. He does not say, "Ye *were* my people;" for they are his people still.

> "Mine is an unchanging love,
> Higher than the heights above;
> Deeper than the depths beneath;
> Free and faithful, strong as death."

Even in carrying out his threats of punishment, Jehovah does not act in anger and vindictiveness. He is the Father chastening the child whom he loveth. He does not abandon the disobedient; he subjects them to discipline which may restore them to submission and to filial love.

III. THIS LANGUAGE IS PREDICTIVE OF FUTURE RECONCILIATION. As long as God says, "My people," there is hope for the future. He has not abandoned; he will not abandon. The city may be razed, but it shall be built again. There shall be captivity; but he deviseth means whereby his banished ones shall return. Wounds shall be healed. The grave shall give up her dead. The wanderer shall return, and shall be clasped to the Father's patient, yearning, rejoicing heart. "My people" are mine for ever.

APPLICATION. God in the midst of wrath remembers mercy. When sin is recognized and realized as such, when chastening has answered its purpose, when the disobedient are penitent and the rebellious are submissive, then is there hope. Not in any excellence connected with man's repentance, but in the grace of the Father's heart, in the faithfulness of the Father's promises. Not Israel alone, but mankind at large, are designated by the Eternal "my people." Therefore he who sent his Son to seek and to save that which is lost is described as "the Saviour of all men, specially of them that believe."—T.

Vers. 4—6.—*Covetousness.* It was not for heterodoxy in theology, it was not for remissness in ritual, that Amos chiefly reproached the Israelites. It was for injustice, violence, and robbery; it was for seeking their own wealth and luxury at the expense of the sufferings of the poor. Avarice, or undue love of worldly possessions, is a serious vice; covetousness, or the desiring to enrich self at the cost of neighbours, is something very near a crime, for to crime it too often leads. I. THE MORAL DISEASE OF COVETOUSNESS. The symptoms may differ in different states of society; and there are details in the text which apply rather to the state of society in Samaria of old than to the England of to-day. But the malady is the same, deep-rooted in the moral constitution of sinful men. This sin is: 1. Injurious to the person who commits it. He who sets his affection upon this world's good, who carries his selfishness so far as to deprive, or even to wish to deprive, his neighbour of what is his—far more he who uses fraud or violence to gratify this desire—is working his own ruin. He is subverting the standard of value, by setting the material above the spiritual. He is dragging his aspirations down from the stars above his head to the dust beneath his feet. 2. Mischievous to society. If all men follow the example of the covetous, and long for the possessions of others, then human society becomes a den of wild beasts bent upon devouring one another, and earth becomes a very hell. Instead of being members one of another, in the case supposed, every man sees an enemy in his neighbour, and seeks his harm. The bonds of society are strained, are even broken. 3. Displeasing to God. In the ten commandments a place was found for the prohibition of this spiritual offence: "Thou shalt not covet." This fact is sufficient to show how hateful is this sin in the eyes of the great Lord and Ruler of all. II. THE DIVINE REMEDY FOR COVETOUSNESS. 1. The recognition of the benevolence and bounty of God. From him cometh down "every good gift and every perfect boon." He is the Giver of all, who openeth his hands, and supplieth the need of every living thing. He who would share the Divine nature must cherish an ungrudging and liberal spirit. 2. The remembrance of the "unspeakable Gift," and of the incomparable sacrifice of the Redeemer. Our Saviour's whole aim was to impart to men the highest blessings, and in the quest of this aim he gave his life for us. His constraining love alone is able to extirpate that selfishness which in human nature is the very root of covetousness. 3. The adoption of the counsels and the submission to the spirit of Christ. It was his saying, "It is more blessed to give than to receive."—T.

Ver. 7.—*The memory of God.* This language is actual truth, although it is based upon and accords with the experience of created intelligences. Memory is one of the primitive endowments of intellect, admitted to be such even by philosophers, who are very loth to admit that the mind of man can possess any such endowments. A man who should never forget would indeed be a marvel, a miracle. But it would be inconsistent with our highest conceptions of God to suppose it possible for anything to escape his memory. In his mind there is, of course, neither past nor future, for time is a limitation and condition of finite intelligence. To the Eternal all is present; all events to him are one eternal now. I. A GENERAL TRUTH CONCERNING THE DIVINE NATURE AND GOVERNMENT. Nothing is unobserved by God, and nothing is forgotten by him. All men's actions as they are performed photograph themselves indelibly upon the very nature of the Omniscient and Eternal. Nothing needs to be revived, for nothing ever becomes dim. II. A SOLEMN TRUTH CONCERNING THE CONDUCT AND PROSPECTS OF THE SINFUL. Parents forget the wrong-doing of their children, and rulers those of their subjects. Hence many evil deeds escape the recompense which is their due. But Jehovah, who "remembered" (to use the expression necessarily accommodated to our infirmity) all the acts of rebellion of which the chosen people had been guilty, does not lose the record of any of the offences committed by men. On the contrary, they are written "in a book of remembrance"—a book one day to be unrolled before the eyes of the righteous Judge.

III. A PRECIOUS ASSURANCE CONCERNING THE GOOD PURPOSES AND ACTIONS WHICH GOD DISCERNS AND REMARKS IN HIS PEOPLE. Thus we find saintly men of old in their prayers beseeching the Lord to remember them: "Remember me, O Lord, for good;" "Remember me with the favour thou showest unto thy people." He who said, "I know thy works," who said, "I will never forget any of their works," is a Being to whom we may safely commend ourselves and all that is ours which he himself creates and which he approves.

APPLICATION. 1. In our confessions let us be frank and open with God, who searcheth the heart, and who forgetteth nothing. It would be folly to suppose that he forgets our sins; it would be wickedness to strive to forget them ourselves. "If we confess our sins, he is faithful and just to forgive." 2. In our prayers for pardon let us bear in mind that there is a sense in which he will "remember no more" the offences of his penitent and believing people. He will treat us as if he had forgotten all our rebellion, and as if he remembered only our purposes and vows of loyalty.—T.

Ver. 10.—"*A bitter day.*" There is something incongruous in this language. Day is the bright and beauteous gift of God, and its sunlight and all the glory it reveals may justly be taken as the emblem of happiness and prosperity. The light is sweet; the day is joyous. Yet here there is depicted a *bitter* day! The context makes it evident that this is attributable to sin, which makes all sweet things bitter, and all bright things dim.

I. THE BITTER DAY OF ISRAEL CONTRASTS WITH BYGONE DAYS OF SWEETNESS. Festivals and songs are mentioned in the context as distinctive of the religious life of the chosen people. And in times of national plenty and prosperity there had never been wanting abundance and even luxury, mirth and music, festivity and joy. These things have vanished into the past now that the "bitter day" has dawned.

II. THE BITTER DAY OF ISRAEL IS MARKED BY CIRCUMSTANCES OF TERRIBLE DISTRESS. The sun goes down, the land is darkened, mourning and lamentation are heard, sackcloth is worn, the hair is shaved off the heads lately anointed for the banquet and wreathed with flowers; the signs are those of "mourning for an only son." The fallen and wretched condition of the nation could not be depicted more graphically. The prophet-artist is skilful to heighten the dark colours which are expressive of Israel's woe.

III. THE BITTER DAY OF ISRAEL IS THE RESULT OF ISRAEL'S SINS. What is called misfortune and calamity is often really punishment. There was nothing accidental in what befell this nation. On the contrary, Israel brought disaster upon itself by unfaithfulness, disobedience, rebellion. As the people had sown, so they were to reap. Under the government of a just God it cannot be otherwise. The fruit of sin cannot be otherwise than bitter.

IV. THE BITTER DAY OF ISRAEL IS SUGGESTIVE OF LESSONS OF WISDOM TO EVERY NATION. The rule of a righteous God is a fact not to be disputed. The retributive consequences of that rule are not to be evaded. Let not the people imagine a vain thing, or the rulers take counsel together against the Lord.—T.

Ver. 11.—*Famine of the Word of God.* There are many blessings which are not suitably valued until they are withdrawn and missed. It is so with bodily health, with political liberty, with domestic happiness. And the prophet assumes that it will be found the same with the Word of God. When it is possessed—when the Scriptures are read and the Gospel is heard—it is too often the case that the privilege is unappreciated. But what must it be to be shut off from all communication with Heaven! And such, it was foretold, was to be the lot of Israel in the days of retribution and calamity which were about to overtake Israel.

I. THE WORDS OF GOD ARE TO THE SOUL AS BREAD AND WATER TO THE BODY. Man's bodily constitution is such that food and drink are a necessity to health and even to life; to be even partially starved is to be disabled and to be rendered wretched. Even so, the truth, the righteousness, the love of God, are the necessary aliment of the spiritual nature. "Man shall not live by bread alone, but by every word that proceedeth out of the mouth of God." Fellowship with God by his Word is indispensably necessary in order that a high, holy, and acceptable service may be rendered.

II. A FAMINE OF THE WORD OF GOD IS TO BE DREADED AS DETRIMENTAL TO SPIRITUAL

LIFE AND WELL-BEING. 1. If the knowledge of God himself be withheld, there is for man no solution of all the mysteries of the universe, the mysteries of his being. 2. If the Law of God be concealed, there is no sufficient guide through human life. 3. If the gospel of Christ be withheld, there is no peace for the conscience, no sufficient inspiration for duty, no assurance of immortality. 4. If revelation be denied, there is no power, no principle sufficient to guide and to govern human society. (*Vide* ' The Eclipse of Faith,' by the late Henry Rogers, where a chapter " The Blank Bible," sets forth the consequences which may be supposed to follow upon the disappearance of the Holy Scriptures.)

III. THOSE WHO POSSESS THE WORD OF GOD SHOULD BY THESE CONSIDERATIONS BE INDUCED TO STUDY IT AND TO USE IT ARIGHT. Neglect of the Divine Word may not in our case entail the actual deprivation foretold in the text. But it certainly will entail an indifference and insensibility to the truth, which will be equally injurious and disastrous. *Now* the Word is ours ; let us listen to it with reverence and faith ; let us obey it with alacrity and diligence. " Walk in the light while ye have the light, lest darkness come upon you."—T.

Vers. 1—3.—*Ripeness for judgment.* " Thus hath the Lord God showed unto me : and behold a basket of summer fruit. And he said, Amos, what seest thou ? And I said, A basket of summer fruit," etc. The text suggests three general truths.

I. WICKED NATIONS GROW RIPE FOR JUDGMENT. The " basket of summer fruit," now presented in vision to Amos, was intended to symbolize that his country was ripe for ruin. This symbol suggests : 1. That *Israel's present moral corruption was no hasty production.* The ripe fruit in that basket did not spring forth at once ; it took many months to produce. It came about by a slow and gradual process. Men do not become great sinners at once. The character of a people does not reach its last degree of vileness in a few years ; it takes time. The first seed of evil is to be quickened, then it grows, ripens, and multiplies until there is a crop ready for the sickle. 2. That *Israel's season for improvement was past and gone.* The ripened fruit in that basket had reached a stage in which improvement was impossible. The bloom was passing away, and rottenness was setting in. Nations become incorrigible. The time comes when it may be said—The harvest is past, all cultivation is impossible. What boots your sowing seed under the burning sun of July or August ? The fructifying forces of nature will not co-operate with you. 3. That *Israel's utter ruin was inevitable.* Nothing awaited that " basket of summer fruit " but rottenness. Its decomposition was working, and would soon reduce it to putrescent filth. So it was with Israel.

II. TRUE PROPHETS ARE MADE SENSIBLE OF THIS RIPENESS. God gives Amos a vision for the purpose. " Thus hath the Lord God showed unto me : and behold a basket of summer fruit. And he said, Amos, what seest thou ? And I said, A basket of summer fruit. Then said the Lord unto me, The end is come upon my people of Israel." God always gives his true ministers a clear vision of the subjects of their discourse. This clearness of vision is in truth their call and qualification for their Divine mission. Men, alas ! often assume the work of the ministry whose mental vision is so dim that they are unable to see anything with vivid clearness ; hence they always move in a haze, and their language is circumlocutory and ambiguous. Amongst the vulgar, those who should be condemned for their obtuseness get credit for their profundity. To every true teacher God says at the outset, " What seest thou ? " Hast thou a clear vision of this basket of summer fruit ? Hast thou a clear idea of this subject on which thou art about to discourse ? Thus he dealt with Moses, Elijah, Daniel, Paul, John.

III. ALMIGHTY GOD MAKES HIS PROPHETS SENSIBLE OF THE RIPENESS OF A PEOPLE'S CORRUPTION IN ORDER THAT THEY MAY SOUND THE ALARM. Why was Amos thus divinely impressed with the wretched moral condition of the people of Israel ? Simply that he might be more earnest and emphatical in sounding the alarm. " The end is come upon my people of Israel ; I will not again pass by them any more. And the songs of the temple shall be howlings in that day, saith the Lord God : there shall be many dead bodies in every place ; they shall cast them forth with silence." What was the calamity he was to proclaim ? 1. *Universal mourning.* " The songs of the temple shall be howlings." Where the shouts of mirth and the songs of joy had been heard, there should be nothing but the howlings of distress. The inevitable tendency of sin is to turn songs of gladness into howlings of distress. 2. *Universal death.* "And there shall be many dead bodies in every place; and they shall cast them forth with silence." The reference is to sword, pestilence, and famine multiplying the dead so rapidly as to render impossible the ordinary decencies and ceremonies at funerals. "Cast them forth with silence."

CONCLUSION. How stands our country? Is not its moral depravity ripening in every direction? Is it not filling up its measure of iniquities, treasuring up wrath against the last day? Does it not become all true teachers to sound the alarm? The time seems past for crying, "Peace and safety." Destruction is at hand; the fields are white for harvest.—D. T.

Vers. 4—10.—*Avarice.* "Hear this, O ye that swallow up the needy, even to make the poor of the land to fail," etc. The prophet here resumes his denunciatory discourse to the avaricious oppressors of the people. The verses may be taken as God's homily to greedy men. "Hear this." Hush! pay attention to what I am going to say. Listen, "ye that swallow up the needy." The words suggest three remarks concerning avarice.

I. IT IS EXECRABLE IN ITS SPIRIT. 1. It is *sacrilegious.* "When will the new moon be gone, that we may sell corn? and the sabbath, that we may set forth wheat?" Bad as Israel was, it still kept up the outward observances of religion, yet these observances they regarded as commercial inconveniences. In their hearts they wished them away, when they seemed to obstruct their greedy plans. With sacrilegious spirit, they treated religious institutions as worthless in comparison with sordid gain. Avarice in heart has no reverence for religion. 2. It is *dishonest.* "Making the ephah small, and the shekel great, and falsifying the balances by deceit." It is always overreaching, always cheating; it generally victimizes the poor; it makes its fortunes out of the brain and muscles, the sweat and life, of the needy. 3. It is *cruel.* "Ye that swallow up the needy, even to make the poor of the land to fail. . . . That we may buy the poor for silver, and the needy for a pair of shoes." Avarice deadens all social affections, steels the heart, and makes its subject utterly indifferent to all interests but its own; it will swallow up, or as some render it, gape after, the needy just as the wild beast pants after its prey. "Greedy men are a generation whose teeth are as swords, and their jaw-teeth as knives, to devour the poor from off the earth, and the needy from amongst men" (Prov. xxx. 14).

II. IT IS ABHORRENT TO JEHOVAH. "The Lord hath sworn by the Excellency of Jacob, Surely I will never forget any of their works." Some render the "Excellency of Jacob" the "Pride of Jacob," and suppose the expression to mean that Israel professed to regard him as its Glory; and therefore it is by himself that he swears, for he can swear by no one greater. God observes all the cruelties which avarice inflicts upon the poor. Nothing is more abhorrent to his benevolent nature than covetousness. One of the leading principles in his moral code is, "Thou shalt not covet thy neighbour's house," etc. Against no sin did his blessed Son preach more earnestly. "Take heed, beware of covetousness," said he (Luke xii. 15). He closes the gates of heaven against covetousness. "The covetous shall not inherit the kingdom of heaven" (1 Cor. vi. 10). 1. It is *repugnant to his nature.* His love is disinterested, unbounded love, working ever for the good of the universe. Greed is a hideous antagonist to this. 2. It is *hostile to universal happiness.* He created the universe in order to diffuse happiness; but greed is against it. (1) It is against the happiness of its *possessor.* The soul under the influence of covetousness can neither grow in power nor be gratified in desire. Avarice is an element of hell. It is in truth one of the fiery furies of the soul. (2) It is against the happiness of *society.* It prompts men to appropriate more of the common good than belongs to them, and thus to diminish the required supplies of the multitude. It is the creator of monopoly, and monopoly is the devil of social life.

III. IT IS A CURSE TO SOCIETY. See what punishment comes on the land through this! "Shall not the land tremble for this," etc.? Observe: 1. How God makes nature an avenging angel. He makes "the land tremble." He "toucheth the hills, and they smoke;" pours out waters as a flood. He can make the world of waters deluge the earth as the overflowing Nile at times inundates the land of Egypt. He can (to use human language) roll back the sun. "I will cause the sun to go down at noon." 2. How God makes a multitude to suffer on account of the iniquities of the few. "And I will turn your feasts into mourning, and all your songs into lamentations; and I will bring up sackcloth," etc.

CONCLUSION. Avoid covetousness. It is the chief of the principalities and powers of darkness. It may be considered the great fountain whence all the streams of crime and misery flow forth. It is eternally opposed to the virtue and happiness of the universe. The fable of Midas in Grecian mythology is strikingly illustrative of this tremendous evil. Bacchus once offered Midas his choice of gifts. He asked that whatever he might touch should be changed into gold. Bacchus consented, though sorry that he had not made a better choice. Midas went his way rejoicing in his newly acquired power which he hastened to put to the test. He could scarcely believe his eyes when he found a twig of an oak, which he had plucked, become gold in his hand. He took up a stone, and it changed to gold. He touched a sod; it did the same. He took an apple from a tree; you would have thought he had robbed the garden of the Hesperides. His joy knew no bounds; and when he got home he ordered the servants to set a splendid repast on the table. Then he found to his dismay that whether he touched bread, it hardened in his hand, or put a morsel to his lips, it defied his teeth. He took a glass of wine, but it flowed down his throat like melted gold. In utter terror, fearing starvation, he held up his arms shining with gold to Bacchus, and besought him to take back his gift. Bacchus said, "Go to the river Pactolus: trace the stream to its fountain-head; there plunge your head and body in, and wash away your fault and its punishment." Hence Midas learned to hate wealth and splendour.—D. T.

Vers. 11—13.—*Soul-famine.* "Behold, the days come, saith the Lord God, that I will send a famine in the land, not a famine of bread, nor a thirst for water, but of hearing the words of the Lord," etc. The Israelites now despised the message of the prophets, and by a just retribution, in addition to all their other calamities, they should experience a total withdrawal of all prophetic communications. In whatever direction they might proceed, and whatever efforts they might make to obtain information relative to the issue of their trouble, they should meet with nothing but disappointment. The subject of these words is soul-famine, and they suggest three general remarks.

I. THAT THE PROFOUNDEST WANT OF HUMAN NATURE IS A COMMUNICATION FROM THE ETERNAL MIND. This is implied in the Divine menace of sending a worse famine than the mere want of bread and water. They were *special* communications from himself, not the ordinary communications of nature, that Jehovah here refers to. And man has no greater necessity than this; it is the one urgent and imperial need. Two great questions are everlastingly rising from the depths of the human soul. 1. *How does the Eternal feel in relation to me as a sinner?* Nature tells me how he feels in relation to me as a creature; but nature was written before I fell. 2. *How am I to get my moral nature restored?* I have a sense of guilt that is sometimes intolerable; the elements of my nature are in eternal conflict; I have sadly terrible forebodings of the future. Now, the special Word of God can alone answer these questions. These are the problems of men the world over. God's Word is to the human soul what food is to the body— that which alone can strengthen, sustain, and satisfy. But as the soul is of infinitely greater importance than the body, the Divine Word is more needed than material food.

II. THAT THE GREATEST DISEASE OF HUMAN NATURE IS A LACK OF APPETITE FOR THIS COMMUNICATION. Which is the greater want of the body—the want of food, or the want of appetite for food? The latter, I trow, for the latter implies disease. It is so with the soul. The vast majority of souls have lost the appetite for the Divine Word. They are perishing, shrivelling up, for the lack of it. The desire is gone. They die, not for the want of the food, but for the want of appetite. As a rule, the starvation of souls is not for the lack of food, but for the lack of appetite. The worst of this disease is (1) men are not conscious of it; (2) it works the worst ruin.

III. THAT THE GREATEST MISERY OF HUMAN NATURE IS A QUICKENED APPETITE AND NO SUPPLIES. "They shall wander from sea to sea, and from the north even to the east, they shall run to and fro to seek the Word of the Lord, and shall not find it." 1. *The appetite will be quickened sooner or later.* Sometimes—would it were ever so!—it is quickened here, where supplies abound. Hear Job's cry, "Oh that I knew where I might find him!" And hear Saul's cry at Endor, "Bring me up Samuel." Oh for one word from his lips, one loving sentence from the mouth of the great Father! "Bring me up Samuel." 2. When the appetite is quickened and there is no supply, *it is an inexpressible calamity.* Such a period will come. "The days shall come," says Christ, "when ye shall desire to see one of the days of the Son of man, and ye shall not see it" (Luke xvii. 22). And again, "Ye shall seek me, and not find me: for where I am, thither ye cannot come" (John vii. 34). Oh miserable state of immortal souls, to be crying to the heavens, and those heavens to be as hard as brass!—D. T.

Ver. 14.—*Religious sincerity.* "They that swear by the sin of Samaria, and say, Thy god, O Dan, liveth; and, The manner of Beersheba liveth; even they shall fall, and never rise up again." "The sin of Samaria" means the idolatry of Samaria. In Samaria they worshipped the golden calf as the chief object; but it would seem there were other inferior idols. The god of Dan was the golden calf set up by Jeroboam in Dan (1 Kings xii.). "The fulfilment," says Delitzsch, "of these threats commenced with the destruction of the kingdom of Israel and the carrying away of the ten tribes into exile in Assyria, and continues to this day in the case of that portion of the Israelitish nation which is still looking for the Messiah, the Prophet promised by Moses, and looking in vain because they will not hearken to the preaching of the gospel concerning the Messiah who appeared as Jesus." The words suggest a thought or two in relation to religious sincerity.

I. THAT RELIGIOUS SINCERITY IS NO PROOF OF THE ACCURACY OF RELIGIOUS CREED. These Israelites seem to have been sincere in their worship of the golden calf; "they swore by it." That dumb idol to them was everything. To it they pledged the homage of their being. Yet how blasphemously erroneous, how contrary to the expresss mandate of Jehovah, "Thou shalt have none other gods but me"! How contrary to the dictates of common sense and all sound reasoning! Idolatry, in every form and everywhere, is a huge falsehood. Hence sincerity is no proof that a man has the truth. There are millions of men in all theologies and religions, who are so sincere in believing lies, that they will fight for their lies, make any sacrifice for their lies, die for their lies. Error, perhaps, can number more martyrs than truth. Saul of Tarsus was sincere when he was persecuting the Church and endeavouring to blot the name of Christ from the memory of his age. "I verily thought with myself, that I ought to do many things contrary to the name of Jesus of Nazareth," etc. (Acts xxvi. 9). Hence sincerity is not necessarily virtuous. A man is sincere when he is faithful to his convictions; but if his convictions are unsound, immoral, ungodly, his sincerity is a crime. The fact that thousands have died for dogmas is no proof of the truth of their dogmas.

II. THAT RELIGIOUS SINCERITY IS NO PROTECTION AGAINST THE PUNISHMENT THAT FOLLOWS ERROR. "They shall fall, and never rise up again." The sincerity of the Israelites in their worship in Bethel and at Dan prevented not their ruin. There are those who hold that man is not responsible for his beliefs—that so long as he is sincere he is a truthful man, and all things will go well with him. In every department of life God holds a man responsible for his beliefs. If a man takes poison into his system, sincerely believing that it is nutriment, will his belief save him? Error leads evermore to disappointment, confusion, and oftentimes to utter destruction. To follow error is to go away from reality; and to leave reality is to leave safety and peace.

CONCLUSION. Whilst there is no true man without sincerity, sincerity of itself does not make a man true. When a man's convictions correspond and square with everlasting realities, then his sincerity is of incomparable worth.—D. T.

EXPOSITION.

CHAPTER IX.

Vers. 1—10.—§ 6. *The fifth vision displays the Lord standing by the altar* and commanding the destruction of the temple (ver. 1). No one shall escape this judgment, flee whither he will (vers. 2—4); for God is Almighty (vers. 5, 6). Their election shall not save the guilty Israelites; still they shall not be utterly destroyed (vers. 7—10).

Ver. 1.—I saw the Lord. It is now no longer a mere emblem that the prophet sees, but actual destruction. He beholds the majesty of God, as Isa. vi. 1; Ezek. x. 1. **Upon** (or, *by*) **the altar**; *i.e.* the altar of burnt offering at Jerusalem, where, it is supposed, the whole nation, Israelites and Judæans, are assembled for worship. It is natural, at first sight, to suppose that the sanctuary of the northern kingdom is the scene of this vision, as the destruction of idolatry is here emblemized; but more probably Bethel is not meant, for there were more altars than one there (ch. iii. 14), and one cannot imagine the Lord standing by the symbol of the calf-worship. **Smite.** The command is mysteriously addressed to the destroying angel (comp. Exod. xii. 13; 2 Sam. xxiv. 15, etc.; 2 Kings xix. 35). **The lintel of the door**; τὸ ἱλαστήριον (Septuagint); *cardinem* (Vulgate); better, *the chapiter* (Zeph. ii. 14); *i.e.* the capital of the columns. The word *kaphtor* is used in Exod. xxv. 31, etc., for the knop or ornament on the golden candlesticks; here the idea is that the temple receives a blow on the top of the pillars which support it sufficient to cause its overthrow. The LXX. rendering arises from a confusion of two Hebrew words somewhat similar. **The posts**; *the thresholds*; i.e. the base. The knop and the threshold imply the total destruction from summit to base. **Cut them in the head, all of them**; rather, *break them* [*the capital and the thresholds*] *to pieces upon the head of all*. Let the falling building cover them with its ruins. The Vulgate renders, *avaritia enim in capite omnium*, confounding two words. Jerome had the same Hebrew reading, as he translates, *quæstus eorum, avaritia*, as if giving the reason for the punishment. The overthrown temple presents a forcible picture of the destruction of the theocracy. **The last of them** (ch. iv. 2); *the remnant*; any who escape the fall of the temple. **He that fleeth**, etc. All hope of escape shall be cut off.

Ver. 2.—The thought of ver. 1 is further expanded, the notion of flight being, as Jerome says, dissected. For **dig**, the LXX. reads, "be hidden;" but the expression implies a breaking through (Ezek. viii. 8). **Hell** (*Sheol*) is supposed to be in the inmost part of the earth (comp. Ps. cxxxix. 7, 8; Obad. 4). **Take them.** To receive punishment.

Ver. 3.—**The top of Carmel.** Among the woods and thickets. There are no caves on the summit of Carmel. "Amos tells us that in his day the top of it was a place to hide in; nor has it changed its character in this respect. . . . I would not have been prompted to place 'the top of Carmel' third in such a series of hiding-places, yet I can fully appreciate the comparison from my own experi-

ence. Ascending from the south, we followed a wild, narrow wady overhung by trees, bushes, and tangled creepers, through which my guide thought we could get up to the top; but it became absolutely impracticable, and we were obliged to find our way back again. And even after we reached the summit, it was so rough and broken in some places, and the thorn-bushes so thickset and sharp, that our clothes were torn and our hands and faces severely lacerated; nor could I see my guide at times ten steps ahead of me. From such biblical intimations, we may believe that Carmel was not very thickly inhabited" (Thomson, 'The Land and the Book,' Central Palestine, p. 237, etc.). Other writers speak of the occurrence of caves and deep valleys in the Carmel range. **In the bottom of the sea.** Both this and **heaven** (ver. 2) are impracticable hiding-places, and are used poetically to show the absolute impossibility of escape. **Serpent** (*nachash*, elsewhere called *leviathan* and *tannin*, Isa. xxvii. 1), some kind of sea-monster supposed to be venomous. Dr. Pusey mentions that certain poisonous hydrophidæ are found in the Indian and Pacific Oceans, and may probably infest the Red Sea and the Persian Gulf.

Ver. 4.—**Captivity** itself, in which state men generally, at any rate, are secure of their lives, shall not save them from the sword (Lev. xxvi. 33; Deut. xxviii. 65, etc. comp. Tobit i. 17, 18; ii. 3, where we see that the murder of captives was not unusual). The prophet looks forward to the Assyrian deportation. **For evil.** The people are indeed subject to God's special attention, but only in order to punish them (Ps. xxxiv. 15, 16; Jer. xliv. 11).

Ver. 5.—To confirm the threats just uttered, the prophet dwells upon God's omnipotence, of which he gives instances. He who will do this is **the Lord God of hosts.** There is no copula in the Hebrew here. (So ch. iv. 13; v. 8.) This title, *Jehovah Elohim Zebaoth*, represents God not only as Ruler of the heavenly bodies, but as the Monarch of a multitude of heavenly spirits who execute his will, worship him in his abiding-place, and are attendants on and witnesses of his glory (see note on Hag. i. 2). **Shall melt**; σαλεύων (Septuagint); comp. Ps. xlvi. 6; xcvii. 5; Micah i. 4; Nah. i. 5. The expression denotes the destructive effects of the judgments of God. **Shall mourn.** The last clauses of the verse are a repetition of ch. viii. 8, with some slight variation.

Ver. 6.—**Stories**; ἀνάβασιν (Septuagint); *ascensionem* (Vulgate); *upper chambers*, or the stages by which is the ascent to the highest heavens (comp. Deut. x. 14; 1 Kings viii. 27; Ps. civ. 3). **His troop** (*aguddah*); *vault.* The word is used for "the bonds" of the yoke in Isa. lviii. 6; for "the bunch" of hyssop in Exod. xii. 22. So the Vulgate here renders *fasciculum suum*, with the notion that the stories or chambers just mentioned are bound together to connect heaven and earth. But the clause means, God hath founded the vault or firmament of heaven upon (not *in*) the earth, where his throne is placed, and whence he sends the rain. The Septuagint renders, τὴν ἐπαγγελίαν αὐτοῦ, "his promise." So the Syriac. **The waters of the sea.** The reference is to the Deluge (ch. v. 8; Gen. vii. 4, 11).

Ver. 7.—Israel's election to be God's people should not save them, unless their conduct corresponded with God's choice. If they obeyed not, they were no better in his eyes than the heathen, their delivery from Egypt had no more significance than the migration of pagan nations. Here is a contrast to ch. vi. 1, etc. The children of Israel were now no dearer than the children of the Ethiopians (*Cushites*). The Cushites are introduced as being descendants of the wicked Ham, and black in complexion (as Jer. xiii. 23), the colour of their skin being considered a mark of degradation and of evil character. The Philistines from Caphtor; *from Cappadocia* (LXX. and Vulgate). This rendering is mistaken. The immigration spoken of took place before the Exodus (see Deut. ii. 23; Jer. xlvii. 4); and Caphtor is either Crete (see Dillman on Gen. x. 14) or the coast-land of the Delta, "which was occupied from an early period by Phœnician colonists, and thus came to be known to the Egyptians as *Keft ur*, or 'greater Phœnicia,' Keft being the Egyptian name of Phœnicia" (*Monthly Interpreter*, iii. 136). Mediæval Jewish writers identified it with Damietta (Conder, 'Handbook to the Bible,' p. 237). The Syrians (*Aram*, Hebrew) from Kir; τοὺς Σύρους ἐκ βόθρου, "the Syrians out of the ditch" (Septuagint); *Syros de Cyrene* (Vulgate); see note on ch. i. 5. "Aram" here probably means the Damascenes, Damascus shortly before the time of Moses having been occupied by a powerful body of immigrants from Armenia (Ewald, 'Hist. of Israel,' i. 286, 311, Eng. transl.).

Ver. 8.—**The sinful kingdom.** The kingdom of all Israel and Judah, the same as **the house of Jacob** just below, though a different fate awaits *this*, regarded as the covenant nation, whose are the promises. **Destroy it**, etc., as was threatened (Deut. vi. 15). **Saving that.** In spite of the destruction of the wicked people, God's promises hold good, and there is still a remnant who shall be saved (Jer. xxx. 11).

Ver. 9.—**For, lo!** He explains how and why the whole nation is not destroyed. **I will sift.** Israel is to be dispersed among the nations, tried and winnowed among them by affliction and persecution, that the evil may fall to the ground and perish, and the good be preserved. The word rendered "sift" implies "to shake to and fro;" and this shaking shall show who are the true Israelites and who are the false, who retain their faith and cleave to the Lord under all difficulties, and who lose their hold of true religion and assimilate themselves to the heathen among whom they dwell. These last shall not return from captivity. **The least grain**; Hebrew, *tseror*, "pebble;" so the Vulgate, *lapillus;* Septuagint, σύντριμμα, "fragment." It is used in 2 Sam. xvii. 13 of small stones in a building; here as hard grain in distinction from loose chaff (Keil). The solid grain, the good wheat, are the righteous, who, when the chaff and dust are cast away, are stored in the heavenly garner, prove themselves of the election, and inherit the promises (comp. Isa. vi. 13; Ezek. xx. 38; Matt. iii. 12). **Fall upon the earth;** *i.e.* perish, be lost (1 Sam. xxvi. 20).

Ver. 10.—**If any are to be saved, it will not be the sinners; they need not flatter themselves that their wilful blindness shall secure them. The evil shall not overtake.** They lulled themselves into a false security, and shut their ears against the warnings of the prophets; but that would avail them nothing. **Prevent;** come upon suddenly, surprise.

Vers. 11—15.—Part IV. Epilogue. The Establishment of the New Kingdom and the Reign of Messiah. The Kingdom shall embrace all Nations (vers. 11, 12), shall be enriched with Superabundant Spiritual Blessings (vers. 13, 14), and shall endure for ever (ver. 15).

Ver. 11.—**In that day.** When the judgment has fallen. The passage is quoted by St. James (Acts xv. 16, 27), mostly from the Greek, in confirmation of the doctrine that the Church of God is open to all, whether Jew or Gentile. **The tabernacle** (*sukkah*): hut, or tent (as Jonah iv. 5); no palace now, but fallen to low estate, a "little house" (ch. vi. 11). The prophet refers probably to the fall of the kingdom of David in the ruin wrought by the Chaldeans. Interpreted spiritually, the passage shadows forth the universal Church of Christ, raised from that of the Jews. Pusey notes that in the Talmud Christ is called "the Son of the fallen." **The breaches.** The house of David had sustained breaches under the hands of Jeroboam and Joash, and in the severance of the ten tribes at the hands of Assyrians and Chaldees; these should be repaired. Unity should be restored, the captives should return, and another kingdom should be established under another

David, the Messiah. Judah's temporary prosperity under Uzziah and Hezekiah would have been a totally inadequate fulfilment of the prophecy. Prophecies of the temporal and spiritual are, as usual, blended together and run up into each other. **His ruins.** The destroyed places of David. **I will build it;** Hebrew, *her.* The whole Jewish Church (comp. Jer. xxxi. 4; xxxiii. 7). **As in the days of old.** The days of David and Solomon, the most flourishing times of the kingdom (2 Sam. vii. 11, 12, 16). In the expression, "of old," Hebrew, "of eternity," may lurk an idea of the length of time that must elapse before the fulfilment of the promise. Septuagint, Ἀνοικοδομήσω αὐτὴν καθὼς αἱ ἡμέραι τοῦ αἰῶνος, "I will build it up as are the days of eternity." This seems to signify that the building is to last for ever.

Ver. 12.—**That they** (the true children of Israel) **may possess the remnant of Edom;** *i.e.* those who were nearest in blood, and yet most hostile of all men. David had subdued the Edomites (2 Sam. viii. 14; 1 Kings xi. 16), and Amaziah had inflicted a great slaughter upon them (2 Kings xiv. 7); but later they recovered their independence (2 Kings xvi. 6, where "Edomites" should be read for "Syrians;" 2 Chron. xxviii. 17), and were actively hostile against the Jews. It was on this account that they were emphatically denounced by Obadiah. "The remnant" is mentioned because, according to the threat in ch. i. 11, 12, they would be punished so that only a few would escape. The Septuagint gives, Ὅπως ἐκζητήσωσιν οἱ κατάλοιποι τῶν ἀνθρώπων [τὸν κύριον, Alexandrian], "That the remnant of men may earnestly seek the Lord," regarding Edom as a representative of aliens from God, and altering the text to make the sense more generally intelligible. This version, which reads "Adam," *men,* instead of "Edom," is endorsed by St. James. **Which are called by my Name;** "over whom my Name hath been called" (Septuagint). This is closer to the Hebrew; but the meaning is much the same, viz. all those who are dedicated to God and belong to him being by faith incorporated into the true Israel. (For the phrase, comp. 2 Sam. xii. 28; Isa. iv. 1; and to illustrate the idea, refer to Deut. xxviii. 10; Isa. xliv. 5; Ps. lxxxvii. 5, 6.) The Messianic kingdom shall be established in order that salvation may be extended to all nations who embrace it. **Saith the Lord;** *is the saying of Jehovah.* This is added to show the immutability of the promise. The covenant-God himself hath predicted it.

Ver. 13.—The prophet expatiates upon the rich blessings which shall follow the establishment of the kingdom. Under the figure of a supernatural fertility are represented the victories of grace (comp. Isa. xi. 6; Ezek. xxvi. 10, etc.; xxxiv. 25, etc.). The blessing is founded on the Mosaic promise (Lev. xxvi. 5). **The ploughman shall overtake the reaper.** Ploughing and harvest shall be continuous, without sensible interval. **The treader of grapes him that soweth seed.** The vintage should be so abundant that it should last till sowing-time. **The mountains shall drop sweet wine.** This is from Joel iii. 18. **And all the hills shall melt.** As Joel says, "shall flow with milk," in this promised land "flowing with milk and honey." Septuagint, πάντες οἱ βουνοὶ σύμφυτοι ἔσονται, "all the hills shall be planted" with vines and olives. For, as Corn. à Lapide quotes, "Bacchus amat colles" (Virg., 'Georg.,' ii. 113). The hyperbolical expressions in the text are not to be taken literally; they depict in bright colours the blessings of the kingdom of Messiah. Material and temporal blessings are generally represented as closely connected with spiritual, and as figurative of them. Such predictions, understood literally, are common in the so-called Sibylline Books; see *e.g.* lib. iii. 743, etc., where, among other prodigies, we have—

Πηγὰς τε ῥήξει γλυκερὰς λευκοῖο γάλακτος.

One is reminded of the golden age depicted by Virgil in his fourth eclogue. Trochon cites Claudian, 'In Rufin.,' i. 381, etc.—

"... nec vomere sulcus adunco
Findetur; subitis messor gaudebit aristis.
Rorabunt querceta favis; stagnantia passim
Vina fluent, oleique lacus."

Ver. 14.—**I will bring again the captivity;** *i.e.* I will repair the misery which they have suffered. The expression is here metaphorical, and does not necessarily refer to any restoration to an earthly Canaan. **Shall build the waste cities** (Isa. liv. 3). All these promised blessings are in marked contrast to the punishments threatened (Deut. xxviii. 30, 33, 39; compare similar promises in Isa. lxv. 21, etc.).

Ver. 15.—The blessing shall last for ever. **They shall no more be pulled up.** This was not true of the literal Israel; it must be taken of the spiritual seed, planted in God's land, the Church of Christ, against which the gates of hell shall not prevail. "Lo," says Christ, "I am with you alway, even unto the end of the world" (Matt. xxviii. 20)

HOMILETICS.

Vers. 1—4.—*A quest which none may elude.* We have here a vivid picture of a dreadful subject. The prophet makes a new departure in his mode of figuration. In other visions we saw the judgments of Heaven painted in terror-moving forms; the mighty forces of nature let loose and working destruction on sinners of men. Here we see, not judgments merely, but the Judge himself, active for destruction, fulminating his thunders, brandishing his two-edged sword, and spreading devastation where his anger rests. It is true all natural forces are his instruments, and their results his work. But they do not so reveal themselves to our sense. It is Scripture that shows us an omnipotent God in the forces of nature, and in every disaster they work a judgment from his hand.

I. THE GOD OF ISRAEL STANDING ON AN IDOL-ALTAR. Not the altar of God at Jerusalem, but the altar for calf-worship at Bethel, is probably here referred to. *God's standing on the idol-altar is not for purposes of fellowship.* That would be a moral impossibility. "What concord hath Christ with Belial? And what agreement hath the temple of God with idols?" Not light and darkness are less compatible, not fire and water more inherently antagonistic, than the great God, who "is all in all," and the idol which is "nothing in the world." *Neither is it in token of tolerance.* Between the two can be no peace, no truce, no parley. "God is a jealous God," and can have no rival. His sovereignty and supreme greatness make him necessarily intolerant here. There can be no Dagons on any terms where the ark rests. *It is for purposes of destruction only.* "There, where, in counterfeit of the sacrifices which God had appointed, they offered would-be-atoning sacrifices and sinned in them, God appeared standing, to behold, to judge, to condemn" (Pusey). When God approaches sin, it is only to destroy it. Sometimes he destroys it in saving the sinner; sometimes the sin and the sinner, hopelessly wedded, are destroyed together.

II. IDOLATERS' JUDGMENT BEGINNING AT THEIR IDOL-SHRINE. "Smite the lintel," etc. This is the natural course. The lightnings of judgment strike the head of the highest sin, and strike it in the provision made for its commission. And there is a fitness in this Divine order. 1. *It stops the worship.* With the appliances destroyed, the observances could not go on. The interruption of sin is an intelligible and appropriate object of Divine judgment. The most effectual punishment of criminal indulgence is a visitation that stops it perforce. If not cured, at least the evil is stayed. 2. *It reveals the Divine hand.* Two plagues had passed on Egypt without any very deep impression having been made. But when Moses smote the dust, and it became lice on man and beast, the magicians said unto Pharaoh, "This is the finger of God." The miracle stopped at once the entire ceremonial of their national worship by making all the priests unclean. The idols were confounded, and Jehovah's power revealed. When a man finds his sufferings in the seat of his sins, he has materials for identifying them as the visitation of God.

III. THIS JUDGMENT FOLLOWING THEM INTO ALL THEIR RETREATS. (Vers. 2, 3.) Driven in terror from their idol-shrines, men seek escape in diverse ways, according to their diverse characters and surroundings. But it is a vain quest. The God who is omnipresent to infallible saving effect in the case of his saints (Ps. cxxxix. 8—12) is so also to the inevitable destruction of the ungodly. One climbs the heaven of proud defiance, to be brought ignominiously down (Jer. xlix. 16; Obad. 4). Another "breaks through into the hell" of abject fear and self-abasement, to be dragged forth into the intolerable light. The Carmel of philosophic nescience presents no cave or grove impenetrable by the hounds of righteous judgment. Even the sea of deeper sinful indulgence has a serpent of avenging providence in its depths, from whose bite there is no escape.

IV. THIS JUDGMENT REACHING THEM THROUGH THE INSTRUMENTALITY OF ALL NATURAL CAUSES. The "sword," as representing human agency, and the "serpent," as representing the agency of natural causes, are both set in motion by God's command. The causes of nature are to God as the bodily organs to the brain, viz. servants to do his bidding. He "acts himself into them." Human wills are accessible to the will of the Supreme, and move with it as the tides with the circling moon. The Assyrian warring against Israel for his own reasons is, nevertheless, the rod of his anger in the hand of Israel's God. This fact gives moral significance to many events that seem purely natural. The drunkard's bloated body, the sensualist's shattered health, the spendthrift's ruined fortunes, are results of natural laws, it is true, but of these directed and combined by supernatural power, and accomplishing Divine moral ends. The evil that comes through nature comes from its God.

Ver. 4.—*The lidless eye.* God is not an absentee. He sits at the helm of things. He administers the affairs of the world which he has made. All creatures he takes cognizance of, determines their destiny, controls their actions. His kingdom ruleth over all. And this rule is moral. Under it condition takes the colour of character. God is pure to the pure, froward to the froward (Ps. xviii. 26). This transgressors know to their bitter cost.

I. GOD'S EYE FOLLOWS THE WICKED. In one sense his "eyes are upon the righteous" (Ps. xxxiv. 15). On the wicked they rest in a very different sense. 1. *In heedfulness.* Divine omniscience is an uncomfortable fact which the wicked try not to realize. "They seek deep to hide their counsel from the Lord." Their whole aim is to get away from him; to be able to think thoughts he shall not know, and cherish desires he shall not sift, and do works he shall not observe (John iii. 20; Isa. xl. 27). But the project is futile (Jer. xxiii. 24; Ps. xxxiii. 13; Prov. xv. 3). God is everywhere, sees everything, fills heaven and earth. No dispensation of inadvertency is possible. God will not ignore. He cannot be inattentive. Events of whatever kind, and everywhere, are infallibly submitted to his cognizance as the movements of the clouds above are faithfully mirrored in the glassy lake. He fills all things, and all that happens happens in his presence. 2. *In perfect insight.* "I the Lord do search the heart." Noticing things, God sees them through and through, discerns their character, and appraises their moral value. The mind and heart of man are no mystery to him. No slightest motion of either eludes his perfect knowledge. The purpose before it comes forth in action, the thought before it has matured into a purpose, the fancy before it has taken shape in evil desire,—all these are open to his eye. Even to the heathen he was *totus oculus,* a Being "all eye." He knows all things eternally, immeasurably, immutably, and by a single act; and men and their works and words and wishes are continually in his sight. 3. *In uncompromising displeasure.* God is passible. He can be affected by the actions of his creatures. His possession of genuine character ensures his genuine feeling. The moral perfection of that character ensures his feeling appropriately. "There must be so much or such kind of passibility in him that he will feel toward everything as it is, and will be diversely affected by diverse things according to their quality" (Bushnell). Therefore "he is angry with the wicked every day." Sin is to him as smoke to the eyes and vinegar to the teeth. It pains him inevitably, and leads to that infinitely pure recoil of his nature from evil, and antagonism to it, in which his wrath consists.

II. GOD'S INFLUENCES FOLLOW HIS EYE. "I set mine eye upon them for evil," etc. God's look brings evil consequences where it falls on evil things. 1. *To feel is with God to act.* Much human feeling comes to nothing. No action is taken on it. Its very existence may remain unspoken. Not so with God. It is a result of his perfection that his mental or moral attitude toward any object is his active attitude toward it also. Disposition associates itself inevitably with suitable action. Feeling against sin, he must also act against it. His very feeling is equivalent to action, for his volition is power, and to will a thing is to bring it to pass. 2. *God's action exactly answers to his feeling.* If he regard sin as evil, he will not treat it as good. His attitude towards it must be one all round, and therefore rigorous all round. And so it is. Whatever mystery may be about certain cases, there is no mystery about the connection between all suffering and sin. In sickness, in sorrow, in anxiety, in doubt, in all forms and degrees of pain, God's eye and hand are on sinners for evil. Until sin becomes congenial to his nature, it cannot become satisfactory to the sinner.

III. GOD'S MERCY WARNS THE SINNER OF BOTH. He makes no secret of his attitude and way in reference to sin. Both are made known to those whom they most concern. 1. *This course is merciful.* It gives the sinner an advantage. He sees the moral quality of sin as hateful in God's sight, and its inevitable result as provoking his hostile action. He can neither sin ignorantly nor incur the penalty unawares. Forewarned, it is his fault if he is not forearmed. 2. *It is moral.* It tends to deter from sin, and so to save from its penal consequences. The thought that it is under God's eye ought to make sin impossible, and does make it more difficult. The knowledge that it ends inevitably in ruin does much to stay the transgressor's hand. 3. *It is judicial.* Sin done consciously under God's eye, and deliberately in defiance of his wrath, is specially guilty. The warning which being heeded might have deterred from sinning will greatly aggravate the guilt of it if disregarded. The truth will be, as we treat it, a buoy lifting us out of the sinful sea, or a millstone sinking us deeper in its devouring waters.

Vers. 5, 6.—*The image of the Deity in "great nature's open eye."* God's wrath "is revealed from heaven against all ungodliness." And it is terrible as it is great. Impotent anger is ridiculous, but the wrath of Omnipotence overwhelms. Whatever, therefore, illustrates the power of God adds terror to his threat. And such is the effect of this passage. The stern purport of the previous commination is emphasized by the moving picture it presents of the Divine majesty and resistless might. Omnipotent resources will push forward to full accomplishment the purposes of Omniscience against doomed and abandoned Israel. We have here—

I. GOD'S NAME REVEALING HIS CHARACTER. This is the object of a name. It distinguishes the bearer from others, and this by expressing some leading characteristic. 1. *The Lord.* This is the word invariably substituted by the Jews for *Jehovah* in the reading of the Hebrew Scriptures. It is a name of authority, and means "the supreme Lord." The Lord is over all. He is Governor and Judge in one. He does as it pleases him. He disposes of all matters, and settles all interests without appeal. He reckons with none, and none can call him to account. 2. *Jehovah.* This is a verb, third person, signifying "he is," and another form of the name "I am," by which God revealed himself to Moses. Its root-idea is that of "underived existence;" then, as arising out of this, "independent action;" and then, as the corollary of both, "eternity and unchangeableness" (see Fairbairn). It is thus the proper name of God to man; self-existent himself, the Author of existence to all persons and things, and manifesting his existence to those capable of knowing it. Jehovah is the concrete and historical name of God. As revealed by it, he exists by his own energy, and makes to be all things that are. Absolute and undetermined, he determines absolutely all things outside himself. Unseen and invisible, he comes forth—concretes himself, as it were—in the works which his hands have made. 3. *Jehovah of hosts.* This title appears first in 1 Sam. i. 3, and, as has been remarked, "simultaneously with the foundation of the Jewish monarchy." It may mean Lord of (Israel's) armies (Ps. xliv. 9), or of celestial beings (Ps. cxlviii. 2), or of the heavenly bodies (Isa. xl. 26), or, more probably, of all three. In this wide sense we "see in the title a proclamation of the universal sovereignty of Jehovah, needed within the nation, lest that invisible sovereignty should be forgotten in the visible majesty of the king; and outside the nation, lest Jehovah should be supposed to be merely a national deity" (Kirkpatrick, on 1 Samuel). This is the God whose eye is for evil on Israel—God supreme, God absolute, and God in special relation to the hosts of Israel who had forsaken him, to the heavenly bodies which they worshipped, and to the angel-hosts, the ministers to do his will on those whom he would visit in wrath.

II. GOD'S OPERATIONS REVEALING HIS WAY. What God does is a criterion of what he can do. His all-pervading activity will include in its sweep the accomplishment of the destiny again and again announced. 1. *He occupies the sky.* "Who buildeth his stories," etc. There were, according to a rabbinical theory, seven heavens, the seventh containing the throne of the Eternal, symbolized by Solomon's throne of ivory and gold, the six steps leading up to which symbolized in turn the six celestial regions below the highest heaven (1 Kings x. 18—20). In terms of this mystic theory is the expression, "stories of the heaven." Heaven is conceived of as a giddy height, approached by aerial steps or stages, all of them the handiwork of God. He stands on the "cloud-capped towers." He dwells in the "airy palaces." He walks on the "fleece-like floors." He makes the different levels of the firmament steps between his throne and the earth below. 2. *He metamorphoses the earth.* (Ver. 5.) God's word brought order out of chaos at first. "He spake, and it was done," etc. By the same word, turning order into chaos again, shall all things be dissolved (2 Pet. iii. 10, 11). It is little for the word that makes and unmakes, that created and will dissolve the frame of nature, to move in earthquake upheaval the solid crust of earth till it mimicks the roll of the sea, or "Nile's proud flood" in its rise and fall. 3. *He distributes the waters of the sea.* The sea is the most stupendous natural object. There is majesty in all its moods, and awe in its very presence. Hence in the mythology a god was allocated to it, brother to Zeus, the god of heaven and earth, and second only to him in power. And God's "way is in the sea." He rules its waves. He regulates its myriad currents and restless tides. Its great throbbing pulse beats but at his will. He holds its waters in the hollow of his hand, and concentrates or disperses them as it pleases him. He is a God, then, "whose wrath is terrible." Every force of nature he not alone controls, but wields an instrument of his will. In ch. v. 8 the same fact is pled as an inducement to seek his favour, which here appears as a reason to dread his wrath. As the same locomotive will drive the train before it or draw it after it at the engineer's will, so the fact of the omnipresent energy of God is fitted alike to alarm and to attract, but in either case to bring the sinner to his feet.

III. PHYSICAL CONVULSIONS THE COUNTERPARTS OF MORAL CONVULSIONS. Events in the two worlds happen according to similar if not identical laws. To a discriminating eye, the one set rises up in the likeness of the other, created so by God. "He daily buildeth his stories in the heavens when he raiseth up his saints from things below to heavenly places, presiding over them, ascending in them" (Pusey). "He toucheth the earth, and it melteth," when he stretches out his hand in wrath on its inhabitants, and men's hearts fail them for fear. "He calleth to the waters of the sea, and poureth them out over the earth," when he makes the wicked the rod of his anger to overrun and vex society (Ps. xciii. 3, 4). Verily the God who makes the heavens his throne, the earth his footstool, the elements his playthings, and men and angels his ministers, is a Being in whose favour is life and whose power is terrible.

Vers. 7—10.—*The exalted brought low.* "Think not to say within yourselves, We have Abraham to our father." And yet the blind and infatuate Israel were always saying it. They said it in view of every imminent catastrophe. They said it in abbreviation of all argument. They said it in lieu of fit and seasonable action. They made it an amulet to hang around their neck when they rushed purblind into rebellious action. They ran into it as into an intellectual joss-house, where any absurdity was raised to the dignity of a god. This last support of their false security the prophet in this passage knocks away. They had acted altogether out of character, and now—

I. APOSTATE ISRAEL CAN ONLY TAKE RANK WITH THE HEATHEN IN GOD'S ESTIMATION. National election was, no doubt, a pledge of national preservation, but only in connection with national faithfulness; for: 1. *A spiritual relation with the unspiritual is impossible.* "What fellowship hath righteousness with unrighteousness?" It is a moral impossibility. They are moral opposites and incompatible in the nature of things. Becoming assimilated to the heathen, Israel contracted themselves out of the covenant, and became "afar off," even as they. 2. *A relation, when it is repudiated on either side, virtually terminates.* Israel had said, "We will not have this Man to rule over us;" and the relation of favour on the one side and fealty on the other could not survive the step. God must cease to be their God when they ceased to be his people. "God chose them that they might choose him. By casting him off as their Lord and God, they cast themselves off and out of his protection. By estranging themselves from God, they became as strangers in his sight" (Pusey). 3. *Acts done because of a spiritual relation existing lose their meaning when it is broken off.* "Have I not brought Israel," etc.? They might think that, after bringing them out of Egypt, God could never disown them, however unfilial and unfaithful. But had not the circumstances of their idolatry and corruption altered the case? Theirs was not the only exodus. He had brought "the Philistines out of Caphtor, and the Syrians out of Kir;" yet these nations were aliens, and to be destroyed (ch. i. 5). If Israel conformed itself to these in character and way, then Israel's exodus would lose its significance, and be no more than events of a like kind in their distant past. What the father did for the son is no binding precedent for the case of the prodigal.

II. ACCORDINGLY, ISRAEL SHALL FARE AS THE HEATHEN DO WHO FORGET GOD. Grouping Israel like to like with heathen, God's attitude must be the same to both. They shall be treated : 1. *As the objects of God's displeasure.* He is angry with the wicked every day. He is angrier with those of them who sin against light and privilege. He is angriest with the spiritual renegades whose disaffection is guilty in proportion to the strength of the ties it sets aside. 2. *As the victims of his destroying judgments.* (Ver. 8.) "And I will destroy it off the face of the earth." Strange words from a God visibly in covenant. But the covenant was broken. The theoretically "holy nation" was actually a "sinful kingdom." Israel's character was not the character to which covenant promises referred. Heathenish in corruption, what but the bolts forged for their pagan kin could fall upon their heads? 3. *This in the character of defiant transgressors.* (Ver. 10.) "Not because they sinned aforetime, but because they persevered in sin until death" (Jerome, in Pusey). Sin may be forgiven, but impenitence never. The unpardonable sin is unforsaken sin.

III. THE JUDGMENT THAT SHALL DESTROY THE WICKED MASS SHALL LEAVE A RIGHTEOUS REMNANT. (Ver. 8.) "Except that I shall not utterly destroy the house of Jacob." God ordains no indiscriminate destruction. His bolts strike his enemies. Of his friends : 1. *Not one shall perish.* "Not even a little grain falls to the ground." The Divine nature, of which the righteous are partakers, is indestructible. The life of the saint is a living Christ within him (Gal. ii. 20). Christ "is alive for evermore" (Rev. i. 18), and says to all in whom he is as their life, "Because I live, ye shall live also." In a mixed community the righteous sometimes die for the fault of the wicked ; but their death is precious in God's sight (Ps. cxvi. 15), and "not an hair of their head shall perish." 2. *They shall be sifted out of the mass.* (Ver. 9.) In these graphic words the righteous minority are corn, and the corrupt masses the chaff. The nations are the sieve, and the Divine judgments the shaking of it. The result is not destruction of the grain, but separation between it and the chaff. "In every quarter of the world, and in well-nigh every nation in every quarter, Jews have been found. The whole earth is, as it were, one vast sieve in the hands of God, in which Israel is shaken from one end to the other. . . . The chaff and dust would be blown away by the air; . . . but no solid corn, not one grain, should fall to the earth" (Pusey). So in other cases. God's judgments winnow men, discerning clearly between clean and unclean. When the storm is over, the seaworthy vessels are easy of identification, for they alone survive. 3. *Their own sinfulness shall be sifted out of them.* "What is here said of all God doth daily in each of the elect. For they are the wheat of God, which, in order to be laid up in the heavenly garner, must be pure from chaff and dust. To this end he sifts them by afflictions and troubles" (Pusey). Suffering is not purifying *per se.* But the suffering of the righteous is (Heb. xii. 11; 1 Cor. iv. 17). It subdues the flesh, deepens our sense of dependence on God, spiritualizes our thoughts, and tests, and by testing strengthens, faith (1 Pet. i. 7). In the night of suffering come out the stars, guiding, consoling, irradiating the soul.

> "Then fear not in a world like this,
> And thou shalt know ere long—
> Know how sublime a thing it is
> To suffer and be strong."

Vers. 11, 12.—*The rebuilding of the waste places.* "God hath not cast away his people, which he foreknew," as the cumulative series of woes announced might seem to indicate. As a people they conspire, rebel, and cast him off, and as a people they are scattered, decimated, and disowned. In their corporate character they cannot longer survive. But there were individuals among them who had either remained loyal or come back to their allegiance, and these stood in a different position. Not only would they be spared, but made the nucleus of a new people, and their existence the occasion of a new dispensation. Such is the burden of these verses. The sinners are destroyed, and a new prosperity blooms for the faithful remnant that survives. The waifs of the national wreck are drawn in safety from the waves, and the desolated land is renovated for their home.

I. THE RESTORATION OF DAVID'S HOUSE. David's house here is not merely the dynasty of David, but the kingdom of David, and this as a type of the kingdom of Christ. Its restoration, in the ultimate sense, is accomplished only in the establishment of the Messianic kingdom which it symbolized. "The raising up of the fallen hut of David commenced with the coming of Christ and the founding of the Christian Church by the apostles" (Keil). Interpreting the passage thus, the rabbis adopted "the Son of the fallen" as one of the titles of Christ. 1. *This house has degenerated into a fallen hut before its true dignity is reached.* Judah shrinks into a petty province, the royal line is represented by a carpenter's wife, and the Jewish Church is a little flock with many a black sheep, ere the set time to favour Zion comes. "Strange comment on human greatness, that the royal line was not to be employed in the salvation of the world until it was fallen. The royal palace had to become the hut of Nazareth ere the Redeemer of the world could be born, whose glory and kingdom were not of this world" (Pusey). 2. *Its restoration will be to a state of ideal perfection.* The "breaches" would be repaired, and the "ruins" rebuilt, with the effect of making it "as in the days of old;" *i.e.* restoring it so as to embody the original design. This restoration to an as yet unrealized ideal could be only spiritual, and the Restorer Jesus Christ. The "hut" into which the "palace" had deteriorated (2 Sam. v. 11) was transformed into a far more glorious structure when Christ sat "upon the throne of David to order it," etc. (Isa. ix. 7; Luke i. 32, 33). The ideal of the Davidic kingdom is realized in the Christian Church; there fully, and there only. 3. *This restoration will be a work of Divine power.* "In the days of these kingdoms shall the God of heaven set up a kingdom which shall never be destroyed" (Dan. ii. 44). The Church, composed of Spirit-quickened men, is the creature of God as no political kingdom can be. Redeemed by Jesus Christ, quickened by the Holy Ghost, made one in the white heat of heavenly grace, it is altogether a Divine thing. Every energy it has is God-given; every grace is Spirit-wrought. In this is the special glory of the Jerusalem which is above. And when, among the ruins of a Hebrew monarchy, there rises, radiant in the beauties of holiness, the kingdom of our God, then indeed the bricks are changed to hewn stones, and the sycamores to cedars, and the palace of David is rebuilt as in the days of old.

II. THE WIDE CIRCLE OF INTERESTS TO BE ADVANCED BY THIS RESTORATION. "The restoration was not to be for themselves alone. No gifts of God end in the immediate objects of his bounty and love. They were restored in order that they, the first objects of God's mercies, might win others to God" (Pusey). Those brought in were to be: 1. *Gentiles as well as Jews.* (Ver. 12.) James, in his speech at the council of Jerusalem (Acts xv. 14—17), declares the fulfilment of this prophecy in the calling of the Gentiles. Edom, as the nation most hostile to the Jews and furthest from David's house, is put by a natural figure for the whole Gentile world. The "remnant of Edom," whether mystic or natural, are the few called in each case out of the many (Matt. xx. 16; ch. i. 12). "All the nations," etc., is a fuller and more literal statement of the ingathering of "the fulness of the Gentiles," when God brings his sons from afar, and his daughters from the ends of the earth. The gospel kingdom is to be the universal kingdom, "filling the whole earth," covering it with the knowledge of God, and making it, as the home of righteousness, a transfigured place. 2. *The Gentiles by means of the Jews.* "That they may take possession," etc. It is in Abraham and his seed that the nations are blessed. In our spiritual freedom and fulness of privilege we may not forget that Christ who founded the Church, the apostles who preached the kingdom of God and organized it, and the holy men who wrote the Scriptures as they were moved by the Holy Ghost, were, almost without exception, Jews. It is thus that "out of Zion has gone forth the law, and the word of the Lord from Jerusalem." To those we owe to the Jews there are no earthly obligations parallel, and the time of their graffing in again is one for which by every tie we are bound to pray. 3. *Both these in virtue of a Divine appropriating act.* "And all the nations upon which my Name is called;" *i.e.* appropriated, or marked as God's own (Gen. xlviii. 16; Deut. xxviii. 9, 10; Jer. xv. 16). Those whom God saves are such as he has graciously chosen to be his own. "Whom he did foreknow them he also called." Salvation is the evolution of an external plan, which in turn is the expression of Divine electing love.

III. GOD'S PURPOSE IN THIS MATTER POTENTIALLY A FACT. "Saith Jehovah who doeth this." 1. *The Divine energy is the efficient cause of events.* Second causes are not independent of or co-ordinate with the First Cause, but the instruments in its hands. Behind all and in all is the Divine Omnipotent energy, the ultimate cause, direct or indirect, of whatever is. 2. *The Divine word pledges the exercise of this Divine energy.* God's word is absolute truth. It cannot be broken. If it goes before, the corresponding act will follow. As well divorce the lightning from the thunder as the work from the word of God. When he says, and what he says, and as he says, he does infallibly. 3. *The Divine will constitutes the Divine energy.* God wills all things into existence. His choosing that a thing shall be brings it to pass. What a source of unfailing consolation is this fact to the gracious soul! Its rich future is assured. Omnipotent power and unchanging truth have the issue in hand, and miscarriage is not to be named.

Vers. 13—15.—*Out of the shadow into the sun.* Israel's atmosphere has cleared. The thunders are silent. The storms are blown out. The clouds are scattered. The shadow of " the great doom's image " has lifted. And now the sun comes out in the clear shining after rain. We look forth on a new land of promise, a land from which the curse of God and the track of the destroyer have disappeared. The ruins are rebuilt. The waste places bloom. The fields throw teeming crops, beyond the harvester's power to gather. The erewhile sinful and down-trodden people are prosperous and pure and free. It is a scene of idyllic beauty and peace—a happy *finale* to the dark storm-times that have gone before. This time will be—

I. A TIME OF TEEMING PLENTY. Figures of unheard-of fertility and abundance are multiplied. 1. *Seed-time and harvest should overlap.* " The ploughman shall overtake the reaper," etc. With a certain difficulty of defining the exact idea here, the general purport of the language is plain. The teeming crops could scarcely be gathered till another seed-time had come, or else growth would be so quick that the harvest would begin as soon as the seed-time was over. So Shakespeare—

> " Spring come to you at the farthest
> In the very end of harvest."

This rich promise was not now recorded for the first time. Conditionally on obedience, it had been made by the mouth of Moses seven centuries before (Lev. xxvi. 5). But, absolutely made, it assumes a new value now. And as the events in it are altogether impossible in the natural world, it must obviously be taken in a spiritual sense. The plenty, like the previously threatened famine (ch. viii. 11), was not to be one of bread and water, but " of hearing the words of the Lord." In the spiritual sphere the seed-time and the harvest may come together. The man who goes forth with seed may return with sheaves (Ps. cxxvi. 6). Indeed, the Samaritan fields were " white unto harvest " (John iv. 35), when, as yet, the sowing had only begun. In such a case poetic figure becomes literal truth, and Zion, as soon as she travails, brings forth (Isa. lxvi. 7, 8). 2. *The mountains should drop wine spontaneously.* The vineyards of Israel were on the mountain-slopes. Of the plethora of over-rich grapes with which they would be loaded many would burst, and in the spontaneous discharge of their juice the mountains would literally " drip new wine." This process, in its spiritual analogue, is more wondrous and delightful still. Spiritual plenty has its inevitable and enriching overflow. " Freely have ye received, freely give." Spiritual character is always imparting of itself in spiritual influence. From the gracious lip there drops continually the new wine of " a word in season." And the religious life, " lived not for ourselves," is a tide of helpful action beating perpetually on the shore of others' lives. 3. *The hills should dissolve themselves in the products they yield.* This is the force of the expression, " All the hills shall melt." The rich earth throws its own substance into the teeming crops it bears. The richer it is the larger proportion of its substance is expended in this process. Pure leaf-mould would, in this way, almost totally disappear, transforming itself entirely into grain or fruit. In the spiritual sphere self-surrender for others is a law of life. Christ gave himself, and Christians give themselves, for men. " I will very gladly spend and be spent for you " (2 Cor. xii. 15) is the philosophy, not alone of Paul's, but of all Christian living. The gracious heart expends itself in helpful action. The sum-total of philanthropic effort in the world is just the concreted spiritual energy of the godly company.

II. A TIME OF NATIONAL RESTORATION. (Ver. 14.) Each term here has a spiritual reference, and the whole has an ultimate spiritual fulfilment. This comes: 1. *Generally, in the breaking of every yoke by Christ.* Sin is bondage—enthralment by the devil, the world, and the flesh. Ceremonialism was bondage—subjection to "weak and beggarly elements" in symbolic and wearisome observance. From both Christ comes a Liberator. He "makes an end of sin" in every aspect; "destroying the devil," "delivering from this present evil world" (Gal. i. 4), and fulfilling his righteousness in men "who walk not after the flesh." He abolishes type, substituting for it the thing typified: for the shadow, the substance; for the Law, "grace and truth." 2. *For individuals, when the Son makes them free.* Spiritual bondage cannot survive believing union with Christ. His blood dissolves the chains of guilt. His Spirit breaks the bonds of indwelling sin. Acceptance with God is not conditioned on an impossible obedience to the whole Law, "for we are not under the Law, but under grace" (Rom. vii. 6). The life of self-surrender is not made burdensome by a carnal nature, "for the law of the Spirit of life in Christ Jesus hath made us free from the law of sin and death." The conditions of the life of joyous fellowship are presented in the inwrought spirit of adoption, and the "Abba, Father" of the free, on Spirit-opened lips (Rom. viii. 15, 21; John iv. 18). They are free indeed, whom, trebly loosing thus, the Son makes free. 3. *For the nation, when brought into the Church during the millennial era.* Their conversion in the latter days is distinctly and repeatedly foretold (Hos. iii. 4, 5; Rom. xii. 12, 15, 23; 2 Cor. iii. 16). National restoration this may not strictly be, but it is more than equivalent to it. When the long-wandering return, when the hearts cold and embittered for ages glow with heavenly love, when the veil drops that hung on mind and sense, when the broken-off branches are set again in the good old olive tree, a spiritual fulfilment will have come of Amos's words, more glorious than any literal or local one, as the glory of the second temple exceeds the glory of the first.

III. A TIME OF RESETTLEMENT IN THEIR OWN LAND. (Ver. 15.) In three classes of events, come or coming, we have as many steps in the fulfilment of this promise. 1. *The return from the Babylonish exile.* The captivity was God's final, because effective, disciplinary measure. Israel was thoroughly sickened with heathen gods and heathen ways. Osiris and Isis in Egypt, and Baal and Ashtaroth in Palestine, had won, almost without wooing, an attachment which, in Babylon, Bel and Nebo could not so much as stir. The last and bitterest prescription had succeeded, and soon the patient, cured abroad, was ordered home. Amidst tremendous difficulties, Jerusalem was repaired, the temple rebuilt, and the land in a measure resettled, and so an approximate fulfilment of Amos's glowing prophecy realized (Ezra vii. 13, etc.). 2. *The calling of the Gentiles.* They are the spiritual Israel, the true children of Abraham (Gal. iii. 7—9). They throw off the yoke of the mystic Babylon; "possess the kingdom for ever" (Dan. vii. 8—22); "inherit the earth," as their own land; repair the ruins, and restore the spiritual wastes left by sin; and they revel in "the feast of wines on the lees," etc. "Throughout the world Churches of Christ have arisen which, for the firmness of faith, may be called *cities;* for the gladness of hope, *vineyards;* and for the sweetness of charity, *gardens*" (Pusey). 3. *The future restoration of the Jews to Palestine.* This is foretold (Ezek. xxviii. 25; xxxvi. 28; xxxvii. 25). God does the work (Ezek. xxxiv. 11—13) through Gentile agency (Isa. xlix. 22; lxvi. 20). "They are to be nationally restored to the favour of God, and their acceptance publicly sealed by their restoration to their land" (David Brown, D.D.). Converted Israel will be eminent alike in character and influence in the millennial Church (Isa. lix. 21; lxvi. 19; Ezek. xxxix. 29; Micah v. 7). Held again by the old people, her cities rebuilt, her grandeur restored, her broad acres reclaimed and fertile, and, above all, Jesus Christ on the throne of the nation's heart, Palestine will be indeed "the glory of all lands."

IV. ALL THIS SECURED BY INFALLIBLE GUARANTEE. There is no romancing with inspired men. What they say is coming, as God is true. The pledge of this is: 1. *God's character.* "Saith Jehovah," *i.e.* "the One who is." He is Reality as against the seeming, Substance as against the typical, Veracity as against the deceiving, Faithfulness as against the changeful. As being Benevolent he is true, human happiness depending on confidence in his character. As Independent he is true, being above all possible temptation to deceive. As Unchangeable he is true, falsehood being essentially a change of character. As Omnipotent he is true, the use of moral agents in free and yet infallible execution of his purposes being possible only as his Word is a revelation of his thought. 2. *His existing relation.* "Thy God." Not a God unknown. Not a God apart. Not a God untried. In his present attitude, his covenant relation, his past deeds, in all such facts is "confirmation strong." The God they connect themselves with is a God to trust. His perfections are the strands, and his relation their twining together, in the cord of confidence not quickly broken, which binds the soul to his eternal throne.

HOMILIES BY VARIOUS AUTHORS.

Vers. 1—4.—*Inevitable judgment.* The thought of the Divine omniscience is a welcome thought to the friend, the child of God. But to the impenitent transgressor no thought is so distasteful, so distressing. If he cannot persuade himself that there is no God, he at all events hopes that the Divine eye does not rest upon him, that he is overlooked and forgotten. This vain refuge of sinners is discovered and destroyed by the revelation of this prophecy. The idolatrous temple shall be dismantled, the idolatrous altar shall be overthrown, when the Lord enters into controversy with unfaithful Israel. And in that day the sinful and deluded worshippers and priests shall be scattered. Whether slain or carried into captivity, none shall escape the eye or elude the chastening hand of the God who has been defied or forgotten. Every individual shall be dealt with upon the principles of eternal justice.

I. The foolish and vain endeavours of sinners to avoid the recompense of their iniquity. The language of the prophet is vigorous and poetical. He pictures the smitten and scattered Israelites as delving into the abyss, as soaring to the heights of heaven, as hiding in the caves of Carmel, as crouching beneath the waters of the ocean; and all in vain. This figurative language represents the sophistry and the self-deception and the useless wiles and artifices by which the discovered sinner seeks to persuade himself that his crimes shall be unpunished.

II. The omnipresence of the righteous Judge. We are reminded of that ancient acknowledgment, "Thou God seest me!" as we read this declaration, "I will set mine eyes upon them." The psalmist, in the hundred and thirty-ninth psalm, has given us the most wonderfully impressive description which is to be found even in sacred literature of the omnipresence and the omniscience of God. Next to that description, for vigour and effectiveness, comes perhaps this passage of the prophecies of Amos. At every point and at every moment the universal and all-comprehending Spirit is in closest contact with every created intelligence; and that presence which may be discerned in operation wherever any work of God in the realm of nature is studied, is equally recognizable in the intellectual, the spiritual kingdom. Every conscience is a witness to the ever-present, all-observing Deity.

III. The consequent certainty of the carrying out of all the regal and judicial decisions of the Divine Ruler. The circumstances of Israel led to the application of this great principle to the case of the sinful and rebellious. It was a painful duty which the prophet had to perform, but as a servant of God he felt that there was no choice left him. It was his office, and it is the office of every preacher of righteousness, to say unto the wicked, "Thou shalt surely die."—T.

Ver. 7.—*National pride and presumption.* It is usual for nations to boast of their history, their position, their great qualities, their good fortune, their invincibility. We know this from our own observation of the nations of modern times. And in this respect all ages seem alike. There were, no doubt, very peculiar grounds for self-confidence and boastfulness on the part of the Jews. Yet such dispositions and habits were again and again censured and condemned by the inspired servants of Jehovah.

I. It is a broad general fact that the movements of nations are under the guidance or superintendence of the almighty Ruler. Amos is directed to point out that what was true of Israel in this respect was equally true of the Cushites, the Philistines, and the Syrians. In the case of all these nations there had been remarkable migrations and settlements. The hand of God is recognized in one as much as in the other. The Hebrews are sometimes charged with narrowness and vanity in their interpretations of Divine providence. Doubtless many of them may be justly so charged. But the language of Amos is a proof that the enlightened Jews took a far wider view. There is no contradiction between general and special providence. The nations of men, because they are men, are subject to the control and direction of God. Not one tribe is unworthy of his regard. In what manner, and to what extent, the great Ruler interposes in the political affairs of peoples it is not for our limited wisdom to decide. But the petty notion that one favoured nation enjoys the protection and guidance of Heaven, whilst other nations are neglected and uncared for, is utterly inconsistent with the teaching of the text.

II. THE GUIDANCE AND PROTECTION WHICH NATIONS HAVE ENJOYED IN THE PAST IS NO GROUND OF EXEMPTION FROM THE OPERATION OF THE MORAL GOVERNMENT OF GOD. There were those in Israel who deemed it incredible that a nation so favoured as theirs had been could possibly be called upon to experience defeat, conquest, captivity, disaster. But the fact is that great privileges simply place men upon a higher level of responsibility. To whom much is given, of them will much be required. Unfaithfulness is the one great ground of censure, condemnation, punishment. Israel had sinned in separating from Judah, in setting up rival altars at Dan and Bethel, in introducing an alien religion, idolatrous sacrifices and worship, in giving way in times of prosperity to luxury, pride, covetousness, and ambition. All the mercies accorded to their forefathers could not release the Israelites from the obligation to maintain the pure religion of Jehovah, and to keep his laws and ordinances. Nor could they be a ground for exemption from the action of those laws of Divine government which are universal in their operation, and disciplinary and morally beneficial in their tendency. The Captivity and the dispersion were conclusive proofs that there is no favouritism in the administration of God's rule; that his laws are not to be defied with impunity by the most privileged of nations. Presumption is irrational and foolish, and is the sure, swift road to destruction.—T.

Ver. 9.—*Sifting and salvation.* If any prediction could convince the reader of the Old Testament that the prophets spoke and wrote under a supernatural inspiration, surely this prediction must possess this virtue. The history of Israel, not only in times immediately following upon those of Amos, but throughout the centuries which have since elapsed, is just a fulfilment of this language. How picturesquely and forcibly is the truth presented under this similitude, so natural as employed by one familiar with all the processes connected with husbandry!

I. THE PROVIDENTIAL SIFTING APPOINTED FOR THE HOUSE OF ISRAEL. 1. It has been determined by the Divine Ruler and Lord. "I will command," says Jehovah. Men may trace the history of the Jews with the design of showing that all the events which have occurred to that people are explicable upon ordinary principles, that Israel drops into its place when marshalled by the enlightened philosopher of history. But beneath all such theory there is an explanation which satisfies the intelligence of the thoughtful and devout student of God's Word: the Lord has ordered it. 2. It has taken place in different lands, and throughout lengthened periods. "Among all the nations," was the expression of the inspired prophet. The successive invasions of Palestine, the conquest of Israel and then of Judah, the captivity into the East, the settlements in Assyria and in Persia, the partial restoration to the land of promise, the subjection of Palestine to successive conquerors, and its subjugation by the Romans, the dispersion among the Gentiles, the scattering of the sons of Israel amongst the nations, alike in the East and the West,—these are but some of the more salient points in a history the most remarkable, the most romantic, and yet the most painful, in the annals of mankind. 3. It has been ordained for a purpose of a moral and beneficial character. Sifting is for the purpose of separating the chaff and refuse from the pure grain. A process of sifting, winnowing, tribulation (in the literal meaning of that word), has been going on throughout the ages. Even yet the purposes of God are very partially accomplished, for the process is continued; nor is there any sign of its immediate termination.

II. THE DIVINE PRESERVATION OF THOSE SUBJECTED TO THIS TRIAL. Not a grain shall drop out of sight and perish. It is a wonderful paradox—sifting and salvation, trial and protection, scattering and gathering, alike experienced. Yet the marvellous story of the chosen people supports to the letter this ancient representation. It is the simple, actual, literal truth. 1. This protection is apparent in the preservation of the Israelites during the Oriental captivity. This was even made to minister to the religious purity and enlightenment of a nation previously inclined to fall into idolatrous worship. 2. We recognize it equally in the preservation and the national or tribal distinctness of the Jews in the ages which have elapsed since the destruction of Jerusalem. The corn has been sifted, but the grain has not been lost. "Whom he scattereth he shall gather." 3. There is a fulfilment of this inspired declaration in the individual conversions to God which have from time to time taken place among those who have been trained among the unbelieving and rebellious. As a nation Israel has never ceased to endure chastening. But members of the community, individual sons and daughters of Jacob, have again and again been seen to turn unto the Lord whom their fathers grieved by their ingratitude and insensibility. Precious grains have thus been preserved and gathered into the garner and saved. 4. Such cases are an earnest of a more complete fulfilment of the prediction. So—such is the assurance of the Christian apostle—" all Israel shall be saved."—T.

Ver. 10.—*The folly of self-confidence.* The conduct of these Israelites, and their fate, may well stand as a beacon of warning to all who have heard the Word of God with indifference and unbelief.

I. THE REASONS WHICH SHOULD PROMPT THE SINNER TO CONCERN. 1. The voice of his own conscience assures him of guilt and ill desert. 2. The warnings of Scripture should not be lost upon him, and revelation abounds with such warnings uttered upon the highest authority. 3. The examples of the impenitent who have been overtaken by judgment and destruction enforce the faithful admonitions of Holy Writ.

II. THE EXPLANATIONS OF THE SINNER'S SELF-CONFIDENCE AND PRESUMPTION. It is unquestionable that there are many who say, "The evil shall not reach nor overtake us." How can this be accounted for? 1. The voice of conscience may be silenced or unheeded. 2. The warnings of Scripture may be utterly disregarded. 3. The sinner may think rather of those instances in which judgment has been delayed than of those in which it has been hastened and fulfilled.

III. THE WISDOM AND DUTY OF IMMEDIATE REPENTANCE. 1. God's Word will certainly be verified. 2. No human power can save the impenitent. 3. The time of probation is short, and may nearly have expired.—T.

Ver. 11.—*The reconstruction of the tabernacle of David.* The reference is probably not to that tabernacle which was replaced and superseded by the temple of Solomon, but to the house of David. The booth or hut may well serve as an emblem of the depressed state of the Jewish monarchy and people, not simply as they were in the time of Amos, but as the prophet foretold that they should be in days about to come. The language is very expressive, and depicts a restoration very complete. Breaches shall be closed, ruins shall be repaired, the structure shall be rebuilt. The fortunes of the people of David must indeed be dark for a season, but a brighter day shall surely dawn.

I. THE MOST GLORIOUS FULFILMENT OF THIS PROPHECY WAS IN THE ADVENT OF THE DIVINE SON OF DAVID. Jesus was recognized by the people as the descendant and successor of their national hero. They shouted, "Hosanna to the Son of David!" He himself made the claim, only that he asserted that he was not only David's Son, but also David's Lord. Like David, he was "after God's heart;" like David, he sang praises unto God in the midst of the Church; like David, he overcame the enemies of Jehovah and of his people; like David, he reigned over the nation of Israel. But unlike David, he was Divine in his nature and faultless in his character; unlike David, he was rather a spiritual than a worldly Conqueror; unlike David, he was King, not over one people, but over all mankind. In Christ the true Israel has found more than the Israel "according to the flesh" lost in David's removal.

II. THE MAIN PROOF OF THIS FULFILMENT OF PROPHECY IS TO BE FOUND IN THE ESTABLISHMENT OF THE MESSIAH'S SPIRITUAL KINGDOM. Time has given an interpretation to this language which was impossible beforehand. How truly the house of David has been more than rebuilt, the kingdom of David more than re-established, is apparent to every observer of what has occurred in the Christian centuries. The kingdom of the Redeemer is : 1. Spiritual. In which respect it is more admirable and more glorious than that of David, which was founded upon the sword, and whose sway was over, not the heart, but the outward life. 2. Universal. For whilst David reigned over a strip of Syrian territory, Christ's empire is vast, and is widening year by year. " The kingdoms of this world shall become the kingdoms of our Lord and of his Christ." 3. Everlasting. The few brief glorious years of David's reign were prophetic of that sway which shall endure for ever. Of Christ's kingdom " there shall be no end."—T.

Vers. 13—15.—*The golden age.* Nothing short of inspiration can account for such a close to such a book. Throughout his prophecies Amos has been exposing national sinfulness, threatening Divine chastisement, picturing the degradation, the desolation, the captivity of the kingdoms of Israel and of Judah. How comes it that he is able to transcend this distressing representation? to look beyond these gloomy clouds? to discern, whether far or near, the vision of a smiling earth, a happy people, a splendid prosperity, an eternal joy? It is not the force of human reasoning; it is not the impulse of delusive hope. No; it is the presence of the Divine Spirit that has purged the prophet's spiritual vision, so that he sees the glory yet to be; it is this that touches the prophet's tongue, so that the wail of sorrow and distress is changed into the shout of triumph and the song of joy.

> " The world's great age begins anew,
>   The golden years return;
> The earth doth, like a snake, renew
>   Her winter weeds outworn;
> Heaven smiles, and faiths and empires gleam
>   Like wrecks of a dissolving dream."

I. THE PICTURE OF PROSPERITY. The inspired poet presses into the service all the resources of nature laid open to him by long years of observation and of fellowship. We notice as depicted : 1. The fruitfulness of the soil. The crops of corn, the summer vintage, follow each other in quick succession. From the laden vineyards and adown the sunny slopes flow rivers of delicious wine. The boughs of the trees are weighed down with fruit. For the tillers of the soil and the dwellers in the cities there is " enough and to spare." 2. The peopling of the towns and villages. The banished ones have returned. The once-silent streets resound with the noise of traffic, with the voices of men, with the songs of the happy. 3. Security and perpetual possession. No longer do the dwellers in the fenced cities arm themselves and man their walls against the foe; no longer do the husbandmen dread the incursions of marauders. Quiet resting-places and a sure habitation are secured by the goodness of Providence. Earth seems transformed into primæval Paradise.

II. THE REALITY WHICH THIS PICTURE REPRESENTS. 1. By many interpreters this vision of peace and happiness is deemed predictive of national prosperity still awaiting the scattered children of Israel. The land of promise shall again flow with milk and honey. Jerusalem shall again be the seat of a mighty kingdom. The hills of Judah and the plains of Ephraim shall again be tilled by the children of Jacob. A converted Israel shall—from the Mediterranean to the Jordan, and from the Jordan to the desert, from the heights of Lebanon to the river of Egypt—witness to the faithfulness of the Eternal, to the Messiah long rejected, but now and henceforth to be held in honour and to be served with devotion. Planted, and no more to be plucked up, the chosen people shall flourish like the green bay tree, like the cedar in Lebanon. 2. Other interpreters pass straight from this vision of prosperity and gladness to the spiritual prospect which it opens up to the eyes of the believers in God's Word, of the disciples of Christ. There is peace of which the seat is the conscience, the heart, of man. There is plenty for the satisfaction of man's deepest wants. There is a sure abiding-place for the faithful in the care and love of the Eternal. There is a kingdom which is " righteousness, peace, and joy in the Holy Ghost." There is a city of which every renewed man becomes a denizen, nay, an immortal citizen. There is prosperity in which the poor, the feeble, the despised may share. And there are songs of gladness and of thanksgiving in which all the redeemed and saved shall join.—T.

Ver. 9.—*The winnowing of God.* " For, lo, I will command, and I will sift the house of Israel among all nations, like as corn is sifted in a sieve, yet shall not the least grain fall upon the earth." Introduction: The free use made by Amos of all the scenes in nature. We may learn from the text three lessons.

I. THAT AMONG THOSE CALLED BY A RELIGIOUS NAME THERE EXISTS A GREAT DIVERSITY OF CHARACTER. " I will sift . . . as corn is sifted." If corn were gathered as manna was—pure, unmixed with deleterious or useless elements—no sifting would be needed. But it grows with other growth, thistles, poppies, darnel, etc., and it seems impossible to keep the field perfectly clean. In the physical, as in the moral, world the false grows beside the true, and the evil beside the good; and God's own law is, " Let both grow together until the harvest." Indeed, during their growth it is difficult to distinguish these. You may mistake tares for wheat, fool's parsley for the garden herb, poisonous fungi for edible mushrooms, and so forth, and only discover your error by serious or even fatal consequences. The mystery of the coexistence of good and evil, then, runs through nature. It is seen in character. " All are not Israel who are of Israel," or are called by that sacred name. Let us now exemplify this from a comparison of the times of Amos with our own. 1. *Idolaters were among the prophet's hearers.* They had deliberately turned from Jehovah. They held that it was a wise policy on the part of Jeroboam I. to prevent the people going to Jerusalem. They were convinced that the calves at Bethel gave a centre to their national life; and therefore, from motives political and worldly, many of them said, " These be thy gods, O Israel." Knowing as they did the history of their fathers, and the laws and ceremonies of the Mosaic institutes, they sinned against the light. Yet they still called themselves " Israel," and they were not marked out by external sign from the true people of God. No brand was on their foreheads, no curse fell on their homes, no fire of judgment overwhelmed them with destruction; but they were amongst the sleek, successful men of Samaria. In this Christian land, and in our Christian congregations, may still be found those who have forsaken God and made unto themselves other gods. Sometimes, for example, a man deifies wealth. His thoughts are concentrated on it, and his full energies are directed to its attainment. To claims made on his generosity he turns a deaf ear; over scruples about the forsaking of righteousness and mercy he rides roughshod. If at last he succeeds he says, " It is my power, and the might of my hand, that has wrought this." Yet prayerless, godless, as such men are, they still call themselves by the Christian name. 2. *Amos spoke to others who were simply indifferent to religion.* They considered that the questions debated between the true and false prophets were professional questions, with which they had no personal concern. Worshipping neither the calves nor Jehovah, their wish was to glide quietly through life, winning for themselves such enjoyment as was possible. Describe the attitude of many towards religion in our day—occasionally attending worship, knowing nothing of the meaning of it, and taking their chance as to the unseen future. They are known, not to us, but to God. 3. *Some in the days of Amos had the character as well as the name of " Israel."* They dared not, could not, go up to Jerusalem. But their families were instructed in the Scriptures. They thought of the old days when Jehovah was universally acknowledged as the Lord, and, like Jacob, they prayed in an agony of supplication, " I will not let thee go, except thou bless me." These belonged not only to the " kingdom " but to the " house " of Israel, on which God would have mercy. (See the promise to this effect, distinguishing between the " kingdom " and the " house," in ver. 8.) Such are still to be found. In business, because of their integrity and charity, their name is as ointment poured forth. In the homes, as instructors of their children, they are preparing blessings for the world. In the sanctuary their praises wing their way to heaven, and in prayer they are princes "having power with God." Now, these differing characters were and are *mingled*, as are the tares and wheat. They are even *united*, as are the chaff and the corn, and therefore the day of sifting and separation must come. It has not come yet. When corn is ripening and flowers are blossoming it is useless to send in the weeders. When the reapers are busy their scythes must cut down all growths alike. There is no time then for separation, but it comes at last. You see a heap of winnowed corn in the granary; the weeds have been burned, the straw is gone, and all the chaff is scattered. So Israel was to be scattered by persecution, war, and captivity; but not one grain of God's wheat should fall upon the ground. (Text.)

II. THAT THERE ARE TESTING-TIMES IN WHICH SUCH DIVERSITY ASSERTS ITSELF. The earth is here represented as a great sieve, in which Israel should be ceaselessly tossed, that the evil might be lost and the good saved. The process is still carried on. There are testing-times here, and there will be a testing-time hereafter. 1. *Preaching*, for example, sometimes so disturbs conscience, that on self-examination the man sees what is true and false in his character. Many a hearer has thus been led to ask, " Am I as the chaff which the wind driveth away ? " 2. *Affliction* is a sieve for testing character. Job was an example of this. His distresses revealed him to himself and to his friends ; and not a grain of wheat (of that which was worth preserving) was lost. Show how this is still true of the afflicted. Illness, bereavement, losses, etc., lead to serious thought, and while they sometimes destroy unfounded hopes, they give more confidence in that " hope which is the true anchor of the soul, sure and steadfast." 3. *Temptation* is a revealer of character. Compare the text with our Lord's words, "Simon, Simon, behold, Satan hath desired to have you, that he may sift you as wheat : but I have prayed for thee, that thy faith fail not." What a revelation to Peter of his weakness and presumption was his denial ! Illustrate by the story of the two houses, built, the one on the rock, the other on the sand (Matt. vii. 24—27). Thus we may test ourselves. If the opportunity offers itself to gratify some passion secretly, without the least risk of detection, is the reply, "How can I do this great wickedness, and sin against God ? " or is the opportunity gladly seized to enjoy " the pleasures of sin for a season " ? 4. *Persecution* tests character. It is easy to deceive ourselves when all our associations are religious. But let these be changed for worldly, sceptical, or immoral surroundings, and the reality of our religious life is proved. Then, either we say, " We must obey God rather than man," and our character is ennobled by the struggle, or the old prayer is omitted, the old Bible neglected, and the old influences blotted out of memory. All such tests as we have mentioned are sent in mercy, to lead to self-examination, and, if need be, to repentance ; but Christ draws the veil of the future, and tells us further of a day when the secrets of all hearts shall be disclosed, and : 5. *When the judgment of God*, according to equity, will be declared. You may escape all other trials, but you will not escape that. Affliction may leave you untouched. Amidst persecution and temptation your reputation may be unscathed. But death will scatter all delusions, and from it, and from that judgment to which it leads, there is no escape (see ver. 3, " And though they hide themselves in the top of Carmel," etc.). On that day there shall be " the manifestation of the sons of God ; " the secret life will be commended, and the quiet service recompensed. With others the vain show will be over, the veil of outward respectability rent asunder, and the words will be heard, "Depart from me, ye that work iniquity ! " Then there will come the separation, as between the sheep and the goats, the tares and the wheat, the corn and the chaff. Men may have met in the same church, heard the same gospel, lived in the same home, yet above the portal of heaven is this inexorable law, " And there shall in no wise enter into it anything that defileth, . . . but they that are written in the Lamb's book of life." Still the words hold good, " Whosoever believeth on him shall not perish, but have everlasting life ; " " How shall we escape if we neglect so great salvation ? " " Among thy saints may I be found," etc. !

III. THAT OVER THE TESTING PROCESS GOD WATCHES AND RULES SO THAT NOTHING TRUE AND NOTHING GOOD MAY BE LOST. " For, lo, I will command . . . yet shall not the least grain fall upon the earth " (comp. Mal. iii. 3). Our text is true in a much broader sense than that in which we have attempted to deal with it. 1. *In changes amongst the nations*, where there seems little but confusion and unrest, God rules. He is testing and purifying his own people. Not a grain of his purpose will fall to the earth. " Heaven and earth shall pass away, but my Word shall not pass away." 2. *Movements take place in ecclesiastical life.* One system makes room for another. The Old Testament economy with its ceremonies, the apostolic Church with its simplicity, the mediæval Church with its superstitions, etc., all were changed, yet of all the praises and prayers offered through past ages not a grain fell to the earth. 3. *In dogmatic theology changes are still going on.* Formularies and phrases die out, but the truth in them is not lost. Christ lives and reigns still, and " of his dominion there shall be no end." That which is saved by God is " the grain," that which has life in it ; and planted in the earth, it shall be developed in new forms of strength and beauty.

CONCLUSION. Therefore, amidst the wreck and the fall of much that seems precious, let your hearts as Christian men be quiet from fear of evil. Have trust in God, who commands and controls, and believe that amidst all his cares you are not forgotten, amidst all these perils you will be safe. Because good is stronger than evil, and Christ is mightier than our adversary, the words of his promise are true to all believers, "They shall never perish, neither shall any pluck them out of my hand."—A. R.

Vers. 1—4.—*Great sins, great calamities, great efforts.* "I saw the Lord standing upon the altar," etc. "This chapter commences with an account of the fifth and last vision of the prophet, in which the final ruin of the kingdom of Israel is represented. This ruin was to be complete and irreparable; and no quarter to which the inhabitants might flee for refuge would afford them any shelter from the wrath of the omnipresent and almighty Jehovah." The prophet in vision sees the Almighty standing upon the altar, and hears him give the command to smite the lintel of the temple door that the posts may shake; in other words, to destroy the temple. The temple here is not, I think (though the allusion is uncertain), the temple at Jerusalem, the temple of true worship, but the temple of idolatrous worship. The passage suggests three remarks.

I. THAT UNDER THE RIGHTEOUS GOVERNMENT OF GOD GREAT SIN EXPOSES TO GREAT CALAMITY. How terrible the calamities here referred to! The Israelites, when threatened by the Assyrians, would flock in crowds to Bethel and implore protection from the golden calf. But the very place where they sought protection would prove their ruin. Jehovah says, "Smite the lintel of the door, that the posts may shake: and cut them in the head, all of them; and I will slay the last of them with the sword," etc. The sin of these Israelites in their idolatrous worship was great. They were the descendants of Abraham, the friend of God. As a people, they were chosen of God and blessed with a thousand opportunities of knowing what was right and true in doctrine and in practice. Yet they gave themselves up to idolatry. Hence these terrible calamities. The greater the sin, the greater the punishment. "Unto whom much is given of him shall be much required;" "He that knoweth his Lord's will and doeth it not, shall be beaten with many stripes;" "It will be more tolerable for Sodom and Gomorrah," etc.

II. THE CONSCIOUSNESS OF APPROACHING CALAMITIES WILL STIMULATE TO GREAT EFFORTS FOR ESCAPE. "Though they dig into hell, thence shall mine hand take them; though they climb up to heaven, thence will I bring them down." There are here supposed attempts at escape. There is the supposed attempt to get into hell—Sheol, the dark realm of shadows, where they could conceal themselves. There is an attempt to climb Mount Carmel, twelve hundred feet in height, there to conceal themselves under the shadows, intricacies, and the crowded forests of oak, pines, laurels, etc., and also in the deep caves running down to the sea. Men in view of great dangers always seek refuge. The sinner here, when he finds death approaching, what strenuous efforts does he employ in order to escape the monster's touch! On the great day of retribution sinners are represented as crying to the rocks and mountains to fall on them.

III. THE GREATEST EFFORTS TO ESCAPE MUST PROVE UTTERLY FUTILE WHEN GOD HAS GIVEN THE SINNER UP. "Though they dig into hell, thence shall mine hand take them," etc. There are many similar passages to these in the Bible, such as the following: "If I ascend up into heaven, thou art there: if I make my bed in hell, behold, thou art there" (Ps. cxxxix. 8); "Though his excellency mount up to the heavens, and his head reach unto the clouds; yet he shall perish for ever like his own dung: they which have seen him shall say, Where is he?" (Job xx. 6, 7); "Though Babylon should mount up to heaven, and though she should fortify the height of her strength, yet from me shall spoilers come unto her, saith the Lord" (Jer. li. 53); "Though thou exalt thyself as the eagle, and though thou set thy nest among the stars, thence will I bring thee down, saith the Lord" (Jer. xlix. 16). Whatever the efforts of the sinner in the prospect of approaching danger, there is no escape for him. God is everywhere, and everywhere all-seeing, all-just, and almighty.

CONCLUSION. The only way to escape utter ruin is to renounce your sin, and commit yourself unto the safe keeping of him who is the Redeemer of mankind.—D. T.

Vers. 5—10.—*God as the Administrator of justice.* "And the Lord God of hosts is he that toucheth the land, and it shall melt, and all that dwell therein shall mourn," etc. These words present God to us as the Administrator of justice.

I. HE DOES IT WITH THE GREATEST EASE. The administrators of justice in connection with human government have often to contend with difficulties that baffle and confound them. But the Almighty has no difficulty. "He toucheth the land, and it shall melt." By a mere touch he can punish a whole nation, nay, destroy the world. Whence come earthquakes and volcanoes? Here is their cause: "He toucheth the hills, and they smoke." Never can there be any miscarriage of justice with God. He bears it right home in every case. He has no difficulty about it. He toucheth the clouds, and they drown the world; he kindles the atmosphere and burns cities, etc.

II. HE DOES IT WITH ALL THE POWERS OF NATURE AT HIS COMMAND. "It is he that buildeth his stories in the heaven, and hath founded his troop in the earth." His throne is on high, above all the forms and forces of the universe, and all are at his call. From those heights which he has built, those upper chambers of the universe, he can pour floods to drown a world, or rain fires which will consume the universe. Every force in nature he can make with ease an officer to execute his justice.

III. HE DOES IT DISREGARDFUL OF MERE RELIGIOUS PROFESSION. "Have not I brought up Israel out of the land of Egypt? and the Philistines from Caphtor, and the Syrians from Kir?" Jehovah here repels the idea which the Israelites were so prone to entertain, that because he had brought them out of Egypt and given them the land of Canaan, they were peculiarly the objects of his concern, and could never be subdued or destroyed. He now regarded and would treat them as the Cushites, or Ethiopians, who had been transplanted from their primal location in Arabia into the midst of the barbarous nations of Africa. The Almighty, in administering justice, is not influenced by the plea of profession. A corrupt Israelite to him was as bad as an Ethiopian, though he calls Abraham his father. "Think not to say . . . that ye have Abraham to your father." Conventional Christians are in the eyes of God as bad as infidels or heathen. He judgeth not as man judgeth, by the outward appearance; he looketh at the heart.

IV. HE DOES IT WITH A THOROUGH DISCRIMINATION OF CHARACTER. "Behold, the eyes of the Lord God are upon the sinful kingdom, and I will destroy it from off the face of the earth; saving that I will not utterly destroy the house of Jacob, saith the Lord." There were some good people amongst the Israelites, men of genuine goodness; the great Judge would not destroy them. "I will not utterly destroy the house of Jacob. . . . I will sift the house of Israel among all nations, like as corn is sifted in a sieve," etc. He would burn up the chaff, but save the wheat. Evermore will the Almighty Judge recognize and tenderly guard the virtuous and the good, however humble their position in life. He will not destroy the righteous.—D. T.

Vers. 11—15.—*The restoration of the true moral theocracy.* "In that day will I raise up the tabernacle of David that is fallen, and close up the breaches thereof; and I will raise up his ruins, and I will build it as in the days of old," etc. In the previous verses we have had to notice the destruction of the sinful kingdom; in this paragraph we have the establishment of the true kingdom—the true moral theocracy. "In that day," *i.e.* when the judgment has fallen upon the sinful kingdom, and all the sinners of the people of Israel are destroyed. "The Israelites," says Dr. Henderson, "now disappear from the scene, in order to give place to a brief and prominent exhibition of the restoration of the Jews from their repressed condition during their anticipated captivity in Babylon." The Apostle James, at the first ecclesiastical council at Jerusalem, quotes this prophecy (Acts xv. 16, 17)—not, however, in its identical phraseology, but in its general meaning—and applies it to the establishment of Christ's kingdom in the world by the admission of the Gentiles into it. The old Hebrew world was for ages governed by a theocracy. God was their King. He had under him and by his appointment human rulers and other functionaries; but they were simply his instruments, and he was their King. That form of government has passed away; but it was symbolical: it was the emblem of a higher theocracy that is to be established, not over the Jews merely, but over the Gentiles and over the whole world. It was to stand for ever. We shall use these words as an illustration of this theocratic government. Four thoughts are suggested concerning it.

I. IT ROSE FROM THE HUMBLEST CONDITION. "In that day will I raise up the tabernacle of David that is fallen." "The fallen hut of David" (Delitzsch). Not the magnificent palace of David, which the monarch built for himself on Mount Zion (2 Sam. v. 11). "It is striking that Amos, prophesying in Israel, closes with a promise, not to the ten tribes primarily, but to the royal house of David, and to Israel only through its restoration. Strange comment on human greatness, that the royal line was not to be employed in the salvation of the world until it was fallen. The royal palace had to become the hut of Nazareth ere the Redeemer of the world could be born, whose glory and kingdom were not of this world, . . . who came to take from us nothing but our nature that he might sanctify it, our misery that he might bear it for us" (Pusey). Ay, this true moral theocracy had in truth a humble origin! Its Founder, who was he? The Son of a poor Jewish peasant, who commenced his life in a stable. Its first apostles, who were they? They were amongst the poorest of the poor. In its origin, indeed, its symbols are the little stone, the grain of mustard seed, and the few particles of leaven.

II. HEATHENS ARE SUBJECT TO ITS AUTHORITY. "That they may possess the remnant of Edom, and of all the heathen, which are called by my Name, saith the Lord that doeth this." The old theocracy was confined to the Jews; this one, this moral theocracy, is to extend to the heathen. Even Edom—the old and inveterate foe of the theocratic people, who may be regarded as the representative of the whole heathen world—is to be subjected to it. It shall "inherit the Gentiles." It is to have the heathen for its inheritance, and the uttermost parts of the earth for its possession. The Bible assures us, in language most explicit and of frequent occurrence, that the time will come when from the rising of the sun to the going down of the same his Name—that is, the Name of this great moral King, Christ—shall be great among the Gentiles. Or, in the language of Daniel, "When the kingdom and dominion, and the greatness of the kingdom under the whole heaven, shall be given to the people of the saints of the most High, whose kingdom is an everlasting kingdom, and all dominions shall serve and obey him" (Dan. vii. 27).

III. ABUNDANT MATERIAL PROVISIONS WILL ATTEND IT. "Behold, the days come, saith the Lord, that the ploughman shall overtake the reaper, and the treader of grapes him that soweth seed; and the mountains shall drop sweet wine, and all the hills shall melt." "The metaphorical language here employed is at once in the highest degree bold and pleasing. The Hebrews were accustomed to construct terraces on the sides of the mountains and other elevations, on which they planted vines. Of this fact the prophet avails himself, and represents the immense abundance of the produce to be such that the eminences themselves would appear to be converted into the juice of the grape." Just as this moral theocracy extends, pauperism will vanish. With the kingdom of God and his righteousness all necessary material good comes. "Godliness is profitable unto all things." Let this theocracy, which means the reign in human hearts of Christliness, extend, and the earth "shall yield her increase, and God, even our own God, shall bless us."

IV. LOST PRIVILEGES ARE RESTORED AS IT ADVANCES. "I will bring again the captivity of my people of Israel, and they shall build the waste cities, and inhabit them; and they shall plant vineyards, and drink the wine thereof; they shall also make gardens, and eat the fruit of them." Three blessings, which man has lost through depravity, are here indicated. 1. *Freedom.* "I will bring again the captivity," or rather, "I will reverse the captivity," give them liberty. Man in a state of depravity is a slave—a slave to lust, worldliness, etc. This moral theocracy ensures freedom to all its subjects. "Ye shall know the truth, and the truth shall make you free" (John viii. 32). 2. *Prosperity.* "Shall build the waste cities, and inhabit them; and they shall plant vineyards, and drink the wine thereof." One of the sad evils connected with man's fallen depravity is that he does not reap the reward of his labours. He builds cities and plants vineyards and makes gardens for others. Through the reign of social injustice he is prevented from enjoying the produce of his honest labours. Under this theocracy it will not be so. What a man produces he will hold and enjoy as his own. 3. *Settledness.* "I will plant them upon their land, and they shall no more be pulled up out of their land which I have given them, saith the Lord thy God." Unregenerate man has ever been restless, homeless, unsettled. He stands not on a rock, but rather on planks floating on surging waters ; he is never at rest.   All the subjects of the true theocracy are established.   " God is their Refuge and Strength."

CONCLUSION.   Let us have faith in this predicted future of the world.   This faith can alone sustain us in our arduous work; this faith has ever been the nerve of all the great men who have toiled for the world's good.

" Poet and seer that question caught
    Above the din of life's fears and frets ;
It marched with letters, it toiled with thought,
    Through schools and creeds which the earth forgets.
And statesmen trifle and priests deceive,
    And traders barter our world away ;
Yet hearts to the golden promise cleave,
    And still at times ' Is it come ? ' they say.

" The days of the nations bear no trace
    Of all the sunshine so far foretold ;
The cannon speaks in the teacher's place,
    The age is weary with work and gold ;
And high hopes wither, and memories wane,
    On hearths and altars the fires are dead ;
But that brave faith hath not lived in vain,
    And this is all that our watcher said."

(Frances Brown.)

D. T.

HOMILETICAL INDEX

TO

THE BOOK OF AMOS

—◦◇◦—

OBADIAH

EXPOSITION BY

W. J. DEANE

HOMILETICS BY

J. R. THOMSON

HOMILIES BY VARIOUS AUTHORS

A. C. THISELTON
D. THOMAS

THE BOOK OF OBADIAH

INTRODUCTION

§ I. Subject of the Book.

THE Book of Obadiah is occupied with one subject—the punishment of Edom for its cruel and unbrotherly conduct towards Judah at the time of some great national calamity, merging at the end in a prophecy of the restoration of Israel. We must not suppose, however, that Obadiah intends to limit his utterances to a denunciation of the Edomites. His words are not exclusively intended for their case. While what he says concerning their destruction is to be regarded as literally true, they are also taken as the type of nations hostile to God, and their overthrow prefigures the universal judgment on Gentiles, which should usher in the establishment of the kingdom of God, the sovereignty of Jehovah over all the world. The work consists of two parts—one (vers. 1—16) telling of the destruction of Edom, and the causes thereof; the other (vers. 17—21), of the salvation and final victory of Israel. It commences with a proclamation of Jehovah to the nations to come and do battle against Edom. Relying on the impregnable nature of her seat among the rocks of Petra, she fears no foe, yet thence the Lord shall bring her down. She shall suffer no mere predatory inroad, but shall be totally stripped and plundered. The allies in whom she trusted shall prove treacherous, and laugh her credulity to scorn. The wise men for whom she was widely celebrated shall fail to save her in that day; all her valiant chiefs shall become faint-hearted, and utter desolation shall be her portion. Why is Edom thus afflicted? It is in retribution for the wrong which she did to Israel, the covenant nation, to whom she was united by closest ties of kindred. When Judah was reduced to low estate, Edom rejoiced in her sister's calamity, beheld her disaster with malicious satisfaction, and sided with her enemies in the plunder and murder of the wretched inhabitants of Jerusalem. Such conduct the Edomites will, as the prophet foresees, repeat at the first opportunity; and for this, when God visits the heathen, they shall be marked out for destruction, and shall receive the measure which they meted to others. The last five verses comprise the second part of the prophecy. On Mount Zion there shall be those that escape, and deliverance shall be given to the house of Jacob. The Israelites shall be agents in God's hand for the accomplishment of his vengeance; they shall expel the invaders of their country, and spread abroad on every side; the dispersed among the Gentiles shall return to their fellow-countrymen; and the great consummation shall arrive when " the kingdom shall be the Lord's."

The relation of Edom to Israel had for the most part been of the most unfriendly character. Quarrels between relatives are proverbially bitter; this was the case with these two nations. The hostility showed itself in the refusal to allow Israel to pass through their land on the way to Canaan; it led to wars with Saul (1 Sam. xiv. 47) and with David, who must have had good reason for his very severe treatment of them when he put to death all the males (2 Sam. viii. 13, 14, Revised Version; 1 Kings xi. 15, etc.). Hadad, an Idumean chief, was one of Solomon's most inveterate opponents (1 Kings xi. 14—22); and though the Edomites were for many years kept under by stern measures, yet they rebelled whenever they saw a hope of success. Thus they joined with Moab and Ammon in an invasion of Judæa in the time of Jehoshaphat (2 Chron. xx. 22); under Jehoram they regained their independence, massacred the Judæans who were in their borders, and, in alliance with Philistines and desert tribes, plundered the king's palace in Jerusalem and slew his sons (2 Chron. xxi. 8, 17; Joel iii. 19; Amos i. 11). Some years later, however, they were successfully attacked by Amaziah, their stronghold Sela, or Petra, was taken, and the population was put to the sword, twenty thousand being slain in battle or butchered afterwards (2 Kings xiv. 7; 2 Chron. xxv. 11, etc.). Yet they were never completely subdued; they were always on the watch to smite Judah and to carry away captives (2 Chron. xxviii. 17). When Nebuchadnezzar besieged Jerusalem, they gladly joined the invaders (Ezek. xxxv.; xxxvi. 5), helped to plunder the city and to cut off stragglers who endeavoured to escape. This hostile attitude of Edom towards God's people is the ground of the judgment denounced by Obadiah.

The following eloquent passage from Dean Stanley's ' Lectures on the Jewish Church ' (ii. 556) shows the attitude of Edom, and the feeling evoked by it in the breast of the Jews: " Deepest of all was the indignation roused by the sight of the nearest of kin, the race of Esau, often allied to Judah, often independent, now bound by the closest union with the power that was truly the common enemy of both. There was an intoxication of delight in the wild Edomite chiefs, as at each successive stroke against the venerable wall, they shouted, ' Down with it, down with it, even to the ground!' They stood in the passes to intercept the escape of those who would have fled down to the Jordan valley; they betrayed the fugitives; they indulged their barbarous revels on the temple hill. Long and loud has been the wail of execration which has gone up from the

Jewish nation against Edom. It is the one imprecation which breaks forth from the Lamentations of Jeremiah; it is the culmination of the fierce threats of Ezekiel; it is the sole purpose of the short, sharp cry of Obadiah, it is the bitterest drop in the sad recollections of the Israelite captives by the waters of Babylon; and the one warlike strain of the evangelical prophet is inspired by the hope that the Divine Conqueror should come knee-deep in Idumean blood."

The territory occupied by the Edomites extended from the southern end of the Dead Sea to the Elanitic Gulf, and comprised an area of about two thousand square miles. Though it was a mountainous district, and well deserved its biblical names of "the mount of Esau" and "Mount Seir," there was no want of fertile soil in its valleys and terraces. The ancient capital appears to have been Bozrah, a city that lay a few miles south of the Dead Sea. But at the time of Obadiah's prophecy this had been supplanted by the celebrated Sela, or Petra, the peculiar position of which place, with its difficult access, its rock-hewn dwellings, and natural defences, had tended to encourage in the Edomites a spirit of independence and security, which taught them to defy attack and to spurn all attempts at subjection.

There has always been great difficulty in visiting the modern representatives of the Edomites, though some few enterprising persons have penetrated their fastnesses, and given to the world the results of their investigations. A late traveller who has succeeded in inspecting Petra has described his visit in the *Century Magazine*, November, 1885, from which the following extracts are taken: "Petra is identified with the Hebrew Selah, 'a Rock,' the Amorite, Edomite, and Moabite stronghold (Judg. i. 36; 2 Kings xiv. 7; Isa. xvi. 1). Strabo (xvi. 663; v. 15, edit. Did.) tells us of Petra as a city shut in by rocks in the midst of the desert, yet supplied abundantly with water, and important as a place of transit for Oriental productions. The city lay in a narrow valley, surrounded by precipitous hills. On the eastern and western sides the cliffs rise almost perpendicularly to the height of six or seven hundred feet. On the north and south the natural barriers are less formidable, and may, in places, be passed by camels. Many recesses, or small lateral valleys, open into the main valley. The circuit of the entire depression, including these lateral valleys, is about four miles. . . . The site of Petra lies half-way between the Gulf of Akabah and the Dead Sea, about seventy miles, as the vulture flies, from each. It has been said that there is but one entrance to Petra. Yet there is a 'back door,' so to speak, through which some travellers have made their way into the city, and by means of which they have also more suddenly made their departure. The real approach is through a narrow gorge (Wady Mousa) some two miles long, of which the gateway faces the east. This is reached from Palestine by way of Moab, east of the Dead Sea, and from the south by the route I took [viz. across the Red Sea, a few miles south of Suez; down the desert to Mount Sinai; thence north and east to the head of the Gulf of Akabah]. The back door may be gained from north or south by way of the Wady Arabah—the vast desert waste which lies between the Gulf of Akabah and the Dead Sea, into which it opens near the base of venerable Mount Hor. . . . Breaking our way through the jungle on the further side of the stream [the Sik], we found ourselves in the very heart of the necropolis of Petra. . . . It may be useful to remind the reader, before we enter Petra proper, that all its principal structures, be they tombs, palaces, or temples, are excavated from the rock, and not constructed of quarried stone. The sides of the mountains are cut to smooth perpendicular faces, which are occupied by unbroken ranges of temples and of homes for the living and the dead. The interiors behind the ornate fronts are but caves squared by the old stone-cutter, and are lighted only by their doors. Continuing our advance, we followed the stream a few rods, and descending as the pass narrowed, the entrance of the frightful chasm, seen afar off at sunrise, was reached at last. What an impregnable gateway! Spanning it is a fine buttressed arch, resting upon rock-cut foundations. Beneath this a little stream gurgles. We followed it through the only entrance—the 'front door' of Petra. The top of the northern wall of the defile was once inhabited. Excavations, bridges, terraced gardens, and various other evidences remain upon it of the industry and artistic taste of a wonderfully persevering people. When we had come fairly inside the gorge, we found it at times so narrow that two of us could not walk abreast. Its perpendicular sides vary in height from four hundred to seven hundred feet, and frequently, without absolutely meeting, they overhang to such a degree that the sky is shut out from the sight for a hundred yards at a stretch. On every side, more than a yard above the stream-bed, channels are cut in the rock as conduits for water, and in some places terra-cotta pipes are found cemented in these channels. Tiny niches abound also, cut in the sides of the gorge— old pagan divinities, no doubt. The growth of oleanders becomes more dense as the gorge descends. Green caper plants dangle from the crevices, and here and there a graceful tamarisk is found in the shade. The tiny brook, the Sik, follows the whole way. The quarried stone scattered along the path indicates that the floor of the fissure was once paved. At every turn we saw evidences of indefatigable effort, and of how lavishly labour was expended by the people who lived in Petra in its days of power. For nearly two miles we followed the semi-subterranean passage. The path-way now descended; the water grew deeper, the opposing thicket more impassable, the scene more grand. . . . Emerging from the gorge into an open area, we stood face to face with the strange edifice (the Khuzneh). . . . The colour is a delicate rose-pink, like that of the buildings further on in the city, almost unbroken by waves of other hue. . . As the inner gate of the city beyond the Khuzneh was entered, to the right and left wondrous architectural fancies loomed up. On the left is a group of square-cut edifices, seeming at first like gigantic steps, but out of which varied façades appear upon a closer view. On the right is a trio of tombs and temples hewn from the end of a range of cliffs, the last one looking like a great grim warder at the city gate. Beneath are numberless excavations, each one of which, from its appearance, might have been used first as a home for the living before being appropriated as a tomb. . . . Now emerging into the expanse of the little valley, the full glory of the Edomite capital burst upon us. Nature built these stupendous walls, and man adorned them with patient workmanship, each artist vying with his fellow in shaping these rainbow cliffs into forms of beauty."

The fulfilment of Obadiah's prophecy may be briefly summarized. It is most probable that, after the fall of Jerusalem, and notwithstanding the assistance which they gave to Nebuchadnezzar on that occasion, the Edomites were subdued by that monarch some five years later. History fails to assert this fact in unmistakable terms, but it is satisfactorily inferred from other considerations. Jeremiah prophesies (xxv. 9; xxvii. 3—6) that the Chaldeans shall attack this country as well as Egypt (xliii. 8—13), and Josephus ('Ant.,' x. 9. 7) narrates how they warred against Cœle-Syria, the Ammonites, and Moabites, and then proceeded to invade Egypt. It is highly improbable that they left Petra unconquered in their rear, more especially as in all likelihood Edom joined with Ammon and Moab in resisting this aggression. Rather, the ruin mentioned by Malachi (i. 3, 4), " They shall build, but I will throw down," was then inflicted, and their " mountains were made a desolation, and their heritage given to the jackals of the wilderness." At this time the Nabathæans, an Arabian tribe, and possibly sent thither by Nebuchadnezzar, took possession of Petra; and thus, according to Obadiah's word, the heathen rose up against her in battle, seized her stronghold, and brought her down to the ground. Antigonus, one of the generals of Alexander the Great, conquered this people and despoiled Petra, B.C. 312. The Edomites, who had established themselves in Southern Palestine, suffered heavy defeats at the hands of Judas Maccabæus (1 Macc. v. 3, 65); John Hyrcanus compelled them to submit to the Mosaic Law (Josephus, 'Ant.,' xiii. 9. 1); Alexander Jannæus completed their ruin (ibid., 15. 4). The scanty remains of the people which existed at the siege of Jerusalem were almost entirely put to the sword ('Bell. Jud.,' iv. 5, etc.; v. 6. 1); the few survivors of the massacre took refuge among the tribes of the desert, and were absorbed in their community, so that Origen could say that in his time their name and language had wholly perished ('In Job.').

§ II. AUTHOR.

Of Obadiah, the author of this prophecy, nothing whatever is known. Not even his father's name is given in the title of the book, which is simply, "the vision of Obadiah." The name itself (in Greek, 'Αβδιού or 'Οβδιού, sc. 'Ορασις: in Latin, Abdias) signifies "Servant" or "Worshipper of Jehovah," and was common among the Hebrews; but the attempt to identify the prophet with any of the persons so called in Holy Writ is entirely unsuccessful, and has arisen rather from the natural desire to know more concerning this holy man than from any special evidence or probability. Persons of the same name (though sometimes in different form) are found in 1 Kings xviii. 3; 1 Chron. iii. 21; vii. 3; viii. 38; ix. 16, 44; xii. 9; xxvii. 19; xxxiv. 12; Ezra viii. 9; Neh. x. 5; 2 Chron. xvii. 7; xxxiv. 12; but none of these has any pretension to be considered our prophet. The contents of his prophecy prove that he belonged to the kingdom of Judah, and St. Ephrem asserts that he came from Sichem. His tomb was shown at Samaria in St. Jerome's time.

§ III. Date.

The age in which Obadiah lived and prophesied is a matter of great dispute, and, after all that can be said, must be considered as only probably ascertained. The most varying opinions have been held. While some regard him as the earliest, or among the earliest, of the minor prophets, others place him after the destruction of Jerusalem in the time of Captivity; and Hitzig sets his date as late as B.C. 312. The interval between the various dates amounts to six hundred years. "That is," says Dr. Pusey ('Minor Prophets,' p. 227), "just as if men doubted, *from internal evidence,* whether a work were written in the time of William the Conqueror or in that of Cromwell; of St. Louis or Louis XVIII.; or whether Hesiod was a contemporary of Callimachus, and Ennius of Claudian; or the author of the 'Nibelungen Lied' lived with Schiller." The elements for determining this controversy are not very satisfactory. First, there is the position of the book in the Hebrew Bible. If this were proved to be strictly chrono-logical, the question might be thus decided, and Obadiah might be regarded as prophesying about the age of Amos, next to whom he is arranged. The Septuagint places his book between Joel and Jonah, setting Micah before the former; and this order would give an approximately similar date. In the Hebrew arrangement the exilian or post-exilian prophets certainly occupy the last place; and Obadiah, occurring among the older seers, between Amos and Jonah, would appear to belong to an earlier age. But it is objected that this position is due to his prophecy being an expansion of the prediction about Edom in the concluding words of Amos (ix. 12), and has no bearing whatever upon his date. Though we can by no means concede this, and are disposed to lay great weight on the arrangement of the Hebrew canon, we must be guided by other considerations in deter-mining the question. The contents of the book supply two further aids. In ver. 11 Obadiah alludes to the capture of Jerusalem; and if we knew for certain to what event he refers, we should at once be in a position to settle the difficulty. We gather from his language that Jerusalem was taken and plundered; that her soldiers were sent into captivity; that her citizens were sold as slaves; and that Edom joined with the invaders, cut off stragglers, and rejoiced in the calamity of Judah. Nothing is said of the total destruction of the city and the temple, nothing of the people recovering their lost home; they are supposed to be still occupying their own country (vers. 17—19), and thence extending their kingdom. Now, we read in the Old Testament of three, or perhaps four, occasions on which Jerusalem was taken. The first capture by Shishak, in the reign of Rehoboam (1 Kings xiv. 25; 2 Chron. xii. 2), was not attended with such evils as are noted in our prophecy, and took place at a time when the Edomites, being subject to Judah, could not have acted in the manner specified.

The second occasion belongs to the reign of Jehoram, when the Philistines and Arabians (the latter being a loose designation of the roving tribes of the wilderness and the inhabitants of the country south of Judæa) invaded Judah, plundered much treasure from the house of the king, and carried away his wives and all his children save his youngest son, Jehoahaz (2 Chron. xxi. 16, 17; comp. 2 Kings viii. 20, etc.). The description is brief, and further details are wanting; but it can scarcely be doubted that other captives were taken besides the royal family; and that if the palace of the king was sacked, the city and its inhabitants could not have got off scatheless. Amos (i. 6, 9, 11) is probably alluding to the same event when he speaks of the injuries perpetrated by the Philistines, Phœnicians, and Edomites; and Joel (iii. 3—6), when he complains that the Phœnicians sold the Judæans into captivity to the sons of the Grecians, and (iii. 19) foretells the desolation of Egypt and Edom for their violence against the children of Judah in their (the Jews') land. It is objected that "the house of the king," in 2 Chron. xxi. 17, does not mean the royal palace, but only the camp where was the king's temporary abode, because in the following chapter we read, "The band of men that came with the Arabians to the camp had slain all the eldest" children. But this proves nothing; the sons may have been killed in the camp (though the account does not say so), and the invaders may have gone on to Jerusalem, now left unguarded, and plundered it. Nor is it likely that they would have found much substance in a temporary camp. It is true that the Edomites are not expressly named among the allied peoples who took part in this raid; but they may well be included in the vague term "Arabians;" and at any rate the latter could not have attacked Judah without their consent, which they were ready to give at this particular time, when they had just recovered their freedom from the rule of David's line, and were glad of an opportunity of vengeance. Of the animosity and active hostility of Edom a further proof is afforded by Ps. lxxxiii., composed, perhaps, in the time of Hezekiah, where among the nations confederate against Israel are mentioned "the tabernacles of Edom and the Ishmaelites."

The third occasion when Jerusalem suffered at the hands of enemies was when Joash King of Israel defeated Amaziah, and brake down the wall of the city (2 Kings xiv. 8, etc.; 2 Chron. xxv. 17, etc.). But this cannot be the catastrophe to which Obadiah refers, as he calls the invaders strangers and foreigners, and describes the calamity as much greater than the partial disaster then incurred.

The fourth capture of Jerusalem is its final destruction by the Chaldeans. Now, the language of Obadiah does by no means adequately depict this terrible catastrophe. There is no mention of Assyrians or Babylonians. The utter destruction of the city and temple, and the dissolution of the kingdom, are nowhere stated or implied. Compare our prophet's words with those of Jeremiah and Ezekiel describing the overthrow, and how tame and insufficient they seem in the face of such utter ruin! Could any true patriot have said only thus much, and have omitted so many points which added intensity to the disaster? What are the strongest expressions used? The fatal time is called thrice, "the day of their calamity;" twice, "the day of distress;" once, "the day of their destruction" and "disaster," when "foreigners entered the gates, and cast lots upon Jerusalem, and carried away her substance." Pillage and rapine are intimated, but nothing more. Where is any similar reproach to that of the psalmist, "Remember, O Lord, the children of Edom in the day of Jerusalem, who said, Rase it, rase it, even to the foundation thereof!" (Ps. cxxxvii. 7)? Could Obadiah have failed to recall this cruel cry of the Edomites in detailing their offences against his people, if he were referring to their conduct at the Chaldean invasion? Then, again, there is no trace in our prophecy of any wholesale deportation of the people or of the desolation of the land. The nation is regarded as still seated in its own country, and adding to its possessions (ver. 17); not as returning from captivity. These considerations seem to point to the conclusion that Obadiah refers, not to the final destruction of Jerusalem, but to some previous calamity; and none that we are acquainted with coincides with the expressions with which he describes it, except the capture by the Philistines and Arabians in the time of Jehoram, which may possibly simplify the chronological difficulty by affording a *terminus a quo*, especially if any reason could be found for regarding this event as recent when Obadiah wrote.

But if we regard this calamity of Jerusalem as the event which the prophet has in view, we cannot, of course from this fact alone, settle the disputed question of his date. It is plain that the language employed in vers. 11 and 16 implies that the event is passed; and our Authorized Version, by a mistranslation of the intervening passage, emphasizes this inference. Thus in vers. 12, etc., we have, "Thou shouldest not have looked on the day of thy brother; . . . neither shouldest thou have rejoiced over the children of Judah," etc. It is certain that this rendering is grammatically wrong, and that *al* with the future can only be prohibitive; the words, therefore, ought to be translated, "Do not look," etc. (Μὴ ἐπίδῃς, Septuagint; *Non despicies*, Vulgate; "Ne intuearis," Mont.). This rendering makes the reference future; and it is said that, if Obadiah were speaking of a past event, he would not give an eightfold injunction not to do something which had already been done. It is not God's wont to warn when it is too late to repent. In answer to this, to argue that the prophet, in poetical form, is describing the past as future, seems scarcely sufficient. Rather, the truth appears to be this: In ver. 11 he is, as we concluded before, alluding to a definite capture of Jerusalem; in the following verses he is warning the Edomites not to act in the manner specified when calamity has overtaken Judah. Judging from what they had done formerly, he surmises that they will repeat the same conduct whenever occasion shall arise. He knows well how bitter and unwearied is Edom's hostility against Judah; he has seen how she behaved in the late invasion, how she sided with the enemy and made her gain from her sister's misfortune; and he urges her to act not again in this way. His prophetic eye looks forward to the future calamity that shall befall his country; from the view of the disaster which he had witnessed under Joram, he rises to the vision of a greater and more complete ruin; one is a type and prophecy of the other; and the behaviour of Edom in the former case is a rehearsal of what she will do in the latter. If the prophet's words, though nominally addressed to the Edomites, were not intended as a warning to them, and, as is most probable, never came under their notice, we may regard them as virtually foretelling their action and consequent punishment, and hence imparting comfort to the faithful few with the hope of a glorious future. The punishment which he invokes is, doubtless, primarily the consequence of their recent conduct; but the prediction embraces other crimes of a similar nature, which will increase the penalty when the moment for its judgment shall arrive. Thus far we have seen reason to decide that Obadiah wrote, not directly after the Chaldean invasion, but after the raid of the Philistines and Arabians, while the catastrophe was still present to men's memory. Again, the enemies are an indefinite mass composed of heathen tribes, not a determinate foe such as the Chaldeans. And the captives are not taken to the far east, but to the north, to Phœnicia, and to western regions. Of fugitives to Egypt no mention is made. With the Chaldean invasion in his view, Obadiah could not have used these expressions. There is another consideration which makes for the same inference, and that is his relation to other prophets. The coincidence of thought and expression between Obadiah and Joel cannot be accidental. One must have been acquainted with the other; or both must have had recourse to a third original. Thus Joel says (ii. 32), "In Mount Zion and in Jerusalem there shall be those that escape, as the Lord hath said;" and Obadiah (ver. 17), "In Mount Zion there shall be those that escape." Joel iii. 2, 3, "Whom they have scattered among the nations, and parted my land; and they have cast lots upon my people;" Obad. 11, "Foreigners entered into his gates, and cast lots upon Jerusalem." Joel iii. 4, 7, "I will return your recompense upon your own head;" Obad. 15, "Thy recompense shall return upon thine own head." "The day of the Lord is near" (Joel iii. 14; Obad. 18); "Jerusalem shall be holy" (Joel iii. 17); "Mount Zion shall be holy" (Obad. 17); "Edom shall be a

desolate wilderness, for the violence done to the children of Judah " (Joel
iii. 19) ; " For the violence done to thy brother Jacob shame shall cover
thee, and thou shalt be cut off for ever" (Obad. 10).   That Joel borrowed
from Obadiah, Keil considers proved by the expression in Joel ii. 32 (according to the numbering of the English Version), " as the Lord hath said,"
where, as we have seen above, he repeats Obadiah's words, which occur
nowhere else.   This, however, is not conclusive, as Joel may be merely
asserting his own claim of Divine authority, and may not necessarily be
quoting another prophet's utterance.   Many other critics incline to the
opinion that Joel rests on Obadiah ; if this could be demonstrated, the dispute concerning the date of the latter might be approximately settled.   But
this opinion is at best presumptive, and depends on such allegations as
that Obadiah never imitates predecessors, except in the one case of an
allusion to Balaam's prophecy (vers. 4, 18, etc.) ; that he is more original
than Joel ; and that it is not probable that in his short book he should
have had recourse to others for ideas and expressions.

The relation between Obadiah and Jeremiah is capable of more satisfactory determination.   There are nine verses in the former (vers. 1—9) which
are found in the latter (Jer. xlix. 7—22).   In the former these occur con-
secutively, and form one connected whole ; in the latter they are dispersed
over a wider space, and disunited by the insertion of other thoughts.   The
prophecy of Obadiah against Edom is an orderly and regular production,
with a beginning, middle, and conclusion, passing on naturally to the climax ;
Jeremiah denounces Edom at various times and in various manners, but
his prediction has no internal unity, and is not worked up into a perfect
whole.   Jeremiah, too, has on other occasions borrowed largely from his
predecessors.   It is impossible that Obadiah should have prefaced his work
with the words, " The vision of Obadiah," and " we have heard tidings from
the Lord," if he was taking such large extracts from previous writings.
A careful inspection of the two prophets (noting especially how Jeremiah
has softened the ruggedness and changed the unusual expressions in
Obadiah) will lead to the conclusion that Obadiah is the original from
whom Jeremiah borrowed, just as he introduces verses from Isaiah in
his denunciation of Moab (comp. Jer. xlviii. 43, 44 with Isa. xxiv. 17, 18 ;
and generally Jer. xlviii. with Isa. xv., xvi.), and a passage from Amos
(i. 4) in the judgment of Damascus (Jer. xlix. 27).   Thus the prophecy
of Obadiah was anterior to that of Jeremiah, whose utterance against
Edom belongs to the fourth year of Jehoiakim (Caspari, pp. 14, etc.).
The question still remains—How long anterior ?   Some intimation of the
truth may be gleaned from the fact that there are found in Obadiah
phrases and sentences common to Amos and Joel, but nothing from writers
later than these.   If these prophets cited Obadiah, *cadit quæstio ;* if he
quoted them, why did he refer to no later writings ?   The presumption is
that he lived close to their time.

From what has been said, we conclude that Obadiah is one of the earliest of the minor prophets, that he lived about the time of Jehoram, and prophesied at latest (as Dr. Pusey thinks) during the minority of Joash.

§ IV. GENERAL CHARACTER.

There can be no doubt that the style of Obadiah is remarkably original. In his very diction he deviates from the beaten track, using many words and forms which occur nowhere else. Though his language is simple, it is very suggestive, full of thought, and pregnant with meaning. Pure and idiomatic, it breathes a high antiquity, unmixed with later forms, and distinct from that of the greater prophets. There is a vigour, and terseness, and a rapidity, which carry the reader along, and place him by the prophet's side in fullest sympathy. Obadiah delights in interrogation and apostrophe, in vivid detail, and concise statement. He is often highly poetic, never monotonous. What force and pathos are there in the sustained description of the injuries inflicted by strangers on Jerusalem, ending in the sudden address to Edom, "Thou wast as one of them" (ver. 11)! What power in the warning against malicious pleasure at a neighbour's disaster, with its oft-repeated expression, "in the day" (vers. 12—14)! What solemnity in the summing up of the prophecy, "And the kingdom shall be the Lord's"! A regular sequence of thought runs through the whole book. To find in this very uniform and consistent prophecy nothing but literary patchwork, as Graf and Ewald, for instance, have done, is a groundless neologian fancy. These critics suppose that the former part of the prophecy (vers. 1—10) was an extract from an older seer—the true Obadiah or an unknown writer; that the latter portion belongs to the time of the Captivity, and was added by the compiler. The sagacity that thus arbitrarily dissects the work is singularly at fault in this case. It requires only an unprejudiced eye (even if we exclude a belief in the predictive element) to see that our book is one whole, that its parts progress equably and uniformly, that the conclusion follows naturally on what precedes; so that if we had to find one special characteristic of the prophecy, we should say that it is distinguished by the close connection of its members without break or interruption.

§ V. LITERATURE.

Among mediæval commentators upon Obadiah we may mention Hugo à S. Victore, whose interpretation is wholly mystical. Ephraem Syrus has left a commentary on this prophet. Luther's 'Enarrationes in Abdiam' are well known. Other works are those of Bishop Pilkington, 'Exposition;' Pfeiffer, with a Latin translation of the Commentary of Arbanabel (Vittemb., 1670); Raynoldi (1613); Leusden (Utrecht, 1657); the text, Hebrew and Chaldee, with the notes of Jarchi, Aben-Ezra, and Kimchi; Crocius (Bremæ, 1673), with rabbinical interpretations; Bishop Horsley, 'Critical Notes;' Hendewerk, 'Obadiæ Proph. Oraculum' (1836); Caspari, 'Der Prophet Obadja' (Leipzig, 1863); Seydel (Leipzig, 1842); T. T. Perowne, in 'Cambridge Bible for Schools and Colleges.' An Armenian Version was published by A. Acoluthus, in 1680, and a Syriac by Grimm, in 1799.

§ VI. Arrangement in Sections.

The book divides into two parts.

Part I. (Vers. 1—16.)   The destruction of Edom, and the cause thereof.

§ 1. (Vers. 1—9.)   The heathen nations are summoned to take vengeance on Edom.   In spite of her impregnable position, they shall bring her low and strip her of her wealth, being aided and encouraged by her own allies.

§ 2. (Vers. 10—14.)   This punishment falls upon her as the result of the malice and unfriendliness which she has displayed towards Israel in the time of her calamity, in that she rejoiced at her sister's disaster and took part with her enemies.

§ 3. (Vers. 15, 16.)   For this cause Edom shall be remembered in the day of the Lord; she shall suffer at the hands of the heathen what she inflicted on others.

Part. II. (Vers. 17—21.)   The restoration of Israel.

§ 1. (Vers. 17—20.)   The house of Jacob shall be delivered, and shall add to its possessions, and spread far and wide.

§ 2. (Ver. 21.)   Salvation shall come to Zion, and "the kingdom shall be the Lord's."

THE BOOK OF OBADIAH

EXPOSITION.

Vers. 1—16.—Part I. The Destruction of Edom, and the Cause thereof.

Vers. 1—9.—§ 1. *The heathen nations are summoned to take vengeance on Edom. In spite of her impregnable position, they shall bring her low and strip her of her wealth, being aided and encouraged by her own allies.*

Ver. 1.—The vision of Obadiah. This is the title of the book, declaring from whom and through whom the revelation comes (Isa. i. 1). Under the word "vision" in prophetic language is included, not only what the seer saw, the mental picture presented to his inner senses, but also all that he is commissioned to disclose or enunciate. **Thus saith the Lord God concerning Edom.** The prophet declares that God speaks through him. One might have expected that the actual words of Jehovah would follow here instead of tidings heard from him. And this difficulty has led some to suppose these introductory words spurious or the insertion of a later hand, others to include them and the rest of the verse in a parenthesis, so as to begin the "vision" with God's words in ver. 2. But these suggestions are unnecessary. The prophet, as the mouthpiece of God, calls his own words the message of the Lord—signifies that what had been revealed to his mind he was bound to communicate to others as a direct warning from God. The Edomites were the descendants of Esau, and bound by ties of blood to the Israelites; but they had always been their most bitter enemies (Amos i. 11). They are regarded as a type of the powers of the world hostile to true religion, whose end is destruction. **We have heard.** "We"—I myself and other prophets; or the Judæans, the prophet identifying himself with his countrymen. Septuagint, ἤκουσα, "I heard;" so Jer. xlix. 14; Arabic,

"ye have heard." **A rumour;** *a report* (Isa. liii. 1); ἀκοὴν (Septuagint); *auditum* (Vulgate). It means here "tidings" (comp. Matt. xxiv. 6, ἀκοαὶ πολέμων : and Rom. x. 16, 17). **An ambassador;** *a messenger;* as though the prophet saw the minister of God's wrath going forth among the heathen to rouse them to war against Edom. Perowne thinks that there is an allusion to the composite character of Nebuchadnezzar's army with which he attacked the Edomites. The Septuagint renders, περιοχήν : so the Syriac, Chaldee, and Symmachus translate "message." This rendering is explained by the following clause. **The heathen** (*goyim*); *the nations,* as vers. 2, 15. **Arise ye, and let us rise.** This has been taken as if "arise ye" were the herald's message, and "let us rise" the response of the nations echoing his words; but it is more forcible to consider the whole clause as the message, the ambassador joining himself with the heathen as their leader and comrade in the war of vengeance. Vers. 1—9 are incorporated in Jer. xlix. 7—22.

Ver. 2.—Behold, I have made thee small. Here is the effect of the summons. So in Jer. xlix. 15, "For, lo, I will make thee small." Jehovah is the Speaker, and he regards the future as past. What he determines is as good as accomplished. At this time the Edomites were a powerful nation, and possessed an almost impregnable seat at Petra. **Small;** in numbers, territory, honour.

Vers. 3, 4.—Edom had prided herself in the strength of her position; but this shall not secure her from destruction when the Lord wars against her.

Ver. 3.—Hath deceived; Septuagint, ἐπῆρε, "elated;" Vulgate, *extulit.* The pointing varies. In ver. 7 Jerome translates the word by *illudere.* **The clefts;**

Septuagint, ὀπαῖς: Vulgate, scissuris. The word occurs in the parallel passage, Jer. xlix. 16, and in Cant. ii. 14, where it has the meaning of "refuge." **Of the rock.** This may be Sela, or Petra, as 2 Kings xiv. 7. The country inhabited by the Edomites lay on the eastern side of the Arabah, and extended from the south end of the Dead Sea to the Elanitic Gulf. It was a region of mountain and valley, difficult, and in many parts inaccessible from the west. Rock-hewn dwellings are found everywhere in these hills, the Edomites, when they expelled the aboriginal Troglodytes (Deut. ii. 12, 22), having adopted their habitations and excavated new ones on the same model throughout the whole district. These were useful, not only as being secure from hostile attack, but as cool retreats in the summer of that scorching tract, and offering a warm shelter in winter when fuel was scarce. Petra, the capital, lay completely hidden at the end of a rocky defile some two miles long, and could easily be defended against an enemy by a handful of men. (For a description of this remarkable place, see the Introduction, § I.)

Ver. 4.—**Though thou exalt thyself as the eagle.** The Hebrew gives "nest" as the subject of both clauses, thus: "Though thou exaltest . . . and settest thy nest." Job (xxxix. 27, 28) speaks of the eagle making its nest in the highest rocks. The metaphor is found in Numb. xxiv. 21; Hab. ii. 9. **Will I bring thee down** (Amos ix. 3). The seizure of Petra by the Nabathæans is the judgment referred to in this part of the prophecy; the complete ruin is mentioned later (vers. 18, etc.).

Vers. 5, 6.—To prove the completeness of the destruction that shall befall Edom, the prophet supposes two cases of despoiling in which something would be left behind. It will be far worse than any mere raid of thieves; nothing will be spared.

Ver. 5.—**Thieves . . . robbers.** The former are ordinary thieves who pilfer secretly; the latter are robbers who act with violence, or members of a marauding expedition. **How art thou cut off!** An interposed ejaculation of the prophet, sympathizing with the Edomites for the utter desolation which he sees in vision. Septuagint, Ποῦ ἂν ἀπερρίφης; "Where wouldst thou have been cast away?" taking a different reading; Vulgate, Quomodo conticuisses? "How wouldst thou have been silent?" i.e. for fear. **Till they had enough.** Would they not have taken such plunder as they wanted, and then decamped? The grape-gatherers would leave some bunches untouched, which escaped their notice. There

is no reference to the charitable law in Lev. xix. 10; Deut. xxiv. 21, which would not affect, or be known unto, these grape-plunderers.

Ver. 6.—Obadiah contemplates Edom's ruin, in retribution of her plundering Jerusalem, and speaks of it as past. **How are the things of Esau searched out!** literally, how are thy things searched out, Esau! i.e. the people and property that belong to Esau. The enemy leave no place unexamined. So in Zeph. i. 12 the Lord says, "I will search Jerusalem with candles." (For "Esau" as equivalent to "Edom," see Gen. xxv. 30.) **His hidden things** (matspon, ἅπαξ λεγόμενον); hidden treasures; Septuagint, τὰ κεκρυμμένα αὐτοῦ. Jeremiah (xlix. 10) gives, "secret places." Keil notes that Petra was a great emporium of the trade between Arabia and Syria, and that in it great treasures were stored (Diod. Sic., xix. 95).

Ver. 7.—In this dire calamity Edom shall be deserted by her friends and allies—a punishment for her behaviour to her sister Judah. **The men of thy confederacy.** The LXX. and the Vulgate annex these words to the following clause. The allies intended may be Moab, Ammon, Tyre, and Zidon, who joined together to resist Nebuchadnezzar, and were smitten by him (Jer. xxvii. 3); or, as Perowne thinks, the Chaldeans themselves, who, though the Edomites had aided in the attack on Jerusalem, afterwards turned against them. **Have brought thee even to the border;** Septuagint, Ἕως τῶν ὁρίων ἐξαπέστειλάν σε, "They sent thee forth unto thy borders;" Vulgate, Usque ad terminum emiserunt ii. Keil and others explain this to mean that the Edomites send ambassadors to their allies, asking help, but these messengers are conducted back to the frontier with their request not granted, because the allies are unwilling to entangle themselves in the fate of Edom. It is easier to understand the passage in this way—Thy very allies have assisted the enemy in expelling thee from thy borders, and refusing to receive fugitives who came to them. **The men that were at peace with thee.** Either the same as "the men of thy confederacy," or the neighbouring Arabian tribes who resorted to Petra for commercial reasons (comp. Judg. iv. 17). The phrase here, literally, the men of thy peace, is found in Ps. xli. 9 and Jer. xxxviii. 22. **Have deceived thee,** by not bringing the expected help; and have **prevailed against** thee, by actual violence. **They that eat thy bread.** The Hebrew is simply, "thy bread," i.e. the men of thy bread. Vulgate, qui comedunt tecum; the LXX. omits the words. The expression (comp. Ps. xli. 9) implies the closest friendship, especially in Eastern lands, where such a tie is of general obligation. Have laid a wound under thee; rather, *lay a snare under thee;* Septuagint, ἔθηκαν ἔνεδρα ὑποκάτω σου, "they set snares under thee;" Vulgate, *ponent insidias subter te* (comp. Ps. lxix. 22). Another interpretation is this: "As thy bread (which they as friends were bound to offer) they lay a sling under thee," *i.e.* prepare an ambush for thee, like Jael did for Sisera. Pusey notes the climax in this verse—not confederates only, but friends; not friends only, but familiar friends, indebted to them. Those banded with them should expel them from their country; those at peace should prevail against them in war; those who ate their bread should requite them with treachery. There is none understanding in him; *i.e.* in Edom. The shock of this defection of allies and the sudden destruction that has overwhelmed them have deprived the Edomites of their wonted sagacity and prudence. They know not whither to turn or what to do. The following verse expands this thought.

Vers. 8, 9.—Their vaunted wisdom and their boasted courage shall fail, for God shall take them away. "Quem Deus vult perdere, prius dementat."

Ver. 8.—In that day; when Edom is abandoned by its friends. Destroy the wise men out of Edom. God shall take their wisdom from them, so that they shall be no more able to offer prudent counsel or suggest plans of safety (Isa. xix. 11—16; xxix. 14; xlvii. 12, 13). The Edomites were celebrated for wisdom or practical philosophy (comp. 1 Kings iv. 30; Jer. xlix. 7; Baruch iii. 22, 23). Mount of Esau (vers. 9, 19, 21). Mount Seir—a designation of Edom from the nature of the country. Ver. 9.—O Teman; Septuagint, οἱ ἐκ Θαιμάν, "those from Thæman;" Vulgate, *a meridic,* taking the word as an appellative; so the Chaldee. The southern district of Idumea was so called (see note on Amos i. 12). One of Job's friends, and the cleverest of them, was a Temanite (Job ii. 11). To the end that. This judicial blindness is inflicted in order that all may perish. By slaughter. Murder at the hands of the enemy. The LXX., Vulgate, and Syriac connect these words with the following verse. But the Masoretic punctuation, as in the Anglican Version, is doubtless correct (see Keil).

Vers. 10—14.—§ 2. *The cause of Edom's destruction.* This punishment falls upon her as the result of the malice and unfriendliness which she has displayed towards Israel in the time of calamity, in that she rejoiced at her sister's disaster and took part with her enemies.

Ver. 10.—For thy violence against thy brother Jacob. The special action to which Obadiah alludes, and which he particularizes in the following verses, occurred at the time of the invasion of Judæa by Philistines and Arabians during the reign of Jehoram, when the Edomites sided with the enemy, and acted as the prophet intimates (2 Chron. xxi. 16, etc.; see Introduction, § III.). The iniquity of such conduct is aggravated by the fact that the victim was the "brother Jacob," who was commanded not to hate the Edomites (Deut. xxiii. 7). This enjoined friendship was not reciprocated by the descendants of Esau. Whether from envy at the superior privileges of Israel, or from other causes, the Edomites, from the time of Moses, had always been actively hostile to the Israelites. They had been subdued by David, but had lately rebelled and secured their independence, and were always looking for an opportunity of revenging themselves on their conquerors (comp. Amos i. 11; Ezek. xxv. 12; xxxv. 5). Shame shall cover thee. Shame for the destruction that hath overtaken thee (Micah vii. 10). Thou shalt be cut off for ever (comp. Mal. i. 4; see Introduction, § I.). Terrible retribution fell on Idumea in the time of the Maccabees (see 1 Macc. v. 3; 2 Macc. x. 15, etc.; Josephus, 'Ant.,' xii. 8. 1). Before that time they had been dispossessed of Petra by the Nabathæans.

Ver. 11.—The injuries complained of were committed lately, and the prophet could speak of them as well known (see note on ver. 10). In the day that thou stoodest; literally, *in the day of thy standing,* without note of time, but implying a past event here. On the other side. The words may denote either malicious unconcern, as Ps. xxxviii. 11 (12), or hostile opposition, as 2 Sam. xviii. 13. Besides the direct application to recent events, the clause intimates the usual attitude of the Edomites toward Israel. In the day that the strangers —Philistines and Arabians (2 Chron. xxi. 16)—carried away captive his forces; rather, *carried away his substance,* as ver. 13; Gen. xxxiv. 29; Deut. viii. 17; Isa. viii. 4. Foreigners. The same as "strangers." Both words are usually applied to heathen enemies. Cast lots upon Jerusalem. Divided the captives and spoil of Jerusalem by lot (2 Chron. xxi. 17; comp. Joel iii. 3; Nah. iii. 10). Nothing is said of the total destruction of Jerusalem or the wholesale deportation of the inhabitants to Babylon, so that Obadiah cannot be referring to the

Chaldean conquest. Thou wast as one of them; literally, *thou, too, as one of them.* In this expression the past is set before the mind as present.

Ver. 12.—The prophet complains of the malignant neutrality of the Edomites. Thou shouldest not have looked. In this and the two following verses, *al* with the future is wrongly translated. It should be rendered throughout, "do not look," "do not rejoice," etc. Obadiah, in view of the past behaviour of Edom, and looking forward to another and more fatal conquest of Jerusalem, warns the Edomites against repeating this malicious conduct. Septuagint, μὴ ἐπίδῃς. Gaze not with pleasure, feast not thine eyes (Micah vii. 10). The day of thy brother; *i.e.* when some great event befell him—explained further in the next clause. Compare "the day of Jerusalem" (Ps. cxxxvii. 7). In the day that he became a stranger; Septuagint, ἐν ἡμέρα ἀλλοτρίων, "in the day of strangers;" Vulgate, *in die peregrinationis ejus.* The Anglican and Vulgate Versions signify, "in the day that he was carried captive into strange lands;" but most probably the expression should be rendered, "in the day of his calamity." Rejoiced over (comp. Job xxxi. 29; Prov. xvii. 5; Micah vii. 8). Spoken proudly; literally, *make thy mouth great;* Septuagint, μὴ μεγαλορρημονῇ, "do not boast;" Vulgate, *non magnificabis os tuum.* Utter a flood of mocking words, probably accompanied with derisive grimaces. There is a climax in this verse—first the complacent look, then the malicious pleasure, then words of insult and derision.

Ver. 13.—In this verse it is the making common cause with the enemy in the plundering of Jerusalem that is complained of. Thou shouldest not have entered. *Do not enter;* so below, "do not look," "lay not hands" (see note on ver. 12). The gate of my people; *i.e.* Jerusalem, the capital, as Micah i. 9. In the day of their calamity, repeated thrice with sorrowful emphasis, as making the Edomites' conduct more reproachful. Yea, thou shouldest not have looked. Hebrew, "look not thou also" —thou, as well as the alien enemies. What is natural in them is a crime in thee (comp. Ps. xxii. 17). Their affliction; Septuagint, τὴν συναγωγὴν αὐτῶν, "their gathering"—a different reading from the Masoretic. Substance, as in ver. 11. This was a further aggravation; they helped to plunder Jerusalem. Septuagint, Μὴ συνεπιθῇ ἐπὶ τὴν δύναμιν αὐτῶν, "Do not set upon their host;" Vulgate, *Et non emitteris adversus exercitum ejus.* This implies a warning against being instigated by the enemy to attack the Jewish forces. But the rendering in the text is doubtless correct.

Ver. 14.—The climax of injury is the cutting off of fugitives, and delivering them into captivity. Neither shouldest thou have stood in the crossway; *and stand not thou in the crossway.* The Edomites, as neighbours, would know all the passes into the wilderness by which the Judæans would seek to escape. Neither shouldest thou have delivered up; *and deliver not up;* Septuagint, μηδὲ συγκλείσῃς, "shut not up;" Vulgate, *et non concludes.* So Pusey, "shut not up," *i.e.* with the enemy, driving them back upon their pursuers (comp. Ps. xxxi. 8). The Hebrew word implies both meanings—"to deliver over to confinement;" and the meaning here is—do not seize on the people to give them over into captivity (comp. Amos i. 6, 9). Those of his that did remain. Those whom the invaders had spared.

Vers. 15, 16.—§ 3. The warning given in the first section (vers. 1—9) is supplemented by the announcement that *in the day of the Lord, Edom and all the enemies of Israel shall be remembered, and shall suffer just retribution, meeting with the fate which they had inflicted on others.*

Ver. 15.—The day of the Lord. This is not primarily the final day of judgment, but the time when "Jehovah reveals his majesty and omnipotence in a glorious manner, to overthrow all ungodly powers, and to complete his kingdom" (Keil). It is announced by Joel i. 15; ii. 1, 31; Zeph. i. 14; but the notion of a judgment to fall on Gentile nations, and to issue in the establishment of the kingdom of God, was familiar long before. Balaam had seen it in dim vision (Numb. xxiv. 17—24); Hannah had anticipated the destruction that would accompany it (1 Sam. ii. 9, 10); so had David (2 Sam. xxiii. 5—7) in his last words; it is clearly predicted in the Psalms (see Ps. ii. and cx.) (Knabenbauer). Is near. Because every such judgment upon individual nations is typical of the great day and preparative of it. As thou hast done, it shall be done unto thee (comp. Judg. i. 7; Ps. cxxxvii. 8; Jer. l. 15). This law of retribution was the ideal of heathen justice, according to the Rhadamanthian rule, "If a man should suffer what he hath done, then there would be strict justice" (Aristotle, 'Eth. Nic.,' v. 5.3). Thy reward (Joel iii. 7 [iv. 7, Hebrew]); better, *that which thou hast performed*—thy work or dealing. Upon thine own head. Like a stone cast towards heaven (comp. Ps. vii. 16; Esth. ix. 25).

Ver. 16.—As ye have drunk. There are two interpretations of this passage. By the first, the people addressed are considered to be the Jews, and the word "drunk" is taken metaphorically in both clauses (see note on Nah. iii. 11). The meaning is then this—As ye Jews, who are upon my holy mountain, the people of election, have not escaped from suffering the wrath of God, so all the nations shall feel the same, and that to a much more terrible extent. Confirmatory of this explanation is the language of Jeremiah, who (xxv. 15—29) bids all the nations to drink the cup of God's wrath, beginning at Jerusalem and passing on to Edom, and then says, in answer to any who refuse the offered draught, " Lo, I begin to bring evil on the city which is called by my name, and should ye be utterly unpunished ? " The same notion is found also in Jer. xlix. 12 and Lam. iv. 21, etc. But there are objections to this view of the passage. The previous verse enunciated the doctrine of retribution ; this verse confirms the former with the words, " for as ye," etc. It would be no proof of the *lex talionis* on the Edomites to cite what had happened to the Jews. What is wanted is an assertion that what they had done should be repaid to them in like coin. Besides, the prophecy is nominally addressed to the Edomites, not to the Jews, and it would be most harsh to change the subject suddenly here. " Upon my mountain " cannot be equivalent to " ye who are upon my mountain ; " nor is such an expression ever used to signify " Judæans." It is best, therefore, to take the clause as referring to the Edomites and their comrades, who, after their victory, indulged in unseemly revelry, and profaned the mountain hallowed by God's presence in the temple with their idolatrous festival. The " drinking " in this first clause is literal ; in the following clause it is figurative. Septuagint, ἔπιες, " thou didst drink," which makes the connection of the subject here with that in ver. 15 more evident, and it has probably been altered by the translators for that purpose. So shall all the heathen drink continually. The prophet plays on the word "drink." The nations shall drink, not wine, but the wrath of God (Ps. lxxv. 8; Jer. xxv. 15). The nations are spoken of here because Edom is taken as a type of all nations hostile to God, and the retribution that falls on him is extended to all who assume his attitude towards God's people (Keil). *Continually;* Vulgate, *jugiter,* perpetually, in uninterrupted succession. The LXX. has οἶνον, by a mistaken reading. They shall swallow down; drink a full draught; Septuagint, καταβήσονται, " they shall go down." They shall be as though they had not been. They shall drain the wrath of God till they utterly perish, till, as nations, they exist no more (comp. Ezek. xxvi. 21 ; xxvii. 36). Septuagint, καθὼς οὐχ ὑπάρχοντες, " as if not being " (comp. Ecclus.

xxxviii. 11 ; xliv. 9). (For the accomplishment of this prophecy against Edom, see Introduction, § I.)

Vers. 17—21.—Part II. The Restoration of Israel.

Vers. 17—20.—§ 1. *While judgment falls upon heathen nations, the house of Jacob shall be delivered, shall add to its possessions, and spread far and wide.*

Ver. 17.—Upon Mount Zion. Once desecrated by the idolatrous revelry of the Edomites and the other nations, now the seat of Jehovah (Joel iii. 17) and his kingdom. Deliverance (*peletah*); Septuagint, σωτηρία. Abstract for concrete, and to be rendered, " those that escape," or " those that are saved ; " *i.e.* a remnant that shall escape destruction (comp. Joel ii. 32; Amos ix. 8). There shall be holiness ; rather, *it* (Mount Zion) *shall be holy ;* so Septuagint, καὶ ἔσται ἅγιον : Hebrew, *kodesh,* " a sanctuary," where the heathen shall not come (Isa. lii. 1 ; comp. Joel iii. 17 [iv. 17, Hebrew] ; Rev. xxi. 27). The house of Jacob. Judah and Benjamin, the holy seed, in whom the kingdom of the Lord should be established (comp. ver. 18). The northern kingdom is not mentioned. Shall possess their possessions ; Septuagint, Κατακληρονομήσουσιν ὁ οἶκος Ἰακὼβ τοὺς κατακληρονομήσαντας αὐτούς, " The house of Jacob shall take for an inheritance those who took them for an inheritance ; " Vulgate, *Possidebit domus Jacob eos qui se possederant.* These versions must have used a different punctuation from that of the Masoretic text— *morishehem* for *morashehem* (comp. Numb. xxiv. 18, 19). The Hebrew pronoun is ambiguous, and " their possessions " may mean either those that the Jews themselves had lost, or those of the Edomites. But nothing is said of Israel being carried away captive and losing its country ; and, though the prophet may have looked forward to such a catastrophe and to a future restoration, this is not the subject here. The possessions referred to are those of the enemy represented by the Edomites, and those which the Jews had lost since the days of David and Solomon ; and " the house of Jacob " signifies, not merely the earthly kingdom of Judah, but " the people of God, who are eventually to obtain the dominion of the world " (Keil) ; Mark xvi. 15.

Ver. 18.—The last clause of the preceding verse is here expanded and more fully explained. The house of Jacob . . . the house of Joseph. The kingdoms of Judah and Israel, the two and the ten tribes united once more. In Ps. lxxvii. 15 the whole people are called " the sons of Jacob and Joseph." So elsewhere. The reunion of the tribes is mentioned in Hos. i. 11; Ezek. xxxvii. 19; Zech. x. 6. The future salvation is to be for all. For stubble, which the Israelites used rather than wood for lighting fires and heating ovens (Matt. vi. 30). (For the image of fire consuming the ungodly as stubble, see Exod. xv. 7; Isa. v. 24; Nah. i. 10.) They shall kindle in them. This may mean, the Israelites "shall burn among" the Edomites; but more probably is merely a repetition of what has gone before : the Jews shall consume the Edomites. There shall not be any remaining. This refers to the total annihilation of the Edomites under John Hyrcanus (Josephus, 'Ant.,' xii. 8. 6; xiii. 9. 1), and is a punishment quite distinct from their defeat at the hands of the Nabathæans predicted in vers. 1—9 (see Introduction, § I.). The LXX. gives, οὐκ ἔσται πυροφόρος (πυρφόρος, Alex.); St. Jerome reads, πυροφόρος, which he translated frumentarius. Many of the Fathers read, πυρφόρος: thus, too, the Arabic and Coptic Versions. Schleusner, sub voce, thinks that the LXX. had in view the Greek proverb, οὐδέ πυρφόρος, which is used to express the idea that not even a single survivor remains (see Herod., viii. 6). For the Lord hath spoken it (Joel iii. 8).

Ver. 19.—Judah and Benjamin between them shall possess the whole territory that once belonged to the children of Israel. In Josh. xv. 21, 33, 48, the inheritance of Judah is distributed into three portions—the south, the plain, and the mountains; the same divisions are noticeable here (see note on Zech. vii. 7). They of the south. The inhabitants of the Negeb, "the dry country"—the southern part of Judah, shall take possession of Idumea (Amos ix. 12). They of the plain. Of the Shephelah, or "low land" —the maritime plain and the country held by the Philistines (2 Chron. xxviii. 18; Zeph. ii. 7). And they shall possess. The Judæans not already mentioned, i.e. those of the mountains, shall take the territory of the ten tribes. The fields of Ephraim, and the fields of Samaria. The country and the capital. Septuagint, τὸ ὄρος Ἐφραὶμ καὶ τὸ πεδίον Σαμαρείας, "the Mount of Ephraim and the Plain of Samaria." Others translate, "Ephraim shall possess the field of Samaria," considering that otherwise Ephraim would be excluded from the restored kingdom, and Judah would inherit the territory of Ephraim, in violation of the covenant (Briggs, 'Messianic' Prophecy,' p. 317). But the Israelites proper were merged in the Judæans at the return; and if Benjamin possesses Gilead, it is not unnatural that Judah should extend northward to Samaria. And Benjamin shall possess Gilead. Benjamin, the other portion of the house of Jacob, whose territory originally

reached to the river, shall possess all the territory on the other side of Jordan. Thus the restored people shall, in accordance with the promise in Gen. xxviii. 14, "spread abroad to the west, and to the east, and to the north, and to the south" (comp. Isa. liv. 1—3). Obadiah sees the twelve tribes, once more united, extending their territory on every side; and, to make this evident, he gives certain examples, using Judah and Benjamin as equivalent to "the people of God," and their enlargement as denoting the majestic progress of the kingdom of God.

Ver. 20.—And the captivity of this host of the children of Israel shall possess that of the Canaanites, even unto Zarephath; Septuagint, Καὶ τῆς μετοικεσίας ἡ ἀρχὴ αὕτη τοῖς υἱοῖς Ἰσραὴλ, γῆ τῶν Χαναναίων ἕως Σαρεπτῶν, "And this shall be the beginning of the captivity of the children of Israel, the land of the Canaanites as far as Sarepta." This would imply that the Ephraimites should be the first to go into exile, and on their return should occupy the territory of the Canaanites on the north. But ἀρχὴ may mean "domain." Vulgate, Et transmigratio exercitus hujus filiorum Israel, omnia loca Chananæorum usque ad Sareptam. The general meaning is that Jewish captives, who have been taken to other lands, shall return and possess the cities of the south. The sentence in the Hebrew is incomplete. Our translators supply, "shall possess." Pusey (in agreement with the Chaldee, and virtually with the Septuagint) renders, "which are among the Canaanites;" and this seems to be correct, making "shall possess the cities of the south" the predicate of both clauses. So the first portion of the verse means, as Henderson says, the number of Israelitish captives which were found in Phœnicia, into which they had been sold at different times as slaves (comp. vers. 11, 14; Joel iii, 6, 7). This host. Not a general deportation, but only the portion of the people referred to. From this expression some have inferred that Obadiah himself was one of this body. This is possible, but not necessary. The captives who are among the Canaanites, even unto Zarephath; as far as Zarephath, were probably placed there for safe keeping before being sold into Greece and other countries. Zarephath ("Melting-house"), the Sarepta of St. Luke (iv. 26), now Surafend or Sarafend, and celebrated in the history of Elijah (1 Kings xvii. 9, etc.), lay between Tyre and Sidon, a little inland, and was a town of some importance, as its ruins prove. The captivity of Jerusalem. The captives from Jerusalem. Which is in Sepharad; Septuagint, ἕως Ἐφραθά, "as far as Ephrathah;"

Vulgate, *quæ in Bosphoro est.* The name occurs nowhere else in the Bible, and its identification cannot be established. Jerome suggests, in his commentary, that it is the Assyrian for "boundary," and not a proper name at all. The Peshito and the rabbins and modern Jews interpret it as "Spain." Keil supposes it to be "Sparta;" Pusey, "Sardis." For this last explanation some ground has been found in an inscription of Nakshi-Rustam, where a place called *Çparda* occurs in a list of tribes between Cappadocia and Ionia; and *Çparda* is considered to be the Persian form of *Sardis* (see Schrader, 'Keilinschr.,' p. 445, etc.). A further confirmation of this identification is found in the complaint of Joel (iii. 6 [iv. 6, Hebrew]), that the Phœnicians had sold Israelites "unto the sons of the Grecians." Professor Sayce, in a note to G. Smith's 'History of Babylonia,' p. 156, places "Saparda" on the Black Sea. It may be questioned, however, whether some town nearer Judæa is not intended. Ewald would read "Sepharam," a town in North Palestine. The two bodies of captives **shall possess the cities of the south.** The Negeb. The cities are named in Josh. xix.

Ver. 21.—§ 2. The prophet sums up his prediction: with the conquest of the Gentiles *salvation shall come to Zion in all its fulness.* **Saviours.** The LXX. incorrectly takes the word passively, translating it ἀνασῳζόμενοι, "they that are saved;" so Aquila, Theodotion, and the Syriac; Symmachus rightly, σώζοντες: Vulgate, *salvatores.* The judges are so called in Judg. iii. 9, 15 (comp. 2 Kings xiii. 5; Neh. ix. 27). The judges had a twofold character—they were deliverers and governors, as in

the present case. Here the immediate reference is to Zerubbabel and the valiant Maccabees, who severely punished the Idumeans (2 Macc. x. 15, etc.; Josephus, 'Ant.,' xiii. 9. 1). But all these "saviours" are types and forerunners of the Messiah, "the Saviour which is Christ the Lord." **Shall come up.** Not from exile, but simply as ascending a hill, and taking their seat there. **Mount Zion.** The seat of the kingdom of God, in contrast with "the mount of Esau," the type of the enemies of Israel and of God. **To judge;** LXX., τοῦ ἐκδικῆσαι, "to take vengeance on." But the "judging" is not only the taking of vengeance on Edom and that which it represents, the expression includes the notion of governing; so that the prophet looks forward to the time when the heathen shall submit themselves to the dominion of the people of God, and, as the following clause foretells, "the kingdoms of this world are become the kingdoms of our Lord, and of his Christ" (Rev. xi. 15). **The kingdom shall be the Lord's.** No earthly accomplishment could fulfil this great announcement. The kingdom can be Jehovah's; he can show himself as Ruler of the world, and be acknowledged as such by the nations, only under Christ. This is "the sceptre of Judah" of which Jacob spoke (Gen. xlix. 10); this is the throne of David which was to be established for ever (2 Sam. vii. 16); this is what all the prophets foresaw, what we are still expecting, what we daily pray for, as we say, "thy kingdom come"—when "the Lord shall be King over all the earth, and there shall be one Lord, and his name one" (Zech. xiv. 9).

HOMILETICS.

Ver. 1.—*The servant of Jehovah.* The names given by the Hebrews were usually significant. The appellation of this prophet was very commonly used, and is indicative of the fervid and practical piety of the Israelitish people. Obadiah means "the Servant or Worshipper of Jehovah."

I. THE NAME IS DESCRIPTIVE OF PERSONAL PIETY. Whilst the ungodly and irreligious are servants of sin, the pious are emphatically the Lord's bondsmen and devotees. 1. Piety involves relation to a living God. The personality of the Deity is assumed in this designation. 2. Piety is practical in its character. The Lord's people offer service to him whom they profess to revere, consecrating their powers to secure the ends which are approved by him. 3. Piety is voluntary and cheerful in its nature. In a sense all men are under Divine authority. But the giving of a name like this implies a distinction among men, a willing devotion on the part of the pious to the holy service of the Supreme.

II. THE NAME IS DESCRIPTIVE OF OFFICIAL RELATION AND ACTIVITY. It is true that there are those who are incapacitated for service, who yet are God's in heart. "They also serve who only stand and wait." Yet, in the case of men possessed of ordinary faculties, and enjoying ordinary opportunities, the felt obligation will express itself in obedience and in zeal and energy. 1. The servant of the Lord receives his instructions from his Master, with whom he is in intimate communication. 2. The servant of the Lord is the agent in conveying the Master's will to his fellow-men. This was especially the vocation of the prophet, who spoke forth the mind of the Almighty to the righteous and to the wicked, whether they would hear or forbear.

Ver. 1.—*The vision.* The designation sometimes given to the prophet, "the seer," corresponds with language which is in many places employed to denote the act of communion with God, by which the honoured servant was qualified for discharging his sacred office. The process and its results are thus brought very strikingly before our mind.

I. THE REVELATION. There is something to be seen, something which is hidden from the minds of ordinary men, something from which, therefore, the veil must be withdrawn, if the spiritual eye is to gaze upon it. How God makes himself, his character, his purposes, known to those whom he selects for this special privilege, we do not know. But, unless Scripture is misleading and deceptive, such a revelation has taken place. Especially to the prophets, things otherwise unseen, unknown, have been revealed.

II. THE INSIGHT. Unless there is an eye, the light shines in vain; indeed, light is but an undulation of ether which it needs the susceptible optic nerve to appreciate. And in order that God may make his counsels known to men, there must be not only objective revelation, but subjective inspiration. The spiritual faculty needs to be quickened, that in God's light we may see light. The action of the Holy Spirit upon the mind of the prophet brought that mind into a receptive state, so that the Divine rays occasioned human illumination. The prophet *saw* the mind, the will, the intentions, of the Eternal.

III. THE PROPHECY. Because the spiritual eye discerned the spiritual reality, the seer became the prophet. What his eyes had seen he was thus enabled to communicate for the information, the warning, the encouragement, of his fellow-men.

Vers. 3, 4.—*The deceptiveness of human pride.* The prophecies of Obadiah were mainly addressed to the Edomites, the descendants of Esau, a wild and warlike people who inhabited the mountainous region to the south of the Dead Sea. Their hostility and treachery towards their kinsmen, the descendants of Israel, were the occasion of the threatenings with which this book abounds. Fancying themselves secure and impregnable in their singular mountain fastnesses, they deemed their neighbours altogether incapable of chastising their perfidy and enmity. But man is only man, and not God; and this lesson Obadiah brings before the inhabitants of Idumea in the glowing and poetical language of the text.

I. SELF-EXALTATION. This was the state of mind in which the Edomites defied the people of Jehovah. Their homes were literally in the clefts of the rocks, where caves sheltered them at an elevation above those passing through the defile below, which seemed to secure their exemption from the assaults of their foes. They compared themselves with the eagle, which chooses the loftiest peaks for his dwelling-place. Nay, they seemed to disdain the earth, and to dwell among the stars. All this is indicative of human pride. Men too often flatter themselves that physical strength, mental powers, social position, political alliances, raising them above the common herd, raise them also above the common lot.

II. SELF-CONFIDENCE. "Who," say the Edomites, "who shall bring us down to the ground?" Men measure their strength with their fellow-men, and draw from the comparison most delusive conclusions. Because they are superior to one, they fancy themselves superior to all; and because they believe themselves above the reach of human enemies, they believe themselves above the reach of God himself. It is a sin to which strong natures are especially exposed. The powerful and the prosperous are tempted to place confidence both in their own wisdom and ability and in their own good fortune. But "let him that thinketh he standeth take heed lest he fall."

III. HUMILIATION. We are assured upon the highest authority that "a haughty spirit cometh before a fall." In the plenitude of their power and pride, the Edomites heard a voice from heaven saying, "I will bring thee down." A retributive providence is a reality. Even the heathen believed in Nemesis, and regarded boastfulness as tempting adversity. The instrument employed in humbling the proud may be human, as in the case of the Edomites, but the power that chastises is Divine. It is ever true under the government of God that he abases the proud and gives grace unto the lowly.

Ver. 7.—*The treacherous betrayed.* The Edomites had turned against their own kinsmen, the children of Israel, had leagued with Israel's enemies, and aided in bringing about Israel's calamities. They had chosen for their allies heathen nations in their own vicinity, relying upon their fidelity and support. The prophet is inspired to assure them that the confederacies they have formed shall fail them, that the friends in whom they have trusted shall prove false, and that Edom shall suffer the reward of perfidy in desertion and subjection.

I. To DESERT AND TO INJURE THE FRIENDS OF GOD IS TO INCUR THE DISPLEASURE OF GOD. The sons of Israel were the chosen and beloved people, and, notwithstanding their frequent unfaithfulness, they were the objects of Divine regard and interest and love. Those who attacked the Israelites attacked him who was in reality their King. Israel was a theocracy, and the anger of the King was enkindled against those who, like these Edomites, treated with injustice the beloved nation.

II. To FORM A LEAGUE WITH GOD'S ENEMIES WILL NEVER CONDUCE TO PROSPERITY: THEY WILL BECOME INSTRUMENTS OF DIVINE RETRIBUTION. The Edomites were attacked, wounded, disgraced, and despised by the very people whose friendship they had courted in preference to that of God's own chosen nation. Their confidence was in vain; the prop upon which they leaned proved a spear to pierce them. Their fancied wisdom brought them to utter perplexity and ruin.

APPLICATION. No alliance with wicked men can serve any holy purpose. It may promise well, but the reality will not correspond with the promise. The friendship of sinners is illusive, seductive, and vain. "The companion of fools shall be destroyed."

Vers. 8, 9.—*Wisdom and power of no avail against God.* Of all their possessions men are most prone to rely upon and to boast of their physical prowess and their intellectual sagacity. It is thought that great power, directed by consummate prudence and wisdom, is of all things earthly the most trustworthy, the most unfailing. Yet warnings are in Scripture often addressed to men to dissuade them from an undue confidence even in gifts and qualities so rare and admirable as these. The sons of Esau are in this passage admonished that, if they trust to their own wisdom and their own strength for safety, protection, and deliverance, their trust shall be disappointed.

I. HUMAN POWER AND WISDOM ARE ALWAYS IN THEMSELVES VERY LIMITED. What is the might of man when compared with the great forces of nature—the earthquake, the tempestuous sea, etc.? And before how many speculative difficulties and practical problems does the wisdom of man confess itself utterly baffled! It is strange that whilst, looking at the general law, men are always ready to confess their physical and intellectual impotency, when they come to particular cases calling for strength and wisdom they are so ready to confide in that which they have every reason to distrust.

II. HUMAN POWER AND WISDOM ARE OFTEN MISDIRECTED. Good in themselves, and admirable instances of the creative skill of God himself, these qualities are especially liable to abuse. Such is the case when power is employed in the cause of injustice and oppression, when wisdom is misused to defeat the designs of truth and charity. Often in the history of other nations than Edom has this misuse been exhibited. We are too prone to admire and extol strength and sagacity superior to our own; but it is better to ask—How have these gifts been used? By what principles have they been guided?

III. HUMAN POWER AND WISDOM WILL CERTAINLY BE BROUGHT TO NOTHING IF OPPOSED TO THE COUNSELS OF GOD. Man's power may be great; God's is irresistible. Man's wisdom may be profound, but God's is omniscient. Hence when that which is finite opposes itself to that which is infinite, the result can only be disastrous for man. Edom found this to be so; and the experience of Edom has been the experience of multitudes in every age.

APPLICATION. "Let not the wise man glory in his wisdom, neither let the mighty man glory in his might; . . . but let him that glorieth glory in this, that he understandeth and knoweth me, that I am the Lord which exercise loving-kindness, judgment, and righteousness in the earth."

Vers. 10—14.—*A neighbour's cruelty.* The prophet deeply feels the injury which Esau has inflicted upon Israel, and the language of this passage gives evidence of a heart deeply aggrieved and wronged and distressed. We have, indeed, in these verses an example of the length to which the cruelty of man can go.

I. THE DETAILS OF THIS CRUELTY. 1. Edom is charged with siding with foreigners against Jerusalem in the day when the city was assaulted and taken. 2. And with rejoicing over Judah's misfortunes, and mocking at her calamities. 3. And with sharing in the spoils of the city when the capture took place. 4. And even with cutting off the retreat of the wretched fugitives.

II. THE AGGRAVATION OF THIS CRUELTY. If a stranger, a "natural enemy" (as men say), had done this, it would have been bad enough. But the Edomites were of the same descent with the Jews; these being sons of Jacob, those of Esau. The point is given to the sting by this fact. It is with "violence against thy brother Jacob" that Edom is charged. "Man's inhumanity to man" is the most sad and depressing spectacle that earth affords. When natural kindred and affinity bind men together, those who snap those ties and assail their brethren are monsters of iniquity.

III. THE PENALTY OF THIS CRUELTY. This was plainly published by Obadiah. "Thou," said he to Edom—"thou shalt be cut off for ever." The laws of God cannot be violated with impunity. The relations which God has fashioned cannot be outraged without involving the guilty in the awful consequences of their sin. "The way of transgressors is hard."

Vers. 15, 16.—*The "lex talionis."* The principle of government or of retribution known as the *lex talionis* was known to the Hebrews as well as to other nations. "It was said by them of old time, An eye for an eye, a tooth for a tooth." Passages in Ezekiel contain threatenings of a retribution similar to that which in this passage is denounced upon Edom.

I. THE AUTHOR AND THE OCCASION OF THIS RETRIBUTION. "The day of the Lord" is an expression frequently occurring in the prophetic writings, and always denoting a season of retribution appointed by a righteous God. The day when iniquity is rampant, when injustice is perpetrated and is apparently unnoticed, is the day of *man*. But as surely as the universe is governed by a Being of rectitude, so surely shall the cause of equity and truth be vindicated; and the time of such vindication, come when it may, is the day of the *Lord*.

II. THE METHOD AND MEASURE OF RETRIBUTION. "As thou hast done, it shall be done unto thee." Edom had deserted her friends; she should be deserted. Edom had spoiled her neighbours; she should be spoiled. And this doom was threatened, not upon Edom only, but upon "all the heathen," *i.e.* upon all who shared Edom's guilt. Whether this was to happen by the working out of what we call a natural law, or by a special interposition of Providence, we are not told, and this is immaterial. History records very many instances in which this principle has operated, in which this doom has been inflicted.

III. THE HIGHER DIVINE PRINCIPLE WHICH TEMPERS THIS OF RETRIBUTION. Our Lord Jesus has taught us that the *lex talionis* is not an adequate principle of human conduct. Much less can it be deemed the perfect and final law of the Divine government. Mercy triumphs over wrath. Where there is true repentance on man's part, there is ready forgiveness on God's part. If this were not so, the human race would long ago have perished; if this were not so, we should not now be rejoicing in the Saviour of our souls, the Saviour of mankind.

Ver. 17.—*Restoration.* It is a peculiarity of the Hebrew prophets that, however gloomy might seem to them the immediate future of their nation, they ever saw beyond the darkness into the glorious light of the future. Opinions have differed, and still differ, as to the reference of many of their predictions of coming prosperity and blessedness. Some refer those visions to a time not long subsequent to the prophet's own time. Others still look for their literal fulfilment in the political history of Israel in the future. Whilst others believe that the visions were not of mere earthly peace and prosperity, but of the spiritual kingdom of Christ and of the true Israel of God, the Church of the living God. Certainly such language as that of the text, whatever be its literal application, contains promises which Christians alone can fully realize.

I. ONE ELEMENT IN RESTORATION IS DELIVERANCE. The return of the captives and exiles to their native soil, their much-loved city, is a picture of the restoration of sinners to the favour and fellowship of the God whom they had angered and alienated. God deviseth means whereby his banished ones shall return. Christ is the Redeemer, and deliverance is his great work. His people are the saved, the rescued, the emancipated, the restored.

II. ANOTHER ELEMENT IN RESTORATION IS HOLINESS. The captivity of the Jews had removed them from their metropolis and from their temple, the holy place of their God. At the same time, the heathen had polluted and defiled the sanctuary of Jehovah. The return from exile was to be the occasion of the restoration of the holy people to the holy house, and the restoration of the sanctuary to its sacred uses. In the Church of the Redeemer the Spirit of holiness takes up his abode. It is filled with sacred services and observances. "Holiness becometh thy house, O Lord, for ever."

III. ANOTHER ELEMENT IN RESTORATION IS THE ENJOYMENT OF SECURITY AND PLENTY. "The house of Jacob shall possess their possessions." The lands and houses which the people had inherited from their forefathers had been occupied by strangers. But upon the restoration the Hebrews took possession of their ancient homes and fields, and abode in peace and enjoyed plenty. In this their position was an emblem of that into which Christ's redeemed people are introduced by his grace. All things are theirs. They possess the privileges of the gospel and the peace of the Spirit, and theirs is the blessed hope of an inheritance incorruptible, undefiled, and unfading.

Ver. 21.—*Empire founded on salvation.* The two conceptions which are united in this verse are united, not only in the history of Judah, but in the dispensation of Divine grace as revealed in the gospel of Jesus Christ. Israel had many saviours; Moses was the first and greatest; the judges followed. In the later periods of Jewish story, Zerubbabel and Judas Maccabæus wrought somewhat similar deliverance for their countrymen. In fact, from first to last revelation is the history of salvations, all pointing on to the one great salvation to be wrought, not for one nation only, but for all mankind. And as the Hebrew deliverers established the kingdom, and brought about the reign of righteousness and the prevalence of peace, so upon his great work of deliverance by. Christ God has founded that kingdom which is "righteousness, peace, and joy in the Holy Ghost."

I. CHRIST IS A SAVIOUR WITH A VIEW TO HIS BEING A KING. His earthly manifestation was as a pitying Deliverer; his heavenly session is as a mighty Lord. In a sense, he purchased his dominion by his sacrificial death.

II. CHRIST'S PEOPLE ARE SAVED IN ORDER THAT THEY MAY BE SUBJECTS. In the first instance, those who receive the gospel behold Christ as a Redeemer. But in saving them the Lord acquires rights over them; these rights they recognize, and their subjection and obedience become the note of their interest in his redemption.

III. THE EARTH IS THE SCENE OF A SAVIOUR'S GRACE THAT IT MAY BECOME THE SEAT OF HIS EMPIRE. From Zion Jehovah judged the mount of Esau. God gives to his Son the heathen for his inheritance. Not by a physical, a military, but by a moral conquest Christ takes possession of our humanity. And he is Lord of all.

HOMILIES BY VARIOUS AUTHORS.

Vers. 1, 2.—*The vision of Obadiah.* "The vision of Obadiah. Thus saith the Lord God concerning Edom; We have heard a rumour from the Lord, and an ambassador is sent among the heathen, Arise ye, and let us rise up against her in battle. Behold, I have made thee small among the heathen : thou art greatly despised." We are now about to study the smallest book in the Old Testament. It comes behind the others in length, but in nothing else. In its weighty character as an inspired writing it is equal to any of the rest. Let us, then, ponder it in our hearts. May the Holy Spirit guide us into all the truth this sacred portion contains! May he open our eyes, that we may behold wondrous things out of this word!

I. WE MAY BEGIN BY ASKING WHO OBADIAH WAS. Some have thought he was the pious steward of King Ahab; but this idea is not in keeping with the evident date of the prophecy. There are many other persons of this name in Scripture, but the prophet cannot be identified with any one of them. We read of Obadiah of the tribe of Judah (1 Chron. iii.); another of the tribe of Issachar (1 Chron. vii.); another of Benjamin (1 Chron. viii.); another of Levi (1 Chron. ix.); another of Gad (1 Chron. xii.); another of Judah (2 Chron. xvii.); another of Zebulun (1 Chron. xxvii.). We find, also, an Obadiah—a Levite—in the time of Josiah (2 Chron. xxxiv.); another a companion of Ezra (Ezra viii.); and yet another a priest in the time of Nehemiah (Neh. x.). The name, therefore, was in very common use among the Jews; and this, not only because it had been borne by some who were distinguished for their upright character, but because it had a most instructive significance.

II. WE ASK THE MEANING OF THE NAME. It means "a Servant," or "a Worshipper of the Lord." Let us note the import of both these. 1. "*A Servant of the Lord.*" Here we may each long to be similarly designated. David said, "O Lord, I am thy servant;" and the reason he gave for this was that his bonds had been broken by God. "Thou hast redeemed me from the slavery of Satan. Thou hast brought me into the glorious liberty of thy people. I now yield myself to thee. I am thy servant." And so Moses was called "the servant of God." And so, too, we meet with such words as these: "Abraham, my servant;" "David, my servant;" "Daniel, servant of the living God;" "James, a servant of God;" "Paul, a servant of Jesus Christ." This blessed service is perfect freedom. Christ himself came among us as the girded Servant. "I am among you as he that serveth." He was Jehovah's righteous Servant. His disciples, therefore, can never rise above his example. They serve the living and true God. "Ich dien." It was not always so. Before the bonds were loosed there was only slavery to sin and Satan and the world, but the emancipation has come. The freed ones serve their Redeemer-God. In faith, in love, in holiness, in patience, in meekness, in joyfulness, they serve, they work, they wait. 2. The second meaning of the name is "*a Worshipper of the Lord.*" And shall we not, every one, aim to be this? It implies much. Let us think about it. In New Testament light, worship means *access to God*. We are brought near by the blood of Christ's cross. It is *filial nearness*. We may come with holy boldness by the blood of Jesus. It includes *prayer* in Christ's Name. "Whatsoever ye shall ask the Father in my Name, he will give it you. Ask, and ye shall receive." Worship includes *praise*. "Whoso offereth me praise, he glorifieth me;" "Praise is comely;" "Praise ye the Lord." Worship includes the *yielding of ourselves to God*. "I beseech you by the mercies of God, that ye present your bodies living sacrifices." Worship includes the *consecration of our substance to God*. Of old his people were told not to come before him empty. They were to present their firstfruits unto him. They were first to consecrate, then enjoy. Giving was therefore a part of worship. It ought to be so now. Worship of Jehovah also involves a complete turning away from idols. There are idols of the heart. Covetousness is idolatry. There are many idols besides those of wood and stone. To be truly an Obadiah, a worshipper of Jehovah, we must say with Ephraim, "What have I to do any more with idols?" And one thought more on this point. In seeking to bear the designation of our prophet, let us remember this canon laid down by the blessed Saviour: "God is a Spirit, and they that worship him must worship him *in spirit and in truth*." Thus, then, we see that much is implied by the designation, "a worshipper of the Lord." May we each be both "a servant" and "a worshipper" of the living God!

III. We may now proceed to observe that THE GREAT AUTHOR OF THE BOOK IS GOD HIMSELF. Obadiah was the ambassador, the messenger, but the words are God's. Ver. 1, "Thus saith the Lord God." It is this "*Thus saith the Lord*" which gives such supreme importance to every word of the Bible. The histories, the prophecies, the precepts, the invitations, the warnings, the exhortations, the revelations, the whole from Genesis to the end, all come to us with the words of power, "Thus saith the Lord." Some minds may be perplexed as to what is said of creation; some are exercised as to what is revealed about the judgment day, and of the Divine wrath upon the wicked; others have difficulty in understanding the moral government of the world; but the docile, humble-minded believer takes this book as from the hand of God. On the top of every page he sees, as it were, written in letters of golden light, "Thus saith the Lord." Where the word of a king is there is power. We have here the words of the King of kings. "By the Word of the Lord were the heavens made, and all the host of them by the breath of his mouth." That same Word upholds all things by its glorious power. And here we have that Word in writing, and it is God's great revelation of his will. It is the chief means by which the Holy Spirit quickens the dead in trespasses and sins, and revives the drooping graces of his saints. "By thy Word thou hast quickened me." If you want any other proof of the power of the Word, read in the Revelation of the doings of him who was clothed in a vesture dipped in blood, and whose name is "The Word of God." St. John was inspired to write five books. In the opening chapter of the first he describes the Word made flesh, and dwelling among us. In the closing chapters of the last book he describes the Word in the blood-dyed vesture. It is the union of these truths which gives such power to the written Word. God has spoken to us by his Son. "The testimony of Jesus is the spirit of prophecy." Let us, then, take heed how we hear. We all need to be attentive to the Word. Oh that Christ's high-priestly prayer were true of each of us, "I have given unto them the words which thou gavest me, and *they have received them.* . . . Sanctify them through thy truth: thy Word is truth"! Let us seek to "*receive*" all the words which have been given us. "*They have received them.*" May this be true of us, and may we be *sanctified* more and more by the Word! "Sanctify them through thy truth: thy Word is truth."

IV. And now let us ask—WHAT IS THE SUBJECT OF THIS PROPHETIC BOOK? It is twofold. It tells of *judgment* upon the house of Esau, and *mercy* upon the house of Jacob. We shall hope to return to this subject again, but for the present let us note what a summary we have here of all revelation. We have, as it were, the pillar of the Lord—a light to Israel, a black cloud to the Egyptians. "He that believeth shall be saved, and he that believeth not shall be condemned." The righteous shall walk therein; the transgressors shall fall therein. Esau, despising his birthright, barters it for a mess of pottage. Jacob, taking hold of God's strength, wrestles with the angel of the covenant, and is called Israel; for as a prince he has wrestled with God, and prevailed. In the one case we see wickedness apparently mighty and dominant, building on the heights, but brought down and made very small. In the other we have Zion, once feeble and down-trodden and despised, made triumphant and glorious by the grace, and love, and wisdom, and power of him who loved us, and washed us from our sins in his own blood, and made us priests and kings unto God. If we notice the story of Esau, we see him in Genesis despising his birthright and hating his brother. In Numbers we see the two nations. Israel is marching to Canaan. Esau withstands him. The King of Edom prevents the progress. In this Edom seems the stronger. In St. Matthew's Gospel we note the birth of Christ and the advance of the spiritual Israel. Then we find Herod the Edomite opposing with no little success. He commands the destruction of all the young children in Bethlehem. A true Edomite —a red man—a man of blood. But as we get to the close of the sacred Word we see that the house of Esau has disappeared. Zion is all-triumphant. Within the pearly gates all is joy, and light, and rest, and glory for evermore. Nothing that defileth can enter. The hosts of the true Israel are safe for ever. The great "Thus saith the Lord" by Obadiah the prophet has received its complete fulfilment. Let us, then, be sure of this—that whatever seeming strength falsehood and wickedness may possess, in the end truth only shall prevail; the kingdom which is "righteousness, peace, and joy in the Holy Ghost" only shall predominate, and in a little while it shall be known that "the Lord God omnipotent reigneth." "The kingdom shall be the Lord's" (ver. 21).—A. C. T.

Vers. 1—4.—*Edom subdued.* "The vision of Obadiah Thus saith the Lord God concerning Edom; We have heard a rumour from the Lord," etc. We have said that, although there are so many Obadiahs mentioned in Scripture, the prophet cannot be identified with any of them. The sacred writers were never ready to put themselves into prominence. They had their message to deliver. They had their solemn work to perform. They had Jehovah to glorify. They were content to be no more than a *voice* crying in the wilderness. Who wrote Joshua? Who wrote Judges? Who wrote the books of Samuel, or the Kings, or Chronicles, or Esther? It was sufficient for the writers that they were used by the Spirit of God. They were ambassadors, not kings. They were servants, not masters. They were the instruments, not the musicians. They were the vessels, not the fountain of living water. The ambassador simply delivers the message of the king. The servant only waits on the guests of the master. The instrument merely gives forth the sounds struck by the musician. The vessel only bears the refreshing draught of the well of life. Obadiah, like John the Baptist, was ready to decrease, that Christ might increase. The morning star heralds the day, then melts before the sunshine. Herein is a lesson of great importance to all workers for Christ.

I. Let us proceed to notice GOD'S DENUNCIATION OF EDOM. Edom was a great adversary of Israel. For instance, we find in Ps. cxxxvii. that Edom joined Babylon in seeking the destruction of Jerusalem: ver. 7, "Remember, O Lord, the children of Edom in the day of Jerusalem; who said, Rase it, rase it, even to the foundation thereof!" The geographical position of Edom made it a formidable enemy, and apparently invincible. Lying south of the Dead Sea, its lofty range of red hills, called Mount Seir, stretched a hundred miles from north to south, by twenty east to west. Bozrah was the capital of the eastern division, and Sela, or Petra (both names mean "a rock"), was the capital of the southern division. The habit of the eagle to select high and lonely pinnacles for its dwelling-place gives force to the words of our fourth verse, "Though thou exalt thyself as the eagle, and though thou set thy nest among the stars, thence will I bring thee down." In Ps. lx. 9 we are led to a period in David's history when that king besieged Edom. As he looks up at the fortified cities among impregnable rocky heights, he seems to despair of victory. "Who will bring me into the strong city? Who will lead me into Edom?" Could he not himself be the leader? Had he not slain Goliath and routed the Philistines? Had he not fought with the lion and the bear to save a lamb of the fold? Where, too, were his mighty men?—Joab, captain of the host? Adino, who lifted his spear against eight hundred? Eleazar, whose sword imbedded itself in his hand? Benaiah, who slew an Egyptian with his own spear? If the muster-roll be called, is there no one to take the lead, and scale the dizzy heights, and subdue the great strongholds? David looks away from himself, away from his men, away from all human strength, and he says, "Wilt not *thou*, O God?" He answers the question in the best and surest way. And we know that God *did* give David the victory (see 2 Sam. viii. 14). *We*, too, have our enemies. We have our fortresses of Edom. Who will enable us to conquer? Where are the weapons mighty to the pulling down of strongholds? Nay, where is he whose goings forth are upon the white horse of war, conquering and to conquer? The answer is brought to us. The warfare is accomplished. "We are more than conquerors through him who loved us." Isa. lxiii. 1, "Who is this that cometh from *Edom*, with dyed garments from Bozrah? this that is glorious in his apparel, travelling in the greatness of his strength?" Then comes the answer. "I that speak in righteousness, mighty to save." Yes, he who is the Lord our Righteousness is the Lord our Saviour—mighty to save to the uttermost. Sin and Satan have been conquered. Edom is subdued. Then comes forth the Conqueror, red in his apparel. "Who is this . . . with dyed garments from Bozrah? I that speak in righteousness, mighty to save."

II. I will ask you now to pass from the general denunciation of Edom to THE PARTICULAR SIN WITH WHICH EDOM IS CHARGED. "The pride of thine heart hath deceived thee." Building like the eagle in the pinnacles of the rocks, setting his nest among the stars, Edom said in his heart, "Who shall bring me down to the ground?" Thus the pride of his heart deceived him. And to many individuals, as well as nations, does the herald of Jehovah bring the message, "The pride of thine heart hath deceived thee." Pharaoh, lifting himself high, asks, "Who is the Lord, that I should serve him?" The answer comes, "The pride of thine heart hath deceived thee." Nebuchadnezzar, looking in self-elation upon Babylon, asks, "Is not this great Babylon which I have built?" The answer comes, "The pride of thine heart hath deceived thee." Belshazzar, banqueting with his lords, and drinking wine from the vessels of the temple, sees the dreadful handwriting upon the wall, and the message comes, "The pride of thine heart hath deceived thee." Herod makes an oration, and gives not God the glory due to his Name. The silent death-warrant comes to him, "The pride of thine heart hath deceived thee." And as with these kings, these representatives of multitudes, so with all classes. The commercial man, gathering wealth and speculating in the markets, suddenly comes down with a crash: the pride of his heart hath deceived him. The professional man, scorning many an honest tradesman, runs into lavish expense, and brings ruin to his family: the pride of his heart hath deceived him. The young man coming into a small estate suddenly launches out into extravagance. He must be as others who have twice his income. He wants to make a dash in the world. He knows more about horses than the way of holiness and the gospel of salvation. He is a stranger to grace. The throne of grace, the covenant of grace, the God of all grace, he knows nothing about. With scarcely twenty-four hours' illness, he is summoned into eternity. He dies without hope. The pride of his heart hath deceived him. The man of high culture, priding himself upon his intellectual attainments, ignoring Bible revelation, and spurning sermons and tracts, he is ready to laugh at humble piety. His habitation is high. He dwells amongst the stars. His nest is with the eagles. He saith in his heart, "Who shall bring me down to the ground?" But what does God say? "The pride of thine heart hath deceived thee." Ay, and there is a moral man, a very Pharisee, who thanks God he is so much better than the publicans and the like. That man is lifted up with his doings. How carefully he pays tithe of his mint, anise, and cummin! How scrupulous about his phylactery! What a parade he makes of his religion! He says in his heart, "Who shall bring me down to the ground?" So the pride of his heart hath deceived him. He that exalteth himself shall be abased. We do well to remember Edom. We must keep in mind that pride of heart is very deceitful. Nature's fortifications, the world's fortifications, social fortifications, moral fortifications, are unavailing if we presume to do without God. Edom built among the stars, but God brought him down to the ground. Pride of heart is the herald of ruin. It is often so even in this world. And those proud ones who are brought to the ground here *may thank God for the valley of humiliation.* Let us all learn to humble ourselves under the mighty hand of God, that he may exalt us in due time. Let us be clothed with humility. "God resisteth the proud, but giveth grace to the humble." The only fortress we can boast of is the cleft Rock of Ages. Here we have safety and joy and peace. Here we may securely hide until all calamities be overpast. Happy those who can say with David, in Ps. ix., "In the Lord put I my trust: how say ye to my soul, Flee as a bird to your mountain?" The true believer needs no foreign helps. The Lord is an all-sufficient Fortress and Shield. The Christian knows whom he trusts, and therefore does not make haste. "With Jehovah I have taken shelter: how say ye to my soul, Flee, sparrows, to your hill?" (Bishop Horsley). May the Holy Spirit give us all to know this happy security!—a security which made the Apostle Paul speak with so much meaning, so much force, so much personal experience, "I knew a man in Christ." A delightful, peaceful knowledge. Only one thing is better. "To depart and to be *with* Christ . . . is far better."—A. C. T.

Ver. 6.—"*The things of Esau searched out.*" "How are the things of Esau searched out!"

I. We may consider ESAU AS THE TYPE OF THE SELF-CONFIDENT. Lifted up, dwelling amongst the stars, wise in his own eyes, he knows not his perilous condition. There are thousands and thousands like this. They say, in the language of Laodicea, "I am rich, and increased with goods, and have need of nothing." They little see themselves as God sees them. They are blind, and know not that they are miserable and poor; but God searches them out. "I know thy works." No one can elude the all-seeing gaze of the Omniscient. "Adam, where art thou?" Thus the Judge of all men comes making manifest the secrets of the heart. Hiding like Adam in the trees of the garden, or dwelling like Edom in the rocks, is only self-delusion. Shall not God search it out? There are many, like Saul, who are so self-complacent that they say, "I have kept the commandment of the Lord." When the stern prophet asks, "What meaneth then this bleating of the sheep in mine ears, and the lowing of the oxen which

I hear?" Some may remind us of the young man who, on hearing the command-ments, said he had kept them all; but when Christ searched him through and through, he left Christ's presence, preferring his earthly possessions to heavenly riches. His heart was as a great stone, which, when disturbed, revealed numberless creeping things which at once shrank from the light and hastened away into new darkness. How are the things of Esau searched out! The disclosure must come. It is inevitable. "There is nothing covered that shall not be revealed, neither hid that shall not be known." It may not be in this world, it may not be until the day—the great day—of judgment, but it *must* come. The things of Esau must be searched out, the folly of self-confidence must be made manifest.

II. In the next place, we may consider ESAU AS THE TYPE OF THE WORLDLY. We know how the first of the race bartered his birthright for a mess of pottage. And the race yet lives. There are yet multitudes carnally minded, who reject joint kinship with Christ for the sake of some mess of pottage, or some cup of pleasure, or some glittering toy, or the incense of human honour. How many are ready to exclaim, when we offer them the religion of Christ, that it would endanger their success in the world! So Demetrius, the silversmith, alarmed his fellow-craftsman by telling them that Chris-tianity would jeopardize their profits. "Sirs, ye know that by this craft we have our wealth." The world so fills the vision of such persons that they have no eyes for Christ, no eyes for heaven, no eyes for the coming glory, no eyes for immortality. They have eyes and see not; ears have they, and hear not. Like the raven in the Flood, they prefer the dead carcases to the security of the ark. Like Ishmael, they are ready to mock at those who differ from them. They ridicule the walk of faith. The cross of Christ is to them foolishness. Shall not God visit for these things? To be carnally minded is *death*. They are like the fabled vessel drawing nigh to the loadstone rock. They get nearer and nearer, when, lo! every bolt and nail is drawn out to the magnet, and the ship is an utter wreck. "How are the things of Esau searched out!" The worldly policy of multitudes may seem for a while to prosper, but the end of these things is death. Some years ago a woman was executed for murder. The fatal deed had been committed to obtain a five-pound note. When the coveted note was gained it was found to be only a pretence. It was called a five-pound "Bank of Elegance" note. Yet for this poor sham the miserable young woman risked her life and took the life of another. What an illustration of Esau's barter—a birthright for a mess of pottage! An inheritance incorruptible is forfeited for some gilded toy. "The wages of sin is death." "How are the things of Esau searched out!"

III. In the next place, we may consider ESAU AS THE TYPE OF THE UNSYMPATHIZING AND CRUEL. In ver. 10 the prophet says, "For thy violence against thy brother Jacob shame shall cover thee, and thou shalt be cut off for ever." This unsympathizing, hard-hearted, cruel spirit is directly opposite to that of Christ. The laws of the king-dom call to gentleness, meekness, brotherly kindness, charity. Christ hath left us an example, that we should follow his steps. He is the gentle Jesus. He is the tender Shepherd. He is the Brother born for adversity. He gave *himself* for us. His mercy is everlasting. He is the sympathizing High Priest. It is clear, then, that the sin of Esau was very great. Jacob from his dying couch denounced the cruelty of Simeon and Levi, although by grace the latter was called to high privileges in Israel. "Instru-ments of cruelty are in their habitations. O my soul, come not thou into their secret; unto their assembly, mine honour, be not thou united!" And in a little while he adds, "Cursed be their anger, for it was great, and their wrath, for it was cruel." But here we have the inveterate cruelty of centuries. The hatred of Esau against Israel had survived many generations. An unyielding, deadly, cruel antagonism to the Jews had been a leading characteristic of Edom. Esau's cruelty was of a most unnatural type. And it had grown worse and worse. The prophet tells us he first looked on Jacob's calamity, then laughed, then insulted, then plundered, and then imprisoned and murdered. We have, then, in Esau a type of the unsympathizing and cruel. And is not the red hand of Esau, the cruel, blood-dyed hand of Esau, at work in our own day? What are the fearful atrocities, the horrible cruelties, the maimings, the murders, the hellish plots, the demon-like machinations? What mean the heart-rending tears and sorrows of widows and orphans? What mean the distress and poverty of multitudes of ladies—Ireland's matrons and daughters? What mean the blight and ruin so common in the land? O my soul, come not thou into the secret! Esau's cruelty and blood-guiltiness were never so bad as the crimes, unpunished and undetected, of our own day. And shall not God search them out? "Verily there is a God that judgeth the earth." Let us for ourselves pray to be kept from the beginnings of all hatred, malice, and uncharitableness. God is love. May we have his mind! May we show ourselves the children of him who maketh his sun to shine on the just and on the unjust! "For if ye love them which love you, what reward have ye? do not even the publicans the same? . . . Be ye therefore perfect, even as your Father which is in heaven is perfect."—A. C. T.

Ver. 7.—*Unholy alliances.* "All the men of thy confederacy have brought thee even to the border: the men that were at peace with thee have deceived thee, and prevailed against thee; they that eat thy bread have laid a wound under thee." Companionship is of Divine appointment. The Lord God chose it in his wisdom for *himself*, and so created angels and men. He might have lived in majestic solitude, in all the sublimity of his one eternal presence; but no, he created angels that excel in strength, hearkening to the voice of his word, and he made man in his own likeness. Companionship, then, is after the Divine mind. Of the first Adam God said, "It is not good for man to be alone." Of the second Adam it is written, "Of him the whole family in heaven and earth is named." So with wideness of meaning the psalmist declares that "he setteth the solitary in families." We know the value of association. Individuals make up households, households linked together make up kingdoms, and kingdoms united are a bulwark of society. But there are two kinds of companionship. "He that walketh with wise men shall be wise, but a companion of fools shall be destroyed." Our text tells us of Edom's unholy alliance, which was probably with Arabian tribes. "The men that were at peace with thee have deceived thee; . . . they that eat thy bread have laid a wound under thee." The marginal reading is more exact, "the men of thy peace . . . the men of thy bread." Here, then, was a confederacy ruinous to Edom. "All the men of thy confederacy have brought thee even to the border: the men of thy peace have deceived thee; the men of thy bread have laid a wound under thee." Edom in extremity expected help, but, instead of that, the allies send his ambassadors back to the frontier, as much as to say, "Shift for yourselves. We are not going to help you. Look within your own borders." And thus, too late, Edom sees the folly of confederacy with Arab tribes. Now he is held up to us as a beacon of warning, assuring us of the disappointing character of worldly confederacy. "Cursed is the man that trusteth in man, and maketh flesh his arm, and whose heart departeth from the Lord" (Jer. xvii. 5). Esau had been like a weak clematis clinging to a broken reed. In the time of the storm the feebleness of the support was manifest. They only are safe who can say, "The Lord is my Stay." Esau had rejected the Lord, and therefore, although exalted amongst the stars, was brought down to the ground. The men of his peace had deceived him. The men of his bread had laid a wound under him. Would that nations and individuals acknowledged in life and practice that salvation is of the Lord! All human alliances are poor and inadequate. In the time of our greatest need this will most be seen. Recall the dying words of Julius Cæsar to Brutus, whose wound had been the worst of all. Recall the Earl of Strafford's words, when he found the king (after many assurances that he would never do so) had signed his death-warrant, "Put not your trust in princes, nor in any of the sons of men." Recall Cardinal Wolsey's last words, "Had I but served God as faithfully as I have served my king, he would not, in mine old age, have abandoned me to my enemies." "The men of thy peace," says the prophet, "have deceived thee; the men of thy bread have laid a wound under thee." Men who refuse the help and succour of the everlasting arms, of everlasting Love, and everlasting Strength, will find that wherein they trusted a festering wound, bringing pain, and anguish, and dishonour, and shame. True union is strength, but it must be with right characters and on right principles. The ungodly are described in Prov. i. 14 as saying, "Cast in thy lot among us; let us all have one purse." They allure to a false confederacy. Better have no purse at all than be allied to the ungodly. Look at the lonely Elijah. How sternly, how heroically, isolated! He refuses to share in the one purse of evil-doers. He will trust God for food. He who feeds the ravens can make even the ravens feed his prophet. Elijah will not come into the secret of the wicked. Unflinching champion, he knows that the purse of the ungodly is a bag with holes, and their cisterns hold no water, and their hopes are bounded by time, and their joys are gilded and unreal; and beyond death all is darkness, darkness—densest, deepest darkness. True wealth, true joy, true greatness, true glory, are for those who are heirs of God, joint-heirs with Christ. "Woe to them that go down to Egypt for help . . . to strengthen themselves in the strength of Pharaoh, and to trust in the shadow of Egypt!" There are many who do so; but what is God's message to Edom? "All the men of thy confederacy have brought thee even to the border: the men of thy peace have deceived thee; the men of thy bread have laid a wound under thee." How truly has even a heathen moralist, as well as an inspired apostle, warned us that "evil communications corrupt good manners"! In the Book of Kings we read of Jehoshaphat allying himself to Ahab in battle. It nearly cost Jehoshaphat his life. But afterwards we see that he had profited by the dear-bought experience. When he built ships to go to Ophir for gold, Ahaziah the son of Ahab said, "Let my servants go with thy servants in the ships," and Jehoshaphat would not. If we have been amongst those who have had worldly associates, let us learn wisdom. Let us walk with the wise. Let us choose for companions those who fear the Lord, and speak often one to another, to whom the Lord hearkens, and concerning whom he says, "They shall be mine in that day when I make up my jewels." In Acts iv. we read that the apostles, being released from prison, went to their own company. Their absence from the godly was by restraint. Prison walls and chains kept them. As soon as ever they were free to choose they went to "their own company." That company was characterized by love to Christ. It was formed of the disciples of the Crucified. Men "took knowledge of them, that they had been with Jesus." That company had common hopes and joys and interests. Their home was heaven. Their heritage was glory. Their Father was God. The company of the Lord's people here on earth are destined to inherit everlasting felicity. The child of God, when he is set free from the last ties that bind him to earth, goes to his "own company;" he goes to heaven, where Christ is gathering to himself those who have made a covenant with him by sacrifice. Let us ask ourselves about the companions of our life's pathway. Let us remember the folly of Edom, and let us remember the inspired counsel, "My son, if sinners entice thee, consent thou not." Let us remember, too, the feast at Enrogel. In 1 Kings i. we read of the splendid entertainment given by Adonijah to his distinguished guests. Amongst those present were some who held the highest positions, military and ecclesiastical. Very merry was the gathering; very loud were the flatteries; very gratifying was everything to the prince. Surely with Joab, Abiathar, and many others on his side, he would soon wear the crown. But the banqueting is suddenly stopped. A messenger in breathless haste makes an announcement. Those who had just been shouting, "God save King Adonijah!" now undergo a change of feeling. They all rise to their feet and hasten away. The prince is left alone. His so-called friends think not of his safety, but only of their own. They all disappear. Adonijah, a short time before admired, praised, flattered, crowned, the centre of a thousand hopes, is now alone. His guests had no true affection for him. They had no bond of love to bind them. The confederacy was for their selfish ends. They fawned for place. Now they see the prince cannot help them, and so they pass away. The banquet-hall is deserted; one solitary man is riveted to the spot. The men of his confederacy have deceived him; the men of his bread have laid a wound under him. Adonijah learns too late the folly and disappointment of worldly alliances. May we all profit by the Spirit's warning! Let us resolve to follow Jesus, and unite our interests with those who are his. Once there came one to the Saviour, asking, "Master, where dwellest thou?" Jesus answered, "Come and see." Let us make for Christ's home in glory. Let us cast in our lot with his people, who through grace "come up from the wilderness, clear as the sun, fair as the moon, and terrible as an army with banners."

> "Come, let us join our friends above
> That have obtained the prize,
> And on the eagle-wings of love
> To joy celestial rise.

" E'en now by faith we join our hands
With those that went before,
And greet the blood-besprinkled bands
On that eternal shore.

"Oh that we now might grasp our Guide!
Oh that the word were given !
Come, Lord of hosts, the waves divide,
And land us all in heaven."

(C. Wesley.)

A. C. T.

Vers. 8, 9.—*False confidences.* "Shall I not in that day, saith the Lord, even destroy the wise men out of Edom, and understanding out of the mount of Esau? And thy mighty men, O Teman, shall be dismayed, to the end that every one of the mount of Esau may be cut off by slaughter." The wise, the mighty!—who shall stand when these fall? Edom made great boast of its *wise* men and its *mighty* men, but it was a vain confidence. "Thus saith the Lord, Let not the wise man glory in his wisdom, neither let the mighty man glory in his might, let not the rich man glory in his riches : but let him that glorieth glory in this, that he understandeth and knoweth me, that I am the Lord which exercise loving-kindness, judgment, and righteousness, in the earth : for in these things I delight, saith the Lord." Edom was long famous for its wisdom. Eliphaz, the principal friend of the patriarch Job, was a Temanite. This Eliphaz, in some respects, was a representative of human wisdom. He oftentimes laid down false principles, or misapplied right ones, but was always ready to boast that he knew more than others. It is great folly to be wise in one's own conceits. God asks, "Shall I not destroy the wise men out of Edom ?" In Jer. viii. he says, "The stork, the turtle, the crane, and the swallow observe the time of their coming, but my people know not the judgment of the Lord." How do ye say, "*We are wise*"? The birds, when the chilly winds of autumn come, take care to migrate to a warmer clime where winter will not destroy, but ye make no preparation for the future. How do ye say, "*We are wise*"? Would it be wise for a merchant never to look into his affairs? Would it be wise for a captain of a ship to see a great storm coming, and make no preparation? Would it be wise to proceed, on a long journey and have no provision? How do ye say, "*We are wise*"? There are multitudes to whom this question must be put. The vainly wise men of Edom still exist—men who might truly learn wisdom from the little things spoken of in Prov. xxx.: "The ants are a people not strong, yet they prepare their meat in the summer; the conies are but a feeble folk, yet make they their houses in rocks [they know where to hide]; the locusts have no king, yet go they forth all of them by bands [they know that unity is strength]; the lizard taketh hold with her hands, and is in kings' palaces;" it has wisdom of patient, painstaking labour. The proud self-confidence of Edom had nothing of true wisdom about it. It was displeasing to the heart-searching God. "Shall I not even destroy the wise men out of Edom?" Then, too, we have the mighty men of Teman denounced. They were of those who gloried in their might. They trusted in nature's strength. With Pharaoh, they were ready to ask, "Who is Jehovah?... I will pursue, I will overtake, I will divide the spoil ... I will draw my sword, my hand shall destroy them." "Thou didst blow with thy wind, the sea covered them; they sank as lead in the mighty waters." With Saul, they rose, girt with strong armour and sword and spear; but the prophet comes and says, "The kingdom is given to another." With Samson, they shake themselves to put forth strength as at other times, but soon in the prison of the enemy we hear the exceeding bitter cry of the blind captive, "My weakness! my weakness!" With the Assyrian king, they exclaim, "With the multitude of my chariots I am come up to the height of the mountains, to the sides of Lebanon, and will cut down the tall cedars thereof, and the choice fir trees thereof: and I will enter into the lodgings of his borders, and into the forest of his Carmel." But God says, "I will put my hook in thy nose, and my bridle into thy lips, and I will turn thee back by the way by which thou camest." And thus we see the vanity of the mighty man glorying in his might. "Thy mighty men, O Teman, shall be dismayed." Now, it will be asked, if the wise must not glory in his wisdom, nor the mighty in his might, where shall we obtain a wisdom worth seeking? Where shall we find the secret of a God-given strength? I will now answer these inquiries.

I. WHERE SHALL WISDOM BE FOUND? That of Edom will not do. The wisdom of this world is insufficient for an immortal soul. We mostly need, not the wisdom of this world, nor of the princes of this world, but that wisdom of God which none of the princes of this world knew, for had they known it, they would not have crucified the Lord of glory. Where shall wisdom be found? St. Paul tells us it is a revelation of the Spirit of God. Where shall wisdom be found? The Scriptures, by the power of the Spirit, "make us wise unto salvation." Behold in Jesus the Wisdom of God. Observe, we say not—See in him great wisdom, but—See in him infinite wisdom; see in him the Wisdom of God. All that can come forth from God is in the blessed Jesus. He is the Wisdom of God. In his Person you have perfect God and perfect man—the heavenly and the earthly, the perfect embodiment and revelation of Wisdom. In his Person, his words, his work, his life, death, and resurrection, behold the Wisdom of God. And remember that "he of God is made unto us Wisdom." Yes; this is the wonder of wonders, this is the gracious answer to the question, "Where shall wisdom be found?" "He of God is made unto us Wisdom;" "Let not the wise man glory in his wisdom, ... but let him glory in the Lord," "who is the Wisdom of God and the Power of God."

II. THE POWER OF GOD. This will bring us to the reply to the second inquiry— Wherein may we find power? The mighty man is not to glory in his might. The *mighty* men of Teman, as well as the wise of Edom, are denounced. What is the source of strength that cannot decay? St. Paul understood when he said, "I can do all things through Christ who strengtheneth me." In Christ we have righteousness and strength. When we are weak in ourselves, we are strong in him. He is not only the Wisdom of God, but the Power of God. God's power to save, God's power to bless, God's power to raise, sanctify, glorify, is Christ—"*Christ the Power of God.*" Is there a soul you want saved? Christ is the Power of God. Is there a tried and afflicted one you desire to be comforted? Christ is the Power of God. Is there one you want taught, guided, succoured, blest? Christ is the Power of God. Do you in your own soul want soul-weanedness, heavenly mindedness, spirituality? Christ is the Power of God. Do you want power to overcome, power to be holy, power to be faithful? Christ is the Power of God. Do you want fears banished, sorrow healed, anguish soothed, and death conquered? Christ is the Power of God. He must be mighty to save. He must be all—able to renew and bless. Christ is the Almighty.

III. We may now LOOK AGAIN AT OUR SCRIPTURE. We have seen that it shows the evil of all false confidence. It declares human wisdom and human power untrustworthy. It shuts us up to Christ, the Wisdom of God and Power of God. And it presses upon our hearts this important question, "What is our hope?" It calls us to see whether we are building on the mountains of Esau or the Rock of Ages. We are warned that every one of the mount of Esau shall be cut off. All refuges of lies shall be swept away. The foundation of God only standeth sure, and none other foundation can any man lay than that which is laid, which is Jesus Christ. Oh, let us rejoice in the sure Foundation! Let us declare plainly that all our hopes are founded on Jesus Christ, that the foundation of our trust is Christ, the foundation of our happiness is Christ, the foundation of our glorious expectations is Christ. On him as our Foundation we may rest secure. The gates of hell cannot prevail against us. The Rock of Ages is immovable, the covenant is inviolable, the promises are unalterable, and the Divine love is eternal, and when the mountains of Edom and all other false confidences shall for ever perish, "the righteous shall shine as the sun in the kingdom of their Father for ever and ever."—A. C. T.

Vers. 10—14.—*Edom's cruelty.* Here one of the great sins of Edom is denounced in very forcible language. Notice the succession of pointed sentences. "Thou shouldest not have looked on the day of thy brother." The *eyes* were in the transgression. Hagar, we read, could not look upon Ishmael in his distress. But Edom could look on afflicted Jacob. "Thou shouldest not have rejoiced over the children of Judah in the day of their destruction." The *emotions* were in the transgression. "Love rejoiceth not in iniquity." "Thou shouldest not have spoken proudly in the day of distress." The *tongue* was in the transgression. We are told in Ps. cxxxvii. how the children of Edom cried, "Down with it, down with it, even to the ground!" "Thou shouldest not have entered into the gate of my people in the day of their calamity." Their *feet* were in the transgression. Like those whose picture the psalmist drew, "their feet were swift to shed blood." And as their thoughts, their emotions, and their words were evil, so were their *deeds*. They were all wrong. "Thou shouldest not have looked on their affliction. Thou shouldest not have laid hand on their substance. Thou shouldest not have stood in the crossway, to cut off their escape. Thou shouldest not have delivered up thy brother a captive to his enemies." A solemn series of charges. One unbrotherly act after another. "Thou shouldest not;" "Thou shouldest not;" "Thou shouldest not." Contrast all these condemning words, "Thou shouldest not;" "Thou shouldest not," with the reiterated words of St. John in his First Epistle, "Let us love one another, for love is of God. He that loveth not knoweth not God, for God is love." We must surely feel that we want more of the spirit that St. John inculcates. Love does not flourish in the Church's garden as it ought. Envy, hatred, and malice are ever springing up, marring the plants of the Lord's own planting. What shall we think of the elder brother whose character is described in Luke xv.? Is not that unfraternal, unsympathetic, unloving elder brother yet alive? Or the priest and Levite of Luke x., are they not still amongst us? And where wounded misery lies bleeding, are not the priest and Levite found passing away on the other side? Nay, is not Edom—Edom red with blood, Edom cruel as the grave, Edom fierce and untamed as a leopard—is not Edom still alive? Who will say that the religion of Christ would not make more progress in heathendom were the whole of Christendom more under its beneficent power? We read in Numb. xx. of Edom withstanding Israel in their march to Canaan. There is much of this antagonism to the progress of truth now. Then comes the reminder of relationship, and its consequent obligations: "Thus saith thy *brother* Israel, Let us pass to Canaan through thy borders." But Edom opposes: "Thou shalt not pass through." Hatred instead of good will, resistance instead of assistance, antipathy instead of sympathy, the spirit of Edom instead of the spirit of love,—these are the baleful hindrances to the Church's progress. Contrast this character of Edom with that of Christ. In Heb. iv. 15 we are told of the fraternal sympathy of our High Priest—sympathy with our infirmities, sympathy with our sorrows, sympathy with our conflicts, sympathy with our struggles, loving, tender, brotherly sympathy. In Prov. xvii. he is called "the Brother born for adversity"— born for it. The gospel is throughout a story of a Brother born to sympathize with adversity. Young man, he has sympathy with you. Child of poverty, he has sympathy with you. Bereaved one, he has sympathy with you. Tempted one, he has sympathy with you. He is the great Sympathizer. In the ages past he was "afflicted in all their afflictions;" and now we have not a High Priest who cannot sympathize with us. See how he is presented to us in the Gospels. See him going about doing good; see him drying the widows' tears; see him healing poor lepers; see him blessing little children; see him opening blind eyes; see him raising the fallen; see him feeding the hungry; see him teaching the ignorant; see him casting out devils; see him blessing the wretched; see him saving the lost. Oh, what sympathy! Oh, what a "Brother born for adversity"! Let us follow in his steps. It must not be enough that we are unlike Nero, who sent Christians to the lions. It must not be enough that we are unlike Edom, who hated his brother Jacob. It must not be enough that we are unlike persecuting Rome in the time when God's faithful martyrs were made to seal their testimony in fire and blood. We are to be Christ-like. We are to take as our example the loving, the forgiving, the tender, the compassionate, the meek, the long-suffering *Christ*. Instead of being like Edom, whose every power went out in unfraternal cruelty, we must bring our powers, our faculties, our emotions, our hearts, our lives, to be sanctified, controlled, and governed by the Holy Spirit of Christ.—A. C. T.

Ver. 11.—*Edom as Babylon.* "Even thou wast as one of them." Edom, although claiming Abraham and Isaac for his forefathers, was so unfraternal to Israel that when Jerusalem was captured by the Babylonians, he shared in the hostility. His cry was, "Rase it, rase it, even to the ground!" To this our text makes reference. "Even thou wast as one of them." And what Obadiah thus says to Edom, he might often stand and say to some of *us*. How many who have been nursed in privileges and taken a place as servants of the God of Abraham, have been found, like Balaam, amongst the enemies of the Lord! "Even *thou* wast as one of them." How often the inquiry might come to those who ought to be bearing holy witness for God, "What doest thou here, Elijah?" The words may well convey a warning to us, for even the most godly have often fallen from their steadfastness. Let us note some examples by way of fixing this warning upon our hearts.

I. WE ALL DENOUNCE DRUNKENNESS. We all sadly mourn the condition of inebriates. Alas! there was a time when Obadiah might have stood in attitude of condemnation before the Patriarch Noah, and said, "Even *thou* wast as one of them."

II. WE SCORN THE LIAR. But there was a time when Abraham became untruthful. Obadiah might have appeared before him, and said, "Even *thou* wast as one of them."

III. WE ABOMINATE IMPURITY. But there was a time when Obadiah might have stood before David, as did the Prophet Nathan, and said, "Thou art the man!" "Even *thou* wast as one of them."

IV. WE DEPLORE RASH SPEAKING AND HOT AND HASTY WORDS. Time was when Obadiah might have come to the meek and holy Moses, and said, "Even *thou* wast as one of them."

V. WE OFTEN LOOK WITH FEELINGS OF DISDAIN UPON THE PROUD. And yet there was a time when Obadiah might have said to the good King Hezekiah, "Even *thou* wast as one of them."

VI. WE ARE EVER READY TO ADMIT THE TURPITUDE OF DENYING CHRIST. But see Obadiah standing before Simon Peter, and we catch his awful words, "Even *thou* wast as one of them."

VII. CONTENTION AMONGST BRETHREN IS ANOTHER EVIL WHICH WE DEPRECATE. Obadiah might have pointed to Barnabas, the "son of consolation," and said to him, "Even *thou* wast as one of them."

VIII. THE SIN OF UNBELIEF IS ANOTHER FEARFUL EVIL. But all the early disciples fell for a time into this sin. Obadiah might have said first to one, then another, "Even *thou* wast as one of them."

IX. A MURMURING SPIRIT IS ANOTHER EVIL WHICH THE CHRISTIAN SHOULD AVOID. St. Paul learned in whatsoever state he was, therewith to be content. The psalmist says his soul was as a weaned child. But we turn to the prophet of fire. We find the great Elijah under a juniper tree, murmuring at his lot. "Even *thou* wast as one of them."

Enough. We see plainly that the Scriptures warn us of the frailty of our nature and the deceitfulness of our hearts. And, if we reflect at all, we must see that repeatedly Christian professors lack consistency. Christian principle and Christian practice should never be at variance. But what is the fact? How often the Christian in business walks so unworthy of his high calling that our prophet seems to speak to him, "Even *thou* wast as one of them." Or we look into society, and we find in some Christians so much worldly conformity, that to one after another Obadiah might come, and exclaim, "Even *thou* wast as one of them." Let me ask those Christians who spend several afternoons in the week in visiting, and yet scarcely ever drop a word for their Lord and Master—Do you think that Obadiah's expostulation is not for you : "Even *thou* wast as one of them"?

Let us learn, therefore, these three lessons. 1. *First*, to live watchfully. "Let him that thinketh he standeth take heed lest he fall." Snares and dangers will beset us as long as we are in the world. What some may call only the shadows upon the mountains may prove conquering foes (Judg. ix. 36). We all need the restraining grace of Christ. "Hold thou me up in my goings, that my footsteps slip not." 2. *Secondly*, to be careful about companionship. Edom's unfraternal antagonism was fed by the company he kept, till he was even "as one of them." Those who "mingle with the heathen" will not be slow to "learn their works." "Blessed is the man that walketh not in the counsel of the ungodly . . . but his delight is in the Law of the Lord." 3. *Lastly*, to walk holily before God. St. Peter's exhortation should be kept in mind, "Giving all diligence, add to your *faith* [faith is the root—add to the root] heroic, manly courage; and to courage *knowledge* [self-knowledge, Bible-knowledge, the knowledge of Christ;

for knowledge is power for working and for waiting, for doing and for suffering]; and to knowledge *temperance* [temperance, or self-control, is an urgently needed grace]; and to temperance *patience* [we are all called to endure; we must not expect that we can be Christians without any trouble; Christ's soldiers must learn to endure hardness]; and to patience *godliness* [piety, devotion]; and to godliness *brotherly kindness* [Edom knew nothing of brotherly kindness; this brotherly kindness is love to the brethren— love to the godly]." And one more grace is enjoined, "Add to brotherly kindness *charity* [love to everybody]." Thus, in walking holily before God, we shall, by the power of his Spirit, keep from the sin of Edom, "Even thou wast as one of them "— one of the Babylonians; and all will take knowledge of us that we are the God-Man's disciples. The ointment of the right hand bewrayeth itself. We are Christ's. His we are, and him we serve. He was as one of us (sin only excepted), that we might be one with him for ever.—A. C. T.

Ver. 15.—*Recompense is sure.* "As thou hast done, it shall be done unto thee." Herein we have an immensely important principle laid down. Sowing and reaping always correspond. "Whatsoever a man soweth, that shall he also reap." All actions are seeds, many of which bear fruit in this world, and many in the next. "As thou hast done, it shall be done unto thee." Edom had been merciless and cruel, and the prophet says, "Thy reward shall return upon thine own head." In like manner we find mystic Babylon denounced in Rev. xviii. 6 (I give the new version as more exact and expressive): "Render unto her even as she rendered, and double unto her the double according to her works: in the cup which she mingled, mingle unto her double." Here you see the principle in force—rendering to Babylon as she rendered; doubling to her as she doubled; mingling for her as she mingled. We cannot overestimate the immense importance of this principle. In this life nations and individuals are constantly exemplifying the solemn truth which it involves. We should therefore all carefully remember that we are seed-sowing, and sooner or later must come the harvest. God told Edom, "Thy reward shall be upon thine own head. For as ye have drunk upon my holy mountain, so shall all the heathen drink continually." So Edom drank the cup at the hands of Babylon; Babylon drank it at the hands of the Medes; the Medes and Persians drank it at the hands of the Macedonians; the Macedonians drank it at the hands of the Romans; the Romans, in their turn, drank it at the hands of the barbarians (Dr. Pusey). Thus as they had done, it was done to them. Their reward returned upon their own head. In Ezek. xxxv. 15 we have a similar denunciation of Edom: "As thou didst rejoice at the inheritance of the house of Israel, because it was desolate, *so will I do unto thee*: and thou shalt be desolate, O Mount Seir, and all Idumea, even all of it." It is, you will notice, exactly the same kind of denunciation. In Prov. xxvi. 27 God says, "Whoso diggeth a pit shall fall therein: and he that rolleth a stone, it will return upon him." And in Ps. ix. 15 we are told, "The heathen are sunk down in the pit that they made: in the net which they hid is their own foot taken." In Numbers we find Moab plotting to curse Israel, and the curse came upon himself. In Judges we read of Adoni-bezek taken in battle, and maimed in his hands and feet. Adoni-bezek acknowledged that he had himself maimed three score and ten petty princes. His words are not dissimilar to our text, "As I have done, so God hath requited me." He confessed that the law of Nemesis had reached him. The end of Haman will occur to us. Haman dug a pit, and fell therein himself. He set a stone rolling, and it returned upon him. He perished upon the gallows which he prepared for Mordecai. In Ps. xviii. David says, "With the froward thou wilt show thyself froward." He clearly means that Jehovah will be sternly opposed to the sinner's frowardness. A similar passage is in Lev. xxvi., "If ye walk contrary unto me, then will I walk contrary unto you." The stubborn will gain nothing by their obstinacy. God will render to nations and individuals according to their ways. They shall be filled with the fruit of their own doings. The enemies of Daniel were devoured by the lions which they intended for his destruction. The accusers of the three Hebrews were consumed by the fiery furnace which they kindled for *them.* The plotters of mischief were taken in their own wickedness and filled with their own ways. "As thou hast done, it shall be done unto thee." In the case of Jezebel we have a terrible example of this kind. In the place where Jezebel caused the dogs to lick the blood of

Naboth, the dogs licked her blood. Well said Eliphaz, "I have seen that they who plough iniquity, and sow wickedness, *reap the same.*" The Jews, who were made to serve "strange" masters, were told that it was for serving "strange" gods. And our Lord himself has said, "With the same measure that ye mete it shall be measured to you again." Society has been likened to the echoing hills. It gives the speaker his words back again, doleful groan for groan, and joyous song for song. Thus "with the same measure that ye mete it shall be measured to you again." Jacob, who deceived his father, was in turn, and similarly, deceived by his sons. The Egyptians killed the Hebrew children; the God of the Hebrews slew the firstborn of Egypt. "As thou hast done, it shall be done unto thee." The words, we know, were addressed to Esau, and we have had abundant proof of the truth of the principle which they involve. But let us briefly notice the converse. "Whatsoever a man soweth, that shall he also reap." If the ungodly cannot sow hemlock, nightshade, and darnel, without reaping the same, so God's servants cannot sow seeds of kindness, seeds of truth, seeds of light, seeds of heavenly blessing, without reaping in due season. The great harvest of well-doing, like that of evil-doing, is indeed hereafter, but it has its tokens and firstfruits even now. Let us notice, for example, our adorable Redeemer's beatitude, "Blessed are the merciful: for they shall obtain mercy." We know that the merciful are those who upon gospel principles are sympathetic, helpful, loving, and kind. We know also that hereafter Christ will say to those on his right hand, "Come, ye blessed, . . . inherit the kingdom. . . . I was an hungered, and ye gave me meat: I was thirsty, and ye gave me drink: I was a stranger, and ye took me in: naked, and ye clothed me: I was sick, and ye visited me: I was in prison, and ye came unto me. . . . Verily I say unto you, Inasmuch as ye did it unto one of these my brethren, even these least, ye did it unto me." Hereafter, it is clear, the merciful will obtain mercy. But at present the like principle is at work. "As thou hast done, it shall be done unto thee." The kind and merciful *now* enjoy much blessedness; the unmerciful are *now* unblest. A man whose sympathies are all dried up lives in a region of wintry blight. He walks in no glorious sunshine and in no joyous liberty. He knows nothing of the bliss that comes from open-hearted sympathy. There is darkness within. Darkness covers the face of the deep, and the Spirit of God does *not* move on the face of the waters. But the merciful man, the man who is kind and sympathizing, the man who is forgiving and for-bearing, the man who has a kind excuse for others, the man who looks on the charitable side of a case, the man who thinketh no evil,—that man will reap here as well as here-after. In his straits and afflictions he will find, as a general rule, the stream of kindness flow back again. The world will learn mercy by his mercy, and show some feeling for one whose wont was to sympathize with adversity. "The merciful man doeth good to his own soul" (Prov. xi. 17). The widow of Sarepta and the woman of Shunem, for kindness to the Lord's prophets, received a prophet's reward. The alms of Cornelius brought good to his own soul. God is not unrighteous to forget your work and labour of love. "As thou hast done, it shall be done unto thee." Now this is one of the original principles of the creation of God. God said, "Let the earth bring forth grass, the herb yielding seed, and the fruit tree yielding fruit, *after his kind.*" The vine yielded grapes; the fig tree, figs; the olive tree, olives. The principle was universal. So it is in the moral world. "What a man soweth, that shall he also reap." There is no altering the law naturally, morally, or spiritually. If a mother spoils a child, we know what the harvest will be. If a man takes to intemperate habits, we know what the harvest will be. And we all expect an idle, indolent man to come to disgrace and shame. Let no one be deceived. "God is not mocked . . . whatsoever a man soweth, that shall he also reap." Often and often souls have been deceived. Eve was deceived, Jacob was deceived, Ahab was deceived, David was deceived; but as they sowed, they reaped. God was not mocked. And so with us. Our words, our actions, our habits, are seeds —seeds that will spring up. *Oh, what will the harvest be?* In this life there is, as I have shown, no little reaping ever going on. Nations and individuals are constantly learning the meaning of God's words to Edom, "As thou hast done, it shall be done unto thee." But the great harvest is at the end of the world. The Lord of the harvest is at hand. My text, which I have said, has a present fulfilment, especially amongst nations, will have its complete accomplishment with regard to individuals when Christ's judgment-throne is set up. Then shall every man receive the things done in the body.

Every one shall receive—that is, carry away with him—the things done in the body, according to that he hath done, whether it be good or bad. The bad—the sins—must each be as a scorpion-sting throughout eternity. Every sinner will be his own hell. The memory of his sins will be perpetual torment. In days when men argue against a future hell, it may be asked—Who will argue that justice must extinguish the memory and take away the remorse of the sinner's wilful transgressions? The recollection of the unpardoned sins of a lifetime will in itself be terrible. Let us, in this day of grace, when Jesus of Nazareth passeth by, offering salvation and everlasting life, let us every one come to him without delay. Let us accept his forgiving mercy, that our sins may be blotted out. Let us yield to the guidance of his Holy Spirit. And let us put on the Lord Jesus Christ, that we may be able to stand in the judgment. Henceforth may this be our language—

> " Jesus, thy blood and righteousness
> My beauty are, my glorious dress;
> 'Midst flaming worlds in these arrayed,
> With joy shall I lift up my head " !

A. C. T.

Ver. 17.—*Safety, sanctity, and sufficiency.* " But upon Mount Zion shall be deliverance, and it shall be holy; and the house of Jacob shall possess their possessions." What a burst of heavenly sunshine! What an effusion of joyous light! What music from the throne of God! What an evangel at the fourth watch of the night! What a smile of Divine love for the cast-down and sorely afflicted captive! Safety, sanctity, sufficiency. The inspired prophet here sets forth some of the richest treasures of the grace of God. They tell of deliverance from Babylon and restoration by Cyrus; they expand to the later deliverance from the Idumeans by the Maccabees; and, what especially applies to *us*, they stretch to the glorious salvation wrought for captive sinners by the Lord and Saviour Jesus Christ. Safety, sanctity, and sufficiency,—these are fully set before us in the gospel. They are the heritage of those who have come to Mount Zion, to the city of the living God. Let us prayerfully study them.

I. SAFETY. " Upon Mount Zion shall be deliverance." 1. *This is deliverance from the Law.* "There is no condemnation to them who are in Christ Jesus." "The law of the Spirit of life in Christ Jesus hath made us free from the law of sin and death." The ten thousand condemning voices of the Law are silenced by the Deliverer. Christ has met the Law's requirements. His people are free. They are free indeed. The old handwriting against them was cancelled by the cross. The debt is paid. We are not under Law, but under grace. 2. *This is deliverance from sin.* "He shall be called Jesus: for he shall save his people from their sins." Yes, from the penalty, from the power, and from the presence of their sins. What a glorious deliverance! 3. *This is deliverance from Satan.* "The Seed of the woman has bruised the serpent's head." Christ has vanquished our deadly foe. Now, if we resist the devil, he will flee from us.

> " Captivity is captive led,
> Since Jesus liveth who was dead."

4. *This is deliverance from the world.* He who said, "Be of good cheer; I have overcome the world," prayed that his people might be kept from the evil in the world. Through him we are more than conquerors. "This is the victory that overcometh the world, even our faith." 5. *This is deliverance from death.* "O death, where is thy sting?" He that trusteth in Christ shall never die. That which we call death is to the servant of God the gate of life. The Christian is promised that he shall not taste of death. The death he undergoes is only the death of pain, of sickness, of sorrow, of sin, of *death.* To depart is to be with Christ, which is far better than remaining here —far better.

> " For ever with the Lord:
> Amen, so let it be.
> Life from the dead is in that word,
> 'Tis immortality."

"Upon Mount Zion shall be deliverance."

II. In the next place, WE FIND SANCTITY PROMISED. "It shall be holy." In its present-day application this promise sets forth the sanctification of God's Israel. It is not sufficient to realize deliverance; we are to seek holiness. Joshua's captains were not only to put their feet upon the necks of the five kings of the enemy, but they were to go forward and possess the whole of Canaan. Deliverance from foes in the cave of the heart is only preparatory to further conquests and higher attainments. We are delivered from our enemies that we may serve God without fear, "in holiness and righteousness all the days of our life." "It shall be holy." The Christian's sanctification is twofold. 1. He is sanctified as *set apart for God*. Like the vessels of the sanctuary, he is consecrated to holy uses. It was Belshazzar's great sin that he took the vessels of the temple and put them to a profane use. God's people are to be vessels unto honour, meet for the Master's service, resting on the heavenly Eliakim. Not their own; a separate people; sanctified or set apart by God the Father. 2. The other view of the Christian's sanctification is *the blessed hallowing of the Holy Spirit*. This is a progressive work. We are to grow in grace, and in the knowledge of our Lord and Saviour. We are to add to our faith. We are to be going from strength to strength. We are to press towards the mark. We are to be changed from glory to glory by the Spirit of the Lord. "Upon Mount Zion shall be deliverance, and it shall be holy." May we now seek to be filled with the Spirit of holiness!

III. The third great promise of my text is SUFFICIENCY. "The house of Jacob shall possess their possessions." Here is all-sufficiency in all things. It is as the heir entering upon his inheritance. "My beloved is mine, and I am his;" "All things are ours, the world, life, death, things present, things to come,—all are ours." In possessing our possessions we enter upon the unsearchable riches of Christ. His salvation ours; his pardon ours; his joy ours; his rest ours; his kingdom ours; his angels ours; his home ours; his glory ours. Christ himself ours; Christ in us the Hope of glory; Christ for us the Pledge of glory; crucified together with him; raised together with him; seated together with him; glorified together. Oh, the unsearchable riches of the Christian! May we learn to possess our possessions, to use our talents, to enjoy our privileges, to rise to our dignity, to realize our standing, to pass through the length and breadth of our Canaan! Ours a righteousness which is Divine; a peace which surpasseth understanding; a joy which is unspeakable; a love which passeth knowledge; a kingdom which cannot be moved; a crown of glory that fadeth not away. Oh, let us go up and possess! Safety, sanctity, sufficiency. Eternal safety, Divine sanctity, all-sufficiency in all things. "Upon Mount Zion shall be deliverance, and it shall be holy; and the house of Jacob shall possess their possessions."—A. C. T.

Ver. 18.—*Truth triumphant.* "And the house of Jacob shall be a fire, and the house of Joseph a flame, and the house of Esau for stubble, and they shall kindle in them, and devour them; and there shall not be any remaining of the house of Esau; for the Lord hath spoken it."

I. WHAT IS HERE PROMISED CONCERNING GOD'S HERITAGE APPLIES TO THE WHOLE CHURCH OF THE FIRSTBORN. Truth may appear to lose many a battle, but in the end it will assuredly prevail. Edom, long hostile to God's ancient Israel, is likened to stubble before the flames. Happy the people who are on the conqueror's side. When Israel was in Egypt, captive and down-trodden, it seemed impossible that they could ever march forth to liberty and Canaan. But the time came when they sang of victory, and Pharaoh and his captains were as stubble before the flame. When Asa found the vast hosts of the Ethiopians coming against him, it might have appeared impossible to subdue them. But Asa knew the secret of power. The Ethiopians were soon as stubble before the flame. When the Moabites, Ammonites, and Edomites were confederate against Jehoshaphat, it seemed as if the might and greatness were on the side of the enemy, but good King Jehoshaphat gave himself to prayer and praise—believing prayer, and joyous and confiding praise. The enemies were soon as the stubble before the flame. And so in the end truth itself shall prevail. Foes may be mighty and gospel doctrines may seem to make slow progress, but the time must come when "the earth shall be full of the knowledge of the Lord as the waters cover the sea." That was a wondrous vision once seen by St. John: war in heaven—Michael and his angels fought against the dragon and his angels, and the dragon was cast out, and his angels with him. "So let all thine enemies perish, O Lord: but let them that love thee be as the sun when he goeth forth in his might." The Church of God has often been likened to a worm, yet it is to thresh the mountain, and is seen in sacred song as "fair as the moon, clear as the sun, and terrible as an army with banners." Thus weakness is girt about with strength, because God himself fights his people's battles, and is one with them. "He that seeketh thy life seeketh my life;" "He that toucheth you toucheth the apple of mine eye." All-conquering oneness. This secret of conquest may be seen by comparing our text with Isa. x. 17. In our text the word is, "The house of Jacob shall be a fire, and the house of Joseph a flame, and the house of Esau for stubble;" but the word in Isaiah is, "The light of Israel shall be for a fire, and his Holy One for a flame: and it shall burn and devour his thorns and his briers in one day." Thus the Lord espouses the cause of his people; so that in all things they are more than conquerors through him who loved them.

II. WHAT IS THREATENED IN OUR TEXT RESPECTING ESAU APPLIES TO ALL THE ENEMIES OF GOD. As it is said that the house of Esau shall be as stubble consumed by the flame, so in New Testament language the ungodly are likened to chaff which shall be burned with unquenchable fire. It is a dreadful thing to be found amongst the enemies of God. St. Paul, we read, wept because there were men who were enemies of the cross of Christ. A man who is hostile to the atonement of the Saviour shows he refuses to be reconciled to God. The message of reconciliation has come to us. The way of peace is proclaimed to us. The gospel of God's grace is set before us. The path of life is revealed. Salvation is offered without money and without price. When we were enemies Christ died for us. Now, the promise is, "peace by the blood of the cross." And some spurn the cross. The apostle might well weep. Angels might well weep. The Saviour himself wept over such. There cannot be hope for a man who remains an enemy of the cross of Christ. The house of Esau shall be as stubble. The ungodly are as the chaff. There cometh One "whose fan is in his hand, and he will throughly purge his floor, and gather his wheat into his garner, but *burn up the chaff with unquenchable fire.*" And not only is this part of our text applicable to all the enemies of God; it reminds us of the overthrow of all that is evil. Every plant that the Father hath not planted shall be rooted up. Truth shall prevail over error. Light shall conquer darkness. Eternal day shall chase away the shades of night. Goodness shall prove stronger than sin. The Seed of the woman shall bruise the serpent's head. All things shall be subdued unto Christ. "He must reign till he hath put all enemies under his feet. The last enemy that shall be destroyed is death." Ere a little, and the song shall be heard, "The Lord God omnipotent reigneth." Voices as of many waters, voices as of mighty thunders, voices loud and strong, voices of angels, voices of the redeemed of men, joyous coronation-voices, shall soon unite in proclaiming the once despised Man of sorrows "KING OF KINGS AND LORD OF LORDS. And he shall reign for ever." "For the Lord hath spoken it."—A. C. T.

Vers. 19, 20.—"*Rehoboth.*" "And they of the south shall possess the mount of Esau; and they of the plain the Philistines: and they shall possess the fields of Ephraim, and the fields of Samaria: and Benjamin shall possess Gilead. And the captivity of this host of the children of Israel shall possess that of the Canaanites [or rather, 'the captivity,' etc., 'which are among the Canaanites' (Pusey, following the Chaldee, etc.)], even unto Zarephath; and the captivity of Jerusalem, which is in Sepharad, shall possess the cities of the south." Here we have wideness at last; *Rehoboth* after narrowness, strife, contention, and hatred (Gen. xxvi.). The house of Jacob is shown us stretching forth in all directions—north, south, east, and west; the promises long looked for fulfilled; Jacob, long pent in, now enjoying a large room. The cries in narrowness have been answered in wideness. *Rehoboth* is inscribed on Judah's banner, and little Benjamin shares the plenteousness. They of the south have no Edomite enemy; nay, the mount of Esau is their possession. They of the plain have no Philistine foe; their own borders reach to the coast. Over Philistia they triumph. The giants of Gath lie in the dust. The men of Ashdod and Ekron, who sang the praise of Dagon, are no more. Ashkelon and Gaza are silent in death. They of the plain possess the whole territory of the Philistines, with the sea for their only border. But much more than this. They extend northward. They take in Ephraim.

No more shall Ephraim vex Judah. They also take in Samaria. No more shall it be heard that the Samaritans have no part with the Jews. And more still. Benjamin shall possess Gilead, thus stretching to the east. It shall have a portion on both sides of Jordan. And, further, Judah shall receive into fellowship those who were carried away captive from them. Some in Zarephath in Zidon, labouring as slaves in the smelting-house, and the captivity of Jerusalem shall possess the cities of the south. Thus the inspired prophet, from the sacred mount of vision, amongst other blessings, notices these five: (1) liberty after captivity; (2) peace after war; (3) wideness after straits; (4) a portion on both sides of Jordan; (5) unity after divisions and discord. With what joy must Obadiah have seen all these rich blessings unfolded before him! *Liberty!* Oh what a history of captivity and bondage was that of the Jews! *Peace!* Their national life hitherto had been one of war. *Wideness!* Up to this they had been sorely straitened and hemmed in in veriest narrowness. *A portion on both sides of Jordan!* Hitherto they had had their lot on the western side only. *Unity!* They had been torn by divisions. They had been weakened, impoverished, and desolated by divisions. How pleasant, therefore, the prospect of Judah receiving into its bosom multitudes of the captivity of Israel! All one at last. One fold under one Shepherd. A delightful prospect. Obadiah, like another Moses, must have viewed the scene with patriotic joy and hallowed fervour and gratitude. And now for the spiritual application of the passage to ourselves.

I. GLORIOUS LIBERTY IS PROCLAIMED TO US. Christ sets his people free. He came to lead captivity captive. He opens the prison to those who were bound. His Word is the perfect law of liberty. The Apostle Peter's deliverance from prison is like a picture of the deliverance wrought for the soul of man. We were in the dark dungeon, fast bound in misery and iron. Light shone in the prison. A friendly hand smote us. A voice bade us arise. The fetters fell off. We were led forth from the darkness of death into the light and liberty of the children of God. Or we may say, in the language of David (Ps. cxxvi. 7), "Our soul is escaped as a bird out of the snare of the fowlers: the snare is broken, and we are escaped." Joyous liberty, blessed liberty, glorious liberty of the children of God.

II. PEACE IS OURS. The peace of the very God of peace. Secure tranquillity through the blood of the everlasting covenant. "Comfort ye, comfort ye my people, saith your God. Speak ye comfortably to Jerusalem, and cry unto her, that her warfare is accomplished, that her iniquity is pardoned;" "Peace to him that is far off, and to him that is near." Peace always and by all means.

III. WIDENESS IS OURS. "Thou hast known my soul in adversities; ... thou hast set me in a large room." The Lord brings his people into a wealthy place. "Rehoboth" is written on the gospel. "Rehoboth" is written on the work of Christ. "Rehoboth" is written on the wells of salvation. On the joys, the glories, the promises of covenant grace, the letters are written as with Calvary's blood—"Rehoboth." Room enough and to spare (Job xxxvi. 16).

IV. A PORTION ON BOTH SIDES OF JORDAN IS OURS. The Christian has the promise of the life that now is as well as that which is to come. All things are ours. The world, life, death, things present, things to come, the blessings of the throne and the blessings of the footstool, the upper springs and the nether springs,—all are ours. Oh, let us pity the men who have their portion only in this life! Let us pray for those whose hearts and treasures are where the rust and moth are. Let us seek to influence for good all those who have no portion on both sides of Jordan.

V. Finally, THE CHURCH IS CALLED TO UNITY. We are to endeavour to keep the unity of the Spirit. There are many stones, but one temple. There are many children, but one household—one family. There are many branches, but one Vine. There are many members, but one body. The Communion feast teaches this oneness. Our Lord's great intercessorial prayer was that his people all might be one. The Holy Spirit, the Spirit of love and concord, calls us to oneness. The divisions of Christians must grieve the Spirit.

> "Our little systems have their day;
> They have their day, and cease to be;
> They are but broken lights of thee,
> And thou, O Lord, art more than they."

Oh for another Pentecost, that the Church of to-day might be as the Church of the first days, and the Redeemer's words be exemplified "That they all might be one, *that the world may believe that thou hast sent me*"!—A. C. T.

Ver. 21.—*Saviours and judges.* "And saviours shall come up on Mount Zion to judge the mount of Esau." "Saviours and judges;" "Mount Zion and the mount of Esau:" what contrasts! And note the saviours are made the judges. The saviours on Mount Zion are made the judges of the mount of Esau. If we follow up these lines they bring us to the true centre of full salvation and perfect judgment. Almighty and most merciful *Saviour, thou* most worthy *Judge* eternal, give us now of thy Holy Spirit that we may profitably study thy Word.

I. "SAVIOURS SHALL COME UP ON MOUNT ZION TO JUDGE THE MOUNT OF ESAU." Temporal deliverance had often been wrought for Israel, and still greater things would God accomplish. In Judg. ii. 16 we have an early use of two words of our text. "Nevertheless the Lord raised up judges, which saved them out of the hands of those that spoiled them." In Judg. iii. 9 we read, "When the children of Israel cried unto the Lord, the Lord raised up a deliverer [saviour] to the children of Israel, even Othniel." Again, in ver. 15, "When the children of Israel cried unto the Lord, the Lord raised them up a deliverer, Ehud the son of Gera." In Neh. ix. 27 we read, "In the time of their trouble, when they cried unto thee, thou heardest them from heaven; and according to thy manifold mercies thou gavest them saviours, who saved them out of the hand of their enemies." Here, then, we see that in temporal deliverances the twofold office was entrusted to one individual. The judges were often called saviours, and the saviours were often called judges. Thus we see the primary meaning of Obadiah's prophecy, "*Saviours* shall come up on Mount Zion to *judge* the mount of Esau." In the deliverance wrought by such as Judas Maccabæus and others we see the primary fulfilment of the words.

II. In another view of the text we may remark that AS TOPICALLY MOUNT ZION STOOD OVER AGAINST THE MOUNT OF ESAU, SO SPIRITUALLY GOD'S HOLY HILL STANDS OPPOSED TO THE MOUNTAINS OF THIS WORLD—the mountains of human pride, the mountains of human misery, the mountains of error, the mountains of unbelief, *all* the dark mountains of sin. And every such mountain shall be judged and brought low, even to the dust. A time is coming when the mountain of the Lord's house shall be established upon the tops of the mountains. At present great mountains of evil may seem to overshadow Zion, but ere long they shall become a plain. Our God can make even the worm to thresh the mountain—the least of his servants to "leap from Bashan," to "overcome troops," and "out of weakness" to become strong. "Saviours shall come up on Mount Zion to judge the mount of Esau."

III. Another reflection is this: THE CHILDREN OF ZION ARE TO BE SAVIOURS NOW; THEY SHALL BE JUDGES HEREAFTER. 1. *Saviours.* We are called to rescue the perishing. "He which converteth the sinner from the error of his way, shall save a soul from death" (Jas. v. 20). But, as saviours, we must see well to our own souls. St. Paul's words to Timothy are very weighty: "Take heed unto thyself, and unto the doctrine: continue in them, for in doing this, thou shalt both save thyself, and them that hear thee." In seeking to win souls we must take care that our own souls are won. In caring for others' vineyards, we must not neglect our own. This said, we return to the doctrine that *the saved are to be saviours.* We once had our part with the destroyer; now we are to be a blessing. We are to seek to save the lost. Moses calls to Hobab; Andrew finds Peter; Philip, Nathanael; the woman of Sychar brings her neighbours to Christ. Thus the saved are saviours. Noah calls others into the ark. Abraham invites Lot to Canaan. Rahab brings her relations under the shelter of the scarlet line. Joshua commands his household. Job sacrifices and prays for his friends. Isaiah lifts up his voice for the remnant. Jeremiah weeps and prays. Daniel fasts and makes supplication. The mothers of Salem bring their children to Christ, that he should bless them. Saviours ascend on Mount Zion. May we all know what it is thus to rise—thus to ascend, and walk on God's high places! 2. The children of Zion shall hereafter be *judges.* They shall "judge the world." They shall "judge angels." They shall sit with Christ on his throne. They shall not only be manifested at the judgment-seat of Christ, but shall share in the decisions of the Lamb. For the present they "judge not," unless it be *themselves,* or in the sense of testimony as regards the evil that is in the world. Through the cross of Christ the world has been crucified to them, and they are crucified to the world. " And this is the judgment, that the light is come into the world, and men loved the darkness rather than the light; for their works were evil." The Christian has now to bear witness to this judgment, but the full and great assize is future.

IV. We may now turn our thoughts to THE LORD JESUS CHRIST. He is the almighty and most merciful Saviour; he is the most worthy Judge eternal. 1. Let us think of him as a *Saviour.* " Behold, I stand at the door and knock." He comes to the sinner's heart. He knocks by his Word, by his providence, by his Spirit. He has knocked long. The heart, like the inn at Bethlehem, has no room for Christ, or the bolts of ignorance and unbelief bar him out. How long shall he be kept away? He may have given his last knock. You and I need a Saviour. Shall we not welcome him? Shall we not accept his offer? Oh, " how shall we escape, if we neglect so great salvation?" 2. Let us think of him as a *Judge.* " Behold, the Judge standeth at the door." If we open not to the Saviour, we must open to the Judge. I have read of a man of immense wealth who built for himself a magnificent mansion, and then shut himself up in it. His sovereign, passing that way, asked for admission. He refused it. Time went on. A change took place. There had come a great depreciation of West Indian property. The proud man, who would not receive his king, saw his gates yield to the law-officers of the crown. " Behold, the Judge standeth at the door." If we welcome not the knocking Saviour, how can we meet the Judge? May the Holy Spirit be our Helper, that we may have boldness in the day of judgment, and not be ashamed at Christ's appearing! May we say with Luther—

> " Beneath the cross I view the day
> When heaven and earth shall pass away,
> And so prepare to meet him " !

A. C. T.

Ver. 21.—*The kingdom.* " The kingdom shall be the Lord's." What fulness of brightest morning glory after a long night of blackest darkness! The kingdom longed for, the kingdom prayed for, the kingdom promised, the kingdom prophesied of, shall be the kingdom *come. The* kingdom. Not many kingdoms, but one. Now there are many, and these diverse from each other, and often at war one with another. The Prophet Daniel spoke of this when he said, " The Lord God shall set up a kingdom which shall never be destroyed." The fulfilment is presented to us in Rev. xi. 15, " The seventh angel sounded; and there followed great voices in heaven, and they said, The kingdom of the world is become the kingdom of our Lord, and of his Christ: and he shall reign for ever and ever." " The kingdom shall be the Lord's." *Now* the world lieth in the wicked one. The kingdom is Satan's. Look at its sins, its miseries, its darkness, its degradation, its ruin. The kingdom is Satan's. See the heathen world bowing to wood and stone, or worshipping devils. Look at the vast millions carried away by the Mohammedan delusion. Turn to the multitudes hardened by Jewish infidelity. View so-called Christendom, with teeming myriads rejecting the truth. See also the millions that have not so much as the profession of any religion. Is not Satan the prince of this world? Is not the great enemy of souls usurping the seat of power? Oh, then, as we think of Israel not gathered home; as we think of Babylon drunk with the blood of saints; as we think of the infidelity and ignorance which stalk abroad in the professing Church and in the world; as we think of war and bloodshed deluging the earth; as we think of nations discomfited by the frailties of human governments; as we think of the Church torn by contentions; as we think of Rachels weeping for their lost ones; as we think of the tears which bedew the cheeks of orphans and widows; as we think of the sorrows in our hospitals; as we think of the bitter poverty in our large cities; as we think, too, of the groans of the poor brute creation; and as we think of the sad partings, the great disappointments, the strong animosities, and the cruel wrongs common to earth;—shall we not pray for the fulfilment of our text? shall we not cry, " Thy kingdom come "? shall we not exclaim, with St. John, " Come, Lord Jesus: come quickly "? It is a cry for the end of toil, the end of suffering, the end of tears, the end of temptations, the end of sin, the end of gloom, the end of darkness, the end of death. It is a loud cry for the song of heaven to be heard, "Now is come salvation and strength, and the kingdom of God, and the power of his Christ." It is an earnest longing to join in the Hallelujah chorus of the great multitude, as the voice of many waters, and as the voice of mighty thunderings, saying, "Alleluia: for the Lord God omnipotent reigneth!" "The kingdom shall be the Lord's." At present, although the kingdom of *nature* is his, creation groans, being burdened. At present the kingdom of *providence* is his, but man keeps blotting the pages of history, and things are not as they ought to be. At present the kingdom of *grace* is his, but his grace is often frustrated, and the subjects of his grace live far below their privileges and high calling. Ere long, and the three kingdoms shall be no more imperfect. They shall be consummated in the full Christocracy—"the kingdom shall be the Lord's." The kingdom of glory shall come, and shall have no end. In closing our study of the Book of Obadiah let us carry with us the sweet echoes of its last words. May the Holy Spirit, in all the vicissitudes of earth, keep us in mind that "the kingdom shall be the Lord's"! Ere long, and he shall come whose right it is to reign. In the interval before the advent let us be alive to our duty.

I. LET US BE READY FOR IT. No one who is impenitent and unbelieving can be ready. Like Ethelred, he is all unready. To be prepared for Christ's coming, we must be washed in his blood, justified by his righteousness, and sanctified by the Spirit of holiness.

II. LET US BE LOOKING FOR IT. Let us say with St. Paul, "We wait for the Saviour, the Lord Jesus Christ, who shall fashion anew the body of our humiliation, that it may be conformed to the body of his glory." Let us mount our *heimwehfluh* in longing expectation and hope. Christ's disciples are to be not only servants, but *like* unto servants who wait for their lord. The servant who expects his lord, has him in mind, and is on the look-out, lest, coming suddenly, his lord finds him sleeping.

III. LET US BE WORKING FOR IT. The absent Saviour has given to every man his work. Each one has something to do. Every true disciple is a worker, called to prepare the way of the Lord—to make some crooked path straighter, some rough place smoother, some mountain lower, some valley higher. "The kingdom shall be the Lord's."

IV. LET US BE LIVING FOR IT. "What manner of persons ought ye to be?" How weaned! How unworldly! How heavenly-minded! How Christ-like! For "the kingdom shall be the Lord's."

V. LET US BE PRAYING FOR IT. "That it may please thee shortly to accomplish the number of thine elect, and hasten thy kingdom."

> "Come, then, and added to thy many crowns
> Receive yet one, the crown of all the earth,
> Thou who alone art worthy."

VI. LET US BE GLAD. We ought to rejoice. We ought to lift up our heads. Advent bells are ringing. The sound of the bells on our High Priest's robe may be heard as he comes forth to bless. Hallelujah! "The kingdom shall be the Lord's."—A. C. T.

Ver. 1.—*God and bad men.* "The vision of Obadiah. Thus saith the Lord God concerning Edom; We have heard a rumour from the Lord, and an ambassador is sent among the heathen, Arise ye, and let us rise up against her in battle." Of the history of Obadiah we literally know nothing. His name, which signifies "Worshipper of Jehovah," and his short prophecy afford the only information concerning him. From vers. 11 to 14, which are thought to contain an allusion to the exultation of the Edomites over the final capture and plunder of Jerusalem, we might with some confidence infer that he flourished after the destruction of Jerusalem by the Chaldeans. In all probability he must have lived near the time of Jeremiah; and indeed there is almost a verbal agreement between his utterances in vers. 1—8 and those contained in Jer. xlix. If we take this view we might suppose that his prophecy was delivered between the year B.C. 588, when Jerusalem was taken by the Chaldeans, and the termination of the siege of Tyre by Nebuchadnezzar. As to his prophecy, it is the *shortest* in the Bible: one chapter comprehends all. Its *subject* is the destruction of Edom on account of its cruelty to Judah, Edom's brother, and the restoration of the Jews. Its *style* is marked by animation, regularity, and clearness. These words of the first verse suggest two thoughts concerning God and bad men.

I. THAT GOD MAKES A REVELATION CONCERNING BAD MEN. Here is a revelation concerning Edom, the enemy of God and his people. Isaac had two sons by Rebekah— Esau and Jacob. Esau was called Edom, "red," in memory, it is said, of the red pottage for which he sold his birthright (Gen. xxv. 30). Observe: 1. The *forms* of the revelation. (1) As a *vision*. "The vision of Obadiah." The prophet was a seer. The Eternal revealed himself to the eyes of his soul. He who would be a true minister of God must see the thing before he speaks it. "That which we have seen and handled," says the apostle. Man has other eyes than those that are in his forehead. He has a faculty for seeing the invisible and the eternal; this distinguishes him from the brute. (2) As a *report*. "We have heard a rumour from the Lord." The word "rumour" means "report." "We have heard a report from Jehovah." He heard as well as saw. The soul has ears to catch the echoes of eternal thought. God in times past spake to the fathers by the prophets; and now, as in olden times, speaks by symbols and sayings, by appealing to the eye and the ear. 2. The *character* of this revelation—a message. "An ambassador is sent among the heathen." Did he mean by the ambassador, himself, or any other prophet or prophets, or some celestial minister? It does not matter. The message is the thing—a message from Jehovah to the nation. God sends his messages to the nations in many ways and by many agents. 3. The *subject* of the revelation. "Arise ye, and let us rise up against her in battle." The object of the message was to stir up the Assyrians, and afterwards the Chaldeans, against Edom. But our proposition is that God makes a revelation concerning bad men; and the subject of that revelation embraces at least two things. (1) *That their sins will ruin them.* This the Almighty has revealed over and over again in the Bible, and in every chapter of human history and experience. The burden of all is, "The wages of sin is death." (2) *That evangelical repentance will save them.* "Let the wicked forsake his way, and the unrighteous man his thoughts: and let him return unto the Lord, and he will have mercy upon him; and to our God, for he will abundantly pardon" (Isa. lv. 7). These two subjects are the great burden of God's revelation to bad men.

II. THAT GOD PUNISHES BAD MEN BY BAD MEN. He now sent a messenger amongst the nations. What for? To stir up the Assyrians and Chaldeans—both bad people— to wreak vengeance on corrupt Edom. Why does he employ bad men for this awful work of retribution? He could do it without any secondary agency at all, or, if he chose to employ any instrumentality, could use the forces of nature and the monsters of the forest alone to do the work; why employ bad men to punish bad men, fiend to punish fiend? By doing so: 1. He reveals in the *most powerful way to the victim the enormity of his sin.* The torture which his fellow-man brings on him he is made to feel is but a slight stroke of that fiend of depravity which has set his own soul against his Maker. 2. He reveals his own *absolute power over the workings of the human heart.* Thus he maketh "the wrath of men to praise him," etc. (Ps. lxxvi. 10). He makes even the devil himself to carry out his will. But though God employs bad men to punish bad men by rapine, plunder, and bloody wars, it is not by his instigation; they act by their own free will. He is not the Author of evil. All good proceedeth from him, and all evil is overruled by him for the order and blessedness of the universe. The devil is not less a devil because he inflicts the penalties of justice on men.—D. T.

Vers. 2—5.—*Pride.* "Behold, I have made thee small among the heathen: thou art greatly despised. The pride of thine heart hath deceived thee," etc. These words may be taken as suggesting and illustrating one of the chief sins of all sinners, viz. *pride,* that which poets tell us "peoples hell and holds its prisoners there." The words suggest three facts in relation to pride.

I. THAT THE MOST DESPICABLE PEOPLE ARE OFTEN THE MOST DISPOSED TO PRIDE. Edom, which is charged with the sin of pride, is here described as "small among the heathen" and "greatly despised." Not only were they a small people, small comparatively in numbers, wealth, and influence, but despised. They became contemptible in the estimation of their contemporaries. Small things and small men are not always despicable, for God made the small as well as the great. It is the moral character that creates and deserves contempt. Now, small and despicable as were these Edomites, they were nevertheless *proud*. It is often, if not ever, so. The smaller the men the more disposed to pride. The man small in *body* is often swollen out with ideas of the comeliness of his person; the man small in *intellect* is the same. The men who rate themselves as great thinkers, scholars, authors, preachers, are invariably small-brained men. Men of great intellect and lofty genius are characteristically humble. An old writer has observed that "where the river is the deepest the water glides the smoothest. Empty casks sound most; whereas the well-fraught vessel silences its own sound. As the shadow of the sun is largest when his beams are lowest, so we are always least when we make ourselves the greatest."

II. THAT PRIDE EVERMORE DISPOSES TO SELF-DECEPTION AND PRESUMPTION. 1. To *self-deception*. "The pride of thine heart hath deceived thee." Pride is a wonderful artist; it magnifies the small; it beautifies the ugly; it honours the ignoble; it makes the truly little, ugly, contemptible man appear large, handsome, dignified in his own eyes. It is said that Accius, the poet, who was a dwarf, would have himself painted as tall and commanding in stature. In truth, it makes the man who is a devil at heart appear to himself a saint. Witness the Pharisee in the temple. 2. To *presumption*. "Thou that dwellest in the clefts of the rock, whose habitation is high; that saith in his heart, Who shall bring me down to the ground?" The Edomites are here taunted with the confidence that they placed in their lofty and precipitous mountain, and the insolence with which they scouted any attempt to subdue them. A proud man always presumes on strength, reputation, and resources which he has not. Whilst he stands on quicksand he fancies himself on a rock. "Thou sayest thou art rich, and increased with goods, and hast need of nothing; whereas," etc. (Rev. iii. 17). Ah! self-deception and presumption are the twin offspring of pride.

III. THAT THE MOST STRENUOUS EFFORTS TO AVOID PUNISHMENT DUE TO PRIDE WILL PROVE FUTILE. Two things are taught here concerning its punishment. 1. Its *certainty*. "Though thou exalt thyself as the eagle, and though thou set thy nest among the stars, thence will I bring thee down, saith the Lord." Here these sinners are assured, by a bold hyperbole, that whatever attempts they made to avoid retribution, they would fail. If, like the eagle, they towered high into the air, far up among the clouds, nestled among the stars, and made the clouds their footstool, the fowler of retribution would bring them down. All attempts on behalf of the impenitent sinner to avoid punishment must fail when the day for justice to do its work has come. 2. Its *completeness*. "If thieves came to thee, if robbers by night (how art thou cut off!), would they not have stolen till they had enough? if the grape-gatherers came to thee, would they not leave some grapes?" The spoliation which thou shalt suffer shall not be such as that which thieves cause, bad as that is; for these, when they have seized enough, or all they can get in a hurry, leave the rest; nor such as grape-gatherers cause in a vineyard, for they, when they have gathered most of the grapes, leave gleanings behind; but it shall be utter, so as to leave thee nothing. The exclamation, "How art thou cut off!" bursting in amidst the words of the image, marks strongly excited feeling. The contrast between Edom, where no gleanings shall be left, and Israel, where at the worst a gleaning is left, is striking (Isa. xvii. 6; xxiv. 13). Retribution strips the sinner of everything; nothing is left but sheer existence, and that existence intolerable.

CONCLUSION. Beware of pride, then. The primal cause of all sin, all pain, and all woe to come, the great fountain-head of evil, is pride. It must lead to ruin. "Pride goeth before destruction, and a haughty spirit before a fall."

> "He that is proud eats up himself. Pride is
> His own glass, his own trumpet, his own chronicle,
> And whatever praises itself but in
> The deed, devours the deed in the praise."
> (Shakespeare.)

D. T.

Vers. 6—9.—*God in retribution.* "How are the things of Esau searched out! how are his hidden things sought up! All the men of thy confederacy have brought thee even to the border," etc. Man is essentially a dependent being. The ineradicable and ever-operative sense of his dependence urges him to lean his being on some object for rest and safety. His sin is that he puts his confidence on objects unworthy and unsafe. "Some trust in chariots, some in horses," etc. The Edomites, it is suggested here, trusted to the insecure. Here we have God *in retribution destroying the grounds of the sinner's confidence.*

I. DID THEY TRUST TO THEIR MATERIAL DEFENCES: THESE WERE WORTHLESS. "How are the things of Esau searched out! how are his hidden things sought up!" The reference is to the hiding-places to which they resorted in cases of danger. The country of the Edomites was pre-eminently favourable for such concealment and shelter. The cities of Edom consisted of houses mostly cut in the rocks. "The great feature of the mountains of Edom is the mass of red bald-headed sandstone rocks, intersected, not by valleys, but by deep seams. In the heart of these rocks, itself invisible, lies Petra" (Stanley). "Petra is unique. The whole Edomite country, from Eleutheropolis to Petra and Selah, hath small habitations (*habitatiunculæ*) in caves. And on account of the oppressive heat of the sun, as being a southern province, hath underground cottages. Hence the aborigines whom Edom expelled were called Horites, *i.e.* dwellers in caves." Nations may trust to their material defences, their armies, navies, fortifications; but they are as stubble to the raging fire when justice begins its work. Individuals may trust to their wealth, to material science and medical skill, to preserve their bodily lives; but when justice sends forth its emissary, death, what are these defences? Nothing, less than nothing, vanity.

II. DID THEY TRUST TO THEIR PLEDGED CONFEDERATES: THESE WERE WORTHLESS. "All the men of thy confederacy have brought thee even to the border: the men that were at peace with thee have deceived thee, and prevailed against thee; they that eat thy bread have laid a wound under thee: there is none understanding in him." Those confederates were probably Moab, Ammon, Tyre, and Zidon, with whom the Edomites joined in resisting Nebuchadnezzar; but these failed them, probably turned against them; and even their friends who were at peace with them and ate their bread deceived them in their hour of trial. "To no quarter could the Idumeans look for aid. Their allies, their neighbours, their very dependants, so far from assisting them, would act treacherously towards them, and employ every means, both of an open and covert nature, to effect their ruin." How often it happens, that when men get into adverse circumstances, their old allies, professed friends, those who have often partaken of their hospitality, not only fail them, but turn against them! "Cursed be the man that trusteth in man, and maketh flesh his arm" (Jer. xvii. 5). He that trusteth even to his firmest friends leaneth on a broken reed.

III. DID THEY TRUST TO THE WISDOM OF THEIR GREAT MEN: THIS WAS WORTHLESS "Shall I not in that day, saith the Lord, even destroy the wise men out of Edom, and understanding out of the mount of Esau?" "The Idumeans confided not only in the natural strength of their country, but in the superiority of their intellectual talent. That they excelled in the arts and sciences is abundantly proved by the numerous traces of them in the Book of Job, which was undoubtedly written in their country. They were indeed proverbial for their philosophy, for the cultivation of which their intercourse with Babylon and Egypt was exceedingly favourable, as were likewise their means of acquiring information from the numerous caravans whose route lay through their country, thus forming a chain of communication between Europe and India" (Henderson). Yet what is the wisdom of man to trust in? "He taketh the wise in their own craftiness." The wisdom of the wise is but foolishness; it is a miserable thing to trust in. Trust not in human wisdom; not in the wisdom of statesmen, scientists, ecclesiastics, theologians.

IV. DID THEY TRUST TO THE POWER OF THEIR MIGHTY MEN: THIS WAS WORTHLESS. "And thy mighty men, O Teman, shall be dismayed, to the end that every one of the mount of Esau may be cut off by slaughter." Delitzsch renders this, "And thy heroes despair, O Teman." Teman was the proper name of the southern portion of Idumea, called so after Tema, a grandson of Esau. Men trust in their heroes. At the banquets of public societies, companies, corporations, how does this confidence come out in the inflated cant of the speakers on the occasion, in relation to the army or the navy! A false confidence this also! God, by a breath of pestilence, can wither all the armies of Europe in an instant.

CONCLUSION. There is nothing in which the sinner trusts, nothing in matter or mind, in force or skill, that can stand for one instant before the retributive stroke of justice. Though some trust in chariots and some in horses, let us trust in the Name of the Lord. Men who trust in anything short of God are like the man who in a thunderstorm takes shelter under a tree, whose tall branches attract and receive the shock of the lightning which scorches him to ashes.—D. T.

Vers. 10—16.—*Social cruelty*: 1. *A sin against the Creator.* "For thy violence against thy brother Jacob shame shall cover thee, and thou shalt be cut off for ever," etc. Social cruelty is the grand subject of these verses, and the cruelty is that which one brother perpetrates on another—Esau on Jacob. "Wrong or violence is all the more reprehensible when it is committed against a brother. The fraternal relation in which Edom stood towards Judah is still more sharply defined by the name Jacob, since Esau and Jacob were twin brothers. The consciousness that the Israelites were their brethren ought to have impelled the Edomites to render helpful support to the oppressed Judæans. Instead of this, they not only revelled with scornful and malignant pleasure in the misfortune of the brother nation, but endeavoured to increase it still further by rendering active support to the enemy. This hostile behaviour of Edom arose from envy at the election of Israel, like the hatred of Esau toward Jacob (Gen. xxvii. 41), which was transmitted to his descendants and came out openly in the time of Moses in the unbrotherly refusal to allow the Israelites to pass in a peaceable manner through their land (Numb. xx.)" (Delitzsch). These verses present to us social cruelty in three different features—as a *sin against the Creator ; perpetrated against a brother, specially offensive to God; as working in various forms from generation to generation.* We shall devote a brief homiletical sketch to each of these. This passage implies, first, that social cruelty is a sin against the Creator; and the truth of this will appear from four subjects of thought.

I. THE CONSTITUTION OF THE HUMAN SOUL. Social cruelty is opposed to the normal condition of the human spirit. He who will study his own spiritual constitution will not fail to observe three great facts in relation to this subject. 1. *The existence of social love.* Social sympathy is one of the primary elements of our nature : its instinct is to render service to others and to seek their good will and fellowship. The malign is not inherent in man. Cruelty in him is not innate, as in the tiger and the bear. We are made to love and to be loved. 2. *The instinctive condemnation of cruel acts.* Never in the history of a soul has it instinctively approved of acts of cruelty as perpetrated either by itself or others. Conscience thunders against all such deeds: on the benevolent, and on the benevolent only, it smiles. 3. *Innate craving for social approbation.* The soul not only deprecates the ill will and loathing of society, but yearns deeply and always for its approbation. But this can only be attained by benevolent deeds. Now, inasmuch as the constitution of the soul is an expression of the Divine will, and that constitution is against cruelty, cruelty is an outrage on the Divine order.

II. THE COMMON RELATION OF ALL TO GOD. He is the Father of all men. No one of the human race is nearer to him than another. Each is his offspring and bears his image. And between all there is, therefore, the relationship of brotherhood. It cannot be the will of the great Father that his children should act as wild beasts, inflicting cruelty on each other, and thus harass his benevolent ears with the groans and shrieks of his offspring. What human father does not deprecate one of his children inflicting an injury on another, and does not ardently desire that each should work for the other? Are we more loving than he who made us? Does the brooklet contain more than the ocean?

III. THE COMMON INTEREST OF CHRIST IN THE RACE. Christ took on him the nature of man. He was the Son of man, not the Son of Jew or Gentile, rich or poor, bond or free, but the Son of *man.* The nature of all men was in him. He wore the nature of every man, he propounded doctrines for every man, he enacted laws for every man, he tasted death for every man. He was not ashamed to call us brethren. He loved the world, and gave himself for it. How abhorrent, then, must it be to him and to his blessed Father for one man to inflict cruelty upon another!

IV. THE UNIVERSAL TEACHING OF THE BIBLE. The whole Decalogue, as reduced and enforced by Christ, consists in loving God with all our hearts, and our neighbour as ourselves. And everywhere in the New Testament are we exhorted to "be kindly affectioned one to another," to "recompense to no man evil for evil."

CONCLUSION. How obvious it is, then, that social cruelty in all its forms is a sin against the Creator! The man who injures his fellow-creature is a rebel against the government of the universe.—D. T.

Vers. 10—14.—*An old sin.* "For thy violence against thy brother Jacob shame shall cover thee, and thou shalt be cut off for ever. In the day that thou stoodest on the other side, in the day that the strangers carried away captive his forces, and foreigners entered into his gates, and cast lots upon Jerusalem, even thou wast as one of them," etc. These words present to us an old sin in one or two aspects.

I. HERE IS AN OLD SIN WORKING IN THE HISTORY OF POSTERITY. "For thy violence against thy brother Jacob," etc. What was the sin? "And Esau hated Jacob because of the blessing wherewith his father blessed him: and Esau said in his heart, The days of mourning for my father are at hand; then will I slay my brother Jacob" (Gen. xxvii. 41). Envy was the sin; and this envy towards Jacob, or Israel, was transmitted from generation to generation. The spirit of envy that was kindled in the heart of Esau towards his brother Jacob glowed and flamed with more or less intensity for ages in the soul of Edom towards the descendants of Jacob. Edom continued to be the inveterate foe of Israel. Neither a man's sinful passion nor his deed stops with himself. Like a spring from the mountain, it runs down posterity, often gathering volume as it proceeds. No sinner liveth to himself. One man's sins may vibrate in the soul of another a thousand ages on. This is shown in almost every chapter of the history of nations. The fire of vengeance which the cruelty of one nation kindles in its victim will not expire at the conquest. It will burn on until it breaks out in fury, and wreaks vengeance upon its own conqueror. Hence he that taketh the sword always perishes by the sword. This fact should: 1. *Impress us with the awfulness of our existence.* It is true that in one sense we are little beings, occupying but a small space in the universe, and soon pass away and are forgotten; still there goes forth from us an influence that shall never end. We throw seed into the mind of the world that will germinate, grow, and multiply indefinitely, and yield harvests of misery or joy. 2. *Impress us with the duty of every lover of the universe to protest against sin in individuals.* A man may say, "What does it matter to you that I sin?" My reply is, "It does matter to me as a benevolent citizen of the universe. If your sin merely damned yourself, it is sad enough; but it does not end there; its pernicious influence on the universe is inconceivably great and calamitous."

II. HERE IS AN OLD SIN REPROBATED BY GOD IN THE HISTORY OF POSTERITY. God's eye traced it from Esau down. How does he treat it? He reprobates it. "For thy violence against thy brother Jacob shame shall cover thee, and thou shalt be cut off for ever. In the day that thou stoodest on the other side, in the day that the strangers carried away captive his forces, and foreigners entered into his gates, and cast lots upon Jerusalem, even thou wast as one of them. But thou shouldest not have looked on the day of brother," etc. Delitzsch renders the words, "Look not at the day of thy brother," and regards vers. 12—14 as a prohibition; others do not acknowledge the authority for that rendering. These Edomites, it would seem from the words, did stand on the other side without rendering help in the day when the stranger entered Jerusalem; they did "rejoice" over the children of Judah at that period; they did "speak proudly" in the day of distress; they did "enter into the gate" of God's people in the "day of calamity;" they did "lay hands on their substance" on that day; they did stand in the "crossway" and "cut" those off "that did escape." The omniscient eye saw all this. The Jews appeal to him to recompense the cruelty of these Edomites. "Remember, O Lord, the children of Edom in the day of Jerusalem; who said, Rase it, rase it, even to the foundation thereof!" (Ps. cxxxvii. 7). For all this God says shame should come on them, and shame did come. They are blotted from the history of the living. God condemns sin wherever it is, however it comes, and whatever its pedigree. It may be asked—If it were the envy of Esau that thus came down from age to age in his posterity, and worked these deeds of crime, where is the justice of God in reprobating them? They only inherit the iniquities of their fathers. We answer: 1. Sin is essentially abhorrent to Jehovah. It is the "abominable thing" which he hates: 2. The very essence of sin is its freeness. Sin is not a forced act; no deed performed by a man against his will has any moral character, or can in a moral sense be either good or bad. The posterity of Esau were not compelled to cherish and develop the envy of their great progenitor. Each one could have quenched it. Each, no doubt, felt it to be contrary to his moral nature, and that it ought to be expelled. The Almighty knew that each man was free; hence his reprobation of sin wherever found.—D. T.

Vers. 10, 11.—*Social cruelty: 2. Perpetrated against a brother, specially offensive to God.* "For thy violence against thy brother Jacob shame shall cover thee, and thou shalt be cut off for ever," etc. The cruelty here is not the cruelty merely of one man against another, but of one who is in close natural relationship to the other—children of the same parents. Strange as it may be, it is nevertheless a fact that a brother's enmity is often the most savage and unrelenting. How can this fact be accounted for? From the greater amount of his natural love. True, the greater amount of love a man has in him, the greater capacity he has for wrath. Wrath is but love in flames. The measure of a creature's love determines his power of anger. The little shallow lake cannot yield that amount of boiling steam which the ocean can produce. No love, no hatred; small love, small hatred; large love, large hatred. A brother is supposed naturally to have more love in him towards his brother than any other. Hence, when this love is kindled into wrath, it is often terribly furious. But the truth contained in the text is this, that a brother's cruelty is specially offensive to Jehovah. It is for "thy violence against thy brother Jacob shame shall cover thee, and thou shalt be cut off for ever." But why should it be specially offensive?

I. BECAUSE THE OBLIGATION TO LOVE IS STRONGER. It is the duty of all men to love one another, but more especially the duty of a brother to love his brother. Children of the same parents are specially bound by nature to be one in sympathy and in heart.

II. BECAUSE THE CHIEF HUMAN INSTITUTION IS OUTRAGED. What is the chief human institution? That of a family. Schools, governments, Churches, are not to be compared to the family institution. The government of the family is the model government; the school of the family is the model school; the Church of the family is the model Church. But when the members of this family become cruel to each other, this human institution is outraged.

III. BECAUSE THE TENDEREST HUMAN LOVES ARE WOUNDED. When brother inflicts injury on brother, parental hearts bleed, and sisters are struck with an agony of grief.

CONCLUSION. We wonder not, then, that cruelty towards brothers is more offensive to God than any other cruelty. Solomon has said that a "brother offended is harder to be won than a strong city: and their contentions are like the bars of a castle" (Prov. xviii. 19). The closer the relationship, in case of dispute, the wider the breach and the more difficult the reconciliation. A really offended brother is often harder to win back to friendship than the taking of a strong city or the breaking of the bars of a castle. Take the case of Cain and Abel, Joseph and his brethren, Absalom and Amnon. In all these cases nothing less than death was plotted and sought. Why is this? Why is a brother's anger so implacable? 1. Great love has been wounded. The more love, the greater capability of indignation. How strong the love of a real brother! 2. Great services have been ill requited. What attentions a true brother shows! how numerous, delicate, and self-sacrificing! If the object of all has proved utterly unworthy of them, how intense his chagrin, how poignant his distress! 3. Great hopes are frustrated. The offended brother anticipated a brother's sympathy, counsel, friendship, through all the checkered scenes of life. These hopes are shattered, and the wreck is vexatious beyond measure. 4. Great reluctance on the offender's side to acknowledge the fault and seek reconciliation. Strange as it may seem, it is yet true —a man would sooner offer an apology to any one than to his relations, especially to brothers.—D. T.

Vers. 12—16.—*Social cruelty: 3. As working in various forms from generation to generation.* "But thou shouldest not have looked on the day of thy brother in the day that he became a stranger," etc. Here we have a sketch of the workings of this cruelty towards Judah when he was in great distress, suffering, and peril.

I. CRUELTY HAS VARIOUS FORMS OF WORKING. Look at the forms here. 1. The *lack of sympathy* when Judah was in distress. "Thou shouldest not have looked," etc. Greatly did Judah need Edom's sympathy at this time. "Strangers carried away captive their forces;" Babylon entered their country and their city and carried them away as captives. Foreigners entered into his gates and cast lots upon Jerusalem. The city, after a long siege, was broken up; and the great officers of the King of Babylon came and sat at the gates and cast lots on the spoils of Jerusalem. It was indeed a "day of calamity," as it is three times expressed in these verses. Terrible and never to be forgotten was that day when Babylon came with all its forces into Judæa, entered the city, and bore away as captives the inhabitants. Now, in their distress, how did Edom their brother act? They stood and looked carelessly on. Want of sympathy with suffering is a sin in the sight of God. Heaven denounces men, not only for the evil they actually perpetrate, but for the neglect of the good they ought to accomplish. These Edomites were like the priest and the Levite. 2. *Positive rejoicing* when Judah was in distress. It is said, "they rejoiced over the children of Judah in the day of destruction," they "spoke proudly in the day of distress." They seem to have gloated over their afflictions. 3. *Participation in the work of their enemies.* They laid their hands on their substance, they cut off those that did escape, they delivered up those that did remain in the day of their distress. Social cruelty ever has had, and still has, many forms of working. Cold indifference, malignant rejoicing, as well as positive inflictions. See the charge brought against the Edomites on this occasion (Ps. cxxxvii. 7; Ezek. xxv. 12).

II. OMNISCIENCE OBSERVES IT IN ALL ITS FORMS. God's eye was on the Edomites, noted not only their positive acts, but the workings of their inner souls. Sin in all its operations is evermore under the eye of Omniscience. He knows the way each spirit takes. He searcheth all hearts, and understandeth all their thoughts. The ways of man are before the eyes of the Lord, and he pondereth their doings; they "are in every place, beholding the evil and the good." This fact, for an incontrovertible fact it is, should be practically realized. And if practically realized it will have a fourfold effect on the soul. 1. It will stimulate to great spiritual activity. When the eye of an intelligence falls right on us, the glance stirs the soul. What soul could sleep if it felt the eye of God ever resting on it? 2. It will restrain from the commission of sin. Did we feel his eye ever on us, should we yield to temptation? "Thou God seest me" is a powerful preventive. 3. It will excite the desire for pardon. God has seen all the errors and sins of the past, and they are great in number and enormity. Since he sees them, they must be either punished or absolved. 4. It will brace the soul in the performance of duty. Moses "endured as seeing him who is invisible." He knows our trials and our difficulties. Therefore let us be magnanimous under trial and brave in danger. Of God all-seeing, "What can escape his eye, deceive his heart omniscient?"

III. A JUST AND TERRIBLE RETRIBUTION AWAITS IT IN ALL ITS FORMS. "The day of the Lord is near upon all the heathen: as thou hast done, it shall be done unto thee: thy reward shall return upon thine own head," etc. Retribution is a settled law in the material universe. "With what measure ye mete, it shall be measured to you again." There is a rebound in every sin. No crime has ever been committed that does not come back with a terrible rebound on the soul of the author. "They shall drink, and they shall swallow down." To swallow up and to be swallowed up is the world's destiny.—D. T.

Ver. 15.—*Social retribution.* "For the day of the Lord is near upon all the heathen: as thou hast done, it shall be done unto thee: thy reward shall return upon thine own head." We have above furnished outlines of three homilies on the first sixteen verses of this chapter. *Social cruelty* we considered as the grand subject of the whole. This was presented: 1 *As a sin against the Creator.* And this was proved by the constitution of the human soul; the common relation of the race to God; the common interest of Christ in the race; and the universal teaching of the Bible. 2. *As when perpetrated against a brother, specially offensive to God.* And three reasons were mentioned for this —the obligation to love a brother is stronger; the chief human institution is outraged; and the tenderest human loves are wounded. 3. *As working in various forms from generation to generation.* In this view it was shown that cruelty has various forms of working; that Omniscience observes it in all its workings; and that a terrible retribution awaits it in all its forms. Now *social retribution* is the subject before us, and this subject we have touched on already. There are two great popular errors concerning the subject of retribution. 1. *That retribution is reserved entirely for the future state.* That the future state will be a state of retribution—a state in which every man shall be rewarded according to his works—must be admitted by every thoughtful student of the Bible. But retribution is not only future; it is here; retribution is an eternal principle of the Divine government; it follows sin at all times and for ever. The men and nations whose acts are registered in the Bible proclaim the grand truth, "Behold, the righteous shall be recompensed in the *earth:* much more the wicked and the sinner" (Prov. xi. 31). "Bishop Butler, in accordance with the same doctrine, lays it down as an axiom that this life is the allotted and appointed period of retributive justice. Having assumed this as an undoubted fact, he proceeds to infer therefrom the certainty of the future judgment. How many masters in Israel arrive at the same wholesome conclusion on quite opposite premisses—the entire absence of systematic retributive justice during this life! 'We find,' he says, 'that the true notion of the Author of our nature is that of a Master or Governor, prior to the consideration of his moral attributes. The fact of our case, which we find by experience, is that he actually exercises dominion or government over us at present, by rewarding and punishing us for our actions in as strict and proper a sense of these words, and even in the same sense, as children, servants, subjects, are rewarded and punished by those who govern them.'" Did not retributive justice strike our first parents and Cain at once? Did it not strike the antediluvian world, Sodom and Gomorrah, etc.? Another popular error concerning retribution is: 2. *That it is a special infliction of God.* We do not say that God may not break through the established order of things to inflict punishment, nor that he has not done so; for the Bible furnishes us with instances to the contrary. All we say is—this is not the general rule. Divine punishments are natural events. Divine justice works as naturally as Divine goodness. Sin and punishment are indissolubly linked as cause and effect. The text suggests two thoughts in relation to *social retribution.*

I. THAT IT IS OFTENTIMES A RETURN TO THE OFFENDER OF THE SAME KIND OF SUFFERING AS HE INFLICTED ON HIS VICTIM. "As thou hast done, it shall be done unto thee: thy reward shall return upon thine own head." The bitter cup thou hast given to thine enemy shall come round to thee, and of its dregs thou shalt drink. This principle is stated by Christ. "With what measure ye mete, it shall be measured to you again." The Bible is full of examples of this principle. Isaac told a lie, affirming that his wife was his sister; and he is told a lie by his son Jacob, who declared himself to be Esau. Jacob had deceived his aged parent in relation to Esau; his sons deceive him with regard to Joseph. He had embittered the declining years of his aged sire; his children embittered his. Again, Joseph was sold by his brethren as a bond-servant into Egypt; in Egypt his brethren are compelled to resign themselves as bond-servants to him. All history is full of examples, and everywhere in modern society illustrative cases may be selected. The deceiver himself is deceived, the fraudulent is himself cheated, the hater is himself hated, the cruel is often ruthlessly treated. Thus "as thou hast done, it shall be done unto thee."

> "Hear the just law, the judgment of the skies;
> He that hates truth shall be the dupe of lies."
> (Cowper.)

II. THAT IT OFTEN APPEARS TO COME AS A SPECIAL VISITATION OF ALMIGHTY GOD. "The day of the Lord is near upon all the heathen." All days are his days. But it is not until the guilty conscience is smitten with a sense of sin that it sees him and feels that the day is full of God. Electricity pervades the universe, is ubiquitous; but men become conscious of it and talk of it only when it flashes in lightning and sounds in thunder. So with God's justice. It is everywhere; but when the guilty conscience feels its punitive touch it calls it the day of judgment. The righteous are *now* going into life eternal, every righteous deed is a step onward; the wicked are *now* going into everlasting punishment, with every sin they tramp downward.

CONCLUSION. Learn that no soul can sin with impunity; that every sin carries with it punishment. "The gods are just, and of our pleasant vices make whips to scourge us."

It may be, indeed, through the deadness of your conscience and the superabundant mercies of this life, that you feel not the retributive lash as you will feel it at some future time; but retribution is working here.

> " We still have judgment here that we but teach
> Bloody instructions, which, being taught, return
> To plague the inventor. This even-handed justice
> Commends the ingredients of our poisoned chalice
> To our own lips."

(Shakespeare.)

D. T.

Ver. 17.—*The true Church; or, the community of the good*: 1. *A beneficent power.* " But upon Mount Zion shall be deliverance, and there shall be holiness ; and the house of Jacob shall possess their possessions."   Obadiah here commences his predictions respecting the restoration of the Jews from Babylonish captivity, their reoccupation of Caanan, and the reign of the Messiah. While the surrounding nations were to disappear, the Jews should regain possession of the land of their fathers. Mount Zion may be taken here as the symbol of the true Church of God, that is, the community of godly men existing on this earth. In this sense it is referred to in Hebrews. Here the whole passage may be taken as representing this true Church, or godly community, in three aspects—as a beneficent power ; a consuming power ; and an aggressive power. The subject of the sketch is on the Church as the beneficent power, which we have in the seventeenth verse. Three thoughts are suggested by the words concerning the Church as a beneficent power.

I. IT IS CONNECTED WITH DELIVERANCE. " Upon Mount Zion shall be deliverance." Mount Zion was the asylum for those who had escaped. In Mount Zion shall be the *escaped.* From Babylonian captivity and suffering they returned to Mount Zion, or Jerusalem, and were safe. There they enjoyed their old protection. In the true Church there is spiritual safety ; it is a refuge that is built upon a rock, and the gates of hell cannot prevail against it. It is watched by the infinite love and guarded by the almighty power of Christ ; its blessed Keeper never slumbers nor sleeps. Oh, ye imperilled spirits pursued by the powers of hell, led by the devil captives, and sold under sin, flee to this Mount Zion, this true Church of God, this community of godly men, which is at once the organ and the residence of Christ.

II. IT IS CONNECTED WITH PURITY. " There shall be holiness." Moral pollution, or sin, is the source of all the calamities that befall men. Mount Zion is a consecrated spot. If there is holiness anywhere it is in connection with that community of men called the Church, which embraces the principles, cherishes the spirit, follows the example of the Son of God. True, the members are not perfect yet ; but they are in the process of cleansing, and are already holy as compared with the pollutions of the ungodly world.

III. IT IS CONNECTED WITH ENJOYMENT. " And the house of Jacob shall possess their possessions." " Though the houses of Jacob and Joseph are here spoken of separately, it was not the intention of the prophet to teach that the two kingdoms of Judah and Israel would be re-established. Yet the special mention of Joseph clearly shows that the ten tribes were to return at the same time, and jointly with Judah and Benjamin, to possess the land of Palestine and the neighbouring regions (see Isa. xi. 12—14; Hos. i. 11). The restored Hebrews would unitedly subdue the Idumeans ; which they did in the time of John Hyrcanus, who compelled them to be circumcised, and so incorporated them with the Jews that they henceforward formed part of the nation." The word " possess " here means *enjoy*—enjoy their possessions. The community of the true Church alone enjoy their possessions. They are a happy people ; all things are theirs ; they are full of joy ; they even glory in tribulation. " Blessed are the people that know the joyful sound ! " (Ps. lxxxix. 15).—D. T.

Ver. 18.—*The true Church ; or, the community of the good*: 2. *A consuming power.* " And the house of Jacob shall be a fire, and the house of Joseph a flame, and the house of Esau for stubble, and they shall kindle in them, and devour them ; and there shall not be any remaining of the house of Esau ; for the Lord hath spoken it." There is a fire in the true Church. Notice—

I. The characteristics which this fire displays. What is the fire? The fire of *truth*, that burns up error; the fire of *right*, that burns up wickedness; the fire of *love*, that burns up selfishness. "I am come," said Christ, "to kindle a fire upon the earth." "Is not my Word like a fire?" 1. The fire in the Church is *a strong fire*. It has burnt an enormous amount of wickedness in every form, age, and land. It has burnt through the fiercest storms of centuries. 2. It is *an extending fire*. Its flames are ever advancing, they reach further to-day than ever. The most splendid systems of men, ethical, theological, and philosophic, however brilliant, have been but sparks compared to this; they have burnt on a little and gone out in darkness. 3. It is *a steady fire*. It does not flare and flash, but burns its way silently wherever it goes. 4. It is *an unquenchable fire*. Men have tried to put it out, oceans of infidelity and depravity have been poured upon it, but it burns on.

II. The materials which this fire consumes. "Stubble." What is moral depravity in all its forms—theoretical and practical, religious, social, political? What is it, however old, however decorated with worldly power and grandeur? What is it? "*Stubble*." It is not a rock, that stands fixed amidst the surges of time; not a tree, that has roots that may grow for ever; it is mere stubble, dry, sapless, worthless "stubble," ready for the fire. Error to truth, wrong to right, malice to love, is but stubble to fire.

Conclusion. God speed this fire until the whole world of wickedness shall be destroyed, until its heavens be dissolved, its earth burnt up, and its elements melt with fervent heat, and there come out of it "a new heaven and a new earth wherein dwelleth righteousness"!—D. T.

Vers. 19, 20.—*The true Church; or, the community of the good: 3. An aggressive power.* "And they of the south shall possess the mount of Esau; and they of the plain the Philistines: and they shall possess the fields of Ephraim, and the fields of Samaria: and Benjamin shall possess Gilead," etc. By the "south" or southern part of Palestine is here meant those who should occupy it; and by the "plain," those who should occupy the low country along the shore of the Mediterranean. "According to the relative positions of those who should take possession of the different parts of the Holy Land was to be the enlargement of their territory by the annexation of the adjoining regions which had formerly been occupied by allies or hostile powers. As there is no subject specified before the country of Edom and the country of Samaria, it seems to be intimated that the regions of Ephraim and Samaria were to be occupied by the Jews and the Israelites jointly, without any regard to tribal distinctions; and the reason why the tribe of Benjamin is mentioned is merely on account of the proximity of Gilead to the territory which it originally possessed" (Elzas). "The promise here," says an old expositor, "no doubt has a spiritual signification, and had its accomplishment in the setting up of the Christian Church, the gospel Israel, in the world; and shall have its accomplishment more and more in the enlargement of it, and the additions made to it, till the mystical body is completed. When ministers and Christians prevail with their neighbours to come to Christ, to yield themselves to the Lord, they possess them. The converts that Abraham had made are said to be the souls that he had gotten (Gen. xii. 5). The possession is gained, not *vi et armis*—by force and arms; for the weapons of our warfare are not carnal, but spiritual; it is by the preaching of the gospel, and the power of Divine grace going along with it, that this possession is got and kept." That the true Church is an aggressive power will appear from considering the *gospel*, which is at once its inspiration, its life, and its instrument. Consider, therefore—

I. The elements of which the gospel is composed. It is made up of two great elements, "grace and truth," that is, eternal reality and Divine benevolence. "Grace and truth came by Jesus Christ." To show the aggressiveness of these two principles, two facts may be stated. 1. That the human soul is made to *feel their imperial force*. It is true that the soul in its unregenerate state is ruled by directly opposite elements —error and selfishness. But even error has power over it only so long as it regards it as reality, and selfishness influences it under the guise of love. It is the truth when made clear to it that comes with a conquering power; it is love or grace that transports its heart. The human soul is made for these two elements. 2. That the human soul is bound to *yearn after these elements as its highest good*. Its deep hunger is for truth and for reality, for benevolence, or love. It has no natural hunger for error, no natural hunger for selfishness. 3. That the human soul is everywhere *restless without these elements.* It is only as the soul gets truth and grace into it that it becomes settled, calm, self-united. These are facts connected with the human soul, and these facts show the aggressiveness of the gospel.

II. THE PROSELYTIZING SPIRIT WHICH THE GOSPEL ENGENDERS. As soon as ever the gospel takes real possession of a soul, that soul becomes intensely solicitous to spread it abroad. It becomes what Jeremiah describes as a "fire in the bones." Peter said, "We cannot but speak the things which we have seen and heard." Paul said, " The love of Christ constraineth us ; because we thus judge," etc. " Necessity is laid upon us." Every genuine recipient, then, of the gospel becomes a missionary, a propagandist, a moral knight, to battle against the mighty hosts of error and selfishness. Each member of the true Church, or godly community, becomes, by a moral necessity, a soldier of the cross.

III. THE TRIUMPHS WHICH THE GOSPEL HAS ALREADY ACHIEVED. Compare the influence of the gospel in the world now to what it was when Christ was on earth. It was then confined to one lonely soul, the soul of Jesus of Nazareth ; it is now in the possession of millions. The springlet has become an Amazon ; the grain has covered islands and continents; the little stone has grown into a mountain that bids fair to fill the earth.

CONCLUSION. Such thoughts as these tend, we think, to demonstrate the essential aggressiveness of the true Church. It will one day take possession of all heathendom, with its "mount of Esau," the "plains of the Philistines," the "fields of Ephraim," and the " fields of Samaria," and what Canaanites there are as far as Zarephath.—D. T.

HOMILETICAL INDEX

TO

THE BOOK OF OBADIAH

———◆———

JONAH

EXPOSITION BY

W. J. DEANE

HOMILETICS BY

J. R. THOMSON

HOMILIES BY VARIOUS AUTHORS

J. E. HENRY

W. G. BLAIKIE

G. T. COSTER

A. ROWLAND

D. THOMAS

THE BOOK OF JONAH

INTRODUCTION

§ I. Subject of the Book.

THE Book of Jonah is not a prophecy, but an account of the prophet's mission to Nineveh to announce its speedy destruction. It is concerned chiefly with Jonah's own personal feelings and history in relation to this mission. Possessed with the national hatred of idolatrous Gentiles, and fearing that God, in his great long-suffering, might, after all, spare these Assyrians to whom he was sent, and that thus his prediction would be discredited and a heathen nation saved, he attempted to escape the unwelcome errand. Mingled with this apprehension there may have been a personal dread of ill treatment at the hands of the cruel and ferocious Assyrians, who would have little respect for an alien prophet, and would probably punish his pretensions with torture and death. But this consideration would have had small influence had his heart been right. He is bold enough when he comes to himself. He knew his duty, but at the present moment determined to avoid its fulfilment. Accordingly, he fled to Joppa and took ship for Tarshish. The providence of God followed him. A violent storm arose, and the crew of the vessel, surmising that it was sent by Heaven as a judgment, cast lots in order to discover who was the guilty person among them. Jonah, being thus designated, confesses the truth, and at his own earnest request is cast into the sea. He is, however, not drowned. A huge fish swallows him, and after three days vomits him forth, and he lands safely on the shore. He then humbly obeys the will of God, sets out, and executes his mission to Nineveh. The king of that city, having heard probably of his strange deliverance from the deep, and believing him to be a messenger from Heaven, ordered a general fast, and by timely repentance averted the threatened doom. Jonah, from national idiosyncrasies, grudging the mercy thus conceded to a heathen nation, showed his displeasure in a marked manner. A better lesson was taught him by a little incident. A gourd, under whose grateful shade he had sat the live-

long day, withered away, and left him exposed to the burning Eastern
sun; and he grieved bitterly over the gourd. Then God shows him how
unreasonable he is in lamenting for this plant, in whose growth he had no
hand, which rose in a night and perished in a night, and yet in being angry
that he, the God of mercy, should have pity on this great city filled with
half a million of souls.

Of the moral corruption of Nineveh, which was the occasion of the
threatened punishment, other prophets speak. "Woe to the bloody city!"
says Nahum (iii. 1); "it is all full of lies and robbery; the prey departeth
not;" "Upon whom hath not thy wickedness passed continually?" (iii.
19). "This is the joyous city," cries Zephaniah (ii. 15), "that dwelt
carelessly, that said in her heart, I am, and there is none else beside me."
"The annals of Assyria," says Layard ('Nineveh and Babylon,' p. 631),
quoted by Trochon, "are nothing but a register of military campaigns,
spoliations, and cruelties. Their monuments display men of a calm and
unmoved ferocity, whose moral and mental qualities are overborne by the
faculties of the lower, brutal nature."

In the book before us we can trace three stages leading to the final
lesson. The first is Jonah's conversion, with its various scenes, ending in
his acquiescence in the Divine call and his second mission. Then follow
the solemn annunciation to Nineveh, and the repentance of king and people.
Lastly we have Jonah's displeasure at the non-accomplishment of the
predicted overthrow, and the better lesson which God vouchsafes to teach
him. These parts, and every portion of them, are replete with most
important truths and types and figures. It is this didactic and symbolical
character that has caused the book to be inserted among the prophets. In
its history there is, indeed, concealed prophecy of the highest importance
which our eyes are open to discern. To the Jew, perhaps, the chief lesson
which it was meant to teach was the capacity of the Gentiles for salvation,
and that God designed to make them partakers thereof. This was a truth
hard to be learned. The Israelites had been often warned that the Gentiles
were ordained to be the punishers of their disobedience and apostasy;
hence they looked upon them as bitter enemies, incapable of salvation,
and cherished all the prophecies concerning their final overthrow, overlooking or misinterpreting those that spoke of their conversion and
entrance into the kingdom of God. The possibility of the admission of
aliens to the privileges of Abraham's seed had now to be enforced. Other
prophets enunciated this great truth in plain words or under dark sayings;
Jonah acted it, expressed it in action. He was forced to show that it was
his duty to sympathize with others who wished to turn to God; to help, not
to impede, their efforts. He is made to exhibit the unreasonableness and
impiety of a spirit like that of the elder brother in the parable of the
prodigal son, who is jealous of the mercy bestowed upon the returning
penitent. In his great candour he places even the heathen sailors in the
category of possible believers: they cry to the Lord, fear him, offer sacri-

fice, and make vows unto him. So, in this view, the history is levelled against the bigotry and exclusiveness of the Jews which come forward so prominently in later times. God has compassion on all men; "In every nation he that feareth him, and worketh righteousness, is accepted with him" (Acts x. 35).

Another object of the history is to teach the nature and efficacy of true repentance. Under this head we are presented with the examples of Jonah himself and the Ninevites. Not that the prophet takes any pains to explain his own conduct or to soften its asperities. He deals with facts and results. The storm, and the lot that points him out as the guilty person on board the ship, awaken in him a sense of his crime in fleeing from his appointed work; the wonderful deliverance vouchsafed fills him with gratitude and remorse, and makes him ready, when restored to his office, to execute the renewed mission as God commanded. The repentance of the people at the mere announcement of Jonah is used by Christ himself to accentuate the obstinate impenitence of the Jews under unusual privileges and advantages (Matt. xii. 41). And to his own contemporaries the prophet, by this history, read a solemn, if silent, warning; he contrasts the submission of these Gentiles, who had so little light and knowledge, with the hardness and obstinacy of the Israelites, who had the Word of God and the light of his presence among them. It is as though he was using to them the words of Christ, "I tell you, except ye repent, ye shall all likewise perish" (Luke xiii. 3), or enforcing the sad comparison that Isaiah (lxv. 1, 2) makes, "I have spread out my hands all the day long unto a rebellious people;" and "I am sought of them that asked not for me; I am found of them that sought me not." But there is another object in this history. It is a type and prophecy of the resurrection of Christ and the issues of that momentous fact. On this feature the Saviour himself shed clear light. "As Jonas was three days and three nights in the whale's belly, so shall the Son of man be three days and three nights in the heart of the earth" (Matt. xii. 40). The Jews themselves taught from this history the resurrection of the body. We can see, however, much more in it. Not merely the resurrection of the flesh, nor merely the resurrection of Christ, are here adumbrated; the Divine plan of salvation is unfolded, as expressed in the words of St. Paul before Festus (Acts xxvi. 23), "That Christ should suffer, and that he should be the first that should rise from the dead, and should show light unto the people, and to the Gentiles." It was not till Jonah had, as it were, died and risen again that he preached repentance to the Ninevites. So Christ had said, "Except a grain of wheat fall into the earth and die, it abideth by itself alone; but if it die, it beareth much fruit" (John xii. 24); "And I, if I be lifted up from the earth, will draw all men unto myself" (John xii. 32). Thus after his resurrection Christ went forth in his Church to make disciples of all nations, and to embrace both Jew and Gentile in the kingdom of God. The mission of Jonah has its place in the gradual development of this design; it gives a sketch of that picture which was one day to be filled up to perfection. By it, on the one hand, the Gentile learned something of the attributes of the true God—his omnipotence, justice, and mercy; and, on the other, the Jew was taught tolerance and charity, and the rigid spirit of pride and exclusiveness received a plain rebuke.

Some critics consider the book to have been written with an apologetic purpose, to show a correct view of the functions of the prophet and the characteristics of prophecy. Many prophecies had remained unfulfilled; many had received a very partial and indefinite fulfilment. Jonah's history emphasizes the truth that all such pre-announcements are conditional, and their issues are liable to be modified and altered by circumstances, and that such variations detract nothing from the Divine nature of the prediction.

It remains to mention another view of the mission of Jonah which considers it to have been of a political rather than a religious character (see Dr. Smith's 'Student's Old Testament History,' p. 468; and Kalisch, 'Bible Studies,' pt. ii.). According to this supposition, Jonah was sent to Nineveh to warn the king against attacking or interfering with Israel. The Assyrians at this time had made frequent inroads upon Syria, and it was probable that they would ere long turn their arms against Samaria. God's forbearance with his rebellious people had been markedly exhibited; lately he had given assurance that "he would not blot out their name from under heaven" (2 Kings xiii. 23), and now he sends a prophet to urge Assyria to desist from its meditated enterprise against Israel. In support of this notion it is argued that the crime of which Nineveh repented could not have been idolatry; for this certainly was not abandoned on account of the preaching of Jonah; and there is no evidence whatever of any religious reformation at this period. The only effect that is admissible is the relinquishment of a design which the king had learned was displeasing to a Divinity whom he saw reason to reverence. But all this is pure assumption. There is not a trace of any political bearing in the whole transaction. Jonah is bidden (ch. i. 2) to "go and cry against Nineveh; for their wickedness is come up" unto the Lord. And when at length he executes his mission, his only word is, "Yet forty days, and Nineveh shall be overthrown" (ch. iii. 4). What need was there of fasting and sackcloth, if the only change desired was the abandonment of a certain military expedition? How could this people be held up as an example of repentance, if they only altered the direction of their arms at the prophet's request? No doubt the lust of conquest, and the cruelty, spoliation, and injustice to which it gave occasion were some of the sins which called for vengeance; but we have no ground for narrowing Jonah's mission to a prohibition of a threatened attack on Israel. The vices of a great and luxurious city, drunk with conquest and exulting in its material strength, were flagrant enough to draw down the vengeance of Heaven; and the providence of God is grandly displayed in offering a hope of repentance to this great people by the word of a prophet from his own chosen nation.

§ II. AUTHOR.

There is no good reason to doubt that the hero, if not the author, of this book was that Jonah, son of Amittai, the prophet whose comforting prophecy was recounted in the days of Jeroboam the Second (2 Kings xiv. 25). The names of Jonah and Amittai occur nowhere else in the Old Testament, and it is incredible that there should have been two distinct persons named Jonah, both prophets, both sons of Amittai. Jonah means "a Dove;" Amittai, "True." Jerome, in his commentary, interprets Jonah to mean "Grieving;" but the former explanation is correct. From the significa-tion of Amittai arose the very improbable opinion that our prophet was the son of the widow of Sarepta, whom Elijah raised to life, because she said, on receiving him restored at the prophet's hands, "Now I know that thou art a man of God, and that the word of the Lord in thy mouth is *truth* (*emeth*) " (1 Kings xvii. 24). Other suggestions, equally unfounded, are that he was the boy who attended Elijah to the wilderness, or the young man who was sent to anoint Jehu, or the husband of the Shunammite woman who extended hospitality to Elisha. Of the facts of Jonah's life nothing is known but what his own book supplies. The notice in Kings adds the only other piece of information about him which we possess, viz. that he was born at Gath-hepher, a place in Zebulun (Josh. xix. 13), about three miles north-east of Nazareth, separated by a wady from the traditional Cana of Galilee. It is identified with the modern village of *Meshed*, and the monument of Neby Yunas, the Prophet Jonah, is still shown there. Another tradition places his tomb at Nineveh, but there is no ground for supposing that, after his mission was accomplished, he stayed on and died there.

As to the actual writer of the book, a grave controversy exists. Most modern critics of the advanced school unhesitatingly deny the traditional view, which regards the prophet as the author, though their arguments are not thoroughly convincing. For instance, doubts have been thrown on the genuineness of the book because it is written throughout in the third person. But there is nothing unusual in this. Classical scholars will recall the 'Anabasis' of Xenophon and the 'Commentaries' of Cæsar, concerning whose genuineness no question has ever been raised, though they are written in the third person. The same may be said of Thucydides, and Josephus, and Frederick the Great, as Hengstenberg has pointed out ('Auth. de Pent.,' ii. 107, etc.). We have many instances of the kind close at hand. Amos, in the midst of his prophecy, inserts the historical interlude concerning his persecution at the hands of Amaziah, in the third person (vii. 12, etc.). There are many passages in other prophets where the same use may be noticed; *e.g.* Isa. vii. 3; xx. 2, 3; Jer. xx. 1, 3; xxvi. 7, etc.; Dan. i.—vii.; Hag. i. 1, 3, 12; ii. 1, 10, 20. Besides this, the candour of the history shows it to have been written by the person whose story it relates. It is true that the book does not profess to have been written by Jonah himself; but surely a Jewish writer, imbued with the national respect for the prophetical character, would never have allowed himself to exhibit a seer in such an unfavourable light. The bigotry, selfishness, petulance, and disobedience, which are so plainly attributed to Jonah, could have been set forth by no one but by himself. His weaknesses and errors are allowed to remain unexplained and unsoftened; the writer makes no attempt to put a favourable construction upon his failings; he leaves the prophet lying under God's reproof. Surely no one but himself would have done this; no one but himself could have shown this unique impartiality, this holy indifference to men's praise or blame. The calm, dispassionate narrative betrays one who is telling the story of his own actions, accurately and humbly, in order to teach a great lesson. The personality is wholly absorbed in this design. He writes for the instruction of others. He records his own weaknesses and prejudices as a warning to other prophets who should be placed in like circumstances. If we can get over other difficulties connected with language, history, etc., we shall not be unreasonable in regarding Jonah as responsible for the narrative, though it may have been modified by a subsequent editor. We may thus regard the story as being the confession of his repentance, the token that he sincerely grieved for his fault, and desired to make amends by exhibiting it in its full heinousness with its punishment and consequences.

We gather the character of Jonah from his own words and actions. He is narrow-minded and prejudiced; a bigoted patriot, incapable of taking a comprehensive view of his unexampled mission. He thinks more of himself and his own reputation than of the moral good of those to whom he is sent; he would rather let the heathen perish than see them repent and spared, and so bring discredit upon his prediction. So that his prophecy held good, he cared nothing for the fate of the Ninevites; compared with the maintenance of the veracity of the prophetical utterance, the overthrow of a heathen city was of small account. Instead of at once obeying, he reasons and looks to consequences. With the utmost trust in God's mercy and loving-kindness, he is not satisfied with blindly following the Divine leading, but must interpose his own self-willed action, as though he had more zeal for God's honour than God himself had. It is not, perhaps, fear for his own safety that holds him back. He is bold enough to be willing to incur death as an atonement for his fault. But in his eager desire to uphold the honour of God, he shrinks from a task which may give occasion for the heathen to exult over a God who threatens but does not strike. Yet, with all his faults, his narrow insularity, his rash impetuosity, his hasty anger, Jonah's is a grand character, and may be compared with that of St. Peter, which in many respects it greatly resembles. His faults were those of his era and his country; his virtues were such as God loves in every age, such as we Christians do well to learn and to emulate. We may grieve for his self-will and capriciousness and bigotry; we may strive to imitate his truth and honesty, his courage and zeal.

§ III. Date.

The date of the historical Prophet Jonah is determined chiefly by internal evidence. We have seen that he is the prophet whose message is mentioned in 2 Kings xiv. 25. Speaking of Jeroboam II., the historian says, "He restored the coast of Israel from the entering of Hamath unto the sea of the plain, according to the word of the Lord God of Israel, which he spake by the hand of his servant Jonah, the son of Amittai, the prophet, which was of Gath-hepher." Of this "word" we have no further knowledge; but it seems to have been uttered or remembered at a time of great national distress; for the account proceeds (vers. 26, 27), " For the Lord saw the affliction of Israel, that it was very bitter: for there was not any shut up, nor left at large, nor was there any helper for Israel. And the Lord said not that he would blot out the name of Israel from under heaven: but he saved them by the hand of Jeroboam the son of Joash." Whether the affliction named belongs to Jeroboam's time or to a period antecedent, it is plain that Jonah prophesied either in the very early part of that king's reign or before his accession. The date of Jeroboam's reign, as now corrected by Assyrian chronology, is B.C. 799—759, or, as others say, B.C. 790—749; and he seems to have won his great victories over the Syrians soon after he came to the throne, when that people were weakened by the constant attacks of the Assyrians. The state of things depicted in ver. 26 of the above-cited chapter is found to have existed in the time of Jehoahaz, when the King of Syria oppressed the Israelites: "Neither did he leave of the people to Jehoahaz but fifty horsemen, and ten chariots, and ten thousand footmen; for the King of Syria had destroyed them, and had made them like the dust by threshing " (2 Kings xiii. 4, 7). Such a crisis called for an assurance of God's protection; and it may well be believed that the prophecy of Jonah was then uttered to comfort the despairing people in their dire necessity. It is thus parallel to the celebrated prediction of Elisha, when, in his last sickness, he sent for Joash, the father of Jeroboam, and gave him promise of three victories over the Syrians (2 Kings xiii. 14—19). Probably after Elisha's death Jonah came into greater prominence as a prophet of the Lord, and his words were treasured up and remembered. From these considerations we are warranted in setting his date at B.C. 800 or a little earlier, among the first of the minor prophets, somewhat senior to Amos and Hosea.

As to the time of his arrival in Nineveh, nothing can be exactly settled. The Assyrian annals record no event which throws light on the matter. From B.C. 810 to 781 the throne was occupied by Vul-nirari, or Iva-lush, or Rimmon-nirari, as his name is variously read by different interpreters. This monarch made various military expeditions, which he recounts in his

annals. Among them he mentions the conquest of the land of the Hittites,
Phœnicia, the cities of Tyre and Sidon, the land of Omri, the kingdom of
Israel, Edom, and the Philistines. These probably merely acknowledged
his superiority by the payment of an annual tribute. His successor, Shalmaneser III. (B.C. 781—770), had great difficulty in maintaining his position
against the rising power of Armenia, though he found time for one attack
on Syria. The following period, during the reigns of Asshur-danil and
Asshur-nirari, or Asshur-lush, up to B.C. 750, was one of internal commotion and distress, and allowed no leisure for foreign conquest. It is very
probable that Jonah's mission was executed towards the close of Jeroboam's
reign, when the Assyrian monarchy was weakened by revolt, and the
country was suffering from plague and famine. Both king and people
were thus more disposed to listen to the warning of a man of God, and to
endeavour to avert imminent ruin by timely, though superficial, repentance.
Possibly, too, the preaching of Jonah may have synchronized with the
famous eclipse which happened on June 15, B.C. 763, as mentioned in the
Assyrian records, and which was regarded as a very evil omen.

Some critics, who cannot away with the miraculous portion of this book,
have endeavoured to throw discredit upon it by assigning to it a date later
than Jonah's time, some giving it a post-exilic origin, others assigning it to
the Maccabean age. They seek for proof of this assertion in the language
employed, and in the use made of the Psalms in Jonah's prayer. The
complete refutation of this hypothesis may be seen in Keil's and Dr. Pusey's
commentaries. We here need only say that the so-called late Aramaisms
cannot be proved to be unknown to the earlier Hebrew, and the only non-
Hebraic word, *taam*, is a Syriac expression which Jonah heard at Nineveh
in the sense of "decree," and introduced into his own narrative. The
phrases in the prayer (ch. ii.), which are also found in the Psalms, are
either taken from those written by David and his contemporaries, which,
of course, were well known long before Jonah's day, or (in the case of the
two in ver. 7 and ver. 2) may have been borrowed by the authors of the
Psalms (Ps. cxlii. 3; cxx. 1) from Jonah. And as to the statement in
ch. iii. 3, that "Nineveh was an exceeding great city," from which Kuenen
deduces the inference that the book was written after its destruction, we
need only remark that the observation is introduced parenthetically, to
explain the reason for the time that the prophet took in traversing it, and
that it merely asserts that, at the period of Jonah's visit, Nineveh was of
large extent. Such criticisms have no weight, and, as Dr. Pusey says, perhaps somewhat too harshly, "are founded, not on the study of the language,
but on unbelief."

§ IV. General Character.

The Book of Jonah is a history, not a prophecy; it is inserted among
the prophets, partly because its author bears this title (2 Kings xiv. 25), but
chiefly because of its didactic and symbolical purpose. But in it there is

no moralizing, no reflection; it is simple narrative, verging here and there into poetry, as in the prayer from the fish's belly, and where the subject suits such variation. The tale is told graphically, and has quite a dramatic interest, advancing in regular stages to the conclusion, and leaving an impression upon the mind as though its various scenes had been enacted before the eyes of the reader. There is not a word too much; all that is essential to the understanding of the transaction is said, and nothing more. There is no trace of additions, interpolations, various authorities. The prayer (ch. ii.) bears the stamp of genuineness, being not a cry of repentance or a petition for preservation, which a forger or romancer would have introduced, but a thanksgiving, an expression of hope and trust, which alone suits the prophet's character (Schegg). There is a wonderful simplicity in the narrative, though it deals largely with the supernatural. The miracles of the fish and "the gourd" are introduced naturally. Such interpositions of God need no explanation in Jonah's view; they are the not unusual workings of Providence, such as he had heard of in the case of Elijah, such as happened often to the great Prophet Elisha. All is unforced, uniform, plain; vivid, indeed, and picturesque, but without effort, and effective rather from its truth, reality, and naturalness, than from elevation of language or rhetorical artifice.

The miraculous element in the book has led many critics to doubt its historical character, and to consider it as romance, allegory, or parable. The miracles, they say, are so prodigious, so wanting in sufficient motive, as to be utterly incredible, and to prove that the writer manifestly intends his work to be regarded as a fiction with a didactic purpose, like some of those writings which are preserved in our Apocrypha. Others see in it only a dream; others, again, regard it as a Jewish adaptation of a Greek or Babylonian myth; others explain away the supernatural portion of the story, as *e.g.* that Jonah was saved by a vessel which was called, or bore as its emblem, a sea-monster. Against all these suggestions we must place the fact that the work comes before us as history; and we need very strong arguments to dislodge us from this position. Such, however, are not produced; and we should have heard nothing of them were it not for the unbelief in the supernatural which underlies all such criticism, or a tendency to reject, *primâ facie*, all narratives which do not meet the standard of evidence which modern critics set up and worship. Of course, there is in itself nothing repugnant to reverence in considering the book as an inspired allegory intended to set forth certain great spiritual truths, as, for instance, the temporary death of the Jewish nation and its resurrection anew to a national existence (Wright, 'Biblical Essays,' p. 70); but does the work confirm such view? We think not.

In the first place, it is plain that the Jews themselves regarded the book as historical. Tobit (xiv. 4—6, 15) bases his advice to his son upon the certainty of the fulfilment of Jonah's prediction. Josephus ('Ant.,' ix. 10. 1, 2) recounts the story as containing all that is known of the Prophet

Jonah. The details are quite in keeping with the localities and the date of the narrative. This will appear in the course of the Exposition. The mention of the size of Nineveh and the extent of its population is proved by recent investigations to be perfectly correct. Could our blessed Lord have referred to Jonah's incarceration in the fish's belly as a sign of his own three-days' sojourn in the grave, had the story been an allegory and nothing more? Could he further have used the comparison of the Ninevites' conduct with that of the men of his own time, had the former been an imaginary people existing, for the nonce, only in fiction? Critics may say that Christ was speaking uncritically and merely using an illustration from a well-known allegory (comp. Ladd, 'Doctrine of Scripture,' i. 67, etc.), but they forget the full bearing of this reference. As Perowne puts it forcibly, "The future Judge is speaking words of solemn warning to those who shall hereafter stand convicted at his bar. Intensely real he would make the scene in anticipation to them, as it was real, if then present, to himself. And yet we are to suppose him to say that ... the fictitious characters of a parable shall be arraigned at the same bar with the living men of that generation."

Again, if the book is a parable, why is the didactic purpose not presented more prominently and directly? If an allegory, can any example be produced of a sacred canonical writer using prodigious miracles as the vehicle of his teaching? In a narrative of facts the psalm (ch. ii.) is introduced naturally; it is given as composed by Jonah under the circumstances related. In an allegory it is quite out of place, marring the unity of the work, and intruding an element which does not harmonize with the other parts. And if a person had to be selected on whom to hang this fictitious narrative, is it conceivable that the Jewish author should have fixed on an eminent and well-known prophet to represent in so unfavourable a light? Would he have been so wanting in common reverence as to affix to a celebrated man of God these traits of disobedience, waywardness, folly, narrowness, and peevishness? Plainly, the only way to account for the prophet being represented in this light is to consider that he acted in the way mentioned, and that the book is the plain narrative of his conduct, whether in its present form written wholly by himself, or partly by some later editor from his record.

Lastly, the miraculous portion of the story is not dragged in unnecessarily, and is not unparalleled by other transactions in Holy Scripture. Jonah's mission was unusual and most important; both the prophet himself and those with whom he was brought into contact needed to be convinced that God's providence was ordering all things, and that the powers of nature and the destinies of men were at his absolute disposal. The storm, the fish, the repentance, the gourd, are parts of this Divine lesson; and where God interferes there must needs be the supernatural. We must doubt the miraculous element in the histories of Elijah and Elisha, if we dispute the reality of the wonders in the biography of Jonah.

That was an age of miracles. God was manifesting his power against idolatry, and showing himself as the Guide and Support of his servants. Some prophets proclaimed him by word, some by action. Among the latter Jonah takes his natural place. Assyria had a great future before it. It is not improbable that on its repentance at the preaching of Jonah depended its continued existence and its subsequent pre-eminence. It was ordained that the Semitic people of Assyria should prevail over the children of Ham in Egypt. This would not have been the case had Nineveh's fall not been postponed for a time. Though Jonah saw not the full bearing of his mission, and, regarding it in a narrow, prejudiced spirit, tried to avoid its execution, really it was a factor in the world's history, and momentous issues hung thereon. Hence arose the extraordinary exhibition of supernatural agencies. As in the era of Moses and Elijah, and in the early days of Christianity, a great crisis demanded a baring of the Almighty's arm and evident tokens of his interference in the affairs of men.

§ V. Literature.

The Book of Jonah has been published in Chaldee, Syriac, Æthiopic, and Arabic, with glossaries by Professor W. Wright. Among commentaries on the book may be mentioned those of Ephraem Syrus; Basil; Theophylact; Calvin, 'Lectures;' J. Brentius; Luther; J. Ferus (1554, often reprinted); Dereser (Bonn, 1786); Kaulen, 'Lib. Jonæ Proph.' (1862); Bishop Hooper, 'Sermons;' Archbishop Abbott, 'An Exposition' (1600, 1845); Gerhard, 'Annotationes' (Jena, 1676); Pfeiffer, 'Prælectiones' (Leipzig, 1686); Leusden, with the commentaries of Jarchi, Aben-Ezra, Kimchi, and Jophi (Utrecht, 1692); Von der Hardt, 'Ænigmata Prisci Orbis;' Helmstad (1723); Grimm, 'Der Proph. Jon. übersetzt' (Düsseldorf, 1789); H. Martin (London, 1866); W. Drake, 'Notes;' Redford, 'Studies' (1885); Kleinert (Bonn, 1871); Archdeacon Perowne, in 'The Cambridge Bible for Schools.'

§ VI. Arrangement of the Book in Sections.

The four chapters into which the book is divided make four natural divisions of the whole work.

Part I. (Ch. i.) The mission of Jonah. His disobedience and punishment.

§ 1. (Ch. i. 1—3.) Jonah is sent to Nineveh; he tries to avoid the mission, and takes ship to Tarshish.

§ 2. (Ch. i. 4—10.) A great storm arises, which the crew discover to have been sent on account of Jonah's sin.

§ 3. (Ch. i. 11—16.) At his own request, Jonah is cast into the sea, which immediately becomes calm.

§ 4. (Ch. i. 17.) He is swallowed alive by a great fish, and remains in its belly three days and three nights.

Part II. (Ch. ii.) Jonah's prayer and deliverance.

§ 1. (Ch. ii. 1—9.) Jonah, in the belly of the fish, offers a prayer of thanksgiving for his rescue from death by drowning, in which he sees a pledge of further deliverance.

§ 2. (Ch. ii. 10.) The fish casts him up on the shore.

Part III. (Ch. iii.) Jonah's preaching in Nineveh; the repentance of the Ninevites.

§ 1. (Ch. iii. 1—3.) Sent again to Nineveh, Jonah obeys the command.

§ 2. (Ch. iii. 4.) He delivers his message.

§ 3. (Ch. iii. 5—9.) The Ninevites believe God and repent.

§ 4. (Ch. iii. 10.) The threatened destruction is averted.

THE BOOK OF JONAH

EXPOSITION.

CHAPTER I.

Vers. 1—17.—Part I. The Mission of Jonah. His Disobedience and Punishment.

Vers. 1—3.—§ 1. *Jonah is sent to Nineveh to cry against it; but he tries to avoid the mission, and to this end takes ship to Tarshish.*

Ver. 1.—**Now;** or, *and.* Some have argued from this commencement that the Book of Jonah is a fragment, the continuation of a larger work; but it is a common formulary, linking together revelations and histories, and is continually used in the Old Testament at the beginning of independent works; *e.g.* Josh. i. 1; Judg. i. 1; 1 Sam. i. 1; Esth. i. 1; Ezek. i. 1. **Jonah the son of Amittai** (2 Kings xiv. 25). (See Introduction, § II.)

Ver. 2.—**Nineveh,** the capital of the kingdom of Assyria, is first mentioned in Gen. x. 11, as founded by Nimrod. It stood on the left bank of the river Tigris, where it is joined by the Khosr, opposite to the present town of Mosul. The Assyrians had already become known in Syria. In B.C. 854 Shalmaneser II. had defeated at Karkar twelve kings confederate against him, among whom is reckoned Ahab King of Israel. Long before his time, Tiglath-Pileser I. had made a great expedition to the west, captured a town at the foot of Lebanon, and reached the coast of the Mediterranean Sea. Jehu was compelled to pay tribute to the Assyrians; and Rimmon-nirari, who reigned from B.C. 810 to 781, held the suzerainty of Phœnicia, Samaria, Edom, and Philistia. Jonah, therefore, knew well what his country might expect at the hands of this people. **That great city.** It is thus called in ch. iii. 2, 3; iv. 11; and the epithet is added here in order to show to Jonah the importance of his mission. The size of Nineveh is variously estimated according to the sense attached to the name "Nineveh." This appellation may be restricted to Nineveh proper, or it may comprise the four cities which lay close together in the immediate neighbourhood of each other, and whose remains are now known as the mounds of *Kouyunjik,* on the south-west, directly opposite to Mosul; *Nimrud,* about eighteen miles to the south-east; *Karamless,* twelve miles to the north; and *Khorsabad,* the most northerly, about the same distance both from Karamless and Kouyunjik. Khorsabad, however, was not built till some hundred years after Jonah's time (Schrader, 'Keilinschr.,' p. 448). These cities are contained in an irregular parallelogram of some sixty miles in circumference. The following account of Nineveh proper is derived from Professor Rawlinson, 'Ancient Monarchies,' i. 252, etc.: "The ruins consist of two principal mounds, Nebbi-yunus and Kouyunjik. The Kouyunjik mound, which lies nearly half a mile north-west of the others, is very much the more considerable of the two. Its shape is an irregular oval, elongated to a point towards the north-east. The surface is nearly flat; the sides slope at a steep angle, and are furrowed with numerous ravines worn in the soft material by the rains of some thirty centuries. The greatest height above the plain is ninety feet, and the area is estimated at a hundred acres. It is an artificial eminence, computed to contain 14,500,000 tons of earth, and on it were erected the palaces and temples of the Assyrian monarchs. The mound of Nebbi-yunus is at its base nearly triangular, and covers an area of nearly forty acres. It is loftier, and its sides are more precipitous than Kouyunjik, especially on the west, where it abutted on the wall of the city. The mass of earth is calculated at six and a half millions of tons. These two vast mounds are both in the same line, and abutted on the western wall of the city, which was some two and a half miles in length. Anciently it seems to have immediately overhung the Tigris, but the river has now receded to the west, leaving a plain of nearly a mile in width between its bank and the old rampart which evidently once followed the course of the river-bank. The western wall is joined at right angles by the northern rampart which runs in a straight line for seven thousand feet. At its other extremity the western wall forms a very obtuse angle with the southern, which impends over a deep ravine, and runs in a straight line for about a thousand yards, when it meets the eastern wall, which is the longest and the least regular of the four. The entire length of this side is sixteen thousand feet, or above three miles. It is divided into two portions by the stream of the Khosr-su; which, coming from the north-west, finds its way through the city and then across the low plain to the Tigris. The town is thus of an oblong shape, and the circuit of its walls is somewhat less than eight miles, and the area which they include is eighteen hundred acres. This, at the computation of something less than one hundred inhabitants per acre, would ascribe to Nineveh a population of one hundred and seventy-five thousand souls" (Rawlinson, 'Anc. Mon.,' i. ch. i.). Cry against it. The message is given in ch. iii. 4. Thus the knowledge of the true God is made known among the Gentiles. Their wickedness; *i.e.*, as Pusey notes, their evil-doing towards others, as in Nah. iii. 19 (see Introduction, § I.). Is come up before me, and appeals for punishment, as Gen. iv. 10; xviii. 20, 21; Septuagint, Ἀνέβη ἡ κραυγή τῆς κακίας αὐτῆς πρὸς μέ, "The cry of its wickedness is come up unto me."

Ver. 3.—Tarshish; probably, *Tartessus*, a Phœnician city on the south coast of Spain, and therefore in the opposite direction to Nineveh. He was sent to the far east; he flees to the distant west. From the presence of the Lord; literally, *from the face of Jehovah*. This may mean, from God's special presence in Jerusalem or the Holy Land, as banishment from Canaan is called "casting out of his sight" (2 Kings xvii. 20, 23; xxiii. 27); or, from serving the Lord as his minister (Deut. x. 8), Jonah preferring to renounce his office as prophet rather than execute his mission. The former seems the most natural explanation of the phrase. Kimchi says that Jonah supposed that the spirit of prophecy would not extend beyond the land of Israel. He could never have thought to escape from God's all-seeing eye. His repugnance to the duty imposed upon him arose partly from national prejudice, which

made him loth to interfere in Gentile business, and partly, as he himself says (ch. iv. 2), because he feared God's compassion would spare the Ninevites on their repentance, and that thus his prediction would be discredited, and mercy shown to heathens already inimical to Israel, if not known to him as the future conquerors of his people. Joppa. This is the modern *Jaffa* (called Japho in Josh. xix. 46), a town on the sea-coast thirty miles in a north-westerly direction from Jerusalem. "Jaffa," says Dr. Thomson ('The Land and the Book,' p. 8, etc.), "is one of the oldest cities in the world. It was given to Dan in the distribution of the land by Joshua, and it has been known to history ever since. It owes its existence to the low ledge of rocks which extends into the sea from the extremity of the little cape on which the city stands, and forms a small harbour. Insignificant as it is, and insecure, yet, there being no other on all this coast, it was sufficient to cause a city to spring up around it even in the earliest times, and to sustain its life through numberless changes of dynasties, races, and religions, down to the present hour. It was, in fact, the only harbour of any notoriety possessed by the Jews throughout the greater part of their national existence. To it the timber for both the temples of Jerusalem was brought from Lebanon; and no doubt a lucrative trade in cedar and pine was always carried on through it with the nations who had possession of that goodly mountain. Through it, also, nearly all the foreign commerce of the Jews was conducted, until the artificial port of Cæsarea was built by Herod. . . . The harbour, however, is very inconvenient and insecure. Vessels of any considerable burden must lie out in the open roadstead—a very uneasy berth at all times; and even a moderate wind will oblige them to slip their cables and run out to sea, or seek anchorage at Haifa, sixty miles distant. . . . The roadstead is liable to sudden and unexpected storms, which stir up a tumultuous sea in a very short time. . . . The landing also is most inconvenient, and often extremely dangerous. More boats upset, and more lives are lost in the breakers at the north end of the ledge of rocks that defend the inner harbour than anywhere else on this coast." Went down into it; ἀνέβη [ἐνέβη, Alex.] εἰς αὐτό, "went up into it" (Septuagint). Went on board; or, as Jerome says, sought a hiding-place in the ship (comp. ver. 5). With them. With the crew. Jonah had told them (ver. 10) that he was flying from God's service, but, knowing and caring nothing about Jehovah, they took him on board when he paid his fare, and thought nothing of his private reasons for joining them

Vers. 4—10.—§ 2. *Jonah's foolish flight is arrested.* In the midst of his fancied security God sends a great storm, and the ship is placed in imminent jeopardy. The crew try all means to save the ship, and at length cast lots to discover by this means for whose sake the tempest has been sent. The lot points out Jonah as the guilty person.

Ver. 4.—Sent out; Septuagint, ἐξήγειρε, "raised;" literally, *cast forth*, or *hurled*, a great wind, like the Euroclydon of Acts xxvii. 14, and what is called nowadays a Levanter. Pusey quotes Josephus's account of the harbour of Joppa and the neighbouring sea, which, he says, is rendered very dangerous by the sudden rise of "the black north wind" ('Bell. Jud.,' iii. 9. 3). Here we see wind and storm fulfilling God's word (Ps. cxlviii. 8). As Tertullian says—

"Si Dominum in terris fugiens, invenit in undis."

"Flying the Lord on earth, he found him in the sea."

Was like to be broken; literally, *thought to be dashed in pieces.* Wordsworth contrasts the living consciousness and apprehension of the ship with the lethargy of the prophet now lying fast asleep in the hold (ver. 5). Septuagint, ἐκινδύνευε τοῦ συντριβῆναι, "was in danger of being broken up."

Ver. 5.—The mariners (*mallachim*). Those who have to do with the *salt* sea. The word is used by Ezekiel (xxvii. 9, 27, 29). **Cried every man unto his god.** They were either Phœnicians from different localities, or men of various nations; hence the multiplicity of their gods. The heathen are represented throughout the book as devout and sincere according to their lights. **They cast forth the wares;** Septuagint, ἐκβολὴν ἐποιήσαντο τῶν σκευῶν, "cast out the furniture, or wares," as Acts xxvii. 18, 19; Vulgate, *miserunt vasa.* They threw overboard probably both all spare tackling and movables, and the cargo. The freight may have been corn, which was exported in considerable quantities from Joppa (comp. Ezek. xxvii. 17), or manufactured articles from Tyre, which were exchanged with Spain for silver and other metals. **To lighten it of them;** literally, *to lighten from against them;* i.e. to ease the ship of its burden, or to ease them of their trouble, as Exod. xviii. 22. The LXX. takes the former interpretation, τοῦ κουφισθῆναι ἀπ' αὐτῶν, "that it might be lightened of them;" Vulgate, *ut alleviaretur ab eis.* **The sides of the ship.** The innermost parts (*interiora*, Vulgate) of the ship; τὴν κοίλην (Septuagint); "the hold" (comp. 1

Sam. xxiv. 3). Jonah hid himself there before the storm arose. The Hebrew word for "ship" (*sephinah*) is found nowhere else, and, probably from its derivation (*saphan*, "to cover"), implies that the vessel was decked. **He lay, and was fast asleep;** ἐκάθευδε, καὶ ἔρεγχε, "was asleep and snoring" (Septuagint); *dormiebat sopore gravi* (Vulgate). The word used implies a very deep sleep, as that of Sisera (Judg. iv. 21) or of the Assyrians (Ps. lxxvi. 6). He was fatigued and worn out with mental anxiety, and now being, as he thought, secure, and longing for solitude, he lay down to sleep, unconscious of danger. Contrast this sleep in the storm with that of Christ (Mark iv. 38), and that of the apostles who slept for sorrow (Luke xxii. 45).

Ver. 6.—The shipmaster; literally, *the chief of the ropemen;* Vulgate, *gubernator;* Septuagint, ὁ πρωρεύς, "the look-out man." The captain. **What meanest thou, O sleeper?** How canst thou sleep so soundly when our danger is so imminent? If thou canst help us in no other way, at least ask the aid of Heaven. It was the duty of a prophet of the Lord to take the lead in prayer; but here the prophet's stupor is rebuked by the heathen's faith. **Call upon thy God.** The sailors' prayers had not been answered, and they arouse Jonah, noting something special about him, perhaps his prophet's dress, or observing that he was an Israelite, and therefore a worshipper of Jehovah, of whose power they had heard. **If so be that God will think upon us.** They use the word "God" with the article, *ha Elohim,* as if they had, in spite of their polytheism, a dim notion of one supreme Deity. Vulgate, *Si forte recogitet Deus de nobis;* Septuagint, ὅπως διασώσῃ ὁ Θεὸς ἡμᾶς, "that God may save us." From the apparent use of the Hebrew word (*ashath*) in Jer. v. 28 in the sense of "shining," some translate here, "if perchance God will shine upon us," *i.e.* be favourable to us. But the meaning given in the Anglican Version is best supported. So the psalmist says, "The Lord thinketh upon me" (Ps. xl. 17), implying that God succours and defends him.

Ver. 7—Finding the storm still violent, the crew come to the conclusion that it is sent by Heaven in punishment of some crime committed by one on board; and they proceed to cast lots to discover the guilty person. Jonah doubtless had meantime complied with the captain's request, but, as the sailors saw, without visible effect. The belief that temporal calamities are often connected with the presence of culprits, and are sent in judgment, is found in classical authors. Thus Plautus, 'Rudens,' ii. 6. 21—

"Pol minume miror, navis si fracta est tibi,
    Scelus te et sceleste parta quæ vexit bona."

"Little I wonder if the ship is wrecked
    Which carries thee and thy ill-gotten
    wealth."

(Comp. Æschylus, 'Electr.,' 1354; 'Theb.,'
598; Horat., 'Carm.,' iii. 2. 26, etc.) The
misfortune of the Israelites at Ai was consequent on the sin of Achan (Josh. vii.).
Let us cast lots. (On the Christian view of
"lots," see Dr. Pusey's Commentary, pp. 270,
271.) Jerome says here, "The fugitive was
taken by lot, not by virtue of the lots,
especially of the lots of heathen men, but by
the will of him who guided the uncertain
lots." **For whose cause;** Septuagint, τίνος
ἕνεκεν. The unusual nature of the tempest
showed them that it was sent in judgment.
Commentators cite the story of Diagoras told
by Cicero ('De Nat. Deor.,' iii. 37). **The lot
fell upon Jonah.** Prov. xvi. 33, "The lot
is cast into the lap; but the whole disposing
thereof is of the Lord" (comp. 1 Sam. x.
20, etc.; xiv. 41; Acts i. 26).

Ver. 8.—The mariners having, as they supposed, discovered the culprit, proceed calmly
to investigate his guilt; amid the roaring of
the tempest and the peril that surrounded
them, they give him every opportunity of
clearing himself or confessing his crime.
For whose cause. Some manuscripts of the
Hebrew and the Greek omit this clause as
unnecessary; but, as Keil remarks, it is not
superfluous, the sailors thereby wishing to
induce Jonah to confess his guilt with his
own mouth. In their excitement they crowd
question upon question, asking him about
his business, his journey, his country, his
parentage. Jerome notes the pregnant
brevity of these inquiries, and compares
Virgil, 'Æneid,' viii. 112, etc.—

"Juvenes, quæ causa subegit
Ignotas tentare vias? quo tenditis? inquit.
Qui genus? unde domo? pacemne huc fertis
    an arma?"

" Warriors, what cause constrained you thus
        to tempt
A path untrodden? Whither are ye bound?
What is your race? Where dwell ye?
    Peace or war
Come ye to bring?"

(Comp. Hom., 'Od.,' i. 170.) **What is thine
occupation?** His occupation, they thought,
might have been one to excite the wrath of
the gods; or his country and family might
have been exposed to the hatred of Heaven;
hence the succeeding questions.

Ver. 9. **I am an Hebrew.** This is the
name used by foreigners in speaking of
Israelites, or by Israelites in speaking of
themselves to Gentiles (see Gen. xiv. 13;
xxxix. 14; xli. 12; Exod. i. 16; 1 Sam. iv.

6, for the former use; and for the latter,
Gen. xl. 15; Exod. ii. 7; iii. 18). Convinced that God had miraculously pointed
him out as the culprit on whose account the
storm was sent, and goaded by the stings
of conscience, Jonah loses all his previous
indecision and spiritual stupor, and in
a manly and straightforward way confesses
the truth without disguise. The LXX.,
reading differently, renders, Δοῦλος Κυρίου
εἰμὶ ἐγώ, "A servant of Jehovah am I."
This makes a tautological statement with
the next words, and leaves one of the
sailors' questions unanswered. **I fear the
Lord.** I worship, reverence (σέβομαι, Septuagint) Jehovah, who is not a local deity like
the false gods whom you adore, but the
Creator of heaven and earth, the Maker and
Ruler of sea and dry land. So Abraham
calls the Lord the God of heaven (Gen.
xxiv. 7), and Daniel (ii. 37, 44) uses the
same expression (comp. Ps. xcvi. 5; Jer.
x. 11).

Ver. 10.—**Exceedingly afraid.** They understand now the greatness of Jehovah and the
terrible risk incurred by one who offends
him. There was a widespread acknowledgment of the power of Jehovah among the
heathen (see Exod. xv. 15; Josh. v. 1;
1 Sam. iv. 7; and comp. Judith v. 21). **Why
hast thou done this?** better, *What is this that
thou hast done?* (Gen. iii. 13). This is not
a question of inquiry, for he had already
told them that he had fled from the presence of the Lord; but rather an exclamation of horror and amazement at his folly
and sin. That one who worshipped the
Almighty Creator should disobey his command seemed to them outrageous and
inexcusably criminal. The prophet does
not spare himself in giving the history of
the transaction. To be thus rebuked by
heathen sailors must have added to the
poignancy of his remorse. **The presence
of the Lord** (see note on ver. 3).

Vers. 11—16.—§ 3. *On hearing Jonah's
confession, the sailors appeal to him, as a
worshipper of Jehovah, to tell them what to
do to him that the storm may cease. He
bids them cast him into the sea, which, after
some demur and after renewed efforts to
escape, they proceed to do. Upon this the
storm immediately abates.*

Ver. 11.—**What shall we do unto thee?**
They recognize that the tempest was sent
as a judgment on account of Jonah's sin; at
the same time, believing him to be a prophet
of Jehovah, under whose wrath they were
suffering, they ask his advice in this
emergency; if it was a crime to receive him,
what shall they do to him to expiate the
offence and to appease the anger of God?

That the sea may be calm unto us; literally, *may be silent from upon us*, so as no longer to bear down upon us (comp. Mark iv. 39). **Wrought, and was tempestuous**; literally, *was going and was tempestuous*; Septuagint, Ἐπορεύετο καὶ ἐξήγειρε μᾶλλον κλύδωνα, "The sea was moving and lifting the surge still more;" Vulgate, *ibat et intumescebat*. That is, according to the Hebrew idiom, "grew more and more tempestuous" (comp. Exod. xix. 19; Prov. iv. 18).

Ver. 12.—Jonah, brought to a better mind, perhaps divinely inspired, pronounces his own sentence. "I know," he says, "that the fault is mine, and deserves death, therefore **take me up, and cast me forth into the sea**." He will not be his own executioner, but will patiently bear a death righteously inflicted by others, whose safety he was endangering by his continued presence.

Ver. 13.—The generous sailors, however, are loth to execute this sentence on a prophet of the Lord, and make a supreme effort to reach the land, and thus obviate this severe alternative. **Rowed hard**; literally, *digged* (Job xxiv. 16; Ezek. xii. 7); Septuagint, παρεβιάζοντο, "used violent efforts." They endeavoured to force their way through the waves with oars, as the use of sails was impracticable. The expression is like the classical phrases, *infindere sulcos, scindere freta, arare aquas*, and our "to plough the main." **To the land**; *to get them back to land*. The wind was off shore, and they had taken down the sails, and tried to row back to the harbour. Τοῦ ἐπιστρέψαι πρὸς τὴν γῆν, "to return to the land" (Septuagint). **The sea wrought** (see note on ver. 11).

Ver. 14.—**They cried unto the Lord.** They prayed no longer to their gods, as before (ver. 5), but unto Jehovah, the God of Jonah. **Let us not perish for this man's life.** Let us not incur death for taking this man's life. They seem to know something of the Noachic law that punished murder (Gen. ix. 5, 6). **Lay not upon us innocent blood.** Charge us not with the guilt of shedding innocent blood (Deut. xxi. 8). **For thou, O Lord, hast done as it pleased thee** (1 Sam. iii. 18). The whole affair has happened according to thy will. The tempest, the lot, the sentence, are all the working of thy providence. The prophet throughout brings into prominence the contrast between the behaviour of these heathen and his own, and would teach his nation a lesson thereby.

Ver. 15.—**They took up**, with a certain reverence. **Ceased from her raging**; literally, *stood from its anger*; Septuagint, ἔστη ἐκ τοῦ σάλου αὐτῆς, "stood from its tossing." The sudden cessation of the storm showed that it had been sent on Jonah's account, and that the crew had not sinned by exe-

cuting the sentence upon him. Usually it takes some time for the swell to cease after the wind has sunk: here there was suddenly a great calm (Matt. viii. 26).

Ver. 16.—**Feared the Lord.** They recognized the supernatural element in the transaction, and conceived an awe and fear of Jehovah, who had wrought these wonders. **Offered a sacrifice unto the Lord.** Many commentators think that they sacrificed on reaching shore, as they had thrown the cargo overboard, and would have had no animal to offer. The Chaldee renders accordingly, "They said that they would offer sacrifices." But the text implies that they sacrificed immediately on the cessation of the storm. They may naturally have had some animal on board fit for offering. **And made vows.** Vowed to make other offerings when it was in their power. Henderson compares Virgil, ' Æneid,' iii. 403, etc.—

"Quin, ubi transmissæ steterint trans
    æquora classes
Et positis aris jam vota in litore solves."

"And when thy fleet hath safely crossed
    the seas,
And, raising altars on the shore, thy vows
Thou shalt perform."

It has been supposed that these sailors embraced Judaism and became proselytes. At any rate, they showed themselves in the light of believers on this occasion.

Ver. 17.—§ 4. *Cast into the sea, Jonah is swallowed alive by a great fish, in whose belly he remains unharmed three days and three nights.* **Had prepared**; Septuagint, προσέταξε, "appointed;" so in ch. iv. 6, 7, 8 (comp. Job vii. 3; Dan. i. 10, 11). The fish was not created then and there, but God so ordered it that it should be at the place and should swallow Jonah. The prophet seems, from some expressions in his psalm (ch. ii. 5), to have sunk to the bottom of the sea before he was swallowed by the fish. **A great fish**; Septuagint, κῆτος (Matt. xii. 40). There is nothing in the word to identify the intended animal, and to call it "a whale" is simply a mistranslation. The white shark of the Mediterranean (*Carcharias vulgaris*), which sometimes measures twenty-five feet in length, has been known to swallow a man whole, and even a horse. This may have been the "great fish" in the text (see Dr. Pusey on Jonah, pp. 257, etc.). **Was in the belly of the fish.** God used the natural agency of the fish, but the preservation of Jonah's life in the animal's belly is plainly supernatural. It is, indeed, analogous to the life of the child in its mother's womb; but it has besides a miraculous element which is unique, unless it was an actual death and revivification, as in the case of Lazarus. Also God ordained this transaction as a type of the resurrection of Christ. **Three days and three nights;** *i.e.,* according to Hebrew usage, parts of the days and nights; *i.e.* one whole day, and parts of the day before and after this. Jonah was released on the third day (comp. Matt. xii. 40 with 1 Cor. xv. 4; and Esth. iv. 16 with **v. 1).** The historical nature of this occur-rence is substantiated by Christ's reference to it as a figure of his own burial and resurrection. The antitype confirms the truth of the type. It is not credible that Christ would use a mere legendary tale, with no historical basis, to confirm his most solemn statement concerning the momentous fact of his resurrection.

HOMILETICS.

Ver. 2.—*A city's sin.* By its very nature sin is individual, personal; for it is the estrangement of the spiritual being and life from God. Yet, as men live in communities, and as these communities possess moral qualities and habits determined by the character of the component units, there is such a thing as the sin of a tribe, of a city, of a nation. This is more obvious when it is remembered that states are personified in their rulers and representatives, whose words and actions must be taken as those of the community at large. The Scriptures, from the record of the Tower of Babel downwards, exhibit national responsibility as connected with national error and unfaithfulness. Among the lessons of this Book of Jonah, this lesson regarding a nation's moral life and accountability is not the least valuable.

I. A CITY'S SIN IS COMPATIBLE WITH ITS POLITICAL GREATNESS. Nineveh was "that great city." It was situated upon the noble river Tigris; it boasted a splendid and ancient history; it was of enormous extent, being, according to the historians, eighteen leagues in circumference; it had a population reckoned by hundreds of thousands; in short, it was one of the greatest and most famous of the cities of the ancient East, and was the capital of one of the most powerful of kingdoms. Recent discoveries have familiarized us with the civic life of the population of the city of Nineveh. Yet the wickedness of Nineveh was great. Magnitude, population, wealth, luxury, splendour, power,—all are, alas! consistent with forgetfulness of God, and with rebellion against his authority who is King of kings and Lord of all the nations upon earth. How signally was this the case with pagan Rome! And are there not cities in professedly Christian lands, the abodes of power and of pleasure, whose sin cries aloud unto God?

II. A CITY'S SIN IS OFTEN DISREGARDED BY HUMAN OBSERVERS, AND EVEN BY RULERS. The citizens take pride in their "gorgeous palaces," their "solemn temples," in magnificent public works, in stately ceremonies, in all the complicated apparatus of civilization, luxury, refinement, and enjoyment. The men in authority are content if outward order is observed, if regulations of police are respected, if the reports of health are satisfactory, if trade flourishes. But it is often forgotten that beneath this outward show of prosperity there may exist moral corruption and religious indifference, or even defiant infidelity. God may not be glorified; he may be hated and disobeyed. And yet no concern may be awakened, no contrition felt.

III. A CITY'S SIN IS OBSERVED BY THE ALL-SEEING GOD. What graphic language is this, "Their wickedness is come up before me"! Under this old Hebrew idiom a great religious truth is discernible. Nothing escapes the notice of him who searcheth the hearts of the children of men. Not only so. God looks upon the sins of the citizens, not as a statistician or a politician might look. He is *grieved* with men's irreligion; he is "angry," *i.e.,* "with the wicked every day." We must not attribute to the Deity any emotions which would be unworthy of a human ruler. But it is not derogatory to God, it is honouring him, to think of him as distressed and dissatisfied with human rebellion, and to remember that his regard is that of a wise and righteous Ruler, who is concerned for the spiritual state of those whom he rules for their own good and for his glory.

IV. A CITY'S SIN MUST BE MET BY A RIGHTEOUS TESTIMONY, REBUKE, AND WARNING. It must not be forgotten that men's sins are often attributable to evil example, to common custom, to the force of habit, to forgetfulness and carelessness. For this reason is it needful that the preacher of righteousness should exhibit a just and lofty standard of national and individual virtue; that he should faithfully expose and denounce prevailing errors, follies, and injustice; and that he should remind men of their amenability to the tribunal of an Omniscient and Almighty Ruler. **There is too** little of this frank and fearless treatment of social corruption; the pulpit is to blame for this; and it is to be desired that Christian preachers should hear the Word of the Lord bidding them go and "cry against" the wickedness of great cities, and warn the citizens of the ruin they are bringing upon themselves. And above all is it important that the wicked should be summoned to repentance, and that the penitent should be directed to that Saviour who is the assurance of Divine pity, and the channel of Divine forgiveness, to all who come to him with contrite sorrow and with lowly faith.

Ver. 3.—*Fleeing from the Lord.* There is something wonderfully simple in this language, and something wonderfully childish and *naive* in the action here described. Yet when Jonah, who should have gone eastward, turned his face towards the west, when he went down to the port of Joppa and took ship for Tarshish, though he was acting in a way sinful in itself and most disastrous for him, he was teaching for all time and for all readers of Scripture a lesson of human infirmity which is to us chiefly precious as preparing the way for a lesson of human repentance and of Divine forgiveness and acceptance.

I. THE MOTIVE WHICH LEADS MEN TO WISH TO FLEE FROM THE PRESENCE OF THE LORD IS BAD. There are various impulses which may tend to drive men away from the all-searching eye of the Supreme. Some, like Jonah, may wish to avoid a service to which they cherish repugnance; for which, perhaps, they feel personally disqualified. Others may wish to hide their sins from One who, they know well, must regard them with displeasure. In any case, though the degree of culpability may vary, the motive is unworthy. The child should hide nothing from the Father; the Christian should never ask—Where shall I hide from thy presence? but should rather rejoice in the nearness, the interest, the favour, of his Maker and Saviour.

II. THE METHOD WHICH MEN ADOPT IN ORDER TO FLEE FROM THE PRESENCE OF THE LORD IS ABSURD. Change of place cannot take us out of the territory of the Omnipresent King. Jacob found that when at Bethel; the Lord was in that place, though he knew it not. Jonah learned that God's hand held in its hollow the raging sea; the same hand that fashioned the dry land from which he fled. It is now more common for those who would flee from God to betake themselves to the society of the profane, the licentious, the ungodly; thus they seek at least to banish the thought of God, if they cannot escape from his all-regarding eye.

III. THE IMPOSSIBILITY OF FLEEING FROM THE PRESENCE OF THE LORD IS OBVIOUS. That is to say, obvious to all who reflect upon the nature and the attributes of the Eternal. And it is well that all who are tempted to wish that relations between themselves and their Creator were suspended should reflect upon this impossibility. In God we live and move and have our being. We may forget him, but he does not overlook us. We may be out of harmony with his highest purposes, but we cannot cease even for one moment to be subjects of his kingdom, whether contented or discontented, loyal or rebellious.

IV. THE CONSEQUENCES OF ENDEAVOURING TO FLEE FROM THE PRESENCE OF THE LORD ARE AFFLICTING. In his favour is life. It is well to walk in the light of the Lord. They who depart from God forsake their true happiness. The presence of the Lord of all is necessary in order to strength and success in our work. A messenger from God above all men needs the consciousness of the Divine favour; for him to flee from God is to sacrifice his life, to throw up his vocation, and, except God have mercy upon him, to destroy his spiritual prospects.

V. GOD'S FORBEARANCE AND COMPASSION MAY BRING BACK THOSE WHO TRY TO FLEE FROM HIM. The narrative tells not only how Jonah fled, but how God followed him; how God did indeed chasten his servant, but did not forsake him; how Providence overruled his sinful conduct and secured his spiritual good. We need not despond, even if we have, as it were, turned our back upon God. "He restoreth our soul." He so reveals his grace that, instead of fleeing from his presence, we come to find in that presence fulness of joy.

Ver. 4.—*Nature and God.* There is a Hebrew directness and energy in this language describing the storm which overtook the unfaithful prophet. Some would be satisfied to say that we have here simply a poetico-theological expression descriptive of a natural phenomenon. But surely the Hebrew idiom here employed is the vehicle of a great truth. The Lord does send the wind and raise the tempest; and the Lord also calms the waters and stills the storm.

I. THE ATHEISTIC VIEW IS THAT NATURE IS A REALITY AND GOD A FICTION. Many scientific, and non-scientific, readers too will say—The storm did arise, but this was in accordance with natural laws, and there is no room and no need for the hypothesis of a Deity. Facts are facts, and regularities and uniformities are undeniable; but with explanations, with personal agencies, we have nothing at all to do.

II. THE PAGAN VIEW IS THAT NATURE IS THE OUTWARD EXPRESSION OF THE PRESENCE AND ACTIVITIES OF INNUMERABLE DEITIES. According to the heathen, the sea and the land, the woods and the fountains, had their several deities, whose actions accounted for all changes. In the tempest, Jonah's fellow-voyagers cried every man unto his god. The mood of the deity might vary, his purpose might change.

III. THE SUPERSTITIOUS VIEW IS THAT NATURE IS GENERALLY INDEPENDENT OF GOD, BUT IS SOMETIMES VISITED BY A DIVINE INTERFERENCE. When all things proceed in an even course, it is supposed that there is no need to presume a Divine presence. But when anything happens which is unusual, this is taken to be an evidence of the interposition of a superior Power. The calm is Nature's work, the storm is God's. A capricious, arbitrary Providence is the superstitious man's deity.

IV. THE RATIONAL AND RELIGIOUS VIEW SEES GOD IN AND BEHIND NATURE IN ALL HER CHANGES. God is the Author of Nature's laws. "The sea is his, and he made it; and his hands formed the dry land." Divine purpose, intelligence, wisdom, benevolence, are to the thoughtful and pious mind manifest in all the scenes and operations which Nature presents to us. We need not be pantheists, and identify God and Nature, in order to see and to glorify God in all his works.

Ver. 6.—*Danger and devotion.* The conduct of the seamen, who themselves, when encompassed by danger and when threatened by death, both called upon their gods and besought Jonah to imitate their prayers and vows, may have been superstitious in its accessories, but it was certainly right in principle.

I. DANGER REMINDS US OF OUR OWN POWERLESSNESS. In the presence of the great forces of nature—the hurricane, the earthquake, the volcano—man feels his own physical feebleness and helplessness. He is mightier than all these forces in that he can think and feel, purpose and act, whilst they blindly and unconsciously work out a higher will. But in his body he is incapable of resisting, of measuring himself against, these tremendous powers.

II. DANGER REMINDS US OF THE UNCERTAINTY AND BREVITY OF HUMAN LIFE. By some "accident" from without, or by some "disorder" within, the life of the body will certainly be brought to a close. The lightning may smite or the waves may swallow up the healthiest frame—may close the most useful and beneficent life. The treacherous sea, as in this narrative, threatens to engulf the mariner and the passenger.

"To thee the love of woman has gone down,
    Brave hearts and true are gathered to thy breast."

III. DANGER DRIVES THE SINNER TO SEEK GOD'S MERCY. To many the hour of peril is the only hour of prayer. Lips that have only used the name of the Eternal Majesty in ribald profanity, when white with fear utter that name in earnest entreaty for pity and for deliverance. When human help is vain, then the godless call upon the great Helper, God. How worthless such prayer often is experience sadly teaches. "The river past, the saint forgot." Yet it is well that men should be awakened, however rudely, from their self-sufficiency and false security.

IV. DANGER DRAWS FORTH THE CONFIDENCE AND THE PRAYERS OF THE PIOUS. How many are the records of shipwreck which tell of the peace and trust, the fortitude and hope, of the true Christian, when those around have abandoned themselves to despair! He who believes the gospel knows that God "thinks upon him," and knows that he so thinks upon his own for good. It *may* be that an unexpected deliverance will be wrought; but it *will* be the case that, whatever the Father above may suffer to happen to the body, the soul shall be safe in heavenly keeping unto life eternal.

Ver. 9.—*A good confession.* What an insight this story gives us into the life and habits of travellers in ancient times! Curiosity is always entertaining; but the inquisitiveness of these seamen bound for Tarshish, as they questioned their passenger regarding his occupation, his race, and his religion, is a revelation of their character, and affords an opportunity to the prophet to avow his religious faith. Jonah was not willing to obey God; yet he was not slow to confess God. There is much to admire in his language.

I. IT WAS AN INTELLIGENT CONFESSION. God is to many little more than a name; religion merely a form of words. There are those who are satisfied to name the name of their hereditary deity. Jonah's acknowledgment was accompanied by statements which prove his faith to have been something more than traditional. He described the Jehovah whom he worshipped as the God of heaven, the Maker of the sea and of the land. The words remind us of the opening of the Apostles' Creed. To confess God truly is to recognize his attributes and his method of dealing with the sons of men. It is not enough to utter mechanically a form of words.

II. IT WAS A BOLD CONFESSION. Instead of being alarmed by the dangers of the deep, the prophet seemed now to recover the self-possession which he had lost. In the presence of the angry elements and the anxious sailors, and above all in the presence of the Lord of nature and of man, Jonah confessed his God. Was there in this conduct something of the spirit embodied in the words, "Though he slay me, yet will I trust in him"?

III. IT WAS A REVERENT CONFESSION. "I fear the Lord;" *i.e.* revere, worship, and honour him. They who know him aright may well offer to him the veneration and adoration which angels delight to present. Who would not fear his great Name? Alas! that the name of God should ever pass irreverent lips!

IV. IT WAS, HOWEVER, A CONFESSION WHICH WAS INCONSISTENT WITH THE PROPHET'S CONDUCT, AND WAS THEREFORE HIS CONDEMNATION. How was it that he, who so honourably confessed his God in the tempest, had fled from that God, and disobeyed his plain commands? Could he use this language and not feel that it censured himself for so acting as he had done? It is well that we should verbally acknowledge God, that we should sincerely confess his right over us. But it may be that when we recite our Creed, and make our confession, we shall learn to think of our frequent inconsistencies with the profession which we avow. The knowledge of God may bring us to the knowledge of ourselves; and confession may lead to penitence, and so to reconciliation.

Ver. 12.—*Self-sacrifice.* Whatever difficulties the facts of this narrative may occasion in the mind of the reader, it must be admitted that it abounds with principles of the deepest interest and value. How could the lesson of self-devotion, of self-sacrifice, be more impressively taught than in the language of Jonah recorded in this verse? The unquestionable realities of federal human life, and of substitutionary suffering and sacrifice, are brought before us in a vivid and impressive form.

I. DIVINE PROVIDENCE APPOINTS THAT THE WRONG-DOING OF MEN SHOULD INVOLVE SUFFERING TO THEIR FELLOW-CREATURES. "For my sake," said Jonah, "this great tempest is upon you." No observer of human life can doubt that the greatest sufferers are not always the greatest sinners; they are often those who are brought into trouble, sorrow, and affliction through the conduct of those connected with them. The child suffers for the father's sins; the wife, for the husband's improvidence; the people, for their rulers' selfishness and negligence. We may not be able to explain this fact, we may not be satisfied with explanations of it which other people accept; but it would show an ignorance of human life to question its reality.

II. THE SAME PROVIDENCE APPOINTS THAT SUFFERINGS WILLINGLY UNDERGONE BY MEN SHOULD BE THE MEANS OF BENEFIT TO OTHERS. "Cast me forth," said Jonah, "into the sea; so shall the sea be calm unto you." Here again we are brought into contact with an undoubted fact in human society. The sufferings, hardships, and self-denial of parents are the means of comfort, culture, and well-being to their children. Great men benefit society by means of their labours, their self-sacrifice. Few persons reap a harvest of gladness and peace and prosperity, the seed of which has not been sown with toil and with tears. It is the highest exercise of patriotism to devote one's self to death for the country's weal; and the highest exercise of benevolence, when called upon by duty, to die for the welfare of humanity.

III. BOTH THESE PRINCIPLES ARE MOST CONSPICUOUSLY EXEMPLIFIED IN THE SACRIFICE OF OUR DIVINE REDEEMER. 1. The sins of men brought Jesus to the cross of Calvary. 2. The sufferings of Jesus bring men to the enjoyment of the Divine favour. "By his stripes we are healed."

Vers. 13, 14.—*Effort and prayer.* It has always been acknowledged that there was in the conduct of these heathen sailors something peculiarly generous. Although they believed themselves to have been brought into danger by the companionship of Jonah, although he himself invited them to cast him overboard and so secure their safety, this they would not do until they had exhausted every means of deliverance.

I. IN TIMES OF DIFFICULTY AND DANGER WE ARE SUMMONED TO EXERT ALL OUR POWERS FOR OUR ESCAPE AND PRESERVATION. There is a false piety which is true fatalism, which is content with prayer and indisposed to effort. But such is not the piety sanctioned in Scripture. Courage, effort, perseverance,—these are the qualities which are always mentioned with commendation. In fact, effort is the use of the natural powers with which our Creator has endowed us, the employment of the means which Providence has put within our reach. In striving for safety and for success men are honouring God. Endeavours may be unsuccessful, but it is better to fail while doing our very best than to fail by sloth and negligence.

II. IN TIMES OF DIFFICULTY AND DANGER THERE IS NO RESOURCE SO PROPER AND SO PRECIOUS AS PRAYER. The conduct of these heathen sailors, as here described, is beyond all praise. What they did was to put forth every effort for their own and their fellow-voyager's safety, and then to commend themselves to the guidance and the mercy of the Most High. With their slender knowledge they could not have prayed with much intelligence; but they prayed with much good feeling towards man, with much submission towards God, and with much fervour. The lesson is obvious. Whilst we can work it is well to work in a prayerful spirit, with dependence upon God. When we can no longer work, when human effort is of no avail, then it is well to call upon God and to leave ourselves entirely in his hands.

Ver. 16.—*Fear, sacrifice, and vows.* Times of danger are often times of devotion; but times of deliverance are not always times of thanksgiving. It is to the credit and honour of these seamen that when the storm ceased they acknowledged Jehovah as the Author of the calm, as the God of salvation. Three aspects of religious exercise are here presented to us.

I. REVERENCE. We cannot say that there was no superstition in the feelings and the conduct of these mariners. Probably the piety of most good men has an element of superstition. In any case, they feared the Eternal, feeling themselves to be in the presence and at the disposal of him who holds the waters in the hollow of his hand.

II. SACRIFICE. It was a thank offering, no doubt, which they presented. If they were sincere, this sacrifice was a symbol of the consecration of their whole nature, their whole life, unto God.

III. VOWS. Mercy experienced in the past should lead to the expectation of mercy in the future. The season of deliverance is a suitable season for resolutions and for vows. But be it remembered, "Better is it that thou shouldest not vow, than that thou shouldest vow and not pay."

HOMILIES BY VARIOUS AUTHORS.

Vers. 1—3.—*A despicable deserter.* "God looketh on the heart." And none but God can. It is an obscure and tortuous place—"deceitful above all things, and desperately wicked: who can know it?" Its chaos and darkness, transparent to the Divine Spirit, are impenetrable to any creature's eye. Even the new heart is not all new. Persistent among the grace-germs are *bacteria* of sin, inseparable and morbific. In Jonah this baneful combination is obvious. He neither loved God supremely nor his neighbour as himself. If he had, the action here recorded could never have been done, nor the feelings which prompted it have found a home in his heart. To fly from God's service because it involved the helping of *men* is a course consistent it may be with grace, but only with grace alloyed, inchoate, and overlaid with the mind of flesh.

I. In God's army it is either desertion or duty. "Jonah rose up to flee from the presence of the Lord." There was a Divine presence from which Jonah was not so ignorant as to attempt escape. He shows familiarity with the Book of Psalms (ch. ii. 2—9), and doubtless knew with the psalmist (Ps. cxxxix. 7—10) that there was no place outside God's omnipresence. But there was a special presence of God in the land of Israel. He was present in gracious hearts, and in the ordinances and offices of the Church. This special and gracious presence Jonah, like Jacob (Gen. xxviii. 16), seems to have considered peculiar to the Holy Land. He had a notion probably that the institutions arising out of it were purely local also, and that flight to heathen Spain would break the spiritual connection and void his prophetic office. His flight was "not from God's presence, but from standing before him as his minister . . . he renounced his office" (Pusey). And the act was logical in one aspect, however criminal. Enlistment in God's service means something. It is not playing at campaigning. It is not a kind of spiritual autumn manœuvres, which merely give spice to a periodical outing. It incurs responsibility and involves obedience.

> "I slept, and dreamed that life was beauty.
> I woke, and found that life was duty."

That all must find who are spiritually awake. There is work for all, and his task for each. And it has got to be done. In the Divine code stand the regulations of the service, and they are not to be trifled with. Idleness is out of the question; insubordination is not to be named. Jonah felt this. "He rose up to flee." He could not point-blank refuse, and stand his ground. Do something he must, when the word went forth. He will not preach, and so he has got to fly. It is so always. A man cannot remain at his post and strike work. The eye of the Master would look him through, and his presence compel obedience. The mutineer is in the same hour a deserter. He can maintain the one character only by adopting the other. Our spiritual duties arise out of our spiritual relations, and are at the same time their necessary expression. The alternative with us is "both or neither." Refuse God's work, and you put yourself out of his service.

II. Bigotry is an inevitable weakener of the moral sense. Some think Jonah refused to summon the Ninevites to repentance for fear they might take him at his word. Their reformation just now would not have suited his views. As heathen he disliked them, and as wicked he could use them as a foil for wicked Israel. Nineveh penitent, on the other hand, after one Divine warning, would have contrasted strongly with Israel impenitent after centuries of prophetic appeal, and he dreaded the repentance which would have been the occasion of such a damaging comparison. But this is clearly an exaggeration of Jonah's feeling in the matter. No prophet of God, no servant of God, could connive at sin against God in order to the destruction of men. To do so would be incompatible altogether with the religious character. Still, Jonah would have been more or less than a Jew if he had not been a bigot. He would not wantonly have compassed Nineveh's ruin. But being a bigot, and an egoist as well, he was so indifferent to the fate of the heathen city as to be ready to sacrifice it rather than risk the lowering of his own prophetic reputation. In all this we see the tokens of a weakened moral sense. Bigotry is an unequalled hardener of the heart. It is narrow, cold, sour, and carping. It denies or belittles all good outside its own ecclesiastical circle. Whilst blind to extern religious excellence, it is indifferent to extern religious attainment. It takes covert pleasure in the sins and weaknesses of rival Churches; it would regard their failure and collapse with mean complacency; and it would almost as lief see men remaining in sin as reformed by effort not its own. The tendency to look every man and Church on our own things is a natural one, and grows. And it necessarily involves the other tendency, its obverse, to look away from the things of others. This is the very antipodes of the "mind of Christ." That believes in the dignity of man as man. It sets a unique value on human life. It regards the question of a human destiny as one of stupendous interest. It makes the securing of it a personal concern. It never asks, "Am I my brother's keeper?" for the fact is with it an axiomatic truth. Loving its neighbour as itself, its moral attitude inspires its active one—" do good to all." It regards life as wasted if not lived for men, and the time as lost in which it does not " save some."

III. INGLORIOUS DUTY IS MOST IN DANGER OF BEING LEFT UNDONE. Jonah had an idea how his mission would end. As a prophet, he knew that Nineveh would repent, and on repentance be spared, his prophecy to the contrary notwithstanding (ch. iv. 2). And the prospect was humbling to his self-love. The affair could bring him little credit. He was simply to deliver an empty threat, a threat the utterance of which would serve God's purpose, and so prevent the necessity of carrying it out. How was he to get up a prophetic reputation by performing such a task? Warnings heeded and predictions fulfilled are the chief credentials of a prophet. The first is both in itself and in its practical results, by far the more important. But the second is more of a personal interest to the prophet as involving his credibility more directly. Hence in proportion as he is " yet carnal " and self-seeking it will bulk more largely in his regard. A Paul could say, " We preach not ourselves, but Christ Jesus the Lord," and mean it thoroughly. But the perfect self-sinking of the apostolic rule was an unscaled height to the egotistic prophet. He wanted a name and official distinction more than the exhibition of God's mercy and the reformation of wicked men. Accordingly, he refused to assume an equivocal position, although he knew, and because he knew, it would lead to these prime results. And servants his counterparts are still found in God's work. The men who " do good by stealth, and blush to find it fame " no doubt exist. But the blushes traceable to this source are a small proportion of the blushes current. He has reached a high spiritual level who so lives to God that personal considerations are as nothing in his work. Position and visibility, to say nothing of considerations more sordid still, are elements in the situation, hard to keep subordinate, harder still to ignore, when the Christian worker is making choice of fields. A place in the most distant mission field may single out a worker from the crowd, and the missionary pioneer finds temptations to pose before the Church as strong as beset the brightest metropolitan star. The large giver, moreover, or the great organizer, has as many temptations to self-seeking as either. It is so through all departments of activity and in all the walks of life. The work that brings fortune and fame will have thousands competing for a chance to do it. The only duty in practical danger of being shirked is the duty to be followed into obscure places, and done with only the eye of God to note our faithfulness.

IV. RETREAT FROM GOD IS RESOLUTE, AND AIMS AT ENTIRE ISOLATION. Jonah started at a run. He evidently meant to get away, and threw all his energy into the effort. He went, too, in a direction exactly the opposite of the one in which he had been sent. God had said, " Go north-east," and he went south-west. He set out, moreover, for the remotest place he knew of, Spain being the " far West " of those early times. He went about it also in the most business-like way, going to Joppa, the great seaport, and booking a berth on one of the great ships of Tarshish, to break which was the *magnum opus* of the east wind (Ps. xlviii. 7). All which things are no doubt an allegory. The sinner's drawing near to God is done at a snail's pace. Loving this sinful world, he hangs back long before he starts. Answering feebly as yet to the drawing of grace, and breaking cord after cord in the tearing of himself away, the motion toward God at first is slow and painful, like that of a weak oarsman against a rapid stream. But like a stone down hill, and drawn by mighty gravitation, the motion away from God is by leaps and bounds (Rom. vii. 19, 22, 23). You have seen at the docks the seamen straining at the windlass, as, after minutes of strenuous effort, they have pulleyed a bale of merchandise high in air. And you have seen, when they let go the winch, how swiftly the handle flies and, as the rope unrolls, the bale comes rushing down. And such is retrogression in contrast to progress in the religious sphere. So much more quickly do men fall than rise, that a few days' backsliding is enough to neutralize the growth of years. Then so opposite to God is the sinful heart that its departure from him is absolute turning back. Swerving would be bad, aberration would be worse, but regression is worst of all; and such is religious backsliding. It is spiritual tergiversation. The renegade turns his back on right, and takes a way the very opposite. He obeys Satan and follows sin, the antipodes respectively of God and good. If God's way be light, his is darkness; if upwards, his is downwards infallibly

Then there is no spiritual half-way house. God in his mercy may arrest him on the way, but the renegade starts for Tarshish, the spiritual remotest point. A stone detached from the house-top has no stopping-place short of the ground. Turn your back on God and heaven, and Satan and hell are, humanly speaking, your destination. Moreover, defection from God is not an aimless drifting, but intelligent and of purpose. It is a course wittingly taken and studiously kept. The deteriorated moral nature presses head and hand into its service, to survey and construct the road by which it would reach the shrine of its chosen idol. At the Joppa of occasion, advisedly sought, is chartered the ship of ways and means, to bring us to the Tarshish of accomplished sin, the goal of our godless hearts.

V. A MAN WILL ALWAYS FIND CIRCUMSTANCES FAVOURABLE TO THE COURSE HE HAS RESOLVED TO TAKE. Jonah found a ship about to sail to his destination, got accommodation on board, and had the means to provide a berth. Things seem as if arranged on purpose to facilitate his flight. Had it been otherwise, we sometimes think the prophet's "Hegirah" might have been stopped earlier, and a good deal of suffering saved. But that would be a shallow philosophy of human action. Physical surroundings cannot thus shape our moral course. Intelligence makes its own use of them all. Purpose is formed; action is decided on; and then the circumstances are examined to see what mode of action they can most easily be made to help. The ship, the berth, and the passage-money to Tarshish were available to many besides Jonah, yet he only prostituted them to the purpose of shirking duty. They lent themselves to his project, because the project had, in the first place, been adjusted to them. So if a thief finds an open window, and no policeman in sight, the circumstances are said to favour a burglary. If a would-be murderer finds the same state of things, then we say the circumstances favour assassination. But if a man who would neither kill nor steal finds them so, they favour no project of his, and so are either put right or passed unheeded. Circumstances favour neither good nor evil particularly, but each man makes use of those that fit his own purpose, and passes the others by. We hear often of wicked men who are the victims of circumstance. And there are some such, no doubt. But the cases are fewer and logically weaker than you might think. Here are two country youths apprenticed in town among a godless set. One turns out a profligate, and friends pity him and say, "He got into bad hands : what better could we expect in such a place?" But the other, with the same surroundings exactly, turns out, as often happens, an honest tradesman and a godly man. And if you examine you will find that he has honest men for his friends, and Christian people for his associates, and enjoys beneficial influences in every relation of life. In other words, he is in a new set of circumstances altogether, favourable to the religious life, and which his own conduct has drawn around him. The circumstances have not made the men, but the men have practically made the circumstances. And so we reason out the truth which God reveals, "To the pure all things are pure," etc. (Titus i. 15). We are greater than our environment. "Each man creates his own world. . . . The soul spreads its own hue over everything; the shroud or wedding garment of nature is woven in the loom of our own feelings. This universe is the image and counterpart of the souls that dwell in it. Be noble-minded, and all nature replies—I am divine, the child of God ; be thou too his child and noble. Be mean, and all nature dwindles into a contemptible smallness" (Robertson). "If any man be in Christ, he is a new creature : old things are passed away ; behold, all things are become new." To you and me the world will be a new world when we are new creatures in Christ. It is not what it was, but a transfigured thing, when we view it "the eyes of our understandings being enlightened," and make all its elements tributary to a new life in Christ.— J. E. H.

Vers. 4—10.—*An effective hue and cry.* We see here a man who ought to run for God endeavouring to run away from him, and also how he speeds. The flight was illogical, a fatuous attempt to get outside the sphere of omnipresence, as much of our sin is a practical endeavour to get, or imagine ourselves, beyond the cognizance of omniscience. And it was made in the blindness of egoism and carnal self-will—the qualities which are generally to be found at the bottom of ministerial unfaithfulness to the message of God. A lorry off the lines attracts attention, when a whole train on them might pass unnoticed. A large proportion of the heterodoxy extant originates in or is exaggerated by a desire to catch the public eye. The evil it does to the souls of men will go on so long as there are nominal servants who have a private interest dearer to them than the Master's work. And the personal disappointment and suffering and failure of the prophet are the experiences bound to be repeated in all cases of spiritual renegadism like it.

I. THEY RUN HARD WHOM GOD'S JUDGMENTS CANNOT OVERTAKE. Jonah scarcely hoped to get away from God. But he did expect to get away from his work. It lay north-east, and he went south-west. He was determined not to be near the place where duty lay, lest by any chance he should be compelled to do it. In this he succeeded for the time, and he succeeded still more fully in getting morally and spiritually away from the Most High. Not depths of sea or wilds of desert could have taken him so far from God as the moral elements implied in that flight. But he found that desertion, however possible, can never be satisfactory. God's authority is not to be run away from. He makes storms his artillery, and thunders after the run-away. He makes heathen sailors his officers, and captures him in his flight. He makes a fish's belly his dungeon keep, and puts him in durance there. Do not for a moment dream of evading God. If you run away from his spade, you run against his sword. You can run away from sobriety, but not from the white liver and empty purse and premature grave that drunkenness brings. You can run away from purity, but not from the debilitated frame, and the cloyed appetite, and the hell of a strengthening lust with failing power to feed it. You can run away from charity, but not from the heart-hardness and bitterness and gnawing unrest of all loveless souls. Disobedience accomplished means judgment on the way, and judgment on the way means judgment ahead of the transgressor, and waiting for him as the angel for wretched Balaam (Rom. ii. 3).

II. THE JUDGMENTS SENT AFTER THE GUILTY OFTEN FALL ON THE INNOCENT AS WELL. "Sin," says Chrysostom, "brings the soul into much senselessness." It brought Jonah to think that he could play off nature against its God, and escape him by the help of his own winds and tides. It brought him to pit one of the great ships of Tarshish—the East Indiamen of that time—against God's east wind (Ps. xlviii. 7). But mighty merchantman or tiny skiff, it is all one to the hurricane's blast. The prophet, so far from getting out of trouble himself, got others into it (vers. 4, 5). The sailors suffered fatigue and alarm; the ship-owners suffered loss of freight; other vessels near suffered dilapidations; indeed, many interests were harassed before Jonah himself was reached. That is the rule with all sin. In almost every offence against the second table of the Law our neighbour suffers first. Then, after the offender begins to suffer, his suffering in turn involves the family and social circles in which he is. The spendthrift's poverty, the debauchee's disease, the felon's disgrace, go down infallibly to children, and it may be children's children. Sinning against God you are indirectly sinning against man, and sinning against one man, you are practically sinning against all his friends and all your own. Such a following of evils does the transgressor drag after him in an ever-lengthening train.

III. THOSE WHO HAVE BEEN THE OCCASION OF GREAT PUBLIC EVIL ARE OFTEN THE LEAST CONCERNED ABOUT IT. Jonah was the coolest man on board while the big storm was raging. It was due to him, sent after him, meant to arrest his thought and step, and yet, when hardy sailors were frightened, and ignorant heathen were driven to pray, the erewhile God-fearing landsman was making himself comfortable below, and curled up fast asleep. So the men who provoked the Flood were cool and calm about it, even when Noah and his family were flying to the ark. To the Sodomites also righteous Lot, preparing to fly the coming doom, seemed but as one that mocked. The hardness produced by recent rebellion had not yet worn off. The murderer does not regret his crime nor fear the gallows while his blood is up. The excitement sustains him for a time in reckless disregard of both. But when he has had time to cool down and think, when he gets the cold iron on his wrists, and sees the outer world through iron bars, when dreams recall his victim's death-struggle or forecast the scaffold and the dangling rope, then his crime begins to look like itself, and his doom to put on its proper terrors. Jonah was still in the earlier stage. He did not see his sin yet, and he was too hot and rebellious to fear the punishment. After sin and before repentance there is an interval of unnatural insensibility, and in this interval Jonah's sleep was taken. It is a horrid sight to see judge and jury and the court affected to tears, and the criminal as hard as iron. Yet that is the analogue of a state into which we have only to defy God in order to fall.

IV. A PRAYERLESS BACKSLIDER IS AN ASTONISHMENT EVEN TO A HEATHEN. (Ver. 6.) The skipper, a responsible man, and pious according to his lights, thinks Jonah, sleeping there in the crash of the storm, must be either sick or mad. Prayer, whether to false gods or the true, is a universal and instinctive religious act. And so when the great wind-guns began to boom and the billowy mitrailleuses to roar in chorus, when the helpless vessel tossed like a log and creaked and strained as about to break, then began every man to cry unto his god. Even the heathen could see that it was the thing to do, and the time to do it; and when the only worshipper of the true God aboard lies silent and indifferent, the captain and crew are alike astonished. Yet it is just what a little knowledge of the human character in its relation to spiritual things would lead us to expect. The iron that has been heated soft, and cooled again in water, is harder than ever. The process has simply tempered it. So the man who has been softened in the fires of grace, and plunged again into the waters of sin, is a harder man than he was at first (Heb. vi. 4). There are Canas and Chorazins among us, and it will be more tolerable for the Tyres and Sidons in the judgment than for them.

V. IT IS IN THE CRISES OF LIFE THAT FALSE CONFIDENCES FAIL AND THE TRUE GOD COMES TO THE FRONT. The captain sees appeal to his own gods to be vain, and he surmises that prayer to the God of Israel might be more successful. "Call upon thy God, if so be that God will think upon us." He knew of the true God as distinguished from the gods many whom he served, but only in extremity does he think of approaching him in prayer. The other gods were fair-weather deities, good enough so long as you wanted nothing from them. But only the God who holds the winds in his fists will serve now. And thus, in a new sense, the extremity of man is the opportunity of God. Beliefs, moralities, observances, are made so many substitutes for the Christ of God. And they do to live with after a fashion. But you never knew a man to die comfortably with them. The last hour is apocalyptic. It unveils things. The bubble of conceit in personal merit bursts. The filthy rags fall off. The soul is flung naked, loathsome, undone, before the majesty of God. Take God in Christ for your trust this hour, and you will never know the withering curse on him that "maketh flesh his arm."—J. E. H.

Vers. 11, 12.—*A voluntary surrender.* Matters so anomalous up to this point are beginning now to resume their normal aspect. The prophet had been behaving in a most inconsequential and erratic way. His flight had been utterly out of character. He ran away from a duty in the doing of which piety would have met philanthropy, and both have had ample scope. His sleep through the storm which his own sin provoked, when death was imminent, and even the heathen sailors called in terror on their gods, was, if possible, more eccentric still. Most unaccountable of all, perhaps, was the declaration, "I fear the Lord," so sincerely made when in the very act of setting his command at naught. But now the craze is passing off. Like the prodigal at a corresponding stage of his career, we see the prophet coming to himself. The reign of law is coming back, and mind and conscience and will fall into line and begin to act by rule. These verses exhibit to us the workings of the backslider's mind in his return to God. We see—

I. THAT CALAMITY HAS COMPELLED HIM TO THINK. The sinner is seldom logical. If he were, he would be a sinner no longer. There are no valid premises to which a sinful act will stand in the relation of a conclusion. If Jonah had reasoned out the matter before he started on his flight, he would not have started at all. He adopted on impulse a course the folly of which a single moment's consideration would have shown. And he avoided this consideration as long as he could. It was only the impossibility of getting further that compelled him to face the question, "Why did I come so far? And was it wisely done?" It is almost invariably the practical results of a line of conduct that lead us to examine as to its intrinsic wisdom. We consult our taste in the first instance. What promises immediate pleasure or profit comes to our judgment so highly recommended by the fact, that few questions are asked.   No one supposes that the drunkard takes the moral, economic, or hygienic measure of his disastrous habit before he forms it.   He has a lively feeling that it is pleasant, and suits his taste, and he waives the consideration of other points till a more convenient season.   It is only when his habit has brought misfortune that he really faces the question whether it is a good one or not.   With his mouth full of the bitter fruit, he naturally begins to form an idea of the character of the tree.   If the fruiting had never come, the appraising would have been left undone.   There is to every sinner a day when he cannot but think.   He is happy if the needs-be **overtakes** him at the outset of his straying ere yet return has become impossible.

II. THOUGHT HAS CONVINCED HIM OF SIN.   We can read a sense of guilt in every word of the arrested fugitive.   His mind has awaked.   In thought he has faced the situation.   And his thought has not been barren.   It has brought forth conviction. It would have been weak indeed if it had not.   The fact of sin is patent to ordinary intelligence.   And so to a certain extent is its demerit.   To declare its existence and quality is the function of natural conscience ; and what is conscience but reason dealing with moral truth ?   Of course, its diagnosis of sin is inadequate.   The awful demerit of sin done against an infinite and holy God cannot be reached by mere force of think-ing.   It takes an enlightened eye to see it as it is, an opened heart to realize the whole truth regarding it.   You must know God, in fact, in order to know sin, which is an offence against him.   This, no doubt, Jonah did.   There was a mote for the time being in his spiritual eye, but it had been opened once for all to see God.   He came, there-fore, to the contemplation of his sin with a measure of spiritual insight.   And all may come to it similarly furnished.   Obey the call of Scripture to " consider."   Make a sincere attempt to examine yourself.   Turn your eye inward, desiring honestly to know yourself as sinful in God's sight.   You won't be left to your own unaided efforts and to failure.   God awaits the beginning of such action to strengthen it.   He awaits the attempt at such action to help it.   He waits the aim at such action to move to attempt it in the strength of grace.   It follows from the connection between wanting and getting in the spiritual sphere—" examine, and you shall know ; " for the Spirit con-vinces the world of sin, and that by guiding into all truth the searchers after its hidden treasures.

III. CONVICTION HAS DRIVEN HIM TO CONFESS.   There is a natural egoism in men that is unfavourable to confession.   You get it out of them only by a difficult process as men get water out of a still.   And the reasons of this are obvious.   One is that men are more or less unconscious of their own moral state.   They do not realize sin.   They deem it an outrage to have guilt charged home.   In the impudence of their uncon-sciousness they would bandy words with God himself (Mal. iii. 8).   Here is evident failure to discern the sinfulness of sin.   And failure is due as much to pride as to incapacity.   Men are naturally prejudiced in their own favour.   Faults that others see well enough they ignore, or weakly disapprove what others utterly condemn.   They abide in darkness because they hate the light (John iii. 19).   Given a man who cannot see his sin if he would, and who would not if he could, and you have a case in which confession need not be named.   Even grant a measure of conviction, and confession does not necessarily follow.   When sin is realized in a certain degree, the sinner's tongue is unloosed, and he tells it out with shame to God.   But it does not follow that he will do it before his fellow-men.   That means a great deal more, is harder to do, and more reluctantly done.   It is greater humiliation.   It involves stronger reprobation.   It implies deeper self-abasement.   When it is honestly done conviction may be held to be at its intensest ; in fact, to be true and adequate.   Jonah's repent-ance had now come to this advanced stage (vers. 10, 12).   " When the whip of God and the rod of his justice had overtaken Jonah, so that he now sees heaven and earth to be against him, down comes his proud heart: the sleeper now awaketh ; the runaway crieth, *Peccavi ;* contrition and confession come now tumbling upon him " (Abbot).   Confession of our faults is an essential part of true repentance.   To deny them is to lie, to conceal is to bolster up.   When a transgressor is either sullenly silent or volubly apologetic, he has not broken with his sin.   He could bear to speak the truth about it if he had definitely cast it off.   Hence God makes confession **a** criterion of sincerity and a condition of pardon (Lev. xxvi. 40—42; Jer. iii. 12, 13).

Hence, on occasion of sin, Aaron (Numb. xii. 11), and Saul (1 Sam. xv. 24), and David (2 Sam. xii. 13), and Josiah (2 Kings xxii. 11, 13, 19), and Rehoboam (2 Chron. xii. 6, 7, 12), and Manasseh (2 Chron. xxxiii. 12, 13), and Hezekiah (2 Chron. xxxii. 26), and Peter (Mark xiv. 72), and others whose sincerity Scripture certifies, whilst it records the fact of their pardon, made free and heart-stricken confession of their fault before God and men. Sin confessed means sin discovered and reprobated and disowned. The man flings it off in the very act, declares himself at once its victim and foe. There is philosophy, therefore, and the fitness of things in the Divine deliverance, prescription and promise hand in hand, that "whoso confesseth and forsaketh his sins shall have mercy."

IV. HIS NEW ATTITUDE TOWARD SIN INCLUDES WILLINGNESS TO SUFFER FOR IT. The world is sometimes surprised and puzzled by a voluntary confession of murder. The self-accused criminal has been hitherto undetected and secure. People may have had their suspicions, and drawn their inferences, but it was impossible to trace the crime home. Yet at last, when investigation had been given up, and the very memory of the crime died out, the murderer comes of his own accord, confesses his crime, and delivers himself up to justice. And, the wonder and puzzlement of shallow people notwithstanding, the act is perfectly logical. The anomaly is not that he has delivered himself up at last, but that he did not do it at the first. There is an instinctive sense of justice in a man, that recognizes the unfitness of a sinner going scot-free. He feels that sin produces a moral derangement which cannot continue, and which it takes punishment to readjust. He feels at war with the nature of things until this has been done. He thinks if he had once endured the penalty the balance of things would be restored, and a foundation for future peace be laid. And he actually finds it so. The very fact of telling out his guilt has already lightened the load, and there is a new restfulness in the thought that now he is going to make some amends. *It is to this principle that the doctrine of the cross appeals.* In Christ crucified the demand of our nature for punishment proportioned to our sin is met. We see our transgressions avenged on him, in him our penal responsibilities met, and our full amends made. Our faith in Christ is, in one aspect, our instinctive clutching at the peace of the punished minus the preliminary pain. The same principle disarms and softens chastisement. Humility feels it is deserved. Intelligence sees it is necessary. And godly sorrow for sin welcomes it as a key to the dwelling of peace from which transgression had strayed. A willingness like Jonah's to accept the meed of sin is no mean criterion of our attitude towards it, and of our whole moral bent.

V. HE THOUGHT THAT THE EVIL CONSEQUENCES OF HIS SIN COULD ONLY BE REMOVED BY HIS ENDURING ITS PUNISHMENT. There was a feeling among the sailors that some action must be taken in reference to Jonah (ver. 11). Their present relation to him had involved them in a storm; what but a new relation to him could bring the calm? And the prophet himself is of the same opinion. He considers himself the mountain which attracts the storm, and that, if he were cast into the sea, its great occasion would be gone. What is this but the practical application of a revealed principle, "He that doeth wrong shall receive for the wrong which he hath done"? The axiom applies to the righteous and the wicked alike, if in a different sense. The sin of wicked Saul is visited with punishment as final rejection and ruin. The sin of righteous David is visited with punishment as fiery trial eventuating in a contrite heart. Heathen Philistia and chosen Israel sin in almost equal degree, yet "the remnant of the Philistines" perishes (Amos i. 8), whilst "the remnant of Israel" is by suffering saved (Isa. i. 8; Rom. ix. 27; xi. 5). And among natural and spiritual men alike the principle holds, cutting this way and that, with double edge: for believing sin, "the rod;" for unbelieving sin, "the sword;" for all sin, wrath in God and anguish in man (Rom. i. 18; ii. 9). A recognition of this fact would solve some mysteries of suffering, and put an end to many "offences" and complaints. A man sins in his youth against God, and others, and his own body. By the grace of the Spirit he is brought in a little to repentance and the higher life. Is, therefore, his wrong-doing undone? By no means. In some physical ailment, in some raked-up imputation, in some injured fellow-creature, it rises before him when his hair is white. And he is surprised at this. He thought that, after repentance and pardon, his sin was done with for ever. But it is not so. Sin once done cannot be undone. It leaves its mark on the sinner—in mind, or body, or estate, or social relations, but leaves it inevitably somewhere. The wood from which a nail has been drawn can never be as if the nail had not been driven. The nail-hole is there, and there remains, do what we will. When, as with Jonah, the sin is against God directly, it has no physical concomitant, and the punishment in its physical aspect can show no connection with it. But it is neither more nor less the doing of God and the result of sin on that account. And, although in regions out of sight, a radical and natural connection still exists between penalty and crime. Its moral necessity and significance and tendency remain the same. Hence the certainty of its coming and the folly of striving to evade its stroke. Not till law natural and moral has had its amends, and all injured interests been recouped, can escape for the law-breaker come. Come then it fitly and fairly may, and come then, and only then, it will (Ps. lxxxix. 30—33). 1. *It is not enough to confess sin in general, we must confess it in particular.* There is a kind of impersonal guilt which many will freely acknowledge, by whom personal guilt is altogether ignored. If we say generally, "Your nature is corrupt," they will own it without hesitation and without emotion. If we say, "Your conduct is bad," they will deny the impeachment and resent it. That was not Jonah's way. He unaffectedly confessed guilt as to the matter in hand. And it is not the way of true conviction. You confess and deny in one breath; deny in the particular what you confess in the general; which amounts to saying that a certain number of whites will make a black. But the fact is your acknowledgment is mechanical and formal, and therefore worthless. The denial, on the other hand, is intelligent and in earnest, and the deliberate expression of your mind and feeling. Accordingly, your confession as a whole means just what it says, and that is—nothing. 2. *Mercy should move us to confession of sin as strongly as judgment.* Who will say that it was altogether the severity of God in punishing at last, and in no degree his goodness in refraining till now, that led the prophet to repentance? Not so speaks the Scripture (Rom. ii. 4). Mercy touches a bad heart and breaks it, a cold heart and warms it, a closed mouth and opens it. That is its normal, and ought to be its actual, effect on you. Your mercies have been neither few nor small. They supply a basis for the inspired appeal, "We beseech you, brethren, by the mercies of God," etc. They supply an impulse more than adequate to bring you to the kingdom. If you have resisted them, what will persuade you? The resources of grace have been well-nigh expended. God's time of striving has almost run out. Strive to enter while you see the gate ajar, or the clang of its closing bolts may be the knell of your immortal soul.—J. E. H.

Vers. 13—16.—*Storm-stilling extraordinary.* We see in this passage, under favourable circumstances, the workings of the heathen mind in its first glimpses of God. And the study is one of lively interest, and important withal. The sailors have, innocently and involuntarily, been made actors in a drama that is not unlike to turn out a tragedy. A stranger, pursued by the vengeance of his (to them) unknown God, has got on board their ship, and mixed them up in his troubles to the extent of bringing them to the very brink of death. From their standpoint it was rather a hard case. They might well have felt resentment and given the cold shoulder to the not guiltless occasion of their evil plight. Their prudence, their considerateness, their conscientiousness, and their ultimate devoutness are qualities that come on us as an agreeable but complete surprise. There is a philosophy of these qualities, however, which it will be worth our while to endeavour to trace out.

I. THEY SHOWED AN ENLIGHTENED REGARD FOR HUMAN LIFE. They might well have been excused if, in imminent danger of death through the guilty Jonah's presence in their ship, they had jumped at his proposal to throw him overboard. They knew, for he—an inspired prophet—had told them, that he had deserved it by his crime, and that to do so would calm the sea forthwith. Yet they make no movement in that direction, but redouble their efforts at the oar in their last desperate attempt to reach the land. This course was unlike a heathen crew. Heathenism has always been reckless about shedding blood. It is the Bible that teaches, and believers in it who recognize, the sacredness of human life. Its command, "Thou shalt not kill," is illustrated and enforced by its history and entire legislation. The murderer was to suffer death, though he should be dragged to it from the very horns of the altar (Numb. xxxv. 31; 1 Kings ii. 29). The very ox that took a human life must die, and might not be eaten (Exod. xxi. 28). Even the man who slew another by misadventure made his life forfeit to the avenger of blood if he were caught outside the city of refuge (Deut. xix. 5). Blood, in fact, according to Scripture, must have blood (Gen. ix. 5, 6). There is no other satisfaction for it. The value of it cannot be expressed in any earthly currency. Even the whole world is no compensation for a lost life (Mark viii. 36). Those principles find little place in the consciousness of heathendom. It is filled with "the habitations of cruelty." You will get no heathen nation in any age exhibiting either in private life or public an adequate sense of the inviolability of human life. It is evident that in the case before us the sailors have been impressed by the Divine portents on the occasion, and under their impulse act for a time on a higher than the heathen plane. Not in their heathenism, but in the theism it is for the time in contact with, must we look for the explanation of their humane and generous conduct. The knowledge of God is early and inevitably practical. By it "grace is multiplied," and the "pollutions of the world" escaped (2 Pet. i. 2; ii. 20).

II. THEY RECOGNIZED THE BELIEVING LIFE AS SPECIALLY SACRED. It will be conceded that, other things being equal, the life of a believer is more important than that of an unbeliever. Not only has it elements and functions which are all its own, but these are intrinsically more excellent than any others. God treats it as precious in a peculiar sense (Ps. lxxii. 14; cxvi. 15), keeping count of the very hairs of his people's heads (Matt. x. 30), and using (1 Cor. iii. 21, 22; 2 Cor. iv. 15), and even sacrificing, the lives of the wicked for their preservation (Isa. xliii. 4). He also safeguards it by a double rampart of threat and promise. The death or the hurt of the saints he will avenge with punishment worse than death (Luke xviii. 8; Matt. xviii. 7); whilst even a cup of water to the least of them shall meet with eternal recognition and reward (Matt. x. 42; xxv. 40). Of the inviolable sacredness of the saint's life the sailors had evidently an intuitive idea. "Although himself accuse himself, and lay his fault plain before them, although winds and waves did confirm it, although the lot thrown did assure it, although in words he did desire to be cast into the water, yet those who should have done it do so ill like of the matter, that if sails or oars can serve they will back again to the land—rather leave their intended journey than use any violence towards him" (Abbot). It was not on the score of his humanity merely that Jonah was so tenderly dealt with. The hurricane, the power and wrath of God speaking in it, Jonah's revealed connection with both, his acknowledgment and denunciation of his fault, and the meek manhood of his offer to die that they might live, were all circumstances to awe and soften them. "Disobedient though he may be, Jonah they perceive is God's prophet, and his servant still. Revering his God, they respect him. They feel that it is a solemn thing to have to do with anything that this God marks as his own—marks as his own even by his displeasure. Hence they pause" (Martin). This is godliness in its normal operation, and realizing its "promise of the life that now is" by surrounding it with an invisible yet inviolable guard.

III. THEY SHAPED THEIR CONDUCT IN THE EMERGENCY AS FAR AS POSSIBLE BY GOD'S. "Thou, O Lord, hast done as it pleased thee" (ver. 14). They would have spared the prophet's life had the thing been possible. It is only when Providence fights against them, and logically shuts them up to it, that they accept the inevitable, and throw him overboard. As their words imply, they "assume that to be righteous which God will have to be done; and because they see him will it, and that he will take no nay, therefore they know it is just, and accordingly yield unto it" (Abbot). The rule of right is God's will. The expression of this in a particular case supersedes the general law. "Thou shalt not kill" and "Thou shalt not steal" are canons in the universal moral code. Yet Abraham would have killed Isaac, and Samuel killed Agag, whilst Israel spoiled the Egyptians at the command of God. Then, from the general law forbidding homicide, was excepted the whole class of cases in which it was necessary for self-defence; and to take spoil in war, or as much food from a neighbour's field as would save the life, was excepted from the general law forbidding theft. On the same principle the execution of Jonah was legalized by the expressed will of God to that effect, and became to the sailors an act of simple duty. And their course was exemplary. Obedience to God is the highest morality. Whatever is done so is done well. It may seem anomalous and unfit. But that is only on the surface. Some of the finest passages in literature are least obviously conformable to grammatical rule.

The conformity is there, and in the highest sense; it is only the tyro who cannot see it. So with actions done in the highest moral plane. The actor is too intent on doing what God says to look after the minor congruities. But the thing he does has an essential and fundamental rightness which lifts details into a new connection where they also become appropriate. "Whatsoever the Lord saith, that will we do." The men who accentuate the "whatsoever," and do it honestly, are seldom favourites with the crowd, but they have scaled the loftiest moral heights, where the voice of human opinion is neither listened for nor heard.

IV. THEY FOUND DELIVERANCE IN FOLLOWING GOD'S LEAD. (Ver. 15.) Attempts at escape in every other direction were made persistently, but all in vain. The ship-lightening, the prayers to idols, the strenuous rowing, were so many exercises in the bootless task of fighting against God. Against the wind and tide of his purpose no human power can sail. "God was pursuing this matter to his own appointed issue, and would allow no effort, however well meant, to baffle his purpose" (Martin). This obvious fact the sailors are compelled at length to recognize. Reluctantly they give up their unavailing struggle, and take the course to which all along events had been conspiring to shut them up. And on the instant the face of affairs is changed. The elemental war is hushed in peace. The hurricane in which earth and heaven reeled becomes the calm as of a tropical night. The waters which had "gaped at their widest to glut him" swallow their prey, and forthwith cease their raging. How easy the end if we only take God's way! How swift the transition from impossibility to attainment! Yet it is just the transition from man's way to God's. Have we not all experiences on which by analogy the event may throw light? Aiming at a legitimate object, we adopt what seems to us a fitting course. But we never get on in it. Disappointment awaits us at every step. Disaster springs on us from every covert. It seems as if men and things were joined together in a universal conspiracy to baulk us. Discouraged at last, and bitter at heart, we take without definite intention or expectation a step in a new direction, and which circumstances seem to thrust upon us; and lo, before we are aware, and almost without an effort, our object is attained. God works, not against means but with them, not apart from means, but by them; yet everywhere and always he works his own will in his own way. As we recognize that way and take it, are we on the moral rectilineal—the shortest line between our present and God's future.

V. THEY ARE FINALLY WON TO GOD'S SERVICE BY THE EXHIBITION OF HIS CHARACTER. In the incidents of the day the sailors read a revelation of God. "The storm they clearly saw was in his hand; a reason for it, they saw, was in his heart. And that reason they saw as clearly as they saw the storm. His hand they saw was almighty. His heart they saw was righteous. They even became executioners of his wrath. It was a solemn initiation into the knowledge of his name" (Martin). And what but the revelation of God's character wins men to his service everywhere (Ps. xxxvi. 7; Rev. xv. 4; 2 Cor. v. 14, 15)? Conversion has many elements leading up to and meeting in it. There is the truth, the instrument in all saving change. There is the Holy Spirit interpreting the truth and bringing it home. But there is something else to which both refer. The power of the truth, even as applied by the Holy Ghost, must lie in the subject-matter of it, and that subject-matter is God (John v. 39; Rom. i. 16). God is the Infinite Beauty. God made manifest means men attracted, all minds dazzled, and all hearts won (Ps. ix. 10). His character commands confidence and challenges fealty. He is one whom to know is to trust, whom to see is to love and choose. It is on this fact that inspiration founds in a familiar maxim of the kingdom (John xvii. 3). Knowledge of God is salvation, for every saving grace inheres in it or goes with it.

VI. THEIR RELIGIOUS LIFE GAVE EVIDENCE OF ITS GENUINENESS BY FOLLOWING SCRIPTURAL LINES. (Vers. 14—16.) Prayer, fear, sacrifice, and vows;—what essential element in religious life or worship do not these exercises cover (Acts ii. 21; Heb. ix. 22; Ps. iii. 10; Isa. xliv. 5)? In prayer is the coming to God for the things that are his gift if they come at all. In sacrifice is the coming symbolically by atonement, the only coming to which blessing is promised. Fear epitomizes the attitude and line of action in which practical religion may be summed up. A vow is a testimony that the ideal life is consecration—a pledge that they will freely give who have received so freely. We wonder at the propriety and fitness of the sailors' entire action. They had no Bible. They learned nothing from the prophet. Yet they took a distinctly scriptural course. They rendered God service in God's appointed way. Does it not seem as if they were somehow taught by his Holy Spirit; their minds enlightened, their hearts renewed, their activity shaped by almighty grace? As to salvation without the Bible, we must say, with a leading Reformation Symbol, that "there is no ordinary possibility" of it; but might it not be going too far to say that it is absolutely and in the nature of the case impossible? The rule is "salvation by faith, and faith by hearing;" but if the rule does not cover the case of infants, why must it be taken to cover that of all other human beings? The mere light of nature is doubtless insufficient to give saving knowledge of God; but saving enlightenment can hardly be held impossible in a mind to which God has access direct. Humility and charity will alike refuse to mark out a path for him whose "footsteps are not known." *It is ill trying to make the voyage of the religious life with a spiritual Jonah on board.* Yet the Church is full of such would-be navigators. There is the Jonah of a demoralizing occupation—occupation having to do, *e.g.*, with gambling, or betting, or drunkenness, or fraudulent manufacture, and it must be thrown overboard or the ship of personal religion will go down. There is the Jonah of some pet sin, which, like Herod to Herodias, we cling to and prefer to Christ; and if we would escape the lake of fire we must "pluck it out and cast it from us." There is above all the Jonah of an unbelieving heart. Men will have a religion without self-surrender; will do anything and everything but yield themselves to God. Yet they must do this, or all else is vain. Unbelief is in its nature fatal, cuts off the dead soul from its life in Christ. We ask you one question—Will you give yourself now and here to Christ? If you answer, "Yes," you are a saved man. If you answer, "No," we need pursue the inquiry no further, for heaven is as inaccessible to you as if Christ the Way to it had never come.—J. E. H.

Ver. 17.—"*The sign of the Prophet Jonas.*" God sees the end from the beginning. He means it from the beginning. He is moving towards it from the beginning. There are no isolated events. Each is connected with a series leading up to it. The series is so long that we cannot see its earlier steps, much less observe their direction. But nothing is surer than that from the first they have a trend toward that one which is their ultimate effect. In proof of this we have only to select a series on which we have the light of Scripture, such as that leading up to the work of Christ. There are many such series. One leads up to his birth, another to his education, another to his sufferings, another to his death; and so on. And these series lead up to it in various ways. There is a prophetic series, and a typical series, and a contributory series, and a causal series. And there are events which lead up to it in two or three of these capacities at once. Such an event is the one recorded here, as the New Testament Scriptures repeatedly affirm. Consider this event—

I. As A MIRACLE. It was clearly outside the natural order. The shark or other sea-monster was "prepared" by God. It swallowed Jonah, contrary to its habit, without crushing him between its teeth. He remained alive in its stomach for days, contrary to all known physical laws. He was cast out safely on land, contrary to all natural probabilities. Seeing, as he could not but see, God's hand in the whole thing, Jonah would learn from it: 1. *The Divine resistless purpose.* Throwing off allegiance, he fled from duty like a man resolved on any terms to get away. But God went after him in a way that showed he meant to have his work done. The fugitive was stopped by wind and wave and conspiring circumstances as by an adamantine wall, impossible to break through. He knew now that God was a God who cannot be baulked, and who will have his way. The same lesson we all need to learn. Much rebellion arises out of a half-conscious expectation that God at last will give way, and our disobedience be all condoned. And half the afflictions we suffer are to cure us of our wilfulness and conceit of irresponsibility. They teach us that God's arm, not ours, is strongest—that his will, not ours, must rule. When we have appropriated and endorsed the sentiment, "Not as I will, but as thou wilt," our life-sky will clear, and the thunder-clouds that threatened a deluge will discharge themselves in fertilizing showers. 2. *The Divine consistent character.* Severity was conspicuous up to the point of the prophet's immersion.

After that everything spoke of goodness. There are qualities in God fitted each in its own way to move men to his service (2 Cor. v. 11; Rom. xii. 1). They moved Jonah. His humble, believing, thankful prayer in the monster's maw is a revelation of their effect on his moral nature. And godly lives the world over and all history through are effects due to the same cause (Ps. vii. 17; Rom. ii. 4). Severity and goodness are just Divine moral excellence facing two different ways (Rom. xi. 22). Both have the same infinitely glorious perfection behind them, and are forceful with its inherent essential energy. 3. *The Divine effective way.* God had not interfered in the matter of Jonah's disobedient flight until things had gone a certain length. He allowed him to reach Joppa, and get on board a ship, and start for Tarshish. The sinful act was completed before the punishment began. But the moment it was morally complete the stern "Thus far and no further" was spoken. And how masterly the strategy, and resourceful the strength of God appeared! The elements, the lower animals, and man alike become his ministers, and stop the runaway before and on either side. And then the measures as a whole are so exactly yet variously apposite to the purpose of checking insubordination, and compelling execution of the original command! Jonah would know more about the God with whom he had to do, and the considerations moving to implicit obedience, than he ever knew before. It is not in the Divine dealings as an exhibition of mere force, but of force directed unalterably to ends of justice and mercy, that them in proportion as God's perfections come out in them and shine. Men are moved by them in proportion as God's perfections come out in them and shine.

II. AS A TYPE. On this point we have for an interpreter Christ himself (Matt. xii. 40). "Jonah was in the fish's belly, so was Christ in the grave; Jonah came forth from thence, so did Christ rise again; his (Christ's) rising doth bring our rising, his resurrection ours, because he was the firstfruits of all those that do sleep (1 Cor. xv. 20)" (Abbot). The analogy between Jonah's sojourn in the deep and Christ's in the grave is such as to fit one to be a type of the other. The analogy holds: 1. *In the time of the sojourn.* It was three days in each case. In the case of Christ we know that two of these days were incomplete. He was buried in the evening of the first day, and rose on the morning of the third day. Rhetorical speech is necessarily in round numbers, and our Lord states the truth broadly without attempting to elaborate details. Why three days was the period fixed on either in type or antitype we cannot tell. It is pertinent to notice, however, that three and four are mystic numbers, and together make up seven, the number of perfection. Then three days were sufficient, and no more, to establish the fact of death in the case of Christ, and the reality of the miracle of preservation in the case of Jonah. Details of Scripture are important because they record details of a Divine procedure which are purposeful through and through. 2. *In the capacity in which each sojourned.* Jonah was in the fish's belly as Christ was in the grave, in payment of the penalty of sin. Moreover, each by accomplishing this saved men from death. "Each of the processes is an atonement, an expiation, a sacrifice, pacifying the Divine Judge, satisfying Divine justice, abolishing guilt, restoring peace, effecting reconciliation" (Martin). But here the analogy ends. The type suffered for sins of his own, the blessed Antitype for sins of others. The type saved men from death of the body, the Antitype saved them from death eternal. Well might he say, on a memorable occasion, "a greater than Jonah is here"! 3. *In the analogous experience of the two.* The experiences were not identical. Christ literally "died and rose again according to the Scriptures." Jonah did not actually die and rise. But he did virtually. His natural life was forfeit, and was only saved by a miracle equal to that of resurrection. His life in the deep was a supernatural life, and, therefore, practically a new one. Indeed, he applies the words "hell" (*Sheol*) and "corruption" (*shachath*) to his condition, the same words which Scripture applies to Christ's sojourn in a state of death (ch. ii. 2—6; Ps. xvi. 10; Acts ii. 31). He uses them doubtless in a figurative sense, but by using them at all he treats himself as virtually a dead man. Like those of Hezekiah and Lazarus and the widow's son (Isa. xxxviii. 5; John xi. 44; Luke vii. 15), the life of Jonah from that hour was God-given and new. So may be your life or mine. If God has saved you alive when men despaired of your recovery, or when but for some interposition which we call an accident it was forfeit by natural laws, then you are even as Jonah, and your remaining life, like his, is in a special sense and measure consecrate (Rom. xii. 1). 4. *That with each it was the gate to a new life.* The life of Jonah after his virtual resurrection was a new one, and greatly higher than the old. He emerges from the sea a new man, in a new relation to God, with a new purpose of heart, and a new life-career opening out. "His old life is cancelled; all its guilt obliterated; all its evils interruptive of Divine fellowship and blessing abolished—left behind in the depths of the sea. He is dead to the past; and it has no more hold on him, no more evidence against him, no more wrath in store for him" (Martin). A prominent element in this new life was the preaching to Gentile Nineveh. But for it that heathen city would have perished for lack of knowledge. So also the resurrection-life of Christ is new (Rom. vi. 10). Living always to God, he lives to him now in a new sense. "He was raised from the dead by the glory of the Father." And as he rose no bond of law kept hold on him any more; no condemnation laid its taint upon him any more; the glory of his Father's unmingled and eternal favour shone upon him now for evermore; and in his Father's favour he had life, his risen and eternal life" (Martin). In short, the risen Saviour's life is life in a new sphere, and a new relation and to new purpose. By that life, moreover, he enters the door which by his death he opened (Eph. ii. 11—17)—the door of access to the Gentile world (Matt. xxviii. 16—20; Acts i. 5—8). The risen Saviour gives the Scriptures to be preached to the ends of the earth, and the apostles and teachers to preach them, and the Spirit to apply them, and the Church to embody them in her Christ-like life. And thus is negotiated a wider repentance than of Nineveh, and with greater results. "God hath also to the Gentiles granted repentance unto life."

III. As a sign. A sign is a miracle viewed from the evidential standpoint, a Divine work regarded as authenticating a Divine truth. Jonah's entombment served this purpose (Matt. xii. 39). 1. *It was a sign to the Ninevites.* (Luke xi. 30.) Jonah in Nineveh would be full of his unparalleled adventure. He would tell the people of his virtual death and rising again by the hand of God. And would not the amazing story credential the prophet as beyond dispute the messenger of God? He would declare to them how the miracle of judgment which had consigned him to the deep had been, if possible, outdone by the miracle of mercy which had saved him "from the belly of hell." And would he not be thus a sign at once of God's resistless vengeance on sin, and his unspeakable mercy to the penitent? From such a God the Ninevites would know what they had to expect in the one character and in the other. 2. *It was the archetype of the sign of the resurrection.* (Matt. xii. 40.) The miracles of Christ were all signs. The effect of them was to certify his Divine mission, and bring men to faith in his Name (Matt. xxvii. 54; John xi. 45). On many, however, they were practically thrown away. The Jews clamoured for a sign, while signs were being wrought before their very eyes. To this blind demand of insuperable unbelief there would be one further concession. The sign of the Prophet Jonah would be repeated in the Person of Christ by the resurrection on the third day. This was an unchallengable sign of the Divine mission of our Lord (Rom. i. 4). If the dead One rose, then undoubtedly that dead One must have been the Son of God (1 Cor. xv. 14). The resurrection of Christ was the Father's sign-manual to the Son's claim to a Divine character and an accepted work. It was a sign, too, of the Divine attitude toward sin. Taken in connection, as it must be, with the death and burial, the whole was, like Jonah's miraculous experience, a graphic attestation of wrath against sin, removed as soon as satisfied, but inappeasable till then. If God "spared not his own Son," whom will he spare? If the sin laid on Christ is punished to the full, how much more the sin that remains on the sinner! And then, if Christ rises into a new life the moment his assumed connection with sin ends by death, shall not we, dead to our sin by the body of Christ, be raised together with him to "walk in newness of life"? The sign of the Prophet Jonah is everything to us. It means Christ credentialled, salvation finished and attested, and a sure hope springing of the resurrection unto life.

1. *See how far God's judgments may follow deserters.* Generally they include misfortune, often sickness, and sometimes death. The principle is that they must be efficacious, and so they go on till they reach their object. The distance you have gone away from God is the measure of the length to which his judgments will follow you (Col. iii. 25). 2. *See how easily God can turn the destroyer into a preserver.* Instead of killing Jonah, the fish saves his life. The Divine afflictive agencies operate in like manner. They wound only to heal; destroy the flesh "that the spirit may be saved

in the day of Jesus Christ." Your judgments are your mercies. Let the Divine mercy they reveal be your call to the duty you owe, your recall to the service you forsake (Ps. lxxxix. 30—33; Rev. iii. 19). 3. *Realize the high things to which this sign of the Prophet Jonas calls you.* The death of Christ was for the death of your sin, his life from the dead for the life of your soul (Rom. vi. 4; Eph. v. 14).—J. E. H.

Vers. 1—3.—*Jonah's call and flight.* "Now the word of the Lord came unto Jonah the son of Amittai, saying," etc.

I. THE MAN. Jonah is introduced without a word of explanation, except (implicitly) that he was a prophet of the Lord. So also Elijah (1 Kings xvii. 1). Their previous history is assumed. God's servants are treated as all waiting on him to receive his orders, so that "he says to this one, Go, and he goeth, and to another, Come, and he cometh." This is the true idea of servants; they "look unto his hand" (Ps. cxxiii. 2); "stand in his house" (Ps. cxxxiv. 1); "stand before him" (Jer. xv. 1). We have a little more information about Jonah (see 2 Kings xiv. 25). In the New Testament we have a twofold view of Jonah—a sign to the Ninevites (Luke xi. 30, 32), and a type of Christ (Matt. xii. 40). This book is short, but of remarkable interest. "It is long and it is short; short if we respect the smallness of the volume, but long if we respect the copious variety of excellent observations that are therein to be found: as the horribleness of sin, which was able within forty days to pluck down an utter desolation on so famous a city as Nineveh; God's love in forewarning them that dwelt in that place that they might be spared; the prophet's foul fall, and his strange punishment for it; his offwardness from God, and God's favourable inclination evermore to him; the regard which the King of Nineveh and his people did bear to God's judgments when they were denounced; the free pardon of the Lord and his remitting of their sin upon their repentance" (Archbishop Abbot).

II. THE CALL. 1. *Its source.* Directly and clearly from God—the only source of spiritual authority—an authority not to be gainsaid or trifled with. Unlike any other authority, to it implicit obedience is due.

"Theirs not to make reply;
Theirs not to reason why."

2. *Its rousing note.* Arise! Implies summons to unusual exertion—the commission that follows needs great energy—it is not to be executed in a listless frame—"wherefore gird up the loins of your mind." Some duties are of such a kind that unusual self-excitation is needed for them (see Heb. xii. 1). "The very first word he hears is 'Arise.' It is a word used before another verb as a term of excitement. Arise! I know you have difficulties, in yourself, in your people, in the mission to Nineveh; arise, therefore, gird up your loins, stir up thy strength and go!" (Rev. A. Raleigh, D.D.). How differently has the command to arise been dealt with by different men! Moses hesitates, pleads off, at last agrees (Exod. iv.). Jeremiah urges his youth (i. 6). Paul confers not with flesh and blood (Gal. i. 16). Our Lord sets his face steadfastly to go up to Jerusalem (Luke ix. 51). 3. *Its sphere.* "Go to Nineveh, that great city." The prophet is sent outside the boundaries of Israel; he is a foreign missionary —the first foreign missionary after Elijah, who was sent among the Phœnicians. The field is Nineveh, probably the greatest and richest city of the world at that time. As missionary to Nineveh, Jonah occupies a remarkable position—through him God is to assert his claim as the God, not only of the Jews, but of the whole earth. He is to declare himself Lord of Nineveh and of all countries, and summon its inhabitants to their allegiance to him. "Suddenly, without note or warning, without preface, without explanation, assuming sovereign state as God Most High over all the earth; Jehovah, remanifesting, if not reassuming his universal supremacy, conducts, on the scale of most amazing miracle, a movement of his ceaseless government, as it extends over all nations; and that it may not fail to compel the attention of all succeeding ages, he adorns that movement with the most marvellous and romantic incident, with one of the most striking if not perplexing developments of human character, especially as occurring in a man of God, and with the symbolic death and resurrection of the agent under whose hand that movement is conducted—a death and resurrection on the very type of Messiah's; for Jonah was three days and three nights in the whale's belly, even as the

Son of man was three days and three nights in the heart of the earth" (H. Martin, D.D.). 4. *Its purport.* "Cry against it; for its wickedness is come before me." "He must *cry* against Nineveh, not whisper in the ear as if it were to one, not speak softly as to a few, but cry as unto all: this is a general proclamation. This word 'cry' is used in Scripture when men are fast asleep and lulled in their sins, and awake not with a little; so that as Elijah said to the Baalites, they were to 'Cry aloud, because Baal might be sleeping, and must be awaked;' so the minister must cry aloud, that men may be raised from their drowsiness in sin" (Abbot). "The wickedness of Nineveh" consisted in pride, ambition, oppression, cruelty, sensuality. The Ninevites were very merciless, and practised most horrible cruelties on captives, even of the highest rank. This wickedness had come before God, denoting that it had become full (Gen. xv. 16), therefore intolerable. Yet to this merciless people Divine mercy was to be shown. Great cities apt to become great in sin—the power of sin becomes concentrated—one sinner encourages another—sin can be more easily hid—or, it may become very shameless—it is the duty of God's servants to cry against the wickedness of such cities, their drunkenness, licentiousness, greed, sabbath-breaking, etc., and proclaim God's wrath against their sins.

III. The call refused. Jonah fulfilled the command to arise—but not to go against Nineveh. He shrinks from duty—"He should have risen to cry, but he rose to fly" (Abbot). His reasons were probably various—one is afterwards referred to by him (ch. iv. 2). Shirking duty because it is irksome and disagreeable, is too common. In ordinary life, irksome employments, when not patiently accepted, breed negligence, idleness, drunkenness, love of illicit pleasure, etc. Here is a lesson for the young—at school, or when beginning business or trade. In religious life, disagreeableness of duty is often a stumbling-block—often makes us unfaithful; we neglect to warn others because the task is disagreeable. As the remedy for this, learn to regard duty ever as the command of God, who will strengthen and carry through all who trust him. "Jonah rose up to flee unto Tarshish from the presence of the Lord." He could hardly have believed that Tarshish was out of God's presence, but he acted as if he thought so. It was away from his *immediate* and manifested presence. There is a tendency in many to act as if God were in some places, not in others—as if God were in the church or religious meeting, but not in the market-place, and as if they might act there as his enemies act. Edmund Burke said the humanity of England was "a thing of points and parallels." Some break the sabbath abroad as they would not do at home. Many fly from the company of godly people, because not willing to think of God. Lurking unbelief in this. Omnipresence of God a lesson for both old and young. God is sometimes represented by conscience. Fatal is the wish to escape from God—it would be to leave all that is bright, holy, gladdening, for ways of darkness, filth, misery. If we say to God, "Depart from us" (Job xxi. 14), he will say to us, "Depart from me" (Matt. xxv. 41). Jonah's effort to escape from God's presence seemed successful— "he found a ship going to Tarshish." Providence seemed to favour him; but this was a narrow view—providence must be interpreted widely. "We cannot expect smiles of approbation from Heaven any longer than we can say with Abraham's servant, 'I being *in the way*'" (Jones of Creaton). "So he paid the fare thereof." He had the money ready—another apparently favourable providence, and he paid it at once, for men do not grudge expense to carry out their own will, however reluctant often to spend it to carry out God's. See the costliness of sin—yet the devil's taxes are usually paid cheerfully. Picture Jonah afloat in the Mediterranean—his conflicting feelings —relief, yet no relief—like a modern criminal escaping to America, with an evil conscience and dread of the telegraph—his expedition insane. "Whither can I go from thy presence?" (Ps. cxxxix.). No hiding *from* God (Jer. xxiii. 24; Rev. vi. 16). Only hiding-place *in* God (Ps. xxxii. 7). The great lesson is this—indefeasible obligation of God's will, and man's alienation from it and disposition to resist it (Rom. vii.). Hence the need of watching and prayer: "Teach me to do thy will!"—W. G. B.

Vers. 4—6.—*The fugitive arrested.* "But the Lord sent out a great wind into the sea, and there was a mighty tempest in the sea, so that the ship was like to be broken," etc. "Woe unto him that striveth with his Maker!" God is never at a loss for means of conquering opposition and bringing erring men to their senses—he arrests Balaam by means of a sword, David through a parable, Peter by a look, the Philippian jailor by an earthquake, Jonah by a storm. All nature is at his command. "The whole world full of invisible couriers, robed and ready for their service."

I. THE STORM SENT OUT BY GOD. Connection between the physical and moral world is so adjusted that the former accomplishes purposes of moral government. Storms in a sense are results of fixed law, yet instruments of Divine will—"stormy wind fulfilling his word" (Ps. cxlviii. 8)—fitted to show men their helplessness and dependence—to reprove them for rebelling against him whose their breath is, and whose are all their ways. Many things else have same purpose—illness, frustration of plans, etc. "In the day of adversity, consider." Sin often causes storms—"in one's heart, in families, in Churches, in towns, and in nations (Jas. iv. 1)" (Jones). The storm was adjusted so as to answer precisely the purpose of God. The ship was not actually broken, but like to be broken—literally, "thought to be broken"—vivid image, as if creaks and groans were those of a living thing, as if the ship itself dreaded destruction.

II. CONDUCT OF THE MARINERS. "Then the mariners were afraid." Mariners usually an intrepid race—"a stiffer kind of men than most are"—are now afraid. Fear drives to prayer. In a storm the forces against man are overwhelming; in such a case fear becomes inevitable, and prayer an instinct. "No man," it has been said, "was ever an atheist in a shipwreck." Herein is testimony to the existence of God—man in conscious helplessness invokes a higher Power. The mariners took a double course—they both prayed and used the means available for the safety of the ship. 1. They cried *every man to his god*. Ignorance and superstition may mingle with more genuine feelings. "I think we have no ground for uttering one word of reproach or blame against these men. They would contrast but too favourably with many a ship's crew that sails out of London or Liverpool. These poor heathen men prayed to their gods. Many a British sailor only swears and curses by his. They did what they could. They were true to the best instincts of the human mind" (Raleigh). The prayer of fear is not necessarily the prayer of faith; fear may be the beginning of a godly life, but is not its essence; love is the essence of true religion and of true communion with God; "perfect love casteth out fear." If fear sets us at first to pray for ourselves, our families, our Church, our country, it must advance to something higher. 2. "They cast forth the wares that were in the ship into the sea, to lighten it of them." How worthless are all earthly possessions in comparison of life! "Skin for skin, yea, all that a man hath, he will give for his life;" "What shall it profit a man, if he gain the whole world, and lose his own life?" There are moments when utter worthlessness of all earthly things irresistibly flashes even on the worldly mind. Would that men thought oftener of this! Contrast the security of the Christian treasure—immovability of the Christian hope.

III. CONDUCT OF JONAH. "But Jonah was gone down into the sides of the ship; and he lay, and was fast asleep." Apparently he avoided prayer when the mariners took to it—he could not pray. "If I regard iniquity in my heart, the Lord will not hear me;" "Your sins have separated between you and your God." A guilty conscience makes prayer impossible, till a break-down takes place, and contrition bursts out. Note the misery of Jonah—he cannot bear to see the men praying while he himself cannot pray—he goes down to the sides of the ship. "The most wretched man in the world is the man who is afflicted, and cannot pray." He was fast asleep. This was not unnatural —he had been under a great strain; now comes a recoil. Sisera slept in the tent of Jael—the disciples in the garden of Gethsemane. Jonah's sleep was not a sign of insensibility, but a proof of the terrible constraint under which he had been acting. He had utterly exhausted himself in his struggle with God, and the very storm cannot keep him awake. Yet surely this was a strange sight—the heathen mariners praying, and the servant of God sleeping. This, indeed, was typical of the purpose for which God had sent him to Nineveh, viz. that the repentance of Nineveh might be a reproof to Israel; so the prayers of these heathen were a reproof to Jonah—he was provoked to jealousy by them that were not God's people. Sometimes the Church is rebuked by the world; at least a contrast to the crooked ways, cross temper, and ungracious talk of professing Christians is sometimes found in the integrity, gentleness, and charity of some who make no profession. Earnestness of heathen in their religious observances is often a reproof to Christians. "Why should the Church allow the world to bear away the palm in reference to any one element of excellence whatsoever—candour, courtesy, charity, kindliness, large-mindedness, liberality, self-denial, any virtue what-soever? Why should there be one single department of what is good—good in any sphere, moral, physical, social, scientific, concerning which the world can with any show of fairness profess to school the Church, or say, Stand aside, for we are more at home here than you?" (Martin).

IV. CONDUCT OF THE SHIPMASTER. The absence of Jonah in time of prayer had arrested attention, and was felt to be strange and unseemly. Even the world expects Christians to do their duty. Shipmaster reproves him sharply, cries aloud against *him*, "What meanest thou, O sleeper?" for his sleep was not the sleep that God gives to his beloved. A rebuke often applicable still to many other classes—to all at ease in Zion, to neglecters of the great salvation, to open transgressors, to worldlings, to forgetters of God, to those who think not of righteousness, temperance, and judgment to come! "Arise, call upon thy God, if so be that God will think upon us, that we perish not." Jonah is called to prayer—earnest prayer; he must "arise"—a recumbent attitude not suitable for such prayer—rather the attitude of Jacob wrestling at Peniel. A reason is given why Jonah should pray, but a hesitating reason, "if so be"—if there be even a chance of prayer prevailing; this is very different from the full assurance of faith. Faith knows that God will hear, and that he ever thinks upon his own, and that they cannot perish, in the deepest sense of the word. "My sheep hear my voice, and I know them, and they follow me, and they shall never perish." The name and work of Christ, unknown to this mariner, give confidence in prayer. The heathen mariner is here the preacher to the prophet, not the prophet to the mariner. "Let us listen to his awaken-ing call. These words of his *have* aroused many a sleeper besides Jonah. . . . Hear them, sleeping soul, to-day. What meanest *thou*, O sleeper?—sleeping here in this great battle-field, where souls are lost and won? In this vineyard of noblest work, where God-given talents are doubled or forfeited for ever? In this treacherous sea of life, girt round with storms which might so easily break the strongest ships that float? What meanest thou?—sleeping now, with noonday lights above thee, and about thee men who strive and men who pray? . . . While the gates of heaven and hell stand open, the murky shadows of the one gathering in deeper folds, the joy-bells of the other waiting to peal?" (Raleigh). Oh the unreasonableness of spiritual sleep—sleep of unbelief—sleep of backsliding! "Now it is high time to awake out of sleep" (Rom. xiii. 11).—W. G. B.

Vers. 7—10.—*The fugitive convicted.* "And they said every one to his fellow, Come, and let us cast lots, that we may know for whose cause this evil is upon us. So they cast lots, and the lot fell upon Jonah," etc. The prayers of the mariners, and Jonah's prayer, if indeed he tried to pray (although that is hardly likely; see ch. iv. 2, "*Then* Jonah prayed"), led to no abatement of the storm. God's purpose was not to be accomplished in that way—Jonah was not to be restored in so easy a manner. But prayer may *seem* to be unanswered while it is answered—it is a link in a chain. A much more profound discipline had yet to be passed through in order that Jonah might be restored and the great purpose of his mission to Nineveh attained. Let us trace the next steps in the development of the providential plan.

I. THE MARINERS RESOLVE TO CAST LOTS. (Ver. 7.) This is a striking step. They might have given themselves up for lost, perhaps drowning their feelings, as sailors have often done, in intoxication (if that be not an exclusively modern practice); but they resolved to make another effort to save their lives and their ship. This proceeded on the belief that this storm was caused by some man's sin; and to find out who was the offender they determined to cast lots. A dangerous generalization, to ascribe a calamity to one man's sin, though in this case correct. Perhaps there were unusual circumstances in the storm that led them to reason thus. "If anything should happen *strangely*, as while we are in this mortality we may very well expect, we can take no better course than these shipmen presently to fear lest iniquity be the author of it " (Abbot). Casting lots was a peculiar device to ascertain a secret; *religious* use of lots, however, is very different from the careless appeal to the lot often made (see Josh. vii. 16; 1 Sam. x. 21; Acts i. 26). The lot becomes legitimate only when all the ordinary methods of settling a difficulty have failed, and nothing remains but to make a solemn appeal to God.

II. THE LOT FALLS UPON JONAH. Picture his anxiety while the lot was being cast—his despair when it fell on him. This seems to have brought him to a sense of his sin: it was God's voice, "Thou art the man!" Jonah now broke down, prostrated by the little arrow from God's quiver. In walking through a hospital after a battle, two remarks are sometimes made—How easy to kill! and—How difficult to kill! Some bodies almost entire, yet killed; some fearfully shattered, yet alive. So we say—How difficult it is to humble! and—How easy it is to humble! difficult for man, easy for God; man may reason, expostulate, apply truth, yet the offender may not in any degree be touched by it. A word, a look, a lot from God, makes one quite prostrate and helpless. What a power of rebuking and prostrating God may use at the last day!

III. JONAH QUESTIONED. All eyes are fixed on Jonah with eager curiosity to ascertain what he had done. The running fire of questions indicates desire for light on the strange transaction. They were chiefly anxious to know his *crime*, his *occupation*, and his *country*; either his personal guilt, or the guilt connected with his occupation, if it was an unlawful one, or with his country, or with his people; for there might be some horrible sin, perhaps committed of old by the people of his country, exposing them and him through them to the wrath of the gods. Why did they not act at once on the decision of the lot, and throw Jonah overboard? Probably they desired confirmation of it; it must be a painful transaction, and they would like more authority for the step they were to take. It would be satisfactory to get Jonah to confess. It might throw light on the origin of storms, and be a useful hint for the future.

IV. JONAH'S ANSWER. The nobler aspect of Jonah's character now comes out—perfect ingenuousness and honesty; he knows his fate—death stares him in the face—yet there is no shrinking or fencing of any kind. He tells them: 1. He is a Hebrew, a member of the race that had so much to do with the powers above. 2. The God whom he worships is the God that made the sea and the dry land, and has absolute power over both. 3. He has fled from his presence, has offended him, and now God is showing his displeasure. Humiliating position, yet not without a certain grandeur—Jonah under the rebuke of God, his own conscience, and the heathen mariners. In reference to the mariners, he who might have been expected to bring them blessing has brought them trouble. His mouth is shut; he can say nothing for himself. There is something very striking in his undergoing the condemnation of the *mariners*. He had been afraid, apparently, of the bad opinion of the Ninevites, and had shunned his commission; but now he encounters the bad opinion of the mariners—with nothing to fall back on—his conscience and his God both against him. Yet there is a grandeur in his honest confession, in his attitude of thorough humility; there is a noble truthfulness now about him; he conceals nothing, though he must be the victim.

V. EFFECT ON THE MARINERS. They were exceedingly afraid. They felt a sense of the reality and nearness of a supernatural power—the power of the God who made the sea and now raises it in storm. The supernatural must be always very impressive—must have subduing effect whenever God is felt to be near, as in time of pestilence. The men now felt God near, in character of the righteous, holy Judge, punishing an offender—not like heathen gods, jesting at sin, but in terrible earnest against it. They seemed to have been impressed, and converted to God, for the soul may move very rapidly; deep impressions may be made very suddenly in time of great excitement. A great lesson to Jonah; if these rough heathen sailors were so deeply impressed by the fear of God, might not the Ninevites have been so too? They said to Jonah, "Why hast thou done this?" Strange aspect of sins of God's servants in eyes of world! God's servants have no cloak for their sins. The question must have cut Jonah to the quick. He could only echo it in blank amazement—Why *have* I done this? Observe the hollowness of all apologies for sin in the hour of judgment; sin, however sweet in the mouth, is bitter in the belly; "lust, when it is finished, bringeth forth death." The horror and misery of the ship's company are a type of the effects of sin, of one sin, by a servant of God. "Who can understand his errors? Cleanse thou me from secret faults. Keep back thy servant also from presumptuous sins." O sin, what a monster art thou! what tragedies come out of thee! how dost thou involve others in ruin, as the drunkard's family! God give us a true sense of it, and teach us to hate it in every form, and guard against its minutest seeds, lest, like the dragon's teeth, they breed against us hosts of armed men! Let each one often put the question, in reference to his sins, "Why hast thou done this?" Sinned against God and man, and against thine own soul, and against thine own children? Better we should put the question and answer it in time, than wait till God puts it in the day of judgment.—W. G. B.

Vers. 11—17.—*The offender sacrificed.* "Then said they unto him, What shall we do unto thee, that the sea may be calm unto us? for the sea wrought, and was tempestuous," etc. A new stage of spiritual progress has been reached—yet the sea not calm. There had been prayer—but no calm followed; now there is frank confession of sin, and doubtless repentance, and acknowledgment of God even by the men, but the sea still wrought, and was tempestuous. Was it "no use" to pray and repent? No; but God's plan was a large one, not yet completed. See the danger of impatience and despair when a blessing is delayed: "Though the vision tarry, wait for it."

I. JONAH IS MADE HIS OWN JUDGE. "Then said they unto him, What shall we do unto thee, that the sea may be calm unto us?" They seem to have felt, "There is one God, and Jonah is his prophet." Fearing God, they recognized the claims of his servant, and appealed to him to pass judgment on himself—"What shall we do unto thee?" Doubtless they had their own ideas, but they respected him as a prophet, and were slow to lay hands on him, and thought that, as a servant of God, he would know best what would appease his wrath. "I see chiefly in this language an appeal to the true God and the true man. Wherever the knowledge of God is clearly and truly communicated, heathenism and idols have no chance. . . . Let God be clearly known as he is revealed, and, with very few exceptions, men cannot *but* believe on him. . . . So, too, when the true man appears among men, although it may be, as in this case, coming out of untrueness and unfairness, staggering back through the storm and penalty that he may at least die in the right way, men must yield that man reverence. The image of God is shining in him once more. He is a living and true man— son of the living and true God—'What shall we do unto thee?'" (Raleigh).

II. THE SELF-IMPOSED SENTENCE. "Take me up, and cast me into the sea." The coward now become a hero shows a noble and self-sacrificing spirit—contrast to former spirit. And now comes to the front the instinct of retribution. Jonah does not propose that he should be granted an opportunity to go to Nineveh and execute his commission; he felt that he was causing death to others—it was just that he should die to prevent them from dying: "I know that for my sake this great tempest is upon you." But he will not be his own executioner: "Take me up, and cast me into the sea." No man is entitled to take away his own life; no countenance either in nature or in Bible to suicide. Jonah's death must be a judicial act, executed by others. "Cast me forth into the sea, for that is the will of God; it is my will also, for I cannot endure to see you in such danger and distress any longer on my account. You have already lost your goods because of me, and you have been for some time in peril of your lives; that you may suffer no more, take me up, and cast me into the sea" (Jones).

III. ANOTHER PULL FOR LIFE. "Nevertheless the men rowed hard to bring it to the land." These men gain upon us—rough seamen by profession, tinged by Oriental barbarity in all likelihood, they become generous, and eager to save Jonah. Jonah's humility, candour, and ready self-sacrifice had impressed them: "They rowed hard to bring the ship to land." A self-sacrificing spirit draws men's hearts—turns the heathen —Livingstone's influence with natives of Africa due in no small measure to this feature —remember the self-sacrifice of our Lord: "I, if I be lifted up from the earth, will draw all men unto me." "Every good thing in our spirit and action has a tendency to reproduce itself in others who are in any way related to it, especially, of course, if it is called forth for their advantage. Jonah is true and noble at length. The sailors, having responsive qualities in themselves, are nobler for his nobleness, are more self-forgetful because, when the moment of stress came, he did the noblest thing a man could do for fellow-men—offered his life for theirs" (Raleigh). Another step is thus gained in moral progress—"the men" have become full of reverence toward God, and full of regard for his prophet—but to no purpose apparently; "for the sea wrought, and was tempestuous against them." A sacrifice is indispensable. (In the men "pulling hard" some have found an emblem of sinners trying to save themselves before they resort to God's way of sacrifice; but this lesson seems far-fetched.)

IV. THE MARINERS PRAY TO GOD. " Wherefore they cried unto the Lord, and said, We beseech thee, O Lord, we beseech thee," etc. The tender conscience and devout feeling of the mariners are very remarkable. Observe : 1. Vehemence of their prayer : "They *cried* "—they beseech God once and again. 2. They appeal to God's justice : " Let us not perish for this man's life." 3. Their concern for life : " Lay not upon us innocent blood." Shedding of blood was little thought of in those times—massacre of innocent and guilty alike were common enough. 4. Their submissiveness to God : " For thou, O Lord, hast done as it pleased thee." Thou hast shown thy sovereign will in the past; let it rule us now. Most profitable lesson for us all : " In all thy ways acknow‑ ledge him, and he shall direct thy paths " (Prov. iii. 6). Especially in reference to any step that, once taken, cannot be recalled. For if they threw Jonah overboard, it was an irrevocable act.

V. JONAH IS CAST FORTH. " So they took up Jonah, and cast him forth into the sea : and the sea ceased from her raging." They took him up, tenderly and respectfully, not pitching him overboard in a tumultuous manner. The prophet offers no resistance ; one great heave, and he is engulfed ; in a little moment the sea closes on him—the men gazing after him with sorrowful, anxious faces, thinking, perhaps, " Poor man ! where is he now ? " It is an awful testimony to the righteousness of God ; one offence has for‑ feited Jonah's life. No wonder they are anxious. But their anxiety does not last long ; God reveals himself at once, and very wonderfully : " The storm ceased from her raging." The men are relieved from a double anxiety—anxiety about the storm, and anxiety whether or not they have done right. " Thus died Jonah, to them, at least, the death of a criminal pursued by justice ; yet the death of a repentant and righteous man ; in death triumphing over death ; committing himself to God in singular meekness and faith ; acknowledging the justice of his doom, and relying on Divine pardon and pro‑ tection ; committing his body to the sea and his soul to the God whom he feared, the God of heaven, and of the sea, and of the dry land " (Martin).

VI. THE EFFECT UPON THE MEN. At last the storm ceases. What neither prayers, nor repentance, nor the change in the mind of the men had accelerated by one iota comes at once and completely after the sacrifice of one man. Fresh token of nearness of God ; but not this time vindicating his justice or executing his wrath ; showing his mercy and his love. Great power of mercy and love to move the heart : " The men feared the Lord exceedingly." Awed by his presence, reassured by his mercy, they " offered a sacrifice unto the Lord, and made vows ; " showed their deep sense of obligation, and took steps to keep it up. The vow was probably to be performed at some future time. Thus they took precautions against evanescence of grateful feeling —a useful lesson. Men " soon forget his mercies ; " vows tend to keep sense of them alive in after‑times.

VII. JONAH NOT LOST. " The Lord had prepared a great fish to swallow up Jonah." " Praise the Lord from the earth, ye dragons, and all deeps." God had shown himself the Lord of inanimate nature ; now he shows himself Lord of animate nature. The storm had been his messenger ; now his messenger is the fish. This is duly in accordance with the idea of God which the whole transaction and the whole book present. Jehovah claims to be not only the God of the Hebrew, but the God of Nineveh, and of the whole earth. He is the God of heaven, " which hath made the sea and the dry land." " The earth is the Lord's, and the fulness thereof ; " " So is this wide and great sea, wherein go things creeping innumerable, both large and small beasts." He shows his sovereignty over the land by " preparing a great fish." He bends it to his own purposes—makes the devouring monster a means of protection and preservation. The whole story has a supernatural air. If the presence of the supernatural be once admitted, the *form* of miracle is a mere matter of detail. Objections arising from the apparently *grotesque* character of this miracle are obviated if it be considered that God wished to convince Jonah of his power to protect and preserve him even in Nineveh, amid hordes of furious enemies, roused perhaps to fury by his message. He that had protected him in the body of the fish, surging up and down through the depths of the stormy sea, was able to protect him at Nineveh. The unusual character of Jonah's mission justifies an unusual miracle. God's manifold resources of preservation—Noah in the ark—Moses in the cradle of bulrushes—Elijah by the ravens—Jesus by flight into Egypt—Paul through his nephew finding out conspiracy. Many more are found in Christian biography. All the powers of nature, all creatures rational and irrational, men, devils, and angels, are subject to him; and now subject to Christ: God "hath put all things under his feet, and given him to be Head over all things to the Church, which is his body, the fulness of him that filleth all in all."—W. G. B.

Ver. 1—ch. iv. 11.—*Characteristics of Jonah.* The weaknesses, the secrets of character, as well as the possibilities of a man are discovered in life's crises. Jonah's great mission to Nineveh has revealed him to us; and who can tell how much it revealed him to himself?

I. HE WAS A MAN OF STERN TRUTHFULNESS. This book was virtually written by him. This is the testimony of antiquity; is attested by some linguistic peculiarities in the original, and by the striking details in the narrative, that only could have been known to Jonah himself. Sad and monitory is that narrative; but be it remembered that *he* writes it. And mark *how.* He conceals nothing, extenuates nothing; says the bitter worst about himself. There is no effort at explanation, no colour of apology, no relieving light. If his conduct *should* be a warning, *let* it be a warning. It is not difficult to "speak truth" to and about others. It is agreeable even to some. But to "speak truth" about *one's self*—there is the difficulty. Truth about one's wrong-doing, one's wrong spirit. The black truth, without any attempt at apology or explanation. Few can do it. Jonah did it. How men hide themselves from themselves! How they tone down their evil deeds! Their sin is not as other men's. Not so with Jonah. He seeks not, even covertly, mercy from the reader. Enough for him to "find mercy of the *Lord.*"

II. HE WAS A MAN OF IMAGINATION. He is ever in triumphant exaltation or despairing depression; ever in extremes. And a very little matter could remove him from one to the other. To the imaginative life has brighter lights *and* deeper shadows than to other men; quicker transitions, darker sorrows. Sorrows, too, are *imagined* that never come. Something is missed; it is deemed lost; hence vexation and annoyance. All needless; the thing is soon found. A friend is expected, is delayed; all kinds of disasters are fancied to have befallen him. Oppressive, foolish fancies! A temperament this that often hinders from action. Molehills swell into mountains, and little bushes into burly lions. That seems in some cases even to exonerate from action; men so enamoured of deeds *imagined*, that the deeds in reality are never done. Men sunken into mere day-dreamers. Every temperament brings its own special temptation. And the imaginative, so easily gladdened or saddened, need much to pray for "the peace of God." We *can* rest from the undue excitements and wearing vexations of imagination as we "rest in the Lord."

III. JONAH WAS A MAN OF NARROW RELIGIOUS SYMPATHIES. His selfish care for his prophetic reputation, fearing lest the preservation of the Ninevites should stigmatize him as a false prophet, made him cruel. His intense uncharitable patriotism made him long for the destruction of Nineveh, his country's enemy. Patriotism that binds us to our birthland, the scenes of memory, and of our nation's history, is well. But it is sadly, terribly *ill* when a man thinks that he can only truly love his own country by longing for the humiliation and harm of all others. God is the God of *all* the nations; the gospel is for "every creature"—is to be passed on by us to those as yet unblessed by us. The story of Jonah warns us against the narrowing influence of professional and national feeling. How noble, in the comparison, is Paul, willing for Israel's sake to be "accursed," and yet the apostle of the Gentiles!

IV. JONAH WAS A MAN OF AN IRASCIBLE TEMPER. Uncorrected, it may be, in early life. Correction always comes sooner or later; better sooner than later. He was one soon angry, and who could be *very* angry. Not a pleasant man to live with. A complaining man, and fond of something to complain of. Fretful, dark, moody. Quick in a quarrel, and one who dared to quarrel with God's goodness. A man with a spirit of contradiction, who stood by what he said. "Did I not say so? I said it in my own country." Unlovable Jonah! A man's temperament is with him from the beginning, and abides with him, through all changes, to the end. But temper can be corrected, and become better; be uncorrected, and become worse. It is to be watched; resisted with "all prayer," if evil. Let temper, as well as cares, be carried to God. *He* can subdue it, curb its anger to peace, charm its darkness to cheerfulness.

V. WITH ALL HIS SIN, JONAH WAS A SERVANT OF THE LORD. The "root of the matter" was in him. We have gleams in this dark narrative of the better nature within him. Pleasant to believe that his later life (of which we have no record) was calm with a patience and beautiful with a charity unknown before; that "at the even-time there was light." Here, through all time, he is seen as the great *missionary*-prophet, and as, of all the prophets, the great Christ-type. On earth he had much to learn—much concerning his own folly, impatience, sin; much of God's wisdom, forbearance, perfection. And *now*, clear from sin, is he not learning the lesson still? For to know God is the blessed lesson of eternity. And its song (as was Jonah's here) is, "Salvation is of the Lord." In that song may we join at length and for ever, with him and all "the goodly fellowship of the prophets"!—G. T. C.

Vers. 1, 2.—*Jonah God's messenger.* In these words we have important instruction as to God's messengers.

I. THEIR CONTINUITY. The first word of this book is the Hebrew conjunction "and:" "*And* the word of the Lord came unto Jonah." Thus begin other books of the Old Testament. How significant! The Divine messages stand not alone; they are connected with those sent before. So with the Divine messengers. Did the word of the Lord come to Abraham, Moses, Elijah? *And* also to Jonah! He shows poorly in comparison with them, yet he too was in "the goodly fellowship of the prophets." We may have slight gifts and narrow opportunities, *still* we may be God's messengers and in the line of the greatest of the past. Each humblest Christian worker can say, "To *me also* is this grace given."

II. THE DIFFICULTIES OF GOD'S MESSENGERS. Jonah had many. This was a *novel* work to which he was bidden. A *great* work—one man to warn the millions of Nineveh. A work he could devolve on no other, and in which he was to have no human helper. He had to say a "hard saying." Not a sermon *concerning* Nineveh—that he could have preached at home; nor *to* Nineveh; but with fearless cry *against* it—the city of violence, of manifold vengeance-clamouring wickedness. But his great difficulty was within him, in an unwilling mind that soon revealed itself in rebellious life. We too have difficulties as God's messengers. In the way we have to go, the people we have to address, their callous unconcern in the message we have to bear—"warning every man." But *our* greatest difficulty is within. To be promptly obedient. Not to hesitate, delay, argue against. Oh, to watch against the reluctant will! *There* is the fontal evil. No audible voice, such as may have come to the prophets, do we need to-day. The Spirit of Christ is with us, speaking in Scripture-illumined conscience, and in the fresh strong convictions of the soul. Let us hear and promptly heed them, willing to bear or do all to which he calls.

III. THE PRIVILEGE OF GOD'S MESSENGERS. With all his faults Jonah is clothed with honour. He carried God's messages to men; he was "Jonah the *prophet*." We too may bear his messages, and by every right word and true deed *are* doing it. How privileged thus are we! Then let us "*arise, go.*" Let nothing hinder, remembering *whose* servants we are. "Arise, go" to cottage, school-class, bed of the afflicted, to warn, entreat—in all bearing God's messages; to business, to do it as in Christ's very presence; to scenes of rest, by purity and cheerfulness to witness for God the All-holy, the All-happy One; to trials, temptations, to be in Christ's strength stronger than all of them. "Arise, go to" all the work given you to do, and go to *finish* it: to sorrows, that through them you may reach the realms of rest; to death, through it to arrive at the land of life; through all to *him* our Master and Lord. "Where he is there we shall be also."—G. T. C.

Ver. 3.—*Jonah the fugitive.* I. THE MOTIVES THAT IMPELLED HIM TO FLIGHT. We cannot know *all* that prevailed with him. If we knew just *where* the call found him, and "the spirit of his mind," *then* we might be less surprised at his flight. Had he been "restraining prayer"? yielding to self-indulgence? or falling to the idolatry of his own judgment—confident that he knew his own powers, what he could best do, where best labour? *not* in all things seeking that higher wisdom which is our only safe and unerring guidance? Anyway, such a man as Jonah falls only by little and little. There are many steps to reach a spiritual catastrophe. Let us be warned, then, against the *first* steps, however secret, that lead from God. Among the things that wrongly influenced him to flight we may suppose: 1. The *novelty* of the work. To be a prophet to a heathen people, to go *to* them as God's messenger, was striking into a new line of duty. How different from work in Israel amid familiar surroundings! 2. It was work afar off, involving a long journey of several hundred miles. Those, too, were days of slow travelling, and Jonah too, perhaps, a poor traveller. 3. The difficulties of the work would only be beginning when Nineveh was reached. That he, a solitary man, a foreigner, should, in that city of insolent pride and pitiless violence, denounce judgment upon it, was indeed a stupendous work—something to *do and* to shrink from. 4. His little success at home was not encouraging. Jeroboam may have been quickened by his prophecies to military effort and victories, but Jeroboam was still an idolater. And idolaters, as a whole, were his people. What can Jonah expect, then, in Nineveh? 5. But if the Ninevites repented, then (for they would surely be saved) Jonah would be discredited. "He had foretold doom, and, lo! deliverance." 6. *Why* should Nineveh, Israel's enemy, be spared? All the small blind patriot in Jonah kindled into revolt against the work to which he was bidden. *Let* Nineveh perish! And have we no excuses for flight from duty? Such a *novel* work, or so new to us! So far away from all our experiences! Beset with countless difficulties! Amid dangers, too, perhaps! And little likelihood of success in it! *Must* the work be done? Then others must do it! Excuses may be many, valid *reasons* there can be none, for neglecting the duty which God bids us to do.

II. THE FAVOURABLE-SEEMING CHARACTER OF CIRCUMSTANCES IN JONAH'S FLIGHT. He left Gath-hepher; went down to the coast. No accident stopped him. In Joppa no illness delayed him. The sea was peaceful. He found just the ship he wished, and bound *whither* he desired. There was room for him on board. He had money enough for the passage; "so he *paid* the fare." He went aboard. What could be better? Not into the book of providence must we look to know the right way from the wrong. In *themselves*, prosperity is no proof of the Divine favour, nor adversity of the Divine displeasure. We have a "sure word" to guide us. And had Jonah tested his conduct by God's word, he would have *known*, in spite of all that seemed favourable, that he was going "the way of transgressors." Have you success in wrong? It is none the less wrong. *Things* are not really, permanently favourable if *God* is unfavourable. Are we right with him? Then *all* things, storm as well as shine, shall be right with *us*. "Even the *night* shall be light about us."

III. JONAH'S SPIRITUAL DEGRADATION IN FLIGHT FROM DUTY. "He went down to Joppa." *Literally*, down from the mountains of Zebulun, down to Joppa, and, having secured his berth, "*down* into it." *Spiritually*, how he had been going down! *Down* from his moral elevation as a prophet. *Down* from the heights of *fellowship*. *Down* from the highlands of *peace*. *Down* from Divine service in which he had been as "upon the top of the mountains." *Down*, ever less noble, beautiful, Divine! Men may "go up" in society, wealth, local influence, and yet morally be *going down*. By every act of duty *done* we ascend; by each *neglected* we morally *descend*. Having the Word of the Lord, may we have his *Spirit* too, that daily we may cheerfully respond to the heavenly voice that says, "Come up higher"!—G. T. C.

Vers. 4—6.—*Jonah reproved*. I. A TEMPESTUOUS PROVIDENCE REPROVED HIM. Jonah, aroused, creeps on deck. What a scene met him! The sea in horrible tumult. The fury of the wind. The ship

"... up and down
From the base of the wave to the billow's crown!"

The bronzed sailors wondering what would be the end! The storm is reproving him. No miraculous wind, perhaps. *Still*, God's servant with strong reproof: "Guilty Jonah, awake! arise! return! To thy God; to thy work! Duty may be left; it can never be escaped till *done!*" *Sleep* had been a part of his flight. Now he was awake. Was conscience awake? *Could* he think? *What* did he think? Or was he *still* escaping from *himself* in the very tumult of the tempest that came to awake him? To not a few *life* is like a long slumber. Thought, imagination, love, are asleep; their noble possibilities awake only to the gains and joys of this little spot of earth and fleeting day of time. But not without reproving storms, of loss, trouble, affliction, bereavement. It is well that the man suffer loss that he be not lost. The voice of circumstances is the voice of God.

II. THE EXAMPLE OF THE SAILORS REPROVED JONAH. They, each man of them, prayed. Each to his favourite god. Earnestly, with faith in the efficacy of prayer, they "*cried* every man unto his god." Prayerless Jonah (how can the backslider pray?) is reproved by those praying sailors. Their prayer is one of ignorance, ignorant earnestness. He has no prayer at all; and he, too, a prophet of the Lord! And how the heathen's passionate cries to his god rebuke *our* restraint of and coldness in prayer! How the full-hearted earnestness of (it may be) the illiterate Christian reproves our heartless accuracies and formal worship! How the backslider is shamed by the cry of the penitent! "Arise, call upon thy God!"

III. THE APPEAL OF THE CAPTAIN REPROVED JONAH. *He*, respectful in all his surprise and suppressed indignation, goes down and *himself* awakes Jonah. A heathen, he is faithful in all his ship. Not man or boy aboard but he calls to prayer. And even the strange passenger must be called as well. A *pattern* master this. He had a religious as well as secular care for those under him; was not ashamed to show his earnest spiritual interest in this strange Hebrew. A pattern for all masters and mistresses on sea and land. Jonah should have been reprover, and he is reproved; a teacher, and is being taught; prayerless, when he should have been leading others in prayer. "What meanest *thou*, O sleeper?" Thou, backslider to-day, why sleep? Awake to thy peril! Call upon the great Deliverer! He will think upon you. His thought shall be salvation. You shall not perish.—G. T. C.

Vers. 7—10.—*Jonah detected.* I. JONAH DETECTED BY THE LOT. *Heathens* cast that lot; *still* the *disposal* of it was of the Lord. *He* guided the fateful token, and so it fell to Jonah. *Now* that the Divine Spirit is given to those that seek him, we are released from dependence upon the indications of the lot. But still by things as little-seeming as lot-casting, backsliders are discovered to themselves if not to others. A cock-crow detected the recreant Peter. And now by some memorial of better days, an old letter perhaps, a book inscribed with a once-cherished Christian name, or a time-yellowed ticket of Church-membership, the backslider is self-detected. Oh the upbraiding days that are no more! Oh, reproaching light of the irrevocable years! Now he has sinned away the light, has grieved out of his heart the joy of the Lord. "The *lot* fell upon Jonah," and he was detected.

II. JONAH DETECTED BY THE SAILORS' MANY QUESTIONS. "Thine occupation?" A prophet! But so faithless to the prophetic call, so unworthy of the prophetic name! "Whence comest thou?" From Gath-hepher; from high, if perilous, mission to Nineveh, seeking, as he tells them, to flee from the presence of the Lord, to escape (how guilty! how futile!) from the great universal presence. "What thy country?" The land of privilege, the Holy Land! "Of what people art thou?" Of the people of God, the people chosen to be the depository of the Divine truth, and the witnesses to the Divine character. Questions these to go home. Backslider, "what thine occupation"? You have been, it may be, a Christian worker, a teacher of the young, a speaker of the truth. And not now. Why not? "Whence comest thou?" From a pious early home? From scenes of Christian activity and service that miss you, that know you no more? "What thy country, thy people?" A citizen of this Christian country, with such opportunities to *be* a Christian man and to *do* Christ's work among men, and yet you act as if gospel light had never shone to you, as if the news of salvation had never sounded in your ears.

III. JONAH DETECTED BY THE SAILORS' UNANSWERABLE QUESTION. "Why hast thou done this?" was the question that pierced deepest of all. It was unanswered. Jonah could not attempt excuses, and *reason* for his flight there was none. Backslider, once you could find time for Christian service; you had joy in it; you were a blessing; you were blest. Not so now. You have withdrawn from Christian work. "Why hast thou done this?" What valid reason can you give? Once you were in fellowship with God's people. Not so now. The world's spell is on you. You are intent on making a position, pushing the fortune of your family; pleasure is your pursuit, ambition your aim. But were you not happier in the former days than in these?

"Why hast thou done this?" Once you tasted that the Lord was gracious; now you are far out on the godless, reckless deep, where there is no peace. Why is this? "Speechless" you must be. For such guilty flight *reason* there can be none.—G. T. C.

Vers. 11—16.—*The sailors' conduct.* Look at those swarthy sailors. They were among Jonah's teachers; they, too, may be among ours. From age to age in this chapter they sail the sea—Jonah's friends; ours also if we will let them be, having much to say to us if we have but ears to hear. Mark—

I. THEIR REVERENCE. There is nothing rough and rude about them. The storm has subdued them. What they hear from Jonah affects them. Is it not the hour of their conversion? They cease from idolatry and worship Jehovah. Hearing of Jehovah as God of heaven, earth, and sea, they were "exceedingly afraid." He must indeed be the Lord! And that Jonah should have sought to flee from him! "What shall we do unto thee?" they ask; for through Jonah they would learn the will of *God* concerning him. They have no grudge against him, no scorn for him, no words of insult, no deed of violence. They reverence his God, and so show kindness to *him*. A pattern in this to us. Have we an offending brother—one who has offended us? Let us wrong not ourselves, nor wrong him, the better man in him, by bitterness. The wrong-doer will have self-reproach enough, bitter memories enough.

II. THEIR SELF-DENYING GENEROSITY. Those sailors did what they could to save the prophet. When Jonah was at his best they were at *their* best. His unselfishness called out theirs; their nobility answered to his. Thus is it ever. Be kind, pure, generous, and you will help others to show kindness, and to be pure and generous. What inspiration is there in goodness! Supremely is this seen in our blessed Lord. What an encouragement to copy him that we may quicken others!

> "Honour to those whose words or deeds
> Thus help us in our daily needs,
>   And by their overflow
>   Raise us from what is low."

III. THEIR PRAYERFULNESS. As heathens they had "given themselves to prayer." Hearing of Jehovah, they pray to *him*. They cannot save Jonah; but before they do the deprecated deed "they cried unto the Lord"—*all* of them, earnest, importunate. They recognized *God* in this series of events; they would be submissive to him; they would be clear of this man's blood; they would take no step without prayer. Nor let us. Let it be the "key of the morning and the bolt of the night." When have we *not* requests to offer? needs to be supplied? When do we not need *God?*

IV. THEIR GODLY FEAR ATTESTED. At the sight of the sudden great calm "the men feared the Lord exceedingly." Their fear, their faith, evidenced itself. By "a sacrifice unto the Lord" they expressed in act thankfulness for the past and present; by their "vows," their resolution of service in the time to come. As *from themselves* must have come the knowledge of the sacrifice offered and vows made, we may believe that that sacrifice to Jehovah was the first of many, and that the vows made were paid; otherwise they had not cared to have remembered or spoken of them. In these days of Christian light may *we* offer a *daily* sacrifice of our time, means, faculty, influence, to him who for us "even dared to die," and in *his* strength perform the many vows that we have made.—G. T. C.

Ver. 17—ch. ii. 10.—*Jonah's "De profundis."* Here the prophet is, as he is called in the Koran, "the man of the fish." God had pity on him, and sent him into an awful school-house that he might "come to himself." A strange character was his, and a strange chastisement came upon him. God's power was his keeper—*his* power "who hath a bridle for the lips of every disease, and a hook for the nostrils of death." The external history of the man through that imprisonment is unwritten. Not so the history of his heart.

I. SEE JONAH AT PRAYER. He had slept in the ship; he is awake in the fish. He prays; he feels his misery; he sees his sin. The *man* is awake. In the terrible darkness of adversity he longs for the light of the Lord. In what *solitude* was he! Far from light of day, human voices, human sympathy. Yet *there* he could pray. We can pray anywhere. Jeremiah could pray in the miry pit, Daniel in the lions' den, and Jonah in the fish amid the paths of the seas. He was in sad and extreme case. He was as a dead man out of mind; yet he can pray. What distress is ours? Our hopes may be "ready to perish." But think of Jonah! *He* could have recourse to prayer. So can we. The greatest of all was Jonah's Friend. In losing his liberty he has found his God. He prays "unto the Lord *his* God." "O Lord *my* God" (ver. 6), he cries. *We*, too, have the greatest of all as our Friend. None need despair with such a Helper.

II. JONAH'S PRAYER WAS A CRY. Whether a vocal cry or not, it was the cry of his soul. In this second chapter we have a well-arranged prayer. If not the exact order, we have here the *substance* of the requests he cried unto the Lord. What agony and horror may be in a human cry! In cries from the sea when perishing men call for a lifeboat! Jonah cried to *God*. What tears in his words! what distress in his tones! What hope for him, as "out of the belly of hell" (the unseen world, the place of the dead) he cried? Already he seemed numbered with the dead. The sense of God's displeasure was the soul of his affliction. "All *thy* billows and waves passed over me." Was God *favourably* there? "I said, I am cast out of thy sight." That was the pang. He had sought to escape God's presence; now he mourned the Divine absence. He had no enjoyment in his prayer, yet it was accepted. The prayer of agony ends in the voice of singing.

III. JONAH'S PRAYER WAS ONE OF FAITH. "I will look again," he said—mentally look again—"toward thy holy temple." How much the "temple" included—the Law, worship, sacrifices! towards these he looked, and thus overcame his fears. Down there, in those depths, in that living tomb, by that "look" this man becomes one of the heroes of faith. He, too, like a prince prevailed. That look was seen. God was pleased with it, and accepted it. *Still* God sees a look when the *soul* is in it. Though no word be spoken, we can look unto him and be saved.

IV. JONAH'S PRAYER WAS ONE OF THANKFULNESS. In this prayer he recalls and makes his own words from the Book of Psalms. Some of the old cries of David became the new cries of Jonah. And, marvellously preserved, his prayer was praise; and, in view of his deliverance, he vowed unto the Lord. And his vow was kept. The very subsequent writing of this chapter warrants our belief of that. And what of the vows *we* have made in times of peril? "Vow and *pay*." Say, "I have opened my mouth unto the Lord, and I cannot go back."

V. JONAH'S PRAYER WAS ONE OF UTTER DEPENDENCE ON GOD. Such was his spirit, such his prayer. With "salvation is of the Lord" it ended. And by that he seems to have meant that he left all with God. He was in the best hands. In his own time and way God would save him. If *he* will, creatures will act contrary to their natures, as did this fish in not hurting Jonah. *It* God had "prepared" or appointed; and now its work was done, the prophet penitent, saved not only from death, but also from trusting in "lying vanity," "the deceitful promise of his own will and his own way," no longer "forsaking his own mercy," even God, but cleaving to him. *Now* "the Lord spake unto the fish, and it vomited Jonah upon the dry land." And the prophet is a saved man —saved body *and* soul, the word, his creed and Te Deum, upon his lips, "Salvation is of the Lord." Still, "he must save, and he alone." Jesus, and no other, "shall save his people from their sins."—G. T. C.

Ver. 17 with ch. ii. 10; iii. 3 (cf. Matt. xii. 39—41).—*Jonah a prophetic sign of Christ.* I. IN BOTH WE SEE A MARKED JUDGMENT OF GOD. The storm, the detection, the punishment, were all from God. Jonah was *the* sinner on board. Christ, "without sin," "*became* sin for us." He suffered at the hands of wicked men; yet "the *Lord* laid on him the iniquity of us all." "He was wounded for *our* transgression." The vast world-vessel went plunging on to destruction, the storm unappeased while the sin was unpunished. On!—

> "When lo! upon the reeling deck a weary stranger stands,
> And to the dark devoted crew stretches his suppliant hands;
> From the face of God, from the face of God, from the face of God ye flee;
> 'Tis the blast of the breath of his nostrils that shakes this stormy sea.
> But take ye me and cast me into the troubled deep,
> And the wrath that is roused against you will be pacified, and sleep."

Yes, *he* is our Peace! "For the transgression of my people was he stricken."

II. JONAH, IN HIS BURIAL, WAS A SIGN OF CHRIST. Very unlike was the sea-monster bearing away the prophet to the rock-tomb that received the body of our Lord; yet in this they were alike, that they had been *unused* as tombs before. *Prepared* were both for the event that has made both eternally memorable. "The *Lord* had prepared" the fish. *Joseph*, unwittingly acting out the Divine purpose, had prepared the rock-hewn tomb. He may have meant it for himself. God meant it for his Son. This Isaiah had foretold: "He made his grave with the *rich*." The *time* of Jonah's and our Lord's burial agreed. So our Lord's resurrection on the third day was "according to the Scriptures"—to his own word, and his predictive type. Jonah, cast into the deep, seemed done with. An end of *him!* So, to many, with Christ, when the loving Marys and "those lords of high degree" bore him to the tomb. In his living tomb Jonah miraculously lived. And though Christ's body was dead, where was *he? Still* living; "doing good;" preaching the glad tidings in the unseen world (1 Pet. iii. 19).

III. JONAH'S RESURRECTION WAS A SIGN OF CHRIST'S. God "spake unto the fish," and it cast the living prophet to the shore. So "God raised from the dead" the Lord Jesus. Thus he *reversed* the marked judgment that, in suffering and death, had come upon his Son. He was now "highly exalted" as Prince and Saviour. Moral resurrections attest Christ's. "Witnesses to Christ's resurrection" are all saved men and women. They are "risen with Christ;" and by his Spirit rise.

IV. JONAH'S MISSION TO THE GENTILES WAS A TYPE OF CHRIST'S. Jonah was sent to the Ninevites. Christ arose to be a Saviour "to the uttermost parts of the earth." To all nations. For every creature. His mission—by many voices and ministers—is going on. *Its* continuance declares *his*. Its moral victories—over ignorance, superstition, sin—attest *his* royal and almighty power. "All power hath been given unto me." *Jonah himself*, raised from such a grave, was *the sign* to the Ninevites. *Christ* is the Sign of Christianity. Often, alas! spoken against and rejected. Happy those—only those—who accept and glory in him!—G. T. C.

Vers. 1, 2.—*The call of Jonah.* We may fairly identify Jonah, the son of Amittai, with the prophet who preached in Israel during the reign of Jeroboam II. (see 2 Kings xiv. 23—27). His name signifies "a Dove," and it well expressed his mournful and brooding temperament. Amittai means "the Truth of God," and it has been wisely said by a great Puritan divine, "I would that truth were every preacher's father." The narrative is exceedingly simple, and the Hebrew remarkably pure; while the lessons taught by the book are of profound significance, and far in advance of those we might have expected in that age of the world's history. The revelation of God's infinite goodness shines radiantly throughout. 1. He was merciful to the *Ninevites*, who were regarded as being outside the covenant; but were warned, converted, and saved. 2. He was merciful to *Jonah*, not cursing him for his wilful disobedience, but preserving him from peril into which his own foolish precipitancy had plunged him; graciously giving him a new commission in spite of his failure; teaching him gently, after a sinful outburst of temper; and closing the narrative of his life by a question of infinite tenderness. 3. He was merciful to the *sailors*, who had been heathen all their lives, but who, on turning towards him, found his deliverance near and complete.

I. THE PROPHET'S CALL. "The word of the Lord came unto Jonah." 1. *It was a Divine call.* Without it no service should ever be attempted; with it no service should be avoided. To go and preach to Nineveh would never have arisen as a conception of duty in the heart of a patriotic Israelite in those days. The generosity of the thought was Divine, not human. We, too, should listen for the words of our God, and wait for his commission. If we are true Israelites, we shall not precede the cloud, but follow it. The attitude of those who would be true prophets should be that of Samuel, when he said, "Speak, Lord; for thy servant heareth." 2. *It was a secret call.* Jonah was not commissioned by courtiers, or by ecclesiastics, or by a popular assembly. Probably his proposed expedition was unknown to all of these. It is a frequent experience with a Christian to get instruction as to what he should do, when he enters into the closet, shuts to the door, and prays to the Father who seeth in secret.

II. THE PROPHET'S SPHERE. Nineveh was at this time in the zenith of its glory. Rich, corrupt, and godless, it was the centre and focus of evil. 1. *The sphere was dangerous.* Even in these gentler times, and amidst more phlegmatic people, moral courage is required by those who rebuke popular sins. But an Eastern mob would be likely to handle very roughly any foreigner who dared to threaten their city for its sins. Jonah had no fear of this, however, and so far sets a noble example of heroism. 2. *The sphere was uncongenial.* These Ninevites were dreaded and hated by the people of Israel. Even under the Christian dispensation we see frequent evidences of national jealousy and antipathy, which prevent willingness to benefit other nations; and many a man would be rebuked as unpatriotic who earnestly sought the well-being of foreigners. How much more intense was such a feeling under the former dispensation! But God had room in his Fatherly heart for other peoples besides the race he had chosen for a peculiar purpose. Whenever the elect nation came into contact with others, God gave to those others some revelation of himself. He revealed himself to the Egyptians through Joseph and Moses; to the Philistines, through the sacred ark; to the Assyrians, through Elisha; and to Nebuchadnezzar and Belshazzar, through Daniel. Those who are inspired by God's Spirit overlook the barriers of race. The apostles did so, and were glad that God had given even to the Gentiles repentance unto life. Personal prejudices and dislikes may also sometimes hinder us in carrying on our divinely appointed work. Let us pray for willing minds and obedient hearts, that uncongenial spheres may be bravely filled.

III. THE PROPHET'S DUTY. 1. *He was to denounce the wickedness of the people.* Both Nahum and Zephaniah refer to the sins of Nineveh. Its inhabitants were luxurious, riotous, addicted to witchcraft, cruel, and idolatrous. Sins vary in form, but not in nature. The vices of our own time we should specially denounce with unsparing courage. 2. *He was to proclaim the nearness of God.* They knew not the truth revealed to Jonah: "Their wickedness is come up before me." Similar was the statement made about the murder of Cain and the sin of Sodom. God sets all our sins in the light of his countenance. 3. *He was to announce a coming judgment.* "Yet forty days, and Nineveh shall be overthrown" (ch. iii. 4). 4. *He was to be ready to receive and convey every message God gave him.* "Preach unto it the preaching that I bid thee." This should be the constant attitude of all religious teachers.—A. R.

Ver. 3.—*The prophet's disobedience.* Scripture never seeks to palliate the sins of the saints, but reveals them in all their wickedness. Jonah's disobedience is exhibited in the strongest light, as being resolute and prompt, following immediately on the Divine command. He had been told to make his way to Nineveh, which lay north-east of his home, and he instantly started in the opposite direction, being determined to go as far west as he could. He "went down" from the mountain district of Zebulun, where he lived, "to Joppa"—now known as Jaffa, a port on the Mediterranean. There he found a vessel on the point of sailing for Spain, which was much larger and safer than the ordinary coasters, as we may judge, not only from the length of the voyage undertaken, but from such a verse as this: "Thou breakest the ships of Tarshish with an east wind;" the destruction of these great vessels by storm being evidently considered a special proof of Divine power. Tarshish was an ancient city of Spain, proverbial for its wealth, and was the exporter to Tyre, to Judæa, and other lands, of silver, iron, tin, and lead. It was known to the Greeks and Romans as Tartessus. In that distant place, mingling with the crowds which thronged its streets, occupied by the fresh strange scenes which would surround him, Jonah hoped to escape from his duty and to drown the voice of conscience. His folly and sin are suggestive of warning to all who are tempted to disobey their God.

I. MANY, LIKE JONAH, FLEE FROM THE WAY IN WHICH GOD WOULD HAVE THEM GO. The expression, "to flee . . . from the presence of the Lord," should be rendered "to flee . . . from being before the Lord," *i.e.* from standing in his presence as his servant. Jonah knew perfectly well that he would never be beyond the reach of God's sight and power. The truths celebrated in Ps. cxxxix. he sincerely believed. But he resolved no longer to act as God's messenger and prophet. He felt sure that his message of warning was meant to bring Nineveh to repentance, and that then the merciful God would spare the city, which, with far-seeing prescience, the prophet perceived would be the destroyer of his country. If the sins of its inhabitants were so great, they deserved to die; and if their growing power was shattered, he cared not how, a threatening danger would be averted from his native land. Just as some Englishmen, jealous of the rising power of the United States, would not have lifted a finger to avert its destruction in the late civil war, so Jonah felt about Nineveh. He determined that he at least would not be the messenger to avert its destruction; so he fled as far as he could from the appointed sphere. Examples of similar conduct are to be seen amongst us. 1. *God calls men to private prayer.* They hear of its benefits; they are conscious that it is a duty and a privilege. Yet they avoid solitude, or they plunge into an interesting book, or they yield themselves to sleep, just when the opportunity comes for praying to the Father who seeth in secret. 2. *God calls men to his service.* The work requires to be done, but they shut their eyes to it, or they leave it to others, or so absorb their time in business that God's service is neglected. 3. *God calls men to give themselves to him.* At times they are almost persuaded to be Christians. But they leave the sphere in which good influences surround them, and wander away into the far country as the prodigal did.

II. IT IS NOT ALWAYS EASY TO AVOID THE GOD-APPOINTED WAY. Jonah felt that he could not remain where he was. He wished to divert his mind by travel, and to make it so difficult to journey to Nineveh that he could quiet his conscience in Tarshish by saying, "The distance is too great." Money, time, and trouble were necessary to his disobedience. Every wrong-doer has had some such experience. Around most of us God mercifully puts a protecting hedge of holy influences, which it is difficult and painful to break through. Those who are brought up in Christian homes do not find it easy to snap the bonds of love which have held them, and to get rid of the sacred memories of a hopeful childhood. They feel shocked and ashamed when they first witness scenes of vice and hear words of evil. Doubts and fears trouble them, especially at the beginning of a downward course, though all too soon they learn even to rejoice in iniquity. All such feelings and associations are among the God-appointed means for saving us from sin.

III. GOD DOES NOT RESISTLESSLY STOP THOSE WHO ARE DETERMINED TO GO WRONG. Jonah had no accident on his journey down to Joppa. He found the very ship he wanted at anchor in the harbour. He paid the fare and embarked for his destination, and when the anchors were raised and the vessel sailed out to sea, he felt that he had nothing more to do but wait, while the breeze that filled the sails would soon carry him to a distant land. Those who mean to leave the ways of unrighteousness do not meet with insuperable difficulties. They may be sometimes troubled with self-reproach, but meantime outward circumstances may appear even to favour their downward progress. If only they can stifle convictions and cast scruples to the winds while they resolutely make their way to scenes of gaiety and sin, God will work no miracle to prevent them. And the time may come when even the inward monitor is silent; for God's voice has been heard saying, "Ephraim is joined to his idols: let him alone."—A. R.

Vers. 4—6.—*The Divine interposition.* When man forsakes God, he who is infinite in mercy does not forsake man. No sooner had Adam fallen than Divine love planned a scheme of redemption. Through all the ages the voice of God has been summoning men to repentance; and in the fulness of time his only begotten Son came to seek and to save that which was lost. He deals as lovingly with individuals as with the race. Jonah was an example of this. Had a favourable voyage taken him to his destination, or had a sudden tempest drowned him in the depths of the sea, we should only have known of him as a disobedient prophet. But God dealt mercifully with him. He sent a tempest which aroused him from lethargy, brought his sin before him through the remonstrances of heathen, provided for him a means of escape, and gave him a new commission as his servant. These are the facts we should now consider.

I. GOD SOMETIMES SENDS A STORM TO AROUSE A WRONG-DOER. On entering the ship, Jonah went below deck; partly, no doubt, to avoid curious inquiries, and partly to rest after the long and hurried journey he had taken. Soon he sank into a heavy sleep—fit emblem of the lethargy of sin. The tempest, or rather its effect on the sailors, aroused him. Many have experienced tempests within or in their outward life which have led them afterwards to say, "He restoreth my soul." Anxieties have been so terrible, that in an agony the convicted have cried, "Lord, save, or I perish." Illness has come so suddenly, and death has seemed so near, that the awakened soul has asked, "What shall I do to be saved?" The forsaking of friends, the death of relatives, the failure of business, have been employed by God again and again to arouse moral thoughtfulness, and save the soul from destruction. Let us learn the lessons which such tempests can teach us. "What meanest thou, O sleeper? Arise, and call upon thy God, if so be that God will think upon us, that we perish not."

II. GOD EMPLOYS UNLIKELY AGENTS TO BRING A WRONG-DOER TO REPENTANCE. The man who uttered the words just quoted was a heathen shipmaster, whom a Jew would despise as a Gentile dog or as an ignorant idolater. Yet but for him Jonah might have slept on till the vessel foundered. It has often been so. Naaman, the distinguished Syrian general, was taught by a slave-girl. David was instructed by Abigail. The Pharisees and scribes were rebuked by the hosannas of little children in the temple. God chooses the foolish things of the world to confound the wise, and weak things to destroy things which are mighty. If we see no reason for fear or for seriousness in the tempest of life, he may arouse us by means we despise. A single phrase in a sermon which is far from eloquent, a leaflet or tract without any pretension to literary charm, an earnest word from an inferior in rank or education, the trustful prayer of a lisping child,—may be used of God, as was the summons which came to Jonah from a superstitious heathen.

III. A MAN MAY BE IN GREAT DANGER WITHOUT BEING CONSCIOUS OF IT. Jonah slept. Perhaps he dreamed of happier days and of distant scenes. These seemed real to him, but the realities actually around him—the storm, the ship, the sailors—were as if they did not exist. He did not know his danger, and had forgotten in sleep his sad disobedience. Even to the sailors his sleep seemed the result of infatuation or of senselessness, and they asked (not, "What meanest thou?"), "What aileth thee, O sleeper?" —as if there was something abnormally wrong with him, as indeed there was. But more strange, more fatal, is the sleep in which so many lie who believe themselves to be awake. Shrewd in business, eager in pleasure-seeking, successful in study, all that they see appears for the time to be the only reality. But, like Jonah, they are in dreamland. Heaven and hell, death and judgment, an enemy of souls, and a Saviour from sin, are recognized by others, not by them. Urge all such to awake, and arise from the dead, that Christ may give them light. "Now is the accepted time; now is the day of salvation."

IV. GOD'S WAY OF SALVATION IS THE ONLY ONE. It was useless for the sailors to row hard in the hope of bringing the ship to land, and equally useless for them to cast the cargo overboard. There was no safety for them or for Jonah except by the way ordained by God. Strange as it seemed to them and to us, Jonah, in all his sinfulness and helplessness, was to be cast into the sea, where none but God could save him. If the story has no other lesson, it at least teaches us the impotency of human effort to battle successfully with the storms of life. The struggles some make in their unaided strength to win salvation are vain as the efforts of these who "rowed hard to bring the ship to land." The endeavour to get rid of besetting sins without prayer for grace is as ineffectual as the casting overboard of the burden in the ship. A simpler, stranger, means of salvation is provided for us. As Jonah was cast helpless and alone into the sea, for God to save in his own way, so we are called to such implicit trust as will prompt us to cast ourselves wholly upon Christ, in whom we shall find eternal rest. —A. R.

Vers. 1—3.—*God speaking to man in mercy, and man fleeing from God in disobedience.* "Now the word of the Lord came unto Jonah the son of Amittai, saying, Arise, go to Nineveh, that great city, and cry against it; for their wickedness is come up before me." This is a strange book. It is not the record of a dream, nor the sketch of an allegory, but the history of a man written by himself. True, he speaks in the third person; but so did many of the old prophets, so did the Apostle Paul, and so have many great men. Intellectual children are prone to use the personal pronoun *I*; great intellectual men prefer writing of themselves in the third person. Speeches and books bristling with *I* are generally the effusions of little souls. We have here his name and that of his father, the one signifying "Dove," and the other "the Truth of God." Names of old were sometimes commemorative, sometimes predictive. Names now signify little. Men by great and noble deeds can, and often do, throw into the commonest names a meaning that will radiate through centuries. In these words we have two things worthy of attention—God speaking to man in mercy, and man fleeing from God in disobedience.

I. GOD SPEAKING TO MAN IN MERCY. 1. Here he *speaks.* "The word of the Lord." His word to Jonah, like his word to all men, was *clear, brief, weighty, practical.* 2. Here he speaks to an *individual.* He speaks to all men in nature, conscience, history; but in sovereignty he singles some men out for special communications. In times past he spake "unto the fathers by the prophets." 3. Here he speaks to an individual for the sake of a *community.* "Arise, go to Nineveh, that great city." Why does God call it a "great" city? To men it was considered "great"—great in numbers, pomp, pretensions, masonry. But to God it could only be great in *sin,* for sin is a great thing to God; it is a black cloud in his universe; it is the "abominable thing" which he hates. For the sake of this city, in order to effect its moral reformation, and therefore to save it, Jonah receives a commission. "Arise," shake off thy languor, quit thyself for action, go down to this city, and "cry against it." Be *earnest.* The danger is great, near at hand, and appoaching every minute. Observe here two things: (1) Man's distinguishing faculty. What is that? The power to **receive,** to *appreciate,* and to *work out* the ideas of the Infinite. No other creature on earth has this power. (2) God's method of helping humanity. God enlightens, purifies, and ennobles man by man. We have this "treasure in earthen vessels."

II. MAN FLEEING FROM GOD IN DISOBEDIENCE. "But Jonah rose up to flee unto Tarshish, from the presence of the Lord." Here is a threefold revelation of man. 1. His *moral freedom.* God did not coerce Jonah, did not drive him to Nineveh. He merely commanded him to go, and Jonah resisted the Divine command. Man has the power to resist God—a greater power this than can be found in all the heavenly orbs or in the whole history of material organisms. This power invests man with all but infinite importance, links him to moral government. "Ye do always resist the Spirit of God." 2. His *daring depravity.* He dares to attempt extricating himself, not only from his obligations to God, but from his very "presence." Alas! men have not merely the power but the disposition to oppose God. This is their guilt and their ruin; it is what men are doing everywhere, trying to break the shackles of moral responsibility, trying to elude the Infinite. 3. His *egregious folly.* See the folly. His endeavouring to escape from God was: (1) Not merely an impulse, but a *resolution.* Had it been a sudden wish, it would have been bad. But here is a resolution. He "rose up." He rallied and marshalled his energies. (2) Not merely a resolution, but an *effort.* He "went down to Joppa." The probability is that he went with the greatest speed to Joppa—the Jaffa of our day. Though a descent, it was rather a long journey, and would take him two or three days. When he reached the spot, how long he was about the quays in search of a suitable vessel! (3) Not merely an effort, but a *persevering* effort. It was not one, or two, or three spasmodic efforts, and then over. He continued his journey from his home to Joppa, then he searched on the quays for a vessel; and when he found, as he thought, a suitable vessel, he "paid the fare thereof." Ah! what fares men pay in the career of sin! And when he had paid the fare thereof, he "went down into it," and there he thought himself safe. How inexpressibly foolish was all this, not only in the nature of the case, but according to *results!* All the efforts, as the sequence shows, not only proved futile, but brought him to the utmost distress.

CONCLUSION. The two things that you have in these verses are always going on—God in mercy speaking to man, and man in terror fleeing from God. Oh, how wrong, how foolish, the attempt to flee from the Infinite! "Whither shall I flee from thy presence?"—D. T.

Ver. 6.—*A rousing voice to moral sleepers.* "What meanest thou, O sleeper? arise, call upon thy God, if so be that God will think upon us, that we perish not." The incident referred to in the text is this—Jonah was sent to Nineveh on a mission of mercy, sent to warn the corrupt population of their impending doom, and to call them to immediate repentance. The Divine message was not to the prophet's mind; he was displeased, and instead of going direct to Nineveh, he went down to Joppa, and found a ship going to Tarshish. He paid the fare, embarked, and hasted away. While on the deep a terrible tempest arose. "The Lord sent out a great wind into the sea, and there was a mighty tempest in the sea, so that the ship was like to be broken." As the tempest raged Jonah was asleep, "fast asleep." So the shipmaster came to him and said unto him, "What meanest thou, O sleeper?" etc. *Moral indifferentism* is the curse of the world. Three practical appeals to the morally indifferent are suggested.

I. JONAH WAS IN IMMINENT PERIL. So are you. It is said that the ship was "like to be broken." The perils of shipwreck have often been graphically depicted; but they surpass the conceptions of all but those who have struggled in their ghastly horrors. But what are the perils of material shipwreck to the perils of a corrupt and disobedient soul? To have the body buried in the depths of the ocean is a trifle compared with the burial of the soul under the black, booming billows of moral depravity and guilt. The buried body becomes unconscious of its position, and sleeps itself into the calm bosom of its mother nature; but the soul becomes burningly conscious of its terrible situation, and struggles in vain to rise from the abyss. What is hell? I know not. I want no rolling thunders of Divine vengeance, no material fires burning on for ever, to impress me with its awfulness. A soul buried in the black ocean of its own depravity, with a conscience intensely alive to its hopeless condition, struggling in vain to release itself, is the hell of all hells. Careless sinner, you are in danger of this hell! Your moral circumstances will soon be changed, a tempest is brooding, it increases with every sin. Every star in your heavens will soon be extinguished, and the sea on which you are now gliding along will be lashed into fury and will engulf you in ruin.

II. JONAH WAS UNCONSCIOUS OF HIS PERIL. So are you. Whilst the tempest was raging and the vessel ready to sink, he was "fast asleep." Carless sinner, you are unconscious of your danger! You say to yourself, "Peace, peace," when there is no peace. If you were aware of your position, you would give no sleep to your eyes, no slumber to your eyelids. 1. Jonah's unconsciousness was *foolish*. So is yours. How unwise was the prophet to sleep under such circumstances! He should have been on deck, alert, all ear and eye, and with hands ready to grapple with the emergencies of the terrible hour. But your folly is greater, inasmuch as your peril is more tremendous. 2. Jonah's unconsciousness was *wicked*. So is yours. For the sake of his companions on board, he ought not to have been "fast asleep;" it indicated a shameful lack of interest in his fellow-men. Your indifferentism is wicked. You ought to be spiritually alive and awake, not only for your own sake, but also for the sake of those around you who are in similar peril.

III. JONAH HAD A MESSENGER TO WARN HIM OF HIS PERIL. So have you. "The shipmaster came to him, and said unto him, What meanest thou, O sleeper? arise, call upon thy God, if so be that God will think upon us, that we perish not." There are certain points of analogy between this "shipmaster" and the godly ministers that are warning you. 1. He believed in the *existence and power of God*. So do they. "Call upon thy God, if so be that God will think upon us." Great dangers seldom fail to strike the idea of God into the hearts of men, whatever their creed or character. This man believed, not only that a God existed, but that that God had raised a tempest, and had the power to subdue it. The Christly men that warn you every Sunday from the pulpits also believe in this God. 2. He believed in the *efficacy of human prayer*. So do they. The shipmaster said to Jonah, "Call upon thy God." Whatsoever speculative scientists may say about prayer, one thing is clear—that it is an instinct of the soul, not a mere doctrine of the Bible; it is a law of nature, not a mere ceremony of religion. What soul does not pray when in conscious contact with overwhelming dangers? Your ministers believe in prayer; they pray for you, and urge you to pray for yourselves. 3. He believed it to *be his duty to sound the warning*. So do they. What right had he to interfere with the sleeping prophet, to break his slumber, and to summon him to prayer? The instincts of nature authorized him, nay, bound him to do so. Your ministers have a right to warn you; they are bound to warn you. They are commanded to "cry aloud, to lift up their voice like a trumpet." Do you say, when godly men speak to you about your moral condition, "What business have they to interfere? My soul is my own; if I choose to throw it away, what matters it to them?" It does matter to them. You are not your own, you are not an isolated unit, you are a member of the spiritual universe; you have, therefore, no right to be dishonest, corrupt, ungodly, and throw your soul away. You were made to serve the universe, not to curse it; you cannot sin without injuring others. Every true man is bound to protest against your conduct, and to demand from you, in the name of God and this universe, an *immediate* reformation.

CONCLUSION. The following fact, recorded in the ' Biblical Treasury,' is worthy of note as an illustration : "A traveller who was pursuing his journey on the Scotch coast, was thoughtlessly induced to take the road by the sands as the most agreeable. This road, which was safe only at low tides, lay on the beach, between the sea and the lofty cliffs which bound the coast. Pleased with the view of the inrolling waves on the one hand and the abrupt and precipitous rocks on the other, he loitered on the way, unmindful of the sea which was gradually encroaching upon the intervening sands. A man, observing from the lofty cliffs the danger he was incurring, benevolently descended, and arresting his attention by a loud halloa, warned him not to proceed. 'If you pass this spot, you will lose your last chance of escape. The tides are rising. They have already covered the road you have passed, and they are near the foot of the cliffs before you ; and by this ascent alone you can escape.' The traveller disregarded the warning. He felt sure he could make the turn in the coast in good time ; and, leaving his volunteer guide, he went more rapidly on his way. Soon, however, he discovered the real danger of his position. His onward journey was arrested by the sea ; he turned in haste, but to his amazement he found that the rising waters had cut off his retreat. He looked up to the cliffs ; but they were inaccessible. The waters were already at his feet. He sought higher ground, but was soon driven off. His last refuge was a projecting rock ; but the relentless waters rose higher and higher ; they reached him ; they rose to his neck ; he uttered a despairing shriek for help, but no help was near, as he had neglected his last opportunity for escape. The sea closed over. It was the closing in upon him of the night of death."—D. T.

EXPOSITION.

CHAPTER II.

Vers. 1—10.—Part II. JONAH'S PRAYER AND DELIVERANCE.

Vers. 1—9.—§ 1. *Jonah, in the belly of the fish, offers a prayer of thanksgiving for his rescue from death by drowning, in which he sees a pledge of further deliverance.*

Ver. 1.—Then Jonah prayed. These were his feelings when he sank in the waters and while he lay in his mysterious prison ; he may have put them into their metrical form after his deliverance. The grammatical arrangement, and especially the language of ver. 7, seem to speak of a deliverance already experienced rather than of one expected. As this "prayer" does not suit an allegory, and as no one but Jonah could have known its substance, we have here an argument for his authorship. It is rather a thanksgiving than a prayer— like that of Hannah (1 Sam. ii. 1). When he realizes that he was saved from drowning, he uttered his gratitude, and saw that he might hope for further rescue. How he passed the three days we cannot tell ; some have thought he was unconscious ; but this is, perhaps, hardly consistent with the notice of his "praying," and with the action of his great Antitype, who, during his sojourn in the unseen world, "preached to the spirits in prison" (1 Pet. iii. 19). **His God.** He

acknowledges Jehovah as his God. He had proved himself his by inspiration, by chastisement, and now by mercy (Pusey). The following prayer contains ample reminiscences of the Psalms, which would be familiar to a devout Israelite. Those quoted are mostly what have been considered to belong to David's time, if their date is really ascertained. But it is a matter of controversy, incapable of settlement, whether Jonah or the psalmist is the original.

Ver. 2.—He introduces the prayer with the fact that he cried to God in distress and was heard. **By reason of mine affliction** ; better, *out of my affliction*. This may be a reminiscence of Ps. cxx. 1 or Ps. xviii. 6 ; but from such coincidences nothing can be established concerning the date of the book. Like circumstances call forth like expressions ; and the writers may have composed them quite independently of one another. Hell (*Sheol*). The unseen world (Ezek. xxxii. 21). He was as though dead when thus engulfed (comp. Ps. xviii. 5). **Cried I** (Ps. xxviii. 1, 2). **Thou heardest my voice** (Ps. cxxx. 1, 2).

Ver. 3.—He describes his danger and distress. **Thou hadst cast** ; rather, *thou didst cast*, the sailors being the agents of the Divine will. Septuagint, ἀπέρριψας. The deep ; βάθη, "depths" (Septuagint) ; Exod. xv. 8. **In the midst** ; literally, *in the heart* ; Septuagint, καρδίας θαλάσσης : Vulgate, *in* *corde maris.* This defines more closely the previous expression. **The floods**; literally, **the river.** This may mean the current (as in Ps. xxiv. 2), which in the Mediterranean Sea sets from west to east, and, impinging on the Syrian coast, turns north; or it may have reference to the notion, familiar to us in Homer, which regarded the ocean as a river. **All thy billows and thy waves;** πάντες οἱ μετεωρισμοί σου καὶ τὰ κύματά σου, "all thy swellings and waves" (Septuagint); *omnes gurgites tui, et fluctus tui* (Vulgate). The former are "breakers," the latter "rolling billows." The clause is from Ps. xlii. 7, Jonah transferring what is there said metaphorically to his own literal experience, at the same time acknowledging God's hand in the punishment by speaking of "*thy* billows" (comp. Ps. lxxxviii. 6, 7).

Ver. 4.—Jonah confesses that he at first fully expected death; but faith and hope soon triumphed over despondency. **I am cast out of thy sight.** This was his thought when what is mentioned in ver. 3 happened unto him. The words are a reminiscence of Ps. xxxi. 22, altered somewhat to suit Jonah's circumstances. The psalmist says, "I said in my haste." Jonah says simply, "I said," without any limitation; and for "I am cut off," Jonah uses, "I am cast out." Septuagint, ἀπῶσμαι—a strong term, implying banishment with violence. *Out of thy sight;* literally, *from before thine eyes;* i.e. from thy protecting care (comp. 1 Sam. xxvi. 24; 1 Kings viii. 29). He who had fled from the presence of the Lord in Canaan fears that he has forfeited the favour of God. **Yet I will look again toward thy holy temple.** I will turn in prayer to that holy place where thou dost manifest thy presence. The Jews were wont to turn towards Jerusalem when they prayed (comp. 1 Kings viii. 30, etc.; Dan. vi. 10; Ps. xviii. 6; xxviii. 2). Some think that Jonah expresses a hope of worshipping again in the temple; but the turn of expression in the text hardly warrants this. Others refer the term to the heavenly temple, as they do in ver. 7; Ps. xi. 4; xviii. 6.

Vers. 5, 6.—In parallel clauses, Jonah describes still more vividly the horrors that surrounded him.

Ver. 5.—**Compassed me about.** Not the same word as in ver. 3. Septuagint, περιεχύθη μοι, "was poured around me." **Even to the soul**; so as to reach his life (comp. Ps. xviii. 5; lxix. 1, 2; Lam. iii. 54). **The depth closed me round about.** The verb is the same as in ver. 3, translated there, "compassed me about." Vulgate, *abyssus vallavit me.* **The weeds** (*suph*); sea-weed. Jonah sank to the bottom before he was swallowed by the fish. The LXX. omits the word.

The Vulgate gives *pelagus*, which is probably derived from the fact of the Red Sea being called "the Sea of Suph," the term being thence applied to any sea.

Ver. 6.—**The bottoms of the mountains;** literally, *the cuttings off*, where the mountains seem to be cut off by the ocean floor; the roots of the mountains. Εἰς σχισμὰς ὀρέων, "the clefts of the mountains" (Septuagint); Ps. xviii. 15. **The earth with her bars;** *as for the earth, her bars were about me;* return to it was shut out for me; the gate by which I might return was locked behind me. He adds, for ever, as it was to all appearance, because he had no power in himself of returning to earth and life. **Yet;** in spite of all, I am preserved. **From corruption** (*shachath*); as Job xvii. 14; *de corruptione* (Vulgate); so the Chaldee and Syriac; Septuagint, Ἀναβήτω ἐκ φθορᾶς ἡ ζωή μου (Alex.), Ἀναβήτω φθορὰ ζωῆς μου (Vatican), "Let my life arise from destruction;" or, "Let the destruction of my life [*i.e.* my destroyed life] arise." Jerome refers the word to the digestive process in the fish's stomach; it is probably merely a synonym for "death." The marginal rendering, "the pit," *i.e.* Sheol, is also etymologically correct (comp. Ps. xxx. 3). **My God.** He thankfully acknowledges that Jehovah has proved himself a beneficent God to him.

Ver. 7.—His prayer was heard. **When my soul fainted within me**; literally, *was covered*—referring, says Pusey, to that physical exhaustion when a film comes over the eyes, and the brain is mantled over. The clause is from Ps. cxlii. 3 or cxliii. 4. **I remembered the Lord.** That was his salvation (Ps. cxix. 55). He turned in thought to thine holy temple (ver. 4), the sanctuary where God's presence was most assured, like the psalmist in the wilderness (Ps. lxiii. 2), or like the exiles by the waters of Babylon when they remembered Zion (Ps. cxxxvii.).

Ver. 8.—Jonah contrasts the joy and comfort arising from the thought of God with the miserable fate of idolaters. **They that observe** (Ps. xxxi. 6); court, pay deference to, reverence. **Lying vanities**; Septuagint, μάταια καὶ ψευδῆ, "vain things and false." Idols (comp. Jer. xviii. 15; Hos. xii. 11; 1 Cor. viii. 4). **Their own mercy**; *i.e.* their state of favour with God—the mercy shown to them, as "the mercies of [shown to] David" (Isa. lv. 3); or God himself, the Fountain of mercy and goodness (Ps. cxliv. 2). Henderson translates, "forsake their Benefactor."

Ver. 9.—But I—who know better than idolaters, and who have learned a new lesson of trust in God—I will sacrifice. Pusey notes that the Hebrew denotes rather, "I fain would sacrifice," as it depended, not on him, but on God, whether he was able to worship again in the Holy Land. His sacrifice of thanksgiving (Lev. vii. 12, etc.) should be offered with prayer and praise (Ps. xlii. 5). That which I have vowed (Ps. l. 14; lxvi. 13). Salvation is of the Lord. This is the conclusion to which his trial has brought him, the moral of the whole canticle (Ps. iii. 8; cxviii. 14, 21; Rev. vii. 10). The LXX. and the Vulgate join this clause to the preceding, thus: "That which I have vowed I will pay to the Lord for my salvation." This is tame, and not in strict accordance with the Hebrew.

Ver. 10.—§ 2. *The fish casts up Jonah alive on the shore.*

Ver. 10.—Spake unto the fish. The punishment having done its work, the fish is impelled by some secret influence to eject Jonah on the dry land, on the third day after he was swallowed (ch. i. 17). Some, who regard the Book of Jonah as an historical allegory, see in these three days an adumbration of the period of the Babylonish captivity, during which Israel was buried in darkness, and from which she rose to a new and happier life. They compare, as referring to the same transaction, Jer. li. 34, 44 and Hos. vi. 1, 2 (see Dr. C. H. H. Wright, 'Exegetical Studies,' pp. 53, etc.). Upon the dry land. Probably on the coast of Palestine, whence he had started.

HOMILETICS.

Ver. 1.—" *Out of the depths.*" Never surely was prayer offered in so strange a place as this! Men have often prayed upon the sea, but Jonah is represented as praying from the ocean depths.

I. No PLACE IS UNSUITABLE FOR PRAYER. It is well to pray in stately cathedrals and in consecrated chapels, in the humble meeting-house and at the "domestic altar." But the persecuted have prayed upon the remote hillside, and in "dens and caves of the earth." And let it be remembered, that God's will is that "men should pray everywhere, lifting holy hands" to heaven. In the thronged street, the busy market, the legislative hall, the court of justice, in the field of battle, and upon the island where the shipwrecked mariner finds a refuge,—in every place God may be sought and found. If Jonah cried "out of the fish's body," and was heard, is there reason for silence, for refraining from prayer, in any spot where we may find ourselves?

II. ACCEPTABLE PRAYER PROCEEDS FROM NECESSITY. There are those who have never prayed before, who have been driven to supplication by their needs. And many, whose prayers have often been formal, have learned to pray in earnest when they have been plunged into the overwhelming ocean of affliction. None ask so urgently as those who are in want; and one purpose of Providence in permitting men to suffer need may well be this—to call forth entreaties and supplications which shall be sincere, profound, and urgent.

III. ACCEPTABLE PRAYER IS THE OFFSPRING OF A SUBMISSIVE MIND. Rebellion, and even murmuring, are incompatible with a prayerful spirit. It proves that Jonah was not wholly bad that, in his affliction, he did not resent the Lord's treatment, he did not "kick against the goad." He rather behaved and quieted himself as "the weaned child." It is well to acknowledge that justice and mercy are in all the Lord's dealings with his people. Many have been taught by experience to say with the psalmist, "Before I was afflicted, I went astray;" "It is good for me that I have been afflicted." Trouble is not designed to lead God's people to cry *against* the Lord, but *unto* the Lord. To complain is both foolish and sinful; but they are happy who endure.

IV. ACCEPTABLE PRAYER IS THE UTTERANCE OF FAITH AND HOPE. Even in the depths of the sea Jonah did not lose his faith in the oversight, the care, the goodness of the Lord. He believed that the Lord had overwhelmed, and that the Lord could rescue him. He who brought him into the depths could bring him out of the depths. The believing prayer which the prophet is recorded to have offered in his extremity is a model to all those who because of their iniquities and transgressions have been afflicted. Have faith in God, and hope in his mercy—such is the lesson which this verse teaches.

V. PRAYER FROM THE DEPTHS IS HEARD IN THE HEIGHTS AND ANSWERED. Jonah's subterraneous, subaqueous dungeon became a temple. God was present when his servant prayed. When submission and faith took the place of disobedience and rebellion, the Most High was willing to deliver the captive, to pardon the sinner, to employ again the unfaithful fugitive.

Vers. 2, 3.—*Affliction and prayer.* Doubtless the language of this psalm of thanksgiving was the result of subsequent meditation, for it is evidently a studied composition, resembling in passages several of the sacred Hebrew odes. But the sentiments were those actually experienced by the prophet when in the most humiliating position. In his experience was much which may prove very instructive and helpful to ourselves. I. DEEP AFFLICTION. The language of ver. 3, literally descriptive of Jonah's state and sufferings, is tinged with poetical feeling, and, like similar passages in the Psalms, is emblematic of the afflictions which, at some periods of human life, are the appointed experience of God's people. The deep waters of trouble must be passed through; the mighty billows must roll over the spirit. Sorrow submerges and apparently overwhelms even the child of God; how much more the impenitent and disobedient! II. EARNEST PRAYER. How, indeed, can prayer be other than earnest, if it be offered from "the belly of hell"? Those afflictions are, indeed, a blessing which prompt such supplications as those which came from Jonah's lips. Far from human succour, and perhaps from human pity, the afflicted lift their voice, and cry, by reason of their afflictions, unto the Lord. There is something very instructive in the language used by Jonah, attributing his affliction to the Being upon whom he was calling, "*Thou* hadst cast me into the deep, . . . *thy* billows and *thy* waves passed over me." In this way the distressed may learn the lesson which the wisdom and the love of God would teach. III. GRACIOUS DELIVERANCE. When in Scripture it is said that God hears, we may usually understand more than is expressed. He hears to answer, to rescue, to save. The Omnipresent did not lose sight of his servant even when he was beneath the waves of the ocean; and the All-gracious was not inattentive to his supplication, though offered from the depths where weeds were about the suppliant's head. If there are those who fear lest their situation or their circumstances should shut them out from the regard and interest of the Supreme, they may well take courage when they think of the experience of the prophet, who called upon the Lord from the depths, and was heard and was delivered.

Ver. 4.—*Looking toward the temple.* It is remarkable that in two passages of this prayer the prophet should allude to the temple. Although he was from Northern Palestine, and lived whilst Judah and Israel were distinct kingdoms, it does not seem open to question that his allusion is to the sacred edifice at Jerusalem, where Jehovah manifested his presence and favour, and received the worship of his people. Yet the temple must have been referred to, not so much as a material edifice, as in the light of the symbol of the manifestation of the presence and the favour of the Most High. I. TO LOOK TOWARD THE TEMPLE IS TO BE REMINDED OF THE EXISTENCE OF GOD. As the sight of a house may remind us of the friend who dwells there, as the sight of a palace may lead us to think of the king,—so to look toward the temple is to look to God. Jonah may have been tempted to say, "There is no God;" or, "If there be a God, he regards not me." When he turned in heart to the temple, such thoughts vanished, and God's existence became a reality to him. II. TO LOOK TOWARD THE TEMPLE IS TO SEEK THE FAVOUR OF GOD. The temple was the place where sacrifices were offered and accepted; where God showed himself to be gracious to his covenant people, where sin was pardoned, and the penitent sinner was received into acceptance. And Jonah knew, even from the very commission he was unwilling to fulfil, that God delighted in mercy, and was long-suffering and compassionate. He had incurred Divine displeasure, but he began to feel that he was not beyond the reach of Divine commiseration and help. III. TO LOOK TOWARD THE TEMPLE IS TO EXPECT THE DIVINE INTERPOSITION AND DIRECTION. The pious Jews sought Jehovah in his house, consulted the oracle, invoked guidance, implored blessing. And when Jonah directed the gaze of his heart towards the dwelling-place of his God, it was with the well-formed expectation that, however impossible it was for him to make a way of escape for himself, God would surely do this upon his behalf. There is no depth from which he cannot lift us; no recess from which he cannot draw us forth; no sorrow of which he cannot relieve us; no sin which he cannot pardon. Of how many of God's people may it be said, "They looked unto him, and were lightened, and their faces were not ashamed"!

Ver. 7.—*Remembering the Lord.* The circumstances in which Jonah was placed were such as give very peculiar value and interest to this declaration. And it appears that this act of recollection was the turning-point in his experience; for hitherto his troubles had increased, whilst henceforth his prospects began to brighten.

I. THE OCCASION OF THIS REMEMBRANCE. 1. External adversity may have prompted him to a kind of remembrance which in his prosperity he had not cultivated. 2. Mental exhaustion and distress caused him to realize his helplessness, and the vanity of expecting human aid. When his "soul fainted within" him, then he called to mind the God whom he had disobeyed.

II. THE CHARACTER OF THIS REMEMBRANCE. 1. Jonah, no doubt, remembered God's commands and his own rebellion. 2. He must also have remembered the revelation of Divine mercy which had been vouchsafed him. And whilst the former recollection must have awakened penitence, this may well have shed into his soul a ray of hope.

III. THE FRUIT OF THIS REMEMBRANCE. 1. It prompted to prayer. They who forget God will not call upon God; but they who remember his promises may well lift up their hearts to him. 2. It was thus the means of securing the Divine regard and the Divine deliverance. God heard the prophet's cry, though uttered from the ocean's depths, and when he heard, he came to the rescue of his servant. "The Lord is mindful of his own." We may for a time forget his faithfulness, but when we call to mind his nearness and his grace, he remembers us even in our low estate.

Ver. 8.—*The vanity of idolatry.* Jonah had been brought into association with idolaters in the person of the mariners of the ship out of which he had been cast. It may be that this fact accounts for the reference in this passage to those who worship other gods than the Lord. The more he experienced the faithfulness and goodness of Jehovah, the more was he convinced that there was none other entitled to reverence, confidence, and prayers.

I. THE DESCRIPTION HERE GIVEN OF IDOLATERS. They are such as "observe lying vanities." The Hebrews, whether pious or not, were monotheists, and regarded with contempt the idolatrous superstitions of their neighbours. The language of irony occurs in several places of Old Testament Scripture when allusion is made to the impotence of the gods of the nations. Yet it may be profitably remembered by ourselves, who may have no immediate connection with professed idolaters, that whatever men substitute for God, as the law of life and the object of devotion and trust, will surely deceive all those who put their faith therein.

II. THE FATE HERE FORETOLD OF IDOLATERS. Their "mercy," their "goodness," is the God whom they forget, and to whom they are so infatuated as to prefer the "lying vanities" here censured. They who quit the Lord prepare for themselves a terrible fate. In God is salvation; out of him is destruction. There is something appalling in the doom which is here described as overtaking those who, when the Saviour may be found, turn their back upon him, in order to seek and to serve other gods. Such are said to "forsake their own mercy." They act against their highest interests; they refuse the richest blessing; they abjure their truest Friend.

Ver. 9.—*Piety triumphant.* The remarkable fact connected with this sublime hymn of confidence and adoration is this—it was uttered while deliverance was yet in the future. The prophet sings of God's goodness while he is still experiencing God's chastisement, and promises offerings whilst the favour which they are to acknowledge is as yet in the future. In these closing words of the hymn there is a tone of exultation and of triumph, which evinces singular confidence and singular hope.

I. THANKSGIVING. There are some circumstances which render gratitude natural and easy. But it is a triumph of faith when the afflicted can acknowledge the good hand of God, when they can discern mercy in chastening, when they can see the hand of a Father in the hand that smites. One thing is certain—whatever be our position, our experience, we owe gratitude as a debt due to him who is ever forbearing and gracious.

II. SACRIFICE. According to the religious customs of his country and his age, the prophet vowed to offer an outward expression of his loyalty and gratitude to God, by presenting a sacrifice in the temple or at some consecrated altar. His life had been spared; his deliverance was near; he looked forward to an opportunity of "offering burnt offerings" upon the altar of Jehovah. The spiritual reality of which such an act is the symbol is the consecration of heart and life unto the God of all grace and salvation.

III. PRAISE. Thanksgiving looks mainly to the benefits received; praise, to the Bestower. "Salvation unto the Lord!" such is the joyful and adoring cry with which this hymn is brought to a close. It is well, when we have acknowledged favour and long-suffering enjoyed, to turn away from ourselves, and to fix our thoughts, our sentiments of affectionate and adoring devotion, upon him whose attribute is mercy, and whose work is salvation.

HOMILIES BY VARIOUS AUTHORS.

Vers. 1—4.—*A unique oratory.* "Then Jonah prayed unto the Lord his God," etc. The key-note of this passage is struck in the first verse. It is the fish, by God's hand made Jonah's preserver instead of his destroyer, that inspires the praise-prayer of the whole chapter. God did not come to help till the prophet had, in imagination, faced the worst; but still he came in time. In the very moment of imminent death he stepped in a Deliverer. And he delivered in his own inimitable way. Natural laws cannot serve his purpose, and he accomplishes it against them. "The ravens furnish Elijah's table; the lions are tame and quiet while Daniel is in the den; the violence of fire is gone when believers are in the furnace; the sea, which acts according to its nature towards Pharaoh and his host, is a wall on the right hand and on the left to Moses and to Israel; and the devouring shark preserves Jonah's life" (Rev. Thomas Jones, *in loc.*). And now the prophet realizes that God, after all, is his Friend. He is bringing life out of the jaws of death, converting the voracious sea-monster into a kind protector. And thus, by judgment and mercy in turn, the obdurate heart is broken, and the sturdy apostate brought to his knees and the praise-song of the restored. We see here—

I. HOW AFFLICTION OPENS THE MOUTH WHICH SIN HAD SHUT. Jonah's defection was deliberate and persistent. Not for a trifle would he cry, *Peccavi!* Not by an ordinary obstacle would he be arrested in his course. He seceded most determinedly. He kept his purpose in unabated strength, through a forty-mile tramp on foot. He overcame difficulty with resourceful energy. He slept calmly, going on his way, amidst the crash of an appalling hurricane. He sat sullen and made no sign when even heathen sailors called upon their gods, and wondered at his self-composure. But flesh is flesh, and at length the word came true, "In their affliction will they seek me early." God has weapons that pierce even armour of proof. The invasion of fiery serpents did it for incorrigible Israel (Numb. xxi. 7). The cut of the Assyrian slave-lash did it for graceless Manasseh (2 Chron. xxxiii. 12, 13). The death of Bathsheba's child did it for David, after a great crime and a whole year of impenitent hardness (2 Sam. xii. 13, 16). The Babylonish exile did it for Israel, as Isaiah expresses, "Lord, in trouble they have visited thee; they poured out a prayer when thy chastening was upon them." And the experiences of a shark's interior did it for Jonah. He would not surrender sooner, but resistance is out of the question now. The victory rests with God. The fires of his judgment have softened the apostate's iron will. Yet not the Divine severity only, but severity and goodness together have operated here as "the medicine of the mind." It was not imminent death alone but this with miraculous life out of death that broke the hideous spell, and opened the lips so stubbornly sealed. It is a wrong way of looking at things to contrast, where both have operated, the value of severity and goodness as motive powers in the religious sphere. Neither probably would be effective by itself. The severity before the goodness did not conquer, and neither, probably, would the goodness, had not the severity gone before. The effect does not flow from the last of the series of its causes, but from the series as a whole.

II. HOW A REVIVING FAITH CAN TRIUMPH OVER SENSE. To sense the prophet's case was desperate. On the platform of natural laws the circumstances forbid hope, and would logically shut the mouth of prayer. Yet their effect is directly the reverse. The prophet only begins to pray at the moment when all seems past praying for. And this is the paradoxical but characteristic way of faith. It triumphs over sense, reverses its verdict, overbears its testimony, realizes in actual possession its theoretic impossibility. "Take the case of Abraham and the character and commendation of his faith. 'Against hope he believed in hope.' Appearances were all against him. Sensible realities all contradicted, and in themselves alone destroyed, his expectation. Had his hope rested on sense, on reason, on nature, on time, it must have failed and sunk for ever. But he did not rest on nature. He did not argue. He believed; and his faith destroyed the hope-destroying power of sense" (Rev. Hugh Martin, D.D., *in loc.*). It is the business of your faith and mine to do likewise. We are surrounded by influences and circumstances altogether adverse to the attainment of our soul's salvation. Lusts are strong. Tempers are violent. Habits are tenacious. Example is corrupting. Toil is engrossing. Pleasure is ensnaring. The world, alike when it smiles and frowns, is our soul's foe. But faith is there—keen-eyed conquering faith. It sees through opacity and discovers the invisible. And it knows things very different from what they seem. Beneath the currents of sense, whose trend is away out to sea, it discerns the tidal wave of unseen influence moving in steady flow toward the celestial shores (2 Cor. i. 9; iv. 8—11). God, in his wise and stimulative dealing, "may clothe all circumstances and all his dispensations towards us with appearances of opposition and hostility, in order that we may flee to the anchor of his pure and simple Word, and lean on it without any other help, or rather against all adverse power" (Martin).

III. HOW NATURALLY PRAYER CLOTHES ITSELF IN THE WORDS OF SCRIPTURE. Jonah's prayer was original in the sense that the thoughts called forth the words. But the words themselves are largely borrowed from the Psalms. Most of these had then been written, and, as the Church's Psalter, would be familiar to a prophet of God. And naturally his devotional feelings appropriate their inspired and so fitting words. His prayer "is the simple and natural utterance of a man versed in Holy Scripture, and living in the Word of God" (Keil). What Scripture says is best said. It contains at once the warrant and the definition of prayer, and the actual words in which it was offered by holy men of old. What more natural or fitting than that a man should use these for himself as at once unerring and appropriate! "Let the Word of God dwell in you richly." There is nothing else can support faith, or so well formulate its prayer. And then as to the Psalms, where in Scripture is there to be found such a concentrated wealth of devotional matter as there? "They appear to me a mirror of the soul of every one who sings them" (Athanasius). "The Psalter deserves to be called the praise of God, the glory of man, the voice of the Church, and the most beneficial confession of faith" (Ambrose). "Not without good grounds am I wont to call this book an anatomy of all parts of the soul, since no one can experience emotions whose portrait he could not behold reflected in its mirror" (Calvin). The artist goes to the Louvre, and the scholar or antiquarian to the British Museum, because he finds there the objects he studies in greatest variety and profusion. And so the pious, in search of devotional materials of the most precious kind, resorts inevitably to the Book of Psalms. There are found portrayed, as from the life, the hopes and fears, the moods and frames, the faith and ardour, of their own soul. There they find words that interpret their case and express the very spirit of their aspiration. And so in all time, and over all the world, the saintly praise and pray and vow "with the words of David and Asaph the seer."

IV. HOW POINTEDLY GOD PUNISHES DEFECTION BY ENDORSING IT. Jonah was a spiritual deserter. He struck work, abandoned his post, and so practically vacated his office and abjured God's service. He seemed resolved to have done with the whole thing. And he succeeded but too well, as now to his cost he feels. God has taken him at his word. Figuratively speaking, he has got the "Chiltern Hundreds." He is no longer prophet of God, or servant, or companion. His punishment rises on him in the likeness of his sin. He has fled from God, and now he complains of the separation. "I am cast out of thy sight," *i.e.* banished from covenant territory, the sphere of God's protection and care. So with Peter. He says, "I know not the Man," and he is virtually and formally a stranger from that moment. Only after three times confessing the Lord whom he had three times denied is he spiritually reinstated, restored to forfeited office, and authorized to feed the sheep. This is a terrible aspect of spiritual renegadism. God accepts it as an accomplished fact. You break away, and are let go. You forsake God, and he casts you off. It is a fearful power this you have of putting a whole infinity between yourself and God, between your sin and his righteousness, between your want and his gifts, between your desolate heart and his everlasting consolations. Yet it is a power proper to a moral being, a power it is of the insignia of your manhood to have, and yet an utter renunciation of it to use.

V. How THE REMINISCENCE OF A FORMER FELLOWSHIP HELPS TO DRAW BACK TO GOD. Jonah could look back to a gracious state and consciousness. He had walked in the light of God's countenance. He knew the joy of his presence and the life in his favour. As part of the thought, "I am cast out from before thine eyes," these things would come up to mind. He must remember their quality in bewailing their loss. And they were a fragrant memory, the very cream and flower of the goodness he had tasted. Would they not bulk large among the influences drawing the wanderer back? "As new-born babes desire the sincere milk of the Word, . . . if so be ye have tasted that the Lord is gracious." Yes! there is the secret. If a man has come and tasted, he will be moved to come back and feast. The final apostasy from God of a true believer would be against the nature of things. "His seed remaineth in him." The life that has had God in it once can never be without him again. The void would be intolerable. And so, like the child that for a time has left its mother's knee, the backslider has survivals of precious memories that bring him back to God.

VI. How THE TEMPLE IS THE CENTRE OF THE RETURNING PENITENT'S REGARDS. (Ver. 4.) The temple was the national meeting-place with God, the spot which "he had chosen to place his Name there." "There was the mercy-seat, the ark of the covenant, and the Divine presence; there the tribes of Israel met to worship the Lord, and there the God of Israel came to meet and bless his people. No wonder Jonah's eyes should be fixed on this house, which was the glory of all lands, the sun in the world of mercy, and the centre of true worship" (Jones, *in loc.*). In the spiritual sphere worship underlies work. When Jonah ceased to labour, he had already ceased to pray. As in every case of suspended animation, it was failure of the heart's action that had paralyzed his hand. And now the converse process begins, and first of all pulsation is re-established. The heart resumes its normal action and beats for God. To approach him in worship, and resume fellowship with him in his holy ordinances, is the first sacred exercise to which his hope springs. It is so always. The stay-at-home Christian is never a worker for God. No heart for the sanctuary, no hand for the plough. The very breath of the religious life is to say, "My soul thirsteth for God, for the living God; when shall I come and appear before God?" 1. *Wherever you are, God has placed you.* Jonah says, "Thou hast cast me into the deep . . . thy billows and thy waves passed over me." Privilege and calamity are both God's. He sends them, and bounds them, and is revealed in them. Judgments viewed as accidents have no disciplinary value and no moral aspect. The rod is reforming only when we see it in our Father's hand. 2. *You cannot be in any place where it is not fitting you should seek God.* Jonah cried out of "the belly of hell." What pit, then, is so deep, what fall so low, what evil case so desperate, that in it and from it we may not call on God? "Is any afflicted, let him pray;" "Whosoever shall call on the Name of the Lord shall be saved." 3. *God is again "my God" in the thought of the returning penitent.* (Ver. 1.) With the child's reawakened love comes back the revived filial instinct. God is "my Father" to the prodigal from the moment he comes to himself. Blessed be his gracious Name, that such things can be! If you have renounced the life for self, you may call God your own this hour. The thought is a new backbone to faith. God "waits to be gracious." He is with you the moment you wish it, and for you the moment you submit, and yours in present possession the moment the soul's appropriating hand is stretched forth.

" O Saviour, precious Saviour,
  Whom yet unseen we love;
O Name of might and favour,
  All other names above:
We worship thee, we bless thee,
  To thee alone we sing;
We praise thee and confess thee,
  Our holy Lord and King."

                            J. E. H.

Vers. 5—10.—*Deliverance waiting on the assured hope of it.* It is an obvious remark that all men are ingenuous with God. There is no thought of trying to mislead his judgment or escape his lidless eye. They know that he knows them, knows them truly, knows them thoroughly. Accordingly, when religious profession is false and religious converse is suppressive, and other religious acts are hollow and formal, secret prayer, if it be offered at all, is both honest and open. Only tell us what a man says into the secret ear of God, and you have told us all that is in his heart—have revealed what microscope could not detect, nor scalpel lay bare. It is in this way that our text is apocalyptic. It unveils for us the inner life of Jonah as this is done by no other portion of his book. And the revelation raises him not a little in our estimation. It shows him at bottom a regenerate and saintly man. It reveals a beaten path between his soul and God's throne, a path unused during a wayward hour, but resorted to instinctively when disaster has come and has sobered him into thought. Learn here—

I. THE ESSENTIAL SOLITUDE OF SUFFERING. (Vers. 5, 6.) We find matter around us of different degrees of density, from the light volcanic ash to the heavy metallic ore. But men of science tell us that no material substance is absolutely solid. In the closest-grained rock, in the diamond itself, the ultimate particles are not in actual contact. They approach each other inconceivably close, but when attraction has brought them thus far, a mysterious repulsion intervenes and forbids that they should altogether touch. This fact of the material world has, no doubt, its counterpart in the world of spirit. There is an individuality about the soul that cannot be destroyed. We may be united to others by the closest ties. We may be of one mind, and one heart, and one taste, and one aim. We may thus approach men and be approached by them on many sides, and feel in union, and, to many effects and purposes, be in union with each other. But it is plain that we never coalesce, never actually touch. The shock of personal disaster proves this. Then all ties seem loosened and fall away. Friends drift apart. We are thrown in upon ourselves. Others cannot follow us into the depths. We are in a relation to the event into which no one else can come. In the last appeal we have to meet it alone. It was so with Christ (John xvi. 31, 32). Disciples, friends, kinsmen,—with none of them could the Redeemer share the pangs of death. He had to die alone. Even the earlier thought, " I am not alone, the Father is with me," gave way in the hour of mortal agony to the question of sore amaze, " My God, my God, why hast thou forsaken me?" It was so with Jonah. He was pressed by a feeling of utter isolation. The depths closed over him. The earth with her bars was about him. This he felt, and in proportion as he felt it did he realize that he was cut off from his kind, engulfed in the horrors of a living grave, and left to face them all alone. " I shall die alone." " Yes; and alone you live. No soul touches another soul except at one or two points, and those chiefly external—a fearful and lonely thought, but one of the truest life. Death only realizes that which has been the fact all along. In the central deeps of our being we are alone" (F. W. Robertson).

II. THERE IS AN ANTICIPATIVE POWER IN ALL TRUE FAITH. (Vers. 7, 9.) Jonah's prayer has really no petition in it. It becomes in the offering a song of praise. Still in the shark's maw, with the sea grass around his head, and going down through the deep sea caves to the foundations of the mountains, he speaks as a man delivered, and knowing only occasion of thanks. This is the grand attitude and achievement of faith. It sees the end from the beginning. It expects the end because there has been a beginning. It anticipates the end at the beginning, and deals with it as an accomplished fact. " Thou *hast* brought up my life from corruption, O Lord my God." " I know nothing more sublime in all the range of recorded human utterances. What could dictate assured and triumphant language like this, but marvellous, miraculous faith? His deliverance is not yet come; yet faith speaks of it as if it were. O noble faith! it is in thy power to bring in the deliverance that is still future, with the sweetness of that which is already present, and the sureness of that which is already past" (Rev. Hugh Martin, D.D.). This quality of Jonah's faith appeared also in that of Paul. Crying for deliverance from indwelling sin, he forestalls the event, and prepays the thanks (Rom. vii. 24, 25). So surely is prayer answered, so infallibly does needed help accrue, that from an adequate faith the gratitude may go up when as yet the blessing has not come down. And there is this prophetic realizing power in all faith. It "is the substance of things hoped for, the evidence of things not seen." It carries in its head the jewel of hope; and where the one reaches the other shines. Faith trusts God that he can do all things, and hope looks for the doing of them. The potential deliverance seen by faith becomes actual deliverance in the eye of hope. And so to the believing soul "the things that shall be" already are, and the present is bright with the borrowed light of not yet risen suns.

III. IT IS JUST IN THE MOMENT OF REALIZED HELPLESSNESS THAT THE THOUGHT OF GOD COMES TO A SOUL. (Ver. 7.) Jonah, as is evident, had up till now forgotten God. Not only so, but he had deliberately driven and persistently kept him out of his thoughts. The bursting of a fearful storm impressed him so little that, if left alone, he would have slept it through. The rude piety of the sailors, calling every man upon his god, sent no responsive thrill through him. The captain's reproachful summons to arise and pray was disregarded or ignored. Even the ominous lot-casting, on the issue of which his life hung, was watched with apparent calm. His self-possessed and iron obstinacy died hard. But it died. Angry Omnipotence will not be denied; and God took measures that not even Jonah's hardihood could survive. The prophet broke down. Flesh and heart failed together. And then he came back to first principles, and remembered God. God, if they knew it, is the one need of human hearts. "Every finite spirit is inherently related to the Infinite, in him to live, and move, and have its being. It wants the knowledge of God, the society of God, the approbation of God, the internal manifestation of God, a consciousness lighted up by his presence, to receive of his fulness, to be strong in his might, to rest in his love, and be centred everlastingly in his glory" (Horace Bushnell, D.D.). But the natural man has no idea of this. Conscious of incompleteness, he knows not in what it consists. And he prescribes at random for his own case. He absorbs himself in business, he struggles up the path of ambition, he plunges into mad indulgence, he runs breathless from sensation to sensation, seeking rest and satisfaction, and finding none. Everything gets stale and tiresome, and the soul finds itself unprovided for and orphan still. Not seldom the man spends his days thus in feverish search of good, and dies unsatisfied and unfed at last. But sometimes, in the providence of God, disaster comes at this stage. He is losing his idol. He is being robbed of all he loved, or abandoned of all he trusted in. He is being brought to the grave's mouth by a resistless Providence. It becomes with him a question of God's help or none. And shut up to it thus, he chooses it, albeit only as a last resource. "I cried unto the Lord with my voice. In the day of my trouble I sought the Lord" (Ps. cxvi. 3, 4). This is the natural history of the soul's resort to God. It is the last resort. All other help has been tried and found wanting before the sinner turns to him. What grace, that he waits till then! that while every conceivable earthly nostrum is being tried, the Balm of Gilead is kept in store, and is available in the extremest hour! Truly a God "long-suffering and slow to wrath, and plenteous in mercy," is our God, who wearies not at our long wandering, and welcomes even the latest return.

IV. THE SIGHT OF GOD AND THE SIGHT OF SIN INVOLVE EACH OTHER. (Ver. 8.) Jonah had lost sight of God and of his own guiltiness together. In his conduct up to this point we see the most astounding oblivion of both. And now the two matters come to mind together, suggesting a logical connection between them. And so there is. Sin is a conscious offence against God. Its antagonism to him is its essential element. Accordingly, the sense of it will come and go with the thought of God, and will be adequate as this is adequate. You cannot remember the offence and yet forget the offended Being. Neither can you realize God as near and cognizant without a consciousness of your moral attitude toward him. The thought of sin and the thought of

God, in fact, bring up each other. And not only is the fact of sin, but the extent and evil of it are revealed in the revelation of God. Contact with the plumb-line betrays the curve in the bowing wall. So, side by side with God's ideal holiness, sin looks itself and looks its worst (Job xlii. 5). When a man sees his sinfulness, he has also, as the condition of it, got a glimpse of God. To Jonah his late conduct seems nothing now but the pursuit of lying vanities. He had no fruit in it. Every promise of good it held out had been falsified. He had not escaped. He had not improved matters in any way. He had only intensified existing evils and involved himself and others in new troubles. And that is a true picture of sin the world over and all history through. It is a following of delusive phantasies, and a running away from our own mercies. Its prospective blessings burst like bubbles in our hands—the hands that, but for it, would have been full of the choicest gifts of God.

V. The receiving of spiritual good is followed by a desire to make some return. (Ver. 9.) Gratitude is a universal duty, and ought to be a universal grace. All men receive blessing from God, and as a consequence owe him thanks. Of the gratitude due, however, they fall far short. Some good things come *incognito*, and are thus received unthankfully. Other good things, God's free gifts, are traced to some earthly source, and so produce no thankful feeling. And then the multitude of life's mercies, so obviously Divine, are yet so common that their origin is forgotten, and they are received as a matter of course. But spiritual gifts can never be ungratefully received. They are too conspicuously gracious to be taken as a matter of right. They are too immeasurably great to be lightly deemed of. They involve the gift of a new heart itself, in which gratitude is a native growth, because grace has made it God-like. There are no thankless Christians. Ingratitude possibly means the spiritual nature absent or in abeyance, and points, where we find it, to previous spiritual deformement. Such deformement Jonah had suffered during the continuance of his rebellious freak. Now that religious principle had resumed the sway in his soul, the gratitude is restored that had been exiled during the spiritual interregnum. And everywhere and always the heart that has been blessed to saving effect is one in which infallibly is mooted the question of making grateful return.

VI. Divine deliverance is always timed to arrive when there is ripeness for it. (Ver. 10.) Deliverance any sooner would have been too soon. It would have anticipated repentance, and so have left the erring prophet unreclaimed. It would, in fact, have defeated the object for which the entire disciplinary course had been adopted. It could not therefore occur in a divinely ordered life-history. God's providence never counterworks his scheme of grace. The one is adjusted to the other. His backsliding Jonahs are converted before his disciplinary whales vomit them forth. See you to the repentance, and God will see to your relief. Refining silver, at a certain stage the molten metal becomes for an instant so still and bright that the refiner can see his image in it as in a glass. And this, it is said, is the moment to pour it out, to anticipate which or delay beyond it is to spoil the whole experiment. In the visitations of his hand, God sits, we read, "as a refiner and purifier of silver," to "purify the sons of Levi, and purge them as gold and silver" (Mal. iii. 3). No fear that he will spoil the process by taking you out of the fire a single moment out of date. He will keep you under discipline till he sees his image in your purified soul, and in that moment precisely will remove his hand.

> " He that from dross would win the precious ore,
>   Bends o'er the crucible an earnest eye,
> The subtle searching process to explore,
>   Lest the one brilliant moment should pass by
> When, in the molten silver's virgin mass,
> He meets his pictured face as in a glass.
>
> " Thus in God's furnace are his people tried,
>   Thrice happy they who to the end endure.
> But who the fiery trial may abide?
>   Who from the crucible come forth so pure
> That he whose eyes of flame look through the whole
> May see his image perfect in the soul?"

(J. Montgomery.)

Vers. 1—7.—"*De profundis:*" *distress and prayer.* "Then Jonah prayed unto the Lord his God out of the fish's belly," etc. Unexampled position of Jonah—no details given, and hints somewhat obscure; evidently he retained measure of consciousness, but for how long we know not—seems to have been conscious of moving through the water before being swallowed by the fish—miracle of his preservation corresponds to that of the three Hebrews in the furnace (Dan. iii. 27), or of the burning bush (Exod. iii. 2, 3)—element of apparent destruction becomes supernaturally element of preservation—this record of his feelings composed after his deliverance—a record of the conflict of sight and faith—to sight, the situation desperate—faith pierces to the unseen, finds support, and finally triumphs. The prayer is a singular combination of midnight darkness and noonday light.

I. THE SITUATION. Described in many expressions, some of awful intensity: "By reason of mine affliction;" "out of the belly of hell;" "in the deep, in the midst of the seas;" "The floods compassed me about, all thy billows and thy waves passed over me;" "out of thy sight;" "The depths closed me round about, the weeds were wrapt about my head;" "I went down to the bottom of the mountains, the earth with her bars were about me for ever." Situation seemed absolutely hopeless—physical surroundings the most frightful ever known—each, too, appeared a token of Divine displeasure—apparently as little hope for the soul as for the body.

II. ITS SOURCE—FROM GOD. For it was not a chance that had befallen Jonah; it was all God's doing: "*Thou* hadst cast me into the deep; all *thy* billows and *thy* waves passed over me." God had pursued him ever since he turned his back on him; raised the storm against him; caused the lot to fall on him; cast him into the deep; entombed him in the fish; shut him up, as it were, in despair. Yet he utters no word of reproach; God is justified when he speaks, and clear when he judges (Ps. li. 4).

III. CONSTERNATION OF HIS SOUL. The first effect was to paralyze him. "I said, I am cast out of thy sight;" "My soul fainted within me." Horrors of his situation unexampled, escape impossible; shut up a helpless prey to the most appalling forms of destruction—Omnipotence itself crushing him: "It is a fearful thing to fall into the hands of the living God."

IV. THE DAWN. "When my soul fainted within me I remembered the Lord." The darkest hour of night is that which precedes the dawn—out of the very depths of helplessness and desolation faith begins to rise. Far more beautiful than the fabled sight when the goddess of beauty rose from the ocean foam is the sight of Jonah's faith rising from the depths, both literal and spiritual. The moment of *utter helplessness* is often the turning-point in spiritual experience—at first, in justification (Rom. iii. 19, 21), afterwards in recovery from backsliding (Hos. ii. 14), and in sanctification (Rom. v. 20).

> "Nothing in my hand I bring;
> Simply to thy cross I cling;
> Naked, come to thee for dress;
> Helpless, look to thee for grace;
> Foul, I to the fountain fly;
> Wash me, Saviour, or I die!"

1. In "remembering God," Jonah recognized him as "the Lord his God;" his by national covenant, by personal choice (the fruit of Divine grace), and by his prophetic call and consecration; his, though he had attempted to flee from his presence, for does he not say, "Turn, O backsliding Israel, and I will heal your backsliding" (Jer. iii. 12, 22)? The God who first chose him in all his unworthiness must have an interest in him still. So the psalmist cried; so Jesus afterwards in the like spirit, "My God, my God, why hast thou forsaken me?" 2. He looked towards God's temple. Why? Because of the promise virtually given to Solomon (1 Kings viii. 38). He builds on God's word, "Remember the word unto thy servant, upon which thou hast caused me to hope" (Ps. cxix. 49). He thinks of the temple, the sacred ark, the mercy-seat, the overshadowing cherubims, the promise to Moses, "There I will meet with you, and I will commune with you from above the mercy-seat" (Exod. xxv. 22). He takes hold of this—steadies his soul upon it—shaking off the impression of his horrible surroundings, and enters into peace. What a change!—the belly of hell turned into the gate of heaven, the howl of despair changed into the hallelujah of delight.

See here an encouragement to spirit of faith—in Jonah all lights extinguished except faith—in lowest depths, "let Israel hope in the Lord, for with the Lord there is mercy, and with him is plenteous redemption." Even when we are the authors of our own troubles, when we are in the depths by reason of sin, *nil desperandum!* "O Israel, thou hast destroyed thyself, but *in me* is thy help."—W. G. B.

Vers. 2—10.—*Triumph, thanksgiving.* "And said, I cried by reason of mine affliction unto the Lord, and he heard me; out of the belly of hell cried I, and thou heardest my voice," etc. This is one of the most striking instances in all Scripture of the benefit of believing prayer.

> "Lord, what a change within us one short hour
>   Spent in thy presence will prevail to make!
> What heavy burdens from our bosom take!
> What parched lands refresh as with a shower!
> We kneel, and all around us seems to lower;
>   We rise, and all, the distant and the near,
>   Stands forth in sunny outline, brave and clear.
> We kneel, how weak; we rise, how full of power!
> Why therefore should we do ourselves this wrong,
>   That we are ever overborne with care?
> That we should ever weak or heartless be,
>   Anxious or troubled, when with us in prayer,
> And joy, and strength, and courage, are with thee?"
>
> (Trench.)

In the brighter part of Jonah's prayer we notice his—

I. GRATEFUL RECOGNITION OF PRAYER AS ANSWERED. (Vers. 2, 7.) Happy effect of *certainty* as to this. There are grounds for such certainty: 1. When prayer is offered *trustfully,* poured as into the ear of a Father, who has promised to hear such prayer. Answer to be *expected,* since God is true and never can deceive us. 2. When the evil dreaded is actually averted, or the benefit asked is sent. Unbelief says it would have been so at any rate; faith says, "My prayer came in unto thee, into thine holy temple." 3. When the heart is filled with a sense of the goodness and love of God and his trustworthiness even before the answer comes, it may be felt that the prayer is heard. Confidence in God as Hearer of prayer is a most valuable Christian grace—ever associated with deep humility—infinitely removed from presumption and boasting.

II. HUMBLE ACKNOWLEDGMENT OF PAST GUILT AND FOLLY. (Ver. 8.) "They that observe lying vanities forsake their own mercy." This is what he had done. Human devices contrary to will of God are "lying vanities;" empty, they bring no satisfaction; lying, they promise peace and safety, but bring misery and horrible troubles. So Eve found, so Pharaoh, so Israel when they went after ways of heathen. So Jonah himself. So all who forsake Fountain of living waters and hew out to themselves broken cisterns that can hold no water. Worldly devices to get happiness apart from God are indeed "vanity of vanities." Soul of man cannot be satisfied with husks. For God's servants to follow them is to forsake their own mercy. It is for prodigal son to change father's house for society of rioters and harlots: "Many sorrows shall be to the wicked: but he that trusteth in the Lord, mercy shall compass him about" (Ps. xxxii. 10). The way of duty is ever the way of safety, peace, and comfort; neglected duty is a sure forerunner of trouble; an evil conscience can never be the harbinger of sweet content.

III. PUBLIC EXPRESSION OF THANKSGIVING AND CONSECRATION. (Ver. 9.) Sacrifice —thanksgiving—vows. This is to be done openly and publicly at the proper place. No concealment by Jonah of what had taken place. He would at once proclaim his own guilt, and declare himself a monument of God's grace. Genuine repentance carries spirit of self-abasement, conscious indebtedness to God—eagerness to be more consecrated to him. The spring of this feeling—"salvation is of the Lord." God's saving mercy keeps alive in redeemed hearts the sense of infinite obligation, and prompts to every suitable recognition. No other spiritual dynamic like this—all active obedience, all the labour of love, all patient endurance spring from this; whatever our mercies, we have the duty of grateful remembrance of them, and active consecration to

God in connection with them. *Jonah is disentombed* (ver. 10). "And the Lord spake unto the fish, and it vomited out Jonah upon the dry land." At length the purpose of the chastisement is served, therefore it is removed. The great fish continues under God's control, and having carried Jonah safely through the deep, deposits him on the dry land. "As you see the foamy track the creature leaves behind gradually melting into the quiet green of the sea; as you turn and look at the prophet, washing himself from the filth of his living grave, and then standing upon the shore, inhaling the fresh breeze, rejoicing in heaven's blessed light, and—to prove and feel himself alive, to make sure that all was not a dream—shouting, perhaps, in a loud voice, 'Salvation is of the Lord,' say, 'God helping me, I shall never despair. Never. For I see that the heaviest judgment may ripen into mercy. The darkest night may have a morning. The deepest grave has a resurrection-portal. A voyage wrapped in whirling storm, and horrible with engulfing dangers, may yet end in safety on a sunny shore'" (Raleigh). *Jonah a sign*: 1. To *the Ninevites*. His history a twofold picture-lesson to them. (1) Of the consequence of spurning the authority of the God of the Hebrews; for he is no local deity, but Lord of earth and sea, of all creatures and all their actions, and has showed he could signally punish and humble Jonah on the very element to which he had betaken himself for safety from this God. It was before this God the iniquities of Nineveh had come. How must he view these? (2) Of the pardoning, restoring, and preserving mercy of God to the penitent—God not inexorable —if Nineveh should repent, it, like Jonah, would experience God's mercy. 2. To *the men of Christ's generation*. (1) *In his humiliation*. The Jews asked of Christ a sign (Matt. xii. 40)—some great display of power *in the heavens*. He refused; the only sign to be given would be precisely opposite, viz. that of Jonah—a sign not in heaven, but beneath the surface of the earth. As Jonah suffered humiliation for his own sin, so Jesus would suffer humiliation for the sin which he bore. Reality of his Messiahship was to be shown in his death and burial, and continuing for the same period as Jonah under the power of death. Divine, saving power of Jesus is connected with his humiliation as Sin-bearer. "As if Jesus had said, 'The signs which are to discover themselves in me are to grow darker, and not brighter: they are to be derived, not from the heavens above, but from the depths beneath—from the very chamber of the dead; yet am I not less on that account the Ambassador of Heaven; yea, surpassing Jonah in the depth of my humiliation, I still more surpass him in the dignity of my character; and the inhabitants of the heathen city, which repented at his preaching, will assuredly rise up in judgment to condemn the impenitent of this generation'" (Fairbairn). (2) *In his exaltation*. This view is rather implied than expressed by our Lord. Jonah escaping from the fish is a type of Christ rising from the dead. The Ninevites were moved to repentance by means of the type; they must have heard Jonah's history and been greatly impressed by it. The Jews had the antitype—the literal resurrection of Christ from the dead, but were not moved by it. Herein is a great lesson for all—listen to the Divine Messenger, who liveth and was dead, and is alive for ever, and hath the keys of hell and of death! "Though our Lord's pointing to the sign of Jonah, with the assurance that no other would be given them, might at first seem to betoken only trouble and disaster to his mission, yet the more thoughtful and discerning minds would not fail to discover, on further reflection, that there was also couched under it a promise of encouragement and success far beyond anything that had hitherto appeared. He was to become to the world the sign that Jonah was to Nineveh only when he entered on the resurrection-life, and in his Name repentance and remission of sins were preached to the people. And hence the great stress laid upon the fact of the resurrection by the first heralds of the gospel, and the wonderful effect produced by it upon those who heard them, not simply on account of the proof it afforded of the truth of Christ's pretensions to be the Son of God, but also, and still more, for the impressive attestation, the living witness it gave of the placability of God, and of the holy earnestness of his desire that sinners would repent and live. Precisely as in the case of Jonah, though in a manner unspeakably more solemn and affecting, the things that had befallen Jesus and the condition in which he now presented himself through his ambassadors to the people, were seen to be a singular and most magnificent provision of love on the part of God to reach their consciences, and to avert, ere it might be too late, the doom of condemnation which Divine justice had suspended over their heads" (Fairbairn).—W. G. B.

Ver. 2.—*The value of affliction* (*as seen in Jonah's prayer*). It: 1. Brings the man to himself. To *soul*-consciousness, to *God*-consciousness. When "in the shadow of a great affliction, the soul sits dumb." Chastened, he feels his need of chastisement, and knows from whom it comes. "*Thy* waves;" "*thy* billows." 2. Brings the consolation of Scripture to the man. From various psalms of sorrow (now remembered) Jonah quotes. By sorrow he enters into the sorrows of others. Affliction "opens up the mine of Scripture, before seen only on the surface." 3. Brings the man to God. He "cries" to him. He comes to him. He feels that "sorrow's crown of sorrow" is in being "cast out of God's sight." 4. Brings the assurance of salvation to the man. Thus, divinely blest, affliction is good. The soul, then, triumphant over trouble, can exclaim, "Salvation is of the Lord;" "O Lord my God."—G. T. C.

Ver. 8.—"*Lying vanities.*" 1. Vanities. Vanities are vain things—things that deceive. Such are idols. All things are idols that men trust out of God. Jonah had *his* idol— it was his false love for his country. How many idols!—ambition, pride, strength, wealth, influence, self, self-will. And men *observe* them as gods. But they are all "lying." They deceive. Their promises fail. *One only* is "faithful who has promised" us happiness. 2. The consequence of observing these lying vanities. Men who observe them "forsake their own mercy." How much they leave! Mercy! It is to all; but not to all alike. "Their own." In turning to any idol, men forsake *God,* "whose property is always to have mercy."—G. T. C.

Ver. 9.—*Thankfulness.* "Thankfulness opens the door of mercy, sets God's goodness free to be good to us, prepares us to receive blessing." It should be cultivated. It should be expressed. "The *voice* of thanksgiving." Jonah was thankful. He had strong reason indeed to be. He *paid* the vows he had made. "Be *ye* thankful." Every mercy is an incentive to thankfulness. And God's mercies, "new every morning and repeated every evening," and pauseless in their coming, "cannot be reckoned up." And all crowned by the gift of Christ. "Thanks be unto God for his unspeakable Gift." "Thanksgiving is thanksliving."

> "Let never day nor night unhallow'd pass,
> But still remember what the Lord hath done."

G. T. C.

Ver. 7.—*The prophet's prayer.* The contrast which Jonah depicts between his own conduct and that of the heathen with whom he came in contact is very unfavourable to himself. He appears as a coward fleeing from his duty, and cruel enough to prefer that the Ninevites should be destroyed rather than that his accuracy should be impugned. But the idolatrous sailors prayed in the storm as best they could, and they were humane enough to try to save him, even after they had been told to cast him overboard (ch. i. 13). It is not only noteworthy that Jonah wrote thus, but also that a book which compared a Jew so disadvantageously with the heathen should have been preserved by the Jewish people, who were notoriously proud and bigoted. Describe the event narrated in the preceding chapter. Point out the use our Lord made of it to typify his own death and resurrection. Pass on to apply the prophet's experience to what is represented by it among ourselves.

I. THE NEGLECT OF APPOINTED SERVICE IS A SIN. The command given to Jonah was plain enough, but he wilfully disobeyed it. Some of the excuses he may have made to conscience may be profitably suggested. 1. "*I have already done my share of service; let another undertake this.*" He had faithfully conveyed his message to King Amaziah, and had doubtless proved his fidelity on other occasions, but he shrank from this new summons from God. Past service does not relieve us of present responsibilities. The indolence or the failure of others will not justify us in ignoring duty. 2. "*It is useless to preach to the Ninevites; they would laugh me to scorn.*" Ignorant of the true God as they were, it certainly was hardly to be expected that they would humble themselves before him at the bidding of a stranger preaching in their streets. Yet often those we deem to be the most hopeless are the most ready to listen. Even if they were not, it is at our peril that we refuse to obey a God-given impulse to speak to them. 3. "*These Ninevites are the foes of my country; let one of their own citizens be raised up to warn them.*" National hostility and personal prejudice have done much to hinder God's work in all ages.

II. SUCH SIN IN GOD'S PEOPLE IS FOLLOWED BY CHASTISEMENT. 1. *Chastisement does not always follow sin.* Sometimes it precedes and prevents it. Paul's thorn in the flesh was sent, not because he was exalted above measure, but lest he should be. But often an affliction is intended to bring a sinner to a right state of mind about sin already committed. 2. *Chastisement gives us time to think.* Jonah acted on impulse, and hurriedly fled to Joppa. When cast into the sea he imagined that all was over with him; but when he was miraculously preserved he had opportunity to reflect on his own wrong-doing and on God's marvellous mercy. So the ill health which prevents work, the family affliction which keeps us within doors, the failure which sets us free from an accustomed sphere,—give us time to think of neglected duties and to recover strength by prayer. 3. *In chastisement God is near.* Jonah felt that he was not beyond Divine help. "My prayer came in unto thee." Compare Peter in prison, and Paul in the storm, and John in Patmos, and Bunyan in jail. Listen to the words of Bradford, "I thank God more of this prison and of this dark dungeon than of any parlour, yea, than of any pleasure ever I had; for in it I find God, my sweet God always." Jonah was cast out as Adam was from Paradise, and as Job was from his home, that he might learn, through prayer, to suffer and be strong.

III. CHASTISEMENT, RIGHTLY RECEIVED, BRINGS ABOUT REPENTANCE. 1. *In order to this it was necessary for Jonah to recognize God's hand in this event.* He felt it was not the result of chance nor of human action. Hence he does not say, "The sailors cast me into the deep," but "*thou*" (ver. 3); nor does he speak of "the waves and billows of the sea," but "*thy billows and thy waves*" (ver. 3). We too must learn to look beyond second causes, such as an unfortunate step or a man's injustice, and see God as the Disposer of all events. 2. *This thought led Jonah to true repentance.* He did not despair, although there seemed no hope of deliverance. He did not pray to be delivered from danger, but earnestly thanks God for his rescue from the sea, and praised him in the belly of the whale that he had been so good and merciful. The reality of his repentance was shown in this, that he gratefully and bravely did the work he had formerly refused. His vow made in trouble was faithfully kept. Pliny advised one who wished to please the gods to be the same when well as he had vowed to be when sick. A lesson for us.

IV. SUCH REPENTANCE UNDER CHASTISEMENT LEADS TO ACCEPTABLE PRAYER. His prayer shows that he had not given up hope, that he still believed that Jehovah was his God, and would do what was best with him. Strangely and soon the prayer was answered.

CONCLUSION. *We may obtain mercy as Jonah did.* We may find that the very instrument of death becomes the preserver of life, as the great fish proved an ark of safety to Jonah; and as he was cast upon the shore, so a trouble may cast us on the shore of duty, and death will cast us on the shore of heaven.—A. R.

EXPOSITION.

CHAPTER III.

Vers. 1—10.—Part III. JONAH'S PREACHING IN NINEVEH; THE REPENTANCE OF THE NINEVITES.

Vers. 1—3.—§ 1. *Jonah is sent a second time to Nineveh, and obeys the command.*

Ver. 1.—**The second time.** He is forgiven and restored to his office, and the commission formerly given is renewed. Commentators have supposed that he went up to Jerusalem to pay his vows, and that the word of the Lord came unto him there. But all unnecessary details are omitted from the account, and we know nothing about this matter. The beginning of the next verse, "arise," seems to imply that he was then in some settled home, perhaps at Gath-hepher.

Ver. 2.—That great city (see note on ch. i. 2). Preaching; rendered "cry" in ch. i. 2; Septuagint, κήρυγμα. This time the proclamation is unto it, as interested in the message, not "against it," as doomed to destruction (Pusey).

Ver. 3.—**Arose, and went.** He was now as prompt to obey as formerly to flee. **Was;** *i.e.* when Jonah visited it. Nothing can be argued from the past tense here as to the date of the composition of the book. It is a mere historical detail, and cannot be forced into a proof that Jonah wrote after the destruction of Nineveh. **An exceeding great city;** literally, *a city great to God;* πόλις μεγάλη τῷ Θεῷ (Septuagint); great before God—in his estimation, as though even God must acknowledge it. So Nimrod is called (Gen. x. 9) "a mighty hunter before the Lord;" and Moses, in Acts vii. 20, is said to have been "beautiful to God." The expression may also mean that God (*Elohim*, God as Governor of the world) regarded this city with interest, as intended in the Divine counsels to perform an important part. For he is not the God of the Jews only, but also of the Gentiles (Rom. iii. 29). **Of three days' journey;** *i.e.* in circumference—about sixty miles (see note on ch. i. 2). Or the writer may mean that it took Jonah three days to visit the various quarters of this huge place. The area of the vast quadrangle containing the remains of the four cities comprised under the name *Nineveh* is estimated by Professor Rawlinson at two hundred and sixteen square miles. We ought, however, to omit Khorsabad from this computation, as it was not founded till Sargon's time, B.C. 710.

Ver. 4.—§ 2. *Jonah, undeterred by the danger of the enterprise, executes his mission at once, and announces the approaching destruction of the city.* **Began to enter into the city a day's journey.** Jonah commenced his day's journey in the city, and, as he found a suitable place, uttered his warning cry, not necessarily continuing in one straight course, but going to the most frequented spots. At the time of Jonah's preaching the royal residence was probably at Chalah; *i.e.* Nimrud, the most southern of the cities. Coming from Palestine, he would reach this part first, so that his strange message would soon come to the king's ears (ver. 6). **Yet forty days.** "Forty" in Scripture is the number of probation (see Gen. vii. 4, 12; Exod. xxiv. 18; 1 Kings xix. 8; Matt. iv. 2). The LXX. has, ἔτι τρεῖς ἡμέραι, "yet three days," owing probably to some clerical error, as writing γ′ instead of μ′. St. Augustine ('De Civit.,' xviii. 44) endeavours to explain the discrepancy mystically as referring to Christ under different circumstances, as being the same who remained forty days on earth after his resurrection, and who rose again on the third day. **Shall be overthrown.** This is the word used for the destruction of Sodom (Gen. xix. 25, 27; Amos iv. 11). The prophet appears

to have gone on through the city, repeating this one awful announcement, as we read of fanatics denouncing woe on Jerusalem before its final destruction (Josephus, 'Bell. Jud.,' vi. 5. 3). The threat was conditional virtually, though expressed in uncompromising terms. In the Hebrew the participle is used, "Yet forty days, and Nineveh overthrown," as though he saw at the end of the specified time the great city lying in ruins. One sees from Isa. xxxvi. 11, 13, that Jonah could readily be understood by the Assyrians.

Vers. 5—9.—§ 3. *The Ninevites hearken to the cry of Jonah, believe in God, and repent.*

Ver. 5.—**Believed God;** *believed in God,* which implies trust and hope; Vulgate, *crediderunt in Deum.* They recognized Jonah as God's messenger; they recognized God's power as able to execute the threat, and they had confidence in his mercy if they repented. This great result has seemed to some incredible, and has occasioned doubts to be cast upon the history. But, as we have seen in the Introduction, Jonah's mission occurred probably at a time of national depression, when men's minds were disposed to expect calamity, and anxious to avert it by any means. Other considerations led to the same result. They had heard much of the God of the Hebrews, much of the doings of his great prophets Elijah and Elisha; and now they had in their midst one of these holy men, who, as they were informed, had been miraculously preserved from death in order to carry his message to them; for that it was thus that Jonah was "a sign unto the Ninevites" (Luke xi. 30) seems most certain. They saw the Divine inspiration beaming in his look, dictating his utterance, animating his bearing, filling him with courage, confidence, and faith. The credulity with which they received the announcements of their own seers, their national predilection for presages and omens, encouraged them to open their ears to this stranger, and to regard his mission with grave attention. Their own conscience, too, was on the prophet's side, and assisted his words with its powerful pleading. So they **believed in God, and proclaimed a fast.** Spontaneously, without any special order from the authorities. Before the final fall of Nineveh, the inscriptions mention, the then king ordered a fast of one hundred days and nights to the gods in order to avert the threatened danger (see a note by Professor Sayce, in G. Smith's 'History of Babylon,' p. 156). **Put on sackcloth** (comp. Gen. xxxvii. 34; 1 Kings xxi. 27; Joel i. 13). The custom of changing the dress in token of mourning was not confined to the Hebrews (comp. Ezek. xxvi 16).

Ver. 6.—**For word came;** *and the matter came;* ἤγγισεν ὁ λόγος, "the word came near" (Septuagint). The tokens of penitence mentioned in ver. 5 were not exhibited in obedience to any royal command. Rather, as the impression made by the prophet spread among the people, and as they adopted these modes of showing their sorrow, the news of the movement reached the king, and he put himself at the head of it. The reigning monarch was probably either Shalmaneser III. or one of the two who succeeded him, Asshur-danil and Asshur-nirari, whose three reigns extended from B.C. 781 to 750. **His robe** (*addereth*); the word used for the "Babylonish garment" in Josh. vii. 21. The magnificence of the Assyrian kings' attire is attested by the monuments. **Sat in ashes** (comp. Job ii. 8; Esth. iv. 3).

Ver. 7.—**He caused it,** etc.; literally, *he caused proclamation to be made, and said,* i.e. by the heralds. **The decree.** The word used here (*taam*) is an Accadian term, which had become naturalized in Assyria, Persia, and Babylonia, and was applied to a mandate issued with royal authority. It is found in Dan. iii. 10, 29; iv. 6; Ezra iv. 8, etc. Jonah introduces it here as being the very word employed in describing the proclamation. **And his nobles.** The monarchs of Assyria were absolute; and if the king in the present case associated the magnates with himself, he did it in an humility occasioned by alarm, and because he saw that they were of the same mind as himself (comp. Dan. vi. 17). **Saying.** The decree extends from here to the end of ver. 9. **Man nor beast;** *i.e.* domestic animals, horses, mules, distinct from **herd and flock.** These great cities contained in their area immense open spaces, like our parks, where cattle were kept. The dumb animals were made to share in their masters' fast and sorrow, as they shared their joy and feasting; their bleating and bellowing were so many appeals to Heaven for mercy; the punishment of these innocent creatures was a kind of atonement for the guilt of their lords (comp. Hos. iv. 3; Joel i. 20; and note how the brute creation is said to share in the happiness of paradise regained, Isa. xi.). The commentators quote Virgil,' Ecl.,' v. 24, etc., where, however, the point is that the grief of the shepherds hinders them from attending to the wants of their flocks. Herodotus (ix. 24) mentions an instance of the Persians cutting the manes and tails of their horses and mules in a case of general mourning (comp. Eurip., 'Alcest.,' 428, etc.; Plut., 'Alex.,' 72).

Ver. 8.—**Let man and beast be covered with sackcloth.** As we put trappings on horses in funerals. The LXX. wrongly makes this verse give an account of the execution of the edict instead of being part of the edict itself; thus: "And men and beasts were clothed with sackcloth," etc. **Cry mightily;** *i.e.* let man cry mightily; Septuagint, ἐκτενῶς, "with intensity;" Vulgate, *in fortitudine.* **Let them turn every one from his evil way** (Jer. xxv. 5; xxxvi. 3, 7). The edict recognizes the truth that outward acts of penitence are worthless without moral reformation—a truth which the Jews themselves had been very loth to admit (see Isa. lviii.). **And from the violence that is in their hands.** The acts of violence that their hands have committed (Job xvi. 17; Ps. vii. 3). This is the special sin of the Assyrians, always grasping after empire, oppressing other nations, and guilty of rapine and avarice at home (see Isa. x. 13, 14; xxxvii. 24, etc.; Nah. ii. 11, 12; iii. 1).

Ver. 9.—**Who can tell?** (2 Sam. xii. 22). An expression of hope that the Divine wrath may be averted by the timely repentance. It is the same form of words as in Joel ii. 14, "Perhaps God would thereby indicate that he had himself put it into their mouths" (Pusey; comp. Jer. xviii. 11). **If God;** *i.e.* the one God, whom the king and his people now acknowledge as supreme, like the idol-worshippers at Carmel, when they fell on their faces, crying, "Jehovah, he is the God" (1 Kings xviii. 39).

Ver. 10.—§ 4. *God accepts this repentance, and the threatened destruction is averted.* **God saw their works.** There is no notice in the inscriptions of this "repentance," or of any change in the polytheistic worship of the Ninevites. But the existing records of this period are singularly meagre, and show a state of calamity and depression, of internal commotions and famine. Nor is it usual in the monumental history to find mention of any events but wars and the execution of material works; moral reformations are not recorded. **God repented of the evil** (Exod. xxxii. 14). This is an anthropopathical mode of speaking; God acted as if, taking man's view of the transaction, he repented. The sentence was conditional, as Jonah well knew (ch. iv. 2), in accordance with the great principle laid down in Jer. xviii. 7, etc., viz. that if a nation against which sentence is pronounced turn from its evil way, the sentence shall not be executed. God does not change, but he threatens that man may change (see note on Amos vii. 3; and observe the same principle applied to individuals, Ezek. xxxiii. 8, 13—16). **He did it not.** The evil day was postponed. This partial repentance, though it was not permanent and made little lasting impression on the national life, showed that there was some element of good in these Assyrians, and that they were not yet ripe for destruction. It has been considered to be a proof of the unhistorical character of the Book of Jonah that no mention of any of the incidents is made in the Books of Kings and Chronicles; but there is nothing strange in this. Those records never touch external politics except as closely connected with Israel's fortunes; and, derived as they were from national annals, it would have been unnatural for them to have narrated events happening so far away, and not likely to be introduced in the documents on which their history was founded.

HOMILETICS.

Ver. 2.—*City preaching.* In Palestine there were no great cities. The population was scattered through pastoral regions or gathered in small and unimportant towns. This fact gave a character to the national life of the Hebrews and to their national religiousness. It was a strange experience for a Jew like Jonah to be brought into contact with city life upon a grand, colossal scale. We modern Englishmen are more familiar with this development of human existence and activity. We need to study the relations of religion to city life, its occupations, temptations, and opportunities.

I. THE PREACHER IN A GREAT CITY NEEDS TO HAVE HIS IMAGINATION AND HIS HEART FILLED WITH AN IMPRESSION OF ITS MAGNITUDE AND IMPORTANCE. In the view of the Almighty all things earthly may well seem diminutive; yet Jehovah is represented as commissioning Jonah to preach unto Nineveh—"that great city." The population, the wealth, the industry, the political importance of a metropolis should be pondered by one who is required to discharge a public ministry among its inhabitants. Thus he will be more likely to rise to the due height of seriousness, of sympathy. He who labours in "an exceeding great city" needs to fill his soul with a conviction of the spiritual necessities and the spiritual possibilities of such a population.

II. THE PREACHER IN A GREAT CITY NEEDS TO FULFIL A MINISTRY OF WITNESS. "Cry unto it the cry." Such is the exact language in which Jehovah commissioned his servant. In the university, the private chapel, the select and cultivated congregation, there may be room for argumentative, emotional, poetical, or philosophical preaching. What a great city needs is a voice, a cry, a preaching, in the proper sense of that word. A plain and powerful witness to man's sin and need, to God's grace and power to save, a summons to repentance and surrender,—such is what the population of a great city for the most part needs.

III. THE PREACHER IN A GREAT CITY NEEDS AN UNMISTAKABLE DIVINE COMMISSION AND MESSAGE. "The preaching that *I bid thee*,"—such was to be the burden of the prophet's utterances. It is only the Word of the Lord which should be proclaimed by the minister of religion in any position, in all circumstances. But when standing in the midst of a great metropolis, how can a man, justly sensible of his own ignorance and powerlessness, proceed in his ministry, unless he is assured that the Lord has sent him, unless he can commence his testimony with the preface, "Thus saith the Lord"?

Ver. 5.—*National repentance.* No doubt repentance is an individual exercise of heart; yet when the bulk of a community is pervaded by similar sentiments, it may be a national exercise also. Such seems to have been the case with the population of Nineveh; Jonah's witness was believed by one and by another, until belief became general; and, as penitence, fear, and supplication spread from man to man, the city seemed moved by one common impulse, leading the whole population to the feet of God.

I. SUCH REPENTANCE BEGINS IN FAITH. The inhabitants of the great city credited the message of the Hebrew prophet; that is, they believed that the Supreme Ruler and Judge was displeased with them because of their sinfulness; that they were liable to the punishment which the godless, the vicious, the criminal deserve; and perhaps also that, notwithstanding their dangerous condition, there was some hope for them in the Divine mercy, if they would but turn unto God. Certainly the gospel of Christ does not ask the sinner to yield his belief merely to the tidings of God's justice and holiness; it invites him also to give credence to its offers of salvation.

II. SUCH REPENTANCE MANIFESTS ITSELF IN CONTRITION AND IN ALL THE SIGNS

OF SINCERE REGRET AND DISTRESS BECAUSE OF SIN. There is something very affecting in the spectacle of a nation mourning and lamenting because of a great bereavement, when an honoured sovereign, a trusted minister, a mighty warrior, passes away. But the pathos and the moral significance of that national mourning are far greater which is prompted by a general consciousness of sin, by a conviction of national wrong-doing, by humiliation before an omniscient and righteous God. The tokens of such contrition, as recorded in the text to have been displayed in Nineveh, were appropriate to that time and community, and accorded with the customs of the East. But whatever be the manifestations of sorrow, the first essential is that it be real, as in the sight of the heart-searching God.

III. SUCH REPENTANCE PERVADES THE WHOLE COMMUNITY. In most cities are individuals who sigh and cry for the abominations done by the people. Even a few are as salt to preserve the mass from corruption. For the sake of a very few a city may be spared the doom deserved. But a nation in mourning for sin is a sight as sublime as it is affecting. Nineveh is in this respect an example to other sinful cities. The king led the way, and his subjects followed. Even the least, the lowest, joined in the solemn act of penitence. Such repentance is indeed repentance unto life; it cannot be unheeded or unrewarded by Heaven.

Ver. 6.—*A king's contrition.* It is an illustration of the power of truth, of the commanding majesty of the faithful and fearless preacher, which we witness in this narrative. An unknown Hebrew, with nothing to recommend him, nothing to enforce attention, comes to a foreign city, passes through the public places, reproaches the citizens for their sins, denounces destruction upon the inhabitants as the punishment due to them because of their wickedness. And what is the result? Is it neglect, or derision, or incredulity? On the contrary, the people feel the justice of the rebukes, acknowledge their ill desert, humble themselves before God, and entreat mercy, forbearance, pardon. What a testimony to the reality of the moral law, to the authority of conscience! Jonah preaches, and the king of a mighty empire divests himself of the insignia of power and rule, abases himself before God in sackcloth and ashes!

I. KINGS ARE SOMETIMES THE LEADERS OF THEIR PEOPLE IN SIN. Surrounded by everything that can minister to selfish gratification, beset by flatterers, possessed in some instances of absolute power, it is not to be wondered at that the occupants of thrones are often the foremost in cruelty, in vice, in self-indulgence. They may be to blame, but in a just estimate their perilous circumstances will be considered. Their temptations are many, and their faithful friends are few.

II. KINGS ARE ACCORDINGLY SOMETIMES RESPONSIBLE FOR THE MISERIES OF THEIR SUBJECTS. When royal ambition has led to culpable warfare and slaughter; when headstrong purposes have issued in national disaster, impoverishment, and disgrace; when luxury in palaces has entailed hunger upon the occupants of hovels;—in such cases sovereigns have a terrible account to render to him who is no respecter of persons, who is King of kings and Lord of lords.

III. KINGS ARE SUITABLY EMPLOYED IN HEADING EVERY ELEVATING AND PROFITABLE MOVEMENT. Happily there are many examples of such conduct on the part of those occupying the very highest stations. Institutions and agencies for imparting knowledge, for refining life, for relieving suffering, are better deserving the "patronage" and the attention of royalty than schemes of pleasure or methods of destruction.

IV. WHEN KINGS AS WELL AS SUBJECTS HAVE SINNED IT BECOMES ALL TO UNITE IN SACRIFICES OF CONTRITION AND IN VOWS OF REFORMATION. The frank, dignified, right-minded conduct of the King of Nineveh raises him in our esteem. No man is disgraced by admitting his faults. And every man, even though he be a king, is in his right place when low on his knees in penitence and in prayer.

Vers. 7, 8.—*Ceremonial and moral repentance.* It must have been a striking and picturesque spectacle that was presented by Nineveh when the decree of the king and nobles was carried out, when a general fast was observed, when sackcloth and ashes were worn by man and beast, and when general prayer ascended in a mighty cry to Heaven. But to the reflective mind it must have been still more interesting to observe the population turning from their evil ways and refraining from acts of violence.

I. THE OUTWARD SIGNS OF PENITENCE AND CONTRITION ARE GOOD WHEN, AND ONLY WHEN, THEY ARE THE EXPRESSION OF GENUINE FEELING AND PURPOSE. We feel this to be the case with reference to ordinary human sorrow. The mere garb and semblance of mourning, being but conventional, is of little value. It is felt to be appropriate when the mourner can say—

> "I have that within which passes show,
> These but the trappings and the signs of woe."

How much more do the religious interest and value of " sackcloth and ashes," " fasting and prayers," depend upon the sincerity of the emotions thus expressed !

II. RESOLUTIONS TO REFORM AND AMEND ARE THE BEST EVIDENCE OF THE GENUINENESS AND ACCEPTABLENESS OF REPENTANCE. It is very much to the credit alike of the prophet and of those to whom he preached, that the Ninevites should have felt and expressed the absolute necessity of moral amendment in order to the enjoyment of forgiveness, favour, and acceptance with God. There must have been something searching in Jonah's preaching, and something very responsive in the heart and conscience of the Ninevites, to have produced such a state of mind as that here indicated. It is especially observable that the citizens turned " every one from his evil way." The ways of sin are devious, numerous, and varied ; sinners have turned every one to his own way ; true repentance shows itself in a resolve on the part of each individual offender to forsake his own sins. " Violence," whether proneness to national schemes for attacking other peoples, or assaults upon peaceful citizens, seems to have been the prevailing sin ; for of this, it is said, the people chiefly repented.

APPLICATION. The whole nature, body and soul, is implicated in sin ; and the whole nature accordingly should concur in repentance.

Ver. 9.—*Hoping for mercy.* The pathos of this question is increased as we call to mind the ignorance of the Ninevites regarding the true God. Their own religion was as likely to conceal as to make known the real character of the Deity. And what they had heard from Jonah was but very slender ground upon which to proceed in their approaches to Heaven. Hence the uncertainty, the commingling of fear with hope in the language they employed : " Who can tell," etc. ?

I. THE NEED OF MERCY. This appears from considering (1) human sin ; (2) Divine justice ; and (3) the express threatenings of the Divine Word. All this was very apparent in the case of the Ninevites, and accounts for their attitude of contrition and supplication. But the same holds good of men of every nation and in every state of society.

II. THE GROUND OF HOPE. 1. With the Ninevites this could have been nothing but some instinct in their own heart. A Creator who has implanted pity in the breasts of his creatures cannot surely be destitute of that quality himself. 2. With those to whom the gospel is preached the case is otherwise ; they have not to ask, " Who can tell ? " for the Lord of all has made himself known to them as delighting in mercy, and has given his own Son to be the Mediator and the Pledge of mercy.

III. THE OBJECT OF ENTREATY. 1. With regard to God, the aversion of his anger. Applying human language to the infinite God, the suppliants hoped for his turning and repentance. 2. With regard to themselves, the suppliants desired that they might not perish, that the doom deserved and threatened might not come upon them, that, in a word, they might be saved. It is not easy to form any judgment as to the measure in which desire for spiritual blessing entered into the prayers of the men of Nineveh. But enlightened Christians are constrained to feel that the salvation which they seek is not merely release from suffering and penalty, but restoration to the favour and the obedience of God.

Ver. 10.—*Man's repentance and God's.* The simplicity with which this great fact is recorded is quite in accordance with the usual style in which the Old Testament is written. Inspired men wrote of God as they would have written of a great king. Thus only, indeed, can we receive or communicate intelligible ideas regarding the Supreme. It is easy to criticize such statements as that of this text by calling them "anthropopathic ; " but the fact is that it is not degrading but exalting the conception of God to attribute to him, not merely reason and will, but the capacity of the highest, purest, and tenderest emotions.

I. HUMAN REPENTANCE THE CONDITION OF THE DIVINE. 1. Repentance involves the turning with loathing from the paths of sin. Yet this is very difficult to account for. How, why, should those who have addicted themselves to sin, because of its pleasantness or its profitableness, regard it in a quite different, a contrary light? 2. Repentance involves an apprehension of the majesty and justice of the moral law. Whilst men look earthward they will never repent, *i.e.* of sin itself; but when they direct their gaze heavenward, and perceive the splendour and beauty of an eternal, an inflexible law of right, then, by comparison with that, their own sin seems odious and degrading.

II. DIVINE REPENTANCE IS THE RESPONSE TO THE HUMAN. 1. The repentance attributed to God does not involve any real change in the character or the purposes of God. He ever hates the sin, and pities and loves the sinner; this is so both before and after the sinner's repentance. 2. Divine repentance is therefore the same principle acting differently in altered circumstances. If the prospect of punishment answers the same purpose as that intended by the punishment itself, there is no inconsistency in its remission; for punishment is not an end, it is only a means to goodness, to the reign of the law of righteousness. 3. Divine repentance is apparent in the forgiveness and acceptance of the contrite sinner. 4. And also in the moral influence which it exercises over the hearts of those who are reconciled. Gratitude is excited, love is awakened, consecration is elicited, obedience is confirmed.

APPLICATION. It is to be observed that these great principles of the Divine government are exhibited in all their power in the gospel of our Lord Jesus Christ. In the cross God summons mankind to repentance; in the cross God shows how he himself can repent.

HOMILIES BY VARIOUS AUTHORS.

Vers. 1—3.—*Peremptory reiteration and prompt obedience.* We see Jonah entering here on the second stage of his strange career. And it is adjusted logically to the first. His recent experiences and their resulting sentiments form an obvious preparation for the duty next to hand. He has sinned and suffered and repented. He has deserted, and been captured and surrendered unconditionally. He has prayed, and been forgiven and set free. And it is natural that duty should be faced from a different standpoint henceforward. He is in another mind now, and ready for a new departure in personal effort and official tactics. And the opportunity to make it is promptly furnished.

I. THE SPIRITUAL DESERTER'S RETURN IS FOLLOWED BY HIS RE-ENGAGEMENT. Jonah had discarded much and been stripped of more. He had refused to act, and had *ipso facto* forfeited his commission. Now with a return to his right mind there is reinstatement in his lost calling, and re-employment in his forsaken work. We account for this on the principle that: 1. *There is forgiveness with God, that he may be feared.* There is a forgiveness that only encourages transgression. Such is weak forgiveness, implying a want of firmness in the forgiver, on which there is the temptation to make further aggressions. Such is careless forgiveness, that takes no hostages for the future, nor even makes terms. Such is inequitable forgiveness, in which principle is ignored, and the offence hushed up without regard to the claims of justice. But the Divine "more excellent way" of pardon is at once equitable and defined and strong. Amends for the past and amendment for the future are both exacted sternly. God forgives when he has punished, and on the unbending condition that the offence cease. Then punishment is mingled with so much of mercy, and requirement is sweetened by such promise of grace, that gratitude mates with reverence, and obedience is the firstborn issue of the happy tie. The insubordinate, mutinous Jonahs having been ironed and subdued, are at length released, that in after-action they may exemplify obedience unquestioning and without a semblance of the old self-will. 2. *Spiritual office attaches to existing spiritual relation.* The Divine government is paternal. God's officers are first of all his children. Their fitness for the discharge of spiritual functions is due to their previous endowment with spiritual gifts. If unspiritual men and whilst unspiritual they may be formally in office, but are incapable of spiritual work. When Jonah fell for the time being out of the spiritual connection, he ceased to be a prophet of God. He could not be at once a recruiter and a deserter, an ambassador and a rebel. Now he has come back, and in resumed spiritual relations he finds the condition of restored religious functions. He may again speak for God now that again he is on God's side. No man goes legitimately on God's errand who cannot do it *con amore*. Spiritual officers are to be sought exclusively by promotion from the spiritual ranks. Every true shepherd has been first of all a sheep in God's fold, and to each relation has come in by Christ, the Door.

II. GOD'S PROGRAMME IS STEREOTYPED, WHATEVER ELSE MAY CHANGE. (Ver. 2.) God has not changed, although Jonah has. The prophet's mutinous outbreak has not moved him a hairbreadth from his purpose. What he meant at first he means still, and will have. So the prophet is brought back exactly to the point at which he had broken away, and told to begin where he had left off. 1. *God is moved still by the same compassion for the doomed.* "That great city." The repetition of these words on each occasion of the mention of Nineveh is significant. It shows that God had regard to the fact of its size; that all through the arrangement of measures for its warning he was moved by the thought of its teeming population given over to death. Hence it is styled in ver. 3 " a great city to God," *i.e.* in his estimation, and in ch. iv. 11 the Divine compunction is directly connected with the existence of its hundred and twenty thousand children, not yet responsible, but bound to perish with it. The Divine compassion is a glorious factor in human life. Its attitude is catholic. It embraces in wide paternal arms the heathen that knows not God, the infant that could not know him if revealed. Its outflow is unstinted, averting myriad evils altogether, softening the inevitable, indemnifying the past by the amends of rich compensatory good. Believe in God's pity. It is a splendid fact. It is hunger's provision, and pain's anæsthetic, and misery's comforter, and humanity's good Samaritan in the darkest reaches of its Jericho-journey, and the most calamitous experiences by the way. 2. *God's prescribed step remains the fitting one to take.* What other methods it was within the resources of Divine omnipotence to use for the conversion of the Ninevites, we cannot tell. What we know is that the proclamation of the truth was the ordinary method, and that God keeps to it. " The sword of the Spirit," with which he pierces the soul and kills its sin, is the " Word of God." "The foolishness of preaching" is that special presentment of the Word by which in all ages it has pleased God to save them that believe. And there is, if we could see it, the perfection of fitness in this ordinance. Truth is light revealing things as they are and as they ought to be. Truth is motive, presenting considerations that move intelligence to seek that better state. Truth is force, conveying to the soul and constituting in it the Divine omnipotent energy in the strength of which the new man arises, and the new life is lived. Truth is comfort, unfolding the soul-rest and joy of the free which climb the throne of being when the new *regime* of righteousness begins. Then truth preached with the living voice and personal element is all this and more. To the influence proper to the abstract truth is added its influence as concreted in a human life. As light it is intensified by the added ray of an illustrative experience. As power it is reinforced by the impulse of a co-operant human will. As comfort it is at once confirmed and sweetened by personal testimony and fellow-feeling. There is no conceivable substitute in the enginery of grace for the personal preaching to sinners of the word of life. 3. *Repentance is best proved by obedience in the matter at which there was stumbling before.* Jonah had passed through a severe discipline for the conquest of his self-will. Whether or not it was really overcome, this reiterated commission would test. And there was a needs-be that the point should be settled. All judgment is " unto righteousness; " to bring us to it if afar from it, to restore us to it if we have strayed. And it is this, not in the general, but in the particular. It is to check particular faults and produce the opposite virtues. In this object God will see that it succeeds. He cannot fail as men fail. His chains must bind. He gives no disputable instructions, nor moves to their observance by futile action. In tow of his disciplinary privateers, when they return to port, will be found, as a prize of war, every skulking craft that had been trying to do the enemy's work. The proof that his measures have not been nugatory is the circumstantial realization of their purpose. The iniquity he visits with the rod he must see put away. The forsworn task he enforces with the strong arm he must see done. "God looks upon men when he has afflicted them and has delivered them out of their affliction, to see whether they will mend of that fault particularly for which they were corrected; and therefore in that thing we are concerned to see to it that we receive not the grace of God in vain" (Matthew Henry).

III. THE DISCIPLINED SERVANT IS AN IMPROVED SERVANT. (Ver. 3.) The stern discipline has done its work at last. The rebellious fit is over, and the unruly servant is pliant to his Master's will. What evils of terror and pain and agony he might have escaped if he had only done this at first! But God bends all things to his purpose, and Jonah's rebellious freak among the rest. His message to Nineveh is not only done, but better done than it could possibly have been at first. 1. *Jonah is better prepared for it than he was.* He has sinned and been forgiven, has suffered and been delivered, has prayed and received an answer. And each experience is of the nature of a qualification for the better doing of his work. "Rejoicing in the sweetness of a fresh and full reconciliation; lightened in spirit by tasting in God a mercy larger than he could formerly have thought of; cleansed from the darkness that brooded over his soul, and the countless images of terror and of evil which rose up before him while he was fleeing from his God in rebellion, and his God was pursuing him in wrath" (Martin), he would approach his Master's work as never before. Reverence for a God so great and good, and gratitude to a God so merciful and kind, would spring together and work together the new mind and way. Affliction, moreover, had left its mark on him. He was subdued and chastened. He knew experimentally his impotence and God's omnipotence. He could speak by book of the terrors of the Lord, and the fatuity of hoping to defy him and escape. And his preaching would have a reality and vividness about it attainable only by way of his late experience. Then "he had called upon the Lord in circumstances almost fitted to shut out the possibility of hope." If there be a case on record pre-eminently fitted to confirm the declaration, "Men ought always to pray, and not to faint," it is his. Would he not resume his post with livelier loyalty and implicit sense of duty, when he could resume it with the blessed protestation, "I love the Lord, because he hath heard the voice of my supplication: because he hath inclined his ear unto me, I will call upon him as long as I live"? (Martin). 2. *He does it implicitly.* (Ver. 3.) "So Jonah arose, and went unto Nineveh." Submission is now as thorough as at first self-will was resolute. The change is excellent, and its occurrence a vindication of the treatment that has brought it about. An infinitely wise and holy will is God's. The ideal of a man's life is to believe in that will, and will it, and find his joy in doing it. From irreconcilable variance to absolute harmony with that ideal is Jonah's change, a change that means his spiritual readjustment. It will mean no less to us all. "The felicity of heaven greatly consists in perfect submission in all things to the government of Jehovah the Saviour. The misery of this world is the want of that temper of mind; the very end and design of grace is to restore us to it; and so far as we are under the influence of the grace of life, we are brought back to it; the more grace the more submission; and grace will not cease its operation in the saints till every thought is brought into captivity to the obedience of Christ" (Jones). A man following absolutely the lines of the infinitely perfect will; a man moving thereon with fullest faith and sympathy and zest; a man starting therein as a child starts for the haven of a mother's arms; a man incapable of other thought than following them to the highest good, and till his life's end;—that is a man in the highest sense, and to the highest spiritual effect. 3. *He goes closely by his instructions.* (Ver. 3.) "According to the word of the Lord." This terse record is instinct with suggestiveness. He went because he was told, and where he was told, and when he was told, and as he was told, and to do the thing he was told, and in the way he was told. His conduct now was exemplary as before it was intolerable. And his case is typical. His instructions were the preacher's instructions for all lands and times. "Preach the preaching that I bid thee." It was this Moses preached (Deut. xviii. 18), and Jeremiah (Jer. i. 7), and Paul (1 Cor. xi. 23), and Christ himself (John vii. 16; xii. 50). It is this we must preach. What else is worth preaching, or can or dare be preached? As to the substance of his message, the preacher has no discretionary power. He is not to preach science, nor philosophy, nor sentiment, nor his own notions, nor human knowledge. He is rightly to divide the Word of life. That is all.

"There is not the greatest minister, not the most learned or acute, but must observe this rule; not James, not John, not Peter, not all the troop of the apostles, may once vary from this: he who shall bring other doctrine, let him be accursed by us; he who speaketh of himself, let him be refused by us; howsoever godly or holy he do pretend himself, yet if he decline that word which should be his direction, let him be declined by us" (Abbot). Here is an admirable maxim for universal use, "according to the Word of the Lord." It is good, and wise, and true, and pertinent to every case, and the key to every puzzle of life. Are you a sinner? there is salvation for you, full, and free, and present, and "according to the Word of the Lord." Are you a seeker? expect to find, for salvation is in Christ, and of those that come to him there are none cast out, "according to the Word of the Lord." Are you a saint? then fight and persist and hope; for that you are "kept by the power of God," and will yet "reap if you faint not," is "according to the Word of the Lord."—J. E. H.

Vers. 4—10.—*A heathen city in sackcloth.* Let us try to realize the scene. An Eastern city sleeps in the rosy morning light. Its moated ramparts tower a hundred feet in air, and, dotted with fifteen hundred lofty towers, sweep around it a length of over sixty miles. Already the gates are open for the early traffic, and conspicuous among the crowd a stranger enters. The stains of travel are on his dress, and he looks with curious awe at the figures of winged colossal bulls that keep silent symbolic guard over the gate by which he passes in. Within, things new and strange appear at every step. The houses, sitting each in its own grounds, are bowered in green. The streets are spanned at intervals with triumphal arches, whose entablature is enriched by many a sculptured story. On every eminence is a palace, or monument, or idol temple, guarded by symbolic monsters in stone, and adorned in carving of bas-relief with sacred symbols. The markets fill, the bazaars are alive with multifarious dealing, soldiers and war-chariots parade the streets, and the evidences of despotic power and barbaric wealth and heathenish worship, with their inevitable accompaniments of luxury, corruption, and violence, abound on every side. The stranger is deeply moved. Surprise gives place to horror, then horror warms into righteous indignation; and with trumpet voice and dilating form and eye of fire he utters the words of doom, "Yet forty days, and Nineveh shall be destroyed." Through street, and park, and barrack, and bazaar the direful message rings. There is momentary incredulity, then swift alarm, then utter consternation. Like wildfire the news, and with it the panic spreads. It reaches the nobles in their palaces. It penetrates to the king upon his throne. It moves society to its depths. And the result is the scenes of mourning and self-abasement our text records.

1. REPENTANCE COMES READILY TO UNTUTORED MINDS. Never did preacher see better or speedier fruit of his labours than Jonah did in heathen Nineveh. By a single sermon but a few sentences long he sent the entire city into penitence and sackcloth. Granted that there was much to account for this in the preaching itself. It was bold and oracular and explicit, and spoken with the conviction that is most of all contagious. It was enforced by such a narrative of his own recent history as made him nothing less than a sign to the men of Nineveh (Luke xi. 30). Granted too "the great susceptibility of Oriental races to emotion, the awe of one Supreme Being which is peculiar to all the heathen religions of Asia, and the great esteem in which soothsaying and oracles were held in Assyria from the very earliest times" (Keil). Yet still the repentance, so widespread, so real, so sudden, has in it something phenomenal in the religious sphere. Not thus did the prophets and their utterances move the Jews. They "beat one, and killed another, and stoned another," and disregarded all as a general rule (Matt. xxi. 35). A greater than Jonah, the Truth himself, spoke to them, and spoke in vain (Matt. xii. 41). Unbelieving and lengthened contact with truth had no doubt produced the exceptional hardness of the Jewish nature. The works done in vain in the gospel-hardened Chorazin or Bethsaida would, as we know, have brought Tyre and Sidon to repentance in dust and ashes. Even filthy Sodom would have cleansed its way, and been spared on earth, had it seen the mighty works by which Capernaum was yet utterly unmoved (Matt. xi. 20—24). So when the soil of the Jewish nature, plied with the truth-seed till trodden hard by the sowers' feet, refused utterly to produce, the apostles found a fertile seed-bed in the virgin soil of the Gentile mind (Acts xiii. 44—48). An analogous fact is the success of Christ among the common

people (Mark xii. 37), when the scribes and Pharisees, who were more familiar with revelation, remained uninfluenced almost to a man (John vii. 48, 49). It would seem as if Divine truth, like potent drugs with the body, is effective most of all in its first contacts with the soul. Lengthened and frequent contact with truth, if it does not regenerate, only thickens the spiritual skin, and much hearing means little heeding as a general rule.

II. REPENTANCE IMPLIES A BELIEF OF THE TRUTH. (Ver. 5.) Belief of the truth is a logical first step to every religious attainment (Heb. xi. 6). Truth is the revelation of things as they are—of character, of destiny, of duty. Until that has been received there can be no spiritual beginning. While not only danger but the disease itself is disbelieved in, the patient will take no step toward cure. "He that cometh to the Lord must believe that he is." This is the least modicum of knowledge conceivable in any intelligent comer. So he that comes away from sin must believe that sin is. Unless he does, and until he does, he has no reason for moving. He that comes by repentance and faith, moreover, must believe in the propriety and dutifulness of these acts. Forecasting the possible result of Timothy's ministry in the turning of the wicked, Paul says, "If God peradventure will give them repentance to the acknowledging of the truth." This aspiration brings out the point exactly. Repentance and the acknowledging of the truth imply and involve each other. Impenitence is largely the result of incredulity. If a man really believed what God says about sin—its demerit, deformity, and destroying character—the grief and hatred and turning which constitute repentance must arise. The impenitent man either does not believe God at all, or he gives him a weak and heedless credence that is never acted on, and so is practical disbelief. Let God's word of dogma, God's word of promise, be truly and adequately believed, and God's word of precept will be infallibly obeyed. A man may contemplate his sin indifferently and commit it with even pulse, but the power to do so means that the Scripture testimony against it has been silenced, or the witness put out of the court of conscience altogether. "It is to be observed that faith operates differently according to the matter believed. When faith looks to the redeeming love of Christ, faith worketh by love. 'We love him who first loved us.' When faith looks to the infinite wrath of God, faith worketh fear, and we 'flee for refuge to the hope set before us.' When faith looks at Christ, bearing in his love the wrath from which he calls us to flee, faith worketh by grief; and, 'looking on him whom we have pierced, we mourn.' And all these operations of faith—love, fear, grief—enter into that repentance unto salvation which true faith produces" (Martin).

III. REPENTANCE IS AT ONCE DEEPENED BY FEAR AND SWEETENED BY HOPE. The Ninevites feared to "perish" through the "fierce anger" of God, yet hoped he might "turn away" from it and "repent." Fear is a rather ignoble emotion, but it is not without its place and power in the religious sphere. A man's *life*, in the widest sense, is his most precious trust. To gain the whole world would not compensate for the loss of it. Hence the universal instinct of self-preservation. "All that a man hath will he give for his life." And by appealing to this instinct, as it so often does, the Scripture assumes its lawfulness (Luke xiii. 3; Matt. x. 28). The loss of soul and body in hell is a loss unparalleled and irreparable, and which it would be madness not to fear. The Ninevites feared it. Their dread of it was a chief cause of the penitence they showed. And naturally so. To a man as yet unspiritual, the bearing of his sin on his own fate is the supreme consideration. When he becomes better he will be amenable to higher motives, but fear as opposed to carnal security is always a prominent factor in the early stages of the religious life. But the Ninevites' repentance did not spring from fear alone; it based on hope as well. "Who can tell," etc.? (ver. 9). The hope here was far from assured. It was a mere glimmer in the soul. Yet still it was hope. Escape was deemed not impossible,—that was all. And there was a shadow of ground for hope, which the keen eye of the doomed did not fail to detect. They had an intuitive idea that God would make some difference between a penitent city and an impenitent one. Then the catastrophe was not to come for forty days, and, in the granting of so long a respite, they would see the door left open for a possible change before its close. Besides, Jonah's own deliverance in a more dire extremity still, and of which he evidently told them in his preaching (Luke xi. 30), would suggest the possibility of a like escape to them with like repentance. If the preacher had been saved in the very moment of imminent death, the fact was ground of hope to the people who had forty days' reprieve. Thus the faith in which the Ninevites' repentance originated "wrought by fear and hope combined. The evil dreaded was sufficient to break and humble all their pride. And the hope they entertained was sufficient to prevent their fear from turning into mere despair" (Martin). It is the element of hope in it that marks off the sorrow which worketh only death from the sorrow which worketh repentance to salvation. There is a persuasion of men which bases on the terrors of the Lord, and a beseeching of them also by the mercies he has shown. And what is this but to make fear and hope the limbs of a stable arch to carry the repentance "that needeth not to be repented of"?

IV. REPENTANCE INCLUDES GRIEF FOR THE PAST AND REFORMATION FOR THE FUTURE. The Ninevites "put on sackcloth," etc., and "turned them every one from his evil way." There was compendious logic in this. Sackcloth and ashes were the conventional livery of abasement and grief (2 Cor. vii. 9, 10), and these have a distinct place in the spiritual connection (Joel ii. 13). But they must be spiritual. Not the result of wounded pride, or baffled purpose, or ruined prospects. These things are utterly carnal. They involve no sense of sin's demerit, no horror of its impurity. They are merely aspects and expressions of selfishness. Every detected rogue can see that he has blundered in his sinning, and from that standpoint grieves. Saul does it, exclaiming, in the bitterness of failure, "I have played the fool exceedingly." But the sorrow "after a godly sort" is a radically different thing, and done in a different spiritual atmosphere altogether. And David crying with contrite and humbled spirit, "I acknowledge my transgression, and my sin is ever before me," is a perfect moral contrast. His is a sorrow that has God in it. Sin is viewed in its relation to God, from God's standpoint, and with feelings like to God's. Job sorrowed thus with God when he said, "Now mine eye seeth thee; wherefore I abhor myself," etc. Such sorrow has hope in it, and so "the promise and potency" of a reformed life. Under its impulse the Ninevites "turned every one from his evil way." Reformation is the work meet for repentance —the crystalline form revealing the genuine metal. "Numbers will do everything in religion but turning from sin to the Saviour; and where this is not done, all the rest is lost labour—their religion is hypocrisy, their hope is mere delusion, and their latter end is bitterness and woe; for all who refuse to depart from sin must perish in sin. In vain shall we fast for sin, if we do not fast from sin; and what blessings can all our prayers bring down while we refuse to turn from our evil ways?" (Jones).

V. REPENTANCE CRIES TO GOD IN PRAYER. The words of Jonah were like an earthquake in the vast city. From king to beggar there was consternation and dismay. The destroying armies of heaven were at hand. Men can neither disbelieve, nor doubt, nor resist, nor fly, nor survive. What remains but to submit and beg for mercy—the last resort of the sinner, but the very first command of God? And so the king descends from his throne, and the beggar rises from his straw, and a stricken universal cry for help goes up in the ear of Heaven. In such an exercise true repentance is at home. Prayer is the spontaneous, the instinctive expression of the soul's new-found need. A true sense of sin, together with an apprehension of God's mercy in Christ which all genuine repentance includes, leads logically to prayer. Given a sick man thoroughly alarmed, and a willing physician accessible, and the application for help will infallibly follow.

> "On bended knees, replete with godly grief,
> See where the mourner kneels to seek relief;
> From his full heart pours forth the gushing plea,
> 'God of the lost, be merciful to me!'
> The light of life descends in heavenly rays,
> And angels shout and sing, 'Behold, he prays!'"

VI. REPENTANCE IS TO BE NATIONAL WHEN THE SIN IS NATIONAL. The Ninevites' was a "public, general, royal fast." So when the Divine judgments menaced Jerusalem in the reign of Jehoiakim, all the people proclaimed a fast (Jer. xxxvi. 9). Then it was observed by all the people in accordance with a royal edict. So Jehoshaphat "feared and proclaimed a fast throughout all Judah" (2 Chron. xx. 3) when Moab and Ammon invaded the kingdom. In the nature of the case, the repentance must correspond to the transgression. The people must repent who have sinned, and in the character and relations in which the sin has been committed. That their action in the matter was suggested

and shaped by royal edict detracted in nothing from the value of the Ninevites' repentance. The obligations of religion rule every relation of life. Each community ought
to be religious, and the rulers of each to consider their office sacred to the accomplishment of this result. Monarchs should reign for the glory of God, and they do so when
they "take order" for the observance of religious worship with due regard to the prerogatives of the Church, and to the right of private judgment. "It is an evil and
dangerous principle that would exempt the rulers of a kingdom from being in subjection
in their public capacity to the Word of Christ, and from being under obligation in their
government to rule for the promotion of his kingdom. It strikes at the root of all
family as well as national religion; and while it would confine Christ to the separate
consciences of individual men, it would refuse him the right to govern the households
and communities into which in Providence they are combined" (Martin). The practical
lesson of this is read to us by Jesus Christ (Luke xi. 32). The existence of saints in
the world is a virtual condemnation of all the sinners. With similar privileges and
opportunities, why are these spiritually changed, and those not? Unless the believers
have done more than their duty, the unbelievers have fallen woefully short. Every
saint in a Christian congregation will stand up in the judgment a silent but damning
witness against its unconverted members who remain so under equal inducements to
repentance. And the case is worse when the balance of privilege was on the unbelievers'
side. It was so as between Nineveh and Israel. The one was brought to repentance
by means incomparably less than those which had proved entirely inoperative with the
other. It will be so as between each of them and us, if we are blind to our greater light,
and insensible to our more potent spiritual agencies. "A greater than Jonah is here"—
greater in person, greater in office, greater in power, and greater in influence. Have we
resisted him? Have we withstood his mightier striving? Then who so inexcusable,
who so hopeless, as we? What guilt so deep, what condemnation so great, as ours
(Heb. x. 28)?—J. E. H.

Vers. 1—4.—*Jonah's second call.* "And the word of the Lord came unto Jonah the
second time, saying, Arise, go unto Nineveh, that great city, and preach unto it the
preaching that I bid thee," etc.

I. REINSTATEMENT OF THE PROPHET. "The word of the Lord came unto Jonah
the second time." Jonah's rebellion had had a twofold effect on his relations to God—
broken up his personal fellowship with him, and suspended his official function as a
prophet. God's grace restored him both personally and officially, as afterwards in the
case of Peter; but, as in this case, the restoration of the first did not necessarily include
that of the second. Servants of God who have fallen need a second call to public service; it needs to be shown that God trusts them with his work again. It is natural
for ministers who have been publicly dealt with and censured to desire to be reponed;
but this cannot be rightly done without some token that God again calls them.

II. THE NEW COMMISSION. "Arise, go unto Nineveh, that great city, and preach
unto it the preaching that I bid thee." We know not where Jonah was—where he
had been landed—what had happened in the interval. Imagination can picture the
prophet on the shore making for Gath-hepher, and probably arriving there. Again the
message is preceded by the word of stimulation, "Arise;" brace thyself, prepare for
arduous work; and this time it would bring a lesson of warning—remember how easily
you were turned aside before! The work was not to be made easier out of regard to the
prophet's proved weakness, but the prophet must seek a higher strength. The greatness of Nineveh is again dwelt on—"Nineveh, that great city"—"an exceeding great
city, and great unto God" (ver. 3). "Think of a whole vast city, full of this humanity,
of this God-breathed life; and is it surprising that a great city should be great unto
God? What flashings of intellectual lights in one day!—as many almost as the
separate rays of the sun. What throbbings of moral or immoral purpose, the moral
faculty acting in each! What a sighing of wandering spirits, unconsciously or blindly
seeking the lost portion! What a swell and heave of the great tide of animated life
composed of the blended individual streams! London is like a great and wide sea of
life. The daily agitations which stir in her bosom are felt in feebler pulsings even in
far-off shores; and in multitudes which no man can number her thoughts and acts, and
in these her checkered moral history, are going up to God's heaven. Such was Nineveh

of old, and for such reasons as we have named, it was still, as at first, a city great to God" (Raleigh). The message is somewhat different from before: "Preach the preaching [literally, 'cry the cry'] that I bid thee." This may either mean, "the cry that I will bid thee at the time," or "the cry that I already bade thee." Either Jonah was to go, like an admiral, with sealed orders to be opened at a certain place; or he was to say what he had been ordered to say before, but had shrunk from saying. The latter view is probably correct—a further trial of Jonah's sincerity and submissiveness—in the very matter which had dissatisfied him before, he was called to place himself in God's hands, and to engage to do precisely as God would direct. In all cases, true meaning is "the preaching that I bid thee." It is a simple message from God; it becomes effectual when it is given as such. All very well to be able to reconcile it with reason and commend it to the conscience, and to set it forth with the enrichments of learning and the embellishments of art; but there is danger lest its true simple nature be thereby disguised; nothing should be allowed which prevents it from being presented as a simple message from God: "the preaching that I bid thee." "How often did our Lord disclaim the authorship of all that he said, and assign it continually to the Father! 'Jesus answered them, and said, My doctrine is not mine, but his that sent me; the words that I speak unto you, I speak not of myself' (John vii. 16). Himself personally cognizant of all truth, he acts as the Church's Teacher under the responsibility and within the exact limits of his office. Officially ordained the Father's Ambassador, he confines himself to a declaration of the Father's words. . . . Exactly as the Father had said unto him, so he speaks" (Martin).

III. THE OBEDIENCE OF THE PROPHET. "So Jonah arose, and went unto Nineveh, according to the word of the Lord." "How different every way from what he was when he fled to Tarshish! We see him no more consulting with flesh and blood, but yielding prompt obedience to the heavenly call. No more running away, but asking, 'Lord, what wilt thou have me to do? Here am I; send me.' The Lord saith, 'Go to Nineveh;' he instantly goes without gainsaying or resistance" (Jones). "In the present case, Jonah would resume his commission with a new obedience; with a meekness, a faith, a courage, to all of which his punishment and pardon had been the signal means of disciplining him. He would resume his work and mission with another spirit—(1) as a sinful man, whose sin had been eminently forgiven; (2) as a prayerful man, whose prayer had been eminently answered; (3) as an afflicted man, whose affliction had been eminently blessed" (Martin). "The Word says, 'Arise,' and Jonah arose; the Word says, 'Go,' and Jonah went. It is beautiful. It is grand. We must not indeed exaggerate. For we know that there is something dark and bitter in this man still, which will break out again. But meantime, and in this act of obedience, so far as we see it, there is a grandeur like that of an angel—a simplicity like that of a child" (Raleigh).

IV. THE MESSAGE DELIVERED. "And Jonah began to enter into the city, a day's journey, and he cried, and said, Yet forty days, and Nineveh shall be overthrown." Jonah in Nineveh—what a contrast to Gath-hepher, Joppa, or even Jerusalem! What temples! what tombs! what monuments!—what new impressions of its vastness and power! Perhaps new impressions of its horrible treatment of those who opposed themselves to it. It was no uncommon sight to witness a row of prisoners, each impaled alive on an iron spike; or men of mark flayed alive; or captives, with hooks in nose, dragged by halters, carrying the bleeding heads of their kings or nobles. Anyhow, pictures of such things abounded. They made no undue impression on Jonah. "Strong in faith," he went boldly forward and delivered the message. "He cried, and said"—lifted up his voice like a trumpet—under the windows of the rich, in the resorts of the poor—before the proud military array—before nobles and judges and all. His message was more specific and startling than before. Stern, but faithful and honest preaching; no flattery; no shrinking from exposure of the true mind of God. They might do with him as they pleased; he had not a single friend in that vast multitude—no protection but God's—nevertheless, he would proclaim the message. As John Knox said long afterwards, "I am in the place where I am commanded of God to speak the truth; and the truth I will speak, impugn it whoso list." Contrast the feeling of Jonah now and when he fled to go to Tarshish. His soul tumultuous and agitated then, in peace and serenity now. "He that saveth his life shall lose it, and he that loseth his life for my sake shall find it." Acknowledge the reality of Divine protection and strength—sense of peace and proof of it, for, after all, fidelity to God is the true policy. "Them that honour me, I will honour" (1 Sam. ii. 30).—W. G. B.

Vers. 5—9.—*The repentance of Nineveh.* "So the people of Nineveh believed God, and proclaimed a fast, and put on sackcloth, from the greatest of them even to the least of them," etc. Here is Jonah in Nineveh alone against the world. Oh, the moral grandeur of the sight!—resting on God alone—"according to his faith it was to him" —marvellous success of his preaching, through Divine power working in him and through him. Observe the contrast to Noah and to Lot. He is like John the Baptist —a torch, setting all on fire. We notice the effects of his crying the cry which God bade him.

I. THE PEOPLE OF NINEVEH BELIEVED GOD. (Ver. 5.) Apparently "the people" were first impressed—deep religious impressions commonly begin with them, and rise from them to the upper class—"the common people heard Jesus gladly." There are many hindrances among men of wealth and station to religious impression, but Providence gives compensations—"the poor have the gospel preached unto them." They believed God. They saw in Jonah only a messenger—the messenger of God, who made the earth and the sea. Probably they had heard his history, for "Jonah was a sign to the Ninevites." Before one, in whose person there had been given such tokens of the Divine power, both to punish and to save, they stood in awe. "The busy crowd is by-and-by arrested; a solemn awe steals over the minds of the people, they press around the preacher to know who and whence he is, and why he utters such an ominous cry in their streets; and hearing as they now do, that, so far from lightly denouncing this doom against them, he had already, at the hazard of his life, shrunk from executing the charge committed to him, that he had been cast out for his wilful resistance into the mighty deep, and miraculously restored only that he might be sent forth anew to utter the cry they now heard of approaching destruction—learning all this concerning Jonah and his burden, how solemn and perilous must their situation have appeared in their eyes!" (Kitto). He whom they now heard proclaiming his warning was the messenger of that God who had roused the storm and cast him overboard; who had prepared the great fish to swallow him, keep him alive within its huge body, and then vomit him on the dry land; and who had sent him back to deliver his message, "Yet forty days, and Nineveh shall be destroyed." The whole community were actuated by a common feeling. "Word came to the king." All ranks and classes were moved by the message of the strange preacher; all realized that the anger of God and the coming destruction of the city were awful calamities; as of the Pharisees at John's baptism, the question might have been asked, "Who hath warned you to flee from the wrath to come?" When God makes his voice heard, he bows the hearts of the people like the heart of one man.

II. PROCLAMATION OF A FAST. An external token of distress is deemed fitting— heathen fasts extended to animals as well as men. "It was a custom among the ancient heathen to withhold food from their cattle as well as from themselves in times of mourning and humiliation; in some instances they cut off the hair of their beasts as well as their own" (Kitto). Attitude of the king, great and noble (ver. 6)—all his pride and vain-glory laid aside—he humbles himself openly before God—contrast this with spirit of Sennacherib afterwards (2 Kings xviii., xix.)—kings never so great as when they pay honour to him by whom kings reign—the King of Nineveh rose above all shame and vanity, saw only the dread reality, and acted accordingly. Kings are in their noblest attitude when leading their people to honour God.

III. PRAYER DEMANDED. "Let them cry mightily unto God." All their own gods are to be set aside—this God only is to be recognized. No one seems to have said a word for the Assyrian gods—"Our God is in the heavens: he hath done whatsoever he hath pleased" (Ps. cxv. 3). Prayer is often derided by the world—in time of pressing danger the praying people are the wise, the patriotic, the true people. Real prayer is no barren form—"let them cry mightily to God"—throw their whole souls into the exercise—pray as for dear life. The true idea of prayer is beseeching God's mercy— beseeching it as the one only resource—what alone can save from misery and ruin.

IV. MORAL REFORMATION DEMANDED. "Let them turn every one from his evil way, and from the violence that is in their hands." The humiliation of the people more than external—" Let the wicked forsake his way, and the unrighteous man his thoughts" (Isa. lv. 7)—instinctive recognition of the holiness of God—it is unholy acts and an unholy spirit that excite his displeasure (see Isa. lviii. 5—7). *Violence* specified—the rapacious cruelty which characterized the people, and the cry of which had come up before God. When once conscience was roused, it would condemn these acts of violence very loudly. Interesting and beautiful sight—all classes hastening to put away their evil ways, and reversing them, doing the very opposite to what they had been wont to do.

> "Sinners listened to Jonah,
> And each one confessed his sins.
> The polluted city heard him,
> And quickly put off its abominations.
> Masters also heard him,
> And proclaimed freedom to their bondmen: . . .
> At the voice of Jonah honourable women
> Brought down their pride in sackcloth:
> The repentance was indeed sincere
> When haughty women put on humility! . . .
> The gay laid restraint upon their eyes,
> That they might not gaze on women.
> Women laid aside their ornaments,
> That those who looked on them might not stumble."
>
> (Ephraem Syrus, translated by Burgess.)

Abiding picture of what ought to be the attitude of kings and people in times of national calamity—sin is then felt to be a curse and a poison : " Search us, O God, and know our hearts; try us, and know our thoughts, and see if there be any wicked way in us, and lead us in the way everlasting."

V. REASON FOR THESE STEPS. (Ver. 9.) "Who can tell if God will turn and repent, and turn away from his fierce wrath, that we perish not?" Only a possibility— "Who can tell?" But in time of extreme peril a possibility ought to be acted on. "We cannot plead this on the score of justice, neither can we ply his faithfulness with any specific assurance of mercy, given to meet the necessities of our case; we have nothing to encourage us but the general character of God himself, as manifested in his dealings with men on earth. But still we have that, and the matter is not altogether hopeless. For why should God have sent his prophet to admonish us of sin, and fore-tell his impending judgment—a prophet too who has himself been the subject of singular mercy and forbearance? If destruction alone had been his object, would he not rather have allowed us to sleep on in our sinfulness? And why in particular should these forty days have been made to run between our doom and our punishment? Surely this bespeaks some thought of mercy in God; it must have been meant to leave the door still open to us for forgiveness and peace" (Fairbairn). The proclamation and the reason for it were not perfect—did not go beyond the spirit of fear and trembling—but the Ninevites acted on their light. "If there be first a ready mind, it is accepted according to what a man hath, and not according to what he hath not " (2 Cor. viii. 12). Who-ever faithfully follows the light he has may look for more—" to him that hath shall be given." It is interesting to think how Jonah's prophecy would affect the young, and it is the property of childhood to receive testimony with full belief in it. Possibly the emotion of the children may have helped to move the parents. Prospect of speedy death is naturally more terrible to young than old. The following picture of the scene by Ephraem Syrus may be quoted :—

> "The children inquired while weeping
> Of their fathers, in the midst of their tears,
> 'Narrate to us, O parents,
> How many days yet remain
> From the time which that Hebrew preacher
> Hath determined for us?
> And what hour he hath indicated
> When we shall go down below to Sheol?

And in what day will it be
That this fair city shall be destroyed?
And further, when will the last day be,
After which we shall not exist?
When will the season arrive,
When mortal pangs shall seize on all of us?
And when, throughout the world
Shall fly the tidings of our ruin?
And the passing spectators shall gaze upon
The city overthrown upon its masters?'

"When the parents listened to these things
From the mouth of their little ones,
Their tears most bitterly
Overflowed, and suffused their children,
And dropped at the same time on the persons
Of the speakers and the hearers.
And the fathers were not able
To find utterance through sighing;
For their grief had closed up
The straight path of words;
And their speech was interrupted
By the weeping of their beloved ones."

Read the analogy between threatened destruction of Nineveh and destruction of sinners at the last day. Reasons for repentance in one case infinitely stronger in other. Natural indifference and unbelief of men in reference to the latter. Accumulated guilt of those who refuse him that speaketh from heaven. "The men of Nineveh will rise up in the judgment with the men of this generation, and condemn it; for they repented at the preaching of Jonah: and behold, a greater than Jonah is here." (1) They had but one preacher, and that a stranger. (2) They heard but one message, and it was wrath. (3) They had but a vague hope of mercy.—W. G. B.

Ver. 10.—*God repenting.* "And God saw their works, that they turned from their evil way; and God repented of the evil, that he had said that he would do unto them; and he did it not." Merciful character of God vindicated. "He retaineth not anger for ever, because he delighteth in mercy;" "I said, I will confess my transgression unto the Lord; and thou forgavest the iniquity of my sin;" "If we confess our sins, he is faithful and just to forgive us our sins, and to cleanse us from all unrighteousness."

I. THE CAUSE OF THE CHANGE. "God saw their works, that they turned from their evil way." He not only heard their professions, but saw from their acts that these were real; they believed God—believed that on account of their sins his "fierce anger" rested on them, and they showed their faith by their works; and the particular kind of works was their turning from their evil way—not resorting to matters of will-worship, such as self-mutilation or making children pass through the fire, not stretching forth hands or making many prayers, but abandoning the sin that had offended God; not giving money to build or ornament temples or buy God's favour, but tearing the idol from their hearts—turning from their evil way. The real test of repentance is giving up sin—favourite sin, pleasant sin—sins of sensuality and indulgence and display; giving them up as acts, and trying to give them up as objects of desire; seeking to have the heart cleansed as well as the hands; to have the natural love of them subdued by the thought that they excite against us the fierce wrath of God; and in our case, under the light of the gospel, by all the considerations derived from the cross of Christ, and God's display of love and grace in him. Was the repentance of Nineveh complete, inward, spiritual? This is not said, nor is it necessary to believe it was. Probably it did not last long. It was repentance, however, according to their light and circumstances—the expression of deep national concern for sins that had come up before God, and against which God had sent his prophet to testify. It was an acknowledgment of the God of Jonah as the God of the whole earth—a submission of themselves to him—such submission as would have saved Egypt and Pharaoh, had it been made, in Moses' time, with accompanying tokens of sorrow and sincerity. Higher quality of repentance is demanded from an *individual* than from a *nation*; fellowship of reconciled God with the individual is much more intimate and spiritual than with the nation; such fellowship is impossible, save in case of regenerate hearts; in "repentance unto life" there must be genuine hating of what God hates, and loving what he loves.

II. THE CHANGE ON THE PART OF GOD. "God repented of the evil, that he had said he would do unto them; and he did it not." It is frequently objected that this implies *fickleness* on the part of God, as if he were mutable—as if he were a son of man that he should repent. But fickleness or mutability implies change of action *while circumstances remain the same;* immutability *demands* change of action when circumstances change. Immutability is tested by *principles* on which one acts rather than on the outward *actions* one performs; hence there is no fickleness on part of God in opposite actions, as when he placed man in Paradise and afterwards drove him forth. When God said by Jonah, "Yet forty days, and Nineveh shall be destroyed," he meant *that* Nineveh—Nineveh if it continued the same, black with guilt, impenitent, unreformed. He did not mean that *another* Nineveh would be destroyed—Nineveh fasting, penitent, transformed. At the end of forty days old Nineveh did not exist; the corruption that would have drawn down the Divine judgment was removed—in a sense that old Nineveh *was* destroyed—it had passed away. Consequently, the denunciation ceased to be applicable; the doom threatened was not inflicted. This was the whole amount of the change on the part of God. The phrase, "God repented," is an anthropomorphism; God acted as man would have done if he had repented—regarded it no longer as a case for infliction of judgment. God's denunciations of judgment are directed rather against states of mind and conduct than particular places or communities—implying, usually, a chance of repentance. In some cases the time for repentance had passed, and denunciation of doom became absolute—as in the case of our Lord weeping over Jerusalem. In rejecting him they had filled up the measure of their iniquities. Their house was left desolate. "We are ever to guard against assigning human imperfection to God. But we are equally to guard against assigning to him such a character or nature as would render living, intelligible, friendly intercourse between him and his people impossible. But impossible utterly all such intercourse may be, if I may not speak to God in the same forms and phrases and feelings in which I would offer a request, or state my case to a fellow-man, though of course retaining unreserved submission and unlimited adoration of the Mighty One of Israel. My adoration unbounded; my surrender of myself to God unreservedly;—these are tributes to the searchless glory of his Godhead which I may not withhold, and yet profess to worship him. Nevertheless, with these I must ·be allowed, in condescension to my weakness, to ask God to be 'attentive to the voice of my supplications;' to 'behold and visit me;' to 'stretch out his hand' for my help; to 'shine upon me with the light of his countenance;' to 'awake;' to 'arise;' to 'draw near;' to 'come and dwell with me.' All these expressions and requests are after the manner of men. I must be allowed to spread out my sorrow and my trial before him, precisely as if my design and expectation were to work on his feelings, and move and induce him in his pity to deliver me" (Martin).

III. NINEVEH IS SPARED. Picture the city as the fortieth day approached; when it dawned; afterwards, when it passed away and Nineveh remained. Picture universal relief and joy—old and young—congratulations—life appearing before them with a new brightness—the day breaks, and the shadows flee away. Symbol of what may be realized when the anger of God due to sin is averted: "In that day thou shalt say, O Lord, I will praise thee: though thou wast angry with me, thine anger is turned away, and thou comfortest me" (Isa. xii. 1). "What, then, must we expect will be the sweet surprise and transport of the *departed soul* on his first entrance into glory; when translated of a sudden from this material world to the world of spirits; from among men into the immediate presence of God? What must be his sensations, delight, and astonishment, when first conducted into the presence of the Saviour reigning on the throne of heaven? What will be his feelings when he sees around the throne a company which no man can number, all arrayed in white robes, and wearing brilliant crowns that never fade; all in transport of joy, singing of redeeming love, and celebrating the praises of the Lamb that was slain, and their voices like the sound of many waters? When the soul first joins this company, and reviews the dangers it has escaped in the world below, its love will kindle into a burning flame, and its song will be eternal."—W. G. B.

Vers. 1—4.—*Jonah in Nineveh.* I. A GREAT RESTORATION. After his recreancy to duty, who had been surprised if Jonah had been thrust out of the prophet's office? The guilt of his flight, the moral insensibility into which he had sunken, rendered him, many would think, unfit to be God's spokesman to men. But God had mercy on him. And saved, he had presently the assurance of it. He was reinstated in the prophet's office, and solemnly commissioned anew to the prophet's work. A "*second* time" bidden go, he went. It was a great restoration, and openly marked by the great errand on which he was sent. The *work* showed that the worker was restored. For that *still* the backslider is recovered. Not for mere personal enjoyment in religion. Not merely to have the assurance of individual safety. But also to "show" what great things God hath done for him. Was Peter restored? Let him prove it: "Feed my sheep, . . . my lambs." So was Jonah comforted; restored, he had the *assurance* of it in the renewed commission, "Go to Nineveh."

II. A GREAT SPHERE FOR WORK. God himself, in giving this commission, spoke of Nineveh as "that great city." Jonah knew from human testimony that the city was great. But *God* says it is. Then let Jonah be ready for difficulties. It is no little work to which he is bidden. And is the greatness of Nineveh mentioned *only* to prepare him for the magnitude of the task before him? Is there not *implied* therein a reason, should the people repent, for the Divine compassion? "Should not I spare Nineveh, that great city?" (ch. iv. 11). In a town, with its many homes, families, cares, virtues, vices,—how much to impress a human imagination, to affect a human heart! But in great cities, throbbing with restless life, each man of the millioned multitude with his own history, his own destiny, how the solemn interest is deepened! Great cities are *great to God*. *Religion* is the only protection of city or state. The repentance of the Ninevites averted the doom of Nineveh; its wealth, valour, fame, availed not to effect this. This punishment of nations *as such* comes in this world. The sins of nations have destroyed them. May our own nation know the time of its visitation, that it perish not!

III. A GREAT EXAMPLE. Jonah is here seen at his best. There is a moral sublimity in his promptitude. "Arise, go." He went. The difficulty of obedience always grows by delay. It may be hard at the beginning, but it will be easier then than ever after. "God loveth a cheerful giver," *whatever* be the gift. *Bold* was Jonah. Wisely bold. *As soon as* Nineveh was reached he began his solemn cry. Bold, *though alone*. He had no human companion to encourage him, to help him. Bold, to utter the cry of woe. *Destruction* was the burden of his oft-repeated message. Nothing in *that* to gather affection to him—loving, joyful attention. May his courage be ours! *We* have *glad* tidings to tell; and no such lonely path to tread as he. With such a message, and with the viewless presence of the Messenger, we may well be of good courage.—G. T. C.

Ver. 2.—*The preaching that God bids.* 1. Not the message of our own imagination. 2. Not what men desire and what will be palatable to them. 3. But what *God* bids. To the messenger he gives the message—from his Word; by his Spirit. His gospel—not altered, not added to, not diminished—is to be preached "to every creature." With faithfulness, simplicity, persistence—whether men hear or whether men forbear. Like Luther, "I can do no other; God help me!"—G. T. C.

Vers. 5—9.—*Jonah's successful ministry in Nineveh.* With a quick and marvellous success was Jonah's ministry crowned. Doubtless the Ninevites knew how he had sought to escape his mission to them, and all the perilous and miraculous consequences of his flight. This seems clearly implied in our Lord's words, who says that Jonah was "a sign unto the Ninevites." And he only could be this in so far as they were acquainted with his history. He was "a sign" that Jehovah was not to be trifled with. If he, a *friend* of Jehovah, had been punished, what might the *enemies* expect? "A sign" also of Jehovah's *mercy* as well as justice. If *he* had been saved, might not they?

If their case had been utterly hopeless, why had he come at all? So, though they had seen no miracle, they "believed God." That doom was at hand; doom that might—who could tell?—be averted, if they "battered the gates of heaven with storms of prayer." They proclaimed a fast; "the *people*;" for then, as always, national repentance and reformation worked its way *upward*. Here, from the people, at length reaching the nobles and the king. *He*, too, was a man and in peril, and, like his subjects, must repent. And, by royal proclamation, all were bidden fast, be clad in sackcloth; the creatures, too, dependent on them, by their mute misery were to share in the national humiliation. Above all, let the people "cease to do evil," and show a changed heart by an altered life. The humiliation of the Ninevites was—

I. ROOTED IN FAITH. "They believed God." What were Asshur and their many gods to them now? Jehovah was the *living* God. All else were dead. They believed in his power to punish; and also (though doubt may have mingled with their faith) that if they turned from their evil way, *he* would turn from the fierceness of his anger, and they should perish not. Not "idle words" were Jonah's. Not heard with critic ear. Not questioned, much less opposed. Jonah—who was he? God's messenger. They believed *God*. Hence their repentance. Had they *not* believed, they had been *un*repentant. How they rebuke many among us to-day! Those who have heard *many* of God's messengers: why turn they not from their evil way? Because they believe not God. This is the capital count in the Divine indictment against man. He makes God a liar. He believes not the testimony God has given in his Son. The terrible testimony against sin as the dark, dreadful evil it is. The gracious testimony to his unutterable love, that only *could* be truly vocal as it spoke in the sorrow, sufferings, and death-agonies of his Son. Did man believe with the heart this, it would be to repentance—to righteousness. "Believe God." Rooted in faith, the conduct of the Ninevites was—

II. FRUITFUL IN REPENTANCE. True belief and true repentance are ever connected as root and fruit.

> "If faith produce no works, I see
> That faith is not a living tree."

The Ninevites fasted, put on sackcloth, cried mightily to God. And is the *expression* of our repentance to be the same as theirs? Are we to fast? If given to the pleasures of the table, to fulness of bread, *abstinence* will be well. *Whatever* hinders the soul must be avoided. If gay clothing is a temptation to us, we must watch against *that* peril. The *soul* must be supreme. Let *it* "cry mightily." Cry that it *may be* truly repentant. For "godly sorrow" is the gift of God. The doom coming on the Ninevites was averted. By what? Not the fasting; not the sackcloth; not even the mighty crying, though a whole city was at prayer. God saw their works, that they turned from their evil way" (ver. 10). That plucked them from the peril. There was *repentance*—a change of mind; *reformation*—a change of life. All is nothing without that. Turn from all evil. Have you wronged another? Confess it; make restitution. Be the changed mind seen in the changed life. The way of sin is an *evil* way and ends in evil. Turn from it. "Lord, make me pure and holy, but not now," prayed the unconverted Augustine. It must be *now*. Turn from sin, and "who can tell if God will turn?" "Tell?" You *know*—as did not the Ninevites—the glorious gospel, that God waits to be gracious; that for Christ's sake he will forgive you. Be not shamed and condemned by the repentant Ninevites. "They repented at the preaching of Jonah; and, behold, a greater than Jonah is here."—G. T. C.

Ver. 10.—*Missions to the heathen.* 1. The heathen are capable of salvation. 2. God purposes their salvation. 3. The Jews were the divinely appointed first preachers of salvation to the Gentile heathens. Jewish Jonah, the first of the prophets, was sent to heathen Nineveh. "A real example" this "of the genius of the gospel." And the Jewish apostles were sent to preach Jesus Christ to "every creature." *He* died for *all!*—G. T. C.

Ver. 10.—*God repenting.* It is *another* people in Nineveh that God now looks down upon. These have "ceased to do evil." "*God* saw their works, that they turned from their evil way." Then is the threatened doom to come? No; "God repented of the evil, that he had said that he would do unto them; and he did it not." And yet in other Scriptures God is said *not* to repent. Words can only faintly portray a *human* friend. How feeble, then, are all words to declare God! Words that *seem* to us to contradict each other are necessary to convey to us a fuller, clearer view of him. If in one Scripture God is said not to repent, or "change his mind" (as the word means), that is true. If in another he is said to do so, that is also true. The Scripture fearlessly declares both. It makes no attempt to harmonize them. We may be unable to do so. And yet we may *believe* both; confident that they *are* in harmony if *we* cannot harmonize them. *Men* repent, or change their mind, in reference to *sin*. *God* repents, or changes his mind, in reference to the *sinner*.

I. In his own nature God is changeless. What changes there are in earth and sky, the seasons, human life and experience! "*Man* continueth not in one stay." With God "is no variableness, neither shadow of turning." He never ceases to be almighty, omniscient, "the only wise God." He says, "I am the Lord, I change not" (Mal. iii. 6). This was the Divine message by Balaam to Balak: "God is not a man, that he should lie; neither the son of man, that he should repent; hath he said, and shall he not do it?" etc. (Numb. xxiii. 19, 20). In other words, no enchantment, no divination, could avail against Israel. What were Balak's bribes to God? He *could* fulfil his promises to Israel—for he was almighty; he *would*, for he was faithful. Further, in various Scriptures (Gen. vi. 3; Jer. xviii. 7; as well as here) we are taught—

II. That God repents, or changes his mind. Some would limit this to God's altered dealings with men; to his *acts*, never to his feelings. They hold that in his feelings he is ever the same to men; that none of the affections found in us have any counterpart in him; that he looks down upon all human changes—sorrows, joys, conflicts, defeats, triumphs—cold, calm, unmoved, immovable! What! a God only thought, only will? No mercy, no pity, no sympathy, no love? Unlovely creed! "God is love." Then he has the *feelings* of love, without, indeed, the imperfections that may mingle with ours. He is "the Father of our spirits." *Our* emotions are the image of his; in *him* "without spot," or defect, "or any such thing." It is no mere figure of meaningless speech that speaks of him as "angry with the wicked," as "pitying them that fear him," as rejoicing over his penitent creatures; as *repenting* concerning Nineveh. With no idle threatening was Jonah sent to the Ninevites. God then *meant* destruction. And had the people not repented, it would have come. But the very threatening was blessed to them. They saw the greatness of their sin in the greatness of the imminent punishment. And when their state of rebellion and defiance ceased, their city came into a new relation to God, "and room was made for the word to take effect; 'the curse causeless shall not come.'" God knew that the city would be spared. Yes. But he also knew that, *when* spared, it would be another city—a city not of violent rebels against him, but of penitent subjects. God is *righteous* in all his ways. He rewards every man according to his works. It was in accordance, then, with his *nature*, that when the Ninevites turned from their evil courses with true heart-sorrow, *he* should turn from the fierceness of his anger. There is *warning* here. God's threatenings are not to be trifled with. Remember the destroyed sinners "in the days of Noah;" ultimately these very Ninevites; and the Jew, "tribe of the wandering foot and weary breast," is witness to-day through all lands to the fact that when a warned nation repents not, God is faithful to his warning. And so with the individual. Let the warned sinner "*flee* from the wrath to come." What *consolation*, too, in this narrative! God is "not willing that any should perish; but that all should come to repentance." How willing—how revealed in Christ, who came to "call sinners to repentance"! Turn from sin. God will turn to you. From afar he will see you. He will run to meet you. He will kiss into forgetfulness all your sins. He waits to be gracious. "He delighteth in mercy."—G. T. C.

EXPOSITION.

CHAPTER IV.

VERS. 1—11.—JONAH'S DISPLEASURE, AND ITS CORRECTION.

VERS. 1—4.—§ 1. *Jonah is grieved at the sparing of Nineveh, the expectation of which had led to his former flight, and complains of God's clemency.*

Ver. 1.—It displeased Jonah exceedingly; literally, *it was evil to Jonah, a great evil.* It was more than mere displeasure which he felt; he was vexed and irritated. The reference is to what is said in the last verse of the preceding chapter, viz. that the predicted destruction was not inflicted. How the knowledge of this reprieve was conveyed to the prophet we are not informed. It probably was made known to him before the expiration of the forty days by Divine communication, in accordance with the saying in Amos iii. 7, "Surely the Lord will do nothing, but he revealeth his secret unto his servants the prophets" (see ver. 5). Various reasons have been assigned for this displeasure. (1) Personal pique, lest, his prediction having failed, he should be liable to the charge of being a false prophet. (2) Zeal for the honour of God, whose knowledge of the future might be discredited among the heathen, when they saw his own servant's words unfulfilled. (3) Because he saw in this conversion of Gentiles a token of the ruin of his own people, who remained always hardened and impenitent. (4) A mistaken patriotism, which could not endure to find mercy extended to a heathen nation which had already proved hostile to Israel and was destined to oppress it still further. This last seems to have been the real ground of his annoyance. So deep was this, that he would gladly have seen the sentence executed even after the city had repented (comp. ver. 11, "Should not I spare Nineveh," *i.e.* which thou wouldst have me even now destroy?) He was very angry; Septuagint, συνεχύθη, "was confounded." His vexation increased unto anger.

Ver. 2.—He prayed. He carried his complaint to God, and was prepared to submit it to him, even while he questioned the wisdom of his clemency. I pray thee (*anna*); Vulgate, *obsecro.* A particle of entreaty, "Ah! I pray thee." Was not this my saying? Was not this what I said to myself, viz. that God would spare Nineveh if it showed signs of repentance? My country. Palestine, where the original message reached him. I fled before; lite-

rally, *I anticipated to fly;* Septuagint, προέφθασα τοῦ φυγεῖν, "I made haste to flee;" Vulgate, *præoccupavi ut fugerem.* I hastened to fly before I should be reduced to seeing my mission rendered nugatory. For I knew. Joel knew the character of God, and how that he threatened in order to arouse repentance, and that he might be able to spare (see Exod. xxxii. 14; xxxiv. 6, 7). The description of God's mercy agrees with that in Joel ii. 13 and Neh. ix. 17.

Ver. 3.—Take . . . my life from me (comp. ver. 8). Jonah throughout represents himself as petty, hasty, and self-willed, prone to exaggerate matters, and easily reduced to despair. Here, because his word is not fulfilled, he wishes to die, though he will not take his own life. In a different spirit Moses (Exod. xxxii. 32) is ready to die for his people's sake, and Elijah asked for death because his zeal for God had apparently wrought no effect (1 Kings xix. 4).

Ver. 4.—Doest thou well to be angry? Septuagint, Εἰ σφόδρα λελύπησαι σύ; "Hast thou been greatly grieved?" Vulgate, *Putasne bene irasceris tu?* The English Version is doubtless correct. God bids him consider with himself whether his anger is reasonable. The version of the LXX., however grammatically permissible, is somewhat pointless.

Ver. 5.—§ 2. *Jonah, not yet abandoning his hope of seeing the city punished, makes for himself a hut outside the walls, and waits there to see the issue.* Went out of the city. It is best so rendered, and not in the pluperfect. It must have been before the end of the forty days that Jonah perceived that Nineveh would escape. And now, from God's expostulation with him in ver. 4, he seems to have conceived the expectation that some catastrophe would still happen; as though God had told him that he was too hasty in his judgment, that he could not know the mind of God, and that because he did not strike immediately he was not to conclude that he would not strike at all. On the east side of the city. The opposite side to that by which he had entered, and where the high ground enabled him to overlook the town, without necessarily sharing in its destruction. A booth. A tent constructed of branches interlaced, which did not exclude the sun (Lev. xxiii. 42; Neh. viii. 14, etc.). What would become of the city. He still expected that some calamity would befall the Ninevites, perhaps with the idea that their repentance would prove so imperfect and temporary that God would punish them after all.

Vers. 6, 7.—§ 3. *God causes a plant to spring up in order to shade Jonah from the sun; but it is made soon to wither away and leave him exposed to the scorching rays.*

Ver. 6.—Prepared (vers. 7, 8); *appointed* (see note on ch. i. 17). **A gourd;** Hebrew, *kikaion* (here only in the Old Testament); Septuagint, κολοκύνθη, "pumpkin;" Vulgate, *hedera;* Aquila and Theodotion, κυκεών. Jerome describes this as a shrub called in Syriac *elkeroa*, and common in the sandy regions of Palestine. It has large leaves and grows to a considerable height in a very few days, so that a mere shrub becomes quickly a small tree. The scientific name of this plant is *Ricinus communis;* in Egyptian, *kiki;* in Assyrian, *kukanitu*. A drawing of it is given in Dr. Pusey's 'Commentary,' p. 260. It is also known by the name of the *Palma Christi*, and from its seeds is expressed "castor oil." But it is very doubtful whether this is the plant intended. Certainly the *ricinus* is never used in the East as a protection against the sun, for which its straggling, open growth renders it unsuitable; while the gourd, as Mr. Tristram testifies ('Land of Israel,' p. 37), is used universally to form trellises for shading arbours and summer-houses, and affords a most effectual screen. "Orientals," says Dr. Thomson ('The Land and the Book,' p. 15), "never dream of training a castor-oil plant over a booth, or planting it for a shade, and they would have but small respect for any one who did. It is in no way adapted for that purpose, while thousands of arbours are covered with various creepers of the general gourd family." With this testimony it is well to be satisfied. Whatever the plant was, its growth was abnormal in the present case, though the rapidity with which it developed was merely a quickening of its ordinary powers, in due accordance with its nature and character. **From his grief;** Septuagint, ἀπὸ τῶν κακῶν αὐτοῦ, "from his evils;" Vulgate, *ut . . . protegeret eum.* The Hebrew word is the same as in ver. 1, and it refers, not so much to the physical discomfort occasioned by the heat, but rather to the condition of his mind, the vexation and disappointment under which he was suffering. **Was exceeding glad;** literally, *rejoiced a great joy;* ἐχάρη χαρὰν μεγάλην (Septuagint). The candour and simplicity of the writer throughout are very remarkable. He may have seen in this providential shelter an intimation that God approved of his intention to wait and see the issue.

Ver. 7.—Prepared (see note on ver. 6). **A worm.** Either a single worm which punctured the stem and caused the plant to wither, or the word is used collectively, as in Deut. xxviii. 39, for "worms." A single

warm night, with a moist atmosphere, will suffice to produce a host of caterpillars, which in an incredibly short time strip a plant of all its leaves. **When the morning rose.** At the very earliest dawn, before the actual rising of the sun (comp. Judg. ix. 33). Jonah seems to have enjoyed the shelter of the gourd one whole day. The withering of the plant came about in a natural way, but was ordered by God at a certain time in order to give Jonah the intended lesson.

Vers. 8—11.—§ 4. *Jonah grieves bitterly for the loss of the gourd; and God takes occasion from this to point out the prophet's inconsistency and pitilessness in murmuring against the mercy shown to Nineveh with its multitude of inhabitants.*

Ver. 8.—A vehement east wind; Septuagint, πνεύματι καύσωνι (Jas. i. 11) συγκαίοντι, "a scorching, burning wind;" Vulgate, *vento calido et urenti* (Hos. xiii. 15). The word translated "vehement" is also rendered "silent," *i.e.* sultry. Pusey and Hitzig rather incline to think it may mean the autumn or harvest wind. Either interpretation is suitable, as, according to Dr. Thomson, there are two kinds of sirocco, equally destructive and annoying — the violent wind, which fills the air with dust and sand; and the quiet one, when scarcely any air is stirring, but the heat is most overpowering ('The Land and the Book,' p. 536, etc.). **Beat upon the head.** The same word for the effect of the rays of the sun as in Ps. cxxi. 6 and elsewhere. Trochon quotes Ovid, 'Metam.,' vii. 804—

"Sole fere radiis feriente cacumina primis."

"The sun with earliest rays
Scarce smiting highest peaks."

Rich, 'Koordistan,' i. 125, "Just as the moon rose, about ten, an intolerable puff of wind came from the north-east. All were immediately silent, as if they had felt an earthquake, and then exclaimed, in a dismal tone, 'The sherki is come.' This was indeed the so-much-dreaded sherki, and it has continued blowing ever since with great violence from the east and north-east, the wind being heated like our Bagdad saum, but I think softer and more relaxing. This wind is the terror of these parts." "Few European travellers," says Layard ('Nin. and Babyl.,' p. 366), "can brave the perpendicular rays of an Assyrian sun. Even the well-seasoned Arab seeks the shade during the day, and journeys by night, unless driven forth by necessity or the love of war" (quoted by Dr. Pusey, *in loc.*). **He fainted** (see note on Amos viii. 13, where the same word is used of the effects of thirst; comp. ch. ii. 7). His position on the east of the city (ver. 5) exposed him to the full force of the scorching sun and wind. **Wished in himself to die**; literally, *asked for his soul to die;* Septuagint, ἀπελέγετο τὴν ψυχὴν αὐτοῦ, "despaired of his life" (1 Kings xix. 4). The expression implies that he asked God to grant him his life to do with it what he liked. In his self-will and impatience he still shows his dependence upon God. He may have had in his mind the precedent of his great master Elijah, though his spirit is very different (see note on ver. 3 above). **Better for me to die.** His wish for death arose from his now assured conviction that God's mercy was extended to the heathen. He argued from the sudden withering of the gourd that he was not to stay there and see the accomplishment of his wishes, and, in his impatience and intolerance, he would rather die than behold Nineveh converted and saved.

Ver. 9.—**God said.** Keil and others have noted the variety in the use of the names of God in this passage (vers. 6—9). The production of the gourd is attributed to Jehovah-Elohim (ver. 6), a composite name, which serves to mark the transition from Jehovah in ver. 4 to Elohim in vers. 7 and 8. Jehovah, who replies to the prophet's complaint (ver. 4), prepares the plant as Elohim the Creator, and the worm as ha-Elohim the personal God. Elohim, the Ruler of nature, sends the east wind to correct the prophet's impatience; and in ver. 10 Jehovah sums up the history and teaches the lesson to be learned from it. **Doest thou well to be angry?** The same tender expostulation as in ver. 4. **I do well to be angry,** even unto death. I am right to be angry, so that my anger almost kills me. Deprived of the shelter of the gourd, Jonah is immediately depressed, and in his unreasoning anger defends himself against the reproaches of God's voice within him. Septuagint, Σφόδρα λελύπημαι ἐγὼ ἕως θανάτου, "I am greatly grieved even unto death," which reminds one of our Lord's words in the garden (Mark xiv. 34).

Ver. 10.—**The Lord.** Jehovah, closing the story, and driving home the lesson with unanswerable force, the prophet himself being the judge. **Thou hast had pity;** *thou on thy part hast spared;* Septuagint, σὺ ἐφείσω. **For the which thou hast not laboured;** Septuagint, ὑπὲρ ἧς οὐκ ἐκακοπάθησας ἐπ' αὐτήν, "for which thou sufferedst no evil." The more trouble a thing costs us, the more we regard it, as a mother loves her sickly child

best. **Neither madest it grow.** As God had made Nineveh into a "great city." **Which came up in a night, and perished in a night;** literally, *which was the son of a night, and perished the son of a night.* The allusion, of course, is to the extraordinary rapidity of the growth and destruction of the gourd.

Ver. 11.—**Should not I spare Nineveh?** The contrast between the feeling and conduct of God and those of the prophet is very forcible. Thou hast compassion for a plant of little worth, in whose growth thou hast had no concern, to which thou hast no right; should I not pity a great city which is mine, which I have permitted to grow into power? Thou hast compassion on a flower which sprang up in a day and withered in a day; should I not pity this town with its teeming population and its multitude of cattle, the least of which is more worth than any senseless plant, and which I uphold daily with my providence? **Six score thousand persons that cannot discern between their right hand and their left hand;** *i.e.* children of tender years, who did not know which hand was the strongest and fittest for use; or, metaphorically, who "had no knowledge between good and evil" (Deut. i. 39), at present incapable of moral discernment. This limitation would include children of three or four years old; and, taking these as one-fifth of the population, we should set the inhabitants at six hundred thousand in number. The multitude of these innocent children, who must needs perish if the city were destroyed, is an additional reason why it should be spared. A still further claim for compassion is appended. **And also much cattle.** God's mercy is over all his works; he preserveth man and beast (Ps. xxxvi. 6; cxlv. 9), and as man is superior to other animals, so are cattle better than plants. The book ends abruptly, but its object is accomplished. Jonah is silenced; he can make no reply; he can only confess that he is entirely wrong, and that God is righteous. He learns the lesson that God would have all men saved, and that that narrow-mindedness which would exclude heathen from his kingdom is displeasing to him and alien from his design. "For thou hast mercy upon all; for thou canst do all things, and winkest at the sins of men in order that they should repent. For thou lovest all the things that are, and abhorrest nothing that thou hast made; for never wouldst thou have made anything if thou hadst hated it. . . . But thou sparest all; for they are thine, O Lord, thou Lover of souls" (Wisd. xi. 23, etc.).

HOMILETICS.

Vers. 1—3.—*Repining at God's mercy.* A more mixed character than Jonah's it would not be easy to imagine. God's treatment of him, God's language to him, prove that he was regarded as a servant, as a prophet, of the Lord. His own prayers and thanksgivings indicated a nature in happy fellowship with the Eternal. Yet how lacking in human charity, in true submissiveness, in unselfishness! True to nature, the portrait is one very suggestive to the thoughtful reader, who is anxious to escape self and to serve God. I. THE CAUSE OF REPINING. 1. Jonah's fear was realized. 2. Jonah's plans were defeated. 3. Jonah's self-importance was wounded. His sin lay here—he thought little or nothing of the Ninevites, much or altogether of himself. So devoted was he to his own dignity, so filled with a sense of the importance of men's estimate of himself, that he had no pity, no thought, for those to whom he was commissioned. The real explanation is here hinted of much of the repining, murmuring, discontent, which prevail among those professedly religious. Men would complain less frequently and bitterly, did they think less of themselves and more of their fellow-men, were they more ready to forget themselves in desiring and seeking the welfare of others. II. THE FRUIT OF REPINING. 1. Anger and displeasure. 2. Vexation and dejection. Moses and Elijah, before Jonah, had asked that life might be taken away. Ardent souls, when disappointed, are prone to despondency. But it is one thing to despond because labour is unsuccessful; another thing to despond because men are saved. Because Nineveh was spared, Jonah fain would die. Had Nineveh perished, he would have been willing to live. III. THE SIN OF REPINING. This appears from the fact, so plainly stated by Jonah himself, that the Divine forbearance and mercy were made the ground of dissatisfaction and complaint. If men murmur at the exercise of God's most gracious attributes, they can have no clearer proof of their want of sympathy with what is best, and no plainer indication of the urgent duty of repentance and humiliation.

Ver. 2.—*The long-suffering of God.* The magnificent description of the Divine character is given in language familiar to the pious Hebrews, as is apparent from its almost exact coincidence with other passages of Old Testament Scripture. Nothing could more conclusively contradict the common impression that the old covenant was one of justice only and not of mercy. The language, occurring as it does in close connection with the repining of the prophet, appears strangely out of place. It is surprising that Jonah could have spoken thus of God without feeling himself reproved and silenced. How could he have reflected upon the mercy and kindness of God, and have continued to cherish regret because his threats were not fulfilled, because a great city was spared? I. THE BENEVOLENT ATTRIBUTES OF GOD. By a redundancy of language, testifying to the depth of appreciation felt, the Lord is declared to be: 1. Gracious. 2. Merciful. 3. Of great kindness. II. THE ACTIONS IN WHICH GOD EXPRESSES HIS BENEVOLENT ATTRIBUTES. 1. He defers the execution of his just indignation against sinners. The narrative gives an impressive instance of this; but it is the lesson of all history. 2. He changes his purposes of wrath into purposes of mercy. Such was the case with Nineveh. Such is the case with humanity at large.

Ver. 4.—*Anger rebuked.* The Prophet Jonah was a singularly complex being. On the one hand, he evidently reverenced and trusted the Lord; yet, on the other hand, he acted disobediently, and cherished feelings which were in the highest degree discreditable to one who enjoyed his opportunities of knowing the Divine character and purposes. The inquiry, the expostulation, of the text indicates God's displeasure with his servant; yet the form in which it shapes itself shows that God wished rather that Jonah should rebuke himself, that his conscience should be awakened to condemn the attitude which he had assumed. I. ANGER IS IN ITSELF AN EMOTION WHICH MAY BE EITHER GOOD OR EVIL. God himself is represented in his Word as having been angry with the wicked; and a righteous anger or indignation with wrong-doers is now and again in the Scripture narrative mentioned with approval. Indeed, a nature to which anger is foreign cannot but be lacking in moral fibre. On the other hand, into how many sins have men been led by giving way to foolish anger?—*i.e.* to anger either altogether unwarranted or unjustifiable in the degree in which it has been cherished. An angry man can seldom decide with justice or act with consideration.

II. ANGER IS NEVER JUSTIFIABLE WHEN OCCASIONED BY THE ACTION OF A RIGHTEOUS AND GRACIOUS GOD. Now, Jonah saw that the Divine Ruler was "slow to anger" with the Ninevites; yet he himself was quick to indignation and wrath. Anger like Jonah's questions the justice of the Divine proceedings. He who is angry with the plans and purposes of the Eternal sets himself up as a judge of that Being who is Judge of all. There may be occasions for anger with fellow-men; but anger with the Creator and Ruler of all is never defensible or excusable. It evinces a sad lack of modesty and of true submissiveness.

III. ANGER IS ALWAYS BLAMABLE WHEN IT IS OCCASIONED BY THE RELIEF AND SALVATION OF MEN. The plain truth concerning Jonah's anger is this—it arose because the Ninevites were not overwhelmed with destruction. If the city had perished, the prophet would have felt satisfaction in contemplating such a fate. Because the city was spared, and (as he thought) his authority was discredited, he gave way to wrath. A more selfish and unamiable temper has never been exhibited.

IV. THERE IS ALWAYS REASON TO SUSPECT THE JUSTICE OF ANGER WHEN IT ACCOMPANIES SOME HUMILIATION OR MORTIFICATION OF SELF. Plainly Jonah thought more of himself than of those to whom he ministered, or he would not have given way to anger because his word of prophecy was not literally fulfilled. Men sometimes endeavour to deceive themselves, to persuade themselves that their wrath is stirred by some infraction of right, when, all the time, the true secret of their anger is to be found in personal mortification. A lesson this of the importance of being upon our guard against the insidious temptation to vanity and self-importance.

Ver. 7.—*The withering of earthly consolation.* If Jonah's vexation and anger were due first to the sparing of Nineveh, and the mortification of his self-importance, similar emotion was excited within him by the deprivation of personal comfort which was appointed by Divine providence.

I. IN TIMES OF TROUBLE GOD APPOINTS DIVINE CONSOLATIONS FOR HIS PEOPLE. The gourd, or palmcrist, which the Author of nature caused to grow up over Jonah's booth, was "for a shadow over his head, to deliver him from his grief." Such a refuge, shelter, shadow, Providence often appoints for those who are in distress. Some unexpected provision for want, some gracious alleviation of suffering, some marvellous deliverance from impending danger, reveals the thoughtful and loving care of the Most High.

II. GOD IN HIS MERCY THUS TURNS SORROW INTO GLADNESS. "Jonah was exceeding glad of the gourd." It was itself beautiful to behold, and its cool shelter was refreshing, and it was a pleasant and welcome emblem of Divine care and kindness. Many have been made glad according to the days in which they have been afflicted, to the years in which they have seen evil. Of many once storm-tossed and imperilled it may be said, "They are glad because they be quiet." It is right to rejoice when Eternal Mercy rescues and delivers those who are in trouble and distress.

III. CONSOLATIONS ARE OFTEN SHORT-LIVED AND DISAPPOINTING. The caterpillars which smote the palmcrist in a few hours robbed Jonah of his comfort, so that his new, dawning joy was overcast with clouds of gloom. And this withering was an emblem of the transitory nature of all earthly happiness and prosperity. The comforts which God sends he takes away, lest we should set our hearts upon created good. Health fails, property is lost, friends die, bright prospects are clouded, hopes perish. Nothing continueth in one stay.

> "This world is all a fleeting show,
>   For man's illusion given;
> The smiles of joy, the tears of woe,
> Deceitful shine, deceitful flow:
>   There's nothing true but heaven."

IV. THE PRIVATION OF EARTHLY COMFORTS IS INTENDED TO LEAD MEN TO SEEK THEIR HIGHEST GOOD IN GOD. Such discipline does not, indeed, produce this effect upon all men; many are hardened, some are driven to despair, by adversity. But with regard to the truly pious, it may be said that, when the gourd withers, the Giver is as firmly trusted and as warmly loved as when the shelter was thick and green.

> "Though vine nor fig tree neither
> 　Their wonted fruit should bear;
> Though all the field should wither,
> 　Nor flock nor herd be there;
> Yet God the same abiding,
> 　His praise shall tune my voice;
> For while in him confiding,
> 　I cannot but rejoice."

Ver. 8.—*Desire to die.* Deep was the mortification, the disappointment, the dejection, which, more than once, found expression in this wish. It is not an uncommon thing for those whose hearts are blighted, whose prospects are clouded, for whom life has but few attractions left, to wish rather to die than to live.

I. THE EXPLANATION OF THIS WISH. 1. The burden of bodily suffering or weakness, or of mental anguish, may be such as is very hard to bear; and men may wish to lay it down even though with it they lay down the load of life. 2. The memory of trouble, calamity, disaster, may be so distressing that even annihilation has been desired rather than an ineffaceable record of woe. The Christian cannot desire extinction of being, but he may hope that, in passing hence, he may steep his soul in Lethe's oblivious waves. 3. The apparent hopelessness of the earthly prospect tempts men to wish to die. To many who are advanced in life, crippled in body, ruined in circumstances, disappointed in life-plans, this earthly existence seems to present no prospects; death seems a relief.

II. THE BLAMABLENESS OF THIS WISH. 1. It implies a habit of discontent and of murmuring. Our circumstances are appointed or permitted by a kind Providence; to wish to escape them is to wish to avoid the discipline ordained for us by our heavenly Father. The Christian pilgrim should be prepared cheerfully, or at least patiently, to finish his path, even to the journey's end. 2. It implies an undue desire for rest. Men's notions of heaven are often carnal and selfish; they look forward to release from labour and service; and sometimes they wish to die that they may enjoy the sweets of repose. But it should be the desire and expectation of all Christians, that they may serve God day and night in his temple. Surely one attraction of the future state for the holy nature is this—it will afford opportunity for higher and purer service.

III. THE COUNTERACTIVE TO THIS WISH. This is to be found in perfect submissiveness to the holy and perfect will of God. Whilst he has work for his people to do on earth, earth is the best place for them; when he wishes them to enter upon heavenly service, he himself will call them hence.

Vers. 10, 11.—*The breadth of the Divine pity.* The close of this very remarkable book is deserving of attention and admiration, as evidently gathering up and exhibiting the purpose for which this composition was designed. Of all things apprehensible by us nothing is equal in interest to the character of the Supreme Ruler and Lord. This is depicted in this closing passage of the narrative and prophecy in the most attractive, encouraging, and glorious colours.

I. GOD'S PITY CONTRASTS WITH MAN'S HARDNESS AND SEVERITY. Jonah, though a prophet of the Lord, would have witnessed the destruction of Nineveh with equanimity and even satisfaction. It might have been supposed that a sinful and fallible being would have been more compassionate. But for the supreme illustration of pity we must look to the Father of all.

II. GOD'S PITY IS EXCITED BY THE SPECTACLE OF A GREAT AND POPULOUS COMMUNITY IN DANGER OF DESTRUCTION. Nineveh was at the other end of the scale, so to speak, from the palmcrist which grew up and perished in a few hours. It was an ancient, vast, populous, powerful, famous city. "Should I not spare," asked God of Jonah, "Nineveh, that great city?" There is in this language something which appeals to our heart. God is represented in the most amiable and attractive light. Such sentiments as these will be cherished by God-like men, by those Christ-like hearts that sympathize with him who beheld Jerusalem, and wept over it.

III. GOD'S PITY IS INTENSIFIED BY THE SPECTACLE OF LITTLE CHILDREN EXPOSED TO DESTRUCTION. By those who are described as unable to discern between their right hand and their left we may well understand babes and young children who had not sinned. Yet these were in danger of being overtaken by the one common calamity and ruin. The tender heart of the All-Father was touched by the possibility of such a catastrophe. And when it was possible to avert it—in harmony with the principles of the Divine government, and so as not to endanger the spiritual interests of humanity —it was a joy to the heart of God to spare the city and the babes of the city's household.

APPLICATION. 1. Let the hearers of the gospel take advantage of the sparing mercy of the Lord. 2. Let the preachers of the gospel proclaim the sparing mercy of the Lord. 3. Let all Christians sympathize with, delight in, and imitate, the sparing mercy of the Lord.

HOMILIES BY VARIOUS AUTHORS.

Vers. 1—4.—*A misanthrope's case against Divine benevolence.* It takes a good deal to make a man of God perfect. After a whole life's discipline the old man of sin will sometimes show his baleful features at the window of the soul. Jonah has just been figuring to our mind as a changed character, returned to his allegiance, going God's errand promptly, and doing his work with faithful zeal. But here he forfeits our good opinion, almost before it has had time to form. The patient's cure has been only seeming, or else he has suffered a bad relapse. At any rate, the narrative leaves him on a spiritual level as low or lower than it found him. He began by quarrelling with a particular command of God, and he ends by quarrelling with his moral government as a whole. If there be a point of religious progress scored at all in connection with the matter, it is the exceedingly minute one that at first he tried to defeat the Divine purpose, and at last, and with an ill grace, he submits to its execution as inevitable. And it may be noted, as a qualifying consideration, that sanctification is the work of a lifetime; and therefore we can look for no very material change in the few days which the narrative of the book covers.

I. A MAN WHO HAS FOUND MERCY HIMSELF MAY YET PRACTICALLY GRUDGE IT TO OTHERS. Misanthropy is Satanic. The devil hates men utterly and intensely. And the man, if there be such, who hates men instinctively, and would destroy them unprovoked, is less human than diabolical. Jonah was not such a man. There were considerations, and paltry ones, for which he would have sacrificed all the souls in Nineveh, but, apart from these, he wished them no ill. 1. *One of these considerations was supplied by egoism.* As the prophet and mouthpiece of God, he had predicted the destruction of the city, even to the naming of the day, and his credit required that the event should now occur. If it did not, his prophecy failed, and his reputation as a prophet suffered, both with the Ninevites and with his own people. The prospect of this he could not stand. In his miserable and guilty self-seeking he preferred the destruction, soul and body, of a million people, to the possible discrediting of his prophetic claims. Such heartlessness in a believing man seems well-nigh incredible. But it is far from unparalleled. Every Christian worker approaches it who works for his own credit or advantage, and not for the salvation of men. He may not be conscious of the fact, or he may fail to realize the significance of it, but he virtually and practically prefers that men should perish rather than that he should be deemed a failure. His reputation as a Christian worker, and his success in that character, is more to him than the salvation from sin of all to whom his words may come. 2. *Another consideration sectarianism provides.* To Israel in its wickedness a whole line of prophets had preached, with no result whatever, save their own extermination (Acts vii. 52), and the announcement of inevitable doom on the obdurate race (Amos v. 27; vii. 17). The Ninevites' deliverance, establishing as it would the genuineness of their turning from sin, would bring into unfavourable contrast the obstinate impenitence of Israel, would emphasize the needs-be of her approaching ruin, and would amount to the preservation and encouragement of the very heathen power by which she was to fall. Then the over-throw of Nineveh by an angry God would have been a terrible example to quote to Israel, and a rod to conjure with when calling on them to fly the wrath of God; whilst its escape the prophet's careless countrymen might wrest to their own destruction, and from it argue that the vengeance denounced would likely never fall. There is an attitude of indifference toward the perishing, into which an analogous spirit of sectarianism sometimes causes believers to fall. The question of their salvation gets mixed up with some question of denominational loss or discredit. We desire their conversion, and desire to be the means of it. But we don't desire it supremely or disinterestedly. We don't desire it apart from all denominational considerations. The idea of their remaining a while longer in sin would be almost as tolerable to us as that some rival sect should win their gratitude and adherence by helping them into the kingdom. This is, at bottom, the spirit of Jonah exactly. It is putting an earthly and narrow interest before the eternal life of souls. It is a spirit unworthy the Christian character, and a shameful stigma on the Christian name. 3. *A further consideration may be found in the surviving misanthropy of a half-sanctified nature.* God desires infinitely the highest well-being of men (Ezek. xxxiii. 11). And men, in proportion as they are God-like, desire it too (Rom. ix. 1—4). The sinful nature, which is largely selfish, is being taken away, and the gracious character, which is essentially benevolent, is being inwrought. But neither process is complete on earth, and the missionary spirit, which is their joint issue, is proportionally weak. It was so with Jonah. He shows the old nature strong still in pride and petulance and ingratitude, and why not in lovelessness, its characteristic vice? Such a man is incapable of understanding the tender and gracious heart of God, which loves men absolutely and infinitely, and acts in every respect in character. He is incapable of desiring supremely the highest good of men, for he has never climbed to the high spiritual level in which to apprehend his own. A half-sanctified man is considerably more than half selfish, and a good deal less than half benevolent. If we would know what it is to travail for men's salvation, we must rise to a love of God baptized into the likeness of the Divine love out of which it springs.

II. GOD'S CHARACTER IS CONSTANT, WHATEVER ELSE MAY CHANGE. (Ver. 2.) Jonah changed, and the Ninevites changed, and God's treatment was changed accordingly; but the Divine character and rule of action remained the same throughout. 1. *He acted strictly in character in this case.* Jonah's language seems to imply a charge of weakness against the Divine dealing with Nineveh. On no other assumption can we understand his quoting in such a connection, and with disapproval, God's own revelation of the character in which he desired to be known (Ezek. xxxiv. 6). And the supposition is strengthened by the fact that, whilst he gives literally the clauses that speak of God's mercy, he leaves out the clause that speaks of his justice (Exod. xxxiv. 7), and substitutes for it a sentiment of his own. But justice and mercy met in the whole transaction. The Ninevites were mercifully spared, yet not unjustly. They might in justice have been destroyed, but not in mercy (Isa. lv. 7; Jer. xxxi. 20). Therefore Jonah absurdly makes it a charge against God that he is what he had always gloried in declaring himself to be. So blind and stupid can a sulky servant be. God need not overact his merciful character in order to offend such people; it is his mercy itself with which they have a quarrel. 2. *The prophet himself affirms the Divine consistency.* "God," we are told, "repented of the evil," etc.; and Jonah says, "I knew that thou art a gracious God . . . and repentest thee of the evil." The thing that Jonah knew he would do he did. His action was normal and entirely consistent—such action as he has always taken, and will take, in a like case. He repented, in fact, yet did not change. He did what it would be a change to cease from doing in the circumstances. He threatened Nineveh sinning, as he threatens all, and then he spared it turning, as he spares men in every age. His repentance, so called, is his method co-ordinating itself with the changing conditions of life, and is simply an aspect of his immutability.

III. THE PRAYER OF THE SELF-SEEKER IS OF NECESSITY ILL-ADVISED. (Ver. 3.) Jonah's prayer was *bona fides*. It is as a believer he prays. His spiritual instinct brings him in his unhappiness to a throne of grace. "He does not seek a refuge from God. He makes God his Refuge" (Martin). He shows a surly sincerity in unreservedly stating what is working in his mind; and "so long as all can yet be declared unto the Lord, even though it be your infirmity, there integrity still reigns" (Martin). Yet, barring the quality of sincerity, this prayer lacks almost every other element of acceptable worship. 1. *It is inappropriate in its matter.* (Ver. 3.) It is not absolutely and necessarily wrong to pray for death. Paul, persecuted and afflicted, had "a desire to depart and be with Christ." It is easily conceivable that a believer, broken down and prostrated with incurable disease, should pray for death as the sole available release. It would be nothing unbecoming if a ripe saint, whose life-work is done, and who longs for rest, should make its early coming a matter of prayer. But Jonah was neither past living usefully nor, in his present temper, ready to die. His death, if allowed, would have advanced no interest either of his own or of others. His work was, humanly speaking, far from being done, and his life, if he put a noble interpretation on it, might be of great importance in the world. He was stupidly wanting to fling away from him, instead of prizing and using it, one of God's most precious gifts, and his own most sacred trust. The desire to die, which some consider the cream of all piety, is as often mistaken as appropriate, and far less often a duty than a sin. In such cases men "ask and receive not, because they ask amiss." 2. *It is improper in spirit.* One can easily see that Jonah was in no praying mood. He was angry and insolent. His prayer was really a contentious manifesto—the joint issue of arrogance and discontent. As such it was utterly offensive to God, and itself a new sin in his sight. The spirit of it, however, made it harmless, as it secured the refusal of its mischievous request. Our union with Christ is a condition of successful prayer (John xv. 7). The guarantee of its acceptability is our dwelling in Christ: the cause of its fitness is his Word dwelling in us. The Spirit helps the believer's infirmities, and in these qualities we have the outcome of his work (Rom. viii. 26). The very gist of prayer is a leaving of ourselves in the hands of God. Its inquiry is, "Lord, what wilt thou have me to do?" and its request is, "Lord, here am I; send me." Such a request is offered in terms of our Father's will, and, being offered in Christ, is ideal prayer to God. But the prayer of wilfulness, of fretfulness, of carnal suggestion in any shape, is lacking in every element that God regards or can accept. "For let not such a one think that he shall receive anything of the Lord."

IV. GOD ANSWERS A FAULT-FINDING PRAYER BY REBUKING THE SPIRIT OF IT. The rule is that believing prayer is answered (Matt. xxi. 22; Mark ii. 24). It is a special qualification of the rule that the answer comes in the form of things agreeable to God's will. Jonah's prayer had enough of faith in it to secure an answer, and yet enough of folly to necessitate an answer very different from the one desired (ver. 4). There was wonderful condescension here. Jonah makes an insane request, and it is mercifully ignored. He makes it in a sinful way, and gets the thing he was most in need of—an admonition. The words imply: 1. *Are you angry on sufficient grounds?* An enumeration of the antecedents of his anger would have covered Jonah with confusion. His contemptibly egotistic refusal to prophesy, as it was his business to do, had not so much been punished, as forcibly overcome, and then forgiven. His life, jeopardized, in the natural course of events, by his own infatuate conduct, had, by a miracle of mercy, been given back to him from the grave's mouth. His recent ministry so tardily exercised had been blessed beyond a parallel, to the saving of a mighty city and the glorious illustration of the mercy and grace of God. These grounds of feeling are the only grounds which, as a servant of God, he could consistently regard. The others, which bore on possible results to his own official prestige, and Israel's moral attitude and fate, were purely speculative, might prove unfounded altogether, and whether or not should have no place in a spiritual mind. A true prophet is a man who speaks for God unquestioningly, who acts for God undauntedly, who is in fullest sympathy with his gracious purposes, and who knows no personal considerations in his work. Well might God ask, "Art thou wiser than I?" "Is thine eye evil because I am good?" If a servant may have an interest antagonistic to his master's; if a man "may make his own narrow capacity the measure by which to judge of the Divine will and the Divine procedure" (Martin); if the salvation of a million strangers is nothing in the balance against a possible hurt to a few of our own friends;—then Jonah was fitly angry, and we, in a like case, may fitly be angry also. The words also imply: 2. *Is your anger itself a right thing?* The will of God is the ultimate reason of things. The way of God is unchallengeably right. The office of censor over him does not exist. There is no provision in his scheme of government for our being angry, and no place in the chain of cause and effect at which it could come in. We do it solely on our own responsibility, in violation of the Divine harmonies, and at our own risk and loss. It settles nothing outside ourselves, influences nothing, and has no right of way across the field of providence. God is supreme, and men are in his hands, and all duty in relation to his government is, "Thy will be done." The question of men's salvation is God's question in the last appeal. He sits at the helm. He settles who shall be saved, and whether any shall be saved (Rom. ix. 11, 16, 22, 23). The conversion of sinners is but the evolution of his purpose; the glorification of saints the realization of his plan. Is not this good tidings for the lost? Seeking God as he thinks with all his heart, the anxious sinner fancies sometimes that he is willing and God is not, and that the question to be solved is the question of overcoming a certain Divine inertia, and getting God's consent to his entrance into life. The idea is a delusion of Satan, and has ruined more lives than could be told. " Ye will not come unto me that ye might have life." That is Christ's way of it. " As I live, saith the Lord God, I have no pleasure in the death of the wicked; but that the wicked turn from his way and live." That is God's gospel, the glorious and precious truth. God's willingness to save is infinite. He waits to be gracious. It is you that are not willing. You think you are, and you may be in some respects. But you are not willing perfectly and all round. There is a secret reservation lurking somewhere. Search well and see. If you had ever been wholly willing for a single instant, you would that instant have been across the threshold and in the kingdom. If you are wholly willing now, it is the golden hour of your life, for it is the beginning of the new life in Christ.—J. E. H.

Vers. 5—11.—*Divine mercy formulating its own apologetic.* God is patient and persistent to a marvel. He sticks to men whom we would unhesitatingly cast off, and bears with them when, to our mind, patience has ceased to be a virtue. His keen eye sees ground for hope where we should utterly despair; and he goes on dealing with cases that we should regard as quite beyond treatment. The case of Jonah was one in point. He displayed a mulish obstinacy, and a tenacious and assertive self-will, on which anything short of the strong arm seemed only labour thrown away. Yet God is neither disgusted nor discouraged. He does not cease to strive; neither does he resort to the violence that would seem so fitting. His mildly suasive measures go on, and go on calmly and confidently, as to infallible success. Verbal expostulation has failed, but that is only one agency of exhaustless Divine resource. The symbolic method of teaching still remains, and may prevail, and God mercifully tries it on the refractory prophet before he will either say, "Cut him off!" or, "Let him alone!" We learn here—

I. HOW TENACIOUSLY A SERVANT OF GOD MAY CLING TO A MUTINOUS PROJECT. (Ver. 5.) Jonah's leaning toward the destruction of Nineveh was not mere caprice. It was largely selfish. That event would have been to him equivalent to a new credential of office. The heathen abroad and Israel at home he could have referred to it as a miraculous authentication of his word, and a new feather in his official cap. Accordingly, his preference went and his influence tried to work in that direction. In this mind he left the city. He would not mingle with the people. Their abject attentions while dreading death, and their possible ridicule if it did not come, would be alike distasteful. His mission, moreover, was practically fulfilled, and he had no very definite business to detain him longer; whilst there would be a natural desire to be out of the city when its fateful hour should arrive. There was, however, a reason for his departure a good deal less to his credit than any of these. He went to see " what would become of the city." Here was watching for souls in hideous, baleful travesty. He was watching for their salvation, it is true, but watching for it in protesting anger and fear. He cannot bring himself to believe that it will take place; and he climbs the hills overlooking the city from the east to watch developments with a mind divided between anger, curiosity, and misgiving. And here he displayed the deliberation and resource that we observed on other occasions. Anticipating inconvenience from the burning heat, he built himself a rustic arbour in which he could sit in the pleasant shade and comfortably await the end. It is humiliating to think that questions of earthly interest, questions even of personal convenience, will compete successfully at times with the question of men's salvation, for the first place in the attention of God's people. Words have, for some paltry personal consideration, been left unspoken, interviews unsought, measures unattended to, on which, humanly speaking, the question of some one's eternity hung. Those who know God and speak for him want to realize that their doing so is the paramount consideration, with which there is no other matter that may for a moment come into competition. A Paul "counts not his life dear unto him that he might finish the ministry received of the Lord Jesus, to testify the gospel of the grace of God" (Acts xx. 24). On no lower level can we, as regards the perishing, "walk in love as Christ also loved us."

II. How God in providence blesses sinners against his grace. (Ver. 6.) Jonah had just complained of the great lenity of God. But he is only quarrelling with his own mercy. He is the very first, as he was the very last, to profit by that lenity himself. The God who offended him by pitying penitent Nineveh gave him unmingled gratification by pitying his rebellious self, and bringing him in his self-made discomfort prompt relief. And the gourd that grew so timely and served so well may be taken as a type of the Divine compensatory arrangements in connection with human life. 1. *These always come.* God does not forget his people, and cannot disregard their troubles. He heeds and he helps them. Wherever there is the burning sun of calamity there is the gourd of some ameliorating circumstance. They do not intermit; if they did our well-being, our very life, would intermit also. They do not fluctuate with our allegiance; if they did they would be at the ebb perpetually. They flow down in a continuous steady stream. "No father like God; none feel for his children like him; none so forgiving and ready to relieve; when none else will pity them, he will; and in the face of manifold provocations the Lord remembereth mercy. When they become sufferers, the Father's bowels of compassion melt over them. We have a High Priest that is soon touched with the feeling of our infirmities" (Jones). 2. *They always suit.* Appropriateness must characterize a "good and perfect gift," such as all God's are. They are not at right angles to our need, but along the line of it. There is a destroying angel to rout a besieging army (2 Kings xix. 35), a flowing spring to quench a dying woman's thirst (Gen. xxi. 19), an earthquake to shake open prison doors (Acts xvi. 26), and "sufficient grace" to make a thorn in the flesh endurable (2 Cor. xii. 8, 9). In fact, God's helpful action bears directly on our sufferings and their alleviation. We get sometimes what we ask for, and always what we need. And we get it too at the moment we need it most. "The sea is opened when Israel is hemmed in on every side; the manna comes down when they have no bread; and the water flows from the rock when they are ready to die with thirst (Ps. xxvii. 10) " (Jones). 3. *They do for us what our own skill and contrivance have failed to do.* Jonah's booth proved insufficient shelter, and in the hour of its proved inadequacy the gourd grew. God allows us to build our own booth first. We try our hand at improving our earthly lot, to find that we cannot command success. We lay deep plans and put forth stupendous efforts, and then flounder and stick fast. At last God, who has been awaiting such a juncture, steps in, and, by some unthought-of incident, the blocked path is opened, and the thing is done. The testimony of God's people everywhere has been that, not their own brain or arm, but "the good hand of the Lord," has opened their path and made their life's prosperity. 4. *They are often appreciated without being traced to their source.* "Jonah was exceeding glad of the gourd." And well he might. It intercepted the broiling sunshine, and converted physical distress into luxurious ease. Yet he rejoiced in its grateful shade without considering it to be God's gift or a blessing to thank him for. It is so that many of our mercies are received. They are welcomed and prized and rejoiced in. We are exceeding glad of them, and more than enough are exercised about them. "I become exceeding glad of my gourd. My heart entwines around it. This pleasing prospect; this budding hope; this successful movement; this welcome visitant, the golden-haired little one within my earthly home, crowing in my arms, searching my eye for the kindling glance of joy and love, and dancing gleefully on finding it;—ah! in many a form my gourd may grow; and I am exceeding glad of my gourd, even when I quarrel with God" who gives it (Martin). But our best of blessings we do not trace to their heavenly source. We take them unheeding as to whence or where they come. It is a fault of our life, and a chief cause of our ingratitude and lack of love, that God's gifts are treated often as our own gains, and so are godlessly enjoyed. They are understood only when God is seen in them, and rightly used when used as from his hand; but, received with the dry eye of ingratitude, or with the shut eye of insensibility, they are deforced of their Divine element, and to us are God's gifts no longer.

III. HOW GOD CONFERS SOME GIFTS ONLY TO TAKE THEM AWAY AGAIN. (Ver. 7.) Jonah got his time of the gourd, but it was a short time. For one day he reclined luxuriously beneath its shadow; the next came the worm, and his shelter was gone. It is so with many comfortable earthly things. God gives them in mercy, and seeing them either inappreciated or idolized, he in further mercy takes them away. They "perish in the using." At best they could only last a lifetime; often they do not last so long. They are flowers that only bloom to wither, mists that melt away as soon as the sun is risen. And, whilst this is true of them as a class, it is specially true of some varieties. "When things come to us in haste, they as hastily part again; when riches come too quickly they quickly take their flight; sudden glories decay suddenly; the fruit which is soonest ripe is found to be soonest rotten" (Abbot). There is in the sudden removal of valued blessings a needful assertion of the Divine control. The things we have are not our own. We hold them at God's pleasure. And he emphasizes this fact occasionally by taking away the thing or the good of it, when we are just settling down for a whole life's enjoyment. Then we make idols of our mercies sometimes. We put the gift into the Giver's place. The most effectual cure for this is to be left without it. Our Father bestows his favours "not with a view to make man happy in the possession of them, but to win upon man, and to allure his heart to himself by his gifts. Abraham's servant did not bestow the jewels of silver and jewels of gold and raiment on Rebekah to make her joyful in a heathen land, but to win her heart to Isaac" (Jones).

IV. CALAMITY SHOWS MEN HOW BADLY THEY COULD DO WITHOUT GOD'S GIFTS. (Ver. 8.) The withering of the gourd and the rising of the hot sirocco were timed to synchronize. And there was disciplinary value in the adjustment. The loss of a gift becomes a lesson by emphasizing what and how much it means. Had the gourd remained, the heat would have been little felt. Had not the sirocco followed, the withered gourd might never have been missed. The concurrence of the two events and their obvious adjustment to each other reveal the hand of God, and point the lesson of the providence beyond mistaking. So misfortunes often march on us in companies, and support each other. One trial prepares the way of another, and lays bare the breast for its darts to penetrate. The discipline of grace is a lengthened process, and advances stage by stage to its lofty end of lust killed and a transfigured life.

V. FROM OUR ATTITUDE TOWARD OUR LOVED OBJECTS WE MAY ARGUE UP TO GOD'S ATTITUDE TOWARDS HIS. (Vers. 10, 11.) Our creation in the Divine image involves this, and all parabolic teaching takes it for granted. The soul is a miniature of God, and the order of coming to pass in it is "after God." Hence the unanswerableness of the question with which the parable and the book both close. 1. *The things we love are paltry.* A gourd against a city, a worthless plant against half a million of immortal souls. Such is a sample of the contrast between the objects of God's compassion and of ours. May we not argue that the compassion itself in the one case and the other is in still profounder contrast? God's love and mercy have reference to a lost race. Ours, unless in so far as we are God-like, refer to some trifling earthly object. Let the fact be realized, and the lesson is learned—a lesson of admiration and awe, and lowly gratitude and love. 2. *We have but a limited interest in the things we prize.* The gourd did not belong to Jonah. He "did not make it grow." He got the use of it for a while, but that was all. So the things we have are not our own. They are left with us as a loan, and held as a brief trust. Our attachment to them has no element of ownership in it, and is therefore destitute of a fundamental excellence. But God loves souls as his property and portion, and with a view to the fruition of them through all eternity. His is indeed a sublime affection—a "love which passeth knowledge." 3. *We have done but little for them.* (Ver. 10.) "For which thou hast not laboured." We love what costs us something. It is to the sickly child, which has cost her years of anxiety and care, that the mother's heart cleaves in most intense affection. Labour and sacrifice for an object bind us to it by a special tie. Created by our skill and effort, it is our offspring in a sense, and dear accordingly. This tie was absent in the case of Jonah. He had not produced, nor contributed to the production of, the much-lamented gourd. But what had God not done for Nineveh? His were the lives forfeited, his the blessings menaced, his the repentance which led to the reprieve. In pitying Nineveh God was pitying the work of his own hands, an object in which he held, as a vested interest, all that he had done for it and meant to do. 4. *They are of brief endurance.* "Which came up in a night, and perished in a night." The time element is an important one in all attachments. The longer they have been growing the firmer they are. Jonah's gourd was lost almost as soon as found, and could not have been the object of any settled regard. But Nineveh had been in God's heart since before the world began, and many in it were to be his joy after time had ceased to be. His love had in it the incomparable strength of continuance, an aspect of "the power of an endless life." What an overwhelming argument for acquiescence in the Divine purpose of mercy! And how often, in the giving and taking away again of some form of earthly good, does God press home the argument on men who are quarrelling with his will! My gourd, like Jonah's, may have grown and flourished, "to the end, perhaps, that it may wither and droop and die; and that my heart, untractable, may at last, by losing it, be taught to feel that, if the object which my poor foolish love fastens on be hard to part with, how infinitely wrong in me to desire God to abandon those purposes which his infinitely wise will hath cherished from eternity, and which he hath bound in with and wrapt around my destiny at once to bless and train me!" (Martin).

Learn from this how to conceive of the value of the souls of men. They are the priceless things. God's masterpieces as to their origin, they are unparagoned as to intrinsic excellence; whilst, as to their place and function, they are the crown jewels of Christ, and the objects for which all heaven is a place prepared. Let saint and sinner mark this well. To barter away our soul is a transaction which will not profit us, though we "gain the whole world" instead. To love our neighbour as ourself, and in doing so supremely to love his soul, is "more than all whole burnt offerings and sacrifices." To love God supremely is to combine in ideal ratio the love of self and the love of souls. They are the "children of the Highest," whose hearts are the home of such affection, and they have in its presence the fruition of their inheritance begun.—J. E. H.

Vers. 1—4.—*Jonah's displeasure.* "But it displeased Jonah exceedingly, and he was very angry," etc. This is not a wholly unexpected manifestation of character in Jonah. His was evidently a strange character, full of contradictory elements. A prophet of the Lord, who can yet run away from his work—influenced by high considerations in the main, yet yielding to a low desire for personal comfort—can sleep in a storm while pagans are at prayer—yet susceptible of profound contrition and repentance—frankly owns himself the cause of the storm—had ignominiously consulted for his comfort, but now generously sacrifices his life—in depth of his humiliation becomes wonderfully penitent, trustful, and obedient. Notwithstanding these contradictions, we should, perhaps, hardly have expected another outbreak of his lower nature, after so striking a Divine discipline and subjugation, and so remarkable a display of honesty, courage, self-sacrifice: it is a surprise to find him again quarrelling with God's appointment, discontented, hard, unmerciful, excited and grieved at the respite of Nineveh. There is a certain inconstancy in impulsive natures; there is a desperate activity of the lower propensities; hence our need of Divine guidance, a continual need—God alone is able to keep the very best from falling. "Let him that thinketh he standeth take heed lest he fall."

I. JONAH'S DISPLEASURE. (Ver. 1.) Proposed change of translation, making words to express *grief* rather than resentment, is hardly called for. Evidently Jonah lost self-control, and gave way to violent excitement. Here is another proof of the honesty of Bible narrative. It gives a faithful picture of human infirmity—"the law of sin in the members warring against the law of the mind." It would be a very untrue representation if faults corrected once, even by God, were represented as subdued for ever. The most distressing experience of true Christians is the renewed activity of their infirmities and corruptions even after profound humiliation and true contrition. "Who can understand his errors? cleanse thou me from secret faults. Keep back *thy servant* also from *presumptuous sins*; let them not have dominion over me" (Ps. xix. 12, 13).

II. REASON ASSIGNED FOR IT. (Ver. 2.) God too merciful—his mercy on this occasion judged out of place. Jonah's truthfulness as a prophet seemed to be compromised; he was made to appear foolish in the eyes of men—the whole of the painful experience he had gone through shown to be unnecessary; he would have to return home without bringing word to his people of the great catastrophe by which they would have been compelled to regard God's will. Jonah finds confirmation of the thought that had influenced him at first—God too merciful to inflict great judgments; he seems to find a reason for his original rebellion, and, with irreverent honesty, vindicates himself before God. A very great aggravation of his sin, that what he disliked in God was his graciousness to sinners. The mood of mind which Jonah is represented as expressing openly often has a lurking existence, not less mischievous because half concealed. Mercy of God is sometimes thought to be excessive. So thought Jews when Gentiles were to be admitted to Christian Church. Possibly this transaction was designed to foreshadow that event—Jonah's strong feeling a foreshadow of narrow Jewish jealousy. On a wider theatre, man's terrible selfishness is apt to prevail even over all considerations of mercy; for instance, a merchant interested in fall of price of grain is apt to be grieved for good weather and plentiful harvest—the heir of a rich man (possibly of his father) disappointed when he recovers from serious illness—the heart is apt to grieve at the good of a neighbour, especially of a rival—some one has said, " There is something even in the troubles of our friends which is not altogether displeasing to us"—a state of war is sometimes desired because of impulse to be given to certain branches of trade: in all such cases, the aspect of selfishness is simply hideous—men may well shrink from looking at such pictures of themselves—yet such feelings are by no means uncommon. What surprises in case of Jonah is that, after showing himself a very paragon of self-sacrifice, the selfish feeling should have been so strong, and that he should have given such open expression to it.

III. JONAH'S PRAYER. (Ver. 3.) He asked to be relieved of his life, which had become too burdensome to him. See here the sad prevalence of carnal spirit—no acknowledgment of higher wisdom of God, of the way in which good might be brought by him out of what seemed to Jonah to be evil. See, too, the sinfulness of a despairing spirit in servant of God—not unnatural in men of world—complications and miseries may arise which overwhelm—misery may be too absolute to bear, and every succeeding step may only aggravate it—dreadful condition of human spirit when absolute misery closes upon it. Such should never be the condition of a servant of God while in possession of his reason—sense of Divine providence, and assurance of protection and guidance should repel it—it is unbelieving men that ask, " Is life worth living?" Unbelief and suicide go together. Observe, in Jonah's case, effect of tolerated sin on his spiritual condition—he loses trust in God—does not see how God can save him even from himself—makes no such request, but only asks him to take away his life. Sometimes it seems so impossible to do right, that we are willing to give up all in despair. " If the light that is in thee be darkness, how great is that darkness!"

IV. GOD'S REMONSTRANCE. (Ver. 4.) " Doest thou well to be angry?" Oh the gentleness of the Divine method!—Jonah's thoughts are thrown in upon himself—no Divine denunciation, but Jonah made, as it were, judge in his own case, asked to sit over himself and say if his feeling was right. Resemblance of this to the method of our Lord —his way of putting questions, compelling thought, and constraining a just decision. See his method of dealing with Simon the Pharisee (Luke vii. 42). Facility with which God may judge us, by making us judges of ourselves. Difference of our actions as regarded by us, and as seen from God's point of view. It is from God's point of view their criminality is most clearly shown. Hence the sense of unworthiness we feel when we bend the knee, and pour out our spirit before God at night. The actions that at the time seemed right enough assume aspect of sin when looked at, as it were, with God's eyes. In the present case no such effect was made on Jonah; he himself comes before God in sullen, selfish spirit. Even God's question does not subdue him. Summing up the sins of Jonah's spirit in this transaction, we notice : 1. His limiting God. There was but one way, in his view, in which the right thing could be done. Nineveh must be destroyed. To that he had made up his mind, and his whole moral nature was shaken when it appeared that God had another way. 2. His refusing to believe in the efficacy of Divine forbearance. Rough methods of dealing alone are believed in by many—slaves treated with fearful violence—the terrors of the Inquisition brought down on heretics—offence of many at the clemency of Lord Canning after Indian Mutiny—Ireland must be scourged with fire and sword—scoundrels, said Carlyle, must suffer the unmitigated doom of scoundrels. God's methods more merciful —he seeks to win, to humble, to reclaim, to convert. 3. His readiness to sacrifice a vast community to carry out his own idea. His want of regard for human life— a common feeling of the time—in Jonah's view all that vast mass of life was not to be considered, provided a blow was struck that would vindicate his authority, and impress his people. 4. Impatience of spirit, giving birth to rash desires and prayers. Loss of self-control is a very humiliating experience in one who desires to be a servant of God. "He that ruleth his spirit is better than he that taketh a city" (Prov. xvi. 32). But "he that hath no rule over his own spirit is like a city that is broken down, and without walls" (Prov. xxv. 28). How unlike Jonah was now to what he had been before!—W. G. B.

Vers. 5—11.—*God's remonstrance with Jonah.* "So Jonah went out of the city, and sat on the east side of the city, and there made him a booth, and sat under it in the shadow, till he might see what would become of the city," etc. Jonah appears to have gone out of the city and taken up his abode in the booth *before* he knew that Nineveh was to be spared. As Noah entered the ark before the Flood came, and waited for the moment when the judgment of Heaven would verify the warnings of a hundred and twenty years, so Jonah entered his booth before the expiry of the forty days, and waited the moment when the judgment of Heaven would verify *his* warning. We can imagine him speculating on the form the judgment would take: "what would become of the city"—whether it would perish as Sodom and Gomorrah perished, or as the Tower of Babel, or as the walls of Jericho had fallen down in presence of the ark. That something was to happen he appears not to have had the slightest doubt; this may account for his mortification when he found that, after all, the city was to be spared. The revulsion of feeling after his mind had been wound up to the highest pitch of expectation, and the sense of having been befooled before men, may explain the vehemence of his feeling. In rebuking Jonah it pleased God to do so by means of an acted parable—the parable of the gourd.

I. THE GOURD (or *Palma Christi, palmcrist,* as some suppose) PREPARED. (Ver. 6.) Further indication how God is Lord of the whole earth and all therein. This book shows God controlling *things inorganic* (winds and waves, ch. i., and the east wind, ch. iv. 8); *vegetables* (the gourd); *things fortuitous* (the lot); *animals* (the great fish); *reptiles* (the worm); also *men*, both Jonah and the Ninevites. The great object, both of the transactions themselves and of this record of them, is to vindicate the universal sovereignty of God, both natural and moral. The gourd partly natural, partly super- natural; God's purpose in it was to deliver Jonah from his grief. So far as supernatural, a pleasant token that God had not forsaken him. Natural effect to ward off sun, cool the air, prevent feverish irritation, keep mind and body calm and cool. Jonah probably suffered much before it grew up, but would feel immediate relief when it came. Learn herein God's ability to effect important results by simple means—influence of mind on body, and body on mind: "Jonah was exceeding glad of the gourd."

II. THE GOURD DESTROYED. (Ver. 7.) Again an important result due to a trifling cause—a worm. Figuratively and spiritually, "the worm Jacob threshing mountains" (Isa. xli. 15). Apparent collisions and contradictions in nature—one force seems to destroy what another creates—as if there were a Siva as well as a Brahma—in the plan of God all work together—it was alike of God to prepare the gourd and to destroy it—the purposes of Divine discipline often require opposite influences at different times, but all are to be regarded as parts of a gracious plan: "I will sing of mercy and of judgment" (Ps. ci. 1); "All things are yours, whether the world, or life, or death, or things present, or things to come" (1 Cor. iii. 22).

III. JONAH'S VEXATION. (Ver. 8.) Aggravation of his uneasiness by the vehement east wind—whatever comfort of mind might have come through the remarkable origin of the gourd was counteracted by this wind, which seemed a token of God's displeasure —combined distress of body and mind in Jonah—impulsiveness of his nature again apparent—contrast between his two faintings—at ch. ii. 7, "when my soul fainted within me, I remembered the Lord;" here "he fainted, and wished in himself to die"—Jonah his own reprover. The great lesson—we should sit loose to creature comforts, like the gourd—thankful for them while we have them, not repining, and, above all, not despairing, when we lose them. Habakkuk's spirit the model, "Although the fig tree shall not blossom," etc. (iii. 17)—Jonah walked by sight, not by faith; he should have said, "When heart and flesh faint and fail, God is the Strength of my heart, and my Portion for evermore."

> "But O, thou bounteous Giver of all good,
> Thou art of all thy gifts thyself the sum!
> Give what thou mayst, without thee we are poor,
> And with thee rich, take what thou wilt away."

"It is impossible to help 'moralizing' on the worm and the gourd. . . . They are felt inwardly to be emblems, too faithful, of the swift-coursing, closely linked joy and sorrow of this mortal life. The *fine plant*, leafy-green, type of our comforts, successes, joys. The *single* day of shade it furnished to the heated prophet . . . transiency of our pleasure. The *worm* . . . a small and mean creature, may be a very formidable enemy. The *place* of its operations probably under the soil . . . agents unknown to us may smite in secret the sources of prosperity. The *time*—morning—human helps and hopes often wither at any season when most needed. *Utter loss* . . . warning not to set our affections on anything which *can* be utterly lost. . . . The *preparation*, indicating how God orders trials for our good" (Raleigh abridged). "Is it not a blessing when the gourds wither? Is it not a mercy in God to sweep them away, even though the heart should be half broken by the loss? . . . Many will bless God for ever because their gourds were withered. Had the gourd not withered, the soul would not have been saved; and the withering of the gourd therefore makes the anthem of the saved the louder" (Tweedie, 'Man by Nature and by Grace').

IV. GOD'S REMONSTRANCES. (Ver. 9.) Repetition of an old question, and, as before, without evoking a suitable answer. We may note man's self-justifying tendency—especially tendency to excuse passion; excitement of passion is sometimes so great that even a question from God fails to convict—Jonah's mood is so completely self-justifying, that he justifies his wish to die—as if his suffering was really beyond what could be borne. Observe the unbecoming attitude and spirit before God; the true attitude of sinners is that in Rom. iii. 19, "that every mouth might be stopped, and all the world become guilty before God." Silence is the true condition of the sinner, as far as justifying pleas concerned; or, when silence is broken, such words as the publican's, "God be merciful to me a sinner."

V. DIVINE APPLICATION OF THE GOURD-HISTORY. (Vers. 10, 11.) Unexpected, yet felicitous, adaptation of the physical to the moral—light thrown on a dark providence —a foreshadow of revelations of many enigmas of providence yet to come. The argument is *ad hominem*: If Jonah would have spared his gourd, why should God not spare Nineveh? It is also *à fortiori*: If the fate of the gourd, a perishing and trifling thing, was an object of concern to Jonah, *much more* must the fate of such a city as Nineveh be an object of concern to God. Observe the force of the how much more— the *numbers* so different—the *relative endurance* of the two objects—the *labour* bestowed on them—the one *sensitive* beings, the other not. The special reason for sparing Nineveh; it contained more than a hundred and twenty thousand infants, and also much cattle. God's regard for children is here set forth—in these Eastern countries lives of children were little thought of—infanticide was common—in some countries (Moab, etc.) children were made to pass through the fire to their gods—massacres of children common (Judg. ix. 5; 2 Kings ii. 1)—their lives precious in eyes of God, even though pagan and uncircumcised—a foreshadow of the gospel view: "of such is the kingdom of heaven"—children may peradventure ward off great calamities— children in great cities are often neglected—immense proportion of deaths occurs under the age of five—mostly due to preventible causes—hence sanitary reform becomes a great duty—laws of healthy upbringing of children are most important— spiritual and moral oversight not less so—the New Testament rule is, "Bring them up in the nurture and admonition of the Lord." God's regard for cattle—he likes to see them enjoying life—shrinks from what needlessly entails or destroys it—thoughtless and needless infliction of suffering and death on animals is a great sin in God's eye. The prophet is silenced now—he opens not his mouth.

The narrative ends somewhat abruptly; but leaves two great truths full in view—the littleness of man; the greatness of God. The littleness even of a good man, one who in his deliberate judgment and inmost soul honoured God, and sought to serve him, but was very excitable, and could not subdue the poor impulses of the lower part of his nature. The greatness of God, Lord of the earth and the sea, caring for his creatures, not willing that they should perish, but that they should be saved. Especially the greatness of God in clemency, compassion, sparing mercy; for the very attributes that Jonah depreciated are as real as they are noble: " a gracious God and merciful, slow to anger, and of great kindness, and repentest thee of the evil." This is emphatically the gospel aspect of God's character : "just, and the Justifier of him that believeth in Jesus "—rich in mercy and great in love, sending his Son into the world, " that whosoever believeth in him should not perish, but should have everlasting life." Let us cherish the view of the Divine character that Jonah disparaged ; it is the only hope for us sinners. And again let us remember how the men of Nineveh have not passed entirely off the scene, for, as our Lord said, " The men of Nineveh shall rise up in judgment against the men of this generation, and shall condemn them; for they repented at the preaching of Jonah; and, behold, a greater than Jonah is here."—W. G. B.

Vers. 1—5.—*Jonah's grief.* There "sat" Jonah, watching, displeased with the Ninevites' preservation, grieved at the gentle dealings of their Preserver. And God's only rebuke of him was the gentle question, " Doest thou *well* to be angry ? " In his mood and conduct let us read our own.

I. OUR DISPLEASURE. Have *we* never been displeased with God's ways? It may have been as patriots. It is easy to be resigned to judgments that come upon our country's enemies. We must beware—beware lest we encourage in ourselves the belief that the great work of God among nations to-day is to do all for the glory of England. Jonah was displeased that his country's enemies should be spared. Yet God spared them. In our own personal history have we never been displeased with God?—displeased that prosperity has been denied us, who could so wisely have used it? displeased that losses and afflictions have impoverished us, when they seemed so much more *needed* by others who have been free from them? displeased to lose our *one* child, when in other homes the many are spared? displeased, it may be, that even the one has been denied us? Have we never charged God foolishly?

II. OUR GRIEF. Jonah was " very grieved " that the Ninevites should be spared. Better, he deemed, that they should perish. Better for Israel thus to be quit of an enemy. Better for God, as thus vindicating his righteousness. Better for Jonah himself —thus accredited as a prophet of truth. Grieved; but what is he doing with his memory? He, such a sinner against the light, had been spared; then why not these repentant heathen? Ungrateful Jonah! But why wonder at him ? Have we not forgotten the Divine goodness? Have we not been grieved at God's dealings? Even in his work how thwarted! How little credit do we get to what we expected! And the work does not prosper in *our way*. Have we never been grieved, angry, with God?—that that great and good man should be taken away in the midst of his days? that that youth of high promise should be cut down when the bright bud was just showing the brilliant flower? that God's work, where most successful, should be threatened with hindrance and *be* hindered? that our work for him should be obstructed, and we get so little commendation for it when we had deemed we deserved it so much? Grieved—and therein the evil—by regarding *God* as at fault.

III. OUR WAYWARD PRAYER. Jonah longed to die. His work seemed to fail because Nineveh was spared. Fail? No; it was a transcendently glorious success. A sublime and ever-memorable proof of the Divine mercy. An abiding encouragement to all coming workers for God. So our work, when *we* count it a failure, may in God's eyes be " not in vain." How we bear ourselves in severe trials of faith will show what spirit and character we are of. Let no wayward prayer be ours. In our peevishness and distrust and vexation God says, " Doest thou well to be angry ? " *He* is ever right.

His way is perfect. " Consider Jesus, *lest* ye be wearied and faint in your minds."
What is our grief to his ?

> " O brothers, let us leave the shame and sin
> Of taking vainly, in a plaintive mood,
> The holy name of *grief !*—holy herein,
> That, by the grief of *One*, came all our good."

As with him so with us—the way of the cross is the way to the crown.—G. T. C.

Vers. 6—8.—*Jonah and the gourd.* Welcome was the broad shadow of the gourd
rising round the booth and above it ! The great glare in subdued green light streamed
through the leaves to the calmed and cooled and comforted prophet. Just now he
wished to die. *Now* he was willing to live—" exceeding glad of the gourd." Short-lived
was his gladness. Worm-smitten, the gourd withered. A day of beauty and value, and
then the end of *it*. And now, unsheltered by the plant, exposed to branding sun and
burning wind, Jonah longed again to die. Note here : *Divine discipline.* The gourd, worm,
wind, divinely sent, have each a ministry for the prophet. He needs *correction* if he is
to amend. They are to teach him. But such is the Divine pitifulness that there comes—
I. THE LESSON OF REFRESHMENT. There was sent the gourd " to deliver him from
his grief." He *needed* a shadow. It was given, and the plant shielded him from the
oppressive, life-exhausting heat. The gloom of his mind had been increased by the
heat of the booth ; the outer had aggravated the inner weariness. In the coolness of
the gourd he was calmed and soothed. The mind affects the body, *and* the body the
mind. " Heaviest the heart is in a heavy air." Much mental and even spiritual
depression must be put to the account of physical causes. Jonah sheltered was
cheered and refreshed ; gloom became gladness. Did he rejoice in the gourd ? How,
then, must God rejoice to spare his human creatures ! And did Jonah meanwhile,
" glad of the gourd," with, we may hope, thankfulness to God for it, think that after
all God was favourable to his bitter longing for the punishment if not utter destruction of Nineveh though repentant ? If so, he thought wrongly. Outward prosperity
is no proof of the Divine approval. In doing wrong, in feeling wrong, all may seem
to go well with us ; *still*, it is none the less wrong. Are *we* in accordance with Divine
truth and righteousness—our will in harmony with the Divine ? *Then all* providences
are in reality friendly, and " even the night is light about us."
II. THE LESSON OF BEREAVEMENT. Did Jonah pity, miss, and mourn for the gourd ?
Shall not God have pity on the myriads in Nineveh ? That was the lesson of his loss
to the prophet. But how reluctant to learn it ! We may be bereaved of our strength,
competence, loved ones. Ah ! how *God* is bereaved ! " Shall a man rob God ? "
What multitudes do—of their love, loyalty, service ! He appeals to each. " How can
I give thee up ? " he says. He may take away his gifts. It is the more fully to give
us himself. All earthly gourds will wither. But for all who will, there is an abiding
shelter from every storm ; a *living* shelter—Christ. In him, though the tempests come
of sorrow, bereavement, death, we have peace, safety, and eternal life.—G. T. C.

Vers. 10, 11.—*An argument from human pity to Divine mercy.* Jonah is met on
his own ground. From *his* human compassion comes the irresistible enforcement of
the argument for the Divine mercy. Mark the contrasts.
I. PITY ON THE GOURD ; PITY ON NINEVEH. Useful had been the gourd to Jonah.
It had made life tolerable ; it had gladdened him. He had saddened to see it wither,
sorrowed to see it dead. He had pity on it ; his pity would have spared it. Nor was
he wrong. It is *well* to be unwilling to see aught that has cheered us perish. But if
he was right in his desire to spare that plant, " should not I spare Nineveh ? " asked
God. Should a plant be more than a great city ? *God's* great thought is upon *men*.
How the Divine pity moved over repentant Nineveh ! How the blessed Redeemer
longed to save Jerusalem ! On his last visit, with what other eyes than those of his
disciples did he look upon it !

> " *They* shout for joy of heart,
> But he the King, looks on as one in grief ;
> To heart o'erburdened weeping brings relief,
> The unbidden tear-drops start."

II. Pity on the short-lived gourd; pity on the Ninevites, immortal creatures. That gourd had but the life of a day. Then "the grace of the fashion of it perished." So frail! But look at those multitudes in Nineveh. Few there had so brief a life as the gourd. And all of them were heirs of immortality, passing to an eternal destiny. How the *human* transcends all lower forms of life! Did Jonah pity the short-lived plant? Shall not God pity the ever-living multitude in the city?

III. Pity on the gourd that had cost Jonah nothing; pity on the vast population that God had made and upheld. The gourd "came up over" Jonah; unsought, unhelped by him—*came* to him. He brought it not; he kept it not in life. He had done nothing for it, yet how he mourned its decay! Mark the principle implied in this contrast! This—that we show our value of a thing by the labour we expend upon it. This also—that our sense of the value of a thing, our love to it, *grows* in proportion to our labour for it. How much God had done for the Ninevites! They were all his creatures. If he had not "laboured for" them, he had made them. He was the Fountain of their life. They lived because he held them in life. He could not lightly let them perish; he was their Maker. Jonah had "not made" the gourd to "grow." But God had made the Ninevites to grow; had built them in strength, fed, clothed, preserved them. And, as with us, the more we do for another, the more we love him; so with God and those Ninevites. They were dear to him, and ever dearer because of what he had done for them.

IV. Pity on the one plant; pity on the many-peopled city. *One* plant called out Jonah's yearning tenderness. But what was that to a *man?*—a man made in God's image, "endued with sanctity of reason," dowered with immortality? A man? Here was a city full of men. *God* knew the number. But in this plea he only gives the number of the children. They in their helplessness and innocence were pleas with him for the preservation of the city. Beautiful, effectual priesthood of children! They are unconscious yet mighty intercessors for us. One hundred and twenty thousand of them are in Nineveh. That is a reason why God should spare it. Better that they should live than die. Heaven, to one who has known God's grace and accepted it, temptation and overcome it, who has "served his generation," will be a nobler world than to an infant caught in his unconsciousness to its unexpected bliss. "And much cattle." Not an animal in Nineveh but is worth more than the gourd. Man's Maker is *its* Maker. And he who made man made it *for* man. The very cattle are a plea for the preservation of the city.

Conclusive, unanswerable appeal! Jonah, so ready with his replies, is now speechless. He *saw* that God's way was right. Let *our* pity to things and persons remind us of God's mercy. A mercy almighty and "to everlasting." A mercy revealed in Christ. A mercy to *be accepted.* If not, if rejected, if trifled with till life is trifled away—where, where can we look? There is one Saviour, and no other!—G. T. C.

Ver. 11.—*The unconscious priesthood of children.* The Ninevite little ones effectually, though unwittingly, interceded with God for the preservation of Nineveh. And are not little children *still* unconscious intercessors with God? 1. By their innocence. *They* have not sinned after the similitude of Adam's transgression. 2. By their dependence. Their dependence on God makes them the dearer to God; their dependence on their parents makes their parents the dearer to him. 3. By their undeveloped moral possibilities. What a work in the earth *they* may do for God! "I heard the voice of the Lord, saying, Whom shall I send, and who will go for us? Then said"— Ninevite babe and suckling—"spare me, teach me," and then in the future "send me." —G. T. C.

Ver. 11.—*God's consideration for animals.* The "much cattle" in Nineveh a plea with God for the preservation of the city. And *still*, be animals where they may: 1. God has made them. 2. He preserves them. "His full hand supplies their need." 3. He dowers them with beauty, or swiftness, or strength, with sensibility and sagacity. 4. He makes them of varied serviceableness to man, and has given man authority over them. "Thou madest him to have dominion over all sheep and oxen; yea, and the beasts of the field." 5. "He regardeth the life of the beast;" complacently, in their "lower pleasures;" pitifully, in their "lower pains;" constantly and minutely, "not one falleth on the ground" without him.   6. He would have them preserved from cruelty and needless destruction (Exod. ix. 19).   7. It is God-like to care for the lower animals.

> "He prayeth well who loveth well
> Both man, and bird, and beast.
> He prayeth best who loveth best
> All things both great and small;
> For the dear God, who loveth us,
> He made and loveth all."

G. T. C.

Vers. 6—8.—*The gourd, the worm, and the east wind.*   Jonah was not faultless after his prayer and penitence.   He undertook his work, and boldly proclaimed his message in Nineveh.   His success was beyond expectation.   The whole city was moved, and all the inhabitants fasted, repented, and prayed.   And in the mercy which is ever his delight, God averted the threatened disaster.   "But it displeased Jonah exceedingly, and he was very angry."   He was indignant that his message should appear to be unfulfilled, and angry when he found that he had been the means of saving from destruction the most dangerous foes of his own country.   Any one who reads the history of Europe at the beginning of this century will understand this feeling.   It was with an awful sense of dread that our grandfathers heard that Napoleon had swept into Russia at the head of six hundred and fifty-seven thousand veterans, expecting to return flushed with victory to complete his work of devastation.   When the news came that of all that great host only eighty-five thousand men had escaped from the horrors of war and frost and famine, a jubilant shout of thanksgiving went up to Heaven, led by the Christian Church !   Sinful though Jonah's feeling was, it was not unnatural, and he sat himself down within view of the city, hoping and praying that at least some smaller disaster would befall it.   Our text shows how graciously God sought to bring him to a better state of mind.   The withering of the gourd, like the withering of the fig tree, was intended to be an epitome of human experience.   Let us learn from it—

I. THAT ALL OUR EARTHLY COMFORTS ARE OF GOD'S PROVIDING.   When Jonah set himself to watch what would become of the city, he made for his shelter a booth, formed of the interlaced branches of trees, which imperfectly kept off the heat of the sun.   And God prepared a gourd, whose broad leaves spread over the booth till good protection was given from the scorching heat, which even seasoned Arabs dared not brave; and Jonah was exceeding glad of it.   There was never more danger than there is now of the non-recognition of God's hand in nature and in history.   The clearness with which we see natural phenomena tends to make less credible what is only spiritually discerned.   But happy is the man who finds every blessing sweetened to him by the thought, "God gave me this."   The great purpose of all his dealings with us is to bring us to thought about himself.   Sometimes he turns us back to duty, as Jonah was turned, by a storm; and sometimes he brings us back to a right mind, as Jonah was brought, by a blessing—strangely coming, and then as strangely going.

II. THAT OUR EARTHLY BLESSINGS ARE OF SHORT DURATION.   Their brevity is as much God's appointment as their existence.   Notice the emphatic declarations in our text: "*The Lord* prepared a gourd;" "*The Lord* prepared a worm;" "*The Lord* prepared a vehement east wind."   In other words, the blessing and the cause of its removal both emanated from him.   1. *The gourd withered when Jonah reckoned most confidently on enjoying it.*   It is so with our blessings too.   Examples: The wealth amassed with such difficulty seems secure at last, but unexpectedly it vanishes.   The child nursed through all the perils of a weakly childhood dies in the fulness of manhood's strength, etc.   2. *The gourd withered from a small and secret cause.*   A worm at the root killed it.   Little things, preventible things, as we think them, often cause our losses.   We may be ruined by some one we never saw, and of whom we never heard.   A noble reputation may be blasted by a silly slander.   Yet there is no awful fate blindly striking hither and thither; there is no hostile power supreme over human events.   Of every loss we may say, "The Lord gave, and the Lord hath taken away; blessed be the Name of the Lord."

III. THAT TROUBLES SELDOM COME ALONE. It was bad enough to lose the shelter of the gourd, but it was worse to find a vehement east wind springing up just after it withered—not one like ours, cutting in its keenness, but one singularly depressing and relaxing in its effects. It came over the burning desert sands; it drank up fire by the way; it dried the skin, and filled the pores with dust, and beat upon the wayfarer like the blast of a furnace. Jonah found it the more unbearable because his shelter was gone. Sorrow comes on sorrow—financial anxiety, domestic bereavement, impaired health, unexpected loss, following each other till our souls are overwhelmed. But God is patient with us, in spite of our angry thoughts; he pities our passionate weeping, and waits till we can say with him who in his agony prayed yet more earnestly, "Thy will, not mine, be done."

CONCLUSION. While Jonah was pitying the gourd whose beautiful leaves were withered, and was grieving over the loss of its shade, God pointed him from it to Nineveh, and said, "If you sorrow over this, how much more do I sorrow over that? You have not laboured for this gourd, but I have laboured for that city. The gourd could never be worth much, but what might not Nineveh be if only its people were redeemed from sin?" Thus would he point us from the contemplation of life's sadness to the contemplation of its sin. He would remind us that as we would sacrifice anything to save the life of one we love, so he has given his only Son to save us from sin and death eternal.—A. R.

Vers. 6—8.—*Emblems of man's earthly good, and God's disciplinary procedure.* "And the Lord God prepared a gourd, and made it to come up over Jonah, that it might be a shadow over his head, to deliver him from his grief. So Jonah was exceeding glad of the gourd," etc. I shall use these verses as presenting an emblem of man's earthly good, and an emblem of God's disciplinary procedure.

I. AS AN EMBLEM OF MAN'S EARTHLY GOOD. I take the "gourd" to represent this. What this plant was, whether it was, as some suppose, a kind of cucumber, which sprang swiftly from the soil, and covered the booth which Jonah had reared and under which he sat, or a kind of ivy that crept up and overshadowed his dwelling, or some plant of more rapid growth and more luxuriant foliage, it matters not. We are told the Lord "prepared" it. It was some indigenous plant, characterized by a speedy growth and abundant leafage, and whose growth, perhaps, was stimulated by a Divine infusion of an unusual amount of vegetative force. It was a great blessing at the time to Jonah. It screened him from the rays of the Oriental sun, and refreshed his sight with its verdure. And it is said that "Jonah was exceeding glad of the gourd." He felt that it was good. Now, this gourd was like man's earthly good in three aspects—in its development, its decay, and destruction. 1. *In its development.* (1) It came out of the earth. The gourd was not a plant sent down directly from heaven. It grew out of the soil. So with all our worldly good. From the earth come all our granaries, our wardrobes, our houses, and all that blesses our material existence. It is all out of the earth. (2) It came out of the earth by Divine agency. It was not the less a Divine gift because it seemed to grow in a natural way. God produced it. He "*prepared*" it. All the earthly good we possess, even that for which we have laboured with the greatest skill and persistent industry, is the gift of God. He it is that gives us our daily bread, and that furnishes us with food and raiment. 2. *In its decay.* "But God prepared a worm when the morning rose the next day, and it smote the gourd that it withered." Not long, perhaps only a few hours, had the gourd spread its shady and refreshing influence over Jonah's dwelling-place before the worm began to gnaw at its vitals and soon smote it. Mark the decaying agent, a "worm." (1) How *mean!* It was not some huge quadruped of the wild, or some royal bird from the craggy cliffs or towering forests, but a worm. The work of destruction is very easy. We are crushed "before the moth." (2) How *prompt!* Decay commenced at once. "When the morning rose the next day" it had done its work. The worm of decay begins its work with the commencement of our earthly good. It gnaws at the foundation of mansions as soon as they are built, at friendships as soon as they are formed, at life as soon as it begins. "As soon as we begin to live we all begin to die." This worm of decay is working everywhere. (3) How *secret!* It works unseen, underground. It gnaws at the vital roots. It is an unseen agent. Who sees the worm that strips the trees in autumn, that steals strength from the strongest animal, and gnaws away the life of the youngest? Verily man and all his earthly good is being "destroyed from morning to evening." 3. *In its destruction.* "God prepared a vehement east wind; and the sun beat upon the head of Jonah, that he fainted, and wished in himself to die." "This wind," says an old expositor, "was not as a fan to abate the heat, but as a bellows to make it more intense." It may be that this vehement east wind was that terrible simoom which was common in that land, and which smote the four corners of the house in which Job's children were. How desolate is the prophet now! The burning beams of the sun are beating on his head. His booth is destroyed, his gourd is withered to the roots, and the east wind like a breath of fire is drying up the current of life. His existence became intolerable. He wished in himself to die. Here, then, is a picture of our earthly good. However abundant in its nature and delicious in its enjoyment, like this gourd it must go from us. The worm will gnaw out its existence and the east wind will utterly destroy it, and when it is gone and we are stripped of everything but sheer existence, unless Christ is formed in us the Hope of glory, our life will be intolerable, and we shall seek for death as our only relief.

II. As an emblem of God's disciplinary procedure. The Eternal, in order to get Jonah into a right state of mind, employs a variety of agency. It is suggested: 1. *That God disciplines man by facts.* Precepts and theories are powerless in the human soul compared with actual facts. "I have heard of thee," says Job, "by the hearing of the ear, but now mine eye seeth thee." Nature is a system of facts. Human life is an experience of facts, the Bible is a record of facts, and by facts God disciplines the human soul. The gourd was a fact, the worm was a fact, the east wind was a fact, and these facts went down to the centre of Jonah's soul. 2. *That these facts are varied in their character.* Here was the pleasant and the painful. The gourd, how pleasant! the simoom and burning sun, how painful! So now God employs the *pleasurable* and the *painful* to discipline our souls to virtue. He employs the *small* and the *great.* Here was the insignificant worm and vehement wind. "Lo, all these things worketh God oftentimes with man, to bring back his soul from the pit, to be enlightened with the light of the living" (Job xxxiii. 29, 30). 3. *That these facts are adapted to their end.* Jonah did not wish that mercy should be shown to the Ninevites. He desired their destruction. This was his state of mind, and a bad state of mind it was, and God dealt with it by giving him a lesson in personal suffering. He taught him what suffering was.

Conclusion. 1. Let us not trust in *earthly good.* It is but a mere gourd. It must wither and rot. "All flesh is grass." Trust in righteousness. "Trust in him that liveth for ever." 2. Let us *improve under the disciplinary influences of Heaven.* Life is a moral school, a school in which the great Father seeks to make his children meet for the "inheritance of the saints in light."—D. T.

Vers. 9—11.—*God reasoning with man.* "And God said to Jonah, Doest thou well to be angry for the gourd?" etc. The whole Book of Jonah develops at least the following truths: 1. *That the regard of Heaven, even under the old dispensation, was not confined to the Jews.* Jonah was sent to Nineveh, a city far away from Judæa, whose population had neither kinship nor sympathy with the Jewish people. It is represented as a bloody city, full of lies and robbery, its ferocious violence to captives is portrayed in its own monuments. The opinion that once prevailed very extensively in the Christian world, and which still prevails to a certain extent, that the Eternal Father confined his interest and communications entirely to the descendants of Abraham, is without foundation; Nineveh, Egypt, and Babylon were as dear to him as Jerusalem. He revealed himself to Pharaoh as well as to Moses, and to Nebuchadnezzar as well as to Daniel. 2. *That wickedness, if persisted in, must end in ruin.* "Arise," says Jehovah to Jonah, "go ... to Nineveh, and cry against it; for their wickedness is come up before me." And because of its wickedness it was on the verge of destruction. So it ever is, sin leads to ruin. "The wages of sin is death." 3. *That true repentance will rescue a people from their threatened doom.* Though the ruin of Nineveh seemed all but settled to take place in about forty days, yet because it repented the terrible doom was averted. "When God saw their works, that they had repented of their evil ways, he repented of the evil he said he would do unto them; and he did it not" (ch. iii. 10). It is ever so. "Let the wicked forsake his way, and the unrighteous man his thoughts: and let him return unto the Lord, and he will have mercy upon him; and to our God, for he will abundantly pardon." Amongst the many remarkable and suggestive passages in this book, not the least striking and significant is that which I have now selected for meditation. I shall employ it to illustrate the amazing interest God takes in mankind. This is seen—

I. IN HIS REASONING WITH A MAN WHO IS IN A BAD TEMPER. That the "High and Holy One that inhabiteth eternity" should notice individual man at all is a condescension transcending our conceptions, but that he should now enter into an argument with one who is under the influence of a bad temper is still more marvellous. Jonah was "angry," and the intensity of his anger became so intolerable that he wished to die. "Therefore now, O Lord, take my life, I beseech thee; for it is better to die than to live." Why was he angry? 1. *Because of the Divine compassion shown to the Ninevites.* Jonah had proclaimed their destruction in forty days, and fully perhaps did he expect that the truthfulness of his word would be attested by the fact. But the forty days passed away, and no thunderbolt of destruction came; it was preserved, and preserved by God because it repented. It seems that he would sooner have seen Nineveh in ruins than have had his word falsified before the people. His vanity was wounded. He thought more of his own reputation than of the lives of a teeming population. "Doest thou well to be angry?" The question implies a negative. "No; thou doest ill; thine anger is a sinful anger." There is a righteous anger; hence we are commanded to "be angry and sin not." Indignation against falsehood and meanness and selfishness and impiety is a holy passion—a passion that must often flame out in all pure hearts in passing through a world of corruption like this. This, however, was not the anger of Jonah; his anger implied vanity, heartlessness, and irreverence. 2. *Because of the loss of a temporal blessing.* The gourd that grew up in a night and mantled his tent with its luxurious leafage, thus sheltering him from the rays of the burning sun, was felt by him one of his greatest temporal blessings. "He was exceeding glad of the gourd." That was now taken from him, the worm gnawed it to death, and as the hot simoom rushed at him, and the rays of the burning sun beat upon his head, he deeply felt its loss, and he was angry; he was angry with God for depriving him of this blessing. He was thus angry with the Almighty for showing compassion to the Ninevites, and also for depriving him of this temporal blessing. His anger seems to have been not a passing emotion, not a momentary flame, but a fire that rendered his life unbearable. "Let me die," he says. The passions of the soul have often extinguished the natural love of life and snapped the mystic cord that unites the body to the soul. Now, is it not wonderful that the great God should condescend to reason with a man in such a state of mind? Man is wont either to shun the individual who is indignant with him, or to hurl anathemas at his head. Not so the Infinite Father. Calmly and lovingly he reasons with his indignant enemy. "Come now, and let us reason together, saith the Lord: though your sins be as scarlet, they shall be as white as snow."

II. IN HIS REASONING WITH A MAN WHO IS IN A BAD TEMPER IN ORDER TO IMPRESS HIM WITH THE REALITY OF HIS COMPASSION. "Then said the Lord, Thou hast had pity on the gourd, for the which thou hast not laboured, neither madest it grow; which came up in a night, and perished in a night: and should not I spare Nineveh, that great city, wherein are more than six score thousand persons that cannot discern between their right hand and their left hand; and also much cattle?" The Almighty here argues from Jonah's pity for the gourd—the plant—to his compassion for Nineveh. The argument is from the less to the greater. If you, Jonah, feel pity for that mere vegetable production which you had for a few hours only, and which you yourself did not produce, conceive of my compassion for the inhabitants of Nineveh. The comparison here implied between the plant and Nineveh may be expressed in three questions. 1. *What is this one plant to the men that inhabit Nineveh?* What is the grandest production in the vegetable world, the most stately and symmetrical tree towering as the king of the forest, to one human being? The tree is the production of the earth, cannot think of its Creator, cannot itself alter its own position, is the mere creature of external influences, and must exhaust itself by its own growth; but man is the offspring of the Infinite, capable of tracing his existence to its Source, having the power to move as he pleases, and endowed with powers inexhaustible, and ever-increasing development! But if a plant is nothing to one man, what is it to the thousands of men that are found in Nineveh? You, Jonah, would have spared the one plant: shall not I spare the million of men? 2. *What is this one plant even to the unconscious infants in Nineveh?* "Wherein are more than six score thousand persons that cannot discern between their right hand and their left hand." What is one plant to a hundred and twenty thousand unconscious infants? Out of those infants will grow sages, poets, saints, kings and priests unto God. What men, in visiting cities, concern themselves with the babes that breathe therein? And yet the purest, divinest, most influential portion of the population are the babes. The great Father regards the infant population. His blessed Son, when here, took babes in his arms, and said, "Of such is the kingdom of heaven." Even one babe is of more worth in the universe than the whole vegetable kingdom. 3. *What is one plant to even the irrational creatures in Nineveh?* "Also much cattle." Though the cattle are below children in the scale of being, they are greater than plants. They are endowed with sensibilities; they have locomotive powers; and for their use the vegetable kingdom exists. God has an interest in the brute creation. "He openeth his liberal hand, and supplies the need of every living thing." He feeds the cattle on the hills, makes provision for the finny tribes of ocean, feeds the fowls of heaven, and prepares nourishment even for the world of microscopic existences. If God thus regards those creatures, with what kindness should we treat them, taking care that they suffer not, either from want of food or the cruelty of man! Such is a brief and imperfect sketch of the argument here employed to impress Jonah with God's compassion for Nineveh. To use the language of another, "It is very beautiful; if you linger over it, planting your feet in the steps of it, touching the several links of it as you pass along, you will say it is beautiful. The skilfulness with which it is introduced, the forbearance with which it is conducted, the condescending regard to the prophet's infirmities, the recognition of human excellence, the delicate allusions, the precious truths hidden in them, the accumulation of force as the argument goes on, the comprehensive linking of the different worlds of life to each other—plants, animals, infants, men—the easy transition from one to another, the abruptness of the close, too, indicating in its own way the completeness of the triumph,—all these proclaim the argument Divine."

CONCLUSION. What subject is more suited to cheer and sustain our hearts amid the somewhat saddening associations connected, for instance, with the closing of the year, than the truth that the great God is lovingly interested in mankind? Every year as it passes bears away objects once most dear, the companions of our youth, and the dear friends of our riper years. And how dark, dreary, and depressed we might feel without the assurance that amidst all these changes and bereavements the great Father lives on, and feels the deepest and most vital interest in our weal! Though years, as they roll on, take away from us, and from our world, those whom we have known and loved, the great Father continues here. He has not withdrawn from the world and left it in an orphan state, dreary and desolate. He is here—here with every human being, here reasoning with the thoughtless, enlightening the ignorant, consoling the sad, strengthening the weak, guiding the perplexed, restoring the lost.

> "God liveth ever!
> Wherefore, soul, despair thou never!
> What though thou tread with bleeding feet
> 　A thorny path of grief and gloom,
> Thy God will choose the way most meet
> To lead thee heavenward, to lead thee home;
> 　For this life's long night of sadness
> 　He will give thee peace and gladness.
> 　　Soul, forget not in thy pains,
> 　　God o'er all for ever reigns."

D. T.

HOMILETICAL INDEX

TO

THE BOOK OF JONAH

MICAH

EXPOSITION BY

W. J. DEANE

HOMILETICS BY

S. D. HILLMAN

HOMILIES BY VARIOUS AUTHORS

E. S. PROUT   A. ROWLAND

D. THOMAS

THE BOOK OF MICAH

INTRODUCTION

§ I. SUBJECT OF THE BOOK

THE Book of Micah, in our present Hebrew copies and in the Latin Vulgate, stands sixth among the minor prophets; in the Septuagint it is placed third. Collected apparently into one volume in the last year of the prophet's life, it contains a number of prophecies uttered, perhaps, at different times, but yet connected together by logical sequence, and displaying a certain symmetrical arrangement. Caspari suggests that he thus gathered the notes of his various discourses, and read them in the ears of the people, in order to assist Hezekiah's great reformation. Threatening and promise alternate in these addresses, upbraiding and pleading, judgment and mercy. There is very much that is common with Isaiah, and the actual words in both are often identical. Being contemporaries, and confronted with the same circumstances, the two prophets naturally use corresponding expressions in dealing with similar subjects. In his account of the moral corruption that prevails, Micah agrees thoroughly with Isaiah, though he differs from him in not touching on politics, and in taking a more hopeless view of the reformation of Israel; in his Messianic anticipations he is as clear and precise as the evangelical prophet himself. Both he and Isaiah look to the great world-empire as fatal to Israel, though Micah calls it in one place (ch. v. 5, etc.) by the current name of Assyria, and in other passages, Babylon.

The state of Judah before Hezekiah's reformation was most unsatisfactory. Apart from the idolatry which was at the bottom of all the evil that prevailed, we gather from the prophet's denunciations that the chiefs of the nation were proud, luxurious, unscrupulous, and cruel; the peasants were ground down by exactions and deprived of their legal rights. And the improvement in religion which Hezekiah effected had not extended very deep, nor produced that real impression which we are wont to assume. "High places" still remained; practical unbelief widely existed; coincident with the worship of Jehovah a virtual idolatry was practised. Looking sadly on all this evil, Micah knew to what result it tended, and his warnings were embittered by the consciousness that the punishment which he foretold was righteously deserved, and would not now be averted by timely repentance.

The book is arranged, for rhetorical purposes, into three prophetical addresses, consisting of words uttered originally at various times, as the Spirit within moved the prophet to speak. The three portions have a generally distinctive character and a certain inward connection. The first is chiefly of a threatening nature; in the second, Messianic hopes predominate; the third is hortatory, urging to repentance under God's chastening hand, in remembrance of past mercies and promised salvation.

Micah begins with a grand description of the coming of the Lord to judge Israel and Judah for their sins and idolatry, when Samaria, as first in wickedness, shall be first to fall before the avenging enemy; and then a similar fate shall happen to Jerusalem and Judæa (whose towns are not mentioned in strictly geographical order), with the deportation of their inhabitants. The sins of the grandees have brought this judgment upon them. There are found in them oppression, injustice, and violence. The false prophets only pander to their evil lusts, and lull them into false security; and the penalty of all this guilt shall be removal from their present home. But God will not cast them off altogether; for they shall yet one day be restored in triumph (ch. i., ii.).

In the second part the prophet, showing the necessity of the judgment, more particularly rebukes the cruelty and rapacity of the great men; denounces woe on the false prophets who led the people astray; on the priests who taught for hire; on the judges who sold their sentences, and the diviners who practised their cheating art for lucre. In requital for these enormities, Zion the royal seat, Jerusalem the holy city, and the temple the house of God, should be brought to desolation. Then a contrast is introduced. This triple overthrow shall be compensated by a triple restoration. The people shall return from captivity, and the Lord's house shall be raised on high, and the nations shall flock unto it to learn piety and true religion; Jerusalem shall be inhabited again, increased and beautified; the royal power shall again be seated in Zion; Jehovah himself shall reign there in the midst of universal peace, having overthrown all the peoples who once rejoiced in Judah's calamity. The Redeemer shall be born in Bethlehem; his kingdom shall extend to the ends of the earth; but all idolatry, all trust in the arm of flesh, must be removed before the great consummation shall occur (ch. iii.—v.).

In the last part, which differs from the preceding portions in being of a more subjective character, Jehovah is represented as holding a controversy or lawsuit with his people, justifying his conduct, and listening to their rejoinder, which is so far from being satisfactory that judgment is pronounced upon them. Then, in touching words, Micah, identifying himself with the people, acknowledges the justice of the sentence, while he bewails its infliction; he repents of the sins which have occasioned this punishment, looks patiently to God, and puts his sole trust in him, and, in answer to his prayers, is rewarded by the promise of deliverance. The book concludes with a triumphal song, celebrating the victory which God will achieve, and praising the mercy and faithfulness which he always has shown to his people (ch. vi., vii.).

Such is a general sketch of the contents of this book. We may note, besides, that in it are contained many special predictions; viz. the destruction of Samaria by Shalmaneser and his successor Sargon (ch. i. 6, 7); the invasion of Judah by Sennacherib (ch. i. 9—16); the overthrow of Jerusalem and the temple (ch. iii. 12; vii. 13); the deportation to Babylon (ch. iv. 10); the return from exile; the peace and happiness under a theocratic government, and the spiritual supremacy of Israel (ch. iv. 1—8, 13; vii. 11, 14—17); the Ruler born at Bethlehem, of the family of David (ch. iv. 8; v. 2); and, as it seems, the destruction of Nineveh and Babylon (ch. v. 5, 6; vii. 8, 10). To Isaiah and Micah belong the two clearest and most unmistakable prophecies of the Messiah. Isaiah describes his birth of the Virgin; Micah pointed out the place of his birth so plainly that when the Wise Men came inquiring where the King of the Jews was born, the answer was given to Herod without hesitation, " In Bethlehem of Judæa; for thus it is written by the prophet " (Matt. ii. 5). Further, Micah declares that the time of Messiah shall be one of profound peace (ch. iv. 1—7), using the same words as Isaiah (ii. 2, etc.). He intimates that the glory of Messiah shall be won by suffering (ch. iv. 8—13); he speaks of his work and his power (ch. v. 1—3); and he depicts the kingdom of Messiah in its exterior and interior organization (ch. v. 4, 8, etc.).

§ II. Author.

The name Micah (Μιχαίας: Μειχαίας, Sin.; Michaeas or Micha, Vulgate), a shortened form of Michaia (Jer. xxvi. 18), and in its original shape Michajahu, is not uncommon in the Old Testament (Judg. xvii. 1; 2 Chron. xiii. 2; xvii. 7; Jer. xxxvi. 11, etc.); but none of the other persons so called are of much note in the sacred story save Micaiah the son of Imlah, who prophesied so boldly in the days of Ahab (1 Kings xxii.). It is probably to distinguish him from this last-named personage that the minor prophet is termed " Micah the Morasthite," i.e. a native of Moresheth-Gath. The LXX., indeed, in ch. i. 1, treat the appellation as a patronymic, τὸν τοῦ Μωρασθεί (Μωραθεί, Alex.); but in Jer. xxxiii. 18 (xxvi. 18, Hebrew) they give Μιχαίας ὁ Μωραθίτης: and there is no doubt that the latter rendering is correct. Moresheth, elsewhere (Josh. xv. 44; 2 Chron. xi. 8), as some say, called Mareshah, was noticed by St. Jerome as a small village near Eleutheropolis. It is now known as Mer'ash, a village on a tel about a mile south-east of Beit-Jibrin, which Dr. Thomson (' Land and the Book,' pp. 210, 214, etc.), after Robinson, identifies with Eleutheropolis, and considers with great plausibility, to be the site of the more ancient Gath. "Micah refers to Moresheth as though it was a suburb of Gath (ch. i. 10, 14). By coupling the two names together, he wrote Moresheth-Gath, probably in order to fix the place of the less-known suburb by the name of the main city."

The name *Micah* signifies, "Who is like Jehovah?" We are reminded by it of the challenge in Moses' song (Exod. xv. 11), "Who is like unto thee, O Lord, among the gods? who is like thee?" and it is doubtless with reference to his own name that the prophet introduces the announcement of God's great mercy with the words, "Who is a God like unto thee?" (ch. vii. 18). The name of Micah's father is not given, so that he was probably of mean origin, most likely a peasant, as Amos; and no events of his life are recorded. Whatever can be known about him must be gathered from his own writings; and this is very little. He was a Judæan, and prophesied at Jerusalem. This latter fact we infer not only from the mention of the kings Jotham, Ahaz, and Hezekiah, under whom he is said to have exercised his ministry, but from the circumstance that he condemns chiefly the corruptions of the city, and makes Zion the central point of his prophecies, as it was the main seat of the evils against which he contended. He suffered great opposition at the hands of the false prophets (ch. ii. 6), who were now beginning to exert that disastrous influence which culminated in the time of Jeremiah. Disobedience to God's enactments had always been common, but organized hostility to God's prophets had not hitherto been the normal state of things. Micah was destined to exercise his powers under obloquy and contradiction. He seems, however, to have gone to the grave in peace, before the fall of Samaria, in the early part of Hezekiah's reign. His birthplace was, according to Jerome (Ep. 86, 'Ad Eustoch.'), also the place of his burial, on the site of which, in Christian times, a church was built. Sozomen ('Hist. Eccles.,' vii. 28) relates that his remains and those of Habakkuk were discovered, in the reign of Theodosius, at a place called Berathsatia (probably the same as Morasthi), ten stadia from Cila, his tomb being called by the ignorant natives, in their own dialect, *Nephsameemana*, which he interprets μνῆμα πιστόν, "monumentum fidele."

§ III. Date.

The superscription of our book states that Micah prophesied "in the days of Jotham, Ahaz, and Hezekiah, kings of Judah." Modern critics see reason to doubt whether this title, as well as the similar ones in Hosea and Isaiah (which, however, contain the name of Uzziah), are genuine. They deem them to be later additions introduced by an unknown editor. In the present case the superscription is confirmed by the contents of the book. Jotham came to the throne in B.C. 757; Hezekiah died in 697; and thus the greatest limit attributed to his ministry would be sixty years; while the interval from the last year of Jotham to the first of Hezekiah, B.C. 742—726, allows a period of sixteen years as the minimum duration of his prophetical activity. In either case he is contemporary with Isaiah, and with the latter portion of the ministry of Amos and Hosea. We have a testimony concerning his date in Jer. xxvi. 18, where certain elders of the land appeal to the case of Micah as one who asserted unpopular truths in the time of Hezekiah, without incurring the charge of blasphemy. "Micah the Morasthite," said they, "prophesied in the days of Hezekiah King of Judah, and spake to all the people of Judah, saying, Thus saith the Lord of hosts; Zion shall be ploughed like a field," etc., quoting ch. iii. 12. But this assertion need not be taken as necessarily restricting all his utterances to Hezekiah's reign. The elders had a traditional report that his prophecies originated in that period; "He was habitually prophesying," is their expression; but that no part of the collection was published before that time cannot be proved by this particular reference. It seems probable that the various prophecies, orally delivered on different occasions, were committed to writing and gathered into one volume in the earlier years of King Hezekiah. There really is no sufficient reason for doubting the accuracy of the superscription. The contents of the book are quite consistent with what we know of the condition of the Jewish people in the reigns enumerated. The mention of "the high places" still existing, and the corruption and demoralization of the people (ch. i. 5; ii.), points to the reigns of Jotham and Ahaz as the period when the first section of the book was originally delivered (see 2 Kings xv. 35; xvi. 4; 2 Chron. xxviii. 4, 25). The prophecy of the destruction of Samaria (ch. i. 6) must have been delivered before the final capture of that city by the Assyrians, B.C. 722, in the fourth or sixth year of Hezekiah. Other allusions serve to supply an approximation to the date of different portions of the prophecy. We have seen that ch. iii. was uttered in Hezekiah's day. In ch. v. 10 Micah declaims against the chariots and horses of Judah, which were doubtless accumulated during the prosperous reign of Uzziah, and on which his successor Jotham prided himself (2 Chron. xxvi. 11—15; xxvii. 4—6; Isa. ii. 7). When he bitterly complains of "the statutes of Omri," and "the works of the house of Ahab" (ch. vi. 16), he is denouncing the king who is expressly stated to have "walked in the ways of the kings of Israel" (2 Kings xvi. 3). It is more likely to have been in Ahaz's time than in Jotham's that idolatrous rites were practised in Jerusalem itself; for the latter is commended because he walked in the steps of his father Uzziah, and "ordered his ways before the Lord his God" (2 Kings xv. 34; 2 Chron. xxvii. 2, 6); and the allusion to human sacrifice (ch. vi. 7) befits the time of Ahaz, who sacrificed his own sons to Moloch (2 Kings xvi. 3; 2 Chron. xxviii. 3), and whose example was probably followed by others. That half-service, too, of which Micah complains (ch. iii. 11; vi. 6), when the people, in the midst of their idolatry and wickedness, yet in some sort "leaned upon the Lord," exactly suits the character of Ahaz, who, though he copied heathen altars, resorted to the brazen altar to inquire of the Lord (2 Kings xvi. 15), and offered thereon the lawful sacrifice. The prophecy of the destruction of Jerusalem, delivered first under Jotham, was repeated under Hezekiah, and it is to its impressive effect at that time that the elders in Jeremiah allude. Doubtless, too, in those early years of Hezekiah his ministry came to an end. The denunciations of idolatry would not have been uttered after the great, though partial, reformation of religion, which, indeed, could not have been fully carried out till Samaria was destroyed; for otherwise Hezekiah's messengers would not have been able unhindered to invite all Israel to join in the celebration of the Passover (Pusey). Of the parallel passages, ch. iv. 1—5 and Isa. ii. 2—5, it has been much debated which is the original and which the copy; but there seems to be no valid reason for supposing that Micah received the words from Isaiah; and as the passage in the former book occurs in close connection and contrast with what immediately precedes, while in Isaiah the connection is not obvious, most critics believe that the words were originally delivered by Micah; or it may be, as Ewald and others suggest, that both prophets adapted to their own purposes an older prophecy current in their days. That there is a close connection between Isaiah and Micah is obvious. It may be that the two prophets addressed different classes of the populace—Isaiah delivering his messages to the higher, Micah to the lower, with which by descent his sympathies were closely connected; but they worked harmoniously together, strengthening the hands of Hezekiah, and confirming the faithful in their difficult course of obedience and trust.

Some critics have attributed ch. vi. and vii. to another hand and a later date. Certainly they do not suit the time of Hezekiah; but they may have been composed earlier, under other circumstances, and placed where they are now found, not as fitting their present position chronologically, but as aiding the rhetorical arrangement of the book, enforcing the previous menaces and confirming the promised triumph. Other passages, the genuineness of which is disputed, will be noticed in the Exposition.

§ IV. General Character of the Work.

The style of the Book of Micah is remarkable. It is rough, as befitting its peasant author, but it is certainly not uncultivated; rugged, perhaps, but pure, clear, and intelligible. It abounds in tropes, figures, paronomasias. It contains sudden transitions of subjects, persons, numbers, genders, which denote in the writer a quick temper and an excitable mind, carried away by inward impulse, and restrained by no formal rules of composition. Micah is at times bold, severe, stern, uncompromising; at times tender, sorrowful, loving, sympathetic. In him mercy rejoices against judgment. Brief and concise in his description of misery, he dilates with exuberance on the blessings that are to follow the day of darkness. He delights in comparing God's tenderness and regard for his people with a shepherd's care for his flock. Those who should head the resistance to the great world-power are " seven shepherds " (ch. v. 5). His last prayer to God is, " Feed thy people with thy rod, the flock of thine heritage " (ch. vii. 14). He does not so much preach repentance as set forth God's dealings to persons who knew that he pardons as well as punishes. It is this strong conviction of the intimate connection between sin and punishment, repentance and forgiveness, which occasions those startling transitions that meet us, as we have said, so continually; where, with the simple conjunction "and," and with no further logical dependence, the prophet contrasts wickedness with its results, punishment with blessing, mercy with comfort. There is wonderful energy in the various forms of his addresses. The last two chapters "take the form of a magnificent colloquy, and are indeed the first prophetic piece of a purely dramatic plan and execution" (Farrar). Elsewhere at one time he commands, at another he entreats; now he uses dialogue, now denunciation; he addresses the whole people under a female designation, then he expostulates with individuals; here he speaks concerning a place, there directly to it; one while he speaks in his own person, and again in that of his nation; he describes a calamity as past in one passage, as future in another. As regards his language, it is measured and rhythmical, the cadences are varied, the grouping is harmonious. A remarkable analysis of these divisions and cadences, both in Micah and other prophets, may be seen in Dr. Pusey's 'Commentary,' pp. 273, 293. The verbal plays and allusions in the description of the calamities that are to overtake Judah (ch. i.) are unequalled in vigour and abundance, and must have fallen with peculiar force upon hearers familiar with the places mentioned, and comprehending with awed intelligence the meaning of the denunciation.

One obvious fact characterizing the book (which it is well to mention in view of neologian theories) is that it exhibits an accurate acquaintance with the Pentateuch, that the author had those writings before him when he put his prophecy into its present shape. The many allusions to the history, the actual expressions sometimes used, prove this beyond question. The Exposition will show it abundantly. Further, other books of the canon were known to Micah besides those of Moses. He refers to Joshua's division of the promised land (ch. ii. 4; vi. 5), to David's lament over Saul and Jonathan (ch. i. 10), to his predecessor's challenge (ch. i. 2; 1 Kings xxii. 28). He introduces words taken from the Psalms (e.g. ch. ii. 1; iii. 2, etc.; vii. 2, 7, etc.) and the Proverbs (e.g. ch. vi. 9, 11). He adopts images and language from Amos (ch. ii. 3, 6, 11; iii. 6). It must be added that the text of Micah is in an unsatisfactory state, having suffered much from corruptions. Many attempts have been made to improve it by reference to the ancient versions; but little success has attended these efforts, as the versions themselves seem to have been founded upon imperfect copies, and the conjectures of critics have not afforded much material help.

§ V. Literature.

Of the earlier commentators on Micah it is sufficient to mention Ephraem Syrus and Theophylact. Later commentators are these: Bibliander, 'Comm. in Micham' (1534); Luther; Gilby, 'Comm. upon Micha' (1551); Chytræus, 'Explicatio Michæ'

(1565); Brentius, 'Comm. in Michæam' (1580); Pocock, 'Works,' vol. i. (1740); Justi, 'Micha neu übersetzt' (1799, 1820); Hartmann, 'Micha neu übers.;' Caspari, 'Über Micha den Morasth.' (1852); Thomas, Genève (1853); Dr. Cheyne, in 'Cambridge Bible for Schools and Colleges' (1885); T. Sharpe, 'Micah, a New Translation' (1876); Kleinert, translated in Lange's 'Commentary on Old Testament;' Orelli, in 'Kurzgef. Komm.' (1888); Rygsel, 'Untersuchungen,' etc. (1887); J. Taylor, 'The Massoretic Text,' etc. (1890).

§ VI. ARRANGEMENT OF THE BOOK IN SECTIONS.

Part I. (Ch. i., ii.) Threatenings and judgments on Israel and Judah, with prediction of eventual deliverance.

§ 1. (Ch. i. 2—4.) Introduction to the prophet's address. The nations are bidden to attend.

§ 2. (Ch. i. 5—7.) Judgment denounced on Israel for its sins.

§ 3. (Ch. i. 8, 9.) Micah mourns because the punishment reaches to Judah.

§ 4. (Ch. i. 10—15.) That kingdom's fate exemplified by the fate of certain of her cities.

§ 5. (Ch. i. 16.) Zion is called to mourn for her captivity.

§ 6. (Ch. ii. 1—5.) Threat justified by the sins of oppression of which the princes were guilty.

§ 7. (Ch. ii. 6—11.) Threat further vindicated, with a glance at the false prophets who taught the people to love lies.

§ 8. (Ch. ii. 12, 13.) Promise of deliverance and restoration.

Part II. (Ch. iii.—v.) Denunciation of the crimes of the grandees, followed by a promise of the glorification of Zion, the birth of Messiah, and the highest exaltation of the people.

§ 1. (Ch. iii. 1—4.) Sins of the rulers, and their punishment.

§ 2. (Ch. iii. 5—8.) Sins of the false prophets.

§ 3. (Ch. iii. 9—12.) Recapitulation of the sins of the three classes—grandees, priests, and prophets; consequent destruction of Zion and the temple.

§ 4. (Ch. iv. 1—5.) The glory of the temple-mountain, and realization of happiness.

§ 5. (Ch. iv. 6, 7.) All Israel included in this restoration.

§ 6. (Ch. iv. 8—10.) Revival of the kingdom of David, after calamity and captivity.

§ 7. (Ch. iv. 11—13.) Zion overcomes all enemies in God's strength.

§ 8. (Ch. v. 1—4.) After Zion's degradation, Messiah shall be born and bring the world into subjection.

§ 9. (Ch. v. 5, 6.) Under his rule shall be peace.

§ 10. (Ch. v. 7—9.) He shall give his people as conquerors and saviours to the nations.

§ 11. (Ch. v. 10—15.) He shall destroy the instruments of war, and put down idolatry everywhere.

Part III. (Ch. vi., vii.) Punishment is the consequence of sin; repentance is the only ground of hope of participating in the covenant mercies.

§ 1. (Ch. vi. 1—5.) God's controversy with his people for their ingratitude.

§ 2. (Ch. vi. 6—8.) The people ask how to please God, and are referred to the moral requirements of the Law.

§ 3. (Ch. vi. 9—12.) God sternly rebukes prevailing sins.

§ 4. (Ch. vi. 13—16.) He threatens punishment.

§ 5. (Ch. vii. 1—6.) Israel's penitential acknowledgment of the general corruption.

§ 6. (Ch. vii. 7—13.) Confession of faith in God; assurance of the fulfilment of the promised restoration.

§ 7. (Ch. vii. 14—17.) The people pray for this restoration, and the Lord assures them that his mercies shall not fail, and hostile nations shall be humbled.

§ 8. (Ch. vii. 18—20.) Praise of God's mercy and faithfulness.

THE BOOK OF MICAH

EXPOSITION.

CHAPTER I.

Ver. 1—ch. ii. 13.—Part I. THREATEN-
INGS AND JUDGMENTS ON ISRAEL AND JUDAH,
WITH PREDICTION OF EVENTUAL DELIVER-
ANCE.

Ver. 1.—The *inscription*, or heading of
the book, conveying the prophet's authority.
The word of the Lord. The expression
applies to the whole contents of the book, as
in Hos. i. 1 and Zeph. i. 1. It is often used
for some particular message to a prophet,
as Jer. i. 4, 11; ii. 1; Ezek. iii. 16. Micah
the Morasthite; *i.e.* Micah of Moresheth-
Gath (ver. 14), a village in the lowland of
Judæa, near Eleutheropolis, some twenty
miles south-west of Jerusalem (see Introduction, § II.). In the days of Jotham,
Ahaz, and Hezekiah. Thus Micah was a
contemporary of Isaiah, though his ministry
did not begin as soon or last as long as
that prophet's (see Isa. i. 1); he was a little
later than Hosea and Amos, who prophesied
under Uzziah, the father of Jotham. Kings
of Judah are mentioned because the
prophet's mission was to Judah, as the line
of election; but, like Amos, he prophesied
against Samaria also. However divided,
the two nations are regarded as one people.
Which he saw. What he saw in vision or
by inward illumination he here relates in
words. Thus the prophecies of Isaiah,
Obadiah, Nahum, etc., are called "visions."
Concerning Samaria and Jerusalem. Samaria
comes first, as being ripe for punishment,
and the first to feel the avenger. The
capitals of the two kingdoms Israel and
Judah stand for the people themselves.

Vers. 2—4.—§ 1. *Introduction to the
prophet's address. The nations and earth
itself are summoned to attend the solemn
announcement.*

Ver. 2.—Hear, all ye people; rather, *all*
ye peoples; Septuagint, λαοί. All nations
are summoned to come and witness the
judgment, and to profit by the warning.
So Micaiah, son of Imlah, the bold denouncer
of false prophets in the age of Ahab, had
cried, "Hear, ye peoples, all of you"
(1 Kings xxii. 28). So Moses, in his song
(Deut. xxxii. 1), calls on heaven and earth to
listen to his words (comp. Isa. i. 2). These
expressions are not mere rhetorical figures;
they have a special application. Whatever
happens to Israel has a bearing on the
development of the kingdom of God; the
judgments on the chosen people are not only
a warning to the heathen, but bring on the
great consummation. All that therein is;
literally, *the fulness thereof;* Vulgate, *pleni-
tudo ejus;* Septuagint, πάντες οἱ ἐν αὐτῇ,
"all ye that are therein" (Ps. xxiv. 1).
Let the Lord God (*the Lord Jehovah*) be
witness against you. Let God by his judgments against you, viz. Israel and Judah,
confirm my denunciation (comp. Deut. xxix.
24). From his holy temple; *i.e.* from heaven,
as ver. 3 shows (1 Kings viii. 30; Ps. xi. 4;
Hab. ii. 20).

Ver. 3.—Here follows a grand description,
in figurative language, of the course of
Divine judgment, and of God's awful majesty
and resistless power. Out of his place. It
is as though the sins of Israel had roused
him to action. God is hidden except when
he displays his power in judgment and
mercy (see note on Zech. xiv. 3). Will
come down. An anthropomorphic expression, as Gen. xviii. 21. The high places.
As though descending from heaven, God
first came upon the tops of the mountains
(see note on Amos iv. 13; comp. Deut.
xxxii. 13). The phrase would imply God's
absolute sovereignty over the universe.

Ver. 4.—The description of God's advent
to judgment is founded on the idea of a
terrible storm and earthquake, perhaps
accompanied with volcanic eruption, though

evidence of such eruptions in the historical period is not forthcoming. The description recalls the awful revelation at Sinai (Exod. xix.). **Shall be molten;** either by the lightning or the showers of rain that descend from heaven. The mountains, the type of stability and strength, fall away at the presence of the Judge. Septuagint, σαλευθήσεται, "shall be shaken;" Vulgate, *consumentur* (Judg. v. 4, 5; Ps. xviii. 7, etc.; lxviii. 8; xcvii. 4, 5; Amos ix. 5). **Be cleft;** Septuagint, τακήσονται, "shall melt." The valleys shall be hollowed out into channels by the force of the water, which falls in torrents. **As wax** (Ps. lxviii. 2; xcvii. 5). This belongs to the first clause, "the mountains," etc. **As waters.** This belongs to the second clause. The cloven plains shall melt away as waters disappear down a precipice. The idea that underlies this description is that the inanimate creation shares in the effects of the judgment on man, and is used as an instrument in his punishment.

Vers. 5—7.—§ 2. *Judgment is denounced on Israel for its sin.*

Ver. 5.—The prophet shows the cause of this punishment. **Transgression;** better, *apostasy*, which the people's trangression really was. **Jacob.** Here the ten tribes and Judah—the whole of the covenant people. In the latter part of the verse the term includes only the ten tribes, called often Israel or Ephraim. **All this.** The manifestation of God's power and wrath described in vers. 3 and 4. **The house of Israel.** The ten tribes. **Is it not Samaria?** She is naught but sin. He names the capitals of the two kingdoms as the source and centre of the idolatry and wickedness which pervaded the whole country. Samaria was built by Omri, a king who "wrought evil in the eyes of the Lord, and did worse than all that were before him;" and in it his son Ahab erected a temple to Baal (1 Kings xvi. 32), and it became the chief seat of idolatry in the land. **What are the high places?** The prophet seems to say that Jerusalem is no longer the Lord's sanctuary, but a collection of unauthorized or idolatrous shrines. These were buildings or altars erected in conspicuous spots, contrary to the enactments of the Mosaic Law (Deut. xii. 11—14), and used more or less for idolatrous worship. With a strange perversity, the Jews mixed the pure service of Jehovah with the rites of heathen deities. Even the best kings of Judah were unable wholly to suppress these local sanctuaries (see 2 Kings xii. 3; xiv. 4, etc.). They were found even in Jerusalem itself (Jer. xxxii. 35), especially in the time of Ahaz (2 Kings xvi. 4). The **parallelism of this clause** with the preceding being thought defective ("high places"

being not parallel with "apostasy"), the Septuagint reads, ἡ ἁμαρτία, "the sin," followed by the Syriac and the Targum. One Hebrew manuscript confirms the reading; but it is probably unauthorized, and has been ignorantly introduced The prophet defines the sins of Samaria and Jerusalem. The sin of the former is apostasy; that of the latter, unauthorized worship. Instead of "what" in both places the Hebrew gives "who," implying that there is a personal cause, the two capitals being personified. Hezekiah's partial reformation had not taken place when this was uttered.

Ver. 6.—**I will make.** This prophecy, therefore, was delivered before the destruction of Samaria in the fourth year of Hezekiah. **As an heap of the field;** or, *into a heap of the field*, like a heap of stones gathered off a cultivated field (comp. Isa. v. 2). Septuagint, εἰς ὀπωροφυλάκιον ἀγροῦ, "the hut of a fruit-watcher." **As plantings of a vineyard;** *into the plantings*, etc.; *i.e.* into mere terraces for vines. Such shall be the utter ruin of the city, that on its site vines shall be planted. The prophet here uses a description of complete destruction which is a regular formula in Assyrian inscriptions, where we read of cities being made into "a rubbish-heap and a field." The expression occurs, *e.g.*, in a monument of Tiglath-Pileser (see Schrader, 'Keilinschr.,' p. 449). **I will pour down the stones thereof into the valley.** Samaria stood on a hilly platform (1 Kings xvi. 24), with a sheer descent on every side, and when it was overthrown its stones were hurled into the valley surrounding it, as may be seen to this day. "When we looked down," says Tristram ('Land of Israel,' p. 136), "at the gaunt columns rising out of the little terraced fields, and the vines clambering up the sides of the hill once covered by the palaces of proud Samaria, who could help recalling the prophecy of Micah? Not more literally have the denunciations on Tyre or on Babylon been accomplished. What though Sebaste rose, under Herod, to a pitch of greater splendour than even old Samaria, the effort was in vain, and the curse has been fully accomplished. In the whole range of prophetic history, I know of no fulfilment more startling to the eye-witness in its accuracy than this." **Will discover;** *will lay bare* (Ps. cxxxvii. 7; Ezek. xiii. 14).

Ver. 7.—**Graven images.** The stone idols (Isa. x. 10). Septuagint, -ὰ γλυπτά. **The hires thereof.** The word properly means, "the wages of prostitution." Idolatry is viewed as spiritual fornication, and the offerings made to the idol-temples are reckoned to be harlot-gifts. Hosea speaks in the same way (ii. 5, 8, 12; ix. 1; comp. Isa.

xxiii. 17; Ezek. xvi. 31). There may be allusion to the shameful practices consecrated with the name of religion, the proceeds of which went to the support of idolatry (see Baruch vi. 43; Herod., i. 199; Strabo, xvi. 1). Idols; more costly *images*, made probably of or plated with precious metals. For she gathered it; rather, *them*, the images and idols, from the offerings made by idolaters, spiritual fornicators, hence called the hire of an harlot. They shall return to the hire of an harlot. The treasures obtained by idolatry shall go to another idolatrous people, viz. the Assyrians; the dedicated offerings in the temples at Samaria shall be carried off to Nineveh to adorn the temples there (comp. Dan. i. 2; v. 3; Ezra i. 7). The sentence seems to be a kind of proverbial saying, like the Latin, *Male parta, male dilabuntur*. Schegg compares the German, *Wie gewonnen, so zerronnen*, and *Unrect Gut that sein Gut*. The judgment on Samaria was executed by the Assyrians. Three times in his short reign of less than six years did Shalmaneser IV. invade Israel. Shortly after his accession, having reason to suspect the fidelity of Hoshea, he " came up against him " (2 Kings xvii. 3), and so overawed him by the exhibition of his superior power that the King of Israel submitted without a struggle, " became his servant, and gave him presents," or rendered him tribute. But Hoshea's allegiance was not yet secured. Encouraged by the enterprise and success of the Ethiopian monarch So, or Shebek, who had defeated and slain the Egyptian king, and established himself firmly on the throne of Upper Egypt, Hoshea, in reliance on Egyptian aid, again threw off the yoke of Assyria, and refused the customary tribute. His punishment was speedy and sharp. Shalmaneser had no difficulty in making himself master of his person, " shut him up and bound him in prison." On a fresh act of rebellion, of what nature we are not informed, Shalmaneser made his third attack. This time he was everywhere resisted, and ended by laying siege to Samaria itself. Before this city his forces were detained for more than two years; nor was it till B.C. 722, when apparently his own reign had come to an end, that Samaria was taken, his successor Sargon claiming the conquest as appertaining to his first year (Rawlinson, 'Ancient Monarchies,' ii. ch. ix.).

Vers. 8, 9.—§ 3. *Micah mourns because the punishment extends to Judah also.*

Ver. 8. — I will wail. The prophet marks the destruction of Samaria with these outward signs of mourning, in order that he might affect the minds of his own countrymen, and show how he grieved over their sins which should bring like punishment. The word rendered " wail " means " to beat " the breast. Septuagint, κόψεται : Vulgate, *plangam*. Stripped and naked. The former epithet the LXX. translate ἀνυπόδετος, as if it meant " barefoot;" and they refer the verse to Samaria, not to Micah. The two epithets contain one notion; the prophet assumes the character, not merely of a mourner, who put off his usual garments, but that of a captive who was stripped to the skin and carried away naked and despoiled (comp. Isa. xx. 2—4; xlvii. 2, 3). Dragons; Septuagint, δρακόντων : Hebrew, *tannim*, "jackals " (Job xxx. 29; Mal. i. 3), whose mournful howling is well known to all travellers in the East. Owls; Septuagint, θυγατέρων σειρήνων, " daughters of sirens;" Vulgate, *struthionum*. The bird is called in Hebrew *bath yaanah*, which some explain " daughter of the desert," or else refer to roots meaning either "to cry out " or "to be freed." Doubtless the ostrich is meant. Concerning the fearful screech of this bird, Pusey quotes Shaw, 'Travels,' ii. 349, "During the lonesome part of the night they often make a doleful and piteous noise. I have often heard them groan as if they were in the greatest agonies."

Ver. 9.—Her wound; *her stripes*, the punishment inflicted on Samaria. Incurable (comp. Jer. xv. 18). The day of grace is past, and Israel has not repented. It is come. The stripe, the punishment, reaches Judah. To the prophetic eye the Assyrians' invasion of Judæa seems close at hand, and even the final attack of the Chaldeans comes within his view. The same sins in the northern and southern capitals lead to the same fate. He is come. He, the enemy, the agent of the " stripe." The gate of my people. The gate, the place of meeting, the well-guarded post, is put for the city itself (comp. Gen. xxii. 17; Deut. xxviii. 52; Obad. 11). Pusey thinks that Micah refers to something short of total excision, and therefore that the invasion of Sennacherib alone is meant (2 Kings xviii. 13). But the fore-shortened view of the prophet may well include the final ruin.

Vers. 10—15.—§ 4. *The judgment on Judah is exemplified by the fate of certain of its cities, whose names the prophet connects with their punishment in a series of paronomasias.*

Ver. 10.—Declare ye it not at Gath. This phrase from David's elegy over Saul (2 Sam. i. 20) had become a proverbial saying, deprecating the malicious joy of their hostile neighbours over the misfortunes that befell them. Gath is mentioned as the seat of the Philistines, the constant and powerful enemy of Judah. (For its situation, see note on Amos vi. 2.) The paronomasias in this passage, which seem to modern ears artificial and puerile, are paralleled in many writings both Hebrew and classic, and were natural to a people who looked for mystical meaning in words and names. Thus Gath is taken to signify "Tell-town," and the clause is, "In Tell-town tell it not." Weep ye not at all; Vulgate, lacrymis ne ploretis; i.e. "weep in silence," or "hide your tears," that the enemy may not know your grief. As in each of the other clauses a town is mentioned, some editors would here read, "In Acco ('Weep-town') weep not"—Acco being the later Ptolemais, the modern St. Jean d'Acre, and taken here to represent another foreign city which would rejoice at Judah's misfortunes (see Judg. i. 31). The Septuagint alone of all the versions seems to countenance this reading, by translating, Οἱ Ἐνακεὶμ μὴ ἀνοικοδομεῖτε, "Ye Enakim, do not rebuild," which has been resolved into οἱ ἐν Ἀκεὶμ, supposed to be an error for οἱ ἐν Ἀχί. The objections against this reading may be seen in Keil and Pusey. There is a play on the words in both these clauses (as in the following five verses), which is not seen in the English Version, begath al taggidu, and bako al tibeku. Knabenbauer imitates the paronomasia in Latin, "Cannis ne canite; Anconæ ne angamini;" Ewald and Schegg in German, "In Mölln meldet nicht; in Weinsberg, weinet nicht;" Reuss in French, "N'allez pas le dire à Dijon! N'allez pas pleurer à Ploermel!" In these puns, as we should call them, the prophet is far, indeed, from jesting. "He sees," says Dr. Cheyne, "like Isaiah, in Isa. x. 30, a preordained correspondence between names and fortunes;" and he wishes to impress this on his countrymen, that the judgment may not come upon them unwarned. In the house of Aphrah; better, at Beth-le-Aphrah, i.e. "House of dust;" Vulgate, in domo pulveris. The site of Aphrah is unknown. Some identify it with Ophrah in Benjamin (Josh. xviii. 23), four miles north-east of Bethel; others, with Ophrah in Philistia (1 Chron. iv. 14). Most of the towns named below lie in the Shephelah. Keil notes that the word is pointed with pathach here for the sake of the paronomasia. Roll thyself in the dust; sprinkle dust upon thyself. This was a common sign of mourning (comp. 2 Sam. xiii. 19; Jer. vi. 26). The Hebrew text (in contradistinction to the margin, Keri) gives, "I roll myself," or "I have besprinkled myself," the prophet identifying himself with the people. But as in all the subsequent passages, not what the prophet does, but what the inhabitants do, is the point impressed, the reading of the Keri is here to be preferred. Vulgate,

pulvere vos conspergite. The Septuagint has an inexplicable rendering, κατὰ γέλωτα γῆν καταπάσασθε, "against laughter sprinkle earth," which Brenton translates, "sprinkle dust in the place of your laughter." With this section (vers. 10—15) should be compared Isa. x. 28—32, which describes the alarm occasioned by Sennacherib's invasion of Judah from the north-east, as Micah represents his progress to the south-west.

Ver. 11.—Pass ye away. Leave your house. Thou inhabitant of Saphir. The Hebrew is "inhabitress," the population being personified as a virgin (comp. 2 Kings xix. 21; Isa. xlvii. 1). "Saphir" means "Fair city." It is placed by Eusebius ('Onomast.') between Ascalon and Eleutheropolis; it is now identified with some ruins named Suâfir, five miles south-east of Ashdod. Having thy shame naked; "in nakedness and shame" (Pusey); Vulgate, confusa ignominia. The prophet contrasts the shame of their treatment with the meaning of their city's name, "Go, Fair-town, into foul dishonour." Septuagint, κατοικοῦσα καλῶς τὰς πόλεις αὐτῆς, "fairly inhabiting her cities." St. Jerome, in despair of explaining these Greek renderings, says here, "Multum Hebraicum a LXX. interpretatione discordat, et tantis tam mea quam illorum translatio difficultatibus involuta est, ut si quando indiguimus Spiritus Dei (semper autem in exponendis Scripturis sanctis illius indigemus adventu), nunc vel maxime eum adesse cupiamus." Zaanan is supposed to be the same as Zenan, mentioned in Josh. xv. 37. The meaning of the name is doubtful. It is taken to signify "abounding in flocks" or "going out." Came not forth; or, is not come forth. The paronomasia seems to lie rather in sound than sense, and is variously explained, "The inhabitants of Flock-town went not forth with their flocks." "The dwellers of Forth-coming came not forth," i.e. to flee, or to fight, or to aid their brethren; or did not escape destruction. Vulgate, Non est egressa quæ habitat in exitu; Septuagint, Οὐκ ἐξῆλθε κατοικοῦσα Σεννάάρ, "She who dwelt at Sennaar came not forth." In the mourning, etc. These words are best joined with the following clause, thus: The mourning of Beth-ezel taketh from you its standing; i.e. refuge or shelter. Beth-ezel is explained, "House at one's side." "Neighbour-town;" so the prophet would say, "Neighbour-town is no neighbour to you," affords you no help. But various other explanations are given. e.g. "Lamentation makes its sure abode at Beth-ezel from your calamity." This may, perhaps, be supported by the rendering of the LXX., Λήψεται ἐξ ὑμῶν πληγὴν ὀδύνης, "She shall receive of you the stroke of anguish." Dr. Cheyne connects the whole verse with one idea, " Zaanan would willingly take to flight, but the sound of the mourning at Beth-ezel (which might mean, ' the house, or place, at one's side ') fills them with despair." Taking Beth-ezel to mean " House of root," others would interpret, on account of the public sorrow, " The ' house of root' affords no firm home for you." Others, again, "The lamentation of 'The near House' will not stop near it, but pass on to other places." Beth-ezel is probably the *Azal* of Zech. xiv. 5, the *beth* being dropped, as is often the case. It was in the neighbourhood of Jerusalem (see note on Zechariah, *l.c.*).

Ver. 12.—Maroth ; *bitterness.* Its site is unknown ; but it was in the immediate neighbourhood of Jerusalem. Ewald suggests that it is the same as Maarath (Josh. xv. 59), *hod. Beit Ummar,* six miles north of Hebron. Waited carefully for good ; waited, expecting succour. But the better translation is, *writhed in anguish on account of good,* which they have lost, whether property or liberty. But evil came ; *for* (or, *because*) *evil is come.* Unto the gate of Jerusalem (comp. ver. 9). The prophet refers to the invasion of the Assyrian kings, Sargon or Sennacherib, also mentioned by Isaiah (xxii. 7), and the haughty message (Isa. xxxvi. 2).

Ver. 13.—Lachish. A very strong and important city of the Canaanites, *hod. Um Lâkis,* about fourteen miles north-east of Gaza, which was captured by Sennacherib after a long siege (2 Kings xviii. 14; Isa. xxxvi. 2; xxxvii. 8). In the British Museum there is a bas-relief, brought from Assyria, representing Sennacherib seated on his throne while the spoil of the city of Lachish passed before him (Sayce, ' Fresh Light from the Monuments,' pp. 123, 125). Bind the chariot to the swift beast. Harness your horses to your chariots, that ye may flee and escape destruction. The phrase is like the Latin, *currum jungere equis.* The paronomasia here lies in the sound, " Inhabitant of Lachish, harness your *rekkesh* " ("runner," "courser"). "Inhabitant of Horse-town, harness your horses." Septuagint, ψόφος ἁρμάτων καὶ ἱππευόντων, "a sound of chariots and horsemen ; " Vulgate, *tumultus quadrigæ stuporis* — renderings which the present Hebrew text does not support. She was the beginning, etc. How Lachish came to adopt the idolatry of Israel, and how she infected Judah, we know not. A connection between Jerusalem and Lachish is found in the case of Amaziah (2 Kings xiv. 19), but nothing bearing on religion is mentioned. The whole clause is translated by Calmet, Keil, etc., thus : " It was the beginning of sin to the daughter of Zion that the iniquities of Israel were found in thee " (comp. ch. vi. 16; Amos viii. 14). The particular transgressions meant may be

the idolatry of Jehoram (2 Chron. xxi. 6) and Ahaziah (2 Chron. xxii. 3, 4).

Ver. 14.—Therefore. Because Judah has adopted the evil practices of Israel. The prophet here addresses Judah, and continues to do so to the end of the chapter. Shalt thou give presents to Moresheth-Gath. The "presents" intended are parting gifts, farewell presents. The word is used (1 Kings ix. 16) for the dowry given to a daughter when she is married. The meaning, therefore, is that Judah must relinquish all claim to Moresheth. The paronomasia is explained in two ways. As *Moresheth* may mean " possession," the prophet may be understood to say, " Thou shalt give up possession of Gath's possession." Or the play of words may depend upon the similarity of sound between *Moresheth* and *Meorasah,* "Betrothed " (Deut. xxii. 23), " Thou shalt give dismissal (bill of divorcement) to the city once betrothed to thee." Moresheth-Gath, Micah's birthplace, is placed just south of Beit Jibrin, or Eleutheropolis, about twenty-five miles from Gaza (see Introduction, § II.). The addition of Gath to the name of the town is meant to mark its situation as in the immediate neighbourhood of that well-known city. So we have Bethlehem-Judah (Judg. xvii. 7), Abel-Maim or -Maachah (1 Kings xv. 20 ; 2 Chron. xvi. 4). Septuagint, Δώσει ἐξαποστελλομένους ἕως κληρονομίας Γέθ, "He shall cause men to be sent forth even to the inheritance of Geth ; " Vulgate, *Dabit emissarios super hereditatem Geth.* To give *shilluchim* the sense of " messengers " seems to be unprecedented. The houses of Achzib shall be a lie (*achzab*), a lying, deceiving brook, which disappoints the hope of the wayfarer, like " fundus mendax " (Horat., ' Carm.,' iii. 1. 30). Septuagint, οἴκους ματαίους, " vain houses ; " Vulgate, *domus mendacii.* The city shall be yielded to the enemy and lost to the Judæans. Achzib (Josh. xv. 44), *hod. Ain Kezbeh,* eight miles north of Adullam, is probably the same as Chezib (Gen. xxxviii. 5), where Shelah, Judah's son by Tamar, was born. The kings of Israel. " Israel " is here equivalent to Judah, having, according to the prediction of vers. 6, 7, lost its political existence (comp. 2 Chron. xxviii. 19, where Ahaz is called King of Israel).

Ver. 15.—Yet will I bring an heir unto thee, O inhabitant of Mareshah. " Mareshah " sounds like *Morashah,* the Hebrew word for "inheritance ; " so the play is, " I will bring an inheritor who shall claim your Heritage-town." The " heir " is the Assyrian king, Sargon, into whose possession the city shall pass. Mareshah (Josh. xv. 44; 2 Chron. xiv. 9) was near Achzib, one mile south-east of Beit Jibrin, and is now called *Mer'ash*. **He shall come**, etc. ; better, *the glory of Israel shall come to Adullam*; i.e. the nobility (comp. Isa. v. 13) of Israel shall fly for refuge to such places as the cave of Adullam, David's asylum (1 Sam. xxii. 1, 2). So the Vulgate. The LXX. has, Κληρονομία ἕως 'Οδυλλὰμ ἥξει ἡ δόξα τῆς θυγατρὸς 'Ισραήλ, " The inheritance shall come to Odullam, even the glory of the daughter of Israel." But Rosenmüller, Henderson, Pusey, and others take the sentence as in the Authorized Version, making " the glory of Israel " in apposition with " Adullam," and understanding by " he " the heir or enemy. One knows no reason why Adullam should be honoured with the above-named title; so the rendering given above is preferable. There is probably a paronomasia intended, " The glory of the Lord shall set (*ad olam*) for ever." The city of Adullam, hod. *Aid-el-Mah*, lay in the valley of Elah, ten miles north-west of Hebron, half-way between Sochoh and Keilah. It was of great antiquity, being mentioned as the birthplace of Hirah, the friend of Judah (Gen. xxxviii. 12), and one of the cities fortified by Rehoboam (2 Chron. xi. 7). In its neighbourhood is the celebrated cave, Mughâ et Khureitun, which is pointed out as the traditional hold of David, and which has been carefully explored by Mr. Tyrwhitt Drake, of the Palestine Exploration Fund (see Thomson, 'Land and the Book,' pp. 332, etc.).

Ver. 16.—§ 5. *The prophet calls upon Zion to mourn for her captivity.* **Make thee bald.** The Hebrew word implies " to make the back of the head bald." Micah addresses Zion as the mother of the children who are to be led into captivity. Shaving the head in sign of mourning seems to have been retained as a traditionary custom in spite of the prohibition of the Law against certain forms which the practice assumed (see Lev. xix. 27; Deut. xiv. 1; and for the actual custom, comp. Isa. iii. 24; Jer. vii. 29; and the note on Amos viii. 10). **Poll thee.** Cut off thy hair, nearly synonymous with the word in the former clause. **Thy delicate children;** literally, *the children of thy delights;* i.e. the children who are a joy and comfort to thee, the citizens of thy kingdom (comp. ch. ii. 9). **As the eagle** (*nesher*). The vulture is meant, either *Vultur percnopterus*, common in Egypt and Palestine, which is bald on the front of the head and neck, or more probably *Vultur fulvus*, the griffon vulture, whose whole head and neck are destitute of true feathers (see 'Bible Educator,' ii. 247). **Into captivity.** This cannot refer exclusively to the Assyrian invasion, wherein very few captives were taken, but must look forward to the Babylonian deportation in ch. iv. 10. The latter calamity alone is parallel to the destruction of Samaria announced in vers. 6, 7 of this chapter.

HOMILETICS.

Ver. 1.—*True spiritual teachers.* A preface is often regarded as of comparative unimportance, and many readers ignore it and pass on to the perusal of the work itself. Let not this preface to the Book of Micah be thus summarily dismissed. Every word of God is " profitable." This introductory verse is very suggestive of teachings bearing upon holy service in the cause of God in our own age. The Hebrew prophets were not merely foretellers; they were also the religious educators of the people amongst whom they laboured. We are reminded here that—

I. TRUE SPIRITUAL TEACHERS ARE ENTRUSTED WITH A REVELATION FROM GOD. Note: 1. *This revelation is given in the form of words.* " The word of the Lord that came to Micah." Thoughts may be communicated by utterance, actions, and in writing. In the olden time God communicated his thoughts to Moses on the mount and to the Israelites by the living voice, and to the seers by dreams and visions. In all times he has unfolded his thoughts in actions (Ps. xix. 1, 2). To us he reveals his thoughts in the *written Word.* And it is just in proportion as, taught by the Divine Spirit, we enter into the meaning of the Word of God, and recognize in its teachings a message committed unto us to deliver, that we are qualified to be teachers of spiritual truth (2 Cor. v. 18, 19). 2. *This revelation comes to us stamped with Divine authority.* " The word of the *Lord.*" There was no tone of uncertainty about the utterances of the Hebrew seers; nothing that was speculative, theoretical, problematical, in what they said; nothing that could be described as the creation of their own fancy and imagination. Whilst each prophet retained his own individual peculiarities and natural gifts, so that a pleasing variety meets us in their writings, each announcement was accompanied by " *Thus saith the Lord.*" In our own day all the resources of sanctified genius and endowment should be laid upon the altar of service to God; but let all uncertainty be dismissed. The messenger must not betray a hesitating tone, as though doubtful whether he has any message to deliver. He has glorious certainties to announce, an authoritative message to declare; and, with confident and unwavering trust, should go forth and publish the bright realities of our faith. 3. *This revelation is made very real to the inner consciousness of the teacher.* "The word of the Lord that came to Micah," "which he saw concerning Samaria and Jerusalem." It was an inward experience with the prophet, a deep inwrought conviction. The word of the Lord took possession of his very soul, and became part and parcel of his very being, touching, quickening, inspiring his whole nature. The circumstances of his nation, too, were vividly presented to him, and the events to be fulfilled were as real as though they had already taken place or were transpiring before his eyes. "Which he saw." The same expression is used with reference to Amos (i. 1) and Habakkuk (i. 1). So still: "That which we have heard," etc. (John i. 1—3). A deeper experimental acquaintance with the truth to be proclaimed would impart to the heralds of it a holier earnestness, and would clothe them with mighty energy and irresistible power. "Let your heart take in by its secret veins that which comes pure from Heaven in showers of blessing: so shall its issues, so far as your influence extends, contribute to fertilize the wilderness" (Arnot). And the heart must be in sympathy with those to whom the truth is to be communicated. The circumstances of his nation pressed upon the heart of Micah. So Ezekiel (iii. 15) and Paul (Rom. x. 1). George Fox said, "I prayed to God that he would baptize my heart into the sense of *all conditions*, so that I might be able to enter into the needs and sorrows of *all*."

II. TRUE SPIRITUAL TEACHERS HAVE OFTEN BEEN RAISED UP AND PREPARED FOR THEIR WORK IN RETIRED AND OBSCURE PLACES. "The word of the Lord that came to Micah *the Morasthite*." Many of the Hebrew prophets sprang from humble and retired localities. Elkosh, Gath-hepher, Tishbe, Abel-Meholah, Anathoth, Moresheth-Gath,— how comparatively insignificant and unknown these places appear! and yet out of them respectively came Nahum, Jonah, Elijah, Elisha, Jeremiah, and Micah. Country life has its special advantages by way of preparing the mind and heart for holy service. It affords a better opportunity for getting the spirit affected with the power and goodness of God as expressed in his works; for scenes of natural beauty are continually unfolded to the view, and of which the citizen is deprived. "God made the country, man the town." Quiet retirement, too, is more available, securing thus facilities for meditation, reflection, and heart-communion. There is so much less to distract and divert the attention than is presented amidst life in the great centres. Yet he who lives in retirement, if designed for prominent service, will not fail, even in his remoteness from the activities of city life, to inform himself concerning the character of the age in which he lives, and to keep himself abreast with it, but will be observant of "the signs of the times," and will familiarize himself with these, even as Micah, away in Moresheth-Gath, was familiar with the moral and spiritual condition of his people, and with the doings of kings and nobles, prophets and priests. It is often a source of discouragement to some engaged in service to God that they are called upon to work in very *retired* spheres, and they ardently long for more scope and wider influence. It should be no slight consolation to such that their spheres, though retired, may nevertheless afford them far-reaching power for good. Perchance under their care may be those whom God has designed for very influential service, and that through their ministry these are being prepared for their life-work; and that in due course, leaving the village and going forth to their mission in city or town, at home or it may be in some far-off land, they will carry with them holy influences which have been exerted upon them by one who may never be known to fame, but whose "witness shall be in heaven, and whose record shall be on high."

III. TRUE SPIRITUAL TEACHERS WILL ADAPT THEMSELVES TO THE AGE THEY ARE TO SEEK TO INFLUENCE. "The word . . . in the days of Jotham, Ahaz, and Hezekiah, kings of Judah." An examination of the period indicates that it was an age: 1. *Thoroughly corrupt.* Nobles, priests, prophets, had alike corrupted their way. Micah denounced with holy boldness the sins of the times (ch. ii. 1, 2, 7—11; iii. 1—4, 5, 7). 2. *Manifestly formal.* In sublime diction Micah enforced the spirituality of genuine worship and the practical character of sincere piety (ch. vi. 6—8). 3. *Utterly unpatriotic.* With loyal spirit he recalled the past of their national history, which should have stirred their hearts anew (ch. ii. 12; vi. 4, 5; vii. 14, 15, 20). 4. *Setting in darkness.* The cup of iniquity was fast filling. The fate of Samaria was sealed. Jerusalem also was reserved for desolation. But whilst declaring the coming judgments, Micah also declared the Divine mercy to the penitent (ch. vii. 18), and, whilst announcing the approaching ruin, he looked beyond the gathering darkness and the falling shadows, and saw by faith " the mighty Child" appearing in the obscure village of Bethlehem in an age to come, and who should prove himself "a Shepherd more royal even than David," and who should usher in "a peace even more universal than that of Solomon" (ch. v. 2). And so did this distinguished seer adapt himself to the age he was commissioned to serve. And in like manner, he who would work successfully in the present day must fully consider the nature of the times, and the special needs of men. Failure does not always arise from want of ability, but often from lack of adaptation. The thing done is good enough *in itself*, but is not suited to the occasion. There is a Hindu proverb, " The chariot is weak at sea, and the ship on land." In no respect did the Divine Master, the great Prophet of the Church, more thoroughly excel all other instructors than in the marvellous suitability of all his methods and utterances to the deepest needs of those amongst whom he laboured.

Learn : 1. To depend upon God for the teaching of his Spirit, and to receive the truth from him. 2. To gather up strength in retirement for future service. 3. To seek to be inspired with holy courage, so as to declare all the counsel of God. 4. To strengthen your hearts amidst present difficulties and darkness by the prospect of that full and complete salvation which shall be accomplished by Christ.

Vers. 2—7.—*The Divine judgments against Israel.* Micah was a prophet of Judah, and had special reference in his prophecy to that kingdom. Still, he referred also to the kingdom of Israel. In these verses he directed attention to the tribulations speedily to come upon the kingdom of Israel; and, whilst his words have reference to "the dead past," they suggest lessons for all times. Consider—

I. THE DIVINE JUDGMENTS AGAINST THE KINGDOM OF ISRAEL AS HERE PREDICTED. Note : 1. *Their occasion.* (Ver. 5.) The secular historian has his account of the causes of the calamities which overtook the Jewish people. He traces these to lust of power and dominion on the part of the ancient monarchies, Assyrian, Chaldean, Babylonian, by which they were attacked and conquered. But the true spiritual teacher probes deeper, and seeks to get at the root of it all, and finds this to be *sin*—national transgression (ver. 5). There were three stages in the downward progress of the nation. (1) *Degeneration in worship.* Jeroboam, influenced by mere political considerations and worldly policy, set up, at Dan and Bethel, new seats of national worship, and represented the Divinity under the outward figure of the sacred calf. Thus did he "sin and make Israel to sin." (2) *Degeneration in the form of worldliness.* The reign of Omri was marked by the nation's growth in pride and self-sufficiency, in the arts and luxuries of life. He founded Samaria, and made it the capital of the country. "The town sloped down from the summit of the hill. A broad wall with a terraced top ran round it. It stood amidst a circle of hills commanding a view of its streets and slopes, itself the crown and glory of the whole scene. Its soft, rounded, oblong platform was, as it were, a vast luxurious couch, in which its nobles rested, securely propped and cushioned up on both sides, as in the cherished corner of a rich divan" (Stanley's 'Jewish Church,' ii. 239, 240). (3) *Degeneration resulting from foreign alliances,* and specially the union of Ahab to Jezebel, and the consequent establishment in the land of the Phœnician worship, the heathen temples rising, and worship to Ashtaroth and Baal being presented side by side with the degenerate worship offered to the God of heaven. These evils wrought their natural effects in the moral degradation of the land, calling for those Divine judgments which the prophet here declared to be impending. Drunkenness and revellings prevailed (Hos. iv. 11; vii. 5); immorality reigned (Hos. iv. 13; vii. 4; Amos ii. 7); oppression, swearing, lying, theft, murder, were crimes of constant occurrence (Hos. iv. 1, 2). 2. *Their necessity.* (Ver. 3.) "For, behold, the Lord cometh out of his place"—a striking sentence employed to express the necessity that existed for retribution to be exercised. "God's place" is his mercy. He is love. He is good and gracious. It is his nature to show compassion. Let all prominence be given to this characteristic of our God. We cannot dwell too much upon it, and can never exhaust the rich theme. "God is love," and mercy is "his place." But there are times when there is a stern necessity for him to "come forth out of his place." He is not only loving, he is also righteous, and he is righteous because he is loving. True love excludes partiality, and true justice requires that men be dealt with according to their actions ; so that, if God would be true to his character as a God of love, both the recompense of the good and the punishment of the evil is demanded. We are to warn men of the terrible and far-reaching consequences of sin, and whilst joyfully proclaiming "the acceptable year of the Lord," we are also to declare with true solemnity the fact of "the day of vengeance of our God." Whilst delighting to speak of mercy as his dwelling-place, we must also declare that there is the necessity for him "to come forth out of his place" to vindicate the right and to punish the wrong. 3. *Their severity.* (Vers. 3, 4.) This is set forth here in striking metaphor. God is represented as treading upon the high places, the pride of the haughty being as the dust beneath his feet. His judgments are described as fire, under the influence of which the mountains should be molten and the valleys be cleft; whilst as wax melts before the fire, and as the rushing waters, poured over a steep place, no more return, but are scattered in spray and dissipated in vapours, so should the evil-doers at length be brought to nought. Samaria, the centre of the nation, and the source whence proceeded noxious and pestilential influences, should be brought to utter desolation (vers. 6, 7). This stern sentence was literally fulfilled (see Porter's 'Giant Cities of Bashan,' p. 227; Stanley's 'Jewish Church,' ii. 311, 312). 4. *Their equity.* The prophet, like other seers, summons the nations and the earth to bear testimony to the rightness which marks all God's judgments (ver. 2). The acknowledgment of the universe shall be that the Divine judgments are "true and righteous altogether."

II. THE BEARING OF THE STORY OF ISRAEL'S GUILT AND FALL UPON NATIONAL LIFE IN THE PRESENT DAY. 1. It warns us that if we use the pre-eminence God has assigned to us as a nation, simply with a view to our own aggrandizement and the furtherance of our own selfish ends, if, instead of worshipping him, and living with a single eye to his glory, we prostrate ourselves before wealth and luxury, ease and sloth, human reason and human applause, God will be against us, and will come forth "out of his place" to judgment, and national decay and death will assuredly follow. A haughty Frenchman once taunted an English captain, saying, "When will you English fetch Calais again?" The captain replied, "When your sins shall weigh down ours!" 2. It reminds us how essential it is, in order to national prosperity, that the sovereign should be a pattern of every virtue; that rulers should not only be men of wisdom and foresight, but also God-fearing; and that religion, spiritual and practical, should characterize all classes of the community. 3. It indicates to us the forbearance of God in sparing our nation, despite all the defections which have marked us as a people, and should lead us to repentance and a new life. And this must be personal and individual. "He who would reform the world must first improve himself." Then let us each "fear God, and keep his commandments," and so prove good citizens of the land we love. And conscious of our weakness, as Nature in all her helplessness offers herself to the kindly influence of the sun and the refreshing effects of the shower, so let us offer our hearts to the quickening and fertilizing influences of God's Spirit, that as Nature becomes clothed with verdure, so we may abound in all holy graces, and in us the Lord and God of all the nations of the earth be abundantly glorified!

Vers. 5, 9, and 13 (last clauses).—*The contagiousness of sin.* Great prominence should be given in Christian teaching to the sad and solemn fact of sin. Would we lead men to prize the redemption wrought by our Lord Jesus Christ, and to appreciate his unutterable love expressed in his "obedience unto death," we must seek to bring home to them a sense of that sinfulness, from the thraldom and evil consequences of which he came to deliver all who trust in him. The Hebrew prophets present to us in this respect an example well worthy of imitation. We find in their writings bright allusions to the deliverance to be wrought "in the fulness of time" by the Messiah, whose heralds they delighted to be, and whose "day" they "saw afar off;" but accompanying these words of hope were heart-searching utterances, now indignant and scathing, and anon tender, pathetic, wailing, all designed to bring home to the con-science and heart a keen sense of evil-doing, and to lead men to bow themselves low in penitence for the wrong they had done. We have brought very conspicuously before us in these verses the *contagious influence of sin*. Observe—

I. THE MISCHIEF IS HERE TRACED, IN THE FIRST INSTANCE, TO LACHISH. (Connect vers. 9 and 13.) Lachish was one of the most powerful of the cities of Judah. It was strongly fortified, and formed the cavalry depôt for the nation. Sennacherib spared no effort to reduce it, and, when he had succeeded, he sent from it his boastful and contemptuous message to Hezekiah. The Assyrian monuments represent the taking of this city by the Assyrians, and indicate how that the victors regarded this as a great triumph. Geographically, no city of Judah was more remote from the kingdom of Israel than this; yet it was through this city that the idolatry of Israel found its way into Judah. Lachish was "the beginning of sin to the daughter of Zion: for the transgressions of Israel were found in her." How this came to pass we can only conjecture. Rehoboam fortified Lachish. Maachah, his favourite wife, cherished a warm attachment to the worship of foreign divinities, and may, through this channel, have introduced this foreign worship into her country; and in this way probably Lachish became "the beginning of sin to the daughter of Zion." And, the gates once opened, the pernicious influence spread, until, despite certain attempts at reformation, the land became thoroughly infected, and the poison so prevailed that we read, "Her wound is incurable," etc. (ver. 9).

II. Another influence that operated in bringing about this morally diseased condition of Judah was THE ALLIANCE FORMED BY JEHOSHAPHAT WITH THE HOUSE OF OMRI, AND WHICH RESULTED IN THE MARRIAGE OF JEHORAM, SON OF JEHOSHAPHAT, WITH ATHALIAH, DAUGHTER OF AHAB. Athaliah was a wicked, powerful woman, possessed of fierce determination, cool and calculating, yet of dauntless, resolute spirit. She heard of the overthrow of her father's house, and of the sad end of Jezebel, and the intelligence but strengthened her resolve that the worship of Baal, uprooted in Samaria, should have a home in Jerusalem. And this she secured for it, with all its pernicious influence (Stanley's 'Jewish Church,' ii. 334, 335).

III. THE REMAINING POWERFUL PERNICIOUS INFLUENCE IS TO BE FOUND IN THE ACCESSION OF AHAZ TO THE THRONE. It was during his reign that Micah prophesied; and when we think of the superstitious character of Ahaz, how that he caused new idolatrous sanctuaries to rise on every hand, established the worship of Moloch under the very walls of Jerusalem, and devoted his son to sacrifice, casting him into the fire, need we wonder at the prophet crying with deep distress, "What are the high places of Judah? Are they not Jerusalem?" Beginning at Lachish, in the very extreme border of the land, the contagious influences spread until the whole nation, even to its very centre, had become infected (ver. 9). So is it ever. There is the commencement of the downward course, "the beginning of the sin," leading on to general depravity and defilement.

Learn: 1. To be watchful against "the beginnings" of evil. 2. Christ suffered "without the gate," that he might deliver us from sin and bless us by turning us from our iniquities (Acts iii. 26). 3. Into "the new Jerusalem" there entereth not anything that defileth or worketh abomination, or maketh a lie; but there all God's perfected ones, freed from the curse and blight of sin, shall serve him in holiness and love for ever.

Ver. 8.—*The prevalence of sin the source of grief to the good.* I. THE FACT. The good in all ages have mourned over sin and its consequences (Ps. cxix. 136; Jer. ix. 1; Luke xix. 41, 42). In ver. 8 we have pictured to us the distress of one thoroughly noble and good, true and patriotic, occasioned by the prevailing ungodliness and the calamities of which he had to speak. With a vivid sense of the evils of the times and of the coming judgments, this prophet (as others before him) flung aside his mantle and went about beating his breast, and pouring forth wild shrieks and lamentations. By "the dragons" is meant "the jackals," and by "the owls" is intended "the ostriches." Of the former we read, "The jackals make a lamentable howling noise, so that travellers unacquainted with them would think that a company of people, women or children, were howling one to another" (Pococke). And of the latter, another writes, "During the lonesome part of the night they often make a doleful and piteous noise. I have often heard them groan as if they were in the greatest agonies" (Shaw's

'Travels'). So that when the prophet speaks of making "a wailing like the jackals, and mourning like the ostriches," he intimates that he would give way to the intensity of grief and distress, in view of the prevailing iniquity and its prospective punishment.

II. THE CAUSES. This grief arises from : 1. Regard for the honour of that holy and perfect Being against whom all sin is directed. 2. Esteem for his pure and holy Law, of which Law all sin is a violation. 3. Love of righteousness. 4. Deep compassion for those who are thus led captive by evil.

III. THE LIMITATIONS. The manifestation of this grief should be restrained when its expression would furnish occasion to the enemies of God to blaspheme (ver. 10). Quoting the expression from David's elegy, "Tell it not in Gath," Micah bids the good, "weeping to weep not," the idea being that prudence should mark them even in their sorrow over sin; that a restraint should be placed by them even upon their mourning over the prevailing evil, rather than by their demonstrations of sorrow they should cause the adversaries of God and of his people to blaspheme and triumph. We should be prepared to endure much, instead of, by giving way, presenting an advantage to the foes of God, and furnishing them with the opportunity of pouring contempt upon his Name.

Vers. 11—16.—*Sorrow following in the train of evil.* I. THIS TRUTH IS SET FORTH IN THESE VERSES IN POETICAL LANGUAGE. The prophet does not mention the land of Judah, but he singles out a number of places in the country, and addresses them by name, employing phraseology calculated to produce a strong impression concerning the grief and sadness that should overspread the nation. We may fittingly compare with this a similar passage in the book of Micah's contemporary, Isaiah (x. 28—32). In both passages these distinguished seers described, in terms of pathetic sadness, the sorrows which should come upon the land in consequence of the nation's guilt. The trials thus predicted did not, however, come in all their intensity so speedily, for the nation, under the influence of Hezekiah, bowed itself low in penitence, and proceeded to reform the prevailing evils. The Assyrian army was, in consequence, divinely checked in its onward march; the destroying angel accomplished his work of terrible destruction in the camp of the Assyrians, and a respite was granted to Judah (Isa. xxxvii. 36).

II. THIS TRUTH, THUS ILLUSTRATED, ADMITS OF THE WIDEST APPLICATION. Sorrow ever follows in the course of evil. A life of obedience to God's revealed will is the only way in which happiness, real and lasting, may be secured. The rabbins say that "when Adam had tasted the forbidden fruit, *his head ached.*" The highest authority has declared that "the way of transgressors is hard," and that "whatsoever a man soweth that shall he also reap" (Gal. vi. 7). An old writer has compared a life of worldliness to one on the stream, and following the river's course. He passes through very lovely scenery. There are the sweet meadows, green woods, the fertile pastures, magnificent buildings, strong forts, famous cities, but at last he comes to *the salt sea.* So the stream of worldliness may yield you many a passing delight, but the end to which it conducts is truly desolate (Thomas Adams). Have we not served sin long enough? All time is too long that is given to that service. It is enough. The time past shall suffice us in which to have wrought the will of the evil one. We cast ourselves at thy feet, O Lord; deliver us from the power and dominion, the shame and sorrow, of sin; and help us to live the manly and godly life!

HOMILIES BY VARIOUS AUTHORS.

Ver. 2.—*The Lord God a witness against sinners.* God never leaves himself without witness among men. He bears witness perpetually *to* them—by the gifts of his hand (Acts xiv. 17), by the still small voice within, and by the voice of his messengers. God has borne and still bears witness *to us* on behalf of Christ. This may be illustrated from John v. 31—39, where our Lord speaks of three ways in which the Father testified on his behalf. 1. By the mission of John the Baptist, representing preachers and teachers. 2. By his works (to us, miracles of grace, converts to Christ). 3. By the written Word. We have to add God's witness : 4. By the resurrection of Christ (Acts

xvii. 31). 5. By the gift of the Holy Spirit (Acts v. 32). In all these ways God is bearing witness *for us*. So even in his chastisements (1 Cor. xi. 32). But if we heed not these testimonies *for us*, we must be prepared at any time to hear the voice of God's providence calling for judgments (vers. 3, 4), and thus witnessing *against us*. When such judgments fall, God will be able to testify: (1) That we have had abundant privileges. Illustrate from 1 Sam. xii. 6—15. (2) That we have had fair warning and have neglected it, as did Samaria (2 Kings xvii.), and Judah (2 Chron. xxxvi. 11—21), and the later Jews (Acts xiii. 46). (3) That his judgments are so righteous that God can summon all people to observe and justify them (cf. Deut. xxix. 24—28). "It is a bitter case when our provoked Lord is provoked to go out of doors to the streets with his beloved's faults." They proceed from the very temple of his holiness (cf. Rev. xv. 3—6, where the songs of vindication and the angels of vengeance are coupled together). God never hesitates to give reasons for his judgments (Prov. i. 24—27; Jer. xxix. 23; Mal. ii. 14; iii. 5). Such judgments as fall now are but predictions and earnests of the great judgment awaiting the ungodly. God, who will then be a witness against us, warns us now of some of the ways in which he will then testify. He will bring as witnesses: (1) The Law (John v. 45). (2) The gospel (John xii. 47). (3) Our outward privileges. Illustrate from Josh. xxiv. 26, 27. So there may be cited against us—the pulpit from which we heard the Word, and the preacher who in it "testified repentance towards God," etc. (Acts xx. 21). (4) The less privileged of our brethren (cf. Luke xi. 31, 32). (5) Our misused talents (Jas. v. 1—4). (6) Our words (Matt. xii. 37). (7) Our consciences (John viii. 9; Rom. ii. 15). If true now, how much more then! Lest God should be a witness against us then, we must, by repentance, faith, and obedience, secure his testimony now, like Enoch (Heb. xi. 5; cf. Ps. cxlvii. 11). Then we shall have the testimony of our brethren (Rom. xvi. 6—13; 3 John 3—6) and of our own consciences (2 Cor. i. 12), and shall be able to anticipate without fear the final verdict of God (Rom. viii. 33, 34).—E. S. P.

Ver. 5.—*Sins in the metropolis.* God's interposition by judgment is threatened on account of the nation's sins. The greatness of their privileges involved special responsibilities and chastisements (Amos iii. 2). These sins are traced to their sources in the capitals of the two kingdoms. A metropolis is a centre of influence for good or for evil. This may be illustrated by the histories of both the Hebrew kingdoms. The northern kingdom had in succession three capitals: (1) Shechem, where the apostasy of Israel began (1 Kings xii. 25—33). (2) Tirzah, the home of Jeroboam (1 Kings xiv. 17), the scene of civil strife (1 Kings xvi. 9, 17, 18), and of the court of Omri of sinister memory (ch. vi. 16), for half his reign. (3) Samaria, the seat of monarchy for two hundred years. Among the sins specially charged by the prophets against Samaria we find pride (Isa. ix. 9), luxury and licentiousness (Isa. xxviii. 1—4; Amos vi. 1—6), incorrigible treachery (Hos. vii. 1), contemptuous disregard of God and his worship (Hos. viii. 5; Amos viii. 14), oppression of the poor (ch. iii.; Amos iv. 1). In Judah the high places were an offence to God, which even good kings did not entirely suppress, so that Jerusalem may be said to have been responsible for them, and did not escape the infection (2 Chron. xxviii. 1—4, 23—25) nor the denunciations of the prophets (Isa. i., v.; xxviii. 14—19). We are thus reminded of—

I. THE RESPONSIBILITIES ATTACHING TO A METROPOLIS. It is: 1. The seat of government, where kings and rulers live and exert great personal influence, and where laws are passed which, if bad, may corrupt the national conscience and deprave social life. 2. One chief centre of public opinion, where the most educated and cultivated congregate. 3. The fountain of fashion. 4. The gathering-place of the rural population, where the opinions and practices of the citizens may be speedily imbibed. Illustrate from the influence of Paris during the second empire, culminating in the craze for war, which brought ruin on the country in 1870; or from the influence of Constantinople and its pachas on the present condition of the Turkish empire. Such capitals are centres of corruption, like diseased lungs where the blood is deteriorated rather than purified.

II. LESSONS ARE SUGGESTED FOR ALL CLASSES OF RESIDENTS IN A METROPOLIS. 1. For the court, lest they be like Jeroboam, "who made Israel to sin." 2. For legislators. Illustrate from the demoralizing effects of many of our past licensing acts.

3. For editors of newspapers and other leaders of public opinion. It was these who were, to a large extent, responsible for the Crimean War. 4. For the leaders of fashion, who may foster habits of extravagance, of peril to health, or even of cruelty in matters of dress. 5. For men of business; the exchanges of the metropolis giving a tone to the commercial customs of the country. 6. For artisans, whose trades unions may help or injure their fellow-workmen scattered in the provinces. 7. For preachers, whom many gather from all parts to hear, and who may give a tone to the preaching of the country. 8. For Church members. Heresy or worldliness in metropolitan Churches may soon spread among rural Churches maintaining a simpler faith and practice (cf. Matt. v. 14, 16; Rom. i. 8).—E. S. P.

Vers. 1, 2.—*Divine revelation.* "The word of the Lord that came to Micah the Morasthite in the days of Jotham, Ahaz, and Hezekiah, kings of Judah, which he saw concerning Samaria and Jerusalem. Hear, all ye people; hearken, O earth," etc. Micah calls himself a Morasthite because he was a native of Moresheth-Gath, a small town of Judæa. He prophesied in the days of Jotham, Ahaz, and Hezekiah, kings of Judah, and his prophetic mission commenced soon after that of Isaiah. He was contemporary with him, as well as with Hosea and Amos. His prophecies were directed to Samaria, the capital city of Israel, and also to Jerusalem. Hence we find denunciations against Samaria mingled with prophecies concerning Judah and Jerusalem. One of his predictions, it seems, saved the life of Jeremiah, who would have been put to death for foretelling the destruction of the temple, had not Micah foretold the same thing a hundred years before. The book is commonly divided into three sections—ch. i. and ii.; ch. iii. to v.; ch. vi. and vii. Each of these opens with a summons to hear God's message, and then proceeds with expostulations and threatenings, which are followed by glorious promises. His style is bold, fiery, and abrupt, and has not a little of the poetic grandeur of Isaiah. His sudden transitions from one subject to another often make his writings difficult to explain. "It is not," says Delitzsch, "a little remarkable that Micah should adopt as the first sentence of his prophecy that with which his namesake concluded his denouncement against Ahab" (1 Kings xxii. 28). Hengstenberg is of opinion that "he quoted the words designedly, in order to show that his prophetic agency was to be considered as a confirmation of that of his predecessor, who was so zealous for God, and that he had more in common with him than the bare name." We may take these words as suggesting certain thoughts concerning *Divine revelation,* or the Bible.

I. IT IS THE "WORD OF THE LORD." What is a word? 1. *A mind-manifesting power.* In his word a true man manifests himself, his thought, feeling, character; and his word is important according to the measure of his faculties, experiences, attainments. Divine revelation manifests the mind of God, especially the moral characteristics of that mind—his rectitude, holiness, mercy, etc. 2. *A mind-influencing power.* Man uses his word to influence other minds, to bring other minds into sympathy with his own. Thus God uses his Word. He uses it to correct human errors, dispel human ignorance, remove human perversities, and turn human thought and sympathy into a course harmonious with his own mind.

II. IT IS "THE WORD OF THE LORD" MADE TO INDIVIDUAL MEN. It "came to Micah the Morasthite." It did not come to all men of his age and country in common. It came to him and a few more. Why certain men were chosen as the special recipients of God's word is a problem whose solution must be left for eternity. If it be said—The men to whom God made special communications were men whose mental faculties, moral genius, and habits specially qualified them to become recipients, and if all men had the same qualifications, all would have Divine communications, the difficulty is not removed by this; for it might still be asked—Why have not all men such qualifications? The fact remains that "Holy men of God spake as they were moved by the Holy Ghost."

III. IT IS "THE WORD OF THE LORD" MADE TO INDIVIDUAL MEN FOR ALL MANKIND. "Hear, all ye people; hearken, O earth, and all that therein is!" God did not speak to any individual man specially in order that the communication might be kept to himself, but that he might communicate it to others. He makes one man the special recipient of truth that he may become the organ and promoter of it. God's Word is for the world, and the man who has it should give it forth. God enlightens, renovates, and saves man by man.—D. T.

Vers. 3—7.—*God's procedure in relation to sin.* "For, behold, the Lord cometh forth out of his place, and will come down, and tread upon the high places of the earth," etc. This is a highly figurative and sublime representation of the Almighty in his retributive work, especially in relation to Samaria and Jerusalem. He is represented as leaving his holy temple, coming out of his place, and marching with overwhelming grandeur over the high places of the earth, to deal out punishment to the wicked. "Behold, the Lord cometh forth out of his place, and will come down, and tread upon the high places of the earth. And the mountains shall be molten under him," etc. "The description of this theophany," says Delitzsch, "is founded upon the idea of a terrible storm and earthquake, as in Ps. xviii. 8. The mountains melt (Judg. v. 4; Ps. lxviii. 8) with the streams of water which discharge themselves from heaven and the valleys split with the deep channels cut out by the torrents of water. The similes 'like wax,' etc. (as in Ps. lxviii. 2), and 'like water' are intended to express the complete dissolution of mountains and valleys. The actual facts answering to this description are the destructive influences exerted upon nature by great national judgments." The reference may be to the destruction of the King of Israel by Shalmaneser, and the invasion of Judah by the armies of Sennacherib and Nebuchadnezzar, by the latter of whom the Jews were carried away captive. The passage is an inexpressibly grand representation of God's *procedure in relation to sin.* Let us look at this procedure in two aspects.

I. AS IT APPEARS TO THE EYE OF MAN. The Bible is eminently anthropomorphic: it presents God to man in human attributes and modes of operation. Two thoughts are suggested: 1. God, in dealing out retribution, appears to man in an *extraordinary position.* "He cometh forth out of his place." What is his place? To all intelligent beings the settled place of the Almighty is the temple of love, the pavilion of goodness, the mercy-seat. The general beauty, order, and happiness of the universe give all intelligent creatures this impression of him. But when confusion and misery fall on the sinner, the Almighty seems to man to come out of his " place "—to step aside from his ordinary procedure. Not that he does so; but in man's view he seems to do so. The Immutable One does not change his purpose. His purpose is benevolent, though in carrying it forward it necessarily brings misery to those who oppose it. Judgment is God's strange work (Isa. xxviii. 21). He comes out of his place to execute it. 2. God, in dealing out retribution, appears to man in a *terrific aspect.* He does not appear as in the silent march of the stars or the serenity of the sun; but as in thunder-storms and volcanic eruptions. "The mountains shall be molten under him, and the valleys shall be cleft, as wax before the fire." Though the Almighty is as benign and serene when bringing deserved suffering upon the sinner as he is when filling heaven with gladness, yet to the suffering sinner he always seems terrific. He seems to be rending the heavens, cleaving the mountains, and tearing the earth to pieces. God is evermore presented to an intelligent creature according to the moral state of his soul.

II. AS IT AFFECTS A SINFUL PEOPLE. In God's procedure in relation to sin, what disastrous effects were brought upon Samaria and Jerusalem! 1. God, in his procedure in relation to sin, brings *material ruin* upon people. "Therefore I will make Samaria as an heap of the field, and as plantings of a vineyard: and I will pour down the stones thereof into the valley, and I will discover the foundations thereof." It means utter ruin. Sin brings material destruction upon a people, brings on commercial decay, political ruin, destroys the health of the body, and brings it ultimately to the dust. Sin brings material ruin. 2. God, in his procedure in relation to sin, brings *mental anguish* upon a people. "And all the graven images thereof shall be beaten to pieces, and all the hires thereof shall be burned with the fire, and all the idols thereof will I lay desolate." A disruption between the soul and the objects of its supreme affections involves the greatest anguish. The gods of a people, whatever they may be, are these objects, and these are to be destroyed. "The graven images thereof shall be beaten to pieces." The divinities, the fanes, the priests—all shattered. Such is the ruin which sin brings on a people.

CONCLUSION. Mark well that God has a course of conduct in relation to sin; or rather, that God, in his beneficent march, must ever appear terrible to the sinner and bring ruin on his head. It is the wisdom as well as the duty of all intelligent creatures to move in thought, sympathy, and purpose as God moves—move with him, not against him. To move with him is to see him in all the attraction of Fatherhood; to move against him is to see him in all the horrors of an infuriated Judge.—D. T.

Vers. 8, 9.—*Moral incurableness.* " Therefore I will wail and howl, I will go stripped and naked: I will make a wailing like the dragons, and mourning as the owls. For her wound is incurable; for it is come unto Judah; he is come unto the gate of my people, even to Jerusalem." These verses have been thus translated : " Therefore will I lament and howl; I will go spoiled and naked; I will keep lamentation like the jackals, and mourning like the ostriches. For her stripes are malignant; for it comes to Judah, reaches to the gate of my people, to Jerusalem." Micah's intention is not only to exhibit publicly his mourning for the approaching calamity of Judah, but also to set forth in a symbolical form the fate that awaits the Judæans. And he can only do this by including himself in the nation, and exhibiting the fate of the nation in his own person. " Wailing like jackals and ostriches is a loud, strong, mournful cry, those animals being distinguished by a mournful wail." We shall take these words as suggesting the subject of *moral incurableness.* Samaria and Jerusalem were, in a material and political sense, in a desperate and hopeless condition. Our subject is *moral incurableness*, and we make two remarks concerning it.

I. IT IS A CONDITION INTO WHICH MEN MAY FALL. 1. *Mental philosophy shows this.* Such is the constitution of the human mind, that the repetition of an act can generate an uncontrollable tendency to repeat it; and the repetition of a sin deadens altogether that moral sensibility which constitutionally recoils from the wrong. The mind often makes habit, not only second nature, but the sovereign of nature. 2. *Observation shows this.* That man's circle of acquaintance must be exceedingly limited who does not know men who become morally incurable. There are incurable liars, incurable misers, incurable sensualists, and incurable drunkards. No moral logician, however great his dialectic skill, can forge an argument strong enough to move them from their old ways, even when urged by the seraphic fervour of the highest rhetoric. 3. *The Bible shows this.* What did Solomon mean when he said, " Speak not in the ears of a fool, for he will despise the wisdom of thy words" (Prov. xxiii. 9)? What did Christ mean when he said, " Give not that which is holy to the dogs, neither cast ye your pearls before swine"? And again, " If thou hadst known, even thou, at least in this thy day, the things which belong unto thy peace ! But now they are hid from thine eyes"? We often speak of retribution as if it always lay beyond the grave, and the day of grace as extending through the whole life of man; but such is not the fact. Retribution begins with many men here; the day of grace terminates with many before the day of death. There are those who reach an unconvertible state; their characters are stereotyped and fixed as eternity.

II. IT IS A CONDITION FOR THE PROFOUNDEST LAMENTATION. At the desperate condition of his country the prophet is brought into the most poignant distress. " Therefore I will wail and howl, I will go stripped and naked : I will make a wailing like the dragons, and mourning as the owls." Christ wept when he considered the moral incurableness of the men of Jerusalem. "O Jerusalem, Jerusalem !" etc. There is no sight more distressing than the sight of a morally incurable soul. There is no building that I pass that strikes me with greater sadness than the Hospital for " Incurables;" but what are incurable bodies compared to *morally incurable* souls? There are anodynes that may deaden their bodily pains, and death will relieve them of their torture; but a morally incurable soul is destined to pass into anguish, intense and more intense as existence runs on, and peradventure without end. The incurable body may not necessarily be an injury to others; but a morally incurable soul must be a curse as long as it lives. Were we truly alive to the moral state of wicked men around us, we should be ready to break out in the words of the prophet, " Therefore I will wail and howl, I will go stripped and naked," etc.—D. T.

Ver. 13.—*Be quick.* " Bind the chariot to the swift beast." These words are addressed to the inhabitants of Lachish. " This place appears to have formed the link of idolatry between Israel and Judah. Lying in the Shephelah, a fortified place of great importance, she was the first city in Judah that was led away by the sin of Jeroboam; and from her the infection spread till at length it reached Jerusalem itself. In the prospect of a sudden attack, it behoved the inhabitants to use all despatch in removing their families and what property they could take with them to a distance. Lachish was besieged by Sennacherib before making the threatened attack on Jerusalem" (2 Kings xviii. 14). Our subject is *promptitude in action.* " Bind the chariot to the swift beast."

I. BE QUICK IN YOUR MATERIAL ENGAGEMENTS. Man has material duties; these are as sacred and as binding as spiritual ones. Indeed, the distinction between the secular and the spiritual is not real, but fictitious. A man should be quick in all his legitimate temporal engagements, whatever they may be. Whatever is to be done must be done at once. "Be diligent in business." By quickness I do not mean the hurry of confusion, but adroit expertness, skilful promptitude. As Shakespeare says, "What the wise do quickly is not done rashly." 1. *The quicker you are, the more you will accomplish.* An expert man will accomplish more in an hour than a slow man in a day. 2. *The quicker you are, the better for your faculties.* The quick movement of the limb is healthier than the slow; the quick action of the mental faculties is more invigorating than the slow. As a rule, the quick man is in every way healthier and happier than the slow. 3. *The quicker you are, the more valuable you are in the market of the world.* The skilful man who cultivates the habit of quickness and despatch increases his commercial value every day. Those trades unions that enact that all of a craft should be paid alike, however they work, enact an absurdity and an injustice. One quick and skilful man may accomplish as much in one day as six slow men, though equally clever. Be quick, then, in business. "Bind the chariot to the swift beast."

II. BE QUICK IN YOUR INTELLECTUAL PURSUITS. You have an enormous amount of mental work to do, if you act up to your duty and discharge your mission in life. You have manifold faculties to discipline, numerous errors to correct, vast and varied knowledge to attain. "The soul without knowledge is not good" (Prov. xix. 2). No, not good either to itself or others. Be quick. 1. *The quicker you are, the more you will attain.* The more fields of truth you will traverse, the more fruits you will gather from the tree of knowledge. Some men in their studies move like elephants, and only traverse a small space. Others, like eagles, sweep continents in a day. The quick eye will see what escapes the dull eye; the quick ear will catch voices unheard by the slow of hearing. 2. *The quicker you are, the better for your faculties.* It is the brisk walker that best strengthens his limbs, the brisk fighter that wins the greatest victories. It is by quick action that the steel is polished and that weapons are sharpened. Intellectual quickness whets the faculties, makes them keen, agile, and apt. "Bind the chariot to the swift beast."

III. BE QUICK IN YOUR SPIRITUAL AFFAIRS. 1. *Morally you have a work to do for your own soul.* It is in a ruined state, it is like the "field of the slothful" and the "vineyard of the man void of understanding" of which Solomon speaks; it needs cultivation. The work is great and urgent. 2. *Morally you have a work to do for others.* There are souls around you demanding your most earnest efforts, etc. (1) Be quick; the work must be done during your life here, if ever done. (2) Be quick; your life here is very short and uncertain. (3) Be quick; the longer you delay, the more difficult it is to do. Be quick: "Whatsoever your hand findeth to do, do it with your might; for there is no knowledge nor device in the grave whither we are all hastening." "Bind the chariot to the swift beast."

> "Oh, let all the soul within you
> For the truth's sake go abroad;
> Strike! let every nerve and sinew
> Tell on ages—tell for God."
>
> (A. C. Coxe.)

D. T.

EXPOSITION.

CHAPTER II.

Vers. 1—5.—§ 6. *The prophet justifies his threat by recounting the sins of which the grandees are guilty.*

Ver. 1.—The prophet, himself one of the people, first inveighs against the sins of injustice and oppression of the poor. **Devise . . . work . . . practise.** A gradation. They are not led into these sins by others; they themselves conceive the evil purpose in their own heart; then they prepare and mature their scheme by reflection; then they proceed to execute it. **Work evil;** *i.e.* prepare the means for carrying out their conception (comp. Isa. xli. 4). **Upon their beds.** At night, the natural time for reflection (comp. Job iv. 13; Ps. iv. 4; xxxvi. 4). **Is light.** Far from shrinking from the light of day in putting into effect their evil projects, they set about their accomplishment as soon as ever the morning allows them. **Because it is in the power of their hand.** Their might makes their right. (For the phrase, comp. Gen. xxxi. 29; Prov. iii. 27.) As the word *el* may be taken to mean "God" as well as "power," some render here, "For their hand is their god," comparing the boast of Mezentius in Virgil, 'Æneid,' x. 773—

"Dextra mihi Deus et telum quod missile libro."

The Vulgate has, *Quoniam contra Deum est manus eorum;* LXX., Διότι οὐκ ἦραν πρὸς τὸν Θεὸν χεῖρας αὐτῶν, "Because they lifted not up their hands unto God." So the Syriac, with the omission of the negative.

Ver. 2.—They carry out by open violence the fraud which they have devised and planned (comp. Isa. v. 8; Amos iv. 1). **Covet fields.** Compare the case of Ahab and Naboth (1 Kings xxi.). The commandment against coveting (Exod. xx. 17) taught the Jews that God regarded sins of thought as well as of action. The Law forbade the alienation of landed property and the transfer of estates from tribe to tribe (Lev. xxv. 23—28; Numb. xxxvi. 7). A rich man might buy a poor man's estate subject to the law of jubilee; but these grandees seem to have forced the sale of property, or else seized it by force or fraud. **Oppress;** Vulgate, *calumniabantur.* The Hebrew word involves the idea of violence.

Ver. 3.—The sin shall be followed by its appropriate punishment. As they devised evil, God will devise a penalty. **This family.** The whole people (Amos iii. 1). **An evil.** A chastisement, a judgment (Amos iii. 6). **Ye.**

The prophet suddenly addresses them, the "family." **Your necks.** He speaks of the calamity as a heavy, galling yoke, from which they should be unable to free themselves (comp. Hos. x. 11). This yoke is their conquest and exile at the hands of foreigners (comp. Jer. xxvii. 12). **Haughtily. With head erect.** Septuagint, ὀρθοί. Their pride shall be brought low. **This time is evil;** full of calamity, which is announced in the following verses. The words occur in Amos v. 13, but the evil there spoken of is moral (comp. Eph. v. 16).

Ver. 4.—**In that day.** The evil time mentioned in ver. 3. **A parable** (*mashal*); probably here "a taunting song." The enemy shall use the words in which Israel laments her calamity as a taunt against her (Hab. ii. 6). **And lament with a doleful lamentation.** The Hebrew gives a remarkable alliteration, *Nahah nehi niheyah;* Septuagint, Θρηνηθήσεται θρῆνος ἐν μέλει, "Lament a lamentation with melody;" Vulgate, *Cantabitur canticum cum suavitate;* "Wail a wail of woe" (Pusey). The Syriac coincides with the LXX. By taking the three words as cognates, we get a very forcible sentence; but most modern commentators consider *niheyah* not a feminine formation, but niph. of the substantive verb *hayah;* hence the words would mean, "Lament with the lamentation;" "It is done," they shall say; "we are utterly spoiled." Thus Cheyne. The lamentation begins with "It is done," and continues to the end of the verse. The verbs are used impersonally—"one shall take up," "one shall lament," "one shall say;" but it is plain that the last two refer to the Jews who shall utter the given dirge, which in turn shall be repeated as a taunt by the enemy. **We are utterly spoiled.** According to the second of the explanations of the preceding clause, these words expand and define the despairing cry, "It is done!" In the other case, they are the commencement of the lamentation. Septuagint, Ταλαιπωρίᾳ ἐταλαιπωρήσαμεν, "We are miserably miserable." The complaint is twofold. First, the once flourishing condition of Israel is changed to ruin and desolation. Secondly, **He hath changed** (*changeth*) **the portion of my people.** This is the second calamity: he, Jehovah, passes our inheritance over to the hands of others; the land of Canaan, pledged to us, is transferred to our enemies. Septuagint, κατεμετρήθη ἐν σχοινίῳ, "hath been measured with a line." **How hath he removed it** [the portion] **from me?** This is better than the alternative rendering, "How doth he depart from me?" **Turning away he hath divided our fields;**

rather, *to an apostate he divideth our fields.*
The apostate is the King of Assyria or
Chaldea; and he is so named as being a
rebel against Jehovah, whom he might have
known by the light of natural religion
(comp. ch. v. 15; Rom. i. 20). This was
fulfilled later by the colonization of Samaria by a mixed population.

Ver. 5.—**Therefore thou.** Because thou,
the tyrannical, oppressive grandee (vers. 1,
2), hast dealt with thy neighbour's land
unjustly, therefore **thou shalt have none
that shall cast a cord** (*the line*) **by lot** (*for
a lot*); i.e. thou shalt have no more inheritance in Israel. The "line" is the measuring-
line used in dividing land, as Amos vii. 17.
The reference is to the original distribution
of the land by lot in Joshua's time (see
Josh. xiv. 2, etc.). **In the congregation of the
Lord.** The Lord's own people, whose polity
was now about to be dissolved. Hitzig,
Reuss, and Orelli suppose that this verse
contains a threat against Micah himself on
the part of the ungodly Jews, intimating
that they will punish him for presuming to
prophesy against them, and that he shall
die without leaving ch'ldren. But this
seems far-fetched and inadmissible.

Vers. 6—11.—§ 7. *The threat announced in
ver. 3 is further vindicated and applied to
individual sinners, with a glance at the
false prophets who taught the people to love
lies.*

Ver. 6.—**Prophesy ye not**; literally, *drop
ye not,* as Amos vii. 16 (where see note).
The speakers are generally supposed to be
the false prophets who wish to stop the
mouths of Micah and those who are like-
minded with him. This is probably correct;
but these are not the only speakers; the
people themselves, the oppressing grandees,
who side with the popularity-hunting seers,
are also included (see note on ver. 12).
Say they to them that **prophesy**; rather,
thus they prophesy (*drop*). Micah uses their
own word sarcastically, "Do not be always
rebuking;" "Thus they rebuke." The rest
of the verse belongs to the same speakers,
and should be rendered, "They shall not
prophesy of these things; reproaches never
cease." The great men and the false
prophets complain of the true prophets that
they are always proclaiming misfortune and
rebuking the people, and they bid them
leave such denunciations alone for the future.
The passage is very difficult, and its interpretation has greatly exercised commentators; the above is virtually the explanation
of Ewald, Hitzig, Caspari, and Cheyne.
Orelli makes the two last clauses Micah's
answer to the interdict of the adversaries,
"Should one not prophesy of these things?

Should reproaches (against the true
prophets) never cease?" We prefer the
interpretations given above, and consider
the prophet's reply to be given in the next
verse.

Ver. 7.—The prophet answers the interdict of the speakers in the preceding verse
by showing that God's attributes are unchanged, but that the sins of the people
constrain him to punish. **O thou that art
named the house of Jacob.** Other renderings
of these words are given, viz. "Ah! what a
saying!" or, "Is this a thing to be said, O
house of Jacob?" The versions of the LXX.,
'Ο λέγων οἶκος 'Ιακὼβ, κ.τ.λ., and of the
Vulgate, *Dicit domus Jacob,* do not suit the
Hebrew. If we adopt the rendering of the
Authorized Version, we must consider that
Micah addresses those who gloried in their
privilege as the family of Jacob, though they
had ceased to be what he was, believing and
obedient. "O ye who are only in name and
title the chosen nation" (comp. Isa. xlviii. 1;
John viii. 33, 39). Professor Driver (*Expositor,* April, 1887) obtains the very suitable
meaning, *Num dicendum,* "Shall it be said,
O house of Jacob, Is the ear of the Lord
shortened?" etc., by the change of a vowel-
point. Somewhat similarly Orelli, "Is this
the speech of the house of Jacob?" viz.
—Should Jehovah be impatient (as these
threats declare him to be)? or were these his
doings? The following clause is Jehovah's
answer to the objection. **Is the Spirit of the
Lord straitened?** or, *shortened.* Is he less long-
suffering than Jehovah of heretofore? Will
you accuse Jehovah of impatience? "Shortness" of spirit is opposed to longanimity (see
Prov. xiv. 29). **Are these his doings?** Are
these judgments and chastisements his usual
doings—that which he delights in? Is the
cause of them in him? Is it not in you (Lam.
iii. 33; Ezek. xxxiii. 11; ch. vii. 18)? **Do
not my words do good,** etc.? This may be
Jehovah's answer to the previous questions,
or Micah's refutation of the complaint. The
Lord's word is good, his action is a blessing,
but only to him who does his commandments
(Ps. xviii. 25, 26; xxv. 10; ciii. 17, etc.;
Luke i. 50).

Ver. 8.—**Even of late; but of late;** literally,
yesterday, implying an action recent and repeated. Septuagint, ἔμπροσθεν, "before;"
Vulgate, *e contrario.* The prophet exemplifies the iniquity which has led God to
punish. They are not old offences which
the Lord is visiting, but sins of recent and
daily occurrence. **My people is risen up as
an enemy.** A reading, varying by a letter
or two, is rendered, "But against my people
one setteth himself." But there is no valid
reason for altering the received text; especially as, according to Ewald, the present
reading may be taken in a causative sense.

"They set up my people as an enemy," *i.e.* the grandees treat the Lord's people as enemies, robbing and plundering them. This translation obviates the difficulty of referring the words, "my people," in this verse to the oppressor, and in ver. 7 to the oppressed. According to the usual view, and retaining the authorized rendering, the meaning is that the princes exhibit themselves as enemies of the Lord by their acts of violence and oppression, which the prophet proceeds to particularize. Septuagint, Ὁ λαός μου εἰς ἔχθραν ἀντέστη, "My people withstood as an enemy." Ye pull off the robe with the garment; *ye violently strip off the robe away from the garment.* The "robe" (*eder*) is the wide cloak, the mantle sufficient to wrap the whole person, and which was often of very costly material. The "garment" (*salmah*) is the principal inner garment, or tunic. There may be an allusion to the enactment which forbade a creditor retaining the pledged garment during the night (Exod. xxii. 26, etc.). Septuagint, Κατέναντι τῆς εἰρήνης αὐτοῦ τὴν δορὰν αὐτοῦ ἐξέδειραν, "Against his peace they stripped off his skin." From them that pass by securely as men averse from war. This is probably the correct translation. The grandees rob those who are peaceably disposed, perhaps strip their debtors of their cloaks as they pass quietly along the road. The versions vary considerably from the received Hebrew text. The LXX. (with which the Syriac partially agrees) has, Τοῦ ἀφελέσθαι ἐλπίδας συντριμμὸν πολέμου, "To remove hope in the destruction of war;" Vulgate, *Eos qui transibant simpliciter convertistis in bellum.* From this rendering Trochon derives the paraphrase—Ye treat them as if they were prisoners of war. Hitzig considers that the reference is to fugitives from the northern kingdom who passed through Judæa in their endeavour to escape the evils of the war, leaving wives and children in the hands of the Judæans. But these treated the refugees harshly.

Ver. 9.—The women of my people. The prophet refers to the widows, who ought to have been protected and cared for (comp. Isa. x. 2). The LXX., with which the Arabic agrees, renders, ἡγούμενοι λαοῦ μου, "the leaders of my people." Have ye cast out. The word expresses a violent expulsion, as Gen. iii. 24. Their pleasant houses; literally, *the house of their delights* (ch. i. 16). The house which was very dear to them, the scene of all their joys. My glory. All the privileges which they enjoyed as God's people and his peculiar care are called "the ornament" of the Lord (comp. Ezek. xvi. 14). The "glory" is by some commentators, but not so appositely, referred to vesture exclusively. These fatherless children had been

ruthlessly stripped of their blessings, either by being forced to grow up in want and ignorance, or by being sold into slavery and carried away from their old religious associations. For ever. The oppressors never repented or tried to make restitution; and so they incurred the special woe of those who injure the poor, the fatherless, and the widow (Pusey). The Septuagint has no connection with the present Hebrew text of this verse, reading, Ἐγγίσατε ὄρεσιν αἰωνίοις, "Draw ye near to the everlasting hills," and previously introducing a gloss, Διὰ τὰ πονηρὰ ἐπιτηδεύματα αὐτῶν ἐξώσθησαν, "They were rejected because of their evil practices." Jerome explains the Greek mystically, despairing of the literal interpretation in its present connection.

Ver. 10.—Arise ye, and depart. The prophet pronounces the oppressors' punishment—they shall be banished from their land, even as they have torn others from their home. This is not your rest. Canaan had been given as a resting-place to Israel (Deut. xii. 9, 10; Ps. xcv. 11), but it should be so no longer. Because it is polluted. The land is regarded as polluted by the sins of its inhabitants. The idea is often found; *e.g.* Lev. xviii. 25, 28; Numb. xxxv. 33; Jer. ii. 7. It shall destroy you, even with a sore destruction. The land is said to destroy when it ejects its inhabitants, as though the inanimate creation rose in judgment against the sinners. The Revised Version, with Keil and others, translates, *Because of uncleanness that destroyeth, even with a grievous destruction;* Septuagint, Διεφθάρητε φθορᾷ, "Ye were utterly destroyed;" Vulgate, *Propter immunditiam ejus corrumpetur putredine pessima.* The Authorized Version is correct.

Ver. 11.—Such prophets as speak unwelcome truths are not popular with the grandees; they like only those who pander to their vices and prophesy lies. This was their crowning sin. If a man walking in the spirit and falsehood do lie. "The spirit and falsehood" may be a hendiadys for "a spirit of falsehood," or "a lying spirit," as 1 Kings xxii. 22 (comp. Ezek. xiii. 2, 3, 17). But it is better to render, *If a man walking after (conversant with) the wind and falsehood do lie.* Wind is symbolical of all that is vain and worthless, as Isa. xxvi. 18; xli. 29. The Septuagint introduces a gloss from Lev. xxvi. 17, Κατεδιώχθητε οὐδενὸς διώκοντος, "Ye fled, no one pursuing you," and translates the above clause, πνεῦμα ἔστησε ψεῦδος: "spiritus statuit mendacium, *i.e.* finem posuit mendacii" (St. Jerome); Vulgate, *Utinam non essem vir habens spiritum, et mendacium potius loquerer.* I will prophesy unto thee, etc. These are the words of a false prophet. "Prophesy," "drop," as ver. 6. **Of wine and of strong drink.** Concerning temporal blessings, dwelling on God's promises of material prosperity (Lev. xxvi. 4, etc.; Deut. xxviii. 4, 11) in order to encourage the grandees in self-indulgence. **He shall even be the prophet of this people.** Such a one is the only prophet to whom the great men, the representatives of "this people," will listen.

Vers. 12, 13.—§ 8. *Promise of restoration and deliverance.*

Ver. 12.—The prophet, without any preface, introduces abruptly a promise of restoration after exile, a type of the triumph of Messiah. Some commentators, indeed, regard this and the following verse as the language of the false prophets; others, as a denunciation of punishment, not a promise of deliverance; others, as a late interpolation. But the style is entirely Micah's (comp. ch. iv. 6, 7), the promise is a true one, and such-like sudden transitions are common in the prophetical books (comp. *e.g.* Isa. iv. 2—6; Hos. i. 10; xi. 9; Amos ix. 11); so that we need not resort to the hypothesis that some connecting link has dropped out of the text, or that the clause is misplaced; and we are fully justified in considering the paragraph as inserted here in its right position, and as predictive of the restoration of the Jews after captivity. Micah would seem to imply—I am not; indeed, as one of the false prophets who promise you earthly good without regard to your moral fitness for receiving God's bounty; neither am I one who has no message but of woe and calamity; I, too, predict salvation and happiness for a remnant of you after you have been tried by defeat and exile. **I will surely assemble.** This presupposes dispersion among the heathen, such as is foretold in ch. i. 8, etc.; ii. 4, etc. **O Jacob, all of thee.** The promise extends to the whole nation, whether called Jacob or Israel, as ch. i. 5; but still only a **remnant,** *i.e.* that portion of the nation which should make a good use of adversity, and turn to the Lord with sincere repentance (comp. Isa. x. 20, etc.; Jer. xxxi. 8; Ezek. xxxiv. 11, etc.; Zeph. iii. 12, etc.). Some see in the term "remnant" an allusion to the people that were left in the northern kingdom after the fall of Samaria. **As the sheep of Bozrah.** There were two or more towns so named—one in Sidon, for which see note on Amos i. 12; and another, *hod. Buzrah,* on the south border of the Hauran. This is mentioned in Jer. xlviii. 24, as one of the cities of Moab, a district celebrated for its flocks (2 Kings iii. 4); hence "sheep of Bozrah" may have become a proverbial saying. **Many** commentators take *Botsrah* as an appellative, meaning "fold," in agreement with the Vulgate, *quasi gregem in ovili,* and Chaldee, as well as Aquila and Symmachus. The parallelism in the following words seems to favour this view. The LXX. reads differently, rendering, ἐν θλίψει, "in trouble." Thus, too, the Syriac. **As the flock in the midst of their fold;** rather, *as a flock in the midst of its pasture.* They shall make great noise, etc. Like a numerous flock bleating in its fold, so shall the returned Israelites be, prosperous and happy, celebrating their salvation with praise and exultation (comp. Ezek. xxxiv. 31). Septuagint, Ἐξαλοῦνται ἐξ ἀνθρώπων, "They shall leap forth from among men," which St. Jerome explains as meaning that the repentant Israelites shall rise above worldly things and aspire to heaven.

Ver. 13.—**The breaker is come** (*gone*) **up before them.** Micah depicts Israel's redemption under the figure of release from captivity. The passage is clearly Messianic, and can neither be considered an interpolation nor tortured into a declaration of the siege and ruin of Samaria or Jerusalem. "One that breaketh" is a liberator, a leader that overcomes all obstacles which oppose Israel's return. There may be an allusion in the first instance to a human leader, such as Zerubbabel, in analogy with Moses and Joshua in old time, but the real conqueror intended is generally regarded as Messiah. The Breaker-up is supposed to be a title of the Messiah well known to the Jews (see Pusey; and Pearson, 'Exposition of the Creed,' art. vii., note y[1]). This interpretation is rejected by Professor Driver (*Expositor,* April, 1887), who considers the "breaker-up" to be "either a leader or a detachment of men, whose duty it was to break up walls or other obstacles opposing the progress of an army." But is not this to introduce an agency unknown to these times? Was there any special body of men trained and maintained for this particular duty? This "breaker-up," according to Dr. Driver's conception, "advances before them, breaking through the gates of the prison in which the people are confined; they follow, marching forth triumphantly through this open way; their king, with Jehovah at his side (Ps. cx. 5), heads the victorious procession (Exod. xiii. 21; Isa. lii. 12)." **They have broken up;** *broken forth,* or *through.* The captives co-operate with their leader. **Have passed through the gate,** etc. The prophet speaks of a solemn, regular removal, like the Exodus from Egypt, which no human power can oppose. **Their king.** The same as Jehovah in the next clause (Isa. xxxiii. 22). He shall lead the host, as he headed the Israelites when they left the house of bondage (Exod. xiii. 21). The prediction may look forward to the final gathering of Israel, which St. Paul seems to contemplate when he writes, "And so all Israel shall be saved" (Rom. xi. 26).

HOMILETICS.

Vers. 1—11.—*Delineations of deep transgression, righteous retribution, and Divine equity.* We have in these verses three pictures, drawn by a master-hand, and very suggestive of practical teaching.

I. A PICTURE OF DEEP TRANSGRESSION. (Vers. 1, 2, 8, 9.) Observe delineated in it: 1. *The abuse of privilege.* (Ver. 1.) What a boon is night! "The season of repose; the blessed barrier betwixt day and day," when the hum and bustle, the anxiety and fatigue, of business is suspended, when the tired artisan rests from his toil; when the voyager on the wide sea forgets awhile the perils of the main; when the warrior ceases for a time to hear the roar of the cannon and to face the foe; and when all nature is hushed to slumber, save the weary watchers by the bed of suffering, and wakeful, loving mothers tending their dear ones in their quiet nests. We bless God for the day with its early sunrise, its noontide glory, its evening shades; but we bless him also for the night, with her sable mantle, her vague solitude, her quiet rest. And this high privilege was grossly abused. "Woe to them that devise iniquity, and work evil upon their beds!" (ver. 1). It was not that evil thoughts unwillingly invaded their minds, but that they deliberately planned evil—they devised it. It is one thing for evil thoughts to enter the mind in its quiet hours unbidden; it is quite another to entertain these; and worst of all is it to "devise" these, and in the very seasons given to man for rest, to be found plotting and contriving harm. So has it ever been with the ungodly, that they have abused God's best gifts (Ps. xxxvi. 4; Prov. iv. 16). 2. *The non-improvement of opportunity.* (Ver. 1.) Each morning comes bearing to us a new gift of time from our God. With our waking hours comes the Divine call to fresh service. Strength has been gathered up, now to be expended in the improvement of the opportunities of holy service which will assuredly arise. Happy they who begin the day with God, and then go forth to hallow every engagement of life, and to use for him every opportunity which may be given—

> "True hearts spread and heave
> Unto their God, as flowers do to the sun:
> Give him thy first thoughts, so shalt thou keep
> Him company all day."

The grave charge here urged was that with the breaking of the day they went forth to renew their evil deeds; that the fresh strength imparted to them by God became employed by them against him; the evil plotted by them in the night they went forth with the morning's dawn to commit; the energies which ought to have been consecrated to God they devoted to dark and daring deeds of impiety. "When the morning is light, they practise it, because it is in the power of their hand" (ver. 1). 3. *The perversion of power.* (Vers. 2, 8, 9.) Both Micah and Isaiah laid stress upon the prevailing sin of covetousness, leading the mighty and influential to pervert the power and influence they possessed, to the injury of the feeble and obscure, oppressing and tyrannizing over them. Thus they are charged here with (1) unscrupulously depriving them of their inheritance (ver. 2); (2) stripping of their raiment peaceful, unoffending persons (ver. 8); (3) driving widows from their houses, and causing fatherless children to suffer from want and neglect (ver. 9). In this way the sad picture of shameless sin here presented to us is rendered increasingly dark through the prevailing sin of covetousness, leading to harsh oppression and grievous wrong. 4. *The wilful rejection of light and preference of darkness.* (Vers. 6, 11.) To the true prophets of the Lord, who sought to bring home to them a sense of their guilt, and to lead them to return unto the Lord, they said, "Prophesy ye not" (ver. 6), whereas to lying spirits they would readily give heed (John iii. 19, 20).

II. A PICTURE OF MERITED CHASTISEMENT. (Vers. 3, 4, 5, 10.) The main feature in this picture is the illustration it affords of the retributive character of the Divine chastisement for sin. Observe: 1. They had "devised" evil against others; now

God would "devise" evil against them (ver. 3). 2. They had oppressed others; now they should be oppressed (ver. 3), and even their own sad elegies, wrung from them through their sorrow, should be taken up and repeated against them in sheer mockery by their oppressors (vers. 4, 5). 3. They had voluntarily chosen their false prophets and had welcomed their lying words, and they should now get no comfort from the words of hope which, in the dark days, should be spoken by the true prophets, and which should prove consolatory to the remnant of God's people who had remained faithful (ver. 6). 4. They had cast out the widows and the fatherless, and they should be themselves cast out (ver. 10). We look on this picture of coming chastisement, and we learn from it that retribution follows sin; we see in it an Old Testament illustration of the New Testament assurance that "whatsoever a man soweth, that shall he also reap" (Gal. vi. 7, 8).

III. A PICTURE OF THE DIVINE EQUITY. (Ver. 7.) God, through his prophet, expostulated with the people who had acted so unworthily, who bore the name of Israel, but who so dishonoured their pious ancestry; and declared to them that his ways were not unequal; that rectitude and mercy characterized all his operations; that through all he had been seeking their good; that it was not his will that the threatened woes should befall them; that this was entirely their own act; and that neither their sins nor their sorrows could truthfully be charged upon him. There are many such passages scattered throughout the prophetical writings, in which God deigned to expostulate with the erring—passages which are inexpressibly tender and touching (Jer. ii. 5; Isa. v. 4; xliii. 22, 25). So Christ to the Jews of his day, when they took up stones to stone him, asked, "For which of these works do ye stone me?" (John x. 32). And the same Divine voice expostulates with us in our sinfulness; and our response should be, "Unto thee," etc. (Dan. ix. 6, 7). These Divine expostulations are the arrows of conviction coming from God to the hearts of men, and which, unlike the poisoned arrows of the ancients that carried death in their flight, carry mercy and life into the human soul.

Ver. 7.—*God's ways vindicated.* In this verse three important questions are asked, and in the answers to these lies the clear vindication of God's ways in his dealings with transgressors.

I. "IS THE SPIRIT OF THE LORD STRAITENED?" *i.e.* when his judgments overtake men for their sins, is this to be regarded as a token that God's loving-kindness and long-suffering have failed? No; his compassions never fail. "His mercy endureth for ever." What, then, is the explanation? It is that such Divine judgments are imperatively demanded. They are so: 1. *In vindication of the Divine rectitude.* If sin went unpunished, the Divine righteousness might, indeed, be questioned. It was this consideration, and not a spirit of vindictiveness which called forth "the imprecatory psalms," in which chastisement was invoked upon the workers of iniquity. 2. *In the interest of the wrong-doers themselves.* It is not for the advantage of transgressors themselves that they should be allowed to go on unblushingly in sin. The Divine long-suffering may operate in checking and bringing such to a stand; in chastening them with a view to their reformation. 3. *In order to the promotion of the well-being of society at large.* Jehovah is the sovereign Ruler; the universe is his domain; and it may be essential, in order to the good of the race, that he should at times interpose in judgment. "When his judgments are abroad in the earth, the inhabitants thereof learn righteousness" (Isa. xxvi. 9).

II. "ARE THESE HIS DOINGS?" *i.e.* is God the Author and Cause of the evils men have to experience when they stray from righteousness? No; he cannot be; these are to be traced to the wrong-doers themselves, and are the outcome of their misdeeds. The sinner is his own punisher. The woes which befall him he has worked out for himself. "Judas fell from the ministry and apostleship, that he might go to *his own place.*" "Men meet with all sorts of bitter, painful, and bad things in their life, just because they are bitter, painful, and bad themselves, and do not see that this is the root of their misery" (Bushnell).

III. "DO NOT MY WORDS DO GOOD TO HIM THAT WALKETH UPRIGHTLY?" Assuredly; and hence, if this good is missed, must it not be because there is a lack of obedience in those who miss it, so that the responsibility is entirely theirs?

Ver. 7.—*The beneficial influence of God's words upon the obedient.* By the "words" of God we understand the utterances of his gracious mind. These were communicated unto the fathers by the prophets; in "the fulness of time" they were made known by his Son; to us they are given in the Scriptures of eternal truth. Their influence upon us depends upon our attitude towards them and upon the spirit we cherish. If our aim is to live a godly life, and to pursue the path of rectitude and obedience, they will prove truly helpful to us.

I. GOD'S "WORDS" "DO GOOD" TO THE UPRIGHT IN HEART, AS IT RESPECTS THEIR PERSONAL AND INDIVIDUAL LIFE. They become thus benefited: 1. *Physically;* being preserved by these teachings from those excesses into which the ungodly often fall (Ps. xci. 16; cxix. 95). 2. *Mentally;* their minds being directed to the sublimest themes, by meditating upon which their intellectual faculties become purified and strengthened. Men possessed of the highest intellectual endowments have acknowledged their deep indebtedness to the holy words of God, and have accepted them with the profoundest reverence and the warmest gratitude. 3. In the darkest seasons of their life "God's words" have cheered and comforted them, and through the sanctifying influence of these they have been rendered in times of severest trial so tranquil, and so calm in death that it may be said—

> "The night-dews fall not gentlier on the ground,
> Nor weary, worn-out winds expire so soft."

II. GOD'S "WORDS" "DO GOOD" TO THE UPRIGHT IN HEART, AS IT RESPECTS THEIR SOCIAL RELATIONSHIPS. 1. Their healthful influence is experienced in the home-life of the obedient. In such homes, selfishness, coldness, jealousy, anger, strife, are avoided; and love, sympathy, union, harmony, are continually cherished. God's words are daily recalled to mind, and the voice of praise and prayer continually ascends to their Author. "Good" is thus experienced. There is written on such abodes, in characters legible and golden, the inscription, "Peace." Day by day the members of such households become united in a firmer bond to each other and to God. Yea, it is theirs to enjoy in the home of earth constant foretastes of the home of heaven. 2. And their healthful influence is experienced in the intercourse of *man with man.* God's words give special enforcement to the principle of mutual regard which should be cherished by the children of men. In proportion as the power of his utterances is realized will the servant be led to promote the best interests of the employer, and the employer to act generously towards even the humblest in his service. The holy teachings of our God impel those who truly accept them to minister to the necessities of the distressed, and to endeavour to alleviate human suffering and woe. Love is indeed the essence of all that he has spoken. And abounding in loving teachings for the guidance of its recipients in their social and everyday life, God's "words" promote the good even of those who unconsciously come within the range of their influence.

III. GOD'S "WORDS" "DO GOOD" TO THE UPRIGHT IN HEART, AS IT RESPECTS THEIR POLITICAL INFLUENCE. The men who are under the sway of these pure words which God hath spoken are the true promoters of the national weal. Nations, in order to their real prosperity, need to hear and heed the voice of God speaking to them as to Israel of old, and saying, "And now what doth the Lord require of thee but to fear the Lord thy God, to walk in all his ways . . . *for thy good?*" (Deut. x. 12, 13).

Vers. 12, 13.—"*Glorious things*" *spoken of the true Israel.* No member of "the goodly fellowship of the prophets" had a more vivid sense of the ultimate enfranchisement from all evil, awaiting the race, to be effected by the Messiah in due course, than was possessed by "Micah the Morasthite." Even as in the opening portion of his prophecy, he lingered, in thought and expression, upon the prevailing ungodliness, marking on every hand confusion and strife and wrong, he could yet see coming "the age of gold," when peace and harmony, purity and righteousness should secure the victory; and of that glorious age, lo! he here sings. Just what the oasis is to the surrounding desert, or the silver lining to the dark cloud, or the momentary pause in the storm, when for an instant the noise of the waves is stilled, telling of the coming calm, that these two verses seem to be to the first three chapters of this book of Scripture, and by their bright and hopeful tone the hearts of "the remnant" who deplored the abounding iniquity of the times became, we doubt not, lifted up with devout thankfulness and inspired with renewed strength. Are we to understand these bright passages scattered throughout this prophecy, and alluding to a glory to be realized in the future, as referring simply to happier days to be experienced by the Jewish nation, or are they to be regarded as having a more comprehensive range? Whilst believing firmly that a glorious destiny is before the Hebrew nation, and that the working out of that destiny shall be not only for its own spiritual good, but also for the enrichment of the world (Rom. xi. 12), yet we should lose much of the force of the prophetic Scriptures in their allusions to "the latter-day glory," by limiting their utterances thus. We should not half realize the depth of meaning underlying these verses by simply regarding the passage as setting forth that the Jews, after a period of captivity in Babylon, should return again to their own land. Prophecy was designed to prepare the way of the Lord Christ. And, thus viewed, it was marked by progressive stages. The work began in the revelation made through Moses of the will and Law of God. Then, after a time, followed the era of Samuel, who, with his contemporaries and successors, laboured to maintain true religion in Israel, chosen of God as the nation through whom his purposes of mercy were to be unfolded. And following these, we come to the age of written prophecy, in which the holy seers, whilst not neglecting the claims of their own nation, took a wider range of vision and looked forward to a new covenant affecting all nations, and to the coming of the Messiah as One who should establish a spiritual kingdom, whose claims were to be urged upon all the world, and unto whom men of every nation and kindred and tribe should turn, thus forming the spiritual Israel over whom the Messiah should reign in righteousness (see Dr. Payne Smith's 'Prophecy a Preparation for Christ'). Micah notably belonged to this more advanced period of the prophetic development, and hence his bright anticipations of the glorious future are to be understood as having this wider scope. He was contemporary with Isaiah, who constantly represented the Lord as reigning over the whole earth, and even the far-distant lands as bringing unto him their tribute. We are led to ask—How did they gain these broad and far-reaching conceptions of all the nations as gathering together, and becoming loyal to the God of the Hebrews, and becoming one as being alike citizens of the heavenly King? It was not natural for them to cherish such a notion as this. It involved their breaking away from their national traditions, and it did violence to all their prejudices as Jews. The Hebrews regarded themselves as the elect of God, chosen by him out of every nation to the highest dignity and honour. How, then, did this conviction, of the world-embracing character of the blessings of the Messiah's reign become developed in the minds, and expressed in the burning words of enthusiasm, by the tongues of men who shared in the national bias? There is no explanation of this remarkable phenomenon save one, even that they had it wrought in them, and were led to embrace it and proclaim it by the inspiration of God's own Spirit (Gal. i. 12). "Glorious things" are here spoken of the true Israel, the spiritual kingdom of the Redeemer, the Church of the living God. Observe—

I. ENLARGEMENT. (Ver. 12.) The good in the land were but few. The vast multitudes of the people, of all sorts and conditions, had corrupted their way. They had turned aside to the practice of iniquity in all its forms. It seemed as though true piety would soon be extinguished in the land. The hearts of the few who amidst the prevailing faithlessness were found faithful were naturally despondent and depressed. And the words of hope here spoken by the prophet were specially designed for the comfort and help of such. God, by the mouth of his holy prophet, reminded such that as there would be, in consequence of the nation's guilt, the scattering and the dispersing, so there should come a time of revival and regathering. The true Israel should not perish. As the shepherd gathers together the scattered members of his flock, so "the remnant according to the election of grace," now to be dispersed through sins not their own, should be watched over in their exile, and eventually be gathered as forming part of the Messiah's flock. Nor they alone; but as in the early days of their national history, the more they were persecuted the more they multiplied and grew, so, as the result of the sorrows now in store, there should be secured a great spiritual increase. Yea, further, whilst "all Israel should be saved," "the fulness of the Gentiles" should also come in. And hence the obedient should be so multiplied in number that they should be as "the sheep of Bozrah," the wealth of which consisted in the abundance of its flocks and herds; indeed, so numerous should they be, that they should make "great noise by reason of the multitude of men" (ver. 12). There are times when we get depressed and sad at heart in holy service, and specially when we mark the vast portions of the human race as yet untouched by the sacred and saving influences of God's truth. We cry, "How long, O Lord, how long? Why is his chariot so long in coming?" But, courage! it will not be ever thus. The Divine purpose is to flood the world with the light of truth, and to gather a multitude out of every nation, and kindred, and tongue, and people. There shall be enlargement. The Messiah "shall see of the travail of his soul, and be satisfied." "Of the increase of his kingdom there shall be no end." This is sure; it is certain; it cannot fail. "The mouth of the Lord hath spoken it."

II. SECURITY. "As the flock in the midst of their fold" (ver. 12). One of the most impressive and encouraging of the figures of speech employed in Scripture to reveal to us the Divine character is that in which the Lord is referred to as the Shepherd folding the flock in his care. True, the figure is suggestive of much that is calculated to humble us; for if he is our "Shepherd," then are we "the sheep of his pasture," and as such are very helpless ourselves, in the midst of the dangers by which we are surrounded, and very prone by reason of our weakness to wander from the fold; but then the beautiful simile encourages us, assuring us that the Lord will be our Strength in weakness, that he will defend us amidst every peril, and that in all our strayings he will follow us with a view to restoring us by his power and grace. Since he is "the Shepherd of Israel," his people are secure "as sheep in the midst of their fold." And this protection will be afforded to "his own," even amidst the gloomiest experiences of their life. There are times when even the best of men are called upon "to walk in darkness," having "no light." And what is needed in such seasons is the spirit of holy trust, a trust which will repose unswervingly in the good Shepherd's faithfulness and love, and which will take comfort in his rod and staff, in the tokens of his presence, the conviction of his sovereign sway, and the assurances of his Word. So Micah would have the tired, yet true-hearted, in his day feel; and so should such in all ages realize, that in the care of God they are as secure from harm as "the flock in the midst of their fold," watched over by the faithful shepherd's continual care.

III. DELIVERANCE. (Ver. 13.) The passage indicates that not only shall there be protection afforded in the times of peril, but also deliverance out of danger. It is in this connection that Micah here introduces into the words of hope he was uttering an allusion to the Messiah. He referred to him as "the Breaker," going on before his servants, overcoming and breaking through every hindrance to their advancement; they following him and through him becoming themselves triumphant. "The Breaker is come up before them," etc. (ver. 13).

IV. HONOUR. "And the Lord at the head of them" (ver. 13). Through all it was their privilege and distinction to be associated with the Lord Most High. The true Shechinah-glory was theirs. And when at length the conflict should be past, and the time of "storm and scattering" should have ended, the all-presiding Love would still be at their head, their everlasting Light, their eternal Glory. "His name shall be in their foreheads" (Rev. xxii. 4); "They shall be his people, and he will be their God." They shall dwell with him, and he abide with them; and from the constant experience of his love and favour their blessedness shall perpetually flow, and flow on for evermore. Thus this messenger of the Lord appears to have turned away his thoughts for a moment from the burden of woe he was delivering, and to have fixed his mind upon that brighter era which should at length dawn upon the world sin had darkened and defiled. We do well also to keep that era in view, and in anticipation of it "in patience to possess our souls."

Ver. 13.—*The Breaker.* In these words the prophet represents the Messiah as going before his people, removing every barrier, overcoming every obstruction, preparing the way for them, and bringing them through every difficulty. This representation was frequently made by the Jewish prophets, and the title, "The *Breaker-through*" was familiar to the Jews as one of the titles of the Messiah.

I. THIS TITLE HAS ITS APPLICATION TO THE MESSIAH IN HIS RELATIONSHIP TO THE

UNIVERSAL CHURCH. The ultimate victory and glory of the Church of God is assured. Such is God's eternal purpose, and which by his sovereign power he will eventually accomplish. Obstacles to the fulfilment of this purpose are continually arising. Impediments are placed in the way. Active opposition has been offered to the advancement of the kingdom of truth and righteousness. "The kings of the earth set themselves," etc. (Ps. ii. 2). Or when not thus actively engaged against the truth they have often taken such measures in the interests of their own worldly policy as have seriously impeded the progress of truth. Hoary systems of idolatry also have long held sway over millions of the human race, and the glory due unto the Lord has been given to "graven images." Yet "the counsel of the Lord standeth sure," and the purpose he has purposed shall be accomplished. And with respect to its accomplishment the Messiah is "the *Breaker-through.*" He, "the Leader and Commander of his people," shall go before them, casting down the imaginations and frustrating the designs of the evil, "opening the blind eyes, bringing out the prisoners from the prison, and them that sit in darkness out of the prison-house." Every mountain shall become a plain before him. He shall go on conquering and to conquer, until at last there shall rise the cry of victory, "The kingdoms of this world," etc. (Rev. xi. 15).

II. THIS TITLE HAS ITS APPLICATION TO THE MESSIAH ALSO IN THE RELATIONSHIP HE SUSTAINS TO HIS SERVANTS INDIVIDUALLY. It is a title which may be accounted precious, not only to the Church of God as a whole, but also to each servant of the Lord. It is interesting to notice how that Christ, in one of his memorable discourses, associated this thought, of his going before his servants with a view to their being brought through every difficulty, with his references to himself as "the good Shepherd;" so that in the recorded words of Jesus (John x. 3, 4) we find the very same association of figures of speech which were here employed by Micah; for Christ said of himself as the Shepherd, "He calleth his own sheep by name, and *leadeth them out;*" "He goeth before them, and *they follow him.*" And may not the writer of the Epistle to the Hebrews have had the words Micah here employed, and the words of Christ alluded to, in mind when he wrote of the Saviour as being "the Forerunner" of his people (Heb. vi. 20)? Christ has gone before his servants, and has gained the victory over their spiritual foes. He has conquered the *evil one.* In his life he conquered, for not once did the adversary gain the ascendancy over him; and in his death he conquered, for then "he spoiled principalities and powers, and made a show of them," etc. (Col. ii. 15). He has conquered the *world,* and could say to his disciples, "I have overcome the world." And he has conquered *death and the grave,* fulfilling the triumphant declaration, "O death! I will be thy plagues! O grave! I will be thy destruction" (Hos. xiii. 14; Isa. xxv. 8). Thus he is, in the interests of each of his servants, "*the Breaker.*" By his victory he has so weakened the strength of our spiritual adversaries as to render the conflict comparatively easy to us. We have to encounter foes already defeated by our Lord. We have to face enemies already dispirited by failure, and who know assuredly that the time of their triumphing is short. Beautiful representation of the Messiah this! "The *Breaker,*" who removes all difficulty out of the way of his servants; who has gone before them to clear the ground, to cast down every obstruction, to make "the crooked things straight, and the rough places plain," that "the glory of the Lord may be revealed." Let us hear his voice saying to us, as he thus leads us on, "Follow me;" and be it ours (1) cheerfully, (2) trustingly, (3) and courageously to obey the great Captain's call, and to enter through him into honour, glory, and immortality!

HOMILIES BY VARIOUS AUTHORS.

Vers. 1—3.—*Deliberate sins bringing predestined punishments.* We see here—

I. THE GENESIS OF CRIME. Three stages are described. 1. *Sinful desires are cherished in the heart.* These sinners "devise iniquity," think over it (Ps. vii. 14), imagine it (the same word as in 1 Sam. xviii. 25, referring to Saul's thought and plan to secure David's death), dwell on it; for wickedness is "sweet in their mouth" (Job xx. 10—12). Illustrate from the licentious thoughts of David (2 Sam. xi. 2, 3) or Amnon (2 Sam. xiii. 1, 2), the covetous thoughts of Ahab (1 Kings xxi.), or the envious and revengeful thoughts of Haman (Esth. iii. 5, 6 ; see Jas. i. 14, 15). Here sin is not traced during its growth. From its birth St. James passes on to its maturity: "The sin, when it is full grown, bringeth forth death." But Micah points out stages in its growth. 2. *Plans of wickedness are deliberately contrived.* They "work," prepare or fabricate, "evil upon their beds." In their hours of rest they "cannot cease from sin." On their beds, where they might enjoy the sleep of God's beloved, where in wakeful hours they might commune with God and their own hearts (Ps. iv. 4; xvi. 7; lxiii. 6; civ. 34), they plot their crimes (Ps. xxxvi. 4; Prov. iv. 16). If they want allies they hesitate not to secure the aid of the false witness, the procuress, the dishonest lawyer, the bribed judge. Illust.: Jezebel; the priests (Matt. xxviii. 11—14); the assassins (Acts xxiii. 12—15). 3. *The plot is executed in a crime.* They act promptly, early, showing no signs of repentance or reflection (Jer. viii. 6); in the daylight, without shame (Esth. vi. 4; Matt. xxvii. 1, 2)—"swift to shed blood," or defraud, or debauch. Might constitutes their right; "impiously mighty and mighty in impiety," "because it is in the power of their hands." "Dextra mihi Deus" (Virgil). They are reckless of the ruin caused to an innocent man or a whole family robbed of their heritage (Neh. v. 1—5), or of their head (1 Kings xxi. 13), or of the flower of the flock, some beloved child more precious than any heritage (2 Sam. xii. 1—9).

II. Its INEVITABLE CONNECTION WITH RETRIBUTION. While sinners are coveting, plotting, plundering, God is watching, devising, and framing punishment. This is: 1. *Predestined*; on the ground of deliberate sin. God's "therefores" have all the force of demonstrative reasoning (Prov. i. 31; Isa. lxv. 12, etc.). 2. *Hard to be borne.* Compared to a yoke. Contrast the yoke of the Father's discipline (Lam. iii. 27), and of the Redeemer's service (Matt. xi. 29, 30). If these yokes are contemptuously cast away, the evil yoke of punishment, a "yoke of iron," is prepared (Deut. xxviii. 48; Jer. xxviii. 14). 3. *Inevitable.* See the striking figures in Amos ix. 1—4 and Zech. xiv. 16—18 (God's manifold instruments of punishment); cf. 1 Tim. vi. 9, 10. 4. *Humiliating.* "Neither shall ye go haughtily." How often the retribution on the proud or the extortioner is strikingly appropriate to their sin ! Man's skill in successful sinning is outmatched by God's wisdom in punishing (Job ix. 4). When God's wisdom and power are both arrayed against us, it is an evil time indeed. 5. *Utterly disastrous.* A revolution in their entire circumstances (ver. 4). Thus the consequences of sin may be irreparable in this world; but the gospel of the grace of God tells of a forgiveness whereby sin may be righteously forgiven, and the eternal consequences may be cut off (Isa. xliii. 25; John v. 24).—E. S. P.

Ver. 6.—*An impious veto; a fatal withdrawal.* We adopt as our rendering of this difficult verse, "Prophesy not; they shall indeed prophesy; they shall not prophesy to these; shame shall not depart." We see here—

I. AN IMPIOUS VETO. Men may seek to put their veto on a faithful messenger in various ways. 1. *By seeking to persuade him to utter smooth words.* Thus Micaiah's integrity was first assailed (1 Kings xxii. 13). So, too, in the later days of Amos (ii. 12, where the corruption of prophets as well as of Nazarites is suggested) and of Isaiah (xxx. 9—11). 2. *By direct veto, supported by threats,* uttered or implied, as in the case of Amos (vii. 10—13). 3. *By direct persecution.* Micaiah was imprisoned; Jezebel "cut off the prophets of the Lord," and sought to slay Elijah. Conspiracies were formed against the liberty and the life of Jeremiah (xx. 1, 2; xxvi. 8, 9). God's faithful witnesses are always odious to "the beast" and those who bear his mark (Rev. xi. 7—10). Successive steps in this impious veto are seen in the experience of Christ's apostles (Acts iv. 1—3, 18—21; v. 17, 18, 26—40). 4. *By stubborn neglect or haughty contempt.* These are virtually a veto on faithful preachers (cf. Isa. xxviii. 9—12; liii. 1). It is as though their hearers said, "Spare your breath," or in still ruder phrase, "Shut up !" For they actually prefer such teachers as those alluded to in ver. 11, who encourage them in sin and delusion (Deut. xxix. 19, 20). The contempt with which preachers and their messages are often regarded are a temptation to abandon the work. They say, "Drop not" (Hebrew), which seems almost equivalent to "Drivel not." We hear of "the decay of preaching," and know by how many it is neglected. To say, "We do not care to hear your message," is much the same as to say, "Prophesy not." And the neglect of God's truth by courteous and even complimentary hearers is a sore temptation to an earnest preacher who watches for souls not for smiles (Ezek. xxxiii. 30—32). To this impious veto a reply comes in the form of—

II. A FATAL WITHDRAWAL. We hear three sharp, decisive messages. 1. "*They shall prophesy.*" God's servants shall continue to do so under the constraint of both a Divine command and an irresistible impulse. Both these are illustrated in the history of Jeremiah, who shrank from his mission (i. 5—19; xv. 10; xx. 7, 8), yet undertook it (ii. 1), and returned to it again and again (xv. 15, 16; xx. 9). St. Paul is another example (Acts xxvi. 16—20; Gal. i. 15, 16; see too Acts xx. 24; 1 Cor. ix. 16). Men's impiety shall not frustrate God's purposes. 2. "*They shall not prophesy to these.*" The ministry shall be withdrawn (Ps. lxxiv. 9; Amos viii. 11—13; and see 1 Macc. iv. 46; ix. 27; xiv. 41); or, if continued, it will be of no avail because of the hardness of heart of the hearers (Ezek. iii. 24—27). Both these threats are illustrated by the treatment of the gospel by the Jews, and of the Jews by the apostles (Acts xiii. 46, 47; xxviii. 23—28). Many now are subject to a similar sentence. They nominally attend some pastor's ministry, but practically are without it, because deaf to the message it brings to them. Then the threat against God's ancient vineyard is fulfilled, "I will also command the clouds that they rain no rain upon it" (Isa. v. 6). Showers of blessing are dropping on others, but their hearts are dry, like Gideon's fleece when the floor around was soaked with dew. 3. "*Shame shall not depart.*" By silencing God's messengers they hoped to silence the reproaches of conscience and the shame they felt at the prophet's rebukes. But in vain. The fact of the withdrawal of the messengers was itself a shame to the people; like the withdrawal of an ambassador because he had been shamefully treated (illust.: 2 Sam. x. 1—4; Roman ambassador insulted at Tarentum; and cf. Luke x. 16). This shame was the fruit of their own doings, and was thus bound up with their future history. It became more and more aggravated, owing to the degrading influence of sin. The wrath of God abode on them, whereas, by repentance and faith, it might have been removed (cf. John iii. 36 with ix. 41). The final issue of shameful sin must be a resurrection "to shame" and "condemnation" (Dan. xii. 2; John v. 29).—E. S. P.

Ver. 7.—*Judgment, God's strange work; mercy, his delight.* Adopting as our translation, "O thou, called the house of Jacob, is the patience of Jehovah short? Are these his doings? Do not his words do good to him that walketh uprightly?" we learn two truths respecting God.

I. JUDGMENT IS GOD'S "STRANGE WORK." 1. *The people are reminded of this by their very name.* It is a great honour but a grave responsibility to have a good name and ancestry (John viii. 39; Acts iii. 25). What sacred associations clustered around the name, "house of Jacob"! The personal history of their ancestor Jacob gave great significance to the name, "God of Jacob" (Ps. xlvi. 11). The history of Jacob shows that he had to do with a God who is forbearing to sinners; who enters into covenant with men, and renews that covenant even with the unworthy children of godly parents; who is the Hearer of prayer, and condescends to represent himself as being overcome by it; who bestows eternal life on those who die in faith (Exod. iii. 6; Matt. xxii. 31, 32). Similar lessons might be learned from God's treatment of "the house of Jacob" which name they gloried in. They could look back to a long catalogue of mercies (Ps. lxxviii., cv., cvi.). Yet the very fact that they bore this name made more glaring the contrast between it and their real character (vers. 5, 6; Hos. xii. 2—7; John viii. 33—40; Rom. ii. 17—29). Apply to the name we English bear as a Christian nation. 2. *An appeal is made to their judgments as to the character of God.* "Is the patience of Jehovah short?" Let God testify to them (Exod. xxxiv. 6, 7), and Moses respond (Numb. xiv. 17—20), and David take up the strain (Ps. ciii. 8—10), and the long lives of the ungodly, and late repentances confirm the Divine words, and their own consciences confess that Jehovah is a long-suffering God. 3. *They are reminded that God is not responsible for sin, and has no pleasure in punishment.* "Are these his doings?" We take it as a moral axiom that God is not responsible for sin, unless the sun can be held responsible for the shadows caused by opaque objects (Jas. i. 13; 1 John i. 5). At the best, sin is the corruption of what God made good; *e.g.* selfishness is depraved self-love; envy is fallen emulation; and so with other sins. In regard to punishment we know that "he doth not afflict willingly." He presides over his own laws and executes his threats; but it is sin, not God, who is the great destroyer. "*Evil* shall slay the wicked" (Ps. xxxiv. 21).

II. MERCY IS GOD'S DELIGHT. "Do not my words do good," etc.? The special reference seems to be to God's words through his prophets, so that it was a glaring sin as well as folly to try to silence God's prophets (ver. 6), whose words were so wholesome (Jer. xv. 16), because they revealed God's Name, and therefore the path of peace and safety (Ps. ix. 10). The prophets would have grievously misrepresented God's Name if they had spoken comfort to the wicked in their wickedness (Isa. iii. 10, 11). Contrast Zedekiah with Micaiah and Elijah in their conduct towards Ahab; and cf. Ezek. xiii. with Ps. xviii. 25, 26; xxxiv. 15, 16. To us God's words do good still more abundantly. The psalmist's words, "Thou hast magnified thy word above all thy Name," are true of the revelation of God in "the word of the truth of the gospel." Yet even the gospel, though offering mercy to the vilest, can do good only to those who deal truly with it and thus walk uprightly. The perversion of the greatest blessing may be the most fatal curse. The word of life will be the word of judgment (John xii. 48); ministers may become a "savour of death," and Christ a stone that shall grind to powder. "When the gospel becomes deadly to a man, it is a terrible thing; to die of a gospel plague is a terrible way of dying" (John Howe). The revelation of God's delight in mercy by Christ's sacrifice for sinners makes it possible for the vilest to walk uprightly. But salvation is from sin itself. Character is essential to heaven, or even God could not make it heaven to us.—E. S. P.

Ver. 10.—*Sin, the great disturber.* It has been so from the beginning; it will be so to the very end.

I. SIN WAS THE DISTURBER OF THE EARLIEST EARTHLY PARADISE. It was not the serpent or the temptation, but Adam's sin, that destroyed our first parents' rest. They might have known of the presence of the tempter, have seen his trail, heard his hiss, and been conscious of his solicitations, and yet have continued in the rest of unbroken confidence in God. But when sin entered their hearts, rest fled, and guilt, shame, and fear took its place. If allowed to remain in the garden, it would no longer have been an Eden, a Paradise to them. The groans of creation begin to mingle with the reproaches of their own hearts. But the voice is heard, "Arise, and depart," etc. (Gen. iii. 22—24).

II. SIN EJECTED THE FIRST INHABITANTS OF CANAAN. Even then it was "the glory of all lands," a splendid inheritance (Gen. xiii. 10; Numb. xiv. 7, 8; Deut. viii. 7—9). But sin of the foulest kind was there. Vice and crime rendered real rest impossible. The land is represented as stained, saturated with sin, no longer able to tolerate any further iniquity (cf. Gen. xv. 16); but ready to "spue out" its inhabitants (Lev. xviii. 24—28; xx. 22, 23). The summons went forth—Arise, and depart, yet not to exile, but to utter destruction.

III. SIN CHANGED THE REST OF CANAAN INTO A LAND OF UNREST TO THE CHOSEN NATION. Canaan was promised as one of God's rests—not the highest, but none the less real (Deut. xii. 9; Ps. xcv. 11). What a rest it might have been, enriched with its natural resources, blessed with peace and brotherhood among the tribes, and crowned with the assurance of Divine protection (Exod. xxxiv. 24; Deut. xii. 10). A dim vision of the fulness of rest they might have enjoyed was seen in the reign of Solomon the peaceful (1 Kings iv. 25). But throughout their whole history they allowed sin to mar their inheritance and break in upon their rest. There were periods of special demoralization, as in the days of the judges and of the later kings. They cast out the fatherless and the widow (ver. 9), they plundered the peaceable (ver. 8), they indulged in some of the abominations of the old Canaanites (1 Kings xxii. 46; 2 Kings xxiii. 7). They could therefore have no rest themselves, but were doomed to exile (Rev. xiii. 10). The land is represented as once more taking sides with God and turning against those who abused his goodness. The false report of the spies (Numb. xiii. 32) received a fulfilment, as Moses foretold (Lev. xxvi. 18—35) and Ezekiel described (xxxvi. 13—19), as though an earthquake or a flood drove the sinners far away (Amos viii. 8). Illust.: Pompeii. So has it been in the history of nations ever since (wars, slavery, despotism, revolutions, etc.). Illustrate from the Indian chief with his tribe fleeing from his foes, till, on the banks of a splendid river, he stuck his spear into the ground, exclaiming, "Alabama!" "Here we rest!" But in vain.

IV. SIN BREAKS THE REST OF THE HAPPIEST HOME. A young bride and bridegroom may think they have reached the goal of earthly happiness. But unless Christ occupies in their hearts the place which he claims, and which he alone can fill, they may soon learn that sin is a great disturber, even in a domestic Eden. Augustine's words are found to be true, " O God, thou hast made us for thyself, and our heart is restless till it rests in thee." Sickness, suffering, death, and other fruits of sin stir up their nest (Deut. xxxii. 11), and remind them that their rest is polluted and therefore insecure.

V. SIN INVADES AND DISTURBS EVEN THE ADOPTED FAMILY OF GOD. For "death passed upon all men, for that all have sinned," so that "ourselves also which have the firstfruits of the Spirit, groan within ourselves" (Rom. v. 12; viii. 23). We rejoice to know that "here we have no continuing city," because it is polluted. But already we know of a rest *in* Christ (Matt. xi. 28, 29; Heb. iv. 3), which will be perfected into a rest *with* Christ (Heb. iv. 9), when we shall have completely "escaped the corruption which is in the world by lust," and be made fully "partakers of the Divine nature" (2 Pet. i. 4). To us the summons, "Arise, and depart," will be the signal of emancipation; the curse will be changed into a blessing, for we shall "depart to be with Christ, which is far better."—E. S. P.

Ver. 13.—*God the great Bond-breaker.* There is a marked contrast between the tone of vers. 10, 11 and that of vers. 12, 13. God delights in such contrasts. He loves to turn from threats to promises. Judgment is his strange work; mercy is his delight. The dispersion of his people is a painful necessity, their restoration is a joy to him. Hence the jubilant tone of the concluding verses of this chapter. The great Bond-breaker is God himself. Apply—

I. TO THE BREAKING OF THE BABYLONISH BONDAGE. Cyrus was a bond-breaker. In a certain sense the words are applicable to him (Ezra i. 2—4, etc.). But above him was the greater Deliverer, whom Cyrus himself recognized, who had long before predicted deliverance (Isa. xlv. 1—6), and who now puts it into the heart of the Persian monarch to act as his servant. Before God interposed, the captives were but as a flock of sheep (ver. 12) whom a fold, not to say a fortress, could restrain. Till the seventy years of destined captivity were fulfilled no breaker could release that flock; but then "the man that executeth my counsel from a far country" appeared (Isa. xlvi. 9—11). When God broke through, it was an easy thing, even for those timid sheep, to pass through or to break through any gate (like Peter passing the iron gate of his prison). As they streamed forth from Babylon, Zerubbabel, "the Prince of Judah" (Ezek. i. 8), led them. But there was another invisible Leader, of a nobler royalty than Zerubbabel —"their King," who went before them (Isa. xlix. 8—10; lii. 12). See Exod. xiii. 21: there the symbol was visible; now the invisible King was seen by the eye of prophetic faith. Learn to recognize the Divine hand in all national deliverances; as did David (2 Sam. v. 20), and Queen Elizabeth at the destruction of the Armada (medal and its inscription, "Afflavit Deus, et dissipuntur "), and godly monarchs in later days.

II. TO DELIVERANCE FROM THE BONDAGE OF SIN. "The Word" was the Divine Deliverer of Israel from Babylon (Isa. lxiii. 9), and is so of us. The Jews recognized "the Breaker" as a title of Messiah their Prince. In this work of spiritual deliverance he was foretold, and now is revealed as: 1. *A Bond-breaker.* (Isa. xlii. 7; xlix. 8, 9, 24, 25.) 2. *A Leader and Commander.* (Isa. lv. 4.) 3. *A Redeemer at the cost of conflict.* (Isa. lxiii. 1—6.) 4. *A Shepherd-King* (Ezek. xxxiv. 23, 24); who gains supremacy by dying for the flock he seeks to deliver (John x. 11, 27—30; Heb. ii. 9—15). 5. *A Saviour from foes within as well as oppressors without.* (Matt. i. 21; Titus ii. 14.) 6. *Who shall save all Israel at last.* (Isa. lix. 20, 21; Rom. xi. 26.) In both these deliverances the redeemed have their appointed work. Israel was bidden to humble themselves in repentance (Lev. xxvi. 40—42), to pray in faith (Jer. xxix. 12, 13), and to accept the Lord as their Redeemer and Leader (Hos. i. 11). And we, too, are commanded to repent, to "believe in the Name of his Son Jesus Christ" (Acts xvii. 30; 1 John iii. 23), and thus to work "the work of God" (John vi. 29). Then Christ our Bond-breaker will, for us, break through the power of evil habit, of this present evil world, and of the infernal oppressor of our souls.

"The world, with sin and Satan,
In vain our march opposes;
By faith we shall break through them all,
And sing the song of Moses."

E. S. P.

Vers. 1—4.—*Avarice.* "Woe to them that devise iniquity, and work evil upon their beds! when the morning is light, they practise it, because it is in the power of their hand," etc. The prophet, in the preceding chapter, foretold the judgment that would befall both kingdoms on account of their apostasy from the living God. He begins this chapter by denouncing the rapacious avarice of their leading men. Oppression is one of the greatest social crimes; alas! one that has been prevalent in every age and land; a crime this, too, which the Bible denounces with great frequency and with terrific force. Avarice, or greed, is the spring and spirit of all oppression. In the text we have this rapacious avarice presented to us in three aspects.

I. SCHEMING IN THE NIGHT. The avaricious men "devise iniquity and work evil upon their beds." When avarice takes possession of a man, it works the brain by night as well as by day. It keeps the intellectual faculties busy in the stillness of nocturnal hours. What schemes to swindle, defraud, and plunder men are fabricated in this London of ours every night upon the pillow! Perhaps there is no passion that takes a stronger hold upon man than this, and that moves his intellect with such concentration and constancy. It has been called "the great sepulchre of all other passions."

II. WORKING IN THE DAY "When the morning is light, they practise it, because it is in the power of their hand." Delitzsch renders this, "In the light of the morning they carry it out, for their hand is their god." The idea is, perhaps, that which they esteem most is the worldly gain of their avaricious labour. So it ever is; gain is the god of the greedy man. He sacrifices all his time and labour on its altar. Before it he prostrates his soul. Your avaricious man in the day trots about the streets, the shops, the markets, like a hungry hound in search of food. Shakespeare compares such a man to a whale, which plays and tumbles, driving the poor fry before him, and at last devours them all at a mouthful. Such whales have I heard of on the land, who never leave gaping till they've swallowed the whole parish—church, steeple, bells, and all.

III. SUFFERING IN THE JUDGMENT. "Therefore thus saith the Lord; Behold, against this family do I devise an evil, from which ye shall not remove your necks," etc. Judgment comes at last; and in the judgment, as these words give us to understand, the punishment will correspond with the sin. "Because they reflect upon evil," says Delitzsch, "to deprive their fellow-men of their possessions, Jehovah will bring evil upon this generation, lay a heavy yoke upon their necks, under which they will not be able to walk loftily or with extended neck." Ay, the time will come when the avaricious millionaire will exclaim, "We be utterly spoiled." "Go to now, ye rich men, weep and howl for your miseries that shall come upon you," etc. (Jas. v. 1).—D. T.

Ver. 7.—*God's truth.* "O thou that art named the house of Jacob, is the Spirit of the Lord straitened? are these his doings? do not my words do good to him that walketh uprightly?" "Thou called house of Jacob, is the patience of Jehovah short then? or is this his doing? Are not my words good to him that walketh uprightly?" Such is a modern translation. We prefer the translation of Henderson, as follows: "What language, O house of Jacob! Is the Spirit of Jehovah shortened? Are these his operations? Do not my words benefit him that walketh uprightly?" These words seem to be a reply to an objection raised against the prophets in the preceding verse. The objector did not approve of predictions so terribly severe. "It is not strange," says Matthew Henry, "if people that are vicious and debauched covet to have ministers that are altogether such as themselves, for they are willing to believe that God is so too." There are people in all congregations who revolt at the proclamation of any doctrines from the pulpit that chime not in with their love of ease and their cherished notions, and especially so if such doctrines are unfamiliar to their ears. They desire the old things to be iterated without end, and with as little change of form and note as possible. The text may be taken as a reproof to such. It says two things to them.

I. THAT THE SPIRIT OF DIVINE TRUTH CANNOT BE RESTRAINED. "Is the Spirit of the Lord straitened?" There is no limit to truth; it is an ocean that has no shore, a field whose ever-springing seeds are innumerable. Men's theological systems, even the largest of them, have narrow limits. They are, as compared to Divine truth, only as a barren rood to a fertile continent; a little sand-pool to the mighty Atlantic. It is not "straitened." It has no limit. To every true minister this Spirit has something fresh to suggest, and which he is bound to propound and enforce. "The Lord hath yet more light and truth to break forth from his Word."

II. THAT THE PRACTICE OF DIVINE TRUTH CANNOT BUT DO GOOD. "Do not my words do good to him that walketh uprightly?" Though you have never heard the particular truth before, though it may be too severe to please you, though it may clash with all your prejudices and wishes, if you practise it, it will do you good. 1. *It is to be practised.* It is not fitted merely for speculation, systematizing, controversy, and debate; it is for inspiring the activities and ruling the life. It is a code rather than a creed; it is not something to play about the brain, the imagination, or the emotions, but to possess, permeate, and transform the whole life. It must be incarnated, made flesh, and dwell in the land. 2. *When practised it is a blessing.* "Do not my words do good to him that walketh uprightly?" Yes, they do good—when they are translated, not into languages and creeds, but into living deeds. A man gets good only as he builds up a noble character. But what is a good character? It is made up of good habits, and good habits are made up of good acts, and good acts are but the forms and expressions of God's words and ideas.—D. T.

Vers. 8, 9.—*Sin an antagonist.* "Even of late my people is risen up as an enemy: ye pull off the robe with the garment from them that pass by securely as men averse from war. The women of my people have ye cast out from their pleasant houses; from their children have ye taken away my glory for ever." This chapter refers to the character and doings of Israel during the last nine years of Ahaz. A very dark period in Israelitish history was this. "We are told in 2 Chron. xxviii. 24, 25 that Ahaz shut up the doors of the temple, and erected altars in every corner of Jerusalem. We may safely conclude, from the language of Micah (ii.) and Isaiah (xi.), that when he did so, abominations of every kind overran the land. A prophet like Micah was no longer permitted to speak. The testimony of Isaiah (vii., viii.) had borne no fruit; the fruitlessness of invoking the aid of Assyria had taught him no better. Ahaz did not repent, like Manasseh, but persisted in his evil ways. What a melancholy course of conduct! Like Uzziah, Ahaz was denied honourable burial (2 Chron. xxviii. 27). The prophet here, in denouncing the sins which were then most prevalent in Judah and Ephraim, alludes expressly to the acts of oppression and violence then common, and tells them that for these they would be driven out of the land." The verses lead us to look at sin in the aspect of an *antagonist,* and suggest—

I. THAT IT IS AN ANTAGONIST TO THE DIVINE. "Even of late [margin, 'yesterday'] my people has risen up as an enemy." "It is not stated," says Delitzsch, "against whom the people rise up as an enemy; but, according to the context, it can only be against Jehovah." Sin is an antagonist to God; it lifts up the soul in hostility against its Maker. We are told that the carnal mind is at enmity with God; it is not only alienated from him, but in deadly opposition to him. Unregenerated men say that they are not conscious of any enmity in their hearts towards their Maker; on the contrary, sometimes they feel a passing glow of gratitude and adoration for him. But it is the conduct of a man that proves the settled state of his heart. What though a man may say that he has no unkind feeling towards me, on the contrary, that he has some amount of respect; if he pursues a course of conduct that he knows is in direct opposition to my wishes, interests, and reputation, can I believe him? I judge his state of heart towards me, not by his words, but by his habitual conduct. Thus men prove their enmity to God; they pursue a course of life which they know is repugnant to his nature, hostile to his government, and injurious to the order and happiness of his universe. 1. *This enmity is most unjustifiable.* Enmity sometimes admits of justification, but never in this case. "They hated me without a cause." There is nothing in his character or procedure to justify one spark of animosity in any intelligent creature in the universe towards him. 2. *This enmity is most wicked.* It is against reason and justice. The character and relations of God are such as to demand the supreme love of all his intelligent creatures. 3. *This enmity is most miserable.* Enmity to God is the fountain of all the misery in the universe; it is the root of all the cursed passions of the soul. The soul's salvation is in love, its damnation is in enmity.

II. THAT IT IS AN ANTAGONIST TO THE HUMAN. "Ye pull off the robe with the garment [margin, 'over against the garment'] from them that pass by securely as men averse from war." Not content with the outer garment, ye greedily rob passers-by of the ornamental robe fitting the body closely and flowing down to the feet; and this you do, not to enemies, but to friends, to those who are "averse from war." More, "The women of my people have ye cast out from their pleasant houses." The widows of the men slain by you in battle you have deprived of their homes. They "devoured widows' houses." This was not all. "From their children have ye taken away my glory for ever." The orphan children you have despoiled. In all this there is the manifestation of sin, as an antagonist to human rights and human happiness. Sin puts man against his brother; hence the slanders, quarrels, litigations, wars, that are rife in every human society. John says, "If a man love God, he will love his brother." The converse of this is true too. If a man hate God, he will hate his brother.

CONCLUSION. Look at sin as an antagonist to God and man, shun it with horror, and battle against it with all the force of your being. This is the great battle of life.—D. T.

Ver. 10.—*The soul's exodus.* "Arise ye, and depart; for this is not your rest: because it is polluted, it shall destroy you, even with a sore destruction." "The prophet, having overthrown, in vers. 7—9, the objection to his threatening prophecies by pointing to the sins of the people, now repeats the announcement of punishment, and that in the form of a summons to go out of the land into captivity, because the land cannot bear the defilement consequent upon such abominations" (Delitzsch). This injunction does not mean either of the three following things: 1. It does not mean the termination of our mortal life. Life is a talent which we should guard. Suicide is a crime. 2. It does not mean neglect of material interests and duties. We are commanded to be diligent in business, etc. 3. It does not mean absolute retirement from the world. The life of the hermit is a sin against our social affections, the claims of our species, and the commands of the Bible. What, then, shall we take it to mean? The rising of the soul above the dominant materialism of this life. It is the setting of the "affections upon things above." It is the exodus of the soul from the Egypt of a dominant materialism. There are three reasons suggested here for this moral exodus of the spirit.

I. THERE IS NO REST FOR THE SOUL IN A DOMINANT MATERIALISM. "This is not your rest." There are four forms in which this dominant materialism exists amongst us, and in neither of which can the soul find rest. 1. *There is the gross, sensual form.* The sensualist and the voluptuary live in this; but they have no rest. Ask the epicurean and the debauchee. 2. *There is the thoroughly secular form.* The man who is absorbed in the work of making money lives here; but he finds in it no rest. Ask the man who has become the creature of business, etc. 3. *There is the intellectual form.* The region of mere flesh wisdom, flesh arts, and flesh literature—poetry and novels that appeal to the flesh. There is no rest for the soul here. Ask Byron, Burns, Dryden, Churchill, etc. 4. *There is the religious form.* There is a fleshly religion amongst men—a religion of pictures, music, pompous rites and ceremonies, all appealing to the senses. There is no rest for the soul here. Let it "arise, then, and depart."

II. THERE IS POLLUTION FOR THE SOUL IN IT. To allow the material in any form to rule us is a sin. 1. *Reason shows this.* Mind was made to govern matter; the senses were made to be the servants, not the sovereign, of the soul. 2. *Conscience testifies this.* Conscience is everlastingly protesting against the dominion of the flesh. 3. *The Bible declares this.* The carnal mind is enmity against God (Rom. viii. 7).

III. THERE IS DANGER TO THE SOUL IN MATERIALISM. "It shall destroy you." "Be not deceived; God is not mocked: for whatsoever a man soweth, that shall he also reap. For he that soweth to his flesh shall of the flesh reap corruption" (Gal. vi. 7, 8). For to be carnally minded is death. The work of soul-destruction is going on every moment; the soul decays in this state. Force of intellect, discrimination of judgment, freedom of will, sensibility of conscience, elasticity of soul, are being destroyed.

CONCLUSION. Arise, then! The voice of philosophy, the voice of history, the voice of the Bible, and the voice of departed saints, all combine in the injunction, " Arise, and depart !"—D. T.

Ver. 11.—*Israel's popular preacher.* " If a man walking in the spirit and falsehood do lie, saying, I will prophesy unto thee of wine and of strong drink; he shall even be the prophet of this people." Henderson's translation of this verse is worth quoting: " If any one conservant with mind and falsehood lie, saying, I will prophesy to thee of wine and strong drink, even he shall be the prophet of this people." This is Micah's idea as to the kind of prophet, or, as we should say, pulpit, the men of Israel would willingly and unanimously accept. Now, if we look a little into the sketch here of this *popular* preacher, we shall find that he was marked by two things which always tend to make a preacher generally acceptable to thoughtless men in every age.

I. BY EMPTINESS OF MIND. " If a man walking in the spirit and falsehood do lie," or, as in the margin, " walk with the wind, and lie falsely." He has nothing in his mind but wind, vain conceits, vapid notions; no deep thought, no rich store of information, no well-digested belief or profound conviction. He walks with the wind. His movements are the swellings of wind, his voice the echoes of wind. Now, the kind of preacher that the Israelites desired is the kind of preacher that is in general request almost everywhere. What thoughtful man of any extensive acquaintance with the religious world does not know that, as a rule, the less brain, intelligence, conviction, a preacher has—if he possesses the gift of passion, voice, and utterance—the more attractive he will be to the people in general? He is the man who attracts the crowd. The causes of this are obvious. The more empty a man is, the more *fluent* he is. The pauses in speech necessitated by thoughtfulness are never pleasing to the thoughtless; they like the rattling flow. The empty mind has generally a glib tongue. Again, the more empty a man is, the more *dogmatic.* The thoughtful man can only suggest and hint, and cautiously and reverentially submit his doctrines. For, as a thinker, he has touched difficulties and mysteries at every point; he can only speak with modesty. This, to the people, is more or less distasteful; they want dogmatism, positiveness, assurance, amounting to audacity. This the empty man can give. The more empty a man is, the more *somnific.* The people do not like mental effort in their pews; what they want is gentle titillation and spiritual dreaminess. This the empty man can and does supply.

II. BY MINISTERING TO PLEASE. " I will prophesy unto thee of wine and of strong drink." These prophets would accommodate themselves to their hearers' tastes and habits, and sanction their indulgences. They would not disturb their consciences nor strike against their prejudices, but talk to them in such a way as to leave them satisfied with themselves. The preacher who can do this, who can enunciate his discourses in such a way as to avoid interference with the tastes, habits, and pleasures of the people, will always be popular. Oh, it is sad to think of the thousands of sermons that are preached every year by our clergy and our ministers which interfere in no measure with the sinful delights of the people, which leave them in the full indulgence of their wine, strong drink, and other carnal gratifications !

CONCLUSION. Such a preacher as this popular preacher is, for many reasons, the greatest curse to his race. I see but little hope for the progress of Christianity or for the spiritual reformation of mankind, until the pulpits of Christendom are closed for ever against such men. Oh, haste the time when none shall assume the solemn office of preacher but those who, by the manifestation of the truth, " commend themselves to every man's conscience in the sight of God " (2 Cor. iv. 2)!

> " I venerate the man whose heart is true,
> Whose hands are pure, whose doctrine and whose life,
> Coincident, exhibit lucid proof
> That he is honest in the sacred cause.
> To such I render more than mere respect,
> Whose actions say that they respect themselves."
>   (Cowper.)

                                            D. T.

Vers. 12, 13.—*Gospel work.* "I will surely assemble, O Jacob, all of thee; I will surely gather the remnant of Israel; I will put them together as the sheep of Bozrah, as the flock in the midst of their fold: they shall make great noise by reason of the multitude of men. The breaker is come up before them: they have broken up, and have passed through the gate, and are gone out by it: and their king shall pass before them, and the Lord on the head of them." "I will surely gather thee entirely, O Jacob; I will surely collect the remainder of Israel; I will put them together like the sheep of Bozrah, like a flock in the midst of their pasture: they shall be in commotion, because of the multitude of men. The Breaker is gone up before them, they break through and pass to the gate, they go out at it; the king passeth on before them, even Jehovah at their head" (Henderson). The prophet here passes from threats to promises, from a dark present to a bright future. The future was to embrace two things. 1. *A grand gathering.* Jacob and the remnant of Israel were to be "gathered" as a mighty flock in the fruitful and lovely region of Bozrah. The scene of the gathering would be like the rich pastures of Bozrah, and the numbers of the gathered would be enormous. "They shall make great noise by reason of the multitude of men." 2. *A triumphant deliverance.* "The breaker is come up before them." Who is the breaker? If reference is here made to Jewish bonds, it was to Moses; if to Babylonish captivity, it was to Cyrus; if to the bondage of the devil, it was to Christ. We shall apply the words to illustrate the grand work of the gospel. "The fulfilment of this prophecy," says Delitzsch, "commenced with the gathering together of Israel to its God and King by the preaching of the gospel, and will be completed at some future time, when the Lord will redeem Israel, which is now pining in dispersion, out of the fetters of its unbelief and life of sin. We must not exclude all allusion to the deliverance of the Jewish nation out of the earthly Babylon by Cyrus; at the same time, it is only in its typical significance that this comes into consideration at all, viz. as a preliminary stage and pledge of the redemption to be effected by Christ out of the spiritual Babylon of this world." Taking the words, then, as an illustration of gospel work, two thoughts are suggested.

I. UNIFICATION. "I will put them together as the sheep of Bozrah." Men are morally divided; there is a schism in the great body of humanity. Men have not only lost interest in their fellows, but an antipathy prevails amongst them. They are scattered abroad in different countries, under different governments, and in connection with different religions and interests. The great work of the gospel is to bring men together, to gather them together in some moral Bozrah, to unite them in the fold of Christ. How is this to be done? Not by any political compact, or ecclesiastical concordat, or social organization. These things can never unite souls together; they have been tried a thousand times, but failed. There is only one way, and that is the presentation of an object of *supreme moral attraction to all men.* That object the gospel presents; it is Christ. It was predicted that unto him should the gathering of the people be, and that he should gather together in one the children of God that are scattered abroad. And he himself said, "I, if I be lifted up . . . will draw all men unto me." There is in him what is not found anywhere else—that which can attract with equal power all souls, and centralize in him the strongest sympathies of all hearts. Men can only become socially united to each other in brotherly love by first becoming united to Christ. The true union of souls is like the union of planets having one centre of light, life, and rule. As a matter of philosophy, I proclaim that there is nothing but the gospel that *can* hush the discords, heal the divisions, and terminate all wars and strifes amongst men; and historically I declare nothing else *has* ever done anything *successfully* towards it.

II. EMANCIPATION. "The breaker is come up before them: they have broken up, and have passed through the gate." Men everywhere are in moral bondage. They are the slaves of sin and the devil. "Carnal, sold under sin." Moral bondage is the worst of all bondage; it is a bondage (1) connected with self-compunction; it is a bondage (2) of the soul, the self; it is a bondage (3) that death cannot terminate. Who shall free man from this bondage? Who is the Moses that will take us out of this Egypt, the Cyrus that will free us from this Babylon? There is One, and but One—Christ. He is the "Breaker." He snaps the chains, breaks open the prison gates, and lets the soul into the true light and liberty of life. He came to preach liberty to the captive, and to open the prison doors of them that are bound.

CONCLUSION. Blessed gospel, speed thy work! Bring all the scattered sections of the world together, and unite them together by uniting them to one common centre—Christ. Break the moral chains that bind the faculties, sympathies, and souls of men to sin and the devil. Bring on the moral jubilee of the race, and let the clarion-blast of liberty be heard through all the land.—D. T.

EXPOSITION.

CHAPTER III.

Ver. 1—ch. v. 15.—Part II. DENUNCIATION OF THE CRIMES OF THE GRANDEES, FOLLOWED BY A PROMISE OF THE GLORIFICATION OF ZION, THE BIRTH OF MESSIAH, AND THE HIGHEST EXALTATION OF THE PEOPLE.

Vers. 1—4.—§ 1. *Sins of the rulers, and their punishment.*

Ver. 1.—The prophet denounces the sins of the rulers, false prophets, and priests; and begins with the injustice and oppression practised by the great men. And I said. The new address is thus introduced as being analogous to the denunciations in the preceding chapter, which were interrupted by the promise of deliverance, to which there is no reference here. O heads of Jacob; synonymous with princes of the house of Israel (comp. ver. 8; ch. i. 5). Micah addresses the heads of families and the officials to whom the administration of justice appertained. These magistrates and judges seem to have been chiefly members of the royal family, at any rate in Judah; see Jer. xxi. 11, 12 (Cheyne). Septuagint, οἱ κατάλοιποι οἴκου 'Ισραήλ, "ye remnant of the house of Israel." Is it not for you to know judgment? Ye, of all men, ought to know what is just and fair, and to practise it (compare the opening of the Book of Wisdom).

Ver. 2.—The good . . . the evil; *i.e.* goodness and wickedness. Septuagint, τὰ καλά, τὰ πονηρά (Amos v. 14, etc.; John iii. 20; Rom. i. 32). Who pluck off their skin from off them. They are not shepherds, but butchers. We have the same figurative expression for merciless extortion and pillage. Ezekiel makes a similar complaint (xxxiv. 2—4). Cheyne sees in this and the following verse a possible allusion to cannibalism as at least known to the Israelites by hearsay or tradition. There is a passage in Wisdom (xii. 5) which somewhat countenances the idea that the Canaanites were guilty of this enormity, but it is probably only a rhetorical exaggeration of the writer. In the present passage the terms seem to be simply metaphors taken from the preparation of meat for human food. Such an allusion is natural in the mouth of one who had just been speaking of Israel as a flock (ch. ii. 12).

Ver. 3.—The idea of the last verse is repeated here with more emphasis. The people are treated by their rulers as cattle made to be eaten, flayed, broken up, chopped into pieces, boiled in the pot (comp. Ps. xiv. 4). (For an analogous figure, see Ezek. xxxiv. 3—5.)

Ver. 4.—The merciless shall not obtain mercy. Then, when the day of chastisement has come, "the day of the Lord," of which, perhaps, the prophet spoke more fully when he originally delivered this address. He will not hear them. A just retribution on those who refused to hearken to the cry of the poor and needy (comp. Ps. xviii. 41; Prov. i. 28; Jer. xi. 11; Jas. ii. 13). As they have behaved themselves ill in their doings; *according as they have made their actions evil,* or *because they have,* etc.; ἀνθ' ὧν (Septuagint).

Vers. 5—8.—§ 2. *Sins of the false prophets who led the people astray.*

Ver. 5.—Concerning the prophets (ch. ii. 11). These are the lying prophets of whom Jeremiah complains (Lam. ii. 14). That bite with their teeth, and cry, Peace. Very many commentators take the phrase, "bite with the teeth," to mean "eat," so that the clause signifies that the prophets when bribed with food predict peace and happiness to people. The antithesis of the following clause seems to require this explanation, which is further supported by the Chaldee. But it is quite unprecedented to find the word translated "bite" (*nashakh*) in the sense of "eat," or as it is taken here, "to have something to eat;" wherever it occurs it means "to bite like a serpent," to wound (see Gen. xlix. 17; Numb. xxi. 8, 9; Amos v. 19; ix. 3). The parallelism of the succeeding member does not compel us to put a forced interpretation upon the word. These venal seers do vital harm, inflict gravest injury, when they proclaim peace where there is no peace; by such false comfort they are really infusing poison and death. He that putteth not into their mouths. If any one does not bribe them, and so stop their evil mouths. They even prepare war against him. The Hebrew expression is, "they consecrate" or "sanctify war." There may be allusion to the religious rites accompanying a declaration of war (Jer. **vi.** 4; Joel iii. 9); but Micah seems to mean that, if the customary bribes are withheld, these prophets announce war and calamity as inevitable; they proclaim them in God's name, as speaking with his sanction and under his inspiration (comp. Jer. xxiii. 16, etc.; Ezek. xiii. 19; see note on Zeph. i. 7).

Ver. 6.—**Night shall be unto you, that ye shall not have a vision.** The Hebrew is, "from," or "without a vision." Septuagint, ἐξ ὁράσεως, "out of vision;" Vulgate, *pro visione.* Hence some interpret this as spoken to the false prophets, who, to punish their lying prophecies and pretended revelations, shall be overwhelmed with calamity. But it is best taken as still addressed to the rulers, and Micah tells how that in the time of their distress there shall be no prophecy to direct them (comp. 1 Sam. xxviii. 6; Prov. i. 28; Lam. ii. 9). "Night shall be unto them without a vision." "Night" and "darkness" are metaphors for calamity, as in all languages. **That ye shall not divine; *without divination.*** Septuagint, ἐκ μαντείας, "out of prophecy." Parallel and identical in meaning with the preceding clause. **The sun shall go down over the prophets;** *i.e.* over the false prophets. The sun of their prosperity shall set. Micah seems to derive his imagery from the phenomena of an eclipse (comp. Jer. **xv.** 9; Amos viii. 9). **The day.** The time of their punishment (ch. ii. 4; Amos v. 18).

Ver. 7.—**Shall the seers be ashamed.** The false prophets shall be ashamed because their oracles are proved to be delusive. **They shall all cover their lips;** *the upper lip;* i.e. the face up to the nose, in sign of mourning and shame (see Lev. **xiii.** 45; Ezek. xxiv. 17, 22). It is equivalent to covering the head for the same reason, as Esth. vi. 12; Jer. xiv. 4. Septuagint, Καταλαλήσουσι καὶ αὐτῶν πάντες αὐτοί, taking the verb to mean "shall open" (not "cover") their lips against them. **For** there is **no answer of God.** There was no revelation (Ps. lxxiv. 9; Ezek. vii. 26). Septuagint, Διότι οὐκ ἔσται ὁ ἐπακούων αὐτῶν, "Because there shall be none that hearkeneth unto them."

Ver. 8.—Micah contrasts his own powers and acts with those of the false prophets. **I am full of power by the Spirit of the Lord.** Micah asserts that he speaks and acts by the direct inspiration of God; he claims three gifts bestowed upon him by the Holy Spirit to enable him to effect his purpose. The first of these is "power"—such might imparted to him that his words fall with force and proclaim their Divine origin (comp. Luke i. 17; Acts i. 8). The second gift is **judgment**—the righteous judgment of God;

this fills his mind and comprises all his message. The third gift is **might,** *i.e.* a holy courage that enables him to face any danger in delivering his testimony (comp. 2 Tim. i. 7). In these points he is in strong contrast to the false prophets, who were not inspired by the Spirit of God, spake not with power, called good evil, and evil good, were timid and time-serving. **Jacob . . . Israel.** The two are identical as in ver. 1, and the clauses in which they occur contain the same thought repeated for emphasis' sake.

Vers. 9—12.—§ 3. *Recapitulation of the sins of the three classes—rulers, priests, and prophets, with an announcement of the destruction of Zion and the temple.*

Ver. 9.—The prophet exemplifies his courage by delivering in full the denunciation with which he commenced (ver. 1; see note there). **Hear this.** What follows. **Pervert all equity.** Ye, who by your position ought to be models and guardians of justice and equity, violate all laws, human and Divine, make the straight crooked, distort every notion of right (comp. Isa. lix. 8).

Ver. 10.—**They build up Zion with blood** Blood is, as it were, the cement that binds the building together. They raise palaces with money gained by extortion, rapine, and judicial murders like that of Naboth (1 Kings xxi.; comp. Jer. xxii. 13, etc.; Ezek. xxii. 27; Hab. ii. 12). Cheyne thinks this to be a too dark view of the state of public morals, and would therefore consider "blood" to be used for violent conduct leading to ruin of others, comparing Isa. i. 15; lix. 3; Prov. i. 11. In these passages, however, actual bloodshed may be meant; and we know too little of the moral condition of Judaea at this time to be able to decide against the darker view.

Ver. 11.—**Judge for reward.** The very judges take bribes (Isa. i. 23; Ezek. xxii. 12), which the Law so stringently forbade (see Exod. xxiii. 8; Deut. xvi. 19, etc.). **The priests thereof teach for hire.** The priests were bound to teach and explain the Law, and decide questions of religion and ritual (Lev. x. 11; Deut. xvii. 11; xxxiii. 10; comp. Hag. ii. 11, etc.). This they ought to have done gratuitously, but they corruptly made it a source of gain. **Divine for money.** The accusation in ver. 5 is repeated. These false prophets sold their oracles, pretending to have a suitable revelation when paid for it (Ezek. xxii. 28; Zeph. iii. 3, 4). **Yet will they lean upon the Lord.** These priests and prophets were worshippers of Jehovah and trusted in him, as though he could not forsake his people. They had faith without love, divorced religion from morality, made a certain outward conformity serve for righteousness and truth. Is not the Lord among us? (Exod. xvii. 7). As though the very fact that they had in their midst the temple, wherein Jehovah's presence was assured, would protect them from all harm, whatever their conduct might be. Such presumptuous confidence is reproved by Jeremiah (vii. 4, 8, etc.; comp. Amos v. 14, and note there).

Ver. 12.—This is the prophecy quoted by the elders to King Jehoiakim (Jer. xxvi. 17, etc.). It may have been delivered before Hezekiah's time originally, and repeated in his reign, when it was productive of a reformation. The denunciation is a mournful contrast to the announcement in ch. ii. 12; but it was never completely fulfilled, being, like all such judgments, conditioned by circumstances. Therefore . . . for your sake. For the crimes of rulers, priests, and prophets. Shall Zion . . . be ploughed as a field. Three localities are specified which destruction shall overtake—Zion, Jerusalem, and the temple. Zion means that part of the city where stood the royal palace. The prophecy relates primarily to the destruction of the city by the Chaldeans, when, as Jeremiah testifies (Lam. v. 18), Zion was desolate and foxes walked upon it. The expression in the text may be hyperbolical, but we know that the ploughing up of the foundations of captured cities is often alluded to. Thus Horace, 'Carm.,' i. 16, 20—

" . . . imprimeretque muris
Hostile aratrum exercitus insolens."

(Comp. 'Propert.,' iii. 7, 41; and, for the whole passage, Isa. xxxii. 13, 14.) "The general surface of Mount Zion descends steeply eastwards into the Tyropœon and Kidron, and southwards into the Valley of Hinnom. The whole of the hill here is under cultivation, and presents a most literal fulfilment of Micah's prophecy" (Thomson, 'The Land and the Book,' p. 540). "From the spot on which I stood," says Dr. Porter, "I saw the plough at work in the little fields that now cover the site of Zion" ('Illustrations of Bible Prophecy,' p. 17). Jerusalem shall become heaps. The city proper shall become heaps of ruins (Jer. ix. 11; Neh. ii. 17; iv. 2). Septuagint, ὡς ὀπωροφυλάκιον ἔσται, "as a storehouse for fruits," as in Ps. lxxviii. (lxxix.) 1. The mountain of the house. The mountain on which the temple was built, Mount Moriah, and therefore the temple itself, no longer mentioned as the Lord's dwelling-place. As the high places of the forest; or, as wooded heights, returning, as it were, to the wild condition in which it lay when Abraham offered his sacrifice thereon. In the time of the Maccabees, after its profanation by the heathen, the account speaks of shrubs growing in the courts as in a forest or in one of the mountains (1 Macc. iv. 38). Such was to be the fate of the temple in which they put their trust and made their boast.

HOMILETICS.

Vers. 1—12.—*The abuse of influence.* God has imparted to all men the power of influencing others. We daily exert an influence either for good or for evil. They who know us, and who come into contact with us, are the better or the worse as the result of such knowledge and association. The nature of our influence depends upon our own character. Whether this subtle power we all possess is to result in good or ill depends altogether upon what we are ourselves. Let the life be pure and holy, fed and sustained by those hidden springs which take their rise in the throne of God, and then a healthy and helpful influence will assuredly follow, as effect follows cause. The extent of the range of a man's influence depends very much upon the social position he occupies. The more prominent a man is among his fellows, the wider will be the circle of his influence. In every community there will be, of necessity, positions of special prominence to be occupied. To desire to occupy these for the sake of being prominent, and accounted great, is indeed a very poor ambition; but to desire to reach these in the hope of gaining and using for good the additional influence thus acquired; whilst "rising in the world," to be also ascending the heights of holiness and goodness, and in ascending thus to reach out the hand of help to others and to assist them to climb above the mists of error and sin, is an aspiration that is truly noble; and happy is it for communities when such men rise. When good men are exalted "the city rejoiceth." These verses present to us a painful example of the opposite of all this. Note we have here—

I. GREAT INFLUENCE GROSSLY ABUSED. Three influential classes in the kingdom of Judah are specially referred to. 1. *The princes;* i.e. the ruling class, the judges and magistrates, these functions being exercised by members of the royal family (Jer.

xxi. 11, 12). 2. *The priests;* i.e. members of the Jewish priesthood, taking part in the services of the temple, and also in teaching the people. 3. *The prophets;* i.e. not the men who were specially inspired of God, like Micah, but men who claimed to possess a desire to work for God, who were trained in "the schools of the prophets," and who became a very numerous class in the land, and took an important part in the education of the community. In these three classes we have comprehended the most influential men in the land; men who, by virtue of their position, ought to have exerted the wisest and most salutary influence upon the people. But instead of this the very opposite was actually the case. They who should have been "the salt of the earth" were "as salt which had lost its savour." The princes, instead of righteously administering the Law, sought their own enrichment. They accepted bribes ("The heads thereof judge for reward," ver. 11), and they utterly sacrificed the rights and interests of the people. "They built up Zion with blood" (ver. 10), *i.e.* they reared their luxurious palaces and increased their own store of wealth by perverting equity, and by unrighteous decisions. Their unjust judgments, their extortions and oppressions, so pressed upon the people that the very life-blood of the nation was drained. Under the expressive figure of cannibalism, the seer describes the effect of their rapacity (vers. 2, 3). The prophets also were utterly mercenary. If the bribe was only given, they prophesied as desired. "They caused the people to err, biting with their teeth [*i.e.* feeding upon the bribe] and crying, Peace" (ver. 5); but only let the bribe be withheld, and they altered their tone and became the heralds of evil tidings (ver. 5). Nor were the priests behind in cherishing the same spirit. "The priests teach for hire" (ver. 11). The support of the Jewish priesthood was provided for by special Divine arrangement. The tenth in Israel was apportioned to the sons of Levi as their inheritance (Numb. xviii. 20; Deut. xviii. 2). But though thus provided for, such was their greed that, "producing the answer of God upon the receipt of money, they sold the grace of the Lord for a covetous price" (Jerome). And so did these prominent and distinguished classes in the kingdom of Judah abuse the great influence which had been bestowed upon them. History repeats itself; and there have been times in the development of other nations which have presented the counterpart to that which is here recorded respecting the kingdom of Judah (see, for example, the state of Europe during the age preceding "the Reformation," as described by D'Aubigné, 'History of the Reformation,' bk. i. ch. iii.).

II. THE ABUSE OF INFLUENCE RESULTING IN CALAMITY. 1. *To the abusers themselves.* The prophet declared that the day of retribution would duly come, and that in that day of Divine manifestation in judgment (1) the rulers should be requited for their evil deeds "measure for measure" (ver. 4), and in the time of trial should find no help in God, for he would hide his face from them (ver. 4); (2) the false priests and prophets should be overtaken by judicial blindness (ver. 6), shame and confusion should be theirs, as the coming events brought to light the falsity of their declarations (ver. 7), and the Divine oracles would be silent in that day (ver. 7). 2. *To the nation.* The land they were seeking to "build up" by unrighteous deeds should be brought to nought, and the responsibility of its overthrow would rest upon them. "Therefore shall Zion for *your sake* be ploughed as a field," etc. (ver. 12).

Learn: 1. The blessing of influence well directed. 2. The boon those who in high places exert such an influence confer upon a community. 3. The need of constant intercession with God on behalf of the leaders of a nation, in order that peace and prosperity may reign. "I exhort," etc. (1 Tim. ii. 1, 2).

Vers. 1—12.—*Avarice.* There is nothing wrong in a man's seeking to acquire riches. Money is good. Its possession is to be desired, since it carries with it the means of surrounding its possessor with the comforts of life, and at the same time gives him the ability to impart good to those who are less favoured and in circumstances of need. The very endeavour also to secure this calls into exercise such qualities as industry and thrift, which are truly commendable. It is rather the love of money, and the inordinate desire for it for its own sake, that merits condemnation. Worldly treasure becomes the greatest possible curse when it is accounted by men the chief good. It will buy up everything else. Time, intellect, justice, truth, conscience, the most sacred rights of humanity, will be bartered for this; and every true well-wisher of the race will endeavour to stem the ever-swelling torrent, and to present motives to turn the energies and enterprises of the world into another and higher direction. This chapter may be viewed as illustrative of the deplorable evils and the fatal results of this spirit of avarice.

I. THE DEPLORABLE EVILS CONNECTED WITH AVARICE. 1. *It saps the foundations of equity.* (Ver. 1.) These rulers understood the Law, but being so thoroughly possessed by the mercenary spirit, they failed to administer it righteously—were partial in their decisions, favouring those who offered the most tempting bribe, and thus caused the legal administration in the land to become rotten and corrupt. 2. *It leads to oppression and cruelty.* (Vers. 2, 3, 10.) The one concern of the princes was to enrich themselves and to find themselves surrounded with all luxuries and splendours ; and hence they cared not to what lengths of extortion and fraud and oppression they went, or what suffering might be involved, if only they could compass this end. 3. *It renders its subject unfaithful in the discharge of the most sacred trusts.* No trust can be more sacred than that committed to the man who is constituted a teacher of spiritual truth, and upon whom it devolves to direct men in the ways of righteousness and God ; but here (ver. 5) we have such catching the spirit of covetousness, and, as the result, proving altogether faithless to God and to the consciences of men, prophesying, "peace" to those who bribed them, and "war" to those who withheld the mercenary gift. 4. *It excites the spirit of self-confidence and self-sufficiency.* These leaders of the people, whilst acting thus at variance with the true and the right, yet finding their ill-gotten gains increasing in their hands, boasted that evil could not reach them (ver. 11).

II. THE FATAL RESULTS OF AVARICE. 1. *Loss of the Divine favour.* For " covetousness is idolatry," and God will not give his glory to another (ver. 4). 2. *Non-apprehension of spiritual realities.* (Ver. 7.) 3. *Complete frustration of their designs.* The palaces they had built up with blood, and the city they had defiled by their iniquity, should come to nought, and in its overthrow all that they had unrighteously sought to secure for themselves should perish (ver. 12). They who boast that they are " full and increased in riches, and have need of nothing," are in reality the most needy and desolate. Spenser, in ' The Faëry Queene,' has described their true condition—

> " Most wretched wight whom nothing might suffice,
> Whose greedy lust did lack in greatest store,
> Whose need had end, but no end covetize,
> Whose wealth was want, whose plenty made him poor,
> Who had enough, yet wishèd evermore."

Ver. 8.—*Worldly and spiritual power : a contrast.* In this verse the prophet seems to place himself in contrast with the false prophets to whom he had referred. They, and the priests and rulers with whom they were in association, may be taken as representing the worldly power of that age, whilst he represented that spiritual power which is inspired in the true servants of God by the working of his own Spirit. It is instructive, in reading this chapter, to contrast these worldly and spiritual forces.

I. THE FORMER IS POWER OFTEN EMPLOYED TO CRUSH ; THE LATTER IS POWER EVER EXERTED TO SAVE.

II. THE FORMER IS POWER BRINGING BLIGHT UPON THOSE WHO COME UNDER ITS INFLUENCE ; THE LATTER IS POWER THE EXERCISE OF WHICH EVER RESULTS IN BLESSING.

III. THE FORMER IS POWER THE PUTTING FORTH OF WHICH IS PROMPTED BY SELFISHNESS ; THE LATTER IS THE OUTCOME OF LOVE.

IV. THE FORMER BRINGS SHAME AND DISHONOUR UPON THOSE WHO EMPLOY IT ; THE LATTER YIELDS TO ITS POSSESSORS PRESENT DISTINCTION, AND SHALL SECURE TO THEM IMPERISHABLE RENOWN.

Vers. 8—12.—*Gifts for Divine service.* I. THEIR NATURE. (Ver. 8.) 1. " *Power.*" (Ver. 8.) Weak as the prophet felt himself to be, he was conscious of a Divine influence resting upon him and inspiring him, clothing him with holy energy and irresistible might. His mind and heart had been brought into an enjoyment of the highest and holiest fellowship with the Invisible and Eternal. His soul was animated by the inward witness of the Father's love. His whole nature was quickened so that the spirit, instead of being ruled by the body, had the body as its willing instrument, and all acting in concert with the will of God. God dwelt in him and he in God. His spiritual life was healthy and vigorous. His was the strength of a man who felt that he had been called to engage in a work demanding peculiar gifts and endowments in order to its successful discharge, but that all he thus wanted God would bestow, so as to render him efficient; and hence he was ready for service—full of inward strength, "full of *power*." 2. "*Judgment*." (Ver. 8.) The reference is not to judgment in the sense of being able to discriminate *character* (although *this* is very desirable), but judgment in the sense of enlightenment to understand the message to be delivered. Here was a messenger who knew what to say; who did not go forth with a sense of uncertainty, but as one who had received his message and was prepared without hesitation to deliver it. 3. "*Might*." The idea is that of *courage*. He not only knew what to say, but was ready to say it *fearlessly*. Humble in origin, born and trained up in obscurity, he cowered not even before princes and nobles, but rather caused *them* to tremble by the holy boldness with which he declared unto them "all the counsel of God."

II. THEIR SOURCE. (Ver. 8.) "But truly I am full of power by *the Spirit of the Lord*." These words betray no egotism on the part of the prophet. Had he simply affirmed himself to be a man of power, he had doubtless laid himself open to the charge of manifesting that "self-praise" which is "no recommendation;" but the qualifying sentence entirely frees him from the charge—"by *the Spirit of the Lord*." He was inwardly strong; he was enlightened to know what he ought to utter in God's name, and he was prepared to go forth and to say it with unflinching courage, because there rested upon him "an unction from the Holy One," and he was inspired by God's own Spirit.

III. THEIR EXERCISE. "He declared unto Jacob his transgression," etc. (ver. 8). With an inspiring consciousness of the presence with him of the Lord he served; with a clear perception of the character of the age and of the announcements he was to make in God's name, and with a boldness no adverse force could intimidate, because divinely sustained, he went forth to his appointed service, reproved the rulers for their unrighteous judgments and their acceptance of bribes, and their acts of cruelty and oppression (vers. 9, 10), chastised the priests and prophets for degrading, by their mercenary conduct, the high functions they were called upon to discharge (ver. 11), and predicted the coming overthrow of the nation, fastening upon these guilty leaders the responsibility of occasioning the impending doom (ver. 12). The history of the Church of God through all ages tells of men thus inspired by God's Spirit with "power" and "judgment" and "might;" and hence who nobly fulfilled their commission. Peter on the Day of Pentecost, Paul before kings and governors, Luther before the Diet of Worms, Knox carrying on the work of Reformation in Scotland, Whitefield and the Wesleys in the work of revival—there rested upon the heads of these true servants of the living God the tongues of heavenly fire; their arms were nerved by the might of omnipotence, and there dwelt in them the wondrous spiritual force that shall yet regenerate the world. There are difficulties connected with service to God in the present as in all past times; yet these should not dishearten or daunt us, but in the Divine strength we should courageously meet these and contend against them until they are all overcome. It betrays the possession of a weak faith, and seems to indicate that he does not realize what Divine resources are available to him, if a man in his work for God sits down before the difficulties of his position as a worker, dispirited and fretful. Shall we manifest less courage in reference to spiritual service than men exhibit in the ordinary pursuits of life? Shall we acknowledge ourselves baffled and beaten when the mighty energy of God's own Spirit is available, and may be ours if we will? There was exhibited on one occasion at the Royal Academy a striking picture of a gallant knight mounted on his charger and approaching a dark cavern. His steed was represented as drawing back through fear, and the dogs following as shrinking through terror; but lo! the knight wears a countenance untouched by alarm. There may be perils ahead, but he recks not, for his hand grasps the cross and his trust is in the living, loving Lord. Let our trust be thus centred, and no difficulty lying before us, or no antagonism against which we may have to contend in holy service, shall be able to daunt us, but we shall say, "Who art thou, O great mountain?

before Zerubbabel thou shalt become a plain." We should " covet earnestly the best gifts," and above all seek to be " endued with power from on high."

Ver. 10.—*National stability.* I. THE ENDEAVOUR TO SECURE NATIONAL STABILITY IS LAUDABLE AND TO BE COMMENDED. Princes, nobles, leaders of the people of all classes, ought to seek to *build up* Zion and Jerusalem; and earnest, enthusiastic effort directed to this end is honourable and worthy of all praise.

II. THIS RESULT CAN ALONE BE GAINED BY RIGHTEOUS MEANS. National strength and stability has its very foundations in truth, rectitude, justice, and goodness.

III. THE ADOPTION OF ANY OTHER METHODS MUST INEVITABLY RESULT IN DISGRACE AND DECAY. These rulers built up Zion with " blood," *i.e.* oppression, wrong, cruelty; and Jerusalem with "iniquity," perverting all that was true and right; and hence, despite the semblance of outward prosperity, the process of decay and dissolution was going on, and became at length completed in the ruin of the nation (ver. 12).

IV. THEY ARE THE TRUE PATRIOTS WHO LIFT UP THE VOICE OF WARNING, AND WHO EXPOUND AND ENFORCE THE PRINCIPLES OF RIGHTEOUSNESS. To adopt this course specially in a worldly, self-indulgent age is sure (1) to *render the teacher unpopular with many*; (2) hence it requires *holy courage and daring*; (3) which will be possessed in proportion as the man is "*moved by the Holy Ghost.*"

Ver. 11.—*The ministry viewed in relation to "hire."* The Jewish priests and prophets were the teachers of the people in matters of religion and morals. They exercised "the teaching faculty;" and this must form a prominent feature in those who devote themselves to the work of the ministry in every age (1 Tim. iii. 2; Col. i. 28; 2 Tim. ii. 15; 2 Cor. iv. 2). The power of the pulpit in these modern times depends very largely upon the maintenance of its teaching efficiency. The men the Church requires as its ministers are such as will come forth week by week not to utter a number of weary platitudes, but to enforce living truths, and to present these in forms fresh and new. Note—

I. SUCH "LABOURERS" ARE "WORTHY OF THEIR HIRE." The support of the Jewish priesthood was arranged under the Law (Deut. xviii. 2); the prophets also received temporal gifts in recognition of their services (1 Sam. ix. 7, 8). In the New Testament this principle of pecuniary acknowledgment being made for spiritual service is distinctly enunciated (Luke x. 7; 1 Cor. ix. 7, 14).

II. TO RENDER THIS SERVICE FOR THE SAKE OF THE "HIRE" IS SELF-DEGRADING, AND IS AN OFFENCE TO GOD AND THE GOOD. 1. *It leads to mere officialism.* 2. *It results in the perversion of truth,* the character of the message being made to depend upon the nature of the bribe and the desire to gratify those who offer it. 3. *It gives rise to sheer hypocrisy.* "Yet will they" (*i.e.* hypocritically) "lean upon the Lord and say, Is not the Lord among us?" (ver. 11). 4. *It awakens vain self-confidence.* "None evil can come upon us" (ver. 11). 5. *It incurs fearful responsibility.* "The blood of souls" will be required of such. The ruin of Zion and Jerusalem was here fastened upon such. "Therefore shall Zion *for your sake,*" etc. (ver. 12). How honourable is the work of the faithful minister of truth! How essential it is that they who engage in it should experience the Divine call, and should guard well their hearts so that they may be true to themselves and may render acceptable service to others! Whatever their "hire" here may be, how glorious is the reward awaiting all who are found true in this calling; for "when the chief Shepherd appears they shall receive the crown of life" (1 Pet. v. 4).

Ver. 12.—*The desolating effects of sin.* The Book of Micah may popularly be considered as consisting of three sections—the first setting forth national guilt and corruption (ch. i.—iii.); the second (ch. iv. v.) as presenting glimpses of a brighter and better age; and the third (ch. vi. vii.) as unfolding the nature and importance of sincere and practical religion, and the Divine mercy to all who thus turn to God and serve him with all their hearts. The verse before us closes the first part of the prophecy, and presents to us the culmination of a course of impiety and iniquity. We have described here that "death" which "sin when it is finished" ever "bringeth forth" (Jas. i. 15). Notice—

I. THE HISTORICAL FACT OF THE MATERIAL DESOLATION WHICH WAS TO RESULT FROM THE PREVAILING NATIONAL TRANSGRESSION. (Ver. 12.) Observe: 1. *This prophecy was doubtless oft repeated by the prophet.* That it was uttered by him during the reign of Hezekiah is clear from Jeremiah (xxvi. 17, 19). But it had probably been uttered by him previously, for the words which follow (ch. iv. 1—3), and which are closely connected with them, were quoted by Isaiah from Micah during the earlier reign of Jotham (Isa. ii. 2—4). The prophets enforced their teaching by constant reiteration. "To write the same things," etc. (Phil. iii. 1). 2. *The faithful utterance of this "dark saying" was the means of working a temporary reformation.* (See Jer. xxvi. 17, 19.) It might have exposed the seer to the greatest peril. To declare such evil omens at a time when the prosperity of the land was reviving under the wise rule of Hezekiah might have involved the prophet in suffering, and even death. But, happily, it had its desired effect; it caused the king and the people to bow before God in humiliation, and "judgment" against the evil works which had been wrought "was not executed speedily" (Jer. xxvi. 19). 3. *Though thus delayed, the destruction of the land was ultimately effected.* Dean Stanley observed in reference to this prediction by Micah, "The destruction which was then threatened has never been completely fulfilled. Part of the south-eastern portion of the city has for several centuries been arable land, but the rest has always been within the walls. In the Maccabean wars (1 Macc. iv. 38) the temple courts were overgrown with shrubs, but this has never been the case since" ('Jewish Church,' ii. 464). It is possible to be too literal in our interpretations, and the facts of history are simply sufficient to indicate how entirely that which Micah predicted (ver. 12) has come to pass (see Richardson's 'Travels,' p. 359; Keith on 'Prophecy,' p. 257; Porter's 'Handbook,' p. 92).

II. CONSIDER THIS AS SYMBOLICAL OF THAT SPIRITUAL DESOLATION WHICH IS EVER THE OUTCOME OF EVIL. It is the natural tendency of sin to render the transgressor desolate in heart; indeed, a man cannot indulge in a course of evil without his inner self, his spiritual being, becoming waste. A man yields to the sin of avarice, and perhaps as the result of its indulgence he gains his hundreds and thousands, gets the best of many a bargain, and at length amasses a fortune; but then he loses peace of mind, kindliness of heart, the joy resulting from cherishing all generous impulses, and probably also his soul; so that whilst in the worldly sense he has succeeded, he has prospered at a terrible sacrifice, even the withering of his highest and noblest powers; he has "got on," has "risen in the world," but his heart is left void and desolate. So also is it with *unholy ambition.* We think of Sennacherib saying to Hezekiah, "Where are the gods of Hamath?" etc. (Isa. xxxvi. 19, 20), thus proclaiming defiantly his victories; or of Herod sitting upon his throne, arrayed in gorgeous apparel, making his oration to the people, and priding himself in their flattery as he heard their cry, "It is the voice of a god, and not of a man" (Acts xii. 21, 22); and whilst on the one hand we see in them representatives of the lovers of power, of outward show, of flattery and applause, we see on the other hand men who, amidst all these outward pretences, were inwardly empty, waste, desolate. And there may be this spiritual desolation amidst much of apparent good. It does not follow that because a man is becoming thus spiritually desolate, his heart is necessarily closed against all that is good, or that because a man is susceptible of some good he is not spiritually becoming waste. There may be love of kindred with all those praiseworthy acts to which this may prompt. There may be large and generous sympathies. Attention, too, may even be paid to religious observances; and yet with all this the heart may be closed to the heavenly influences of the Spirit of God, and may be found at length a moral waste (Prov. iv. 23). Think of the inestimable value of that Sacrifice, the design of which was the putting away of sin and the raising to honour and dignity those whom sin had covered with ignominy and had plunged into ruin. Our very desolation has rendered us the objects of the special concern of the Most High (John iii. 16). Trusting to Christ, we become delivered from sin with all its thraldom and misery. And the happy era shall at length dawn, to which we look forward with longing, expectant hearts, when the entire moral aspect of the universe shall be changed. and "the desert rejoice and blossom as the rose."

HOMILIES BY VARIOUS AUTHORS.

Ver. 8.—*God's gift of a faithful ministry*. The expression, "But truly (אוּלָם)," implies a contrast to what precedes. The false prophets were in alliance with the tyrannical princes, and were destined to humiliation and to the utter loss of whatever power they once possessed. But Micah, conscious of a Divine calling and of fidelity to it, can point to himself as an illustration of God's precious gift of a faithful ministry. Note—

I. ITS QUALIFICATIONS. The fundamental one is: 1 *The indwelling of the Spirit of God*. The true prophet or minister magnifies his office, but does not exalt himself. He traces all he has to God, as does St. Paul (1 Cor. xv. 10; 1 Tim. i. 12—16). Pretenders to the prophetic or pastoral office were "sensual (ψυχικοί), not having the Spirit," inspired only by the spirit of the world, or of self; but true ministers can use St. Paul's words (1 Cor. ii. 12), for they are relying on their Divine Master's promise of the Holy Spirit. 2. Hence *spiritual power*. It may be special and superhuman, such as prophets and apostles enjoyed. But the more valuable power is that which enables us to witness for Christ (Acts i. 8), to exert a holy influence (2 Cor. iii. 2, 3), and to preach "in demonstration of the Spirit and of power." Power is a general term; the Divine Spirit manifests his presence by a diversity of gifts appropriate to special necessities. Two of these are mentioned here as needed by the prophet and, in truth, by every faithful minister. 3. *Judgment*, including such thoughts as these—a clear sense of God's equity in his dealings (Ezek. xviii.), an impartial utterance of God's sentences (Jer. i. 16—19), and therefore discrimination in all his messages and in his treatment of his hearers, "doing nothing by partiality," "rightly dividing the Word of truth," "warning every man and teaching every man." Such a ministry will emit light as well as heat, will show discretion as well as zeal. 4. *Moral courage*. "Might," such as the apostles sought and received (Acts iv. 29—31; cf. Eph. vi. 19, 20; Col. iv. 4; 2 Tim. i. 7). All these gifts are needed in a high degree—"full," etc. "However the Lord may bless the meanest gifts of such as be honest, yet neither are ministers to be empty vessels nor swelled with ostentation, but a large measure of real furniture is to be sought after." All these qualifications were more or less fully manifested in the true prophets of God; *e.g.* Elijah (Ecclus. xlviii. 1), Isaiah (lviii. 1), Jeremiah (vi. 11, 27), Ezekiel (iii. 8—11), and many others.

II. ITS DIFFICULTIES. The main difficulty here suggested arises from its relation to the sins of men. 1. The burden of the Lord laid on ministers requires them to be willing to be used in the disagreeable task of convicting communities and individuals of sin. This may be traced in the long prophetical and apostolical succession of God's true ministers, including such illustrious names as Moses, Samuel, Nathan, Elijah, Daniel, John the Baptist, Peter, and Paul. We too must be prepared to show to the Church and to individuals their sins in trade, their transgressions of the royal law in their conduct, whether towards servants or masters. Thus we may seem to many "men of strife," or even enemies (Gal. iv. 16). 2. But we do not successfully "show" to men their transgressions unless they are induced to abandon their sin and accept God's method of deliverance. We seek to *take men alive* out of the snare of the devil (see 2 Tim. ii. 24—26, Revised Version). It is a terrible thing to convict a man of sin, and yet fail to save him, thus increasing his condemnation.

III. ITS ENCOURAGEMENTS. 1. *Frequent successes*. We learn from Jer. xxvi. 17—19 that Micah's message on this occasion led to the conversion of Hezekiah, or to the reawakening of his zeal as a reformer. The Christian minister's song of victory is often heard (2 Cor. ii. 14). 2. *Constant Divine approval*. Sometimes a sense of failure causes a feeling of isolation and of heart-sickness, such as Jeremiah often felt. But even then we can fall back on the sense of the abiding presence of God (John xvi. 32), and of his approving smile (Isa. xlix. 4, 5).—E. S. P.

Vers. 9—11.—*Spurious faith*. The prophet at once vindicates the claim he has just made (ver. 8). We have here—

I. AN UNSPARING EXPOSURE OF SINS IN HIGH QUARTERS. All classes are involved, and to each class the most scandalous characteristic offences are imputed. 1. *Civil rulers.* They are open to bribes, in direct violation of Exod. xxiii. 8, and therefore pervert judgment. These sophists on the judgment-seat make "the worse appear the better reason;" and at length reach such a stage of iniquity that they "abhor judgment," and "call evil good," etc. (Isa. v. 20; cf. 2 Pet. ii. 14). In the striking figure of Isaiah (lix. 14), "truth is fallen in the street, and equity cannot enter." Their crimes are set out in detail in vers. 1—4. Meanwhile they are building fine mansions or laying out estates, but at the price of blood, like Ahab (1 Kings xix.) or Jehoiakim (Jer. xxii. 13—19); or they are wronging the poor, though the consequences may be fatal; as in modern society some of the "heads thereof" connive at social systems in government or in business, by which the poor are defrauded of their claim to a livelihood. "The bread of the needy is their life; he that defraudeth him thereof is a man of blood. He that taketh away his neighbour's living slayeth him: and he that defraudeth the labourer of his hire is a bloodshedder" (Ecclus. xxxv. 21, 22). 2. *Ecclesiastical leaders.* The priests' duty was to teach the Law (Lev. x. 11; Deut. xvii. 11; xxxiii. 10), but they too needed *douceurs*, or fees or bribes. They probably misinterpreted the Law from the same motive as did Eli's sons (1 Sam. ii. 12—17). "So Arian bishops, themselves hirelings, by false expositions of Scripture countenanced Arian emperors in their persecution of the faithful" (Pusey). So, too, persecuting priests and prelates in more recent days. 3. *Prophets.* These religious teachers were raised up to promote a reformation; but they too had been dragged down to the level of other teachers. Divine prophecy had been corrupted into divination, as in the case of Balaam, and covetousness was universal (ver. 5; and cf. Ezek. xiii. 1—6). An instructive parallel may be found in the case of the regular clergy of the mediæval Church, who were gradually degraded to the low moral level of the secular clergy. We are reminded of the odiousness of a mercenary ministry. Thus all classes were combined in a conspiracy of unrighteousness (as in Ezek. xxii. 23—31), and the love of money was the root of all this evil.

II. An indignant protest against unwarranted faith in God. They flatter themselves: 1. *That they may lean upon the Lord.* Deaf to all past teachings, blind to the danger signals which history has erected, they insult God by leaning upon him, and expecting him to support their vile souls and pampered bodies (cf. Deut. xxix. 19, 20). They further take for granted: 2. *That the Lord is among them.* Though invisible to sense, and sending repeated protests, they assume his favourable presence. They trust in lying words, saying, "The temple of the Lord are these," as though the temple of the Lord and the Lord of the temple were identical. In a church at Innsbruck, on the tabernacle containing the consecrated wafer are the words, "Ecce tabernaculum Dei." If this daring perversion of Scripture had proclaimed a truth, what a false confidence for an unworthy communicant; as though "Corpus Christi" and "Christ in you" were the same! "There standeth One *among you* whom ye know not" may be true, but in a new sense; if not to sanctify, to condemn. 3. *That no evil will befall them.* As though God's protests and a guilty conscience were not in themselves evils and the forecast shadows of coming doom. So deceitful and desperately wicked is the heart of man. These truths may be applied to many "*nominal* Christians." (1) Ambitious monarchs or statesmen, "building up" their country by huge standing armies, or navies, or palaces, at the cost of grinding taxation, leading to semi-starvation and loathsome disease as among the Italian peasantry, or of tyrannical extortions from Egyptian felaheen, or of a merciless conscription as in Germany, driving some of her best sons from her shores. (2) Landlords amassing fortunes from rack-renting the fever-slums of London, or confiscating the fruits of the tenants' industry in Ireland. (3) Drink-sellers fattening on the pauperism of their wretched customers, or carrying liquid poisons to tribes just emerging from barbarism. (4) Hireling preachers or priests, prophesying smooth things to unrighteous aristocrats or plutocrats, or lulling guilty consciences by the opiate of the sacrament. Such men of expediency crucified even the Son of God that Zion might be "built up" (John xi. 48; see Jer. v. 30, 31). To that final question an answer is found in ver. 12.—E. S. P.

Vers. 1—6.—*Civil rulers.* "And I said, Hear, I pray you, O heads of Jacob, and ye princes of the house of Israel; Is it not for you to know judgment? Who hate the good, and love the evil; who pluck off their skin from off them, and their flesh from off their bones," etc. The punishment threatened in this chapter is against the authorities of Israel, against the princes who turn right into wrong and slay the people, against false prophets who lead the people astray and confirm them in their sin, and against the priests in connection with both princes and prophets. The passage before us is directed to the princes and the rulers. These are represented as radically corrupt, hating good and loving evil, and cruelly oppressive: "Who pluck off their skin from off them, and their flesh from off their bones." And more than this, "they eat the flesh of my people, and flay their skin from off them." They are represented not only as slaying the people, robbing them of the means of existence, but devouring them, treating them like cattle, which are first killed and then boiled in the pot for food. All this, of course, is strong figure used to make a strong impression. We have two things worthy of notice concerning civil rulers.

I. WHAT CIVIL RULERS OUGHT ALWAYS TO BE. They ought always to "know judgment," that is, always practically to know the right. The ruler who has not a practical knowledge and love of the right is out of his place; he is a usurper. There is such a thing as right in the universe. What is the standard of right? Not public sentiment, not human law, but the Divine will. God's being is the foundation of right; God's will is the standard of right; God's Christ is the completest revelation of that standard. The man who is not Christly in character is more or less despicable everywhere, but nowhere so much as on a throne. Are we not commanded to honour the king? Yes, but the command implies that the king is honourworthy. Reason, conscience, and the Bible call upon us to loathe and despise moral corruption on a throne.

> "He, a king,
> A true right king, that dare do aught save wrong,
> Fears nothing mortal but to be unjust;
> Who is not blown up with the flattering puffs
> Of spongy sycophants; who stands unmoved
> Despite the jostling of opinion."
>
> (Marston.)

II. WHAT CIVIL RULERS OFTEN ARE. What were these rulers? 1. *They were morally corrupt.* These rulers were of those who "hate the good and love the evil." They were in heart radically wrong, corrupt to the very core, hating good. 2. *They were socially cruel.* They treated the people as the butchers and the cooks treat beasts—kill them, boil them for their own use. How often, even in the history of England, have rulers treated the people as mere cattle for food! 3. *They were divinely abandoned.* "Then shall they cry unto the Lord, but he will not hear them: he will even hide his face from them at that time." The Monarch of the universe is no "respecter of persons." Princes are no more in his eyes than paupers; and he will treat both according to their character, their responsibility, and their merits. He has often roused nations to send their rulers howling into infamy and ruin. After all, the existence of corrupt kings is to be ascribed to the ignorance, the cowardice, and servility of the people. Let the peoples of the earth advance in intelligence, moral discernment, and independency, and such rulers will disappear. Corrupt rulers are like glowworms, that in the night seem brilliant, but in the day contemptible grubs. Weak, ignorant, and tyrannic kings appear glorious in the night of popular ignorance, but abhorrent as the day of mental intelligence advances.—D. T.

Vers. 5—7.—*False prophets.* "Thus saith the Lord concerning the prophets that make my people err, that bite with their teeth, and cry, Peace; and he that putteth not into their mouths, they even prepare war against him. Therefore night shall be unto you, that ye shall not have a vision," etc. The following is the version of Delitzsch: "Thus saith Jehovah concerning the prophets who lead my people astray, who bite with their teeth and preach peace. And whoever should put nothing into their mouths, against him they sanctify war. Therefore night to you because of the vision, and darkness to you because of the soothsaying; and the sun will set over the prophets, and the day blacken itself over them. And the seers will be ashamed and the soothsayers blush, and all cover their head, because there is no answer of God."

"Here he attacks the false prophets, as before he had attacked the 'princes.' 'That make my people err'—knowingly mislead my people, by not denouncing their sins as incurring judgments. 'That bite with their teeth, and cry, Peace;' *i.e.* who, so long as they are supplied with food, promise peace and prosperity in their prophecies. 'And he that putteth not into their mouths, they even prepare war against him.' Whenever they are not supplied with food, they foretell war and calamity: they sanctify war, *i.e.* proclaim it as a holy judgment of God, because they are not fed. 'Therefore night shall be unto you, that ye shall not have a vision; and it shall be dark.' Calamities press on you so overwhelmingly as to compel you to cease pretending to divine (Zech. xiii. 4). Darkness is often the image of calamity (Isa. viii. 22; Amos v. 18; viii. 9). 'Then shall the seers be ashamed, and the diviners confounded: yea, they shall all cover their lips.' The Orientals prided themselves on the moustache and beard. To cover the upper lip, therefore, was a token of shame, mourning, and sorrow (Lev. xiii. 45; Ezek. xxiv. 17). 'Cover not thy lips,' *i.e.* assume not the usual token of one mourning (Ezek. xxiv. 22). They shall be so ashamed of themselves as not to dare to open their mouths, or boast of the name of prophet. 'For there is no answer of God.' They shall no more profess to have responses from God, being struck dumb with calamities" (Fausset). False prophets are here brought under our attention again, and three things are suggested concerning them.

I. THEY ARE DECEIVING. God says, they "make my people err." Preachers often make their hearers err. 1. *In theology.* They propound ideas, crude and ill digested, concerning God, Christ, moral conditions and relations, utterly inconsistent with truth. 2. *In worship.* The forms they propose to use in worship, the rules they enjoin for it, are often such as to give the people wrong ideas as to what worship really is. 3. *In morality.* Their standard of duty is often wrong; hence wars are sanctioned, priestly exactions and assumptions encouraged and maintained. Ah me! how the preachers make men err on these great subjects!

II. THEY ARE AVARICIOUS. They "bite with their teeth, and cry, Peace." Greed governs them in all their ministries. They are ever hungering after gain; pelf with them is a passion. Their eyes are ever on pew-rents, offerings, tithes, etc. If their greed is offended, they "prepare war against" the offender; they raise an opposition strong and deadly against him. They are "greedy of filthy lucre."

III. THEY ARE CONFOUNDED. Confounded in *darkness.* "Night shall be unto you, that ye shall not have a vision; and it shall be dark unto you, that ye shall not divine; and the sun shall go down over the prophets, and the day shall be dark over them." They were blind leaders of the blind, and they themselves fall into the ditch. Confounded in *shame.* "Then shall the seers be ashamed, and the diviners be confounded." Jehovah ignores them. "There is no answer of God." "Those," says Matthew Henry, "who deceive others are but preparing confusion for their own faces."—D. T.

Vers. 8—12.— *The true prophet.* "But truly I am full of power by the Spirit of the Lord, and of judgment, and of might, to declare unto Jacob his transgression, and to Israel his sin. Hear this, I pray you," etc. It is supposed that this chapter belongs to the reign of Hezekiah; if so, the mournful state of matters which it depicts belongs to the time preceding the reformation. These words lead us to consider *the true prophet.*

I. THE WORK OF A TRUE PROPHET. "To declare unto Jacob his transgression, and to Israel his sin." It is a characteristic of all true prophets, that they have a keen moral sense to discern wrong, to loathe it, and to burn at it. No man is a true prophet who is not roused to thunder by the wrong. It has been charged against the preachers of England that it is not wrong that rouses them, but little dogmas that agree not with their theology, sects that unite not with their Church, policies that interfere with their income and position. We fear this is too true. The crimes of the people of England are not denounced by the pulpit as they should be—the vice in high places, the injustices perpetrated under the name and sanction of law, the cupidity of traders, the swindlings of joint stock company men, by which they become millionaires and win a seat in the Parliament of the nation. These things are not held up as they should be for public execration, in the broad sunlight of eternal truth.

Where have we men now to " declare unto Jacob his transgression, and unto Israel his sin"? 1. *This is a painful work.* It will incur the disfavour of some, and rouse the antagonism of the delinquents. Still, it must be done—done as John the Baptist did it, who denounced his countrymen as a " generation of vipers;" done as Christ did it, who levelled his terrible " woes" at the heads of the great criminals of his age. 2. *This is an urgent work.* No work is more needed in England to-day. To expose wrong goes a great way towards its extinction. Honeyed words in the pulpit we have enough, tawdry disquisitions, and sensational inanities. God multiply men of the stamp of John the Baptist and of the Apostle Peter, who on the Day of Pentecost charged home the terrible crime of the crucifixion to the men he addressed!

II. THE POWER OF A TRUE PROPHET. " Truly I am full of power by the Spirit of the Lord, and of judgment, and of might." There is no egotism in this. A powerful man knows his power, and will ascribe it to the right Source—the "Spirit of the Lord." Micah's power was moral; it was the might of conscience, moral conviction, of invincible sympathy with eternal right and truth. This is a very different power to that of mere intellect, imagination, or what is called genius. It is higher, more creditable, more influential, more God-like. What does the man who has it care for the smiles or frowns of his audiences? He sets his face like a flint. The praises of his fellow-men affect him no more than the twitterings of a sparrow would an eagle; their frowns, no more than the yelpings of a cur affect the monarch of the forest.

III. THE FIDELITY OF A TRUE PROPHET. This is seen here in three things. 1. *In the class he denounces.* " Hear this, I pray you, ye heads of the house of Jacob, and princes of the house of Israel." He struck at the higher classes of life. " Heads of the house of Jacob, and princes of the house of Israel." Ah me! how little we pulpiteering cowards here in England address ourselves to the crimes of the upper classes! The low, the helpless, the destitute, we are always lecturing. Do your ecclesiastical lords lecture royalty, think you? I read their fulsome flatteries often, but their denunciations never. The prophet's fidelity is seen: 2. *In the charges he makes.* " They build up Zion with blood, and Jerusalem with iniquity." (1) He charges them with extortionate cruelty. " The civic rulers only are addressed in ver. 9, viz. those who were charged with the administration of justice and of the affairs of the state, but who did the very opposite—who abhorred justice and made the straight crooked because they passed sentence for bribes. They thereby build Zion with blood, etc., *i.e.* obtain the means of erecting splendid buildings by cruel extortions, partly also by actual judicial murder, as Ahab, and after him Jehoiakim, had done" (Delitzsch). Building up Jerusalem by blood is something like building up churches by beer. It is not uncommon now for large brewers, from the enormous profits of their pernicious craft, to build up magnificent temples for God. What an outrage on decency! What an insult to omniscient Purity! (2) He charges them with base mercenariness. " The heads thereof judge for reward, and the priests thereof teach for hire, and the prophets thereof divine for money." He saw mercenariness on the bench, inspiring the judge; mercenariness at the altar, inspiring the priests; mercenariness in the pulpit, inspiring the preachers. *Money* was the motive power of all. With all this mercenariness, still they " leaned upon the Lord," that is, professed to worship the one true and living God, and ignorantly and presumptuously concluded that he would be ever amongst them, and that consequently no great evil would overtake them. The prophet's faithfulness is seen: 3. *In the doom he proclaims.* " Therefore shall Zion for your sake be ploughed as a field, and Jerusalem shall become heaps, and the mountain of the house as the high places of the forest." The prophecy was never literally fulfilled till the destruction of Jerusalem by the Romans, when the ground on which the city stood was ploughed up, in token of its utter demolition, and no city was to be built there without the emperor's leave. " It is," says an old writer, " the wickedness of those who preside in them that brings the ruin. It is for your sake that Zion shall be ploughed as a field; you pretend to build up Zion, but, doing it by blood and iniquity, you pull it down. The sin of priests and princes is often the ruin of states and Churches. *Delirant reges, plectuntur Achivi;* the kings act foolishly, and the people suffer by it."

CONCLUSION. Such is the true prophet.—D. T.

EXPOSITION.

CHAPTER IV.

Vers. 1—5.—§ 4. *The prophet suddenly announces the future glory of the temple mountain and the ideal happiness of the people.*

Ver. 1.—But. There is no adversative particle here; the verse is merely connected with what precedes without any expressed contrast. What is implied is that it was impossible that the temple, to which God's high promises attached, should lie waste for ever. The passage, vers. 1—3, occurs in Isa. ii. 2—4. The question as to which prophecy is the earlier cannot be settled. Possibly both prophets borrowed the language of some earlier work, as Isaiah is thought to have done on other occasions, *e.g.* Isa. xv. and xvi., the community of ideas leading them to the same source of testimony. **In the last days;** literally, *at the end of the days;* Cheyne, "in the days to come." It is the usual phrase to designate the time of Messiah, unto which the prophet's thoughts are directed, and for which all preceding events and periods are a preparation (Jer. xxiii. 20; Hos. iii. 5; comp. 1 Cor. x. 11; 1 Tim. iv. 1). Septuagint, ἐπ᾽ ἐσχάτων τῶν ἡμερῶν, "at the last days." The phrase may often suitably be rendered, "in latter days," as spoken not absolutely, but relatively to preceding times. **The mountain of the house of the Lord.** Mount Moriah, the ruin of which was foretold (ch. iii. 12). But the term here seems to include Jerusalem itself. **Shall be established,** firmly and permanently (as 1 Kings ii. 45), no longer subject to ruin and devastation. **In the top of the mountains;** better, *on the head of the mountains.* The idea is that the temple mountain shall be raised above, and stand forth prominently from the lower hills that surround it and form its basis (comp. Ezek. xl. 2; Zech. xiv. 10; Rev. xxi. 10). The prophet speaks as if he contemplated a physical change, expressing thereby with singular force the notion that the worship of the true God (of which the temple was the symbol) shall be promulgated among all nations of the world; that from the old Jewish centre of religion a new order of things shall arise, not transitory, nor local, but extending to all time and pervading the utmost parts of the earth. **And people** (*peoples*) **shall flow unto it.** The prophet beholds the nations of the world coming up in formal procession to join in the service of the temple. Thus is adumbrated the comprehension of all nations in the Catholic Church. Isaiah says "all nations" in the parallel passage (comp. Zeph. ii. 11 and Zech. viii. 22, and notes there).

Ver. 2.—The prophet further explains his last statement. The new revelation shall be so conspicuous and so attractive that all men shall hear, and desire to become partakers of it. **Many nations.** In contrast to the one nation from whom the Law emanated. They shall exhort one another to resort to the great religious metropolis, *i.e.* to the true religion. **Of his ways.** His plans in the moral government of the world, and the way in which he would have men walk in order to please him. **For the law** (*torah*)**;** *teaching, direction;* not the Mosaic Law, but a rule of life (Prov. vi. 23). This is the reason given by the prophet for the eagerness of the nations to resort to Jerusalem. They would seek instruction at the hand of those authorized to give it (see note on ch. iii. 11). **The word of the Lord.** The revelation of Jehovah, the gospel. **From Jerusalem.** It is obvious that in a defined sense the gospel sprang from Jerusalem, the place where Christ exercised his ministry, died, rose, ascended; where the apostles received their commission and the gift of the Holy Ghost (Luke xxiv. 47; Acts i. 8); the gospel being not set up in opposition to the Law, but being its fulfilment and development.

Ver. 3.—The effect of this reception of true religion shall be universal peace. **He shall judge among many people;** or better, *between many peoples.* The Lord shall be the Arbiter to whom all disputes shall be referred, as in the next clause. When his reign is acknowledged and his Law obeyed, all war and all causes of war shall cease. The gospel is a gospel of peace and love, and when "the kingdoms of this world are become the kingdoms of our Lord and his Christ" (Rev. xi. 15), peace and love shall everywhere abound. (For the phrase in the text, comp. Judg. xi. 27; 1 Sam. xxiv. 12, 15.) **Rebuke strong nations afar off.** The word rendered "rebuke" means here "decide concerning," "act as umpire for." The arbitration of the sword shall no more be resorted to. The words "afar off" are omitted in the similar passage of Isaiah. **Beat their swords into ploughshares;** *i.e.* they shall practise the arts of peace instead of war. Literally, the short broad sword of the Israelites might readily be converted into a share, and the spear forged into a pruning-hook (comp. Hos. ii. 18; Zech. ix. 10). Martial has an epigram entitled "Falx ex ense" (xiv. 34)—

" Pax me certa ducis placidos curvavit in
usus :
Agricolæ nunc sum, militis ante fui."

The reverse process is seen in Joel iii. 10,
where ploughshares are beaten into swords.
Thus Virgil, 'Georg.,' i. 508—

"Et curvæ rigidum falces conflantur in
ensem."

(Comp. Ovid, 'Fast.,' i. 699, etc.)
Ver. 4.—This verse is omitted in Isaiah.
They shall sit every man under his vine.
This image of plenty and security is derived
from the account of the material prosperity
of Israel in the days of Solomon (1 Kings
iv. 25), in accordance with the Mosaic
promise (Lev. xxvi. 4, etc.). It passed into
a proverb expressive of peace and happiness
(comp. Zech. iii. 10 ; 1 Macc. xiv. 12). **The
mouth of the Lord of hosts.** The great
promise is thus confirmed (Isa. lviii. 14).
The LXX. usually renders this expression in
Jeremiah and the minor prophets by Κύριος
παντοκράτωρ, elsewhere by Κύριος σαβαώθ,
and Κύριος δυνάμεων. It means, " the Lord of
the powers of heaven and earth," the idea
being originally that God was the Leader of
the armies of Israel.
Ver. 5.—This verse gives the reason why
Israel is thus strong and safe. In the
parallel passage in Isaiah (ii. 5) it is converted into an injunction to the house of
Jacob. **All people will walk ;** rather, *all
nations walk.* Every one in the name of
his god. "To walk" is generally used of
moral and religious habits (*e.g.* 2 Chron.
xvii. 4 ; Ps. lxxxix. 31 ; Ezek. v. 6, etc.);
so here the meaning is that all other
nations adhere to their false gods, and
frame their life and conduct relying on the
power and protection of these inanities, and,
by implication, shall find their hope deceived. **And we will walk in the name of
the Lord our God.** This is the secret of
Israel's strength. The heathen can never
prevail against the true believers who put
their whole trust in the Lord, and live in
union with him. By saying *we,* the prophet
identifies himself with the faithful people.
For ever and ever. The Church shall never
fail. Heathen powers last for a time ; the
kingdom of Messiah is everlasting.

Vers. 6, 7.—§ 5. *In this promised restoration all Israel is included, if they choose to
accept the offer.*

Ver. 6.—**In that day.** The Messianic age
of ver. 1. **Her that halteth ;** Septuagint, τὴν
συντετριμμένην, "her that is bruised ;" Vulgate, *claudicantem.* Under the image of a
flock footsore and dispersed, the prophet
signifies the depressed condition of the
exiled Hebrews (comp. ch. ii. 12 ; Zeph.

iii. 19). It is the sick and afflicted here who
are to be gathered together, the remnant,
that is (ver. 7), wherever found, which
turns to the Lord in repentance and humility.
Ver. 7.—**I will make her that halted a
remnant.** The " remnant " is " the election,"
that portion of Israel which accepts the
offered redemption (Rom. ix. 27 ; xi. 5) ; and
God declares that he will treat this section,
now miserable and depressed, as sharers in
the Messianic promises (see note on Zeph.
iii. 19). As commonly, the restoration from
captivity and the privileges of Messiah's
kingdom are combined in one foreshortened
view. But this " remnant " shall be made
into a strong nation, which no power shall
overthrow (Isa. xi 14 ; lx. 22). **The Lord
shall reign over them.** Not through an
earthly representative, but by himself (comp.
Isa. xxiv. 23 ; lii. 7 ; Obad. 21 ; Zech. xiv. 9).
In Mount Zion. This prophecy does not
necessarily point to any literal earthly fulfilment, but rather to the establishment of
Christ's spiritual kingdom, and the revelation of that new Jerusalem which St. John
saw " descending out of heaven from God "
(Rev. xxi. 10).

Vers. 8—10.—§ 6. *After a certain period
of calamity and captivity the kingdom of
David shall be revived.*

Ver. 8.—**And thou, O tower of the flock**
(*migdal-edar*). There was a village with a
tower so called near Bethlehem (Gen. xxxv.
21), and it is thought that Micah refers to
it as the home of David and as destined to
be the birthplace of Messiah. But the context compels us to consider the expression
as a periphrasis for Jerusalem, which the
prophet here addresses, declaring that the
royal power shall be restored to her. It is
evidently the same place as the strong hold
(*ophel*, " the hill ") of the daughter of Zion.
The name " Ophel " is affixed to the southern
spur of Moriah, opposite to the Mount Zion,
from which it was separated by the Tyropœon Valley. It was fortified by Jotham
(2 Chron. xxvii. 3) and Manasseh (2 Chron.
xxxiii. 14), and on it were the king's house,
i.e. the old palace of David, and " the tower
that lieth out," or the upper tower (see Neh.
iii. 26, 27). This is probably the " flock-
tower " mentioned in the text (comp. Isa.
xxxii. 14, where Ophel and the watch-tower
are named together); and it is so called as
having been originally a place of refuge for
flocks, or of observation for shepherds. Micah
uses the two expressions to represent the
power and dominion of Jerusalem. The propriety of the use of the term " flock-tower "
is seen when we remember that David was
a shepherd before he was king, and that the
Israelites are the sheep of the Lord's pasture.
The reference to a flock in the preceding

verses may also have influenced the prophet's thought. Owing to a slight variation in the reading, the LXX. renders *Ophel* by αἰχμώδης, "dark;" so Jerome, "nebulosa;" Aquila, σκοτώδης: Symmachus, ἀπόκρυφος. These translators would refer the term to the ruinous condition of the tower. **The first dominion shall come,** *i.e.* the former, original empire, such as it was in the days of David and Solomon, and which had been lost in later times. The LXX. adds, ἐκ Βαβυλῶνος: and hence the Greek expositors explain the passage as referring to the siege of Jerusalem by the Chaldeans. **The kingdom shall come to the daughter of Jerusalem.** The verb "shall come" is better taken with the "first dominion," and this clause in apposition to the former, "the kingdom of" or "the reign over the daughter of Jerusalem." Sovereignty over Jerusalem, or, as others take it, that appertains to Jerusalem, represents rule over the whole country. In Messiah the glory and power are restored to the throne of David (Luke i. 32, 33).

Ver. 9.—Before this glorious revival the prophet foresees calamity and exile in the nearer future; yet he bids the people not to despair. **Why dost thou cry out aloud?** The prophet hears the cry of Zion, and asks the cause. Septuagint, 'Ἱνατί ἔγνως κακά; "Why knowest thou evils?" from a variation in reading. **Is there no king in thee?** Hast thou lost thy king? Is this the reason of thy sorrow? The allusion is to the captivity of Jehoiachin and Zedekiah (2 Kings xxiv., xxv.). The loss of the king, the representative of the help and favour of God, was a token of the withdrawal of the Divine protection (comp. Lam. iv. 20; Hos. xiii. 10). **Thy counsellor.** A synonym for "king." Cheyne notes that the root of *melech* ("king") in Aramaic means "to counsel." In Isa. ix. 6 Messiah is called "Counsellor." The Septuagint, treating the word as a collective, renders, ἡ βουλή σου, "thy counsel." **Pangs,** etc. The comparison of sorrow of heart to the anguish of labour pains is very common (comp. Isa. xiii. 8; Jer. vi. 24; l. 43; Hos. xiii. 13).

Ver. 10.—**Be in pain.** The anguish is not to be resisted, but shall end, like birth-pains, in deliverance. Septuagint, Ὤδινε καὶ ἀνδρίζου καὶ ἔγγιζε, "Be in pain, and do bravely, and draw near," which is like Æneas's encouragement to his friends (Virgil, 'Æneid,' i. 207)—

"Durate, et vosmet rebus servate secundis."

For now shalt thou go forth. The prophet leaves his metaphor, and announces that the people shall "go forth" into captivity. He says "now," as having the scene before his eyes. They must leave their city, live shelterless in the open country, be carried to a distant land, even to Babylon. **Shalt dwell in the field;** *i.e.* while they are making their way to the place of their captivity. **Thou shalt go even to Babylon.** This is simple prophecy, and could have been known to Micah only by inspiration. In his day Assyria was the enemy whom Israel had to dread (as ch. v. 5, 6), Babylon being at this time in the position of a conquered country, and not becoming again powerful and independent for another century. So Isaiah prophesied of the captivity to Babylon (xxxix. 3—8), if modern critics have not shaken our faith in the genuineness of that chapter. Micah does not define the time of the Captivity, or the agents; he notes merely the place whither the Jews were at last to be deported. Even in this case "Babylon" may have its typical import, and be taken to represent the great world-power arrayed against the chosen race; and the prophecy may look forward to other fulfilments in succeeding ages. Some commentators think that Babylon is here mentioned as the most distant country known, or as a portion of the Assyrian empire. Others suppose that Sargon transported some Israelitish captives to Babylon to replace the rebellious Babylonians whom he exiled to Palestine (' Records of the Past,' vii. 29; 2 Kings xvii. 24; comp. 2 Chron. xxxiii. 11), and that thus Micah was naturally led to represent the Judæans as following their brethren. Whichever explanation we take, there is no reason to consider that the reference to Babylon is the interpolation of a late editor of the prophetic writings. **There shalt thou be delivered.** In Babylon deliverance shall arise. This prophecy was first literally fulfilled in the return from captivity under Cyrus; it is further fulfilled, under Christ, in the rescue of the true Israelites from the bondage of sin and the world.

Vers. 11—13.—§ 7. *Rescued from Babylon, Zion overcomes all enemies in the strength of God.*

Ver. 11.—**Now also;** *and now.* A new scene is presented in contrast to the view in vers. 1—4. **Many nations are gathered against thee.** Primarily the Assyrians are meant (Isa. xxxiii. 3), whose armies were composed of various nationalities (Isa. xxii. 6; see below, ch. v. 5). Pusey thinks that the reference is rather to the attacks of petty enemies, *e.g.* in Maccabean times, and in the Samaritans' opposition to the rebuilding of the temple. Cheyne would place vers. 5—10 in a parenthesis, and connect the present with the ideal description in vers. 1—4. **Let her be defiled;** *i.e.* profaned, despoiled of her boasted holiness and inviolability. LXX., ἐπιχαρούμεθα, "we will rejoice." The Vulgate, *lapidetur*, points to her punishment as an adulteress, which does not suit the context. **Let our eye look upon Zion.** The heathen anticipate with malicious pleasure the sight of the humiliation of Jerusalem (comp. Obad. 12, 13).

Ver. 12.—But the enemies who came to exult over Zion do not know God's design while blindly working it out. God's people are not to be destroyed, but their adversaries. **They know not the thoughts of the Lord.** The heathen, who were the instruments of God's wrath against his people, knew nothing of his purpose in thus afflicting them, nor perceived that they themselves were drawn together for punishment. **He shall gather** (*hath gathered*) **them as the sheaves into the floor.** Their blindness is proved by their not perceiving till too late that God has brought them together before Jerusalem, as sheaves are brought into the threshing-floor, in order to be broken up and destroyed (comp. Isa. xxi. 10; Jer. li. 23). The metaphor is carried on in the next verse. Various are the explanations of this prophecy. Many commentators see in it a reference to the destruction of the army of Sennacherib (2 Kings xix. 35); others discern a defeat of the Scythians after the return from captivity; others, again, place it in the times of the Maccabees; and others interpret it of the defeat of the mystical adversaries of God's Church adumbrated in Ezek. xxxviii.; Zech. xii.; and Rev. xx. But the prophet has not one definite event in view, but looks forward to the general conflict between the powers of the world and the Church, of which the historical events and material enemies were the types. Certain historical circumstances may exactly suit the prediction, but they do not exhaust it. And indeed we do wrong to seek for minute and definite fulfilment of particular predictions. Such utterances are often conditional and are modified by subsequent circumstances. The prophets are concerned with great moral truths and the righteous government of the world, and are not always to be interpreted with literal exactness.

Ver. 13.—**Arise.** Shake off thy sorrow and fear and despair. **And thresh.** Tread thine enemies underfoot, now that they are gathered in the floor, as the oxen tread out the corn (Isa. xli. 15, etc.; Jer. li. 33.) **Thine horn.** The horn is an emblem of power and victory, as appertaining to the wild ox, the most powerful animal in Canaan (Deut. xxxiii. 17; 1 Kings xxii. 11.) The metaphor of threshing is dropped for the moment, but resumed in the next clause. **Hoofs.** In allusion to the mode of threshing mentioned above (Deut. xxv. 4; 1 Cor. ix. 9). **People;** *peoples.* Israel shall crush all the nations that rise up against her. **I** (*God*) **will consecrate.** So the Masoretic text; but the second person, which the ancient versions give, is preferable. Septuagint, ἀναθήσεις, " thou shalt dedicate;" Vulgate, *interficies.* **Thou,** Zion, shalt devote **their** gain unto the Lord. This consecration, or devotion, to the Lord in the case of living things involved death, the restitution to the Lord of the life which he had given (see Lev. xxvii. 21, 28, 29; Zech. xiv. 21). Thus the spiritual Israel, purified by suffering, and redeemed, shall consecrate to the Lord the power of the world; and all the wealth and might of earth shall be subservient to the glory of the kingdom of God.

HOMILETICS.

Vers. 1—8.—*The Messiah's spiritual kingdom.* These verses call us away from the contemplation of sin and its effects as set forth in the previous chapters, and bid us turn our thoughts to the golden age that rose before the prophet's vision, and animated and cheered his heart in the dark days in which his lot was cast. We live in happier times. Much that was to him only *distant expectation* has become fully realized by us. " Blessed are our eyes," etc. (Matt. xiii. 16, 17). Still, favoured as we are, the kingdom of Christ has not, even in our own day, attained unto the highest perfection. The noontide splendour of his rule has not yet been reached. The cross has brought the crown, and the Lord Christ now reigneth as King in Zion; but " we see not yet all things put under him." There are still many difficulties and discouragements, and there is much to sicken and sadden the hearts of all to whom his Name is precious, and his truth and kingdom dear. And amidst all this we do well, like this seer, to look on to the ultimate complete triumph which the Christ shall assuredly win, and by this bright vision to gain the renewal of heart and hope. We have indicated here—

I. CERTAIN CHARACTERISTICS OF THE MESSIAH'S KINGDOM. 1. *Its spirituality.* We shall assuredly lose sight of the beauty of these prophetic descriptions if we give to them a literal and material significance. This, indeed, is what the Jews themselves did, and hence the true Messiah was by them " despised and rejected." " As upon the figure of David the prophetic figure of the Messiah is developed, so upon the figure of Jerusalem is the prophetic figure of the holy community of the future" (Lange). Connecting ver. 1 with the last verse of the previous chapter, we are reminded that whilst the material kingdom was marked to fall, and should, in due course and as the result of national guilt, decay and pass away, yet this mournful apostasy of the chosen race should be rendered in the Divine wisdom "the riches of the world" (Rom. xi. 11, 12). The old economy should eventually disappear, but the new dispensation should follow. The long-promised Messiah should appear and establish a spiritual kingdom, the subjects of which should be renewed and sanctified men; to which kingdom higher privileges and honours should be attached than Judaism had ever presented, and the influence of which should extend to the wide world. 2. *Its pure and righteous principles of government.* "For the Law shall go forth of Zion," etc. (ver. 2). These have been framed with a due regard to the interests of all the subjects; they are not only designed to regulate the outward conduct and actions of men, but they go deeper and affect the heart and the secret springs of action. The great law of the kingdom is love—love to God and to man. "Love is the fulfilling of the Law" (Rom. xiii. 10). 3. *Its comprehensiveness.* "Peoples shall flow unto it" (ver. 1); "And many nations shall come" (ver. 2). Judaism was marked by its exclusiveness. Its privileges were confined to a particular nationality. But lo! it is here declared that the kingdom of the Messiah should be world-embracing. It shall become indeed "a great nation," for "unto it" all peoples and tribes "shall flow." The King whom Jehovah has "set upon his holy hill of Zion," and who shall "reign in righteousness," shall sway his sceptre at length over a ransomed, regenerated, happy world. 4. *Its perpetuity.* "It shall be abidingly established" (ver. 1). "The Lord shall reign over them in Mount Zion *from henceforth, even for ever*" (ver. 7). The kingdoms of this world are unenduring. "They all shall perish." They rise, progress, attain unto their zenith, and then decline and pass away. Egypt and Tyre, Assyria and Babylon, Greece and Rome, powers that once dominated the world, their glory is laid in the dust, their pomp has passed away like a dream, their works survive only in chambers of antiquity, and their deeds have only a record in historical lore. So perishes the glory of this world! But this spiritual kingdom of the Lord Christ lives and shall never fail. Its throne shall never be shaken, its riches shall never be impoverished, its glory shall never be dimmed. "Thy kingdom is an everlasting kingdom," etc. (Ps. cxlv. 13). 5. And hence, *its pre-eminence.* "It shall be exalted above the hills" (ver. 1). It shall attain unto heights such as no worldly power has ever reached, and its King shall enjoy distinction and honour such as earthly monarchs have never known. "He shall be exalted and extolled, and be very high" (Isa. lii. 13); "And he shall bear the glory" (Zech. vi. 13).

II. THE INFLUENCE OF THE MESSIAH'S RULE. It is here predicted that this should be of the most healthy and beneficent nature. Under his sway : 1. *Enthusiasm should be enkindled.* "Come, and let us go up," etc. (ver. 2). Men drawn to him in the spirit of whole-souled devotion should seek to lead others to participate with them in the enjoyment of the blessings he imparts. "The love of Christ" has "constrained" men to the consecration of all their energies to his service. So Paul (Acts xx. 23, 24). Xavier said, "You say they will kill me by poison. It is an honour unto which such a poor sinner as I dare not aspire; but I am ready to die ten thousand deaths for the salvation of a single soul." In our own day we have seen men thus impelled to go forth to distant and uncivilized tribes; and when they have been stricken down by fever ending in death, lo! others have been found ready to be "baptized for the dead." 2. *Knowledge should be diffused.* "And he will teach us," etc. (ver. 2). The true Messiah is also "the true Light," "the Light of men," "the Light of the world." He came to rule, but his rule should be an enlightened one. Where his influence touches there is light. He dissipates the darkness of error, superstition, idolatry; and his enlightening power shall extend until "the knowledge of the Lord shall cover the earth" (Isa. xi. 9). 3. *Obedience should be rendered.* "And we will walk in his paths" (ver. 2). The connection between this and the preceding sentence is very intimate. All true knowledge is designed to affect the conduct and life. Knowing and doing are closely related (John xiii. 17). How purifying and elevating Christ's moral influence upon the world has proved! Wherever the influence of his truth is felt, there, as sure as day succeeds night, a higher morality becomes developed. 4. *Peace should be established.* (Ver. 3.) The Messiah is "the Prince of Peace" (Isa. ix. 6). "Glory to God in the highest," etc. (Luke ii. 14), was the song of angels as they welcomed his advent. Strange, then, that men should ascribe to his religion the prevalence in the world of war and conflict. His religion has often been made the pretext for entering into deadly strife; but underlying this there has been some ambitious design which has been the real though concealed cause. The growing disposition amongst the nations to seek peaceful solutions of existing difficulties, and not to draw the sword until these have been exhausted, is an effect of the influence of the principles of Christ upon society at large. The universal dissemination of his truth shall be followed by the complete fulfilment of this glowing prediction (ver. 3). 5. *Security should be realized.* (Ver. 4.) In the Assyrian monuments representations are given of men in a reclining posture, with the vines in rich profusion over their heads, suggestive of quiet and rest and freedom from everything calculated to disturb and alarm. And this is the idea expressed here. Fear had taken possession of the hearts of those whom the prophet was addressing. They thought with sadness and dismay of the awaiting judgments to follow national sin. The enemy had come well-nigh to the gates; but lo! the seer cheers them by the prospect of happier days which should at length dawn upon them. As it had been with the nation in the peaceful days of Solomon, so he declared it should be in a spiritual sense under the rule of the Messiah. "Such is that most quiet fearlessness which the law of Christ bringeth as being the law of charity, peace, and concord." 6. *Restoration should be effected.* (Vers. 6, 7.) Into the enjoyment of these high blessings even they should be brought who had erred from God's ways, who had "halted" in his service, and had divided their allegiance between him and Baal. They must, in consequence of their sin, be "driven out" and "afflicted" and "cast off;" yet in their exile he would watch over them, seeking them in his deep compassion, "devising means that his banished be not expelled from him" (2 Sam. xiv. 14), and in his own time and way these should be brought in with "the fulness of the Gentiles," to form "a strong nation" over whom he would reign for ever and ever (vers. 6, 7).

III. THE CERTAINTY OF THE REALIZATION OF ALL THUS EXPRESSED. The seer throughout uses the language of holy confidence. And he was warranted in this; for: 1. *Such is the Divine purpose.* The issue is divinely guaranteed. God has promised the kingdom to his Son. 2. *This Divine purpose has been repeatedly expressed.* "For the mouth of the Lord hath spoken it" (ver. 4). 3. *That which God has purposed and declared,* his power can and will fulfil. Despite the humble circumstances and conditions through which the chosen of Heaven would have to pass, "the kingdom should come to the daughter of Jerusalem"—"the *first* or *former* dominion;" *i.e.* the rich spiritual honour which had been promised to David's line should be bestowed (ver. 8), for such was the Divine will and which the Divine power would assuredly accomplish. Our hope for a bright future rests upon the same foundation. And as God requires us to put him in remembrance of his Word, we will say, "For Zion's sake," etc. (Isa. lxii. 1); and will cry in the words of our own Milton, "Come forth out of thy royal chamber, O Prince of all the kings of the earth! Put on the visible robes of thy imperial majesty; take up that unlimited sceptre which thy Almighty Father hath bequeathed thee; for now the voice of thy bride calls thee, and all creatures sigh to be renewed."

Ver. 2.—*Enthusiasm in religion.* I. THE SPIRIT OF ENTHUSIASM IN RELATION TO RELIGION IS EMINENTLY DESIRABLE. It is so: 1. *As indicating the possession of loving devotion to God.* 2. *As prompting to endeavour with a view to the spiritual well-being of others.* (Ver. 2, "Come, and let us go up," etc.; John i. 41, 42, 45, 46; iv. 28, 29.) 3. *As being contagious.* For, all aglow themselves, they will be the means of inspiring others with the same fervour.

II. THIS SPIRIT, UNLESS UNDER WISE CONTROL, MAY PROVE INJURIOUS. It may seem a very simple matter to invite others to God, to say to them, "Come, let us go up," etc.; but it is possible, by undue familiarity of approach, or by extravagance of language, to alienate those it is desired to win.

III. THIS SPIRIT IS IN SAFE KEEPING IF ITS POSSESSOR CULTIVATES THE DISPOSI-

TIONS HERE EXPRESSED (ver. 2), viz. : 1. *Of seeking to understand God's truth more clearly.* "And he will teach us of his ways." The consciousness of his imperfect attainments will keep him humble, and preserve him from mere dogmatism and self-conceit. 2. *Of endeavouring to be obedient in heart and life to God's will.* "And we will walk in his paths." His realization of the importance of ethical practical life will preserve him from either thinking or advocating the false notion that piety consists in profuse verbal declarations and mere outward professions.

Ver. 2.—*Higher spiritual life.* "Let us go up to the mountain of the Lord." We are too prone to be content with living at a very low level of spiritual attainment. We need to hear and heed the voice of God's own Spirit addressing us through our own consciences, and through all the holy influences encompassing us, and bidding us leave the ordinary plain on which we have been content to dwell, and to ascend the mount of the Lord, and thus to rise to the nobler heights of spiritual privilege and goodness. "Let us go up," etc.

I. WHAT IS THIS HIGHER SPIRITUAL LIFE? It is a life of obedience to God and of faith in him. It is a life of holy and hallowed fellowship with the invisible. It is a life sustained and strengthened by hidden Divine springs. It is not perfect life, but life characterized by constant *endeavour after* the perfect. It is a life characterized by the patient endurance of trial, the successful resistance of temptation, and the cheerful performance of duty. It is a life animated by hopes entering "within the veil," and in which is increasingly realized union with the spiritual world.

II. HOW MAY IT BE REACHED? 1. *The ministration of the truth is designed to this end.* The advancement of the good in Divine knowledge and in the varied graces of the Christian character is one aim of the Christian ministry (Eph. v. 11—13). 2. *The commonest duties of our daily life* may be so discharged as to be made to contribute to our spiritual elevation. The aim should be to make every duty subservient to the great end of our spiritual advancement. 3. *The sorrowful experiences of our life* are all designed to secure to us "more life and fuller." These constitute the threshings of the spiritual man by means of which God would separate his servants from evil, and enable them to enter into the higher joys of his kingdom. 4. And this soul-elevation is to be secured not only by receiving, but also by imparting, *holy influences.* We rise ourselves as we invite others to rise; as we speak to them the encouraging word, and hold out to them the helping hand. Ruskin reminds us that the name which of all others is most expressive of the being of God is that of "the Helpful One," or, in our softer Saxon, "the Holy One." And we may each know what one has beautifully called *the holiness of helpfulness* (Dr. Robert Collyer's 'The Life that now is,' pp. 63, 64).

III. WHAT ADVANTAGES WILL ACCRUE FROM ITS ATTAINMENT? 1. *There will be greater enjoyment in connection with religious privileges than can otherwise be experienced.* 2. *Tranquillity will possess the heart amidst the disappointments, changes, and bereavements of life.* 3. *A clearer apprehension of the truth of God will be gained.* (Ver. 2.) 4. *More effective service to God in the world will be rendered.* Certain saints of God belonging to the past are sometimes set forth as having been specially eminent, and as though the same altitude could not be reached nowadays; whereas we are to be " followers " of such (Heb. vi. 12), and the " helps " they used are as available to us. Use them, and say—

> " Go up, go up, my heart!
> Be not a trifler here ;
> Ascend above these clouds,
> Dwell in a higher sphere.
> Let not thy love go out
> To things so soiled and dim :
> Go up to heaven, and God
> Take up thy love to him."

Ver. 2.—*God our Teacher.* " And he will teach us of his ways." How?

I. BY WORKING IN OUR HEARTS THE SPIRIT OF TRUE HUMILITY. There must be humility in order that we may apprehend spiritual things. We must become " as little children " would we enter the kingdom of truth. And this disposition is fitting ; for what, after all, are we but children in relation to such knowledge ? " Embryos we are all." Too many, forgetting this, and cherishing the opposite spirit, misapprehend or pervert the meaning of God's truth. Pride of intellect is cherished, and, strong and dogmatic in their adherence to false intellectual conceptions, they miss the highest truth. " The meek will he guide in judgment, and the meek will he teach his way." " As low trees and shrubs are free from many violent gusts and blasts of wind which shake and rend the taller trees, so humble souls are free from those gusts and blasts of error that rend and tear proud lofty souls." " The high tide quickly ebbs." " The valleys laugh with fatness when the hills are bare." " I thank thee, O Father," etc. (Matt. xi. 25, 26).

II. BY CONSTRAINING US TO CHERISH THE SPIRIT OF HEARTY OBEDIENCE. By the gentle constraints of Divine love the will is brought into harmony with the higher and perfect will of God ; and to the man thus obedient there is unfolded the glorious treasures of Divine wisdom and knowledge. " The secret of the Lord is with them that fear him, and he will show them his covenant " (Ps. xxv. 14); " Then shall we know, if we follow on," etc. (Hos. vi. 3).

III. BY IMPARTING UNTO US SPIRITUAL DISCERNMENT. The heart being rendered humble and obedient, light springs up within; a spiritual insight is imparted; the unction of the Holy One rests upon the man; higher perceptions are his; he apprehends and understands truths which formerly were unperceived or distorted by him. " Pure in heart," he " sees God ; " spiritually minded, he discovers spiritual things. God's ways stand revealed to him, and God's Word is no longer a dead letter, but is instinct with life and power to his soul. Then, with an earnest desire to enter into the full significance of spiritual realities, and with a deep consciousness of our own weakness and need of guidance, we do well to cry, " Lead us in thy truth and teach us ; " and to rejoice in the encouraging assurance, " And he will teach us of his ways."

Ver. 2.—*Obedience to the Divine will.* " And we will walk in his paths." The idea is—living obediently to the will of God. Observe—

I. GOD HAS REVEALED HIS WILL UNTO MAN. "The Law has gone forth," etc. (ver. 3). The revelation of what God requires of his creatures has been given (1) in the commandments unfolded to Moses on Sinai ; (2) in the full and perfect exposition of those commandments given in the teaching of Christ ; (3) in the complete transcript of them presented in the Divine Teacher's spotless character and life.

II. TO OBEY THAT WILL INDICATES THE POSSESSION OF TRUE PIETY. Sincere piety does not consist in outward observances, although these have so high a value that we are not to " forsake the assembling of ourselves together " for Christian fellowship and teaching; nor does it consist in Church association, although there are many advantages resulting from Christians banding themselves together that thus they may be helpful to each other in the spiritual life, and by combined action the more effectually do God's work; nor does it consist in the repetition of a Creed, however admirably conceived and expressed, and however desirable it may be for us to be well grounded in the foundation-doctrines of our holy religion; but it consists in obedience to the will of God, and in seeking, like the great Exemplar, to act in harmony with God's holy Law.

> " Nor name, nor form, nor ritual,
> But simply *following thee."*

III. IN THIS OBEDIENCE LIES THE TRUEST WELL-BEING BOTH OF THE INDIVIDUAL AND OF THE RACE. Walking in these paths, it is found that they are " right paths," that they yield " peace" and " pleasantness; " " mercy and truth " also abound to the obedient, whilst the wide adoption of this course by the children of men is pointed to as the token of the coming of " the latter-day glory." " A world-wide Christ-likeness is the great necessity. If, in imitation of him, there were truth on every tongue and kindness in every heart, gentleness in every spirit and obedience to God in every will, purity in every life and blamelessness in every character, the bloom and blessedness of Eden would be seen to-morrow." Too many, alas ! still resolve that " they will walk every one in the name of his god " (ver. 5); but our hope for humanity lies in the growing number whose feet are being turned into "the ways of righteousness," and who are impelled to say, "And we will walk in his paths." "We will walk in the Name of the Lord our God for ever and ever" (ver. 5).

Vers. 9—13; ch. v. 1.—*Through trial to triumph.* There is a very natural connection between these and the previous verses. The seer has presented a glowing picture of the ultimate triumphs of the Messiah's kingdom. In choicest language he has unfolded the nature of the Messiah's rule, and the beneficent effects to be secured thereby. And now he reminds us that this victory should be won by suffering—that God's order is *through trial to triumph.* Notice—

I. THE EXPERIENCE OF SORROW AS PREPARATORY TO JOY; OF CONFLICT AS PRE-PARATORY TO VICTORY. (Vers. 9—13; ch. v. 1.) Whatever view may be taken as to the true application of these verses, it is very clear that they refer to deep sorrow, through which the nation must pass before the manifestation of the true spiritual King whose coming is so clearly indicated in the chapter following. Captivity must be experienced; conflict must be engaged in with "many nations;" loss of rulers and leaders must be sustained; war and siege must be felt. Yet all these should prove but preparatory to the experience of joy and victory; they should be but as the pangs preceding birth; out of and following these throes there should come the establishment of a kingdom which should never be moved, and which their *material* kingdom, now being so shaken, even in its most prosperous and peaceful days only faintly symbolized. And this is ever the Divine order of procedure. It is the all-wise appointment of God that his servants should pass through trial and be made perfect through suffering. He takes the seed and plants it in rough soil, and as the result he causes to arise beauteous flowers. The tear often precedes the smile. The thick cloud gathers over our heads, and lo! afterwards the triumphant arch spans the sky, telling of the Divine faithfulness and love. We must suffer would we ultimately reign; we must bear the cross would we wear the crown. God's servants are *soldiers,* and the soldier must "endure hardness" (2 Tim. ii. 3), and engage in sharp conflict ere he reaps the warrior's reward. His followers are *trees of righteousness,* and God prunes his trees that "they may bring forth much fruit" (John xv. 2).

II. STIMULATING THOUGHTS AMIDST THESE DARKER EXPERIENCES OF LIFE. Several such thoughts are suggested here. 1. *There's "a needs be" for these sorrows.* (Ver. 10.) It is here declared that there was a necessity for the sorrows here predicted. The trials are referred to as experiences that *must be,* and that could not be *avoided.* The travail must be endured, the captivity must be experienced, the discipline must be passed through. The nation had woefully transgressed, and only thus could it be purged and purified. As the crushing of the seed results in a more abundant increase, so the oppression of God's servants should result in the upspringing of "the peaceable fruits of righteousness." "Of sorrow, sanctity is born." Here is one solution of "the mystery of suffering." It is designed to work purification; it is a healthful discipline. It is not that our Father-God is wanting in sympathy that we have to pass through adverse scenes, but because his sympathy is so large and so perfect that it extends to the whole of our being. When he says, "Be in pain," etc. (ver. 10), it is not that he does not feel with us, but rather because his sympathy is so large that he deigns to lift us up to a higher level, and to lead us to attain unto a purer and more perfect character and life; and hence, whilst "he will not break the bruised reed, nor quench the smoking flax," he will also "send forth judgment unto victory" (Isa. xlii. 2, 3). 2. *There is an overruling Providence.* (Vers. 11, 12.) In these verses the heathen nations are represented as encouraging each other to make a decisive onslaught upon the favoured people, and as speaking as though their plans could very easily be executed, the overthrow of Judah be effected, and they gaze with satisfaction upon the downfall and desolation (ver. 11). But there was a higher than any mere human power swaying the destinies of the peoples of the earth. The Lord God omnipotent was reigning. He had his purposes and plans of which the nations took no account, but which nevertheless were to be developed. And in the unfolding of these all the dark designs of the evil would be overruled, and whilst the nation of his choice should thus be tried as by fire, and so have its dross consumed, they who, prompted by their own mercenary and ambitious ends, assaulted it, should be brought to utter confusion and shame (ver. 13). The world still abounds in evil-doers who are pursuing their own ends, and that they may gain these are ever planning and contriving harm; but it may well comfort and strengthen our hearts, amidst the anxiety and distress such occasion, that there is still an overruling Providence guiding human affairs, and that under God's all-wise and loving direction good only shall eventually come to the good, whilst the counsel of the wicked shall perish, and the arm of their power be broken. 3. *There is the Divine abiding presence.* This is implied in ver. 9. The prophet, abounding in deepest sympathy with his people in their calamities, would, nevertheless, have them feel that they were not left utterly destitute; that, though earthly rulers had failed them, there was One who ever abides, and who, if they but trusted him, would bear them safely through all. He who had been the King and Guide of their nation before earthly monarch had ever been appointed over it (1 Sam. xii. 12) would not forsake them now that human supports had given way, but would make their present sorrows to end in higher joy than they had formerly experienced (Hos. xiii. 9, 14). Nor need we fear in the time of trouble, so long as it remaineth that "the Lord of hosts is with us," etc. (Ps. xlvi. 7). 4. *There is ultimate deliverance.* (Ver. 10.) The Lord would assuredly "turn again the captivity of Zion" (Ps. cxxvi. 1—6). Through fire and through water they should be brought out into a wealthy place (Ps. cxvi. 12). Weeping might endure for a night, but joy should come in the morning (Ps. xxx. 5). And so with his servants in every age. The way he would have us take, despite all its difficulties and discouragements, shall bring us at length to the palace and to our crown.

HOMILIES BY VARIOUS AUTHORS.

Vers. 1, 2.—*A new Mount Zion.* The threat of ch. iii. 12 has been fulfilled. Mount Zion, the glory of the nation on account of its situation, its buildings, its history, and its religious associations (Ps. xlviii.; cxxii., etc.), has become as a forest, or as desolate heaps of ruins. But while the prophet gazes through the tears which patriotism and piety bring to his eyes, as in some dissolving view a new vision unfolds itself before him. Instead of a ploughed field and a ruinous mound, he sees an exceeding high mountain, a glorious city, and countless multitudes flocking towards it. It is the new Mount Zion.

I. Its ELEVATION. There were other hills or mountains that already were or soon would be of note among men, such as the "high places" of a corrupt worship in Judæa and Samaria, the huge artificial hill of Babylon sacred to Belus, the acropolis of Athens, the seven hills of Rome. But this Mount Zion was founded on the summits of the world's loftiest heights, and towered above them all. Thus the mountain is seen to be spiritual and the elevation figurative. It is a vision of "the latter days," of the days of the Messiah, when the new kingdom of God is set up. Because it is "the mountain of *the house of the Lord,*" it is thus exalted. Illustrate from Ezekiel's vision of the "very high mountain" (xl. 2), and the sublime conclusion of it, "Jehovah-Shammah" (xlviii. 35; and cf. 1 Tim. iii. 15). "This mountain of the Church of Christ transcends all laws, schools, doctrines, religions, synagogues, and philosophies, which seemed to rise among men like mountain-tops" (Corn. à Lapide, in Pusey). It is "a city set on a hill."

II. Its CONGREGATION. The prophet sees a stream of worshippers ascending that hill; not an unfamiliar sight in the old days of the literal Zion. But much earnestness is needed to scale this lofty mountain. And it is a miracle of grace that not only the chosen people of God, but "the peoples" of the world lying in wickedness, should be attracted by a Church so lofty and so pure. For, as the prophet watches, he sees strange companies gathering, of varied colours, costumes, and languages—negroes from Ethiopia, Chinese from the land of Sinim, and pale-faced strangers from the western isles of Europe. Contrast the mountain-like tower of Babel, man's scheme of unity, issuing in dispersion, and this Mount Zion, God's way of union, attracting a congregation from all kindreds and peoples and tongues (Isa. lv. 8, 9). The prophet hears their language as they encourage one another, "Come ye," etc. They thus confess: 1. *Their ignorance.* "He shall teach us of his *ways*"—a comprehensive term (Ps. xxv. 4, 8, 9). 2. *Their dissatisfaction.* Their old paths had been "broad;" "destruction and misery" had been in them.　Henceforth they desire to walk in other "paths," in God's way of holiness.　3. *Their confidence;* that the God of Jacob alone was both able and willing to supply their need.　The prophet foresaw what Christ still more clearly predicted (Matt. viii. 11, 12), and what we are seeing in these days of missionary enterprise.

III. Its EMANATIONS.　As light and heat stream from the sun, and fragrance from the flowers, so from this new Mount Zion, this city of God, there stream forth the very blessings which the nations need—truth, light, life.　It is a Divine power that first draws this congregation towards the Church of Christ (John vi. 44, 45).　And the blessings they need and receive are summed up in two terms.　1. *"The Law."*　They receive it as a rule of life, as an ideal of daily conduct.　It goes forth as a stream of blessing which can turn the wastes of heathen life into a paradise.　But more than law is needed: 2. *" The Word of the Lord."*　This is a more comprehensive term.　It includes the revelation of his will, his mercy and grace, " the word of the truth of the gospel."　This goes forth with all the attractiveness of a message of mercy (Luke xxiv. 47, etc.), but also with all the authority of a law (Acts xvii. 30; 1 John iii. 23).　The preaching of the cross proves itself the power of God.　This word of the Lord has free course and is glorified.　No wonder that such blessings follow as are described in the following verses.—E. S. P.

Vers. 3, 4.—*" The peaceable fruit of righteousness."*　The wonders of Micah's vision (vers. 1 and 2) are not yet at an end.　He sees a succession of the most improbable and incredible events, as the nations return from their pilgrimage to the new Mount Zion to their distant capitals and homesteads.　With those distant and " strong " heathen nations there are associations of horror and dread in the minds of the Hebrews, especially of the godly among them.　Illustrate this from what we know through Hebrew prophets and historians of the Gentile nations near and afar off; *e.g.* border wars and frequent invasions of the Philistines (2 Chron. xxi. 16, 17), Edomites, Ammonites, Moabites, and others (Ps. lxxxiii.; and cf. the impressive messages of judgment in Amos i. and ii.).　Egypt, at one time their oppressor or invader (2 Chron. xii.), later on their untrustworthy ally, always the home of degrading idolatries (Isa. xix.; xxx. 1—7).　Assyria, the seat of a relentless despotism, the captors of their northern brethren, casting its war-cloud over Hezekiah's kingdom (Nah. iii.).　Beyond these were the mountaineers of Media, the barbarous tribes of the far north, " Meshech and Tubal," and the sons of Greece in the distant west.　The gloomy vision of Ezekiel (xxxii.) graphically describes how the sword and bloodshed are bound up with the histories of these and other nations.　All these are seen welcoming a new King, who "shall reign in righteousness," new legislation and new customs.　The strangest of all these new customs is that "the peoples that delight in war" are seen changing their weapons into instruments of peace, and enjoying a tranquillity equal to that of the palmy days of Solomon.　The mystery is explained by the fact that the word of the Lord had gone forth from Jerusalem.　We learn—

I. THE GOSPEL OF GOD PREPARES FOR THE REIGN OF GOD.　1. *It reveals God's love.* It thus comes as a revelation, startling, almost incredible to heathens, in whose minds lust not love, hatred not mercy, are bound up with their thoughts of God.　That central verse of the New Testament (John iii. 16), a " miniature Bible," as Martin Luther called it, applied by the Spirit of God, has broken many a rocky heathen heart, and opened the way for the blessings that God's love has prepared for sinful souls (1 John iv. 19).　2. *It inspires men's hope.*　Those who were once living " having no hope, and without God in the world," find that all things are become new.　All the most bright and buoyant emotions, love, hope, joy, are called forth by the gospel of God.　The brightest visions of a golden age in the future which heathen poets have sung about are seen to be possible under the reign of a righteous and merciful God.　They are " saved by hope."　3. *It awakens men's consciences.*　An educational process ensues. The dormant conscience is awakened; the blind conscience sees the light of truth; the blunt conscience is made sensitive and tender.　Thus gradually things which were tolerated in the individual or the community are branded as unchristian, or even infamous.　Illustrate from 1 Cor. v. and vi.　In those whose spiritual education is most advanced, every thought is brought " into captivity to the obedience of Christ." Thus gradually the average standard of morality is raised first in the Church and then in the nation, and the gospel of God is seen to have prepared the way for the reign of God.

II. THE REIGN OF GOD WILL BE A REIGN OF PEACE. War is a terrible defiance of God and of his authority, and yet it is one of the most popular forms of wickedness. The press, the clubs, "the forces," often make it hard even for a government calling itself Christian to resist the gusts of popular passion which sweep nations into war. Even as late as 1882 we were told that on board the ironclads off Alexandria the countenances of the officers fell as the sight of a flag of truce made it possible that after all their new guns might not be tested by a bombardment. Yet even this unclean spirit will be exorcised by the power of the gospel of Christ, which has already been at work in many ways; e.g. "the truce of God" in the Middle Ages, providing for the suspension of hostilities during Advent, Lent, and other seasons; the sparing of the lives of prisoners; the care and kindness shown towards the wounded; the power of the public opinion, even of a minority, to restrain governments from hastily rushing into war; the introduction of arbitration, in which the British Government set so honourable an example at Geneva in 1872. In such cases it may be said that God, through the judgments of upright men, is called to "judge between many peoples," and "reprove" even strong nations when they wronged their neighbours. Thus gradually war will be banished, even as duelling and other abominations have been. "Fraternity" will be one of the watchwords of the future, and war will be regarded as fratricide. Lucian says of Christians, "Their first Lawgiver persuaded them that they are all brethren." Christianity is working towards the restoration of that ideal. Then Solomon's days shall be reproduced in more than their ancient glory. New princes of Sheba and Seba shall offer gifts at the court of the Prince of Peace, whose subjects shall "dwell safely, and be quiet from fear of evil." The glorious visions of Ps. lxxii.; Isa. lx., etc., shall be fulfilled, "for the mouth of the Lord of hosts hath spoken it."

Learn: 1. That the only hope of true national righteousness is in the reign of Christ. 2. That the Christian who witnesses for unpopular truths is the noblest among patriots. 3. That the sanctification of individual souls through the power of the gospel is the surest method of securing the ultimate and universal reign of Christ on earth.—E. S. P.

Vers. 6, 7.—*The restoration of Israel.* It is the Gentile nations for whom the blessings of "the last days" have just been predicted (vers. 2—4). The new Mount Zion of the Messiah's days will have a magnetic power on "the East and the West" (Matt. viii. 11; John xii. 32). But Israel, through whom these blessings reach the nations, shall not be excluded from a share in them. Yet the form of the prediction reminds us of the abject condition of God's ancient people and of the gradual extension of the glories of Messiah's reign over them.

I. THEIR ABJECT CONDITION. They are described as: 1. *Halting.* This was the result of internal infirmity or of injury from without, or of both. The Jewish people at the advent were suffering both from ecclesiastical and moral corruptions, which made them figuratively like the folk at Bethesda, "halt, withered, impotent." 2. "*Driven out.*" Multitudes had been driven out of their heritage in Palestine by the decrees of conquerors or the oppressions of foreign tyrants. Centuries before, Jeremiah had declared, "Israel is a scattered sheep; the lions have driven him away: first the King of Assyria hath devoured him; and last this Nebuchadrezzar King of Babylon hath broken his bones" (l. 17). In subsequent centuries similar captivities or oppressions were endured at the hands of the Ptolemies, the Seleucidæ, the Idumeans, and the Romans. Those who remained were as strangers in their own fatherland. And soon a far more fearful catastrophe scattered them from one end of the heavens to the other, after the destruction of their city by the Romans.

> "But we must wander witheringly
>   In other lands to die;
> And where our fathers' ashes be
>   Our own must never lie:
> Our temple hath not left a stone,
> And Mockery sits on Salem's throne."
>   (Byron.)

3. *" Stricken of God, and afflicted."* Unfaithful " shepherds " among their own rulers (Ezek. xxxiv. 1—6) or heathen conquerors were the scourges; but " shall there be evil in a city, and the Lord hath not done it ? " Devout men recognized this, and uttered such penitential wails as we find in Ps. xliv., lxxiv.; Lam. i., ii., etc.

II. THEIR RESTORATION. The establishment of the new kingdom of God—Christ's kingdom—on Mount Zion was itself a pledge of the restoration of the Jews and of their participation in its blessings. For it could not be that Christ should reign over the Gentile nations and leave " his own people " (John i. 11) to perish finally in unbelief. This would be opposed both to the ancient promises of God (Isa. xlv. 17 ; lix. 20, 21, etc.) as well as to the predictions and the heart of Christ (Matt. xxiii. 37—39). Yet there are stages in this process of restoration. 1. *The halting ones are restored, but they are only a remnant.* (Cf. ch. v. 3, 7, 8.) The immediate effect of the establishment of Christ's kingdom was seen in a great religious revival among the Jews from Pentecost onwards. But all the converts were but a remnant of the nation which, because of its unbelief, was " broken off " (Rom. xi. 1—5, 17—20). Yet in the fact of the salvation of the few the Apostle Paul sees the pledge of the final salvation of the many. 2. *The banished ones shall be made a strong nation.* Trace St. Paul's inspired argument in Rom. xi. till he arrives at the sublime conclusion in vers. 32—36. The nation's restoration to God will be accompanied by a restoration to their own land (Zech. xii. 10—14; xiv. 8—11, etc.). 3. *" The Lord shall reign over them in Mount Zion."* We look for the restoration of Israel to their Saviour and to their land as one of the marvellous evidences of the truth of the prophetic word which God is reserving for the scepticism of these latter days. We need not anticipate a literal and local throne of Christ at Jerusalem. But the Lord Christ, being enthroned in the hearts of his long faithless yet much beloved people, will as truly " reign over them in Mount Zion " as though they had his glorified humanity always manifested in their midst. And then his reign shall be " from henceforth, even for ever." " I the Lord will hasten it in his time."

> " O come, O come, Emmanuel,
> And ransom captive Israel,
> That mourns in lonely exile here
> Until the Son of God appear.
> Rejoice, rejoice : Emmanuel
> Shall come to thee, O Israel ! "

E. S. P.

Vers. 9, 10.—*Discipline and deliverance.* A glorious future has been held up to the view of the Jewish nation (vers. 6—8). It is like the ideals of peace and blessedness presented to all in the Word of God; like the visions of the heavenly glory set before even the most ungodly. Such promises are attractive; even the godless Jews in Micah's time would exult in the thought of " the former dominion," the days of David and Solomon returning to Zion. But the vision again changes. Cries of pain and distress are heard. There passes before the prophet's mind a view of the discipline and chastisement which must fall on the disobedient nation before the promised blessings can be enjoyed.

I. THE SALUTARY DISCIPLINE. In brief, vivid words a succession of calamities is sketched. 1. *Their monarchy is overthrown.* " Is there no king in thee ? " Jehoahaz, Jehoiakim, Jehoiachin, and Zedekiah in succession were dethroned by foreign conquerors, and carried into exile. Many national promises and blessings were bound up with the name and family of David (2 Sam. vii.), so that the loss of their king was no ordinary loss. He was their chief stay and " counsellor " (cf. Isa. ix. 6), " the breath of their nostrils " (Lam. iv. 20). No wonder their consternation and distress : " pangs," etc. (cf. Ps. lxxxix. 38—51). Thus one step in Divine discipline then and now may be the striking down to the ground of the chief objects of our confidence, the earthly props which we seek to substitute for God. 2. *They are humiliated before their foes.* They " go forth out of the city; " some in a vain attempt to escape, like Zedekiah and his troops (2 Kings xxv. 4—6); others as prisoners of war from a city which has capitulated and is being sacked by its conquerors. Illustrate from Lam. v. 1—16. They are driven forth into " the field; " without shelter even from the elements unless in tents (contrast their former " ease in Zion," Amos vi. 1—7, etc.); without the protection of the old towers and bulwarks in which they had prided themselves (Ps. xlviii. 12, 13); without weapons or leaders, and thus exposed to any indignities that these conquerors choose to inflict upon them. Thus may it be with those whose way God "turneth upside down," stripping them of all their old sources of security—money, position, friends; turning them out of the "nest" in which they expected peacefully to spend the remainder of their days. Illustrate from contrasts in Job xxix. and xxx. 3. *They are carried captive " even to Babylon."* Babel in early days had been a symbol of a godless world-power. It does not rise again on the Hebrew horizon till the days of Isaiah and Micah. Making friendly overtures to Hezekiah, it is presented to his view, by his faithful seer, as a distant, mysterious, but formidable foe of the future— *ignotum pro mirifico* (Isa. xxxix.). As the ten tribes had been carried captive to Halah and Habor and adjacent districts, so should Judah be taken "*even to Babylon.*" Thus is it in God's discipline with his prodigals now. They may find themselves in " a far country," brought down to the lowest depth of humiliation, shut out from all earthly help, shut up to God. And even now, in the midst of the pleasures of sin, prophetic voices within may warn them : " Thou shalt go forth . . . thou shalt go even to ——." The dreadful possibilities of judgment, whether in this world or another, may at times mar their peace. For, unlike the servants of God, they dare not say, " Things to come . . . *are ours.*" 4. *In the house of bondage pangs of sorrow must be borne.* " Seventy years!"—a long lifetime of captivity. " Tribulation ten days!" a time of discipline indefinite to us, though fixed by the counsel of God. Those pangs will be " resistless, remediless, doubling the whole frame, redoubled till the end for which God sends them is accomplished, and then ceasing in joy" (Pusey). For the very term " daughter of Zion " suggests hope. It is a term of friendliness, like " Father of spirits " (Heb. xii. 9), which reminds us of the essential relations between us and our God, and gives us a pledge that in wrath he will remember mercy (cf. Isa. lvii. 16).

II. "THE END OF THE LORD." Then and there the end for which the trials are sent will be reached, and deliverance will come. As with their king Manasseh, so shall it be with the nation. In their affliction they will seek the Lord (Jer. xxix. 10—13). 1. *They shall be delivered.* Set free from the burden of their sins, a burden too grievous to be borne; purged from idolatry; blessed with a revival of religion, as shown by a renewed regard to God's Law through the gracious work of his own " free Spirit " (Ezek. xxxvi. 16—27). 2. *They shall be redeemed from the hand of their enemies.* God will visit them as their *Goel,* their Kinsman-Redeemer, who has not forgotten or forsaken them (Jer. xxx. 8—11). By the manifestation of his righteous grace and irresistible power they shall be " redeemed without money " (Isa. lii. 3), restored to their land and to the enjoyment of ancient privileges. Such is " the end of the Lord " in the discipline of life. The revelation of the Fatherhood of God in the Person of Christ and in his sacrificial death for the redemption of sinners assures us that he chastens " for our profit, that we may be partakers of his holiness." But it is only by sitting at his feet and learning of him, and thus being " exercised " by our trials, that we can hope to win from them " the peaceable fruit of righteousness " (Heb. xii. 9—11).—E. S. P.

Vers. 1—4.—*The gospel age.* " But in the last days it shall come to pass, that the mountain of the house of the Lord shall be established in the top of the mountains," etc. " The last days " is an expression frequently used in the Old Testament. It points to the future, beginning with the Christian dispensation and running on to its close. It means the times of the Messiah. The patriarchal times had passed away, the Mosaic epoch was on the wane, and would soon vanish. The times of the Messiah, or " the last days," would succeed, and run on to the end of time. This prophecy, with scarcely any variation, is found in Isa. ii. Whether Isaiah borrowed it from Micah, or Micah from Isaiah, or both from some older prophecy, does not appear. One thing seems certain, that the prophecy has never yet been fulfilled in the history of the world, and that its accomplishment must be in some distant period—" the last days." It enables us to make certain remarks concerning the true religion of the gospel age.

I. THE TRUE RELIGION OF THE GOSPEL AGE WILL BECOME A GREAT POWER. " The mountain of the house of the Lord." Referring particularly to the temple that was built on Mount Moriah, and called the mountain of the Lord's house. The temple was the greatest thing in the religion of the Jews; it was the "mountain" in their scenery. The true religion is to become a mountain. The little stone will become a mountain, and fill the whole earth. In truth, the true religion, where it exists, is the biggest thing. In the individual soul it is the largest thing. It is the dominant power, it is the mountain in the scenery of a good man's experience. Let all men possess it, and then it will be to the whole world what it is to the individual. In sooth, true religion is either everything or nothing; supremacy is its essence—the supreme thought, the supreme love, the supreme aim. Two things are here stated about this mountain. 1. *It is to become established.* How is it to be established? By civil authority, legislative enactments? Our foolish forefathers have thought so, and many of the dolts of this generation think so too. But this to the last point is unphilosophic and absurd. The weakness of religion in Christendom to-day may be ascribed to the futile attempts of unwise and ambitious men to establish it by law. You may as well endeavour to govern the planetary universe by the ten commandments as to establish religion by civil laws. 2. *It is to become conspicuous.* "In the top of the mountains." It will be seen from afar—the most elevated power of the world. It will be the chief thing in the markets, professions, and governments of the world, high up on the top of all.

II. The true religion of the gospel age will become universally attractive. "And people shall flow unto it." "This is a figurative expression, denoting that they shall be converted to the true religion. It indicates that they shall come in multitudes, like the flowing of a mighty river. The idea of the flowing of the nation is of the movement of many people towards an object like a broad stream on the tides of the ocean, and is one that is very grand and sublime" (Barnes). In this period the social element will be brought into full play in connection with true religion. Men will stimulate each other to inquire after truth. "Come, and let us go up to the mountain of the Lord." 1. *They will study its laws in order to obey them.* "He will teach us of his ways, and we will walk in his paths." In those good times that are coming, men will study God's ways, and not man's theories, and study these ways, not as a matter of intellectual speculation, but in order to obey them, to walk in his ways. Religion in those days will be practical; it will be the law of every one's life, the great regulative force of society. 2. *They will study its laws at the fountain-head.* "For the Law shall go forth of Zion, and the Word of the Lord from Jerusalem." Jerusalem was the fountain-head of Christianity. Christ commanded his disciples to tarry at Jerusalem until they should be endued with power from on high. There also he commanded that the first sermon should be preached, a sermon concerning repentance and remission of sins; and there Peter opened his commission in his wonderful Pentecostal discourse. In those days men will go for religious instruction, not to *patristic, puritanic, Anglican,* or any other theological school, but to the fountain-head, to Jerusalem, where it is fresh and pure, most potent in spiritual stimulation and suggestion. Men in these days have gone far away from the theology of Jerusalem. In that theology there are none of those miserable dogmas that are now preached, but *facts* concerning a Person, and that Person none other than the *Son of man and the Son of God.*

III. The true religion of the gospel age will become powerful to terminate all wars. 1. *Here is the destruction of war.* "Beat their swords into ploughshares, and their spears into pruning-hooks." The arts of war destroyed, in their stead will flourish the arts of peace. The sword and spear, what ills of immeasurable enormity they have inflicted upon the race! Implements of hell, instruments by which all the infernal passions of the human heart have been excited and gratified. War is antichrist. 2. *Here is the establishment of peace.* "Shall sit every man under his vine and under his fig tree." The words, "sit under his vine," are taken from 1 Kings iv. 25, etc. Most incredible must this prediction have been to the men of Micah's time; but it will be accomplished, for the mouth of the Lord of hosts hath spoken it. If he has spoken it and it does not come to pass, it must be for one of three reasons: (1) Insincerity; which cannot be entertained. (2) Change of purpose; which is equally inadmissible. (3) Unexpected difficulties; which is an absurdity when applied to Omniscience.—D. T.

Ver. 5.—*Man's religious nature.* "For all people will walk every one in the name of his god, and we will walk in the Name of the Lord our God for ever and ever." It is trite to say, what has been said a thousand times, that man has a religious nature. Albeit the practical recognition of the fact is of immense importance; without it, more than half the history of the world would be inexplicable, all methods for its true improvement would be futile, and man would pass through this world to another without a God or any hope for a future. This verse suggests the wrong and the right development of this nature.

I. THE WRONG DEVELOPMENT. What is that? Idolatry. "All people will walk every one in the name of his god." Polytheism proper is, and generally has been, the most popular religion in the world. Men have gods which they have made, palpable objects which they fashioned after an ideal, and the ideal not unfrequently of the most base and loathsome kind. And they walk after these gods. The mariners in Jonah's vessel, when the storm came on, cried every man unto his god. Whence the cause of polytheism? The one great cause, which comprehends all others, is depravity. Depravity: 1. *Involves moral corruption.* What are heathen gods, as a rule, but the deification of the lower passions and vices of mankind? 2. *Involves carnality.* Depraved men are so carnal that they have no idea of *real* things which have not size and form and tangible properties. Hence they want a god they can see and handle and touch. 3. *Involves thoughtlessness.* Polytheism cannot stand reasoning. It is supported by the thoughtless millions through the craft and sophistry of the priests. Every true thought will shatter a heathen deity.

II. THE RIGHT DEVELOPMENT. What is that? Practical monotheism. "We will walk in the Name of the Lord our God for ever and ever." 1. *This is rational.* The one God is the sum total of all moral properties, the Proprietor of all resources, and the Bestower of all the existences and all the blessings therewith. What can be more rational than to walk in his way? In truth, it is the only true rational way in life. 2. *This is obligatory.* No man is bound to walk in the name of an idol; nay, he is commanded not to do so. But every man is bound to walk in the Name of the Lord— bound on the ground of his supreme excellence, his relations to man, and the obligation springing therefrom. 3. *This is blessed.* To walk in his Name is to walk through sunny fields abounding with all beauty and fruitfulness.—D. T.

Vers. 6—8.—*The moral monarchy of Christ in the world.* "In that day, saith the Lord, will I assemble her that halteth, and I will gather her that is driven out, and her that I have afflicted; and I will make her that halted a remnant, and her that was cast far off a strong nation : and the Lord shall reign over them in Mount Zion from henceforth, even for ever. And thou, O tower of the flock, the strong hold of the daughter of Zion, unto thee shall it come, even the first dominion; the kingdom shall come to the daughter of Jerusalem." Whether the subject of these verses is the restoration of the Jews after the Babylonish captivity or the gathering of men by Christ into a grand spiritual community, is a question on which there has been considerable discussion among biblical scholars, and therefore should preclude anything like dogmatism on either side. I am disposed, however, to entertain the latter idea, because it seems most in accordance with the previous verses, in which there is an undoubted reference to the gospel age, and because it gives the passage a wide practical application. Delitzsch says, "'In that day' points back to the end of the days. At the time when many nations shall go on pilgrimage to the highly exalted mountain of the Lord, and therefore Zion-Jerusalem will not only be restored but greatly glorified, the Lord will assemble that which limps and is scattered abroad." We shall take the words, then, as illustrating certain facts connected with the *moral monarchy of Christ in the world.*

I. IT EMBRACES AMONGST ITS SUBJECTS THE MOST WRETCHED AND SCATTERED OF MEN. "In that day, saith the Lord, will I assemble [gather] her that halteth [that which limpeth], and I will gather her that is driven out [that which was thrust out], and her that [which] I have afflicted; and I will make her that [that which] halted [limps] a remnant, and her that [that which] was cast far off a strong nation : and the Lord shall reign over them in Mount Zion from henceforth, even for ever." Christ was sent to the lost sheep of the house of Israel (Matt. x. 6), and his invitation was to all that are "weary" and "heavy laden." The Church of Christ from the beginning has comprised those who were the most afflicted, the most scattered, and the most distressed of mankind. It has been and is the grand asylum for the tried and the sorrowful and those who are counted "the offscouring of all things" (1 Cor. iv. 13). 1. *Christ's moral monarchy knows nothing of favouritism.* It does not treat men according to their physical condition, social status, or temporal circumstances. It has *respect to souls.* It is as much interested in the soul of the pauper as in that of the prince, the soul of the slave as in that of the sovereign. Human monarchies have ever been taken up with man in his material relations. The more wealthy and influential a man is, the more favours will worldly kings bestow; the indigent and the homeless are only regarded as beasts of burden. Not so with Christ as the Monarch. Every soul to him is a matter of profound practical interest. 2. *Christ's moral monarchy is remedial in its design.* It brings all the miserable together in order to rid them of their sorrows. By working into human souls right principles of action and expelling wrong ones, it indirectly, though most efficiently, heals all the temporary woes of mankind. "Seek first the things from above, and all others shall be added unto you." "Godliness is profitable unto all things, having the promise of the life which now is, as well as of that which is to come."

II. IT ESTABLISHES ITSELF AS THE GUARDIAN OF MEN FOR EVER. "And thou, O tower of the flock, the strong hold of the daughter of Zion," etc. The address to the "tower of the flock" shows that, as the most wretched and scattered of men will be brought into a great community, so shall the reign of the daughter of Zion be restored, *i.e.* the Jews be converted and brought in with the Gentiles. The watch-tower spoken of by Isaiah (xxxii. 14) is most likely the tower here referred to by Micah. "Flock-tower" is a good expression, inasmuch as it indicates the watchfulness of Christ as a moral Shepherd, the great Shepherd of souls. It is said here that "the kingdom shall come to the daughter of Jerusalem." It did so come; it began with the Jews. "He came to his own, and his own received him not." Although on his last visit to Jerusalem the common people did receive him as their King: "Hosanna to the Son of David!" What a Guardian, what a "Bishop of souls," is Christ! 1. *He knows all his sheep.* Each of the millions is known to him—his idiosyncrasies, imperfections, necessities, etc. 2. *He has ample provision for all his sheep.* His provisions are adapted to all, and are inexhaustible. 3. *He has power to protect all his sheep.*

CONCLUSION. Thank God this moral monarchy of Christ is established on our earth! The kingdom of God is come unto us. Thousands of all grades and classes have entered into it, and they have found it to be "righteousness, peace, and joy in the Holy Ghost." Would that it were universal! It will be so one day. It is not so yet, because, being moral, men have the power of resisting it.—D. T.

Vers. 9—13.—*The moral regeneration of the world.* "Now why dost thou cry out aloud? is there no king in thee? is thy counsellor perished? for pangs have taken thee as a woman in travail. Be in pain, and labour to bring forth, O daughter of Zion," etc. The prophet here, without doubt, refers to the carrying away of the Jews to Babylon. He refers to the consternation in which the Jews would be placed on the approach of the Chaldean army. The questions relative to a "king" and a "counsellor" (ver. 9) are, it is thought, put forth in bitter irony, in order to provoke an answer. "Is there no king in thee? is thy counsellor perished?" The answer, perhaps, would be, "Yes, we have a king, and we have counsellors, but they are utterly worthless; they have power neither to protect us from the terrible calamities nor to invent means for our escape." The metaphor of the parturient woman seems intended to shadow forth the agony of their consternation at the idea of going forth from the city of Jerusalem, being located in the open country, and afterwards conveyed to Babylon. After this comes the promise of emancipation. "There the Lord shall redeem thee from the hand of thine enemies." Their restoration is metaphorically represented by a travailing woman. Whilst it is unfair to attach to Scripture a wrong interpretation, it is perfectly fair to use its passages as symbols of truths applicable to man in all ages and all lands. These words may serve to illustrate, therefore, some points in relation to the *moral regeneration of the world.*

I. THE STATE OF MANKIND REQUIRES IT. "Is there no king in thee? is thy counsellor perished?" It was more serious for the Jewish people to be deprived of a king than for any other people, for their king was theocratic; he was supposed to be the voice and vicegerent of God. The prophet means to say that when the Chaldeans would come and carry them away, they would have no king and no counsellors. Now, men in an unregenerate state: 1. *Have no king.* A political ruler is to man, as a spiritual energy, only a king in name. He does not command the moral affections, rule the conscience, or legislate for the inner and primal springs of all activity. Such a king is the deep want of man; he wants some one to be enthroned on his heart, to whom his conscience can render homage. No man in an unregenerate state has such a king; he has gods many and lords many, of a sort, but none to rule him, and to bring all the powers of his soul into one harmonious channel of obedience. 2. *Have no counsellor.* Society abounds with counsellors who proffer their advice; but some of them are wicked, most of them worthless, few, if any, satisfactory, that is, to conscience. What the soul wants is not the mere book counsellor—though it be the Bible itself—but the *spirit* of that book, the spirit of reverence, love, Christ-like trust. Such a spirit, when it comes to us, will guide us into all truth; it is the " unction from the Holy One." 3. *Have no ease.* " Pangs have taken thee as a woman in travail." The unregenerate soul is always liable to consternation, remorse; it often writhes in agony. " There is no peace, saith my God, to the wicked." Now, moral regeneration brings the man a true King, a true Counsellor, a true Peace—a peace " that passeth all understanding."

II. IT IS OPPOSED BY FORMIDABLE ANTAGONISTS. "Many nations are gathered against thee." The nations here referred to are those that composed the army of Nebuchadnezzar, or those that joined it in the attack against the Jews. What formidable opponents there are to the conversion of man! 1. *The depraved elements of the soul.* Unbelief, selfishness, carnality, etc. These are Canaanites that battle mightily against the moral Joshua. 2. *The corrupt influence of society.* How much, in this country and this age especially, is there struggling against man's regeneration—custom, fashion, amusements, pleasures! And then, too, acting through all these forces within and without, there are the principalities and powers of darkness; so that it comes to pass that it is no very easy thing to effect the regeneration of men; there are nations of moral forces battling against it.

III. IT IS GUARANTEED BY THE WORD OF ALMIGHTY GOD. " They know not the thoughts of the Lord," etc. The enemies of the Jews were utterly ignorant of God's purpose to deliver his people from Babylonish captivity. " They had not the most distant idea that the object of Jehovah, in permitting his people to be so treated, was to recover them from idolatry, and thus prepare them for a triumphant restoration. The metaphor taken from the process of threshing out grain is frequently used by the prophets to denote the complete destruction of a people." 1. *Man in ignorance fights against God's purpose.* The Chaldeans and all the enemies of the Jews did so now. Men are always doing this. " Had they known it, they would not have crucified the Lord of glory." 2. *Man, in fighting against God's purpose, brings ruin on himself.* It is here predicted that the enemies of the Jews should be as " sheaves," and that the Jews themselves should be strengthened. " I will make thine horn iron, and I will make thy hoofs brass." " When God," says an old writer, " has conquering work for his people to do, he will furnish them with strength and ability for it—will make the horn iron and the hoofs brass; and when he does so, they must exert the power he gives them, and execute the commission: even the daughter of Zion may arise and thresh." The nations thought to ruin Christianity in its infancy, but it was victorious over them. Those who persisted in their enmity were broken to pieces (Matt. xxi. 44), particularly the Jewish nation; but multitudes by Divine grace were joined to the Church, and they and their substance were consecrated to the Lord Jesus, the Lord of the whole earth.—D. T.

EXPOSITION.

CHAPTER V.

Vers. 1—4.—§ 8. *After Zion's degrada-tion Messiah shall be born, and shall bring the world into subjection.*

Ver. 1.—This verse is joined to the pre-ceding chapter in the Hebrew. Jerusalem is addressed, as in ch. iv. 9, 11, not the invading army. The prophet returns to the view of the misery and humiliation ex-pressed in that passage. **Gather thyself in troops;** or, *thou shalt gather thyself*, etc. Jerusalem must collect its armies to defend itself from the enemy. **O daughter of troops.** Jerusalem is thus named from the number of soldiers collected within her walls, from whence marauding expeditions were wont to set forth. Pusey considers that she is so called from the acts of violence, robbery, and bloodshed which are done within her (ch. ii. 8; iii. 2, etc.; Jer. vii. 11). Keil thinks the prophet represents the people crowding together in fear. It is more natural to refer the expression to the abnormal assemblage of soldiers and fugitives within the walls of a besieged city. Septuagint, 'Εμφραχθήσε-ται θυγάτηρ ἐμφραγμῷ, "The daughter shall be wholly hemmed in;" Vulgate, *Vastaberis, filia latronis*. **He hath laid siege.** The enemy is spoken of by an abrupt change of person (comp. Isa. i. 29). **Against us.** The prophet identifies himself with the besieged people. **They shall smite the judge of Israel,** etc. "The judge" repre-sents the supreme authority, whether king or other governor (Amos ii. 3); but he is called here "judge," that the sacred name of king may not be spoken of as dis-honoured. To smite upon the cheek is the grossest insult (comp. 1 Kings xxii. 24; Job xvi. 10; Luke xxii. 64). When Zion is thus besieged, and its rulers suffer the utmost contumely, its condition must look hopeless. Such a state of things was realized in the treatment of Zedekiah (2 Kings xxv.), and in many subsequent sieges of Jerusalem. But the underlying idea is that Israel shall suffer dire distress at the hands of her enemies until Messiah comes, and she herself turns to the Lord. The LXX. translates *shophet*, "judge," by φυλάς, "tribes," but the other Greek translators give κριτήν.

Ver. 2.—At the time of Zion's deepest distress, and when her earthly king is suffering the grossest degradation, reduced as it were to the shepherd-house at Bethle-hem, a Deliverer shall arise thence who shall do wonderful things. This passage was quoted by the Sanhedrin to answer

Herod's question where the Christ was to be born (Matt. ii. 5, 6; comp. John vii. 42). **But thou, Bethlehem Ephratah.** Ephratah (Ephrathah, or Ephrath), "fruitfulness," is another name for Bethlehem, "House of bread" (Gen. xxxv. 19; 1 Sam. xvii. 12; Ruth i. 2); from its position it is also called Bethlehem Judah (Judg. xvii. 7), being situated in the tribal lot of Judah, about five miles south of Jerusalem, and thus distinguished from a town of the same name in Zebulun (Josh. xix. 15). Septuagint, Καὶ σὺ, Βηθλεέμ, οἶκος 'Εφραθά [τοῦ 'Εφραθά, Alex.], "And thou, Bethlehem, house of Ephrathah." The rest of the clause is best translated, *too little to be among the thou-sands of Judah*. Each tribe was divided into "thousands," which would be equiva-lent to clans, with its own head. Probably the reckoning was made of fighting men (see note on Zech. ix. 7; and comp. Numb. i. 16; x. 4; Josh. xxii. 21, 30; 1 Sam. x. 19). Bethlehem, called in the text Bethle-hem Ephratah for solemnity's sake, was a small place (κώμη, John vii. 42), of such slight importance as not to be named among the possessions of Judah in Josh. xv., or in the catalogue of Neh. xi. 25, etc. Yet out of thee shall he (one) come forth unto me that is to be **Ruler in Israel.** In spite of its insignificance, this birthplace of David shall be the birthplace of Messiah. "Shall come forth" is spoken sometimes of birth and descent, as in Gen. xvii. 6 and xxxv. 11; at other times it contains merely the notion of proceeding from, as in Jer. xxx. 21. In the present case both ideas are suitable. *Unto me* (Jehovah is speaking). To my praise and glory, to do my will. Micah by these words would recall the announcement con-cerning David made to Samuel, "I have provided me a king" (1 Sam. xvi. 1), and thus show the typical relation of David to the Messiah (Keil). **Whose goings forth have been from of old, from everlasting.** The mean-ing of the word rendered "goings forth" (*motsaoth*) is somewhat doubtful. Septua-gint, ἔξοδοι: Vulgate, *egressus*. The Fathers see in it a declaration of the eternal genera-tion of the Son: he who was born in time at Bethlehem hath an eternal existence. In this case the plural form of the word is a plural of majesty, or an abstract expres-sion (comp. Ps. cxiv. 2, "dominions;" Isa. liv. 2, "habitations"). To Christians, who believe in the mystery of the Holy Trinity, the plural would express the continual generation of the Son from the Father from everlasting and to everlasting, never begin-ning and never ending; as the Council of Lateran says, "Without beginning, ever and without end, the Father begetting, the Son being born (*nascens*), and the Holy Ghost proceeding." Many commentators take the "goings forth" to be the ancient promises, the revelations of the Angel of the covenant to the patriarchs, the various preparations made in type and history for the appearance of the great Son of David in due time; but this is a forced interpretation of the word. Granted that Micah's contemporaries understood the prophecy to state merely that a Saviour should arise from the lineage of David who traced his descent from hoar antiquity, and might be said to have lived in the days of old, this fact (if it be a fact) does not preclude us, with our more perfect knowledge, from seeing a deeper meaning in the inspired utterance, an adumbration of the nature of that Prince whom Isaiah calls "Everlasting" (ch. ix. 6), the Word who "was in the beginning with God" (John i. 1, 2). We may note certain contrasts in these two first verses. Zion, "the daughter of troops," is contrasted with the mean and insignificant Bethlehem; yet the former shall be shamefully handled, the latter highly honoured; that one's king shall be dethroned and disgraced, this one's Ruler is from everlasting and to everlasting.

Ver. 3.—**Therefore;** *i.e.* because God hath designed to punish before delivering, and this deliverance is to arise from the little Bethlehem, not from Jerusalem. This presupposes that the house of David will have lost the throne and have been reduced to a low condition. **Will he give them up.** Jehovah will give up the people to its enemies; this is the way in which the house of David shall come to low estate. **She which travaileth hath brought forth.** Many commentators have taken the travailing woman to be the afflicted community of Israel, or Zion; but we may not altogether reject the old interpretation which regards this as a prophecy of the birth of Christ from the Virgin, in accordance with the received Messianic exposition of Isaiah's great prediction, "Behold, the virgin shall conceive" (Isa. vii. 14). Such an announcement comes in naturally after the announcement of the Ruler coming forth from Bethlehem. Israel shall be oppressed until the time ordained when "she who is to bear" shall bring forth. Then (rather, *and*, i.e. until) **the remnant of his brethren shall return unto (*with*) the children of Israel.** The remnant of his brethren are the rescued of the Judæans, who are the brethren of Messiah according to the flesh; these in a literal sense shall return from exile together with the others, and in a spiritual sense shall be converted and be joined with the true Israelites, the true seed of Abraham.

Ver. 4.—**He shall stand.** The Ruler, Messiah, shall stand as a good shepherd, guiding and ordering his flock, watchful and ready to aid and defend (comp. Ezek. xxxiv. 23; John x. 11). Septuagint, στήσεται καὶ ὄψεται, "shall stand and see." **Feed;** *i.e.* his flock. Septuagint, ποιμανεῖ τὸ ποίμνιον αὐτοῦ. **In the strength of the Lord,** with which he is invested and which he displays in the care of his people. **In the majesty of the Name of the Lord his God.** Messiah shall rule in all the power and glory with which God hath revealed himself on earth (comp. Isa. ix. 6; Matt. xxviii. 18; John i. 14). **They shall abide;** Septuagint, ὑπάρξουσι, "they shall be." The children of Israel shall sit, dwell, in rest and peace in their own land (ch. iv. 4; Lev. xxvi. 5, 6; Joel iii. 20; Amos ix. 14, 15). The Vulgate, from a different pointing of the Hebrew, renders, *convertentur*. With this the Chaldee and Syriac agree. But this idea is already expressed in ver. 3. **Now shall he be great.** When the prophecy is fulfilled and Messiah is feeding his flock, his dominion shall extend unto the ends of the earth (comp. Mal. i. 11, 14; Ps. ii. 8; lxxii. 8; Luke i. 32).

Vers. 5, 6.—§ 9. *Under Messiah's rule shall be peace.* Cheyne considers these verses to have been inserted by an afterthought, either to explain the "many nations" and "many peoples" of ch. iv. 11, 13, or to rectify the omission of the period of foreign rule. This may be reasonably allowed; but it is not necessary to the explanation of the paragraph, which is merely a further description of Messiah's kingdom.

Ver. 5.—**And this Man shall be the Peace;** *and he shall be Peace;* Vulgate, *et erit iste Pax.* This same Ruler will not only bring peace, and be the Author of peace, but be himself Peace; as Isaiah (ix. 5) calls him "Prince of Peace," and St. Paul (Eph. ii. 14) "our Peace." Peace personified (comp. Zech. ix. 9). It is best to put a full stop here, and remove the colon at "land" in the next clause. There may be an allusion to Solomon, the peaceful king, who erected the temple and whose reign exhibited the ideal of happy times. Septuagint, καὶ ἔσται αὐτῇ εἰρήνη, "and to her shall be peace." **When the Assyrian shall come.** The prophet, in this and the following verses, shows what is that peace which Messiah shall bring. Asshur is named as the type of Israel's deadliest foe, and as that which even then was threatening the kingdom: witness Sennacherib's invasion in Hezekiah's time, when the angel of the Lord smote the alien army with sudden destruction (2 Kings xix.). The prophecy looks forward to a far-distant future, when the world-power is arrayed against God's people; the details (as often in such prophecies) do not exactly suit the actual facts in contemporary history. **Then shall we raise against him seven shepherds.** We, the Israel of God, shall be enabled to repel the enemy. "Shepherds," *i.e.* princes, and those in abundance. "Seven" is the perfect number, representing completeness and rest. **And eight principal men;** or, *princes among men,* appointed by the Ruler as his subordinates and representatives. These are said to be "eight," to imply their great number: there should be a super-abundance of able leaders. (On a similar use of numbers, see note on Amos i. 3.) The LXX. renders, ὀκτὼ δήγματα ἀνθρώπων, "eight attacks of men," reading differently.

Ver. 6.—**They shall waste.** The word rendered "waste" (*raah*) is capable of two interpretations according as it is derived. It may mean "to break" or "to feed;" and in the latter sense may signify either "to eat up" or "to be shepherd over," as the Septuagint, ποιμανοῦσι. The addition, **with the sword,** however, limits the explanation, whichever verb we refer it to. These leaders shall not only defend their own land against the enemy, but shall carry the war into the hostile territory, conquer it, and rule with rigour (for the phrase, comp. Ps. ii. 9; Rev. ii. 27; xii. 5). True religion has always a war to wage with error and worldliness, but shall conquer in the power of Christ. **The land of Nimrod.** This is taken by some commentators to mean Babylon, the other great enemy of the Church of God. But Babylon is nowhere in Scripture called "the land of Nimrod," though Nimrod is connected with Babel in Gen. x. 10; and the term is better explained here as a synonym of Assyria, used to recall the "rebel" (so *Nimrod* is interpreted) who founded the first empire (Gen. x. 8—12), and gives the character to the kingdom of this world. **In the entrances thereof;** literally, *in the gates thereof;* i.e. in the cities and fortresses, corresponding to the "palaces" of ver. 5 (comp. Isa. iii. 26; xiii. 2; Nah. iii. 13). Septuagint, ἐν τῇ τάφρῳ αὐτῆς, "with her trench;" Vulgate, *in lanceis ejus,* which, if the Hebrew be taken as Jerome reads it, will be in close parallelism with the words in the preceding clause, "with the sword." **Thus** (*and*) **he shall deliver us.** Israel has to undergo much tribulation and many struggles, but Messiah shall save her.

Vers. 7—9.—§ 10. *The people under Messiah's rule have a mission to execute; they are to be not only conquerors, but saviours also.*

Ver. 7.—First, Israel in God's hands shall **be an instrument of life and health to the** nations. **The remnant of Jacob.** The faithful, Messianic Israel, as ch. iv. 7; Isa. x. 21. **Many people;** rather, *many peoples* (ch. iv. 11, 13); so in ver. 8. The LXX. inserts, ἐν τοῖς ἔθνεσιν, "among the nations," as in ver. 8. **As a dew from the Lord.** Converted Israel shall act as Messiah himself in refreshing and stimulating the nations. Receiving grace from him, she shall diffuse it to others. (For the metaphor of dew thus used, comp. Deut. xxxii. 2; Hos. xiv. 6.) It is especially appropriate in a country where from May to October the life of herbage depends chiefly on the copious dews (comp. Gen. xxvii. 28; Deut. xxxiii. 13, 28; Hag. i. 10). **As the showers upon the grass.** The dew is called "showers" as appearing to descend in a multitude of drops. **That tarrieth not for man, nor waiteth for the sons of men.** This refers to the dew, which is wholly the gift of God, and is not artificially supplied by man's labour, as Egypt is "watered by the foot" (Deut. xi. 10). So grace is God's free, unmerited gift, and will come upon the nations in his good time and way. The LXX. has here a curious rendering, Καὶ ὡς ἄρνες ἐπὶ ἄγρωστιν, ὅπως μὴ συναχθῇ μηδεὶς, μηδὲ ὑποστῇ ἐν υἱοῖς ἀνθρώπων, which Jerome explains of the obdurate Gentiles who continue in unbelief, "as lambs upon the grass, that none may assemble nor withstand among the sons of men."

Ver. 8.—Secondly, **Israel shall be a terrible power** among the nations, and invincible in strength. "Nova theocratica agit suaviter et fortiter" (Knabenbauer). **As a lion.** The Lamb of God is also the Lion of the tribe of Judah (Rev. v. 5; Numb. xxiii. 24), and he "is set for the fall and rising again of many" (Luke ii. 34). In his irresistible strength Israel shall overcome all enemies. So Judas Maccabæus is compared to a lion (1 Macc. iii. 4).

Ver. 9.—The prophet's exulting prayer for the success of his people. **Thine hand shall be,** etc.; rather, *let thine hand be lifted up;* and so in the next clause, "let thine enemies be cut off." The phrase, "high be thy hand upon, or over," recalls the expression in Exod. xiv. 8, "The children of Israel went out with an high hand" (comp. Numb. xxxiii. 3; Isa. xxvi. 11; and our idiom, "to get the upper hand"). (For the promise contained in the prayer, see Isa. lx. 12.)

Vers. 10—15.—§ 11. *Messiah shall destroy all the instruments of war, and put down all idolatry, having taught his people to rely upon him alone.*

Ver. 10.—**In that day.** When Messiah's kingdom is established. Micah depicts the interior perfection of the Church, as he had before explained its relation to external nations. **Horses . . . chariots.** The things most used in attack and defence, and forbidden by God as betraying distrust in his providence (comp. Deut. xvii. 16; Isa. ii. 7; Zech. ix. 10). In the reign of the Prince of Peace all war shall cease (Isa. ix. 4—6).

Ver. 11.—**Cities.** Abodes of luxury and pride. From Messiah's kingdom all pomp and vain-glory shall be shut out. **Strong holds.** Such defences shall not be needed nor allowed (comp. Isa. ii. 15; Zech. ii. 4, 5).

Ver. 12.—**Witchcrafts.** Magic and sorcery, which were much practised in Syria and Palestine, as in Chaldea, the literature of which country consists in great part of spells and charms. It is to the belief in the efficacy of such incantations that we owe the episode of Balak and Balaam (Numb. xxii. —xxiv.), and the enactments in the Law; e.g. Deut. xviii. 10, etc. (comp. Isa. ii. 6; xlvii. 12). Septuagint, τὰ φάρμακά σου, "thy poisons;" Vulgate, *maleficia.* **Soothsayers**; properly, *cloud-diviners,* or *storm-makers;* either persons who professed to divine by means of the shape and colour of clouds, or, as the old Scandinavian witches, charlatans who assumed the power of causing and directing storms. Cheyne compares the common name of sorcerers among savages, "rain-makers."

Ver. 13.—**Graven images,** of stone or metal (Lev. xxvi. 1). **Standing images;** Septuagint, τὰς στηλάς σου, "thy columns;" Vulgate, *statuas tuas.* These are stone images or pillars dedicated to false gods

(1 Kings xiv. 23). A pillar to mark a place consecrated to the worship of the Lord was allowed (see Gen. xxviii. 18; xxxi. 13, 45; Isa. xix. 17). It was when this custom degenerated into idolatry that it was sternly denounced (Deut. xvi. 22; xxvii. 15, etc.).

Ver. 14.—**Thy groves** (*Asherim*); Exod. xxxiv. 13; Deut. vii. 5, etc. Asherah was a Canaanitish goddess, whose worship was celebrated with licentious rites. She corresponds to the Ashtoreth of the Phoenicians and Ishtar of the Assyrians, and seems to have been adored as the goddess of the productive power of nature. Her symbol was a tree or a wooden post. **So** (*and*) **will I destroy thy cities;** *i.e.* those cities which have been the centres of idolatry, or are especially connected with such worship (comp. Amos v. 5). The word rendered "cities" has by some been translated, and by others has been so altered as to be translated, "adversaries;" but there is no variety in the reading, or in the rendering of the ancient versions (except the Targum); and, explained as above, it is no mere repetition of the thought in ver. 11.

Ver. 15.—The time of Messiah is the era when judgment shall fall on the obdurate heathen. **Such as they have not heard;** rather, *which have not hearkened,* which are disobedient. Septuagint, "Because they hearkened not" (comp. Isa. lxvi. 15—18; Joel iii. 9, etc.; Zeph. iii. 8; Hag. ii. 22; 2 Thess. i. 7—10). It is implied that some of the heathen will hearken to the revelation of Jehovah by the Messiah.

HOMILETICS.

Ver. 2.—*Bethlehem Ephratah.* I. THE NAME OF THE PLACE IS VERY SUGGESTIVE. Bethlehem; *i.e.* "House of bread." Ephratah; *i.e.* "*Fruitfulness.*" Both thus signified plenty, abundance, fertility. They were most appropriate as designating the spot, for fertility has been and is still characteristic of that locality. "It is now a large village, beautifully situated on the brow of a high hill, which commands an extensive view of the surrounding mountainous country, and rises in *parterres* of vineyards, almond groves, and fig plantations, watered by gentle rivulets that murmur through the terraces; and is diversified by towers and wine-presses" (Kitto's 'Cyclopædia,' art. "Bethlehem," vol. i. p. 326; see also Porter's 'Handbook,' p. 206). The place in its rich fruitfulness was symbolical of that spiritual abundance which should be secured to the world by him who is "the Bread of life" (John vi. 33—35), and the seed-corn to fall into the ground and die, and thus to bring forth much fruit (John xii. 24).

II. THE LOWLINESS OF THE PLACE IS ALSO SUGGESTIVE. From Numb. i. 5—16 and x. 4 we learn that each of the tribes of Israel had its thousands of fighting men, each thousand having its appointed leader; whilst from the Book of Joshua we gather that this appointment was continued after the settlement of Canaan (xxii. 21, 30). So insignificant, however, was Bethlehem that it could make but a small contribution towards this arrangement, and hence was "least among the thousands of Judah." Yet upon this lowly place honour was to be conferred in the birth there of the world's Redeemer. The small was to become great, and the mean exalted. Around its plains the glory of the Lord should shine, and the songs of angels should resound, chanting the natal-song, " Glory to God in the highest," etc. (Luke ii. 14). And if a humble *village* through its connection with the Christ of God became thus exalted, much more surely shall human hearts and lives. Associated with him, they who, judged by the world's standards, are accounted mean and despicable, secure to themselves present dignity and eternal honour.

III. THIS PROPHECY RESPECTING THE MESSIAH'S LOWLY BIRTHPLACE LIVED IN THE MEMORIES AND HEARTS OF GOD'S ANCIENT PEOPLE. Two striking confirmations of this are given in the Gospels. 1. In connection with the visit of the Magians to Jerusalem. Herod in his alarm gathered the Jewish Sanhedrin together, and imperiously demanded information from the priests and scribes as to where, in accordance with Jewish traditions, the Messiah was to be born. And their reply (Matt. ii. 5, 6) indicates that they had in their memory this prophecy by Micah; whilst the readiness with which they replied to the inquiry of Herod manifests how clearly this prophecy had become impressed upon the Jewish mind. 2. In connection with Christ's appearance in Jerusalem at "the Feast of Tabernacles." His hearers, moved by his marvellous teaching, began to acknowledge him as the Messiah, when lo! the Pharisees cried, " Shall Christ came out of Galilee ? Hath not the Scripture said that Christ cometh of the seed of David, and out of Bethlehem, where David was ? " (John vii. 42). It is evident that these Pharisees knew all about this ancient prediction, and that they expected the Messiah, in accordance with it, to appear in Bethlehem. Note—

IV. THE REMARKABLE FULFILMENT, IN THE ORDER OF PROVIDENCE, OF THIS NATIONAL EXPECTATION. The decree went forth from Cæsar Augustus that all the Roman world should be enrolled (Luke ii. 1). The emperor, in issuing the decree, thought only of his imperial authority and the glory of the empire; but God was working through all, and making the earthly kingdom to serve the heavenly, and bringing about the fulfilment of the prophecy that in Bethlehem the Christ should appear. So, earthly princes and potentates, statesmen and diplomatists, are ever at work, thinking only of the interests of their own nations; but above all is the God of nations, the supreme Ruler, sitting on the throne of his majesty in perfect repose, and overruling all to the accomplishment of his purposes of love and mercy towards the whole race (Prov. xxi. 1; xvi. 33).

Ver. 2.—*The nature of the Messiah's rule.* " *That is to be Ruler in Israel.*" In the first verse Micah had spoken of the failure of earthly rulers. "The judge of Israel should be smitten with a rod upon the cheek." The rulers who had so lamentably failed in their administration should come to nought, but there should rise up in the time appointed "a King to reign in righteousness," and who should establish a kingdom which should never be "moved." Unfortunately, however, in the Jewish mind, the nature of this kingdom took a visible shape; and they anticipated that the Messiah should establish a kingdom which should be marked by regal splendour and worldly power. Hence, when he appeared, the appeal was made to him to free them from paying tribute to Cæsar (Matt. xxii. 17—22); to sit in judgment, and to settle disputes (Luke xii. 13; John viii. 2—11); and they sought to take him by force, and to compel him to set up his throne (John vi. 15). And it is easy to understand how that, cherishing these mistaken notions, the Christ of God became an enigma to them; and that, disappointed in the course he pursued, they turned aside from him, cherished hostility towards him, and even cried, "Away with him! crucify him!" But, for all this, in the spiritual sense predicted by Micah and others, he was the true King of Israel, and his claim can be fully vindicated. He was "Ruler in Israel" in a far higher and nobler sense than David and his successors had ever been the sovereigns of the people. The functions which Jesus declined to fulfil were, after all, the lesser and inferior functions of the King of Israel. The higher functions were those which the Lord God himself had fulfilled in relation to the Jewish nation, and before that nation in the pride of its heart had demanded an earthly ruler. God had been their King. David and his successors were but Jehovah's deputies, and were appointed by him to discharge the lesser and secondary functions; but there were higher functions, which Jehovah alone had fulfilled. It was he who by his appointment and power had separated that people from among the nations, and it was he who of his infinite wisdom framed those Divine laws by which the people thus separated were to be governed, and in obedience to which they were to find happiness and security. And Christ Jesus became in the highest sense "the Ruler in Israel," in that he came to gather a people to his praise out of the wreck and ruin sin had wrought among the nations, and to give them that Christian law of rectitude and righteousness, of mercy and love, the embodiment and perfecting of all previous revelations, and in following which there should be experienced the truest peace and the most abiding joy. He came to set up on earth "the kingdom of heaven," and to establish amongst men a Divine and heavenly rule. His is not a kingdom of the senses, but of the spirit; it consists not in "meat and drink," but in "righteousness, peace, and joy in the Holy Ghost" (Rom. xiv. 17). He is "the Ruler," and the principles of his rule are such as, finding a lodgment in the heart and drawing the soul to him in loving loyalty and devotion, renders it true and good, holy and happy. And all that is needed in order to render the world sin has blighted bright and blessed, is that his rulership be universally acknowledged and his reign be established in every human soul.

> "Hark the glad sound, the Saviour comes,
> The Saviour promised long;
> Let every heart prepare a throne,
> And every voice a song."

Ver. 2 (last clause).—*The eternal "goings forth" of the Christ of God.* "When he says his beginnings are from the beginning, from the days of antiquity, he shows his pre-existent nature, as when he says he will go forth as Ruler to feed his people Israel he shows his temporal birth" (Chrysostom). "Going forth is here opposed to going forth—a going forth out of Bethlehem to a going forth from eternity; a going forth which then was still to come, to a going forth which had been long ago, from the days of eternity. The word expresses pre-existence, an eternal existence backwards as well as forwards, the incommunicable attribute of God" (Pusey, *in loc.*). The expression here naturally leads us to think of the words with which St. John commences his Gospel (i. 1). We can offer no explanation as to how this could be. We fully acknowledge the difficulty, and which lies within the Divine nature itself. We bow before the mystery. "God is great, and we know him not." Reason is baffled when it inquires concerning the Divine Personality; but where reason cannot penetrate, *faith* can reverentially and tranquilly rest. And certainly the Prophet Micah here, and the Evangelist John in the prologue to his Gospel, claimed no more for the Messiah than the Christ claimed for himself (comp. John vi. 62; viii. 58; xvii. 5, 24; Rev. i. 8). This eternal Son of God is presented to us here in his Divine manifestations; for the seer speaks of "his *goings forth.*"

I. TRACE THESE "GOINGS FORTH." We may do so: 1. *In creation.* In view of his oneness with God, *this* is declared to have been his work (John i. 3; Col. i. 16, 17). 2. *In providence.* In reading the Old Testament in its allusions to the Divine care exercised over eminent saints of God, we find a Divine exalted Personage occasionally referred to as manifesting himself to such—to Abraham (Gen. xviii.); to Jacob (Gen. xxxii. 24, 30) to the Israelites through Moses (Exod. xxiii. 20, 21); to Joshua (Josh. v. 13—15). There are insuperable difficulties if we simply regard these as angelic ministries expressive of the Divine care over the good as the God of providence. It would not have been said in reference to any angel, "Provoke him not, for he will not pardon your transgressions;" nor would any mere angelic intelligence have accepted the adoration of Joshua, but would have said, "See thou do it not: for I am thy fellow-servant," etc. (Rev. xxii. 9). The most reasonable conclusion is that these were the "goings forth" in providence of the pre-existent Son of God. 3. *In grace.* (1) In the counsels of the Godhead. Man by transgression mournfully departed from his God. He lost the Divine favour and the light of the Divine countenance. And when his condition became helpless and hopeless, lo! Divine interpositions with a view to his salvation. And it was in the depths of the compassion of the eternal Son of God that the stream of Divine mercy took its rise, and which shall flow on to bless the whole world; and from him, "the Sun of Righteousness," has emanated the cheering ray of hope to ruined man. Nor, in speaking thus of the love of the eternal *Son,* do we slight the love of the eternal *Father.* Observe, in this verse God, speaking of his Son, says,

" He shall come forth *unto me*," meaning surely that Christ, in his incarnation, with all that was thus involved of mercy and grace, would, in rescuing and restoring man, fulfil the Divine purpose and accomplish the Divine will. The Divine Father is no wrathful Being, needing to be appeased by the sacrifice of his Son. The Father "so loved the world, that he *gave*," etc. (John iii. 16). The eternal Spirit, too, strives and pleads with men. There never has been schism in the eternal counsels. The mercy that saves us had its origin in the free and unbought love of the Godhead. (2) In the life and work of the incarnate Christ. The life of Jesus is the most wonderful ever lived in the flesh. The lives of patriarchs, prophets, and righteous men through all ages pale in the presence of this life. "Grace and truth came by Jesus Christ." "His goings forth have been from of old, from everlasting;" but none of his manifestations has ever equalled that which took place when he clothed himself in the veil of our mortal flesh, and enabled man, through his perfect character and self-sacrificing work, to behold expressed in their very midst the glory of the Lord.

II. CONNECT THESE "GOINGS FORTH" WITH WHAT WAS PREDICTED HERE RESPECTING THE ADVENT OF CHRIST. As we behold him in his eternal existence and glory, Creator of all things, the Giver of life, the Imparter of light, manifesting himself in all the departments of the Divine operation; and then think of him as condescending to the limitations and conditions of our humanity, humbling himself to "the poor manger" at Bethlehem, and "the bitter cross" at Calvary, we are filled with wonder; yet love also inflames and inspires our souls. With profoundest gratitude and holiest joy we raise our carols. As we think of him as "the Ancient of days" and also the Babe of Bethlehem, our hearts are drawn to him, and we are impelled to adopt as our own the strain of Micah's great contemporary Isaiah, and to sing exultantly, "For unto us a Child is born," etc. (Isa. ix. 6).

Ver. 3.—*Success ; but in God's own time.* There is a certain degree of ambiguity about these words, yet amidst this we find certain practical teachings very clearly enunciated.

I. WE ARE REMINDED OF DELAYS IN THE DIVINE WORKING. Seven hundred years must elapse ere the predictions respecting the advent of the Redeemer should be fulfilled and "the time" come. God's purposes in grace, as well as in nature and providence, are developed gradually. He makes demands upon human patience, bidding us wait. He often, by slow processes, brings to pass that which he has planned. "Rest in the Lord," etc. (Ps. xxxvii. 7).

II. WE ARE REMINDED OF THE WITHDRAWAL OF PRIVILEGE. "Therefore will he give them up until," etc. The favoured people had slighted the privileges which God had so richly bestowed upon them. He had not dealt so graciously with any other nation, but the blessings granted they had failed to improve, and hence these were now to be withdrawn. God had delivered them from their foes, but now they were to go into the land of captivity. The precious symbols of his near presence with them were no longer to be seen. The voice of prophecy, too, should soon become silent. Through sad and solemn losses they were to be led to look with ardent hope to the coming of "the Consolation of Israel."

III. WE ARE REMINDED HERE OF ULTIMATE GLORIOUS INCREASE. "Then the remnant of his brethren shall return unto the children of Israel." Some limit these words to *the conversion of the Jews*, and understand by "the children of Israel" the true spiritual Israelites like Simeon and Anna, who waited for the advent of a spiritual Redeemer, and regard the words as intimating that to these in Messianic times there should be gathered "the remnant of Christ's brethren," *i.e.* the more spiritually minded amongst *his own nation* who should be constrained to welcome him to their hearts, and to consecrate themselves to his service. According to this interpretation the prophecy received its partial fulfilment in the conversion of the Jews in apostolic times, and shall yet be more completely fulfilled when the Jewish nation shall be brought in, and when "all Israel shall be saved." Others, however, give the words a yet wider meaning, and understand by "brethren" all who "hear the Word of God and keep it," and who are obedient to the will of Christ's Father and theirs, whether they be Jews or Gentiles; and see in these words a pre-intimation in prophetic times of the coming of that happy era when "the Ruler in Israel" shall sway his sceptre over a ransomed and redeemed world. And to that bright day of God we look on with longing hearts. Dawn upon our darkened world it surely will. God has not totally "given up" and abandoned our sin-stricken and sin-stained world. Even his withdrawals are with a view to the spiritual good of his children, and are followed, when the discipline is accomplished, by brighter and more glorious manifestations of his love and grace. "At the Name of Jesus every knee shall bow, and every tongue shall confess him Lord." His kingdom shall come, and his "will be done on earth, even as it is done in heaven."

Ver. 4.—*The ministering Christ.* The whole of this chapter is more or less occupied with graphic descriptions of the Christ of God drawn ages before he appeared, and setting forth his nature, his work, and his influence upon the world and the race. A little child has been called " an unsolved problem." We dare not be so bold as to attempt to forecast the future of any child. This, however, is done here respecting the "Babe of Bethlehem." Distinct Divine pre-intimations were given concerning the destiny of this mighty Child, and to which he has proved himself gloriously true. Here he is presented to us as *the ministering Christ.* We have predicted here—

I. THE HOLY MINISTERING LIFE OF THE CHRIST OF GOD. "And he shall stand and feed," etc. (ver. 4). It was thus declared that the very coming of Christ would be a descent with a view to helpfulness. In his advent the lofty would descend to the low, the strong to the feeble, for the express purpose of ministering unto them in order that he might lift up the fallen and restore the erring, and strengthen the weak by his own great might and love. This ministering character of the life of the Christ who was to appear was set forth by this and other Hebrew seers under the figure of a shepherd tending his flock. This was natural in view of the national history. The Jewish people gloried in David as one raised from the sheepfold to the throne, and rejoiced in him as their shepherd-king. Hence with appropriateness the prophets referred to "great David's greater Son " under this simple yet beautiful emblem. The allusions, too, were in harmony with the destined birthplace of the Messiah—a locality so thoroughly pastoral in its character, and upon the plains of which district the Eastern shepherds kept constant watch. The emblem is admirably suggestive of the character and work of the Messiah, setting forth : 1. His *gentleness;* the weak, the tired, the tempted, the erring, being tended by him with patient love (Isa. xl. 11). 2. His *watchfulness.* "He shall *stand*," etc. (ver. 4) ; the posture indicating alertness, readiness to protect and defend. 3. His *succours.* He should "feed" the flock, supplying abundantly the spiritual wants of his people, and fully satisfying the longings and aspirations of their hearts. The records of the evangelists indicate how truly "ministering" in character the life of Christ was, and how that the most trusty shepherd watching over the flock committed to his charge but faintly images his wondrous care (Matt. xx. 28). His followers are to emulate his example, and to live ministering lives (Matt. xx. 26, 27). He, as "the Man Christ Jesus," pursued his course of holy service "in the strength of the Lord, in the majesty of the Name of the Lord his God." And this Divine influence is available to all his servants.

II. THE PROSPERITY OF ALL WHO AVAIL THEMSELVES OF HIS MINISTERINGS AND WHO COMMIT THEMSELVES UNTO HIS CARE. "And they shall *abide.*" 1. The thought of *rest* is suggested. "And they shall abide;" literally, " sit." The idea is the same as in Ps. xxiii. 2, "He maketh me to lie down," etc. Delightful repose—rest for the weary. The pastures of sin are dry and parched, and its waters are troubled, and man seeks in vain therein freedom from unrest ; but when the heart reposes in Christ, then it knows what it is to lie down on the pastures of tender grass, and by the waters of quietness. 2. The thought of *security* is also suggested. They shall sit without fear of harm overtaking them, because he " stands," their Guardian against all intrusion and invasion, ready as their champion to defend them from all peril, and to maintain their cause. So shall they dwell at rest and in security, and true prosperity be theirs perpetually. "And they shall *abide.*"

III. THE HONOUR WITH WHICH THE MINISTERING CHRIST, BY REASON OF HIS CONDESCENDING AND GRACIOUS SERVICE, SHALL BE CROWNED. "For now shall he be great unto the ends of the earth." "For *now.*" The far-distant future was present to the prophet's gaze as he uttered these words, and he referred to it as though it had already come. His faith had peered beyond the centuries intervening before the advent of the Messiah, and had rendered that event very real to him; and now he took by faith a yet wider range of vision, and looked on to the ages following the advent, and saw the ever-growing, ever-widening influence and honour the Christ should enjoy, and even beheld this as extending to earth's remotest bounds. Long and weary ages had passed since the prophet of God uttered this prediction; and we to-day, in the partial fulfilment of his words, have every ground of encouragement to look on to their complete accomplishment. What name is so powerful to inspire within men the holiest emotions, and to move them to devoted consecration, as that of Jesus Christ? He is indeed "great" in the marvellous influence he exerts upon human hearts and lives; and despite all the discouragements which meet us in Christian service, we find this influence widening, and behold cheering signs of the coming of that bright day in which all the ends of the earth shall see his salvation, and the assurance of the angel Gabriel to Mary be fully realized (Luke i. 32, 33). Let us make room for One who comes with such eager gladness to bind up the world's wounds, and to pour into them the balm of his healing love. Let us yield to his holy and heavenly ministerings, and cast ourselves upon his loving, gentle care. True happiness and peace shall then be ours. The path of usefulness shall open out before us here, and in the day of his complete triumph we shall be sharers with him in his victory, and when his glory shall be revealed we also shall be glad with exceeding joy (1 Pet. iv. 13).

Vers. 5, 6.—"*The Prince of Peace.*" Solomon as well as David was a type of Christ; and just as Micah, when he said (ver. 4), "He shall stand and feed," etc., probably thought of the shepherd-youth, raised to the throne of Israel, as typical of Israel's spiritual King, who would eventually appear and bring heavenly strength and succour to a needy world, so when he added respecting the Messiah, "*And this Man shall be the Peace,*" he thought of the peaceful rule of Solomon, and saw in this a symbol of that spiritual tranquillity which the Christ, the greater than Solomon, should, through his appearing, bring to human hearts, and ultimately to the world at large. And the same characteristic of the Messiah was present to the mind of Isaiah, and found expression in one of the titles employed by him in that remarkable cluster of designations (see Isa. ix. 6), so rich in spiritual significance—"*The Prince of Peace.*" The text applies to—

I. THE DISTRACTIONS WHICH ARISE TO US IN OUR PERSONAL LIFE. 1. In our *sinfulness* we find peace in Christ. Sin is attended by distraction. It separates from God, the true Source of rest. It creates inward disquiet; for whilst when we do right conscience approves, "in whisper gentle and secret, like the murmur of a brook beneath the foliage," yet when we do wrong its accusations prey upon the spirit as with a fever's strength. And there is no deliverance from all this disquietude but in Christ (Matt. xi. 28; Rom. v. 1). 2. In our *sorrowfulness* we find peace in Christ. He traverses the stormy seas of sorrow, and these adverse waves obey his voice. Amidst all the strifes and struggles of our life occasioned by our darker experiences he can give our spirits rest. Though in the world we must have tribulation, yet in him we have peace. 3. In our *intellectual questionings and doubtings* we find peace in Christ. The spirit of inquiry is rife in this age. Increased light is being shed upon various questions, and may necessitate the laying aside of opinions and forms of thought long cherished. But, amidst this shaking and uprooting, the historical Christ remains, and his words, so charmingly simple and clear, so confident and reassuring, abide for ever. And reposing with childlike trust in him and in his utterances, in which he has revealed to us the true way of life here, and has assured us of a blessed immortality with him hereafter, all mental unrest ceases, and our minds stayed thus shall ever be kept at perfect rest. "And this Man shall be the Peace."

II. THE DIFFERENCES WHICH PREVAIL BETWEEN CHRISTIAN COMMUNITIES. 1. *From within.* There will be such differences. Truth is many-sided, and our mental constitution varies. But amidst these diversities there is a centre of unity—*Christ himself.* Sharing his spirit, and being under the inspiration of his love, men become united in heart, and, despite their differences, are made one through the possession of a common life and love. This is the true unity, the being one in life, and therefore in spirit, aim, endeavour, and in sympathy with our Father who is in heaven, and with his Christ, who came to save his people from all selfishness and sin, and to establish a universal brotherhood amongst men. It was for this that the great Intercessor prayed in his memorable high-priestly prayer (John xvii. 21). 2. *From without.* Vers. 5 and 6 clearly refer to assaults from without. Whether we take the reference to Assyria metaphorically or literally, the allusion must be to external attacks. And God in Christ is the Refuge and Strength of his Church, and amidst these will keep her in perfect peace whilst she rests in him (Ps. xlvi.).

III. THE CONFLICTS BETWEEN NATIONS. It is mournful to reflect upon the method adopted, even by civilized and enlightened nations, in order to settle the disputes which arise between them. The appeal is made to the arbitrament of the sword. The heart sickens at the very thought of the battle-field, with all the suffering and desolation connected with it, and yearns with ardent desire for the coming of that bright day of God in which such strife shall cease. And our assurance of its coming rests upon Christ. Peace is a distinguishing characteristic of his holy gospel, which shall at length universally be accepted (Jas. iii. 17; Gal. v. 22), and the acceptance of which shall be followed by peoples dwelling in amity and concord (Isa. xi. 6—9; ch. iv. 3). Christ's disciples should be eminently distinguished by this spirit of peace. No contentious jarring spirit, out of tune, and hence marring the harmony of the concert, should be found amongst them, but all their voices should be in agreement, thus producing the sweetest music (Ps. cxxxiii.).

Vers. 7—15.—*The spiritual influence of good men symbolized.* By "the remnant of Jacob" is intended the good who were to be found in the land of Judah; for in the most corrupt times God has ever had a people to show forth his praise. The expression may be taken as descriptive of good, holy, spiritual men; and it is here declared that these shall exert among the nations a gracious influence. Notice—

I. THE SPIRITUAL INFLUENCE OF GOOD MEN IS HERE SET FORTH BY MEANS OF SYMBOLS. 1. This is likened to the influence of *the dew and the rain* (ver. 7). The symbol is suggestive of the preservative influence of the good. We know what a wasteful, scorching drought means to the natural world. Hills and dales, fields and downs, are arrayed in robes of sorrow. Branches that were covered with leaves have become "withered sprays." Meadows that were clothed with grass have become converted into "short, unmowed hay." Flocks once skipping about are pining through hunger and thirst. Earth's fruits are become "abortive," and her clods "stark and dry." Clouds of dust sweep over her plains, and from her banks the river seems to shrink. And thus desolate spiritually had the world been but for the influence of good men. Between the time of "the early and latter rains" vegetable life in Palestine was entirely dependent upon the dew. It was this which kept vegetation from becoming dry and withered, and preserved the land from drought and desolation. And even so the influence of good men in the world is preservative. Bad as the world is to-day morally and spiritually, it is not so bad as it would have been save for the influence exerted by those who are under the motive force of pure and holy principles. This preservative influence of the good is silent, quiet, noiseless in its operation. How gentle is the dew, and how copious when all is calm and tranquil! And how gently the rain falls from heaven in the refreshing shower, penetrating deeply into the thirsty land! There is suggested quiet power, yet very effectual withal. So is it with the influence of the good. In the olden time here referred to, when princes and nobles, priests and prophets, had corrupted their way, a remnant was to be found among the people, unknown ones for the most part, but who nevertheless by their holy virtues and heavenly graces kept piety alive, and whose influence upon society was as that of the dew upon the parched, needy ground. So shall it ever be that our God shall not be left without faithful witnesses to honour and glorify his great Name. 2. The other symbol employed here is that of *the lion* (vers. 8, 9). This suggests the thought of courage, boldness, fearlessness, together with destructive strength and might. "The remnant of Jacob" are ever such as dare to do right, who resolutely follow their convictions, who possess a strong sense of justice and rectitude, and who act upon this at all risks and costs. They "trust in God and do the right." They are unyielding where true principle is at stake. "The wicked fleeth," etc. (Prov. xxviii. 1). And ultimately the victory is with such.   The unprincipled shall be subdued and go down before them, as surely as sheep yield before the beasts of the forest.

II. THIS MORAL AND SPIRITUAL INFLUENCE OF GOOD MEN THUS SET FORTH IS DIVINELY DERIVED.   It cometh *"from the Lord"* (ver. 7).   He alone can impart to us the quiet, refreshing, reinvigorating power typified by the dew and the showers; and he alone can make us valiant in the maintenance and defence of truth and righteousness.   We need hence to be found constantly looking unto him, that, divinely strengthened and sustained, it may be manifest that we belong to "the remnant" through whom it is his purpose to fertilize and bless the world.

III. IN ORDER TO THIS BENEFICENT INFLUENCE BEING EXERTED THERE MUST BE PURITY OF HEART AND SEPARATION FROM EVIL.   (Vers. 10—14.)   God's ancient people were placed in the most favourable circumstances for being the medium of good to other nations and tribes; but, forgetful of their "high calling," they yielded to the contaminating influences of the world around, and even exceeded the heathen nations in the practice of sin, and hence their honour was laid in the dust, and they were threatened with national decay.   And for the comfort of "the remnant" the assurance was given that there should be brought about the purification of the Church (vers. 10—14).   True spiritual influence is ever the outcome of true spiritual excellence. Would we be influential for good, we must "follow after holiness."   We must be watchful over our lips that we offend not with our tongues.   All self-seeking, strifes, jealousies, must be put away from us.   "Let every one that nameth," etc. (2 Tim. ii. 19).   Then "God will bless us," and through us others (Ps. lxvii.).

IV. THIS SPIRITUAL INFLUENCE SHALL ULTIMATELY PREVAIL.   (Ver. 15.)   Whilst evil sometimes appears victorious, the cause of truth and righteousness shall finally triumph.   This chapter, which begins with declaring the coming of "the Babe of Bethlehem," ends with a solemn declaration of the final discomfiture of all who oppose the sway of this "Ruler in Israel" (ver. 15).   Array not yourselves "against the Lord and his Anointed."   His foes shall become his footstool.   "Kiss the Son" (Ps. ii. 12).

HOMILIES BY VARIOUS AUTHORS.

Ver. 2.—*A new David: the lowliness and majesty of the Messiah.*   Thoughts respecting the lowliness of the Messiah cluster around the reference to his birthplace. Bethlehem was so small and unimportant that it was "little to be among the thousands of Israel."   It was like one of our *hamlets*, not even attaining to the dignity of a *parish.*   From this village there went forth a youth unknown to fame, and almost unnoticed among his own kindred (1 Sam. xvi. 11; Ps. lxxviii. 70, 71).   Even after the establishment of David on the throne, his birthplace was allowed to remain in its former insignificance; or, if honoured for a time, sank into obscurity again (as Micah testifies), just as the royal family of David itself sank into such a low estate that it could be compared to the stump of a tree cut down and giving little promise of a renewed vigorous vitality (Isa. xi. 1).   This lowly condition of both the home and the house of David corresponds to the debased condition of the Jewish Church at the time of the advent.   It was "despised," "hated," "afflicted" (Isa. lx. 14, 15).   In that hamlet Jesus, the Christ, was born.   Now note the contrasts that have followed.   1. Bethlehem has become one of the most notable places in the world—a theme for poets, a subject for artists, a goal for pilgrims.   Its names have received a new and higher significance.   Bethlehem has become a "house of bread" for a dying world; Ephratah has been "fruitful" in the richest blessings for the human race.   2. The family of David is now, through Jesus Christ, the most exalted family of the earth.   Contrast the Ptolemies, Cæsars, and other royal names.   3. The Jewish Church sprang to a new life.   It has taken a place of supreme influence among the nations, not simply through Christ himself, but through the works and writings of his apostles and evangelists.   Great as these blessings are already, we shall see greater things than these.   "The kingdom" shall be restored, "yea, the former dominion shall come" (ch. iv. 8).   For ages there had been "no king" (ch. iv. 9), at the best only a temporary "judge" (ver. 1).   Israel still held as its ideal king *David the great.*   Its ideal should be more than realized.   A new David shall come forth "unto me," and in

God's Name and strength shall rule (ver. 4). Victory is promised under figures suggested
by existing foes (vers. 5—9). In those spiritual triumphs of Jesus Christ we shall see
the fulfilment of the predictions of his everlasting dominion. And in these victories of
grace his nation will take a share, and will be still further glorious in the eyes of God
and man (Isa. lx., lxvi., etc.). The prediction of a Ruler so mighty, yet of such lowly
origin, prepares for the description of a still greater glory. And the fact of the power
and influence in the world of the Babe of Bethlehem prepares us to receive, nay, more,
requires us to believe in, *his Divine dignity.* The "coming forth" from Bethlehem can
only be explained by previous "goings forth." These words declare: (1) The pre-
existence of the Messiah (John viii. 58). (2) His previous manifestations and operations—in creation (John i. 3), providence (Col. i. 17; Heb. i. 3), and as the Divine
Angel of Jehovah (Gen. xviii., etc.). (3) Eternal existence. Because thou art "from
everlasting," therefore "thou art God" (Ps. xc. 2; John i. 1). Nothing but the truth
of the Deity of Christ can explain the predictions of him or unlock the mysteries of his
character and his life. The more lowly his origin and all the facts of his earthly life,
the more inexplicable his present majesty, unless we acknowledge him as personally
Divine.—E. S. P.

Vers. 7—9.—*The gentleness and terribleness of the people of God.* "The remnant of
Jacob" is the faithful few who remain loyal to God's truth and the duty of the day,
whether in the times of Elijah (1 Kings xix. 18), Uzziah (Isa. i. 9), or Christ (Rom.
xi. 5). The people of God, the Church of Christ dispersed among the "peoples" of the
earth, have a twofold aspect—*gentleness* and *terribleness.* This twofold aspect is seen
in God (Exod. xxxiv. 6, 7; Ps. xviii. 25, 26; Isa. viii. 13, 14), in Christ (Isa. xxviii.
16; Matt. xxi. 42—44; Luke ii. 34), who is both a "Lamb" and a "Lion;" and
therefore in his people who are called into fellowship with himself. They are—
I. GENTLE TO BLESS. Notice the figures. 1. "*A dew from the Lord.*" The dew is
of heavenly origin, and comes fresh from the hand of God (Job xxxviii. 28; cf. John
i. 13; iii. 3, "from above"), reflecting God's light, transparent and glistering (cf. Matt.
v. 16; 2 Cor. i. 12; Phil. ii. 15, 16), evanescent and apparently one of the frailest of
nature's forces, yet powerful to quicken and sustain life that would otherwise perish
(cf. 1 Cor. i. 26—28; iv. 15; 2 Cor. iv. 12; Jas. v. 19, 20). Such spiritual qualifications in individuals made the Church of Christ a life-giving power. Issuing from
Judæa, Christ's disciples were as dew to the parched and perishing Roman world, both
by their teaching (Deut. xxxii. 2) and still more by the testimony of the wondrous
beauty of their lives (Ps. cxxxiii. 3). Therefore they were scattered abroad—John
to Asia, Thomas to India, Paul to Rome, etc.—that the life-giving dew might be conveyed to the distant "peoples" of the earth. 2. "*The showers upon the grass.*" Christ
"shall come down like rain," etc. (Ps. lxxii. 6), not only by his individual blessings,
but through his people. Like the rain, they "tarried not for man." Once the vision
was seen and the appeal heard before the mission was commenced (Acts xvi. 9); yet
even then, as elsewhere, the prophecy was fulfilled in the disciples as well as the
Master, "I am found of them that sought me not" (Isa. lxv. 1). Nor did they
depend upon or "wait for the sons of men" (1 Cor. iii. 5—7). By both proclaiming
and living God's Word they became identified with the promise, and sharers in the
blessing of the old Messianic predictions (Gen. xxii. 18; Isa. lv. 10, 11).
II. TERRIBLE TO VANQUISH OR DESTROY. Courage and fearlessness are implied, such
as were promised (Luke xxi. 15) and enjoyed (Acts iv. 13—21; v. 29—42, etc.). But
the lion is not always on the defensive. The Church of Christ, with its new doctrines,
maxims, morals, and threats of a wrath to come, was terrible to the pagan world of the
first century, with its foul gods, its godless creeds, its nameless immoralities, its
revolting cruelties and crimes. The contrast of the "dew" and the "lion" may be
marked even in the apostles' teaching both to heathen and to professing Christians
(Acts xvii. 24—31; xxiv. 24, 25; 2 Cor. v. 11, 20; xiii. 1—11; 2 Thess. i. 6—10).
Its one object was to vanquish souls by destroying sin and bringing them into
captivity to Christ. It trod down its foes and "went forth conquering and to
conquer" (cf. Acts xxi. 20; Rom. xv. 19; 2 Cor. ii. 14), till, less than two hundred
years later, Tertullian could speak of the Christians thus: "We are but of yesterday,
and we have filled every place among you—cities, islands, fortresses, towns, market-

places, the very camp, tribes, companies, palace, senate, forum ; we have left nothing to you but the temples of your gods " ('Apology,' c. 38). In a similar way the Church of the Reformation was terrible to the corruptions of the papacy, which it sought to " tear in pieces " with weapons not carnal, but spiritual. And to-day the true Church of Christ, with its lofty standards and ideals, is hateful to the world with its maxims of expediency and fraud, its sins and shams ; and to many also who would claim the sacred name of Christian. Such foes of Christ and his people must submit (Isa. lx. 14) or perish (Isa. lx. 12). The Church of God will at last be terrible in the day of the destruction of those who love darkness rather than light, and who will be driven away in their wickedness. " The saints shall judge the world " (1 Cor. vi. 3 ; Jude 14, 15 ; Rev. xix. 11—15) ; " Let thine hand be lifted up," etc. (ver. 9).—E. S. P.

Ver. 2.—*The promise of Messiah.* "But thou, Bethlehem Ephratah, though thou be little among the thousands of Judah, yet out of thee shall he come forth unto me that is to be Ruler in Israel ; whose goings forth have been from of old, from everlasting." This is one of the most definite of the Messianic prophecies. In the previous verse Micah foretells a period of deep degradation. The people of God would troop together before the invader, as sheep huddle together before a snowstorm. All resistance would prove vain. The judge would be smitten on the cheek, *i.e.* righteous rule and self-rule would perish. But when things were at their worst a new Ruler would arise. He would come, not from the city of Jerusalem, but from the village of Bethlehem, so small a place that it was never reckoned amongst "the thousands" (the chief divisions of the tribe) of Judah. Yet he who came from that obscure birthplace would be " he whose goings forth have been from of old, from everlasting." This prophecy was universally regarded as applicable to the Messiah. It was quoted by the scribes in their reply to Herod (Matt. ii. 6) ; and at a later period, when it was popularly supposed that Jesus was of Nazareth, it was used as an argument against those who believed him to be the Christ (John vii. 42, etc.).

I. WHENCE CAME THE PROMISED KING ? 1. *In his origin he is Divine.* "His goings forth," etc. The prophet and the New Testament concur in asserting the pre-existence and Divinity of our Lord. Jehovah, speaking through the prophet, says, " he shall come forth unto *me*," *i.e.* as a son is born to his father ; and the disciples heard a voice from heaven, saying, "This is my beloved Son," etc. Micah says, "His goings forth have been from of old ; " and in harmony with this John declares, " In the beginning was the Word," etc. Divinity was a necessity to the Redeemer-King. He could not save humanity if he was simply part of it. He could not suffer as the spotless Lamb of God if it was true of him as of us, "Behold, I was shapen in iniquity," etc. In order to assume a true humanity he was " born of a woman ; " but the active cause of his earthly being was not in man, but in God. Hence Gabriel said, " That holy thing that shall be born of thee shall be called the Son of the Highest." "The Word was made flesh," etc. Signs of his Divine origin may be seen in the accompaniments oi his birth—the angels' song ; the effect of the emperor's edict in bringing Joseph and Mary to Bethlehem ; the star seen in the east ; the Scripture evidence (Matt. ii. 6) unwittingly adduced by the scribes ; the general expectation which presaged the advent, as the fragrance of the spice islands foretells to the sailor that they are near. The Babe of Bethlehem was the Son of God. 2. *In his birth he was human.* In spite of its association with David and with Ruth, Bethlehem never became great. From the first God chose "things despised." To a people like the Jews, to whom names were never without significance, these in the text would be suggestive. *Bethlehem,* the " House of bread," was the birthplace of him who spoke of himself as "the Bread of life" (John vi.). *Ephratah,* the old and still the poetic name of the village, signifying "the Fruit-field," was connected with him who was the Seed-corn of the world's life (John xii. 24). Had he been born in Jerusalem, an earthly policy might have sought to use him ; but being born in Bethlehem, only loyal hearts welcomed him ; so that the cradle, like the cross, tested men. Further, had Jerusalem been his birthplace, it might have been considered the world-centre of his kingdom, which we know is "not of this world."

II. WHAT IS THE NATURE OF HIS RULE? 1. *He reigns by lawful right.* If he is "from everlasting," we should approach him with reverence. Insistence on Christ's humanity has been of advantage in making him less a theological abstraction, and more manifestly our Brother; but there is some danger of our forgetting his royal dignity. The familiar expressions, "dear Jesus," "my Jesus," etc., are too lightly used of our Lord. Nor are we justified in speaking of him as one superior to other teachers merely in his moral excellence and mental power. Ours should be the reverence of Thomas, who exclaimed, "My Lord and my God!" 2. *He reigns by the power of love.* Because he will only rule thus he lost, and is losing, an earthly kingdom. If he appeared in the glory of his power, defiance would break down, hesitation would cease. Yet he is satisfied that instead of this men should be stirred by an exhortation the effect of which may soon pass. Why? Because he only cares for willing service; he would not weaken moral responsibility, and would only have that sway which is deepest and widest, because truest. His is not the power of a tyrant who is repressing by force the aspirations of his people, but the influence of a father who bids his child do something which he is free to leave undone, though he is confident the child, for love's sake, will do more than he says. 3. *He reigns for the welfare of his people.* Note the association of "feed" and "rule" in Scripture. David had training for the exercise of royal power, and at the same time saw a type of it, in his care for the sheep at Bethlehem. Show how Christ used the figure of the shepherd to denote his work and sacrifice. Contrast his reign and its issues with that of many an earthly monarch.

III. WHO ARE THE SUBJECTS OF HIS SWAY? Not always those whom we should expect. Not the scribes, with their knowledge and preparation and responsibility as religious leaders. Not the Jewish people, who did not find their expectations fulfilled in the Babe of Bethlehem, the Lad of Nazareth, the Prophet of Galilee. "He came unto his own, and his own received him not." Who are the "Israel" now—heirs of the promises? The men who have come from a far country like the Magians, because they seek holiness and truth; the women like Mary, whose hearts are big with hope of "sweeter manners, purer laws;" the children who pray with all their hearts, "Thy kingdom come;" the busy men like Joseph, who are struggling with temptation, and wanting help and hope outside themselves; the sinful and outcasts, who find rest at Jesus' feet, etc. These are the heirs of Jacob, who at Bethel gained his name "Israel;" for they see in Christ the ladder that reaches heaven, though its foot rests on earth; they pledge themselves to serve him, and in agonizing prayer say, "I will not let thee go, except thou bless me."

CONCLUSION. May we have given to us of God some thought which shall be to us what the star in the East was to the Wise Men, that we may say, "Where is he who is born to be King? for *we* have seen his star . . . and have come to worship him"!—A. R.

Ver. 1.—*The Church of God.* "Now gather thyself in troops, O daughter of troops: he hath laid siege against us: they shall smite the judge of Israel with a rod upon the cheek." The prophet, as if fearful that his previous promises would be somewhat too reassuring, so that the people would lose the due impression of the perils to which they would be exposed, here reminds them of the calamities which would befall them before the promised prosperity would be realized. "O daughter of troops!" Jerusalem was so called on account of the numerous troops that it possessed. "He hath laid siege against us." That is, the enemy hath—the invading army. "He shall smite the judge of Israel with a rod upon the cheek." Zedekiah, the judge or king of Israel (Amos ii. 3), was so insulted by the Chaldeans as if he had been smitten on the cheeks. To smite on the cheek was esteemed by the Orientals the greatest affront. This insult, we know, was offered by the nation to him who is the "Prince of the kings of the earth." "I gave my back to the smiters, and my cheek to them that plucked out the hair. I hid not my face from shame and spitting" (Isa. l. 6). It is perfectly legitimate to take these words as a symbolical portrait of the Church of God. Look at it—

I. AS MILITANT IN ITS CHARACTER. Jerusalem is addressed as "daughter of troops." As Jerusalem was a military city, containing a great body of soldiers within her walls, so is the Church on earth; it is military. The life of all true men here is a battle; all are soldiers, bound to be valiant for the truth. They are commanded to fight the good fight, to war the good warfare. They are to "wrestle not against flesh and blood, but against principalities and powers, and spiritual wickedness in high places." The warfare is *spiritual, righteous, indispensable, personal.* No one can fight the battle by proxy.

II. As PERILOUS IN ITS POSITION. "He hath laid siege against us." The dangerous condition of Jerusalem, when the Chaldean army surrounded its walls in order to force an entrance, is only a faint shadow of the perilous position of the Church of God. It is besieged by mighty hosts of errors and evil passions, and mighty lusts that "war against the soul." Hosts of enemies are encamped round every human soul. The siege is planned with strategic skill and with malignant determination. How it becomes every spirit to be on its watch-tower, fully armed for the fight of defence! "Wherefore take unto you the whole armour of God," etc. (Eph. vi. 13).

III. As INSULTED BY ITS ENEMIES. "They shall smite the judge of Israel with a rod upon the cheek." Were the enemies of Christianity ever more insolent than in this age? And their insolence, we regret to state, has been encouraged by the brainless utterances and doings of religious fanatics. The argumentative opponents of conventional evangelicism seem to me more insulting in their spirit and behaviour than ever.

IV. As SUMMONED TO ACTION. "Now gather thyself in troops." The men of Jerusalem are here commanded by Heaven to marshal their troops and to prepare for battle, since the enemies are outside their walls. Far more urgent is the duty of the Church to collect, arrange, and concentrate all its forces against the mighty hosts that encompass it. "Let us not sleep as do others;" "let us quit ourselves like men," etc. "Gather thyself in troops."

> "Sounds the trumpet from afar!
> Soldiers of the holy war,
> Rise! for you your Captain waits;
> Rise! the foe is at the gates.
>
> "Arm! the conflict has begun:
> Fight! the battle must be won;
> Lift the banner to the sky,
> Wave its blazing folds on high."

D. T.

Ver. 2.—*Christ.* "But thou, Bethlehem Ephratah, though thou be little among the thousands of Judah, yet out of thee shall he come forth unto me that is to be Ruler in Israel; whose goings forth have been from of old, from everlasting." For the sake of continuity we here transfer thoughts on this passage which have appeared before. Our subject is Christ, and the text leads us to consider—

I. HIS BIRTH AS THE SON OF MAN. Two remarks are suggested here. 1. *He was born in obscurity.* "But thou, Bethlehem," etc. Bethlehem Ephratah, where Jacob says, "Rachel died by me in the land of Canaan in the way, when yet there was but a little way to come into Ephrath: . . . the same is Bethlehem" (Gen. xlviii. 7), or Bethlehem-Judah, so called to distinguish it from Bethlehem in Zebulon. It is a few miles south-west of Jerusalem. Bethlehem means "the House of bread;" Ephrath means "Fruitful;" both names referring to the fertility of the region. "Though thou be little among"—though thou be scarcely large enough to be reckoned among, etc. It was insignificant in size and population, so that in Josh, xv. 21 it is not enumerated among the cities of Judah; nor in the list in Neh. xi. 25. Under Rehoboam it became a city (2 Chron. xi. 6). "He built even Bethlehem." The scribes' quotation of Micah, in answer to Herod's inquiry prompted by the Wise Men of the East, who asked, "Where is he that is born King of the Jews?" (Matt. ii. 6), seems to contradict Micah, "thou art not the least," but the contradiction is only seeming. What is meant in Matthew is that though "thou art least in worldly importance, thou art morally greatest, inasmuch as thou art the birthplace of the Messiah." Why was this Illustrious One thus born in such obscurity? He had what no other man ever had—the power of selecting his own parentage and birthplace. He might have been born of royalty and nursed in a palace. No doubt there was the highest reason for this. It was a protest to the ages against the popular and influential opinion that human dignity consists in birth and ancestral distinctions. 2. *He was born according to Divine plan.*

"Out of thee shall he come forth unto me." Unto whom? Jehovah. The *fact* of his birth, the *scene* of his birth, the *object* of his birth, were all according to a Divine plan. "He shall be called Great, and . . . the Son of the Highest." "Behold my Servant, whom I uphold, mine Elect, in whom my soul delighteth." "He shall come forth unto me" (1) according to my will; (2) to do my will. 3. *He was born to an empire.* "To be Ruler in Israel." He is the Prince of Peace, on whose shoulder the government is laid. He is a Ruler. Not a *temporal* ruler; temporal rule is but a shadow. He is to rule thought, intelligence, soul. He is the greatest king who governs mind; and no one has obtained such a government over mind as he who, eighteen centuries ago, "came forth out of Bethlehem Ephratah." His kingdom is increasing every day. "Gird thy sword upon thy thigh, O most mighty," etc. Speed the time when the "kingdoms of this world shall become the kingdoms of our Lord and of his Christ," etc.

II. His history as the Son of God. "Whose goings forth have been from of old, from everlasting," or, as Delitzsch says, "whose goings forth are from olden time, from the days of eternity." Micah does not announce here the eternal generation of the Son from the Father, or of the Logos from God, the *generatio Filii æterna*, as the earlier orthodox commentators suppose. Eternal generation, humanly speaking, is a theological fiction, a philosophical absurdity. He who was before all time. "I was set up from everlasting;" "In the beginning was the Word;" "He was fore-ordained before the foundation of the world, but was manifested in these last times;" "Glorify thou me with thine own self, with the glory which I had with thee;" "Whose goings forth have been of old, from everlasting." "Goings forth!" What for? To furnish immensity with innumerable worlds, and to people them with sentient and intelligent beings, to participate in the infinite bountihood of God. As the Son of God, he never has had a beginning and has always been active. "The Father worketh hitherto, and I work." His activity explains the origin and phenomena of the universe. "By him were all things created."

> "Oh, who can strive
> To comprehend the vast, the awful truth
> Of the eternity that hath gone by,
> And not recoil from the dismaying sense
> Of human impotence? The life of man
> Is summed in birthdays and in sepulchres;
> But the eternal God hath no beginning;
> He hath no end. Time had been with him
> For everlasting, ere the Dœdal world
> Rose from the gulf in loveliness. Like him
> It knew no source; like him 'twas uncreate.
> What is it, then? The past eternity!"
>
> D. T.

Vers. 3, 4.—*Christ as the great Shepherd of mankind.* "Therefore will he give them up, until the time that she which travaileth hath brought forth: then the remnant of his brethren shall return unto the children of Israel. And he shall stand and feed in the strength of the Lord, in the majesty of the Name of the Lord his God; and they shall abide: for now shall he be great unto the ends of the earth." "Therefore will he give them up, until the time when a travailing woman hath brought forth: and the remnant of his brethren will return, together with the sons of Israel. And he will stand and feed in the strength of Jehovah, in the majesty of the Name of Jehovah his God; and they will dwell: for now will he be great to the ends of the earth" (Delitzsch). The following quotation from Delitzsch on this passage we think the best commentary: "Therefore (*lâkhēn*), *i.e.* because the great Divine Ruler of Israel, from whom alone its redemption can proceed, will spring from the little Bethlehem, and therefore from the degraded family of David (Caspari). This is the correct explanation; for the reason why Israel is to be given up to the power of the nations of the world, and not to be rescued earlier, does not lie in the appearance of the Messiah as such, but in his springing from little Bethlehem. The birth of the Messiah in Bethlehem, and not in Jerusalem, the city of David, presupposes that the family of David, out of which it is to spring, will have lost the throne and have fallen into poverty.

This could only arise from the giving up of Israel into the power of its enemies. Micah had already stated clearly enough, in what precedes, that this fate would fall upon the nation and the royal house of David, on account of its apostasy from the Lord; so that he could overlook this here, and give prominence to the other side alone, viz. to the fact that according to the counsel of God the future Deliverer and Ruler of Israel would also resemble his royal ancestor David in the fact that he was not to spring from Zion, the royal city built on high, but from the insignificant country town of Bethlehem, and that for this very reason Israel was to remain so long under the power of the nations of the world." These words may be regarded as presenting to us *Christ as the great Shepherd of mankind ;* and looking at them in this light the following points come up to notice.

I. HIS INTRODUCTION TO THE WORLD AS A SHEPHERD. "Therefore will he give them up [that is, leave them to suffer their calamities], until the time that she which travaileth hath brought forth." Christ came into the world through sufferings that may be fairly represented as parturient. The whole Jewish nation groaned and travailed together until he came; and although the throes of his mother are perhaps specially referred to here, the Hebrew people through all preceding times had struggled in agony in order to give birth to the Messiah. Herein is a mystery—the world's Deliverer came into the world through suffering. And does not all the good we have come out of anguish? Every true enjoyment, like every birth, implies previous pain. "Through much tribulation" we enter into kingdoms. "Our light afflictions, which are but for a moment," etc.

II. HIS QUALIFICATION FOR HIS WORK AS A SHEPHERD. "He shall stand and feed in the strength of the Lord, in the majesty of the Name of the Lord his God." Observe: 1. *His attitude.* "He shall stand." The word "stand" here may mean one of two things—either a commanding position, by which he can *observe* and *direct all,* or *stability,* indicating his endurance and unswerving perseverance. He is settled and fixed in his work as a Shepherd. Both these ideas are true. It is true that Christ, as a Shepherd, has a commanding view of all, and a controlling power over all; and it is also true that he stands immovable as a Shepherd. "He shall not fail nor be discouraged, until he hath set judgment in the earth" (Isa. xlii. 4). 2. *His Divinity.* "In the strength of the Lord, in the majesty of the Name of the Lord his God." He is endowed with the strength of Omnipotence, he is invested with the majesty of God himself. He is "Almighty to save," he is the "Image of the invisible God." Here is a competent Shepherd!

III. HIS BENEFICENCE IN HIS WORK AS A SHEPHERD. He "shall feed in the strength of the Lord." The word "feed" means both "feed" and "rule;" indeed, feed implies rule, for human souls can scarcely be nourished without a wise and merciful control. "He shall feed his flock like a shepherd : he shall gather the lambs with his arm, and carry them in his bosom, and shall gently lead those that are with young" (Isa. xl. 11); "They shall not hunger nor thirst, neither shall the heat or the sun smite them; for he that hath mercy on them shall lead them, even by the springs of water shall he guide them" (Isa. xlix. 10).

IV. THE EXTENSION OF HIS FAME ON THE EARTH AS A SHEPHERD. "For now shall he be great unto the ends of the earth." His authority on the earth as a spiritual Shepherd is limited to-day, but is wider than it has been; and it will widen and widen until it fills the earth. His Name will one day be above every name on the earth. All other names will be esteemed as mean and contemptible unless they reflect his.

CONCLUSION. "All we like sheep have gone astray," etc. But a Shepherd from heaven has come to seek and restore us. Would that all heard and responded to his voice! "Come unto me, all that are weary and heavy laden."

> "Good Shepherd, hasten thou that glorious day,
> When we shall all in the one fold abide with thee for aye!"

D. T.

Vers. 5, 6.—*An invasion.* "And this Man shall be the Peace, when the Assyrian shall come into our land: and when he shall tread in our palaces, then shall we raise against him seven shepherds, and eight principal men. And they shall waste the land of Assyria with the sword, and the land of Nimrod in the entrances thereof: thus shall he deliver us from the Assyrian, when he cometh into our land, and when he treadeth within our borders." "And this same shall be the peace when the Assyrian shall invade our land, and tread our palaces, we will raise against him seven shepherds, and eight anointed men. And they shall afflict the land of Assyria with the sword, and the land of Nimrod at the entrances thereof; and there shall be deliverance from the Assyrian, when he shall invade our land, and when he shall tread our borders" (Henderson). Assyria is here made the representative of all the foes of Israel in all ages, who shall see the destruction of all its enemies at the Messiah's appearance. "*Seven shepherds and eight principal men.*" Seven expresses perfection; seven and eight are an idiom for a full and sufficient number. "And they" (that is, these seven and eight shepherds) "shall waste the land of Assyria with the sword, and the land of Nimrod in the entrances thereof." The land of Nimrod means Babylon, including Assyria, to which it extended its borders. "Thus shall he deliver us from the Assyrian, when he cometh into our land." As the Assyrians invade our borders, so shall their own borders and entrances be invaded. "*He.*" Who? The Messiah, mentioned in the fifth verse, "This Man shall be the Peace." We have here two things.

I. A TERRIBLE INVASION. The Assyrian, which, as we have said, may be regarded as the representative of all the enemies of Israel, enters the Holy Land, takes Jerusalem, and treads in the "palaces" of the chosen people. A faint picture is the Assyrian of the hellish invader of human souls. He breaks his way through all bulwarks, enters the sacred territory, and treads even in the palaces of the intellect and heart. Satan is a strong man armed, that enters the human soul and "keepeth his palace." Moral invasion is the worst of all invasions.

II. A TRIUMPHANT DEFENDER. There are "seven shepherds, and eight principal men" who now hurled back the Assyrian invader, entered his own territory, and carried war into the midst. Who is the Deliverer? "This Man shall be the Peace." The Man mentioned in the preceding verses, "whose goings forth have been of old, from everlasting." He did it. 1. *He did it successfully.* "Thus shall he deliver us from the Assyrian." "When a strong man armed keepeth his palace, his goods are in peace: but when a stronger than he shall come upon him, and overcome him, he taketh from him all his armour wherein he trusted, and divideth his spoils." Christ will one day ruin this moral Assyrian; as "lightning falleth from heaven he shall fall." He will hurl him from the habitation of men. 2. *Christ, in doing this, uses human instrumentality.* "Seven shepherds, and eight principal men." Christ destroys the works of the devil by the instrumentality of men. (1) The instrumentality that he employs may seem to us very feeble. "Seven shepherds, and eight principal men," against unnumbered hosts of the enemies. "He chooseth the foolish things of the world to confound the wise," etc. (1 Cor. i. 27). (2) Though the instrumentality may seem feeble, it was sufficient. The work was done. "Not by might, nor by power, but by my Spirit, saith the Lord" (Zech. iv. 6).—D. T.

Vers. 7—9.—*God's people, their tender and terrible aspect in the world.* "And the remnant of Jacob shall be in the midst of many people as a dew from the Lord, as the showers upon the grass, that tarrieth not for man, nor waiteth for the sons of men." Two things are here predicted concerning the Jews after their restoration from Babylon. 1 Their influence upon the nations would be *as refreshing dew.* "Their signal victories against such formidable armies, attracting attention to him whom they worshipped, and to whom they ascribed their success. During the existence of the new Jewish state, the members of the theocracy had much intercourse with foreigners, multitudes of whom became proselytes to the faith of Jehovah, and were thus prepared to receive the gospel when preached by the apostles" (Henderson). 2. Their power on the nations would be as *terrible as the lion's on the herds of the flock.* It will not, I think, be unfair to use the passage to illustrate the twofold aspect of the people of God in this world—the tender and terrible, the restorative and the destructive. Like Israel of old, godly men in every age have only been a remnant, a very small minority of the generation in which they lived. It will not always be so. Speed the day when they shall become, not merely the majority, but the whole. Notice—

I. THE TENDER ASPECT OF GOD'S PEOPLE IN THE WORLD. They are spoken of here as "dew." *Silent* in its fall, *beautiful* in its appearance, *refreshing* in its influence. Three things are suggested concerning this "dew." 1. *It is Divine.* It is "from the Lord." All that is quickening and refreshing in the thoughts, spirits, character of good men on this earth descends from heaven. "Every good and perfect gift cometh down from the Father of lights," etc. (Jas. i. 17). 2. *It is copious.* "As the showers upon the grass." There have been seasons when those spiritual influences have descended on men with plenitude and power, such as on the Day of Pentecost. Would it were so now! The moral heavens seem, alas! closed, and only a few drops fall here and there. 3. *It is undeserved of men.* "That tarrieth not for man, nor waiteth for the sons of men." Man has something to do in bringing down those moral showers. Though he is powerless to unseal the natural clouds and bring down the rain, these moral showers do not descend altogether independent of his efforts. Good men in this world are to their generation what the gentle dew and the fertilizing shower are to the thirsty earth. Their speech distils as dew and their influence descends on the souls of men like rain upon the new-mown grass.

II. THE TERRIBLE ASPECT OF GOD'S PEOPLE IN THE WORLD. The same men as are represented under the metaphor of dew are here spoken of as a "lion." Bold, terrible, and destructive. Elijah was a lion in his age, so was John the Baptist, so was Luther, so was Latimer, etc. Indeed, every good man has these two aspects, the tender and the terrible—gentle, sympathetic, succouring towards the weak in goodness, but strong in indignation towards wrong wherever found. Christ, the great Model, who did not "cause his voice to be heard in the street," hurled his fulminations on the ears of hypocrites. In truth, love—which is the essence of all goodness—is constantly taking these two forms. The same love which whispers in the softest tones of pity, often comes out in the fiercest thunder and lightning: no wrath is so terrible as the wrath of love. Every good man is like the pillar that guided the children of Israel through the wilderness; it gleamed a guiding light to the Hebrews through the sea, but threw a shadow of confounding darkness to the Egyptians who assayed to follow.

CONCLUSION. This subject suggests: 1. *A picture of the unregenerate world.* There are some germs of goodness in its soil that require the fertilizing influence of Heaven to quicken and develop; and there are some things in it so pernicious and baneful that it requires all the courage, force, and passion of moral lions to destroy. 2. *A picture of the completeness of moral character.* A complete character is not all "dew" or all "lion," but both combined.—D. T.

Vers. 10—15.—*God's depriving dispensation towards men.* "And it shall come to pass in that day, saith the Lord, that I will cut off thy horses out of the midst of thee, and I will destroy thy chariots: and I will cut off the cities of thy land, and throw down all thy strong holds." "The prophet now returns to times near his own, and predicts the beneficial moral changes that were to be effected in the condition of his countrymen by the Babylonish conquest and captivity. They had, contrary to the express command of the Lord (Deut. xvii. 16), kept up a formidable body of cavalry and war-chariots, trusted in their fortified cities, encouraged sorcery, and indulged in abominable idolatry. These were all to be removed when the Jewish state was broken up; and after God had employed the heathen in punishing his apostate people, they in their turn should be punished for their obstinate adherence to idol-worship, notwithstanding the testimony borne against their conduct by the Jews who lived among them." The grand subject of these words is *God's depriving dispensation towards men.* Here the Almighty is represented as taking away from Israel many things they greatly valued—"horses, chariots, cities, soothsayers, witchcrafts, graven images, groves," etc. God's providence deprives as well as bestows. "The Lord gave, the Lord hath taken away." He is constantly taking away from men. In relation to his depriving dispensations I offer two remarks.

I. THEY ARE VERY PAINFUL. The things here referred to were the dearest things to the hearts of Israel. They loved them, they trusted in them, and they would feel life to be perilous, if not intolerable, without them; yet they were to be taken away. The things he takes away are of two classes. 1. The *temporally valuable.* Here chariots and horses and cities are taken away. These are valuable. Whatever is dearest to the heart—property, friends, health, fame—is the most painful to lose. And is not the Almighty constantly, in his providence, taking these things from men? He takes from the rich man his property, the strong man his health, the ambitious man his power, the social man his dearest friends. And such deprivations are the constant sources of human sorrow and anguish. All temporal good must go—chariots, horses, cities, etc. The other class of things he takes away are: 2. The *morally vile.* Here are "witchcrafts, soothsayers, graven images," etc. Whatever man indulges in that is wrong—false worship, all the sorceries of intellectual or physical pleasure—must go, the sooner the better. It is well when all that is morally wrong is taken from us in this world.

II. THEY ARE VERY USEFUL. It is often well to be stripped of temporary good; it is always necessary to be stripped of the morally wrong. All is done in mercy for the soul. God takes away temporal property from a man in order that he may get spiritual wealth; and often does a man's secular fall lead to his spiritual life. He takes away physical health from a man in order that he may get spiritual; and often do the diseases of the body lead to the cure of the soul. Did we understand things thoroughly, see them as we shall when we have done with this mundane system, we should often acknowledge more mercy in God's depriving than in his bestowing providences. Ever should we remember that the great end of all his dealings with us is our spiritual advancement in intelligence, holiness, power, and blessedness. "Lo, all these things worketh God with man, that he may bring him back from the pit in order to enlighten him with the light of the living" (Job xxxiii. 30).

CONCLUSION. Though I know not the future—and no one does—I know that severe depriving providences are ahead, but that mercy underlies the whole.

> "And so beside the silent sea
> I wait the muffled oar;
> No harm from him can come to me
> On ocean or on shore.

> "I know not where his islands lift
> Their fronded palms in air;
> I only know I cannot drift
> Beyond his love and care.

> "And thou, O Lord, by whom are seen
> Thy creatures as they be,
> Forgive me if too close I lean
> My human heart on thee."
>
> (J. G. Whittier.)

D. T.

EXPOSITION.

CHAPTER VI.

Ver. 1—ch. vii. 20.—Part III. In this address, which is later than the preceding parts, the prophet sets forth the way of salvation: PUNISHMENT IS THE CONSEQUENCE OF SIN; REPENTANCE IS THE ONLY GROUND FOR HOPE OF PARTICIPATING IN THE COVENANT MERCIES.

Vers. 1—5.—§ 1. *God's controversy with his people for their ingratitude.*

Ver. 1.—Hear ye now. The whole nation is addressed and bidden to give heed to God's pleading. **Arise, contend thou.** These are God's words to Micah, bidding him put himself in his people's place, and plead as advocate before the great inanimate tribunal. **Before the mountains;** *i.e.* in the presence of the everlasting hills, which have as it were witnessed God's gracious dealings with his people from old time and Israel's long ingratitude (comp. ch. i. 2).

Ver. 2.—Hear ye, O mountains. Insensate nature is called upon as a witness. (For similar appeals, comp. Deut. iv. 26; xxxii. 1; Isa. i. 2; Jer. xxii. 29.) **The Lord's controversy.** So God calls his pleading with his people to show them their sin and thankless unbelief; as he says in Isa. i. 18, "Come, and let us reason together" (comp. Hos. iv. 1; xii. 2). **Ye strong** (*enduring*) **foundations of the earth.** The mountains are called everlasting (Gen. xlix. 26; Deut. xxxiii. 15), as being firm, unchangeable, and as compared with man's life and doings, which are but transitory. The LXX. offers an interpretation as well as a translation, Αἱ φάραγγες θεμέλια τῆς γῆς, " Ye valleys, the foundations of the earth." **With his people.** It is because Israel is God's people that her sin is so heinous, and that God condescends to plead with her. He would thus touch her conscience by recalling his benefits. So in the following verses.

Ver. 3.—**O my people.** The controversy takes the form of a loving expostulation ; and thus in his wonderful condescension Jehovah opens the suit. **What have I done unto thee ?** What has occasioned thy fall from me ? Hast thou aught to accuse me of, that thou art wearied of me ? Have my requirements been too hard, or have I not kept my promises to thee (comp. Isa. xliii. 23, etc. ; Jer. ii. 5)? **Testify.** A judicial term: make a formal defence or reply to judicial interrogatories ; depose (Numb. xxxv. 30) (Pusey).

Ver. 4.—God answers his own question by recounting some of his chief mercies to Israel. He has not burdened the people, but loaded them with benefits. **I brought thee up,** etc. The Exodus was the most wonderful instance of God's intervention ; and to it the prophets often refer (comp. Isa. lxiii. 11, etc. ; Jer. ii. 6 ; Amos ii. 10). **Out of the house of servants ;** *of bondage,* quoting the language of the Pentateuch, to show the greatness of the benefit (Exod. xiii. 3, 14 ; Deut. viii. 14, etc.). **I sent before thee.** As leaders of the Lord's flock (Ps. lxxvii. 20). **Moses,** the inspired leader, teacher, and lawgiver. **Aaron,** the priest, the director of Divine worship. **Miriam,** the prophetess, who led the praises of the people at their great deliverance (Exod. xv. 20), and who probably was charged with some special mission to the women of Israel (see Numb. xii. 1, 2).

Ver. 5.—The Lord reminds the people of another great benefit subsequent to the Exodus, viz. the defeat of the designs of Balak, and the sorceries of Balaam. **Consulted.** United with the elders of Midian in a plot against thee (see Numb. xxii. etc.). **Answered him.** There ought to be a stop here. The answer of Balaam was the blessing which he was constrained to give, instead of the curse which he was hired to pronounce (comp. Josh. xxiv. 10). **From Shittim unto Gilgal.** This is a fresh consideration, referring to mercies under Joshua, and may be made plainer by inserting " remember " (which has, perhaps, dropped out of the text), as in the Revised Version. Shittim was the Israelites' last station before crossing the Jordan, and Gilgal the first in the land of Canaan ; and so God bids them remember all that happened to them between those places—their sin in Shittim and the mercy then shown them (Numb. xxv.),

the miraculous passage of the Jordan, the renewal of the covenant at Gilgal (Josh. v. 9). *Shittim ; the acacia meadow (Abel-Shittim),* hod. *Ghor-es-Seisaban,* was at the south-eastern corner of the *Ciccar,* or Plain of Jordan, some seven miles from the Dead Sea. *Gilgal* (see note on Amos iv. 4). **That ye may know the righteousness** (*righteous acts*) **of the Lord.** All these instances of God's interposition prove how faithful he is to his promises, how he cares for his elect, what are his gracious counsels towards them (see the same expression, Judg. v. 11; 1 Sam. xii. 7).

Vers. 6—8.—§ 2. *The people, awakened to its ingratitude and need of atonement, asks how to please God, and is referred for answer to the moral requirements of the Law.*

Ver. 6.—**It is greatly** doubted who is the speaker here. Bishop Butler, in his sermon " Upon the Character of Balaam," adopts the view that Balak is the speaker of vers. 6 and 7, and Balaam answers in ver. 8. Knabenbauer considers Micah himself as the interlocutor, speaking in the character of the people ; which makes the apparent change of persons in ver. 8 very awkward. Most commentators, ancient and modern, take the questions in vers. 6 and 7 to be asked by the people personified, though they are not agreed as to the spirit from which they proceed, some thinking that they are uttered in self-righteousness, as if the speakers had done all that and more than could be required of them ; others regarding the inquiries as representing a certain acknowledgment of sin and a desire for means of propitiation, though there is exhibited a want of appreciation of the nature of God and of the service which alone is acceptable to him. The latter view is most reasonable, and in accordance with Micah's manner. **Wherewith ;** *i.e.* with what offering ? The prophet represents the congregation as asking him to tell them how to propitiate the offended Lord, and obtain his favour. **Come before :** *go to meet,* appear in the presence of the Lord. Septuagint, καταλάβω, " attain to." **Bow myself before the high God ;** literally, *God of the height,* who has his throne on high (Isa. xxxiii. 5 ; lvii. 15); Vulgate, *curvabo genu Deo excelso ;* Septuagint, ἀντιλήψομαι Θεοῦ μου ὑψίστου, " shall I lay hold of my God most high." **Calves of a year old.** Such were deemed the choicest victims (comp. Exod. xii. 5 ; Lev. ix. 2, 3).

Ver. 7.—**Thousands of rams,** as though the quantity enhanced the value, and tended to dispose the Lord to regard the offerer's thousandfold sinfulness with greater favour. **Ten thousands of rivers** (*torrents,* as in Job xx. 17) of oil. Oil was used in the daily meal offering, and in that which accompanied every burnt offering (see Exod. xxix. 40; Lev. vii. 10—12; Numb. xv. 4, etc.). The Vulgate has a different reading, *In multis millibus hircorum pinguium;* so the Septuagint, ἐν μυριάσι χιμάρων [ἀρνῶν, Alex.] πιόνων, "with ten thousands of fat goats;" so also the Syriac. The alteration has been introduced probably with some idea of making the parallelism more exact. **Shall I give my firstborn?** Micah exactly represents the people's feeling; they would do anything but what God required; they would make the costliest sacrifice, even, in their exaggerated devotion, holding themselves ready to make a forbidden offering; but they would not attend to the moral requirements of the Law. It is probably by a mere hyperbole that the question in the text is asked. The practice of human sacrifice was founded on the notion that man ought to offer to God his dearest and costliest, and that the acceptability of an offering was proportioned to its preciousness. The Hebrews had learned the custom from their neighbours, *e.g.* the Phœnicians and Moabites (comp. 2 Kings iii. 27), and had for centuries offered their children to Moloch, in defiance of the stern prohibitions of Moses and their prophets (Lev. xviii. 21; 2 Kings xvi. 3; Isa. lvii. 5). They might have learned, from many facts and inferences, that man's self-surrender was not to be realized by this ritual; the sanctity of human life (Gen. ix. 6), the substitution of the ram for Isaac (Gen. xxii. 13), the redemption of the firstborn (Exod. xiii. 13), all made for this truth. But the heathen idea retained its hold among them, so that the inquiry above is in strict keeping with the circumstances. **The fruit of my body;** *i.e.* the rest of my children (Deut. xxviii. 4).

Ver. 8.—The prophet answers in his own person the questions in vers. 6 and 7, by showing the worthlessness of outward observances when the moral precepts are not observed. **He hath showed thee;** literally, *one has told thee,* or, *it has been told thee,* i.e. by Moses and in the Law (Deut. x. 12, etc.). Septuagint, Εἰ ἀνηγγέλη σοι; "Hath it not been told thee?" **What doth the Lord require of thee?** The prophets often enforce the truth that the principles of righteous conduct are required from men, and not mere formal worship. This might well be a comfort to the Israelites when they heard that they were doomed to be cast out of their country, and that the temple was to be destroyed, and that the ritual on which they laid such stress would for a time become impracticable. So the inculcation of moral virtues is often connected with the prediction of woe or captivity. (For the prophetic view of the paramount importance of righteousness, see

1 Sam. xv. 22; Ps. xl. 6, etc.; l. 8, etc.; Isa. i. 11—17; Jer. vi. 20; Hos. vi. 6, etc.; see on Zech. vii. 7.) **To do justly.** To act equitably, to hurt nobody by word or deed, which was the exact contrary of the conduct previously mentioned (ch. ii. 1, 2, 8; iii. 2, etc.). **To love mercy.** To be guided in conduct to others by loving-kindness. These two rules contain the whole duty to the neighbour. Compare Christ's description of genuine religion (Matt. xxiii. 23). **To walk humbly with thy God.** This precept comprises man's duty to God, humility and obedience. "To walk" is an expression implying "to live and act," as the patriarchs are said to have "walked with God," denoting that they lived as consciously under his eye and referred all their actions to him. Humility is greatly enforced in the Scriptures (see *e.g.* Isa. ii. 11, etc.). Septuagint, ἕτοιμον εἶναι τοῦ πορεύεσθαι μετὰ Κυρίου, "to be ready to walk with the Lord;" Vulgate, *Solicitum ambulare cum Deo;* Syriac, "Be prepared to follow thy God." But our version is doubtless correct.

Vers. 9—12.—§ 3. *Because Israel was very far from acting in this spirit, God sternly rebukes her for prevailing sins.*

Ver. 9.—**The Lord's voice** (Isa. xxx. 31; Joel ii. 11; Amos i. 2). These are no longer the words of the prophet, but those of God himself, and not spoken in secret, but **unto the city,** that all may hear the sentence who dwell in Jerusalem. **The man of wisdom shall see thy Name;** *i.e.* he who is wise regards thy Name and obeys thee, does not simply hear, but profits by what he hears. The reading is uncertain. Others render, "Blessed is he who sees thy Name;" but the construction is against this. Others, "Thy Name looketh to wisdom" (or prosperity), has the true wisdom of life in sight. The versions read "fear" for "see." Thus the LXX., Σώσει φοβουμένους τὸ Ὄνομα αὐτοῦ, "Shall save those that fear his Name;" Vulgate, *Salus erit timentibus Nomen tuum;* Syriac, "He imparts instruction to those that fear his Name;" Chaldee, "The teachers fear his Name." This reading depends upon a change of vowel-pointing. Orelli renders, "Happy is he who fears thy Name." The Authorized translation, which seems on the whole to be well established, takes the abstract noun "wisdom" as equivalent to "the wise," or "the man of wisdom." For similar expressions, Henderson refers to Ps. cix. 4; Prov. xiii. 6; xix. 15. The prophet parenthetically announces that, however the bulk of the people might receive the message, the truly wise would listen and profit by it. **Hear ye the rod.**

Observe the rod of God's anger, the threatened judgments (so Isa. ix. 4 [3, Hebrew]; x. 5, 24). The power of Assyria is meant, The LXX. renders differently, Ἄκουε φυλή, "Hear, O tribe;" so the Vulgate, *Audite, tribus*. And who hath appointed it. Mark who it is who hath ordained this chastisement. It is from the Lord's hand. Septuagint, Τίς κοσμήσει πόλιν; "Who will adorn the city?" with some reference, perhaps, to Jer. xxxi. 4, "Again shalt thou be adorned with thy tabrets;" Vulgate, *Et quis approbabit illud?* This implies that few indeed will profit by the warning.

Ver. 10.—The reproof is given in the form of questions, in order to rouse the sleeping conscience of the people. Are there yet the treasures of wickedness in the house of the wicked? Do the wicked still continue to bring into their houses treasures obtained by wrong? The old versions compare this ill-gotten wealth to a fire which shall consume the homes of its possessors. Septuagint, Μὴ πῦρ καὶ οἶκος ἀνόμου θησαυρίζων θησαυροὺς ἀνόμους; "Is there fire and the house of the wicked treasuring up wicked treasures?" Vulgate, *Adhuc ignis in domo impii thesauri iniquitatis?* So the Syriac; the Chaldee keeps to the Masoretic reading. The scant measure; literally, *the ephah of leanness*. The ephah was about three pecks. According to Josephus (' Ant.,' xv. 9. 2), it contained one Attic medimnus, which would be nearly a bushel and a half. Fraudulent weights and measures are often denounced (Lev. xix. 35, etc.; Deut. xxv. 14, etc.; Prov. xx. 10, 23; Amos viii. 5). Vulgate, *Mensura minor iræ plena*, where the Hebrew has, that is abominable. Such frauds are hateful to God, and are marked with his wrath.

Ver. 11.—Shall I count them pure? literally, *Shall I be pure?* The clause is obscure. The Authorized Version regards the speaker as the same as in ver. 10, and translates with some violence to the text. It may be that the prophet speaks as the representative of the awakened transgressor, "Can I be guiltless with such deceit about me?" But the sudden change of personification and of state of feeling is very harsh. Hence some follow Jerome in regarding God as the speaker, and rendering, "Shall I justify the wicked balance?" others, the Septuagint, Syriac, and Chaldee, Εἰ δικαιωθήσεται ἐν ζυγῷ ἄνομος; "Shall the wicked be justified by the balance?" Cheyne is inclined to read the verb in the second person, "Canst thou (O Jerusalem) be pure?" since in the next verse the prophet proceeds, "the rich men thereof" (*i.e.* of Jerusalem). If we retain the present reading, "Can I be innocent?" we must consider the question as put, for effect's

sake, in the mouth of one of the rich oppressors. Jerome's translation is contrary to the use of the verb, which is always intransitive in kal.

Ver. 12.—The rich men thereof; *i.e.* of the city mentioned in ver. 9. They have just been charged with injustice and fraud, now they are denounced for practising every kind of violence. And not only the rich, but all the inhabitants fall under censure for lying and deceit. Their tongue is deceitful; literally, *deceit;* they cannot open their mouth without speaking dangerous and destructive lies.

Vers. 13—16.—§ 4. *For all this God threatens punishment.*

Ver. 13.—Will I make thee sick in smiting thee; literally, *have made the smiting thee sick;* i.e. incurable, as Nah. iii. 19, or, "have made the blows mortal that are given thee." The perfect is used to express the certainty of the future. The Septuagint and Vulgate read, "I have begun [or, will begin] to smite thee."

Ver. 14.—Thou shalt eat, etc. The punishment answers to the sin (which proves that it comes from God), and recalls the threats of the Law (Lev. xxvi. 25, etc.; Deut. xxviii. 29, etc.; comp. Hos. iv. 10; Hag. i. 6). Thy casting down shall be in the midst of thee; *i.e.* thy humiliation, thy decay and downfall, shall occur in the very centre of thy wealth and strength, where thou hast laid up thy treasure and practised thy wickedness. But the meaning of the Hebrew is very uncertain, and the text may be corrupt. The LXX. had a different reading, συσκοτάσει ἐν σοι, "darkness shall be in thee." The Syriac and Chaldee interpret the word rendered "casting down" (חשׁ, which is found nowhere else) of some disease like dysentery. It is most suitable to understand this clause as connected with the preceding threat of hunger, and to take the unusual word in the sense of "emptiness." Thus, "Thy emptiness (of stomach) shall remain in thee." Jeremiah (lii. 6) speaks of the famine in the city at the time of its siege. Thou shalt take hold; rather, *thou shalt remove (thy goods)*. This is the second chastisement. They should try to take their goods and families out of the reach of the enemy, but should not be able to save them. The LXX. interprets the verb of escaping by flight. That which thou deliverest. If by chance anything is carried away, it shall fall into the hands of the enemy (comp. 2 Kings xxv. 4, 5; Jer. lii. 7, 8).

Ver. 15.—Here is another judgment in accordance with the threatenings of the Law (Deut. xxviii. 33, 38, etc.; comp. Amos v. 11; Zeph. i. 13; Hag. i. 6). Shalt not reap.

The effect may be owing to the judicial sterility of the soil, but more likely to the incursions of the enemy. Trochon quotes Virgil, ' Ecl.,' i. 70—

" Impius hæc tam culta novalia miles habebit ?
    Barbarus has segetes? en, quo discordia cives
    Produxit miseros ! his nos consevimus agros ! "

Tread the olives. Olives were usually pressed or crushed in a mill, in order to extract the oil; the process of treading was probably adopted by the poor. Gethsemane took its name from the oil-presses there. The oil was applied to the person for comfort, luxury, and ceremony, and was almost indispensable in a hot country. **Sweet wine.** Thou shalt tread the new wine of the vintage, but shalt have to leave it for the enemy (comp. Amos v. 11). The Septuagint has here an interpolation, Καὶ ἀφανισθήσεται νόμιμα λαοῦ μου, " And the ordinances of my people shall vanish away," which has arisen partly from a confusion between Omri, the proper name in the next verse, and *ammi*, " my people."

Ver. 16.—The threatening is closed by repeating its cause : the punishment is the just reward of ungodly conduct. The first part of the verse corresponds to vers. 10—12, the second part to vers. 13—15. **The statutes of Omri.** The statutes are the rules of worship prescribed by him of whom it is said (1 Kings xvi. 25) that he " wrought evil in the eyes of the Lord, and did worse than all that were before him." No special " statutes " of his are anywhere mentioned;

but he is named here as the founder of that evil dynasty which gave Ahab to Israel, and the murderess Athaliah (who is called in 2 Kings viii. 26, " the daughter of Omri ") to Judah. The people keep his statutes instead of the Lord's (Lev. xx. 22). **The works of the house of Ahab** are their crimes and sins, especially the idolatrous practices observed by that family, such as the worship of Baal, which became the national religion (1 Kings xvi. 31, etc.). Such apostasy had a disastrous effect upon the neighbouring kingdom of Judah (2 Kings viii. 18). **Walk in their counsels.** Take your tone and policy from them. **That I should make thee.** " The punishment was as certainly connected with the sin, in the purpose of God, as if its infliction had been the end at which they aimed " (Henderson). The prophet here threatens a threefold penalty, as he had mentioned a threefold guiltiness. **A desolation**; ἀφανισμόν (Septuagint); *perditionem* (Vulgate). According to Keil, " an object of horror," as Deut. xxviii. 37; Jer. xxv. 9. Micah addresses Jerusalem itself in the first clause, its inhabitants in the second, and the whole nation in the last. **An hissing**; *i.e.* an object of derision, as Jer. xix. 8; xxv. 18, etc. **Therefore (and) ye shall bear the reproach of my people.** Ye shall have to hear yourselves reproached at the mouth of the heathen, in that, though ye were the Lord's peculiar people, ye were cast out and given into the hands of your enemies. The Septuagint, from a different reading, renders, Καὶ ὀνείδη λαῶν λήψεσθε, " Ye shall receive the reproaches of nations," which is like Ezek. xxxiv. 29; xxxvi. 6, 15.

HOMILETICS.

Vers. 1—5.—*The memories of the way.* Truly affecting are those portions of Scripture in which God is represented as expostulating and pleading with erring men (Hos. vi. 4; xi. 8; Isa. i. 16—20; Jer. ii. 1—14). The opening verses of this chapter are of the same character. God testifies, and in so doing calls upon the mountains and hills and strong foundations of the earth which have stood from age to age to bear him witness and confirm his testimony (ver. 2). " O my people," he cries, " what have I done unto thee," etc. ? What sadness, what piercing grief, what ineffable sorrow, is implied in these words ! Truly God grieves over sinning men. He is not impassive, but is infinitely sensible to the sins and sorrows of men, and every transgression strikes a pang into the heart of the Divine Father. Surely this sorrow of Divine love over the evils inflicted by man upon himself through sin should lead us back to God in humility, in penitence, and in submission to his authority and will. How remarkable is the faculty of memory, strengthening the affections, aiding progress, increasing enjoyment, and alleviating sorrow ! Well may the poet sing of " the morning star of memory." The prophet desired his people to review the past of their national history, that by these " memories of the way " they might be impelled to " return unto the Lord." Concerning these memories, note—

I. THEIR REMARKABLE VARIETY. There were memories of: 1. *Wondrous deliverances.* From Egyptian bondage (ver. 3); from the curse pronounced by Balaam (ver.

4). 2. *Heavenly guidance.* " I sent before thee Moses " (ver. 4)—the distinguished leader and lawgiver. 3. *Sacred fellowship.* "Aaron" (ver. 4)—their high priest and intercessor, who led them in thought into "the holiest of all." 4. *Grateful adoration.* "Miriam" (ver. 4), with timbrel and dance inspiring them to celebrate in rapturous praise God's redeeming mercy. 5. *Continuous interposition.* "From Shittim unto Gilgal" (ver. 5), *i.e.* from the desert unto the promised land; by miracle, type, prophecy, and promise, they were continually experiencing Divine help and encouragement. So with us; mercies temporal and spiritual have been bestowed upon us in infinite variety; whilst in number they have been more than could be counted.

II. THEIR INTENDED INFLUENCE. These remembrances and memories of God's great goodness are designed to lead men to " *know the righteousness of the Lord* " (ver. 5), and to give him the unswerving confidence of their hearts. Through all his dealings with the children of men he has been calling them to repentance, faith, newness of life, the putting away of cherished sin, the detaching themselves from ungodly associations, the breaking away from habits of evil, the experience of the most satisfying good, and to the purest and noblest service.

III. THEIR EMPHATIC TESTIMONY. The Most High, in deigning to expostulate with erring men, makes his appeal to these (ver. 3). He asks, " O my people, what have I done unto thee ? " And must not this be our answer, " Nothing but good ; good, only good " ? " Wherein have I wearied thee ? " he asks. And must we not reply, " Thy commandments are not grievous; yet surely we have wearied thee by the way in which we have slighted and neglected them, and have failed to yield to them the true obedience of our hearts and lives ? " " Testify against me," says God. " Nay, we can only testify against ourselves. ' To thee, O Lord, belongeth mercy, but unto us shame and confusion of face ' " (Dan. ix. 7). " I beseech you therefore, brethren, by the mercies of God," etc. (Rom. xii. 1). Then all must be well with us here, and at last we shall enter the land of light and rest and fulness of joy, where, with memory never failing, and with gratitude rising ever higher, we shall reflect upon the entire course along which we have been guided and upheld by him whose mercy and love endure for evermore.

Vers. 6—8.—*Man's spiritual need, and its supply.* These verses form one of the most striking passages in the Old Testament Scriptures. Let any one inquire as to the nature of true religion, and he may find the exposition of it expressed here with marvellous vigour and terseness of speech, and with a completeness leaving nothing to be supplied. The false conception respecting true religion as consisting in that which is external is swept clean away as with a besom, and the loftiest view concerning it is set before us in diction so simple that it cannot be misunderstood and in tone so earnest that it cannot fail to come home to the conscience and the heart.

I. THERE UNDERLIES THESE WORDS THE THOUGHT OF MAN'S DEEP NEED OF GOD. To " come before the Lord " and to " bow before the most high God " is a necessity of humanity. Uncentred from God, the children of men are ever craving after some unattained good, and which alone consists in the Divine favour and blessing. They turn to objects that are unworthy and that can never meet the wants of their higher nature. They seek satisfaction in that which is material, in cherishing attachment to the outward, the fleeting, the unreal ; even as these people of Judah turned to luxury, ease, and self-indulgence; and the result is and ever must be miserable disappointment. Or they turn to objects such as are really worthy—wealth, scholarship, oratory, political and civic honours; but anticipating getting more out of these than they had any right to expect, there is failure and consequent disquietude. " He hath showed thee, O man, what is good." God has declared that true heart-rest can alone be found in himself. " Thou hast formed us for thyself, and our heart is disquieted till it resteth in thee " (Augustine). Consider—

II. THE IMPOSSIBILITY OF FINDING THE SATISFACTION OF THIS DEEP NEED OF THE SOUL IN A MERELY FORMAL AND EXTERNAL SERVICE. It is a great thing when a true reformer succeeds in making an impression. When evils have become deep-rooted, when men have become accustomed to perverted ways, there is an indifference and callousness about them which it is difficult indeed to overcome. And the distinction of this Hebrew seer is seen in the success he achieved where so many have signally failed. By the force of his own personal character, combined with the simplicity and vividness, the mingled severity, tenderness, and the intense earnestness of his language, he succeeded in rousing many to a sense of their sinfulness, and in awakening within them desires and aspirations after a truer life, and impelling them to cry, "Wherewith shall I come," etc.? (ver. 6). But mark what followed. Micah prophesied in the reign of Hezekiah, and the history shows that the people rested in outward reformation and external forms. They cried, "Shall I come before him with burnt offerings ... rivers of oil?" (vers. 6, 7); i.e. shall I bring the costliest and choicest sacrifices, and cause the oil which accompanies the offerings to flow plenteously? "Shall I" (following the practice of the heathen) "give my firstborn," etc.? (ver. 7). And they acted in the spirit of these inquiries. The interest in the temple and its services became revived, the Law was read, the sacrifices renewed, the fasts and feasts once more observed, and the threatened judgments were delayed. But all this was only temporary, there was outward reformation, but unaccompanied by inward renewal; the observance of external forms and the resting in these instead of in God; so that the spiritual unrest continued, and the process of national decay went on, whilst the voice of God was heard uttering the strongest denunciations, saying, "To what purpose," etc.? (Isa. i. 11—15). Beware of cherishing a merely formal piety, of honouring God with your lips whilst your hearts are far from him, of resting in outward reformation and external worship (Ps. li. 16, 17; John iv. 23, 24).

III. THIS NEED OF THE HEART IS MET IN THE POSSESSION OF SINCERE AND GENUINE PIETY. Such piety is described (ver. 8) as consisting in doing justly, loving mercy, and walking humbly with God. It is spiritual in its nature, and has its seat in the heart. Possessing a heart renewed, trustful, and obedient to the Divine will, God will dwell with us, will be our chief joy, and in all places and at all seasons will manifest himself to us. So shall we at all times and under all circumstances find tranquillity and peace. So shall we sing—

"Without thee life and time are sadness,
    No fragrance breathes around;
But with thee even grief is gladness,
    The heart its home hath found."

Ver. 8.—*The Divine response to the cry of humanity.* "He hath showed thee, O man, what is good." "Who will show us any good?" (Ps. iv. 6) is the cry of humanity, and has been its reiterated inquiry all through the ages of the world's history. And not only has man ceaselessly raised the question, but he has sought its solution, and has thus fallen into errors, which are corrected by the response God has given to this aspiration of the human spirit. We turn, in our darkness, to his unerring Word, and we find light shed upon this otherwise dark problem.

I. IT CORRECTS THE NOTION THAT "GOOD" IS TO BE SOUGHT AND FOUND IN MATERIAL THINGS BY SHOWING THAT IT IS TO BE OBTAINED ALONE BY THE SPIRIT RESTING IN GOD.

II. IT CORRECTS THE NOTION THAT "GOOD" MAY BE OBTAINED BY EXTERNAL OBSERVANCES AND SACRIFICES, BY SHOWING THAT IT DEPENDS UPON THE STATE OF THE HEART, AND LIES IN OBEDIENCE AND SELF-SURRENDER TO THE DIVINE WILL.

III. IT CORRECTS THE NOTION THAT "GOOD" IS THE MONOPOLY OF ANY CLASS OR NATION, BY APPEALING TO MAN AS MAN. "He hath showed thee, *O man*, what is good."

Ver. 8.—*True piety: its clear delineation.* "And what doth the Lord require of thee," etc.?

I. To "DO JUSTLY." He requires that rectitude and uprightness should characterize us in all our relationships. We are not to oppress or defraud. We are not to seek to damage the reputation of another, or by word or deed to endeavour to lessen the good opinion which has been formed respecting him. The golden rule is to be acted upon, and we "do unto others as we would that they should do unto us."

II. To "LOVE MERCY." There are two ideas here—that of forgiveness, and that of compassion. Mercy is forgiveness towards the erring and benevolence towards the tried; over both the sinful and the suffering she spreads her wing. This quality is truly royal in its character. "Sweet mercy is nobility's true badge." It is indeed

God-like and Divine, and cannot be exercised without securing to us real happiness. " It is twice blessed," etc. It is well for men to be upright towards their fellow-men, to " do justly ; " but let this be joined to " loving mercy," we seeking thus to smooth each other's path through life. We respect the man whose conduct is regulated in accordance with strict justice ; but we can love the man who rises higher than this, and who, whilst doing that which is just, is also large-hearted and generous.

III. To " WALK HUMBLY WITH THY GOD." To walk with God is to make it our fixed purpose and determination to live to him ; to devote ourselves to his service. To walk with God is to acknowledge him as our Sovereign and our Father ; to set him ever before us ; to live a life of hallowed communion with him ; to make his glory the great object and end of life ; to seek to do only those things which are well-pleasing in his sight. To walk with God is to have our mind and will brought into subjection to his ; to strive to do all he would have us do and to be all he would have us be ; to endeavour more and more to resemble him, and to have taken from us whatever in us is contrary unto him. To walk with God is to love him ; to rejoice in his presence ; to feel ourselves attracted towards him ; to value nothing more than his favour ; to deprecate nothing more than his displeasure. To walk with God is to have him dwelling continually in our hearts ; ever to seek his approval ; ever to make it the great business of life to glorify and to honour him. And in all this true humility is to mark us as we think of his greatness and our own littleness and unworthiness. True piety thus covers the whole range of human duty ; it embraces our duty towards God and towards our fellow-men. The fulfilment of this is " required " of us, and in such obedience lies the evidence that we are the possessors of sincere and vital godliness.

Ver. 8.—*True piety : its exalted character.* " And what doth the Lord require of thee," etc. ? The standard God has set up for human conduct is very high. His law covers the whole range of man's relationships, and demands lofty attainments. Note—

I. PIETY AS DEFINED IN THE TEXT IS VERY EXALTED IN ITS NATURE. See this : 1. *In its eminently practical character.* It is to enter into all the concerns of our daily life. It does not ignore the emotional in man, but it insists upon holy feeling being transmuted into holy service to God and to man. 2. *In its being synonymous with morality.* The distinction often drawn between " a religious man " and " a moral man " has no recognition here. God's Law has two tables—the one having reference to our obligations to God, and the other to our duties to man ; and, correctly speaking, the term " morality " can only be applied to those who are endeavouring to heed both these requirements, and he has no claim to it who regards only one of these tables, and that the lesser, and who virtually excludes God from his own Law. And the converse is also true. As there can be no true morality apart from piety, so also there can be no true piety apart from morality ; in other words, that these cannot practically be separated. Profession and life must go together, and be in harmony ; it is the union of religion and morality that constitutes the life of true and vital godliness.

II. THE CONTEMPLATION OF THIS EXALTED NATURE OF TRUE PIETY IS CALCULATED TO EXERT A DEPRESSING INFLUENCE UPON OUR HEARTS. When we reflect upon the Divine requirement in the light of our own actions and conduct, we feel how infinitely and painfully short we have fallen below what we ought to have been. The standard set up is so lofty that we fear we shall never reach it. " It is high, we cannot attain unto it," we cry, and almost feel despairing and hopeless.

III. BUT WITHAL THERE ARE GLORIOUS ENCOURAGEMENTS. 1. *The Divine purpose.* What encouragement lies in the thought that he who has revealed this perfect Law for human conduct, and who has the hearts of all men at his own disposal, will not rest until by the power of his grace and Spirit he has so touched and elevated the life of man as that the ideal shall become actual, and the race be delivered, fully and for ever, from guilt and sin. 2. *The obedience of Christ.* In accordance with this Divine purpose, God gave his own Son, and the Christ appeared amongst men. Think of the life he lived, and how complete a transcript of the Divine Law it was ! And whilst he exemplified that Law in his life, in his voluntary surrender to the stroke of death as a sacrifice for human guilt he put lasting honour upon it. By that memorable death he declared silently the purity of the Divine Law, and attested the righteousness of the penalty attached to its violation. It has been truly said that "man convinced of sin is ready to sacrifice what is dearest to him rather than give up his own will and give himself to God" (W. Robertson Smith). It is easier to offer "to come before him with burnt offerings, with calves of a year old," than to lay our proud wills at his feet and to yield to him our hearts. But as we contemplate the obedience of Christ and his yielding himself up for us, and see in him expressed the great Father's love, that which was difficult becomes light—we own ourselves subdued, we view sin now in the light of the cross, and see its loathsomeness, and desire to be more entirely delivered from its practice, whilst as we contemplate God's Law, under the influence of the feelings and emotions thus excited within us, we are impelled to cry in all the fulness of a consecrated heart, "I delight in the Law of God after the inward man!" (Rom. vii. 22); "O how I love thy Law!" (Ps. cxix. 97).

Vers. 9, 13—15.—*Divine chastisement.* I. A SOLEMN DECLARATION OF COMING CHASTISEMENT. (Vers. 13—15.) The form this chastisement would assume is suggestive of the thought of *utter disappointment.* Their gain should be turned into loss; their expectations should be completely frustrated; all that they hoped to realize as the result of their deceptions and extortions should fail them, even as the brook fails the parched traveller when coming to it to slake his burning thirst, lo! he finds it dried up. They should be made desolate because of their sins (ver. 13). Surrounded for a time, and through their ill-gotten gains, with all material comforts, they should no more be satisfied by these than he can be upon whom disease has fastened its deadly grasp (ver. 13). Nor should these material comforts abide. Internal conflicts and foreign invasion should result in their impoverishment. The toil of the sowing had been theirs, but they should not experience "the joy of harvest;" they had trodden the olives and had pressed the grapes, but they should not rejoice in the oil that makes the face to shine, or the wine that makes glad the heart of man (vers. 14, 15). They had broken God's Law, and the judgment threatened in that Law they must now inevitably experience (Lev. xxvi. 16; Deut. xxviii. 30, 38). II. THIS CHASTISEMENT APPOINTED BY GOD. (Ver. 9.) "The Lord's voice crieth unto the city," bidding men hear him who had "appointed" the judgment (ver. 9). "*I* will make thee sick," etc. (ver. 13). Their sin was allowed to work out its evil consequences upon them, that they might be led to see how evil a thing it was. God turns events into teachers, and sorrows into discipline. He allows the reeds upon which men were leaning to break, and the earthly pleasures upon which their hearts were set to yield only the bitterness of gall and wormwood, that thus they may be led to look to him, the unfailing Spring. It is not by chance that trials meet the children of men in the pathway of life. It is the Divine arrangement that men should be thus met, if perchance they may be impelled to turn away from an unsatisfying world, and be led to seek in him their chief good. Sometimes we are so wayward that we will not pause in our wandering until God reveals the peril that is in our path. The prodigal had to feel shame and hunger before "he came to himself." So we need at times to be startled and chastened into obedience. Even God's chastisements are love. "Whom the Lord loveth he chasteneth," etc. (Heb. xii. 6—8); "As many as I love I rebuke and chasten" (Rev. iii. 19). III. THE WISDOM OF RECOGNIZING GOD IN THESE ADVERSE EXPERIENCES OF LIFE. "And the men of wisdom," etc. (ver. 9). We show the possession by us of this wisdom when we (1) accept our life-sorrows as coming to us with this wise and loving intent; (2) when we calmly and trustingly bow to the Divine will in the seasons of grief; (3) When we cherish solicitude that the gracious ends designed may be fulfilled in us; and (4) when, our bonds "loosed," and the sorrow overpast, the grateful acknowledgment, springing from our inmost souls, breaks forth from our lips, "It is good for me that I have been afflicted" (Ps. cxix. 71); "Before I was afflicted I went astray," etc. (Ps. cxix. 67).

Vers. 10—12.—"*Weighed in the balances, and found wanting.*" Having expounded the nature of true piety, the prophet proceeds in these verses to apply the principles thus enunciated to the case of his people, endeavouring by means of searching inquiries to bring home to their hearts a sense of their guilt and depravity.
I. WE HAVE HERE AN ILLUSTRATIVE EXAMPLE OF HUMAN CONDUCT WHEN TESTED BY

THE DIVINE REQUIREMENTS BEING FOUND WANTING. Notice in this case: **1.** *Dishonesty in trade as opposed to "doing justly."* Rectitude in all the transactions of life was repeatedly insisted upon in the Law of God as given by Moses (Lev. xix. 35, 36; Deut. xxv. 14, 15). Disregard of this requirement was an indictment constantly brought against the Jewish people by their faithful seers (Amos viii. 4—6; Ezek. xlv. 9, 10; Hos. xii. 7, 8). To be engaged in trade has been regarded by some as a badge of social inferiority. No right-minded man could speak or even think thus. All honest trades are honourable. None need be ashamed of their callings because these belong to the shop and the mart. The dishonour lies in fraud, trickery, deceit, and sharp practice; but let all these be eschewed, and the principles of uprightness and honour prevail, and the humblest trade, conducted on these lines, is thereby ennobled. "Royalty in her robes of state is not so majestic as Commerce clothed in spotless integrity and commanding unlimited confidence. Victory, raising her trophies from the spoils of a conquered army, is not so glorious as Commerce, patiently and perseveringly, slowly but surely, gaining its end by scorning and disdaining the arts which promise a speedy but treacherous elevation" (Dr. Robert Halley). **2.** *Oppression and violence as opposed to "loving mercy"* (ver. 12). Men, making haste to be rich, fall into many hurtful snares (1 Tim. vi. 9), and one of these is that of oppressing those less favoured than themselves. They become hard, and are led to take undue advantage of those who are needy and who can in any way be made tributary to their interests. Provision against this was made in the Law of Moses (Deut. xxiv. 10—22). This provision of that Divine law, which so marvellously met every circumstance and condition of life, the prophet charged his people with disregarding. "The rich men thereof are full of violence" (ver. 12; Isa. i. 23; v. 7; Amos v. 11; Mal. iii. 5). The love of mercy was sacrificed to the love of gain. Man, consumed by lust of wealth, used his fellow-men as mere stepping-stones, trampling them beneath his feet. **3.** *Degeneration in speech as altogether incompatible with "walking humbly with God."* (Ver. 12.) Very glorious is the power of utterance, the ability to give audible expression, with clearness and perspicuity, to the thoughts which may be filling our minds and stirring our very souls.

> "And when she spake
> Sweet words, like dropping honey, she did shed:
> And 'twixt the pearls and rubies softly brake
> A silver sound that heavenly music seemed to make."
>
> (Spenser's 'Faëry Queene.')

Speech is a very sure index to character. "Out of thine *own mouth* will I judge thee" (Luke xix. 22). "A bell may have a crack, and you may not see it, but take the clapper and strike it, and you'll soon perceive that it is flawed." Degradation is stamped, not only upon the physical form of savage tribes, but also upon the very language they employ. When, as the result of a long course of transgression or of prolonged banishment from civilization, noble thoughts and high spiritual conceptions have dropped away from them, there has attended this the loss even of the very words by which these thoughts and conceptions are expressed, so that the language of such people has become woefully impoverished. Clearly, then, would we have our speech right, we must get our hearts right. "The weights and wheels are in the heart, and the clock strikes according to their motion. Truth in the inward parts is the certain cure for all evil in the tongue." The prevailing degeneracy over which this seer so deeply mourned is indicated in his words, "The inhabitants thereof have spoken lies, and their tongue is deceitful in their mouth" (ver. 12). And, this being the case, they were utterly unfitted for complying with the requirement that they should walk humbly "with their God;" for only "the pure in heart" can have fellowship with him. "Weighed" thus "in the balances" of the requirements of God's pure Law, they were "found wanting."

II. ALTHOUGH DIFFERING IN DEGREE, YET IT IS TRUE UNIVERSALLY THAT HUMAN CONDUCT, PROVED THUS, WILL NOT STAND THE TEST. God's Law is "holy, just, and true," and man is by nature and practice so sinful that, judged by that high standard, "every mouth must be stopped, and the whole world appear guilty before God" (Rom. iii. 19).

III. THE CONSCIOUSNESS OF THIS SHOULD LEAD US TO WELCOME THE CHRIST OF GOD,

WHOSE ADVENT THIS PROPHET PREDICTED, AND TO REJOICE IN HIS WORK ON OUR BEHALF. We cannot meet God on the ground of obedience to his pure Law. If we take that stand, then he righteously and imperatively requires that the whole Law be kept; and this is impossible to us, since even if we were capable of perfect obedience in the future, this would not atone for the failures of the past. The true meeting-place is not Sinai, but Calvary (2 Tim. i. 9; Rom. iii. 20—26).

Ver. 16.—*The influence of evil men.* These are the last recorded words of Micah declarative of coming judgment; and they are deeply impressive as setting forth the influence exerted by evil men.

I. ITS PERPETUITY. "For the statutes of Omri are kept, and all the works of the house of Ahab, and ye walk in their counsels" (ver. 16). God had separated this people from among the nations, and had specially favoured them with a revelation of his will. He had given unto them his pure Law. Their fathers had gathered in the olden time at Sinai, that

> "Separate from the world, their breast
>   Might duly take and strongly keep
> The print of heaven to be ex1 rest
>   Ere long on Zion's steep."
>
> (Keble.)

God had conferred signal honour upon them in constituting them the depositaries of his truth, and his witnesses unto the ends of the earth. They were bound by the most sacred obligations, the most solemn vows repeatedly renewed, and by pains and penalties too, "to keep his statues" and "to obey his commandments." But they lamentably failed to fulfil their high mission, and the failure is in no small degree traced in these records to the influence of their kings. Jeroboam, Omri, and Ahab stand out conspicuously in the history of the kingdom of Israel as having sinned and caused Israel to sin, and the evil influence thus exerted spread to the kingdom of Judah, and descended from generation to generation. One hundred and seventy years had passed since the death of Ahab, nearly two hundred since the death of Omri, and about two hundred and thirty since the death of Jeroboam; yet their pernicious influence was still felt, and the people were keeping their statutes instead of God's, and walking in their ways instead of in "the way of holiness." It is clear, then, that, whilst we may by a true life be helpers, even to those who come after us, in all that is good, we may also, by the perversion of this power, prove hinderers to them, and keep them back from the highest bliss. Evil deeds as well as good actions have the stamp of permanence upon them. "Being dead," men "yet speak" for ill as for good. You cannot limit the influence of wrong-doing to the men who commit it. Generations yet unborn will experience the dire effects of the sins men are committing now. "For the statutes of Omri" (ver. 16).

II. ITS PERNICIOUSNESS. "That I should make thee," etc. (ver. 16). The injurious effects thus wrought in a nation are here specially set forth. 1. It leads on to national decay. "That I should make thee a desolation" (ver. 16). 2. It excites the contempt of the adversaries. "And the inhabitants thereof an hissing" (ver. 16). 3. It lays spiritual honour in the very dust, and causes the foes of God and of his truth to blaspheme. "Therefore ye shall bear the reproach of my people" (ver. 16; Ezek. xxxvi. 20; Ps. lxxxix. 4; xliv. 13—16).

HOMILIES BY VARIOUS AUTHORS.

Vers. 1—5.—*A protest and a retrospect.* The serious state of the case between Jehovah and his people is shown by this appeal to the hills and mountains. As though among all the nations none could be found impartial enough to be umpires, or even witnesses, inanimate nature must supply its testimony. (Illustrate from Job xii. 7, 8; Isa. i. 2, 3; Luke xix. 40; 2 Pet. ii. 16.) The mountains have stability; not so the favoured nation. They have survived many generations of God's ungrateful beneficiaries, and have been witnesses of the blessings those thankless ones have received. The cliffs of Horeb have echoed back the precepts and promises of Jehovah, and the gentler tones of his "still small voice," but his people have remained deaf to his appeals. Hence—

I. A PROTEST. Before Jehovah passes judgment he permits himself to be regarded as the defendant if his people can venture to bring any charge against him. He knows that nothing but unrighteous treatment on his part could justify them in departing from him. Hence the appeal in Jer. ii. 5, and the similar remonstrances of Christ in John viii. 46 and x. 32. Nothing but intolerable grievances can justify a national revolt or a desertion of the paternal home. Had God "wearied" Israel by unreasonable treatment? The whole history of the nation refutes the suggested libel. Or can we make any such charges against God? What can they be? 1. *Undue severity?* Can "*my people*" (what a sermon in that mere term!) say so (Job xi. 6; Ps. ciii. 10; Dan. ix. 7)? 2. *A harsh and trying temper?* The very opposite is the spirit of "the Father of mercies" (Ps. cxlv. 8, 9). 3. *Unreasonable exactions of service?* No; he can make the appeal, "I have not caused thee to *serve* with an offering, nor wearied thee with incense" (Isa. xliii. 23). His "yoke is easy;" "His commandments are not grievous." 4. *Negligence in his training of us?* Far from it; he can declare, "What could have been done more?" etc. (Isa. v. 1—4). Forbearance, loving-kindness, and thoughtful consideration have marked God's conduct throughout. The case against God utterly breaks down. Instead of desiring to remonstrate, or even "reason with God," as at one time Job did, every reasonable soul, hearing God's words and catching some vision of his glory, must acknowledge, as that patriarch did, "I abhor myself, and repent in dust and ashes" (cf. Job xiii. 3; xlii. 5, 6). The way is cleared. O God, thou art justified when thou speakest, and clear when thou art judged. And now God's messenger may take up his parable, like Samuel (1 Sam. xii. 7), and God himself may make the appeal in vers. 4, 5.

II. A RETROSPECT. Jehovah selects specimens of his gracious dealings with them from their early history. He reminds them of: 1. *A grand redemption.* (Ver. 4.) We, too, as a nation can speak of great deliverances from political and ecclesiastical bondage. See T. H. Gill's hymn—

> "Lift thy song among the nations,
> England of the Lord beloved," etc.

And for each of us has been provided a redemption from a worse than Egyptian bondage, through "Christ our Passover, sacrificed for us." 2. *Illustrious leaders.* Moses, their inspired lawgiver and the friend of God (Numb. xii. 8); Aaron, their high priest and intercessor; Miriam, a singer, poet, prophetess. What memories of "the loving-kindnesses of the Lord" these names would recall—the Paschal night, the morning of final deliverance and song of triumph by the Red Sea, the manna, the plague stayed, etc.! We, too, can look back on our illustrious leaders in English history. And in common with the whole of Christendom, "all things are yours, whether Paul or Apollos, or Cephas"—the apostles, the martyrs, the preachers, the poets of the past—"all are yours" by right, if not by actual enjoyment. 3. *Foes frustrated.* (Ver. 5.) "Remember *now*"—a word of tender appeal, as though God would say, "Oh, do remember." Balak was a representative foe, striving against Israel, first by policy (Numb. xxii.), then by villainy (Numb. xxv.), and finally by violence (Numb. xxxi.). Again the parallel may be traced in national and individual history. 4. *Curses turned into blessings.* (Deut. xxiii. 5.) So has it been with many of the trials of the past. "*Remember* from Shittim unto Gilgal" (cf. Numb. xxv. 1 and Josh. iv. 19). What a contrast! Sins forgiven; reproach "rolled away" (Josh. v. 9); chastisements blessed; the long-looked-for land of promise entered. All these blessings show us "the righteous acts of the Lord." They remind us of the successive acts of God's righteous grace. They make sin against him shamefully ungrateful as well as grossly unjust. Oh, that the goodness of God may lead to repentance! that he may overcome our evil by his good! that "the love of God which is in Christ Jesus our Lord" may constrain us to live henceforth, not to ourselves, but to him!—E. S. P.

Vers. 6—8.—*The essentials of godliness.* If the questions of vers. 6 and 7 are those of Balak and the answers are Balaam's, they remind us of how a man may know and explain clearly the path of righteousness and peace, and yet neglect it. Balaam may prophesy; Demas may preach; Judas may cast out devils; but "I never knew you; depart from me ye that work iniquity!" Or if we regard the questions as proposed, either by the nation convicted of sin (vers. 1—5), or by any one sin-stricken soul, we learn the same truths. It is the old controversy, older than Balak, between God and man, as to the grounds of man's acceptance with God and the essential requirements from man by God. We see—

I. ANXIOUS QUESTIONS. (Vers. 6, 7.) These questions remind us of: 1. *Man's sense of distance from God.* He is not consciously walking "with God," like Enoch; "before God," like Abraham. 2. *His conviction that he cannot come to God by any right or merit of his own.* "Wherewith?" He cannot come just as he is, empty-handed. He has no right of entry to the court of the Divine King. 3. *And that if he comes at all he must "bow," as an inferior, conscious of absolute dependence.* This "consciousness of absolute dependence" (Schleiermacher's definition of religion), which is shared by all intelligent creatures, is intensified by the consciousness of sin. Sin has as its shadow *guilt,* and the brighter the light the clearer and darker the shadow. That shadow projects itself into the mysterious future. A sense of desert of punishment and "a certain fearful looking for of judgment" are the attendants of sin, though there may be no meltings of godly sorrow from a sense of its base ingratitude. Thus sin is the great separater; man feels it; God declares it (Isa. lix. 1, 2). Hence there follow suggestive inquiries as to the means by which acceptance with God may be obtained. Shall they be "burnt offerings"? There was a germ of truth in this thought (cf. 2 Sam. xxiv. 24). Burnt offerings were entirely devoted to God. They might be precious in quality, like "calves of a year old," or multiplied in quantity ("thousands of rams," etc.). These burnt offerings were designed to denote God's right to our entire surrender, but could be no substitute for that surrender. They might be signs of eager desire for acceptance, though at a high price. But in themselves they could bring no sense of access to God and of peace with him. Then comes the suggestion of a sacrifice infinitely more costly ("my firstborn," etc.). To a parent a child's life is more precious than his own. If the sinner can be forgiven and accepted only at such a price, shall it be paid? Terror-stricken, deluded consciences have answered, "Yes;" but the peace has not come. While some of these proposals are detestable to God, all of them are worthless. Unless the man himself is right with God, no sacrifice can avail. Yet many would rather sacrifice health, life, wife, child, than give up sin which is the great separater. Sinful man can ask such anxious questions as these, but he cannot answer them. His suggestions land him in deeper guilt, or at the best leave him in blank despair.

II. REASSURING ANSWERS. (Ver. 8.) These come from God himself. Every fragment of *gospel*—news of good, is news from God. It was given not now for the first time. God had spoken at sundry times and in divers manners by Moses and the earlier prophets. All previous revelations of Law and grace were means of showing men "what is good." In regard to man himself, God from the beginning has testified that his only real "good" is real godliness. This was the sum of his requirements (see Deut. x. 12, 13, etc.). He did not seek for something from themselves, but for themselves and for the fruit of his Spirit within them. There were *false methods* by which "that which is good" was sought, such as heathen sacrifices and austerities. There were *inadequate methods,* such as God's own appointed system of sacrifices and services, when emptied of the spirit of self-surrender they were designed to foster and of the teaching they contained of the need of "better sacrifices" (Heb. ix. 23). These symbolical educational sacrifices were but part of a process which was to issue in man's acceptance by God, that thus man might render to God what he required, and might know and "prove what is that good and acceptable and perfect will of God" (cf. Heb. x. 1—10, 19—25). Looking closely at ver. 8, we see a summing up of both Law and gospel. 1. "*To do justly.*" Elementary morality is here linked with all that is Divine. To do *justly* is not only to do what is just, but because it is just, and with an earnest desire to be right with God. The "righteousness" which "the righteous Lord loveth" (Ps. xi. 7) is more than the outward act. And yet these most elementary acts of righteousness were neglected by many then (vers. 10—12 and ch. vii. 3) as well as now, who proposed anxious questions about their acceptance with God or even professed to have found satisfactory answers to them. 2. *"To love mercy."* Mercy is more than justice, just as "a good man" is more than a merely "righteous" one (Rom. v. 7). The lack of it may arise from hardness of character, or from never having passed through the temptations by which some have fallen. To cultivate the love of mercy will bring us nearer to God, and will make it easy for us to scatter blessings around our path, even to the unthankful and the evil (Prov. xxi. 21; Matt. v. 7; Luke vi. 32—36). Such a disposition is incompatible with spiritual pride. But lest a just and benevolent man should be tempted to pride himself and to rely on his outward conduct, we are reminded of God's last requirement. 3. *"To walk humbly with thy God."* Here the first table of the Decalogue and the law of the gospel are combined. "Walk *with* God." How can the sinner, except he be reconciled (Amos iii. 3)? Hence the need of peace in God's appointed way. This way to us is not the way of self-righteousness or the way of ceremonies and sacraments, but it is the way of faith in God's own appointed and accepted atonement (Rom. iv. 4, 5; 1 John iii. 23). To "submit" to this righteousness of God requires a humbling of many a proud heart. And if we have welcomed reconciliation as God's free gift through Christ, we shall ever after walk humbly with our God as his grateful, happy children. Such a humble walk will make justice and mercy easier to us. When Luther was asked what was the first step in religion, he replied "Humility;" and when asked what was the second and the third, answered in the same way. Therefore walk humbly, as a learner; as a pensioner; as a pardoned and joyous child, "looking for the mercy of the Lord Jesus Christ unto eternal life" (Titus ii. 11—14).—E. S. P.

Ver. 9.—*The voice of the rod.* God's voice has often called to Jerusalem in mercy and in warning; now it cries in judgment—it is *the voice of the rod.* Notice—

I. THE SINS THAT CALL FOR IT. In the context many of the chief national sins are once more enumerated, such as ill-gotten gains (ver. 10), false weights and measures (vers. 10, 11), oppression of the poor by the petty magnates of the city (ver. 12), habitual fraud and falsehood (ver. 12). Apply these illustrations to some of England's national sins. But as though these were not enough, there were added thereto the sins of the darkest period of the northern kingdom, viz. from Omri to Jehu (see ver. 16 margin, "He doth much keep," *i.e.* does diligently keep such statutes as these rather than the statutes of Jehovah, which his people are exhorted diligently to keep, Exod. xv. 26, etc.). These sins included the establishment of idolatry and all the immoralities associated with Baal-worship, the persecution of God's faithful servants (1 Kings xviii. 13; xix. 10; xxii. 27), and oppression even by the highest (*e.g.* Naboth). In the days of Ahaz the kingdom of Judah sank to such a level as this. All these evils were concentrated at Jerusalem, so that it is to this city the rod appeals.

II. THE MESSAGES IT BRINGS. Some elements of distinct retributive justice are discernible. 1. Uneasiness, from consciousness of guilt, while pursuing and seeking to enjoy their nefarious courses (ver. 11 margin, "Shall I be pure," etc.?). Conscience may be like an Elijah confronting Ahab in Naboth's vineyard. Illust.: Shakespeare's Richard III. 2. As they defrauded the poor, so should they be bitterly disappointed when seeking the fruit of their own labour (ver. 14; Eccles. vi. 1, 2). 3. Their labour would be for the benefit of others, and all their efforts to secure it for themselves would be as much frustrated as were the toilsome labours of those whom they had defrauded (vers. 14, 15). For they can save nothing from the hand of God. 4. Thus their wounds would be incurable (ver. 13), and their ill-gotten gain a treasure of wrath (Jas. v. 1—4). 5. These luxurious and delicate ones should become a scandal and a reproach to all around them (ver. 16).

III. THE SPIRIT THAT WILL SILENCE IT. 1. *Recognizing God's hand as holding it.* He "hath appointed it." (Illustrate from Isa. x. 5; Jer. xlvii. 6, 7; so now Amos iii. 6.) 2. *Listening to God's voice speaking through it.* Their great sin in the past has been the disregard of God's voice (Isa. xlviii. 18; Jer. xiii. 15—17). The voices of entreaty and warning were not heard, so now the voice of chastisement speaks. Yet even in the time of such chastisement there might be hope (Prov. i. 24—27, 33; and see Lev. xxvi. 40—45). 3. *Honouring God's Name.* "The man of wisdom shall see thy Name." God's Name declares his character, and it is his character as a holy God that requires the punishment of the unrighteous (Exod. xxxiv. 7). So long as men persist in sin, they must remain under the wrath of God. Sinning and punishment are inseparable. Till sinners "see God's Name" by recognizing its meaning and learning that they can honour it by nothing but a renunciation of sin, the voice of the rod must be heard even through the ages of eternity.—E. S. P.

Vers. 6—8.—*Man's yearning for his Maker.* The prophet supposes that his earnest appeals have had some effect—that the people are stirred from their senselessness, and are beginning to feel after God. Overwhelmed with a consciousness of sin, they dare not approach him as they are. Their hesitation and their self-communing are like those of the prodigal in the far country when he came to himself. The sense of distance between the finite and the infinite, between the sin-stained and the holy, is oppressive and painful, and it finds expression in the words of our text.

I. THE ANXIOUS INQUIRY. "Wherewith shall I come before the Lord, and bow myself before the high God?" Whether men wish to do so or not, they are bound by the inexorable laws of God to appear before him. They *may* come as sinners, casting themselves upon his mercy, as David and the publican came; but they *must* come, on the last great day, as responsible creatures, to give an account of the deeds done in the body, whether they are good or bad. It is not as a race, or even as families, that judgment will be received by men, but by each in his individual capacity. Hence the wise man asks himself, "Wherewith shall *I* come before the Lord?" 1. *This implies belief in a personal God.* There is no conception here or elsewhere in Scripture of the world being ruled by an impersonal Power, by a tendency which makes for righteousness. Such theories are in the long run destructive of the sense of personal accountability, and therefore fatal to the basis on which moral law rests. 2. *This implies conviction of sin.* Else why this nameless dread, and this notion of sin offering? It matters not how it is aroused, whether by tender touches of Divine love or by fervid appeals by inspired messengers; nor is it of consequence whether the sins were those of omission or of commission; but in some form, and by some means, a sense of sin is aroused in most men by the power of the Holy Spirit, whose office it is to "convince the world of sin, of righteousness, and of a judgment to come." 3. *This implies willingness to make some sacrifice.* Even the heathen have had the innate consciousness that without the shedding of blood there is no remission. The Jews had a divinely ordained and most elaborate system of sacrifice, which kept this idea before their minds, in all the changeful conditions of life. But they were taught that it was not these outward and visible offerings which atoned for sin. "Thou desirest not sacrifice, else would I give it," etc. "Lebanon is not sufficient to burn," etc. "The sacrifices of God are a broken spirit: a broken and a contrite heart, O God, thou wilt not despise."

II. THE SATISFACTORY ANSWER. With ever-increasing fulness it came, until at last the voice of the Lord Jesus was heard saying, "I am the Way, the Truth, and the Life; no man cometh unto the Father, but by me." 1. *Christ Jesus has offered an atonement for us.* "Once, in the end of the world, he hath appeared to put away sin by the sacrifice of himself." He has not repealed the moral law; he has not abolished the necessity for means of moral culture; he has not quenched the Divine wrath; but he has revealed (not created) the Divine purpose, and has commended (not purchased) the Divine love. "God commendeth his love toward us, in that, while we were yet sinners, Christ died for us." 2. *Christ Jesus has brought God near to us.* In him God is manifest in the flesh. "He that hath seen me hath seen the Father." (1) By seeing him we can understand what God is. The unseen power which pulsates through this boundless universe is too vast for our appreciation; but revealed in the Lord Jesus, we know him to be a Person, speaking to us in wisdom and love. (2) Through Jesus we know that God is love. He inspires hope and trust in those who are alienated and afraid. A display of Divine glory would terrify us; but we are encouraged to draw near by One who appeared as the Babe of Bethlehem, as the patient Teacher of the disciples, as the gracious Friend of the sinful and distressed. 3. *Christ Jesus attracts us to God.* Arousing gratitude and confidence, he is the great magnet of human hearts. "And I, if I be lifted up, will draw all men unto me."

III. THE DIVINE REQUIREMENT. "He hath showed thee, O man, what is good; and what doth the Lord require of thee, but to do justly, and to love mercy, and to walk humbly with thy God." This is not required as a means of our justification, but as an evidence of it. It does not exclude the work of Christ, but presupposes it. But, on the other hand, it effectually refutes the notion that the elect can live as they list. They are only "predestined to be conformed to the image of his Son." 1. "*To do justly*" involves the discharge of fairly demanded duties both towards God and towards man. We are unjust in our dealings with God when we withhold time and wealth and influence which we are able to devote to him. We are unjust as servants when we render mere eye-service; unjust as employers when we look only "on our own things." Buyers and sellers, statesmen and diplomatists, need all hearken to this law. 2. "*To love mercy*" is to go beyond the strict rights which others may claim of us in the exercise of generosity and pity. "Blessed is he that considereth the poor," etc.; "If thine enemy hunger, feed him." 3. "*To walk humbly with God*" implies fellowship, constant and real. Reverence and seriousness in the treatment of the Divine revelation; consciousness of the infinitude of truth, and our incapacity to grasp it; lowly submission to our Father's will, when it is contrary to our own wishes; and steadfast progress in the Christian life, as we walk hand-in-hand with him, are all involved in walking humbly with our God.

> " Walking in reverence
>   Humbly with thee,
> Yet from all abject fear
>   Lovingly free ;
> E'en as a friend with friend,
> Cheered to the journey's end,
>   Walking with thee."

A. R.

Vers. 1—5.—*Man in the moral court of history.* "Hear ye now what the Lord saith; Arise, contend thou before the mountains, and let the hills hear thy voice. Hear ye, O mountains, the Lord's controversy and ye strong foundations of the earth : for the Lord hath a controversy with his people, and he will plead with Israel," etc. There are three things here very striking and deserving our solemn attention.

I. HERE IS A CALL ON MAN TO GIVE AUDIENCE TO ALMIGHTY GOD. "Hear ye now what the Lord saith." These are the words of the prophet who speaks in the name of Jehovah, and on his behalf. Such an audience as this is: 1. *Natural.* What is more natural than for the child to hang on the lips and attend to the words of his parent? How much more natural for the finite intelligence to open its ears to the words of the Infinite! It is more natural for the human soul to look up, listening, to the great Father-Spirit, and to receive communication from him, than for the earth to thirst for the sunbeam and the shower. The human soul is made for it. 2. *Binding.* Of all duties it is the most primary and imperative. The great command of God to all is, "Hearken diligently to me; hear, and your soul shall live" (Isa. lv. 2, 3). The conscience of every man tells him that his great duty is to hear God in all the operations of nature, in all the events of life, in all the teachings of the Bible, in all the monitions of the soul. God is always speaking to man. Would that the human ear was ever open to his voice! 3. *Indispensable.* It is only as men hear, interpret, digest, appropriate, and incarnate God's Word that they can rise to a true, a noble, and a happy life. "Hear ye now," then, "what the Lord saith." "*Now.*" In the scenes of retribution whither you are hastening, you will be bound to hear his voice, whether you wish or not.

II. HERE IS A SUMMONS TO INANIMATE NATURE TO HEAR THE CONTROVERSY BETWEEN GOD AND MAN. "Arise, contend thou before the mountains, and let the hills hear thy voice. Hear ye, O mountains, the Lord's controversy, and ye strong foundations of the earth : for the Lord hath a controversy with his people, and he will plead with Israel." "It is not unusual," says an eminent biblical scholar, "with the prophets to make appeals respecting the enormity of human guilt to the inanimate part of creation, as if it were impossible for it not to inspire them with life, and call them forth as intelligent witnesses of what had taken place in their presence (see Deut. xxxii. 1; Isa. i. 2; Jer. ii. 12, 13). By a similar personification, the mountains and durable foundations of the earth are here summoned to appear in the court of heaven. Jehovah, however, instead of bringing forward the charge, abdicates, as it were, his right, and leaves it to the guilty party to state the case. In the appeal to lofty and ever-during mountains, in which the puny affairs of man could excite no prejudice, and which might therefore be regarded as quite impartial judges, there is something inexpressibly sublime." The appeal to inanimate nature: 1. *Indicates the earnestness of the prophet.* He would seem to speak with such vehement earnestness as if he would wake the dead mountains and hills to hear his voice, and shake the very " foundations of the earth " with his thunders. He would cry aloud and spare not. Every minister should be earnest. " Passion is reason " here. 2. *Suggests the stupidity of the people.* Perhaps the prophet meant to compare them to the dead hills and mountains. As firmly settled in sin were they as the mountains, as hard in heart as the rocks. 3. *Hints the universality of his theme.* His mission had no limitation; his doctrine was no secret, it was as open and free as nature.

III. HERE IS A CHALLENGE TO MAN TO FIND FAULT WITH DIVINE DEALINGS. "O my people, what have I done unto thee? and wherein have I wearied thee? Testify against me." His challenge: 1. Implies that they could bring nothing against him. " What have I done unto thee?" which means, "I have done nothing. I have not treated you with injustice, I have laid on you no intolerable burdens, I dare you to charge me with any act unrighteous or unkind." What fault has the sinner to find with God? 2. Declares that he had done everything for them. He here reminds them of: (1) His delivering them from Egyptian bondage. "I brought thee up out of the land of Egypt, and redeemed thee out of the house of servants." (2) What he did for them on the way to Canaan. "I sent before thee Moses, Aaron, and Miriam." Moses the lawgiver, Aaron the priest, and Miriam the prophetess. (3) What he did for them in Canaan. "O my people, remember now what Balak King of Moab consulted," etc. He not only furnished them with inspired teachers, but counteracted the designs of false ones, as in the case of Balaam, who was engaged by Balak to curse them, but was inspired by Heaven to bless them. If the Israelites could find no fault with God, and if he did so much for them, how stand we here in this country and in this age under the full light of the gospel dispensation? What more could he have done for us than he has? etc.

CONCLUSION. Sinner, you are in the great moral court of the universe, you are arraigned before your Judge, you are commanded to listen to his voice. Inanimate nature around is a witness against you in this court; the very timbers of the wall will cry out against you. You are commanded to give a full explanation of your conduct. If you have any fault to find with the Almighty, bring it forth. If you have not, ponder until your heart breaks into penitence and gratitude at the memory of his wonderful mercies to you.—D. T.

Vers. 6—8.—*Fellowship with God.* "Wherewith shall I come before the Lord, and bow myself before the high God? shall I come before him with burnt offerings, with calves of a year old? Will the Lord be pleased with thousands of rams, or with ten thousands of rivers of oil?" etc. We raise from these words three general observations—

I. THAT A LOVING FELLOWSHIP WITH THE GREAT GOD IS THE ONE URGENT NEED OF HUMANITY. "Wherewith shall I come before the Lord?" The language is that of a soul convinced of its sin, and roused to a sense of the importance of friendship with the Almighty. "Wherewith shall I come?" Come *I must*; I feel that distance from him is my great sin and misery. 1. *Loving fellowship with the great God is essential to the happiness of moral intelligences.* *Reason* suggests this. All souls are the offspring of God; and where can children find happiness but in the friendship, the intercourse, and the presence of their loving Father? *Conscience* indicates this. Deep in the moral souls of all men is the yearning for intercourse with the Infinite. The hearts of all " cry out for the living God." The *Bible* teaches this. What mean such utterances as these: " Come now, and let us reason together;" " Return to the Lord;" " Come unto me," etc.? Not more impossible is it for a planet to shine when cut off from the sun, a river to flow when cut off from the fountain, a branch to grow when severed from the root, than for a soul to be happy apart from God. "In thy presence is fulness of joy." 2. *Man, in his unregenerate state, is estranged and far away from God.* He is represented as a lost sheep wandering in the wilderness away from the fold, as the prodigal son remote from his father's house and in a far country. How far is the human soul, in its unregenerate state, from God? How far is selfishness from benevolence, error from truth, pollution from holiness, wrong from right? The moral space or gulf that lies between is immeasurable.

II. THAT SACRIFICES THE MOST COSTLY ARE UTTERLY INSUFFICIENT TO SECURE THIS FELLOWSHIP. "Shall I come before him with burnt offerings, with calves of a year old?" Such offerings were presented under the Law (Lev. i., etc.). "Will the Lord be pleased with thousands of rams, or with ten thousands of rivers of oil?" This also was enjoined in Leviticus. Oil was to be poured on the meat offering. "Shall I give my firstborn for my transgression, the fruit of my body for the sin of my soul?" The Jews offered many human sacrifices in the valley of Hinnom. They caused their children to pass through the fire in honour of Moloch. The idea is—Are there any sacrifices I can make, however costly and however painful, in order to commend me to the favour and friendship of Almighty God? The interrogatory implies a negative— No. Offer the cattle upon a thousand hills: can they be a satisfaction for sin? Can they commend you to Infinite Love? All are his. How men came at first to suppose that human sacrifices could be acceptable to God is one of the greatest enigmas in history. "Though a man give his body to be burned, without charity he is nothing." Two things are here presented. 1. *The great cry of a sin-convicted soul is for God.* No sooner is conviction of sin struck into the human soul, than it turns itself away at once from the world to God: "I want God; I have lost him; God I must have; oh that I knew where I might find him!" 2. *Worldly possessions, in the estimation of a sin-convicted soul, are comparatively worthless.* He is prepared to make any sacrifices. Holocausts, thousands of rams, ten thousands of rivers of oil; what are they? Nothing in comparison with the interests of the soul. "What shall it profit a man if he gain the whole world," etc.? It feels this when convicted of sin.

III. THAT MORAL EXCELLENCE IS THE ONE METHOD BY WHICH THIS FELLOWSHIP CAN BE OBTAINED. "He hath showed thee, O man [Hebrew, 'Adam,' the whole race, Jew and Gentile alike], what is good; and what doth the Lord require of thee, but to do justly, and to love mercy, and to walk humbly with thy God?" This moral excellence consists of two parts, social and religious. 1. *That which refers to man.* (1) "Do justly;" "Whatsoever ye would that men should do to you, do ye even so to them." "Render to all men their due." (2) "Love mercy." Mere justice is not enough, there must be tender commiseration for the suffering; the poor and the distressed must be remembered. Mercy must not only be shown, but loved. To help the needy must be delight. 2. *That which refers to God.* "Walk humbly with thy God." Walking with God implies consciousness of the Divine presence, harmony with the Divine will, progress in Divine excellence. This is moral excellence—the moral excellence that God has revealed to all men, Jew and Gentile, the entire race, and which he requires from all; and this is the condition of fellowship with him. How is this moral excellence to be attained? it may be asked. Philosophically, I know but of one way —faith in him who is the Revelation, the Incarnation, the Example of all moral excellence—Jesus Christ.

CONCLUSION. Learn from this what religion is—how transcendent! It is the soul going away from sin and the world to God. Not merely to temples, theologies, ceremonies, but to God; and to him, not through intellectual systems or ceremonial observances, but through a true life, both in relation to man and God.—D. T.

Ver. 9.—*God's voice to cities.* "The Lord's voice crieth unto the city, and the man of wisdom shall see thy Name: hear ye the rod, and who hath appointed it." We raise three remarks from this verse.

I. THAT GOD HAS A "VOICE" TO CITIES. "The Lord's voice crieth unto the city." The city meant here is Jerusalem. He speaks to a city: 1. Through its *commerce.* The failures that follow fraud, indolence, chicanery. 2. Through its *mortality.* The funeral processions that darken the streets, the cemeteries that lie within and around. 3. Through its *churches.* The sermons that are preached, the agents that are employed to enlighten the ignorant, to comfort the distressed, reclaim the lost. Heavenly Wisdom "standeth at the corner of the streets; she crieth aloud," etc.

II. THE WISE IN CITIES RECOGNIZE THE VOICE. "The man of wisdom shall see thy

Name." "And wisdom has thy Name in its eye" (Delitzsch). "And he who is wise will regard thy Name" (Henderson). The idea seems to be this—that the wise man will recognize God's voice. Job says, "God speaks once, yea twice, and they perceive it not." The crowds that populate cities are deaf to the Divine "voice." The din of passion, the hum of commerce, the chimes of animal pleasures, drown the voice of God. But the wise man has his soul ever in a listening attitude. Like young Samuel, he says, "Speak, Lord; for thy servant heareth." Abraham heard the voice of God concerning Sodom, Daniel concerning Babylon, Jonah concerning Nineveh, Jeremiah concerning Jerusalem. "I will hear what the Lord God will say"—this is the language of wise men.

III. THE JUDGMENT OF CITIES IS IN THAT VOICE. "Hear ye the rod, and who hath appointed it." The rod is the symbol of judgment. "O Assyrian, the rod of my anger, the staff in their hand is my indignation" (Isa. x. 5). 1. *God warns cities.* (1) He warns them of ultimate temporal ruin. All cities must go—go with Nineveh, Greece, Babylon, Rome, Jerusalem. London, Paris, Petersburg, New York, etc., all must go as these have gone. It is only a question of time. (2) He warns them of spiritual danger. "The soul that sinneth, it shall die." This is his voice to every citizen. Here is the "rod"—the warning—over all cities. 2. *His warning should be attended to.* "Hear ye the rod." The only way to escape is attention. Hear it, and flee for refuge; hear it, and thunder it abroad to alarm the careless; hear it before it is too late. "If thou hadst known the things that belong to thy peace in this day! but now are they hid from thine eyes" (Luke xix. 42).

> "Heaven gives the needful, but neglected, call.
> What day, what hour, but knocks at human hearts,
> To wake the soul to sense of future scenes?
> Deaths stand, like Mercuries, in every way,
> And kindly point us to our journey's end."
> (Young.)

D. T.

Vers. 10—15.—*Civic sins.* "Are there yet the treasures of wickedness in the house of the wicked, and the scant measure that is abominable? Shall I count them pure with the wicked balances, and with the bag of deceitful weights? For the rich men thereof are full of violence," etc. In these verses we have specified a sample of the crimes which abounded in the city, and which would bring on the threatened judgment. The passage leads us to make two remarks concerning *civic sins,* or the sins of a city.

I. THEIR VARIETY. 1. *Here is fraud.* "Are there yet the treaures of wickedness in the house of the wicked, and the scant measure that is abominable?" "Are there still in the house of the wicked treasures of wickedness and the scanty ephah?" (Henderson). This sin is described in Amos viii. 5, "When will the new moon be gone, that we may sell corn? and the sabbath, that we may set forth wheat, making the ephah small, and the shekel great, and falsifying the balances by deceit?" Fraud is one of the most prevalent crimes in all cities. Perhaps in no city was it ever more prevalent than it is in London to-day. Our commercial immorality is that at which thoughtful men stand aghast. 2. *Here is violence.* "The rich men thereof are full of violence." Strong in every age has been the tendency of rich men to oppress the lower classes by unrighteous exactions of service, by oppressive enactments. Wealth has a tendency to make men arrogant, haughty, heartless, often inhuman. The tyrant in man, as a rule, grows with the increase of his wealth. 3. *Here is falsehood.* "The inhabitants thereof have spoken lies, and their tongue is deceitful in their mouth." Unveracity is a crime, and a crime most prevalent in all cities. There is scarcely a trade or profession carried on without deception. Fortunes are made by lies. Men are everywhere deceiving each other. Such are samples of the crimes prevalent in Jerusalem.

II. THEIR RETRIBUTION. All these crimes are offensive to the Ruler of the universe, and by the law of retribution bring dire results upon the population. God says, "Shall I count them pure with the wicked balances?" It is said in Ps. xviii. 26 that with the "pure God will show himself pure; but with the froward he will show himself froward." And what are the results? Several are here specified. 1. *Disease.*

"Therefore also will I make thee sick in smiting thee." Crime is inimical to physical health and strength. The diseases that prevail in cities are, in most cases, traceable to their crimes. In every sin there is a germ of physical disease, a something which tends to disturb the nerves, taint the blood, and sap the constitution. 2. *Desolation.* "In making thee desolate because of thy sins." What is desolation? It is not the mere loss of property, friends, or the external means of physical enjoyment. A man may have all these and yet be desolate. It is the awful sense of lonesomeness, desertion. A desolate man is one who neither loves nor is loved; and sin produces this state. Few states of mind are more awful or more crushing than the sense of aloneness. 3. *Dissatisfaction.* "Thou shalt eat, but not be satisfied." Of whatever a sinful man partakes, however delicious the viands, however choice and costly the provisions, he has no satisfaction of soul. He has in connection with, and in spite of, all a hunger deep, gnawing, unappeasable. Sin and satisfaction can never coexist. 4. *Disappointment.* "Thou shalt sow, but thou shalt not reap; thou shalt tread the olives, but thou shalt not anoint thee with oil; and sweet wine, but shalt not drink wine." A sinful soul can never get out of its labour that which it expects. He toils hard for enjoyment, but all the toils are fruitless; enjoyment is not won. The autumn comes, and the fruits are gathered in—the wheat, the olives, the sweet wine; but they do not bring him what he has struggled for—true enjoyment. He has laboured for that which satisfieth not. 5. *Destruction.* "Thy casting down shall be in the midst of thee; and thou shalt take hold, but shalt not deliver; and that which thou deliverest will I give up to the sword." Henderson's translation of this seems to me good: "Thou shalt be inwardly depressed; thou mayest remove, but thou shalt not rescue, or what thou rescuest I will give to the sword."

CONCLUSION. Mark the law of retribution. "Be not deceived; God is not mocked: for whatsoever a man soweth, that shall he also reap;" "Be sure your sin will find you out." Not more certain is it that the rivers flow to the ocean, the planets follow the sun, than that suffering follows sin. Sins brings with it disease, desolation, dissatisfaction, disappointment, destruction.—D. T.

Ver. 16.—*Omri and Ahab: lessons worth study.* "For the statutes of Omri are kept, and all the works of the house of Ahab, and ye walk in their counsels; that I should make thee a desolation, and the inhabitants thereof an hissing : therefore ye shall bear the reproach of my people." On the long dark roll of human infamy there are few darker names than those of Omri and Ahab. The former, who at first was an officer in the army of Israel (1 Kings xvi. 30), through blood and slaughter took possession of the throne of Israel, which he held polluted and disgraced for twelve long years. He built Samaria and made it the capital of the ten tribes. Ahab was his son and his successor, and rivalled even his father in immorality and impiety. He established the worship of Baal as the national religion. I draw three lessons from this passage.

I. THAT THE RELIGIOUS SENTIMENT IN MAN IS OFTEN TERRIBLY PERVERTED. Omri and Ahab were not only idolaters themselves, but established idolatry in their country. They worshipped Baal, the god that was worshipped by the Carthaginians, the Babylonians, the Assyrians, and others—the god, it is supposed, who is sometimes called Moloch, to whom the Ammonites made their cruel and bloody sacrifices. For the service of this god Ahab established a numerous hierarchy of priests. The religious sentiment in man is perhaps the fundamental element of his nature. Man is made to worship, and to worship the one true and living God only. But so blinded is his intellect, so debased his nature, so utterly corrupt, that, instead of worshipping the infinitely Great, he falls down before the infinitely contemptible. The perversity of the religious sentiment: 1. *Explains the errors, crimes, and miseries of the world.* Man's strongest love is the spring of all his activities, the fontal source of all his influence. When this is directed to an idol, the whole of his life is corrupted. 2. *Reveals man's absolute need of the gospel.* There is nothing but the gospel of Christ that can give this sentiment a right direction.

II. THAT OBEDIENCE TO HUMAN SOVEREIGNS IS SOMETIMES A GREAT CRIME. The worship of Baal was enacted by the "statutes" of Omri and enforced by the practice of Ahab. If the establishment of a religion by law can make it right, it was right that the people should worship Baal. But it was not right; it was wrong. A human law, enacted by the greatest sovereign in the world with the sanction of the most illustrious statesmen, if it is not in accord with the eternal principles of justice and truth, as revealed in God's Word, should be repudiated, renounced, and transgressed. "Whether it is right to obey God rather than man, judge ye."

III. THAT THE CRIMES OF EVEN TWO MEN MAY EXERT A CORRUPTING INFLUENCE UPON MILLIONS IN FUTURE GENERATIONS. The reigns of Omri and Ahab were ages before the time when Micah lived. Notwithstanding, their enactments were still obeyed, their examples were still followed, and their practices were still pursued. The wickedness of these two men was now, ages after, perpetrated by a whole nation. How great the influence of man for good or evil! Verily one sinner destroyeth much good. From one corrupt source may flow a stream of polluting influence that shall roll down all future times, widen and deepen in its course, and bear thousands' on its bosom to crime and ruin.

> "Our many deeds, the thoughts that we have thought,
> They go out from us thronging every home;
> And in them all is folded up a power
> That on the earth doth move them to and fro;
> And mighty are the marvels they have wrought
> In hearts we know not and may never know."
> (F. W. Faber.)

D. T.

EXPOSITION.

CHAPTER VII.

Vers. 1—6.—§ 5. *Israel's penitential acknowledgment of the general corruption.*

Ver. 1.—Woe is me! (Job x. 15). Micah threatens no more; he represents repentant Israel confessing its corruption and lamenting the necessity of punishment. I am as when they have gathered the summer fruits; literally, *I am as the gatherings of the fruit-harvest.* The point of comparison is only to be inferred from the context. At the fruit-harvest no early figs are to be found, and (in the next clause) after the vintage no more grapes; so in Israel there is none righteous left. The Septuagint gives a plainer exposition, 'Εγενήθην ὡς συνάγων καλάμην ἐν ἀμητῷ, "I became as one that gathereth straw in harvest;" so the Vulgate, *Factus sum sicut qui collegit in autumno racemos vindimiæ,* joining the two clauses together. My soul desired the first-ripe fruit; better, *nor early fig which my soul desired.* The holiness and grace of more primitive times are wholly absent from this later period (see Hos. ix. 10, where a similar figure is used; compare also Christ's dealing with the barren fig tree, Matt. xxi. 18, etc.). The first-ripe figs were proverbially sweet and good (see Isa. xxviii. 4; Jer. xxiv. 2; and Hosea, *loc. cit.*).

Ver. 2.—This verse explains the preceding comparison; the grape and the early fig represent the righteous man. The good man; LXX., εὐσεβής, the godly, pious man. The Hebrew word (*khasidh*) implies one who exercises love to others, who is merciful, loving, and righteous. Is perished out of the earth; has disappeared from the world (comp. Ps. xiv. 2, 3; and especially Isa. lvii. 1). They all lie in wait for blood. They all practise violence and rapine, and meditate how they may pursue their evil designs, even to the shedding of blood. LXX., πάντες εἰς αἵματα δικάζονται, which narrows the charge to one special kind of iniquity, viz. committing judicial murders. They hunt every man his brother with a net. They ought to love their brethren, their fellow-countrymen, partakers of the same hope and privileges (Lev. xix. 18). Instead of this, they pursue them as the fowler traps birds, or the hunter beasts. The word rendered "net" (*cherem*) is in most versions translated "destruction." Thus, Septuagint, ἐκθλίβουσιν ἐκθλίβῇ: Vulgate, *ad mortem venatur;* so the Syriac and Chaldee. In the present connection it is best taken as "net" (Hab. i. 15).

Ver. 3.—That they may do evil, etc.; rather, *both hands are upon* (equivalent to "busy with") *evil to do it thoroughly.* This clause and the rest of the verse are very obscure. Cheyne supposes the text to be corrupt. Henderson renders, "For evil their hands are well prepared;" so virtually, Hitzig, Pusey, and the Septuagint. Caspari agrees rather with the Vulgate (*Malum manuum suarum dicunt bonum*), "Hands are (busy) upon evil to make (it seem) good," which looks to that extremity of iniquity when men "call evil good, and good evil" (Isa. v. 20). The general meaning is that they are ready enough to do evil, and, as the next clause says, can be bribed to do anything. **The prince asketh**; makes some nefarious demand of the judge, some perversion of justice at his hands, as in the case of Naboth (1 Kings xxi.). **The judge asketh** (*is ready*) **for a reward.** The judge is willing to do what the prince wishes, if he is bribed for it. LXX., Ὁ κριτὴς εἰρηνικοὺς λόγους ἐλάλησε, "The judge speaks words of peace" (comp. ch. iii. 11; Isa. i. 23; Zeph. iii. 3). **He uttereth his mischievous desire;** or, *the mischief of his soul.* The rich man speaks out unblushingly the evil that he has conceived in his heart, the wicked design which he meditates. **So they wrap it up;** better, *and they weave it together.* The prince, the judge, and the rich man weave their evil plan together, to make it strong and right in others' eyes. The passage is altered in meaning by a different grouping of the Hebrew letters, thus: "The prince demandeth (a reward) to do good; and the judge, for the recompense of a great man, uttereth what he himself desireth. And they entangle the good more than briars, and the righteous more than a thorn-hedge." The LXX. carries on the sense to the next verse, Καὶ ἐξελοῦμαι τὰ ἀγαθὰ αὐτῶν ὡς σὴς ἐκτρώγων, "And I will destroy their goods as a consuming moth."

Ver. 4.—**The best of them is as a brier;** hard and piercing, catching and holding all that passes by. The plant intended by the word *chedek* is a thorny one used for hedges (Prov. xv. 19). Under another aspect thorns are a symbol of what is noxious and worthless (2 Sam. xxiii. 6), or of *sin and temptation.* **The most upright is sharper** (*worse*) **than a thorn-hedge.** Those who seem comparatively upright are more injurious, tangled, and inaccessible than a hedge of thorns. In punishment of all this corruption, the prophet points to the day of judgment. **The day of thy watchmen.** The day of retribution foretold by the prophets (Isa. xxi. 6; Jer. vi. 17; Ezek. iii. 17). **And** (*even*) **thy visitation;** in apposition with the **day,** the time, and explanatory of punishment. **Cometh;** *is come*—the perfect tense denoting the certainty of the future event. Septuagint, Οὐαί, αἱ ἐκδικήσεις σου ἥκασι, "Woe! thy vengeance is come." **Now shall be their perplexity.** When this day of the Lord comes, there shall be confusion (Isa. xxii. 5); it shall bring chastisement before deliverance. The prophet here, as elsewhere, changes from the second to the third person, speaking of the people generally. Septuagint, Νῦν ἔσονται κλαυθμοὶ αὐτῶν, "Now shall be their weeping;" so the Syriac. Pusey notes the paronomasia

here. They were as bad as a thorn-hedge (*merucah*); they shall fall into perplexity (*mebucah*).

Ver. 5.—Such is the moral corruption that the nearest relations cannot be trusted: selfishness reigns everywhere. The prophet emphasizes this universal evil by warning the better portion of the people. **Friend . . . guide.** There is a gradation here, beginning with "neighbour," or "common acquaintance," and ending with "wife." The word rendered "guide" means "closest, most familiar friend," as in Ps. lv. 13 (14, Hebrew). Our version is sanctioned by the Septuagint, ἡγουμένοις, "leaders;" and the Vulgate, *duce;* but the context confirms the other translation (comp. Prov. xvi. 28; xvii. 9). Our Lord has used some of the expressions in the next verse in describing the miseries of the latter day (Matt. x. 21, 35, 36; xxiv. 12; comp. Luke xii. 53; xxi. 16; 2 Tim. iii. 2). **Keep the doors of thy mouth.** Guard thy secrets. (For the phrase, comp. Ps. cxli. 3.) **Her that lieth in thy bosom.** Thy wife (Deut. xiii. 6; xxviii. 54).

Ver. 6.—**For the son dishonoureth;** Septuagint, ἀτιμάζει: Vulgate, *contumeliam facit;* literally, *treats as a fool, despises* (Deut. xxxii. 6, 15). (For the rest of the verse, see Matt. x. 21, 35, etc.) **Men of his own house.** His domestic servants (Gen. xvii. 27). Henderson, referring to this dissolution of every natural tie, compares Ovid, 'Metamorph.,' i. 144, etc.—

"Vivitur ex rapto; non hospes ab hospite tutus,
 Non socer a genero; fratrum quoque gratia rara est;
 Imminet exitio vir conjugis, illa mariti;
 Lurida terribiles miscent aconita novercæ;
 Filius ante diem patrios inquirit in annos;
 Victa jacet pietas."

Vers. 7—13.—§ 6. *Israel expresses her faith in God, though she suffers grievous tribulation, and is confident in the fulfilment of the promised restoration.*

Ver. 7.—**Therefore I;** rather, *but as for me, I,* etc. The prophet speaks in the name of the ideal Israel. Though love and confidence have disappeared, and the day of visitation has come, and human help fails, yet Israel loses not her trust in the Lord. **Will look;** gaze intently, as if posted on a watch-tower to look out for help. **Will wait** with longing trust, unbroken by delay. **The God of my salvation.** The God from whom my salvation comes (Ps. xviii. 46; xxv. 5; xxvii. 9; Hab. iii. 18). **My God will hear me.** My prayer is sure to be answered (Isa. xxx. 19).

Ver. 8.—Israel in her sorrow and captivity asserts her undiminished confidence in the

Lord. **O mine enemy.** The oppressor of the Church, the worldly power, is represented at one time by Asshur, at another by Babylon. God uses these heathen kingdoms as agents of his vengeance. **When I fall**; *have I fallen; if I have fallen;* i.e. suppose I have suffered calamity and loss (Amos v. 2). **Sit in darkness.** Darkness is another metaphor for distress (Ps. xxiii. 4; Isa. ix. 2; Lam. iii. 6; Amos v. 18). **The Lord shall be a light unto me,** giving me gladness and true discernment (comp. Ps. xxvii. 1; xcvii. 11). The distinction between darkness and the full light of day is more marked in Eastern countries than in our Northern climes.

Ver. 9.—**I will bear the indignation of the Lord.** However long may be the delay before relief comes, Israel will patiently bear the chastisements inflicted upon her, because she knows that they are deserved. This is the language of the penitent people, owning the justice of the sentence, yet trusting to the covenant God, who in wrath remembers mercy. **Until he plead my cause.** Until God considers that the punishment has done its work, and takes my cause in hand, and judges between me and the instruments of his vengeance. **Execute judgment for me.** Secure my rights, violated by the heathen, who misuse the power given them by God. **The light** (see note on ver. 8). **His righteousness** (ch. vi. 5); his faithfulness to his promises exhibited in the destruction of the enemies and the restoration of his people. For this conception of the Divine righteousness, Cheyne compares 1 John i. 9, "He is faithful and righteous to forgive us our sins."

Ver. 10.—**She that is mine enemy.** The worldly power is here personified, as so often "the daughter of Jerusalem." **Shall see it.** She shall see that Israel was not conquered because God was powerless to save. **Where is the Lord thy God?** The Assyrians always attributed their success in arms to the assistance of their gods and the superiority of their deities to those of the conquered nations (comp. Isa. x. 9—11; xxxvii. 10—13). Thus the inscription of the palace of Khorsabad begins, "The gods Assur, Nebo, and Merodach have conferred on me the royalty of the nations. . . . By the grace and power of the great gods, my masters, I have flung my arms, by my force I have defeated my enemies" ('Records of the Past,' vol. ix.). (For taunts like that in the text, see Ps. xlii. 3; lxxix. 10; cxv. 2; Joel ii. 17). **Mine eyes shall behold her.** Israel shall behold the destruction of the enemy. **As the mire of the streets** (Isa. x. 6; Zech. x. 5).

Ver. 11.—The prophet here addresses Zion, and announces her restoration. In the day that **thy walls are to be built;** rather, *a day for building thy walls (gader) cometh.* Zion is represented as a vineyard whose fence has been destroyed (Isa. v. 5, 7). The announcement is given abruptly and concisely in three short sentences. In that day shall the **decree be far removed.** The decree (Zeph. ii. 2) is explained by Hengstenberg and many commentators, ancient and modern, to be that of the enemy by which they held Israel captive. Keil and others suppose the law to be meant which separated Israel from all other nations, the ancient ordinance which confined God's people and the blessings of the theocracy to narrow limits. This is now to be set aside (comp. Eph. ii. 11—16), when heathen nations flock to the city of God. Caspari, Hitzig, Cheyne, and others translate, "shall the bound be afar off," i.e. the boundaries of the land of Israel shall be widely extended (comp. Isa. xxxiii. 17, which Cheyne explains, "Thine eyes shall behold a widely extended territory"). Wordsworth obtains much the same meaning by taking the verb in the sense of "promulgated," and referring the "decree," as in Ps. ii. 7, 8, to God's purpose of giving to Messiah the utmost parts of the earth for a possession. The building of the walls does not indicate the narrowing of the limits of the theocratic kingdom. Whether *chok* be taken to signify "decree" (*lex*, Vulgate) or "boundary," the effect of its removal afar is seen by the next verse to be the entrance of foreign nations into the kingdom of God. The LXX. favours the first interpretation, 'Αποτρίψεται [ἀπώσεται, Alex.] νόμιμά σου [σου omit, Alex.] ἡ ἡμέρα ἐκείνη, "That day shall utterly abolish thy ordinances."

Ver. 12.—**He shall come**; *they shall come.* Men shall flock to Zion as the metropolis of the new kingdom (ch. iv. 2). The countries named are those in which the Jews were dispersed (see Isa. xi. 11). Micah embraces in one view the restoration of Israel and the conversion of the heathen (comp. Isa. xix. 24; xxvii. 12, 13). **Assyria.** The type of the greatest enemy of God. **The fortified cities**; rather, *the cities of Mazor,* the strong land, i.e. Egypt. The usual term for Egypt is Mizraim; but Mazor is found in 2 Kings xix. 24; Isa. xix. 6; xxxvii. 25. Cheyne compares the Assyrian name for this country, *Muçar.* **From the fortress**; *from Mazor*; Septuagint, ἀπὸ Τύρου, "from Tyre" or Tsor. **Even to the river.** From Egypt to the Euphrates, which was the river *par excellence* (Gen. xv. 18). **From sea to sea.** Not necessarily from the Mediterranean to the Dead Sea or to the Persian Gulf (as Joel ii. 20), but generally, from one sea to another, from the earth as bounded by the seas; so, from mountain to mountain; *i.e.* not from Lebanon to Sinai, or from Hor (Numb. xx. 22) to Hor (Numb. xxxiv. 7), which is too limited, but from all lands situated between mountain-barriers, which are the bounds of the world (comp. Isa. lx. 3, etc.).

Ver. 13.—Notwithstanding the land shall be desolate. Very many commentators consider the land of Canaan to be here intended, the prophet recurring to threatenings of judgment before the great restoration comes to pass ; but it is best to regard the clause as referring to all the world, exclusive of Canaan. While the Messianic kingdom is set up, judgment shall fall upon the sinful world. " For the nation and kingdom that will not serve thee shall perish ; yea, those nations shall be utterly wasted" (Isa. lx. 12; comp. Rev. xii. 12). And the material world shall suffer with its inhabitants (Gen. iii. 15, 18 ; vi. 13 ; xix. 25 ; Isa. xxxiv, 4, etc.). Their doings. Their evil deeds, especially the rejection of Messiah.

Vers. 14—17.—§ 7. *The prophet in the name of the people prays for this promised salvation, and the Lord assures him that his mercies shall not fail, and that the hostile nations shall be humbled.*

Ver. 14.—Feed thy people with thy rod. The prophet prays to the Shepherd of Israel (Gen. xlix. 24 ; Ps. lxxx. 1), beseeching him to rule and lead his people, and to find them pasture. The " rod " is the shepherd's staff (Lev. xxvii. 32 ; Ps. xxiii. 4). The flock of thine heritage. So Israel is called (Ps. xxviii. 9 ; xcv. 7 ; comp. Zeph. iii. 13). Which dwell solitarily; or, *so that they dwell;* separate from all other nations, religiously and physically, by institution and geographical position. Compare Balaam's words (Numb. xxiii. 9; also Deut. xxxiii. 28). It was Israel's special characteristic to be holy, *i.e.* set apart, and it was only when she observed her duty in this respect that she prospered (see Exod. xxxiii. 16). In the wood (*forest*) in the midst of Carmel. The forest would isolate the flock, and secure it from interference. The chief pasture-lands west and east of Jordan are named, and the whole country is included in the description. (For Carmel, see note on Amos i. 2.) Bashan and Gilead were also celebrated for their rich pasture. " Bulls of Bashan " were a proverb for well-fed animals, and a metaphor for bloated, proud aristocrats (Deut. xxxii. 14 ; Ps. xxii. 12 ; Ezek. xxxix. 18 ; Amos iv. 1). Gilead was so excellently adapted for cattle that Reuben and Gad were irresistibly drawn to settle there (Numb. xxxii. 1, 5 ; 1 Chron. v. 9 ; see the parallel to this passage in Isa. lxv. 9, 10, and Ezek. xxxiv. 13, 14). As in the days of

old ; usually taken to refer to the time of Moses and Joshua, but also and more probably, to that of David and Solomon, which realized the ideal of peace and prosperity (comp. ch. iv. 4).

Ver. 15.—According to (*as in*) the days. The Lord answers the prophet's prayer, taking up his last word, and promising even more than he asks, engaging to equal the wonders which marked the exodus from Egypt. That great deliverance was a type and foreshadowing of Messianic salvation (comp. Isa. xliii. 15, etc.; li. 10 ; 1 Cor. x. 1, etc.). Unto him; unto the people of Israel (ver. 14). Marvellous things ; Septuagint, Ὄψεσθε θαυμαστά, " Ye shall see marvellous things." Supernatural occurrences are meant, as Exod. iii. 20; xv. 11 ; Ps. lxxvii. 14. We do not read of any special miracles at the return from captivity, so the people were led to look onward to the advent of Messiah for these wonders.

Ver. 16.—Shall see. The heathen shall see these marvellous things. Be confounded at (*ashamed of*) all their might. Hostile nations shall be ashamed when they find the impotence of their boasted power. Compare the effect of the Exodus on contiguous nations (Exod. xv. 14, etc.; Josh. ii. 9, 10). They shall lay their hand upon their mouth. They shall be silent from awe and astonishment (Judg. xviii. 19 ; Job xxi. 5 ; Isa. lii. 15). Their ears shall be deaf. Their senses shall be stupefied by the wonders which they see—that which Job (xxvi. 14) calls " the thunder of his mighty deeds." There may also be an allusion to their wilful obstinacy, and unbelief.

Ver. 17.—They shall lick the dust like a serpent (Gen. iii. 14 ; Isa. lxv. 25). The enemies of God's people " shall lick the dust " (Ps. lxxii. 9), shall be reduced to the utmost degradation (Isa. xlix. 23). They shall move out of their holes, etc.; rather, *they come trembling out of their close places* (or, *fastnesses,* Ps. xviii. 46), *like crawling things of the earth.* They who prided themselves on their security shall come forth from their strongholds in utter fear, driven out like snakes from their lairs (comp. Ps. ii. 11 ; Hos. xi. 10, etc.). They shall be afraid of (*whine with fear unto*) the Lord our God. They shall be driven by terror to acknowledge the God of Israel. The expression is ambiguous, and may mean servile fear, which makes a man shrink from God, or that fear. which is one step towards repentance ; the latter seems intended here, as in Hos. iii. 5, where, as Pusey says, the words, " and his goodness," determine the character of the fear. Because of (or, *before*) thee. It is the heathen who are still the subject, not the Israelites (Jer. x. 7).

The sudden change of persons is quite in the prophet's style.

Vers. 18—20.—§ 8. *The book ends with a lyric ode in praise of God's mercy and faithfulness.*

Ver. 18.—In view of the many provocations and backslidings of the people, Micah is filled with wonder at the goodness and long-suffering of God. Who is a God like unto thee? The question seems to recall the prophet's own name, which means, "Who is like Jehovah?" and the clause in Moses' song (Exod. xv. 11), "Who is like unto thee, O Lord, among the gods?" Such comparisons are made from the standpoint of the nations who believe in the real existence of their false gods. That pardoneth iniquity (comp. Exod. xxxiv. 7; Numb. xiv. 18). Passeth by the transgression; Septuagint, ὑπερβαίνων ἀσεβείας, "passing over iniquities;" Vulgate, *transis peccatum*. To pass by, or pass over, is to forgive, as Amos vii. 8. There is probably an allusion, as Jerome says, to the night of the Exodus. As the destroying angel passed over the Israelites and destroyed them not, so God spares his people, imputing not their iniquities unto them. The remnant (ch. ii. 12; iv. 6, 7). The true Israel, which is only a remnant (Isa. x. 21; Rom. ix. 27). He retaineth not his anger for ever (Ps. ciii. 9). The word rendered "for ever" is translated by Jerome *ultra*, and by the Septuagint εἰς μαρτύριον, *i.e.* to testify the justice of his punishment. He delighteth in mercy. As the Collect says, "O God, whose nature and property is always to have mercy and to forgive" (comp. Wisd. xi. 24).

Ver. 19.—He will turn again, and have compassion upon us. The verb "turn again," joined with another verb, often denotes the repetition of an action, as in Job vii. 7; Hos. xiv. 8, etc.; so here we may translate simply, "He will again have compassion." He will subdue; literally, *tread underfoot*. Sin is regarded as a personal enemy, which by God's sovereign grace will be entirely subdued. So, according to one interpretation, sin is personified (Gen. iv. 7; comp. Ps. lxv. 3). Cast all their sins into the depths of the sea. Thou wilt blot out and bury completely and for ever, as once thou didst overwhelm the Egyptians in the Red Sea (Exod. xv. 1, 4, 10, 21). The miraculous deliverance of the Israelites at the Exodus is a type of the greater deliverance of the true Israelites in Christ (Ps. ciii. 12; 1 John i. 7; comp. Isa. xliii. 25).

Ver. 20.—Thou wilt perform (literally, *give*) the truth to Jacob, and the mercy to Abraham. Jacob and Abraham are mentioned as the chiefs and representatives of the chosen family; and "the truth" (*i.e.* God's faithfulness to his promises) and "mercy" are equally given to both, separately assigned only for the sake of the parallelism. Knabenbauer compares such passages as Ps. cxiv. 1, "When Israel went forth out of Egypt, the house of Jacob from a people of strange language" (Ps. cv. 6; Isa. xli. 8; lxiii. 16, etc.). The general meaning, therefore, is that God will perform the promises made to the forefathers, as Luke i. 72, etc. Hast sworn, as in Gen. xxii. 16, etc.; xxviii. 13, etc.; Deut. vii. 12. With the close of the ode Hengstenberg compares Rom. xi. 33—36. Thus the checkered prophecy ends with the glow of faith and happy hope.

HOMILETICS.

Vers. 1—13.—*The good in degenerate times.* We are not to understand these verses as referring specially to the prophet himself. In ch. i. 8, 9 we have his own lamentation in view of the prevailing ungodliness; here "the speaker is not the prophet, but the true Israel, *i.e.* Israel within Israel, personified" (Cheyne). God has never left himself without witnesses. Even in the most corrupt and degenerate times he has had a people to show forth his praise. It was so in the age to which this book of Scripture refers. Widespread though the depravity was, "a remnant" continued faithful, true, loyal to God and obedient to his will; and Micah here speaks simply as the mouthpiece of these, setting forth their sadness in view of the abounding wickedness, yet withal their unshaken confidence in the triumph of truth and righteousness; whilst then, as the prophet of the Lord, he declared that this confidence should not be disappointed, but the victory anticipated be most surely won. Notice here, concerning the Church of God—

I. HER BITTER DISAPPOINTMENT. (Vers. 1—6.) 1. *The desire for spiritual excellence was ardently cherished.* This aspiration of the good is here expressed figuratively. "My soul desired the first-ripe figs" (ver. 1). These were accounted the choicest and sweetest, and were very refreshing and very welcome to the weary traveller, and hence were chosen as the symbol of spiritual excellence. So elsewhere in the prophetical writings (Hos. ix. 10; Jer. xxiv.). The meaning, then, is that the good longed for the prevalence of piety in the nation, and to see the people bringing forth the fruits of righteousness. This is the aspiration of the good in every age. As the sculptor ardently desires to see the rough block transformed into the perfect statue, or the artist to see the bare canvas before him covered with the creations of his genius, or the horticulturist to see the waste field transformed into a garden of delight, and bearing, in infinite variety, the flowers and fruits; so all good men yearn to see the spiritual transformation of the world. " My soul desired the first-ripe figs " (ver. 1). 2. *This ardently cherished desire was unrealized.* (Ver. 1.) The verse brings vividly before us the sense of disappointment arising from the spiritual barrenness and unproductiveness that prevailed in the land. The scene presented was not that of an abundant harvest, but of a land bare and barren, whose best days were of yore, in which so little good remained as to be but like gleanings when the vintage is over, not even a cluster remaining. " I am as when they have gathered," etc. (ver. 1). And as further illustrating this disappointment, a graphic description is given of the prevailing spiritual desolation. (1) Mortality and martyrdom had impoverished the land in the removal from it of the tender, the trusty, the true (ver. 2; Isa. lvii. 1). (2) Anarchy reigned, with its accompanying violence, treachery, and injustice (vers. 2, 3). (3) The administration of justice had become a burlesque, its administrators working together, " wrapping it up," weaving it together so as to keep up the form, and to appear just, whilst really seeking their own selfish ends (ver. 3), and even " the best " amongst them being " hard and piercing," even as a briar, and " the most upright " being as " a thorn-hedge which, set for protection, inflicts injury " (ver. 4). (4) Friendship, " sweet'ner of life and solder of society," had become insincere and unreal; yea, even the most sacred relationships of life had become perverted, and natural affection sacrificed and changed to hate (vers. 5, 6). 3. *This non-realization occasioned bitter disappointment.* " Woe is me ! " (ver. 1). A life of piety is marked by the experience of true joy (Ps. i. 1—3; Prov. iii. 17). Yet it is not always sunshine even with the good. " If we listen to David's harp, we shall hear as many hearse-like harmonies as carols " (Bacon). And a very large ingredient in the cup of sorrow to the good is occasioned by the contemplation of the blighting effects of sin. As looking around them, and despite their endeavours to disseminate truth and righteousness, they see multitudes walking according to the world's maxims, cherishing its spirit and reaping its sad harvest, sorrow fills their hearts, and they become desponding and sad. And hence the lament of the Church in view of her small numbers and the general corruption, as here expressed, " Woe is me ! " etc. (ver. 1).

II. HER UNSWERVING CONFIDENCE. (Vers. 7—10.) 1. *This confidence rested in God.* " Therefore I will look unto the Lord " (ver. 7). In times of seeming nonsuccess in holy service we should cherish unswerving trust in the God of truth, and having faithfully discharged our duty, should commit the rest unto him. 2. *This confidence was expressed in patient waiting for God.* He had " spoken good concerning Israel," and had declared " glorious things " respecting Zion, the city of God. And in the dark days his servants were prepared patiently to wait for the fulfilment of these, even as the mariner waits for fair winds and favourable tide, or as the watchman waits through the long night for the coming of the day. " I will wait for the God of my salvation " (ver. 7). 3. *This confidence was sustained by inspiring hope.* " My God will hear me." So did hope cast her bow of promise across the stormy cloud and kindle the bright star in the dark sky. 4. *This confidence triumphed even in the midst of adversity.* The world was very evil, and the good in the land were few. Iniquity appeared to be victorious, and might to triumph over right. The hearts of the pious, full of patriotism and of the love of God, were sad; yet their reliance was unshaken and unswerving. Dark days were before them, severe chastisement must be experienced, and they would soon feel the rod of the oppressor and be exposed to the taunts of the heathen, who would mockingly ask, " Where is the Lord thy God ? " But they could rest in the assurance that the Lord would be their Light in darkness; that he would interpose on their behalf, bringing them forth out of the gloom into the light, covering their foes with shame, and vindicating his own righteousness. " Rejoice not against me," etc. (vers. 8—10).

III. HER ASSURED VICTORY. (Vers. 11—13.) In these verses, speaking, not as the mouthpiece of the good but prophetically as the seer, Micah delivers the assurance he was inspired by God to utter, and bearing upon the time to come. His words, as rendered in the Authorized Version, are somewhat obscure, but we gather from them that a brighter future should dawn upon the world sin had darkened and defiled, and of that glorious era he here speaks. And as his people, in the days when they " sat by the rivers of Babylon, and wept as they remembered Zion," and thought of the desolation sin had wrought, turned to these and similar assurances of the golden age yet to come, who can tell to what an extent they became nerved afresh and inspired with renewed courage and hope! Even so let those to-day who grieve, with the good through all ages, over the blighting effects of sin, rejoice in the prospect of the ultimate victory. "Lift up your heads . . . redemption draweth nigh." Now death reigns and sin triumphs; but ere long grace shall reign through righteousness unto eternal life. Every throe of sorrow is bringing us nearer to the time of the world's full deliverance from the power of evil. The triumph is sure. "The Lord God Omnipotent reigneth." This suggestive paragraph closes with a note of warning. "Notwithstanding," etc. (ver. 13). There is a glorious future awaiting the Church of God, but meanwhile the work of judgment must be perfected. Notwithstanding the bright prospect here unfolded, sin will assuredly work its dire effects. The triumph of righteousness carries with it the defeat of unrighteousness. One of the poets sings of a bell suspended on the Inchcape rock, that the sound might warn the sailors of their nearness to danger; and tells how pirates cut the bell so as to silence the sound; and how that subsequently these same pirates struck upon the very rock which they had deprived of its means of warning them. Let us not thus treat this note of warning, but be constrained to "break off sin by righteousness," as it reminds us that "God is not mocked," and that "whatsoever a man soweth, that shall he also reap."

Ver. 7.—*Waiting for God.* "I will wait for the God of my salvation." The good, personified, are here represented as declaring that they would place themselves in harmony with the wise and holy will of God; that they would trustingly acquiesce and quietly endure, drawing from intimate personal relationship to God that holy inspiration which would enable them in the dark days now before them, with true heroism to encounter every difficulty, and with calm resignation to bear every sorrow, and to find in so doing tranquillity and peace. "I will wait," etc. (ver. 7).

I. OUR CIRCUMSTANCES IN LIFE OFTEN CALL FOR THE EXERCISE OF THIS SPIRIT OF PATIENT WAITING FOR GOD. It is the method of our God by slow processes to bring to pass all that he has designed, whether in nature, in providence, or in grace. His purposes are gradually evolved. His delays are for wise and gracious reasons. Hence, instead of fretting and repining and growing impatient under adversity, as though some strange thing were happening to us, it behoves us to "rest in the Lord," and so be cheerful even in the night and under the shadow of the cloud, assured that to those rightly exercised by sorrow "tribulation worketh patience, and patience experience, and experience hope" (Rom. v. 3, 4).

II. THE CHERISHING OF THIS SPIRIT ENNOBLES HUMAN CHARACTER. 1. *You see in such a case a man who is continually gaining triumphs where multitudes are worsted and defeated.* There are many who can do, but who cannot bear. They can actively serve God and strive to promote the interests of men, but they cannot passively yield themselves up to the will of God, and, without resentment, bear the reproaches of those who seek their hurt. And certainly the man who is able to do this is the more royal. Who can doubt the wisdom of Solomon when he said, "He that ruleth his spirit is better than he that taketh a city" (Prov. xvi. 32)? 2. *You see in such a case a man who is clearly under the influence of high Christian motives.* The influences which impel a man calmly and trustingly to submit to God's all-wise but often inscrutable appointments, are not human, but Divine. There is nothing in mere earthly considerations that is at all calculated to inspire this patience. It is only as we bring the realities of eternity to bear upon our present experiences that we become lifted up to a higher realm, and are enabled patiently to endure.

III. BY THIS PATIENT WAITING GOD IS GLORIFIED AND SERVED. The thought of service to God is too often restricted to *active endeavour.* It is overlooked that he may be served by us passively as well as actively; by quiet resignation to his will as well as by open and earnest toil in seeking the good of others. "They also serve who only stand and wait." Great was the service rendered by the Man Christ Jesus as he traversed the cities and villages of Palestine, going about doing good, and speaking of the things pertaining to the kingdom of God; but yet higher service was rendered by him as with holy resignation he acquiesced in the great Father's will and "endured the cross, despising the shame."

IV. This waiting for the Lord shall in no wise lose its reward. There shall be ultimate deliverance; salvation shall come, and the thankful acknowledgment shall be, "Lo, this is our God; we have waited for him, and he hath saved us: this is the Lord; we have waited for him, we will evermore be glad and rejoice in his salvation" (Isa. xxv. 9).

Vers. 8, 9.—*From darkness into light.* "When I sit in darkness, the Lord shall be a Light unto me. . . . He will bring me forth to the light." The Bible is "the heart-book of the world." In order to the unravelment of its deep spiritual teaching, we must study it in the light of our own soul-experiences—of our joys and sorrows and needs. It is one thing to be able to understand the volume in the meaning of its words and the construction of its phrases and forms of expression; but it is quite another thing to feel that it is ours to enter into the inward experiences of God's saints of old, through whom he speaks to us in these wondrous pages—experiences by which he has fitted them to be his messengers of help and hope to the world; and to enter into these we must bring our hearts as well as our intellects to the study of the book, and endeavour to trace the application of its teachings to the wants and aspirations of the human spirit. Notice in the human experience here described—

I. Darkness. The adverse influences of life are thus symbolized. We are constantly attended by these. It must be so. Human life is a pilgrimage, and no traveller can expect to reach the end of his journey without feeling weary and worn. It is a voyage, and hence we must encounter storms. The world is a stage, and we are the players, and although to outward appearances it may seem that we are acting our respective parts with ease, who can tell what anxiety is encountered *behind the scenes?* These adverse influences meet us in life's daily duties. They are often occasioned by differences in temper and disposition, giving rise to misunderstanding; or by the temporal circumstances being straitened; or by prolonged and tedious suspense in reference to the success or failure of certain projects; or by baffled hopes and expectations. They come to us in the form of the sorrows of life. There is failure of health, with the anxious days and weary nights it brings to the household. There is bereavement, with its attendant grief and gloom. There are also cruel misrepresentations, malicious censures, unjust reproaches (ver. 10). And these adverse influences follow in quick succession.

> "When sorrows come, they come not single spies,
> But in battalions."

They fill the heart with sadness, and there settles down upon the troubled spirit the darkness of night. "I sit in darkness."

II. Light in darkness. Light is revealing, restoring, gladdening, in its effects. Under its influence that which was before concealed becomes manifest to us; new life is put into us, and joy and gladness become inspired within. So shall it be with the good in a spiritual sense. In their gloomiest seasons these gracious influences shall be experienced by them by reason of the presence with them of the Lord their God. It is not so much that the Lord will cause light to break in upon them (although that is gloriously true), as that he himself will be with them as their Light. "When I sit in darkness the Lord shall be a Light unto me;" "The Lord is my Light and my Salvation" (Ps. xxvii. 1); "In his favour is life" (Ps. xxx. 5). Light in darkness, springing from the conscious presence of the Lord, is the thought here expressed. And in the next verse is the additional, yet closely related thought of—

III. Passing out of darkness into the light. "He will bring me forth to the light" (ver. 9). So has it been in the past in the experience of the good. Jacob (comp. Gen. xlii. 36 with xlv. 26—28); Elijah (comp. 1 Kings xix. 4 with vers. 5—8, 18); the Shunammite (comp. 2 Kings iv. 20 with ver. 37); the Captivity (comp.

Ps. cxxiii. with Ps. cxxvi.). So still to all trusting hearts; and so hereafter, "The Lord shall be thine everlasting Light, and the days of thy mourning shall be ended" (Isa. lx. 20).

Vers. 14—17.—*Prayer and its response.* How mysteriously great is the privilege of prayer! How wonderful that finite creatures may thus draw near to the Infinite, carrying their needs into the Divine presence, breathing their desires into the ear of God, and obtaining from him all required mercy and grace! We think of the patriarch who, weary and worn with his wanderings, slept, with a stone for his pillow, and we speak of the ladder he beheld connecting the spot where he lay with the very throne of God, as his *vision ;* but the thought of *prayer* changes this into a blessed *reality,* for communication between earth and heaven has been established, and thus human spirits rise to God, and enrichments descend from him to satisfy men's deepest needs! Prayer, in the highest conception of it, is a thoughtful communion with God. It is intercourse with God. It is sympathetic contact with him. It is an exercise in which we engage that we may have fellowship with the Invisible, and may thus understand the Divine will, and become increasingly disposed to become obedient thereunto. Helpful, indeed, is the influence we derive from communion with the pure and holy amongst men ; then say how elevating must be contact with him who is perfect in purity, the Eternal Spirit! But prayer is also supplication. We have wants. God has constituted us dependent beings. Needs, both temporal and spiritual, press upon us at times with a heavy weight. And prayer is the soul, deeply conscious of these necessities, coming to God with intense desire seeking their supply. Our supplications, however, should rise beyond our own individual wants. Prayer should be presented by us on behalf of others. In this holy exercise we should seize upon interests broader than those pertaining to our own personal life, and, with a true concern, should bear these up before the throne of God. As the great Intercessor pleads for us before his Father's throne, so we also in our measure are to be intercessors for men. The Prophet Micah comes before us in these verses as exercising this intercessory function. Note here—

I. THE DEVOTED SEER PLEADING WITH GOD ON BEHALF OF HIS PEOPLE. (Ver. 14.) Observe : 1. He makes mention of their peculiar relationship to the Most High : (1) As being his chosen servants. "Thy people;" "the flock of thine inheritance." (2) As separated from the nations to his praise: "which dwell solitarily." 2. He recalls the former manifestations to them of the Divine goodness in the bestowment of rich blessings. "The days of old." 3. He supplicates the Divine Shepherd to be with them in the dark days now before them, sustaining them and enriching them with plenty (ver. 14).

II. THE DIVINE RESPONSE TO THE EARNEST SUPPLICATION OF THE PROPHET. 1. The prophet was assured that there should be deliverance wrought for his people by Divine interposition (ver. 15). 2. It was declared to him that the foes who would triumph over them should ultimately be covered with confusion and shame (vers. 16, 17). Intercessory prayer is still an essential part of the ministry of the Church ; it is mighty and prevailing ; it commands and wields the forces of heaven. "The effectual fervent prayer of a righteous man availeth much" (Jas. v. 16).

Vers. 18, 19.—*The forgiving God.* No words could possibly have been more appropriate than these by way of bringing this brief book of prophecy to a close. When we think of the degenerate character of the age in which this prophet lived, and when we remember that he had constantly to deal with human guilt and depravity, to declare the Divine judgments, and to endeavour by warnings and threatenings to bring home to men a sense of their sinfulness,—what could be more fitting than that, in closing his contribution to the Divine oracles, he should expatiate, as he does here so impressively, upon Jehovah as being *the forgiving God.* His design in these verses clearly was to extol the grace and mercy of the Lord his God. As he thought of the Divine forgiving love, he felt that with the Most High none can compare. With warmest admiration, combined with the profoundest adoration, he asks, "Who is a God like unto thee, that pardoneth iniquity, and passeth by the transgression of the remnant of his heritage?" (ver. 18). And instead of attempting to answer his own inquiry, he indicates what his answer would be by enlarging yet further upon God's pardoning grace: "He retaineth not," etc. (vers. 18, 19). Let us reflect upon the incomparableness of the Lord our God, viewed as the Divine Forgiver. Consider—

I. WHAT THIS DIVINE FORGIVENESS IMPLIES. 1. *The great fact of sin.* There are those who have endeavoured to explain away this solemn fact of sin; who contend that there is not to be found in man any intentional preference of wrong to right; that what we call sin is something predicable of society rather than of the individual; that man himself is right enough, but lacks the science required to organize society rightly; and that what we call sin is after all only the development of these discordant causes in society. See Bushnell's reply to this, setting forth on this theory our inconsistency in blaming the persons by whom sinful acts have been wrought, and in censuring ourselves when we have done unworthy acts, etc. ('Nature and the Supernatural,' ch. v.). There is no escape from admitting the great fact of sin. The Word is unerring as it declares that "all have sinned, and come short of the glory of God" (Rom. iii. 23); that "there is none that doeth good, no, not one" (Rom. iii. 12); and that "every mouth must be stopped, and the whole world stand guilty before God" (Rom. iii. 19). 2. *The Divine interposition with a view to the deliverance of the race from this terrible blight.* We can form no true conception of the Divine forgiveness unless these facts of personal guilt and transgression, and of the Divine interposition in order to our deliverance, are kept prominently before us. And even at this stage our admiration is called into exercise, and we cry, "Who is a God like unto thee?" This is intensified as we consider—

II. WHAT THIS DIVINE FORGIVENESS INCLUDES. It includes deliverance from the sad consequences of sin. Note what these are. 1. *Mark the consequences of sin to the individual.* (1) There is *loss of power.* Every spiritual defeat is attended by the weakening of moral strength. (2) There is *disquietude of conscience.* (3) *Separation from God.* There can be no communion where there is contrariety of nature. "How can two walk together except they be agreed?" (4) *Suffering and death.* The connection between the spirit and the body is so intimate that the body necessarily suffers through the disorganization sin has wrought in the soul. 2. *Consequences resulting to society.* These also are sad and distressing. "The bad inheritance passes, and fears, frauds, crimes against property, character, and life, abuses of power, oppressions of the weak, persecutions of the good, piracies, wars of revolt, wars of conquest, are the staple of the world's bitter history. It is a pitiless and dreadful power, as fallen society must necessarily be" (Bushnell, 'Nature and the Supernatural,' p. 123). The Divine forgiveness means deliverance from all these sad consequences of evil. It is not a bare pardon merely, but it carries with it enfranchisement from the blighting effects of evil. There is the impartation to the forgiven of a Divine power, an inward spiritual force to enable them to resist the evil and downward tendencies; the lost power is restored, and which is mighty in "subduing our iniquities" (ver. 19). There is the impartation to the forgiven of peace of conscience; the discordant and disturbing elements are hushed; the harmonies are restored. There is the experience of renewed communion with the Eternal. The soul, accepted and renewed, would ever abide at the feet of the Lord. There is oneness and agreement now, and hence fellowship is possible and practicable, yea, is felt to be desirable and essential. "Blessed are the pure in heart: for they shall see God." And whilst suffering and death remain, yet by a Divine alchemy the character of these life-sorrows becomes entirely changed, and they cease to be viewed as harsh inflictions, but are accepted as the loving discipline by which the Divine Father renders the character perfect and entire, whilst "the sting of death" having been taken away, the terror also is gone. And as men become thus brought into this holy experience will the regeneration of the world and its complete deliverance from evil be brought to pass. What a fulness of meaning, then, there is when God is spoken of as "pardoning iniquity"! And as we think how that this forgiveness carries with it all the privileges, honours, and enjoyments here and hereafter of the spiritual life, our admiration of him who has made all this possible to the individual and the race rises higher still, and we cry with wondering and adoring love, "Who is a God like unto thee?"

III. WHAT THIS DIVINE FORGIVENESS INVOLVES. 1. It has involved on the part of God all that is comprehended in the gift and work of his Son Jesus Christ; for it is through Christ alone that this forgiveness of sin is secured. "In him have we redemption through his blood, even the forgiveness of our sins" (Col. i. 14).   It involved the heavenly Shepherd's coming forth to seek his lost and fallen world. "The Son of man is come to seek and to save that which was lost" (Luke xix. 10).   Lo ! the Christ of God, the Gift of the Father's love, clothed himself in our humanity, obeyed the Law we had broken, atoned for sin in the death of the cross, that we might not perish, that we might exchange the wilderness for the fold, be lifted out of the lost condition into hope, dignity, and character here, and be raised hereafter to immortal purity, peace, and joy.   The power of human language is too weak adequately to describe the love of God as expressed even in the minutest of his doings; but in reference to this seeking the erring, with a view to their restoration, it signally fails, and we can only adoringly cry, "Who is a God like unto thee ? "   2. On the part of *man* this Divine forgiveness involves *penitence and faith.*   "Repent ye, and believe the gospel" (Mark i. 15).   On conditions thus simple the vilest transgressor may find mercy of the Lord.   And if there is another thought which leads us to feel this pardoning love of God to be the more wonderful, it is the remembrance that he has not only provided the pardon, but even condescends to plead with men, that they may be led to fulfil the righteous conditions and to receive the boon (Isa. i. 18; Rev. iii. 20).   Let us not repel him who has come to bless us by turning us away from our iniquities, but rather give him a hearty greeting.   Then, with this ancient seer and with the forgiven through all ages, we shall cry, with hearts overflowing with love and praise, "Who is a God like unto thee ? " (vers. 18, 19).

Ver. 20.—*The Divine promises and their fulfilment.* These words bear upon them the impress of deep human experience.   They form the crowning testimony of a man who had long proved the reality of that which they affirm.   In closing his book of prophecy he would, with all his heart and soul, affix his seal to the bright declaration that God is ever faithful and true.   Jehovah was to him a living reality, the centre of his affections and the strength of his heart.   "He endured as seeing him who is invisible."   And Divine, indeed, is that trust in the eternal Lord which fires the soul and nerves it for entering into "the holy war;" which stands the warrior in good stead, and proves invulnerable whilst he engages in the strife; and which also, when the good soldier, having fought well and grown grey in the service, begins to lay aside his armour and quietly to await the summons to the presence and joy of the Lord he has served, proves his consolation and support.   Micah doubtless had in mind the rich promises given by God, first to Abraham, and then reiterated to Jacob, that they should be blessed and multiplied, and that through their line lasting blessings should flow to all the families of the earth (Gen. xxii. 16—18; xxviii. 13, 14).   Notice—

I. HE REPRESENTS THE DIVINE PROMISES AS CHARACTERIZED BY "MERCY" AND "TRUTH."   "The truth to Jacob, and the mercy to Abraham" (ver. 20).   The expression is, at first sight, rather peculiar; yet it may easily be explained.   By "mercy" we understand favour shown to the undeserving.   Grand hero as Abraham was, there was nothing in him to merit such distinguishing honour as was conferred upon him.   The choice was altogether traceable to the abounding mercy and grace of God.   So also with Jacob, who, at the outset of his career, was about as unlovely as man could well be.   Then why, it may be asked, the change in the form of expression?   Why not "the mercy to Abraham" and "the mercy to Jacob"?   Why "the mercy to Abraham" and "the truth to Jacob"?   Simply to introduce the additional thought of "truth."   "Truth" here means the bringing into clearer light that which had been partially hinted at.   "What was free mercy to Abraham became, when God had once promised it, his truth" (Pusey).   And his revelation of truth became clearer and brighter, until at length he appeared in whom both "grace and truth" came in their unveiled clearness and their unrestricted fulness.

II. HE TRACES THESE DIVINE PROMISES AS HAVING THEIR SOURCE AND SPRING IN THE ETERNAL LOVE OF GOD.   "From the days of old," *i.e.* from eternity, God has cherished the loving purpose of enriching us thus.   It is not "a modern project, but an ancient charter."

III. HE REJOICES IN THE ASSURANCE THAT THESE DIVINE PROMISES SHALL BE UNDOUBTEDLY FULFILLED.   "Thou wilt perform," etc.   This assurance rested on *the Divine pledge* ("which thou hast sworn unto our fathers"), and which the faithful Promiser is both able and willing to redeem.   "He cannot deny himself" (2 Tim. ii.

13). In building the temple of Solomon two pillars were set up in the porch of the edifice—the left one being called Boaz, *i.e.* " In God is strength ; " and the other on the right being named Jachin, *i.e.* " He will establish "—thus beautifully associating together the thoughts of God's ability and his willing resolve to bless. Let these thoughts dwell in our minds respecting him, for on these pillars our faith and hope may ever securely rest.

HOMILIES BY VARIOUS AUTHORS.

Vers. 1, 2.—*A moral dearth in the land.* The prophet, speaking in the name of the godly remnant of the land, laments their terrible isolation. We are thus reminded of the sad condition of a land in which there is a dearth of good men. For: 1. *They are the choice fruit of the land*—wholesome, fragrant, delicious. The ideal Israel is compared to "grapes" and "the first ripe in the fig tree" (Hos. ix. 10). The Lord " taketh pleasure " in such ; they satisfy the hunger of the Divine heart for godliness in the creature (Ps. cxlvii. 11; cxlix. 4 ; Prov. xi. 20). So far as they share the spirit of Christ, they are, like him, " beloved of God," and should be attractive to men. 2. *They are the salt of the earth*—the one element that preserves from universal corruption. The picture presented to us is the gradual dying out of the godly; they "cease" (Ps. xii. 1), they "perish" (Isa lvii. 1). Some few remain, "two or three in the top of the uttermost bough," which were not touched, or those unripe which were but imperfect and poor, or those which had fallen, " and thus were fouled and stained, and yet were not utterly carried away." The promise, "Instead of thy fathers shall be thy children " (Ps. **xlv.** 16), is no longer fulfilled. The sons and daughters of the godly do not rise up to fill their places in the Church. The few godly survivors are heard lamenting and longing for the pious companions of former days; " my soul desireth the first-ripe fig " (*desiderio tam cari capitis*). The fewer the good that remain, the more difficult it is for them to retain the fervour of their piety. Embers dispersed soon die out. It is hard to keep up a June temperature under December skies. From this dearth of the godly many evils follow. There is a loss of confidence, first in spiritual fellowship, and then in social relations (ver. 5). There is a loosening of the most sacred family bonds. Depravity and degradation become deeper and darker (vers. 3, 4). The little remnant of God's servants are increasingly depressed and discouraged: " Woe is me! " (cf. Ps. cxx. 5 ; Isa. vi. 5). This results from constant contact with sin and from the heart-sickness which it causes; "great heaviness and continual sorrow in my heart " (Rom. ix. 2). Thus we learn : 1. The greatest calamity to a nation is not war, pestilence, or famine, but the withholding of the Spirit of grace to convert the hearts of men, and consequently the dying out of the righteous. The famine of bread is bad ; the famine " of hearing the words of the Lord " is worse. But worst of all is the dearth of living witnesses for God in the land. 2. The winning of souls to God is the greatest wisdom and the most enlightened patriotism. 3. The welfare of a nation is bound up with the living God, the true Church, and believing prayer.—E. S. P.

Ver. 3.—*Earnest sinners.* A contrast is suggested between various grades of evildoing. Some are not so much active as passive in sin. They drift; they are led ; when sinners entice them they " consent," perhaps reluctantly at first. For want of resisting power they are found walking " in the counsel of the ungodly." Ere long they bestir themselves to gratify some sinful desire. At first they are half-hearted in the service of sin, for memory and conscience still restrain them. " Their heart is divided," and it is only one hand they stretch out to grasp the forbidden fruit. Their other hand has still hold on the book of the Law of their God which they learned at their mother's knee. They soon find that they cannot serve two masters. The book of God is dropped ; the hand that held it, released from the mysterious magnetic power which the Bible exerts on those that study it, is stretched out to co-operate with its fellow in deeds of sin. Practice makes perfect; the appetite grows by what it feeds upon ; and soon the transgressor, who not so long ago blushed even at the enticements to sin that were addressed to him, now is foremost among those who " do evil with both hands earnestly." In these earnest sinners we note the following points. 1. *Unity of purpose.* They are men of one idea—how to please themselves. As they have abandoned all thought of seeking their pleasure in doing the will of God, and doing "good unto all men," they concentrate their energies, "both hands," on gratifying every desire whatever the cost may be. 2. *Perversion of conscience.* We are reminded of this by Jerome's rendering, "They call the evil of their hands good." They speak of the evil done as "well done." They could hardly be so earnest in sin unless they had in some way perverted conscience. Some of the forms of iniquity disclosed in vers. 3—6 imply this. And certainly this is one of the most fatal results of sinning. Acts of sin form habits of sinning which react on the judgment and pervert it till the doom is incurred, "Woe unto them that call evil good, and good evil!" etc. (Isa. v. 20). 3. *A conspiracy of men of influence.* We expect a certain amount of crime and moral obliquity in what has been called the *residuum* of society; but profligacy in high places is a scandal and "a reproach to any people." See Jeremiah's experience (v. 1—5). Wherever the infection began, it has spread now to the court and the judgment-hall: "Death is entered into our palaces." There is such a dearth of good men (vers. 1, 2) that the restraint of their protests, or even of the silent testimony of their presence, is awanting. The princes expect bribes, or "black mail." The judges judge for reward. The testimony of contemporaneous and later prophets on this point is very strong (Isa. i. 23; Ezek. xxii. 27; Hos. iv. 18; Amos v. 12). And they veil these crimes under milder names. The prince *demands*, but calls it "asking." The judge's *bribe* is called a reward for service rendered. The great man hesitates not to "utter his mischievous desire" in the presence of meaner men, who, he knows, will be ready enough to carry it out, if they can thus curry favour with him or earn money, though it be the price of blood; "thus they weave it together" (Revised Version). Illustrate by the conspiracy of Ahab, Jezebel, and the elders and nobles in the robbery and murder of Naboth. 4. *We see this infection extending to the most sacred scenes of family life.* What a terrible picture is suggested by vers. 5, 6! The great men who have conspired in crime carry the contagion home with them. They cannot leave their sin on the threshold, like an infected garment. Their children catch the plague. Even a wife is not above suspicion. Thus curses come home to roost. The sins of the fathers are visited upon the children. Families are demoralized. "The end of those things is death." Learn: 1. *Earnestness is not in itself an excellent thing.* The devil is terribly in earnest, "going about as a roaring lion," etc. (1 Pet. v. 8). False teachers are sometimes more earnest than the true. "They zealously seek you in no good way" (Gal. iv. 17). Earnestness may be as glowing as a fire, and as destructive. 2. *Earnest sinners should be a motive and stimulus to the servants of Christ.* If they are so eager in the work of destruction, what manner of persons ought we to be in the work of salvation? Yet some move neither hand, but stand all the day idle. Others are half-hearted, and therefore ply their work with but one hand, not devoting all their faculties to him whom they own as both Redeemer and Lord. Illustrate from King Joash's interview with Elisha (2 Kings xiii. 14—19). Loyalty to our Saviour-King demands concentration of energy and enthusiasm of devotion, that we may do good "with both hands earnestly."—E. S. P.

Ver. 7.—*A soul shut up to God.* The word "therefore," or the term in the Revised Version, "but as for me," marks the transition from a terrible necessity to a priceless privilege. It was a time when it was needful to be suspicious of those who ought to have been worthy of unlimited confidence. Neither a companion nor a familiar friend, nor even a child or a wife, could be trusted (vers. 5, 6). Such had been the experience of many in the past. Samson had been betrayed by his tribesmen, his friend, his father-in-law (Judg. xiv. 20), and her that "lay in his bosom." David had found his confidence betrayed by the men of Judah (1 Sam. xxiii. 12, 19), by Joab (2 Sam. iii. 22—39), by Ahithophel, and by Absalom. As it was in the days of Micah, so would it be in the days of Jesus Christ, when many of his disciples would go back and walk no more with him, and when an apostle would betray him. No wonder that some of his servants are called to a similar experience (Matt. x. 24, 34—36). The prospect *manward* is thus dark and depressing in the extreme. Note what a disintegrating and destructive force sin is. It not only separates between man and God (Isa. lix. 2), but has a tendency to alienate friends, to break up families, to destroy human confidences, and gender a pessimism which finds expression in the passionate, though not deliberate, verdict of the psalmist, "All men are liars." If we cannot repose confidence in others, can we trust in ourselves? Our consciousness of sin and utter failure forbids this (vers. 8, 9; Jer. xvii. 9). Thus we are utterly shut up to God. A military man, suffering from some obscure disease of the mind, was in the habit of promenading in a certain track on the ramparts, after sunset. When he walked eastward, and had nothing but the dark sky to look on, extreme dejection oppressed his clouded mind. But no sooner did he turn towards the west, where his eyes caught the brightness left by the sun that had set, than hope and peace revived in his heart. There are times when, if we look anywhere but towards God, our Sun, we may feel ready to despond or despair. Then we know what it is to be shut up to God. "But as for me, I will look unto the Lord." That look implies hope: "I will wait;" and faith: "My God will hear me." When we thus look, wait, trust, our thoughts may express themselves in the following thoughts about God, and our "meditation of him shall be sweet."

I. How MUCH WE HAVE IN GOD. 1. *His name, Jehovah, describes his nature.* He is the eternal, unchangeable, faithful, covenant-keeping God. He revealed himself by that new name when he came as the Redeemer of his distressed people. And this Jehovah is "my God." Martin Luther remarks, "There is a great deal of divinity in the pronouns." The theology taught in the term "*my* God" is worth more than all the lectures ever given on "the attributes." 2. *The figures employed for God remind us of the treasure we have in him.* Look, for example, at a single group of figures in the sixty-second psalm. There God is described as "my Rock," on which I can safely rest and securely build; as "my high Tower" (Revised Version); "my strong Habitation, whereunto I may continually resort" (Ps. lxxi. 3); and therefore as "my Refuge," where I may be safe from the sword of the avenger of blood, or from any other foe. The city of Metz prided itself in the name "La Pucelle," the virgin-fortress; but in October, 1870, its fair fame was tarnished by its fall, and its inhabitants were at the mercy of their foes. But no such disaster can ever overtake those who can say of the Lord, "He is my Refuge and my Fortress, my God; in him will I trust."

II. How MUCH WE MAY EXPECT FROM GOD. "My soul, wait thou only upon God; for my expectation is from him." Among the blessings we may expect are the two crowning mercies which the prophet claims by faith. 1. *Answers to prayer;* which will be definite, appropriate, decisive ("My God will hear me"), such as God's servants of old received; e.g. Jacob (Gen. xxxii.), Moses (Numb. xiv. 13—20), Asa (2 Chron. xiv. 11, 12), Jehoshaphat (2 Chron. xx.). These prayers will bring: 2. *Deliverance;* for "my God" is "the God of my salvation." Thus in the midst of dangers from without or from within we can say, with the psalmist, "I shall not be greatly moved" (Ps. lxii. 2). Like the rocking-stones on the Cornish coast, we may at times be slightly shaken but not "greatly moved;" *moved,* but not *removed.* Like the magnet, we may oscillate for a time, and be slightly affected by changing conditions, but never greatly moved from our purpose of witnessing faithfully for God and his truth. Yet our confidence in regard to our stability is not in ourselves, but in our God, in "the love of God which is in Christ Jesus our Lord."

III. How WORTHY HE IS OF UNLIMITED CONFIDENCE. "I will look;" "I will wait;" "My soul, wait thou *only* upon God;" "Trust in him at all times." "It is comparatively easy," says Dr. Edward Payson, "to wait upon God, but to wait upon him only—to feel, so far as our strength, happiness, and usefulness are concerned, as if all creatures and second causes were annihilated, and we were alone in the universe with God, is, I suspect, a difficult and rare attainment." This is the unlimited confidence to which we aspire. Then we may not only wait *upon* God, but wait *for* God, leaving the time and method of our deliverance to him (Ps. xxxvii. 7—9; cxxx. 5, 6). Then we shall not only be shut up to God, but shut in with God (Ps. xci. 1). With God on our side we are in the majority. "How many do you count me for?" asked an ancient commander of an officer who was alarmed at the disparity of the forces they could array against the foe. "I will fear no evil, *for thou art with me.*"

> "Be thou my God, and the whole world is mine;
> Whilst thou art Sovereign, I'm secure;
> I shall be rich till thou art poor;
> For all I fear and all I wish, heaven,
> Earth, and hell are thine."

E. S. P.

Vers. 8, 9.—*God the Vindicator of the penitent.* The truths here taught might be applied to the people of Israel, with whom the prophet identifies himself, when humbled before exulting foes like the Edomites (Obad. 8—15) or their Chaldean conquerors. Light came to them in Babylon, through the witness borne by Daniel and his friends, the ministry of Ezekiel, the favour of Cyrus, and above all by their deliverance from the curse of idolatry before their restoration to their land. They may be applied also to a Church in a depressed or fallen state. A godly remnant could yet look forward to deliverance and revival. *E.g.* Sardis (Rev. iii. 1—5). We may also use the words as describing the experience of a sinner humbled before God and man. Notice—

I. HIS PRESENT STATE. 1. *He has fallen.* Then he had stood before. He has been no hypocrite, but a pilgrim on the highway from the City of Destruction to the Celestial City. Like Christian in Bunyan's immortal allegory, he has been confronted by Apollyon. In the struggle he has been wounded in the head, the hand, and the foot. "Then Apollyon, espying his opportunity, began to gather up close to Christian, and, wrestling with him, gave him a dreadful fall; and with that Christian's sword flew out of his hand." Prostrate and powerless, he seems "drawn unto death and ready to be slain." 2. *He sits in darkness.* A hardened sinner in such a crisis may have a light, such as it is ("Walk in the light of your fire, and in the sparks that ye have kindled," Isa. l. 11). But the fallen Christian is heard bemoaning himself (Job xxix. 2, 3). The sun, the light of God's countenance, is gone. It is a night of mist. Not even a star of promise can be seen except when the mist is for a moment or two dispersed before a rising breath of the Divine Comforter, who, though grieved, will not depart. 3. *He is exposed to the indignation of the Lord.* He cannot attribute his darkness to sickness or nervous depression. In the gloom caused by conscience he sees the shadow caused by the righteous anger of God (Isa. lix. 1, 2). "*Therefore* we wait for light, but behold obscurity; for brightness, but we walk in darkness." "For our transgressions are multiplied," etc. (vers. 9, 12). 4. *He has to bear the scorn of men.* His enemies rejoice. This makes the cup of bitterness overflow. The self-righteous formalist thanks God he is not as other men, *or even as this Christian.* The profligate man finds one more excuse for asserting that there is no such thing as real religion (cf. Ps. xxxv. 15, 16, 21, 25). We can imagine the morbid curiosity in the streets of Jerusalem, when it began to be whispered that a dark deed had been committed in the palace of King David, and that Uriah's death had been procured by foul means. Would not the men of Belial mock at the royal psalmist—seducer—murderer (2 Sam. xii. 14)? How the soldiers and the servants round the fire within the judgment-hall must have chuckled while Peter was weeping without! The world may hold its most riotous carnival, not when martyrs are burning at the stake, or their dead bodies are lying in the street of Sodom, but when the Saviour is wounded in the house of his friends, and the Church is mourning over the lost reputations of its fallen members (Luke xvii. 1).

II. THE GROUNDS OF HIS CONFIDENCE FOR THE FUTURE. The fallen Christian looks forward to rising again. He anticipates a new day when the Sun of Righteousness shall again rise on him. He speaks boldly (ver. 8). This is either the grossest presumption or the noblest faith. It is like Samson's boast, "I will go out as at other times;" or like David's trustful anticipation, "Then will I teach transgressors thy ways," etc. That these words are no vain vaunting we learn from the grounds of his confidence. 1. *He resolves quietly to endure God's chastening strokes.* Such submission is one sign of genuine repentance. Illust.: The Jews in captivity (Lev. xxvi. 40—42, "and they then accept the punishment of their inquity; then will I remember my covenant," etc.); Eli (1 Sam. iii. 18); David, all through his long chastisement (see *e.g.* 2 Sam. xii. 20; xv. 25, 26; xvi. 11; cf. Job xxxiv. 31; Lam. iii. 39; Heb. xii. 5—7). 2. *He puts his trust entirely in God.* He has just before (ver. 7) spoken of himself as shut up to God. Again he returns to him and repeatedly expresses his faith, "The Lord shall be a Light unto me: he shall plead my cause: he will bring me forth to the light." His godly sorrow and cheerful submission are signs that there is a mystic film, a spiritual cord that binds him, even in his fallen state, to his Father-God. And he has promises to plead (Ps. xxxvii. 24; Prov. xxiv. 16). Illust.: Jonah (ii. 3, 4), St. Paul (Rom. vii. 24, 25). Grievous as are the sins of God's adopted children, they are provided for: "My little children, these things write I unto you, that ye sin not. And if any man sin"—if any one of you little children sin, grievous and aggravated as *your* sin may be—" we have an Advocate with the Father, Jesus Christ the righteous : and he is the Propitiation *for our sins*" (1 John ii. 1, 2). God vindicates such a penitent. He restores his soul. He renews his peace. He re-establishes his tarnished reputation. He puts a new song in his mouth (Ps. xl. 1—3 ; Isa. xii. 1, 2 ; lvii. 18, 19).—E. S. P.

Ver. 13.—" *The fruit of their doings*." This expression is a most suggestive one. It occurs three times in the Prophet Jeremiah. In Jer. xvii. 10 God declares, as one of the signs of his omniscient, heart-searching power, that he can not only recompense each individual according to his *ways*, but " according to the *fruit of his doings*." In Jer. xxi. 14 a similar declaration is addressed to the royal house of David : " I will punish you according to the fruit of your doings." And in Jer. xxxii. 17—19 the prophet expresses his admiration at the discriminating omnipotence of God—" great in counsel, and mighty in work : for thine eyes are open upon the ways of the sons of men : to give unto every one according to his *ways*, and according to the *fruit of his doings*." Our text calls for *exposition* and admits of *illustration*.

I. EXPOSITION. An act is one thing ; the fruit of that act is another thing. By fruit we understand that which is the natural result of the acts we perform. Those natural results under the reign of moral law we might foresee. Acts, like trees, bring forth fruit " after their kind." For such fruit we are held responsible. Responsibility varies according to knowledge acquired or attainable. A child's falsehood, though fraught with lifelong disasters, is less criminal than the less injurious lie of an adult. But we cannot disconnect our acts and their fruit. We cannot kill them in the seed, or nip them in the bud, or blight them in the flower ; they will bear fruit of some kind. We are not held responsible for what we may call the accidental issues of our acts. Our good may be evil spoken of. The most unjustifiable inferences may be drawn from our words or deeds. Our Lord's teaching has been the occasion of discord in families and strife in states (Matt. x. 34—36). St. Paul's doctrine was perverted (Rom. iii. 8). A clear judgment is needed to discern what will be the natural effect of our conduct. We may not, dare not, leave our influence on others out of the account. We must use the enlightening Word, and pray for the aid of the illuminating Spirit, that we may acquire an enlightened conscience. And then we must seek so to live that the fruit of our doings will bring honour to God and be for our own " praise and honour and glory at the appearing of Jesus Christ."

II. ILLUSTRATION. Our first class of illustrations will be those in which the fruit of our doings, like the fruit of the tree in the garden, is " good " and " pleasant to the eyes," and " to be desired " as food for the soul through all eternity. 1. *The life and work of Jesus Christ.* The " good Master" " went about doing good." He did the will of him that sent him, and in doing it " became obedient unto death, even the death of the cross." What is the fruit of these doings ? Eternity alone can reveal. His reward will be according to it—according to the glory brought to God and the blessedness to men (Isa. liii. 11, 12). 2. *The characters and labours of devoted servants of Christ.* The life and work of Christ is a pattern and an encouragement to all his followers (Luke vi. 40). Sow now the seed of Christian living and doing. It may seem to be lost, like the seed cast on the surface of flooded lands, but you shall find it after many days. You may die without seeing the fruitage in this life ; you may rest from your labours, but your works will follow you (Gal. vi. 7—9). Incidents confirming this frequently come to light. At a Unitarian anniversary in New England a few years ago, one of the ministers, speaking of the small results of his work, added, " It must be remembered where my field is. The Connecticut valley is the home of Jonathan Edwards, and though he has been dead a century, he is a great name and a power for orthodoxy through all that country to-day." A devoted pastor, Rev. Thomas Hall, laboured for twenty-seven years at Heckmondwike, Yorkshire, amid great discouragement because he saw so little fruit from his labours. His successor could report that for a long time after his death most of those who were added to the fellowship of the Church acknowledged their indebtedness to their deceased pastor for their first religious impressions or some other special spiritual help. Take courage, fellow-labourers. If you seem to have laboured in vain, you can add, "My judgment is with the Lord, and my work with my God" (Isa. xlix. 4). He will recompense you according to the natural results of your life's work, "the fruit of your doings" (Isa. iii. 10). Yet this fruit must vary with the quality of our work (see this lesson taught in 1 Cor. iii. 8—15). But the truth of our text has its shady as well as its sunny side. 3. *A nation will be recompensed according to its national sins and the fruit of them.* Illust.: Great Britain and the opium traffic. Even national repentance and reformation may not avert some of the disastrous consequences of past transgressions. Colonial slavery has left some of its foul stains on the present generation. 4. *Sinners must await "the harvest" which is "the end of the world" before they can receive the just recompense of their deeds.* William Cowper, in a letter to John Newton, alluding to the translation of Homer on which he was engaged, says very truly, "An author had need narrowly to watch his pen, lest a line should escape it which by possibility may do mischief when he has been long dead and buried. What we have done when we have written a book will never be known till the day of judgment; then the account will be liquidated, and all the good that it has occasioned will witness either for or against us." Homer himself supplies an illustration of this. We are told it was the 'Iliad' that did much to mould the character of Alexander of Macedon. The life of Alexander was the inspiration of two other notorious warriors—Julius Cæsar and Charles XII. of Sweden. In contrast to the posthumous influence of Jonathan Edwards, there stands on record the baneful effect on a village in Berkshire of the infidel, wit, and libertine, Lord Bolingbroke. He died in 1751; but he had so poisoned the minds of the poor villagers against religion, that three quarters of a century afterwards "the fruit of his doings" was most distinctly to be traced. Nor need our acts be flagrantly evil to bring forth bitter fruit. The neglect of duty tends to make others neglect it, and thus to leave that duty altogether undone. The neglect of "assembling ourselves together" in public worship tends to the dissolution of such assemblies and the abandonment of such worship. The fruit of secret discipleship would be the dying out of Christian Churches. What can be the fruit of sin but sorrow, suffering, loss? "The harvest shall be a heap in the day of grief and of desperate sorrow" (Isa. xvii. 11). Even though sin be forgiven through repentance and faith, the consequences of misused or wasted years will remain. And as those consequences, ever widening, cannot be summed up till the great day of God, "we must all be made manifest before the judgment-seat of Christ; that each one may receive *the things done in the body,* according to what he hath done, whether it be good or bad." Let us therefore "make it our aim . . . to be well-pleasing unto him" (2 Cor. v. 9, 10).—E. S. P.

Vers. 18, 19.—*Matchless mercy.* "The Lord thy God turned the curse into a blessing unto thee, because the Lord thy God loved thee." These words of Moses receive a striking illustration in the fact that every one of the "minor" prophets who threatens judgments against Israel ends by promises of deliverance which anticipate the days of the Messiah. In none is this more strikingly seen than in Micah. In this chapter the prophet, who has been lamenting the universal corruption of the people (vers. 1—6), finds comfort in God alone, to whom he looks with submission and hope, and obtains an assurance of renewed Divine favour when the chastisement is past (vers. 7—13). This encourages him to pray (ver. 14). His prayer is answered by a promise of deliverance such as God accomplished for his people in Egypt (vers. 15—17). Upon this he breaks forth in adoration of God's *matchless mercy,* and anticipates the fulfilment of promises which would only be realized by the coming of the long looked-for Deliverer (vers. 18—20; and cf. Luke i. 70—75). This matchless mercy is shown both in God's essential character and in his treatment of sinners. Each clause suggests some fresh thought on this attractive subject.

I. "WHO IS A GOD LIKE UNTO THEE?" The reference to the Exodus (ver. 15) reminds us of Moses' words (Exod. xv. 11). If there is none like God, "glorious in holiness, fearful in praises, doing wonders," what wonder can be so great as deliverance from sin? If even ungodly men are charmed into adoration for a brief period at some deliverance from danger, how profoundly and unceasingly should we adore and glorify God for salvation from sin, which is a more dreadful evil than cholera, lunacy, or death! Notice how a question like this is often asked or answered; *e.g.* in regard to God's power (Deut. xxxiii. 26), his faithfulness (1 Kings viii. 23), his deliverance of the oppressed (Ps. xxxv. 10), his condescension to the lowly (Ps. cxiii. 5, 6). In a word, in his character and in all his dealings he stands alone (Ps. lxxxix. 6—8).

II. "THAT PARDONETH INIQUITY." This is as essential a part of God's character as is maternal love in a mother's heart. When Moses said to God, "I beseech thee, show me thy *glory*," the answer was, "I will make all my *goodness* pass before thee, and I will proclaim the Name of the Lord before thee" (Exod. xxxiii. 18, 19). And when the sublime proclamation was made, one of the essential elements of Jehovah's character, as revealed in his Name, was "forgiving iniquity and transgression and sin" (Exod. xxxiv. 5—7). God loves to be reminded of his Name, and to see that it is that on which our hopes of pardon rest; *e.g.* Numb. xiv. 17—20; Ps. xxv. 11; lxxxvi. 5, 15; cxxx. 4; Dan. ix. 9.

III. "AND PASSETH BY THE TRANSGRESSION OF THE REMNANT OF HIS HERITAGE." This denotes a continual action on the part of God. Isolated acts of pardon would not meet the case. He comes with his eyes as a flame of fire, and yet he does not "mark iniquities" (Ps. cxxx. 3; and cf. Numb. xxiii. 21). What he commends he practise (Prov. xix. 11). Yet not because of any laxity in his relations to sin, but because of his righteous grace. Such declarations of Divine mercy as the Old Testament is full of can only be perfectly understood when read in the light of the New Testament, and of the atoning sacrifice of Christ, "for the redemption of the transgressions that were under the first covenant;" "Whom God set forth to be a Propitiation, through faith, by his blood, to show his righteousness, because of *the passing over* of the sins done afore-time, in the forbearance of God" (Rom. iii. 25; Heb. ix. 15).

IV. "HE RETAINETH NOT HIS ANGER FOR EVER, BECAUSE HE DELIGHTETH IN MERCY." In the midst of words of grace we have a distinct recognition of anger as one of God's perfections. So in Exod. xxxiv. 7, "that will by no means clear the guilty." If he were not angry with sinners he would be less perfect. This truth needs to be emphasized in the present days of superficial views of sin. But if he were to retain his anger for ever, it would be fatal (Isa. lvii. 16). So "he will not always chide," etc.; he "will not cast off for ever; but though he cause grief, yet will he have compassion according to the multitude of his mercies" (Ps. ciii. 9; Lam. iii. 31, 32). And this "because he delighteth in mercy." In its literal sense "he is bent on mercy." Proofs of this crowd on us from every side. We see it in the history of Israel (Neh. ix. 16—19, 26—31; Ps. lxxviii.), in the cross of Christ (1 John iv. 10), in the long lives of many of the most impenitent (Rom. ii. 4), and in the experience of those who are now rejoicing in salvation (Eph. ii. 4—7; Titus iii. 4—7). It is therefore a joy to God to forgive and save. The parables of Luke xv. 1—10 remind us of this. The pearl of parables that follows might be called, not "The prodigal son," but "The long-suffering and rejoicing father."

V. "HE WILL TURN AGAIN, HE WILL HAVE COMPASSION UPON US." In our idiom "He will again have compassion on us." When God sent Jesus Christ "preaching peace" to Israel, it was no new thing. It was the latest and sublimest illustration of a Divine habit (Heb. i. 1). In the wilderness-days, "he, being full of compassion, forgave their iniquity, and destroyed them not: yea, many a time turned he his anger away, and did not stir up all his wrath" (Ps. lxxviii. 38). Thus God treated them all through their history. See the summary of the later history of Judah in 2 Chron. xxxvi. 14—16, ". . . till there was no remedy," etc. But he again had compassion; he turned again their captivity, according to his promises by Moses (Deut. xxx. 1—6). And though they crucified the Christ, and were "broken off," they are still "beloved for the fathers' sake." God will again have compassion on them (Zech. xii. 10—14; xiii. 1). "And so all Israel shall be saved." These repeated acts of the mercy in which God delights may encourage the vilest to appeal for forgiveness, "according unto the multitude of thy tender mercies" (Ps. li. 1).

VI. "HE WILL SUBDUE OUR INIQUITIES." He will tread them down, trample them underfoot. One of the marked peculiarities of the Divine forgiveness is the result on the sinner himself. No one pardons with such a good effect on the sinner pardoned. Some are disappointed in those they forgive. Not so God. Whenever he remits sin he reforms the sinner. His salvation being from the love and the power as well as the punishment of sin, a sinner cannot grasp the pardon and neglect the purity. Nor does he desire to. The most sacred motives forbid. The promise of pardon is accompanied with the assurance of the purifying Spirit (Ezek. xxxvi. 25—27; Rom. viii. 1, 2; 1 Cor. vi. 11). Sin is a serpent to be crushed under the heel (Rom. xvi. 20). It is a foe to be conquered, and who shall be conquered because we are " not under the Law, but under grace " (Rom. vi. 14). The victory is God's, though the blessedness of it is ours (Ps. xcviii. 1), " *He* will subdue our iniquities."

VII. "THOU WILT CAST ALL THEIR SINS INTO THE DEPTHS OF THE SEA." This indicates the completeness of the Divine salvation. Elsewhere we have the promise (Ps. ciii. 12). Hezekiah says, " Thou hast cast all my sins behind my back," so that the accuser cannot get them without going behind the very throne of God; and God himself will never turn to see them. Here the figure is still more striking; sins cast, not in the shallows, subject to the tidal waves which might throw them up into sight again, but into the depths of the sea (cf. Jer. l. 20). Other figures are used to teach the same truth—the cloud blotted out, never to be seen again (Isa. xliv. 22); sin forgotten, even by God himself (Isa. xliii. 25). Such is God's matchless mercy in pardoning sin. And when our sins are finally subdued as well as pardoned, cast into the depths of the sea, while we are standing on the eternal shore, justified, sanctified, glorified, then we shall sing the final song, " Thanks be to God who giveth us the victory through our Lord Jesus Christ." And because we are already being saved by a God of such matchless mercy, in whom we have placed our trust, we have no fear as to the issue (Rom. viii. 38, 39).

> " We lift our hands exulting
> In thine Almighty favour,
> The love Divine, which made us thine,
> Shall keep us thine for ever."

E. S. P.

Vers. 18, 19.—"*A pardoning God*." In the days of Micah the social and religious condition of Jerusalem was deplorable. All through the country evils prevailed, but they were worst at its centre. Instinctively the vicious make their way to a crowded city. If vice is condemned in the nation, its disgracefulness is less conspicuous in a crowd; and if vice is not condemned, the city affords the best opportunities for the gratification of unholy desire. It still needs courage and wisdom to recognize and combat evils prevailing in great cities, and God still requires knights of the cross who will fight, not as of old for the grave of Christ, but for his Church. Micah was one of these. The prevalent sins of the prophet's days were threatening the existence of society, loosening the ties which gave unity to the nation, and dividing into factions members of the same family. The wealthy were sucking the very life-blood of the poor, and the judges openly asked for bribes, without the smallest sense of shame; so that the prophets were not only the teachers of truth, but also the tribunes of the people. Unbelief in God lay at the root of such wrong-doing, for unless rulers recognize responsibility to him, one of the greatest safeguards against their abuse of authority is destroyed. Persuading themselves that God was such a one as themselves, idolatry prevailed, and although the temple still stood and its worship was as gorgeous as ever, unreality and hypocrisy rendered such religion worse than useless. A few voices were lifted up boldly against this condition of things. Isaiah and Micah stood side by side in their protests, and did much to stem the tide of iniquity. With all their vigorous denunciation of sin, however, hope was constantly held out to the sinner, and never was the mercy of God more clearly set forth than in the words of our text. Seven hundred years after this prophet's death, Wise Men from the East came to Jerusalem inquiring for him who was born to be the King of the Jews and the Light of the world. They were answered in the words of Micah, and it was through following his directions that they saw and worshipped the infant Jesus. Even in our day we may say, " He being dead yet speaketh." While the splendid orations of Cicero and Demosthenes have no influence over modern society, and the speeches recorded by Tacitus and Thucydides have only their marvellous literary value, the words of this ancient prophet meet our necessities, give us guidance and comfort, emboldening us to trust in the mercy of a pardoning God. The subject of *Divine pardon* suggested here will now have our consideration.

I. THE PREROGATIVE OF PARDON IS CLAIMED BY GOD FOR HIMSELF. He knew the needs of his children, and therefore proclaimed his pardoning love from the first. Even amid the terrors of Sinai he revealed himself as a God "pardoning iniquity." David was emboldened to come into his presence, after the commission of most grievous sins, praying, "Have mercy upon me, O Lord, according to thy loving-kindness," etc. He pardons of his own free-will, because, as Micah says, "he delighteth in mercy," and with a perfect knowledge of what is worst in us, he declares his willingness to forgive all who are penitent. This power he has delegated to no man. If Jesus had simply been human, the Pharisees would have been justified in saying, "This man blasphemeth," when he forgave the sins of the paralytic. Nor did our Lord's declaration to his apostles, "Whose sins soever ye remit, they are remitted unto them," endue them with a super-natural or exclusive privilege. Their right was only ministerial and declarative, and is shared by all those who, by Divine grace, have been made "kings and priests unto God."

II. DIVINE PARDON SEEMS THE MORE WONDERFUL WHEN COMPARED WITH MAN'S FOR-GIVENESS. "As the heavens are higher than the earth, so are my ways higher than your ways," etc. Suppose the case of an *employé*, who, having robbed his master, is detected, but on evidence of sincere contrition is reinstated in his position. His restitution is accompanied by hard terms, he is watched suspiciously, and his employer considers that he has been exceptionally generous to restore him at all. Contrast this with what our Lord tells of God's pardoning love in his parable of the prodigal son. Instead of being refused, his father sees him "when a great way off;" instead of angry reproaches, he has "compassion upon him;" instead of cold reserve, he falls on his neck, and kisses him; instead of suspicion, there is gladness, and all the house is filled with music and dancing. Or take, as another contrast, the reception given at home to a girl who has gone wrong, with the touching story of our Lord's love to the woman who was a sinner. And Jesus says, "He that hath seen me hath seen the Father." "Who is a God like unto thee, that pardoneth iniquity?"

III. DIVINE PARDON IS PROFFERED FOR ALL KINDS OF SIN. Different words are used here and elsewhere in order to show that no sort of wrong-doing is exempt from pardon; so that the moral and the vicious, those who have sinned inwardly or out-wardly, may alike be encouraged to return to the Lord. "*Transgression*" is an act of evil committed against a Law acknowledged to be holy. It signifies stepping across a line which is drawn and visible. "*Iniquity*" is the inward tendency which responds to suggestions of evil; which we cannot root out, and which makes self-reformation hopeless. "*Sins*" are acts done from wrong motives. All these it is promised shall be done away with on our repentance.

IV. DIVINE PARDON IS COMPLETE AND THOROUGH. 1. "*Thou wilt cast all their sins into the depths of the sea.*" If we drop a knife into a tidal pool, we can see it and regain it; but if we sail out of sight of land, and drop it overboard in the "depths of the sea," it is gone for ever. So completely gone are our forgiven sins. 2. "*He will subdue our iniquities.*" If our nature is not sanctified, we shall only do again our evil deeds. All our affections and thoughts must be subjected to the Divine will, and this can only be the result of God's own work.

CONCLUSION. *How can God be just, and yet our Justifier?* This mystery, which lies at the root of his moral government, finds its only answer in the cross of Christ. God's laws are eternal and inexorable. He cannot swerve from absolute righteousness. Sin must bring shame, misery, and death, here and hereafter. If, therefore, God had said all shall be overlooked, the penalty shall be removed, the Law repealed, it would appear to myriads of intelligent beings (compared with whose multitude the human race is as nothing) that the Law was either unjust in its enunciation or unjust in its repeal. Yet a sense of the perfect integrity of God is the foundation of his creature's bliss. But the Son of God became the Son of man. He gathered up into himself all the sympathies, powers, and sufferings of our race. He stood forth as our Represen-tative, vindicating the Law by his obedience, and dying on the cross for transgressors. This would evoke grander reverence for Law than if the race had been punished; and such a display of love wins all hearts from disobedience.

> "My faith would lay her hand
> On that dear head of thine,
> While like a penitent I stand,
> And there confess my sin."

A. R.

Vers. 1—6.—*The wail of a true patriot on the moral corruptions of his country.*
"Woe is me! for I am as when they have gathered the summer fruits, as the grape-gleanings of the vintage: there is no cluster to eat: my soul desired the first-ripe fruit," etc. In these verses the prophet bewails the moral condition of his country. The picture he draws of its wickedness is a very hideous one. It answers not only to the character of the people in the reign of Ahaz, but to their character under the reign of other kings and in other times. Take the words as presenting the wail of a true patriot over the moral corruptions of his country. "Woe is me!" etc. He means to say, "It is with me as one seeking fruit after the harvest, grapes after the vintage; there is not one cluster." There are several things that he bemoans.

I. THE DEPARTURE OF EXCELLENCE FROM HIS COUNTRY. "The good man is perished out of the earth." Who are the good men referred to here is not known. The statement is put in general terms, and may imply merely that there are no good men to be found in the country. Or do the words, as some think, point especially to Hezekiah, Josiah, or to good men unknown to fame? They had, however, departed. Whether they had emigrated to distant lands or gone into the great eternity, is not said. The latter is the more probable idea. In any case, the departure of such men is a great loss—a loss which true patriots may well bemoan. Good men are the "lights of the world." They are the "salt of the earth." Their influence penetrates the mass, counteracts its tendency to corruption, removes its moral insipidity, gives it a new spirit—a spirit pungent and savoury. They are the conservators of the good and the peaceful reformers of the bad. "Perished out of the earth." It does not say, "perished out of being." They had left the land, but not the universe. They were thinking, feeling, active still. There is a sense, indeed, in which they could not perish out of the land. Good men leave behind them principles, ideas, a character, which will live and spread and work to the end of time.

II. THE RAMPANCY OF AVARICE IN HIS COUNTRY. The workings of avarice are indicated in the latter end of the second and two following verses. 1. *Here we have its working amongst the general community.* "They all lie in wait for blood; they hunt every man his brother with a net." To get wealth for themselves was with them such a furious passion, that the rights and lives of others were disregarded. Their avarice was as ravenous as the passion of a wild beast. Nay, they looked upon men only as victims for their prey. Does not this avarice work thus in English society? Man has come to value man just in proportion as he can render him service, enrich his exchequer, and advance his aggrandizement. What nets are spread out in every street, in every mart and office, in every journal, in order to catch men! "They hunt every man." 2. *Here we have its working amongst the higher classes.* "That they may do evil with both hands earnestly, the prince asketh, and the judge asketh for a reward; and the great man, he uttereth his mischievous desire: so they wrap it up." The idea seems to be this—that the "great man," the "prince," for some corrupt motive, seeks the condemnation of some innocent person; and the "judge," for a bribe, gratifies his wish. A judge from avarice will pronounce an innocent man guilty. All this is done very industriously "with two hands." The business must be despatched as soon as possible, lest some event should start up to thwart them; and when it is done "they wrap it up." "So they wrap it up." Avarice, like all sinful passions, seeks to wrap up its crimes. But the Authorized Version is probably wrong, and the rendering should be "they weave it together," *i.e.* join in plotting (see Exposition).

III. THE MISCHIEVOUSNESS OF THE BEST IN HIS COUNTRY. "The best of them is as a briar: the most upright is sharper than a thorn-hedge." There is a gradation of wickedness of the men in the country, but the best of them is like a prickly thorn and worse than a thorn-hedge. The prophet is so struck with this that the thought of retribution takes hold of him, and he says, "The day of thy watchmen and thy visitation cometh; now shall be their perplexity."

IV. THE LACK OF TRUTHFULNESS IN THE COUNTRY. "Trust ye not in a friend, put ye not confidence in a guide," etc. "Place no faith in a companion; trust not a familiar friend; from her that lieth in thy bosom guard the doors of thy mouth. For the son despiseth the father, the daughter riseth up against her mother, the daughter-in-law against her mother-in-law; a man's enemies are the members of his own family"

(Henderson). All social faith was gone; a man had lost all confidence in his brother. Social scepticism and suspicion prevailed in all circles. No faith was to be put in a friend. The very lips were to be sealed. No confidence in the wife, no longer was she to be treated as an object of trust. No confidence in the son, the daughter, or the mother. The nearest relations were counted as enemies. "A man's enemies are the men of his own house."

CONCLUSION. Such were the evils over which this patriotic prophet pours forth his lamentations. What right-hearted man would not bewail such a moral corruption in his country? Jeremiah said, "Oh that mine head were waters, and mine eyes a fountain of tears, that I might weep day and night!" etc. Paul said, "Would that I were accursed!" etc. Christ said, "O Jerusalem, Jerusalem!" etc. It is the characteristic of a true patriot that he feels a deeper concern for the moral state of his country than for its educational or commercial condition.—D. T.

Vers. 7—9.—*The possibilities of godly men falling into great trouble.* "Therefore I will look unto the Lord; I will wait for the God of my salvation: my God will hear me. Rejoice not against me, O mine enemy: when I fall, I shall arise; when I sit in darkness, the Lord shall be a light unto me," etc. The prophet, having reverted in the preceding verses of this chapter to the wickedness of his people, which he had before depicted in most dark and dreadful colours, here proceeds to represent them in their state of captivity, reduced to repentance, and yearning for that Divine interposition which would involve the complete destruction of their enemies. I take the words as exhibiting the *possibilities of godly men.*

I. THE POSSIBILITY OF GODLY MEN FALLING INTO GREAT TROUBLE. "Rejoice not against me, O mine enemy: when I fall, I shall arise." Who is the enemy here referred to scarcely matters, whether Babylon, Edom, or some other persons or peoples. All godly men have ever had their enemies. All who have ever endeavoured to lead a godly life have suffered persecution in some mode and measure. Two things are referred to here concerning the trouble. 1. *It was a "fall."* Godly men are liable to many falls—falls from health to sickness, from wealth to poverty, from social friendship to desolation; but the greatest fall is *moral*—the fall of character. To this the best of men are liable, *e.g.* Moses, David, Peter. 2. *The trouble was a "darkness."* "When I sit in darkness." Light and darkness are frequently used for prosperity and adversity. There are many things that darken the soul. Disappointment is a cloud, remorse is a cloud, despair is a cloud. Some of these clouds often mantle the mental heaven in sackcloth. Godly men are often permitted to walk in darkness and to have no light.

II. THE POSSIBILITY OF GODLY MEN BEING GLORIOUSLY SUSTAINED IN TROUBLE. "Therefore I will look unto the Lord; I will wait for the God of my salvation," etc. The godly man has a power within him, with the Divine help, of lifting his soul above the *crushing* cares, sufferings, and sorrows of life. "Rejoice not over me, O mine enemy: when I fall, I shall arise; when I sit in darkness, the Lord shall be a light unto me." How does he do it? 1. *By looking at God.* "Therefore I will look unto the Lord." The man who fastens his eyes on the sun becomes unconscious of the small things around him. The soul which feels God to be the grand object in its horizon can scarcely fail to be buoyant and courageous. 2. *By waiting upon God.* "I will wait for the God of my salvation." He is sure to come to my deliverance; it is only a question of time, and I will wait. As the farmer in the snows and storms of winter waits for the vernal season, certain that it will come, so the godly man, in trial, waits for God's approach. 3. *By trusting in God.* "My God will hear me." He has promised to do so; he has done so before; he is a prayer-hearing God. He has said, "Unto that man will I look," etc. 4. *By submitting to God.* "I will bear the indignation of the Lord, because I have sinned against him." I will not repine nor rebel under my suffering; I will bow to his will, for I deserve punishment, as I have sinned against him. The sufferings I endure are insignificant compared to the sins I have committed. 5. *By hoping for God.* "He will bring me forth to the light, and I shall behold his righteousness." "Weeping may endure for a night, but joy cometh with the morning." Thus it is possible for godly men to rise in courage and even triumph in the greatest calamities. Sunk in the deepest affliction, they may look their enemies in the face and say, "Rejoice not against me, O mine enemy : when I fall, I shall arise." Though I am now down, I shall rise again.   Blessed hope !

> "It whispers o'er the cradled child
>   Fast locked in peaceful sleep,
> Ere its pure soul is sin-beguiled,
>   Ere sorrow bids it weep.

> "It soothes the mother's ear with hope,
>   Like sweet bells' silver chime,
> And bodies forth the unknown scope
>   Of dark, mysterious Time !

> "'Tis heard in manhood's risen day,
>   And nerves the soul to might,
> When life shines forth with fullest ray,
>   Forewarning least of night.

> "It speaks of noble ends to gain,
>   A world to mend by love
> That tempers strength of hand and brain
>   With softness of the dove.

> "It falls upon the aged ear
>   Though deaf to human voice,
> And when man's evening closes drear,
>   It bids him still rejoice.

> "It tells of bliss beyond the grave,
>   The parted souls to thrill—
> The guerdon of the truly brave
>   Who fought the powers of ill."
>   (*Household Words.*)
>   D. T.

Ver. 10.—*Religious persecutors.* "Then she that is mine enemy shall see it, and shame shall cover her which said unto me, Where is the Lord thy God? mine eyes shall behold her : now shall she be trodden down as the mire of the streets." "And may mine enemy see it, and shame cover her who hath said to me, Where is Jehovah thy God?   Mine eyes will see it ; now will she be for a treading down like mire in the streets " (Delitzsch). "Although, for example, God had given up his nation to the power of its enemies, the nations of the world, on account of its sins, so that they accomplished the will of God by destroying the kingdoms of Israel and Judah and carrying away the people into exile ; yet they grew proud of their own might in so doing, and did not recognize themselves as instruments of punishment in the hand of the Lord, but attributed their victories to the power of their own arm, and even aimed at the destruction of Israel with scornful defiance of the living God.   Thus they violated the rights of Israel, so that the Lord was obliged to conduct the contest of his people with the heathen, and secure the rights of Israel by the overthrow of the heathen power of the world " (ibid.).   The words present to us a few thoughts concerning *religious persecutors.*

I. THEIR HUMILIATING VISION.   "Then she that is mine enemy shall see it, and shame shall cover her."   "See" what?   The deliverance, the exaltation which God wrought for the victims.   Few things are more painful to a malign nature than to witness the prosperity and happiness of the object of its intense aversion.   Every beam of delight in the hated one falls as fire on the soul-nerves of the hater.   Witness Haman and Mordecai.   It is destined that every ungodly persecutor shall witness one day the happiness of the godly whom he has tormented.   The songs of the martyr shall fall on the ears of the human demons that forged his chains, kindled his fires, and tortured him when living.   "There shall be weeping and gnashing of teeth, when ye shall see Abraham, and Isaac, and Jacob, and all the prophets, in the kingdom of God, and you yourselves thrust out."   Another thing in the passage presented to us concerning religious persecutors is—

II. THEIR TAUNTING SPIRIT.   "Where is the Lord thy God?"   Scorn is one of the leading elements in the soul of the persecutor. "My tears," said David, "have been my food day and night, while mine enemies continually say, Where is now thy God?" Again, "Mine enemies reproach, saying daily unto me, Where is thy God?" Again, "Wherefore should the heathen say, Where is their God?" How this taunting spirit was shown in those who persecuted and put to death the Son of God! "They that passed by reviled him, wagging their heads, and saying, Thou that destroyest the temple, and buildest it in three days, save thyself. If thou be the Son of God, come down from the cross" (Matt. xxvii. 40). The taunting spirit is generally *malific*. It is fiendish, has in it the venom of hell. The taunting spirit is generally *haughty*. "Proud and haughty scorner is his name" (Prov. xxi. 24). The taunting spirit is generally *ignorant*. He who deals in ridicule generally lacks the power of information and argument.

III. THEIR UTTER RUIN. "Now shall she be trodden down as the mire of the streets." There is a God that judges on the earth, and his retributive forces are ever on the heels of crime. The blood of martyrs cries to heaven, and stirs these forces to action. "How long, O Lord, holy and true, dost thou not judge and avenge our blood on them that dwell on the earth?" (Rev. vi. 10).

> "Avenge, O Lord, thy slaughtered saints, whose bones
> Lie scattered on the Alpine mountains cold;
> Ev'n them who kept thy truth so pure of old,
> When all our fathers worshipped stocks and stones,
> Forget not: in thy book record their groans
> Who were thy sheep, and in their ancient fold
> Slain by the bloody Piedmontese that rolled
> Mother with infant down the rocks. Their moans
> The vales redoubled to the hills, and they
> To heaven. Their martyr'd blood and ashes sow
> O'er all th' Italian fields, where still doth sway
> The triple tyrant; that from these may grow
> A hundredfold, who, having learned thy way,
> Early may fly the Babylonian woe."

(Milton.)

D. T.

Vers. 11, 12.—*The good time coming.* "In the day that thy walls are to be built, in that day shall the decree be far removed. In that day also he shall come even to thee from Assyria, and from the fortified cities, and from the fortress even to the river, and from sea to sea, and from mountain to mountain." The prophet here speaks in the name of Israel, and seems to exult in the expectation of the full restoration of Jerusalem. Her walls would be rebuilt, and her scattered citizens would be gathered unto her from Assyria to Egypt, from sea to sea, and from mountain to mountain. "The most natural construction," says Henderson, "is that the decree of God respecting the political changes that were to take place was not to be confined to Babylon, but was to be extended to all the countries round about Judæa, in consequence of which great numbers would become proselytes to the Jewish faith." The words may be used to illustrate two things concerning the *good time coming*.

1. IT WILL BE A TIME FOR REBUILDING THE RUINED. "In the day that thy walls are to be built." The walls of Jerusalem are referred to—the walls of fortification, protection; these are to be rebuilt. Daniel said that they were to be rebuilt in troublesome times (Dan. ix. 25). There is, however, a more important rebuilding than this —a rebuilding that is going on, and will go on, until the great moral city shall be complete. 1. *The human soul is a building.* It is a temple, a "spiritual house" reared as a residence for the Eternal, a home for the Holy Ghost to dwell in. It is "a city whose Builder and Maker is God." 2. *The human soul is a building in ruins.* The walls are broken down; its columns, arches, roof, rooms, all in ruins. 3. *The human soul is a building to be rebuilt.* Christ is to be the Foundation-stone, etc. "Ye are built together for a habitation of God through the Spirit" (Eph. ii. 22). This rebuilding is going on according to a plan of the great moral Architect; is being worked out by agents that know nothing of the plan. It will be completed one day; the top-stone will be brought forth one day, with shouts of "Grace, grace!" (Zech. iv. 7). This new

Jerusalem established on earth, what a magnificent city it will be! The words may be used to illustrate another thing concerning the good time coming.

II. IT WILL BE A TIME FOR REGATHERING THE SCATTERED. "In that day also he shall come even to thee from Assyria, and from the fortified cities, and from the fortresses even to the river, and from sea to sea, and from mountain to mountain." "All," says an old writer, "that belong to the land of Israel, whithersoever dispersed and however distressed, far and wide over the face of the whole earth, shall come flocking to it again. He shall come even to thee, having liberty to return and a heart to return from Assyria, whither the ten tribes were carried away, though it lay remote from the fortified cities and from the fortress—those strongholds in which they thought they had them fast; for when God's time comes, though Pharaoh will not let the people go, God will fetch them out with a high hand. They shall come from all the remote parts, from sea to sea, and mountain to mountain, not turning back for fear of your discouragements, but they shall go from strength to strength, till they come to Zion." The human family, which Heaven intended to live as one grand brotherhood, has been riven into moral sections, antagonistic to each other, and scattered all over the world. The time will come when they shall be gathered together, not, of course, in a local sense, but in a spiritual—in unity of sentiment, sympathy, aim, soul. All shall be one in Christ. They will be gathered in spirit together from the four winds of heaven.

CONCLUSION. Haste this good time! May the chariot-wheels of Providence revolve with greater speed!

> "One song employs all nations; and all cry,
> 'Worthy the Lamb, for he was slain for us!'
> The dwellers in the vales and on the rocks
> Shout to each other, and the mountain-tops
> From distant mountains catch the flying joy;
> Till, nation after nation taught the strain,
> Earth rolls the rapturous Hosanna round."
> (Cowper.)

D. T.

Ver. 13.—*Man's ruin the fruit of his own conduct.* "Notwithstanding the land shall be desolate because of them that dwell therein, for the fruit of their doings." Here is a prediction of what would take place before the advent of those glorious events pointed out in the preceding verses. There will be a dark night before the morning, a great storm before the calm. The subject here is—*Man's ruin the fruit of his own conduct.* The reason why the land should be "desolate" before the coming of the glorious times is here stated—"for the fruit of their doings." That man's ruin springs from his conduct is demonstrated by universal experience as well as by the Word of God. "O Israel, thou hast destroyed thyself . . . O Israel, return unto the Lord thy God; for thou hast fallen by thine iniquity" (Hos. xiii. 9; xiv. 1). It is the man who heareth the sayings of Christ and doeth them not that will be ruined at last. "Whatsoever a man soweth, that shall he also reap." Assuming it to be a fact that man's ruin is evermore the fruit of his own conduct, four things follow.

I. THAT HIS MISERY WILL BE IDENTIFIED WITH REMORSE. Morally it is impossible for a man to ascribe his ruin to his organization, to circumstances, or to any force over which he has no control. He must feel that he has brought it on himself; and this feeling it is that makes his miserable condition a very hell. The suffering of remorse is the soul of suffering. "A wounded spirit who can bear?"

II. THAT IN HIS SUFFERINGS HE MUST VINDICATE THE DIVINE CHARACTER. Forced to see and feel that all his sin and miseries spring from his own conduct, he will be compelled to say, "Just and right art thou," etc. (Rev. xv. 3). Into the deepest heart of such God speaks the words, "They hated knowledge, they despised all my reproof; therefore shall they eat the fruit of their own way, and be filled with their own devices" (Prov. i. 29). All their misery is but the eating of the fruit of their own doings; they reap that which they have sown. As fruit answers to seed, as echoes to sound, their calamities answer to their conduct.

III. THAT HIS SALVATION FROM RUIN REQUIRES A CHANGE OF LIFE. Men's conduct is fashioned and ruled by their likings and dislikings, their sympathies and antipathies; in other words, if their conduct is bad, it can only be made good by a change of heart. "Marvel not that I said unto you, Ye must be born again."

IV. THAT CHRISTIANITY IS THE ONLY SYSTEM THAT CAN MEET HIS CASE. The mission of Christianity is to change the heart, to renew the life, and effect a spiritual reformation. This it is *designed* to do, this it is *fitted* to do, this it has done, this it is doing; and no other system on earth is capable of accomplishing this work.—D. T.

Ver. 14.—*A prayer.* "Feed thy people with thy rod, the flock of thine heritage, which dwell solitarily in the wood, in the midst of Carmel: let them feed in Bashan and Gilead, as in the days of old." Here is a prayer addressed by the prophet to Almighty God. It is brief, but beautiful, beautiful in spirit and style. It has a prophetic aspect. This prayer recognizes three things.

I. AN INTERESTING RELATION BETWEEN GOD AND HIS PEOPLE, FLOCK AND SHEPHERD. The Jews, here as elsewhere, are metaphorically referred to as a flock, and Jehovah as their Shepherd (Ps. lxxx. 1; xcv. 7, etc.). "The Lord is my Shepherd;" "I am the good Shepherd." What a Shepherd is he! 1. He is the *absolute Owner* of the flock. "My sheep are mine, and I know them." "All souls are mine." How incalculably valuable is one soul!—a free, ever active, influential, undying spirit! How rich is this Shepherd, to own untold millions of such! 2. *He has a perfect knowledge of the flock.* He knows what they are, what they have been, what they will be through all the future. "I know my sheep," etc. (John x.). 3. *He has an infinite love for the flock.* The good Shepherd hath laid down his life for them. 4. *He has abundant supplies for the flock.* Though their wants are varied, numerous, urgent, ever-recurring, he is able to meet them all. "I give unto my sheep eternal life, neither shall any pluck them out of my hands;" "He is able to do exceeding abundantly more than we can ask or think" (Eph. iii. 20); "Feed thy people with thy rod," or staff. It recognizes—

II. THE TRYING CONDITION IN WHICH GOD'S PEOPLE ARE SOMETIMES FOUND. "Which dwell solitarily in the wood, in the midst of Carmel." The primary reference is to their captivity in Babylon. (For another view, see Exposition.) They were as sheep in the forest or wood; in danger of being lost in the thickets or being devoured by beasts of prey. Human souls in this world are in a moral wilderness; beset with perils on every hand. "They are scattered on the mountains as sheep having no shepherd." Two facts render this condition peculiarly distressing. 1. *It is caused by self.* Souls have not been driven away into moral captivity. "All we like sheep have gone astray." 2. *It is undeliverable by self.* No soul ever found its way back to God by its own unaided efforts; hence Christ came to "seek and to save the lost."

III. THE IMPORTANCE OF RESTORATION TO FORMER ENJOYMENTS. "Let them feed in Bashan and Gilead, as in the days of old." The regions of Bashan and Gilead, on the east of the Jordan, were celebrated for their rich pasturage, and on this account were chosen by the tribes of Reuben and Gad and the half-tribe of Manasseh (Numb. xii.; Deut. iii. 17). Morally, the great need of man is the restoration of normal rights, normal virtues, normal enjoyments.

"Good Shepherd, hasten thou that glorious day,
When we shall all
In the one fold abide with thee for aye!"

D. T.

Vers. 15—17.—*The ultimate deliverance of man from sin.* "According to the days of thy coming out of the land of Egypt will I show unto him marvellous things. The nations shall see and be confounded at all their might: they shall lay their hand upon their mouth, their ears shall be deaf. They shall lick the dust like a serpent, they shall move out of their holes like worms of the earth: they shall be afraid of the Lord our God, and shall fear because of thee." In this passage there is an answer to the prophet's prayer. It contains a Divine assurance that wonders analogous to those displayed in the deliverance of the Jews from Egypt would be vouchsafed in their deliverance from Babylonish captivity; and that the display of those wonders would lead to the utter confusion and ruin of the "nations" who were their enemies. They would feel that all their strength was contemptible impotence in the presence of

God's great power. This deliverance, thus described, resembles the ultimate deliverance of man from sin and ruin in two respects.

I. IT INVOLVES THE EXHIBITION OF THE MARVELLOUS. There were "marvellous things" shown when the Hebrews were delivered from Egypt; marvellous things when they were brought out of Babylonian captivity; but these marvellous things are but mere shadows of the marvels displayed in the moral redemption of mankind. The *incarnation of Christ*; the wonders that his mighty hand performed; the extraordinary phenomena connected with his death, his resurrection, and ascension to heaven; the revolutions in the moral character and institutions of mankind;—all these are, in truth the wonders of the wonderful, the marvels of the marvellous.

II. IT INVOLVES THE CONFUSION OF ENEMIES. "The nations shall be confounded at their might, they shall lay their hand upon their mouth," etc. As Egypt and Babylon were confounded, humbled, and terrified at God's marvels in their deliverance, so will all the spiritual foes of Christ be ultimately overwhelmed at the wonders displayed at the redemption of the world. Matthew Henry's remarks on this passage are worth quoting. "1. Those that had exulted over the people of God in their distress, and gloried that when they had them down they would keep them down, shall be confounded when they see them thus surprisingly rising up; they shall be confounded at all the might with which the captives shall now exert themselves, whom they thought for ever disabled. They shall now lay their hands upon their mouths as being ashamed of what they have said, and not be able to say any more by way of triumph over Israel. Nay, their ears shall be deaf too, so much so that they shall be ashamed at the wonderful deliverance; they shall stop their ears as being not willing to hear any more of God's wonders wrought for that people whom they had so despised and exulted over. 2. Those that had impudently confronted God himself shall now be struck with a fear of him, and thereby brought, in profession at least, to submit to him. They shall lick the dust like a serpent; they shall be so mortified as if they were to be sentenced to the same curse the serpent was laid under (Gen. iii. 14). They shall be brought to the lowest abasements imaginable, and shall be so dispirited that they shall tamely submit to them. They shall lick the dust of the Church's feet (Isa. xlix. 23). Proud oppressors shall be made sensible how mean and little they are before the great God; and they shall with trembling and the lowest submission move out of the holes into which they had crept, like worms of the earth as they are, being ashamed and afraid to show their heads; so low shall they be brought and such abjects shall they be when they are abased. When God did wonders for his Church, many of the people of the land became Jews because the fear of the Jews and of their God fell on them (Esth. viii. 17). So it is promised here that they shall be afraid of the Lord our God, and shall fear because of thee, O Israel! Forced submissions are often feigned submissions; yet they redound to the glory of God and the Church, though not to the benefit of the dissemblers themselves."—D. T.

Ver. 18.—*The incomparableness of God illustrated in his forgiveness of sin:* 1. *The nature of his forgiveness.* "Who is a God like unto thee, that pardoneth iniquity, and passeth by the transgression of the remnant of his heritage?" The prophet here—anticipating the full deliverance, not only of the Jews from Babylonian captivity, but probably of humanity itself from the curse of sin through Jesus Christ—breaks forth in a sublime strain of praise and admiration in relation to the *incomparable* character of God. "Who is a God like unto thee?" The subject of the two verses (18, 19) is *Divine forgiveness*, its *nature*, its *source*, and its *completeness*. We shall confine ourselves now to the *nature* of Divine forgiveness. God's forgiveness here is represented in the words, he "passeth by the transgression of the remnant of his heritage." This does not mean that God is unobservant of sin, for all things are naked and open unto him; nor that it is not an offence to him, for it is "an abomination in his sight," but that he regards it in no fault-finding spirit, but with a noble generosity. As loving parents are disposed to overlook much in their children of which they cannot approve, the great Father is disposed to overlook much. "He is not strict to mark iniquity." He passes it by, pursues his benevolent march as if it did not exist. Theology, which has thrown a haze over many of the bright things of revelation, has clouded this, one of its most glorious orbs. Forgetting that the Bible is a popular book, using language in accommodation to our habits of thought and expression, it has constructed its theories upon the etymology of words. The truth and pertinence of this remark will be seen if, at the outset, we consider the very diversified forms in which the Bible represents to us the doctrine of Divine forgiveness. Generally, indeed, I find it set forth under figures corresponding to the aspects in which sin stands before the mind of the writer at the time. For example—

I. WHEN SIN APPEARS AS A DEBT, AN UNFULFILLED OBLIGATION, THEN PARDON IS SPOKEN OF AS A CANCELLING. Thus in the forty-third chapter of Isaiah Jehovah is represented as saying, "I, even I, am he who blotteth out thy transgressions;" and Peter, on the Day of Pentecost, exhorts his vast auditory to "repent, that their sins may be blotted out." When a man has paid his debts, or when some one else has discharged them, the creditor takes his pen in hand and strikes from the ledger both the name of the debtor and the amount. But sin is a debt in a very figurative sense, and therefore such representations of pardon must not be taken in a literal meaning.

II. WHEN SIN APPEARS AS AN ESTRANGEMENT FROM GOD, THEN FORGIVENESS IS REPRESENTED AS RECONCILIATION. But as the estrangement is not mutual, it being exclusively on man's part; in the reconciliation there is no mutual change of mind. God *cannot* change, and *need* not change, to be reconciled to the sinner.

III. WHEN SIN APPEARS AS AN INDICTMENT, FORGIVENESS IS SPOKEN OF AS A JUSTIFICATION. But justification can in the nature of the case have but a very remote resemblance to the forensic term as used by men. In civil justification, for instance, the charge has been found false, the accused demands justification as a *right*, and retires from the court with a high sense of insulted innocence.

IV. WHEN SIN APPEARS AS A POLLUTION, FORGIVENESS IS REPRESENTED AS A CLEANSING. Hence we read of Christ's blood cleansing from all sin. But it is only in a very figurative sense that you can employ the word "washing" to the mind, which is an invisible and impalpable power.

V. WHEN SIN APPEARS AS A DISEASE, FORGIVENESS IS REPRESENTED AS A HEALING. "I will heal your backsliding;" "I am come to bind up the broken-hearted."

VI. WHEN SIN APPEARS AS AN OBSTRUCTION BETWEEN THE SOUL AND GOD, FORGIVENESS IS REPRESENTED AS A CLEARING. The mountains are levelled, the clouds are dispersed, the foes are crushed and are buried as Pharaoh and his host were buried in the depths of the sea. There are three points of contrast between Divine forgiveness and human. 1. *In human governments forgiveness is exercised with most cautious limitations.* Human sovereigns, however generous their natures, can only bestow pardon on a few out of numerous criminals. Were forgiveness to become general, the power of the government to maintain order would be weakened. There is no such limitation to the exercise of this prerogative in God. He offers pardon to *all*. 2. *In human forgiveness there is no guarantee against future criminality.* The prisoner pardoned by a human sovereign may be inspired by gratitude and prompted perhaps to resolve upon a life of future obedience, and yet his heart remain unchanged. The principles that led to his crime may still be in him, and, being there, they may break forth again. But in Divine forgiveness it is not so. The pardoned man is a changed man: he has a new heart put within him—a heart inspired with such love to the Sovereign as will secure a joyous and constant obedience. 3. *Human forgiveness can never put the criminal in such a good position as he had before his transgression.* He has his freedom as before, but he has not his self-respect, he has not the same standing in society; his contemporaries will never look upon him in the same light again. Some will shun him, others will suspect him, and few will venture to give him their confidence and their love. But in Divine forgiveness the criminal is raised to a higher status even than that of innocence. I know not whether the angels would have been his servants had he never fallen; but after his forgiveness they become so. They rejoice with him on his conversion, they cheer him on his pilgrimage, they bear him on their pinions to their heavenly scenes. He is brought into an "innumerable company of angels." We see partially from his state in Eden what relations man would have entered into with his Maker had he never sinned; but I believe that he never would have had what the pardoned sinner has—the honour of seeing his Maker, in the Person of Jesus, on the throne of the universe, gazed on by every eye and worshipped by every heart.—D. T.

Ver. 18.—*The incomparableness of God illustrated in his forgiveness of sin* : 2. *The source of his forgiveness.* "He retaineth not his anger for ever, because he delighteth in mercy." Anger in God is not passion, but principle; not antagonism to existence, but to the evils that curse existence. His anger is but love excited against everything that tends to disturb the harmony, cloud the brightness, and injure the happiness of his creation. "Fury is not in me," etc. (Isa. xxvii. 4). Here is the source of forgiveness: "He delighteth in mercy."

I. FORGIVENESS IS A MERCIFUL ACT. It is not an act of equity, but of compassion; not of justice, but of love. It is the prerogative of mercy. "The Lord passed by before him, and proclaimed, The Lord, The Lord God, merciful and gracious, long-suffering and abundant in goodness and truth, keeping mercy for thousands, forgiving iniquity and transgression and sin." Again, "The Lord is long-suffering and of great mercy, forgiving iniquity and transgression." It is mercy that cancels the debt, blots out the cloud, effects the reconciliation, cleanses the stain, and heals the disease. "Not by works of righteousness which we have done," etc. All the redeemed in heaven acknowledge this: "Unto him that loved us, and washed [loosed] us from our sins in his own blood," etc. (Rev. i. 5).

II. THIS ACT OF MERCY IS THE DELIGHT OF GOD. "He delighteth in mercy." Mercy is a modification of benevolence. It always implies misery, for if there were no misery there would be no mercy. Whilst God does not delight in misery, he delights in removing it. What greater delight has a loving parent than in restoring to health and vigour a diseased and suffering child? To a true soul the delight of moral restoration is even greater than this. A noble father has perhaps more delight in the virtues and fellowship of the son whom he has been the means of raising from moral depravity to spiritual purity and power, than in those of the one who has always pursued the virtuous way. It is thus with him from whom all human love proceeds, he delights in mercy. Will not the song of the redeemed have more music in his ear than the lofty strains of those who have never fallen? He delights to welcome to his bosom and his home his returning prodigals. 1. *If he delights in mercy, then hush for ever the pulpits that blasphemously represent him as malign.* The God that you have in the Calvinian theology is not the God of the Bible, but the God of ill-natured, morose, and vindictive souls. Hence the masses of England turn away in horror from some modern pulpits. "He delighteth in mercy." Let us declare this! "Let the wicked forsake his way," etc.; "Come, let us reason together," etc.; "Come unto me, all ye that are weary and heavy laden," etc. 2. *If he delights in mercy, then let no sinner despair on account of the enormity of his sins.* Let all the sins of the world be embodied in one man's life; let that one man return to God, and he will "*abundantly* pardon" him. He will do it, not reluctantly, not half-heartedly, but with aboundings of joy. He will rejoice over you. "There is more joy in heaven over one sinner that repenteth," etc. 3. *If he delights in mercy, may we not hope that one day there will come an end to all the misery of the moral universe?* "He retaineth not his anger for ever." Who shall say but in some distant future, by some way not revealed, every discord in the moral universe shall be hushed, every prison opened, all sufferers delivered, and all hells quenched? What generous heart would not a thousand times rather believe in this, if they could, than in eternal torment or utter extinction?—D. T.

Ver. 19.—*The incomparableness of God illustrated in his forgiveness of sin* : 3. *The completeness of his forgiveness.* "He will turn again, he will have compassion upon us; he will subdue our iniquities; and thou wilt cast all their sins into the depths of the sea." The reference is here, perhaps, to the destruction of Pharaoh and his host. "He will destroy their sins as he destroyed them, and buried them in the depths of the sea" (Exod. xv. 4, 10).

I. THE ENTIRE SUBJUGATION OF ALL SINS. "Sin," says Henderson, "must ever be regarded as hostile to man. It is not only contrary to his interests, but it powerfully opposes and combats the moral principles of his nature and the higher principles implanted by grace; and, but for the counteracting energy of Divine influence, must prove victorious. Without the subjugation of evil propensities, pardon would not be a blessing. If the idolatrous and rebellious disposition of the Jews had not been subdued during their stay in Babylon, they would not have been restored." Sin is the enemy of all enemies. If it is in us, it sets the holy, happy heavens against us. Take it from us, and hell becomes our minister for good. This God subdues. In truth, Divine forgiveness is the destruction of sin in us, nothing else. It is not something outside; it is all within.

II. THE ENTIRE SUBMERSION OF ALL SIN. "Thou wilt cast all their sins into the depths of the sea." Forgiveness is deliverance from sin. How strong is the imagery employed in the Bible to represent the completeness of this deliverance! It is as the "blotting out of a thick cloud." See that dark mass of cloud up yonder; how it hides the sun and chills the air! A breeze has sprung up, and it is gone—the sky is azure, the scene is bright, and the flowing air warm with life. That cloud can never come again; no more may thy sins. It is as the throwing of them behind God. "Thou hast cast all my sins behind thy back." Who knows where the back of God is? I see his face in nature. His smiles are the beauty of the world. I see his face in Jesus, "the Brightness of his glory." But where is his back? It is the fathomless abyss of nothingness. It is a separation as far as the east is from the west. Tell me the distance from the east to the west, and I will tell you the distance which the pardoned sinner is from sin. It is a casting them into the "depths of the sea." Not on the shore, to be washed back by the incoming waves, but into the "depths." Into the abysses of some mighty Atlantic, where no storms shall stir them up, no trump shall wake them from their graves. "In those days, saith the Lord, the iniquity of Israel shall be sought for, and shall not be found." But where are they buried? In the forgetfulness of infinite love. "I will remember their sin no more." Can Infinite Intelligence forget? Yes, and his forgetfulness is one of the radiant attributes of his character. Does not all true forgiveness involve forgetfulness? Those who say they forgive and cannot forget, lack the faculty of forgiveness; as yet, Heaven has not endowed them with the power of granting absolution. It is of the very nature of love to hide injuries. Charity covereth sins. God has the power of forgetting injuries, because he is *Love*. I see the power of love in hiding injuries working everywhere in nature. The sea hastes to cover up the wounds which ruthless ships have ploughed into its noble bosom. The tree, bleeding with the sores which the woodman has inflicted, loses no time in its efforts to conceal the marks of violence it has received. Day by day goes on, until the year comes round, when, amidst its luxuriant foliage you look in vain for the old scars. And thus, as the waves of the sea and the flowing sap, love ever works. It hastes to cover up from the eye of memory the injuries it has received. How soon the love of a wife buries in forgetfulness any injuries she has received from the man she loves too well! The countless pains which the thoughtlessness and waywardness of children in their early days inflict upon the parental heart are soon buried in the sea of parental love. Love digs in the heart of parents a grave for the wrongs, and builds a museum for the virtues of their children. All this is of God, God-like. Infinite love "passeth by the transgression." He leaves it behind him as he proceeds, in the majesty of his goodness, to diffuse wider and wider for ever the blessedness of his own being.—D. T.

HOMILETICAL INDEX

TO

THE BOOK OF MICAH

NAHUM

EXPOSITION BY

W. J. DEANE

HOMILETICS BY

T. WHITELAW

HOMILIES BY VARIOUS AUTHORS

S. D. HILLMAN

D. THOMAS

THE BOOK OF NAHUM

INTRODUCTION

§ I. Subject of the Book

THE prophecy of Nahum, as the title asserts, is concerned with one subject alone. It is "the burden of Nineveh;" it announces the fate of that evil city. In the Greek Bible it is placed immediately after Jonah, as being the complement of that book. Jonah had preached repentance to Nineveh, and the people had hearkened to his voice, but had soon relapsed into their old sins; and now Nahum pronounces their sentence. Their pride, oppression, idolatry, and especially their defiance of God's sovereignty, are severely rebuked, and the certain and complete destruction of the nation is plainly announced.

The prophecy is composed of three strophes, answering almost exactly to the three chapters into which it is divided. It begins (ch. i.) with stating God's purpose to inflict punishment on Nineveh. The Lord is just and severe, long-suffering, indeed, as the continued existence of Assyria proves, yet the certain Avenger of wrong-doing. Who has ever withstood his power? Earth and sea, and all the inhabitants thereof, bear witness to his irresistible might. And Nineveh must perish, in spite of its riches and its armies, because it has exalted itself against God and his people. Thus the Lord's justice shall be revealed and established, when be brings ruin on his enemies and happiness to his children. Then (ch. ii.) the prophet announces more in detail the destruction of Nineveh. She shall be besieged, she shall struggle in vain, she shall be taken and plundered and utterly wasted. Comparing her future ruin with her past splendour, the prophet is lost in admiration of the equity and wisdom of God, who doeth all these things. What is the cause of this calamity he then proceeds to state (ch. iii.). Assyria had become notorious for cruelty, treachery, rapine, idolatry. It had seduced other nations to follow its steps. And now its might should save it no more than its strength had saved Thebes, so lately captured. Its towers and fortresses should fall, its soldiers should lose heart, its palaces be consumed with fire, its inhabitants be put to the sword, and the Assyrian empire, lately so formidable and strong, should become a byword of derision among all people.

This prophecy, so precise and assured, was the result of no human prevision; it was the outcome of no glance of a far-seeing statesman's eye. It was something more definite than a general confidence in God's moral government, and the ultimate triumph of righteousness. When Nahum prophesied Assyria was at the height of its prosperity. No enemy in its neighbourhood was left unsubdued; the distant Egypt had submitted to its arms; Phœnicia and Cyprus owned its sway; Judæa paid annual tribute; commercial enterprise had drawn unto it the riches of all nations. No one at this epoch could have foreseen the speedy end of this prosperity. Nahum needed a single-hearted courage and a full persuasion of the truth of his mission to denounce the crimes of this flourishing kingdom, and to proclaim its coming downfall. In fifty years the end came. A combination of enemies overthrew this mighty empire. On the death of Assurbanipal matters began to assume a dangerous attitude. Egypt rose against its former conqueror; Babylon revolted; the Medes, now become a powerful monarchy, prepared to attack Nineveh. The reigning monarch (whose name is uncertain), the successor of Assurbanipal, himself marched against the latter, sending Nabopolassar to recover Babylon. The Medes were defeated, and for a time driven back. Nabopolassar also was successful, and received as a reward for his services the title of King of Babylon. Here he managed affairs so skilfully, and strengthened himself so effectually, that, after fifteen years, he found himself able to throw off the Assyrian yoke, and to establish his own independence. The Medes, meantime, under Cyaxares, had recovered from their late defeat, and were only deterred from attacking Nineveh by an inroad of the Scythians into their own country. In order to strengthen his position, Nabopolassar made alliance with all the enemies of Assyria, and became the ruling spirit of a strong confederacy, which comprised Medes and Persians, Egyptians, Armenians, and other nations, all animated with the fierce desire of revenging themselves on Assyria. Josiah of Judah, as a tributary prince, was drawn into the contest, and fell at Megiddo, while endeavouring to arrest the advance of the Egyptian army. About B.C. 612 the allied forces attacked Nineveh, but were repulsed with loss. Victory for some time hovered over the Assyrians; but the enemy, reinforced from Bactria, proved irresistible. The Ninevites, fearing for their final safety, attempted to escape from the city. They were, however, overtaken, and again shut up within their walls. Here they valiantly defended themselves for more than two years, when a circumstance, against which no remedy availed, laid them at the mercy of the besiegers. An unusually heavy and long-continued flood of the river Tigris carried away a large section of the huge rampart that surrounded the city. Through the gap thus formed the enemy forced their way within the walls and captured the place. The king, rather than fall into the hands of his implacable foes, gathered his wives and his treasure into the palace, and burned himself with them there; the town was sacked, and a great number of the inhabitants were massacred. Thus fell Nineveh, B.C. 608, according to the prophecy of Nahum, so that, a few years afterwards, Ezekiel could say (xxxii. 22, 23), "Assyria is there and all her company: his graves are about him: all of them slain, fallen by the sword: whose graves are set in the sides of the pit, and her company is round about her grave: all of them slain, fallen by the sword, which caused terror in the land of the living."

§ II. Author.

Of the Prophet Nahum nothing definite is known but what he himself says. His name, which means "Comforter," does not occur elsewhere in the Bible, but is found, according to Gesenius ('Mon. Phœn.,' pp. 134, 137), in Phœnician inscriptions, and under the form Νάουμος in one of Bœckh's Greek inscriptions ('Corp. Inscript.,' iv. 3). He calls himself "the El-koshite" (ὁ Ἐλκεσαῖος). This is not a patronymic, but signifies "a native of Elkosh," or Elcesi, which, as Jerome says ('Prol. in Nah.'), was a small village in Galilee, well known to the Jews, but in his time showing very few traces of ancient buildings. It is supposed to be represented by the modern El-Kauzeh, a village a little eastward of Ramah in Naphtali. That Nahum was a native of Galilee is perhaps intimated by the name Capernaum, which is interpreted, "village of Nahum," and by the fact that he shows special interest in the northern portion of the Holy Land, in his mention of Carmel, Lebanon, and Bashan, as languishing under the rebuke of God. It is probable that, when Esarhaddon repeopled the northern province with a mixed population imported from his own dominions, Nahum with many of his countrymen removed to Judæa. This may have given direction to his oracle. There is, however, nothing provincial in his language to serve as an indication of his locality, but we should judge that he must have removed from Galilee to Judæa, and uttered his prophecy in the latter province. A late tradition, mentioned by Asseman ('Bibl. Orient.,' i. 525; iii. 352), and adopted by some modern writers, maintains that Nahum was born in Assyria of parents who had been carried thither after the capture of Samaria, and that his sepulchre was to be found at Alkush, ten miles north of Mosul, on the left bank of the Tigris, in which spot also, as the story goes, were buried Jonah, Obadiah, and Jephthah. "It is a place," says Layard ('Nineveh,' i. 233), "held in great reverence by Mohammedans and Christians, but especially by Jews, who keep the building in repair, and flock here in great numbers at certain seasons of the year. The tomb is a simple plaster box, covered with green cloth, and standing at the upper end of a large chamber. The house containing the tomb is a modern building. There are no inscriptions, nor fragments of any antiquity about the place." The story arose some two thousand years after the prophet's time, and was probably inverted to account for his knowledge of Assyrian affairs, which was supposed to denote a resident and eye-witness, or else was founded simply on the similarity between the name of the village and that of his birthplace. Elkosh and Alkush were near enough in sound to suggest identity, and mediæval tradition, credulous and uncritical, fastened upon the Assyrian village as the scene of Nahum's birth and labours, and it became a shrine for pilgrims' honour, with no more reason than in the case of Jonah and Obadiah. And as to Ewald's opinion that Nahum was born of parents living in captivity there, we have only to say that the Israelites were not deported to Assyria under Tiglath-Pileser, but into Media, Babylon, and Mesopotamia. That no one living in Canaan at that time could have exhibited Nahum's acquaintance with Nineveh and its people, is an assertion utterly groundless. The knowledge displayed is not necessarily that of an eye-witness, and was doubtless also possessed by many Jews who had mixed with Gentiles, or had become acquainted with the foreign soldiers who had too often forced their way into the Holy Land. And if it be said that the prophecy is concerned wholly with Assyria, and contains little or no mention of Judæa, which could scarcely have been the case if the writer had been resident in the latter country, it must be answered that the whole tenor of the utterance is to demonstrate the destruction of the power hostile to Judah, the type of the most brutal form of heathendom, and to comfort the Hebrews with the assurance of final victory. But, say the critics, Nahum employs Assyrian words, which a Judæan could never have used. It is true that three such expressions have been found in ch. ii. 7 and iii. 17, but they prove nothing in favour of the assumption. The first, *huzzab*, as it is given in our version, may be considered a Hebrew word taken as a verb, and rendered, "it is decreed," or "it is decided," but is more probably an appellative, as shown in the Exposition; the second is probably also a Hebrew word, derived from *nazar*, "to separate," and meaning "the crowned," or "the levied for war;" the third, *taphsar*, occurs in Jer. li. 27, and is an Assyrian official title, which might well be known in Judæa, and is here used most appropriately. There is nothing, therefore, to negative the general opinion that Nahum was a native of Palestine, and exercised his prophetical office in that country.

§ III. Date.

The time when Nahum prophesied has always, till quite lately, been considered most uncertain, and critics have variously assigned it to dates differing as widely as those of Jehu and Zechariah. Ewald regards him as a prophet of the Captivity, arguing that the prominence given to Assyria, and the merely cursory mention of Judah, could have proceeded only from a seer who was himself an exile from the promised land, and probably resident in the country which he denounces. It is obvious to remark that, commissioned as he was to prophesy against Nineveh, he must necessarily make this the chief subject of his utterances; and, in reality, comfort and encouragement to Judah from the central part of his prophecy, to which all the denunciations of the enemy converge. A majority of critics have considered him to have prophesied during the reign of Hezekiah, and to have been a contemporary of Micah and Isaiah. The place assigned to his work in the Hebrew canon affords support to this opinion, which is supposed to be further confirmed by the language of ch. i. 11, 12, which, it is said, alludes to the invasion of Judæa by the Assyrians ; and that of ch. ii. 13, which, it is affirmed, hints at the mission of Rabshakeh (Isa. xxxvi.). It must be allowed that the allusions are most obscure if regarded as concerned with those facts (see the Exposition, *in loc.*). One thing is certain, viz. that Nahum prophesied after the deportation of the ten tribes. The words of ch. ii. 2 (" The Lord hath turned away the excellency of Jacob, as the excellency of Israel," etc.) can refer to nothing else than that event. Another point is that there are many passages in Nahum and Isaiah which are so similar that one prophet must have copied from the other; but which was the original, which the borrower, cannot be settled by a mere comparison of the writings. But all surmises as to the prophet's date have been set at rest of late years by certain discoveries in the Assyrian inscriptions (see Schrader, p. 450, etc.). In ch. iii. 8 our prophet speaks of the capture and destruction of No-Amon, and the deportation of its inhabitants, as a recent and well-remembered event. No is Thebes, in Upper Egypt, called by the Greeks Diospolis, the capital of that part of the kingdom; and we now learn from the cuneiform records that Assurbanipal, the son and successor of Esarhaddon, took that city in his second expedition against Urdamani, or Rud-Amon, the successor of Tirhakah, and carried the inhabitants away. This invasion took place soon after the death of Tirhakah, which occurred B.C. 664. So we may reckon the date of Nahum's prophecy to have been within ten years of the fall of Thebes, during the reign of Manasseh, whose name was suppressed in the title of the book, owing to that king's evil reputation.

As an instance of destructive criticism, we may note that Hitzig and others, knowing no corroborative evidence concerning the capture of No, at once concluded that the passage in Nahum which asserted this fact was an interpolation deserving of no credit. The inscriptions have happily proved the veracity of the prophet, and the rashness of his critics.

§ IV. General Character.

Among the minor prophets Nahum holds the highest place. His prophecy is a poem, stately, orderly, and impressive, all the parts of which are well arranged and mutually conducive to the unity of the whole. It is eminently tuneful and rhythmical, the words " re-echoing to the sense," and hurrying the hearer away with the speaker in complete sympathy. The style is full of force, the colouring brilliant, the picturing lifelike. The majestic opening, in which are described the attributes of God, his mercy and justice, is equalled by the vivid representation of the sack and ruin of Nineveh, which he paints as if passing before his own eyes. The language is pure and classical, with a certain originality in words and forms which separates it from other writings. It is true that here and there may be found remembrances of Joel and Isaiah; but these expressions may be derived from sources common to all the prophets, and from which, unconsciously as it may be, they drew some materials. And this incidental indebtedness does not diminish the character of originality in treatment and execution which is claimed for Nahum's work. The variety of illustration, the force of imagery, the elegance of diction, the clearness of style, in spite of rapidity of transition, give a unique character to this poem, and differentiate it from all others in the collection. There are no Messianic references; nor is there room for any lengthened array of moral and religious ideas; but these are entwined in forcible, if concise, terms God's existence, justice, and providence are everywhere asserted, witnessed to by the past, expected in the future; and from the coming judgment is drawn a lesson of comfort for the chosen people.

§ V. LITERATURE.

The special commentaries on Nahum are chiefly these: Bibliander (Zurich, 1534); Peritus (Coimbre, 1582, etc.); Gesner, 'Explicatio' (Wittemberg, 1565); Augustin de Quiros (Seville, 1622); Crocius (Brême, 1620); Ursin, 'Hypomnemata' (Francfort, 1652); Hufenreffer (Stutgard, 1663); Tarnovius (Rost., 1623); Van Höke, 'Explicatio' (1709); Kalinsky, 'Observationes' (Breslau, 1748); Agrek (Upsal, 1788); Greve (1798); Grimm, 'Erklärung' (Düsseldorf, 1790); Svanborg (1806); Bodin (Upsal, 1806); Frühn, 'Curæ' (Rostoch, 1806); Justi (Leipzig, 1820); Hölemann 'Illustratio' (Leipzig, 1842); O. Strauss, 'Nahumi de Nino Vaticinium' (Berlin, 1853); also G. Strauss, 'Nineveh und das Wort Gottes' (Berlin, 1855); Vance Smith, 'The Prophecies relating to Nineveh and the Assyrians' (London, 1857); Breiteneicher, 'Nineveh und Nahum' (Munich, 1861); Reinke, 'Aelt Version' (Munster, 1867); B. B. Edwards, 'Translation of Nah.,' in *Biblioth. Sacra*, v. 551.

§ VI. ARRANGEMENT IN SECTIONS.

Part I. (Ch. i. 1—15.) The judgment upon Nineveh decreed by God.
  § 1. (Ch. i. 1.) The heading of the book.
  § 2. (Ch. i. 2—6.) The Divine justice is described, and the irresistible power of God illustrated by his control of the material world.
  § 3. (Ch. i. 7—11.) But the wrath of God falls not on those who trust in him; it is reserved for his enemies generally.
  § 4. (Ch. i. 12—15.) And especially for Nineveh, which shall be utterly destroyed, while Zion shall rejoice at the joyful news of its ruin, and keep her feasts in safety.
Part II. (Ch. ii. 1—13.) The execution of the decree; the destruction of Nineveh.
  § 1. (Ch. ii. 1—8.) Nineveh shall be besieged, because God is about to exalt his people by taking vengeance on the enemy, whose defence is of no avail.
  § 2. (Ch. ii. 9—13.) The city is plundered, and lies waste in terrible contrast with its former excellency.
Part III. (Ch. iii. 1—19.) The cause of the judgment—the sins of the city, which bring inevitable punishment.
  § 1. (Ch. iii. 1—7.) The crimes that have brought this fate upon Nineveh.
  § 2. (Ch. iii. 8—13.) The ruin can be no more averted than was that of No-Amon.
  § 3. (Ch. iii. 14—19.) In spite of all its efforts and all its resources, it will meet with a terrible end.

THE BOOK OF NAHUM

CHAPTER I

Vers. 1—15.—Part I. THE JUDGMENT UPON NINEVEH DECREED BY GOD.

Ver. 1.—§ 1. *The heading of the book.* The book has a double title, the first giving the object of the prophecy, which otherwise would not be evident; the second, its author, added to give confidence in its contents. **The burden;** *massa* (Hab. i. 1)—a term generally used of a weighty, threatening prophecy (Isa. xiii. 1), though translated by the LXX. λῆμμα here, and elsewhere ὅρασις and ῥῆμα. Some prefer to render it "utterance," or "oracle." The word is capable of either meaning. It almost always (except, perhaps, in Zech. xii. 1) introduces a threat of judgment. **Of Nineveh.** The denunciation of this city is the object of the prophecy. The effect of Jonah's preaching had been only temporary; the reformation was partial and superficial; and now God's long-suffering was wearied out, and the time of punishment was to come. (For an account of Nineveh, see note on Jonah i. 2.) Some critics have deemed one part of the title an interpolation; but the connection of the two portions is obvious, and without the former we should not know the object of the prophet's denunciation till ch. ii. 8. **The book of the vision.** This is the second title, in apposition with the former, and defining it more closely as the book in which was written the prophecy of Nahum. It is called a "vision," because what the prophet foretold was presented to his mental sight, and stood plainly before him (comp. Isa. i. 1). **The Elkoshite;** *i.e.* native of Elkosh, for which, see Introduction, § II.

Vers. 2—6.—§ 2. *The prophet describes the inflexible justice of God, and illustrates his irresistible power by the control which he exercises over the material world.*

Ver. 2.—**God is jealous, and the Lord revengeth**; better, *Jehovah is a jealous and avenging God,* as Exod. xx. 5; Deut. iv. 24; Josh. xxiv. 19. The threefold repetition of the name of *Jehovah* and the attribute "avenging" gives a wonderful force to this sublime description of the Divine character. God is here called *jealous* (ζηλωτὴς, Septuagint) anthropopathically, as ready to defend his honour against all who oppose him, as One who loves his people and punishes their oppressors. **Is furious;** literally, *master of fury,* as Gen. xxxvii. 19, "master of dreams." The Lord is full of wrath (comp. Prov. xxii. 24; xxix. 22). The word used implies a permanent feeling, like the Greek μῆνις. **He reserveth wrath.** The Hebrew is simply "watching," "observing" for punishment. Septuagint, ἐξαίρων αὐτὸς τοὺς ἐχθροὺς αὐτοῦ, "himself cutting off his enemies;" Vulgate, *irascens ipse inimicis ejus.* God withholds his hand for a time, but does not forget. All this description of God's attributes is intended to show that the destruction of Assyria is his doing, and that its accomplishment is certain.

Ver. 3.—**Slow to anger** (Exod. xxxiv. 6, 7). Nahum seems to take up the words of Jonah (iv. 2) or Joel (ii. 13). God is long-suffering, not from weakness, but because he is **great in power,** and can punish when he will. **Will not at all acquit the wicked;** literally, *holding pure will not hold pure;* i.e. he will not treat the guilty as innocent. Ἀθωῶν [Alex., ἀθῶον] οὐκ ἀθωώσει (Septuagint); *Mundans non faciet innocentem* (comp. Exod. xx. 7; xxxiv. 7). **The Lord hath his way,** etc. The prophet grounds his description of the majesty and might of God upon the revelation at the Exodus and at Sinai (see Exod. xix. 16—18; Ps. xviii.; xcvii.). **The clouds are the dust of his feet.** Large and grand as the clouds look to us, they are to God but as the dust raised by the feet in walking. As an illu tration of this statement (though, of course, the fact was utterly unknown to Nahum), it has been remarked that recent scientific discovery asserts that clouds owe their beauty, and even their very exi-tence, to the presence of dust-particles in the atmosphere. The aqueous vapour, it is said, condenses on these particles, and thus becomes visible.

Ver. 4.—The great physical changes and convulsions in the world are tokens of God's wrath on sinful nations. **He rebuketh the sea, as at** the passage of the Red Sea (Exod. xiv. 21; Ps. cvi. 9). This is a sign of omnipotence (comp. Luke viii. 24). **All the rivers.** A generalization from the miracle at the Jordan (Josh. iii.; comp. Ps. cvii. 33; Isa. l. 2). Septuagint, ποταμοὺς ἐξερημῶν, " making rivers desolate; " Vulgate, *flumina ad desertum deducens.* **Bashan** (see note on Amos iv. 1). **Carmel** (see on Amos i. 2). **Flower of Lebanon.** This district was famous, not only for its cedars, but also for its vines and flowers (comp. Hos. xiv. 7; Cant. iv. 11). These three regions are mentioned as remarkable for their fertility, and they occur most naturally to the mind of a native of Galilee, as was Nahum. They also geographically are the eastern, western, and northern boundaries of the land. They are used here proverbially to express the truth that God can cause the most luxuriant regions to wither at his word.

Ver. 5. — **The mountains quake.** The mountains, the very emblems of stability, tremble before him (Amos viii. 8). **The hills melt;** Οἱ βουνοὶ ἐσαλεύθησαν, " The hills were shaken " (Septuagint). The hills dissolve like wax or snow at his presence (see Amos iv. 13; Micah i. 4). Burned; Septuagint, ἀνεστάλη, "recoils," "is upheaved," as by an earthquake. This rendering has the greatest authority. **The world;** *i.e.* the habitable world, and all living creatures therein (Joel i. 18—20). Nature animate and inanimate is represented as actuated by the terror of conscious guilt.

Ver. 6.—**Who can stand?** (Ps. lxxvi. 7; Joel ii. 11; Mal. iii. 2; comp. Rev. vi. 17). **His fury is poured out like fire** (Deut. iv. 24); like the brimstone and fire that destroyed Sodom and Gomorrah (Gen. xix. 24), or like the molten lava that issues from a volcano (Jer. vii. 20). Septuagint (reading differently), ὁ θυμὸς αὐτοῦ τήκει ἀρχάς: *consumit principatus* (Jerome). **Are thrown down;** rather, *are rent asunder* (comp. 1 Kings xix. 11; Jer. xxiii. 29). If such is the power of God, how shall Assyria resist it?

Vers. 7—11.—§ 3. *The prophet prepares the way for proclaiming the punishment of*

Nineveh by declaring that the wrath of God falls not on those who trust in him, but is reserved for his enemies.

Ver. 7.—**The Lord is good.** The Targum adds unnecessarily, "for Israel" (Ps. xxv. 8). He is "good," in that he is **a strong hold in the day of trouble,** as in the perilous time when the Assyrians attacked Judæa (comp. Ps. xxvii. 1; Jer. xvi. 19). **He knoweth;** loves and cares for (Ps. i. 6; xxxvii. 18; comp. 2 Tim. ii. 19; and see note on Amos iii. 2).

Ver. 8.—**With an overrunning flood.** This may be merely a metaphor to express the utter devastation which should overwhelm Nineveh, as the invasion of a hostile army is often thus depicted (comp. Isa. viii. 7; Dan. xi. 26, 40); or it may be an allusion to the inundation which aided the capture of the city (see note on ch. ii. 6). **Of the place thereof;** *i.e.* of Nineveh, not named, but present to the prophet's mind, and understood from the heading (ver. 1). (For the utter destruction of Nineveh, comp. Zeph. ii. 13, etc.) The LXX. has, τοὺς ἐπεγειρομένους (" those that rise up "). The Chaldee has a similar reading, with the meaning that God would exterminate those who rise up against him. **Darkness shall pursue his enemies.** So the Septuagint and Vulgate. But it is better rendered, *He shall pursue his enemies into darkness,* so that they disappear from the earth. If this is the meaning of the clause, it resembles the termination of many Assyrian inscriptions which record the defeat of a hostile chieftain: "and no one has seen any trace of him since."

Ver. 9.—The prophet suddenly addresses both Jews and Assyrians, encouraging the former by the thought that God can perform what he promises, and warning the latter that their boasting (comp. Isa. x. 9, etc.; xxxvi. 20) was vain. **What do ye imagine against the Lord?** *Quid cogitatis contra Dominum?* (Vulgate). This rendering regards the question as addressed to the Assyrians, demanding of them what it is that they dare to plot against God; do they presume to fight against him, or to fancy that his threats will not be accomplished? But the sentence is best translated, *What think ye of the Lord?* Τί λογίζεσθε ἐπὶ τὸν Κύριον; "What devise ye against the Lord?" (Septuagint). This is addressed not only to the Jews in the sense, "Do ye think that he will not accomplish his threat against Nineveh?" but to the Assyrians also. **He will make an utter end.** This denunciation is repeated from ver. 8 to denote the absolute certainty of the doom. **Affliction shall not rise up the second time.** The Assyrians shall never again have the power of oppressing Judah as they have **ruined Israel** there shall be no repetition of Sennacherib's invasion. Septuagint, Οὐκ ἐκδικήσει δὶς ἐπιτοαυτὸ ἐν θλίψει: *Non vindicabit bis in idipsum* (Jerome). From this text the Fathers take occasion to discuss the question how it is that God does not punish twice for the same sin.

Ver. 10. -**While they be folden together as thorns.** The clause is conditional: "Though they be interwined as thorns." Though the Assyrians present an impenetrable front, which seems to defy attack. (For the comparison of a hostile army to briers and thorns, see Isa. x. 17; xxvii. 4; Henderson.) **And while they are drunken as drunkards;** *and though they be drunken with their drink,* regarding themselves as invincible, and drenched with wine, and given up to luxury and excess. There may be an allusion to the legend current concerning the destruction of Nineveh. Diodorus (ii. 26) relates that, after the enemy had been thrice repulsed, the King of Nineveh was so elated that he gave himself up to festivity, and allowed all his army to indulge in the utmost licence, and that it was while they were occupied in drunkenness and feasting they were surprised by the Medes under Cyaxares, and their city taken. An account of such a feast, accompanied with sketches from the monuments, is given in Bonomi, ' Nineveh and its Discoveries,' p. 187, etc. We may compare the fate of Belshazzar (Dan. v. 1, etc.). **They shall be devoured as stubble fully dry;** like worthless refuse, fit only for burning (Exod. xv. 7; Isa. v. 24; Joel ii. 5; Obad. 18). The LXX. renders this verse differently, " Because to its foundation it shall be dried up (χερσωθήσεται: *redigentur in vepres,* Jerome), and as bind-weed (σμίλαξ) intertwined it shall be devoured, and as stubble fully dry."

Ver. 11.—The reason of the destruction and of the punishment is told. **There is one come out of thee.** Nineveh is addressed; and we need not refer the words entirely to Sennacherib and his impious threats, but may take them generally as expressing the arrogant impiety of the Assyrians and their attitude towards Jehovah. **A wicked counsellor;** literally, *a counsellor of Belial;* i.e. of worthlessness. The expression, perhaps primarily applied to Sennacherib, also regards the plans prepared by the Assyrians for destroying the people of God, a type of the world arrayed against piety.

Vers. 12—15.—§ 4. *The destruction of Nineveh is emphatically announced, and Zion is depicted as rejoicing at the news of its ruin, and celebrating her feasts in safety.*

Ver. 12.—**Thus saith the Lord.** An expression used to introduce a solemn declaration. **Though they** (the Assyrians) **be quiet.** *Shalem* has this meaning elsewhere, as Gen. xxxiv. 21; but this is unsuitable here, where it must be translated, "in full strength," "unimpaired," "complete," like the thorn-hedge in ver. 10. Vulgate, *Si perfecti fuerint.* Though they be unbroken in strength, and likewise (*on that account*) many in number. Septuagint, Τάδε λέγει Κύριος, κατάρχων ὑδάτων πολλῶν, "Thus saith the Lord, ruling over many waters." So the Syriac and Arabic. Jerome interprets "the waters" to mean the heavenly powers (Ps. cxlviii. 4). Yet thus (though such is their state) shall they be cut down. The verb is used of the mowing of a field or the shearing of sheep, and implies complete destruction. **When he shall pass through;** better, *and he shall pass away.* The number is changed, but the same persons are meant, spoken of as one to show their insignificance and complete annihilation. Septuagint "Thus shall they be dispersed [διασταλήσονται: *dividentur,* Jerome], and the report of thee shall no more be heard therein." The following clause is not translated. **Though I have afflicted thee.** The Lord addresses Judah, referring to the oppression of Judæa by the Assyrians in the times of Ahaz and Hezekiah (2 Kings xvi. 18; 2 Chron. xxviii. 20, etc.; xxxii.). **I will afflict thee no more;** according to the promise in ver. 9. This is further confirmed in what follows.

Ver. 13.—**His yoke.** The yoke of Assyria, probably referring to the vassalage of Judah (2 Kings xviii. 14; 2 Chron. xxxiii. 11). (For the metaphor of " yoke " denoting subjugation, comp. Lev. xxvi. 13; Jer. xxvii. 2; Ezek. xxxiv. 27.) Jeremiah (xxx. 8) seems to use these words of Nahum to announce the deliverance of Israel from captivity. **Burst thy bonds in sunder;** by the final overthrow of the Assyrian power (Ps. ii. 3; Jer. ii. 20).

Ver. 14.—**Concerning thee.** The prophet addresses the Assyrian, and announces God's purpose concerning him. **That no more of thy name be sown.** There is no special reference to Sennacherib in this or the next clause, but the prophet means that the Assyrian people and name shall become extinct. **Out of the house of thy gods** (Isa. xxxvii. 38, where the murder of Sennacherib in the temple of Nisroch is mentioned). An account of the religion of the Assyrians will be found in Layard,' Nineveh and its Remains,' vol. ii ch. 7. **Graven image;** carved out of wood or stone. **Molten;** cast in metal. The two terms comprise every kind of idol, as in Deut. xxvii. 15; Judg. xvii. 3. The Assyrians used to destroy the images of the gods worshipped by conquered nations (2 Kings xix. 18). Bonomi ('Nineveh and its Palaces,' p. 163) gives a picture of soldiers cutting up the image of some foreign deity, and carrying away the pieces. So should it now be done unto their gods. I **will make thy grave.** I will consign thee, O Assyrian, and thy idols to oblivion (Ezek. xxxii. 22, etc.). It is not, "I will make it, the temple, thy grave," as those who see a reference to the death of Sennacherib (2 Kings xix. 37) render it; but, "I prepare thy grave"—I doom thee to destruction. The reason is given: For thou art vile; *quia inhonoratus es* (Vulgate); ὅτι ταχεῖς, "for they are swift" (Septuagint). The word is also translated "light," weighed in the balances, and found wanting, as Dan. v. 27.

Ver. 15.—The second chapter commences here in the Hebrew and Syriac; the Anglican follows the Septuagint, Vulgate, and Chaldee Versions. This seems most agreeable to the method of the prophecy, wherein threat is succeeded by promise, denunciation of the enemy by declaration of comfort to Judah (comp. ch. i. 6, 7, 12, and

13; so here vers. 14 and 15). The prophet announces the joy with which Judah receives the news of the overthrow of Nineveh. **Behold upon the mountains,** etc. Isaiah (lii. 7) uses these words to proclaim the coming of Messiah (comp. Isa. xl. 9; Rom. x. 15). The messengers come from the East across the mountains of Palestine, announcing the fall of Nineveh and the consequent peace and security of Judah—a type of the overthrow of God's enemies and the safety of his Church. There may be an allusion to the custom of spreading tidings by beacon fires. **Keep thy solemn feasts.** Judah is exhorted to resume the observation of her solemnities, which were interrupted during the enemy's occupation of the country, or which could not be properly attended by the distant inhabitants. Judah must offer her praises and thanksgivings for deliverance, and perform the vows which she made unto the Lord in the time of peril. **The wicked** (Hebrew, *Belial*) **shall no more pass through thee.** *Belial* is here the adversary, the opposing army (see ver. 11).

HOMILETICS.

Ver. 1.—*A vision and a burden.* I. THE VISION OF NAHUM. 1. *The person of the prophet.* (1) His name. Nahum, "Consolation"—fitly borne by one whose mission was to be the comforter of God's people. That so many in the Hebrew Church and nation possessed names prophetic of their future destinies points as its explanation to an overruling providence, which in this way kept alive in the hearts of the people a strongly operative belief in a Divine interposition in human affairs. That names are not now in this fashion significant does not prove that God is less cognizant of or interested in mundane matters, but merely shows that such devices are not now required to enable thoughtful persons to detect God's finger in the progress of history. (2) His birthplace. Elkosh; not to be sought for in Assyria, as *e.g.* in the modern Christian village of Elkosh, east of the Tigris and north-west of Khorsabad, two days' journey from Mosul, where the tomb of the prophet is still shown, in the form of a simple alabaster box of modern style (Michaelis, Eichhorn, Ewald, etc.); but in Galilee, perhaps in the present-day village of *Helcesæi* (Jerome, Hitzig, Delitzsch, Keil, etc.). (3) His parentage. Unknown. That his father's name was Elkosh (Strauss) could only be maintained by regarding "the Elkoshite" as a patronymic, and the Elkoshites as a distinct family. Of this, however, Scripture affords no trace. (4) His time. Uncertain. According to Josephus ('Ant.,' ix. 11. 3), Nahum prophesied in the reign of Jotham. But the prophecy itself rather points to a later date—not to the earlier years of Hezekiah, before the destruction of Sennacherib's army (Jerome, Fausset), but to a point of time after that event, and consequently after the conquest of Samaria and the deportation of the ten tribes (Vitringa, Hitzig, Delitzsch, Keil, Nägelsbach in Herzog), more particularly to an age after the destruction of No-Amon, or Thebes (ch. iii. 8), which took place soon after Tirhakah's death, in B.C. 664. Hence B.C. 660, or the last years of Manasseh, may be accepted as the most probable date for Nahum's prophecy (Schrader, 'Die Keilinschriften,' p. 452; Kleinert, in Riehm; Sayce, 'Fresh Light,' etc., p. 154). 2. *The nature of his vision.* (1) Not political foresight merely, since the destruction of Nineveh occurred in B.C. 609—606 (Schrader), *i.e.* a full half-century later than the days of Nahum, which is too broad a chasm to be spanned by purely human sagacity. If the Preacher is not in error (Eccles. iii. 11; viii. 7), Nahum required more than mere natural ability to enable him to predict the downfall of the great Assyrian capital fifty years before it happened. (2) Divine inspiration alone can explain the utterance of Nahum. "The

Lord God will do nothing but he revealeth his secret unto his servants the prophets " (Amos iii. 7). Compare the examples of Abraham (Gen. xviii. 17), Moses (Numb. xii. 6), Samuel (1 Sam. iii. 11), Elijah (1 Kings xviii. 36), Jeremiah (xi. 18), Daniel (ii. 19), etc. The details given in Nahum's prophecy concerning Nineveh are such that they must have been obtained either by direct personal knowledge or by Divine revelation. But inasmuch as the former hypothesis—the ground upon which some scholars and critics locate Elkosh in Assyria—is rendered impossible by the time when Nahum lived (shortly after the destruction of No-Amon), it can only have been by the latter method that he acquired his information.

II. THE BURDEN OF NINEVEH. 1. *The city.* Nineveh; in Assyrian *Ninua,* or *Nina,* equivalent to "Station," "Dwelling," if the word be of Semitic origin; equivalent to "Fish-house" if derived from the Accadian (Delitzsch). A city remarkable for: (1) Its antiquity. Founded by Asshur, who went forth out of the land of Shinar, or Babylon, and builded Nineveh, the present-day *Kouyunjik* and *Nebbi Yunus,* opposite Mosul on the Tigris (Layard, Smith, Schrader); Rehoboth Ir, the site of which is unknown; Calah, represented by the mounds of *Nimrud* (Layard, Smith, Schrader); and Resen, or *Selamiyeh* (Layard, Smith, Schrader), between Calah and Nimroud (Gen. x. 11, 12). "The foundation of Nineveh, the modern Kouyunjik, probably goes back to as early an age as that of Assur (Kalah Shergat, the original capital), but it was not until a much later period that it became an important city, and supplanted the older capital of the kingdom" (Sayce, ' Assyria: its Princes,' etc., p. 22). (2) Its size. Even from earliest times it was regarded as a great city, including Calah, Rehoboth Ir, and Resen, as well as Nineveh proper. In Jonah's day it was "a great city " (i. 1), "an exceeding great city of three days' journey" (iii. 3). This accords both with the statements of classical writers—one of whom gives its circumference as four hundred and eighty stadia, or twelve geographical miles—and with the discoveries of modern research, according to which Nineveh appears to have been used to designate at one time Nineveh proper, at another time the four large prominent cities—Nineveh, equivalent to *Kouyunjik* and *Nebbi Yunus*; Calah, *Nimroud*; Resen, *Selamiyeh*; and Dur-Sargina of the inscriptions, *Khorsabad.* These four cities " formed a trapezium, the sharp angles of which lay towards the north and south, the long sides being formed by the Tigris and the mountains, the average length being about twenty-five English miles, and the average breadth fifteen" (Delitzsch, on Jonah i. 1). "The circumference of these four quarters or towns has been given by the English Jones at almost ninety English miles, which may correspond to a circuit of three days' journey" (Schrader, ' Die Keilinschriften,' p. 448). (3) Its population. In Jonah's time it contained over a hundred and twenty thousand young persons at and under seven years of age (Jonah iv. 11), which would give a population of six hundred thousand (Niebuhr, Delitzsch, Keil) or seven hundred thousand (Schrader) souls—a number exceeded by many modern cities. (4) Its wealth. Nahum speaks of Nineveh as having multiplied her merchants above the stars of heaven (ch. iii. 16); and that this was so her situation "at the culminating point of the three quarters of the globe, Europe, Asia, and Africa " (O. Strauss), might naturally lead one to expect. That Nineveh contained immense stores of gold and silver (ch. ii. 9) accords with the statements of ancient writers, which represent the spoil of Nineveh as having been unparalleled in extent. So completely also was it plundered that "scarcely any fragments of gold and silver have been found in its ruins " (Kitto's ' Cyclopædia,' iii. 334), thus verifying the prediction that she should be "empty, and void, and waste " (ch. ii. 10). (5) Its power. The crowned ones, *i.e.* nobles, and the marshals, *i.e.* the captains, of Nineveh were as plentiful as the locusts and great grasshoppers (ch. iii. 17); in which case what must have been the number of the common soldiers? To these—the levied and selected ones (for war) and the soldiery—rather than to the princes and commanders, according to another interpretation (Keil), the prophet's language refers. The shields and scarlet coats of her mighty men, the rattling of her war-chariots, and the prancing of her horses are vividly depicted (ch. ii. 3; iii. 1); as well as the fierceness and destructiveness of her warfare (ch. ii. 11, 12). (6) Its wickedness. This, which in Jonah's time was so aggravated as to call forth against it a threatening of Divine punishment (Jonah i. 2; iii. 4, 8, 10), was not less conspicuous in the days of Nahum. The " bloody city, full of lies and rapine" (ch. iii. 1), had fully justified her designation by the manner in which she had deceived and destroyed the nations, Syria, Phœnicia, Philistia, Israel, and even Egypt. 2. *The burden.* This, which refers to Nahum's oracle concerning Nineveh, appropriately describes: (1) Its momentous character. A burden on the prophet's soul until it was uttered, it forthwith became a weight of doom upon the city against which it was pronounced. (2) Its certain fulfilment. Laid upon the bloody city by Jehovah's hand (ch. ii. 13; iii. 5), it would inflict a grievous wound and cause a bruise for which there should be no healing (ch. iii. 19).

LESSONS. 1. The argument from prophecy for the inspiration of the Scriptures. 2. The superiority of the Christian dispensation, whose messenger was not a prophet of Jehovah, but the Son of God (Heb. i. 1). 3. The excellence of the gospel, which contains a burden, not of wrath, but of mercy.

Vers. 2—6.—*The wrath of God—a warning.* I. NECESSARY AS TO ITS EXISTENCE Based upon the character of God as a jealous God. Jealous: 1. *For his own glory,* and therefore admitting of no rival claimant to man's worship and homage (Exod. xxxiv. 14; Deut. iv. 24). 2. *For his holy Law,* and therefore shut up to punish iniquity (Exod. xx. 5; Deut. v. 9; xxix. 20; Josh. xxiv. 19). 3. *For his own people,* and therefore impelled to take vengeance on their adversaries.

II. RIGHTEOUS AS TO ITS CHARACTER. Directed only and always: 1. *Against his adversaries;* i.e. against those who decline to do him homage, and show this by worshipping idols. 2. *Against those who dishonour his holy Law* by their disobedience and unrighteousness. 3. *Against those who oppress and tyrannize over his people,* as the Assyrians had done and were doing.

III. FURIOUS AS TO OPERATION. The wrath of Jehovah is not a trifle. Nahum speaks of it as something that has fury in it (vers. 2, 6). The prophets generally represented it as terrible in its forth-flashing against sin and sinners (Deut. xxix. 28; 2 Chron. xxviii. 13; Isa. xiii. 9; Jer. xxi. 5; Zeph. i. 18; Zech. vii. 12). Christ did not view it as of small moment (Luke xxi. 23; xxii. 22). Reason does not warrant the idea that it will be slight and easy to bear, it being the anger of a great and holy God.

IV. SLOW AS TO MANIFESTATION. It does not spring forth readily. Scripture distinctly testifies that God is slow to anger (ver. 3). 1. *Jehovah himself claimed that such was his character,* (1) when he spake to the people at Mount Sinai (Exod. xx. 6); and (2) when he declared his Name to Moses (Exod. xxxiv. 6). 2. *The Bible throughout concedes to him this character.* Moses (Numb. xiv. 18), David (Ps. lxxxvi. 15), Jonah (iv. 2), Micah (vii. 18), Nehemiah (ix. 17), alike proclaim it. In the New Testament, Paul (Rom. ix. 22) and Peter (2 Pet. iii. 9, 15) entertain the same idea. 3. *Experience sufficiently confirms the Divine claim and the Scripture representation.* The providential treatment of the world, of the antediluvian race, of Israel and Judah, of Nineveh and Babylon, of unbelievers in Christendom and of idolaters in heathendom, —the best evidence that God is not willing that any should perish.

V. CERTAIN AS TO INCIDENCE. 1. *His character such as to demand this.* "He will by no means clear the guilty." If he did he would contradict the representations of his character, falsify his word, and endanger his government. Hence his long-suffering cannot arise from any secret sympathy which he has with sin, but must spring solely from his own inherent mercifulness. 2. *His power sufficient to secure this.* If Jehovah is slow to anger, this proceeds not from any defect in his ability to execute wrath upon his adversaries. He is of great power—a truth explicitly set forth in Scripture (Gen. xviii. 14; Exod. xv. 11; Deut. vii. 21; Job ix. 4; Ps. lxxxix. 8, etc.), and amplified and illustrated by Nahum, who depicts that power in a threefold way. (1) By its character as supernatural. "The Lord hath his way in the whirlwind and in the storm, and the clouds are the dust of his feet" (ver. 3). As such it is mysterious, violent, and swift, inscrutable as to origin, immeasurable as to vehemence, incalculable as to velocity. (2) By its effects as irresistible. Nothing can stand before it; not the most uncontrollable element in nature, the sea, which with its dashing billows and moaning waters is to the human mind a striking emblem of power. "He rebuketh the sea and maketh it dry, and drieth up all the rivers" (ver. 4)—an allusion to the drying up of the Red Sea and of the Jordan for the Israelites to pass over (Exod. xiv. 22; Josh. iii. 17). Jehovah's supremacy over the sea a frequent theme with Scripture writers (Job

ix. 8; xxxviii. 8, 11; Ps. xxix. 3; lxv. 7; lxxiv. 15; Isa. xliv. 27; li. 10). Not the freshest and most vigorous, of which Bashan, Carmel, and Lebanon are cited as examples —these languish and fade, their beauty decaying and their fruitfulness departing when he directs against them the fury of his wrathful power (ver. 4; cf. Ps. cvii. 34). Not the most solid and stable, the mountains, the hills, the earth, the world, all of which quake, melt, and burn at his presence (ver. 5; cf. Ps. lxviii. 8; Micah i. 4; Isa. lxiv. 1). Not the most exalted and wise, the living creatures that dwell upon the surface of the globe, beasts and men, both of which are upheaved with terror before the mani-festations of Jehovah's power (Joel i. 18, 20; Hos. iv. 3; Ps. lxv. 8). APPLICATION. "Who can stand before his indignation? and who can abide in the fierceness of his anger?" (ver. 6).

Vers. 7, 8.—*Consolation in God.* I. IN HIS LOVE. "The Lord is good." 1. *Revealed in his Word.* (1) Made known to Moses (Exod. xxxiii. 19; xxxiv. 6); (2) proclaimed by David (Ps. lii. 1; c. 5; cxix. 68); (3) announced by Jeremiah (Lam. iii. 25); (4) confirmed by Christ (Matt. xix. 17). 2. *Attested by his works.* (1) In creation, God having made the earth to be an abode of happiness for innumerable myriads of creatures: "the earth is full of the goodness of the Lord" (Ps. xxxiii. 5). (2) In providence, by his being good unto all (Ps. cxlv. 9), and making all things work together for good to his people (Rom. viii. 28). (3) In grace, by the gift of his Son to be man's Redeemer (Rom. viii. 32; 2 Cor. ix. 15), and by the various blessings of salvation he for Christ's sake bestows upon them—pardon, peace, adoption, holiness, light, strength, life, heaven. 3. *Experienced by his saints.* From the beginning of time downwards, good men have been partakers of, and delighted to bear testimony to, the goodness of God, saying, like David, "The Lord is my Shepherd," etc. (Ps. xxiii. 1); "He hath dealt bountifully with me" (Ps. xiii. 6); confessing, like Solomon, "There hath not failed one word of all his good promise" (1 Kings viii. 56); acknowledging, like Jacob, "He hath fed me all my life long unto this day" (Gen. xlviii. 15). 4. *Illustrated by his Son.* The highest, clearest, and fullest evidence that God is good was furnished by Jesus Christ, who was good in himself (John x. 11), and went about continually doing good (Acts x. 38). II. IN HIS POWER. "He is a Stronghold in the day of trouble." 1. *Accessible.* (1) To all troubled ones, amongst his believing people (Ps. xlvi. 1; Prov. xiv. 26; Isa. xxv. 4), and amongst mankind generally, if they care to avail themselves of it (Ps. xci. 9). (2) From every quarter of the globe, from every rank and condition of society. Jehovah the God, not of the Jew only, but also of the Gentile (Rom. iii. 29); not of the rich and learned and outwardly virtuous, to the exclusion of the poor, ignorant, and degraded, nor of these to the disadvantage of those—with him is no respect of persons (2 Chron. xix. 7; Rom. ii. 11; Eph. vi. 9; Col. iii. 25). (3) In every form of calamity—in the day of national adversity, such as had often befallen Israel undivided (Exod. xiv. 10; Judg. vi. 1, 2; x. 9; 1 Sam. iv. 2), and Judah in separation (2 Chron. xiv. 9; xx. 1; xxxii. 1), and such as was soon to threaten the latter again, if not from the Assyrian, from the Babylonian power; in the day of domestic tribulation, such as overtook Job (i. 13—19), David (2 Sam. xv.- -xviii.), Jacob (Gen. xlii. 36), Jairus (Matt. ix. 18), the centurion (Luke vii. 2), the widow of Nain (Luke vii. 12), the nobleman (John iv. 46), and the household of Bethany (John xi. 1); in the day of personal affliction, which may be either spiritual like the distress which fell on David (Ps. xxxviii. 3), or material like that which overtook Lot (Gen. xix. 29), bodily like that which struck Hezekiah (Isa. xxxii. 1), or mental like that which crushed Jeremiah (ix. 1), occasional like that which happened to Manasseh (2 Chron. xxxiii. 12), or perpetual like that which was the lot of Paul (2 Cor. iv. 10). 2. *Impregnable.* This inevitable, considering what kind of a fortress it is—Divine, and by what munitions it is guarded, the royal battalion of the Divine attributes, by Jehovah's omnipotence, omniscience, omnipresence, faithfulness, wisdom, holiness, love. Against this manifestly no weapon can prevail. "Mine omnipotency shall be your guard. I am God Almighty, your Almighty Protector, your Almighty Benefactor. What though your enemies are many? More are they that are with you than they that are against you; for I am with you. What though they are mighty? they are not almighty," etc. (Alleine's 'Heaven Opened,' pp. 256, 257). 3. *Sufficient.* Every succour the soul needs in its day of trouble is found in God, and found completely—for the soul's guilt, pardon (Isa. i. 16; xliii. 25); for its pollution, cleansing (Ezek. xxxvi. 25); for its anxiety, peace (Isa. xxvi. 3; Matt. xi. 28); for its weakness, strength (Isa. xlv. 24); for its darkness, light (Ps. cxviii. 27; 1 Pet. ii. 9; 1 John i. 5); for its death, life (Isa. xxv. 8; Rom. iv. 17).

III. IN HIS KNOWLEDGE. "He knoweth them that put their trust in him." He knoweth them: 1. *Collectively.* All that belong to the body of his believing people he exactly and always knows, so that he can think and speak of them as his people (Isa. xxxii. 18; 2 Tim. ii. 19), as Christ does of those who are his (John x. 14). 2. *Individually.* Not in the mass merely, but separately and singly, he knows them (2 Sam. vii. 20; Ps. cxxxix. 1; 1 Cor. viii. 3, Heb. iv. 13), as Christ also calls his own sheep by name (John x. 3). 3. *Thoroughly.* (1) Their characters—seeing that he searches the heart (1 Kings viii. 39; Jer. xvii. 10; Ps. cxxxix. 2; Luke xvi. 15; Acts i. 24; xv. 8; 1 Thess. ii. 4). Hence he can never err as to their persons. (2) Their conditions—since nothing can be hid from him, neither person (Jer. xxiii. 24; Hos. v. 3) nor thing (Ps. cxxxix. 15; Jer. xvi. 17), but both alike are manifest in his sight (Heb. iv. 13). Hence he can never mistake as to their circumstances, but must always understand precisely what they need. 4. *Efficiently.* Different from the wicked, whom he knows afar off (Ps. cxxxviii. 6), *i.e.* as persons estranged from and hostile to them that put their trust in him he knows appreciatively and helpfully, so as to love, cherish, protect, and assist them. "Though the Lord be high, yet hath he respect unto the lowly"—to their persons to love them, to their characters to admire them, to their wants to supply them, to their souls to save them.

CONCLUSION. Note: 1. The characters of those for whom this consolation exists—they put their trust in God. Remark upon the simplicity and efficacy of faith. 2. The evil fate of them who, being destitute of faith, are his enemies—they shall be destroyed by an overrunning flood, their habitations swept away, their persons engulfed, their hopes disappointed, their projects defeated, their ambitions scattered to the winds; they shall be pursued by (or into) darkness (see next homily).

Ver. 8.—*Pursued by* (Authorized Version), *into* (Revised Version), *darkness.* I. A WOEFUL FATE. 1. *The picture.* That of a defeated enemy pursued by a victorious general who comes up behind his foes like the shades of night upon a wearied and dispirited traveller stumbling forward upon an uncertain and perilous way, as Abraham fell upon the kings by night and smote them, and pursued them unto Hobah (Gen. xiv. 15); or, who drives them on before him into the gloom of night, where they encounter unforeseen dangers and perish, as the kings of Sodom and Gomorrah did when chased by Chedorlaomer's troops (Gen. xiv. 10). 2. *The interpretation.* The defeated enemy is the sinner; the pursuing conqueror is either darkness, meaning those calamities which God has ordained to follow sin, or God himself, by whom the sinner shall be chased into such disastrous overthrow. In either case, with darkness behind or darkness before—and, in reality, it is both behind and before—the condition of God's enemy is pitiful indeed.

II. A CERTAIN DOOM. Pursued by or into darkness. There is no "peradventure" about the lot of the ungodly. What is here predicted is not contingent, but absolute; not what ought to be merely, or what may be only, but what shall be. 1. *God's Word hath declared it.* "The wicked shall be silent in darkness," etc. (1 Sam. ii. 9); "The eyes of the wicked shall fail," etc. (Job xi. 20); "He shall be driven from light into darkness" (Job xviii. 18); "Let their way be darkness and slippery places" (Ps. xxxv. 6); "The candle of the wicked shall be put out" (Prov. xxiv. 20); "The children of the kingdom [who have become God's enemies] will be cast into outer darkness," etc. (Matt. viii. 12)—"And the Scripture cannot be broken" (John x. 35). 2. *God's character requires it.* If his love and mercy make it sure that none who return to him will be rejected (Isa. lv. 7; Jer. iii. 22; Hos. xiv. 4), his holiness and justice render it equally imperative that the impenitent and unbelieving, the rebellious and disobedient, should be punished with everlasting destruction from the presence of God and from the glory of his power (Rom. i. 18; 1 Cor. vi. 9; 1 Pet. iii. 12). 3. *Sin itself ensures it.* Every action that a man performs carries in its own bosom its reward or punishment. "The wages of sin is death," just as certainly as "the fruit of holiness" is "everlasting life" (Rom. vi. 21—23).

III. A JUST RETRIBUTION. To be pursued by or into darkness is a fitting lot for those who in their lifetime rather have loved the darkness rather than the light. 1. *The law of moral retribution demands that this shall be so.* "Whatsoever a man soweth that shall he also reap" (Gal. vi. 7). He that walks in darkness here cannot hope to walk in light yonder; he who does the deeds of darkness on earth will not likely begin to do deeds of light in heaven. 2. *The character of the wicked makes it certain that this shall be so.* No being can act otherwise than in accordance with its nature. Mere change of place suffices not to alter one's nature. No reason to think that passing from one form of existence to another will effect any radical transmutation of one's being. Hence they who have died in darkness will (in all probability) continue to dwell in darkness.

LESSONS. 1. Forsake sin. "Have no fellowship with the unfruitful works of darkness." 2. Follow holiness. "Walk as children of the light."

Vers. 9—14.—*A wicked counsellor.* I. His PERSON. 1. *The Assyrian power.* Represented in Hezekiah's reign by Sennacherib; in Manasseh's (Nahum's time) by Esarhaddon or Assurbanipal; in each successive reign by the ruling sovereign. 2. *The unbelieving world.* Of this Assyria was now the symbol, as in former times Egypt had been, as in later days Rome was (John xv. 18; Jas. iv. 4). 3. *The unrenewed heart.* The carnal mind is enmity against God (Rom. viii. 7).

II. His CHARACTER. 1. *Powerful.* The Assyrian in Nahum's age was "in full strength" (ver. 12), a well-organized and firmly knit confederacy like "tangled thorns" (ver. 10), which were dangerous to touch, and a multitudinous people (ver. 12) in comparison with which Judah was but a handful. The same elements of power coexist in the unbelieving world—force (Eph. ii. 2), order (Eph. vi. 12), numbers (1 John v. 19)—in comparison with which the Church of God is weak, disunited, and small. The individual transgressor also not unfrequently exhibits an energy, a determination, and a capacity to enlist others upon his side which are wanting in the followers of God and Christ. 2. *Self-reliant.* Like drunkards drenched in drink (ver. 10), the Assyrians were foolishly confident, and believed themselves to be invincible. In like manner, the unbelieving world in general and the individual sinner in particular, are of opinion that they are more than sufficient to cope with any form of calamity that may assail them, and to ensure their own safety against any foe, bodily or ghostly, earthly or unearthly, human or Divine. 3. *Vile.* (1) The Assyrian court was notorious for its gluttony and revelry, especially in the days of Assurbanipal. The world also runs to strange excess of riot in eating and drinking (Rom. xiii. 13; 1 Pet. iv. 4). (2) The Assyrian people were worshippers of idols (ver. 14); and the world of to-day has its idols before which it delights to prostrate itself and present homage. (3) The Assyrian kings were tyrannical, cruel, and oppressive; and so also is the world.

III. His DESIGNS. 1. *Evil.* "He counselleth wickedness" (ver. 11)—in particular oppression of the people of Jehovah (ver. 13). Such was the aim of Assyria towards Judah; such is the aim of the world towards the Church; and of the unbeliever towards the believer. 2. *Impious.* His wicked counsels are also directed "against the Lord" (vers. 9, 11). This was the spirit of Assyria as represented by Rabshakeh in the time of Hezekiah (2 Kings xviii. 28—35; 2 Chron. xxxii. 11—17; Isa. xxxvi. 7, 14, 15, 18—20; xxxvii. 10—13); and of Herod, Pontius Pilate, the Gentile world, and the unbelieving Jews in the days of Christ (Ps. ii. 1; Acts iv. 25—28); and is the spirit still of the unrenewed heart (Rom. viii. 7). 3. *Vain.* The fruits of a corrupt "imagination" (vers. 9, 11), they will prove idle and worthless. Assyria's schemes for the subjugation of Judah came to nought; so resulted in defeat those of Herod and of Pilate, of the Jews and of the Gentiles against the holy Child Jesus; and so will terminate in shame those of wicked men generally against the truth.

IV. His DOOM. 1. *Certain.* The decree had gone forth against Assyria when Nahum spoke. "The Lord hath given commandment concerning thee, that no more of thy seed be sown" (ver. 14). A similar decree has gone forth against the ungodly world (2 Pet. iii. 7; 1 John ii. 15—17), and against unbelievers as individuals

(Phil. iii. 19; 1 Thess. i. 9). 2. *Complete.* Of Nineveh Jehovah was to make "a full end," so that no second affliction should be required to destroy them (Calvin, Hitzig), or should be able to proceed from them (Keil, Fausset) against Judah (ver. 9); the Assyrians were to be "destroyed utterly as dry stubble" (ver. 10), "to be cut down and pass away," so that Jehovah should no more (at least by their hand) afflict his people (ver. 12); the royal house was to come to an end, no more of that name being sown (ver. 14); the very divinities of Assyria and Nineveh were to be exterminated (ver. 14). More complete ruin was inconceivable; so will all the enemies of God and Christ be utterly destroyed (Jer. xii. 17; Ps. xxxvii. 38; Matt. xxi. 41; 2 Pet. ii. 12).

LESSONS. 1. The danger of forming designs against either God or his people. 2. The wisdom of taking warning in time before it is too late. 3. The certainty that, when God begins the work of judgment, he will also make an end.

Ver. 15.— *Glad tidings for God's people.* I. THE DESTRUCTION OF A POWERFUL FOE. 1. *The historical allusion.* The "wicked one" whom Nahum represents as "utterly cut off" was the power of Assyria, whose certain and complete annihilation he has just predicted (ver. 14), and now depicts as accomplished. 2. *The spiritual application.* Capable of being applied to every deliverance wrought by Jehovah for Judah, in particular to her deliverance from Babylonian captivity, it is specially true of that emancipation which was wrought for mankind sinners by the destruction of the Church's greatest foe, the prince of the power of the air, over whom Christ triumphed through his cross. This the first note of the gospel message that Christ hath destroyed death, and him that hath the power of death, the devil (Heb. ii. 14).

II. THE PROCLAMATION OF A BLESSED PEACE. 1. *The scene depicted.* The prophet represents heralds as appearing on the mountains encircling Jerusalem with the joyous announcement that the ancient and terrible enemy she feared was overthrown, and could no more invade her land or oppress her people, and that henceforth she might dismiss all anxiety and be at peace. 2. *The sense intended.* The prophet wished to convey the thought that when once the power of Assyria was broken there would be no cause of alarm—that Judah might rest at ease, and prosecute her national career without fear of being disturbed by hostile invasion. 3. *The symbol interpreted.* As the destruction of Nineveh meant peace for Judah, so the overthrow of Satan and the powers of darkness means peace for God's believing people. This the second note of the gospel message. After the work of redemption the publication of peace (Acts x. 36; Eph. ii. 14—17). As Judah's duty was to behold the peace-messengers upon the mountains of Judah, and to believe their message, so the duty of the New Testament Church is to recognize him whom God hath sent, and to receive his gospel of peace.

III. AN INVITATION TO A JOYOUS FEAST. 1. *The feasts referred to.* These were the three principal feasts enjoined upon the Hebrew Church by Moses—the Feast of the Passover, commemorative of the nation's deliverance from Egypt; the Feast of Harvest, in which the firstfruits of the field were presented to the Lord; and the Feast of Ingathering, when the labours of the year were happily concluded by the safe storing of the well-filled sheaves. In addition were other feasts which need not now be mentioned. The above-named three were pre-eminently gladsome in their causes and their forms. They gave expression to the nation's thankful joy in thinking of the Divine mercifulness, the Divine faithfulness, and the Divine goodness—first, in sparing them and making them a nation; next, in faithfully keeping with them his covenant of seed-time and harvest; and, thirdly, in making such abundant provision for their wants, of all which they had been made partakers. Hence they fitly stood as types of the great feast of salvation to which God's believing people are invited in consequence of Christ's atoning and redeeming work, and in which God's mercy, faithfulness, and goodness are expressed—that feast of fat things full of marrow, and of wines on the lees well refined, of which Isaiah speaks (xxv. 6), that feast to which Christ alluded in his parables of the wedding banquet (Matt. xxii. 2) and of the great supper (Luke xiv. 16), and that feast which is symbolized in the Lord's Supper (1 Cor. v. 8). 2. *The invitation given.* (1) To whom addressed? To Judah, God's ancient people; and, while in one sense the overtures of the gospel are extended to all, in another they belong only to them who believe and are God's people through faith in Christ Jesus. (2) On what based? Not on any merit or good works on the part of Judah, as *e.g.* on Judah's prowess in defeating her ancient enemy, but solely on the fact that Jehovah had done so ; and the people of God in the Church of Christ are invited to participate in the joyous banquet of salvation, and to celebrate their New Testament feast, not because of any worthiness in themselves, or because of any share they have had in overthrowing their arch-foe (since they have had none), but exclusively because their adversary hath been destroyed for them—because God's right hand alone hath gotten him the victory (Ps. xcviii. 1).

IV. A SUMMONS TO A PLEASANT DUTY. 1. A *becoming* duty. The payment of Judah's vows meant her performance of the engagements she had come under to be faithful and obedient to Jehovah, observing his worship, and keeping his commandments. To do this had been her duty from the first, though she had often failed in it ; to return to it now after experiencing Jehovah's mercy was in the highest degree proper. 2. A *necessary* duty. Without this Judah would not be truly grateful for her deliverance, her outward observance would be insincere and hypocritical, and her inner life would be practically unchanged. So the highest evidence a soul can give of its thankfulness for Divine mercy, of its own heartfelt sincerity, and of its genuine conversion and regeneration, is obedience. 3. An *agreeable* duty. What should be easier or more delightful than service which springs from love ? So to gracious souls God's commandments are not grievous, and hearts constrained by the love of Christ find that his yoke is easy and his burden is light.

Learn : 1. The possibility of extracting gospel truths from Old Testament Scriptures. 2. The clearer light which shines in the Christian records concerning God's gracious work of redemption. 3. The larger responsibilities that rest upon such as have experienced the salvation of Christ.

HOMILIES BY VARIOUS AUTHORS.

Ver. 1.—*The messenger of judgment.* Notice here—

I. THE MESSENGER : HIS PERSONALITY. "Nahum the Elkoshite." 1. *His name.* "Nahum," signifying "Consolation ;" and whilst this scarcely accords with the character of his mission as the proclaimer of Divine judgments, yet, interspersed with the heavy tidings concerning Nineveh, we have here very tender and consolatory words addressed by him to his own afflicted nation (vers. 7, 12, 13—15). 2. *His birthplace.* He was "the Elkoshite," a native of Elkosh, a village of Galilee. This has been questioned, and a tradition has been appealed to representing that he belonged to the Captivity, and was born at Alcosh, a town near Mosul. It has been urged, however, that much of the phraseology he employs, together with certain familiar references to places, connects him unmistakably with North Palestine.

II. THE CHARACTER OF HIS MESSAGE. "The burden of Nineveh." 1. It was a message to be delivered to a heathen nation. Like the message of Jonah, to which it has been fittingly described as being "the complement and the counterpart," it indicates that God holds wider relations with mankind than the Jews were prepared to admit ; and that all nations and peoples lie within the range of his providence and power. 2. It was a message full of dark forebodings. It told of impending judgment and of national destruction and desolation. The sombre announcements were unrelieved even by a single word of hope being addressed to the guilty nation. The Ninevites had previously recognized the Divine righteousness, and upon their repentance had experienced the Divine clemency ; but this had been followed by relapse into the grossest iniquity, and there remained now only the experience of the threatened ruin—the nation should be "utterly cut off." " The burden of Nineveh " was also the burden of Nahum. His few words recorded here addressed to his own people are sufficient to indicate that he was a man of refined susceptibilities ; and to such a man his commission must have been indeed oppressive. Yet he would not shrink, but would faithfully fulfil his trust. Whilst the mercy and love of God should be the constant theme of the modern teacher, yet the great and solemn fact of his retributive justice must not be ignored. There is to be declared "all the counsel of God " (Acts xx. 27).

III. THE DIVINE AUTHORITY WITH WHICH HE WAS INVESTED. A plain man unfolding such teachings respecting a mighty heathen power might well be required to furnish his credentials. And we have his authority expressed in the words, " the vision of Nahum." A Divine insight had been imparted unto him; there had been given him "visions and revelations of the Lord," and of his terrible doings about to be wrought. Such apprehension of spiritual realities is absolutely essential in order to constitute any man a messenger of God to his age (1 Cor. ii. 10—16; 1 Pet. i. 12; 1 John iv. 14).

IV. THE PERMANENT RECORD OF HIS SOLEMN TEACHING. "The book of the vision," etc. (ver. 1). This is the only form in which mental thoughts and conceptions can be lastingly perpetuated. The matchless works of the great masters in painting, sculpture, and architecture, which have excited the admiration of the whole world, can have but a limited existence; no copy equal to the originals can be made; and in the waste and wear of time these must inevitably pass away; whereas the literary productions of men of genius will continue to live on; for time does not impair that art by which books are reproduced and the circle of their influence extended. The Bible is a collection of books; and the remarkable unity combined with progressiveness traceable therein furnish a very convincing evidence of its Divine origin. Written prophecy forms a most important feature in this development of truth. It was not only necessary that the prophets should labour (as they did so earnestly) to maintain religion amongst the people who had been chosen of God and separated to his praise, but also that, as the work of prophecy advanced, there should be indicated and recorded how that the Lord was working among the nations, Hebrew and heathen alike, and bringing about the fulfilment of his all-wise and gracious purposes. And viewed under this aspect, "the book of the vision of Nahum the Elkoshite" fills an important niche, whilst its grave words of admonition and warning may well lead evil-doers to reflection and penitence, and its occasional words of hope to the pious and God-fearing may serve, in troublous times, to keep their hearts in quietness and assurance.—S. D. H.

Vers. 2—6.—*The Divine vengeance.* In engaging in work for God, the worker must not be unmindful of the terrible consequences resulting from despising the riches of Divine mercy and grace. There is, assuredly, such a thing as retribution following a course of alienation from God's ways. It must be so. The very love of God renders the punishment of the ungodly absolutely essential. Objectors sometimes point to the scriptural teaching concerning the future of the impenitent as indicating that the God of the Bible is unlovely and severe. But surely, where there is love there will also be found regard for justice. There is a mawkish sentimentalism about the teaching which dwells upon the love of God to the exclusion of all regard for his rectoral character. There is much of this teaching prevalent to-day. It is the recoil from extreme Calvinism, and, as is usual in such cases, the very opposite extreme is reached. It is impossible to indicate the extent to which the intense sense of God possessed by the Reformer of Geneva gave strength to his work; and let God be realized by us as "infinite Justice, infinite Love, and infinite Truth, blended in one indivisible ray of whitest light," and the thought of his all-embracing sovereignty and wise and perfect administration will be found full of comfort and inspiration to our hearts. And so long as he is righteous, sin, unrepented of and unabandoned, must be followed by bitter results; and hence, whilst joyfully proclaiming "the acceptable year of the Lord," we must also declare the coming of "the day of vengeance of our God." In these verses—

I. LIGHT IS CAST UPON THE NATURE OF THE DIVINE VENGEANCE. Our conceptions of the Divine Being are sometimes assisted by our ascribing to him certain characteristics belonging to the children of men. Analogy, however, in this direction must not be pressed too far, or we may be led to form very erroneous views concerning our God. We have in these verses a case in point. Nothing is more strongly to be condemned in men than the cherishing by them of the spirit of jealousy and of vengeance; yet this is here ascribed to God. "The Lord is jealous, and the Lord revengeth," etc. (ver. 2). But then "jealousy" and "vengeance" mean something very different when applied to man from what is intended when the same terms are used in reference to God. By jealousy on the part of man we understand envy, but by the same word in reference to God we are reminded of his regard for the maintenance of truth, his holy concern for the upholding of righteousness. And by vengeance on the part of man we understand revenge, a determination that satisfaction shall be given for the injury we consider has been done to us; whereas the same word as applied to God carries with it no such idea of vindictiveness, but simply a pure desire that the cause of justice and rectitude may be established and secure complete vindication. Since this brief book of prophecy has almost exclusive reference to the Divine judgments to fall upon the Assyrians, it is all-important that we clearly understand at the outset that Divine vengeance has absolutely no malice in it, and is ever exercised in the maintenance of righteousness. This is indicated in the next verse in three particulars (ver. 3). 1. *The Divine slowness.* "The Lord is slow to anger." Vindictiveness will not brook delay; human vengeance reckons with its victims at the earliest moment; revenge burns; passion rages; but the Divine vengeance delays, that perchance, through penitence, the blow may not be required to fall. 2. *The restraining of Divine power.* Man, cherishing the spirit of vindictiveness, sometimes lingers because conscious of his want of power to inflict the penalty; but God "great in power" (ver. 3) restrains his might, holds back his avenging hand, that "space for repentance" may be given, and the fact be made manifest that he "desires not the death of the wicked." 3. *The Divine concern for the maintenance of his pure Law.* "And will not at all acquit the wicked" (ver. 3). His vengeance is not vindictive, but is exercised in order that the supremacy of his holy Law may be asserted. He has graciously made provision for the forgiveness of sin and the salvation of transgressors from condemnation (Rom. viii. 1), and they who willfully persist in iniquity must bear the consequences, which will light upon them, not because God is vindictive, but because the honour of his pure Law must be sustained.

II. THIS ASPECT OF THE DIVINE CHARACTER IS SET FORTH IN GRAPHIC IMAGERY. (Vers. 3—6.) For sublimity and grandeur this passage stands unrivalled. The Divine vengeance is presented to us here: 1. *In its irresistibleness.* Like the whirlwind, it sweeps everything before it (ver. 3). 2. *In its terribleness.* In vivid symbolical language all nature is represented as full of terror at the Divine manifestations (ver. 5). 3. *In its destructiveness.* Desolation is brought about—the sea and the rivers are dried up at the rebuke of the Lord; the rich pastures of Bashan, the beautiful gardens of Carmel, and the fragrant flowers and fruitful vines and stately trees of Lebanon languish (ver. 4); as a devouring fire this vengeance consumes in every direction (vers 5, 6); yea, so mighty is it that the very rocks crumble to pieces when it is put forth (ver. 6).

III. THIS VIEW OF OUR GOD IS PRESSED HOME UPON OUR HEARTS BY EARNEST INQUIRY. "Who can stand before his indignation? and who can abide in the fierceness of his anger?" (ver. 6). The design of the questions is to quicken conscience. They contain and suggest the answers. Humbled in the very dust of self-abasement, we cry, "Enter not into judgment with thy servants, O Lord; for in thy sight shall no man living be justified" (Ps. cxliii. 2).—S. D. H.

Ver. 7.—*The Divine goodness.* "The Lord is good." The word "good" is used here in the sense of the desire to promote happiness. The prophet affirms that "the Lord" possesses this disposition—that whilst he is powerful he exerts this power in saving, not in destroying, "judgment" being "his *strange* work;" that whilst his presence fills all space, and his omniscient eye penetrates all, he is concerned, in his watchfulness, that none of the creatures he has formed should lack the blessings his bounteous hand has to bestow; and that as he is eternal in his duration, so the streams of his bounty shall ever continue to flow. "The Lord is good." This inspiring truth was revealed even from the earliest times, and is inscribed in Scripture upon every page. Abram in the vision by night (Gen. xv.), Jacob in his weary wanderings (Gen. xxviii. 10—22), and Moses in "the holy mount" (Exod. xxxiii. 19), were alike favoured with special revelations of it. The very thought of God thus woke up within the psalmist the faculty of song, and led him to strike his lyre and to sing with holy fervour, "Thou, Lord, art good and ready to forgive" (Ps. lxxxvi. 5); "They shall abundantly utter the memory of thy great goodness," etc. (Ps. cxlv. 7); "Oh, taste and see," etc. (Ps. xxxiv. 8). And prophets unite with psalmists in bearing this testimony (Jer. xxxiii. 11; Isa. lxiii. 7). Very different was the conception formed by the heathen. We think of the tyranny, caprice, and revenge supposed to characterize heathen deities, the acts of cruelty ascribed to them, the impurity of heathen rites, and the wearisomeness of heathen penances, and we rejoice that the voice from heaven has

spoken unto us, and that the truth which heathen worshippers did not know has been
so clearly revealed to us in the bright assurance, " The Lord is good." " The Lord is
good." Nature, with her ten thousand voices, bears emphatic testimony here. Benevolence marks all the operations of the Creator's hands. All his works declare his goodness. The majestic sun, the full-orbed moon, the stars countless in number and
sparkling in the vault of heaven, the refreshing and fertilizing shower, the gentle
breeze, the woods re-echoing with the notes of little songsters, the varied landscape, the
carpeted earth, the tinted flowers, all seem to speak and to say, " The Lord is good."
" O Lord, how excellent is thy Name in all the earth ! " (Ps. viii. 1) ; " O Lord, how
manifold," etc. ! (Ps. civ. 24). " The Lord is good." As in creation so in providence, the
same testimony is borne. Specially is this so in the Divine dealings with men, supplying his wants, ministering to his necessities, scattering blessings in his path, and daily,
yea, hourly, sustaining and preserving him from peril and danger. His goodness, too,
is seen in that he is " kind even to the unthankful," and bestows his favours not only
upon " the just " but also upon " the unjust," sustaining even those who live in rebellion
against him. Nor does the fact that whilst the ungodly often seem to " prosper in
their way," " waters of a full cup are wrung out to his people," militate against the
declaration of this text ; for God's providence takes into account the *entire welfare* of
his servants, and adverse scenes may be necessary in order to the promotion of this ;
and, the discipline accomplished, deliverance shall be theirs, whilst the arm of the
oppressor shall be broken (vers. 12, 13). " The Lord is good." This truth, impressed
upon the pages of the Old Testament, receives its highest exemplification in the records
of the New. In him whose advent prophets predicted, and whose work was shadowed
forth in type and symbol, and in the free redemption he has wrought ; in the seeking
and self-sacrificing love and the compassionate mercy and grace of God as thus expressed,
we see the noblest, purest, brightest token that " the Lord is good." In this Divine
goodness, ever watchful to guard us ; almighty, and hence equal to every emergency of
our life ; immutable too, and therefore an unfailing dependence amidst the mutations
and fluctuations of our earthly lot,—let us rest with unswerving trust, until at length,
every bond sundered, we, as " the ransomed of the Lord, come to Zion with songs and
everlasting joy upon our heads," there with adoring gratitude to reflect upon the
memory of his great goodness, and to praise him for his mercy and grace and love for
evermore.—S. D. H.

Ver. 7.—*God our Stronghold.* Great, indeed, is the honour sustained by the man
who fulfils the mission of being a comforter to others, who is enabled to minister to
sorrowing and stricken ones, who watches with them in their Gethsemanes, and by his
gentle words and tender sympathy imparts consolation to their wounded hearts. " I
dwelt as a king in the army ; as *one that comforteth the mourners* " (Job xxix. 25). No
service makes a greater demand upon a man than this, yet he has an abundant reward
for the self-sacrifice involved, in beholding the objects of his regard no longer in
" ashes," but raised out of the dust and made comely ; no longer with disfigured
countenance through grief, but radiant with joy ; no longer arrayed in gloom, but clad
in the beautiful garments worn on festal days (Isa. lxi. 2, 3). Nahum, whilst the
minister of condemnation to the Ninevites, was also the minister of consolation to his
own people in their sadness and sorrow. Only a few of his words to Israel are recorded,
but they are words full of consolation and hope. Here he pointed to God as the Stronghold of his servants. " He is a Stronghold in the day of trouble " (ver. 7). We have
here—

1. A COMMON UNIVERSAL EXPERIENCE. " Trouble." Man is born to this. Trials
arise ; conflicts must be engaged in ; the cares and anxieties of life press ; hopes are
frustrated ; injustice triumphs ; slander blights ; sickness, disease, death, prevail ; our
best and dearest pass away from our view ; graves are opened ; the tears fall fast ; and
immunity from all this is granted to none, *each* must pass through dark experiences
and encounter adverse influences : this is the discipline of life.

> " In this vain world the days are not all fair ;
> To suffer is the work we have to do ;
> And every one has got a cross to bear,
> And every one some secret heart-ache too."

II. A DEEP INWARD NEED ARISING OUT OF THIS EXPERIENCE. It is implied here that man circumstanced thus needs help. He knows not how to bear the ills of life unaided and alone. He who has to face the pitiless storm needs to be robed to resist the stress of adverse weather, and he who has to confront the foe requires to be armour-clad. This need of the sorrowing heart cannot be supplied by earthly sources. The world's cheer then comes to the man like songs to a heavy heart, and he has no taste for its music. Scepticism can cast no bow of promise across the cloud; whilst human philosophy may counsel the cherishing of the spirit of indifference, but which under the pressure it is impossible to cultivate.

III. THIS NEED AMPLY MET IN GOD. "He is a Stronghold in the day of trouble." The figure is a very striking one. There stands the castle with its thick walls and buttresses and its brave defenders ready to resist any attack. The foes attempt a landing, and the inhabitants, old and young, hasten to the fortress. The drawbridge is lifted, the moat is filled with water, and all are safely lodged in the stronghold, and in the day of visitation are securely guarded and safely kept. Even thus is it with the good in " the day of trouble." So David cried, "Thou hast been a Shelter for me and a Strong Tower from the enemy" (Ps. lxi. 3, 4). God was his "Light and his Salvation" (Ps. xxvii. 1), his "Pavilion" (Ps. xxvii. 5), the Solace of his every grief as well as the Centre of his every joy. He loved him, he trusted him, he knew that the dearest experience in life is the experience of God's love and care. So Hezekiah and his people when threatened by Sennacherib. The Assyrian army gathered in all its strength around "the city of God," and Jerusalem became as a mountain shaken by the swelling of the sea, portions of which were crumbling and falling through the violence of the waves, and the whole of which seemed ready to be borne entirely away; yet the king and his subjects were calm and tranquil; they committed their cause to "the Strong One," and rested in his protection, and cried with holy fervour, "God is our Refuge and Strength," etc. (Isa. xxxvi.; xxxvii.; Ps. xlvi.). And let us only realize that Jehovah is to us a living Presence, the Source of our inspiration, the Strength of our hearts and our abiding Portion, and we shall give to the winds all craven fear, and in our darkest seasons shall sing—

> "A sure Stronghold our God is he,
> A timely Shield and Weapon:
> Our Help he'll be, and set us free
> From every ill can happen.
> And were the world with devils filled,
> All eager to devour us,
> Our souls to fear shall little yield,
> They cannot overpower us."

S. D. H.

Ver. 7.—*The Divine regard for trusting hearts.* "And he knoweth them that trust in him." Something more than mere acquaintance is involved here; the meaning undoubtedly is that he intimately and lovingly regards those who commit themselves and their way unto him, and will tenderly care for them and promote their weal; yea, still more, even that he knows and cares thus for such *personally and individually,* not overlooking any of them in the multitude, but regarding thus each and every such trusting heart.

I. THIS TRUTH ADMITS OF AMPLE CONFIRMATION. There is something very wonderful in this thought. Is it not almost past conception that he who has the direction of all worlds dependent upon him, and whose dominions are so vast, should look upon his servants in this small world of ours, separately and with loving regard, and should interest himself in our personal concerns? So too, awed and humbled as we stand in the midst of the vast and mighty works of God, we feel impelled to cry, "When I consider thy heavens," etc. (Ps. viii. 3). Yet that it is so is abundantly confirmed in the teachings of Scripture. 1. *See this truth taught in type.* Call to remembrance the breastplate of the Jewish high priest, that splendid embroidered cloth which covered his breast, and in which were set precious stones bearing the names of the tribes of Israel. And did not those precious stones, worn so near the heart of the high priest, symbolize the truth that all sincere servants of God are dear unto him; that he not only bears them up in his arms with an almighty strength, but bears them also upon his heart with the most tender affection? 2. *See this truth taught in prophecy.* It is therein declared that there is nothing so impossible as that God should forget his trusting children. " Zion said, The Lord hath forgotten me, and my Lord hath forsaken me" (Isa. xlix. 14, 15). And in response to this fear the Lord declared that this could never be, and that his love and care are even more enduring than that of mothers. "Can a woman," etc.? (Isa. xlix. 15); "I have graven thee upon the palms of my hands" (Isa. xlix. 16). Undying remembrance surely! The name is inscribed there, never to be obliterated, a ceaseless memorial before his face. 3. *The New Testament unites with the Old* in bearing this bright testimony; for does not Christ, as the good Shepherd, declare that "he calleth his own sheep by name, and leadeth them out"? do we not read also the assurance, "The Lord knoweth them that are his" (2 Tim. ii. 19)? yea, is it not even affirmed that this Divine knowledge and care respecting the good shall be perpetuated evermore (Rev. vii. 15—17; xxi. 3, 4)?

II. THIS TRUTH IS CALCULATED TO EXERT A STRENGTHENING AND STIMULATING INFLUENCE. This thought, if more intensely realized by us, would prove helpful in many ways. 1. *It would render us less dependent than we are upon human supports.* What over-anxiety is felt by us at times in reference to the success of our plans and projects, or for the continuance to us of those in whom our prosperity, humanly speaking, centres! But if we grasped fully the assurance here expressed, we should be led to depend less upon earthly sources and more upon him who has loved us with an everlasting love; who, though unseen by us, ever encompasses our path, and who, in the season of their deepest extremity, will guide and strengthen all who stay themselves on him. 2. *It would give increased reality to the sacred exercise of prayer.* We too often draw nigh unto God as though we were seeking One who, because he is invisible, is necessarily at an infinite distance from us, and who may or may not regard our cry, and perhaps it is not too much to say that we sometimes draw nigh without any distinct apprehension of the Being to whom we profess to come, and whose aid we invoke; but then we should indeed feel prayer to be a reality and not a merely formal exercise, and by such intimate and hallowed communion should renew our spiritual strength. 3. *It would strengthen and aid us in our conflicts with sin.* In this strife we sometimes suffer defeat; and in our endeavours after the Christian character and life we are painfully conscious at seasons of failure. How cheering in such circumstances is the thought that all our aspirations after truth and purity and goodness are known unto our God; that he is acquainted with all the circumstances of our case; that he is conscious we have not designedly strayed from him; and that he follows us, with loving regard, in all our wanderings, with a view to bringing us back to his fold!—S. D. H.

Vers. 8—15.—*Antagonism to God and his rule.* Nahum doubtless prophesied during the reign of Hezekiah, and shortly after the defeat of Sennacherib by the destroying angel of the Lord (Isa. xxxvii. 36). That memorable event, it would appear, was present to his mind and is referred to in these verses, although his thoughts were also carried on to the future and to the complete and final overthrow of the Assyrian power in the destruction of the capital, and which forms the theme of the succeeding chapters. The latter part of this first chapter may be regarded as introductory to the description to be given of the ruin of Nineveh; and in the mind of the seer, as he wrote these verses, the events which had recently transpired and darker events yet to come were associated together. The significance of the conflicts waged by Sennacherib against Hezekiah lies very materially in the fact that his enterprises were designedly antagonistic to *the God of the Hebrews.* It is not simply an ambitious sovereign seeking to extend his dominions and to spread his conquests that is presented to us here, but a mortal man, invested with regal honour, resolved upon measuring his strength with that of the Supreme Ruler. The historical records we possess bearing upon the career of this Assyrian king present him to us as one who thought he could "outwit Divine wisdom, and conquer omnipotence itself" (2 Kings xix. 10—13; Isa. xxxvi. 13—20); and viewed thus they become suggestive to us of important teachings bearing upon that moral antagonism to God and his authority which unhappily prevails in every age. Concerning this opposition to the Most High and his rule, note—

I. ANTAGONISM TO GOD HAS ITS ORIGIN IN A DEPRAVED HEART. Evil thoughts and vain imaginings, self-sufficiency and self-conceit, revellings and drunkenness, all betoken an evil heart, and these are here associated with the action of Assyria. "For thou art vile" (ver. 14); "a wicked counsellor" (ver. 11), etc. So in every age. Men with hearts alienated from all that is true and right desire not the knowledge of his ways, and say unto him, "Depart from us;" and "they set themselves against the Lord, and against his anointed, saying, Let us break their bands asunder, and let us cast away their cords from us" (Ps. ii. 2, 3).

II. ANTAGONISM TO GOD REVEALS ITSELF OPENLY IN THE ACTIVE OPERATIONS OF EVIL MEN. As here: 1. Unprincipled leaders are forthcoming (ver. 11). 2. Combinations are formed. "Though they be entire, and likewise many" (ver. 12); "While they be folden together" (ver. 10). 3. Plots are conceived. "They imagine evil against the Lord" (ver. 11). 4. Mischief is wrought. "The yoke" of Assyria was upon Judah, and because of the threatened invasion the hearts of the good Hezekiah and his subjects failed, and were in sore distress. The Assyrians were as "thorns" to Judah (ver. 10). And so evil men, antagonistic to God and to the principles of his rule, are ever a blight and a curse.

III. ANTAGONISM TO GOD CAN ONLY END IN DEFEAT AND DISHONOUR. In the case of Assyria this discomfiture was: 1. *Divinely inflicted.* "I will make thy grave" (ver. 14). 2. *Sudden*—so far as the proud, vaunting Sennacherib and his hosts were concerned (Isa. xxxvii. 36). 3. *Complete.* "He will make an utter end" (ver. 9). 4. *Permanent.* "The Lord hath given a commandment concerning thee, that no more of thy name be sown" (ver. 14). "So let all thine enemies perish, O Lord; but let them that love him be as the sun when he goeth forth in his might" (Judg. v. 31).—S. D. H.

Vers. 8—15.—*Spiritual redemption symbolized.* The expression in ver. 11, "a wicked counsellor," is rendered in the margin "counsellor of Belial." "Belial" is used in the Old Testament to indicate sensual profligacy (Judg. xix. 22; xxii. 13; 1 Sam. ii. 12); and in the New Testament as a synonym for Satan (2 Cor. vi. 15). The term was here (ver. 11) applied to Sennacherib; and the deliverance of Judah from the vauntings and oppressions of this mighty and evil Assyrian monarch described in these verses (8—15) may be taken as serving to illustrate the spiritual deliverance of men. There is thus suggested—

I. DELIVERANCE FROM SERVITUDE. Assyria had been a bitter scourge to Judah. Through the action of his predecessors, Hezekiah found himself the vassal of this heathen power, and his attempts to free himself from the yoke had only resulted in his fetters being fastened the more securely; until now, by Divine interposition, the power of the oppressor was broken (ver. 13). So sin yielded to becomes a tyranny. It gains an ever-increasing power over its subjects. The fetters of habit become forged about them that they cannot release themselves. There is no slavery like that of sin—only the grace of God can sunder the fetters and free us from the galling yoke; but "made free" thus, we become "free indeed" (John viii. 34—36).

II. DELIVERANCE FROM SORROW. "Affliction shall not rise up the second time" (ver. 9); "Though I have afflicted thee, I will afflict thee no more" (ver. 12). The promise was conditional. The people humbled themselves before God in penitence, and it was implied that they should not be afflicted again if they continued in God's ways. In this they failed—the reformation proved but partial; still, God never afflicted them again through Assyria. So suffering is disciplinary, and "made free from sin" there accompanies this deliverance from sorrow. The character of life's trials become changed to the good; they are not looked upon as harsh inflictions, but as lovingly designed by the All-wise and All-gracious.

III. DELIVERANCE RESULTING IN PRIVILEGE. "O Judah, keep thy solemn feasts, perform thy vows" (ver. 15). Whilst under the yoke of Assyria, there had been the restriction of their religious privileges, but now these could be renewed and enjoyed without restraint, and the ransomed of the Lord could return to Zion with songs, and pay their vows unto the Lord, and keep the sacred festivals. Spiritual freedom is with a view to holy and joyous service. The Emancipator becomes enthroned in the hearts of the enfranchised; they love him supremely; his service is their delight; they become bound to him in loving loyalty and devotion for ever.

IV. DELIVERANCE PROCLAIMED IN THE SPIRIT OF HOLY GLADNESS. (Ver. 15.) Let the countenance be lighted up with joy as the announcement of the "good tidings" is made. With a glad heart let the proclamation be published that, through the abounding mercy and grace of God, it is possible for sinful men to become delivered from condemnation and freed from the slavery of sinful habit, and to soar to that higher and holier realm where God is, and to exchange the miserable chains of evil for those golden fetters which only bind to the holy and the heavenly. There can be no more exalted or joyous service than that engaged in by the man who stands upon the mountains ringing this great bell, that, guided by its sound, the imperilled traveller may make his way across the snowy wastes, to find in Christ a sure and safe retreat from the storm and tempest. "Behold upon the mountains," etc. (ver. 15; Isa. xl. 9).—S. D. H.

Vers. 1, 2.—*Great sins bringing great ruin.* "The burden of Nineveh. The book of the vision of Nahum the Elkoshite. God is jealous, and the Lord revengeth; the Lord revengeth, and is furious; the Lord will take vengeance on his adversaries, and he reserveth wrath for his enemies." But little is known of Nahum, whose name signifies "Comfort." He was a native of Elkosh; generally supposed to be a Galilæan village. He lived probably in or about the year B.C. 650. The burden of his prophecy is the destruction of Nineveh, which destruction was predicted by Jonah a century before. Nineveh was destroyed about fifty years after this prophecy was uttered, and so complete was its overthrow that the very site where it stood is a matter of conjecture. The prophecy, though divided into three chapters, is a continuous poem of unrivalled spirit and sublimity, and admirable for the elegance of its imagery. "The third chapter is a very striking description of a siege—the rattle of the war-chariot, the gleam of the sword, the trench filled with corpses, the ferocity of the successful invaders, the panic of the defeated, the vain attempts to rebuild the crumbling battlements, final overthrow and ruin." The opening words suggest two remarks.

I. THAT THE GREAT SINS OF A PEOPLE MUST EVER BRING UPON THEM GREAT RUIN. The population of Nineveh was pre-eminently wicked. It is represented in the Scriptures as a "bloody city," a "city full of lies and robberies;" its savage brutality to captives is portrayed in its own monuments, and the Hebrew prophets dwell upon its impious haughtiness and ruthless fierceness (Isa. x. 7, 8). In this book we have its "burden," that is, its sentence, its doom; and the doom is terrible beyond description. It is ever so. Great sins bring great ruin. It was so with the antediluvians, with the inhabitants of Sodom and Gomorrah. It was so with the Jews in the time of Titus. Thirty-seven years after the crucifixion of our Lord, the Roman general, with a numerous army, laid siege to their city, and converted it into a scene of the greatest horrors ever witnessed on this earth. The principle of moral causation and the eternal justice of the universe demand that wherever there is sin there shall be suffering; and in proportion to the amount of sin shall be the amount of suffering. "Unto whomsoever much is given, of him shall be much required."

II. THAT THE GREAT RUIN THAT COMES UPON GREAT SINNERS PRESENTS GOD TO THE "VISION" OF MAN AS TERRIBLY INDIGNANT. "God is jealous, and the Lord revengeth; the Lord revengeth, and is furious; the Lord will take vengeance on his adversaries, and he reserveth wrath for his enemies." The passions of man are here ascribed to God. In this form of speech the Eternal Spirit is often represented in the Bible as having feet, hands, ears, mouth; but as he has none of these, neither has he any of these passions. It is only when terrible anguish comes upon the sinner that God *appears* to the observer as indignant. The God here was the God who only appeared in the "vision" of Nahum—the God as he appeared to a man of limited capacity and imperfect character. Jesus *alone* saw the absolute God. "No man hath seen God at any time; the only begotten Son who is in the bosom of the Father, he hath declared him." The God of Jesus of Nazareth had no jealousy, no vengeance, no fury. He was love. "Fury is not in me, saith the Lord" (Isa. xxvii. 4) If God has anger, it is the anger of principle, not passion—the anger of love, not malevolence. It is indeed but another form of love: love opposing and crushing whatever is repugnant to the virtue and the happiness of the universe.

CONCLUSION. Beware of sin. Ruin must follow it. "Be sure your sins will find you out."—D. T.

Ver. 3.—*The patience of God.* "The Lord is slow to anger, and great in power, and will not at all acquit the wicked." These words suggest two thoughts concerning God's patience.

I. HIS PATIENCE ALWAYS IMPLIES GREAT POWER. "The Lord is slow to anger, and great in power." This is a remarkable expression. It seems as if the prophet meant, God is "slow to anger" because he is "great in power;" if he had less power he would be less patient. A man may be "slow to anger," slow to deal out vengeance, because he lacks power to do so. But God is "slow to anger" because he has abundance of power. In order to see the power revealed in his forbearance towards sinners in this world, think of four things. 1. *His exquisite sensibility.* There are some men "slow to anger" because they have not the susceptibility of feeling an insult or offence; their patience, such as it is, is nothing but a natural stoicism. Many men are lauded for their calmness under insults, who are rather to be pitied for their natural insensibility, or denounced for their moral callousness. But the great God is ineffably sensitive. He is sensibility itself. He is love. He feels everything. Every immoral act vibrates, so to speak, on his heart-chord; and yet he is "slow to anger." 2. *His abhorrence of sin.* It is the "abominable thing" which he emphatically hates. His whole nature revolts from it. He feels that it is antagonism to his will and to the order and well-being of the universe. 3. *His provocation by the world.* Multiply the sins of each man in one day by the countless millions of men that populate the globe; then you will have some conception of the provocation that this God of exquisite sensibility, of an ineffable hatred to sin, receives every day from this planet. One insult often sets man's blood ablaze. Surely, if all the patience of all the angels in heaven were to be embodied in one personality, and that personality were entrusted with the government of this world for one day, before the clock struck the hour of midnight he would set the globe in flames. 4. *His right to do whatever he pleases* He could show his anger if he pleased, at any time, anywhere, or anyhow. He is absolutely irresponsible. He has no one to fear. When men feel anger there are many reasons to prevent them from showing it; but he has no such reason. How great, then, must be his "power" in holding back his anger! His power of self-control is infinite. "He is slow to anger, and of great power." "The Lord is not slack concerning his promise, as some men count slackness; but is long-suffering to usward, not willing that any should perish, but that all should come to repentance" (2 Pet. iii. 9).

II. HIS PATIENCE PRECLUDES NOT THE PUNISHMENT OF THE IMPENITENT. "And will not at all acquit the wicked." That is, the impenitent wicked. However wicked a man is, if he repents he will be acquitted. "Let the wicked forsake his ways, and the unrighteous man his thoughts," etc. (Isa. lv. 7). 1. To "acquit" the impenitent would be an *infraction of his law.* He has bound suffering to sin by a law as strong and as inviolable as that which binds the planets to the sun. "The wages of sin is death;" "Sin, when it is finished, bringeth forth death." Sin leads to ruin: this is a law. 2. To "acquit" the impenitent would be a *violation of his word.* "The wicked shall be turned into hell, with all the nations that forget God;" "Unless ye repent, ye shall all likewise perish;" "I will laugh at your calamities, and mock when your fear cometh." 3. To "acquit" the impenitent would be to *break the harmony of his universe.* If inveterate rebels and incorrigible sinners were acquitted, what an impulse there would be given in God's moral empire to anarchy and rebellion!

CONCLUSION. Abuse not the patience of God; nay, avail yourselves of it. While he forbears, and because he forbears, repent! "Despisest thou the riches of his goodness and forbearance and long-suffering; not knowing that the goodness of God leadeth thee to repentance?" (Rom. ii. 4).—D. T.

Vers. 3—6.—*God's power.* "The Lord hath his way in the whirlwind and in the storm, and the clouds are the dust of his feet. He rebuketh the sea, and maketh it dry, and drieth up all the rivers," etc. Here is a description of God's power unrivalled in its sublimity and soul-stirring force. " Power belongeth unto God." It is absolute, inexhaustible, ever and everywhere operative. " He fainteth not, neither is weary." His power is here presented in two aspects.

I. As OPERATING IRRESISTIBLY IN NATURE. 1. *It works in the air.* " The Lord hath his way in the whirlwind and in the storm, and the clouds are the dust of his feet." He is in the " whirlwind " and in the " storm," and has his way in the clouds. As men walk on the dust of the earth, he walketh upon the clouds of heaven. He creates the whirlwind and the storm; he controls the whirlwind and the storm; he uses the whirlwind and the storm. " He maketh the clouds his chariot, and rideth upon the wings of the wind." He awakes the tornado and simoom, he forges the thunderbolts, and he kindles the lightnings. 2. *It works in the sea.* " He rebuketh the sea, and maketh it dry, and drieth up all the rivers." There is undoubtedly an allusion to the Red Sea and the Jordan. " He holdeth the winds in his fists, and the waters in the hollow of his hands." His " way is in the sea," and his " path in the great waters." The billows that rise into mountains, as well as the smallest wavelets that come rippling softly to the shore, are the creatures of his power and the servants of his will. 3. *It works on the earth.* " Bashan languisheth, and Carmel, and the flower of Lebanon languisheth." No spots in Palestine were more fruitful than these three; they abounded in vigorous vegetation and majestic forests. But their life and their growth depended on the results of God's power. All the blades in the fields, all the trees in the forest, would languish and wither did his power cease to operate. Nor is his power less active in the inorganic parts of the world. " The mountains quake at him, and the hills melt, and the earth is burned at his presence, yea, the world, and all that dwell therein." " He looketh on the earth, and it trembleth: he toucheth the hills, and they smoke." He piles up the mountains, and again makes them a plain; he kindles the volcanoes and quenches them at his pleasure. God's power is seen in all the phenomena of the material world. How graphically and beautifully is this presented in Ps. civ.! The fact that God's power is ever acting in the material universe is: (1) The most *philosophic* explanation of all its phenomena. The men who ascribe all the operations of nature to what they call laws fail to satisfy my intellect. For what are those laws? (2) The most *hallowing* aspect of the world we live in. God is in all. " How dreadful is this place! it is none other than the house of God." Walk the earth with reverence. " Take your shoes from off your feet, for the place whereon thou standest is holy ground."

II. As IRRESISTIBLY OPPOSED TO THE WICKED. " Who can stand before his indignation? and who can abide in the fierceness of his anger? his fury is poured out like fire, and the rocks are thrown down by him." The mightiest rocks are but as pebbles in his hands. " He taketh up the isles as a very little thing; he weigheth the mountains in scales, and the hills in a balance " (Isa. xl. 12, 15) His anger, as we have said, is his determination to crush the wrong; and there is no power in the universe that can thwart him in this. Who can stand before this? Were all the creatures in the universe to stand up against it, the attempt would be as feeble and as futile as the attempt of a child to turn back the advancing tides with his little spade. Sinner, why attempt to oppose him? You must submit, either against your will or by your will. If you continue to resist, the former is a necessity. He will break you in pieces like a potter's vessel. The latter is your duty and your interest. Fall down in penitence before him, yield yourselves to his service, acquiesce in his will, and you are saved.—D. T.

Vers. 7, 8.—*Opposite types of human character, and opposite lines of Divine procedure.* " The Lord is good, a Stronghold in the day of trouble; and he knoweth them that trust in him. But with an overrunning flood he will make an utter end of the place thereof, and darkness shall pursue his enemies." The previous verses were introductory to the subject which the prophet now takes up, namely, the safe keeping of the Jews by Jehovah, in view of the tremendous attack the King of Nineveh was about making on their country and their city, and also to announce the terrible doom of Nineveh, the capital of the Assyrian foe. In these verses there is a very striking and significant contrast (1) between the characters of men, and (2) between the lines of Divine procedure in relation to them. Here we have—

I. Two opposite types of human character. 1. *Here we have the friends of God.* There is here a twofold description of them. (1) "They trust in him." This is the universal character of the good in all ages. Instead of placing their chief confidence in the ever-changing creature, they centre it in the immutable Creator. They trust his love ever to provide for them, his wisdom as their infallible guide, and his power as their strength and their shield. "Blēssed is the man that trusteth in the Lord." (2) He acknowledges them. "And he knoweth." This means that he recognizes them as his loyal subjects and loving children, his people. In Hos. xiii. 5 he saith, "I did know thee in the wilderness," which means, "I did acknowledge thee, and took care of thee!" The words imply the cognizance of special sympathy with the just. He knows them; they are always in his mind, his heart. "Can a mother forget her sucking child," etc.? 2. *Here we have the enemies of God.* "Darkness shall pursue his enemies." The men who misrepresent our characters, oppose our expressed wishes, seek to undermine our influence, and are ever in association with those who are opposed to us—such men, whatever may be their professions of regard and friendship, we are bound to regard as enemies. Is it not so with men in relation to God? Those who pursue a course of life directly opposite to the moral laws of Heaven, whatever they may say, are his enemies. How numerous are God's enemies! These two great classes comprehend the human race to-day. The race may be divided into very numerous classes on certain adventitious principles, but on *moral* grounds there are but two—God's friends and God's enemies.

II. Two opposite lines of Divine procedure. God's procedure is very different towards these two opposite classes of men. 1. *He affords protection to the one.* When the hosts of Sennacherib were approaching Jerusalem, Hezekiah the king, under Divine inspiration, said to the people, "Be strong and courageous, be not afraid nor dismayed for the King of Assyria, nor for all the multitude that is with him: for there be more with us than with him: with him is an arm of flesh; but with us is the Lord our God to help us, and to fight our battles. And the people rested themselves upon the words of Hezekiah King of Judah" (2 Chron. xxxii. 7, 8). Thus it is ever. God is always the Refuge and Strength of his people in times of tribulation. As a Refuge, he is: (1) *Ever accessible.* However suddenly the storm may come, the refuge is at your side, the door is open. "I will never leave thee," etc. (2) *Ever secure.* The sanctuary once entered, no injury can follow. Amidst the most violent convulsions of nature, the wreck of worlds, the shatterings of the universe, there is no endangering the security of those who avail themselves of this refuge. 2. *He sends destruction to the other.* "But with an overrunning flood he will make an utter end of the place thereof, and darkness shall pursue his enemies." The image of a flood which breaks through every barrier is not unfrequently used in the Bible to represent overwhelming armies of invasion. The primary allusion here, no doubt, is to the way which Nineveh was captured by means of the Medes and Babylonians. A flood in the river, we are told, broke down the wall for twenty furlongs. The rolling tide burst its barriers, bore away the defences of the city, and opened an easy and unexpected way for the invading armies. On all finally impenitent men destruction must come as irresistibly as a flood. The destruction, however, of existence, conscience, or moral obligations would be the destruction of all that would make existence worth having.

Conclusion. The grand question of every man is—How do I stand in relation to God? If I am his friend, his procedure is in my favour, it guards me and blesses me every step. If I am his enemy, his procedure is not in my favour, not because he changes, but because I put myself against him, and it must be my ruin if I change not. As he proceeds in his beneficent and undeviating march, he showers blessings on the good, and miseries on the evil, and this for ever.—D. T.

Vers. 9, 10.—*Sin.* "What do ye imagine against the Lord? He will make an utter end: affliction shall not rise up the second time. For while they be folden together as thorns, and while they are drunken as drunkards, they shall be devoured as stubble fully dry." These words suggest a few thoughts concerning sin.

I. The essence of sin is suggested: it is hostility to God. It is something directed against the Lord: it is opposition to the laws, purposes, spirit of God. "The carnal mind is enmity against God; for it is not subject to the law of God, neither indeed can be" (Rom. viii. 7). It involves: 1. The basest *ingratitude;* for to him we owe everything. 2. The greatest *injustice;* for he has supreme claims to our devotion and obedience. 3. *Impious presumption.* Frail worms raising their heads against the Infinite!

II. THE SEAT OF SIN IS SUGGESTED: IT IS IN THE MIND. "What do ye imagine against the Lord?" Sin is not language, however bad; not actions, however apparently wicked. Words and deeds are no more sin than branches are the sap of the tree. They are the mere effects and expression of sin. Sin is in the mind—in the deep, secret, mute thoughts of the heart. God's legislation extends to thought, reaches it in the profoundest abyss. "As a man thinketh in his heart, so is he" (Prov. xxiii. 7). Christ, in his sermon on the mount, taught this. Adultery, robbery, murder, are all perpetrated on the arena of the heart. How necessary the prayer, "Create within us clean hearts, O God"!

III. THE FOLLY OF SIN IS SUGGESTED: IT IS OPPOSITION TO OMNIPOTENCE. "What do ye imagine against the Lord? He will make an utter end: affliction shall not rise up a second time." "How mad is your attempt, O Assyrians, to resist so powerful a God! What can ye do against such an Adversary, successful though ye have been against all other adversaries? Ye *imagine* ye have to do merely with mortals, and with a weak people, and that so you will gain an easy victory; but you have to encounter God, the Protector of his people" (Fausset). In opposing him: 1. He *will completely ruin you.* "He will make an utter end: affliction shall not rise up the second time." The literal meaning of this is that the overthrow of Sennacherib's host was so complete that Judah's affliction caused by this invasion would never be repeated. The man who opposes God will be utterly ruined. 2. *He will completely ruin you, whatever the kind of resistance you may offer.* "For while they be folden together as thorns, and while they are drunken as drunkards, they shall be devoured as stubble fully dry." You may be combined like a bundle of thorns, offering resistance; you may have all the daring and temerity of drunkards, albeit you "shall be devoured as stubble fully dry." All this was realized in the destruction of his enemy. Oh the folly of sin! Fighting against God is a mad fight. "What do ye imagine against the Lord," then? Sinners, submit.—D. T.

Vers. 11—14.—*Corrupt kings.* "There is one come out of thee, that imagineth evil against the Lord, a wicked counsellor. Thus saith the Lord; Though they be quiet, and likewise many, yet thus shall they be cut down, when he shall pass through," etc. These words suggest a few thoughts concerning human kings and kingdoms.

I. HUMAN KINGS ARE SOMETIMES TERRIBLY CORRUPT. "There is one come out of thee, that imagineth evil against the Lord, a wicked counsellor." This evidently means Sennacherib, the King of Nineveh. He was one of the great moral monsters of the world. "He invaded the land of Judah with an immense army, besieged Lachish, and having reduced that city, threatened to invade Jerusalem itself. Hezekiah, dreading his power, sent him an obsequious embassy, and by paying three hundred talents of silver and thirty talents of gold, purchased an inglorious peace. But no sooner had Sennacherib received the money than, disdaining his engagements, he prosecuted the war with as much vigour as if no treaty had been in existence, sending three of his generals and a powerful army to besiege Jerusalem. Being informed that Tirhakah King of Ethiopia joined by the power of Egypt, was advancing to assist Hezekiah, he marched to meet the approaching armies, defeated them in a general engagement, ravaged their country, and returned with the spoil to finish the siege of Jerusalem. Hezekiah, in the extremity of his distress, implored the succour of Heaven; and the insolence and blasphemy of Sennacherib drew upon the Assyrians the vengeance of God. And, in perfect accordance with the prophecy of Isaiah, the sacred historian informs us that the angel of the Lord slew, in one night, one hundred and eighty-five thousand of the Assyrian army." Such is a brief and very partial sketch of this monster. Alas! he is only a type of the vast majority of men who have found their way to thrones! They have been in all ages the chief devils of the world. There are kings that have powers ordained of God; but such kings, and those only, are "a terror to evil-doers and a praise to those that do well." We are commanded to honour the king; but such a king as this Sennacherib, who can honour? A king, to be honoured, must be honourworthy; he must be just, ruling in the fear of the Lord.

II. CORRUPT KINGS OFTEN RUIN THEIR KINGDOMS. "Though they be quiet, and likewise many, yet thus shall they be cut down, when he shall pass through. Though I have afflicted thee, I will afflict thee no more." These words seem to be addressed to Judah concerning the utter destruction that will befall their enemies, and their consequent deliverance from all fear from that quarter. It was here said they should be destroyed: 1. *Notwithstanding their military completeness.* "Though they be quiet." The word "quiet" means *complete.* No doubt the military organization, discipline, and equipment of Sennacherib's mighty army, as he led them up to attack Jerusalem, were as complete as the intelligence, the art, and the circumstances of the age could make them. Notwithstanding this, ruin befell them. 2. *Notwithstanding their numerical force.* "Likewise many." Their numbers were overwhelming, yet how complete their destruction! They were "cut down," and their name ceased. Nineveh has been long since blotted from the earth. The account given of the destruction you have in 2 Kings xix. 35, "And it came to pass that night, that the angel of the Lord went out, and smote in the camp of the Assyrians an hundred fourscore and five thousand: and when they arose early in the morning, behold, they were all dead corpses." Then followed, in due course, the complete destruction of Nineveh itself by the forces of the Medes and Babylonians. So utterly was it destroyed, that even the references of classical writers to it are to a city that is long since extinct. It was a wonderful city; it stood, according to the account of some, on an area ten times the size of London; its walls a hundred feet high, and so broad that three chariots could be driven on them abreast. It had fifteen hundred towers, each two hundred feet in height. In 1842 Botta began to excavate, and three years afterwards Layard commenced his interesting and successful explorations. The remains which were discovered by these excavators filled the world with astonishment. "A city, an empire, had risen from the silent slumber of ages; its kings could be numbered, and its tongue mastered; while its history, manners, customs, and dwellings formed an unexpected revelation, wondrous in its variety and fulness." Who brought all this ruin on this grand old city? Sennacherib, a ruthless despot and a bloody warrior, and his successors, as savage as himself. And what cities and empires have been ruined by such men in all ages! Who broke up ancient dynasties? Despots. And in modern times who has brought all the suffering, the disorder, and the spoliation that has befallen France during the last sixty years? Despots. Until despotism is put down, such will continue to be the case.

III. THE RUIN OF CORRUPT KINGDOMS IS A BLESSING TO THE OPPRESSED. "For now will I break his yoke from off thee [that is, 'thee, Judah'], and will burst thy bonds in sunder." "Yoke" here refers to the tribute imposed upon Hezekiah King of Judah by Sennacherib (2 Kings xviii. 14). And so it ever is—when despotism has fallen, the oppressed rise to liberty. What teeming millions of men are groaning, not only in Asiatic countries, but in European countries, under the tyranny of despots! These arrogant, haughty autocracies must fall, as Assyria and other ancient despotisms fell, before the yoke shall be taken from the neck of the oppressed, and their bands burst asunder.

CONCLUSION. 1. *Realize the truth of prophecy.* When Nahum uttered these fearful predictions in relation to Nineveh, Nineveh shone in unabated splendour, and stood in unabated strength; but after a very few generations had passed away the predicted ruin came, and Nineveh has long since been buried in the oblivion of centuries. Have faith in the Word of God. Heaven and earth shall pass away, but not one jot or tittle of his Word shall fail to be accomplished. 2. *Realize the importance of promoting education among the people.* By education I do not mean what is merely technical or scientific, but chiefly moral. The education that teaches the people the sense of personal independency and responsibility, the duty of self-respect, the inalienable right of private judgment, and a liberty of action circumscribed only by the rights of others. It is when such an education as this spreads among the peoples of the world that despotisms will moulder to dust. When men shall know the moral truth, the moral reality, then the truth shall make them free.

> "It's coming yet for a' that,
> That man to man the warld o'er
> Shall brithers be for a' that."

D. T.

Ver. 15.—*Three things worthy of note.* "Behold upon the mountains the feet of him that bringeth good tidings, that publisheth peace! O Judah, keep thy solemn feasts, perform thy vows: for the wicked shall no more pass through thee; he is utterly cut off." A mighty army has gone up against Nineveh, and so certain it is that it will be utterly destroyed that the prophet speaks of it as past. He has seen the "messenger" upon the mountain proclaiming deliverance to Judah. The "mountains" are those round Jerusalem, on which the hosts of Sennacherib had lately encamped, and the messenger of peace scales the mountains that his welcome presence may be seen. How transporting the message must have been! Sennacherib, the disturber of the nations, is no more, and Jerusalem is delivered. The first clause of this verse is applied in Isa. lii. 7 to the message of peace brought to the world through Jesus Christ. There are three things here worthy of note.

I. PEACE PROCLAIMED. "Behold upon the mountains the feet of him that bringeth good tidings, that publisheth peace." Glorious to the ears of the men of Jerusalem must have been the intelligence that their great enemy was destroyed, that the Assyrian hosts were crushed, and now peace was come. A proclamation of peace is indeed "good tidings." A proclamation of *national* peace is "good tidings." What country that has been engaged in a bloody campaign, in which its commerce has been all but ruined, the flower of its manhood destroyed, and its very existence imperilled, does not hail with rapture the proclamation of peace? But the proclamation of *moral* peace is still more delightful. Paul quotes these words, and applies them to the ministers of the gospel. "How beautiful are the feet of them that preach the gospel of peace, and bring glad tidings of good things!" (Rom. x. 15). As there is no war so painful, so terrible, as a moral war, the war of a soul with itself, with the moral instincts of the universe, and with the will of its God; so no tidings are so delightful to it as the tidings of peace, peace brought through Jesus Christ, the "peace that passeth all understanding." "My peace I give unto you, . . . not as the world giveth give I unto you."

II. WORSHIP ENJOINED. "O Judah, keep thy solemn feasts, perform thy vows." "During the Assyrian invasion the inhabitants of Judah were cut off from all access to the metropolis; now they would be at liberty to proceed thither as usual, in order to observe their religious rites, and they are here commanded to do so." Observe: 1. *War disturbs religious observances.* War, which has been called the totality of all evil, is an enemy to the progress of religion. It not merely arrests the march of the cause of truth and godliness, but throws it back. It is said in Acts ix. 31, "Then had the Churches rest throughout all Judæa and Galilee and Samaria, and were edified; and walking in the fear of the Lord, and in the comfort of the Holy Ghost, were multiplied." The storm of persecution which Stephen had invoked and Saul aided had abated, and the Christian religion advanced. As peace in nature is the time to cultivate your ground and sow your seed, peace in the nation is the time to promote growth in religion and virtue. 2. *In war men are disposed to make religious vows.* When dangers thicken around, and death seems close at hand, the soul naturally turns to Heaven, and vows that, if life is preserved, it shall be devoted to God. When peace comes they are called upon to "perform" their "vows." But alas! how often are such vows neglected! and we are told (Eccles. v. 5) it is better not to vow, than to vow and not pay. Worship is a duty ever binding.

III. ENEMIES VANQUISHED. "For the wicked shall no more pass through thee; he is utterly cut off." Here is encouragement. Sennacherib is gone; Nineveh is in desolation. They will "no more pass through thee." The time will come with all good men when their enemies shall be utterly vanquished. "The God of peace shall bruise Satan under your feet shortly." What a blessed time for the world, when the wicked shall no more "pass through" it! This will be its millennium.

> "Peace is the end of all things—tearless peace;
> Who by the immovable basis of God's throne
> Takes her perpetual stand; and, of herself

Prophetic, lengthens age by age her sceptre.
The world shall yet be subjugate to love,
The final form religion must assume;
Led like a lion, rid with wreathed reins,
In some enchanted island, by a child."

(Bailey.)

D. T.

EXPOSITION.

CHAPTER II.

Vers. 1—13.—Part II. THE EXECUTION OF THE DECREE; THE DESTRUCTION OF NINEVEH DESCRIBED.

Vers. 1—8.—§ 1. *Nineveh shall be besieged, because God is about to exalt his people by taking vengeance on the enemy, whose defence, howsoever formidable, is of no avail.*

Ver. 1.—Nahum addresses Nineveh, and forewarns her of the siege she was about to undergo (see Introduction, § I.). He that dasheth in pieces; *the disperser; qui dispergit* (Vulgate); ἐμφυσῶν, " panting " (Septuagint). The mixed army that invested Nineveh is so called from its effect on the inhabitants of the neighbouring lands. Others translate it, " the maul," or " hammer "—an appellation of Cyaxares, which reminds one of Charles Martel and Judas Maccabæus. Is come up before thy face. Placing his forces in thy sight, that thou mayest see his power and thine own danger. Keep the munition. The prophet urges the Ninevites to guard their fortress well. Some connect this clause with the preceding: " the disperser is come to maintain the siege; " as the Vulgate, *qui custodiat obsidionem.* But the other interpretation is more forcible, and suits the rest of the verse. The LXX., reading differently, gives, ἐξαιρούμενος [+ σε, Alex.] ἐκ θλίψεως, " one delivered from affliction." Watch the way, by which the enemy approaches. Make thy loins strong. Gather up thy strength, the loins being regarded as the seat of strength (2 Chron. x. 10; Job xl. 7; Ezek. xxix. 7; 1 Pet. i. 13). So weak, effeminate people were called in Latin *elumbes,* " loinless." Fortify thy power mightily; Ἀνδρίσαι τῇ ἰσχύϊ σφόδρα (Septuagint). Make yourselves as strong as possible (comp. Amos ii. 14).

Ver. 2.—This ruin shall fall on Nineveh because God is mindful of his chosen people, whom Assyria has oppressed. Hath turned away. It should be rendered, *returneth to,* or *restoreth, bringeth back; reddidit* (Vulgate); Isa. lii. 8; Hos. vi. 11. The excellency of Jacob, as the excellency of Israel. The Lord restores the glory and honour of Jacob, the nation in its political aspect, and the high privileges of the spiritual Israel, the chosen people of God (comp. Obad. 18). For. Asshur is visited because Judah has had its full measure of punishment. The emptiers have emptied them out. The plunderers (the enemy) have plundered the Jews. And marred their vine branches. The heathen have cut off the members of Israel, the Lord's vineyard. (For the metaphor " vine," comp. Ps. lxxx. 8, etc.; Isa. v.; Jer. xii. 10.) Not only from what is read in the Bible (*e.g.* 2 Kings xv. 19; xvi. 7, etc.; xvii. 3; xviii. 14), but from the details in the cuneiform inscriptions, we learn that the Assyrians were a constant danger and annoyance to Israel, and harassed continually both the southern and northern provinces.

Ver. 3.—The prophet describes, as though himself an eye-witness, the army advancing against Nineveh. The shield of his mighty men is made red. " His heroes " may be either God's heroes, as sent by him to war against the evil city, or those of the " dasher in pieces " of ver. 1. The shields of the early Assyrians were usually circular or oval in shape, formed of wicker-work, with a central boss of wood or metal. In the latest period they were made straight at bottom and rounded only at top (Rawlinson's ' Anc. Mon.,' i. 440). Some bronze shields have been brought to England from Nineveh; these are circular, about two feet and a half in diameter, the rim bending inwards, and forming a deep groove round the edge. The handles are of iron, and fastened by six bosses or nails, the heads of which form an ornament on the outer face of the shield (Layard, 'Discoveries,' p. 194). There were used also in sieges tall oblong shields, sufficient to protect the entire body, constructed of wicker-work or the hides of animals (Bonomi, ' Nineveh and its Discoveries,' p. 320, etc.). The shields are said to be " made red," either because they were really so coloured (though the monuments have not confirmed this opinion), or else because of the polished copper with which they were sometimes covered (Josephus, 'Ant.,' xiii. 12. 5). Septuagint, pointing differently, ὅπλα δυναστείας αὐτῶν ἐξ ἀνθρώπων, " the arms of their power from among men." Are in scarlet. The word rendered " scarlet " is found nowhere else.

Septuagint, mistaking the word, ἐμπαίζοντας ἐν πυρί, "sporting in fire;" Vulgate, *in coccineis*. It is derived from the term applied to the *coccus,* or worm which was used in dyeing to give to cloth a deep scarlet colour (Henderson). Some have seen in the colour of the soldiers' garments an emblem of the Divine wrath of which they were the appointed ministers. This colour was much affected by combatants in old times as in modern days. Professor Edwards quotes Ælian, ' Var. Hist.,' vi. 6, " It was necessary to enter into battle clothed in purple, that the colour might denote a certain dignity, and if drops of blood from wounds were sprinkled on it, it became terrible to the enemy " (comp. Xen., ' Cyrop.,' i. 3. 2). Red or purple seems to have been the favourite colour of the Medes and Babylonians (Ezek. xxiii. 14), blue or violet that of the Assyrians (Ezek. xxiii. 6; xxviii. 23, etc.) (Orelli). The chariots shall be **with flaming torches;** literally, *are with fire of steels;* i.e. flash with steel, and so the clause should be translated, as in the Revised Version. Commentators generally refer the description to the steel bosses of the wheels; but the Assyrian chariots (and those of the Medes and Chaldeans were not dissimilar) were conspicuous for shining metal, hung round with gleaming weapons and figures of the heavenly bodies, carrying bright-armed warriors, the horses covered with trappings, which flashed under the sunshine, and fastened to poles of glittering steel. There is no trace in the monuments of chariots armed with scythes, which seem to have been unknown before the time of Cyrus. They are first mentioned in 2 Macc. xiii. 2 (see Livy, xxxvii. 41). The word *peladoth,* translated " torches," is an ἅπαξ λεγόμενον. The LXX. renders it, αἱ ἡνίαι, "the reins," whence Jerome obtained his version, *igneæ habenæ curruum;* but it means, "things made of iron or steel," and by critics uninstructed in monumental discoveries was naturally referred to the scythes with which chariots were armed in later times, instead of to the gleaming metal with which they were adorned. **In the day of his preparation.** When the Lord marshals the host for battle, as Isa. xiii. 4. **The fir trees shall be terribly shaken;** i.e. the spears with their fir or cypress shafts are brandished. So Homer often calls the spear " the ash," from the material of which the handle was made (comp. ' Il.,' xvi. 143; xxii. 225, etc.). The Septuagint rendering is very far from the present text, Οἱ ἱππεῖς θορυβηθήσονται, "The horsemen shall be thrown into confusion." Nor is the Vulgate any better, *Agitatores consopiti sunt,* which is explained to mean that the invaders are so carried away by their courage and fury, that they act as if

intoxicated. " Sensus utique non spernendus," says a Roman Catholic commentator, " at unum desidero, ut scil. ex verbo ipso fluat "—which is certainly not the case. The text is possibly corrupt. and might be corrected from the Septuagint. Certainly there seems to be no other passage in the Hebrew Scriptures where the metaphor of " cypress " is used for " a spear." After the mention of the chariots, it is not unnatural that the writer should proceed, " and the riders are in active motion," urging their horses with hand and whip and gesture (see Knabenbauer, *in loc.*).

Ver. 4.—**The chariots shall rage in the streets.** The chariots rave, dash madly (Jer. xlvi. 9) about the open ways in the suburbs, or in the plains of the country. The description still appertains to the besiegers, who are so numerous that to the Ninevites, looking from their walls, their chariots seem to dash against one another. **They shall seem**—their appearance is—**like torches.** Thus is described the gleaming of the chariots and the armour (see on ver. 3; 1 Macc. vi. 39, " Now when the sun shone upon the shields of gold and brass, the mountains glistered therewith, and shined like lamps of fire ").

Ver. 5.—The prophet turns to the Ninevites and their preparations for defence. **He shall recount his worthies;** *he remembers his nobles.* The King of Nineveh calls to mind the mighty captains who have often led his armies to victory, and sends them to defend the walls (comp. ch. iii. 18). The LXX., anticipating the next clause, adds here, καὶ φεύξονται ἡμέρας, " and they shall flee by day." **They shall stumble in their walk.** In their fear and haste, or half-drunken, they totter and stumble as they hasten to the walls of the city. **The defence shall be prepared;** literally, *the covering is prepared.* If this refers to the operations of the Ninevites, it means some kind of breastwork or fascine erected between the towers; but it most probably depicts the sight that meets their eyes from the walls. They see the besiegers bringing up their mantelets and towers. As used by the Assyrians, the machine called " the covering " is either a wooden tower or a wicker mantelet in which was suspended a battering-ram. It stood on four or six wheels, and the larger sort had archers posted in the various stories, both to annoy the enemy and to defend the engine. The rams were provided with lance-headed extremities, and must have rather picked at and loosened the courses of bricks of which the walls were composed than battered them down (see Bonomi, ' Nineveh and its Palaces,' pp. 160, 234, 243, etc.; Layard, ' Nineveh,' ch. v. p. 376, etc., figs. 57, 58). The Septuagint rendering applies rather to the besieged, Ἑτοιμάσουσι τὰς προφυλακὰς αὐτῶν, "They shall prepare their defences."

Ver. 6.—All defence is vain. The prophet describes the last scene. The gates of the rivers shall be (are) opened. The simplest explanation of this much-disputed clause is, according to Strauss and others, the following: The gates intended are those adjacent to the streams which encircled the city, and which were therefore the best defended and the hardest to capture. When these were carried, there was no way of escape for the besieged. But, as Rosenmüller remarks, it would have been an act of folly in the enemy to attack just that part of the city which was most strongly defended by nature and art. We are, therefore, induced to take "the gates of the rivers," not literally, but as a metaphorical expression (like "the windows of heaven," Gen. vii. 11; Isa. xxiv. 18) for an overwhelming flood, and to see in this a reference to the fact mentioned by Diod. Sic. (ii. 27), that the capture of Nineveh was owing to a great and unprecedented inundation, which destroyed a large portion of the fortifications, and laid the city open to the enemy. "At the north-west angle of Nineveh," says Professor Rawlinson, "there was a sluice or flood-gate, intended mainly to keep the water of the Khosr-su, which ordinarily filled the city moat, from flowing off too rapidly into the Tigris, but probably intended also to keep back the water of the Tigris, when that stream rose above its common level. A sudden and great rise in the Tigris would necessarily endanger this gate, and if it gave way beneath the pressure, a vast torrent of water would rush up the moat along and against the northern wall, which may have been undermined by its force, and have fallen in" (Rawlinson, 'Ancient Monarchies,' ii. p. 397, edit. 1871). The suggestion that the course of its rivers was diverted, and that the enemy entered the town through the dried channels, has no historical basis. Dr. Pusey explains the term to mean the gates by which the inhabitants had access to the rivers. But these would be well guarded, and the opening of them would not involve the capture of the city, which the expression in the text seems to imply. The LXX. gives, Πύλαι τῶν πόλεων διηνοίχθησαν, "The gates of the cities were opened." The palace shall be (is) dissolved; or, melteth away. Some take this to signify that the hearts of the inhabitants melt with fear, or the royal power vanishes in terror. That the clause is to be taken literally, to denote the destruction of the royal palace by the action of the waters, seems to be negatived by the fact that the Assyrian palaces were built on artificial mounds of some thirty or forty feet in elevation, composed of sun-dried bricks united into

a solid mass, and were thus secured from the effects of an inundation (see Bonomi, 'Nineveh and its Discoveries,' p. 129, etc.). There is evidence, too, that fire played a great part in the destruction of the temples and palaces (see note on ch. iii. 13).

Ver. 7.—And Huzzab. The Anglican rendering (which has the authority of the Jewish commentators, and is endorsed by Ewald and Rückert) takes Huzzab as an appellative, either the name of the Queen of Nineveh, or a symbolical name for Nineveh itself, as Sheshach, Pekod, and Merathaim were for Babylon (see Jer. xxv. 26; l. 21; li. 41; Ezek. xxiii. 23), which was formed or adopted by Nahum for the purpose of describing its character. Huzzab may mean "established," "set firm" (Gen. xxviii. 12), and confident in its strength; pual from natsab, "to set," "to fix" (Wordsworth). We may dismiss the idea that Huzzab is the name of the queen. Such a personage is unknown to history; and there is no reason why she should be mentioned rather than the king; and persons are not introduced by name in prophecy except for some very special reason, as Cyrus (Isa. xliv. 28). The alternative rendering, "it is decreed," adopted by Keil, Pusey, and many modern commentators, is unexampled, and comes in baldly, and not at all according to the prophet's manner. Henderson joins the clause with the preceding, thus: "The palace is dissolved, though firmly established." The Septuagint gives, Ἡ ὑπόστασις ἀπεκαλύφθη, "The hidden treasures are revealed," or, "The foundation is exposed;" Vulgate, Miles captivus abductus est. It seems best to take Huzzab as an appellative representing either Nineveh or Assyria, as the country between the Upper and Lower Zab (Rawlinson, in 'Dictionary of the Bible'), or as meaning "firm," "bold." Thus Egypt is called Rahab, "arrogant" (Isa. xxx. 7); the King of Assyria, Jareb, "contentious" (Hos. v. 13); Jerusalem, Ariel, "God's lion" (Isa. xxix. 1). Shall be led away captive; better, is laid bare. She, the queen of nations, is stripped of her adornments and ignominiously treated. She shall be brought up. She is carried away into captivity. "Brought up" may mean brought up to judgment, as ch. iii. 5; Isa. xlvii. 2, 3 (Pusey). Her maids shall lead her; rather, her handmaids moan. The inhabitants of Nineveh, personified as a queen, or the lesser cities of her empire, follow their mistress mourning. As with the voice of doves (comp. Isa. xxxviii. 14; lix. 11; Ezek. vii. 16). They shall not only show the outward tokens of sorrow, but shall mourn inwardly in their hearts, as the LXX. renders the whole clause, καθὼς περιστεραὶ φθεγγό-μεναι ἐν καρδίαις αὐτῶν, "as doves moaning in their hearts." **Tabering;** beating on a tabret. (For smiting the breast in token of sorrow, comp. Luke xviii. 13; xxiii. 48; Homer, 'Il.,' xviii. 31, Χερσὶ δὲ πᾶσαι Στήθεα πεπλήγοντο.)

Ver. 8.—The prophet compares the past and present condition of Nineveh. **But Nineveh is of old like a pool of water;** *and* (or, *though*) *Nineveh hath been like a pool of water all her days.* Others, altering the points in accordance with the Septuagint and Vulgate, translate, "But as for Nineveh, her waters are like a pool of water." This is what she has come to, for "her waters" represent herself. She is compared to a pool or reservoir (Neh. ii. 14; iii. 15) from the multitude of her inhabitants gathered from all parts of the world, and streaming unto her, both as tributary and for commercial purposes (comp. Jer. li. 13; Rev. xvii. 1, 15). **Yet they shall flee away.** In spite of their numbers, the multitudes represented by "the waters" fly before the enemy. In vain the captains cry, **Stand, stand.** They pay no attention. **None shall look back.** No one of the fugitives turns round or gives a thought to anything but his own safety.

Vers. 9—13.—§ 2. *The city is plundered, and henceforth lies waste, in terrible contrast with its former excellency.*

Ver. 9.—The prophet calls on the invaders to come and gather the spoil of the city, which God gives into their hands. **Take ye the spoil.** Fabulous stories are told of the amount of the precious metals stored in Nineveh and Babylon. "Sardanapalus is said to have placed a hundred and fifty golden beds, and as many tables of the same metal, on his funeral pile, besides gold and silver vases and ornaments in enormous quantities, and purple and many-coloured raiments (Athen., lib. xii.). According to Diodorus, the value of the gold taken from the temple of Belus alone by Xerxes amounted to above 7350 Attic talents, or £21,000,000 sterling money" (Layard, 'Nineveh,' ii. 416, etc.; comp. Dan. iii. 1, where the size of the golden image or pillar, sixty cubits high and six cubits broad, shows how plentiful was gold in these countries). Bonomi: "The riches of Nineveh are inexhaustible, her vases and precious furniture are infinite, copper constantly occurs in their weapons, and it is most probable a mixture of it was used in the materials of their tools. They had acquired the art of making glass. . . . The well-known cylinders are a sufficient proof of their skill in engraving gems. Many beautiful specimens of carving in ivory were also discovered. . . . The condition of the ruins is highly corroborative of

the sudden destruction that came upon Nineveh by fire and sword.. . . . It is evident from the ruins that both Khorsabad and Nimroud were sacked and then set on fire. Neither Botta nor Layard found any of that store of silver and gold and 'pleasant furniture' which the palaces contained; scarcely anything, even of bronze, escaped the spoiler" ('Nineveh and its Discoveries,' pp. 334, 336). **There is none end of the store;** Vulgate, *Non finis est divitiarum;* Septuagint, Οὐκ ἦν πέρας τοῦ κόσμου αὐτῆς, "There was no end of her ornament." **And glory out of all the pleasant furniture;** literally, *vessels of desire.* It is plainer to translate, *There is abundance of all precious furniture.*

Ver. 10.—**She is empty, and void, and waste.** *Bukahum' bukah, um' bulakah.* The three words are of very similar meaning and sound, and express most forcibly the utter ruin of the city. A Latin commentator has endeavoured to imitate the Hebrew paronomasia by rendering them, "vacuitas, evacuatio, evanidatio"—a translation more ingenious than classical. The paronomasia is better rendered by "vastitas, vastitia, vacuitas," and the German, "leer und ausgeleert und verheert." "Sack and sacking and ransacking" (Gandell). An analogous combination of words is found in Isa. xxiv. 3, 4; xxix. 2, 3; Ezek. xxxiii. 29; Zeph. i. 15. Septuagint, ἐκτιναγμὸς, καὶ ἀνατιναγμὸς, καὶ ἐκβρασμός, "thrusting forth and spurning and tumult." **The heart melteth.** A common expression for fear and despondency (Josh. vii. 5; Isa. xiii. 7; Ezek. xxi. 7). **The knees smite together** (Dan. v. 6). So in Homer continually, λύτο γούνατα. **Much pain is in all loins.** The anguish as of childbirth. Septuagint, ὠδῖνες, "labour-pains," in contrast with the injunction in ver. 1 (comp. Isa. xiii. 8; xxi. 3; Jer. xxx. 6). **Gather blackness** (Joel ii. 6); or, *withdraw their colour;* i.e. wax pale. But the Hebrew rather implies that the faces assume a livid hue, like that of coming death. Hence the LXX. renders, ὡς πρόσκαυμα χύτρας, as the burning of an earthen vessel, which is blackened by the fire; and Jerome, *sicut nigredo ollæ* (comp. Jer. xxx. 6).

Ver. 11.—The prophet asks, as if in consternation at the complete collapse of the great city—Where is the site of Nineveh? **Where is the dwelling (den) of the lions?** The lion is a natural symbol of Assyria, both from that animal's cruel, predatory, ravenous habits, and from its use as the chief national emblem. Nergal, the war-god, has a winged lion with a man's face as his emblem. See the figure in Rawlinson, 'Anc. Mon.,' i. 173, who adds (p. 308) that the lion is accepted as a true type of the people, blood, ravin, and robbery being their characteristics in the mind of the prophet. **The feeding-place of the young lions** may mean the subject lands whence they took their prey. **And the old lion;** rather, *the lioness.* The lion is designated by different names, which may, perhaps, refer to the various satraps and chieftains of the Assyrian kingdom. There are the full-grown male lion, the lioness, the young lion able to seek its own food, and the whelp too young to find its own living. Instead of "the lioness," the LXX., Vulgate, and Syriac, reading differently, give, τοῦ εἰσελθεῖν, *ut ingrederetur,* "that the lion's whelp should enter there." **And none made them afraid.** They lived in perfect security, without fear or care, irresistible in might (Lev. xxvi. 6; Micah iv. 4; Zeph. iii. 13).

Ver. 12.—**The figure of the lion is continued,** and this verse, in loose apposition to the preceding, may be best explained by continuing the interrogation in thought—Where is now the lion that used to tear in pieces, etc.? **The lion did tear in pieces enough for his whelps.** The Assyrian monarch provided for his children and dependents by plundering other nations. **His lionesses** may mean his wives and concubines. It was the custom both with the Persians and Assyrians to assign towns and provinces to their favourites. Xenophon ('Anab.,' i. 4. 10) mentions certain villages as set apart for the girdle of Queen Parysatis. A Lapide quotes Cicero, 'Verr.,' ii. 3. 33, "They say that the barbarian kings of the Persians and Syrians [*i.e.* Assyrians]

are wont to have many wives, to whom they assign cities in this fashion—this city is to provide a girdle for her waist, that a necklace, that again to dress her hair; and so they have whole nations, not only privy to their lusts, but also abettors of them" (see Arnold's note on Thucydides, i. 138; comp. 2 Macc. iv. 30).

Ver. 13.—**I am against thee.** The destruction shall be surely accomplished, because God himself directs it. Literally, *I to thee* (ch. iii. 5; Jer. li. 25; Ezek. xxxviii. 3). **The Lord of hosts** (*sabaoth*), Lord of the forces of heaven and earth, and therefore omnipotent. Κύριος παντοκράτωρ (Septuagint). **I will burn her chariots in the smoke.** "Chariots" stand for the whole apparatus of war and military power. Septuagint for "chariots" gives πλῆθος, "multitudes." **Thy young lions.** Thy fighting men, the metaphor being continued. **Cut off thy prey.** Thou shalt no more be able to pillage other countries. **Thy messengers.** These are the heralds who carried the king's commands to his lieutenants, or those, like the imperious Rabshakeh (2 Kings xviii. 17, etc.; xix. 23), who summoned nations to surrender, and imposed tributes. "O Nineveh," writes St. Jerome, "thou shalt suffer all that has been spoken. I the Lord will burn to ashes thy chariots, and will cause thy nobles and satraps to be devoured by the sword; never again shalt thou lay countries waste, nor exact tribute, nor will thy emissaries' voice be heard throughout thy provinces."

HOMILETICS.

Vers. 1—10.—*A predicted invasion.* I. THE ENEMY DESCRIBED. **1.** *His violence.* Nahum calls him "a dasher in pieces" (ver. 1), and represents his warriors as "mighty" and "valiant" (ver. 3)—epithets which apply with fitness and force to the Medo-Babylonian army under Cyaxares and Nabopolassar. **2.** *His boldness.* He comes up against Nineveh, not stealthily and under cover of darkness, but openly, pitching his tent opposite the city gates. His fearless attitude was a proof that God was secretly impelling him, using him against Assyria as formerly Assyria had been used against other nations. **3.** *His invincibility.* Nineveh may "keep the munition, watch the way, make her loins strong, fortify her power mightily,"—all will be in vain. The onset of this terrible assailant will be practically resistless. Whether irony (Fausset) or poetry (Keil), the meaning is the same, that Nineveh's utmost exertions will not be able to ward off her ruin. **4.** *His fierceness.* With crimson-coated soldiers, bearing red-coloured shields and shaking terribly tall spears of fir, and with chariots flashing with the gleam of steel plates, his appearance was fitted to inspire terror (ver. 3). "The chariots of the Assyrians, as we see them on the monuments, glare with shining things made either of iron or steel, battle-axes, bows, arrows, and shields, and all kinds of weapons" (Strauss). **5.** *His impetuosity.* The swiftness and the fury of his attack are vividly described (ver. 4). His chariots the prophet represents as raging, driving on madly, through the streets, as crowding the broad spaces in such a fashion as to jostle against and threaten to run down one another, as flashing to and fro like torches, as running hither and thither with the celerity of lightning.

II. THE ATTACK EXPLAINED. **1.** *The Assyrian oppression of Israel.* "The emptiers," *i.e.* the Assyrians, "have emptied out" the Israelites, and "marred their vine branches." They had done so by their devastation and depopulation of the northern kingdom (2 Kings xvii. 6), and by their repeated invasions of the southern (Isa. x. 5—11; 2 Chron. xxxii. 1). Now the time was come when they themselves should be emptied (ver. 10) and their branches marred (Ezek. xxxi. 12). Jehovah had employed the Assyrian as the rod of his anger to punish Israel and Judah; but he had never concealed his purpose, when this was done, "to punish the fruit of the stout heart of the King of Assyria, and the glory of his high looks" (Isa. x. 12). 2. *The Divine remembrance of Israel.* Having promised never to forget her or finally cast her off (Isa. xliv. 21; xlix. 16; Ps. lxxxix. 33, 34), he had returned to the excellency of Jacob as to the excellency of Israel (Keil), or had brought again the excellency of Jacob as the excellency of Israel (Revised Version). Both renderings are admissible, and both conduct to the same goal. The doom of Nineveh was certain because Jehovah was about to restore Judah to her ideal excellence as "Israel," and this he was to do by himself, returning to her as if she were an ideal Israel.

III. THE RESISTANCE BEGUN. 1. *Suddenly.* Nineveh at length realizes her danger and bethinks herself of her warriors : "He remembereth his worthies" (ver. 5). Assyria had good generals and valiant troops; to these she now turns. 2. *Hastily.* Not a moment is lost. Men and marshals hurry to the wall. No time to trifle when such enemies as Cyaxares and Nabopolassar thunder at the gates. 3. *Vigorously.* The defence (Authorized Version), mantelet (Revised Version), or movable parapet, literally, the covering one, the *testudo* or tortoise (Keil), is prepared—probably "either a movable tower with a battering-ram, consisting of a light framework covered with basket-work, or else a framework without any tower, either with an ornamented covering or simply covered with skins and moving upon four or six wheels" (Keil). 4. *Blindly.* Their energy and haste only lead to confusion : "They stumble in their march." The more haste, the less speed.

IV. THE CONQUEST COMPLETED. 1. *The capture of the city.* This was effected by forcing the gates in the city wall : "The gates of the rivers are opened" (ver. 6). These were the gates leading from the river into the city (Luther, Keil), rather than the dams or sluices through which the waters of the river were admitted into the canals which protected the palace. 2. *The demolition of the palace.* "The palace is dissolved," not by the inundation of water from the river (Fausset), since the palaces were usually "built in the form of terraces upon the tops of hills, either natural or artificial, and could not be flooded with water" (Keil); but by the inrush of enemies against it. The prophet means that "there will be no impediment to hinder the approach of enemies, for all the fortresses will melt away, and that of themselves, as though they were walls of paper, and the stones as though they were water" (Calvin). 3. *The deportation of the queen.* "And Huzzab is uncovered," etc. (ver. 7). This may signify either that the consort of the king is seized, degraded, and borne off into inglorious exile (Ewald), or that Nineveh, personified as a queen, is now covered with shame, and that she who had formerly been established is now swept off into captivity (Keil, Fausset, Calvin). In the former case the handmaids who accompany her, mourning with the voice of doves and beating on their breasts (literally, "hearts") are the ladies of her court; in the latter, they are most probably the inhabitants who bewail the fate of their once famous city and kingdom (Calvin, Keil). 4. *The flight of the inhabitants.* "They," *i.e.* the masses of the people, "flee away" (ver. 8). (1) Most unexpectedly, since "Nineveh hath been of old like a pool of water," so strong, impregnable, and inaccessible to any foe, as well as so prosperous and flourishing that the thing least to be anticipated was that its inhabitants should flee from it. (2) Most determinedly, however, they do so, giving no heed to the few patriotic men who call upon them to remain. "Stand, stand, they cry; but no one looketh back" (ver. 8). 5. *The spoliation of the treasure.* (1) The quality of the treasure—silver, gold, pleasant furniture. "The Assyrians were celebrated for their skill in working metals. Their mountains furnished a variety of minerals—silver, iron, copper, and lead, and perhaps even gold" (Layard's 'Nineveh,' ii. 415). (2) The quantity of the treasure : "none end of the store." That gold, silver, and precious vessels should have been abundant in Nineveh is sufficiently explained by remembering, in addition to the mines just mentioned, the enormous tribute received and rich spoils carried off from conquered nations ('Records of the Past,' vol. i. 37, etc., 59, etc.). **6.** *The desolation of the scene.* "She is empty, and void, and waste" (ver. 10)—the effect of this description being heightened in Hebrew by the combination of three synonymous and similarly sounding words, *būqâh umebhūqâh umebullâqâh.* Emptied of her population and despoiled of her treasure, she became a total ruin. According to Strabo, when Cyaxares and his allies took the city, they utterly destroyed it (Layard's 'Nineveh,' ii. 159, 204). **7.** *The horror of the vanquished.* "The heart melteth and the knees smite together, and anguish is in all loins, and the faces of them all are waxed pale" (ver. 10). "Hence we may learn how foolishly men boast of their courage, while they seem to be like lions; for God can in a moment so melt their hearts that they lose all firmness" (Calvin).

LESSONS. **1.** The retributions of Divine providence (ver. 1). The destroyers of others may expect themselves to be destroyed (Isa. xxxiii. 1). **2.** The hopelessness of defending one's self against the invasions of Heaven (ver. 1). "Who would set the thorns and briars against me in battle?" (Isa. xxvii. 4; cf. 'Herod.,' ix. 16, "Whatever necessarily comes from God, it is impossible for man by any contrivance to turn aside"). **3.** The true ideal of a nation's greatness (ver. 2)—the dwelling of Jehovah in her midst (Ps. xlvi. 5). **4.** The utter vanity of all earthly glory (ver. 8). The world's strength, riches, honours, are all destined to perish (1 John ii. 17). **5.** The horrors of the wicked when the terrors of judgment come upon them (ver. 10). "Then shall they say to the mountains and the rocks, Fall on us," etc. (Rev. vi. 16).

Vers. 11—13.—*The parable of the lion's den.* I. THE DESCRIPTION OF THE DEN. **1.** *Its site.* Nineveh, the capital of the Assyrian empire. (1) Old, extending over centuries at least. (2) Capacious, having caves in it for its prey, and room in it for the lion, lionesses, and lion's whelps to walk about. (3) Strong, surrounded on two sides by water and seemingly impregnable—a secure retreat, in which its inhabiting wild beasts felt themselves safe. **2.** *Its occupants.* The lions above referred to. (1) The old lion—the King of Assyria. (2) The lionesses—the queens and concubines of the reigning prince. (3) The lion's whelps, or young lions—his sons, princes, nobles, and warriors. **3.** *Its prey.* The spoils of the nations. Syria, Phœnicia, Philistia, Israel, Judah, and even Egypt had felt the might of Assyria and contributed to swell the ravin she had stored in her cities.

II. THE DESTRUCTION OF THE DEN. **1.** *Its certainty.* According to Nahum, Jehovah was against Nineveh, and that was enough to secure its overthrow. "The face of the Lord is against them that do evil," etc. (Ps. xxxiv. 16). Besides, his uttered threatening, "I will burn her chariots [*i.e.* all her military armament] in the smoke," rendered her doom inevitable. The word of Jehovah can as little fail in threatening as in promise. **2.** *Its celerity.* So little difficult would be the task to Jehovah, that he would not need fire, but only smoke, to consume the power of Nineveh. "In short, the prophet shows that Nineveh would be, as it were in a moment, reduced to nothing, as soon as it pleased God to avenge its wickedness" (Calvin). **3.** *Its completeness.* (1) Her warriors should be destroyed: "The sword shall devour thy young lions." (2) Her spoliations should cease: "I will cut off thy prey from the earth." (3) Her emissaries should be silent: "The voice of thy messengers shall no more be heard," exacting tribute from the nations thou hast conquered.

Learn: **1.** That Jehovah is against sin in nations no less than in individuals. **2.** That national wickedness is the certain prelude to national ruin.

HOMILIES BY VARIOUS AUTHORS.

Vers. 1, 2.—*God the Vindicator of the oppressed.* I. THE OPPRESSION OF THE CHOSEN PEOPLE BY THE ASSYRIANS. **1.** *This is expressed figuratively.* "The emptiers have emptied them out" (ver. 2), had exhausted their resources, as the contents of a vessel poured out until every drain had been withdrawn, so had both Israel and Judah been impoverished by the Assyrians. "And marred their vine branches." Ancient Israel was often described as God's vineyard (Isa. v. 1; Ps. lxxx. 9). This vineyard the foe had ruthlessly invaded, casting down and injuring its fruit-bearing trees. **2.** *These* *figurative representations are sustained by historical fact.* The more familiar we become with Assyrian history the more do we trace in that vast heathen power the prevalence of the haughty, overbearing spirit. Its rulers and people vainly supposed that national greatness consisted in the possession of might to be used in oppressing other nations and peoples. To be able to depict upon the walls of the palaces of Ninus battle-scenes indicative of military triumph, accompanied by great spoil and cruel chastisement inflicted upon their adversaries, seems to have been their highest ambition. Their whole relationship to Israel and Judah was based upon this principle. The favoured of Heaven, having forsaken their God, and hence lost his protecting care, turned in their exigencies to Assyria for aid, but only to find, in this supposed helper against their foes, a more powerful enemy. In this way the kingdom of Israel was first made tributary to Assyria by Pul (2 Kings xv. 17—20), and, soon after, its tribes were carried away into captivity by Shalmaneser (2 Kings xvii. 3—23), whilst the kingdom of Judah in like manner became compelled to acknowledge the lordship of Tilgath-Pilneser (2 Chron. xxviii. 16—21). Hezekiah sought to cast off the Assyrian yoke, but this only resulted in the nation, in Nahum's time, being brought into circumstances of extreme peril (2 Kings xviii. 13—17), and from which eventually supernatural help alone was able to deliver it (Isa. xxxvii. 36).

II. DIVINE INTERPOSITION PROMISED ON BEHALF OF THE OPPRESSED. (Ver. 2.) Such interposition had in a measure but recently taken place (Isa. xxxvii. 36). "The angel of death" had "breathed in the face of the foe," and had caused "the might of the Gentile" to "melt like snow," and the oppressor to return humbled to his capital (Isa. xxxvii. 37). The time, however, for the complete and final interposition of Heaven had not yet arrived. Still, it *should* come. The seer, in rapt vision beheld it as though it had been then in operation, and for the encouragement of the oppressed he declared that the Divine eye observed all that was being endured, that the Lord Almighty still regarded them with favour (ver. 2), and would yet make them "an eternal excellency, a joy of many generations" (Isa. lx. 15).

III. THIS DIVINE INTERPOSITION EVENTUALLY TO BE EXPERIENCED VIEWED AS CARRYING WITH IT THE ENTIRE OVERTHROW OF THE OPPRESSOR. (Ver. 1.) Asshur should in due course be brought low, and the yoke of bondage should fall from off the necks of the captives. In "the day of visitation:" 1. *Agents should not be wanting to carry out the Divine behests.* The defection of the Assyrian general, the forces of the King of Media, and the overflowing of the Tigris, should all combine to bring about the accomplishment of the Divine purpose; and these forces are here personified as "the dasher in pieces" (ver. 1). 2. *Resistance should be in vain.* They might "keep the munition, watch the ways," etc. (ver. 1), but all to no purpose. The proud power must inevitably fall, and in its overthrow proclamation be made that it is not by means of tyranny and oppression and wrong-doing that any nation can become truly great and lastingly established, but by the prevalence in its midst of liberty, virtue, and righteousness. Nineveh in her downfall

> ". . . seems to cry aloud
> To warn the mighty and instruct the proud;
> That of the great, neglecting to be just,
> Heaven in a moment makes a heap of dust."

S. D. H.

Vers. 3—13.—*The downfall of Nineveh, as illustrative of the Divine and the human elements in revelation.* There are two elements in the Bible, the Divine and the human. God speaks to us in every page, nor does he speak the less emphatically, but all the more so, in that he addresses us through men possessing throbbing hearts, and who were passing through experiences like our own. We honour the volume as being in the highest sense God's Word, nor do we honour it the less in this respect because we rejoice that he has been pleased to make holy men the medium of communicating his will. The account given in these verses of the predicted ruin of Nineveh must be taken as a whole, and in the graphic picture here presented to us we have strikingly illustrated this twofold character of the Scriptures of eternal truth.

I. THE ACCOUNT CONTAINED HERE OF THE PREDICTED OVERTHROW OF NINEVEH SERVES TO ILLUSTRATE THE DIVINE ELEMENT IN REVELATION. Nahum flourished in the reign of Hezekiah (B.C. 725—696), and Nineveh was destroyed between B.C. 609 and 606). He lived and prophesied thus say a hundred years before the occurrence of the events he so vividly described, and when the Assyrian power was in the zenith of its prosperity. His announcements were very distinct and definite, and by placing these and the records of secular historians given at a subsequent period side by side, we see how minutely the predictions of this seer have been fulfilled, and that hence, in making these, he must have been God's messenger, uttering, not his own thoughts, but those which had been communicated to him by " visions and revelations of the Lord." In ch. i. 10 we read, " For while they be folden together as thorns, and while they are drunken as drunkards, they shall be devoured as stubble fully dry." The secular historian writes, " While all the Assyrian army were feasting for their former victories, those about Arbuces, being informed by some deserters of the negligence and drunkenness in the camp of the enemies, assaulted them unexpectedly by night, and falling orderly on them disorderly, and prepared on them unprepared, became masters of the camp, and slew many of the soldiers and drove the rest into the city " (Diodorus Siculus, bk. ii. p. 80). In ch. ii. 6 we read, " The gates of the rivers shall be opened, and the palace shall be dissolved." The secular historian writes, " There was an oracle among the Assyrians that Nineveh should not be taken till the river became an enemy to the city ; and in the third year of the siege, the river, being swollen with continual rains, overflowed part of the city, and broke down the wall for twenty furlongs. Then the king, thinking that the oracle was fulfilled, and the river had become an enemy to the city, built a large funeral pile in the palace, and collecting together all his wealth and his concubines and eunuchs, burnt himself and the palace with them all, and the enemy entered at the breach that the waters had made, and took the city " (Diodorus Siculus, bk. ii. p. 80). In ch. ii. 9 the prophet, as though addressing the adversaries of Nineveh, said, " Take ye the spoil of silver, take the spoil of gold : for there is none end of the store and glory out of all the pleasant furniture ; " and the same secular historian already quoted informs us that the conquerors carried many talents of gold and silver to Ecbatana, the royal city of the Medes. No language could be more explicit than that in which Nahum predicted the *total* destruction of the city (ch. ii. 10—13 ; iii. 7, 15—17). The Prophet Zephaniah used words equally plain (ii. 13—15). Their utterances would have appeared very strange to the Ninevites at the time they were spoken ; as strange, indeed, as similar utterances would appear if addressed at the present time to the inhabitants of our own metropolis ; but they were true nevertheless, and the facts of history furnish abundant confirmations. For upwards of two thousand years after its overthrow, Nineveh lay buried in the earth. History and tradition indicated its probable site, and the mounds to be found in the supposed districts, and out of which the Turks obtained materials for building purposes, of evident antiquity, invited research ; and within a very recent period such research has been carried on, the long-buried palaces of the kings of Assyria have been discovered, huge sculptures have been carefully dug out of the mounds, and the national museums both of France and England are now enriched with these long-lost works of art, testifying not only to the ancient splendour of the Assyrian empire and its capital, but also to the truthfulness of the prophetical records, and to the prophets as speaking and writing under the inspiration of the Almighty, and as being indeed the messengers of him who has said, " I am God, and there is none like me, declaring the end from the beginning, and from ancient times the things that are not yet done " (Isa. xlvi. 9, 10).

II. The account contained here of the predicted overthrow of Nineveh serves to illustrate the human element in revelation. Holy Scripture is remarkable in its variety—not variety in purpose, for this is single throughout, but variety in expression. History, prophecy, poetry, parable, proverb, miracle, biography, vision, epistle, are all laid under tribute. As there is a Divine element in the Bible, so also there is a human element therein. Whilst upon the writings of each of its contributors there is unmistakably the impress of the operation of the Spirit of God, there is likewise, throughout the whole, clear indications of the preservation of those natural gifts and endowments which the respective writers possessed. There was no suspension of the powers of the men who were honoured of God in communicating to their fellow-men a knowledge of his will ; but rather there was the retention of their own individual peculiarities and natural qualities, whilst the Divine Spirit operated through these and turned these to the most useful account. Biblical critics are agreed in recognizing "the classic beauty and the finished elegance" of the style of Nahum, and in assigning to this writer a place in the first rank of Hebrew literature. "The variety in his method of presenting ideas discovers much poetic talent in the prophet. The reader of taste and sensibility will be affected by the entire structure of the poem, by the agreeable manner in which the ideas are brought forward, by the flexibility of the expressions, the roundness of his turns, the delicate outlines of his figures, by the strength and delicacy, and the expression of sympathy and greatness, which diffuse themselves over the whole subject" (De Wette's Introduction). "Nahum of all the prophets has the most impassioned style; and in none is found the change of numbers, of persons addressed, and of suffix-relations, with such frequentness and immediateness as in him. At the same time, his language has wonderful energy and picturesque beauty. The painting does not embrace merely single rhythms and groups of words, but whole series; and in connecting his thoughts, he shows, with all his vehemence, great and varied skill" (Kleinert). His description of the siege and fall of Nineveh, contained in this chapter (vers. 3—13), is wonderfully vivid. As we read the account, even at this distant date, the stirring scenes seem to live again, and to pass in review before us. We see the attacking warriors in their scarlet attire and with their chariots armed with sharp instruments of steel (ver. 3), and the defenders of the city, suddenly startled, hastening their preparations, their chariots in the hurry jostling against each other in the streets, and the gallants summoned by the king hastening to the ramparts, which the foe is seeking with battering-rams to cast down (vers. 4, 5). We behold the overflowing of the river, facilitating the advance of the enemy, and paralyzing the people by reason of the popular tradition now seemingly being fulfilled (ver. 6). We witness the inhabitants brought low in shame and dishonour, moaning like a captive woman (ver. 7), or fleeing for their very life in hopelessness and despair, conscious that resistance is vain (ver. 8). We view the spoiling of the city—the conqueror carrying away the gold and the silver to the Median capital, the trophies of victory (ver. 9). Finally, we picture to ourselves the prophets of the Lord gazing upon the waste and desolation, reflecting upon the proud being abased, their offspring cut off, their gains confiscated, their boastful messengers silenced, and ascribing all the terrible reverses thus experienced to the righteous retribution of the Lord of hosts (vers. 10—13); and we feel, as we linger upon the scene thus graphically portrayed, that whilst rejoicing in this volume of revelation as having been given by inspiration of God, and as containing Divine lessons abounding both in encouragement and warning, we may well prize it also even on the lower ground of its literary merit, and heartily rejoice in the infinite variety of human powers and endowments here consecrated to the presentation of the loftiest and grandest spiritual teaching.—S. D. H.

Ver. 13.—*Man incurring the Divine displeasure.* "Behold, I am against thee, saith the Lord of hosts." This attitude of God towards man—

I. IMPLIES WRONG DOING ON MAN'S PART. God is not thus adverse to man for naught. "His delights are with the sons of men" (Prov. viii. 31). Sin alienates man from God, and causes God to be righteously displeased with man.

II. INVOLVES MAN IN PRESENT DISTRESS. Man cannot be at ease whilst under the ban of Jehovah. "In his favour is life" (Ps. xxx. 5). Separation from him through sin means disquietude and unrest. "The worst troubler in the world is a wilful heart." "Conscience makes cowards of us all." "The heart melteth, the knees smite together" (ver. 10).

III. RESULTING IN ULTIMATE RUIN TO SUCH AS WILFULLY PERSIST IN SIN. God is *the Lord of hosts.* All power is his. "Who shall stand when he is angry?" (Ps. lxxvi. 7). All have sinned, and hence have incurred the displeasure of him who "is of purer eyes than to behold iniquity;" but in Christ, whose day the seers saw afar off, God is reconciled to man; so that the distress and ruin indicated can alone result from man refusing to be reconciled unto God.—S. D. H.

Ver. 13 (with ch. i. 15).—*The messengers of Nineveh and the messengers of Zion: a comparison.* " And the voice of thy messengers shall no more be heard " (ver. 13) ; " Behold upon the mountains the feet of him that bringeth good tidings, that publisheth peace ! " (ch. i. 15). Messengers, differing very materially in their character and mission, are referred to in these words. The messengers of Nineveh and the messengers of Zion are alluded to in these passages. A comparison of these respective messengers may prove suggestive and useful in its application to certain developments in these modern times. From the Second Book of Kings and the Second Book of Chronicles we learn that the heralds or messengers of Nineveh cherished the spirit of blasphemy with reference to the God of heaven. The faith of the pious Hebrews consisted in the recognition of the one living and true God, and of his providential care over all his creatures ; and it was against this bulwark that the emissaries of Assyria constantly directed their assaults in words foul and filthy (see Rabshakeh's appeal to the Jews, 2 Kings xviii. 33—35 ; and his letter, 2 Chron. xxxii. 17). The great and distinguishing characteristic of the messengers of Zion was loyalty to the God of heaven. Their feet stood upon the mountains, and their voice proclaimed to the people, " Behold your God ! " (Isa. xl. 9); " Thy God reigneth ! " (Isa. lii. 7). In the present age there are messengers who boldly declare their non-acceptance of the teaching that recognizes the Divine Being and his working, and who seek to disseminate their views, and in doing so are not particular if they blaspheme the God of heaven. And whilst there are such messengers in the world doing their injurious work, there are also those who are thoroughly loyal to the King of kings, who delight to show forth his praise, to tell the story of his love in the gift and work of Christ, and to seek to draw men in loving obedience to his authority and will. Note certain contrasts, then, suggested ; thus—

I. CAPTIVITY IN CONTRAST WITH FREEDOM. The messengers of Nineveh approached Jerusalem, to which Sennacherib was laying siege, but they bore no tidings of liberty. They claimed *full submission,* and declared that even this must be followed by captivity in a strange land (2 Kings xviii. 31, 32). The assurance of ultimate deliverance came from the messengers of the Lord (ch. i. 12, 13). Sin is bondage. Evil passions, habits, desires, are fetters; a life of alienation from the true and the right is a life of hard bondage. Transgressors are slaves. And scepticism has nothing to offer such by way of helping them to escape. The messengers may expatiate to such a one upon the nobleness of virtue, may sound in his ears some wise sayings of sages and philosophers, may remind him of the injury he is inflicting upon himself, and bid him " be a man," and " turn over a new leaf." But he is down ; he is conscious of moral inability; he lacks inward strength. Lo! the messengers of Zion come. They tell him of the great Father's unwearying love, the Saviour's obedience unto the death of the cross, the energizing and sanctifying Spirit ready to gird him with all-sufficient strength, the elder Brother who has proved his trials and his tears, and who is prepared to be near him in every season of need as his " strong siding Champion." He feels the tidings to be " good ; " is bowed low in penitence; his eye of faith turns to the hill called Calvary, and rises to the everlasting hills whence cometh help; the fettered soul is released, is free, for the messengers on the mountains have proclaimed deliverance to the captive, and the opening of the prison to the bound (Isa. lxi. 1).

II. STRIFE IN CONTRAST TO PEACE. The messengers of Nineveh to Judah had nothing conciliatory to convey ; they told only of contention and strife. The assurance that peace should ultimately be enjoyed came to the anxious King of Judah from God's messengers, who published peace. The messengers of scepticism have no proclamation of peace to make; their work is altogether destructive; contumely is their delight; to seek to unsettle the minds of men and to shake their faith is their poor mission. It is the privilege, however, of the messengers of Zion to proclaim those spiritual and eternal verities in which the heart may securely and tranquilly repose, and to point to him who can quell every storm and give rest unto the soul.

III. GLOOM IN CONTRAST TO GLADNESS. Hezekiah and his people were in extremity; it was to them a time of " trouble ; " but not a ray of hope came to them through the messengers of Nineveh. Their worst fears were confirmed; the foe was unrelenting. Their hope was in God, and in the words spoken by his holy prophets. So in the extremities of life—in sickness and sorrow, and specially at life's close, hope springs not from unbelief, but from the words God has addressed to us through his servants. The gospel has no rival in such seasons. Scepticism has no voice then, or, if it speaks, it but deepens the prevailing gloom; but the good tidings God has revealed dispels our sadness and fills the soul with immortal hopes. Happy messengers, who are thus enabled to "comfort all that mourn," etc. (Isa. lxi. 2)!

IV. SHAME IN CONTRAST TO HONOUR. The voice of all messengers who blaspheme the holy Name of God "shall be no more heard," for God will put them to silence; but voices publishing his love and grace shall go sounding on through the ages—the bright succession of proclaimers shall not cease. Growing numbers shall be raised up who shall find their way to all nations and kindreds and tribes, until the glad tidings shall reach every shore, and the knowledge of the Lord shall fill the earth (Isa. xi. 9).—S. D. H.

Ver. 1—ch. iii. 19.—*Wicked nations:* 1. *They are often allowed to exist on this earth until they reach a terrible degree of wickedness.* "He that dasheth in pieces is come up before thy face: keep the munition, watch the way, make thy loins strong, fortify thy power mightily," etc. We take these two chapters together, (1) because they treat of one subject, viz. the destruction of Nineveh; (2) because scarcely any detached verse would supply suggestions for a practical discourse; and (3) because our purpose in these sketches is not critical, but homiletic. The critical part has been admirably done by Henderson, Keil, and others, and is found in the Exposition. We shall therefore endeavour to gather up all that is practical in these two chapters under three general headings. 1. *That nations are often allowed to exist on this earth until they reach a terrible degree of wickedness.* 2. *That it is the decree of Heaven that, however long they exist, the time must come when they shall be utterly destroyed.* 3. *That Providence often employs one wicked nation to inflict ruin upon another.* We shall devote a separate sketch to each of these propositions. Our subject now is that nations are often allowed to exist on this earth until they reach a terrible degree of wickedness. Assyria, the nation referred to here, was one of the oldest kingdoms in the world; it could count its age by centuries. Generation after generation came through centuries, played their part, and passed away, whilst Assyria stood. Its beginning is so far back that it is lost in obscurity. An early reference to it in Scripture will be found in Numb. xxiv. 22. Reference to its capital, Nineveh, and its founder, Asshur, we have also in Gen. x. 11. Our proposition suggests two questions—

I. WHAT WERE ITS LEADING CRIMES? From these chapters we can infer a few. 1. *Rapacity.* The city is described as the dwelling-place of lions. "Where is the dwelling of the lions?" etc. (ch. ii. 11, 12). "The point of comparison is," says Keil, "the predatory lust of its rulers and warriors, who crushed the nations like lions, plundering their treasures and bringing them together in Nineveh." As lions prowl about with ravenous instincts in search of their prey, and are utterly regardless of the sufferings and agonies they inflict, so long as they gain their object, so the King of Assyria and his minions went forth to rifle and to ruin distant countries, in order to augment their wealth and promote their aggrandizement. This rapacity seems to have been their habit; the city was a dwelling-place of lions. What an enormity is this!— man preying upon man like predatory beasts. The spirit of this rapacity lives too strongly in modern nations. It is seen, not only in aggressive wars, but in trade and commerce—the strong everywhere preying on the weak for the sake of gain. 2. *Cruelty.* The lion instinct was so prevailing in the population, that the very city is called "the bloody city" (ch. iii. 1). The golden rule, "Do unto others as you would have others do unto you," was trampled in the dust. Instead of respect being paid to the rights of men, life itself was cheaply held; their feet were "swift to shed blood." It lived by rapine. Its cruelty is handed down in its sculptures, where we have lions of every form, winged and unwinged. Cruelty is the worst stage of depravity. When all social love in the human breast gives way to malevolence, what have you but a devil? There are men in every age and country whose chief pleasure is to inflict torture. Atrocities are being perpetrated to a greater or less extent in all ages and lands. "Beasts," says our great dramatist, "are not cruel save when urged by hunger;" but men are often so, and into a cruel nature it is impossible to work the humane and generous.

> "You may as well use question with the wolf,
> Why he hath made the ewe bleat for the lamb;
> You may as well forbid the mountain pines

> To wag their high tops, and to make no noise
> When they are fretted with the gusts of heaven;
> You may as well do anything most hard,
> As seek to soften that (than which what's harder?)—
> A cruel heart."

3. *Imposture.* The city is represented as "full of lies and robbery" (ch. iii. 1), or, as Keil renders it, "full of deceit and murder." Falsehood and violence were rampant. The imposture or falsehood is expressed in the fourth verse, "Because of the multitude of the whoredoms of the well-favoured harlot, the mistress of witchcrafts, that selleth nations through her whoredoms, and families through her witchcrafts." "The idolatrous practices of the Ninevites, and the means which they employed to seduce others to worship their gods, are here represented as the principal cause of their destruction. At the same time, the commerce, luxury, etc., which they carried to the greatest height, are not to be excluded; for in making contracts and treaties with the more powerful of their neighbours, they not only employed these as inducements, but did not scruple to deliver into their power nations and tribes that were unable to help themselves (comp. Joel iii. 3, 6, 8; Amos i. 6). The metaphor of an unchaste female, and the seductive arts which she employs, is not unfrequent in the prophets" (Henderson). The cunning and deceptive policy is here called whoring or love-making, because it was that selfishness which wraps itself up in the dress of love, but under the appearance of love seeks only the gratification of its own lust. It was a mistress of this art, and by it sold nations, deprived them of their independence and liberty. Such are some of the crimes here referred to, of which the Assyrians were pre-eminently guilty —rapacity, cruelty, imposture. These imply every species of moral evil, and moral evil in its most inhuman and ungodly aspects. Where these are there is no rectitude, no benevolence, no moral order, no true religion.

II. WHY WAS SUCH A NATION ALLOWED TO EXIST SO LONG? It was wicked from the beginning: why did not righteous Heaven crush it at the outset? Why was such a monster of iniquity allowed to perpetrate such enormities in the world from age to age? The question is similar to that which Job asked, "Wherefore do the wicked live, become old, yea, are mighty in power?" (Job xxi. 7). Without presuming to penetrate the mind of God, or give the reason, we can see some important purposes which the continuation of the existence of wicked men in this world answers. It serves to show: 1. *The freedom of the human soul.* The natural tendency of all the blessings and beauty of life, the spirit of grandeur and beneficence that runs through all nature, are against wickedness and in favour of virtue and holiness. Notwithstanding this, men are wicked. They have a power to resist the Divine, to pervert the good, and outrage their own natures. Here is freedom of nature. Men are not bad by necessity; they are bad by their own free determination. 2. *The wonderful forbearance of God.* Though wickedness is to the last degree repugnant to his holy nature, and though by a volition he could annihilate a universe of sinners, through his infinite love he forbears. "The Lord is not slack concerning his promise, as some men count slackness, but is long-suffering to us-ward, not willing that any should perish, but that all should come to repentance" (2 Pet. iii. 9). 3. *The existence of a future state of retribution.* Under the righteous government of God such a state of things cannot go on for ever. There must come an end, a balancing of the world's accounts, and an administration of justice to every soul. Human society is in an abnormal state; like water in a flood, it is hurrying onward to a more settled destination. "The mills of God grind slowly."—D. T.

Ver. 1—ch. iii. 19.— *Wicked nations:* 2. *However long they exist, they will be utterly destroyed.* "He that dasheth in pieces," etc. "The Scripture," says Sherlock, "takes notice of a certain measure of iniquity, which is filling up from one generation to another, till at last it makes a nation or family ripe for destruction. And although these persons on whom this vengeance falls suffer no more than their own personal sin deserved, yet, because the sins of former generations, which they equal or outdo, make it time for God utterly to destroy them, the punishment due to the sins of many generations is said to fall upon them" (Gen. xv. 16; 2 Kings xxiv. 3, 4; Matt. xxiii. 32—36). So thorough was the destruction of Nineveh, that its very site for ages was a matter of conjecture. The wonderful discoveries of Botta in 1842, followed up by

Layard in 1845, not only determined its site, but disclosed the dwellings, ornaments, history, manners, of the inhabitants of the old Assyrian metropolis. Now, in the prophecy which Nahum gives, we learn that its destruction reveals several things.

I. THE FRUITLESSNESS OF THE MOST STRENUOUS EFFORTS OF RESISTANCE. "Keep the munition, watch the way, make thy loins strong, fortify thy power mightily" (ch. ii. 1). This is supposed by some to be ironical, and to mean—Do your utmost to resist, concentrate all your forces, bring them into vigorous play, it will be utterly worthless. No doubt Nineveh, in her extremities, strove to the utmost to crush the invader and to preserve her own existence. But all efforts failed; its doom was sealed, its time had come, it had filled up the measure of its iniquity. There is no resisting God's judgment when it comes. "There is no discharge in that warfare." We learn from this prophecy that its destruction reveals—

II. THAT THE SAME VIOLENCE WITH WHICH IT DESTROYED OTHERS WAS NOW EMPLOYED FOR ITS OWN DESTRUCTION. Nineveh was a city of blood, full of lies and violence, the dwelling-place of ravenous lions, which had preyed upon other nations and ruined them. Now this violence is brought to bear upon them. "With what measure ye mete, it shall be measured to you again." See the description given of its conquerors (ch. ii. 3; iii. 2, 3), "The shield of his mighty men is made red," the emblem of slaughter. "The chariots shall be with flaming torches," their wheels rolling with such velocity that they flash lightning from the stones. They "rage in the streets," jostle against each other, and "run like the lightnings," and there are the "noise of the whips," the "rattling of the wheels," the "prancing of the horses," the flashing of the swords and the glittering spears. Crowds are struck down, "a great number of carcases," there is "none end of their corpses; they stumble upon their corpses," etc. The Bible is full of the doctrine of retributive justice; it abounds with examples of sinners receiving back in punishment the very same evils that they have inflicted on others. "Every man shall be rewarded according to his works." How often it happens in the government of the world, that the deceiver is punished by deceit, the ambitious by ambition, the avaricious by avarice, the violent by violence "His mischief shall return upon his own head, and his violent dealing shall come down upon his own pate."[1]

III. THE WORTHLESSNESS OF ITS CHIEF METHOD OF DEFENCE. "The gates of the rivers shall be opened, and the palace shall be dissolved" (ch. ii. 6). "The river wall on the Tigris (the west defence of Nineveh) was 4530 yards long. On the north, south, and east sides there were large moats, capable of being easily filled with water from the Khos-ru. Traces of dams, gates, or sluices, for regulating the supply, are still visible, so that the whole city could be surrounded with a water barrier. Besides, on the east, the weakest side, it was further protected by a lofty double rampart, with a moat two hundred feet wide between its two parts, cut in the rocky ground. The moats, or canals, flooded by the Ninevites before the siege to repel the foe, were made a dry bed to march into the city, by the foe turning the water into a different channel, as Cyrus did in the siege of Babylon" (Maurer). This, however, is not substantiated. "In the earlier capture of Nineveh by Arbaces the Mede and Belsis the Babylonian, Diodorus Siculus states that there was an old prophecy, that it should not be taken till the river became its enemy; so, in the third year of the siege, the river, by a flood, broke down the walls twenty furlongs, and the king thereupon burnt himself and his palace and all his concubines and wealth together; and the enemy entered by the breach in the wall" (Fausset). It is often thus with the sinner, that the very things on which he relies contribute to his ruin. It may be wealth, physical strength, genius, morality, etc.; but when judgment comes, these, like the Tigris, "flee away."

IV. THE INEVITABLENESS OF ITS UTTER RUIN. The reason of it was, "I am against thee, saith the Lord of hosts" (ch. iii. 5). "Art thou better than populous No?" (ch. iii. 8—10)—the Egyptian name for Thebes, the possession of Ammon. The populousness of Thebes and its wonderful natural productions did not save it from ruin. Her "strength" was "infinite," yet she was "carried away into captivity;" if she could not resist, neither canst thou. "How vain," says a modern expositor, "are all the defences of sinners when the Lord is against them! No-Ammon, or Thebes,

[1] See a little volume entitled, 'The Retributive Justice of God commencing in this Life,' by Rev. J. Langley (Hatchards and Co.).

was one of the grandest and most magnificent cities of the earliest ages. Yet her rampart and sea-wall, with her seemingly infinite strength, were of no avail to save her young children from being dashed in pieces and all her great men from being bound in chains. Such was to be the doom of Nineveh likewise. God acts on the same unchanging principle in all ages, and in the case of all nations. Unrighteousness towards man and impiety and idolatry towards God bear the same bitter fruits everywhere, however for a time transgressors may seem to prosper. Let us as a nation remember that our safety consists, not in our fleets and armies, nor even in the 'multiplication of our merchants above the stars of heaven' (ch. iii. 16). Riches, like the cankerworm or the grasshopper (ver. 17), certainly make themselves wings, they fly away (Prov. xxiii. 5). The strongholds (ver. 12) on which we rely would fall before the invader as easily as the ripe fruit into the mouth of the eater, if God were against us. The nobles and captains who are the glory of England would soon be abased in the dust (vers. 17, 18). Our security therefore depends on our godliness. Wickedness persevered in continually (ver. 19) would bring on us a grievous wound, not to be healed, and the very nations now in alliance with us would clap their hands over us, exulting in the tidings of our fall. Let us therefore repent of our sins as a nation, as families, and as individuals, and 'bring forth worthy fruits of repentance.'"
—D. T.

Ver. 1—ch. iii. 19.—*Wicked nations: 3. Providence often employs one wicked nation to inflict ruin upon another.* "He that dasheth," etc. "He that dasheth in pieces is come up before thy face." "The disperser hath come up before thee" (Henderson) ; "A dasher in pieces comes against thee" (Keil). Who is "he that dasheth in pieces"? The Medo-Babylonish army. This mighty army, under the command of Cyaxares and Nabopolassar, composed of Medes and Babylonians, wrought the terrible destruction so graphically predicted in these chapters. And beneath its triumphant power Nineveh fell, between B.C. 626 and 608—fell to rise no more. Both these powers —the Medes and the Babylonians—were pre-eminently wicked, as bad in every respect, if not worse, than the Assyrians. These were the battle-axe with which God broke in pieces the Assyrian power. As a rule, in the government of the world, God employs one wicked nation to destroy another. Who destroyed Edom and Egypt, and Persia and Moab, and Greece and Rome? These were all destroyed by the hands of wicked men. Why this? Why does not the Almighty punish wicked nations by some other way? Why does he not destroy them without any instrumentality whatever, by a mere volition ; or, if he employs instrumentality, why not the blind forces of nature, or wild beasts, or poisonous reptiles? Why should he employ wicked men as his instruments? The method clearly answers certain purposes.

I. IT MAKES THE PUNISHMENT APPEAR MORE TERRIBLE. Who would not sooner die by a flash of lightning, or a pestilential blast, or a predatory beast, than in deadly conflict with a man with whom he has measured his strength? In such a death passions are roused that burn in the centre of the soul, and a terrible humiliation is felt. A wicked man can have no greater tormentor than a wicked man. The greatest tormentors of fiends are fiends. In punishing wicked men in this way the Almighty declares to their consciences that they are so wicked that the wicked shall destroy them. Those of their own flesh and blood and character shall wreak vengeance on their head.

II. IT REVEALS THE ENORMITY OF SIN. Man was made to love his brother. His social instincts, his physical relationships, and the law of interdependence, as well as the laws of God, demonstrate this. But when you see him flaming with malign emotions towards his fellows, and wrestling in a deadly conflict, what a revelation of the enormity of sin! The battle-field is at once the product and the type of hell. Such a manifestation of sin is surely hideous enough to make us stand aghast with horror and hate.

III. IT SHOWS GOD'S MASTERY OVER HUMAN ACTIONS. The wicked engage in bloody wars, and thus become the instruments in administering the just penalties of sin ; not to obey the Divine will, but to gratify their own avarice, ambition, malice, and greed. They do not serve Providence *by* their will, but *against* it. God is such a Master of human souls that he "maketh the wrath of man to praise him." It is not optional with man whether he shall serve God or not; serve him he must; the option is whether he shall serve him willingly or unwillingly, as an agent or as an instrument. God links the devil himself to that providential chariot which is bearing on his great purposes to their fulfilment.

CONCLUSION. Two things should be remembered in connection with this subject. 1. That the *wickedness* of nations does not necessarily imply *wickedness* in all their members. There are good men in every nation under heaven, even in the worst. There are Noahs, Lots, Daniels, Jobs, amongst the corruptest people. 2. That the *ruin* of nations does not necessarily imply the *ruin* of all their members. Nations are but assemblages of individuals—abstractions, nothing more. They have no future existence; there is no Egypt, Persia, Assyria, Babylon, Greece, Rome, Germany, Italy, England, etc., in eternity. Nor are there any Churches there, Papal or Protestant, Conformist or Nonconformist. "Public bodies and communities of men, as such, can only be rewarded and punished in this world. This world is the only season for national punishments."

> " The individual culprit may sometimes
> Unpunished to his after-reckoning go.
> Not thus collective man; for public crimes
> Draw on their proper punishment below :
> When nations go astray, from age to age
> The effects remain, a fatal heritage."
> (R. Southey.)

D. T.

EXPOSITION.

CHAPTER III.

Vers. 1—19.—Part III. THE CAUSE OF THE JUDGMENT—THE SINS OF THE CITY, WHICH BRING INEVITABLE PUNISHMENT.

Vers. 1—7.—§ 1. *The prophet specifies the crimes which have brought this ruin upon Nineveh.*

Ver. 1.—The bloody city; literally, *city of bloods*, where blood is shed without scruple (comp. Ezek. xxiv. 6, 9; Hab. ii. 12). The cruelty of the Assyrians is attested by the monuments, in which we see or read how prisoners were impaled alive, flayed, beheaded, dragged to death with ropes passed through rings in their lips, blinded by the king's own hand, hung up by hands or feet to die in slow torture (see Bonomi, pp. 168, etc., 190, etc., 225). Others have their brains beaten out, or their tongues torn out by the roots, while the bleeding heads of the slain are tied round the necks of the living, who are reserved for further torture (Layard, 'Nineveh and Babylon,' p. 456 ; Rawlinson, 'Ancient Monarchies,' ii. 503, etc., edit. 1864). The royal inscriptions recount with exultation the number of the enemies slain and of captives carried away, cities levelled with the ground, plundered, and burnt, lands devastated, fruit trees destroyed, etc. **It is all full of lies**; ὅλη ψευδής, "all lie" (Septuagint). The Assyrians used treachery in furthering their conquests, made promises which they never kept, to induce nations to submit to their yoke. Such, doubtless, were those of Rabshakeh (Isa. xxxvi. 16). Rawlinson, " Falsehood and treachery . . . are often employed by the strong, as furnishing short cuts to success, and even, where the moral standard is low, as being in themselves creditable (see Thucyd., iii. 83). It certainly was not necessity which made the Assyrians covenant-breakers; it seems to have been in part the wantonness of power—because they 'despised the cities, and regarded no man' (Isa. xxxiii. 8); perhaps it was in part also their imperfect moral perception, which may have failed to draw the proper distinction between craft and cleverness" ('Ancient Monarchies,' i. 305). **Robbery**; rather, *rapine*, or *rending in pieces*. The figure applies to the way in which a wild beast kills its prey by tearing it to pieces. So the three crimes of Nineveh here enumerated are bloodshed, deceit, and violence. In the uncertainty concerning the word (*pereq*) rendered "robbery," which only occurs in Obad. 14, where it means "crossway," the LXX. translates, ἀδικίας πλήρης, "full of unrighteousness." The Vulgate is correct, *dilaceratione plena.* **The prey departeth not.** They go on in the same way, gathering spoil into the city, never ceasing from this crime. The monuments continually record the booty that was brought to Nineveh (see, for instance, the 'Annals of Assurbanipal,' *passim;* 'Records of the Past,' vol. ix.; Schrader,

'Keilinschr.,' 195, etc., 216, 233, etc.; comp. Isa. xxxiii. 1). Septuagint, Οὐ ψηλαφηθήσεται θήρα, which gives a sense contradictory to the text, "Prey shall not be handled."

Ver. 2.—The noise of a whip. The prophet describes the advance of the investing army. He hears the cracking of the whips of the charioteers, and the rattling of the wheels of the chariots, and the galloping horses, and the chariots bounding over the plain. Probably all the expressions in this verse refer to chariots and to horses yoked to them, which varied in number from one to three. The whip was a simple thong attached to a short handle. Comp. Virg., 'Georg.,' iii. 106, etc.—

". . . illi instant verbere torto
Et proni dant lora ; volat vi fervidus axis ;
Jamque humiles, jamque elati sublime videntur
Aera per vacuum ferri, atque adsurgere in auras."

Ver. 3.—The horseman lifteth up. The Hebrew is more vivid, the words standing in pairs, as if describing the successive onsets of the enemy. So Pusey. It is best to render, "horsemen making to rear ;" or as Septuagint, ἱππέως ἀναβαίνοντος, "horseman mounting ;" so the Vulgate ; Henderson. Horsemen are seen in the most ancient sculptures of Nimroud, and in the bas-reliefs of Kouyunjik (comp. Judith ii. 15 ; Ezek. xxiii. 6 ; Layard, 'Nineveh,' ii. 356). **Both the bright sword ;** better, *and the flaming sword* (Gen. iii. 24) ; literally, *the flame of the sword*. **And the glittering spear ;** literally, *the lightning flash of the spear* (Hab. iii. 11). These are the arms of the foot-soldiers. **A multitude of slain.** The effect of the assault is described. So numerous are the corpses that one cannot help stumbling over them ; the invaders themselves are impeded by the heaps of dead bodies which they have to mount. The LXX. connects this verse with the following, thus : "They shall grow weak in their bodies by reason of the multitude of their fornications."

Ver. 4.—The cause is given that has brought this punishment. **Because of the multitude of the whoredoms.** This term is commonly applied to idolatry, the swerving from the true God and turning to false deities ; and it is thought that it cannot be used in that sense here, as Assyria had always worshipped idols, and could not be said to have forsaken or proved false to the Lord. Hence Hitzig, Keil, and others refer the term to the treacherous friendship and crafty politics by which Nineveh ensnared other states, seeking really only her own interests (comp. Isa. xxiii. 17). But this habit of treachery has been already mentioned in ver. 1 (where see note) ; and, as

Knabenbauer remarks, the Assyrians used no meretricious blandishments to effect their conquests, but the cruel arts of war and the stern ordeal of the sword. It is scarcely probable that the prophet would omit idolatry among the crimes of the Assyrians that called for vengeance, as all their wars were carried on in the name of their gods, and the monarchs professed to be under Divine protection and influence. The term "whoredom" is applied to the idolatry, not only of the Israelites, but to that of Jezebel (2 Kings ix. 22), who was always a heathen. The idolatry of the Assyrians may very well be so called, because it was a wilful ignoring of the light of nature and natural religion (see Wisd. xiii. 1 ; Rom. i. 19, etc.). They were careful, too, wherever they carried their arms, to erect there symbols of their deities, and to compel conquered nations to receive them and pay them Divine honour. With this idolatrous worship was associated that gross immorality which even Herodotus (i. 199) termed utterly disgraceful (comp. Baruch vi. 43). Rightly is Nineveh called the well-favoured harlot ; for her splendour and magnificence were unsurpassed, dazzling all beholders and hiding the rottenness that lay below the surface. **The mistress of witchcrafts.** She was skilful in employing every art to seduce nations to her side. We hear much of magic in connection with Babylon and the Chaldeans, but not in reference especially to Assyria. The expression here is metaphorical, alluding to the secret practices which she employed to gain her ends and to make her rule attractive (comp. Rev. xviii. 2, 3). **That selleth nations.** Depriving them of freedom and making them tributary, or, in some cases, actually selling the inhabitants as slaves (comp. Deut. xxxii. 30 ; Judg. ii. 14 ; Joel iii. 3 ; Amos i. 6, 7). **Families.** Not only nations in the aggregate, but smaller bodies, individuals, so that none escape. Septuagint, λαούς, "peoples."

Ver. 5.—I am against thee (see note on ch. ii. 13). The Lord will punish Nineveh with the utmost ignominy, treating her ("the whore," ver. 4) like a harlot or adulteress. **Thy skirts.** The borders of the long flowing dress which added to her pomp (comp. Isa. xlvii. 2, etc. ; Jer. xiii. 26 ; Lam. i. 8). **Upon** (*before*) **thy face.** So that thou mayst know thine own shame. **I will show the nations.** All men shall see what thou really art, like an adulteress haled before the congregation.

Ver. 6.— The metaphor is continued. Nineveh shall be like a vile woman exposed to the insults and ill treatment of the rabble (comp. Ezek. xvi. 37, etc.). **A gazing-stock.** That all may see thee and take warning. LXX., εἰς παράδειγμα, "for

a public example," which recalls Matt. i.
19.

Ver. 7.—**Shall flee from thee.** As an object
of disgust, or fearing to be involved in thy
ruin (Rev. xviii. 10, 15). **Who will bemoan
her?** No one will pity her for her well-
deserved chastisement (Jer. xv. 5). **Whence
shall I seek**, etc.? Truly, nowhere in all
the world (comp. Isa. li. 19).

Vers. 8—13.—§ 2. *The ruin of Nineveh
can be averted no more than was that of
No-Amon.*

Ver. 8.—**Art thou better than populous
No?** " Better " probably means here more
prosperous. " Populous No " ought to be
rendered, *No-Amon*, i.e. No of the solar
god Amon. This is the celebrated Thebes,
in Upper Egypt, called in Egyptian Pa-
Amun, " the House of Amun," and in the
inscriptions Ni, which is the same word as
No. The name Amon is attached because
that god was particularly worshipped there.
The LXX. has, μερίδα Ἀμμών (" a portion of
or for Ammon "), translating the word "No."
St. Jerome, misled by his Hebrew teacher,
renders, " Alexandria populorum," as if
Thebes stood on the site of the much later
city of Alexandria; whereas we see from
Assurbanipal's annals that he was forty
days marching from Memphis, where he defeated Rudammon, to Thebes (see G. Smith,
'Assurbanipal,' p. 55). On the grandeur and
magnificence of this city, Denon (quoted by
Rawlinson, 'Ancient Monarchies,' i. 309,
note 7), writes, " On est fatigué d'écrire, on
est fatigué de lire, on est épouvanté de la
pensée d'une telle conception; on ne peut
croire, même après l'avoir vu, à la réalité de
l'existence de tant de constructions réunies
sur un même point, à leurs dimensions, à la
constance obstinée qu'a exigée leur fabrica-
tion, aux dépenses incalculables de tant de
somptuosité" ('Egypte,' ii. 226). " In the
long and rich valley of the Lower Nile, which
extends above five hundred miles from Syene
to Memphis, almost any situation might
furnish a site for a great city, since, except
at Silsilis and at the Gebeleïn, the valley
is never less than two miles wide, the soil is
always fertile, good quarries are always at
hand, and lavish Nature is so bounteous with
her gifts that abundant sustenance can at
any point be obtained for a large population.
But in this wealth of eligible sites, there
are still degrees of eligibility—spots which
Nature has distinguished by special favour,
and, as it were, marked out for greatness and
celebrity. Such a position is that which
the traveller reaches when, passing through
the gorge of the Gebeleïn, he emerges upon
the magnificent plain, at least ten miles in
width, through which the river flows with
a course from south-west to north-east for a

distance of some forty miles between Erment
and Qobt. Here, for the first time since
quitting the Nubian desert, does the Nile
enter upon a wide and ample space. On
either side the hills recede, and a broad
green plain, an alluvium of the richest description, spreads itself out on both banks of
the stream, dotted with *dom* and date palms,
sometimes growing singly, sometimes collected into clumps or groves. Here, too,
there open out on either side, to the east
and to the west, lines of route offering great
advantages for trade, on the one hand with
the Lesser Oasis and so with the tribes of
the African interior, on the other with the
western coast of the Red Sea and the spice
region of the opposite shore. In the valley
of Hammamât, down which passed the
ancient route to the coast, are abundant
supplies of *breccia verde* and of other valuable
and rare kinds of stone, while at no great
distance to the right and left of the route lie
mines of gold, silver, and lead, anciently
prolific, though exhausted now for many
ages. Somewhat more remote, yet readily
accessible by a frequented route, was the
emerald region of Gebel Zabara, where the
mines are still worked" (Rawlinson, 'Ancient
Egypt,' ii. 124, etc.). Thebes was situated
on both banks of the Nile, the principal
portion lying on the east; the Necropolis
and Memnonia were on the west. It seems
never to have been surrounded with a wall
(notwithstanding its " hundred gates "), the
river and canals forming a sufficient defence.
At the present time the ruins are some
twenty-seven **miles** in circuit, including
Luxor and the remains of the great temple
at Karnak. **The sea.** The Nile formed its
rampart. Great rivers are called seas in the
poetical books. Thus Isa. xix. 5; xxvii.
1; Jer. li. 36. **Her wall was from the sea;**
or, *of the sea.* The sea was her wall. Septuagint, ὕδωρ τὰ τείχη αὐτῆς, "water her
walls."

Ver. 9.—**Ethiopia and Egypt** were **her
strength.** Urdamaneh, or Rudammon, in
whose time this capture of No-Amon took
place, was son and successor of Tirhakah,
who is called expressly King of Ethiopia
(2 Kings xix. 9; Isa. xxxvii. 9). *Egypt.*
The Egyptians proper, combined with the
Ethiopians, formed the kingdom of Egypt
under the twenty-fifth, the Ethiopian
dynasty. **And it was infinite.** The power
of Egypt was boundless, its forces innumerable (see 2 Chron. xii. 3). Pusey
notes a remark of Cato (in Steph. Byzant.
ap. Boch., iv. 27) that the Egyptians connected with Thebes amounted to seven
millions. In Isa. xviii.—xx. Ethiopia and
Egypt are represented as combined against
Assyria, and conquered by it (Wordsworth).
Septuagint, Οὐκ ἔστη πέρας τῆς φυγῆς,

"There was no limit of the flight." This is thought by Jerome to be connected with the previous verses, and to refer to Nineveh. **Put and Lubim were thy helpers.** No-Amon is here suddenly addressed. Put, or Punt, designates either a part of Arabia or that part of the coast of Egypt opposite to it (see Ebers, ' Ægypt. und die Büch. Mos.,' p. 64, etc.). Lubim are the Lybians, dwelling on the west of the Canopic mouth of the Nile. Thus the enumeration of the forces of Thebes is regularly arranged, beginning with the south, Ethiopia, then through Egypt proper to the north, and then to the provinces on the east and west (Knabenbauer). The Vulgate translates the two terms, *Africa et Libya.* The LXX. combines them in one, Λίβυες. These peoples are named together elsewhere: *e.g.* Jer. xlvi. 9; Ezek. xxvii. 10; xxx. 5; xxxviii. 5.

Ver. 10.—**Yet was she carried away.** In spite of her strong position and infinite resources, Thebes was captured and despoiled; and shall Nineveh fare better? Surely not. This capture of Thebes took place B.C. 664, and must have been in men's minds when Nahum wrote his prophecy. The Assyrians twice took Thebes in the days of Assurbanipal. The first time it is merely recorded that the soldiers, under the commander of the satraps, made a slaughter in the city. The second capture is thus described in the monarch's own tablet (Brugsch, ' Egypt,' i. 272—275, Eng. transl.): "Urdamaneh fled alone, and entered Thebes, the city of his kingdom . . . I directed my march in pursuit of him. I came to Thebes. He saw the strength of my army, and left Thebes, and fled to the city of Kipkip. Of that whole city (Thebes), with thanksgiving to Asur and Istar, my hands took the complete possession. Silver, gold, metals, stones, all the treasures of its palace whatsoever, dyed garments of berom and linen, great horses [elephants?] men and women, great and small, works of zakah [basalt?] and marble, their kelal and manzas, the gates of their palace . . . I tore away and carried to Assyria. I made spoil of the animals of the land without number, and carried them forth in the midst out of Thebes. I caused a catalogue to be made of the spoil. I returned in safety to Nineveh " (see a different version in G. Smith, ' Assurbanipal,' p. 52, etc.). **Were dashed in pieces.** The prophet describes the usual treatment of captured cities (comp. 2 Kings viii. 12; Ps. cxxxvii. 9; Isa. xiii 16). **At the top of all the streets.** In the most public places, where many streets converge (Lam. ii. 19). **Cast lots.** The victors divided the nobles among themselves by lot (see note on Obad. 11). **Were bound in chains.** We find in the Assyrian

monuments delineations of captives with their arms bound together by a rope held by a soldier, sometimes men, sometimes women and children; the women are tearing their hair in despair (see Bonomi, ' Nineveh and its Palaces,' pp. 226, 277). In a bas-relief at Khorsabad captives are led by a rope fastened to a ring in the lip (comp. 2 Kings xix. 28; see Rawlinson, ' Anc. Mon.,' i. 304; Layard, ' Nineveh,' fig. 60, and vol. i. p. 376).

Ver. 11.—**Thou also shalt be drunken.** Nahum makes the application: The fate of Thebes shall be thine, O Nineveh. Thou shalt drink to the full the cup of God's wrath (see note on Obad. 16; and comp. Jer. xxv. 15, 17, 27). The metaphor indicates the effect of some overwhelming calamity that makes men reel with terror or stupefies them with amazement. **Thou shalt be hid;** *thou shalt be powerless,* or *reduced to nothing;* Ἔση ὑπερεωραμένη, "Thou shalt be despised"(Septuagint); *Eris despecta* (Vulgate). Nineveh, which was taken and destroyed between B.C. 626 and 608, was so effectually " hidden " that its very site was discovered only in late years, and its monuments have only been partially disinterred after immense labour. **Thou also shalt seek strength because of the enemy;** or, *thou also shalt seek a stronghold from the enemy.* As the Egyptians fled for refuge from one place to another (see note on ver. 10), so shall the Assyrians attempt in vain to escape the enemy. History records that they endeavoured to effect a retreat from Nineveh during the siege (see Introduction, § I.).

Ver. 12.—Shall be like (*are*) **fig trees with the first-ripe figs.** The Assyrians' fortresses are as ready for destruction and as easy to destroy as ripe figs are ready to fall from the tree at the least shake of the eater (Isa. xxviii. 4).

Ver. 13.—The reason why the fortresses are so readily taken is now given. **Are women.** The Assyrians were essentially a brave nation, but they should be now no more able to resist the enemy than if they were women (comp. Isa. xix. 16; Jer. l. 37; li. 30). **The gates of thy land.** The various approaches and passes which lead into Assyria (comp. Jer. xv. 7; Micah v. 6). So Strabo (xi. 12. 13) speaks of certain mountain passes as "the Caspian gates," and Xenophon (' Anab.,' i. 4. 4) mentions " the gates of Cilicia and Syria." The famous defile that led into Greece was called Thermopylæ. The **fire shall devour thy bars.** Hitzig, Keil, and others take the " bars " metaphorically, meaning the forts and castles which defend the passes; but the literal sense is the most natural, as in the parallel passage, Jer. li. 30 (see note on Amos i. 5). It was the Assyrians' custom to set fire to the gates of any city that they attacked (see Bonomi, 'Nineveh and its Palaces,' pp. 178, 185, 192). "It is incontestable," says Bonomi, in another place, "that, during the excavations, a considerable quantity of charcoal, and even pieces of wood either half-burnt or in a perfect state of preservation, were found in many places. The lining of the chambers also bears certain marks of the action of fire. All these things can be explained only by supposing the fall of a burning roof, which calcined the slabs of gypsum, and converted them into dust. . . . It must have been a violent and prolonged fire to be able to calcine not only a few places, but every part of these slabs, which were ten feet high and several inches thick. So complete a decomposition can be attributed but to intense heat" (ibid., p. 213).

Vers. 14—19.—§ 3. *In spite of all its efforts and all its resources, Nineveh shall meet with a terrible end.*

Ver. 14.—Nahum ironically bids the Ninevites prepare for the siege they were about to sustain. **Draw thee waters for the siege.** The drinking water necessary for a long siege is meant. This injunction is not particularly applicable to Nineveh, which from its situation was abundantly supplied with water, unless there was danger that the enemy would divert the courses of the rivers. But the warning would come home with peculiar force to the inhabitants of Jerusalem, among whom Nahum prophesied (2 Kings xx. 20; Isa. xxii. 11; xxx. 20). **Fortify thy strong holds;** *strengthen thy fortresses.* Repair all defects in thy defences (2 Chron. xi. 11). The mode of doing this in the Assyrian fashion is then denoted. **Go into clay, and tread the mortar.** The soil round Nineveh was of a tenacious quality; and when moistened with water and kneaded either with feet or hands, with the addition usually of a little chopped straw, was easily formed into bricks. These, even without the aid of fire, became dry and hard in the course of a few days. But it is plain from the investigations of ruins that the Assyrians used both kiln-baked and sun-dried bricks, though the mass of the walls was usually composed of the latter, the more durable material being employed merely as an accessory (see Bonomi, 'Nineveh and its Palaces,' p. 9; Layard, 'Nineveh,' ii. 252). Xenophon, 'Anab.,' iii. 4. 11, speaks of the brick wall (πλίνθινον τεῖχος) of a town he calls Mespila. **Make strong the brick-kiln.** There is an uncertainty about the meaning of the last word (*malben*), which occurs only in two other places (2 Sam. xii. 31 and Jer. xliii. 9). In the latter passage it may possibly mean "a square" or "open quadrangle." Jerome has, *tene la-*

terem; the LXX., κατακράτησον ὑπὲρ πλίνθον, "make them strong above (equivalent to 'stronger than') brick," connecting it with the following verse. Some translate it, "brick-mould." If the Anglican Version is correct, the prophet bids them repair their kilns, unused in the days of prosperity, when they had no need to look to the security of their walls. Virtually the same sense is elicited by rendering, "lay hold of the brick-mould."

Ver. 15.—**There.** In the very place where thou hast taken all these precautions. **Shall the fire devour thee.** That fire played a great part in the destruction of Nineveh is asserted by historians and proved by the remains of the city discovered in modern times (see note on ver. 13; also Herod., i. 106; Diod. Sic., ii. 25—28; Athen., xii. 529). The fate of the last king, who burnt himself and his palace, is a well-known story (see Justin, 'Hist.,' i. 3; Eusebius, 'Chron.,' i. 9; xiv. 3; xv. 7; Syncell., 'Chron.,' i. 396, edit. Dind.) (Knabenbauer). **The sword shall cut thee off.** While fire destroys the buildings, the sword shall devour the inhabitants of the city. **The cankerworm;** literally, *the licker* (Joel i. 4). The locust in its earlier stage is thus described (see ver. 16). The figure implies that the destruction of Nineveh should be sudden and complete, as that wrought on vegetation by an inroad of locusts. **Make thyself many.** Collect thine armies, gather hosts as innumerable as the locusts, it will be all in vain. The "cankerworm" represented the enemy; the "locusts" represent the Assyrians themselves.

Ver. 16.—Its extensive commercial relations shall not save it. **Thou hast multiplied thy merchants.** Nineveh was most favourably situated for carrying on commerce with other countries. The roads from Asia Minor, Syria, Egypt, and Phœnicia, that led into Media, Persia, and the interior of Asia, converged at Nineveh, and brought thither merchandise from all lands; and the Assyrians themselves exported their own produce and manufactures to the far West. Among these are enumerated textile fabrics, carpets, dyed attire, and embroidered work, carvings in ivory, gems, spices (see Rawlinson, 'Anc. Mon.,' ii. 179, etc.; Layard, 'Nineveh,' ii. 414, etc.). **The cankerworm spoileth;** or, *spreadeth itself* for plunder; Vulgate, *expansus est;* Septuagint, ὥρμησεν, "attacked." The cankerworm (see note on ver. 15) are the enemy, who spread themselves over the rich produce of Nineveh, and then **flee away** laden with spoil. Pusey makes the cankerworm represent Nineveh. She spread herself everywhere wasting and plundering, and now she is gone, has disappeared. But the former explanation better suits the comparison in ver. 15, where "the licker" is the enemy; and it is most natural that the prophet should allude to the fate of that commercial wealth which he has just mentioned, as in previous verses he contrasts the riches and power of Nineveh with the ruin that awaits them.

Ver. 17.—**Thy crowned.** The word *minnezar* is found only here, and, as its derivation is uncertain, it has received various interpretations. The Anglican Version derives the word from *nezer*, "a diadem," and "the crowned" are the officials of upper rank. "High officers of state in Assyria were adorned with diadems, closely resembling the lower band of the royal mitre, separated from the cap itself. Very commonly the head was encircled with a simple fillet or hoop, probably of gold, without any adornment" (Gosse, 'Assyria,' p.463, quoted by Strauss; see the figures in Bonomi, p. 319). Others derive it from *nazar*, "to separate," in the signification of "those separated or selected for war." Septuagint, ὁ συμμικτός σου: i.e. the band of mixed mercenary troops—a rendering in which Wordsworth acquiesces. Knabenbauer (referring to Strassmaier's Assyrian vocabulary) considers the word to be a transliteration (*ss* being resolved into *ne*) of the Assyrian *ma-as-sa-ru*, which means "guardian," or some inferior officer. With this agrees the Vulgate *custodes*. **As the locusts;** i.e. in multitude. That the number of captains and superior officers would be very great may be conjectured from the inscriptions which sometimes enumerate the captives carried off from conquered countries. Thus in the account of the capture of some insignificant nation, the then king boasts that he took away 13,000 fighting men, 1121 captains, and 460 superior officers (Strauss, *in loc.*). The prophet's meaning is that if the officers, etc., are so numerous, the multitude of soldiers and civilians must be truly immense. **Thy captains.** *Taphsar* is an Assyrian word, occurring only in Jer. li. 27. It is probably the same as *dupsarru* or *dipsarru* of the inscriptions, and is taken to signify "a scribe" (see Schrader, p. 424). Such officials are often represented on the monuments (see Layard, ii. 184), and seem

sometimes to have been of high or priestly rank. Jerome translates, *parvuli tui*, though in Jeremiah, *loc. cit.*, he retains the Assyrian word. The Septuagint omits it. **Great grasshoppers;** *swarms of locusts* (Amos vii. 1). **Which camp in the hedges in the cold day.** Locusts become torpid in cold weather; so the captains and princes of Nineveh are paralyzed and useless in the day of calamity. **They flee away.** Thus the Assyrian army perishes and leaves no trace behind. The LXX. adds, "Woe unto them!"

Ver. 18.—**Thy shepherds.** The princes and counsellors, on whom the safety of the state depends. **Slumber.** Sleep the sleep of death—slain in the war (Ps. lxxvi. 6). **O King of Assyria.** The power and evil of Nineveh personified, not any particular king. **Shall dwell in the dust;** *are lying*, or *are at rest*, in death; Septuagint, Ἐκοίμισε τοὺς δυνάστας σου, "Put to sleep thy mighty men" (comp. Euripides, 'Hec.,' 473, where κοιμίζειν is used in the sense of "to slay"); Vulgate, *sepelientur*. **Is scattered upon the mountains.** Their shepherds being dead, the flock, the herd of common people, is scattered abroad and perishes, because **no man gathereth them**—there is no one to collect them. "The mountains" referred to are those which shut in Assyria on the north.

Ver. 19.—**There is no healing of thy bruise;** *there is no assuaging of thy hurt* (Revised Version; Jer. x. 19). The ruin is irretrievable; no one shall restore the destroyed kingdom (see Zeph. ii. 13, 14). **Thy wound is grievous;** *Pessima est plaga tua* (Vulgate); Ἐφλέγμανεν ἡ πληγή σου, "Thy wound is inflamed." The "wound" is the stroke or plague inflicted by God (Lev. xxvi. 21). **Shall clap the hands over thee.** All who hear of thy destruction will rejoice over it (Ps. xlvii. 1; Lam. ii. 15). **Thy wickedness.** The cruelty and oppression of Nineveh have been universally felt. If Edom is the type of insidious foes of the Church's own household, Nineveh is the emblem of open, blaspheming infidelity, arrayed in powerful opposition against God's people. In the overthrow of this kingdom there is a prophecy of the destruction of all anti-Christian powers, which shall be utterly crushed in the latter days.

HOMILETICS.

Vers. 1—7.—*Woe to Nineveh.* I. THREATENED. (Ver. 1.) 1. *By the prophet.* Jonah (iii. 4) had once before announced the destruction of the Assyrian capital, which threatening, however, was averted by the repentance of its inhabitants; Nahum's prediction was literally fulfilled, because Nineveh in due time filled up the measure of its iniquities. 2. *In the name of God.* Had Nineveh's doom been pronounced only by Nahum's lips, it had been harmless; but Nahum was the mouthpiece of Jehovah, who already had declared himself against the great and wicked city (ch. ii. 13), and a second time repeats the fact, "Behold, I am against thee, saith the Lord of hosts" (ver. 5). There is a wide difference between God's threatenings and man's.

II. DEPICTED. (Vers. 2, 3.) 1. *The advance of a hostile force.* "The noise of the whip [of charioteers urging on their steeds], and the noise of the rattling of wheels [of war-chariots in motion], and prancing horses [*i.e.* horses leaping up and starting forward as they feel the spurs dug into their sides], and jumping chariots [*i.e.* springing up as they dash along the rugged ground]." 2. *The attack upon the city.* "The horseman mounting [or, 'charging,' *i.e.* causing his steed to leap up and advance against the city]; and the flashing sword and the glittering spear; " rather than " the horseman lifteth up the bright sword and the glittering spear" (Authorized Version). 3. *The appearance after battle.* "A multitude of slain, and a great heap of carcases." So numerous, indeed, are the fallen, that "there is none end of the corpses, and they," the Medo-Babylonian invaders, "stumble upon their corpses," *i.e.* the dead bodies of the Assyrians.

III. JUSTIFIED. (Vers. 1, 4.) By the character of Nineveh. 1. *A city of blood;* literally, " of bloods," *i.e.* of bloodshed or murder, alluding to the barbarous and inhuman character of her warfare. 2. *A city of deceit.* Referring to the vain promises of protection with which she beguiled the nations to put their trust in her—promises which she never kept any more than did Egypt. 3. *A city of oppression.* "The prey departeth not." She is never done rending in pieces and tearing some nation or people. 4. *A city of seductions.* A city of witchcrafts, the prophet comparing her brilliance and prosperity, by which she fascinated surrounding powers and secretly drew them to seek her favour, to the grace and beauty with which a harlot attracts and bewitches passers-by.

IV. EMPHASIZED. (Vers. 5, 6.) By Jehovah, who declares that her doom will be : 1. *Certain ;* since he, Jehovah, is against her : " Behold, I am against thee, saith the Lord of hosts." 2. *Shameful ;* since he will treat her, not as a chaste matron, but as a polluted harlot, whose skirts are thrown above her head, that her person may be exposed (Isa. xlvii. 3; Jer. xiii. 22; Ezek. xvi. 37—41; Hos. ii. 3). 3. *Visible ;* since he will cause the nations to see her nakedness, and the kingdoms to behold her shame.

V. ATTESTED. (Ver. 7.) By two things. 1. *The horror of the nations.* "It shall come to pass that all they that look upon thee shall flee from thee." Not so much in disgust (Keil) as in terror (Ezek. xxxi. 16); cf. the effect produced by the fall of Tyre (Ezek. xxvi. 21; xxvii. 35), and of the mystical Babylon (Rev. xviii. 10). 2. *The absence of helpers.* Her fate was so richly deserved that no one interposed to ward off the stroke. In her hour of sorrow no one bewailed her; in her moment of weakness no one assisted her (Isa. li. 19).

Learn: 1. That greater woes have been pronounced against sinners in general than were uttered against Nineveh—read the woes of Christ in the Gospels (Matt. xxiii. 13, 14, 15, etc.; xxvi. 24; Luke vi. 24, 25, 26; xi. 42, 46). 2. That these woes will no more fail in their fulfilment than did those directed against Nineveh. God's word never returns to him void (Isa. lv. 11). 3. That God's judgments upon the wicked will eventually vindicate themselves in all men's eyes as just. "Salvation and honour and power," etc. (Rev. xix. 1, 2).

Vers. 8—13.—*The story of No-Amon.* I. THE BRILLIANT CITY. 1. *Its sacred name.* No-Amon, in Egyptian, *Nu-Amun,* or "Dwelling of Amun ;" in Greek, Θῆβαι, or Thebes, with which corresponded the Egyptian *Ta-ape,* or "City of Thrones." Originally the capital of a nome, it subsequently rose to be a royal city. It became the residence of the Theban dynasty of Pharaohs. Homer describes it as having had a hundred gates ('Iliad,' ix. 383). 2. *Its impregnable situation.* "Among the rivers [or, 'canals']." " In all the long course of the Nile there is no site that can compare with that of Thebes," writes Stanley Leathes. At Thebes "the mountains (Libyan and Arabian) open out a great amphitheatre, such as a king would choose to build his capital therein." " Nothing more lovely than this great amphitheatre, with its border of yellow sand and rampart of cliffs, can be seen in all the land of Egypt" ('Picturesque Palestine,' etc., iv. 190, 191). With the Nile running through, and canals formed round it, the city enjoyed a strong natural position. 3. *Its military strength.* (1) Its native forces, those of Egypt and Ethiopia, were practically numberless. (2) Its foreign auxiliaries, Put and Lubim, or the Libyans in the north of Africa and those contiguous to Egypt, were reliable.

II. THE DISASTROUS OVERTHROW. 1. *Its unexpected occurrence.* "Yet was she carried away." Notwithstanding her regal magnificence and boasted strength, she was captured and destroyed. Of this humiliation of Egypt's proud capital the monuments afford express information. Rudammon, the nephew (son of his sister) and successor of Tirhakah of Egypt, sat upon the throne. In an expedition against Egypt and Ethiopia, Assurbanipal of Assyria (B.C. 665) marched his forces first against Memphis, which Rudammon incontinently left, and then against Thebes, into which the alarmed fugitive had fled to save his life. The Assyrian king thus relates the issue of his campaign : " After Rudammon the road I took ; I went to Thebes, the strong city ; the approach of my powerful army he saw, and Thebes he abandoned, and fled to Kipkip. That city (Thebes), the whole of it, in the service of Assur and Ishtar, my hands took ; silver, gold, precious stones, the furniture of his palace, all there was ; garments costly and beautiful, great horses, people male and female, two lofty obelisks covered with beautiful carvings . . . a hundred talents their weight, set up before the gate of a temple ; with them I removed and brought to Assyria. Its spoils unnumbered I carried off. From the midst of Thebes, over Egypt and Ethiopia, my servants I caused to march, and I acquired glory. With the tributes peacefully I returned to Nineveh, the city of my dominion " (' Records of the Past,' i. 67, 68 ; cf. Schrader, 'Die Keilin-schriften,' p. 449). 2. *Its frightful severity.* In addition to the information supplied by the Assyrian conqueror, the sacred narrative declares that it was accompanied by heart-rending excesses. (1) The population of the gay capital were exiled. "She went into captivity." The deportation of conquered peoples into strange lands was then a customary practice, and seemed the only means that sovereigns like Shalmaneser, Tiglath-Pileser, Assurbanipal, and Nebuchadnezzar had for keeping them in subjection (2 Kings xvii. 6). (2) The young children were ruthlessly massacred—they were " dashed in pieces at the top of all the streets." These were probably butchered to avoid trouble and inconvenience upon the march. This inhuman practice was likewise frequent in ancient warfare (2 Kings viii. 12; Isa. xiii. 16; Hos. xiii. 16). (3) The princes and nobility were degraded. They were parted among their conquerors by " lot " and " bound in chains; " after which they were borne off into slavery.

III. THE PROPHETIC WARNING. The fate of No-Amon will one day overtake Nineveh. 1. *Righteously.* "Thou also shalt be drunken." Nineveh will be made to drink of the cup of Jehovah's wrath on account of her sins (Isa. li. 17, 21 ; Obad. 16). As Jehovah dealt with the Egyptian capital, so will he deal with the Assyrian. "The particle 'also' is here emphatical; it was introduced that the Ninevites might know that they could not possibly escape the punishment which they deserved; for God continues ever like himself " (Calvin). 2. *Resistlessly.* "Thou also shalt seek a stronghold because of [or, 'a defence against'] the enemy." Nineveh would call in vain for allies to help her against the terrible Medo-Babylonian power, as No-Amon had fruitlessly looked to surrounding peoples for aid against Nineveh. 3. *Easily.* "All thy fortresses shall be like fig trees with the first-ripe figs; if they be shaken, they fall into the mouth of the eater." The ramparts of Nineveh will go down at the first touch of the foe. "Hence a useful doctrine may be deduced : whatever strength men may seek for themselves from different quarters, it will wholly vanish away; for neither forts, nor towers, nor ramparts, nor troops of men, nor any kind of contrivances will avail anything; and were there no one to rise against them, they would yet fall of themselves " (Calvin). 4. *Surprisingly.* "Behold, thy people in the midst of thee are women : the gates of thy land are set wide open to thine enemies." The very last thing Nineveh would ever dream of would be that her warriors, hitherto invincible, would become faint-hearted as women, and that her fortresses would be as easily passed through as opened gates. Yet exactly these two things were what should happen to Nineveh. 5. *Utterly.* "The fire hath devoured thy bars," and " thou shalt be hid." Nineveh should perish in flames and pass away as if she had never been, her very site for centuries remaining unknown.

LESSONS. 1. The worthlessness, for nations and cities, as for individuals, of purely material glory. 2. The certain ruin of nations, cities, and individuals who do not build on the only permanent foundation of righteousness. 3. The frequency with which, in the history of nations, no less than of private persons, coming events cast their shadows before.

Vers. 14—19.—*The fall of Nineveh.* I. PREPARATIONS FOR A SIEGE. (Ver. 14.) In anticipation of the impending attack upon their capital, the inhabitants of Nineveh are exhorted by Nahum (ironically) to provide for their safety. 1. *For their sustenance.* This they should do by laying up within their city a plentiful supply of water for drinking, so as to enable them to withstand a prolonged siege. "Draw thee water for the siege." This, in a land like Assyria, would be likely to give way earlier than bread. It is only in seasons of exceptional scarcity arising from long-continued drought, or from such calamities as occur in war, that men come to estimate correctly the value of water. 2. *For their defence.* This, on the other hand, they should do by strengthening their fortresses; for which again they would need an abundant store of bricks. Hence the prophet's exhortation, still satirical in its tone, "Strengthen thy fortresses; go into the clay, and tread the mortar, make strong the brick-kiln." The Assyrians, like the Egyptians, as the monuments attest, prepared their bricks with clay, which they mixed with straw, and sometimes burnt, at other times merely drying them in the sun (Layard, 'Nineveh,' ii. 252); and quantities of these would be required, when the evil day arrived, to repair the breaches that might be made in the walls, or to construct an inner line of defence when the outer should be taken.

II. RESULTS OF THE SIEGE. (Ver. 15.) 1. *The burning of the city.* "There," in the midst of thy fortifications, "the fire shall devour thee." That Nineveh perished by fire is attested equally by ancient writers and by the state of the ruins. 2. *The slaughter of its inhabitants.* "The sword shall cut thee off, it shall devour thee like the cankerworm." The thought is that, even should the people of Nineveh be as numerous as a swarm of locusts, yet should they be swept away as completely as every green blade is swept away by the "cankerworm," or "licker," *i.e.* by the locust (Joel i. 4; ii. 3). 3. *The plundering of its treasures.* "Thou hast multiplied thy merchants above the stars of heaven: the cankerworm or ['licker,' *i.e.* the army of the enemy] spoileth, and flieth away." "As soon as the soldiers entered a captured city they began to plunder, and then hurried away the spoil. They led off the horses, carried forth on their shoulders furniture, and vessels of gold, silver, and other metals; and made prisoners of the inhabitants, who probably became the property of those who seized them" (Layard's 'Nineveh,' ii. 377). That Nineveh was a rich city may be inferred from the spoils she had taken from surrounding nations during her career of conquest, as well as from her favourable position for commerce. The costly produce of India was conveyed through Nineveh and Babylon towards the West (Layard, 'Nineveh,' ii. 414). That Nineveh, who had so often despoiled others, should be herself despoiled was an instance of just retribution. 4. *The annihilation of its army.* "Thy crowned are as the locusts, and thy marshals [or, 'scribes'] as the swarms of grasshoppers which camp in the hedges in the cold day," etc. (ver. 17). Whether the "crowned" ones should be understood as signifying the princes of Nineveh (Calvin, Gesenius, Fausset), or the warriors in general, whom it represents as "levied," "selected," "picked" (Keil); and whether the "marshals" here spoken of should be regarded as "military leaders," and thus as practically synonymous with the "crowned" ones, or as common soldiers, though of a special excellence (Keil);—it is probable that the destruction of the army of Assyria is that which the language is designed to set forth. Though the war-force of Nineveh should be as numerous as the locusts, or as swarms of grasshoppers, which pitch their camps in the walls at nights and in cold weather, yet they would as completely vanish as do these insects when the sun ariseth. 5. *The destruction of its nobility.* "Thy shepherds slumber, O King of Assyria: thy worthies are at rest." Assyria's princes and great men, her "royal counsellors, deputies, and generals" (Keil), should be slain and lie in still death. With grim satire the prophet represents them as having sunk into peaceful slumber after the labours of a long and busy day. Perhaps he intended to recall the scene which had once been witnessed before Jerusalem, when the stout-hearted (of Sennacherib's army) were spoiled, when they "slept their sleep," and "none of the men of might found their hands," when at the rebuke of Jacob's God "both the chariot and horse were cast into a deep sleep" (Ps. lxxvi. 5, 6). 6. *The dispersion of its people ;* i.e. of such of them as had escaped the sword. "Thy people are scattered upon the mountains, and there is none to gather them" (ver. 18). Compare the language of Micaiah to Ahab with reference to the result of the battle of Ramoth-Gilead (1 Kings xxii. 17). 7. *The exultation of the nations.* "All that hear the bruit of thee clap the hands over thee" (ver. 19). Wherever the report of Nineveh's overthrow should penetrate, it would awaken no compassion. As all nations had suffered from her wickedness, so would they rejoice in her humiliation. None would seek to help her or raise her up. Hence her downfall would be final; there would be no assuaging of her hurt; her wound would be grievous, would be dangerously bad, would be incurable.

Learn: 1. That the day of doom can be averted as little by ungodly men as by wicked nations. 2. That the resources of civilization—commerce and gunpowder—are powerless defences against Heaven's artillery. 3. That nothing and no one can upraise what God has overthrown. 4. That God's righteousness in judging the wicked— whether individuals or nations—will ultimately vindicate itself in the eyes of all.

HOMILIES BY VARIOUS AUTHORS.

Vers. 1—7.—*The guilt and ruin of Nineveh.* We have here—
I. A MOURNFUL REVELATION OF NATIONAL GUILT AND DEPRAVITY. (Vers. 1, 4.) The Assyrians are here charged with: 1. *Unrighteous war.* (Ver. 1.) There may be times in a nation's history when war becomes a dire necessity; but all war prompted, not by the desire to defend against unworthy aggression, but by unholy ambition, aggrandizement, lust of conquest and glory, deserves the severest reprobation. And such were the wars of the Assyrians, and which secured to their capital the unenviable appellation here used, "the bloody city," *i.e.* "city of bloods," founded and built up by strife and bloodshed. 2. *Cunning craftiness.* "It is all full of lies" (ver. 1). It gained its unrighteous ends by deceit. Like "the strange woman" (ver. 4), who bedecks herself in showy attire, puts on winsome manners, and resorts to bewitching arts, in order to attract, and then conducts her victim to the very "chambers of death," so Assyria, under show of friendship, brought other powers under her yoke, and effected their overthrow. With cunning craftiness she lay in wait to deceive, so as to enrich herself at the expense of others. 3. *Continuous spoliation.* "It is full of robbery" (ver. 1); "The prey departeth not" (ver. 1). Nineveh was great in barbaric splendour, and abounded in costly treasures; but this was secured by spoils taken in war and by tribute extorted from feebler nations unable to resist her encroachments; by robbery she thus continually made additions to her stores. This iniquity was perpetrated despite professed penitence and reformation resulting from the ministry of Jonah ; and now the cup was full. Hence we have—
II. A SOLEMN DECLARATION OF IMPENDING DIVINE JUDGMENT RESULTING IN NATIONAL RUIN AND SHAME. Observe: 1. *The intimate connection between the sin and the shame.* "Because of," etc. (ver. 4). The war so graphically described (vers. 2, 3) was declared by the prophet as the outcome of the national guilt. 2. *The marked retributive nature of the Divine judgment.* (1) Assyria had delighted in war: by war she should fall (vers. 2, 3). (2) She had practised deceit: her real character should be exposed to her confusion and disgrace (ver. 5). (3) She had triumphed over other nations, and in her victory had shown no consideration towards the vanquished: she should herself now be humiliated, and be made a gazing-stock (ver. 6). (4) She had blasphemed the God of Israel: now he would be against her, and would bring all this ruin upon her (vers. 5, 6). 3. *The entire absence of sympathy towards her in her reverses.* (Ver. 7.) No regret should be felt at her fall. No sympathy should be expressed. From her shades men should flee (ver. 7). She should be thought of only as a beacon and a warning—"to point a moral." She should be utterly "desolate"— "cut off" and "laid waste" (ver. 7). This is the end of evil-doing (Job xviii. 17; xxvii. 23; Prov. x. 7; Eccles. viii. 10; Jer. xvii. 13).—S. D. H.

Vers. 8—13.—*No-Amon, a sign.* There are certain great principles regulating the Divine government, and these are abiding. The seer spoke in harmony with these when he declared beforehand the ruin of Nineveh. Men, through unbelief, are slow to accept these principles and to acknowledge the inevitable results of their working. They are deceived by *present appearances.* They reason from things as they are, and conclude that, where there is material prosperity, this will of necessity continue. Such was the difficulty with which Nahum had to contend. Assyria in his day was the dominant power, acknowledged and, on account of its tyranny and ambition, dreaded by all. How, then, could the Hebrews credit the announcements of this prophet? Nahum felt their difficulty, and hence, in enforcing his teaching, he wisely turned from the future to the past, and, by referring to what God had done, he indicated what might yet be expected. He appealed to No-Amon as a sign. Consider—

I. No-Amon a sign to the people of Judah concerning Nineveh. By "No" (ver. 8) is intended the renowned city of Thebes, the capital of Upper Egypt, called No-Amon, from the idol Ammon enshrined there and represented in the Egyptian monuments by a ram or by a man seated on a chair and with a ram's head. The sign thus chosen by the prophet by way of enforcing his teaching was singularly appropriate. Could Nineveh boast of remarkable natural advantages? So could No-Amon (ver. 8). "It was situate among the rivers," etc. It was surrounded by the Nile and its canals (rhetorically here called "the sea," and actually so called still by the Bedouins), and which served as a natural fortification or bulwark. Could Nineveh pride herself in the multitude of her hosts ready to do her bidding? So could No-Amon. In this respect "her strength was infinite" (ver. 9). Cato computed the number of Egyptians connected with Thebes at seven millions. Could Nineveh glory in her foreign alliances? So could No-Amon (ver. 9). Yet despite all these advantages, No-Amon suffered defeat, and experienced the cruelties attendant thereon (ver. 10). The reference is not to the complete destruction of No-Amon (which was mainly effected by Cambyses, B.C. 525, and entirely completed by Ptolemy Lathyrus, B.C. 81), but to the expedition of Sargon against Egypt (Isa. xx. 3, 4), B.C. 714. Profane history gives no record of this; but the inscriptions on the monuments found in the palace at Khorsabad, built by Sargon, mention Egypt in connection with the wars of that king, and, when clearly deciphered, appear likely to strikingly confirm the scriptural representations (see Spiegel's 'Nineveh and Assyria' in Herzog's 'Cyclopædia'). And as No-Amon, despite her resources, suffered at the hands of Assyria, so in the time to come should Assyria, notwithstanding her present glory, suffer through the foes who should rise up against her. Complete destruction should overtake her, and the records of her past triumphs and glories lie hidden under the mounds (ver. 11). No power enabling her to withstand the enemy should be available (ver. 11). Her strongholds when assailed should prove like fig trees with the first-ripe figs, which fall without effort on his part into the eater's mouth (ver. 12). Her proud warriors should be in her midst as weak and timid women, their hearts failing them for terror. Her gates should be thrown wide open, and their bolts consumed by fire (ver. 13).

II. No-Amon and Nineveh a sign to modern nations. No-Amon, which in Nahum's day had only been partially subjugated by the Assyrians, subsequently fell beneath the power of the conqueror, and so "proud Thebes," "the world's great empress on the Egyptian plains," came to nought. Nineveh, too, which in his time was great indeed in worldly glory, has likewise passed away, and is no more seen. Solemn impressions must be excited within the minds of reflecting men when they are privileged to visit the sites of these ancient despotisms, and to gaze upon the relics of departed greatness (see Stanley's 'Sinai and Palestine,' Introd. xxxviii.—xlv.; Wilkinson's 'Ancient Egypt,' iii. 266, 329, 330; Layard's 'Nineveh and its Remains,' i. 6, 7. A voice comes to us from the colossal statues, the decorated palace halls, and the royal tombs of No-Amon; and from the uncovered mounds at Nimroud and Khorsabad, and which seems to say to us: 1. "*The Word of our God shall stand for ever.*" (Isa. xl. 8.) 2. National stability is not secured merely by (1) *strong natural defences;* (2) *influential foreign alliances;* (3) *vast accumulated treasure;* (4) *great military prowess and success.* 3. *Permanent influence, whether for individuals or for nations, has its foundation laid in righteousness and in the fear and love of God.* (Ps. cxliv. 15; lxvii.)—S. D. H.

Vers. 14, 15.—*Human efforts as directed against the Divine purpose.* We have furnished us in these verses an illustration of human effort as directed against the accomplishment of the purpose of God. Sometimes this course is taken by men unconsciously, but it was scarcely so in this instance. We know that the Assyrian power in the time of Sennacherib boldly defied the God of heaven, and it seems with the lapse of time to have gone from bad to worse. It was the Divine will that at length the arm of Assyria should be broken, and that its haughty and oppressive rule should cease; and the prophet here set forth how that, in the day of trial, human strength should do its best in order to avert the destruction divinely intended to be wrought. Some regard ver. 14 as simply indicating the fact that the Assyrian power would maintain a prolonged defence; whilst others view the prophet as speaking ironically, and as mocking the vain endeavours of the defenders of Nineveh, just as Isaiah ridiculed the makers of idols (xliv. 9—20). Be this as it may, he certainly declared here prophetically that human effort should be enlisted against the overthrow divinely purposed, and that this should utterly fail; the fire should devour, and the sword should cut them off; yea, as destructive as the locusts should the instruments of the Divine vengeance prove (ver. 15). We may find all this suggestive as applied to man's hostile action in relation to the Divine working in the spiritual realm.

I. IT IS AN UNDOUBTED FACT THAT HUMAN EFFORT IS DIRECTED AGAINST THE ACCOMPLISHMENT OF THE DIVINE PURPOSE IN GRACE. That purpose is the entire subjugation of evil—the recovery of a lapsed world to allegiance to Heaven, and hence its restoration to holiness and happiness. This benevolent purpose of our God is repeatedly expressed in his Word (Ps. ii. 6; Isa. lii. 10; John xii. 32; Rev. xi. 15). The redemptive plan rests upon it, the unfailing consciousness that he was fulfilling the Divine counsels sustained the Christ as he pressed on with his glorious toil (Heb. xii. 2), and the mighty hope supports his followers in all holy service. Yet such is the aversion of the hearts of men by nature, that against this glorious and loving will of our God human effort has from age to age been directed. The antagonism has taken various forms—persecution, idolatry, scepticism, worldliness; all these forces have been employed in order to bring the counsel of God to nought. Note—

II. THE WEAKNESS OF HUMAN EFFORT AS THUS DIRECTED. So weak, indeed, are such endeavours, that in spite of them the Supreme Ruler sits on the throne of his majesty in perfect repose. He views with calm composure and without even a momentary apprehension and with scornful contempt, this plotting and working of evil-doers (Ps. ii. 4, 5).

III. THE VANITY OF ALL SUCH ENDEAVOURS. They must inevitably prove ineffectual. So has it been, and so shall it be. Monumental pillars were raised to the memory of Diocletian, in that "he had everywhere abolished the superstition of Christ, and had extended the worship of the gods;" yet to-day this "superstition of Christ," as they called it, is everywhere spreading. The crescent shall wane before the cross; and despite the baneful influences of scepticism and worldliness, the Christ shall become enthroned in every heart. "The burial-place of Christianity cannot be pointed out; it is not; for the living have no tomb." Its adversaries may "draw waters for the siege, fortify their strongholds," etc. (ver. 14), but they shall surely be defeated (ver. 15), for "*the Lord God omnipotent reigneth.*"—S. D. H.

Vers. 16—18.—*The instability of material greatness.* We have vividly described here—

I. MATERIAL GREATNESS. This consisting in: 1. *Extensive commercial relations.* "Thou hast multiplied thy merchants," etc. (ver. 16). "The point at which Nineveh was situated was certainly the culminating point of the three quarters of the globe—Europe, Asia, and Africa; and from the very earliest times it was just at the crossing of the Tigris by Nineveh that the great military and commercial roads met which led into the heart of all the leading known lands" (Strauss, quoted by Keil and Delitzsch, 'Commentary on Minor Prophets,' vol. ii. note p. 38). "The lists of plunder or of tribute carried off during the world-empire of Egypt, before it was displaced by Assyria, attest the extensive imports or manufactures of Nineveh; the titles of 'Assyrian nard, Assyrian amomum, Assyrian odours, myrrh, frankincense, involve its trade with the spice countries; domestic manufactures of hers apparently were purple and dark-blue cloaks, embroidery, brocades, and these conveyed in chests of cedar; her metallurgy was on principles recognized now; in one practical point of combining beauty with strength she has ever been copied" (Pusey on 'Nahum,' p. 394). 2. *Vast military resources*. (Ver. 17.) "Thy crowned are as the locusts, and thy captains as the great grasshoppers." By the term here rendered "crowned" some have understood subordinate princes (see Sennacherib's boast, Isa. x. 8), and by "captains" military officers; but it has been urged with force that such interpretations hardly agree with the comparison to locusts, the number of vassal princes and military officers being comparatively small; and that probably the terms are technical for certain classes of the soldiery (Keil and Delitzsch, *in loc.*). The comparison of these to the locusts and grasshoppers indicates the vast hosts of warriors Assyria could command in her expeditions. 3. *Influential counsellors and commanders*. (Ver. 18.) The "shepherds" and "nobles" were the king's counsellors, and the commanders of his armies, the government of the kingdom devolving upon the former, and its defence upon the latter. In all that constitutes the material strength of a people Assyria was great. Notice—

II. THE INSTABILITY OF MATERIAL GREATNESS. The prophet, looking on to the future, declared that these material tokens of greatness would all fail in the day of trial which was inevitably before them. All these outward indications of prosperity and power would then fade away. The merchants, like the cankerworms in the fields, would remain whilst they could secure any gains, but would seek some safe retreat in the time of national calamity (ver. 16). Their military forces should then perish and be no more, even as the locusts with the shining of the sun depart, leaving no trace behind (ver. 17). Their counsellors, too, should sleep the sleep of death (ver. 18), and their commanders lie beneath the dust of the earth (ver. 18). And even so everything that is connected with material glory is unenduring. Seneca related how that one known to him was raised above the inordinate love of the world by the sight of a Roman triumphal procession. When the scene ended he said, "I have seen all this pomp and magnificence put in such order and passing slowly along; yet it is all gone: why should I esteem that which is so momentary?"

"For all that in this world is great and gay
Doth as a vapour vanish and decay."

III. THE HOPELESSNESS OF THOSE WHO HAVE THIS AS THEIR SOLE DEPENDENCE. "Thy people is scattered upon the mountains, and no man gathereth them." Nothing remains in such a case but irretrievable ruin. They only are safe whose repose is placed in the higher and heavenly Source of help. "Put not your trust in princes, nor in the son of man," etc. (Ps. cxlvi. 3—6).—S. D. H.

Ver. 19.—*Hopelessness*. "There is no healing of thy bruise; thy wound is grievous." Nothing can be more distressing than the consciousness of powerlessness in the presence of the deepest human need; to witness from the seashore the wreck, and to be utterly unable to save the shipwrecked mariners; to be sure that some one is in the burning edifice, and yet for it to be impossible to reach him and to bring him out; to stand before an audience alarmed by some needless cry, and to see the rush towards the doors, and to be unequal to checking it; or even to be by the bedside of one in life's youth or manhood's prime, and to hear that disease has, humanly speaking, prematurely seized its victim, and that medical help cannot cure, but only, and that for a time, alleviate. This position is occupied by many an earnest-hearted worker for God and the good of souls, in relation to the moral salvation of men. Nahum sustained it in reference to the Ninevites. He saw in them a people wrecked through the adverse winds and tempests of evil, consumed by the fires of unholy passion, on the mad rush to ruin and death, diseased through and through so that recovery was impossible; and hence, unable to heal, he cried in the sadness of his heart, "There is no healing of thy bruise; thy wound is grievous" (ver. 19). So Isaiah said, "Ye will revolt more and more: the whole head is sick," etc. (i. 5, 6). So still. Note—

I. THIS STATE OF MORAL HOPELESSNESS IS NOT REACHED ALL AT ONCE, BUT IS BROUGHT ABOUT BY DEGREES.

II. IT IS NOT BROUGHT TO PASS THROUGH DIVINE HELP AND STRENGTH BEING UNAVAILABLE.

III. It cannot be excused on the ground of there being a lack of warnings and expostulations.

IV. It is entirely self-caused; the transgressor brings himself into this state of hopelessness; the sinner is his own destroyer. "Take heed lest ye be hardened through the deceitfulness of sin" (Heb. iii. 12, 13).—S. D. H.

Ver. 19.—*The overthrow of evil-doers a source of thankful joy.* "All that hear the bruit of thee shall clap the hands over thee: for upon whom hath not thy wickedness passed continually?" These last words in the Book of Nahum are truly impressive. The messenger closes his brief prophecy in the same tone in which he commenced it, the vengeance of God being still his theme. At the outset he declared the solemn fact; at the end he applies the truth thus announced to the particular case in hand. "The magnificent dirge" forming this third chapter "is one sustained shout of wild exultation that the oppressor has fallen at last. The naked discrowned corpse of the glorious city is cast out to the scorn and disgust of the world. No spark of pity mingles with the prophet's delight. In this storm of indignation and vengeance the spirit of prophecy in the northern kingdom breathes its last. Under this doom Nineveh vanishes from view, to be no more seen till in our day the discovery of her buried remains has given new life to the whole of this portion of sacred history" (Stanley's 'Jewish Church,' ii. 315, 316). The theme suggested by this final utterance of Nahum is *the overthrow of evil-doers a source of thankful joy.* Wherever the report of the fall of Nineveh should reach it should occasion a sense of relief and should excite rapturous delight. "All that hear the bruit of thee shall clap the hands," etc. (ver. 19). This satisfaction, providing it does not arise from revenge, may be amply justified. See this in that—

I. The fall of wrong-doers means a diminution of suffering. It is to this that the prophet specially alludes when he says, "For upon whom hath not thy wickedness passed continually?" meaning that through her guilt she had proved a bitter scourge to all who had come under her influence, and that hence there would be general thanksgiving at her fall in that the tyranny would cease.

II. The fall of wrong-doers means the triumph of righteousness. The true-hearted, as they witness the prevalence of iniquity, and as they see on every hand hollowness and insincerity, treachery and malice, envy and jealousy, slander and calumny, tyranny and oppression, are led ardently to long for the time when sin shall be completely vanquished, and when right shall be victorious; and since the discomfiture of wrong-doers brings on the final triumph, they rejoice in this, though with a chastened joy, thankfulness for the victory of the right being blended with pity for transgressors.

III. The fall of wrong-doers vindicates the Divine rectitude. The honour of their God is very precious to the hearts of the faithful and true. This is often impugned when manifest injustice and wrong seems to pass unpunished. The sceptical appeal to such inequalities, and ask tauntingly, "Where is now thy God?" "Is there a God that judges in the earth?" And when, in the history of men and of nations, God interposes in judgments and vindicates his rectitude, his servants cannot but praise and give thanks.

Note: 1. From the discomfiture and defeat which must eventually be the outcome of evil-doing, God would save men. "He willeth not the death of the sinner." 2. How benevolent the ministry of those who seek men's deliverance from evil! 3. How great the folly of not heeding the call to righteousness given through them! 4. How intense will be the joy of the redeemed Church of God when our poor sin-stricken humanity shall be completely healed, and the full conquest over sin be gained by "the Lord and his Christ"!—S. D. H.

HOMILETICAL INDEX

TO

THE BOOK OF NAHUM

HABAKKUK

EXPOSITION BY

W. J. DEANE

HOMILETICS BY

T. WHITELAW

HOMILIES BY VARIOUS AUTHORS

S. D. HILLMAN   D. THOMAS

THE BOOK OF HABAKKUK

INTRODUCTION

---

§ I. SUBJECT OF THE BOOK

NAHUM had comforted Judah with the assurance that the power of Assyria should be overthrown, though for a time it was permitted to afflict the people of God. Habakkuk warns Judah of another great empire which was commissioned to chastise her backslidings (in spite of the partial reformation under Josiah), but which should itself suffer the vengeance which its iniquities merited. The predicted fate of Nineveh had lulled the Judæans into a false security, so that they forgot the dangers that threatened them, and, though they were no longer guilty of idolatry or selfish luxury, they relapsed into carelessness, forgetfulness of God, and various evil practices. Habakkuk is commissioned to show them that punishment was waiting for them at the hands of the Chaldeans, from whom as yet they had not realized their danger, though Isaiah (xxxix. 6, etc.) had forewarned Hezekiah that his treasures should be carried to Babylon and his sons be servants in the palace of the king. The Chaldeans were hitherto little known in Judæa, and prophecies referring to them made but slight impression on the hearers. It was not, indeed, till Nineveh had fallen that Babylon, long an appanage of Assyria, secured its independence, and entered on its short but brilliant career of conquest. Nabopolassar, who had treacherously joined the Medes and aided in the capture of Nineveh, obtained the hand of the Median king's daughter for his son Nebuchadnezzar, and received, as the reward of his treachery, not only Babylonia itself, but a large portion of the Assyrian territory, including the suzerainty over Syria and Palestine. Thus the way was prepared for the interference of the Chaldeans in Jewish affairs. The overthrow of Pharaoh-Necho, King of Egypt, at Carchemish by Nebuchadnezzar left the Babylonian monarch free to punish the revolt of Jehoiakim, and to continue the hostile measures which culminated in the destruction of Jerusalem and the deportation of the Jews.

The prophecy of Habakkuk is an organic whole, divided into two parts, the first of which is a colloquy between God and the prophet, in which is announced the judgment coming upon Judah through the instrumentality of the Chaldeans; the second is a magnificent ode celebrating the punishment of God's enemies and the salvation of the pious. After announcing his office and mission, the prophet (ch. i.) expostulates with God on the iniquity and corruption which abounded in Judæa, and complains that it has not sooner been checked and the righteous released from suffering at the hands of the wicked. God answers that the day of retribution is at hand, for he commissions the Chaldeans, a fierce, rapacious, warlike nation, to punish the sinful people. Terrified at this account of the Chaldeans, the prophet beseeches the Lord not to punish unto death, and not to involve the good in the fate of the evil, and asks how God, in his holiness, can look calmly on the wickedness of those whom he uses as the instruments of his vengeance. The prophet (ch. ii.) waits for the answer to his expostulation; and God graciously replies, and bids him write the oracle plainly that all may read, because, though the fulfilment may be delayed, it is absolutely certain. The law of his kingdom is that the just shall live by faith; that righteousness has the promise of life and is life, but the proud and evil shall perish. This asserts the doom of the Chaldeans in general terms; and then their fall is announced in more particular form, under five special "woes," arranged strophically, and supposed to be uttered by the nations whom they had oppressed. They are thus denounced for insatiate ambition, covetousness, cruelty, drunkenness, and idolatry. So if the evils among the Jews are about to meet with chastisement, yet destruction awaits the oppressing Chaldeans, and God's justice is confirmed. The psalm that follows (ch. iii.) illustrates and, as it were, recapitulates the substance of the previous portion. Habakkuk professes himself greatly terrified at the judgment announced, and prays the Lord, while carrying out his threat, to remember mercy. Then he depicts the coming of the Lord to judge the world and to bring salvation to the righteous. He describes the theophany wherein God showed his majesty and power, and made the nations and inanimate nature to tremble. He delineates the judgment against the enemies of the Church, first symbolically, by the agitation of material things at the Lord's presence, and then properly, by its effect on the ungodly in this world. And through all runs a stream of consolation in that salvation is promised to the righteous amid the wreck of evil men. He ends the ode by describing the effects of this manifestation on the people of God, viz. fear at the coming chastisement, and hope and joy at the future salvation.

§ II. AUTHOR.

The writer of this book calls himself "Habakkuk the prophet;" and that is all that we are told of him for certain in Holy Scripture. The name signifies "Embracing," and is taken personally to mean either "one who embraces " or " one who is embraced." The latter seems more probable. St. Jerome explains it also in the sense of one who wrestles with God, as Jacob, in prayer. But this sense is not generally allowed, and many commentators assume that the appellation is virtually equivalent to Theophilus, "Beloved of God." The name is written by the LXX. Ἀμβακούμ. Other forms also occur. In the apocryphal addition to Daniel, entitled ' Bel and the Dragon,' a prophet in Jewry, named Habakkuk, carries food to Daniel in the den of lions; and the title of this legend in the Septuagint itself (not in Theodotion) is, " Part of the prophecy of Habakkuk, the son of Jesus, of the tribe of Levi." But the whole account is plainly unhistorical, and its connection with the canonical writer cannot be maintained for a moment. In calling himself a "prophet" Habakkuk claims Divine inspiration and mission, and to have exercised his office in his appointed sphere. Whether he was called from some other occupation, as Amos, or whether he was trained in the schools of the prophets, is unknown. Some ground for supposing him to have been a Levite is given by the musical direction in ch. iii. 1, and the conclusion of the psalm, "For the chief musician on my stringed instruments," which would perhaps imply that he was qualified to take part in the temple services, and himself accompanied his hymn with instrumental music. But recent critics have thrown grave doubt on this inference (see Exposition). Legend has supplemented the silence of authentic history concerning the life of Habakkuk by certain details, some of which may have some elements of truth. Thus rabbinical tradition asserts that he was the son of the Shunammite woman whom Elisha restored to life. This, of course, is altogether unfounded. Christian writers, too, have not been backward in developing hints into facts. Pseudo-Epiphanius ('De Vit. Prophet.') and Pseudo-Dorotheus (' Chron. Pasch.,' p. 250) assert that Habakkuk was of the tribe of Simeon, and born in a place called Bethitouchar, perhaps Bath-Zacharias, famous in the history of Judas Maccabæus (1 Macc. vi. 32), that at the capture of Jerusalem by Nebuchadnezzar he fled to Ostracine, a town on the sea-coast of Egypt, some sixty miles east of Pelusium, and remained there till the Chaldeans departed, when he returned to his own country, and died two years before the end of the Captivity. His tomb is said to have been long shown at Keilah in the hill-country of Judah, and at Chukkok in Naphtali.

§ III. Date.

The time when Habakkuk prophesied can be gathered only from hints scattered in the book itself; and the limits thus obtained are a period before Babylon had obtained its independent position and so was able to menace its neighbours, and of course before the invasion of Judah, B.C. 605, twenty years later. Modern critics who do not believe in the possibility

of supernatural prediction, at once settle the question of the prophet's date
by affirming that his assertion concerning the punishment of Jerusalem at
the hands of the Chaldeans must have been uttered after the event, or else
so short a time previous, that natural acuteness could foresee the result
so certain to occur.   But this does not dispose of his prediction touching
the overthrow of Babylon, which human foresight could not have taught;
and if we must allow the predictive element in one case, why must we
refuse it in another?   But neglecting the theories of these critics, as
based on an erroneous principle, we find very great difficulty in coming
to any satisfactory decision.   Two theories are upheld by great names
respectively.   The first assigns our prophet to the time of Manasseh,
immediately succeeding Nahum—a theory which is countenanced by the
position of the book in the Hebrew and Greek canon.   The general
iniquity of which Habakkuk complains may certainly be predicated of that
period in Jewish history.   That the Chaldeans had not yet invaded the
land, and that their appearance was not expected, we learn from ch. i. 5,
" I will work a work in your days, which ye will not believe, though it be
told you."   The words, " in your days," imply, says Pusey, that he is
speaking to adults, many of whom would survive the invasion of Nebuchadnezzar, in the fourth year of Jehoiakim, and who, if he prophesied
about the close of the reign of Manasseh, would be about sixty years old at
the time of the Chaldean attack.   Some time later, when the Babylonian
empire was well established, it would have been nothing incredible that
destruction should menace Judæa from that quarter.   It seems probable,
too, that Zephaniah, who executed his office in the days of Josiah, adopted
some of the words of Habakkuk (comp. ch. ii. 20 with Zeph. i. 7).   Jeremiah
likewise made use of his prophecy (Jer. iv. 13; Zeph. iii. 3; and ch. i. 8).
Habakkuk, on the other hand, employs the language of Isa. xi. 9 in ch. ii. 14.
These arguments would apply with equal force to the earlier part of Josiah's
reign.   Thus critics would place our prophet between B.C. 650 and 635,
according to the usual reckoning, or about B.C. 626 in revised chronology.
And this seems the most probable opinion.   The other theory makes him a
contemporary of Jehoiakim, between B.C. 609 and 598, grounding the opinion
upon the idea that his account of the violence and oppression committed
by the Chaldeans could only have been written by one familiar with their
proceedings, and that it would have been injudicious prematurely to fill the
minds of the people with fear of these foreign invaders.   This is further
supported by the tradition mentioned above, that he lived to see the
Babylonian exile.   The force of these arguments will not be allowed by
any one who believes in the supernatural inspiration of the prophets of God.

§ IV. General Character.

There is something very striking in the style of Habakkuk.   In grandeur
and magnificence it is perhaps equalled by other of the prophets; language

as pure, power as concentrated, may be found elsewhere; but the extended colloquy between God and the prophet, and the exquisitely beautiful ode which forms the conclusion of the prophecy, are unique. The introduction of the majestic theophany is as bold in conception as it is sublime in diction. We know not whether most to admire the idea set forth, or the images under which it is developed. How terrible are the threatenings and announcements! how bitter the derision! how sweet and tender the promises of mercy and love! The past, the present, and the future are presented in vivid colours. Difficult, almost impossible, as it was for a prophet, confined to one circle of ideas, to be original, Habakkuk has given a new form to old conceptions, and brightened the notions of earlier seers with the splendour of imagery all his own, and with harmonious diction which is surpassed by no other sacred poet. The final ode may be set beside the two grand psalms, the eighteenth and the sixty-eighth, and will not suffer by the comparison.

§ V. Literature.

Among the works specially devoted to the elucidation of the prophecy of Habakkuk we may note the following: The Jew Abarbanel, whose commentary was translated into Latin by Sprecher (1709); Agellius (1597); De Thou; Jansen d'Ypres, 'Analecta in Habac.;' Dugué, 'Explication' (1734). The above are Roman Catholic commentators. Among Protestants may be mentioned Capito (1526); Chyrtæus, 'Lectiones' (1592); Marbury, 'A Commentarie' (1650); Tarnovius, 'Comm.' (1623); Kalinsky; Monrad (1759); Kofod (1792); Faber (1779); Wahl, Translation and Notes (1790); Wolff (1822); Delitzsch, 'Der Proph. Hab. ausgelgt' (1843); Gumpach (1860); Reinke, 'Der Proph. Hab.' (1870).

§ VI. Arrangement in Sections.

The book consists of two parts.

Part I. (Ch. i., ii.) Judgment upon the evil, in the form of a colloquy between the prophet and God.

§ 1. (Ch. i. 1.) The inscription of the book.

§ 2. (Ch. i. 2—4.) The prophet complains to God of the iniquity rife in the land, and its consequences.

§ 3. (Ch. i. 5—11.) God answers that he will send the Chaldeans to punish the ill-doers with a terrible vengeance; but these, his instruments, shall themselves offend by pride and impiety.

§ 4. (Ch. i. 12—17.) The prophet beseeches the Lord not to suffer his people to perish, seeing that he is in covenant with them, but to remember mercy even during the affliction at the hand of these rapacious oppressors.

§ 5. (Ch. ii. 1—3.) The prophet, waiting for his answer, is bidden write the oracle in plain characters, because its fulfilment is certain.

§ 6. (Ch. ii. 4.) The great principle is taught that the proud shall not continue, but the just shall live by faith.

§ 7. (Ch. ii. 5.) The character of the Chaldeans in some particulars is intimated; their destruction is announced under the form of five " woes."

§ 8. (Ch. ii. 6—8.) For rapacity.

§ 9. (Ch. ii. 9—11.) For avarice, violence, and cunning.

§ 10. (Ch. ii. 12—14.) For founding power on blood and devastation.

§ 11. (Ch. ii. 15—17.) For base treatment of subject nations.

§ 12. (Ch. ii. 18—20.) For idolatry.

Part II. (Ch. iii.) Psalm or prayer of Habakkuk.

§ 1. (Ch. iii. 1.) The title.

§ 2. (Ch. iii. 2.) The prooemium, in which the prophet expresses his fear at the coming judgment, and prays God in his wrath to remember mercy.

§ 3. (Ch. iii. 3—15.) He depicts in a majestic theophany the coming of God to judge the world, and its effect, symbolically on material nature, and properly on evil men.

§ 4. (Ch. iii. 16, 17.) It produces in the people of God, first, fear and trembling at the prospect of chastisement.

§ 5. (Ch. iii. 18, 19.) And next, hope of salvation and joy in God.

THE BOOK OF HABAKKUK

———⋄———

EXPOSITION.

CHAPTER I.

Ver. 1—ch. ii. 20.—Part I. JUDGMENT UPON THE EVIL, IN THE FORM OF A COLLOQUY BETWEEN THE PROPHET AND GOD.

Ver. 1.—§ 1. *The inscription of the book.* **The burden** (see note on Nah. i. 1). **The prophet** (ch. iii. 1). This title, which is added in the inscriptions only to the names of Haggai and Zechariah, and cursorily to that of Jeremiah (xlvi., xlvii., l.), implies that he exercised the practical office of prophet, and was well known; and, as Pusey thinks, Habakkuk appended it here on account of the form in which his prophecy is cast, as being addressed almost entirely to God or the Chaldeans, not to his own people. **Did see.** In prophetic vision (see note on Amos i. 1).

Vers. 2—4.—§ 2. *The prophet complains to God of the iniquity of his own nation, and its consequences.*

Ver. 2.—**Shall I cry**; Septuagint, κεκρά-ξομαι. The Hebrew is taken to imply that the prophet had long been complaining of the moral depravity of Judah, and calling for help against it. There is no reference here, as Ewald fancies, to acts of violence committed by the Chaldeans, who, in fact, are announced as coming to chastise the wickedness of the chosen people (ver. 6). **And thou wilt not hear!** The continuance of evil unchecked is an anomaly in the prophet's eye; and, putting himself in the position of the righteous among the people, he asks how long this is to last. Even cry out unto thee of **violence**; better, *I cry out unto thee, Violence.* A similar construction is found in Job xix. 7; Jer. xx. 8. "Violence" includes all manner of wrong done to one's neighbour. Septuagint, Βοήσομαι πρὸς σὲ ἀδικούμενος, "I will cry unto thee being wronged," as if the wrong was done to the

prophet himself. So the Vulgate, *Vociferabor ad te vim patiens.* But Habakkuk doubtless speaks in the person of the righteous, grieved at the wickedness he sees around, and the more perplexed as the Law led him to look for temporal rewards and punishments, if in the case of individuals, much more in that of the chosen nation (Lev. xxvi., *passim*).

Ver. 3.—**Why dost thou show me**—*Why dost thou let me see* daily with my own eyes —iniquity abounding, the very evil which Balaam says (Numb. xxiii. 21) the Lord had not found in Israel? **Cause me to behold grievance.** This should be, *Dost thou look upon perverseness?* He asks how God can look on this evil and leave it unpunished. The LXX. and the Vulgate translate the word *amal* "trouble," or "labour;" Keil, "distress." In this case it means the trouble and distress which a man inflicts on others, as wrong-doing seems to be generally spoken of. **Spoiling and violence are before me.** "Spoiling" is robbery that causes desolation. "Violence" is conduct that wrongs one's neighbour. The two words are often joined; *e.g.* Jer. vi. 7; Amos iii. 10. Vulgate, *prædam et injustitiam.* These are continually coming before the prophet's eyes. **There are that raise up strife and contention**; better, *there is strife, and contention is raised.* This refers to the abuse of the Law by grasping, quarrelsome nobles. Septuagint, "Against me judgment hath gone, and the judge receiveth bribes." So the Syriac and Arabic. The Vulgate gives, *Factum est judicium, et contradictio potentior,* where *judicium* is used in a bad sense.

Ver. 4.—**Therefore.** Because God has not interfered to put an end to this iniquity, or because of the want of righteous judges, the following consequences ensue. **The Law is slacked.** The Law, *Torah,* the revealed code which governed the moral, domestic, and political life, "is chilled," is benumbed

(Gen. xlv. 26), is no longer of any force or efficacy, is become a dead letter. Διασκέδασται, "is dispersed" (Septuagint); *lacerata est* (Vulgate). **Judgment doth never go forth**; *i.e.* right is powerless, as if it had never been; justice never shows itself in such a case. Septuagint, οὐ διεξάγεται εἰς τέλος, "proceedeth not effectually;" so the Vulgate. The rendering, "goeth not forth unto victory," given by the Syriac, is not so suitable; "**unto truth**" is a mistake arising from referring the word to a wrong root. **Doth compass about.** In a hostile sense, with threats and treachery (Judg. xx. 43; Ps. xxii. 13). Septuagint, καταδυναστεύει, "prevails;" Vulgate, *prævalet adversus.* **Therefore.** Because the righteous are unable to act as they desire, being opposed by the wicked. **Wrong judgment proceedeth**; rather, *judgment goeth forth perverted.* **Right**, or what is so called, when it does come forth, is distorted, wrested, so as to be right no more.

Vers. 5—11.—§ 3. *To this appeal God answers that he will send the Chaldeans to punish the evil-doers with a terrible vengeance; but these, his instruments, shall themselves offend by pride and impiety.*

Ver. 5.—**Behold ye among the heathen;** *the nations.* God, in answer, bids the prophet and his people look among the nations for those who shall punish the iniquities of which he complains. I will use a heathen nation, he says, as my instrument to chastise the sinners in Judæa; and you shall see that I have not disregarded the evil that is rife among you. Some commentators suppose that the impious are addressed; but Habakkuk spoke in the name and person of the righteous, and to them the answer must be directed. The LXX. gives, Ἴδετε, οἱ καταφρονηταί, "Behold, ye despisers," which is justifiable. St. Paul quotes the Greek Version, Acts xiii. 41, in his sermon at Antioch in the Jewish synagogue, warning those who despised the gospel. This was sufficiently close to the Hebrew for his purpose. **And regard, and wonder marvellously.** They are to wonder because the work is as terrible as it is unexpected. The LXX. (quoted by St. Paul, *loc. cit.*) adds, καὶ ἀφανίσθητε, "and perish," or rather, "be stupefied by astonishment," die of amazement. **I will work;** *I work.* The pronoun is not expressed, but must be supplied from ver. 6. It is God who sends the avengers. **In your days.** The prophet had asked (ver. 2), "How long?" The answer is that those now living should see the chastisement (see Introduction, § III.). **Which ye will not believe.** If ye heard of it as happening elsewhere, ye would not

give credit to it; the punishment itself and its executors are both unexpected (comp. Lam. iv. 12).

Ver. 6.—The executors of the Divine vengeance are now plainly announced. **I raise up.** God does it; he uses the power and passion of men to work out his designs (1 Kings xi. 14, 23; Amos vi. 14). **The Chaldeans;** *Kasidim.* By this appellation the prophets signify the soldiers or inhabitants of Babylon, which won its independence and commenced its wonderfully rapid career of conquest after the fall of Nineveh, between B.C. 626 and 608. At the time when Habakkuk wrote the Chaldeans had not appeared in Judæa, and no apprehension of danger from them was entertained. **Bitter and hasty.** The former epithet refers to their cruelty and ferocity (comp. Isa. xiv. 6; Jer. vi. 23; l. 42). They are called "hasty," as being vehement and impetuous in attack and rapid in movement. **Which shall march through the breadth of the land;** *which marcheth through the breadths of the earth.* The statement explains the general character of the Chaldeans, and points to the foreign conquests of Nebuchadnezzar. LXX., Τὸ πορευόμενον ἐπὶ τὰ πλάτη τῆς γῆς (comp. Rev. xx. 9).

Ver. 7.—**They.** The Hebrew is singular throughout. The disposition of the people, as of one man, is depicted. **Terrible;** exciting terror, as Cant. vi. 4, 10. **Their judgment and their dignity shall proceed of themselves;** *his judgment and his eminence are from himself.* The LXX. translates the two nouns κρίμα and λῆμμα: Vulgate, *judicium* and *onus.* The meaning is that the Chaldeans own no master, have no rule of right but their own will, attribute their glory and superiority to their own power and skill (comp. Dan. iv. 30). They are like Achilles in Horace, 'Ep. ad Pison.,' 121, etc.—

"Impiger, iracundus, inexorabilis, acer,
    Jura neget sibi nata, nihil non arroget
      armis."

Hitzig quotes Æschyl., 'Prom.,' 186, Παρ' ἑαυτῷ τὸ δίκαιον ἔχων, "Holding as justice what he deemeth so."

Ver. 8.—**Their horses, etc.** Jeremiah (iv. 13) compares their horses to eagles (comp. Job xxxix. 19, etc.). The punishment predicted in Deut. xxviii. 49, etc., is to come upon the Jews. We often read of the cavalry and chariots of the Chaldeans (Jer. iv. 29; vi. 23; Ezek. xxiii. 23, 24). **Evening wolves.** Wolves that prowl for food in the evening, and are then fiercest (Jer. v. 6; Zeph. iii. 3). Septuagint (with a different pointing), "wolves of Arabia." **Their horsemen shall spread themselves.** The verb is also rendered, "bear themselves proudly," or "gallop." Septuagint, ἐξιπ- πάσονται. The Anglican Version seems correct, implying that the cavalry, like Cossacks or Uhlans, swept the whole country for plunder. The verbs throughout vers. 8—11 should be rendered in the present tense. **From far.** From Babylonia (Isa. xxxix. 3). The preceding clause was of general import; the present one refers to the invasion of Judæa. **As the eagle** This is a favourite comparison of Jeremiah, as quoted above (comp. also ch. xlviii. 40; xlix. 22; Lam. iv. 19).

Ver. 9.—**They shall come all for violence.** All, every one of the invaders, come for violence—to repay that violence of which Habakkuk complained (ver. 2). Septuagint, Συντέλεια εἰς ἀσεβεῖς ἥξει, "An end shall come upon the impious;" Vulgate, *Omnes ad prædam venient.* **Their faces shall sup up as the east wind.** The word translated " shall sup up" occasions perplexity, being an ἅπαξ λεγόμενον. The Anglican rendering is virtually supported by other versions, *e.g.* Symmachus, Chaldee, and Syriac. The Vulgate, too, gives, *facies eorum ventus urens,* which Jerome explains, " As at the blast of a burning wind all green things dry up, so at the sight of these men all shall be wasted." This is the meaning of the Anglican Version, which, however, might be improved thus: *The aspect of their faces is as the east wind.* The Revisers have, *Their faces are set eagerly as the east wind,* which does not seem very intelligible. Other renderings are, " the endeavour," or " desire of their faces is directed to the east," or " forwards." (This rendering has the support of Orelli and others.) " The crowd of their faces," as equivalent to " the multitude of the army," which is not a Hebrew phrase found elsewhere. Septuagint, ἀνθεστηκότας (agreeing with ἀσεβεῖς in the first clause) προσώποις αὐτῶν ἐξεναντίας, " resisting with their adverse front." The effects of the east wind are often noted in Scripture; *e.g.* Gen. xli. 6, 23; Job xxvii. 21; Hos. xiii. 15. **They shall gather the captivity as the sand.** " He collects the captives as sand "—a hyperbolical expression to denote the numbers of captives and the quantity of booty taken. The mention of the east wind brings the thought of the terrible simoom, with its columns of sand.

Ver. 10.—**And they shall scoff,** etc.; *it,* or *he, scoffeth at kings.* The Chaldean nation makes light of the power and persons of kings. Compare Nebuchadnezzar's treatment of Jehoiakim (2 Chron. xxxvi. 6; 2 Kings xxiv. 1, 3; Jer. xxii. 19) and Jehoiachin (2 Kings xxiv. 12, 15). **They shall deride every strong hold.** The strongest fortress is no impediment to them. **They shall heap dust.** This refers to the raising of a mound or embankment for the purpose of attacking a city (comp. 2 Sam. xx. 15; 2 Kings xix. 32; xxv. 1). In the Assyrian monuments one often sees representations of these mounds, or of inclined planes constructed to facilitate the approach of the battering-ram (see Bonomi, 'Nineveh and its Palaces,' pp. 181, 188, etc.; Layard, ' Nineveh,' etc., ii. 369).

Ver. 11.—**Then shall his mind change;** Τότε μεταβαλεῖ τὸ πνεῦμα (Septuagint); *Tunc mutabitur spiritus* (Vulgate). From the ease and extent of his conquests the Chaldean gains fresh spirit. But it is best to translate differently, *Then he sweepeth on as a wind.* The Chaldean's inroad is compared to a tempestuous wind, which carries all before it. **And he shall pass over.** This is explained to mean, he exceeds all limits in his arrogancy, or he passes onward through the land. The former interpretation regards what is coming, the latter keeps to the metaphor of the wind. **And offend.** He is guilty, or offends, as the next clause explains, by attributing his success to his own prowess and skill. Thus the prophet intimates that the avenger himself incurs God's displeasure, and will suffer for it. Septuagint, καὶ ἐξιλάσεται, which St. Cyril interprets to mean that the Lord will change his purpose of punishing the Jews, and will have mercy on them—a notion quite foreign to the purport of the sentence. **Imputing this his power unto his god;** more literally, *this his power is his god;* Revised Version, *even he whose might is his god.* He defies the Lord, and makes his might his god. (For such pride and self-glorification, comp. Isa. xiv. 13; xlvii. 7. etc.; Dan. iv. 30.) Thus Mezentius, the despiser of the gods, speaks in Virgil, 'Æn.,' x. 773—

" Dextra mihi deus et telum, quod missile libro,
    Nunc adsint !"

Comp. Statius, 'Theb.,' iii. 615—

    " Virtus mihi numen, et ensis,
      Quem teneo."

Vers. 12—17.—§ 4. *The prophet, in reply, beseeches the Lord not to suffer his people to perish, seeing that he has deigned to be in covenant with them, but to remember mercy even during the affliction at the hand of their rapacious enemies.*

Ver. 12.—Habakkuk calls to mind God's immutability and his covenant with Israel. **Art thou not from everlasting,** etc.? An affirmative answer is expected. This is one ground of confidence in the corrective nature of the chastisement. God is Jehovah, the covenant God, who has been in personal relation to Israel from time immemorial, and is himself eternal. **Mine Holy One.** He speaks in the person of the righteous people, and he refers to God's holiness as a second ground of hope, because, although God must punish sin, he will not let the sacred nation, the chosen guardian of the faith, perish utterly. And then he expresses this confidence : **We shall not die.** We shall be chastened, but not killed. The Masorites assert that the present reading is a correction of the scribes for "thou wilt not die," which the prophet wrote originally, and which was altered for reverence' sake. But this is a mere assumption, incapable of proof. Its adoption would be an omission of the very consolation to which the prophet's confidence leads. **Thou hast ordained them** (*him*) **for judgment.** Thou hast appointed the Chaldean to execute thy corrective punishment on Israel (comp. Jer. xlvi. 28). Others take the meaning to be—Thou hast predestined the Chaldean to be judged and punished. This is not so suitable in this place. **O mighty God ;** Hebrew, *O Rock*— an appellation applied to God, as the sure and stable Resting-place and Support of his people (Deut. xxxii. 4, 15, 37 ; Ps. xviii. 2 ; xxxi. 3 ; Isa. xvii. 10). **Thou hast established them** (*him*) **for correction.** Thou appointedst the Chaldean, or madest him strong, in order to correct thy people. He is, like the Assyrian, the rod of God's anger (Isa. x. 5). Septuagint, Ἔπλασέ με τοῦ ἐλέγχειν παιδείαν αὐτοῦ, "He formed me to prove his instruction." This, says St. Jerome, is spoken in the person of the prophet announcing his call and office.

Ver. 13.—**Thou art of purer eyes than to behold evil** (comp. ch. i. 3). God cannot look with complacency on evil (Ps. v. 5, 6). **Iniquity ;** Septuagint, πόνους ὀδύνης, "labours of pain." Injustice and the distress occasioned by it. God's holiness cannot endure the sight of wickedness, nor his mercy the sight of man's misery. And yet he permits these evil men to afflict the holy seed. This is the prophet's perplexity, which he lays before the Lord. **Them that deal treacherously.** The Chaldeans, so called from their faithless and rapacious conduct (Isa. xxi. 2 ; xxiv. 16). **More righteous.** The Israelites, wicked as they were, were more righteous than the Chaldeans (comp. Ezek. xvi. 51, etc.). Delitzsch and Keil think that the persons intended are the godly portion of Israel, who will suffer with the guilty.

Ver. 14.—The prophet appeals movingly to God by showing the indignity with which the people are treated. **As the fishes of the sea.** Dumb and helpless, swept off by the fisherman. **That have no ruler over them.** None to guide and protect them (comp. Prov. vi. 7 ; xxx. 27). So the Jews seem to be deprived of God's care, and left to be the prey of the spoiler, as if of little worth, and no longer having God for their King (comp. Isa. lxiii. 19, Revised Version). The "creeping things" are worms, or small fish (Ps. civ. 25).

Ver. 15.—**They take up all men with the angle ;** *he bringeth up all together with the hook* (Amos iv. 2). The net. Any kind of net. Septuagint, ἀμφίβληστρον, "cast-net." The drag (σαγήνη). The large drag-net. At their own pleasure, unhindered, the Chaldeans make whole nations their prey, their fishing implements being their armies, with which they gather unto themselves countries, peoples, and booty.

Ver. 16.—**Therefore they sacrifice unto their net.** This is spoken metaphorically, implying that the Babylonians recognized not God's hand, but attributed their success to the means which they employed (comp. ver. 11 ; Isa. x. 13 etc.). There is no trace in the monuments of the Chaldeans paying divine honours to their weapons, as, according to Herodotus (iv. 62), the Scythians and other nations did (see Justin, 'Hist.,' xliii. 3 ; and Pusey's note here). What a man trusts in becomes a god to him. **Their portion is fat ;** *his portion is rich.* He gains great wealth. **Their meat plenteous ;** *his meat dainty.* He is prosperous and luxurious.

Ver. 17.—**Shall they therefore empty their net ?** Because they have had this career of rapine and conquest, shall God allow them to continue it ? Shall they be permitted to be continually emptying their net in order to fill it again ? The idea is that they carried off their booty and captives and secured them in their own territory, and then set out on new expeditions to acquire fresh plunder. The question is answered in the next chapter, where the judgment on the Chaldeans is pronounced. **And not spare continually to slay the nations ?** And cease not to send forth his armies and to found his empire in the blood of conquered nations. The Septuagint and Vulgate have no interrogation, the assertion being made by way of expostulation.

HOMILETICS.

Ver. 1.—*A prophet's burden.* I. THE PROPHET. 1. *His name.* Habakkuk— "Embracing," which might signify either "one who embraces" or "one who is embraced." Accepting the former sense, Luther notes the suitability of the prophet's name to his office. "He embraces his people (in his prophecy), and takes them to his arms; *i.e.* he comforts them, and lifts them up as one embraces a poor weeping child or man, to quiet it with the assurance that, if God will, it shall be better soon;" though probably the name rather points to the character of the prophet's faith, which cleaved fast to the Lord amid the perplexity of things seen (Pusey). 2. *His person.* A Jewish prophet, belonging to the tribe of Levi, and officially qualified to take part in the liturgical service of the temple (ch. iii. 19). Beyond this nothing is known of his history, the Jewish legends concerning him (consult Introduction) being absolutely worthless. 3. *His date.* Uncertain. Before the arrival of the Chaldeans in Judah (ver. 6), and therefore before the third year of Jehoiakim (Dan. i. 1); but whether in the reign of Manasseh (Hävernick, Keil, Pusey), or in that of Josiah (Delitzsch), or in that of Jehoiakim (De Wette, Ewald, Umbreit, Hitzig, Bleek, Kleinert), is open to debate. That the Assyrians are not mentioned as a power seems to indicate that by this time Nineveh had fallen (B.C. 606), which speaks for the third of the above dates; that the predicted judgment (ver. 5) was to be so unlikely as barely to be credible favours a time while Babylon was yet subject to Assyria, and therefore a date in the reign of Manasseh. The moral and spiritual degeneracy of the age in which Habakkuk lived (vers. 1—4) harmonizes less with the reign of Josiah than with that of Manasseh or Jehoiakim. The latter is supported by the fact that the Chaldeans appear to be depicted as already on their march (ver. 6); the former by the circumstance that the judgment is represented as not immediately at hand, but only as certain to happen in the days of those to whom the prophet spoke (ver. 5).

II. THE BURDEN. 1. *Its contents.* As Nahum had predicted the destruction of Nineveh and the Assyrian power, which had carried the ten tribes into captivity (2 Kings xvii. 6), so Habakkuk declares (1) the judgment about to come upon the degenerate nation of Judah through the instrumentality of the Chaldeans; and (2) the overthrow of the Chaldeans for their insatiableness, ambition, cruelty, treachery, and idolatry. 2. *Its form.* In the first two chapters the prophet sets forth his message in the form of a conversation between himself and Jehovah, the prophet addressing Jehovah in the language of complaint (vers. 1—4) and challenge (vers. 12—17), and Jehovah in return replying to his complaint (vers. 5—11) and to his challenge (ch. ii. 2—19). In the third chapter Habakkuk appends a prayer, which begins by supplicating mercy for the afflicted people of God (ch. iii. 1, 2), and quickly passes into a sublime description of Jehovah's coming in the glory of the Almighty (ch. iii. 3—11) for the destruction of his foes (ch. iii. 12—15) and the salvation of his people and his anointed (ch. iii. 13). "The whole of the prophecy has an ideal stamp. Not even Judah and Jerusalem are mentioned, and the Chaldeans who are mentioned by name are simply introduced as the existing possessors of the imperial power of the world, which was bent upon the destruction of the kingdom of God, or as the sinners who swallow up the righteous man" (Keil). 3. *Its style.* The lofty sublimity of this brief composition, as regards both thought and expression, has been universally recognized. "His language is classical throughout. . . . His view and mode of presentation bear the seal of independent force and finished beauty" (Delitzsch). "Habakkuk bears not merely the prophet's mantle, but also the poet's wreath adorns his honourable head. He is a Jeremiah and an Asaph in one" (Umbreit). "As regards force and fulness of conception and beauty of expression, he was certainly one of the most important among the prophets of the Old Testament" (Kleinert). 4. *Its origin.* No more in his case than in Nahum's was this political foresight, but inspiration. If this prophecy proceeded from the age of Manasseh, political foresight is simply out of the question as its explanation; if from the first years of Jehoiakim, it will be time enough to admit that political foresight could certainly predict a Babylonian invasion at a year's distance when it has been shown that modern statesmen can infallibly tell what shall be on the morrow. And, of course, if political foresight could not certainly predict the Babylonian invasion at one year's distance, still less could it announce a Babylonian overthrow at a distance of more than half a century. Political foresight, then, being an insufficient hypothesis, Divine inspiration should be frankly admitted. Like Nahum, Habakkuk "saw" the burden he delivered. In the New Testament the book is cited as inspired (Rom. i. 17; Gal. iii. 11; Acts xiii. 40, 41; Heb. x. 38).

Learn : 1. That future events are known to God—Divine foreknowledge. 2. That God can reveal these to men, should he so please—the possibility of revelation. 3. That those whom God selects to be his messengers nevertheless retain their individual and characteristic modes of thought and expression—inspiration not mechanical or uniform.

Ver. 2.—*The lamentation of a good man.* I. OVER THE RELIGIOUS DEGENERACY OF HIS AGE. Not merely for himself, but as the representative of the godly remnant of Judah, Habakkuk expostulates with Jehovah concerning the wickedness of the times in which he lived. The picture he sets before Jehovah is one of deep national corruption, such as existed in the days of Jeboiakim (Jer. xx. 8 ; xxii. 3, 13—17). A picture of wickedness. 1. *Great.* (1) Violence was abroad, as it had been in the days before the Flood (Gen. vi. 11), in the time of David (Ps. lv. 9), and even later in the reigns of Jotham and Ahaz (Micah ii. 2 ; vi. 12), practising spoliation, causing distress, and producing devastation, as it did in the long-past era of the patriarch of Uz (Job xxiv. 1—12), evoking strife and contention, perhaps partly through the natural resistance of good men defending their property, but just as likely through the spoliators quarrelling over their prey, leading to deceit and treachery in order to gain its unhallowed end, " the wicked compassing about the righteous," and " plotting against the just" (Ps. xxxvii. 12). (2) Iniquity abounded, and that amongst a people whose ideal vocation was holiness (Numb. xxiii. 21); immoralities whose source was a perverse heart (Matt. xv. 19); such practices as were inconsistent with the professions and privileges of those who did them ; iniquity, or that which was unequal, and therefore contrary to law and truth. (3) The Law of God was fallen into disrespect. The Torah, or Divine, revealed Law, " which was meant to be the soul, the heart of political, religious, and domestic life" (Delitzsch), was slacked ; it was benumbed or chilled, paralyzed through the moral and spiritual apathy of the nation, which gave it no response and yielded to it no obedience. (4) Human justice was itself perverted. Just because men's hearts had declined from the love of God, and had ceased to respect his Law, judgment seldom or never proceeded forth against evil-doers ; or, if it did, it went forth perverted. When criminals were brought to trial, they could always secure a verdict in their favour. 2. *Public.* It was not merely a degeneracy, eating its way secretly into the vitals of the nation; the disease had already come to the surface. Vice and irreligion were not practised in private. Iniquity flaunted its robes openly in the eyes of passers-by. The prophet saw it, looked upon it, felt himself surrounded by it. Spoiling and violence were before him ; and sinners of every description around him. 3. *Presumptuous.* It was wickedness perpetrated, not merely against God's Law, but by God's covenanted people, in the face of remonstrances from God's prophets, and under the eye of God himself. The prophet states that Jehovah as well as he had beheld the wickedness complained of. 4. *Inveterate.* It was not a sudden outburst of moral and spiritual corruption, but a long-continued and deeply rooted manifestation of national degeneracy, which had often sent the prophet to his knees, and caused him to cry for Divine interposition.

II. OVER THE SEEMING INDIFFERENCE OF GOD. 1. *A frequent phenomenon.* During the long antediluvian period Jehovah, apparently without concern, allowed mankind to degenerate; though he saw that the wickedness of man was great in the earth (Gen. vi. 5), it was not till one man only remained righteous before him that he interposed with the judgment of a flood. From the era of the Flood downwards he " suffered all nations to walk in their own ways " (Acts xiv. 16). Job (xxiv. 12) observed this to be the method of the Divine procedure in his day, Asaph in his (Ps. l. 21), Habakkuk in his; and to-day nothing can be more apparent than that it is not a necessary part of Heaven's plan that " sentence against an evil work " should be " executed speedily." 2. *A perplexing mystery.* That God cannot be indifferent to sin, to the wickedness of nations or to the transgressions of individuals, is self-evident; otherwise he could not be God (Ps. xi. 7 ; cxi. 9 ; cxlv. 17 ; Isa. lvii. 15 ; 1 Pet. i. 15 ; Rev. iv. 8). But that, loving righteousness and hating iniquity, he should seem to make no effort to protect, vindicate, strengthen, and diffuse the one, or to punish, restrain, and overthrow the other,— this is what occasions trouble to religious souls reflecting on the course of providence (Job xxi. 7 ; Ps. lxxiii. 2). The solution of the problem can only be that, on the one hand, he deems it better that righteousness should be purified, tested, and established by contact with evil, while, on the other hand, it seems preferable to his wisdom and love that wickedness should have free scope to reveal its true character, and ample opportunity either to change its mind or to justify its final overthrow (see homily on vers. 12—19).

III. OVER THE MANIFEST FRUITLESSNESS OF HIS PRAYERS. An experience: 1. *Strange.* Habakkuk had cried long and earnestly to Jehovah about the wickedness of his countrymen. If rivers of waters ran not down his eyes because they kept not Jehovah's Law, as the psalmist tells us was the case with him (Ps. cxix. 136), and Jeremiah (ix. 1) wished that it could have been with him, long processions of groanings ascended from his bosom to the throne of God on that very account. Doubtless, also, he expostulated with Jehovah about his seeming indifference, saying, "How long, O Lord, will this wickedness prevail? and how long wilt thou be silent?" Yet was there "no voice, nor any that answered him," any more than if he had been a worshipper of Baal (1 Kings xviii. 26); and this although Jehovah was pre-eminently the Hearer of prayer (Ps. lxv. 2), and had invited his people to call upon him in the day of trouble (Ps. l. 15). 2. *Common.* It is not wicked men alone whose prayers are denied—men like Saul (1 Sam. xxviii. 6), and the inhabitants of Judah in the days of Isaiah (i. 15) and of Jeremiah (xi. 14), but good men like Job (xxx. 20) and David (Ps. xxii. 2) as well. As the Syro-Phœnician woman cried after Jesus, and was answered never a word (Matt. xv. 23), so many prayers ascend from the hearts of God's people to which, for a time at least, no response returns. 3. *Valuable.* Fitted to test the faith and sincerity of the petitioner, it is also admirably calculated to teach him the sovereignty of God in grace as well as in nature, to show him that, while God distinctly engages to answer prayer, he undertakes to do so only in his own time and way.

Learn: 1. That no good man can be utterly indifferent to the moral and spiritual character of the age in which he lives. 2. That good men should bear the highest interests of their country before God upon their hearts in prayer. 3. That good men should never lose faith in two things—that God is on the side of righteousness, even when iniquity appears to triumph; and that God hears their prayers, even when he delays to answer or appears to deny them.

Vers. 5—11.—*Judgment on the wing.* I. ITS CHARACTER DESCRIBED. (Ver. 5.) 1. *Its subjects.* The land and people of Judah (ver. 6). These, though Jehovah's covenanted people, had declined from his worship, departed from his ways, dishonoured his Name. It was in the covenant that, under such circumstances, they should be chastised (2 Sam. vii. 14; Ps. lxxxix. 30); and Jehovah is never unmindful of his covenant engagements (Ps. cxi. 5), if men are of theirs (2 Tim. ii. 12, 13). 2. *Its Author.* Jehovah. "The Judge of all the earth" (Gen. xviii. 20), "his eyes behold and his eyelids try the children of men" (Ps. xi. 4), communities and nations no less than individuals (Ps. lxvii. 4). As "justice and judgment are the habitation of his throne" (Ps. lxxxix. 14), so "all his ways are judgment" (Deut. xxxii. 4), and "the works of his hands are verity and judgment" (Ps. cxi. 7). As the least significant occurrence (Matt. x. 29), so the most momentous, cannot happen without the Divine permission. The Supreme is behind all second causes. He regulates the rise and fall of nations and kings (Job xii 23; Ps. lxxv. 7), the ebb and flow of ocean (Job xxxviii. 11), the movements of the heavenly bodies (Job xxxviii. 31—33), the growth and decay of flowers (Isa. xl. 7). When Nineveh is overthrown and Babylon raised up, Jehovah, unseen but all-powerful, is the prime Mover. When Judah or Israel is chastised, it is Jehovah's hand that holds the rod. 3. *Its certainty.* Being matter of clear and definite promise on the part of Jehovah: "I will work a work;" "Behold, I raise up the Chaldeans." So certain is Jehovah's future judgment of his enemies (Mal. iii. 5; Acts xvii. 31). This, like that, has no basis but Jehovah's announcement. That this will not fail may be inferred from the accomplishment of that. 4. *Its vicinity.* Close at hand. "Behold, I work a work in your days" obviously meant that within a generation at furthest the Divine stroke should descend on Judah, and that every person in the nation should regard it as near. In the same way are Christians directed to think of the judgment of the great day as at hand (Jas. v. 9; 1 Pet. iv. 7; Rev. xxii. 12), though of that day and of that hour knoweth no man (Mark xiv. 32) more than this, that it is certain (Job xxi. 30; Ps. l. 4; Dan. vii. 10;

Matt. xxv. 32; Heb. ix. 27). 5. *Its strangeness.* It should be both startling and incredible. (1) Startling. As to its Author, Jehovah; as to the quarter whence it should proceed, from among the heathen; as to the power by which it should be inflicted, the Chaldeans, when they might rather have expected the Assyrians (if Habakkuk prophesied under Manasseh) or the Egyptians (if he flourished in the first years of Jehoiakim); as to the suddenness with which it should spring forth, there being at the time when Habakkuk wrote no tokens of its coming discernible on the horizon. So will the judgment of the great day surprise the ungodly world and a sleeping Church (Matt. xxiv. 27—44; xxv. 6; 1 Thess. v. 2, 3; Rev. xvi. 15). (2) Incredible. So unlikely did a Chaldean invasion of Judæa seem, that Jehovah felt nothing but an actual experience of the same would ever convince his people of it. A simple fore-announcement of it would not suffice to carry conviction of its reality to their mind, although, of course, it should. That this was true, the reception accorded to Jeremiah's prediction of Nebuchadnezzar's appearance before Jerusalem showed (Jer. v. 12; xx. 7, 8; xxvi. 8—11). Up to the moment when the Chaldean armies arrived neither Jehoiakim nor his people would allow that a Chaldean conquest was so much as possible. Events, however, proved them to be in error. So the antediluvians knew not till the Flood came and took them all away (Matt. xxiv. 39). So shall the coming of the Son of man be (2 Pet. iii. 1—10).

II. ITS INSTRUMENT INDICATED. (Vers. 6—11.) This was the Chaldean or Babylonian power, at the time subject to Assyria, and not risen to the ascendency it afterwards enjoyed under Nebuchadnezzar and his successors. The prophet depicts it when raised up, not only into a nation, but against Judah by a sevenfold characteristic. 1. *Its natural disposition.* He calls it "a bitter and hasty nation," *i.e.* fierce and rough, heedless and rash, and represents it as marching through the breadth of the earth, impelled by covetousness, and making a way for itself by sheer brute force and violence—taking possession of dwelling-places not its own. 2. *Its formidable appearance.* "They are," or he, *i.e.* the nation, is, "terrible and dreadful," by its very name and much more by its aspect and actions inspiring terror in the breasts of beholders. 3. *Its presumptuous self-sufficiency.* "Their judgment and dignity proceed from themselves;" *i.e.* conscious of its own strength, it determines for itself its own rule of right, and ascribes to itself its elevation above the other nations of the earth. This putting of self instead of God in the place of honour and seat of authority is the essence of all sin. Wicked men walk after the counsels and in the imaginations of their own evil hearts (Jer. vii. 24), and are prone to arrogate to themselves what should be rendered to God, viz. the glory of their successful achievements (Deut. viii. 17; Judg. vii. 2). 4. *Its military strength.* (1) Its horses swifter than leopards, lighter of foot than panthers, which spring with the greatest rapidity on their prey, and fiercer than evening wolves, or wolves going forth at eventide after having fasted all day—an emblem of ferocity applied to the judges of Judah (Zeph. iii. 3). (2) Its horsemen or warriors coming from afar and spreading themselves abroad—"Neither distance of march shall weary nor diffusion weaken them" (Pusey)—darting upon its foes like an eagle hasting to devour, a bird to which Nebuchadnezzar is compared (Jer. xlviii. 40; Lam. iv. 19; Ezek. xvii. 3; Dan. vii. 4). (3) Both bent upon violence and having their faces set eagerly as the east wind, *i.e.* either set towards the front with determination, or like the east wind for devastation. Thus the characteristics of Babylonian warfare were—swiftness of movement, simultaneousness of action in the different parts of the army, unanimity of purpose, determination and ferocity, qualities the existence of which in them the monuments sufficiently attest. 5. *Its warlike achievements.* (1) The deportation of subjected populations. "They gather captives as the sand," *i.e.* "countless as the particles which the east wind raises, sweeping over the sand wastes, where it buries whole caravans in one death" (Pusey). (2) The defiance of all opposition. "Yea, he scoffeth at kings, and princes are a derision unto him." So Nebuchadnezzar did with Jehoiakim, Jehoiachin, and Zedekiah (2 Kings xxiv. 15; xxv. 6, 7; 2 Chron. xxxvi. 5—21). (3) The capture of every stronghold. No fortress could withstand the Babylonian conqueror. Not even Tyre, "whose very name (Rock) betokened its strength" (Pusey). The most impregnable garrison seemed only to require that he should heap up a little dust against it, and it was taken. 6. *Its daring impiety.* Rushing on like a swollen torrent, like his own **Euphrates when it** overflows its banks, sweeping across the land like a tempestuous wind over the sandy desert, it overleaps all barriers and restraints both Divine and human, and stands convicted before God as a guilty transgressor. 7. *Its shameless blasphemy.* The culmination at once of its offence and of its guilt is that it deifies its own might, saying, " Lo, this my strength is my god!" Such was the spirit of Nebuchadnezzar (Dan. iv. 30) and of Belshazzar (Isa. xiv. 14); such will be that of the future antichrist (2 Thess. ii. 4).

Learn : 1. That if God's people sin they must look for chastisement (Deut. xi. 28 ; Ps. lxxxix. 32). 2. That if God's people are chastised for their offences, God's enemies cannot hope to escape punishment for theirs (1 Pet. iv. 17, 18). 3. That God can always lay his hand upon an instrument wherewith to inflict punishment upon his people (Isa. x. 5). 4. That wicked men and nations whom God employs in the execution of his judgments do not thereby escape responsibility for their own actions (Isa. x. 12). 5. That the deification of self is the last delusion of a foolish heart (Gen. iii. 5).

Vers. 12—17.—*The triumph of faith.* I. HABAKKUK'S GOD. (Vers. 12, 13.) 1. *Eternal.* From everlasting (Ps. xciii. 2), and therefore to everlasting (Ps. xc. 1); hence immutable (Mal. iii. 6), without variableness or shadow cast by turning (Jas. i. 17), in respect of his being (1 Tim. i. 17), character (Isa. lxiii. 16 ; Ps. cxi. 3), purpose (Job xxiii. 13), and promise (Heb. vi. 17). 2. *Holy.* In himself the absolutely and the only stainless One (Exod. xv. 11 ; Isa. vi. 3), and in all his self-manifestations (Job xxxiv. 10), in his ways and works (Ps. cxlv. 17) as well as words (Ps. xxxiii. 4), equally immaculate, and necessarily so, since an unholy Divinity could not be supreme, he is "of purer eyes than to behold evil," and "cannot look upon iniquity" with indifference, and far less with favour (Ps. v. 4 ; Jer. xliv. 4). 3. *Omniscient.* Inferred from the fact that he beheld all the evil that was done beneath the sun, both in Judah by his own people (ver. 3) and among the nations by the Chaldeans (ver. 13). Omniscience a necessary attribute of the Supreme, and one much emphasized in Scripture (Prov. xv. 3; Job xxviii. 24 ; 2 Chron. xvi. 9 ; Jer. xxxii. 19 ; Heb. iv. 13). 4. *Omnipotent.* This implied in his supremacy over the nations, raising up one power (the Chaldeans) and putting down another (Judah), giving the peoples into Nebuchadnezzar's net, and again hurling down Nebuchadnezzar's grandson from his seat of power. Also suggested by the designation "Rock," given him by Habakkuk, who meant thereby to teach the strength and steadfastness of Jehovah in comparison with the idols of the heathen, and his ability to shelter and defend those who trusted in him (Deut. xxxii. 4, 15, 18, 30, 31, 37 ; Ps. xviii. 2 ; xxviii. 1 ; xxxi. 3, etc.). 5. *Gracious.* He was such a God as had entered into covenant with the prophet, who accordingly styled him "my God," "mine Holy One." "My" is faith's response to God's grace in offering himself to man as a God (Exod. xx. 2).

II. HABAKKUK'S PERPLEXITY. (Vers. 13—17.) 1. *A great mystery.* (1) Concerning Judah. Why God, being what he was, from everlasting, holy, etc., should suffer his people, who with all their faults were more righteous than their oppressors, to be trodden down, butchered, and driven off into captivity by the Chaldeans! Why, when he saw them humiliated and destroyed, he held his peace! Strange inconsistency of the human heart, especially when touched by grace. A little before (ver. 3) the prophet had been concerned at God's silence about the wickedness of Judah; now, when God has spoken of raising up against that wickedness the Chaldean army, he is troubled that God should allow such cruelty to be perpetrated against the people of whom he had complained. (2) Concerning the Chaldeans. Why God, being what he was, unchangeably pure and just as well as resistlessly powerful, should permit the heathen warrior to work such havoc among the nations of the earth, to practise such deception towards and cruelty against them (ver. 13), to angle them up like fishes out of the sea or catch them in his net (ver. 15), to deprive them of their heads by carrying away their kings, and so to make them like the finny tribes that have no rulers over them (ver. 14) ; and not only so, but to exult in his conquests and depredations, as if these were exclusively the result of his own power and skill ; to "sacrifice unto his net, and burn incense unto his drag" (ver. 16), thus making might his god (ver. 11), and practically deifying himself. 2. *An old problem.* Habakkuk's perplexity was the same which from time immemorial has troubled thoughtful men, the dark enigma of providence—why good men should so frequently be crushed by misfortune, and wicked men so often crowned with prosperity. This mystery was a source of anxiety to Job (xii. 6; xxi. 7—13), David (Ps. xvi. 14, 15), Asaph (Ps. lxxiii. 1—13), Jeremiah (xii. 1), the Preacher (Eccles. vii. 15; viii. 14), in the olden times; has caused much stumbling to good men since, and probably will do so while the world lasts. 3. *A valuable discipline.* Distressing as this mystery is, it is nevertheless not without its uses to such as are exercised thereby. It assists them to understand the sovereignty of God, that he giveth not account of any of his matters (Job xxxiii. 13); to realize their own limited and imperfect vision, which can only see in part, not in whole (Job xxxvii. 21; 1 Cor. xiii. 9), only the middle and neither the beginning nor the end of God's work in providence; to cultivate those virtues of patience, humility, trustfulness, which are essential elements in all true goodness (Ps. xxxvii. 3—5); and to seek their portion in God himself (Ps. xvi. 5) rather than in earthly things (Ps. xvii. 14), in the future world rather than in the present life (Col. iii. 2).

III. HABAKKUK'S CONSOLATION. (Vers. 12—17.) 1. *Concerning the righteous.* (1) Jehovah being what he was, it was impossible his people should be either cut or cast off. Habakkuk argued that Judah could not perish—"We shall not die"—because God lived and was holy. Jehovah sustained the argument by answering, in Mal. iii. 6, "I am the Lord, I change not; therefore ye sons of Jacob are not consumed;" and Christ acknowledged its validity when he said to his disciples, "Because I live, ye shall live also" (John xiv. 19). This implies not exemption from physical suffering or death, as doubtless many Judæans perished in the Chaldean conquest, but protection from that future and eternal death which is the last penalty of unrepented and unforgiven sin. This the main consolation of a believer under suffering, that his covenant God hath said, "My mercy will I keep for him for evermore" (Ps. lxxxix. 28), and that Christ hath declared, "My sheep shall never perish" (John x. 28). (2) This being so, their sufferings must be designed only for their correction, not for their destruction, and accordingly should be regarded rather as fatherly chastisements than as penal inflictions. Habakkuk perceived that the Chaldean had been "ordained for judgment" and "raised up for correction," not commissioned for extermination. So the Christian discerns that "tribulation worketh patience," etc. (Rom. v. 3); that "our light affliction, which is but for a moment, worketh for us a far more exceeding, even an eternal weight of glory" (2 Cor. iv. 17); that present chastisements are intended for our future profit, "that we might be partakers of his holiness" (Heb. xii. 10), and that they might yield to us "the peaceable fruits of righteousness" (Heb. xii. 11); and in short, that suffering is the royal road to moral and spiritual perfection (Heb. ii. 10). 2. *Concerning the wicked.* Jehovah being what he is, the wicked cannot be allowed to go on always as they are. "Shall he," the Chaldean, "therefore empty his net" to fill it again? Is this process of angling and dragging for men and nations to go on for ever? Shall he "not spare to slay the nations continually"? the prophet asks; meaning by the question, "No, verily, this must come to an end." And those who have reflected deepest on the problem have perceived that, at the longest, the triumph of the wicked is but short (Job xx. 5; Ps. xxxvii. 35, 36; lxxiii. 18—20), and that their experience of prosperity, however long it may be, will only in the end aggravate their misery, unless before the end they repent of their wickedness, and turn to God in faith, humility, love, and righteousness. "The immortal gods," wrote Julius Cæsar, in his 'Gallic War' (i. 14), "are accustomed, the more heavily to pain by reverse of fortune those of whom for their wickedness they wish to be avenged, to grant to them in the mean while a larger share of prosperity and a longer period of impunity."

Learn: 1. That the good man's best comfort in affliction and stay in adversity is the character of God (Deut. xxxiii. 27; Isa. lii. 21; 2 Cor. i. 3). 2. That with God silence is not to be understood as equivalent to consent (Ps. l. 21). 3. That it is God's custom to make men reap as they have sown, to reward perverseness with perverseness, and iniquity with iniquity (Ps. xviii. 26; Matt. vii. 2; Gal. vi. 7). 4. That governments tend to the good order of society, and are to be respected and obeyed even when not perfect (Rom. xiii. 1, 2). 5. That the reign of wickedness will one day terminate (Ps. cxlv. 20; Matt. xxi. 11; 1 Cor. xv. 25).

HOMILIES BY VARIOUS AUTHORS.

Ver. 1.—*The title.* This introduces us to the writer and his work. Note—

I. HIS NAME. *Habakkuk*; i.e. "One who embraces" — a name singularly appropriate in its significance to the man who "rested in the Lord, and waited patiently for him" through the dark days. Luther applied the name to the prophet's regard for his people, "embracing them, taking them to his arms, comforting them, and lifting them up as one embraces a weeping child, to quiet it with the assurance that, if God will, it shall be better soon." Jewish tradition has identified him with the son of the Shunammite woman (2 Kings iv. 18), and with the watchman sent by Isaiah to the watch-tower (xxi.) to look towards Babylon. But with these and other merely fanciful and utterly unreliable traditions the silence of Scripture very favourably contrasts. It makes him known to us through his teaching. It is the message rather than the messenger that is presented to us here; yet through the message we get to know the man so intimately that he becomes to us quite a familiar presence.

II. HIS OFFICE. "Habakkuk *the prophet.*" This title clearly indicates that he had been appointed to the prophetical office. Many men in Old Testament times uttered certain prophecies, as for instance Moses, David, Solomon, Daniel, but we do not find the title "the prophet" appended to their names, it being given simply to such as were specially chosen and. set apart to this office. The closing words of the book (ch. iii. 19) have led some to regard him as belonging to one of the Levitical families, and as appointed to take part in the liturgical services of the temple; but of this we cannot speak with any degree of certainty, though probably it was so.

III. HIS PROPHECY. This is described as "the burden which Habakkuk the prophet *did see.*" The phrase is peculiar, but the meaning is clear. He saw a vision of coming events, in which solemn Divine judgments would be executed both against his own people and their oppressors; and the scene of impending woe oppressed his spirit and lay as a heavy weight upon his soul. Still, dark as the outlook was, and oppressed in heart as he felt himself to be amidst the mysteries of life viewed in relation to the Divine government, he maintained throughout unswervingly his trust in God; and which so clearly pervaded his spirit and so repeatedly revealed itself in his expressions as amply to justify the representation that he is "eminently the prophet of reverential, awe-filled faith." Viewed from a literary standpoint, his prophecy may well exite our profoundest interest. Critical writers with one consent bear testimony to the beauty of his contributions to these sacred oracles. Ewald calls the book "Habakkuk's Pindaric Ode." Delitzsch says of it, "His language is classical throughout, full of rare and select words and turns, which are to some extent exclusively his own, whilst his view and mode of presentation bear the seal of original force and finished beauty." Pusey observes, "Certainly the purity of his language and the sublimity of his imagery is, humanly speaking, magnificent; his measured cadence is impressive in its simplicity." But valuable as this composition is in this respect, its great charm consists in the spirit of holy trustfulness which it breathes. As we ponder over its contents we feel at every stage our lack of confidence in our God reproved, and are impelled to cry, "Lord, we believe: help thou our unbelief" (Mark ix. 24); "Lord, increase our faith" (Luke xvii. 5).—S. D. H.

Vers. 2—4.—*The elegy.* In this brief and plaintive strain we have—

I. AN EARNEST HEART REFLECTING UPON THE PREVAILING INIQUITY. Whatever may have been the exact date of this prophecy, it is clear that the writer stood connected with the close of the kingdom of Judah, the eve of the Captivity, and that he presents to us, in a few graphic touches, a vivid description of the depravity then prevailing in the land. He bitterly laments over: 1. *The insecurity of property.* "Spoiling and violence are before me" (ver. 3). 2. *The strifes of parties and factions.* "And there are that raise up strife and contention" (ver. 3). 3. *Laxity in the administration of the Law.* "The Law is slacked, and judgment doth never go forth" (ver. 4). 4. *The good suffering unjustly at the hands of the evil.* "The wicked doth compass about the righteous" (ver. 4). 5. *The openness and audacity of wrong-doers in this evil course.* He speaks of all this iniquity as being patent to the observer. Sometimes, " vice, provoked to shame, borrows the colour of a virtuous deed ; " but in this instance there was no attempt at concealment or disguise, and no sense of shame. "Spoiling and violence *are before me* " (ver. 3).

II. AN EARNEST HEART YEARNING FOR THE ESTABLISHMENT OF RIGHTEOUSNESS, AND IMPATIENT OF DELAY. The life of piety is undoubtedly the happy life (Ps. i. 1). Still, it is not always sunshine, even with the good. There are times in their experience when the sky becomes overcast, and when they become depressed and sad at heart. Although possessing " the firstfruits of the Spirit," the pledge and the earnest of the enjoyment at length of a fulness of blessing, they often " groan within themselves " (Rom. viii. 23). And a very large ingredient in the cup of sorrow the good have to drink is that occasioned by beholding the blighting effects of sin. As they witness men unprincipled in their dealings, impure in their speech, dishonourable in their transactions, and as they note the pernicious influence and effects of such conduct, their hearts are rendered sad, and they are constrained to long ardently for the time when sin shall be completely vanquished, when it shall be banished from this fair universe of God, and when there shall come in all its perfection the reign of truth and righteousness, peace and love. This spirit runs through the prophet's mournful strain (vers. 2—4). We recognize it also in the words of David, " Oh let the wickedness of the wicked ! " etc. (Ps. vii. 9), and of Jeremiah (xiv. 8, 9), and impelled by it many are crying to-day, " Why is his chariot so long in coming ? Why tarry the wheels of his chariot ? "

III. AN EARNEST HEART DIRECTING ITS IMPASSIONED APPEAL TO GOD IN PRAYER. (Ver. 2.) The seer did not question the Divine rectitude, but his spirit was perturbed at the delay, and he yearned with a holy impatience for the vindication of the honour of his God. And under such conditions no course is so commendable as that of pouring our plaint into the ear of Infinite Love. Prayer at such seasons will be found helpful : 1. In tranquillizing the spirit, quieting and subduing agitation, and imparting a sense of restfulness and peace. 2. In linking our human weakness to God's almighty strength, and thus fitting us for renewed service to him. " Toil, pain, doubt, terror, difficulty,—all retreat before the recognition of a great life-purpose wrought out in entire dependence upon Heaven." 3. In causing light to shine through the dark cloud of mystery, helping us to understand the Divine plan (Ps. lxxiii. 16, etc.), and so preparing the way for our exchanging the mournful elegy for the rapturous melody of thankful and adoring praise.—S. D. H.

Vers. 5—11.—*The Divine working against evil and its doers.* We have expressed here God's response to the impassioned appeal addressed to him by his servant. There is much that is suggestive in these words as bearing upon the Divine working against those who practise sin and who persist in its commission. Note—

I. THAT GOD IS NOT INDIFFERENT WITH RESPECT TO PREVAILING UNGODLINESS. The seer had asked, " How long ? " (ver. 2). He was impatient of delay. But whilst there is this lingering on the part of God, so that "judgment against an evil work is not executed speedily " (Eccles. viii. 11), this is owing to the Divine long-suffering and patience, and does not arise from indifference and unconcern being cherished by the Most High in reference to iniquity. Wrong-doing is ever before him, is closely observed by him. It is the source of displeasure to him who is perfect in purity, and the requital of it will assuredly be experienced by transgressors. Though it may tarry, it will surely come. " I will work a work," etc. (ver. 5).

II. THAT GOD, IN THE ORDER OF HIS PROVIDENCE, IN EXECUTING HIS JUDGMENTS, OVERRULES THE ACTIONS OF EVIL MEN, AND CAUSES THESE TO FULFIL HIS RIGHTEOUSNESS. The verses contain a wonderfully graphic account of the Chaldeans who were to be the instruments of the Divine chastisement of Judah (compare with them Isa. xiv. 6, 16, 17), and whilst in reading them, so vivid is the portrayal, that we seem to see the Chaldean horsemen sweeping through the land like the simoom, causing death and desolation to follow in their track, we also have presented to us certain traits most clearly indicative of their gross wickedness. (1) Their proud ambition to possess the dwelling-places that were not theirs (ver. 6); (2) their fierceness and cruelty (ver. 7); (3) their self-sufficiency (ver. 7); (4) their scorn and contempt (ver. 10) and their blasphemy (ver. 11);—all pass in review before us. And these were chosen to be the executors of the Divine judgments! "For, lo, I raise up the Chaldeans" (ver. 6). The meaning is that God, in his providence, would permit "that bitter and hasty nation" to be a scourge to his chosen people on account of their transgression. The Chaldeans, in seeking their own ends, should be made to fulfil the Divine behests. Man is wondrously free to act; and he often does act without any regard to truth and righteousness. The world, indeed, is full of evil-doers acting according to their own devices; but "he that sitteth in the heavens" is guiding and directing all to the accomplishment of his own high purposes and to the fulfilment of his holy and gracious will.

III. That God, in operating against evil and its doers, sometimes employs unexpected agents. "The Hebrew state was at this time in close alliance with the Chaldean state, an alliance so close and friendly that the Hebrew politicians had no fear of its rupture. Yet it was in this wholly unexpected form that the Divine judgment was to come upon them. The Chaldeans in whom they trusted, on whom they leaned, were to give the death-blow to the dynasty of David." All the material and moral forces of the universe are under the Divine control, and in ways and by means little anticipated his retributions often overtake his adversaries.

IV. That this Divine working against evil and its doers receives but tardy recognition and acknowledgment from man. (Ver. 5.) The retributions have to light upon them ere they will believe. "They cry, Peace and safety: till sudden destruction comes upon them" (1 Thess. v. 3). So has it been in the past, and so, upon the authority of Christ, will it be in the future (Matt. xxiv. 27—29). Still, amidst this unconcern and unbelief, the duty of the messenger of God is clear. He must "cry aloud." He must bid men "behold," "regard," and "wonder," and then, "whether they hear or forbear," "he has delivered his soul."—S. D. H.

Ver. 12.—*The inspiration of hope.* Hope is the expectation of future good. The cherishing of this spirit, even as it respects the affairs of everyday life, yields strength and courage, whilst the centering this in the glorious realities God has revealed imparts joy and gladness to the heart. To the man of piety hope is the helmet, serving as a protection and defence in the day of conflict, and the anchor rendering his spirit peaceful and secure amidst the storms of life.

I. Consider the prophet's reasoning in this verse in its application to himself and his nation, and note how the inspiration of hope fired his soul. 1. The seer directed his thoughts to the contemplation of the character of his God. Two aspects of this were vividly present to his mind. (1) *God's eternal duration.* "Art thou not from everlasting?" etc. (ver. 12). (2) *His infinite purity.* "Mine Holy One" (ver. 12). 2. Associated with these thoughts concerning God in the mind of the prophet we have the recognition of the relationship sustained by this Eternal and Holy One to himself and the nation whose interests lay near and pressed with such weight upon his heart. He and his people were the chosen of Heaven. God had entered into covenant relations with them. They had been the objects of his ever-gracious care and providential working. He had not dealt thus with any other people. They could call him *theirs.* "O Lord *my* God, *mine* Holy One" (ver. 12). 3. And by associating together these thoughts of God and of his relationship to his people he gathered, in the troublous times upon which he had fallen, the inspiration of hope. One great difficulty with him arose from the threatened extinction of his nation. He had mourned over the national guilt, and had sought earnestly in prayer the Divine interposition. The response, however, to his impassioned cry unto God was different from what he had expected. The revelation made to him of the approaching Chaldean invasion of his country seemed to carry with it the complete annihilation of the national anticipations, and the utter desolation and extinction of those who had been specially favoured of God. Surely, thought he, this cannot be. God is eternal; his purposes must be fulfilled. Then "we shall not die" (ver. 12). God is holy. Then evil cannot ultimately be victorious. It could only be for chastisement and correction that the threatened trials should come. "O Lord, thou hast ordained them for judgment; and, O mighty God, thou hast established them for correction" (ver. 12). And by such reasoning hope became the balm of healing to his troubled heart, the bow of promise cast across his stormiest cloud, the bright star kindled in his darkest sky.

II. OBSERVE THAT THE PROPHET'S REASONING ADMITS OF A MORE EXTENDED RANGE OF APPLICATION, AND HAS AN IMPORTANT BEARING UPON THE IMMORTALITY OF MAN. Jehovah is "from everlasting." He is "the eternal God;" hence, our immortal destiny: "We shall not die." Surely the Divine Father will not allow his children to fade away and be no more. Certainly, he whose tender love to his children the love of human parents so faintly images, will not dwell through the eternal ages and "leave himself childless when time shall end."

> "Souls that of his own good life partake,
> He loves as his own self; dear as his eye
> They are to him; he'll never them forsake;
> When they shall die, then God himself shall die:
> They live, they live in blest eternity."
>
> (Henry More.)

It may be said that this reasoning, however concise and seemingly conclusive, is after all based upon probability. We grant it, and whilst refusing to undervalue its worth, we thankfully turn even from these beautiful words of the noble prophet, "Art thou not from everlasting, O Lord my God, mine Holy One? we shall not die," and fix our thoughts upon the assurances, so authoritative and so certain, of the world's Redeemer. "Let not your heart be troubled," etc. (John xiv. 1—3); "I am the Resurrection," etc. (John xi. 25, 26); "Because I live, ye shall live also" (John xiv. 19).—S. D. H.

Ver. 12.—*The benefits of life's adversities.* "O Lord, thou hast ordained them for judgment; and, O mighty God, thou hast established them for correction." This is a second inference drawn by the prophet. He not only inferred, from what he knew of the Divine character, that his people should not be *utterly destroyed* by the adversities which were about to overtake them—"We shall not die"—but also that these coming judgments should be made to *work for their good.* "O Lord, thou hast ordained," etc. (ver. 12). God's chastisements are not directed to the overthrow but to the salvation of those upon whom they are inflicted. He chastens men sore, but does not give them over unto death. The dark scenes through which the frail and erring children of men are led are designed to contribute to their weal. How? Well, they operate in various ways.

I. THEY TEACH US THAT WE ARE NOT TO EXPECT TO HAVE OUR OWN WILL, BUT THAT THERE IS ONE HIGHER THAN OURSELVES, TO WHOSE WILL WE MUST ALL BOW.

II. THEY LEAD US TO REFLECTION, AND ARE THE MEANS OF REVEALING TO US OUR PAST SHORTCOMINGS AND FAILINGS.

III. THEY RENDER US MORE SUSCEPTIBLE TO RECEIVING THE TEACHINGS OF GOD'S OWN SPIRIT.

IV. THEY RAISE OUR THOUGHTS FROM EARTH TOWARDS GOD AND HEAVEN.

V. THEY BRING US BACK WHEN WE HAVE WANDERED FROM OUR GOD, AND ARE THE MEANS OF RESTORING TO US THE WARMTH AND FERVOUR OF TRUE PIETY. Whilst, therefore, suffering considered in itself is not good, yet instrumentally it is desirable, and, if we are rightly exercised by it, will help us to attain unto a holier and more heavenly life. So David (Ps. cxix. 71, 67). So Manasseh (2 Chron. xxxiii. 11—13). It is because we are so slow to learn the lessons our sorrows are intended to teach us that it is "through much tribulation" that we are to enter the kingdom prepared for the saints of God. We need these threshings of the inner spiritual man in order that the chaff may be separated from the wheat, and we become thus prepared for the heavenly garner. Let us accept all our griefs as precious tokens of the Divine Father's love, and make them our convoy to bear us up to him.—S. D. H.

Ver. 16.—*The pride of human sufficiency.* The reference is to the Chaldeans. They would, in due course, invade Judah, and should be successful in their invasion. The "sinful nation" should fall into their hands as fish into the net of the angler; and, intoxicated by their success, they should congratulate themselves upon their achievements and adore their military prowess and skill, and their weapons of war, as though these had won the victory. "Therefore they sacrifice," etc. (ver. 16). They should be lifted up with the pride of human sufficiency. Observe—

I. SUCCESS IS EVER SECURED AS THE BESTOWMENT OR BY THE PERMISSION OF GOD. 1. *Temporal success is thus gained.* The age in which we live is an age of earnest toil, of restless activity. It is becoming more and more felt that a man cannot expect to make headway apart from continuous, energetic work. And this is a healthy "sign of the times." It reminds us that life is too valuable a gift to be frittered away. It contrasts, strikingly and pleasingly, with those periods in which ease, luxury, and sloth were deified and adored. There is dignity in labour. The danger lies in the non-recognition of God as the Bestower of the prosperity secured, and in ascribing the success achieved wholly to ourselves. The true spirit is that which prompts the acknowledgment, "All things come of thee" (1 Chron. xxix. 14). The Lord is "Giver of all." Success is sometimes achieved by bad men. By fraud, oppression, reckless speculation, and by taking mean advantage, "the portion" of such is "made fat" and "their meat plenteous;" and in such cases all this is through the all-wise although often inscrutable permission of the Most High. 2. *Spiritual success is also thus gained.* In holy service we are but the instruments employed by God. The power is his, and the honour should all be laid at his feet. Baxter, when complimented at the close of his career upon the usefulness of his writings, said, "I was but a pen in the hand of my God, and what honour is due to a pen?"

II. MEN, FORGETFUL OF THIS AND TRACING TO THEMSELVES THE SUCCESS ACHIEVED, BECOME ELATED WITH THE PRIDE OF HUMAN SUFFICIENCY. "Therefore they sacrifice unto their net," etc. (ver. 16). "They say in their heart, My power and the might of mine hand hath gotten me this wealth" (Deut. viii. 17). So Pharaoh said, "My river is mine own, and I have made it for myself" (Ezek. xxix. 3). So Nebuchadnezzar said, "Is not this great Babylon, that I have built," etc. (Dan. iv. 30). Pusey refers in illustration of this to certain North American Indians, "who designate their bow and arrow as the only beneficent deities whom they know;" to the Romans sacrificing to their military standards; and to the French referred to in the *Times* during the Franco-German War as "almost worshipping the mitrailleuse as a goddess." And this is still our peril. Because our possibilities are so great, we think that we can win all blessings for ourselves. Everywhere we see the worship of our human powers and means—the workman worshipping the strength of his arm and the deftness of his fingers, the man of business worshipping his skill and acuteness, and the man of science, human knowledge. Nor is the Church of God free from this spirit: for there is far too much of trusting to forms and ceremonies, to worldly alliances, to machinery and organization, as though these were the great essentials, and far too little of "looking up unto the hills whence cometh her help."

III. ALL SUCH GLORYING IS VAIN. 1. *It reveals self-ignorance.* For no one who really understands himself could possibly cherish this spirit. 2. *It leads to oppression.* The man who has exalted notions of his own powers and doings is likely to be proud and overbearing in his conduct towards others. 3. *It is offensive to God.* "He resisteth the proud, but giveth grace unto the humble" (Jas. iv. 6). "In all our ways, therefore, let us acknowledge him," and as we prosper in our course ascribe the success gained to his favour and blessing. In the language of Keble, let us say—

"Should e'er thy wonder-working grace
        Triumph by our weak arm,
    Let not our sinful fancy trace
        Aught human in the charm:

"To our own nets ne'er bow we down,
        Lest on the eternal shore
    The angels, while our draught they own,
        Reject us evermore."

S. D. H.

Vers. 13—15, 17; ch. ii. 1—4.—*Dark problems and man's true attitude in relation to them.* I. THE MYSTERY CONNECTED WITH THE DIVINE OPERATIONS. (Vers. 13—15, 17.) The prophet in these words expressed the perplexity of his mind and the consequent sadness of his heart. He had bitterly mourned over the prevailing guilt of his people, and had earnestly appealed to Heaven to vindicate the right. The Divine response, however, filled him with distress. That Divine chastisement should be inflicted upon his country he understood and approved, but that the Chaldeans, who were still greater transgressors, should be permitted to run over the land, and to lead his people into captivity, baffled and perplexed him. Yea, more; whilst the good in his land were but few, yet there were to be found such; and how could it be that these should suffer, and suffer at the hands of the heathen who were so gross and iniquitous? Surely, thought he, this scarcely accorded with the thought of the Divine purity, and of the rectitude of God's providential government. And hence he cried in his perplexity, "Thou art," etc. (vers. 13—15, 17). There is mystery in the Divine operations; dark problems confront us as we reflect upon the Divine working. "How unsearchable are his judgments, and his ways past finding out!" (Rom. xi. 33); "Thy way is in the sea;" i.e. "far down in secret channels of the deep is his roadway;" "Thy footsteps are not known;" i.e. "none can follow thy tracks" (Ps. lxxvii. 19). One man enjoys the endowment of reason; another is left a helpless lunatic. One has all things and abounds; another is well-nigh destitute of the common necessaries of life. One has "no changes;" another is being continually subjected to adverse influences. We see the mother dying just after she has given birth to her child; we behold the young and the beautiful passing "out of sunshiny life into silent death;" we behold the earnest toiler stricken down in the very prime of life, whilst useless and injurious lives are preserved and "burn to the socket." The sceptic asks us to reconcile all this with the thought of God's wise and loving rulership, and, failing this, to join him in his indifference and practical atheism; but to do so would be to go contrary to the deepest convictions of our hearts, and to the clearest testimony of our consciences. We will rather seek to cherish a faith which will pierce the mists, and enable us, despite such anomalies, to recognize the goodness and the love of God.

II. THE TRUE ATTITUDE IN RELATION TO THESE DARK PROBLEMS. 1. *The attitude of prayer.* The seer took all his fears and forebodings, his difficulties and discouragements, his doubts and perplexities, to God in prayer (vers. 13—15, 17). As we pray light often is cast upon the hidden path. 2. *The attitude of expectancy.* "I will stand upon my watch," etc. (ch. ii. 1). We are to "wait patiently for the Lord," and there is ever to enter into this waiting the element of watchfulness. We are to look for further light, even here, upon the works and ways of our God, and we shall assuredly miss this unless we cherish the spirit of holy expectation. "Many a proffered succour from heaven goes past us because we are not standing on our watch-tower to catch the far-off indications of its approach, and to fling open the gates of our hearts for its entrance" (Maclaren). 3. *The attitude of trust.* "The just shall live by his faith" (ch. ii. 4). It is not in the process, but in the issue, that the wisdom and rightness of the Divine operations will be fully manifested, and for the issue we must trustfully wait. Tennyson sings—

> "Who can so forecast the years,
> And find in loss a gain to match?
> Or reach a hand through time to catch
> The far-off interest of tears?"

In God's economy there is a gain to match every loss. Tears do bear interest; only we cannot "forecast the years," and see the gain; we cannot reach forth and seize in advance "the interest of tears." But however far off, it is there. We shall know more and more, even in the present life, as God's purposes concerning us develop, that all things are working together for our good (Rom. viii. 28), whilst at length standing upon the heights of eternity, and gazing back upon the past and seeing in the perfect light, the perfect wisdom, and the perfect love, we shall cry with adoring gratitude, "He hath done all things well!"—S. D. H.

Vers. 1—4.—*The cry of a good man under the perplexing procedure of God.* "The burden which Habakkuk the prophet did see. O Lord, how long shall I cry, and thou wilt not hear! even cry out unto thee of violence, and thou wilt not save!" etc. Of Habakkuk nothing is known for certainty. The fifth and sixth verses of the first chapter tell us that he prophesied before that series of invasions by the Chaldeans which ended in the destruction of Jerusalem and the captivity of the people—probably between 640 and 610 years before Christ. He was therefore contemporary with Jeremiah and Zephaniah. The book treats of the wickedness of the Jews, the infliction of punishment upon the Chaldeans, and the destruction of the latter in their turn. It has also a splendid ode, composed by the prophet in anticipation of their deliverance from Babylonish captivity. His work is quoted by the apostles (Heb. x. 37, 38 ; Rom. i. 17 ; Gal. iii. 11 ; Acts xiii. 41), hence it was regarded as having Divine authority. His style, in dignity and sublimity, is not surpassed by any of the Hebrew prophets. He is original. His utterances are bold and animated; his descriptions graphic and pointed. The lyric ode contained in the third chapter is esteemed by most biblical critics as one of the most splendid and magnificent in the whole compass of Hebrew poetry. The prophet sets forth the cause of the Chaldean invasion, and the great wickedness that abounded in the Jewish nation during his time. This was the burden of his discourse. "The burden which Habakkuk the prophet did see." What was the burden ? The heavy judgments impending over his nation. He saw it like a mountain with his prophetic eye; nay, he felt it as a mountain in his heart. This doom hanging over the Jewish people was indeed an intolerable weight. The text contains the *cry of a good man under the perplexing procedure of God*—" O Lord, how long shall I cry !" There seem to be two elements in his perplexity.

I. GOD'S APPARENT DISREGARD TO HIS EARNEST PRAYER. "O Lord, how long shall I cry, and thou wilt not hear !" Under the pressure of "the burden" that was resting on his heart, viz. the moral corruption and the coming doom of his country, it would seem that he had often cried unto the Almighty and implored his interposition; but no answer had come. How often have good men in every age felt that God disregarded their supplications ! They cried and cried, but no answer came. The heavens seemed like brass; the oracles were hushed. It was thus with the Syro-Phœnician woman. Christ for a time not only treated her application with seeming indifference, but he even repulsed her. Why are not the prayers of good men immediately answered? In reply to this question three undoubted facts should be borne in mind. 1. *That importunity of soul is necessary to qualify for the appreciation of the mercies sought.* It is not until a man is made to feel the deep necessity of a thing that he values it when it comes. If we obtained from the Almighty what we required by one cry, or even by a series of mere formal applications, the boon would be of doubtful service ; it would scarcely be appreciated, and would fail to fire the soul with the sentiments of devout gratitude and praise. It is not what God gives a man that does him good; it is the *state of mind* in which it is received that transmutes it either into a blessing or a curse. "How long shall I cry !" How long? Until the sense of need is so intensified as to qualify for the reception and due appreciation of the blessing. 2. *That the exercise of true prayer is in itself the best means of spiritual culture.* Conscious contact with God is essential to moral excellence. You must bring the sunbeam to the seed you have sown, if you would have the seed quickened and developed ; and you must bring God into conscious contact with your powers, if you would have them vivified and brought forth into strength and perfection. True prayer does this ; it is the soul realizing itself in the presence of him " who quickeneth all things." 3. *That prayers are answered where there is no bestowment of the blessing invoked.* We know not what to pray for ; and were we to have what we seek, we might be ruined. Acquiescence in the Divine will is the highest answer to all true prayer. Christ prayed that the cup should pass from him. It did not pass from him ; but, instead, there came to him the spirit of acquiescence in the Divine will : "Not my will, but thine be done." This is all we want. Acquiescence in the Divine will is the moral perfection, dignity, and blessedness of all creatures in the universe. With these facts let us not be anxious about the apparent disregard of God to our prayers.

II. GOD'S APPARENT DISREGARD TO THE MORAL CONDITION OF SOCIETY. "Why dost thou show me iniquity, and cause me to behold grievance ? for spoiling and violence are before me : and there are that raise up strife and contention. Therefore the Law is slacked, and judgment doth never go forth : for the wicked doth compass about the righteous ; therefore wrong judgment proceedeth." The rendering of Delitzsch is both faithful and forceful, "Why dost thou let me see mischief, and thou lookest upon distress? Devastation and violence are before me; there arises strife, and contention lifts itself up. Therefore the Law is benumbed, and justice comes not forth for ever: for sinners encircle the righteous man: therefore justice goes forth perverted." The substance of this is the old complaint, " Wherefore doth the way of the wicked prosper? wherefore are all they happy that deal very treacherously?" (Jer. xii. 1). Two facts should be set against this complaint. 1. *The good have the best of it, even in this life.* Goodness is its own reward. Take two men—one who enjoys the love and fellowship of God, but who is destitute of this world's good and lives in poverty; the other, in whose heart reign the elements of wickedness, but who has an abundance of the things of this life. Ask which of the two is the happier. The former, without doubt. Benevolence is the fountain of happiness, and selfishness the fountain of misery in both worlds. In this world give me poverty and piety rather than riches with wickedness. 2. *That the evil will have the worst of it in the next life.* There is no doubt about this. The parable of the rich man and Lazarus teaches this. " When the wicked spring as the grass, and when all the workers of iniquity do flourish, it is that they shall be destroyed for ever" (Ps. xcii. 7).

Conclusion. Pray on, brother. " Pray without ceasing." Thy prayers are not lost. Let not God's apparent disregard to the supplications of his people and the moral condition of society perplex thy judgment and disturb thy peace. Wait the great explaining day. " What thou knowest not now thou shalt know hereafter."—D. T.

Vers. 5—10.—*The doom of a nation of conventional religionists.* " Behold ye among the heathen, and regard, and wonder marvellously: for I will work a work in your days, which ye will not believe, though it be told you. For, lo, I raise up the Chaldeans, that bitter and hasty nation; which shall march through the breadth of the land," etc. In these verses we have the doom of a nation of *conventional religionists.* The Jews were such a nation; they prided themselves in the orthodoxy of their faith, in the ceremonials of their worship, in the polity of their Church. " To them pertained the adoption, and the glory, and the covenants, and the giving of the Law, and the service of God, and the promises" (Rom. ix. 4). But they had now become abhorrent to their Maker. He was weary of them, and he threatens them with a terrible doom; the doom was so terrible that " ye will not believe, though it be told you." The doom threatened was terrible in many respects.

I. IT WAS TO BE WROUGHT BY THE INSTRUMENTALITY OF A WICKED NATION. " I will work a work in your days, which ye will not believe, though it be told you. For, lo, I raise up the Chaldeans, that bitter and hasty nation, which shall march through the breadth of the land, to possess the dwelling-places that are not theirs." " Nabopolassar had already destroyed the mighty empire of Assyria, and founded the Chaldeo-Babylonian rule. He had made himself so formidable that Necho found it necessary to march an army against him, in order to check his progress; and, though defeated at Megiddo, he had, in conjunction with his son Nebuchadnezzar, gained a complete victory over the Egyptians at Carchemish. These events were calculated to alarm the Jews, whose country lay between the dominions of the two contending powers; but, accustomed as they were to confide in Egypt and in the sacred localities of their own capital (Isa. xxxi. 1; Jer. vii. 4), and being in alliance with the Chaldeans, they were indisposed to listen to, and treated with the utmost incredulity, any predictions which described their overthrow by that people" (Henderson). Observe that God employs *wicked* nations as his instruments. " Lo, I raise up the Chaldeans." " I will work a work," he says; but how? By the Chaldeans. How does he raise up wicked nations to do his work? 1. *Not instigatingly.* He does not inspire them with wicked passions necessary to qualify them for the infernal work of violence, war, rapine, bloodshed. God could not do this. The diabolic passions are in them. 2. *Not coercively.* He does not force them to it; in no way does he interfere with them. They are the responsible party. They go forth on the bloody message with a consciousness of freedom. How, then, does he " raise " them up? He permits them. He could prevent them; but he allows them. He gives them life, capacity, and opportunities; but he does not inspire or coerce them. Now, would not the fact that the destruction of the Israelites would come upon them from a heathen nation, a nation which they despised, make it all the more terrible?

II. IT WAS TO BE WROUGHT WITH RESISTLESS VIOLENCE. 1. *The violence would be uncontrolled.* "Their judgment and their dignity shall proceed of themselves." They recognize no authority, and proudly spurn the dictates of others. "They recognize no judge save themselves, and they get for themselves their own dignity, without needing others' help. It will be vain for the Jews to complain of their tyrannical judgments, for whatever the Chaldeans decree they will do according to their own will: they will not brook any one attempting to interfere" (Fausset). 2. *The violence would be rapid and fierce.* "Their horses are swifter than the leopards." A naturalist says of the leopard that it runs most swiftly, straight on, and you would imagine it was flying through the air. "More fierce than the evening wolves." These ravenous beasts, having skulked all the day away from the light of heaven, get terribly hungry by the night, and come forth with a fierce voracity. Like the swift leopards and the ravenous wolves, we are here told, these Chaldeans would come forth. Yes, and swifter and more ravenous than the wolves, like the hungry eagle on its pinions that "hasteth to eat." What a terrible description of their doom! Alas! into what a monster sin has transformed man! he becomes leopard, wolf, eagle, etc.

III. IT WAS TO BE WROUGHT WITH IMMENSE HAVOC. "Their faces shall sup up as the east wind, and they shall gather the captivity as the sand. And they shall scoff at the kings, and the princes shall be a scorn unto them: they shall deride every stronghold; for they shall heap dust, and take it." As the east wind, they would sweep through the country, like the simoom, spreading devastation wherever it passed; and like that wind would bear away the Jews into captivity, thick as the sand. "They shall scoff at the kings, and the princes shall be a scorn unto them." They would regard all the great magnates of Judæa with a haughty contempt, and treat them with derision. And so would they be in their bloody expedition. They would regard their very conquering power as their god, and worship their success.

CONCLUSION. All this was to come upon a nation of *conventional reglionists.* All peoples whose religion is that of profession, letter, form, ceremony, are exposed to a doom as terrible as this.—D. T.

Vers. 12, 13.—*The eternity, providence, and holiness of Jehovah.* "Art thou not from everlasting, O Lord my God, mine Holy One? we shall not die. O Lord, thou hast ordained them for judgment; and, O mighty God, thou hast established them for correction," etc. In this passage the prophet refers to the eternity, the providence, and the holiness of the Jehovah of the Jewish people.

I. HE REGARDS HIS ETERNITY AS AN ARGUMENT FOR THEIR PRESERVATION. "Art thou not from everlasting, O Lord, my God, mine Holy One? we shall not die." "However terrible and prostrating the Divine threatenings may sound, the prophet draws consolation and hope from the holiness of the faithful covenant God, that Israel will not perish, but that the judgment will be only a severe chastisement" (Delitzsch). "Art thou not from everlasting?" The interrogatory does not imply doubt on his part. The true God is essentially eternal; he "inhabiteth eternity." He is without beginning, without succession, without end. The loftiest thoughts of the loftiest intelligence are lost in the idea of his eternity. From his eternity the prophet argues that his people will not perish: "We shall not die." There is force in this argument. His people live in him. Their life is hid in God, and so long as he endures they may hope to continue. Christ said to his disciples, "Because I live, ye shall live also." Man's immortality is not in himself, but in God. If he has purposed that we shall live for ever, he is eternal, and will never change his mind or die.

II. HE REGARDS HIS PROVIDENCE AS A SOURCE OF COMFORT. "O Lord, thou hast ordained them for judgment; and, O mighty God, thou hast established them for correction." "Jehovah, for judgment thou hast appointed it, and, O Rock, thou hast founded it for chastisement" (Delitzsch). Whatever evil of any kind, from any quarter, comes upon the loyal servants of God, comes not by accident; it is under the direction of the All-wise and the All-beneficent. These Chaldeans could not move without him, nor could they strike one blow without his permission; they were but the rod in his hand. All the most furious fiends in the universe are under his direction. He says, concerning the mighty tide of wicked passions, "Hitherto shalt thou come, and no further." Is not this a source of comfort under suffering and oppression? Whatever mischief men design to inflict upon his people, he purposes to bring good out of it: and his counsel shall stand.

III. HE REGARDS HIS HOLINESS AS AN OCCASION FOR PERPLEXITY. "Thou art of purer eyes than to behold evil, and canst not look on iniquity: wherefore lookest thou upon them that deal treacherously, and holdest thy tongue when the wicked devoureth the man that is more righteous than he?" Jehovah is the Holy One. His holiness is essential, underived, indestructible, reflected in all consciences. He is of "purer eyes than to behold evil." His eyes do behold iniquity. There is no sin that comes not within his glance. What the prophet means, I presume, is—Thou art of "purer eyes" than to behold iniquity with satisfaction. It is that "abominable thing" which God hates. Now, this holiness was the occasion of perplexity to the prophet. As if he had said, "Since thou art holy, why allow such abominations to take place? why permit wicked men to work such iniquities, and to inflict such suffering upon the righteous?" This has always been a source of perplexity to good men. That a holy God, who has the power to prevent such iniquities, should allow them to occur, abound, and continue, is one of the great mysteries of life.

CONCLUSION. Let us, in all our troubles, like the prophet, look to the Everlasting One, and hold firmly the conviction that, notwithstanding the abounding of evil in the world, He is the *Holy One*, and is of "purer eyes" than to approve of wickedness.

> "Courage, brother, do not stumble;
>   Though thy path be dark as night
> There's a star to guide the humble;
>   Trust in God, and do the right.
>
> "Let the road be rough and dreary,
>   And its end far out of sight;
> Foot it bravely, strong or weary:
>   Trust in God, and do the right.
>
> "Perish policy and cunning,
>   Perish all that fears the light;
> Whether losing, whether winning,
>   Trust in God, and do the right.
>
> "Trust no party, sect, or faction;
>   Trust no leaders in the fight;
> But in every word and action
>   Trust in God, and do the right.
>
> "Simple rule and safest guiding,
>   Inward peace and inward might,
> Star upon our path abiding:
>   Trust in God, and do the right.
>
> "Some will hate thee, some will love thee,
>   Some will flatter, some will slight;
> Cease from man, and look above thee:
>   Trust in God, and do the right."

(Norman McLeod.)

D. T.

Vers. 14—17.—*Rapacious selfishness in power.* "And makest men as the fishes of the sea, as the creeping things, that have no ruler over them. They take up all of them with the angle, they catch them in their net, and gather them in their drag: therefore they rejoice and are glad," etc. In Nebuchadnezzar you have rapacious selfishness in power. He is here represented by implication as treating the Jewish people as a fisherman treats the fish in the sea. His aim is to catch them by "angle," "net," and "drag," and turn them to his own vile use. "These figures are not to be interpreted with such speciality as that the net and fishing-net answer to the sword and bow; but the hook, the net, and the fishing-net, as the things used for catching fish, refer to all the means which the Chaldeans employ in order to subdue and destroy the nations. Luther interprets it correctly. 'These hooks, nets, and fishing-nets,' he says, 'are nothing more than his great and powerful armies, by which he gained dominion over all lands and people, and brought home to Babylon the goods, jewels, silver and gold, interest and rent of all the world'" (Delitzsch). In these verses we have a specimen of *rapacious selfishness in power*. Selfishness is the root and essence of sin. All unregenerate men are therefore more or less selfish, and rapacity is an instinct of selfishness. Selfishness hungers for the things of others. Whilst this rapacious selfishness is general, mercifully it is not always *in power*, otherwise the world would be more of a pandemonium than it is. It is ever tyrannic and ruthless in the measure of its power. Here we find it in the power of an absolute monarchy, and it is terrible to contemplate. Four things are suggested.

I. IT PRACTICALLY IGNORES THE RIGHTS OF MAN AS MAN. "And makest man as the fishes of the sea, as the creeping things, that have no ruler over them." The Babylonian tyrant did not see in the population of Judæa *men* possessing natural endowments, sustaining moral relationships, invested with rights and responsibilities similar to his own fellow-men, but merely "fishes;" his object was to catch them and turn them to his own use. It is ever so with selfishness: it blinds man to the claims of his brother. What does the selfish landlord care for the *man* in the tenants and labourers on his estate? He only values them as they can subserve his interests. What does the selfish employer care for the *man* in those who work in his service and build up his fortune? He treats them rather as fishes to be used than as brethren to be respected. What does the selfish despot care for the moral humanity of the people over whom he sways his sceptre? He values them only as they can fight his battles, enrich his exchequer, and contribute to his pageantry and pomp. What were men to Alexander? What were men to Napoleon, etc.?

II. IT ASSIDUOUSLY WORKS TO TURN MEN TO ITS OWN USE. "They take up all of them with the angle, they catch them in their net, and gather them in their drag; therefore they rejoice and are glad." Thus they take up all of them, some with the hook one by one, others in shoals as in a net, others in a drag or enclosed net. Ah me! Human life is like a sea—deep, unresting, treacherous; and the teeming millions of men are but as fishes, the weaker devoured by the stronger.

> " . . . the good old rule
> Sufficeth them, the simple plan
> That they should take who have the power,
> And they should keep who can."

> (Wordsworth.)

The mighty ones use the hook to oppress individuals one by one, the net and the drag to carry multitudes away. To a rapacious selfishness in power the man is lost in the labourer, the clerk, the *employé*, the sailor, the soldier, the subject, etc. Men, what are they? To its eye they are goods, chattels, beasts of burden, "fishes"—nothing more. As the fisherman works by various expedients to catch the fish, the selfish man in power is ever active in devising the best expedients to turn human flesh to his own use.

III. IT ADORES SELF ON ACCOUNT OF ITS SUCCESS. "Therefore they sacrifice unto their net, and burn incense unto their drag; because by them their portion is fat, and their meat plenteous." They glory even in their crimes, because these result in success. They admire their own dexterity and prowess. The selfish man says to himself, "My power and the might of mine hand hath gotten me this wealth" (Deut. viii. 17). According to the measure of a man's selfishness is his propensity to self-worship. The more selfish a merchant, a scholar, a religionist, an author, a preacher, etc., is, the more prone to praise himself for his imaginary success. Because men are everywhere selfish, they are everywhere "sacrificing unto their net, and burning incense unto their drag." The selfish statesman says, "There is no measure like mine;" the selfish sectarian, "There is no Church like mine;" the selfish author, "There is no book like mine;" the selfish preacher, "There is no sermon like mine."

> "To our own nets ne'er bow we down,
> Lest on the eternal shore
> The angels, while our draught they own,
> Reject us evermore."

> (Keble.)

IV. IT REMAINS INSATIABLE, NOTWITHSTANDING ITS PROSPERITY. "Shall they therefore empty their net ? " etc. An old author thus paraphrases the language : "Shall they enrich themselves and fill their own vessels with that which they have by violence and oppression taken away from their neighbours ? Shall they empty their net of what they have caught, that they may cast it into the sea again to catch more ? And wilt thou suffer them to proceed in this wicked course ? Shall they not spare continually to slay the nations ? Must the number and wealth of nations be sacrificed to their net ? "

CONCLUSION. What an awful picture of the world we have here ! All unregenerate men are selfish. Men are everywhere preying on men; and, alas ! often those who most lament the universal selfishness are the most selfish. Like the ravenous birds which seem to bewail the sheep when dying, they are ready to pick out their eyes when their opportunity comes. " Where every man is for himself," says an old author, " the devil will have all." This selfishness is the heart of stone in humanity, which must be exchanged for a heart of flesh, or the man will be damned. What but the gospel can effect this change ? Oh that those who call themselves Christians would cherish and exemplify that disinterestedness which alone gives title to the name ! "I would so live," said Seneca, " as if I knew I had received my being only for the benefit of others."—D. T.

EXPOSITION.

CHAPTER II.

Vers. 1—3.—§ 5. *The prophet, waiting for an answer to his expostulation, is bidden to write the oracle in plain characters, because its fulfilment is certain.*

Ver. 1.—Habakkuk speaks with himself, and, mindful of his office, waits for the communication which he confidently expects (Jer. xxxiii. 3). **I will stand upon my watch** (Isa. xxi. 6, 8). As a watchman goes to a high place to see all around and discern what is coming, so the prophet places himself apart from men, perhaps in some secluded height, in readiness to hear the voice of God and seize the meaning of the coming event. Prophets are called "watchmen" (comp. Ezek. iii. 17; xxxiii. 2, 6; Micah vii. 4). **The tower;** *i.e.* watch-tower, either literally or metaphorically, as in the first clause. Septuagint, πέτραν, "rock." **What he will say unto me;** *quid dicatur mihi* (Vulgate); τί λαλήσει ἐν ἐμοί, "what he will speak in me" (Septuagint). He watches for the inward revelation which God makes to his soul (but see note on Zech. ii. 0). **When I am reproved;** *ad arguentem me* (Vulgate); ἐπὶ τὸν ἔλεγχόν μου (Septuagint); rather, *to my complaint,* referring to his complaint concerning the impunity of sinners (ch. i. 13—17). He waits till he hears God's voice within him what answer he shall make to his own complaint, the expostulation which he had offered to God. There is no question here concerning the reproofs which others levelled against him, or concerning any rebuke conveyed to him by God—an impression given by the Anglican Version.

Ver. 2.—Jehovah answers the prophet's expostulation (ch. i. 12, etc.). **Write.** That it may remain permanently on record, and that, when it comes to pass, people may believe in the prophet's inspiration (John xiii. 19; comp. Isa. viii. 1; xxx. 8; Jer. xxx. 2; Rev. i. 11). **The vision** (see ch. i. 1: Obad 1). The word includes the inward revelation as well as the open vision. **Upon tables;** *upon the tables* (Deut. xxvii. 8); i.e. certain tablets placed in public places, that all might see and read them (see Isaiah, *loc. cit.*); Septuagint, εἰς πυξίον, "a boxwood tablet." The summary of what was to be written is given in ver. 4. This was to be "made plain," written large and legibly. Septuagint, σαφῶς. **That he may run that readeth it.** The common explanation of these words (unfortunately perpetuated by Keble's well-known hymn, "There is a book, who runs may read "), viz. that even the runner, one who hastens by hurriedly, may be able to read it, is not borne out by the Hebrew, which rather means that every one who reads it may run, *i.e.* read fluently and easily. So Jerome, "Scribere jubetur planius, ut possit lector currere, et nullo impedimento velocitas ejus et legendi cupido teneatur." Henderson, comparing Dan. xii. 4, "Many shall run to and fro, and knowledge shall be increased," interprets the clause to signify that whosoever reads the announcement might run and publish it to all within his reach. "'To run,'" he adds, "is equivalent to 'to prophesy' in Jer. xxiii. 21," on the principle that those who were charged with a Divine message were to use all despatch in making it known. In the passage of Daniel, " to run to and fro," is explained to mean " to peruse."

Ver. 3.—For. The reason is given why the oracle is to be committed to writing. Is yet for an (the) appointed time. The vision will not be accomplished immediately, but in the period fixed by God (comp. Dan. viii. 17, 19; xi. 27, 35). Others explain, "pointeth to a yet future time." But at the end it shall speak. The verb is literally "breathes," or "pants;" hence the clause is better rendered, and it panteth (equivalent to hasteth) towards the end. The prophecy personified yearns for its fulfilment in "the end," not merely at the destruction of the literal Babylon, but in the time of the end—the last time, the Messianic age, when the world-power, typified by Babylon, should be overthrown (see Daniel, loc. cit.). And not lie; it deceiveth not; οὐκ εἰς κενόν, "not in vain" (Septuagint). It will certainly come to pass. Wait for it. For the vision and its accomplishment. Because it will surely come. The author of the Epistle to the Hebrews (x. 37) quotes the Septuagint Version of this clause, applying it to the last coming of Messiah : Ὅτι (plus ὁ, Hebrew) ἐρχόμενος ἥξει, καὶ οὐ μὴ χρονίσῃ (οὐ χρονιεῖ, Hebrew) ; so the Vulgate, Veniens veniet, et non tardabit. The original passage does not primarily refer to the coming of Messiah, but as the full and final accomplishment of the prophecy doubtless belongs to that age, it is not a departure from the fundamental idea to see in it a reference hereto. It will not tarry ; it will not be behindhand ; it will not fail to arrive (Judg. v. 28 ; 2 Sam. xx. 5).

Ver. 4.—§ 6. The great principle is taught that the proud shall not continue, but the just shall live by faith. The prophecy commences with a fundamental thought, applicable to all God's dealings with man. Behold, his soul which is lifted up is not upright in him; literally, behold, puffed up, his soul is not upright in him. This is a description of an evil character (especially of the Chaldean) in opposition to the character delineated in the following hemistich. One who is proud, presumptuous, thinks much of himself, despising others, and is not straightforward and upright before God, shall not live, shall not have a happy, safe life; he carries in himself the seeds of destruction. The result is not expressed in the first hemistich, but may be supplied from the next clause, and, as Knabenbauer suggests, may be inferred from the language in Heb. x. 38, 39, where, after quoting the Septuagint rendering of this passage, Ἐὰν ὑποστείληται, οὐκ εὐδοκεῖ ἡ ψυχή μου ἐν αὐτῷ, the writer adds, "But we are not of them that shrink back (ὑποστολῆς) unto perdition." Vulgate, Ecce, qui incredulus est, non erit recta anima ejus in semetipso, which seems to confine the statement to the case of one who doubts God's word. But the just shall live by his faith. The "faith" here spoken of is a loving trust in God, confidence in his promises, resulting in due performance of his will. This hemistich is the antithesis to the former. The proud and perverse, those who wish to be independent of God, shall perish; but, on the other hand, the righteous shall live and be saved through his faith, on the condition that he puts his trust in God. The Hebrew accents forbid the union, "the just by faith," though, of course, no one can be just, righteous, without faith. The passage may be emphasized by rendering, "As to the just, through his faith he shall live." This famous sentence, which St. Paul has used as the basis of his great argument (Rom. i. 17; Gal. iii. 11; comp. Heb. x. 38), in its literal and contextual application implies that the righteous man will have perfect trust in God's promises, and will be rewarded by being safe in the day of tribulation, with reference to the coming trouble at the hands of the Chaldeans. When the proud, greedy kingdom shall have sunk in ruin, the faithful people shall live secure. But the application is not confined to this circumstance. The promise looks beyond the temporal future of the Chaldeans and Israelites, and unto a reward that is eternal. We see how naturally the principle here enunciated is applied by the apostle to teach the doctrine of justification by faith in Christ. The LXX. gives, Ὁ δὲ δίκαιος ἐκ πίστεώς μου ζήσεται, i.e. "by faith in me." The Speaker is God. St. Paul omits μου. Habakkuk gathers into one sentence the whole principle of the Law, and indeed all true religion.

Ver. 5.—§ 7. The character of the Chaldeans in some particulars is intimated. The general proposition in the former hemistich of ver. 4 is here applied to the Chaldeans, in striking contrast to the lot of the just in the latter clause. Yea also, because he transgresseth by wine. This should be, And moreover, wine is treacherous. A kind of proverbial saying (Prov. xx. 1). Vulgate, Quomodo vinum potantem decipit. There is no word expressive of comparison in the original, though it may be supplied to complete the sense. The intemperate habits of the Babylonians are well attested (see Dan. v. 3, 4; Quint. Curt., v. 1, "Babylonii maxime in vinum et quæ ebrietatem sequuntur effusi sunt;" comp. Her., i. 191; Xen., 'Cyrop.,' vii. 5. 15). They used both the fermented sap of the palm tree as well as the juice of the grape, the latter chiefly imported from abroad. "The wealthy Babylonians were fond of drinking to excess; their banquets were magnificent, but generally ended in drunkenness" (Rawlinson, 'Anc. Mon.,' iii. 450, edit. 1865). Neither the Septuagint, nor the Syriac, nor the Coptic Version has any mention of wine in this passage. The Septuagint gives, ὁ δὲ κατοιόμενος καὶ καταφρονητής, "the arrogant and the scorner." He is a proud man, neither keepeth he at home; a haughty man, he resteth not. His pride is always impelling him to new raids and conquests. This is quite the character of the later Chaldeans, and is consistent with the latter part of the verse. The comparison, then, is this : As wine raises the spirits and excites men to great efforts which in the end deceive them, so pride rouses these men to go on their insatiate course of conquest, which shall one day prove their ruin. The verb translated "keepeth at home" has the secondary sense of "being decorous;" hence the Vulgate gives, Sic erit vir superbus, et non decorabitur ; i.e. as wine first exhilarates and then makes a man contemptible, so pride, which begins by exalting a man, ends by bringing him to ignominy. Others take the verb in the sense of "continueth not," explaining that the destruction of Babylon is here intimated. But what follows makes against this interpretation. The LXX. gives, Ἀνὴρ ἀλαζὼν, οὐθὲν μὴ περάνῃ, which Jerome, combining with it his own version, paraphrases, "Sic vir superbus non decorabitur, nec voluntatem suam perducet ad finem; et juxta Symmachum, οὐκ εὐπορήσει, hoc est, in rerum omnium erit penuria." Who enlargeth his desire as hell; Hebrew, Sheol. Hell is called insatiable (Prov. xxvii. 20 ; xxx. 16; Isa. v. 14). Is as death, which seizes all creatures and spares none. People ; peoples.

Vers. 6—8.—§ 8. The destruction of the Babylonians is announced by the mouth of the vanquished nations, who utter five woes against their oppressor. The first woe : for their rapacity.

Ver. 6.—All these. All the nations and peoples who have been subjugated and barbarously treated by the Babylonians (comp. Isa. xiv. 4). A parable. A sententious song (see note on Micah ii. 4). A taunting proverb. The Anglican Version combines the two Hebrew words, which stand unconnected, into one notion. So the Vulgate, loquelam ænigmatum. The latter of the two generally means "riddle," "enigma ;" the other word (melitzah) is by some translated, "a derisive satirical song," or "an obscure, dark saying ;" but, as Keil and Delitzsch have shown, is better understood of a bright, clear, brilliant speech. So the two terms signify "a speech containing enigmas," or a song which has

double or ambiguous meanings (comp. Prov. i. 6). Septuagint, Πρόβλημα εἰς διήγησιν αὐτοῦ. Woe (Nah. iii. 1). This is the first of the five "woes," which consist of three verses each, arranged in strophical form. Increaseth that which is not his. He continues to add to his conquests and possessions, which are not his, because they are acquired by injustice and violence. This is the first denunciation of the Chaldeans for their insatiable rapacity. How long ? The question comes in interjectionally—How long is this state of things to continue unpunished (comp. Ps. vi. 3; xc. 13)? That ladeth himself with thick clay; Septuagint, βαρύνων τὸν κλοιὸν αὐτοῦ στιβαρῶς, "who loadeth his yoke heavily ;" Vulgate, aggravat contra se densum lutum. The renderings of the Anglican and Latin Versions signify that the riches and spoils with which the conquerors load themselves are no more than burdens of clay, which are in themselves worthless, and only harass the bearers. The Greek Version seems to point to the weight of the yoke imposed by the Chaldeans on them ; but Jerome explains it differently, "Ad hoc tautum sævit ut devoret et iniquitatis et prædarum onere quasi gravissima torque se deprimat." The difficulty lies in the ἅπαξ λεγόμενον abtit, which forms an enigma, or dark saying, because, taken as two words, it might pass current for "thick clay," or "a mass of dirt," while regarded as one word it means "a mass of pledges," "many pledges." That the latter is the signification primarily intended is the view of many modern commentators, who explain the clause thus: The quantity of treasure and booty amassed by the Chaldeans is regarded as a mass of pledges taken from the conquered nations a burden of debt to be discharged one day with heavy retribution. Pusey, "He does in truth increase against himself a strong pledge, whereby not others are debtors to him, but he is a debtor to Almighty God, who careth for the oppressed (Jer. xvii. 11)."

Ver. 7.—That shall bite thee. As thou hast cruelly treated others, so shall they, like fierce vipers (Jer. viii. 17), bite thee. Henderson, Delitzsch, Keil, and others see in the word a double entendre connected with the meaning of "lending on interest," so the "biting" would signify "exacting a debt with usury." Such a term for usury is not unknown to classical antiquity; thus (quoted by Henderson) Aristoph., 'Nub.,' 12—

Δακνόμενος
Ὑπὸ τῆς δαπάνης καὶ τῆς φάτνης καὶ τῶν χρεῶν.

"By the expenditure deep bitten,
And by the manger and the debts."

Lucan., 'Phars.,' i. 181, "Hinc usura vorax,

avidumque in tempore fænus." The "biters" rising up suddenly are the Persians who destroyed the Babylonian power as quickly and as unexpectedly as it had arisen. **Vex;** literally, *shake violently*, like διασείσητε (Luke iii. 14), or like the violent arrest of a creditor (Matt. xviii. 28); Septuagint, οἱ ἐπιβουλοί σου, "thy plotters;" Vulgate, *lacerantes te.* So of the mystic Babylon, her end comes suddenly (Rev. xviii. 10, 17). Ver. 8.—The law of retaliation is asserted. **All the remnant of the people** (*peoples*) **shall spoil thee.** The remnant of the nations subjugated and plundered by the Chaldeans shall rise up against them. The downfall of Babylon was brought about chiefly by the combined forces of Media, Persia, and Elam (Isa. xxi. 2; Jer. l. 9, etc.); and it is certain that Nebuchadnezzar, at one period of his reign, conquered and annexed Elam; and there is every probability that he warred successfully against Media (see Jer. xxv. 9, 25; Judith i. 5, 13, etc.); and doubtless many of the neighbouring tribes, which had suffered under these oppressors, joined in the attack. **Because of men's blood.** Because of the cruelty and bloodshed of which the Babylonians were guilty. **For the violence of** (*done to*) **the land, of the city** (see ver. 17). The statement is general, but with special reference to the Chaldeans' treatment of Judæa and Jerusalem, as in Isa. xliii. 14; xlv. 4; Jer. li. 4, 11. Jerome takes "the violence of the land," etc., to mean the wickedness of the Jews themselves, which is to be punished. He is led astray by the Septuagint, which gives, διὰ . . . ἀσεβείας γῆς, "through . . . the iniquity of the land."

Vers. 9—11.—§ 9. *The second woe: for their avarice, violence, and cunning.*

Ver. 9.—**That coveteth an evil covetousness to his house;** better, *gaineth evil gains for his house.* The "house" is the royal family or dynasty, as in ver. 10; and the Chaldean is denounced for thinking to secure its stability and permanence by amassing godless gains. **That he may set his nest on high.** This is a figurative expression, denoting security as well as pride and self-confidence (comp. Numb. xxiv. 21; Job xxxix. 27, etc.; Jer. xlix. 16; Obad. 4), and denotes the various means which the Chaldeans employed to establish and secure their power (comp. Isa. xiv. 14). Some see in the words an allusion to the formidable fortifications raised by Nebuchadnezzar for the protection of Babylon, and the wonderful palace erected by him as a royal residence (see Rawlinson, 'Anc. Mon.,' iii. 340, etc., edit. 1865). It is certain that Nebuchadnezzar and other monarchs, after successful expeditions, turned their attention

to building and enriching towns, temples, and palaces (see Josephus, 'Cont. Ap.,' i. 19. 7, etc.). **From the power of evil;** *from the hand of evil;* i.e. from all calamity. Ver. 10.—The very means he took to secure his power shall prove his ruin. **Thou hast consulted shame to thy house.** By thy measures thou hast really determined upon, devised shame and disgrace for thy family; that is the result of all thy schemes. **By cutting off many people** (*peoples*). This is virtually correct. The verb in the present text is in the infinitive, and may depend upon the verb in the first clause. The versions read the past tense, συνεπέρανας, *concidisti.* So the Chaldee and Syriac. This may be taken as the prophet's explanation of the shameful means employed. **Hast sinned against thy soul** (Prov. viii. 36; xx. 2). Thou hast endangered thy own life by provoking retribution. The Greek and Latin Versions have, "Thy soul hath sinned." Ver. 11.—Even inanimate things shall raise their voice to denounce the Chaldeans' wickedness. **The stone shall cry out of the wall.** A proverbial expression to denote the horror with which their cruelty and oppression were regarded; it is particularly appropriate here, as these crimes had been perpetrated in connection with the buildings in which they prided themselves, and which were raised by the enforced labour of miserable captives and adorned with the fruits of fraud and pillage. Compare another application of the expression in Luke xix. 40. Jerome quotes Cicero, 'Orat. pro Marcello,' 10, "Parietes, medius fidius, ut mihi videntur, hujus curiæ tibi gratias agere gestiunt, quod brevi tempore futura sit illa auctoritas in his majorum suorum et suis sedibus" (comp. Eurip., 'Hippol.,' 418, Τέρεμνά τ' οἴκων μή ποτε φθογγὴν ἀφῇ: Ovid, 'Metam.,' ii. 696, "Tutus eas: lapis iste prius tua furta loquetur"). Wordsworth sees a literal fulfilment of these words in the appalling circumstance at Belshazzar's feast, when a hand wrote on the palace wall the doom of Babylon (Dan. v.). **And the beam out of the timber shall answer it.** "The tie-beam out of the timber work shall" take up the refrain, and "answer" the stone from the wall. The Hebrew word (*kaphis*) rendered "beam" is an ἅπαξ λεγόμενον. It is explained as above by St. Jerome, being referred to a verb meaning "to bind." Thus Symmachus and Theodotion translate it by σύνδεσμος. Henderson and others think it means "a half-brick," and Aquila renders it by μᾶζα, "something baked." But we have no evidence that the Babylonians in their sumptuous edifices interlaced timber and half-bricks (see Pusey, p. 419, note 23). The

LXX. gives, κάνθαρος ἐκ ξύλου, a beetle, a worm, from the wood. Hence, referring to Christ on the cross, St. Ambrose ('Orat. de Obit. Theod.,' 46) writes, "Adoravit illum qui pependit in ligno, illum inquam qui sicut scarabæus clamavit, ut persecutoribus suis peccata condonaret." St. Cyril argues that tie-beams were called κάνθαροι from their clinging to and supporting wall or roof. Some reason for this supposition is gained by the fact that the word canterius, or cantherius, is used in Latin in the sense of "rafter."

Vers. 12—14.—§ 10. *The third woe: for founding their power in blood and devastation.*

Ver. 12.—The Chaldeans are denounced for the use they make of the wealth acquired by violence. That buildeth a town with blood (Micah iii. 10, where see note). They used the riches gained by the murder of conquered nations in enlarging and beautifying their own city. By iniquity. To get means for these buildings, and to carry on their construction, they used injustice and tyranny of every kind. That mercy was not an attribute of Nebuchadnezzar we learn from Daniel's advice to him (iv. 27). The captives and deported inhabitants of conquered countries were used as slaves in these public works (see an illustration of this from Koyunjik, Rawlinson's 'Anc. Mon.,' i. 497). What was true of Assyria was no less true of Babylon. Professor Rawlinson (ii. 528, etc.) tells of the extreme misery and almost entire ruin of subject kingdoms. Not only are lands wasted, cattle and effects carried off, the people punished by the beheading or impalement of hundreds or thousands, but sometimes wholesale deportation of the inhabitants is practised, tens or hundreds of thousands being carried away captive. "The military successes of the Babylonians," he says (iii. 332), "were accompanied with needless violence, and with outrages not unusual in the East, which the historian must nevertheless regard as at once crimes and follies. The transplantation of conquered races may, perhaps, have been morally defensible, notwithstanding the sufferings which it involved. But the mutilations of prisoners, the weary imprisonments, the massacre of non-combatants, the refinement of cruelty shown in the execution of children before the eyes of their fathers,—these and similar atrocities, which are recorded of the Babylonians, are wholly without excuse, since they did not so much terrify as exasperate the conquered nations, and thus rather endangered than added strength or security to the empire. A savage and inhuman temper is betrayed by these harsh punishments, one that led its possessors to

sacrifice interest to vengeance, and the peace of a kingdom to a tiger-like thirst for blood . . . we cannot be surprised that, when final judgment was denounced against Babylon, it was declared to be sent in a great measure 'because of men's blood, and for the violence of the land, of the city, and of all that dwelt therein.'"

Ver. 13.—Is it not of the Lord of hosts? Hath not God ordained that this, about to be mentioned, should be the issue of all this evil splendour? That the people shall labour in the very fire; rather, *that the peoples labour for the fire;* i.e. that the Chaldees and such like nations expended all this toil on cities and fortresses only to supply food for fire, which, the prophet sees, will be their end (Isa. xl. 16). Jeremiah (li. 58) applies these and the following words to the destruction of Babylon. This is indeed to weary themselves for very vanity. Babylon, when it was finally taken, was given over to fire and sword (comp. Jer. l. 32; li. 30, etc.).

Ver. 14.—The prophet now gives the reason of the vanity of these human undertakings. For the earth shall be filled, etc. The words are from Isa. xi. 9, with some little alterations (comp. Numb. xiv. 21). This is one of the passages which attests "the community of testimony," as it is called, among the prophets. To take a few out of many cases that offer, Isa. ii. 2—4 compared with Micah iv. 1—4; Isa. xiii. 19—22 with Jer. l. 39, etc.; Isa. lii. 7 with Nah. i. 15; Jer. xlix. 7—22 with Obad. 1—4; Amos ix. 13 with Joel iii. 18 (Ladd, 'Doctrine of Scripture,' i. 145). All the earth is to be filled with, and to recognize, the glory of God as manifested in the overthrow of ungodliness; and therefore Babylon, and the world-power of which she is a type, must be subdued and perish. This announcement looks forward to the establishment of Messiah's kingdom, which "shall break in pieces and consume all these kingdoms, and shall stand for ever" (Dan. ii. 44). We must remember how intimately in the minds of Eastern heathens the prosperity of a nation was connected with its local deities. Nothing in their eyes could show more perfectly the impotence of a god than his failing to protect his worshippers from destruction (comp. 2 Kings xviii. 33, etc.). The glory of Jehovah and his sovereignty over the earth would be seen and acknowledged in the overthrow of Babylon, the powerful, victorious nation. As the waters cover the sea. As the waters fill the basin of the sea (Gen. i. 22; 1 Kings vii. 23, where the great vessel of ablution is called "the sea").

Vers. 15—17.—§ 11. *The fourth woe: for base and degrading treatment of subject nations.*

Ver. 15.—Not only do the Chaldeans oppress and pillage the peoples, but they expose them to the vilest derision and contumely. The prophet uses figures taken from the conduct produced by intemperance. That giveth his neighbour drink. The Chaldeans behaved to the conquered nations like one who gives his neighbour intoxicating drink to stupefy his faculties and expose him to shame (comp. ver. 5). The literal drunkenness of the Chaldeans is not the point here. That puttest thy bottle to him. If this translation is received, the clause is merely a strengthened repetition of the preceding with a sudden change of person. But it may be rendered, "pouring out, or mixing, thy fury," or, as Jerome, "mittens fel suum," "adding thy poison thereto." This last version seems most suitable, introducing a kind of climax, the "poison" being some drug added to increase the intoxicating power. Thus: he gives his neighbour drink, and this drugged, and in the end makes him drunken also. For the second clause the Septuagint gives, ἀνατροπῇ θολερᾷ, subversione turbida, and the versions collected by Jerome are only unanimous in differing from one another. That thou mayest look on their nakedness. There seems to be an allusion to the case of Noah (Gen. ix. 21, etc.); but the figure is meant to show the abject state to which the conquered nations were reduced, when, prostrated by fraud and treachery, they were mocked and spurned and covered with ignominy (comp. Nah. iii. 5, 11). So the mystic Babylon is said to have made the nations drink of her cup (Rev. xiv. 8; xvii. 2; xviii. 3).

Ver. 16.—Just retribution falls on Babylon. Thou art filled with shame for glory. Thou art satiated, indeed, but with shame, not with glory. Thou hast revelled in thy shameless conduct to the defenceless, but this redounds to thy dishonour, and will only add to the disgrace of thy fall. The Septuagint joins this clause with part of the following : " Drink thou also fulness of shame for glory." Drink thou also the cup of wrath and retribution. Let thy foreskin be uncovered. Be thou in turn treated with the same ignomiuy with which thou hast treated others, the figure in ver. 15 being here repeated (comp. Lam. iv. 21). It is otherwise translated, " Be thou," or " show thyself, uncircumcised." This, in a Jew's eyes, would be the very climax of degradation. The Vulgate has consopire, from a slightly different reading. The LXX., Καρδία σαλεύθητι, καὶ σείσθητι, " Be tossed, O my heart, and shaken." The present text is much more appropriate, though the Syriac and Arabic follow the Greek here. The cup of the Lord's right hand. Retributive vengeance is often thus figured (comp. Ps. lx. 3; lxxv. 8; Isa. li. 17, 22; Jer. xxv. 15, etc.). Shall be turned unto thee. God himself shall bring round the cup of suffering and vengeance to thee in thy turn, and thou shalt be made to drink it to the dregs, so that shameful spewing (foul shame) shall be on thy glory. The ἅπαξ λεγόμενον kikalon is regarded as an intensive signifying "the utmost ignominy" (ἀτιμία, Septuagint), or as two words, or a compound word, meaning vomitus ignominiæ (Vulgate). It was probably used by the prophet to suggest both ideas.

Ver. 17.—For the violence of Lebanon shall cover thee; LXX., ἀσέβεια τοῦ Λιβάνου: iniquitas Libani (Vulgate). It would be plainer if translated, "the violence against," or "practised on, Lebanon," as the sentence refers to the devastation inflicted by the Chaldeans on the forests of Lebanon (comp. Isa. xiv. 8; xxxvii. 24). Jerome confines the expression in the text to the demolition of the temple at Jerusalem in the construction of which much cedar was employed; others take Lebanon as a figure for Palestine generally, or for Jerusalem itself; but it is best understood literally. The same devastation which the Chaldeans made in Lebanon shall "cover," overwhelm, and destroy them. And the spoil of beasts, which made them afraid. The introduction of the relative is not required, and the passage may be better translated, And the destruction of beasts made them (others read "thee") afraid. Septuagint, "And the wretchedness of the beasts shall affright thee." Jerome, in his commentary, renders, "Et vastitas animalium opprimet te." The meaning is that the wholesale destruction of the wild animals of Lebanon, occasioned by the operations of the Chaldeans, shall be visited upon this people. They warred not only against men, but against the lower creatures too; and for this retributive punishment awaited them. Because of men's blood, etc. The reason rendered in ver. 8 is here repeated. Of the land, etc., means "toward" or "against" the land.

Vers. 18—20.—§ 12. The fifth woe: for their idolatry.

Ver. 18.—The final woe is introduced by an ironical question. The Chaldeans trusted in their gods, and attributed all their success to the divine protection; the prophet asks—What good is this trust? What profiteth the graven image? (comp. Isa. xliv. 9, 10; Jer. ii. 11). What is the good of all the skill and care that the artist has lavished on the idol? (For "graven" or "molten," see note on Nah. i. 14.) And a (even the) teacher of lies. The idol is so termed because it calls itself God and encourages its worshippers in lying delusions, in entire contrast to Jehovah who is Truth. From some variation in reading the LXX. gives, φαντασίαν ψευδῆ, and Jerome, "imaginem falsam" (comp. Jer. x. 14). **Trusteth therein.** The prophet derides the folly which supposes that the idol has powers denied to the man who made it (Isa. xxix. 16). **Dumb idols;** literally, *dumb nothings.* So 1 Cor. xii. 2, εἴδωλα τὰ ἄφωνα (comp. 1 Cor. x. 19; Ps. cxv. 5, etc.). There is a paronomasia in the Hebrew, *elilim illemim.*

Ver. 19.—The prophet now denounces the folly of the maker and worshipper of idols. With this and the following verses compare the taunts in Isa. xliv. 9—20. **The wood.** From which he carves the image. **Awake!** Come to my help, as good men pray to the living God (comp. Ps. xxxv. 23; xliv. 23; Isa. li. 9). **Arise, it shall teach!** The Hebrew is better rendered, *Arise! it teach!* i.e. shall *this* teach?—an emphatic

question expressing astonishment. Vulgate, *Numquid ipse docere poterit?* The LXX. paraphrases, καὶ αὐτό ἐστι φαντασία, "and itself is a phantasy." It is laid, over. "It" is again emphatic, as if pointed at with the finger. Hence the Vulgate, *Ecce iste coopertus est;* and Henderson, "There it is, overlaid," etc. The wooden figure was encased in gold or silver plates (see Isa. xl. 19; Dan. iii. 1).

Ver. 20.—The prophet contrasts the majesty of Jehovah with these dumb and lifeless idols. **His holy temple.** Not the shrine at Jerusalem, but heaven itself (see Ps. xi. 4, and note on Micah i. 2). **Let all the earth keep silence before him.** Like subjects in the presence of their king, awaiting his judgment and the issue to which all these things tend (comp. ver. 14; Ps. lxxvi. 8, etc.; Zeph. i. 7; Zech. ii. 13). Septuagint, Εὐλαβείσθω ἀπὸ προσώπου αὐτοῦ, κ.τ.λ., "Let all the earth fear before him."

HOMILETICS.

Vers. 1—3.—*The prophet upon his watch-tower.* I. THE OUT-LOOKING PROPHET. (Ver. 1.) Having spread out before Jehovah his complaint, Habakkuk, determined to stand upon his watch-tower or station himself upon his fortress, and to look forth to see what Jehovah would speak within him, and what reply in consequence he should give to his own complaint. The words indicate the frame of mind to be cherished and the course of conduct to be pursued by him who would hold communion with and obtain communications from God. There must be : 1. *Holy resolution.* No soul can come to speaking terms with God without personal effort. Certainly God may speak to men who make no efforts to obtain from him either a hearing or an answer, but in general those only find God who seek him with the whole heart (Ps. cxix. 2). Prophets frequently received revelations which they had not sought (Gen. xii. 7; Exod. iii. 2; xxiv. 1; Isa. vi. 1; Ezek. i. 1; Dan. vii. 1), but as often the Divine communications were imparted in answer to specific seeking (Gen. xv. 13; Exod. xxxiii. 18; Dan. ix. 2; Acts x. 9). In the same way may God discover himself, disclose his truth, and dispense his grace to individuals, as he did to Saul of Tarsus (Acts ix. 1—6), without their previous exertions to procure such distinguished favours; but in religion, as in other matters, it is the hand of the diligent that maketh rich (2 Pet. i. 10). 2. *Spiritual elevation.* He who would commune with God must, like Habakkuk, "stand upon his watch-tower, and station himself upon his fortress," not literally and bodily, but figuratively and spiritually. It is not necessary to suppose that Habakkuk went up to any steep and lofty place in order the better to withdraw himself from the noise and bustle of the world, and the more easily to fix his mind on heavenly things and direct his soul's eye Godward. Abraham certainly was on the summit of Moriah when Jehovah appeared to him; Moses was called up to the top of Sinai to meet with God (Exod. xxiv. 1; xxxiv. 2); Jehovah revealed himself to Elijah upon the mount of Horeb (1 Kings xix. 11); Balaam went to "an high place" to look out for a revelation from God (Numb. xxiii. 3); the disciples were on the crest of Hermon when Christ was transfigured before them (Matt. xvii. 1); and even Christ himself spent whole nights in prayer with God among the hills (John vi. 15). Local elevation and corporeal isolation may be usefully employed to aid the heart in abstracting itself from mundane things; yet this only is the elevation and isolation that brings the soul in contact with God (Matt. vi. 6). When David prayed he retired into the inner chamber of his heart (Ps. xix. 14; xlix. 3) and lifted up his soul to God (Ps. xxv. 1). 3. *Confident expectation.* Habakkuk believed that his prayers and complaints would not pass unattended to by God. He never doubted that God would reply to his supplications and interrogations. So he that cometh to God must believe that he is, and that he is the Rewarder of them that diligently seek him (Heb. xi. 6). It was David's habit, after directing his prayer to God, to look up expecting an answer (Ps. v. 3), and it ought to be the practice of Christians first to ask in faith (Jas. i. 6), and then to confidently hope for an answer (Matt. xxi. 22 ; Mark xi. 24 ; 1 John v. 14). 4. *Patient attention.* Though Habakkuk had no doubt as to the fact that God would speak to him, he possessed no assurance either as to the time when or as to the manner in which that speaking would take place. Hence he resolved to possess his soul in patience and keep an attentive outlook. So David waited on and watched for God with patient hope and close observation (Ps. lxii. 5 ; cxxx. 5). So Paul exhorted Christians to "continue in prayer, and watch in the same with thanksgiving " (Col. iv. 2). Many fail to obtain responses from God, because they either are not sufficiently attentive to discern the tokens by which God speaks to his people, or lack the patience to wait till he chooses to break silence. 5. *Earnest introspection.* The want of this is another frequent cause of failure on the part of those who would but do not hear God speak. Habakkuk understood that if God answered him it would be by his Spirit speaking in him, and that accordingly he required not to watch for "signs" in the firmament, in the earth, or in the sea, but to listen to the secret whisperings that he heard within himself. So David exhorted others to commune with their own hearts upon their bed (as doubtless he himself did), if they would know the mind of God (Ps. iv. 4); and Asaph, following his example, observed the same godly practice (Ps. lxxvii. 6). While God has furnished lessons for all in the pages of nature and revelation, it is in the domain of the inner man, enlightened by his Word and taught by his Spirit, that his teaching for the individual is to be sought.

II. The In-speaking God. (Ver. 2.) Habakkuk had not long to wait for the oracle he expected ; and neither would modern petitioners be long without answers were their waiting more like Habakkuk's. Three things were announced to the prophet. 1. *That he should receive a vision.* Jehovah would not leave his dark problem unsolved, would afford him such a glimpse into the future of the Chaldean power as would effectually dispel all his doubts and fears, would unveil to him the different destinies of the righteous and the wicked in such a way as to enable him calmly to endure until the end ; and exactly so has the Christian obtained in the Bible such light upon the mystery of Providence as helps him to look forward to the future for its full solution. The vision about to be granted to Habakkuk was (1) definite, *i.e.* for an appointed time, and so is the vision now granted to the Christian for a time as well known to God (though not to the Christian) as any moment in the past has been ; (2) distant, *i.e.* to be fulfilled after a longer or shorter interval, and so has the day of the clearing up of the mystery of providence for the Christian been " after a long time ; " but still (3) certain, *i.e.* it would surely come to pass, and so will all that God has revealed in Scripture concerning the different destinies of the righteous and the wicked come to pass. Heaven and earth may pass away, but not God's Word (Matt. xxiv. 35). 2. *That he should write the vision.* Whether a literal writing upon a tablet (Ewald, Pusey) was intended, as Isaiah (viii. 1 ; xxx. 8) and Jeremiah (xxx. 2) were directed to write down the communications received by them from God ; or whether it was merely a figurative writing (Hengstenberg, Keil) that was meant, as in the case of Daniel (xii. 4) ; the intention manifestly was that Habakkuk should publish the vision he was about to receive—publish it in terms so clear and unambiguous that persons who only gave it a casual glance would have no difficulty in understanding it. This has been done, not with reference to Habakkuk's vision merely, but as regards the whole Bible, which is not only " all plain to him that understandeth " (Prov. viii. 9), but is able to " make wise the simple " (Ps. xix. 7), and guide in safety " the wayfaring man, though a fool " (Isa. xxxv. 8). The object contemplated by the writing (literal or figurative) of Habakkuk's vision was (1) the comfort of God's people in Judah during the period of waiting that should intervene between then and the day of their enemy's overthrow ; and (2) the interpretation of the vision when the incidents occurred to which it referred. The same purposes are subserved by the Word of God, and especially by those prophetic parts which foretell the destruction of the enemies, and the salvation of the people, of God. 3. *That he should wait for the vision.* It might be delayed, but it should come. Hence he should possess his soul in patience. So should Christians wait patiently for the coming of the Lord for their final redemption and for the overthrow of all the Church's foes (Jas. v. 8). The contents of the vision are narrated in the verses which follow.

LESSONS. 1. The dignity of man, as a being who can converse with God; the condescension of God in that he stoops to talk with man. 2. The duty and the profit of reflection and meditation; the sin and loss of those who never commune with their own hearts. 3. The simplicity of the Bible a testimony to its divinity; had it been man's book it would not have been so easy to understand. 4. The certainty that Scripture prediction will be fulfilled; the expectation of this should comfort the saints; the realization of this will vindicate God.

Vers. 4, 5.—*The unjust man and the just: a contrast.* I. THEIR CHARACTERS. 1. *The unjust man.* (1) Proud or "puffed up" in soul. The heart the seat and source of all sin (Jer. xvii. 9; Mark vii. 21); pride its origin and essence (Ps. x. 4; lii. 7; Prov. xvi. 5; Mal. iv. 1). Arrogant haughtiness and self-sufficiency characteristic of the carnal heart (Rom. i. 30; Eph. iv. 17). These qualities had marked the Assyrian (Isa. x. 12), and were to distinguish the Chaldean (ver. 5) conqueror. They discover themselves in all who oppose or decline from the spirit of Christ (1 Cor. v. 2; Phil. ii. 3; 3 John 9). They will eventually culminate in antichrist (2 Thess. ii. 4). (2) Wicked or ungodly in life. His soul, being thus puffed up with pride, is not " upright" or "straight" within him; is not free from turning and trickery; does not in its thoughts, feelings, words, and actions adhere to the straight path of integrity, but loves "crooked ways" and devious roads, and thus turns aside unto iniquity (Ps. cxxv. 5). Again true of the Chaldean, whose iniquities—drunkenness, boasting, restless ambition, insatiable lust of conquest, relentless oppression—are specifically enumerated (ver. 5), it holds good also of the natural heart and carnal mind (Jer. xiii. 10; 2 Tim. iii. 2). (3) Rejected or "condemned" by God. This implied in the fact that he is not a just or "justified" man. 2. *The just man.* (1) Believing in soul. As pride or trust in self is the animating principle of the wicked, so is faith or trust in God that of the good. Faith the root of all moral and spiritual excellence in the soul. As the proud soul stands aloof from God, the humble heart cleaves to God, as " that which is straight, being applied to what is straight, touches and is touched by it everywhere." (2) Upright in life. As pride leads to disobedience, faith leads to obedience. Hence Paul speaks of "the obedience of faith" (Rom. i. 5), *i.e.* such obedience as is inspired by faith. The soul that trusts God, walks in his ways, avoids sin, and endeavours to order his conversation aright (Ps. l. 23; 1 Pet. ii. 5). Faith and holiness are in the gospel scheme inseparably connected (John xv. 8; Rom. ii. 13; Eph. ii. 10; Titus iii. 8). (3) Accepted by God. Paul in Romans (i. 17), and the writer to the Hebrews (x. 38), by quoting this statement from Habakkuk, teach that the "just" and the "justified" are one—that the just in the Scripture sense of that expression are those legally and spiritually righteous before God.

II. THEIR DESTINIES. 1. *That of the unjust—death.* Though not stated, this may be inferred. (1) The soul of which the inward essence is pride and self-sufficiency is destitute of spiritual life, is dead. "Swollen with pride, it shuts out faith, and with it the presence of God" (Pusey); and "without faith it is impossible to please God" (Heb. xi. 6). (2) The man who lives in sin is dead while he liveth (1 Tim. v. 6)—dead in trespasses and sins (Eph. ii. 1), and so long as he remains a stranger to the principle of faith which the breath of God's Spirit alone can awaken in the unrenewed, he must continue "dead," *i.e.* incapable of actions spiritually good. (3) The sinner not accepted before God is of necessity condemned by God; and to be under condemnation is to be "legally dead." 2. *That of the just—life.* Not necessarily life physical and temporal, because the "justified" die no less than their neighbours (Heb. ix. 27); but (1) life legal and judicial—"he that believeth shall never come into condemnation" (John iii. 18; v. 24; Rom. viii. 1); (2) life moral and spiritual, which Scripture connects with faith in God and in his Son Christ Jesus as a stream with its fountain, as a tree with its root, as an effect with its cause (Acts xv. 9; xxvi. 18; 2 Thess. i. 11; Gal. ii. 20); and (3) life indestructible and eternal, this being always a quality ascribed to the life which the justified man receives through his faith (John iii. 36;

v. 24; xi. 26; 1 John ii. 25; v. 11; 1 Tim. i. 16; vi. 12; Titus i. 2; iii. 7). All other life but that which Christ bestows is temporal and perishing.

Vers. 6—8.—*A parable of woes*: 1. *Woe to the rapacious!* I. THEIR PERSONS IDENTIFIED. 1. *The Chaldean nation*, in its kings and people, who were animated by a lust of conquest, which impelled them upon wars of aggression. 2. *The enemies of the Church of God and of Jesus Christ*, whether national or individual, in whom the same spirit dwells as resided in the Babylonian power. God's promises and threatenings in the Bible have almost always a wider sweep and a larger reference than simply to those to whom they were originally addressed.

II. THEIR SIN SPECIFIED. Spoliation, robbery, theft, plunder. A wickedness: 1. *Unjust*; as all theft is. In heaping up the spoils of plundered nations, the Chaldean was increasing what was not his; and the same is done by those who store up money or goods gotten by fraud or oppression. What men acquire by violence or guile is not theirs. How much of the wealth of modern nations and of private persons is of this character may not be told; to assert that none is may be charity, but is not truth. The practices complained of by James (v. 4—6) have not been unknown since his day. 2. *Insatiable*; as the lust of possession is prone to be. The plundered nations are depicted as asking—How long is this devastating power to go on despoiling peoples weaker than himself? Is his career of rapine never to be arrested? Will his thirst for what belongs to others never be quenched? So "he that loveth silver shall not be satisfied with silver, nor he that loveth abundance with increase" (Eccles. v. 10). The passion for heaping up ill-gotten gains grows by what it feeds on. Those who determine to enrich themselves at the expense of others seldom know when to stop. Almost never do they cry, "Enough!" till retribution, overtaking them, strips them of all. 3. *Vain*; as all sin will ultimately prove to be. The foreign property taken by the Chaldean from other nations, the prophet characterizes as "pledges" exacted from them by an unmerciful creditor, perhaps intending thereby to suggest that the Chaldean would be "compelled to disgorge them in due time" (Keil). The idea, true of all man's earthly possessions (Job i. 21)—

> "Whate'er we fondly call our own
>   Belongs to heaven's great Lord;
> The blessings lent us for a day
>   Are soon to be restored,"

—is much more applicable to wealth acquired by fraud or oppression (Jer. xvii. 11). The day will come when, if not by the robbed themselves, by God the rightful Owner of the wealth (Hag. ii. 8) and the strong Champion of the oppressed (Ps. x. 18), it will be demanded back with interest (Job xx. 15).

III. THEIR PUNISHMENT DESCRIBED. 1. *Certain.* "Shall not all these take up a parable against him?" The overthrow of the Chaldean is so surely an event of the future that the very nations and peoples he has plundered, or the believing remnant amongst them, will yet raise a derisive song over his miserable and richly merited fall; and just as surely will the rapacious plunderer of others be destroyed, and his destruction be a source of satisfaction to beholders (Prov. i. 18, 19). 2. *Heavy.* The wealth he has stolen from others will be to him as a "burden of thick clay" that will first crush him to the earth, making the heart within him wretched and the spirit sordid and grovelling, and finally sink him into a hopeless and cheerless grave (Eccles. ii. 22, 23; vi. 2; Ps. xlix. 14). 3. *Sudden.* Retribution should fall upon the Chaldean in a moment—his biters should rise up suddenly, and his destroyers wake up as from a sleep to harass him (ver. 7); and in such fashion will the end be of "every one that is greedy of gain and taketh away the life of the owners thereof" (Prov. i. 19); he may "spend his days in wealth," but "in a moment he shall go down to the grave" (Job xxi. 13); he may "heap up silver as the dust, and prepare raiment as the clay," but he shall "lie down and not be gathered;" he shall "open his eyes, and behold! he is not" (Job xxvii. 16, 19). 4. *Retributive.* The Chaldean should be spoiled by the nations he had spoiled. So will violent and rapacious men reap what themselves have sowed. How often is it seen that money goes as it comes! Acquired by speculation or gambling, it is lost by the same means. He who robs others by violence or fraud not unfrequently is himself robbed by another stronger or craftier than he. "Whatsoever a man soweth," etc. (Gal. vi. 7).

LESSONS. **1.** " Provide things honest in the sight of all men " (Rom. xii. 17). **2.** " Do violence to no man " (Luke iii. 14). **3.** " If thou do that which is evil, be afraid " (Rom. xiii. 4).

Vers. 9—11.—*A parable of woes:* 2. *Woe to the covetous!* I. THEIR AIM. 1. *Personal comfort.* Suggested by the term "nest," which for the Chaldean meant Babylon with its palaces, and for the individual signifies his mansion or dwelling-place (Job xxix. 18). Josephus ('Ant.,' x. 11. 1) states that Nebuchadnezzar built for himself a palace " to describe the vast height and immense riches of which would be too much for him (Josephus) to attempt; " and Nebuchadnezzar himself tells us in his inscription that he constructed " a great temple, a house of admiration for men, a lofty pile, a palace of his royalty for the land of Babylon," " a large edifice for the residence of his royalty," and that within it were collected as an adornment " trophies, abundance, royal treasures " (' Records of the Past,' v. 130, etc.). Men who set their hearts on riches mostly do so under the impression that these will add to their comfort and increase their happiness—to them comfort and happiness being synonymous with large, beautiful, and well-plenished houses (Ps. xlix. 11). 2. *Social distinction.* Pointed at by the word "high," in which notions of elevation and visibility are involved. For one rich man that covets wealth to augment his bodily comfort or mental gratification, ten seek it for the lustre in others' eyes it is supposed to give. The upper classes in society are the wealthy; the under or lower classes are the poor. None notice the wise man who is poor (Eccles. ix. 16); the rich fool stands upon a pedestal and receives the homage of admiring crowds (Prov. xiv. 20). The same delusive standard is employed in estimating the greatness of nations. Wealth is commonly accepted by the world as the true criterion of rank. Rich nations take precedence of poor ones. In God's sight money is the smallest distinction that either country or person can wear. 3. *Permanent safety.* Stated by the clause, " that he may be delivered from the power [or, ' the hand '] of evil." The Babylonian sovereigns as individuals and as rulers held the delusion that the best defence against personal or national calamity was accumulated treasure (Prov. x. 15; xviii. 11). Nebuchadnezzar in particular used his " evil gain " for the fortification of his metropolis, building around it " the great walls " which his father Nabopolassar had begun but not completed, furnishing these with great gates of ikki and pine woods and coverings of copper, to keep off enemies from the front, and rearing up a tall tower like a mountain, so rendering it, as he supposed, " invincible" (' Records of the Past,' v. 126, etc.). In a like spirit men imagine that " money is a defence" (Eccles. vii. 12), and that he who has a large balance at his banker's need fear no evil. But " riches profit not in the day of wrath " (Prov. xi. 4); and just as certainly as Nebuchadnezzar's "eagle's nest " was not beyond the reach of the Persian falconer, so neither will the wicked man's silver and gold be able to deliver him when his end is come (Jer. li. 13; Ezek. vii. 19; Zeph. i. 18).

II. THEIR SIN. 1. *Against God.* This evident from the nature of the offence, which God's Law condemns (Exod. xx. 17), as well as from the evils to which it leads—oppression, pride, self-sufficiency, and self-destruction. 2. *Against others.* In carrying out its wicked schemes covetousness usually involves others in ruin. It impelled the Chaldean to cut off many peoples. It drives those whom it inspires to deeds of violence, robbery, oppression, and murder (Prov. i. 19; 1 Tim. vi. 10). 3. *Against themselves.* The covetous burden their own souls with guilt; and so, while professing to seek their own happiness and safety, are in reality accelerating their own misery and destruction.

III. THEIR FATE. 1. *Disappointment.* Whereas the covetous man expects to set his house on high, he usually ends by involving it in shame (Prov. xv. 27); instead of promoting its stability, as the result of all his scheming he commonly accomplishes its overthrow (Prov. xi. 28). 2. *Vengeance.* Likening the covetous nation or man to a house-builder, the prophet says that " the stone shall cry out of the wall, and the beam out of the timber shall answer it," as it were uniting their voices in a solemn cry to Heaven for vengeance on the avaricious despoiler. Almost literally fulfilled in the history of Belshazzar (Dan. vi. 24—28), the words are often verified in the experiences of communities and individuals who are destroyed by that very prosperity in which they have trusted (Prov. i. 32).

LESSON. " Take heed, and beware of covetousness " (Luke xii. 15).

Vers. 12—14.—*A parable of woes: 3. Woe to the ambitious!* I. Tʜᴇ ᴄʀɪᴍɪɴᴀʟᴛʏ ᴏғ ᴛʜᴇɪʀ ᴀᴍʙɪᴛɪᴏɴ. 1. *The object aimed at.* To build towns and establish cities. Not necessarily a sinful project, unless the motive or the means be bad. City-building may have originated in a spirit of defiance against Jehovah (Gen. iv. 17), though this is not certain ; but cities may be, as they often are, centres and sources of incalculable blessing to mankind. If they help to multiply the forces of evil, they also serve to intensify those of good. Cities promote the good order of society, stimulate intellectual life, increase the privileges, opportunities, and comforts of individuals, and so tend to accelerate the march of civilization, by quickening movements of reform and com- bining against public evils. Hence, though "God made the country," and " man made the town " (Cowper), it need not be assumed that city-founding is against the Divine will —it can hardly be, since he himself has prepared for us a city (Heb. xi. 16). Only as there are cities and cities, so are there diversities in the modes of their construction. 2. *The means resorted to.* Blood and iniquity. Murder, bloodshed, transportation, and tyranny of every kind the Babylonian sovereigns employed to enrich their capital and strengthen their empire ; and one is not sure whether in modern times cities are not sometimes built and kingdoms strengthened by similar methods, viz. by wars of aggression against foreign peoples, and by the enforcement of sinful treaties upon unwilling but weak governments. With regard to individuals, there is no room for doubt that often they build the houses of which a city consists in the way here indicated, if not by bloodshed exactly, at least by iniquity, paying for them by ill-gotten gains, and erecting them by means of under-paid labour.

II. Tʜᴇ ᴠᴀɴɪᴛʏ ᴏғ ᴛʜᴇɪʀ ᴀᴍʙɪᴛɪᴏɴ. 1. *The fact of it.* They, *i.e.* the peoples (nations or individuals), who build towns and cities as above described, " labour for the fire" and " weary themselves for vanity ;" *i.e.* exert themselves to erect buildings that the fire will one day consume, and weary themselves in producing structures that will one day be laid in ruins. What is here said about Babylon is true of all earthly things (2 Pet. iii. 10), and ought to moderate the strength of men's desires in running after them. 2. *The certainty of it.* It is already determined of the Lord of hosts. It is part of his counsel that permanence shall not attach to anything here below (1 John ii. 17), and least of all to the productions of iniquity. Individuals may be allowed to wait for their ultimate overthrow till the day of death or the end of the world, but cities and nations, having no future, are usually visited with doom in the present. The overthrow in time of nations and empires that are built up by bloodshed and iniquity may be safely counted on. Nineveh, Babylon, Rome, are examples. 3. *The reason of it.* "The earth shall be filled with the knowledge of the glory of God." That is to say, because this is the destiny of the world, the goal towards which all things terrestrial are moving, it is impossible that the ambitious projects of man should be allowed per- manently to succeed. All superstructures, however solidly built, must be overthrown, all organizations, however compactly formed, must be broken up, that hinder the advancement of that happy era which Jehovah has promised. Hence the triumph of Babylon will come to an end, and with that the glory of Jehovah will shine forth with a brighter degree of effulgence. Men will see in that a display of Jehovah's character and power never witnessed before. The knowledge of his glory will take a wider sweep and extend over a larger area than before. The same principle demanded the overthrow of Rome, and demands the final destruction of all God's enemies, that the knowledge of his glory may cover the earth as the waters cover the sea.

Learn : 1. The sin and folly of ambition. 2. The beauty and wisdom of humility.

Vers. 15—17.—*A parable of woes: 4. Woe to the insolent!* I. Wᴀɴᴛᴏɴ ᴡɪᴄᴋᴇᴅ- ɴᴇss. 1. *Symbolically set forth.* The image employed is that of giving to one's neighbour drink from a bottle with which " vengeance," " fury," or " wrath," or, according to another interpretation, " poison," has been mixed, in order to intoxicate him, that one might have the devilish enjoyment of looking on his nakedness, as Ham did on that of Noah, or generally of glorying in his shame. To infer from this that the bare act of giving to a neighbour drink is sinful, is not warranted by Scripture (Prov. xxxi. 6 ; Eccles. ix. 7 ; 1 Tim. v. 23), and is going beyond the intention of the prophet, who introduces the " picture from life," not as an instance of one sort of wickedness in itself, but as a symbol of another sort of wickedness on the part of the

Chaldean. Still, the action selected by the prophet has in it several elements of wickedness which are worthy of consideration. If the mere giving of drink to another is not sinful (Prov. xxxi. 6), the doing so out of malice ("adding venom or wrath thereto") is, while the sin is aggravated by practising deception in connection therewith ("mixing poison therewith"—"drugging the wine," as the modern phrase is), and intensified further by the motive impelling thereto (to be able to gloat over the neighbour's degradation), and most of all condemned by being done against a neighbour to whom one owes not wrath but love, not casting down but lifting up, not exulting in his shame but rejoicing in his welfare. The words can hardly be construed into a condemnation of those who give and take wine or other drinks in moderation and to the glory of God; but they unquestionably pronounce him guilty in God's sight who deliberately and maliciously makes his fellow-man drunk in order to enrich or amuse himself at that fellow-man's expense. 2. *Historically acted out.* (1) By the Chaldean, who drew the nations of the earth into his power by means of poisoned flatteries. Enticed to place themselves beneath his tutelage, these nations ultimately fell into his power, and were by him oppressed, degraded, and insulted. (2) By modern nations, who to enrich themselves enforce upon weaker tribes treaties and traffic (whether of opium or of strong drink) which lead to their moral enfeeblement. (3) By private individuals, who for their own gain or pleasure hurl their neighbours with sublime indifference into gulfs of misery and shame.

II. APPROPRIATE PUNISHMENT. 1. *Of Divine sending.* Jehovah's goblet, of which he had caused the nations to drink, should be handed round to the Chaldeans and other guilty nations and individuals, who should all be compelled to drink of it (Ps. lxxv. 8). 2. *Of terrible severity.* It should be as shameful as that which the Chaldeans had inflicted upon the nations. It should cause him also to be drunken, and should expose his foreskin to others (cf. Isa. xlvii. 3). It should cover his glory with shame as when the attire of a drunken man is bespattered with his vomiting. Of sinners generally it is written that "shame shall be the promotion of fools" (Prov. iii. 35). 3. *Of retributive character.* The wickedness of the Chaldean should return upon his own pate. The violence he had done to Lebanon (the Holy Land or the fair regions of the earth generally) should rebound upon himself. The destruction of the beasts, *i.e.* practised upon wild animals which, by their incursions, cause men to assemble against them, should crush the Chaldean who had become as a ferocious beast (Pusey); or the destruction inflicted by the Chaldean on the wild beasts of Lebanon and other districts by cutting down the wood thereof for military purposes or for state buildings, should return upon them with avenging fury (Keil). The same law of retribution obtains in the punishment of sinners generally (Matt. vii. 2).

Learn: 1. The sin of drunkenness. 2. The greater sin of making others drunk. 3. The acme of sin, exulting in the moral overthrow of others. 4. The certainty that none of these acts of sin will go unpunished. 5. The fitness that this should be so.

Vers. 18, 19.—*A parable of woes:* 5. *Woe to the idolatrous!* I. IDOLATRY AN ABSURDITY. It must ever be so. The notion that any figure fashioned by man out of wood or stone, silver or gold, however carved or gilded, can either be or represent the Infinite and Eternal One, carries the stamp of unreason on the face of it (Ps. cxv. 4—8; Isa. xliv. 19; Jer. x. 5).

II. IDOLATRY A FRAUD. Set up as gods, and worshipped as such, graven and molten images are a hideous imposition upon man's credulity, being (1) lifeless,—"There is no breath at all in the midst of them;" (2) speechless,—the carved wood and graven stone are alike "dumb" (1 Cor. xii. 2), and only fools would say to them, "Arise, and teach!" (3) truthless,—in so far as they can be supposed to impart instruction being veritable "teachers of lies;" and (4) valueless,—of no use or profit to any one on earth and beneath the sun (Jer. x. 5).

III. IDOLATRY A RUINATION. It brings with it a woe upon all who are deluded by it. It entails upon them God's curse (Deut. xxvii. 15) and endless sorrow (Ps. xvi. 4) and everlasting death (Rev. xxi. 8).

LESSON. "Little children, keep yourselves from idols" (1 John v. 21).

Ver. 20.—*The temple of Jehovah.* I. THE HOLY TEMPLE. 1. *Its material dimen-*

sions. The universe. "Do not I fill heaven and earth? saith the Lord" (Jer. xxiii. 24). "The Lord of heaven and earth dwelleth not in temples made with hands," but in that which his own hands have fashioned (Acts xvii. 24). He "filleth all in all" (Eph. i. 23). 2. *Its inner shrine.* Heaven, the habitation of his holiness (Deut. xxvi. 15; Isa. lxiii. 15), his dwelling-place (1 Kings viii. 43; 2 Chron. vi. 33), the throne of his glory (Ps. xi. 4; Isa. lxvi. 1), the place of his immediate presence (Ps. xvi. 11; xvii. 15), the abode of the redeemed (Ps. lxxiii. 24; Rev. iv. 4), his temple proper (Rev. vii. 15; xvi. 1). 3. *Its distinctive designation.* Holy, as being the temple of a holy God, which only the holy in spirit can enter, and in which holy services alone can be performed.

II. THE INDWELLING DEITY. 1. *His name.* Jehovah, the Self-existent and Immutable One. "I am that I am" (Exod. iii. 14). 2. *His attributes.* Omnipresence, since he is in his holy temple (Exod. xx. 24; Jer. xxiii. 24); omniscience, since all are before him (Ps. lxvi. 7; Prov. v. 21; xv. 3). 3. *His character.* Gracious, since he condescends to receive the homage of worshippers, and to hold communication and correspondence with them.

III. THE SILENT WORSHIPPERS. 1. *Their persons.* "All the earth;" *i.e.* all the inhabitants thereof. If all are not as yet (Ps. lxxiv. 20; 1 Cor. x. 20), all ought to be (Exod. xx. 3; xxxiv. 14; Matt. iv. 10), and all one day will be (Ps. xxii. 27; Isa. xi. 9; ch. ii. 14; Rev. xv. 4) worshippers of the one living and true God. 2. *Their attitude.* "Before him"—in his presence, beneath his eye, before his throne, at his footstool. God's worshippers should strive to realize the immediate presence of him whom they worship (Ps. li. 11; xcv. 2; c. 2). 3. *Their devotion.* "Silence;" expressive of reverence before his majesty (Ps. lxxxix. 7), of submission beneath his authority (Ps. xxxi. 2), of trust in his mercy (Ps. cxxx. 5), of expectant waiting for his utterances whether of commandment or promise (Ps. lxxxv. 8).

Learn: 1. That the highest glory of the universe is God's presence in it. 2. That man's truest hope springs from the vicinity of God. 3. That the finest worship may at times be inaudible. 4. That God oftenest speaks to those who are waiting to hear him.

HOMILIES BY VARIOUS AUTHORS

Ver. 3.—*Waiting for the vision.* In this chapter we have set forth the doom of Babylon. The prophet had given to him glimpses of the future as affecting the adversaries of his people. The Divine voice within him gave assurance that the power of the oppressor should at length be broken. He saw the solution of the dark problem which had perplexed him so much concerning the victory to be gained over his people by the Chaldeans. The triumphing of the wicked should be short, and should be followed by their utter collapse. Yet there would be delay ere this should come to pass. The darkness which brooded over the nation should not be at once dispersed; indeed, it should even become more dense in the working out of the Divine purposes. Defeat must be experienced, the Captivity must be endured, and the faithful and true must suffer in consequence of sins not their own. Still, ultimately, "light should arise," and meanwhile, so long as the gloom continued, it behoved him and his people to trust and not be afraid, assured that in God's time the vision of peace and prosperity should dawn upon them. "Though it tarry, wait for it," etc. (ver. 3). The truth suggested is that even the best of men have to experience seasons of darkness—times when everything appears adverse to them, but that it shall not be ever thus with them, that brighter scenes are before them, and that hence their duty in the present is tranquilly and trustfully to wait the development of God's all-wise and gracious purposes. This teaching admits of various applications.

I. TEMPORAL CIRCUMSTANCES. These are not always easy and prosperous. Sources of perplexity may at any moment arise. There may come slackness of trade; new rivals may appear, causing sharp and severe competition; losses may have to be sustained; and in this way, from a variety of causes, "hard times" may have to be passed through. And under such circumstances we should trust and not be afraid, knowing that all our interests are in our loving Father's keeping. He has promised us

a sufficiency. " His mercies are not the swift, but they are the sure, mercies of David."
We must not be less hopeful and trustful than the little red-breast chirping near our
window-pane, even in the wintry weather. " Behold the fowls of the air," etc. (Matt.
vi. 26). Then, " though the vision," etc.

II. LIFE'S SORROWS. These have fallen upon men at times with a crushing weight.
All has appeared dark ; not a ray of light has seemed to penetrate the gloom. Yet
still they have found that, whilst the vision of hope has been deferred, it has been
realized at last, filling their hearts with holy rapture. Jacob lived long enough to see
that neither Joseph nor Benjamin had been really taken from him, and that those
circumstances which he regarded as being against him were all designed to work out
his lasting good. Elijah cast himself down in the wilderness and slept. And, lo !
angel-guards attended him and ministered unto him, new supplies of strength were
imparted, the sunshine of the Divine favour beamed upon him, and he who thought he
ought to die under a lonely tree in the desert was ultimately altogether delivered from
experiencing the pangs of the last conflict, and was borne in triumph to the realms of
everlasting peace. The Shunammite had her lost child restored ; the exiled returned at
length with songs unto Zion. The Egyptians painted one of their goddesses as standing
upon a rock in the sea, the waves roaring and dashing upon her, and with this motto,
" Storms cannot move me." What that painted goddess was in symbol we should
seek to be in reality, unmoved and unruffled by the tempests which arise in the sea of
life, assured that there awaits us a peaceful and tranquil haven. Then, " though the
vision," etc.

III. SPIRITUAL DEPRESSION. The Christian life is not all shadow. It has its sunny
as well as its shady side. The good have their seasons of joy—seasons in which,
believing, they can rejoice with joy unspeakable and full of glory. Yet they have
also their seasons of depression. There is " the midnight of the soul," when the vision
of spiritual light and peace and joy tarries ; and it is then their truest wisdom to trust
and to wait, assured that in due time God will make them glad by lifting upon them
" the light of his countenance." " Who is among you that feareth the Lord ? " etc.
(Isa. l. 10) ; " Though the vision," etc. (ver. 3).

IV. CHRISTIAN WORK. The great purpose of this is the deliverance of men from the
thraldom of sin. The vision we desire to behold an accomplished reality is that of the
dry bones clothed afresh, inspired with life, and standing upon their feet, an exceeding
great army, valiant for God and righteousness. But the vision tarries ! Spiritual death
and desolation reign ! What then ? Shall we despair ? Shall we express doubt as to
whether the transformation of the realm of death into a realm of spiritual life shall
ever be effected ? No ; though the vision tarry, we will wait for it, knowing that it
will surely come ; for " the mouth of the Lord hath spoken it." So Robert Moffat
laboured for years without gaining any converts from heathenism, but at length a few
were won, and he commemorated with these the death of Christ. " Our feelings,"
he wrote, " were such as pen cannot describe. We were as those that dreamed while
we realized the promise on which our souls often hung (Ps. cxxvi. 6). The hour had
arrived on which the whole energies of our souls had been intensely fixed, when we
should see a Church, however small, gathered from amongst a people who had so long
boasted that neither Jesus nor we his servants should ever see Bechuanas worship
and confess him as their King." And so shall the faith and patience of all workers for
God be rewarded, since the issue is guaranteed and the harvest-home of a regenerated
world shall be celebrated amidst rapturous joy.—S. D. H.

Ver. 4 (last clause).—*The life of faith.* There are two forms of life referred to in
Scripture—the life of sense, and the life of faith. These differ in their bent (Rom. viii.
5), and also in the issues to which they tend (Rom. viii. 13). The sincerely righteous
man, " the just," has tested both these. Time was when he lived the former, but,
satisfied as to its unreality, he now looks not at the things which are seen, but at
those which are unseen (2 Cor. iv. 18). His motto is Gal. ii. 20. " The just shall live
by his faith." These words are quoted by St. Paul (Rom. i. 17 ; Gal. iii. 11), and also
by the writer of the Epistle to the Hebrews (x. 38). The New Testament writers
were diligent students of the Old Testament, and we may learn from their example
not to treat those more ancient writings as being of comparative unimportance. They,

however, use this expression of the Prophet Habakkuk in a somewhat different sense from that in which he employed it, and apply it to the exposition and enforcement of the important doctrine of "justification by faith." The thought possessing the mind of the seer was that the righteous man exercises an implicit confidence in God; and adopting this course is preserved and protected, and experiences tranquillity and happiness under every circumstance of life. In reflecting upon his words our attention may appropriately be directed to some of the circumstances in which "the just" may be placed, with a view to indicating how that, under these, their faith in God strengthens and sustains them, and enables them truly to live.

I. "The just shall live by their faith" in times of DECLENSION IN RELIGION. Such declension prevailed in the age to which this prophet belonged. The mournful words with which his prophecy commences indicate this (ch. i. 2—4). Many similar times of declension have risen among the nations, and when the falling away from the true and the right has been widespread. So also has it been with Christian communities. Watchfulness has been neglected, and prayer has been restrained; there has been a lack of the spirit of Christian unity and concord; there has been the fire upon the altar, but, alas! it has been in embers; the lamp has been burning, but it has given only a flickering light. "The just," under such circumstances, are grieved as they view the state of religion around them, but whilst sad at heart in view of such declension and of the way in which it dishonours God, they are also inspired with confidence and hope. Their trust is in him. They know that with him is "the residue of the Spirit." Whilst praying the prayer of this prophet, "O Lord, revive thy work" (ch. iii. 2), they can also, like him, express this confident assurance, "For the earth shall be filled," etc. (ch. ii. 14). And so it comes to pass that in the season of declension in religion, when many around have lost the fervour of their love and loyalty to God and to righteousness, "the just shall live by his faith."

II. "The just shall live by their faith" in times of NATIONAL CALAMITY. Chastisement follows transgressions to nations as well as to individuals. Judah had wandered from God, and, lo! he permitted them to fall into the hands of the Chaldeans; and it was the mission of Habakkuk to foretell the approaching Captivity. National calamities have been experienced by our own people. Sometimes it has come to us in the form of *war*. The appeal has been made to the arbitrament of the sword; and even although we have been victorious, the triumph has been secured at an enormous sacrifice of life, with all the bitter suffering to survivors thus involved. Or *pestilence* has prevailed. The destroying angel has swept over the land, sparing neither the old nor the young, and numbering thousands among his victims. And in the midst of these faith grasps the rich promises of God and rests unswervingly on him. Let the Chaldean warriors come on horses swifter than the leopards and more fierce than the evening wolves, let them in bitterness and haste traverse the breadth of the land, resolved to possess the dwelling-places that are not theirs, let them scoff at kings and scorn princes and gather the captivity as the sand, still the hearts of the faithful shall be upborne, for in the time of national calamity, and when hearts uncentred from God are breaking, "the just shall live by his faith."

III. LEAVING THE EXACT CONNECTION OF THE TEXT, THE TRUTH CONTAINED IN IT RECEIVES ILLUSTRATION FROM THE VARIED CIRCUMSTANCES IN WHICH THE GOOD ARE PLACED HERE. Take the two extremes of prosperity and adversity. 1. Some enjoy great temporal prosperity. The temptations of such are (1) pride, (2) worldliness, (3) indolence, (4) selfishness, and yielding to which they lack those higher joys and nobler aspirations in which consists the true life. Walking by faith, the good man is preserved from yielding to the influence of these temptations. *Strong in faith,* he will see that all his prosperity is to be ascribed to him who giveth power to get wealth, and thus pride will be laid low. *Strong in faith,* he will realize that there are other treasures, incorruptible and unfading, and with mind and heart directed to the securing of these, he will think less of this world's pomp and vanity and show. *Strong in faith,* he will feel that he has a work to do for God, and that the additional influence prosperity has secured to him ought to be held as a sacred trust to be used to God's glory, and hence he will be preserved from seeking merely his own ease and enjoyment. And *strong in faith,* he will view himself as a steward of all that he has, and will therefore seek to be God's almoner to the needy around him. So shall he live by his faith. 2. Others have to pass through adverse scenes; and the faith that strengthens in prosperity will also sustain amidst life's unfavourable influences. Resting in the Lord and in the glorious assurances of his Word, his servants can outride the severest storm, quietly acquiescing and bravely enduring. Ruskin remarks that there is good in everything in God's universe, that there is hardly a roadside pond or pool which has not as much landscape in it as above it, that it is at our own will that we see in that despised stream either the refuse of the street or the image of the sky, that whilst the unobservant man knows simply that the roadside pool is muddy, the great painter sees beneath and behind the brown surface what will take him a day's work to follow, but he follows it, cost what it will, and is amply recompensed, and that the great essential is an eye to apprehend and to appreciate the beautiful which lies about us everywhere in God's world. And this is what we want spiritually—the *eye of faith*, and then shall we see, even in the most opposite of the experiences which meet us in life, God's gracious operation, and the vision shall thrill us with holy joy. "The just shall live by his faith." This life of faith is a life characterized by true blessedness. There can be no real happiness whilst we are opposing our will to the will of God; but if our will is renewed by his grace, if we are trusting in the Saviour and following him along the way of obedience to the Divine authority and of resignation to the Divine purpose, then amidst all the changing scenes of our life our peace shall flow like a river, and we shall experience joy lasting as God's throne.—S. D. H.

Vers. 6—8.—*Covetousness*. In the remaining portion of this chapter the prophet dwells upon the sins prevailing amongst the Chaldeans, and indicates the misery these should entail. His utterances, taken together, form a satirical ode directed against the Chaldeans, who, though not named, are yet most clearly personified. In the general statement respecting them in ver. 5 allusion is made to their rapacity, and the first stanza in the song is specially directed to this greed, which was so characteristic of that nation. The words of the prophet suggest to us respecting the sin of covetousness, that—

I. It is unsatisfying in its nature. It is compared (ver. 5) to Hades and death, that crave continually for more. "The covetous man is like Tantalus, up to the chin in water, yet thirsty." Necessarily it must be so, for "a man's life consisteth not in the abundance of the things that he possesseth" (Luke xii. 15). Wealth can only yield satisfaction in proportion as it is acquired, not for its own sake, but to be consecrated to high and holy purposes. George Herbert sings—

> "Be thrifty, but not covetous. Get, to live:
> Then live and use it: else it is not true
> That thou hast gotten."

II. It leads to injustice and oppression. The covetous man "increaseth that which is not his" (ver. 6). He disregards the rights of others. He uses all who come within his power with a view to his own aggrandizement. Self is the primary consideration with him, and influences all his movements. "He oppresseth the poor to increase his riches," and out of their grinding poverty and want he grows fat. He is ready to take any mean advantage so as to add to his own stores. He demands heavy security of the debtor, and exacts crushing interest, and "ladeth himself with thick clay" (ver. 6), *i.e.* "loadeth himself with the burden of pledges."

III. It incurs sure retribution. Whether this sin is committed by individuals or nations, it is alike "woe" unto such; for there shall assuredly follow Divine judgments. Habakkuk represents the Chaldeans as one who had gathered men and nations into his net (ch. i. 14—17), and as having "spoiled many nations" (ver. 8), and Jeremiah confirms these representations of their rapacity by describing them as "the hammer" (l. 23) and the destroyer (li. 25) of the whole earth; and they also declare that there should overtake them certain retribution for the wrongs they had thus done and the sorrows they had thus occasioned, and that the spoiler should be at length spoiled (vers. 7, 8). In the destruction of the Chaldean empire by the Medes and Persians we have the fulfilment of the threatenings, whilst, at the same time, we hear the voice of God speaking to us in the events of history and saying, "Take heed, and beware of covetousness!"—S. D. H.

Vers. 9—11.—*Corrupt ambition.* Ambition may be pure and lofty, and when this is the case it cannot be too highly commended. It is "the germ from which all growth of nobleness proceeds." "It is to the human heart what spring is to the earth, making every root and bud and bough desire to be more." Headway cannot be made in life apart from it, and destitute of this spirit a man must be outstripped in the race. Ambition, however, may take the opposite form, and it is to ambition corrupt and low in its nature that these verses refer. Observe indicated here concerning such unworthy ambition—

I. ITS AIM. The concern of the rulers of Babylon was to secure unlimited supremacy, to reach an eminence where, secure from peril and in the enjoyment of ease and luxury, they might, without restraint, exercise despotic control over the nations. "That he may set his nest on high, that he may be delivered from the power of evil" (ver. 9). False ambition, whether in individuals or nations, is directed to the attainment of worldly distinction, authority, and power, and has its foundation in pride and self-esteem.

II. ITS UNSCRUPULOUSNESS. "They coveted an evil covetousness to their house" (ver. 9), totally disregarding the sacredness of property and the rights of man. Their acts were marked by oppression, plunder, and cruelty; they impoverished feebler nations and even "cut off many people" (ver. 10) in seeking the accomplishment of their selfish purposes. So is it ever that "such ambition breaks the ties of blood and forgets the obligations of manhood."

III. ITS ISSUE. The prophet indicates that all this self-seeking and self-glorying must end in disgrace and dishonour. 1. The very monuments reared thus in the spirit of pride should bear adverse testimony. In the language of poetry he represents the materials which they had obtained by plunder and which they had brought from other lands into Chaldea, to be used in the construction of their stately edifices, as protesting against the way in which they had been obtained and the purposes to which they had been applied (ver. 11). 2. Shame and ruin should overtake the schemers and plotters themselves. "Thou hast sinned against thy soul" (ver. 10). Whatever their material gain, they had become spiritually impoverished by their course of action. They had degraded their higher nature and had incurred guilt and condemnation. 3. All connected with them should share in the disgrace and dishonour. "Thou hast consulted shame to thy house" (ver. 10); "God visits the iniquities of the fathers upon the children, unto the third and fourth generation of them that hate him" (Exod. xx. 5); "He that is greedy of gain troubleth his own house" (Prov. xv. 27). Men who have sought, by grasping and extortion, or by war and conquest, to establish and perpetuate a high reputation, have, through their unrighteous deeds, passed away in ignominy, leaving to their posterity a tarnished and dishonoured name. "The house of the wicked shall be overthrown; but the tabernacle of the upright shall flourish" (Prov. xiv. 11).—S. D. H.

Vers. 12—14.—*The two kingdoms: a contrast.* Reference is made in these verses to two kingdoms—the kingdom of Babylon and the kingdom of God; and this association serves to indicate several points of contrast.

I. THE GLORY OF THE KINGDOMS OF THIS WORLD IS MATERIAL; THE GLORY OF THE KINGDOM OF GOD IS SPIRITUAL. The glory of Chaldea centred in its magnificent city of Babylon, so grand in its situation, its edifices, it defences, and in the stores of treasure it contained, its greatness consisting thus in its material resources; but the glory of the kingdom of God is spiritual. It is "the glory of the Lord" that constitutes its excellence—all moral beauty and spiritual grace abounding therein.

II. THE KINGDOMS OF THIS WORLD HAVE OFTEN BEEN FOUNDED AND ESTABLISHED BY MEANS OF WRONG-DOING; THE KINGDOM OF GOD IS FOUNDED AND ESTABLISHED IN PURE RIGHTEOUSNESS AND TRUE HOLINESS. The Chaldeans, by their superior might and powers, conquered other tribes, and with the spoils of war and the forced labour of the conquered they reared their cities. They "built a town with blood, and established a city by iniquity" (ver. 12); but "a sceptre of righteousness is the sceptre of God's kingdom."

III. HUMAN TOIL IS INVOLVED IN THE INTERESTS OF BOTH; yet notice, by way of contrast: 1. Toil in the interests of earthly kingdoms is often compulsory and is rendered reluctantly—aliens who had fallen as captives into the power of the Chaldeans were made to labour and serve; but toil in the interests of God's kingdom is ever *voluntary* and is rendered *lovingly* and *without constraint*. 2. Toil in the interests of earthly kingdoms is often *toil for that which shall be destroyed, and which shall come to nought.* "The people shall labour in the very fire, and the people shall weary themselves for very vanity" (ver. 13), *i.e.* they should labour in erecting edifices which should be consumed by fire, and thus their toil prove in vain; but *toil in the interests of God's kingdom shall prove abiding and eternal in its results.* 3. The workers of iniquity, no matter how earnest their toil, should be *covered eventually with dishonour and shame*—"Woe to him!" etc. (ver. 12)—but all true toilers for God and righteousness shall be *divinely approved and honoured.*

IV. THE PROSPERITY OF MATERIAL KINGDOMS IS UNCERTAIN; WHEREAS THE TRIUMPH OF GOD'S SPIRITUAL KINGDOM IS ASSURED. "The knowledge of the glory of the Lord shall cover the earth."

V. EARTHLY KINGDOMS ARE LIMITED IN EXTENT; BUT THE SPIRITUAL KINGDOM OF OUR GOD SHALL ATTAIN UNTO UNIVERSAL DOMINION. "The earth shall be filled with the knowledge of the glory of the Lord as the *waters cover the sea.*"—S. D. H.

Vers. 15—17.—*God's retributive justice.* It is a Divine law that "whatsoever a man soweth that shall he also reap" (Gal. vi. 7). God is just, and hence will cause retribution to be experienced by evil-doers. A striking illustration of the operation of this great law is presented in these verses. Consider—

I. THE COURSE THE CHALDEANS HAD ADOPTED TOWARD OTHERS. (Ver. 15.) The reference in this verse is not to the sin of drunkenness. That sin is a distressing and degrading one, and they are true lovers of their kind who seek to lessen its ravages, to deliver men from its thraldom. It has proved a blight to the children of men all down the ages. The Chaldeans were notorious for it; revellings, banquetings, excess of wine, marked them all through their history, and specially signalized the close of their career. The prophet, however, here simply used this vice as a symbol in order to set forth vividly the course the Babylonians had adopted towards others, and specially to indicate their deceitfulness. Drink drowns the reason, and places its victim at the mercy of any who are mean enough to take advantage of him. And the thought the prophet wished to convey here (ver. 15) seems to be that as a man, desiring to injure another, persuades him to take stimulant, and thus, whilst professing good intentions, effects his evil purpose, so had the Chaldeans intoxicated feebler powers by professions of friendship and regard, drawing them into alliance, and then turning upon them to their discomfiture and ruin. And he proceeds to indicate—

II. THE COURSE GOD WOULD ADOPT TOWARDS THEM. (Vers. 16, 17.) And in this he traced the Divine retribution of their iniquity. He saw prophetically that: 1. As they had taken advantage of others, so others should in due course take advantage of them (ver. 16) and bring them to shame. 2. As they would lay waste his country and take his people into captivity, so subsequently they should themselves be brought to nought, and their empire pass out of their hands (ver. 17; comp. Isa. xiv. 8, in which the fir trees and cedars are made to rejoice in the overthrow of Babylon). Our prophet had been perplexed at the thought of the Chaldeans as being the instruments of the Divine justice in reference to his own sinful people, but the mystery was clearing away, and in the final overthrow of Babylon he here foreshadowed, he traced another token that "the Lord is righteous in all his ways."—S. D. H.

Vers. 18—20.—*Worship, false and true.* The prophet, in recounting the sins of the Chaldeans, finally recalled to mind the idolatry prevailing amongst them. He thought of the temple of Bel, "casting its shadow far and wide over city and plain," and of the idolatrous worship of which it was the centre, and he broke forth in words expressive of the utmost scorn and contempt, and then closed his song by pointing to him who alone is worthy to receive the devout adoration and adoring praise of all the inhabitants of the earth. Notice—

I. HIS EXPOSURE OF THE WEAKNESS AND FOLLY OF IDOLATRY. (Vers. 18, 19.) 1. He appealed to *experience.* His own people unhappily had been betrayed into idolatry, and he asked them whether they had ever profited thereby (ver. 18). 2. He appealed to *reason*. The maker of anything must of necessity be greater than that which he fashions with his own hands and as the result of his own skill; hence what greater absurdity could there be than for the maker of a dumb idol to be reposing his trust in the thing he has formed (ver. 18)? 3. He denounced the *idol priests*, who, by using dumb idols as their instrument, made these "teachers of lies" (ver. 18). 4. He declared the hopelessness resulting from reposing trust in these. "Woe unto him!" etc. (ver. 19). 5. He indulged in scornful satire (ver. 19). This verse may be fittingly compared with Elijah's irony of speech addressed n Carmel to the prophets of Baal (1 Kings xviii. 27). The verse is more effectively rendered in the Revised Version—

> "Woe unto him that saith to the wood, Awake!
> To the dumb stone, Arise!
> Shall this teach! Behold, it is laid over with gold and silver:
> And there is no breath at all in the midst of it."

The weakness and folly of idolatry as practised in heathen lands is readily admitted by us; yet we are prone to forget that the idolatrous spirit may prevail even amongst those who are encompassed by influences eminently spiritual. Love of the æsthetical may lead us to become sensuous rather than spiritual in worship. Attachment to science may cause us to slight the supernatural and to deify nature. Desire for worldly success may result in our bowing down in the temple of Mammon; so that the counsel is still needed, "Little children, keep yourselves from idols" (1 John v. 21).

II. HIS PRESENTATION OF JEHOVAH AS BEING SUPREME AND AS ALONE ENTITLED TO THE REVERENT HOMAGE OF HUMAN HEARTS. "But the Lord is in his holy temple: let all the earth keep silence before him." 1. The contrast presented here is truly sublime. From impotent idols the seer raises his thoughts and directs attention to the living God. 2. The temple in Jerusalem was the recognized dwelling-place of God. The prophet saw looming in the distance the invasion of his country by the idolatrous Chaldeans, followed by the destruction of the temple and the desecration of all he held so sacred in association with it. Still he was assured that through all the coming changes Jehovah would remain the Supreme Ruler and Controller. Unconfined to temples made with hands, their overthrow could not affect his rule. "His throne is in the heavens;" he reigns there; and fills heaven and earth, dominating the universe, and guiding and overruling all to the accomplishment of his all-wise and loving purposes. "The Lord is in his holy temple." 3. Our true position as his servants is that of reverentially waiting before him, acquiescing in his will, trusting in his Word, assured that, despite the prevailing mysteries, the end shall reveal his wisdom and his love. He says to us, "Be still, and know that I am God." Then let no murmuring word be spoken, even when clouds and darkness seem to be round about him; the processes of his working are hidden from our weak view, but the issue is sure to vindicate the unerring wisdom and infinite graciousness of his rule. Happy the man who is led from doubt to faith, who, like this seer, beginning with the complaint, "O Lord, how long shall I cry, and thou wilt not hear!" etc. (ch. i. 2), is led through calm reflection and hallowed communion to cherish the conviction that "the Lord is in his holy temple, and that all the earth should keep silence before him."—S. D. H.

Vers. 1—3.—*Man's moral mission to the world.* "I will stand upon my watch, and set me upon the tower, and will watch to see what he will say unto me, and what I shall answer when I am reproved. And the Lord answered me, and said, Write the vision, and make it plain upon tables, that he may run that readeth it. For the vision is yet for an appointed time, but at the end it shall speak, and not lie: though it tarry, wait for it; because it will surely come, it will not tarry." The prophet, after his supplicatory cry, receives a Divine command to write the oracle in plain characters. because it was certain, although it would not be immediately fulfilled. The first verse is a kind of monologue. The prophet holds conversation with himself; and he resolves to ascend his watch-tower, and look out for a Divine revelation. It is thought by many critics that the watch-tower is not to be regarded as something external, some lofty place commanding an extensive view and profound silence, but the recesses of his own mind, into which he would withdraw himself by devout contemplation. I shall use the words of the text to illustrate man's *moral mission to the world.* Wherefore are we in this world? Both the theories and the practical conduct of men give different answers to this all-important problem. I shall take the answer from the text, and observe—

I. OUR MISSION HERE IS TO RECEIVE COMMUNICATIONS FROM THE ETERNAL MIND. "I will stand upon my watch, and set me upon the tower, and will watch to see what he will say unto me." That man is constituted for and required to receive communications from the Infinite Mind, and that he cannot realize his destiny without this, appears evident from the following considerations. 1. *From his nature as a spiritual being.* (1) He has an *instinct* for it. He naturally calls out for the living God. As truly as the eye is made to receive light, the soul is made to receive thought from God. (2) He has a *capacity* for it. Unlike the lower creatures around us, we can receive the ideas of God. (3) He has a *necessity* for it. God's ideas are the quickening powers of the soul. 2. *From his condition as a fallen being.* Sin has shut out God from the soul, created a dense cloud between us and him. 3. *From the purpose of Christ's mediation.* Why did Christ come into the world? To bring the human soul and God together, that the Lord might "dwell amongst men." 4. *From the special manifestations of God for the purpose.* I say special, for nature, history, heart, and conscience are the natural orders of communication between the human and the Divine. But we have something more than these—the Bible; this is *special.* Here he speaks to man at sundry times and in divers manners, etc. 5. *From the general teaching of the Bible.* "Come now, and let us reason together," etc.; "Behold, I stand at the door," etc. But how shall we receive these communications? We must ascend the "tower" of quiet, earnest, devout thought, and there must "watch to see what he will say."

II. OUR MISSION HERE IS TO IMPART COMMUNICATIONS FROM THE ETERNAL MIND. "Write the vision, and make it plain upon tables, that he may run that readeth it." From this we may conclude that writing is both an ancient and a divinely sanctioned art. Thank God for books! That we have to *impart* as well as to receive is evident: 1. *From the tendency of Divine thoughts to express themselves.* It is of the nature of religious ideas that they struggle for utterance. What we have seen and heard we cannot but speak. 2. *From the universal adaptation of Divine thoughts.* Thoughts from God are not intended merely for certain individuals or classes, but for all the race in all generations. 3. *From the spiritual dependence of man upon man.* It is God's plan, that man shall be the spiritual teacher of man. 4. *From the general teaching of the Bible.* What the prophets and apostles received from God they communicated. "When it pleased God to reveal his Son in me, immediately I conferred not with flesh and blood," etc. (Gal. i. 16).

III. OUR MISSION HERE IS TO PRACTICALLY REALIZE COMMUNICATIONS FROM THE ETERNAL MIND. "Though it tarry, wait for it," etc. The Divine thoughts which we receive we are to realize in our daily life, practically to work out. Here, then, is our moral mission. We are here, brothers, for these three purposes; not for one of them only, but for all. God is to be everything to us; he is to fill up the whole sphere of our being, our "all in all." We are to be his *auditors,* hearing his voice in everything; we are to be his *organ,* conveying to others what he has conveyed to us; we are to be his *representatives,* manifesting him in every act of our life. All we say and do, our looks and mien, are to be rays reflected from the Father of lights.

CONCLUSION. From this subject we may learn: 1. *The reasonableness of religion.* What is it? Simply to receive, propagate, and develop communications from the Infinite Mind. What can be more sublimely reasonable than this? 2. *The grandeur of a religious life.* What is it? The narrowness, the intolerance, the bigotry, the selfishness of many religionists lead sceptics to look upon religion with derision. But what is it? To be a disciple of the all-knowing God, a minister of the all-ruling God, a representative of the all-glorious God. Is there anything grander? 3. *The function of Christianity.* What is it? To induce, to qualify, and enable men to receive, communicate, and to live the great thoughts of God.—D. T.

Ver. 4.—*The portraiture of a good man.* "Behold, his soul which is lifted up is not upright in him: but the just shall live by his faith." Whether the man whose soul is represented as "lifted up" refers to the unbelieving Jew or to the Babylonian, is an unsettled question amongst biblical critics; and a question of but little practical moment. We take the words as a portraiture of a good man.

I. A GOOD MAN IS A HUMBLE MAN. This is implied. His soul is not "lifted up." Pride is not only no part of moral goodness, but is essentially inimical to it. It is said that St. Augustine, being asked, "What is the first article in the Christian religion?" replied, "Humility." "What is the second?" "Humility." "And the third?" "Humility." A proud Christian is a solecism. Jonathan Edwards describes a Christian as being such a "little flower as we see in the spring of the year, low and humble in the ground, opening its bosom for the beams of the sun, rejoicing in a calm rapture, suffusing around sweet fragrance, and standing peacefully and lowly in the midst of other flowers." Pride is an obstruction to all progress and knowledge and virtue, and is abhorrent to the Holy One. "He resisteth the proud, but giveth grace to the humble."

> "Fling away ambition,
> By that sin fell the angels; how can man, then,
> The image of his Maker, hope to win by 't?"
> (Shakespeare.)

II. A GOOD MAN IS A JUST MAN. "The just shall live by his faith." To be good is nothing more than to be just. 1. Just to *self*. Doing the right thing to one's own faculties and affections as the offspring of God. 2. Just to *others*. Doing unto others what we would that they should do unto us. 3. Just to *God*. The kindest Being thanking the most, the best Being loving the most, the greatest Being reverencing the most. To be just to self, society, and God,—this is religion.

III. A GOOD MAN IS A CONFIDING MAN. He lives "by his faith." This passage is quoted by Paul in Rom. i. 17 and Gal. iii. 11; it is also quoted in the Epistle to the Hebrews (x. 38). What is faith? Can you get a better definition than the writer of the Hebrews has given in the eleventh chapter and first verse?—"Faith is the substance of things hoped for, the evidence of things not seen." This definition implies three things. 1. That the things to which faith is directed are invisible. "Things not seen." These things include things that are contingently unseeable and things that are essentially unseeable, such as thought, mind, God. 2. That some of the invisible things are objects of hope. "Things hoped for." The invisible has much that is very desirable to us—the society of holy souls, the presence of the blessed Christ, the manifestations of the infinite Father, etc. 3. That these invisible things faith makes real in the present life. "The substance of things hoped for, the evidence of things not seen." The realization of the hopeable. Now, it is only by this faith that man can live a just life in this world; the man who lives by sight must be unjust. To be just, he must see him who is invisible.—D. T.

Ver. 5.—*Moral wrong: some of its national phases.* "Yea also, because he transgresseth by wine, he is a proud man, neither keepeth at home, who enlargeth his desire as hell, and is as death, and cannot be satisfied, but gathereth unto him all nations, and heapeth unto him all people." No doubt Habakkuk was reviled like the other prophets on account of his terrible predictions, as recorded in the preceding chapter (vers. 6 and 11). From this verse to the nineteenth the prophet unfolds new visions concerning the national crimes committed by Babylon, and the consequent national calamities approaching. This verse gives some of the national phases of moral wrong as they appeared in Babylon. Evil, like good, is one in essence, but it has many forms and phases. The branches that grow out of the root, whilst filled with the same sap, vary widely in shape and hue. In this verse we have three of its forms.

I. DRUNKENNESS. "He transgresseth by wine;" or, as some render it, "moreover, the wine is treacherous." This is one of the most loathsome, irrational, and pernicious forms which it can assume. Drunkenness puts the man or the woman absolutely into the hands of Satan, to do whatsoever he wills—lie, swear, rob, murder, and luxuriate in moral mud. "A drunken man is like a fool, a madman, a drowned man; one draught too much makes him a fool, the second mads, and the third drowns him" (Shakespeare). It is the curse of England. It fills our workhouses with paupers, our hospitals with patients, our jails with prisoners, our mad-houses with lunatics, our cemeteries with graves. Moral wrong took this form in ancient Babylon, and it takes this form in England to-day to an appalling extent. Woe to our legislators, if they do not put it down by the strong arm of the law! Nothing else will do it.

II. HAUGHTINESS. "Is a proud man." Babylon became inspired with a haughty insolence. She regarded herself as the queen of the world, and looked down with supercilious contempt upon all the other nations of the earth, even upon the Hebrew people, the heavenly-chosen race. Nebuchadnezzar expresses the spirit of the kingdom as well as his own, when he says, "Is not this great Babylon, that I have built for the house of the kingdom by the might of my power, and for the honour of my majesty?" (Dan. iv. 30). It is suggested that the Chaldeans' love of wine had much to do in the developing of this haughty spirit. We read (Dan. v.) that Belshazzar at his feast drank wine with the thousands of his lords, his princes, his wives, his concubines. "Wine is a mocker;" it cheats a beggar into the belief that he is a lord. "Strong drink is raging;" it lashes the passions into furious insolence. It is fabled that Accius the poet, though he was a dwarf, would be pictured a giant in stature. Pride is an evil that leads to ruin. "Pride goes before destruction, and a haughty spirit before a fall."

III. RAPACITY. Two things are suggested concerning the rapacious form it assumed in Babylon. 1. It was *restless*. "Neither keepeth at home." Not content with its own grandeur, wealth, and luxuries, it goes from home in search of others; goes out into other countries to rifle and to rob. 2. It is *insatiable*. "Who enlargeth his desire as hell [that is, 'as Sheol, the grave'], and is as death, and cannot be satisfied." "Hell and destruction," that is, the grave and death, says Solomon, "are never full." The grave cries for more and more, as its tenants multiply by millions. The earth seems to hunger and to gape for all the dust that enters into the frames of men. So it was with the Babylonian despot, though he gathered unto him all nations, and heaped unto him all peoples, his greed and ambition remained unsatiated and insatiable. "This," says an old writer, "is one of the crying sins of our land, insatiable pride. This makes dear rents and great fines; this takes away the whole clothing of many poor to add one lace more in the suits of the rich; this shortens the labourer's wages, and adds much to the burden of his labour. This greediness makes the market of spiritual and temporal offices and dignities, and puts well-deserving virtue out of countenance. This corrupts religion with opinions, justice with bribes, charity with cruelty; it turns peace into schism and contention, love into compliment, friendship into treason, and sets the mouth of hell yet more open, and gives it an appetite for more souls." Such are some of the forms that moral wrong took in Babylon, as indicated in these words. But these are not the only forms, as we shall see in proceeding through the chapter. Does not moral wrong assume these very forms here in England? Drunkenness, haughtiness, rapacity,—these fiends show their hideous shapes everywhere, and work their demon deeds in every circle of life.—D. T.

Vers. 6—8.—*National wrongs ending in national woes. No.* 1. "Shall not all these take up a parable against him, and a taunting proverb against him, and say, Woe to him that increaseth that which is not his! how long? and to him that ladeth himself with thick clay! Shall they not rise up suddenly that shall bite thee, and awake that shall vex thee, and thou shalt be for booties unto them?" etc. In these verses, up to the nineteenth inclusive, the prophet denounces upon the Chaldeans and Babylonians five different woes. One for their pride and insatiableness (vers. 6—8); another for their covetousness, etc., which would become the cause of their corruption (vers. 9—11); another for the bloody and cruel means which they had employed for gratifying their thirst for acquiring possessions not their own (vers. 12—14); and fourth, for their wickedness, etc., which would be recompensed to them (vers. 15—17); and the fifth, for their trust in idols, which would redound to their shame (vers. 18, 19). We shall take each of the five sections separately under the title, *National wrongs ending in national woes.* Notice—

I. THE NATIONAL WRONGS. 1. *Dishonest accumulation.* "Woe to him that increaseth that which is not his!" Babylon grew wealthy. Its treasures were varied and all but inexhaustible. But whence came they? Came they by honest industry? Were they the home produce of diligent and righteous labour? No; from other lands. They were wrested from other countries by violence and fraud. Even the golden and silver vessels used at the royal feast were taken out of the temple which was at Jerusalem. "No more," says an old writer, "of what we have is to be reckoned ours than what we came honestly by. Nor will it long be ours, for wealth gotten by vanity will soon diminish." Take away the ill-gotten wealth of the nations of Europe—wealth gotten by fraud and violence—and how greatly will they be pauperized! How much of our national wealth has come to us honestly? A question this worth the impartial investigation of every man, and which must be gone into sooner or later. 2. *Dominant materialism.* "And to him that ladeth himself with thick clay." Although some render this "ladeth himself with many pledges," our version, which gives the word "clay," will cover all. The burning and insatiable desire of Babylon was for *material* wealth; and the men or the nation who succeed in this, only lade themselves with "thick clay." It is a bad thing for moral spirits to be laden with "thick clay." See the individual man who so pampers his animal appetites until he becomes a Falstaff. His spirit is laden with "thick clay." See the nation whose inspiration is that of avaricious merchandise, and whose god is mammon; its spirit is laden with "thick clay." Ah me! what millions are to be found in all civilized countries who are buried in "thick clay"! Clay is everything to them. 3. *Extensive plunder.* "Thou hast spoiled many nations." The first monarchy we read of in Holy Scripture is that of the Assyrians, begun by Ninus, of whom Nineveh took name, and by Nimrod, whom histories call Belus, and after him succeeded Semiramis his wife. This monarchy grew, by continual wars and violences on their neighbours, to an exceeding height and strength; so that the exaltation of that monarchy was the ruin of many nations, and this monarchy lasted, as some write, *annos* 1300. 4. *Ruthless violence.* "Because of men's blood, and for the violence of the land, of the city, and of all that dwell therein." "The terms ' men,' ' land,' ' earth, 'city,' " says Henderson, "are to be understood generally, not restricted to the Jews, their country and its metropolis." What oceans of the blood of all countries were shed by these ruthless tyrants of Babylon!

II. THE NATIONAL WOES. All these wrongs, as all other wrongs, run into woes. Crimes lead to calamities. What are the woes connected with these wrongs, as given in these verses? 1. *The contempt of the injured.* "Shall not all these take up a parable against him, and a taunting proverb against him, and say, Woe to him that increaseth that which is not his! how long? and to him that ladeth himself with thick clay!" The *woe* comes out in a derisive song, which continues to the end of the chapter. Dishonesty and low animalism must ever sink the people amongst whom they prevail into bitter contempt. Scarcely can there be anything more painful than the contempt of others when it is felt to be deserved. To be sneered at, laughed at, ridiculed, scorned,—is not this bitterly afflictive? Jeremiah predicted that one part of the punishment should be that he should be laughed to scorn. 2. *The avenging of the spoiled.* "Because thou hast spoiled many nations, all the remnant of the people shall spoil thee." Here is retaliation—plunder for plunder, blood for blood. Divine retribution often pays man back in his own coin. "With what measure ye mete, it shall be measured to you again."

CONCLUSION. Ever under the righteous administration of Heaven *woes* tread closely on the heel of *wrongs.* More certainly than the waves of the ocean follow the moon must suffering follow sin. To every crime there is linked a curse, to every sin a suffering, to every wrong a woe. Be sure that "your sins will find you out."—D. T.

Vers. 9—11.—*National wrongs ending in national woes. No.* 2. "Woe to him that coveteth an evil covetousness to his house, that he may set his nest on high, that he may be delivered from the power of evil! Thou hast consulted shame to thy house by cutting off many people, and hast sinned against thy soul. For the stone shall cry out of the wall, and the beam out of the timber shall answer it." Notice—

I. THE NATIONAL WRONGS HERE INDICATED. 1. *Coveting the possessions of others.* "Woe to him that coveteth an evil covetousness to his house!" "An evil covetousness!" There is a good covetousness. We are commanded to "covet earnestly the best gifts" (1 Cor. xii. 31). But to hunger for those things which are not our own, but the property of others, and that for our own gratification and aggrandizement, is the sin which is prohibited in the Decalogue, which is denounced in the Gospel as a cardinal sin, and which is represented as excluding from the kingdom of heaven. The covetous man is a thief in spirit and in reality. 2. *Trusting in false securities.* So "that he may set his nest on high, that he may be delivered from the power of evil." The image is from an eagle (Job xxxix. 27). The royal citadel is meant. The Chaldeans built high towers like the Babel-founders, to be delivered from the power of evil. They sought protection, not in the Creator but in the creature, not in moral means but in material. Thus foolishly nations have always acted and are still acting; they trust to armies and to navies, not to righteousness, truth, and God. A moral character built on justice, purity, and universal benevolence is the only right and safe defence of nations. "Though thou exalt thyself as the eagle, and though thou set thy nest against the stars, thence will I bring thee down, saith the Lord" (Obad. 4). 3. *Sinning against the soul.* "And hast sinned against thy soul," or against thyself. Indeed, all wrong is a sin against one's self—a sin against the laws of reason, conscience, and happiness. "He that sinneth against me wrongeth his own soul." Such are some of the wrongs implied by these verses. Alas! they are not confined to Babylon or to any of the ancient kingdoms. They are too rife amongst all the modern kingdoms of the earth.

II. THE NATIONAL WOES HERE INDICATED. "Woe to him that coveteth an evil covetousness to his house!" etc. What is the woe connected with these evils? It is contained in these words, "The stone shall cry out of the wall, and the beam out of the timber shall answer it." Their guilty conscience will endow the dead materials of their own dwellings with the tongue to denounce in thunder their deeds of rapacity and blood. Startling personification this! The very stones of thy palace and the beams out of the timber shall testify. "Note," says Matthew Henry, "those that do wrong to their neighbour do a much greater wrong to their own souls. But if the sinner pleads, 'Not guilty,' and thinks he has managed his frauds and violence with so much art and contrivance that they cannot be proved upon him, let him know that if there be no other witnesses against him, the *stone shall cry out of the wall* against him, and the *beam out of the timber* in the roof *shall answer* it, shall second it, shall witness it, that the money and materials wherewith he built the house were unjustly gotten (ver. 11). The stones and timber shall cry to Heaven for vengeance, as the *whole creation groans under* the sin of man, and waits to be delivered from *that bondage* of *corruption.*" Observe: 1. That mind gives to all the objects that once impressed it a *mystic power of suggestion.* Who has not felt this? Who does not feel it every day? The tree, the house, the street, the lane, the stream, the meadow, the mountain, that once touched our consciousness, seldom fail to start thoughts in us whenever we are brought into contact with them again. It seems as if the mind gave part of itself to all the objects that once impressed it. When we revisit, after years of absence, the scenes of childhood, all the objects which impressed us in those early days seem to beat out and revive the thoughts and feelings of our young hearts. Hence, when we leave a place which in person we may never revisit, we are still tied to it by an indissoluble bond. Nay, we carry it with us and reproduce it in memory. 2. That mind gives to those objects that impressed us when *in the commission of any sin* a terrible power to start remorseful memories. This is a fact of which, alas! all are conscious. And hence those stones and timbers, stolen from other people, that went to build the palaces, temples, and mansions in Babylon, would not fail to speak in thunder to the guilty consciences of those who obtained them by violence or fraud. No intelligent personal witness is required to prove a sinner's guilt. All the scenes of his conscious life vocalize his guilt.—D. T.

Vers. 12—14.—*National wrongs ending in national woes. No. 3.* "Woe to him that buildeth a town with blood, and stablisheth a city by iniquity! Behold, is it not of the Lord of hosts that the people shall labour in the very fire, and the people shall weary themselves for very vanity? For the earth shall be filled with the knowledge of the glory of the Lord, as the waters cover the sea." Notice—

I. THE NATIONAL WRONGS INDICATED IN THESE VERSES. The great wrong referred to in these verses is the accumulation of gain by wicked means. "Woe to him that buildeth a town with blood, and stablisheth a city by iniquity!" In itself there is nothing improper in building towns, establishing cities, and accumulating wealth.

Indeed, all these things are both legitimate and desirable. But it is stated that these Babylonians did it : 1. *By violence.* "With blood." Men's lives were sacrificed for the purpose. "By iniquity." Justice was outraged in the effort. 2. *By cruelty.* "Labour in the very fire." These wrongs we have already explained in the preceding sections. (But see a different explanation of "labour in the fire" in the Exposition.)

II. THE NATIONAL WOES INDICATED IN THESE WORDS. What is the woe ? Disapprobation of God. 1. *These wrongs are contrary to his nature.* "Is it not of the Lord of hosts ?" or, as Keil renders it, "Is it not beheld from Jehovah of hosts that the people weary themselves for fire, and nations exhaust themselves from vanity ?" He does not desire it. Nay, it is hostile to his will, it is displeasing to his nature. The benevolent Creator is against all social injustice and cruelty. His will is that men should "do unto others as they would that men should do unto them." 2. *These wrongs are contrary to his purpose for the world.* His purpose is that the "earth shall be filled with the knowledge of the glory of the Lord." To this end the kingdom of the world which is hostile to him must be destroyed. "This promise," says Keil, "involves a threat directed against the Chaldean, whose usurped glory must be destroyed in order that the glory of the universe may fill the whole earth." What a glorious prospect ! (1) *This world, in the future, is to enjoy the greatest blessing.* What is that ? The knowledge of the glory of God. Knowledge in itself is a blessing. The soul without it is not good (Prov. xix. 2). It is not the mere knowledge of the *works* of God. This is of unspeakable value. Not merely the knowledge of some of the *attributes* of God. This is of greater value still. But the knowledge of the *glory* of God, which means the knowledge of God himself, "whom to know is life eternal." (2) *This world, in the future, is to enjoy the greatest blessing in the greatest abundance.* "As the waters cover the sea." He shall flood all souls with its celestial and transporting radiance.—D. T.

Vers. 15—17.—*National wrongs ending in national woes.* No. 4. "Woe unto him that giveth his neighbour drink, that puttest thy bottle to him, and makest him drunken also, that thou mayest look on their nakedness! Thou art filled with shame for glory : drink thou also, and let thy foreskin be uncovered : the cup of the Lord's right hand shall be turned unto thee, and shameful spewing shall be on thy glory," etc. "This," says Henderson, "is the commencement of the fourth stanza. Though the idea of the shameless conduct of drunkards here depicted may have been borrowed from the profligate manners of the Babylonian court, yet the language is not to be taken literally, as if the prophet were describing such manners, but, as the sequel shows, is applied allegorically to the state of stupefaction, prostration, and exposure to which the conquered nations were reduced by the Chaldeans (see Isa. li. 17—20 ; and comp. Ps. lxxv. 8; Jer. xxv. 15—28; xlix. 12; li. 7; Ezek. xxiii. 31, 32; Rev. xiv. 10; xvi. 19; xviii. 6). Notice—

I. THE NATIONAL WRONGS. What are the wrongs referred to in this passage ? 1. *The promotion of drunkenness.* "Woe unto him that giveth his neighbour drink !" The Babylonians were not only drunkards, but the promoters of drunkenness. The very night on which this prophecy was fulfilled, Belshazzar drank wine with a thousand of his lords. More than once in these homilies we have had to characterize and denounce this sin. Who are the promoters of drunkenness ? *Brewers, distillers, tavern-keepers,* and, I am sorry to add, *doctors,* all of whom, with a few exceptions, recommend intoxicating drinks. In doing so these men inflict a thousand times as much evil upon mankind as they can accomplish good. 2. *The promotion of drunkenness involves indecency.* "That thou mayest look on their nakedness." It is the tendency of drunkenness to destroy all sense of decency. A drunkard, whether male or female, loses all sense of shame.

II. THE NATIONAL WOES. "Woe unto him that giveth strong drink !" What will come to those people ? 1. *Contempt.* "Thou art filled with shame for glory. . . . The cup of the Lord's right hand shall be turned unto thee." As the Chaldeans had treated the nations they had conquered in a most disgusting manner, so they in their turn should be similarly treated. "With what measure ye mete, it shall be measured to you again." 2. *Violence.* "For the violence of Lebanon shall cover thee." Stripped of all figure, the meaning of this is that the sufferings which Babylon inflicted upon Palestine, represented here by Lebanon, would return to them. Here is retribution. Babylon had given the cup of drunkenness, and in return should have the cup of fury and contempt.—D. T.

Vers. 18, 19.—*National wrongs ending in national woes.* No. 5. "What profiteth the graven image that the maker thereof hath graven it; the molten image, and a teacher of lies, that the maker of his work trusteth therein, to make dumb idols? Woe unto him that saith to the wood, Awake; to the dumb stone, Arise, it shall teach! Behold, it is laid over with gold and silver, and there is no breath at all in the midst of it." We have said that the prophet denounces upon the Chaldeans, in vers. 6—19 of this chapter, five different woes of a most terrible nature. We have noticed four of them. This is the fifth and the last; and it is denounced on account of their idolatry. We have seen no translation of the text more faithful to the original than this, the Authorized Version. The note of Henderson on the text deserves quotation. "These verses expose the folly of idolatry, to which the Babylonians were wholly addicted. It might be supposed, from all the other stanzas having been introduced by a denunciatory הוי, 'woe!' that a transposition has here taken place, and that the nineteenth verse ought to be read before the eighteenth; and Green has thus placed them in his translation. But there is a manifest propriety in anticipating the inutility of idols, in close connection with what the prophet had just announced respecting the downfall of Babylon, before delivering his denunciation against their worshippers themselves." Now, idolatry, as it prevails in heathen lands, idolatry proper as we may say, is universally denounced by the professors of Christianity everywhere. We need not employ one word to expose its absurdity and moral abominations. But its *spirit* is rampant in all Christendom, is *rife* in all "Christian Churches," as they are called; and it is the spirit, not the form, that is the guilty and damnable part of idolatry. We raise, therefore, three observations from these verses.

I. THAT MEN OFTEN GIVE TO THE WORKS OF THEIR OWN HANDS THE DEVOTIONS THAT BELONG TO GOD. These old Chaldean idolaters gave their devotions to the "graven image" and to the "molten image" that men had carved in wood and stone or moulded from molten metals. It was the works of their own hands they worshipped. They made gods of their own productions. This was all they did; and are not the men of England, as a rule, doing the same thing? They yield their devotions to the works of their own hands. It may be wealth, fame, fashion, pleasure, or power. It is all the same. Are men's sympathies in their strong current directed towards God or towards something else? Do they expend the larger portion of their time and the greater amount of their energies in the service of the Eternal, or in the service of themselves? This is the question; and the answer is too palpable to the eye of every spiritual thinker. Exeter Hall may "weep and howl" over the idolatry prevailing in India, China, and other heathen parts; but thoughtful Christ-like souls are showering in silence and solitude their tears on the terrible idolatry that reigns everywhere in their own country.

II. THAT MEN OFTEN LOOK TO THE WORKS OF THEIR OWN HANDS FOR A BLESSING WHICH GOD ALONE CAN BESTOW. These old idolaters said to the "wood, Awake; to the dumb stone, Arise!" They invoked the dead forms they themselves had made, to help them, to give them relief, to render them happy. Now, it is true that men do not say formal prayers to wealth, or fashion, or fame, or power; yet to these they look with all their souls for happiness. A man's prayer is the deep aspiration of his soul, and this deep aspiration is being everywhere addressed to these dead deities; men are crying for happiness to objects which are as incapable of yielding it as the breathless gods of heathendom. "There is no breath at all in the midst of it." Men who are looking for happiness to any of these objects are like the devotees of Baal, who cried from morning to evening for help, and no help came.

III. THAT IN ALL THIS MEN ENTAIL ON THEMSELVES THE WOES OF OUTRAGED REASON AND JUSTICE. "Woe unto him that saith to the wood, Awake; to the dumb stone, Arise!" 1. *It is the woe of outraged reason.* What help could they expect of the "molten image, and a teacher of lies"? What answer could they expect from the "dumb idols" that they themselves had made? What relief from any of the idols, though overlaid with gold and silver? "There is no breath at all in the midst of it." How irrational all this! Equally unreasonable is it for men to search for happiness in any of the works of their hands, and in any being or in any object independent of God. 2. *It is the woe of insulted justice.* What has God said? "Thou shalt have no other gods before me;" "Thou shalt worship no graven image;" "Thou shalt love me with all thy heart," etc. All this devotion, therefore, to the works of our own hands, or to any other creature, is an infraction of man's cardinal obligation. "Will a man rob God?" Go, then, to the men on 'Change, who are seeking happiness from wealth—to the men in scenes of fashionable and worldly amusements, who are seeking happiness from sensual indulgences and worldly applause—and thunder, "Woe unto him that saith to the wood, Awake; to the dumb stone, Arise!"

> " And still from him we turn away,
> And fill our hearts with worthless things;
> The fires of avarice melt the clay,
> And forth the idol springs!
> Ambition's flame and passion's heat
> By wondrous alchemy transmute
> Earth's dross, to raise some gilded brute
> To fill Jehovah's seat."
>
> (Clinch.)
>
> D. T.

Ver. 20.—*Silence in the temple.* "The Lord is in his holy temple: let all the earth keep silence before him." "In striking contrast," says Dr. Henderson, "with the utter nihility of idols, Jehovah is here introduced, at the close of all the prophecy, as the invisible Lord of all, occupying his celestial temple, whence he is ever ready to interpose his omnipotence for the deliverance and protection of his people and the destruction of their enemies (comp. Isa. xxvi. 21). Such a God it becomes all to adore in solemn and profound silence (Ps. lxxvi. 8, 9; Zeph. i. 7; Zech. ii. 13)." We take these words as suggesting three great subjects of thought.

I. THE UNIVERSE IS THE TEMPLE OF GOD. Men practically ignore this fact. To some the world is only as a great farm to produce food; to others, a great market in which commodities are to be exchanged in order to amass wealth; to others, a great chest containing precious ores which are to be reached by labour, unlocked and brought into the market; to others, a great ball-room in which to dance and play and revel in sensuous enjoyment. Only a few regard it as a temple. But few tread its soil with reverent steps, feeling that all is holy ground. What a temple it is! how vast in extent! how magnificent in architecture! how stirring are its national appeals!

II. THE TEMPLE IS FILLED WITH THE DIVINE PRESENCE. "The Lord is in his holy temple." He is in it, not merely as a king is in his kingdom or the worker in his works; but he is in it as the soul is in the body, the fountain of its life, the spring of its activities. Unlike the human architect, he did not build the house and leave it; unlike the author, he did not write his volume and leave his book to tell its own tale; unlike the artist, he did not leave his pictures or his sculpture to stand dead in the hall. He is in all, not as a mere *influence*, but as an absolute, almighty *Personality.* " Do not I fill the heaven and earth? saith the Lord."

III. HIS PRESENCE IN THE GREAT TEMPLE DEMANDS SILENCE. "Keep silence before him." It would seem as if the Divine nature revolted from bluster and noise. How *serenely* he moves in *nature!* As spring by universal life rises out of death without any noise, and as the myriad orbs of heaven roll with more than lightning velocity in a sublime hush. How serenely he moves in *Christ!* He did not cause his voice to be heard in the streets. His presence, consciously realized, will generate in the soul feelings too deep, too tender for speech. Were the Eternal to be consciously felt by the race to-day, all the human sounds that fill the air and deaden the ears of men would be hushed into profound silence.

> " Never with blast of trumpets
> And the chariot-wheels of fame
> Do the servants and sons of the Highest
> His oracles proclaim;

But when grandest truths are uttered,
And when holiest depths are stirred,
When our God himself draws nearest,
The still, small voice is heard.
He has sealed his own with silence :
His years that come and go,
Bringing still their mighty measures
Of glory and of woe—
Have you heard one note of triumph
Proclaim their course begun?
One voice or bell give tidings
When their ministry was done?"

D. T.

EXPOSITION.

CHAPTER III.

Vers. 1—19.—Part II. Psalm or Prayer of Habakkuk.

Ver. 1.—§ 1. *The title.* **A prayer.** There is only one formal prayer in the ode, that in ver. 2; but the term is used of any devotional composition; and, indeed, the whole poem may be regarded as the development of the precatory sentences in the proœmium (see the inscriptions in Ps. xvii.; lxxxvi.; xc.; cii.; cxlii.; and the last verse of Ps. lxxii., the subscription of Book II.). (For other hymns in the prophetical books, see Isa. xxxiv. and xxxv.; Ezek. xix.; Jonah ii.; Micah vi. 6, etc.; and as parallel to this ode, comp. Deut. xxxiii. 2, etc.; Judg. v. 4, etc.; Ps. lxviii. 7, etc.; lxxvii. 13—20; cxiv.; Isa. lxiii. 11—14.) **Of Habakkuk the prophet.** The name and title of the author are prefixed to show that this is no mere private effusion, but an outpouring of prophecy under Divine inspiration. **Upon Shigionoth** (comp. title of Ps. vii.); Septuagint, μετὰ ᾠδῆς, " with song; " Vulgate, *pro ignorantiis.* For this latter rendering Jerome had etymological ground, but did not sufficiently consider the use of *shiggayon* in Ps. vii., where it indicates the style of poetry, nor, as Keil shows, the fact that all the headings of Psalms introduced, as the present, with *al*, refer either to the melody, or accompaniment, or style in which they were to be sung. The Revised Version gives, " set to Shigionoth; " and the expression is best explained to mean, in an impassioned or triumphal strain, with rapid change of emotion, a dithyrambic song—a description which admirably suits this ode.

Ver. 2.—§ 2. *The proœmium, in which the prophet expresses his fear at the coming judgment, and prays God in his wrath to remember mercy.* **Thy speech;** or, *the report of thee;* the declaration made by God in the preceding chapters concerning the punishment of the Jews and the destruction of the Chaldeans. The LXX., regarding the ambiguity of the Hebrew, gives a double rendering, εἰσακήκοα τὴν ἀκοήν σου, and κατενόησα τὰ ἔργα σου, " I heard thy report," and " I considered thy works." Pusey considers that both meanings are intended, viz. both what God had lately declared, and all that might be heard of God, his greatness and his workings. **Was afraid.** The revelation of God's interposition makes the prophet tremble. **Revive thy work.** God's work is the twofold judgment spoken of above; and the prophet prays God to " quicken " and make it live, because, though it brings temporary distress upon his countrymen, it will also cause the destruction of their enemies, and re-establish the Jews and crown them with salvation, and make the glory of God known to all the earth. Dr. Briggs (' Messianic Prophecy,' p. 234) translates, " Jahveh, I have heard the report of thee; I fear, Jahveh, thy work. In the midst of the years revive him (Israel)." He explains God's " work " to be his acts in theophany— his judgment, especially as in ver. 16, the cause of fear to the psalmist. **In the midst of the years.** The " years " are the period between the announcement of the judgment and its final accomplishment (ch. ii. 3); the prophet prays that God would manifest his power, not merely at the extreme limit of this epoch, but earlier, sooner. This overthrow of the world-power forms, as it were, the central point of history, the beginning of a new age which shall culminate in the Messianic kingdom. **Make known.** Let all the earth know and acknowledge thy work. The LXX. have given two or more versions of this passage, one of which is remarkable. Thus they read, " In the midst of two animals (δύο ζώων) thou shalt be known; when the years draw nigh thou shalt be well known; when the time is come thou shalt be revealed." The rendering, " two animals," arises from a confusion of words:

but many of the Fathers, who were conversant with the Greek Scriptures, saw herein a reference to the incarnation of our blessed Lord, as lying in the stable at Bethlehem between the ox and the ass, which was the mystical explanation of Isa. i. 3, "The ox knoweth his owner, and the ass his master's crib." Others interpreted the two animals of the two thieves between whom Christ was crucified; or of angels and men; or Jews and Gentiles; or the two Testaments; or Moses and Elias. Others again accented the word ζῶων so as to understand "two lives," the present and the future, in the midst of which the Judge shall appear; or the life of Christ before his death and after his resurrection. There is a great truth underlying most of these interpretations, namely, that this magnificent hymn is concerned with the victories of Christ and his Church. **In wrath remember mercy.** When thine anger is displayed by sending the Chaldeans against us, remember thy mercy, and make a speedy end of our misery, and mitigate our enemies' cruelty (comp. ch. i. 13; and vers. 9, 13, 18, 19 of this chapter). The LXX. gives a double version, "In the troubling of my soul, in wrath, thou wilt remember mercy."

Vers. 3—15.—§ 3. *The prophet or the congregation depicts in a majestic theophany the coming of God to judge the world, and its effect symbolically on material nature, and properly on evil men.*

Ver. 3.—In this episode Habakkuk takes his imagery from the accounts of God's dealings with his people in old time, in Egypt, at the Red Sea, at Sinai, at the Jordan, in Canaan; he echoes the songs of Moses and Deborah and the psalmist; and he looks on all these mighty deeds as anticipative of God's great work, the overthrow of all that opposes and the establishment of the kingdom of Messiah. **God** (*Eloah*) **came from Teman.** The words are connected with Moses' description of the Lord's appearance at Sinai (Deut. xxxiii. 2; comp. Judg. v. 4). As he then came in glory to make a covenant with his people, so will he appear again in majesty to deliver them from the power of evil and to execute judgment. The verbs throughout are best rendered in the present. The prophet takes his stand in time preceding the action of the verb, and hence uses the future tense, thus also showing that he is prophesying of a great event to come, symbolized by these earlier manifestations. Habakkuk here and in ch. i. 11 uses the word *Eloah*, which is not found in Jeremiah, Ezekiel, or the other minor prophets; it occurs once in Isaiah, twice in Deuteronomy, and frequently in Job.

There is no ground for the contention that its employment belongs to the latest stage of Hebrew. **Teman;** i.e. Edom; Vulgate, *ab Austro* (see notes on Amos i. 12 and Obad. 9). In Moses' song the Lord is said to come from Sinai. Habakkuk omits Sinai, says Pusey, which was the emblem of the Law, and points to another Lawgiver, like unto Moses, telling how he who spake the Law, God, should come in the likeness of man. **The Holy One.** A name of God (ch. i. 12), implying that he will not let iniquity pass unpunished, and that he will preserve the holy seed. **Mount Paran.** The mountainous district on the north-east of the desert of *Et-Tih.* The glory of the Lord is represented as flashing on the two hilly regions separated by the Arabah. They both lay south of Canaan; and there is propriety in representing the redeemer and deliverer appearing in the south, as the Chaldean invader comes from the north. The LXX. adds two translations of the word "Pharan," viz. "shady," "rough;" according to its etymology it might also mean "lovely." **Selah;** Septuagint, διάψαλμα. This term occurs also in vers. 9, 13, and frequently in the Psalms, but nowhere else, and indicates some change in the music when the ode was sung in the temple service. What is the exact change is a matter of great uncertainty. Some take it to indicate "a pause;" others, connecting it with *salah*, "to lift up," render it "elevation," and suppose it means the raising of the voice, or the strengthening of the accompaniment, as by the blast of trumpets. The meaning must be left undetermined, though it must be added that it is always found at the end of a verse or hemistich, where there is a pause or break in the thought, or, as some say, some strongly accented words occur. **His glory covered the heavens.** His majestic brightness spread over the heavens, dimming the gleam of sun and stars; or it may mean his boundless majesty fills the highest heavens and encompasses its inhabitants. **His praise.** This is usually explained to signify that the earth and all that dwell therein, at this glorious manifestion, utter their praise. But there is no allusion as yet to the manner in which the appearance is received, and in ver. 6 it produces fear and trembling; so it is best to take "praise" in the sense of "matter of praise," that glory "which was calculated to call forth universal adoration" (Henderson).

Ver. 4.—**His brightness was as the light;** *brightness appeareth like light.* The sunlight is meant, as Job xxxi. 26; xxxvii. 21; Isa. xviii. 4. **He had horns coming out of his hand;** *i.e.* rays of light on either side. The comparison of the first rays of light to the horns of the gazelle, according to Keil, is common in Arabic poetry (comp. Exod. xxxiv. 29, 30). In the original passage, Deut. xxxiii. 2, we read, "At his right hand was a fiery Law unto them"—a reference to the two tables of stone, perhaps resplendent with light. The "hand" in our text is a general expression, and is not to be taken with any special reference to lightning launched by the hand (which is not a scriptural expression), nor to works effected by God's agency, but simply as signifying that the light of his presence streamed forth from both sides, *i.e.* everywhere. **There** was the hiding of his power. There, in that ineffable light, was the hiding-place of his majesty. He clothes himself with light as with a garment (Ps. civ. 2), and the splendour is the mantle of that presence which eye of man cannot behold (Exod. xxiv. 17; 1 Tim. vi. 16). Farrar quotes Ps. xviii. 11, "He made darkness his secret place;" and Milton—

"Dark with excess of light his skirts appear."

Septuagint, Ἔθετο ἀγάπησιν κραταιὰν ἰσχύος αὐτοῦ, which rendering has arisen from taking the adverb *sham* as a verb (*sam*), and mistaking the meaning of the following word.

Ver. 5.—After describing the splendour of the theophany, the prophet now turns to the purpose and effects of God's appearing. He comes to avenge and judge, therefore **before him went the pestilence.** Before him stalks plague, to punish his enemies and the disobedient, as in Egypt, in Canaan (Exod. xxiii. 27; 1 Sam. v. 9, 11); and among his own people (Numb. xi. 33; xiv. 37, etc.; Lev. xxvi. 25). For "pestilence" the LXX. reads "word." **Burning coals went forth at his feet.** "Fiery bolts" followed his advance, "hailstones and coals of fire" (Ps. xviii. 12, 13); as in Ps. xcvii. 3, "A fire goeth before him, and burneth up his enemies on every side." But, regarding the parallelisms of the hemistiches, it is better to take *resheph* in the sense of "fever heat," as in Deut. xxxii. 24; scorching fever follows in his train. Jerome translates the word, *diabolus,* looking on the evil spirit as the agent of the Divine vengeance. The Jews, he says, had a tradition that Satan was called *Reseph,* from the speed of his movements. The LXX. has, "It (the word) shall go forth into the plains," which Jerome interprets, "shall make the crooked straight and the rough ways smooth."

Ver. 6.—**He stood, and measured the earth.** God takes his stand, and surveys the earth which he is visiting in judgment. As his glory filled the heavens, so now he with his presence paces the earth, measuring it, as it were, with his foot. He con-

siders, too, **all the doings** of the children of men, and requites them accordingly. Vulgate, *Stetit, et mensus est terram.* So the Syriac. On the other hand, the LXX. gives, Ἔστη καὶ ἐσαλεύθη ἡ γῆ, "The earth stood and quaked." Thus the Chaldee, and many modern commentators, "rocketh the earth." This rendering seems to anticipate what follows, and is not so suitable as the other, though it is quite admissible. **Drove asunder.** Dispersed and scattered. Septuagint, διετάκη ἔθνη, "nations melted away." Others translate, "made to tremble" (Exod. xv. 15, etc.). **The everlasting mountains.** Mountains that have lasted as long as creation, and are emblems of stability and permanence (Deut. xxxiii. 15). **Were scattered;** or, *were shattered* (comp. Micah i. 4; Nah. i. 5). **His ways are everlasting.** This is best taken alone, not as connected grammatically with the preceding clause, and epexegetical of the "hills and mountains," which are called God's "ways," *i.e.* his chief creative acts, as Job xl. 19; Prov. viii. 22; but it means that, as God acted of old, so he acts now; "The ancient ways of acting are his" (Prov. xxxi. 27). "He reneweth his progresses of old time" (Delitzsch). The eternal, unchangeable purpose and operation of God are contrasted with the disruption of "the everlasting hills." The Greek and Latin Versions connect the words with what precedes. Septuagint, Ἐτάκησαν βουνοὶ αἰώνιοι πορείας αἰωνίας, "The everlasting hills melted at his everlasting goings;" Vulgate, *Incurvati sunt colles mundi ab itineribus æternitatis ejus,* where the idea seems to be that the high places of the earth are God's paths when he visits the world.

Ver. 7.—As God moves in his majesty the various nations are struck with fear, as of old were the peoples that heard of the Exodus (see Exod. xv. 14—16). **I saw.** In prophetic vision (1 Kings xxii. 17). **The tents of Cushan;** LXX., σκηνώματα Αἰθιόπων, "the tents of the Ethiopians;" Vulgate, *tentoria Æthiopiæ.* "Cushan" is not Chushan-Rishathaim, the Mesopotamian king mentioned in Judg. iii., but is a lengthened form of Cush (as *Lotan* for *Lot,* Gen. xxxvi. 20), the biblical name for Ethiopia. Here the African country is meant, lying along the west coast of the Red Sea. **In affliction.** Panic-stricken. The prophet particularizes what he had said above generally of the nations hostile to the people of God. **The curtains; the tent curtains;** Vulgate, *pelles.* Both "tents" and "curtains" are used by metonymy for their inhabitants. **Midian.** The country on the Gulf of Akaba, the eastern arm of the Red Sea. Ethiopia and Midian are named, as God is supposed to advance from the south.

Ver. 8.—Interrupting his description of the theophany, the prophet asks the motive of this wrathful revelation. This is done, not with expectation of an answer, but giving life and vigour to the composition. Such sudden transitions are not uncommon (comp. Judg. v. 12; Ps. lxxviii. 19, etc.). Was the Lord displeased against the rivers? *Was it against the rivers, O Jehovah? was thy wrath kindled against the rivers?* Was God angry with inanimate nature, when he showed his power, for instance, in the Nile and the Jordan and the Red Sea? God meant more by these acts. He showed his supremacy over all creation, and his will to save his people and to crush all opposition to the execution of his great design (see Ps. cvi. 9; cxiv. 3, etc.). That thou didst ride upon thine horses. The prophet speaks of the Lord as a Leader of a mighty host which came with chariots and horses to defend the Israelites and to crush their foes (comp. Ps. xviii. 10). And thy chariots of salvation. "And," which is not in the Hebrew, is better omitted, the clause being an explanation of "thine horses." The chariots come for the salvation, *i.e.* the deliverance, of Israel (ver. 13). Some translate, "Thy chariots are salvation;" as the Septuagint, καὶ ἡ ἱππασία σου σωτηρία: and Vulgate, *et quadrigæ tuæ salvatio.* It comes to the same thing, whichever rendering we adopt.

Ver. 9.—The prophet continues his description of the Lord as "a man of war" (Exod. xv. 3). Thy bow was made quite naked. The sheath of the bow was laid aside to make it ready for use. In the Assyrian monuments the bow-case forms part of the quiver, and holds only the lower half of the bow (Rawlinson, 'Anc. Mon.,' ii. 55, edit. 1864). It was fastened to the side of the chariot or carried at the back of the archer. (For the general sense, comp. Deut. xxxii. 40, etc.; Ps. xlv. 5.) In the Revelation (vi. 2) he that sits on the white horse has a bow. According to the oaths of the tribes, even thy word; *i.e.* thou doest all this to confirm the promises of deliverance and salvation made to the tribes of Israel. This sense is satisfactory; but the Hebrew text is corrupt, and cannot be explained with any certainty. The Revised Version gives, "The oaths to the tribes were a sure word;" in the margin, "Sworn were the chastisements (Hebrew, 'rods') of thy word." Thus Dr. Briggs: "Sworn are the rods of thy word." Orelli translates, "Oaths, rods of the word," and explains the clause to mean that the Lord comes to execute the denounced punishment, which proceeds from his mouth like chastising rods. The word *mattoth* is translated "tribes" (as in 2 Chron. v. 2) or "rods." Keil contends

for the latter, as instruments of chastisement, rendering, "Rods are sworn by word." Henderson, taking the words as a military signal, curiously translates, "'Sevens of spears' was the word." Pusey supports the Authorized Version, which, indeed, gives a good sense, and is probably correct. It is virtually supported by Jerome, who has, "Suscitans suscitabis arcum tuum, juramenta tribubus quæ locutus es," "Thou wilt awaken the oaths," which, so long as the evil prospered, seemed to be forgotten and sleeping. The LXX. omits the word rendered "oaths," and translates *mattoth*, σκῆπτρα, thus: Ἐντείνων ἐνέτεινας τόξον σου ἐπὶ σκῆπτρα, λέγει Κύριος, "Thou didst surely bend thy bow against sceptres." Selah. A pause ensues before the introduction of a new series of natural phenomena, accompanying the Lord's epiphany (see on ver. 3). The next clause would be more fitly joined with ver. 10. Thou didst cleave the earth with (or, *into*) rivers. This refers to some catastrophe like that which happened at the Flood, when "the fountains of the great deep were broken up" (Gen. vii. 11; comp. Ps. lxxvii. 16). Others think that the allusion is to the miracles at the Red Sea, or Sinai, or Rephidim in the wilderness, as in Ps. lxxiv.; lxxviii.; cv. But though the prophet glances at such particular circumstances, his scope is more general.

Ver. 10.—The mountains saw thee, and they trembled; literally, *were in pain*, Septuagint, ὠδινήσουσι. The words point to the phenomena of an earthquake, as Sinai shook at the presence of the Lord (Exod. xix. 18; Ps. cxiv. 6). So Virgil, 'Æn.,' vi. 256—

"Sub pedibus mugire solum, et juga cœpta moveri
Silvarum . . .
Adventante dea."

For "mountains," the LXX. reads, "peoples." The overflowing of the water passed by; *the torrent of water passed along.* Cataracts of rain fell, as in the Deluge. "The windows on high are open, and the foundations of the earth do shake" (Isa. xxiv. 18). Those who confine the reference to past events see here an intimation of the passage of the Jordan (Josh. iii. 15, 16). The deep uttered his voice. The mass of waters in the ocean and under the earth roars mightily as it bursts forth (Gen. xlix. 25; Deut. xxxiii. 13). His hands. Its waves (Ps. xcviii. 8). Septuagint, ὕψος φαντασίας αὐτῆς, "the height of its form."

Ver. 11.—The sun and moon stood still in their habitation; or, *stand still*, or *withdraw into their habitation.* They hide themselves in the tabernacles whence they are said to emerge when they shine (Ps. xix. 4, etc.). Overpowered with the splendour of God's presence, the heavenly luminaries hide their light in this day of the Lord (comp. Isa. xiii. 10; Joel ii. 2, 10, 31; iii. 15; Amos v. 20; Matt. xxiv. 29). The miracle of Joshua (Josh. x. 12, etc.) may have suggested some of the language here, but the idea is quite different. **At the light of thine arrows they went;** *i.e.* the sun and moon fled away discomfited at the glory of God's weapons, his arrows gleaming with light. The idea may be that, in the absence of the sun and moon, the terrific scene was illuminated only by flashes of lightning. "Lightnings" are sometimes called God's "arrows," as in Ps. xviii. 14; lxxvii. 17, etc.; but the image here is rather of the arms of a warrior. Many supply the relative in the sentence, and render, "arrows which shoot along." This seems to be unnecessary, and is not supported by the versions. There is no special reference to the hailstorm at Bethhoron, which discomfited the Canaanites, but enabled the Israelites to pass on to victory (Joshua, *loc. cit.*). It is the terror of the judgment that is adumbrated, when the Lord shall come in flames of fire (2 Thess. i. 8), and the heavens shall be dissolved, and the elements shall melt with fervent heat (2 Pet. iii. 12).

Ver. 12.—**Thou didst march through the land in indignation;** *thou treadest the earth in fury.* The mighty Judge stalks over the earth (ver. 6; comp. Judg. v. 4; Ps. lxviii. 7). It is a general statement, and not to be confined to the successes of Joshua and the destruction of the Canaanites. Septuagint, Ἐν ἀπειλῇ ὀλιγώσεις γῆν, with the alteration of a letter, "Thou wilt bring low the land with threats." **Thou didst thresh the heathen** (*nations*) in anger; Septuagint, ἐν θυμῷ κατάξεις ("thou wilt break in pieces") ἔθνη. Jerome here renders the verb, *obstupefacies;* but elsewhere, as Isa. xxviii. 28; Hos. x. 11; Amos i. 3, he uses *triturare,* which gives the best meaning. The kindred figure is found in Micah iv. 13; Isa. lxiii. 1, etc.

Ver. 13.—**Thou wentest forth.** The prophet specifies the end which these manifestations were designed to effect. God is said to "go forth" when he intervenes for the aid of his people, as Judg. v. 4; 2 Sam. v. 24; Isa. xlii. 13. **For salvation with thine anointed;** *In salutem cum Christo tuo* (Vulgate); τοῦ σῶσαι τὸν χριστόν σου (τοὺς χριστούς σου, Alex., Sin.), "to save thine anointed" (Septuagint). If the signification of the word "with" (*eth*) be pressed, the passage is taken to mean that, as God manifested himself in old time for the salvation of his people with his chosen " Christ," Moses; so he will hereafter reveal

his power for the destruction of the Chaldeans with his chosen "Christ," Cyrus. But this is too definite, and cannot be shown to be intended. The "anointed one," again, is not the nation of Israel, for the term is always applied to a single individual and never to the people collectively; so here it is the theocratic king who is meant—first, the representative of David; and secondly, the Messiah. God reveals himself for the salvation of his people in union with the work especially of his anointed Son, Christ. This is how the passage is taken by Eusebius ('Dem. Evang.,' iv. 16), Εἰς σωτηρίαν λαοῦ σου σὺν Χριστῷ σου. It must be confessed, however, that most modern commentators translate, "for the salvation of thy anointed," taking the last expression (contrary to all usage) to mean the Israelites, as being a kingdom and nation of priests (Exod. xix. 6). In this case the present clause is merely a repetition of the preceding one. **Thou woundedst the head out of the house of the wicked;** *thou dashest in pieces the head.* As in the following clause the metaphor of a house is plainly employed, "the head" must be taken for the gable or topmost ridge. "The house of the wicked" is an allegorical description of the Chaldaic dominion and its king; and the prophet declares that God will smite with destruction both the ungodly monarch and the kingdom that opposes itself. Some commentators see here an allusion to the primeval sentence (Gen. iii. 15); others to the destruction of the Egyptians' firstborn; others to the incident of Jael and Sisera (Judg. v. 26). If the prophet's language was influenced by any of these matters, his view and his oracle are concerned with the mighty future. The LXX. has, "Thou wilt cast death upon the heads of the evil." **By discovering** (literally, *making naked*) **the foundations unto the neck.** "By" is better omitted. Keil supposes that "the neck" is the central part of the house, looking from the gable downwards; though why this should be so called is not apparent; and the wording of the original, "the foundations even to the neck," compels us to connect the two words together, and will not allow us to interpret "the neck" of some higher part of the building. The general meaning is plain—the metaphorical house is destroyed from summit to base, the destruction beginning at the gable is carried on to the very foundations. According to this view, "the neck" should mean the very lowest basis of the walls. Henderson (after Capellus and others) suggests that we should read "rock," a word derived from the same root. Septuagint, Ἐξήγειρας δεσμοὺς ἕως τραχήλου, "Thou didst raise chains unto the neck." It is possible that the mention of "the head," just above, has led the prophet to use the term "neck" in order to express the utter destruction of the whole body. Selah. Another solemn pause ensues.

Ver. 14.—**Thou didst strike through with his staves;** *thou didst pierce with his own spears.* Thou dost turn on the Chaldeans and all thine enemies the destruction which they intended for others. The people meet with the same fate as the royal house (ver. 13); Vulgate, *maledixisti sceptris ejus,* which seems to be a mistranslation. **The head of his villages** (פְּרָזָו). There is a difficulty in arriving at the meaning of this last word. The LXX. renders it, "mighty men;" Jerome, "warriors;" Chaldee, "army;" Delitzsch and many modern critics, "hordes" or "inhabitants of the plain;" others again, "rulers" or "judges." The most probable version is either "warriors" or "hordes." The head, *i.e.* collectively the heads of his warlike troops. **They came out** (or, *who rush)* **as a whirlwind to scatter me** (see the description of the Chaldees, ch. i. 6, etc.). The prophet identifies himself with his people. (For the figure of the whirlwind, comp. Isa. xli. 16; Jer. xiii. 24; Hos. xiii. 3.) Dr. Briggs renders, "Thou dost pierce with his rods the chief, when his rulers are rushing in to scatter me." **Their rejoicing was as to devour the poor secretly;** or, *as in ambush, to devour the helpless.* They exult in acting the part of robbers and murderers, who lurk for the defenceless and afflict the poor (Ps. x. 8, etc.). *As* is equivalent to "as it were." Vulgate, *Sicut ejus qui.* "The poor" are primarily the Israelites, and then all meek worshippers of God.

Ver. 15.—The Exodus is the type of the deliverance of God's people. **Thou didst walk through** (*didst tread*) **the sea with thine horses;** literally, *thou treadest the sea, thy horses,* the horses being explanatory. The prophet takes his imagery from Exod. xv. 1—19. He represents God as a warrior in his chariot, leading the way through the waters to the destruction of his enemies and to the salvation of his own people. **Through the heap of great waters;** or, *upon the surge of mighty waters.* The verse may also be rendered, *Thou treadest the sea—thy horses (tread) the heap of great waters* (Ps. lxxvii. 19). Past mercies and deliverances are types and pledges of future.

Vers. 16, 17.—§ 4. *The contemplation of the Divine judgments produces in the people of God at first, fear and trembling at the prospect of chastisement.*

Ver. 16.—**When I heard.** "When" is better omitted. "I heard" the report of thee (ver. 2). The LXX. refers to ch. ii. 1,

rendering, "I watched." If the former part is the pæan of the congregation, the present is the prophet's own utterance expressive of his dismay at the prospect before him. **My belly trembled.** My inmost part, my inward self, trembled with fear (comp. Isa. xvi. 11). **My lips quivered at the voice.** My lips quivered with fear at the voice of God that sounded in me (ch. ii. 1), proclaiming these awful judgments. The word rendered "quivered" (*tsalal*) is applied to the tingling of the ears (1 Sam. iii. 11; 2 Kings xxi. 12), and implies that the prophet's lips so trembled that he was scarcely able to utter speech. The LXX. renders, "from the voice of the prayers of my lips." **Rottenness entered into my bones.** This is an hyperbolical expression, denoting that the firmest, strongest parts of his body were relaxed and weakened with utter fear, as if his very bones were cankered and corrupted, and there was no marrow in them. **And I trembled in myself.** The last word (*tachtai*) is rendered variously: "under me," according to the Greek and Latin Versions, *i.e.* in my knees and feet, so that I reeled and stumbled; or, "in my place," on the spot where I stand (as Exod. xvi. 29). **That I might rest in the day of trouble;** better, *I who shall rest in the day of tribulation.* The prophet suddenly expresses his confidence that he shall have rest in this affliction; amid this terror and awe he is sure that there remaineth a rest for the people of God. This sentiment leads naturally to the beautiful expression of hope in the concluding paragraph (ver. 17, etc.). Keil and others render, "tremble that I am to wait quietly for the day of tribulation;" that I am to sit still and await the day of affliction. But Pusey denies that the verb (*nuach*) ever means "to wait patiently for," or "to be silent about;" its uniform signification is "to rest" from labour or from trouble. Thus the Septuagint, Ἀναπαύσομαι ἐν ἡμέρᾳ θλίψεως, "I will rest in the day of affliction;" Vulgate, *Ut requiescam in die tribulationis.* **When he cometh up unto the people, he will invade them with his troops.** This should be, *When he that invades with bands comes up against the people;* i.e. in the day when the Chaldeans attack the Israelites (comp. 2 Kings xxiv. 2, where the word "bands" is also used). Septuagint, Τοῦ ἀναβῆναι, εἰς λαὸν παροικίας μου: "To go up against the people of my sojourning;" Vulgate, *Ut ascendam ad populum accinctum nostrum,* which is thus explained: "I will bear all things patiently, even death itself, that I may attain to the happy company of those blessed heroes who fought for their country and their God." It is obvious to remark that this is a gloss, not on the original text, but on the erroneous version.

Ver. 17.—The prophet depicts the effects of the hostile invasion, which are such as to make the natural heart despair. *Although the fig tree shall not blossom.* The devastations of the enemy leave the country bare and uncultivated. The Chaldeans, like the Assyrians and Egyptians, cut down and burnt the fruit-bearing trees of the countries which they invaded (comp. Deut. xx. 19; Isa. ix. 10; xxxvii. 24; Jer. vi. 6). The trees most useful and abundant in Palestine are mentioned (comp. Deut. vi. 11; Hos. ii. 12; Joel i. 7; Micah iv. 4; vi. 15, etc.). *The labour of the olive shall fail;* literally, *shall lie.* The "labour" is the produce, the fruit. Though the yield shall disappoint all expectation. The use of the verb "to lie" in this sense is found elsewhere; *e.g.* Isa. lviii. 11; Hos. ix. 2. So Horace, 'Carm.,' iii. 1. 30, "Fundus mendax;" and 'Epist.,' i. 7. 87, "Spem mentita seges." *The fields;* the corn-fields (Isa. xvi. 8). *The flock shall be cut off from the fold.* There shall be no flocks in the fold, all having perished for lack of food. "Omnia hæc," says St. Jerome, "auferentur a populo, quia inique egit in Deum creatorem suum."

Vers. 18, 19.—§ 5. *In spite of the terror produced by these judgments, the true Israelite is blessed with hope of salvation and joy in the Lord.*

Ver. 18.—*Yet I will rejoice in the Lord.* Unshaken in confidence, the prophet, representing the faithful Israelite, expresses his unbounded joy at the prospect of salvation which opens to him beyond the present affliction. The psalmist often thus shows his exulting faith (see Ps. v. 7; xiii. 6; xvii. 14, 15; xxxi. 19). *I will joy.* I will shout for joy; my joy shall express itself outwardly. *The God of my salvation* (see note on Micah vii. 7). The God who judges the nations to procure the final salvation of his people. Septuagint, Τῷ Θεῷ τῷ σωτῆρί μου, "God my Saviour;" Vulgate, *In Deo*

Jesu meo. From this gloss of St. Jerome some of the Fathers have argued for the existence in this passage of a revelation of the incarnation of Christ and the redemption wrought by him.

Ver. 19.—*The Lord God is my strength;* more accurately, *Jehovah, the Lord, is my strength,* from Ps. xviii. 32; comp. Ps. xxvii. 1. He will make my feet like hinds' feet (Ps. xviii. 33). He makes me active and swift-footed as the gazelle, as a lusty warrior (2 Sam. i. 23; ii. 18) should be. So by the help of God I shall be superior to my enemies. *He will make me to walk upon mine high places.* The expression is used properly of God (Micah i. 3), and elsewhere, says Keil, to denote the victorious possession and government of a country (see Deut. xxxii. 13; xxxiii. 29). Here it signifies that believing Israel shall overcome all opposition and dwell in safety in its own land. *To the chief singer* (*musician*) *on my stringed instruments* (*neginoth*). This is a musical direction, answering to the heading in ver. 1, and implies that the ode is committed to the conductor of the temple music, to be by him adapted for the public service to the accompaniment of stringed instruments. Such directions are elsewhere always found at the beginning, not the end, of psalms (see Ps. iv.; vi.; liv.; lv.; lxvii.; lxxvi.). It has been thought that the suffix of the first person, "my stringed instruments," denotes that Habakkuk had a right to take part in the temple service, and was therefore a Levite; but it is very doubtful whether this suffix is not a clerical error, as Kuenen and Ewald suppose, or merely paragogic. Certainly neither the Greek, Latin, nor Syriac Versions afford it any confirmation. These versions make the subscription part of the ode. Thus LXX., Ἐπὶ τὰ ὑψηλὰ ἐπιβιβᾷ με, τοῦ νικῆσαι ἐν τῇ ᾠδῇ αὐτοῦ, "He maketh me to mount upon the high places, that I may conquer by his song;" Vulgate, *Super excelsa mea deducet me victor* (*victori,* Cod. Amiat.) *in psalmis canentem.*

HOMILETICS.

Ver. 2.—*The prayer of an alarmed prophet.* I. THE PROPHET'S ALARM. 1. *Its cause.* The report of Jehovah; *i.e.* the communication received from Jehovah concerning the punishment of Judah and the destruction of Chaldea. Habakkuk not the first man that had been afraid at the hearing of God's voice (Gen. iii. 10; Exod. iii. 6), at the thought of his presence (Job xxiii. 15), at the manifestation of his power (Ps. lxv. 8), at the contemplation of his judgments (Ps. cxix. 120). Nor will they who hear the fame of his doings in the past or the announcement of his "judgments to come," as both of these are unfolded in Scripture, fail to be similarly affected. Like the Canaanites before the advance of Joshua and his host, their hearts will melt in them for fear (Josh. ii. 11). What excited terror in the breast of Habakkuk was the prospect Jehovah's "report" opened up before him! Though a pious man and a prophet, he was at the same time a philanthropist and a patriot, who could not contemplate without a shudder the decimation of his people or the desolation of his country; and neither can the Christian anticipate without apprehension those chastisements that are promised to himself for correction of his backslidings, and to the Church for her recovery from doctrinal aberration or spiritual declension. It may be better to fall into God's hands, because his mercies are great, than to fall into those of man (2 Sam. xxiv. 14); but in any case it is a fearful thing to fall for judgment into the hands of the living God (Heb. x. 31). Again, the fierce whirlwind of retribution, which in the end should throw down the eagle's nest of Chaldean pride and blow up the crackling flames in which its palaces and temples were to be destroyed, raised within him awe-inspiring conceptions of the omnipotence of Jehovah which made him tremble, even though the downfall of Chaldea meant the deliverance of Judah; and so, although the final destruction of the ungodly will be to the saints a cause of rejoicing (Rev. xviii. 20), it will also inspire them with a solemn awe of the Divine holiness and justice, majesty and power. 2. *Its cure.* Prayer. Different from Adam, who, having heard God's voice, ran from God, Habakkuk, in his alarm, betook himself to God. Hiding from God, the custom of sinners; hiding in God, the comfort of saints (Ps. cxliii. 9). Suitable for all times (Eph. vi. 18; Phil. iv. 6; 1 Thess. v. 17), prayer is specially appropriate for bad times (Ps. l. 15). In addition to the promise that God will be a Refuge for the oppressed, a Refuge in times of trouble (Ps. ix. 9), and to the fact that good men in all ages have found him so (Ps. xlviii. 3; xci. 2; Jer. xvi. 19), the practice of pouring one's fears (Ps. xxxiv. 4) as well as complaints (Ps. cxlii. 2) and requests (Phil. iv. 6) into the ear of God seems justified by this, that he who by his judgment causes, is by his wisdom and mercy best able to remove alarms.

II. THE PROPHET'S PRAYER. 1. *Its fervour.* Intimated by the repetition of the term "Jehovah," and by the three short sentences of which the prayer is composed. Souls labouring under strong emotion commonly express themselves in brief and broken ejaculations, rather than in long and polished periods. 2. *Its tenor.* A threefold petition. (1) For the acceleration of Jehovah's work. "O Lord, revive thy work in the midst of the years." The work referred to was the purification of Judah by means of the Chaldean exile, and the salvation of Judah by the ultimate overthrow of her oppressor. It was thus a picture of God's work in all ages—the deliverance of the individual believer and of the Church in general, first through the afflictions and trials of life from the moral defilement of sin; and second, through the overthrow (by Christ's cross and rule) of the enemies of both from the legal and spiritual bondage of sin. The prophet craved that Jehovah might not defer the completion of Judah's redemption till the end of the time which had been appointed for this purpose, but that he might cause his work to live (not suffer it to go to sleep, but quicken and revive it), so that it might be finished in the midst of the years, and Judah's reformation and emancipation brought about long before the stipulated period had arrived. Thus his prayer was one the believer might offer for himself, that God would perfect that which concerned him (Ps. cxxxviii. 8), would carry on his work of grace within him (Phil. i. 6), making all things work together for his good (Rom. viii. 28), causing tribulation to work in him patience, etc. (Rom. v. 3), and afflictions to yield him the peaceable fruits of righteousness (Heb. xii. 11), as well as to work out for him a far more exceeding, even an eternal weight of glory (2 Cor. iv. 18); and would crown that work by completely effecting his deliverance from the curse and power of sin, from the terror of death, the darkness of the grave, the misery of hell. It was also a petition which the Church might present for herself, that she might be purified, extended, completed, glorified, not after long waiting, but soon, in the middle of the years. "Even so, come [quickly], Lord Jesus" (Rev. xxii. 20). (2) For the manifestation of Jehovah's glory. "In the midst of the years make it known." Make it known, the prophet meant, that the work of punishing and purifying Judah by means of exile in Babylon is thy work; so shall it comfort Judah and awe Babylon. Make it known that the deliverance of Judah by means of the overthrow of Babylon is thy work; so again shall Judah rejoice and the nations of the earth be afraid. The believer and the Church may also ask that God's work in dealing with them should be manifest, not to themselves merely, but to the world at large. This would both sustain them and impress the world.

Until affliction is seen to be God's work, it does little good to the soul; till the world perceives that God is in the Church, it will not cease to persecute and hinder the Church. (3) For the dispensation of Jehovah's mercy. Habakkuk's plea was not merit. He knew well that what he asked could not be granted on the score of justice.

> " 'Tis from the mercy of our God
> That all our hopes begin."

Lessons. 1. That God's voice should excite alarm even in the hearts of good men is no mean proof of the fallen state of mankind generally. 2. It is a good sign of grace when an alarmed soul betakes itself to God. 3. The pre-eminence which belongs to redemption over all the other works of God. 4. The only power that can awaken dead souls or revive unspiritual and decadent Churches is God. 5. The chief hope of man lies in the mercy of Heaven, not in the goodness of himself.

Vers. 3—5.—*An ideal theophany*: 1. *The onward march of the Deity.* I. His Person designated. 1. *God, or Eloah, the Strong or Powerful One.* A name for the Supreme used for the first time by Moses (Deut. xxxii. 15) to portray God as the Creator of Israel, and employed by Habakkuk "to designate God as the Lord and Governor of the whole world" (Keil). Omnipotence an essential attribute of Divinity (Gen. xvii. 1; Josh. iv. 24; 1 Chron. xxix. 12; Job xxxvi. 5; xlii. 2; Ps. lxii. 11); the impotence of heathen idols was the best proof that they were no gods (Isa. xlv. 20; Jer. ii. 28). 2. *The Holy One.* An appellation given to God at least three times in the Psalter (Ps. lxxi. 2; lxxviii. 41; lxxxix. 18), twice in Jeremiah (l. 29; li. 5), once in Ezekiel (xxxix. 7), once in Hosea (xi. 9), twice in Habakkuk (i. 12; iii. 3), and occurring frequently in Isaiah. Equally with strength is purity an indispensable quality in the Supreme; and this no less than that in an infinite measure and degree. An unholy God could not be all-powerful, all-wise, all-just, or all-good. Holiness the guarantee and guardian of the other attributes of his nature. Least of all could an unholy God be either a Saviour or a Judge of men.

II. His glory depicted. 1. *Its extent.* All-pervading, irradiating the entire universe, covering the heavens and spreading over the earth (Ezek. xliii. 2). What is here declared of the material or symbolic presence of Deity is true of his real, though unseen, presence (Ps. viii. 1; xix. 1; Isa. vi. 3). 2. *Its brightness.* Resembling the light, *i.e.* the sun, to which Scripture likens God himself (Ps. lxxxiv. 11), and Christ (Mal. iv. 2; John ix. 5), who is God's Image (2 Cor. iv. 4), the Brightness of his Father's glory, and the express Image of his Person (Heb. i. 3). In exact accordance with the prophet's thought, God is represented as covering himself with light as with a garment (Ps. civ. 2), and as dwelling in the light which no man can approach unto (1 Tim. vi. 16); while Christ is ever set forth as the highest expression of the uncreated glory of the Supreme (John i. 14). 3. *Its manifestation.* Emitting rays or shooting forth beams ·on all sides, like the rising sun (Keil, Delitzsch), an emblem suggestive of the partial and gradual, though universal, manner in which the Divine glory unveils itself to intelligent spectators on earth (Job xxvi. 14). 4. *Its power.* Emanating from his hand, like rays darting forth from the sun's disc, or like horns shooting out from the head of a gazelle (Pusey, Fausset). The allusion may have been to the lightnings which flashed forth from the cloud upon Mount Sinai (Exod. xix. 16); but the underlying thought is that one principal aspect of God's glory is the exhibition of power which he furnishes to men in the material creation (Isa. xl. 26, 28), in the phenomena of nature (Job xxxvi. 22, etc.), and in the scheme of grace (1 Cor. i. 24). 5. *Its essence.* Hidden, unsearchable, unfathomable, the above-mentioned coruscations of his glory being not so much unveilments as concealments of his ineffable Personality, not so much exhibitions as hidings of his power. That which may be known of God from the outshinings of his glory is the fact, not the fulness, of his power and Godhead. The grand truth symbolized by the cloudy pillar infolding brightness, viz. that Israel's God was a God that, while discovering, yet hid himself (Isa. xlv. 15), was in the Incarnation exemplified and emphasized (cf. John i. 14 with vii. 27), and is receiving confirmation by every advance the human mind makes in knowledge (Job xi. 7—9; xxvi. 9; xxxvii. 23; Ps. cxlv. 3; cxlvii. 5; Isa. xl. 28; Rom. xi. 33). Agnosticism a witness to the truth here stated.

III. His ADVANCE DESCRIBED.   1. *The quarter whence he comes.*   Teman and Paran, *i.e.* the country south of Judah or Idumea, and Paran the desert region lying between Judah and Sinai (see Exposition).   Separated only by the Wady-el-Arabah, the two localities were intended to indicate the Sinaitic region as the spot whence this sublime theophany of the future should proceed.   In so defining its starting-point, the prophet probably wished to suggest a variety of thoughts, as *e.g.* that the future glorious manifestation of Jehovah was rendered possible, and even probable, by what had in the past occurred at Sinai; that it would proceed in the line of that earlier theophany, and be a carrying out of the Divine policy therein revealed—a policy of mercy and judgment, of salvation and destruction; and that in it, as in the ancient Apocalypse, both the power and the holiness of God would be signally displayed.   True of the Divine advent in the overthrow of Babylon, these thoughts were also realized in the advent of the fulness of the times, and will be conspicuous in the final advent at the close of human history.   2. *The purpose for which he comes.*   To execute judgment upon the ungodly world, and so to effect the deliverance of his people.   This was to be the object of his interposition in the overthrow of Babylon, as it had been in the destruction of Egypt; this was the end aimed at in the first coming of the Saviour, the redemption of his Church by the annihilation of her foes; this will be the purpose of his appearing at the end of the world, to complete the redemption of his people by completing the punishment of the ungodly.   3. *The attendants by whom he is served.*   Pestilence in front, and fiery bolts in the rear, signifying that God will be accompanied with sufficient instruments to effect his purpose.   "Death and destruction of all sorts are a great army at his command" (Pusey).

Learn: 1. The certainty of a future manifestation of Jehovah in the Person of the glorified Christ.   2. The double object for which that glorious manifestation of Christ will take place.

Vers. 6, 7.—*An ideal theophany: 2. The wonderful acts of the Deity.*   I. MEASURING THE EARTH, AND DRIVING ASUNDER THE NATIONS.   1. *Measuring the earth;* i.e. either surveying it with his all-seeing glance whereat there is universal consternation (Fausset), or measuring it out among the peoples on its surface, as Joshua partitioned the Holy Land after its conquest among the tribes (Pusey).   Both ideas are historically true, no Divine interposition of any magnitude occurring among earth's inhabitants without bringing with it to thoughtful minds a conviction that the hand and eye of God are at work, and leaving after it, as a result, a rearrangement of the map of the globe.   The marginal reading, "shaking the earth," causing it to reel (Delitzsch, Keil), as David says it trembled on the occasion of Jehovah's coming down on Mount Sinai (Ps. lxviii. 8), presents also a valuable truth that the Divine providential government of the world, especially when it takes to deal with long-established iniquity for the purpose of punishing and destroying the same, is calculated to inspire awe among earth's inhabitants (Ps. xcix. 1), as it did when it broke the pride of Egypt (Exod. xv. 14), as it was to do when it overthrew the Chaldean power, and as it will do when it hurls the mystical Babylon to the abyss (Rev. xviii. 19).   This the thought contained in the parallel clause.   2. *Driving asunder the nations.*   "He beheld and drove asunder [or, 'made to tremble'] the nations."   He so paralyzed them with fear that he drove them asunder, rendering combination amongst them impossible.

II. SCATTERING THE MOUNTAINS AND BOWING THE HILLS.   Not the lesser heights of comparatively recent formation, but the primeval altitudes, whose hoary peaks have witnessed the passing by of millenniums, and whose roots go down amid the granite bars of the earth (Ps. xc. 2).   These by his encampment on their summits he causes to crumble, resolve themselves into dust, and vanish into nought (Nah. i. 5; Micah i. 4).   The image may point to "the convulsions on Mount Sinai and to the earthquake which announced the descent of the Most High" (Adam Clarke), but it signifies the utter impossibility of even the strongest forces of nature, whether in matter or in man, resisting the advance of God, and that because his ways are older than even the everlasting hills (Ps. xc. 2), are the only things on earth to which everlastingness belongs.   "The everlasting ways of the everlasting God are mercy and truth" (St. Bernard, quoted by Pusey).

III. TERRIFYING THE HEATHEN AND PUNISHING THE ADVERSARIES OF HIS PEOPLE.

In prophetic vision Habakkuk beheld the impression made upon the neighbouring nations through which Jehovah passed on his march from Teman to the Red Sea—the Cushites or African Ethiopians on the west "in affliction," and the Midianites towards the east, "trembling." A different interpretation makes Cushan the Mesopotamian king, Chushan-Rishathaim, who oppressed Israel eight years in the time of the Judges (Judg. iii. 8—10), and Midian the last enemy who seduced Israel into sin when on the borders of the promised land (Numb. xxv. 17), and came up against them after they had settled in it (Judg. vi. 4—11). In this case the prophet selects the judgments executed upon these—upon the first by Othniel, upon the second by Gideon—as typical of the inflictions that would fall upon Jehovah's enemies at his future coming.

Learn: 1. The sovereignty of God over men and kings. 2. The duty and wisdom of recognizing God's hand in the movements of nations and in the phenomena of nature. 3. The impossibility of defeating the ultimate realization of God's purposes, whether of judgment or of mercy.

Ver. 8.—*An ideal theophany: 3. The terrible wrath of the Deity.* I. ITS VISIBLE MANIFESTATIONS. The prophet conceives Jehovah as "a warlike hero equipped for conflict," depicts him as marching forth against his enemies, and throwing all nature (especially its rivers and seas, emblems of the earth's populations) into consternation, and inquires of him what had been the cause of his vehement displeasure. The form of the question suggests that Jehovah's anger had not been directed against inanimate nature, but that the commotions visible in the rivers and the seas were only symbols of his wrath against men. II. ITS SECRET DESTINATION. It was aimed at a threefold purpose. 1. *The destruction of his enemies.* Of these the rivers and seas were merely emblems (ver. 14). 2. *The salvation of his people.* Jehovah's horses and chariots were horses and chariots of salvation (ver. 13). "The end of God's armies, his visitations and judgments, is the salvation of his elect, even while they who are inwardly dead perish outwardly also" (Pusey). 3. *The vindication of his own honour.* His bow had been (and was to be) made quite bare, *i.e.* drawn from its scabbard in fulfilment of the oaths he had given to the tribes —first to Abraham, then to Isaac, next to Jacob, and afterwards to David—that he would deliver them from the hand of their enemies (Luke i. 73—75); or, accepting the marginal translation, because "sworn were the chastisements [literally, 'rods'] of his word," *i.e.* because the threatenings he had uttered against his people's enemies (Deut. xxxii. 40—42) were as sure as the promises of deliverance bestowed upon his people themselves.

Learn: 1. That the wrath of God is as much a reality as the love of God is. 2. That the destruction of God's enemies is as sure as is the salvation of his friends. 3. That in both God will be glorified.

Vers. 9—16.—*An ideal theophany: 4. The glorious interposition of the Deity.* I. NATURE'S HOMAGE TO THE JUDGE. (Vers. 10, 11.) Jehovah's presence on that great and terrible day will be attested by a succession of marvels. 1. *Wonders in the earth.* (1) The cleaving of the earth with rivers (ver. 9) may point to the bursting forth of waters from the deep places of the earth, which are again opened as at the Flood (Gen. vii. 11) through violent convulsions, or to the overflowing of the land by the agitated and swollen waters, as also happened on the occasion of that appalling catastrophe (Gen. vii. 11, 17, 19). (2) The trembling of the mountains, which writhe as if in pain, may contain an allusion to earthquakes and similar cataclysms. 2. *Wonders in the sea.* "The tempest of waters passed by, the deep uttered his voice, and lifted up his hands on high" (ver. 10). These words possibly allude to what occurred both in the Flood and in the dividing of the Red Sea and the Jordan. 3. *Wonders in the sky.* "The sun and moon stood still in their habitation: at the light of thine arrows they went, at the shining of thy glittering spear" (ver. 11), as they did in the time of Joshua, when Jehovah fought for Israel against Gibeon (Josh. x. 13). Compare the description in the Apocalypse of the great day of the wrath of the Lamb (Rev. vi. 12—16). II. THE WRATHFUL PROCEDURE OF THE JUDGE. 1. *Marching through the land in indignation.* The land referred to is in the foreground Chaldea, and in the background the whole earth, which, no less than Babylon, will have become an object of Divine displeasure. 2. *Threshing the nations in anger.* Not the Chaldean people only, but all the peoples who, like them, shall have become the oppressors of God's heritage, all the nations that have not known or served God, will experience the strokes of his anger. 3. *Wounding the head of the house of the wicked, laying bare the foundation even to the neck.* The wicked one is first the Chaldean king, the head of the Chaldean power, and lastly that wicked one whom Christ will destroy with the brightness of his coming (1 Thess. iv. 8). The image is that of complete destruction (see Exposition). 4. *Piercing with his own staves the head of his warriors* or hordes. These were the Chaldean troops, whom the prophet saw coming up against himself and Israel as a whirlwind to scatter them, as highway murderers lying in wait to devour the poor secretly, but whom he also beheld falling upon and destroying one another, wounding themselves with their own swords (cf. 1 Sam. xiv. 20; 2 Chron. xx. 23, 24). So will God's enemies in the end consume and devour one another. 5. *Overcoming every obstacle that might be supposed to hinder his purpose,* viz. the execution of wrath upon his foes, or the deliverance of his people.

III. THE MERCIFUL PURPOSE OF THE JUDGE. This was (and always will be) the salvation of his people and of his anointed, *i.e.* of his people Israel and Judah with their Davidic king, then of his believing Church with its anointed Head. If God executes judgment upon the ungodly, it is because otherwise the salvation of the godly cannot be secured.

LESSONS. 1. The certainty of a day of judgment. 2. The terrifying aspect to the wicked of the glory of God. 3. The infinite fierceness of the wrath of the Almighty. 4. The ability of God to execute his purposes both of judgment and salvation. 5. The graciousness towards believers of all God's interpositions.

Vers. 17—19.—*Sorrowing, yet rejoicing.* I. THE CASE SUPPOSED. A complete failure of all creature comforts. 1. *Extremely unusual.* Even the worst are seldom reduced to the bare boards of absolute privation (Ps. cxlv. 9; Matt. v. 45). David confesses in old age that he had "never seen the righteous forsaken, nor his seed begging bread" (Ps. xxxvii. 25). 2. *Not impossible or unknown.* Persons, and these by no means always the ungodly, but sometimes the good, the excellent of the earth, the pious, the people who fear God and keep his commandments, who believe in his Word and delight in his ways, have been known to be placed in circumstances of utter destitution, such as Habakkuk so touchingly describes. Whether Habakkuk himself was in it, he expected that he might be, as he foresaw that many of his countrymen would be when the terrible Chaldean invasion came. Job had experience of such a situation as Habakkuk portrayed (Job i. 13—22); Paul (2 Cor. xi. 27) and many others both before and since have known it. 3. *Always sad.* No blossom on the fig tree, no fruit upon the vine, no harvest from the olive trees or corn-fields, no flocks in either fold or stall. Everything gone. Every prop and stay taken—money scattered to the winds by unsuccessful trading, household furniture arrested and sold to pay debt, means of earning a livelihood gone, friends vanished just at the moment when most required, children laid down with sickness when money to pay for medical relief is wanting, health precarious through age or infirmity. When a case like this occurs it is sad. 4. *Yet it might be worse.* It would be if a Christian were to lose not the creature comforts merely, but the Creator himself, from whom these comforts flow. Let a man lose what he may, so long as he has God and Jesus Christ, the Bible and the throne of grace, with the gift of forgiveness and the hope of heaven, he is not utterly undone.

II. THE RESOLUTION TAKEN. To "rejoice in the Lord." 1. *Sensible.* If a man loses three-fourths of his fortune, it may be natural to grieve over what is lost, but it cannot fail to strike one as more sensible to make much of and rejoice in what remains. So a good man, when he sees his creature comforts taken from him, will show himself a wise man by letting these go without too great indulgence in sorrow and cleaving to the Creator, who is infinitely more precious than all besides. 2. *Satisfactory.* What remains to the good man after the departure of creature comforts is the best part of his estate. It is the part he can least want; he might do without his fig trees, etc., but not without his God; and the part that is most satisfying—fig trees, etc., might feed the body, but only God can support a soul; and the part that is most permanent—the only part that is permanent, all earthly things being subject to decay. 3. *Sanctifying.* No man can make and keep it without becoming holier and better because of it. He who rejoices in God will gradually grow like God. 4. *Profitable.* It will come back to him who adopts it in blessings upon his head. If any man will delight in God, God will delight in him, will rejoice over him to do him good.

III. THE CHERISHED EXPECTATION. That God would perfect his salvation. 1. *By imparting to him strength.* "Jehovah, the Lord, is my Strength." The man who used these words had made three great discoveries : (1) that man's strength at the best is little better than weakness—in the domain of the body, and in that of the mind, but chiefly in that of the spirit; (2) that the source of all strength, whether physical, intellectual, or spiritual, for the human being, is God (Zech. x. 12; 2 Cor. iii. 5; ix. 8; x. 4; Eph. iii. 20; Col. i. 11); and (3) that this Divine strength is indispensable for enabling the soul to cling to God in the day of trouble and season of calamity (Phil. i. 6; ii. 13; 1 Pet. i. 5). 2. *By inspiring him with alacrity or zeal.* "He maketh my feet like hinds' feet;" *i.e.* maketh them lithe and nimble, active and steady, skilful to climb, and tenacious to hold on like those of the female deer, which quickly scents danger, and bounds along with safety among the crags and cliffs of its native haunts. The language is descriptive of one who, in the season of adversity, in the hour of trial, temptation, and danger, is quick to discern, eager in adopting, and steadfast in pursuing the path of duty, which for him, as for all, is the path of safety. Moreover, the man who rejoices in God will commonly find himself advised in due season of the approach of danger, assisted in ascertaining the path of duty, and strengthened both to enter upon and adhere to it. 3. *By exalting him to safety.* "He maketh me to walk upon mine high places." The man who can rejoice in God will sooner or later find that God has begun to exalt him beyond common men : (1) has set him on a high place of safety beyond the reach of condemnation ; (2) is setting him upon a high path of moral and spiritual elevation; and (3) will set him in the end upon a high throne of glory.

Learn : 1. The vanity of creature comforts. 2. The sweetness of Divine comforts. 3. The secret of true happiness. 4. The certainty of final glory.

HOMILIES BY VARIOUS AUTHORS.

Ver. 1.—*Prayer and praise.* This chapter records the remarkable " prayer " or " ode " of Habakkuk. The superscription contained in the first verse and a cursory glance at the chapter as thus described may be found suggestive of important teachings respecting the sacred exercises of prayer and praise. Note—

I. THE TEACHINGS CONCERNING PRAYER. 1. We do well to solicit present blessings. " In the midst of the years make known " (ver. 2); *i.e.* he sought the Divine manifestation in mercy to be granted to his people *in his own day.* 2. We should recount God's goodness in the past. The prayer abounds in reminiscences of God's favour as bestowed upon his chosen in the days of yore. 3. The comprehensive nature of prayer. This prayer of Habakkuk contains (1) petition; (2) adoration; (3) devout contemplation of God in his character and works; (4) review of his providential doings; and, (5) pervading the whole, the spirit of confiding and joyous trust.

II. THE TEACHINGS CONCERNING PRAISE. 1. The desirability of employing in this exercise the devout compositions of God's servants in past ages, which have been preserved in his Word. 2. The appropriateness of the language of prayer as the medium of expressing praise to God. "The prayers of David the son of Jesse" are contained and expressed in his Psalms. "The prayer of Habakkuk" is also "an ode" set to music, and used at his suggestion in the liturgical services of the temple. 3. The importance of cultivating correct musical expression in the presentation of the sacrifice of praise to God. The tones should be in harmony with the character of the thoughts and sentiments of the words being sung. This is probably the meaning of the expression, "upon Shigionoth" (ver. 1), *'al shigyônôth* meaning "in wandering measures," the tones to be varied according to the character of the thoughts and words. The term "Selah," used by him (vers. 3, 9, 13), and the direction, "To the chief singer on my stringed instruments," with which he closes his book, also indicate the carefulness in execution the prophet would have exercised. All true worship to God must proceed from humble and trusting hearts, and be presented "in spirit and in truth," and this is perfectly compatible with regard for all that is cultured and artistic in method. Our motto should be, "The best for the Lord."—S. D. H.

Ver. 2.—*Prayer for revival.* The revival of God's work stands intimately connected with prayer. The Holy Spirit is the Author of all true quickening of the Divine life in the souls of men, and his renewing and sanctifying influences are secured in response to earnest supplication (Ezek. xxxvi. 37; Mal. iii. 10; Acts i. 14; ii. 1). "It is visionary to expect an unusual success in the human administration of religion unless there were unusual omens. Now, an emphatic spirit of prayer would be such an omen. And if the whole or greater number of the disciples of Christianity were, with an earnest unfailing resolution of each, to combine that Heaven should not withhold one single influence which the very utmost effort of conspiring and persevering supplication would obtain, it would be the sign of a revolution of the world being at hand" (John Foster). Observe—

I. PRAYER FOR REVIVAL INVOLVES AN INTELLIGENT APPREHENSION OF THE STATE OF THE AGE, AND THE CHURCH IN THE AGE, IN WHICH IT IS OFFERED. The language of the prophet in the former part of his prophecy indicates the possession by him of an insight into the character and needs both of the Hebrew nation and Church in his day; and this acquaintance prepared his mind and heart for pleading so earnestly for a revival of God's work. Our own age and the state of religion in it claims our thoughtful regard. Reflection upon it will show the imperative need there is for the possession of a higher measure of spirituality, consecration, Christian intelligence and courage, and will impel the utterance of the earnest cry, "O Lord, revive thy work" (ver. 2)

II. PRAYER FOR REVIVAL WILL BE PROMPTED BY ANXIOUS CONCERN IN VIEW OF THE EVIL CONSEQUENCES RESULTING FROM THE PREVAILING DEGENERACY. "O Lord," cried the prophet, "I have heard thy speech, and I was afraid." Jehovah had spoken unto him in vision, unfolding the terrible judgments which should overtake his people in consequence of their apostasy, and this vision of coming Divine chastisement filled him with terror; and with the real concern of a true patriot in view of the disastrous issue to which, through the prevailing iniquity, the national interests were tending, he implored Divine interposition and help ("O Lord, revive," etc.). The Christian patriot in our own land has reason for anxious solicitude as he views the present in its relation to the future. He knows that there is danger lest the *temporal prosperity* enjoyed in this age should result in the cherishing of pride, in conformity to the world, and in apathy in holy service; and lest the *intellectual activity* prevailing should lead to the weakening of conviction, the cherishing of doubt, and resulting in complete indifference in relation to spiritual realities. All this occasions him serious concern, which is intensified as he beholds multitudes in whom these dire effects have been already wrought; and in this spirit of solicitude he is led to the throne of grace, and to cry with impassioned earnestness, "O Lord, revive thy work."

III. PRAYER FOR REVIVAL IS EVER DIRECTED TO THE SECURING OF SPIRITUAL RESULTS. "In wrath remember mercy" (ver. 2). The seer knew by revelation that his nation, owing to its sinfulness, should be overtaken by judgment, and should fall into the power of the Chaldeans; and in his prayer he did not ask for the reversal of this. Divine wrath must follow transgression, but he prayed that in the midst of this God would "remember mercy," in other words, that he would so interpose as to sanctify the dark experiences looming in the future, drawing his erring people nearer to himself, so that they might trustfully pass through the painful discipline in store for them, and come out of it at length purified as gold. And so ever true prayer for revival seeks the spiritual renewal of men; it solicits the manifestation of the Divine mercy in delivering the plants of his own planting from the blighting effects of sin, and in causing them to abound in all holy excellence and grace. .

IV. PRAYER FOR REVIVAL IS IMPATIENT OF DELAY. It seeks a present blessing. "In the midst of the years, in the midst of the years make known" (ver. 2); *i.e.* without lingering, without postponement, forthwith, in the seer's own time. "How long, O Lord, how long?" "Thy kingdom come;" "It is time for thee to work."—S. D. H.

Vers. 3—18.—*God in history.* On reading these verses containing the ode of Habakkuk we find that they abound in historical allusions. The prophet recalled to mind the Divine interpositions both in mercy and in judgment which had taken place in the bygone days, and in the light of them contemplated the position and prospects of his people in his own time. This course was a very customary one with the Hebrew bards. They were eminently patriotic, and delighted to touch upon the national experiences of sorrow and conflict, of joy and triumph; and, indeed, to such an extent did they carry this, that an acquaintance with the facts of Jewish history is essential in order that we may apprehend the meaning and appreciate the beauty of their poetic strains. But whilst thus national, these sacred songs, in that they refer to principles which are of general application, and to experiences which are common to humanity, are felt by us to be universal in their character, and to belong unto us as well as to the Hebrews, that in reference to them "there is neither Jew nor Greek," in that they are calculated to instruct and edify, to stimulate and strengthen us all. Viewing in this light the celebrated "ode" of Habakkuk here recorded, we see illustrated in it the great fact of God's working in human history, together with the design and influence of this Divine operation.

I. SEE ILLUSTRATED HERE THE FACT OF THE DIVINE WORKING IN HUMAN HISTORY. Looking back, the prophet traced this working: 1. In the giving of the Law on Sinai (comp. vers. 3, 4, with Deut. xxxiii. 2; Judg. v. 4, 5; Ps. lxviii. 8; Teman being another name for Seir). The manifestation of "the eternal light" is thus fittingly compared to the rising of the sun, heaven and earth reflecting his glory. The coming of God in judgment was the thought which, in the circumstances, was necessarily the most vividly present to the prophet's mind; and his allusion here to the manifestation of God in his infinite purity served as an appropriate prelude to this. 2. In the plagues which fell upon the Israelites in the desert, as the result of their disobedience (comp. ver. 5 with Deut. xxxii. 24). The plague is referred to as going before God, like the ancient shield-bearer before the warrior (1 Sam. xvii. 7), or the courier before the man of rank (2 Sam. xv. 1); and pestilence as coming after, as an attendant following his master. 3. In the effects produced upon the Midianites by the advance of the hosts of God's chosen (comp. vers. 6, 7 with Exod. xv. 13—15). 4. In the dividing of the Red Sea and the passage of the Jordan (comp. ver. 8 with Exod. xv. 8; Ps. cxiv. 3—5). Ver. 8 clearly has reference to these Divine interpositions, although the poet, rising with his theme, looked beyond those events and took a wider sweep, and beheld God as going forth, the Divine Warrior in his chariot of salvation, to put his foes to confusion and to effect deliverance for his own. 5. Expressions also are used in vers. 11—15 which, though somewhat veiled, doubtless suggested to the Hebrews, as they raised this song of praise, the sun standing still in Gibeon, and the moon in the valley of Ajalon, in the time of Joshua's victory over the Amorites (ver. 11); the tragedy of the slaughter of Sisera, the representative of the head of the Canaanitish tribes (vers. 13, 14); and the complete discomfiture of the Canaanites (ver. 12). So that the "ode" sets forth God's hand in the events connected with the Jewish nation, and in this way illustrates most forcibly the great fact of the Divine working in human history through all the ages.

II. SEE EXPRESSED HERE THE DESIGN OF THE DIVINE WORKING IN HUMAN HISTORY. This is ever wise and good (ver. 13). God rules over all, making all events contribute to the working out of his purposes of love and mercy in the interests of the whole race. Earthly rulers pursue their own ends, and are prompted by considerations of glory and ambition, but their working is in subjection to the Divine control. "The king's heart," etc. (Prov. xxi. 1). Nothing can befall us, whether individually or nationally, without the permission of our heavenly Father—nothing, too, which he cannot or will not overrule to the advancement of our highest interests.

> "All change changing
>   Works and brings good;
> And though frequent storms, raging,
>   Carry fire and flood;
> And the growing corn is beaten down,
>   The young fruits fall and moulder,
> The vessels reel, the mariners drown
>   Awing the beholder:

Yet in evil to men is good for man.
Then let our heart be bolder,
For more and more shall appear the plan
As the world and we grow older."

(T. T. Lynch.)

By a process of **Divine** evolution, God causes the upheavings and commotions of all kinds which occur in the history of the world to result in the good of humanity; and whilst there is occasion for us, as we note his hand in human history, to say to him with reverence and awe, " In anger thou marchest through the earth; in wrath thou treadest down the nations" (Revised Version), yet we find abundant reason for adding, in the spirit of true adoration, " *Thou goest forth for the salvation of thy people, for the salvation of thine anointed* " (ver. 13).

III. SEE SUGGESTED HERE THE INFLUENCE THIS THOUGHT OF THE DIVINE WORKING IN HUMAN HISTORY EXERTS UPON LOYAL HEARTS. 1. In view of God's terribleness in judgment which marks his working in human history, such are filled with sacred awe. The prophet represents his whole being as convulsed with terror as he thought of the retributions God would, in righteousness, inflict (ver. 16). 2. In view of God's gracious purpose, in all his interpositions to save, restore, and bless the race, such are inspired with holy joy. Hence, strange paradox! whilst oppressed in spirit they are also glad in heart. " They tremble and rejoice," and this is their rapturous song in the night, expressive of their whole-souled trust through all, " Although the fig tree shall not blossom," etc. (vers. 17—19).—S. D. H.

Ver. 4 (last clause).—*The Divine concealments.* " The hiding of his power."

I. IN THE CONTEMPLATION OF THE NATURE AND OPERATIONS OF OUR GOD WE ARE MET BY THE DIVINE CONCEALMENTS. He is a God " that hideth himself" (Isa. xlv. 15); " He doeth great things past finding out," etc. (Job ix. 10); " He giveth no account of any of his matters" (Job xxxii. 13); " He maketh darkness his secret place" (Ps. xviii. 11); "How unsearchable," etc.! (Rom. xi. 33). 1. We realize this as we think of his Being and perfections. " Who by searching," etc.? (Job xi. 7). He is veiled to us by the very covering of his splendour. " Who coverest thyself," etc. (Ps. civ. 2). 2. And we also realize this as we think of his *working*. Mystery meets us in every department of his operations. The scientist and the theologian alike become baffled in their researches, the former having to admit his partial failure as he strives to penetrate the mystery of the universe, and the latter being perplexed at the seeming inequality of God's ways in the providential government of the world, and feeling himself enclosed as with a veil when he ventures to inquire into the high themes of revelation. " There is the hiding of his power." Notice—

II. CERTAIN COURSES ARE OPEN TO US IN VIEW OF THIS GREAT FACT. 1. There is that which is pursued by the sceptic. He reasons—God cannot be known; therefore all thought on the part of man concerning him is needless and vain; all worship of him is folly; all structures reared by his servants to his honour mean waste; his very existence is but a possibility. Here we have the old atheism, banishing God from his universe; the old atheism, only arrayed in a newer and more subtle guise, 2. There is, however, "a more excellent way." Though our God is infinitely beyond our poor stretch of thought, yet he may be known by us. Beyond the comprehension of human reason he is nevertheless present to faith, and deigns to reveal himself to the pure and loving heart. And we do well to remember this, and to repose the trust of our hearts in him, and then to set ourselves to inquire whether, after all, the partial obscurity of the Divine nature and operations may not be wisely and graciously as well as necessarily designed. And pursuing this course, such quieting thoughts as the following, bearing upon the Divine concealments, will be suggested to us. (1) That our personal well-being is advanced by this partial concealment which characterizes our God. It would not be well for us to have complete knowledge of him or his purposes and plans, since then there would be no room for the exercise of faith, patience, resignation; life would cease to be a time of discipline; and there would be no scope for trial and no stimulus to earnest and thoughtful inquiry. (2) That these Divine concealments, whilst they are for our good, also contribute to the advancement of the Divine glory. " It is the glory of God to conceal a thing " (Prov. xxv. 2). It is in this way that he makes his power felt; that he indicates his superiority to man and his independence of him (Isa. xl. 13, 14). (3) That whilst much is thus concealed, everything essential to man's salvation is clearly unfolded.

III. GOD SOMETIMES CAUSES LIGHT TO FALL UPON HIS HIDDEN WAYS AND REVEALS HIMSELF AND HIS OPERATIONS MORE FULLY TO THE VIEW. 1. It has been so in reference to the sacred Scriptures. During the lapse of ages God gradually drew back the veil, revealing more of his will than had been unfolded before. 2. It has been so in the working out of the purpose of redeeming mercy. In the cross of Christ there was expressed the power as well as the wisdom of God; but there was the hiding of this Divine power. The spectators of the scene at Calvary saw only the weakness, and the cross was suggestive to them of shame and reproach and dishonour; but there was power there, although hidden, which soon began to be felt, one of the criminals crucified at the side of the Saviour being the first to experience it. The macerated body of the Redeemer was taken down from the cross, and laid in the sepulchre hewn out of the rock; and again there was the hiding of God's power, and it seemed as though death had conquered; but with the dawn of the first day of the week this power became revealed—the mighty Victor rose, despite seal and guard, the earnest and pledge of the ultimate resurrection of all his saints. 3. And it has been so in human experience. In the dark days of sorrow there has been realized " the hiding of God's power ; " but there has followed the revelation of his loving purpose and the making clear to troubled hearts that in all " his banner over them was love." And this shall be made still more manifest hereafter, for the eternal day shall break, and the shadows flee away for ever !—S. D. H.

Vers. 17, 18.—"*Songs in the night.*" The thought underlying these intensely human words is that of holy and triumphant joy manifesting itself on occasions when in the ordinary course of things the very opposite experience might naturally have been expected. The writer was under the elevating influence of sincere piety, and his rapturous outburst sets forth the truth that true religion excites within its recipients such thoughts, inspires within them such emotions, and imparts to them such confidence, as to enable them, even when all is adverse in their experience, to rejoice and shout aloud for joy. These songsters can break forth in song, not only in fair weather, when the sun is shining and the sky is clear and blue, and when all nature is full of exhilaration, but also when the sun is withdrawn, and when no rift can be traced in the dark clouds.

I. THE GOOD IN CIRCUMSTANCES OF EXTREMITY. 1. The language employed is figurative, and strikingly suggests to us circumstances of the deepest human need. The fruit of the fig tree was an extensive article both of food and commerce. The vine was diligently cultivated from the earliest times, and, with its rich clusters of grapes and its refreshing shade, became a very appropriate symbol of prosperity; whilst the olive, living from age to age, and yielding an abundant supply of oil, was also typical of abundance. Hence the failure of all these indicates the deepest affliction, the direst calamity (Ps. cv. 33), and the picture of desolation is rendered still more complete when, in addition to these, the bread-corn is represented as ceasing, and the flocks and herds as being cut off (ver. 17). 2. These adverse circumstances befell the nation, and, as the result of the Chaldean invasion, the direst woes had to be experienced. 3. The children of men still have to pass through such dark seasons. There is extremity arising from (1) temporal want occasioned by reverses in circumstances; (2) slander, charges having no foundation in truth, being made and resulting in mistrust and alienation; (3) mental depression, the strong man being brought down to the weakness of the child, the sturdy oak becoming feebler than the bruised reed; (4) bereavement, home being rendered " desolate as birds' nests, when the fledglings have all flown."

II. THE GOOD, CIRCUMSTANCED THUS, STAYING THEMSELVES UPON GOD, AND ON HIM AS WORKING IN ALL FOR THEIR SALVATION. " In God," " the God of my salvation " (ver. 18). The thought which appears specially to have been present to the mind of the prophet was that of adversity as being God's loving discipline to result in the perfecting of the tried, and resulting in their salvation : " the God of my salvation." A picture called " Cloudland," by a German painter, viewed at a distance appears a mass of gloom and cloud, but on closer inspection every cloud is an angel or an angel's wing; and so our sorrows, when interpreted in the light of this gracious design of our God, become changed into blessings. The thought that God is with us in our darkest experiences, working for our salvation and to secure to us the highest good, that the narrow path through which he, our Captain, causes us to fight our way will bring us to "the prize of our high calling," is indeed inspiring, and grasping it we may well press on, raising high our banners, and cheering the way and the conflict with music and song.

III. THE GOOD, THUS RESTING IN GOD AND APPREHENDING HIS GRACIOUS DESIGN, BEING RENDERED TRANQUIL AND TRIUMPHANT AND INSPIRED WITH HOLY JOY. "Yet will I rejoice in the Lord, I will joy," etc. (ver. 18). The joy of the wicked ceases when the fig trees cease to blossom, and the vines to yield their fruit (Hos. ii. 11, 12), for it lies upon the surface; but the joy of the holy lies deep in the soul, and is a settled and abiding possession, and triumphs under the darkest circumstances of life. Illustrations: David (Ps. xlii. 7—9); Asaph (Ps. lxxiii. 2, 24, 25); Paul and Silas (Acts xvi. 25). Resting in God and apprehending his loving working in our life-experiences, he will prove himself our Strength and Song, and will become our Salvation.—S. D. H.

Ver. 19 (first clause).—*God our Strength.* "The Lord God is my Strength."

I. THE LORD GOD IS OUR STRENGTH IN THE CONFLICT WITH SIN. Men are drawn into sin in the hope of securing some personal gratification; they yearn after some unattained good, some unrealized satisfaction, and they yield to the enticements of evil in the hope of securing that for which they are thus craving. But the man whose hope is in God, and to whom he is his "exceeding joy," has parted with these earthly yearnings; in proportion as the higher and the eternal have gained an influence over him, this attachment to the lower and the fleeting has been rooted out. With hearts uncentred from the true God, the Chaldeans craved worldly dominion, and in seeking this "rejoiced to devour the poor secretly" (ver. 14), whereas Habakkuk with God as his Portion was as unaffected by the vanities of earth as dwellers inland are by the noise of the distant sea. So the good, rejoicing in God, are unallured by the baits of temptation, and are rendered strong to war against evil.

II. THE LORD GOD IS OUR STRENGTH IN THE MIDST OF THE ADVERSE SCENES OF LIFE. Man, seeking his satisfaction in earthly things, must be feeble indeed when these fail him, since, with thoughts and affections centred in these, as they depart they leave him without comfort and in a state of orphanage. But he who has sought and found his satisfaction in God has remaining with him, when things seen and temporal have taken their flight, the unseen and the eternal to cheer and gladden his soul. Hence he is strong, and in the light of the Divine teaching and the Divine love can calmly look at his sorrows until, interpreted thus, they become to him light afflictions which are but for a moment, and which work for him a far more exceeding and eternal weight of glory.

III. THE LORD GOD IS OUR STRENGTH IN HOLY SERVICE. Such service is ever attended with difficulties and discouragements, and it is only as we lift up our eyes to the everlasting hills, rejoicing in God and becoming strengthened by him, that we can grapple with these and overcome them. It was this prophet's strong faith and delight in his God that enabled him to prove himself so true a witness in the corrupt age in which his lot was cast. It has ever been the case that the men who have been the most effective workers for God have been the men to whom his living Presence has been an intense reality.

IV. THE LORD GOD WILL CONTINUE TO BE THE STRENGTH OF HIS PEOPLE WHEN THEIR TIME OF SERVICE SHALL CLOSE. Whether this prophet lived to see the devastation of his country which he predicted, we cannot tell, the accounts of his life being so meagre and for the most part apocryphal. We know, however, that, from the state of mental doubt and distress in which he was when he commenced his prophecy (ch. i. 2), he fought his way to unswerving trust in God; for his brief prophecy, opening with the expression of his ardent yearning for more light in reference to the mystery of God's ways, closes with notes of triumphant confidence and hope. Often, doubtless, as his faith became strengthened, did he feel himself in life to be so raised and elevated through his hope and joy in God, as to be like the hind bounding joyously to the high places: and raised above the tumults of earth, though not in heaven, yet in "heavenly places" he communed with his God. Even so we should believe that, as his life terminated, he calmly departed in peace, having seen God's salvation. And all faithful servants of Heaven shall find that when heart and flesh fail, God will be the Strength of their hearts and their Portion for ever. Happy, then, in life and in death such as can say from their inmost souls, "The Lord is my Strength."—S. D. H.

Vers. 1, 2.—*God devoutly addressed.* "A prayer of Habakkuk the prophet upon Shigionoth. O Lord, I have heard thy speech, and was afraid: O Lord, revive thy work in the midst of the years, in the midst of the years make known; in wrath remember mercy." This chapter is considered to be one of the most magnificent compositions of the inspired volume. It was intended undoubtedly to impart consolation in view of the tremendous calamities which were approaching from the Babylonian invasion. "It exhibits," says Dr. Henderson, "a regular ode, beginning with a brief but simple exordium, after which follows the main subject, which is treated in a manner perfectly free and unrestrained, as the different topics arose one after the other in the excited mind of the prophet, and finishes with an epigrammatic resumption of the point first adverted to in the introduction." The whole chapter presents to us God in three aspects—as *devoutly addressed*, as *poetically portrayed*, and as *triumphantly enjoyed*. These two verses present him to us in the first aspect—as devoutly addressed. "A prayer of Habakkuk the prophet upon Shigionoth." Henderson renders the word "shigionoth," "with triumphant music," which indicates that the ode was in all probability intended for the liturgical service in the temple, but to be set to the freest and boldest music. Perhaps the prophet himself was an accomplished musician, as well as a bard of the first order. Three things are to be observed in relation to this devout address.

I. IT WAS COMPOSED FOR GENERAL USE. It is not an *extemporaneous* address; it is a settled form of devotion. Prearranged forms of devotion are both scriptural and expedient. There is a set form given to the priests for blessing the people in Numb. vi. 23—26. Ps. xcii. is called "a psalm for the sabbath," Ps. cii. "a prayer for the afflicted." Hezekiah commanded the Levites to "praise the Lord in the words of David, and of Asaph the seer," which is Ps. cvi. And Christ himself gave his disciples a form of prayer. Whilst it is scriptural, it is also *expedient*. It is absurd to suppose that a minister can properly lead the devotions of a congregation by impromptu utterances. The well-known apathy of congregations under the influence of extemporaneous prayers shows it cannot be done. For the *individual* himself, the extemporaneous prayer is all that is needed, for it is the "soul's sincere desire, uttered or unexpressed." But to get a whole congregation into the channel of devotion, a prearranged form seems desirable.

II. IT WAS IN PROSPECT OF A TERRIBLE CALAMITY. "O Lord, I have heard thy speech, and was afraid." Terrible was the calamity now looming on the vision of the prophet. The Chaldean army was approaching; the ruthless troops would soon be in his country, sack Jerusalem its metropolis, and bear his countrymen away into captivity. In view of this calamity the prayer is addressed. The threatened judgments of hell may well drive men into the presence of God to sue for mercy. "Call upon me in the day of trouble," etc. Surely, if men fully realized the predicted judgments that will fall on this world, prayer would be the habitude of their souls.

III. IT WAS FOR A REVIVAL OF DIVINE WORK. "Revive thy work in the midst of the years, in the midst of the years make known; in wrath remember mercy." Keil thus renders the passage: "Jehovah, thy work in the midst of thy years call to life, in the midst of the years make it known." This may mean—Perfect the work of delivering thy people; let not thy promise lie as it were dead, give it new life by performing it. Do it now, in the midst of the years, when our calamities are at their height, when thy wrath seems to be at high tide and terrible. Now, "revive thy work." Three thoughts are suggested: 1. *The work of human deliverance is the work of God.* This is true of all deliverances—personal, domestic, national, temporal, and *spiritual.* He alone can effectually deliver man. 2. *This work of God may appear to decline.* The perils may thicken, the disease grow more desperate, and all things seem as if God had given up his work. This is often the case with religion in the soul. 3. *This decline of God's work can only be overcome by his intervention.* "Revive thy work."—D. T.

Vers. 3—15.—*God poetically portrayed and practically remembered.* "God came from Teman, and the Holy One from Mount Paran. Selah," etc. The Bible contains many grand songs and odes. There is the song that Moses taught Israel to sing (Exod. xv. 1). There is the triumphant song of Deborah and Barak (Judg. v.). There is the song of Hannah, the mother of Samuel (1 Sam. ii. 1). There is the song of David bewailing the death of Saul and Jonathan (2 Sam. i. 19), and his song of thanksgiving after the communication of Nathan respecting the building of the temple (2 Sam. vii. 18). There is the song of Hezekiah after he had received comfort in his sickness and recovered his health (Isa. xxxviii. 9—20). There is the song of the blessed Virgin, *Magnificat;* the song of Zacharias, *Benedictus;* the song of Simeon, *Nunc dimittis.* But this song of Habakkuk stands in peerless splendour amongst them all. Here the majesty of God in Jewish history is *poetically portrayed* and *practically remembered.*

I. POETICALLY PORTRAYED. God is here presented, not as he is in himself—the Absolute One, whom "no one hath seen or can see," nor as he appears to philosophical or logical minds, but as he appears to a lofty imagination divinely inspired. To the prophet's imagination he appears as coming from Teman and Mount Paran, which refers to the visible display of his glory when he gave the Law upon Mount Sinai amidst thunders and lightnings and earthquakes. Then, indeed, his glory covered the heavens. People at a distance witnessed the splendour of his appearance and shouted his praise. He seemed encircled in surpassing radiance; his brightness was as the light; he "had horns coming out of his hand," and there was the "hiding of his power." Henderson renders it, "Rays streamed from his hand, yet the concealment of his glory was there." The idea, perhaps, is that the brightness that was seen was not his full glory, but mere scintillations or emanations of those infinite abysses of his unrevealed and unrevealable glory. What is revealed of God is as nothing compared with the unrevealed. "Before him went the pestilence, and burning coals went forth at his feet." Or, as Keil renders it, "Before him goes the plague, and the pestilence follows his feet." The reference is, perhaps, to the plagues which he brought upon the Egyptians in order to obtain the deliverance of his people. "He stood, and measured the earth: he beheld, and drove asunder the nations; and the everlasting mountains were scattered, the perpetual hills did bow: his ways are everlasting." "He stands, and sets the earth reeling: he looks, and makes nations tremble, primeval mountains burst in pieces, the early hills sink down: his are the ways of the olden time" (Keil). "While," says Henderson, "Jehovah is marching forth to the deliverance of his people, he stops all of a sudden in his progress, the immediate effects of which are universal consternation and terror." "I saw the tents of Cushan in affliction: and the curtains of the land of Midian did tremble." "When he drove asunder the nations of Canaan," says an old writer, "one might have seen the tents of Cushan in affliction, and the curtains of the land of Midian trembling, and all the inhabitants of the neighbouring countries taking alarm. He struck consternation into the heart of his enemies." "Was the Lord displeased against the rivers? was thine anger against the rivers? was thy wrath against the sea, that thou didst ride upon thine horses and thy chariots of salvation? The bow was made quite naked, according to the oaths of the tribes, even thy word? Thou didst cleave the earth with rivers." "'Was it against rivers, O Jehovah, against the rivers, that thy wrath was kindled? that thou ridest hither upon thy horses, thy chariots of salvation? Thy bow lays itself bare. Thou splittest the earth into rivers.' The ode, taking a new turn, now passes from the description of the coming of God to an address to God himself. To the mental eye of the prophet God presents himself as Judge of the world, in the threatening attitude of a warlike hero equipped for conflict, so that he asks him what is the object of his wrath. The question is merely a poetical turn given to a lively composition, which expects no answer, and is simply introduced to set forth the greatness of the wrath of God; so that in substance it is an affirmation. The wrath of God is kindled over the rivers, his fury over the sea" (Keil). The riding upon horses is a figurative representation of the celerity of his triumphant progress. "The mountains saw thee, and they trembled: the overflowing of the water passed by: the deep uttered his voice, and lifted up his hands on high." "The mountains saw thee, they were in pain: the inundation of water overflowed; the abyss uttered its voice, it raised its hands on

high." "The mountains being the most prominent objects on the surface of the globe,
Habakkuk reiterates in a somewhat prominent form what he had expressed in the sixth
verse in order to preserve the impression of the tremendous character of the transactions
to illustrate which they had been figuratively introduced" (Henderson). "The sun
and moon stood still in their habitation: at the light of thine arrows they went, and at
the shining of thy glittering spear" (see Josh. x. 12, 13). Some, however, suppose
that the reference here is to the surpassing splendour of the Divine manifestation, that
the heavenly orbs withdraw altogether from the fear and horror that pervade all nature,
which are expressed in the mountains by trembling, and in the waters by roaring, and
in the sun and moon by obscuration. God is here viewed as a warrior whose darts are
so brilliant that sun and moon pale before them. "Thou didst march through the
land in indignation, thou didst thresh the heathen in anger." The special reference here
may be to his march in leading the children of Israel through the wilderness, and
smiting down his enemies. "Thou wentest forth for the salvation of thy people, even
for salvation with thine anointed; thou woundedst the head out of the house of the
wicked, by discovering the foundation unto the neck." "Having described, in language
of the most sublime and terrible import, the manifestations of Jehovah in reference to
his enemies, Habakkuk now proceeds to specify in express terms the end which they
were designed to answer, viz. the deliverance and safety of the chosen people, and then
depicts their fatal effects in the destruction of every hostile power" (Henderson).
"'Thou didst strike through with his staves the head of his villages: they came out
as a whirlwind to scatter me: their rejoicing was as to devour the poor secretly. Thou
didst walk through the sea with thine horses, through the heap of great waters.' Thou
goest out to the rescue of thy people, to the rescue of thine anointed one: thou dashest
in pieces the head from the house of the wicked one, laying bare the foundation even
to the neck. Thou piercest with his spears the head of his hordes which storm hither
to beat me to powder, whose rejoicing is as it were to swallow the poor in secret. Thou
treadest upon the seas: thy horses upon the heap of great waters. The Lord, at
whose coming in the terrible glory of the majesty of the Judge of the world, all nature
trembles and appears to fall into its primary chaotic state, marches over the earth, and
stamps or tramples down the nations with his feet (compare the kindred figure of the
treader of the wine-press in Isa. lxiii. 1, 6). Not all nations, however, but only those
who are hostile to him; for he has come forth to save his people and his anointed one.
The perfects in vers. 13—15 are prophetic, describing the future in spirit as having
already occurred" (Keil). Now, all this sublime representation of God is *poetic*,
highly poetic. It is the characteristic of poetry that it ascribes to one class of objects
attributes that belong to another; and in this ode we find attributes ascribed to the
Creator which belong to the creature. For example, he is here represented as moving
from one place to another, from Teman and from Paran; as standing, "he stood," etc.;
as conquering his enemies by human weapons; as riding upon horses and driving in
chariots; and as fired with indignation. All this is human. The Infinite One does not
move from place to place, does not stand in any one spot, knows no rage, fury is not in
him. Whilst in this ode the attributes of the creature are applied to the Creator, we
find also the attributes of the living ascribed to dead and insentient existences. The
mountains are here represented as writhing and in pain, the deep as uttering its voice
and lifting up its hands. But whilst we take this as a poetic representation, we must
not fail to notice some of the grand truths which it contains. 1. *That God's glory
transcends all revelations.* The brightness of the Shechinah, in which he appeared on
Sinai and elsewhere to the Jews, however effulgent, was but a mere scintillation of the
infinite splendour of his Being, the mere "hiding of his power." All his glory as seen
in nature, both in the material and spiritual universe, is but as one ray to the eternal
sun. 2. *That God's power over the material universe is absolute.* He makes the
mountains tremble, and the seas divide, and the orbs of heaven stand still. In the
Apocalypse the refulgent glory of the judgment-throne is represented as causing
the material universe to melt away before it. And before a full manifestation of himself,
what are mountains, rivers, sun, and stars? Mere vapours on the wings of the storm.
3. *That God's interest in good men is profound and practical.* All his operations, as
here poetically described, are on behalf of his chosen people. Though he is high, he has
respect to the lowly, and to that man he ever looks who is of a contrite and humble spirit.

II. PRACTICALLY REMEMBERED. Why did the prophet recall all these Divine manifestations made to the Hebrew people in past times? Undoubtedly to encourage in himself and in his countrymen unbounded confidence in him at the critical and dangerous period in which they were placed. The Chaldean hosts were threatening their ruin, the political heavens were black with thunder-clouds under which his countrymen might well shiver and stand aghast. Under these perilous circumstances he turns to God; he calls to mind and portrays in vivid poetry what he had been to his people in ancient times. 1. *He recalls the fact that God had delivered his people in ancient times from perils as great as those to which they were now exposed.* From the Egyptians, the Canaanites, the Philistines, etc. 2. *That God had done this by stupendous manifestations of his power.* Manifestations of his power in the sea, in the mountains, in the orbs of heaven, etc. 3. *That what God had done for his people he would continue to do.* "His ways are everlasting," or, as Keil renders it, "His are ways of the olden times." The idea, perhaps, is that he has an eternal plan, fixed and settled. What he has done for them he will still do. Thus the prophet remembered the days of old, and took courage.—D. T.

Ver. 16.—*Horror of God.* "When I heard, my belly trembled; my lips quivered at the voice: rottenness entered into my bones, and I trembled in myself, that I might rest in the day of trouble: when he cometh up unto the people, he will invade them with his troops." "Having finished the poetic rehearsal of the mighty acts of Jehovah on behalf of his people in ancient times, which he had composed in order to inspire the pious with unshaken confidence in him as their covenant God, Habakkuk reverts to the fear which had seized him on hearing of the judgments that were to be inflicted upon his country by the Chaldeans" (Henderson). Our subject is *horror of God;* and we offer three remarks on this state of mind.

I. IT IS AN ABNORMAL STATE OF MIND. The benevolent character of God, and the moral constitution of the soul are sufficient to show that it was never intended that man should ever dread his Maker or be touched with any servile feelings in relation to him. Unbounded confidence, cheerful trust, loyal love,—these are the normal states of mind in relation to the Creator. How has the abnormal state arisen? The history of the Fall shows this, "I heard thy voice in the garden, and was afraid." Having sinned, a sense of guilt came to the conscience, and conscience under the sense of guilt invested almighty love with attributes of terror. Horror of God springs from a sense of guilt.

II. IT IS AN UNNECESSARY STATE OF MIND. God is not terrible. There is nothing in him to dread. "Fury is not in me." He is love. His voice to man: 1. In all *nature* is, "Be not afraid." The smiling heavens, the blooming earth, the warbling songsters of the air, in all he says to man, "Be not afraid." 2. In all *true philosophy* is, "Be not afraid." All things which true philosophy looks into show benevolence or intention, and breathe the genius of love. 3. In all *true Christianity* is, "Be not afraid." Corrupt Christianity, it is true, makes him horrific; but the Christianity of Christ reveals him in love and in love only. In Christ he comes down in man to man, and demonstrates his love.

III. IT IS A PERNICIOUS STATE OF MIND. Horror is a *pernicious* state of mind in every way. It is pernicious to the *body.* The language of the text implies this, "When I heard, my belly trembled; my lips quivered at the voice: rottenness entered into my bones, and I trembled in myself." The prophet's alarm drove back the blood from the extremities to the heart, his flesh grew cold, contracted, his voice quivered, and his very bones seemed to rot. Horrific feeling is inimical to physical health. But dread of God is even more pernicious to *soul.* 1. It *destroys its peace.* Fear shakes every power of the soul as the winds shake the leaves of the forest. 2. It *depresses its powers.* All the faculties of the soul shrink and shiver under the influence of fear, as the herds of the mountain at the approaching thunder-storm. 3. It *distorts its views.* Fear of God gives men horrid ideas of him. It has forged all the theologies, both in heathendom and Christendom, that have frightened men. It is fear that has given men that Calvin Deity which frightens the millions away from the glorious gospel of the blessed God.

CONCLUSION. Let us preach to men the God of Christ, the God who says to all men, "It is I: be not afraid."—D. T.

Vers. 17—19.—*The possibilities in the life of a good man.* "Although the fig tree shall not blossom, neither shall fruit be in the vines; the labour of the olive shall fail, and the fields shall yield no meat; the flock shall be cut off from the fold, and there shall be no herd in the stalls: yet I will rejoice in the Lord, I will joy in the God of my salvation," etc. "The desolation here so graphically and forcibly described is that which was to be effected by the Chaldeans, whose army would consume or destroy the best and most necessary productions of the land; not only seizing upon the cattle and devouring the fruits of the earth, but so injuring the trees as to render them incapable of yielding any produce. The passage contains the most beautiful exhibition of the power of true religion to be found in the Bible. The language is that of a mind weaned from earthly enjoyments, and habituated to find the highest fruition of its desires in God. When every earthly stream is dried up, it has an infinite supply in his all-sufficient and exhaustless fulness." Our subject is—*The possibilities in the life of a good man.*

I. The GREATEST MATERIAL DESTITUTION IS POSSIBLE TO A GOOD MAN. It is possible for the fig tree not to blossom, etc. Man lives by the fruits of the earth. These may fail from one of two reasons. 1. From *human neglect.* It is the eternal ordinance of God, that what man wants from the earth for his existence he must get from it by labour—skilful, timely, persevering labour. The earth gives to the brute what he wants without his labour, because the brute is not endowed with qualifications for agricultural work. But man must labour, and this arrangement is wise and beneficent. It promotes health, imparts vigour, and develops faculties both intellectual and moral. Let man cease to cultivate the soil, and the earth will fail to support him either with the right animal or vegetable productions. 2. *From Divine visitation.* The mighty Maker can, and sometimes does, wither the fruits of the earth, destroy the cattle of the fields. He does this sometimes without instrumentality, by mere volition; sometimes with the feeblest instrumentality—locusts, worms, etc.; sometimes with human instrumentality—war, etc. We say the greatest material destitution is *possible* to a good man. Possible? It is frequent. In all ages some of the best men have been found in the most destitute circumstances. Even Christ himself had nowhere to lay his head; and the apostles, what had they?

II. THE HIGHEST SPIRITUAL JOY IS POSSIBLE TO A GOOD MAN. "I will rejoice in the Lord, I will joy in the God of my salvation." "Spiritual joy," says Caleb Morris, "is a free, full, and overflowing stream, that takes its rise in the very depth of the Divine essence, in the immutability, perfection, abundance, munificence, of the Divine nature. While there is a God, and that God is happy, there is no necessity that there should be any unhappy Christians." What is it to "joy in God"? 1. *It is the joy of the highest contemplation.* The joys of contemplation are amongst the most pure and elevating which intelligent creatures can experience. These rise in the character according to their subjects. The highest subject is God, his attributes and works. 2. *It is the joy of the most elevating friendship.* The joys of friendship are amongst the chief joys of earth; but the joys of friendship depend upon the purity, depth, constancy, reciprocity of love; and friendship with God secures all this in the highest degree. 3. *It is the joy of the sublimest admiration.* Whatever the mind admires it enjoys, and enjoys in proportion to its admiration, whether it be a landscape or a painting. Moral admiration is enjoyment of the highest kind, and this in proportion to the grandness of the character. Admiration of Divine excellence is the sublimest joy. "I will joy in God." To joy in God is to bask in sunshine, is to luxuriate in abundance, is to revel in the immensity of moral beauty, is to dwell with God.

III. THE HIGHEST SPIRITUAL JOY IN THE MIDST OF THE GREATEST MATERIAL DESTITUTION IS POSSIBLE TO A GOOD MAN "Although" every material blessing is gone, "I will rejoice." Good men have always been enabled to do so. They have been happy in poverty, exultant in prisons, and even triumphant in the martyr's flames. Having God with them, they have had the reality without the forms, they have had the crystal fountain rather than the shallow and polluted streams. Like Paul, they have "gloried in tribulation," etc. All things have been theirs. In material destitution they felt: 1. In God they had *strength.* "The Lord God is my Strength." "As thy day, so shall thy strength be." 2. In God they had *swiftness.* "He will make my feet like hinds' feet." The reference is here, perhaps, to the swiftness with which God would enable him to flee from the dangers which were overtaking his country. It is, however, a universal truth that God gives to a good man a holy alacrity in duty. Duty to him is not a clog or a burden, but a delight. 3. In God they had *elevation*. "He will make me to walk upon mine high places." "They that wait upon God shall renew their strength; they shall mount up with wings as eagles," etc., up upon the mountains, far too high for any enemies to scale. "God, willing more abundantly to show unto the heirs of promise the immutability of his counsel, confirmed it by an oath : that by two immutable things, in which it was impossible for God to lie, we might have a strong consolation, who have fled for refuge to lay hold upon the hope set before us" (Heb. vi. 17, 18).—D. T.

HOMILETICAL INDEX

TO

THE BOOK OF HABAKKUK.

ZEPHANIAH

EXPOSITION BY

W. J. DEANE

HOMILETICS BY

S. D. HILLMAN

HOMILIES BY VARIOUS AUTHORS

T. WHITELAW   J. S. CANDLISH

D. THOMAS

THE BOOK OF ZEPHANIAH

INTRODUCTION.

§ I. SUBJECT OF THE BOOK.

THE prophecy of Zephaniah has been called by Kleinert the *Dies iræ* of the
Old Testament; and there is much truth in this designation. It is, indeed,
replete with announcements of judgment to come; it is wholly occupied
with this subject and its consequences, and exhortations founded thereon;
not that this is the final object of the prophecy, but it is introduced
uniformly as being the means of establishing righteousness in the earth,
making God's power known, purging out the evil, and developing the
good. The prophet is inspired with the idea of the universal judgment
which shall affect the whole world; he sees this anticipated by particular
visitations on certain heathen nations; he sees heathendom generally overthrown; he warns his own countrymen of the punishment that awaits
them; and he looks forward to the salvation of Israel when all these things
have come to pass. The book is one continuous prophecy divided into
three parts; it contains, perhaps, many utterances condensed into one
systematic whole, which comprises the threat of judgment, the exhortation
to repentance, and the promise of salvation.

The prophet begins abruptly with announcing the judgment upon the
whole world, upon idolaters, and specially upon Judah for its iniquity; he
describes the terrible character of this judgment, and upon whom it shall
fall, viz. the chieftains who affect Gentile habits and oppress others, upon
the traders who exact usury, upon the faithless who have no belief in
Divine providence (ch. i.). Having depicted the day of the Lord, he
exhorts the people to repentance, and urges the righteous to persevere that
they may be protected in the time of distress. He gives a reason for this
exhortation by a more extended announcement of the Divine judgment
which shall fall upon nations far and near—Philistines, Moabites, Ammonites,
Ethiopians, Assyrians, yea, and upon Jerusalem herself, whose princes,
judges, and prophets shall be justly punished. This display of vengeance
shall lead to a reverential awe of the Name of the Lord, and prepare the

way for the pure worship of God (ch. ii. 1—iii. 8). This introduces the announcement of Messianic hopes. The nations shall serve the Lord with one accord; Israel shall return from its dispersion, purified and humbled, the evil being purged away; it shall be safe under God's special care, and shall rejoice in happiness undisturbed; the oppressor shall be destroyed, and the holy nation shall be "a name and a praise among all people of the earth" (ch. iii. 9—20).

The prophecy of Zephaniah is in some respects supplementary to that of Habakkuk. The latter had foretold the punishment of Judah through the Chaldeans; the former shows how the judgment will affect, not the Jews only, but pagan nations also, yea, the whole earth; but he does not name nor accurately describe the instruments of this vengeance. This reticence has given occasion to much speculation on the part of critics. Those who believe in the predictive element of prophecy, and acknowledge the inspiration of Divine foreknowledge in the utterances of the prophets, have no difficulty in seeing the fulfilment of the announced judgment in the action of the Chaldeans, whom Zephaniah, in agreement with the general and comprehensive character of his oracle, does not specifically name. But Hitzig and those who reject all definite prophecy take much pains to discover an enemy to whom the prophet could allude without resorting to supernatural knowledge. They find this convenient invader in the horde of Scythians who, as Herodotus relates (i. 103—106), burst into Media, went thence towards Egypt, were bought off by Psammetichus, and on their return a few stragglers plundered a temple at Ascalon. This inroad is reported to have happened about the time that the prophecy was uttered. But Herodotus's account of the Scythians, when carefully examined, is proved to be full of inaccuracies; and even this gives no support to the figment of their attack on the Jews, of whose existence they were probably unaware, nor to any destruction of the nations mentioned by Zephaniah effected by them. Whether it was revealed to the prophet that the Chaldeans were to be the executors of the Divine vengeance, or whether the exact instruments were not identified in his view (the law of moral government being present to his mind rather than any definite circumstances), the fact remains that he announces certain events which we know were not fulfilled by any proceedings of Scythians, but were exactly accomplished by the Chaldeans (see note on ch. i. 7).

The peculiarity in Zephaniah's prophecy is the extension of his view to all lands and nations, their spiritual concerns, their future condition. While cursorily announcing the fate of Jerusalem, he dwells chiefly upon the exercise of God's power upon the exterior kingdoms of the world, and how they are ordained to work out his great purposes.

§ II. Author.

Of Zephaniah we know absolutely nothing but what he himself mentions in the superscription of his book. No information can be gathered from the contents of the prophecy, where the writer's personal history is wholly unnoticed.   He calls himself " the son of Cushi, the son of Gedaliah, the son of Amariah, the son of Hizkiah."   As it is usual to mention only the name of the father, it has been inferred that the genealogy is carried up to the fourth generation because Hizkiah, *i.e.* Hezekiah, was a celebrated personage, and most probably the famous King of Judah.   But the inference is not undoubted.   Hizkiah is not called "King of Judah" in the genealogy, which would naturally have been done had he been the ancestor intended, as in Prov. xxv. 1; Isa. xxxviii. 9.   There is room enough, indeed, between Hezekiah and Josiah for the four specified descents, though only three are named in the case of Josiah himself; but the name Hezekiah was not unknown among the Jews, and we cannot assume without further support that the person here mentioned is the king.   It is fair to argue that the insertion of the genealogical details shows that the prophet was of distinguished birth; but further it is impossible to go with any certainty.

The name of the prophet is variously explained, as " The Lord hath hid," or " The Lord hath guarded," or " The Lord's Watch-tower."   Keil is generally followed in interpreting it as " He whom Jehovah hides, or shelters."   The LXX. writes it Σοφονίας: Vulgate, *Sophoniah*.   There were others who bore this name (see 2 Kings xxv. 18; 1 Chron. vi. 36; Zech. vi. 10, 14).   The details given by Pseudo-Dorotheus and Pseudo-Epiphanius (' De Vit. Proph.,' xix.), among which is the assertion that he was a member of the tribe of Simeon, have no historical basis.

§ III. Date.

Zephaniah, in the inscription of his book, states that he prophesied "in the days of Josiah the son of Amon, King of Judah;" and this assertion has never been seriously disputed.   The only question is in what part of that king's reign did he exercise his office.   Josiah reigned thirty-one years, according to the usually received dates—from B.C. 640 to B.C. 609.   The destruction of Nineveh, which Zephaniah foretold, took place quite at the end of Josiah's reign, and his prophecy must have been uttered some time before this event.   No other data for determining the question exist save what may be gathered from internal evidences.   And these are most uncertain, depending chiefly upon inferences drawn from the great reformation effected by the good king.   Did he prophesy before this reformation was begun, or after it was effected, that is to say, in the first or second half of Josiah's reign?   A third alternative may be added—Was it during the progress of this religious amelioration?   Those who assign the prophecy to the earlier period, before the king's eighteenth year, when his vigorous measures produced their happy results, rely upon the fact that the prophet speaks as though idolatry and the disorders which Josiah repressed were still rampant, even the members of the royal family being implicated in the general iniquity. It is inconceivable, they say, that Zephaniah should have taken this gloomy view, and have entirely omitted all mention of the young prince's noble efforts to effect a change for the better, had this attempt already been commenced. All this points to a time when Josiah was still a minor, and before he had begun to assert himself in the direction of affairs. On the other hand, it is contended that certain statements in the body of the work prove that the reformation was being carried on at the time when it was composed: the public worship of Jehovah existed (ch. iii. 4, 5), and this side by side with that of Baal and with many idolatrous practices (ch. i. 4, 5); there were priests of Jehovah as well as priests of false gods at the same time. Nor can we reason from Zephaniah's silence concerning reforms that none had been essayed; for Jeremiah, who began to prophesy in the thirteenth year of Josiah, is quite as strong as Zephaniah in his denunciations of idolatry, the fact being that, though it was publicly abolished, it was still practised extensively in secret. Others, again, claim a still later date for the prophecy, because it speaks of the extermination of the *remnant* of Baal (ch. i. 4), which implies that the purification had already been effected, and that only isolated instances still existed; the prophet also speaks of and refers to the Mosaic books as well known to his hearers (comp. ch. i. 13, 15, 17; ii. 2, 5, 7, 11; iii. 5, 19, 20), which could only have been after the discovery of the " book of the Law " in Josiah's eighteenth year (2 Kings xxii. 8). It must be noted that on this occasion reference was made to the Prophetess Huldah, not to Zephaniah (2 Kings xxii. 14). Hence some suppose that he was dead at this time.

From this brief recapitulation of arguments it will be seen that each of the three theories mentioned above has much to be said in its favour; and that the only safe conclusion to adopt is this—that although the present book, as now displayed in the sacred canon, forms one connected whole, it is composed of prophecies uttered at various times and gathered by their author into a volume and arranged on a definite plan. Its place in the canon is the same both in the Hebrew and Greek, and coincides with the chronological order to which it is assigned.

§ IV. General Character.

Some critics have spoken disparagingly of the style of Zephaniah's prophecy, as being prosaic and bearing no comparison with any of the other Hebrew poets. There is some truth in this criticism; but the censure is exaggerated and unjust. Of the remarkable purity of his language there can be no doubt; and if his rhythm is at times faulty, judged by the standard of the highest models, and sinks into prose; if he is wanting in sublimity and elegance; it must be allowed that he is always easy and full of life, often vehement, fiery, and severe, and that the force and conciseness of his utterances leave a definite impression on the mind which needs no rhetorical artifice to make it permanent. Like other prophets, he connects himself with his predecessors by employing their language, not from poverty of idea, not from " declension in the originality of prophets of this date," but because he designs to give, in a compendious form, " the fundamental thoughts of judgment and salvation which are common to all the prophets " (Keil). He predicts judgment; the particular instrument he leaves untold. The destruction, not the destroyer, is the subject of his oracle. His future is vague, and extends even to the end of time; particular period or special agent is beyond his scope to name. He culls isolated expressions and striking words from his predecessors, Isaiah. Joel, Amos, and Habakkuk; he avails himself of their language with respect to judgment to come, and God's love for the righteous among the people, and applies it to his own purpose (see Pusey, p. 441). The peculiar nature of this prophecy, its comprehensiveness and universality, has been well intimated by Bucer, who says, " Si quis desiderat secreta vatum oracula brevi dari compendio, brevem hunc Zaphanjam perlegat."

§ V. Literature.

Of special commentaries on Zephaniah the most noteworthy are the following: M. Bucer, 'Sophon. Proph.' (Argent., 1528); Laren, 'Tuba Zeph.' (Magdeb., 1653); Jansen., 'Analecta in Sophon.;' Tarnovius, 'Comment.' (Rost., 1623); Nolten, 'Dissert. Exeget.' (1719); 'Comment.' (Franc., 1724); Cramer, 'Scyth. Denkmäler' (1777); Von Coeln, 'Spicilegium' (Bresl., 1819); P. Ewald, 'Zeph. übersetzt' (Erlang., 1827); Strauss, 'Vaticin. Zeph. Comment. Illustr.' (Berlin, 1843); Reinke, 'Der Proph. Zeph.' (Munst., 1868).

§ VI. Arrangement in Sections.

The book is divided into three parts.
Part I. (Ch. i.) The judgment upon all the world, and upon Judah in particular.
    § 1. (Ch. i. 1.) Title and inscription.
    § 2. (Ch. i. 2, 3.) The prelude, announcing the judgment upon the whole world.
    § 3. (Ch. i. 4—6.) This judgment will fall specially upon Judah and Jerusalem for their idolatry.
    § 4. (Ch. i. 7—13.) The judgment is described as regards its objects, viz. the princes, the traders, the irreligious and profligate.
    § 5. (Ch. i. 14—18.) The near approach and terrible nature of this judgment.
Part II. (Ch. ii. 1—iii. 8.) Exhortation to repentance and to perseverance.
    § 1. (Ch. ii. 1—3.) Let all examine their ways before the day of the Lord comes, and let the righteous specially seek the Lord more earnestly, that they may be safe in the judgment.
    § 2. (Ch. ii. 4—7.) The exhortation is supported by the announcement of the punishment on various nations, which shall prepare the way for the acceptance of true religion; and first the punishment shall fall on the Philistines.
    § 3. (Ch. ii. 8—10.) Then upon the Moabites and Ammonites.
    § 4. (Ch. ii. 11.) Jehovah destroys idolatry, that pure religion may reign over all the earth.
    § 5. (Ch. ii. 12—15.) The judgment shall fall on the Ethiopians and Assyrians.
    § 6. (Ch. iii. 1—5.) If God punishes the heathen, he will not spare the hardened sinners in Judah.
    § 7. (Ch. iii. 6—8.) This is the only way left to secure salvation for Israel and the whole world.

THE BOOK OF ZEPHANIAH

EXPOSITION.

CHAPTER I.

Vers. 1—18.—Part I. The Judgment upon all the World, and upon Judah in Particular.

Ver. 1.—§ 1. *Title and inscription.* **The word of the Lord** (see note on Micah i. 1). Zephaniah, "Whom the Lord shelters" (see Introduction, § II.). **The son of,** etc. The genealogy thus introduced shows that the prophet was of illustrious descent; or it may be inserted to distinguish him from others who bore the same name. **Hizkiah.** The same name which is elsewhere written in our version *Hezekiah.* Whether the great King of Judah is here meant may well be questioned (see Introduction). Other prophets have prefixed their genealogies to their books (see Zech. i. 1; and in the Apocrypha, Baruch i. 1). **In the days of Josiah.** Zephaniah here gathers into one volume the denunciations and predictions which he had uttered during the reign of Josiah, both before and _after the great reformation effected by that good king (2 Kings xxiii.).

Vers. 2, 3.—§ 2. *The prelude, announcing the judgment upon the whole world.*

Ver. 2.—I will utterly consume; literally, *taking away I will make an end.* Jeremiah (viii. 13) uses the same expression. The prophet begins abruptly with this announcement of universal judgment before he warns Judah in particular of the punishment that awaits her, because his position is that the way to salvation is through chastisement. Vulgate, *congregans congregabo,* where the verb must be used in the sense of "gathering for destruction." **All things.** More expressly defined in the following verse. This awful warning recalls the judgment of the Flood and the pre-

liminary monition (Gen. **vi. 7**). **From off the land;** *from the face of the earth,* not the land of Judah alone. **Saith the Lord;** *is the saying of Jehovah.* The prophet in this is merely the vehicle of the Divine announcement.

Ver. 3.—Man and beast, etc. This is not mere hyperbole to express the utter wasting and destruction that were impending, but points to the mysterious connection between man and the lower creation, how in agreement with the primal curse even material nature suffers for man's sin (Gen. iii. 17; Rom. viii. 22). If we expect a new heaven and a new earth, we know that God will show his wrath against the old creation defiled with sin (2 Pet. iii. 10; comp. Jer. iv. 25; ix. 9, etc.; Hos. iv. 3). **And the stumbling-blocks with the wicked.** Not the sinners only shall be swept away by this judgment, but also all offences, all causes of stumbling, whether idols or other incentives to departure from truth and right. Septuagint, καὶ ἀσθενήσουσιν οἱ ἀσεβεῖς, "and the ungodly shall be weak;" Vulgate, *et ruinæ impiorum erunt.* These versions seem to have missed the point. **I will cut off man.** It is *on* man's account that this judgment is sent—a truth which the prophet enforces by reiteration.

Vers. 4—6.—§ 3. *The judgment will fall especially upon Judah and Jerusalem for their idolatry.*

Ver. 4.—I will also stretch out mine hand. This expression is used when God is about to do great things or inflict notable punishment (see Exod. iii. 20; xv. 12; Deut. iv. 34; Isa. v. 25; Jer. li. 25, etc.). **Judah.** In so far as Judah was rebellious and wicked, it should incur the judicial punishment. Judgment was to begin at the house of God (1 Pet. iv. 17), the sin of the chosen people being more heinous than that of heathens. Hence it is added, **upon all the inhabitants of Jerusalem**, because, having in their very midst the temple of God, with its services and priests, they ought especially to have abhorred idolatry and maintained the true faith. **The remnant of Baal**; *i.e.* the last vestige. One cannot argue from this expression that the reform was already carried so far that Baal-worship had almost disappeared. The next verse shows that idolatry still flourished; but the term implies merely that God would exterminate it so entirely that no trace of it should remain. The LXX. has, "the names of Baal," τὰ ὀνόματα τῆς Βάαλ (Hos. ii. 17). (For Josiah's reform of these iniquities, see 2 Kings xxiii. 4, etc.) **The name of the Chemarims** (*Chemarim*). The word means "black-robed," and is applied to the idolatrous priests whom the kings had appointed to conduct worship in high places (2 Kings xxiii. 5; Hos. x. 5). "The name," says Dr. Pusey, "is probably the Syriac name of 'priest,' used in Holy Scripture of idolatrous priests, because the Syrians were idolaters." Not only shall the persons of these priests be cut off, but their very name and memory shall vanish (Zech. xiii. 2). **With the priests** (*kohanim*). Together with the legitimate priests who had corrupted the worship of Jehovah (ch. iii. 4; Jer. ii. 8; Ezek. viii. 11).

Ver. 5.—**That worship the host of heaven upon the house-tops.** In this verse two classes of false worshippers are mentioned, viz. star-worshippers, and waverers. The worship of the sun, moon, and stars was a very ancient form of error, the heavenly bodies being regarded as the representatives of the powers of nature and the originators of events on earth (see Deut. iv. 19; xvii. 3; Job xxxi. 26, 27; 2 Kings xvii. 16). It was especially prevalent in the time of Manasseh (2 Kings xxi. 3). On the flat roofs of the houses, which were used as places of meditation, recreation, or conference (comp. Josh. ii. 6; 1 Sam. ix. 25; 2 Sam. xi. 2; Acts x. 9), they erected altars for family worship of the heavenly bodies. Here they both burned incense (Jer. xix. 13) and offered animal sacrifices (2 Kings xxiii. 12). "In Syrian cities," says Dr. Thomson, "the roofs are a great comfort. The ordinary houses have no other place where the inmates can either see the sun, smell the air, dry their clothes, set out their flower-pots, or do numberless other things essential to their health and comfort. During a large part of the year the roof is the most agreeable place about the establishment, especially in the morning and evening. There multitudes sleep during the summer" ('The Land and the Book,' p. 39). **Them that worship and**

that, etc.; rather, *the worshippers who*, etc. These were people who endeavoured to blend the worship of God with that of Baal, or halted between two opinions (1 Kings xviii. 21). **Swear by the Lord**; rather, *swear to the Lord*; i.e. bind themselves by oath to him, and at the same time swear **by Malcham**; *swear by their king*, Baal, or Moloch; call upon him as god. Septuagint, κατὰ τοῦ βασιλέως αὐτῶν, "by their king." But it is, perhaps, best to retain the name untranslated, in which case it would be the appellation of the god Moloch, who could hardly be omitted in enumerating the objects of idolatrous worship (see Jer. xlix. 1, 3; and notes on Amos i. 15; v. 26).

Ver. 6.—**Them that are turned back from the Lord.** This is a third class, viz. apostates and open despisers. Those who follow him no more, renegades who have left his service. The Vulgate renders the original by, *qui avertuntur de post tergum Domini*. **Those that have not sought the Lord.** These are the indifferent, who do not trouble themselves about religion. The chief classes mentioned in these two verses are three, viz. the open idolaters, the syncretists who mingled the worship of Baal with that of Jehovah, and those who despised religion altogether.

Vers. 7—13.—4. *The judgment is described with regard to those whom it will affect, viz. the princes, the traders, the irreligious and profligate.*

Ver. 7.—This judgment, so fearful, is near at hand, and must needs occasion the utmost terror and dismay. **Hold thy peace at the presence of the Lord God**; literally, *Hush, from the face of the Lord Jehovah!* εὐλαβεῖσθε (Septuagint); *silete a facie Domini Dei* (Vulgate). The expression is like Hab. ii. 20. The reason of this silent awe is next given. **For the day of the Lord is at hand.** The day of judgment is thus called (Joel i. 15; Isa. xiii. 6; Amos v. 18, 20; Obad. 15). **The Lord hath prepared a sacrifice.** The words are from Isa. xxxiv. 6 (comp. Jer. xlvi. 10; Ezek. xxxix. 17, 19). The sacrifice is the guilty Jewish nation. The punishment of the wicked is regarded as a satisfaction offered to the Divine justice. **He hath bid his guests;** *he hath consecrated his called.* The "called ones" are the strange nations whom God summons to execute his vengeance. Septuagint, ἡγίακε τοὺς κλητοὺς αὐτοῦ. These are said to be "sanctified," as if engaged in a holy war, when summoned to punish those who had become as heathen. So those who are called to chastise Babylon are termed "my sanctified ones" (Isa. xiii. 3), as being the instruments appointed and set apart to carry out this purpose (comp. **Jer. xxii. 7**; li. 27, 28; Micah iii. 5). The particular agents intended are not specified by the prophet, whose mission was not directed to any such definition. He has to speak generally of the judgment to come, not of those whom God should employ to inflict it. We know from other sources that the Chaldeans are meant, they or the Assyrians being always announced as the executors of God's vengeance on his rebellious people. The notion, adopted by Ewald, Hitzig, and others, that the prophet refers to some supposed invasion of Scythians which took place about this time, would never have been started had not such authors desired to eliminate the predictive element from prophetic utterances. The vague account of Herod., i. 105 gives no support to the assertion that the Scythians invaded Palestine in Josiah's reign; nor is there a trace of any knowledge of such irruption in Zephaniah or Jeremiah (see Introduction, § I.).

Ver. 8.—The prophet names the **three** classes of people who shall be smitten in this judgment. First, the princes. **In the day of the Lord's sacrifice** (see note on ver. 7). God is speaking; so the name of the Lord is employed instead of the pronoun (comp. Lam. iii. 66). **I will punish**; literally, *visit upon* (ver. 12; Amos iii. 14). **The princes.** The heads of tribes and families, nobles and magistrates. **The king's children** (*sons*); Septuagint, τὸν οἶκον τοῦ βασιλέως, "the house of the king." The royal family, not specially the sons of Josiah, who, if they were then in existence, must have been mere children, but princes of the royal house. The reference may be particularly to the sons of the king reigning when the judgment fell (see 2 Kings xxv. 7). The king himself is not mentioned as subject to the judgment, inasmuch as he was pious and obedient (2 Chron. xxxiv. 27, etc.). In the mention of these "children" Keil finds proof of the late origin of the prophecy. **Such as are clothed with strange apparel.** This clause must represent the sin for which the princes are "visited." "Strange" apparel means "foreign" apparel, and this implied foreign manners and habits. The Israelites were reminded by their very dress that they were a peculiar people, consecrated to God's service (Numb. xv. 37, etc.; Deut. xxii. 12). These nobles, however, assumed the dress of the Egyptians and other nations with which they came in contact, and, despising their own national customs, copied the manners and vices of foreigners (comp. Isa. iii. 16—24; Ezek. xx. 32; 1 Macc. i. 11—15).

Ver. 9.— **Those that leap on** (*over*) **the threshold.** These are the retainers of the princes, etc., named in ver. 8. There is no allusion to the circumstance of the priests of Dagon abstaining from treading on the threshold of their temple in consequence of what happened to the idol at Ashdod (1 Sam. v. 5). It is inconceivable that this merely local custom, which demonstrated the impotence of the false god, should have been imported into Judah. where, indeed, the worship of Dagon seems never to have made any way. The following clause explains the meaning which the Latin version intimates, *Omnem qui arroganter ingreditur super limen*—all those who, carrying out their masters' wishes, violently invade the houses of others and pillage them of their contents. The expression, "to leap over the threshold," seems to have been a common term for burglary and stealing with violence. **Which fill their masters' houses.** These retainers plunder and steal in order that they may increase their masters' treasures. The king (though not Josiah) may be meant, the plural being the plural of majesty, or the idol-temples. The LXX., followed by Jerome, renders, "who fill the house of the Lord their God." This is plainly erroneous, as there is no question here about the temple at Jerusalem. **Violence and deceit**; *i.e.* the fruits of, what they have extorted by, violence and fraud (Jer. v. 27).

Ver. 10.—The second class which shall be smitten, viz. the traders and usurers, the enemy being represented as breaking in upon the localities where these persons resided. **The fish gate.** This is generally supposed to have been in the north wall of the city towards its eastern extremity, and to have been so called because through it were brought the fish from the Jordan and the Sea of Galilee, and there was a fish-market in its immediate neighbourhood (see Neh. iii. 3; xii. 39; 2 Chron. xxxiii. 14). It was probably on this side that the Chaldeans entered Jerusalem, as Zedekiah seems to have escaped from the south (Jer. xxxix. 4). The LXX. has, ἀπὸ πύλης ἀποκεντούντων, which Jerome notes as a mistake. **From the second** district, the lower city upon the hill Acra, to the north of the old town, Zion. This is so called, according to one rendering, in 2 Kings xxii. 14 and Neh. xi. 9. **A great crashing.** Not merely the crash of falling buildings, but the cry of men when a city is taken and the inhabitants are put to the sword. **The hills**, on which the greater part of the city was built. Keil thinks that the hills surrounding the lower city are meant, viz. Bezetha, Gareb, etc., as the hearer of the cry is supposed to be on Zion.

Ver. 11.—**Maktesh**; *the Mortar*; Septuagint, τὴν κατακεκομμένην, "her that is broken down." The word is found in Judg. xv. 19 of a hollow place in a rock, and it is here used in the sense of "valley," and probably refers to the Tyropœum, or part of it, the depression that ran down the city, having Acra and Zion on its west side, and Moriah and Ophel on its east, and extended south as far as the pool of Siloam. It does not seem a very appropriate appellation for a lengthy valley like the Tyropœum, nor is there any trace of such a name being applied to it elsewhere. It may have been a name affixed to a certain locality where a bazaar was situated or certain special industries had their seat; or it may have been invented by Zephaniah to intimate the fate that awaited the evil merchants, that they should be, as it were, brayed in a mortar by their enemies. **The merchant people;** literally, *people of Canaan*. So Septuagint and Vulgate (comp. Hos. xii. 7; Hist. of Susannah 56; Zech. xiv. 21). The iniquitous traders are called "people of Canaan," because they acted like the heathens around them, especially the Phœnicians, who were unscrupulous and dishonest in their transactions. **Are cut down;** *are silenced;* Vulgate, *conticuit* (Isa. vi. 5; Hos. x. 7). **They that bear** (*are laden with*) **silver.** Those who have amassed wealth by trade and usury. The LXX. has, οἱ ἐπηρμένοι ἀργυρίῳ, "those who are elated with silver;" St. Jerome, *involuti argento*.

Ver. 12.—The third class which shall be smitten, viz. the profligate and riotous. **I will search Jerusalem with candles** (*lights*). No evil-doer shall escape. The enemy whom God summons to execute his wrath shall leave no corner unsearched where the debauchees hide themselves (comp. Luke xv. 8). Jerome and commentators after him refer to Josephus's account of the last siege of Jerusalem for a parallel to these predicted proceedings of the Chaldeans. Here we read how princes and priests and chieftains were dragged from sewers, and pits, and caves, and tombs, where they had hidden themselves in fear of death, and were mercilessly slain wherever they were found (Josephus, 'Bell. Jud.,' vi. 9). **The men that are settled on their lees;** *i.e.* confirmed, hardened, and inveterate in their evil habits. The metaphor is derived from old wine not racked off, which retains all its flavour and odour, and becomes thick and viscid (see Isa. xxv. 6; Jer. xlviii. 11). The LXX. paraphrases, Τοὺς καταφρονοῦντας ἐπὶ τὰ φυλάγματα αὐτῶν, which Jerome renders, *qui contemnunt custodias suas.* **That say in their heart.** They do not openly scoff at religion, but think within themselves these infidel thoughts. **The Lord will not do good,** etc. Just what God says of idols (Isa. xli. 23). These "fools" (Ps. xiv. 1) deny God's moral government of the world; they will not see the working of Divine providence

in all that happens, but, secure and careless in their worldly prosperity, they assign all events to chance or natural law, placing Jehovah in the same category as the idols worshipped by heathens (comp. Job xxii. 12, etc.; Ps. x. 4, etc.; xciv. 7).

Ver. 13.—**Their goods;** literally, *their strength;* their wealth in which they trusted shall become the prey of the enemy, and thus they shall learn that God ruleth in the affairs of men. **They shall also build houses,** etc. They shall prove in their own case the reality of the punishment threatened in the Law (Lev. xxvi. 32, etc.; Deut. xxviii. 30, 39; comp. Amos v. 11; Micah vi. 15).

Vers. 14—18.—§ 5. *To arouse the self-confident sinners, the prophet here enlarges upon the near approach and terrible nature of this coming judgment.*

Ver. 14.—Having signified the victims of the judgment, Zephaniah recurs to what he had said in ver. 7, and enforces upon his hearers its near approach. **The great day of the Lord** (Joel ii. 1, 11). Even the voice of the day of the Lord. The day is so close at hand, that the sound of its coming can be heard. Some translate, "Hark! the day of Jehovah." **The mighty man shall cry** (*crieth*) **there bitterly.** There, on the battle-field, the hero is panic-stricken, and cries out for fear. The Greek and Latin Versions connect "bitter" with the former clause. Thus the Vulgate, *Vox dies Domini amara;* Septuagint, Φωνὴ ἡμέρας Κυρίου πικρὰ καὶ σκληρὰ τέτακται, "The voice of the day of the Lord is made bitter and harsh."

Ver. 15.—**That day is a day of wrath;** Vulgate, *Dies iræ, dies illa*, words which form the commencement of the famous hymn. The better to describe the terrible nature of the judgment, the prophet crowds together all available expressions of terror and calamity. First, it is a day when God's anger shall blaze forth (Isa. ix. 18). **Of trouble and distress.** In its effects upon sinners (Job xv. 24). **Of wasteness and desolation.** As if things returned to the primeval chaos (Gen. i. 2; comp. Job xxx. 3; xxxviii. 27, where there is a similar combination; see note on Nah. ii. 10). **Of darkness and gloominess** (Joel ii. 2; Amos v. 18, 20). **Of clouds and thick darkness** (Deut. iv. 11; comp. Hab. iii. 11).

Ver. 16.—**A day of the trumpet and alarm.** "Alarm" means "the sound of alarm." Among the Jews trumpets were used to announce the festivals (Numb. xxix. 1), and to give the signal for battle or of the approach of an enemy (Jer. iv. 5, 19; Ezek. xxxiii. 4). Here it is the signal of destruction (Amos ii. 2). **The fenced cities.** The strongest fortresses shall feel the irresistible attack (Micah v. 11). **The high towers.** These are the turrets built at the angles of the walls for the better defence of the city, and to annoy the besiegers (ch. iii. 6). LXX., ἐπὶ τὰς γωνίας τὰς ὑψηλάς, "upon the lofty angles;" Vulgate, *super angulos excelsos.* Others take the words to mean "the battlements" on the walls. Henderson quotes Tacitus's description of the later walls of Jerusalem, "Duos colles immensum editos claudebant muri per artem obliqui aut introrsus sinuati, ut latera oppugnantium ad ictus patescerent" ('Hist.,' v. 11).

Ver. 17.—In this storming of cities and universal ruin, sinners shall perish without hope. **I will bring distress upon men.** I will drive them into the utmost straits (comp. Deut. xxviii. 52, 53). **They shall walk like blind men.** Not knowing where they go in their terror and confusion, seeking a way of escape and finding none (see Deut. xxviii. 29, on which this passage is founded; comp. Job v. 14; Isa. lix. 10). **Because they have sinned,** as shown in vers. 4—12. **Their blood shall be poured out as dust.** The point of comparison is rather in the worthlessness than in the abundance of dust. Bloodshed is as little regarded as dust that is trodden under foot (comp. 2 Kings xiii. 7). The comparison with water is found elsewhere (cf. Ps. lxxix. 3). **Their flesh as the dung.** The verb from the preceding clause may be taken by zeugma with this clause; then the meaning is that their dead bodies are left unburied to rot on the ground (Jer. ix. 22). Or the substantive verb may be supplied (comp. Job xx. 7).

Ver. 18.—**Neither their silver,** etc. They cannot bribe this enemy; their wealth cannot win for them immunity (Isa. xiii. 17; Ezek. vii. 19). **The fire of his jealousy** (ch. iii. 8). The whole earth (for, as we have seen in ch. i. 2, 3, the judgment is universal) shall be punished in the wrath of the Lord, who will not have the honour which is due to him given to any other. **He shall make even a speedy riddance;** more closely, *he shall make an end, yea, a speedy end* (comp. Nah. i. 8; Isa. x. 23, which our text imitates). (For the sudden and unexpected arrival of the day of the Lord, see Luke xvii. 26, etc.)

HOMILETICS.

Vers. 1—3.—*The prophet and his times.* I. HIS PEDIGREE. (Ver. 1.) This is the solitary instance in which the lineage of a prophet is traced back in Scripture four generations. The reason would seem to be in order to indicate his relationship to Hezekiah, the pious King of Judah. Note: 1. The honour connected with a pious ancestry. 2. The perpetuity of the influence of a good life.

II. HIS AUTHORITY. This was not derived from his royal descent, but from his being under the inspiration of the Almighty. "The word of the Lord which came unto Zephaniah" (ver. 1). The words of those high in rank are often invested with a value they do not intrinsically possess, but the utterances of this prince of Judah claim our regard as the words of one taught by the Spirit of God.

III. HIS AGE. He prophesied "in the days of Josiah the son of Amon, King of Judah" (ver. 1). Unhappily, the reforms instituted by the good Hezekiah had not been sustained during the succeeding reigns, so that the nation, both politically and spiritually, had relapsed into a thoroughly corrupt state by the time that the boy-king Josiah came to the throne. Consecrated from early life to the service of the true God, the youthful monarch devoted the energies of his early manhood to the rooting out of idolatry from his land, and to the restoration and re-establishment of the temple and its services. Zephaniah, doubtless, prophesied shortly before this work of reformation commenced, and the influence of his faithful ministry would be helpful to the royal reformer in carrying out his noble work.

IV. THE CHARACTER OF THE MESSAGE WITH WHICH HE WAS DIVINELY ENTRUSTED. This was: 1. Very dark. He was, indeed, a messenger of judgment; the solemn responsibility devolved upon him of announcing "the terrors of the Lord" (vers. 2, 3). The anger of the Lord was kindled against Judah, and though to be delayed until Josiah should be gathered to his rest, it must at length fall (2 Kings xxii. 3—20; xxiiii. 21—27; 2 Chron. xxxiv. 8—33; xxxv. 1—19). 2. Very comprehensive. His predictions of judgment were not limited to Judah, but were directed also against heathen nations—Philistia, Moab and Ammon, Ethiopia, and Assyria (ch. ii.). 3. Yet withal not lacking encouragement; for whilst he told of impending judgment, he called to repentance, unfolded the mercy of the Most High, and indicated how that even the darkest events impending would be overruled for the well-being of the race.

Vers. 4, 5.—*A corrupt priesthood and its pernicious influence.* The work of reformation carried on by Hezekiah was unquestionably great, yet it cannot be correctly described as having been complete. The weeds of idolatry were extensively destroyed by him, yet many roots remained, and, springing up, bore a fresh harvest of evil in the succeeding reigns, so that the godly Josiah found himself confronted with a powerful remnant of idolatry. In dealing with this he must have been materially assisted by the bold denunciations of Zephaniah; and these were fittingly directed first of all against the corrupt priesthood (ver. 4). We have here—

I. AN EXALTED OFFICE. That of the priest. The Jewish priesthood was of Divine appointment, chosen and set apart by God to the most sacred duties, and the whole being typical of the character and mission of the great High Priest who was in the fulness of time to appear. And whilst in his work these functions received their consummation, and the Aaronic priesthood passed away, yet Christ when he ascended upon high "gave gifts unto men," etc. (Eph. iv. 11—13). The work of the ministry is scriptural, noble, honourable. Those divinely called to it have to teach the truth of God, to seek to win men to righteousness and heaven, to lead worshippers to the very throne of the Eternal, to direct the activities of the Church, and to shepherd the flock of Christ. The work is "a good work" (1 Tim. iii. 1), and faithfully to do it is to secure present and eternal honour.

II. THIS HIGH OFFICE CORRUPTED. Those here styled "the Chemarims" were Jewish priests, some of whom were of the tribe of Levi, and others chosen from the lowest of the people, who sold themselves to the faithless kings of Judah, and at their bidding offered polluted rites at the altar of God, and joined with the heathen priests in serving the altars of Baal (2 Kings xxiii. 5; Hos. x. 5). The highest and holiest functions may still be perverted. This is the case when motives other than those of love to God and to the souls of men impel to engaging in ministerial service, or when in rendering such service any compromise is made with error and sin.

III. THE PERNICIOUS INFLUENCE RESULTING FROM SUCH CORRUPTION. "Like priests, like people." Hence, immediately following the allusion to the corrupt priesthood, reference is made to the people as worshipping the host of heaven upon the house-tops (ver. 5). Luther says, "The chemarim produced an erroneous opinion among the people that they were of all others the most assiduous in religion and Divine worship," and if so, their influence over the people would be proportionately increased through their zeal, and no wonder that, following these false guides, idolatry and irreligion so widely prevailed in the land. A faithless and disloyal ministry in any age must prove a blight and a curse.

IV. THE DIVINE JUDGMENTS PRONOUNCED AGAINST THESE FAITHLESS ONES AND THEIR ADHERENTS. Their followers should be visited with retribution, whilst as to these false leaders, they should be "cut off," and their very name be blotted out. Their fate speaks silently and solemnly to all who claim to be ministers of God. His charge to all such is, "Son of man, I have made thee a watchman," etc. (Ezek. ii. 17—21), and this is his promise attached to fidelity, "Be thou faithful unto death, and I will give thee a crown of life" (Rev. ii. 10).

Ver. 5.—*Divided service.* "That worship and that swear by the Lord, and that swear by Malcham." It is not two distinct classes of persons that are here referred to, but one and the same class. The allusion is to such as sought to be identified both with the service of God and the service of Malcham. It is an example of divided service that is here presented to us, an illustration of men attempting that which the great Teacher in a later age declared to be altogether impracticable, even to serve two masters.

I. AN IMPOSSIBLE TASK ATTEMPTED, AND RESULTING IN FAILURE AND SHAME. 1. *The task.* Malcham, or Malkâm, or "king," was a term used for Baal, and who is thus described on the Phœnician inscriptions. The times being corrupt, and idolatry being popular in the land, there were those who, from considerations of policy and interest doubtless, attempted to combine the worship of Jehovah and that of Baal, or Malcham. The same spirit prevails still; men desire to serve both God and mammon, and too much resemble those who were "willing to serve God so that they did not offend the devil." 2. The task is an impossible one; it cannot be accomplished. (1) Scripture proclaims this to be an impossibility (Josh. xxiv. 19—25; 1 Sam. vii. 3; 1 Kings xviii. 21; Ezek. xx. 39). (2) Proverbial sayings of different nations recognize this. "Lay not two saddles on one horse;" "A true subject serves not two sovereigns;" "Ye cannot go east and west at the same time." (3) Men do not attempt this in the ordinary affairs of life, but concentrate their energies upon one purpose. (4) One plain reason accounts for the impossibility, viz. the service of God and that of Malcham, or mammon, or worldliness, are so thoroughly opposite in their nature that there can be no union. "You cannot be heavenly and worldly too. If I am heavenly I sanctify the world, and if I am worldly I debase the heavenly. You are therefore one of two things, and there is no mixture in your character." 3. To attempt it can only result in defeat and disgrace. They who sought to worship God and Malcham were to be "cut off." Their conduct met with the Divine displeasure, and was followed by such manifestations of his disapproval as filled them with confusion and shame. Other instances: Meroz (Judg. v. 23); the young ruler (Matt. xix. 22); Peter in the high priest's hall (Matt. xxvi. 75).

II. A MORE EXCELLENT COURSE OF ACTION. 1. Weigh well the respective claims of God and of Malcham, Christ and mammon. This is the way in which men wisely act in reference to temporal things, and they should also act thus in reference to religion. 2. Yield yourself faithfully, wholly, and irrevocably to the master whose claim you feel to be the strongest. "If the Lord be God, follow him; but if Baal, then follow him." Multitudes, as they have thus reflected upon the claims of Christ, have felt these to be paramount; as they have thought of his bright and beautiful teaching, his wonderful, self-sacrificing human life, and as, gathering at Calvary, they have contemplated his humiliation unto death, they have been constrained to acknowledge his undoubted right to their loving confidence and entire service, and, yielding themselves up to him without reservation, have found in so doing happiness and peace.

Ver. 6.—*The sin of apostasy.* "And them that are turned back from the Lord." Some biblical expositors regard the whole of this verse as referring to one class, even to such as are utterly indifferent and unconcerned in reference to God's claims; whilst other commentators regard this class as referred to in the latter part of the verse, and view the expression, "And them that are turned back from the Lord" as an allusion to those who, having professed loyalty to God and his truth, had allowed themselves to be drawn away and to walk no more with him. Concerning this sin of apostasy, note—

I. THE CAUSES WHICH HAVE RESULTED IN MEN FALLING INTO THIS SIN. 1. *Temporal success.* Favourable progress in the affairs of this life has proved the ruin of many spiritually. They have set their hearts upon their treasures, and have bowed down before the golden image (Deut. xxxii. 15). 2. *Temporal adversity.* "The cares of life," as well as "the deceitfulness of riches," will often choke the Word. The very troubles which should unite men to God by a closer bond (for if all else fail, *he* abides) have been permitted to drive them away from the Source of consolation and help. 3. *Mental difficulties.* Forgetful that Truth is boundless and immeasurable, and that after the most earnest research there must remain profound depths yet to be explored, the inquirer has wanted to understand fully **now**, and, failing in this, has, through pride of intellect, brought himself into a state of mental unsettledness, so that even the plainly declared truths of revelation have lost their charm to him, and he has taken shelter in unbelief. 4. *Worldliness;* by which term is meant love of the untrue and unsubstantial; regard only for the outward, the transient, the unreal; the world becoming invested with ruling power over the man, instead of the man reigning over it. So Paul wrote of Demas, that he had yielded here (2 Tim. iv. 10).

II. THE INTENSE SADNESS ASSOCIATED WITH THIS COURSE OF ACTION. 1. It involves the violation of the most solemn and sacred vows. 2. It is attended by separation from the most holy and helpful associations. 3. It hinders the progress of the cause of God. 4. It grieves and dishonours the Lord.

III. THE SPIRIT WHICH SHOULD BE CHERISHED BY THE FAITHFUL IN REFERENCE TO THOSE THAT ARE TURNED BACK FROM THE LORD. 1. There must be no palliation of their sin. Zephaniah uttered burning words of condemnation with reference to these transgressors, and we shall not really help such by making light of their sin. 2. Yet we should earnestly seek their recovery. We should endeavour by kindness and gentleness to restore these erring ones. Although they may be darkly stained by sin, they are still our brethren. Whilst they have stumbled and fallen in the path, it is in very weakness that we ourselves have trodden it. The tender, loving word may perchance win them back to holiness and to God. In voyaging, some vessels are completely lost,—they go down through the storm, and utterly perish; others arrive at the port, but with masts broken and sails torn through battling with wind and wave; whilst others outride every storm, and with full sail enter the destined haven. Thus was it, one has pointed out, with the three associates of St. Paul who are specially referred to in 2 Tim. iv.; and thus is it in the spiritual life. Demas, wrecked; Mark, overpowered by adverse gales and seemingly crushed, yet rising again and reaching the harbour at length in safety; but Luke, "the beloved physician," holding peacefully and tranquilly on his course all through, and having ministered to him an abundant entrance to the heavenly kingdom (see paper by Dr. Maclaren, *Good Words*, 1877, p. 595). May our course be as the last-named of these disciples, unmarked either by failure or even by temporary estrangement, but being steadfast and immovable! May no place be found by us amongst those "that have turned themselves back from following after the Lord"! May we, escaping the perils of the sea of life—all its shoals and quicksands—reach at last the haven of eternal rest and felicity!

Ver. 6.—*The sin of indifference.* "And those that have not sought the Lord, nor inquired for him." Various classes of transgressors are alluded to in these verses (vers. 4—6). The corrupt priests and their followers, those dividing their allegiance between God and Baal, the backsliders in heart, are all spoken of in brief and forcible sentences. And now, in the expression before us, allusion is made to the unconcerned and indifferent, and who are described as "those that have not sought the Lord, nor inquired for him." This class is, in some respects, the most hopeless of all. An idolater is interested in worship, and may become convinced of his folly in rendering this to "the work of his own hands." The divided heart is partially directed to God, and may be won over to complete loyalty. The backslider may remember the joys he has forfeited, and, by the sacred memories of the past, which even his estrangement cannot obliterate, may be constrained to return unto the Lord. But in proportion as a man is callous and indifferent to the claims of God, he places himself outside the circle within which holy and gracious influences operate. Less fear need be cherished of the pernicious influence of the scepticism of the age than of the fatality attendant upon the spirit of indifferentism to God and his claims which so widely prevails. Observe—

I. THE PREVALENCE OF THIS SPIRIT MAY BE ACCOUNTED FOR. 1. The reason of it is to be found in the fact of *possession*. Nothing is more calculated to lead a man to be indifferent in reference to higher claims than to find property increasing in his hands. The consciousness of independence, the sense of self-sufficiency, and the feeling of comfort, all tend to lead him to think and act as though he had "need of nothing." "A certain man made a great supper, and bade many." One thus invited said, "I have bought a piece of ground, and I must needs go and see it: I pray thee have me excused" (Luke xiv. 16—18). See well to it, ye who have secured the possessions of earth, that ye do not, through the influence of these material things, come short of participation in the true festal joys. 2. Another reason lies in the fact of *familiarity*. Is it not so that our very familiarity with anything is likely to lead us in a sense to be somewhat indifferent to it? A walk may appear long, and may be long; but take it frequently, and the distance will appear to lessen, and in time it will cease to affect you. View constantly the scenery of some charming dale, and however much of quiet enjoyment you will get out of it perpetually if you are a lover of natural beauty, yet you will not be so enthusiastic as a stranger who gazes upon it for the first time. And much of the prevailing indifference concerning God and his truth may be traced to this cause. When King Clovis heard for the first time the story of Calvary, it is said he grew excited, and cried out, "I wish I'd been there with my Franks; I'd soon have settled those Jews!" The novelty charmed the rude king; but men all around us are so familiar with the story that they are not moved thus; and multitudes are so unconcerned respecting these great themes as that they may be described as "those who have not sought the Lord, nor inquired for him." 3. This indifference may also be traced to *custom*. The power of habit is very strong. Men became confirmed in their ways (Jer. xiii. 23).

II. THEY WHO CHERISH THIS SPIRIT RUN THE RISK OF INCURRING INFINITE LOSS. Loss may be incurred unintentionally and through indifference and neglect. You neglect to insure your property, and perchance a fire breaks out and destroys it, and you find yourself thrown back for years to come; or you neglect your health and fail to heed the first symptoms of disease, and it may end in the disease gaining too firm a hold for it ever to be eradicated ; and so spiritual and eternal honour may be forfeited, not wilfully, but through indifference and unconcern.

III. HENCE THE SUPREME VALUE OF THE PRESENT TIME WITH ITS OPPORTUNITIES. Our great dramatist has it—

> "There is a tide in the affairs of men,
> Which, taken at the flood, leads on to fortune
> Omitted, all the voyage of their life
> Is bound in shallows and in miseries."

And it is so that there is a tide in the spiritual affairs of men. Human feelings, sentiments, desires, ebb and flow like the sea; and there are seasons in which this tide sets towards piety ; and such a season, if only improved, "is the accepted time," "the day of salvation." Use it, and it shall not be said that you belong to those "that have not sought the Lord," etc. (ver. 6).

Vers. 7—18.—"*The day of the Lord.*" The reader of this brief book of Scripture, forming his conclusions from this opening chapter exclusively, is likely to get a very false impression respecting the spirit and views of the writer. The chapter deals entirely with sin and its punishment, and, taken alone and apart, conveys undoubtedly a very strong conviction as to the terribleness and severity of God. The seer seems to linger in thought upon the coming judgments, and to reiterate these in every possible form, and even to exult in the retributions which should at length fall upon the sinful nation. His "song" appears to be altogether "of judgment." That we may rightly estimate, however, his spirit and teaching, we should remember : 1. That the great and solemn fact of Divine retribution for sin ought not to be ignored. Whatever theory may be held respecting the doom and destiny of the impenitent, the fact remains stamped on every page of the volume of revelation, in Old and New Testament alike, that sin shall result in chastisement, that man shall reap as he sows. The prophet in this respect is in perfect agreement with all the Bible writers. 2. That the prevailing corruption of his times necessitated a strong insistance, on the part of the prophets, upon the approaching judgments on account of national transgression ; and this also was in harmony with the character of the dispensation. 3. That whilst sternly declaring the Divine punishment to fall upon the nation because of its sinfulness, Zephaniah also, as he proceeded, dwelt very frequently upon the Divine intention to purify through chastisement, and pointed out the gracious purpose of the Most High by means of coming tribulations to sanctify and save. His "song" was "of mercy" as well as "of judgment." Here, however (vers. 7—18), he dwells specially upon the Divine judgments, and points to "the great and notable day of the Lord," "the day of vengeance of our God." These judgments he sets forth—

I. IN STRIKING SYMBOL. (Ver. 7.) Sacrifice was well understood in Jerusalem. Offerings were offered on Jewish altars to the true God, and, when the people had become corrupt, also to Baal. Jehovah now declared by his holy prophet that the people, having proved faithless, should themselves be sacrificed ; they should be the victims, and the heathen who should effect their overthrow would, in so doing, be consecrated to his service. This symbol is used also in the same sense by other prophets (Isa. xxxiv. 6 ; Jer. xlvi. 10 ; Ezek. xxxix. 17).

II. IN VIVID DESCRIPTION. (Vers. 10—13.) The prophet witnesses in imagination, and describes with realistic power, the coming siege and destruction of the city by the Chaldeans. He sees "the fish gate" (ver. 10), the weakest part, assaulted, and hears a loud cry (ver. 10), telling that it has fallen, and that the invaders have gained admission ; whilst "the sound of wailing" coming from the inhabitants of the lower part of the city ("the second," ver. 10) intimates that, having gained an entrance, the foe is carrying on the work of destruction. "A great crashing from the hills" (ver. 10) indicates that the invaders, with their engines of war, are striking against the walls and forts. And as the work of invasion proceeds, he marks how it becomes concentrated upon the mercantile part of the city, "El-Wad," or "The Valley" (called by Zephaniah "Maktesh," or "The Mortar," ver. 11); the merchants being destroyed, their "silver" and "their goods" becoming "a booty;" their houses rendered a desolation, and their vineyards laid waste (vers. 11, 13).

III. IN MOURNFUL SONG. (Vers. 14—18.) Concerning this song it has been well said, "There are no grander verses, none more sombre and tragic, none in which terror is more picturesque, in the literature of the world. They call for little comment. They are to be felt rather than critically analyzed and explained" (Cox, in 'Bible Educator,' vol. ii. 257). The expression, "the day of the Lord," so frequently used in this chapter, is employed in the New Testament with reference to the final judgment (Jude 6). That day will be a day of wrath to those who persist in working unrighteousness (Rom. ii. 8, 9). "Knowing therefore the terror of the Lord, we persuade men" (2 Cor. v. 11); "Be ye reconciled to God" (2 Cor. v. 20).

Vers. 8, 9.—"*No respect of persons.*" I. SOCIETY IS COMPOSED OF VARIOUS GRADES. There are royal personages, "the princes" and "the king's children" (ver. 8); there are "the merchant people" (ver. 11); there are masters and servants (ver. 9); there are nobles in affluence, who can clothe themselves with "strange apparel" (ver. 8); and there are the poor and needy. Nor would it be advantageous to society to break down these distinctions. An equal division of wealth and rank would be found both impracticable and undesirable. What is needed is the cultivation, amongst all sections of society, of the spirit of regard and good will. If the injunctions of God's Word were heeded, wrong-doing would cease, the ruler would not oppress the subject, the employer would not act unjustly towards the employed, nor the employed refuse to abide by just regulations. It is not by breaking down the social distinctions of society that the existing wrongs are to be redressed, but by a wider diffusion amongst all classes of the pure teachings of the religion of peace and love. II. IN EACH OF THESE GRADES THE WORKING OF EVIL MAY BE TRACED. In vers. 8 and 9 this is indicated. Princes, nobles, retainers, menials, alike corrupted their way. Pride in bearing and in attire, the emulating of the vices of the heathen, injustice and wrong, "violence and deceit," prevailed amongst all classes. Sin is a disease, the contagious influence of which spreads through society at large, causing sickliness and ending in moral death. It has been fittingly compared to the Egyptian plague of frogs, for as these coming up from the river afflicted king, nobles, magicians, and people alike, so sin in its varied forms and hurtful influence has been felt by all. III. THE DIVINE JUDGMENTS ON ACCOUNT OF SIN WILL BE RIGHTEOUSLY AWARDED AND WITHOUT PARTIALITY. Princes, nobles, merchants, servants, will be reckoned with according to their works (vers. 8, 9). With God there is "no respect of persons." Here social position and influence screen wrong-doers at times from reaping the just consequences of their evil-doing. However justly the administrators of human law may desire to act, and to remove the reproach that "there is one law for the rich and another for the poor," the fact remains that the former class, when pursued by the hand of justice, can command assistance such as is denied to the latter, and the employment of which has often moderated the sentence inflicted. But the "righteous Lord, who loveth righteousness," will "give to every man according as his work shall be."

Ver. 12.—*Searching Jerusalem with candles.* Jerusalem here stands for the nation at large. The whole land was corrupt and was to fall, and the prophet singles out Jerusalem as being the centre of influence, but his remarks apply to the people generally. We have suggested here— I. PROSPERITY IN WORLDLY AFFAIRS RESULTING IN FALSE SECURITY. Success in secular matters is to be desired. Rightly improved, such prosperity becomes a source of good to its possessors, and through them to their fellow-men. The danger lies in the temptation to pride and self-sufficiency, leading men to "think more highly of themselves than they ought to think." In proportion as men grow rich are they in peril of feeling themselves to be "full," and to "have need of nothing."

II. FALSE SECURITY LEADING TO INDIFFERENCE TO GOD AND HIS CLAIMS. Being "at ease," "their eyes standing out with fatness," "having more than heart could wish," they "lightly esteem" the Lord and ignore his claims. They are not atheists in theory, but they are so in practice; they do not trouble to deny the Divine existence, but they live in total disregard of him to whom they are indebted for all that they possess; they say in their hearts, "The Lord will not do good, neither will he do evil" (ver. 12).

III. INDIFFERENCE TO GOD AND HIS CLAIMS FOLLOWED BY MORAL CORRUPTION AND INIQUITY. Those acting thus are compared to wine that is settled on its lees. "The lees are the refuse of the wine, yet stored up with it, and the wine, unremoved, rests as it were upon them. So do men of ease rest in things defiled and defiling." Taking this course, Judah and the inhabitants of Jerusalem had become corrupt and full of iniquity.

IV. MORAL CORRUPTION AND INIQUITY ABOUT TO BE BROUGHT TO LIGHT THROUGH THE DIVINE SCRUTINY. "And it shall come to pass at that time, that I will search Jerusalem with candles" (ver. 12). In the day of terrors drawing near, "he would go through the city, making diligent search, trying house by house, man by man. As the vintner goes through his cellar, torch in hand; or as the head of the household, taper in hand, searches every nook and corner of his house before Passover, lest any morsel of leaven should be hidden in it; so Jehovah would search Jerusalem *with candles*, hunting the evil out of every dark nook in which they have concealed themselves, suffering none to escape."

V. INIQUITY THUS DIVINELY REVEALED WILL ASSUREDLY BE FOLLOWED BY DIVINE RETRIBUTION. "And I will punish," etc. (ver. 12). Sin cannot go unpunished. The Divine revelation of sin is with a view to this retribution, and serves to vindicate the rectitude of the Most High.

Learn: 1. To guard against the spirit of self-sufficiency and worldliness engendered of ease and luxury. 2. To scrutinize your own conduct, using faithfully with a view to this the torch of (1) conscience, (2) of God's holy Word, (3) and of the perfect example presented in the life of "the Man Christ Jesus." 3. To pray earnestly for deliverance from all that is evil, and to be led into right paths, and so to be preserved from being at last condemned with the world. "Search me, O God, and know my heart," etc. (Ps. cxxxix. 23, 24).

HOMILIES BY VARIOUS AUTHORS

Vers. 1—6.—*A prophet of doom.* I. THE MEANING OF HIS NAME. Zephaniah, "One whom Jehovah hides." Hiding in the day of calamity a blessing promised to them that fear God (Ps. xxxi. 19, 20), who are therefore styled God's hidden ones (Ps. lxxxiii. 4), and may confidently reckon upon God's extending to them his protecting care in the midst of peril (Ps. xxvii. 5), yea, may even boldly flee unto him to hide them (Ps. cxliii. 9).

II. THE DIGNITY OF HIS PERSON. The scion of a kingly house, "the son of Cushi, the son of Gedaliah, the son of Amariah, the son of Hezekiah." Mentioned here, not because they had been prophets, but probably because they had been celebrated persons, perhaps good men, these ancestors of Zephaniah—three of them, like himself, with Jehovah in his name—may have been introduced to show that the prophet, while descended from the good King Hezekiah, belonged to a different branch of the family from Manasseh and Amon; proceeded from the line in which Hezekiah's goodness was transmitted, and thus had more than royal blood in his veins (not always an advantage) —hereditary piety in his soul.

III. THE TIME OF HIS APPEARING. 1. *The age fixed.* (1) "The days of Josiah, the son of Amon, King of Judah;" *i.e.* not before B.C. 640, when Josiah began to reign. (2) Before the fall of Nineveh (ch. ii. 13), which took place in B.C. 625. (3) Probably after Josiah's reformation had begun and before it was completed, since the prophet speaks of a "remnant of Baal" as existing at the time when he began to prophesy. (4) Hence the date of Zephaniah may be placed between Josiah's twelfth and eighteenth years, or between B.C. 628—622 (Hitzig, Keil, and Delitzsch), though by some interpreters (Ewald, Havernick, Pusey) it has been fixed earlier--to wit, prior to Josiah's twelfth year. 2. *Its character declared.* (1) Generally, as regards the whole land of Judah, an age of widely spread, deeply seated, and well-nigh incurable wickedness, of deplorable religious apostasy, of intensely debasing idolatry, of shameless hypocrisy, and of gross worldliness and indifference to Divine things (ver. 4). (2) Particularly, as regards Jerusalem, an age of rebellion, disobedience, irreligion, prayerlessness, unbelief, violence, treachery, desecration of Jehovah's sanctuary, insensibility to correction, and deep-seated immorality (ch. iii. 1—4), with all of which the metropolis and its inhabitants were chargeable (cf. Jer. v.; vi.).

IV. THE SOURCE OF HIS INSPIRATION. "The word of Jehovah." Whether this came to him by direct revelation through voice (Jer. i. 4) or vision (Isa. i. 1; ii. 1), or indirectly by meditation on the moral and political condition of his countrymen as well as on the character of Jehovah and the laws of righteousness by which he governs the universe, is not said and need not be inquired into. It suffices to know that the prophet claimed for his message that it had been expressly given him—put into his heart and mouth—by Jehovah; while his predictions certainly were such as could not have been announced without the aid of Divine inspiration.

V. THE BURDEN OF HIS PROPHECY. Judgment. 1. *Divine.* The instrument is not mentioned; the first cause alone is placed in the foreground—"I will utterly consume;" "I will cut off;" "I will stretch out mine hand." The present-day tendency is to set God in the background, if not to deny his agency altogether, alike in the production of material phenomena and in the superintendence of the social, moral, and political worlds, and to concentrate attention principally, if not exclusively, upon what are merely God's instruments. The prophet's way of looking at men and things accorded more with sound philosophy and true science, not to say sincere religion, than the practice prevailing in many so-called enlightened circles to-day. 2. *Universal.* The judgment should embrace the wide earth. "All"—"man and beast, the fowls of the heaven, and the fishes of the sea, the stumbling-blocks and the wicked"—should be arraigned at Jehovah's bar. If the language pointed not to a general judgment of men and nations at the end of the world, it at least emphasized the thought that no part of the world, no age or nation, could escape the ordeal of appearing before Heaven's tribunal or elude the grasp of Divine retribution. The terms in which Jehovah declares his purpose to visit the wicked with destruction are such as to show that the complete fulfilment of the prophecy can only be reached in the great and terrible day of the Lord at the close of time (cf. Isa. xxiv. 1—23). 3. *Particular.* While enclosing the whole world in its sweep, the threatened judgment should fall with a special stroke upon Judah and the inhabitants of Jerusalem—as it were beginning with the house of God (1 Pet. iv. 17). That the instruments of judgment would be the Scythians of whom Herodotus (i. 15, 103, 106; iv. 10, 12) speaks as having invaded Upper and Higher Asia (Hitzig, Ewald, Bertheau), is not supported by sufficient evidence, whilst the fact that neither Herodotus nor the Old Testament reports any conquest of Jerusalem by them seems decisive against their being considered the executors of Jehovah's wrath. The agents actually employed were the Chaldeans (2 Kings xxv. 9), though it was not Zephaniah's purpose to indicate by whom the judgments should be carried out. 4. *Complete.* Thorough-going; upon both the world in general and Judah in particular. "I will utterly consume all from off the face of the ground, saith Jehovah." (1) As regards the world, the destruction should be as wide-sweeping as had been that of the Deluge (Gen. vii. 21). (2) As regards Judah and Jerusalem, the purgation as effective. "The remnant of Baal should be cut off," *i.e.* root and branch extirpated, or the work of extirpation, if already begun, should be carried forward till not a vestige of the hated idol-worship should be seen. (*a*) First, the idolatrous priests of both kinds should be swept away—the Chemarim, or "the priests whom the kings of Judah had ordained to burn incense in the high places in the cities of Judah and in the places round about Jerusalem" (2 Kings xxiii. 5; Hos. x. 5); and the priests, not "the idolatrous priests in the stricter sense" (Keil), but the unworthy priests of Jehovah who had either secretly or openly favoured the prevailing Baal-worship (Fausset, Farrar). (*b*) Next, the idol-worshippers of both kinds should be cut off—the thorough-paced devotees of the heathen cultus, who worshipped the host of heaven upon the house-tops, and the temporizers who tried to combine the worship of Jehovah with that of Baal, offering oaths of allegiance partly to Jehovah and partly to their king, *i.e.* Baal. (c) And finally, apostates and open despisers of the Jehovah-religion should be punished—those who had turned back from serving Jehovah, and those who had never served him at all (ver. 6).

Learn : 1. The value of an honoured and pious ancestry. 2. The light the Word of God (contained in Scripture) can cast upon the future. 3. The certainty of a day of judgment for men and nations. 4. The impossibility of eluding the just judgment of God. 5. The inevitable ruin of them who will not serve God. 6. The impossibility of trying to serve God and idols. 7. The danger of neglecting religion hardly less than that of apostatizing from it.—T. W.

Vers. 7—13.—*" The day of the Lord's sacrifice."* I. THE INTENDED VICTIMS. 1. *Their persons catalogued.* (1) The royal household. Josiah exempted on account of his piety (2 Kings xxii. 19, 20; 2 Chron. xxxiv. 27, 28)—a testimony at once to Divine faithfulness and to the superior advantage of godliness (Ps. xvii. 7; xci. 9, 10; 2 Pet. ii. 9 ; Rev. iii. 10). But included were the princes, or " the heads of the tribes and families who naturally filled the higher offices of state " (Keil); the king's sons, either Josiah's children, then quite young, Jehoiakim being six and Jehoahaz four years of age, and Zedekiah not yet born; or Josiah's brothers and uncles who were also king's sons ; and the superior servants of the palace, who are probably referred to as those who " leap over the threshold and fill their masters' house with violence and deceit " (ver. 9). (2) The rich merchants of Jerusalem. Described by their residence, their occupation, their prosperity, and their doom. The part of the city in which they were located, named most likely by the prophet himself, Maktesh, or " The Mortar," was " most probably the depression which ran down between Acra on the west, and Bezetha and Moriah on the east, as far as the fountain of Shiloah " (Keil), " the cheese-makers' valley " of Josephus, styled by the present-day inhabitants El-Wâd, or " The Valley." There they traded, lending money upon usury, and were called by the prophet " people of Canaan," because of their resemblance to Canaanitish or Phœnician merchants. With such success had they carried on their business, that they were " laden with silver." Yet were they doomed to be destroyed, ground to pieces, and bruised to death, by the Babylonian conquerors, like corn in a mortar when the pestle descendeth. (3) The irreligious debauchees and rioters of the metropolis generally. Characterized as persons who had settled on their lees, and said in their hearts, " The Lord will not do good, neither will he do evil." (For an explanation of the figure, consult Exposition, and see homily on ver. 12.) The language pointed to those whose material prosperity had been their moral and religious ruin, who, having grown wealthy and luxurious, had also become atheistical at least in practice, saying in their hearts, and acting as if they believed, that either there was no God at all, or if there were, that he was perfectly indifferent to their characters and conduct—a form of infidelity that has seldom lacked representatives among foolish and ungodly men (Job xxii. 12—14; Ps. x. 4 ; xiv. 1, xciv. 6, 7). 2. *Their sins specified.* (1) Of the royal household, two—wearing foreign clothes and leaping over the threshold. The *former* referred to the custom of copying the dress and with that the manners and luxuries of heathen peoples, and in particular, in Josiah's time, of Egypt and Assyria, or Babylon. Among the Egyptians " the dress of the king was most gorgeous, consisting of robes of the most beautiful stuffs and the richest ornaments " (Budge, 'Dwellers on the Nile,' p. 181). Nahum (ii. 3) describes the Assyrian soldiery as arrayed "in scarlet; " while Ezekiel (xxiii. 12, 15) depicts the Assyrian warriors as "clothed most gorgeously," and speaks of the Chaldeans as "girded with girdles upon their loins, exceeding in dyed attire upon their heads." Of course, the sin against which the prophet inveighed was not the mere adoption of Egyptian, Assyrian, or Babylonian habiliments, but the inclination to look to and lean upon, to follow after and copy, these nations in their luxuries and idolatries rather than to remain faithful to Jehovah's Law and worship, which the imitation of their dress revealed. Clothes, according to Carlyle ('Sartor Resartus,' i. 1), are " the vestural tissue which man's soul wears as its outmost wrappage and overall, wherein his whole other tissues are included and screened, his whole faculties work, his whole self lives, moves, and has its being." Hence a person's **dress is** no mean indication of a person's inner self. " Outward dress," says Pusey, "always betokens the inward mind, and in its turn acts upon it." In Isaiah's time the Jerusalem ladies were distinguished for gay attire and wanton hearts (Isa. iii. 16—23). Peter (1 Epist. iii. 3) exhorts Christian women to adorn themselves, "not with that outward adorning of plaiting the hair, and of wearing of gold, or of putting on of apparel, but with the ornament of a meek and quiet spirit." The *latter* of the two sins charged against the royal household, that of leaping over the threshold, is believed (Calvin, Keil, Ewald, Pusey, Farrar) to allude, not to the custom of leaping over the threshold of the king's palace (Hitzig) in imitation of Dagon's priests, who, when they entered their idol's temple in Ashdod, trode not upon its threshold (1 Sam. v. 5); but to the practice, observed probably by "dishonourable servants of the king," of intruding into other people's houses in order to deprive them of their property through violence and fraud, and with the spoils so obtained to enrich the king, whose dependants they were, and whose favour they desired to retain. Should this interpretation be correct, it suggests useful thoughts about the distribution of guilt, or the mutual responsibility of masters and servants for each other's evil deeds. If the king's servants merely carried out the orders of their royal master, they were no less criminal in Heaven's sight than he; if they acted on their own motion, the king who profited by their plunder became a partner of their guilt. (2) Of the merchants, also two—avarice and usury. Had they been merely successful traders who had prospered through honest dealing, they had not been condemned; but they were "laden with silver," acquired through nefarious practices such as deceit and usury. Wealth honourably obtained is no offence against Heaven, and, if righteously employed, may contribute to the happiness and influence of both the individual possessor and the community of which he is a member; riches heaped up by wicked arts are a curse to those who have them, and often go as they have come by violence and fraud. To "provide things honest in the sight of all men" (Rom. xii. 17) should be the aim of all, but especially of Christians. "On the bells of the horses of trade and commerce should be, Holiness unto the Lord" (Zech. xiv. 20). Happy the nation "whose traffickers are the honourable of the earth" (Isa. xxiii. 8). (3) Of the debauchees and rioters, two—self-indulgence and infidelity. "Settled upon their lees," they abandoned themselves to the gratification of their sinful desires and corrupt inclinations, closed their minds and hearts against better things, and proceeded to daring and presumptuous unbelief, denying the Divine providence if not challenging the Divine existence. All sin tends to lead the soul away from God, to cause it first to shut out thoughts of God, and finally to conclude that God has ceased to be.

3. *Their punishments proclaimed.* (1) The sinners of the royal house would be called to account for their iniquities. Though God seemed to be at a distance from them, like a man upon a far journey, he would return and visit upon them the evil deeds of which they had been guilty. Nations no more than individuals, and persons in high station no more than persons in low, can escape the just judgment of God (Rom. ii. 3). (2) The merchants would be despoiled of their unjust gains (Isa. xxxiii. 1), and themselves overwhelmed with ruin (Jer. xvii. 11). If good men are sometimes deprived of wealth at a stroke, as Job was, and thus seem to have no advantage above their wicked neighbours, they are never, as these are, utterly undone by the loss of material possessions. In the fall of their houses they do not themselves perish, but find in God a Portion larger, more satisfying and secure, than their silver or gold (Hab. iii. 17, 18). (3) The debauchees and rioters would be dragged forth from their darkest retreats and requited for their sensuality and unbelief. "The same diligence which Eternal Wisdom used *to seek and to save that which was lost, lighting a candle and searching diligently* till it find each lost piece of silver, the same shall Almighty God use that no hardened sinner shall escape" (Pusey).

II. THE OFFICIATING PRIESTS. 1. *Jehovah himself.* "I will punish;" "I will punish;" "I will search;" and "I will punish," saith the Lord. Whatever subordinate agents or secondary causes may be employed to inflict Divine vengeance upon rebellious nations and wicked men, the hand that directs these agents and wields these causes is God's. He is "the Judge of all the earth" (Gen. xviii. 25), and "shall judge the people righteously" (Ps. lxvii. 4), rendering to every man "according to his work" (Ps. lxii. 11). He "shall bring every work into judgment, with every secret thing, whether it be good or whether it be evil" (Eccles. xii. 14). "He hath appointed a day in which he will judge the world" (Acts xvii. 31). 2. *Jehovah's ministers.* Described as his called and sanctified ones; *i.e.* not personally holy, but specially consecrated for the **work** to which they were appointed. (1) In the case under consideration these were to be the Chaldean armies, which in little more than thirty years were to fall upon Jerusalem, and pour out upon it the vials of Jehovah's wrath (2 Chron. xxxvi. 16, 17). (2) In the world generally the events of his providence are the instruments selected for the execution of his victims (Ps. cxi. 7). (3) The last minister of judgment will be his Son, into whose hands he hath committed all judgment (John v. 22), and before whose tribunal all must appear (2 Cor. v. 10). To him belong the epithets "called" and "sanctified" in their highest sense.

III. THE ENCOMPASSING SPECTATORS. The faithful remnant of Israel, those who still adhered to Jehovah and mourned as did Josiah, Jeremiah, and Zephaniah, Huldah the prophetess, Hilkiah the priest, and others, over the degenerate condition of the nation. So in the world still are God's believing people called to witness, and often actually do witness, the execution of God's judgments upon the ungodly. So in the last day, when the vials of Divine indignation will be outpoured upon the finally impenitent, the saints who have been counted worthy to attain Christ's kingdom and glory will behold the appalling scene, as Abraham beheld the burning of the cities of the plain, and will say, "Hallelujah! salvation, and glory, and honour, and power, unto the Lord our God ; for true and righteous are his judgments" (Rev. xix. 1, 2).

IV. THE RESULTING IMPRESSIONS. Pointed to in the solemn "Hush! be still" (ver. 7), with which the prophet opened his roll of woe. When he summoned the spectators to be silent before the face of Jehovah, he signified that silence was to be the effect produced upon their spirits by the spectacle they were about to witness. And this silence would be one: 1. *Of awe ;* as they contemplated the overpowering revelation of the majesty of God, of his holiness and justice, of his power and fidelity, which would be afforded by his judgments upon the wicked. 2. *Of submission ;* as they recognized the equity of those judgments by which sin was punished, the Divine Law vindicated, and God's glory proclaimed. 3. *Of amazement ;* as they marvelled how ever they who had once themselves been sinful, had through grace escaped those calamities which they saw overtaking the wicked.

Learn : 1. That God deals with men and nations upon the principle of moral retribution. 2. That neither national nor individual wickedness, if unrepented of, can evade its just recompense of reward. 3. That God's judgments upon both will ultimately be approved by all.—T. W.

Ver. 7.—*The soul's silences before the presence of the Lord.* I. A SILENCE OF ADORATION. As becomes a creature in the presence of his Creator (Zech. ii. 13 ; Hab. ii. 20), and a sinner in the presence of the Holy One (Job xl. 4).

II. A SILENCE OF CONTEMPLATION. As befits the soul in those moments in which God reveals himself in nature (Job xxxvii. 14) or in grace (Gen. xvii. 3 ; Exod. xiv. 13).

III. A SILENCE OF EXPECTATION. As a praying soul maintains when looking out for a response to his supplications (Ps. lxii. 1, 5, margin), or a perplexed spirit when waiting for God to clear up the mystery of his providence (Ps. xxxvii. 7, margin).

IV. A SILENCE OF SUBMISSION. As they preserve who recognize the ills of life to proceed from the hand of God (Ps. xxxix. 2 ; Lam. iii. 28, 29).

V. A SILENCE OF APPROBATION. As God's judgments will enforce upon all who behold them (Ps. xlvi. 10).—T. W.

Ver. 8.—*Foreign clothes.* I. A BOND OF INTERNATIONAL UNION. The interchange of commodities among the different peoples of the earth one of the surest means of promoting peace and causing wars to cease.

II. A SIGN OF ADVANCING CIVILIZATION. When a nation's wants multiply beyond its own power directly to meet them, it naturally draws upon the resources of lands and peoples beyond itself. Thus while the existence of these wants marks the upward progress of the nation itself, the effort needed to supply them acts as a stimulus to other peoples to join in the onward march.

III. A SYMPTOM OF DECLINING PATRIOTISM. No truer indication that the national sentiment amongst a people is becoming feeble than the slavish imitation of the manners and customs, speech and dress, of a stronger neighbour.

IV. A SYMBOL OF RELIGIOUS DECLENSION. In this light regarded by the prophet. Egyptian or Chaldean raiment worn by Judæan princes and peasants meant that their hearts were hankering after Egyptian or Chaldean idolatry. So when Christians conform to the world's ways, adopting its maxims and principles, manners and customs, thoughts and feelings, sentiments and practices—all of which should be to them what foreign clothes were to Israel—there is reason to suspect that a backward movement in religion has begun.—T. W.

Ver. 12.—*Settled on one's lees.* I. A PICTURE OF PROSPEROUS EASE. The image—that of wine which has been allowed to settle in its cask, without having ever been drawn off or emptied from vessel to vessel—naturally suggests the condition of one who has become prosperous and affluent, who has never been visited by misfortune, agitated by calamity, or disturbed by affliction, but who through long years has been left to feast and fatten, like an ox in his stall, or (adhering to the metaphor) to fill and settle like a cask of wine.

II. A SYMBOL OF RELIGIOUS (OR, RATHER, IRRELIGIOUS) DEGENERATION. As wine, left upon its lees, retains its flavour—good or bad, as the case may be—so does the soul acquire a moral flavour from the things in which it delights, and on which, as it were, it rests. Nay, as good wine becomes better and bad wine worse from being allowed to settle on its lees, so do pious souls become stronger and more fixed in goodness, but ungodly souls more confirmed and rooted in wickedness, by being suffered to rest, the one on the holy inclinations and the other on the sinful lusts which form the lowest strata respectively of their beings.

III. A PRECURSOR OF APPROACHING DOOM. As bad wine allowed to settle on its lees rapidly deteriorates and reaches such a state of badness as to be unfit for use, so wicked men that settle on their lees, gratifying their sensual desires and venting their atheistical opinions, ultimately sink to such a point of moral degeneration as not to admit of recovery, and as allows nothing to be anticipated for them but swift and sudden destruction.

LESSONS. 1. The danger of prosperity. 2. The value of adversity.—T. W.

Vers. 14—18.—*"The great day of the Lord."* I. RAPIDLY APPROACHING. "The great day of the Lord is near, it is near, and hasteth greatly" (ver. 14). This was true of the Chaldean invasion, then little more than one generation distant—so near, in fact, that the prophet could hear the bitter cry of the mighty man who saw himself confronted by its terrors; and is true of that other and greater day of the Lord, the day of judgment (2 Pet. ii. 9; 1 John iv. 17; Rev. vi. 17), which the Christian is directed always to consider as at hand (Phil. iv. 5; Jas. v. 8, 9; 1 Pet. iv. 7; Rev. xxii. 12), because the exact moment of its coming no one can tell (Matt. xxiv. 36; xxv. 13, 42).

II. TERRIBLY ALARMING. What the Chaldean invasion should prove to the guilty city of Jerusalem and nation of Judah the prophet depicts by heaping together all the images of horror that his mind can conceive or his language express, calling the time of that visitation a day of wrath and fury, in which Jehovah should pour out his indignation upon the land and its inhabitants, letting loose upon them the ferocious warriors of Babylon; a day of trouble and distress, in which men should be hemmed in on every side by calamity and pressed down by anguish, walking like blind men and falling like wounded and dying soldiers; a day of wasteness and desolation, in which fields should be devastated, houses overthrown, and men and women put to the edge of the sword; a day of darkness and gloominess, of clouds and thick darkness, in which not so much as a single star of hope should appear in the political firmament; a day of the trumpet and alarm against the fenced cities and against the high battlements, in which their fortified towns and cities should experience the shock of pitiless assailants. But even more appropriately will these images apply to the day of judgment, when the Lord Jesus Christ shall be revealed in flaming fire and with his holy angels (2 Thess. i. 8).

III. FIERCELY DESTROYING. 1. *Absolutely unavoidable.* "The mighty man crieth bitterly there," "because he cannot save himself, and must succumb to the power of the foe" (Keil). So would it be in the hour of Babylon's descent upon Judah and Jerusalem; so will it be in the day of the revelation of the wrath of the Almighty (Rev.

vi. 15—17). 2. *Utterly consuming.* "Their blood shall be poured out as dust, and their flesh as dung. Neither their silver nor their gold shall be able to deliver them in the day of the Lord's wrath; but the whole land shall be devoured by the fire of his jealousy: for he shall make an end, yea, a terrible end, of all them that dwell in the land" (comp. Ezek. vii. 19). The same doom of utter extermination will overtake the finally impenitent in the day when God awakes in terrible majesty to execute judgment on the ungodly. Of these "God shall make an utter, terrific, speedy destruction, a living death, so that they shall at once be and not be; be, as continued in being; not be, as having no life in God, but only a continued death in misery" (Pusey).

LESSONS. 1. Gratitude to God, who hath made provision through the gospel of his Son for delivering men from the wrath to come. 2. The duty of all to whom that gospel is made known to embrace its provisions and escape from impending peril, while yet the day of mercy lasts. 3. The wisdom of living in constant anticipation of that day, and of perfecting holiness in the fear of the Lord. 4. The urgency of making known to men the gospel, that they may flee from the wrath to come.—T. W.

Vers. 1—18.—*The judgment threatened.* We learn from ver. 1 that Zephaniah received from the Lord his message to Judah in the days of Josiah, the last of the godly and reforming kings, who, after the gross corruption of the preceding reigns of Manasseh and Amon, restored to a large extent the purity of the worship of God, and was the means of bringing about a certain kind and degree of repentance and amendment in the people. Probably, however, the major part of Zephaniah's prophecy belongs to the early part of Josiah's reign, before his greatest public reformation was begun; for there is no allusion to that hopeful work in the book of the prophet, and there is no mention of Zephaniah in the history, where Jeremiah and Huldah the prophetess are described as aiding and guiding the king's efforts to bring the people back to godliness. But the word of the Lord which came to Zephaniah doubtless prepared the way for the work of full reformation, though the messenger may not have been spared to take part and rejoice in it. His message is, first, an announcement of the judgment of Jehovah against the people, which occupies the whole of ch. i.; and ver. 7 may be taken as its central point, containing the lesson of duty, on which all that precedes and follows it converges. We shall best feel the force of this lesson if we begin from the outside of this oracle, the more obvious and manifest appearance of the judgment of Jehovah here announced, which the prophet puts at the beginning and end (vers. 2, 3, 14—18).

I. THE NATURE OF THIS JUDGMENT. At the very outset it is described in a way fitted to startle and alarm; for it is to be of a most sweeping and universal nature (vers. 2, 3). The words remind us of nothing less than the universal deluge, by which the old world was swept away. A destruction like that is impending over Judah. There had been many chastisements sent on the people before; the land had been invaded, the royal treasuries rifled, the country laid waste. No fewer than ten of the twelve tribes of Israel had been not very long before carried away into Assyria. Still, these visitations had been only partial; a remnant had always been left; and many were apt to trust that so it would ever be. Because God had given Israel the land, they thought that some part of it at least must always be theirs. But now they are warned that this is a false confidence, and that, in spite of the gift of the land to Abraham's seed, the corrupt race that now inhabit it shall be utterly cut off. Moreover, this judgment, that is to be so sweeping, is also very near at hand. In the old world the long-suffering of God waited in the days of Noah; but now he has waited long and sent messenger after messenger; and at last the time of delay is nearly exhausted, and the judgment is close at hand, for their iniquity is all but full. The day of the Lord is represented as hasting to meet them; the sound of its coming is already heard, and very soon it will be here. Have not all these lesser judgments been foretastes of it?—the capture of Galilee by Tiglath-Pileser, the removal of the whole northern kingdom by Shalmaneser or Sargon, the invasion of Judah by Sennacherib? and has not each one of these been more sweeping and far-reaching than the former? Are not these signs and harbingers of the great day of the Lord here announced? Then how terrible and irresistible is this judgment (vers. 15—18)! Physical strength and power shall not deliver the guilty nation. There are, indeed, fortified cities in the land, and high towers to bar the entrance of an enemy; and it may seem as if behind these they might defy the invader; but against them shall be raised the sound of the war-trumpet, and the battle-shout of a great host, before which they shall not be able to stand. Skill and wisdom shall not be able to save them. These have often enabled armies very much inferior in numbers to conquer great hosts; but now there shall be perplexity and dismay, and men shall be groping like blind men in the dark, unable to devise any means of resistance or escape, bewildered and disheartened. Wealth sometimes may be used to buy off an invading monarch or army. So in former days kings of Judah had repeatedly obtained relief from foreign foes by giving up to them the treasures of the palace and temple. But in this invasion neither silver nor gold shall be of any avail to deliver them. The prophet does not indicate more particularly from what quarter this terrible invasion shall come—that is left to be made manifest by the event. For the terribleness of the judgment did not arise merely from the fact that it was to be inflicted by a great worldly power, which would be overpowering in force and would not care for bribes; but from this, that that power, whatever it might be, was to be the instrument of Jehovah's wrath against the nation. Israel had often been saved from fierce attacks of mighty nations before, and enabled to defy their rage; but that had not been because of their wisdom or courage, but because they trusted in God, and had his protection. Now, however, there was coming on them the day of the Lord's anger; he was to hide his face from them, and therefore it would be to them a day of such darkness, dismay, and despair. This brings us somewhat nearer the centre and heart of this prophecy, and leads us to consider—

II. The causes of the judgment, announced as so sweeping, near, and terrible. These are the sins of the land, of which a long and dark catalogue is unrolled (vers. 4—12). First comes what was the great besetting sin of ancient times, as it has ever been of men who possess not or will not receive God's revelation of himself, idolatry, the worship of the seen and earthly as Divine, instead of the only true God who is invisible and spiritual, the worshipping and serving the creature more than the Creator. The invisible things of God, his eternal power and Godhead, are seen and understood by the things that are made; for "the heavens declare the glory of God, and the firmament showeth his handiwork." But men, not liking to retain God in their knowledge, keep back this truth in unrighteousness, and come to regard the powers of nature as themselves Divine; and worship the heavens, the earth, the sun, the stars, as gods, instead of regarding them as the works of the true God, who is above them all. Thus they fall into a religion that is purely sensuous, requiring no elevation of the soul above what can be seen and heard and felt—a religion also that is divorced from morality, for when men come to regard the processes of nature as the highest thing that there is, they can see in them no moral law or order. Such was the corrupt religion of the heathen world, left by God to its own way, and against this his revelation to Israel was designed to testify, declaring him to be a Being spiritual and holy, the one living and true God. But the chosen people were ever tempted to fall back to that sensuous and immoral conception of God that found expression in the idolatry of the surrounding nations. Various forms of such idolatry as was then common are here alluded to. There was the Phœnician worship of Baal, which had been introduced long ago by Jezebel into the northern kingdom, and through Athaliah into Judah; and there was also the more recently imported worship of the stars and heavenly bodies, the form of idolatry that prevailed in the Eastern countries with which Judah was now beginning to be acquainted. This worship was performed by burning incense and offering sacrifices on the flat tops of the houses, looking up to the sky and host of heaven. But along with these gross forms of idolatry there is also condemned the corrupt worship of Jehovah. The worship at the high places, with which the kohanim (ver. 4) were connected, was indeed a worship of Jehovah, but had become in course of time thoroughly idolatrous in its character; the pillars or groves placed beside the altars came to be worshipped as symbols of the Deity, and, as in Bethel and Dan, idols were identified with him. Thus the true invisible God was degraded to the likeness of the idols of the heathen, and this worship at the high places had to be utterly condemned and swept away. Another corruption of the pure worship of Jehovah was the combination of it with that of the heathen deities. There were those who worshipped and swore to Jehovah, and at the same time swore by Malcham (ver. 5) their king, i.e. Baal. They thought that they could preserve their allegiance to the God of Israel while yet they paid homage also to Baal. They would thus be halting between two opinions, or trying to make a compromise, which on any view of it must degrade the true God. It could only imply either that Jehovah and Baal were both real powers over their several nations, and so Jehovah would be merely a local or national deity; or else that they were but different names of the same supreme power, which would thus be made a mere nature-power, such as Baal was conceived to be, not the holy God who had revealed himself to Israel. Then the prophet speaks (ver. 6) of what is implied in all this, and lies at the bottom of it all. These corrupt forms of worship were really a forsaking the Lord; and the beginning of the evil lay in ungodliness; they did not seek the Lord, nor inquire for him. Many who might not be guilty of any of the kinds of idolatry that prevailed, might yet be liable to this reproach, which is surely the severest of all. They professed that they knew God, but they did not look to him in their times of trouble, they did not seek to know his will from his Law or his prophets, they did not call on him for help in time of need—he was to them, in fact, but a name or an idea, not a real, living, personal God. If this was all their religion, it was no wonder that they should be easily led to adopt some visible symbol of the Deity, or to cover up the hollowness of their profession by abundance of rites of worship, or to associate their belief in one Lord with the service of the deities of neighbouring countries, which seemed to be more realities to their devotees. Such were the corruptions of religion in Israel. With these were associated great social evils. Along with the foreign religious rites there were introduced also foreign customs, that marred the simplicity of the national character. This appeared most prominently in dress, which is here especially mentioned (ver. 8); but that was doubtless only an outward symptom of much more radical evils. According to the Law, Israel was to be distinguished from other nations by their dress as well as by their religion. Their characteristic dress was to be marked, on the one hand, by simplicity and decency (Lev. xix. 19; Deut. xxii. 11, 12), and on the other hand, by having fringes as a memorial of Jehovah's Law (Numb. xv. 38). But now they were growing ashamed of this outward mark of their religion, and came to adopt the more varied and splendid costume of their neighbours. This probably indicated in general habits of luxury and ostentation, which would naturally begin and be most prevalent among the princes and courtiers, though from them they would spread to other classes. Such selfish indulgence was especially to be condemned at a time when the nation was far from being in a secure or prosperous state. It had suffered serious losses, and barely escaped from imminent dangers; and even now the land was much impoverished compared with its former state, and the great empires around were becoming more powerful and threatening. Surely this was not a time to imitate foreign luxurious customs, and to be ashamed of the ancient and godly simplicity of Israel's manners. Such luxury could only be maintained by the rich and the princes by means of oppression and extortion; and this is another evil described as the cause of the judgment (ver. 9). Those who leap on the threshold may refer, as some think, to the Philistines, who formed, with other foreigners, the royal body-guard; or they may simply indicate, as others think, the eagerness with which the satellites of the princes intruded into the houses of the citizens, in order, by their oppressive exactions, to fill the houses of their masters. Anyhow, the verse indicates that, in order to keep up the splendour and luxury of the court, the people were oppressed, and exorbitant taxes or contributions levied from them by a system of fraudulent charges, or forcible domiciliary visitation. This is the natural accompaniment of a selfish oligarchy in an impoverished and declining state. Then, further, the merchant people in Jerusalem, who seem to have had as their place of business the valley between the hills of the old and new city, are as Canaanites in their transactions; the balances of deceit are in their hand; they have laden themselves with silver by usury and fraud. Such ill-gotten gains seem to be alluded to in ver. 11, and threatened with destruction when the enemy shall burst into the city by the fish gate at the north-west, its most exposed side; when the cry from it shall only be answered by a helpless howling from the new city and crashing from the higher parts, and the hollow valley where merchants most did congregate shall be, as it were, a mortar (Maktesh), in which they shall be trodden down and bruised to pieces by the invading host. At least there is described a prevailing avarice and hasting to be rich, as one of the causes on account of which this crushing judgment comes. Finally, we have set before us the careless self-indulgence of those who are at ease amid all this prevailing evil, who have had no changes, and have no fear of change, who say or think that neither good nor evil, blessing nor judgment, is to be looked for from God (ver. 12). All things continue as they were; and the thought of a present, living God, the Judge of the earth, and the Avenger of wrong, has faded from men's minds. Such are the various forms of evil that are indicated by the prophet as the cause of the judgment which he announces. Can it be said that they are unknown in our day and in ourselves? No doubt the outward forms of idolatry and oppression then rampant are strange and repulsive to us ; but are we free from the tendency to degrade the living God to a mere nature-power, which is the essence of idolatry? And are not ungodliness, neglect of God's spiritual worship, selfish ostentation and luxury, neglect and oppression of the poor, love of money, and careless self-indulgence, but too well known among us? The picture is not one of mere historical or antiquarian interest, but of ever-present moral significance. It teaches us that such evils always lead to ruin, that they lay a nation helpless at the feet of its enemies, and make its continued existence impossible. All history confirms this lesson ; and revelation bids us look beyond all merely historical catastrophes to that final judgment of the Lord which shall, in the fullest sense, be universal, embracing, not one nation only, but all mankind, and searching out each individual, to be confronted with his Judge and with the fruit of his own doings.

III. The lesson of all this is expressed in the words, "Hold thy peace at the presence of the Lord God." (Ver. 7.) This is the first and most urgent duty. The prophet has further directions to give in following discourses; but this is the immediate effect that the announcement of judgment should have. A silence of awe and humility is what becomes men in the presence of God, when he rises up to judgment as the Lord of all the earth. "Be still, and know that I am God," is his voice as the day of the Lord approaches. This implies a recognition, on the one hand, of the reality, and on the other hand, of the justice, of God's judgment. It should be received as a real expression of God's wrath against the sins of men. Let not the evils that come upon nations or individuals in consequence of their sins be regarded as mere accidents, or as only due to the operation of natural laws. They may be brought about immediately by such second causes, but behind all these we are to recognize the mind and will of the living God. He speaks to us as truly by the ordinary courses of nature as by the most stupendous miracle, and if he shows us that earthly conceptions of the Divine degrade and brutalize man, that selfishness and selfish indulgence, luxury and oppression, bring a people to ruin and lay them helpless at the feet of their foes, that is a real and most solemn judgment of God against these things. Let us be silent also as recognizing the justice of this judgment. These things are evil, deserving of abhorrence and destruction; and God, who in his laws of nature appoints ruin to be their consequence, shows himself just and holy. Let us humbly acknowledge this; and in so far as these evils of ungodliness and selfishness have found place in us, let us put our hand on our mouth, acknowledging that we have nothing to answer to God, and are verily guilty in his sight. There is hope for us if we thus confess our sin. There is hope in the very fact that God announces his judgment against our sin. For what is the announcement? It is that God will utterly sweep away the evils that are done in the land ; it is against those that the fire of his wrath is kindled ; and if men will cling to these evils, and hug their sins to their bosom, he will sweep away the wicked with the stumbling-blocks. Both together shall be destroyed, for God will be rid at last of sin. But if any are willing to be separated from their sins, by however humble and painful a process that may be, then the assurance that God will utterly sweep away the evil will have hope for them. The fire that is to devour the whole land is a fire of jealousy as well as of wrath. Because the Lord loves his people with a jealous affection, in spite of all their unfaithfulness, he will, if they but silently trust themselves to him, make the fire of his anger against their sin to purify and perfect them. Thus this coming of the Lord for judgment is the harbinger of final salvation to those who desire to be purged from those evils against which his wrath is revealed. Therefore "let Israel hope in the Lord, for with the Lord there is mercy, and with him is plenteous redemption; and he will redeem Israel from all his iniquity."—C.

Vers. 1—6.—*The Word.* "The word of the Lord which came unto Zephaniah the son of Cushi, the son of Gedaliah, the son of Amariah, the son of Hizkiah, in the days of Josiah the son of Amon, King of Judah. I will utterly consume all things from off the land, saith the Lord. I will consume man and beast," etc. Of Zephaniah we have no information but what is contained in his prophecy. His genealogy is given in the first verse of this chapter. He prophesied in the reign of Josiah, probably between the twelfth and eighteenth years of his reign. In the first chapter he predicts the utter desolation of Judah. In the second, he exhorts his countrymen to repentance in view of the approaching judgments, and threatens the surrounding nations, Philistia, Moab, and Ammon. In the third, after a severe rebuke of Jerusalem, he foretells, in glowing language, its future purification and enlargement, and the destruction of all its enemies. The style is distinguished neither by sublimity nor elegance. He resembles in many respects his contemporary, Jeremiah. He borrows some of the language of former prophets (comp. ch. ii. 14 with Isa. xiii. 21 and xxxiv. 11; ch. ii. 15 with Isa. xlvii. 8). "The genealogy of Zephaniah is given through Cushi, Gedaliah, and Amariah to Hezekiah; for in the original Hebrew the words 'Hizkiah' and 'Hezekiah' are the same. As it was unusual that the descent of prophets should be given with such particularity, it has been assumed with some probability that Hezekiah was the king of that name; though in this case we should have expected the addition, 'King of Judah.' The chemarim are the idol-priests; that is, priests devoted to idol-worship. In 2 Kings xxiii. 5, where the writer is speaking of the reformation under Josiah, the word is translated *idolatrous* priests; in Hos. x. 5, simply *priests*, which is its meaning in the Syriac language. Some have maintained that the invasion of Judah to which Zephaniah refers was that of the Scythians described by Herodotus; but this is very improbable. From the fact that the king's children are included in the threatened invasion—in the Hebrew, 'I will visit upon the princes and the king's children'—some have inferred that they must have been already grown and addicted to idolatrous practices; consequently, that Zephaniah wrote later than the eighteenth year of Josiah. But, as Keil and others have remarked, the mention of the king's children may have been added simply to indicate the universality of the approaching visitation; not to say that the prophetic vision of Zephaniah may have anticipated the sin and the punishment of these king's children, Jehoahaz and Jehoiakim" (Barrows). In these verses we learn two things.

I. THE DISTINGUISHING CAPACITY OF MAN, AND THE WONDERFUL CONDESCENSION OF GOD. 1. *The distinguishing capacity of man.* What is that? To receive the word of Jehovah. "The word of the Lord which came unto Zephaniah the son of Cushi," etc. This Zephaniah, who from the fulness of his genealogy here given, was perhaps a person of note, was, however, mainly distinguished by this—viz. that he received a word from Jehovah. What is it to receive a word from another? Not merely to hear it, to remember its sound, or to write it down, but to *appreciate* its meaning. This is the grand distinction of man as a mundane existence. It is not the reasoning principle that distinguishes man from other creatures on earth, for other creatures possess this in some degree; not the durability of his existence, for other creatures may live as long as he; but the capacity of taking in ideas from the Infinite Mind, to understand and realize God's thoughts. In a sense, there is a greater distance between me as a man and the most intelligent animal on this earth, than there is between me and my Maker. The highest animal cannot take in and understand my thoughts; but I can take in and understand the thoughts of my Maker. "The word of the Lord" comes to every man at times—comes in visions of the night, comes in the intuitions of conscience, comes in the impressions that nature makes on the heart. 2. *The wonderful condescension of God.* How amazing the condescension of God to speak to man! Many of the poor little wretched creatures who are called emperors and empresses would, perhaps, not deign to speak to paupers, to hold converse with them; but the "Lord, though he be high, yet hath respect unto the humble;" "Thus saith the High and Lofty One that inhabiteth eternity, whose name is Holy, To that man will I look who is of a contrite heart."

II. THE MORAL CORRUPTION OF MAN, AND THE EXCLUSIVE PREROGATIVE OF GOD. 1. *The moral corruption of man.* There are three great moral evils indicated in these verses. (1) *Idolatry.* "I will cut off the remnant of Baal from this place, and the name of the Chemarims with the priests; and them that worship the host of heaven upon the house-tops." The remains of Baal-worship, which as yet Josiah was unable utterly to eradicate in remoter places. Baal was the Phœnician tutelary god. His name means *lord* ; and the feminine god corresponding and generally associated with him was Ashtaroth. As he was represented by the sun, so she was the goddess answering to the moon and the rest of the heavenly host. In fact, it was the worship of nature ; a worship to which corresponds the pantheistic and scientific exaltation of Nature and her laws in our own days, as if God were the slave of his own world and its laws, instead of the Lord, Creator, and Sustainer, who can and will modify, alter, and suspend the order of the present system of things, according to his own sovereign pleasure, and in furtherance of the higher moral laws, in subserviency to which the laws of nature exist. From the time of the judges (Judg. ii. 13) Israel had fallen into this idolatry ; and Manasseh had lately set up this idol within Jehovah's temple itself (2 Kings xxi. 3—7): "He reared up altars for Baal, and made a grove [symbol of the goddess Ashtaroth] . . . and worshipped all the host of heaven. . . And he built altars in the house of the Lord, of which the Lord said, In Jerusalem will I put my Name. And he built altars for all the host of heaven in the two courts of the house of the Lord. And he set a graven image of the grove [the symbol of the heavenly host] that he had made in the house, of which the Lord said to David, and to Solomon his son, In this house, and in Jerusalem, which I have chosen out of all the tribes of Israel, will I put my Name for ever." Josiah began his reformation in the twelfth year of his reign (2 Chron. xxxiv. 3, 4, 8), and in the eighteenth had as far as possible completed it. "And the name of the Chemarims with the priests." These chemarim were in all probability subordinate ministers of the idolatrous priests, and their duty was to assist them at the altar. "Them that worship the host of heaven upon the house-tops." The houses in the East had flat roofs, open to the heavens, and there the worship was performed. Idolatry is one of the great sins of the world ; it is confined to no age or land. Its spirit is loving the creature more than the Creator. (2) *Backsliding.* "Them that are turned back from the Lord." Indeed, idolatry is an apostasy, and so is all sin. All sin is a going back from the Lord. "My people have committed two evils ; they have forsaken me the Fountain of living waters, and hewed them out cisterns, broken cisterns, that can hold no water" (Jer. ii. 13). (3) *Indifferentism.* "And those that have not sought the Lord, nor inquired for him." This is the most prevalent of all sins, and is one of the great roots of all immoralities—an utter neglect of religion. Religious indifferentism is the great sin of England to-day. God and his claims are everywhere practically ignored. This indifferentism, like a vast pool of mud, generates all that is morally noxious, pernicious, and vile in our midst. 2. *The exclusive prerogative of God.* What is that? To *destroy.* "I will utterly consume all things from off the land, saith the Lord. I will consume man and beast ; I will consume the fowls of the heaven, and the fishes of the sea, and the stumbling-blocks with the wicked ; and I will cut off man from off the land, saith the Lord." (1) No one *can* really destroy but God. ."I kill, and I make alive." Annihilation is as far behind the power of the creature as is the work of creation. Man may crush the forms of things, but the essences lie infinitely beyond his touch. (2) God has a *right* to destroy human life. He has a right because it belongs to him. He has a right because through sin it has forfeited its existence. (3) His destructive work is as *beneficent* as his sustaining and creating. Destruction is a principle in all nature ; one plant destroys another, one animal destroys another, and there are elements in nature whose work is destruction. From destruction new life and beauty come ; destruction keeps the universe alive, fresh, and healthy.—D. T.

Vers. 7—18.—*The day of war the day of horrors.* "Hold thy peace at the presence of the Lord." These verses present a graphic and soul-stirring description of the horrid day of war which was about to dawn on the Hebrew land. It is called a "day of wrath," a "day of trouble and distress, a day of wasteness and desolation, a day of darkness and gloominess, a day of clouds and thick darkness, a day of the trumpet and alarm against the fenced cities, and against the high towers." No more awful day than the day of war. It is a day when fiends are released from prison and let loose on earth. The war-day is represented here—

I. As a DAY OF ENORMOUS SACRIFICE. "Hold thy peace at the presence of the Lord God: for the day of the Lord is at hand: for the Lord hath prepared a sacrifice." A sacrifice! 1. *It is an enormous sacrifice of life.* Several classes are referred to here as the victims of this war. (1) *Royalty.* "I will punish the princes, and the king's children, and all such as are clothed with strange apparel." The reference is here probably to the princes of the royal house, to the children of the king who would be on the throne at the time of the fulfilment of the prophecy. In 2 Kings xxv. 7 it is said that Nebuchadnezzar slew the sons of King Zedekiah before his eyes. When the savage and bloodthirsty lions of war are let loose, they are regardless of all social distinction; they seize the princes as well as paupers. No class in society, perhaps, as a rule, deserve the destruction more than the rulers of the people. They for the most part create the wars, and often deserve to be struck down. Through all history they have generally been the war-makers. War is their own child, and their child sometimes strikes them down. (2) Another class referred to is the *nobility.* "In the same day also will I punish all those that leap on the threshold, which fill their masters' houses with violence and deceit." Some suppose that there is a reference here to the Philistine custom of not treading on the "threshold," which arose from the head and hands of Dagon being cut off on the threshold before the ark (1 Sam. v. 5). It scarcely matters; reckless men in power are referred to—men that fill their masters' houses with violence and deceit. "The servants of princes," says Calvin, "who have gotten prey like hounds for their masters, leap exultingly on their masters' threshold, or on the threshold of the houses which they break into." War sometimes, and insurrectionary war always, strikes savagely at the higher classes. It plays sad havoc with aristocracies; it sets manors in flames, and treads coronets in the dust. (See another and more probable interpretation in the Exposition.) (3) Another class referred to is that of the *traders.* "Howl, ye inhabitants of Maktesh, for all the merchant people are cut down: all they that bear silver are cut off." Some translate Maktesh, "Mortar," a name employed for the valley of Siloam, from its hollow shape. It was a valley at the eastern extremity of Moriah, where the merchants dwelt. The invading army seizes the wealth of the country. Greedy conquerors have always had a keen eye to this. (4) Another class referred to is the *masses.* "And it shall come to pass at that time, that I will search Jerusalem with candles, and punish the men that are settled on their lees: that say in their heart, The Lord will not do good, neither will he do evil." This is not a bad description of the masses of people in all ages. They are: (*a*) *Unconspicuous.* Pretty well all alike, they do not stand out in the country from the generality. War has no particular aim at them, though it strikes them indiscriminately; still, though unconspicuous, war will find them out. "I will search Jerusalem with candles." (*b*) *Religiously indifferent.* "Settled on their lees." This means crusted, hardened, like wines long left at the bottom undisturbed. "That say in their heart, The Lord will not do good, neither will he do evil." Religious indifferentism has always been the leading characteristic of the masses. Note the sacrifice of life in all these classes—the rulers and the ruled, the rich and the poor, the ignorant and the learned, the innocent and the guilty, the young and the old, all in war form one huge sacrifice of blood. It is overwhelmingly awful to think of the lives that have been sacrificed in war even since the year 1852. In the Crimean War (1854) it is estimated that 750,000 fell; in the Italian War (1859), 45,000; in the war at Schleswig-Holstein, 3000; in the American Civil War, 800,000; in the war between Prussia, Austria, and Italy (1866), 45,000; expeditions to Mexico, Cochin China, Morocco, Paraguay, 65,000; in the Franco-German War, 215,000; Turkey massacres in Bulgaria, 25,000; total, 1,948,000. This is one of the sacrifices that war has made, not only in civilized lands, but even in Christendom during the last thirty-five years; and the perpetrators of these enormities call themselves Christians, professed disciples of him who said, "I came not to destroy men's lives, but to save them;" "If thine enemy hunger, feed him." 2. *It is an enormous sacrifice of property.* "Therefore their goods shall become a booty, and their houses a desolation: they shall also build houses, but not inhabit them; and they shall plant vineyards, but not drink the wine thereof." Who can estimate the amount of property that the wars during the last thirty years have utterly destroyed? The Crimean War cost £340,000,000; the Italian, £60,000,000; the American Civil War, £1,400,000,000;

the Franco-Prussian, £500,000,000; and the comparatively smaller wars, £1,000,000; an amount altogether of £2,400,000,000—a sufficient sum to supply every inhabitant of the globe, not only with the necessaries, but with the comforts and educational advantages of life. "Give me," says Stebbins, "the amount that has been spent in war, and I will purchase every foot of land of the globe. I will clothe every man, woman, and child in an attire that kings and queens might be proud of. I will build a school-house upon every hillside and in every valley over the habitable earth. I will supply that school-house with a competent teacher. I will build an academy in every town, and endow it; and a college in every state, and fill it with able professors. I will crown every hill with a church consecrated to the promulgation of the gospel of peace. I will support in its pulpit an able teacher of righteousness, so that on every sabbath morning the chime of one hill shall answer to the chime of another around the earth's broad circumference; and the voice of prayer and the song of praise shall ascend like the smoke of a universal holocaust to heaven." To talk of the glories of war is to exult in the horrors of hell. I confess that a quivering seizes my nerves, and a chilly sadness comes over my spirits, when I hear men calling themselves Christians, especially ministers, uttering one word in favour of war, whether defensive or aggressive. The man who defends war defends the devil himself.

II. As a day of Divine retribution. All these horrors of war are here represented as judgments from the Almighty. It is called the "day of the Lord." He is represented as having "prepared a sacrifice," referring to the awful sacrifice of life and property; as having summoned his guests—the warriors, men of blood—to battle. Indeed, it is called the "Lord's sacrifice." He is represented as saying, "I will punish the princes;" "I will search Jerusalem with candles;" "I will bring distress upon men." And again, "The whole land shall be devoured by the fire" of his jealousy; "for he shall make even a speedy riddance." In Bible phraseology, the Almighty is often represented as the Author of that which he *merely permits*. He does not *originate* wars. The consciousness of warriors attests this. All the passions of greed, revenge, and ambition, whence all wars spring, are self-generated in the breast of the man of blood. His moral constitution will not allow him to ascribe them to his Maker; he charges them on himself. He feels that he is not their Author, and he knows that they stand in awful contrast with the holy and beneficent will of the almighty Maker of the universe. He does not instigate these abominations, but allows, uses, and controls them. In using war as a punishment for sin, three things are to be observed. 1. *That all who perish in war righteously deserve their fate.* God says here, "I will bring distress upon men, that they shall walk like blind men, *because* they have sinned." War, in its most savage recklessness, does not strike one man down who has not sinned, and whose sin does not deserve death. The penalty of death that comes to men in war would, by the moral laws of the universe, come to them sooner or later in some other form. "It is appointed to all men once to die;" "The wages of sin is death." 2. *That warriors, in executing the Divine justice, demonstrate the enormity of the evil requiring punishment.* Where can sin be seen in aspects so complete in all that is morally horrific, outrageous, and infernal, as in the battle-field? No thoughtful man can gaze on it there without feeling that the righteous Governor of the universe, for the happiness of his creation, is bound to visit it with his hot displeasure. 3. *War, as an officer of Divine justice, reveals the amazing freedom allowed to the sinner in this world, and God's controlling power over hostile forces.* Who will say that man is a slave when he sees the warrior going forth with a free step on a mission directly hostile to the beneficent laws of the universe, the moral institutions of his own nature, and the revealed will of Heaven? He allowed men even to put to death his own Son upon the cross. Here is liberty. Whilst human freedom is revealed, God's controlling power is also most strikingly manifest. "He maketh the wrath of man to praise him." He has servants who serve him *against* their will, as well as servants who serve him *with* their will. Warriors and devils are of the former class. "Ye thought evil against me; but God meant it unto good" (Gen. l. 20); "I have raised thee up for to show in thee my power" (Exod. ix. 16); "Let all the house of Israel know assuredly that God hath made that same Jesus whom ye have crucified both Lord and Christ." Out of the wars and tumults of his enemies he will bring something glorious, a Lord and Christ.

> "Patiently received from thee,
> Evil cannot evil be;
> Evil is by evil healed,
> Evil is but good concealed."
>
> (Charles Wesley.)
>
> D. T.

EXPOSITION.

CHAPTER II.

Ver. 1—ch. iii. 8.—Part II. Exhortation to Repentance and to Perseverance.

Vers. 1—3.—§ 1. *The prophet urges all to examine their ways before the day of the Lord come; and he prays the righteous to seek the Lord more earnestly, in order that they may be safe in the judgment.*

Ver. 1.—Gather yourselves together. So the versions; and this rendering is probably correct. The prophet calls upon his nation to assemble themselves together in order to take mutual counsel or to make general confession and supplication to God. Another rendering, based on some alteration of letters, is, "Set yourselves to be ashamed; yea, be ashamed" (comp. Isa. xlvi. 8). **Yea, gather together.** The LXX. renders the two words, συνάχθητε καὶ συνδέθητε, "be ye gathered and bound together;" "Id est," says Jerome, "estote vobis caritatis vinculo copulati." **O nation not desired;** Vulgate, *gens non amabilis*—a litotes for abominable, hated for its sins, unworthy of God's love and care. The Septuagint rendering, ἀπαίδευτον, "unchastened," points to the meaning affixed by the Chaldee paraphrase, "that does not wish to be converted," having no desire for amendment; like what is said in Jer. ii. 30, "they received no correction." Others render, "which does not turn pale," *i.e.* which is not ashamed, comparing Isa. xxix. 22. The verb *kasaph* seems to have this meaning in niphal, according to Talmudic use; but its usual signification is "to pine" or "long for." The Revised Version gives in the margin, "that hath no longing"—a rendering adopted by Professor Gandell, implying that the people are quite satisfied with their present condition, and have no aspiration for anything better or higher (comp. Hos. xii. 8). This is a very apposite interpretation; but there is no sufficient ground for rejecting the translation of the Authorized Version, which is supported by high authority, is agreeable to the use of the word, and affords a satisfactory sense.

Ver. 2.—Before the decree bring forth. Before the result follows the fiat. The Divine purpose is represented as a woman labouring with child, travailing before it comes to execution. This is thrice repeated in substance, to show the certainty and speed of its arrival. **Before the day pass as the chaff.** "Before" is not in the Hebrew, and the clause is parenthetical, "Like chaff the day passeth." "The day" must be still the day of the Lord, not the day of life or the day of repentance. God brings on the judgment as easily and as quickly as the wind carries the chaff before it. The Septuagint and Syriac join the two clauses together; thus the LXX., Πρὸ τοῦ γενέσθαι ὑμᾶς ὡς ἄνθος παραπορευόμενον, "Before ye become as a flower that passeth away." And Jerome gives, "Priusquam pariat jussio quasi pulverem transeuntem diem," "Before the decree beget the day which passeth by like the dust." The present Hebrew text does not confirm these versions. The figure of the chaff is common (see Job xxi. 18; Isa. xvii. 13; xxix. 5).

Ver. 3.—The prophet here addresses especially the pious among the people, urging them to perseverance in the right way. Ye meek of the earth. The humble, peaceable, religious, among the Israelites are primarily meant; whose character is the direct contrary of the proud, self-confident infidels mentioned above (comp. Isa. xi. 4; Amos ii. 7). But there is no reason why the admonition should not include the heathen who are striving to live after the light of conscience (Isa. xxiv. 5; Rom. ii. 14, etc.). **Which have wrought his judgment.** Who have fulfilled the ordinances of God's Law. **Seek righteousness.** This and the following injunction explain what is meant by "seek the Lord" at the beginning of the verse (Deut. xvi. 20). **Seek meekness.** Persevere in showing a humble, gentle temper. Septuagint, καὶ ἀποκρίνασθε αὐτά, "and answer them." **It may be.** Even the righteous shall scarcely be saved (comp. 1 Pet. iv. 17, 18). **Ye shall be hid.** Ye shall be preserved in the time of judgment (Ps. xxvii. 5; xxxi. 20; Isa. xxxii. 2). This recalls the prophet's name, which is interpreted, "Whom the Lord hides" (comp. Amos v. 14, 15).

Vers. 4—7.—§ 2. *The admonition is enforced by the announcement of the punishment that is about to fall on various nations, which shall prepare the way for the general* *acceptance of true religion; and first the sentence shall reach the Philistines.*

Ver. 4.—There is reason enough why Judah should tremble when the nations around her, such as the powerful and turbulent Philistines, fall before the invading host. Four of the five cities of the Philistines are mentioned, as denoting the whole territory, which again is the representative of the heathen world more definitely particularized later on. Thus the four quarters of the world are virtually specified: the Philistines representing the west, the Moabites and Ammonites (vers. 8—10) the east, the Cushites (vers. 11, 12) the south, and the Assyrians (vers. 13—15) the north. Gaza (see note on Amos i. 6) shall be forsaken; depopulated and desolate. There is a paronomasia in the Hebrew: *Azzah* will be *azubhah.* Some of the other localities are treated in the same manner (comp. Micah i. 10—15, and notes there). Ashkelon a desolation (see note on Amos i. 8). They shall drive out Ashdod. The inhabitants shall be expelled. (For Ashdod, see note on Amos, *loc. cit.*) At the noon day. The hottest part of the day, the most unlikely time for a hostile attack, hence the expression is equivalent to "unexpectedly and suddenly" (comp. Jer. xv. 8). Ekron shall be rooted up. In the Hebrew paronomasia, *Ekron* ("the Deep-rooted") shall be *teaker.* (For Ekron, see note on Amos, *loc. cit.,* where the fulfilment of prophecy concerning that town is noted.) Gaza (see note on Amos i. 7), after being depopulated and again repeopled by Alexander the Great, fell into the hands of Ptolemy, and was destroyed by Antiochus, B.C. 198 (Polybius, 'Reliq.,' xvi. 40; Pusey, p. 457). Often rebuilt, it was as often razed to the ground; and the present representative of the ancient town, Ghuzzeh, stands upon a hill composed of the accumulated ruins of successive cities. Of the condition of Ashkelon, Dr. Thomson writes, "There are no buildings of the ancient city now standing, but broken columns are mixed up with the soil. . . . Let us climb to the top of these tall fragments at the south-east angle of the wall, and we shall have the whole scene of desolation before us, stretching terrace after terrace, quite down to the sea on the north-west. . . . No site in this country has so deeply impressed my mind with sadness. . . . They have stretched out upon Ashkelon the line of confusion and the stones of emptiness. Thorns have come up in her palaces, and brambles in the fortresses thereof, and it is a habitation of dragons and a court for owls (Isa. xxxiv. 11—13)" ('The Land and the Book,' p. 546). "It was for ages," says Dr. Porter, "a great and strong city. Under the Philistines, the Hebrews, the Greeks, the Romans, the Saracens, the Crusaders, it was a place of note. The shattered walls that still surround the site were built by Richard Cœur de Lion. When I first clambered to the top of a broken bastion, a scene of desolation burst suddenly upon my view for which I was not prepared, though I had seen Baalbec and Palmyra, Heliopolis and Memphis. The whole site was before me, and not a fragment of a house standing. One small section was covered with little gardens; but over the rest of the site lay smooth rounded hillocks of drifting sand. The sand is fast advancing—so fast, that probably ere the close of the century the site of Ascalon will have been blotted out for ever" ('Illust. of Bible Proph.,' p. 21). As for Ekron, *hod. Akir,* travellers note that it is now a little village, consisting of about fifty mud houses, without a remnant of antiquity except two large walls; its very ruins have vanished. The omission of Gath, a town at this time of small importance (see note on Amos i. 6), is probably owing to a feeling of the symbolism of numbers, four denoting completion, or the whole, like "the four winds, the four ends of the earth," etc.

Ver. 5.—Woe. The denunciation extends to all Philistia. The inhabitants of the sea coast. Both the Greek and Latin Versions retain the notion of the Hebrew word *chebel:* "Ye who inhabit the measured allotment of the sea." "Philistia," says Sir C. Warren, "consists of an undulating plain from fifty to a hundred feet above the level of the sea, reaching thirty-two miles from Ekron to Gaza, with a breadth of from nine to sixteen miles. To the east of this the hills commence, not the hill-country, but a series of low spurs and undulating ground, culminating in hogs' backs, running nearly north and south, and rising in places to twelve hundred feet above the ocean" ('Survey Memoirs: Jerusalem,' p. 436). The nation of the Cherethites. So in Ezek. xxv. 16. Zephaniah calls the Philistines by this name for the sake of a play on the word, *Cherethites* meaning "Cutters-off," and they were devoted to being "cut off" (*karath*). Part of David's body-guard was composed of the same people (1 Sam. xxx. 14). The name seems to have belonged to a portion of the Philistines who inhabited the southern part of the district. "One of the principal villages of Philistia is now called *Keretiya,* so that the term may apply to the inhabitants of this town—an ancient Cherith not mentioned in the Bible" (Conder's 'Handbook to the Bible,' p. 237). They have been supposed to have emigrated from Crete, but there are no reliable grounds for this theory, though the LXX. in the present passage has, Πάροικοι Κρητῶν, "sojourners of the Cretans;" and the Syriac gives a similar rendering. St. Jerome renders, "gens perditorum," "nation of destroyers." **The word of the Lord is against you.** The sentence is pronounced in the words following. **O Canaan.** O Philistia, which shall be as Canaan, and in like manner exterminated. Canaan means "Lowland," a name which originally was applied to the Phœnician and Philistine tracts on the sea-coast. **I will even destroy thee.** The like threat is uttered by Jeremiah (xlvii. 4, 5) and Ezekiel (xxv. 15—17).

Ver. 6.—**Dwellings and cottages for shepherds;** better, *pastures with caves for shepherds.* In the use of the word *keroth,* "diggings" ("cottages," Authorized Version) there is probably intended another play on the "Cherethites." Neale, "The road from Gaza to Askalon lay along the sea-shore. . . . In the winter months many parts of it are impracticable, owing to the encroachment of the sea. The surf then dashes wildly into the huge caverns worked out of the endless sand-hills that line this coast. These caverns were tenanted, when we passed, by goatherds and their flocks. Thither they resort for shelter from the fierce heat of the noontide sun; and here during the night the goats are penned. There are wells and reservoirs in the vicinity which furnish water for the flocks the whole year round, and the brambles and thorn-bushes that flourish near the seaside form their pasturage" ('Eight Years in Syria,' i. 40, 41). Septuagint, ἔσται Κρήτη νομὴ ποιμνίων, "Crete shall be a pasture of flocks."

Ver. 7.—**And the coast shall be for the remnant,** etc.; *it will be a tract for the remnant.* The district will be the possession of the Jews, who should be restored to their land (Obad. 19). Zephaniah virtually predicts the Captivity and the return, and intimates that the destruction of hostile nations is the means of advancing true religion. **They shall feed** their flocks **thereupon.** Where the Philistine cities stood shall be the pasture-ground of the Israelites' flocks. **Ashkelon.** One city is mentioned as a type of all. **For.** This is the reason why they are permitted to triumph thus. **Shall visit.** In a good sense, to protect and cherish (Exod. iv. 31; Ruth i. 6; Ps. viii. 4; Zech. x. 3; Luke i. 68). **Turn away** (*reverse*) **their captivity.** Bring them back from their exile to their own land (comp. Joel iii. 1; Micah iv. 10). The phrase, however, is often (and possibly here) used metaphorically for the abolishment of misery and the restoration to a happy condition (comp. Deut. xxx. 3; Job xlii. 10 (15); Jer. xxix. 14). The full accomplishment of this prophecy concerning the overthrow of

Philistia is of a spiritual nature, and must be looked for in the Messianic era, when the kingdoms of the world become the kingdom of Christ; and so in the subsequent predictions.

Vers. 8—10.—§ 3. *The punishment shall fall next upon the Moabites and Ammonites, representing the east.*

Ver. 8.—**The reproach of Moab.** As this refers to past actions, it must signify the hostile attitude which Moab always assumed towards Israel. **The revilings of the children of Ammon.** Both these descendants of Lot proved themselves bitter enemies of the Jews. Keil refers to Numb. xv. 30 and Ezek. xx. 27, where the word *gadaph* is used in the sense "to revile or blaspheme by actions." (For the persistent hostility of Moab, see note on Amos ii. 1, and for that of Ammon, the note on Amos i. 13.) **Magnified themselves against their border.** They carried themselves haughtily, showed their pride by violating the territory of the Israelites. This pride and self-exaltation is a leading feature of the character of these two nations (comp. Isa. xvi. 6; Jer. xlviii. 29, etc.). The destruction of the kingdom of Israel and the weakness of that of Judah gave occasion to these neighbours to display their haughtiness and independence. The LXX. has, "my borders." God himself assigned its boundaries to Israel, as to other nations (Deut. xxxii. 8); and to invade these was an offence against him.

Ver. 9.—**As I live.** This is a common formulary to express certainty, God, as it were, pledging his existence to the truth of his declaration (Deut. xxxii. 40; Isa. xlix. 18, etc.). God calls himself, **The Lord of hosts,** therefore able to fulfil his threats; and **the God of Israel,** and therefore ready to punish wrongs done to his chosen people. **As Sodom.** This threat came home with particular force to the Moabites and Ammonites who dwelt in the neighbourhood of the Dead Sea, and had before their eyes this awful proof of the chastisement with which sin meets, and which had happened in the time of their forefather Lot. "There are no settled inhabitants," says Dr. Porter, writing of Moab, "but the hillsides and glens are studded with the ruins of ancient towns and villages. We at length pitched our tents by the lonely fountain of Heshbon. The site of this royal city is commanding— a rounded hill on the edge of a vast plateau, which extends on the south and east to the horizon, and on the west breaks down in steep slopes, jagged cliffs, and wild ravines, to the Dead Sea and Jordan valley, nearly four thousand feet below. The hill was the nucleus of the city. Its sides are covered with ruins, and remains of houses, temples, and other buildings are strewn over a considerable section of the adjoining plain. All is desolate. Not a building, and scarcely a fragment of a wall, is standing; yet, though deserted for centuries, it bears its ancient name. I looked from Heshbon far and wide over the ancient territory of the Moabites, and saw desolation everywhere. The old towns and villages are all deserted and in ruins. In fact, there is not at this moment a single inhabited town or village in Moab, except Kerak, which stands on the extreme southern border. The sites of many were visible—grey mounds dotting the plain" ('Illust. of Bible Proph.,' pp. 24, 25). " The cities, towns, villages, are all in ruins. ... And no attempt is ever made to rebuild or repair; no man ventures to seek even a temporary abode among the ruined cities of Moab. The local Arab avoids the old sites, and seeks rest and security amid rocks and ravines; the powerful desert tribes sweep over the country periodically, and devour and destroy all in their track" (ibid., p. 28). Even **the breeding of nettles**; rather, *a possession of nettles;* a place where nettles only grow. Vulgate, *siccitas spinarum.* The identification of the plant *kharul* is uncertain. In Job (xxx. 7) it is represented as of sufficient growth to conceal fugitives; hence some think it is the wild mustard. Dr. Pusey, relying on a notice of Professor Palmer, considers it to be the mallow, which grows in rank luxuriance in Moab. The LXX., reading *daleth* instead of *mem* in the ἅπαξ λεγόμενον *mimshaq,* rendered " breeding," has Δαμασκὸς ἐκλελειμμένη, " Damascus shall be left." **Salt-pits.** All travellers note the abundance of rock-salt in the vicinity of the Dead Sea (see Deut. xxix. 23; and comp. Ps. cvii. 34; Jer. xvii. 6). **A perpetual desolation.** The prophecy intimates that this country should never recover its prosperity (comp. Ezek. xxv.). **The residue of my people shall spoil them.** A partial fulfilment of this prophecy occurred when Judas Maccabæus smote Ammon (1 Macc. v. 6, etc.), and Alexander Jannæus subdued the Moabites (Josephus, 'Ant.,' xiii. 13. 5); but the prophet looks forward to a spiritual fulfilment under the Messiah, as we see from ver. 11 (comp. Isa. xiv. 1, 2; xlix. 23, etc.). The faithful remnant shall win possession of the heathen strongholds, and convert the nations to Christ, and incorporate them in the Church.

Ver. 10. — **This shall they have.** All these calamities mentioned above shall fall on the Ammonites and Moabites in punishment of their pride and spite and insolence (see note on ver. 8).

Ver. 11.—§ 4. Before passing to the judgment on the nations of the south and north, the prophet shows the object of all these chastisements : *God destroys idolatry in order that pure religion may reign over all the earth.* **The Lord will be terrible unto them.** The Lord shows himself as a terrible God over the Moabites and Ammonites, but only as parts of the heathen world, and with a view to a universal result. This is the purpose of the revelation of himself as Judge. Septuagint, Ἐπιφανήσεται Κύριος ἐπ' αὐτούς, "The Lord will appear against them.' **For he will famish all the gods of the earth.** The verb means literally, "to make lean," and then " to destroy;" hence the LXX., ἐξολοθρεύσει. The word may be chosen in order to express the idea that worshippers will no more be found to offer sacrifices and drink-offerings to the gods (see Bel and the Dragon 6, 12). The nations being destroyed, the gods reverenced by them would vanish and be heard of no more. **Men shall worship him.** Idolatry abolished, men shall learn to worship Jehovah. **Every one from his place.** Every one shall worship God in his own place and country; the Lord shall be universally recognized, and his worship shall no longer be confined to one temple or one land, but wherever men dwell there shall they offer their homage and adoration (comp. Isa. xix. 18, 19; Mal. i. 11, where the same truth is signified). Such passages as Micah iv. 1 and Zech. xiv. 16, which seem to imply that all nations are to come up to the material Jerusalem to pay their devotions, require evidently a spiritual interpretation, and denote that the heathen converted to Christ shall be received into the Church, and join in the worship of the true Israel. **The isles of the heathen;** or, *coasts of the nations;* the most distant countries that lie across the seas (Gen. x. 5; Ps. lxxii. 10; Isa. xi. 11, etc.).

Vers. 12—15.—§ 5. *The judgment shall fall upon the Ethiopians and Assyrians, representing the south and north.*

Ver. 12.—**Ethiopians;** *Cushites.* These are named as the most remote inhabitants of the south with which the Israelites were acquainted (Ezek. xxxviii. 5). **Ye shall be slain by my sword;** *the slain of my sword are they,* the second person being dropped, as one cannot address the dead (Orelli). The Lord's sword is the instrument which he uses to effect his purpose of punishment (comp. Isa. xxvii. 1; xxxiv. 5; lxvi. 16). The Ethiopians are reckoned among the forces of Egypt (2 Chron. xii. 3; Nah. iii. 9, etc.). The prediction had a fulfilment when the Assyrians conquered Egypt, and again under Nebuchadnezzar. It shall have a more sublime accomplishment when the sword of the Spirit shall reduce the utmost south to the dominion of Christ (see Isa. xlv. 14; Ps. lxviii. 31). The commencement of this conversion is seen in the chamberlain of Queen Candace (Acts viii. 27, etc.).

Ver. 13.—**The north,** represented by Assyria, as yet unconquered, and still apparently flourishing. Though this country lay to the north-east of Palestine, its armies attacked from the north, and it is generally represented as a northern power. Its destruction was foretold (Isa. x. 12; Ezek. xxxi. 11, etc.; Nah. i. 14, etc.). In this verse the Hebrew verbs are not in the simple future, but in the imperative or optative mood, "Let him stretch out his hand," etc., as though the prophet were praying that the enemies of his people might be overthrown. **Nineveh.** St. Jerome gives *speciosam*, rendering the proper name according to his notion of its Hebrew etymology. Its proper meaning, in Accadian, would be "Fish-house," *i.e.* house consecrated to the god of fish. (For a description of Nineveh, see note on Jonah i. 2. For the destruction of Nineveh, see the Introduction to Nahum, § I.) **Dry like a wilderness.** The country shall become an arid desert. Assyria was greatly indebted for its remarkable fertility to a very successful system of artificial irrigation, and when this was not maintained, great tracts soon relapsed into a wilderness (Layard, 'Nineveh,' ii. 68). "Cultivation," says Professor Rawlinson, "is now the exception instead of the rule. 'Instead of the luxuriant fields, the groves and gardens of former times, nothing now meets the eye but an arid waste' (Chesny). Large tracts are covered by unwholesome marshes, producing nothing but enormous reeds; others lie waste and bare, parched up by the fierce heat of the sun, and utterly destitute of water; in some places sand-drifts accumulate, and threaten to make the whole region a mere portion of the desert" ('Anc. Mon.,' i. 41).

Ver. 14.—**Flocks; herds.** The prophet describes graphically the desolation mentioned in the preceding verse. The "herds" are not sheep and cattle, as in parallel cases (Isa. xvii. 2; xxvii. 10; xxxii. 14), but all the beasts of the nations—all the wild beasts that infest the country. Septuagint, πάντα τὰ θηρία τῆς γῆς. The Hebrew will hardly bear Keil's rendering, "all kinds of beasts in crowds." (Compare similar predictions, Isa. xiii. 21; xxxiv. 11, 14). The cormorant (*kaath*); probably *the pelican;* Vulgate, *onocrotalus;* the Septuagint gives, χαμαιλέοντες, which word Schleusner thinks to have been interchanged with κόρακες that follows soon afterwards. But in the latter

place Jerome has *corvus.* The pelican is found in the Assyrian monuments under more than one appellation (see 'Transact. of Soc. of Bibl. Archæol.,' viii. 93, etc., and 141). **The bittern** (*kippod*). Most recent critics translate this by "hedgehog" cr "porcupine." The Septuagint has, ἐχῖνοι: the Vulgate, *ericius.* But neither hedgehog nor porcupine utters cries or frequents pools of water, and it may well be doubted whether some marsh-loving bird is not meant. Certainly the following clause suits the habits of a bird better than those of a hedgehog (see 'Bible Educator,' iii. 312, where Dr. Tristram is quoted saying, "As a matter of fact, the bittern is very abundant in these swamps of the Tigris, and in all the marshy grounds of Syria; and its strange booming note, disturbing the stillness of the night, gives an idea of desolation which nothing but the wail of the hyena can equal"). No notice of the bittern seems to be found in the Assyrian monuments, though the mention of the heron is not uncommon. The *kaath* and *kippod* are commonly mentioned together, *e.g.* Isa. xxxiv. 11. **The upper lintels;** "the capitals" of the columns (see note on Amos ix. 1, where the same word *kaphtor* is used). Their **voice shall sing in the windows;** literally, *the voice of the songster in the window.* Birds shall perch and sing in the apertures of the ruined palaces. Vulgate, *Vox cantantis in fenestra;* the LXX. has, Θηρία φωνήσει ἐν τοῖς διορύγμασιν αὐτῆς, "Wild beasts shall cry in the breaches thereof." Others translate, "Hark! it singeth in the windows." There are no traces of windows in any of the Assyrian palaces, even in the case of chambers next the outer walls. If daylight were admitted, it must have entered through openings in the ceilings (Layard, 'Nineveh,' ii. 260). **Desolation shall be in the thresholds.** The word rendered "desolation" (*chorebh*) Jerome notes may be read as meaning "sword," "drought," and "raven;" he adopts the last signification, and translates, in agreement with the LXX., *corvus.* But it seems best to take the term as signifying "desolation;" no human creature shall be found there, only ruin and rubbish. Ewald renders, "Owls shall sing in the windows, crows on the threshold, 'shivered, crushed.'" **For he shall uncover** (*he hath laid bare*) **the cedar work.** God, or the enemy, has so destroyed the palaces that the cedar panelling is exposed to the weather. Jerome has, "Attenuabo robur ejus." We see by Sennacherib's boast (Isa. xxxvii. 24) that the Assyrians imported cedars for building purposes. And we have monumental evidence of the employment of cedar in palaces at least since the time of Assurnazirpal, B.C. 860. Esarhaddon reports that he received cypress and cedar from Lebanon as tribute; and Assurbanipal states that in erecting his palace he used cedar pillars from Sirjon and Lebanon (Schrader, 'Die Keilinschrift. und Alt. Test.,' pp. 183, 453). Neriglissar, King of Babylon, B.C. 559, in rebuilding his palace, records that he "arranged tall cedars for its roof" ('Records of the Past,' v. 142).

Ver. 15.—**This is the rejoicing city.** Such is the fate of this once exulting city, **that dwelt carelessly, secure,** with no fear of danger at hand (Isa. xlvii. 8, on which this passage is founded). **I am, and there is none beside me.** Thus, in effect, Nineveh claimed for herself the attributes of Almighty God. She stands alone, mistress of nations, a type of the powers of this world, which deify themselves and defy the Lord. Septuagint, Οὐκ ἔστι μετ' ἐμὲ ἔτι, "There is no more any after me." **Shall hiss.** In scorn (Job xxvii. 23; Jer. xix. 8; Micah vi. 16). **Wag his hand.** He shall shake or wave his hand with the gesture of dismissal, as if saying, "Away with thee! get thee gone!"—a rehearsal of the awful "Depart ye!" in the final judgment (comp. Nah. iii. **19**).

HOMILETICS.

Vers. 1, 2.—*The evil summoned to repentance.* Having declared fully and faithfully the Divine judgments, the prophet changed his tone, and, turning to another aspect of truth and blending compassion with severity, he tenderly entreated those who had become so estranged from God to return to him with all their hearts. This is how he appeals to his godless fellow-countrymen. "Gather yourselves," etc. (vers. 1, 2). Notice—

I. THE HARDENING EFFECT OF SIN. Evil hardens those who indulge in it, even as the fire hardens the material brought under its influence. You read such words as Jer. ii. 25; xviii. 12; Zech. vii. 12, and you cannot help being impressed with the hardening tendency of sin. So here (ver. 1) note the words, "*O nation not desired.*" The word rendered "desired" means "to turn pale," "to become white with shame." It is the same word used by Isaiah (xxix. 22), "Jacob shall not now be ashamed, neither shall his face now wax pale." Indulgence in sin renders men stubborn and stiff-necked. There is a spiritual condition expressively described as "past feeling." The heart may become hardened, and the conscience seared. "Take heed," etc. (Heb. iii. 13).

II. GOD'S INFINITE CONDESCENSION AND GRACE IN MAKING ANY APPROACH OR APPEAL TO THOSE THUS CONFIRMED IN EVIL-DOING. He might have left such to reap the full consequences of their transgressions, whereas in truth, all down the ages his seeking love has been going out after such with a view to their restoration, and even his chastisements have had the same merciful intention. 1. We see this seeking love of God manifested in ancient time in the raising up of these prophets, men full of faith and power; bold, courageous, daring; and in sending these forth to expostulate with the callous and impenitent, if perchance they might be led "to break off sin by righteousness." 2. In the Incarnation. He who spake in time past to the fathers by the prophets, subsequently spoke unto them by his Son (Heb. i. 1). "The Son of man came to seek and to save that which was lost." 3. In the institution of the Christian ministry, sending forth his ambassadors to proclaim to the estranged the conditions of reconciliation and peace (2 Cor. v. 20).

III. GOD'S CALL ADDRESSED TO EVIL-DOERS IS A CALL TO REPENTANCE. "Gather yourselves together, yea, gather together" (ver. 1); *i.e.* "Bend yourselves," bend low in contrition in view of transgression—repent, and submit yourselves to God. The nature of repentance must be understood in order to this. There enters into it the element of sorrow; the deep humbling of the soul; yet sorrow alone does not constitute it; there must accompany this the breaking away from sin, and the turning unto God. "Repentance towards God, and faith in the Lord Jesus Christ" are sacred and imperative duties and obligations; yet there is no merit in them, but the heart must rest entirely in the mercy of God, which is so large that man has only to bend his heart before God—to be willing—and God's all-regenerating power shall be experienced. Then "bend yourselves, bend, ye people, that do not grow pale" (ver. 1).

IV. THIS SPIRIT OF PENITENCE AND SUBMISSION TO THE LORD GOD SHOULD BE CHERISHED WITHOUT DELAY. (Ver. 2.) A British general, on being asked when he could be ready to take the command of the forces, answered, "Now." He knew as a soldier that the call of duty did not admit of delay. When a course is felt by us to be right, we ought at once to pursue it. "What is 'now'? 'A bright presence.' Wrestle with it, and say, 'I will not let thee go except thou bless me'! 'A sweet garden.' Go, gather in it the fruits of life! 'A true temple.' Bow down in it, and consecrate yourself to him who has placed you within its shrine! 'A living rescue.' Use it, that you may run into the ark of safety! 'A rich banquet.' Now the feast is spread: 'Come, eat, O friends, drink, O beloved! yea, eat and live for ever'!" (Martin Tupper's 'Proverbial Philosophy,' p. 204). "Now is the accepted time; behold, now is the day of salvation" (2 Cor. vi. 2).

Ver. 3.—*The good stimulated to a truer life.* It is a truth admitting of abundant illustration, that even in the most degenerate times God has had a people to show forth his praise. He has not left himself without witnesses. Whilst in this prophet's day there was "the remnant of Baal" (ch. i. 4), there was also "the remnant of the house of Judah" (ch. ii. 7), "the remnant of Israel," that did no iniquity nor uttered lies (ch. iii. 13). "The meek of the earth" clothed with humility and working righteousness (ver. 3).

I. TRUE PIETY INFLUENCES BOTH THE CHARACTER AND CONDUCT OF ITS SUBJECTS. It is an inward grace, manifesting itself outwardly in holy excellence and holy living. 1. *Humility* is the token referred to as indicating its influence upon the character. "Ye meek of the earth." Meekness is power tempered with gentleness—it is the soul restraining, holding back its own power. (1) It manifests itself towards God. He has marked out to man the true way of life; but man has the power to decline to pursue this course. "The meek of the earth" are such as, although conscious of this power, yield themselves up in passive obedience to God, to receive the impress of his Spirit, and to be moulded at his will. (2) And it manifests itself towards man. The possessor of this heavenly grace, in his intercourse with his fellow-men, lays aside all parade and show and ostentation; whilst under wrong, in patience he possesses his soul, and although he may have the power to revenge the wrong done, he holds back this power, ruling his spirit, and proving himself mightier than he who taketh a city. 2. *Rectitude* is the token referred to as indicating the influence of true piety upon the conduct. "Which have wrought his judgment" (ver. 3). It prompts to obedience to God's revealed Law—to righteousness of life—obedience rendered by a heart thoroughly loyal to God and to righteousness, and which, becoming the very habit of the soul, is rendered easy and pleasant.

II. THE GROWTH OF THE SOUL IN HOLY CHARACTER AND CONDUCT IS GRADUAL. The reiterated counsels and exhortations addressed to the good by prophets and apostles indicate that the goal had not been reached. Such are to "go on unto perfection" (Heb. vi. 1), to seek to be continually advancing, ever to be aiming after a purer and holier life. "Nearer, my God, to thee." "Not as though I had already attained," etc. (Phil. iii. 12).

III. THIS PROGRESS IS TO BE SECURED AS THE RESULT OF DIVINE DISCIPLINE AND PERSONAL ENDEAVOUR. 1. *Divine discipline.* In the time of national calamity described by this prophet, and ere long to befall his land, the good as well as the evil would suffer—the sorowful experience would be passed through by all, whilst the Divine discipline thus designed to rouse the indifferent was intended also to purify the good, and to contribute to the perfecting in them the Divine character and life. And such being ever the gracious intention of God, let the good circumstanced thus sing—

> "Great Master, touch us with thy skilful hand,
>   Let not the music that is in us die;
> Great Sculptor, hew and polish us, nor let
>   Hidden and lost thy form within us lie.
> Spare not thy stroke; do with us as thou wilt;
> Let there be nought unfinished, broken, marr'd;
> Complete thy purpose, that we may become
> Thy perfect image, O our God and Lord!"

2. *Personal endeavour.* The seer here stimulated the good to persevering effort so as to attain unto a truer life. "Seek ye the Lord;" "seek righteousness;" "seek meek-

ness." By earnest prayer, by calm reflection and meditation, and by holy service, man is to co-operate with God with a view to his own spiritual growth. "Work out your own salvation with fear and trembling," etc. (Phil. ii. 12).

IV. THEY WHO THUS PROGRESS IN THE DIVINE LIFE SHALL BE RENDERED SECURE IN THE DAY OF CONFLICT AND JUDGMENT. "It may be ye shall be hid," etc. (ver. 3). The "may be" was not intended to express uncertainty with reference to their security, but rather to keep them from becoming too confident and self-reliant. They who continue in the love and service of God cannot but be secure, for their safety is amply guaranteed (Isa. xxvi. 20 ; Ps. xxxi. 20 ; Isa. xxxii. 2).

Vers. 4—7.—*The doom of the Philistines.* The prophet, having declared the judgments to come upon Judah, turned his thoughts to the surrounding heathen nations, and proclaimed the doom they should experience. Several reasons probably influenced him in taking this survey and in calling attention to the chastisements inflicted upon other lands. (1) A desire to make it clear to his people that with God there is no respect of persons ; (2) that wrong-doing works evil issues wherever it is practised; (3) to make vivid to them that the dark clouds of retribution were gathering, and so to rouse them out of their apathy and to stimulate them to return to righteousness of life. In referring thus to the heathen, he began with the Philistines, the natural enemies of his nation. We have here—

I. A SOLEMN DECLARATION OF DIVINE JUDGMENTS TO BE EXECUTED AGAINST EVIL-DOERS. 1. The nation referred to was that of the Philistines. They were very influential in Palestine. Occupying the coast, they were in possession of the trade carried on with Europe and Asia. Besides this transit trade, they had vast internal resources. They were given to agriculture, and hence we read that the Israelites had to go to the Philistines "to sharpen every man his share and his coulter, his axe and his mattock." In their prosperity they built their five great cities, Gaza, Ashdod, Ashkelon, Gath, and Ekron. They were warlike and idolatrous, and through their self-sufficiency and boastfulness, their tyranny and oppression, together with their idol-worship, they became offensive in the sight of Heaven. 2. The judgments here declared as about to overtake them. Their cities should be destroyed, their land rendered desolate, their inhabitants should be removed, the busy tract by the sea, where once trade and commerce flourished, should become pastures and folds for sheep, and where once stood the abodes of prosperous merchants, the humble shepherds should construct their huts (vers. 4—6). 3. The fulfilment is unquestionable ; the word of the Lord by the mouth of his holy prophet has been amply verified. It is true that the Gaza of to-day is a populous town, and hence those ready to carp and cavil have urged that Gaza has not been forsaken. But the ruins which have been found and explored within a mile or two of modern Gaza indicate the site of the ancient city, and tell how that city has indeed, like the others, passed away. "The Word of our God shall stand for ever."

II. A TENDER ASSURANCE OF DIVINE MERCY TO BE MANIFESTED TOWARDS THE FAITHFUL. In terms of exquisite beauty and gracious tenderness he represents the faithful servants of Heaven, "the remnant of Judah," as visited by God in the midst of their dark experiences, brought by him out of captivity and conducted by his guiding hand to the green pastures, where their wants are fully supplied by day, and to quiet resting-places, where by night they may lie down and repose in perfect security, as being under the Divine Shepherd's guardian care (ver. 7). The verse has been taken by some literally, and they have either seen its fulfilment in the return of the pious Jews after captivity in Babylon, or they look on to the fulfilment in the conversion of the Jews and their restoration to their own land ; whilst others are content with recognizing in the words a confident assurance and a beautiful symbolical picture of that ultimate peace and security and abundance which all the ransomed of the Lord shall enjoy. Certain it is that we may take the seer's stern words pronouncing the doom of the Philistines as conveying a clear intimation that evil-doing shall assuredly be followed by Divine retribution, whilst from his words of promise to the faithful we may draw the encouraging and inspiring consciousness that the faithful and God-fearing shall be sustained and comforted in present sorrow, and shall at length emerge out of the gloom and the darkness into the sunshine of a true prosperity.

Vers. 8—10.—*The Divine judgment upon the Moabites and Ammonites.* The Moabites and Ammonites were related to the Israelites by kinship. They were the descendants of Lot—the Moabites by Moab, the elder son of that patriarch, and the Ammonites by Ben-Ammi, or Ammon, his younger son (Gen. xix. 37, 38). With these tribes, in view of this blood-relationship, the Israelites were distinctly forbidden to wage war (Deut. ii. 9, 19). These pastoral tribes, however, did not act thus peaceably toward Israel. They cherished the spirit of hatred in reference to the Israelites, which manifested itself in their revilings and boastings, and also in the incursions they made upon their territory (Isa. xvi. 6; Jer. xlviii. 29). The prophet here proceeds to declare against these tribes the judgments of God. Note—

I. THE PREVAILING SIN OF THE MOABITES AND AMMONITES. *Pride* (ver. 10; Jer. xlviii. 29). This spirit manifested itself (1) in their evil-speaking,—"they reproached and reviled God's people" (ver. 8); (2) in their arrogant and insolent bearing,—they "*magnified* themselves against the people of the Lord of hosts" (ver. 10); (3) in their deeds of oppression and cruelty,—they "magnified themselves against their border" (ver. 8), crossing this and making raids upon Judah, and taking special advantage of those seasons when, through conflict with foreign adversaries, that nation had become enfeebled. This sin of pride, so characteristic of these tribes, is still very prevalent, and lies at the very root of human misery; it leads to the cherishing of false appearances, to inconsiderateness and injustice with reference to the rights of others; it occasions misunderstandings, and then, standing in the way of mutual concession, causes alienation. It inflicts likewise self-injury, carries with it its own chastisement in the unhappy spirit it engenders; it is its own condemnation, for it is evident to all that trees whose boughs do not bend to the ground are not very well laden with fruit; and it ends in ruin, for "pride goeth before destruction," etc. (Prov. xvi. 18).

II. THE SURE PUNISHMENT WITH WHICH THEY WERE TO BE OVERTAKEN ON ACCOUNT THEREOF. (Ver. 9.) 1. Their cities were to be destroyed. Even as Sodom and Gomorrah of old had become engulfed in the Dead Sea, upon which these haughty ones constantly gazed without recalling the past and laying to heart its lessons of warning, so theirs should likewise pass away. 2. Their rich pasture-lands should become barren, and the fertile region changed into a region of nettles and salt-pits and a perpetual desert (ver. 9). 3. Israel, so often oppressed by them and called upon to endure their scorn and contempt, should eventually triumph over them, and take possession of their territory as the spoils of war (ver. 9). 4. This fate should really come to pass, since Jehovah was against them, and was pledged to its accomplishment. "Therefore as I live," etc. (ver. 9). All that his people had suffered through their haughtiness, he had known (ver. 8), and would duly requite. And so ever, since he reigneth, shall pride be subdued and the haughty oppressor be laid in the dust. "He scatters the proud in the imagination of their hearts. He puts down the mighty from their seats, and exalts them of low degree" (Luke i. 51, 52).

> "True dignity abides with him alone
> Who, in the silent hour of inward thought,
> Can still suspect and still revere himself
> In lowliness of heart."

Ver. 11.—*The Divine purpose in reference to the race, and the way of its fulfilment.* A very erroneous notion has been widely entertained respecting God's relations to the peoples of the earth. The representation has been very current that, in selecting the Jewish tribes and constituting these his "peculiar treasure," the Most High left all other nations to their own resources, and that they became practically outcasts from his love and care. We have, however, abundant evidence that such is by no means the teaching of Scripture; that whilst with a view to the revealing and developing of his plan of redeeming mercy he did select the Jewish race, imparting to them special privileges and communicating to them a knowledge of his will, yet that all the nations were likewise under his government and nurture. We think of what is recorded in the Bible respecting Job the Chaldean, Balaam the heathen soothsayer, the mission of Elisha to the woman of Sarepta, and of Jonah to Nineveh, and the Divine revelations made to heathen monarchs, and, with all this before us, we cannot foster the notion that the world outside the pale of Judaism was disregarded by Heaven, but we see clearly that, whilst God was working out his special purposes of love to the race through the medium of " the chosen people," he was also in various ways by his Spirit striving with *all* the children of men. The beauty in the teachings of the Hebrew prophets consists in the fact that they were so ready to acknowledge all this ; that they broke through the narrow boundary of exclusiveness which the Jews guarded so jealously, and told of the Divine working in all lands, and of the Divine intention to bless the entire race. The case of the Prophet Zephaniah is a conspicuous example of this. Whilst declaring the Divine judgments to light upon his own people, he also looked north and south, east and west, and saw the retributions which were to come upon the heathen nations. Nor did he rest here, but, peering still further into the future and apprehending the Divine Ruler as bringing order out of chaos, and out of trial and sorrow working good for the race, he paused in the midst of his dark announcements of coming woe to proclaim this loving design of his God (ver. 11),'whilst at length, having ended his predictions of impending evil, he again turned to this cheering theme, and lingered upon it even to the very end of his prophecy (ch. iii. 8—20).

I. THE DIVINE PURPOSE AS HERE EXPRESSED. This includes: 1. The complete extinction of idolatry. This is most expressly referred to here under the figure of starvation. The gods of the heathen should die through want and neglect. "He will famish all the gods of the earth" (ver. 11). 2. The full establishment of the worship of God. "And men shall worship him every one from his place" (ver. 11). 3. The universal acknowledgment of him by Gentile nations. "Even all the isles of the heathen" (ver. 11). The thought of the universality of this acknowledgment of the true God eventually is seen to be the more decidedly expressed here as we remember that in ancient times whole countries and continents were described as " the isles."

II. THIS DIVINE PURPOSE IS TO BE WROUGHT OUT THROUGH THE OUTWARD DISCIPLINE OF CONFLICT AND TRIAL. "The Lord will be terrible unto them" (ver. 11). Men are to be humbled that God may be exalted. They pursue their own designs, and often care only for the realization of their own selfish ends, but " the Lord sitteth in the heavens," ruling over all, and, through all the conflicts and strifes, the turmoils and trials of individuals and nations, he is bringing to pass his loving purposes, and is leading on to the glory of the latter day.

III. THE THOUGHT OF GOD AS WORKING THUS YIELDS INSPIRATION AND STRENGTH TO TRUE AND LOYAL HEARTS AMIDST THE DIFFICULTIES AND DISCOURAGEMENTS IN HOLY SERVICE. This was to Zephaniah the source of strength. Whilst faithful to his trust as the messenger of judgment he made to his own and to heathen nations the stern announcements of coming tribulation, he paused again and again to reflect upon the thought that these very judgments should be made to contribute to the accomplishment of God's merciful and gracious design to bless and save the race.

Ver. 12.—*The doom of Ethiopia.* We have here simply a passing allusion, yet we do well to pause and reflect upon it. Every word of God is " profitable," and even words which at first glance seem unimportant are found on reflection to be suggestive of holy teaching. We are reminded here—

I. THAT THE DIVINE JUDGMENTS REACH EVEN TO REMOTE PLACES. Ethiopia was in the south, and at the extreme south. Now, Judah had other and nearer foes in that direction. There was Edom and there was Egypt ; but the prophet, in his announcement of coming Divine judgments, carried his thoughts beyond these, and fixed his mind upon those dwelling at the remotest point. "Ye Ethiopians also," etc. (ver. 12). Remoteness will not screen wrong-doers.

II. THAT IT IS PERILOUS TO STAND IN ASSOCIATION WITH THOSE WHO ENGAGE IN EVIL-DOING. These Ethiopians or Cushites had no direct conflict with Judah, but they were in alliance with Egypt ; and through this alliance they would have to suffer in the time of coming retribution. Egypt was specially singled out for judgment because of her oppression, and Ethiopia, as one of her allies, her "helpers," would fall under the retributive chastisements of God (Ezek. xxx. 4, 5). They who ally themselves with transgressors make themselves participators in their crimes, and must expect to be partakers of their plagues.

III. THAT THE EVIL PASSIONS OF MEN ARE MADE TO FULFIL THE DIVINE BEHESTS. War is a terrible evil. In no way are the evil passions of men more surely let loose than in such conflicts; yet by these military conflicts God's purposes have at times been accomplished. Nebuchadnezzar and his forces, invading Egypt and destroying the Egyptians and their allies the Ethiopians, were instruments God employed to work his will. God through his holy prophet declared, "Ye Ethiopians also, ye shall be slain by my sword" (ver. 12).

Vers. 13—15.—*The doom of Assyria.* It was very natural that the prophet, in unfolding the Divine judgments upon heathen nations, should turn his thoughts to the north and to the Assyrian empire. That power was, in his day, at the very zenith of its prosperity, and his own nation was peculiarly exposed to its tyranny and oppression. The Hebrew seers frequently referred to this empire and to the ruin which should eventually overtake it; and whilst Zephaniah's allusion is very brief, limited indeed to three verses, it is nevertheless remarkably graphic and vivid. Observe—

I. THE STERN SENTENCE. (Vers. 13, 14.) 1. It foretold that the prevailing power which was seeking the overthrow of the kingdom of God in Judah should itself be completely destroyed. In a few descriptive touches he set forth the utter ruin which should befall the haughty Assyrian nation. She should be destroyed, and her capital become a dry, desolate waste in the midst of which the beasts of the desert should make their home. Her temples and palaces should lie broken, pelicans and hedgehogs lodging in the fallen capitals, whilst instead of the strains of the men-singers and women-singers, no more to be heard in her palaces, the notes of some solitary bird sitting in the window of some outer wall should alone sound forth. "Desolation" too "should be on the thresholds," and heaps of sand blown from the desert should mingle with the wreck of the city, until at length every trace of the former magnificence should have disappeared. And the acknowledgment should be made that this ruin was merited; the passer-by should hiss with very scorn, and move his hand in token of supreme contempt (vers. 13—15). 2. It declared this ruin to be the result of the Divine working. "And *he* will stretch out his hand," etc. (ver. 13). 3. This stern doom thus pronounced has literally come to pass. Modern research has been amply rewarded in the evidence which has thus been supplied of the fulfilment to the very letter of God's declarations uttered through his holy prophets. "The Word of the Lord endureth for ever."

II. THE SOLEMN REFLECTION. (Ver. 15.) 1. In reading these words we are led to feel that the prophet had a vivid realization of the future, and of the changes which were to take place. He saw "the rejoicing city" full of worldly prosperity, and he saw it likewise in its desolation, and his heart was moved as he reflected upon the instability of mere earthly greatness and might. 2. He traced the coming overthrow of the Assyrian power to its true causes. (1) *Pride.* "That said in her heart, I *am*, and there is none beside me" (ver. 15). (2) *Selfishness.* "*There is none beside me.*" Her interests centred in herself. There was no regard for the rights of others. She sought only her own ends, and sought by oppression and cruelty to make all surrounding nations tributary to her own worldly splendour and prosperity. And fostering this unholy spirit, she "dwelt carelessly," crying, "Peace and safety," wrapt in carnal security, until at length "sudden destruction" came upon her, and she was left in her desolation, silently yet emphatically to proclaim to all after-ages that true prosperity for nations, as for individuals, lies not in material greatness and worldly aggrandizement, but in the cultivation of the fear of God and in rectitude and righteousness of life.

HOMILIES BY VARIOUS AUTHORS.

Vers. 1, 2.—*A call to repentance, addressed to the nation of Judah.* I. THE CONDITION OF THE NATION DESCRIBED. Not its physical or material, but its moral or religious, condition. The former prosperous and fitted to inspire vain thoughts of stability and permanence. Its upper classes devoted to money-making and pleasure-seeking (ch. i. 8, 12; cf. Jer. iv. 30); its lower orders, here not the victims of oppression (ch. i. 9; iii. 1; cf. Jer. v. 27, 28; vi. 6), well-fed and comfortable (Jer. v. 7, 17). The latter degenerate and deserving of severe reprehension. 1. *Irreligious.*

According to the marginal rendering of both the Authorized and Revised Versions, the nation was "not desirous," *i.e.* possessed no longing after Jehovah, his Law, or worship, but had forsaken him, and sworn by them that are no gods (Jer. **v.** 7), offering up sacrifices and pouring out drink offerings unto other divinities in the open streets, and even setting up their abominations in the temple (Jer. vii. 17, 18, 30). For a nation no more than for an individual is it possible to remain in a state of irreligious neutrality or indifference. The people whose aspirations go not forth after him who is the King of nations as well as King of saints will sooner or later find themselves trusting in "lying vanities," or creating divinities out of their own foolish imaginations (Rom. i. 23). Between theism and polytheism is no permanent half-way house for either humanity as a whole or man as an individual. 2. *Shameless.* This translation (Grotius, Gesenius, Ewald, Keil and Delitzsch, Cheyne, and others) depicts the moral and spiritual hardening which results from sin long continued, passionately loved, and openly gloried in, as Judah's apostasy had been (ch. iii. 5). A whole diameter of moral and spiritual being lies between the shamelessness of innocence (Gen. ii. 25) and the shamelessness of sin (Phil. iii. 19). The former is beautiful and excites admiration; the latter is loathsome and evokes reprehension and pity. " A generation," says Pressensé, "which can no longer blush is in open insurrection against the first principles of universal morality " ('The Early Years of Christianity,' iv. 392). 3. *Hateful.* So the Authorized Version, followed by Pusey. The degenerate nation, addicted to idolatry and sunk in immorality, was not desired or loved by God; but, on account of its wickedness, was an object of aversion to God. No contradiction to the truth elsewhere stated that God still loved the people and desired their reformation (Jer. ii. 2; iii. 14); neither is it inconsistent to preach that " God is angry with the wicked every day " (Ps. vii. 11); and that, nevertheless, " he willeth not that any should perish, but that all should turn to him and live " (2 Pet. iii. 9).

II. The duty of the nation defined. To "gather themselves together." The figure, derived from the gathering together or collecting of stubble or dry sticks, " which are picked up one by one, with search and care " (Pusey), points to that work of self-examination which, in nations as in individuals, must precede conversion, and must be conducted: 1. *With resoluteness.* Being a work to which their hearts were naturally not disposed, it could not be entered upon and far less carried through without deliberate and determined personal effort. Hence the prophet's reduplication of his exhortation. To make one's self the subject of serious introspection, never easy, is specially difficult when the object is to detect one's faults and pronounce judgment on one's deeds. 2. *With inwardness.* A merely superficial survey would not suffice. An action outwardly correct may be intrinsically wrong. Hence the individual that would conduct a real work of self-examination must withdraw himself as much as possible from things eternal, take his seat on the interior tribunal of conscience, and gather round him all that forms a part of his being, in addition to his spoken words and finished deeds, the feelings out of which these have sprung, the motives by which they have been directed, the ends at which they have aimed, and subject the whole to a calm and impartial review. 3. *With minuteness.* The things to be reviewed must be taken one by one, and not merely in the mass. Words and deeds, motives and feelings, when only glanced at in the heap, seldom reveal their true characters; to be known in their very selves they must be looked at, considered, questioned, weighed separately. All about them must be brought to light and placed beneath the microscope of conscientious investigation. 4. *With thoroughness.* As each word, act, feeling, motive, so all must be taken. None must be exempted from scrutiny. Nor will it suffice that they be passed through the ordeal of examination once; the process must be repeated and re-repeated till the exact truth is known. " For a first search, however diligent, never thoroughly reaches the whole deep disease of the whole man; the most grievous sins hide other grievous sins, though lighter. Some sins flash on the conscience at one time, some at another; so that few, even upon a diligent search, come at once to the knowledge of all their heaviest sins " (Pusey).

III. The danger of the nation declared. Unless the duty recommended and prescribed were immediately and heartily entered upon and carried through, the judgment already lying in the womb of God's decree would come to the birth, and the day of his fierce anger would overtake them. 1. *The event was near.* Should Judah continue unrepentant, the hour of doom would be on her before she was aware. It was rapidly approaching, like chaff driven before the wind. So will the day of the Lord come upon the wicked unawares (Luke xvi. 34). 2. *The issue was certain.* Like chaff before the wind, too, her people would be driven away to pitiless destruction. The like fate is reserved for ungodly men generally (Ps. i. 4; Job xxi. 18). Nothing can avert the final overthrow of the unbelieving and impenitent, whether nation or individual, but repentance and reformation, not outward but inward, not seeming but real, not temporary but permanent.

Learn: 1. The reality of national no less than of individual wickedness. 2. The responsibility that attaches to nations as well as men. 3. The necessity of self-examination for communities as well as for private persons.—T. W.

Ver. 3.—*An exhortation to the meek, addressed to the believing remnant of Judah.* I. A CHEERING TESTIMONY. 1. *To the existence of a believing remnant.* Dark as the outlook for Judah was, degenerate as the mass of her people had become, there were yet those belonging to her community who either had not apostatized from Jehovah or had reverted to their allegiance (see 2 Kings xxii., xxiii.; 2 Chron. xxxiv., xxxv.). Since "the days that were before the Flood" (Gen. vi. 5—7, 12, 13), God has never wanted a seed to serve him, though oftentimes it has been small, and as in the days of Elijah (1 Kings xix. 10, 18) scarcely perceptible, at least by man. Compare the times after the exile (Mal. iii. 16) and those preceding the birth of Christ (Luke ii. 25). "Even so at this present time also there is a remnant according to the election of grace" (Rom. xi. 5). However discouraging in some respects the present aspect of society may be—what with infidelity in the upper and learned classes, indifference towards religion among the masses, and lukewarmness on the one hand with fanaticism on the other in the Church itself—there are, nevertheless, those who fear God and think upon his Name, who believe in Christ and seek to follow in his steps, who sigh and cry for the irreligion of the age, mourn over the deadness and divisions of the Church, and pray for the coming of that happy era when "the earth shall be filled with the knowledge of the Lord," etc. (Isa. xi. 9). 2. *To the beauty of their characters.* Designated "the meek of the earth." Indicating (1) their patience in enduring the disesteem, scorn, ridicule, and perhaps also oppression, spoliation, and persecution heaped upon them for their nonconformity to general custom in the matter of religion, and for venturing to dissent from common practice in serving Baal; and (2) their humility in maintaining intercourse with others, but especially in communing with God. Such virtues of patience and humility lie at the root of all religion (Matt. v. 3, 5), were exemplified by Jesus Christ (Matt. xi. 29; xxvii. 12; 2 Cor. x. 1; 1 Pet. ii. 23), and are demanded of all his followers (Eph. iv. 2; Col. iii. 12; 1 Pet. ii. 21). 3. *To the piety of their lives.* They had "wrought Jehovah's judgment," *i.e.* had honestly endeavoured to carry out what Jehovah had prescribed as the right thing to do in the matter of worship and duty. This, after all, the ultimate test of sincerity in religion, which signifies not the mere acceptance of certain propositions relating to God, his worship, and his commandment, but the carrying out of God's will in respect of both. Compare what Samuel said to Saul (1 Sam. xv. 22), what Christ explained to his followers (John xiv. 15; xv. 14), and what Paul wrote to the Corinthians (2 Cor. x. 5).

II. AN URGENT ADMONITION. 1. *Its import.* Explained by two clauses: "Seek righteousness, seek meekness." Only in these ways could Jehovah be sought—neither by coveting the material and temporal tokens of his favour, such as health, comfort, protection, prosperity, nor by maintaining the external forms of his worship, however elaborate or costly, but by aspiring after inward and outward, spiritual and moral conformity to his Law (righteousness) and character (meekness). The same sense attaches to the phrase when addressed to Christians, who are exhorted to follow after righteousness and meekness (1 Tim. vi. 11), and to seek both in Christ (Matt. xi. 29; Rom. x. 4). 2. *Its incidence.* Declared by the words, "all ye meek." Addressed to the humble-hearted, first in Judah, and then in the whole world. The obligation to seek Jehovah grounded for both on (1) their relations to Jehovah as his creatures and servants; (2) their own free choice of him as their Lord and King; (3) the nature of religion, which is not an act to be performed once for all, but a habit of soul to be maintained throughout life; and (4) the necessity of attending to their own safety, which could not otherwise be secured than by patient continuance in well-doing (Matt. xxiv. 13; Rom. ii. 7; Rev. ii. 10). 3. *Its urgency.* Proclaimed by the threefold "seek." The like diligence demanded of all in the matter of religion. (1) Because of the majesty of him whose service it is (2 Chron. ii. 5; 1 Tim. vi. 15). (2) Because of its intrinsic excellence as a purely spiritual service (John iv. 24; Rom. xii. 1). (3) Because of the momentous issues involved in it according as it is sincere or insincere (Job viii. 13; Prov. x. 28). (4) Because of the shortness and uncertainty of man's opportunity on earth to make his calling and election sure (Eccles. ix. 10; Eph. v. 16; Phil. iv. 5).

III. An ENCOURAGING CONSOLATION. 1. *A promise of safety for the righteous.* Not a doubtful promise, though introduced by "it may be." From this phrase it cannot be inferred that the prophet was uncertain whether the meek in the land would be protected in the day when Jehovah poured out his wrath upon Judah and Jerusalem; or whether the meek generally would be sheltered in the day of judgment. Merely he intimated that the hiding would be difficult; not the hiding of them by Jehovah, with whom nothing could be hard or easy, but the supplying by them of the moral and spiritual conditions without which God's hiding of them could not come to pass. The ultimate salvation of the meek is guaranteed (Ps. cxlix. 4; Matt. v. 5); but the actual process, in time, of saving them is attended by so many difficulties that there is need for constant watchfulness against the danger of coming short. 2. *A threatening of doom for the ungodly.* If the difficulty of saving the righteous be so great, what possible loophole of escape can there be for the ungodly (Luke xxiii. 31; 1 Pet. iv. 17, 18)? The overthrow of the wicked an additional security to the salvation of the righteous.—T. W.

Vers. 4—15.—*Divine judgments upon heathen nations.* I. THE NATIONS SPECIFIED. 1. *Philistia in the west.* (1) Its situation. "The sea-coast," "the region of the sea," or "the track by the sea." Extending along the Mediterranean, from Gaza in the south to Jaffa in the north, and reaching back to the hill-country of Judah in the west, it consisted of two parallel strips of land; one "of undulating plains, about twelve miles in breadth, bordering on the sea-coast, elevated from fifty to a hundred feet above the sea-level, without distinctive features, and composed of the richest alluvial deposit;" and another "twelve to fifteen miles wide, consisting of a series of hills and spurs from five hundred to eight hundred feet above the sea-level, and broken through by broad valleys" ('Picturesque Palestine,' iii. 151). (2) Its names. "The land of the Philistines," "of the Cherethites," "of Canaan." Of these the first describes it as a land whose inhabitants had been originally "immigrants," Philistia—in Hebrew *Pelesheth,* in the Assyrian inscriptions *Pilastu, Pilasta,* and *Palastav*—being derived from a root signifying "to wander about." The second depicts these inhabitants from a tribe settled in the south-west of the country, the Cherethites, a race of "Cutters," or "Executioners," who had achieved their settlements by means of the sword (Amos ix. 7). Whether they came originally from Crete (Gesenius, Hitzig, Baur in Riehm's 'Handwörterbuch'), which must then be identified with Caphtor (Deut. ii. 23; Jer. xlvii. 5), settling down first on the Egyptian coast (Gen. x. 14), and gradually creeping north towards the Palestinian coast, though extremely probable, is still a matter of debate. The names of Philistine kings preserved in Assyrian inscriptions and bearing a more or less Semitic character suggest that the people must have been of Semitic origin (Schrader, 'Die Keilinschriften,' 2 auf. 167). The third name, Canaan, "Lowland," was probably given to it because that had been its primitive designation, although the appellation afterwards was transferred to the whole country, just as Philistia or Palestine was. (3) Its chief cities. Four mentioned—Gaza, Ashkelon, Ashdod, and Ekron—in the Assyrian inscriptions *Haziti, Iskaluna, Asdudu,* and *Amkaruna.* Their early histories may be learnt from Scripture. Gaza, the modern *Guzzeh,* originally inhabited by the Avim (Deut. ii. 23), and, prior to the conquest of Palestine, by the Caphtorim or Philistines, and a remnant of the Anakim (Josh. xi. 22), was the scene of Samson's feats of strength, imprisonment, and destruction, and the site of a temple of Dagon (Judg. xvi. 1—3, 21—30). Ashkelon, situated on the sea (Josh. xiii. 3), had also been the scene of one of Samson's feats (Judg. xiv. 19). Ashdod possessed a temple of Dagon, in which the captured ark was placed (1 Sam. v.). Ekron, the most northern of the five chief cities, with a temple of Beelzebub (2 Kings i. 2), was the city from which the ark was sent back to Israel (1 Sam. v. 10).   2. *Moab and Ammon in the east.* In the Assyrian inscriptions *Ma'-ab, Ma'aab, Muaba,* and *Bit Ammân.*   Here conjoined probably because (1) of their blood-relationship, the Moabites having been descended from Lot's son Moab (Gen. xix. 37), and the Ammonites from the same patriarch's son Ben-Ammi (Gen. xix. 38); (2) of their geographical contiguity, their territories lying east of the Jordan,—that of Moab south of the Arnon, and stretching from the Dead Sea to the Syrian desert, and that of the Ammonites a little to the north-east, "in a mountainous district not annexed by Israel" (Conder); and (3) of their mutual hostility to Israel, having more than once joined forces in an attack upon the latter (Judg. iii. 13; 2 Chron. xx. 1).   3. *Ethiopia in the south.*   The land of Cush, in Assyrian *Kûsu,* the furthest south territory known to the Hebrews, was probably regarded as embracing Nubian Ethiopia and Arabia (Gen. ii. 13; 2 Chron. xxi. 16; Esth. i. 1; Isa. xviii. 1; Ezek. xxix. 10; xxx. 5).   Its inhabitants, dark-skinned (Jer. xiii. 23), were of a war-like character (Jer. xlvi. 9).   Ethiopians composed part of Shishak's army (2 Chron. xii. 3).   Zerah their king was defeated by Asa (2 Chron. xiv. 9—15; xvi. 8).   "They were a race cognate with the Egyptians, but darker in complexion and coarser in feature—not by any means negroes, but still more nearly allied to the negro than the Egyptians were" (Rawlinson's 'Egypt: Story of the Nations,' p. 315).   4. *Assyria in the north.*   Founded by Asshur (Gen. x. 11), who appears to have given his name first to the city he founded, and then to the empire it began, Assyria had as its capital Nineveh, the modern *Koujunjik.*   (On the history of Nineveh as detailed by the cuneiform inscriptions, see Layard's 'Nineveh;' Sayce's 'Assyria, its Princes, Priests, and People;' and Schrader's 'Keilinschriften').   "The Assyrians were allied in blood and language to the Hebrews, the Aramæans, and the Arabs;" "were a military people, caring for little else save war and trade;" and "if less luxurious than their Babylonian neighbours, were also less humane" (Sayce).   Israel's contact with Assyria began in B.C. 853, with Ahab's contribution of ten thousand infantry and two thousand chariots to assist Benhadad II. of Damascus against Shalmaneser II. of Assyria ('Records of the Past,' iii. 99), and ended with the fall of Nineveh in B.C. 606.

II. THEIR SINS RECORDED.   1. *Idolatry.*   All alike guilty of worshipping false gods —the Philistines of doing homage to Ashtaroth, Dagon, and Beelzebub; the Moabites, to Baalpeor and Chemosh; and the Ammonites, to Moloch; the Ethiopians, most likely to the gods of Egypt, Amen-Ra, Ptah, Osiris, Anubis, Thoth, Isis, Hathor, etc.; and the Assyrians, to the old Babylonian divinities, Bel, Anu, and Ea.   Idolatry regarded as a sin not in Israel alone (Exod. xx. 3—5), but in heathen peoples as well (Ps. xcvii. 7; Rom. i. 25).   2. *Enmity against Israel.*   In this also all had been partakers—the Philistines from the days of the judges (Judg. x. 7); the Moabites and Ammonites from the same period (Judg. iii. 13); the Ethiopians in the times of Rehoboam and Asa (2 Chron. xii. 3; xiv. 9); and the Assyrians under Tiglath-Pileser II., who first invaded the northern kingdom in the reign of Menahem (2 Kings iv. 19).   In particular the Philistines of Gaza, in the days of Jeroboam II., had sold captive Israelites to Edom (Amos i. 6); the Moabites under Mesha the sheepmaster, in the days of Jehoram, son of Ahab, not only revolted against Israel (2 Kings iii. 5), but carried the torch of war into Israelitish territory, defeating the Israelitish king and making many prisoners ('Records of the Past,' 2nd series, ii. 200); while the Assyrians invaded Judah so late as the days of Manasseh, and even deported that king to Babylon (2 Chron. xxxiii. 11).   3. *Pride.*   This more especially the sin of Moab (ver. 10) and of Assyria (ver. 15), of whom the former despised and magnified herself against Israel, and the latter exulted in her own fancied security and superlative greatness.

III. THEIR JUDGMENTS PRONOUNCED.   1. *In character equally severe.*   (1) Deportation of their inhabitants.   The Philistine cities will be overtaken by this fate (ver. 4).   Moab and Ammon shall be involved in a like doom.   The former "shall be as Sodom," and the latter "as Gomorrah" (ver. 9).   Ethiopia shall not escape, but her people shall be "slain by Jehovah's sword" (ver. 12).   Assyria shall suffer similar calamity.   Nineveh will become a desolation, etc. (vers. 13, 14).   (2) Desolation of their lands. The land of the Philistines, the tract by the sea, shall be pastures with caves for shepherds' huts, and folds for flocks (ver. 6).   The territories of Moab and Ammon shall become a possession of nettles and salt-pits and a perpetual desolation (ver. 9).

Nineveh will become dry like a wilderness (ver. 13), and desolation shall be in her thresholds (ver. 14). (3) Occupation of their deserted lands by Israel. "The Philistine coast shall be for the remnant of the house of Judah" (ver. 7). Of Moab and Ammon it is written, "The remnant of my nation shall inherit them" (ver. 9). 2. *In incidence equally certain.* All rested on a common ground, and were pronounced by a common voice, that of Jehovah. "The word of Jehovah was against the land of the Philistines" (ver. 5). Unto Moab and Ammon Jehovah had undertaken to be terrible (ver. 11). Jehovah's sword was to slay the Ethiopians (ver. 12). He should also stretch out his hand against the north, and destroy Assyria (ver. 13). What God directly by his own voice, or indirectly through the voice of another, undertakes to do is as good as done. 3. *In result equally good.* In threatening to destroy the above-mentioned nations— from their number and situation obviously designed to represent the whole heathen world—Jehovah practically engaged that the issue of his judgments would be to famish all the gods of the earth (ver. 11), *i.e.* cut off their worshippers, and so starve or make them lean, and in this way cause them to vanish from the face of the earth. Thus the ultimate result of his punishing the heathen would be (1) to reveal the nothing-ness of idols, whose inability to protect their worshippers would thereby be revealed; (2) to extinguish idolatry, since men would no longer serve divinities that were powerless to save them; and (3) to hasten the conversion of the world, since "all the isles of the nations" would be induced by what they saw to worship Jehovah "every one from his place."

Learn: 1. That God sees and notes the attitudes of nations towards himself and his kingdom. 2. That God is as much against nations that do wickedly as he is against individuals that sin. 3. That the strongest and most flourishing empires can be easily overthrown when God becomes their assailant. 4. That social and political convulsions are all hastening on the era when "the meek shall inherit the earth." 5. That national judgments are a prelude and premonition of the judgments of the great day when "before him shall be gathered all nations."—T. W.

Ver. 3.—*The duty of seeking the Lord.* This may be taken as the key-note of the second discourse of the prophet (ch. ii. 1—iii. 7), in which, after having uttered the solemn threatening of judgment in the former discourse, he gives more explicit directions as to what is the duty of the people in the view of this impending calamity. The call in ch. i. had simply been "Hold thy peace at the presence of the Lord God," *i.e.* to recognize the reality, nearness, and justice of the judgment he announced; but now the prophet gives more particular and express admonitions as to what people should do. What he calls upon them to do is, in one word, to seek the Lord; but in this discourse he enlarges at some length on the grounds and the way of doing so.

I. WHY OUGHT MEN, IN VIEW OF SUCH A JUDGMENT, TO SEEK THE LORD? 1. Because the judgment is universal. It is not merely a local visitation on the land of Israel, in which it alone is to suffer at the hands of some powerful and successful invader. In that case prudence might dictate the propriety of seeking escape by allying themselves with the conquering power, or taking refuge in some other land not exposed to its invasion. It might even be suggested by the idolatrous superstition of those days, that the cause of the triumph or safety of other nations was the power of their gods, and that this might be a reason for worshipping or fearing them. But the judgment is to be from the Lord, the only living and true God, the Creator of heaven and earth, and it is to show itself as such in this that it shall include all nations in its sweep; it is to be on the countries round about, as well as on Judah. The most prominent of the neighbouring nations are mentioned as involved in the calamity—the cities of the Philistines on the sea-coast to the south-west (vers. 4—7), Moab and Ammon on the south-east (vers. 8—10). These had been old hereditary enemies of Israel, and were inclined to rejoice in her calamity, and boast themselves as if their old hatred was now to be gratified. But this very jealousy and pride offend the Lord and bring down his judgment on them too. Then even the more distant nations of the Ethiopians far to the south-west, beyond Egypt, and Assyria in the remote north-east, with the great luxurious and proud city of Nineveh, were to be visited too; so that there would be no quarter of the earth to which Israel could turn for safety (vers. 12—15). So it ever is when God visits men; he makes it to be felt that vain is the help of man, and that there are no devices of human power, or riches, or wisdom, by which his hand can be escaped. It does not always need universal and sweeping judgments to show this; and it is our wisdom to learn the lessons even from single and separate manifestations of the power of God's wrath; or from the records and threatenings of these old judgments and their lessons. 2. But this is only a negative motive; it shows us in what quarters we are not to turn—that we can find no help in man. But the prophet gives also positively a reason why we should seek the Lord, and that is because his judgments are sent with a view to mercy. This is pointed out both in regard to Judah (ver. 7) and in regard to the Gentiles (ver. 11); for not only is the captivity of Judah to be turned back, but all the isles of the heathen are to worship the Lord. Such is ever the design of God's judgments against sin in this world. They are, indeed, expressions of his wrath and foretastes of his curse against sin, and as such they are fitted and intended to produce fear, and to lead men to hold their peace at the presence of the Lord God, and to humble themselves under his mighty hand. But the design of them never is simply to destroy. It may be needful ultimately, for the glory of the Lord, that the sinners be consumed out of the earth, and that the wicked be no more; and that utter destruction shall surely over-take the impenitent, when the Lord shall destroy the stumbling-blocks with the wicked, when "the Son of man shall send forth his angels, and they shall gather out of his kingdom all things that offend, and them which do iniquity, and shall cast them into a furnace of fire" (Matt. xiii. 41, 42). That is the doom solemnly denounced against the impenitent. But is not the very denunciation of it, stern as it is, an act of mercy? It is a warning graciously sent in time, lest that doom should come upon them unforetold and unexpected—a call to them to flee from the wrath to come, a signal of danger ahead, that may lead sinners to arrest their onward and downward course. Now, if the warning in words is thus manifestly merciful, so also are these foretastes of judgment that are but warnings in deed given when those in words have been disregarded. Had Israel listened to the words of the prophets, and turned from their evil ways, it might not have been necessary that God should send on them the judgment of the Captivity; but when they would not take warning from the solemn words of the Lord denouncing judgment, it was needful that they should be made to feel that these were not mere words, and be taught by actual inflictions in deed. But these were also sent in mercy, like the famine that came on the prodigal son in the far land to which he had wandered and wherein he wasted his substance in riotous living. Suffering may pierce the heart which the mere threat of suffering, however solemn and earnest, had failed to touch; and in that case the suffering, as well as the warning of it, has a gracious end. Even to the heathen nations, the judgment is with a view to mercy. Had Israel been faithful to their God and their calling, they would have been a kingdom of priests to spread the knowledge of the true God and of his grace and mercy among the Gentile nations around. But since they would not do this willingly, in the way of faithfully walking in the covenant of their God, he shall bring it to pass that by the judgments they undergo they shall be the means of making known his way in the earth, and his salvation among all nations. The heathen shall learn in the ruin of Israel to recognize the justice of the Lord, and the very nations that destroyed Israel shall be taught that the hand of God is on them too, and that they cannot escape his righteous judgments. "The Lord will be terrible to them; for he will famish all the gods of the earth." When he sent a grievous famine on the far country where the prodigal was, this might lead some of the citizens of that country, as well as the prodigal himself, to see how vain and perishing was the abundance in which they had been trusting, and might constrain him to look to that father's house from which he had gone away; when the heathen mariners in the ship in which Jonah was fleeing from the Lord found that none of their gods could save them from the great storm sent by the Lord against his disobedient servant, they cried to the Lord, and they "feared the Lord exceedingly, and offered a sacrifice unto the Lord, and made vows." So when the heathen nations shall find that the judgments of God against his people for their sin come upon themselves also, and that none of their gods can save them, they too, says the prophet, "shall worship him, every one from his place, even all the isles of the heathen." Thus the judgment, even as regards them, is with a view to mercy; and this is the strong positive reason that all have to seek the Lord. Are you suffering calamity or trouble of any kind, and does conscience tell you that this affliction is not undeserved, nay, that it is the natural consequence and the just punishment of your sin? Then do not on any account let this drive you to despair; do not think that there is no hope for you; do not give way to mere idle grief or vain regret of the past that cannot be recalled; believe and be assured that the suffering has been sent in mercy as well as judgment, that it is a proof that God has not yet pronounced against you that most awful of all sentences, "Ephraim is joined to idols: let him alone" (Hos. iv. 17); and instead of hardening your heart in disobedience, or wringing your hands in despair, let God's judgments move you to "seek the Lord while he may be found, and to call upon him while he is near."

II. But the prophet not only sets forth the strong motives which the impending judgment affords to seek the Lord; he also INDICATES THE WAY IN WHICH THIS IS TO BE DONE. More especially there are two parts of this duty that he emphasizes, the one religious and the other moral, both of which must be combined. 1. The more directly religious duty is humiliation and prayer to God (vers. 1—3a). The somewhat obscure language of ver. 1, in the exact rendering of which scholars differ, seems to indicate, in the way of general humiliation before God, either a public gathering for a day of fasting, such as that described by Joel (ii. 15—17), or more directly the feeling of shame and humiliation arising in the hearts of those who had before been strangers to it. Then the very expression, "Seek the Lord" (ver. 3), describes religious exercises of prayer and worship. If the judgment threatened against Israel, or any Divine judgment, is to have its right and designed effect, there must be a recognition of a personal God and of our personal relation to him. "Seek righteousness, seek meekness." There is something more implied here than merely "a power not ourselves that makes for righteousness." Could we be called to seek such a power in any other way than by seeking righteousness? Yet seeking the Lord is here spoken of as something distinct, though not to be separated, from seeking righteousness; and the anger of the Lord, so repeatedly and emphatically mentioned in vers. 2 and 3, is not to be explained away as a mere figure for the infliction of punishment. The "power that makes for righteousness" is a Person in whose favour lies our only true happiness. Were it not so, the evils that follow on sin would be no call to humiliation or to shame, for they would be the result of a mere law or tendency. But since we have to do with a living Person, who not only punishes but is grieved and displeased at our sins, we have reason not only to fear but to be humbled and ashamed before him. Such feelings are essential to true repentance; they find expression in that confession of sin which everywhere in Scripture is made a requisite for its forgiveness. A true confession implies grief and shame for sin, and an acknowledgment of it, and expression of these feelings to God; and without this, even though the judgments that follow on sin could be removed, God's displeasure and wrath would not be turned away—there would be no reconciliation, and the offender would be no nearer to God than before. But where there is this humiliation before God as the living God with whom we are in a personal relation, then there can be also prayer to him, and this also is implied in the call to seek the Lord. We are not only to turn to him for refuge, as a Power that will save us; we are to speak to him as a Person, and ask him first and chiefly to forgive us for our past sins, and then, if it is his will, to save us from the judgments that they deserve. Such is the religious duty to which the prophet here calls Israel, and this movement of heart-religion must ever enter into the exercises of soul to which we are impelled by God's judgments, if these are to have a salutary effect. 2. But this religious exercise must never be separated from the moral duty here enjoined along with it. Humiliation, confession, and prayer can never be sincere if they remain alone, or if the sense of sin prompts to nothing more than these; for the religious element of repentance, however important it is, cannot be made to supersede the moral. There must be a grief for sin, not only because it has offended God personally, but because of its intrinsic evil; for the offence that it gives to God does not spring from any mere arbitrary command on his part, but from his own essential nature as the perfectly and unchangeably Holy One. Therefore that is no real approach to him that does not imply a hatred of and turning from sin and a seeking after righteousness. Hence the command, "Seek the Lord," is closely connected with "Seek righteousness, seek meekness;" only in this way can the God of Israel, who is essentially holy, be really sought. Righteousness and meekness are the virtues here specially mentioned, for these contain the sum of moral duty, and are opposed to the violence and deceit, the avarice and oppression, that had been depicted in ch. i. as the evils which brought down the judgment of the Lord on Judah and Jerusalem. If we would truly seek the Lord, we must turn from the sins of which we have been guilty, and set about those duties that we have been neglecting. This may be no easy task. It may imply a seeking, a searching of heart with great diligence to detect the hidden roots of evil, a pursuit of holiness with labour and perseverance in order to overcome inbred habits of sin, and to acquire habits of goodness. The character is not to be renewed or changed by a single effort or in one day; it requires a lifelong effort to " put off the old man, which is corrupt according to the deceitful lusts; and put on the new man, which after God hath been created in righteousness and holiness of truth." But the work can and ought to be begun at once, and will be so begun if we really seek the Lord. If we know the Lord as the Holy One, and feel the evil of sin as it is in his sight, then our turning to him in repentance really implies a turning from all sin and a seeking righteousness and meekness. This too must be prompt and immediate. There is no time to be lost; the day of the Lord is at hand, his judgment is announced, his wrath has almost begun to burn, the dark thunder-clouds are as it were big with the approaching storm. Therefore let there be no delay; make haste, and tarry not, before the decree brings forth its terrible execution. Judgment is still, as it were, in the womb of the Divine law and order, but ere long it must break forth, and the day of the Lord's wrath will sweep away all the wicked of the earth as chaff. Before that day comes, yet there is time, time enough to seek the Lord, but no time to waste in dallying with sin or halting between two opinions. Finally, be it remembered that this call is addressed to all alike, to the godly as well as to sinners. It is especially addressed to all the meek of the earth, who have wrought God's judgment, as well as to those who have still to seek righteousness and meekness. For, indeed, those who have most earnestly repented will most feel their need of the ever-fresh and repeated call. That repentance is not genuine which is not virtually continued and actually repeated even to the very end of life, is a principle of Protestant theology, and most important for practical religion. We must not be content in this matter with any past experience or exercises of soul; as long as we have in us or about us anything of the sins that provoke God's anger, our repentance must be continual. The whole of a Christian's life should be a turning from sin to God. In view of the sin that dwells in us, and our continual shortcomings of the righteousness and meekness required by God's Law, we must be constantly humbling ourselves before God and asking his forgiveness; and we must also be striving against sin, making it our earnest effort to abandon all practices and habits that are wrong, to eradicate passions and tempers of mind at variance with God's holy Law, and to acquire and cultivate the qualities required by it. We are to be putting off the old man and putting on the new, constantly day by day. Alas! how often do we forget this! How many days do we spend without conscious striving against sin or effort after holiness! Can we wonder that we should need rebuke and chastening from the Lord if we are thus neglecting what is an essential element of Christian life? Again, this repentance needs not only to be constantly going on as to the principle or power of it, but there are occasions when it needs to be actually renewed. One such occasion is when a believer falls into any grievous sin, such as wounds his conscience and destroys his peace. Then he must not be satisfied with a mere general acknowledgment of sinfulness; he must come once more, as he came at first, to God through Christ and anew, as at first, with the returning prodigal say, " Father, I have sinned," etc.; anew, as at first, turn from his sin to God with full purpose of heart and endeavour after new obedience. No fresh burden of guilt is to be got rid of in any other way than that, and in that way all may be removed. Another occasion when we ought actually to renew our repentance is when we seek to enter into spiritual communion with God. Israel of old was commanded to keep a solemn day of fast and humiliation for sins just before the joyful Feast of Tabernacles, and in regard to the New Testament feast of the Lord's Supper it is said, " Let a man examine himself, and so let him eat of that bread, and drink of that cup." There cannot be faithful self-examination without a remembering and bringing to light of much sin, and that must needs call for humiliation and prayer for forgiveness, and renewed efforts after holiness. But if, thus searching and trying our ways, we turn unto the Lord, and lift up our heart with our hands unto God in the heavens, we shall assuredly find him; we shall experience that mercy which he shows to those who confess their sins, and we shall be made more and more partakers of his holiness. Thus we shall be hid in the day of the Lord's anger, for we shall be able to say to him, "Thou art my Hiding-place; thou shalt preserve me from trouble; thou shalt compass me about with songs of deliverance."—C.

Vers. 1—3.—*Sin and repentance: the bane and the antidote.* "Gather yourselves together," etc. Here is an exhortation to the men of Judah to repent ere the Chaldean invaders approach, and wreak destruction on their land. Two thoughts are suggested.

I. SIN EXPOSES MAN TO RUIN. It was sin, in the form of idolatry and gross immorality, that exposed the Jewish people to the terrible doom that was now hanging over them. Sin is evermore the cause of all human suffering. Corporeal sin brings corporeal suffering; moral sin brings moral suffering; national sin brings national suffering. "Sin, when it is finished, bringeth forth death." 1. *The suffering that follows sin is sometimes very terrible.* It was so now. Sin brings upon a people famines, pestilences, wars, perdition. 2. *The suffering expresses God's antagonism to sin.* "The fierce anger of the Lord," or, as Henderson has it, "the burning anger of Jehovah." God's anger is not a passion, but a principle; and the principle is antagonism, not to the happiness of his creatures, but to their sin and their wickedness. The connection between sin and misery is a beneficent arrangement. It is well that misery should pursue wrong.

II. THAT REPENTANCE DELIVERS MAN FROM RUIN. To prepare for the coming doom, the men of Judah are called upon to repent. "Gather yourselves together, yea, gather together, O nation not desired," which may mean, "not worthy of the grace or favour of God." Some translate it, "not waxing pale," meaning, "being dead to a sense of shame." Others regard the expression as meaning, "not desiring to repent." 1. The *preparation* for repentance. "Gather yourselves together," etc. "Gather yourselves together" in connection; deliberate together as to the best way of securing the friendship and protection of God. "Gather the people, sanctify the congregation, assemble the elders" (Joel ii. 16). It is well for sinners, in the prospect of their doom, to meet and confer concerning their relations to Almighty God. 2. The *nature* of repentance. It is here represented as seeking the Lord. "Seek ye the Lord, all ye meek of the earth;" or, as Henderson renders it, "Seek ye Jehovah, all ye humble of the earth." There are two seekings here. (1) The seeking of *God.* Which is to be understood in a moral sense, seeking his friendship; for in a natural sense he is "not far from every one of us." But we are all away from him in sympathy. (2) The seeking of *meekness.* "Seek righteousness, seek meekness," etc. Indeed, to seek moral excellence is to seek God; and to seek moral excellence is repentance; it is a turning away from the creature to the Creator, from the wrong to the right. "Seek ye the Lord while he may be found, call ye upon him while he is near." 3. The *urgency* of repentance. Do it now. "Before the decree bring forth, before the day pass as the chaff, before the fierce anger of the Lord come upon you, before the day of the Lord's anger come upon you." It will be too late to repent when the judgment comes. "They shall call upon me, and I will not answer;" "Many shall say to me at that day," etc. (Matt. vii. 22).

CONCLUSION. As sin is in the world, judgments are in the world. Retribution, like an invading army, is always marching toward the victim. Repentance is the only means of deliverance. "Except ye repent, ye shall all likewise perish."—D. T.

Vers. 4—7.—*The sinner's baleful influence, and God's disposal of all.* "For Gaza shall be forsaken, and Ashkelon," etc. Here the prophet makes the punishment awaiting the neighbouring states, which he goes on to specify, an argument for immediate repentance. "For Gaza shall be forsaken." Gaza was one of the five principalities of the Philistines, and was situated on the coast of the Mediterranean at the southern extremity of Canaan. "Ashkelon a desolation." This was another of the fenced cities of the Philistines, situated on the shore of the Mediterranean between Gaza and Ashdod. "Ekron shall be rooted up." Another Philistine city, lying north-west of Gath, and north of Ashdod. "Woe unto the inhabitants of the sea-coast!" The Philistines dwelling on the sea-coast south-west of Canaan. "The nation of the Cherethites"—the Cretans, the name applied to the Philistines that sprang from Crete. "O Canaan, the land of the Philistines." They occupied the strip of land on the south shore of the Mediterranean (Josh. xiii. 3). Two facts are here suggested.

I. THAT THE CALAMITIES FALLING UPON ONE SINNER OFTEN INVOLVE OTHERS. It was so now. The ruin that was approaching the Hebrew nation would be most calamitous to the Philistine cities, and indeed to the neighbouring states. Gaza would be "forsaken," Ashkelon would be a "desolation," Ashdod would be "driven out," Ekron would be "rooted up," the inhabitants of the seashore, the Cherethites, the Canaanites, all would be involved. So vital, strong, and numerous are the ties that connect man with man in this world, that the condition of one must affect the condition of others. It is so: 1. With *nations*. At no period in the world's history was it more manifest than now. No one state or kingdom of Europe can be affected without influencing others. What was called "the Eastern question," in that terrible war between the sultan and the czar, affected every part of the civilized world. 2. With *individuals*. A man cannot fail in health, in business, or in character, without painfully affecting others in some way or other. What sufferings the failures of the Gurneys, the Petos, and the Grants have brought upon thousands in this country! This shows: (1) The social connection between man and man. No man can live unto himself. Each man is a link in the great chain of human life; and he cannot move without influencing others. Each man is a link in the great human body; and, if one suffers, all suffer. (2) The duty of each man to look well after his own conduct. A sinner has no right to say he will do what he likes, and that no one may properly interfere with him. If his actions terminated in himself, there might be some reason in such a claim; but as they cannot, and they must affect others, every man, all society, the whole human world, have a right to protest against the sinful conduct of any individual man.

II. THAT THE LOT OF MAN IS AT THE DISPOSAL OF ALMIGHTY GOD. "And the sea-coast shall be dwellings and cottages for shepherds, and folds for flocks. And the coast shall be for the remnant of the house of Judah; they shall feed thereupon; in the houses of Ashkelon shall they lie down in the evening: for the Lord their God shall visit them, and turn away their captivity." "And the line of the sea shall be pastures, with cisterns for shepherds and folds for sheep. Yea, the line shall be for the remnant of the house of Judah, thereupon shall they feed; in the houses of Ashkelon shall they lie down at even; for Jehovah their God shall visit them, and reverse their captivity" (Henderson). Here the Almighty is represented as arranging the future home and circumstances of "the remnant of the house of Judah." Paul at Athens said that God had "determined the times before appointed, and the bounds of their habitation" (Acts xvii. 26). Though we are free and conscious of our freedom, we are at the disposal of One above us. He has appointed: 1. Our *place* in the world. He has set bounds to our habitation "that we cannot pass." 2. Our *period* in the world. "My times are in thy hand." The periods of our birth and death are all arranged by him. "Man's days are determined; the number of his months is with thee" (Job xiv. 5). We are often tempted to imagine that chance rules us. We are struck with the apparent contingency when we look at men's circumstances in connection with their *choice*. None of us has any choice as to the condition, the place, the time, in which we are to be born or brought up. We are struck with the apparent contingency also when we look at men's circumstances in connection with their *merits*. How often do we find feeble-minded men in eminent positions, and men of talents and genius in obscurity! some, by what is called a hit, making fortunes and earning fame, whilst honest industry plods on with little or no success; vice in mansions, and virtue in the pauper's hut! Verily the race is not always to "the swift, nor the battle to the strong." But amidst all this feeling of contingency, and over all, there is the ruling plan of the beneficent God.—D. T.

Vers. 8—10.—*The persecution of the good.* "I have heard the reproach," etc. "The threat now turns from the Philistines in the west to the two tribes in the east, viz. the Moabites and the Ammonites, who were descended from Lot, and therefore blood-relations, and who manifested hostility to Israel on every possible occasion." The passage suggests three facts.

I. THAT GOOD MEN ARE OFTEN SUBJECT TO ANNOYANCES FROM THE UNGODLY WORLD. "I have heard the reproach [abuse] of Moab, and the revilings of the children of Ammon, whereby they have reproached my people [abused my nation], and magnified themselves against their border." These people, the Moabites and the Ammonites, were constantly annoying and abusing the chosen people in the time of Moses. Balak, the King of the Moabites, sought to destroy the Israelites by means of Balaam's curses (Numb. xxii.). And in the time of the judges, both peoples endeavoured to oppress Israel (Judg. iii. 12; x. 7). The charge here probably refers to the hostile attitude assumed by both tribes at all times toward the people of God. Both Isaiah and Jeremiah accused them of annoying them (Isa. xvi. 6; Jer. xlviii. 29). The hostile conduct of Moab and Ammon towards Israel is only a specimen and an illustration of the antagonism of wicked men towards the truly pious. They "reproach" them; they charge them with superstition, fanaticism, cant, hypocrisy. Their revilings are often bitter and constant. "It has been," says an old writer, "the common lot of God's people in all ages to be reproached and reviled on one account or another." There is an eternal enmity between the two seeds—the seed of the serpent and the seed of the woman. The conduct of a truly good man can scarcely fail to exasperate worldly and ungodly people. It condemns their selfishness, their greed, their falsehood, their pleasures. "If the world hate you, ye know that it hated me before," etc.; "If they have called the Master of the house Beelzebub, how much more shall they call those of the household!" "Cain, who was of that wicked one, and slew his brother; and wherefore slew he him? because his own works were evil, and his brother's righteous." In corrupt society, we may lay it down as a truth that the better a man is, the more pure, honest, true, righteous, the more he will be hated and annoyed by his neighbours. The best men, the men of whom "the world is not worthy," are always persecuted.

II. THAT THESE ANNOYANCES ESCAPE NOT THE NOTICE OF GOD. "I have *heard* the reproach of Moab." I have heard the whole, all their calumnies, reproaches, revilings; not a word has escaped me, not a syllable has been lost. Observe : 1. *God's attention to the minute concerns of human life.* He who is the Maker and Manager of the universe, to whom the creation is as nothing and less than nothing, is not indifferent to the utterances of little human creatures on this earth, which is itself a mere speck in space. "I have heard the reproaches."

"He sees with equal eye, as God of all,
A hero perish, or a sparrow fall."

2. *God's special interest in his people.* Good men are his children, as dear to him as the apple of the eye; and whatever happens to them, even a reproachful word, affects him. It is truly consoling, it is energizing, to know that the great Father is interested in all that pertains to us. "Thine eyes are open upon all the ways of the sons of men : to give every one according to his ways, and according to the fruit of his doings" (Jer. xxxii. 19).

III. THAT GOD WILL NOT FAIL TO CHASTISE THE AUTHORS OF SUCH ANNOYANCES. "Therefore as I live, saith the Lord of hosts, the God of Israel, Surely Moab shall be as Sodom, and the children of Ammon as Gomorrah, even the breeding of nettles, and salt-pits, and a perpetual desolation : the residue of my people shall spoil them, and the remnant of my people shall possess them. This shall they have for their pride, because they have reproached and magnified themselves against the people of the Lord of hosts." Mark : 1. The *doom* of those reproachers. "They shall be as Sodom and Gomorrah." "This simile," says Keil, "was rendered a very natural one by the situation of the two lands in the neighbourhood of the Dead Sea. It affirms the utter destruction of the two tribes." Their land is to abound with "nettles and salt-pits," the products and proofs of utter ruin. 2. The *cause* of their doom. "This shall they have for their pride." All the persecutors of the good will meet with a terrible chastisement. Sooner or later God will avenge his own elect. Hence let the godly victims of persecution, when they are "reviled, revile not again ; " "Vengeance is mine, I will repay, saith the Lord;" "Blessed are they which are persecuted," etc. (Matt. v 10).—D. T.

Ver. 11.—*Good things in the future.* "The Lord will be terrible unto them," etc. '' Jehovah is to be feared above all the gods of the earth, for he will cause them to waste away; and all the inhabitants of the maritime regions shall worship him, each from his place.' While announcing the destruction of the surrounding idolatrous nations, the prophet was inspired to predict the gradual but certain destruction of idolatry universally throughout the earth. The period predicted should be one in which all peculiarity of local worship should cease, and Divine worship be acceptable wherever presented in sincerity and truth " (Henderson). The passage reminds us of two good things that are in the future of our world.

I. THE DESTRUCTION OF IDOLATRY. What is idolatry? It is the giving of our supreme affection to creature-objects. It is not confined to the worship of heathen deities, which are for the most part the productions of human invention and art. The spirit of idolatry often exists where heathen idolatry is denounced. Whatever objects a man loves most is his god. In our England and throughout Christendom there are gods many, although they have no recognized temple. Wealth is a mighty god, power is a mighty idol, pleasure is a mighty idol, fame is a mighty idol. Before these idols the vast majority of the civilized world prostrate their souls in the ardour of devotion. The destruction of idolatry, therefore, does not mean the beating to dust or the consuming to ashes the idols that fill the temples of heathendom, but means the withdrawal of man's supreme love from every object short of God. You may burn up all heathen temples, and leave idolatry as rampant as ever. To " famish all the gods of the earth " is to draw man's supreme sympathy from all things except God. This is the great moral famine that is to be desired, to be prayed for and struggled after. The other good thing in the future of our world is—

II. THE ADVANCEMENT OF TRUE WORSHIP. " And men shall worship him, every one from his place, even all the isles of the heathen." Observe : 1. The *object* of true worship. " Men shall worship him," that is, Jehovah. Him, not it—not the universe, but the infinite Personality that created it, the Fountain of all existence, all energy, all love, all blessedness. Him—the Creator of the material, the Father of the spiritual. 2. The *scene* of true worship. " Every one from his place." Wherever he is. The worshipper need not go to any particular scene—no temple, chapel, or cathedral. " From his place." It may be in solitude or in society, on the mountain brow or the seashore. " Neither in this mountain" nor on that mountain, but everywhere. " God is a Spirit." 3. The *extent* of true worship. " Even all the isles of the heathen."

CONCLUSION. What a glorious future awaits the world! How blessed will those ages be when every man of every tribe and clime shall have his heart centred in supreme love upon the one great Father of all!—D. T.

Vers. 13—15.—*National pride and national ruin.* "And he will stretch out his hand against the north, and destroy Assyria; and will make Nineveh a desolation, and dry like a wilderness. And flocks shall lie down in the midst of her, all the beasts of the nations," etc. Dr. Henderson's translation of this passage is not only beautiful, but seems so faithful and clear as scarcely to require any exposition.

> " And he will stretch his hand over the north,
> And destroy Assyria.
> He will also make Nineveh waste,
> An arid region like the desert.
> And flocks shall lie down in the midst of her,
> All the wild beasts of the nations :
> Both the pelican and the porcupine
> Shall take up their abode in her capitals :
> A voice shall sing in the windows,
> Desolation shall be in the thresholds,
> For the cedar work is laid bare.
> This is the exulting city which dwelt securely,
> Which said in her heart,

> I am, and beside me there is none.
> How she is become desolate!
> A resting-place for wild beasts!
> Every one that passeth by her shall hiss,
> He shall shake his head."

Two facts are suggested.

I. THAT MEN ARE OFTEN PRONE TO PRIDE THEMSELVES ON THE GREATNESS OF THEIR COUNTRY. The men of the city of Nineveh—the capital of Assyria—were proud of their nation. It is called the "rejoicing city," and represented as saying, "I am, and there is none beside me." This was the voice of the population. There was much in the city of Nineveh to account for, if not to justify, the exultant spirit of its population. It was the metropolis of a vast empire; it was a city sixty miles in compass, it had walls a hundred feet high, and so thick and strong that three chariots could be driven abreast on them; it had twelve hundred massive towers. The boasting spirit of the men of Nineveh concerning the grandeur of their country is by no means uncommon; it beats in the hearts of modern nations. Italy, Austria, Germany, America, England, each says in its spirit, "I am, and there is none beside me." Nations are egotistic, they exult in their own greatness, they sing their own praises. This spirit of national boasting is *unjustifiable*. There is nothing in a nation of which it should be proud, except moral excellence; and, alas! how little moral excellence there is in the most virtuous kingdom of the earth! On the contrary, how much ignorance, sensuality, worldliness, intolerance, impiety, that should humble us in the dust! It is, moreover, a *foolish* spirit. It is a check to true national progress, and its haughty swaggerings tend to irritate other countries.

II. THAT THE GREATEST COUNTRY MUST SOONER OR LATER FALL TO RUIN. "He will stretch out his hand against the north, and destroy Assyria," etc. This great city, peopled with pompous boasters, became a *receptacle for beasts*. "Flocks shall lie down in the midst of her," etc. "All the beasts of the nations: both the cormorant [the pelican] and the bittern [the porcupine] shall lodge in the upper lintels of it." The wild grim birds that haunt all ruins. Not only a receptacle for beasts, but a *derision to travellers*. "Every one that passeth by her shall hiss, and wag his hand." Such was the doom that came on this great city when Cyaxares and Nabopolassar, 600 years B.C., struck it down. This is the fate that awaits all the nations under heaven, even the greatest. Egypt, Syria, Babylon, Rome, Greece, have risen, prospered, and decayed. The symptoms of decay are manifest in many of the grandest nations of Europe. The more thoughtful amongst us discover those symptoms in the life of our England. England has nothing more to become, they say; the plum is overripe, and it must rot; the tree has exhausted all its latent vitality, and it must wither; the sun has passed the meridian, and it must go down. Thoughtful men point to the sad lack of capacity in our statesmen, the unscrupulous greed of our traders, the grumbling of our artisans, the weakness of our pulpits, the haughtiness of our ecclesiastics, the hollowness of our religion, the infidelities of our scientists, the diminution of our revenue and the increase of our pauperism, the arrogance of one class and the flunkeyism of another, pampered indolence here and starving toil there, jobbery in politics, swindling in commerce, cant in religion, and strikes in trade,—and say these are unmistakable marks of national corruption.—D. T.

EXPOSITION.

CHAPTER III.

Vers. 1—5.—§ 6. *The prophet turns to Jerusalem, and warns her that, if God punishes the heathen, he will not spare the hardened sinners in Judah.*

Ver. 1.—**Woe to her!** This is addressed to Jerusalem, as is seen by vers. 2—4.

Filthy; rather, *rebellious*, i.e. against God. The LXX., mistaking the word, renders, ἐπιφανής, "notable." So the Syriac. Jerome has *provocatrix*. The true sense is seen by the expansion of the term in ver. 2. **Polluted** by her many sins. Jerome, following the Septuagint ἀπολελυτρωμένη, "ransomed," has, *redempta*, which he explains, "Captivitatibus tradita, et rursum redempta." The oppressing city, that acts unjustly and cruelly to the weak and poor. So the three sins for which she is here denounced are that she is rebellious against God, defiled with sin in herself, and cruel to others. The Septuagint and Vulgate translate *jonah* ("oppressing") "dove," which seems singularly inappropriate here, though some try to explain it as applied to Jerusalem in the sense of "silly" or "stupid" (Hos. vii. 11)

Ver. 2.—The voice; *i.e.* of God, as heard in the Law and at the mouth of his prophets (comp. Jer. vii. 24, etc.; ix. 13). Received not correction. They took not to heart the chastisements sent upon them, and did not profit by them. She trusted not in the Lord, but in man. When danger threatened, she relied on human aid, made alliances with the heathen, or else had recourse to idols and prayed for help to false gods, as the next clause complains. She drew not near to her God. She broke the covenant which she had made, would not avail herself of the privilege bestowed upon her, and had no intercourse with the Lord in prayer and worship.

Ver. 3.—Roaring lions. The princes, who ought to protect the people, are ready to tear them in pieces and devour them (Prov. xxviii. 15). Probably the violence and arrogance of the chiefs had increased during the minority of the king. This must have been written before the great reformation. Evening wolves (see note on Hab. i. 8). The judges, whose duty it was to administer justice and to set an example of equity and virtue, are themselves most cruel and rapacious. They gnaw not the bones till to-morrow; *they gnaw no bones in the morning;* that is, they are so greedy that they eat up all their prey at once and leave nothing till the morning. The versions drop the metaphor, and render, "They leave not to the morning" (comp. Ezek. xxii. 27).

Ver. 4.—Her prophets. These are the false prophets, who have no true mission from God (comp. Micah ii. 11; iii. 5). Light; either, *frivolous* or *empty boasters.* The word means properly, "boiling over," like water. Vulgate, *vesani;* Septuagint, πνευματοφόροι, which means, probably, not "inspired by an (evil) spirit," but "carried away by the wind," "light" (comp. Matt. xi. 7). Treacherous persons; literally, *men of treacheries,* who uttered their own fancies as if they were commissioned by God, and so really opposed him whom they professed to represent (Jer. xxiii. 32). Her priests have polluted the sanctuary (*what is holy*). Not the temple only, but all that has to do with God's service, worship, rites, sacrifices; they make no distinction between what is sacred and what is profane (Ezek. xxii. 26).

They have done violence to the Law. Chiefly, doubtless, by distorting its meaning, and neither observing it themselves nor teaching others to keep it.

Ver. 5.—In the midst of this congregation of sinners God is continually manifesting his righteousness; he leaves not himself without witness; and therefore their iniquities are without excuse. The just Lord is in the midst thereof; or, *the Lord in the midst of her is righteous* (Deut. xxxii. 4). His presence was associated with the temple; his moral government was always being manifested. He would not be "just" if he left sinners unpunished. Every morning; Hebrew, "in the morning, in the morning." The phrase is rightly explained in our version (comp. Exod. xvi. 21; Ps. lxxxvii. 5). Doth he bring his judgment to light. His prophets proclaim his perfect justice; his judgments on the heathen manifest it (ver. 8; Hos. vi. 5). It is not from ignorance of the Law that the people sin. He faileth not; or, *it faileth not;* Vulgate, *non abscondetur.* God never ceases thus to act; or, his justice is clear as day. But the unjust knoweth no shame. In spite of this hourly manifestation of God's justice, and the enactments of the Law so well known, the perverse nation will not amend its ways, feels no shame at its backslidings (Jer. iii. 3; vi. 15). The Septuagint Version, according to the Vatican manuscript, is curious here, and in the latter part somewhat like St. Matthew's rendering of Isa. xlii. 3, Καὶ οὐκ ἔγνω ἀδικίαν ἐν ἀπαιτήσει, καί οὐκ εἰς νεῖκος ἀδικίαν (comp. Matt. xii. 20), which Jerome translates, "Nescit iniquitatem in exactione, nec in sempiternum injustitiam," and explains, "When God exacts from every man the sum he has committed to him, he will not be unjust, nor allow injustice to prevail."

Vers. 6—8.—§ 7. *Obdurate and blinded as nations are, these extreme measures are the only way left to secure salvation for Israel and the whole world.*

Ver. 6.—God speaks, showing why he has sent these judgments. I have cut off the nations. The reference is to facts well known to the hearers (though not specified here); such as the ruin of Pentapolis, the destruction of the Canaanites, the defeat of the Chaldeans in Hezekiah's time, the conquest of cities and countries by the Assyrians, and the devastation of Israel itself. Their towers are desolate. Their towers (see note on ch. i. 16), in which they trusted for defence, are overthrown and lie in ruins. Others translate, "street-corners," where people most do congregate. Streets; perhaps, *roads;* signifying the open country.

So Keil. **None inhabitant** (comp. Jer. iv. 7).

Ver. 7.—Taught by such examples, the Jews might have learned to repent and amend their ways. **I said.** God represents himself as reasoning as a man would reason. **Surely thou wilt fear me;** Septuagint, "only fear me." This is the one condition for salvation. Or, according to our version, Judah must learn experience from my threats and visitations, and return unto me. **Thou wilt . . . receive instruction;** Septuagint, "receive ye discipline," accept the correction and learn the lesson which it is meant to teach (Prov. xxiv. 32). **Their** (*her*) **dwelling.** Jerusalem or Judæa. The temple is never called the dwelling-place of the people. This sudden change of person is very common in the prophets. **Howsoever I punished them;** rather, *according to all that I appointed concerning her.* God had ordained certain punishment for Jerusalem if she reformed not. The Anglican Version means that God would never cut them off wholly, however severely he might chastise them. The Hebrew will not carry this; nor are the Greek and Latin Versions quite correct. Septuagint, Οὐ μὴ ἐξολοθρευθῆτε ἐξ ὀφθαλμῶν αὐτῆς πάντα ὅσα ἐξεδίκησα ἐπ' αὐτήν, "And ye shall not be cut off from the face thereof for all the punishment that I inflicted upon it;" Vulgate, *Propter omnia in quibus visitavi eam.* **But they rose early.** Warning, reproof, and chastisement were expended in vain; the people only gave themselves up more ardently to their evil doings. "To rise early to do a thing" is a phrase used to signify the acting with zeal and full purpose (comp. Jer. vii. 13, 25; xi. 7, etc.). **Corrupted all their doings.** Like the inhabitants of the earth before the Flood (Gen. vi. 12; comp. Ps. xiv. 1). The Septuagint rendering is peculiar, Ἑτοιμάζου, ὄρθρισόν, ἔφθαρται πᾶσα ἡ ἐπιφυλλὶς αὐτῶν, "Prepare thyself, rise early, all their produce is spoiled." St. Jerome, moralizing on this, adds, "Nisi præparati fuerimus, non nobis orietur sol justitiæ. Orto autem sole, omnes racemi de vinea Sodomorum dissipantur et pereunt; ut non solum grandes botri, sed etiam quod parvum esse videbatur in nobis, Christi lucerna radiante dispereat."

Ver. 8.—**Therefore.** Because of the outrage done to God's "long-suffering," he must needs punish. **Wait ye upon me;** *wait ye for me.* The exhortation is addressed to the pious among the Jews, as in ch. ii. 3, and is used in a good sense (Ps. xxxiii. 20; Isa. viii. 17), urging them not to despair, but to be patient under the affliction, in the assured hope of salvation. The same expression is used in Hab. ii. 3. **I rise up to the prey.** This is a phrase denoting effort and the effecting of some great object. Jehovah seizes the prey when the nations, roused by judgment inflicted, are converted unto him (Isa. liii. 12; Ps. lxviii. 18). The LXX., pointing the last word differently (עַד), renders, εἰς ἡμέραν ἀναστάσεώς μου εἰς μαρτύριον: "until the day of my rising up for testimony." Jerome, "In die resurrectionis meæ in futurum." The Fathers interpreted this of the times of Messiah—some, of Christ's resurrection from the dead; some, of his rising up to divide the spoil (Gen. xlix. 9, 27. See St. Augustine, 'De Civit.,' xviii. 33; Eusebius, 'Dem. Ev.,' ii. 17; and Jerome and Cyril, *in loc.*). But such interpretations are alien from the intention of the passage, however allowable as glosses. **For my determination is;** literally, *my judgment* (*mishpat*) *is.* My justice is displayed, as ver. 5. The word, according to Keil, never means, "decree" or "decision." **That I may assemble the kingdoms.** Not for utter extermination, but to bring them to a better mind (Isa. xxvi. 9; Joel iii. 11, etc.). **Fire of my jealousy** (ch. i. 18). God will allow no rival anywhere (Nah. i. 2). This is the reason of the severity and universality of the judgment. The Masorites note that this is the only verse in the Bible which contains the whole Hebrew alphabet.

Vers. 9—20.—Part III. PROMISE OF THE CONVERSION OF THE WORLD AND THE HAPPINESS OF ISRAEL.

Vers. 9, 10.—§ 1. *The heathen shall be converted, and shall help in the restoration of Israel.*

Ver. 9.—**Will I turn to the people** (*peoples*) **a pure language** (*lip*). When his judgments have done their work, God will bring the heathen to the knowledge of him. He will purify their lips, which have been polluted with the names of idols and the worship offered to false gods (Ps. xvi. 4; Hos. ii. 17); the confusion of Babel shall be done away, and all shall speak the language of faith in one God. This, of course, points to Messianic times. For "pure lip," the Vulgate has, *labium electum;* the LXX., by a mistake of a letter (*bhedurah* for *bherurah*), γλῶσσαν εἰς γενεὰν αὐτῆς (sc. γῆς), "a tongue for her generation." **With one consent;** literally, *with one shoulder;* ὑπὸ ζυγὸν ἕνα, "under one yoke" (Septuagint); *humero uno* (Vulgate). The metaphor implies that all will help to carry the same burden, and to accomplish the same work, bearing the gospel throughout the world, and being all of one mind in the service of Jehovah (Jer. xxxii. 39; Isa. xix. 23, 24; Rev. xi. 15).

Ver. 10. — **From beyond the rivers of Ethiopia** (*Cush*); *i.e.* from the distant south, a type of the remotest parts of the world (ch. ii. 12). The rivers of Cush (Isa. xviii. 1), are the Nile, the Atbara, and their affluents. **My suppliants, even the daughter of my dispersed, shall bring mine** offering. From the ends of the earth, the Jews who have continued faithful to Jehovah, and have not lost their nationality among the Gentiles, but have considered themselves as belonging to "the dispersion," shall be again received of the Lord, and bring their oblations unto him. This may be the sense intended: but looking to the thought in Isa. lxvi. 20 (where it is said that the Gentiles shall bring the Israelites out of all nations as a meat offering unto the Lord), we had better render the passage as the Revised Version margin, "They shall bring my suppliants, even the daughter of my dispersed, for an offering unto me." The remote Gentiles shall show their faith in God by aiding the Hebrews among them to turn to the Lord; this shall be their offering to the true God, whom they have learned to adore. When they themselves are converted, they shall be evangelists to the Hebrews of the Dispersion. For this work of the Gentiles in converting the Hebrews, Wordsworth compares Cant. iii. 4; viii. 8, 9; Isa. lxi. 5, 6; lxv. 18—21. St. Paul speaks to the same effect in Rom. xi. *Offering* (*minchah*). The pure meal offering (Mal. i. 10, 11, where see notes; comp. Rom. xv. 16; Phil. ii. 17). Dr. Briggs renders, "From beyond the rivers of Cush will be my incense (*athar*); the daughter of Phut will bring a minchah." This brings out the parallelism. The universal worship of Messianic times is expressed in the ceremonial terms of the old dispensation, but has a very real applicableness to the Christian religion (see note on Mal. i. 11).

Vers. 11—13.—§ 2. *Israel, restored to God's favour, shall be cleansed and sanctified.*

Ver. 11.—**In that day.** When the Lord rises to seize the prey (ver. 8), when the Gentiles are converted, and Judah returns to her obedience. **Shalt thou not be ashamed for all thy doings.** God addresses Israel repentant and converted, and assures her that she shall not have to reproach herself any more, **or** to blush for her iniquities, because God blots them out, or because she sins no more as she has done. And the great help to this improvement is the abolition of the cause and incitement to sin. **I will take away out of the midst of thee them that rejoice in thy pride** (*thy proud triumphers*, Isa. xiii. 3). God will cut off all those who gloried in their temporal prosperity without thought of God,

who in the pride of their heart walked as they pleased, deeming themselves accountable to no one, subject to no law. Such shall no longer be found in the holy nation. **Haughty because of** (*in*) **my holy mountain**; *i.e.* in the temple (Isa. xi. 9). They shall no longer exult in the exclusiveness of their privileges, or feel a vain-glorious confidence in their own election, or the sanctity of their temple or its provision of worship. The Gentiles should be admitted to the covenant, and share in their privileges. Here we see adumbrated the nature of the Christian Church, an organized body no longer local, insulated, but Catholic—a spiritual temple open to all believers.

Ver. 12.—A further characteristic of Messiah's kingdom is here unfolded. No worldly pomp or splendour shall be found in it; its members are not proud, conceited, self-reliant. **I will also leave in the midst of thee.** I will leave over, as a remnant saved in the judgment (comp. Rom. ix. 27; Micah ii. 12, and the note there). **An afflicted and poor people.** The two epithets are elsewhere joined together (Job xxxiv. 28; Isa. xxvi. 6) to express the feeling of patience under affliction and inability to help one's self by one's own efforts. The spirit signified is just the contrary of the haughty, complacent, self-satisfied temper previously mentioned (1 Cor. i. 26; Jas. ii. 5). **They shall trust in the Name of the Lord.** All self-confidence shall be abolished, and the religion of the remnant shall be characterized by quiet trust in God.

Ver. 13.—**The remnant of Israel** (see note on ver. 12). Though they claim no worldly eminence, the true Israelites shall be conspicuous for spiritual graces. **Shall not do iniquity.** Their acts shall be just and holy; their daily conduct such as becomes the children of God's election (Lev. xix. 2; 1 John iii. 9). **Nor speak lies.** There shall be no lying prophets there, and all fraud and double-dealing shall be abolished. The proof of their righteous conduct is found in the favour of the Lord and the security in which they shall live. For they shall feed, etc. The remnant is compared to a "little flock" (Luke xii. 32), of which the Lord is the Shepherd (comp. Micah vii. 14). The blessing is that promised to Israel in the Law if she kept the commandments (Lev. xxvi. 5, 6).

Vers. 14—20.—§ 3. *Israel shall be comforted and largely blessed by the presence of Jehovah, and exalted to honour in the eyes of all the world.*

Ver. 14.—In view of the coming blessing, the prophet bursts forth in exultation, yet with a vein of prophecy running through all the canticle. After the late denunciation of woe and judgment, he soothes the faithful with the promise of the grace and peace which the time of Messiah shall bring. **Sing, O daughter of Zion** (Isa. i. 8; Zech. ii. 14; ix. 9). He calls on the restored remnant of Judah to show its joy by outward tokens. **O Israel.** All the tribes are to unite in praising God. This is one of the passages where "Israel" is supposed to have been written by mistake for "Jerusalem." So Jer. xxiii. 6. The LXX. gives, θύγατερ Ἰερουσαλήμ, "daughter of Jerusalem" (see note on Zech. i. 19). The prophet enjoins a triple note of exultation in order to confirm the universal joy. (On the use of the number "three" in this passage, see **Dr. Pusey's** note, p. 480.)

Ver. 15.—In this and following verses the prophet gives the reasons why Zion should rejoice. **Thy judgments.** The chastisements inflicted on thee in judgment, rendered necessary by thy iniquity (Ezek. v. 8). These God has removed; this is the first ground for rejoicing. Septuagint, τὰ ἀδικήματά σου, "thine iniquities." When God removes the punishments, he forgives the sin. **He hath cast out** (*cleared quite away*) **thine enemy.** The enemies who executed the judgment are utterly dispersed. **The King of Israel, even the Lord, is in the midst of thee** (Obad. 21). The theocracy is restored. Under the judgments which fell upon Israel, Jehovah seemed to have left his people; now he is in the midst of them as their King (Isa. xii. 6; lii. 7; Hos. xi. 9). The perpetual presence of Christ in the Church is here adumbrated. **Thou shalt not see evil any more.** So the Septuagint. Another reading adopted by Jerome is, "Thou shalt not fear." In view of the following verse, this seems rather tautological. With God in their midst, the people shall see, *i.e.* experience (Jer. v. 12), no evil (Rev. xxi. 3, 4).

Ver. 16.—**It shall be said.** So obvious to all men shall be the happy and secure position of Zion under God's favour and rule, that they shall join in bidding her cast away fear and exult in the Divine protection. **Fear thou not** (comp. Matt. xiv. 27; xxviii. 5, 10; Luke xii. 7, 32). **And to Zion.** Probably vocative, *O Zion.* **Let not thine hands be slack.** Be not despairing or faint-hearted, but work with energy and confidence (comp. Isa. xiii. 7; Heb. xii. 12); or the sentence may be rendered, "Jerusalem will be called *Fear not,* and Zion, *Let not thine hands be slack.*" In this case we may compare the names *Hephzibah* and *Beulah* given to Jerusalem (Isa. lxii. 4), and *Jehovah-Tsidkenu* (Jer. xxxiii. 16).

Ver. 17.—**In the midst of thee;** better, *is in the midst of thee* (see note on ver. 15). **Is mighty; he will save;** rather, *a Mighty One who will save;* LXX., Ὁ δυνατὸς σώσει

σε, "The Mighty One shall save thee." This is the real ground of confidence: the Lord wills their salvation. **He will rejoice over thee with joy,** now that thy iniquity is purged, and thou art united again to him, as a chaste and comely bride (Isa. lxii. 5; Jer. xxxii. 41; Hos. ii. 19). **He will rest** (Hebrew, *be silent*) **in his love.** This is a human expression, denoting that perfect love which needs no outward demonstration. For the very greatness of his love God rests, as it were, in quiet enjoyment of it. Some take it to mean that in his love for his people he is silent about, makes no mention of, past sins; but this seems less suitable, as this clause is merely an expansion of the preceding one. The Septuagint and Syriac Versions render, "He will renew thee in his love;" and Ewald has proposed to alter the present reading to, "He will do a new thing." But there is no sufficient reason for making the change. **With singing.** Again he gives to his ineffable love outward expression. The LXX. paraphrases accurately, "He will rejoice over thee with delight as on a day of festival" (Isa. lxv. 19).

Ver. 18.—The love which God feels he shows in action. He cares for the exiled and dispersed, and will gather them again and comfort them for all their sorrows. **I will gather them that are sorrowful for the solemn assembly;** or, *far removed from the solemn assembly.* Those who grieve because by their exile from the Holy Land they are debarred from duly attending the periodical festivals, these God will restore, and enable them again to participate in the sacred feasts. The above version and explanation are undoubtedly right, as the Latin Version is certainly wrong, *Nugas, qui a lege recesserant, congregabo;* that is, the light and fickle persons, who have estranged themselves from the Law, God will reclaim, and join them to the congregation of the true Israel; and this, *quia ex te erant,* for their origin's sake, because they are descendants of the chosen people. Who are of thee; *they are of thee,* O Zion. These are the true Israelites; this is why they mourn for the cessation of the festivals, and why they shall be restored to the Holy Land. To whom **the reproach of it** was **a burden;** *i.e.* who felt the desolation of Zion and the reproaches uttered against her by enemies (Ps. cxxxvii.) as a burden grievous to be borne. The Vulgate has, *Ut non ultra habeas super eis opprobrium;* i.e. "That they may be no more a disgrace to thee;" the LXX. reads somewhat differently, Οὐαί, τίς ἔλαβεν ἐπ' αὐτὴν ὀνειδισμόν; "Alas! who took up a reproach against her?"

Ver. 19.—**I will undo all that afflict thee;** *I will deal with* in punishment (Jer. xviii. 23); Vulgate, "I will slay." The restoration of Israel is preceded by the destruction of the enemies of God and the Church. Septuagint, Ποιῶ ἐν σοὶ ἕνεκέν σου ἐν τῷ καιρῷ ἐκείνῳ, λέγει Κύριος, "Dominus dicet ad Sion, Ecce, ego faciam in te propter te, id est, faciam ultionem tuam" (St. Jerome). Her that halteth (Micah iv. 6). The afflicted of Israel, here compared to a lame and footsore flock of sheep. Septuagint, τὴν ἐκπεπιεσμένην, "pressed," like grapes or olives, to extract the juice. Her that was driven out. The exiled and dispersed. I will get them praise and fame; *I will make them to be a praise and a name.* This is in accordance with the promise in Deut. xxvi. 19. In every land where they have been put to shame; literally, *in every land of their shame.* The scene of their shame should be the scene of their glorification. The prophet does not consider that the restored theocracy shall be confined to the geographical limits of the Holy Land; he looks to its dissemination throughout the world. Wide as the dispersion itself shall be the diffusion of the knowledge of God and the admiration of his doings towards Israel (comp. ch. ii. 11; iii. 9; Ezek. xx. 41; xxviii. 25; Zech. viii. 23).

Ver. 20.—Will I bring you again (*in*). He repeats the promise with some slight verbal changes. I will lead you like a flock to the pastures of Zion. People; *peoples.* When I turn back your captivity; *i.e.* when God brings them all home into the spiritual Zion from which they were long exiled (but see note on ch. ii. 7; and comp. Hos. vi. 11; Amos ix. 14). Before your eyes. Most certainly and evidently, so that what they hoped for they shall plainly see (Deut. i. 30; xxx. 3, etc.; Isa. lii. 8, 10). Saith the Lord. All this shall assuredly come to pass, for the mouth of the Lord hath spoken it. In the prophet's eye the restoration from captivity and the times of Messiah are synchronous, or the former is so closely connected in idea with the latter that he speaks of both under one set of terms, applying the same imagery to both.

HOMILETICS.

Vers. 1—8.—*Guilt and retribution.* Having taken a mental survey of the surrounding heathen nations, the seer returns again in thought to his own people. It was, indeed, in their interest that he had been led to take this wide review of God's dealings with men. He desired to make very real to them the Divine law that sin cannot go unpunished, and that national guilt must inevitably be followed by chastisement; yea, more, that if this law operated in heathen lands, much more might they expect to come under it who had enjoyed the special illumination of God's Spirit, to whom he had given his holy oracles, and amongst whom he had raised up a succession of faithful men to guide them into the paths of truth and righteousness. In these verses observe—

I. THE PROPHET PRESENTS A HEAVY INDICTMENT, SETTING FORTH THE GUILT OF JUDAH AND JERUSALEM. 1. This indictment contained certain counts directed against the people in general. They were charged with (1) inward defilement: "filthy and polluted" (ver. 1); (2) outward tyranny: "the oppressing city" (ver. 1); (3) practical atheism. God had spoken unto them, but they had not hearkened unto his voice (ver. 2). He had corrected them, but they did not humble themselves under his chastening hand (ver. 2). He had offered himself to them as the Object of trust, but they withheld their confidence from him, and rested in an arm of flesh (ver. 2). He had intimated his willingness to enter into fellowship with them, and to inspire and strengthen them, but "they drew not near unto him" (ver. 2). He had frustrated and brought to confusion their adversaries, and had covered with confusion and shame the godless nations around them, but instead of being warned by these Divine judgments, executed in their sight against evil-doers, they had themselves wilfully persisted in their iniquity (vers. 6, 7). 2. This indictment contained also certain counts directed against the leaders of the nation in particular (vers. 3, 4). (1) The princes were charged with cruelty, devouring, like roaring lions, those they ought to have protected (ver. 3). (2) The judges were marked by greed and rapacity, and were insatiable as evening wolves, so that justice was perverted, and wrong remained unredressed (ver. 3). (3) The prophets of the people, who claimed to be messengers of God to them, were trifling and insincere, so that no reliance could be placed upon their words (ver. 4). (4) The priests profaned the temple and its services, and dishonoured the Law they were appointed to expound and enforce (ver. 4).

II. THE PROPHET DECLARED THE RIGHTEOUSNESS OF GOD, AND THE CONSEQUENT

RETRIBUTION THAT SHOULD BE EXPERIENCED BY THE EVIL-DOERS. (Vers. 5, 1, 8.) God is righteous (ver. 5). He is so absolutely and essentially. His perfections are all conformed to this, and, when truly contemplated by us, only render his righteousness the more manifest and intense to us. His Law is distinguished by this, and all his doings are guided by this. "He thinks, and feels, and purposes, and acts always according to what ought to be, and never in accommodation to what is; he makes uncompromising rectitude the rule of all his judgments and proceedings in all his dealings with men. He is not facile and bending, open to appeals and appliances from without, but inherently and unalterably righteous" (Candlish). And God being thus essentially and eternally righteous, iniquity cannot go unpunished; and transgressors persisting shamelessly in wrong-doing must reap the due reward of their deeds. In no spirit of vindictiveness, but in strict accordance with this rectitude, so perfect and entire, by which he is characterized, God here, by "the mouth of his holy prophet," pronounced "woe" unto Jerusalem (ver. 1), and declared his "determination" to gather the godless nations and to assemble the rebellious kingdoms, and to pour upon them his indignation, etc. (ver. 8).

III. THE PROPHET INDICATED THE TRUE ATTITUDE OF THE GOOD IN THE LAND WHILST THE PREVAILING INIQUITY WAS REACHING ITS CULMINATION AND WHEN THE JUDGMENTS OF HEAVEN SHOULD FALL. They should wait in the exercise of patience and of hope, assured that out of the chaos wrought by sin God would evolve his purposes of love, bringing good to the race. "Therefore wait for me, saith Jehovah" (ver. 8).

Ver. 9.—*Symbols of the final prosperity of God's spiritual kingdom.* This verse introduces us to brighter scenes. The writer has unfolded the guilt of his own and other nations, and has declared the terrible judgments which, in consequence of the prevailing iniquity, should be experienced; and now, in the closing portion of his prophecy, he seeks to comfort the true-hearted in such troublous times by lingering upon the glorious future of the Church of the living God. His faith pierces the mists and clouds, and apprehends the noble victories to be won in the coming time by the Lord and his Christ, and the halcyon days that lay beyond. We are not to imagine that the ancient prophets realized the *full* significance of the predictions they uttered respecting the glory of "the latter day." They wrote under the inspiration of God's Spirit, and we doubt not there was often a deeper meaning underlying their utterances than even they supposed. Unconsciously they "testified beforehand" of a "glory" such as, if fully seen by them, would have dazzled and bewildered them by its very splendour. We must avoid placing narrow interpretations upon their words in reference to these high themes. It were weak indeed to seek the complete fulfilment of the glowing predictions which form the closing portion of this prophecy in any one nation, and still less in any particular event in that nation's history. The prophets themselves, partial although the light they possessed was, would not thus have restricted their own words, for they recognized and rejoiced in the thought of God as working in the interests of the whole race; and we, with the increased light possessed by us, ought not to be less comprehensive than they. Viewing this verse (ver. 9) in this spirit, we may see set forth in it a striking symbol, the characteristics of the sincere and genuine subjects of the spiritual kingdom of God. Such are distinguished by—

I. PURITY IN HEART AND LIFE. "For then will I turn to the peoples a pure language;" literally, "a purified life" (ver. 9). Degeneracy reveals itself in a marked manner in the evil utterances of men. The filthy jest, the coarse oath, the brutal curse, the foul names, which have often offended our ears as we have walked along the public streets, indicate the depravity of hardened hearts. Equally expressive of this is uncharitable speech, whether taking the form of open reproaches or the cowardly and more dangerous form of secret slander. Double-tongued utterances, too, reveal the wickedness of the human heart—utterances which appear to convey a twofold meaning, good and evil, the good being simply a kind of disguise employed for the purpose of rendering the evil the more effective. And vain and frivolous speech likewise serves to indicate wrongness of heart; "idle words," useless effectless words, words which some spend so much time in dropping from house to house, words very unsavoury to all sensible minds, and which, if they accomplish anything, only work mischief and mistrust. In contrast to this, and as indicating the opposite disposition of mind and heart, we place true speech. "The mouth of a righteous man is a well of life" (Prov. x. 11), "natural, clean, life-giving, refreshing;" "The tongue of the wise useth knowledge aright" (Prov. xv. 2); "A wholesome tongue is a tree of life" (Prov. xv. 4); "The lips of the wise disperse truth" (Prov. xv. 7). Happy they who resemble the character portrayed by George Eliot, in her 'Scenes of Clerical Life,' and of whom she says, "He was the man to give me help and comfort when everything else failed: every word he says seems to have a new meaning. I think it must be because he has felt life more deeply than others, and has a deeper faith. I believe everything he says at once; his words seem to come like rain on the parched ground. It has always seemed to me before as if I could see behind people's words as one sees behind a screen, but in this man it is his very soul that speaks." And since speech thus reveals character, no more appropriate symbol could have been chosen by Zephaniah than this for the purpose of setting forth the Divine renewal in man, and of expressing that purity in heart and life which should characterize the members of the true Church of God in the happier days to which, despite the prevailing gloom, he looked forward so hopefully. "For then will I turn to the peoples a pure language."

II. DEVOUTNESS IN SPIRIT AND DISPOSITION. Purified in heart, they should be rendered devout in spirit. Fellowship with God should be their delight. They should no longer grovel in the dust, but their aspirations should tend towards God and heaven. Delivered from idolatry and superstition and worldliness, they should all "call upon the Name of the Lord" (ver. 9). " From the rising of the sun even unto the going down of the same my Name shall be great among the Gentiles; and in every place incense shall be offered unto my Name, and a pure offering" (Mal. i. 11).

III. UNITY IN PURPOSE AND AIM. "To serve him with one consent," literally "with one shoulder." The symbol was suggested by the thought of a number of men being engaged in bearing a heavy burden. They walk in step, they act together, they stand shoulder to shoulder, the weight is proportionately shared by each; such, indeed, is their agreement and concert that it would seem as though there were but one shoulder among them. And so shall it be with the Church of God eventually. The time shall come when all divisions and strifes shall cease, when all antagonisms, whether real or seeming, shall be no longer traceable amongst good men, when that true unity in heart, in life, and in endeavour shall become manifest, for which the great Intercessor yearned, and for which he prayed as he cried, "That they all may be one" (John xvii. 21—23). Happy era, predicted in this verse, and which, since "the mouth of the Lord hath spoken it," shall assuredly come at length, when all God's servants shall "with one mind and one mouth glorify God, even the Father of our Lord Jesus Christ" (Rom. xv. 6).

Ver. 10.—*The restoration of the Jews.* These words have been regarded by some biblical expositors as having reference to the conversion of the Gentiles. This utterance of Zephaniah in the Old Testament, and the prophecy of Caiaphas recorded in the New (John xi. 51, 52), have been associated together in their minds, and they have thought that by the "dispersed" Zephaniah meant the Gentiles, even as Caiaphas described the Gentiles as "the children of God that were scattered abroad," and that when the prophet alluded to the dispersed "beyond the rivers of Ethiopia," he meant to intimate that the Gentiles even from *the remotest parts* should eventually be brought home to God. Others, including many of the ablest interpreters, take the opposite view. They regard ver. 9 as referring to the Gentiles in their relation to the truth and the kingdom of God, and as intimating the great fact of the calling of the Gentiles, who should be led with one consent to serve the Lord, and then refer to this tenth verse as having special reference to the spiritual restoration of the Jews, who, through the agency of the Gentiles thus converted to God, should at length be brought in (Rom. xi. 30, 31). Accepting this latter interpretation, we have here declared the spiritual restoration of the Jews (ver. 10). Note—

I. THEIR PRESENT POSITION. 1. *Dispersed.* Scattered over the face of the whole earth. "Can you find a country which they can call their own? Can you find a nation in which they are not? In Europe, Asia, Africa, and America, and the furthest islands of the Southern Sea, among bond and free, copper-coloured and yellow, white and black, wherever there are men, there are Jews." 2. *Yearning.*

Crying out to God, longing for the fulfilment of their cherished hopes. In exile they are still his "suppliants," expecting the promised Messiah, and, whilst many of them are embittered against Christianity, there are not wanting numbers who have embraced it, and openly avowed their faith in Christ, whilst many are his disciples "secretly," ready to avow themselves his, only shrinking from the pains and penalties involved, whilst a still larger number are inquiring concerning him, and are easily accessible to the missionary of the cross.

II. THEIR ULTIMATE RESTORATION. 1. The fact of their spiritual recovery is here emphatically declared (ver. 10). From the remotest parts they shall come and surrender themselves as an offering unto God. "All Israel shall be saved." They shall be brought in with the fulness of the Gentiles, and "there shall be one flock, one Shepherd" (John x. 16). Their restoration to their own land is a question of comparative unimportance in view of this spiritual recovery which is so frequently declared in the unerring Word of God (Rom. ix. 1—6, 8, 9; x. 1—4; xi. 1, 9, 11—15, 23—32; 2 Cor. iii. 12—16). 2. It is implied here that this spiritual restoration shall be effected through the agency of the Gentiles. The offering here referred to as to be brought unto the Lord was "the meat offering." The idea expressed here is that, just as the children of Israel presented the meat offering unto God, so the Gentiles themselves, converted to him, should labour for the conversion of the Jews, and, crowned with success in this holy service, should bring these Hebrew converts as a meat offering unto the Lord. And the meaning is still more clear if we remember the signification of the meat offering. It was a sacrifice in which the Jew recognized God's goodness and grace in the bounties of his hand, and acknowledged that these gifts were his by right, and ought to be consecrated unto him. And even so, it is here declared that the Gentiles should recognize God's mercy in bringing home to himself his chosen race, and should present these converts to him as those who were his in virtue of all he had done for them, and who ought to be entirely consecrated to his service. The Church of Christ should ever prove herself a missionary Church, and in these enterprises a conspicuous place should be assigned to work for the spiritual good of God's ancient people, whose "falling away" shall result in "the reconciling of the world," and the restoration of whom shall be "as life from the dead" (Rom. xi. 15).

Vers. 11—17.—*Pictorial representation of the Church of God in the latter age.* Dark days were in store for his people when this prophet prophesied. The Captivity was in prospect, and there would soon be occasion for them, by "the rivers of Babylon," to "weep as they remembered Zion." Still, he would have them remember that it would not be ever thus, but that the time should come in which the ransomed of the Lord should return to Zion with songs and with gladness. In these verses he draws a beautiful picture of the Church of the future. How far his description has been realized in the past in the experience of the Hebrew Church in connection with the return from captivity, it would be impossible for us to indicate; certain, however, is it that, for the full realization of this, we must turn to the future, to the Church of God in the latter age. We do well to unite with the good of all past times in looking on by faith to that bright day of God which shall yet dawn upon the world sin has darkened and sorrow blighted, and to anticipate, with expectant hearts, its glorious appearing. Concerning the Church of the future, we are reminded here of—

I. HER PERFECTED CHARACTER. Her members are represented as : 1. *Purified.* So pure indeed should they be as that "they should not be ashamed for all their doings wherein they had transgressed against God" (ver. 11); *i.e.* they should have "no more conscience of sin" (Heb. x. 2). So completely should they be delivered from the old life of sin that even the remembrance of the sinful past should all be obliterated, and should no more rise before them to disturb and distress. 2. *Humble.* No longer puffed up with spiritual pride, boasting of themselves as being the favoured of Heaven, and glorying in their special advantages of ancestry and country, "they should no more be haughty because of God's holy mountain" (ver. 11), but should be lowly in heart, and clothed with that humility and meekness which is in the sight of God of great price 3. *Trustful.* Resting wholly in "the Name of the Lord, which is a strong tower" (Prov. xviii. 10). "And they shall trust in the Name of the Lord" (ver. 11). 4. *Sincere.* They should reach unto the heights of holy obedience, and which is, indeed, the climax. "The remnant of Israel shall not do iniquity, or speak lies, neither shall a deceitful tongue be found in their mouth" (ver. 13).

II. HER HIGH PRIVILEGES. 1. Deliverance from all sorrow. "Thou shalt not see evil any more" (ver. 15). 2. Enrichment with peace and tranquillity. "For they shall feed and lie down, and none shall make them afraid" (ver. 13). 3. Safety under God's protecting care. "The King of Israel, even the Lord, is in the midst of thee;" "Fear thou not" (vers. 15, 16).

III. HER DIVINE RESOURCES. In the seventeenth verse the love of God towards his servants is declared in words of exquisite beauty and tenderness. "The prophet speaks of the eternal love and joy of God towards his people as an exuberant joy, one which boundeth within the inmost self, and again is wholly *silent in his love*, as the deepest, tenderest, most yearning love broods over the object of its love, yet is held still in silence by the very depth of its love, and then again breaks forth in outward motion, and leaps for joy, and uttereth what it cannot form in words; for truly the love of God in its unspeakable love and joy is past belief, past utterance, past thought" (Pusey). And since he who thus loves is "mighty," the objects of this Divine love need not fear nor grow faint-hearted ever, for their resources are infinite and eternal.

IV. HER RAPTUROUS JOY. "Sing, O daughter of Zion; shout, O Israel," etc. (ver. 14). The joy of the redeemed eventually shall be full and all-sufficing, and, in anticipation of entering into this experience at length, all God's servants, even in the dark days, may well lift up their heads, and "in the darkness raise their carols of high praise."

Ver. 15.—*The abiding presence of God with his Church.* "The King of Israel, even the Lord, is in the midst of thee." This truth was constantly affirmed in the Old Testament with reference to the Jewish Church; and as the Church of God through all ages is one Church, we may take the promises of God to Israel of old as having their application to his Church still. So may we apply to her to-day those assurances contained in the Hebrew Scriptures (Ps. xlvi.; xlviii.), or that contained in the text, or, turning to the New Testament, we may grasp the gracious promise of the God-Man, "Lo, I am with you alway, even unto the end of the world" (Matt. xxviii. 20).

I. INDICATE SOME OF THE WAYS IN WHICH GOD HAS ESTABLISHED THIS TRUTH OF HIS ABIDING PRESENCE WITH HIS CHURCH IN ALL AGES. 1. By having "a remnant" to his praise even in the darkest times. It is an undoubted fact that, whatever dark clouds of persecution, or indifference, or declension may have arisen, God has had all through the season of darkness a people to show forth his praise. These Hebrew prophets, amidst their emphatic testimony against the iniquity prevailing in their times, constantly recognize with thankfulness "a remnant" as remaining true to God and to righteousness. Elijah at Horeb thought himself to be the only servant of Heaven remaining in his corrupt day; but God removed the veil concealing from his view the secret and hidden Church, and, lo, he beheld "an exceeding great army," where he had supposed himself to be the solitary warrior for the truth. "Yet have I left me seven thousand in Israel," etc. (1 Kings xix. 18). In "the dark ages," when the light of Christian truth had become well-nigh extinguished, there were not wanting those who dared to maintain the truth of God in its simplicity and purity. Even within the pale of the Church of Rome in those days there were some who deplored the prevailing corruptions, and who longed for a return to the simplicity in teaching and the purity of life by which the early Christians were characterized; whilst outside her communion were associations of Free Christian societies, as in Lombardy and in the Alps, who were as lights shining in dark places. The Nestorians, "the Protestants of Asia," referred to by Mr. Layard, serve as another illustration, and who, away in the remote valleys of Kurdistan, and entirely separated from intercourse with other Christian communities, have preserved through so many centuries a knowledge of the Christian faith in the purity of its character and the simplicity of its worship. There has ever been "a remnant" true to God, and serving as a clear token of his abiding presence with his Church. 2. By raising up in her midst, and qualifying, men for special service. Whilst we may not "glory in men," we may magnify God's grace and power in them; and it is intensely interesting to note how he has in every emergency raised up his agents to do his work. Moses and Joshua, in relation to the deliverance of the Israelites and their settlement in Canaan; Ezra and Nehemiah, in connection with the return from the Captivity in Babylon; the faithful prophets raised up to declare the judgments of Heaven against idolatrous nations; Luther, Melancthon, Zwingle, called by him to take part in the work of the Reformation; and Owen, Howe, Bunyan, Baxter, Flavel, and others, following, to wield the pen effectively in support of the truth, and so to confirm and to consolidate the work of their predecessors. And by thus raising up men and endowing them with gifts for special service, God has confirmed to his Church the assurance of his abiding presence. 3. By frustrating and bringing to nought the evil designs of her enemies. He has repeatedly proved that "no weapon directed against his Church can prosper," and has made manifest the folly of those who have sought to overthrow the kingdom of truth and righteousness. "The wrath of man shall praise him," etc. (Ps. lxxvi. 10). 4. By opening up new fields for the extension of her influence. India has been placed under British rule, and the opportunity given of making known to its teeming millions "the unsearchable riches of Christ." The exclusiveness that prevented access to the empire of China has passed away, so that the missionary may go through the length and breadth of the land. The heart of Africa has been penetrated, and there is now the prospect of her sable tribes becoming elevated and blessed through Christian influence. And in thus opening up the world for Christian enterprise to bestow upon it all its energy and zeal, God has shown himself as being still with his Church. "The King of Israel," etc. (ver. 15).

II. THE ENCOURAGEMENT THIS THOUGHT OF GOD'S ABIDING PRESENCE WITH HIS PEOPLE IS CALCULATED TO AFFORD TO THEIR HEARTS. 1. In view of the character of the age in which we live, as related to Christian truth. Many are seeking to restore that papal supremacy which has proved such a blight in ages that are past; many are cherishing the spirit of scepticism, and would have us even banish God himself from his universe; and there is also a widespread spirit of indifference in relation to the highest spiritual realities. Yet still we will not despond, for "the Lord of hosts is with us," and as he caused the light to burn and to prevail even in the darkest ages, so he will still work until the light shall shine in every land, and all flesh see together the revealed glory of the Lord. 2. In view of apathy, coldness, and declension in holy service. Such seasons do occur, and such lifelessness and deadness at times falls upon the Church of God and upon Christian communities. Yet God does not forsake us even when we thus grow lukewarm in his service. He is with us still, and will grant us renewal and revival if we will but turn to him with all our hearts. 3. In view of the losses the Church of God is called upon to sustain through the ravages of death. The last foe is ever active. Beneath his unsparing hand the useful as well as the useless fall—the true-hearted worker for God as well as the idler whose life is altogether barren of good. But amidst these changes the chief Shepherd liveth; all holy gifts and heavenly graces are his bestowments, and he will not fail his Church, but will raise up a bright succession of devoted servants to do his bidding and to help on the grand consummation. Hence we will not despair; for "God is in the midst of her; she shall not be moved: God shall help her, and that right early" (Ps. xlvi. 4).

Vers. 18—20.—*Words of help and hope to the exiled and banished.* The closing words of this prophecy, contained in these verses, are amply sufficient to indicate that although the writer was a messenger of judgment, and as such addressed burning words of denunciation to evil-doers, he was also a man full of tenderness—a Barnabas as well as a Boanerges. Whilst, being commissioned by God to reprove the ungodly, he did not spare such, yet he also knew how to speak words of help and hope to the sorrowful and distressed; indeed, we find him here anticipating sorrow, being beforehand with consolation, and providing the balm for wounds yet to be inflicted.

I. THE CASE SUPPOSED. The prophet had spoken of captivity; yet he was conscious that God would restore his people at the close, and bring them from Babylon to their own land. But, whilst confident as to this, he knew that, in the very nature of the circumstances, only a portion of God's people would be privileged thus to return, and that many of them would be dispersed among the heathen in various places, and would be unable to come back with those who should be restored "when the Lord should turn again the captivity of his people." And he also knew that, amongst these scattered ones, there would be those who, in their remote exile, would mourn for the solemn assembly, and whose hearts would be burdened in view of their banishment (ver. 18).

II. The words of help and hope addressed by the prophet to those thus circumstanced. 1. He assured them that the Lord their God would bring to nought their oppressors. "I will undo all that afflict thee" (ver. 19). 2. That the Shepherd of Israel would in his own time regather every member of his flock, however scattered they were, and however feeble some of them might be. "And I will save her that halteth, and gather," etc. (ver. 19). 3. And that in the very lands where they would be put to shame he would eventually secure to them lasting honour and imperishable renown (vers. 19, 20).

III. The prophet an example to teachers of religion in every age. There must be the bold denunciation of wrong, but there should ever accompany this tenderness of spirit, revealing itself in the endeavour to comfort and cheer troubled hearts. And in proportion as this spirit is cherished by us do we resemble the great Prophet of the Church, who was "anointed to comfort those that mourn," etc. (Isa. lxi. 1—3).

HOMILIES BY VARIOUS AUTHORS.

Vers. 1—8.—*Jerusalem the rebellious and polluted; or, the wickedness and woe of a degenerate city.* I. The number and variety of her sins. 1. *Rebellion.* This, marking her attitude towards God, is amplified and detailed as consisting in four transgressions. (1) Disobedience. She had not obeyed Jehovah's voice speaking to her through the Law and the prophets, enjoining on her precepts and imposing on her duties, but, like an ordinary heathen nation, had said, "Who is Jehovah, that we should serve him, or that he should reign over us?" (2) Insubordination. She had not received correction, *i.e.* had not accepted with meek submission the discipline or chastisement Jehovah had laid upon her in consequence of her sins, as for instance when he brought against her Shishak of Egypt (1 Kings xiv. 25, 26), Jehoash of Israel (2 Kings xiv. 13), Sargon or Sennacherib of Assyria (2 Kings xviii. 17; 2 Chron. xxxii. 1), but had resented it, not only adhering to her disobedient ways, but improving on them, "rising early and corrupting all her doings." (3) Unbelief. Not trusting in Jehovah, she had alternately trusted in Assyria and Egypt. Whereas her confidence in Jerusalem's stability and impregnability ought to have rested on the fact that Jehovah had chosen it to place his Name there, had entered into covenant with the nation of which it was the capital, had established in it his worship, and had promised to protect it, she was constantly basing her hopes on a political alliance either with the northern power against the southern, or with the southern against the northern (Isa. xxxvi. 6; Hos. xiv. 3). (4) Irreligion. Having renounced all faith in Jehovah, she had scarcely maintained the pretence of observing his worship—had not drawn near to him, either externally in the way of celebrating those rites he had prescribed, or internally by pouring out her heart before him in supplication of his favour and help. 2. *Pollution.* This declares what the city was in herself. The completeness of her defilement discovered itself in the wickedness of all classes of her population, but more especially of her civil and spiritual rulers. Of the latter, (1) the prophets were light and treacherous persons, vain-glorious boasters, boiling up with their own conceited imaginings, men of treacheries who published their own false dreams as if these had been the true visions of God (Jer. xxiii. 32), and thus caused the people to err (Isa. ix. 16; Micah iii. 5). As they exercised their callings without having themselves been called to these by God (Jer. xiv. 14), they were not his prophets, but hers. Scarcely less polluted were (2) the priests, who, as Jehovah's ministers, ought to have been holy (Lev. xxi. 6; Numb. xvi. 5), but who, through being themselves impure, profaned that which is holy, or defiled the sanctuary and all connected with it—its rites, persons, things, places, sacrifices, and violated the Law (Ezek. xxii. 26) "by treating what was holy as profane." 3. *Oppression.* Revealing her behaviour towards man: her civic dignitaries practised cruelties ferocious and unprovoked upon those over whom they ruled. (1) Her princes in the midst of her, *i.e.* her kings and nobles, like roaring lions rushing on their prey (Prov. xxvii. 15), ground down her poor and unresisting population by excessive taxations and labours. (2) Her judges, in their administration of law and (so-called) justice, were so fixedly bent on their own enrichment, and so insatiably greedy of their evil gains, that they seemed like hungry and rapacious evening wolves which could not leave a bone of their prey till the morning, but must devour it ere the night passed (Hab. i. 8; Jer. v. 6; Ezek. xxii. 27).

II. THE AGGRAVATION AND HEINOUSNESS OF HER SINS. 1. *Against Divine grace.* She had been guilty of all the foregoing wickednesses, though Jehovah had been in the midst of her. That he chose at the first to establish his presence in her was a favour— a special favour; that he remained in her after she had become rebellious, polluted, and oppressive, was more than a special favour—was an exceeding great mercy. 2. *Against Divine example.* In all Jehovah's dealings with her he had shown himself "righteous," even proved that he would not and could not do iniquity; nevertheless, she had not followed in Jehovah's steps, but had turned aside into crooked paths and unclean ways. 3. *Against Divine instruction.* Jehovah had brought his judgment to light every morning by causing his Law to be proclaimed to the nation daily by the prophets. Yet she had rebelled against the light and done the works of darkness. 4. *Against Divine warnings.* She had seen Jehovah cutting off the nations around, throwing down their battlements, and rendering them desolate, "making their streets waste," etc. (ver. 6); and still she had closed her ears against the warnings these providential judgments gave. 5. *Against Divine expectation.* Jehovah had hoped she would fear him and receive the instruction and correction he had intended for her; but she had not done so. Rather she had risen early and corrupted herself, thereby proving herself one of the unjust who know no shame.

III. THE RECOMPENSE AND REWARD OF HER SINS. 1. *A severe penalty.* Woe; and the cutting off of her dwelling. Unless she repented and turned from her evil ways, she would be overwhelmed with the righteous indignation of God, and her place as a nation wiped out—an impressive symbol of the doom threatened against unbelieving and unrepentant sinners under the gospel. 2. *A contingent penalty.* If she feared Jehovah and accepted correction, her dwelling should not be cut off, and the vials of woe should not be outpoured upon her (Jer. xviii. 7). So are God's threatenings against sinners contingent on their continued impenitence. But this presupposed, it becomes: 3. *A certain penalty.* Nothing could avert the woe and the cutting off in Jerusalem's case but repentance and reformation, neither of which she showed; and so when within less than a century it became apparent that there was no remedy, the sluice-gates of wrath were opened, and she was cut off without compassion (2 Chron. xxxvi. 16, 17). So will it be with those under the gospel, who, being often reproved, yet harden their necks—they shall be utterly destroyed, and that without remedy (Prov. xxix. 1).

Learn: 1. The danger of sin. 2. The certainty of judgment.—T. W.

Ver. 5.—*The shamelessness of sin.* I. A DEMONSTRABLE FACT. 1. *Asserted by Scripture.* In addition to the statement of the text, that "the unjust knoweth no shame," may be cited other declarations to the same effect from both the Old (Jer. iii. 3; vi. 15; viii. 12) and the New (Eph. iv. 19; Phil. iii. 19) Testaments. 2. *Proved by experience.* Besides the individuals to whom the above passages allude, persons are often met with in actual life who not only seem, but so far as can be discovered from their behaviour actually are, insensible to shame.

II. A PSYCHOLOGICAL ENIGMA. 1. *Shame the fruit of sin.* Exemplified in the case of Adam and Eve (Gen. ii. 25; iii. 7). Shame is the outward sign of the soul's inward consciousness of guilt. 2. *Sin the death of shame.* If shame does not lead to repentance, and so to the destruction of sin, sin will soon assert its supremacy over shame and lead to its extinction.

III. A SIGNIFICANT PHENOMENON. Teaching: 1. *The possibility of complete spiritual deterioration.* When a soul can no longer feel ashamed on account of sin, when its moral perceptions have become darkened, and its conscience is deadened, the process of spiritual or religious degeneration has reached its lowest point. The soul is practically dead in trespasses and in sins. It has become essentially and permanently unjust. 2. *The impossibility of ultimate redemption.* The soul that cannot blush is at least perilously near the condition of those of whom it is written, "It is impossible to renew them again unto repentance" (Heb. vi. 6).—T. W.

Vers. 8—13.—*The gracious acts of Jehovah; or, Israel's glorious future.* I. THE

RESTORATION OF ISRAEL. (Ver. 8.) 1. *The time indicated.* The day that Jehovah riseth up to the prey; *i.e.* to take for himself as a booty or spoil out of the nations he visits a people who shall desire his salvation and confess his Name. Among those who shall then be captured by Jehovah will be Israel, or at least a remnant thereof, who shall be brought again to their own land. The time thus indicated began with Persia's overthrow of Babylon, to which doubtless the prophet's language primarily refers, continued till the advent of Christ, in whom Jehovah rose up not merely to bring redemption to the pious remnant of Israel (Luke i. 68), but to take out of the Gentiles a people for his Name (Acts xv. 14), and will not terminate till the close of the present era, during which, by the gospel, is being gathered out of all nations and kindreds, peoples and tongues, a people for Jehovah, of whom ancient Israel was but a shadow and a type (Matt. viii. 11; Luke xiii. 29; Rev. vii. 9). 2. *The instrumentality declared.* A work of judgment upon the nations of the earth, which work again commenced with the destruction of Babylon, and will only be finished when Christ appears a second time to execute judgment upon all (Jude 15), and in particular to pour out his wrath upon the impenitent and unbelieving (2 Thess. i. 7, 8; Heb. x. 27; Rev. vi. 17). As in Zephaniah's time Jehovah declared it to be his fixed purpose to hold such an assize of the nations, so has he revealed his intention to hold another and a grander at the end of time (Acts xvii. 31); and as he further maintained (to adopt another rendering) that the holding of such an assize, with what would inevitably result from it, viz. " the devouring of all the earth with the fire of his jealousy," *i.e.* the destruction of his enemies by his judgments, and the salvation of his people by his grace, should be a clear vindication of his righteousness, so does he in respect of the final judgment claim that its decisions will manifest to all the righteous character of himself and his government (Rom. ii. 2, 5; 2 Thess. i. 5; Rev. xvi. 5). 3. *The duty prescribed.* To wait for Jehovah. Addressed, not to the whole wicked and corrupt nation (Hitzig), but to its pious remnant (Keil and Delitzsch, Pusey, Fausset, Farrar), this counsel was in effect: (1) A warning against apostasy. Though Jehovah's judgments should descend upon the nation, they, the meek of the land (ch. ii. 3), were not to discontinue either believing in Jehovah or practising his religion, but were to steadfastly adhere to both. (2) An intimation of mercy. Since, even before the judgment fell, Jehovah counselled them to wait for him after it had fallen, the sense could only be that he had it in contemplation to interpose in his own time for their deliverance. (3) An encouragement to hope. In the darkest hours of their despondency, when the nation's fortunes should be at the lowest ebb, they should not yield to despair, but look expectantly forward to the good time coming. The duty here prescribed that of God's people collectively and individually at all times, but especially in seasons of calamity and affliction.

II. THE ENLARGEMENT OF ISRAEL. (Vers. 9, 10.) 1. *The accession of the Gentiles.* (1) The outward occasion of this turning of the nations to Israel. The visible, historical instrumentality by which it should be brought about has been declared to be the pouring out upon them of Jehovah's indignation. When God's judgments are abroad, the inhabitants' of the world learn righteousness (Isa. xxvi. 9). Nations and communities no less than individuals, and these no less than those, not unfrequently require to be whipped into obedience and chastised into submission. Calamities in the shape of wars and pestilences bring powerful kingdoms and haughty empires to their knees, when nothing else will. Prodigals and profligates need experience of servitude and starvation at the swine's trough, before they will return in penitence to God. (2) The impelling force. Jehovah's grace in turning to them a pure language (literally, " lip "). Not imparting to them instruction through his servants the prophets (Luther, Hofmann), but purifying their lips defiled by the worship of idols (Hitzig, Keil, and Delitzsch). This, again, was only possible by first purifying their hearts, or weaning them from the love of their debasing superstitions. The fountain must be cleansed if the stream running from it is to be pure; the tree must be good if its fruit is to be good (Matt. xii. 33). The prime mover in all religious awakenings and reformations is God (Ezek. xxxvi. 27; John iii. 3, 5; vi. 63; Rom. viii. 2; 1 Cor. xv. 10). (3) The formal expression. Calling upon the Name of the Lord. A phrase used to designate the worship of Jehovah by Abraham (Gen. xii. 8), and of Christ by believers under the gospel (Rom. x. 13). The Name of God signifies his manifested character (Exod. iii. 15; xx. 24; xxiii. 21; John xvii. 6); to call upon his Name, to invoke the help that Name proffers and warrants to expect. (4) The animating Spirit. " To serve him with one consent," or "one shoulder;" signifying that their adherence to Jehovah shall not be purely formal but essentially spiritual, not of outward ceremonial alone but also of inward devotion, not forced and constrained but voluntary and of personal choice, and not fragmentary and isolated but united and combined. 2. *The ingathering of the dispersed* (Jews). These the prophet represents: (1) As objects of Jehovah's affection, even in the countries of their exile. Jehovah speaks of them as his dispersed (men may forget their covenant relationship to God; he never forgets his relationship to them), and as the daughter of his dispersed (cf. ver. 14), a designation of Israel shaped after similar expressions of Isaiah (ii. 8; iv. 4; xxii. 4) and Jeremiah (iv. 11, 31; vi. 2, 14),—God's love to men changes not, though their circumstances and, even their characters may change. (2) As returning to Jehovah's service. From the furthest bounds of their dispersion, even from beyond the rivers (the Nile and the Astaboras) of Ethiopia and from other countries into which they may have been scattered. No spot too distant or condition of existence too abject that one may not find his way back from it to God. In a spirit of penitential entreaty. Jehovah calls them his suppliants, to indicate the mood of mind in which they shall return (Zech. xii. 10). In so doing "he describes the character of all who come to God through Christ" (Pusey). To offer acceptable worship. What Jehovah styles "his offering," was the minchah, or meat offering due to him according to the Law of Moses (Exod. xxix. 41; Lev. ii. 8; Numb. iv. 16), the tribute they owed him as their Divine King (1 Sam. x. 27; 1 Kings iv. 21). According to another rendering (De Wette, Keil and Delitzsch, Fausset, Revised Version margin), the offerers are the Gentiles, and the offering the Jews of the dispersion, whom the former shall bring and present to Jehovah. Though favoured by Isaiah (lxvi. 20) and Paul (Rom xi. 25, 26, 31), it is doubtful if this view of the passage was in the prophet's mind (Hitzig, Pusey).

III. THE ESTABLISHMENT OF ISRAEL. (Vers. 11—13.) 1. *In the enjoyment of spiritual peace.* When the Lord had turned again her captivity, and brought her back to himself with weeping and with supplication (Jer. xxxi. 9; l. 4; Joel ii. 12), she should no longer be ashamed for or "on account of" her past iniquities. Not because these would then have ceased to be reprehensible and fitted to cause shame, but either because they would then have ceased to be (Keil and Delitzsch), or because God would then have forgiven them (Pusey). A new heart and a quiet conscience—two of the first gifts bestowed upon returning penitents. 2. *In the possession of heart-humility.* Then all her proudly exulting citizens should be cut off, and all her haughty leaders abased, so that none should remain in her but an afflicted and poor people, who should no more be haughty in Jehovah's holy mountain. Meekness of mind, lowliness of heart, poverty of spirit, an indispensable characteristic of true religion in the soul (Matt. v. 3; xi. 20; xviii. 4; Col. iii. 12; 1 Pet. v. 5, 6). 3. *In the exercise of living faith.* They, *i.e.* the inhabitants of restored Jerusalem, shall trust in the Name of the Lord. If true religion begets a spirit of lowliness towards one's self, it inspires a feeling of calm and confident trust in God (Ps. ix. 10). 4. *In the pursuit of true holiness.* The members of God's spiritual Israel should neither commit injustice nor tell lies, nor practise deceit of any kind. These again, righteousness and truth, are absolute requirements from all who claim to be possessed of sincere religion (Phil. iv. 8). 5. *In the satisfaction of all her needs.* Like Jehovah's flock, she (Israel) should want nothing (Ps. xxiii. 1). She should have: (1) Food. She should "feed" (Isa. xl. 11). (2) Rest. She should "lie down" (Ps. xxiii. 2; Ezek. xxxiv. 15). (3) Protection. "None should make her afraid" (Ps. xci. 1—7; cxxi. 3—8).—T. W.

Vers. 14—17.—*The reciprocal joy of Israel and Jehovah.* I. THE JOY OF ISRAEL IN JEHOVAH. (Vers. 14—16.) 1. *The character in which Israel is summoned to rejoice.* Indicated by the names in which she is addressed. (1) Daughter of Zion. Zion meaning "sunny," hence "arid," and so "thirsty," or thirsting after God. (2) Israel. Signifying "Prince of God," or one who has power with God, and can prevail. (3) Daughter of Jerusalem. Equivalent to "City of peace." At all events, those whom God calls to rejoice in the fulness of his salvation are those who hunger and thirst after righteousness (Matt. v. 6), those who seek his face and call upon his Name (Rom. x. 12), and those who are possessed of a spirit of peace (Matt. v. 9). 2. *The enthusiasm with which she is invited to rejoice.* Suggested by the threefold call to sing, shout, and be glad. " *Sing,*—it is the inarticulate, thrilling, trembling burst of joy ; *shout,*—again the inarticulate, yet louder swell of joy, a trumpet-blast; and then too, deep within, *be glad,*—the calm even joy of the inward soul ; *exult,* the triumph of the soul which cannot contain itself for joy ; and this with the whole heart, no corner of it not pervaded with joy " (Pusey). 3. *The grounds on which Israel is called to rejoice.* (1) Judgments taken away. The calamities inflicted on her because of her iniquities have been removed (Isa. xl. 2). Meaning, her sins have been pardoned. Believers under the gospel have the same cause for exultation. For them, as for Israel, is no condemnation more (Rom. v. 11 ; viii. 1). (2) Enemies cast out. In the case of Israel this was so far true that henceforth she was no more seriously harassed as a nation after the restoration. Of believers under the gospel it is true that their chief enemy, the prince of this world, has been cast out by Jesus Christ (John xii. 31), while sin, which represents his power in them, will ultimately be expelled from their renewed natures (Gal. i. 4 ; Eph. i. 4 ; v. 27 ; Titus ii. 15). (3) God returned. As her covenant God, —" the Lord thy God ;" rightful King,—" The King of Israel, even the Lord, is in the midst of thee;" powerful Protector,—the Lord thy God is " a Mighty One who will save thee." In the same characters God abides in the Church and dwells in the heart of the believer. (4) Prosperity secured. With Jehovah in her midst she shall no more see or experience evil (Ps. xci. 10). The same true of the Christian believer, in whose heart God dwells (2 Thess. iii. 3 ; 1 Pet. iii. 13). 4. *The signs Israel shows that she does rejoice.* (1) No more fear. " In that day it shall be said to Jerusalem, Fear thou not." So Christ says to his little flock, " Fear not ! " (Luke xii. 32 ; John vi. 20). (2) No more despondency. " O Zion, let not thine hands be slack." Drooping hands are the sign of a fainting heart. Believers are exhorted to faint not (Luke xviii. 1 ; 2 Cor. iv. 16). (3) No more indolence. Slack hands are idle hands ; and no greater enemy to activity in Churches or individuals exists than lack of joy, as nothing stimulates to religious work like the experience of religious joy.

II. THE JOY OF JEHOVAH IN ISRAEL. (Ver. 17.) 1. *The character of this joy.* The joy : (1) Of a conqueror over the prey he has captured (ver. 8) ; Israel in her restoration being a trophy of his prowess. (2) Of an artificer in the work of his hands (ver. 11); Israel in her purified condition being a production of his grace. (3) Of an owner in the value of his possession (ver. 10) ; Jehovah speaking of Israel as " his dispersed." (4) Of a lover in the object of his affection, as *e.g.* of a bridegroom in his bride (Isa. lxii. 5). 2. *The tenderness of this joy.* It was a joy springing out of love to Israel, the joy of one who seeks the happiness of another, rather than of one who glories in his own felicity. In God's joy over Israel is no element of selfishness; it is all sympathy and affection. 3. *The intensity of this joy.* Marked by the gradation of clauses. Beginning with an inward feeling of delight, it swells in volume and deepens in tenderness till it becomes too great for utterance, and the subject of it is " silent in his love," after which it keeps on rising like a tide, till at length it overflows the soul's banks and breaks forth into song. 4. *The spontaneity of this joy.* It is not meant that Jehovah's joy in Israel is occasioned or evoked by Israel's joy in Jehovah, but rather that Jehovah's joy in Israel should prompt and sustain Israel's joy in Jehovah. As " we love him because he first loved us " (1 John iv. 19), so can we only " joy in God through our Lord Jesus Christ " (Rom. v. 11) when we realize that he for Christ's sake is well pleased with us.—T. W.

Ver. 17.—*God and his people.* I. GOD'S RELATION TO HIS PEOPLE. 1. Their covenant God. 2. Their rightful King. 3. Their mighty Saviour.

II. GOD'S PRESENCE WITH HIS PEOPLE. He is in their midst. 1. In the Spirit of his Son. 2. In the Word of his truth. 3. In the ordinances of his Church.

III. GOD'S WORK FOR HIS PEOPLE. Salvation : 1. From the guilt and power of sin. 2. From the danger of ignorance and error. 3. From the temptations and corruptions of the world. 4. From the fear of death and the dominion of the grave.

IV. GOD'S DELIGHT IN HIS PEOPLE. 1. True and tender. 2. Full and deep. 3. Perfect and abiding.—T. W.

Vers. 18—20.—*The turning again of Israel's captivity; or, good news for sin's exiles.* I. LIBERTY FOR THE CAPTIVES. "I will deal with all them that afflict thee," etc. Those members of the Israelitish community who were soon to be carried off into exile and enslaved in a foreign land were to be eventually (in the day when God rose up to the prey) rescued from their oppressors and set free from the reproach of slavery which pressed upon them like a heavy burden. So were the members of the human race captives of sin and Satan, and bondmen in a far-off land of alienation from God, when Christ came to preach deliverance to the captives and the opening of the prison to them that were bound (Isa. xli. 1; Luke iv. 18). So are men by nature sin's captives still (John viii. 34), and the burden of the gospel message still runs, "If the Son shall make you free, then are ye free indeed" (John viii. 36).

II. COMFORT FOR THE SORROWFUL. "I will gather them that sorrow for the solemn assembly." Those about to be exiled in Babylon, especially such among them as should preserve their piety, would regard it as the saddest element in their lot that through banishment they were no longer permitted to take part in the festal assemblies of the nation, in particular in the Feast of Tabernacles, the most joyful of all their celebrations (Hos. xii. 10). To them, therefore, it would come "like cold water to a thirsty soul," or "like good news from a far country," that they should afterwards, "at that time," be restored to their religious privileges, and the fellowship with Jehovah which these signified. So men "in sin," being far off from him whose favour and fellowship alone is life, when they first awake to this thought, are filled with sorrow, and mourn after God, after that reconciliation and communion with him in which alone true happiness can be found (Ps. xxxi. 16; li. 8—12; lxxxv. 4, 6; cxliii. 7, 8). To all such the gospel promises comfort and consolation (Matt. v. 4).

III. GATHERING FOR THE DISPERSED. Many of Israel's sons and daughters should be scattered into far-off lands when Jenovah rose to pour his indignation on the nations (ver. 8). But into whatsoever region they should have wandered, Jehovah would re-collect them in the day when he turned again Israel's captivity. So have men by sin been driven away into many different "far countries"—into conditions of existence where their material environments, dispositions of soul, and habits of life have become widely divergent. But up out of all situations and from all characters God by his grace can bring men who have departed from him and separated from each other, and can form them again into a united community, a holy brotherhood, a spiritual household, a redeemed family. To do this is the aim of the gospel (Eph. ii. 17—22).

IV. GLORY FOR THE SHAMED. Whereas the approaching exile would lead to Israel becoming overwhelmed with dishonour, when the Lord turned again her captivity that dishonour would be wiped out, and she should once more acquire a name and a praise among all the peoples of the earth. This certainly was true of the Jewish people, who, for all their humiliation, rose to a position of commanding influence because of her relation to Jehovah and the Christian Church, to which no nation on earth has ever attained; while Assyria, Babylon, Greece, and Rome, her great world-rivals, and frequently her oppressors, have passed away into comparative oblivion. So, if sin turns man's glory into shame, the gospel of Jesus Christ promises to reconvert man's shame into glory; and this it does by giving to the Christian Church a position and power possessed by no other human institution, and by conferring on the individual believer the glory (1) of a good name; (2) of an influential life; (3) of a peaceful end; and (4) of a blessed future.

LESSONS. 1. "Blessed are the people that know the joyful sound" (Ps. lxxxix. 15). 2. "Go ye into all the world, and preach the gospel to every creature" (Mark xvi. 15).—T. W.

Vers. 9—20.—*The promise of restoration.* Very remarkable is the way in which the most gracious promises are in this book interwoven, and, as it were, wrapped up in threatenings of judgment. This appears in ch. ii. 11, where it is declared that the Lord shall be terrible to the nations that magnified themselves against his people, and shall famish all the gods of the earth, so depriving these nations of their fancied support and confidence; and then it is added that men shall worship him every one from his place, even all the isles of the heathen. The deserved judgment would really prove to be the greatest blessing, leading them from the worship of dumb idols that could not save to that of the living and true God. So it is in the very similar prophecy given here. It is not certain whether ver. 8 is to be understood as a warning given in solemn irony to the ungodly Jews, or an encouragement addressed to the faithful remnant among them ; and so the precise connection of ver. 9 with the preceding context is not quite clear; but in general it is plain that it speaks of the conversion of the peoples to God as the result of the terrible revelation of his judgments against them. Thus we see how true it is that the Lord delighteth not in judgment, but in the midst of wrath remembers mercy. Now, this is no isolated or exceptional case, but an instance of the general principles on which God acts in his dealings with men. It may therefore be taken to illustrate the conversion of sinners to God at any time and in any circumstances. We may notice two things that it shows us: (1) the cause; (2) the results of conversion.

I. THE CONVERSION OF THE PEOPLES IS HERE TRACED VERY DIRECTLY TO THE AGENCY OF GOD. It is his doing, and that not merely indirectly, by the influence of the judgments that he has been threatening to send, but by an inward work of renewal wrought in the people. The judgments of God may convince the heathen of the vanity of their idols, or even show them that they should call on the Name of the Lord, and that they must do so if they are to be delivered; but then how shall they do so? The Lord is revealed as the just God, who will not do iniquity, and every morning doth he bring his judgments to light; but their lips, with which they should call upon him, are impure, they have taken up the names of other gods, they have been full of cursing and bitterness. May they not well feel as Isaiah did, when he saw the vision of the Holy One, that they are undone, for they are men of unclean lips, and dwell among a people of unclean lips? Who can enable such peoples, whose lips are accustomed to falsehood and profanity and uncleanness, to worship the God who is a Spirit, and seeketh such to worship him as will worship him in spirit and in truth? Who but that very God himself, who purged Isaiah's lips, who touched the lips of Jeremiah and put his words in his mouth? It must be he himself who enables them to call on him, by an act of gracious will and mighty power, purifying their lips and opening their mouths. The nature of this act of Divine power and grace is not more particularly described, but the language used suggests a comparison with what is said of Saul after he had been anointed by Samuel to be king over Israel, "God gave [Hebrew, 'turned'] him another heart" (1 Sam. x. 9). It is the same phrase as is used here, and so the meaning is that God will give to the peoples another lip, which shall be pure, instead of their former unclean lip. But a change of lip or language cannot be conceived apart from a change of heart, as, on the other hand, the new heart that God gave to Saul showed itself at once in his language, for when a company of prophets met him, he prophesied among them (1 Sam. x. 10). Out of the abundance of the heart the mouth speaketh ; and so, if the lips are to be pure, filled with the praises of God and calling on his Name, the heart must be changed. Now, this renewal of heart, showing itself in the utterance of the lips, is everywhere in the Bible traced to the Spirit of God as his special work. So it was with Saul. "The Spirit of God came upon him, and he prophesied." This working of the Spirit, too, is of God's sovereign and free grace. It comes on the most unlikely and unworthy objects. "The wind bloweth where it listeth, and thou hearest the sound thereof, but canst not tell whence it cometh or whither it goeth : so is every one that is born of the Spirit." So it was with Saul. He seemed an unlikely person to receive such a gift, and men said "Is Saul also among the prophets?" and the answer was, "But who is their father?" Men receive not the gift by descent from any human ancestry, but by the direct bestowal of God ; and so it may come upon any, and is to come at last, as Joel prophesied, on all flesh, even on the servants and handmaidens. Thus this prophecy is connected with those that point to the great manifestation of the grace and power of God's Spirit that was made at Pentecost, when the disciples of Jesus, speaking with new tongues as the Spirit gave them utterance, testified of the new and pure language that the Lord was to turn to the nations. He will pour out his Spirit on all flesh ; and even those nations that were most alienated from him, and sunk in impurity of heart and life, may receive the heavenly gift. But this, like all the promises of God, is given in Christ. He it is that sends the gift of the Spirit, as he is exalted a Prince and a Saviour to give repentance and remission of sins. Listen, then, to him as he graciously and freely offers it, and comply with his loving call, "If any man thirst, let him come unto me, and drink. He that believeth on me, as the Scripture hath said, out of his belly shall flow rivers of living water. And this spake he of the Spirit, which they that believe on him should receive" (John vii. 37—39). When we seek to determine in theory the exact relation of order between the gift of the Spirit and our faith, we run into difficulties that we cannot solve. But in practice these difficulties need not trouble us, or are solved by our actually coming to Jesus in faith. We need not wait till we are conscious of the renewing influence of the Spirit in order to come to Christ; we may be sure that any impulses that lead us to Christ are from him, and that the Lord's own gracious call is sufficient warrant for us to believe on him, that we may be fully conscious of the indwelling of the Spirit.

II. THE RESULTS OF CONVERSION, AS HERE INDICATED, ARE SEVERAL. 1. "That they may all call upon the Name of the Lord" (ver. 9). The first movement of the renewed heart is towards God; the first utterance of the pure lip is prayer to him. So it was said of Saul, when the Lord arrested him in his career of persecution, "Behold, he prayeth." The tendency of the natural heart is away from God, and the lips are by nature slow and backward to call upon him. But when the Lord changes the heart, and turns to the peoples a pure lip, then they call upon his Name, they comply with the call formerly given by the prophet, to seek the Lord. Instead of endeavouring to hide themselves from his presence, or to find some refuge or defence against his judgments, they are led to see that there is none that can deliver them out of his hand, but that he himself is merciful and gracious, and that if they turn to him and implore his mercy, they shall be delivered. For his name is "the Lord, the Lord God, merciful and gracious, long-suffering and abundant in goodness and truth, keeping mercy for thousands, forgiving iniquity and transgression and sin, and that will by no means spare the guilty" (Exod. xxxiv. 6, 7); and that affords a strong encouragement to all the nations to call upon him. His Name is just the expression of his character, and that is one of grace and love, of mercy and forgiveness; so that even the most sinful may call upon him. 2. "To serve him." The words of the lips, the prayer of faith, may be the first result of the change wrought by God's Spirit in the soul; but that will not remain alone, but, if it is sincere and genuine at all, will lead to service in deeds. They shall not merely honour him with their lips, but shall serve him. He is the Lord, as well as the Saviour, of the world; and when they call upon his Name as their Saviour, they will further give themselves to him as their Lord. They have been refusing to serve him before, saying, "Our lips are our own; who is lord over us?" asserting that they were not in bondage to any man, but their own masters, yet really serving divers lusts and pleasures. But now, weary and heavy laden with the burden of the service of self and sin and the world, they come unto Christ, and take his yoke upon them; they enter that service in which alone is perfect freedom. It is a most essential characteristic of the converted, that they serve the Lord. They count themselves his servants, as Paul, for example, speaking of Christ, says, "Whose I am, and whom I serve." They are not their own, but bought with a price; and they seek to realize this by living, not for themselves, but for him who died and rose again for them. This does not imply that they go out of the world and separate themselves from its active work and affairs, to spend their time wholly and exclusively in exercises of worship. The service that the Lord would have given to him is to be carried on in the world; they are to be "not slothful in business, fervent in spirit, serving the Lord." By diligence in the duties of the calling in which God has placed them, by uprightness and sincerity in word and deed, by letting no corrupt communication proceed out of their mouth, but that which is good for the use of edifying, that it may minister grace to the hearers, by working with their hands that which is good, that they may have to give to him that needeth; and, above all, by walking in love, after the example of Christ, God's servants serve him; and this they are enabled to do by the work of his grace in their hearts. 3. Another result here indicated as flowing from conversion is unity and harmony among the nations. "They shall all call on the Name of the Lord, and serve him with one consent." The invocation of the true God is to be in common, and the service rendered to him a united and harmonious one, "with one shoulder," as the words literally mean, as if bearing the yoke together, and equally taking part in the work. This implies a gathering together of the nations in peace and good will. Idolatry and polytheism ever go hand-in-hand with national exclusiveness and mutual hostility. Each people is supposed to have its own patron gods, each land its own local deities, and the servant of one god naturally becomes the enemy of the people of another. Religion, in this corrupt form, tends to separate men, and set one against another. Ungodliness, too, has much the same tendency. When men recognize and worship no god or power above the earth, their selfish passions and interests set each one against his fellow. But when the one universal Lord and Maker of all is recognized as God, then the consideration that we have all one Father, and that one God created us, forms a tie of brotherhood among all nations. And this is strengthened by the fact that, when his judgments are abroad on the earth against all nations alike, all are invited and encouraged to trust in his mercy and call on his Name. "For the same Lord over all is rich unto all who call upon him." This does away with every ground of separation, as if there were many local or national deities, as the heathen thought; it does away even with the special privileges of the seed of Jacob, which the Jews were apt to abuse, so as to foster a selfish and exclusive pride; for "in Christ Jesus there is neither Jew nor Greek, Barbarian, Scythian, bond, nor free, but Christ is all and in all." True conversion, also, by taking away the ungodliness of the natural heart, removes the great root of selfishness, and gives a ground, a motive, and an example for love to all men. In proportion as men are brought nearer to God are they brought nearer also to one another. He is the Centre and Sun of the universe, and the more the paths of any of the creatures depart from him, the more will they diverge from one another; while the nearer they come to God, the closer will they find themselves drawn to their fellows, who may have started from very distant points and been led by very different ways. These things, then—prayerfulness, diligence in God's service, and brotherly love—may be taken as genuine and sure evidences of that great change that must be wrought in every man ere he can see the kingdom of God—a change that is secret and mysterious in its own nature, though known and recognized by its fruits.—C.

Vers. 1—5.—*A religious city terribly degenerate.* "Woe to her that is filthy and polluted, to the oppressing city! She obeyed not the voice; she received not correction; she trusted not in the Lord; she drew not near to her God," etc. "To give still greater emphasis to his exhortation to repentance, the prophet turns to Jerusalem again, that he may once more hold up before the hardened sinners the abominations of this city in which Jehovah daily proclaims his right, and shows the necessity for the judgment, as the only way that is left by which to secure salvation for Israel and for the whole world" (Keil). We have two things here to look at.

I. A PROFESSEDLY RELIGIOUS CITY TERRIBLY DEGENERATED. Jerusalem is distinguished not so much for the beauty of its architecture, the extent of its population, the measure of its trade and resources, as by its being religious. There the one temple stood; there the worship, with its imposing ritual, was daily performed; there the priests lived and God was specially manifested. But how morally degenerate it became! She is here represented as "filthy," "polluted," and "oppressing." "She obeyed not the voice; she received not correction; she trusted not in the Lord; she drew not near to her God." In this degeneracy all classes of the community seemed to be involved. 1. *The "princes" are mentioned.* "Her princes within her are the roaring lions." Like rapacious beasts, they preyed on all about them, they lived on people, they devoured their property. As a rule, "princes" have too often lived upon the people; they are devourers of their means; they consume everything, and produce nothing. 2. *The "judges" are mentioned.* "Her judges are evening wolves; they gnaw not the bones till the morrow." Or, as Henderson renders it, "they gnaw no bones till the morning." So insatiable are they, that they leave not a single bone till the morning, of the prey that they have caught in the evening. 3. *The "prophets" are mentioned.* These "prophets are light and treacherous persons." In their life and teaching there was no truth, gravity, or steadfastness. They were "treacherous," false to man, and false to God (Jer. xxiii. 32; Ezek. xxii. 28). 4. *The "priests" are mentioned.* These "polluted the sanctuary" by desecrating the sacred place, and outraged the "Law" by distorting its meaning and misrepresenting its genius and aim. Like Hophni and Phinehas, their wicked lives made the sacrifices of the Lord to be abhorred. Such was the degenerate condition into which this holy city is represented as having fallen. How many modern cities to-day, which call themselves Christian, have sunk into a similar degeneracy! London, Paris, Rome, St. Petersburg, etc., are all highly religious in profession, and have religious means in abundance. What is the moral condition, not only of their masses, but of their "princes," their "judges," their "prophets," and their "priests"? Ah me! under the cover of religion there rolls the sea of putrescent depravity. Morally, how much better is London than Bombay, Pekin, or Jeddo?

II. A PROFESSEDLY RELIGIOUS CITY TERRIBLY DEGENERATED, ALTHOUGH GOD WAS SPECIALLY WORKING IN ITS MIDST. "The just Lord is in the *midst* thereof; he will not do iniquity: every morning doth he bring his judgment to light, he faileth not; but the unjust knoweth no shame." In every city, and amongst every people, the just Lord, the righteous Jehovah, is and works—works by the operations of material nature, by the events of human life, by the suggestions of human reason, and the dictates of human conscience. But in Jerusalem he was in a more especial sense, and he wrought in special ways. The temple was his dwelling-place, and the gleaming Shechinah was the symbol of his presence; and specially did he reveal himself to some of its noblest men. And yet, notwithstanding all, Jerusalem sank; with God amongst them working to raise them, they fell lower and lower. What does this teach? 1. *The wonderful freedom which the Almighty allows to wicked men on the earth.* Though he strives to improve them, he does not coerce them. He makes no invasion of their moral agency. 2. *The tremendous force of human depravity.* What a power sin gains over man! It binds him in chains often stronger than adamant. It loads him with a weight which he cannot shake off, but which sinks him deeper and deeper into the abysses of wickedness.

CONCLUSION. 1. Do not hinder Christian propagandism from entering a city because it is nominally Christian. The gospel is wanted there, perhaps, more than anywhere else, more even than in pagan populations. 2. Do not expect that the world will be morally renovated by miraculous agency. Almighty Goodness does not coerce. There is no way by which mere force can travel to a man's soul.—D. T.

Vers. 6—8.—*Terrible calamities in human history.* "I have cut off the nations: their towers are desolate; I made their streets waste, that none passeth by: their cities are destroyed, so that there is no man, that there is none inhabitant. I said, Surely thou wilt fear me, thou wilt receive instruction," etc. In these verses the prophet sums up all that he had said in the preceding verses of this chapter, and thus closes his admonition to repentance with the announcement of tremendous judgments. These verses remind us of three great truths of universal importance, claiming the attention of men wherever they exist.

I. THAT THERE IS A SENSE IN WHICH THE MOST TERRIBLE CALAMITIES IN HUMAN HISTORY MAY BE ASCRIBED TO GOD. Here he is represented as cutting off the nations, destroying their "towers," making their "streets waste," so that "there is no man," and "none inhabitant." What particular nation is here referred to cannot be determined with certainty. We know that he did destroy nations—the Canaanitish nations, also Assyria and Babylon. These calamities are here ascribed to God. In Bible language he is frequently represented as doing that which he only permits. Nations destroy each other, he allows them to do so. Though he does not give them the disposition for the work, he imparts the power and the opportunities.

II. THAT THE GRAND DESIGN OF SUCH CALAMITIES IS THE PROMOTION OF MORAL IMPROVEMENT AMONGST MANKIND. Why did he permit the wreck and ruin of those nations, and all the dire desolations here recorded? Here is the answer, "I said, Surely thou wilt fear me, thou wilt receive instruction." The grand end of all his dispensations with men is to generate within them the right state of mind in relation to himself; in other words, to make them "meet for the inheritance of the saints in light." "Lo, all these things worketh God oftentimes with man, to bring back his soul from the pit, to enlighten him with the light of the living" (Job xxxiii. 29, 30). As the storms, the snows, the frosts, and the cutting winds of winter help to bring on the luxuriant spring, so the calamities in human life contribute to the moral regeneration of mankind.

III. THAT THE NON-REALIZATION OF THIS DESIGN AMONGST A PEOPLE EXPOSES

THEM TO TERRIBLE RETRIBUTION. "But they rose early, and corrupted all their doings." The men of Jerusalem, instead of becoming better for these terrible calamities, grew worse. They "corrupted all their doings." This they did with assiduity. They "rose early." They began their morning with it. "Therefore wait ye upon me, saith the Lord, until the day that I rise up to the prey; for my determination is to gather the nations, that I may assemble the kingdoms, to pour upon them mine indignation, even all my fierce anger: for all the earth shall be devoured with the fire of my jealousy." Or, as Keil renders it, "Therefore wait for me, is the saying of Jehovah, for the day when I rise up to the prey; for it is my right to gather nations together, to bring kingdoms in crowds, to heap upon them my fury, all the burning of my wrath; for in the fire of my zeal will the whole earth be devoured." The Almighty here speaks after the manner of men, as he does almost everywhere in the Bible, in condescension to human infirmities. He speaks as if he were disappointed in the moral results of the calamities which he had sent, and as if his nature now glowed with the fires of his indignation. There is, of course, really no disappointment for him, for he knows the future, and "fury" is not in him.—D. T.

Vers. 9, 10.—*The good time coming.* "For then will I turn to the people a pure language, that they may all call upon the Name of the Lord, to serve him with one consent. From beyond the rivers of Ethiopia my suppliants, even the daughter of my dispersed, shall bring mine offering." Henderson supposes that the poem from this verse to the end of the book relates to Messianic times; that the prophet points to that dispensation of remedial mercy under which we live, and which commenced more than eighteen hundred years ago. We may therefore regard these words as pointing to at least two of the great characteristic blessings that will come to the world during the continuance of the gospel age; and these two are moral purity of language and spiritual unity of worship.

I. MORAL PURITY OF LANGUAGE. "Then will I turn to the people a pure language." Or, as Keil renders it, "a pure lip." Human language is looked upon in different aspects by different men. Some look upon it grammatically, trace its etymology, and arrange its words and sentences according to the conventional rules of speech; some look at it logically, study it in its relation to the law of human reasoning; some look upon it philosophically, view it in relation to the nature of the things it is intended to represent; and some look upon it morally, contemplate it in its relation to the law of conscience and God. Grammatical language is mere conformity to acknowledged rules of speech; logical language, conformity to recognized principles of reasoning; philosophical language is conformity to the order of nature; moral language is conformity to the moral law of God. There is a regular gradation in the importance of these aspects of language. The first is of the least importance; the second and third come next; and the last is the most important of all. It is strange and sad to see that the amount of attention which men pay to these aspects is in the inverse ratio of their importance. The first, the least important, is the most attended to; the second, next; the third, next; and the last, the most important of all, almost entirely neglected. In the department of speech we have more grammarians than logicians, more logicians than philosophers, more philosophers than honest saints. It is *moral* purity of language that is wanted in the world, and that is here promised. Language that shall be used, not without meaning, as it is oftentimes used now, nor to misrepresent meaning, as is often the case. A "pure" moral language implies two things. 1. That the state of the heart should be in accord with Divine reality. 2. That the words of the lip should be in accord with the state of the heart. In other words, purity of soul and veracity of expression.

II. SPIRITUAL UNITY OF WORSHIP. "That they may all call upon the Name of the Lord, to serve him with one consent." "That they may serve him with one accord" (Henderson). Who are to serve him with one accord? The nations, partially specified in the tenth verse. "From beyond the rivers of Ethiopia [Cush] my suppliants, even the daughter of my dispersed, shall bring mine offering." The glorious point to be observed is not that all nations shall worship, for worship will ever belong to the race; but that all nations will worship with *one accord.* There is a oneness in their worship. Unity of worship does not necessarily mean unity of theological opinion or of ritualistic observances; but unity of object, the *same* God in the same *spirit*—reverence, gratitude, adoration.

CONCLUSION. What a glorious future awaits the world! All men morally pure in speech, all men heartily one in worship. Thrice hail the day!—D. T.

Vers. 11—13.—*A sketch of a morally regenerated city.* "In that day shalt thou not be ashamed for all thy doings, wherein thou hast transgressed against me: for then I will take away out of the midst of **thee them** that rejoice in thy pride, and thou shalt no more be haughty because of **my holy mountain**," etc. "These verses," says Henderson, "contain a description of restored and regenerated Israel. The being not ashamed of their sinful practices does not mean their not feeling a compunctious sense of their intrinsic odiousness and demerits, but is expressive of the great change that should take place in the outward condition of the Jews. That condition, into which they have been brought by their obstinate rebellion against Jehovah and his Messiah, is one of disgrace. When recovered out of it, all the marks of shame and infamy shall be removed. The Pharisaic spirit of pride, and the vain confidence in the temple and the temple-worship, which proved the ruin of the nation, shall be taken away. The converted residue shall be a people humble and poor in spirit (Matt. v. 3; xi. 5), and of a truly righteous and upright character; and, having fled for refuge to the hope set before them in the gospel, they shall be safe under the protecting care of their heavenly Father." These verses may be regarded as giving a *sketch of a morally regenerated city.* It is marked by—

I. THE UTTER ABSENCE OF THE BAD. There is an absence of: 1. *Painful memories.* "In that day shalt thou not be ashamed for all thy doings." Thou wilt not need to be ashamed of all thy iniquities, (1) because they are all forgiven; (2) because they will occur no more. Whilst regenerated souls will perhaps ever remember their past iniquities, the memories will not be associated with pain, they will awaken no moral shame. So flooded will the soul be with new loves, hopes, and purposes, that everything painful in connection with the past will be buried in comparative forgetfulness. Departed saints cannot but remember their old sins, but, in view of pardon and purification, the remembrance of them is associated with pleasure, not pain. 2. *Wicked citizens.* "I will take away out of the midst of thee them that rejoice in thy pride," or, "thy proud triumphers." In a thoroughly regenerated city there will be no proud vaunters, no blustering pretenders, no arrogant worldlings. The voices of such men will not be heard; they will not be seen in the streets, in the marts of commerce, the chambers of legislation, or the scenes of recreation. 3. *All crimes.* "The remnant of Israel shall **not** do iniquity, nor speak lies; neither shall a deceitful tongue be found in their **mouth.**" No wrong committed, no lies spoken, no deceit practised. The whole atmosphere of the city cleared of such moral impurities.

II. THE BLESSED PRESENCE OF THE GOOD. "I will also leave in the midst of thee an afflicted and poor people, and they shall trust in the Name of the Lord." Who will be the citizens? 1. *Men of humility.* Delitzsch translates the word "afflicted," "bowed down;" and Henderson, "humble." Humility is evidently the idea. There will be men who are "poor in spirit." Moral humility is moral nobility. The humbler a man is, the nobler and the happier too. "Blessed are the poor in spirit." 2. *Men of piety.* "They shall trust in the Name of the Lord." Their chief confidence will be placed, not in their strength, their wealth, or their wisdom, but in God. They will centre their trust, not in the creature, but in the Creator. 3. *Men of concord.* "They shall feed and lie down, and none shall make them afraid." There will be amongst them no acrimonious disputations, no commercial rivalries, no social jealousies or envyings, no painful divisions of any kind. They will be united as brethren, one in leading thoughts, loves, and aims.

CONCLUSION. This is indeed a model city. What a city this! When shall such a city appear on this earth? Ah! when? It is in the distant future, but it has been gradually rearing from the dawn of the Christian era to this hour. It will, I believe, be one day completed, the "topstone" will be put on with shoutings of triumph.—D. T.

Vers. 14—17.—*Joy, human and Divine.* "Sing, O daughter of Zion; shout, O Israel; be glad and rejoice with all the heart, O daughter of Jerusalem. The Lord hath taken away thy judgments, he hath cast out thine enemy," etc.　Here is a call to the regenerated inhabitants of Jerusalem to exult in the mercy of God, who has wrought their deliverance, at the same time, a beautiful description of the sublime delight with which Jehovah will regard them in the future.　The words bring under our notice joy, human and Divine.

I. THE JOY OF THE REGENERATED MAN.　" Sing, O daughter of Zion; shout, O Israel; be glad and rejoice."　What is the joy?　1. *The joy of gratitude for the deliverance from evil.*　"The Lord hath taken away thy judgments, he hath cast out thine enemy." What is the joy of the slave in the hour of his emancipation, of the prisoner on leaving his cell, of the long-suffering invalid on his restoration to full health?　Far more is the joy of the man who feels himself morally delivered—delivered from the power of sin, and brought into the "glorious liberty of the children of God."　Gratitude is always an element of joy.　2. The joy of *conscious security.*　" Even the Lord is in the midst of thee: thou shalt not see evil any more."　What joy breaks forth in the apostolic challenge, " Who shall separate us from the love of God?" etc.!　Here is the joy of regenerated humanity, the joy of gratitude for the greatest deliverance, the joy of conscious security from all possible dangers.

II. THE JOY OF THE REGENERATING GOD.　" The Lord thy God in the midst of thee [within thee] is mighty; he will save, he will rejoice over thee with joy; he will rest in his love, he will joy over thee with singing."　What is the joy of God? It is the joy of infinite benevolence.　What is the joy of the genuine patriot when he has delivered his country from a power that threatened its utter destruction? What is the joy of a loving physician when he has rescued his patient from the very jaws of death?　What is the joy of a loving parent who has rescued his child from ruin?　Some such joy as this—infinitely superior—is the joy of God over regenerated humanity.　In this joy the redeemed will participate; indeed, it will be their heaven. " Enter into the joy of thy Lord."　" Rejoice over thee with singing."　*Does God sing?*　Yes; in all the happy voices of the universe, especially in the shouts of the redeemed.—D. T.

Vers. 18—20.—*The moral restoration of mankind.*　" I will gather them that are sorrowful for the solemn assembly, who are of thee, to whom the reproach of it was a burden.　Behold, at that time I will undo all that afflict thee," etc.　" The salvation held up in prospect before the remnant of Israel, which has been refined by the judgments and delivered, was at a very remote distance in Zephaniah's time.　The first thing that awaited the nation was the judgment through which it was to be dispersed among the heathen, according to the testimony of Moses and all the prophets, and to be refined in the furnace of affliction.　The ten tribes were already carried away into exile, and Judah was to share the same fate immediately afterwards.　In order, therefore, to offer to the pious a firm consolation of hope in the period of suffering that awaited them, and one on which their faith could rest in the midst of tribulation, Zephaniah mentions, in conclusion, the gathering together of all who pine in misery at a distance from Zion, and who are scattered far and wide, to assure even these of their future participation in the promised salvation" (Delitzsch).　These verses may be taken to illustrate *the moral restoration of mankind.*　Taking them for this purpose, we have the restoration and the Restorer.　We have here—

I. THE RESTORATION.　What is the restoration?　1. *From the deprivation of religious privileges to their enjoyment.*　The Jews, who were in a state that rendered it impossible to celebrate their religious festivals at Jerusalem, are here represented as filled with sorrow or grief when they reflected on the privileges of their ancestors. " By the rivers of Babylon we sat down and wept," etc.　Though unregenerate men may live amidst religious privileges, they are really deprived of them, for they do not possess and enjoy them.　Their moral restoration brings them into that happy enjoyment.　Though the ungodly man holds the gospel in his hand, he is morally exiled from it.　It is more distant from him than was the temple from the Jew in Babylon.　2. *From the sufferings of oppression to the happiness of deliverance.* " Behold, at that time I will undo all that afflict thee: and I will save her that halteth, and gather her that was driven out."　The literal reference is here, of course, to Babylonian tyrants.　By the providence of God these were overcome.　Their power was broken, their counsels confounded, so that they were forced to surrender their prey. "I will save her that halteth, and gather her that was driven out." The Hebrew captives were delivered, and brought back to their own country and city. In moral restoration the power of the oppressor is broken, the soul is delivered from the power of Satan and the bondage of corruption. "Being made free from sin, and become servants to God, ye have your fruit unto holiness, and the end everlasting life." What was the tyranny of Babylon to the Jews, compared to the tyranny of evil over the soul? 3. *From the condition of reproach to that of true honour.* "I will get them praise and fame in every land where they have been put to shame." High above all nations was Israel at one time. The "reproach" brought on them was one of their sorest grievances; that reproach has been partially wiped away, the Jewish people are the most distinguished of the races of the earth, for of them Christ came, who is the glory of his people Israel. When a man is morally restored, he becomes truly honourable, not before. Goodness is moral majesty. There is no true royalty which has not its foundation in moral excellence.

II. THE RESTORER. All the restoration sketched in these verses was effected by whom? Not by Cyrus and his battalions: they were but instruments. It was Jehovah. "*I* will gather;" "*I* will save;" "*I* will get them praise;" "*I* bring you again;" "*I* will make you a name;" "*I* turn back your captivity." So in moral restoration. No one can restore a soul but God. It is his work. 1. A work which he does by moral means. By the gospel. 2. A work which, from the nature of the case, must proceed gradually. 3. A work which will one day be consummated. —D. T.

HOMILETICAL INDEX

TO

THE BOOK OF ZEPHANIAH

———◦◇•———

HAGGAI

EXPOSITION BY

W. J. DEANE

HOMILETICS BY

T. WHITELAW

HOMILIES BY VARIOUS AUTHORS

S. D. HILLMAN   D. THOMAS

THE BOOK OF HAGGAI

INTRODUCTION

§ I. Subject of the Book.

FROM the time when Zephaniah prophesied of judgment to come to the day when Haggai lifted up his voice, some hundred years or more had elapsed. In this interval God had not left himself without witness; the prophets Jeremiah, Ezekiel, and Daniel had carried on the torch of prophecy, and had not suffered the light of inspiration to be extinguished. Meanwhile startling events had happened. That which earlier seers had foretold had come to pass; warnings unheeded had ripened bitter fruit. Israel had long ago been carried into captivity; Judah had suffered a similar fate. For seventy years she had sat weeping by the waters of Babylon, learning a hard lesson and profiting thereby. But the period of punishment came to an end at the appointed moment. God stirred up the spirit of Cyrus King of Elam, to allow and to urge the return of the Hebrews to their own land and the rebuilding of their temple. Not that Cyrus was a monotheist, who believed in one supreme God. This idea, which has long obtained, is proved to be erroneous by the inscriptions which have been discovered, and which may be read in Professor Sayce's 'Fresh Light from the Monuments,' pp. 142, etc. From these it is clear that he was a worshipper of Bel-Merodach, the patron god of Babylon, and that, as it was his first care on the capture of that city to reinstate its deities in their shrines, so his edict respecting the rebuilding of the temple at Jerusalem was a result of his usual policy to adopt the gods of conquered countries, and to win their favour by supporting their worship. That God used him as his instrument for the restoration of the Hebrews proves nothing concerning his personal religion. Unworthy agents often perform most important service. Obeying the king's edict, many of the Jews, assisted by donations and bearing with them the rifled treasures of the temple, B.C. 536, prepared to return to their native land under the leadership of Zerubbabel, a prince of the house of David, and Joshua the high priest They were, indeed, but a small body, amounting, according to the enumeration of Ezra (ii. 64, 65), to 42,360, exclusive of menservants and maidservants reckoned at 7337. But they set to work with vigour on their arrival at Jerusalem, and in the second year of Cyrus, B.C. 534, erected the great altar in its old place, and established regular worship according to the Mosaic ritual. They then proceeded to lay the foundations of a new temple in the second year after their arrival. The prosecution of this undertaking met with unexpected obstacles. The mixed population which had been settled by the Assyrian conquerors in Central Palestine claimed, on the score of brotherhood, to take part in this sacred work. Such a claim could not be entertained. These Samaritans, as they are named, were not of the holy seed, did not worship Jehovah with pure worship, mixed idolatrous rites with their devotions to the true God. It would have been an abandonment of their unique position, treason to their Lord, for the Israelites to have admitted such syncretists to a participation in the erection of the temple. Zerubbabel, therefore, rightly declined their offered assistance. This rejection was bitterly resented. By representations made at court, they endeavoured to hinder the work, and were so successful in their opposition that the building was stopped during the remainder of the life of Cyrus, and during the reign of his successors, Cambyses and Pseudo-Smerdis (Artaxerxes I.). Other causes combined to bring about the suspension of operations. The zeal with which the labour was begun grew cold. The exiles had returned with high hope of happiness and prosperity; they had expected to enter into possession of a home prepared and ready for their reception; in their fervid imagination peace and plenty awaited them, and the blessings promised to obedience in their old Law were to be theirs with little labour or delay. A very different state of things awaited them. Cities ruined and desolate, a land sterilized by want of cultivation, neighbours unfriendly or openly hostile, scantiness of bread, danger, toil,—these were the objects which they had to contemplate. And though the spirit that animated their first enterprise, and the enthusiasm that accompanied a great national movement, excited them to commence the work with earnestness and ardour, their hearts were not sufficiently engaged in its prosecution to enable them to rise superior to inward distraction and outward opposition; and so they grew less interested in the completion of the undertaking, and they acquiesced with stolid complacency in its enforced cessation. They learned to look on the ruins of their holy house with a certain desponding equanimity, and turned to the furtherance of their own personal concerns, contentedly leaving the restoration of the temple to other times and stronger hands than theirs. But a happier condition of affairs arrived under the rule of Darius, the son of Hystaspes, who succeeded to the throne of Persia B.C. 521. The interdict which had stopped the building of the temple was removed, the original decree of Cyrus was discovered and re-enacted, and every assistance was given to the Jews to carry out their original design. Nothing but the will was now wanting. It was the design of Haggai's prophecy to inspire this will, to shame the people into a display of energy and self-denial, and to encourage them to continue their efforts till the whole work was satisfactorily completed.

Steiner and others have questioned the fact that the rebuilding of the temple was begun under Cyrus. They say that no genuine passage in the Book of Ezra gives any countenance to the statement, and that it was only in consequence of the interference of Haggai and Zechariah that the work was first commenced in the second year of Darius, being then carried on without interruption till it was completed four years afterwards. Haggai himself does not expressly mention any earlier attempt at laying the foundation, and indeed places this event in the four and twentieth day of the ninth month of the second year of Darius (ch. ii. 18). But this passage is capable of another interpretation; and the direct statement of Ezra iii. 8, that "in the second year of their coming . . . they began to set forward the work of the house of the Lord," and "the foundation of the house of the Lord was laid" (ver. 11), can only be surmounted by arbitrarily denying the genuineness of this chapter and the authenticity of its details. The grounds of this rejection are weak and inconclusive. When we consider the enormous importance attached to the rebuilding of the temple—which, indeed, was the test of fidelity to the Lord, and the desire to abide by the covenant—it is inconceivable that the good men who guided the nation should allow some sixteen years to elapse before making any attempt to set in hand the good work; so that the very nature of the case confirms the statement of Ezra, while nothing in the books of Haggai and Zechariah really militates against it. On the contrary, there are passages in Haggai which distinctly involve its truth. Thus in ch. ii. 14 it is implied that formal sacrifices were offered before Haggai's public interference, and in ch. ii. 3 that the temple was already so far built that its future appearance and condition could be conceived.

The book comprises four discourses, which make natural divisions, and are accurately dated. The first, uttered on the first day of the sixth month of Darius's second regnal year, contains an exhortation to Zerubbabel and Joshua to take in hand at once the rebuilding of the temple. The people are sternly reproached for their indifference, which they think to excuse by affirming that the time for this work has not yet come, while they expend their energies in increasing their own material comfort. The prophet shows them that the barrenness of their land and the distress which they suffer are a chastisement for this neglect. He concludes with an account of the effect of this expostulation, how that the chiefs and all the people listened to his words, and "came and did work in the house of the Lord of hosts" (ch. i.). The following month witnessed the second address, wherein the prophet comforts those who, contrasting the new with the former temple, depreciated the present undertaking, and assures them that, although its appearance is humbler, the glory of the latter house shall far exceed that of the former, because of the splendid donations of princes, and because of Messiah's presence there (ch. ii. 1—9). The third exhortation was uttered in the four and twentieth day of the ninth month. By certain legal questions concerning the communication of holiness and pollution, Haggai demonstrates that the people's tendency to rest in external righteousness is sinful, and that their lukewarmness in the holy work before them vitiated their worship and occasioned want and misery, which would only be relieved by their strenuous efforts to finish the temple (ch. ii. 10—19). The prophecy ends with a promise to the scion of the house of David, that amid the destruction of the powers of the world, his throne should be exalted and glorified, "for I have chosen thee, saith the Lord of hosts" (ch. ii. 20—23).

The reason why the rebuilding of the temple is made of such singular importance is found in the light in which the house of God is regarded, and the opportunity thus afforded for displaying zeal and fidelity towards God. The temple is the visible token of the Lord's presence with his people, the material sign of the covenant; its restoration showed that the Israelites desired to maintain this relation with Jehovah, and to do their part in the matter. Here alone could the federal relation be renewed and sustained; here alone could the daily worship be duly offered. While the temple lay in ruins, the covenant was, as it were, suspended; for its re-establishment the Lord's house must be rebuilt and adapted to Divine service. And yet this covenant was not simply a revival of the old one in its Sinaitic form; it was a new one, without the visible cloud of glory, without the ark and mercy-seat and the tables of the Law, but one attested by the very presence of Messiah himself, and the laws of which were written in the heart and mind of the faithful. Of this the material building was a symbol, and therefore its reconstruction was an imperative duty.

§ II. Author and Date.

Of the Prophet Haggai we know nothing save what may be gathered from his book and a few words in Ezra. The name Haggai, in Greek Ἀγγαῖος, is explained by St. Jerome to mean "Festive;" for, he says, he sowed in tears that he might reap in joy, when he witnessed the re-erection of the ruined temple. Reinke deems that he was so named because he was born on some great feast-day. He is mentioned with Zechariah in Ezra (v. 1; vi. 14) as prophesying unto the Jews that were in Jerusalem in the name of the God of Israel, urging them to continue the work of rebuilding the house of the Lord. It has been conjectured, from ch. ii. 3, that he had seen the temple of Solomon, that he was one, as Dr. Pusey says, "who had lived among the outward splendour of the former temple, who had himself been carried into captivity, and was now part of that restoration which God had promised." But this idea is not supported by the language of the passage on which it is founded: "Who is left among you that saw the house in her first glory?" If the conjecture were true, he would have been at least eighty years old at the time of his prophecy, the date of which he himself states as the second year of Darius the king, *i.e.* B.C. 520. He continued his addresses at intervals during four months of that year; but whether he lived to see the full result of his labours by the completion of the building in the sixth year of Darius, is uncertain. Jewish tradition makes him to have been a member of the great synagogue, and other accounts, equally unsubstantiated, assign to him an honoured burial in the sepulchre reserved for priests.

Some manuscripts of the Septuagint attribute to Haggai and Zechariah the authorship of Ps. cxxxvii. and cxlv.—cxlviii. To them, too, in the Syriac are assigned Ps. cxxv., cxxvi., cxlv.—cxlvii., and in the Latin Vulgate Ps. cxi. and cxlv. "It may be," says Mr. Wright ('Dict. of Bible,' *sub voce* "Haggai"), "that tradition assigned to these prophets the arrangement of the above-mentioned psalms for use in the temple service, just as Ps. lxiv. is in the Vulgate attributed to Jeremiah and Ezekiel, and the name of the former is inscribed at the head of Ps. cxxxvi. in the LXX." From certain coincidences in style, and for other reasons connected with the minuteness of details given, it has been conjectured that Haggai is the author of that part of the Book of Ezra which extends from ch. iii. 2 to the end of ch. vi., with the exception of the fragment in ch. iv. 6—23. The grounds for this opinion are given in Smith's 'Dict. of the Bible,' i. 607; but they do not seem very conclusive. Pseudo-Epiphanius says ('De Vit. Proph.') that Haggai and Zechariah were the first to sing "Hallelujah" and "Amen" in the second temple, which probably means that they took the lead in chanting the Hallelujah psalms. References to Haggai occur in Heb. xii. 26; Ecclus. xlix. 10, 11; 1 Esdras vi. 1; vii. 3; 2 Esdras i. 40.

§ III. GENERAL CHARACTER.

The language of Haggai is generally considered tame and featureless, indulging in unnecessary repetitions, and rarely rising above the level of ordinary prose. But in estimating the character of his addresses, we must remember that in their present form they are probably only the outline of the original utterances, and that what may seem poor and curt in the summary may have been telling and eloquent in its fuller form when spoken. Even as we have them, the addresses in their simplicity are full of force; outward ornament and rhetorical artifice were not needed in order to set forth the work which the people were expected to perform. Haggai had one distinct message to deliver, and he announced it in plain, unvarnished language, which came home to the hearts of his hearers, not only with conviction, but with persuasive force, so that they did not merely say, "How true!" and do nothing in consequence, but they put their conviction into action, and began at once to build. He is indeed concise, antithetical, and impressive; but the great point is that he gained the end which he had in view. The highest efforts of oratorical power could attempt and effect no more.

§ IV. Literature.

The chief commentaries on Haggai are these: **Abarbanel, Heb. cum Vers. Lat.** a Scherz. (Lips., 1663); Melanchthon, Opp. ii.; Eckius (Salignac, 1538); Pilkington, 'Exposition' (London, 1560); Mercier (Paris, 1581); Grynæus (Genev., 1581), translated into English by C. Featherstone (London, 1586); Tarnovius (Rost., 1624); Raynolds (London, 1649); Pfeffinger (Strasburg, 1703); Köhler, 'Die Weissag. Hag.' (Erlangen, 1860); Moore, 'The Prophets of the Restoration' (London, 1858); Reinke (1868); McCurdy (Edinburgh); Pressel (1870); Archdeacon Perowne, in 'The Cambridge Bible for Schools' (Cambridge, 1886).

§ V. Arrangement in Sections.

The book is divided into four addresses, delivered at specified dates.

Part I. (Ch. i.) The first address: Exhortation to build the temple, and its result.

§ 1. (Ch. i. 1—6.) The people are reproved for their indifference with regard to the erection of the temple, and admonished that their present distress is a chastisement for this neglect.

§ 2. (Ch. i. 7—11.) The prophet urges them to work zealously at the building as the only remedy for the unfruitfulness of the season.

§ 3. (Ch. i. 12—15.) The appeal is obeyed, and for a time the people apply themselves diligently to the work.

Part II. (Ch. ii. 1—9.) The second address: The glory of the new temple.

§ 1. (Ch. ii. 1—5.) The prophet comforts those who grieve at the comparative poverty of the new building, with the assurance of the Divine protection and favour.

§ 2. (Ch. ii. 6—9.) He foretells a future time when the glory of the new temple should exceed that of the old, adumbrating the Messianic era.

Part III. (Ch. ii. 10—19.) The third address: The cause of their calamities, and promise of blessing.

§ 1. (Ch. ii. 10—17.) By an analogy drawn from the Law Haggai shows that residence in the Holy Land and offering of sacrifice do not suffice to make the people acceptable, as long as they themselves are unclean through neglect of the house of the Lord. Hence comes the punishment of sterility.

§ 2. (Ch. ii. 18, 19.) On their obedience the blessings of nature s'all again be theirs.

Part IV. (Ch. ii. 20—23.) The fourth address: Promise of the restoration and establishment of the house of David, when the storm bursts on the kingdoms of the world.

THE BOOK OF HAGGAI

EXPOSITION.

CHAPTER I.

Vers. 1—15.—Part I. The First Address: Exhortation to build the Temple, and its Result.

Vers. 1—6.—§ 1. *The people are reproved for their indifference with regard to the erection of the temple, and admonished that their present distress is a chastisement for this neglect.*

Ver. 1.—**In the second year of Darius the king.** This is Darius Hystaspes, who reigned over Persia from B.C. 521 to B.C. 486. He is called in the inscriptions *Daryavush*, which name means "Holder," or "Supporter." Herodotus (vi. 98) explains it as "Coercer" (ἐρξείης). Hitherto the prophets have dated the time of the exercise of their office from the reigns of the legitimate Hebrew monarchs; it shows a new state of things when they place at the head of their oracles the name of a foreign and a heathen potentate. The Jews had, indeed, now no king of their own, "the tabernacle of David had fallen" (Amos ix. 11), and they were living on sufferance under an alien power. They had returned from exile by permission of Cyrus in the first year of his occupancy of the throne of Babylon sixteen years before this time, and had commenced to build the temple soon after; but the opposition of neighbours, contradictory orders from the Persian court, and their own lukewarmness had contributed to hinder the work, and it soon wholly ceased, and remained suspended to the moment when Haggai, as the seventy years of desolation drew to an end, was commissioned to arouse them from their apathy, and to urge them to use the opportunity which was afforded by the accession of the new monarch and the withdrawal of the vexatious interdict that had checked their operations in the previous reign (see Introduction, § I.; and comp. Ezra iv. 24). **The sixth month,** according to the sacred Hebrew calendar, which reckoned from Nisan to Nisan. This would be Elul, answering to parts of our August and September. **In the first day.** This was the regular festival of the new moon (Numb. x. 10; Isa. i. 13), and a fitting time to urge the building of the temple, without which it could not be duly celebrated. **By;** literally, *by the hand* (as in ver. 3), the instrument whom God used (Exod. ix. 35; Jer. xxxvii. 2; Hos. xii. 11; Acts vii. 35). **Haggai the prophet** (see the Introduction). **Zerubbabel the son of Shealtiel;** Septuagint, Εἰπὸν πρὸς Ζοροβάβελ τὸν τοῦ Σαλαθιὴλ, "Speak to Zorobabel the son of Salathiel." The temporal head of the nation, the representative of the royal house of David, and therefore with the high priest jointly responsible for the present state of affairs, and having power and authority to amend it. The name, as explained, and rightly, by St. Jerome, means, "Born in Babylon," and intimates the truth concerning his origin. He is called Sheshbazzar in Ezra i. 8; v. 14, which is either his name at the Persian court, or is an erroneous transliteration for a synonymous word (see Knabenbauer, *in loc.*). The name is found in the cuneiform inscription, as *Zir-Babilu*. Shealtiel (or Salathiel) means, "Asked of God." There is a difficulty about Zerubbabel's parentage. Here and frequently in this book, and in Ezra and Nehemiah, as well as in Matt. i. 12 and Luke iii. 27, he is called "son of Shealtiel;" in 1 Chron. iii. 19 he is said to be the son of Pedaiah the brother of Salathiel. The truth probably is that he was by birth the son of Pedaiah, but by adoption or the law of the *levirate*, the son of Salathiel. He was regarded as the grandson of Jehoiachin, or Jeconiah. **Governor** (*pechah*). A foreign word, used in 1 Kings x. 15, in Isaiah (xxxvi. 9), and frequently in Ezra, Nehemiah, and Esther, to denote an inferior satrap or subordinate governor. Strassmaier (*ap.* Knabenbauer) notes that in Assyrian the word is found in the form *pachu*, that *pichatu* means "a province," *pachat*, "a district." It seems natural, though probably erroneous, to connect it with the Turkish pashah. But see the discussion on the word in Pusey, 'Daniel the Prophet,' p. 566, etc. Instead of "Governor of Judah," the LXX. here and ver. 12 and ch. ii. 2 reads, "of the tribe of Judah." One of the house of David has the government, but the foreign title applied to him shows that he holds authority only as the deputy of an alien power. Judah was henceforward applied to the whole country. The prophecy in Gen. xlix. 10 still held good. **Joshua.** The highest spiritual officer (Ezra iii. 2, 8; iv. 3). This Joshua, Jehoshua, Jeshua, as he is variously called, was a son of Josedech who, in the time of Nebuchadnezzar, had been carried captive to Babylon (1 Chron. vi. 15), and grandson of that Seraiah who, with other princes of Judah, was slain at Riblah by the Babylonians (2 Kings xxv. 18, etc.). The parentage of Zerubbabel and Joshua is specially mentioned to show that the former was of the house of David and the latter of the family of Aaron, and that even in its depressed condition Israel retained its rightful constitution (see note on Zech. iii. 1).

Ver. 2.—**The Lord of hosts.** Haggai, as the other prophets, always uses this formula in enunciating his messages (see note on Amos ix. 5). Trochon justly remarks that this expression is not found in the earlier books of the Bible—the Pentateuch, Joshua, and Judges. If these books were contemporary with the prophets, the phrase would certainly occur in them (see a valuable note in the Appendix to Archdeacon Perowne's Commentary on Haggai, in 'The Cambridge Bible for Schools'). **This people;** *populus iste* (Vulgate), with some contempt, as if they were no longer worthy to be called the Lord's people (ch. ii. 14). It looks as if they had often before been admonished to proceed with the work, and had this answer ready. **The time is not come;** literally, *it is not time to come* (comp. Gen. ii. 5), which is explained by the new clause, **the time that the Lord's house should be built.** The versions shorten the sentence, rendering, "the time for building the Lord's house has not come." The excuse for their inaction may have had various grounds. They may have said, reckoning from the final destruction of Jerusalem (B.C. 586), that the seventy years' captivity was not complete; that there was still danger from the neighbouring population;

that the Persians were adverse to the undertaking; that the unfruitful season rendered them unable to engage in such a great work; and that the very fact of these difficulties existing showed that God did not favour the design.

Ver. 3.—**Then came the word of the Lord,** etc. The formula of ver. 1 is repeated to give more effect to the Lord's answer to the lame excuses for inaction. This emphasis by repetition is common throughout the book.

Ver. 4.—**For you, O ye;** *for you, yourselves;* such as ye are (see Zech. vii. 5). He appeals to their consciences. You can make yourselves comfortable; you have time and means and industry to expend on your own private interests, and can you look with indifference on the house of God lying waste? **Your cieled houses;** *your houses, and those cieled*—wainscoted and roofed with costly woods (1 Kings vii. 3, 7; Jer. xxii. 14), perhaps with the very cedar provided for the rebuilding of the temple (Ezra iii. 7). Septuagint, ἐν οἴκοις ὑμῶν κοιλοστάθμοις, "your vaulted houses," or, as St. Cyril explains, "houses whose doorposts were elaborately adorned with emblems and devices." They had naught of the feeling of David (2 Sam. vii. 2), "I dwell in an house of cedar, but the ark of God dwelleth within curtains."

Ver. 5.—**Consider;** literally, *set your heart upon* (so ver. 7; ch. ii. 15, 18). **Your ways.** What ye have done, what ye have suffered, your present projects, and the consequences thereof.

Ver. 6.—Their labours for years past had lacked the Divine blessing. Though they had fine houses to dwell in, they had been visited with scanty harvests and weak bodily health. **Ye have sown much, and bring in little;** *but to bring in little* (Hebrew). And this infinitive absolute is continued in the following clauses, giving remarkable force to the words, and expressing an habitual result. We see from ch. ii. 15—17 that these unfruitful seasons had visited them during all the continuance of their negligence (Deut. xxviii. 38). **But ye have not enough** The food which they ate did not satisfy them; their bodies were sickly and derived no strength from the food which they took (Lev. xxvi. 26; Hos. iv. 10) or from the wine which they drank (see note on Micah vi. 14). **But there is none warm.** Perhaps the winters were unusually rigorous, or their infirm health made their usual clothing insufficient to maintain their bodily heat. To put it into **a bag with holes.** A proverbial saying. The money gained by the hired labourer vanished as if he had never had it, and left no trace of benefit. Comp. Plaut., 'Pseudol.,' i. 3. 150—

"In pertusum ingerimus dicta dolium; operam ludimus."

Vers. 7—11.—§ 2. *The prophet urges the people to work zealously at the building ; only thus could they hope for the removal of their present disasters.*

Ver. 7.—(See note on ver. 5.) The repetition of the call to reflection is needed (comp. Phil. iii. 1). Former experience opens the way to the injunction in ver. 8.

Ver. 8.—**Go up the mountain.** The hill-country in the neighbourhood of Jerusalem, whence by their own personal exertions they might procure material for the building. The temple mount is certainly not meant, as if they were to bring wood from it. Nor can Lebanon be intended, as in Ezra iii. 7 ; for the injunction looks to an immediate actual result, and in their depressed circumstances they were scarcely likely to interest the Sidonians and Tyrians to provide cedar for them. There was abundance of wood close at hand, and the "king's forest " (Neh. ii. 8) was in the immediate neighbourhood of Jerusalem. There is no mention of stone, probably because the foundations had long been laid, and the ruins of the old temple supplied material for the new one ; and, indeed, stone was to be had in abundance everywhere ; or it may be that the prophet names merely one opening for their renewed activity, as a specimen of the work required from them. Not costly offerings were desired, but a willing mind. **I will be glorified;** *I will glorify myself* by showering blessings on the house and the people, so that the Hebrews themselves and their neighbours may own that I am among them (comp. Exod. xiv. 4 ; Lev. x. 3 ; Isa. lxvi. 5).

Ver. 9.—He shows the real cause of the calamities that had befallen them. **Ye looked for much, and, lo, it came to little.** Emphatic infinitive, as in ver. 6. "To look for much, and behold ! little." They fixed their expectations upon a rich harvest, and they reaped less than they had sown (Isa. v. 10). And when they had stored this miserable crop in their barns, **I did blow upon it ;** or, *did blow it away* (ἐξεφύσησα, Septuagint), dissipated it as if it were mere chaff, so that it perished. Doubtless, as Dr Pusey observes, they ascribed the meagreness of their crops to natural causes, and would not see the judicial nature of the infliction. The prophet brings the truth home to their conscience by the stern question, **Why ?** And he answers the question for them, speaking with God's authority. **Because of mine house that is waste.** The reason already given in ver. 4, etc., is repeated and enforced. **And** (*while*) **ye run.** Ye are indifferent to the miserable condition

of the house of God, while ye haste with all diligence to your own houses for business or pleasure, being entirely absorbed in worldly interests, or eager only to adorn and beautify your own habitations. Or, your zeal is all expended on your own private dwellings.

Ver. 10.—**Over you.** This would be a reference to Deut. xxviii. 23. But the preposition is probably not local, but means rather, "on your account," *i.e.* on account of your sin, as Ps. xliv. 22. This is not tautological after the preceding "therefore," but more closely defines and explains the illative. **Is stayed from dew ;** *hath stayed itself from dew ;* withholds not only rain, but even dew (comp. Zech. viii. 12). On the importance of dew in the climate of Palestine, see note on Micah v. 7. The dews generally are remarkably heavy, and in the summer months take the place of rain. Dr. Thomson speaks of the dew rolling in the morning off his tent like rain ('Land and the Book,' p. 491). **The earth is stayed from her fruit ;** *hath stayed her fruit ;* according to the threat (Deut. xi. 17).

Ver. 11.—**I called for a drought.** So Elisha says (2 Kings viii. 1) that "the Lord hath called for a famine." There is a play of words in the Hebrew : as they had let the Lord's house lie "waste" (*chareb*) (vers. 4, 9), so the Lord punished them with "drought" (*choreb*). The Septuagint and Syriac, pointing differently, translate this last word "sword," but this is not suitable for the context, which speaks of the sterility of the land only. **The land,** in contradistinction to the mountains, is the plain country. Nothing anywhere was spared. **All the labour of the hands** (Ps. cxxviii. 2, etc.). All that they had effected by long and wearisome toil in the corn-field, the vineyard, etc. (comp. Hos. ii. 9 ; Joel i. 10).

Vers. 12—15.—§ 3. *The appeal meets with respect and attention, and for a time the people apply themselves diligently to the work.*

Ver. 12.—**All the remnant of the people** (ch. ii. 2) ; *i.e.* the people who had returned from the Captivity, who are technically named "the remnant" as being only a small portion of all Israel (Isa. x. 21, 22 ; Zech. viii. 6 ; Micah ii. 12). Others, not so suitably, understand by the expression, all the people beside the chiefs (ver. 14). **Obeyed ;** rather, *listened unto.* The active obedience is narrated in ver. 14. **And the words.** The prophet's words are the voice of the Lord ; and the people heeded the message which the Lord had commissioned him to give. **Did fear.** They showed that true religion which the Bible calls "the fear of the Lord." They saw their faults, perhaps dreaded some new chastisement, and hastened to obey the prophet's injunction (Ezra v. 1, 2).

Ver. 13.—**Then spake Haggai.** God hastens to accept their repentance and to assure them of his protection. **The Lord's messenger.** Haggai alone of the prophets uses this title of himself, implying that he came with authority and bearing a message from the Lord (comp. Numb. xx. 16, where the word "angel" is by some applied to Moses). Malachi's very name expresses that he was the Lord's messenger, and he uses the term of the priest (ii. 7), and of John the Baptist, and of Messiah himself (iii. 1). In the Lord's message (1 Kings xiii. 18). In the special message of consolation which he was commissioned to deliver. The Septuagint rendering, ἐν ἀγγέλοις Κυρίου, "among the angels of the Lord," led some to fancy that Haggai was an angel in human form, which opinion is refuted by Jerome, *in loc.* I am **with you** (ch. ii. 4). A brief message comprised in two words, "I with you," yet full of comfort, promising God's presence, protection, aid, and blessing (comp. Gen. xxviii. 15; xxxix. 2; Josh. i. 5; Jer. i. 8; Matt. xxviii. 20).

Ver. 14.—**The Lord stirred up,** etc. The Lord excited the courage, animated the zeal, of the chiefs of the nation, who had themselves succumbed to the prevailing indifference, and had suffered their ardour to be quenched (comp. 1 Chron. v. 26; 2 Chron. xxi. 16; Ezra i. 1, 5). **They came and did work.** They went up to the temple and began to do the work which they had so long neglected.

Ver. 15.—**In the four and twentieth day of the sixth month.** The first admonition had been made on the first day of this month; the three intervening weeks had doubtless been spent in planning and preparing materials, and obtaining workmen from the neighbouring villages. The note of time is introduced to show how prompt was their obedience, and the exact time when "they came and did work in the house of the Lord" (ver. 14). Some, on insufficient grounds, consider this clause to be an interpolation from ch. ii. 10, 18, with a change of "ninth" to "sixth month." In the Latin Vulgate, in Tischendorf's Septuagint, and in many editions of the Hebrew Bible, the whole of this verse is wrongly annexed to the following chapter. St. Jerome arranges it as in the Authorized Version. It is possible that, as St. Cyril takes it, the words, in the second year of Darius the king, ought to begin ch. ii. The king's reign has been already notified in ver. 1, and it seems natural to affix the date at the commencement of the second address.

HOMILETICS.

Ver. 1.—*Divine revelations.* I. SELECT THEIR OWN TIMES. These are: 1. *Often unexpected.* In the present instance this was probably the case. The band of exiles who, availing themselves of Cyrus's permission (Ezra i. 3), returned to Judah and Jerusalem—nearly 50,000 persons in all (Ezra ii. 64, 65), though Pusey estimates the company of immigrants at 212,000, counting free men, women, children, and slaves—had for sixteen years at least not heard a prophet's voice. The last that had fallen on their ears had been Daniel's in Babylon (Dan. ix. 1), which had predicted the going forth of a commandment to build and restore Jerusalem, and the coming, "seven weeks and three score and two weeks" thereafter, of Messiah the prince (Dan. ix. 25). Now, in the second year of Darius the king (Ezra iv. 24), *i.e.* about B.C. 520, the interval of silence terminated, and the lips of a new prophet were unsealed. That God reserves in his own hands "the times and seasons" of his special supernatural interpositions in human history, while it should keep men alive to every movement of the Divine presence in their midst, ought to guard them against presumption both in making and in interpreting prophecy. 2. *Always appropriate.* The interpositions of Heaven are never *post horam.* The clock of eternity always keeps time. When the hour comes, so does the man. Man often speaks at an inopportune moment; God, never. When Haggai stood forth among the Jews who had returned from Babylon, they were in urgent need of such a messenger from heaven as he proved himself to be. Sixteen years at home in their own land, for a year and a half they had been disheartened about the building of their temple, and had even discontinued work. Some had even begun to lose interest in the restoration of the sacred edifice (ver. 2). Hence they much wanted rousing from indolence and rebuke for unbelief, as well as comfort in sadness and succour in weakness; and all this they received from the new monitor from Jehovah that had arisen in their midst. So have God's revelations ever been as suitable to men's necessities as to time's urgencies. Notably was this the case with his showing of himself to Moses at the bush (Exod. iii. 2), and his disclosure of himself to mankind in the Person of Christ (Gal. iv. 4). 3. *Sometimes suggestive.* This was so in the case under consideration. First, the year in which Haggai appeared was suggestive of the people's sadness; having no more a king of their own to count from, they reckoned the date as that of the second year of Darius, *i.e.* of Darius Hystaspes (*Dârajavus* of the cuneiform inscriptions), who reigned from B.C. 521 to B.C. 486. Next, the month—the sixth of their ordinary Jewish year (corresponding with our August or September), and therefore towards the close of harvest—ought at least, by the comparatively barren fields they had reaped, to have reminded them of their chastisement (vers. 10, 11), and so induced in them a spirit of humility. Lastly, the day of the month, the new moon's day, which the Law had directed to be kept as a day of special sacrifice (Numb. xxviii. 11), which their forefathers had observed as a popular festival (Prov. vii. 20, margin Authorized Version), and marked by religious gatherings at the local sanctuaries (Isa. i. 13, 14; 2 Kings iv. 23), and which probably they also celebrated as a holiday, might have spoken to them of their sin in preserving the outward forms of religion while neglecting its inward spirit, and perhaps also of their duty, to attend with true docility to the admonition which proceeded from the new prophet's lips.

II. FIND THEIR OWN INSTRUMENTS. These also are: 1. *Mostly humble.* Only once did Divine revelation find an organ that was truly exalted, viz. when he who, as the only begotten Son, had been in the Father's bosom, made him known (John i. 18)— although even then it was needful that that Son should empty himself of his glory and veil his Divinity behind a garment of humanity before he could properly accomplish his work (Phil. ii. 6, 7). But in all other instances the instruments selected by Jehovah for the transmission of his will to mankind are humble and lowly in comparison with him whose will they bear (Isa. xl. 18), even when they are angels; how much more when men, as they mostly are! And of these it is seldom the most exalted in rank or wisdom that he selects, but most frequently the lowliest—persons in obscure stations, like Moses when a stranger in Midian (Acts vii. 29—31), like Elisha when holding the plough (1 Kings xix. 19), or like Amos when among the herdsmen of Tekoa (Amos i. 1); and persons of unknown family, like Elijah the Tishbite, or Nahum the Elkoshite, or Habakkuk, of whom almost nothing is known. 2. *Always suitable.* Men frequently err in choosing instruments to execute their will; God, never. He can always discern spirits, while men only think they can. Men judge according to appearance; he, according to the heart. Haggai was, perhaps, not such a vehicle as man would have pitched upon to be the medium of a Divine communication. But for God's purpose he was fitted beyond most. Though not absolutely certain, it is most probable he was an old man of eighty years (Ewald, Pusey), who had seen the first temple in its glory (ch. ii. 3), and who could therefore speak with greater emphasis and solemnity as one standing on the confines of eternity, who knew the vanity of earthly greatness, and could appreciate the superior excellence and desirability of things inward and spiritual. Besides, his very name—Haggai, or " Festive "—fitted him to be the bearer of a message to desponding builders. What they wanted was inspiriting incitement, encouragement, and hope; and of that there was a promise in the old man's designation —Haggai, or "The Festal One"—especially if this only expressed the habitual disposition of his soul. 3. *Generally efficient.* "It has been the wont of critics, in whose eyes the prophets were but poets," writes Pusey, "to speak of the style of Haggai as 'tame' and 'destitute of life and power;'" but, for all that, it was adapted to the object sought to be accomplished. Haggai had no need to complain, as the eloquent Isaiah (first or second), "Lord, who hath believed our report? and to whom is the arm of the Lord revealed?" (Isa. liii. 1); of him it is recorded that his words awoke an immediate response in his hearers' hearts, and "they came and did work in the house of the Lord of hosts, their God" (ver. 14). Man cannot always say of his instruments, however finely polished, that they will never fail; God can always predict of his, however rude, that they will certainly succeed.

III. CHOOSE THEIR OWN RECIPIENTS. These are commonly diverse, as in the present instance. Haggai's message was directed: 1. *To Zerubbabel;* concerning whom may be noted: (1) His names. Sheshbazzar (Ezra i. 8), most probably Chaldean or Babylonian, and perhaps signifying "Worshipper of Fire" (Gesenius); Zerubbabel (Ezra ii. 1), obviously Hebrew, and meaning "Born in Babylon;" and Tirshatha (Ezra ii. 63; Neh. vii. 65), most likely Persian, and equivalent to "The Feared." (2) His descent. Described in the text as the son of Shealtiel, who was the son of Jeconiah the captive (1 Chron. iii. 17, Authorized Version), or, if Assir be taken as a proper name (1 Chron. iii. 17, Authorized Version), the grandson of Jeconiah; or again, if Luke's register be followed (iii. 27), the son of Neri;—Zerubbabel is expressly stated by the chronicler to have been a son of Pedaiah, a brother of Shealtiel (1 Chron. iii. 19). Probably as good a solution of the difficulty as any other is Keil's, that Jeconiah, according to the prophecy of Jeremiah (xxii. 30), had no sons, but only a daughter, who married Neri, a descendant of David, and became by him the mother of Shealtiel and Pedaiah, who accordingly were reckoned sons of Jeconiah, and that Shealtiel having died without issue, his brother Pedaiah married his widow, and raised up for him a son named Zerubbabel. (3) His office. As a descendant of the royal house of Judah, he was the recognized head of the Jewish exiles in Babylon, and as such was by Cyrus appointed governor of the pilgrim band who returned to their native land. 2. *To Joshua;* who also is described by his ancestry as the son of Josedech, who had been carried away by the Chaldeans to Babylon (1 Chron. vi. 15), when his father Zeraiah had been put to death by Nebuchadnezzar (2 Kings xxv. 18—21; Jer. lii. 24—27), and by his office as the high priest of the young community that had returned to Judæa and Jerusalem. As Zerubbabel was their civil, so was Joshua their religious, head; and "together they are types of him, the true King and true Priest, Christ Jesus, who by his resurrection raised again the true temple, his body, after it had been destroyed" (Pusey). 3. *To the people.* Though Haggai's words were directed in the first instance to Zerubbabel and Joshua, they were in the second instance designed for the whole congregation; and that the whole congregation received them, whether directly from the prophet's own lips or indirectly through those of the prince and the priest, is expressly stated (vers. 12, 13).

LESSONS. 1. The possibility of revelation. 2. The human medium of inspiration. 3. The greater privilege of the Christian Church in having as a revealer of the Divine will, not a human prophet merely, but the incarnate Son. 4. The higher responsibility which this entails.

Vers. 2—5.—*The mistakes of the temple-builders: a warning.* I. THEY FAILED TO DISCERN THE SIGNS OF THE TIMES. They imagined the time had not come for them to build the Lord's house, whereas it had fully arrived. 1. *What led them to suppose or say so, though not stated, may easily be inferred.* (1) They were disheartened by the opposition they encountered (see next head). (2) The original grant obtained from Cyrus (Ezra iii. 7) was probably then exhausted. (3) They had been interdicted by a decree of Artaxerxes, or of pseudo-Smerdis (Ezra iv. 23, 24). And (4) they were suffering from bad trade and worse harvests (ver. 6), and consequently were unable to contribute towards the expense of the building. 2. *The indications that the time had fully come were so plain that they should hardly have been misread.* (1) The seventy years during which the whole land of Judah was to lie desolate, and its inhabitants should serve the King of Babylon (Jer. xxv. 11, 12), and at the end of which the exiles should return to their own land (Jer. xxix. 10), had manifestly rolled by. (2) The very deliverer of whom Isaiah had spoken by name, Cyrus (Isa. xliv. 28; xlv. 1), had appeared, and opened the two-leaved gates of Babylon (Ezra i. 2, 3). (3) The sacred vessels which Nebuchadnezzar had carried off to Babylon (2 Kings xxiv. 13), and Jeremiah (xxviii. 3) predicted would again be brought from Babylon, had actually been delivered over into the hands of Zerubbabel by Cyrus (Ezra i. 8). (4) The bad harvests and depressed trade from which they were suffering were a manifest token of the Divine displeasure on account of their negligence, and were no real excuse for their illiberal conduct, since they could obviously find money enough to build ceiled mansions for themselves. (5) The decree of Artaxerxes only forbad the building of the city (Ezra iv. 21), not of the temple; and even though it had been directed against the latter, Artaxerxes himself no longer reigned, having been driven from the throne he had usurped, and his place having been occupied by Darius Hystaspes, so that the repressive edict, had they been anxious, might easily have been revoked. This mistake of the builders has often been committed; as *e.g.* by Moses in Egypt, who misread the signs of the times, and thought the hour had struck for Israel's deliverance, when it had not (Exod. ii. 11—15 ; Acts vii. 25); by the Jewish rulers in Christ's day, who failed to discern in the Galilæan Prophet the manifest tokens of Messiah (Matt. xvi. 3, 4); by the city of Jerusalem, which knew not the day of her visitation (Luke xix. 42); and by the present-day unbeliever, who cannot see that "now is the accepted time, and now is the day of salvation" (2 Cor. vi. 2).

II. THEY WERE TOO EASILY DAUNTED BY OPPOSITION. 1. *The nature and source of this opposition is described in the Book of Ezra* (iv.). Prevented from taking part in the building of the temple, the Samaritan settlers first "weakened the hands of the builders," next "hired counsellors against them," and ultimately obtained an interdict commanding them to cease. It was certainly annoying, but: 2. *They should not have been so easily discouraged.* No enterprise of any moment was ever carried through without encountering difficulties and frequently hostilities, and without calling for patient perseverance in well-doing. How otherwise would Israel have been brought from Egypt at the first, or Judah from Babylon a few years before? 3. *The same mistake is committed still* by those who imagine the spiritual temple of Jehovah, either in the individual soul or in the Church as a whole, can be built without difficulty, without experiencing resistance from enemies within and without, or in any other way than by indomitable perseverance. 4. *" Never despair " and " Never give in " should be the twin mottoes of every one engaged in temple-building for God*—of the individual believer, of the Christian minister, of the foreign missionary.

III. THEY PREFERRED THE MATERIAL AND TEMPORAL TO THE SPIRITUAL AND RELIGIOUS. The ordinary occupations of life had more attraction for them than the duties of religion. To assert that they cared nothing for religion would, perhaps, be wrong, since what had brought them back from Babylon, where for the most part they had comfortable settlements, was a true feeling of piety no less than an ardent spirit of patriotism. Yet were they not long back upon their much-loved ancestral soil before they showed they had brought back with them from Babylon a passion stronger than even their love for religion, namely, devotion to the earthly and material pursuits of life. Their zeal in temple-building was quickly damped, but not so their enthusiasm in ploughing and sowing their fields, in working for wages, in erecting magnificent mansions, sumptuous palaces like those they had seen and perhaps lived in in Babylon, with walls of polished stone and roofs of cedar. With much ease they could see that "the time for building God's house was not come," as they supposed; they had large difficulty in perceiving it was not the season to attend to their ordinary avocations. So do many on becoming Christians carry over with them into their new life "passions for things material and temporal," which, while religious feeling is fresh, are kept in abeyance, but which, the moment this begins to abate, assert themselves to the hindrance of what is properly religious work, and to the detriment of the soul's religious life. This constitutes a third mistake against which Christians should be on their guard.

IV. THEY FOLLOWED THEIR OWN INTERESTS RATHER THAN THE GLORY OF GOD. One cannot help thinking that, had the building of the Lord's house been a matter that concerned their own glory, comfort, or interest, they would not have suffered it to lie waste as they did; but only the honour of the Deity was involved, and what was that to their material advantage and temporal felicity? Was it not of greater moment that they themselves should be well housed, well fed, well clothed, than that even God, who dwelleth not in temples made with hands, and requireth not to be worshipped as though he needed anything, should be well lodged? If it came to the worst, they could do without a temple altogether, could worship in the open air, as they had done since coming from Babylon, but they could not well do without well-stocked farms and finely ceiled houses. And so they let the work, which had only God's glory as its motive, drop, and applied themselves to that which contemplated man's or their own material good. Is it wrong to find in this a parable for Christians? Is not the essence of Christianity just this—that a man, like Christ whom he follows, shall seek, not his own glory, but God's ; shall do, not his own will, but the will of him who hath sent him into the world? Yet among professing Christians are those who cannot see beyond their own little selves, and who imagine that a man's chief duty upon earth, even after having become a Christian, is to do the best he can for himself, whereas it is to do the best he can for God. Acting on the former principle leads to spiritual blindness, to **cowardice, to this**-worldism, all of which are deplorable mistakes; acting on the latter-principle terminates in no such disastrous results, but brings with it to the individual so acting spiritual insight, moral courage, and heavenly-mindedness, three qualities which ennoble all by whom they are possessed.

LESSONS. 1. The duty of discerning the signs of the times. 2. The necessity of combining courage with forethought. 3. The propriety of guarding against the disturbing influence of supposed self-interest.

Vers. 5, 7.—*Considering one's ways.* I. AN EXALTED PRIVILEGE. The faculties of introspection and reflection, which enable man to consider his ways, constitute a lofty endowment, which places him incontestably at the apex of creation. 1. *It distinguishes him from the lower animals.* These may be possessed of capabilities which enable them to perform actions in some degree resembling the fruits of intelligence—it may even be conceded are, in some instances at least, endowed with faculties of memory, imagination, and judgment; but they are wholly devoid of the powers of self-introspection and reflection here ascribed to man. Of the noblest of brute beasts it still remains to be proved that it ever said to itself, "I communed with mine own heart: and my spirit made diligent search" (Ps. lxxvii. 6); or "I thought on my ways" (Ps. cxix. 59). 2. *It sets him in the neighbourhood of God.* The Hebrew psalmist conceived the ideal man as a being only a little short of Divinity (Ps. viii. 5); and though the basis on which he rested this conception was man's manifest dominion over the creatures, yet this arose, as he well knew, out of the fact that man, as distinguished from the lower creatures, had been made in the Divine image (Gen. i. 26); which again, in part at least, consisted in his capacity to consider his ways, or to look before and behind in whatever way he was treading. "Known unto God are all his works from the beginning of the world" (Acts xv. 18); "He declareth the end from the beginning" (Isa. xlvi. 10); and though the Preacher affirms that "no man can find out the work that God maketh from the beginning to the end" (Eccles. iii. 11), yet to each man has been granted the ability to consider the way in which he himself goeth (Eccles. v. 1), and in this high capacity of pondering the path of his feet he possesses an endowment that in him a finite being corresponds to the omniscience of the infinite God.

II. AN URGENT DUTY. The consideration of one's ways required by two things. 1. *Divine commandment.* In addition to the twice-repeated exhortation here addressed to the builders, the admonition frequently occurs in Scripture (Ps. iv. 4; Prov. iv. 26; 1 Cor. xi. 28; 2 Cor. xiii. 5; Gal. vi. 4) to commune with one's own heart, to search and try one's ways, to examine carefully into one's spiritual condition. And this to a good man is enough to constitute an imperative obligation. "Where the word of a king is"—much more where the word of the King of kings is—"there is power." 2. *Present safety.* No one can travel long securely or comfortably along the path of life who does not ponder well at the outset from what point the course he is pursuing starts, who does not frequently pause to notice whither it is tending, and who does not always have an eye upon the where and the how it shall terminate. The man that lives purely by haphazard, that rushes on blindfold into whatever enterprise he takes in hand, whether in business or religion, is sure to come to grief, if not to fall into the ditch. 3. *Future responsibility.* There might be less need for attending to this duty if the issues of our ways and actions always exhausted themselves on earth and in time. But they do not. "We must all appear before the judgment-seat of Christ, and give an account of the deeds done in the body, whether these be good or whether they be bad" (2 Cor. v. 10). The ways of every man project themselves into the unseen beyond. Every man is making his future by the ways he is travelling and the deeds he is doing in the present.

III. A PROFITABLE EXERCISE. Apart altogether from the duty of it, the advantages to be derived from it should go far to recommend this practice. 1. *Self-knowledge.* No one will ever attain to a trustworthy or valuable acquaintance with his own heart who does not frequently undertake a review of "the issues of life" (Prov. iv. 23) that proceed from it. Yet next to the knowledge of God and Christ, which constitute the essence of "life eternal" (John xvii. 2), the knowledge of self is the highest attainment to which one can rise. 2. *Moral discernment.* The power of distinguishing between right and wrong, which belongs to all as an intuitive endowment, is nevertheless susceptible of improvement or deterioration, according as it is exercised or neglected. It may be clarified, intensified, quickened, strengthened; or it may be dulled, darkened, weakened, deadened. Through diligent personal culture the soul may become sensitive to nicest distinctions of right and wrong as an aneroid barometer to smallest variations in the atmosphere; or, through want of use, it may become hard as a fossilized organism or as a petrified log of wood. 3. *Spiritual improvement.* No one is likely to make progress in religion without an intimate acquaintance with his own ways. Without this one may even not suspect that his religion is defective. In proportion as one knows what in himself is dark and needs illumining, or feeble and requires strengthening, or low and demands upraising, or deficient and calls for supplementing, or wrong and wants correcting, will one advance in moral and spiritual attainment. Learn: 1. The dignity of man. 2. The responsibility of life. 3. The duty of circumspection.

Vers. 6—11.—*Hard times.* I. A FREQUENT OCCURRENCE. Poor harvests and profitless trade, famine and idleness, lack of bread and want of employment, nothing to eat and nothing to do. The two commonly go together. Examples of famines were in ancient times those which occurred in Canaan (Gen. xii. 10), in Egypt (Gen. xli. 54), in Samaria (1 Kings xvii. 2; 2 Kings vi. 25), in Jerusalem (Jer. lii. 6); in modern times those which have taken place in India, China, and other parts of Asia. II. A SORROWFUL EXPERIENCE. When the husbandman has laboured, and, perhaps through long-continued drought, has obtained an altogether insufficient return for his labours. When through deficient harvests the people of a country are reduced to a state of semi-starvation. When through this failure in the sources of wealth the wheels of a nation's industry are stopped. When strong men who would willingly work can find no work to do. When wages already scanty are eaten up by exorbitant prices. III. A PROVIDENTIAL JUDGMENT. Hard times: 1. *Are of God's sending.* To say that bad harvests and dull trade are the results of natural (physical and social) laws does not show them to be disconnected with God. The Almighty is behind both nature and society. Jehovah claimed that the state of matters in Judah after the exile was his doing. 2. *Have their occasions, if not their causes, in sin.* Haggai's countrymen had been made to suffer because of their indifference to religion and devotion to self-interest (ver. 9). Were modern nations to reflect more deeply, they might discover connections between their characters and their conditions, their sins and their sufferings. IV. A SALUTARY DISCIPLINE. Intended as all chastisement is: 1. *To arrest attention.* Inconsiderateness a principal sin of men and nations. 2. *To convince of sin.* A remarkable proof of depravity that moral perceptions require to be awakened by physical corrections. 3. *To excite repentance.* Though confessions under the lash are not the same thing as penitence, yet they may and should be, and often are, accompanied by penitence. 4. *To promote amendment.* Though punishment is not exclusively reformatory in its character, yet it is mostly (on earth at least) inflicted with design to benefit the sufferer. LESSONS. 1. Religion in individuals and nations the best defence against hard times. 2. Repentance and prayer the best resort in bad times.

Vers. 12—15.—*Ancient temple-builders.* I. UNIVERSAL ACTIVITY. "They came and did work"—all of them: "Zerubbabel the governor, Joshua the high priest, and all the remnant of the people." There was not an idler amongst them. Every person was engaged at something in connection with the building. The spectacle was: 1. *The reproduction of an old scene,* when in the wilderness of Sinai, orders having been issued for the construction of a tabernacle, "as many as were willing-hearted came, both men and women," and contributed their aid to the work (Exod. xxxv. 20—29). 2. *The foreshadowing of a later scene,* when the infant Church of the New Testament was assembled in the upper room, and "there came a sound from heaven as of a rushing mighty wind, which filled all the house where they were sitting," and "they were all filled with the Holy Ghost, and all began to speak with tongues as the Spirit gave them utterance" (Acts ii. 1—4). 3. *The picture of a (possibly) present scene.* What is wanted is the carrying over of this scene of universal activity into the

Christian Church, and the spectacle of every professing disciple of Jesus Christ contributing his quota of work to the building of that spiritual edifice which is to-day being erected on the foundation of the apostles and prophets, Jesus Christ himself being the chief Corner-stone, for the inhabitation of God through the Spirit (Eph. ii. 20—22). "The kingdom of heaven is as a man taking a far journey, who left his house, and gave authority to his servants, and to every man his work" (Mark xiii. 34).

II. CHEERFUL WILLINGNESS. "They all *came*." Not one required to be coerced or in any way dragged forth against his will. Nobody skulked or came forward with a grudge, but each was readier than his neighbour. So was it in the erection of the tabernacle; so should it be in the building of the Christian Church. Yet how to realize this ideal in the latter case is one of the problems of the day. 1. *The back-wardness of Christians to engage in specifically Christian work is a too evident fact.* It may arise with some from constitutional timidity, with others from undue depreciation of their own ability, with a few from inability to discern a sphere suitable to their supposed gifts, but with most (it is to be feared) from a depressed condition of religion in the soul. The cure for the first may be found in the grace of God (2 Cor. xii. 9); for the second, in a high conception of God's ability (Phil. iv. 13); for the third, in doing the first thing that comes to hand (Eccles. ix. 10); and for the fourth, in a quickening of the soul by the Holy Ghost (Ps. lxxx. 18). 2. *The forwardness of Christians to engage in Christian work might be expected on many grounds.* Gratitude to God, if nothing else, should constrain them (Ps. cxvi. 12). Love to Christ might impel them (2 Cor. v. 14, 15). The nobility of the work might attract them; it would be walking in the footsteps of Christ (Acts. x. 38). The splendour of the reward might induce them (Dan. xii. 3; Matt. xxv. 40; 1 Cor. xv. 58; Rev. ii. 10; xiv. 13). The clamant need there is for such work might move them (1 John v. 19). The good it would do might urge them (Titus iii. 8).

III. ARDENT ENTHUSIASM. They came and *did* work. Not merely "putting in the time," as the workmen's phrase is; or simply dragging on with heartless indifference; or hurrying up the job with utmost speed and in careless fashion, anxious to get it done, no matter how; but toiling honestly and earnestly, with a business-like energy and determination, doing good work, and doing it with a will. Such had been the manner in which the tabernacle-makers worked; such should be the style of working in the Christian Church. 1. *The Founder of the Christian Church was an enthusiastic Worker.* From the commencement of his ministry (Mark iv. 23; John ii. 17) to its close (Luke ix. 51; xii. 50), Jesus was consumed with a burning devotion to his work of glorifying God and blessing men. 2. *The apostles and early preachers of the Christian Church were enthusiastic workers.* The eleven (Mark xvi. 20); the twelve (Acts v. 42); Paul (Phil. iii. 13); Apollos (Acts xviii. 25); Epaphroditus (Phil. ii. 27). 3. *The Christian Church has in almost every age possessed workers of a like spirit.* Ministers, like Augustine, Athanasius, Chrysostom, Cyril, Calvin, Knox, Latimer, Baxter, Wesley, Chalmers; missionaries, like St. Augustine, St. Columba, St. Aidan, St. Mungo, Brainerd, Martyn, Carey, Williams, Moffat, Livingstone; private Christians, like the late Earl of Shaftesbury and others.

IV. INDOMITABLE PERSEVERANCE. Too soon discouraged on the first occasion by the angry speeches and malicious threats of their enemies, on this occasion the temple-builders met their adversaries with a bold front (Ezra v. 11), and rested not until they brought the work to completion (Zech. iv. 7, 9). Perseverance: 1. *A characteristic of all sincere Christian workers.* Exemplified in the history of Jesus, of Peter and John, of Paul, and of others who have followed in their steps. 2. *A necessary condition of all true success in Christian working.* The greater the work, the more does it demand patient perseverance. Enterprises that can be carried through with a rush and an effort are seldom of moment. 3. *A certain guarantee of ultimate success.* The man who perseveres wins—in ordinary life commonly, in religious life certainly.

CONCLUSION. The Christian worker's encouragement. "I am with you, saith the Lord" (ver. 13; cf. Matt. xxviii. 20). 1. For aid, to help you with needed strength in your labours (Ps. cxxvii. 1; Isa. xli. 10; Zech. xii. 1). 2. For protection, to defend you against the machinations of your adversaries (Ezra v. 5; Ps. xci. 1—7; Prov. ii. 7; Zech. ii. 5; 1 Pet. iii. 13; Rev. iii. 10). 3. For approbation, to accept your service when it is finished (ch. ii. 9).

HOMILIES BY VARIOUS AUTHORS.

Ver. 1.—*The introduction.* The Bible student, with a view to the clear understanding of the Old Testament Scriptures, should fix in his mind the order of the prophetical writings. These books of prophecy may appropriately be arranged under three heads. 1. Those which stand related to the Assyrian period, including the books of Jonah, Joel, Amos, Hosea, Isaiah, Micah, and Nahum. 2. Those connected with the Babylonian period, including Habakkuk, Zephaniah, Jeremiah, Daniel, Ezekiel, and Obadiah. 3. Those associated with the return from the exile: Haggai, Zechariah, Malachi. The introduction of this brief prophecy by Haggai suggests to us—

I. THE CHANGES MARKED BY THE REVOLVING WHEEL OF TIME. We are able, through this opening verse, to fix the exact date of this prophecy. It was "in the second year of Darius the king" that Haggai fulfilled this special mission, *i.e.* B.C. 521. Hence upwards of a century had passed away since Zephaniah had declared so faithfully the terrible Divine judgments which should overtake the nation on account of its guilt. His words had proved strictly true, and had been very literally and completely fulfilled. The land had been rendered utterly desolate; its cities had been entirely destroyed; its temple reduced to a heap of ruins; and its people carried away into exile. No King of Judah was referred to by Haggai in commencing his book, for the simple reason that the throne had fallen, and he had to recognize the authority of a Persian sovereign, and to speak of his favoured land as a province of a foreign power (ver. 1). The dispersion, however, had in a measure been followed by the regathering. Zephaniah had prophesied respecting the return of "a remnant," and his prophecy had, in a sense, now been fulfilled, for Cyrus permitted the Jews to colonize their own land, and a number had availed themselves of this permission, and had now spent some years in the land given to their fathers, seeking to repair the waste and desolation which the march of events and the lapse of time had wrought.

II. THE WILL OF GOD AS COMMUNICATED THROUGH HUMAN INSTRUMENTALITY. The returned exiles commenced well. Their first concern had reference to the rebuilding of the house of the Lord, and with all possible speed they laid the foundation of the second temple. They were, however, weak and poor; they laboured amidst untold difficulties and discouragements, and it is not surprising that, their hearts becoming downcast and depressed, their ardour declined and their zeal languished. They needed stimulus; they required some message from the Lord their God declarative of his will and purpose; and this need was supplied, for they heard "a voice from heaven" speaking unto them through Haggai and Zechariah (Hag. i. 1, 2; Zech. i. 1). In every age God has communicated his will and intention through the instrumentality of man. He has made holy men, full of human sympathies, the medium of communicating his purposes. His agents in this instance, as ever, were admirably chosen. Haggai was advanced in life; he had probably seen the former temple; he was a link connecting the old with the new, and brought to bear upon the difficulties of the times a ripened and matured experience; whilst Zechariah was young, and with all the enthusiasm and warmth of youth. They worked together in perfect harmony and for the common good, their prophecies being at times admirably interwoven. There are two elements in the Bible—the Divine and the human. God speaks to us in every page, and he does so all the more emphatically, in that he addresses us through men who possessed throbbing hearts and who passed through experiences like our own.

III. THE RAISING UP IN THE ORDER OF PROVIDENCE OF EFFICIENT LEADERS TO DIRECT GREAT MOVEMENTS. "The word of the Lord came by Haggai the prophet *unto Zerubbabel the son of Shealtiel, Governor of Judah, and to Joshua the son of Josedech, the high priest*" (ver. 1). Zerubbabel, of royal descent from David, and Joshua, who was in the priestly line, had secured the confidence and esteem of the Jewish community in the land of captivity; and the former had won the regard of Cyrus, the Persian monarch; so that when the time for the return came, leaders, esteemed alike by the Jews and their foreign rulers, were prepared to guide the movement and to carry it through successfully. God's work shall never fail through lack of suitable agents to do his bidding, but he will raise up a bright succession of leal-hearted men to carry on his cause, until the ruin and desolation wrought by sin has been completely repaired, and the top-stone of the temple of redeemed humanity be "brought forth" amidst rapturous praise.—S. D. H.

Ver. 2.—*Procrastination.* "This people say, The time is not come, the time that the Lord's house should be built." There are several ways of accounting for the delay which occurred in the work of re-erecting the temple in Jerusalem. 1. In part it arose from the returned exiles being preoccupied in seeking to secure to themselves material prosperity. 2. Then they were daunted by the opposition they had to encounter as they engaged in this work. The powerful neighbouring tribes, being alike antagonistic to the restoration of Jerusalem as the centre of the pure and unadulterated worship of God, combined to place obstacles in the way of the repairers of the breaches. 3. Further, they had grown somewhat accustomed to being without the structure. Comparatively few of them had seen "the first house." 4. It is to be feared also that they had lost, through the changes they had experienced, that strong sense of the need of the Divine abiding presence in their midst. Influenced by such considerations as these, and forgetful that "good is best when soonest wrought," they kept postponing carrying out the great undertaking to which they had pledged themselves, and excused themselves by saying, "The time is not come," etc. (ver. 2). This habit of delay is far too general, and is not limited to any age or race. It prevails widely to-day as in all past times; and in no respect more so than in matters affecting man's relation to God. Time was when man was wholly devoted to his Maker's praise. God formed him in his own image, holy, spotless, pure; but he mournfully fell. He who had been the temple of God became a moral waste. "Ichabod" became inscribed upon the once consecrated spiritual man. . Every power of the soul became corrupt, every propensity became drawn to that which is evil. "The gold became dim, and the most fine gold changed." And the voice of God calls us to the glorious work of rebuilding this temple. He has presented to us, in the perfect life of his own Son, the pattern after which we should seek to raise in ourselves the superstructure of a holy life, and offers us his gracious aid so that we may build into our character the noble materials of truth and virtue, wisdom and love. And it is just at this point that the temptation to delay meets men. 1. They are not insensible to the claims of God, nor are they altogether indifferent about attending to these, but they say, "The time is not come," etc. (ver. 3). 2. They are immersed in other matters at present: (1) the cares of the world; (2) the pursuit of riches; (3) the pleasures of life, absorb them; they are pre-occupied just now; they say, "The time is not come" (ver. 3). 3. They reason that there is the whole future yet before them, and that ample opportunity will be given them in due course. So they go on robbing themselves of "aspirations high and deathless hopes sublime."

> "Procrastination is the thief of time;
> Year after year it steals, till all are fled,
> And to the mercies of a moment leaves
> The vast concerns of an eternal scene."

S. D. H.

Vers. 3—11.—*The stirring appeal.* It must not be supposed that, for purposes of revelation, there was any suspension of the powers of the men who were honoured of God in being the medium of communicating a knowledge of his will; rather there was the retention of their own individual peculiarities and natural gifts, the Divine Spirit operating through these, and turning them to the most profitable account. One beauty of the Bible lies in the fact that, whilst upon the writings of each of its contributors there is unmistakably the impress of the operation of the Spirit of God, there is likewise throughout the whole clear indications of the preservation of those natural endowments which the respective writers possessed, and hence the remarkable variety in style and form of presentation meeting us in the Holy Word, and which constitutes one great charm of the volume. Viewing this particular book of Scripture from this human standpoint, biblical writers have described it as being inferior in respect of literary merit as compared with other prophetical writings; and it must be granted that we find lacking here "the poetical swing" and "the finished beauty" characteristic of "the earlier prophetical diction." The circumstances, however, under which he gave utterance to his message will account for this. It did not devolve upon him to any extent, as it had done upon his predecessors, to make prophetic announcements concerning the future age; his simple mission was to stimulate and stir a lethargic people to renewed action, to reprove them for their neglect of solemn duty, and to impel them to fulfil their trust. And whatever there may be lacking here of poetic genius, the picture presented to us of this noble-hearted man standing " in grey-haired might " amidst the ruins of Jerusalem, and, strong in conviction that the favour and blessing of Jehovah was the great essential in order to the happiness of his people, urging them to acknowledge him in all their ways, and without further delay to rear his sanctuary, is one truly beautiful, and which we could have ill spared from these holy records. Consider his stirring appeal.

I. HIS SUMMONS TO REFLECTION. " Consider your ways " (vers. 5, 7); *i.e.* " Set your heart upon your ways "—your conduct, actions, designs, purposes. Thoughtlessness is the source of so much evil. Men do not always intend to do wrong or to fail in respect of duty, but they do not " give heed." They allow their minds to wander into other courses, and to be preoccupied with other matters.

> " Evil is wrought by want of thought,
> As well as want of heart."

It is in view of men's highest interests, then, that God by his providential dealings, or the ministry of his servants, or the inward voice of conscience, says to them at times, " Consider your ways." We should consider: 1. Whether our ways are true and right. 2. How they stand affected to the claims which God has upon us. 3. The motives by which we are being influenced. 4. The results to which our actions are tending, whether the sowing is such as will yield a harvest of good. The momentous importance of the admonition is seen in its repetition here. Man is wondrously free. He can choose good or evil. This freedom increases his responsibility, and the sense of this should lead to frequent self-examination. " Let each man prove his own work " (Gal. vi. 4).

II. THE WEIGHTY CONSIDERATIONS HE URGED UPON THEIR ARRESTED ATTENTION. Their great excuse for the unwarrantable delay which had taken place in the work of rebuilding the temple was the hardness of the times; and in his stimulating address Haggai kept this excuse before his mind, and completely exposed to them its hollowness, and swept it away by setting before them two important facts. 1. He brought home to them a *sense of their own inconsistency.* Hard though the times were, the fact remained that in these hard times they had built for themselves durable dwellings, and had enriched these with costly adornments; and surely if they could do all this for themselves, they might have done something by way of proceeding with the erection of the house of the Lord (ver. 4). Clearly they had lacked not so much the ability as the disposition to do their duty. 2. Admitting the severity of the times, Haggai pointed out that the way in which to have improved these would have been by their discharging more faithfully their duty to their God. In vivid language he described the depressed state of things then prevailing (ver. 6), but his contention was that God had visited them with such adverse experiences in retribution. They had forgotten his claims, and had selfishly cared only for their own interests; and he, knowing their hearts and observing their ways, had withheld from them the dews of heaven, and had caused drought to prevail, that by failure and loss they might be led to reflection and to a truer and more devoted life (vers. 9—11). When the times are hard—trade slack and commercial depression prevailing—men too often begin retrenchment by withholding from God his due, and long before they sacrifice a single luxury of life will they plead inability to sustain his cause. Wiser far would it be for them to give full recognition to him and to his claims, and, whilst thus honouring him, to look to him for his blessing and the renewal of the temporal blessings of his providence.

III. THE PROMPT ACTION, IN VIEW OF THESE THOUGHTS, UPON WHICH HE SO STRONGLY INSISTED. " Go up to the mountain," etc. (ver. 8). This stirring appeal of the prophet was made on " the sixth month, in the first day of the month " (ver. 1), *i.e.* the new moon's day. That day was a special day amongst the people. A festal sacrifice was offered (Numb. xxviii. 11—15), and a solemn assembly of the people at the sanctuary took place (Isa. i. 13; 2 Kings iv. 23). On this occasion, therefore, we may suppose the people as gathered together on the site of the temple, the bare foundations of which silently testified against their inertness, and the prophet appearing amongst them, addressing words of stern reproof to them, and then bidding them without longer delay go to the mountains and fetch the cedars, and build forthwith the house for God. Such he declared to be the will of God, obedience to which, on their part, would yield pleasure to the Most High, and bring glory to his Name, and would result in the promotion of their own temporal and spiritual well-being (ver. 8).— S. D. H.

Ver. 4.— *The house of the Lord lying waste.* The temple was designed to be the centre of hallowed influence to the Jewish nation. It was the recognized dwelling-place of God, the shrine where, in bright symbol, his glory was specially revealed. The pious Jew rejoiced to repair to it, and wherever his lot might be cast he looked towards it with ardent and longing desire. The desecration of it by the introduction of idolatrous practices into its courts had materially contributed to the nation's collapse. It was of the utmost importance, therefore, that the work of its restoration should be pressed forward with all zest, now that the captives had been permitted to return, and at first it seemed as though this course would have been pursued, but unhappily they soon allowed their zeal to flag, and year after year passed by and nothing was done. The house of the Lord lay "waste." The Divine Teacher, when he came to usher in a new dispensation, declared that God is a Spirit, and is to be worshipped "in spirit and in truth" (John iv. 23, 24). He taught that place has but little to do with worship, and that there is no spot we may not consecrate by our praises and prayers, and render to us "hallowed ground." Still, he constantly resorted to the temple, and we read of his apostles how that they went up to the temple "at the hour of prayer" (Acts iii. 1). The erection and maintenance of Christian sanctuaries is most thoroughly in harmony with his will, and is calculated to promote the truest interests of the race. Close all such sanctuaries, and (1) good men would be left to sigh for the holy fellowship they had lost; (2) spiritual darkness would steal over the land; (3) the streams of true benevolence would rapidly diminish; (4) men in general, losing sight of the common relationship they sustain to the Eternal, would also overlook the interest they ought to feel in each other's weal; (5) iniquity would pass unreproved, and vice unchecked. As lovers of God, our country, and our fellow-men, we do well to sustain Christian sanctuaries, and not to allow them to "lie waste." Notice, "the house of the Lord" may "lie waste"—

I. IN THE SENSE OF THE MATERIAL STRUCTURE BEING NEGLECTED. There should be correspondence in respect of beauty and adornment, comfort and cleanliness, between the houses in which we live and the sanctuary in which we meet for worship, and where this is lacking, the want indicates a wrong state of mind and heart.

II. IN THE SENSE OF ITS PECUNIARY RESOURCES BEING OVERLOOKED, AND THERE BEING THUS STRAITNESS IN RESPECT TO MEETING THE EXPENSES NECESSARILY INCURRED IN ITS MAINTENANCE. Giving should be regarded as an act of worship. "Bring an offering, and come into his courts" (Ps. xcvi. 8). Contributions for the maintenance of the worship of God ought not to be regarded in the light of charitable gifts, but as the discharge of bounden obligation.

III. IN THE SENSE OF ITS SEATS BEING UNOCCUPIED. There is far too much of "waste" in this respect. The growing habit of attending only one of the services on the sabbath, and none during the week-days, needs to be checked. Personal influence should be brought more to bear upon the inhabitants of a locality with a view to securing their presence. "Come, let us go up to the house of the Lord" (Ps. cxxii. 1).

IV. IN THE SENSE OF THE EXERCISES CONDUCTED THEREIN BEING MARKED BY BALD-NESS AND INEFFICIENCY. The services should be marked by culture, variety, heart; the worshippers should throw their whole souls into all its engagements, and render each part of the service "heartily" and as "unto the Lord."

V. IN THE SENSE OF PAUCITY OF SPIRITUAL RESULTS. With a view to the prevention of this, let us "pray for Jerusalem," that its services may yield comfort to the mourning and guidance to the perplexed, and that through these the cold in heart may regain the fervour of their "first love," and "the dead in trespasses and sins" be quickened to a new and heavenly life. "Save now, O Lord; O Lord, we beseech thee send us now prosperity" (Ps. cxviii. 25); "Repair the waste places of Zion" (Isa. lviii. 12); "Build thou the walls of Jerusalem" (Ps. li. 18).—S. D. H.

Vers. 12—15.—*The hearty response.* The human spirit is so backward in respect to the performance of the duties and the fulfilment of the obligations it is under in relation to the higher life, that it requires stimulus, and acts of renewed dedication to the service of God cannot fail to be spiritually helpful. There are moments in life when we become specially impressed as God's servants with a sense of his claims to our most devoted service, and when holy emotions rise within us, moving us to a more unreserved consecration of ourselves to his service. And we do well to make these impressions permanent by placing upon them the stamp of holy resolution. It is wonderful how soon, if we do not take this course, these impressions and emotions vanish. We should therefore foster all holy impulses, and take advantage of at once of all emotions and aspirations which would constrain us to render to the Lord our God a truer service than we have rendered in the past. Such impressions are buds we should not nip, sparks of heavenly fire we should not extinguish, the breathings of God's own Spirit, from the influence of which it is at our peril that we remove ourselves. The interest in these closing verses (12—15) lies in that they present to us a bright example of this wise course being pursued. The earnest address of the aged seer touched the hearts of his hearers; they became painfully conscious of past omission and shortcoming and neglect of duty, and were led to consecrate themselves anew to the service of him who had brought them up out of captivity and to their own land.

I. THE SPIRIT THAT WAS CHERISHED. 1. It was the spirit of obedience. "They obeyed the voice of the Lord their God, and the words of Haggai the prophet" (ver. 12). 2. It was the spirit of reverential fear. "And the people did fear before the Lord" (ver. 12). "Whom God would make strong for his service he first subdues to his fear." 3. This obedient and devout spirit was cherished by *all.* Zerubbabel the governor, Joshua the high priest, and all the remnant of the people alike made this full surrender of themselves to the service of their God (ver. 14).

II. THE EFFECTS THAT FOLLOWED. 1. *The Divine favour was experienced.* Haggai was again commissioned to speak to them in the name of the Lord, and to say to them for God, as his messenger, "I *am with you,* saith the Lord" (ver. 13). The abiding sense of God's presence with them had made the heroes of their nation the men they were. Moses could face the whole Israelitish tribes when they were murmuring against him and against Aaron; David could confront the mail-clad Goliath; Daniel could be steadfast in the performance of his religious duties despite the lions; Ezekiel could utter burning denunciations against ungodly nations;—because they realized in their inmost hearts the consciousness of the presence and power of God. And now this same presence was pledged to them, and in the Divine might they would be able to overcome every obstacle. The promptness with which this assurance was given is instructive. "God is waiting to be gracious, and will meet the returning wanderer even before his hand has begun the work of service." 2. *The spiritual life was quickened.* "The Lord *stirred up* the spirit of Zerubbabel," etc. (ver. 14). He gave new life to them all, so that they were ready with zeal and alacrity and with holy courage to do his bidding. 3. *The good work was advanced.* "And they came and did work in the house of the Lord of hosts, their God" (ver. 14).— S. D. H.

Vers. 1, 2.—*Duty revealed.* "In the second year of Darius the king, in the sixth month, in the first day of the month, came the word of the Lord by Haggai the prophet unto Zerubbabel the son of Shealtiel, Governor of Judah, and to Joshua the son of Josedech, the high priest, saying, Thus speaketh the Lord of hosts, saying, This people say, The time is not come, the time that the Lord's house should be built." Haggai is the first of the three prophets who lived and taught after the restoration of the Jews from the Babylonian captivity. It is generally supposed that he returned with the Hebrew exiles under Zerubbabel and Joshua the high priest, in the year B.C. 536. He prophesied in the reign of Darius Hystaspes, who ascended the Persian throne B.C. 521. He and Zechariah were employed by Jehovah to excite and encourage the

Jews to the rebuilding of the temple. This book consists of four messages, which were delivered in three months of the year B.C. 520, and all refer to the work of temple restoration. His style, being somewhat interrogatory, has much vigour and vehemence. The grand subject of this whole chapter is *duty*—duty *revealed*, duty *postponed*, duty *vindicated*. These two verses direct us to the revelation of duty. Here we have: 1. The *time* of its revelation. Every duty has its time, every true work has its hour. Woe to us if that hour is neglected! 2. The *organ* of its revelation. "Came the word of the Lord by Haggai." God speaks to humanity through individual men whom in sovereignty he appoints. In all ages there are certain great men through whom God speaks to the world. They are his messengers. 3. The *order* of its revelation. Haggai had to deliver the message to men nearest to him, with whom he was most identified, and the men, too, who had the most power in influencing others. To the greatest man in the state, Zerubbabel; to the greatest man in the Church, Joshua. I make two remarks as suggested by this subject.

I. DUTY IS THE BURDEN OF DIVINE REVELATION. The great purpose of Haggai's mission was, in the name of God, to urge his countrymen to the fulfilment of a work which was morally incumbent on them, viz. the rebuilding of the temple. It was the purpose of God that the temple should be rebuilt, and he required the Jews to do that work. He could have restored the structure by a miracle or by the hands of others; but he imposed the building of it on the Jewish people for reasons best known to himself. What was the burden of Haggai's mission is in truth the burden of the whole Divine revelation—*duty*. It contains, it is true, histories of facts, effusions of poetry, discussions of doctrine; but the grand all-pervading substance of the whole is duty; its grand voice teaches, not merely to believe and feel, but *to do*; it regards faith and feeling as worthless unless taken up and embodied in the right act. It presents the *rule* of duty, it supplies the *helps* to duty, it urges the *motives* to duty. This fact shows two things. 1. *That the Bible studies the real well-being of man.* According to our constitution, our strength, dignity, and blessedness consist, not merely in our ideas and emotions, but in our settled character. But what is character? Not an assemblage of beliefs and emotions, but an assemblage of acts and habits. 2. *That unpractised religion is spurious.* There is the religion of *creed*, of *sentimentality*, of *sacerdotalism*, of *routine*. These are all spurious; it is the *doer of the Word* that is blessed; it is the doer of the Divine will that God approves. "Every one that heareth these sayings of mine, and doeth them not," etc. (Matt. vii. 26).

II. DUTY IS INCREASED BY SOCIAL ELEVATION. This is implied in the circumstance that Haggai went directly with the message from God to the most influential men in the state, to "Zerubbabel the son of Shealtiel, Governor of Judah, and to Joshua the son of Josedech, the high priest." The former was one of the head men in the *state*, the commander-in-chief at the head of the Jews in their return from their captivity in Babylon; the latter was the head man in the *Church*, he was the high priest. It was the duty of all the Jews to set to the work; but the obligation of these men, on account of their high position, had an increased force. These men had greater opportunities of knowing the Divine will, and greater facilities for carrying it out. The influence of men in high position is a great talent that God requires to be used. This fact serves two purposes. 1. *To supply a warning to men in high places.* The man who is in a high position, and disregards his great responsibilities, is more an object of pity than envy. "Unto whom much is given, of him much will be required." Elevated positions in life invest men with an immense social power—power which God intended to bless, but which is often used to curse men. 2. *A lesson to ministers.* Let the ambassadors of Heaven carry their messages first, if possible, to men in authority. Do not be afraid; none need your message more; none, if they receive it in faith, can render you better assistance in the great work of spiritual reformation. It is common to lecture the poor on duty. How seldom the Divine voice of duty is made to ring into the hearts of men in authority and power!—D. T.

Vers. 3, 4.—*Duty adjourned.* "Then came the word of the Lord by Haggai the prophet, saying, Is it time for you, O ye, to dwell in your ceiled houses, and this house lie waste?" The seventy years of the Babylonian captivity had passed away. The Babylonian empire had fallen; and Cyrus, the founder of the Persian empire, gave the

Jews permission to return to their land, and commanded them to rebuild the temple of Jehovah in Jerusalem. Hence fifty thousand captives, with their menservants and maidservants, went forth, led by Zerubbabel and by the high priest Joshua, to their own lands. Forthwith on their arrival they commenced restoring the altar of burnt offering and re-establishing the sacrificial worship, and began to lay the foundation of the new temple. The Samaritans speedily interfered and impeded their progress. Because the chiefs of Judah would not accept their co-operation in the undertaking, they set themselves to the work of obstruction. They made the hand of the people of Judah idle, as we read, in frightening them while building, and hiring counsellors against them to frustrate their design, so that the work at the house of God at Jerusalem ceased and was suspended until the second year of the reign of King Darius of Persia (Ezra iv. 24). Hereupon the zeal of the Jews so cooled down that they relinquished the work altogether, and simply began to provide for their own necessities and to build their own houses. Hence Heaven employs Haggai to rouse them again from their wickedness. The subject of these verses is the *adjournment of duty*. "The time is not come, the time that the Lord's house should be built." They do not question the *desirableness* or the *obligation* of the work. This indeed seems to be assumed. During the Captivity, we are told elsewhere that they hanged their harps upon the willows, and wept when they "remembered Zion." Often, perhaps, in those circumstances did they resolve, should they ever be restored, to rebuild that temple which was the glory of the land; but now that they are there on the spot, and the ruins lying before them, their ardour is cooled, and they say, "The time is not come." We see three evils coming out here, which, perhaps, are always connected with the *adjournment of duty*.

I. COWARDICE. They did not say, "We will *not* build the temple, we will leave it to remain in ruins;" they were too cowardly for that. Their consciences rendered them incapable of making such a decision. Men who neglect duty are too cowardly to say, "We will never attend to it, we will never study the Scriptures, worship God." 1. Sin is *cowardice*. 2. Sin is cowardice because *conscience*, the truly heroic element, is ever against it.

II. SELFISHNESS. What was it that prompted them to adjourn this duty? The answer is at hand, *Selfishness*. "Is it time for you, O ye, to dwell in your ceiled houses, and this house lie waste?" They set to work for their own *private* interests. Virtually they said, "We must build houses for *ourselves* first, for all is in ruin about us; we must cultivate our own land first; we must attend to our own business, and after all that is completed we will see to the temple." 1. *Selfishness is a perversion of self-love.* 2. *Selfishness is fatal to self-interest.*

III. PRESUMPTION. "The time is not come." How did they know that? Were they judges of times and seasons? Had they the hardihood to suppose that circumstances can set aside or modify our obligations? Are they imperious enough to plead Providence as a patron of their disobedience? "Go to, now, ye that say, To-day and to-morrow" (Jas. iv. 13). 1. Such presumption is always *guilty*. It implies that we know better than our Maker about times and seasons. 2. Such presumption is always *perilous*. It treads upon an awful precipice.—D. T.

Vers. 5—11.—*Duty divinely vindicated.* "Now therefore thus saith the Lord of hosts; Consider your ways. Ye have sown much, and bring in little; ye eat, but ye have not enough; ye drink, but ye are not filled with drink; ye clothe you, but there is none warm; and he that earneth wages earneth wages to put it into a bag with holes," etc. Their efforts to improve their secular condition were all *unsuccessful*. The ground brought forth little, etc. Why was this? Not because they did not work; not because either the soil or the seed was bad. The reason was a moral one— they neglected the great duty that Heaven had enjoined upon them, the rebuilding of the temple. They neglected this, and the curse of Heaven rested as a mildew upon all their operations. Had they rightly discharged this duty, prosperity would have attended all their efforts. *Real success in any labour, so as to obtain happiness, depends upon the spiritual state of the soul.* This is a point which has, perhaps, seldom occupied your attention; nevertheless, it is a point of overwhelming moment. It is common for men to refer success to industry, ingenuity, fortune, luck, or some such cause; the real cause of success or failure is to be referred to the moral state of the soul.

They were selfish motives that brought secular disasters to the Jews now. The verses teach us that *duty is vindicated by the Divine government.* We offer two remarks here.

I. THAT THE DIVINE GOVERNMENT RECOGNIZES THE SELFISH MOTIVES THAT ACTUATE MEN. Men are governed in everything by motive. Motive is the mainspring that keeps the world in action; motive is the fountain from which all the streams of life proceed; motive is the germ from which springs every branch and leaf of the great tree of character. We judge each other from appearance; God, from motives. God sees theft, blasphemy, and all other crimes where they have never been expressed in words or acts. This Divine inspection of motives argues three things. 1. *The necessity of moral reformation in the world.* If all pertaining to human life springs from motive, and the motives of the world are depraved, then the grand necessity of the world is reformation. Knowledge, civilization, refinement, social order, mercantile prosperity, wholesome legislation,—these will be of no real service where the motives are bad. Hence the great Reformer has said, "Ye must be born again." To accomplish this reformation is the great aim of the gospel. It is the fire to burn up false motives, it is the axe to strike the upas at the roots. 2. *The necessity for attending more to the spiritual than the formal in the Church.* It is not conformity to standards of faith, however scriptural, attention to rituals, however æsthetic and impressive, the repetition of prayers, however beautiful in language, devout in sentiment, and correct in doctrine; it is not, in fact, in any externalism that religion consists or that God delights; it is in holy *motive.* "Neither circumcision . . . nor uncircumcision," etc. (Gal. v. 6). In all true worship man is at once the temple, the sacrifice, and the priest. When will the time come that men shall regard the Church, not as a piece of timber carved into certain forms by the hand of art, remaining the same from age to age, but as a living tree, working itself by the power of its own life into living forms with every season that passes over it? 3. *The possibility of solemn disclosures on the last day.* Here men conceal their real hearts from each other. We only know each other after the flesh. Sometimes here Providence takes off the mask from those whom we thought friends, and we recoil from their hideousness with horror. At the last day all will be uncovered. "The hidden things of darkness will be brought to light" (1 Cor. iv. 5). What a revelation on that day!

II. THAT THE DIVINE GOVERNOR AVENGES THE SELFISH MOTIVES OF ACTION. "Ye looked for much, and, lo, it came to little." The passage shows two ways in which God opposes the labour of selfish men. 1. *He neutralizes the results of their labour.* "I will blow upon it." The man may realize the means which he thought would make him happy; God will hinder it from doing so. One selfish man may get wealth in abundance; another may acquire vast treasures of knowledge; another, immense power in society; yet in all cases there may be unhappiness, because God "blows" upon the whole. In fact, nothing can make a *selfish* man happy. 2. *He renders ineffective the materials of their labour.* Labour always employs three things—*agent, instrument,* and *materials.* The materials of labour are here specified—"light," "air," "water," "earth." On these men operate. Out of these we weave our clothing, of them we construct our dwellings. God acts upon these and renders them all ineffective for happiness. "Therefore the heaven over you is stayed from dew, and the earth is stayed from her fruit. And I called for a drought upon the land." (1) *God directs the universe;* not necessity, not chance. (2) God directs the universe *for mind.* (3) God directs the universe so as to meet the *state of every heart.* "To the pure all things are pure."—D. T.

EXPOSITION.

CHAPTER II.

Ver. 1—ch. ii. 9.—Part II. THE SECOND ADDRESS: THE GLORY OF THE NEW TEMPLE.

Vers. 1—5.—§ 1. *The prophet comforts those who grieve at the comparative poverty*

of the new building with the assurance of the Divine protection and favour.

Ver. 1.—In the seventh month, in the one and twentieth day of the month. The seventh month is Ethanim or Tisri, answering to parts of September and October. The twenty-first was the last and great day of the Feast of Tabernacles (Lev. xxiii. 34, etc.), when it was the custom to celebrate the ingathering of the harvest. The joyous nature of this festival was sadly marred on this occasion. Their crops were scanty, and they had no temple in whose courts they might assemble to pay their vows and offer their thank-offerings. The building which had begun to make some progress only the more showed its poverty. Everything tended to make them contrast the present with the past. But God mercifully relieves their despondency with a new message. **By the prophet Haggai** (see note on ch. i. 1).

Ver. 2.—**Speak now to Zerubbabel.** The message is addressed to the heads of the nation, temporal and spiritual, and to all the people who had returned (see notes on ch. i. 1 and 12).

Ver. 3.—**Who is left among you?** etc. It is quite possible that there should be some old people present who had seen Solomon's temple. Many have thought that Haggai himself was of the number. It was sixty-eight years ago that the temple was destroyed, and we can well believe that its remarkable features were deeply impressed on the minds of those who as boys or youths had loved and admired it. Ezra tells us (iii. 12) that "many of the priests and Levites [when the foundation first was laid] and chief of the fathers, who were ancient men, that had seen the first house, . . . wept with a loud voice." **This house.** The prophet identifies the present with Solomon's temple, as being adapted for the same purposes, to fill the same place in the national life, built on the same hallowed spot, and partly with the same materials. In the Jews' eyes there was one only temple, whatever might be the date of its erection or the comparative worth of its decorations and materials. **First;** *former,* as ver. 9. **How do ye see it now?** (Numb. xiii. 18). In what condition do ye see this house now? **Is it not in your eyes in comparison of it as nothing?** The words, "in comparison of it," ought to be omitted, as not required by the Hebrew idiom. Does it not seem in your eyes as if it had no existence? If the injunction of Cyrus (Ezra i. 3, etc.) had been carried out, the dimensions of the new temple would have exceeded those of the old; but Zerubbabel seems to have been unable, with the small resources at his disposal, to execute the original design, though even so the proportions were not greatly inferior to those of the earlier temple. But the chief inferiority lay in the absence of the splendour and enrichment with which Solomon adorned his edifice. The gold which he had

lavished on the house was no longer available; the precious stones could not be had. Besides these defects, the Talmudists reckon five things wanting in this second temple, viz. the ark of the covenant, with the cherubim and mercy-seat; the holy fire; the Shechinah; the spirit of prophecy; the Urim and Thummim. It was, according to Josephus, only half the height of Solomon's—sixty cubits ('Ant.,' xv. 11. 1), and it appears to have been in many respects inferior to the first building ('Ant.,' iv. 2). Hecabæus of Abdera gives the dimensions of the courts as five hundred feet in length and a hundred cubits in breadth (double the width of the court of the tabernacle), and the size of the altar as twenty cubits square and ten cubits high (see Josephus, 'Cont. Ap.,' i. 22; Conder, 'Handbook to the Bible,' p. 370).

Ver. 4.—**Be strong.** This is repeated three times for emphasis' sake. The same exhortation was given by David to Solomon before the building of the first temple (1 Chron. xxviii. 10; comp. Josh. i. 6, 7, 9). Haggai seems to suggest comfort in the thought that such admonition was needed at that time as well as now when they are so depressed (comp. Zech. viii. 9). **And work;** literally, *and do;* ποιεῖτε: *facite.* The word is used absolutely, as often (comp. Isa. xliv. 23; Amos iii. 6, and note there). Here it means, "Work on bravely, finish what you have begun." **I am with you** (see ch. i. 13, and note there). The consciousness of God's presence gives confidence and strength.

Ver. 5.—According to **the word that I covenanted.** The Hebrew is simply, "the word that I," etc. Hence some have connected it with the verb "do" in the preceding verse, the intervening words being parenthetical. But there is intended no injunction respecting the observation of the old covenant, but a consolatory message under present despondency. Others take it with the verb that follows: "the word and my Spirit remain among you." But it is best to leave the clause in the abrupt fashion in which it is introduced: "(Here is, here stands) the word that I covenanted with you." If anything is supplied, we might insert, "I will confirm." The promise of present help is confirmed by the remembrance of God's former covenant with Israel, that they should be his peculiar people, and possess the right of access to him and a claim on his help (Exod. xix. 5, 6; xxix. 45, 46; Deut. vii. 6; Jer. vii. 23). This clause is entirely omitted by the Septuagint. **So my Spirit remaineth among you;** Revised Version, *and my Spirit abode among you.* But the clause refers to God's presence among them now, which was shown by the revelations made to the prophets, as Haggai and Zechariah, and which exhibits itself in his providential ordering of events, the removal of obstacles, the furthering of the good work. Wordsworth notes that "Christ was with the ancient Church in the wilderness (see 1 Cor. x. 9; Heb. xi. 26); and now, when the eternal *Word* became incarnate, and when the *Holy Spirit* was sent to be *in the midst* of God's faithful people, then this prophecy was fulfilled." **Fear not.** "If God be for us, who can be against us?" (Rom. viii. 31; and comp. Zech. iv. 6).

Vers. 6—9.—§ 2. *The prophet, to reconcile the people to the new temple, and to teach them to value it highly, foretells a future time, when the glory of this house shall far exceed that of Solomon's, adumbrating the Messianic era.*

Ver. 6.—Yet once, it is a little while; ἔτι ἅπαξ (Septuagint); *Adhuc unum modicum est* (Vulgate), The writer of the Epistle to the Hebrews (xii. 26, 27) quotes and founds an argument on this rendering of the LXX. The expression is equivalent to "once again within a little time." **I will shake,** etc. Some difference of opinion exists as to the events here adumbrated. All, however, agree in seeing an allusion to the promulgation of the Law on Mount Sinai, which was accompanied with certain great physical commotions (see Exod. xix. 16; Ps. lxviii. 7, 8), when, too, the Egyptians were "shaken" by the plagues sent on them, and the neighbouring nations, Philistia, Edom, Moab, were struck with terror (Exod. xv. 14—16). This was a great moral disturbance in the heathen world; the next and final "shaking" will be under the Messianic dispensation for which the destruction of heathen kingdoms prepares the way. The Israelites would soon see the beginnings of this visitation, *e.g.* in the fall of Babylon, and might thence conclude that all would be accomplished in due time. The prophet calls this interval "a little while" (which it is in God's eyes and in view of the vast future), in order to console the people and teach them patience and confidence. The final consummation and the steps that lead to it in the prophet's vision are blended together, just as our Lord combines his prediction about the destruction of Jerusalem with details which concern the end of the world. The physical convulsions in heaven and earth, etc., spoken of, are symbolical representations of political revolutions, as explained in the next verse, "I will shake all nations," and again in vers. 21, 22. Other prophets announce that Messiah's reign shall be ushered in by the overthrow or conversion

of heathen nations; *e.g.* Isa. ii. 11, etc.; xix. 21, 22; Dan. ii. 44; Micah v. 9, etc.

Ver. 7.—All nations (Luke xxi. 25, where our Lord refers to the end of this world). But before Christ's first advent there was a general shaking of empires. Persia fell; Alexander's dominion was divided and gradually shattered before the might of Rome; Rome herself was torn with civil wars. The faith in the power of national gods was everywhere weakened, and men were prepared to receive the new revelation of one Supreme Deity, who came on earth to teach and save. Now is mentioned the object or consequence of this shaking of nations. **The desire of all nations shall come.** This is the rendering of the ancient Jewish expositors, the Chaldee Targum, and the Vulgate, which gives, *Veniet desideratus cunctis gentibus.* The words in this case point to a person, and this person can be no one else than the Messiah, for whom "all nations consciously or unconsciously yearn, in whom alone all the longings of the human heart find satisfaction" (Perowne). But there is difficulty in accepting this view. The word rendered "the desire" (*chemdath*) is singular, the verb "shall come" (*bau*) is plural, as if it was said in Latin, *Venient desiderium omnium gentium.* The LXX. translates, Ἥξει τὰ ἐκλεκτὰ πάντων τῶν ἐθνῶν, "The choice things [or, 'portions'] of all the nations shall come." The plural verb seems fatal to the idea of a person being spoken of; nor is this objection answered by Dr. Pusey's allegation that the object of desire contains in itself many objects of desire, or Bishop Wordsworth's refinement, that Messiah is regarded as a collective Being, containing in his own Person the natures of God and man, and combining the three offices of Prophet, Priest, and King. Every one must see that both these explanations are forced and unnatural, and are conformed rather to theological considerations than to grammatical accuracy. *Chemdah* is used for "the object of desire," as 2 Chron. xxxii. 27, where it refers to Hezekiah's treasures, and 2 Chron. xxxvi. 10, "the goodly vessels" of the temple (comp. Jer. xxv. 34; Nah. ii. 9). Nowhere is any intimation given that it is a name applied to the Messiah; nowhere is any such explanation offered of the term so applied. The word is a common one; its meaning is well ascertained; and it could hardly have been understood in any but its usual acceptation without some preparation or further definition. This acceptation is confirmed by the mention of "the gold and silver" in ver. 8. The Revised Version cuts the knot by rendering, "the desirable things;" Perowne affirms that the plural verb denotes the manifoldness and variety of the gifts. This seems scarcely satisfactory. May it not be, as Knabenbauer suggests, that "the desire of all nations" forms one notion, in which the words, "all nations," have a predominating influence, and so the plural ensues by *constructio ad sensum?* The meaning, then, is that all nations with their wealth come, that the Gentiles shall devote their treasures, their powers, whatever they most highly prize, to the service of God. This is what is predicted elsewhere (*e.g.* Isa. lx. 5—7, 11, 13, 17), and it is called, metaphorically, coming with treasures to the temple. To hear of such a glorious future might well be a topic of consolation to the depressed Israelites. (For a further development of the same idea, see Rev. xxi. 24, 26.) **I will fill this house with glory.** There is a verbal allusion to the glory which filled Solomon's temple at the dedication (2 Chron. vii. 1), but the especial mode in which it is to be manifested in this case is not here mentioned. The previous clause would make the reference rather to the material offerings of the Gentiles, but a further and a deeper signification is connected with the advent of Messiah (as Mal. iii. 1), with which the complete fulfilment commenced.

Ver. 8.—**The silver is mine.** All the riches of the world are the Lord's, and he disposes of them as he wills; if he has promised that the Gentiles shall offer their treasures for his service, be sure he will perform his word. There may also be intended a word of comfort for the desponding; they need not grieve because they had but poor offerings to bring to the house; he wanted not gold or silver, for all was his.

Ver. 9.—**The glory of this latter house shall be greater than of the former.** Revised Version, following the Septuagint, "The latter glory of this house shall be greater than the former." "This house" means the temple at Jerusalem, regard not being paid to the special building (ver. 3), whether of Solomon, or Zerubbabel, or Herod. As understood by the hearers, this promise referred to the material riches, the precious things offered by the Gentiles. To us it speaks of the presence of Christ, God incarnate, in the holy city and in the temple itself, and of his presence in the Church, wherein he abides for ever. Here is the complete answer to the complaint of ver. 3. **In this place will I give peace.** Primarily this means in Jerusalem, the place where the temple stood, God would grant peace from enemies, freedom from danger, and quiet enjoyment of promised blessings (comp. Isa. lx. 18; Joel iii. 17; Micah v. 4, 5). But the promise is not fulfilled by this; the peace promised to the spiritual temple is that peace of heart and

conscience which is given by him who is the Prince of Peace (Isa. ix. 6), and which includes all the graces of the Christian covenant (Ezek. xxxiv. 25). The first temple was built by the king whose name is "Peaceful;" the second is glorified by the presence of the "Peace-bringer" (Gen. xlix. 10). At the end of this verse the LXX. has an addition not found in the Hebrew, "even peace of soul for a possession to every one who buildeth, to raise up this shrine."

Vers. 10—19.—**Part III. The Third Address: The Cause of the Calamities which had befallen the People, and a Promise of Blessing.**

Vers. 10—17.—§ 1. *By an analogy drawn from the Law, Haggai shows that residence in the Holy Land and the offering of sacrifice do not suffice to make the people acceptable, as long as they themselves are unclean through neglect of the house of the Lord. Hence comes the punishment of sterility.*

Ver. 10.—**In the four and twentieth day of the ninth month.** The ninth month is Chisleu, answering to parts of November and December. It was now three months from the time the people had commenced to build, and two from the day when the second address was delivered. On the weather at this time depended the hope of the yearly crops. Between the second and third address Zechariah's first prophecy was uttered (Zech. i. 2—6).

Ver. 11.—**Concerning the Law.** Others translate, "for instruction." Ask the priests these two legal questions, such as they were appointed to expound (Deut. xvii. 8, etc.; xxxiii. 10; Mal. ii. 7). By this appeal the prophet makes his lesson sink deeper into the people's mind.

Ver. 12.—**If one bear;** literally, *behold, one beareth,* which is equivalent to "suppose a man bears." Perowne compares Jer. iii. 1, "Lo, a man puts away his wife;" and 2 Chron. vii. 13. **Holy flesh.** The flesh of animals sacrificed to God, which was set apart from profane uses, and might be eaten only by the priests or persons ritually pure (Lev. vi. 26; vii. 15—20; x. 13; comp. Jer. xi. 15). **The skirt of his garment;** literally, *wing of his garment,* as Deut. xxii. 12; 1 Sam. xv. 27. **Any meat;** παντὸς βρώματος: anything eatable. **And said, No.** The priests answered correctly according to Lev. vi. 27. Whatever touched the hallowed flesh became itself holy, but it could not communicate this holiness to anything else.

Ver. 13.—**Unclean by a dead body;** Septuagint, ἀκάθαρτος ἐπὶ ψυχῇ: Vulgate, *pollutus in anima.* These versions are closer to the Hebrew, "unclean by a soul," than

the Authorized Version, but not so intelligible. "Soul" (*nephesh*) is used to mean
a person, and, with the attribute "dead"
understood, a corpse, as Lev. xxi. 1. The
full phrase is found in Numb. vi. 6, 11.
Contact with a dead body produced the
gravest ceremonial uncleanness, which
lasted seven days, and could be purged
only by a double lustration and other rites
(Numb. xix. 11, etc.). This uncleanness
was doubtless connected with the idea that
death was the result of sin. **Any of these.**
The things mentioned in the preceding
verse. **It shall be unclean.** In accordance
with Numb. xix. 22. A polluted human
being communicated his pollution to all
that he touched. It was owing to the
defilement that accompanied contact with
the dead that the later Jews used to whiten
the sepulchres every year, that they might
be seen and avoided (Matt. xxiii. 27, and
Lightfoot, 'Hor. Hebr.,' *in loc.*).

Ver. 14.—**Then answered Haggai, and
said**; *then Haggai continued and said.* He
applies the principles just enunciated to
the case of the Jews, taking the communication of uncleanness first. **So is this people.**
Not, *my people*, because by their acts they
had disowned God (ch. i. 2). This people
is defiled in my sight like one who has
touched a corpse, and not only they themselves, but **so is every work of their hands**;
all their labour, all that they put their
hands to, is unclean, and can win no
blessing. Their pollution was their disobedience in not building the house of God.
They had calmly contemplated the lifeless
symbol of the theocracy, the ruined temple,
and made no determined effort to resuscitate
it, so a blight had rested on all their work.
That which they offer there (pointing to the
altar which they had built when they first
returned, Ezra iii. 2) **is unclean.** They
had fancied that the sanctifying influence
of the altar and its sacrifices would extend
to all their works, and cover all their shortcomings; but so far from this, their very
offerings were unclean, because the offerers
were polluted. They who come before the
Holy One should themselves be holy.
Neither the altar nor the Holy Land
imparted sanctity by any intrinsic virtue of
their own, but entailed upon all an obligation to personal holiness (Wordsworth). The
LXX. has an addition at the end of the
verse, Ἕνεκεν τῶν λημμάτων αὐτῶν τῶν
ὀρθρινῶν, ὀδυνηθήσονται ἀπὸ προσώπου πόνων
αὐτῶν, καὶ ἐμισεῖτε ἐν πύλαις ἐλέγχοντας,
"On account of their morning gains [or,
'burdens'] they shall be pained in the
presence of their labours, and ye hated
those who reproved in the gates." This is
expounded by Theodoret thus: As soon as
morning dawned ye employed yourselves in

no good work, but sought only how to
obtain sordid gain. And ye regarded with
hatred those who reproved you, who sitting
at the gate spake words of wisdom to all
who passed by. The passage is found in
no other version.

Ver. 15—The prophet bids the people
look backwards, and consider how their
neglect had been visited by scanty harvests;
their own experience would teach them this
lesson. **From this day**; viz. the twenty-
fourth day of the ninth month, when this
address was delivered (ver. 10; comp. ver.
18). **And upward**; *i.e.* backward. He bids
them go back in thought fourteen years
when they first intermitted building.
Before a stone, etc. This does not mean
before the building was first begun, but
before they began to build on the foundation
already laid.

Ver. 16.—**Since those** days **were.** The
word "days" is supplied. Revised Version,
"through all that time," viz. the fourteen
years spoken of in ver. 15. Septuagint, τίνες
ἦτε, "what ye were;" the Vulgate omits
the words. **When one came to an heap of
twenty** measures. The word "measures" is
not in the Hebrew; it is supplied by the
LXX., σάτα (equivalent to *seahs*), and by
Jerome, *modiorum.* But the particular
measure is of no importance; it is the proportion only on which stress is laid. The
prophet particularizes the general statements of ch. i. 6, 9. The "heap" is the
collection of sheaves (Ruth iii. 7). This
when threshed yielded only half that they
had expected. **There were** (in fact) but **ten**;
καὶ ἐγένετο κριθῆς δέκα σάτα, "and there were
ten measures of barley." **The press-fat**; *the
wine-fat,* the vat into which flowed the juice
forced from the grapes when trodden out by
the feet in the press. A full account of this
will be found in the 'Dict. of the Bible,'
arts. "Wine-press" and "Wine." **Fifty**
vessels **out of the** press. The Hebrew is
"fifty *purah.*" The word *purah* is used in
Isa. lxiii. 3 to signify the "press" itself,
hence the Authorized Version so translates
it here, inserting "out of," and supplying
"vessels," as "measures" above; but it
probably here denotes a liquid measure in
which the wine was drawn. LXX., μετρητάς
(equivalent to Hebrew *baths*). Jerome,
lagenas; and in his commentary, *amphoras.*
They came and examined the grapes and
expected fifty *purahs,* "press-measures,"
but they did not get even half that they
had hoped. **There were but twenty.** Knabenbauer suggests that the meaning may be—
looking at the crop of grapes, they expected
to draw out, *i.e.* empty (*chasaph*), the press
fifty times, but were egregiously deceived.

Ver. 17.—**I smote you with blasting** and
with mildew. It was God who inflicted

these calamities upon them judicially, according to the threats in Deut. xxviii. 22 (comp. Amos iv. 9, and note there). These two pests affected the corn; the vines were smitten with hail (Ps. lxxviii. 47). **In all the labours** (*work*) **of your hands.** All that you had cultivated with toil, corn, vines, fruit of every sort. **Yet ye turned not to me.** The clause is elliptical, "yet not ye to me." The LXX. and Syriac translate as the Authorized Version, supplying the verb from the parallel passage in Amos iv. 9. The Vulgate (not according to precedent), *Non fuit in vobis qui revertetur ad me.* In spite of these visitations there was not one among them who shook off his idle inaction and worked for the Lord.

Vers. 18, 19.—§ 2. *On their obedience the blessings of nature shall again be theirs.*

Ver. 18.—**Consider now from this day and upward** (see note on ver. 15.) For "upward" Jerome has here *in futurum*, though he translated the same word *supra* in ver. 15. Such a rendering is allowable, and affords a good sense, the prophet directing the people's attention to the happy prospect in the future announced in ver. 19. But it seems best to keep to the same interpretation in two passages so closely allied. The prophet bids the people consider the period from the present, **the four and twentieth day of the ninth** month, when this prophecy was uttered (ver. 10), to the other limit explanatory of the term "upward" or "backward." Even **from the day that the foundation,** etc.; rather, *since the day that*, etc. This is obviously the same period as that named in ver. 15, after the foundation was completed, but before "stone was laid upon stone" of the superstructure (comp. Zech. viii. 9).

Ver. 19.—**Is the seed yet in the barn?** Is there any of your poor crop still left in your granaries? Is it not already expended? "The seed" is here the produce of the seed, the grain (1 Sam. viii. 15; Job xxxix. 12). The corn crop is mentioned first, then the fruit harvest. The Vulgate has, *Numquid jam semen in germine est?* Has the seed begun to grow? Is there any sign of abundance? Yet the harvest shall be prolific. But there is no doubt that *megurah* means "barn," not "sprout." LXX., Εἰ ἐπιγνωσθήσεται ἐπὶ τῆς ἅλω, "If it shall be known upon the threshing-floor." Jerome must have read γῆς for τῆς, as he renders, "Si ultra cognoscetur super terram area." He expounds it thus: So abundant shall be the produce that the threshing-floor shall not recognize its own corn. or that the threshers shall be forced to join floor to floor to make room for all the grain, "et arearum separatio nesciatur in terra." **Yea, as yet;** καὶ εἰ ἔτι

(Septuagint); *et adhuc* (Vulgate); as Judg. iii. 26; Job i. 18. Others translate, "as regards." Though there was no sign of leaf or fruit on the trees, nothing by which one could judge of the future produce, yet the prophet predicts an abundant crop, dating from the people's obedience (Lev. xxvi. 3, etc.; Deut. xxviii. 2, etc.). **From this day will I bless you.** "This day" is the twenty-fourth day of the ninth month (ver. 10). From now the improvement in the season should begin and make itself evident. "Bless" is a term often used for sending fruitful seasons (Deut. xxviii. 8; Mal. iii. 10).

Vers. 20—23.—Part V. THE FOURTH ADDRESS: PROMISE OF THE RESTORATION AND ESTABLISHMENT OF THE HOUSE OF DAVID, WHEN THE STORM BURSTS ON THE KINGDOMS OF THE WORLD.

Ver. 20.—Temporal blessings had been promised to the people generally; now spiritual blessings are announced to Zerubbabel as the head of the nation and the representative of the house of David. **And again;** *and a second time;* ἐκ δευτέρου (Septuagint). This revelation took place on the same day as the preceding one.

Ver. 21.—**Zerubbabel** (see note on ch. i. 1). **I will shake the heavens and the earth.** He repeats the prediction of ver. 6 in this chapter (where see note). This is the general statement, expanded and explained in the next verse.

Ver. 22.—**I will overthrow the throne of kingdoms.** No events in Zerubbabel's time satisfied this prediction, which waits for its fulfilment in the Messianic age (Luke i. 52). "The throne" is used distributively for "every throne of kingdoms;" Septuagint, "thrones of kings." **Of the heathen;** *of the nations.* **Chariots,** etc. Emblems of the military power by which the nations had risen to eminence (Ps. xx. 7; Zech. x. 5). **Shall come down.** Be brought to the ground, perish (Isa. xxxiv. 7). **By the sword of his brother.** The heathen powers shall annihilate one another (Ezek. xxxviii. 21; Zech. xiv. 13).

Ver. 23.—**In that day.** When the heathen nations of the earth are overthrown, Israel shall be safe, and be the more exalted by the Divine favour and protection. **Will I take.** The verb simply serves to introduce the following act as one of importance, and does not signify, "take under my protection" (comp. Deut. iv. 20; 2 Kings xiv. 21; Keil). **My servant.** An honourable title used especially of David (1 Kings xi. 13, etc.; Jer. xxxiii. 21, etc.), and his future successors (Ezek. xxxiv. 23, etc.; xxxvii. 24). **Make thee as a signet.** I will make thee most precious in my sight (comp. Cant viii. 6). Among Orientals the signet-ring was an article of great importance and value (see Rev. v. 1 ; ix. 4 ; and ' Dict. of the Bible,' art. "Seal"). The allusion is particularly appropriate here, because Zerubbabel is set at the head of the nation in the place of his grandfather (?) Jeconiah, whose rejection from the monarchy had been couched in these terms : "As I live, saith the Lord, though Coniah the son of Jehoiakim King of Judah were the signet upon my right hand, yet would I pluck thee thence" (Jer. xxii. 24). The Son of Sirach, in his praise of great men, refers to this promise, "How shall we magnify Zorobabel? even he was as a signet on the right hand" (Ecclus. xlix. 11). The signet, too, is the sign of authority (Gen. xli. 42; Esth. iii. 10); so Zerubbabel has authority delegated to him from God, the type of him who said, "All things are delivered unto me of my Father" (Matt. xi. 27). "The true Zerubbabel, *i.e.* Christ, the Son and Antitype of Zerubbabel, is the signet in the hand of the Father, both passively and actively, whereby God impresses his own majesty, thought, and words, and his own image, on men,

angels, and all creatures " (Corn. à Lapide *ap.* Pusey). **I have chosen thee.** This is not a personal assurance only to Zerubbabel, for neither he nor his natural seed reigned in Jerusalem, or rose to any special eminence in the kingdoms of this world. The fulfilment must be looked for in his spiritual progeny and in Christ. Promises are often made in Scripture to individuals which are accomplished only in their descendants; witness those made to Abraham and the other patriarchs, the prophecies of Jacob to his sons, and many others of a similar nature in the Old Testament. Those large promises made to David in old time, that his seed should endure for ever, that his throne should be as the sun before God (Ps. lxxxix. 36, 37; 2 Sam. vii. 16), were now passed on to Zerubbabel and to his line, because of him was to spring Messiah, in whom alone these wide predictions find their fulfilment. "He shall be great, and shall be called the Son of the Highest : and the Lord God shall give unto him the throne of his father David : and he shall reign over the house of Jacob for ever; and of his kingdom there shall be no end" (Luke i. 32, 33).

HOMILETICS.

Vers. 3—5.—*Past and present.* I. A SUGGESTION—*of the continuity of human history.* Haggai's question assumes that the structure then erecting was not a new edifice (which it really was), but the old building set up again, though in faded splendour, which also it was, inasmuch as it was based on the foundations of the earlier pile. "This house in its former glory " meant that the prophet looked on the two houses as one, and the two eras represented by these houses, not as two distinct and separate periods, but as one continuous period. As it were the national life, for seventy years interrupted by the exile, again flowed on, restoring the temple, reinstituting the religion of Jehovah, and pervading the whole fabric of society. The present was not so much a fresh commencement as a prolongation of the past. And this is true of human history and life in general. No age or individual is entirely disconnected from and independent of the ages and individuals that have gone before. A perfectly new beginning in human history or in individual life has never yet taken place. Even in the Incarnation, the second Adam was connected with the first through his human nature. The civilization of the nineteenth century is built upon the foundations laid by preceding centuries. The maturity of manhood in wisdom or virtue is developed from the gains in knowledge and goodness made in youth.

II. AN ILLUSTRATION—*of the tendency to glorify the past at the expense of the present.* "Who is left among you that saw this house in its former glory ? and how do you see it now ?" asks the prophet; "is it not in your eyes as nothing ?" In certain respects this depreciation of the post-exilic temple, in comparison with the Solomonic, was justifiable—the material splendour of the second building was vastly inferior to that of the first; but in other respects the glory of the latter house would ultimately far eclipse that of the former (ver. 9)—it would be the centre and scene, the instrument and support of a purer worship than had been maintained in the former, and would be honoured by the visit of a greater potentate than Solomon himself, even by the Messenger of the covenant and the Lord of the temple, after whom were going out the desires, not of Israel alone, but of all nations (ver. 7). And just as these aged temple-builders were inclined to disparage the meaner edifice rising upon the foundation of the old structure of cedar wood and gold, and to glorify the old which seventy years before had perished in the going down of their nation before the might of Babylon, so does it seem to be a tendency in human nature to exalt the past and to depress the present, to extol the men and institutions, the characteristics and occurrences of other days at the expense of the present, even when there is as little ground for doing so as there was for the depreciatory remarks of the builders. It is not difficult to account for either this laudation of the past or this disparagement of the present. On the one hand, lapse of years allows the memory of past discomforts, irritations, deficiencies, imperfections, blemishes, to fade away, while present evils obtrude themselves upon the notice and press upon the hearts of the passing generation; on the other hand, the present is too near for its peculiar excellences to be rightly gauged, while the glories of the past, like distant mountains, shine out with augmented splendour. Yet the verdict which prefers the past to the present is incorrect (Eccles. vii. 10). Unless the world is a hopelessly bad world, which it is not (Rom. viii. 20), and the grace of God that bringeth salvation is effete, which is not the mind of Scripture (Titus ii. 11); unless the predictions of the Word of God are to be falsified (Isa. xi. 9; Hab. ii. 14; Rev. xi. 15), which cannot be (Isa. lv. 11; Matt. xxiv. 35), and the aspirations of good men's hearts are to be disappointed, which would be clean contrary to what God has led them to expect (Ps. cxlv. 19);—there can be little doubt that the world is and must be surely but slowly becoming better.

> " For I doubt not through the ages one increasing purpose runs;
> And the thoughts of men are widened by the process of the suns."

> (Tennyson.)

To the widening of the thoughts add the purifying of the hearts and the elevation of the lives of men.

III. AN EXHORTATION—*to earnest diligence in discharge of present duty.* " Yet now be strong, O Zerubbabel, saith the Lord," etc. The duty of the builders was to prosecute the work in which they were engaged, the erection of the temple, even though the temple should be inferior to its predecessor, and the circumstances for its erection less favourable than had been those for the construction of the former— perhaps all the more their duty on that account. So were the present age inferior to the ages which had gone before, the same duty would be incumbent on all ranks and classes—the duty, viz. of working with earnest diligence at one's daily calling, "the trivial round, the common task," if assigned by God, and more especially at the upbuilding of God's spiritual temple in the individual soul and in the world at large. Without this the present age cannot grow better than the past, and is certain to grow worse.

IV. A CONSOLATION—*in the guaranteed fellowship of God.* Jehovah would be with them—always, of course, conditionally if they continued with him (2 Chron. xv. 2). 1. *Not merely externally,* as through his immanent presence he is with all, *but internally,* by his Spirit abiding amongst them as a community, and in their hearts as individuals, as he still does in the midst of his Church and in the souls of believers, when these remain true to him, no matter how degenerate the age may be in which their lot is cast. 2. *Not now for the first time, but as he had ever been* since the day when they came forth from Egypt; without which, indeed, they had never become a nation having access to Jehovah through their priests and sacrifices, and receiving from him revelations and spiritual quickenings through the medium of their prophets (Heb. i. 1); and without which they could not now be prospered in their undertaking. God's Spirit is the secret source and ultimate cause of all good in either Church or nation. 3. *Not of constraint, but willingly,* according to his own covenant engagements, which are never imposed on him by any of his creatures, but always freely proposed and executed by himself—whence they are rightly styled covenants of grace. It is the existence of such a covenant that guarantees the indestructibility and perpetuity of the Christian Church. 4. *Not as an unseen presence only, but as an actively co-operating power,* imparting to them strength for their work as well as boldness in it (see homily on ch. i. 13, 14), both of which would be theirs in proportion as they realized the cheering truth that they were fellow-labourers with God. In like manner also, and for similar ends and purposes, is Christ, by his Spirit, present with his Church (Matt. xxviii. 20; John xiv. 6).

LESSONS. 1. The inheritance of the past a cause of thankfulness. 2. The imperfections of the present a stimulus to duty. 3. The glorious times of the future a reason for cheerfulness and hope.

Vers. 6, 7.—*The shaking of the heavens and the earth.* I. HISTORICAL ILLUSTRATIONS. 1. *At Sinai,* when Jehovah manifested himself to Israel (Exod. xix. 16—19; Ps. lxviii. 7, 8). Preparatory and prophetical. 2. *At the birth of Christ,* when Jehovah appeared on earth in the Person of his Son (Joel ii. 30, 31 : Luke ii. 8—14; Acts ii. 19, 20). Furthering and fulfilling. 3. *At the end of time,* when Jehovah will a third time appear, in the Person of the glorified Christ, to save his people and judge his foes (Isa. xxiv. 19, 20 ; 2 Pet. iii. 10). Culminating and completing. II. SCRIPTURAL INTERPRETATIONS. According to the writer to the Hebrews, "This word, Once more, signifieth the removing of the things that are shaken, that those things which cannot be shaken may remain" (Heb. xii. 27). In other words, the object of each successive Divine interposition has been and will be the abrogation of institutions that have served their day, the correction of errors that have hindered the truth, the alteration of circumstances and conditions that are no longer suited to the new era about to be introduced. 1. At Sinai *were shaken and removed* (1) the polytheism which Israel had in large measure brought with her from Egypt ; (2) the individualism which had hitherto prevented Israel from forming herself into a nation ; and (3) the serfdom which had rendered the realization of Israel's calling impossible ; while *the things that could not be shaken and remained* were (1) the unity of God, or the monotheistic element which still survived in Israel's religion ; (2) the covenant relationship in which Jehovah stood towards Israel ; and (3) the capacity for religion which no amount of oppression had been able utterly to destroy. 2. At the birth of Christ *were shaken and removed* (1) the Mosaic institute which had then served its day, and was even ready to vanish away (Heb. viii. 13); (2) the partition wall between Jew and Gentile (Eph. ii. 14), which had repelled each from, rather than attracted each to, the other; and (3) the externalism and literalism in worship, which had converted it into mere mechanism ; while *the unshakable things that remained were* (1) the covenant of grace which underlay the Mosaic institute, and shone the brighter when that was removed which for centuries had been superimposed upon it ; (2) the brotherhood of man, which was henceforth to be placed in the forefront of the gospel message (Acts xvii. 26 ; Rom. ii. 11 ; iii. 29 ; Col. iii. 11 ; Gal. iii. 26); and (3) the spirituality of religion, which was no more to be confined to either places or seasons, persons or forms, but to find its seat in the heart and its priest in the renewed soul (John iv. 21—24). 3. At the end of time *will be shaken and removed* (1) the present state and condition of things (1 Cor. vii. 31; xv. 50—57; 2 Pet. iii. 10, 12; 1 John ii. 17); (2) the presence and power of sin (Rev. xxii. 3); and (3) the mediatorial sovereignty of Christ (1 Cor. xv. 23); while *as things that cannot be shaken, shall remain* (1) the new heavens and the new earth wherein dwelleth righteousness (2 Pet. iii. 13); (2) the redeemed family of believers (1 John ii. 17); and (3) the eternal supremacy of God, who shall then be all in all (1 Cor. xv. 23). Learn : 1. That nations and individuals mostly advance by means of struggle and commotion. 2. That peace and quietness may often mean stagnation and death rather than progress and life. 3. That truth and right will eventually prevail over falsehood and wrong.

Ver. 7.—" *The desire of all nations."* 1. ALL NATIONS HAVE DESIRED A VISIBLE DIVINITY ; AND SUCH A MANIFESTED OR REVEALED DIVINITY HAS BEEN GIVEN TO MANKIND IN CHRIST. That all nations from the beginning downward have believed in the existence of a Supreme Being has been sufficiently demonstrated by the universality in man of the instinct of worship. Nor have all nations merely wished to possess a god, but the Deity they have longed for has been, not a god remaining always little more than a conception of the mind, an infinitely exalted being with whom they could not enter into fellowship, but a God whom they could look upon, or at least think of, as not far from any one of them, a God who could not only come near to them, but to whom they in turn could come near. The lowest forms of religion that have existed on the earth, the religions of men in most degraded conditions, have made this perfectly apparent no less than the elaborate rites of the cultivated and civilized nations of antiquity. What the savage means by putting a spirit into the various forms of nature by which he is surrounded, or by making an idol of wood or stone, and setting it up before him as an object of adoration; what the untutored child of nature thereby means, viz. to express his belief in a power above himself and above nature, and his desire to bring that invisible power or divinity forth into visibility or nearness; that the old religions of Chaldea, Egypt, and Phœnicia did when they deified the hosts of heaven and the forces of nature, or looked upon these as instruments and embodiments of supernatural powers. In their case it was one more effort of the human mind to fetch God out of the far distance and make him a distinct object of contemplation and worship. Then the later religions that prevailed in Persia, India, Greece, and Rome, with their "incarnations," or beliefs in gods who assumed the likeness of men, evinced the same longing of the human heart for a God at hand rather than afar off, a God visible rather than a god who remained always unseen, a God who might be approached in thought, at least, if not in space, rather than a god who so transcended his worshippers as to be practically inaccessible. And this longing Christianity —whether it be true or no may meantime be left undetermined—meets, as no other religion has done or is likely to do, by placing before man as an object of religious contemplation and worship One who claimed to be the Image of the invisible God, saying, "I and my Father are One," and "He that hath seen me hath seen the Father."

II. ALL NATIONS HAVE DESIRED AN ATONEMENT FOR SIN; AND SUCH ATONEMENT HAS BEEN PROVIDED AS NOWHERE ELSE BY CHRIST AND CHRISTIANITY. It is not meant that everywhere and always men have possessed the same clear, definite, exalted, and correct ideas on the subject of sin, sacrifice, propitiation, atonement, as are presented in the Hebrew or the Christian Scriptures. The most affirmed is that while everywhere men have possessed a deep instinctive longing after God, along with this they have always been more or less conscious of unworthiness and unfitness to enter into fellowship with him, have had a secret conviction that the Deity whom they wished to serve was displeased with them, and that they could not enjoy his favour without the intervention of some atonement or propitiation. Hence, wherever man has been found to have a god, there also he has owned an altar. The practice begun at the gate of Eden, of worshipping the Deity by means of sacrifices, and carried forwad in the altar-building of Abraham and the patriarchs, and finally developed in the Mosaic ritual of priest and victim, has been discovered, on investigation, not to have been confined to these, but to have been followed, with more or less closeness of adherence to the primitive pattern, by every nation under heaven that has shaped for itself a religion. In religions of the most rudimentary type, as well as in those of the highest culture, a place has been reserved for the practice of sacrificing and for the notion of expiation. "The sense of impurity and of the need of expiation," writes Pressensé, "are manifested in the most barbarous modes of worship. We admit that the atonement to which they have recourse is often as cruel as the wrath of the deity whom the worshippers seek to appease. There is a phase in which sacrifice is nothing more than food offered to the gods. But a higher idea soon manifests itself. Remorse comes in, the consciousness of guilt prompts the sacrifice, and the priest who at first was regarded in the light of an enchanter becomes a mediator between man and the deity" ('The Ancient World and Christianity,' p. 12). In addition it might easily be shown that the same ideas of sin, penitence, forgiveness, propitiation, sacrifice, atonement, were present in the religions of ancient Chaldea and of Egypt (ibid., pp. 47, 87). And the inference from all is that, irrespective of age or country, and however overlaid with superstition, the deep conviction of the human heart is that man has sinned against God and requires the assistance of a Mediator who shall in some way make peace with the offended Deity, and secure for the offender forgiveness of his transgressions. Well, here again Christianity steps in to supply this demand of the human heart, to answer this pathetic wail for a Deliverer, for One who can make peace and bring forgiveness—steps in as no other religion known to man does, by exhibiting Jesus Christ as Son of God and Son of man (John i. 49, 51), and therefore as possessed of authority to act as Daysman or Mediator between God and man, laying his hand upon both (Job x. 33; 1 Tim. ii. 5), by discovering him as standing in the room of sinful man (Rom. v. 6), and as making peace by the shedding of his blood (Eph. ii. 14), by presenting him to view as One whose blood is able both to wipe away the guilt of sin and to break its enslaving power. And this, again, is a high certificate in favour of Christianity as the only true religion. For what is a religion worth if it cannot or dare not meet the demands of the human heart and conscience?

III. ALL NATIONS HAVE DESIRED A DIVINE REVELATION, OR AN AUTHENTIC COMMUNICATION OF THE DIVINE WILL; AND THIS CHRISTIANITY MEETS IN A WAY THAT NO OTHER RELIGION HAS DONE OR CAN DO. Not only have men in every age and country believed that God is, and that by means of sacrifices it might be possible to appease his anger and secure his favour; they have also supposed it within their reach to receive trustworthy information from God as to his will and their duty. In the rudest forms of religion, the media through which such Divine communications have been conjectured to come have been signs in the sky above or on the earth beneath. In unusual phenomena of nature, in unaccustomed sights and sounds, in dreams and visions, men have been wont to see indications of a higher will than their own made known to them for the guidance of their earthly lives. As religion has advanced in intelligence and refinement, special persons have come to be regarded as oracles through whom responses from the heavenly world might be obtained, and messages from the unseen received. Priests and priestesses, seers and sages, have been viewed as standing in immediate connection with the Deity, and as serving to transmit to men the utterances he might wish to make known. Then, too, in many of the world's religions, as in those of Egypt and Persia, India and Arabia, that is to say, in the most developed religions of which we have any knowledge, but especially in Parseeism, Brahminism, Mohammedanism, there have been sacred books in which the revelations vouchsafed to mankind through the founders of these religions have been preserved. Now, in all this, irrespective of the truth or falsehood of these religions, a signal testimony arises to the strength and depth of the desire on the part of man to possess some authorized expounder of the Divine will in the shape of man, or book, or perhaps both; and there is no need to say that God has never gratified this desire outside of the Hebrew or the Christian Church; but of this one may be certain, that the longing for a Heaven-sent teacher was not confined to the Hebrews, with their Moses who spake with God face to face as a man talketh with his friend, but existed as well among the Greeks, Plato, in one of his dialogues, putting into the mouth of one of his disputants the ever-memorable words, "It is therefore necessary to wait until one teach us how to behave towards the gods and men," and into that of another, "And when shall that time arrive? and who shall that teacher be? for most glad would I be to see such a man." Just such a man was felt to be one of the world's greatest wants before Christ came; and when he came just such a man appeared. The verdict pronounced by the officers on Jesus, "Never man spake like this Man," has never been reversed; nor is there the least likelihood that it ever will.

IV. ALL NATIONS HAVE DESIRED AN ASSURANCE OF IMMORTALITY; AND THAT ASSURANCE HAS BEEN GIVEN BY CHRIST IN A WAY THAT HAS BEEN DONE BY NO OTHER. Whether apart from Divine revelation the reality of a future life beyond the grave can or could be demonstrated, may be doubtful; but this much is undoubted, that in all ages men have believed in the existence of such a life, and have expressed that belief in their religions. The lowest races by their worship of ancestors, the Egyptians by their elaborate ritual of the Book of the Dead, and the ancient Chaldeans by their mythological narrative of the descent of Ishtar into Hades, each in turn showed that they clung to the idea of the persistence of the human soul after death. But, indeed, the notion that death ends all, though the assertion of some philosophers, and though supposed to be the teaching of science, has never at any period been the faith of the generality of mankind, and has never won the assent of the human heart in its inmost and truest convictions. Nor must it be overlooked that this universal belief in a future state is a clear testimony to the heart's longing for a continued existence beyond the grave, and to the heart's wish for some authentic tidings about that unknown land; and nothing surely can be less in need of demonstration, than that Jesus Christ answers man's inquiries about the future life with a clearness and fulness of information in comparison with which the teaching of all other religions, the Hebrew Scriptures not excepted, is as darkness.

LESSONS. 1. The pre-eminence of Jesus Christ, and of the Christian religion. 2. Gratitude for God's unspeakable Gift. 3. The duty of seeking in Christ satisfaction for the soul's true desires.

Ver. 8.—*The silver and the gold: a sermon on money.* I. A FORGOTTEN TRUTH RESTATED. That God is the sole Proprietor of money : "The silver is mine, and the gold is mine, saith the Lord of hosts" (cf. Joel iii. 5). The proof lies in three things; that the silver and the gold are: 1. *Of God's making.* They belong to him as part of that earth and its fulness which he hath created (Ps. xxiv. 1; l. 12), as David acknowledged in his prayer, "All that is in the heaven and in the earth is thine;" and again, "Of thine own have we given thee" (1 Chron. xxix. 12, 14). 2. *Of God's giving.* God claimed that he had multiplied Judah's silver and gold (Hos. ii. 6); and David owned that "all things," including "riches and honour," were of him (1 Chron. xxix. 12). The same sentiment is involved in the words of the Baptist (John iii. 27), in those of Paul (1 Tim. vi. 17), and in those of James (i. 17). 3. *Of God's keeping.* As no man can obtain wealth from other than God, so with no help but his can man retain the wealth he has got. "Except the Lord keep the city, the watchman watcheth in vain" (Ps. cxxvii. 1). Nor can any one keep it longer than God chooses. At any moment can he recall what he has given.

II. AN IMPORTANT INFERENCE DEDUCED. That no man is the owner of his money, but merely its selected steward, its casual recipient and temporary holder. What Benhadad of Syria said to Ahab of Israel, "Thy silver and thy gold is mine" (1 Kings xx. 3), expresses God's thought concerning millionaires and paupers alike; while the answer of Ahab, "My lord, O king, according to thy saying, I am thine, and all that I have," exactly utters the response which every one possessed of silver and gold, whether much or little, should give to the Divine declaration. Few things are more difficult for men to realize than that that is not their own for which they have laboured, sometimes like galley-slaves, and not unfrequently sinned. The habitual attitude of men towards their silver and their gold is that of the rich farmer in the Gospels, "my fruits," "my barns," "my goods" (Luke xii. 17, 18). A recognition of man's steward-ship in respect of silver and gold would secure three things of immense consequence, both for the religious life of the individual, and for the moral welfare of the world. 1. *A just estimate of money.* As one of God's gifts, it would be highly valued, but as only a gift it would never be regarded as a permanent endowment, or preferred above the Giver. 2. *A proper use of money.* As a trust it would be carefully kept, wisely used (Matt. xxv. 16), faithfully administered (1 Cor. iv. 2), and correctly accounted for (Luke xvi. 2). It would not be prodigally squandered (Luke xv. 13), or in miser fashion hoarded (Matt. xxv. 25), or selfishly expended (Hos. x. 1), but skilfully, lovingly, and unweariedly employed for the Master's glory. 3. *A right feeling with regard to money.* Neither inordinate desire after it (1 Tim. vi. 10), nor over-esteem of one's self on account of it (Hos. xii. 8), would arise in one's bosom; but feelings of contentment with what one has received (Phil. iv. 11; 1 Tim. vi. 6), and of gratitude that one has received any (Gen. xxxii. 10).

Ver. 9.—*The latter glory of "this house;" or, "the glory that excelleth."* I. THE HOUSE 1. *The temple of Zerubbabel,* then building, which, however, was regarded as a continuation of and as one with the temple of Solomon (cf. ver. 3). 2. *The Christian Church,* which on a similar principle of interpretation was viewed as an outcome and development of the Hebrew temple (cf. John ii. 20, 21).

II. THE GLORY. Called by Haggai "the latter glory" of this house, in contradistinction to the earlier or former glory which belonged to it before the Captivity, this can only signify the glory which, in Messianic times, should pertain to the temple when it should have reached its ideal form in the Christian Church, whose "glory," in comparison with that of the Solomonic structure, should be a glory that excelleth. 1. *The glory of spiritual magnificence,* as opposed to that of merely material splendour. The temple of Solomon was, after all, but an "earthly house" of polished stone, carved cedar, and burnished gold; but the temple of Jesus Christ is a spiritual house, constructed of lively stones, or believing souls (1 Pet. ii. 5), "an holy temple" erected out of quickened and renewed hearts "for an habitation of God through the Spirit" (Eph.

ii. 21). 2. *The glory of an indwelling Divinity*, in contrast with that of a merely symbolic residence therein. The ark with its mercy-seat overshadowed by the cherubim, between whose outstretched wings shone the visible glory or the Shechinah —this ark which occupied the holy of holies in the Solomonic temple, was not Jehovah, but only the material token of his presence. Though in the Christian Church there is, as in Zerubbabel's temple there was, no ark, yet the Divine presence fills it. Not only does Paul describe it as a temple which God inhabits (see above), but he represents it as the body of the glorified Christ, the fulness of him that filleth all in all (Eph. i. 23), and even speaks of individual believers as temples of the Holy Ghost (1 Cor. vi. 9) and of the living God (2 Cor. vi. 16); while Christ expressly promises to his Church a perpetual indwelling in their midst, not collectively alone, but individually as well (Matt. xviii. 20; xxviii. 20; John xiv. 17, 23; xv. 4; xvi. 7, 22). 3. *The glory of diffusing spiritual and eternal peace*, as distinguished from a peace which should be merely temporal and temporary. The Solomonic temple was indeed built by one whose name was Peace, whose reign was undisturbed by foreign or domestic wars, and whose spirit was neither military nor aggressive; but it is doubtful if the whole period during which the Solomonic temple stood could with truthfulness be characterized as one of peace (see the books of 2 Kings and 2 Chronicles). Nor could it be asserted that the era of the temple of Zerubbabel was throughout peaceful. "Temporal peace they had now, nor was there any prospect of its being disturbed; . . . (but) in later times they had it not. The temple itself was profaned by Antiochus Epiphanes. . . . Again by Pompey, by Crassus, by the Parthians, before it was destroyed by Titus and the Romans" (Pusey). But the temple of Jesus Christ was the building of One who was by pre-eminence the Prince of Peace (Isa. ix. 6), who came to teach men the way of peace (Luke i. 79), who bequeathed to his disciples as his parting legacy his own peace (John xiv. 27), who died to make peace between God and man through his cross (Eph. ii. 14), and who has since come to men in and through his gospel, preaching peace (Acts x. 36), and by his Spirit shedding peace abroad in the hearts of them who believe (Rom. v. 1; viii. 6; xiv. 17; Gal. v. 22; Phil. iv. 7; Col. iii. 15).

III. THE LESSON. 1. *The certainty of God's Word.* What Haggai predicted has at length been fulfilled. So will all God's promises reach realization. 2. *The superiority of the gospel dispensation.* A dispensation not of letter and form, but of spirit and life; not of condemnation and death, but of justification and glory; not of temporal duration, but of eternal continuance. 3. *The perfectibility of the race.* Human history has hitherto progressed according to the law—"first that which is natural, and afterwards that which is spiritual;" there is no reason to believe it will do otherwise in the future.

Vers. 10—19.—*The parable of the holy and the unclean.* I. THE LETTER OF THE PARABLE. Directed by Jehovah, Haggai proposes two questions to the priests. 1. *Concerning the law of communicated sanctity.* Supposing the case of a man carrying in the skirt of his garment holy flesh, *i.e.* flesh of animals slain in sacrifice, and with his skirt touching bread, pottage, wine, oil, or any meat, the prophet desires to be informed whether the holiness which according to the Law (Lev. vi. 27) was imparted to the skirt extended further so as to reach also anything with which the skirt might come in contact. To this the priests properly answer, "No." 2. *Concerning the law of legal defilement.* Stating a contrary case, that of a person defiled by having himself touched a dead body (Lev. xxi. 11; Numb. xix. 16), Haggai asks whether contact with such a person would render any of the above articles unclean, and is promptly answered that according to the Law it would (Numb. xix. 22).

II. THE INTERPRETATION OF THE PARABLE. "So is this people, and so is this nation before me, saith the Lord." 1. *Any sanctity possessed by the nation could not pass beyond themselves.* The sanctity which they possessed arose from the fact of their having an altar in Jerusalem, which had been built immediately on their return from Babylon, and of their maintaining in connection therewith the festal and sacrificial worship appointed by the Law of Moses (Ezra iii. 1—6). Yet this could not transmit itself to the soil so as to render it holy and cause it to become fruitful in corn and wine and oil, notwithstanding their disobedience in neglecting the building of the temple. On the other hand: 2. *Whatever defilement was on the nation would affect all that belonged to the nation.* But the nation, through its disobedience in neglecting to build the temple, was defiled, since according to Jehovah "to obey is better than sacrifice, and to hearken than the fat of rams" (1 Sam. xv. 22). Hence their uncleanness rendered all about and around them unclean. In particular, it put the land beneath a curse which made its harvests scanty.

III. THE APPLICATION OF THE PARABLE. 1. *To the days before the building of the temple was resumed.* (1) In character those were days of scanty harvests and bad trade (ch. i. 6), of fruitless labours and disappointed expectations. Whereas the farmer might have anticipated from a heap of sheaves twenty measures of wheat, on threshing it out he found only ten; and the vine-dresser who hoped to draw off fifty vessels of wine from the pressing-trough, had to content himself with twenty (ver. 16). (2) The reason of all this was, though it never seemed to strike the people, that Jehovah had, in punishment for their disobedience, smitten the land with blasting and mildew and hail (ver. 17). 2. *To the days since the temple foundation was laid.* Not at the first (Ezra iii. 10), but then, under Haggai, in the four and twentieth day of the ninth month of the second year of Darius (Ezra v. 2; Zech. viii. 9). As yet there was, comparatively speaking, no seed in the barn, and only a small supply of vines, figs, pomegranates, and olives, since the preceding harvest had been bad, so that no evidence as yet appeared that, as regards their condition, any change for the better had begun, nevertheless they were confidently to anticipate that from that day forward Jehovah would bless them.

Learn: 1. The limitations of personal religion. 2. The greater contagion that belongs to sin. 3. The blindness of the human heart to Divine judgments. 4. The certainty that piety will be rewarded. 5. The ability of God to do beyond what reason warrants or sense expects.

Ver. 23.—*Zerubbabel the son of Shealtiel.* I. THE SUBJECT OF A SPECIAL DIVINE CALLING. This alluded to in the words, "I have chosen thee, saith the Lord of hosts." By this was meant, not merely that his birth in Babylon, preservation and growth to manhood, high esteem and favour among his countrymen and with Cyrus, as well as obvious natural abilities, had all come about in accordance with that general providence by which God appoints to all men the times of their coming into life and of their going out at death (Eccles. iii. 1, 2), the bounds of their habitation (Acts xvii. 26), and the particular circumstances of their lot (Ps. xvi. 6); but, in addition to this, that God had specially selected, endowed, and trained him for the office into which he had been thrust, that of leading the people forth from Babylon, and for the work he had now to do, that of laying the foundations, not of a second temple merely, but of a second empire. What Haggai wished to impress upon Zerubbabel was that the position he occupied at the head of the new community was one that had come to him, not by accident, but, as in the earlier cases of Abraham (Isa. xli. 2), Moses (Exod. iii. 10), and Cyrus (Isa. xliv. 28), by Divine appointment. One can imagine the inspiration a thought like that must have imparted to Zerubbabel, the stimulus it must have given to every good impulse of his heart, the elevation and dignity it must have lent to even the least significant action he performed. Similar inspiration, stimulus, and dignity might be enjoyed by all, were all to realize that "the steps of a good man are ordered by the Lord" (Ps. xxxvii. 23), and that for each man's life there is a plan existing in the mind of God, into which each will be surely guided, if only he will meekly put himself into the hand of God (Ps. xxv. 9).

II. THE POSSESSOR OF A LOFTY FAITH. This distinction may be claimed for Zerubbabel, though not assigned a place in the magnificent picture-gallery of Heb. xi.; because it is difficult to see how Zerubbabel, being the man he was, a descendant of the royal line of David, and located where he was in the prosperous city of Babylon, and situated as he was in the manifest enjoyment of the Persian monarch's favour, would have acted as he did, had he not been possessed of faith. In comparison with those who remained behind in Babylon, but a handful set forth to seek the land of their fathers; and it is little probable that Zerubbabel would have cast in his lot with the pilgrims, had he not been persuaded that the movement was of God, that the journey upon which they were about to enter had been marked out for them by Heaven, and that the insignificant and feeble company itself was a true representative of Jehovah's Church upon the earth. That spirit, it may be added, which was present in Zerubbabel, the spirit of faith, which can recognize the superiority of things spiritual and religious to things earthly and secular, that is not ashamed to espouse the cause of truth and righteousness on earth, however humble and obscure, because it is the truth of God, and that is always ready, when the voice of God cries within the soul, "Who will go for us?" to respond, "Here am I, Lord; send me!" lies at the basis of all true greatness in the soul.

III. An example of indomitable courage. Few things rarer, even among Christians, than a fortitude that can brave all difficulties and defy all oppositions, especially in matters of religion. Yet is nothing more indispensable. Thousands of brilliant schemes, private as well as public, in Church as in state, have come to nothing for want of manly resolution to go on with them and carry them through. Had Zerubbabel been a craven, he never would have done so outwardly foolish a thing as join himself with a handful of pilgrims who proposed to quit their comfortable homes and prosperous estates in Babylon, and undertake a long and perilous journey to a promised land on the other side of the Syrian desert. Nor, had he been a weakling, would he have succeeded in carrying these pilgrims in safety to their destination. Traced out on a modern map, it seems not a far journey between Babylon and Jerusalem. Most likely Zerubbabel took the road that Abraham had travelled by when he departed from Ur of the Chaldees, moved northwards to Haran, rounded the head of the Syrian desert, and came down upon Palestine by Damascus. Yet to Abraham, with his comparatively small company, the feat must have been immensely easier than it could have been to Zerubbabel, with fifty thousand heads of families and nearly a quarter of a million souls in all to take charge of. But with the help of God and his own stout heart he did it. It was a feat only second to that of Moses, who brought their fathers out of Egypt, led them through the scorching and fiery wilderness, and set them down at the gate of Canaan. Nor again, unless Zerubbabel had been a hero who was not easily discouraged, could he have brought the temple to completion, working, as he did, with a company of builders who became alarmed at every menace uttered against them by the people of the land, and who threw down their tools on encountering the smallest resistance. So difficult was the task to keep them at their work, and so formidable were the obstacles he had to encounter, that Zechariah, a younger prophet than Haggai, likened the work he had to do to the levelling of a great mountain, encouraging him at the same time with the assurance that it would be levelled, "Who art thou, O great mountain? before Zerubbabel thou shalt become a plain." And become a plain it did. Reinforced by a fresh company of builders who came up from Babylon under the leadership of Ezra, Zerubbabel and his band pushed on the work till it was finished, and the temple received its top-stone with shoutings of "Grace, grace unto it" (Ezra vii. 6—8; Zech. iv. 7).

IV. An illustration of conspicuous promotion. A great honour was conferred on Zerubbabel when chosen by Jehovah to be his servant, and as such appointed the leader of his people. A greater when assured that God would graciously assist him until the task assigned to him had been successfully carried through. The greatest when, in reward for his faithful service, it was promised that he and his would be sharers in the future Messianic glory reserved for Israel; for this is what the clause means, "I will make thee as a signet-ring, O Zerubbabel, my servant." It lends a remarkable interest to this verse of Haggai to be told that in recent excavations upon Temple Hill, a ring has been discovered with the name of Haggai inscribed upon it ('Recent Discoveries on the Temple Hill,' pp. 78—80). In the eyes of Orientals the finger-ring, or signet, was regarded as a valuable possession, to lose which was esteemed a dire calamity. To speak of one as a signet-ring was to assure him of tender regard and watchful preservation. Reversing the threat pronounced against Jeconiah, the last King of Judah, and the grandfather of Zerubbabel (Jer. xxii. 24), Jehovah promises that Zerubbabel shall be as a signet-ring upon his own finger, i.e. shall be indissolubly associated with himself and regarded with sincere affection; and this promise may be said to have been fulfilled, so far as Zerubbabel was concerned, in that he was henceforth inseparably linked with the history of God's people, and in fact constituted an ancestor of Messiah, who afterwards sprang from his line. But as the day when the promised distinction should be conferred on Zerubbabel was expressly specified as the day when the process begun by Jehovah of shaking the heavens and the earth should have been brought to a completion, at which time Zerubbabel should have been long dead, it becomes obvious that the promise must be understood as having reached its highest fulfilment in Zerubbabel's distinguished descendant, who should then be made Jehovah's signet-ring, in reward for a greater work of emancipation and temple-building than had been performed by Zerubbabel.   And in this reward all share who, whether before his coming or since, have been fellow-workers with him by serving the will of God in their day and generation.

LESSONS.   1. The value of great men to their own age and to the world at large. 2. The certainty of a Divine fore-ordination in ordinary life.   3. The impossibility of faithful work on earth losing its reward.

HOMILIES BY VARIOUS AUTHORS.

Vers. 1—9.—*Returning despondency and renewed stimulus.*   In these verses we have the third of the earnest addresses delivered by the devoted seer to these temple-builders.   In the first (ch. i. 3—11) he reproved them for their neglect and stimulated them to the performance of their duty.   In the second (ch. i. 13), in few words, a single pregnant sentence, indeed, he assured them of God's presence with them now that they had repented of their negligence and were prepared to consecrate themselves to the important enterprise.   In this third address (vers. 1—9) he expatiated upon the glory of the second temple.   The people had again become discouraged and depressed, despondent and downcast, and he sought to impel them to fresh endeavour by indicating the brightness and blessedness of the coming times.   Consider—

I. THE CAUSES OF THEIR DESPONDENCY.   This despondency *very soon* again took possession of them.   They had been less than a month engaged in earnest endeavour to carry on the great work when they gave way once more.   It was "on the twenty-fourth day of the sixth month" that, stirred up by the word of God through the prophet, they devoted themselves afresh to the service of rearing the sanctuary for the Lord, and now on the twenty-first day of the seventh month their hands tired and their hearts grew faint.   Why?   1. *The failure of their harvests.*   This was brought conspicuously before them by the fact that "the Feast of Tabernacles" was now going on.   This festival stood out amongst the Jews as "*the* feast," and is described by Jewish writers as "the holiest and greatest feast" of the nation.   It served a double purpose, for whilst it commemorated the goodness of God as manifested to the fathers during their desert-wanderings, it also commemorated his goodness in the harvest just gathered in, and was therefore not only called "the Feast of Tabernacles," but likewise "the Feast of Ingathering." In prosperous times, during its celebration, the holy city wore quite a holiday aspect. It became converted into a vast camp for all the people, and, with a view to make more vivid to them the tent-life of their ancestors in the wilderness, they dwelt for the time being in booths, which they constructed of boughs of olive and palm, pine and myrtle; all the courses of the priests were employed in the religious exercises, bullocks were offered in sacrifice, the Law was read, the trumpets were sounded daily, and each who took part in the commemoration bore in the left hand a branch of citron, and in the right a palm branch entwined with willows and myrtle.   When we remember how that on this occasion, in celebrating this feast, they would have, of necessity, to dispense with many of the usual accompaniments, and also that the blight had been upon their crops, and hence the ingathering had been only scanty (ch. i. 6), we need not be surprised at the depression from which they were suffering.   2. There was, however, another cause of their despondency, viz. *the unfavourable contrast presented as they compared the structure they were rearing with the first temple.*   (Ver. 3.)   There were old men among these returned exiles who had seen the temple of Solomon, and who, when the foundations of this second temple were laid, conscious that the new structure would be very inferior in character to the former building, gave way to demonstrations of grief (Ezra iii. 11—13).   And it would seem that, as the work of reconstruction proceeded, these hoary-headed men continued to revert to the glories of the past, and instituted so many unfavourable comparisons between that age and the times as they were now, that the builders grew weary and faint-hearted in their work.

II. THE CONSIDERATIONS URGED BY THE PROPHET SO AS TO STRENGTHEN THEIR

HEARTS AND TO ENCOURAGE THEM TO RENEWED CONSECRATION. Haggai was aged, yet, unlike his contemporaries, instead of dwelling despondingly upon the past, he looked on hopefully to the future. With prophetic insight he saw the golden age as lying, not in the days of yore, but in the coming time. His thoughts were centred upon Divine blessings to be bestowed richly and bountifully upon the true and faithful, and he sought to animate the drooping faith and hope of the workers by directing their minds to these. He reminded them of: 1. The abiding presence with them of the Lord of hosts, in fulfilment of the covenant made with their fathers (ver. 5). 2. The national upheavings which should take place, and which should be overruled to their good (vers. 6, 7). 3. The halo of glory which should eventually rest upon the shrine they were rearing (vers. 7, 9). 4. The Divine proprietorship of all material resources (ver. 8). 5. The deep and durable tranquillity which should be experienced as the result of the development of the Divine purposes (ver. 9). The sense of despondency is experienced still by those engaged in holy service, and the way to get roused out of this is by anticipating the brighter days that are in store, when rectitude shall mark every character, and truth be on every tongue; when holy virtue shall adorn every life; when the heavenly fruits of "love, joy, peace, long-suffering, kindness, goodness, faithfulness, meekness, temperance," shall everywhere abound, and the Lord of hosts shall have a home and dwelling-place in every heart.—S. D. H.

Vers. 6—9.—*The prophet's Messianic prophecy.* In studying the Old Testament, it is deeply interesting to trace therein the gradual development of the Messianic hope. Three distinct stages are observable. 1. From the promise made at the Fall (Gen. iii. 15) until the death of Moses. The indefinite promise respecting "the Seed of the woman" was made more definite in the promise to Abraham (Gen. xii. 3), and was revealed still more explicitly in "the Prophet" who was declared by Moses as at length to arise, and who should be Law-giver, Ruler, and Deliverer (Deut. xviii. 15). 2. During the reigns of David and Solomon, the idea of the Kingship of the Messiah was developed, and this Divine royalty was the theme of the Messianic psalms. 3. From Isaiah to Malachi we have a yet further unfolding, the Incarnation and Passion of the world's Redeemer being declared (see Liddon's Bampton Lectures on 'Our Lord's Divinity,' lect. ii.). The mission of Haggai had special reference to encouraging the temple-builders in their arduous toil; but the verses now before us (vers. 6—9) connect him with this development of the Messianic anticipation, since only in the light of the Christian age can the full significance of his teaching as contained here be realized.

I. CONSIDER WHAT THIS PROPHECY PROBABLY SUGGESTED TO THE JEWS OF THIS SEER'S OWN TIME. 1. Freedom from the yoke of servitude. These returned exiles were under the power of the Persian monarch; and they would understand their seer (vers. 6, 7) to mean that political agitations would soon occur among the nations, and which their God would overrule to the effecting of their enfranchisement. 2. The temple they were rearing to become enriched with material wealth. "And the desire of all nations shall come," etc. (vers. 7, 8). "*Chemdâh* signifies desire, then the object of desire, that in which a man finds pleasure and joy, valuables. *Chemdath haggōyîm* is therefore the valuable possessions of the heathen, or, according to ver. 8, their gold and silver or their treasures and riches. The thought is the following: That shaking will be followed by this result, or produce this effect, that all the valuable possessions of the heathen will come to fill the temple with glory" (Keil and Delitzsch, on 'The Minor Prophets,' vol. ii. 193, 194). 3. A time of settled peace and prosperity (ver. 9). This restricted apprehension of the meaning underlying the prophet's words would cheer the hearts of the builders and impel them to renewed endeavour.

II. CONSIDER THE PARTIAL FULFILMENT OF THIS PROPHECY DURING THE LATER JEWISH AGE. We know that the national convulsions hinted at in the prophecy did arise—that Persia was subdued by Greece; that Greece was shaken into fragments at the death of Alexander; and that the Eastern world became the prey of Rome; and we know also that whilst these conflicts were going on the Jews prospered, and material wealth flowed into their temple, the heathen, with the decay of their systems, coming and consecrating their possessions to the Lord of hosts. Nor were tokens wanting of the partial fulfilment of the prophecy in its spiritual significance. "Rites and ceremonies retired more into the background; and prayer began to assume its true place in public worship. The religious knowledge of the people was kept up through the regular public reading and distribution of the Scriptures, which were early collected into their present canonical form. Synagogues were established, the people having learnt at Babylon that God's presence might be enjoyed in their assemblies in any place or circumstances. Thus there was kept alive throughout the nation a higher and purer type of religion than it had known in the days when the first temple with its outward splendour and gorgeous ritual excited the admiration of the people, but too seldom led their thoughts to the contemplation of the truths it expressed and prefigured" (McCundy; see Lange's 'Commentary on Haggai,' p. 19).

III. CONSIDER THE COMPLETE FULFILMENT OF THE PROPHECY IN THE CHRISTIAN DISPENSATION. The prophecy is Messianic. Underneath its letter there lies a deep spiritual meaning. The prophet saw, afar off, the day of Christ, and testified beforehand of the latter-day glory of the Lord and his Christ. We see its full accomplishment: 1. In the shaking of the nations by the power of the Divine Spirit. 2. The consecration by the good of all their gifts and endowments to the service of the Lord. 3. The realized spiritual presence of God in Christ with his Church, and which constitutes her true glory. 4. The inward rest and tranquillity all his people shall experience as his bestowment.—S. D. H.

Vers. 4, 5.—*The real presence.* In contrasting the house the builders were now raising for God with the first temple, many a reference was doubtless made by the "ancient men" to "the ark of the covenant" and "the Shechinah," which had been the visible symbols of the Divine presence. What, after all, they would urge, could this new structure be without these precious tokens of the Lord, as being with them in all his majesty and might? Haggai therefore most appropriately laid great emphasis upon the glorious fact that they had with them the spiritual presence of the Lord Most High, who would remain with them, and would faithfully fulfil to them every covenant engagement made with their sires (vers. 4, 5).

I. THE GLORIOUS FACT OF THE REAL PRESENCE OF THE LORD WITH HIS CHURCH. 1. This truth is constantly declared in the oracles of God. 2. It was brought home to the Israelites in the olden times by means of symbolical representations. 3. It was impressed upon these returned captives by the raising up of faithful men to declare the Divine will, and to stimulate them to renewed devotion. 4. It is made manifest to us in the Incarnation of God in Christ. Not only will God in very deed dwell with man upon the earth, but he has even taken man's nature into union with his own. He has come to us, affecting us not only with the glory of his majesty, but revealing to us his very heart, and unveiling to us the intensity of his infinite love.

II. THE INFLUENCE WHICH THE CONSCIOUSNESS OF THIS GREAT TRUTH SHOULD EXERT UPON HIS SERVANTS. 1. It should be to them in times of depression the source of strong consolation. "Be strong" (ver. 4); *i.e.* "Be comforted." 2. It should take from them all craven fear, inspiring them with holy courage: "Fear ye not" (ver. 5). 3. It should impel them to renewed consecrated endeavour: "and work" (ver. 4).—S. D. H.

Ver. 7.—*God's temple filled with glory.* "And I will fill this house with glory, saith the Lord of hosts."

I. VIEW THIS DIVINE PROMISE AS FULFILLED IN THE ADVENT OF CHRIST TO THIS PARTICULAR SANCTUARY FOR GOD. 1. Thither the Child Jesus was taken in his infancy by Joseph and Mary, that they might present him before the Lord. So far as material splendour was concerned, no trace of it was to be seen in this introduction of the Child Jesus to that house. The rich were required to bring a lamb as an offering when they came to present their children thus, but Joseph and Mary were too poor to bring so costly an offering, and hence they brought the humbler gift the Law required. But whilst earthly glory was lacking on this occasion, a higher glory was expressed. See those distinguished servants of God! And as you behold old age gazing with holy joy upon that helpless Babe, regarding him as the Deliverer of Israel, as in imagination you witness the one, Simeon, taking that infant form into his arms, exclaiming

" Lord, now lettest," etc. (Luke ii. 29), and as you behold the other, Anna, " giving thanks to God, and speaking of the Redeemer to all who looked for redemption in Jerusalem " (Luke ii. 38), do you not see the promise realized, " I will fill," etc. (ver. 7) ? 2. When he attained the age of twelve years, we find him again in that temple, sitting as a learner, hearing those who gave instruction there, and asking them questions. We can form no idea as to the nature of the questions he proposed to the masters in Israel ; but when we think of those teachers as being confounded by the questions and answers of that Galilæan Youth, when we remember how that all who heard him were astonished at his understanding, and when we reflect upon the Divine light and knowledge which was then communicated, we see how that on the day when the sorrowing parents were searching diligently for their lost Son, God was fulfilling the promise made ages before to his people, " I will fill," etc. (ver. 7 ; Luke ii. 42—51). 3. Whenever he entered that temple it became filled with the glory of the Lord. This was so, no matter whether he approached it for the purpose of performing some of his mighty works, or to give utterance to his wondrous words, or to drive from the shrine those who were desecrating it and causing it to become a den of thieves. Never did he enter it without imparting to it a glory such as was unknown to the temple of Solomon. That temple in all its glory could not bear comparison with this second, when this latter house was favoured with the visits and the holy influence of the Christ of God ; and it was not until they who ought to have rejoiced in the light he imparted and in the halo his presence shed had rejected and crucified him that the glory departed from this temple as from the former one, and that irreparable ruin was brought upon the house which had been repeatedly filled with the glory of the Lord.

II. VIEW THIS DIVINE PROMISE AS HAVING ITS APPLICATION TO EVERY SANCTUARY IN WHICH GOD IS WORSHIPPED IN SPIRIT AND IN TRUTH. Every such structure is as much God's temple as the Jewish temple ever was. The Christian worshipper may adopt, in reference to the sanctuary to which it is his happiness to repair, such utterances as Ps. lxxxiv. 1 ; lxv. 1, 2 ; cxxii. 1, 2 ; and he can apply to these modern sanctuaries the grand old promise of his God, " And I will fill," etc. (ver. 7). There is but one essential in order that any sanctuary may be filled with glory, *even the presence of Christ,* not the visible, but the spiritual, presence of the Divine Redeemer. Let this be wanting, and it is immaterial how magnificent may be the structure reared or how imposing the outward form. Vestments may be worn, the whole assembly may assume a reverential aspect, the music may be of the most attractive character, the pulpit may be occupied by one who may charm and captivate by his eloquence ; yet if the presence of Christ is not realized, the house will not be lighted up with the true glory ; whereas much of this may be wanting, but if Christ's presence is realized, glory shall fill the place. What a contrast there was between this temple and the upper chamber in which the chosen disciples were assembled, waiting for the fulfilment of the promise of their risen Lord ! And yet, on the second sabbath after the Ascension, a glory filled that upper chamber such as was unknown to the Jewish temple, simply because he who had been driven from the temple, and who, during his appearances there, had been invariably rejected by its worshippers, was a welcome Guest in that upper room. His presence was fully realized there, and hence the place was filled with the Divine glory, and was rendered " the very gate of heaven." The spiritual presence of the Divine Redeemer thus constitutes the true consecration of any building reared for Christian worship and teaching ; this is what is needed in order that any sanctuary in our own day may be filled with God's own glory. Then, clothed with true sincerity of spirit, partaking of his love, his purity, his spirituality, his consecration, walking as he walked, honestly, uprightly, consistently, and so fulfilling the conditions upon which his manifestation depends, may we feel him near, as in the sanctuary, dear to us by hallowed associations, we engage in acts of worship ; near us the Imparter of a Divine life, the Inspirer of all our songs, our prayers, our words, our toils ; the Bestower of large blessings upon us and upon all who come within the range of our influence. " Now therefore arise, O Lord God," etc. (2 Chron. vi. 41).—S. D. H.

Ver. 8.— *The consecration of wealth.* " The silver is mine, and the gold is mine, saith the Lord of hosts."

I. THE DIVINE RIGHT TO EVERYTHING WE POSSESS. God is our Sovereign, and as such he exercises dominion over us, and disposes of us as it seemeth him good. This sovereignty is exercised by him in strict accordance with the principles of wisdom, rectitude, and goodness. This Divine right has reference, not only to ourselves, but extends also to all that we possess. "All things come of him;" we are but stewards of his bounty. The recognition of this fact contributes to a man's real welfare. If a man views his possessions as being his own, he is in danger of that love of money which is the root of all evil. Hence it is with a view to man's spiritual preservation, as well as with a due regard to the benefit of the race and the progress of his cause, that God insists upon his right, saying, "The silver is mine," etc. (ver. 8).

II. THE IMPORTANCE OF THE RECOGNITION OF THIS DIVINE RIGHT ON THE PART OF MAN, AND THE CONSECRATION OF HIS SUBSTANCE TO THE SERVICE OF GOD. 1. *Neglect of this involves loss.* The young ruler an example (Matt. xix. 16—22). "He went away sorrowful, for he had great possessions." He kept his wealth, but at a terrible sacrifice, for he forfeited intercourse with Christ, the joys of the Christly life, and the unfading treasures with which the Saviour was prepared to enrich him.

> "For mark the change! Thus saith the Lord,
> 'Come, part with earth for heaven to-day.'
> The youth, astonished at the word,
> In silent sadness went his way."

2. *Regard to this ensures gain.* Cornelius an example (Acts x. 1, 2). He viewed property as a trust. He rendered unto God his due. His prayers and his alms "came up for a memorial before God." And the result was that God blessed him, granting unto him the ministry of angels, guiding him into truth by his servant, imparting to him the consciousness of his love, and filling him with the graces of his Spirit. Let us readily render unto God his just claim in reference to the possessions of earth (1) when help is required in order to the maintenance of his worship; (2) when the cry of distress, occasioned not by improvidence, but by unavoidable adverse influences, rises into our ears; (3) when fresh openings for doing the work of God both at home and abroad are found, and call for increased liberality that they may be embraced, let God's voice be heard in these, intimating that he has need of those resources which have come to us as his gifts, and let us cheerfully give to him of his own. For who has such right to what we possess of this world's goods as he whose free gifts these are, and who in the bestowment of them has blessed the work of our hands?—S. D. H.

Ver. 9.—*The peace of God.* "And in this place will I give peace, saith the Lord of hosts." Various theories have been propounded concerning how temporal peace and prosperity may be secured to a people. One will tell you that everything turns upon which political party happens to be in power; a second will cry, "Free Trade;" a third will respond, "Protection;" a fourth will dilate upon "the reform of the land laws;" a fifth will enlarge upon the importance of the maintenance of our military prestige, affirming that peace is best guaranteed by being prepared for war; but we may rest assured that the foundations of national peace and prosperity lie deeper far, and are laid in rectitude and righteousness. True peace, and, as a consequence, lasting prosperity, come to a people only in a secondary sense through their rulers and legislators, and men of mark in the various departments: they come primarily through the people themselves. In proportion as they become God-fearing and Christ-like, submissive to the Divine authority and guided by the principles of God's Word, will he bless them and make them prosperous and happy. But there is a higher form of peace than that which is denominated temporal, and to that more exalted blessing the Divine promise contained in this text referred. Temporal peace was now being enjoyed by the returned from exile. They dwelt in quietude, although the subjects of a foreign power. But the Lord of hosts promised them spiritual peace, and assured them that, in association with the sanctuary they were raising to his honour, they should experience inward tranquillity and rest. "In this place will I give peace," etc. (ver. 9).

I. GOD FULFILS HIS GRACIOUS PROMISE TO HIS SERVANTS AS THEY GATHER AT HIS SANCTUARY BURDENED WITH A SENSE OF SIN. In our daily life we are continually contracting fresh sins. We stray from God's ways, undesignedly we err from his precepts, and as the result are rendered restless and disquieted. And coming thus to his house, as we bow in worship, and as we listen to the story of redeeming love, we become humbled in spirit and filled with penitence, and we find peace in Christ. He who controlled the winds and the waves controls also the passions and tumults of the wilder human spirit as he says in gracious tones, " Come unto me, and I will give you rest."

II. GOD FULFILS HIS GRACIOUS PROMISE TO HIS SERVANTS AS THEY GATHER AT HIS SANCTUARY OPPRESSED WITH A SENSE OF SORROW. In every congregation assembled for worship there are to be found sorrowing hearts. " Every heart knoweth its own bitterness," and we little know how many and varied are the trials being experienced by those who form our fellow-worshippers; and as such in their deep need, and oppressed with griefs they could not disclose to others, turn to him who is touched with the feeling of our infirmities, they feel themselves divinely soothed and succoured, and realize the fulfilment of the ancient promise, " And in this place," etc. (ver. 9).

III. GOD FULFILS THIS GRACIOUS PROMISE TO HIS SERVANTS AS THEY GATHER AT HIS SANCTUARY HARASSED THROUGH A SENSE OF MISGIVING AND MISTRUST. Doubts arise within the mind, problems are presented concerning God's truth and his providence that baffle and perplex, and as it was with Asaph in the olden time, so has it been with many since—they have found light cast upon the hidden way as they have come to the sanctuary of God (Ps. lxxiii. 16, 17). And so at all times and under all our experiences he can breathe over us the peace that calms the troubled soul and makes the weary heart at rest.—S. D. H.

Vers. 10—19.—*The past and the future.* Two months had now elapsed since, stimulated by the prophet's glowing words, the temple-builders had resumed their labours (comp. ver. 1 with ver. 10). These months were of great importance with reference to agricultural interests, being the usual season for sowing the seed and planting the vines. That at such a time they should manifest so much zest in the work of rebuilding the temple proved how thoroughly in earnest they were; and this earnestness is the more evident as we remember that the previous harvests having failed, the people must at this time have been in very straitened circumstances. It is not surprising if, whilst engaged in these combined operations, renewed depression took possession of their hearts, and if in sadness they asked themselves what they would do if the next harvest should likewise fail. The address of Haggai recorded in these verses (10—19) was designed either to anticipate or to meet such gloomy apprehensions; and we have only to bear this design in mind, and the meaning of his words, otherwise somewhat ambiguous, becomes very clear.

I. THE CAUSE OF PAST ADVERSITY. 1. He traced this to their own moral defection. The method he adopted was peculiar—it was by means of parables that he sought to make vivid to them their past sinfulness, and which had caused their sorrow. (1) The first parable and its application. He referred them to the priests, bidding them ask whether, if a man carries holy flesh in the lappet of his garment (*i.e.* flesh of animals slain as sacrifices), and he happened to touch any food with the lappet, the food thus touched would become consecrated. The priests, in accordance with the ceremonial Law (Lev. vi. 27), answered, " No " (vers. 11, 12), contending that the lappet of the dress was made holy, but that it was not said in the Law that it could communicate this holiness. So, the prophet implied (ver. 14), was it with his nation. God had chosen their land to set his Name there. His worship had been established in their midst, they had been constituted a favoured people, and their land had been consecrated through this association with the Lord. This, however, did not affect that which had been planted in the soil; the earth was not bound to yield an abundant increase by virtue of these sacred associations. It was only by their being faithful to their high calling, diligently cultivating the soil, and looking up to Heaven for the blessing, that temporal prosperity could be enjoyed, and the lack of this spirit had been the cause of all their sorrow. (2) The second parable and its application. The appeal was again made to the priests, to know whether, if one who had been defiled by contact with a dead body happened to touch anything, the thing thus touched would be unclean. The priests unhesitatingly replied that it would, the declarations of the ceremonial Law upon this point being very explicit (Numb. xix.). So the prophet affirmed that his people, neglecting the claims of Jehovah, had rendered themselves morally unclean, and the blight had consequently rested upon the works of their hands (ver. 14). Their adversity was traceable to their sad defection from holy duty and devotedness to the Lord their God. 2. He intimated that because of this defection God had visited them in judgment. He had in chastisement smitten them with blasting and mildew and hail, rendering their labour so abortive that their sheaves had yielded but a scanty return (vers. 15—17). 3. He recorded the fact that, despite these judgments, they had persisted in their neglect of duty. "Yet ye turned not unto me, saith the Lord" (ver. 17). The prophet's strong faithful speech indicates that there had been amongst these returned captives much of indifference, coldness, and deadness in reference to the work of God, and it was only right that they should be reminded of this, and that by the painful memory of past failure they should be stimulated to more thorough and entire consecration in the future, and to which we may be sure the devoted seer gladly turned. The past is irrevocable and irretrievable. No tears, no regrets, can win it back to us.

> "Thou unrelenting Past!
> Strong are the barriers of thy dark domain;
> All things, yea, even man's life on earth,
> Slide to thy dim dominions and are bound."

The future, however, is available, and hence, leaving the past, with all our shortcomings in relation to it, and rejoicing in God's mercy and in the strength he is so ready to impart, let us "go and sin no more."

II. THE ASSURANCE OF FUTURE PROSPERITY. (Ver. 19.) Their action had now completely changed. They fully recognized God's claims; instead of seeking their own personal and selfish ends, they now consecrated themselves heart and soul to the work of God, striving in every way to advance his glory. The temple rose, and "they finished it according to the commandment," etc. (Ezra vi. 14). And their attitude towards God and his work being thus changed, his attitude towards them became likewise changed. They must still for a while experience the effects of their past neglect in that time must elapse before rich fruitfulness should appear where formerly there had been dearth and barrenness, but they might rest assured of the returning favour of the Lord; yea, from that moment this joy should be theirs. "From this day will I bless you" (ver. 19). So is it in our life, that whilst the cherubim with the flaming sword sternly guard the door of the past, so that there is no possibility of our return (Gen. iii. 24), there is also the angel of the Lord opening up the path before us through the wilderness, and prepared to guide us, if we will, to the brighter Eden that lies beyond (Exod. xxiii. 21, 22).—S. D. H.

Vers. 20—23.—*The final message.* We gather from this last recorded message of this prophet, and addressed to Zerubbabel—

I. THE IMPOSSIBILITY OF JUDGING RESPECTING THE FUTURE FROM PRESENT APPEARANCES. The seer referred to coming commotions and upheavings in national life (vers. 21, 22); but at the time he gave utterance to these intimations all was peace and tranquillity. Rawlinson refers to the Persian empire as spreading over two millions of square miles, or more than half of modern Europe, and this vast power was at this time unassailed. In the opening vision of Zechariah, having reference to this time, the representation made was, "Behold, all the earth sitteth still, and is at rest" (Zech. i. 11). We cannot forecast the future; we know not what a day may bring forth.

II. THE RECOGNITION OF GOD IN THE OVERTHROW OF NATIONS. Repeatedly in vers. 21, 22, the Most High refers to his own action in the convulsions and revolutions to take place. "I will shake," etc. Whilst civil broils and contentions and military conflicts contribute to the effecting of such desolation, these are but agents unconsciously fulfilling the Divine behests. "The Lord God Omnipotent reigneth;" "He changeth the times and the seasons: he removeth kings and setteth up kings" (Dan. ii. 21); "This is the finger of God."

III. THE SECURITY AMIDST ALL THESE CHANGES OF SUCH AS ARE TRULY CONSECRATED TO THE SERVICE OF THE LORD. (Ver. 23.) The signet-ring was a precious token. It was worn by the Eastern prince on one of the fingers of his right hand, and was prized by him above all things. The symbol, as used here, suggests that Zerubbabel the prince, who had so faithfully fulfilled his trust, should be loved and cared for by God; that the Lord would cherish him even as the signet-ring was cherished by its owner. Zerubbabel is regarded by some as a symbolical character, as typical of Christ, the Prince of Peace, who was to come; and such regard this assurance addressed to him as having its application to the Messiah, and as setting forth the Divine Father's delight in him. The emblem may be still further extended in its application. All true and loyal hearts are cared for by him as his chosen ones, and he will preserve them unto his everlasting kingdom.—S. D. H.

Vers. 1—5.—*God's message to his people by Haggai.* "In the seventh month, in the one and twentieth day of the month, came the word of the Lord by the prophet Haggai, saying, Speak now to Zerubbabel the son of Shealtiel, Governor of Judah, and to Joshua the son of Josedech, the high priest, and to the residue of the people," etc. Here is the second Divine message addressed by Haggai to Zerubbabel, Joshua, and the residue of the people. Observe: 1. The Divine message often comes from *one* man to *many.* It now came by Haggai. 2. *All temples* but the temple of nature are to be built by man himself. God could have studded the world with temples; but he has honoured human nature by leaving it to men to do. 3. Any *postponement* of duty is opposed to the will of God. All duty requires the utmost promptitude. The Jews were now dallying with duty. The subject of these verses is—*God requires human labour purely for religious objects.* We have to labour for many things—for material subsistence, for intellectual culture and scientific information, but *in all* for a religion. True labour in every form should be religious. Whatsoever we do in word or deed, we should do all to the glory of God. Three thoughts are here suggested in relation to this subject—

I. THAT THIS LABOUR SHOULD BE STIMULATED BY THE VIEW OF RELIGIOUS DECADENCE. The temple, once the glory of the country, was now in ruins, etc. "Who is left among you that saw this house in her first glory? and how do ye see it now?" Into what a low state has genuine religion sunk in our country! It is cold, formal, worldly, conventional.

II. THAT THIS LABOUR SHOULD BE PERFORMED BY THE MOST VIGOROUS EXERTION. "Be strong, O Zerubbabel, . . . be strong, O Joshua, . . . be strong, all ye people of the land." All the powers of our nature should be concentrated in this work, the work of resuscitation. Why? 1. Because it is *right,* and therefore you may throw your conscience into it. 2. Because it is *worthy* of all your faculties. Call out and honour all the faculties of your nature. 3. Because it is *urgent.* The highest interests of your countrymen and your race depend upon it.

III. THIS LABOUR SHOULD ENLIST THE CO-OPERATION OF ALL. All are called upon here to work. The men in office, and the people. All should unite in this work. It concerns all—young and old, rich and poor. The energies of all should be enlisted in this grand work of religious revival.

IV. THIS LABOUR HAS A GUARANTEE OF DIVINE ASSISTANCE. "For I am with you, saith the Lord of hosts," etc. Those who are engaged in this work are labourers together with God. He is with them, inspiring, directing, encouraging, energizing. Christ says to his disciples, "Lo, I am *with you alway, even unto the end of the world.*"—D. T.

Vers. 6—9.—*The moral progress of the world.* "Thus saith the Lord of hosts; Yet once, it is a little while, and I will shake the heavens, and the earth, and the sea, and the dry land," etc. Humanity is undoubtedly progressing in certain directions—in secular information, in scientific discoveries, in useful and ornamental arts, in the extension of commerce, in the principles of legislation. But whether it is progressing in moral excellence is undoubtedly questionable, and yet there is no real progress without this. The real progress of man is the progress of moral goodness. Three thoughts are suggested by the passage in relation to this moral progress.

I. IT REQUIRES GREAT SOCIAL REVOLUTIONS AMONGST MANKIND. "Thus saith the Lord of hosts; Yet once, it is a little while, and I will shake the heavens, and the earth, and the sea, and the dry land." Perhaps the primary reference here is to the changes which were to be effected in the Jewish system and commonwealth, preparatory to the Christian dispensation. Judaism was, as we know, shaken to its centre by the appearance of Christ. Revolutions in society seem to me essential to the moral progress of the race. There must be revolutions in theories and practices in relation to governments, markets, temples, Churches. How much there is to be shaken in the heaven and earth of Christendom before the cause of true moral progress can advance! May we not hope that all the revolutions that are constantly occurring in governments and nations are only the removal of obstructions in the moral march of humanity? In the clash of arms, in the fall of kingdoms, one ought to hear the words, "Prepare ye the way," etc.

II. IT INVOLVES THE SATISFACTION OF THE MORAL CRAVINGS OF MANKIND. "The desire of all nations shall come." Whether this refers to Christ or not has been questioned. Still, philosophy and history show that he meets all the moral longing of humanity. The moral craving of humanity is satisfied in Christ, and in Christ only. 1. *Man's deep desire is reconciliation to his Creator.* 2. *Man's deep desire is to have inner harmony of soul.* Christ effects this. 3. *To have brotherly unity with the race.* Moral socialism is what all nations crave for. Christ gives this. He breaks down the middle wall of partition. He unites all men together by uniting all men to God.

III. IT ENSURES THE HIGHEST MANIFESTATIONS OF GOD TO MANKIND. "I will fill this house with glory, saith the Lord." 1. *God will be recognized as the universal Proprietor.* "Silver is mine, and gold is mine," etc. In the good time coming, men will feel that all is God's, not theirs. They will act as trustees, not as proprietors. God will be all in all. 2. *God will be recognized as the universal Peace-giver.* "I will give peace, saith the Lord of hosts."—D. T.

Vers. 10—14.—*Human duty.* "In the four and twentieth day of the ninth month, in the second year of Darius, came the word of the Lord by Haggai the prophet, saying, Thus said the Lord of hosts; Ask now the priests concerning the Law," etc. "On the twenty-fourth day of the ninth month of the same year, that is to say, exactly three months after the congregation had resumed the building of the temple (ch. i. 15), and about two months after the second prophecy (ch. ii. 1), a new word of the Lord was uttered through Haggai to the people. [This is the prophet's third address, extending over vers. 10—19.] It was now time, since the despondency which had laid hold of the people a few weeks after the recommencement of the building had been dispelled by the consolatory promises in vers. 6—9, and the work was vigorously pursued, to confirm the people in the fidelity which they had manifested, by bestowing upon them the blessing which had been withdrawn. To this end Haggai received the commission to make it perfectly clear to the people that the curse, which had rested upon them since the building of the temple had been neglected, had been nothing but a punishment for their indolence in not pushing forward the work of the Lord; and and that from that time forth the Lord would bestow his blessing upon them again " (Delitzsch). The passage suggests two facts.

I. THAT THE QUESTION OF HUMAN DUTY IS TO BE DECIDED BY AN APPEAL TO DIVINE AUTHORITY. "Thus saith the Lord of hosts; Ask now the priests concerning the Law." The question, of course, implies two things. 1. *That there is a Divine written law for the regulation of human conduct.* Though the Law here refers to ceremonial institutes which were contained in the Levitical code, there is also a divinely written law of a far higher significance—that moral law which rises out of man's relations, and is binding upon man as man, here and everywhere, now and for ever. 2. *That there are divinely appointed interpreters of this law.* "Ask now the priests." Under the old economy there were men appointed and qualified by God to expound the Law to the people; and in every age there are men endowed with that high moral genius which gives them an insight into the eternal principles of moral obligation. They descry those principles, not only in the words of God, but in his works; they have that ethical and spiritual "unction from the Holy One," by which they know all things pertaining to duty. Thus, then, the question of duty is to be decided. It cannot be decided by the customs of the age, the enactments of governments, or the decrees of Churches. "To the Law and to the testimony." The will of God is the standard of moral obligation.

II. THAT THE DISCHARGE OF DUTY REQUIRES THE SPIRIT OF OBEDIENCE. It was the duty of the Jews now to rebuild the temple; but that duty they discharged not by merely bringing the stones and timbers together and placing them in architectural order. It required further the spirit of consecration. The prophet sought to impress this upon the mind of his fellow-countrymen engaged in this work by propounding two questions referring to points in the ceremonial law. The first had reference to the communication *of the holiness of holy objects to other objects brought into contact with them.* "If one bear holy flesh in the skirt of his garment, and with his skirt do touch bread, or pottage, or wine, or oil, or any meat, shall it be holy?" In other words, whether, if a person carry holy flesh in a lappet of his garment, and touched any food with the lappet, it should become holy in consequence? The priests said, "No;" and rightly. Mere ceremonial holiness cannot impart virtue to our actions in daily life; cannot render our efforts in the service of God acceptable to him. Ritualism without righteousness is morally worthless. The second question was this: "If one that is unclean by a dead body touch any of these, shall it be unclean?" The priests answered and said, "It shall be unclean." "The sum," says an old writer, "of these two rules is that pollution is more easily communicated than sanctification; that is, there are many ways of vice, but only one of virtue, and a difficult one. *Bonum oritur ex integris; malum ex quolibet defectu,* 'Good implies perfection; evil commences with the slightest defect.' Let not men think that living among good people will recommend them to God, if they are not good themselves; but let them fear that touching the unclean thing will defile them, and therefore let them keep at a distance from it."

CONCLUSION. Mark: 1. *The transcendent importance of the spirit of obedience.* What are ceremonial observances, and what are all intellectual or bodily efforts, in connection with religion, apart from the spirit of obedience? Nothing, and worse. "Behold, to obey is better than sacrifice;" "What have I to do with the multitude of thine oblations," etc.? 2. *That man can more easily communicate evil to another than good.* As a legally unclean person could impart his uncleanness to anything, and a legally holy person could not impart his sanctity to anything, so it is suggested that evil is more easily communicated by man to man than good. This is a sad truth, and proved by universal observation and experience. Briars will grow without cultivation, but not roses. A man can give his fever to another easier than he can give his health.—D. T.

Vers. 15—19.—*Man's temporalities.* "And now, I pray you, consider from this day and upward, from before a stone was laid upon a stone in the temple of the Lord," etc. The subject of these verses is *man's temporalities;* or, in other words, his earthly circumstances, his secular condition. And the passage suggests three ideas in relation to this subject.

I. THAT MAN'S TEMPORALITIES ARE AT THE ABSOLUTE DISPOSAL OF GOD. Here the Almighty is represented as at one time, namely, the period during their neglect of rebuilding the temple, withholding from the Jewish people temporal prosperity. But after they had commenced the work in earnest, the stream of prosperity would begin to flow. Here are the words: "Before a stone was laid upon a stone in the temple of the Lord: since those days were, when one came to an heap of twenty measures, there were but ten: when one came to the press-fat for to draw out fifty vessels out of the press, there were but twenty." "It was I that gave you only ten instead of twenty measures, only twenty instead of fifty vessels in the vat. It was I that smote you with blasting and with mildew and with hail." So it ever is. Man's temporal circumstances are at the disposal of God. Out of the earth cometh all man's temporal good; but he can make the earth barren or fruitful as he pleases. He can bind it with frosts, inundate it with floods, or scorch it with heat. Man, cease to pride thyself in thy temporal prosperity!

II. THAT GOD SOMETIMES REGULATES THE TEMPORALITIES OF MAN ACCORDING TO MAN'S MORAL CHARACTER. The Almighty here tells the Jewish people that in consequence of their neglect of his command to rebuild the temple, temporal distress would befall them. He smote them with "blasting" and with "mildew" and with "hail" in all the "labours of their hands." But as soon as they commenced in earnest he said, "From this day will I bless you." The fact that God sometimes and not always regulates man's temporalities according to his moral obedience or disobedience suggests: 1. *That the cultivation of a high moral character is important to man even as a citizen of this earth.* "Godliness is profitable to all things." 2. *That even this occasional expression of God's regard for moral conduct is sufficient to justify* the belief in the doctrine of a future and universal retribution. Antecedently, we should infer that, under the government of an all-wise, all-powerful, and all-just God, man's secular circumstances would be according to his moral worth. It would have been so, had man not fallen, no doubt. It is sometimes so now, as in the case before us. It will be universally so one day—the great day that awaits humanity.

III. THAT THESE FACTS OUR MIGHTY MAKER REQUIRES US PROFOUNDLY TO STUDY. "Now, I pray you, consider from this day and upward." This call to consider the facts is thrice repeated. Consider why the adversity came upon you in the first case, and why the blessing is promised in the second case. It was, in one case, because you neglected your moral duty, and in the second because you began to discharge it. Why should these facts be studied? 1. That we may have a practical consciousness that God is in the world. In all the elements of nature, in all the seasons of the year, in all the varying temperatures and moods of nature, we see God in all things. "The place whereon thou standest is holy ground." 2. That we may have a practical consciousness that God recognizes moral distinctions in human society. Good and evil are not alike to him. The good he sees, he approves; the evil he beholds, he loathes. 3. That we may have a practical consciousness that *retribution is at work in the Divine government.*—D. T.

Vers. 20—23.—*Terrible revolutions.* "And again the word of the Lord came unto Haggai in the four and twentieth day of the month, saying, Speak to Zerubbabel, Governor of Judah, saying, I will shake the heavens and the earth ; and I will overthrow the throne of kingdoms," etc. This is the fourth address. These verses remind us—

I. THAT THE REVOLUTIONS AMONGST MANKIND ARE SOMETIMES VERY TERRIBLE. Here we read of the "shaking of the heavens and the earth," the "crash of thrones," the "destruction of kingdoms," the "overthrow of chariots," etc. What the *particular* revolutions referred to here are cannot be determined. Alas ! we know well enough that such terrible catastrophes have been too common in every age and land. During the last forty years what tremendous revolutions have occurred in Europe and in America ! The political heavens and earth have been shaken to their very centre, and even now the political world throughout Christendom is heaving with earthquakes and thundering with volcanoes. Such revolutions imply the existence and prevalence of two antagonistic moral principles in the world—*good* and *evil.* These are the Titanic chieftains in all the battles, the elemental forces in all the convulsions of the world. It is truth against error, right against wrong, liberty against thraldom, virtue against vice.

II. THAT GOD HAS TO DO EVEN WITH THE MOST TERRIBLE OF THESE REVOLUTIONS. "I will shake the heavens, . . . I will overthrow the throne," etc. "I will destroy the strength," etc. Inasmuch : 1. *As God is eternally against the false and the wrong and the tyrannic, he may be said to be the Author of these revolutions.* 2. *As he can prevent them, he may be said to be the Author of these revolutions.* He does not originate them, but he permits them. He could annihilate all wicked doers by a volition ; he allows them to fight themselves often to death in battling against the right and the true. Hence God permits and controls all human revolutions. This should inspire us with confidence in the most terrible scenes. "The Lord sitteth upon the flood." He sits in serene majesty, controlling all the fury of the battling forces. He "holds the winds in his fist."

III. THAT THE GOOD MAN IS SAFE IN THE MOST TREMENDOUS REVOLUTIONS OF TIME. "In that day, saith the Lord of hosts, will I take thee, O Zerubbabel, my servant, the son of Shealtiel, saith the Lord, and will make thee as a signet : for I have chosen thee, saith the Lord of hosts" (ver. 23). What is here said of Zerubbabel suggests three thoughts. 1. *That good men sustain the highest office.* Zerubbabel was not only a servant, but a "chosen servant." He was selected for the work of rebuilding the temple. The highest honour for moral intelligence is to be the appointed servant of Jehovah. 2. *That good men will receive the highest distinction.* "I will make thee as a signet." A signet indicates : (1) Worth. It was a ring with a seal on it, worn on the finger, as an ornament of great value. Good men are elsewhere represented as God's jewels. (2) Authority. The signet of an Eastern monarch was a sign of delegated authority. A good man is invested with the highest authority—the authority to fight against wrong and to promote right, at all times and in every place 3. *That good men will always be safely kept.* Jehovah says this to Zerubbabel Amidst all evil, "God is my Refuge and Strength, a very present Help in trouble —**D. T**

HOMILETICAL INDEX

TO

THE BOOK OF HAGGAI

———◆◆◆———

ZECHARIAH

EXPOSITION BY

W. J. DEANE

HOMILETICS BY

W. S. LEWIS

HOMILIES BY VARIOUS AUTHORS

W. FORSYTH   D. THOMAS

THE BOOK OF ZECHARIAH

INTRODUCTION

§ I. Subject of the Book

THE prophecy of Zechariah (at least that contained in the first eight chapters) continues and supplements that of his contemporary Haggai. These two prophets were raised up and inspired to animate the flagging energies of the Jews, who, on their return from Babylon (B.C. 536), had begun to rebuild the temple, but were soon disheartened, and at length, owing to opposition of neighbours and adverse circumstances, ceased altogether from the work. Now after sixteen years' intermission, encouraged by the accession of Darius Hystaspes, who looked with favourable eyes on their undertaking, the Jews had an opportunity of resuming their operations. Almost simultaneously with Haggai, Zechariah comes forth to enforce the same lesson, urging them to restore the house of the Lord, and inspiring them with hopes of a glorious future. The rest of the prophecies, if they belong to the same age and author, without special mention of the return from the Captivity, reach to far distant time; they are supposed to speak of the preservation of the temple under Alexander the Great, of the victories of the Maccabees; they certainly speak of the rejection of Christ; they speak of the repentance of the Jews for this rejection, and the final conversion of them and of the Gentiles.

The temple was finished in the sixth year of Darius (B.C. 515); and the latter part of Zechariah's prophecies may have been spoken after that event, and possibly many years subsequent.

The book consists of three parts. The first, after a brief prelude, describes certain visions revealed to the prophet, and ends with a symbolical action typifying the completion and glory of the new temple. The second part comprises an answer to certain questions about the observance of fasts, and a comfortable assurance of the future happiness of Jerusalem. In the final portion the prophet foretells the struggle of God's people against the powers of the world, and Messiah's victory, and announces the conversion of Israel, the destruction of the enemies of the theocracy, and the final exaltation of God's kingdom.

The following is a brief analysis of the book, considered as one harmonious whole, applying to the condition of the chosen people, their dangers and errors, their connection with the powers of the world, God's purposes towards them, and the future that awaits the Church. The first part, consisting of ch. i.—vi., commences with an introduction, giving the title, date, and author's name, followed by a warning from the past and a call to repentance and renewed energy. Then the prophet describes eight visions which came to him on the same night, descriptive of events near at hand and far distant, the interpretation of which is imparted by an angel. In the first vision (ch. i. 7—17) the prophet sees, in a myrtle grove, a rider upon a red horse with attendants. These announce that the whole earth is quiet as yet, unshaken by the storm that is to fall upon it; but God assures the angel that the temple shall be completed, the cities of Judah restored, and Zion comforted. To confirm and explain this promise a second vision is granted (ch. i. 18—21). Four horns, symbols of hostile powers, are destroyed by four craftsmen ("carpenters," Authorized Version). All impediments being thus removed, the various steps to the restoration of the theocracy are revealed. The prophet is shown, in the third vision (ch. ii. 1—13), a man with a measuring-line, who is checked in marking out the ground-plan of Jerusalem by an intimation that the city of the future shall be too large to be compassed by any wall, so abundant will be its population, but that God himself will be her defence and her glory. At this prospect, and at the thought of the affiliation of many heathen nations, Zion is bidden to exult. But the restoration of the material temple would be of no avail without a holy priesthood to minister therein; so the fourth vision (ch. iii. 1—10) exhibits Joshua the high priest engaged in some official duty clad in filthy garments, not in the spotless garb required. But he is pardoned and purified, invested with robes of honour, and reinstalled in his office; and he is promised the Divine protection, and receives an announcement of the advent of Messiah, "The Branch," of whom his office is typical. The spiritual support of the theocracy is next displayed by the vision (the fifth) of the golden candlestick of the holy place (ch. iv. 1—14), which is fed by two olive trees, representing the agencies which convey God's grace to the Church. Zerubbabel is taught to rely upon this, for by it he shall bring his work to completion. The people and the land are now to be sanctified; accordingly, the sixth vision (ch. v. 1—4) represents a huge roll, on which is inscribed the curse against the evil, flying rapidly through the air in token of the speed with which its mission shall be executed. God thus reveals his wrath against sinners in the land. Similarly, in the seventh vision (ch. v. 5—11), the unclean thing, represented by a woman, is caught and confined in an ephah, pressed down by a sheet of lead, and transported out of the Holy Land unto Babylon, the proper home of all that is wicked. The final vision, the eighth (ch. vi. 1—8), discloses four chariots issuing from between two brazen mountains, which are sent as the messengers of God's wrath in the four quarters of the world, till his judgments are satisfied. The destruction of the enemies of God's people is the inauguration of Messiah's kingdom; what glory is reserved for the future temple and who should be the priest to build it up, is set forth by a symbolical action (ch. vi. 9—15). The prophet is directed to take the silver and gold, which some Jews had just brought from Babylon as offerings for the temple, and of them to make crowns, which he was first to place on the head of Joshua, the high priest, the type of Messiah, in whom were united the offices of king and priest, and then to hang them up for a memorial in the temple.

The second part (ch. vii., viii.) is shorter and simpler than the preceding. It is after a silence of two years that the prophet now speaks. A deputation comes to the temple to ask whether the fasts instituted in memory of the calamities of Jerusalem are still to be observed. Zechariah, as chief of the prophets as well as priest, is commissioned to answer. He teaches them that God loves justice and mercy better than outward observances; that they had not listened to previous warnings, and that their hearts were hard even while they fasted. Obedience, he tells them, is the only warrant for blessing from God; and to urge them to this he draws a glowing picture of the prosperity of restored Jerusalem, in whose happiness the once alien nations shall share, esteeming it an honour to be associated with an Israelite.

The interpretation of the rest of the book depends largely upon the view taken of its unity and integrity. If we regard ch. ix.—xi. and ch. xii.—xiv. as written by the same Zechariah as the first part (which seems to me to be the most reasonable hypothesis), the following is the most acceptable explanation of them.

The temple rebuilt and its worship restored, after, it may be, the lapse of many years, Zechariah is inspired to utter the prophecies which compose the third part of his work (ch. ix.—xiv.). He has two "burdens" to deliver, contained respectively in ch. ix.—xi. and xii.—xiv. At the time when these last prophecies were uttered the Jews needed encouragement. Things had not prospered as they hoped; they were still in a depressed condition, vassals of a foreign lord, endangered by the proximity of bitter enemies. The heathen had not come flocking to Jerusalem, eager to embrace the Jewish religion; the temple was not enriched by the gifts of distant nations; their country suffered much from the passage of alien armies which traversed their territory. They had no king; the family of David had fallen into utter insignificance, and their political degradation seemed complete. Now the prophet is commissioned to raise their spirits by a series of fresh communications. And first he gives them hopes of renewed prosperity by foretelling the chastisement of those nations which held territory originally granted to the Israelites—Syria, Philistia, Phœnicia, and over which David and Solomon had actually ruled. So he opens with announcing the judgment on these nations in the neighbourhood, and the preservation of Judæa amid the coming calamities (ch. ix. 1—8). Then shall come to Zion, in meek and lowly fashion, her King, no lordly warrior, but a peaceful Prince, who shall cause the weapons of war to perish, unite in one the divided people, restore the captives, give fertility to the land, and found one universal kingdom (ch. ix. 9—17). Such happy results can be expected only from the God of Israel, not from the idols and teraphim to which once they had recourse. It was for such sins that they had evil rulers set over them; but these shall be removed, and the theocracy shall be established on a firm and lasting foundation, victory and happiness shall be theirs, and the scattered tribes shall be gathered from every part of the world, and serve the Lord in their own chosen land (ch. x.). But there is another side to the picture. They shall not receive this Prince, this Shepherd, when he comes; and punishment falls upon them, first in the north and then in the lowlands and the south. The prophet is bidden to personate Jehovah's Shepherd, and he relates what he himself did in carrying out his commission, the treatment which he received, and how he threw up the office in disgust. The section ends with the prediction of the calamitous rule of "a foolish shepherd," who shall himself be in turn destroyed. The second "burden" is concerned with events chiefly future, but all connected with Israel and the theocracy. The prophet sees Jerusalem surrounded with enemies, but saved by the intervention of Jehovah, who strengthens the people to fight valiantly. This great deliverance shall be followed by a national repentance, which shall be deep and full, resulting in the abolition of the very memory of idols and false prophets, and a general purification (ch. xii. 1—xiii. 6). Recurring to the statement of the rejection of the Shepherd, the prophet shows the result of this sin—the Shepherd smitten, the sheep are scattered, and a remnant only is saved through much tribulation (ch. xiii. 7—9). Then Jerusalem is introduced vanquished, plundered, desolate, when suddenly the Lord comes to her rescue; mighty convulsions of nature accompany his appearance; he raises the holy city to the highest splendour; the enemies perish in terrible fashion; all that are left of the nations shall come hither to worship, and everything henceforward shall be "holiness to the Lord" (ch. xiv.).

"Through the ages, ever since the Christ took his seat on the throne, 'crowned with glory and with honour,' his prediction has been and is being fulfilled. In degree as the kingdom extends and its influence is felt, the curse is lifted from the race, and 'holiness to the Lord' becomes inscribed on those who have been in arms against him, enemies by a mind in evil works. The end is not yet; we see not yet all things put under him. But we see the kingdom advancing, and in due time the mystery of God shall be finished, as he hath declared to his servants the prophets (Rev. x. 7)—that mystery which is also 'the mystery of Christ,' that the Gentiles (τὰ ἔθνη, those outside the Israel of God) are fellow-heirs (with Israel) and of the same body, and partakers of the promise in Christ by the gospel

(Eph. iii. 3—6). This mystery, which was kept secret since the world began, but is manifested now in this latter time, it was given to Zechariah as to other prophets of the former dispensation to make known" (Alexander 'Zechariah's Visions,' pp. 334, 335).

§ II. AUTHOR AND DATE.

The name *Zechariah* was not uncommon among the Jews; more than twenty bore it in the Old Testament. It is interpreted, "The Lord remembers." The prophet calls himself (ch. i. 1) "the son of Berechiah, the son of Iddo," which words the LXX. translates, Ζαχαρίαν τὸν τοῦ Βαραχίου, υἱὸν Ἀδδὼ τὸν προφήτην, as if he was son of Barachias and Iddo, one his natural father, the other his by adoption. But the English Version is doubtless correct in calling him "son of Berechiah," who was son of Iddo. The only objection to this genealogy is that he is termed in Ezra v. 1 and vi. 14, "the son of Iddo;" but the word "son" is used loosely for "grandson," as Laban in Gen. xxix. 5 is called "son" of Nahor, and in Gen. xxxi. 28 Laban calls Jacob's children his "sons." Probably Barachias died young, and Iddo, being more celebrated, and being the immediate predecessor of his grandson, was alone mentioned in the historical books. Iddo was one of the priests who returned from Babylon with Zerubbabel and Jeshua (Neh. xii. 4). Zechariah, therefore, was one of the family of Aaron, and exercised his sacerdotal office in the days of Joiakim, the son of Jeshua (Neh. xii. 12, 16). But he acted as prophet before this, if we can reason on the term "young man" possibly applied to him in ch. ii. 4 (comp. Jer. i. 6). He must have been born in Chaldea, as he commenced his prophetical office eight years after the return, some two months later than his elder contemporary, Haggai, both of these seers having the same object in view—the encouragement of the people in the interrupted work of rebuilding the temple. Jewish tradition makes him a member of the great synagogue, and to have had some share in providing for the liturgical services of the temple. As has been noted in the Introduction to Haggai (§ II.), these two prophets are credited with the production of some eight of the psalms, the contents of which are quite consistent with their supposed authorship. The latest note of time in the prophecy is the fourth year of Darius (ch. vii. 1); but it is with reason conjectured that Zechariah lived to see the temple finished two years later (see Ezra vi. 14, 15). Tradition makes him arrive at extreme old age, dying in Judæa, and being buried in a tomb near to the last resting-place of his fellow-seer Haggai, in the neighbourhood of Eleutheropolis. The sepulchral monument called after him on Mount Olivet is of much later date. Many early writers identified our prophet with the "Zacharias son of Barachias" slain, as our Lord says (Matt. xxiii. 35), "between the sanctuary and the altar." But it is most improbable that the Jews should have committed such a crime at that time, when they had just hearkened to the prophet's voice and done his bidding; there is no hint of any such ending to Zechariah's career in the books of Ezra, Nehemiah, or Malachi, nor is any tendency to such a national crime imputed to his contemporaries. And it is now well recognized that the name Barachias in the text of the Gospel is an interpolation or alteration, and that the incident mentioned has nothing to do with our prophet, but concerns the son of Jehoiada, whose murder is recorded in 2 Chron. xxiv. 20—22.

The first prophecy of Zechariah being uttered in the second year of Darius, and his third in the fourth, the period of the active exercise of his office extended from B.C. 520 to B.C. 518. The headship in the college of priests became his subsequent to this last date, probably on the death of Iddo, his grandfather. It is well pointed out by Dean Perowne ('Dict. of Bible,' iii. 1821, etc.) how important for the due discharge of his special duty was Zechariah's priestly origin. In the history of Israel "too often the prophet had had to stand forth in direct antagonism to the priest." When the latter was a mere formalist, and ignorant of the inner meaning of the holy things which he handled, the former had to recall men's minds to the truth enshrined in the outward ritual. At this time there was danger of apathetic neglect of religion, that the soul and the expression of it would fade entirely away. "At such a time, no more fitting instrument could be found to rouse the people, whose heart had grown cold, than one who united to the authority of the prophet the zeal and the traditions of a sacerdotal family."

Concerning the genuineness of the first eight chapters of the Book of Zechariah, no question has ever been raised. It is quite different with regard to the remainder, the authorship of which has been the subject of dispute since the days of Joseph Mede until the present, and is still undecided. Mede was led to dispute the unity of the book by the fact that in Matt. xxvii. 9 the well-known passage concerning the thirty pieces of silver in ch. xi. 12, 13 is attributed to Jeremiah. Acting on this hint, Mede and his followers found what they considered ample grounds for considering these six last chapters to belong to pre-exilian times, "disputing," as Calmet dryly remarks, "several chapters of Zechariah in order to restore a verse to Jeremiah." Various explanations of the statement in St. Matthew have been offered, e.g. that the name "Jeremiah" is an interpolation, or a clerical error, or that the evangelist quoted from memory, or that the Book of Jeremiah being placed first gave its name to the writings of the other prophets. Any one of these answers would be sufficient to overthrow the argument that is built on this quotation. It cannot be denied that the opposition to the opinion of the unity of our book is of quite modern growth. It was absolutely unknown to antiquity. Neither Jew nor Christian ever disputed the genuineness of these six chapters till some two hundred years ago. It must be remembered that the sacred canon was fixed soon after Zechariah's death, when the question of authorship could most easily have been settled, and there is no proof whatever that the book was not then such as it has reached our hands, and such as all the versions make it to be. The care exhibited in assigning the other prophetical works to their rightful authors, even in the case of the brief prophecy of Obadiah, would surely not be wanting in the case of this long and important oracle. The uniform consensus of antiquity can only be overborne by most cogent arguments. If, indeed, later critics were of one mind on the subject; if, induced by weighty considerations, supported by the new appliances of modern scholarship and fresh discoveries, they were unanimous in affixing a definite date or author to the disputed chapters, there would be, perhaps, sufficient reason to subvert the traditional opinion. But unanimity is remarkably wanting in the theories that have been published. While some affirm merely that the six last chapters are not written by the author of the first eight, others assert that this portion of the book is the work of two authors living at different periods. Many later critics assign ch. ix.—xi. to an anonymous prophet who lived in pre-exilian times, and ch. xii.—xiv. to another Zechariah who flourished just before the destruction of Jerusalem by Nebuchadnezzar. The diversity of date assigned to these supposed authors is wide indeed. Dr. Pusey, in his edition of the 'Minor Prophets,' gives (p. 511, etc.) a curious "Table of dates which in this century have been assigned to Zech. ix.—xiv." By this it appears that the evidence which satisfies one critic that Zechariah wrote in Uzziah's reign (B.C. 770), convinces another that he lived some four hundred and fifty years later—about B.C. 330. The internal evidence which produces such astonishing results must be very uncertain in itself, or be manipulated and interpreted in the loosest manner. The arguments on both sides of the question have been discussed at great length, and will be found set forth in order in the 'Dictionary of the Bible,' and in the works of Dr. Pusey, Dr. Wright, and many others, and succinctly in Archdeacon Perowne's useful edition of 'The Prophet Zechariah.' We add here a brief view of the matter, the objections against the unity of the book and the answers to these objections following one another.

The objections may be classed under two heads, viz.: A, differences in style in the two parts of the book; and, B, historical and chronological references which are inconsistent with the traditionary view of the authorship.

A. *Differences in style.* That there is a marked difference between the style of ch. i.—vii. and the other parts is evident. 1. The first is prosaic, unimaginative, cold; the second is fervid, poetical, lofty, mysterious. But this variety is accounted for by the change of subject. The description of certain visions which really occurred to the writer required a plain, unvarnished narrative, in which flights of imagination and oratorical effects would have been unsuitable. The grand prophecies which follow, uttered probably many years later, and which bear a great similarity to the later Jewish apocalyptic literature, allowed a different treatment. The writer's individuality might here appear; he might bestow care on the form and diction of his communications, and make his language equal his theme. The prophetical inspiration came, it may be, slowly and gradually, giving him time to elaborate the scenes presented and to paint them with the hues of imagination.   Many men write both prose and poetry, and it would often be very difficult to decide from internal considerations that these compositions were the work of the same author.   It must also be observed that the passage ch. ii. 10—13 rises into poetry, while ch. xi. 4, etc., sinks to ordinary prose.   2. Special phrases and idioms which occur in one part are not found in the other.   Thus the introductory formulæ, "The word of the Lord came" (ch. i. 7; iv. 8; vi. 9, etc.), "Thus saith the Lord of hosts" (which occurs very frequently), "I lifted up mine eyes, and saw" (ch. i. 18; ii. 1; v. 1; vi. 1), are never found in the second part; while the phrase, "in that day," which is very common in the latter (e.g. ch. ix. 16; xi. 11; xii. 3, 4, etc.), is entirely absent from the former.   Now, Hosea uses introductory formulæ in the first five chapters of his book, but none in the last nine; yet no one disputes the integrity of that work.   How little dependence can be placed on such variations may be seen by an examination of three of Milton's poems by Professor Stanley Leathes, quoted by Dr. Pusey, p. 505, note 9, by which it appears that in 'L'Allegro' there are 325 words not in 'Il Penseroso,' and 315 not in 'Lycidas,' and that in 'Il Penseroso' there are nearly 440 words not in 'Lycidas.'   Some of the formulæ mentioned are not needed in the second part, and their absence proves nothing.   On the other hand, there are certain rare expressions common to both portions.   Thus: "None passed through nor returned" (ch. vii. 14 and ix. 8); "Sing and rejoice, O daughter of Zion: for, lo, I come" (ch. ii. 10 and ix. 9).   There is a peculiar use of the word "eye" in ch. iii. 9; iv. 10; and ch. ix. 1, 8.   The appellations, "Judah and Israel," "Ephraim and Joseph," are applied to the theocracy (ch. i. 12; ii. 2, 12; viii. 15; and ix. 13; x. 6; xi. 14, etc.).   In both divisions the destruction of the enemies of Israel is predicted (ch. i. 14, 15; vi. 8; and ix. 1—6; xii. 2, etc.; xiv. 14); Messiah is celebrated and highly exalted (ch. iii. 8; vi. 12; and ix. 9, 10); the tribes are invited to return (ch. ii. 6, 7 and ix. 11, 12); the nations shall be converted and join themselves to Israel (ch. ii. 11; vi. 15; viii. 22; and xiv. 16, 17); holiness shall be found pre-eminently in the restored community (ch. iii. 2, etc.; v. 1, etc.; and xiii. 1, etc.; xiv. 20, 21).   We may compare also the promises of abundance, peace, and happiness, in ch. i. 16, 17; ii. 2, 12; iii. 2; viii. 3—5, with those in ch. ix. 8, etc.; xii. 2, etc.; xiii. 1; xiv. 8, etc.; and of the return of the tribes and their consolation in ch. viii. 8, 9 and x. 6, 10 (Knabenbauer).   3. The mention of the prophet's own name or the names of his contemporaries (ch. i. 1, 7; iii. 1; iv. 6; vi. 10, 14; vii. 1, 2, 8); the notes of time (ch. i. 1, 7; vii. 1); the introduction of Satan (ch. iii. 1, 2).   All these things, found in the first part, are absent in the second.   Naturally so.   The earlier section deals directly with contemporary persons and events, the later contains dark prophecies of the future, the date and place of whose delivery were of no practical importance. The course of his predictions did not lead the prophet to speak of Satan in the second part, and the omission of all mention of the evil spirit is equally a feature in the books of other prophets. 4. The absence of visions and the change of figures and imagery entirely separate the second from the former part. But really the answer already given to objection 1 applies equally to this criticism. The changes observed are no more than such as might reasonably be expected from the differing subjects. In the one case the prophet had to narrate visions, and to give practical warnings and exhortations; in the other he was carried away into the distant future, rapt in anticipations of coming glory. What wonder is it that the form of his utterances was altered, and tropes and figures hitherto unused were introduced? We may add, too, that Amos has visions in one part of his book, and in the other only denunciations, and that the first part of our book comprises two chapters in which there are no visions; yet no one has disputed the integrity of the prophecy of Amos, or doubted that the author of ch. i.—vi. of Zechariah and vii., viii., was one and the same. But there is another positive argument for the integrity of the book (which also helps to decide its date) that must not be neglected, and this is the apparent use made in both parts of the earlier and post-exilian prophets. In his opening address, and afterwards, Zechariah refers to "the former prophets" (ch. i. 4—6 and vii. 7, 12), and commentators have gathered numerous such allusions. Thus the mention of the vine and fig tree (ch. iii. 10) seems to come from Micah iv. 4; the remarkable prediction that when the king came to Zion chariots and horses should be cut off from Jerusalem (ch. ix. 10), is also renewed from Micah (v. 10); the exhortation to "flee from the land of the north" (ch. ii. 6, Authorized Version) is founded on that of Isaiah (xlviii. 20), "Flee ye from the Chaldeans;" the words, "Every one that is left of all the nations shall go up from year to year to worship the King, the Lord of hosts, and to keep the Feast of Tabernacles" (ch. xiv. 16), are a remembrance of Isa. lxvi. 23, "From one new moon to another, and from one sabbath to another, shall all flesh come to worship before me, saith the Lord" (comp. Isa. lx. 6—9); the words (ch. xiii. 9), "I will say, It is my people: and they shall say, The Lord is my God," are almost verbally from Hos. ii. 23; the use of the title of the Messiah, "The Branch" (ch. iii. 8; vi. 12), is in accordance with Isa. iv. 2 and Jer. xxiii. 5; xxxiii. 15; the loosing of the exiles from the pit, and the rendering of double unto them (ch. ix. 11, 12), are found in Isa. li. 14 and lxi. 7; ch. ix. 5, in which is announced the desolation of Ashkelon, Gaza, and Ekron, is taken from Zeph. ii. 4; the language (ch. x. 3) concerning "the shepherds" and the "goats" is borrowed from Ezek. xxxiv. 2, 17; from Ezek. xxxiv. comes the whole allegory of ch. xi.; from Ezek. v. 2, 12 is derived the warning (ch. xiii. 8, 9) that two parts of the people shall be cut off, while a third is left in the land; the prophecy of the four chariots (ch. vi.) would be unintelligible without the visions in Dan. ii., vii.; the expression, "the pride of Jordan" (ch. xi. 3), is taken from Jer. xii. 5; xlix. 19. We need not multiply instances further. If these examples are worth anything, and are themselves genuine, they are sufficient to show that the author makes ample use of the prophets that were before him, and likewise, in the second part, quoted largely from post-exilian writers, thus determining, one would infer, his own date.

B. The second head of objections is concerned with *historical and chronological references*. Critics, as we said above, have divided ch. ix.—xiv. among two writers, sometimes assigning ch. ix.—xi. to one, a contemporary of Amos and Isaiah; and the remainder to another, whose date is more uncertain, but at any rate was pre-exilian. Another theory, which places the author in the days of Antiochus Epiphanes, needs no refutation in the face of the only consistent exegesis. The point of the former objection is that the whole part is thought to show indubitable proof that it was written before the Captivity. 1. The kingdom of the ten tribes is supposed to be still standing (ch. ix. 10, 13; x. 6, 7, 10; xi. 14); the prophecy against Damascus, etc. (ch. ix. 1—7), would have been meaningless if the peoples therein denounced had already lost their national existence and suffered punishment for their sins against the Hebrews. But this prophecy may be regarded as especially applicable to the Persian period, and the territory named is that which Persian armies would traverse in their march southwards; it belonged according to promise to the Israelites, and the fate announced for its inhabitants was intended as an assurance to the returned Jews that God watched over them still, and would in the end punish those who usurped their privileges. Nothing can be inferred from the use of the terms "Ephraim," "Judah," and "Israel," for they are employed indiscriminately to express the whole people in or after the Captivity (comp. Jer. xxx. 3, 4; xxxi. 6, 27, 31; xxxiii. 14; Ezek. xxxvii. 16; Ezra i. 3; iii. 1; iv. 1, 3, 4; vii. 13, 14). 2. Idolatry is still practised (ch. x. 2), which was not the case after the return. But it is very probable that the prophet in this passage is referring to past transgressions; nothing is said of idolatry being a sin of his days; though a warning against superstitious practices connected with teraphim and divination may have been needed then, as indeed it might be now in the case of some of the inhabitants of Palestine. 3. The mention of Assyria instead of Babylon in ch. x. 10 shows that the prophecy was composed when Assyria was still a flourishing kingdom. In answer it may be said that the country is referred to whither the tribes had been deported, and where doubtless they had suffered much cruelty at the hands of the Assyrians, though these were now a conquered people. The name "Assyria," too, is used in a loose way for Babylon and Persia in Ezra vi. 22; Judith i. 7; ii. 1 (comp. 1 Esdras ii. 30 and vii. 15). 4. The state of things described in ch. xi. 2, 3, 6, 8, belongs to the period of anarchy after the death of Jeroboam II. (2 Kings xv. 8—16). The description, however, would equally well suit any invasion which occasioned widespread ruin and destruction, and might be applied to the Roman or any other attack; and whatever explanation we give of the cutting off of the "three shepherds," nothing compels us to see in it the violent deaths of Shallum, Zechariah, and a third (?) Menahem—a suggestion which Dr. Pusey calls "even absurd." So it is affirmed that the statements in ch. xiii. 9 and xiv. 2 apply to times before the Captivity; whereas it is plain that the prophet is here speaking of the future, not of the past. To touch briefly on the positive side of the question, we may say that there are details and passages and allusions which could have been written only after the exile. Zechariah mentions governors; he never hints that there was any king in Judæa at the time when he writes; Judah and Israel had been in exile, and some of them still remained in the land of their captivity (ch. ix. 11, 12; x. 6—10); the Jewish nation, Judah and Ephraim, shall wage successful war against "Javan," the Greek rulers of Syria (ch. ix. 13); for the jealousy between the two divisions of the chosen people is ended, and they form one nation, dwelling in Judah and Jerusalem. This could never have been said of pre-exilian times.

Many other alleged proofs of pre-exilian authorship are capable of easy solution, as will be seen by examining their treatment in the Exposition. Suffice it here to say that, while adhering to the traditionary view of the unity and integrity of the book, we lay no great stress on the consideration that Zechariah is the author of the whole; and as long as it is allowed that the writer was gifted with predictive powers, and exercised his prophetical office under the inspiration of God, we deem it a matter of secondary importance whether the words that pass under his name are assigned to one, two, or three authors. It is conjectured that these last chapters had been placed at the end of the minor prophets before Malachi was added to the canon, and thus became appended to Zechariah without further examination. While generally adopting the traditional theory in the Exposition, we have not been unmindful of modern criticism, and, where practicable, have introduced the interpretation which other views of the author's date have constrained some commentators to maintain.

§ III. General Character.

Regarding the Book of Zechariah in its integrity, we meet with great diversity of style, in accordance, as we have seen above, with the varying subject-matter. Visions that came before the prophet's own eyes are narrated in simple prose; in uttering prophecy he rises to a higher level, employing figures and symbols such as Jeremiah and Daniel used, but also showing an originality which gives a peculiar character to his work. The grandest and most powerful passages are found in ch. ix.—xi. These are as fine as any in Hebrew poetry. But in other places the prophet is often harsh, inharmonious; emphasizes by repetition; passes from one point to another abruptly, without connecting link. His parallelisms want the neatness and harmony which are found in earlier writings; his language is tolerably pure and free from Chaldaisms. Many causes have combined to render his oracles difficult of comprehension, so that Jerome speaks of Zechariah as the longest and most obscure of all the twelve prophets. But it must be observed that many of the difficulties found in his work have been imported by commentators themselves. Jewish expositors have refused to acknowledge in his pages a humbled and suffering Messiah; and modern critics, coming to the study with prejudiced notions concerning the prophet's office, have endeavoured to discover sanction for their views in the text, and naturally find the task an arduous one. Scholarship without faith is of little use in interpreting dark places of Scripture.

§ IV. Literature.

The special commentaries on the Prophet Zechariah are very numerous. We select a few out of many that are noteworthy. Among the Jews we have David Kimchi's 'Commentary,' translated by A. McCaul (London, 1837), and other commentaries by Rashi (1713) and Aben Ezra. Of Christian and modern commentators we may mention the following: Grynæus (Geneva, 1581); Ursinus (Frankfort, 1652); W. Pemble, 'Exposition' (London, 1629); Nemethus, 'Proph. Zech. Explic.' (Ultr., 1714); Venema, 'Serm. Acad.' (Leovard., 1787); Blayney, 'A New Translation' (Oxford, 1797); Koester, 'Meletemata' (1818); Stonard (London, 1824); Baumgarten, 'Nachtgesichte Zach.' (Braunschweig, 1854, 1855); Moore, 'Prophets of the Restoration' (New York, 1856); Neumann, 'Die Weissag. d. Sakh.' (Stuttgart, 1860); Kliefoth, 'Der Pr. Sach. übers.' (Schwerin, 1862); Köhler, 'Die Nachexil. Proph.' (Erlangen, 1860, 1865); Von Ortenberg, 'Die Bestundtheile d. Buch. Sach.' (Gotha, 1859); Pressel, 'Comm. zu Hag.,' etc. (Gotha, 1870); Dr. C. H. H. Wright, 'Zech. and his Prophecies' (London, 1879); W. H. Lowe, 'Hebr. Student's Comm. on Zech.' (London, 1882); Dr. W. L. Alexander, 'Zechariah, his Visions and Warnings' (London, 1885); Archdeacon Perowne, in 'Cambridge Bible for Schools' (1886).

Besides the above-named commentators, there are numerous writers who have discussed the question of the integrity of the book, a list of the chief of whom will be found in the 'Dictionary of the Bible,' and a further selection in the Introduction to Dr. Wright's work.

§ V. Arrangement in Sections.

The book consists of three parts.

Part I. (Ch. i.—vi.) A series of eight visions, and a symbolical action.
§ 1. (Ch. i. 1.) Title and author.
§ 2. (Ch. i. 2—6.) The prophet admonishes the people not to follow their fore-fathers' evil example, but to turn to the Lord with all their heart.
§ 3. (Ch. i. 7—17.) The first vision: the horsemen in the myrtle grove.
§ 4. (Ch. i. 18—21.) The second vision: the four horns and the four craftsmen.
§ 5. (Ch. ii. 1—13.) The third vision: the man with the measuring-line.
§ 6. (Ch. iii. 1—10.) The fourth vision: Joshua the high priest before the angel.
§ 7. (Ch. iv. 1—14.) The fifth vision: the golden candlestick.
§ 8. (Ch. v. 1—4.) The sixth vision: the flying roll.
§ 9. (Ch. v. 5—11.) The seventh vision: the woman in the ephah.
§ 10. (Ch. vi. 1—8.) The eighth vision: the four chariots.
§ 11. (Ch. vi. 9—15.) A symbolical action—the crowning of the high priest.
Part II. (Ch. vii., viii.) Answer to a question concerning the observance of certain fasts.
§ 1. (Ch. vii. 1—3.) A deputation comes from Bethel to ask whether a fast instituted in calamitous times was still to be maintained.

§ 2. (Ch. vii. 4—7.) In answer they are told that fasting is in itself an indifferent thing, but is to be judged by the conduct of those who observe it.

§ 3. (Ch. vii. 8—14.) They are further reminded that they had been disobedient in old time, and had been punished by exile.

§ 4. (Ch. viii. 1—8.) The Lord promises to show his love for Zion, to dwell among his people, and to fill Jerusalem with a happy populace.

§ 5. (Ch. viii. 9—17.) The people are exhorted to be of good cheer, for God will henceforth give them his blessing, which, however, was conditional on their obedience.

§ 6. (Ch. viii. 18—23.) The fasts should be turned into joyful festivals, former calamities being forgotten; the heathen should worship the God of Israel, and esteem it an honour to be received into fellowship with the Jewish nation.

Part III. (Ch. ix.—xiv.) The future of the powers of the world and of the kingdom of God.

A. (Ch. ix.—xi.) The first burden.

§ 1. (Ch. ix. 1—8.) To prepare the land for Israel, and to prove God's care for his people, the neighbouring heathen shall be destroyed, while Israel shall dwell in safety and independence.

§ 2. (Ch. ix. 9, 10.) Then shall the righteous King come to Zion in lowly fashion, and inaugurate a kingdom of peace.

§ 3. (Ch. ix. 11—17.) All Israel united into one people shall wage successful war with adversaries, and attain to glory, and increase largely in numbers.

§ 4. (Ch. x. 1, 2.) These blessings are to be asked from the Lord, not from idols or teraphim.

§ 5. (Ch. x. 3, 4.) The evil rulers set over them for their sins shall be removed, and Israel shall be firmly established.

§ 6. (Ch. x. 5—7.) Israel and Judah together shall triumph over their foes.

§ 7. (Ch. x. 8—12.) The scattered people shall be gathered from all parts of the world, and dwell in their own land, under the protection of Jehovah.

§ 8. (Ch. xi. 1—3.) The Holy Land is threatened with judgment.

§ 9. (Ch. xi. 4—14.) The punishment falls because the people reject the good Shepherd, personified by the prophet, who rules the flock and punishes evil-doers in vain, and at last flings up his office in indignation at their contumacy.

§ 10. (Ch. xi. 15—17.) In retribution the people are given over to a foolish shepherd, who shall destroy them, but shall himself, in turn, perish miserably.

B. (Ch. xii.—xiv.) The second burden.

§ 1. (Ch. xii. 1—9.) Hostile nations gather together against Jerusalem, but shall themselves be overthrown; for the inhabitants and their leaders, trusting in the Lord, will overcome all opposition.

§ 2. (Ch. xii. 10—14.) There shall ensue an outpouring of God's Spirit, which shall produce a great national repentance.

§ 3. (Ch. xiii. 1—6.) This repentance will lead to purification from past defilement, and a reaction against idolatry and false prophets.

§ 4. (Ch. xiii. 7—9.) For the smiting of the good Shepherd Israel is punished, passes through much tribulation, by which it is refined, and in the end (though but a remnant) is saved.

§ 5. (Ch. xiv. 1, 2.) Jerusalem is represented as taken and plundered.

§ 6. (Ch. xiv. 3—7.) Then the Lord himself comes to her help, great convulsions of nature accompanying his presence.

§ 7. (Ch. xiv. 8—11.) The land shall be transformed and renewed, and the Lord shall be owned as the sole King of all the earth.

§ 8. (Ch. xiv. 12—15.) Further details concerning the destruction of the enemies: they shall perish by plague, by mutual slaughter, by the sword of Judah.

§ 9. (Ch. xiv. 16—19.) The heathen shall be converted and join with the Hebrews in the regular worship of Jehovah.

§ 10. (Ch. xiv. 20, 21.) Then everything alike shall be holy, and the ungodly shall be wholly excluded from the house of the Lord.

THE BOOK OF ZECHARIAH

EXPOSITION

CHAPTER I.

Ver. 1—ch. vi. 15.—Part I. A SERIES OF EIGHT VISIONS, AND A SYMBOLICAL ACTION.

Ver. 1.—§ 1. *Title of the book, and author.* **The eighth month.** This was called Bul before the Captivity (1 Kings vi. 38), and afterwards Marchesvan (Josephus, 'Ant.,' i. 3. 3); it answered to parts of October and November, and was a time of rain. Haggai had first prophesied two months earlier. **The second year of Darius.** Being now under foreign rule, the prophet uses the regnal years of the king to whom his people were subject (see note on Hag. i. 1). **Son of Berechiah** (see Introduction, § II.). **The prophet.** This appellation belongs to "Zechariah," as the LXX. and Vulgate take it. A comma should be inserted after "Iddo" here and in ver. 7. **Saying.** The visions virtually spoke to him, communicated to him the Lord's will; but first he has to deliver the following warning.

Vers. 2—6.—§ 2. *The prophet admonishes the people not to follow their forefathers' evil example, but to turn to the Lord with all their heart.*

Ver. 2.—Hath been sore displeased; literally, *displeased with displeasure*, which the versions render, ὠργίσθη ὀργὴν μεγάλην: *iratus iracundia* (cf. ver. 15). Not only events connected with their earlier history proved that God had been incensed with their forefathers, but the ruin of their kingdom, and the late Captivity, and the desolation around them, were evidence of the same sad truth.

Ver. 3.—Say thou unto them. The prophet shows why he has reminded them of their forefathers' sins and punishment. **Saith the Lord of hosts.** The expression recurs three times in this verse; it denotes the almightiness and infinite resources of God

(see note **A** in the appendix to Archdeacon Perowne's edition of this prophet). Its constant repetition, as in Haggai, gives a certain heaviness to the prophet's style. **Turn** (*return*) **ye unto me.** He calls the people to repentance, partly, doubtless, with a view to their taking an active part in rebuilding the temple, thus carrying on the exhortations of Haggai, but also with reference to their general indevotion and laxity which Ezra afterwards had to reprove (see Ezra ix. 2). **Saith the Lord of hosts;** literally, (*it is*) *the utterance of Jehovah of hosts.* This is a more threatening form than the mere "saith" in the other two places in this verse. **And I will turn** (*return*) **unto you** (Mal. iii. 7). God promises his favour on their repentance and better conduct; as Haggai had been commissioned to proclaim a return of fruitful seasons as soon as the people obeyed his word and attended diligently to the work before them (Hag. ii. 19). They were called now to attend to the pure worship of the Lord, as the sole condition of prosperity (comp. 2 Chron. xxx. 6; Jas. iv. 8). It has been well observed that when it is said, "Turn ye unto me," etc., we are reminded of our free-will; and when we cry, "Turn us, good Lord, and we shall be turned," we acknowledge the need of God's preventing grace.

Ver. 4.—The former prophets have cried. Omit "have." The prophets referred to are those before the Captivity, both those whose writings are extant, as Hosea, Joel, Amos, etc., and those whose names are mentioned in the historical books, *e.g.* Nathan, Gad, Shemaiah, Azariah, Hanani, Elijah, Elisha, Micaiah (Pusey). (See similar complaints in 2 Kings xvii. 13; 2 Chron. xxxvi. 15, etc.; Jer. xxv. 3—8, which last passage seems to have been in Zechariah's mind.)

Ver. 5.—To compel them to listen to the warning, he asks them, **Your fathers, where are they?** What became of those who paid no heed to the admonitions of the prophets? Have they not suffered dire calamities and perished miserably? And the prophets, do they live for ever? They can teach and threaten no longer. It is true that the seers who warned your fathers are no more, but did not their words come true (see ver. 6)? Jerome referred these words to the false prophets, resting, doubtless, on Jer. xxxvii. 19. But it is more natural to refer them to the "former prophets" mentioned above and in the following verse.

Ver. 6.—**My words.** The words that God put into the mouths of the prophets (Jer. xxxix. 16; Lam. ii. 17). Statutes, usually applied to the Law, which the prophets had to announce and enforce; but it may mean "decrees" which God appointed (Zeph. ii. 2). The LXX. inserts "receive ye" to govern these nouns. **I commanded.** The LXX. adds, ἐν πνεύματί μου, "by my inspiration." **Did they not take hold of your fathers?** *Did they not overtake*, etc.? Did not their threatened chastisements, however long delayed, reach your fathers in the end? **And they returned;** turned, as vers. 3, 4. They turned so far as to acknowledge that the threats had been fully accomplished (see Dan. ix. 5; Ezra ix. 6, etc.). **Thought to do;** παρατέτακται (Septuagint), "designed, purposed to do" (comp. Lam. ii. 17).

Vers. 7—17.—§ 3. *The first vision: the horsemen in the myrtle grove.*

Ver. 7.—In a series of visions it is now shown what is the nature of the restored theocracy, and what shall befall it. Thus were the people comforted by hearing God's purposes of mercy and the great future that awaited Israel. In this first vision it is revealed to Zechariah that the Gentile nations should be overthrown, and that whatever might be the present condition of the Jewish people, God's purpose of mercy toward them was unshaken and would be fulfilled. **The four and twentieth day of the eleventh month, which is the month Sebat.** This month (called here by its Chaldean name) answered to parts of January and February. It was three months since Zechariah had been called to the prophetical office, and five since the building of the temple had been resumed at Haggai's remonstrance. Meantime Haggai had concluded his mission by uttering his final prophecies two months ago, and now Zechariah carries on the revelation. A comparison of the months in the cuneiform inscriptions with the Hebrew will be found in Schrader, 'Keilinschriften,' 379, and in Dr. Wright's note on this verse. **The word of the Lord.** The visions with their explanations are in effect the oracle (see note on ver. 1).

Ver. 8.—**I saw by night;** *in the night;* i.e.

the night of the twenty-fourth day (ver. 7). The visions were seen in this one night at short intervals. There is nothing to make one suppose that they came in dreams (Isa. xxix. 7). The prophet is awake, but whether he sees these scenes with his bodily eyes, or was rapt in ecstasy, cannot be decided. **A man riding upon a red horse.** This is the Angel of Jehovah, mentioned again in ver. 10 and in ver. 11, in both of which places the description, "that stood among the myrtle trees," serves to identify him. He is different from the interpreting angel, and is the leader of the company of horsemen that follow him. Keil and Wright consider that the rider on the red horse cannot be identified with the Angel of Jehovah, because otherwise he would have been represented as standing opposite to the other horsemen to receive the information which they brought him, and they would not have been spoken of as "behind" him. But the expression in ver. 8 may mean merely that the prophet sets his eyes first on the leader and then on the attendants. Or in ver. 10 he is the spokesman who begins the account of the riders' doings, which these themselves complete in ver. 11. Thus there are in the scene only (1) the prophet; (2) the angel-rider and his attendants; and (3) the interpreting angel. The red colour of the horse is supposed to represent war and bloodshed, as in Rev. vi. 4; but this seems unsuitable in this place, where nothing of the kind is intimated, but rather the contrary (ver. 11). It is, indeed, impossible to affix any satisfactory explanation to the colour. If, as we may well suppose, this personage is the Angel of the covenant, who was the leader and guide of the Israelites (comp. Josh. v. 13), his standing in the valley among the myrtles may represent the depressed and humbled condition of the chosen people, which yet was well-pleasing unto God, like the sweet scent of odoriferous myrtles is agreeable to men. **The myrtle trees.** The myrtle is indigenous in the hilly regions of Northern Palestine, and is still seen in the glens near Jerusalem, though no longer on the Mount of Olives, where the returned captives found it when celebrating their first Feast of Tabernacles (Neh. viii. 15). **In the bottom;** *the valley.* Myrtles love such places. "Amantes littora myrtos" (Virgil, 'Georg.,' iv. 124). The term would suit the valley of the Kidron. Others render, "the shady place," or "the tabernacle," but not so appropriately. LXX., ὀναμέσον τῶν [Alex., δύο] ὀρέων τῶν κατασκίων, "between the shady mountains." The Greek translators seem to have borrowed their reading from ch. vi., where the chariots issue from between two mountains of brass. **Behind him were there red horses;** *i.e.*

horses mounted by riders (ver. 11). **Speckled.** It is not clear what colour is meant by this word. The Revised Version gives *sorrel;* Wright, " bay or chestnut;" LXX., ψαροὶ καὶ ποικίλοι : "dapple-grey and spotted;" Vulgate, *varii.* The Septuagint Version is probably a double rendering. The word occurs elsewhere only in Isa. xvi. 8, where it is applied to the tendrils of the vine. What is intended by the different colours of the horses is a matter of great dispute, and cannot be known. There is some reason for considering that they represent the world-powers at this particular period—the Babylonian, the Medo-Persian, the Greek; three of those concerning which Daniel prophesied; the fourth, the Roman, not having yet come in view. The notion of tutelary angels, presiding over countries, was familiar to the Hebrew mind (see Dan. x. 12, 13, 20, 21). These horsemen are evidently not post-couriers, but warriors on military service.

Ver. 9.—**O my lord.** The prophet speaks to the angel of the Lord, who answers briefly, and is succeeded by the interpreting angel. **What are these?** Not " who," but " what;" *i.e.* what do they signify? (comp. Amos vii. 8). **That talked with me;** literally, as the LXX. and Vulgate, *that spake in me.* So vers. 13, 14, and in the following visions. Hence some regard the expression as intimating a communication borne inwardly to the soul without the aid of external organs, or that the angel overpowered and influenced the prophet as the evil spirit possessed the demoniac. But the same term is used, as Dr. Wright points out, in the sense of to commune with a person (Numb. xii. 6, 8; 1 Sam. xxv. 39), and to speak to a person (Hos. i. 2; and perhaps Hab. ii. 1). It may, however, be that the angel of the Lord presented matters objectively, and the prophet's own angel interpreted subjectively. But the Authorized Version is probably correct. **I will show thee.** This he does through the chief angel (ver. 10).

Ver. 10.—**The man that stood,** etc. The rider upon the red horse of ver. 8, the leader of the company of horsemen. **Answered** the question which the prophet had proposed, or answered in response to a sign from the interpreting angel. **They whom the Lord hath sent,** etc. These angelic ministers had been sent to traverse the earth and to report its condition (comp. Job i. 7; ii. 2; Heb. i. 14), and to guide it to the carrying out of God's purposes.

Ver. 11.—**They answered.** Having said who they were, the angel directs them to tell of their doings. **The angel of the Lord.** The " man riding upon the red horse" (ver. 8) is now called " the Angel of Jehovah." This term is usually held to denote a mani-

festation of the Logos, the Second Person of the Holy Trinity, assuming an angelic form or imparting his immediate presence to the revealer of his will. **Sitteth still, and is at rest.** The world was lying in proud security. There was no sign of that shaking of nations which Haggai (ii. 7, 21, 22) had foretold should precede the coming of Messiah and the restoration of Israel. In this second year of Darius, the empire, though suffering from internal disturbances, was outwardly at peace, and was threatened by no enemy at a distance. But the condition of the Jews was sad and disheartening; the temple still unbuilt, the walls of Jerusalem lying in ruins, themselves only a small remnant, exposed to the insults and attacks of jealous neighbours, living on sufferance as subjects of a heathen power, and no sign of the predicted salvation appearing,—this was their state. And the angel sees their despondency, recognizes their disappointment, and intercedes for them.

Ver. 12.—**Answered.** He answered the feeling in the prophet's mind, the unexpressed longing of his heart. **O Lord of hosts.** The angel is the intercessor for the people. So Christ prays to the Father (John xvii.). **How long wilt thou not have mercy,** etc.? He prays that the weary waiting for deliverance may speedily come to an end, and Jerusalem be restored, and Judæa be again inhabited by a happy population. **These three score and ten years.** The predicted seventy years of captivity (Jer. xxv. 11; xxix. 10) were past; it was time that the punishment should cease. There are two computations of this period. The first dates from the first capture of Jerusalem by Nebuchadnezzar, B.C. 606, when Judæa was made tributary to Babylon (2 Kings xxiv. 1; 2 Chron. xxxvi. 6; Dan. i. 1, etc.), unto the return of the company of exiles under Zerubbabel, B.C. 536; the second dates from the final destruction of Jerusalem, B.C. 588, unto the second year of Darius, B.C. 519, when Zechariah saw these visions. However reckoned, the dark period was now over; might they not now expect the commotion among the nations which was to precede their own restitution?

Ver. 13.—**The Lord answered.** The Angel of Jehovah is thus called as the representative of God, whether we regard him as the Logos or a created angel empowered by God (see note on ver. 11). This personage is often seemingly identified with Jehovah (comp. ch. iii. 2; Gen. xviii. 1, 2, 13, 17, 22; Josh. v. 14, 15; vi. 2). He gives the answer to the interpreting angel, which the latter is to convey to the prophet, which he, in turn, was to announce to the people. **Good words,** promising blessing and salvation

(1 Kings xii. 7); and these are comfortable words (Isa. lvii. 18), a message calculated to bring comfort to the people's desponding hearts. What the message is is given in the following verses (14—17).

Ver. 14.—Cry thou (Isa. xl. 6). The prophet has to publish two things: (1) God's love for his people, however humiliated and miserable their present position might be; and (2) the promise of coming prosperity. I am jealous. The term implies ardent love, which cannot bear itself to be slighted, or the object of its affection to be injured (comp. ch. viii. 2, and note there; Numb. xxv. 11, 13; Joel ii. 18). For Jerusalem, as the capital of the kingdom; and for Zion, as the seat of worship.

Ver. 15.—The heathen; the nations, who were God's instruments in punishing Israel. That are at ease. Living in proud security and self-enjoyment (Isa. xxxii. 9, 11; Amos vi. 1; comp. ver. 11). Septuagint, τὰ συνεπιτιθέμενα, "which join in attacking her;" Vulgate, opulentas, "wealthy," their riches giving them self-confidence. I was but a little displeased. God had been angry with his people, it is true, but only in measure, chastising them, like a parent, for their good. Others take "a little" (parum, ὀλίγα) to mean "for a little time," in allusion to the seventy years' captivity. And they helped forward the affliction; or, in the LXX., συνεπέθεντο εἰς κακὰ, "helped for evil;" Vulgate, adjuverunt in malum. They exceeded their part as mere instruments in God's hands, and wished to destroy Israel altogether, or to oppress them beyond the purposed period of their chastisement. A similar complaint is made against the Assyrians (Isa. x. 5, etc.) and the Babylonians (Isa. xlvii. 6).

Ver. 16.—Therefore. Because God loved his people and was incensed with the heathen. I am returned; I return. According to the promise in ver. 3 (see note on ch. viii. 3). A line shall be stretched forth. A measuring-line shall now be used to mark out the city for rebuilding (Job xxxviii. 5). The first proof of God's renewed mercy would be seen in the restoration of the temple, the symbol of the theocracy, and in the revival of the city, the type of national life. The "line" had been used for purposes of destruction (2 Kings xxi. 13; Isa. xxxiv. 11; Lam. ii. 8).

Ver. 17.—Cry yet, saying. This introduces the second part of the prophet's message. The LXX. begins the verse with the words, "And the angel that spake in me said unto me." My cities through prosperity shall yet be spread abroad. "Yet," in this verse, is better rendered again. God calls the cities his, to show his love for Judah; and he promises that they shall not only be reoccupied

by returning immigrants, but increased in extent and number by reason of the enlarged population. So Josephus tells us that in later times Jerusalem had outgrown its walls, and that the fourth quarter, Bezetha, was added ('Bell. Jud.,' v. 4. 2). But it seems best to translate the clause thus: "My cities shall yet overflow with prosperity." Vulgate, Adhuc affluent civitates meæ bonis; LXX., Ἔτι διαχυθήσονται πόλεις ἐν ἀγαθοῖς. Shall yet comfort Zion, for all her afflictions. Shall yet choose Jerusalem (ch. ii. 12 [16, Hebrew]; iii. 2). God will show that the election of Israel remains unimpaired and secure (comp. 2 Kings xxi. 7; 2 Chron. vi. 5). The partial fulfilment of the items of this prophecy are to be found in the rebuilding of the temple, the restoration of Jerusalem by Nehemiah, and the prosperity of Judah under the Asmonean princes. A hint of further blessings is given in the final clause, but their nature is not expressly mentioned.

Vers. 18—21.—§ 4. The second vision: the four horns and the four craftsmen.

Ver. 18.—I lifted up mine eyes, and saw. This vision is closely connected with the former. The prophet had been told that the hostile nations should be punished and scattered; he now is shown this threat being executed. Four horns, belonging to four beasts but dimly seen or wholly invisible. Horns are symbols of strength and power (comp. Ps. lxxv. 4, 5; Dan. viii. 3; Amos vi. 13). Here they mean powers hostile to Israel, and the number "four" (the symbol of completeness) points to the four winds from which they come, i.e. from every side. In the Hebrew ch. ii. begins at this verse.

Ver. 19.—Which have scattered, etc. Some see here an allusion to the prophecy of Daniel concerning the Babylonians, Medo-Persians, Macedonians, and Romans. Against this view it is urged that the prophet is speaking of past events, not of a far-distant future. Others take the four horns to represent Assyria, Egypt, Babylon, and Medo-Persia, all of which had scattered Israel. But it is well to lay no special stress on such explanations of symbolical language, which are at best mere conjectures, liable to be overthrown by a new theory. The word "scattered," which Jerome renders ventilaverunt, means properly, as Wright observes, "to winnow," to separate and scatter by means of the wind. The perfect tense of this verb must not be pressed so as to exclude all notion of coming events. The prophets see at one glance past and future, and combine in one expression far-distant occurrences. Doubtless Zechariah's vision has some relation to

Daniel's, and his description of the powers hostile to the Church of God runs on parallel lines with that of his predecessor. Whether he refers to the same four empires must be left in uncertainty. **Judah, Israel, and Jerusalem.** All the tribes and the capital. According to Ewald, Judah is named first as occupying the place of honour, even as Benjamin is named before Judah in Ps. lxviii. 27, because the capital city lay in its territory. Jerusalem was the centre of worship and government for all the people, the northern tribes being represented by Israel, the southern by Judah. Some critics cancel the word "Israel" here, and there is no doubt that it is often written for "Jerusalem" by mistake (comp. Jer. xxiii. 6 [where see Professor Cheyne's note]; xxxii. 30, 32; li. 49; Zeph. iii. 14; Mal. ii. 11). Grätz supposes that in the present passage the scribe discovered his mistake, and wrote the right word "Jerusalem" after the wrong one "Israel," but leaving the latter still in the manuscript. Of course, there is no proof of this supposition. Some manuscripts of the Septuagint omit "Jerusalem" here.

Ver. 20.—**Four carpenters;** *craftsmen;* Revised Version, *smiths*, in which case "the horns" would be made of iron. The word is applied to workers in wood, stone, and metal; therefore an ambiguous rendering seems most suitable here. LXX., τέκτονας; Vulgate, *fabros.* They represent the human agencies employed by God to overthrow the powers hostile to the Church. Their number is the same as that of the "horns," thus showing their adequacy for the work which they have to execute. It is quite unnecessary to attempt to identify the four "craftsmen." Some take them to be Zerubbabel, Joshua, Ezra, and Nehemiah; or Nebuchadnezzar, Cyrus, Cambyses, and Alexander the Great; or the four evangelists; or generally, angels. We shall be safer if we look upon them merely as God's instruments and servants without further identification.

Ver. 21.—**And he spake.** The interpreting angel spake. **Which have scattered Judah.** The LXX. adds, "and broke Israel in pieces." **Did lift up his head.** These powers laid Judah prostrate. **To fray them.** To terrify the powers symbolized by the four horns, and disturb their self-complacent security (ver. 15). The LXX., mistaking the sense, gives, Τοῦ ὀξῦναι αὐτὰ εἰς χεῖρας αὐτῶν τὰ τέσσαρα κέρατα, "To sharpen them, even the four horns, in their hands." **To cast out;** *to cast down,* to overthrow these proud powers. **Over** (*against*) **the land.** The nations had treated Judah as a wild bull treats things that oppose him, tossing and scattering them to the wind.

HOMILETICS.

Vers. 1—6.—*A timely warning.* "In the eighth month, in the second year of Darius, came the word of the Lord unto Zechariah, the son of Berechiah, the son of Iddo the prophet," etc. Special attention seems invited in the opening verse of this opening prophecy to the question of time. Probably because the time of its utterance was a time of much hope, as shown by the cotemporaneous prophecies of Hag. i. 13—15 ("sixth month"); ii. 1—9 ("seventh month"); and ii. 18, 19 ("ninth month"). Probably also because a time of much hope is a time of much fear; the season of bloom is the season of blight. Accordingly, the whole of this opening message—a kind of prologue to the visions that follow—is one of admonition and warning, a warning which turns (1) on the *present position,* and (2) on the *past experience,* of the Jewish people and Church.

I. PRESENT POSITION. 1. *The fact.* How did they stand before God? As the children of sinners (ver. 2). This is the first thing to be remembered by them, as also by us all (Eph. ii. 3, end). 2. *The significance of the fact;* and that in two opposite directions. (1) As to God's attitude towards them. His favour was turned away from them. As he had been "displeased" with their "fathers," so also, though not irretrievably, with themselves. This implied in the very promise of ver. 3, "I will turn to you." This same truth, again, both in the second commandment, and also in the gracious declaration of Exod. xxxiv. 5—7, is set forth as part of God's uniform rule. (2) As to their (natural) attitude towards God. Their hearts were turned away from him. Hence the exhortation of ver. 3. Their attitude was one even of malignant aversion, if so we may speak, always tending of itself, like certain malignant bodily diseases, to become aggravated and worse. The longer we postpone our repentance the more difficult it becomes. This is the most serious consideration of all.

II. PAST EXPERIENCE. (See vers. 5, 6.) In these they are reminded: 1. *That some things belonging to the past had indeed passed away*, as it were. "Their fathers," *e.g.* who had received so many warnings, and despised them. Even "the prophets" also, who had delivered these warnings, and believed them, had fulfilled their days, and departed. Like a scene in a play, like a picture in a magic-lantern, there was something else in their place. 2. *Some things belonging to the past were still remaining.* The truth of God's Word, for example (see Ps. vi. 6—8). This manifest to their senses. Did not "my words and my statutes take hold of your fathers"? All their recent history, their complete and long-enduring captivity, their partial return, their present condition, an affirmative answer to this question. This same truth acknowledged, too, by those gone. They acknowledged the fact: "As God thought to do, so he did." They acknowledged its justice: "According to our ways, and according to our doings, so hath he" done (comp. Lam. ii. 17, 18; and as to the general principle, Judg. i. 7). This the special triumph of God's Word, that it is vindicated and preached at times by its bitterest foes (Gal. i. 23; John xi. 49—52. Also the saying attributed to Julian the Apostate, "Thou hast conquered, O Galilæan!").

In conclusion, we may note and admire in this passage: 1. *The discrimination of Scripture.* How exactly suited the whole tenor of this passage to the case of those here addressed! Reminding us of the "wise steward," who gives to "every one a portion of meat in due season." Also of the declaration of the apostle, that all inspired Scripture is so variously profitable as to make "the man of God" complete, or perfect, as to all that he needs (2 Tim. iii. 16, 17). 2. *The faithfulness of Scripture.* How different all this from the flattery with which most nations are addressed by their teachers; and which most nations also demand! Contrast "When France is content, Europe is tranquil;" also, as to our own country, the words of the poet—

> "Thou shalt flourish, great and free,
> The dread and envy of them all."

3. *The mercy of Scripture.* Notwithstanding all provocations—all personal, all patrimonial, iniquity—the language of God here is, with outstretched hand (Rom. x. 21), "Be ye reconciled unto me" (2 Cor. v. 20; comp. also Hos. iii., and the emphatic "only" in Jer. iii. 12—14). Note also how greatly this mercy is set forth by the greatness of the faithfulness before named. In the words of our English laureate—

> "He showed me all the mercy,
> For he showed me all the sin."

Vers. 7—11.—*A vision of rest.* "Upon the four and twentieth day of the eleventh month, which is the month Sebat, in the second year of Darius, came the word of the Lord unto Zechariah, the son of Berechiah, the son of Iddo the prophet," etc. Several points in this vision, as in many others, cannot certainly be explained. The nature and significance of the colours of the horses is one of these points. Another is as to the identity or otherwise of the "angel" of ver. 9 with that of the "rider" of ver. 8, who seems undeniably to be the "man" of ver. 10 and the "angel of the Lord" of vers. 11, 12. The idea of identity is favoured by Pusey's rendering, "talked *in* me," compared with Numb. xii. 6—9; Hab. ii. 1; 1 Pet. i. 11; also by the high probability of the person *promising* in ver. 9 being the same as the person *performing* in ver. 10; and by the similar probability that the person *asking* in ver. 12, and the person *answered* in ver. 13, should be one and the same. From these very uncertainties, however, we may, perhaps, learn an incidental truth of importance. We may learn, *e.g.*, that the agents of God are not less manifold, and not less mysterious to us, than his works. Also that whether the "angel of the Lord" speaks to us directly, or only by the instrumentality of one of his accredited servants, it comes to much the same in the end. In the rest of the vision we may notice (1) *the King himself*; (2) *the King's servants*; and (3) *the King's work.*

I. THE KING HIMSELF. Under this head we learn: 1. *His condition.* He appears as a Rider, *i.e.* as one who has left his home and is on a journey for a season. 2. *His rank.* He has many and various attendants, but all "behind him" (comp. Rev. xix. 14, where the rider probably appears on a white horse, because riding in triumph).

3. *His place*; amongst the myrtle trees in the hollow; representing, it is thought, the people of God, humble yet pleasing to him, in their then low estate (see Isa. xli. 19; lv. 13). 4. *His apparent purpose*; viz. to "visit" and save his people (Gen. l. 24; Exod. iii. 16; iv. 31; Luke i. 68).

II. THE KING'S SERVANTS. Of these we find that they are the objects: 1. *Of special inquiry*. Who the Leader is the prophet understands. Who these are that attend upon him he cannot tell, yet much wishes to know, probably because of something very special in their numbers and variety and general appearance of readiness and expectation. "What is it the King means to do with all these?" 2. *Of special explanation*. Explanation very readily given. Your difficulty is natural. Your inquiry is legitimate. "I will show thee what these be." Explanation also very sufficiently given. Who are they? They are persons "sent;" they have a mission indeed to accomplish. Who sent them? The *Lord* himself. For what purpose? For that of special investigation. To investigate where? In all parts of the earth. *This* is why God has visited his people, viz. to learn, by means of these his servants, how things are with them in the world.

III. THE KING'S WORK. The nature and completeness of this are shown to us by his servants' report. For example, we see: 1. *Its great promptitude*. The next thing we hear of this report is of its completion (ver. 11). No time, apparently, has been lost. While the prophet's question has been put and acknowledged, their mission has been accomplished (comp. Dan. ix. 21; Ezek. i. 14). 2. *Its perfection*. They have examined the whole earth. They have examined it all so thoroughly that they challenge any one ("behold") to do more. 3. *Its purport and unanimity*. This is how they all found the world, viz. "sitting still and at rest"—like a weary traveller (so the figure may mean) who has finished his long journey, and taken his seat, and only asks to sit still.

See, therefore, in conclusion, respecting this vision: 1. *How specially encouraging it was at that time*. By the Jews, just then exhorted to recommence the restoration of their temple, two things only were specially required. The one was to know, as to God, that his eye was upon them for good (see Ezra v. 5). The other was to know, as to men, that they would be let alone in their work (Ezra iv. 3). And these, we see, were just the two things of which this vision assures them. With everything to help them in heaven, and nothing to hinder them on earth, what more could they ask? 2. *How instructive for all times*. When any direct work for God, such as that of building his house or enlarging his Church, has to be done, this is how it often pleases him to order the world. So Solomon was raised up as a "man of rest" to build the original temple. So Christ was born, and the foundations of the Christian Church were laid, when all the world was at peace. So we read also in Acts ix. 31. Compare also the language of the Collect for the Fifth Sunday after Trinity; and the connection between vers. 2 and 4 in 1 Tim. ii.

Vers. 12—16.—*A vision of mercy*. "Then the angel of the Lord answered and said," etc. In the last portion (vers. 7—11) we saw Christ, or the Angel-Jehovah, presented to us as a King, exercising visitatorial powers. In the present we seem to read of him under those two other principal aspects in which he is revealed to his people, viz. (1) as their *great High Priest interceding for them* with God; and (2) as their *great Teacher or Prophet instructing and comforting them* in God's name.

I. INTERCESSION. We find this to be: 1. *Exceedingly apposite*. Much had already been done for the remnant of the Captivity; but much also remained. A mere handful (some fifty thousand all told, Ezra ii. 64, 65), compared with the many thousands of Israel, had been brought back; a few scattered centres of population only were to be found in the land, and Jerusalem itself was more like a city of the dead than of the living (compare the description of it in Neh. vii. 4, many years afterwards). This state of things is exactly recognized in the Angel-Jehovah's petition, "How long wilt thou not have mercy on Jerusalem and on the cities of Judah?" (For similar and, probably, nearly contemporaneous request for further mercy after much mercy received, comp. Ps. cxxvi. 4 and 1.) 2. *Very judicious*. See what this intercession allows, viz. the justice of God. "Thou hast had indignation;" and rightly, so it implies. (For similar confessions of God's justice in pleading for mercy, comp. Gen. xviii. 25; Jer.

xii. **1.**) See also what this intercession relies on, viz. on the one hand, God's character, as delighting to exercise mercy (so to speak) as soon as he can; and, on the other hand, on God's faithfulness, as being sure to confine his indignation strictly to the duration specified by him. "These three score and ten years" (see Jer. xxvi. 11, 12). 3. *Very effectual.* This shown by the answer obtained, which consisted, on the one hand, of "good words," *i.e.* words promising good; and on the other hand, of "comfortable words," literally, words "sighing with," or full of sympathy, in the spirit of Rom. xii. 15; Isa. lxiii. 9; and so being all that could be wished for, both in matter and manner.

II. INSTRUCTION. The Angel-Jehovah, having received this reply, then proceeds—either personally or, as some think, through the instrumentality of some subordinate angel—to instruct the prophet accordingly. In this we may notice: 1. *His commission.* The satisfactory answer just received by the Angel-Jehovah the prophet was now to make known in his turn: "Cry *thou.*" He was also to tell it *aloud*, to *proclaim* it: "Cry" (*bis*); comp. Gen. xli. 43; 2 Chron. xxxii. 18, where the same word is employed. And he was to do so being thus commissioned (this also is mentioned twice, vers. 14, 17) in God's name. 2. *His message.* This corresponds, as might be expected, with the "words" of ver. 13. For example, it is a message (1) of great sympathy; being one, we find, in which God identifies himself with the interests of his people (observe "my," in vers. 16, 17), and even speaks of himself as sharing to some extent in their anxieties and purely national jealousies and rivalries. It was no pleasure to him to see other nations at ease, and them in trouble, however deserved. No doubt he had been "displeased" with them (ch. i. 1, 2); but he was still more so with their foes (ver. 15). A message (2) of great hope. Much good, in fact, had begun. Not only had the remnant returned to Jerusalem; God himself also had done so (ver. 16), and that "with mercies;" to stay amongst his people, and not merely to "visit" them. More good was to follow. The "house" now building was to be finished; the rest of the now desolate city to be marked out and finished; and the scattered cities of Judah to be so filled as to overflow ("spread abroad;" comp. ch. ii. 2) on all sides. All this, however apparently unlikely, was, nevertheless (observe "yet" three times), being God's settled purpose, to be accomplished; and the prophet also was to go on saying so until this was the case ("Cry yet," ver. 16).

Do we not see illustrated in all this, finally? 1. *The perfection of the gospel.* "Good words and comfortable words"—"glad tidings of great joy"—so we see it to be. How full of sympathy! How full of hope! Its excellency culminating in this, perhaps, above all, that we have not only such a "Propitiation" (1 John ii. 2), but such a perpetual "Advocate" (1 John ii. 1) and Intercessor to plead it (see also Heb. vii. 25; Luke xxii. 31, 32; xiii. 8, 9; Acts vii. 55). 2. *The certainty of the gospel.* As to its essence and source, on the one hand. As in ver. 13, it is, in effect, the promise of God to his Son (comp. Ps. ii. 7—9; cx., *passim*). As to its conveyance to us, on the other; being, in effect, as in ver. 14, the message of Christ himself to us through those appointed by him. Compare the visions of Christ to Isaiah (vi.; John xii.) and Daniel (x. 5, 6, and references); also John xiv. 26; xvi. 13, 14; Col. iii. 16, etc.

Vers. 18—21.—*A vision of help.* "Then lifted I up mine eyes, and saw," etc. In these verses, and some that follow, certain detached portions of the previous general prophecy seem to be set before us again in greater amplitude and detail—like maps of England, France, and so on, in an atlas, following the general but smaller-scaled map of the whole "quarter" of Europe. In the verses now especially before us, it is the previous message concerning the enemies of God's people (vers. 14, 15) which seems to be thus followed up and enlarged. And the twofold purpose in view seems to be that of reminding his people in this connection (1) of their *special danger;* and (2) of their *special defence.*

I. THEIR SPECIAL DANGER. On this point they are shown: 1. *Its reality.* Though God was sorely displeased with the heathen, though he had done much already to restrain them, so that the earth now was "at rest" (*supra*, ver. 11), and the returned people were able to rebuild his house, he had by no means destroyed them as yet. The four "horns" seen in the vision—the well-known symbols of authority and strength and hostility (Ps. lxxv. 4—7, 10; Jer. xlviii. 25; Deut. xxxiii. 17; 1 Kings xxii. 11) —suffice to prove this. However restrained at that moment, the ability and the disposition to injure were still in existence. 2. *Its peculiar greatness.* This (1) as to *power.* How much evil those same Gentile horns had already done in the past (see end of vers. 19 and 21)! Also perhaps (2) as to *direction;* the "four" horns representing that they had such enemies on all sides (comp. Ps. lxxxiii. 5—8, where every side of Palestine seems to be represented). Or possibly (3) as to *duration;* first one enemy, then another, as in the very similar description of Jer. l. 17; or else with some reference to the four successive world-empires of Daniel's visions, and as meaning to intimate, in that case, that, whichever of such "horns" should be specially exalted for the time, it would be a horn *against them.* So much was their condition, of itself, like that described in Luke x. 3.

II. THEIR SPECIAL DEFENCE. 1. *The fact itself.* This manifest—having such enemies as they had—from their still continued existence. Though "scattered," it was not beyond recovery; though so prostrate that no man could "lift up the head," they were not destroyed (comp. Ps. cxxix. 1, 2). Who could have caused this but Jehovah himself? 2. *The peculiar nature* of this defence. Jehovah restrains the many enemies of his people by "fraying" or frightening them from going too far (comp. Ps. lxxvi. 9, 10; also Gen. xxxv. 5; Exod. xv. 16; 2 Kings xix. 6; 2 Chron. xvii. 10; and to some extent the cases of Abimelech, Gen. xx. 6, 7; and Balaam, Deut. xxiii. 5). 3. The *peculiar instrument* of this defence. Not other "horns" to push against these; not other men of war to overcome these; but artificers only, men of peace. Possibly also artificers of the class engaged in building, as though to intimate that the work of building God's temple was the best defence at that time to God's people. 4. The *peculiar completeness* of this defence. As shown, perhaps, by there being as many in number thus to defend as there were to attack. From whichever side, at whatever time, the attack, there also would be prepared against it this kind of defence (comp. Ps. xxxii. 7, 10).

We see all this abundantly illustrated: 1. *In the subsequent history of the literal Israel.* How often since assaulted! how apparently close, at times, to extermination! how utterly powerless, frequently, in themselves! yet how wonderfully preserved in existence, by similar restraints of their enemies, from that day until this! 2. *In the history of nations and Churches.* It is at least worthy of consideration, in this connection, that since the day when the Reformation found its most congenial home in this island, every projected hostile invader has been restrained from reaching our shores. Also, perhaps, the remarkable (true) prosperity and preservation of the Moravian and Waldensian Churches, are cases in point. 3. *In the history of the spiritual Israel at large.* How many its enemies from the first (Acts xxviii. 22; Luke xxi. 17; Eph. vi. 12)! How incapable of defending itself (Matt. x. 16, as before)! Yet how wonderfully preserved until now; and also, to be preserved to the end (Matt. xvi. 18)! 4. *In the experience of individual believers.* See lives of such men as Luther, Wesley, Whitefield, Simeon, and others. We may almost say of each of such, as just now of the Church at large, "Each man immortal till his work be done." So in truth of every one who truly believes in Christ Jesus. The righteous *scarcely* is *saved,* but he *is* saved, after all.

HOMILIES BY VARIOUS AUTHORS.

Vers. 1—6.—*God's call to repentance.* Repentance is turning from sin unto God. I. THE CALL IS FOUNDED ON GOD'S ABSOLUTE RIGHT TO OBEDIENCE. "Lord of hosts." Sublime title. Thrice used, to give the greater impressiveness. Implies that God's rule is wide as creation. Mark the "host" of stars (Isa. xl. 26). Higher, behold the "angels and principalities and powers" (Ps. ciii. 20, 21). God is Lord of all, and it is this God that claims our homage. To turn *from* him is folly and ruin; to turn *to* him is the highest wisdom and blessedness.

II. URGED BY GOD'S JUDGMENTS ON TRANSGRESSORS. Israel is our "ensample" (1 Cor. x. 11). The sun does not ripen the corn more surely than God's favour attended the Jews when they were steadfast to walk in his ways; nor are thorns and

briars more certain to spring up in a neglected field than God's judgments to fall on
Israel when their hearts were set in them to do evil. God is not changed. The world
is governed now on the same principles as in the past.

III. ENCOURAGED BY GOD'S PROMISES. "Out of the abundance of the heart the
mouth speaketh." So of God's Word. It reveals his heart. There is no bar on God's
part to the sinner's return. He himself has opened the way, and his promise is to
those who turn to him. "I will turn unto you." Here is hope held out, help
graciously offered, joyful welcome assured. We have not only doctrines, but facts.
Great cloud of witnesses, who can say each for himself, like Paul, "I obtained
mercy."

IV. ENFORCED BY THE EXPERIENCES OF LIFE. Every man's life is separate. But
much common. The *brevity* of life. Delay is dangerous. The *confessions* of life.
God's Word is truth. Faithful are his promises and his threatenings. The *monitions*
of life. Voices of the past, of the good, and of the evil, of earth and heaven, all combine and cry with awful and convincing force, "Repent!"—F.

Ver. 5.—*Are we better than our fathers?* I. "FATHERS" IMPLIES SUCCESSIVENESS.
Changes are constant. Not a whole generation together, but men go, as they come,
one by one. Seems common to all existences. Necessary also. If all lived on, there
would not be room for the ever-increasing multitudes. Part of God's great plan for
the education of the race.

II. "FATHERS" IMPLIES INTERDEPENDENCE. There is a close relationship between
fathers and children. Physically, mentally, and even morally, we are to a large
degree what others have made us. "How shall a man escape from his ancestors, or
draw off from his veins the black drop which he drew from his father's or his mother's
life?" (Emerson).

> "'Tis law as steadfast as the throne of Zeus,
> Our days are heritors of days gone by."
>
> (Æschylus.)

And as we have been influenced by the past, so we shall influence the future. Our
children not only receive a certain impress from their birth, but are moulded for good
or evil by the teaching and example of their parents, and by the environment of their
daily life.

III. "FATHERS" IMPLIES RESPONSIBILITY. "Be not as your fathers." There
should be reflection and choice of the good. Whether we are better or worse is a
difficult question. The term "fathers" is indefinite. We should fix some point for
comparison. But where? Our immediate fathers, or those of earlier times? Besides,
difficult to get evidence for a fair comparison. History defective. Tradition unreliable.
The "fathers" stand out like hills enshrouded in mist, or as stars that take a glory
from being far. Besides, who are to judge? Ourselves. Then risk of partiality.
We naturally lean to the party to which we belong. Suppose you take the *old*.
They are apt to side with the past. Their day is over. Their vigour is gone. They
dwell on what has been done. Rarely will you find an old man who does not say,
"The former days were better" (Eccles. vii. 10). Suppose you take the *young*. They
side with the present. The world is all before them. They are eager for the strife.
"Yearning for the large excitement that the coming years would yield." But in any
case, our judgment is liable to be affected by circumstances. Our own state, the love
of society, the spirit of the age, influence us largely (cf. Elijah, 1 Kings xix. 4).
Are we *better than our fathers?* There is no question but *we ought to be*. Progress is
the law. We have the higher advantages. The great thoughts and the great deeds
of others should inspire us. We are the "heirs of all the ages." In some respects we
are certainly better. As to food, clothing, habitations, means of education, political
and social rights, intercourse with other nations, and so forth, there has been an
immense advance. But what availeth this, if morally and spiritually we stand, not
higher, but lower than our fathers? "Christ is our Hope." Individually we are bound
to strive after a better life, and thus we can best influence society. There may be
much in our past that is bad; but it *is* past; and let us take hope. If there are
sins, they are forgiven. If there are bad habits, they have been broken off. If there

are failures, they have been retrieved. We can look on. Stirred with a holy ambition, sustained by precious promises, animated by noble examples, we can press on to the brighter and better days to come. Our standard should be, not the conventional standard of the Church or the day, but the perfect law of Christ (Matt. v. 20—48).—F.

Ver. 5.—*The transitoriness of life.* I. COMPARED WITH THE PERMANENCE OF THE EARTH. Objects of nature remain. There are changes, but they are not so great within the limit of our brief lives as to attract much notice. "One generation passeth away, and another generation cometh; but the earth abideth for ever" (Eccles. i. 4).

II. COMPARED WITH THE CONTINUITY OF THE RACE. The individual withers; families disappear; kingdoms decay and fall; but the race of man remains. Our life is as a tale that is told, but the story of the generations of the past reaches back beyond our ken.

III. COMPARED WITH THE IMMENSE LABOUR BESTOWED ON MEN. What a preparation going before! What long and arduous toils there have been to fit us for our place and our work! and then how short the time we have for accomplishing anything! How often early promise fails, and the dear hopes cherished are disappointed!

IV. COMPARED WITH THE EXPECTATIONS FORMED. What plans, schemings, enterprises! What high ambitions! And yet how little is achieved! Man's promise is always better than his performance. Once, perhaps, we took a forward place; our names were on the lips of many—looked to win great fame. But the end is "vanity."

V. COMPARED WITH THE IMMORTALITY OF GOD'S WORD. Fathers and prophets alike pass away. They cannot continue by reason of death. "All flesh is as grass, and all the glory of man as the flower of grass. The grass withereth, and the flower thereof falleth away: but the Word of the Lord endureth for ever. And this is the Word which by the gospel is preached unto you" (1 Pet. i. 24, 25).—F.

Ver. 6.—*God's Word taking hold.* I. THE FLIGHT. Men strive to get away from God. Some try one device, some another (cf. Adam, Gen. iii. 10; Jonah i. 3; Paul, Acts xxvi. 9). Such conduct is unnatural, wicked, and vain (Ps. cxxxix. 7).

II. THE PURSUIT. The sinner followed. He feels that God knows all, and that the day of reckoning will come. Memory, conscience, Law, Scripture, prophecy of judgment. The officer of justice is on the sinner's track. Any moment he may feel his hand on his shoulder, and hear the awful words, "You are my prisoner."

III. THE OVERTAKING. Certain, for good or for evil. In the day of conviction, of true penitence, or of righteous retribution—amidst the songs of rejoicing angels or the weeping and wailing of lost souls. What has been our experience? God's Word "takes hold," as *truth* of the intellect, as *righteousness* of the conscience, as *love* of the heart. Mark Augustine in the garden at Milan (Rom. xiii. 13, 14); Luther painfully climbing the church steps at Rome (Rom. i. 17). Study Bunyan's 'Grace Abounding.' So of all the redeemed. Happy are we when we recognize that God's Word comes, not as a foe, but as a friend; not to compel by force, but to constrain by love; not to drag us with fear and trembling before the Judge, but to draw us gently to the cross and the Saviour.—F.

Vers. 8—13.—*The Church and Christ.* The vision may suggest—
I. THE HIDDEN RICHES OF THE CHURCH. "Myrtle in the bottom" symbolizes the Church in a low condition. Obscure, despised by the world; but fresh, fragrant, and beautiful in the sight of God. The object of increasing care. Grand future.

II. THE GLORY OF THE CHURCH'S HEAD. Christ supreme. All forces are under his control. The resources of heaven and earth are at his disposal. He is ever on the watch. He scans the horizon with clear, far-seeing eye. He is always quick to do what he deems best for the defence and good of his people. Here is comfort for times of depression and fear. We have our personal troubles. We are distressed because of the state of the Church, and the slow progress of religion in the world. But let us take courage. Christ is Head over all things for the Church. In the darkest hour, when we pray, the heavens are opened. We behold Christ on the throne, and cry with the holy angels, "Alleluia: for the Lord God omnipotent reigneth" (cf. Eph. i. 16—23).—F.

Ver. 11.—*The wonder of indifference.* "'At rest;' *i.e.* secure, proud, and licentious, as if there were no God in heaven" (Wordsworth). May be taken to illustrate a common state of mind as to religion. Indifference seems wonderful when we consider—

I. THE VAST INTERESTS AT STAKE. What questions so deep and urgent as those that concern God and truth and immortality?

II. THE BRIEF TIME FOR DECISION. Life is short. Delay, and youth is gone; delay, and manhood is past; delay, and all is lost. Besides, what uncertainty and what constant interruptions and claims of other things! "The world is too much with us."

III. THE GREAT IMPORTANCE OF EARNESTNESS. See how men act in other matters. Firm and decided. "The children of this world are wiser in their generation than the children of light."

IV. THE CEASELESS ACTIVITY OF THE POWERS OF EVIL. (1 Pet. v. 8.)

V. THE URGENT APPEALS OF GOD. How much of Holy Scripture is taken up with calls, and pleadings, and remonstrances, and beseechings! Then, how often does the voice of God in providence give the deeper force and significance to the warnings of his Word! Surely what lies so near the heart of God should be the chief thing for us. Surely what moved the eternal Son to come to earth should be the supreme interest with us. His mind should be our mind, and our highest blessedness should be to consecrate ourselves, like him, to the service of God and of humanity.—F.

Ver. 15.—*The wrath of God and the wrath of man.* I. GOD'S WRATH IS THE HIGHEST REASON. It is not a mood or passion; not the outburst of arbitrary power; but the calm expression of the Eternal Mind. He who does wrong identifies himself with the wrong, and so far must be an object of indignation. God feels towards things as they are. How different the wrath of man (cf. Jas. iv. 1)!

II. GOD'S WRATH IS THE PUREST JUSTICE. Law must stand. Government and order must be maintained. Else anarchy. But nothing will be done beyond what is necessary for the ends of justice. God's wrath is just, in measure and duration. How different with the wrath of man! Often carried beyond the bounds of right, and becomes oppression. Often continued beyond the limits of justice, and becomes revenge (Isa. xlvii. 6).

III. GOD'S WRATH IS THE HOLIEST LOVE. There is much in the ways of God that we cannot understand, but we should never forget what he himself has taught us as to his Spirit and purpose (cf. Ezek. xxxiii. 11). God's wrath is consistent with pity for the sufferer, mercy for the penitent, and deliverance for the oppressed. In his hand pains are disciplinary, trials are remedial, chastisements are benedictions in disguise. "The end of the Lord is merciful." But with men how often is wrath pitiless and cruel, working evil instead of good, rejoicing in destruction instead of deliverance!

> " Father and Lover of our souls!
> Though darkly round thine anger rolls,
>   Thy sunshine smiles beneath the gloom,
> Thou seek'st to warn us, not confound,
> Thy showers would pierce the hardened ground
> And win it to give out its brightness and perfume."
>   (Keble.)
>   F.

Vers. 18—21.—*The dark and the bright side of things.* Prophet depressed. Heart failing for fear. Roused. Vision twofold. Like the mystic pillar of the wilderness, it is dark and lowering towards God's enemies, but bright and cheering towards his friends.

I. THE POWERS OF EVIL. Beasts dimly seen. "Horses" indicate the strength and malice of the world-powers. The results are terrible. The unity of Israel is broken. Strength dissipated in party conflicts. Gored and tossed and sore oppressed by their enemies. Dispirited, "so that no man did lift up his head." But man's extremity is God's opportunity. Let us feel and confess in true humility our sin, and the justice of our sufferings, and cry mightily to God; then deliverance will surely come.

II. THE POWERS OF GOOD. (Vers. 20, 21.) Cf. Elisha and his servant (2 Kings vi. 17). So here. "Carpenters;" "workmen." 1. *Equal in number.* Four indicates completeness. There will be sufficiency for God's purpose, and yet the number will not be in excess of that on the other side, as if the victory were to be obtained by might and not by right. 2. *Greater in authority.* Law at their back. Ministers of justice. Power not usurped or wrongly used, but employed under the authority of God. 3. *Completer in equipment.* (Ezek. xxi. 36.) Men of free souls, sympathetic hearts, and invincible courage. Men of trained intelligence and executive ability. The right men in the right time.—F.

Vers. 1—6.—*The importance of repentance.* "In the eighth month, in the second year of Darius, came the word of the Lord unto Zechariah, the son of Berechiah, the son of Iddo the prophet, saying, The Lord hath been sore displeased with your fathers," etc. Zechariah and Haggai were contemporaries—prophets of the restoration. The former began to prophesy about two months after Haggai. Like Jeremiah and Ezekiel, he was of priestly descent; a son of Berechiah and grandson of Iddo, the chief of one of the priestly families that returned from exile along with Zerubbabel and Joshua (Neh. xii. 4). He commenced his prophetic labours in the second year of Darius Hystaspes, B.C. 520. The most remarkable portion of the book consists of the first six chapters, where we have a record of a series of extraordinary visions, all of which seem to have been vouchsafed to the prophet during one night. The two succeeding chapters (vii. and viii.) contain an answer to a question which the inhabitants of Bethel proposed, respecting the observance of a certain fast. The remaining six chapters contain a variety of predictions. The authenticity of these chapters is denied by some scholars, and doubted by many more. His style is varied, sometimes almost colloquial; at other times sublimely poetic, abounding with gorgeous symbols. The subject suggested by these words is—*the importance of repentance.* There are three grounds in this passage on which this subject is urged.

I. FROM THE DIVINE DISPLEASURE TOWARDS THE IMPENITENT MEN OF THE PAST. "The Lord hath been sore displeased with your fathers." This "may be interpreted as bearing reference to the whole of their previous history. They had all along shown a mournfully strong and inveterate propensity to depart from God and from his ways. They had needed incessant repetitions of Divine admonitions, entreaties, promises, and threatenings; and many a time all had proved unavailing. Jehovah bound them to himself with 'cords of love.' But 'they brake the bands asunder, and cast away the cords from them.' They chose their own ways; they followed the wicked devices of their own hearts. They thus provoked him to anger; they drew down upon themselves his judicial visitations. From one of these visitations the people whom the prophet now addressed had but recently, in the faithfulness and mercy of a covenant-keeping and compassionate God, been delivered. And I cannot doubt that to *that* most recent manifestation of the Divine displeasure Zechariah specially referred. Their fathers had by their sins brought that heavy seventy years' judgment upon themselves. And he who in justice had executed the judgment, had returned in mercy, and rescued them from their second bondage" (Dr. Wardlaw). Now, the displeasure of God to sinners of the past is here referred to in order to induce the Jews to repent of the selfish negligence which they had evinced concerning the building of the temple (Hag. i. 2—7). The argument here is the kind called enthymeme, in which one premiss only is expressed, and the consequent proposition is left to be supplied by the reader. It means this: the great God has been displeased with your fathers on account of their sins, and he will be displeased with you except you repent. This is an argument that preachers may well urge at all times. They may call up to their hearers the judgments that have fallen on the wicked of the past ages, in order to urge reformed life on the existing generation.

II. FROM GOD'S ASSURANCE OF A WELCOME TO ALL THAT TRULY REPENT. "Say thou unto them, Thus saith the Lord of hosts; Turn ye unto me, saith the Lord of hosts, and I will turn unto you, saith the Lord of hosts." Blessed truth this! Proved: 1. *By his invitation to the impenitent.* "Come now, and let us reason together, saith the Lord," etc.; "Let the wicked forsake his way, and the unrighteous man his thoughts: and let him return unto the Lord," etc.; "Him that cometh unto me I will in no wise cast out." The infinite Father is infinitely more ready to welcome true penitence than the father of the prodigal to welcome the return of his long-lost son. 2. *By the experience of mankind.* Manasseh, David, Saul, Bunyan, and millions more returned to him, and he not only received them, but rejoiced over them. This being the case, how powerful is the exhortation here, "Be not as your fathers, unto whom the former prophets have cried, saying," etc.! Your fathers, who rejected the call of my prophets of the past, bad as they were, would not have met with their terrible fates had they returned to me. Be not like them; take warning from the past.

III. FROM THE TRANSITORINESS OF HUMAN LIFE, WHETHER WICKED OR GOOD. "Your fathers, where are they? and the prophets, do they live for ever?" By "the fathers" here undoubtedly reference is to those spoken of in the former verses with whom the Almighty is displeased. These have disappeared; they have vanished from the earth. The prophets, too, the good men who spoke to them and whose call they rejected, useful men as they were, they did not live for ever. The impenitent hearers and their faithful preachers are both gone. How solemnly true this is! All pass away from the stage of life, whether good or bad, useful or mischievous. The life of a generation is but a vapour that will endure for a little and then vanish away. What an argument this: 1. *For the wicked to repent!* Impenitent hearers of the gospel, you will soon be gone. Ere another century passes over this globe, your bodies will be in the dust and your spirits in the awful Hades of retribution; therefore listen and repent. Ye preachers of the gospel, what an argument this: 2. *For faithfulness and for persevering zeal!* You will soon have finished your mission. A few more sermons, and all will be over. "The prophets, do they live for ever?" etc. "Fathers," the ungodly men of the past, where are they? Ah! where are they? Echo answers, "Where?"—D. T.

Vers. 7—17.—*The first vision: God's government of the world.* "Upon the four and twentieth day of the eleventh month, which is the month Sebat, in the second year of Darius, came the word of the Lord unto Zechariah, the son of Berechiah, the son of Iddo the prophet, saying, I saw by night, and behold a man riding upon a red horse," etc. About three months after the call of Zechariah to the prophetic office, he had no less than seven, or, as some count, eight visions in *one night.* And this night, we are told, was in the twenty-fourth day of the eleventh month, *i.e.* "the month Sebat, in the second year of Darius." Exactly five months before this night the rebuilding of the temple would be resumed. Amongst the various manners in which God revealed himself to men of old, visions were perhaps the most frequent and impressive. He sometimes employed articulate sounds, sometimes the Urim and Thummim, sometimes the apparitions of the dead, sometimes internal suggestion. In some direct way he touched the springs of thought. But here in *one night* he appears to the prophet in many distinct visions. The visions were marked by these four characteristics. They were: 1. *Mental.* Unlike all other creatures on the earth, so far as we know at present, man has an inner visual organ; he can see with his mind. This is seen in poets, such as Milton, Spenser, etc.; allegorists, such as Bunyan, etc. 2. *Symbolic.* Strange and grotesque objects were seen. These objects were all symbolic; they had a spiritual significance. 3. *Divine.* All men, unless they are utterly destitute of the poetic sentiment, have visions sometimes, not only sleeping but waking visions. But seldom, perhaps, are these visions Divine. 4. *Prophetic.* They point here to the future of God's moral kingdom upon the earth. Men of lofty, sanctified genius often in their visions have a glance of "things that are to come." This vision seems to give us a look into God's moral government of the world. It takes us behind the veil of phenomena, and shows us principles and agencies that move, fashion, and control all. Three facts are suggested in relation to God's government in the world.

I. IT IS CARRIED ON IN CONNECTION WITH MYSTERIOUS AGENCIES. What did the prophet see? "I saw by night, and behold a man riding upon a red horse, and he stood among the myrtle trees that were in the bottom; and behind him were there red horses, speckled, and white." It is idle to attach special ideas to each of these objects; the grand idea is that God has ministers in his empire fully equipped for his work, and prompt to obey his behests. Who are these? *Unfallen angels.* These by millions stand near his throne, ready to do his bidding. In relation to these agents two thoughts are suggested. 1. *That they are under the command of a trans-*

cendent mind. Most expositors regard the man on the red horse, and who stood among the myrtle trees, as no less a personage than the Angel of the covenant, the great Messiah. The subsequent verses sustain this idea. This same man appeared to Abraham in the plains of Mamre, to Jacob before his meeting with Esau, to Moses at the burning bush, to Joshua at Jericho, with the sword drawn in his hand. Here he is on the "red horse," emblem of war. He is a great moral Chieftain. 2. *That there are varied orders.* "Behind him were there red horses, speckled, and white." This is the troop that followed the man. When the eyes of Elisha's servant were opened, he beheld a "mountain full of horses and chariots of fire round about Elisha." Horses are emblems of force and fleetness. In Christ's army there are hosts, mighty in power and swift in motion. "Are they not all ministering spirits?" How infinitely varied are God's ministers—varied in kind and measure of faculty, in experience, attainment, and aspect too—thrones, principalities, powers, and dominions! 3. *That the whole world is their sphere of action.* "These are they whom the Lord hath sent to walk to and fro through the earth." (1) They "go to and fro" through the earth. They are ever journeying; some are swift as lightning in their speed; some of them are "full of eyes," and see all things. (2) They know the state of the world. "We have walked to and fro through the earth, and, behold, all the earth sitteth still, and is at rest." "At rest," not in the rest of righteousness, not in the repose of goodness, but in carnal security and sin.

II. THAT IT HAS NOT ONLY DIFFICULTIES, BUT AN INTERPRETER ALSO. "Then said I, O my lord, what are these?" Observe: 1. *The difficulties of God's government.* "*What are these?*" The prophet understood not these strange appearances; and in amazement he exclaims, "What are these?" What thoughtful man has not asked such a question as this concerning the Divine government over and over again? "What are these? What are these elements, forces, laws, existences, events? What are they? Are they messengers of mercy or of justice? O my lord, what are these?" We are all moving in mystery. 2. *The interpreter of God's government.* Who answered the question? "The man that stood among the myrtle trees answered and said, These are they." Some other creature, the angel that talked with him, was asked first; but the answer came not from him, but from the Man Christ Jesus. In Rev. v. 2 "a strong angel" is represented as crying with a loud voice concerning the mysteries of God's government, inquiring who was worthy to "loose the seals;" but no one was found in heaven, in earth, or under the earth, able to "open and read the book." There was only one found: "It was the Lamb in the midst of the throne." Christ is the only Interpreter of God. He is the *Logos.*

III. THAT IT IS ESPECIALLY CONCERNED IN THE INTERESTS OF HIS PEOPLE. His people are supposed to be here represented by the "myrtle trees." The Jewish Church at this time was not like a forest of stately cedars, but a grove of myrtles, fragile and obscure. 1. *These seem to be the centre of Divine operations on the earth.* Now, in the myrtle trees is the man "riding upon a red horse." And in the myrtle trees were the "red horses, speckled, and white"—the whole troop was there. The "myrtle trees" seemed to be the centre of all the agents. From it they started on their mission, and to it they returned. The true Church is the temple, the residence of God himself. 2. *The object of special intercession.* "Then the angel of the Lord answered and said, O Lord of hosts, how long wilt thou not have mercy on Jerusalem, and on the cities of Judah, against which thou hast had indignation these three score and ten years?" The duration of their captivity in Babylon. Who is the angel that makes this appeal? It was he that "ever liveth to make intercession for us." "If any man sin, we have an Advocate with the Father, Jesus Christ the Righteous." 3. *The subjects of the Divine communication.* "The Lord answered the angel that talked with me with good words and comfortable words." The prophet is here commissioned to proclaim: (1) God's *zeal* on behalf of Jerusalem. "Cry thou, saying, Thus saith the Lord of hosts." (2) His *displeasure* for the enemies of Jerusalem. "I am very sore displeased with the heathen." His merciful purpose was to bestow blessings on Jerusalem. "Therefore thus saith the Lord," etc.

CONCLUSION. Though we are far enough from presuming to have given a correct interpretation of the passage, or of maintaining that the thoughts we have suggested are contained in it, we conscientiously believe that the ideas are scriptural, and adapted for spiritual usefulness. The subject of God's government in the world is one of the sublimest that can engage the human mind, and is beset with difficulties that often baffle the profoundest thinkers. It is our happiness to know that, small as is our planet in comparison with millions of other orbs that people immensity, and insignificant as are its human tenants, the infinite Father superintends it in wisdom and in love. —D. T.

Vers. 18—21.—*Second vision : four horns and four carpenters.* " Then lifted I up mine eyes, and saw, and behold four horns. And I said unto the angel that talked with me, What be these? And he answered me, These are the horns which have scattered Judah, Israel, and Jerusalem," etc. This is the second vision that the prophet had that night. The " horn " in the Bible is a symbol of power (Amos vi. 13). The horns here represent possibly those worldly kingdoms which had been, or were to be, opposed to the Jewish people, namely, Babylon, Persia, Greece, and Rome. These four were symbolized in the colossal figure which filled the imagination of Nebuchadnezzar in his dream. Whom do the " four carpenters " symbolize, or, as some translate it, the "four smiths"? Undoubtedly, those instruments by which the moral Governor of the world overcomes all the enemies of truth and right. The interpreting angel says, in relation to these four smiths, or workmen, that they had " come to fray," or terrify and cast down, the hostile powers represented by the horns. This vision presents to us *the cause of right on the earth,* and suggests two thoughts in relation to it.

I. THAT THE CAUSE OF RIGHT ON THE EARTH HAS STRONG ANTAGONISTS. Here are four horns, four mighty powers, all of which are in dead hostility to the covenant people. They are represented as those who have " scattered Judah, so that no man did lift up his head." The enemies of the true *scatter* and *crush.* Though Babylon, Persia, Greece, and Rome have long since passed away, the horns, or the mighty powers of evil, are still here, and are at work. What are they? *Reigning materialism* is a horn; *practical atheism* is a horn; *intolerant superstition* is a horn; and *dominant selfishness* is a horn. All these mighty forces are ever at work in order to destroy the cause of right and truth upon the earth. They are the " principalities and powers of darkness," against which all that is righteous, true, and pure upon the earth have to wrestle for existence.

II. THAT THE CAUSE OF TRUTH UPON THE EARTH HAS DIVINE DEFENDERS. Here are four carpenters, or smiths, who appear to "fray them, to cast out the horns of the Gentiles." Mark, the defenders were: 1. *Men,* not angels. God saves man by man. Who were the first apostles? 2. *Working* men. Toilers, labourers. It is man as man, not philosopher, poet, king, millionaire, that has to battle for the right. The greatest moral victories have been won by men in the lower walks of life. 3. They were *skilled* men. These men had a trade; they were craftsmen; they had been trained to the work they undertook. There is a skill required in order to strike effectively at the errors and wrongs of life. Stupid men, however good their intentions, accomplish but little, if anything, in the noble cause. They must be men of good natural sagacity, and that sagacity trained by the Spirit of God. A man to convert souls must have as much aptitude for the work as the carpenter has in order to shape the wood to his purpose, or the smith to mould and shape the metals.

CONCLUSION. Thank God that if the " horns " are here, there are carpenters here also to bring them to ruin, and to build up the blessed kingdom of truth and righteousness. —D. T.

EXPOSITION.

CHAPTER II.

Vers. 1—13.—§ 5. *The third vision: the man with the measuring-line.*

Ver. 1.—(Heb. ii. 5.) I lifted up mine eyes again (comp. ch. v. 1; vi. 1; Dan. viii. 3). This third vision makes a further

revelation of God's mercy to Israel. Consequent on the destruction of enemies shall be the growth and development of the chosen people till the time of their final glory (comp. ch. i. 16). There is some difficulty in arranging the details of this vision, depending in great measure on the decision we arrive at with regard to the identification of the "young man" of ver. 4. Those who, as Theodoret, Hitzig, Schegg, Trochon, Wright, Perowne, etc., consider him to be the man with the measuring-line of ver. 1, do not explain why the message should be given to him instead of to the prophet who had asked for information. Nor is it at all certain that the measurer is meant to be regarded as having made a mistake in attempting to define the limits of what was practically unlimited—viz. the restored Jerusalem—and was stopped accordingly in his proceedings. It seems preferable, with Jerome, Cornelius à Lapide, Pusey, Keil, Knabenbauer, etc., to regard the "young man" as Zechariah himself. Then the vision is thus presented: The prophet sees a man with a measuring-line; he asks whither he is going, and is answered that he was going forth to measure Jerusalem. Upon this the interpreting angel leaves the prophet's side to receive the explanation of the man's proceedings, and is met by a superior angel, who bids him hasten to tell the prophet the meaning of the vision. **A man.** Probably an angel in human form, as ch. i. 8. **A measuring-line.** This is not the same word as that in ch. i. 16; but the idea there proposed is taken up here, and its fulfilment is set forth (comp. Ezek. xl. 3; Rev. xi. 1; xxi. 15, 16).

Ver. 2.—**What is the breadth thereof.** The man measures to see what shall be the dimensions of the restored city, for from ver. 12 it is apparent that the building is not yet completed, nor are we to think that the rebuilding of the material ruined walls is meant.

Ver. 3.—**Went forth.** The interpreting angel leaves the prophet, and goes away to meet another angel who advances from the opposite side. Septuagint, εἱστήκει, "stood." **Another angel went out;** *went forth,* the word being the same as before. This latter angel, sent by God with a revelation, is superior to the interpreter, as the latter receives the message from him to deliver to the prophet.

Ver. 4.—**And said unto him;** *i.e.* the second angel said to the interpreter. **Run.** He was to hasten and deliver the message, because it was a joyful one and calculated to allay the prophet's solicitude. **This young man.** The Prophet Zechariah. The term applied to him is thought to show that he was still young when the vision appeared; but the word is used also for minister, or servant, or disciple, without necessarily defining the age. Others, not so suitably, consider that the measuring angel is meant, who is thus stopped in his intention of measuring Jerusalem, as being ignorant of God's counsels. **Jerusalem shall be inhabited as towns without walls.** Jerusalem

shall be as open villages in a plain country. The word *perazoth* is used in Ezek. xxxviii. 11, meaning "unwalled villages," where men dwelt "without walls, having neither bars nor gates." So Esth. ix. 19, where it means, "country towns," in contrast to the metropolis, which was walled and fortified. The idea in the text is that Jerusalem in the future shall be so extended that walls shall no longer contain its inhabitants, but they shall spread themselves in the open country on every side. It is certain that the city did greatly increase in after-time, if we may believe Aristeas's account in his famous letter to his brother Philocrates; and the annunciation of this prosperity would be a comfort to the prophet (comp. Josephus, 'Bell. Jud.,' v. 4. 2). But no material increase of this nature satisfies the prophecy, which can only have its fulfilment in the spiritual Jerusalem, whose Builder is Christ, in whose light the nations of them that are saved shall walk (Rev. xxi. 24; see Isa. xlix. 18, etc.; liv. 2, 3). This open condition implies not only extent, but peace and safety also. The reason of this quiet security is given in the next verse. Septuagint, Κατακάρπως κατοικηθήσεται Ἱερουσαλήμ, "Jerusalem shall be abundantly inhabited."

Ver. 5.—**A wall of fire.** She will not need walls. God will be her protection, not only defending her from attack, but consuming the enemy who may presume to assault her (comp. Deut. iv. 24; Ps. lxviii. 2). **The glory;** εἰς δόξαν ἔσομαι (Septuagint). God will make his glory conspicuous by the mighty deeds he will do in Jerusalem and the providential care he will take of her. He shall be known to be dwelling there, as he revealed his presence by the pillar of fire and the Shechinah (comp. Isa. lx. 1, 2, 19).

Ver. 6.—**The superior angel of ver. 4** continues to speak. He calls on all the Hebrews still in dispersion to come and share this glorious state and escape the punishment which was about to fall upon the hostile kingdom. The exaltation of Jerusalem is connected with the downfall of her enemies. **Ho, ho, come forth, and flee;** Hebrew, "Ho, ho! and flee," or, "flee thou" (comp. Isa. xlviii. 20; Jer. li. 6, 45.) A great number of the exiles had remained in Babylonia, having established themselves there, according to the injunction in Jer. xxix. 5, etc., and grown rich. These people had refused to exchange their present prosperity for the doubtful future offered by a return to their desolate native land. But they are now called upon to "flee" from the danger that menaced the country of their adoption. Babylon is said to have been twice taken in the reign of Darius (see note on ver. 7). **The land of the north;** *i.e.*

Babylonia (comp. Jer. i. 14; iv. 6; xxiii. 8). We should have called the Babylonians an Eastern people if we had dwelt in Palestine; but they always invaded this land from the north, and the great caravan route entered the country from the same quarter, so they were deemed to be a northern power. I have spread you abroad as the four winds (Ezek. xvii. 21). The Jews had been dispersed through all parts of the extensive Babylonian empire, and that with a violence which is compared to the force of the combined winds of heaven. Keil, Wright, and others regard the words as a promise of future extension only to be obtained by a return to the promised land, translating, "I will spread you," the perfect of the text being taken to express prophetic certainty. But it is surely incongruous to comfort the dispersed Jews by the promise of a still wider dispersion. This appears to be as erroneous as the Septuagint rendering of the verb, συνάξω, "I will gather."

Ver. 7.—Deliver thyself. Escape from the danger. O Zion. The exiled Jews are thus designated. Septuagint, Εἰς Σιὼν ἀνασώζεσθε, "Go to Zion, and save yourselves." That dwellest (thou that dwellest) with the daughter of Babylon. The inhabitants of Babylon are called "the daughter of Babylon," in analogy with the common phrases, "the daughter of Zion," "the daughter of Jerusalem" (comp. Jer. xlvi. 19). There is some reproach implied in the clause, as if these Jews were content to dwell and remain in this heathen city. The immediate danger that menaced Babylon arose from two severe rebellions, in the course of which the city was twice taken. The first revolt was headed by Nidinta-Bel, B.C. 519, who was slain by Darius at Babylon. The second took place under Arakha, B.C. 514; he was defeated by a general of Darius, named Intaphernes, taken prisoner and crucified. A record of these occurrences is found in Darius's inscription on the rock at Behistun, translated in 'Records of the Past,' vol. i. The merciless Persians would doubtless treat the inhabitants of the captured city with their wonted cruelty.

Ver. 8.—After the glory hath he sent me. After glory (there is no article in the original), i.e. to win honour, hath Jehovah sent me — the superior angel who speaks. As the words, "thus saith the Lord," precede, we should have expected, "have I sent thee," but such change of persons, and indirect address, are common in Hebrew (comp. ch. xiv. 5). The angel is sent to get glory over the heathen by taking vengeance on them (comp. Exod. xiv. 18). Such judgments are often represented to be inflicted by angelic agency (Gen. xix. 13; 2 Kings xix. 35; Ezek. ix.). The apple of his eye.

The language is human. Israel is very precious to God; and they who vex and harass him are as they who hurt that which God prizes inestimably, and which a mere touch offends and injures. The word rendered "apple" is usually considered to mean "aperture," or "gate," the pupil being the entrance to the visual organ; but Dr. Wright regards it rather as a natural word of endearment, like the Latin, pupa, pupilla, indicating "a doll," "little maiden of the eye." Similar, though not identical, expressions occur in Deut. xxxii. 10; Prov. vii. 2; Ps. xvii. 8.

Ver. 9.—I will shake mine hand upon (over) them. The angel reports Jehovah's message now in the first person, or speaks as the representative of Jehovah. The action of shaking the hand over a nation is one of menace (Job xxxi. 21; Isa. xi. 15; xix. 16). Shall be a spoil to their servants; to their slaves, those who once served them. This was true only in a spiritual sense, when the nations were won over to the true faith (see ver. 11; and comp. Isa. xiv. 2; xlix. 22, etc.; Ezek. xvi. 61). Septuagint, τοῖς δουλεύουσιν αὐτοῖς, "to them that serve them." Ye shall know, etc. (ch. iv. 9; vi. 15). When this comes to pass, the Israelites shall recognize and own the Divine mission of God's messenger.

Ver. 10.—Sing and rejoice. The Jews released from Babylon, and the whole Jewish nation, are bidden to exult in the promised protection and presence of the Lord. Lo, I come; Septuagint, ἰδοὺ ἐγὼ ἔρχομαι. So Christ is called, ὁ ἐρχόμενος, "he that cometh" (Matt. xi. 3). I will dwell in the midst of thee (ch. viii. 3; ix. 9). Not merely the rebuilding of the temple is signified, and the re-establishment of the ordained worship (though without the Shechinah), but rather the incarnation of Christ and his perpetual presence in the Church. Κατασκηνώσω ἐν μέσῳ σου (Septuagint), which recalls John i. 14, "The Word was made flesh, and dwelt (ἐσκήνωσεν) among us" (comp. Isa. xii. 6; Ezek. xliii. 9; xlviii. 35; Mal. iii. 1).

Ver. 11.—Many nations shall be joined (shall join themselves) to the Lord; "shall fly for refuge unto the Lord" (Septuagint). My people; unto me for a people; Septuagint, "shall be unto him for a people" (comp. ch. viii. 20). No mere conversion of individuals among the heathen satisfies this promise. Whole nations shall become the Lord's people. That title shall be shared with Israel by countless multitudes (comp. Isa. ii. 2, 3; xi. 10; Micah iv. 2; Zeph. ii. 11). I will dwell, etc. The promise of ver. 10 is repeated for assurance' sake. The LXX. has, "And they shall dwell in the midst of thee." Thou shalt know (as ver. 9).

Ver. 12—Shall inherit Judah. The Lord, though it is true that many other nations shall be converted, shall take Judah (*i.e.* the whole Jewish nation) as his portion, in accordance with Deut. xxxii. 9. In the holy land. This expression is not found elsewhere applied to Judæa, nor is it to be confined to that nation here. Every land is holy where the Lord dwells. The conversion of the heathen should emanate from Judæa (Luke xxiv. 47), and spread through all the world, and thus the earth should be holy ground. Shall choose Jerusalem again; Revised Version, "shall yet choose Jeru-

salem" (comp. ch. i. 17). This points to Christ as King of the spiritual Zion.

Ver. 13.—Be silent; *hush* (comp. Hab. ii. 20; Zeph. i. 7, and notes there). In the expectation of these mighty events, men are called upon to wait in awe and reverence. He is raised up; *he hath arisen.* He had seemed to sleep when he let his people be trodden down by the heathen; but now he, as it were, waketh and cometh from heaven, his holy habitation (Deut. xxvi. 15), to inflict the threatened judgment on the nations, and to succour his own people (comp. Ps. xliv. 23, etc.).

HOMILETICS.

Vers. 1—5.—*A vision of safety.* "I lifted up mine eyes again, and looked, and behold a man with a measuring-line in his hand," etc. We have here another case of repetition and expansion. In the end of ch. i. 16 we had a brief promise of the full restoration of Jerusalem as a city—a place of dwellings with dwellers therein. In the present passage we have the same promise expressed at more length. In other words, we are asked to observe (1) how *immediate its application;* (2) how *emphatic its repetition;* and (3) how *profound its significance.*

I. How IMMEDIATE ITS APPLICATION. So immediate, in fact, that the first steps towards its accomplishment had already begun. Whatever may have been previously resolved on in private in regard to building operations, the first visible and overt step in those operations themselves is that of measuring and staking the ground. The very children understand the meaning of that. Jehovah, accordingly, in the opening verses of this chapter, accommodates himself to this truth. The prophet sees manifestly (he "lifted up his eyes, and looked"), but apparently much to his surprise ("behold"), a man with a measuring-line in his hand. Where is he going? so the prophet asks; and is told—He is going to "Jerusalem" with his line. For what purpose? To "measure" it, to survey it as for building, to ascertain its length and its breadth. What does all this amount to? It amounts to "business," as we should now express it. Consultation, deliberation, decision,—the time for all these is now past. It is the time for doing, for actual fulfilment. The work, in one sense, therefore, as we said, has begun. Compare "The hour is coming, and now is," in John iv. 23; v. 25; also Luke xii. 49.

II. How EMPHATIC ITS REPETITION. This shown: 1. *By the dignity of the speaker.* Two angels are now spoken of (vers. 3, 4), about whom and their respective doings much difference of interpretation exists. If, however, we assume the "young man" of ver. 4 to be the prophet himself (see Pusey, *in loc.*; and comp. Jer. i. 6; 2 Kings ix. 4, "the young man the prophet"), it seems clear that the one of these angels, speaking as he does (in ver. 5) in Jehovah's name, is that Angel-Jehovah mentioned before in ch. i. 11, 12, and afterwards in ch. iii. 1; as also that it is this same Angel who commissions the other to communicate to the prophet the declaration of ver. 4. No speaker, therefore, in regard to dignity, can go beyond him (Matt. xxi. 37; Heb. i. 5). 2. *The earnestness of the action.* (1) On this great Speaker's part, "going forth," as with some special purpose in view. (2) On the other angel's part, going forth to "meet him," as though to learn his will as soon as possible. (3) In the command given, to "run and speak," as men do who carry good tidings (2 Sam. xviii. 27). 3. *The explicitness of the language.* Jerusalem was to more than recover (ver. 4) its former population and size. Now its population and dwellings were much too few for its ancient limits. By-and-by they should be as much too many. What evidence this of increase! What a picture of security, of population, of wealth (comp. Gen. xiii. 2; xxiv. 35; Job i. 3)! What a promise, in short, of blessing and good!

III. How PROFOUND ITS SIGNIFICANCE. The features already noticed, however striking, were only, as it were, on the surface. There were others deeper and still more worthy of notice which accounted for these. 1. *How came Jerusalem to be thus secure and enlarged?* Because the Lord Jehovah himself was as "a wall of fire round about;" such a defence, *i.e.*, as would not only keep the enemies out, but also destroy them if they essayed to draw near (comp. Ps. cxxv. 2, a psalm, like cxxvi., probably belonging to this time; 2 Kings vi. 17). 2. *How came Jerusalem to be thus protected and favoured?* Because God himself had returned to dwell in her; and to do so, moreover, as her peculiar "glory." These two points illustrated by Ps. xlvi. 5; and Acts ii. 5—11; viii. 27, 28. This, in short, was why there should be so many other inhabitants in Jerusalem, viz. because of this most glorious Inhabitant of all.

We are reminded by this subject yet further: 1. *How swift and willing is the service of the angels of heaven.* Compare the word "run," etc., with Dan. ix. 21, 23; Ezek. i. 14; and Ps. ciii. 20, 21. This described by the poet—

> "Thousands at his bidding speed,
> And post o'er land and ocean."

This partly at the root, perhaps, of the common notion that angels have wings. This also a thing to be imitated and aimed at by us. "Thy will be done on earth, as it is in heaven." 2. *How blessed the effects of the presence of Christ.* As to safety (Matt. viii. 24—26); as to success (Matt. xviii. 19, 20); as to comfort (Mark ii. 19); as to hope (Col. i. 27, "Christ among you, the Hope of glory"); as to all that constitutes heaven (1 John iii. 2; John xiv. 3; xvi. 24).

Vers. 6—9.—*A promise of triumph.* "Ho, ho! come forth, and flee from the land of the north, saith the Lord," etc. Soon after the time of the deliverance of this prophecy, Babylon suffered greatly at the hands of Darius. The primary reference of the verses before us is to this fact, in the judgment of some—vers. 6, 7 being an urgent call to flee from that city and land, and vers. 8, 9 a solemn prediction of the calamities about to come upon it, uttered in support of that call. It will, perhaps, be safer for us to use the passage in a general way, and as showing to us (1) *Zion's perpetual duty towards God*; and (2) *God's constant devotion to Zion.*

I. ZION'S DUTY TOWARDS GOD. God's people called here by that name because the prophet has been speaking specially of Jerusalem, and because the "time to favour Zion," as the life-centre of their whole community, had now come. Being so named, observe: 1. *To what they are called*; viz. to be separated from Babylon, and her doings, and, to a certain extent, from her people (comp. Rev. xviii. 4; Isa. xlviii. 20; 2 Cor. vi. 17; 2 Chron. xix. 2, etc.). 2. *How they are called to this*; viz. (1) with a very loud call ("Ho, ho!"), as though overcome with slumber, and not aware of the danger arising, as with persons sleeping through cold, from the peculiar insidiousness of the things of this world (Matt. xiii. 28; 1 Tim. vi. 9); also (2) with a very urgent call, as though to "flee" for their lives (Gen. xix. 17); and, once more, (3) with a peculiarly imperative call, "Thus saith the Lord." 3. *Why they are called to it.* (1) Partly on account of their experience in the past. Because of their previous lack of separation from God's enemies (see Hos. vii. 8; iv. 17), God had spread them abroad, or completely scattered them, as by the four winds of heaven, leaving no corner untouched (compare the similar effect produced by the different figure of 2 Kings xxi. 13). (2) Partly on account of their then present condition. The people specially addressed seem to have been those belonging to Zion, who were dwelling in Babylon (ver. 7) at that time, where the name of Jehovah was scorned and despised (Ps. cxxxvii. 3, 4; 2 Kings xviii. 35), and where they were specially exposed, therefore, to the temptations here referred to (Dan. i. 5, 8; iii., *passim*). Avoid her snares; avoid her fate (see Jer. l. 8, 9; li. 6, 45).

II. GOD'S DEVOTION TO ZION. If God thus calls upon his people to be peculiarly his (1 Pet. ii. 9), he is ready and willing, on his part, to be peculiarly theirs. "*After the glory*" just previously spoken of—*i.e.* (perhaps) *besides* being the invisible glory and defence, as there described, of his Zion—there were two further things he would do. 1. *He would openly identify himself with their cause.* He would let it be seen; he would "send" the Messenger-Jehovah himself to proclaim it, that they were part of himself, as it were—nothing more intimately so, in real truth (see end of ver. 8; and comp. Deut. xxxii. 10; also Exod. iv. 22; Acts ix. 4; Matt. xxv. 40). 2. *He would as openly manifest himself against their enemies.* "I will shake my hand over them," and spoil those that spoil thee (comp. vers. 9 and 8). This a special proof of the presence of God with his servants, and of their mission to speak in his Name (end of ver. 9). So of Moses (comp. Exod. iii. 21, 22; xii. 35, 36); of Barak (Judg. v. 12); of Christ himself (Ps. lxviii. 18; Eph. iv. 8; Col. ii. 15).

All this: 1. *A glorious picture of the state of God's people at the time of the end.* (1) As to their nearness to God (see such passages as Ps. lxvii. 6, 7; Rev. xxi. 2, 3; xxii. 4). (2) As to their separation from evil (Ezek. xliii. 7; Rev. xxi. 27; xxii. 3; ch. xiv. 20, 21). (3) As to their triumphs in Christ (Rev. xxi. 4; 1 Cor. xv. 52—57; Ps. cx.; Heb. i. 13; x. 13, etc.). 2. *An instructive lesson as to the great thing to be aimed at by us now.* (Cant. ii. 16; John xv. 4, etc.; compare also what is shown of the importance of "holding the Head," in Col. ii. 19, and context; and of being "found in Christ," in Phil. iii. 9.)

Vers. 10—13.—*The benefits of God's presence.* "Sing and rejoice, O daughter of Zion: for lo, I come, and I will dwell in the midst of thee," etc. In these verses the prophecy takes us back to a thought twice touched on already (see ch. i. 16; ii. 5), viz. the manifested presence of God with his people. Three times over in the present passage is this same thought referred to (observe "I will dwell," both in vers. 10 and 11; and "habitation," in ver. 13). Taking this, therefore, as the main idea of the passage, we may learn from it, in a general way, how such a presence of God in Christ is connected (1) with the *extension* of his *kingdom;* (2) with the *stablishment* of his *people;* and (3) with the *confutation* of *unbelief.*

I. THE EXTENSION OF HIS KINGDOM. "Many nations shall be joined to the Lord in that day." So says the Angel-Jehovah here as the Representative and Equal of Jehovah. In what day? The "day" so often referred to of his "dwelling" or being amongst them. "Joined," in what manner? So as to become his "people" themselves. The illustrations of this general principle, whatever be the special application thereof primarily intended in this passage, are many and close. Compare the command ("make disciples") and the promise ("I am with you") of Matt. xxviii. 19, 20; also the connection, in Rom. xi. 12, 15, between the restoration of Israel to God's favour (equivalent to his presence among them) and the conversion of the world; also Ps. lxvii. throughout; Gen. xlix. 10; 1 Cor. xiv. 25; Isa. xlv. 14; Zech. viii. 23.

II. THE STABLISHMENT OF HIS PEOPLE. "Thou shalt know that the Lord of hosts hath sent me." 1. This partly due to the *direct results* of the manifested presence of Christ. Contrast the language of Cleophas ("we trusted," Luke xxiv. 21), when he supposed Christ to be absent, with the language of the disciples, not long before, in his presence (John xvi. 30). 2. Partly due to its *indirect effects* as referred to just now. It greatly confirms our own faith in Christianity when we see strangers brought to believe it. The more widely a remedy is found to succeed, the more our trust in it is augmented. This truth seems recognized or implied in such passages as Rom. i. 13; Acts xi. 22, 23; Col. i. 3—6, 23, etc.

III. THE CONFUTATION OF UNBELIEF. "Be silent, O all flesh." All "flesh and blood" —human nature at large. Compare, after the presence and power of the Captain of the Lord's host (Josh. v. 13—15) had been so signally manifested in the events recorded in Josh. x., how we read in the twenty-first verse of that chapter, that "none moved his tongue against any of the children of Israel" (see Exod. xi. 7; Ps. lxxvi. 7—9; Zeph. i. 7; Hab. ii. 20). Also Rom. xi. 33—36, where we have the same arising of God to manifest his presence by restoring Israel to his favour (note expressions, "choose Jerusalem again," and "raised up," in vers. 12, 13), and the same call to "silent awe and reverential contemplation" (Wardlaw) of his greatness. May we not also compare what is said in the prophecy of Enoch as quoted in Jude 14, 15? When "every eye shall see him" (Rev. i. 7) every mind shall believe.

CONCLUDING THOUGHTS. 1. *How deep the foundations of gospel truth!* Some of the most vital of these are connected with the Person and office of Christ, viz. as already referred to, his being at once the appointed Messenger and the personal Equal of God. Observe how each of these separate lines is woven into the whole tenor and structure of the passage before us. Three times over the person speaking is described as being "sent" (vers. 8, 9, 11); yet nowhere can we find any distinction as to authority between the speaker and Jehovah himself. So far from this, in fact, as to lead to an appearance of utter confusion between him who is sent and him who sends; like the apparent confusion to be found in the language of the Angel-Jehovah in Gen. xxii. 11, 12. A confusion, however, which, when viewed in the more explicit light of New Testament teaching, becomes comparatively clear, and even natural. How striking, because —on the human writer's part—how undesigned a coincidence! 2. *How peculiarly important in these days the duty of preaching the gospel "afar off"!* The best answer to sceptical questionings at home is to be found in missionary conquests abroad. Other religions, being the inventions of particular "races," suit those races alone. Christianity suits "every creature" (Mark xvi. 15), because the Creator's own work.

HOMILIES BY VARIOUS AUTHORS.

Vers. 1—5.—*Measuring the Church.* "Jerusalem" stands for the Church. The "man" (ver. 1) seems the same person who is afterwards spoken of as "young," and who is implicitly rebuked for taking in hand a task beyond his powers. The passage suggests for consideration—

I. MAN'S IDEA OF THE CHURCH AS CAPABLE OF STRICT DEFINITION AND MEASUREMENT. There has always been a disposition to fix and limit the boundaries of the Church. 1. *Irrational.* The visible Church may be defined, but not the invisible. Truth is not to be measured by our belief, or godliness by the piety of the party to which we belong, or the community of the good by the little systems of our day. 2. *Presumptuous.* This work cannot be done by man. He has neither the capacity nor the means. "We mete out love as if our eye saw to the end of heaven." It demands higher powers—a purer eye, a deeper insight, a more far-reaching vision. Even Elijah failed, and Peter greatly erred. Only the Lord himself knoweth them who are his. 3. *Injurious.* Mistakes must occur. Some excluded who ought to have been included, and others included who should have been excluded. Hence evil both to the judge and to the judged—pride, injustice, uncharitableness. See Saul "breathing out threatenings and slaughter." Mark John, the beloved disciple, wanting to call down fire on the Samaritans. Behold the Corinthian Church—sample of many others down to our own day—torn by factions and blighted by party spirit. How often, in the world, have grievous wars arisen from paltry questions as to boundaries! So the Church has suffered incalculable evils from "profane and vain babblings" and questions which minister strife.

II. GOD'S IDEA OF THE CHURCH AS TRANSCENDING ALL HUMAN LIMITATIONS. God is the Supreme and only Judge. He sees things as they are. He knows not only the outward works, but the heart, and the end from the beginning. In the woman whom Simon the Pharisee despised our Lord saw a true penitent. In the man who was casting out devils in his name he discerns an ally, though he followed him not openly as a disciple. In the devout Cornelius he acknowledged a true worshipper and servant of God, though he was as yet unknown to the apostles. His love overflows the letter of our Creeds and the boundaries of our Churches. And as in the past, so in the future. The picture is grand and inspiring. It foreshadows the glory of the latter day. Here is: 1. *Vast extension.* (Vers. 6, 7.) The Church is like a city that outgrows its walls, that absorbs the outlying villages and hamlets, that gradually includes the whole land in its benign embrace. As Jerusalem, so the Church, in the day of prosperity, would far surpass all former bounds. 2. *Inviolable security.* The figure is vivid and striking. It recalls the story of the prophet (2 Kings vi. 15—17) and the more ancient records of Moses and of Israel in the wilderness. The true defence is not material, but spiritual—not of the world, but of God. 3. *Divine blessedness.* The life and splendour of the Church are in the inhabitation of God. This secures the supremacy of goodness, and the brotherhood of man in Christ Jesus. God is in the midst. "God is Light," "God is Love," God is Holiness; therefore the people will live and move and have their being in light and love and holiness. It will be the days of heaven on earth.—F.

Vers. 6—9.—*The exiles' return.* "Return." This call implies—

I. KNOWLEDGE OF THEIR CONDITION. In the dark days we are apt to say, "Doth God know?" This is our weakness. The cries of the poor, the needy, and the oppressed are ever heard on high.

II. CONTINUED INTEREST IN THEIR WELFARE. Israel, though scattered, was not forsaken. Affliction witnesses both as to our sin and God's mercy. If God did not care, he would let us go on in sin. But because he loves and pities us and yearns for our home-coming, he ceases not to cry, "Return."

III. ADEQUATE MEANS PROVIDED FOR THEIR RESTORATION. God does not require the impossible. His commands are promises. The way is open. The exiles are free to come back. Welcome and peace are assured on the word of the Lord. But self-effort is needed. We must ourselves act.

IV. GRANDEST ENCOURAGEMENT TO OBEDIENCE. The best reasons to convince the judgment. The most powerful motives to sway the heart. God appeals: 1. To the *sense of right.* What should be the best and the noblest? "We needs must love the highest when we see it." 2. The *feeling of brotherhood.* The old unity might be restored. The Jews looked back with pride to the days of David and Solomon. So of the Church. 3. *Their consciousness of the real dignity of their being.* They were precious in God's sight. Specially protected and dear "as the apple of his eye." Such thoughts fitted to raise our hearts, to inspire us with worthier ideas of our nature and destiny (1 John iii. 1). 4. *Their hope of better times.* Obedience would bring blessedness.—F.

Vers. 10—13.—*The joys of the Church in her great Head.* "It is a great jubilee of joy to which Zion is invited. Thrice besides is she invited with the same word (Isa. liv. 1; Zeph. iii. 14, 15; Isa. xii. 6), and all for the restored and renewed presence of God" (Pusey).

I. THE GLORY OF HIS PRESENCE. Absenteeism is a sore evil among men, but the King of Zion is always in residence.

II. THE VASTNESS OF HIS DOMINION. Not material but moral. Souls. "The riches of his inheritance in the saints." Far and wide. People of every kindred and tongue. Constant accessions of territory, till the uttermost parts of the earth are possessed.

III. THE SPLENDOUR OF HIS ACHIEVEMENTS. The cross means death to evil and life to good. As when our Lord was in the world, wherever he went he brought light and blessing, so it is still. There is joy in heaven over every sinner that repenteth, and this joy is shared by the saints on earth.

IV. THE BLESSEDNESS OF HIS REIGN. He rules not by force, but by love. The homage of his subjects is from the heart, and their service is freely and joyously rendered. The honours of his kingdom are not to the noble and the great of the earth, but to the good. At last the old word is fulfilled, "In his days shall the righteous flourish" (Ps. lxxii. 7).—F.

Vers. 1—5.—*Third vision: an interesting future for the world.* "I lifted up mine eyes again, and looked, and, behold, a man with a measuring-line in his hand. Then said I, Whither goest thou? And he said unto me, To measure Jerusalem, to see what is the breadth thereof, and what is the length thereof," etc. Here is the third vision which the prophet had the same night. It is a continuation of the subject of the former one, namely, the rebuilding and reoccupation of Jerusalem and the temple. Observe: 1. *What he saw.* "A man with a measuring-line in his hand." In Ezek. xl. 3; xli., xlii., you have the same image. Who was this man? The general impression is that it was the Messiah in human form. He is the great Moral Architect, the Builder of the great temple of truth in the world. Then the prophet sees angels. "Behold, the angel that talked with me went forth." Who was this angel? The interpreter. Then there is another angel he sees, who went out to meet him. Who is he? Some suppose, the same as the "man with the measuring-line." In addition to this he sees a young man. "Run, speak to this young man." Who is this young man? He is generally believed to be the prophet himself; and Christ is here represented as commissioning an angel to run and speak. 2. *What he says to him.* "Whither goest thou?" The "man with the measuring-line" excites his curiosity. His appearance, gait, speed, as he carried the measuring-line in his hand, would naturally give occasion to the question. 3. *What he heard.* He heard the answer to his question : "To measure Jerusalem, to see what is the breadth thereof, and what is the length thereof." He heard the commission given to the angel : "Run, speak to this young man." He heard a description given of Jerusalem : "Jerusalem shall be inhabited as towns without walls," etc. And he heard the Divine promise made concerning it : "For I, saith the Lord, will be unto her a wall of fire round about." This part of his vision may be fairly taken to illustrate the future increase, security, and glory of good men on the earth.

I. THE FUTURE INCREASE OF GOOD MEN ON THE EARTH. Two remarks are suggested concerning the extent of genuine religion. It is : 1. *Measurable only by the Divine.* Who had the "measuring-line"? Not a mere man, not any created intelligence, but the God-Man, the Messiah. Men cannot measure the growth of piety in the world. They attempt it, but make fearful mistakes. They deal in statistics, they count the number of Churches in the world and the number of professed worshippers. But piety cannot be measured in this way. When you have summed up the number of temples and the number of professed worshippers, you have not approached a correct estimate as to the amount of genuine piety in the world. Have you scales by which to weigh genuine love? any numbers by which to count holy thoughts, aspirations, and volitions? any rules by which to gauge spiritual intelligence? Have you any plummet by which to fathom even the depths of a mother's affections? No one but God can weigh and measure the holy experiences of holy souls. By his method of measurement he may discover more piety in a humble cottage than in crowded tabernacles and cathedrals. He hath the true "measuring-line," and no one else. Hence endeavour not to determine the usefulness of a minister by the numbers of his congregation or the funds contributed by them. 2. *Unrestricted by material bounds.* "Jerusalem shall be inhabited as towns without walls for the multitude of men and cattle therein." The literal idea is that so many shall be its inhabitants that all could not be contained within the walls, but shall spread out in the open country around (Esth. ix. 19), and so secure shall they be as not to need shelter behind walls for themselves and the cattle. So hereafter Judæa is to be "the land of unwalled villages" (Ezek. xxxviii. 11). We are told that "the earth shall be full of the knowledge of the Lord, as the waters cover the sea."

II. THE FUTURE SECURITY OF GOOD MEN ON THE EARTH. "For I, saith the Lord, will be unto her a wall of fire round about." "A wall of fire." Who shall penetrate a massive wall of fire? But that wall is God himself, omnipotent in strength, immeasurably high. "I heard a great voice out of heaven saying, Behold, the tabernacle of God is with men, and he will dwell with them, and they shall be his people, and God himself shall be with them, and be their God;" "And the city had no need of the sun, neither of the moon, to shine in it : for the glory of God did lighten it, and the Lamb is the light thereof" (Rev. xxi. 3, 23). Conventional Christians talk about the Church being in danger. Are the stars of heaven in danger? The true Church is founded on a rock, and the gates of hell cannot prevail against it. Omnipotence is the Guardian of the good. "He shall give his angels charge over thee," etc.

III. THE FUTURE GLORY OF THE GOOD MEN ON THE EARTH. "And will be the Glory in the midst of her." The reference here is to the Shechinah and the mercy-seat. Good men are the recipients and the reflectors of Divine glory. They are the temples for the Holy Ghost to dwell in, and they reveal more of him than the whole material universe. Holiest souls are his highest manifestations.—D. T.

Vers. 6—9.—*Soul-exile.* "Ho, ho, come forth, and flee from the land of the north, saith the Lord : for I have spread you abroad as the four winds of the heaven, saith the Lord," etc. This is a call of Jehovah to the Jews in Babylonian captivity to return to their own land. Cyrus had made a way for them, and publicly proclaimed their deliverance. There are expressions in these verses, as indeed in almost every verse of the book, the exact meaning of which cannot be settled : it is idle to attempt to interpret their precise significance. For example, what is meant by "I have spread you abroad as the four winds of heaven"? Some say that it means that the proclamation was to be made to every part of the land. Some, that it refers to the extent of their dispersion, that they had been scattered by the four winds of heaven. But what matters it? Again, what is meant by "After the glory hath he sent me unto the nations which spoiled you"? Some suppose the prophet to be the person who here speaks of himself as being sent. Others, the angel mentioned in ver. 4. Some read the words, "after the glory," "to win glory." And again, what is meant by "Behold, I will shake mine hand upon them, and they shall be a spoil to their servants"? The expression, perhaps, is indicative of a threatening attitude of Jehovah when about to inflict punishment upon his enemies. Dr. Wardlaw says of vers. 8, 9, "That the simplest and most natural interpretation is that which makes them refer to the fulfilment of the promise in ver. 5, 'I will be the Glory in the midst of her.'" When this has been fulfilled—when Jehovah's house has been built, and he has returned and taken possession of it, and become anew the glory of his people and his city—then, says the speaker, "He hath sent me unto the nations which spoiled you,"— words of which, in this connection, the most appropriate interpretation seems to be that Jehovah hath given him a commission against those nations. These words may be fairly taken to illustrate *the moral exile of humanity.* As the Jews in Babylon were exiled from their own land, souls are away from God in the "far country" of depravity. The point suggested is *the reluctance of the exile to return.* This reluctance is here seen—

I. IN THE EARNESTNESS OF THE DIVINE APPEAL. "Ho, ho, come forth, and flee from the land of the north, saith the Lord." Though Providence, through the interposition of Cyrus, had removed all physical obstacles to their return, still they had such lingering attachments to the land of their captivity that they seemed loth to break away. Hence the appeal of the Almighty to "flee from the land of the north." Is not this an illustration of the moral state of sinners? Though their way to return back to God has been made clear by Christ, yet return they will not. Hence how earnest and persevering the Divine call! What is the voice to humanity of the Almighty Word, the voice sounding through nature, through all history, and especially through Christ? Does it not amount to this, "Let the wicked forsake his way, and the unrighteous man his thoughts: and let him return unto the Lord," etc.? "*Return*" is the word. "Flee from the land of the north." It is the land of corruption, the land of tyranny.

II. IN THE POTENCY OF THE DIVINE REASONS. Several things are suggested by God as reasons why they should attend to his call and "*return.*" 1. *The greatness of their separation.* "I have spread you abroad as the four winds of the heaven." You ought to be one people, united as loving brethren—united in spirit and aim, in a common worship and a common purpose of life; but you are divided far apart. You are not in one part of the country, but at every point of the compass—east, west, north, south. Do not be separated any more. Gather together into one fold. Is not this a good reason why sinners should return to God? So long as they are away from him they are divided amongst themselves. They are not only apart from each other, they are not only without sympathy with each other, but in antipathy. What a motive this to "return"! 2. *The tender interest of God in them.* "He that toucheth you toucheth the apple of his eye." Some regard this as meaning, "He that injures you injures himself;" as if the words meant, "He that toucheth you toucheth the pupil of his own eye." There is a great truth in this. He that *injures another injures himself thereby.* This is a law manifestly just and eternally irrevocable. You cannot wrong another without wronging yourself. But although this is a truth, the words, I think, convey something more than this; they convey the idea of God's tender interest in his people. It is a charming figure. The eye is one of the most intricate and delicate structures in the human frame; and the pupil of the eye—the opening by which the light of heaven enters for the purposes of vision—the most sensitive, as well as important, part of that structure. Nothing can more finely convey the idea of the exquisitely tender care of Jehovah for the objects of his love. Such interest the Bible teaches with frequency and fervour. Hence we read, "In all their affliction, he is afflicted." We read, "As a father pitieth his children," etc. We read, "Can a woman forget her sucking child?" We read, "He is touched with a feeling of our infirmities," etc. What an argument is this for man's moral return! If the Almighty Father is so tender towards us, ought we not to hurry home to his presence! The father of the prodigal son represents the universal Father of mankind. "When he was yet a great way off, his father saw him," etc.   3. *The opposition of the Almighty to their enemies.* "For, behold, I will shake mine hand upon them." This can be the language of no other than Jehovah, and yet is the language of one who speaks of "*Jehovah*" as having "*sent him.*" There does not appear to be any reasonable explanation of this but our considering the speaker as the Divine Angel of the covenant. This is a strong reason why they should "return." They need not be afraid, therefore, of their enemies. God is against them. Is not this a good reason why sinners should return to him? They need not dread their enemies, whether they be men or devils. God says, "I will shake mine hand upon them."

CONCLUSION. Why should sinners be so reluctant to return to God? What made the Jews so reluctant " to flee from the north"—to break away from Babylon and return to their own land? Was it *indolence?* Did they so love ease as to dread exertion? Was it *love of the world?* Had they established prosperous businesses, and amassed such property as to tie them to the spot? Was it *old association?* Had they formed acquaintances in which they were interested, associates whose services promoted their private advantage, and whose fellowship yielded pleasure to their social natures? Perhaps each of these acted—*indolence, love of the world, old associations.* And do not all these act now to prevent sinners from coming out of moral Babylon (see Rev. xviii. 4)?—D. T.

Vers. 10—13.—*The joy of the millennial Church.* "Sing and rejoice, O daughter of Zion: for, lo, I come, and I will dwell in the midst of thee, saith the Lord," etc. "The daughter Zion, or the Church of the Lord, delivered out of Babylon, is to rejoice with joy, because her glorification is commencing now. The Lord comes to her in his angel, in whom is his Name (Exod. xxiii. 21) and his face (Exod. xxxiii. 14), *i.e.* the Angel of his face (Isa. lxiii. 9), who reveals his nature, to dwell in the midst of her. This dwelling of Jehovah, or of his Angel, in the midst of Zion, is essentially different from the dwelling of Jehovah in the most holy place of his temple. It commences with the coming of the Son of God in the flesh, and is completed by his return in glory (John i. 14; Rev. xxi. 3). Then will many, or powerful nations, attach themselves to Jehovah, and become his people (cf. ch. viii. 20, 21; Isa. xiv. 1). This kingdom of God, which has hitherto been restricted to Israel, will be spread out and glorified by the reception of the heathen nations which are seeking God (Micah iv. 2). The repetition of the expression, ' I dwell in the midst of thee,' merely serves as a stronger asseveration of this brilliant promise" (Keil). These words may be fairly taken to represent the *joy of the millennial Church.* The words, as we have seen, point to the bright periods when Messiah's kingdom shall so extend as to embrace "many nations." Three remarks are suggested concerning this joy. It is *righteous, reasonable,* and *reverential.*

I. IT IS RIGHTEOUS. It is not only divinely authorized, but commanded. "Sing and rejoice, O daughter of Zion." Often we are informed by religious teachers that joy is a *privilege,* but seldom told that joy is a *duty.* But joy is in truth as much a duty as honesty; for he who has commanded us not to steal has also commanded us to " rejoice evermore." It is as truly a sin against Heaven to be spiritually gloomy and sad as to be socially false and dishonest. "Sing and rejoice, O daughter of Zion." Similar commands are found elsewhere on the pages of Holy Writ. "Break forth into joy, sing together" (Isa. lii. 9); "Cry out and shout, thou inhabitant of Zion" (Isa. xii. 6); "Rejoice evermore" (1 Thess. v. 16); "Rejoice in the Lord alway: and again I say, Rejoice " (Phil. iv. 4). God in nature says to all, " Be happy." God in Christ says to all, "Be happy." " These things have I spoken unto you, that your joy may be full." *Gratitude* is joy; and ought not gratitude to fill every soul? *Admiration* is joy; and ought not every soul to be filled with admiration of the Divine excellence? *Love* is joy; and ought we not to love all creatures with the love of benevolence, and the Creator with the love of adoration?

II. IT IS REASONABLE. What is righteous is of course always reasonable. True morality is true policy. But here are reasons suggested for this joy. What are they? 1. *The presence of God.* "Lo, I come, and I will dwell in the midst of thee, saith the Lord." The highest happiness of an intelligent creature is the presence of the object it supremely loves. "In thy presence is fulness of joy." To be with God is to be with the Fountain of all joy. 2. *The increase of the good.* " Many nations shall be joined to the Lord in that day." There is a bright prospect for the true Church; though it has been and still is small, uninfluential, and despised, it is destined to grow, extend its boundaries, and embrace nations. The stone shall become a mountain and fill the whole earth. Is not this a good reason for joy—to see the clouds of error in the human sky breaking, dissolving, vanishing, and the Sun of truth rising, spreading, and penetrating the whole earth with its life-giving beams? Is not this a sublime reason for life-giving joy—" Many nations shall be joined to the Lord," as the branches are joined to the roots of the tree, as the members of the body are joined to the head? 3. *The restoration of the Jews.* " And the Lord shall inherit Judah his portion in the holy land, and shall choose Jerusalem again." As all the language of this book is highly figurative, to give a literal meaning to this expression is neither necessary nor just. It is not a literal but a spiritual restoration that is meant. Paul's words are a commentary on this (Rom. xi. 25—32), " For I would not, brethren, that ye should be ignorant of this mystery, lest ye should be wise in your own conceits; that blindness in part is happened to Israel, until the fulness of the Gentiles be come in. And so all Israel shall be saved: as it is written, There shall come out of Zion the Deliverer, and shall turn away ungodliness from Jacob: for this is my covenant unto them, when I shall take away their sins. As concerning the gospel, they are enemies for your sakes: but as touching the election, they are beloved for the fathers' sakes. For the gifts and calling of God are without repentance. For as ye in times past have not believed God, yet have now obtained mercy through their unbelief: even so have these also now not believed, that through your mercy they also may obtain mercy. For God hath concluded them all in unbelief, that he might have mercy upon all."

III. IT IS REVERENTIAL. " Be silent, O all flesh, before the Lord: for he is raised up out of his holy habitation." " The Lord is in his holy temple: let all the earth keep silence before him." The profoundest emotions of the soul are always mute. Superficial feelings are noisy and chattering. The shallow stream babbles amongst the hills. The deep river rolls by unheard. There are emotions of a pleasurable kind, that go off in the boisterous laugh, or the jocund song, or the sentimental hymn. But deep joy is silent as the stars. The real lover of art has joy in gazing at a magnificent piece of art, but his joy is inarticulate. The real lover of nature has deep joy in surveying some landscape of unparalleled grandeur. It is a joy that cannot go out in laughter, or speech, or song; it is silent. It is so with the godly soul. In the presence of the supremely beautiful it is filled with a joy that cannot speak, " a joy unspeakable, but full of glory."

CONCLUSION. Are we " joined to the Lord," loyal subjects of his great spiritual empire? If so, we might well be happy.—D. T.

EXPOSITION.

CHAPTER III.

Vers. 1—10.—§ 6. *The fourth vision: Joshua the high priest before the angel.*

Ver. 1.—**He showed me.** The Septuagint and Vulgate give, " The Lord showed me." Some suppose that it was the interpreting angel who showed this vision; but his duty was to explain, not to present, the visions. So in ch. i. 20 it is the Lord who shows the " four craftsmen." This vision is closely connected with the last. In that it was declared that the Lord would again dwell in Jerusalem, and visit his people with blessings. But to fit them for the presence and favour of Jehovah they must be pure. To this end they must have a holy priest-

hood to train them in righteous ways, to oppose the attacks of the adversary, and to intercede for them effectually. The removal of their impurity is represented in the fourth vision. **Joshua the high priest** (see note on Hag. i. 1). The name is written Jeshua in Ezra ii. 2, etc. He was the first of the high priests after the Captivity, succeeding, as by hereditary right, his father Josedech, who died in Babylon. For his services in re storing the temple he is praised among great men in Ecclus. xlix. 12. **Standing before the angel of the Lord.** Joshua is the representative of the priesthood, and through that also of the whole people. The angel of Jehovah (see notes on ch. i. 11, 13) is the representative of and endowed with attributes of Jehovah, the Friend and Leader of Israel. The phrase, "standing before," is used in a ministerial sense, as of a servant rendering service to a superior (Gen. xli. 46; 1 Kings xii. 6, 8), and a priest or Levite performing his official duties (Deut. x. 8; Ezek. xliv. 15); also, in a judicial sense, of a person appearing before a judge, either as plaintiff (Numb. xxvii. 2; 1 Kings iii. 16) or defendant (Numb. xxxv. 12). Many commentators find in this scene a judicial process, Joshua appearing before the angel as before his judge; and Ewald supposes that it adumbrates his actual accusation at the Persian court. The mention of the adversary at the right hand (Ps. cix. 6) is supposed to confirm this interpretation. But it is obvious that the adversary might stand at the right hand, not as a formal accuser in a trial, but in order to resist and hinder Joshua's proceedings; the angel, too, is not represented as sitting on a throne of judgment, but standing by (ver. 5), and there is no further intimation of any judicial process in the vision. It is therefore best to conceive that Joshua is interceding for the people in his official capacity in the presence of the representative of Jehovah. The locality is not specified; it may have been before the altar, which, we know, was built and used at this time. The special mention of his garments implies that he was engaged in official duties in a consecrated spot; but the place is immaterial. Satan; the adversary, or accuser. The personality of Satan is here plainly recognized, as in Job i. 6, etc.; ii. 1, etc., rendered by the LXX. in all these places, ὁ διάβολος (see Appendix B, in Archdeacon Perowne's 'Commentary on Zechariah'). At his (Joshua's) right hand. Not as a judicial accuser, but as an enemy to resist his efforts for the good of the people, and to thwart his interests with the angel of the Lord. To resist him; to act the adversary to him. The verb is cognate to the noun above. From what follows we must suppose that Satan objects against Joshua both his own personal sin and the transgressions of the people whose burden he bore (comp. ver. 9, where his sin is called "the iniquity of the land," which would include the guilt which had led to the Captivity, their dilatoriness in building the temple, and all their backslidings since the return).

Ver. 2.—The Lord said. The Angel of Jehovah speaks. The appellations are often here used interchangeably. The Lord rebuke thee. The Lord's rebuke falls with effect where it is directed; it paralyzes the hostile power (comp. Ps. cvi. 9; Nah. i. 4). Satan's accusation may have been well founded, but it sprang from malice, and was directed against the people whom God was receiving into favour, and therefore it was rejected

and rendered innocuous. Some commentators have supposed that St. Jude is alluding to this passage when (ver. 9) he quotes the words of Michael contending about the body of Moses, "The Lord rebuke thee;" but it is more probable that Jude is referring to some rabbinical tradition, or to the apocryphal 'Assumption of Moses' (see the matter examined in Dissertation I. of Dr. Gloag's 'Introduction to the Catholic Epistles'). That hath chosen Jerusalem (ch. i. 17; ii. 12). God's election of Israel and renewed acceptance of her is the reason why Satan's accusation is rejected (Deut. vii. 7, 8). She is not to be abandoned to the consequences of her sins, nor were God's gracious purposes towards her to be frustrated. "God hath not cast away his people, which he foreknew;" and, "Who shall lay anything to the charge of God's elect?" (Rom. viii. 33; xi. 2, 29). This. This man, Joshua, saved from his father's and grandfather's fate (see on Hag. i. 1), a type of the deliverance of Israel. A brand plucked out of the fire. Israel had been already punished by defeat, captivity, distress, and misery. From these evils, which had almost destroyed her, she had been delivered; and the deliverance would be completed; she should not be cast again into the fire (see Amos iv. 11, and note there). The expression is proverbial (comp. 1 Cor. iii. 15; Jude 23).

Ver. 3.—Clothed with filthy garments. The soiled, or dark mourning garments represent not so much the low estate to which the Aaronic priesthood had been reduced, as the defilements of sin with which Joshua was encompassed, especially, perhaps, his error in allowing his descendants to intermarry with heathens (Ezra x. 18). But the sin was not only personal; he appeared laden with the guilt of the priesthood and his people. He is a type of Christ in this. Christ, indeed, was without sin; yet he bare our sins in his own body on the tree, and was made sin for us (Rom. viii. 3; 2 Cor. v. 21). Some consider that the soiled garments denote the mean address in which an accused person appeared in court. But this is to import a Roman custom (comp. Livy, ii. 54; vi. 20) into Hebrew practice. Others deem it incongruous to make a high priest violate the decency of his office by officiating in unclean apparel. But the violation of propriety was a requirement of the vision, that thus the defilement of sin might be symbolical. He stood before the angel. To ask his aid and protection (ver. 4).

Ver. 4.—He answered. The Angel of Jehovah answered the mute petition of Joshua. Those that stood before him. The attendant angels, who waited on the Angel of Jehovah to do his pleasure (see note on ver. 1). **Take away the filthy garments.** This symbolized remission of sins and restoration to favour, as the following words explain. **I will clothe thee with change of raiment;** Revised Version, *with rich apparel.* The word *machalatsoth* occurs also in Isa. iii. 22, and may mean either "change of raiment," or "costly raiment;" or the meanings may be combined in the sense of "festal robes," only worn on great occasions and changed after the occasion. They are used here as symbols of righteousness and glory. Not only is the sin pardoned, but the wearer is restored to the full glory of his state. The LXX. makes the words to be addressed to the attendants, "Clothe ye him in a robe flowing to the feet" (ποδήρη, the word used for Aaron's priestly garment, Exod. xxviii. 4; Ecclus. xlv. 8).

Ver. 5.—**I said.** If this is the true reading (which Ewald doubts), we must consider that the prophet, excited by what has passed, cannot stand by as a mere spectator, but feels constrained to take part in the scene, and to request that the change of garments may be completed by the addition of the fair head-dress. The LXX. omits the word, continuing the address to the attendant. The Vulgate has, *et dixit.* So the Syriac and the Targum and some few manuscripts. But the received reading is confirmed, as Dr. Alexander points out, by the change in the mood of the following verb from the imperative to the optative, "let them put," "would that they put." There is nothing incongruous in the prophet thus intervening in his own person. Thus Isaiah, in the midst of a solemn vision, gives vent to his feelings (Isa. vi. 5), and St. John in the Apocalypse often mingles his own sentiments and actions with what he beheld (comp. Rev. v. 4; x. 9; xi. 1). **Mitre** (*tsaniph*); Septuagint, κίδαριν: so the Vulgate, *cidarim.* This is not the same word as that used in Exod. xxviii. 4, etc. (which is *mitsnepheth*), for the official head-dress of Aaron, though it is probably a synonym for it; and the prophet's wish is to see Joshua not only reinstated in his office and dignity, but found holy also. For the fair linen mitre, or tiara, was that which bore upon its front the golden plate inscribed, "Holiness unto the Lord" (Exod. xxviii. 36—38), and therefore showed that he was qualified to intercede for the people. **Stood by.** The Angel of Jehovah continued standing in his place, contemplating, sanctioning, and directing what was being done.

Ver. 6.—**Protested.** Solemnly and earnestly admonished, adjured. Διεμαρτύρατο (Septuagint); Gen. xliii. 3; 2 Kings xvii. 13. The Angel sets before Joshua his duties, and urges him to keep in the right way, promising to him and to the nation blessing and honour, and proceeding to prophesy of a great future.

Ver. 7.—**Walk in my ways.** God's ways are his commandments, as the next words explain (comp. 1 Kings iii. 14). **Keep my charge.** The Vulgate retains the Hebraism, *Custodiam meam custodieris* (comp. Gen. xxvi. 5; Mal. iii. 14). The charge means the laws and ordinances of the Mosaic institution. **Then.** The apodosis rightly begins here, though Kimchi and others make it commence at "I will give thee," taking the following two clauses as denoting parts of his duties, the observance of which conditioned his acceptance. **Thou shalt also judge my house.** The mention of "my courts" in the following clause requires that "house" here should mean, not people or family, but, in a more restricted sense, the temple, looked upon as the spiritual centre of the nation. If the high priest kept the ordinances and commandments, he should rule and order Divine worship, and "judge," *i.e.* govern, the ministers of the sanctuary. **Keep my courts.** He was to preserve the temple, and that which the temple represented, from all idolatry and ungodliness. This duty, as Hengstenberg observes, is introduced as a reward, because it was an honour and a privilege to be entrusted with such an office, and the greatest favour which God could confer upon man. **Places to walk.** The LXX. takes the word as a participle, translating, ἀναστρεφομένους, "persons walking;" so the Syriac; Vulgate, *ambulantes.* This is explained to mean that God will give him, out of the band of angels (ver. 4), some to accompany and aid him in his ministrations. But the word is best taken as a noun meaning "walks," "goings." The Revised Version gives, "a place of access" in the text, restoring the Authorized Version in the margin; but there seems to be no good reason for the Revised rendering. The translation," goings," "walks," gives much the same signification, and is consonant with the use of the word elsewhere (comp. Neh. ii. 6; Ezek. xlii. 4; Jonah iii. 3, 4). It means that Joshua should have free access to God. The gloss of the Targum, that it is here intimated that the high priest should be admitted to the company of the angels after the resurrection, is unsuitable, as the other parts of the promise have respect to this present world. **Among these that stand by;** *i.e.* among the attendant angels who wait upon God to do his will, and a company of whom were gathered round the Angel of Jehovah in the vision (see ver. 4). It is natural piety to believe that the hosts of heaven join in the worship of the Church on earth, and assist godly ministers with their presence and fellowship. Here is adumbrated that access to God which the Christian enjoys in Christ (John xiv. 6; Eph. ii. 18). This is more fully revealed in the next verse.

Ver. 8.—**Hear now**; ἄκουε δή (Septuagint). Joshua is called upon to give all his attention to the important announcement that follows, which promises a very great boon in the future. **Thy fellows that sit before thee.** His fellow-priests, who took their orders from him and sat with him in council (comp. 2 Kings iv. 38; Ezek. viii. 1, etc.). These priests were not seen in the vision. Keil considers that the address, to which Joshua's attention is called, begins at "Thou and thy fellows." **For** (or, *yea*) **they are men wondered at**; Septuagint, διότι ἄνδρες τερατοσκόποι εἰσί, "men observers of wonders;" Vulgate, *Quia viri portendentes sunt* (see Isa. viii. 18). The phrase would be better rendered, "men of portent, sign, or type." Revised Version gives, "men which are a sign," *i.e.* who foreshadow some future events, whose persons, office, duties, typify and look forward to good things to come. **I will bring forth my Servant the BRANCH.** This is why they are called typical men, because God is making the antitype to appear. The word rendered "branch" (*tsemach*) is translated by the Septuagint ἀνατολήν, which is used in the sense of "shoot" as well as "sunrise" (see Jer. xxiii. 5; Ezek. xvi. 7; xvii. 10), and by the Vulgate, *orientem.* So the Syriac and Arabic (comp. Luke i. 78). Most interpreters rightly see here a reference to the Messiah. Some few have fancied that Zerubbabel and Nehemiah are meant; but the appellation, "my Servant Branch," has already been applied in prophetical language to Messiah, and cannot be distorted to any inferior subject, such as a mere civil ruler. Messiah is often called the Lord's "Servant," *e.g.* Isa. xlii. 1; xliii. 10; lii. 13, etc. And the terms, "Branch," or "Rod," or "Shoot," referring to Messiah, are found in Isa. iv. 2; xi. 1; Jer. xxiii. 5; xxxiii. 15. From the depressed house of David a scion should spring, in whom all that was prophesied concerning the priesthood and kingdom of Israel should find its accomplishment.

Ver. 9.—**For behold.** This gives the reason why the "Branch" is brought forth; the Church is to be firmly established and all iniquity to be abolished. **The stone that I have laid** (*set*) **before Joshua.** In the vision a stone is seen lying at the feet of Joshua, either the foundation-stone of the temple, say the commentators, or the cornerstone, or the coping; or, as the Talmud testifies, a stone that rose some three fingers' measure above the ground, and upon which the high priest used to set the censer of incense. But it was more probably none of these, but some rough, unhewed block, not yet polished or fitted into its place. What does it represent? Many critics of note answer at once, the Messiah. He who was above called "Branch" is now called the "Stone." And certainly this term is applied unto him in prophetical language, as in Isa. xxviii. 16; Ps. cxviii. 22; and references are made to the appellation in the New Testament as to a well-known title, *e.g.* Matt. xxi. 42; Eph. ii. 20. But there are objections to taking this as the primary sense. As Knabenbauer points out, it is not likely that in one verse the Lord's Servant Branch is said to be destined to be brought forth, and in the next the same is called the stone which is set before Joshua and has to be graven by a hand Divine. Besides, if both terms mean Messiah, we have the very lame conclusion: I will bring Messiah because I have already placed him before Joshua. The stone, too, is represented as somewhat under the management of Joshua, and needing graving and polishing, neither of which facts apply to the Messiah. Putting out of sight other interpretations which are all more or less inadmissible, we shall be safest in considering the stone to represent the theocracy, the spiritual kingdom of Israel, now indeed lying imperfect and unpolished before Joshua, but ordained to become beautiful and extensive and admirable. So Daniel (ii. 35, 45) speaks of the stone cut out of the mountains without hands, which filled the whole earth, a figure of the Church and kingdom of God, small in its beginning, but in the end establishing its rule over the world. **Upon one stone;** LXX., ἐπὶ τὸν λίθον τὸν ἕνα, "upon the one stone." The stone is termed "one" in contrast with the number seven that follows. **Shall be** (*are*) **seven eyes.** Upon this stone the eyes of God are directed in watchful care (comp. ch. iv. 10; and for the phrase, see 1 Kings viii. 29; Ps. xxxiii. 18; xxxiv. 15; Jer. xxxix. 12). "Seven" is the number of perfection, and may denote here the infinite care which God takes of his Church, even as St. John in the Revelation (i. 4; v. 6) beheld the Lamb "having seven eyes, which are the seven Spirits of God sent forth into all the earth." The expression is metaphorical, and we are not to suppose, with Ewald, that the eyes were graven on the stone, or that Zechariah derived his notion from the tenets of Zoroaster or the degrees of rank in the Persian court. There may be an allusion to the seven gifts of the Spirit with which Messiah is anointed (Isa. xi. 2), and which animate and strengthen his body, the Church. **I will engrave the graving thereof.** As God engraved the tables of the Law (Exod.

xxxii. 16). I will cut and polish this rough stone to fit it for its place in the temple. The verb is used of the bold engraving and ornamentation of stone-work, the finishing which it undergoes to perfect its preparation (comp. 1 Kings vii. 36; 2 Chron. ii. 7; iii. 7). Those who regard the stone as typifying the Messiah, see in this clause an intimation of the Passion of Christ, who "was wounded for our transgressions." The LXX. has, "I dig a trench," which Jerome explains of the wounds of Christ on the cross. **I will remove the iniquity of that land.** The shaping of the stone involves the bestowal of purity and holiness. God will pardon the inhabitants of the land of Israel, and make them a holy nation (Jer. xxxiii. 7, 8). But the promise stretches far beyond the limits primarily assigned to it. **In one day.** The day when Christ died for the sins of men. There is an allusion to the great Day of Atonement, when the high priest went once a year into the holy of holies with the blood of sacrifice. This, however, was an imperfect reconciliation, and had to be repeated annually. "But Christ being come an High Priest of the good things to come . . . through his own blood entered in once for all (ἐφάπαξ) into the holy place, having obtained eternal redemption. . . . Now once at the end of the ages hath he been manifested to put away sin by the sacrifice of himself" (Heb. ix. 11—26; comp. Heb. vii. 27; x. 10).

Ver. 10.—**Shall ye call every man his neighbour**, etc. In this cleansed and purified kingdom shall be found peace, happiness, and plenty, recalling the prosperous days of Solomon (1 Kings iv. 25). (For a similar picture of prosperity, see Micah iv. 4, and note there.) This is fulfilled in Christ, who says to his true disciples, "Peace I leave with you, my peace I give unto you" (John xiv. 27). Dr. Wright notes, "We are told in the Talmud ('Yoma,' vii. 4) that when, on the great Day of Atonement, the high priest had performed the various duties of that solemn day, he was escorted home in a festive manner, and was accustomed to give a festal entertainment to his friends. The maidens and youths of the people went forth to their gardens and vineyards with songs and dances; social entertainments took place on all sides, and universal gladness closed the festival of that solemn day."

HOMILETICS.

Vers. 1—5.—*The priesthood restored.* "And he showed me Joshua the high priest," etc. Here begins a new vision, which, like that described in ch. ii. 1—4, takes us back to the date of utterance. In that we saw the restoration of the ancient city Jerusalem. In this we seem shown the restoration of the ancient Levitical priesthood. For seventy years the functions of that priesthood appear to have been in abeyance. Nowhere in Daniel and Ezekiel do we read of sacrifices being offered by the children of the Captivity. It was desirable, therefore—possibly necessary—to have those functions restored (compare, perhaps, the restoration of Peter's apostleship in John xxi. 15—17). Understood as describing a kind of heavenly council called for this purpose, the present vision sets before us (1) the *offender*; (2) the *adversary*; (3) the *Advocate*; and (4) the *decision*.

I. THE OFFENDER; viz. Joshua the son of Josedech, the lineally descended high priest of that day (1 Chron. vi. 3—15; Ezra iii. 2), and, therefore, the proper and natural representative of the priesthood which had lapsed. As such we see him here: 1. *Appearing in guilt.* This shown, of course, by the "filthy garments" (Isa. lxiv. 6) in which he is clothed, and by which may be understood more especially those sins of himself and of his predecessors and people by which, in a measure and for a season, the former priesthood had been forfeited. 2. *Coming up to be judged.* This shown by his "standing" (as noticed both in vers. 1 and 3; comp. Acts xxv. 10; Rom. xiv. 10) before the Angel-Jehovah, his proper Judge (comp. John v. 22; Rom. xiv. 10). Such, be it remembered, in each respect, if without a Saviour, is the condition of us all.

II. THE ADVERSARY. As his name (margin of ver. 2), so his work in this place (comp. Job i. 9—11; ii. 4, 5; Rev. xii. 10). This a great aggravation of the evil of Joshua's case. It is one thing to be guilty and deserving of punishment. It is another, and even worse, to have a powerful and malignant adversary claiming, as it were, the actual infliction of that punishment upon us. Sin itself cries out for justice against the offender (Gen. iv. 10; Heb. xii. 24). The adversary cries out against the *injustice* of allowing him to be spared (2 Sam. xix. 21).

III. THE ADVOCATE; viz. the Judge—*i.e.* Jehovah himself (see beginning of ver. 2). This greatly to be admired (comp. Ps. xxxii. 7, "*Thou* art my Hiding-place;" also Ps. cxix. 114). Note, also, the two cogent pleas which this great Advocate (1 John ii. 1) urges. These are: 1. *The settled purpose* of God in this matter. God had long ago "chosen Jerusalem." He must not now be asked to reject it. 2. The *past action* of God in this matter. Having already so far begun to deliver as to "pluck this brand from the burning," it would be inconsistent of him now to go back (comp. 1 Sam. iii. 12; also the great maxim of Rom. xi. 29). Even to ask anything opposed to that is to incur the "rebuke" of Jehovah.

IV. THE DECISION. It is very complete. It embraces, as we should describe it in New Testament language: 1. The "*justification*" of Joshua, or the acceptance of his *person*. This signified, as we are expressly told here, by the change of his raiment (see also Isa. lxi. 10; Luke xv. 22; Rev. xix. 8). 2. The "*sanctification*" of Joshua, or the acceptance of his *ministrations*. This represented by that "fair mitre," which—either at the request of the prophet, or, as some take it, of the great Angel himself, who, in any case, is described as "standing by" and assenting—was next placed on Joshua's head; and in which mitre also (though the word is different) there seems (see Pusey, *in loc.*) a reference to that "beauty of holiness" described in Exod. xxviii. 36—38. So completely now was that fulfilled of which we read in Ezek. xx. 41, and which was afterwards described in Mal. iii. 4.

Two very remarkable omissions may be noted, to conclude. These illustrate: 1. The *wonderful freeness* of God's mercy. We find nothing whatever offered to God by Joshua and Israel towards recovering these lapsed privileges. Nothing whatever, also, is demanded of them as a necessary condition thereto. The whole thing is spoken of as a matter of grace or favour from beginning to end. 2. The *wonderful fulness* of God's mercy. No mention is made, in the account of this great transaction, of the precise nature of the accusations and charges brought by the adversary against Joshua. Whatever they are, they are treated as done with; and done with altogether. Their very memory, as it were, is to perish. So, "I will not *remember* their sins," in Isa. xliii. 25 (see Jer. xxxi. 34; also, in a somewhat different connection, Ezek. xviii. 22; xxxiii. 16). "To err is human; to forgive, Divine." Especially so to forgive in this manner (compare, "Who is a God like unto thee?" in Micah vii. 18—20).

Vers. 6—10.—*The priesthood eclipsed.* "And the angel of the Lord protested unto Joshua," etc. The ancient Jewish priesthood, as we saw in our last, being fully restored, what was to become of it in process of time? The answer to this was partly conditional, partly not so. If faithfully discharged by Joshua and his fellows and successors, that priesthood would be for many generations a thing of honour and blessing. In any case, it would ultimately be altogether eclipsed by another priesthood of a far more glorious kind. Such seems to be the full purport of the rest of this chapter. We may consider the *conditional promise* in the first place, and the *unconditional* in the second.

I. THE CONDITIONAL PROMISE. (Vers. 6, 7.) Under this head we may notice: 1. *The marked solemnity of its manner.* By whom made? The Angel-Jehovah. In what attitude? That of standing, as most impressive (see Pusey, *in loc.*). With what language? That of protestation, and protestation in God's name. 2. *Its twofold condition.* Being, on the one hand, apparently personal—"walking in God's ways," and, on the other, apparently ministerial—keeping God's "charge" or ordinances (compare "Take heed to thyself, and to the doctrine," of 1 Tim. iv. 16; also Acts xx. 28). 3. *Its threefold blessing.* The preceding conditions being observed, Joshua and those after him, representing the restored priesthood, should have the honour and privilege (1) of administering justice, and so being a blessing to God's people or "house" (compare the semi-civil position occupied afterwards by Ezra the priest, Ezra viii. 11, etc., specially vers. 25, 26; also x. 4; also, in New Testament, by Caiaphas and others, and, in the history of Josephus, by Jaddua and others); (2) of taking charge of God's courts, and leading his worship and service—a blessing this, indeed, as shown by such passages as 1 Sam. ii. 28; Ps. cxxxiv.; also lxxxiv. 10 and xxvii. 4; and, (3) as we understand it, of taking rank, after death, even with those holy angels who were then in attendance, and whose appointed place of honour and dignity was close to God's throne (see ch. iv. 14; vi. 5; Luke i. 19; Matt. xviii. 10).

II. THE UNCONDITIONAL PROMISE. However things might turn out with this Joshua (or Jesus) and his successors regarding this restored Levitical priesthood, they were but "men of marvellous signs" (so Pusey and others). In other words, they were but types and figures of a far greater and holier " Jesus "—a Priest who was some day to be " brought forth." This Priest, while like these in some respects, was to differ from them in many others. For example, besides being a Priest who was to be " brought forth " and to supersede these, he was also to be : 1. *From a wholly different line;* viz. that of " David " and Judah (see Heb. vii. 13, 14). 2. *In a very different position.* Not merely a Judge (see *supra*) as well as Priest, under Persian or other chief rulers, but a King (compare what is said of the " Branch " in Jer. xxiii. 5 ; also ch. vi. 12, 13). 3. *Of a far superior nature.* Divine, *i.e.*, as well as human (compare, once again, what is said of the " Branch " in Jer. xxiii., as " *Jehovah* our Righteousness;" also what is said here of the " stone " and the " seven eyes," with Dan. ii. 34, 35, 44, 45; Zech. iv. 10; Rev. iv. 5; Col. ii. 9). 4. *Doing a far higher work;* viz. partly because suffering in his own glorious Person (as shown by the " graving " engraven on this " stone "), and not merely offering sacrifice ; partly, also, because " removing iniquity " fully and once for all (" in one day "), and not merely partially and for a time (Heb. x. 11—14; ix. 13, 14); and partly because, by so doing, he brought in perpetual peace (comp. ver. 10 with Gen. xiv. 18; Ps. lxxxv. 10; Isa. xxxii. 17; Rom. v. 1).

The whole passage, thus interpreted, serves to illustrate : 1. *A peculiar feature of Holy Writ.* We can hardly believe that the prophet himself understood all that we have now gathered from his words. This taught us about the Old Testament prophets generally in 1 Pet. i. 10, 11, and almost necessarily implied, in fact, in the Divine inspiration of Scripture. This exemplified also in the case of bad men (Numb. xxii. --xxiv.; John xi. 51, 52) when " carried away " (φερόμενοι, 2 Pet. i. 21) by the Spirit of God. Even in the case of demoniac inspiration (so to describe it), something like this is true, the speech of the man or woman possessed expressing more than they themselves can be supposed to mean or to know (Mark i. 23, 25; Acts xvi. 16, 17). 2. *The great object of Holy Writ;* viz. to testify of the " Branch," the " Day-spring " (Luke i. 78, see margin), the " Lord our Righteousness " (comp. John v. 39; Luke xxiv. 25—27; 1 Pet. i. 11, as before; 1 Tim. iii. 15). Always, as here, the Scriptures seem to hasten away from what is temporary and conditional to what is eternal and, in one sense, unconditional, viz. to those sufferings and subsequent glories of the Incarnate Word which the apostle seems to understand by that remarkable expression, " the sure mercies of David " (Isa. lv. 3; Acts xiii. 34). So true is that which we find written in Acts x. 43 and in the end of Rev. xix. 10.

HOMILIES BY VARIOUS AUTHORS.

Vers. 1—5.—*Satan and Christ.* Joshua was the representative of the people, not personally, but in his public character. What was done to him in a figure was to be done to them and for them in fact. The great object was to restore confidence in God and in his servants, and to raise the hopes of the people that the work of grace would triumph in spite of all opposition.

I. THE POWER OF SATAN TO RESIST. The adversary. Cunning and strong. Maliciously working as he has done from the beginning, to keep man apart from God. But his power is usurped, and his devices are doomed to exposure and defeat. He may plead in the guise of justice, but it is not from love of right. He may work upon a guilty conscience, but it is not to lead to penitence, but to engender fear and distrust, and to widen the breach between the soul and God.

II. THE POWER OF CHRIST TO REDEEM. 1. *Founded in righteousness.* He is the true " Daysman." 2. *Inspired by love.* He has vindicated his claim to plead for us because he died for us. Whom he " chooses " he will never forsake. 3. *Adequate to the greatest emergency.* He is able to " rebuke " the adversary ; to " rescue " the prey from the hands of the mighty ; to " restore " the lost purity, and the failing confidence, and the faltering service. He was manifested to " destroy the works of the devil." In this there is hope for the sinner, comfort for the downcast believer, encouragement to all true servants of the Lord.—F.

Vers. 1—5.—*Three things which concern the soul.* I. GUILT. " Filthy." The outward symbolizes the inward. Satan pleads that there is no remedy. He would anticipate the day of doom. "Let him that is filthy be filthy still." But all is not lost.

II. MEDIATION. Christ our Representative. Pleads for us on the ground of his sacrifice. Pledges himself to raise us from our low and lost estate. Not only removal of guilt, but restoration of character. He is stronger than the strong man, and rejoices to rescue the prey from his hands.

III. HOLY SERVICE. Begins with conversion. But there must be renewed consecration. Satan resists. Pleads at the bar of conscience, to crush the rising hopes of the heart; at the bar of God, to hinder, if he can, the return of the soul to its true allegiance and service. All obstacles to good are of the devil. Christ is for us, therefore let us not be afraid. Highest encouragements. God's love. Christ's work of grace. The Holy Spirit the Sanctifier.—F.

Ver. 5.—We may take this as *a picture of Christ and the soul.* "Stood by."
I. TENDER CONCERN. The beginnings of life are full of interest. So it is with the budding of the flower; the lispings of infancy; the first tokens of love. How carefully the gardener watches the germinating of some rare seed! With what tender solicitude friends wait for the signs of returning health to the loved one brought low by disease! So in an infinitely higher way as to our Lord. Our souls are precious in his sight (Luke xv. 20; John i. 48).
II. HOLY SATISFACTION IN THE DEFEAT OF THE GREAT ENEMY. Sympathetic. Ever on the alert. Ready to interpose effectively at the right moment. The wilderness, Gethsemane, Calvary, testify to his love and mighty power. His victory was our victory. Every sinner converted, every backslider restored, every believer strengthened and fitted for higher service, is to the shame of Satan and to the glory of Christ.
III. EXULTING JOY IN THE RESCUE OF SOULS. "Standing" implies continued interest. Lasts all through, from the first struggle to the final victory (cf. Stephen, Acts vii. 36). Christ's love never faileth, and his joy is the joy of eternity and of God. "He shall see of the travail of his soul, and be satisfied."—F.

Vers. 6, 7.—"*If*" and "*then;*" or, the great things of God's promises. I. THE GREAT IN CHARACTER. How described. 1. *Obedience.* Life regulated by the Divine will. "Walk in my ways." 2. *Fidelity of service.* Life devoted to God's glory. So Moses (Heb. iii. 5).
II. THE GREAT IN HONOUR. Not place, or outward distinction, or arbitrary rewards. "Knighthoods and honours borne without desert are titles but of scorn" (Shakespeare). Three things. 1. "*Judge my house.*" 2. "*Keep my courts.*" 3. "*Walks among those that stand by.*" Dignity. Power with God and power with man. Society of the noblest.
III. THE GREAT IN BLESSEDNESS. Freedom of soul. Holy living. Harmonious development. Grandest fellowship. Immortal hope. The promises of God are gracious in character, elevating in purpose, faithful in fulfilment.—F.

Ver. 8.—*Portents.* "Men wondered at." There are times when there are signs in the heavens and on the earth—prodigies which rouse attention. So in society. There are men who stand out from others. Their characters have a special significance. Their lives are prophecies. Perhaps most of the great men of the Bible were of this sort. So here—
I. REPRESENTATIVE OF THEIR GENERATION. They breathe the spirit of the age. The evil and the good, of their times, are seen in them at the highest. "There were giants in those days."
II. ADUMBRATE GREAT FORCES. Powers have been at work for long that come out. Embodied. We see the height to which corruption may rise. Intellect without conscience, passion without principle, power without God. Or it may be otherwise. Men of genius and resolution faithful to the truth, ardent for the good of their brethren —reformers, professors, martyrs, whose glory was to live not to themselves, but to God.
III. FORESHADOW COMING JUDGMENT. Like Pharaoh, they have been raised up for God's glory. Like the Jews, they are "ensamples" of God's judgments. What they

do, what they suffer, what they enjoy, are as forecasts and foreshadowings of what will be, on to the perfect end. Often such men obtain a certain worship. "There is so much of chance in warfare, and such vast events are connected with the acts of the single individual, that the proper temperament for generating and receiving superstitious impressions is naturally produced" (Coleridge). But they are "for our admonition, upon whom the ends of the world have come."—F.

Vers. 8—10.—*Messiah's mission.* I. THE TIME OF HIS COMING DIVINELY FIXED. There was the ancient promise, and long-waiting generations came and went. Manifold changes. Overturning of kingdoms and dynasties. The old stock of David seemed as good as dead. But life preserved. "Branch" destined to spring and bud in his season. There is "a time to every purpose" (Eccles. iii. 1). Christ came "in the fulness of time."

II. THE CHARACTER OF HIS WORK DIVINELY APPOINTED. "Servant." Christ came to do the will of the Father. As the Law was hidden in the ark, so the law of God was hidden in his heart. What God ordained, he freely chose. What God commanded, he delighted to carry out. He never wavered, never wearied. Why? Because the work given him to do accorded both with eternal righteousness and the highest good of man. Faithful even to the death of the cross.

III. THE RESULTS OF HIS MINISTRY DIVINELY SETTLED. Removal of sin. Upbuilding of the Church of God in the strength of righteousness and the beauty of holiness and the joys of love. What he began he would surely finish. Solomon's temple was "finished," and king and people rejoiced with great joy. Zerubbabel's temple was also to be "finished," and this should be a sign and seal of the forgiveness of past iniquity, and of the outshining of God's favour on the land. So these prophesy of greater things to come. Christ's exulting cry on the cross, "It is finished!" proclaimed the opening of heaven to all believers, the new heaven and the new earth, and the restitution of all things.—F.

Vers. 1—6.—*The good man on earth in his intercessory function.* "And he showed me Joshua the high priest standing before the Angel of the Lord, and Satan standing at his right hand to resist him," etc. Our prophet here delivers to the Jews who had been restored from Babylon a vision which he had witnessed, in order to encourage them in the work of rebuilding the temple. The scene of the vision seems to have been the precincts of the temple. He saw Joshua, the high priest, standing before the Lord on their behalf, robed in "filthy garments." He saw "Satan," the great enemy of humanity, oppose him in his intercessory engagements; but Satan was, nevertheless, rebuked by Jehovah; and the seer heard a Divine voice commanding the "filthy garments" to be taken away from the priest, declaring the removal of his iniquity, commanding a "mitre" to be put on his head, ordering him to be clothed in a new raiment, and promising him other blessings if he would but "walk" in the "ways" of God. Regarding the vision as a symbolical revelation of Joshua, in his *representative* aspect as the high priest of the Jewish people then existing, we feel authorized to infer from it two or three ideas touching the *intercessory functions of good men while on earth.*

I. THAT THE GOOD MAN, IN HIS INTERCESSORY FUNCTIONS ON EARTH, HAS TO BEAR BEFORE GOD THE MORAL IMPERFECTIONS OF HIS RACE. Joshua had on "filthy garments." This was evidently intended to represent the corrupt state of the Jewish people. The seventy years' captivity had not purified them; for now, instead of setting themselves to the work of rebuilding the house of the Lord, they were taken up with their own personal concerns, and excusing themselves by saying, "The time is not come" (Hag. i. 2). Here, then, is a *characteristic feature* of a good man's intercession while on earth. He has to bear the imperfections of his fellow-creatures before God. *Intercession* itself we consider to be an obligation resting on all minds, in all worlds, for ever. *Prayer*, either for self or others, is not confined to earth. What is prayer for self but a living *sense of dependence* upon God? And where is there a virtuous mind in the universe without this sense? This, indeed, lies at the root of all true religion. And what is prayer for others, or intercession, but a deep, loving sympathy with them, a desire for their highest interests? And does not this *benevolent* feeling lie at the basis of all moral excellence? There is not a saint nor an angel in heaven, we suppose, who does not desire the progress of kindred spirits; and what is this but intercession? But that which *distinguishes* the intercession *on earth* is that we have to remember the *moral corruption of our race*. In heaven there is no *defilement*. All there are clad either in the robes of pristine holiness or in garments washed and made white by the cleansing influences of redemptive love. But here all are in " filthy garments " —garments stained by sensuality, worldliness, idolatry, falsehood, and dishonesty. Here the pious parent has to appear before God for sinful children, the minister for sinful people, and the pious sovereign for a sinful nation.

II. THAT THE GOOD MAN, IN HIS INTERCESSORY FUNCTIONS ON EARTH, HAS TO CONTEND WITH A MIGHTY SPIRITUAL ANTAGONIST. The prophet saw Satan standing at his right hand to resist him. The existence of some mighty spirit or spirits, who are determined foes of truth, virtue, and the happiness of man, is rendered more than probable by a number of considerations, independent of the testimony of the Bible. Such, for example, as the *general belief of the race, the conflicting phenomena of the moral world, the unaccountable opposite impressions of which all are conscious*. But the Bible is most clear on this subject. Under various names, " the serpent," " the devil," " the god of this world," " the prince of the power of the air," this great enemy of the race is brought under our notice. Now, this enemy stood up to resist Joshua in his intercessions. And who will say that he is not now specially active with the good man, when he draws near to God? In how many ways may he hinder our prayers? Sometimes he may suggest to us, even in the very time of our prayers, doubts as to the existence of God; we may be tempted to ask—Are we sure there is a God? May not the idea be a delusion, for who has ever seen or heard him? Or, granting his existence, he may suggest whether he would condescend to attend to the affairs of an individual. We may be tempted to the supposition that he takes care of the great but overlooks the little; or that the universe is so thoroughly and absolutely under a system of laws, that he will not interpose on behalf of any of his creatures. Or, granting that he does exist, and that he attends to the prayers of some, Satan may suggest that I am too worthless for his notice, that it is presumptuous for me to address his awful majesty; I am too great a sinner ever to be attended to. In such suggestions as these Satan may be said to stand up against us when we appear before the Lord. This, again, is a peculiarity of our intercessory functions on earth. In heaven, we presume, no enemy will intrude on our devotions, no Satan will stand up to resist as we appear before God. No power there to darken our faith with cloudy doubts, nor to cool the ardour of our devotions!

III. THAT THE GOOD MAN, IN HIS INTERCESSORY FUNCTIONS ON EARTH, HAS THE SPECIAL ASSISTANCE OF A DIVINE HELPER. Whilst Satan stood up against Joshua, there was One who stood up for him—the Lord, called also "the Angel of the Lord." Who is this? All acknowledged expositors are agreed in concluding this to be Jesus Christ, the Saviour of the world. And he, indeed, is man's great spiritual Helper. He is our Advocate, our Intercessor. He helps us in our prayers, he attracts us to the throne of grace. "Seeing that we have a great High Priest, who has passed into the heavens." His Spirit makes intercession within us, awakens in us those desires which agree with the will of God. The scene illustrates two thoughts concerning the help rendered. 1. *It was rendered sympathetically.* "Is not this a brand?" etc. Consider the suffering to which the petitioners have been subject. Christ is full of sympathy. "We have not a high priest," etc.; "Him that cometh unto God through him he will in no wise cast out." 2. *The help was rendered effectually.* The old " filthy garments," the emblems of impurity and guilt, were taken away, and he was clothed in other garments; that is, their guilt was removed, they were restored from their degradation. And the " mitre," the emblem of dignity, was put on his head. They were raised once more to the glory of an independent nation. See: (1) That if you would effectually help your race, you must appear before God as an intercessor. Other means are also to be employed. Promote general knowledge, advance the arts, help on commerce, above all, diffuse the gospel of Jesus; but, in connection with all, you must appear before God, as Joshua did for Israel. It is in this way you will change the world's " filthy garments," and get for them the " raiment " of purity and the " mitre " of honour. (2) That if you would effectually appear before God, you must have the help of Jesus Christ. What is the vision before us but an adumbration of a common fact in the spiritual history of *every* praying man? Ever as we attempt to approach the everlasting Father in devout thought and worship, do we not find some opposing force like this Satan, or rather, this Satan himself, "standing" "at our right hand to resist" us? What is to be done? Are we to retire?—cease all endeavour to commune with the loving Parent of our souls? God forbid! Our doom is sealed in midnight and anguish, should this be so. There is no happiness for any finite spirit but that which flows from intercourse with the eternal Fountain of good. Our only hope is in getting him, the great Mediator, with us, who shall repel our foe—drive him from our presence with the words, "The Lord rebuke thee, O Satan!"—D. T.

Ver. 7.—*The Bible and true greatness.* "Thus saith the Lord of hosts; If thou wilt walk in my ways, and if thou wilt keep my charge, then thou shalt also judge my house, and shalt also keep my courts, and I will give thee places to walk among these that stand by." The words direct us to the Bible and true greatness.

I. THE BIBLE DIRECTS US TO THE SPHERE OF TRUE GREATNESS. The promise made to Joshua here is. "Thou shalt also *judge* my house, and shalt also keep my courts." The words convey this idea: *Great authority.* By the house of God is here probably meant the people of Israel; and the keeping of God's courts, the regulation of the temple. The literal meaning here is that Joshua's piety should be rewarded by the long continuance of his exalted office of High Priest. Godliness raises: (1) *To dignified positions.* It makes us "kings and priests unto God." (2) *To high fellowship.* "I will give thee places to walk among *these that stand by.*" With the general consent of commentators, the angels of God are meant by "these that *stand by.*" The angels of God minister in his house. They are "ministering servants." We are come "to an innumerable company of angels." Good men are brought by religion into fellowship with those lofty intelligences.

II. THE BIBLE PRESENTS TO US THE PATH OF TRUE GREATNESS. "If thou wilt walk in my ways," etc. Two things are stated here as the conditions of elevation. 1. *Obedience.* "If thou wilt walk in my ways." God has ways for men to walk in. His ways are his laws. "Blessed are they who walk in the Law of the Lord." Walking in his ways implies: (1) The abandonment of our own ways. "Let the wicked forsake his way." (2) The entrance on God's ways. Walking in them implies that we are on them, and the way into them is by faith in Christ. He is the "Door." (3) Progress in God's ways. We must add to our faith, virtue; to virtue, knowledge, etc. (2 Pet. i. 5). 2. *Fidelity.* "Keep my charge." We have all a trust committed to us. Our time, talents, and possessions are all given in trust. We are not owners of them, but stewards. "It is required of a steward that he be found faithful." Paul felt, as he was leaving the world, that he had finished his course, and kept the faith. Such is the path to greatness—the *only* path, the *sure* path.

III. THE BIBLE GIVES US A GUARANTEE FOR TRUE GREATNESS. "Thus saith the Lord of hosts." The word of God is the pledge. 1. His word has been *fulfilled in the experience of the good in all ages.* All who have walked in God's ways and kept his charge have reached this sublime elevation. They are the illustrious heroes of the ages; and they have high authority in the empire of God. 2. His word can *never fail of its accomplishment.* "Heaven and earth shall pass away," etc.

Brother, art thou walking in the ways of God? If so, grand distinctions await thee. "Be thou faithful unto death, and I will give thee a crown of life."—D. T.

Vers. 8—10.—*The world's wants and God's provisions.* "Hear, now, O Joshua the high priest, thou, and thy fellows that sit before thee: for they are men wondered at: for, behold, I will bring forth my Servant the BRANCH," etc. It is admitted by most acknowledged expositors of Holy Scripture that the sacerdotal institutions of the Mosaic system were typical of gospel realities; they were, as St. Paul has it, the "shadows of good things to come." This passage undoubtedly points to the Messiah and his times. Joshua, here called "the high priest," is a type of Christ, who is represented as "my Servant the BRANCH." A name by which he is designated in other parts of the Bible. Thus, for example: "There shall come forth a rod out of the stem of Jesse, and a Branch shall grow out of his roots," etc. Again, "In that day shall the branch of the Lord be beautiful," etc. And again, "Behold, the days come, saith the Lord, that I will raise unto David a righteous Branch," etc. Indeed, the men who are here spoken of as those who "sit before" Joshua, "men wondered at," are typical men. This, indeed, is the meaning of the expression, "men wondered at," which some translate, "men appointed " (Isa. viii. 18), that is, typical men. Literally, the reference is to the members of the subordinate priesthood; and as the high priest, Joshua, was the type of Christ, these men were the types of his disciples in every age. I shall take the words as presenting *the world's wants and God's provisions.*

I. THE WORLD WANTS A MORAL HELPER, AND IN THE GOSPEL ONE IS PROVIDED. Morally, man is enslaved, diseased, exiled, lost to the great uses and purposes of his being. God has provided a great Helper, here called his "Servant the BRANCH." In Isaiah (xlii. 1) we have these words, "Behold my Servant whom I uphold, mine elect, in whom my soul delighteth." He is *the* "Branch," God is the Root, and all holy souls are branches, deriving their life, beauty, and fruitfulness from him; but Christ is the "Branch," the oldest Branch, the largest Branch, the strongest Branch, the most fruitful Branch, etc. He is the Branch on which there hang clusters of perennial fruits for the "healing of the nations."

II. THE WORLD WANTS DIVINE GUARDIANSHIP. "Behold the stone that I have laid before Joshua; upon one stone shall be seven eyes." What is here meant by the "stone"? Not the foundation-stone of the temple, which was now being rebuilt, for that had been laid long before. "The stone," says Keil, "is the symbol of the kingdom of God, and is laid by Jehovah before Joshua, by God's transferring to him the regeneration of his house and the keeping of his courts (before, *liphne* in a spiritual sense, as in 1 Kings ix. 6, for example). The seven eyes which watch with protecting care over this stone are not a figurative representation of the all-embracing providence of God; but, in harmony with the seven eyes of the Lamb, 'which are the seven Spirits of God' (Rev. v. 6), and with the seven eyes of Jehovah (ch. iv. 10), they are the seven-fold radiation of the Spirit of Jehovah (after Isa. xi. 2), which show themselves in vigorous action upon this stone, to prepare it for its destination." Perhaps the meaning is that upon the kingdom of Christ, here symbolized by the stone, God's eyes are fixed (*engraven*) with deep and settled interest. "The eye is the natural hieroglyphic for knowledge; and 'seven,' as every reader of the Bible is aware, is the number used to denote completeness, perfection. Seven eyes denote the perfection of observant knowledge; and as the 'eyes of Jehovah' mean Jehovah's observation and knowledge, his 'seven eyes' express the perfection of both—omniscient observation." Two thoughts are suggested. 1. *God has a special interest in Christ and his followers.* His eyes are on the "stone," there in all their completeness—seven. He has a *general* interest in the universe, but a special interest here. His eyes, which "run to and fro through all the earth," glance with a wonderful tenderness upon the "stone." 2. *God has a settled interest in Christ and his followers.* The eyes are said to be *engraven* on the stone, not written in ink, not painted with colour which time would erase, but cut into its very heart; the stone itself must moulder before the engraving is destroyed. "Who shall separate us from the love of Christ?" "The mountains shall depart, and the hills be removed," etc.

III. THE WORLD WANTS MORAL PURIFICATION, AND IN THE GOSPEL IT IS PROVIDED. "I will remove the inquity of that [this] land [that is, Palestine] in one day." The "iniquity of that land," the land of the Jews, was multiform, aggravated, immeasurable; but in one day provision should be made for its removal, the day on which Christ died upon the cross. "The work of the Messiah had a primary respect to Israel. The offer of salvation was to the Jew first." "Unto you first, God, having raised up his Son Jesus, sent him to bless you, in turning away every one of you from his iniquities" (Acts iii. 36). These words of Peter to the Jews of his day are a commentary on those before us. The great want of man is moral purification. Thank God, "Christ came to put away sin by the sacrifice of himself."

IV. THE WORLD WANTS SPIRITUAL REPOSE, AND IN THE GOSPEL IT IS PROVIDED. "In that day, saith the Lord of hosts, shall ye call every man his neighbour under the vine and under the fig tree." "When iniquity is taken away," says Matthew Henry, "(1) We reap precious benefits and privileges from our justification, more precious than the products of the vine or the fig tree (Rom. v. 1). (2) We repose in a sweet tranquillity, and are quiet from the fear of evil. What should terrify us when iniquity is taken away, when nothing can hurt us? We sit down under Christ's shadow with delight, and by it are sheltered from the scorching heat of the curse of the Law. We live as Israel in the peaceable reign of Solomon (1 Kings iv. 24, 25), for he is the Prince of Peace."—D. T.

EXPOSITION.

CHAPTER IV.

Vers. 1—14.—§ 7. *The fifth vision: the golden candlestick.*

Ver. 1.—The angel that talked with me. The interpreting angel is meant. **Came again, and waked me.** It is thought that the angel, who is said (ch. ii. 3) to have gone forth, now rejoined the prophet and renewed his colloquy with him. But the expression in the text is probably only equivalent to "aroused me again" (comp. Gen. xxvi. 18; 2 Kings i. 11, 13, etc.). Absorbed in awe and wonder at the contemplation of the preceding vision, the prophet had fallen into a state of exhaustion and torpor, as Daniel slept after his great visions (Dan. viii. 18; x. 8, 9), and the apostles were heavy with sleep on the Mount of Transfiguration (Luke ix. 32). From this mental prostration the angel arouses him to renewed attention. Or what is meant may be that the change wrought on the faculties by the Divine influence was as great as that between natural sleeping and waking.

Ver. 2.—What seest thou? The angel does not show the vision to the prophet, but makes him describe it, and then explains its import. This vision of the candlestick, with its seven lamps fed by two olive trees, signifies that the work of rebuilding the temple, and preparing the way for the Church of the true Israel, was to be accomplished by relying, not on human resources, but on Divine aid. Thus were Zerubbabel and his people roused to perseverance and energy in their good work, of which the final success is assured. **I have looked;** ἑώρακα (Septuagint), "I have seen." **A candlestick all of gold.** The candelabrum as described differs in some particulars from that in the tabernacle, though the same word, *menorath*, is used in both cases (Exod. xxv. 31; xxxvii. 17, etc.). In Solomon's temple there were ten candelabra (1 Kings vii. 49), which were carried away to Babylon when Jerusalem was taken (Jer. lii. 19). The single candelabrum of Zerubbabel's temple is mentioned in 1 Macc. i. 21; iv. 49, 50. The one sculptured on the arch of Titus may be a truthful representation of that in Herod's temple, but probably is not the same as that in the second edifice (comp. Josephus, 'Ant.,' xiv. 4. 4). The candelabrum in the vision differed from the original one in three particulars: it had a central reservoir; it had also seven pipes; and it was supplied with oil by two olive trees. **With a** (*its*) **bowl upon the top of it.** The "bowl" (*gullah*) is a reservoir for oil placed at the top of the candelabrum; and from it tubes led the oil for the supply of the lamps. In the tabernacle each lamp was separate, and trimmed and filled by the ministering priests; the mystic lamps needed no human agency to keep them supplied. They were fed by the "bowl." The word is translated in the Septuagint, λαμπάδιον: in the Vulgate, *lampas*; hence some have supposed that, besides the seven lamps, there was another large light in the centre; but the Greek and Latin rendering is mistaken, the word meaning "a fountain" (Josh. xv. 19), or "a ball" (1 Kings vii. 41), or "a round bowl" (Eccles. xii. 6). **And seven pipes to the seven lamps, which are upon the top thereof.** The Hebrew is, literally rendered, *seven and seven pipes to the lamps which are upon its top.* The LXX. translates, Καὶ ἑπτὰ ἐπαρυστρίδες τοῖς λύχνοις τοῖς ἐπάνω αὐτῆς, "And seven vessels for the lamps which are upon it;" so the Vulgate, *Septem infusoria lucernis, quæ erant super caput ejus.* These versions imply that there was one supply pipe to each of the lamps, which seems most natural. In this case, the first "seven" in the text must be an interpolation. Commentators who regard the present reading as correct have taken various ways in explaining it. Some multiply the number into itself, and make the pipes forty-nine; but this is unwarranted by Hebrew usage (Henderson). Others add the numbers together, making fourteen; but here again the copulative *vau*, which implies diversity, is an objection. The Revised Version has, "There are seven pipes to each of the lamps," taking the words distributively; but the number of tubes seems here to be unnecessarily large. Dr. Wright considers that there were two pipes to each lamp, one set connecting each to the central bowl, and one connecting the several lamps together. One, however, does not see of what particular use the second set is. Dr. Wright, p. 84, gives a drawing of the candelabrum with its appurtenances, according to his notion of the vision. The Authorized Version seems to give the correct idea of the passage, whether we arrive at it by rejecting the first "seven," or by considering that it is repeated for emphasis' sake, as Cornelius à Lapide and Pressel think: "Seven are the lamps upon it—seven, I say, and seven the pipes." Take it as we may, the point is that the oil is well and copiously supplied to the several lights.

Ver. 3.—**Two olive trees.** These, as explained in ver. 12, discharged the oil from their fruit-bearing branches into conduits which led to the central reservoir. Without man's agency the oil is separated from the berry and keeps the lamps constantly supplied (comp. Rev. ii. 4).

Ver. 4.—**What are these, my lord?** The question may refer to the two olive trees, which were a novelty to the prophet, who, of course, was well acquainted with the form and use, if not the symbolism, of the candelabrum. But it may also be taken as desiring information about the whole vision.

Ver. 5.—**Knowest thou not?** The angel speaks not so much in surprise at the prophet's slowness of comprehension (comp. John iii. 10) as desirous of calling his most serious attention to the coming explanation.

Ver. 6.—**This is the word of the Lord unto Zerubbabel.** The Lord's message unto Zerubbabel is the purport of the vision, viz. that his work will be accomplished through the grace of God alone. **Not by might.** Septuagint, "not by great might;" but the Vulgate, "not by an army." The word is almost synonymous with the following, translated **power**; and the two together mean that the effect is to be produced, not by any human means, however potent. Doubtless Zerubbabel was dispirited when he thought how much there was to do, how feeble the means at his disposal (Neh. iv. 2), and how formidable the opposition; and nothing could better reassure him than the promise of Divine aid. **But by my Spirit.** The angel does not say expressly what is to be done; but the purpose that filled the minds of Zechariah and Zerubbabel applied the word. The operations of the Spirit are manifold, and his aid alone could bring these mighty things to pass. The oil is a figure of the grace of the Holy Spirit; and as the lamps are not supplied by human hands, but directly from the olives, so the good work now undertaken shall be supported by Divine means (see on ver. 14).

Ver. 7.—**Who art thou, O great mountain?** The "mountain" is a figurative expression to denote the various difficulties that stood in Zerubbabel's way and impeded the carrying out of his great design. **Before Zerubbabel.** The Vulgate affixes these words

to the former part of the clause, but the accent is in favour of the Authorized Version. Thou shalt become a plain; literally, *into a plain!* A command. All obstacles shall be removed (comp. Isa. xl. 4; xlix. 11; Matt. xvii. 20; Luke iii. 4, 5). Septuagint, τοῦ κατορθῶσαι (intrans.), "that thou shouldst prosper;" "ut corrigas" (Jerome). **He shall bring forth the headstone thereof.** "He" is evidently Zerubbabel. He shall commence and put the finishing stroke to the work of rebuilding the temple. Many commentators take this stone to be the one that completes the building, "the top-stone." But it may well be questioned whether a building like the temple could have any such stone. An arch or a pyramid may have a crowning stone, but no other edifice; nor is there any proof that such a top-stone was known or its erection celebrated. It may be a mere metaphor for the completion of the work. It is better, however, to take it as the corner-stone, to which we know great importance was attached (comp. Job xxxviii. 6; Ps. cxviii. 22, etc.). This stone, on which the building rests, Zerubbabel will bring forth from the workshop; as the next verses say, his hands have laid the foundation. That action, already past, is represented as future, the regular commencement of the work under Zerubbabel's direction being intimated, and its happy conclusion promised. Septuagint, Καὶ ἐξοίσω τὸν λίθον τῆς κληρονομίας, "And I will bring forth the stone of the inheritance"—the meaning of which is obscure, though Jerome explains it by considering it an allusion to Christ. **With shoutings,** crying, **Grace, grace unto it!** All the by-standers, as the stone is placed, shout in acclamation, "God's favour rest upon it!" (Ezra iii. 10). The LXX. seems to have mistaken the sense, rendering, Ἰσότητα χάριτος χάριτα αὐτῆς, "The grace of it the equality of grace" (John i. 16); and to have led St. Jerome astray, who translates, "Et exæquabit gratiam gratiæ ejus," and comments thus: "We all have received of his fulness, and grace for grace, that is, the grace of the gospel for the grace of the Law, in order that the Israelites and the heathen who believe may receive equal grace and a like blessing." The Targum recognizes here a Messianic prophecy: "He will reveal the Messiah whose Name is spoken of from all eternity, and he shall rule over all the kingdoms."

Ver. 8.—**The word of the Lord came unto me.** The word came through the interpreting angel, as is clear from the expression in ver. 9, "The Lord hath sent me unto you." He explains more fully what had been already announced figuratively.

Ver. 9.—**Have laid the foundation.** Zerubbabel had commenced the rebuilding in the second year of the return, in the second month (Ezra iii. 8); it had been hindered by the opposition of the neighbouring people (Ezra iv. 1—5, 24), and was not resumed till the second year of Darius. **Shall finish it.** The temple was finished in Darius's sixth year (Ezra vi. 15). **Thou shalt know,** etc. The truth of the angel's mission would be proved by the event, viz. the successful issue (comp. ch. ii. 9, 11; vi. 15; Deut. xviii. 22). The completion of the material temple was a pledge of the establishment of the spiritual temple, the Church of God.

Ver. 10.—**For who hath despised the day of small things?** The "small things" are the weak and poor beginning of the temple (Hag. ii. 3); as the Targum glosses, "on account of the edifice, because it was small." Small as the present work was, it was a pledge of the full completion, and was therefore not to be despised. So the question is equivalent to, "Can any one, after these promises and prophecies, presume to be doubtful about the future?" **For they shall rejoice,** etc. The subject of the verbs is that which comes last in position, the seven eyes of Jehovah; and the verse is best translated thus: "For (*i.e.* seeing that) these seven eyes of Jehovah, which run through all the earth, behold with joy the plummet in the hand of Zerubbabel." The work is not contemptible, since the Lord regards it with favour, watches, and directs it. The LXX. and Vulgate (followed nearly by the Authorized Version) make the despisers the subject of the verbs, and lamely dissociate the final clause entirely from the preceding. The version given above is in accordance with the Masoretic accentuation. **The plummet;** literally, *the stone, the tin;* τὸν λίθον, τὸν κασσιτέρινον (Septuagint); *lapidem stanneum,* "the stone of tin" (Vulgate). Tin is not found in Palestine; it was imported by the Phœnicians in great abundance, and from them the Jews obtained it. The supply must have come from Spain or Britain. With **those seven.** The preposition is an interpolation of the Authorized Version. It should be, "even these seven," explaining who are "they" at the head of the clause. **The eyes of the Lord.** The "seven eyes" have been already mentioned (ch. iii. 9, where see note). They are expressive of God's watchful providence and care. **Which run to and fro.** This clause further enforces the previous image (2 Chron. xvi. 9; Prov. xv. 3).

Ver. 11.—**Then answered I.** The prophet had received a general explanation of the vision; he had probably understood that the candelabrum represented the theocracy, of whose restoration and life the temple was the symbol and vehicle. One point was still obscure, and he asks, **What are these two olive trees?** (ver. 3). To this question no answer is immediately forthcoming, the answer being delayed in order to augment the prophet's desire of understanding the vision, and to induce him to make the question more definite.

Ver. 12.—The prophet perceives the chief point in the mystic olive trees, so he alters his question the second time, asking, **What be these two olive branches?** (*shibbolim*); Vulgate, *spicæ,* "ears," as of corn, so called, as Kimchi supposes, because they were full of berries, as the ears are full of grains of corn. **Which through the two golden pipes,** etc.; rather, *which by means of two golden tubes are emptying the golden oil out of themselves.* The oil dropped of itself from the fruit-bearing branches into two tubes, spouts, or channels, which conveyed it to the central reservoir. The Revised Version renders, "which are beside the two golden spouts;" like the Vulgate, *quæ sunt juxta duo rostra aurea.* The LXX. has, οἱ κλάδοι . . . οἱ ἐν ταῖς χερσὶ τῶν δύο μυξωτήρων ("beaks," "noses") τῶν χρυσῶν—where "in the hands" or "by the hands" may be a Hebraism for "by means of." **The golden** oil; Hebrew, *the gold.* The oil is so called from its colour. The Greek and Latin versions lose this idea altogether. *In quibus sunt suffusoria ex auro* (Vulgate); "leading to the golden vessels" (Septuagint).

Ver. 13.—**Knowest thou not?** (comp. ver. 5). The angel wishes to impress upon the prophet whence came the power of the theocracy and the Divine order manifested therein.

Ver. 14.—**The two anointed ones;** literally, *the two sons of oil;* so the Revised Version; Vulgate, *filii olei;* Septuagint, υἱοὶ τῆς πιότητος, "sons of fatness" (comp. Isa. v. 1). By them are intended the two powers, the regal and the sacerdotal, through which God's help and protection are dispensed to the theocracy. Oil was used in appointing to both these offices (comp. Lev. xxi. 10; 1 Sam. x. 1). The expression, "son of," in many cases denotes a quality or property, like "son of Belial," "son of might;" so here Dr. Alexander considers that "sons of oil" means people possessed of oil, oil-bearers, channels through which the oil flowed to others. Zerubbabel and Joshua are representatives of the civil and priestly authorities, but the text seems expressly to avoid naming any human agents, in order to show that the symbol must not be limited to individuals. Nor, indeed, must it be confined to the Jewish Church and state; it looks forward to the time when Jew and Gentile shall unite in upholding the Church of God. **That stand by the Lord of the whole earth;** *i.e.* ready as his ministers to do him service. There is a reference to this passage in Rev. xi. 4, where the "two witnesses" are called "the two olive trees . . . standing before the Lord of the earth" (Perowne). The vision, as we have seen, prefigures primarily the completion of the temple and the restoration of its worship, and secondly the establishment of the Christian Church by the advent of Messiah. The several parts of the vision may be thus explained. The candelabrum is a symbol of the Jewish Church and theocracy, in accordance with the imagery in the Apocalypse, where the seven candlesticks are seven Churches (Rev. i. 20). It is made of gold as precious in God's sight, and to be kept pure and unalloyed; it is placed in the sanctuary, and has seven lamps, to indicate that it is bright with the grace of God, and is meant to shed its light around at all times, as Christian men are bidden to shine like lights in the world (Matt. v. 16; Phil. ii. 15). The oil that supplies the lamps is the grace of God, the influence of the Holy Spirit, which alone enables the Church to shine and to accomplish its appointed work. The two olive trees are the two authorities, viz. the civil and sacerdotal, through which God communicates his grace to the Church; these stand by the Lord because, instituted by him, they carry out his will in the ordering, guiding, extending, and purifying his kingdom among men. The two olive branches remit their oil into one receptacle, because the two authorities, the regal and priestly, are intimately connected and united, and their action tends to one end, the promotion of God's glory in the salvation of men. In Messiah these offices are united; he is the channel of Divine grace, the source of light to the whole world.

HOMILETICS.

Vers. 1—7.—*The Church revived.* "And the angel that talked with me came again, and waked me," etc. The imagery of these verses is twofold; but their subject seems one. By the "candlestick" expressly mentioned in ver. 2 (comp. Rev. i. 13; ii. 1; also Matt. v. 14, 15; Phil. ii. 15), and by the temple tacitly referred to in ver. 7, we understand, spiritually, the same thing, viz. in the first instance certainly the Jewish Church of that time. And what this twofold imagery seems intended here to set before us respecting this Church is (1) the *secret*, and (2) the *completeness* of its restoration to life.

I. THE SECRET OF ITS RESTORATION TO LIFE. Under this head we have set before us the question: 1. *Of Church work.* What is the great duty of a Church in this world? Is it not, like a lamp or candlestick, to give light, to be a continued witness to men respecting things unseen and eternal—a standing testimony in favour of truth and righteousness, and against error and sin? in other words (Art. XX.), "a witness and keeper of Holy Writ"? See again references *supra;* and note, in connection with this duty of spiritual light-giving on the part of a Church, the various grounds of the praise or blame administered in Rev. ii. and iii. 2. *Of Church needs.* The returned remnant of the Captivity, with their altar again set up (Ezra iii. 3), their feasts again begun (Ezra iii. 4), their temple in course of re-erection (Ezra iii. 10; vi. 14), and their ancient priesthood again restored (Zech. iii. 1—5), had now become such a witness. They were a "candlestick" or lamp again "lighted." How unequal in themselves to so important an office! How weak, how inexperienced, also how greatly endangered! Above all, how greatly needing that sacred unction, or "oil," of God's grace, of which we are told here (comp. also Acts x. 38)! 3. *Of Church supplies.* How ample, according to the vision described in vers. 2, 3, the provision made for supplying this revived lamp with this oil! What besides is meant by the different features of this vision the prophet knows not (ver. 4), and the angel tells not, at present. But, at any rate, they seem to signify that abundant provision is made. (1) For supplying such oil. There are "two" olive trees, *e.g.*, to yield a double supply. Two "trees," also, things always growing and always producing, and able to yield, therefore, a continual supply. (2) For storing it up, viz. in the "bowl" placed at the "top," whence it could naturally flow out and down as required. (3) For distributing it in every needed direction, viz. by means of the twice-seven pipes (or even, as some take it, the seven-times-seven pipes), to the seven lamps of which we are told. So mysterious, yet so sufficient, was the secret source of life in this case. Let Zerubbabel, as the successor of David, and earthly guardian of his Church, know this for his comfort (see ver. 6).

II. THE COMPLETENESS OF THIS RESTORATION. In the seventh verse, as noted before, the figure is changed. The Church of the restored Captivity is before us now under the metaphor of a building inhabited by God himself, as often in God's Word (see Heb. iii. 6; 2 Cor. vi. 16; Eph. ii. 21, 22; 1 Tim. iii. 15; 1 Pet. ii. 5). And the purport of this change seems that of representing, not only as before the adequacy, but also now the actual effectiveness, of the provision here made. It should eventually be with that spiritual house as with the material house which they were then building as its image and type. This true: 1. *As to external obstacles.* The greatest of these, even if like a " great mountain " itself in bulk, should become, " before Zerubbabel "—having the Spirit of God on his side—like a plain. 2. *As to final victory.* To use a well-known modern expression, there should be "the crowning of the edifice" of the Church. All that the pre-Captivity Jewish Church had really been in the world this restored Church should now be, up to the very " headstone "—the last stone to be put in its place—with every mark of triumph (" shoutings ") and favour (" grace ") as well (ver. 7).

Observe, in conclusion : 1. *How strikingly these promises were fulfilled.* Besides all that we read concerning the days of the Maccabees (as referred to probably in Heb. xi. 35—38), how much more spiritual life remained in the Jewish Church even to the times of the gospel! See indications of this in Luke ii. 25, 38; Matt. xxvii. 53; Mark xv. 43; Acts ii. 5, etc. See indications, also, as to the extent to which the witness or " light " of this Church had told on the Gentile world in Luke vii. 5 ; John xii. 20; Acts x. 1; xiii. 43, 50 (τὰς σεβομένας); xvii. 4, 17. 2. *How great a lesson this teaches.* There was nothing in this case but the secret working of God's Spirit thus to keep this Church in existence ; no " might," no " power." On the contrary, many obstacles—persecutions, enemies, corruptions, and so on. So plain is it how much can be done (and done only) in the way of Christian organization, labour, and progress by the sacred oil of God's Spirit. " Utilis lectio, utilis eruditio, sed magis utilis unctio, quippe quæ docet de omnibus."

Vers. 8—14.—*The Church sustained.* " Moreover the word of the Lord came unto me, saying, The hands of Zerubbabel have laid the foundation of this house," etc. These verses continue the metaphors of the previous portion, but in the opposite order. Vers. 1—7 begin with the " olive trees " and end with the " house ; " vers. 8—14 begin with the " house " (vers. 8—10) and conclude with the " trees." We may look on this latter passage, therefore, as a kind of additional message (" moreover," ver. 8) on the same general subject and to the same general purport as before. The principal difference is in connection with the questions of order and depth. As we learned before not a little, first as to the secret, and secondly as to the completeness, of the restored life of the Jewish Church, so here we learn very much more (1) as to that same *completeness,* and (2) as to that same *secret,* of this same restored life.

I. ITS COMPLETENESS. As conveyed, we suppose, by what is said respecting the material "house " (or typical Church) then in process of erection. We find this described in vers. 9, 10. And of the promise contained therein we may notice : 1. *How peculiarly explicit it is.* Not only is the work which Zerubbabel had begun to be finished; it is to be finished by " his hands," and therefore, of course, in his time. Not only, again, is it to be so far finished as to be capable, as it were, of habitation and use ; but so far finished as to be ready for that most absolutely ultimate of all building processes, the process of testing the work done. How graphic the description of this! " They shall see the plummet in the hands of Zerubbabel." 2. *How exceedingly deliberate it is.* To start the work of erecting this temple—to begin such a true spiritual Church-restoration—was a great thing. To accomplish it, a still greater. If accomplished, indeed, that of itself would be a sufficient proof of a true mission from God (see the end of ver. 9; also, to some extent, 2 Sam. vii. 12, 13). Especially would this be so in that " day of small things," when even well-wishers—persons ready to " rejoice " in such a thing, if really accomplished—as it were " despised " the idea. All this was known, all this was recognized, when the promise was given. 3. *How fully assured it is.* Was there not One " sent " to accomplish this, even that Angel-Jehovah represented by the " stone " of ch. iii. 9 ? And was there not sent also, of necessity, together with him, a full supply of all that was necessary to accomplish these wonders? (See end of ver. 10, and the reference there to "those seven" eyes to be found on that "stone;" also Rev. v. 6; 2 Chron. xvi. 9; and compare end of ver. 6 in this chapter.) To secure that "stone" is to secure that sevenfold blessing, and all it involves.

II. ITS SECRET. A yet further point, in regard to this, seems revealed to us in that which comes next. It is not enough to have the blessing referred to, so to speak, in reversion. If the Church is to shine as a living witness, some channel of communication must be in existence by which it can be always supplied therewith without fail. To understand the emblem employed (as before described in ver. 3) to represent this, we may notice: 1. *The prophet's ignorance of its meaning.* See this five times referred to, viz. in vers. 4, 5, 11, 12, 13. Whatever he meant, therefore, it is evidently something the nature of which is so far occult and secret that even the eyes of a prophet might fail to discern it at first. 2. *The angel's surprise at his ignorance.* "Knowest thou not?" (see vers. 5 and 13; and comp. John iii. 10; Mark iv. 13; Rom. vi. 3, 16; vii. 1). The prophet ought to have discerned it, although he did not. 3. *The explanation that follows.* (Ver. 14.) An explanation which seems to show us: (1) Why the *prophet* ought to have understood the emblem, viz. because it represented an ordinance carefully ordered and arranged, even that of certain persons "anointed" for special service; an ordinance, also, ancient and settled ("stand by," as a custom or habit); an ordinance of most extensive import, even affecting the whole earth. (2) What *we* may understand thereby; viz. that God always maintains in the world a succession of *special* witnesses for him, who "stand by" him, as it were, so as to be informed of his will, and who are "anointed," as it were, so as to keep alive in turn the *general* witness of his Church (see 2 Cor. v. 18—20; iv. 7; 2 Tim. ii. 2; Gen. xviii. 17; Amos iii. 7); and who also, either as being always sufficient in number (2 Cor. xiii. 1, and references; also Rev. xi. 3, 4), or else as being usually divided, as were Zerubbabel and Jeshua, in the spirit of Luke x. 24 and 1 Tim. v. 17, are set forth to us as "two" in number. In these ways it is that it pleases God always to keep alive the life of his Church (1 Cor. i. 21).

See illustrated here also, in conclusion: 1. *God's great love for his people.* He gives his Son for them in order, afterwards, to give them his Spirit as well (John iv. 10; Gal. iv. 4—6). He buys these earthen vessels for a sum beyond cost, in order, then, to fill them with an ointment which is also beyond cost! 2. *God's great care for his Church.* Whatever the objects of the "ministry of angels," God has entrusted specially to men the duty of keeping alight among men the "candlestick" of his truth. How often this light has been all but extinct (Gen. vi. 5—8; xii. 1 compared with Josh. xxiv. 2; 1 Sam. iii. 1; vii. 3; 1 Kings xix. 10, 14; Ps. xii. 1; Isa. liii. 1; Micah vii. 2; Rev. xi. 7—10)! Yet how wonderfully preserved throughout; and to be preserved to the end (Matt. xvi. 18)!

HOMILIES BY VARIOUS AUTHORS.

Vers. 1—7.—*The Church in three aspects.* I. SYMBOLICALLY REPRESENTED. (Vers. 2, 3.) Candelabrum.

II. DEVOUTLY CONTEMPLATED. (Ver. 5.) Humble, earnest, reverent inquiry.

III. DIVINELY INTERPRETED. 1. *The unity of the Church.* 2. *The spiritual use of the Church.* 3. *The Divine care of the Church.* 4. *The future glory of the Church.* The Church should be: (1) *Receptive* of the Divine. (2) *Communicative* of the Divine. "They empty themselves," etc. Freely, constantly, rejoicingly. (3) *Reflective* of the Divine. Life and work. Not only true of the Church as a whole, but of every individual member. "Let your light shine before men."—F.

Ver. 2.—*On seeing.* The question, "What seest thou?" suggests—

I. THE SLUMBER OF THE SOUL. (Ver. 1.) Want of consciousness and activity. Delusions (Isa. xxix. 7). Peril (Mark xiii. 36).

II. THE AWAKENING OF THE SOUL. (Ver. 1.) "The angel" may be taken to illustrate the various ministries employed by God to quicken and rouse his people. *Providence.* Loss of health, property, friends, and such-like incidents. *Word of the truth.* Law and gospel. *The Spirit of Christ.* (1 Kings xix. 11, 12; John xvi. 8—13; Rev. i. 10—20.)

III. THE GLORIOUS THINGS REVEALED TO THE AWAKENED SOUL. The question. Mark: 1. *The time.* When the soul was awakened; not before (Isa. l. 4; Luke ix. 32). 2. *The purpose.* To stimulate activity. "I have looked." Must use our own faculties. 3. *The result.* Manifold things revealed. As *we* are, so will our sight be. Press the question, "What seest thou?" *In nature.*

> "O lady, we receive but what we give,
> And in our lives alone does nature live."
>   (Coleridge.)

Human life. Life all confused and dark, a maze without a plan, or the hand of God. *Holy Scriptures.* God. Truth. Immortality. Christ. "*We see Jesus*" (Heb. ii. 9).—F.

Ver. 5.—*The learner and the learned.* I. THE SPIRIT OF THE LEARNER. *Humility.* The first thing to know, as the ancient sage said, is that we know nothing. *Love of truth.* For its own sake. To be sought for as hidden treasure—with ardour and delight. *Obedience.* Not merely readiness to receive, but courage to act. Faithful carrying out of principles. Progress. Step by step, in the spirit of self-sacrifice. "When first thine eyes unveil, give thy soul leave to do the like" (Vaughan).

> "Study is like the heaven's glorious sun,
>   That will not be deep-search'd with saucy looks;
> Small have continuous plodders ever won,
>   Save base authority from others' books."
>   (Shakespeare.)

II. THE SPIRIT OF THE LEARNED. 1. *Wisdom.* Not mere knowledge, but insight into character, and capacity to turn knowledge to the best account. 2. *Kindness.* Hence patience with ignorance and prejudice. Loving endeavour to give to others what has been good and a joy to themselves. 3. *Faithfulness.* Not hiding what should be told; not making compromises of principle; not striving for the mastery, but for the victory of truth. 4. *Humility* is as much the character of the learned as of the learner (cf. Newton likening himself to a child gathering shells).

> "Were man to live coeval with the sun,
> The patriarch-pupil would be learning still,
> And dying leave his lesson half unlearnt."
>   F.

Ver. 6.—*The secret of power.* Power is indispensable. It is not in numbers, or organization, or method. These are good, but not enough. It is not of man, though it is by man. Must look higher. It is of God. Life is from life. The highest life can only come from the highest life. "Not by might," etc. Apply to—

I. THE MINISTRY OF THE CHURCH. Talent, culture, wide sympathies, zeal and eloquence, not enough. Even truth not enough. Need more. "My Spirit." There must be a right relation to God. There must be the quickening of the soul with the life of God—the energizing and elevating of the natural powers to the highest capacity and use. This influence is necessary both for preachers and hearers.

II. THE WORSHIP OF THE CHURCH. In the Church God draws near to us and we draw near to God. As a Father to his children he speaketh unto us; as children *unto a Father* we should speak unto him. 1. Praise. 2. Prayer. 3. Hearing of the Word. 4. Communion. 5. Times of refreshing. It is only as we are quickened from above that our worship is hearty and true (cf. John iv. 23), acceptable to God, and profitable to ourselves.

III. THE WORK OF THE CHURCH. Life must precede work. As individuals, in the society to which we belong, and in our daily life, we are called to serve God. Every one has his place and his work. It is as we carry out faithfully the duty committed to us that the cause of the Lord will prosper, and "his kingdom come" at home and abroad.—F.

Vers. 7—10.—*Encouragement to Christian workers.* I. THOUGH THE WORK BE DERIDED, IT IS GOD'S WORK. Therefore we are sure it is right and good. We can throw ourselves into it with all our heart. Patience. What is of God cannot fail.

II. THOUGH THE DIFFICULTIES BE GREAT, THEY ARE CAPABLE OF BEING OVERCOME. Difficulties are a *test.* They show what spirit we are of. They separate the chaff from the wheat. Remember "Formality" and "Hypocrisy" in the 'Pilgrim's Progress.' Difficulties are a *challenge.* They put us on our mettle. Courage mounteth with occasion. Once we can say, "It is our duty," nothing should daunt us (Acts v. 29; xx. 24). In A.D. 1800 Napoleon wanted to cross the Alps with his army into Italy. He asked Marescot, chief of the engineers, "Is it possible?" He replied, "Yes, but with difficulty." "Let us, then, set out," was the order of the great captain (1 Cor. ix. 25). Difficulties are our *education.* It is not ease but effort that makes men. "Our antagonist is our helper," said Burke. "He who has battled, were it only with poverty and hard toil, will be found stronger and more expert than he who could stay at home from the battle, concealed among the provision-waggons, or even resting unwatchfully, abiding by the stuff" (Carlyle). So it is in all spheres of activity. "To overcome, we must conquer as we go." Difficulties lead us to a deeper and truer appreciation of our dependence upon God (Rom. v. 3—5; viii. 31, 37).

III. THOUGH THE PROGRESS BE SMALL, ULTIMATE SUCCESS IS CERTAIN. God's Word is sure. He is truth, and cannot lie. He is love, and cannot betray. He is almighty, and cannot be defeated. The laying of the foundation-stone, in his Name, implies the completion of the structure; and, by faith, we already hear the shoutings and the jubilant cries as the work is finished. "Grace, grace unto it!"—F.

Vers. 1—10.—*Man as a student of the Divine revelation and a doer of Divine work.* "And the angel that talked with me," etc. "It is needful to keep in mind that all these successive scenes were presented to the mind of the prophet in vision; and that each vision was distinct, forming a whole of itself, independently of the scenery of those which preceded it, although not so as to preclude connection in the lessons taught, and occasional reference (such as we shall find in the one now before us) to the earlier in the latter. The fourth in the series of visions, then, was now closed; and at the close of it, the prophet represents himself as having fallen into a kind of reverie arising from its disclosures, or from some particular part of them, by which his mind was absorbed and unconscious of aught that might be passing around him. From this state he was roused, as the first verse indicates, by the touch and the voice of the ministering angel, and his attention arrested to a new scenic representation, and the explanation of its meaning" (Wardlaw). I have to confess that the more I look into this vision, as well as into the previous visions, the more I feel my utter inability to attach a satisfactory meaning to all the strange and grotesque symbols that are presented. And my sense of inability has been deepened as I have examined the explanations that have been put forth by biblical critics—some most fanciful and absurd, and many most conflicting. Indeed, it requires a Daniel to interpret dreams; the objects in a dream are generally so unnatural, grotesque, shadowy, and shifting, that men seldom try to attach any definite idea to them. I may regard this passage as setting before us man in two aspects, viz. as a student of the Divine revelation, and as a doer of the Divine purposes.

I. AS A STUDENT OF THE DIVINE REVELATION. "I have looked, and behold a candlestick all of gold, with a bowl upon the top of it, and his seven lamps thereon, and seven pipes to the seven lamps, which are upon the top thereof: and two olive trees by it, one upon the right side of the bowl, and the other upon the left side thereof. So I answered and spake to the angel that talked with me, saying, What are these, my lord?" This candelabrum made of gold, with a bowl on the top, its seven lamps and seven pipes, etc., is taken by most expositors to represent the Church of God, and popular preachers go on to draw analogies between the candlestick and the Church. Of course, this is easy work. But the Church of God, as the phrase is, has not, alas! been very golden or very luminous. The *ideal* Church is all this. The candlestick may, I think, fairly represent the Bible, or God's special revelation to man: that is *golden*, that is *luminous*, that is *supernaturally supplied* with the oil of inspiration. In fact, in the passage, the interpreting angel designates this candlestick, not as the Church, but as the "word of the Lord unto Zerubbabel." I make two remarks concerning this revelation. 1. *It has in it sufficient to excite the inquiry of man as a student.* The prophet, on seeing these wonderful objects, exclaimed, "What are these, my lord?" He seemed to feel as Moses felt in relation to the burning bush, when he said, "I will now turn aside, and see this great sight, why the bush is not consumed." What wonderful things are in this Bible! It is a museum of wonders; and the greatest of all wonders is God manifest in the flesh. 2. *It has an interpreter that can satisfy man as a student.* The angel to whom the prophet directed his inquiry promptly answered. "Then the angel that talked with me answered and said unto me, Knowest thou not what these be? And I said, No, my lord. Then he answered and spake unto me, saying, This is the word of the Lord unto Zerubbabel, saying, Not by might, nor by power, but by my Spirit, saith the Lord of hosts." The prophet here displays two of the leading attributes of a genuine student of the Divine. (1) *Inquisitiveness.* He inquires; and because he inquires, he receives an answer. Had he not inquired, the object would have remained an unmeaning symbol. The Bible is an unmeaning book to the great masses of mankind, because they do not inquire into its significance. Truth is only got by genuine inquiry. (2) *Ingenuousness.* The first reply of the interpreting angel to the prophet was, "Knowest thou not what these things mean? and he said, "No, my lord." At once he confesses his ignorance. "Let us," says Dr. Wardlaw, "imitate the twofold example—both that of inquisitiveness and that of ingenuousness. Let us be on the alert in our inquiries after knowledge; and in order to our acquiring it, never foolishly, and to save our pride and vanity, affect to have what we have not." The man who develops these two attributes in relation to God's Word, has a Divine Interpreter at his side, namely, the Spirit of God, who will lead him into all knowledge.

II. AS A DOER OF THE DIVINE WILL. Man has not only to study, but to work; not only to get Divine ideas, but to work them out. "Then he answered and spake unto me, saying, This is the word of the Lord unto Zerubbabel, saying, Not by might, nor by power, but by my Spirit, saith the Lord of hosts. Who art thou, O great mountain? before Zerubbabel thou shalt become a plain: and he shall bring forth the headstone thereof with shoutings, crying, Grace, grace unto it! Moreover the word of the Lord came unto me, saying, The hands of Zerubbabel have laid the foundation of this house; his hands shall also finish it; and thou shalt know that the Lord of hosts hath sent me unto you." The work of the prophet was to convey a message from God to Zerubbabel, and the message he conveyed was a message to work. Man is to be a "worker together" with God. I offer two remarks concerning man as a worker out of the Divine will. 1. *That though his difficulties may appear great, his resources are infinite.* Zerubbabel, in rebuilding the temple, had enormous difficulties. Those difficulties hovered before him as mountains. But great as they were, he was assured that he had resources more than equal to the task. "Not by might, nor by power, but by my Spirit, saith the Lord of hosts." By this is meant, not that human might and power are not required, or are utterly useless, but Divine might would give aid to all honest-effort and endeavour. The difficulties in a good man's path of duty rise oftentimes like mountains before him; but let him not be disheartened; those mountains are nothing compared with the might that is guaranteed. "If ye have faith as a grain of mustard seed, ye shall say unto this mountain, Remove hence to yonder place; and it shall remove," etc. 2. *That though his efforts may seem feeble, his success will be inevitable.* (1) The *feebleness* of human efforts is here *implied.* "Who hath despised the day of small things?" (*a*) It is *common* to despise small things. Proud man will only honour what seem to him great things—conventionally great. A small house, a small business, a small book,—these are despised. (*b*) It is *foolish* to despise small things. All great things were small in their beginnings. London was once a little hamlet; the oaken forest once an acorn. We do not know what really are small things; what we consider small may be the greatest things in the universe. (*c*) It is *contemptible* to despise small things. Truly great souls never do so. (2) The *success* of feeble efforts is here *guaranteed.* "He shall bring forth the headstone thereof with shoutings, crying, Grace, grace unto it." Literally, the promise is that Zerubbabel, notwithstanding all the difficulties he had to contend with in rebuilding the temple, should see it completed, should see the crowning stone laid on the building, amid the hosannahs of the people: "Grace, grace unto it!" So it will be with every genuine work to which a true man puts his hand in the name of God. It will be finished; there will be no failure, success is inevitable. "As I live, saith the Lord, the whole earth shall be filled with my glory" (Numb. xiv. 21).—D. T.

Vers. 11—14.—*The olive trees and the candlesticks: model religious teachers.* "Then answered I, and said unto him," etc. This is not another vision, but an explanation of the one recorded in the preceding verses. The explanation is that the two branches of the olive tree which, by means of the two tubes of gold empty their oil, is that they represented "two anointed ones," or sons of oil. Perhaps Joshua and Zerubbabel are particularly referred to. "Because," says Henderson, "when installed into office they had oil poured upon their heads as a symbol of the gifts and influences of the Holy Spirit, which alone could fit them rightly to discharge their important functions. Their services to the new state were of such value that they might well be represented as furnishing it, instrumentally, with what was necessary for enabling it to answer the purpose of its establishment." I shall take these two "anointed ones" as types of model religious teachers. Three things are suggested.

I. THEY HAVE A HIGH ORDER OF LIFE IN THEM. They are represented by the olive branches. There are few productions of the vegetable kingdom that are of such a high order as the olive. Though not large, seldom rising higher than thirty feet, it has a rich foliage, beautiful flowers, abundant fruit, and withal is filled with precious oil. One tree contains often not less than a thousand pounds of precious oil. Its fatness was proverbial (Judg. ix. 9); it is an evergreen, and most enduring. In short, it is marked by great beauty, perpetual freshness, and immense utility. It was one of the sources of wealth in Judæa, and its failure was the cause of famine. The emblems of a true teacher are not dead timber or some frail vegetable life, but an olive tree. Religious teachers should not only have life, but life of the highest order. They should be full of animal spirits, full of creative genius, full of fertile thought, full of Divine inspiration. Men whose vitality is of a low order are utterly disqualified to be public religious teachers. They should not be reeds, fragile, and with temporary foliage, but like a "green olive tree in the house of God." The curse of the modern pulpit is its lack of *vitality, freshness,* and *power.*

II. THEY COMMUNICATE THE MOST PRECIOUS ELEMENTS OF KNOWLEDGE. They "empty the golden oil out of themselves." Whether the expression "golden" here signifies merely the richness of its colour or the preciousness of its property, it scarcely matters. It has been observed by modern travellers that the natives of olive countries manifest more attachment to olive oil than to any other article of food, and find nothing adequate to supply its place. Genuine religious teachers feed the lamp of universal knowledge with the most golden elements of truth. They not only give the true theory of morals and worship, but the true theory of moral restoration. What a high value Paul set on this knowledge! "I count all things but loss for the excellency of the knowledge of Christ Jesus my Lord." What are the true genuine religious teachers doing? They are pouring into the lamps of the world's knowledge the choicest elements of truth.

III. THEY LIVE NEAR TO THE GOD OF ALL TRUTH. "Then said he, These are the two anointed ones, that stand by the Lord of the whole earth." They "*stand,*" a position of dignity; "*stand,*" a position of waiting —waiting to receive infallible instructions, ready to execute the Divine behests. All true religious teachers live *consciously* near to God. To "stand by the Lord of the whole earth" is one thing, to be *conscious* of it is another. All "stand by" him; but few of the race are practically conscious of the position, and these few alone are the true teachers.

CONCLUSION. Let us, who are engaged in the office of public teaching, try ourselves by these criteria. The olive tree gave what it had in it—gave out its nature. So must we. Manufactured discourses, intellectual speculations, rhetorical flourishes,—these have no oil.—D. T.

EXPOSITION.

CHAPTER V.

Vers. 1—4.—§ 8. *The sixth vision: the flying roll.*

Ver. 1.—Then I turned, and lifted up mine eyes; *i.e.* I lifted up mine eyes again, and saw the vision that follows. The prophet had seen, in the fourth vision, how in the new theocracy the priesthood should be pure and holy; in the fifth how the Church should be restored; he is now shown that sinners should be cut off, that no transgression should be left in the kingdom of God. **A flying roll;** *volumen volans* (Vulgate); comp. Ezek. ii. 9, 10. The Hebrews used parchment and leather scrolls for writing; the writing was divided into columns, and when completed the document was rolled round one or two sticks and kept in a case. In the present vision the scroll is unrolled and exhibited in its full length and breadth, showing that it was to be made known to all. Its flight denotes the speedy arrival of the judgment, and, as it is seen in the heaven, so the punishment proceeds from God. Theodotion and Aquila render the word, διφθέρα, "leather;" the Septuagint, by mistake, δρέπανον, "a sickle."

Ver. 2.—He said. The angel-interpreter spoke (ch. iv. 2). **The length thereof,** etc. Taking the cubit at a foot and a half, the size of the roll is enormous, and may well have aroused the prophet's wonder. The dimensions given correspond to those of the porch of Solomon's temple (1 Kings vi. 3), twenty cubits long by ten broad. These are also the dimensions of the holy place in the tabernacle, and of Solomon's brazen altar (2 Chron. iv. 1). The careful statement of the size of the roll indicates that some special meaning is attached to these measurements. We do not know that any symbolical signification was recognized in the porch of the temple; but these dimensions may well contain a reference to the sanctuary and the altar, as Knabenbauer explains, "The curse is of the same measure as that altar which was the instrument of expiation and reconciliation, and as that sanctuary which was the entrance to the holy of holies." Others consider that the curse is pronounced according to the measure of the sanctuary, *i.e.* according to the Divine Law; or that all might thus know that it came from God, and that the possession of the temple did not secure the people from vengeance unless they were pure and obedient.

Ver. 3.—This is the curse. The roll contained the curse written upon it on both sides. (For the curse of God upon guilty nations, comp. Isa. xxiv. 6; Dan. ix. 11.) **Earth;** *land;* for Judæa is meant. The curse was ready to fall on all who might come under it by their transgressions. This would be a warning also to exterior nations. **Every one that stealeth . . . every one that sweareth.** Thieves and perjurers are especially mentioned as incurring the curse. Perjury is a chief offence in one table of the Law, theft in the other; so these sins may stand for all offences against the Decalogue (comp. Jas. ii. 10, etc.). But probably they are named because they were particularly rife among the returned Jews. During their long sojourn in Babylon they had engaged in commercial pursuits and had fallen into the lax morality which such occupations often engender. These bad habits they had brought with them and practised in their new home (comp. ch. viii. 17, and note there). **Shall be cut off as on this side according to it;** Revised Version, *shall be purged out on the one side* (margin, *from hence*) *according to it;* Ewald, "driven hence like it." The reference is to the two sides of the roll, answering to the two tables of the Decalogue. Sinners shall be "cleansed away," *i.e.* utterly consumed, according to the tenor of the roll. The Vulgate has *judicabitur;* the LXX., ἕως θανάτου ἐκδικηθήσεται, "shall be punished unto death." **That sweareth;** *i.e.* falsely, as is plain from ver. 4; Septuagint, πᾶς ὁ ἐπίορκος, "every perjurer."

Ver. 4.—I will bring it forth. God will not keep the curse confined and inoperative (Deut. xxxii. 34, etc.), but it shall enter into **the house of the thief.** The curse shall not fall lightly and pass quickly by, but shall fix its abode with the sinner till it has worked out its fell purpose. **It shall remain;** *it shall pass the night*—take up its lodging; LXX., καταλύσει. **With the timber thereof,** etc. A hyperbolical expression of the terrible effects of Divine vengeance, which consumes utterly like a devouring fire—an adumbration of the destruction at the day of judgment (comp. Deut. iv. 24; Mal. iii. 2; Matt. iii. 12).

Vers. 5—11.—§ 9. *The seventh vision: the woman in the ephah.*

Ver. 5.—Went forth. While the prophet meditated on the last vision, the interpreting angel retired into the background or among the company of angels; he now comes into view again to explain a new revelation closely connected with the former. **That goeth forth.** That comes into sight from the surrounding darkness. As the preceding vision denoted that sinners should be extirpated, so the present vision shows how iniquity itself, the very principle of evil, should be removed from the Holy Land.

Ver. 6.—**What is it?** The prophet did not clearly discern the object, or his question may mean, "What does it signify?" **An ephah;** *the ephah,* as "the curse" (ver. 3). The ephah was the largest of the dry measures in use among the Jews, and was equal to six or seven gallons. It was, of course, too small to contain a woman. The LXX. calls it simply "the measure;" the Vulgate, *amphora;* and it must be considered as an imaginary vessel of huge size. It may have a tacit reference to dishonest dealings (comp. Amos viii. 5; Micah vi. 10). **This is their resemblance;** literally, *this is their eye.* The Authorized Version explains the meaning accurately. "Eye" is often used for that which is seen, as in Lev. xiii. 55, where the Authorized Version has "colour;" and Numb. xi. 7, where in reference to the manna we read, "The eye thereof was as the eye of bdellium" (comp. Ezek. i. 4, 16). So here the meaning is: This ephah and this whole vision represent the wicked in the land. Some take "the eye" to mean the object of sight, that to which they look. But the ephah was not set forth for all the people to examine. The LXX. and Syriac, from some variation in the reading, have ἀδικία, "iniquity," and some critics have desired to adopt this in the text. But authority and necessity are equally wanting.

Ver. 7.—**There was lifted up a talent of lead.** As the prophet gazed, the leaden cover of the ephah was raised, so that the contents became visible. The word rendered "talent" (*kikkar*) denotes a circle. It is used in Gen. xiii. 10, 12, for the tract of country of which the Jordan was the centre, and in 1 Sam. ii. 36 for a round loaf. Here it means a disc or circular plate which formed the cover of the round shaped ephah. In the next verse it is called, "the weight of lead." **And this is a woman that sitteth in the midst of the ephah;** *and there was a woman sitting,* etc. When the leaden lid was raised one woman (*mulier una,* γυνὴ μία) was seen in the measure. She is called "one," as uniting and concentrating in her person all sinners and all sins.

Ver. 8.—**This is wickedness.** This woman is the personification of wickedness. It is very common to find backsliding Israel represented as a faithless and adulterous woman (comp. Isa. i. 21; Jer. ii. 20; Hos. ii. 5; and the parable of the two women in Ezek. xxiii.). **He cast it;** *her*—the woman. As the woman rose, or tried to rise, from the ephah, the angel flung her down into it.

It is possible, as some commentators suppose, that the ephah into which wickedness is thrust represents the measure of iniquity which, being reached, constrains God to punish (see Gen. xv. 16, where the dispossession of the Amorites is postponed till their iniquity is full). **The weight of lead;** literally, as the LXX., *the stone of lead;* Vulgate, *massam plumbeam.* This is the cover of the ephah, that which is called the "talent of lead" in the preceding verse. This heavy cover the angel cast upon the mouth of the ephah, in order to confine the woman therein (comp. Gen. xxix. 2, which passage may explain why the cover is called "a stone"). Dr. Wright and some other commentators, referring the passage to theft and perjury alone, consider that the woman held in her hand the leaden weight with which she weighed her gains, and was sitting in the ephah which she used in her traffic; so that she represents dishonesty in the matter of weight and measure. She is punished by the means of the instruments she had used unrighteously; the weight is dashed upon her lying mouth, and the ephah, her throne, is made the vehicle that carries her out of the land. But it seems a mistake to confine the iniquity mentioned to the two special sins of theft and perjury; nor would the talent and the ephah be natural instruments of stealing and false-swearing; and the point of the vision is not the punishment of wickedness, but its expulsion from the land. It is true that the pronominal suffix in the mouth thereof is feminine, and that the LXX. makes it refer to the woman, τὸ στόμα αὐτῆς. But it may equally refer to *ephah,* which is also feminine.

Ver. 9.—**Then lifted I up mine eyes.** This is the conclusion of the vision. **And looked;** *and saw.* **There came out** (*forth*) **two women.** These two women who now come in sight have been supposed to represent the Assyrians and Babylonians, who were the agents in the deportation of Israel; or else are considered abettors of the woman in the ephah, who for a time save her from destruction. This latter supposition proceeds on the erroneous idea that wickedness is herein rescued from punishment, whereas the notion that underlies the whole vision is that the Holy Land is purged of wickedness. That the two nations hostile to Israel are represented is an untenable suggestion; for why should they carry off iniquity from Jerusalem and fix it in their own land? Probably by the two women carrying away the evil woman is signified (if the details are capable of explanation) that iniquity brings with it its own destruction and works out its own removal. **The wind was in their wings.** They were borne along so quickly that they seemed to be carried by the wind; or the wind helped their flight. **A stork;** Septuagint, ἔποπος, "the hoopoe;" Vulgate, *milvi*. The Authorized Version is certainly correct. The stork is common enough in Palestine, and is reckoned among unclean birds in the Pentateuch (Lev. xi. 19; Deut. xiv. 18), for which cause some have thought it is here introduced as bearing the sin-laden ephah. But its introduction more probably has reference to its migratory habits, the power and rapidity of its flight, and, as some think, to its skill in constructing its nest.

Ver. 11.—**To build it** (*her*) **an house.** The LXX. refers the pronoun to the ephah, but it seems more natural to refer it to a person, the woman. The feminine gender of the original would apply to either. She is carried away from Judæa to have a permanent dwelling in a land more suited to her. Pusey thinks that possibly a temple may be intended, "a great idol-temple, in which the god of this world should be worshipped." **In the land of Shinar;** *i.e.* the ideal land of unholiness, where the world-power first arrayed itself against God in the attempt at Babel. Septuagint, ἐν γῇ Βαβυλῶνος (Gen. xi. 2, etc.). *Shinar*, equivalent to *Sumer* in the Assyrian monuments, denotes Lower or Southern Babylon; *Accad*, Upper or Northern Babylon. **And it shall be established.** The house shall be firmly fixed there. Others render, "when it is ready." **And set there.** The gender shows that the woman is meant, not the house: "And she shall be set there in her own place." Thus from the spiritual Zion all wickedness shall be abolished (ch. iii. 9) and sent to its own place prepared for the enemies of God and holiness. Doubtless, too, a warning is here conveyed to those Jews who still lingered in Babylon, that they were dwelling in a land accursed of God, and were liable to be involved in the fate which pursues ungodliness. Orelli and some others see in these two visions an analogy to the two goats on the Day of Atonement, of which one was sacrificed for the sins of the people, and the other bore away their iniquity to the demons' abode, the wilderness (Lev. xvi.).

HOMILETICS.

Vers. 1—4.—*The reassertion of the Law.* "Then I turned, and lifted up mine eyes, and looked, and behold a flying roll," etc. Most of the distinguishing privileges first given to Israel after leaving Egypt for Canaan were gradually restored to Israel on its partial restoration to Palestine after the captivity of Babylon. This illustrated, as noted before, as to the altar (Ezra iii. 3); the daily sacrifice (Ezra iii. 5); the Feast of Tabernacles (Ezra iii. 4); the tabernacle or the temple itself (Ezra iii. 10; vi. 15). This also illustrated, as we have just seen, as to the revival of the Levitical priesthood (ch. iii. 1—5); and also as to the rekindling of that temple "candlestick" which typified the restoration and maintenance of the Jewish Church as a witness for God amongst men (ch. iv. 1—3, 11—14). In the present passage we think we perceive a similar reassertion and, as it were, restoration of that written statement of man's duty and God's will which was given originally on Mount Sinai, on the two tables of stone; this second proclamation differing from that, however, according to the differences of the exigency and time. This we hope to show by considering the vision before us (1) as to its *general nature*; and (2) as to its *special characteristics*.

I. ITS GENERAL NATURE. As with the original Decalogue, so we are shown here in vision: 1. A message in *writing* from God; a message, therefore, like the other, peculiarly deliberate and explicit in its character, and peculiarly permanent in its form (Exod. xxxiv. 1; 2 Cor. iii. 7; see also Isa. viii. 1; Jer. xxxvi. 18; xxx. 2; Luke i. 3, 4; Acts xv. 23, etc.). 2. A message of *judgment*; in other words, containing a "curse," or solemn declaration of anger against sin and wrong-doing (Deut. xxvii. 26; Jer. xi. 3, 4; Gal. iii. 10). 3. A message of great *breadth* and *extent*, being written on a roll of the same dimensions (so it has been noted) as the sanctuary, or temple, and applying, therefore (so it may be intended), to the whole duty of man (see again Gal. iii. 10); or else, possibly, showing that this proclamation of God's will, like the former one, had to do especially with his "house" (1 Pet. iv. 17; Amos iii. 1, 2). 4. A message, however, of *universal applicability*, as shown by its "flying" over the whole earth," or land (comp. Rom. ii. 9, 12—16). 5. A message of a *twofold* purport or form—the words written on one side of the "roll" referring to a commandment contained in the first table of the Decalogue, and those written on the other to a commandment in the second. On all these points we see there is a more or less marked similarity between those tables of stone and this flying roll.

II. ITS SPECIAL CHARACTERISTICS. These to be seen, if we mistake not, somewhat remarkably: 1. *In the special transgressions here denounced;* being just those to which we have reason to believe, from other sources, that the post-Captivity Israelites were especially prone. Note, *e.g.*, in the first table of the Law, with regard to the sin of "false swearing," what evidences we find (as in Rom. ii. 17, 23, 24, and elsewhere) of their falsely professing supreme reverence for the very Name of Jehovah, even using a periphrasis instead of it, as in Mark xiv. 61; but how few evidences, if any—so different from pre-Captivity times—of open violations of the first and second commandments; and what an extreme solicitude, if to some extent a blind one, as to the outward observance of the fourth (Luke xiii. 14; John v. 16; ix. 16, etc.). Note also, in the second table of the Law, with regard to the sin of "stealing," how many evidences we have, after the return from Babylon, of the special prevalence of that cruel spirit of covetousness which lies at the root of all theft (see Neh. v. 1—13; Mal. iii. 5, 8—10; Luke xii. 15; xvi. 14; xx. 46, 47; to say nothing of the modern history of the Jews since the destruction of Jerusalem). 2. *In the special punishment here threatened,* viz. just that which persons prone to such transgressions would be afraid of the most. The great objects aimed at by such in their lip-worship and fraud (observe connection of thought in beginning of Luke xx. 47) would be the establishment and enrichment of themselves and their "houses." Instead of this, the very opposite, viz. the total destruction thereof, is described figuratively, but most graphically, as being the result. God himself should "bring forth" the appointed evil or "curse," which should reach its appointed *place;* and stay there its appointed *time;* and thoroughly perform there its appointed *work,* destroying not the house only but its very materials (ver. 4). How strikingly suitable, how emphatic a method of re-enacting his Law!

See, in conclusion, from this view of the passage: 1. *The immutability of God's Law.* In every successive dispensation alike, obedience to it is demanded. In the patriarchal, under Noah. In the legal, under Moses. Here, also after the Captivity; and that in closest connection, as just seen, with prophecies about the priesthood of Christ, and the work of his Spirit. And not less so, finally, in the gospel itself, with its blaze of mercy and love (Matt. v. 17—20, etc.; Rom. iii. 31; viii. 4; Titus ii. 12, 13; iii. 8). 2. *The elasticity of its application.* In each several case God causes those parts of it which are most needed to be most emphasized too. So in the instance before us, as we think we have shown. So also, under Noah, as shown by comparing Gen. vi. 13; ix. 5, 6. Compare, again, as to Moses, the length and emphasis of the second commandment with Exod. xxxii. 1—6, and the subsequent history of the nation. And see, finally, under the gospel, how specially suited such language as that in Matt. xxii. 36—40 was to the mere formalism of those times.

Vers. 5—11.—*The vindication of Law.* "Then the angel that talked with me went forth, and said unto me, Lift up now thine eyes," etc. The last vision was one of warning. This, as we take it, is one of judgment. The subject appears, however, to be the same. What the prophet previously dreaded and threatened he now describes as fulfilled. In other words, in a mystical fashion, and in language (it may be) only partially understood by himself, he foretells how the warning just uttered by him would be, on the one hand, *completely despised* by the Jewish people and Church; and, on the other hand, *completely vindicated* by the course of events.

I. THE WARNING DESPISED. This is predicted, in vision, by certain similitudes, which convey to our minds: 1. *The idea of measure.* An "ephah," a common measure, sometimes put (according to some, see Deut. xxv. 14, margin) as a representative of all measures, is seen "going forth." What for, except to be used? And how used, unless for measuring? As also—if Dr. Pusey is right in speaking of it as the largest measure in use—for measuring something of very unusual magnitude. 2. *The idea of national sin.* Of sin, by what is said of the contents of this ephah, viz. (ver. 8), "This is wickedness." Of nationality, by its being presented to us under the figure of a woman (see Isa. xxxvii. 22; Ezek. xvi. 2, 4; and other Scriptures; and comp. Isa. iii. 26 with the figure and legend of "Judæa Capta" on the coin struck in commemoration of the destruction of Jerusalem), and perhaps, also, by the remarkable declaration in end of ver. 6. 3. *The idea of repletion.* This large measure being so filled up as only to require the closing up of its mouth; and that with so heavy a closing as a "talent of lead," as though never requiring to be opened again. See what our Lord long after-wards said to the Jews in Matt. xxiii. 32 (comp. Gen. xv. 16), with apparent reference to this very prophecy, and, as some think (Matt. xxiii. 35), to this very prophet. Also compare what is said concerning the sin of "stealing," in ver. 4 of this chapter, with what our Saviour also said to the Jews of that day in Matt. xxi. 13; and see Dan. viii. 23; 1 Thess. ii. 16.

II. THE WARNING FULFILLED. This seems shown us by the following emblems: 1. *The emblem of captivity.* The "woman," or nation, with its "wickedness," being, as already noted, shut up in the ephah. 2. *The emblem of settled purpose.* As exhibited by the appearance of "two" persons to effect the same thing. Compare such passages as Amos iii. 3; Gen. xix. 1; xli. 32; and note how "two" angels declare both the resurrection and the second coming of Christ (John xx. 12; Acts i. 10). 3. *The emblem of irresistible removal.* The "two women" spoken of are naturally able to overcome and lift up the one in the ephah (Eccles. iv. 9, 10). The same idea may also be conveyed by their having the "wings of a stork," the most familiar of all birds of migration (Jer. viii. 7); also by their having "the wind" in their wings, their natural strength being made stronger still (so this may mean) by the appointed course of events (comp. Ps. cxlvii. 18; cxlviii. 8); also once more, perhaps, by the ephah being so "lifted up from the earth" that nothing earthly could have the power to prevent its removal. 4. *The emblem of permanent stay.* The ephah being taken to "Shinar," or Babylon, a land of long captivity to Israel in the past (Jer. xxix. 4, 5), and having a house "built" for it there, and being "established" there on a base of its own. All which seems to have been fulfilled when the Romans came, after the "filling up" of the sins of the Jews by their rejection of Christ, and took away their "place and nation" (John xi. 48), carrying them away captive by irresistible might and evidently Divine assistance into their long exile in the great city of that mystical "Babylon," which is also, spiritually, "called Sodom and Egypt" (Rev. xi. 8; xiv. 8; xvii. 1, 5, 18, etc.), and settling them there (so it possibly means) on a "base" of their "own," *i.e.* in a kind of life and under a Divine dispensation peculiar to themselves (comp. Numb. xxiii. 9, end).

We see, in this prophecy so viewed, in conclusion: 1. *The cumulative nature of sin.* As nations and men continue in disobedience, so also, and even more, does the amount charged against them, as by a terrible kind of compound interest, continue to increase. The sins of yesterday greatly aggravate the sins of to-day. Besides passages *supra*, see Rom. ii. 5; Jas. v. 3; Deut. xxxii. 3, 4. 2. *The necessary limits of sin.* Sin, in its ultimate essence, is simply rebellion against God (1 John iii. 4; Ps. li. 4). Even in the case, therefore, of Israel, who was dealt with in especial mercy and love, there must be some boundary beyond which the accumulation of sin cannot be allowed to proceed. What becomes, else, of God's rule? What of his holiness too? *Judex damnatur cum nocens absolvitur* (see Gen. xviii. 25, end). 3. *The ultimate issue of sin.* If not repented of, if not atoned for, what can this issue be except "banishment"? And what can such banishment mean except "death" (Matt. xxv. 41; Ps. xvi. 11; Rom. vi. 23; Prov. xxix. 1)?

HOMILIES BY VARIOUS AUTHORS.

Vers. 1—4.—*Retribution.* I. PROVOKED. Sin is the transgression of the Law. Here two kinds singled out. 1. Sins against the second table. "Stealeth." Fraud, injustice of all kinds. False to man. 2. Sins against the first table. "Sweareth." Profanity. Self-will. False to God. These are samples of sins infinite in number and variety. Bold and flagrant offences, opposed to all law and order, defiant of God.

II. PROCLAIMED. Symbolically set forth. Sin will be judged, not according to custom or public sentiment, but by the measure of the sanctuary, the eternal Law of God. "Flying roll." 1. Broad enough to cover all offences. 2. Swift to seize all transgressors in its fatal embrace. The warning comes in mercy. "Flee from the wrath to come." See refuge under the shadow of the cross. Justice pursues the sinner, but it stops satisfied at Calvary.

III. INFLICTED. Sooner or later judgment will come. Inevitable and sure, just because God is God. Society must be purified. The bad will have to give place to the good. The earth will end with Eden, as it began.

> " My own hope is, a sun will pierce
> The thickest cloud earth ever stretched;
> That, after last, returns the first,
> Though a wide compass round be fetched;
> That what began best can't end worst,
> Nor what God blessed once prove accurst."
>
> (Browning.)

F.

Vers. 5—11.—*Worldliness in the Church.* I. SADLY PREVALENT. "This is their eye"—what they mind and what they lust after. There is a climax. First two classes of sinners are figured, next one great indistinguishable mass. Then " wickedness " is personified, as one woman. This teaches how *worldliness* is: 1. Common. 2. Absorbing. 3. Debasing—corrupting all that is beautiful and fair.

II. SPECIALLY OFFENSIVE. Bad in the world; infinitely worse in the Church. 1. Opposed to the Spirit of Christ. 2. Incompatible with the service of God. 3. Obstructive to the progress of the gospel.

III. RIGHTEOUSLY DOOMED. Even now restrained. Limited as to place and power. But the end cometh. The judgment set forth implies: 1. *Disinheritment.* They defrauded others, and will themselves be impoverished. Like Satan, cast out. Like Esau, lose their birthright. 2. *Banishment.* Judgment based on sympathies. What is right in law is true to feeling. Society cleansed. The bad go with the bad. Ungodliness is driven to the land of ungodliness. Captivity leads to captivity. Judas went " to his own place." 3. *Abandonment.* Judgment swift, thorough, irresistible. There is a terrible retention of character. "The wicked are driven away in their wickedness : but the righteous hath hope in his death."—F.

Vers. 1—4.—*The flying roll: Divine retribution:* "Then I turned, and lifted up mine eyes, and looked, and, behold, a flying roll. And he said unto me, What seest thou? And I answered, I see a flying roll : the length thereof is twenty cubits, and the breadth thereof ten cubits," etc. This is the sixth vision of the series of visions which the prophet had during the night. He now saw a "flying roll." We have mention made of such rolls by Ezra, by Isaiah, by Jeremiah, and by Ezekiel. Ezra speaks of search being made in "the book of rolls," the depository of the public archives or records, and of a "roll" being found there in which was recorded the decree of King Darius respecting the Jews ; and Jeremiah speaks of "a roll of a book." The book might be considered as consisting of several "rolls," over each other, and forming one volume. This is illustrated by the *book* which John saw "in the right hand of him that sat on the throne," which was "sealed with seven seals," and of which the contents were brought to view as each of the seals was unfolded. "The ancients wrote on a variety of materials—the papyrus, or paper-reed, the inner bark of particular trees, and the dressed skins of animals, forming a kind of parchment. These, when written, were rolled up, for convenience and for preservation of the writing, either singly or in a number over each other. The roll seen by the prophet was a 'flying roll,' but not flying through the air in its rolled-up state. It was expanded, and was of extraordinary size. Reckoning the cubit at a foot and a half, it was *ten yards* in length by *five* in width, the measurement being guessed by the prophet's eye" (Wardlaw). "This is the curse that goeth forth over the face of the whole earth." This is the explanation given by the interpreting angel. Without presuming to give an accurate interpretation of all the particulars of the symbolic representation, I think it may be fairly and usefully employed to exhibit the sublimely awful subject of *Divine retribution.* And this subject it serves to illustrate in two aspects.

I. AS FOLLOWING SIN. Notice : 1. *The particular sins which retribution pursues.* They are : (1) *Theft and sacrilege.* "Every one that stealeth." Stealing, here, refers not only to any property taken from man, but especially to the appropriation of worldly wealth to the decoration of their "ceiled houses," instead of applying it to the rebuilding of God's house. Hence Jehovah said, "Ye have robbed me in tithes and offerings.

Ye are cursed with the curse, even this whole nation" (Mal. iii. 8). This is the worst of all robberies. In fact, it embraces all robberies, the applying to our own selfish purposes what belongs to God. (2) *Perjury and false swearing.* Their sacrilegious conduct appears to have been sustained by false oaths, which increased the heinousness of their offence. The sins here noted are not mere specimens, but root or fountain sins. The "flying roll" of Divine retribution followed sin with its curses. There is a curse to every sin, and this is not vengeance, but benevolence. It is the arrangement of love. 2. *The way in which just retribution pursues them.* (1) *Openly.* The roll is spread open, and is written in characters that are legible to all. Divine retribution is no secret to man. It is not some intangible, hidden, occult thing. It is open to all eyes. Every man must see the "flying roll," not only in the history of nations and communities, but in his own domestic and individual life. The "flying roll" hovers over every sin. (2) *Rapidly.* Retribution is swift. It is a "flying roll." No sooner does a man commit a sin than he suffers in some form or other. The Nemesis is at the heels of the criminal. Retribution follows sins swifter than the sound of the swiftest thunder-peal follows the lightning-flash. (3) *Penetratingly.* "I will bring it forth, saith the Lord of hosts, and it shall enter into the house of the thief, and into the house of him that sweareth falsely by my Name." Wherever the sinner is, it will find him out. No mountain so high, no cavern so deep, no forest so intricate and shadowy, as to protect him from his visitation. "The flying roll" will reach the sinner everywhere. "There is no darkness or shadow of death where the workers of iniquity may hide themselves."

II. As ABIDING WITH SIN. "It shall remain in the midst of his house." Not only does it rule the house of the sinner, "it remains in the midst of it," like a leprosy, infecting, wasting, consuming, destroying. It is a curse that embitters every sweet, and gives more than twofold intensity to every bitter. It dooms to destruction the man and all his possessions. And from this world it must accompany and follow him to another, and settle with him there for ever. "The special reference made to their houses, with the 'stones thereof and the timber thereof,' forcibly points to the care which they had been taking of their own accommodation, in comfort and elegance, while Jehovah's was neglected" (Wardlaw). It abides in the house to curse everything, even the timber and the stones. Guilt, not only, like a ravenous beast, crouches at the door of the sinner, but rather, like a blasting mildew, spreads its baneful influence over the whole dwelling. The sin of one member of a family brings its curse on the others. The sins of the parents bring a curse upon the children. "Between parents and children," says Jeremy Taylor, "there is so great a society of nature and of manners, of blessing and of cursing, that an evil parent cannot perish in a single death; and holy parents never eat their meal of blessing alone; but they make the room shine like the fire of a holy sacrifice; and a father's or a mother's piety makes all the house festival, and full of joy from generation to generation."

CONCLUSION. Sinner, wouldst thou escape the tremendous curses which Heaven has written on this "flying roll," this book of Divine retribution? Then abandon a sinful life, exorcise the sinful temper, inhale the spirit of him who came to put away sin from humanity and to destroy the works of the devil.—D. T.

Vers. 5—11.—*A materialistic community.* "Then the angel that talked with me went forth, and said unto me, Lift up now thine eyes, and see what is this that goeth forth. And I said, What is it? And he said, This is an ephah that goeth forth," etc. Here is another (the seventh) vision in the wonderful series of visions which the prophet had that night. This is one of the strangest of the whole, one, perhaps, admitting of no certain interpretation—a "*woman in the ephah.*" We know what an "ephah" was. It was the greatest measure of capacity which the Hebrews had for dry goods, and was about the size of a cubic foot. It contained about an English bushel. The woman is generally regarded, and with probable accuracy used, as the symbol of a Jewish community—a community that had become by this time most mercenary. Mammon was their god. The interpreting angel said, "*This is wickedness.* And he cast it into the midst of the ephah; and he cast the weight of lead upon the mouth thereof." "Because it was wickedness or abhorrent worldliness that this woman symbolized, the angel threw her down in the midst of the ephah, and threw the weight of lead on the mouth of it" (Henderson). Utter mercenariness is an abhorrent object to an angel's eye. The prophet still looks, and what does he see? "Then lifted I up mine eyes, and looked, and, behold, there came out two women, and the wind was in their wings; for they had wings like the wings of a stork: and they lifted up the ephah between the earth and the heaven." The meaning of this new scene may easily be discovered. The ephah, with the woman in it, is carried away between earth and heaven, *i.e.* through the air. Women carry it, because there is a woman inside; and two women, because two persons are required to carry so large and heavy a measure, that they lay hold of it on both sides (הָאִשָּׁה with the א dropped; cf. Gesenius, 74, 3, A. 4). These women have wings, because it passes through the air; and a stork's wings, because these birds have broad pinions, and not because the stork is a bird of passage or an unclean bird. "The wings are filled with wind, that they may be able to carry their burden with greater velocity through the air. The women denote the instruments or powers employed by God to carry away the sinners out of his congregation, without any special allusion to this or the other historical nation. This is all that we have to seek in these features, which only serve to give distinctness to the picture" (Keil and Delitzsch). "Then said I to the angel that talked with me, Whither do these bear the ephah? And he said unto me, To build it an house in the land of Shinar: and it shall be established, and set there upon her own base." There is no necessity for regarding Shinar here as designating any particular geographical spot, such as the land which Nimrod founded. The idea may be that this utter worldliness bears men away for ever from the Divine scenes of life. The most practical use I can turn this mysterious passage to is to employ it to illustrate the condition of a truly materialistic community.

I. SUCH A COMMUNITY IS ENCASED BY THE MATERIAL. This woman, the emblem of the worldly Jews, was not only "in the midst of the ephah," but was closely confined there. "He cast the weight of the lead upon the mouth thereof." To an utterly worldly man matter is everything. He is utterly shut out from the spiritual; there is no glimpse of it, no interest in it. Like the woman in the ephah, he is encompassed by that which shuts him in. The bright heavens and the green fields of the spiritual world are over and around him, but they are nothing to him. He is in the ephah. 1. Your *secular scientist* is in the ephah. He sees nothing but matter, believes in nothing but matter. 2. Your *sensuous religionist* is in this ephah. He judges after the flesh. He lives in the horrors of Sinai, in the tragedies of Calvary; his talk is of blood, and fire, and crowns, and white robes, etc. The spiritual is shut out from him, or rather he is shut out from it. 3. Your *man of the world* is in this ephah. All his ideas of *wealth, dignity, pleasure,* are material. He judges the worth of a man by his purse, the dignity of a man by his pageantries, the pleasures of a man by his luxuries. Verily a sad condition this for humanity. For a soul that was made to realize the invisible, to mingle with the spiritual, to revel in the infinite, to be shut up like this woman in the ephah of materialism, may well strike us with shame and alarm.

II. SUCH A COMMUNITY IS BEING DISINHERITED BY THE MATERIAL. This woman in the ephah, emblem of the worldly Hebrew, is borne away from Palestine, her own land, into a foreign region; borne away by two women who had "wings like a stork, and whose wings were full of wind." Materialism disinherits man. His true inheritance as a spiritual existent is "incorruptible, undefiled, and fadeth not away." But materalism carries him away from it—away to the distant and the gross. 1. *The process was rapid.* No bird so fleet with wing and foot as the stork, and with this fleetness this woman in the ephah was borne. How rapidly do animalism and worldliness bear away the spirit of man from the realm of spiritual realities, from a love of the true and the beautiful! 2. *The process was final.* "And he said unto me, To build it an house in the land of Shinar: and it shall be established, and set there upon her own base." "To be carnally minded is death." "He that soweth to the flesh shall of the flesh reap corruption." Materialism bears the soul away into the "bondage of corruption." Well might the apostle say, "Many walk, of whom I have told you often, and now tell you even weeping, that they are enemies to the cross of Christ; whose end is destruction, whose god is their belly, and whose glory is in their shame, who mind earthly things" (Phil. iii. 19). "As you love your soul," says Mason, "beware of the world; it hath slain its thousands and ten thousands. What ruined Lot's wife? The world. What ruined Achan? The world. What ruined Haman? The world.

What ruined Judas? The world. What ruined Simon Magus? The world. What ruined Demas? The world. And, 'What shall it profit a man, if he shall gain the whole world, and lose his own soul?'"—D. T.

EXPOSITION.

CHAPTER VI.

Vers. 1—8.—§ 10. *The eighth vision: the four chariots.*

Ver. 1.—**I turned, and lifted up mine eyes** (see note on ch. v. 1). **Four chariots.** These are war-chariots. The angel explains, in vers. 5, etc., what these chariots mean, how that they represent God's judgments on sinners in all the world. Though evil is removed from the Church, God's vengeance pursues it wherever it is located. If we compare this vision with the first (ch. i. 8—11), we shall see that the quiet there spoken of is here broken, and that the shaking of the nations, which is to accompany Messiah's advent (Hag. ii. 7), has begun. That the four chariots are to be identified with the four powers of Daniel's visions (ii. and vii.)—the Babylonian, Medo-Persian, Macedonian, and Roman—is an opinion that does not commend itself. These four kingdoms and their fate have been already symbolized in the horns of the second vision (ch. i. 19—21), and it is most unlikely that they should be again introduced under a different figure. This would mar the orderly development of the revelation. And how could these kingdoms, such as they were, be said to issue from the seat of the theocracy and to be attentive to God's commands? Further, how could the chariots symbolize the kingdoms which were to be the objects of punishment, when at the same time they are themselves the instruments which inflict the chastisement? Neither does the angel's explanation suit this notion; for kingdoms are nowhere found under the figure of winds, and such a symbol would have been unintelligible to the prophet without further elucidation. **Two mountains.** The Hebrew has the article, "the two mountains," two well-known mountains. The scene of the vision is Jerusalem or its neighbourhood; hence the two mountains mentioned are thought to be those of Zion or the temple-mount, and Olives (comp. ch. xiv. 4; Joel iii. 16). It is impossible to identify them: and probably nothing more is meant than that the chariots came forth from a defile between the two mountains which appeared in the vision. **Mountains of brass;** or, *copper.* These impregnable, undecaying mountains represent the immovable, invincible nature of the theocracy and of God's decrees respecting it. From it the chariots go forth, because for the sake of God's kingdom and to promote its objects the world-powers are destroyed (Knabenbauer) (Isa. lxvi. 15). The number "four" represents completeness; the judgment shall leave no quarter unvisited.

Ver. 2.—**Red horses** (see note on ch. i. 8). The colours of the horses are significant, though the symbols are not undisputed. "Red" symbolizes bloodshed and war (Isa. lxiii. 2; Rev. vi. 4); "black," sorrow and mourning (Isa. l. 3; Jer. iv. 28; Rev. vi. 5); "white," victory and joy (Eccles. ix. 8; Rev. vi. 2; xix. 11). What the colour of the horses in the fourth chariot means is very doubtful (see below on ver. 3).

Ver. 3.—**Grisled and bay;** rather, *speckled, strong;* Septuagint, ἵπποι ποικίλοι ψαροί, "horses pied and dapple-grey." But ψαρὸς is explained by the Scholiast in Aristophanes, 'Nub.,' 1225, as "swift;" and possibly the LXX. used it in that sense here. The Vulgate has *fortes;* Aquila, καρτεροί. One would have expected a colour to be named, but why these are specially mentioned as strong or active is seen in ver. 7. The word *beruddim,* "speckled," occurs only in Gen. xxxi. 10, 12, where it has no symbolical character. As it denotes a combination of colours, probably spots of white on a dark ground, it may signify a quality of a mixed nature, thus indicating a visitation of war and pestilence, the sword and famine.

Ver. 5.—**The four spirits of the heavens.** Both the Septuagint and Vulgate render, "the four winds of heaven;" and this is doubtless correct. It was a familiar symbol to the Jews. The winds are often introduced in executing God's will on sinners (comp. Ps. civ. 4; cxlviii. 8; Jer. xlix. 36; Dan. vii. 2). **Which go forth from standing before the Lord** (comp. Job i. 6; ii. 1). The winds are supposed to be God's servants, waiting his pleasure to be sent forth on his errands. The Septuagint and Vulgate translate, "which go forth to stand before the Lord." This denotes merely their usual obedience; but the text implies that the prophet sees them moving from their usual expectant attitude, and hastening forth to do God's commands.

Ver. 6.—The angel now (vers. 6, 7) indicates the various destinations of the chariots, except the first with the red horses. Why this is omitted has never been satisfactorily explained. Some regard ver. 7 as giving the destination of this chariot, by making a slight change in the word rendered "bay" in the Authorized Version, which would cause it to mean "red." The Syriac, indeed, which omits the word in ver. 3, translates it here by "red." If we retain the Masoretic reading, we must let this difficulty remain unsolved, and suppose that the angel explains only part of the vision, leaving the rest for the prophet's meditation. **The black horses which** are **therein**; literally, *that wherein are the black horses, they go forth,* etc.; which is equivalent to "the chariot wherein are the black horses goeth forth." So the Revised Version. **The north country**, Babylonia (see note on ch. ii. 6). **After them**; *behind them.* The white horses go to the same quarter; and thus is indicated the overwhelming destruction that was coming on Babylon, and the victory and triumph of the conquerors over it. **The south country**; *i.e.* Egypt (Isa. xxx. 6; Dan. xi. 5), another hostile power, also, perhaps, Edom and Ethiopia. One chariot only is seen to go towards it, drawn by the speckled horses that denote a mixed judgment, perhaps of war and pestilence (see on ver. 3). The north and south symbolize the whole earth and the powers hostile to the true Israel.

Ver. 7.—**The bay**; rather, *the strong*, as in ver. 3; the horses in the fourth chariot, whose special mission needed peculiar powers. Septuagint, οἱ ψαροί: but the Vulgate, *qui erant robustissimi.* **Sought to go.** These agents desired a wider sphere, and asked permission to extend their action, and to **walk to and fro through the earth.** Famine and pestilence, which this chariot symbolizes, come at different times and in different places mysteriously and unexpectedly "as arrows shot from the hand of God (Ezek. v. 16) on the objects of his displeasure" (Alexander). LXX., Καὶ ἐπέβλεπον [S², Καὶ ἐζήτουν καὶ ἐπέβλεπον] τοῦ πορεύεσθαι τοῦ [Α, καὶ] περιοδεῦσαι τὴν γῆν, "And looked to go and compass the earth."

Ver. 8.—**Then cried he upon me.** The angel cried aloud (like a herald announcing a proclamation, Jonah iii. 7), to call the prophet's attention to what was coming, which was of most immediate consequence to his people. This angel speaks as in the person of God. **Have quieted my spirit**; literally, *have caused my spirit to rest;* LXX., ἀνέπαυσαν τὸν θυμόν μου, "quieted my anger," *i.e.* by satiating it. Many commentators take the clause as equivalent to "have caused my wrath to rest upon the land" (comp. John iii. 36), referring to Judg. viii. 3; Prov. xvi. 32; Eccles. x. 4, for the use of the word "spirit" (*ruach*) in the sense of "anger." Others see here an intimation of mercy and grace to the Jews still resident in Babylonia. But it is plain

that the vision is one of judgment; and the Spirit of the Lord is a Spirit of judgment and vengeance (Isa. iv. 4), which destroys evil that good may flourish.

Vers. 9—15.—§ 11. *A symbolical action— the crowning of the high priest.*

Ver. 9.—The preceding visions having come to an end, they are now confirmed by a public act which should show the glory of the future temple, the acceptance of the members of the theocracy, and the King and Priest who was to come. **Came unto me.** This was probably on the morning after the night of visions, or as soon as he had divulged them to the people.

Ver. 10.—**Take of them of the Captivity.** The verb is in the infinitive for the imperative, "take thou from the Captivity;" what he is to take is noted in the next verse. "Those of the Captivity" are certain envoys sent by the Jews who still dwelt in Babylon (Ezek. i. 1; iii. 11), bearing gifts for the temple. These messengers the prophet was to visit at the house of Josiah, their host. **Heldai**; or, *Cheldai*, in **ver. 14** "Helem" or "Chelem," "The Enduring One" (Keil); "The Lord's Word" (Pusey). The name occurs in 1 Chron. xxvii. 15. **Tobijah**; "The Lord is good," a well-known name. **Jedaiah**; "God careth." The name is found in 1 Chron. ix. 10; xxiv. 7. The LXX. explains the names in symbolical fashion, Παρὰ τῶν ἀρχόντων, καὶ παρὰ τῶν χρησίμων αὐτῆς, καὶ παρὰ τῶν ἐπεγνωκότων αὐτήν, "From the chief men, and from its good men, and from those that have understood it." **Which are come from Babylon.** This clause in the Authorized Version is transposed from its place in the Hebrew, which is at the end of the verse, where it refers to the house of Josiah, and should be rendered, "to which," or "whither they have come from Babylon." Septuagint, Τὸν οἶκον Ἰωσίου . . . τοῦ ἥκοντος ἐκ Βαβυλῶνος, "The house of Josiah . . . who came from Babylon." **The same day.** There was to be no delay; the transaction was to be carried out "on that day," the day made known to the prophet, and by himself in person. **The house of Josiah the son of Zephaniah.** He was, perhaps, treasurer. At any rate, at his house the envoys were entertained, and there were stored the contributions which the Jews in exile had sent to their brethren in Jerusalem. Josiah is the same person as Hen, according to the Authorized Version and the Vulgate, in ver. 14 (where see note). He was probably son of the Zephaniah mentioned in 2 Kings xxv. 18 as in the second rank of priests among those who were deported to Babylon (comp. Jer. xxi. 1; xxxvii. 3).

Ver. 11.—**Silver and gold.** That which had been brought from Babylon. However unwilling the Jews were to let the Samaritans take part in the good work, they were quite ready to receive contributions from their brethren in the dispersion, and likewise from heathen kings and princes (see Ezra vi. 8, etc.; vii. 15, etc.). **Make crowns.** The prophet was to get the crowns made (comp. Exod. xxv., *passim*). The plural may here be used intensively for "a noble crown," as in Job xxxi. 36; or it may signify the two metals of which the crown was made, two or more wreaths being intertwined to form it. It is certain that only one crown was to be made, and that that was to be placed on Joshua's head. There is no mention of Zerubbabel in the passage; so the plural cannot be taken to intimate that there was a crown for the high priest and a crown for the princely ruler, as Ewald and Bunsen assert. These critics, followed by Hitzig and Wellhausen, supply the passage thus: "on the head of Zerubbabel and on the head of Joshua." Zerubbabel had no kingly position. Rather, all mention of Zerubbabel is expressly excluded, in order to denote that in the Person of him whom Joshua symbolized, the offices of priest and king were united (Ps. cx.). We may note that in Rev. xix. 12 Christ is said to have on his head many crowns, by which is meant a diadem composed of many circlets. The high priest's mitre is never called a crown. That which was placed on Joshua's head was a royal crown, a token of royal dignity, not his own, but his whom he represented— Christ the eternal Priest, the universal King.

Ver. 12.—**Speak unto him, saying.** The prophet is to explain to Joshua the meaning of this public act. **Behold the Man whose name is The BRANCH**; literally, *behold the man, BRANCH is his name* (see note on ch. iii. 8). The Targum has, "Behold the Man, Messiah is his name." It is plain that the term "Branch" or "Shoot" (LXX., Ἀνατολή: Vulgate, *Oriens*) could not be addressed to Joshua; indeed, the very form of the sentence, "his name," not "thy name," shows this. All who saw the transaction and heard the words must have understood that they had reference to the "Shoot" of David, the Messiah that was to come, to whom was committed the regal and priestly dignity. **And he shall grow up out of his place**; Septuagint, Καὶ ὑποκάτωθεν αὐτοῦ ἀνατελεῖ, "And from beneath him he shall spring up;" Vulgate, *Et subter eum orietur;* Drake, "He shall sprout forth from under himself;" Revised Version margin, "And it (or they) shall bud forth under him;" Hitzig, Ewald, "From under him there shall be sprouting." But there is no need to alter the rendering of the Authorized Version, which indicates that the shoot shall grow from its own soil, that Messiah shall

arise in his own country and nation, and shall spring from a lowly origin to the highest glory (see Isa. xi. 1; liii. 2). **He shall build the temple of the Lord.** He should build, not the material temple whose foundations Zerubbabel had laid, but the spiritual temple of which the tabernacle and the temple of Jerusalem were only the type and shadow—that new sanctuary which Ezekiel beheld (xli.), a house not made with hands, the Church of the living God (Eph. ii. 20, etc.; 1 Pet. ii. 5).

Ver. 13.—**Even he shall build.** A forcible repetition of the preceding statement, laying stress on the Person, "*He*, and no one else, shall build." The clause is omitted by the Septuagint. **He shall bear the glory.** The word rendered "glory" is used to denote royal honours here, as in 1 Chron. xxix. 25; Jer. xxii. 18; Dan. xi. 21. Messiah shall have regal majesty. Compare the many passages where the glory of Christ is spoken of; *e.g.* John i. 14; ii. 11; xvii. 5; Luke ix. 32; xxiv. 26; Heb. ii. 9; Rev. v. 12, etc. **Shall sit and rule upon his throne** (comp. ch. ix. 10). Thus Christ says, "All power is given unto me in heaven and in earth" (Matt. xxviii. 18; see Luke i. 32). **And he shall be a Priest upon his throne;** Septuagint, Καὶ ἔσται ἱερεὺς ἐκ δεξιῶν αὐτοῦ, "There shall be a Priest upon his right hand." The Authorized Version is doubtless correct, as the clause is intended to declare that Messiah should, like Melchizedek, combine the offices of Priest and King (Ps. cx. 4; Heb. v. 6, 10). **The counsel of peace shall be between them both.** The two offices or dignities are meant, which are combined in one person. The Messiah, in his two offices of Priest and King, has one common design, to bring peace to his people (Isa. ix. 6; Micah v. 5, where see note). Other interpretations are unsuitable. Thus: There shall be harmony between Joshua and Zerubbabel; but the two are nowhere mentioned together in the paragraph, and, indeed, the statement would be superfluous. There shall be perfect concord between the two offices; but a person is spoken of, not an abstraction. Others explain the "counsel of peace" to be between Jews and Gentiles, or the returned and the exiled Jews; but neither of these have been named. Pusey takes it to mean, "between the Father and the Son;" but there is nothing in the passage to lead to this. Knabenbauer expounds it of those who alone are mentioned in the text, Messiah and Joshua, seeing in it an exhortation to the latter to make the type correspond to the Antitype, so that all may see that there is perfect harmony between them.

Ver. 14.—**The crowns shall be . . . for a memorial.** The crown was to be taken from

Joshua's head and deposited in the temple as a memorial of this prophecy, and of the zeal of those who had come from far to bring offerings to the Lord, and likewise of the hospitality of Josiah, who had received them into his house. That such "gifts" were dedicated in the temple is well known (see Judith xvi. 19; 2 Macc. v. 16; ix. 16; Josephus, 'Bell. Jud.,' ii. 17. 3; 'Ant.,' xvii. 6. 3; xix. 6. 1; Philo, 'Legat. ad Cai.,' § 40, ii. p. 592). **Helem** is the same as *Heldai* (ver. 10), whether he bore both names, or whether, as is probable, this is a mere mistake of a copyist. **To Hen.** The Authorized Version considers this as a proper name. In this case it would be another name for Josiah. But it is really an appellative, and the rendering should be, "for the kindness of the son of Zephaniah." The crown would be also a memorial of his kindness in receiving and entertaining these exiles (comp. Matt. x. 41). The LXX. explains the names as in ver. 10, though not quite in the same way, Ἔσται τοῖς ὑπομένουσι, καὶ τοῖς χρησίμοις αὐτῆς, καὶ τοῖς ἐπεγνωκόσιν αὐτήν, καὶ εἰς χάριτα υἱοῦ Σοφονίου, καὶ εἰς ψαλμὸν ἐν οἴκῳ Κυρίου, "The crown shall be to them that endure,

and to its good men, and to those that have understood it, both for a favour to the son of Sophonias, and for a psalm in the house of the Lord."

Ver. 15.—**They that are far off**; οἱ μακράν (Septuagint); comp. Eph. ii. 13, 17. The Jews who had come from Babylon to Jerusalem are a figure of the conversion of distant nations and their offerings to the Church (see Hag. ii. 7, and note there). **Build in the temple of the Lord.** They shall join in building up the spiritual temple, the universal Church of Christ. Ye shall know, etc. (ch. ii. 9, 11; iv. 9). The Angel of Jehovah is speaking in Jehovah's name (ver. 9). What takes place in the case of this material temple shall be a token and a prelude of the great fulfilment in Messianic times. **If ye will diligently obey.** Neither the restoration of the temple nor the advent of Messiah's kingdom was in itself doubtful; but the people's share in the former, and their participation in the blessings of the latter, depended on the preparation of the heart, obedience, zeal, and holiness (Dan. xii. 10; Mal. iv. 1, 2; John i. 12; 2 Tim. ii. 11, 12).

HOMILETICS.

Vers. 1—8.— *The ministry of angels.* "And I turned, and lifted up mine eyes, and looked, and, behold, there came four chariots out from between two mountains." This, the last of the present series of visions, is perceptibly similar in several points, to the first (ch. i. 7—11). We find mention in both, *e.g.*, of "horses;" of the variety of their colours; of the prophet's inquiry respecting their meaning; of some of them going to and fro on the earth; and of final "quiet" (ver. 8) or "rest" (ch. i. 11). If we were right, therefore, in understanding the first as a "vision of angels," we may do the same, of course, of this last. This idea is confirmed by the frequent way in which "chariots," as here spoken of, are employed in Holy Scripture as descriptive of the angels of God (see Ps. lxviii. 17; Deut. xxxiii. 2; Acts vii. 53; 2 Kings ii. 11; vi. 17); as also by what is said of those seen as "standing by the Lord of the whole earth" (1 Kings xxii. 19; Dan. vii. 10; Luke i. 19; also ch. iv. 14, *supra*, where we, perhaps, have an example of the placing of men on an angelic level; Ps. viii. 5; Luke xx. 36). Taking this general view of the passage, it may be understood as giving us instruction (1) respecting the *nature* of the angels; and (2) respecting their *work*.

I. THEIR NATURE. We are shown in this vision, for example: 1. How *mighty* they are. They are represented as chariots of war—chariots of "fire," in other places—probably because such chariots, in old days, were, like artillery in these days, the most formidable "arm" of an army (see Judg. i. 19; iv. 3; 2 Chron. xviii. 30, 31; and note how angels, whether elect or fallen, are spoken of in Rom. viii. 38; Eph. i. 21; vi. 10; 2 Pet. ii. 11). 2. How *orderly*. Each separate emblematical "colour" being distinguished from the others, and each coming forth in its turn. May we not trace similar ideas of perfect order and symmetrical arrangement, and consequent facility in ascertaining numbers, in Rev. v. 11; Dan. vii. 10 (comp. Mark vi. 40, 44; and the words of the collect, "the services of men and angels in a wonderful order")? 3. How *diverse*. This, also, seems intimated by what is said of the different "colours" of the horses. This also we can easily understand to be true. If the varieties of men are so many, who yet are all "men," however diverse (Acts xvii. 26), why not of the angels also? why not of the angels much more, being innumerable (Heb. xii. 22)?

This same truth seems intimated to us also in Col. i. 16; and, perhaps, of evil angels, in Mark ix. 29. A legitimate subject this for meditation and praise, though not for intrusion (Col. i. 18). 4. *How diversely employed.* Like "the four winds of heaven," *e.g.*, some go in this direction, some in that. Also some are to follow, some to precede. Some, again, to move in one direction only; some in every direction, "to and fro." Angels, in short, like the stars of the mighty firmament, and apparently bearing, therefore, the same name, "the host of heaven" (Gen. ii. 1; Ps. xxxiii. 6; Luke ii. 13; Job xxxviii. 6), are, as it were, some fixed, and some revolving; some of one light, some of another; some larger, some smaller; some single, some double or treble; some nearer, some more remote (1 Cor. xv. 41).

II. THEIR WORK. However mighty or diverse these angels, all that they here do is seen to be: 1. *In strict subordination to God's purposes.* These mystical "chariots" only run, as it were, "between," and not over the mountains—the unsurmountable and undecaying "brass" mountains of God's settled arrangements (see Micah iv. 13). Even of the mightiest angels Acts iv. 28 holds good. 2. *In strict obedience to God's directions.* Observe what is said in ver. 7 of those who "sought to go," but till expressly allowed, did *not* go, "to and fro" (comp. Dan. ix. 23; Heb. i. 14, "sent forth;" and see, even of evil angels, Luke viii. 32). 3. *To the complete satisfaction of God's Son.* See the emphatic declaration of the Angel-Jehovah in ver. 8. This is true, even if we understand that verse (with some), "These have made my anger to rest on the north country." Why else does this Divine Angel employ this word "my"? Why proclaim this fact thus "aloud" (Pusey; comp. Ps. ciii. 20, 21; Matt. vi. 10)? 4. *For the sake of God's friends.* What is this "north country" on which God's anger is thus caused to abide? What but that great enemy of his Zion—that mystic Babylon, or "Shinar," by banishment in which (see last chapter) he had punished his Israel for their sin? Compare this predicted fate of the future "Babylon" with that of the literal as described in Isa. xlvii. 6—9, and elsewhere; and compare ch. i. 15, and perhaps Rev. xviii. 5, 6.

From the whole, we may see, to conclude: 1. *The exceeding complexity of God's government.* How many instruments—what varied agents, both in heaven and earth—he employs (comp. Dan. iv. 35)! Much as there is to admire in that visible "cosmos" of which men have discovered (under one aspect) so much; how much more there is when we include also that invisible "cosmos" (Gen. xxviii. 12; John i. 51), of which revelation informs us! It is, in fact, only less marvellous than its Maker himself. 2. *The exceeding simplicity of its general principle.* So far as explained to us, it all turns on one point, viz. "Israel's" calling and work. This shown here of the literal Israel. This still more true of the spiritual. See two last references again; also such passages as 2 Cor. iv. 15; 1 Cor. iii. 21; Eph. iii. 10, 11. Note, also, how this principle was laid down once for all in Gen. xii. 3; and how it corresponds with and is partly explained by the remarkable declaration of Eph. i. 23.

Vers. 9—15.—*The ministry of Messiah.* "And the word of the Lord came unto me, saying," etc. The series of striking visions which we have now been considering had a kind of "prologue" in ch. i. 1—6. We seem to have the corresponding "epilogue" here. It turns on the fact of the arrival (probably about the same season, no special note of time being given as in ch. vii. 1) of certain visitors at Jerusalem, with offerings for the temple, from a "far" country, viz. "Babylon" (see vers. 10 and 15; and comp. Isa. xxxix. 3). And what we seem invited to notice, respecting these visitors, is (1) the *welcome*; (2) the *instruction*; and (3) the *promotion* which they received.

I. THE WELCOME ACCORDED THEM. This is shown in several ways. 1. *As to their persons.* They are mentioned by name (ver. 10; comp. Exod. xxxi. 2; xxxiii. 12; 1 Kings xiii. 2; Isa. xlv. 3; John x. 3), including the name of the man who appears to have given them hospitality in his "house" (Matt. x. 41). Also, if it be true, as some suppose from comparing vers. 10 and 14, that two among them had more names than one, the second name in each case being one assumed because containing in it, like all the rest (see Pusey), the name of Jehovah or Jah (comp. Dan. i. 7; iv. 8; v. 12; Micah iv. 5), it is, perhaps, worthy of notice that their names seem mentioned in full; thus showing, further, it may be, how God is pleased to notice and honour the very least thing that is done by us in remembrance of his Name (Mark ix. 41). 2. *As to their offerings.* These are not only not refused, but openly accepted—a very great point, and by no means such a matter of course as we are sometimes inclined to suppose (Gen. iv. 4, 5; Numb. xvi. 15; Exod. xxv. 2; xxx. 16; xxxv. 5, etc.). Also, when accepted, these offerings are honoured, and put to very dignified use, being employed to make "crowns" (ver. 11) for God's chief minister then upon earth (compare, in some respects, the box of ointment mentioned in Mark xiv. 3—9).

II. THE INSTRUCTION VOUCHSAFED THEM. See what God says of Joshua, when thus adorned, as a type or sign (comp. ch. iii. 8), in vers. 12 and 13. With these two crowns on him, he seems to represent to us: 1. *The appearance of the coming Messiah in his humiliation.* We see him here (1) as a man ("Behold the Man!" ver. 12; John xix. 5); and, therefore, as sharing to the full man's nature and circumstances ("growing up;" comp. Isa. liii. 2; Luke ii. 51, 52). We see him here (2) as the Representative Man, the Son of man ("The Branch," ver. 12), engaged, as such, in doing man's work, viz. in saving men or bringing them to glory (Heb. ii. 10, 11); in other words, in "building" God's "temple," or Church (Matt. xvi. 18). 2. *The appearance of the coming Messiah in his glory.* For example, we see him here (1) as a Builder or Teacher, doing all by himself. "*Even he*" (ver. 13). He, indeed, being such as he is! He, alone, having no one else with him (see Isa. lxiii. 3, 5)! More especially and clearly we see him (2) as both King and High Priest. This also foreshadowed by the case of Melchizedek (Gen. xiv. 18; Ps. cx. 4; Heb. vii. 14). This signified here by the interpretation apparently given to the two "crowns" in ver. 13 ("sitting and ruling on his throne," and being "a priest on his throne"); and possibly, also, by the intimation at the end of that verse, of perfectly harmonious co-operation, in his case, of these generally divided and even incompatible offices. This afterwards accomplished, as to his priestly office, when, by being "lifted up" on the cross, he drew all men to himself (John xii. 32, where note also the connection between the inquiry of the Greeks, so "far off," in vers. 20—23, and the "glorifying" of the Son of man in the subsequent verse); and, as to his kingly office, in that primary "building" up of his Church by the bestowment of the gifts mentioned in Acts ii. 33 and v. 31. Then most manifestly did he "bear" that twofold "glory" referred to here in ver. 13.

III. THE SPECIAL PROMOTION CONFERRED ON THEM. As shown by the final destination of their offerings. After doing their duty, as "crowns" to Joshua, in a typical way, they were to have a perpetual place amongst the treasures of God's house (ver. 14). This: 1. *As a "memorial."* (Ver. 14.) Future visitors should learn from them how these first visitors (as they appear to have been) had been welcomed. Possibly this may even help to account for the world-wide habit which afterwards prevailed amongst the Jews in this respect (Acts ii. 1—11, etc.; and compare, perhaps, Rom. xvi. 5; Eph. ii. 12). 2. *As a pledge.* Placed in the restored temple, these crowns would be a kind of standing prophecy: (1) Of the future calling of the Gentiles, when those now "afar off" should not only come and be welcomed, but should even help to "build" the true temple of God. (2) Of the coming glory of Messiah. Then, *i.e.* when this ingathering of the Gentiles (Gen. xlix. 10) has taken place, says the Angel-Jehovah here (in ver. 15), ye shall know that the Lord of hosts hath sent me unto you (compare two clauses of Luke ii. 31). 3. *As a warning.* "Ye shall know," if willing to know—so it means (see end of ver. 15; and comp. Dan. xii. 10; John vii. 17).

See how these various considerations show the *unity of the Bible.* 1. As to its *structure.* Joshua, or Jesus, after the Exodus, brings the Israelites, as Moses could not do, into rest. Another "Jesus," after the Captivity, typifies, in ch. iii. 6—10, the two natures of Christ; and, in this passage, his two offices of King and Priest. In the "fulness of time" a third "Jesus" arises, in whom all these things are fulfilled. Is there no evidence, in all this, of "design"? 2. As to its *subject.* Wherever we penetrate far enough beneath the surface, we find this one "Rock." Must it not, therefore, like the granite in geological formations, be the foundation of all? 3. As to its *source.* To what are we to attribute such singular unity of teaching, at such very different times, and in such very different circumstances, except virtual unity of origin, or of supervision, to say the least? Is not the true and only explanation in such passages as 2 Pet. i. 21; 1 Cor. xii. 6—11?

HOMILIES BY VARIOUS AUTHORS.

Vers. 1—8.—*The world ruled in the interest of Christianity.* I. THE POWERS OF THE WORLD ARE UNDER THE CONTROL OF GOD. East and west, north and south, all the world over, God is supreme. He is the Lord of all forces, the Ruler of all events, the Arbiter of all destinies. War, famine, pestilence, may be the result of natural causes, but, all the same, they are his servants; they come and go at his command; they accomplish what he pleases.

> "Happy the man who sees a God employed
> In all the good and ill that chequer life."
> (Cowper.)

II. THE POWERS OF THE WORLD ARE CONTROLLED BY GOD IN THE INTEREST OF CHRISTIANITY. God takes a direct and living interest in his people. He is Enemy of their enemies, and the Friend of their friends. "All things work together for good to them who love God." And there is nothing arbitrary in this. God is not partial, but just. As he is God, he must act as God. The true and the righteous and the holy must ever receive the protection and the blessing of the True and the Righteous and the Holy One. God's government is marked by immutability of counsel, variety of method, universality of range, sovereignty of sway, and beneficence of result. How grand and benign must be the end that satisfies the mind of the Eternal! "Quieted my spirit."—F.

Vers. 9—15.—"*Messiah the Prince.*" "Behold."
I. THE COMING MAN OF THE AGES. "Branch." Lowliness, and yet dignity. The heathens fabled that the Titans were sons of heaven and earth. Here is what they vainly imagined. "Grew up." Natural development. Perfection of humanity. Long the cry was, "He cometh." We see his shadow in every sacrifice. Find his presence in every prophecy. Hear his footfall in every promise. He was the Hope of Israel, and the Desire of all nations.
II. CHARGED WITH THE NOBLEST MISSION. "Build"—personally and instrumentally. Many whom he honours as "fellow-workers." Temple slowly rising. Grandeur and beauty gradually unfolding. Implies the union and fellowship of men as "living stones" in the great temple of humanity.
III. DESTINED FOR THE GRANDEST EMPIRE. "The glory." 1. *Priest.* Power with God. "For ever, after the order of Melchizedek." 2. *King.* Power with men. The rule of righteousness and love. 3. *The recompense of his sufferings.* "Sit and rule." First the cross, then the crown (cf. Heb. x. 12, 13; 1 Pet. i. 11).
IV. DESIGNATED FOR IMMORTAL HONOUR. Heaven is the perfect state. What do we see there? Let St. John declare (Rev. v. 6). Even on earth, what honour to Christ! Every day, and especially on the Lord's day, what prayers in his Name! what offerings to his praise and glory! In how many lands, by what various voices, with what measureless love, is his name breathed forth! "Behold the Man!" Let each heart answer, with adoring gratitude and joy, "My Lord and my God!"—F.

Vers. 1—8.—*God's government of the world.* "And I turned, and lifted up mine eyes, and looked, and, behold, there came four chariots out from between two mountains; and the mountains were mountains of brass," etc. This is the last in the series of visions, which amount in all to eight, during that one night. All are so obscure that the more scholarly and enlightened the expositor, the less disposed will he be to regard his interpretation as absolutely correct. Certainly this is not more easy of interpretation than the preceding ones. The objects which were now revealed to the prophet's vision are various and strange. 1. He sees four chariots. It does not say expressly whether they were chariots of war bearing the warrior out to battle or home in triumph, or whether they were chariots used for private or public conveyances; but it is implied that they were war-chariots. 2. He saw these four chariots proceeding from two mountains. These were not mountains of earth or stone, but mountains of brass; mountains, therefore, having peculiar solidity and strength. 3. He saw these chariots drawn by horses of different colours. In the first chariot we have red horses; in the second, black; in the third, white; and in the fourth, grisled or piebald grey. Now, the prophet seemed utterly unable to understand the meaning of these objects. But he is anxious to do so, and he addresses the interpreting angel, and says, "What are these, my lord?" Here is the answer: "And the angel answered and said unto me, These are the four spirits of the heavens, which go forth from standing before the Lord of all the earth," etc. The chariots, then, are the four "spirits," or winds, as the margin has it. Some translate the word, "celestial spirits," and suppose that angels are referred to. The "four winds" probably represent the invisible agencies by which the Almighty is pleased to carry on the government of the world. These spirits stand before the Lord of all the earth, and are in his presence, at his disposal, ever ready to execute his behests. My purpose in these sketches is not speculative, but practical. Were it speculative, I should find a wide and fertile field for hypothetical thought. For example, a large variety of opinions exist concerning the four chariots and horses and their charioteers. Some suppose that they represent the great monarchies of the ancient world—the Chaldean, the Grecian, and the Roman. Some, indeed, have supposed them to refer to the four Gospels. And some have supposed them to refer to the history of the Church after Constantine—the *first*, to the wars of invaders of the Roman Empire, and the wars of controverted doctrines and opinions; the *second*, to the blackness of darkness, the ignorance, oppression, and misery of papal domination; the *third*, to the light and knowledge, the joy and triumph, of the Reformation; and the *fourth*, to the mixed condition of things, the confusion of false doctrine and true, right and wrong precepts, holy and unholy rites of worship, subsequent to that great revolution. But I take the vision to illustrate *God's government of the world*; and it illustrates four facts concerning that government—its variety, immutability, universality, and supremacy.

I. VARIETY. This is suggested by the colour of the steeds that bear onward the chariots of his plans. The "*red* horses," emblem of war and bloodshed. The "*black*," emblem of calamity, distress, and mourning. The "*white*," emblem of gladness and prosperity. The "*grisled*" and "*bay*," or piebald, a mixture of events, prosperity and adversity, friendship and bereavement, sorrow and joy, etc. Has not this variety characterized the providence that is over man from the beginning until this hour? It is not only seen in every page of the history of nations and Churches and families, but in the history of individuals. The experience of every man is more changeable than the weather. There is a constant alternation—the red, the black, the white, the mixed. These changes are useful. 1. *They break the monotony of life.* They tend to keep the heart of humanity on the alert. There is but little opportunity for moral sleep. 2. *They create a desire for a state of certainty.* They prompt a search for a "city that hath foundations, whose Builder and Maker is God." This is not our rest.

II. IMMUTABILITY. These chariots move between two "mountains of brass." Though they are borne by a variety of steeds, and move rapidly towards every point of the compass, and carry a variety of events wherever they go, they are overshadowed and hedged in by the immutable, represented by mountains of brass. God's immutable counsels of decrees keep all the motions and commotions, all the convulsions and revolutions of the world in their place. As the ocean, amidst all its ebbings and flowings, rage and fury, is bound to obey the moon, which remains serenely settled in her orbit, so all the agitations of the earth are bound to obey the immutable decrees of Heaven. Thank God, that in this changing world of ours there are mountains of brass, things that cannot be shaken. "All flesh is grass, . . . but the word of our God shall stand for ever;" "My counsel shall stand, and I will do all my pleasure."

III. UNIVERSALITY. These chariots, borne by these varied coloured steeds, rolled towards every point of the globe, some to the north and some to the south. They walked "to and fro through the earth." Yes; through the earth—through every part of it. Not a spot unvisited or ignored. God's providence embraces all, matter and mind, great and small, good and evil. All we have, and all that every creature has, is borne to us in these chariots; they bear to us our trials and our joys. Hence we should bow with resignation under all our sorrows, and shout with gratitude in all our enjoyments. Hence, too, we should practically realize our dependence upon him in every moment of our life. "Give us this day our daily bread," etc.

IV. SUPREMACY. "These are the four spirits of the heavens, which go forth from standing before the Lord of all the earth." He is at the head of all. No evil spirit moves without his permission and control; no good spirit without his inspiration and guidance. He is the Lord of all the earth. How great must he be who manages all things!

> "All good proceedeth from him, as sunbeams from the sun;
> All evils fall before him; his will through all is done."

Let us trust him with an unbounded confidence. Let us obey him with loving loyalty. "Of him, and by him, and to him are all things." "He is over all, God blessed for ever."—D. T.

Vers. 9—15.—*The matchless Man in history.* "And the word of the Lord came unto me, saying, Take of them of the Captivity, even of Heldai, of Tobijah, and of Jedaiah, which are come from Babylon, and come thou the same day." The crowning, the work, and the position of Joshua spoken of in these verses are obviously employed to symbolize some coming Man who would be matchless in all history. Concerning this matchless Man, we are here taught—

I. THAT HE IS ONE WHOM HEAVEN COMMANDS THE PEOPLE TO HONOUR. "And the word of the Lord came unto me, saying, Take of them of the Captivity, even of Heldai, of Tobijah, and of Jedaiah, which are come from Babylon, and come thou the same day, and go into the house of Josiah the son of Zephaniah; then take silver and gold, and make crowns, and set them upon the head of Joshua the son of Josedech, the high priest." The prophet is commanded to go to certain of the more distinguished men who had returned from Babylonian captivity, representative men and envoys it may be. He was to take these men, whose names are here given, who were entertained in the house of another distinguished man, here called Josiah the son of Zephaniah. From that house the silver and gold which they had brought from Babylon were to be taken, with which crowns were to be made and placed upon the head of Joshua the son of Josedech, the high priest. By the general consent of expositors, this was a mere symbolical transaction—a transaction pointing to some great Man whom Heaven will require all men to crown with the highest dignity. The spirit of hero-worship is so strong in human nature that the servile multitudes of all times have been ready to fall down and render homage to most unholy characters. They hoist flags, ring bells, shout hurrahs, in honour of the laurelled butchers, crowned despots, and gorgeous millionaires. This is one of the worst features of human depravity, one of the greatest obstructions to the progress of men and nations. But here is a character symbolized by the name of Joshua, to whom the people are called upon by *God himself* to render honour. Who is this Man? Can you find him anywhere amongst the millions of your contemporaries in any land, or on the page of the history of the people of any time? anywhere but in the records of the four evangelists—the Man Christ Jesus? "When he bringeth in the First Begotten into the world, he saith, Let all the angels of God worship him." And all heaven worships him. "I heard the voice of angels round about the throne," etc.

II. THAT HIS PEDIGREE WAS STRIKINGLY SINGULAR. "Thus speaketh the Lord of hosts, saying, Behold the Man whose name is The BRANCH; and he shall grow up out of his place, and he shall build the temple of the Lord." He is a "Branch;" he has root somewhere; he has life, and he grows. It is here said, "He shall grow up out of his place." The reference is to some Man who grows on the earth, who is not of the earth. What man on the earth can be said to have grown out of his place? The earth is the place of all men during their stay here. It is their native home. Only one such Man we know of—the illustrious "Son of Mary." He came down from heaven and tabernacled on this earth, which was not his place. And here he grew in body and mind, in the favour of God and man. Though there was nothing congenial with his Spirit here, still he grew and became the Prince of life, the Conqueror of death, and the moral Commander of the race. A great soul, dominated by a supreme sympathy with the Supremely Good, can grow anywhere, in its place or out of it. It can subordinate the most hostile external elements and forces to its own will and interests.

III. THAT HE IS ONE WHOSE MISSION IS SUBLIMELY GLORIOUS. "He shall build the temple of the Lord," etc. Zerubbabel was now engaged in the work of rearing the material temple at Jerusalem; and a more glorious work than this is not given to man than to promote the public worship of God. The progress of nations is dependent upon morality, and morality is the growth of genuine religion. Philanthropy springs from piety; it is only as philanthropy grows that humanity can advance. Hence no work so transcendently important as that of promoting public worship, building temples, etc. Hence it is added here, " He shall bear the glory." The true promoter of public worship bears with him in every honest effort the glory, compared with which the glory of every other department of human labour pales into dimness. The building of the material temple is but the emblem of the rearing of the great spiritual temple. And the Man here referred to is the Builder of that. There is one and only one, and that is Christ. He is not only the Builder, but the Creator of the materials, and himself the Foundation of the whole. " Other foundation can no man lay than that which is laid, that is Jesus Christ." In doing this he bears the glory. " Now is the Son of man glorified." God is glorified in him. " God hath highly exalted him, and given him a name which is above every name," etc. St. Peter gives a beautiful description of this temple when he says, " To whom coming, as unto a living stone, disallowed indeed of men, but chosen of God, and precious, ye also, as lively stones, are built up a spiritual house, an holy priesthood, to offer up spiritual sacrifices, acceptable to God by Jesus Christ." Christ is the great Builder of the moral temple of the world, and no one else.

IV. THAT HE IS ONE WHOSE POSITION AND FUNCTIONS ARE TRANSCENDENTALLY EXALTED. He is on a throne. " He is exalted far above all heavens." But he is there : 1. *As a priestly King.* On behalf of humanity before God, he holds the reins of universal dominion. 2. *As a glorious Reconciler.* " The counsel of peace shall be between them both." What does this mean ? Not that there is a covenant of peace between him and his Father. They were never at variance. And to suppose any contract or covenant between them is to derogate Infinite Majesty. The " counsel of peace " between the Infinite Father and his alien and rebellious children. He is the Mediator between God and man. He is the Reconciliation, the Atonement. (But see in the Exposition (ver. 13) another explanation, and one more conformable to the context.)

V. THAT HE IS ONE WHOSE POWER TO ATTRACT OTHERS TO HIS ENTERPRISE IS IMMENSELY GREAT. " And they that are far off shall come and build in the temple of the Lord, and ye shall know that the Lord of hosts hath sent me unto you." "There can," says Dr. Wardlaw, " be no doubt here; to you who were far off, and to them that were near are the very terms of distinction between Gentile and Jew, which, in addressing the former, the apostle uses. ' I will bring my sons *from far*,' says Jehovah, ' and my daughters from the ends of the earth.' The Gentiles were to be themselves stones in the building, and agents in the rearing of it. And this was fulfilled in the beginning of the gospel, in the ministerial activity and usefulness of many a Gentile convert; and it is fulfilling to this day in every Gentile nation where Christianity has formed a settlement, and in every heathen country to which missionaries are carrying the message of salvation, and gathering sinners into the Church of God. For that Church of God is his temple (the members of it, how widely soever scattered, being all ' builded together for an habitation of God through the Spirit '), in which ' spiritual sacrifices ' will be offered to him—' acceptable through Jesus Christ,' in all time and for ever! "

CONCLUSION. " Behold the Man ! " What manner of man is he ? He stands alone, the majestic cedar amongst the saplings of the race, the sun amidst the satellites. He is the " Wonderful."—D. T.

EXPOSITION.

CHAPTER VII.

Ver. 1—ch. viii. 23.—Part II. The Answer to a Question concerning the Observance of Certain Fasts.

Vers. 1—3.—§ 1. *A deputation comes from Bethel to ask whether a fast instituted in memory of the calamity of Jerusalem was still to be observed.*

Ver. 1.—**In the fourth year of King Darius.** This happened, then, B.C. 518, nearly two years after the visions had occurred (ch. i. 7). In two years more the temple was finished (Ezra vi. 15), and the work of rebuilding was now proceeding vigorously; it seemed a fit opportunity for inquiring whether, in this period of comparative prosperity and success, it behoved the people to continue the fast appointed in sadder times. **The word of the Lord came.** This is the usual formula for introducing a revelation (ch. i. 1), but it is here placed in a peculiar position, dividing the date into two parts. Keil connects the last clause, which gives the day of the month, with the next verse; but this is against the traditional accentuation, and is not required by the wording of ver. 2. The prophet first gives the date generally when the word came to him, and then defines it more accurately. **Chisleu;** *Chislev* (Neh. i. 1). This month corresponded to parts of November and December.

Ver. 2.—**When they had sent unto the house of God.** The Vulgate supports this version, *Et miserunt ad domum Dei;* the LXX. gives, Καὶ ἐξαπέστειλεν εἰς Βαιθὴλ Σαρασὰρ καὶ Ἀρβεσεὲρ ὁ βασιλεὺς καὶ οἱ ἄνδρες αὐτοῦ, "And Sarasar and Arbeseer the king and his men sent to Bethel"— which is far from clear. But the temple is never called *Beth-el*, while a mission to the town Bethel would be unmeaning. So "Bethel" is to be taken as the subject of the sentence, thus: "Now Bethel (*i.e.* they of Bethel) sent." The persons named may be taken either as the deputation or as the persons meant by "they of Bethel." The former seems most likely to be intended. The Bethelites sent these men to Jerusalem to make the inquiry. The exiles returned each to his own city, as we read in Ezra ii.; among them were many people of Bethel (Ezra ii. 28; Neh. vii. 32), which town they rebuilt (Neh. xi. 31). They seem to have tacitly acquiesced in the spiritual supremacy of Jerusalem, notwithstanding the associations connected with their own city. **Sherezer.** The names of the deputies are Assyrian; they seem to

have retained them on their return. *Sherezer*, equivalent to Assyrian *Sar-usur* or *Asur-sar-usur*, "Asur protect the King," is the name borne by a son of Sennacherib (2 Kings xix. 37). **Regem-melech;** "Friend of the King." The first half of the word is probably Assyrian (see Schrader, 'Die Keilinschr. und Alt. Test.,' pp. 206, 417). **And their men.** Certain persons associated with them in the business. **To pray before the Lord;** literally, *to stroke the face of the Lord* (ch. viii. 21, 22; Exod. xxxii. 11); so Latin, *mulcere caput.* Hence it means, "to entreat the favour of God" for their city. This was one object of their mission. The other purpose is mentioned in the next verse.

Ver. 3.—**The priests.** They were addressed as interpreters of the Law (see Hag. ii. 11, and note there). **Which were in;** rather, *which belonged to.* **The prophets.** Such as Zechariah, Haggai, and perhaps Malachi, through whom God communicated his will. **Should I weep in the fifth month?** The use of the first person singular to express a community or a people is not uncommon; here it means the Bethelites (comp. Numb. xx. 18, 19; Josh. ix. 7; 1 Sam. v. 10, 11). Weeping was the accompaniment of fasting (Judg. xx. 26; Neh. i. 4; Joel ii. 12). This fast in the fifth month, the month of Ab, had been established in memory of the destruction of Jerusalem by Nebuchadnezzar. The temple was burnt on the ninth or tenth of the month (see 2 Kings xxv. 8, 9; Jer. lii. 12, 13). The only fast-day enjoined by the Law of Moses was the great Day of Atonement on the tenth day of the seventh month, Ethanim (Lev. xxiii. 26, etc.). But the Jews added others in memory of certain national events (see Judg. xx. 26; 1 Sam. vii. 6; Isa. lviii. 3, etc.). In ch. viii. 19 mention is made of four extraordinary fasts instituted and observed during the Captivity, viz. on the ninth day of the fourth month, in memory of the capture of Jerusalem by the Chaldeans; in the fifth month, in remembrance of the burning of the temple and city; in the seventh month, in consequence of the murder of Gedaliah (Jer. xli. 1, 2); and in the tenth month, in memory of the commencement of the siege of Jerusalem by Nebuchadnezzar (see note on ch. viii. 19). **Separating myself.** Abstaining from food and pleasure. Vulgate, *vel sanctificare me debeo,* such separation or abstinence being regarded as a consecration to the Lord. The LXX. has not understood the passage, rendering, Εἰσελήλυθεν ὧδε ἐν τῷ μηνὶ τῷ πέπτῳ τὸ ἁγίασμα, "The sanctification hath come in here in the fifth month."

These so many years. All the seventy years of exile. There is, perhaps, some Pharisaical complacency in this assertion.

Vers. 4—7.—§ 2. *In answer to the inquiry, the delegates are told that fasting is in itself an indifferent thing, but is to be estimated by the conduct of those who observe it.*

Ver. 4.—**Then came the word of the Lord.** This formula marks the several portions of the answer to the inquiry (see ver. 8; ch. viii. 1, 18). The present verse takes up the sentence in ver. 1, interrupted by the explanation of the object of the deputation (vers. 2, 3).

Ver. 5.—**Unto all the people of the land.** The message was not for Bethel only, but for all the restored Jews, for whose satisfaction the question had been asked. **And to the priests.** The prophet was to make known to the priests God's will in this matter, it not being a mere ritual question. **Fifth** month (see note on ver. 3). The original question referred only to this fast; the answer embraces also another fast appointed by human authority. **The seventh** month. This fast was instituted in consequence of the murder of Gedaliah, B.C. 587, just seventy years ago, when the greater part of the remnant of the Jews, contrary to the prophet's warning, fled into Egypt to escape the punishment of the crime (2 Kings xxv. 25, 26; Jer. xli. 2, 16, etc.). **Did ye at all fast unto me?** It was not by God's command, or to do him honour, that they fasted; not from hearty repentance or sorrow for the sins which had brought ruin upon their city and country; but from vexation at the calamity itself, and in a self-righteous spirit, with some idea of gaining merit by this punishment of the body; and God was not constrained by this formal observance to show them favour. **Even to me.** (For the forcible repetition of the pronoun, comp. Gen. xxvii. 34; Prov. xxii. 19; Hag. i. 4.)

Ver. 6.—**When ye did eat**, etc.; better, *when ye eat and when ye drink.* As in your fasts, so in your rejoicings and your daily life. **Did not ye eat for yourselves,** etc.? literally, *Is it not ye who are eating and ye who are drinking?* There the matter ends; it is self that is concerned, and there is no reference to God (comp. 1 Cor. viii. 8; x. 31).

Ver. 7.—Should ye **not hear the words,** etc.? A verb must be supplied. "Do ye not know the words?" or "Should ye not obey the words?" Syriac, Septuagint, and Vulgate, "Are not these the words?" **By the former prophets** (ch. i. 4). It had been a common cry of the prophets from early times that men must not put their trust in the observance of outward ceremonies, but attend to the cultivation of moral obedience and purity (see 1 Sam. xv. 22; Prov. xxi. 3; Isa. i. 11, 12, 16, 17; lviii. 3, etc.; Jer. vii. 22, 23; Hos. vi. 6; Micah vi. 8, where see note). **When Jerusalem was inhabited.** Before its destruction and the deportation of its inhabitants. He recalls the former prosperity to their memory, contrasting it with the present low estate, to remind them of all they had lost in punishment of disobedience. **The south** (*Negeb*). The southern part of Judæa was so called (see on Obad. 19; and comp. Numb. xiii. 17; Josh. xv. 21). **The plain** (*Shephelah*); *the low land*, along the coast of the Mediterranean (Josh. xv. 33; 1 Macc. xii. 38). The above districts comprise two of the three divisions of Judæa (Judg. i. 9); the third, the mountain or hill country (Luke i. 39), is intended in the expression, "Jerusalem and the cities round about her." There was still a great dearth of population in the country, and the towns were not half inhabited, nor was the land half cultivated.

Vers. 8—14.—§ 3. *The people are further reminded that they had been disobedient in old time, and had been punished by exile.*

Ver. 8.—**Unto Zechariah.** The prophet speaks of himself in the third person, as in ch. i. 1. A further explanation of God's answer is next given. Some critics suppose that this verse is an interpolation, and that vers. 9, 10 are " the words" referred to in ver. 7.

Ver. 9.—**Thus speaketh;** *thus saith.* The Lord hath always so said, and saith so now. Revised Version, *thus hath the Lord of hosts spoken, saying.* **Execute true judgment;** literally, *judge ye judgment of truth;* i.e. judge according to truth without bias or partiality. The same phrase occurs in Ezek. xviii. 8. Exhortations to this effect are often found; *e.g.* Exod. xxiii. 6, etc.; Deut. xxiv. 14; Isa. i. 17; Jer. vii. 5—7; xxii. 3. **Show mercy.** Kindness and love in general. **Compassions.** Pity for the afflicted.

Ver. 10.—**Oppress not the widow,** etc. (Exod. xxii. 21, 22; Deut. x. 18, 19); Vulgate, *nolite calumniari,* where *calumniari* is used in the sense "to vex, torment." **Imagine evil against his brother in your heart.** God's Law forbids even a thought of revenge or injury against a neighbour, for this is only the first step to wrong-doing (comp. Micah ii. 1). Septuagint, Κακίαν ἕκαστος τοῦ ἀδελφοῦ αὐτοῦ μὴ μνησικακείτω ἐν ταῖς καρδίαις ὑμῶν, "Let none of you remember in your hearts the malice of your brother."

Ver. 11.—**Pulled away the shoulder;** *they gave a stubborn, refractory shoulder,* like an ox which refuses to have the yoke put on his neck, or draws back when it feels the weight (Neh. ix. 29; Hos. iv. 16). **Stopped their ears.** Made their ears heavy. Τὰ ὦτα αὐτῶν ἐβάρυναν (Septuagint); Isa. vi. 10; lix. 1. Three degrees of obduracy are named in this verse: they refused to listen; they resisted the warners; they exhibited open contempt for them. The full climax is given in the next verse.

Ver. 12.—**They made their hearts as an adamant stone.** They made their hearts as hard as a stone which could receive no cutting or engraving; no message from God could find entrance; and this from their wilful obstinacy. The word rendered "adamant," *shamir*, probably means "diamond," a stone so hard, says Jerome, as to break all metals to pieces, but to be itself broken by none; hence it is called *adamas*, "unconquerable." Ezekiel (iii. 9) notes that it is harder than flint (comp. Jer. xvii. 1). The LXX., paraphrasing, gives, Τὴν καρδίαν αὐτῶν ἔταξαν ἀπειθῆ, "They set their heart disobedient." **The Law.** The various enactments of the Mosaic system. **In his Spirit;** rather, *by his Spirit.* The teaching which the Spirit of God inspired the prophets to deliver (comp. Neh. ix. 30; 2 Kings xvii. 13; Micah iii. 8). And for the succession of prophets from Solomon to the Captivity, see note on Amos ii. 11; and to those there enumerated, add Iddo, Shemaiah, Hanani, Micaiah, Huldah.

Ver. 13.—**As he cried.** As the Lord called to them by the prophets. Just retribution fell upon them (Prov. i. 24, etc.; Isa. lxv. 12, 13; lxvi. 4). **So they cried,** and I would not hear; rather, *so they shall cry, and I will not hear.* God will be deaf to their cry, and will give them up to their own ways (Jer. ii. 28). In the protasis Jehovah is spoken of in the third person, in the apodosis he speaks in the first.

Ver. 14.—**I scattered them;** *I will scatter them.* What had happened in the past is a sign of what shall befall them in the future in punishment of like obduracy. The form of the sentence denotes that God is recounting what he had said to the people in past time; hence it is best to translate the verbs in the future tense. **Scattered them with a whirlwind;** Septuagint, ἐκβαλῶ αὐτούς, "I will cast them out;" Vulgate, *dispersi eos* (comp. Job xxvii. 21; Amos i. 14). **Nations whom they knew not.** This is the usual phrase for people of strange tongue (Deut. xxviii. 33; Jer. xvi. 13). **Thus the land was desolate.** This was the result of God's threatenings. Some make the words of Jehovah continue to "nor returned," but the punctuation is against them. **After them;** *i.e.* after they were carried away in captivity. **No man passed through nor returned.** No one went to and fro—a picture of extreme desolation (comp. Isa. xxxiii. 8; Jer. ix. 12; and for the phrase, see ch. ix. 8; Ezek. xxxv. 7). **For they laid the pleasant land desolate.** The pronoun refers to the disobedient Jews, their sin being the cause of the desolation; or the verb may be taken impersonally, "So the pleasant land was made desolate." "The pleasant land" is literally, "the land of desire." Septuagint, γῆν ἐκλεκτήν (Ps. cvi. 24; Jer. iii. 19).

HOMILETICS.

Vers. 1—7.—*Hypocrisy unmasked.* "And it came to pass in the fourth year of King Darius, that the word of the Lord came unto Zechariah," etc. In the latter half of the last chapter we were told of an embassy to Jerusalem, which met with acceptance and honour. In the present passage we read of another, which meets with just the opposite treatment. The question asked by these messengers is not answered at all in this chapter. Not only so, those who ask it are indirectly rebuked for so doing. Why this remarkable difference of behaviour? Not in the *surface*, but in the *sub-surface*, view of affairs. So we will now try to point out—

I. THE SURFACE VIEW. At first sight what can appear more thoroughly deserving of approval than the inquiry here mentioned? This so, whether we consider: 1. *Its object.* What the men desire, apparently, is simply to know God's will—a desire which we find, in so many other cases, so very warmly approved (Acts ii. 37; ix. 6; xvi. 30; Luke iii. 10, etc.). 2. *Or its subject.* They would learn God's will as to "fasting," *i.e.* as to one department of the proper worship of God. What, apparently, more proper and right (comp. Ps. cxvi. 12; Micah vi. 6, 7; and contrast Numb. xv. 30; 1 Kings xii. 33; Col. ii. 18, 23)? 3. *Or its method;* viz. that of going to God's "house" (vers. 2, 3), and consulting his regular teachers, the "priests" (Lev. x. 11; 2 Chron. xv. 3; Hag. ii. 11; Mal. ii. 7), and his occasional and extraordinary teachers, the "prophets" (Jer. vii. 25; xxv. 4, etc.). 4. *Or its special occasion.* Seventy years, as predicted (Jer. xxv. 11), having now elapsed (viz. from B.C. 588 to 518) since that burning of the temple on the tenth day of the fifth month (Jer. lii. 13), in commemoration of which this fast of the fifth month had been instituted; and the renewed building of the temple, commenced in the second of Darius (Ezra iv. 24; v. 1, 2), having now (in this fourth of Darius, see ver. 1) so far advanced that the priests could live in it (see ver. 3), what more natural and apparently opportune than this inquiry about the propriety of observing this fast any longer (comp. Dan. ix. 1—3)?　5. *Or its special channel*, so to describe it.　How peculiarly befitting, to all appearance, the particular messengers sent! And that, whether we understand them (with some) to be persons sent by the inhabitants of "Bethel" (translated in our version, "the house of God," in ver. 2), a place so long and notoriously connected with idol-worship and the contempt of God's will (see 1 Kings xii. 32, 33; 2 Kings xvii. 28; Amos vii. 13); or whether, with others, judging from the Assyrian turn of their names (comp. 2 Kings xix. 37; and contrast ch. vi. 10), we suppose that they were Jews of the Captivity come up in person to make inquiry. In either case, such an inquiry, from such persons, seems eminently deserving of praise—at first sight.

II. THE SUB-SURFACE VIEW.　Nevertheless, in all this same "fasting," about which they inquire, this Scripture, when further examined, shows us that their conduct had been only deserving of blame.　This true, inasmuch as their conduct, during all that time, had been : 1. *Never wholly in the right.*　"Fasting" is only valuable as an outward sign of repentance; but their repentance, during all "those seventy years" (ver. 5), had never been true repentance, *i.e.* "repentance toward God."　Note, "Did ye at all fast unto me, even to me?" in ver. 5; and comp. Acts xx. 21; also the "sorrow κατὰ Θεόν" of 2 Cor. vii. 10, and the sorrow of David (Ps. li. 4) and the prodigal (Luke xv. 18), for the *evil* of sin, with the sorrow of Saul (1 Sam. xv. 30), apparently for its *consequences* alone.　2. *Always eminently in the wrong.*　Their solicitude, when engaged in their fastings, had not really been about God's pleasure and will; but it had been, and that most thoroughly, concerning their own; as much so, in fact, as when, at other times, they had eaten and drunk (ver. 6).　So completely, we see, in some cases, may mere abstinence from food be one of the "sins of the flesh" (comp Matt. vi. 16 and Isa. lviii. 3—7).　3. *Always inexcusably in the wrong.*　(1) *For having sinned thus against light.*　Long ago and often (see beginning of ver. 7) God's "prophets" had warned their fathers against thus drawing nigh unto him with their lips only (Isa. xxix. 13); and they had the remembrance and the record of this as their guide. (2) *For having sinned thus against experience.*　When these prophets had so spoken all was happy and bright, "Jerusalem" and the "cities round about" "inhabited" fully and in "prosperity," as also at that time, even those comparatively barren and country districts, "the south and the plain."　How awfully different their condition during "those seventy years"! How loudly, therefore, their own experience, and, as it were, their own land itself, had admonished them! And yet how entirely in vain !

May not all this illustrate, further, for our own admonition? 1. *The exceeding deceitfulness of formalism.*　All God's people (they speak as one man in ver. 3), and even, apparently, all God's ministers (the "priests," ver. 5), being deceived thereby, in this instance, to so great an extent, and for so many years, and in such circumstances of trial (comp. John xviii. 28 with xii. 10, "Lazarus *also*;" and Matt. xxvii. 4, 6). 2. *The exceeding penetration of God's Word.*　Unmasking thus, and making plain, and bringing to light all these deeply hidden deceits (comp. Heb. iv. 12, 13; also Luke xii. 2; Matt. ix. 4; 1 Cor. xiv. 25; Ps. l. 21, end; Ps. xc. 8).　How easy, in short, to deceive ourselves! How impossible to mock God (see Gal. vi. 7) !

Vers. 8—14.—*Hypocrisy warned.*　"And the word of the Lord came unto Zechariah, saying, Thus speaketh the Lord of hosts," etc.　The severe rebuke of the previous verses seems followed up in these verses by a very solemn yet very merciful warning, intended apparently to save the Jews from the various evils to which their hypocrisy had exposed them.　The language of God to their fathers, as referred to in ver. 7, appears still (note "thus *spake*," according to Pusey, Wardlaw, and others, in ver. 9) the theme of discourse.　And three successive points of importance, in connection with this language and its consequences, seem described to us here, viz. (1) a most *gracious purpose*; (2) a *stubborn refusal*; and (3) a *terrible doom.*

I. A MOST GRACIOUS PURPOSE.　What was it really that, by the "former prophets" (ver. 7), God had demanded of men? Under one aspect, as before shown by us, "repentance towards" himself. Under another aspect, so it seems here explained in vers. 9, 10, only what was good for themselves. How many blessings, *e.g.*, if God's laws had been really kept, and their fathers had only done as God asked of them, would have been found in the land! We may describe them as being chiefly four, viz. (1) perfect and universal *fairness* of dealing; (2) perfect kindness and *generosity* of dealing, as in brotherly love; (3) *special and peculiar kindness* of dealing to those ("the stranger," etc.) needing it most; and (4) total absence, in any cause whatever, of *ill will in the heart.* Could anything have been better? So true is it (Rom. vii. 12), that "the Law" is not only "holy," or worthy of God; and "just," or fair in its require-ments; but "good," also, or kind in its object, and intended, in fact, for men's highest benefit (compare, as a partial illustration, Mark ii. 27; and, in one sense also, Ezek. xx. 11, 13, 21; and especially Deut. vi. 24; x. 12, 13).

II. A STUBBORN REFUSAL. How had this message of goodness and mercy been received in the days referred to? 1. *With every outward sign of dishonour.* Such as (1) marked indifference, "refusing to hearken" (comp. Isa. xxx. 9—11); (2) open aversion, "pulling away the shoulder," as though saying, when special effort was made to gain their attention, "I am giving attention to something else;" and (3) utter con-tempt, "stopping their ears," as much as to say, "I had rather hear nothing than listen to you" (comp. Acts xxii. 22). 2. *With every inward feeling of rebellion to correspond.* This shown: (1) By their dread of its power. Notwithstanding their extreme unwillingness to hear, something of the meaning of God's gracious message would reach their understandings. Even if so, if they could help it, it should not penetrate to their consciences. So well were they aware of its power (see the words in ver. 12, "As an adamant stone, *lest* [in this sense] they should hear"). What a testimony on their part! What a precaution! (2) By their defiance of its authority. How many, as here implied, its claims to reverential submission! As being essentially a "law," or command; as containing "words" of command from the "Lord of hosts" himself, whom so many obeyed; as being his command in so express a manner, because delivered by messengers known to be appointed and inspired by himself (see, again, ver. 12). All this in addition to the fact above noted of its being a message for "good." Yet to all this their unconquerable, *i.e.* "adamant," obstinacy refused to submit.

III. A TERRIBLE DOOM. When such condescending goodness met with so perverse a return, what could ultimately ensue but "great wrath"? According to the moral laws of God's spiritual kingdom, which are as fixed, could we only believe it, as the natural laws of his physical creation, here was a clear case of cause and effect. This is declared to us: 1. *By the nature of the judgments.* See how they correspond to the offence. Israel had refused to hear God. So God now refuses to hear them (ver. 13; Mark iv. 24; Gal. vi. 7, 8; Hos. viii. 7). 2. *By the sentence of the Judge.* God speaks of all that afterwards came upon them as being inflicted (1) by his authority ("*I* scattered them," etc.; (2) on their account ("The land was made desolate *after* them"); and even, (3) in a certain sense, by the instrumentality of their transgressions ("*They* laid the land desolate;" comp. also Hos. xiii. 9; Mal. i. 9).

From this review of that portion of the past history of Israel here referred to, we get a sample of many other histories as they will appear at the last. This is true: 1. *Of many individual lives.* Lifelong entreaty, lifelong forbearance, lifelong rebellion, followed up by more than lifelong death, impossible as that sounds,—such will be in brief, and yet in full also, the history of many a soul. 2. *Of many individual communities;* both nations and Churches. How many cities, kingdoms, empires, and races, once great on the earth, might have all that is really essential to their history told in a precisely similar way (see, for one example, Gen. xiii. 13; xviii. 20, 21; xix. 9; 2 Pet. ii. 8; Jude 7)! See a succession of examples in the succession of world-empires in Daniel. See, also, as to religious communities, similar lessons taught by comparison of past and present condition of some of the Apocalyptic Churches. 3. *Of the whole world of the ungodly.* What a long history of gracious messages and of stubborn refusals will be found at the end of the whole completed history of the race of Adam and Eve (Rom. iii. 19, end; Jude 14, 15)!

HOMILIES BY VARIOUS AUTHORS.

Vers. 1—14.—*God and men.* I. THE UNITY OF GOD'S PURPOSE. God's thoughts do not vary, though he varies his methods. His end for nations and individuals is always the same—advancement, not merely in knowledge and culture, but in moral goodness.

II. THE MERCIFULNESS OF GOD'S WARNINGS. At no time hath God left himself without witnesses. By word and providence and in countless ways his warnings come. We see this in the past. (Ver. 7, "former prophets.") So in the present. Every mercy has a voice calling for thankfulness. Every chastisement has a summons to moral thoughtfulness and prayer. There is no excuse for continuance in sin.

III. THE RIGHTEOUSNESS OF GOD'S JUDGMENTS. Persistence in transgression must bring punishment. God's laws fulfil themselves. Every rejection of God's counsels, every refusal of God's offers, every slighting of God's love, works for evil, blinding, hardening, alienating, bringing dire ruin nearer. Judgment is God's strange work, but it must come. "The pleasant land laid desolate."—F.

Ver. 3.—*Shall we fast?* This question has been often asked down to our own day.

I. There are NATIONAL FASTS. These are rare, and only appointed under very solemn circumstances. In 1853, when cholera prevailed, the Presbytery of Edinburgh (Church of Scotland) suggested to Lord Palmerston, then Home Secretary, the propriety of ordering a national fast. His lordship, in his reply, recommended observance of natural laws rather than fasting. If this were attended to, all would be well. Otherwise pestilence would come, "*in spite of all the prayers and fastings of a united but inactive nation.*" He does not seem to have understood that the two things were quite compatible. Prayer and inaction is folly; but prayer and action is the highest wisdom. Surely there is something grand and beautiful in a whole nation bowed in humility and supplication before the Most High. (Buckle, vol. ii., has a characteristic notice of this, where he falls into the odd mistake that in Scotland "fasting" meant abstinence from food!)

II. Then there are CHURCH FASTS. These are only binding on the members of the several Churches that appoint them. In Scotland it has for long been customary to have *fast-days* in connection with the sacrament of the Lord's Supper; but as to this there is now a change. First their enforcement under penalties ceased; then the rigour of their observance was given up; then, from the necessities of modern life, and the knowledge that they were often the occasion of more evil than good, they have come in many cases to be discontinued. The question is one of Christian expediency, and requires to be dealt with both with wisdom and gentleness.

III. Besides these there is PRIVATE FASTING. As to this, no rule can be laid down (cf. Rom. xiv. 5, 6). But certain principles should be kept in view, such as that fasting has no virtue in itself; that what may be good for one Christian may not suit another; and that the great end of all such observances is spiritual good, "room to deny ourselves," a path "to bring us daily nearer God."—F.

Ver. 7.—*God's education of the people.* I. THE MORAL RELATIONSHIP OF THE PEOPLE. We are not absolutely separate existences. Related through birth, custom, association, and in other ways, we are connected, we are parts of one great whole. Hence in a large degree we are what others have made us. This must be taken into account as a factor in life.

II. THE CONTINUOUS SPIRITUAL EDUCATION OF THE PEOPLE. The past speaks to us as well as the present. We learn from the dead as well as the living. Above all, we have the Bible. It is God's book, for it is man's book. In it God speaks to us. Shows us what he was, and therefore what he is; what he has done, and therefore what he will do. Reveals the laws and principles of government, and thus makes manifest his will, and that the only way to reach our true destiny is by loving and doing his will.

III. THE GROWING RESPONSIBILITY OF THE PEOPLE. Increased knowledge. Larger experience. Grander opportunities. More may be learned, and therefore *ought* to be learned. Better lives may be lived, and therefore *ought* to be lived. Greater things may be done for the good of others and for the advancement of the cause and kingdom of the Lord, and therefore greater things *ought* to be done. Privilege is the measure of responsibility.—F.

Ver. 11.—*The history of ungodliness.* I. GERM. The question is—Self or God, our own will or God's will. Must be settled. Pressed by prophet after prophet. The answer shows the state of the heart. "Refused to hear."
II. PROGRESS. There is growth in evil, as in good Stages. "First the blade, then the ear, then the full corn in the ear." 1. *Wilful refusal.* "Pulled away the shoulder." Sinners will not submit to be guided by the higher will. Angry and fretted, they will not bow to God's yoke. 2. *Insolent rejection.* "Stopped their ears." Warnings and counsels are in vain. Pride rises to insolence. Refusal, to determined opposition and rebellion. 3. *Settled obduracy.* (Ver. 12.) This implies a steady process. The bad is more and more gaining the mastery. Every fresh victory brings the time nearer when the evil becomes "unconquerable" (Greek *adhámas*).
III. CONSUMMATION. (Ver. 13.) The end is come. 1. Ruined character. 2. Blasted life. 3. Hopeless future.

> "Oh! where is that mysterious bourne,
>   By which our path is crossed,
> Beyond which God himself hath **sworn**
>   That he who goes is lost?
>
> "How far may we go on in sin?
>   How long will God forbear?
> Where does hope end, and where **begin**
>   The confines of despair?
>
> "An answer from the skies is sent,
>   'Ye that from God depart,
> While it is called to-day, repent,
>   And harden not your heart.'"
>
> (Alexander.)

F.

Vers. 1—7.—*Religious beliefs that are right; religious services that are wrong.* "And it came to pass in the fourth year," etc. The preceding visions and symbolic actions recorded in this book occurred, we are informed, in the eighth month of the second year of King Darius. What is here recorded appears to have taken place in the ninth month of the fourth year of that king's reign—about two years later. The ninth month is here called Chisleu, and corresponds with the latter part of November and the first part of December. What was the prophet doing during these two years? We hear nothing of him, although we doubt not he was busy in his prophetic labours. Indeed, we are informed in the Book of Ezra (vi. 14) that the elders of the Jews builded, and they prospered through the prophecy of Haggai the prophet, and Zechariah the son of Iddo. Their prophetic words stimulated the activities and prompted the efforts of the builders. Here is an account of a commission composed of two men, called Sherezer and Regem-melech, distinguished personages, no doubt, still remaining in Babylon, sent as envoys to the house of God, that is, the temple at Jerusalem; and their work there was "to pray before the Lord, and to speak unto the priests." It would be well, perhaps, to give Dr. Henderson's translation of these two verses; and his translation agrees with that of Keil: "And it came to pass in the fourth year of Darius the king, that the word of Jehovah was communicated to Zechariah on the fourth day of the ninth month, which is Chislev, when Babel sent Sherezer Regemelech and his men to conciliate the regard of Jehovah." Looking at these words homiletically, they present two subjects for thought—*religious beliefs that are right*, and *religious services that are wrong.*
I. RELIGIOUS BELIEFS THAT ARE RIGHT. There are three beliefs implied in this commission entrusted to Sherezer. What are they? 1. *The efficacy of prayer.* They

were sent "to pray before the Lord," or, as in the margin, "to entreat the face of the Lord." That men can obtain by prayer to the Supreme Being what they could not obtain without it is one of the fundamental and distinctive faiths of humanity. Instead of being against the law of nature, it is one of the most uniform and settled laws of the moral world. Hence all men pray in some form or other. Prayer springs out of the sense of man's dependence upon his Creator; and that sense is built upon a fact beyond dispute or doubt. 2. *The intercession of saints.* These men were sent to pray before the Lord, not merely for themselves, but for others. Those who sent them proved thereby their faith in the power of man to intercede with God on behalf of his fellow. The intercession of saints is not a doctrine merely of the Roman Church; it is an instinctive belief in the human soul. Men not only implore the Deity for those whom they love, but others implore them to pray for them. How natural it is for a father to pray for his son! how natural, too, for a son to ask the father to pray for him, and friend to ask friend the same! Intercessory prayer is also a law of nature. 3. *The special ability of some men to solve the religious questions of others.* This Sherezer and Regemmelech appealed unto the "priests which were in the house of the Lord of hosts, and to the prophets, saying, Should I weep in the fifth month, separating myself, as I have done these so many years?" They wanted a certain religious question answered, and they appealed to a certain class of religious men who they believed had the power to do so. The question they asked was one of a selfish character, "Should I weep in the fifth month, separating myself, as I have done these so many years?" From this it would seem that for seventy years during the period of their captivity they had, on certain days, wept, fasted, and humbled themselves before the Lord. Now that many had returned to their own land, and others were returning, they wanted to know whether all this fasting and humiliation would still be required. Would that which was done in Babylon be required in Jerusalem? Would not they in their own land be exonerated from such humiliations of soul? This was the question, and this question they addressed to the priests and the prophets. And they did it because they believed they had the special qualification to solve such problems. This also is an instinctive belief. All communities of men in all times and lands have had a certain class amongst them whom they regarded as qualified more than all others to answer the religious questions of the soul. Hence the existence of priesthoods. It may be that Heaven has never left in any age or country, any race, tribe, or community without such men amongst them, men gifted above their fellows, with a broad moral vision, far-reaching intellect, and even prophetic genius. God teaches man by man.

II. RELIGIOUS SERVICES THAT ARE WRONG. The Jews had performed religious services; they had "fasted," they had "mourned in the fifth and seventh month, even those seventy years." This was right enough so far as the form is concerned; but in spirit the service was wrong, hence here is the reproof: "Then came the word of the Lord of hosts unto me, saying, Speak unto all the people of the land, and to the priests, saying, When ye fasted and mourned in the fifth and seventh month, even those seventy years, did ye at all fast unto me, even to me? And when ye did eat, and when ye did drink, did not ye eat for yourselves, and drink for yourselves?" 1. *Their services were selfish.* Mark the reproof: "Did ye at all fast unto me?" Was it not from selfish motives that ye did all this? Was it not with a view of obtaining release and securing my favour for yourselves? It is not because you have done the wrong thing against me. "It was not to me, even to me." The wrong you had done me was not thought of. Your outrages on morality, on the harmony of the universe, were not thought of at all. How much of the popular religion is of this type? The Almighty might well say to the conventional Churches of Christendom—You rear temples, you contribute property, you preach sermons, you offer prayers, you sing hymns; but it "is not unto me," it is not to *me*, it is all self. Whether you fast or feast in your religious services, it is all for "*yourselves*; it is not for me, not for me." *Religious services that are wrong,* where are they not? 2. *Selfish motives the Almighty had always denounced.* "Should ye not hear the words which the Lord hath cried by the former prophets, when Jerusalem was inhabited and in prosperity, and the cities thereof round about her, when men inhabited the south and the plain?" Always has the Lord Almighty denounced a selfish religion (see Isa. lxvi. 1—3; Jer. xxv. 3—7; Amos v. 21, 27, etc.).—D. T.

Vers. 8—14.—*Religion, genuine and spurious.* "And the Word of the Lord," etc. From this passage we infer three facts.

I. GENUINE RELIGION IS PHILANTHROPIC. (Isa. i. 16, 17; lviii. 6, 7; Matt. v. 44.) "Thus speaketh the Lord of hosts, saying, Execute true judgment, and show mercy and compassions every man to his brother," etc. Here is the ritual, the manifestation, the proof of genuine religion, and it is practical philanthropy. The sign and evidence of genuine religion is not in ceremonial observances or mere devotional exercises, but in the spirit of Christly morality, in doing good to men. St. John says, "We ought to lay down our lives for the brethren, and that because Christ laid down his life for us" (1 John iii. 16). Our love to God is to be shown in the same way as God has shown his love to us, by *self-sacrifice*, and self-sacrifice for our *brother man.* What is the true and healthy development of our love to God? The Church has too often acted as if its development was entirely *theological;* hence the battling for dogmas. It has too often acted as if its development was *devotional,* as if psalmody and prayers were the only true expression. It has too often acted as if *pros lytizing* was the true development of love to God; hence the zeal to make converts to its faith. The text teaches, however, that *self-sacrificing* benevolence is the true development. "Whoso hath this world's good," etc. The case supposed by the apostle is that of a brother in distress, looked on by a brother possessing this world's goods, and rendering no help. John intimates that a *man* seeing his brother in need, having the power to help, and not helping him, cannot be a Christian. He may be a great theologian, a great pietist, a great propagandist, but no *Christian.*

II. SPURIOUS RELIGION IS INHUMAN. "But they refused to hearken, and pulled away the shoulder, and stopped their ears, that they should not hear." This religious people not only neglected to do what they were commanded to do towards their fellow-men, but the very reverse of that, "they refused to hearken," etc. The most inhuman force in the world is a spurious religion. All history shows this. Read the history of martyrdom as given by Fox or any other authentic historian. A spurious religion murdered the Son of God himself. A more cruel class of men I know not than religious men whose religion is not that of power, love, or a sound mind. Such men are ever ready to damn those who agree not with their narrow dogmas. Their dogmas make them as heartless as fiends. It makes their "hearts as an adamantine stone."

III. THAT AN INHUMAN RELIGION HAS A TERRIBLE DOOM. "Therefore it is come to pass, that as he cried, and they would not hear; so they cried, and I would not hear, saith the Lord of hosts." God will make inquisition here for blood. "The cries of the persecuted and neglected enter into the ears of the Lord God of sabaoth." "Go to now, ye rich men, weep and howl for your miseries that shall come upon you. Your riches are corrupted, and your garments are moth-eaten. Your gold and silver is cankered; and the rust of them shall be a witness against you, and shall eat your flesh as it were fire. Ye have heaped treasure together for the last days. Behold, the hire of the labourers who have reaped down your fields, which is of you kept back by fraud, crieth; and the cries of them which have reaped are entered into the ears of the Lord of sabaoth. Ye have lived in pleasure on the earth, and been wanton; ye have nourished your hearts, as in a day of slaughter. Ye have condemned and killed the just; and he doth not resist you" (Jas. v. 1—6). Because the religion of the Jews had become inhuman, Jehovah permitted them to be carried away into Babylon. "I scattered them with a whirlwind among all the nations whom they knew not. Thus the land was desolate after them, that no man passed through nor returned: for they laid the pleasant land desolate." God will ever harden himself against those who have hardened themselves against their fellow-men. "With what measure ye mete, it shall be measured to you again."—D. T.

EXPOSITION.

CHAPTER VIII.

Vers. 1—8.—§ 4. *The Lord promises to show his love for Zion, to dwell among his people,* and to fill Jerusalem with a happy populace.

Ver. 1.—**Again**; rather, *and.* This chapter contains the second half of the Lord's answer concerning fasting, merging into prophecy.

Ver. 2.—**Thus saith the Lord of hosts.** This formula occurs ten times in this chapter, thus enforcing the truth that all the promises made to Zion come from the Lord himself, and are therefore sure to be fulfilled. **I was jealous;** *I am jealous,* as ch. i. 14 (where see note). **With great fury.** Against her enemies (ch. i. 15). "Zelus" is defined by Albertus Magnus: "amor boni cum indignatione contrarii." One side of God's love for Zion is shown in the punishment of her enemies. Knabenbauer likens this zeal or jealousy of God to the pillar of fire at the Exodus—light and protection to the Israelites, darkness and destruction to the Egyptians (Exod. xiv. 20).

Ver. 3.—**I am returned** (ch. i. 16); *I return.* When Jerusalem was taken and given over to the enemy, God seemed to have deserted her (Ezek. x. 18; xi. 23); but now the restoration of the exiles, the rebuilding of the temple, the voice of prophecy, showed that the Lord had returned, and that now he **will dwell in the midst of Jerusalem** (ch. ii. 10). **A city of truth;** *city of truth;* no longer full of lies and treachery and infidelity. God dwelling therein, it shall be "the faithful city" (Isa. i. 26), in which all that is true and real shall flourish (comp. ver. 16; Zeph. iii. 13). **The holy mountain.** The hill whereon the temple is built shall be called the holy mountain, because the Lord dwelt in the sanctuary. The prophecy in this and the following verses received a partial fulfilment in the days between Zerubbabel and Christ; but there is a further accomplishment in store.

Ver. 4.—**There shall yet old men . . . dwell** (*sit*), etc. A picture of happy security and plenty, in vivid contrast to the desolation deplored in Lam. ii.; v. In the days of the Maccabees it is noted, among other tokens of peace and prosperity, that "the ancient men sat all in the streets, communing together of good things" (1 Macc. xiv. 9). **For very age;** Hebrew, *for multitude of days.* People shall reach the utmost limits of human life. According to the old Law, length of days was the reward of obedience (Gen. xv. 15; Exod. xx. 12; Deut. iv. 40), and an early death was inflicted as a punishment of sin (Deut. xxviii. 20; Ps. liv. 23; lxxviii. 33). Such promises are made also in Messianic times (Isa. lxv. 20), though in a different sense.

Ver. 5.—**Full of boys and girls.** Jerusalem and the other cities had long been strangers to any such happy sight. Large increase of population is a blessing often promised in the latter days (Hos. i. 10; Micah ii. 12). Perowne remarks that our

Lord alludes to the games of children in the market-places as a familiar incident in his days (Matt. xi. 16, 17; comp. Jer. vi. 11).

Ver. 6.—**In these days;** rather, *in those days.* If what is promised in vers. 3—5 seems incredible to those who shall see the fulfilment. **The remnant.** The returned Jews and their posterity (Hag. i. 12—14). **Should it also be marvellous in mine eyes?** Certainly not. Nothing is impossible with God.

Ver. 7.—God promises to bring his dispersed people home again—a promise only yet partially fulfilled. **My people.** A title of honour (Hos. ii. 23). **From the east country, and from the west country.** Two regions are named, symbols of the whole world (comp. Ps. l. 1; Mal. i. 11). The return of the captives from Babylon was a prelude of the future restoration of the dispersed, when all Israel shall be saved (Rom. xi. 26). (See a similar promise, Isa. xliii. 5, 6; comp. John xi. 52.)

Ver. 8.—**In the midst of Jerusalem.** As the centre of worship (see ch. ii. 4, and note there). **In truth and in righteousness.** The words belong to both parts of the preceding clause: God will deal truly and righteously with them, but they must deal truly and righteously with him. If they are faithful to their obligations, God would be unto them all that he had promised to be.

Vers. 9—17.—§ 5. *The people are exhorted to be of good cheer, for God will henceforth give them his blessing, which, however, was conditional on their obedience.*

Ver. 9.—**Let your hands be strong** (comp. Hag. ii. 15—19). Be of good courage for the work before you (Judg. vii. 11; Isa. xxxv. 3; Ezek. xxii. 14). **By** (*from*) **the mouth of the prophets, which** were. Who came forward as prophets. These prophets, who prophesied after the foundations of the temple were laid, were Haggai and Zechariah; they are thus distinguished from the pre-exilian seers mentioned in ch. vii. 7. The same prophets who encouraged you in your work at first are they who have spoken to you words of promise in those days. **That the temple might be built;** Revised Version, *even the temple that it might be built.* This could not be predicated of the first foundation, which was followed by a long period of inaction (Ezra iv. 24), only terminated by the vigorous exhortations of the prophets, which led to a resumption of the work that might be called a second foundation of the temple.

Ver. 10.—The prophet reminds the people of the sad condition of affairs during the cessation of the good work, and how things began to improve directly they showed diligence and zeal. **There was no hire for man,** etc. Either the yield was so small that no labour of men or beasts was needed to gather it in, or the general poverty was so great that labourers could not get their wages nor the oxen their well-earned share of provender (Hag. i. 11; ii. 17, 18). **Neither was there any peace . . . because of the affliction;** rather, *because of the adversary.* They could not go about their usual occupations, or pass in safety from place to place, on account of the enemies that compassed them about (Ezra iv. 4). The rendering of the Authorized Version is supported by the Septuagint and Vulgate, but the word (*tsar*) is often used for the concrete, "adversary." So the Syriac here. **I set all men every one against his neighbour.** There were internal dissensions as well as outward opposition. God had allowed this for his own wise purposes.

Ver. 11.—**But now I will not be.** God's attitude towards the people had already changed in consequence of their diligence in the work of restoration. Perowne renders, "Now I am not." **The residue;** *the remnant;* the returned Jews (ver. 12; Hag. i. 12). **The former days.** In the time of their inactivity, when a curse rested upon them and upon their land. The curse was now removed, and a marked amelioration had set in (Hag. ii. 15—19).

Ver. 12.—**The seed shall be prosperous;** literally, (*there shall be*) *the seed of peace.* The crops sown shall be crops of peace, safe and secure, in contradistinction to the threat in Lev. xxvi. 16, that the seed should be sown in vain, for it should be devoured by an enemy (Knabenbauer). Or, more generally, all farming labours shall succeed and prosper. Jerome's paraphrase is, "There shall be universal peace and joy;" Septuagint, "But I will show forth peace." Another way of understanding the words which has found much favour with modern commentators is to take the clause in apposition with the words immediately following; thus: "The seed (*i.e.* growth) of peace, the vine, shall give its fruit." But there is no especial reason why the vine should be called "the seed of peace." It is not peculiar among fruit trees for requiring a time of peace for its cultivation. And the term "seed" is very inappropriate to the vine, which was not raised from seed, but from cuttings and layers. Perowne also points out that such a rendering destroys the balance of the three following clauses, which explain and expand the general statement that agriculture shall prosper. Dr. Alexander takes "the seed of peace" to be that from which peace springs; *i.e.* that peace should be radically established

in the land, and from this fact the results following should ensue. This affords a very good sense; but it is probably a metaphor quite unintended by the prophet. The Syriac reads differently, "The seed shall be safe." **The remnant** (see on ver. 11). **To possess;** *to inherit;* Septuagint, κατακληρονομήσω (Rev. xxi. 7). This promise recalls the blessings in the old Law (Lev. xxvi. 4, etc.; Deut. xxxiii. 28; Ps. lxvii. 6).

Ver. 13.—**As ye were a curse among the heathen.** As your fate was used as a formula of imprecation among the heathen; *e.g.* "May your fate be that of the Jews" (see examples of this, 2 Kings xxii. 19; Isa. lxv. 15; Jer. xxiv. 9; xxix. 22). The other way of taking the expression as meaning the object of curse (*i.e.* as the heathen once used to curse you), is not so suitable. **Judah . . . Israel.** This expression includes the twelve tribes, of all of which some members had returned, and continued to return, from the Captivity. They were united now and formed one nation (see note on ch. ix. 10). **So will I save you.** In as open and significant a manner will I show that I am delivering and favouring you. **Ye shall be a blessing.** This must be taken correspondingly to the former phrase, being a "curse;" ye shall be used as a formula for blessing; *e.g.* "God make thee as Ephraim and as Manasseh" (Gen. xlviii. 20; comp. Ruth iv. 11, 12). **Fear not** (Zeph. iii. 16). "If God be for us, who can be against us?" (Rom. viii. 31; comp. Numb. xiv. 9). **Let your hands be strong** (see note on ver. 9). The LXX. takes the paragraph differently and erroneously: "And it shall be that in like manner as ye were a curse among the nations, O house of Judah and house of Israel, so will I save you, and ye shall be a blessing," *i.e.* a cause of blessing, Ἦτε ἐν κατάρᾳ . . . ἔσεσθε ἐν εὐλογίᾳ.

Ver. 14.—**The ground of the promise is the will of God, who cannot deceive. As I thought to punish you;** *as I purposed to do evil to you;* i.e. to the nation whose continuity is thus intimated (comp. Hag. ii. 5; and for a similar contrast of punishment and blessing, see Jer. xxxi. 28). **I repented not.** God carried out the dread decree to the full (ch. i. 6; 2 Chron. xxxvi. 16). (For the phrase applied to God, comp. Numb. xxiii. 19; Jer. iv. 28; Jonah iii. 10, where see note.) Vulgate, "I pitied not."

Ver. 15.—**So again have I thought,** etc. The past chastisement, which happened as it was threatened, is a guarantee of the fulfilment of the promised blessing. But there is a condition to be observed, which is set forth in the two next verses. The LXX. has, "So have I ordered and purposed." In these special blessings Judah and Jerusalem alone were to share at the first; Israel's happy time (ver. 13) was to come later.

Ver. 16.—**These are the things.** To secure the fulfilment of the promise of good, they must do the will of God (ch. vii. 9, etc.). **Truth.** This was to be observed in all conversation and transactions with their neighbours. St. Paul quotes this injunction (Eph. iv. 25). **Execute the judgment of truth and peace**; literally, *judge ye truth and the judgment of peace.* So the Septuagint and Vulgate. Practise perfect equity in judgments, and so decide, according to truth and justice, as to secure peace and concord between the parties concerned. **In your gates.** Where the judges sat, and justice was administered (Deut. xvi. 18; xxi. 19; see note on Amos v. 10).

Ver. 17.—**Let none of you imagine** (see note on ch. vii. 10, where these words occur). **Love no false oath.** The prevalent sins at this time were not idolatry, but cheating and lying and injustice, vices learned in the land of exile, where they had turned their energies to traffic and commerce (see ch. v. 2—4, and note on ver. 3 there).

Vers. 18—23.—§ 6. Here follows the direct answer to the question originally proposed. *The fasts should be turned into joyful festivals, former calamities being forgotten. Then the change extending its influence, the heathen shall worship the God of Israel, and esteem it an honour to be received into fellowship with the Jewish nation.*

Ver. 19.—**The fast of the fourth** month, etc. (For the occasions of these fasts, see note on ch. vii. 3.) Jerome gives the later Jewish traditions concerning them. The fast of the seventh day of the fourth month commemorated the breaking of the two tables of the commandments by Moses, as well as the first breach in the walls of Jerusalem; that of the fifth month was observed in memory of the return of the spies sent to explore Canaan, and the consequent punishment of forty years' wandering in the wilderness, as well as of the burning of the temple by the Chaldeans; that in the tenth month was appointed because it was then that Ezekiel and the captive Jews received intelligence of the complete destruction of the temple. **Joy and gladness.** The observance of these fasts seems, by the Lord's answer, to have been neither enjoined nor forbidden; but as for their sins their festivals had been turned into mourning (Amos viii. 10), so now their fasts should be turned into joyful feasts, and former miseries should be forgotten in the presence of the blessings now showered upon them. **Therefore love the truth and peace.** This is the condition of the fulfilment of the promise (ver. 16; ch. vii. 9), here again forcibly impressed.

Ver. 20.—**It shall yet come to pass, that there shall come people;** *peoples.* The sight of the prosperity of the Jews shall induce surrounding nations to join in the worship of Jehovah. The same truth is expressed in Ps. cxxvi. 1—3. Perowne thinks that vers. 20, 21 refer to the tribes of Israel; but it seems unnatural to suppose the prophet asserting that it will *yet* happen that Israelites will seek the Lord, when there is no reason to think that they had not done so in some fashion, or that they would need the previous deliberation mentioned in the next verse. **Many cities.** So the LXX. and Vulgate. Others translate, "great, or, populous cities;" but this is less suitable.

Ver. 21.—**The inhabitants of one city shall go to another.** The LXX. has, "The inhabitants of five cities shall go unto one;" Vulgate, "The inhabitants go one to another." **Let us go speedily.** The Hebrew is an imperfect followed by an infinitive absolute—an idiom which implies combination, *Let us go on and on, continually.* So Pusey and Wright. **To pray before the Lord;** *to entreat the favour of the Lord* (see note on ch. vii. 2). The Gentiles would be moved, not only to make pilgrimages to the great annual festivals, but to seek to know the Lord, and how to worship him acceptably. **I will go also.** The inhabitants answer willingly to those who exhort them. It is quite unnatural to take the clause to mean (as Drake does), "I, Zechariah, will go too, to see the alteration in the mode of observing these fast-days."

Ver. 22.—**Many people** (*peoples*) **and strong nations.** This explains ver. 20 more fully. The Jews were not actuated by the missionary spirit, yet even before Christ's advent their religion had spread into all parts of the world, as we see from the catalogue of proselytes in Acts ii. 9—11. Intimations of the same fact are given in Ezra vi. 21; Esth. viii. 17. **To seek the Lord of hosts in Jerusalem;** *i.e.* to keep the solemn festivals observed there (comp. Isa. ii. 2; lxvi. 20—23; Micah iv. 1, and note there). The literal fulfilment of this prophecy is not to be looked for. It declares the future conversion of the Gentiles, and their being made one with Israel in the Church of Christ, "one fold under one Shepherd" (John x. 16).

Ver. 23.—**Ten men.** The number ten is used for a large indefinite number (comp. Gen. xxxi. 7; Lev. xxvi. 26; 1 Sam. i. 8). **Out of all languages** (*the languages*) **of the nations.** The diversity of languages shall not hinder the unity in the faith (comp. Isa. lxvi. 18; Rev. v. 9; vii. 9). **Shall take hold** of the skirt of him that is a Jew. Taking hold of the skirt implies a desire to share the privileges, and to be united in fellowship with (comp. Isa. iv. 1; Hag. ii. 12). St. Cyril considers the idea to be that the heathen shall cling to the Jews like children holding their fathers' dress for support and guidance. In "the man that is a Jew" St. Jerome discerns the Messiah. We will go with you. The picture presented to the mind by this verse is of a Jew journeying to Jerusalem from some distant country to keep a solemn festival, and a number of Gentiles clinging round him, asking permission to accompany him on his journey, because they have learned how good the Lord has been to his countrymen. But the ideal intended is much more than this. Salvation, indeed, is of the Jews; it began to be announced at Jerusalem; it was preached by the Jewish apostles; its founder was of the seed of David. But the true Israelites are not merely those who are of the natural posterity of Abraham, but all true Christians united under Christ, the Head. To their number all who would be saved must be joined (comp. Rom. iv. 11; Gal. iii. 7, 29; iv. 26, etc.).

HOMILETICS.

Vers. 1—8.—*Assurance of favour.* "Again the word of the Lord of hosts came to me." When warning is carried too far, it degenerates into threatening, and defeats its own end, producing despair instead of desire to escape. It is probably on this account that the solemn warning with which ch. vii. concludes gives place, in this chapter, to an animating series of encouragements and promises. (For somewhat similar transitions, see Heb. vi. 9; Isa. i. 18, etc.) In the verses now immediately before us, we have the beginning of these encouragements in a gracious *assurance of favour* to the remnant addressed by the prophet—an assurance conveyed to them in the way (1) of *emphatic repetition;* (2) of *graphic detail;* and (3) of *copious addition.*

I. EMPHATIC REPETITION. We have such repetition: 1. *Of the feelings of Jehovah towards the enemies of his Zion.* He had described himself before (ch. i. 14) as looking with an eye of displeasure and jealousy on the comparative "ease" of those foes. We have the same idea here (in ver. 2) in a still more forcible shape. "I was jealous for Zion with great fury." What can go beyond that? 2. *Of the purposes of Jehovah towards Zion herself.* On this point, also, God's former declaration (as found in ch. i. 16; ii. 10) is repeated and enforced. Not only would God again dwell in her, as prophesied before; but he would do so in such a manner as to make her a city of truth and holiness (ver. 3; and comp. Jer. xxxi. 23). All this as though to impress on his people how deliberately he had spoken. "I know what I said, and I mean it; I meant even more than I said." Such is the purport, such also the effect, of repetition like this. It is the natural language of steadfast purpose and conscious power to fulfil. Some persons think, accordingly, that the Epistle to the Ephesians is, virtually, such a repetition of that to the Colossians; and that the same holds good about the two Epistles to the Galatians and Romans.

II. GRAPHIC DETAIL. A previous prophecy (ch. ii. 4) had declared that Jerusalem should be inhabited as "towns without walls." Vers. 4 and 5 of the present chapter amplify this description under three principal ideas of great beauty and force. 1. *The idea of restoration and order.* Instead of being a city of waste places (compare sixty years afterwards, Neh. vii. 4, margin), we see it a city of populous "streets." This a wonderful touch. In a growing neighbourhood, where every new building is an event, we think most of the houses; in a completely built city, where there is no room for more buildings, we think most of the thoroughfares. 2. *The idea of safety and peace.* In times of warfare and tumult the first to succumb to violence and privation and terror are the aged. Streets, therefore, full of such (ver. 4) tell a twofold tale. Had there not been long peace in the past, these aged ones would not have survived. Were there not assured peace in the present, they would be in flight or concealment, and not in the streets. 3. *The idea of gladness and joy.* What happier sight on this earth than that described in ver. 5, in its comparative innocence, its abundant life, its musical utterances, its sweet faces and smiles, its graceful figures and movements, and the untold wealth of tender love and delighted looks, of which, in so many different homes, it gives proof! How all this detail would help men to realize what God's promises meant!

III. COPIOUS ADDITION. Did these visions seem very marvellous in the eyes of those to whom they were shown? Almost too good, in fact, to be true. Let such persons remember: 1. *That they were not too marvellous for God's power.* Often had God shown this kind of thing to be true (see Gen. xviii. 14; Jer. xxxii. 6—17, where note connection with the subject of restoration after Captivity, as in this instance). Let such persons understand of these promises: 2. *That they were far beneath God's power, in real fact.* Besides the remnant now brought back from the Captivity, he would bring others as well; not only those from the east, but those from the west (ver. 7); not only also (ver. 8) those who were his people already, but those who should become so in the fullest manner. Most probably much of the meaning of this would be concealed at that time from the prophet's understanding, but even to see such distant peaks "afar off" (Heb. xi. 13), and above the clouds, as it were, would be a great help on the road.

Two important lessons derivable to conclude. 1. *How to receive God's Word,* viz. as something not only *perfectly sure,* but also as something *wonderfully significant* and *overflowingly full.* It is with the secrets of grace as with those of nature; they can never be fully described, never altogether exhausted (see Eccles. iii. 11; viii. 17; Rom. xi. 33; Ps. xxxvi. 6; lxxvii. 19; and especially what is said in Job xi. 6, of the "secrets of wisdom," that they "are double to that which is"). 2. *How to set forth God's truth,* viz. as having both a sombre side and a bright one. Some are now preaching the gospel as though no such thing as repentance and judgment were mentioned in the Bible. Others confine themselves to repentance and judgment, as though there were no pardon or love. The right "proportion" (Rom. xii. 6) is shown us in our present passage combined with our last, and in such Scriptures as Ps. ci. 1; Rom. ii. 3—11, etc.

Vers. 9—17.—*Evidence of favour.* "Thus saith the Lord of hosts; Let your hands be strong," etc. In the beginning of these verses we have the opposite of that with which the previous verses concluded. There God confirmed his people in hoping for certain comparatively proximate blessings by assuring them of other and greater blessings which he designed afterwards to bestow. Here he confirms their hopes of what is more distant by pledging himself, as it were, to what is nearer. And this he does, we shall find, by drawing their attention (1) to the *mercies of the present;* and (2) to the *judgments of the past.*

I. THE MERCIES OF THE PRESENT. (Vers. 9—13.) Three things, especially, to be noted regarding these. 1. *How marked their character!* Great temporal mercies (ver. 12) are to be "now" (ver. 11)—abundant produce both in the open "ground" and cultivated enclosure, abundant blessing both in the soil itself and in that which came on it. These also all the more notable for coming after a widely different state of things, when, besides utter want (ver. 10), even for those most desirous to work, there was the common concomitant of such evils, viz. home dissension and strife; and that, wherever men were and whatever they did (see also Hag. ii. 16, 17, describing those same evil days). Who could avoid seeing and admiring so blessed a change? 2. *How striking their connection!* This happy change in their circumstances had taken place simultaneously with a corresponding change in their doings. From the very day when, as it were, for the second time they "laid the foundation" of God's house (ver. 9; Ezra iv. 24; v. 1, 2), God had begun to prosper thus the work of their hands. "Before" then (ver. 10) was trouble; but "now" (ver. 11) "I am not" (so some) as before. This, too, we find occurring (see Hag. i. 9—11; ii. 15—19) in accordance with express promise to this effect. 3. *How hopeful their bearing!* What was all this but plain evidence of a corresponding change, as it were, up above? And what might not be expected in future, such being the case? Even all promised in ver. 13, viz. that God's people should become as conspicuous now for their prosperity as formerly for their adversity (see also Jer. xxiv. 9; xxv. 18; xlii. 18, etc.). Much as when, from the very day on which a certain remedy is first employed, a sick man begins to improve. How easy then to believe the physician's assurance that he shall ultimately become better than ever!

II. THE JUDGMENTS OF THE PAST. This conviction further confirmed by going still further back in their history. For doing so shows: 1. *The steadfastness of God's purposes.* (Vers. 14, 15.) When the state of things is such as to call for judgment, ye have seen how the thought of such judgment is carried out by *me* (comp. 1 Sam. iii. 12). Learn from this, when things, as at present, are different, to rely on the same steadfastness on my part. 2. So to describe it, *the easiness of God's terms.* All that he asks on their part, in order to ensure on his part the full accomplishment of his purposes of mercy, was that (as in the case of their fathers) which would be for their good. See previous remarks on ch. vii. 9, 10; and note that we have here, in vers. 16, 17, the same thoughts and almost words as before, followed up, however, by two remarkable additions which seem specially meant for those times—the mention of false swearing (comp. ch. v. 4); and the implied assurance that, if these evils were persisted in, they would stop the current of God's love. "All these things, being hurtful to you, are hateful to me. Therefore, on every account, do them not."

Do we not see here, in conclusion: 1. *The unchangeableness of God's nature?* His dealings with men vary often and widely; his character, never. He is always true to his purpose; never, as men are, turned from it by caprice. The very variety of his dealings helps to demonstrate this. The very same sunshine which melts the ice hardens the clay. See this illustrated by the opposite effects of mercy and favour, hardening some (Isa. xxvi. 10; Eccles. viii. 11, etc.) and melting others (Ps. cxxx. 4; cxvi. 1, 12); also of affliction or chastisement, humiliating some (Luke xv. 17—19; 2 Chron. xxxiii. 12) and exasperating others (Gen. iv. 13; 2 Chron. xxviii. 22; Rev. ix. 20, 21). 2. *The certainty of God's promises?* Established, as we see, by God's very judgments, what wider base can they have (comp. Mal. iii. 6; also Ps. cxix. 52, " I remembered thy judgments of old, and comforted myself")? In this way, how many (apparently) unlikely things combine to preach Christ! Even the thunders of Sinai itself (see in one sense, Gal. iii. 24)! Other things, perhaps, more articulately as it were, but none with more power.

Vers. 18—23.—*Pre-eminent favour.* "And the word of the Lord of hosts came unto me, saying, Thus saith the Lord of hosts; The fast of the fourth month," etc. The close of this chapter gives an answer at length to the question asked in ch. vii. 3. And this answer consists—unlike the intervening stream of mingled denunciation, warning, and encouragement—of an almost unbroken outburst of promise and hope. The only apparent exception, in fact, is to be found in the six brief words of admonition at the close of ver. 19. How far this abundance of promise was fulfilled in the experience of the literal Israel of the past, how far in that of the spiritual Israel of Christ's Church, and how far it yet remains to be verified in the case of either or both,— has been debated often and much. Taken simply as they stand (which is clearly the first thing to do with them), we may consider the words as setting before us (1) the *future happiness of Judah;* (2) the *eminence of Jerusalem;* and (3) the *future dignity of the Jew.*

I. THE FUTURE HAPPINESS OF THE PEOPLE OF JUDAH. We shall appreciate this best by noting: 1. *Their recollections* at the time of this prophecy. For seventy years they had been accustomed, on four different annual occasions (see ver. 19), to fast and weep in remembrance of four different and dreadful stages in their overthrow as a nation, viz. in the tenth month, in remembrance of the opening of the siege of Jerusalem (Jer. lii. 4); in the fourth month, in remembrance of its capture (Jer. lii. 6); in the fifth, in remembrance of the burning of the temple (Jer. lii. 12—16); and in the seventh, in remembrance of the flight of the last residue of the "seed royal," and army, and prophets, and people from Palestine into Egypt (2 Kings xxv. 25, 26; Jer. xli. 1—xliii. 7). What a succession, what a continual aggravation, what a climax, of ill! 2. *Their experience.* They had now got so far (as we noted on ch. vii. 3) that a remnant of the people had returned, and the temple had begun to rise again, and its full restoration seemed only a work of time. This being so, that fifth-month day of humiliation, which was connected with the destruction of the temple, appeared no longer in place. Why should they longer commemorate a loss which they had already begun to efface? 3. *Their prospects.* Why, indeed, seeing the time was coming (ver. 19) when all the calamities commemorated by all the four Captivity fasts here referred to would be so completely outbalanced by corresponding blessings as to call for " cheerful feasts " rather than fasts? Only let them "love truth and peace," and all their losses would be forgotten, as in the case mentioned in Gen. xli. 51.

II. THE FUTURE EMINENCE OF JERUSALEM. This capital of Israel was to become "yet" (*i.e.*, however apparently unlikely, however apparently delayed) the religious capital of the world. As foretelling this, we have portrayed to us here: 1. *A great journey resolved on.* We see (1) many pilgrims assembling together, people who have "cities" and settled habitations ("inhabitants," *bis*) of their own, leaving those cities to visit this (comp. Heb. xi. 8—10, 14—16; xiii. 14). These pilgrims have (2) a common purpose, the inhabitants of one city inviting those of others, and volunteering themselves, to go up (Ps. cxxii. 1). They have also (3) a very earnest purpose: let us go "perseveringly" (Pusey), till we obtain what we seek—till our feet actually "stand" (Ps. cxxii. 2) where we desire. And they have, finally, (4) a most suitable and laudable purpose, even that of finding that presence of Jehovah which is to be found in that city alone; and are not seeking to reach it merely as a means of reaching something beyond. 2. *A great journey accomplished.* (Ver. 22.) The pilgrims have arrived at last. How mighty in number! "Many people shall come;" and come to seek God. How mighty also in significance! "Strong nations," who might have come as invaders, are here as suppliants before God (comp. Isa. lx. 3, 11, etc.; ii. 2—4; and the almost identical passage in Micah iv. 1—8, noting specially "the first dominion").

III. THE FUTURE DIGNITY OF THE JEW; *i.e.* of every individual enjoying, in those days, the natural citizenship of this illustrious city. Even when far from its walls, every such citizen (something as with those referred to in Acts xvi. 37, 38; xxii. 25—29, etc.) would be almost as much an object of homage as that city itself. Note what is here shown: 1. As to the *depth* of this homage, men being willing even to sink their own distinctive names in that of an Israelite, even as a woman does when she marries (comp. Ruth iii. 9; Isa. iv. 1; and contrast Pilate's indignant question in John xviii. 35). 2. *Its extent.* How *many* would do thus! viz. as many as ten to each Jew. How manifold, also, they would be! viz. out of "all languages" upon earth. Wherever their dwelling, whatever their diversities of race, training, customs, or speech, they would break through all to do this. 3. *Its foundation.* On the one hand, negatively. The homage paid to this "citizen" is *not* due to anything else but his being "a Jew." On the other hand, positively. This homage *is* paid to him because, as being such, he is believed to be peculiarly favoured of God (see end of ver. 23; and Numb. x. 29, 32; and contrast John iv. 20; see also end of ver. 22).

Two brief lessons to conclude. 1. *As to Israel now.* Let us ever think of God's ancient people with peculiar tenderness and respect. With tenderness, as is only proper, because of their having "seen better days." With respect, as is only becoming, considering their "great expectations." Whatever the exact application of the present prophecy, of this much we are sure (Rom. xi., *passim*). Who, indeed, may not be proud of the name mentioned in John i. 47? 2. *As to ourselves.* When will the Jews be thus honoured? When they truly seek God. So, therefore, of us, in our turn. We must never forget what it took Peter so much trouble to learn (Acts x. 34, 35).

HOMILIES BY VARIOUS AUTHORS.

Vers. 1—23.—*The future glory of the Church.* God speaks. Formerly stern rebuke; here sweet encouragement. Glowing picture of the good time coming.

I. GOD'S ABIDING LOVE TO HIS CHURCH. There are times when it would seem as if God had cast off his people. "Has God forgotten to be gracious?" Here is the answer. "I am jealous," etc. There is real, intense, and abiding attachment. Words of good cheer verified by facts. "I am returned," etc.

II. GOD'S GRACIOUS PURPOSE TO RESTORE HIS CHURCH. God's withdrawal was because of sin. But for a season. When we return to God, he will return to us. The very righteousness that obliges him to punish the impenitent, binds him to bless the penitent. The light will shine more and more. Times of revival are times of refreshment. The release of the captives pledges freedom to all. The return of the exiles prophesies of the final restoration.

III. GOD'S DELIGHT IN THE PROSPERITY OF HIS CHURCH. (Vers. 4—6.) Sweet and ravishing picture. So far fulfilled in the heroic times of the Maccabees (1 Macc. xiv.

8—12). Finds a grander fulfilment under the gospel, and will be perfectly fulfilled in the latter days.

IV. GOD'S FAITHFULNESS IN FULFILLING HIS PROMISES TO HIS CHURCH. There are things which seem too great to be possible—too good to be true. It may be so with man, but not with God. Eternal Wisdom cannot err. Absolute truth cannot alter. Omnipotent love cannot fail.—F.

Ver. 21.—*The soul's response to the gospel call.* "I will go also." This resolution is—

I. PERSONAL. "I." Religion is a thing between the soul and God. We are brought face to face with Christ in the gospel. Free and responsible. Must decide for ourselves.

II. RESULT OF CONVICTION. Many careless, some anxious, others almost persuaded. He who says, "I will go," has considered the question, and made up his mind on evidence which to him is satisfactory and convincing. "God is with you."

III. PROMPTLY AND THOROUGHLY CARRIED OUT. Not a mere thought, or impulse, or sentiment. Not the result of transitory feelings in times of excitement. But the expression outwardly of the change wrought within—of the heart won to Christ (Ps. cxix. 59, 60).

IV. FORTIFIED BY THE SYMPATHY AND APPROVAL OF ALL THE GOOD. We crave sympathy. Alliance with others gives courage, especially at the outset. The fellowship of the saints intensifies our best emotions and increases our purest joys.

V. LEADING TO A TRUE AND NOBLE LIFE.—F.

Ver. 23.—*Right representation.* Much depends on whether religion is rightly represented. In order to be attractive, the representation should be—

I. AGREEABLE TO REASON. An irrational religion cannot stand. Christ and his apostles constantly appeal to the moral judgment.

II. CONGRUOUS TO MAN'S NECESSITIES. There is a certain condition of things. The feeling and the cry of sin. The craving for reconciliation with God. Aspirations after holiness. The longing for confirmed tranquillity. The gospel must be shown to meet these needs.

III. IN HARMONY WITH THE SPIRIT OF CHRIST. Christ *is* the gospel. Those who witness for Christ must take heed that their witness is true. We behold in Christ utter truth, disinterested love, self-sacrificing earnestness, supreme sympathy with God.

IV. CONFIRMED BY THE CHARACTER AND LIFE OF ITS PROFESSORS. Conduct is the test of faith. The truth is identified with its advocates. To get others to believe, we must show that we believe ourselves. Life is better than doctrine. To do good, we must be good. Gehazi would never have won Naaman. Lot failed to move his sons-in-law. At home and abroad, Christianity is suffering from the faithlessness of Christians.

V. VERIFIED BY THE DIVINE EFFECTS WHICH IT PRODUCES. "God is with you" (cf. 1 Cor. xiv. 25). The gospel is its own best witness.—F.

Vers. 1—6.—*The blessed community of men yet to appear on the earth.* "Again the word of the Lord of hosts came to me, saying, Thus saith the Lord of hosts; I was jealous for Zion with great jealousy, and I was jealous for her with great fury," etc. This chapter does not commence a new subject, but continues the subject of the preceding one. The awful consequences of disregarding the will of Heaven had often been set forth by the prophets; and here, in this chapter, we have the assurance of the renewal of Divine favour to those who had returned from the Captivity. Without concerning ourselves with "times and seasons," it is clear that in this section of Scripture there is sketched a state of human society which has never yet existed on the earth, and which is not likely to appear for many centuries, if not millenniums hence. It is to this *community*, as herein pictured, that I desire to call the attention of my readers. The following facts are eminently noteworthy in relation to this *blessed community*.

I. HERE IS A COMMUNITY SPECIALLY INTERESTING TO THE GREAT GOD. "Again the word of the Lord of hosts came to me, saying, Thus saith the Lord of hosts; I was jealous for Zion with great jealousy, and I was jealous for her with great fury." The rendering of Dr. Henderson is worth citation : " And the word of Jehovah was communicated to me, saying, Thus saith Jehovah of hosts: I have been jealous for Zion with great zeal, yea, with great indignation have I been jealous for her." Jerusalem was a city in which God had chosen " to put his Name ; " there was his temple, there were the ark, the mercy-seat, and the memorials of his power and goodness in the history of Israel. This city had been destroyed by the Babylonian invaders, and during the whole period of its ruin Jehovah's hand was on it and its scattered and exiled people. During all this time, he says, "I was jealous for Zion with great jealousy." Instead of losing interest in his persecuted people, his feelings were intense concerning them. The Eternal is interested in all the works of his hand, interested in men even in their state of infidelity and rebellion; but *specially* interested in those whom he regards as his people. "To this man will I look, even to him that is poor and of a contrite spirit, and that trembleth at my word ; " " As a father pitieth his children, so the Lord pitieth them that fear him " (Isa. lvii. 15; Ps. ciii. 13).

II. HERE IS A COMMUNITY IN WHICH THE ALMIGHTY SPECIALLY RESIDES. "Thus saith the Lord ; I am returned unto Zion, and will dwell in the midst of Jerusalem." Jerusalem was in a very particular sense the dwelling-place of God (Exod. xxix. 45; Lev. xxvi. 12). There shone the symbol of his presence for centuries ; there he communed with his people from off the mercy-seat ; there lived and laboured the priests whom he had chosen to represent his will. But he dwells with his people in a more *real* and *vital* sense than this. Know ye not that " ye are the temple of the living God, as God hath said, I will dwell in them and walk in them, and I will be their God, and they shall be my people " ? There are two senses in which the Almighty dwells with good men. 1. *By his sympathy.* The loving mother dwells with her loved child ; yes, though separated by continents and seas. Jehovah's sympathies are with his children. 2. *By his presence.* The loving parent cannot always be personally with the loved child. In person they may be as far asunder as the poles. But God's presence is always with his people. "I will never leave thee, nor forsake thee." What a blessed community that must be, where God not only by his sympathies but by his presence dwells !

III. HERE IS A COMMUNITY DISTINGUISHED BY REALITY AND ELEVATION. 1. *Reality.* " And Jerusalem shall be called a city of truth." What is moral reality ? A *practical correspondence of the sympathies and life with eternal facts.* All whose thoughts, affections, and conduct are not in accord with the immutable moral laws of God, live in fiction, " walk in a vain show ; " and in this state most, if not all, communities are found. Alas! "THE CITY OF TRUTH" is not yet established, it is in a distant future. 2. *Elevation.* " And the mountain of the Lord of hosts the holy mountain." Where are the communities of men now found in a moral sense ? Down in the hazy, boggy, impure valleys of carnalities and falsehoods. But this community is up on the holy mountain ; it is in a place of high moral exaltation.

IV. HERE IS A COMMUNITY IN WHICH THE VERY AGED AND THE YOUNG LIVE IN SOCIAL ENJOYMENT. "Thus saith the Lord of hosts; There shall yet old men and old women dwell in the streets of Jerusalem, and every man with his staff in his hand for very age." The promise of long life was esteemed one of the greatest blessings in the Jewish theocracy (Exod. xx. 12; Deut. iv. 40); and in Isa. lxv. 20—22 this is promised as one of the signal blessings of Messianic times. Through bloody wars and general disregard of the laws of health, only an insignificant minority of the human race reach old age. Blessed is that community in which aged people abound, ripe in wisdom, goodness, and experience. But not only are the very aged in this community, but the young. "The streets of the city shall be full of boys and girls playing in the streets thereof." No sight is more refreshing, more morally inspiring to the true-hearted of all ages, even to the oldest, than a community of guileless, bright, and blithesome children. They are the latest emanations and revelations of Infinite Love to the world. They are to adults as flowers growing on the sides of the dry and dusty walks of life. Beautiful city this ! The children not filthy, half-starved, diseased arabs in crowded alleys, but bright creatures gambolling in the sunny streets.

V. HERE IS A COMMUNITY WHOSE ESTABLISHMENT, THOUGH INCREDIBLE TO MAN, IS CERTAIN TO GOD. " Thus saith the Lord of hosts; If it be marvellous in the eyes of the remnant of this people in these days, should it also be marvellous in mine eyes ? " As if the Almighty had said, "The creation of such a social state amongst you may appear an impossibility; but it is not so to me." Indeed, to create such a community as this on the earth, to make the whole globe a kind of Jerusalem, whose members shall be all holy and all happy, does appear so wonderful that even the most believing amongst us are often filled with doubt. How far off is such a state of things from the present! How imperceptibly slow does the Christly reformation proceed! How vast and mighty is the reign of error and wrong everywhere! and how difficult to believe that the time will come "when the kingdoms of this world shall become the kingdoms of our Lord and of his Christ"! Still, God has promised it; and what he has promised he is able to accomplish. Let us live and labour in faith. "Let us be steadfast, unmovable, always abounding in the work of the Lord, forasmuch as we know our labour is not in vain in the Lord."—D. T.

Vers. 7, 8.—*A twofold Divine restoration.* "Thus saith the Lord of hosts; Behold, I will save my people ['out of the land of the rising and the land of the setting' (Keil)] from the east country, and from the west country; and I will bring them, and they shall dwell in the midst of Jerusalem: and they shall be my people, and I will be their God, in truth and in righteousness." "The east and the west are here put as parts for the whole. The meaning is, 'I will deliver my people from regions whither they have been scattered.' Were there any reason to believe that the prophecy has respect to a restoration of the Jews yet future, there would be a singular propriety in the use of הַשֶּׁמֶשׁ מְבוֹא, 'the setting of the sun,' the Jews being now, for the most part, found in countries to the west of Jerusalem; but there is every reason to conclude that it has an exclusive reference to what was to take place soon after it was delivered. Vast numbers were carried away captive after the time of Alexander. Not fewer than a hundred thousand were carried by Ptolemy, and were settled in Alexandria and Cyrene" (Henderson). We shall use these words as suggesting a *twofold Divine restoration—temporal and spiritual.*

I. HERE IS A DIVINE TEMPORAL RESTORATION. "And I will bring them, and they shall dwell in the midst of Jerusalem." There is no sound reason for believing that the people here mentioned as those that were brought "from the east country and from the west" refer to the Jews in the far future, who, some suppose, will be restored to Jerusalem at last. I know of no authority for supposing that such a restoration will ever be effected. Nor does the passage point, I think, to the universal conversion of the Jews to Christianity in the last times. The reference is manifestly to those Jews who had been scattered abroad over various countries through the Babylonian Captivity and other disastrous causes. The point is that the restoration here promised is a *temporal* restoration to their own land and city. They had been exiled for many long years, and deeply did they deplore in a foreign land their expatriation. "By the rivers of Babylon we sat down," etc. The Almighty by Cyrus restored them. And he is constantly restoring his people to those temporal blessings they have lost. He restores often (1) to lost *health*; (2) to lost *property*; (3) to lost *social status*. He is the temporal Restorer of his people. In all their distresses he bids them look to him. "Call upon me in the day of trouble," etc.

II. HERE IS A DIVINE SPIRITUAL RESTORATION. "And they shall be my people, and I will be their God, in truth and in righteousness." This may mean, "I will become their God in good faith, or in reality, both on their side and mine." This is incomparably the most important restoration. In truth, all temporal restorations are of no permanent value without this. Observe: 1. *Man may lose his God.* He may be without "God in the world." Indeed, the millions are in this state. "They feel after him, if haply they may find him." 2. *The loss of God is the greatest loss.* A man separated from God is like a branch separated from the root, a river from the fountain, a planet from the sun. 3. *Restoration to God is the transcendent good.* He who can say, "The Lord is my Portion," possesseth all things. This restoration the Almighty is effecting now in the world. "He is in Christ reconciling the world unto himself."—D. T.

Vers. 9—15.—*A Divine call to a Divine work.* "Thus saith the Lord of hosts; Let your hands be strong, ye that hear in these days these words," etc. This paragraph is promising and cheerful; it is at once intended and suited to animate the builders of the temple and to stimulate them to resolute diligence in their work. It accords with that of Haggai (see Hag. i. 2—6; ii. 15—19) respecting Heaven's displeasure at their apathy in God's work and their eagerness in their own. In the words we have a *Divine call to a Divine work*. This call is urged on two considerations.

1. THE WRETCHEDNESS CONSEQUENT ON THE NEGLECT OF DUTY. "Thus saith the Lord of hosts; Let your hands be strong, ye that hear in these days these words by the mouth of the prophets, which were in the day that the foundation of the house of the Lord of hosts was laid, that the temple might be built." The "prophets" here referred to were undoubtedly Haggai and Zechariah (see Ezra v. 1, 2). The words which they addressed to the people were words of stimulation and encouragement to arise and rebuild the temple. The prophet here reminds them, as an inducement to set in earnest to the work, of the wretched condition of the people before the work began. "For before these days there was no hire for man, nor any hire for beast; neither was there any peace." That is, "before the days" the building commenced: They were then destitute of three elements essential to the well-being of any people. 1. *Industry*. "There was no hire for man, nor any hire for beast." The people were purposeless, lazy, and in a state of general lethargy and collapse. No great project inspired their interest, engrossed their intention, enlisted and marshalled their powers. The lack of industry is a curse to any people; it is an injury to health, as well as an obstruction to material and social progress. 2. *Peace*. "Neither was there any peace to him that went out or came in because of the affliction." The lack of earnest occupation naturally led to intestine broils and contentions. Nothing is more natural and more common than for people without employment to wrangle and dispute with one another. "Satan finds some mischief still for idle hands to do." Men who are full of business have no time to quarrel. 3. *Social unity*. "For I set all men every one against his neighbour." In biblical phraseology, the Almighty is frequently represented as doing that which he only permits. It would be unreasonable and even blasphemous to suppose that the God of love and peace exerts himself in any way to inspire his human creatures with hostility towards one another. But for reasons known to himself, and which we are bound to regard as wise and kind, he often allows these feelings to rise and express themselves in malignant recriminations and bloody wars. He originates good, and good only; and the evil which he permits, he overrules for good, and for good only. The general truth here taught is that, so long as duty is neglected by men, certain terrible evils must ensue. Hence the Divine call, "Thus saith the Lord of hosts; Let your hands be strong." Go with courage and energy into the work which is Divinely enjoined.

II. THE IMPROVEMENT WHICH ENSUES ON THE RESUMPTION OF DUTY. "But now I will not be unto the residue of this people as in the former days, saith the Lord of hosts. For the seed shall be prosperous," etc. This means, "But now, as you have resumed the work and rebuilt the temple, I will bless you." There are three blessings here promised. 1. *Temporal prosperity*. "For the seed shall be prosperous; the vine shall give her fruit, and the ground shall give her increase, and the heavens shall give their dew." Material nature is in the hands of God, and he can at any moment make it a curse or a blessing to man. Here he promises to make it a blessing. "Godliness is profitable unto all things," etc. 2. *Social usefulness*. "And it shall come to pass, that as ye were a curse among the heathen, O house of Judah, and house of Israel [comprehending the whole of the Jewish people[1]]; so will I save you, and ye shall be a blessing." The expression, "a curse among the heathen," may mean either that they were "cursed" *by* the heathen—objects of their denunciation—or that they were a curse *to* the heathen by the influence of their corrupt example. The latter seems to me the most likely idea. (See another explanation of the phrase in the Exposition.) The whole of the Jewish people, prior to the Captivity—with a few exceptions—were sunk into almost the lowest depths of moral corruption. But now it is promised that on the resumption of the great duty which Heaven had enjoined upon them, they should be a "blessing." So it ever is; the disobedient are a curse

---

[1] The "house of Israel," or ten tribes, as distinguished from the "house of Judah," shared in the happy fulfilment of the prophecy. It follows that they also returned to Palestine in the very days to which it refers (Henderson).

to any community; the obedient are evermore a blessing. "No man liveth to himself." We must either bless or curse our race. 3. *Divine favour.* "For thus saith the Lord of hosts; As I thought to punish you, when your fathers provoked me to wrath, saith the Lord of hosts, and I repented not: so again have I thought in these days to do well unto Jerusalem and to the house of Judah: fear ye not." Where there was Divine displeasure there would be Divine favour.

CONCLUSION.   On these two grounds men may always be urged to duty. Duty neglected brings misery on a people; duty resumed and faithfully prosecuted will utterly reverse the experience, turn the distressing into the joyous, the destitution into abundance, the discordant into the harmonious, the pernicious into the beneficent. Listen, then, to the voice of Heaven! "Thus saith the Lord of hosts; Let your hands be strong," etc.—D. T.

Vers. 16—23.—*A universal revival of genuine religion.* "These are the things that ye shall do; Speak ye every man the truth to his neighbour," etc. The whole of this paragraph may be taken as setting forth a *universal revival of genuine religion;* and, looking at it in this light, we have here two things: the *essential prerequisites;* and *the signal manifestations* of a universal revival of genuine religion.

I. THE ESSENTIAL PREREQUISITES. We discover in these verses four prerequisites or preparatories for a universal revival of genuine religion. 1. *There must be truthfulness in speech.* "These are the things which ye shall do; Speak ye every man the truth to his neighbour." Truthful speech is somewhat rare in all social circles, and in all departments of life. Fallacious statements abound in markets, senates, courts, and even families. Men are constantly deceiving one another by words. It is not so *easy* a matter to speak truthfully as one might think. To speak is easy enough; but to speak *truthfully* is often very difficult. Truthful speaking involves two things. (1) *Sincerity.* To speak a true thing insincerely is not to speak truthfully. A man must conscientiously believe that what he speaks is true, before he can be credited with veracity. There is more truthful speaking in the man who is telling a falsehood sincerely than there is in the man who is telling the truth in insincerity. (2) *Accuracy.* A man may speak with sincerity, and yet, from ignorance or mistake, may not speak according to fact; and unless he speaks according to fact, he can scarcely be said to speak truthfully. His speech unintentionally conveys falsehood. Hence, truthful speaking requires a strong sense of right,—and an adequate acquaintance with the subjects of the speech. Considerable effort is herein demanded—effort to discipline the conscience and to enlighten the judgment. But difficult as truth-speaking is, it is incumbent. "Every man should be swift to hear, but *slow to speak.*" 2. *There must be rectitude in conduct.* "Execute the judgment of truth and peace in your gates." In the East the courts of justice were held at the gates of the city; and perhaps the primary reference here is to the pronouncing of judgment on cases that were righteous and tended to peace. But rectitude of life is even more important and urgent than rectitude in judgment. In fact, scarcely can a man be morally qualified to sit as a judge in a court of justice who is not righteous in all his life and conduct; and yet, alas! it is not uncommon, even here in England, to have men of the lowest morality enthroned on the bench of justice. The great law of social life is, "Whatsoever ye would that men should do to you, do ye even so to them." 3. *There must be benevolence in feeling.* "Let none of you imagine evil in your hearts against his neighbour." We must not only keep our hands from evil, but we must watch over our hearts that they imagine not any evil against our neighbour. Mischief must be crushed in the embryo. "Charity thinketh no evil," and this charity must be cultivated. 4. *There must be abhorrence of falsehood.* "Love no false oath." If the oath is false, whether sworn by others or yourself, do not bind yourself to it, recoil from it with horror and abomination. Don't espouse a falsehood because it is sworn to; nay, repudiate it the more resolutely and indignantly. A strong reason is here assigned for a practical respect to all these injunctions; it is this—God abhors the opposites. "For all these are things that I hate, saith the Lord" (see Prov. vi. 19). Whatever God hates, we should hate.

II. THE SIGNAL MANIFESTATIONS. It is suggested that where these prerequisites are found, *i.e.* where a revival takes place, three things are manifest. 1. *An increased pleasure in religious ordinances.* "Thus saith the Lord of hosts; The fast of the fourth month, and the fast of the fifth, and the fast of the seventh, and the fast of the tenth, shall be to the house of Judah joy and gladness, and cheerful feasts." "The fast of the fourth month was on account of the taking of Jerusalem (Jer. xxxix. 2; lii. 5—7); that of the tenth was in commemoration of the commencement of the siege (Jer. lii. 4). The Jews are distinctly informed that these fasts should be turned into festivals of joy" (Henderson). The idea is, perhaps, that these fast-days are no longer seasons of mourning and penitential confession, but seasons of rejoicing. The first sign of a true revival of religion, in an individual or a community, is a new and happy interest in the ordinances of religion. 2. *A deep practical concern for the spiritual interests of the race.* "Thus saith the Lord of hosts; It shall yet come to pass, that there shall come people, and the inhabitants of many cities: and the inhabitants of one city shall go to another, saying, Let us go speedily to pray before the Lord, and to seek the Lord of hosts: I will go also." There will be a mutual excitation amongst the people to seek the one true and living God. Not only shall the inhabitants of one house go to another house, but the inhabitants of one city shall go to another city and say, "Let us go *speedily* to pray before the Lord." "*Speedily;*" there is no time to be lost; religion is for all, and for all an urgent duty. 3. *A universal desire to be identified with the people of God.* "In those days it shall come to pass, that ten men [a definite number for an indefinite multitude, indicating many rather than a few] shall take hold out of all languages of the nations, even shall take hold of the skirt of him that is a Jew." The Jew (the representative of the people of God), to him men shall go, they shall lay hold of the "skirt" of his garment—an expression conveying the idea either of anxious entreaty or conscious inferiority. Dr. Henderson says, in relation to this, "The prophecy is generally regarded as having respect to something yet future, and is often interpreted of the instrumentality of the Jews when converted in effecting the conversion of the world. I can find no such reference in the passage. 'Jerusalem' cannot be understood otherwise than literally, just as the term 'Jew' is to be so understood; but according to our Lord's doctrine respecting the new dispensation, that city is no longer the place where men are exclusively to worship the Father (John iv. 21—23). Incense and a pure offering are now presented to his Name in every place where his people assemble in the name of Jesus and with a view to his glory (Mal. i. 10, 11). It was otherwise before the advent of Christ. Jerusalem was the place which Jehovah had chosen to put his Name there; and thither all his true worshippers were expected to come to the great festivals, in whatever country they might reside. Thus the treasurer of Candace went all the way from Abyssinia (Acts viii. 27), and thus numbers from all parts of the Roman empire assembled in that city at the first Pentecost after our Saviour's resurrection. As the Hellenistic Jews and the Gentile proselytes travelled along in companies, they could not but excite the curiosity of the pagans through whose countries and cities they passed; and, celebrated as the metropolis of Judæa had become for the favours conferred upon it by some of the greatest monarchs of the times immediately gone by, and for the prosperity and warlike prowess of the Jewish people, it was impossible that it should not attract the attention of the surrounding nations to the character and claims of the God who was there adored, and who accorded such blessings to his worshippers. Men, for ages, had to go to the Jew for the true religion; the Gentiles in the apostolic times received it from the Jew; Christ and his apostles were Jews; but in these times the Jews have to come to the Gentiles for the true religion. Still, inasmuch as the Bible is a book of the Jews, Jewish histories, poetries, moralities, etc., and inasmuch as the grand Hero of the book was a Jew, it will, perhaps, ever be true that all nations shall take hold of the Jew in order to 'seek the Lord' with success."

CONCLUSION. When will this universal revival of religion take place? The signs are scarcely visible anywhere. We can only hasten it by attending to the prerequisites—truthfulness in speech, rectitude in conduct, benevolence in feeling, and abhorrence of falsehood.—D. T.

EXPOSITION.

CHAPTER IX.

Ver. 1—ch. xiv. 21.—Part III. The Future of the Powers of the World and of the Kingdom of God.

Ver. 1—ch. xi. 17.—A. The First Burden.

Vers. 1—8.—§ 1. *To prepare the land for Israel, and to prove God's care for his people, the neighbouring heathen shall be chastised, while Israel shall dwell in safety and independence.*

Ver. 1.—The burden (see note on Nah. i. 1). (On the circumstances connected with this prophecy, see Introduction, § I.) Destructive critics attribute ch. ix.—xi. to an anonymous prophet, whose utterances have been by mistake appended to the genuine work of Zechariah. We have given reasons for disputing this conclusion in the Introduction, § II. In (*upon*) the land of Hadrach. This expression is found nowhere else, and has occasioned great trouble to the commentators. But Assyrian inscriptions have cleared away the difficulty, and shown that it was the name of a city and district near Damascus, called in the monuments *Hatarakha* or *Hatarika* (see Schrader, 'Keilinschr. und das Alt. Test.,' p. 453). Expeditions against this place are mentioned as occurring in various years, *e.g.* B.C. 772, 765, 755 (see G. Smith, 'Assyrian Canon,' pp. 46, etc., 63; 'Records of the Past,' v. 46; Schrader, pp. 482, 484, etc., 2nd edit.). Damascus shall be the rest thereof. The "burden" shall light upon Damascus in wrath, and settle there (comp. Ezek. v. 13). This district should be the first to suffer. The LXX. has, Καὶ Δαμασκοῦ θυσία αὐτοῦ, "In the land of Sedrach and Damascus is his sacrifice." When the eyes of man, etc.; literally, *for to Jehovah (is, or will be) the eye of man and of all the tribes of Israel.* This gives the reason why Hadrach and Damascus are thus united. Because Jehovah has his eye on men and on Israel. Septuagint, "because the Lord looketh upon men" (comp. ch. iv. 10; and ver. 8 below). We may thus translate, "For to Jehovah is an eye over man," etc. He sees their evildoings and their oppression of Israel, and therefore the judgment falls upon them (comp. Jer. xxxii. 19). The Authorized Version intimates a conversion of the Gentiles, of which, however, the context says nothing; and there is no sense in saying that judgment shall fall upon a particular nation when, or because, the eyes of all men look to the Lord. Wright explains thus: When the wrath of God falls on Damascus, the eyes of the

heathen, as well as those of Israel, will look to the Lord, and they will marvel at the judgment and the close fulfilment of the prediction. This would be a very sound and probable exposition of the passage if the expression, "the eye of man being towards Jehovah," can mean that man marvels at his doings. All the tribes of Israel. God watches over them to guard them from evil (Deut. xi. 12; Ezra v. 5; Ps. xxxiii. 18).

Ver. 2.—And Hamath also shall border thereby; Revised Version, *and Hamath also which bordereth thereon.* Hamath, which is near unto Damascus, shall share in the Divine judgment. The Authorized Version probably means that Hamath shall be the companion of Damascus in punishment. (For Hamath, see note on Amos vi. 2.) These Syrian towns, as well as those below in Phœnicia and Philistia, shall be visited, because they were all once included in the territory promised to Israel (see Gen. xv. 18; Exod. xxiii. 31; Numb. xxxiv. 2—12; Deut. xi. 24; and comp. 2 Sam. viii. 6, etc.; 1 Kings iv. 21; viii. 65; 2 Kings xiv. 25). The judgment was inflicted by Alexander the Great after the battle of Issus, B.C. 333, when Damascus was betrayed into his hands and plundered of all its enormous treasures. Tyrus and Zidon. Tyre was taken after a siege of seven months, its walls were demolished, its houses burnt, ten thousand of its defenders were massacred, the women and children sold as slaves; and it never rose to greatness again. Zidon, originally the chief city of the country, had long been eclipsed by its daughter, Tyre: it submitted to Alexander without a struggle. Though it be very wise; or, *because she is very wise.* The pronoun refers to Tyre, the mention of Zidon being, as it were, parenthetical. In spite of, or because of, its boasted wisdom, Tyre should suffer heavy punishment. The wisdom of Tyre is spoken of in Ezek. xxviii. 3, 4. Wright, as the LXX., makes the clause refer to both cities, "though they be very wise." Vulgate, *Assumpserunt quippe sibi sapientiam valde.*

Ver. 3.—Tyrus (*Zor*) did build herself a strong hold (*mazor*). Wright endeavours to imitate the paronomasia, "Tyre built for herself a *tower.*" It was in her strong fortifications and her amassing of riches that Tyre showed her worldly wisdom. The city was built partly on the mainland, and partly on an island nearly half a mile distant, which rose abruptly out of the water in rocky precipices, and was surrounded with walls a hundred and fifty feet high. The insular portion of the town was that which so long mocked the Macedonian's utmost efforts, which were only successful when he had united the island to the mainland by erecting an enormous mole between them. This causeway has now become an isthmus of some half-mile in width, owing to accumulations of sand and *débris*. As the dust (comp. 2 Chron. ix. 27; Job xxvii. 16).

Ver. 4.—Will cast her out; *will take possession of her;* i.e. will conquer her by the hands of her enemies, as Josh. viii. 7; xvii. 12. Septuagint, κληρονομήσει, "will inherit;" Vulgate, *possidebit;* Ewald and Hitzig render, "will impoverish her." **Will smite her power in the sea.** "Power" here includes all that made Tyre proud and confident—her riches, her fleets, her trade, her fortifications. God declares that she shall be smitten there as she stood in the midst of the sea, which formed her bulwark, and which should soon dash over her ruins. The LXX. translates, "shall smite into the sea." Zechariah seems here to have a reminiscence of Ezek. xxvii. 32, "What city is like Tyrus, like the destroyed in the midst of the sea?" (comp. Ezek. xxvi. 4). With fire (comp. Amos i. 10). The city was burned by Alexander (see note on ver. 2. The siege is narrated by Arrian, ii. 15—24; Quint. Curt., iv. 2, etc.; Diod. Sic., xvii. 46, etc.).

Ver. 5.—**Ashkelon shall see it.** The ruin of so mighty a city as Tyre naturally filled neighbouring people with dismay. The prophet directs his attention to Philistia, and threatens its chief cities. The cities are enumerated in the same order as in Jer. xxv. 20. Gath is omitted, as in Amos i. 6—8 and Zeph. ii. 4. It seems never to have recovered its destruction by Uzziah (2 Chron. xxvi. 6). (For Ashkelon, Gaza, and Ekron, see note on Amos i. 6.) Her **expectation shall be ashamed.** The hope of aid from Tyre shall not be fulfilled. After the fall of Tyre, Alexander continued his march southwards towards Egypt, subduing the cities on his way. The siege of Gaza delayed him some months; and when it was taken, it shared the treatment of Tyre. Its governor, one Batis, a eunuch, was tied alive to the conqueror's chariot, and dragged round the walls, in cruel imitation of the fate of Hector. **The king shall perish from Gaza.** No particular king is meant; but the prediction says that henceforward no king should reign in Gaza. In contrast with the Eastern policy of allowing conquered nations to retain their own rulers as tributary sovereigns, Alexander always deposed or slew reigning monarchs, and consolidated his empire by replacing them with governors of his own. The various chastisements are meted out by the prophet among the various cities, though they equally apply to all.

Ver. 6.—**A bastard.** The word (*mamzer*) occurs in Deut. xxiii. 2 (3, Hebrew), where it may possibly mean "a stranger." It is generally considered to signify one whose birth has a blemish in it—one born of incest or adultery. In Deuteronomy the LXX. renders, ἐκ πόρνης, "one of harlot-birth;" here, ἀλλογενής, "foreigner." The Vulgate has *separator*, which is explained as meaning either the Lord, who as Judge divides the just from the unjust, or the Conqueror, who divides the spoil and assigns to captives their fate. Here it doubtless signifies "a bastard race" (as the Revised Version margin translates); a rabble of aliens shall inhabit Ashdod, which shall lose its own native population. The Targum explains it differently, considering that by the expression is meant that Ashdod shall be inhabited by Israelites, who are deemed "strangers" by the Philistines. **Ashdod** (see note on Amos i. 8). **The pride.** All in which they prided themselves. This sums up the prophecy against the several Philistine cities. Their very nationality shall be lost.

Ver. 7.—Personifying Philistia, the prophet declares that she shall cease to practise idolatry, and shall be incorporated in Israel. **I will take away his blood out of his mouth.** This refers to the practice of drinking the blood of sacrifices as an act of worship, or of eating the victims with the blood—a practice strictly forbidden to the Israelites (see Lev. iii. 17; vii. 26; xvii. 10, 12; and comp. Gen. ix. 4). **Abominations.** Sacrifices offered to idols, and afterwards eaten. The two clauses intimate the entire abolition of idolatry. Many see in this prediction a reference to the doings of the Maccabees; how, *e.g.*, Judas destroyed the altars and idols in Azotus (1 Macc. v. 68); Jonathan again took that city, and burned it and the neighbouring towns, and, besieging Ashkelon, was received with great honour by the inhabitants, and confirmed in the possession of this place and Ekron (1 Macc. x. 84, etc.); and Simon stormed Gaza (? Gazara, a place near Ashdod), cleansed the houses of idols, "put all uncleanness out of it, and placed such men there as would keep the Law" (1 Macc. xiii. 47, 48). But though such events partially fulfil the prophecy, the seer looks forward to a greater issue, and in these comparatively petty details beholds the working of the great principle that all nations shall be subdued to the faith. **He that remaineth, even he, shall be for our God;** better, *he too shall be left* (or, *a remnant) for our God.* The Philistine shall become a choice and elect remnant unto the God of the Israelites, and no longer regarded as alien and impure. **As a governor;** Septuagint, χιλίαρχος, "head over a thousand," which the word *alluph* means (ch. xii. 5, 6). It is used of the chiefs of Edom in Gen. xxxvi. 15, 16, etc., where the Authorized Version gives "dukes." The tribes of Israel were divided into thousands, consisting of families, each of which was held together by closer affinities than the mere tribal bond (see note on Micah v. 2). The meaning is that the Philistine shall be admitted into the commonwealth of Israel as one of her chiefs. **Ekron as a Jebusite.** "Ekron" is equivalent to "the Ekronite," who again stands in the place of all the Philistines. The Jebusites were the ancient possessors of Zion, who held their position till the days of David, and, when at last conquered by him (2 Sam. v. 6, etc.), were incorporated into his nation, and, as we may infer from Araunah's conduct, adopted his religion (2 Sam. xxiv. 22; 1 Chron. xxi. 23). God promises here that the Philistines, like the Jebusites, shall be absorbed into the Jewish Church. Mr. Drake ('Speaker's Commentary,' *in loc.*) curiously renders, "He shall be as Eleph (Josh. xviii. 28) in Judah, and Ekron as Jebusi," explaining that the cities of Philistia were to be incorporated into Judæa. The conquests of Alexander conduced to the conversion of the heathen and their reception into the Church of God; and the general principle enunciated by all the prophets was thus abundantly confirmed. But it is not easy to discover the exact historical fulfilment of the latter part of this prophecy, concerning the merging of the Philistines in the Jewish nation. Josephus ('Ant.,' xiii. 15. 4) tells us that, about B.C. 100, the Jews held most of their cities, destroying some whose inhabitants refused to become proselytes. In the time of our Lord, by reason of intermarriage and social intercourse, the Philistines had ceased to be regarded as a separate nation; and a little later Philistia, far from being considered as alien and hostile, under the form Palestine, gave its name to the whole country. Christianity, too, made rapid progress in this district, so that the psalmist's words received herein a fulfilment, "Behold Philistia, and Tyre, with Cush; this one was born there" (Ps. lxxxvii. 4).

Ver. 8.—While the heathen world suffers the judgment of God, he protects his own people. **I will encamp about** (*for the protection of*) **my house.** God's house, or family, is the kingdom and Church of Israel, as Hos. viii. 1. Septuagint, Ὑποστήσομαι τῷ οἴκῳ μου ἀνάστημα, "I will erect a fortification for my house." **Because of the army.** It may also be translated "against," or "from;" *i.e.* to defend it from the hostile army. Others, pointing differently, render, "as a garrison," or "rampart." **Because of** (*against*) **him that passeth by,** etc. Against

all hostile attacks. The phrase, "**him that passeth by and him that returneth**," is used of an enemy making incursions, or attacking at various points (see note on ch. vii. 14). The Vulgate gives the whole clause thus: *Circumdabo domum meam ex his, qui militant mihi euntes et revertentes,* "I will defend my house with a guard chosen from those who serve me and do my will," *i.e.* angels. But this seems far from the signification of the Hebrew. Pusey restricts the meaning to the proceedings of Alexander, who passed by Judæa on his way to Egypt, and returned by the same route, without doing any injury to Jerusalem. Here comes in the Talmudic story related by Josephus ('Ant.,' xi. 8). The Jews "repaid the protection of Persia with a devoted loyalty, which prompted them to refuse the demand of submission made by Alexander during the siege of Tyre. He marched to chastise them after the fall of Gaza, and the beautiful city had already risen before his view on the hill of Zion, when he found the high priest Jaddua waiting his approach at the watch-station of Sapha, clad in his robes of gold and purple, and followed by a train of priests and citizens in pure white. The conqueror bowed in reverence to the Holy Name upon the high priest's frontlet; and, being asked by Parmenio the reason of his conduct, said that in a dream at Dium, he had seen the God of Jaddua, who encouraged him to pass over into Asia, and promised him success. Then entering Jerusalem, he offered sacrifice in the temple, heard the prophecy of Daniel about himself, and granted certain privileges to all the Jews throughout his empire. The desire to honour a shrine so celebrated as the Jewish temple is quite in accordance with the conduct of Alexander at Ilium and Ephesus, Gordium and Tyre. The privileges he is said to have conferred upon the Jews were enjoyed under his successors, and some minor matters have been adduced in confirmation of the story. On the other hand, the classical writers are entirely silent on the subject, and the details of Josephus involve grave historical inconsistencies. It seems not an unreasonable conjecture that the story is an embellishment of some incident that occurred when the high priest came to Gaza to tender the submission of the Jews. But we must not dismiss it without a remark on the vast influence which the conquests of Alexander had in bringing the Jews into closer relations with the rest of Asia, and so preparing them to fulfil their ultimate destiny as Christians" (P. Smith, 'History of the World,' i. 60, etc.). Oppressor. The word is used for "taskmaster" in Exod. iii. 7. Septuagint, ἐξελαύνων, "one who drives away;" Vulgate, *exactor.* This latter rendering would imply that Israel would no longer have to pay tribute to foreign nations, but should henceforward be independent. For now have I seen with mine eyes. It is as though, during Israel's calamities, God had not looked upon her; but now he notices her condition, and interposes for her succour (comp. Exod. ii. 25; iii. 7, 9; Acts vii. 34). This is done by sending the personage mentioned in the following section.

Vers. 9, 10.—§ 2. *Then shall the righteous King come to Zion in lowly fashion, and inaugurate a kingdom of peace.*

Ver. 9.—The prophet invites Jerusalem to rejoice at the coming of the promised salvation in the Person of her King; no mighty earthly potentate and conqueror, like Alexander the Great, but one of different fashion (comp. Zeph. iii. 14). Thy King cometh unto thee. St. Matthew (xxi. 5) and St. John (xii. 15) see a fulfilment of this prophecy in Christ's triumphal entry into Jerusalem on the first day of the week in which he was crucified. All attempts to disprove the Messianic import of this passage have been unavailing. Even critics who refer this part of Zechariah (ch. ix.—xi.) to an unknown author writing in the time of Hezekiah, allow that it is replete with Messianic ideas, and can be applied to no hero of Jewish story or event of Jewish history. There is no other "King" of Israel to whom it can refer. Our blessed Lord himself, by his abnormal actions on Palm Sunday, plainly assumed the part of the predicted King, and meant the people to recognize in him the promised Messiah (see the full discussion of the subject in Dr. Pusey's notes, pp. 556, etc.). Thy King. A king of thine own race, no stranger, but one predestined for thee. He who was foretold by all the prophets, who was to occupy the throne of David, and reign for ever (Ps. ii. 6; xlv. 1, 6, 7; Isa. xxxii. 1). Unto thee. For thy good, to bless thee (Isa. ix. 6). Just. Righteous in character and in practice, ruling in equity (Ps. lxxii. 1—4, 7; Isa. xi. 2—4). Having salvation; Septuagint, σώζων, "saving." Vulgate, salvator; so the Syriac and Chaldee. The genius of the language requires the participle to be taken passively, as it is in two other passages where it occurs (Deut. xxxiii. 29; Ps. xxxiii. 16). The context has seemed to some to demand that it be understood in an active sense, thus contrasting him who came to save with the haughty Grecian conqueror, whose progress was marked by bloodshed. But the usual meaning of the word affords a satisfactory sense. The King who comes is "saved," endowed with salvation, either as being protected and

upheld by God (Ps. xviii. 50; cx. 1, 2, 5; Isa. xlii. 1; xlix. 8), or as being victorious and so able to aid his people. In this latter view, the active sense is included in the passive. His own deliverance is a sure sign of the deliverance of his people. Lowly; Septuagint, πραΰς, "meek;" Vulgate, pauper—meek and lowly, as Christ himself says (Matt. xi. 29), far removed from warlike pomp and worldly greatness. The word is also rendered "afflicted," and would then be in accordance with the description in Isa. lii. 13—liii. 5; Ps. xxii. 6. Riding upon an ass. In illustration of his poor or afflicted estate; it is this, and not merely the peacefulness of his reign, that is meant by this symbolical action, as we see by the following clause, where the youthfulness of the animal is the point enforced. And (even, and that) upon a colt the foal of an ass; such as she-asses bear, and one not trained; as the evangelist says, "whereon never man sat." Christ sat upon the foal. In old times judges and men of distinction rode upon asses (Gen. xxii. 3; Judg. v. 10; x. 4); but from Solomon's days the horse had been used, not only in war, but on all state occasions (Jer. xvii. 25); and the number of horses brought back on the return from Babylon is specially mentioned (Ezra ii. 66). So to predicate of a King that he would come to his capital riding, not on a war-horse, but on a young, unbroken ass, showed at once that he himself was not to be considered a victorious general or a worldly potentate, and that his kingdom was not to be won or maintained by carnal arms. This is signified more fully in the following verse, which describes the character and extent of Messiah's kingdom.

Ver. 10.—I will cut off the chariot. All the apparatus of war will be removed, Messiah's rule being not established by physical force, or maintained by military defences. The Jews seem to have used war-chariots from the time of Solomon, who, we are told, had fourteen hundred of them (1 Kings x. 26). Ephraim . . . Jerusalem. The former term denotes the kingdom of the ten tribes; the latter, that of Judah; the two together comprising the whole Israelite nation. From the use of these terms here it cannot be concluded that the author wrote at a time when the two kingdoms existed side by side. In the first place, the description of the whole people is given poetically, and must not be taken to have more significance than is intended; and secondly, in ch. viii. 13, which is confessedly post-exilian, the "house of Judah," and the "house of Israel" are distinguished. Dr. Cheyne notes, too, that in Ezekiel (xxxvii. 15—28), who prophesied during the Captivity, the ten tribes are distinguished by the name of

Ephraim, and pertinently asks why such term may not be also used by one who wrote after the Captivity. **The battle bow** stands **for all weapons of war.** That Messiah's kingdom should be peaceful and peace-bringing, see the prophecies (Ps. lxxii. 7; Isa. ii. 4; ix. 4—7; comp. Micah v. 10, 11). **He shall speak peace unto the heathen.** He will extend this peace to all the world, teaching the heathen to receive his spiritual rule, to compose their differences, to lay aside their arms, and live as one united family (comp. Eph. ii. 17). **From sea even to sea.** Geographically, the phrase means from the Dead Sea on the east to the Mediterranean on the west, as in Exod. xxiii. 31 and Ps. lxxii. 8, from whence our passage is derived. Poetically, an Eastern sea, perhaps, is supposed to bound that side of the earth. **From the river** even **to the ends of the earth.** From the Euphrates unto the utmost limits of the world (see Amos viii. 12; Micah vii. 12). Both expressions obtain an unlimited signifiance, and show the universal extent of Messiah's kingdom; for in him, according to the promise made to Abraham, all the families of the earth should be blessed.

Vers. 11—17.—§ 3. *All Israel, united into one people, shall wage successful war against adversaries, and attain to high glory, and increase largely in numbers.*

Ver. 11.—**As for thee also.** The prophet addresses the daughter of Zion, the covenant people (comp. vers. 10, 13). "Also" is inserted to intimate that this deliverance is given in addition to the blessings promised in the two preceding verses. All who are living far from their native Zion are invited to come to her and partake of her good things. By (*because of*) **the blood of thy covenant.** The covenant is that made at Sinai, sealed and ratified by blood (Exod. xxiv. 4—8), which still held good, and was the pledge to the nation of deliverance and help. This was a token of that everlasting covenant sealed with the blood of Christ, by which God's people are delivered from the bondage of sin (comp. Matt. xxvi. 28; Heb. ix. 15; x. 14—23; xiii. 20). **I have sent forth;** *I send forth*—the prophetic perfect. The Greek and Latin Versions render, "thou sentest forth," not so correctly. **Thy prisoners.** Those members of the nation who were still oppressed or captives in foreign lands, as Babylon and Egypt (comp. Obad. 20; Joel iii. 6, etc.; Amos i. 6, 9, etc.). **The pit wherein is no water.** "Pit," or cistern, is a common name for a prison (Gen. xl. 15; Exod. xii. 29; Jer. xxxvii. 16). The absence of water may be notified either to imply that the tortures of thirst were

added to the horror of the situation, or to intimate that the prisoners were not hopelessly drowned therein. We Christians see in this paragraph a figure of the redemption of a lost world by the blood of Christ.

Ver. 12.—The prophet calls on the prisoners to avail themselves of the offered deliverance. **Turn you to the strong hold.** Return ye to Zion, the city defended by God (ch. ii. 5), and able to afford you a safe asylum. (For the spiritual meaning, see Luke iv. 18–21.) **Ye prisoners of hope.** Captives who have good hope of deliverance because they are still in covenant with God. Septuagint, δέσμιοι τῆς συναγωγῆς, "prisoners of the synagogue." Pusey remarks that "hope" here and nowhere else has the article, and that what is meant is "the Hope of Israel," that of which St. Paul spoke (Acts xxvi. 6, 7 and xxviii. 20). **Even to-day.** In spite of all contrary appearances. Septuagint, ἀντὶ μιᾶς ἡμέρας παροικεσίας σου, "for one day of thy sojourning." **Double.** A double measure of blessing in compensation for past suffering (Isa. xl. 2; lxi. 7). There ought to be a full stop at the end of this verse, as in the Revised Version.

Ver. 13.—The Lord proceeds to explain the promised blessings in detail. **First is** signified the victorious resistance of the Maccabees against the Seleucidæ—a figure of Messiah's victory over all the enemies of God. **When** (*for*) **I have bent Judah for me.** The verbs are in the prophetical perfect, and may be rendered future. By a grand figure God is represented as a warrior armed for battle, who uses his people for the weapons of his warfare. The Hebrews speak of "treading" the bow, where we say "bend," because they used the foot in bending it. In the present case Judah is God's bow. **Filled the bow with Ephraim.** Ephraim is the arrow (comp. Ps. cxxvii. 4, 5). Judah and Ephraim, the united people, are God's instruments, and fight against the world-power in his strength. **And raised up;** better, *and I will stir up;* Septuagint, ἐξεγερῶ: Vulgate, *suscitabo.* **Greece;** *Javan.* Not a vague term for the far west, whither some prisoners had been carried, but to be taken strictly as the appellation of Greece. Nothing but inspiration could have enabled Zechariah and Daniel to foresee the rise of the Macedonian dynasty, and the struggle between the Jews and the Syro-Grecian power in Maccabee times, which is here plainly announced. The earlier the date assigned to this part of Zechariah's prophecy, the more incredible is it that any mere human sagacity or prescience should have enabled a man to foretell these events, or to see in Greece a power arrayed in conflict with the people of God. **And made thee;** rather, *and I will make* *thee.* God will make his people into a hero's sword to execute vengeance on the enemy.

Ver. 14.—**The Lord shall be seen over them.** To encourage the chosen people in the contest, the Lord shall make his presence manifest as their Leader. **His arrow.** God's arrows are the judgments which he inflicts upon his enemies, which come forth suddenly as the lightning flash, and cannot be avoided (Ps. xviii. 14; Hab. iii. 11). **Shall blow the trumpet.** As the signal of battle and calamity (Numb. x. 9; Judg. vii. 19, 20; Ezek. vii. 14; Amos iii. 6; Zeph. i. 16). **Whirlwinds of the south.** He shall come upon the enemy and sweep them away with irresistible force. Storms from the south were the most violent, coming from the Arabian desert (Job xxxvii. 9; Isa. xxi. 1; Hos. xiii. 15). Septuagint, Πορεύσεται ἐν σάλῳ ἀπειλῆς αὐτοῦ, "He shall go in the surge of his menace."

Ver. 15.—**Shall defend them;** ὑπερασπιεῖ αὐτούς, "shall put his shield over them" (Septuagint). There are numerous examples, in the Books of Maccabees, of God's special interposition in his people's favour, and thus far and in part fulfilling this prophecy (see 1 Macc. iii. 16—24; iv. 6—16; vii. 40—50; 2 Macc. ii. 21, 22; iii. 24, etc.; v. 2—4; xi. 8; xii. 11, 15, 22, 28, 37; xv. 7, etc.). **They shall devour.** The prophet seems to have had in view Numb. xxiii. 24, where Israel is compared to a lion, eating of the prey and drinking the blood of the slain. So here he says they shall "devour," *i.e.* the flesh of their enemies (comp. Micah v. 8). **Subdue with sling-stones.** So the Vulgate, and virtually the Septuagint, taking the case of the noun as instrumental; but it is best to take it as accusative of the object, as in the margin of the Authorized Version, "They shall tread down the stones of the sling." The "sling-stones" are the enemies, as in the next verse "the stones of a crown" are the Jews; and the sentence means that the Jews shall tread their enemies underfoot like spent sling-stones, which are of no account. Or it may signify simply and without metaphor that they shall despise the enemies' missiles, which shall fall harmless among them (Job xli. 28, 29). **They shall drink** the blood of the slain, like lions. **Make a noise.** As men exhilarated with wine. Vulgate, *Bibentes inebriabuntur quasi a vino* (Isa. xlix. 26; Ezek. xxxix. 17—19). **Shall be filled like bowls.** They shall be filled with blood like the sacrificial vessels in which the blood of victims was received (ch. xiv. 20). **The corners of the altar.** The blood was also sprinkled on the corners or sides of the altar (Lev. i. 5, 11; iii. 2). There may be included the notion that the war against God's

enemies was a sacred war, and accepted by him as a sacrifice. In the Maccabean struggle the bloodshed was often very considerable (see 1 Macc. vii. 32, 46; xi. 47; 2 Macc. viii. 30; x. 17, 23, 31, etc.).

Ver. 16.—**Shall save them.** He shall give them a positive blessing beyond mere deliverance from enemies. Keil, "Shall endow them with salvation." **As the flock of his people;** so the Vulgate; literally, *as a flock, his people;* Septuagint, ὡς πρόβατα λαὸν αὐτοῦ. He will tend his people as a shepherd tends his flock (Ps. lxxvii. 20; c. 3; Jer. xxiii. 1; Ezek. xxxiv. 2, 8, etc.), So Christ calls himself the "good Shepherd," and his followers "little flock" (John x. 11; Luke xii. 32). **Stones of a crown.** The valuable gems set in crowns and diadems, or in the high priest's official dress. The people shall be in God's sight as precious as these in the eyes of men, and shall be highly exalted. The Septuagint and Vulgate render, "sacred stones;" and Knabenbauer thinks that by the term is meant the temple of God, which shall arise or shine in the Holy Land, as a reward for its faithful defence. But the sense given above is satisfactory and simpler. **Lifted up as an ensign upon his land;** better, as the Revised Version margin, *glittering upon his land.* "His" may refer to Jehovah, or Israel; probably the latter is meant. The "land" is the crown or diadem in which the precious stones, the redeemed people, are set. They shall be raised to the highest possible glory and honour. If the words be taken in the sense of "raised on high over his land," they must be considered to indicate that the crown which contained the gems shall be raised aloft in victorious triumph.

Ver. 17.—**His goodness.** The goodness, *i.e.* the prosperity, of Israel or the land. Revised Version margin, "their prosperity." If the affix "his" is referred to Jehovah, the nouns "goodness" and "beauty" must be taken, not as his attributes, but as gifts bestowed by him, the prosperity and beauty which he confers. But it is more suitable to the context to consider the reference to be to the people, who in the next clause are divided into young men and maidens, and to take the "goodness," or goodliness, as appertaining more especially to the former, and the "beauty" to the latter. **His beauty** (comp. Ezek. xvi. 14). (For the Messianic interpretation, see Ps. xlv. 2; Isa. xxxiii. 17.) **Corn . . . new wine.** This is an expression often found to denote great abundance and prosperity. The two are distributed poetically between the youths and maidens (Deut. xxxiii. 28; Ps. lxxii. 16; Jer. xxxi. 12, 13; Joel ii. 18, 19). **Make . . . cheerful;** literally, *make sprout.* It probably refers to the increase of population occurring in times of plenty. This outward prosperity is a symbol of God's favour and the uprightness of the people. In these things, too, we may see adumbrated the spiritual blessings of the gospel, which are, as corn and wine, to strengthen and refresh the soul.

HOMILETICS.

Vers. 1—6.—*A visitation of judgment.* "The burden of the word of the Lord in the land of Hadrach," etc. Whatever view is taken of the exact time of the fulfilment of the glorious promises with which the last chapter concludes, it was necessarily a time still future when those promises were uttered. Other things of a very different nature were first to occur. On some of these, accordingly, as constituting a kind of "burden" (ver. 1) on some of the lands and people contiguous to Israel, the tongue of the prophet, in the verses before us, next speaks—something, probably, after the fashion of Luke xix. 11; 2 Thess. ii. 3. Most commentators believe that what he thus predicts was fulfilled in connection with the Syrian conquests of Alexander the Great. Certainly we shall find this predicted "visitation of judgment" to correspond very strikingly with the history of those conquests in three principal ways, viz. in regard (1) to the *circumstances* it came in; (2) to the *path* it followed; and (3) to the *marks* it left.

I. THE CIRCUMSTANCES IT CAME IN. It was a time when the "eyes of man," and especially (so Pusey, *in loc.*) "of all the tribes of Israel," should be "toward the Lord." This seems to describe, first and generally, a condition of expectation and wonder— perhaps also of fear (see Luke xxi. 26). Secondly, and more particularly, and it may be of the "tribes of Israel" especially, a spirit of trust and reverence (see Ps. v. 3; 2 Chron. xx. 12; Ps. cxlv. 15; cxxiii. 2; Isa. xvii. 7, 8). If so, we may find that in the history supposed to be referred to which corresponds in both respects very exactly. How certainly great, for example, was the expectation and wondering fear of the inhabitants of the East at large, after the astounding victory of Alexander at Issus, when he first sent his general and turned his attention to Syria and Damascus! How exceedingly natural, also, that the marvellous speed and completeness of his triumph should remind "the tribes of Israel" of Dan. viii. 1—8, 20, 21, and so fix their eyes on their own Jehovah in adoration and trust! This almost certain, indeed, if we believe what Josephus tells us of the prophecies of Daniel being afterwards shown to Alexander.

II. THE PATH WHICH THIS VISITATION FOLLOWED. Three principal stages are mentioned in the prophecy. 1. *Where the "visitation" began;* viz. (see ver. 1) in the land of Damascus and Hadrach, a principal city, as only lately known (see Pusey), of Syria, towards the north-east. 2. *Where it went next;* viz. to Tyrus and Zidon (vers. 2—4), cities of Phœnicia, travelling west. 3. *Where it went last;* viz. to the cities of the Philistines (vers. 5, 6), travelling south. Three corresponding stages are also traceable in the history referred to. So Pusey writes ('Daniel the Prophet,' pp. 277, 278), "The selection of the places and of the whole line of country corresponds very exactly to the march of Alexander after the battle of Issus, when the capture of Damascus, which Darius had chosen as the strong depository of his wealth, etc., opened Cœle-Syria; Zidon surrendered; Tyre was taken; Gaza resisted, was taken, and, it is said, plucked up." Also Eichhorn, as there quoted, "All the chief places, which Alexander, after the battle of Issus, either took possession of or conquered, are named one by one—the land of Hadrach, Damascus and Hamath, Tyre and Zidon, Ashkelon, Gaza, Ekron, and Ashdod."

III. THE MARKS IT LEFT. Here, again, in the prediction, the description is threefold. In the country of Hadrach and Damascus and their neighbouring city Hamath ("Hamath, which bordereth thereby," so some), the great mark was the abiding character of the visitation, or "burden." There judgment was to come first, and there to remain. In the case of Tyrus (Zidon being only mentioned parenthetically), the result, notwithstanding all her wisdom (Ezek. xxviii. 2, 3), strength, wealth, and power, would be her total overthrow and destruction by fire. In the cities of Philistia the results would be fear, sorrow, disappointment; in one case, the loss of the ruler (ver. 5); in another (ver. 5), the loss of inhabitants; in all, the abasement of "pride." More briefly still—"subjugated," "ruined," "humbled"—so would this visitation, according to this *prediction*, leave these three lands. According to the *history*, we read the same. "The *Syrians*, not as yet tamed by the losses of war, despised the new empire; but, swiftly *subdued*, they did obediently what they were commanded" (Q. Curtius, quoted by Pusey). Of Tyre we read, in the pages of history, as to her "trong hold" and her "power on the sea," and wealth, that the inhabitants "determined to resist Alexander, trusting in the strength of the island, and the stores laid up," as also that they "mocked at the king, as though he thought to prevail against Neptune." As to her "wisdom," we read of "unwearied inventiveness of defence," etc. As to the result, that "Alexander, having slain all save those who fled to the temples, ordered the houses to be set on fire." Of Gaza, which had had kings for fifteen hundred years, that Betis, its "king," after a two months' siege, was dragged to death at the chariot-wheels of his conqueror (see further Pusey and Wardlaw, *in loc.*).

This passage, thus interpreted, may seem to illustrate, in conclusion: 1. *The imperfection of man's knowledge.* This city, Hadrach, which turns out to have been most conspicuous and important for many generations, afterwards for many generations is so forgotten that its very name is a riddle. How much beside, therefore, has doubtless been so buried by time that all traces of it are gone! 2. *The perfection of God's knowledge.* He knows even the future infinitely better than we do the past. Doubtless, on this account, there are some touches in this prediction which we cannot appreciate, but which may, however, have been of peculiar interest to devout Jews at this time.

Vers. 7, 8.—*A visitation of mercy.* "And I will take away his blood out of his mouth, and his abominations from between his teeth," etc. The key to this passage seems to be in its very last words (comp. Exod. iii. 7 and end of ver. 6). In the preceding verses we saw how God "visited" the nations bordering on Israel with a "visitation of judgment." Here we seem to read how he visits his own people with a "visitation of mercy." He does so, apparently, in two principal ways, viz. (1) indirectly, by *converting their enemies*; and (2) directly, by *defending themselves*.

I. IN CONVERTING THEIR ENEMIES. (Comp. Prov. xvi. 7.) Of this conversion, as described in ver. 7, three things should be noted. 1. *Its completeness.* This evidenced, partly, by the doing away of that especial outward token of religious distinction connected with "eating the blood" (see Lev. xvii. 10, 11; Ps. xvi. 4; Ezek. xxxiii. 25); and partly, also, by the fact of this greatly prized heathen indulgence being given up when "between the teeth," and so when most enticing and pleasant (comp. Jonah iii. 8, "the violence that is in their hands"). 2. *Its extent.* It would apply to all the Philistines that "remained;" and to all of them, also, in such a manner that every one of them individually ("he that remaineth, even he") should be on the God of Israel's side. 3. *Its importance.* Every individual so gained would be as great a source of strength as a "governor," or captain of a thousand; and every band of them (so the concluding phrase of ver. 7 may signify) as great an advantage as when their originally indomitable enemy, the "Jebusite," became, in the person of Ornan or Araunah, the king-like giver of the very site on which their temple was built (see Josh. xv. 60; Judg. i. 21; 1 Chron. xxi. 15; 2 Sam. xxiv. 18; 1 Chron. xxii. 1). In supposed fulfilment of all this, some have noticed what Josephus relates as to the way in which the Philistines, many years afterwards, identified themselves with the Jews. But we are, perhaps, on safer ground if we notice, with a similar view, how completely, in New Testament times, the Philistines have disappeared from sight as enemies of the Jews; and how much, also, we read of the early triumphs of the gospel in their part of the land (see the mission of St. Peter as related in Acts ix. 32—43; x.; xi. 1—18). Was not Cornelius as important to the Gentile Church as Araunah to the Jewish temple?

II. IN DEFENDING THEMSELVES. Here also three features to be specially marked. Notice: 1. The *completeness* of this defence. In many ways there would be danger: in the mere existence of an "army" or hostile body; in its close proximity to them when in movement, and that, both when "passing by" and also when "returning;" perhaps, also, in the terrible character and exceptional might of that army's commander, as signified by what is twice said here so emphatically about "him" in connection with its movements. From *all* these dangers defence is here promised. 2. *Its secret.* By God's own hand: "I will encamp" (comp. Ps. xx. 7; xxxiv. 7; 2 Kings vi. 17). For the sake of God's own house, some expressly render the words, "about mine house" (comp. Ps. cxxii. 9; 1 Kings viii. 29). 3. *Its results;* viz. comparative freedom from oppression to God's people till their then work should be accomplished. They might be visited; they might be attacked; but they would not, as before, be left to the oppressor's mercy and will. In apparent fulfilment of this part of the prophecy, we may notice, in the pages of history, how Alexander, when engaged in besieging Tyre, demanded the assistance of the Jews; how the high priest, Jaddua, refused on account of his previous oath to Darius; how Alexander threatened Jerusalem in consequence; how, after destroying Gaza, he passed by them to subdue Egypt; how he returned thence, vowing vengeance; how Jaddua and the priests met him, and showed him the prophecies of Daniel; how Alexander is said to have recognized in Jaddua the same man as had long previously appeared to him in a dream; how, on all these accounts, he not only spared the Jews, but promoted them, and laid the foundation of a policy in regard to them which helped to preserve them till New Testament times (see Josephus and other authorities, as quoted by Wardlaw, and by Pusey in 'Minor Prophets,' and 'Daniel the Prophet').

Thus regarded, we seem taught for ourselves: 1. *How* God preserves those that are his—how variously; how wonderfully; how abundantly. Though unarmed themselves, they not only escape, they more than disarm, the vengeance of the conqueror of the world. 2. *Why* God preserves them, viz. because of their connection with his "temple"—in other words, with his Son (comp. John ii. 19—21; Col. ii. 9; 1 Tim. ii. 5; Acts iv. 12; x. 43; xiii. 39, etc.).

Vers. 9—12.—*A joyful kingdom.* "Rejoice greatly, O daughter of Zion; shout, O daughter of Jerusalem," etc. How sudden, how loud, how urgent, is this call to rejoice! No wonder; for in the bare fact announced here there is ample cause to rejoice. "Thy King cometh"—a King of thine own, not an alien king like him just spoken of. This possibly the connection of thought. Still greater the cause for rejoicing in what is said of this King; whether (1) to *Zion herself;* or (2) to her *Gentile neighbours;* or (3) to *mankind at large.*

I. To ZION HERSELF. Consider: 1. *The purpose of his coming,* viz.: (1) To save his people, not to condemn them (Luke ix. 56; John iii. 17, etc.). This the more necessary to specify, because of the righteousness or justice so specially attributed to him in this place. Although "just," he is coming to pardon. (2) To save his people indeed. To save them not only from the guilt, but also from the practice and power of their sins; calling "sinners," but calling them to "repentance." Although coming to pardon, he is just (Rom. iii. 26). 2. *The manner of his coming.* How admirably this corresponds to his purpose! Being a King, he appears (for once at least) in befitting state, riding on an animal never employed before. Being also a Saviour, he comes in mercy and meekness, in the lowliest way a king could.

II. To THE HEATHEN NEIGHBOURS OF ZION. As shown by the description given here: 1. *Of the aspect of his kingdom towards them.* "He shall speak peace to the heathen" (ver. 10). The Jews themselves seem to have expected otherwise; as shown to some extent by such passages as Acts i. 6; Mark x. 37; and specially by the extreme unwillingness of the Apostle Peter to treat any Gentile whatever (Acts x. 4) as otherwise than common or unclean. This "enmity" (Eph. ii. 16) was to be so completely "taken away" that the very weapons of warfare were to be "cut off" and perish. A cause for rejoicing, indeed, when accomplished, both to believing Jews (Acts xi. 18) and to Gentiles (Acts xiii. 48). 2. *Of the extent of his kingdom among them.* "From sea to sea," etc. (ver. 10). The reference, apparently, is to Ps. lxxii. 8; also to the promise to Abraham in Gen. xv. 18; and ultimately to Ps. ii. 8. How this was fulfilled in gospel times we learn from such passages as Acts xi. 26 and xvii. 6; Rom. xv. 19; Col. i. 6.

III. To MANKIND AT LARGE. Whether we consider: 1. *The kind of persons saved.* These would appear (from ver. 11) to be the worst cases of all—persons needing salvation the most. They are described as being persons in prison; as being in its lowest part, perhaps in its "pit;" as being there without means of subsistence; as having their life, in fact, like Joseph in Gen. xxxvii. 24, 27, only *not* gone.   2. *The kind of salvation vouchsafed.*   (1) Its certainty.   A matter of "covenant" (ver. 12)—of a covenant still binding, renewed "to-day;" a covenant made by the greatest of all beings ("do *I* declare"), and in the most solemn of all methods, viz. by shedding of "blood" (see 1 Pet. i. 19, etc.).   (2) Its fulness.   "I will render double unto thee."   Not merely "as the offence" is this "free gift" (Rom. v. 15), though that would be surprising enough.   It is very "much more," even "double" (comp. Isa. xl. 2; lxi. 7).

CONCLUSION.   How great cause, in all this, for us, too, to rejoice!   If the prospect was good, the fulfilment is better (Matt. xiii. 16, 17; Heb. xi. 13, 39, 40; 1 Pet. i. 10—12).   If the mere hope was so bright, how much better the harvest!   How great cause, also, for taking warning!   The fuller the salvation, the greater the peril of rejecting it (Heb. ii. 1—3; x. 28, 29).   The more complete, also, its provisions, the more final.   "There remaineth *no more* sacrifice for sin;" "*Last of all* he sent unto them his Son."

Vers. 13—17.—*A successful campaign.*   "When I have bent Judah for me, filled the bow with Ephraim," etc.   It is clear, from the beginning of these verses, that we have to do here, in some sense, with battle and war.   It is equally clear, from the fact that the persons here mentioned have been described in ver. 10 as specially separated from battle and war, that we have only to do here with such things in some more literal sense.   It seems most probable, therefore, that the "peace" spoken of in the latter portion of the passage must be something equally peculiar in its way.   Let us endeavour to find, in each case, where the peculiarity lies.

I. AS TO WAR.   Under this head we may notice: 1. *The description of the combatants.*   On the one hand, "Judah," "Ephraim," and "Zion," representing probably the Jewish people at large, as specially identified with the worship of Jehovah, the true God (Ps. lxxxvii. 2).   On the other hand, "Greece," as probably representing the heathen at large (ver. 10), in connection with those mythological fictions and philosophical inquiries in which the "sons" of Greece took the lead.   When did these combatants and these systems of thought come into conflict?   Even when God raised up those Jewish apostles of Christ (so it has been answered), who, by the preaching of the cross, attacked and overcame the religion and wisdom of Greece (1 Cor. i. 18—24).   This was most truly a kind of "war," which also spoke "peace" (ver. 10); a war, also, in which the "Word of the Lord out of Zion" (Isa. ii. 3) was as a "sword" (Eph. vi. 17) in God's hand.   2. *The description of the conflict.*   Was not the Lord truly "seen over," or with these combatants for his truth (Mark xvi. 20; Heb. ii. 3, 4)?   Did not God's Word also, as spoken by them, find its mark like an "arrow" (Acts ii. 37; 1 Cor. xiv. 24, 25)?   Did it not shake and overthrow many deeply rooted convictions, like the "trumpet" of Jericho, as though by its sound (Acts xvii. 6)?   And overcome apparently insuperable obstacles as though by a "whirlwind" (2 Cor. x. 4, 5)?   Did not God again specially "defend" these combatants when endangered (Acts v. 23; xii. 1—17; xiv. 20, 21; xvi. 26; xix. 23—41; xxi. 32, etc.)?   Did they not also, with their weapons of peace, "devour and subdue" those weapons of war, "the stones of the sling" (margin), spreading the gospel even when destroyed themselves (Acts xi. 19—21)?   And altogether were they not like men carried along as though with a holy "wine" from the "altar," in their fervour of zeal and success (Acts ii. 13; xxvi. 24; 2 Cor. v. 13)?   In all these respects we seem to have here a faithful description of the earlier conquests of Christ's cross.

II. AS TO PEACE.   Corresponding to this singular and hallowed warfare shall be its hallowed results.   The Church, or congregation of God's believing people, shall be made thereby a new thing on the earth.   1. *Externally;* and that in three ways.   (1) As to members.   Before "that day" the family of God was confined almost entirely to one little people and land.   Now, those thus saved by him should be "as the flock of his people."   (2) As to appreciation.   Like "the stones of a crown," like so many jewels, that is to say, not only most valuable in themselves, also most appreciatingly employed, shall his people then be.   Compare the name of Peter, signifying "a Stone," and such passages as 1 Pet. ii. 5; Rev. ii. 17; iii. 12.   (3) As to effect.   The Church becoming then, like a "standard" or "ensign," something easily seen, readily recognized, and faithfully followed (comp. Cant. vi. 10).   So numerous, so illustrious, so conspicuous, was the New Testament Church, on the one hand, to become. Just so, on the other hand, with all its faults and corruptions, has it actually been! 2. *Internally.* And this, in turn, manifested in three different ways. (1) In a special sense of God's love. "How great is his goodness!" (comp. John iii. 16; 1 John iii. 1; iv. 16, 17; Rom. v. 5; Eph. ii. 4—7). (2) In a special sense of God's perfections. "How great is his beauty!" (Compare such passages as Rom. iii. 25, 26; xi. 33; 1 Cor. i. 24, 25, 30.) (3) In a special consequent sense of satisfaction and rest; and that amongst all. "Corn shall make the young men cheerful, and new wine the maids." Illustrated, perhaps, by such passages as Matt. xi. 28—30; Rom. v. 1, 2; Acts xvi. 34; Rom. xv. 13; 1 Cor. iii. 21—23; and it may be also, if we look to the margin, by Acts ii. 16—18; xxi. 4, 9. Never have all these things been so deeply and so commonly felt in the "Israel of God," as since the days when the apostles first went forth to preach Christ.

From the various predicted changes thus accomplished, we may see, in conclusion: 1. *The supernatural origin of Christianity.* Physically, the Roman conquered the world. Intellectually, the Greek conquered the Roman. Spiritually, the Jew has conquered them both. A little society, formed originally out of the most despised of the nations, and principally, if not exclusively, out of the most despised of its provinces (Acts ii. 7; John vii. 52), has become the ruling society upon earth. Can we help saying as in Ps. cxviii. 23? 2. *The supernatural value of Christianity.* Is there any system to be compared with it as to the blessings it bestows? Can the statement of 1 Tim. iv. 8 be made of any other religion as it can of this one? Can anything else also so completely satisfy all the cravings of our nature (see John iv. 14)?

HOMILIES BY VARIOUS AUTHORS.

Vers. 1—8.—*God's judgments.* I. THE DARK SIDE. "Burden." Word of ill omen to God's enemies. God's eye is on all. Storm gathering. Will soon burst in fury, just, universal, overwhelming. None so small as to be overlooked. None so great as to secure immunity. The wisdom of the wise, the resources of the rich, and the fame of ancient days will prove as vanity.

II. THE BRIGHT SIDE. Eye of kindness. Hand of gracious interposition. Incorporation of Jews and Gentiles in one glorious Church. 1. *Divine protection.* "Encamp," etc. 2. *Righteous freedom.* No more taskmasters, as in Egypt. 3. *Grateful service.*—F.

Ver. 9.—*The ideal King.* I. BEAUTIFUL VISION. Poets in rapt moments have had glimpses of the highest (Ps. xlv. 72). The character, the life and work of a true King, have passed before them as things fair to see. But where is the reality? "Find me the true king or able man, and he has a Divine right over me" (Carlyle).

II. PASSIONATE LONGING. The heart yearns for what is best. The need presses. Circumstances now and again arise that intensify the feeling and the cry. There is so much to be done—evils to remove, wrongs to be redressed, rights and liberties to be secured. Oh for the coming of the true King! "What he tells us to do must be precisely wisest, fittest, that we can anywhere or anyhow learn, the thing which it will in all ways behove us, with right loyal thankfulness and nothing doubting, to do. Our doing and life were then, so far as government would regulate them, well regulated" (Carlyle).

III. IMMORTAL HOPE. There have been kings, good, bad, and indifferent. Some began well, but did little. The best have come far short of the highest standard. The true King "not yet." Still hope. Faith in the possibilities of human nature; above all, faith in the promise of God.

> "Ring out false pride in place and blood,
> The civic slander and the spite;
> Ring in the love of truth and right,
> Ring in the common love of good. . . ●

> "Ring in the valiant man and free,
>   The larger heart, the kindlier hand;
> Ring out the darkness of the land.
> Ring in the Christ that is to be."

F.

Vers. 9, 10.—*The advent of the King.* The accession of a sovereign is a time of rejoicing (cf. Solomon, 1 Kings i. 40). But there may be disappointment. The early promise may fail, and the first joys end in bitterness. Not so with Messiah. The better he is known, the more he is loved. The longer experience of his reign, the greater the satisfaction.

I. THE GREATNESS OF HIS NATURE. Son of man. Son of God. Dignity commanding the highest homage.

II. THE BEAUTY OF HIS CHARACTER. Everything in him that is true and fair and good. He is altogether lovely. 1. *Just.* Fulfils all righteousness. 2. *Merciful.* Stoops to the lowest. Kind to the poorest. Equitable to all. 3. *Humble.* Meek and lowly.

III. THE GLORY OF HIS REIGN. 1. *Empire spiritual.* His kingdom is "within." He writes his laws upon *the heart.* 2. *Based on the free convictions and love of the people.* His subjects do not bow the knee in form, but in truth. They honour him not with mere lip-service or state ceremonials, but with the homage of the heart. 3. *Characterized by righteousness and peace.* "Salvation" is brought by him to all. He not only pardons the rebel, but converts him into a loyal subject. He not only emancipates the slave, but binds him for ever to himself in grateful devotion. He not only rescues the lost, but unites them with all the redeemed in one holy and loving brotherhood. 4. *Destined to universality and immortality.* Of his kingdom there shall be no end.—F.

Vers. 11, 12.—*The sinner in three aspects.* I. SELF-RUINED. Joseph, Daniel, Jeremiah, were cast into "the pit" by wicked hands. The sinner has himself to blame. If there is gloom, chains, and misery, it is because of revolt from God. It is not the body but the soul that is "in prison," and no soul can be imprisoned save by its own deed and consent.

II. GOD-PITIED. Though we have cast off God, he has not cast off us. He is long-suffering and merciful. His voice to us is full of pity and inspires hope. "Prisoners of hope." Why? Specially: 1. As called of God. 2. Roused to a sense of danger. 3. Encouraged to seek deliverance.

III. CHRIST-RESCUED. Refuge is provided. "Stronghold." 1. Near. 2. Open to all. 3. Ample for the reception and defence of all who come. Hence the urgent and loving appeal, "Flee." Happy they who have responded, "who have fled for refuge to lay hold upon the Hope set before us" (Heb. vi. 19)!—F.

Ver. 13.—*Victory through God.* I. THE MARSHALLING OF THE FORCES. The "trumpet" calls to arms. On one side are the armies of heaven, and on the other the hosts of darkness.

II. THE TERRIBLENESS OF THE STRUGGLE. Characterized by: 1. Might, as of a storm carrying havoc far and wide. 2. Fury, as of wild beasts raging and ravening. 3. Deadliness, as of arrows that strike quick, and with fatal effect.

III. THE SPLENDOUR OF THE VICTORY. Complete overthrow of God's enemies. Establishment of his people as a flock, in unity and peace. Human agency, but Divine efficiency. Everything here to rouse ardour, to quicken flagging energies, and to nerve the soul to the highest endeavours, under the eye of the great Captain of our salvation.—F.

Vers. 1—8.—*The dark and the bright side of God's revelation to mankind.* "The burden of the word of the Lord," etc. This chapter begins that portion of the book whose genuineness, though denied by some, is accepted by most unbiassed expositors. As it is our main purpose, in preparing these sketches, to use the statements, whether prosaic or poetic, prophetic or historic, to illustrate truths of universal application, it comes not within our purpose to discuss the questions of genuineness, authenticity, and inspiration.   In the preceding chapters the prophet had in vision seen and said much concerning many of the more remarkable events connected with the continued rule of the Persians ; he advances now to foretell some of the more striking circumstances which would transpire under that of the Greeks, during the military expeditions of Alexander and his successors, so far as they had a bearing upon the affairs of the Jewish people. "He describes," says Dr. Henderson, "in this chapter the conquest of Syria after the battle of Issus (ver. 1), and the progress of the army of Alexander along the coast of the Mediterranean, involving the capture of the principalities of the Phœnicians and Philistines, but leaving the Jews unmolested, through the protecting care of Jehovah (vers. 2—8).   He then contrasts with the character and military achievements of that conqueror the qualities which should distinguish the Messiah and his kingdom, whom he expressly predicts (vers. 9, 10).   After which he resumes the thread of his historical discourse, and describes the wars of the Maccabees with Antiochus Epiphanes, and the victory and prosperity with which they were followed (vers. 11—17)."   These verses may be taken to illustrate the dark and the *bright side of God's revelation to mankind.* Here are threatenings and promises.   The Bible, in relation to humanity, is something like the mystic pillar in the wilderness, as it appeared on the Red Sea ; it threw a radiance on the chosen tribes as they advanced, and a black cloud upon their pursuing foes, overwhelming them in confusion.   Notice, then—

I. THE DARK SIDE OF THE DIVINE WORD.   Notice two things.   1. *In this aspect it is here called a "burden."*   The word " burden " is almost invariably used to represent a calamity.   Thus we read of the burden of Babylon, the burden of Moab, the burden of Damascus, the burden of Tyre, the burden of Egypt, etc.   The general meaning is a terrible sentence.   God's sentence of condemnation is indeed a terrible thunder-cloud. 2. *In this aspect it bears upon wicked men.*   The doomed peoples are here mentioned. They are in " the land of *Hadrach.*"   Whether Hadrach here means the land of Syria or the common names of the kings of Syria, it scarcely matters ; the people of the place of which Damascus was the capital were the doomed ones.   Besides these, there are the men of " Hamath," a country lying to the north of Damascus and joining the districts of Zobah and Rehub.   And still more, there are " Tyrus " and " Zidon," places about which we often read in the Bible, and with whose history most students of the Bible are acquainted.   " Ashkelon," " Gaza," and " Ekron " are also mentioned. These were the chief cities of the Philistines, and the capitals of different districts. All these peoples were not only enemies of the chosen tribe, but enemies of the one true and living God.   History tells us how, through the bloody conquests of Alexander and his successors, this " burden of the word of the Lord " fell with all its weight upon these people.   Observe : (1) That the Bible is heavy with black threatenings to the wicked.   It has not one word of encouragement to such, but all menace ; not one gleam of light, but a dark mass of cloud.   (Quote passages.)   (2) That these black threatenings will inevitably be fulfilled.   All the threatenings here against the land of Hadrach, Hamath, Tyrus, Zidon, Gaza, Ekron, Ashkelon, and the Philistines were fulfilled.

II. THE BRIGHT SIDE OF THE DIVINE WORD.   There is a *beam* of promise here. " And I will take away his blood out of his mouth, and his abominations from between his teeth : but he that remaineth, even he, shall be for our God, and he shall be as a governor in Judah, and Ekron as a Jebusite.   And I will encamp about mine house because of the army, because of him that passeth by, and because of him that returneth : and no oppressor shall pass through them any more : for now have I seen with mine eyes."   The following is Dr. Keil's translation of these verses : " And I shall take away his blood out of his mouth, and his abominations from between his teeth, and he will also remain to our God, and will be as a tribe-prince in Judah, and Ekron like the Jebusite.   I pitch a tent for my house against military power, against those who go to and fro, and no oppressor will pass over them any more ; for now have I seen with my eyes."   The promise in these words seems to be twofold.   1. *The deprivation of the power of the enemy to injure.*   " I will take away his blood from between his teeth," etc.   "The Philistines and other enemies of the Jews," says Scott, " would be deprived of their power to waste them any more ; and the spoils they had taken by violence and the most abominable rapine would be taken away from them as prey from a wild beast." The Bible promises to the good man the subjection of all his foes. "The God of peace shall bruise Satan under your feet shortly;" "The last enemy that shall be destroyed is death." 2. *Divine protection from all their enemies.* "I will encamp about mine house," etc. "They were not to be injured," says Henderson, "by the army of Alexander, on its march either to or from Egypt—a promise which was fulfilled to the letter, for while that monarch punished the Samaritans, he showed great favour to the Jews. Nor was any foreign oppressor to invade their land, as the Assyrians and Chaldeans had done, during the period that was to intervene before the advent of the Messiah, predicted in the verse immediately following. They were, indeed, subject to much suffering, both from the Egyptian and the Syrian kings, especially from Antiochus Epiphanes; but their nationality was not destroyed; and the evils to which they were exposed only paved the way for the Maccabean victories and for the establishment of the Asmonean dynasty. For this preservation they were indebted to the providence of God, which watched over them for good. This is emphatically expressed in the last clause of the verse." The Bible promises eternal protection to the good. "God is our Refuge and Strength," etc.—D. T.

Vers. 9, 10.—*The ideal Monarch of the world.* "Rejoice greatly, O daughter of Zion," etc. "In the former part of this chapter," says Dr. Wardlaw, "we found in the progressive conquests of Alexander the Great and the favour which, in the midst of them, he showed to Jerusalem, the execution of God's vengeance, as here threatened, against the enemies and oppressors of his people, along with his protecting care over his people themselves. By the reference to these speedily coming events, and in them to the career of that mighty prince and warrior—of whom it has been strongly said that, having conquered one world, he sat down and wept that he had not another to conquer—the prophet, under the impulse of inspiration, is rapt into times more distant; and fixing his eye on a King and a Conqueror of a very different description, invites his people, in terms of exulting transport, to hail his coming." That these verses point to the advent of Christ is an opinion entertained both by Jewish and Christian expositors. The references in Matt. xxi. 1—5 and John xii. 12—16 contribute not a little to the confirmation of this opinion. Anyhow, the words depict a Monarch the like of whom has never appeared amongst all the monarchs of the earth, and the like of whom is not to be found on any throne in the world to-day—a Monarch, the ideal of whom is realized in him whom we call with emphasis the Son of man and the Son of God. There are five things here suggested concerning this Monarch.

I. HERE IS A MONARCH THE ADVENT OF WHOM IS A MATTER FOR RAPTUROUS JOY. "Rejoice greatly, O daughter of Zion; shout, O daughter of Jerusalem." What sincere, thoughtful man, in any kingdom on the face of the earth, has any reason to look forward to-day with rapture to the successors of any of the monarchs of the earth? In most cases there are sad forebodings. Christ's advent to the world was announced by the gladsome music of angelic choirs. "Glory to God in the highest," etc. Why rejoice at his advent? Because he will (1) *promote all the rights of mankind;* (2) *remove all the calamities of mankind.*

II. HERE IS A MONARCH THE DIGNITY OF WHOM IS UNAPPROACHED. "Thy King cometh unto thee." "*Thy* King." Thou hast never yet had a true king, and there is no other true king for thee: this is *thy* King. 1. The King who alone has the *absolute right to rule thee.* Thou art his—his property. All thy force, vitality, faculty, belong to him. 2. The King who alone can *remove thy evils and promote thy rights.*

III. HERE IS A MONARCH THE CHARACTER OF WHOM IS EXCEPTIONALLY GOOD. 1. *He is righteous.* "He is just." The little word "just" comprehends all virtues. He who is just to himself, just to his Maker, just to man, is the perfection of excellence, is all that Heaven requires. 2 *He is humble.* "Lowly, and riding upon an ass." Where there is not genuine humility there is no true greatness; it is essential to true majesty. Pride is the offspring of littleness; it is the contemptible production of a contemptible mind. No man ever appeared in history whose humility approached the humility of Christ. "He was meek and lowly in heart;" he "made himself of no reputation." How different is this righteous, humble character from that of human monarchs! How often have their moral characters been amongst the foulest abominations in the foulest chapter of human history!

IV. HERE IS A MONARCH WHOSE MISSION IS TRANSCENDENTLY BENEFICENT. 1.
It is remedial. "Having salvation." Salvation! What a comprehensive word!
Deliverance from all evil, restoration to all good. Worldly monarchs often bring
destruction. They have never the power, and seldom the will, to bring salvation to a
people. Any one can destroy; God alone can restore. 2. *It is specific.* "And I will
cut off the chariot from Ephraim, and the horse from Jerusalem, and the battle bow
shall be cut off: and he shall speak peace unto the heathen." He will put an end to
the "chariot," the "horse," the "battle bow," of war, and "speak peace" to the
nations. Peace! This is what the nations have always wanted. War has been and
still is the great curse of the nations. Here is a King who speaks peace to the nations.
His words one day shall be universally obeyed. "The wolf shall dwell with the lamb,
and the leopard shall lie down with the kid," etc. (Isa. xi. 6—9).

V. HERE IS A MONARCH THE REIGN OF WHOM IS TO BE UNIVERSAL. "And his
dominion shall be from sea even to sea, and from the river even to the ends of the earth."
The language here employed was universally understood by the Jews as embracing the
whole world. He claims universal dominion; he deserves it, and will one day have
it. "The kingdoms of this world shall become the kingdoms of our God and of his
Christ," etc.

CONCLUSION. Learn: 1. The infinite goodness of God in offering to the world
such a King. It is the world's great want. 2. The amazing folly and wickedness of
man in not accepting this Divine offer. Not one-tenth of the human population have
accepted him. What ingratitude is here! and what rebellion! Yes, and *folly* too. It
is his characteristic and his glory as a King that he does not force his way to dominion.
He submits himself to the choice of mankind. This monarchy is a moral monarchy,
a monarchy over thought, feeling, volition, purpose, mind.—D. T.

Vers. 11, 12.—*Historical facts illustrations of spiritual realities.* "As for thee
also, by the blood of thy covenant I have sent forth thy prisoners out of the pit wherein
is no water. Turn you to the strong hold, ye prisoners of hope: even to-day do I
declare that I will render double unto thee." In these verses we have three subjects
which demand and will repay thought.

**I. HERE IS A STATE OF WRETCHEDNESS WHICH REMINDS US OF MAN'S MISERABLE CON-
DITION AS A SINNER.** "As for thee also"—that is, as for thee, daughter of Zion and
Jerusalem—" by the blood of thy covenant"—that is, according to the covenant vouchsafed to thee on Mount Sinai, and ratified by the blood of sacrifices (Exod. xxiv. 8)—
"I have sent forth thy prisoners out of the pit wherein is no water." The Jewish people
are here represented as having been prisoners in a pit without water. "Dungeons
were often pits without water, miry at the bottom, such as Jeremiah sank in when
confined (Gen. xxxvii. 24; Jer. xxxviii. 6). This image is employed to represent the
misery of the Jewish exiles in Egypt, Greece, etc, under the successors of Alexander,
especially under Antiochus Epiphanes, who robbed and profaned the temple, slew
thousands, and enslaved more. In Zechariah's time, the time of the Persian rule, the
practice was common to remove conquered peoples to distant lands, in order to prevent
the liability to revolt in their own lands." Very fairly may this be taken as an illustration of that miserable moral condition in which all unregenerate men are found.
They are in a "pit" of ignorance and depravity, shut out from the true light, and
destitute of true liberty. It is a "pit" in which the soul is. A man's body may be
in a "pit," and yet he may possess light and liberty within. Men have sung in
dungeons ere now. But when the soul is in "a pit," the man himself is enthralled in
darkness and bondage.

II. HERE IS AN ADMONITION WHICH REMINDS US OF MAN'S DUTY AS A SINNER.
"Turn you to the strong hold, ye prisoners of hope." The prisoners here undoubtedly
signify the Jewish exiles who were in bondage in Egypt and Greece and other
countries, and whose restoration is here promised. Though they were prisoners, they
were "prisoners of hope." God was on their side, and had made to them the promise
of redemption. 1. *All sinners are "prisoners of hope."* Though bound by the chains
of guilt and corruption, there is "hope" for them; means of deliverance have been
provided, and millions upon millions of prisoners have reached to the full enjoyment
of that deliverance. There is hope; for—

"While the lamp holds out to burn,
The vilest sinner may return."

2. *They are "prisoners of hope" for whom a "strong hold" has been provided.* If these exiles would return to Jerusalem, they would be safe. Jehovah himself would be their Guard and Defence. Christ is the "Strong Hold" of sinners; he is their "Refuge and Strength;" "Look unto me, and be ye saved, all ye ends of the earth;" "Behold the Lamb of God, which taketh away the sin of the world!" 3. *They are "prisoners of hope" who should flee to the "Strong Hold" at once.* "Even to-day." When the prospect seems most gloomy, when the cloud of despair seems spreading over the heavens, and things are at the worst, "even to-day." This is the "accepted time," to-day is the "day of salvation."

III. HERE IS A PROMISE THAT GIVES ENCOURAGEMENT TO THE SINNER. "I will render double unto thee." As if Jehovah had said to the daughter of Zion—Great as has been thine adversity, thy prosperity shall be doubly greater (Isa. lxi. 7). "Turn you to the Strong Hold," and you shall not only be saved, but more than saved. "Let the wicked forsake his way, and the unrighteous man his thoughts: and let him return unto the Lord, and he will have mercy upon him; and to our God, for he will *abundantly pardon.*"

"God's boundless mercy is to sinful man
Like to the ever-wealthy ocean;
Which, though it sends forth thousand streams, 'tis ne'er
Known, or else seen, to be the emptier:
And though it takes all in, 'tis yet no more
Full and filled full, than when full-filled before."
(R. Herrick.)

D. T.

Vers. 13—17.—*God works amongst the nations in the interests of his people.* "When I have bent Judah for me," etc. "The double recompense which the Lord will make to his people will consist in the fact that he not only liberates them out of captivity and bondage, and makes them into an independent nation, but that he helps them to victory over the powers of the world, so that they will tread it down, *i.e.* completely subdue it. The first thought is not explained more fully because it is contained *implicite* in the promise of return to a strong place, the 'double' only is more distinctly defined, namely, the victory over Javan. The expression, 'I stretch,' etc., implies that the Lord will subdue the enemies by Judah and Ephraim, and therefore Israel will carry on this conflict in the power of its God" (Keil). Referring our readers for minute criticisms on this passage to such authors as Henderson, Hengstenberg, Pusey, and Keil, we note the great facts which it contains.

I. THAT GOD WORKS AMONGST THE NATIONS OF THE EARTH. God is here represented as raising up Zion against Greece. "And raised up thy sons, O Zion, against thy sons, O Greece." The literal reference, it may be, is to the help which he would render the Maccabees, as the heroic leaders of the Jews, to overcome the successors of the Grecian Alexander, Antiochus Epiphanes, and the other Grecian oppressors of Judah. He works with the Jew and the Greek, or Gentile—the two great divisions of mankind. He is in their conflicts and their battles. Three remarks are suggested concerning his work amongst men. 1. *He works universally amongst men.* He works with the "sons" of Zion and the "sons" of Greece. He operates with all, with the remote and the distant, with the little and the great, with the good and the bad; he is in all human history. All good he originates, all evil he overrules. 2. *He works by human agency amongst men.* "When I have bent Judah for me, filled the bow with Ephraim." Ephraim and Judah, which here represent the whole Jewish people, are, by a strong figure of speech, spoken of as the bows and arrows of Jehovah, the military weapons which he would employ in crushing the Grecians under Antiochus Epiphanes. God carries out his purposes with man by the agency of man; wicked kings are his tools, obscure saints are his ministers of state. 3. *He works manifestly amongst men.* "And the Lord shall be seen over them;" or, as Keil renders it, "Jehovah will appear above them." What thoughtful student of human history has not felt disposed to exclaim, as he has passed from page to page, "This is the Lord's doing, and it is marvellous in our eyes"?   We say, "thoughtful student;" for it is only manifest to the spiritually thoughtful. The hearts of others are so thickly veiled with depravity and wickedness that they see him not; they neither recognize his hand nor hear his voice. 4. *He works terribly amongst men.* "And his arrow shall go forth as the lightning: and the Lord God shall blow the trumpet, and shall go with whirlwinds of the south." "Like the lightning will his arrow go forth, and the Lord Jehovah will blow the trumpets, and will pass along in storms of the south" (Keil). "Is there evil in the city, and the Lord hath not done it?" (Amos iii. 6)—done it by permission? He is in the crashings of conflagrating cities, in the booming thunders of contending armies, in the wild whirlwinds of battling kingdoms; with him there is "terrible majesty" as he proceeds on his march in human history.

II. GOD WORKS AMONGST THE NATIONS OF THE EARTH IN THE INTERESTS OF HIS PEOPLE. 1. *He works for their defence.* "The Lord of hosts shall defend them;" or, "shelter them." He guards his saints; they are as the apple of his eye; he is their Shield and Defence. 2. *He works for their victory.* "They shall devour, and subdue with sling-stones," etc. "Jehovah of hosts shall protect them, and they shall devour and tread down the sling-stones, they shall drink, they shall be noisy, as those who drink wine; they shall be full as the bowl, as the corners of the altar" (Henderson). The idea is their complete triumph over their enemies. Hengstenberg observes that there is not the least indication that a spiritual conflict is intended. Quite true, but a spiritual conflict it may illustrate, and its victory too. In such a conflict we are all engaged, and God has promised, if we are faithful, to make us more than conquerors. 3. *He works for their salvation.* "And the Lord their God shall save them in that day as the flock of his people." They shall be restored to the fold and guarded by Jehovah as their Shepherd. God works for the entire salvation of his people—salvation from all evil, salvation to all good. 4. *He works for their glory.* "They shall be as the stones of a crown, lifted up as an ensign upon his land;" or, as Hengstenberg renders it, "For crowned jewels shall they be rising up upon his land." There is true glory awaiting the good. There is a crown of glory laid up in heaven, etc. 5. *He works for their perfection.* "For how great is its goodness, and how great is its beauty! Corn shall make the young men cheerful, and new wine the maids." We accept the rendering of Keil here, which is not only faithful to the original, but in harmony with the context. The prophet is speaking of the high privileges of God's people, and not of the excellences of the Supreme. It is an exclamation of admiration of the high privileges of the godly.

CONCLUSION. As much of the writings of this prophet admit of so many interpretations, and are perhaps impossible fully to understand, we have thought, not only the most useful, but the safest way of treatment to be the employment of statements and phrases to illustrate those spiritual realities which are important to man in all times and places. It is true that God works amongst men, and it is true that he works amongst men in the interests of those who love and serve him. May we be of that number, and thus realize in our experience the fact that "all things work together for good to them that love God, to them who are the called according to his purpose"!—D. T.

EXPOSITION.

CHAPTER X.

Vers. 1, 2.—§ 4. A connecting link between the last section and the next. *The condition for obtaining the promised blessings is that they are to be sought from the Lord, not from idols.*

Ver. 1.—**Ask ye of the Lord rain.** The promise of abundance at the end of the last chapter suggests to the prophet to make a special application to the practice of his countrymen. They must put their trust in God alone for the supply of temporal as well as spiritual bounties. **The latter rain** was due at the time of the vernal equinox, and was necessary in order to swell the maturing grain (comp. Deut. xi. 14). The early rain occurred at the autumnal equinox. It was considered as a special manifestation of God's providential care that these periodical rains were received (see Isa. xxx. 23; Jer. v. 24; Joel ii. 23). So the Lord **shall make bright clouds**; rather, *Jehovah* *maketh the lightnings.* Thunderstorms accompany the periodical rains. Ye must ask of him, and ye shall have. Septuagint, Κύριος ἐποίησε φαντασίας, " The Lord makes flashes " (of lightning?); Vulgate, *Dominus faciet nives,* where the right reading is supposed to be *nubes* (comp. Ps. cxxxv. 7; Job xxxviii. 25, 26). **Give them showers of rain.** Abundant rain, as Job xxxvii. 6. The address is now in the third person. **Grass.** All vegetable food for man and beast, as in Gen. i. 11, 29; Ps. civ. 14; Amos vii. 2.

Ver. 2.—**For.** The prophet supports his exhortation to pray to Jehovah by showing the worthlessness of trust in idols. **Idols;** *teraphim.* What these were is not known for certain. They seem to have been images of human form and sometimes of life size, corresponding in some degree to the lares or penates of the Romans (Gen. xxxi. 19; 1 Sam. xix. 13). They were supposed to be capable of bestowing temporal blessings and giving oracles (Judg. xvii. 5; xviii. 5, 24; Ezek. xxi. 21). **Have spoken vanity.** Gave worthless, misleading responses. The mention of teraphim in this passage is thought to indicate a date anterior to the Captivity; but the prophet is speaking of past events, of the results of these base superstitions in former, not present, time. Three kinds of superstition are mentioned. Septuagint, οἱ ἀποφθεγγόμενοι, "speaking" images. These are the first. Secondly come the soothsayers, **the diviners,** persons who pretended to predict the future (Jer. xxvii. 9; xxix. 8; Ezek. xxi. 21; Hab. ii. 18). **Have told false dreams;** Vulgate, *somniatores locuti sunt frustra;* LXX., τὰ ἐνύπνια ψευδῆ ἐλάλουν, "spake false dreams." The Vulgate seems to be correct, " dreams, *i.e.* dreamers, spake deceit." This is the third class among the practisers of superstitious observances. **They comfort in vain,** when they promise temporal blessings (Job xxi. 34). **Therefore they went their way as a flock.** Because they trusted in these vain superstitions, the Israelites had to leave their own place, were led into exile like a flock of sheep driven away for sale or slaughter (Jer. l. 17). **They were troubled.** They were and are still oppressed by the heathen. **Because there was (*is*) no shepherd.** Because they had no king to guard and lead them, they fell under the power of foreign rulers, who ill treated and oppressed them (Ezek. xxxiv. 5; Neh. v. 15).

Vers. 3, 4.—§ 5. *The evil rulers set over them for their sins shall be removed, and Israel shall be firmly established.*

Ver. 3.—**Mine anger was (*is*) kindled against the shepherds.** These heathen rulers were indeed God's instruments in punishing his people, but they had exceeded their commission, and afflicted Israel in order to carry out their own evil designs, and now they themselves shall be chastised. Some commentators take "the shepherds" to be the rulers of Israel civil and ecclesiastical, comparing Ezek. xxxiv. 2, 5, etc. But the context leads us to consider them as those who took the place of rulers of Israel when she had no shepherd of her own (ver. 2). **I punished (*will punish*) the goats (***bell-wethers***);** literally, *will visit upon; i.e.* chastise. The same word (*paquad*) is used in the next clause in a good sense. The "goats" are the leading men, those powerful for evil, as Isa. xiv. 9. **Hath visited his flock.** The reason why the evil shepherds are punished is because God visits his flock in love and care, to see their state and to relieve them from trouble (Zeph. ii. 7). The house of Judah here includes all the nation, to which it afterwards gave its name. **Hath made (*shall make*) them as his goodly horse.** The Israelites shall not only be delivered from oppression, but God shall use them as a stately war-horse, richly caparisoned, to tread down enemies and triumph over them. So he said before (ch. ix. 13) that he would make Judah his bow and Ephraim his arrow. (For a description of the war-horse, see Job xxxix. 19—25; comp. Rev. vi. 2; xix. 14, where Christ is represented riding on a white horse, and his saints following him on white horses.)

Ver. 4.—The firmness and security of Judah, thus "visited," is announced in terms admitting of further application. **Out of him came forth (*shall come*).** Out of Judah, mentioned in ver. 3. Others, not so suitably, explain, "out of Jehovah," in contrast to Hos. viii. 4. The succeeding figures are taken from the building and furnishing of a house. **The corner.** The corner-stone (Isa. xxviii. 16). From Judah herself shall come the prince on whom the whole edifice shall rest; *i.e.* primarily, she shall be independent of foreign rulers; and secondly, from Judah shall come the Messiah, "the Head-stone of the corner" (Matt. xxi. 42; Eph. ii. 20; Heb. vii. 14). Septuagint (taking the noun as a verb), καὶ ἀπ' αὐτοῦ ἐπέβλεψε, "et ex ipso respexit" (Jerome). **The nail.** The word (*yathed*) is taken for the peg that fastens the cord of a tent, for a nail used in building with timber, or a peg for hanging up arms and utensils on the walls of a house. In whichever sense we take it here, it implies one who consolidates or upholds the political constitution (Isa. xxii. 23, 24). **The battle bow.** The people shall themselves have arms and military skill to protect them against all assailants. **Oppressor**; rather, *ruler*, as Isa. iii. 12; lx. 17. Judah shall have every leader necessary for all emergencies. Septuagint, πᾶς ὁ ἐξελαύνων ἐν τῷ αὐτῷ, "he that expelleth together;" Vulgate, *omnis exactor simul.* If the word be taken in the sense of these versions and the Authorized Version, the clause would mean that the Israelites shall subjugate their enemies, and oppress them, and exact tribute from them. The word (*noges*) usually means "taskmaster."

Vers. 5—7.—§ 6. *Thus equipped, Israel and Judah united shall triumph over their foes.*

Ver. 5.—**Which tread down** their enemies **in the mire of the streets.** "Their enemies" is supplied naturally from the context. Others take the participle "treading" intransitively, "treading upon street mire," the enemy being figuratively denoted by "mire." The Greek and Latin Versions give, "treading the mud in the streets" (comp. Ps. xviii. 42; Micah vii. 10). **They shall fight.** They shall carry on long-continued war successfully because God is with them. **The riders on horses.** The strong force of cavalry arrayed against them shall fall before Israel, and be put to shame. The Israelite forces were for the most part infantry, while the principal strength of their enemies consisted in cavalry (Dan. xi. 40).

Ver. 6.—**House of Joseph**; *i.e.* Israel, or the ten tribes, called Ephraim in the next verse (see note on Amos v. 6). Israel and Judah alike shall share in the contest and the victory, under the protection of God. **I will bring them again to place them.** This is one word in Hebrew, which may mean either "I bring them again," or "I make them dwell." The Authorized Version unwarrantably combines both significations. Septuagint, κατοικιῶ αὐτούς, "I will settle them;" Vulgate, *convertam eos.* It is better taken here, in contrast with "cast off" in a following clause, in the sense of "I will cause them to dwell," *i.e.* in safety and comfort. **As though I had not cast them off.** The happy restoration shall make them forget former troubles and the calamities of their rejection (Isa. xliii. 18, 19). **Will hear them** (ch. xiii. 9; Isa. lviii. 9).

Ver. 7.—They of **Ephraim**; *i.e.* as well as Judah, shall be heroes. Not many members of the northern kingdom returned at first from the Captivity; but the prophet gives the assurance that they shall come and prove themselves mighty warriors. **As through wine.** They shall hasten to the battle cheerfully and exultingly, like men refreshed and strengthened with wine (see

ch. ix. 15; Ps. lxxviii. 65, 66). **Their children shall see it.** Though unable to participate in the struggle, their children shall share the universal joy. **Their heart shall rejoice in the Lord** (Ps. lxiii. 7; Isa. xli. 16; Joel ii. 23; Hab. iii. 18). Attempts have been made to find the fulfilment of these prophecies (ver. 3, etc.) in certain events of Maccabean times. Thus, according to Patritius, the sin for which the Hebrews suffered such distress at the hands of the Seleucidæ (ver. 2) was their imitation of heathen practices mentioned in 1 Macc. i. 13—15 and 2 Macc. iv. 7—17, when the high priest purchased his office by a bribe, and the other priests followed Greek customs. The prophet is supposed to refer specially to this state of things when he says, "They were troubled because there was no shepherd. Mine anger was kindled against the shepherds." But we have shown above that Zechariah is here speaking of the past, not of the future. There is more verisimilitude in discerning the wars and victories of Judas, his brothers and successors, in the allusions of vers. 4—7. The truth is that such descriptions suit many different events, and have various applications. Though their complete fulfilment may be expected only in Messianic times and circumstances, yet we may see many anticipatory and preparative transactions, which are meant to introduce the final accomplishment. The Jewish prophet is not always foretelling certain definite events. Oftentimes he is teaching, warning, and exhorting; and generally he is enunciating great principles, the truth of which shall be clear in the future, rather than predicting particular facts. Not unfrequently commentators have neglected this consideration, and sought too curiously to restrict the prophet's words to some one issue. It may be noted, further, that where the prophetic language concerning the destiny of the restored people seems to be exaggerated and not borne out by subsequent facts, the promises are always conditioned by the moral state of the recipients. If they answered fully and consistently to God's call, the result would be such as was predicted. That the event in all respects did not correspond with the high ideal previously announced must be attributed, not to the prophet's mistake, but to the people's waywardness and disobedience.

Vers. 8—12.—§ 7. *The scattered people shall be gathered from all parts of the world, and dwell in their own land, under the protection of Jehovah.*

Ver. 8.—**I will hiss for them**; σημανῶ αὐτοῖς, "I will signal to them" (Septuagint);

sibilabo eis (Vulgate). The slightest summons will bring them when God wills the return of the dispersed. The "hissing" is the whistling or tinkling with which bees are allured to swarm (Isa. v. 26; vii. 18, 19). **I have redeemed them.** They were virtually delivered from captivity and exile, though all had not taken advantage of the deliverance. **They shall increase as they have increased.** The same promise is made in Ezek. xxxvi. 10, 11. The allusion is to the marvellous growth of the Israelite nation in Egypt (Exod. i. 7, 12). The prophets often announce this fulfilment of the promise made to Abraham (Gen. xiii. 16; xv. 5, etc.) after the return (see Isa. liv. 2; Hos. i. 10; Micah ii. 12).

Ver. 9.—**I will sow them among the people** (*peoples*). The "sowing" here does not mean scattering, but increase, and this was to go on while they were dispersed among the nations. The word is used in the same sense in Hos. ii. 23; Jer. xxxi. 27. This continued dispersion was a part of their discipline, a test of their loyalty to God. **They shall remember me.** In the countries where they are living they shall worship the Lord and observe his Law, and be a witness for him among the heathen. **They shall live with their children** (Ezek. xxxvii. 14). The promised blessing is not for a time only, but perpetual. **Turn again;** *i.e.* return to their own land (Isa. xxxv. 10). It cannot mean, "turn to the Lord," for they are said already to remember the Lord, and their "conversion must precede the promise of life." The next verse describes the return more particularly.

Ver. 10.—**Egypt . . . Assyria.** It is certain that there was a large body of Jews in Egypt at this time (Jer. xliii. 6, 7); and to Assyria the ten tribes, who are here specially mentioned under the name Ephraim, had been deported. Besides this, Assyria is often used loosely for Western Asia or Babylonia, of which, after its submission, it formed a most important feature (see 2 Kings xxiii. 29; Ezra vi. 22; and in the Apocrypha, 1 Esdr. vii. 15; Judith i. 7; ii. 1). In the 'Oracula Sibyllina,' the Assyrians are continually confused with Persians, Babylonians, and other Eastern nations. Egypt and Assyria are here used as types of the countries to which Jews had been banished (comp. Hos. xi. 11). **Gilead and Lebanon.** A designation of the northern district of Palestine, on both sides of the Jordan, in which these tribes had been originally settled. This region had been most exposed to hostile attacks, and was the first to be depopulated. **Place shall not be found for them** (Isa. xlix. 20). Josephus testifies to the teeming population of Galilee in later times ('Bell. Jud.,' ii. 3. 1; iii. 3. 2;

iv. 1. 2; 7. 5). Septuagint, "There shall not even one of them be left behind," *i.e.* in exile.

Ver. 11.—**He shall pass through the sea with affliction.** In bringing his people back the Lord is ready to repeat the miracles of the Exodus. This is the general meaning of the passage; but the details present difficulties. For "he shall pass" the LXX. gives, "they shall pass through." But the reference is plainly to Jehovah, as the following clause shows. The next two words are in apposition, "the sea," "affliction." Revised Version, "the sea of affliction;" Septuagint, ἐν θαλάσσῃ στενῇ, "in a strait sea;" or, as the Hebrew cannot be so translated, "in a sea, a strait;" Vulgate, *in maris freto.* It seems best to take the two words simply as, "the sea, which is affliction." The Red Sea, through which Jehovah led his people, was a figure of the sufferings which they had endured in Egypt, and brought destruction upon their enemies (comp. Exod. xiv. 16, 17, 24, etc.). **Smite the waves** (Exod. xv. 8; Isa. xi. 15, 16; li. 10). **The river.** The Nile. The drying up of the waters of the Nile is a figure of the humiliation of the nations which have been guilty of enslaving the chosen people. The Nile, the representative of Egypt, is mentioned because of the allusion to the bondage in Egypt running through the paragraph. **The pride of Assyria.** Pride is noted as the characteristic of Assyria (comp. Isa. x. 7, etc.; Ezek. xxxi. 3, 10). **The sceptre.** This may refer to the decadence of the power of Egypt, and the transference of royal authority to strangers; but, regarding the immediate context, we had better translate, "the rod of Egypt," and see in it an allusion to the oppression of the taskmasters during the sojourn in that land. All such tyranny shall be at an end (comp. Isa. x. 24).

Ver. 12.—**I will strengthen them in the Lord.** I will strengthen them with myself—with my grace and power. **They shall walk up and down in his Name.** They shall live in obedience to, and dependence upon, the Lord (Micah iv. 5, where see note). The Septuagint reads, "They shall boast themselves." So God will work wonders to deliver his people from the captivity of the devil, destroying all enemies, visible and invisible, which array themselves against him. This is the final fulfilment of the prophecy. The complete restoration from the Captivity is the immediate subject of the prophet's words; and between these two we may see a reference to the conversion of the Jews in the time of Christ and the apostles, which shall go on until the end.

HOMILETICS.

Vers. 1—5.—*The secret of victory.* "Ask ye of the Lord rain in the time," etc. In the last passage the Church of God (in its new Testament form, as we supposed) was presented to us under the figures of an army (ver. 13, etc.); a flock (ver. 16); and a field which the Lord had blessed (ver. 17). In the present verses we find al, these figures again employed: the field (ver. 1); the flock (vers. 2, 3); the army or host (vers. 3—5). It would appear, therefore, that we have also presented to us the same topic of illustration, viz. the New Testament Church; and that, further, under the same circumstances and at the same time as before. The distinction to be noted is, that, in the present passage, we have a deeper view of the subject—the secret nature of that Church being explained and enforced by describing to us (1) *a special gift;* (2) *a grievous failure;* (3) *a signal success.*

I. A SPECIAL GIFT. According to the first verse, there is something to be "asked of the Lord;" something appointed by him, having its proper "time;" something to be hoped for from him: "the Lord shall give;" something to be hoped for by all: "to every one." It is figured to us as "rain." What does it signify? In the present connection, what can it signify but the gift of God's Spirit (Isa. xliv. 3; Joel ii. 28)? How specially were men taught, in New Testament times, to "ask" for this gift (see Luke xi. 9—13, where men nine times over are encouraged in praying for this very blessing; also John iv. 10; vii. 37—39)! How expressly, again, were those "latter" days the appointed "time" for this blessing (Luke xxiv. 49; John xvi. 7; Acts i. 4)! In what abundant "showers," once more, was it given in these primitive times, as it were, "to every one" "in the field" (Acts ii. 17; viii. 17—19; xi. 17; Gal. iii. 2, 3)! These were some of the things which caused the dispensation then commenced to be called "the dispensation of the Spirit"! In short, without this holy "rain" from above, the strictly "Christian" Church could never have come into existence. Much less, of course, could it have continued alive.

II. A GRIEVOUS FAILURE. The state of things in the Jewish Church at the coming of Christ seems described to us next. In one sense that Church, as a body, though free from the grosser idolatry of earlier days, was worshipping "idols" of its own. Its members trusted to merely external rites, and names, and privileges, and professions (Rom. ii. 17—20; Matt. iii. 9; xxiii. 14, 23, 30, etc.). As a consequence, they never obtained (Jer. xiv. 2, etc.), as they never desired, the gift spoken of here. Failing of this, they failed altogether, notwithstanding all their privileges (Rom. iii. 1, 2), as a Church. This evidenced at the time—as apparently here predicted beforehand—in various ways. For example, by the absence among them: 1. *Of solid knowledge and truth.* "The diviners have seen a lie, and have told false dreams" (comp. Matt. xv. 14; xxiii. 16, 19, 24, 26; John ix. 40, 41). 2. *Of saving knowledge and truth.* "They comfort in vain" (see Matt. v. 20; Rom. ix. 31; perhaps also Mark x. 20, 21). 3. *Of proper pastoral oversight.* (See end of ver. 2; and comp. Matt. ix. 36.) Also by the presence among them: 4. *Of special judgments* on those who professed (Matt. xxiii. 2) to be "shepherds" (ver. 3). (See Matt. xxiii. throughout, with its sevenfold denunciation of "woe" on the "scribes and Pharisees.") Was there not "failure," indeed, when such language could be used as that found in Matt. xxiii. 33 and xxi. 13?

III. A SIGNAL SUCCESS. 1. *Its nature.* Being the same as that noted before on ch. ix. 14, 15, viz. success in preaching the gospel of Christ and bringing sinners beneath its power. 2. *Its secret.* This found in the fact that, by the coming of Christ, "the Lord of hosts" (ver. 3) had "visited" his people and "flock" (comp. Luke i. 68, 78, 79; vii. 16; and note, in ver. 5, the expression, "They shall fight, because the Lord is with them"). 3. *Its instruments.* These very notable, (1) as being men of "Judah," or Jews (as all the apostles were); men, *i.e.*, belonging to that very Church and people which, in religious matters, as just now noted, had so egregiously failed. Possibly, also, (2) as being, some of them, men like Saul of Tarsus, who, at first, were "oppressors" (see also John i. 46). And certainly, (3) as being able to "tread down" obstacles, and "confound" opponents in a very marvellous way (see Acts iv. 13; v. 33; vi. 10; ix. 22; xviii. 28; and perhaps, also, xxvi. 28).

How strikingly all this teaches us the absolute need of the Spirit of God! 1. For all true religious *life.* It was the absence of this which made the Jewish Church the dead thing (Luke xvii. 37) that it was, like the old world and Sodom (Luke xvii. 27, 29) when Noah and Lot had gone out of them. All their many other privileges (see Rom. ii. 17—20; iii. 1, 2; ix. 4, 5) were of no avail without this. 2. For all true religious *work.* It was the presence of this, secured by that coming and work of Christ which we have supposed to be referred to in ver. 3 (comp. Acts ii. 33), which encountered and overcame both the Jewish Church and the Gentile world (see Acts i. 8; v. 32; 1 Pet. i. 12). How essential, indeed, was that gift, which more than supplied, in one sense, the presence of Christ himself (John xvi. 7—10)!

Vers. 6—12.—*The restoration of Israel.* "And I will strengthen the house of Judah," etc. The separate mention in this passage (vers. 6, 7) of Judah, Joseph, and Ephraim, taken together with that of Gilead, Lebanon, Egypt, and Assyria, in vers. 10, 11, seems an indication that we now have to do especially with Israel "after the flesh." The previous verses spoke of "the times of the Gentiles," and of the great spiritual conquests to be inaugurated amongst the Gentiles during those times by teacher-warriors of Jewish birth. "Jerusalem" itself, however, in all the mean time, was to be "trodden down of the Gentiles" (Luke xxi. 24). What was to happen to it when that long "tribulation" (Matt. xxiv. 29; Mark xiii. 24) should be over? The present passage seems to reply, teaching us, apparently, that the literal Israel should then be restored (1) to their former *favour;* and (2) to their former *inheritance.*

I. THEIR RESTORATION TO FAVOUR. We may notice: 1. *Its reality;* as shown by the expressions, "I will strengthen" (comp. Ps. lxxx. 14, 15, 17); "I will save;" "I have mercy upon them;" "I will hear them" (comp. Ps. lxvi. 18—20). 2. *Its universality;* as embracing both "Judah" and "Joseph," the two rival and long-divided leading families of Jacob (see Isa. xi. 13, 14; Jer. iii. 18; Ezek. xxxvii. 16, 17, etc.). 3. *Its completeness.* What "Judah" needs, viz. "strengthening," being accomplished for *it;* what "Joseph" needs, as having been more heavily punished, viz. "saving," being accomplished for *it;* and that, in both cases, so effectually as entirely to obliterate the evil past: "They shall be as though I had not cast them off." 4. *Its blessedness.* Causing special rejoicing and exhilaration, like that occasioned through "wine." 5. *Its solidity.* Causing joy in the "heart" (comp. Ps. iv. 7, and context). 6. *Its permanence.* Their "children" sharing in the joy as well as themselves (comp. Isa. lxv. 22, 23, "their offspring with them").

II. THEIR RESTORATION (APPARENTLY) TO PALESTINE. See, generally, ver. 6, "I will bring them again to place them." And observe, more particularly: 1. *The call.* They are to be summoned aloud ("I will hiss," comp. Isa. v. 26), as people living afar off; also as people belonging to God, because "redeemed;" as rightly also belonging to that place in which they had formerly "increased" so amazingly; and possibly, once more, as having been long intended for this very destiny, like seed "sown" (ver. 9) with the ultimate object of reaping a harvest to correspond. 2. *The response.* However "far off," however widely dispersed, when that call is given, they will "remember" that voice, and hear it; and, together with their children (see end of ver. 9), prepare to return. 3. *The return.* In correspondence with this preparation, they are (1) to be "brought out" of the countries of their dispersion, whether lying, like "Egypt," to the south, or lying, like "Assyria," to the north; and (2) are also, in a manner as wonderful and as humbling to their enemies as when the Red "Sea" and the "river" Jordan in former days had been divided and dried up before them, to be "brought into" their ancient possession; and that further, (3) in such exuberant numbers as not only to occupy the trans-Jordanic region of Gilead, but even a territory like that of Lebanon, almost beyond the limits of ancient Israel; and not, even so, to have sufficient room (end of ver. 10; comp. Isa. xlix. 20). 4. *The happy result.* The strength of their enemies (end of ver. 11) being for ever broken, and they themselves being "strengthened in Jehovah," they shall be able to treat the whole land then as fully their own (comp. Gen. xiii. 14—17); they themselves, also, as God's own people, doing everything therein in his Name (Ps. lxvii. 6; Micah iv. 5; Col. iii. 17).

These things may teach us, in conclusion: 1. *To take an ever-increasing interest in Israel's lot.* Whether right or wrong in our view of details, the general principle is undoubted. The future history of the world, as its past history, turns on the history of Abraham's seed (Gen. xii. 3, etc.).   2. *To place ever-increasing confidence in Israel's God.* In whatever circumstances, through whatever vicissitudes, under whatever provocations, how amazingly faithful to his ancient promise (Rom. xi. 1, 28, 29)!

HOMILIES BY VARIOUS AUTHORS.

Vers. 1, 2.—*Prayer for temporal blessings.* I. AGREEABLE TO OUR CIRCUMSTANCES. Dependent. In want. Instinctively turn to God. We have his Word to cheer us; the record of his deeds to comfort us; the testimony of his saints to encourage us.

II. CONDITIONED BY THE NECESSITY OF THINGS. There are limits. Plainly there are things which it would be reasonable, and others which it would be unreasonable and foolish, to ask. "Pray ye that your flight be not in the winter," said our Lord. The flight was a necessity, but the time and manner were within the range of things unsettled. This seems hinted at here by the condition, "in the time of the latter rain."

III. SHOULD BE SUBORDINATED TO OUR SPIRITUAL GOOD. The soul is more than the body. It may not be necessary for us to live, but it is necessary that we should abide in the love of God and do his will. "Rain" is symbolic of spiritual blessings. Only God can give rain, and only God can give the quickening, invigorating, sanctifying influences of the Holy Spirit. "Seek ye *first* the kingdom of God."

IV. SHOULD BE OFFERED IN HUMBLE SUBMISSION TO THE WILL OF GOD. He is infinitely wise and holy and good. Let us trust him, for he cannot will us aught but good.

V. SHOULD BE ACCOMPANIED BY EARNEST USE OF ALL LAWFUL MEANS. It is an old saying that "God helps those who help themselves." Prayer without work is fanaticism and folly; but prayer and work is the highest wisdom and the surest way to success. "Wherefore criest thou unto me?" said the Lord to Moses. "Speak unto the children of Israel, that they go forward" (Exod. xiv. 15).—F.

Vers. 1, 2.—*Parable of the rain.* I. MAN'S GREAT NEED. Without rain the ground is impoverished and dead. So is the soul without God. No good fruit.

II. MAN'S GREAT RESOURCE. Not idols or enchantments, not human devices or philosophies, but appeal to God. He will withhold no good from them that walk uprightly.

III. MAN'S GREAT CONSOLATION. 1. *Sweet.* (Cf. Deut. xxxii. 2.) 2. *Timely.* God does not give in an arbitrary way, but according to his own wise and holy laws. When rain is most needed, it is most appreciated. So in spiritual things (cf. Ps. xliv. 3). 3. *Abundant.* "Showers." Rains sometimes slight, partial, or temporary. Here promise of "abundance of rain" (1 Kings xviii. 41), meeting the needs of all, reaching to the furthest limits of the parched land. 4. *Invigorating and fertilizing.* "To every one grass in the field." Calls for thankfulness and joy.—F.

Ver. 3.—*God's visits to his people.* Indicate—

I. HIS CONCERN FOR THEIR WELFARE.

II. HIS PURPOSE TO DO THEM GOOD.

III. HIS DELIGHT IN THEIR HEALTH AND PROSPERITY. Wordsworth gave as a motto for a dial, "Light, come, visit me." So we should lay open our souls to the coming of God, and welcome his visits.—F.

Vers. 4, 5.—*The strength of states.* I. CAPABLE RULERS. "Corner-stone," on which the fabric rests. The stability of the whole depends on the foundation.

II. JUST ADMINISTRATION. "Nail"—what binds and fixes. The laws must not only be just, but justly applied. Forms of government vary according to the circumstances and needs of the people. There is much truth in Pope's saying, "Whate'er is best administered is best."

III. AMPLE RESOURCES. "Battle bow" may stand for implements of war. Means of defence. The weapons are nothing compared to the men who wield them. True citizens, devoted to the right, giving themselves and their all for the defence of truth and liberty, and for the advancement of the general good.

IV. National independence. Enlightenment. Love of freedom and justice. Purity of domestic life. Superiority to passion and vain-glory. Courage in duty. Power not only to hold their own, but to bear themselves generously towards the vanquished, and to overcome evil with good.

> "What constitutes a state?
> Not high-raised battlements or laboured mound,
>   Thick walls or moated gate;
> Not cities proud, with spire and turret crowned,
> Nor bays, nor broad arm'd ports,
> Where, laughing at the storm, rich navies ride;
> But men, high-minded Christian men."

                                                              F.

Vers. 5—12.—*Redemption.* I. Conflict resulting in victory.

II. Victory resulting in union. This does not always happen. There have been wars that have bred more wars, and victories that have left strong hates and bitter memories prolonged for generations. Besides, union may be based on defeat in the interest of the conqueror and not of the conquered; more formal than real, more a thing of covenants and legal fictions than the free choice of the people. But here it is real and true. The middle wall of partition has been taken away. Enmity has given place to love. Jealousy and strife, to brotherhood and peace.

III. Union resulting in happiness. There have been examples of union with various results. The union of England and Scotland has been productive of the highest good to both countries. The union with Ireland has not been so happy. We see a beautiful example of prosperity under just covenants and laws in the United States of America. Here the highest and best results are foreshadowed. 1. Increase of strength. 2. General freedom. 3. Abounding prosperity.—F.

Ver. 9.—*The hand of God in Jewish history.* I. In their long descent. Origin of nations is generally obscure. As difficult to find as the source of the Nile. The Jews are like their own Jordan. They are the only people that can trace their descent. "Children of Abraham." Two friends were visiting the museum at Berlin. One said how strange it was to look at the intellectual features of Julius Cæsar, and to think of his triumphal march northward when the Britons were but roving barbarians. "Speak for your own ancestors," answered the other, who was a Jew; "as for mine, they were singing the psalms of David, and worshipping God as members of his true Church on earth, centuries before Julius Cæsar was born!"

II. In the vicissitudes of their history. "As the modern traveller surveys the remains of the arch of Titus at Rome, he feels bewildered in endeavouring to realize the distant date of its erection; and yet it commemorates only the last of a long series of Jewish dispersions. You read of the fragments of antiquity dug up from the ruins of Babylon, and your mind is carried still further back than by the Roman arch; but the Jew possibly formed that Babylonian brick, and imprinted on it those arrow-headed characters. The pyramids of Egypt take your imagination still further back; the Jew not improbably helped to build the oldest of them. Time was young when God said to Abram, 'I will make of thee a great nation'" (Dr. Harris). In the various dispersions we see the fulfilment of Scripture (Deut. xxviii. 64—67) and the preparation for the gospel of Christ (Acts ii. 5, 9—11).

III. In the permanency of their character. From Jacob down to our own day we see the same prevailing elements of character. Their very physiognomy is that painted on the walls of Thebes. They are still a separate people. Their purity of blood, their education and training throughout the ages, have raised them high physically and intellectually. In the struggle for existence, they seem an instance of the survival of the fittest.

IV. In the greatness of their destiny. Preserved—but why? Surely for some great purpose. Witnesses for God. Servants of righteousness. Ministers of the cross (Rom. xi. 1—27).—F.

Vers. 10—12.—*The great exodus.* From Egypt—the type (cf. Isa. xi. 11—16).

I. THE GATHERING. So now under the gospel. From far and near they come. **At** the call of Jesus they gather under the banner of the cross.

II. THE PASSAGE. (Ver. 11.) Like children of Israel—pilgrims in the wilderness. Manifold trials. Educated by adversity and prosperity. Course ever onward, under the hand and guidance of God.

III. THE SETTLEMENT. Canaan. Future glory of the Church—in increase **and** prosperity. "Place not found."—F.

Ver. 12.—*Manliness.* Of the true man, we might ask, as Delilah did of Samson, 'Tell me, I pray thee, wherein thy great strength lieth?" The answer includes several things.

I. SELF-MASTERY. Reason must rule, and not passion. The Spirit, not the flesh.

.II. DIVINE INVIGORATION. Need constant aid. The plant thrives by commerce with the sun, so the soul gains energy from God. The prayer of all true men is that favourite one of David, "Quicken thou me."

III. DEVOTION TO THE RIGHT. Doing evil is dissipation of strength. Doing good brings its own recompense. The Sandwich Islanders believed that the souls of the braves slain in war pass into those who slay them, and that therefore the more a man kills the stronger he becomes. This is true spiritually. It was fabled of the giant Antæus that when he touched the earth he renewed his strength; so when we touch right we are renewed after the image of God.

IV. ASSOCIATION WITH THE NOBLEST. To be allied with the bad is not only criminal, but ruinous. Fellowship with the good elevates and ennobles.

V. GROWING NOBLENESS OF CHARACTER. There is the consciousness of advance. Settled principles. Enlarged experience. Progress in faith and godliness. All this prophesies of victory. Peter was far stronger at Pentecost than when he made his great confession; when he wrote his Epistles than when Paul had to withstand him to the face for dissembling at Antioch.

VI. HOPE OF IMMORTALITY. The strength won will never be lost. The life given by God in Christ is everlasting.

> "Whene'er right feelings fire thy languid heart,
> Let them not smoulder out in sighs and songs,
> But flash them into living acts forthwith.
> Thus strength Divine shall nerve thy mortal frame,
> And light from upper worlds shall fall upon thy path."
>
> F.

Ver. 12.—*The true life.* I. HOLY CONSECRATION. "In the Name of the Lord." Sincere and thorough renewal of consecration essential to increase of faith and holiness.

II. HARMONIOUS DEVELOPMENT. "Walking" implies health, freedom, activity. Necessary to the right development of the soul. Not in part, but in all its powers.

III. SPIRITUAL USEFULNESS. Time, talent, opportunity, rightly employed. "Up and down" zeal and diligence in all good.

IV. HAPPY ASSOCIATIONS. We are continually forming associations in life. Places and persons. The result may be good or evil, sad and painful or bright and exhilarating.

V. DELIGHTFUL PROSPECTS. Not only memories to cheer, but the outlook of the future, bright with hope up to the very gates of heaven.—F.

Vers. 1—4.—*God in relation to the good and the bad.* "Ask ye of the Lord rain in the time of the latter rain; so the Lord shall make bright clouds, and give them showers of rain, to every one grass in the field," etc. This chapter is a continuation of the subject with which the former concluded; and the words lead us to observe three facts in relation to the Almighty.

I. HE ATTENDS TO THE PRAYERS OF GOOD MEN. "Ask ye of the Lord rain in the time of the latter rain; so the Lord shall make bright clouds, and give them showers of rain." The abundance of corn promised in the last clause of the preceding chapter depends upon rain, and this rain God will give in answer to prayer. Observe: 1. *God gives rain.* A pseudo-science would ascribe "rain" and "clouds" and "showers" to what they call the laws of nature; but what these laws are, and how they operate, they cannot tell. The Bible, giving us at once an adequate and an intelligible cause, is more philosophical than any meteorological science. "He watereth the hills from his chambers: the earth is satisfied with the fruit of thy works. He causeth the grass to grow for the cattle, and herb for the service of man: that he may bring forth food out of the earth; and wine that maketh glad the heart of man, and oil to make his face to shine, and bread which strengtheneth man's heart" (Ps. civ. 13—15). "Thou visitest the earth, and waterest it: thou greatly enrichest it with the river of God, which is full of water: thou preparest them corn, when thou hast so provided for it. Thou waterest the ridges thereof abundantly: thou settlest the furrows thereof: thou makest it soft with showers: thou blessest the springing thereof. Thou crownest the year with thy goodness; and thy paths drop fatness" (Ps. lxv. 9—11). 2. *The God who gives rain attends to human prayer.* This is wonderful, but not absurd. Wonderful, that the God who created nature, and presides over it, should condescend to listen to the supplications of such an insignificant creature as man. But it is not absurd, because: (1) Man is greater than material nature. (2) Prayer is a settled law of the Divine government. To cry to the Almighty in distress is an instinct of the soul. Prayer, instead of interfering with the laws of nature, is a law of nature.

II. He abominates the character of religious impostors. "For the idols [the household gods] have spoken vanity, and the diviners have seen a lie, and have told false dreams; they comfort in vain: therefore they went their way as a flock, they were troubled, because there was no shepherd. Mine anger was kindled against the shepherds, and I punished the goats." This stands in contrast with the former verse, and is a reason for the duty there enjoined. Their false prophets—attaching themselves to idols and seducing the people to their worship, and those of them who, speaking in Jehovah's name, said, "Thus saith Jehovah," when Jehovah had not spoken, putting in his lips and clothing with his authority the "lies" and "false dreams" by which they sought to entice them from him and from his ways—had ever given promises and "vain comfort," all ending in bitterness and vexation of spirit. They had proved shepherds that only starved and scattered and exposed their flocks, instead of feeding and tending, gathering and protecting, them. "Thus, under such misleading guides, such selfish and unprincipled shepherds, the flock was driven about and 'troubled.' They had 'no shepherd,' no truly faithful shepherd, who took a concern in the well-being of the flock" (Wardlaw). Now, against such impostors, Jehovah says, "Mine anger was kindled." "That the shepherds and the goats," says Hengstenberg, "are the heathen rulers who obtained dominion over Judah when the native government was suppressed, is evident from the contrast so emphatically pointed out in the fourth verse, where particular prominence is given to the fact that the new rulers whom God was about to appoint would be taken from the midst of the nation itself." Are there no religious impostors now, no false teachers, no blind leading the blind, no shepherds fleecing the flocks?

III. He works in all for his people. "Out of him came forth the corner, out of him the nail, out of him the battle bow, out of him every oppressor together." The words teach that all their help came from him. "Out of him came forth the corner," or corner-stone, that upon which the whole building stands firmly. It means that from him comes stability. All stability in moral character, in social order, and political prosperity, is from God. "Out of him the nail." With us a nail is a small thing; but with the Orientals it is not so. It is a large peg in the inside of the room, wrought into the wall when the house was built, and on which are hung the utensils of the household. It means, therefore, support. "Out of him the battle bow." This word is used synecdochically, to represent all effective weapons of war; power to conquer comes from him. "Out of him every oppressor together," or, as Keil renders it, "from him will every ruler go forth at once." Thus God is all in all to the true. Whatever we need comes from him. "Every good and every perfect gift cometh down from the Father."

Conclusion. What a sublime view of the Almighty have we here! He is over all nature, yet listening to the prayers of the true; indignant with religious impostors, yet tolerating their existence and permitting their pernicious influence; sending out from himself all that true souls require to fight bravely and triumphantly the great moral battle of life.—D. T.

Vers. 5—12.—*Victory, unification, and blessedness for the good.* "And they shall be as mighty men," etc. This paragraph is a continuation of the preceding portions of the chapter. The various statements bring under our notice subjects which, if we give them a spiritual application, are of great and permanent interest, viz. the subjects of *victory, unification,* and *blessedness.*

I. VICTORY. "And they shall be as mighty men, which tread down their enemies in the mire of the streets in the battle: and they shall fight, because the Lord is with them, and the riders on the horses shall be confounded." Or, as Hengstenberg renders it, "And they will be like heroes, treading street-mire in the battle: and will fight, for Jehovah is with them, and the riders upon horses are put to shame." "Though the Jews were forbidden by the Law to multiply horses in battle (Deut. xvii. 16), they themselves figuratively are made Jehovah's war-horses (Ps. xx. 7), and so on foot tread down the foe, with all his cavalry (Ezek. xxxviii. 4; Dan. xi. 40). Cavalry was the chief strength of the Syro-Grecian army." This victory was: 1. *Complete.* The enemies were trodden down as "mire in the streets," and were utterly discomfited. 2. *Divine.* "Because the Lord is with them." They became victorious through him. 3. *Reinvigorating.* "I will strengthen the house of Judah, and I will save the house of Joseph, and I will bring them again to place them." They would be strengthened by their victory, not only in wealth and security, but in courage. 4. *Extensive.* "And they of Ephraim shall be like a mighty man, and their heart shall rejoice as through wine: yea, their children shall see it, and be glad; their heart shall rejoice in the Lord." "The prophet had," says Hengstenberg, "occupied himself first of all with Judah, the centre of the people of God. In ver. 6 he proceeds to speak of Judah and Ephraim together. In this verse, and those which follow, he fixes his attention peculiarly upon Ephraim, which looked in the prophet's day like a withered branch that had been severed from the vine. He first promises that descendants of the citizens of the former kingdom of the ten tribes will also take part in the glorious conflict, and then announces the return of the ten tribes from their exile, which was to be the condition of their participating in the battle. Now, all these facts connected with this victory apply to that victory the grandest of all—the victory of all true souls over error and wrong. That victory will be *complete.* "The last enemy that shall be destroyed is death." That victory will be *Divine.* It is the Almighty himself that bruises Satan under their feet. That victory will be *reinvigorating.* Some savages have the belief that the strength of the creature they destroy passes into themselves, and gives new vigour to their frames. Every victory we achieve in morals adds new energy to our souls. This victory will be *extensive.* Millions in heaven have achieved it; millions on earth are achieving it now; the moral conquerors will at last be more numerous than the stars of heaven, or perhaps the sands that gird old ocean's shores.

II. UNIFICATION. "I will hiss for them, and gather them," etc. There is no sufficient reason for regarding this regathering, *re*-collecting of the world-scattered Hebrews as pointing to that far-distant period which some believe in, viz. the universal restoration of the Jews to their own country. Observe: 1. *The ease with which the regathering will be effected.* "I will hiss [or, 'whistle'] for them." The word is understood as referring to a particular whistle used by the shepherd for calling his scattered flock together, or by those who have the care of bees, to bring them into the hive. "As sheep flock together at the well-known call of the shepherd, as bees follow in swarms the shrill note of the bee-master, so should the Lord, by his own means, gather his scattered people from their dispersions, how widely soever distant, and bring them to himself and to their heritage." With what ease God does his work—a mere look, a breath, a word! "He looketh on the earth, and it trembleth; he toucheth the hills, and they smoke." 2. *The regions to which the regathering will extend.* "And I will sow them among the people [or, as some render it, 'Though I have scattered them among the nations']: and they shall remember me in far countries [distant regions]; and they shall live with their children, and turn again." They had been scattered, not only through Egypt and Assyria. It does not say that all Jews shall return, but a great multitude is implied. 3. *The scene at which the regathering will take place.* " I will bring them again also out of the land of Egypt, and gather them out of Assyria; and I will bring them into the land of Gilead and Lebanon." This describes the whole of Palestine, with its two boundaries—the eastern, Gilead beyond Jordan; and the northern, that is, Lebanon. Large as that district is, there will not be room for all. "Place shall not be found for them." 4. *The national catastrophes which the regathering will involve.* "And he shall pass through the sea with affliction, and shall smite the waves in the sea, and all the deeps of the river shall dry up." There is evidently an allusion here to their first deliverance from Egypt; and it means that something similar to that event will occur in the course of their regathering (see Exod. xiv. 4—14). "And the pride of Assyria shall be brought down, and the sceptre of Egypt shall depart away." The idea probably is that as "the haughty boastings of Sennacherib and the sceptred power of Pharaoh proved alike feeble and unavailing against the might of Jehovah in former days, so should all the combined opposition of the most inveterate enemies prove in days to come. Before him—when he had a purpose to fulfil or promise to his people to accomplish—all pride should be abased, all power baffled, all counsel turned to foolishness." Now there is a unification, of which this is but a faint emblem—the unification of the good of all ages. "They shall come from the east, and from the west, and from the north, and from the south, and shall sit down with Isaac and with Jacob." What a blessed union is this! What countless millions will it include, and what overturning of the kingdoms of the world will its full realization involve!

III. BLESSEDNESS. Here is the highest *strength.* "And I will strengthen them in the Lord." 1. Whether this refers to their national strength, their security in their own country, or moral strength—strength of faith in him—or all, one thing is clear, that to be strengthened in the Lord is the highest strength we can have. The greatest blessing of life is strength : *physical* strength, to do with ease and to endure with patience; *intellectual* strength—strength to master with ease all the great problems of life, and to reach a theory of being in which the understanding can repose free from all disturbing doubt. These strengths are blessings ; but *moral* strength— strength to resist the wrong, to pursue the right, to serve Almighty God with acceptance, and to bless the race of man with beneficent influences—this, indeed, is the perfection of our blessedness. This strength, which implies unbounded confidence in the procedure and an unconquerable love for the character of God, is the strength we all need. " Be strong in the Lord, and in the power of his might," says Paul. " He giveth power to the faint, and to them that have no might he increaseth strength." 2. Here is the highest *exercise.* " They shall walk up and down in his Name, saith the Lord." (1) All living men must walk the road that is "up and down." Human life is made up of "ups" and "downs ;" the road is not smooth and level, but rugged and hilly, sometimes up and sometimes down; up to-day and down to-morrow. (2) This road can only be walked happily by walking it in the " Name " of the Lord. A practical recognition of his presence, and of his claims to our supreme reverence and worship. Alas! how few walk this road in the Name of the Lord! They walk it in the name of pleasure, of greed, or of ambition, or, it may be, of intellectual research. Dreary and dangerous is this road without God.

CONCLUSION. Let us battle for this *victory,* cease not a stroke until the foe is beneath our feet ; let us hail this grand *unification* of souls, hail the time when God shall meet and mingle with all noble and Heaven-born spirits. Meanwhile, let us walk this " up-and-down " road of life in the Name of the Lord. " For all people will walk every one in the name of his god, but we will walk in the Name of the Lord" (Micah iv. 5).—D. T.

EXPOSITION.

CHAPTER XI.

Vers. 1—3.—§ 8. Restoration to their own land and material prosperity do not free the Israelites from probation or trouble. The prophet, therefore, darkens his late picture with some gloomy shadows. *The Holy Land is threatened with judgment* (vers. 1—3).

Ver. 1.—**Open thy doors, O Lebanon.** The prophet graphically portrays the punishment that is to fall upon the people. The sin that occasions this chastisement, viz. the rejection of their Shepherd and King, is denounced later (§ 9). Lebanon stood in the path of an invader from the north, whence most hostile armies entered Palestine. The "doors" of Lebanon are the mountain passes which gave access to the country. Some commentators, following an old Jewish interpretation, take Lebanon to mean the temple or Jerusalem; but we are constrained to adhere primarily to the literal signification by the difficulty of carrying on the metaphorical allusions in the following clauses. **That the fire may devour thy cedars.** That the invader may wantonly destroy thy trees which are thy glory and thy boast.

Ver. 2.—**Howl, fir tree.** A species of cypress is intended, or, as some say, the Aleppo pine. It is the tree of which Solomon made floors, doors, and ceiling in his temple (1 Kings vi. 15, 34), and David harps (2 Sam. vi. 5). The prophet dramatically calls on this tree to wail for the fate of the cedar, as being about to suffer the same destruction. **The mighty;** μεγιστᾶνες, "the chieftains" (Septuagint). Trees are being spoken of, and so the primary sense is, "the goodly" (Ezek. xvii. 23) or "glorious trees." Metaphorically, the chiefs of Israel may be intended. **Bashan,** famous for its oaks, is next visited by the invading force, and its trees are felled for the use of the enemy. **The forest of the vintage.** The Authorized Version here follows, very inappropriately, the correction of the Keri. The original reading should be retained and translated, "the inaccessible forest"—an expression appropriate to Lebanon. If Lebanon is not spared, much less shall Bashan escape. LXX., ὁ δρυμὸς ὁ σύμφυτος, "the close-planted wood;" Vulgate, *saltus munitus*, "defenced forest."

Ver. 3.—There is **a voice.** The Hebrew is more terse and forcible, "A voice of the howling of the shepherds!" or, "Hark! a howling," etc. (Jer. xxv. 34, etc.). The destruction spreads from the north southwards along the Jordan valley. **Their glory.** The noble trees in whose shadow they rejoiced. **Young lions.** Which had their lairs in the forests now laid waste (Jer. xlix. 19). **The pride of Jordan.** The thickets that clothed the banks of Jordan are called its "pride" (Jer. xii. 5). The lion is not now found in Palestine, but must have been common in earlier times, especially in such places as the brushwood and reedy coverts which line the margin of the Jordan. The prophet introduces the inanimate and animate creation—trees, men, beasts—alike deploring the calamity. And the terms in which this is depicted point to some great disaster and ruin, and, as it seems, to the final catastrophe of the destruction of Jerusalem by the Romans, the punishment of the rejection of Messiah. This reference becomes plainer as we proceed. It is inadmissible to refer the passage (as some do) to the Assyrian invasions mentioned in 2 Kings xv. 29 and 1 Chron. v. 26. Holding the post-exilian origin of the prophecy, we are bound to interpret it in accordance with this view, which, indeed, presents fewer difficulties than the other.

Vers. 4—14.—§ 9. *The punishment falls upon the people of Israel because they reject the good Shepherd, personified by the prophet, who rules the flock and chastises evil-doers in vain, and at last flings up his office in indignation at their contumacy.*

Ver. 4.—**Thus saith the Lord.** The person addressed is Zechariah himself, who in a vision is commanded to assume the office of the good Shepherd (see ver. 15), and to tend the chosen people, the sheep of the Lord's pasture. God herein designs to show his care for his people from the earliest times amid the various trials which have beset them both from external enemies and from unworthy rulers at home. **The flock of the slaughter;** rather, *the flock of slaughter* —destined for, exposed to, destruction at the hands of their present shepherds (Ps. xliv. 22; Jer. xii. 3; Rom. viii. 36).

Ver. 5.—**Possessors;** or, *buyers.* Those who claimed to be owners by right of purchase. **Hold themselves not guilty.** They are so blinded by self-interest that they see no sin in thus treating the flock. But the expression is better rendered, *bear no blame,* i.e. suffer no penalty, commit this wickedness with impunity. Septuagint, "repent not;" Vulgate, *non dolebant,* which Jerome explains, "did not suffer for it." **Blessed be the Lord.** So little compunction do they feel that they actually thank God for their ill-gotten gains. The prophet is speaking of chiefs and rulers, civil and ecclesiastical, who played into the enemies' hands, and thought of nothing but how to make a gain of the subject people. Our Lord denounces such untrustworthy shepherds (John x. 11—13). Doubtless, too, the expressions in the text refer to the foreign powers which had oppressed the Jews at various times, Egypt, Assyria, etc. Amid all such distresses, from whatever cause, God still had tender care for his people, and punished and will punish their enemies. In this verse the offenders against Israel are of three classes —buyers, sellers, shepherds (see ver. 8). "Shepherd" appears sometimes in the Assyrian inscriptions as a synonym for "prince" (see Schrader, 'Keilinschr.,' p. 453).

Ver. 6.—**The inhabitants of the land.** It is a question whether by this expression is meant the Israelites, or the dwellers on earth generally. In the former case, the verse gives the reason of the calamities depicted in ver. 5, viz. God's displeasure, and expounds the parable of the sheep as meaning men (so Cheyne). In the other case, the signification of the paragraph is that God intends to put an end to the state of things just described, by punishing the oppressing world-powers who had so cruelly executed their office of being instruments of God's judgment on his people. The latter seems the correct exposition; for the people of Israel have just been called the flock of slaughter, and they were to be fed, while these "inhabitants" are to be destroyed; nor could the Israelites be said to have kings, as just below. Thus **for,** at the beginning of the verse, introduces the reason why Jehovah tells the shepherd to feed the flock, because he is about to punish their oppressors; and "the inhabitants of the land" should be "the inhabitants of the earth;" i.e. the nations of the world, among whom the Israelites lived. **I will deliver the men,** etc. God will give up the nations to intestine commotions and civil war, so that they shall fall by mutual slaughter. **Into the hand of his king.** Each of them shall be delivered over helpless unto their tyrant's hands, and God will not interpose to succour them.

Ver. 7.—**And I will feed.** Thus the Greek and Latin Versions; but it should be, So I fed. It is the account of what the prophet did in accordance with the command in ver. 4 (see the end of this verse, "and I fed"). **Even you, O poor of the flock.** There is difficulty about the word rendered "you" (lachen), which may be the personal pronoun, or an adverb meaning "therefore," "therewith," "truly," or a preposition, "on account of;" Vulgate, propter hoc. The best rendering is, I fed the flock therefore,

the poor among the flock. "Therefore" refers to the previous command. It is also rendered "in sooth." The LXX., arranging the letters differently, translates, Ποιμανῶ τὰ πρόβατα τῆς σφαγῆς εἰς τὴν Χαναανίτιν, "I will go and tend the flock of slaughter in the land of Canaan;" some render the last words, "for the merchants." This Jerome interprets to mean that the Lord will nourish the Israelites for slaughter in the land of the Gentiles (but see note on ver. 6). **And I took unto me two staves.** Executing in vision his commission of feeding the flock, the prophet, as the representative of the Shepherd, took two shepherd's staves. The two staves intimate the manifold care of God for his flock from the earliest days, and the two blessings which he designed to bestow (as the names of the staves show), favour and unity. **Beauty;** Κάλλος (Septuagint); Decorem (Vulgate); "Graciousness" (Revised Version margin). It probably means the favour and grace of God, as in Ps. xc. 17. **Bands;** literally, Those that bind; Σχοίνισμα, "Cord;" Vulgate, Funiculum. The name is meant to express the union of all the members of the flock, especially that between Israel and Judah (see ver. 14). These make one flock under one shepherd. **I fed the flock.** This repetition emphasizes the beginning of the verse, and expresses God's care in time past and in time to come also.

Ver. 8.—In executing the office of feeding the flock, **three shepherds also I cut off in one month;** Septuagint, "And I will take away the three shepherds in one month." The article in the Hebrew and Greek seems to point to some known shepherds, three in number, unless we take it as "three of the shepherds." Hence expositors have sought to find historical personages to whom the term might apply. Those who assert a pre-exilian origin for this part of the prophecy, suggest the three kings, Zachariah, Shallum, and Menahem; or, as Menahem reigned ten years, some unrecorded pretender, who started up at the time. Others see some Syrian monarchs in Maccabean times; or the three offices, king, prophet, priest; or the three dynasties that oppressed Israel, viz. the Babylonian, Medo-Persian, and Macedonian. All these interpretations fail in some point; and we are reduced to see herein a reference, as Cheyne says, to "the prompt and vigorous action of Jehovah's Shepherd in dealing with the evil shepherds, as well as in feeding the flock;" the number three being used indefinitely. Or we may find in this number an allusion to the three classes in ver. 5—the buyers, the sellers, and the pitiless shepherds. The oppressors, external and internal, are removed and cut off in one month. To the prophet's eye all this seemed to take place in that short space of time. If anything more is intended, we may, with Keil and others, taking the month as consisting of thirty days, assume that ten days are assigned to the destruction of each shepherd, after each had fulfilled his allotted period—the number ten expressing perfection or completion. **And my soul loathed them;** literally, *but my soul was straitened for them;* i.e. was impatient, weary of them. These words begin a new paragraph, and refer, not to the three shepherds, but to the sheep, the Israelites. The prophet now shows how ill the people had responded to God's manifold care, and mingles with the past a view of their future ingratitude and disobedience which will bring upon them final ruin. God, as it were, was weary of their continual backslidings and obstinate perseverance in evil. (For the phrase, see Numb. xxi. 4; Judg. xvi. 16; Job xxi. 4.) It is the opposite to long-suffering. **Their soul also abhorred me.** They showed their abhorrence by their devotion to idols and their disinclination for all goodness.

Ver. 9.—**I will not feed you.** In consequence of their contumacy, the shepherd abandons the flock to their fate, as God threatened (Deut. xxxi. 17; comp. the very similar passage in Jer. xv. 1—3). Three scourges are intimated in the succeeding words—plague, war, famine, combined with civil strife. **Eat every one the flesh of another** (comp. Isa. ix. 20). Many see here a reference to the awful scenes enacted when Jerusalem was besieged by the Romans, and intestine feuds filled the city with bloodshed and added to the horrors of famine.

Ver. 10.—**Cut it asunder.** The breaking of the staff "Beauty" indicates that God withdraws his grace and protection; he will no longer shield the people from the attack of foes, as the following words express. **My covenant which I had made with all the people;** rather, *with all the peoples.* God calls the restriction which he had laid on foreign nations to prevent them from afflicting Israel, "a covenant." Similar "covenants," *i.e.* restraints imposed by God, are found in Job v. 23; Hos. ii. 20 (18, Authorized Version); Ezek. xxxiv. 25, etc. The restraint being removed, there ensued war, exile, the destruction of the kingdom and theocracy, the subjection of Israel to Gentile nations.

Ver. 11.—**It was broken.** The covenant just mentioned (ver. 10) was broken. **And so the poor of the flock that waited upon me** (*that gave heed unto me*) **knew.** The punishment inflicted on the withdrawal of God's protection had some good result. Though the bulk of the nation took no heed, learned no lesson, yet the humble

and the suffering among them, who paid respect to his words, recognized that what happened was according to God's Word, and knew that all the rest would be fulfilled in due season. This was the effect of the Captivity; it forced the Israelites to see the hand of the Lord in the calamities that had befallen them, and it drove the thoughtful among them to repentance and amendment (Jer. iii. 13, 23; Dan. ix. 3, etc.). The breaking asunder of the first staff refers primarily to the time of the exile, and not to the absolute relinquishment of the flock. One staff is left, and for a time utter destruction is postponed. For "the poor," the LXX. reads, as in ver. 7, "the Canaaneans," meaning probably "merchants." Ewald and others, who hold the pre-exilian date of this prophecy, see here an allusion to the invasion of the Assyrians under Pul (2 Kings xv. 19).

Ver. 12.—**I said.** The prophet is speaking in the person of the great Shepherd. **Unto them.** Unto the whole flock. **Give me my price;** *my wages.* He asks his hire of the flock, because the flock represents men. Acting far differently from the wicked shepherds, he used no violence or threats. He gives them this last opportunity of showing their gratitude for all the care bestowed upon them, and their appreciation of his tenderness and love. The wages God looked for were repentance, faith, obedience, or, in another view, themselves, their life and soul. It was for their sake he required these, not for his own. **If not, forbear.** He speaks with indignation, as conscious of their ungrateful contempt. Pay me what is due, or pay me not. I leave it to you to decide. I put no constraint upon you. So God has given us free will; and we can receive or reject his offers, as we are minded. **So they weighed for my price thirty pieces of silver.** This paltry remuneration displayed the people's ingratitude and contempt. It was the compensation offered by the Law to a master for the loss of a slave that had been killed (Exod. xxi. 32). It was, perhaps, double the price of a female slave (Hos. iii. 2); and the **very** offer of such a sum was an insult, and, says Dr. Alexander, "suggested an intention to compass his death. They despised his goodness; they would have none of his service; they sought to cut him off; and they were ready to pay the penalty which the Law prescribed for the murder of one of so mean a condition." The word "weigh" was used in money transactions even after the use of coined money rendered weighing unnecessary.

Ver. 13.—**The Lord said unto me.** The Lord takes the insult as offered to himself in the person of his representative. **Cast it unto the potter;** Κάθες αὐτοὺς εἰς τὸ χωνευτήριον, "Lay them in the foundry, and I will see if it is approved;" Vulgate, *Projice illud ad statuarium;* the Syriac and Targum have, "Put it into the treasury" (Mal. iii. 10). This involves an alteration of the text, and is in itself an improbable reading, as God could not be made to tell the prophet to throw this despicable wage into his treasury, unless, perchance, it is said ironically. There may be an undesigned coincidence here. In Matt. xxvii. 5 the council discuss the propriety of putting the thirty pieces of silver into the treasury. But taking our present text as genuine, commentators usually consider the phrase as a proverbial expression for contemptuous treatment; as the Greeks said, ἐς κόρακας, as the Germans say, "zum Schinder," "to the knacker," and we, "to the dogs." There is, however, no trace elsewhere of any such proverb, nor do we know how it could have arisen; it likewise does not very well suit the last clause of the verse, "I cast them to the potter in the house of the Lord." If we substitute the supposed analogous expression, "I threw them to the dogs," we see how unseemly would be the proverb in this connection. The rendering of the Jews in old time, adopted recently by Knabenbauer, "Cast them to the Creator," is considered by Dr. Pusey to be unidiomatic, and involves great difficulties. It seems simpler to consider that the command, "cast it to the potter," implies contemptuous rejection of the sum, and at the same time intimates the ultimate destination to which, in the sight of Omniscience, it was directed. The potter is named as the workman who makes the meanest utensils out of the vilest material. That this was ordered and executed in vision is plain; how much the prophet understood we cannot tell. The ambiguous and highly typical order was explained and fulfilled to the letter by the action of Judas Iscariot, as the evangelist testifies (Matt. xxvii. 5—10). A (*the*) goodly price, etc. This is ironical, of course. Such was the price at which they estimated the good Shepherd's services. Cast them to the potter in the house of the Lord. This rejection of the paltry wage took place in the house of the Lord (in the vision), because the insult had been really offered to him, and this was the natural place where oblations would be made; thus the transaction was represented as formal and national. Whether the potter was seen in the temple we know not. The prophet was made to connect him in some way with the business; and we learn from the fulfilment that the potter did in the end receive the money, which was paid for his field applied to an unclean purpose. In Matt.

xxvii. 9 the two verses, 12, 13, with some variations, are quoted as "spoken by Jeremy the prophet." Hence some attribute this part of Zechariah to Jeremiah; and others think that in St. Matthew the present name is a mistake. The probability is that the evangelist did not name any prophet, but that some early transcriber, remembering the purchase of the field in Jer. xxxii.6—12, attributed the quotation to that prophet. Or we may suppose that inspiration did not extend to all minor details, nor save the writers from unimportant errors.

Ver. 14.—**I cut asunder mine other staff.** As the flock, by their contemptuous payment, showed their alienation from the Shepherd, so he now, by his symbolical action, shows his rejection of them, and his surrender of them to anarchy, confusion, and ruin. The breaking of the first staff indicated that God withdrew his defensive care; the breaking of the staff called "Bands" signifies the utter dissolution of all the bonds that held the nation together, the civil and social disunion that paved the way for the victory of the Romans, and issued in the final disruption which sent the Jews wandering through the world. This in the vision is represented as the breaking of the brotherhood between Judah and Israel, the component parts of the nation. Thus was hinted the ultimate rejection of the Jews in consequence of their treatment of Christ, the good Shepherd, who came unto his own, and his own received him not (comp. Matt. xxiii. 36—38). This doom is declared more fully in the next section.

Vers. 15—17.—§ 10. *In retribution for their rejection of the good Shepherd the people are given over to a foolish shepherd, who shall destroy them, but shall himself, in turn, perish miserably.*

Ver. 15.—**Take unto thee yet** (*yet again*) **the instruments of a foolish shepherd** (comp. Hos. iii. 1). The prophet, in vision, is directed to do as he had done before (ver. 4, etc.), and enact the part of a shepherd, taking the dress, scrip, and crook, which were appropriate to the character; but this time he was to represent "a foolish," *i.e.* an evil, shepherd; for sin is constantly denoted by "folly" in the Old Testament; *e.g.* Job v. 2, 3; Ps. xiv. 1; cvii. 17; Prov. i. 7; vii. 22; xiv. 9, etc. (comp. ver. 17).

Ver. 16.—**I will raise up a shepherd in the land.** God explains the reason of the symbolical character which he directed the prophet to assume. He was going to allow the people to be chastised by an instrument whom he would permit to work his will upon them. As this evil shepherd was to arise to punish them for their rejection of

Messiah, he must represent some person or power that existed subsequent to Christ's death. Many consider that he symbolizes the Romans; but these people could not be deemed to exercise pastoral care over the Israelites, nor could their neglect of this (ver. 17) be attributed to them as a sin; nor, again, did their destruction follow upon the overthrow of the Jewish polity (ver. 18). Others see here a prediction of the coming of antichrist; but the character of "shepherd" does not suit his attributes as given elsewhere; at any rate, this cannot be the primary reference of the symbol, though all evil powers that oppose the Church of Christ are in some sense images and anticipations of antichrist. The genuine reference here is to the native chiefs and rulers ("in the land") who arose in the later times of the nation—monsters like Herod, false Christs and false prophets (Matt. xxiv. 5, 11, 12, 24; Mark xiii. 22), hirelings who made merchandise of the flock, teachers who came in their own name (John v. 43), and deceived the people to their destruction. Which shall not visit those that be cut off; or, *those that are perishing.* This foolish shepherd shall perform none of the offices of a good shepherd; he will not care for and tend those that are in danger of death (Jer. xxiii. 2). The young one; rather, *those that are scattered;* Septuagint, τὸ ἐσκορπισμένον: Vulgate, *dispersum* (Matt. xviii. 12). That that is broken. Bruised, or with limb fractured. Feed that that standeth still; literally, *that standeth;* i.e. is sound and healthy. This shepherd attended neither to the diseased nor to the healthy sheep. Septuagint, τὸ ὁλόκληρον, "that which is whole." He shall eat the flesh of the fat.

He thinks only how to get personal advantage from the flock (comp. Ezek. xxxiv, 2—8). Tear their claws (*hoofs*) in pieces, as some say, by making them traverse rough places, and not caring where he led them; but as such travelling would not specially injure sheep, and as the immediate context is concerned with their treatment as food, it is better to see here a picture of a greedy and voracious man who tears asunder the very hoofs to suck out all the nourishment he can find, or one who mutilates the fattest of his flock, that they may not stray, and that he may always have a dainty morsel at hand.

Ver. 17.—Woe to the idol-shepherd! rather, *woe to the worthless shepherd!* literally, *shepherd of vanity,* or *nothingness,* as Job xiii. 4, "physicians of no value." The LXX., recognizing that no special shepherd is signified, renders, Ὢ οἱ ποιμαίνοντες τὰ μάταια, "Alas for those who tend vanities!" St. Jerome, expounding the verse of antichrist, "O pastor, et idolum!" That leaveth the flock. Thus Christ speaks of the hireling (John x. 12). The sword shall be upon his arm, etc. The punishment denounced is in accordance with the neglect of the shepherd's duties. *The sword* represents the instrument of punishment, whatever it be; the right eye, the severity of the retribution (1 Sam. xi. 2). The arm that ought to have defended the flock shall be withered up as by catalepsy; the eye that should have watched for their safety shall be blinded. This is the judgment on the foolish shepherd. Ewald thinks that the passage ch. xiii. 7—9 is out of place there, and belonged originally to the end of the present chapter.

HOMILETICS.

Vers. 1—6.—*A final warning.* "Open thy doors, O Lebanon," etc. The prophet, after having foretold (ch. x. 6—12) the great future and final glory of the literal Israel, seems here, as it were, to "hark back" to a previous and very different scene, viz.—as most commentators, both Jewish and Christian, believe—to that which should happen in those evil days when Jerusalem should be destroyed. We noted a very similar transition at the beginning of ch. ix. (comp. also Luke xvii. 24, 25; xix. 11, etc.; 2 Thess. ii. 3). In the present case the destruction predicted seems to be of a threefold description. It was to be a destruction of the nation by being a destruction (1) of their *palaces;* (2) of their *princes;* and (3) of the *people* at large.

I. OF THESE PALACES OR CONSPICUOUS PUBLIC BUILDINGS, in which they came afterwards to glory so much (Matt. xxiv. 1; Mark xiii. 1; Luke xxi. 5). To this interpretation of vers. 1, 2 we seem pointed by the peculiar word "doors;" as also by the fact that the "doors" of the Jewish temple, and almost all its inner linings as well, are said to have been made of cypress ("fir") and cedar (see 1 Kings v. 8, 10); and, if so, we may notice: 1. *How thorough is the nature* of the coming destruction. What the "fire" can "devour" will be utterly destroyed in that way. What the fire cannot devour will "come down," or be levelled. Even if the stones remain, that is, the buildings will perish (see Matt. xxiv. 2, end). Also: 2. *How wide its extent. All* the buildings they gloried in would thus perish. They would perish thus, (1) however costly, even though almost built, as it were, of the precious cedar (Jer. xxii. 13, 14); and (2) however varied, whether comparable to "cedar," or "oak," or cypress; and finally (3) however strong, or "mighty," even if comparable (see margin) to a "defenced forest." Nothing would save the whole collection of buildings from being utterly "spoiled" and destroyed. Well might those buildings be called upon, in the bold language of prophecy, to "howl" at such an outlook! And abundantly was all this fulfilled when the Roman ploughshares ploughed the ground on which the temple and fortress of Jerusalem had previously stood.

II. OF THE PRIESTS. These are compared, in ver. 3, to "shepherds" and "young lions," as showing, perhaps, on the one hand, what they ought to be to the commonalty of Israel, and, on the other hand, what they ought to be to its foes (see Ps. lxxviii. 70—72; Gen. xlix. 9, 10). We see: 1. How *complete* their destruction. This evidenced (1) by their "howl" of despair. With the destruction of Jerusalem came that of the whole Jewish polity and liturgical service; and with that also for ever departed all the glory of the then ruling classes of Jewry. How great the emphasis, in this connection, of Matt. xxiii. 38! Also (2) by their "roar" of fury like that of young lions, the "pride," or terror, of the whole valley of Jordan, when driven therefrom by its "swelling" (Jer. xlix. 19). What is there that so excites the deepest anger as the utter humiliation of pride (comp. John xi. 48; xii. 10, 11; Matt. xxvii. 18)? 2. How *just* their destruction, and that also in two separate ways. Namely, (1) by their neglect of others. Though they belonged to the flock, as being its "own" shepherds, appointed to tend and care for it, they "pitied" it "not" (contrast Matt. ix. 36). Though the flock belonged to them, as being, in a sense, its "possessors," instead of preserving the flock they "sell" and "slay" it (see Matt. xxiii., almost *passim*). Also (2) by their satisfaction with themselves. They see no sin in their conduct; "they hold themselves not guilty." They even see cause for thankfulness to God in its results: "Blessed be the Lord; for I am rich" (comp. Luke xii. 1; xvi. 14). Can any men more deserve to suffer than those who "glory" thus "in their shame" (Phil. iii. 19)?

III. OF THE PEOPLE AT LARGE—OF THE "FLOCK." Of this destruction, note: 1. *How solemnly it was predetermined.* The very appellation here given, viz. the "flock of slaughter," signifies as much. Almost all, also, that is said respecting the flock—"I will no more pity;" "I will deliver" to evil; "I will not deliver" therefrom—implies as much. 2. *How terribly it was accomplished.* Whether (1) as to extent—the very "land" itself, as well as its "inhabitants," being "smitten" for their sakes; or (2) as to the agency used, the destruction in question being effected partly by their mutual jealousies and internecine contentions as "neighbours," and partly by their common madness in preferring "Cæsar" to "Christ" as their "king." See the well-known account of Josephus, in which the final overthrow of Jerusalem and the Jews is traced almost equally to the unwilling action of Titus without, and the furious folly of the factions within. Under both aspects it was a marvellous case of political self-destruction, as described in this passage.

In conclusion, there are just two other points to observe and admire, viz.: 1. *How inexhaustible is God's mercy!* In this awful scene of destruction, with all its aggravated guilt, shameless hypocrisy, and suicidal infatuation, the light of that mercy is yet not wholly extinguished. There are some in this "flock of slaughter" who are to be "fed" (ver. 4). So, in the case of the Noachian Deluge, and in that of the destruction of Sodom, there were some to be saved. So it is said, also, that in the fearful, final destruction of Jerusalem—and the fact may possibly be referred to in the words now before us—the Christians were saved by their flight to Pella. 2. *How discriminating are God's judgments!* The people were guilty here as well as their leaders (Jer. v. 30, 31). Therefore the people are visited with anger as well as their leaders (see Isa. xxiv. 2; Hos. iv. 9). The people, however, being less privileged and instructed, are also, in some measure, less guilty (see Jer. v. 4, 5). The people, therefore, though punished as well, are not punished as much (see above, about some of these being "fed;" also below, in ver. 7, about the "poor of the flock;" compare such passages as Matt. xi. 20—24; Luke xi. 29—32). The acknowledgment of David in Ps. li. 4, end, will be the acknowledgment of all "in that day."

Vers. 7—14.—*A final opportunity.* "And I will feed the flock of slaughter," etc. Although the "flock" of Israel was ripe for "slaughter"—as we saw in our last—there was to be, nevertheless, a certain measure of pause before that slaughter began (comp. 1 Pet. iii. 20). Israel should hear again, if only once more, an offer of peace. Our present very difficult passage may, perhaps, be understood as describing how such an offer was made to rebellious Israel—just previously to that destruction of Jerusalem which seems predicted in the preceding verses—by our Lord himself (the good Shepherd) and his apostles. Also it seems to describe to us how that final offer was met. These, accordingly, are the two points on which we would speak; viz. (1) that *momentous offer*; and (2) its *momentous results.*

1. THE NATURE OF THIS FINAL OFFER. This seems to be represented to us: 1. By the good Shepherd's *resolve.* "I will feed the flock"—I will attend to them carefully; I will offer them all they require. Also: 2. By the good Shepherd's *implements.* These are two, we read, called "Beauty" and "Bands." By the one we may, perhaps, understand (see Ps. xc. 17; xxvii. 4; ch. ix. 17, *supra*; Isa. lii. 7) the abounding favour and grace and love of the message of Christ. Though he came to a "generation" altogether deserving condemnation and death (Matt. xii. 34, 39; xxiii. 32, 33; Acts ii. 40), he came not to condemn, but to save (John iii. 17; xii. 47; Luke ix. 56). By the other we may, perhaps, understand the special limitation of the personal message of Christ (Matt. xv. 24); as also, in the first instance, of that of his apostles (Matt. x. 5, 6; Acts xiii. 46). There was *especial* favour—there was almost *exclusive* favour—in this final offer of Christ to "his own" (John i. 11, second clause).

II. ITS MOMENTOUS RESULTS. These appear to have been of two very different kinds. 1. In the case of *the Jewish teachers and people at large* they proved to be of a very painful and calamitous kind. On the one hand, these teachers and people contemptuously rejected the gracious offers of Christ. To them there was no degree whatever of "beauty," either in his character or his teaching (see ver. 8, end; and comp. Isa. liii. 2; John vii. 12, 13; xix. 7; Matt. xxvi. 66; xxvii. 63). By them, therefore, the peculiar favour he offered was utterly scorned (John xix. 15; xviii. 40; and such passages as Acts xiii. 45; 1 Thess. ii. 15, etc.); and he himself, in a certain most remarkable and significant manner, only estimated and valued at the price of a slave (vers. 12, 13; Matt. xxvi. 15; xxvii. 9, 10; Exod. xxi. 32). On the other hand, this being so, both the Saviour's feelings and conduct towards them became changed. Instead of favour there comes "loathing" (or indignation and grief; see Mark iii. 5; Luke xix. 41—46); instead of a special offer of mercy, the coming down of special judgment, in a singularly rapid and terrible manner, on the highest persons or classes amongst them ("three shepherds in one month"); instead of deliverance, utter desertion (ver. 9 compared with Matt. xxiii. 38; Luke xxi. 22—24); and instead of the limitation of favour to them, the manifest transference of it from them to the rest of mankind (Acts xiii. 46; xviii. 6; xxviii. 28; Rom. xi. 11). 2. At the same time, in the case of *the less esteemed and less eminent* portion of the flock of Israel, there were results of a different kind. In their case the Shepherd's gracious offer was not only made, but also received. As he resolved ("I will feed even you, O poor of the flock") in their case, so he did (end of ver. 7; see also Matt. xi. 5; Luke iv. 18; Mark xii. 37). In their case, again, the Shepherd's message was duly honoured and highly prized as being indeed "the Word of the Lord" (ver. 11, end; comp. Matt. xvi. 16; John vi. 68; xvi. 30). Even that comparative and temporary rejection of the Jews, which we suppose to be described in vers. 8, 9, 10, and 14, contributed greatly among the "poor" of the Gentiles to their establishment in this faith (see, again, ver. 11, and such passages as Rom. xi. 11, 25, beginning of 28, 30; 1 Cor. i. 26).

From this view of the passage—or, at any rate, from this review of those undoubted New Testament facts to which we have supposed it to point—two concluding reflections seem to arise. 1. *How obdurate is man's nature!* We have become so familiar with the story of the rejection of Christ by his own people, that it does not always surprise us as it ought. Yet how exceedingly surprising it is! Greater power, greater wisdom, greater goodness, could not possibly have been combined. Should we not also have said, at first, that they could not possibly have been resisted? No wonder the apostle speaks with such evident amazement as he does in John i. 11 (*supra*); see also John xii. 11, 37. 2. *How wonderful are God's ways!* The rejection of Christianity by those to whom it first came has been overruled to furnish its best evidence in the eyes of the rest of mankind. By crucifying their Messiah the Jews crowned him as ours. It reminds us of the words of the poet—

> " From seeming evil still educing good,
> And better thence again, and better still,
> In infinite progression."

Vers. 15—17.—*A picture of antichrist.* "And the Lord said unto me, Take unto thee yet the instruments of a foolish shepherd," etc. After the experience of the good Shepherd comes the description of the bad; after the right "instruments," the wrong ones; after the Christ, the *antichrist,* the person *usurping* the true Christ's position, that is to say, and so *opposing* his work. See (ver. 17) the "idol-shepherd" —the shepherd making himself the object of worship to his flock; and comp. 2 Thess. ii. 4; Luke iv. 7. Which of the "many antichrists" (1 John ii. 18) to appear in "the last time" is here intended primarily, we do not propose to discuss. It seems safer to take the description as applying to all. So interpreted, it may be understood as setting before us (1) their *true calling;* (2) their *chief characteristics;* and (3) their *final doom.*

I. THEIR TRUE CALLING. They are spoken of here (ver. 16) as "raised up" by God. By this we may understand: 1. That they do not come *without the knowledge of God.* By the typical action enjoined on his prophet (ver. 15), God not only shows here that he foreknew the appearance of these various enemies, but he also foretells it. As the prophet is ordered to do in figure, so will they do in fact (comp. Acts i. 16; 2 Thess. ii. 3; 1 Tim. iv. 1; Matt. xiii. 25; and see 1 Cor. xi. 19). 2. Nor yet *without God's will.* It is the natural tendency of corruption to come to a head, as it were, in this manner. An evil movement never continues long without producing evil leaders to guide it. But they cannot be fully developed till God permits (see the story of Jeroboam, 1 Kings xi. 13, 26, 35; xii. 2, 3; 2 Thess ii. 6, 7, 8, beginning).

II. THEIR CHIEF CHARACTERISTICS. These appear to be three. 1. *Shameful negligence.* The things to which, in the position assumed by these idol-shepherds, they ought specially to attend are just those they neglect. Where their flocks are in danger (" cut off "), they forsake them; where weak, as the " young," they pass by them; where "wounded," they do not "heal " them; where unable to walk (standeth still), they do not " bear " them (see John x. 12, 13; Ezek. xxxiv. 4; and contrast Ezek. xxxiv. 16; Isa. xl. 11; John x. 15). 2. *Shameless selfishness.* Instead of feeding the flock, they feed themselves—" eating the flesh of the fat " (see Ezek. xxxiv. 2, 8, end, 10; also such passages as Matt. xxiii. 14; Luke xvi. 14; 2 Pet. ii. 1—3, 15; Jude 11; and contrast 2 Cor. xii. 15—18). 3. *Unblushing cruelty.* (See end of ver. 16, "tear their claws in pieces;" and comp. Ezek. xxxiv. 4, end.) These perverters of God's truth ever become, in due course, the persecutors of God's people (see Rev. xvii. 6; xviii. 24; xix. 2).

III. THEIR FINAL DOOM. Judgment, though often long delayed, will always come upon them at last. The " sword," in due time, will descend. Moreover, this judgment, when it does come, will be found: 1. *Peculiarly just.* It is on the negligent " eye," and the cruel and grasping hand and " arm," that the punishment comes (compare, perhaps, in Ezek. xxxiv. 16, how it is said of the "fat and the strong," which had "fed themselves," " I will feed *them* with judgment"). 2. *Peculiarly awful;* all their *power* being " clean dried up," and all their *light* being " utterly darkened." So 2 Thess. ii. 8; Rev. xviii. 8, 21, etc.; and compare such passages as 2 Kings ix. 35—37; Ps. ii. 9; Isa. xxx. 14; Matt. xxi. 44; and below ch. xiv. 12.

In contemplating these scenes we may frequently notice: 1. *How great is the forbearance of God.* When we see this succession of enemies permitted to arise and prosper in sowing tares in his field, we may well exclaim as in Rom. ix. 22. Not so would man have acted (Matt. xiii. 28). 2. *How great is the goodness of God.* This forbearance is partly for the sake of those who truly believe in his Name (Matt. xiii. 29); and partly, also (more wonderful still), for the sake of those who do not (Rom. ii. 4; 2 Pet. iii. 9). 3. *How great should be the humility of his people.* With our short lives and limited powers and many infirmities both of intellect and of temper, how little we can understand of that widely scattered, often-shifting, far-spreading, long-enduring campaign of good against evil which he thus permits and directs! Well may even an apostle confess as in 1 Cor. xiii. 9, and beginning of ver. 12! And well may he admonish us all, therefore, as in 1 Cor. iv. 5!

HOMILIES BY VARIOUS AUTHORS.

Ver. 2.—*Grief for the fall of a leader.* "Howl." This may be held to express—

I. SENSE OF A GREAT LOSS. The death of a good man is always a loss. But there are differences. Some stand higher than others in society. Not only "firs," but "cedars." Great men leaders in Church and state. Hence more deeply missed and mourned. There is not only loss of their work, counsel, prayers, but of their personal influence. There are times when the feeling is intensified. Some great work to do, some difficult enterprise to be carried out; or a national crisis, demanding the service of the wisest and the best.

II. COMPLAINT OF GRIEVOUS WRONG. Death is the lot of all. When it comes in the order of nature, may grieve, but cannot justly complain. But often death comes not of necessity, but through violence and crime. The "axe," which belongs of right to justice, is seized and foully used by tyrants and assassins. So with many of the prophets and apostles. So often in the history of nations—William the Silent, President Lincoln. So in the Massacre of St. Bartholomew, when so many great and good men were cruelly murdered.

III. PRESAGE OF DIRE CALAMITY. Dark cloud. The stroke falls. Forecasts the storm. Greater disasters. If the first, the noblest, the usefullest are struck down, who shall escape?

"Freedom shrieked as Kosciusko fell."

LESSONS. 1. *Call to activity.* Close ranks. 2. *Challenge to the living to look to themselves.* We must all fall, but how and with what results? Robert Hall said of Robinson that "he fell like a noble tree." We should live so as to be missed. Better be mourned for, as friends and well-doers gone before, than die unhonoured and unblest.—F.

Vers. 5, 6.—*Oppressors and oppressed.* I. GOD'S JUDGMENT ON OPPRESSORS. Power great thing. Test of character. Few able to use it rightly. Even the "wise man" (Eccles. vii. 7) may have his head turned, and act as if "mad." The "shepherds" false to their awful trust. Hence the people became the prey of oppressors. Merciless, avaricious, godless, neither fearing God nor regarding man. Such oppressors are found in various forms. Landlords and other "possessors" have need to take warning. The people were not made for the land, but the land for the people. Property has its duties as well as its rights. "Unto whom much is given, of them shall much be required." "Shall not the Judge of all the earth do right?"

II. GOD'S MERCY FOR THE OPPRESSED. The Bible is on the side of the weak, and not the strong; of the wronged, and not the wrong-doer. Prophet after prophet has spoken on behalf of the poor and the needy, and carried their cause to the throne of the Most High. God acts by means. "*Feed* :" 1. *With the gospel of love.* 2. *With the law of righteousness.* Binding on all. 3. *With the hope of immortality.*

> "We were weary and we
> Fearful, and we in our march
> Fain to drop down and to die;
> Still thou turnedst and still
> Beckonedst the trembler and still
> Gavest the weary thy hand.
> If, in the paths of the world,
> Stones might have wounded thy feet,
> Toil or dejection have tried
> Thy spirit, of that we saw
> Nothing; to us thou wast still
> Cheerful and helpful and firm.

> Therefore to thee it was given
> Many to save with thyself.
> And at the end of thy day,
> O faithful Shepherd, to come,
> Bringing thy sheep in thy hand."
>   (Matthew Arnold.)

F.

Vers. 7—14.—*The true Shepherd.* I. GOD'S IDEA OF THE TRUE SHEPHERD. His character and service. Faithful and disinterested. Not a hireling. He is for the sheep, not the sheep for him. If his recompense left to the free-will of the people, should be adequate and fair. "The workman is worthy of his hire." But the wage should be given in more than material form. "*Themselves.*" Their trust, sympathy, prayers, and hearty co-operation in all good. "I seek not yours, but you," said Paul.

II. MAN'S TREATMENT OF THE TRUE SHEPHERD. 1. *Grossly unjust.* Remuneration mean and paltry. Not measured by the work done, but doled out by selfish and stupid hands. 2. *Basely insulting.* Instead of just appreciation, mockery. Put on the level of a slave. Such remuneration worthy of scorn. *Away with it.* 3. *Darkly menacing.* Take it or leave it. Nothing to us. Starve if you will. Murder is in their hearts. 4. *Reveals the baseness of the heart.* Indicates great social degeneracy. Foreshadows the rejection of the Saviour (Matt. xxvii. 9, 10). Let us endeavour to be true to God's idea.

> "The Christian pastor, bow'd to earth
>   With thankless toil, and vile esteem'd,
> Still travailing in second birth
>   Of souls that will not be redeem'd:
> Yet steadfast set to do his part,
> And fearing most his own vain heart."
>   (Keble.)

F.

Vers. 7—10.—*The two staves.* Acted parable. May be taken to illustrate the two great blessings of Christ's kingdom.

I. THE FATHERHOOD OF GOD. "Beauty" may indicate the covenant of peace. God's grace restraining, preserving, governing. "*Broken.*" Sign of judgment and woe. "Ichabod!" But as whole, emblem of the fatherly love and care of God, and the fairness and beneficence of his rule.

II. BROTHERHOOD OF MAN. National covenant. Union of Judah and Israel. One people under the rule of Jehovah. Fulfilled in part in the restoration; more perfectly, and in a spiritual sense, under the gospel of Christ. His kingdom is one. In him all the kindreds of the earth shall be blessed (Gal. iii. 28; Eph. ii. 14—22).—F.

Vers. 15—17.—*The evil shepherd.* I. CHARACTER. Vain. Selfish. Hypocritical. Greedy of gain and popularity. Worthless for real good. Permitted, but not approved.

II. OFFENCE. 1. *Coldness.* No "pity." His heart is not in his work. 2. *Neglect.* Takes no pains to seek out the poor and needy. Does not "visit." 3. *Unfaithfulness.* No warnings. False teaching. Making gain of godliness. God's ideal of the shepherd lost. God's benign purposes in the ministry of grace frustrated. Souls perish, and their blood calleth from the ground.

> "The hungry sheep look up, and are not fed,
>   But, swoln with wind and the rank mist they draw,
> Rot inwardly, and foul contagion spread:
>   Besides what the grim wolf with privy paw
> Daily devours apace, and nothing fed:
>   But that two-handed engine at the door
> Stands ready to smite once, and smite no more."
>   (Milton, 'Lycidas.')

(Cf. Ruskin's exposition in 'Sesame and Lilies.')

III. DOOM. "Woe." **1.** *Hardened in evil.* Degradation. Judicial blindness. **2.** *Cursed with uselessness.* **3.** *Destined to destruction.*

> " Alas, my brother ! round thy tomb
> In sorrow kneeling and in fear
> We read the pastor's doom,
> Who speaks and will not hear."
> (Keble.)

F.

Vers. 1, 2.—*The cedars, fir trees, and oaks of society.* "Open thy doors, O Lebanon, that the fire may devour thy cedars. Howl, fir tree ; for the cedar is fallen ; because the mighty are spoiled: howl, O ye oaks of Bashan ; for the forest of the vintage is come down." This chapter, it has been said, divides itself into three sections. **1.** The threat of judgment (vers. 1—3). **2.** The description of the good Shepherd (vers. 4—14). **3.** The sketch of the foolish shepherd (vers. 15—17). The expression, "Open thy doors [gates], O Lebanon," is, of course, quite dramatic in style. "The prophet, instead of announcing to Lebanon its future destruction, commands it as the servant of God to open its gates ; the meaning therefore is, 'Thou Lebanon wilt be stormed and devastated by the foe'" (Hengstenberg). Lebanon, here, may be regarded as a symbol of the kingdom of Judah, its cedars as denoting the chief men of the kingdom. We shall take the words to illustrate three subjects in relation to mankind—a variety of distinction, a common calamity, and a natural alarm.

I. A VARIETY OF DISTINCTION. The "cedar" here, the "fir tree," or cypress, and the "oaks," are employed to set forth some of the distinctions that prevailed amongst the Hebrew people. Now, whilst all men have a common origin, a common nature, and common moral obligations and responsibilities, yet in every generation there prevails a large variety of striking distinctions. There are not only the cedars and fir trees, but even briars and thistles. There is almost as great a distinction between the highest type of man and the lowest as there is between the lowest and the highest type of brute. In the great forest of every generation there are a few tall cedars and oaks rising in majesty above all the other trees, down to mere brushwood and even fungi. There are intellectual giants and intellectual dwarfs, moral monarchs and spiritual serfs. This variety of distinction in the human family serves at least two important purposes. **1.** *To check pride in the highest and despondency in the lowest.* The cedar has no cause for boasting over the fir tree or over the humblest plant: it owes its existence to the same God, and is sustained by the same common elements. And what have the greatest men—the Shakespeares, the Schillers, the Miltons, the Goethes—to be proud of ? What have they that they have not received ? And why should the weakest man despond ? He is what God made him, and his responsibilities are limited by his capacities. **2.** *To strengthen the ties of human brotherhood.* Were all men of equal capacity, it is manifest that there would be no scope for that mutual ministry of interdependence which tends to unite society together. There are the givers and the receivers ; the delight of the former is in his gifts, the hope of the latter is in the helps he receives. The strong rejoices in bearing the infirmities of the weak, and the weak rejoices in gratitude and hope on account of the succour received. Between the least and the greatest, therefore, in human society there is ample scope afforded for the full play of the faculties, the sympathies, and the services of all.

II. A COMMON CALAMITY. "Howl, fir tree ; for the cedar is fallen." An expression which implies that the same fate awaits the fir tree. There is one event that awaits men of every type and class and grade, the tallest cedar and the most stunted shrub, and that is, *death.* "All flesh is grass ; " "Wise men die, likewise the fool and the brutish person perish, and leave their wealth to others." **1.** This common calamity *levels all distinctions.* The cedar and the fir tree—if not cut down by the woodman, scathed by the lightning, or uprooted by the tempest—must sooner or later rot, and their dust mingle with the earth ; so with men of all distinctions, the prince and the pauper, the cedar and the bramble in the human forest, must bow to the stroke. "Though his excellency mount up to the heavens, and his head reach unto the clouds, yet he shall perish for ever." **2.** This common calamity should *dematerialize all souls.* Since we are only here on this earth for a few short years at most, why should we live to the flesh, and thus materialize our souls? Here we are only pilgrims, and we should be in quest of "the city that hath foundations, whose Builder and Maker is God." To see the pinions of the noble eagle, made to pierce the clouds and bask high up in sunlight, buried in a foul pool of mud, is a lamentable sight; but ten thousand times more terrible is the sight of a human soul immersed in matter.

III. A NATURAL ALARM. "Howl, fir tree." It is the howl, not of rage, not of sympathy, but of alarm. The principle of alarm here implied is that when the higher falls the lower may well take the alarm. If the cedar gives way, let the cypress look out. This principle may apply to: 1. *Communities.* Amongst the *kingdoms* of the earth there are the "cedar" and the "fir tree." Egypt, Persia, Greece, Rome,—these were cedars; they have "fallen." Let the smaller ones take the alarm. England is a "cedar," but it must fall; it has, I fear, even now the marks of decay on it; its multiplying branches of ambition are exhausting its roots. Its fall, when it comes, will be a just warning to all the smaller states of the world. The same may be said of *markets.* There are the "cedars" in the commercial world, great houses regulating almost the merchandise of the world. Some have recently fallen, others are falling: let the "fir trees" take the alarm and be cautious. 2. *Individuals.* When men who are *physical* "cedars," strong and stalwart, whose build is almost like the gnarled oak, fall, let weaker men take the alarm. When men who are *moral* "cedars," majestic in character and mighty in beneficent influences—great preachers, authors, philanthropists—fall, let the less useful take the alarm, still more the useless. "Howl, fir tree, for the cedar is fallen." This was the text of the funeral sermon which the famous Mr. Jay, of Bath, preached on the equally famous Rowland Hill; and commenting on it he spoke eloquently concerning the impressions made by the death of a man of mark.—D. T.

Ver. 3.—*Bad men in high office.* "There is a voice of the howling of the shepherds; for their glory is spoiled: a voice of the roaring of young lions; for the pride of Jordan is spoiled." We have here two subjects of thought.

I. BAD MEN IN HIGH OFFICE. The men referred to here are called "shepherds," which is a designation of men in power, men who politically and ecclesiastically presided over the people—the leaders. Communities of men everywhere and in all times have had "shepherds," men who guided and ruled them. These "shepherds" have sometimes reached their position irrespectively of the will of the people, sometimes with the will of the people, sometimes against the will of the people. In this country we have a number of "shepherds," politically from the mayor to the queen, ecclesiastically from the assistant curate to the archbishop. The "shepherds" referred to in the text had unfortunately what, alas! the leaders of the people in all ages have too frequently had—an ambitious character. Hence they are here called, "young lions," "a voice of the roaring of young lions;" or, as Keil has it, a "loud roaring of the young lions." They were *hungry, ravenous,* and *rapacious,* fattening upon the people of their charge. Elsewhere they are represented as "ravening wolves." How often have men in high office, both in state and Church, been of this character! Such as they care nothing for the people, only so far as they can make use of them, feed and fatten on them. Observe: 1. *That a man in high office who has a bad character is of all men the most contemptible.* A bad character in a pauper makes him contemptible; but a bad character in a king makes him ten times the more contemptible. When God commands us to honour our parents, and to honour the king, it implies that the parents and the king are honourworthy; if they are corrupt in character, they should be dishonoured and denounced. 2. *That it is the duty of all peoples to promote those alone to high office who have a high moral character.* Alas! they have not done so; hence they have often had unworthy magistrates, judges, kings, bishops.

II. BAD MEN IN HIGH OFFICE GREATLY DISTRESSED. "There is a voice of the howling of the shepherds; for their glory is spoiled: a voice of the roaring of young lions; for the pride of Jordan is spoiled." "The glory of these shepherds being spoiled," says Wardlaw, "signifies the bringing down of all their honour and power, and the wealth and luxury which, by the abuse of their power they had acquired, all becoming a prey to the sacking and pillaging besiegers. The pride of Jordan lay in its evergreens and brushwood with which its banks were enriched and adorned; and these being the covert and habitation of the young lions, the two parts of the figure are appropriate. As the lions howl and roar in dismay and fury when dislodged from their refuges and dwelling-places, whether by the swelling flood sweeping over their lairs, or from the cutting down or the burning of their habitations, so should the priests and rulers of Jerusalem be alarmed and struck with desperation and rage, when they found their city, within whose walls they had counted themselves secure from the very possibility of hostile entrance, laid open to the outrage of an exasperated enemy, and all its resources given up to plunder and destruction—country as well as city thrown into confusion and desolation!" Such rulers may well be distressed. Let them howl: 1. *Because all the keen-sighted and honest men over whom they preside despise them.* Though the hordes of miserable sycophants worship them on account of the glitter and pageantry of their elevated position, the Carlyles, the Thackerays, and the unsophisticated millions regard them with ineffable disdain. 2. *Because the righteous Governor of the world has denounced them.* "Woe unto you, scribes and Pharisees, hypocrites! for ye devour widows' houses, and for a pretence make long prayer: therefore ye shall receive the greater damnation .... Woe unto you, scribes and Pharisees, hypocrites! for ye pay tithe of mint and anise and cummin, and have omitted the weightier matters of the Law, judgment, mercy, and faith: these ought ye to have done, and not to leave the other undone. Ye blind guides, which strain at a gnat, and swallow a camel. Woe unto you scribes and Pharisees, hypocrites! for ye make clean the outside of the cup and of the platter, but within they are full of extortion and excess" (Matt. xxiii. 14, etc.).—D. T.

Vers. 4, 5.—*Oppressed people, and their oppressors.* "Thus saith the Lord my God; Feed the flock of the slaughter; whose possessors slay them, and hold themselves not guilty: and they that sell them say, Blessed be the Lord; for I am rich: and their own shepherds pity them not." Notice two things.

I. HERE IS A DUTY ENJOINED TOWARDS OPPRESSED PEOPLES. "Thus saith the Lord my God; Feed the flock [sheep] of the slaughter." These shepherds, these rulers of the Hebrew people, "slaughtered" the people. Without figure, oppressed peoples are "slaughtered"—slaughtered, though they continue to exist, by unrighteous exactions. Their rights are "slaughtered," their energies are "slaughtered," their liberties are "slaughtered," their independency is "slaughtered," their means of subsistence and advancement are "slaughtered." People "slaughtered" in these respects abound in every state and place in Europe. Alas! millions of them groan out a miserable existence in this highly favoured land of ours. What is our duty to these oppressed ones? "Feed the flock." "Feed" them: 1. *With the knowledge of their rights as men.* Their rights as citizens to make their own laws, their rights as religionists to worship their own God in their own way, to form their own convictions and to work them out according to the dictates of their own conscience. 2. *With the knowledge of the true methods to obtain these rights.* Not by violence and spoliation, but by moral means, by skilful industry, by temperate habits, by economic management, by moral suasion, by skilful, honest, and persevering industry. 3. *With the knowledge of worthy motives by which to obtain these rights.* Teach them that they should struggle for their rights, not for their own selfish aggrandizement, nor for the crushing of others, but in order fully to develop and honour the nature with which Heaven has endowed them. Let the oppressed peoples of Europe be thus fed by a Christly ethical education, and despotism will soon be swept from the face of the earth.

II. HERE IS A SKETCH OF THE AUTHORS OF OPPRESSION. 1. *They are cruel.* "Whose possessors slay them." Not only destitute are they of all practical sympathy for the rights and comforts of the people, but they treat them with a heartless inhumanity, they kill them. 2. *They are impious.* In all their cruelties they "hold themselves not guilty." The greatest despots of the world have ever been ready to justify themselves to their own consciences. Rulers have been found in all ages, and are still found, who, in originating and conducting the most cruel wars, "hold themselves not guilty." In war, the most fiendish of all the fiendish enterprises of wicked humanity, they have no qualms of conscience. 3. *They are avaricious.* "And they that sell them, say, Blessed be the Lord; for I am rich." A miserable greed was their inspiration; they hungered, not only for power, but for wealth; and so base were they in heart that they hypocritically thanked God for the riches which they had won by their cruelty and injustice. "Blessed be the Lord; for I am rich." There are men who say this now, men who say, "Blessed be the Lord; for I am rich," not thinking how the riches have come. The history of fortune-making is too often the history of crime.

CONCLUSION. Let it be ours to "feed," by wholesome knowledge, those who are "slaughtered" by oppression—political slaves and priest-ridden dupes.—D. T.

Vers. 6, 7.—*A terrible doom, and an invaluable privilege.* "For I will no more pity the inhabitants of the land, saith the Lord: but, lo, I will deliver the men every one into his neighbour's hand, and into the hand of his king: and they shall smite the land, and out of their hand I will not deliver them. And I will feed the flock of slaughter, even you, O poor of the flock." These words contain two subjects.

I. A TERRIBLE DOOM. "For I will no more pity the inhabitants of the land, saith the Lord: but, lo, I will deliver the men every one into his neighbour's hand, and into the hand of his king: and they shall smite the land, and out of their hand I will not deliver them." What is the doom? *The abandonment of God.* 1. *This abandonment came after great kindness.* For long centuries he had manifested the greatest kind-ness to the Hebrew people. From their rescue from Egypt down to this hour he had been merciful to them. He warned them, he threatened them, he besought them, he chastised them. Many a time they had provoked him, but still he bore with them. But now he delivers them up. "My Spirit shall not always strive with man." 2. *This abandonment involved inexpressible ruin.* They were given up to the heathen cruelty of one another and to the violence of foreigners. What more terrible fate can befall people than this? If God abandons us, what are we? This will be the doom of the finally impenitent, "Depart from me."

II. AN INVALUABLE PRIVILEGE. "I will feed the flock of slaughter, even you, O poor of the flock." "The Lord is my Shepherd, I shall not want." In Christ, the great God acted thus in a most manifest and impressive way. He came to the lost sheep of the house of Israel. "When he saw the multitudes, he was moved with compassion towards them, because they fainted, and were scattered abroad as sheep having no shepherd." "I am the good Shepherd," said Christ.

CONCLUSION. Thank God, we are not *abandoned* yet. God is with us as a Shepherd. He is seeking the lost and feeding those who are in his fold. "What man of you, having an hundred sheep, if he lose one of them, doth not leave the ninety and nine in the wilderness, and go after that which is lost, until he find it? And when he hath found it, he layeth it on his shoulders, rejoicing. And when he cometh home, he calleth together his friends and neighbours, saying unto them, Rejoice with me; for I have found my sheep which was lost."—D. T.

Ver. 8.—*A mutual dislike between God and man.* "My soul loathed them, and their soul also abhorred me." It would be idle to attempt to ascertain who are intended by the "three shepherds" that were "cut off in one month," and who are here represented as abhorring God and "loathed" by him. In running through the various conflicting explanations, as given by biblical critics, we feel such a task would be utterly hopeless and a waste of time. We take the words in order to illustrate a *mutual dislike between God and man.* That such a mutual dislike exists is proved by the moral history of the world, the consciousness of individuals, and the testimony of the inspired Word. Between God and man there is a mutual moral antagonism. We offer four general remarks on this subject.

I. THIS MUTUAL MORAL ANTAGONISM IS MANIFESTLY ABNORMAL. It is not conceivable that the all-wise and all-loving Maker of the universe would create beings whom he would loathe and who would abhor him. Such an idea is opposed at once to our intuitions and our conclusions. The Bible assures us, in language most explicit and in utterances most frequent, that mutual love, similar to that which exists between the most affec-tionate parents and their children, was that which existed in the pristine state of humanity. God loved man, and man loved God.

II. THIS MUTUAL MORAL ANTAGONISM IMPLIES WRONG ON MAN'S PART. For Infinite Purity and Righteousness to *loathe* the corrupt and the wrong is not only right, but a necessity of the Divine character. He abhorreth sin; it is the "abominable thing" which he hates. This is his glory. But for man to *abhor* him, this is the great sin, the fontal sin, the source of all other sins. To abhor the infinitely Loving and Lovable is, indeed, a moral enormity. They " hated me without a cause."

III. This mutual moral antagonism explains the sin and wretchedness of the world. Why does the world abound with falsehoods, dishonesties, and oppressions, unchastities, cruelties, and impieties? Because human souls are not in supreme sympathy with the supremely Good, because they are at enmity with God, and not " subject to the Law of God." And why all the miseries of humanity? Because God loathes sin.

IV. This mutual moral antagonism argues the necessity for a reconcilia-tion. The great want of the world is the reconciliation of man to the character and the friendship of God. Such a reconciliation requires no change on God's part. His loathing is the loathing of love—love loathing the wrong and the self-made miserable. The change must be on man's part. " God was in Christ reconciling the world unto himself." Christ is the Atonement, the Reconciliation.—D. T.

Vers. 8—11.—*Divine rejection.* " My soul loathed them, and their soul also abhorred me. Then said I, I will not feed you : that that dieth, let it die; and that that is to be cut off, let it be cut off; and let the rest eat every one the flesh of another. And I took my staff, even Beauty, and cut it asunder, that I might break my covenant which I had made with all the people." The subject of these words is *Divine rejection.* A time comes in the history of incorrigible nations and incorrigible individuals when they are rejected of Heaven. David said to Solomon, " And thou, Solomon my son, know thou the God of thy father, and serve him with a perfect heart and with a willing mind; for the Lord searcheth all hearts, and understandeth all the imaginations of the thoughts. If thou seek him, he will be found of thee; but if thou forsake him, he will cast thee off for ever " (1 Chron. xxviii. 9). The text gives us the cause, the result, and the sign of this lamentable event.

I. The cause. " My soul loathed them, and their soul also abhorred me." A mutual moral antagonism (as we have seen) between man and God. " Can two walk together except they be agreed?" The sinners' character becomes so repugnant to the Almighty that his patience is exhausted, and their rejection is the result. " My Spirit shall not always strive with man;" " Ephraim is joined to his idols: let him alone." There is a limit to the Divine forbearance. " How often would I have gathered thy children together, even as a hen gathereth her chickens under her wings, and ye would not!" " Depart from me, I never knew you;" " Because I have called, and ye refused; I have stretched out my hand, and no man regarded; . . . I also will laugh at your calamity; I will mock when your fear cometh."

II. The result. The results here are threefold. 1. *The cessation of Divine mercy.* " I will not feed you." You are no longer my sheep; no longer will I minister to your needs. 2. *Abandonment to self-ruin.* " That that dieth, let it die; and that that is to be cut off, let it be cut off." " The wages of sin is death;" " Sin, when it is finished, bringeth forth death." Let the elements of moral destruction do their work. 3. *Deliver-ance to mutual tormentors.* " And let the rest eat every one the flesh of another." All these results were realized in a material sense in the rejection of the Jewish nation. Josephus tells us that in the destruction of Jerusalem pestilence, famine, and intestine discord ran riot amongst the God-rejected people. These material evils are but faint emblems of the spiritual evils that must be realized by every God-rejected soul.

III. The sign. " And I took my staff, even Beauty, and cut it asunder, that I might break my covenant which I had made with all the people." The Divine Shepherd is represented as having two staves, or crooks; ordinary shepherds have only one. Expo-sitors, in their interpretation of these staves, differ here as in many places elsewhere in this book. Some say they indicate the *double* care that the Divine Shepherd takes of his people; some, the different methods of treatment pursued by the Almighty Shepherd towards his people; some, that they refer to the house of Judah and to the house of Israel, indicating that neither was to be left out in the mission of the work of the good Shepherd; and some that the one called " *Beauty* "—which means grace—represents the merciful dispensation under which the Hebrew people had been placed; and the other staff, called " *Bands,*" the brotherhood between Judah and Israel. One thing seems clear, that the cutting of the staff called "Beauty" asunder was a symbol of their rejection from all future grace and mercy. It may be stated, as a general truth, that all Heaven-rejected souls have signs of their miserable condition. The sign of Samson was loss of strength; "he wist not that the Lord was departed from him," until his strength was put to the test and he failed. What are the general signs? 1. Practical ignorance of God. 2. Utter subjection to the senses. 3. Complete devotion to selfish aims. 4. Insensibility of conscience.

CONCLUSION. Let us not trifle with the patience of God, lest he cast us off for ever; but rather let us earnestly and perseveringly cultivate a stronger and more vital sympathy with him, and a closer identification with his loving heart and benevolent aims.—D. T.

Vers. 12—14.—*A model spiritual teacher.* "And I said unto them, If ye think good, give me my price; and if not, forbear. So they weighed for my price thirty pieces of silver. And the Lord said unto me, Cast it unto the potter: a goodly price that I was prised at of them. And I took the thirty pieces of silver, and cast them to the potter in the house of the Lord." Why these words should have been referred to by the Evangelist Matthew (xxvii. 9, 10), and applied to Christ and Judas, I cannot explain. Nor can any one else, judging from the conflicting interpretations of biblical critics. Matthew not only misquotes the words, but ascribes them to Jeremiah, and not to Zechariah. The probability is that the "thirty pieces of silver" and the "potter's field," in connection with Judas, reminded the evangelist of these words, brought them to his memory, and from his memory he quotes them; for he gives them very incorrectly, neither according to the Greek version nor the original Hebrew. As the words, as they stand here, have an historical meaning entirely independent of St. Matthew's application of them, they may be fairly employed to illustrate a *model spiritual teacher in relation to secular acknowledgments of his teachings.* Three things are suggested concerning the shepherd in this capacity.

I. HE LEAVES THE SECULAR ACKNOWLEDGMENT TO THE FREE CHOICE OF THOSE TO WHOM HIS SERVICES HAVE BEEN RENDERED. "And I said unto them, If ye think good, give me my price; and if not, forbear." He does not exact anything, nor does he even suggest any amount. He leaves the matter entirely to themselves, give or not give, give this amount or that. This is as it should be. Ministers, whilst they have a Divine claim to a secular remuneration of their services, are neither authorized nor are they *disposed,* if they are true teachers, to enforce their claims upon the reluctant. "We have not used this power," says Paul (see 1 Cor. ix. 9—17). It may be asked—Why should the temporal support of the spiritual teacher be left entirely to the choice of the people? 1. Because contributions that are entirely free are *the only proofs to the minister that his services are really valued.* What proof is there in the amounts raised by tithes or rates, or, as in some Nonconformist Churches, by *diaconate guarantees,* that the service of the existing minister has been really valued? 2. Because the contributions that are entirely free are *the only contributions that are of any moral worth.* Those who give from custom or law, or in any way reluctantly, without a "willing mind," have no claim to moral credit; their contributions, however large, are counted worthless in the empire of virtue.

II. HIS SPIRITUAL SERVICES ARE SOMETIMES SHAMEFULLY UNDERRATED. "So they weighed for my price thirty pieces of silver." Thirty shekels. An amount in our money of about £3 3s. 9d. This was the price they put on his services, just the price paid for a bond-servant (Exod. xxi. 32). 1. *Do not determine the real worth of a spiritual teacher by the amount of his stipend.* This is often done: all fools do this. Yet who does not know ministers who get for their labours £100 a year who are of far higher character, and render nobler services than many who get £500, and even £1000? The fact is, the minister who wants a large income, as a rule, must get a large congregation; and he who would get a large congregation must pander to popular prejudices and tastes. 2. *Deplore the backwardness of the world in appreciating the highest services.* The highest service one man can render another is the impartation of those Divine ideas that will most quicken, invigorate, and ennoble his mind. But such services are, alas! the least valued. Men will pay their scullery-maid or their groom a larger sum every year than they pay their minister. "Thirty shekels," £3, for a minister;

£100 for a horse! Curates are starving, whilst cooks, dressmakers, and tailors are getting fat.

III. His INDEPENDENT SOUL REPUDIATES INADEQUATE SECULAR ACKNOWLEDG-MENTS. "And the Lord said unto me, Cast it unto the potter : a goodly price that I was prised at of them. And I took the thirty pieces of silver, and cast them to the potter in the house of the Lord." He felt the insult of being offered such a miserable sum. "Cast it unto the potter"—perhaps a proverbial expression, meaning, "Throw it to the temple potter." "The most suitable person to whom to cast the despicable sum, plying the trade, as he did, in the polluted valley (2 Kings xxiii. 10) of Hinnom, because it furnished him with the most suitable clay." A true teacher would rather starve than accept such a miserable acknowledgment for his services. Your money perish with you!

CONCLUSION. Oh for ministers of this lofty type!—ministers who feel as Paul did when he said, "I seek not yours, but you" (2 Cor. xii. 14).—D. T.

Vers. 15—17.—*Fraudulent shepherds of the people.* "And the Lord said unto me, Take unto thee yet the instruments of a foolish shepherd. For, lo, I will raise up a shepherd in the land, which shall not visit those that be cut off, neither shall seek the young one, nor heal that that is broken, nor feed that that standeth still : but he shall eat the flesh of the fat, and tear their claws in pieces. Woe to the idol-shepherd that leaveth the flock! the sword shall be upon his arm, and upon his right eye : his arm shall be clean dried up, and his right eye shall be utterly darkened." "After Israel has compelled the good Shepherd to lay down his shepherd's office, in consequence of its own sin, it is not to be left to itself, but to be given into the hand of a foolish shepherd, who will destroy it. This is the thought in the fresh symbolical action" (Keil). The "foolish" shepherd means the charlatan, or fraudulent ruler. Here we have—

I. FRAUDULENT SHEPHERDS OF THE PEOPLE DESCRIBED. We learn here : 1. *That their existence is a Divine permission.* "I will raise." In biblical phraseology, the Almighty is frequently represented as doing that which he only permits. Thus he is said to have "hardened Pharaoh's heart." He here practically respects that freedom of action with which he has endowed the human soul. Here, in this scene of probation, he allows it ample scope. Whilst he does not originate aught that is bad in the worst of men, he permits the worst of men to work out the bad that is in them, and to rise sometimes even to the highest positions in human society. In doing this, three purposes are answered. (1) *He inflicts punishment here upon the guilty by the agency of wicked men.* The Herods, the Neros, the Alexanders, the Bonners, and the most corrupt occupants of the papal chair become his instruments in the punishment of a guilty generation. For this purpose, it is intimated, these "foolish shepherds" were now raised up. (2) *He reveals to the universe the enormity of human depravity.* When bad men are allowed to reach the highest offices in Church and state, and give free scope and unrestrained development to all that is bad within them, an opportunity is afforded to all moral intelligences of receiving such an impression of the enormity of moral evil as otherwise would be impossible. (3) *He furnishes the most powerful assurance of future retribution for mankind.* To allow wickedness such liberty as this, liberty to rise to the highest positions, and to gratify its vilest propensities for ever, would be to condemn him in the eyes of the universe as an unrighteous Ruler. 2. *That under the profession of blessing their race, they are its greatest curse.* There are three features of wickedness in the character here described. (1) *Negligence.* "Which shall not visit those that be cut off, neither shall seek the young one, nor heal that that is broken, nor feed that that standeth still;" or, as Keil translates it, "That which is perishing will he not observe, that which is scattered will he not seek, and that which is broken will he not heal; that which is standing will he not care for." The groans of the people affect them no more than the roar of the breaking billows affects the granite cliffs. (2) *Selfishness.* "He shall eat the flesh of the fat." These fraudulent guides and guards of the people feed and fatten on their miseries. (3) *Cruelty.* "And tear their claws [hoofs] in pieces." If the people yield not to their exactions, contribute not to their aggrandizement, they will pounce upon them like hungry hounds, despoil them of their property, rob them of their liberty, and persecute them even unto death. "This," says Dr. Wardlaw, "was not a just character of Herod only, there were many such negligent, selfish, cruel pretenders; **false** Christs and false prophets abounded, abounded then and abound now."

II. FRAUDULENT SHEPHERDS OF THE PEOPLE DENOUNCED. "Woe to the idol-shepherd!" Here is the doom of those "idol-shepherds"—idol because vain and worthless. "The woe pronounced," says an able expositor, "is striking and impressive. 'The sword shall be upon his arm and upon his right eye.' The sword is the sword, doubtless, of the invading foe. The faithless shepherd shall be among its surest victims. The 'arm,' which ought, as the emblem of power, to have been employed in defending the flock, shall be smitten and 'dried up:' he shall lose all power, not only for their protection, but, on account of his neglect of them, for his own. His 'right eye,' which, as the emblem of knowledge and vigilance and foresight, should have guided the flock, and been ever on the watchful look-out after every member of it, shall be 'utterly darkened.' Visited by a righteous God with judicial blindness, he shall grope in the noonday as in the night, deceiving and being deceived, and shall utterly perish in his own delusions."

CONCLUSION. Beware of "wolves in sheep's clothing." "Believe not every spirit, but try the spirits, whether they are of God; because *many false prophets are gone out into the world*."—D. T.

EXPOSITION.

CHAPTER XII.

Ver. 1—ch. xiv. 21.—B. THE SECOND BURDEN.

Vers. 1—9.—§ 1. The prophet proceeds to announce Israel's conflict with heathen powers. *Hostile nations gather together against Jerusalem, but shall themselves be overthrown; for the people and their leaders, trusting in the Lord, overcome all opposition.*

Ver. 1.—**The burden of the word of the Lord for** (*concerning*) **Israel.** This is the title of the second oracle, corresponding to that at the head of ch. ix. Though the literal Israel has been rejected, as we saw in the last "burden," a new people of God arises (Hos. i. 10), the Messianic theocracy, which is also called Israel, whose fortunes the prophet herein delineates, describing its probation, its contests, triumph, and development. The body is like its Head; as the good Shepherd, Christ, was persecuted and rejected, so his members, the true Israelites, suffer at the hand of the world and Satan, before they are finally glorified. Some critics suppose that "Israel" here is written by mistake for "Jerusalem," as possibly in Jer. xxiii. 6 (see note on ch. i. 19). It is best to put a full stop after "Israel," and begin a new sentence with "Thus saith the Lord," or "The saying of Jehovah." **Which stretcheth forth the heavens,** etc. (comp. Isa. xlii. 5; Amos iv. 13). The attributes of God are mentioned here that all may believe that what he has promised, that he is able to perform. He is not only the Creator, but also the Preserver of all things (Ps. civ. 2—4; Heb. i. 3). **Formeth the spirit of man within him.**

God creates the souls of men, and moulds and guides them. In life and death men work out his purposes (Numb. xvi. 22; Heb. xii. 9).

Ver. 2.—**A cup of trembling;** *a bowl of reeling*—a bowl whose contents cause staggering and reeling, ὡς πρόθυρα σαλευόμενα, "as tottering porticoes" (Septuagint); *superliminare crapulæ* (Vulgate). This Jerome explains to mean that any one who crosses the threshold of Jerusalem in hostile guise shall totter and fall. Jerusalem is the capital and type of the Messianic theocracy; the hostile powers of the world crowd round her, like thirsting men round a bowl of wine; but they find the draught is fatal to them; they stagger back discomfited and destroyed. The figure of the cup and drunkenness is often employed to denote the judgment of God upon transgressors, which makes them incapable of defence or escape (comp. Isa. li. 17; Jer. xxv. 15, etc.; li. 39, 57; Hab. ii. 16). **The people;** *the peoples* (so vers. 3, 4, 6). The heathen nations who war against God's people. **When they shall be in the siege,** etc. This gives a good sense, but the Hebrew will not allow it. Septuagint, Ἐν τῇ Ἰουδαίᾳ ἔσται περιοχὴ ἐπὶ Ἱερουσαλήμ, "In Judæa there shall be a blockade against Jerusalem;" Vulgate, *Sed et Juda erit in obsidione contra Jerusalem*, which may mean that Judah shall be among those that besiege Jerusalem, or when Jerusalem is beset Judah shall suffer the same calamity. Pusey and Revised Version render, "And upon Judah also shall it [*i.e.* 'the burden'] be in the siege against Jerusalem." Cheyne, "And also on [or, 'over'] Judah it [*i.e.* the protection and deliverance implied in the first clause of the verse] shall be, in the siege," etc. **Any** interpretation of the passage which makes Judah join with the enemy in attacking Jerusalem is precluded by the very intimate union between Judah and Jerusalem denoted in vers. 4—7, and by the hostility of the nations against Judah. Cheyne's explanation is hardly a natural one, however suitable. Lowe ('Hebr. Stud. Comm.') renders, "And also on Judah [shall fall this reeling] during the siege [which is to take place] against Jerusalem." It seems best to render, with Alexander, "Also against Judah shall it be in the siege against Jerusalem," i.e. not only the mother city, but all the country, shall be exposed to hostile invasion. This suits ver. 5, where the chieftains of Judah are represented as trusting in the valour of the inhabitants of Jerusalem when they are incurring the same danger.

Ver. 3.—**A burdensome stone.** Jerusalem shall prove to all the nations that attack it a weight not only too heavy to lift, but one which, itself remaining unhurt, shall wound and injure those who attempt to carry it. Jerome supposes here an allusion to a custom in the towns of Palestine, which prevailed to his day (and, indeed, in Syria even now), of placing round stones of great weight at certain distances, by lifting which the youths tested their bodily strength. But we do not know that this custom existed in Zechariah's time, and the nations are not gathered together for amusement or display of strength, but for hostile attack. Septuagint, λίθον καταπατούμενον, "a stone trodden down," which reminds one of Luke xxi. 24, Ἱερουσαλὴμ ἔσται πατουμένη ὑπὸ ἐθνῶν. **Shall be cut in pieces;** i.e. by the sharp edges of the stone, or, as the Revised Version, shall be sore wounded. **Though;** rather, and; Septuagint, καὶ ἐπισυναχθήσονται: Vulgate, et colligentur. **All the people** (peoples) **of the earth.** This indicates that the struggle spoken of is no mere local conflict, waged in Maccabean or other times, but the great battle of the world against the Church, which shall rage in the Messianic era.

Ver. 4.—**I will smite every horse with astonishment** (consternation). Cavalry represents the forces of the enemy. Astonishment, madness, and blindness are threatened against Israel in Deut. xxviii. 28; here they are inflicted on the enemy. **Madness.** The riders should be so panic-stricken that they knew not what they did, and shall turn their arms against each other (Hag. ii. 22). **Open mine eyes upon the house of Judah;** i.e. will regard with favour and protect (Deut. xi. 12; 1 Kings viii. 29; Ps. xxxii. 8). **With blindness.** They shall be blinded with terror. The previous threat is repeated with this emphatic addition.

Ver. 5.—**The governors** (chieftains) of **Judah shall say in their heart.** The leaders of Judah have a profound, settled conviction that Jehovah is on his people's side. The **inhabitants of Jerusalem shall be** (are) my **strength.** When they see the enemy discomfited (vers. 2—4) each of them shall have confidence in the Divine election of Jerusalem, foregoing their former jealousy, and see in her success a token of God's protection and their own final victory.

Ver. 6.—**A hearth;** literally, a pan. The victory should be easy and complete. The chieftains of Judah shall be like a chafing-dish full of fire set among dry faggots (comp. Obad. 18; Nah. i. 10). **In a sheaf;** among sheaves. **Jerusalem shall be inhabited again;** rather, Jerusalem shall yet again dwell. Jerusalem is personified as a female. In spite of all the attacks of the enemy, who tried to destroy and remove her, she shall remain firm and unshaken **in her own place.** In Jerusalem, the centre of the theocracy where God has set her. So against the Church the gates of hell shall not prevail, and the persecutions which she suffers increase her stability and add to her numbers.

Ver. 7.—**Shall save the tents of Judah first.** Instead of "first," a preferable reading, supported by the Greek, Latin, and Syriac Versions, is "as in the beginning," or "as in former days." The prophet declares that the open towns and villages of Judah, which can offer no effectual resistance to an enemy like the fortified city Jerusalem, shall be saved by the aid of God, as so often has happened in old time. If "first" be the genuine reading, the meaning is that the country people shall first be saved in order to prevent Jerusalem glorifying herself at their expense. **That the glory . . . do not magnify** themselves **against** (be not magnified above) **Judah.** God will save the chosen nation in such a manner that each part shall have its share in the glory and honour. The leaders, represented by "the house of David" and "the inhabitants of Jerusalem," as the sanctuary of God and a strongly fortified city, shall not be able to exalt themselves as more favoured than the rest of the people. By God's help alone is the victory won, and all alike share in this. The expressions in this verse could not have been written, as some assert, while the dynasty of David reigned.

Ver. 8.—**He that is feeble** (literally, that stumbleth) **among them . . . shall be as David.** God shall endue the inhabitants of Jerusalem with marvellous strength and courage, so that the weakest among them shall be a hero such as David, who killed the lion and bear and overcame the giant (comp. Ps. xviii. 32). **The house of David shall be as**

God (*Elohim*). The chiefs of the theocracy shall be endowed with supernatural might, the expression, "as God," being explained in the next clause. Septuagint, ὡς οἶκος Θεοῦ, "as the house of God," as if it were of the heavenly family. The translators seem to have thought the genuine expression too unqualified. **As the angel of the Lord before them.** Even as the angel of the Lord, who led the Israelites in all their wanderings (comp. Exod. xiv. 19; xxiii. 20; xxxii. 34; Josh. v. 13). We see in this description an intimation of the graces and endowments bestowed upon every faithful member of the Church of Christ.

Ver. 9.—**I will seek to destroy.** It shall be always my aim and my care to destroy the enemies of the Church, that they shall never prevail against it. The words cannot apply to the literal Jerusalem, against which no such confederacy of nations was ever formed.

Vers. 10—14.—§ 2. *There shall ensue an outpouring of God's Spirit upon Israel, which shall produce a great national repentance.*

Ver. 10.—**I will pour.** The word implies abundance (comp. Ezek. xxxix. 29; Joel ii. 28). **The house of David,** etc. The leaders and the people alike, all orders and degrees in the theocracy. Jerusalem is named as the capital and representative of the nation. **The spirit of grace and of supplications.** The spirit which bestows grace and leads to prayer. "Grace" here means the effects produced in man by God's favour, that which makes the recipient pleasing to God and delighting in his commandments (Heb. x. 29). **They shall look upon me whom they have pierced.** The Speaker is Jehovah. To "look upon or unto" implies trust, longing, and reverence (comp. Numb. xxi. 9; 2 Kings iii. 14; Ps. xxxiv. 5; Isa. xxii. 11). We may say generally that the clause intimates that the people, who had grieved and offended God by their sins and ingratitude, should repent and turn to him in faith. But there was a literal fulfilment of this piercing, *i.e.* slaying (ch. xiii. 3; Lam. iv. 9), when the Jews crucified the Messiah, him who was God and Man, and of whom, as a result of the hypostatic union, the properties of one nature are often predicated of the other. Thus St. Paul says that the Jews crucified "the Lord of glory" (1 Cor. ii. 8), and bids the Ephesian elders "feed the Church of God, which he hath purchased with his own blood" (Acts xx. 28; for the reading Θεοῦ, see the critics). St. John (xix. 37) refers to these words of Zechariah as a prophecy of the Crucifixion (comp. Rev. i. 7). The LXX. renders, Ἐπιβλέψονται πρὸς μὲ ἀνθ᾽ ὧν κατωχρήσαντο,

"They shall look to me because they insulted," either reading the last verb differently, or understanding it figuratively in the sense of assailing with cutting words; but there is no doubt about the true reading and interpretation. Vulgate, *Aspicient ad me quem confixerunt.* "Me" has been altered in some manuscripts into "him;" but this is an evident gloss received into the text for controversial purposes, or to obviate the supposed impropriety of representing Jehovah as slain by the impious. That St. John seems to sanction this reading is of no critical importance, as he is merely referring to the prophecy historically, and does not profess to give the very wording of the prophet. A suffering Messiah was not an unknown idea in Zechariah's time. He has already spoken of the Shepherd as despised and ill-treated, and a little further on (ch. xiii. 7) he intimates that he is stricken with the sword. The prophecies of Isaiah had familiarized him with the same notion (Isa. liii., etc.). And when he represents Jehovah as saying, "Me whom they pierced," it is not merely that in killing his messenger and representative they may be said to have killed him, but the prophet, by inspiration, acknowledges the two natures in the one Person of Messiah, even as Isaiah (ix. 6) called him the "Mighty God," and the psalmists often speak to the same effect (Ps. ii. 7; xlv. 6, 7; cx. 1, etc.; comp. Micah v. 2). The "looking to" the stricken Messiah began when they who saw that woeful sight smote their breasts (Luke xxiii. 48); it was carried on by the preaching of the apostles; it shall continue till all Israel is converted; it is re-enacted whenever penitent sinners turn to him whom they have crucified by their sins. Critics have supposed that the person whose murder is deplored is Isaiah, or Urijah, or Jeremiah; but none of these fulfil the prediction in the text. **They shall mourn for him.** There is a change of persons here. Jehovah speaks of the Messiah as distinct in Person from himself. **As one mourneth for his only son . . . for his firstborn.** The depth and poignancy of this mourning are expressed by a double comparison, the grief felt at the loss of an only son, and of the firstborn. Among the Hebrews the preservation of the family was deemed of vast importance, and its extinction regarded as a punishment and a curse, so that the death of an only son would be the heaviest blow that could happen (see Isa. xlvii. 9; Jer. vi. 26; Amos viii. 10). Peculiar privileges belonged to the firstborn, and his loss would be estimated accordingly (see Gen. xlix. 3; Exod. iv. 22; Deut. xxi. 17; Micah vi. 7). The mention of "piercing," just above, seems to connect the passage with the Passover solemnities and the destruction of the firstborn of the Egyptians (see *Expositor*, vol. vi. p. 131, etc.).

Ver. 11.—As if the above comparisons were not strong enough, the prophet presents a new one, referring to an historical event, which occasioned a universal mourning in Jerusalem. **As the mourning of** (*at*) **Hadadrimmon in the valley of Megiddon.** This is generally supposed to refer to the death of King Josiah of a wound received at Megiddo, in the battle with Pharaoh-Necho (B.C. 60J), and to the national lamentation made for him and long observed on the anniversary of the calamity (see 2 Kings xxiii. 29; 2 Chron. xxxv. 20—25). This universal and perennial mourning is a figure of the continual remembrance of the death of Christ in the Church. There is a difficulty about the identification of Hadadrimmon. St. Jerome says it was a place in the Plain of Megiddo, near Jezreel, and known in his day by the name of Maximianopolis. This is supposed to be *Rummáneh*, seven miles north-west of Jezreel, on the southern edge of the Plain of Esdraelon. But the identification is far from certain. The Assyrian name given to the place may, as Lowe suggests, be a confirmation of the post-exilian origin of the prophecy. The site of Megiddo also is undetermined, though Conder suggests *Mujedda*, a ruined city about three miles south of Bethshean. The opinion that the name Hadadrimmon is that of a Syrian or Phœnician god, whose rites were celebrated as those of Adonis ("the weeping for Tammuz" of Ezek. viii. 14), is preposterous; and the idea that the prophet would thus refer to the worship of an abominable idol is one that could have occurred only to disbelievers in revelation. The LXX., mistaking the text, gives, ὡς κοπετὸς ῥοῶνος ἐν πεδίῳ ἐκκοπτομένου, "as mourning for a pomegranate cut off in the plain."

Ver. 12.—**The land.** Not Jerusalem only, but the whole country. **Every family apart.** The mourning should extend to every individual of every family (comp. Ezek. xxiv. 23). **David . . . Nathan.** First the royal family is mentioned generally, to show that no one, however, high in station, is exempted from this mourning; and then a particular branch is named to individualize the lamentation. Nathan is that son of David from whom descended Zerubbabel (1 Chron. iii. 5; Luke iii. 27, 31). **Their wives apart.** In private life the females of a household dwelt in apartments separate from the males, and in public functions the sexes were equally kept distinct (see Exod. xv. 20; Judg. xi. 34; 1 Sam. xviii. 6; 2 Sam. vi. 5).

Ver. 13.—**Levi . . . Shimei.** As before, the priestly family is first mentioned generally, and then individualized by naming Shimei, the son of Gershon, and grandson of Levi, of whom was the family of the Shimeites (Numb. iii. 17, 18, 21). The LXX. gives, "the tribe of Simeon," instead of "the family of Shimei." But there is no reason for singling out this tribe. In one sense, this prophecy began to be fulfilled when a great company of priests were converted by the preaching of the apostles (Acts vi. 7).

Ver. 14.—**The families that remain.** All the families that have not been mentioned already.

HOMILETICS.

Vers. 1—4.—*A wonderful siege.* "The burden of the word of the Lord for Israel, saith the Lord," etc. These three concluding chapters seem to refer to one principal topic ("the burden of the Lord for *Israel*," ver. 1) and to one principal time (see the thirteen-times repeated expression, "in that day"). The general preface or introduction to the special succession of wonders which they announce to us is contained in ver. 1, setting forth, as it does, the wonder-working nature of the God who foretells them, in regard (1) to all above (the "heaven"); (2) all beneath (the "earth"); and (3) all within (the "spirit of man"). See somewhat similar preface to a somewhat similar announcement of wonderful doings in Rev. xxi. 5. After this introduction, in vers. 2—4, we have described to us, as the opening wonder of all, a certain future wonderful "siege." In which description we may notice three principal things, viz. (1) *the many enemies* of the city besieged; (2) *its one Defender;* and (3) *its complete defence.*

I. ITS MANY ENEMIES. Herein, evidently, is to be one leading peculiarity of this "siege" of Jerusalem. It is not only to be a complete investment, "all the people" being "round about" (ver. 2; see also Luke xix. 43), but it is also to be an investment by an exceedingly large assemblage of "peoples . . . gathered together" from all parts of the world. Considering, indeed, the frequent use in these verses (some six times in all) of the expressions "all" and "every," and the apparent definiteness of comprehension of the language in the end of ver. 3, we seem justified in believing that every separate Gentile nation or people will be employed in this siege. All the rest of the world against Jerusalem. Such is what we seem to see here. Such is what we seem to see also in such passages as Ezek. xxxviii. 1—16 (where note special mention, as in ver. 4 here, of "horses" and "horsemen"); Joel iii. 9—17; Rev. xvi. 14—16; xx. 8, 9. Whether or not we consider all these passages to refer to exactly the same times and events, at any rate they illustrate, if they do not apply to, the universal league described here.

II. ITS ONE DEFENDER. With all the rest of mankind against the people of Jerusalem, there can be no man, of course, on their side. But they are not to be on that account without a defender. On the contrary, they will have the best of all, even Jehovah himself. Five times over, and in two separate ways, he gives them to understand this. He declares: 1. *That he will give heed to their case.* "I will open mine eyes upon the house of Judah" (see Ps. xxxiii. 18; xxxiv. 15; Deut. xi. 12; 1 Kings ix. 3; Dan. ix. 18; and ch. ix. 8 above). 2. *That he will give help in their need.* He will give help by "making" Jerusalem (vers. 2, 3) that which it requires to be "made" in this time of extremity. He will give help also by "smiting" those many enemies (ver. 4) who are leagued together for their destruction, and who, therefore, require to be "smitten" on their behalf; and what, of its kind, could be more satisfactory than this double assistance? this weakening of their enemies? this concurrent strengthening of themselves (comp. 2 Sam. iii. 1)?

III. ITS COMPLETE DEFENCE. This twofold assistance was sufficient in degree as well as satisfactory in nature. What it proposed to do, that it did. In particular, God, in this manner: 1. *Bewildered the minds* of all the enemies of Jerusalem. He made Jerusalem, to these enemies, such a cup of trembling and of stupor and slumber that they were not able, and did not dare, in many respects, to attack them. Completely as they seemed, by being "round about" the city, to have it in their power, they were like men appalled and stupefied, and left it alone (comp. Gen. xxxv. 5). 2. Also, when these enemies did find themselves able to devise measures against Jerusalem, God *crushed their efforts.* They were as men trying their strength by endeavouring to lift a heavy stone from the ground, the only result being to crush themselves by its weight. So would Jerusalem be made to do thus to its foes—to all its foes, however numerous. It would not only bruise, but destroy them, as though the sword had "cut" them "in pieces." 3. Besides which, so we may perhaps understand ver. 4, God would himself *overwhelm their spirits.* Having failed so fatally in their efforts, those who survived, and their agents also, in utter panic, folly, and ignorance, would be so far from being able to do further injury that they would themselves be in need of defence. So surpassingly well can that one Defender do for those that are his.

We learn something here, in conclusion: 1. *As to the possibilities of the future.* Who can say that such a gigantic conspiracy of evil against a literally restored and renovated Jerusalem, and such a triumphant delivery from it, may not mark the end of this age? Certainly far greater things, both in the way of manifested evil and good, than have ever been witnessed hitherto, may yet be seen on this earth. 2. *As to the true character of the present.* This last conflict will be but the fully developed result of a long previous conflict of a similar kind. Compare the conspiracy and deliverance in long-ago days described in Ps. lxxxiii. (compare also, on the one side, Acts xxviii. 22; and on the other, Matt. xxviii. 20).

Vers. 5—8.—*A wonderful people.* "And the governors of Judah shall say in their heart, The inhabitants of Jerusalem shall be my strength," etc. In the preceding verses the dominant idea is that of Jerusalem as a city *besieged.* In these we have a vision of it as a city *inhabited* (note end of ver. 6, and the thrice-recurring expression, "the inhabitants of Jerusalem"). And there are three aspects in which, when so regarded, we seem called upon to admire it, viz. (1) as perfectly *safe;* (2) as properly *humble;* and (3) as amazingly *strong.*

I. JERUSALEM SAFE. See: 1. In the end of ver. 6, *how this condition of safety is described.* Jerusalem is spoken of as "inhabited again;" not deserted, *i.e.* as previously, because of the attacks of its foes. Also as "inhabited again in her own place, even in Jerusalem;" as now, therefore, not even claimed as belonging to any but those who had been identified with it for so many generations. 2. *How this description of safety is justified.* (1) It is so if we take ver. 5 as it stands, by the thorough confidence of the "governors" in the people of Jerusalem. They acknowledge this people to be their "strength," not with their lips only, but in their "heart." (2) Such confidence is a great element of safety, especially when combined, as in this instance, with an equal amount of confidence, on the part of both rulers and ruled, in Jehovah himself (see end of ver. 5). (3) For such a combination renders those rulers, like that famous general who spoke of his well-tried army as "able to go anywhere and do anything," an amazing power to their city in the way of protection and defence. At any rate, so it was God made them to be in this instance. Like flame when applied to things most inflammable, so would he make them amidst the foes of his people, viz. equally sure and equally swift to consume. How safe a city when all those who threaten it can thus effectually be destroyed!

II. JERUSALEM HUMBLE. See: 1. *Why this humility was secured;* viz. because of its vital importance. If either the leaders ("the house of David") or the people should begin to "magnify themselves" on account of those effectual means of defence just described, they would at once be in danger again (Prov. xxviii. 26; Jer. xvii. 5, 6, etc.). 2. *How this humility was secured.* The beginning of deliverance was to be in something apart from Jerusalem, as it were. In something, also, that at first sight she might be inclined to despise. Such deliverance will, therefore, be like a "soldiers' victory" in its way. Rather, like that deliverance we read of in 2 Kings vii., which began with certain despised outsiders, and was clearly not their work, but God's. "The *Lord* shall save the *tents of Judah first.*" Observe the triple emphasis in these words.

III. JERUSALEM STRONG. Strong: 1. *Because of the gracious continuance of God's care.* Whatever he had already done for his people, so long as they are enabled to remain truly humble and trustful, that he will go on to do still (see Hos. xiii. 1; Prov. xviii. 12; Isa. lxvi. 2). 2. *Because of the abundant results of God's blessing.* The very feeblest amongst them should be made, in desire and intention, like the very strongest, in that way, previously known (1 Sam. xiii. 14; 1 Kings ix. 4; xv. 3, etc.). The leaders amongst them should be *leaders* indeed—persons deserving to be *followed* as closely and fully as the Angel-Jehovah, of whom we afterwards read, as in 1 Pet. ii. 21, 22; John xiii. 15; Phil. ii. 5; 1 Cor. xi. 1, etc. This state of things (apparently) the complete fulfilment of Deut. xxxiii. 29.

Three things, as illustrated here concerning the prophetical Scriptures generally, may be noticed to conclude. 1. Their *obscurity* in many points. On the one hand, *e.g.,* the specially distinctive mention both of "Jerusalem" and of "Judah," and the singularly local complexion of the end of ver. 6, point us to a literal view of the whole. On the other, the mention of the house of David, which has so long since vanished from sight, and the apparent connection of it with our Divine Redeemer as the true New Testament "David" (Ezek. xxxiv.; xxxvii.; Acts ii. 29—31), point us almost as strongly to a figurative and spiritual interpretation. Who can decide confidently between them till all is decided by the actual fulfilment of the prophecy? 2. Their *plainness* in others. That some exceedingly blessed and glorious condition of things, either in the literal or the spiritual Jerusalem—or, it may be, in both together—is here fore-described, who can doubt? What this condition of things is to depend on, and how to be brought about, also seem very plain. This whole prophecy, in short, is at present, as are so many others, like a "proof before letters." We can only guess at present about the *name* of the landscape which it sets before us, but we can appreciate its *loveliness* to the full. 3. Their *profitableness* in all. So far as obscure, they serve to teach us the three great Christian duties of patience before God, humility as to ourselves, and forbearance towards others. So far as plain, they are fitted to animate our hope and sustain our courage and direct both our faith and our walk (2 Thess. iii. 5; 2 Pet. iii. 14; Rom. xv. 4, etc.).

Vers. 9—14.—*Wonderful sorrow.* "And it shall come to pass in that day, that I will seek to destroy all the nations," etc. There is much that is striking in the apparent connection of this passage with that before. Just when God shall be seen by his people to be "seeking" and bringing about (see ver. 9) the overthrow and destruction of their many enemies, they, on the other hand, will be seen to be overwhelmed with sorrow of heart. Their souls, as it were, will be plunged into darkness at the very breaking of day. The very thing they have hoped for seems close at hand; and, lo! they are as men in despair. Equally remarkable, next, with the time of this sorrow, is its character. So we shall find, whether we consider (1) its peculiar *origin*; or (2) its peculiar *magnitude*.

I. ITS PECULIAR ORIGIN. To what is it due? Not to those causes which bring about the ordinary "sorrow of the world" (2 Cor. vii. 10). On the contrary, being sorrow which is "according to God" (κατὰ Θεὸν, 2 Cor. vii. 10), it has the "things of God" as its cause. In other words, it is occasioned: 1. *By the action of God on the hearts of his people.* He "pours on" them: (1) "The spirit of grace." He gives them, *i.e.*, in overflowing abundance, those gracious influences of the Spirit of holiness by which men are enabled to believe in him as "the God of all grace," and so are encouraged to pray (Rom. viii. 15; Gal. iv. 6). (2) "The spirit of supplications." He gives them, *i.e.*, in similar abundance, those other gracious influences of that same Holy Spirit by which he is pleased both to guide men and also to assist men in their prayers (Rom. viii. 26; Eph. vi. 18; Jude 20). 2. *By the consequent thoughts of God's people about him.* (1) They think of him as having been "pierced" by their sins. This is an especial feature, we know, in "godly sorrow"—its horror at having sinned against God (Ps. li. 4; Gen. xxxix. 9; 2 Sam. xii. 13; perhaps also Isa. xliii. 24, end; Eph. iv. 30). (2) They think of him as having been alienated by their folly. They "mourn for him" like those mentioned in 1 Sam. vii. 2. After their privileges are gone from them, they see, with sorrow, how much they have lost. From none of these sources, we repeat, is man's natural sorrow found to flow forth.

II. ITS PECULIAR MAGNITUDE. Wide waters are generally shallow; deep waters are seldom broad; but here we have both. 1. *Peculiar depth.* On the one hand, (1) there is only one known *kind* of sorrow equally deep. As the shades of life's afternoon thicken around us, it is to our children we look to give us comfort and hope, and to keep up the interest of life in our hearts (Gen. v. 28, 29; John xvi. 21). How peculiarly great, therefore, the sorrow of losing a firstborn and only son (Gen. xxii. 2; xlix. 3; Prov. iv. 3, 4; Luke vii. 12)! The loss bewailed here is like that— loss of all! On the other hand, (2) there had never been but one previous *example* of sorrow equally deep, viz. the sorrow felt on the death of Josiah, almost the very best (2 Kings xxiii. 25; xviii. 5), and certainly the last real, king among the descendants of David— a sorrow the memory of which, in the prophet's own day, had not at all been forgotten, and the sound of which is to be heard still by the world in the Lamentations of Jeremiah (2 Chron. xxxv. 25; Lam. iv. 20). 2. *Peculiar diffusion.* We find this sorrow described as pervading not the city only, but all the "land." We find it affecting every separate "house" amongst the houses of Israel, whether in Church or state (Levi and David[?]), whether well known or only little known (David and Nathan), whether with good antecedents or evil ones (Levi and Shimei; see Deut. xxxiii. 8; 2 Sam. xvi. 5—13); also affecting every "family" of every separate "house;" also every adult member of every family, whether male or female. At once, therefore, in this tempest of sorrow, they were all united, yet all "apart." Even so, with their separate roots, are the "trees of the wood," when all moved by one wind (see Isa. vii. 2).

We see, in all this, something: 1. *To give us comfort and hope.* Without attempting to dogmatize on such a subject, we cannot but see, from this analysis of the passage, what it seems to foretell, viz. the future conversion of the whole people of Israel to belief in the gospel of Christ (comp. 2 Cor. iii. 13—16 with Rom. xi. 25—27; see also John xix. 37; Rev. i. 7; and, in addition to all that has been noted above, see how accurately this application of the passage to a future national recognition of Christ by Israel helps to explain the singular change of person, viz. from "me" to "him" in ver. 10, something the same as in that other passage where the Angel-Jehovah is speaking, viz. Gen. xxii. 12; and note, finally, as to the peculiar time and character of this sorrow, the very remarkable language of Hos. iii. 5, end; while as to the joyful importance of such an interpretation, if correct, see again Rom. xi. 12, 15). 2. *To give us instruction and warning.* Equally great, for example, ought to be our sorrow for sin (Rom. iii. 9, 29). Equally, also, ought it to be founded on our thoughts about Christ (John xvi. 9; Acts ix. 4, 5; Matt. xxv. 40, etc.). And equally, finally, can we only hope to receive it as a gift from above (Acts v. 31; 2 Tim. ii. 25).

HOMILIES BY VARIOUS AUTHORS.

Vers. 1—9.—*The security of Zion.* I. MIGHT OF HER KING. The worlds of matter and of mind are under his control. If so, there is no such thing as chance. Then whatsoever God has promised he will certainly perform. Then to trust and to obey God must be the great end of our being. God's friends are blessed (vers. 2, 4). His enemies, intoxicated by pride, muster for the fight. They are discomfited and driven back in headlong rout. Blindness seizes them, terror overpowers them; they perish, as at the Red Sea and in Midian's evil day (cf. Ps. cxxxii. 18).

II. ENERGY OF HER LEADERS. (Vers. 5—7.) Men of faith and capacity, command-ing the confidence of the people. Bound together by their common faith in God and devotion to the highest interests of humanity.

III. HEROISM OF HER PEOPLE. (Vers. 8, 9.) Strength, Divine in its source, various in degree, adequate for every emergency, making the weak strong, and the strong stronger. A united people, with settled government, equal laws, courageous and faithful for the right. Zion united can stand against every assault, but divided becomes the prey of her enemies. "Pray for the peace of Jerusalem."—F.

Ver. 8.—*True greatness.* I. NOT INHERITED, BUT PERSONAL.
II. NOT IN CIRCUMSTANCES, BUT CHARACTER.
III. NOT IN SELF-AGGRANDIZEMENT, BUT IN SOCIAL USEFULNESS.
IV. NOT BOUND BY HUMAN WEAKNESS, BUT RISING TO THE GLORY OF DIVINE STRENGTH.
V. NOT RESTRICTED TO INDIVIDUALS, BUT THE COMMON POSSESSION OF THE GOOD
VI. NOT LIMITED TO EARTH, BUT LEADING TO THE HONOURS OF ETERNITY.—F.

Vers. 11—14.—*The great mourning.* The scene depicted has reference first of all to the Jews. Already partially fulfilled. But the principles involved are of universal application. Take it to illustrate *true repentance.*

I. GOD FOR ITS CAUSE. Not man, but God. The Father of our spirits acting on our spirit. "The spirit of grace."

II. SINNERS OF MANKIND FOR ITS SUBJECTS. Not angels. We read of their fall, but never of their rising again. For them there seems no place for repentance. Not the righteous. If man were innocent, there would be no need for penitence. But sinners. As all have sinned, repentance is required of all.

III. THE CROSS OF CHRIST FOR ITS INSTRUMENT. On the one hand, how can the sense of sin be brought home to man's conscience? On the other, how can God, con-sistently with his righteousness, show mercy to the sinner? The answer is found in the cross. Here we see, and here alone: 1. The exceeding sinfulness of sin. 2. The exceeding greatness of God's love to sinners. "God commendeth his own love towards us, in that, while we were yet sinners, Christ died for us."

IV. INTENSITY AND THOROUGHNESS FOR ITS GREAT CHARACTERISTICS. 1. *Intensity.* Thought and feeling. Sorrow deep and bitter. 2. *Thoroughness.* Goes to the very root of the matter; real and abiding.

V. REGENERATION OF SOCIETY AS ITS BLESSED RESULT. Society made up of indi-viduals. Change them, and you change all. The whole lump will be leavened. When there is peace with God, purity of life, brotherly kindness and charity, the old glory of the land will be restored.—F.

Ver. 1.—*The universe.* "The burden of the word of the Lord for Israel, saith the Lord, which stretcheth forth the heavens, and layeth the foundation of the earth, and formeth the spirit of man within him." This chapter, and on to ver. 6 of the following, most expositors regard as referring to Israel's conflict and victory, conversion and ultimate holiness. The first verse announces how the conflict against Jerusalem and

Judah will result in the conquest of all enemies. The passage before us suggests a few thoughts concerning the universe.

I. THAT THE UNIVERSE INCLUDES THE EXISTENCE OF MATTER AND OF MIND. The phrase "heavens" and "earth" is used here and elsewhere to represent the whole creation. 1. *It includes matter.* Of the essence of matter we know nothing; but by the word we mean all that comes within the cognizance of our senses, all that can be felt, heard, seen, tasted. How extensive is this material domain! Science shows that it baffles all efforts and methods of mensuration. 2. *It includes mind.* Indeed, mind is here specified. "And formeth the spirit of man within him." Man has a spirit. Of this he has stronger evidence than he has of the existence of matter. He is conscious of the phenomena of mind, but not conscious of the phenomena of matter. Man's mind is only an insignificant part and a humble representative of the immeasurable universe of spirit.

II. THAT THE UNIVERSE ORIGINATED WITH ONE PERSONAL BEING. "The Lord, which stretcheth forth the heavens," etc. It had an origin; it is not *eternal.* The idea of its eternity involves contradictions. It had an origin; its origin is not *fortuitous;* it is not the production of chance. The idea of its springing from chance may live in the region of speculation, but never in the realm of intelligent conviction. It had an origin; its origin is not that of a *plurality of creators;* it has one, and only one—"the Lord." This is the only philosophic account of its origin, "Thou, Lord, in the beginning hast laid the foundation of the earth, and the heavens are the works of thy hands."

III. THAT THIS ONE PERSONAL CREATOR HAS PURPOSES CONCERNING THE HUMAN RACE. "The burden of the word of the Lord for Israel, saith the Lord." This may mean, "the sentence of the word of the Lord concerning Israel." Now, this chapter, this book—nay, a large portion of the Bible—purports to be a revelation of his purpose to mankind. He has not created us without an object, nor placed us on this earth without an object; both in our creation and preservation he has a purpose. This being so: 1. No events in human history are accidental. 2. The grand purpose of our life should be the fulfilment of his will. "Not my will, but thine be done."

IV. THAT HIS PURPOSE TOWARDS MANKIND HE IS FULLY ABLE TO ACCOMPLISH. His creative achievements are here mentioned as a pledge of the purposes hereafter announced. Every purpose of the Lord shall be performed. Has he purposed that all mankind shall be converted to his Son? It shall be done. "There is nothing too hard for the Lord."—D. T.

Vers. 2, 3.—*Sin self-punishment.* "Behold, I will make Jerusalem a cup of trembling unto all the people round about, when they shall be in the siege both against Judah and against Jerusalem. And in that day will I make Jerusalem a burdensome stone for all people: all that burden themselves with it shall be cut in pieces, though all the people of the earth be gathered together against it." There is in this passage a principle by which the Governor of the world punishes malicious men. That principle is this—*the reaction of their efforts to injure others causing injury of themselves.* It is here said that Jerusalem would become confusion and destruction to the men who sought its ruin. It is here said that: 1. Jerusalem would become to them "a cup of trembling," or, as some render it, "a cup of intoxication." It does not say that Jerusalem will put forth any active efforts to wreak vengeance on its enemies, but that its effect upon the enemies would be as an intoxicating cup; it will make them reel and stagger in confusion. The thought of their own malicious conduct towards it would produce an effect upon their own minds that would make them tremble and become confused. 2. Jerusalem would become to them "a burdensome stone." The idea is that, in their endeavours to injure Jerusalem, they would crush themselves. I make three remarks in relation to this punishment by reaction.

I. IT IS WELL ATTESTED. 1. *It is attested by every man's consciousness.* Every man who attempts to injure another feels sooner or later that he has injured himself. There is a recoil and a regret. In truth, the malign passion itself is its own punishment. A man who cherishes anger towards another injures himself more than he can by any effort injure the object of his displeasure. In every malign emotion there is misery. 2. *It is attested by universal history.* It is a law that runs through all history, that the "mischief" of a man "shall return upon his own head, and his violent dealing shall come down upon his own pate" (Ps. vii. 16). The conduct of Joseph's brethren and of Haman may be cited as illustrations; but the conduct of the Jews towards the Messiah is an example for all times, most mighty and impressive. The blows which the old Jewish nation struck on him rebounded on their own heads and ruined them. "Whoso diggeth the pit," says Solomon, "shall fall therein; and whoso rolleth the stone, it will return on him" (Prov. xxvi. 27).

II. It is MANIFESTLY JUST. What man thus punished can complain of the righteousness of his sufferings? He must feel, and feel deeply, that he has deserved all and even more than he endures. Indeed, it is true that the punishment of the sinner is self-punishment; it is the fruit of his own doings. Witness Cain, Belshazzar, Judas, etc.

III. It is ESSENTIALLY BENEFICENT. It serves: 1. To guard men from the injuries of others. 2. To restrain the angry passions of men.

CONCLUSION. Let us in all our conduct to our fellow-men practically recognize the principle that with what measure we mete it shall be measured to us again. "He that rolleth the stone, it shall return upon him." The stone of revenge and malice which you have rolled at another shall come back upon the head of you that rolled it —come back with a terrible momentum, come back to crush you.—D. T.

Vers. 4—9.—*A good time for good people.* "In that day, saith the Lord, I will smite every horse with astonishment, and his rider with madness: and I will open mine eyes upon the house of Judah, and will smite every horse of the people with blindness," etc. These words, which are confessedly difficult if not impossible to interpret correctly (for some say they are to be taken literally, others spiritually; some historically, others prophetically), may be fairly used to illustrate *a good time for good people.* In relation to this good time, I observe—

I. It is A TIME WHEN THEIR ENEMIES SHALL BE VANQUISHED. "In that day, saith the Lord, I will smite every horse with astonishment, and his rider with madness: and I will open mine eyes upon the house of Judah, and will smite every horse of the people with blindness." Here the overthrow of the enemies of Jerusalem is threatened. "The Lord," says Keil, "will throw the mind and spirit of the military force of the enemy into such confusion that, instead of injuring Jerusalem and Judah, it will rush forward to its own destruction. Horses and riders individualize the warlike forces of the enemy. The rider, smitten with madness, turns his sword against his own comrades in battle. On the other hand, Jehovah will open his eyes upon Judah for its protection (1 Kings viii. 29; Neh. i. 6; Ps. xxxii. 8). This promise is strengthened by the repetition of the punishment to be inflicted upon the enemy. Not only with alarm, but with blindness, will the Lord smite their horses. We have an example of this in 2 Kings vi. 18, where the Lord smote the enemy with blindness in answer to Elisha's prayer, *i.e.* with mental blindness, so that, instead of seizing the prophet, they fell into the hands of Israel. The three plagues, *timmâhōn, shiggâʻōn,* and *ʻivvârōn,* are those with which rebellious Israelites are threatened in Deut. xxviii. 28. The house of Judah is the covenant nation, the population of Judah, including the inhabitants of Jerusalem, as we may see from what follows." Now, whether this conquest refers to the triumphs of the Maccabees, or to some wonderful victories of the Jews in some future times, one thing is clear to us, that the *time will come for all good people when their enemies shall be entirely destroyed.* To every good man this victory is promised. "Be thou faithful unto death, and I will give thee a crown of life."

II. It is A TIME WHEN THEIR POWER SHALL BE AUGMENTED. The power here promised is: 1. *The power of unity.* "The governors of Judah shall say in their heart, The inhabitants of Jerusalem shall be my strength in the Lord of hosts their God." "Observe here," says Dr. Wardlaw, "the confidence of the leaders in the people. Without the people's concurrent aid, their counsels and plans and directions could, of course, be of little avail. This the rulers should feel, and should exult in seeing what ground they had for full reliance on them in time of pressure and danger, which implies unanimity and intrepid valour, combined with persevering effort, on the part of the inhabitants. This union and valour would be the 'strength' of their leaders, without which they must find themselves utterly powerless. A divided, dispirited, heartless, dastardly soldiery or populace, is weakness, disappointment, and discomfiture to the best-conceived plans of the most bold, prudent, and experienced leaders." All good people over all the earth will one day be thoroughly united—united, not in opinion, for this would be, if possible, undesirable; but in devotion to Christ, the common Centre. This union is strength, Divine strength, "strength in the Lord of hosts." "Strong in the Lord and in the power of his might." 2. *The power of conquest.* "In that day will I make the governors of Judah like an hearth of fire among the wood, and like a torch of fire in a sheaf; and they shall devour all the people round about, on the right hand and on the left;" or, as Dr. Henderson renders it, "In that day will I make the chiefs of Judah like a fire-pot among sticks of wood, and like a torch of fire in a sheaf, and they shall consume all the people around, on the right hand and on the left." As the fire consumes the wood and the sheaf of straw, so would the men of Jerusalem have power to conquer all the people "round about, on the right hand and on the left." God invests all good men with power to conquer their spiritual foes; this is the power of faith—faith that overcometh the world. This power, though weak in most, is triumphant in many (see Heb. xi.). It shall be all-conquering one day.

III. It is a time when they shall be settled in their home. "And Jerusalem shall be inhabited again in her own place, even in Jerusalem." Jerusalem, in the first instance, stands for the Jews, and in the second instance for the city or the country. It means, therefore, that in this good time—whether it is past or to come—some, if not all, the Jews that were scattered abroad will return and settle in their own home. The language expresses reoccupancy and permanent possession. Those who return—whether from Egypt, Babylon, or elsewhere—will return and settle down in their old home. A time comes for all good people when they shall settle down in a permanent dwelling-place. Here they are "strangers and pilgrims," and have "no abiding city." But a glorious country awaits them, an "inheritance incorruptible, undefiled, and that fadeth not away."

IV. It is a time when they shall be blessed with equal privileges. 1. *They were to have equal honour.* "The Lord also shall save the tents of Judah first, that the glory of the house of David and the glory of the inhabitants of Jerusalem do not magnify themselves against Judah." Dr. Henderson's translation expresses this: "And Jehovah shall deliver the tents of Judah first, in order that the splendour of the house of David and the splendour of the inhabitants of Jerusalem may not be magnified above Judah." 2. *They were to have equal protection.* "In that day shall the Lord defend the inhabitants of Jerusalem; and he that is feeble among them at that day shall be as David; and the house of David shall be as God, as the angel of the Lord before them. And it shall come to pass in that day, that I will seek to destroy all the nations that come against Jerusalem." Here Jerusalem is promised protection against the foe, and "he that is feeble among them at that day shall be as David." "To the Jew, David was the highest type of strength and glory on earth (2 Sam. xvii. 8), a man of war (2 Sam. xviii. 3); such shall the weakest citizen of Jerusalem become (Joel iii. 10)." "And the house of David shall be as God, as the angel of the Lord before them." "The Divine Angel that went before them through the desert, the highest type of strength and glory in heaven (Exod. xxiii. 20; xxxii. 34). The house of David is the prince and his family sprung from David (Ezek. xlv. 7, 9). David's house was then in a comparatively weak state." Now, there is a time coming when all good people shall have distinguished honour and complete protection. They shall settle down in the heavenly Jerusalem; and what a city is that (see Rev. xxi.)!

Conclusion. Though I have not been able to put forth what I feel to be a satisfactory interpretation of these words, or attempted to give to them a spiritual signification, I trust that, in using them as an illustration of the good time coming for the good, I have presented a legitimate and a useful application. A glorious time awaits all good men, in all lands, Churches, nations—a time when they shall be delivered from all evil and be put in permanent possession of all good. Seeing we look for such things, "what manner of persons ought we to be in all holy conversation and godliness?" etc.—D. T.

Vers. 10—14.—*Penitential sorrow.* "And I will pour upon the house of David, and upon the inhabitants of Jerusalem, the spirit of grace and of supplications: and they shall look upon me whom they have pierced, and they shall mourn for him, as one mourneth for his only son, and shall be in bitterness for him, as one that is in bitterness for his firstborn," etc. To whatever particular event this passage refers, the subject is obvious and most important, viz. that of *penitential sorrow*. And five things in connection with it are noteworthy.

I. THE SUBJECTS OF THIS PENITENTIAL SORROW. They are Jews, and not Gentiles. "The house of David, and the inhabitants of Jerusalem"—expressions which designate the whole Israelitish people. The Jewish people had often been reduced to this state of sorrow. When in Babylonian captivity they wept when they "remembered Zion." "The scene," says Dr. Wardlaw, "depicted bears a very close resemblance to those recorded to have taken place on the restoration from Babylon, when Jehovah, having influenced them individually to return to himself, and to set their faces, with longing desire, to the land of their fathers, inclined their hearts, when thus gathered home, to social and collective acts of humiliation and prayer. The prayers of Ezra and Nehemiah on those occasions might be taken as models, in the 'spirit and even the matter' of them, for the supplications of Judah and Israel when brought back from their wider and more lasting dispersions."

II. THE CAUSE OF THIS PENITENTIAL SORROW. "I will pour." The Prophet Joel (ii. 28) refers to this outpouring of Divine influence. "And it shall come to pass afterward, that I will pour out my Spirit upon all flesh." All genuine repentance for sin originates with God. He sends down into human souls the spirit of grace and of supplications. The spirit of grace is the spirit that produces in the mind of man the experience of the grace of God; and this experience works repentance and inspires prayer.

III. THE OCCASION OF THIS PENITENTIAL SORROW. "And they shall look upon me whom they have pierced." "The expression, 'upon me,'" says Hengstenberg, "is very remarkable. According to ver. 1, the Speaker is the Lord, the Creator of heaven and earth. But it is evident from what follows that we are not to confine our thoughts exclusively to an invisible God who is beyond the reach of suffering, for the same Jehovah presently represents himself as pierced by the Israelites, and afterwards lamented by them with bitter remorse. The enigma is solved by the Old Testament doctrine of the Angel and Revealer of the Most High God, to whom the prophet attributes even the most exalted names of God, on account of his participation in the Divine nature, who is described in ch. xi. as undertaking the office of Shepherd over his people, and who had been recompensed by them with base ingratitude." "They shall look upon me whom they have pierced, and they shall mourn for him." The "me" and the "him" are the same Person, and that Person he who says, in ver. 10, "I will pour upon the house of David." In the first clause he is speaking of himself; in the second clause the prophet is speaking of him. The Messiah was pierced, and pierced by the Jews: "They pierced my hands and my feet." A believing sight of Christ produces this penitential sorrow.

> "Alas! and did my Saviour bleed,
> And my Redeemer die?
> Did he devote his sacred head
> For such a worm as I?"

IV. THE POIGNANCY OF THIS PENITENTIAL SORROW. "And they shall mourn for him, as one mourneth for his only son, and shall be in bitterness for him, as one that is in bitterness for his firstborn." "There are few states of deeper and acuter sorrow than this—that which is felt by affectionate parents when bereft of those objects of their fondest affections; the one solitary object of their concentrated parental love; or the firstborn and rising support and hope of their household." As to the poignancy of this grief, it is further said, "In that day shall there be a great mourning in Jerusalem, as the mourning of Hadadrimmon in the valley of Megiddon," etc. Perhaps the greatest sorrow ever known amongst the Jews was the sorrow in the valley of Megiddon, occasioned by the death of King Josiah (2 Chron. xxxv. 24). Jeremiah composed a funeral dirge on the occasion, and other odes and lamentations were composed, and were sung by males and females. But true penitential sorrow is far more poignant than that occasioned by the death of an only son or a noble king. It is tinctured with moral remorse.

V. THE UNIVERSALITY OF THIS POIGNANT SORROW. "And the land shall mourn, every family apart," etc. All the families of the land shall mourn, and all shall mourn "apart." Deep sorrow craves loneliness.

CONCLUSION. There is one event in history—whether such an event is referred to here or not—that answers better to the description here of penitential sorrow than any other in the chronicles of the world; it is the Day of Pentecost. Thousands of Jews assembled together on that day from all parts of the known world. Peter preached to the vast assembly and charged them with having crucified the Son of God. The Holy Spirit came down upon the vast congregation, and the result was that, "When they heard this, they were pricked in their heart" (Acts ii. 37). Far on in the future, it may be, a period will dawn in Jewish history when such penitential sorrow as is here described will be experienced by all the descendants of Abraham.—D. T.

EXPOSITION.

CHAPTER XIII.

Vers. 1—6.—§ 3. *This repentance will lead to purification from past defilement, and a reaction against idolatry and false prophets.*

Ver. 1.—**In that day.** At the time when the great mourning (ch. xii.) takes place, or, more generally, in the Messianic period, when all these things shall be fulfilled. **Shall be a fountain opened,** etc. Shall be opened and continue open. The allusion is to the lustral rites practised in the consecration of the Levites, who were to have "water of sin" sprinkled on them, and to "the water of separation," or "water of uncleanness" (the word found in our passage), used for purposes of legal purification (see Numb. viii. 7; xix. 9). Instead of this merely ceremonial cleansing, there should be in the Christian Church the cleansing of the soul by the blood of Christ (1 Pet. i. 2; 1 John i. 7). Septuagint, Ἔσται πᾶς τόπος διανοιγόμενος, "Every place shall be opened." **The house of David and the inhabitants of Jerusalem** represent the whole nation, as in ch. xii. 10; the cleansing is as universal as the sin (see the announcement in Ezek. xxxvi. 25; xlvii. 1—12; Joel iii. 18). **For sin and for uncleanness.** The latter word is used for the separation on account of uncleanness (Lev. xv. 20, etc.); and the two terms together comprise all guilt and pollution. Ver. 2.—**I will cut off the names of the idols.** Idols should be so utterly abolished that their very names should perish (Hos. ii. 17; Micah v. 12, 13; Zeph. i. 4). The prophet names the two chief sins which had brought ruin on the old theocracy—idolatry and false-prophetism, and declares that these shall not be found in the new theocracy. As these two sins were not specially prevalent after the Captivity, some see in their mention here an argument for the pre-

exilian authorship of this part of Zechariah. But the prophet, grounding his message on past history, does well to give assurance that such lapses shall not happen again. Nor is it altogether certain that the warning against these errors was not needed after the return. There were false prophets in Nehemiah's time (Neh. vi. 14); and we read in the Book of Maccabees that many Jews adopted heathen rites and customs, among which the worship of idols must have been included (1 Macc. i. 11, etc.; 2 Macc. iv. 13, etc.), and the people and even priests contracted marriages with heathen wives (Ezra ix. 2; Neh. xiii. 23); so that there was real danger of relapse. **The prophets.** The false prophets are meant, as is evident from their being associated with idols and the unclean spirit, and from vers. 3—6. The Septuagint has, "the false prophets;" so the Vulgate. **The unclean spirit.** This is the lying spirit which works in the false prophets (see 1 Kings xxii. 19—23), and which we find later denounced by apostles (Acts xvi. 18; 1 Cor. x. 20, 21; 2 Thess. ii. 9, 10; 1 Tim. iv. 1). Septuagint, τὸ πνεῦμα τὸ ἀκάθαρτον (comp. Matt. xii. 43; Rev. xviii. 2).

Ver. 3.—**When any shall yet prophesy;** *i.e.* if any man shall pretend to have predictive powers conferred on him by God. There is here no intimation that true prophecy should cease, as Keil and Köhler suppose; the man is punished, not because he prophesies, but because "he speaketh lies." **His father and his mother.** The passage is grounded on the enactments in Deut. xiii. 6—10 and xviii. 20, which commanded the death of a false prophet or of one who enticed others to idolatry. Here the holy zeal of the parents should put the law in force. This was quite a different state of things from that which obtained in former times. The earlier prophets continually complain of the favour shown to these deceivers (comp. Isa. ix. 15; Jer. v. 31; Micah ii. 11); and we never read of the legal punishment being inflicted after due investigation, the test being the non-fulfilment of the prediction (Deut. xviii. 22). In the new theocracy, so great is the recoil from such pretenders, that their nearest relations shall at once punish them with death without any previous legal process. **Shall thrust him through.** Stab, pierce him, put him to death, as in ch. xii. 10. The gospel deals more tenderly with heretics (Luke ix. 55). "Defendenda religio non est occidendo," says Lactant. ('Div. Inst.,' v. 20), "sed moriendo; religio cogi non potest" (Wordsworth, *in loc.*).

Ver. 4.—**Shall be ashamed.** The falsity of their pretensions being now recognized, these prophets shall be ashamed to utter their oracles in public. **When he hath prophesied;** rather, *when he prophesieth.* **A rough garment;** *a mantle of hair;* Septuagint, δέῤῥιν τριχίνην: Vulgate, *pallio saccino.* Such was the mantle of Elijah (1 Kings xix. 13, 19; 2 Kings i. 8; ii. 13, 14) and of John the Baptist (Matt. iii. 4), and it seems to have become the distinctive badge of the prophet, and was assumed by these pretenders in order to inspire confidence.

Ver. 5.—**I am an husbandman.** The impostor shall confess the truth about himself, and own that he is only "a tiller of the ground (ἄνθρωπος ἐργαζόμενος τὴν γῆν)," as Gen. iv. 2. The abnegation in Amos vii. 14 is quite different in character. **Man taught me to keep cattle;** literally, *man bought* (or, *possessed) me;* Revised Version, *I have been made a bondman.* So eager is he now to hide his false pretensions, that he is willing to be considered a slave, employed from his youth in farm work, and therefore incapable of executing the prophetical office. Vulgate, *Quoniam Adam exemplum meum ab adoloscentia mea;* i.e. "I have followed the example of Adam in tilling the ground and in earning my bread by the sweat of my brow." St. Cyril and some modern commentators hold that the false prophet says this in sorrow and repentance, not with any idea of deceiving; and that herein is exhibited a signal instance of the grace of God in the Messianic period, when even such sinners are converted from the error of their ways.

Ver. 6.—**What are these wounds in thine hands?** or rather, *between thy hands,* i.e. on thy breast; Revised Version, *between thine arms.* Cheyne compares, "between his arms," *i.e.* in his back (2 Kings ix. 24) and "between your eyes," *i.e.* on your foreheads (Deut. xi. 18). Not satisfied with the assertion in ver. 5, the questioner asks the meaning of these wounds which he sees on

his body. Jerome considers these scars to be marks of correction and punishment at the hands of his parents. More probably they are thought to be self-inflicted in the service of some idol, according to the practice mentioned in 1 Kings xviii. 28; Jer. xlviii. 37. Those **with which I was wounded in the house of my friends.** This may be a confession of guilt, the impostor owning that his friends had thus punished him for his pretensions; or, as the word rendered "friends" is generally used in the case of illicit or impure love or spiritual fornication, it may be here applied to the idols whom he served. But it seems most probable that the answer is intentionally false and misleading; as if he had said, "The wounds were not made as you suppose, but are the result of something that happened to me in my friends' house." The LXX. renders, ἃς ἐπλήγην ἐν τῷ οἴκῳ τῷ ἀγαπητῷ μου, "with which I was struck in my beloved house." To see in this passage a reference to our blessed Lord and his crucifixion, though such an opinion has the support of the Roman Liturgy and of many interpreters, is to do violence to the context, and to read into the words a meaning wholly alien from the subject of false prophets, which is the matter in hand.

Vers. 7—9.—§ 4. *For the smiting of the good Shepherd Israel is punished, passes through much tribulation, by which it is refined, and in the end (though reduced to a mere remnant) is saved.*

Ver. 7.—**Awake, O sword.** Zechariah proceeds to show the course of the purification of the people. The mention of the false prophet and the shameful wounds in his flesh leads him to the contrast of the true Prophet and the effects of his "piercing." The abruptness of the commencement of the verse is dramatic, and gives no sufficient cause for supposing that this paragraph ought to be transferred (as Ewald and others desire) to the end of ch. xi. (For a similar apostrophe, comp. Jer. xlvii. 6.) It is introduced here to show that all that happened to the Shepherd was done after the determinate counsel and foreknowledge of God; and as if the sword could never have dared to act thus except it were permitted by the Divine will. The "sword" represents any kind of instrument that inflicts death (comp. Exod. v. 21; 2 Sam. xii. 9; Isa. xxvii. 1). **My Shepherd.** The Shepherd of Jehovah, who is speaking. He is the good Shepherd, the Representative of Jehovah, mentioned in ch. xi. 4, etc., the Messiah, who is identified with Jehovah in ch. xii. 10. The Septuagint has, τοὺς ποιμένας μου, "my shepherds" (Vatican), as if no particular person was indicated, but rather all the leaders of the people of God; but the next clause seems to render the reference definite. **The man that is my fellow.** The word rendered "man" means rather "mighty man;" that rendered "fellow" occurs often in Leviticus, but nowhere else (Lev. v. 21; vi. 2; xix. 11, 15, 17, etc.), and is usually translated "neighbour;" it implies one united to another by the possession of common nature, rights, and privileges. God could speak only of One thus associated with himself, that is, of him who could say, "I and my Father are One" (John x. 30). The term is variously translated by the versions. Septuagint, Ἄνδρα πολίτην μου: Aquila, Ἄνδρα σύμφυλον μου: Vulgate, *Virum cohærentem mihi.* That the Shepherd is Messiah is proved by Christ's application of the following clause to himself (Matt. xxvi. 31). **Smite the Shepherd, and the sheep shall be scattered.** When Christ was apprehended, all the disciples forsook him and fled (Matt. xxvi. 56); and what they did was done by others. Even the faithful few were scandalized at the cross. The command, "Smite the Shepherd," like the apostrophe, "Awake, O sword," shows that it was God's purpose that was being there executed (see John xix. 11; Acts ii. 23). It is also thus intimated that the dispersion of the Jews, and their denationalizing, were results of this rejection and smiting of the Shepherd. This dispersion is further explained in vers. 8, 9, where it is shown that to some it will be ruin, to others salvation. **I will turn mine hand.** "To turn," or "bring back the hand over," is used in a good and a bad sense (comp. Isa. i. 25; Amos i. 8). There is a promise of comfort in the use of the phrase here. **God's hand shall** cover and protect some, while he punishes the others. Those thus protected are called **the little ones,** the humble and meek. This recalls Christ's words to his disciples, "Fear not, little flock; for it is your Father's good pleasure to give you the kingdom" (Luke xii. 32).

Ver. 8.—**In all the land;** *i.e.* Palestine, the country in which the good Shepherd tended his flock (ch. xi.), and which is a figure of the kingdom of God (comp. ch. xii. 12; xiv. 9, 10). **Two parts therein shall be cut off** and die; literally, *the mouth,* i.e. *the portion of two,* as Deut. xxi. 17; 2 Kings ii. 9, where it denotes the double portion inherited by the firstborn. The inheritance is divided into three portions, of which two parts are given over to death. Compare a similar allotment in the case of the Moabites (2 Sam. viii. 2). The doomed portion is supposed to represent the multitudes who perished at the siege of Jerusalem. This may be; but by analogy it stands for those who shall not accept the Messiah or be purified by suffering, even as Christ said, "Many are called, but few chosen" (Matt. xx. 16; comp. Matt. iii. 12). **The third.** This third part represents the faithful among the Jews (Rom. xi. 5), and the Christian Church gathered out of all nations (comp. Isa. vi. 13; and especially Ezek. v. 2, 12).

Ver. 9.—**Through the fire.** This third part, like its Master, passes through much tribulation, and is thereby refined and purified (comp. Ps. lxvi. 10; Isa. xlviii. 10; Jer. ix. 7; Dan. xii. 10; Mal. iii. 3; 1 Pet. i. 6, 7). **Call on my Name.** In their distress they shall turn in faith to Jehovah, as the covenant God, a very present Help in trouble (Isa. lxv. 24). Thus is represented God's dealing with his Church in every age.

HOMILETICS.

Ver. 1.—*The end of sin.* "In that day there shall be a fountain opened," etc. The close of the last chapter described certain persons as pouring forth "a fountain of tears" (Jer. ix. 1). This opens by describing a "fountain" of a different kind—a fountain opened for the especial benefit of those who thus mourned (comp. ch. xii. 10). In this last-mentioned verse their grief is attributed to their looking on him "whom they had pierced." Remembering how distinctly this expression is applied, in John xix. 37, to the death of Christ Jesus, we seem justified in concluding that there is a similar reference here. According to this, therefore, the "fountain" of ver. 1 is a figurative description of that flow of blessings which comes from Christ's cross; and its "opening in that day" to the people described is a similar description of their being then at last enabled to discover and partake of that flow. So "opened," what will be its results? Two principally, both of chief importance, viz. an end of sin (1) in regard to its *guilt*; and an end of sin (2) in regard to its *pollution.*

I. THE END OF ITS GUILT. Sin, as being the transgression of Law (1 John iii. 4; v. 17; Rom. iv. 15; v. 13), involves the displeasure, and that inevitably, of the Lawgiver. If the Law is worth enacting, it is worth enforcing. If not meant, indeed, to be enforced, why was it ever proclaimed? The wiser, also the better, the holier, the higher the Lawgiver, the more this reasoning holds. The greater also, such being the case, and that both in itself and also before him, is the offence of rebelling against him. And it is this "offence," this deadly "offence," that the mystical fountain here described in the first place—providing, as it does, "a full, perfect, and sufficient sacrifice, oblation, and satisfaction for the sins of the whole world"—so entirely brings to an end. See how emphatically this is taught generally in Rom. viii. 1; iii. 25. And see how the same appears to be taught specially concerning Jerusalem and its inhabitants in the future in such passages as Isa. xl. 2; xliii. 25; Jer. l. 20 (see also Dan. ix. 24). *Now* their "iniquities have separated," as described in Isa. lix. 2, "between them and their God, and their sins have made him [margin] hide his face from them, that he will not hear." *Then*, through that "opened fountain," this will all be reversed. No longer separated or concealed from them, he will accept their prayers with "delight" (see John iv. 23, end; Prov. xv. 8).

II. The end of its pollution. Besides being an offence to God, sin is an injury to ourselves. Being altogether unworthy of us in every respect, it brings about, and that immediately, our own degradation and shame. It involves pollution, that is to say, as well as guilt. And it further involves, such being the case, in addition to the before-mentioned separation or alienation of God's favour from us, the separation or alienation of our nature from him. This second evil would seem to be described in our text (see margin) as "separation" for or by means of "uncleanness." How such alienation on man's part through the pollution of sin is evidenced, we may see in Gen. iii. 8; Luke v. 8; Isa. xxx. 11; Rom. i. 28, beginning; and also in that which is assumed respecting us in the gracious appeal of 2 Cor. v. 20. On the other hand, how entirely this second alienation can be overcome by the remedy of our text is seen in 1 John i. 7, end; John xii. 32. And how completely both this and the previously mentioned alienation are to be removed in the case of Judah and Israel at the last, as here described, we may perhaps see in Jer. xxxi. 31—34, especially as quoted and summarized in Heb. x. 16, 17 and elsewhere.

If this interpretation is accepted, we may learn hence for ourselves, in concluding: 1. *The necessity of Christ's death.* In all cases we see it is thus that God has appointed as to doing away with our sins. It is only by the "fountain" in this way provided, and not by any fountain of tears on man's part, however copious, however unexampled, however certainly due even to an influence from above (ch. xii. 10), that the "double cure" of sin can be wrought.

> "Could my tears for ever flow," etc.

2. *The necessity of man's faith.* The necessity, we mean, of course, where there is the capacity for faith in existence. Till that capacity for faith is exercised, no matter what the object of faith, what can it do? Till the "fountain" in this way be "opened" —in other words, be discovered and used—whom can it cleanse? (See Rom. v. 1 and Acts xv. 9 respectively for the two sides of this truth.) 3. *The abundance of God's grace*—whether to pardon or heal. It is not a cistern, not even a well, but a fountain, to which we find it compared (comp. Jer. ii. 13; John iv. 12, 13). No limitation as to supply. No limitation as to use (see Deut. xi. 10, 11).

Vers. 2—6.—*The end of error.* "And it shall come to pass in that day, saith the Lord of hosts, that I will cut off the names of the idols," etc. After the end of sin, the end of that which leads to sin, viz. of error. This gift completes the previous blessings by making them lasting and sure (comp. Ps. lxxxv. 8). This gift also, as we find it described here, is most complete in itself. It is so, whether we consider what is told us (1) as to the future *action of God*, or (2) as to the *action of men*, in bringing error to an end.

I. The action of God. It is promised here that he will put an end to error: 1. *By abolishing its very symbols.* The "names" of idols are the symbols or words by means of which their supposed attributes or connection with different localities are set forth and commemorated; and under which also they are worshipped. Besides numerous classical examples, see in Acts xix. 34 how evidently the people of Ephesus considered it as equivalent to a declaration of their faith to repeat the mere name of Diana. What is promised here, therefore, is that it should be eventually with all systems of error as it is now with many of the singular and subtle heresies which vexed the primitive Church. They are so far forgotten by this time that it is a matter of difficult antiquarian research even to ascertain their true meaning. 2. *By banishing its teachers.* Not only then shall the "tares" of falsehood be "rooted up," but the "enemy" also that sowed them shall be taken away. This, moreover, shall be done so completely that not only the false "prophet," but the "unclean spirit" also, his inspirer and confederate, shall "cease" to exist in the land (comp. 1 Sam. xxviii. 3 end, 9; and see Rev. xvi. 13, 14; xix. 20; xx. 1—3). Error, therefore, at that happy season, shall be twice dead, as it were; gone altogether beyond recollection; gone also beyond recovery.

II. THE ACTION OF MAN. Even should any persons qualified to act as false prophets be still left in existence (see again 1 Sam. xxviii. 7), there will be two further things effectually to prevent them from making use of their gifts. There will be the extent to which, at that time, the false prophet: 1. *Shall be hated by others.* He will be hated (1) by all others, including specially even those who, as having brought him into being, will naturally be the most disposed to befriend or endure him. Also (2) he will be hated by these in the bitterest manner, *their* mouths pronouncing against him, and *their* hands inflicting on him *sentence of death.* And finally (3) he will be hated thus on account of his connection with error (note "*for* thou speakest lies," and "*when* he prophesieth," in ver. 3). Acting also at that time in the same direction, will be the extent to which the false prophet shall be : 2. *Despised by himself.* For example, he will be ashamed (1) of his inward prophetical thoughts or "visions," not thinking more of them as guides to truth than a sensible man does of his dreams. He will be ashamed (2) of his outward prophetical garb, being so far from wishing to have it "seen of men" (Matt. xxiii. 5) that he will never clothe himself in it. And, finally, (3) he will be ashamed of both these things to such an extent as to be willing rather to be regarded as a bondman, or slave (so many understand ver. 5), and ready rather (so we may, perhaps, understand the difficult words of ver. 6) to seek shelter from the imputation of being a prophet in any subterfuge, however absurd. "Call me anything but a teacher of truth. Believe what you will of me except that I profess to be that!"

Whatever the special application of the passage which sets before us such a complete cessation of error, there are two general principles of much importance which seem illustrated thereby. 1. *The increasing light of the future.* Compared with the past, whether Jewish or pagan, how full of light the dispensation that now is (see Matt. xiii. 16, 17; Heb. xi. 13; 1 Pet. i. 10, 11; Acts xvii. 3; xxvi. 18)! Compared with the future, how full of darkness (1 Cor. xiii. 9—12; 1 John iii. 2; Col. i. 12; Rev. xxi. 23; xxii. 4, 5)! Much, indeed, yet remains to be revealed to those described in Ps. xxv. 14. 2. *The great consequent blessedness of the future.* What a scene of distraction, with its "many masters" (see Revised Version, Jas. iii. 1) and discordant outcries (Matt. xxiv. 23—26), not unlike the scene described in Dan. vii. 2, is the present! How profound the tranquillity, how sweet the calm, caused by the cessation of all! Happy, indeed, to have the hope of travelling at last "to where beyond these voices there is peace"!

Vers. 7—9.—*A wonderful sentence.* "Awake, O sword, against my Shepherd, and against the man that is my fellow," etc. The prophet here seems again to "hark back," as at the openings of ch. ix. and xi. (where see remarks and references), from the "glory" that was to "follow" to the "sufferings" that were to precede. At any rate, we have the highest authority (Matt. xxvi. 31, 56) for understanding this passage of the "sufferings" and death of our Lord himself. This being so, how does its language present that great "Passion" to us? As something surpassingly wonderful (1) *in itself;* and (2) *in its results.*

I. WONDERFUL IN ITSELF. Here is a man spoken of—here is a command given respecting him—by the Lord of hosts. 1. *How wonderful the man spoken of!* (1) He is supreme in office. All other men are to him but as sheep. He is to them in the position of a shepherd. He is also recognized and appointed as such ("*my* Shepherd ") by God himself. Nor is there any other whatever so appointed, except by his direction and in a subordinate place (see Isa. xl. 11; John x. 11; Heb. xiii. 20; 1 Pet.

ii. 25; v. 4). (2) He is supreme in nature. He is Jehovah's "fellow," or equal, just as men dwelling together in Palestine as neighbours (see Lev. xix. 15, 17; xxv. 14, 15, etc., where the same word is employed) were fellows, or equals. Higher than this— higher, *i.e.*, than the highest—who can possibly be? 2. *How wonderful the command*, things being thus! (1) Consider its purport; viz. that such a one should be smitten at all; should be smitten also with such a weapon—a weapon of so judicial a nature (Rom. xiii. 4); a weapon of so deadly a character, aiming at life itself (Matt. xxvi. 52). Why should the "sword" be thus called upon to "awake"—as though previously "asleep" and neglecting its duty—against him? Who less deserving, in himself, to suffer thereby? Who more fit, rather, in every way, to employ it (see John v. 22; Acts xvii. 31, etc.)? (2) Consider its Author—the Lord of hosts. The marvel is the same as that we read of in Isa. liii. 10, "Yet it pleased the *Lord* to bruise him; *he* hath put him to grief" (see also Acts ii. 23; Rom. viii. 32). It is the Judge of judges, the eternal Father himself, who bids the sword awake against *him!*

II. WONDERFUL IN ITS RESULTS. For these, as described to us here, are: 1. *Most unexpected*. The immediate result, indeed, that of scattering the sheep, is not at all unexpected. What more likely, what more certain to follow, humanly speaking, from smiting the Shepherd? But the ultimate result, that of saving these "little ones" (so many understand end of ver. 7), that of preserving the sheep by thus slaying their Preserver (comp. John xviii. 8, 9; Matt. xxvii. 42, beginning; Gal. iii. 13; Isa. liii. 5, end), is unexpected indeed. Has not the very idea, indeed, seemed the height of "foolishness" to many (1 Cor. i. 23) who thought themselves "wise"? 2. *Most widely diverse*. This extraordinary method of preserving the flock was not expected to preserve all within reach of its influence. On the contrary, far too many amongst them—something like two to one of them, in fact, all taken together (" in *all* the land ")—would decline to avail themselves of it. (1) Its effect upon these who despise it—for it would have effect upon these—would be their uttermost ruin. The method of deliverance, by being thus inverted, would become their destruction. The weapon of defence, by being turned thus against them, becomes a weapon of death (see 2 Cor. ii. 16, beginning; Luke ii. 34; Heb. ii. 3). (2) Its effect on those who embrace it, on the other hand, would be their uttermost salvation. Observe the various steps. First, they are " left; " that is (see Ezek. ix. 8), not destroyed. Next, they are purified by discipline—*i.e.* saved from the *power* of sin—as metals by fire; and this as thoroughly at the last (comp. Heb. xii. 23, end) as when gold has been "tried" till it requires trying no longer. Concurrently with this, on the other hand, they are saved so thoroughly from the condemnation of sin, that they have full access to God's presence and attention; and when they openly speak of God as their Portion (as such persons will do, Ps. xvi. 5; cxix. 57), are acknowledged by him as his portion in a similar manner (see Ps. lxvii. 6; Jer. x. 16; li. 19; Deut. xxxii. 9; Cant. ii. 16). They are favoured by him, in fact, both secretly and openly too (Matt. vi. 6).

Three brief thoughts to conclude. 1. *How lofty the superstructure* of the gospel salvation! Salvation itself, understood rigorously (as we have noted), is only *not* being lost. Actually, as here described to us, it is all that heart can desire—the heirship of all things through Christ (Rom. viii. 17; Gal. iv. 7; 1 Cor. iii. 22, 23). 2. *How deep its foundations!* Penetrating to the very greatest depths, as it were, of the Divine nature and plans (Rev. xiii. 8). 3. *How certain its truth!* Like that house which the Saviour himself describes (Matt. vii. 24, 25) as being founded on a *rock*—founded, in fact, on that " Rock of Ages," which not all the " ages " can shake (comp. Heb. xii. 27, 28).

HOMILIES BY VARIOUS AUTHORS.

Ver. 1.—*The fountain of grace.* Salvation through Christ. The glorious gospel.

I. THE EVIL. " Sin and uncleanness." All are sinners. Law, facts of life, testimony of conscience, prove our guilt. Sin defiles all that it touches. " Uncleanness," alas! how prevalent, and in manifold forms! 'Twas sin that brought it all into the world. If there were no sin there would be no uncleanness. Need for grief and prayer.

II. THE REMEDY. " Fountain," etc. 1. *Freedom of access.* Open, not shut. None debarred. In the promise of God—by the atoning death of Christ—through the ministry of grace, the fountain has been opened for all (John xix. 34; 1 John i. 7; Heb. ix. 13). 2. *Plenitude of supply.* Not a pool or a cistern, but a fountain, with rich and ample supplies for all. Thousands and tens of thousands have already been blessed, and whosoever will may come, and will find that Christ is mighty to save. 3. *Perennial virtue.* Not like Bethesda, at certain times; but all the year round, and from generation to generation. After many years' absence, I visited the home of my youth. There were sad changes. Friends were gone. None to know me. But under the shade of firs, in the old place, I found the spring where I had often slaked my thirst. It was still the same—the water sweet and refreshing as ever. So Christ is "the Same yesterday, to-day, and for ever."—F.

Ver. 7.—*The sword.* There is here something of heaven and earth. Jehovah speaks. He lays his command on the sword of justice, to awake and "smite." This implies death, and death not of a common sort, but as a judicial act, under the sanction of law. We take the scene to illustrate the *tragedy of Calvary* (Matt. xxvi. 31; John xvi. 32). Three questions may be asked.
I. WHO? The rebellious Babylon, Rome, Jerusalem? No. "The man that is my fellow." Who is this? Search, and where can you find such a one? Abraham was God's friend, but not his "fellow." Prophets and kings, martyrs and confessors, all stand aside. None but Christ answers the description. He is the First and the Last and the only One, in human likeness, who could say, "I and my Father are One."
II. WHY? Justice has its reasons. All that God does must be in accordance with eternal right. But here is mystery. The Man who alone was "without sin," holy and perfect—the solitary man, in human form, who was nearest of kin to God himself —to be dealt with as if he were a transgressor, and as if he had done things worthy of death,—this is exceeding strange. The key is in the term "Shepherd." Implies covenant relationship. Substitution of person and of sufferings. The One for the many; the Shepherd for the sheep.
III. WHAT THEN? We reasonably expect results worthy of such a tragedy. Twofold. 1. *Judgment.* Not only as to the disciples, but the Jewish people. 2. *Mercy.* Tender compassion. Gracious interposition. Glorious resolve. "I will turn my hand upon the little ones." Let us note that there is but one alternative—hand or sword. If we pass by God's hand stretched out to save, we must perish by the sword. "It is a fearful thing to fall into the hands of the living God."—F.

Vers. 1—6.—*The gospel age.* "In that day there shall be a fountain opened to the house of David and to the inhabitants of Jerusalem for sin and for uncleanness. And it shall come to pass in that day, saith the Lord of hosts, that I will cut off the names of the idols out of the land, and they shall no more be remembered," etc. Concerning the preceding chapter and these six verses, Dr. Keil says, "This section forms the first half of the second prophecy of Zechariah concerning the future of Israel and of the world, viz. the prophecy contained in ch. xii.—xiv., which, as a side-piece to ch. ix.—xi., treats of the judgment by which Israel, the nation of God, will be refined, sifted, and led on to perfection through conflict with the nations of the world. This first section announces how the conflict against Jerusalem and Judah will issue in destruction to the nations of the world (ch. xii. 1—4). Jehovah will endow the princes of Judah and inhabitants of Jerusalem with marvellous strength to overcome all their foes (vers. 5—9), and will pour out his spirit of grace upon them, so that they will bitterly repent the death of the Messiah (vers. 10—14), and purify themselves from all ungodliness (ch. xiii. 1—6)." "The day" here is generally supposed by expositors to point to the gospel age; and three remarks are here suggested in relation to this day.
I. IT IS A "DAY" FOR THE ABOUNDING OF SIN-CLEANSING INFLUENCES. "In that day there shall be a fountain opened to the house of David, and to the inhabitants of Jerusalem." This phrase comprehended the whole Jewish nation. To the Jews, washing from sin and ceremonial impurity was an idea with which they were well acquainted. It was enjoined by the Law (Numb. viii. 7; see also Ezek. xxxvi. 25). 1. *That sin and uncleanness are in the world.* This is a fact written in all history.

patent to every man's observation and consciousness. 2. *The removal of sin is the world's great necessity.* Its existence is the cause of all the miseries of the world, physical, social, political, religious. 3. *Provisions for its removal abound.* "A fountain opened." Sin and uncleanness are not an *essential part* of human nature. Men have lived without sin, and men in the other world do now. It is a mere stain on human nature, separable from it, and the means of separation are provided—provided in the gospel. In the mediatory life, teaching, works, death, resurrection, and ascension of the Son of God. In all this he has opened to the world a fountain of influence by which sin is to be cleansed. It is a fountain. This implies: (1) *Abundance.* It is not a rill, a brook, a lake, but a fountain. What is the fountain? Infinite love. (2) *Freeness.* Flowing, ever open to all. (3) *Perpetuity.* The hottest sun does not dry up the fountain. It has an under-connection with the boundless deep.

II. IT IS A "DAY" IN WHICH IDOLATRY SHALL BE UTTERLY ABOLISHED. The spirit of idolatry is *giving to any object that love which belongs only to the Supreme;* and this sin is perhaps as rife in regions where monotheism is professed as in those lands where polytheism holds its empire. The cutting off the "names of the idols" means their utter destruction (see Hos. ii. 17). But you may destroy all the million idols, involving those which are the workmanship of men and those which are the creation of God, before which men have bowed, and yet leave idolatry as rampant as ever. Nothing but the destruction of the spirit will be the destruction of idolatry. Hence we have here suggested a time when men shall give their affection to the Supreme Being, and to him alone, when they shall worship the one true and living God. This is the idolatry the gospel comes to destroy; it is to turn men from idols to the living God. What a blessed age will that be, when all men on the face of the earth shall have their souls centred in love and devotion on the one great and common Father of us all! "In that day a man shall cast his idols of silver, and his idols of gold, which they made each one for himself to worship, to the moles and to the bats" (Isa. ii. 20).

III. IT IS A "DAY" IN WHICH ALL FALSE RELIGIOUS TEACHINGS SHALL CEASE. "And I will cause the prophets and the unclean spirit to pass out of the land," etc. The words here in relation to false prophets suggest the following thoughts. 1. *False religious teachers are great curses to a community.* This is implied in the promise here of their destruction. False teachers in any branch of knowledge, be it historic, scientific, philosophic, literary, or artistic, are for many reasons great evils; but in religion the evils they inflict are inconceivably great. They deceive souls on the most vital of all points. False religious teachers are not merely teachers of pantheism, idolatry, or Mohammedanism, but even those who are nominally teachers of the gospel. The man who gives a wrong interpretation of the gospel is a false teacher, and such men are found even in the pulpits of our England. What blasphemous ideas of God and degrading notions of his blessed Son have we in some of the popular sermons of the age! Whosoever teaches the conventional Christ is false to the Christ of the gospel. 2. *False religious teachers may become objects of indignation even to their nearest relations.* "And it shall come to pass, that when any shall yet prophesy, then his father and his mother that begat him shall say unto him, Thou shalt not live; for thou speakest lies in the name of the Lord: and his father and his mother that begat him shall thrust him through when he prophesieth." It will be, indeed, a blessed time when the people of a country will have a greater love for truth than for their dearest relations, even their very children; when the appearance of a false teacher will awaken such a public indignation as will expose his very life to danger; when men's moral ears will be so attuned to truth, that the very sound of falsehood will become intolerable. Thank God, there is an age of moral reality coming, an age when men will recoil from shams as from "demons vile." 3. *False religious teachers will on this "day" be ashamed to exercise their mission.* "The prophets shall be ashamed." If any false prophets should continue to exercise their function, they will have to do it: (1) With secrecy. "Neither shall they wear a rough garment to deceive." It is said, when Domitian banished philosophers from Rome, many persons shaved off their beards and flung away their cloaks, that they might not be included in the ban. So now the false prophet will be ashamed of his badge, his rough garment, made perhaps of untanned sheepskin, or a Bedouin blanket made of camel's hair, like that of John the Baptist. (2) Disclaiming their profession. "He shall say, I am no prophet, I am an husbandman." If they carry on their work, they will do it under a false character, such as farmers or herdmen. "I belong to that class in society which lies under the least suspicion of aspiring to a function in which knowledge of affairs, dexterity in making use of men's weaknesses, and some literary faculty are needed. Besides, 'men own me from my youth' (for this is the meaning of the words rendered, 'men taught me to keep cattle from my youth'); and so if I had had the will I could never have had the chance of setting up as a prophet. I have not been my own master. Not quite satisfied with this disclaimer, the supposed examiners ask to be allowed to look at his hands, as you can judge roughly of a man's calling by the state of his hands—at least, you can thus judge whether a man is earning his bread with his hands or his head. They at once detect suspicious marks on this man's hands, wounds which they evidently suspect to have been self-inflicted in accordance with some idolatrous rite. Self-mutilation and self-laceration have always been common accessories of pagan worship, and common accompaniments of manifestations of pagan fanatical ecstasy. They are far from uncommon still in heathen and in Mohammedan countries. Permanent marks of a distinctive kind were also frequently made upon different parts of the person, and especially upon the arms, in acknowledgment of allegiance to some particular god (Jer. xlviii. 37), where mourning is thus described: 'Every head shall be bald, and every beard clipped: upon all the hands shall be cuttings.' But the man denies that his wounds have any such significance; they are not, he says, religious marks at all: 'they are wounds which I received in the house of friends,' in some rustic frolic with his boon companions, or as the slave's brand in the house of his master" (Dr. Dods). Should their disclaiming be questioned, they will take shelter in falsehood. "And one shall say unto him, What are these wounds in thine hands? Then he shall answer, Those with which I was wounded in the house of my friends." "The doubting examiner asks him to show him his hands, that he may ascertain if he has the rough hands of a farmer; those hands he shows, but they have nevertheless marks of a prophet on them, and of these very marks he gives a false account." "I was wounded in the house of my friends."

CONCLUSION. Thank God, we live in this gospel age. The sin-cleansing fountain is here, sending forth its streams in all directions. They flow through all the good books we have, through all the good lives we meet with. Let the streams multiply. The fountain will supply streams equal to the exigencies of all. Let us remove obstructions, cut new channels, and strive to let them into every heart. These will multiply in power, and increase in volume, till all idolatry, false teaching, and every other form of iniquity that pollutes the heart of the world, be washed clean away, and the whole world be holy in character, without spot or wrinkle or any such thing.—D. T.

Vers. 7—9.—*God's government of the world.* "Awake, O sword, against my Shepherd, and against the man that is my fellow, saith the Lord of hosts: smite the Shepherd, and the sheep shall be scattered: and I will turn mine hand upon the little ones. And it shall come to pass, that in all the land, saith the Lord, two parts therein shall be cut off and die; but the third shall be left therein. And I will bring the third part through the fire, and will refine them as silver is refined, and will try them as gold is tried: they shall call on my Name, and I will hear them: I will say, It is my people: and they shall say, The Lord is my God." Here we have God's government of the world in two aspects, *bringing penal ruin on many in a community, and remedial discipline upon a few;* appearing as the sword of justice in the one case, and as a refiner's pot in the other. Here we have it—

I. As BRINGING PENAL RUIN UPON MANY. 1. *The destruction of their leader.* "Awake, O sword, against my Shepherd." In the Bible language political religious leaders are represented as shepherds. For example, it was applied to Cyrus (Isa. xliv. 28). The person defined is represented as "the man that is my fellow." Dr. Keil's rendering is, "the man who is my neighbour;" and Dr. Henderson's, "the man who is united to me." Who is this man? On this question there are different opinions. "Calion thought it was Zechariah himself as representative of all the prophets, and that the prophecy referred only indirectly to Christ. Grotius, Eichhorn, Bauer, and Jahne apply it to Judas Maccabæus; Ewald, to Pekah; Hitzig, to the pretended prophets spoken of in the preceding verses." The expression, "my fellow," does not necessarily mean one who is equal in nature and character, but rather one who has fellowship of interests and aims. The poorest labourer in the cause of gospel truth is a "fellow" with the Archbishop of Canterbury, even a fellow-labourer of Christ, and fellow-labourer with God himself. Evangelical writers, however, apply the language to Christ, without much critical examination and without hesitation. They do this mainly on the ground that Christ himself quotes the passage, on the night in which he was betrayed, as an illustration of what was immediately awaiting him. "Then saith Jesus unto them, All ye shall be offended because of me this night: for it is written, I will smite the Shepherd, and the sheep of the flock shall be scattered abroad" (Matt. xxvi. 31). He does not say that the prophecy referred to him, but merely that the passage was about to be illustrated in his history. The Shepherd was to be smitten, and the sheep scattered. This, indeed, is a common fact in the history of the world; when the leader is gone the fold is scattered. Christ was, indeed, about to be smitten —smitten to death, not by the "sword" of Divine vengeance, as is impiously held by some, but by the wrath of his human enemies. "Awake, O sword." "These are words," says an old orthodox expositor, "of God the Father giving orders and commission to the sword of his justice to awaken to his Son." It is the sword of justice that he may die as a criminal on an ignominious tree; awaking to smite him, not with a drowsy blow, but with a mighty one." Dr. Watts has the same idea—

> "The Father plunged his flaming sword
> In his atoning blood."

From all such representations of the benign God of the universe, and the Infinite Father of love, my reason and heart revolt as from a monstrous creed or cursed blasphemy. However, I am not going to debate either the question whether the words were intended for Christ or not, or, if they were, the accuracy or otherwise of the interpretations thus given. Our point is that *God often brings sufferings on a people by striking down their leader.* There are few greater calamities that can befall a people than when nations lose their shepherds and leaders, or when Churches lose their pastors. Even when families lose their heads the loss is incalculable. 2. *The dispersion of the flock.* This comes to most communities when the true leader is taken away. The removal of a leader in a family—a parent—often leads to a scattering of the children. So with the leader in a Church—the pastor; and so with the leader of a nation. When the shepherd has gone, the flock is scattered, and the scattering is a great evil. Unity is strength and harmony; division is weakness and disorder. When communities are broken up and dispersed, the various members often place themselves in antagonism with each other, and rivalries, jealousies, and envyings run riot. 3. *The ruin of multitudes.* "And it shall come to pass, that in all the land, saith the Lord, two parts therein shall be cut off and die; but the third shall be left therein." Probably this refers primarily to the destruction of two-thirds of the inhabitants of Judæa by the Roman arms, and the famine or the pestilence and other destructive influences which are the usual concomitants of all wars. Thus the afflictions of the great majority of the human race, here represented as the two-thirds of a community, come upon them as the retribution of justice—the Divine sword here invoked. They are not disciplinary, but penal. The victims do not morally improve under them, they grow worse. They are "cut off and die."

II. BRINGING REMEDIAL DISCIPLINE TO A FEW. "And I will bring the third part through the fire, and will refine them as silver is refined, and will try them as gold is tried: they shall call on my Name, and I will hear them: I will say, It is my people: and they shall say, The Lord is my God." The very calamities which were penal and utterly ruinous to two-thirds of that population were morally disciplinary and improving to the remaining third. In the one case they were the strokes of the "sword" of justice. In the other the calamities were but fire in the "pot of the refiner." Just as the refiner purifies his silver and his gold by fire, God in mercy spiritually improves his people by the trial and the sufferings which he inflicts. These, taught by the purifying influence of trials: 1. *Pray and are heard.* "Shall call on my Name, and I will hear them." 2. *Are accepted of God as his people.* They acknowledge their relationship. "I will say, It is my people: and they shall say, The Lord is my God."

CONCLUSION. Amidst all the difficulties connected with this passage, this doctrine stands out in sublime prominence—*that afflictions which are penal and destructive to the many are remedial and merciful to the few.* All experience shows this to be true. Two men stand before me. Both are equally afflicted with similar sufferings. The one writhes, murmurs, and rebels under his afflictions; he becomes intensified in his enmity to God. Like Pharaoh, his heart is hardened; he dies a rebel, and is lost. The "sword" of justice has struck him. The other becomes spiritually thoughtful, repentant, resigned, humbled, and devout. The "fire" has purified him, and like David he says, "It is good for me that I was afflicted," and like Paul, "I glory in tribulation."—D. T.

EXPOSITION.

CHAPTER XIV.

Vers. 1, 2.—§ 5. The afflictions of the people and their results are set forth in figure and symbol. *Jerusalem is represented as taken and plundered.*

Ver. 1.—**The day of the Lord**; *a day of* (or, *to*) *Jehovah cometh.* The Greek and Latin Versions have the plural, "days of the Lord come." It is a time when he will specially manifest his glory and power, and be recognized as allowing the trial of his people for wise purposes. It is impossible to fix on any historical fulfilment of this prophecy. The details suit neither Maccabean nor Roman times; the attempt to define exactly the period and matter of its accomplishment has proved a failure, and has led to a mingling of events of very different dates, and to a conglomeration of senses literal, metaphorical, and anagogical, which creates confusion while assuming to explain difficulties. The literal interpretation must be resigned, and the whole prophecy must be taken to adumbrate the kingdom of God in its trial, development, and triumph. **Thy spoil shall be divided.** Jerusalem is addressed; and the prophet intimates that the enemy shall get possession of the capital, plunder it, and divide its spoil among themselves in its very midst with the greatest security, the inhabitants being wholly at the conquerors' mercy.

Ver. 2.—How this shall come to pass is now shown. **For I will gather all nations.** God uses the Gentile nations as his instruments in this trial of his people; they are the fires by which he refines and purifies his elect (Joel iii. 2, 9—11). **The city shall be taken.** The outrages offered to the captive city are such as are indicated in the case of Babylon (Isa. xiii. 16; comp. Lam. v. 11, etc.). **Half of the city.** The term "half" must not be pressed, as if it contradicted the mention of the two-thirds that were to perish, according to the prediction in ch. xiii. 8. It is a mere rhetorical expression. Or it may apply to the city alone, while the other referred to the whole land. **Shall not be cut off.** In the former captivity all the

people were carried away; in this capture of the city a remnant shall be left therein. It is plain from this statement that the prophecy cannot apply to the destruction of the city by the Romans; for, according to the account of Josephus ('Bell. Jud.,' vi. 9), the city itself was razed to the ground, and all the inhabitants were either put to the sword or sold for slaves.

Vers. 3—7.—§ 6. *Then the Lord himself comes to her help, great convulsions of nature accompanying his presence.*

Ver. 3.—**Shall go forth.** God is said to "go forth" when he manifests his power by delivering his people and punishing their enemies (comp. Isa. xxvi. 21; xlii. 13; Micah i. 3). **As when he fought in the day of battle.** The Hebrew is in general terms, "as when he fighteth in a day of battle," or, "slaughter;" Septuagint, καθὼς ἡμέρα παρατάξεως αὐτοῦ ἐν ἡμέρᾳ πολέμου, "as a day of his battle in a day of war;" Vulgate, *sicut præliatus est in die certaminis.* There is nothing in the text to confine the reference to any one special interposition; it refers rather to the general course of God's providence in defending his people, though, doubtless, the prophet has in his mind the crowning act of mercy at the Red Sea (Exod. xiv. 13, 14, 25), which is so often referred to as a typical deliverance (comp. Isa. xi. 11; Jer. xvi. 14; xxiii. 8; Hab. iii. 15; and above, ch. x. 11).

Ver. 4.—**His feet shall stand.** By this theophany he shall come to the aid of his people; nature shall do his bidding, owning the presence of its Maker. **Upon the Mount of Olives . . . on the east.** This mount lay on the east of Jerusalem, from which it was separated by the deep valley of the Kidron, rising to a height of some six hundred feet, and intercepting the view of the wilderness of Judæa and the Jordan ghor. The geographical detail is added in the text to indicate the line of escape which shall be opened for those who are to be delivered. This is the only place in the Old Testament where the Mount of Olives is thus exactly named; but it is often alluded to; *e.g.* 2 Sam. xv. 30; 1 Kings xi. 7; 2

Kings xxiii. 13 (where it is called "the mount of corruption"), etc. **Shall cleave in the midst thereof.** As the enemy are supposed to beset Jerusalem, so as to make escape by any ordinary road impossible, the Lord will open a way through the very centre of the mountain (as he opened a path through the Red Sea), by cleaving the hill in sunder, the two parts moving north and south, and leaving a great valley running east and west, and leading to the Arabah.

Ver. 5.—**Ye shall flee to the valley of the mountains;** *ye shall flee by the valley of my mountains;* i.e. by the ravine made by the cleaving of Olivet into two, which God calls "my mountain," because effected by his special interposition. Septuagint, *Φραχθή-σεται ἡ φάραγξ τῶν ὀρέων μου,* "The valley of my mountains shall be blocked;" Vulgate, *Fugietis ad vallem montium eorum.* The last word is probably an error for *meorum.* Into the chasm thus miraculously formed the remnant shall flee for refuge. **Unto Azal;** *ἕως Ἰασόδ* (Septuagint); *usque ad proximum* (Vulgate); so Symmachus. If Azal, or Azel, be a proper name, it is with some probability identified with Beth-ezel, mentioned in Micah i. 11, a village on the east of Olivet. The meaning in this case is that the valley should extend from the west unto the east side of the Mount of Olives, and that in it the people shall find an asylum, that they might not be involved in the judgments which fall on the enemy. Some take *Azal* to mean "union," and see in it a symbol of the union of the Law and the gospel, or the Jew and Gentile, in one Church—the valley of God's mountain extending to "union;" that is, to enfolding all the faithful (see Wordsworth, *in loc.*). **The earthquake in the days of Uzziah.** This is mentioned in Amos i. 1, but not in the historical books (see note on Amos, *loc. cit.*). The intervention of the Lord is here accompanied by an earthquake, which produces the same panic as on the former occasion, and drives the inhabitants to flight. **Shall come.** To smite his enemies and to defend his people. **All the saints** (*holy ones*) **with thee.** The versions have, "with him;" and thus many Hebrew manuscripts. But such abrupt changes of persons are not uncommon (see note on ch. ii. 8). The "holy ones" are the angels (comp. Deut. xxxiii. 2; Job v. 1; Dan. vii. 10; and the parallel predictions in Matt. xxiv. 30, 31; xxv. 31).

Ver. 6.—**The light shall not be clear, nor dark.** The Greek, Syriac, and Latin Versions have, "There shall not be light, but ('and,' Septuagint) cold and ice." With the absence of light and sun shall come bitter frost, which impedes all activity, and kills life: or, taking the Septuagint rendering, there shall no longer be the interchange of seasons, but one lasting sunshine. It is plain that a time of distress and calamity is intended, and that the passage is threatening and not consolatory, at any rate, at first. There is solid ground for the rendering of the Revised Version margin, adopted by Cheyne and others, which is according to the Khetib, "There shall not be light, the bright ones shall contract themselves;" *i.e.* the heavenly bodies shall contract their light, or be heaped confusedly together, and cease to shine. The prediction in this case may be compared with that in Joel iii. 15; Isa. xiii. 10; and in Matt. xxiv. 29; Rev. vi. 12, 13. The Authorized Version is explained in the margin, *i.e.* "It shall not be clear in some places, and dark in other places of the world"—a gloss which is inadmissible.

Ver. 7.—**One day.** A unique day, unparalleled (comp. Cant. vi. 9; Ezek. vii. 5). **Which shall be** (*is*) **known to the Lord.** Its peculiar character, and the moment of its arrival, are known to God, and God only (Matt. xxiv. 36). **Not day, nor night.** It cannot be called truly the one or the other, because there is darkness in the day and light at night, as the following clause says. This is symbolically explained by St. Ephraem, "It will not be altogether consolation, nor altogether affliction." It is not full daylight, for calamity presses; it is not deep night, because there is hope amid the distress. **At evening-time it shall be light.** In the midst of trouble and danger deliverance shall come. The whole section is a figurative description of the fortunes of the Church militant, even as Christ announced to his disciples: "In the world ye shall have tribulation: but be of good cheer, I have overcome the world" (John xvi. 33); "If they have persecuted me, they will also persecute you" (John xv. 20); "Let not your heart be troubled, neither let it be afraid" (John xiv. 27).

Vers. 8—11.—**§ 7.** *Then shall occur a season of joy. The land shall be transformed and renewed, and the Lord shall be owned as the sole King of all the earth.*

Ver. 8.—**Living waters;** *i.e.* water fresh, pure, and perennial (Gen. xxvi. 19; Jer. ii. 13), a figure of the spiritual blessings and graces bestowed by God upon his Church. **From Jerusalem,** as the centre and representative of the kingdom of God, as in ch. xii. 2. The city itself was, as we know, abundantly supplied with water by many conduits and subterranean channels; but standing, as it does, surrounded by hills higher than itself, it is physically impossible that the waters could literally flow as stated.

The description is symbolical, though the natural features of the country are supposed to be changed in order to preserve verisimilitude (comp. Ezek. xlvii. 1, etc.; Joel iii. 18]. The former (*eastern*) sea . . . the hinder (*western*) sea. The Dead Sea is the eastern sea to one looking to sunrise from Jerusalem; the Mediterranean is the western sea, behind the observer's back. Into every quarter the salutary stream shall flow. In summer and in winter. Neither drought nor frost shall stop their perennial flow. "Alike in times of peace and of persecution those waters shall continue their course" (St. Jerome); Septuagint, "In summer and in spring"—a rendering which seems to indicate the home of the Alexandrian Version.

Ver. 9.—All the earth; *all the land* of Israel (vers. 8, 10)—a type of the kingdom of God in all its extent (Rev. xi. 15, "The kingdoms of this world are become the kingdoms of our Lord, and of his Christ; and he shall reign for ever and ever"). Shall there be one Lord; rather, *Jehovah shall be one.* He shall be universally acknowledged as "the blessed and only Potentate" (1 Tim. vi. 15). His name one. Idolatry shall be abolished, and the one God shall be everywhere adored (comp. ch. xiii. 2; Deut. vi. 4). Men shall no longer attribute operations and effects to various heavenly powers, but shall see and confess that all are derived from and centre in him, and are only different revelations of his ineffable nature and attributes. We do not, indeed, see this prediction yet fulfilled, but the grace to accomplish it is ready and operating; it is only men's perverse wills that impede the gracious purpose of God.

Ver. 10.—All the land shall be turned as a plain. To indicate the exaltation and stability of the centre of the new theocracy, the prophet announces that all the country round Jerusalem shall be turned into a plain, dominated by the metropolis, which stands sublime on a lofty mountain. The Revised Version renders, "shall be turned as the Arabah," *i.e.* as the Jordan ghor, a valley of abnormal fertility. From Geba to Rimmon south of Jerusalem; *i.e.* from the north of Judah to its southern boundary. Geba was a town and district on the edge of the great Wady Suweinit, five miles north of Jerusalem. It is identified with Jeba (1 Sam. xiii. 3), and it formed the northern boundary of the kingdom of Judah (Josh. xviii. 24). Rimmon is described as "south of Jerusalem," to distinguish it from a town of the same name in Galilee (Josh. xix. 13), and from the famous rock Rimmon, to which the Benjamites fled (Judg. xx. 45, 47). It was situated in the territory of Simeon (Josh. xv. 32; xix. 7), and has been identified

with *Umm-er-Rummamin*, a town ten miles north of Beersheba. It shall be lifted up. Jerusalem shall remain exalted on its hill, while all the country around sinks into a plain—a figure representing the spiritual exaltation of the new theocracy. Inha' ited in her place; or, *shall dwell in her place.* Shall occupy her ancient limits, and abide there safely without fear (comp. Jer. xxxi. 38—40; Ezek. xlviii. 15, etc.). From Benjamin's gate, etc. (Jer. xxxvii. 13). It is difficult to define the given boundaries with certainty in every particular. Benjamin's gate is the same as the gate of Ephraim (2 Kings xiv. 13; Neh. viii. 16), so called as leading to the territory of Benjamin, and beyond again to that of Ephraim. It was situated in the north or second wall. From this point the course of the wall is followed, first to the west, and then to the east. The first gate. This was in the eastern part of this wall, and is the same as "the old gate," or "gate of the old town," of Neh. xii. 39. The corner gate (2 Kings xiv. 13; Jer. xxxi. 38) was at the north-west corner, west of the gate of Benjamin, at the angle where the first and second walls approached each other. These dimensions would give the breadth of the city from east to west. The tower of Hananeel (Neh. iii. 1) was at the north-east corner of the north wall, where the citadel Baris or Antonia afterwards stood. The king's wine-presses were probably near "the king's garden" (Neh. iii. 15), at the south-east extremity of the city. They may have been cut out of the rock, as was often the case. This description gives the extent of the city from north to south. Thus Zechariah illustrates the growth and stability of the Church of God by the figure of the earthly city Jerusalem, firmly and orderly built, and inhabited by a teeming population, as the following verse shows. There is no ground for expecting the literal fulfilment of this prediction.

Ver. 11.—Men shall dwell in it. There shall be no fear of exile and captivity, and no necessity to fly from a victorious enemy (vers. 2, 5). Utter destruction; literally, *curse, ban;* LXX. and Vulgate, "There shall be no more anathema." The inhabitants shall not incur the curse which is inflicted on transgressors, idolaters, and their cities by the old Law (see Exod. xxii. 20; Deut. vii. 2; xiii. 12—15; xx. 17; comp. Ezra x 8; Isa. xliii. 28; Rev. xxii. 3). Shall be safely inhabited; or, *shall dwell safely.* Sin being removed, there will be no more occasion for chastisement; and the spiritual Jerusalem shall never be destroyed.

Vers. 12—15.—§ 8. *Having noted the blessings on the true Israelites, the prophet gives further details concerning the destruction of the enemies: they shall perish by plague, by mutual slaughter, by the sword of Judah.*

Ver. 12.—**This shall be the plague.** These are the instruments which the Lord uses when he fights against the nations (not **the people,** as in the Authorized Version), ver. 3. The plague, or smiting (*maggephah*), is some contagious affliction sent by God, as in Exod. ix. 14; Numb. xiv. 37; 1 Sam. vi. 4. **Their.** It is, in the Hebrew, "his flesh, his feet," etc., to show that the general plague extends to every individual. In the last clause the plural is used, "their mouth." With body, eye, and tongue they opposed the holy city, and took pleasure in its discomfiture: in all their members they shall suffer retributive punishment. **While they stand upon their feet.** The flesh of each shall putrefy and moulder away, while he is still alive and arrayed against the city of God. **Holes; sockets.** The eyes had spied out the weak places in the defence, and looked with malicious pleasure on the defeat and fall. **Tongue.** They had blasphemed God, and cried against his holy place, "Down with it, even to the ground!"

Ver. 13.—**A great tumult from the Lord** (ch. xii. 4). A general panic or confusion sent by the Lord, such as befell the Midianites (Judg. vii. 22) and the Philistines (1 Sam. xiv. 20), which ends in mutual slaughter. **They shall lay hold every one,** etc. In this general panic each shall seize his neighbour's hand in fierce contention. The next clause gives the same meaning (comp. ch. xi. 6).

Ver. 14.—**Judah also shall fight at Jerusalem.** The *adversus Jerusalem* of the Vulgate and some Jewish interpreters is a mistake, and introduces a wholly irrelevant idea. The meaning is that the Judæans outside of Jerusalem, the nation at large, rallying to the attack, shall fall on the enemy, now thinned by pestilence and internecine conflicts within the walls of the city, and prevail against them (comp. ch. xii. 6). Septuagint, ʼΙούδας παρατάξεται ἐν ʼΙερουσαλήμ, " Judah shall draw up his forces in Jerusalem." **The wealth of all the heathen** (*nations*) **round about.** The costly booty of the enemy shall fall into Judah's hands. Thus the Church emerges victorious from persecutions, and is enriched and adorned by the means of those who planned her overthrow.

Ver. 15.—**So shall be the plague of the horse,** etc. As was the plague that came on men (ver. 12), so shall be the plague that falls on their beasts and cattle. The brute animals suffer for their owners' sin according to the ban under the old Law (Deut. xiii. 15; comp. Numb. xvi. 32, 33; Josh.

vii. 24, 25). **Tents;** *camps;* Septuagint, παρεμβολαῖς. The verse illustrates the utter destruction which shall befall the enemies of God's Church.

Vers. 16—19.—§ 9. *Warned by these manifestations of God's power, the residue of the heathen shall be converted, and shall join with the Hebrews in the regular worship of Jehovah.*

Ver. 16.—**Every one that is left.** All the heathen that attacked the holy city shall not be destroyed; the remnant saved shall become subjects of the Divine kingdom. **Shall go up.** This is the usual phrase for going to Jerusalem for the purpose of worship (comp. Isa. ii. 2, 3; Micah iv. 2; Luke ii. 42; John vii. 8). The prophet here and in the following clause speaks as a Jew to Jews, who knew and observed only the prescribed form of worship. It is evident that the announcement could never be literally fulfilled; the Gentile world could never come yearly to pay their devotions at Jerusalem. The prediction can only signify that under Messiah's reign the Gentiles shall be converted to true religion and worship God in regular, orderly fashion, the prophet intimating this in terms derived from the old dispensation, which had the Divine sanction. **The Feast of Tabernacles.** The Israelites were required to appear before the Lord three times in the year (Exod. xxiii. 17; Deut. xvi. 16)—at the festivals of the Passover, Pentecost, and Tabernacles. But the Gentiles are here required to present themselves only once. The Feast of Tabernacles is chosen for this occasion owing to its peculiar character and the associations connected with it. It commemorated not only the ingathering of the harvest, but also Israel's sojourn in the wilderness and the Divine protection there accorded to them, and their entrance into the promised land; it was therefore a fitting symbol of the rescue of the Gentiles from the devil's kingdom, and their entry into the Church of God, where they enjoyed the blessings of God's grace and protection. It was also a more catholic feast, in one sense, than the Passover or Pentecost, not being so distinctively Jewish, but one which all nations could keep in gratitude to the Giver of material benefits. We must remember, also, that it was at this feast that our Lord cried (John vii. 37), " If any man thirst, let him come unto me, and drink," and likewise he declared himself to be "the Light of the world" (John viii. 12), wishing us, it may be, to understand that this feast was the one we should need to keep, being the one which specially sets him forth as the Sustainer and Guide through life's pilgrimage.

Ver. 17.—**Will not come up;** *goeth not up.* Those who neglected this yearly worship shall be punished according to the threat in Deut. xi. 16, 17. **No rain.** The failure of periodic rain in Eastern countries meant drought, famine, and widespread distress. In a spiritual sense, rain represents the grace and blessing of God; these are withholden from those who refuse to worship him and wilfully cut themselves off from the Church. The LXX. has, Καὶ οὗτοι ἐκείνοις προστεθήσονται, "These shall be associated with those," *i.e.* shall be reckoned among those enemies whose punishment has been mentioned above.

Ver. 18.—**If the family of Egypt go not up.** Egypt is mentioned as the great typical enemy of God and Israel, and therefore most obnoxious to punishment if it did not obey the call. **That have no rain.** This rendering implies, what is not the fact, that Egypt is without rain, and is not dependent upon rain for its fertility. The expression in the text is elliptical, being merely, "then not on them," and it is obviously natural to supply, "shall there be rain." As the rise of the Nile depends upon the equinoctial rains in the interior, the failure of these would be disastrous. Another way of rendering the passage is to combine the clauses and append a note of interrogation; thus: "Shall there not be upon them the plague wherewith," etc.? The LXX. and Syriac omit the negative, Καὶ ἐπὶ τούτους ἔσται ἡ πτῶσις, "Even upon these shall be the plague."

Ver. 19.—**The punishment;** literally, *sin;* ἁμαρτία: *peccatum;* here obviously the punishment of sin—sin with all its fatal consequences (comp. Numb. xviii. 22; Lam. iii. 39; iv. 6).

Vers. 20, 21.—§ 10. *Then everything alike shall be holy, and the ungodly shall be altogether excluded from the house of the Lord.*

Ver. 20.—**Upon the bells of the horses.** The prophet, describing the holiness of the theocracy, uses imagery drawn from the ritual customs of the Law. "The bells," says Henderson, "were small metallic plates, suspended from the necks or heads of horses and camels, for the sake of ornament, and making a tinkling noise by striking against each other like cymbals."

Probably these plates had the names of the owners engraven on them. The Septuagint gives "bridle," which possibly the unusual word *metzilloth* may mean. **HOLINESS** (*holy*) **UNTO THE LORD;** *Sanctum Domino* (Vulgate); Ἅγιον τῷ Κυρίῳ παντοκράτορι (Septuagint). This was the inscription upon the golden plate on the mitre of the high priest (Exod. xxviii. 36). The affixing of this inscription on the trappings of horses signifies that the commonest things shall become holy, all things that men use for work, profit, or ornament shall be consecrated to God's service. **The pots in the Lord's house.** The "pots" are vessels of inferior sanctity used for boiling the meat of the sacrifice (1 Sam. ii. 14; 2 Chron. xxxv. 13). **The bowls before the altar.** These held the blood of the victims for sprinkling on the altar, and the sacred libations, and were considered of superior sanctity. The prophet announces that now all shall be holy, the lower equal to the highest.

Ver. 21.—The last announcement is amplified. **Every pot.** All the vessels of the country shall be consecrated and used in Divine service. The Levitical distinction shall be abolished, and the Lord's service shall be perfect freedom. Every member of the Church, however humble his station or mean his acquirements, shall be a saint and fit for the Lord's use (comp. 2 Tim. ii. 21). **The Canaanite;** *mercator* (Vulgate). The word is used in the sense of "trafficker," or "merchant," in Job xl. 30 (xli. 6, Authorized Version); Prov. xxxi. 24 (comp. Zeph. i. 11). If any vessel might now be used in God's service, worshippers would no longer be obliged to buy special bowls from those who sold in the temple courts (Matt. xxi. 12). But it is best in agreement with the context to take "Canaanite" to mean any unclean or profane person (comp. Gen. ix. 25; Lev. xviii. 28, etc.). Thus Daniel, in the History of Susanna, ver. 56, addresses the wicked elder, "Thou seed of Chanaan, and not of Juda;" and Isaiah (i. 10) calls the chiefs of Israel "rulers of Sodom," and "people of Gomorrah." Henceforward the "people shall be all righteous" (Isa. lx. 21). There shall be one, holy, Catholic Church. Thus the vision of the golden candlestick (ch. iv.) is fulfilled; and that this should come to pass is the design of God's manifold providences and operations (comp. Rev. xxi. 27; xxii. 15).

HOMILETICS.

Vers. 1—5.—*A signal revelation.* "Behold, the day of the Lord cometh," etc. The "day of the Lord" here referred to seems that of the second coming of Christ. We say this partly because it is a day to be marked by a signal exercise of Jehovah's power against his enemies, "as in the day of battle" (2 Pet. i. 16; 2 Thess. ii. 8; Josh. x. 14, 42); partly, also, because he is then to appear in person in the neighbourhood of Jerusalem (ver. 4), as though in fulfilment of Matt. xxiii. 39; Acts i. 11, 12; and partly, again, because of those who are mentioned here (end of ver. 5) as then to appear in his suite (comp. Matt. xxv. 31; Dan. vii. 10; Jude 14, 15; Rev. xix. 11—16). Understood thus of that stupendous event, the prophecy seems to describe (1) *its immediate antecedents*; and (2) *its primary results.*

I. ITS IMMEDIATE ANTECEDENTS. These appear to be described here only so far as "Jerusalem " is concerned—whether we understand thereby, as some do, the literal city inhabited again and besieged (see above, ch. xii. 2) by the rest of the nations, or that great "spiritual city," the Christian Church (Gal. iv. 26; Heb. xii. 22; Rev. iii. 12). In either (or both) of these senses we see the condition of " Jerusalem " at the time intended (note "then " in ver. 3). For example, we see: 1. *The city itself wholly subdued.* Its bulwarks are all "taken," its separate "houses " "rifled," its choicest treasures boldly divided by the secure and triumphant enemy in its most central positions, and every refuge against the deepest indignities utterly gone. 2 *Its population half destroyed.* When the inhabitants of a neighbourhood are decimated by disease it is awful enough. Here we have a proportion of lost ones just fives times as great! Every second house uninhabited! Every family less by one-half! What all this exactly points to it is hard to say; but there are passages connecting such unexampled excess of trial with the very eve of the Saviour's coming, in Dan. xii. 1; Matt. xxiv. 12, 13; possibly, also, in a spiritual sense, in Luke xviii. 8.

II. ITS PRIMARY RESULTS; viz. as might be expected, very great natural—or else spiritual—convulsions (comp. Hag. ii. 6, and beginning of 7; Mal. iii. 1, 2). Three things to be marked about these. 1. *How mighty they are in nature!* To divide the tideless waters of the upper Red Sea in old days had been much. To do the same by the flowing waters of Jordan (Josh. iii. 16) perhaps more. To separate, as prophesied here, into two districts, and far-removed portions, the solid range of Mount Olivet, more again. At any rate, nothing less. 2. *How momentous in results!* Jerusalem, with Mount Olivet practically gone from " before " it " on the east," where it had stood for so long the most conspicuous object all round about (comp. Ps. cxxv. 2), would be no longer the same place as before. Where once had been a mountain was now a valley; where a barrier, a way of escape—a way of complete escape to " Azal;" either, *i.e.,* as far as needed (so some), or else close at hand (as others). Certainly, if we may judge from the case of Zedekiah (2 Kings xxv. 4, 5), the "way of escape " in previous sieges had been by a very different route. 3. *How easily wrought!* viz. immediately on the Master's arrival, by the mere force of that arrival itself—by the mere touch, as it were, of his feet! Compare—itself not improbably another prediction of the same occurrence—the striking description of Hab. iii. 6; also 2 Thess. ii. 8, " Whom the Lord shall destroy with the brightness of his coming " (or " presence," see margin of Revised Version), as darkness is destroyed, and that instantly, by the mere presence of light.

Observe, from all this, the inevitable consequences of every manifestation of Christ, specially, of course, of the latest of all. 1. *Amazing changes to all.* " Every valley shall be exalted, and every mountain and hill brought low." These will be partly, of course, in the world of feeling and thought. " *Then* shall the righteous shine forth," as they certainly do not at present (see also Matt. xx. 16, and elsewhere; and Acts iii. 20, 21). Partly, also, it is far from improbable, in the world of matter and sense. (See such passages, on the one side, as Ps. lxvii. 6; Ezek. xxxiv. 25, 26; Amos ix. 13; the very ground which was cursed for the first Adam's sake being blessed then for the sake of the second. See, on the other, 2 Pet. iii. 10, etc.) 2. *Exceeding fear to some.* Many then will be found fleeing as though for their lives, even in such a way as they did on the occasion of that appalling earthquake in the days of Uzziah, the terror of which had engraved itself so deeply on the national mind. Never before had there been greater fear than there will be at "that day " (Matt. xxiv. 30; Isa. ii. 19; Rev. vi. 15—17). 3. *Corresponding triumph to others.* How many things which now divide Christ from his people—how many which now separate his people from one another—shall then be things of the past! All his "saints " shall be with him then (ver. 5), and with him for ever (1 Thess. iv. 17). Consequently (1 John iii. 2; 1 Cor. xv. 49), they shall be fully " like him " at last; and therefore, also, like one another;

and therefore, again, divided no more! No longer, when at last in the Master's presence, will they "dispute," as they once did "by the way" (Mark ix. 33, 34).

Vers. 6—11.—*A wonderful day.* "And it shall come to pass in that day, that the light shall not be clear, nor dark," etc. However obscure, in some respects, the opening verses of this passage, the "day" they speak of is to be, very manifestly, a day by itself. How strange, *e.g.*, the character of its light! Is it the light of "day"? or the darkness of "night"? How strange, also, its time—so that it should be, apparently, at its brightest just when the light of day is no more (end of ver. 7)! Altogether, a kind of "day" only fully "known to the Lord" (see, though not in exactly the same connection, Matt. xxiv. 36). Corresponding to this, in other respects also, shall be the character of that day. In particular, "Jerusalem" shall then, as never before, be (1) *a centre of blessing*; (2) *a centre of rule*; and (3) *a centre of strength*.

I. A CENTRE OF BLESSING. This is represented to us under the figure of a flow of "living waters" therefrom (see Joel iii. 18; Ezek. xlvii., *passim*, and especially ver. 9; also John iv. 10; vii. 38) What is remarkable in this case is that the flow of these waters shall be: 1. *In most unusual directions.* Some will flow, naturally enough, along the intervening descent to the "former," or eastern sea; but some also, altogether supernaturally according to the lie of the land, to the "latter," or western sea. Countries and races, that is to say, which at present are hardly sprinkled with gospel influences, and to which at present it seems almost impossible to send them, shall then be overflowed by them as by a flood. 2. *At most unusual seasons.* How sadly intermittent, as things are now, is the flow of Church work! Now in decadence, now restored! Now frozen by indifference, now revived by warmth! Now exhausted by heat, now refreshed by rain (Ps. lxviii. 9)! The flow of these days is to be independent of seasons—rivers all the year through (comp. Rev. xxii. 2).

II. A CENTRE OF RULE. Very naturally does this head follow from that before. Influence of such a gracious character, so universally and constantly in operation, will subdue the whole world in due time. This is what seems foretold in ver. 9. In the present divided rule of the world—and, in some measure, of the Church as well—it is difficult to give hearty subjection to this authority without rebelling against that. Not so when, in all the world, there shall be but one supreme Head. Not so, still more, when the possessor of that supreme authority shall only be known by one name. At present, in many cases, we have vast composite sovereignties, "united kingdoms," "dual empires," at best. The man obeyed here as Emperor of Austria is only obeyed next door as King of Hungary. Not so at all in "that day." The King of "Jerusalem"—Christ in his Church—shall be the one title of that "only Potentate" (see Dan. vii. 13, 14, 27; Rev. xi. 15; xix. 16; Isa. xxiv. 23; also Ps. ii. and cx., *passim*; and Luke i. 32, 33).

III. A CENTRE OF STRENGTH. "Jerusalem" is to be strong then for three different reasons. There shall be: 1. *No facilities for attacking it.* Beginning from the ancient fortress of Geba on the north (Pusey, *in loc.*), down along the whole mountain range to Rimmon in the south, instead of lofty hills sheltering the invaders and dominating the hill of Mount Zion, the "whole land shall be a plain." 2. *Every facility for defending it.* What those other mountains lose, as it were, the hill of Zion shall gain. Remaining still "in her place," but "lifted up" (comp. Isa. ii. 2) far above her former elevation, the holy city shall look down then on the whole subject neighbourhood—every ancient wall and battlement being also restored and elevated together with it, and so made doubly effective as a means of defence. 3. Better still, the knowledge of the possession of these advantages shall prevent *the very thought of attack.* "Men shall dwell there"—shall choose to dwell there—knowing how secure it is from attack. What *had* been so often there shall be never again. "Jerusalem" now is a city which can never be touched. This shall be felt, this shall be acted on, by all without, by all within.

This glorious prospect of that future day of blessing and peace, whether comparatively near or far off, may console us greatly in the days that now are, whether in witnessing: 1. *Their cruel dissensions.* What a scene of selfishness, greed, competition, strife, suspicion, distrust, and violence is that now around us! Worse than a "struggle for existence," it is too often a struggle, even where existence is not imperilled, to keep others down. See how the whole civilized (!) world is standing armed to the teeth, possessed of deadlier weapons, and, consequently, of deadlier determination, than ever. How restful to the spirit to look beyond all this to that described here! 2. *Their cruel disappointments.* Much as these evils have been bewailed and lamented, and often as many men have hitherto tried to relieve them, how little comparative success they have reached! Political endeavours to remedy these evils have only led to worse, as a rule. Even the religion of Jesus, the religion of "liberty, equality, and fraternity," in the very best (and perhaps only possible) sense, has become the occasion, too often, though not the cause, of that which it sought to remove. It is a comfort to know that another hand will itself apply this remedy in due time; and that that will be easily accomplished by him when he comes down from the "mount," which is now impossible to his friends (Mark ix. 14—27).

Vers. 12—21.—*A regenerate world.* "And this shall be the plague wherewith the Lord will smite all the people that have fought against Jerusalem," etc. A regenerate man is not a man without disposition to sin, but a man in whose case that disposition is habitually overcome. In that regenerate world partially described in the previous verses, something very similar is to hold good. All the elements of evil are not then altogether to cease; but there shall be in operation then a new principle of action, which shall prevent them from raising their heads. How exceedingly different a condition of things the full establishment of such a rule will result in seems to be taught us, in these concluding verses, in three different ways; viz. in regard (1) to those who shall hate "Jerusalem;" (2) to those who shall *despise it;* and (3) to those who shall *inhabit it,* in those days.

I. THOSE WHO HATE IT. For such persons there will be, even at that time, as at all previous times, in existence. There will even be some in existence—at any rate, at the very beginning of "that day"—who shall be bold enough to declare war against it. How will it be with such then? Not at all as it is with them now, when they seem so often and so mysteriously to have the "upper hand" (Ps. ix. 19, Prayer-book Version) against God. On the contrary, partly (1) by judgments *within* them, their very bodily organs, as it were, visibly withering away under God's displeasure; partly (2) by judgments *among* them, causing them, as in a kind of frenzy, to lay violent hands on one another; partly (3) by judgments *upon* them, which shall turn their very endeavours to injure "Jerusalem" into means for enriching it; and partly (4) by judgments *around* them, represented as coming even on the poor brutes they employ for their sakes;—God will testify openly what are his feelings and purposes with regard to such doings. In such circumstances, if evil be sometimes desired, it will very seldom be deliberately attempted, and never achieved. How total a contrast, in every respect, to that which we read of in Eccles. viii. 11!

II. THOSE WHO DESPISE IT. Besides that hostility which is open and active, there is that which is passive and half-concealed. Some men do not so much oppose religion as ignore its injunctions. Men disposed to act thus will not be lacking, even in that glorious "day." This illustrated here by a reference to that well-known ancient "Feast of Tabernacles," in which the settled Israelites commemorated the fact of their having been wanderers once in the wilderness (Lev. xxiii. 41—43). Something so far corresponding to this, at any rate, as to be fitly described by the same appellation, will be of universal obligation in the final settlement of that great sabbatical "day" (comp. Heb. iv. 1—9). How will things be with those who despise it and neglect to "come up" (ver. 17)? Not as now (see Matt. v. 45); but rather as it was in those days when Goshen was distinguished for Israel's sake, as by a special command from Heaven, from all the rest of the land. Every such contemptuous nation or "family," whatever the peculiarity of their circumstances and ordinary climate, shall be made to feel then the open displeasure of him who commandeth the clouds. How widely different in those days the language of Heaven! How widely different the conduct, may we not expect, therefore, of the most callous of men!

III. THOSE WHO INHABIT IT. These men shall find Jerusalem then "the holy city" indeed. Speaking here of the future, in language drawn from the usages of his own time; or possibly, as some have supposed, speaking so because there will be a certain measure of return to those usages in the future;—there are three great changes which the prophet bids us expect in the "Jerusalem" of "that day." Its inhabitants will see: 1. *The previously " common " become " holy."* The very bells of the horses being outwardly marked for God's service, like the high priest's mitre was in ancient times (Exod. xxviii. 36—38; see also Isa. xxiii. 17, 18). 2. *The previously holy made holier still.* The ordinary temple "pits," only used of old days for "dressing the victims" (Pusey), being now regarded as like the sacrificial "bowls before the altar," containing the atoning blood itself; and even those vessels outside the "house," which were only so far holy before that they were found in " Jerusalem " (the holy city), or belonged to " Judah " (the holy people), shall now be regarded as fit for employment in the temple worship itself. 3. *The irreclaimably profane for ever shut out.* "The Canaanite," *i.e.*, as representing those who, though not truly the children of promise, yet "would live" amongst them (Judg. i. 35) through all the ages, being never seen there again (comp. Isa. xxxv. 8; Joel iii. 17; Eph. v. 27; Rev. xxi. 27; xxii. 15).

> " Not yet! not yet! The faultless flock,
> The field without a tare,
> Come last of all the blessing sought
> By centuries of prayer!"

How fitting a close of the whole is this thought! How rightly does this chief prophet of the post-Captivity Jerusalem tell us thus, in conclusion, of that far more glorious Jerusalem which is some day to shine forth! It is much the same that the Prophet Daniel does at the end of his prophecy. It is the same also that "St. John the divine" does at the end of his song. They bring their message to an end when they have given us a glimpse of the end which God has in store. It is for us to take care that we are truly numbered with those for whom that "end" is prepared.

HOMILIES BY VARIOUS AUTHORS.

Ver. 5.—*Lessons of the earthquake.* "Speak to the earth, and it shall teach thee." So said Job (xii. 8). The earthquake serves—

I. To IMPRESS US WITH THE GREATNESS OF GOD. There are forces great and terrible. But back of all, and controlling all, is God. So the prophets taught, and so we believe (Ps. lxviii. 8; civ. 32; Job xxv. 9—14; Exod. xix. 18).

II. To HUMBLE US UNDER A SENSE OF OUR UTTER HELPLESSNESS. Many things possible to man. Can tame the wild beasts and subdue the earth. Can make fire and air and water his servants. But there are times when he feels his impotence. When the earthquake comes, can only say, "It is the will of the Lord" (Isa. ii. 19—22).

III. To CONVINCE US OF THE INSTABILITY OF ALL EARTHLY THINGS. The earth seems of all things the most stable. But there comes a crisis, and our old faith is gone for ever. "A bad earthquake at once destroys our oldest associations. The earth, the very emblem of solidity, has moved beneath our feet; one second of time has created in the mind a strange idea of insecurity which hours of reflection could not have produced" (Darwin).

IV. To ADMONISH US OF THE JUDGMENTS THAT ARE COMING UPON THE EARTH. Geologists tell us of internal fires, and the probability of some great catastropho, sooner or later. "Coming events cast their shadows before." Earthquakes are prophecies. Confirmed by Scripture (2 Pet. iii. 10—12).

V. To TEACH US THE PERFECT SECURITY OF GOD'S SAINTS. Come what will, who shall separate us from the love of God? There are things which cannot be moved, and they are the heritage of God's people (Isa. liv. 10; Ps. xlvi.; Heb. xii. 25—29). "We look for a new heaven and a new earth, wherein dwelleth righteousness."—F.

Vers. 6, 7.—*The day of days.* The promise that "at evening-time it shall be light" is suggestive and comforting.

I. THE DAWN. Ordinary light seems withdrawn. Things are seen dimly. Discouragement and fear. Ready to say, "Darkness shall cover us." Call for faith. "God is light." "He will bring the blind by a way that they know not, making darkness light before them" (cf. Isa. l. 10).

II. PROGRESS. Still uncertainty. Neither wholly day nor night. Alternations. Now the sun seems about to break forth, now the gloom returns. Hopes and fears. But on the whole advance. Faith still finds firm footing. Hope brightens. Love never fails. Amidst all the conflicts with science and philosophy, Christianity abides in its power. There is promise of the "perfect day."

III. THE CLOSE. "Evening." After long waiting and many disappointments. When most needed and least expected. Not in the order of nature, but of grace. When the shadows are lengthening and the sun going down, the light shines forth with a sweet and beautiful radiance. Glorious ending to a dark and cloudy day. The history of the Church, and the experience of individual Christians, afford many illustrations. The promise sometimes finds a tender and comforting fulfilment in the last hours of the dying believer. Bunyan tells us of Mr. Fearing, that, at the entrance of the Valley of the Shadow of Death, he was "ready to die for fear." But to him the valley was quiet from troublers. Then Greatheart notes, as something very remarkable, at the departure of this pilgrim, "The water of that river was lower, at this time, than ever I saw it in all my life; so he went over at last not much above wetshod."—F.

Vers. 8—11.—*Living waters.* Emblematic of the gospel.

I. SOURCE. "Jerusalem." Centre of supreme authority and law. The place of holy sacrifice. The city of the great King. Here is God's throne (Rev. xxii. 1). "Salvation is of the Jews." "Of whom as concerning the flesh, Christ came."

II. DIRECTION. There is movement. Not arbitrary, but regulated. Not limited to one land, but for all people. "Beginning at Jerusalem." Such was the law; but from that starting-point the messengers of salvation were to go forth to the whole earth. Water seeks the lowest level, and the gospel comes down to the poorest, the most despised, "the chief of sinners."

III. AFFLUENCE. Rich supply—ample to meet the needs of all. In the wilderness the rock-waters followed the Israelites in all their wanderings. But this river is sufficient "for the whole world."

IV. PERPETUITY. There are rivers that vary. They run part of the year, and then they fail. But this river never fails. Neither the winter's cold nor the summer's heat can affect its flow. There are rivers that have disappeared—like old peoples and old civilizations—but this river runs on throughout the ages with unchanging life and virtue.

V. BENEFICENCE. Vitality. Life and the power of life. What so sweet and refreshing as the streams of pure water? Carry blessings far and wide. So with the gospel. Converting souls. Purifying society. Advancing the world in the highest forms of civilization. Grand future. Universal subjection. Universal homage. "One Lord."—F.

Vers. 9—11.—*The elevation of Zion.* Morally and spiritually (Isa. ii. 2; Micah iv. 1; Ezek. xl. 2).

I. RAISED ABOVE THE STRIFE OF FACTIONS. Sects. Party spirit. Din and strife of tongues. Confusion and every evil work. But for Zion's children there is a purer atmosphere and serener skies.

II. RAISED ABOVE THE CORRUPTIONS OF THE WORLD. We hear much in our day of germs. The air is everywhere infected. The seeds of disease are on every side. But rise higher, and the danger ceases. So of Zion. Drunkenness, illegitimacy, worldliness, and other sins abound, and lower the tone of society. Need to rise nearer to heaven. "Ye are from beneath: I am from above," said our Lord.

III. RAISED ABOVE THE ASSAULTS OF THE WICKED. Storms. Enemies. Temptations. Cry, "Deliver us from the evil." The higher we rise, the greater our safety. The more we resemble Christ, with the more hope can we say, "The prince of this world cometh, and hath nothing in me."

IV. RAISED ABOVE THE VICISSITUDES OF TIME. Dispensations vary. Habits of society alter. Beliefs may change. But eternal truth and righteousness abide. "The true religion is built upon the rock, the rest are tossed upon the waves of time" (Bacon).

"Serene will be our days, and bright
And happy will our nature be,
When love is an unerring light,
And joy its own security."

(Wordsworth.)

F.

Vers. 16—21.—*The great harvest-home.* The Feast of Tabernacles had a threefold reference. It was a memorial of the past, it was a service of thanksgiving, and it was also foreshadowing of the better things to come. Well, therefore, may the prophet make it a symbol of the glory of the latter days, when under Messiah's reign the fulness of the Gentiles should be brought in, and all Israel should be saved. The glowing and beautiful picture may represent the great harvest-home of the world.

I. UNITY OF WORSHIP. No more many gods, but one. No more hostile sects and parties, but the holy Catholic Church of the living God. At last the old promise is fulfilled (Numb. xiv. 21).

II. JOYFULNESS OF SERVICE. The Spirit of Christ reigns. Love and joy and peace are in all hearts. From all lands and peoples come the songs of praise and the services of thanksgiving to the Father of lights, and the Giver of every good and perfect gift.

III. SANCTITY OF LIFE. Society is purified. Every life is consecrated to God. There is no need any more for the law of ordinances, for all things are cleansed. "Holiness" is the law everywhere. 1. *Common life.* 2. *Domestic life.* 3. *Religious life.*

"Ah! when shall all men's good
Be each man's rule, and universal peace
Lie like a shaft of light across the land,
And like a lane of beams athwart the sea,
Thro' all the circle of the golden year?"

F.

Vers. 1—3.—*A sketch on bad men.* "And thy spoil shall be divided," etc. There are three facts here suggested concerning bad men.

I. THAT THEY ARE CAPABLE OF PERPETRATING THE GREATEST ENORMITIES ON THEIR FELLOW-MEN. "The city of Jerusalem shall be taken, and the houses rifled, and the women ravished." In the account given by Josephus of the destruction of Jerusalem by the Romans, we have a record of enormities at which we might well stand aghast. Christ said, concerning this event, "There shall be great tribulation, such as was not from the beginning of the world until this time, no, nor ever shall be." "The particulars," says Dr. Wardlaw, "here noted, are such as usually, it might be said invariably, attend the besieging, the capture, and the sacking of cities; especially when, as in this case, the assailing army has been exasperated by a long, harassing, and wasting defence. The entrance of the unpitying soldiery, the rifling of houses, the violation of women, the indiscriminate massacre, and the division of the spoil, are just what all expect, and what require no comment. And never were such scenes more frightfully realized than at the destruction of Jerusalem, when God in his providence, in judicial retribution, gathered all nations against the devoted city to battle." "All nations," a correct description of the army of Titus, the empire of Rome embracing a large proportion of the then known world, and this army consisting of soldiers of all the different nations which composed it. And, while such was to be the destruction brought upon the "city," the desolation was to extend, and that in different ways, at short intervals, throughout "the land." The fact that men are capable of perpetrating on their fellow-men such enormities, shows: 1. *Man's apostasy from the laws of his spiritual nature.* To love supremely the supremely good, to do unto others what we would have others do unto us, to love and to be loved, seem to us to be truths inscribed upon the very constitution of the soul. They are instinctive truths. But in all such abominations as here recorded, all these are outraged. Men have fallen away from their own nature. Somehow or other they have become denaturalized. 2. *The great work which the gospel has to do in our world.* The great mission of the gospel (and admirably adapted it is to its mission), is morally to renew human nature, to bring it back to its true self and its God. It has done so in millions of instances, it is doing so and will continue to do so until the present abominations shall be unknown amongst the race.

II. THAT WHATEVER ENORMITIES THEY PERPETRATE, THEY ARE EVERMORE INSTRUMENTS IN THE HANDS OF THE WORLD'S GREAT RULER. The period in which these abominations were enacted is in the text called the "day of the Lord," and he is represented as calling the Gentile armies to the work. "I will gather all nations against Jerusalem to battle; and the city shall be taken, and the houses rifled, and the women ravished." If we are to particularize the predicted destruction, and are not satisfied with figurative explanation, we may look to the conquest under Titus, as in some sort fulfilling the announcement. Rome at this time was the mistress of the world, and the army of Titus, who besieged and sacked the holy city, was composed of soldiers of all the nations. These all moved freely, unconscious of any Divine restraint; still they were but the "sword" of justice in his hand—mere instruments. God in his retributive procedure *punishes the bad by the bad.* In this case: 1. *No injustice is done.* The men of Jerusalem deserved their fate. They "filled up the measure of their iniquity." So it was of old with the Canaanites, who were exterminated by Joshua and his triumphant hosts—the aborigines deserved what they received. Joshua was but the sword of justice. No injustice therefore is done. 2. *There is no infringement of free agency.* Good men might revolt from inflicting such enormities upon their fellow-creatures, but it is according to the wish of bad men. They go to it freely. It is the gratification of their malign nature. This is God's retributive method, to punish the bad by the bad. Thus he makes the very wrath of bad men to praise him.

III. THAT ALTHOUGH THEY ARE BUT INSTRUMENTS IN THE HANDS OF THE WORLD'S RULER, HE WILL PUNISH THEM FOR ALL THEIR DEEDS OF ENORMITY. "Then shall the Lord go forth, and fight against those nations, as when he fought in the day of battle." That is, for example, he will fight against Rome, the instrument with which he inflicted just punishment upon the sinners at Jerusalem. By successive irruptions of the barbarous tribes of the north, the glory of Rome was extinguished, and its end hastened. Where is the justice of punishing men whom he employs to execute his own will? Two facts will answer this question. 1. *What they did was essentially bad.* Murder, plunder, rapine, etc., were all violations of his great moral laws, and repugnant to his holy nature. 2. *What they did was in accord with their own wills.* He never inspired them nor constrained them. They were free, and because they committed crimes of their own free accord, eternal justice required their punishment. Of the Divine government, the justice cried, "Awake, O sword!"

CONCLUSION. Do not let the abominations of war and the outrages on justice, truth, and humanity, which are rife in this country of ours, shake our faith in God. "The Lord reigneth; let the earth rejoice;" "The Lord sitteth upon the flood."—D. T.

Vers. 4, 5.—*God in relation to a suffering world.* "And his feet shall stand in that day upon the Mount of Olives, which is before Jerusalem on the east, and the Mount of Olives shall cleave in the midst thereof toward the east and toward the west, and there shall be a very great valley," etc. The men in Jerusalem were in great suffering and imminent peril, and here is a figurative representation of the Almighty in relation to them.

I. HE OBSERVES THEIR TERRIBLE CONDITION. "And his feet shall stand in that day upon the Mount of Olives, which is before Jerusalem on the east." On this Mount of Olives Jesus often stood, and from it he commanded a view of the holy city; on one occasion, from its brow, he beheld the city, and wept over it on account of its approaching doom. But the idea suggested here is that God observes men in all their calamities and dangers. His eye is on them. He watches them with the interest of a Father. This is *especially the case with his people.* We are assured that his eye is ever upon the righteous. Job said, "He knoweth the way that I take." Let us remember, in our greatest trials and sufferings, that he stands on the Mount of Olives. In standing there: 1. *He sees what we have to endure.* 2. *He sees how we behave ourselves in our condition,* whether under our afflictions we are trustful, patient, and submissive, or otherwise; whether in our perils we are making an effort to escape. How comforting it is to feel that the eye of a tender, compassionate Father is ever on us, in all our sufferings, in this world of sorrow, trial, and dangers! "Thou compassest my path and my lying down, and art acquainted with all my ways."

II. HE MAKES A WAY FOR THEIR DELIVERANCE. "And the Mount of Olives shall cleave in the midst thereof toward the east and toward the west, and there shall be a very great valley." "These verses," says Dr. Henderson, "convey in language of the most beautiful poetical imagery, the assurance of the effectual means of escape that should be provided for the truly pious. We accordingly learn from Eusebius that on the breaking out of the Jewish war, the Christian Church at Jerusalem, in obedience to the warning of our Saviour (Matt. xxiv. 16), fled to Pella, a city beyond Jordan, where they lived in safety. As the Mount of Olives lay in their way, it is represented as cleaving into two halves, in order to make a passage for them." It is not necessary to suppose that the Mount of Olives was thus riven asunder. The idea is that the obstruction to their escape, though formidable as a mountain, should be removed. Christ had said, "Let them which be in Judæa flee unto the mountains," etc. It was their duty, therefore, to do so. And here is promised the removal of every obstruction. The Almighty would give them every facility to escape to the refuge. This he does for our suffering race. He makes a way for their escape. He makes the crooked places straight, and the rough places smooth. The way for their escape from guilt, ignorance, and misery, which has been blocked up by mountains of difficulties, he has made straight. The mountains have been cleft asunder, nay, removed. Christ is *the* Way.

III. HE PROVIDES A REFUGE FOR THEIR SAFETY. "And ye shall flee to the valley of the mountains; for the valley of the mountains shall reach unto Azal: yea, ye shall flee, like as ye fled from before the earthquake in the days of Uzziah King of Judah." Mark here three things. 1. *The scene of refuge.* "Azal." Where is this "*Azal*"? No one knows. Its position is a matter of pure conjecture. Nor does it matter. It was some asylum to secure them from danger. God has provided a refuge for sinners. We are exhorted to flee to the Refuge set before us in the gospel. 2. *The impulse of flight.* "Like as ye fled from before the earthquake in the days of Uzziah King of Judah." 3. *The necessity of the flight.* "The Lord my God shall come." Providential dispensations are often spoken of in the Scripture as the coming of the Lord. The destruction of Jerusalem is spoken of as his coming, and here it is assured as a certainty, the ruin was inevitable. "There is not a word," says a modern expositor, "concerning this earthquake as spoken of in Scripture history." The only other allusion to it occurs in the Book of Amos, who was amongst the herdmen of Tekoa, "which he saw concerning Israel in the days of Uzziah King of Judah, and in the days of Jeroboam the son of Joash King of Israel, two years before the earthquake." It must have been something extraordinary, unusually extensive and awful, when it is thus used to date a period, and, at the same time, as having occasioned such a flight from the destruction wrought by it as to render it a suitable comparison for the prophet here. Fear was to be their inspiration in flight. As the people fled panic-stricken from the presence of the earthquake in the days of Uzziah, they were to flee from the dangers at Jerusalem. "Men and brethren, what shall we do?"

CONCLUSION. How thankful should we be to know that God has not deserted humanity in its sins and sorrows! His eye is on it. He has provided a Way for its escape, and a safe Refuge to which it should flee. Our world, bad as it is, is not a God-deserted world.—D. T.

Vers. 6, 7.—*Dark and bright periods in human life.* "And it shall come to pass in that day, that the light shall not be clear, nor dark: but it shall be one day which shall be known to the Lord, not day, nor night: but it shall come to pass, that at evening-time it shall be light." The word rendered "clear" is in the margin "precious," and is in the plural. The word "dark" here is in the margin rendered "thickness." The following translation by Dr. Henderson gives, I think, the meaning: "And it shall be in that day, that there shall not be the light of the precious orbs, but condensed darkness. But there shall be one day, it is known to Jehovah, when it shall not be day and night; for at the time of the evening there shall be light." We have here two distinct periods—one of *unmitigated distress*, the other of *uninterrupted prosperity*.

I. HERE IS A PERIOD OF UNMITIGATED DISTRESS. "Shall not be clear nor dark," or, as it is rendered, "condensed darkness." Dr. Keil gives the same idea as Dr. Henderson, "And it will come to pass on that day, there will not be light, the glorious ones will melt away." This period of unmitigated calamity primarily refers, we have no doubt, to those long centuries of oppression, cruelty, mockery, and scorn, to which the Jewish people have been subjected ever since the destruction of Jerusalem. In the predictions of Joel (ii. 31; iii. 15) referring to the destruction of the holy city and the breaking-up of the Jewish commonwealth, the period is referred to as a period when "the sun shall be turned into darkness, and the moon into blood." The history of the Jews, indeed, for eighteen centuries has been the history of one long starless night. Two remarks are suggested concerning this dark day. 1. *Such a day is the hard destiny of some men.* It is so with *individuals.* There are hundreds and thousands of men in every age and country who pass through life from its beginning to its close with scarcely a ray of hope or a beam of joy. Their life is a day of darkness. It is so with some *nations.* The history of some nations and tribes is little less than a history of crushing oppression, bloody revolutions, and untold cruelties and sufferings. The precious orbs are seldom if ever seen in their political heavens. 2. *Such a day is deserved by most men.* All men are sinners, and deserve this blackness of darkness for ever. The very tendency of sin, in fact, is to quench every light in the firmament of the soul. Thank God, Christ has come a Light to the world, and into that light during our stay here we may all enter.

II. HERE IS A PERIOD OF UNINTERRUPTED JOY. "But it shall be one day which shall be known to the Lord, not day, nor night: but it shall come to pass that at evening-time it shall be light." This is indeed a *unique* day. Even when evening might be anticipated, "it shall be light." 1. *Such a day as this is destined to dawn on every good man.* Heaven is a scene of light. No clouds of ignorance or suffering obstruct the rays, nor will the sun ever go down: "the Lord God is the Light thereof." 2. *Such a day as this is destined to dawn on the world in the future.* Some expositors consider that the millennium is here pointed to—that long bright period when "all shall know the Lord from the least to the greatest." This period is promised, and it must come; for "heaven and earth shall pass away, but not one jot or tittle of his word shall fail to be accomplished." When will it come? It is far off, I know. "It shall be known to the Lord;" "It is not for you to know the times and the seasons," etc.

CONCLUSION. Are there not *dark* and *bright* days in every good man's life? There are days when he walks in darkness, when neither sun nor star appears; and there are days too when all is cloudless and bright. He needs the dark day to prepare him for the full appreciation and enjoyment of the light. As the earth requires the dark cold days of winter as well as the bright and genial days of summer, in order to prepare it to yield the fruits that man and beast require, so doth the human soul require periods of gloom and tempest as well as periods of brightness and calm.—D. T.

Ver. 8.—*The gospel river.* "And it shall be in that day, that living waters shall go out from Jerusalem; half of them toward the former sea, and half of them toward the hinder sea: in summer and in winter shall it be." The "former sea" here means the Dead Sea; the "hinder sea," the Mediterranean. The great populations of the world lie towards the west of Jerusalem, and these are to be refreshed by "living waters." Taking the passage as referring to the gospel, we will notice—

I. ITS NATURE AND ITS RISE. 1. *Its nature.* It is "living water." Water is the most precious element in nature; it may be regarded as the source, the substance, and the sustenance of all life. But then it is not so precious as the gospel. The gospel is often referred to in Scripture as the river of life, the pure *water* of life. It is a living water. Not a dead lake or stagnant pool, but a living stream. 2. *Its rise.* "It shall go out from Jerusalem." The gospel might be said to have commenced at Jerusalem. The apostles were commanded to commence there: "Beginning at Jerusalem." In Peter's sermon on the Day of Pentecost, the river might be said to have broken forth.

II. ITS DIFFUSION AND CONTINUOUSNESS. 1. *Its diffusion.* "Half of them toward the former sea, and half of them toward the hinder sea." It is to go from the east and from the west, from the sun's rising to its setting. The gospel is for all climes. It is world-wide in its provisions, adaptations, and claims. 2. *Continuousness.* "Summer and winter." In all seasons of human life, individually and corporately. (1) It is constant in the *fitness* of its supplies for human wants. Men, through all changes, in all places, and through all times, want Divine knowledge, moral purity, heavenly forgiveness, fellowship with the Eternal. The man will never be born who will not require these things. (2) It is constant in the *fulness* of its supplies for human wants. It is an inexhaustible river. After countless myriads have had their wants supplied, it remains deep and full as ever. (3) It is constant in the *availableness* of its supplies for human wants. Faith is the great condition on which its blessings are communicated, and every man can believe. It is just that act of mind that comes within the power of the child and the adult, the learned and the rude, the savage and the sage, the bond and the free, to perform. How obvious, then, our duty and our interest!

CONCLUSION. How profoundly thankful should we be to Almighty Love for opening in our world such a "living" river as this! and how earnest should we be in our endeavours to let its waters flow into every heart and home and land, the world over!—D. T.

Vers. 9—11.—*The coming moral reign of God on the earth.* "And the Lord shall be King over all the earth," etc. The subject is the coming moral reign of God on the earth. We say *moral,* for physically he reigns everywhere. Morally, alas! his reign depends upon the will of men, and that will is hostile. As a moral Monarch, the Almighty has to be chosen by his subjects. Three things are suggested in the text as to his coming moral reign on the earth.

I. IT IS TO BE EXTENSIVE. "And the Lord shall be King over all the earth." Although in the next verse "all the earth" is rendered "all the land," meaning the land of Judæa, we are authorized to believe that he will one day reign over all the earth; that all souls will bow to his influence, as the ripened fields of autumn to the winds of heaven. His kingdom shall come, and his will be done on earth as it is in heaven.

II. IT IS TO BE EXCLUSIVE. "In that day there shall be one Lord, and his name One." He will be regarded as the one King whose laws all study and obey. The great question of all souls will be, "Lord, what wilt thou have me to do?" No other power will rule the soul where he becomes the moral Monarch.

III. IT WILL BE BENEFICENT. "All the land shall be turned as a plain from Geba to Rimmon south of Jerusalem." Taking vers. 10 and 11, we gather at least two beneficent results of his moral reign. 1. *The removal of all obstructions* to the river of truth. "The land shall be turned as a plain from Geba to Rimmon," etc. That is, from the northern to the southern boundary of Judæa. The levelling of this land would not only leave Jerusalem conspicuous, but allow the "living waters" to have free flow. 2. *The elevation and establishment of the good.* Jerusalem is here represented, not only as being raised and made conspicuous, but as settling down and dwelling securely. "It shall be lifted up, and inhabited in her place." There shall be no more utter destruction; Jerusalem shall be safely inhabited.

CONCLUSION. Who will not pray, "Let thy kingdom come, and thy will be done on earth as it is in heaven"? Let God reign on earth, and all obstructions to the progress of truth will be removed, and his people will be exalted and established for ever.—D. T.

Vers. 12—15.—*The elements by which the Divine government punishes sin.* "And this shall be the plague," etc. In the third verse of this chapter we are told that "the Lord shall go forth and fight against those nations," that is, against those nations comprehended in the armies which destroyed Jerusalem; and we have elsewhere endeavoured to illustrate how God punishes bad men by bad men. This passage is a further illustration of the idea. There are three elements of punishment which Jehovah is represented as employing in these verses—physical diseases, mutual animosity, and temporal losses.

I. PHYSICAL DISEASES. "And this shall be the plague wherewith the Lord will smite all the people that have fought against Jerusalem; their flesh shall consume away while they stand upon their feet, and their eyes shall consume away in their holes, and their tongue shall consume away in their mouth." "This description of the plague-stricken people," says a modern author, "is shocking, but it is not more than what actually occurs" (see Defoe's 'Plague of London'). Kingsley says, "What so terrible as war? I will tell you what is ten times and ten thousand times more terrible than war, and that is outraged nature. Nature, insidious, inexpensive, silent, sends no roar of cannon, no glitter of arms, to do her work; she gives no warning note of preparation. . . . Man has his courtesies of war and his chivalries of war; he does not strike the unarmed man; he spares the woman and the child. But Nature . . . spares neither woman nor child . . . silently she strikes the sleeping child with as little remorse as she would strike the strong man with the musket or the pick-axe in his hand." One could scarcely imagine a more revolting condition of humanity than is here presented—a living skeleton, nearly all the flesh gone, the eyes all but blotted out, the tongue withered. Physical disease has ever been one of the instruments by which God has punished men in this world—pestilences, plagues, epidemics, and so on. But it is not merely a plague amongst the people, but also amongst the cattle, as we see in ver. 15. "And so shall be the plague of the horse, of the mule, of the camel, and of the ass, and of all the beasts that shall be in these tents, as this plague." These words remind us of Byron's description of the destruction of Sennacherib's host.

> "And there lay the steed with his nostril all wide,
> But through it there rolled not the breath of his pride;
> And the foam of his gasping lay white on the turf,
> And cold as the spray of the rock-beating surf."

II. MUTUAL ANIMOSITY. "And it shall come to pass in that day, that a great tumult from the Lord shall be among them; and they shall lay hold every one on the hand of his neighbour." The idea is, perhaps, that God would permit such circumstances to spring up amongst them as would generate in their minds mutual misunderstandings, malignities, quarrellings, and battlings. "They shall lay hold every one on the hand of his neighbour." "Every man's sword shall be against his brother." All the jealousies, envyings, contentions, that are rife in society may be regarded as the means by which sin is punished. Sin punishes sin, bad passions not only work misery, but are in themselves miseries.

III. TEMPORAL LOSSES. "And Judah also shall fight at Jerusalem." Not against Jerusalem. "And the wealth of all the heathen round about shall be gathered together, gold, and silver, and apparel, in abundance." Earthly property men in their unrenewed state have always valued as the highest good. To attain it they devote all their powers with an unquenchable enthusiasm, and to hold it they are ever on the alert, and their grasp is unrelaxable and firm. To have it snatched from them is among their greatest calamities; and how often this occurs in society! By what we call accidents, by a commercial panic, legal flaws, chicaneries, and frauds, rich men frequently are deprived of their wealth, men who are born in palaces often die in a pauper's hovel. "Riches take to themselves wings, and fly away." This is another way in which Heaven punishes sin.

CONCLUSION. See those elements of retribution working everywhere around us. They have worked through all history. Because they are common we do not note them as we ought. We connect them not with the Justice that reigns over the universe. Albeit they are penal forces.—D. T.

Vers. 16—19.—*The public worship of Jehovah.* "And it shall come to pass," etc. Two remarks are suggested here concerning the public worship of Jehovah.

I. IT IS A DUTY BINDING ON ALL PEOPLE. "And it shall come to pass, that every one that is left of all the nations which came against Jerusalem shall even go up from year to year to worship the King, the Lord of hosts, and to keep the Feast of Tabernacles." "Keil thinks the Feast of Tabernacles is mentioned because it was a feast of thanksgiving for the gracious protection of Israel, in its wanderings through the desert, and its introduction into the land flowing with milk and honey, whereby it foreshadows the blessedness to be enjoyed in the kingdom of God. But in rejecting Koehler's observation that there is a reference to the feast as a harvest thanksgiving, he overlooks the fact that, if this harvest reference is not recognized, the punishment threatened in the next verse, the absence of rain, loses its appropriateness. The Feast of Tabernacles was meant to keep them in mind, amidst their abundant harvests, and well-cared-for fields and vineyards, that as in the desert so still it was God who gave the increase. It was therefore a festival most suitable for all the nations to join in, by way of acknowledging that Jehovah was the God of nature throughout the earth, however various might be the aspects of nature with which they were familiar. Besides, there can be little doubt that by the time of Zechariah, and probably long before, this feast had become a kind of symbol of the ingathering of the nations (John iv. 35) " (Dr. Dods). Whilst the thousands neglect public worship, not a few argue against it, they say it is uncalled for and unnecessary. In reply to this, we state, where there is genuine religion : 1. *Public worship is a natural development.* The being we love most we crave an opportunity for extolling ; we want that all shall know his merits. If we are really religious, we love God supremely, and is it not natural to declare our affection in the presence of our fellow-men ? 2. *Public worship is a happy development.* What delights the soul so much as to hear others praise the object we love the most ? This at once gratifies the religious instinct and the social love. Every true worshipper in the great congregation can say it is a good thing to give praise—it is a happy thing. 3. *Public worship is a beneficent development.* There is nothing that tends so much to quicken and ennoble souls as worship, and nothing gives such a vital interest in one soul for another as public worship. In genuine public worship there is a close coming together of souls, an interblending of the deepest thoughts and the purest sympathies, a kind of spiritual amalgamation. "We should, therefore, not forsake the assembling of ourselves together."

II. Its NEGLECT EXPOSES TO TERRIBLE CALAMITIES. "And it shall be, that whoso will not come up of all the families of the earth unto Jerusalem to worship the King, the Lord of hosts, even upon them shall be no rain. And if the family of Egypt go not up, and come not, that have no rain ; there shall be the plague, wherewith the Lord will smite the heathen that come not up to keep the Feast of Tabernacles. This shall be the punishment of Egypt, and the punishment of all nations that come not up to keep the Feast of Tabernacles." Two things are to be observed here. 1. *The greatness of the punishment.* "Upon them shall be no rain." Now, the absence of rain involves every temporal evil you can think of—famine, pestilence, loss of physical enjoyment, loss of health, loss of life. 2. *The fitness of the punishment.* (1) To the offence. "The withholding of the rain," says Dr. Dods, "was not only one of the ways by which idolatry and apostasy were punished under the theocracy, but it was the appropriate punishment of those who refused to acknowledge Jehovah as the Giver of the harvest. This suiting of punishment to offence is a marked characteristic of God's government, and should probably be more used in education than it is (*e.g.* by secluding for a time, from all intercourse with his companions, the boy who has told a lie, and so on). Dante has largely utilized the principle in his great poem. In his vision of the realms of punishment he saw tyrants immersed in blood ; gluttons exposed in all their pampered softness to a sleety tempest of cold, discoloured, stinking hail ; the proud bending for ever under heavy burdens ; schismatics, who have rent the Church, themselves cleft asunder ; those who had pried into the future, and professed prophetic foresight, with faces reversed, unable to see their own way." (2) To the offender. The idea of not having rain would not, perhaps, terrify the Egyptians, for they had the Nile, which supplied them with abundance of water. Hence a plague is threatened to them, and no word to them was more terrible than the word "plague." They had not forgotten the ten plagues inflicted on them in the time of Moses. It was a land of plagues. Thus God punishes. But mark, the punishment was to come because of the neglect of public worship, and the neglect of public worship is punished : (*a*) Now ; by the loss of the highest spiritual enjoyments. (*b*) Hereafter ; by the reproaching of conscience and the banishment from all good.—D. T.

Vers. 20, 21.—*The bright future of the world—the reign of holiness.* "In that day shall there be upon the bells of the horses," etc. Looking at the passage as a portraiture of the future of the world, we are reminded that holiness will be its grand characteristic. There may be, and no doubt there will be, other things—great material and mental prosperity—but holiness will be its salient feature. The holiness will be universal.

I. It will embrace the affairs of common life. "In that day shall there be upon the bells of the horses." It was common amongst ancient nations to have bells on horses for use or ornament, or perhaps for both. It is said that in Alexander's funeral procession the horses had gold bells attached to their cheek-straps. "Holiness unto the Lord," under the Law of Moses had been inscribed on the frontlet of the high priest, and nowhere else; now it was to be even on the bells of the horses, the commonest things of secular life. In this age no horses will be employed in wars and races, they will only be employed for right purposes and in a right way. The men who ride and drive them in state will be holy men, the men who use them in agriculture will be holy men. Horses, which for ages have been unrighteously treated and unrighteously used, in that day will be properly treated and properly employed.

II. It will embrace all domestic concerns. "Every pot in Jerusalem and in Judah shall be holiness unto the Lord of hosts." The idea is that holiness will extend even to the minutest concerns of domestic life, the members of families will be religious. The very pots in which the priests cooked their food should be as sacred as the bowls that caught the victim's blood. Observe (1) that the distinction between the sacred and secular is to be abolished; but (2) not by separation from the world, nor by making all things secular, but by making all things holy, by carrying into all occupations the spirit and delight of God's presence. " 'Holiness to the Lord' is not to be obliterated from the high priest's mitre, so that he might feel as little solemnized when putting on his mitre and entering the holiest of all, as if he were going into his stable to put the collar on his horse; but when he puts the collar on his horse and goes to his day's work or recreation, he is to be as truly and lovingly as one with God as when with incense and priestly garments he enters the holy of holies" (Dr. Dods).

III. It will embrace all religious characters. "In that day there shall be no more the Canaanite in the house of the Lord of hosts." "By 'Canaanite,'" says Dr. Henderson, "is meant 'merchant.' The Phœnicians who inhabited the northern part of Canaan were the most celebrated merchants of antiquity. The word may fairly be regarded as standing for mercenary men—men animated by the mercenary spirit." Such men are ever to be found in connection with religion. The old prophets bewailed this spirit. It was found in the earlier ages of the Christian Church. Men who considered "gain as godliness," the Canaanite or the merchant, do not necessarily belong to mercantile life, but to other avocations as well, and even to the priestly life. Perhaps the mercenary spirit is as rife in priests and ministers now as ever. But in the coming age there will be no more the Canaanite—the mercenary man—in the house of the Lord; all will be holy.

Conclusion. Hail, blessed age! May the chariot of time quicken its speed, and bring this blessed age to this world of depravity and sin!

Note: This closes our sketches on the prophecy of Zechariah. We confess that going through it *seriatim* we have found in various passages, expressions and allusions to which we were utterly unable to put any clear and intelligible interpretation. There is a haze more or less over the whole book, and our endeavour has been, wherever we have caught a glimpse of a great, practical truth, to bring it out and work it into the service of soul-culture. Though we may have failed to give the true meaning to many passages, we know that we have not intentionally misinterpreted any utterance, or turned a phrase or a word to any theological or ecclesiastical predilection, if indeed any such we have.—D. T.

HOMILETICAL INDEX

TO

THE BOOK OF ZECHARIAH

MALACHI

EXPOSITION BY

W. J. DEANE

HOMILETICS BY

E. S. PROUT

HOMILIES BY VARIOUS AUTHORS

R. TUCK   D. THOMAS

THE BOOK OF MALACHI

INTRODUCTION

§ I. Subject of the Book.

THE reformation effected by Nehemiah in the earlier part of his administration had been maintained by his own personal influence and political
authority; and when the strong hand of the governor was for a time
removed, old abuses revived, and even some new laxities and transgressions
were added. In the thirty-second year of Artaxerxes (B.C.433–2) Nehemiah
had been recalled to Babylon or Susa, either because his furlough had expired,
or because he had to make further arrangements for the prolongation of
his command, or simply, as was the Persian custom, to give an account
of his actions, which had been unfavourably represented at court. On
his return at the end of two or three years (Neh. xiii. 6), he found great
cause for sorrow and anxiety. Advantage of his absence had been taken
by the latitudinarian party in the commonwealth to return to those evil
practices and that open disregard of the Law which he had so severely
reprobated twelve years before. Ezra was probably dead, as no further
mention is made of him after Nehemiah's second return from the Persian
court; and, losing the support of this wise and single-hearted scribe,
Nehemiah would have had to stem the torrent of laxity and profaneness
alone, had not God raised up the Prophet Malachi at this crisis. As Haggai
and Zechariah had animated the spirits and rebuked the faint-heartedness
of the earlier pilgrims, so now Malachi comes forward to assist Nehemiah
in this new reformation by boldly and unflinchingly reproving the
delinquencies of priest and people, and announcing the great day of judgment. A prophet was indeed needed at this moment. The spirit of
Pharisaism and Sadduceeism, which in after-years worked such ineradicable
mischief, had already begun to exhibit its evil propensities. On the one
hand, the perfunctory, outward observance of ritual acts with no inward
repentance or devotion, was considered to be all that religion could claim,
all that was needed for acceptance; on the other, a widespread scepticism

was sapping all morality, and teaching men to live impiously and selfishly. The promises set forth by the earlier prophets had, as they reflected, not been fulfilled; they were still in a depressed and humble position; and, contrasting their present state with the splendid prospect spread before them in the restored theocracy, they murmured against God, and questioned his providence and his power. They were impatient for some display of his judgment on the Gentiles, and, not seeing this, they presumed to doubt the righteousness of his rule and ordering. In their impatience they forgot that it was their own negligence, infidelity, and manifold transgressions that withheld God's blessings from them. They might also have observed that the brilliant future predicted was not promised as immediately to succeed the return from captivity; on the contrary, many intimations were given that a long interval lay between the prophecy and its complete fulfilment. Against this evil spirit of unbelief Malachi had to contend; and how vigorously he performed his part, a review of his book will clearly show.

The book is divided into four chapters in the Authorized Version, the Greek, Latin, Syriac, and Arabic Versions; the Hebrew combines our third and fourth chapters into one. But neither arrangement exactly suits the distribution of the subject-matter, which is usually (after Ewald) divided into three parts, consisting respectively of ch. i. 2—ii. 9; ch. ii. 10—16; and ch. ii. 17 to the end. Though thus artificially distributed, the prophecy is one whole, and forms one continuous address, combined, it may be, from many utterances.

The prophet begins by showing Jehovah's love for Israel, and proving it by recalling to memory the differing destinies of Jacob and Esau, how that the descendants of the latter had suffered ruin and desolation, while the Israelites had experienced favour and protection in the past, and should be still more blessed in the future (ch. i. 1—5). Yet they had not responded to his love; yea, the very priests had been foremost in offending him, by polluting his altar and offering unworthy sacrifices; these offerings God wholly rejects, demanding such pure offering as that which shall be presented in the time of Messiah. But the priests have performed their office in a mercenary and perfunctory spirit, and have learned to despise the worship of God; therefore, unless they repent, they shall be punished with curse and rejection; and then, to demonstrate how far they have erred from the right path, the prophet sketches the portrait of the true priest, such as God would have him to be (ch. i. 6—ii. 9). The second part reproves the heathen marriages of priests and people. In defiance of the Law, and regardless that they were thus profaning the covenant, they had repudiated their own legitimate wives in order that they might marry the daughters of the idolatrous heathen. The Hebrew wives had wept and laid their cause before the Lord, and he hears them, and will vindicate his own institution (ch. ii. 10—16). The third part introduces God as the God of judgment. The people had thought to go on their way unpunished;

but the Judge shall come at a time when they look not for him, and shall
punish evil-doers, executing swift judgment upon those who violate their
duty to God and their neighbour, and separating from them the righteous,
that the land may be purified and refined. Did the people complain that
God was tardy in executing his promises? Let them see the cause in their
own transgressions, their many rebellions against his authority, their
neglect of tithes and offerings. If they did their duty, he would reward
them with fertility and abundance. They had dared to say that it was a
vain thing to serve God; they had confounded good and evil; but the
Lord cared for the pious, and would bring them to glory, while he condemned the wicked as stubble to the fire. Therefore let all men observe
the Law of Moses, and let them look for the coming of the great day of
judgment, and the gracious appearance of the Lord's messenger Elijah the
prophet (ch. ii. 17; iv. 6).

The distinctive character of the Messianic prophecies in this book
consists in the announcement of the second Elijah, who should precede the
advent of the Messenger of Jehovah, the Messiah himself, and in the
statement of the universal and everlasting nature of Christ's sacrificial
offering and mediatorial office. Combined with these two declarations is
the account of the effects dependent on the advent of Messiah. That
appearance shall be a day of fire, consuming the evil, purging away the
dross, and making men fit to offer acceptable sacrifice; it will be also a day
of light, bringing health and joy to those who fear God.

§ II. Author and Date.

The name *Malachi* is found nowhere else in Scripture. The LXX., in
the title, calls him Μαλαχίας. It is probably contracted from *Malachijah*,
and means, "Messenger of Jehovah." Such abbreviations are not
uncommon. Thus we find *Abi* for Abijah (2 Kings xviii. 2; 2 Chron. xxix.
1); *Phalti* for Phaltiel (1 Sam. xxv. 44; 2 Sam. iii. 15). So probably
Zabdi is the same as Zabdiel, *Uri* as Urijah. Absolutely nothing is known
of his history; and as the Septuagint (ch. i. 1) reads, instead of "by the
hand of Malachi," ἐν χειρὶ ἀγγέλου αὐτοῦ, "by the hand of his messenger,"
many have doubted whether the name is that of a person or of an office, an
appellation given to an ideal messenger of God. Origen held that the
book was written by an angel; others have argued that Malachi was a
pseudonym for Ezra, who was the real author of the work, though one
would have thought that the style and diction of the two writers were
sufficiently distinct to obviate any such supposition, and it is hardly
possible that the authorship of so distinguished a man should have been
forgotten when the canon was arranged. Besides, to all the prophetical
books the writer's own name is prefixed. The use of a pseudonym
or a symbolical name is unknown; and the authenticity of the contents of the prophecy is always testified by the naming of the author

as one known to his contemporaries and approved by God. Malachi, therefore, is certainly a real person; and though there is no description of him in his book, neither his parentage nor his birthplace being mentioned, yet the same omission occurs in the case of Obadiah and Habakkuk, of whose personality no doubt has ever arisen. That the histories of Ezra and Nehemiah contain no notice of him or his prophetical work is easily accounted for by the fact that he exercised his ministry on or just before Nehemiah's second visit to Jerusalem, of which we have only the barest and most summary account (Neh. xiii. 7—31). From his trenchant references to the priesthood it is conjectured that he was a member of that body; but there is nothing further to support the notion. The absence of all authentic information concerning Malachi has been supplied by tradition. The Talmud states that he was a member of the great synagogue, as Haggai and Zechariah had been; and Pseudo-Dorotheus and Pseudo-Epiphanius assert that he was born in Sopha, or Supha, in the tribe of Zebulun, and died there while still young. No particulars of his life have been handed down even in mythical narrative.

The general period of Malachi's appearance as a prophet is easily determined; but the definition of the exact date has some difficulties. It is plain, from the contents of the prophecy, that it was delivered when the Captivity was well-nigh forgotten, and after the temple was rebuilt and its worship had been for some time duly established; it is also evident that, as the prophet complains of the inferior offerings brought by the people, the time of the royal grant made to Ezra (Ezra vii. 20—26) had expired, and the necessary sacrifices were supplied by the inhabitants themselves. This was done without dispute or apparent reluctance in the earlier part of Nehemiah's administration, according to the engagement introduced by him (Neh. x. 32, etc.). No mention of any infringement of the resolution then passed is made in the Book of Ezra; so it seems most probable that the abuses named crept in after Ezra's death, and during the time when Nehemiah was absent at the court of Persia (Neh. xiii. 6), which may have been an interval of two or three years. That Malachi prophesied during this interregnum, or at any rate at a period when Nehemiah was not acting as governor, has been deduced from the expression in ch. i. 8, where, rebuking the people for daring to sacrifice imperfect animals, he says, "Offer it now to thy governor; will he be pleased with thee, or accept thy person?" Nehemiah, it is contended, prided himself on never having taken anything, even his dues as viceroy, from the people; therefore the governor here mentioned must be some other person. But this is by no means a necessary conclusion. The self-denying practice referred to belongs to the early years of his administration, and may not apply to his later governorship. Further, the refusal to be burdensome to his countrymen did not extend to the non-acceptance of presents, without which no Oriental would come for a formal interview with a superior; and the prophet might well ask whether they would dare to make such offerings to a governor, without any special reference to a particular personage.   But although we cannot build any theory of date on this expression of the prophet, there is other internal evidence which is more determinate.   The great point is that the abuses rebuked by him are just those against which Nehemiah had to contend.   Both of them denounce the corruption of the priests in marrying alien wives (comp. ch. ii. 11 with Neh. xiii. 23); the withholding of the appointed tithes from the Levites (ch. iii. 8 and Neh. xiii. 10); the neglect of and dishonour done to the temple, and its services (ch. i. 12, 13 and Neh. xiii. 4, 5, 11); the repudiation of legitimate wives (ch. ii. 15, 16 and Neh. xiii. 23, 27, whence it may be easily concluded that these foreign marriages were accompanied with divorce and cruelty).   It is true that Malachi does not expressly name the desecration of the sabbath, against which Nehemiah made such strict regulations (Neh. xiii. 15—22), but he denounces the infringement of the Law in the offering of blemished victims, and we cannot doubt that this was only one instance of the same spirit which led to the breaking of the sabbath.   Thus it seems that the prophet and the civil ruler are contending against the same evils, and endeavouring in their different vocations to draw the people to amendment.

From the above considerations we may conclude that Malachi exercised his ministry during the time of Nehemiah's second visit to Jerusalem, B.C. 430–420.

Thus Malachi is the last of the prophets, the author of the final book of the Hebrew canon, and named by Jewish authorities " the seal and end of the prophets."   He exercised his ministry a hundred years later than Haggai and Zechariah.   We may here note that the twelve minor prophets cover a period of four centuries—a space, as Farrar remarks, nearly equal to that from Chaucer to Wordsworth.

§ III. General Character of the Work.

Some critics have characterized Malachi's style as " pedantic, forced, and barren;" but we cannot assent to their somewhat inconsiderate verdict. In contrast with some other prophetical works, Malachi's writings may be considered to be prosaic, and to hold an inferior position, but they have an excellency and orginality of their own which acquit them of all such charges as those above.   The great peculiarity of the style consists in the use made of interrogation and reply.   A dialogue is introduced between God and the people or priests; the questions of objectors or complainants are stated, amplified, and finally answered with withering scorn by the mouth of the prophet.   Thus he is rather a reasoner than a poet; he exhibits the calmness of the practised orator rather than the fire and energy of earlier seers.   But there are tokens that he is still influenced by the ancient prophets, and with all his methodical and artificial forms he models himself upon his predecessors.   Simple, smooth, concise, his diction is easy to understand; if he does not rise to the grandeur and power of other prophets, he is always polished and elegant, and at times even remarkably eloquent. The sketch of the character of the ideal priest (ch. ii. 5—7) is a passage of eminent beauty; and there are a few other places of equal excellence.

§ IV. LITERATURE.

Among the most useful commentaries on Malachi may be cited those of Chyrtæus (Rostock, 1568); Kimchi and Jarchi, 'Commentarii,' Interprete S. M. De Muis (Paris, 1618); Stock (London, 1641); Sclater (London, 1650); Pocock, 'Works,' vol. i.; Venema (Leov., 1759); Bahrdt (Leipzig, 1768); Fischer, with notes on the Septuagint Version (Leipzig, 1779); Packard, 'Book of Malachi expounded' (Edinburgh); Reinke, 'Der Prophet Malachi' (Giessen, 1852, 1856); Koehler (Erlangen, 1865); Dr. Samuel Cox, in vol. iii. of 'The Bible Educator.'

§ V. ARRANGEMENT OF THE BOOK IN SECTIONS.

The book is most conveniently divided into three parts.

Part I. (Ch. i.—ii. 9.) Reproof of the priests for neglect of Divine service.
    § 1. (Ch. i. 1.) Heading and author.
    § 2. (Ch. i. 2—5.) The prophet declares God's special love for Israel.
    § 3. (Ch. i. 6—14.) Israel had shown no gratitude, and the priests had been the chief offenders by offering defective sacrifices and profaning the temple-worship.
    § 4. (Ch. ii. 1—4.) The priests are threatened with punishment.
    § 5. (Ch. ii. 5—9.) In contrast with these, the character of the true priest is sketched.
Part II. (Ch. ii. 10—16.) Condemnation of priests and people for alien marriages and for divorces.
Part III. (Ch. ii. 17—iv. 6.) The day of the Lord.
    § 1. (Ch. ii. 17—iii. 6.) The faithless people doubted God's providence, but the prophet announces the coming of the Lord to judgment, preceded by his messenger. He shall refine his people and exterminate sinners.
    § 2. (Ch. iii. 7—12.) God is faithful to his promises, but the people have been shamefully negligent in the matter of tithes and offerings; let them amend their practice, and they shall be blessed.
    § 3. (Ch. iii. 13—18.) The impious murmuring of the people is contrasted with the conduct of those who fear God, and the reward of the pious is set forth.
    § 4. (Ch. iv. 1—3.) The final separation of the evil and the good at the day of judgment.
    § 5. (Ch. iv. 4—6.) Concluding admonition to remember the Law, lest they should be liable to the curse, to avert which the Lord would send Elijah to promote a change of heart in the nation before his coming.

THE BOOK OF MALACHI

EXPOSITION.

CHAPTER I.

Ver. 1—ch. ii. 9.—Part I. REPROOF OF THE PRIESTS FOR NEGLECT OF DIVINE SERVICE.

Ver. 1.—§ 1. *Heading and author.* **The burden** (Zech. ix. 1; xii. 1; see note on Nah. i. 1). The word of the Lord is heavy and full of threats, but, as St. Jerome notes, it is also consolatory, because it is not " against " but to Israel. By this name the whole covenanted nation is designated, here, perhaps, with some idea of reminding the people of Jacob's faith and patience, and stimulating them to imitate their great ancestor. **By Malachi**; literally, *by the hand of Malachi* (comp. Jer. xxxvii. 2). That Malachi is the proper name of the prophet, and not a mere official designation, see the proof in the Introduction, § II. The LXX. renders, ἐν χειρὶ ἀγγέλου αὐτοῦ, " by the hand of his angel," or " messenger," and some curious theories have been founded on this translation ; *e.g.* that an angel was the real author of the book, or came and explained it to the people. A similar legend once obtained concerning Haggai, called " The Lord's Messenger " (Hag. i. 13). At the end of the verse the LXX. adds, " fix it in your hearts," which Jerome supposes to have been imported hither from Hag. ii. 15.

Vers. 2—5.—§ 2. *The prophet declares God's special love for Israel.*

Ver. 2.—**I have loved you.** The prophet, desiring to bring home to the people their ingratitude, lays down his thesis ; then, in his characteristic manner, repeats the objection of the sceptics in an interrogatory form, and refutes it by plain argument. God had shown his love for Israel by electing them to be his people, and by his treatment of them during the whole course of their history. **Wherein hast thou loved us ?** This was the inward feeling of the people at this time. They doubted God's love and faithfulness. Events had not turned out as they expected. They had, indeed, returned from captivity, and the temple was rebuilt ; but none of the splendid things announced by the prophets had come to pass. They were not great and victorious ; Messiah had not appeared. Therefore they repined and murmured ; they were ungrateful for past favours, and questioned God's power and providence. **Was not Esau Jacob's brother ?** God refutes their unjust charge by referring them to a palpable fact, viz. the different fate of the descendants of the twin-brothers, Esau and Jacob. How miserable the destiny of the Edomites ! how comparatively fortunate the condition of the Israelites ! **Yet I loved Jacob.**

Ver. 3.—**And I hated Esau.** St. Paul quotes these words (Rom. ix. 13) in order to illustrate his position, " that the purpose of God according to election might stand, not of works, but of him that calleth." Even before his birth Jacob was the chosen one, and Esau, the elder, was to serve the younger. This mystery of Divine election has seemed to some to be stated so harshly that they have thought that the words of the text need to be softened, or to be modified by their explanation. Thus they give the glosses, " I have preferred Jacob to Esau ; " " I have loved Esau less than Jacob ; " or they have limited the terms " love " and " hatred " to the bestowing or withholding of temporal blessings ; or they have affirmed that Esau was hated because God foresaw his unworthiness, and Jacob was beloved owing to his foreseen piety and faithfulness. The whole question is discussed by Augustine, ' De Div. Quæst. ad Simplic.,' i. 18 (xi. 433). He ends by saying, " Deus odit impietatem : in aliis etiam punit per damnationem, in aliis adimit per justificationem." But Malachi is not speaking of the predestination of the one brother and the reprobation of the other; he is contrasting the histories of the two peoples represented by them; as Jerome puts it, "In Jacob vos dilexi, in Esau Idumæos odio habui." Both nations sinned; both are punished; but Israel by God's free mercy was forgiven and restored, while Edom was left in the misery which it had brought upon itself by its own iniquity. Thus is proved God's love for the Israelites (Knabenbauer). That it is of the two nations that the prophet speaks, rather than of the two brothers, is seen by what follows. Laid his mountains . . . waste. While the Israelites were repeopling and cultivating their land, and their cities were rising from their ruins, and the temple and the capital were rebuilt, Edom, which had suffered at the hand of the same enemies, had never recovered from the blow, and still lay a scene of desolation and ruin. It seems that Nebuchadnezzar attacked and conquered Edom some few years after he had taken Jerusalem. This event happened during one of his expeditions against Egypt, one of which took place in the thirty-seventh year of his reign, as we learn from a record lately deciphered (see 'Transact. of Soc. of Bibl. Archæology,' vii. 210, etc.). (For Edom and its history, see the Introduction to Obadiah.) Dragons; rather, *jackals* (Micah i. 8); Septuagint, εἰς δώματα ἐρήμου, "for habitations of the desert;" Vulgate, *dracones deserti*, whence the Authorized Version.

Ver. 4.—Whereas; rather, *if*, or *although*; Vulgate, *quod si*. If Edom were to attempt to repair its desolation, the Lord would not permit it—a striking contrast to the national restoration of Israel. We are impoverished; or, as the Revised Version, *we are beaten*; Septuagint, ἡ Ἰδουμαία κατέστραπται, "Idumea has been overthrown." Vulgate, *destructi sumus*. The desolate places; Vulgate, *quæ destructa sunt*, places once inhabited and now deserted. Compare the boast of the Ephraimites (Isa. ix. 9, 10). I will throw down. Edom never recovered its power; it became the prey of the Persians, the Nabatheans, the Jews under the Maccabees, the Macedonians, the Romans; and finally the Mohammedan conquest effected its utter ruin. They (*men*) shall call them, The border of wickedness. Edom shall be called, "The territory of iniquity," its miserable condition attesting the wickedness of the inhabitants thus punished by Divine justice. Hath indignation; Septuagint, παρατέτακται, "hath been set in battle array;" St. Jerome, "My anger is proved by their enduring desolation; and in contrast to the evils experienced by your

brother, ye shall experience the goodness of God towards you."

Ver. 5.—Your eyes shall see. Jacob is addressed. When you see these proofs of God's love for you, you shall leave off murmuring and be ready to praise God for his goodness and power. The Lord will be magnified; better, *the Lord is great*; Septuagint, Ἐμεγαλύνθη Κύριος, "The Lord was magnified." God makes his greatness known. From (*over*) the border of Israel. This means either beyond the limits of Israel, *i.e.* in all the world, or upon Israel, *i.e.* by the protection which he vouchsafes to Israel.

Vers. 6—14.—§ 3. *Israel had shown no gratitude for all these proofs of God's love, and the very priests had been the chief offenders by offering defective sacrifices, and profaning the temple-worship.*

Ver. 6.—A son honoureth his father. The prophet commences with a general principle which every one allows, and argues from that what was the attitude which they ought to assume towards God. A father. God was the Father of Israel by creation, election, preservation, watchful guardianship (see Exod. iv. 22; Deut. xxxii. 6; Isa. lxiii. 16; lxiv. 8, etc.). My fear. The fear, respect, reverence, due to me. O priests. He addresses his reproof to the priests, as the representatives of the people, and bound to lead them to obedience and holiness, and to be a pattern to the flock. Wherein have we despised thy Name? The priests have grown so callous, and have so obscured true religion by Pharisaical externalism, that they profess to be utterly unconscious how they have shown contempt of God. The Name of God is God himself and all that has to do with him.

Ver. 7.—Ye offer polluted bread (*food*) upon mine altar. The prophet answers the priests simply by detailing some of their practices. The "bread" (*lechem*) is not the shewbread, which was not offered on the altar, but the flesh of the offered victims (see Lev. iii. 11, 16; xxi. 6; xxii. 25). This was "polluted" in that it was not offered in due accordance with the ceremonial Law, as is further explained in the next verse. Wherein have we polluted thee? They did not acknowledge the truth that (as St. Jerome says) "when the sacraments are violated, he himself, whose sacraments they are, is violated" (comp. Ezek. xiii. 19; xx. 9; xxxix. 7). The table of the Lord is contemptible. This was the thought of their heart, if they did not give open expression to it in words. The "table of the Lord" (ver. 12) is the altar, on which were laid the sacrifices, regarded as the food of God, and to be eaten by the fire (Ezek. xli. 22; xliv. 16). They showed that they despised the altar by fancying that anything was good enough for offering thereon, as the next verse explains.

Ver. 8.—**If ye offer the blind.** The Law ordered that the victims should be perfect and without blemish (see Lev. xxii. 19—25). Is it not evil? It is more forcible to read this without the interrogation, "It is no evil!" and to regard it as the priests' thought or word, here introduced by the prophet in bitter irony. Their conscience had grown so dull, and they had become so familiarized with constant dereliction of duty, that they saw no wrong in these violations of the Law, and never recalled the people to their duty in these matters. **Offer it now unto thy governor.** The word for "governor" is *pechah*, as in Hag. i. 1 (where see note). It denotes a ruler set over a province by a Persian king. As Nehemiah had refused to be burdensome to the people (Neh. v. 14—18), it is thought that Malachi must have written this when some other person was acting as governor. But Nehemiah's generosity was exhibited in his earlier administration, and he may have thought it right to take the dues under a more prosperous state of affairs. The prophet may be putting the case generally—Would you dare offer such things to your governor? At any rate, the question is not about provisions and dues supplied to the governor and liable to be exacted by him in his official capacity, but about voluntary offerings and presents, without which no inferior would presume to appear before his prince (see Introduction, § II.). To offer to such a one what was mean and defective would be nothing less than an insult; and yet they thought this was good enough for God. **Accept thy person.** Regard thee with favour (Gen. xix. 21; Job xiii. 10; xlii. 8).

Ver. 9.—**Beseech God**; literally, *the face of God.* This is not a serious call to repentance, but an ironical appeal. Come now and ask the favour of God with your polluted sacrifices; intercede, as is your duty, for the people; will he accept you? will he be gracious to the people for your sakes? **This hath been by your means.** These words form a parenthesis, implying that it was from the priests that the evil custom of offering blemished animals proceeded, and they were answerable for the consequences; that their intercessions were vain was the result of their transgressions in these matters. Others interpret, "The thing depends on you," *i.e.* whether God shows favour or not. **Will he regard your persons?** Will he show favour to any one because ye intercede for him? So it might

be translated, *Will he accept any because of you?*

Ver. 10. — The prophet continues his severe reprobation of the priests. **Who is there even among you that would shut the doors for naught, etc.?** Thus rendered, the passage rebukes the mercenary spirit of the priests, who would not even shut the temple door nor kindle the altar fire unless they were paid for it; or else it means that, though all the officers of the temple were remunerated for their most trivial services, yet they were remiss in attending to their duties, and neglected the law of sacrifices. The Latin Version omits the negative in the last clause, *Quis est in vobis qui claudat ostia, et incendat altare meum gratuito?* The LXX., with some little variation in the reading, renders, Διότι καὶ ἐν ὑμῖν συγκλεισθήσονται θύραι, καὶ οὐκ ἀνάψεται τὸ θυσιαστήριόν μου δωρεάν, "Wherefore also among you the doors shall be shut, and my altar shall not be kindled for nothing," *i.e.* God threatens that the temple services shall wholly cease. But it is best to consider the passage as continuing the sarcastic strain of the preceding verse, and saying in effect that it would be better to have no pretence of worship at all than to have it thus profaned. Translate as in the Revised Version, *Oh that there were one among you that would shut the doors, that ye might not kindle fire on mine altar in vain!* The doors are those of the inner court of the temple, where the great altar stood; and the polluted sacrifice is offered " in vain," because it offends God rather than propitiates him. **An offering** (*minchah*). Here not sacrifice in general, as many commentators suppose, because it would be unnatural to take the word in one sense in this verse, and in a different sense in the following, where it is confessedly used in its restricted signification. The term is applied technically to the offering of fine flour combined with oil and frankincense, burnt on the altar (Lev. ii. 1, etc.); though it is also occasionally used even of bloody sacrifices; *e.g.* of Abel's (Gen. iv. 4; comp. 1 Sam. ii. 17). As liturgically employed, it denotes the unbloody offering. So in this verse we may note a kind of climax. God would not accept the victims sacrificed, no, nor even the meat offering, which was naturally pure and unpolluted.

Ver. 11.—**My Name shall be great.** The course of thought is this: God does not need the worship of the Jews and their impious priests; he needs not their maimed sacrifices; his majesty shall be recognized throughout the wide world, and pure worship shall be offered to him from every nation under heaven. How, then, shall he not punish those who, being his elect, ought to have been an example of holiness, and prepared the way for his universal reception? The LXX. treats this circumstance as already occurring at this time, Τὸ ὄνομά μου δεδόξασται, "My Name hath been and is glorified." This could only be said if it was allowed that the heathen in some sense, however blindly and imperfectly, did worship the true God. But the notion cannot be upheld for a moment; and there is a general consensus of commentators in referring the time to the Messianic future, when God's power is acknowledged and worship offered to him, not in Jerusalem alone, but in every place. The participles in this verse may be rendered by presents or futures, but there can be little doubt that a prophecy is intended, and not a statement of a fact—which, indeed, could not be truthfully maintained. When such a future is in store, is this a time for Jewish priests to dishonour Jehovah? **Incense shall be offered unto my Name, and a pure offering** (*minchah*). The universal worship is expressed in the terms of the Jewish ritual (see note on Zeph. iii. 10). The Hebrew is more forcibly rendered, *In every place incense is burned, oblation made unto my Name, and indeed a pure oblation.* Incense is to our minds a type of prayer (Rev. v. 8; viii. 3, etc.); the pure oblation is the symbol of the Christian sacrifice of praise and thanksgiving; and the prophet, rising superior to Jewish prejudices, announces that this prayer and sacrifice shall no longer be confined to one place or one specially favoured country, but be universal, world-wide. The Fathers and mediæval writers, and many modern commentators, see in this verse a prophecy of the Holy Eucharist, the "pure offering" commemorative of Christ's sacrifice, which is found in every nation under heaven where the Name of Christ is adored.

Ver. 12.—**But ye have profaned it;** *ye profane* God's Name. The prophet contrasts the negligence and profanity of the priests with the piety of the Gentile nations, which he foresees. **The table of the Lord** (see note on ver. 7) **The fruit thereof, even his meat.** The food and meat of the altar are the victims offered thereon. By their conduct the priests made both altar and offerings contemptible. Septuagint, Τὰ ἐπιτιθέμενα ἐξουδένωται βρώματα αὐτοῦ, " Its meats that are laid thereon are set at naught; " Vulgate, *Quod superponitur contemptibile est, cum igne qui illud devorat.* This is either a free paraphrase, or for "meat" Jerome must have read a participle, " eating," and taken " that

which eats " the offering to be the fire which consumes it, as " lick up " (1 Kings xviii. 38). Others explain the Vulgate to mean that the priests complain of the scantiness and inferiority of the victims, the flesh of which formed their support. But as this was owing to their own neglect, they were not likely to make it a subject of complaint.

Ver. 13.—**What a weariness is it!** The reference is to the table of the Lord. Despising the altar, and performing their duties without heart or faith, the priests found the services an intolerable burden. Vulgate, *ecce de labore,* which seems to be an excuse of the people, urging that they offer such things as their toil and poverty allow. Septuagint, ταῦτα ἐκ κακοπαθείας ἐστί, which has much the same meaning. The present Hebrew text is represented by the Authorized Version. **Ye have snuffed at it;** *i.e.* at the altar. The phrase expresses contempt. "It" has been supposed to be a "scribes' correction" for "me." The Septuagint and Syriac give, "I snorted at them." **That which was torn;** rather, *that which was taken by violence*—that which was stolen or unjustly taken. Septuagint, ἁρπάγματα: Ecclus. xxxiv. 18 (xxxi. 21), " He that sacrificeth of a thing wrongfully gotten, his offering is ridiculous (μεμωκημένη)." **Lame . . . sick** (see Lev. xxii. 19 —25). **Thus ye brought an** (*bring the*) **offering** (*minchah*). Subject to analogous defects is even your meat offering, the accessory to other sacrifices, and therefore it is unacceptable.

Ver. 14.—**But** (*and*) **cursed be the deceiver.** The curse is fulminated against all who are guilty of these violations of the Law. The prophet mentions two instances out of many. The first is of one who offers a female victim, on pretence that he has no male in his flock. This will be clearer if we translate, with Keil, "And cursed is he who deceives, whereas there is in his flock a male animal." Septuagint, " Cursed is he who was able and had in his flock a male." **And voweth . . . a corrupt** (*blemished*) **thing.** The second case is of one who in some emergency vows an offering, and then pays it by presenting a blemished animal (Lev. iii. 1, 6). With a slightly altered punctuation, some editors give, "a faulty female." **For I am a great King.** This is the reason that they are cursed who dishonour him. **Dreadful.** Held in awe and reverence. Septuagint, ἐπιφανές, "notable." He whom the Gentiles honour will not permit his own people to profane his Name.

HOMILETICS.

Ver. 1.—*Malachi and his burden.* I. MALACHI, THE LAST OF THE PROPHETS OF THE OLD TESTAMENT. He may be compared to: 1. A late evening closing a long day of light and blessing, and which is itself: 2. A midsummer twilight in some northern latitude, bearing on its bosom the new and still brighter day of the gospel. 3. A finger-post pointing across an untrodden waste of time in the direction in which the ages should move onwards towards the advent of their expected King. 4. A faithful minister, the last of a noble succession, resigning his trust (the prophetic gift), but bidding his flock expect to "see greater things than these," and expiring with the gospel on his lips (ch. iv. 2—6).

II. THE PROPHET'S BURDEN. Any word of the Lord is : 1. A burden of responsibility to the bearer (1 Cor. ix. 16, 17). Especially so are messages of judgment with which Malachi was charged. So Jeremiah felt (Jer. xv. 10—21; xx. 8—10), and Paul (Phil. iii. 18), and our Lord Jesus Christ (Luke xix. 41—44). It is thus a test of fidelity (Prov. xxx. 6; Ezek. iii. 17—21) and of courage (Micah iii. 8). 2. Messages of judgment should be felt to be burdens by the sinner because they proceed from a God to whom judgment is "a strange work," yet who hates sin more than suffering, and whose holiness is seconded by his omnipotence. Only by repentance toward God and faith toward our Lord Jesus Christ can the burden be changed into a beatitude, the curse into a blessing.

Vers. 2—5.—*The sovereign love of God.* Remembering that the scriptural sense of "hate" in this and corresponding passages is to love less in comparison, or to reject when there is a competition of claims, we nevertheless learn from this passage—

I. THAT GOD'S LOVE TO INDIVIDUALS AND TO NATIONS IS A SOVEREIGN LOVE. By this we mean that it is a love which bestows special favours, for reasons which cannot be discovered in those that enjoy them, but in the gracious purpose of God. 1. In the case of the two brothers personally we note the following facts : Esau was the elder, yet not the heir of *the* promise. He suffered at the hands of a brother in some respects less noble than himself. He thus lost his father's chief blessing and had to take the remnants, and to be satisfied with a poorer inheritance, while Jacob received " the glory of all lands." 2. The two nations, Israel and Edom, were separated like two rivers issuing from the same fountain, the one destined to be a highway of commerce and a source of fertility, the other to be lost in the sands of the desert. Israel, blessed with a priesthood, a succession of prophets, and a covenant "ordered in all things and sure," in spite of many apostasies ; Edom, allowed to drift into idolatry and crime till it became known as "the border of wickedness," etc. (ver. 4). Such gifts and calling of God cannot be annulled any more than his sentences of judgment can be reversed (ver. 4). In those judgments and in those mercies men shall see the finger of God, and shall stand in awe of the glory of God (ver. 5). These truths applicable to God's dealings with nations now. 3. The salvation of individuals is no less the result of sovereign love, inasmuch as the very beginnings of spiritual life are of God, and are "according to his own purpose and grace," etc. (2 Tim. i. 9). Election is not "an order of merit," but a cord of love. The experience of all Christians confirms the doctrine of God's sovereignty in salvation, though it cannot answer the many questions suggested by God's varied dealings with individuals, or explain the reasons of his eternal purposes. Note St. Paul's "conclusion of the matter" (Rom. xi. 33—36).

II. THAT THIS UNMERITED LOVE OF GOD MAY BE IGNORED BY THE RECEIVERS. "Wherein hast thou loved us ?" This may arise from : 1. Forgetting past mercies under the presence of present trials, like Israel (Ps. cvi. 12—14). 2. Forgetting our present blessings as contrasted with the lot of others. 3. Having an imperfect sense of our absolute dependence on the unmerited mercy of God (Deut. vii. 7, 8). 4. And therefore taking even our spiritual blessings very much as a matter of course, and indulging in self-complacency rather than cultivating grateful humility in view of "the love of God which is in Christ Jesus our Lord" (cf. 1 Cor. iv. 7, 8).

Ver. 6.—*The reverence due to God.* Earthly analogies to Divine relationships are instructive though imperfect. Neither the most absolute master nor the most affectionate father can adequately represent God. Yet God reminds us of the reverence due to himself from the fear and honour expected by them. The appeal should be most powerful to those who, like the priests here appealed to, are in any positions of authority. It should be a most tender plea to all parents. It falls in tones of deepest pathos on those who have received the adoption and the spirit of sons through Jesus Christ. But the appeal binds all to whom in any sense God stands in the sacred relations of " the Father of spirits " (Exod. iv. 22; Deut. xxxii. 6; Isa. lxiii. 16; lxiv. 8). We assume the case of a father who combines that wise authority and tender love which makes him a type of the heavenly Father. A son honoureth such a father—

I. BY OBEDIENCE. This is the first lesson a child must learn. After the early conflicts with self-will, it becomes part of the child-nature. It may rise to self-denial or even heroic self-sacrifice. Illust.: Henry Havelock, as a boy, waiting for hours in a crowded street of London, in obedience to his father, who had forgotten him; or Casa Bianca's son blown up in the French flag-ship at the Battle of the Nile. God is greatly honoured when our obedience is habitual and cheerful, when we " worship " the " sweet will of God," and can say, " I delight," etc. (Ps. xl. 8; cxix. 128).

II. BY LOVE. The instinctive love of an infant makes way for the intelligent affection, founded on esteem, which the youth feels towards a father who has trained him in habits of obedience. Disobedience begets dislike; submission strengthens love. The pruning and training of wise discipline is rewarded by the copious fruits of love. We most honour God when our love is not merely the love of gratitude even for redemption, but of complacent delight in the character of our Father. In that character there are no flaws such as a partial son may nevertheless see in his earthly father (Jas. i. 17). Let him not have to say John v. 42.

III. BY REGARD TO HIS REPUTATION. A boy's eye flashes with indignation if a stranger assails his father's reputation. How do we regard the dishonour done to God by profanity, by reckless criticisms on his character and government, and on the work of Christ (" The Father wounded through the Son ")? Can we say, with Christ, "The reproaches," etc. (Ps. lxix. 9)? Let us beware, however, of the zeal of a Jehu (2 Kings x. 16—31) or of the Pharisees (Matt. xxiii. 15). Let our lives be answers to our prayers, " Hallowed be thy Name."

IV. BY UPHOLDING HIS AUTHORITY. 1. When it has to be exercised in discipline on ourselves (Heb. xii. 5—11). 2. When it is resisted by others. There is a rebellion in the great family of God which requires every true child to take an active part on the side of God. While grieved (Ps. cxix. 158) and indignant (Ps. cxxxix. 21), we shall yet be labourers together with God, that in the spirit of the sinless Son we may seek by all means to save some (1 Pet. iv. 10, 11).

Vers. 7, 8.—*Irreverence—its causes and signs.* Notice how in many places Malachi puts the thoughts of sinners into bold and bald words. He interprets their conduct in speech, that they may see the offensiveness of their thoughts and acts. Sins of the heart may sometimes be best exposed by translating them into unsubmissive or even impious prayers. They cannot endure the light when they are paraded in speech under the scrutiny of our fellow-men. Still less can they tolerate the brightness that proceeds from the throne of grace, where God seeth in secret, that he may answer him " that setteth up his idols in his heart" "according to the multitude of his idols" (Ezek. xiv. 3, 4). In this section the irreverence of the priests and people is exposed by the prophet calling things by their right names. Note—

I. SOME OF THE CAUSES OF IRREVERENCE. 1. Inadequate views of the holiness of God and the sinfulness of men. We forget the names and titles of the God with whom we have to do—" Jehovah," " Lord of hosts," " Master," " Father," " a great King," " glorious in holiness, fearful in praises, doing wonders," etc. We forget our own utter sinfulness and unworthiness as " dust and ashes," " the imagination of whose heart is evil from our youth," to have any intercourse with the Thrice-holy One (cf. Job xl. 3—5). If it is hard to appreciate this, we may be helped by the contrast between what we see in the characters of Christ and of ourselves. Illust.: Peter (Luke v. 8). 2. Familiarity with sacred things. It may " breed contempt." The altar and its offerings were regarded as commonplace or even despicable objects. The worship of God, the table of the Lord, the most sacred acts and objects may be observed and resorted to without the slightest expectation of gaining good. They might be means of grace, but familiarity makes them contemptible. 3. The indolence which shrinks from the effort needed to stir up ourselves to take hold of God (Isa. lxiv. 7). Worship must be a spiritual service; it may be a "conflict" an ἀγών (Col. ii. 1). Indolence may beget irreverence, and will, in its turn, be a sign of it.

II. SOME OF THE SIGNS OF IRREVERENCE. We may copy the evil example of the Jews in bringing blind, lame, sick, or polluted offerings. 1. Formal and half-hearted services. "Blind is the sacrifice of the soul which is not illumined by the light of Christ. Lame is his sacrifice of prayer who comes with a double mind to entreat the Lord" (Jerome; Matt. xv. 8). 2. Superstitious services; e.g. blind obedience to a man claiming to be a priest, which may save the trouble of searching for God with all the heart. Unintelligent worship, perhaps in an unknown tongue, as though a lesson learned by rote would suffice for the Divine Teacher. 3. Offering to God what we should not dare to offer to an earthly superior (ver. 8). As though we would say, "God is not very particular." Yet he requires the very best service we can render. Such conduct is virtual dishonesty, for the intention to sacrifice to God at all implies the sacrificing of our best. Illust.: David (2 Sam. xxiv. 24; cf. Matt. xxii. 37). Note how the revelation of God in Christ shows still more impressively his claims on our highest services. "The Lamb that was slain" is worthy to receive *everything* and *the best of everything* we can offer to him (Rev. v. 12). 4. Still grosser forms of irreverence are seen in the Corinthians feasting at the Eucharist, and thus despising the Church of the living God (1 Cor. xi. 22), and making the table of the Lord contemptible; or in men celebrating a sacred rite as a passport to some secular office; or in getting rid of a base coin at a collection, like "the deceiver" in ver. 14.

Learn: 1. The many subtle forms of a deep-seated sin of the heart (Jer. xvii. 9). 2. The need of radical remedies such as Divine power alone can employ (Luke vi. 43—45; Ps. xix. 12—14).

Ver. 11.—*God's honour secured in spite of his people's sins.* The heartlessness and negligence of the priest leads God to say that the fires of the altar might as well be extinguished, and the temple shut up as it had been in the days of Ahaz; for no offerings would any longer be accepted at their hands, and "Ichabod!" "No glory!" was written on the altar. The godly remnant of the Jews naturally begin to say, "What a dishonour that would be to the God of Israel!" and to ask, like Joshua (vii. 9), "What wilt thou do unto thy great Name?" And even the formalists, who had not entirely cast off God, but wished to keep on speaking terms with him, would shrink from such a public slight being offered to the God of their nation. To all such fears God gives an answer in the declaration and prediction of ver. 11, "My Name shall be magnified; my honour shall be secured, in spite of my people's sins:" (1) *among new and more numerous worshippers;* (2) *by purer and more spiritual sacrifices.*

I. AMONG NEW AND MORE NUMEROUS WORSHIPPERS. It was an inveterate superstition of the Jews that the honour of God was in some way bound up with sacred places or persons. He had taught them in the past that his glory was not attached to the ark, as they thought when they took it into battle (1 Sam. iv.), or to one line of priests (1 Sam. ii. 27—36), or to the tabernacle at Shiloh (Ps. lxxviii. 59—64), or to the temple (Jer. vii. 1—16). He now teaches them that his glory is independent both of the revived priesthood, the restored temple, and the nation brought back from captivity. The temple may be again destroyed; the priesthood may be abolished; the people disinherited. God has a larger temple than the sanctuary on Mount Moriah, or even than the land of promise itself. His temple extends "as far as the east is from the west." His worshippers shall be as numerous as the tribes and the tongues of the heathen world. No longer shall it be especially true that "In Judah is God known; his Name is great in Israel;" "For from the rising of the sun," etc. Comparing this prediction of the kingdom of Christ on earth with others, we are reminded of a few truths respecting the way in which God's honour would be secured among the nations of the earth. His judgments would arouse them (Isa. lix. 18, 19). His free love would seek those who knew him not (Isa. lxv. 1). The atoning sacrifice on the cross would attract their sin-burdened consciences (John xii. 32), and the beneficence of the reign of Christ would allure all classes to accept his dominion (Ps. lxxii. 8—14, especially ver. 12, " For," etc.). Thus the Name of God would be glorified in his Son. Apply this truth: 1. To those who refuse to give to God the glory due unto his Name. So did the Jews in the days of Christ. But God's honour could be secured in other ways (cf. Matt. xxi. 41—43; Luke xix. 37—40). Note in the former and latter parts of Ps. xxii. the contrast between vers. 6—8 and vers. 27—31. "His own received him not," but "the Gentiles glorified the word of the Lord" (Acts xiii. 48; cf. Isa. xlix. 3—9; Matt. viii. 11, 12). 2. To those who are tempted to shrink from honouring God because of the risk to themselves or the sacrifice required at their hands. Illust.: Esth. iv. 10—14. The loss will be only our own (Matt. x. 39). God will find other servants in our place to render the honour he asks at our hands, and to receive that which he bestows in return (1 Sam. ii. 30). 3. To God's faithful servants who are needlessly anxious about his glory in "a day of trouble and of rebuke and of blasphemy;" e.g. Moses (Numb. xiv. 11—21), Joshua (vii. 9). But God is more jealous for his own honour than we can be (Deut. xxxii. 26, 27), and is wiser than we can be in answering the prayer he has taught us, "Hallowed be thy Name."

II. BY PURER AND MORE SPIRITUAL SACRIFICES. 1. By the revelation of God in Christ as "the Saviour of all men," God's Name was truly magnified (Ps. xcvi. and xcviii.). That revelation included a sacrifice, the sacrifice of a sinless soul to suffering in order to do the will of God (Heb. x. 7—10), and thus to offer a propitiation for the sins of the whole world. Thus the prayer was answered (John xii. 28) and the prediction fulfilled (Rom. xv. 8, 9). 2. By the spiritual sacrifices the acceptable services, like fragrant incense, presented by Gentile hearts, e.g. the penitence of the woman of Samaria; the pertinacious prayers of the Syro-phœnician; the marvellous faith of the centurion; the alms and prayers of Cornelius; the unrecorded acts of faith and service of unknown worshippers in the heathen world;—these are accepted by God, while the tainted sacrifices of the Jewish priests are refused. This a warning to all formalists. 3. By pure offerings from all hearts that "in every place call upon the Name of Jesus Christ our Lord, both theirs and ours" (cf. John iv. 21—24). Our hearts were once impure, but have been cleansed by the blood and the Spirit of Jesus Christ. And now we are eager, impatient to express our sense of the greatness and goodness of God by acceptable sacrifices, our " bodies " (Rom. xii. 1), our gifts (Phil. iv. 18), our praises, our good deeds, and any means by which we can "communicate" to others, and thus glorify our Saviour-God (Heb. xiii. 15, 16).

Notice, in conclusion, what an encouragement this truth may be to those who long to give unto God the glory due unto his Name, but are dissatisfied with their own efforts. God's honour will be secured in spite of our failures. These may stimulate us to seek that greater purity by which our offerings may themselves become purer. It will not provoke us to envy, but rejoice our hearts that others are able to render to God more useful service than we do. And if, in the midst of our efforts to offer such pure offerings and fragrant incense as our poor hearts can present, we are called away from this service, we may rejoice to know that God's honour will not suffer because our services are withdrawn. Illust.: In one Roman Catholic convent there is a chapel of "perpetual adoration," where, every hour, night and day, some service is being offered at the altar. So will be the true worship of God throughout the world—universal and perpetual.

HOMILIES BY VARIOUS AUTHORS.

Ver. 1.—*Burdensome prophecies.* "The burden of the Lord to Israel by Malachi." Much of the work of the Old Testament prophets involved a serious strain on feeling, and may appropriately be figured as a "burden" which they were called to bear. A very large proportion of it consists of denunciations, declarations of swiftly coming and overwhelming Divine judgments. Those prophets were, in fact, raised up to meet a condition of society and national life of which God disapproved, and by which God was dishonoured. It should never be forgotten that the prophets belong to the Israelite monarchy, and that was not God's ideal of government for his people. It brought conditions and perils the significance of which the prophets were to declare. Malachi's is the last prophet-voice of the Old Testament times. After him a great prophetic silence fell on the land. No direct utterance came from God for some three hundred years, until John the Baptist appeared. Nothing is certainly known concerning this Prophet Malachi. He is, indeed, only a name, and our interest lies entirely in his message. His name means, "The Messenger of Jehovah," and it calls us to attend to the message rather than to the speaker. We do know something of the times in which he lived, and we can understand what would be the burden of a Jehovah-prophet at such a time. After Nehemiah had been working for some twelve years at the moral reformation of the people of Jerusalem and Judæa, he was recalled to Persia; and immediately on his departure the old evils which he had stoutly resisted came back like a flood. In spite of the presence of Ezra in Jerusalem, it was seen that a reformation enforced by the civil power, rather than as the fruit of individual conviction, had no permanent vitality. When Nehemiah's back was turned, "the tithes due to the temple, the Levites, and the priests were not delivered, and the greatest distress was thus caused to all those who depended on them for maintenance. The choristers, the guards of the gates, and the ordinary Levites alike, were compelled to go back to their homes, and cultivate their fields for a living. Public worship was thus interrupted, and the temple, forsaken by its ministers, was neglected by the people. Nor was the refusal to pay tithes the only sign of an altered spirit. The sabbath was profaned, both in town and country, wine-presses were busy in its sacred hours, and the roads and fields were dotted with the workers taking sheaves to the barn on their heavily laden asses. Jerusalem itself was disturbed by a sabbath fair, to which loads of wine, grapes, figs, and much else were carried in during sacred hours. After all the professed zeal to put an end to mixed marriages, things were rapidly drifting to almost a worse condition than of old. The very priests had rapidly lost their high tone. Their irreverence, indifference, and worldliness shocked the thoughtful. Everything that Ezra and Nehemiah had effected was well-nigh undone." The Prophet Malachi had the "burden" laid upon him of recalling both priests and people to their duties. And this he did partly by vigorous denunciations of surrounding evils, and partly by anticipations of the times of Messiah. The "Coming One" would surely prove to be a stern Rebuker of national sin.

I. THE PROPHET'S MESSAGE WAS A BURDEN TO HIMSELF. Denunciations of wrongdoing and wrong-doers lose their true force when those who utter them *enjoy* their work. Then they put into them a bitter tone, which makes them ungod-like messages. Stern things have still to be spoken for God, but they must be spoken with pathos in the tone, and tears ready to start. No man can deliver a message of judgment aright, unless he feels it to be a burden.

II. THE PROPHET'S MESSAGE SHOULD BE A BURDEN TO THOSE ADDRESSED. A burden of holy concern. It should set them upon grave self-searching. It should burden them with anxiety about their sins, and with earnest efforts to put sin away. If it was not taken as a burden in that sense, it would become a burden as bringing upon them full, unrelieved, Divine judgments.

III. THE PROPHET'S MESSAGE MAY BE THOUGHT OF AS A BURDEN TO GOD. "Judgment is his strange work;" "In all their affliction he was afflicted;" "Have I any pleasure in the death of the wicked?" We are permitted to think that it troubles God to punish his people. He is burdened by the messages which our sin compels him to send.—R. T.

Vers. 2, 3.—*The Lord's love for his people.* The Lord had chosen Israel as his peculiar people, out of pure love and kindness, without any antecedent merit on their side. This love is strikingly exhibited by contrasting the Divine dealings with the two nations, Edom and Israel. Both came into Divine judgment for sin, and love triumphed in the restoration of Israel; but because of Edom's treatment of Israel, it was left to its desolations. The word "hate" is employed, but South properly explains that "hating" is sometimes used comparatively for a less degree of love (Gen. xxix. 31; Luke xiv. 26). The English word "hate" has somewhat changed its meaning. Now it means, "have a personal aversion to," "regard with ill will." But when our Bible was translated, it had a simpler and kinder meaning, "love less," "show less favour to." It is important to note that the reference is not to God's personal feelings to individuals, but to his providential dealings with nations. Still, it stands out prominently that God's ways with Israel had been the indication of selecting love for her.

I. GOD'S LOVE FOR ISRAEL WAS A DISTINGUISHING LOVE. Of Israel, as of Christ's apostles, it could be said, " Ye have not chosen me, but I have chosen you." The race of Abraham is a selected race. It was separated in order to preserve, and to witness for, the great primary religious truths which are essential to the world's well-being, but are imperilled by the free moral experiment of humanity. It was a sign of Divine love that Israel received such a trust.

II. GOD'S LOVE FOR ISRAEL WAS A PATIENT LOVE. And the patience was very severely tried by the wilfulness and waywardness of the loved ones. This can be illustrated from every stage of the history. The patience is seen in this, that God kept on endeavouring to correct by chastisement. Under no provocation did he give them up in despair, and let judgment prove finally overwhelming. Compare the case of Edom, which, as a nation, is lost beyond recovery. That patience of the Divine love is the holiest joy to us still.

III. GOD'S LOVE FOR ISRAEL WAS A TRIUMPHANT LOVE. This is what seems chiefly in Malachi's mind. He wants the people to feel how the love had triumphed in their recovery from captivity, and their restoration as a nation. And these proofs of the Lord's love should have acted as persuasions to the Lord's service.—R. T.

Vers. 4, 5.—*Divine judgments by disappointments.* The Lord's dealings with Edom are here introduced as contrasting with the Lord's dealings with Israel. And one chief point of contrast is this—Israel's expectations will be realized ; but Edom's expectations will be disappointed. "Thus saith the Lord of hosts. They shall build, but I will throw down." There was an exceedingly bitter feeling between Israel and Edom, dating from the time when Edom insultingly refused to allow the passage of Israel through her territory, and so compelled God's people to take the weary and perilous way up the Arabah. Again and again we have hints of the unfriendly feeling between the kindred and neighbour nations ; and that it was continued up to the time of the destruction of Jerusalem by Nebuchadnezzar is indicated by the exclamation of the poet, in Ps. cxxxvii. 7, " Remember, O Lord, the children of Edom in the day of Jerusalem ; who said, Rase it, rase it, even to the foundation thereof." That Jehovah, as God and King of Israel, took its part against Edom is clearly intimated in the prophecy of Obadiah. The point of the passage before us is that on the efforts of Edom to recover itself as a nation no permanency would rest ; whereas if Israel would but be faithful to its obligations, it as a kingdom should be established for ever.

I. FAILURE IN LIFE'S ENTERPRISES IS A SIGN OF DIVINE DEALING WITH US. However we may say that such failure attends (1) particular dispositions ; or (2) imperfect training and culture, it remains true that a deeper explanation is possible. The promise to the good is, " Whatsoever he doeth shall prosper." The judgment on the evil may be, " Whatsoever he doeth shall fail." There is no experience of life more trying than the disappointment of failing again and again. There is no misery like the hopelessness of feeling as if we *could* not succeed, and it is no use to try any more. The man is lost who feels that.

II. FAILURE IN LIFE'S ENTERPRISES MAY BE DIVINE DISCIPLINE, BUT IT MAY BE DIVINE JUDGMENT. Chastisement, to convince that we have done the thing wrongly. Judgment, as in the case of Edom, of some sin committed in early life, the spirit of which we have kept up through the long years. If we fail in life, we should searchingly inquire why God lets us fail.—R. T.

Ver. 6.—*Human claims impressing Divine claims.* The figure of fatherhood is used in Scripture to suggest God's peculiar relation to Israel ; and we are therefore invited to use the family sentiments and responsibilities in the endeavour to realize our obligations to God. Our Lord, in his teachings, made a similar appeal to family feelings: " If ye then, being evil, know how to give good gifts unto your children, how much more shall your Father who is in heaven give good things to them that ask him ? " And the writer of the Epistle to the Hebrews argues in a similar way, " Furthermore we have had fathers of our flesh which corrected us, and we gave them reverence ; shall we not much rather be in subjection unto the Father of spirits, and live ? " It is true that arguments based on human relationships must take due account of human infirmities; but there is an ideal human relationship in every case, which men in their hearts recognize, and the obligations connected with it may always be safely applied to our relations with God. But there is a special point in Malachi's pleading with the priests of his day. In common with Jehovah's people, they came under the children's claims and responsibilities; but, *as priests*, they were children honoured with special trusts. They were favoured children, and were bound to be *model* children. The obligation of the servant to the master is similar to that of the son to the father, but in the case of the child there is the help of personal affection. The two figures may be used to illustrate the point of this passage.

I. A MASTER'S CLAIM ILLUSTRATES THE DIVINE CLAIM. "If I be a Master, where is my fear? saith the Lord." This is taking the lowest ground. There is no necessary *affection* in this relationship. There is simply obligation and duty. A servant is bound to serve. Apply to the priests, who were precisely the servants of Jehovah's house, or temple. He had a right to claim service that would honour him, that would show a cherished sense of reverence and fear, and would make others think highly of him. But just *that* service the priests of the day were failing to render. Still, if no higher relation be realized, God claims our service as his servants.

II. A FATHER'S CLAIM ILLUSTRATES THE DIVINE CLAIM. This is higher ground to take, because it is a relation involving personal affection, and the refusal of the claim is therefore the more unworthy. Work out that if the father-figure as presented in the Old Testament was a great persuasion of the Divine claims, much more must the Father-figure be as revealed in the teaching and Sonship of Jesus Christ.—R. T.

Ver. 7.—*Polluted bread; or, priestly sins.* What was consumed upon the altar was regarded as God's portion, and may, in a figure, be called "the bread of God." "The offerings of the Lord made by fire, and the bread of God, they do offer: therefore they shall be holy" (Lev. xxi. 6). By "polluted bread" we are to understand maimed and blemished sacrifices. The Divine reproach is that the priests show how little value they have for the worship of God, since they do not care in how slight and contemptuous a manner it is performed. The Prophet Malachi deals very largely with the unfaithfulness, the unpriestliness, of the priests of his day. It was at once a sign of a sad condition of morals and religion when the priests failed of their duty; and the way to recover the nation to righteousness, when the priests were recalled to the sense of their obligations.

I. SOCIETY REVEALED IN THE UNFAITHFULNESS OF THE PRIESTS. These may be taken as representing the clergy of the Christian generations. It has always been true that society is reflected in the moral standard of the clergy. This is embodied in the saying, "Like priest, like people;" and it is a wider and more searching truth than is usually apprehended. The clergy are the moral barometers by which the atmosphere of an age is discovered. The priests of Malachi's time declare the moral and religious degeneracy of the people. "The saddest sign of all was the degeneracy of the priesthood which Malachi, though perhaps himself a priest, was specially commissioned to denounce. The lack of all real faith and moral soundness in the very order which ought to have kept alive among the people the essential elements of the spiritual life, was eating like a cancer into the heart of the national sincerity" (Farrar). It may be shown that priestly indifference and unfaithfulness are products and results of neglected personal religious life. So long as priestly duties are instinct with spiritual feeling they will be worthily performed. When personal godliness fails, they become perfunctory, and then if in seeming they are kept up, in reality they deteriorate. It is in maintaining the personal religious life that priests lead the nations.

II. SOCIETY IS RECOVERED BY THE RECOVERY OF THE PRIESTS. Therefore Malachi appeals to them. It may be that the priests are the last to yield to the society evils; but they must always be the first recovered. They must become forces on the side of God in the restoration of moral health to a nation. Revivals are always hopeless things unless their first effect is the spiritual revival of the clergy.—R. T.

Ver. 8.—*The law of acceptable sacrifice.* It must be such as would be acceptable if offered to any earthly official. This, indeed, is but taking low ground, but that the prophet should take this position, and use this argument, is in itself a revelation of the sad condition into which the priesthood of the day had fallen. He could not take high grounds, and make his appeal directly to the holiness of the claims of the infinitely Holy One. "It argues a great contempt of Almighty God when men are less careful in maintaining the decencies of his worship than they are in giving proper respects to their superiors." It should be borne in mind that the Levitical system very rigorously demanded that only sound and clean animals should be presented in sacrifice. It is always necessary to check the meanness of men, which tempts them to put God off with that which they themselves do not greatly value (see Lev. xxii. 22, etc.). The sin of offering the imperfect to God can be tested in two very simple ways.

I. OFFER AN IMPERFECT GIFT TO YOUR FRIEND. For a birthday-time find something you have done with; something you do not care for; something out of taste in your own house, which you are glad to get rid of; something damaged, or soiled, or broken. You send it, saying in your heart, "It is good enough for him." That gift dishonours the friend, and morally degrades you as the giver. If that friend has any spirit, he despises such gifts, and sends the coldest of acknowledgments of their receipt. Is God in Christ our Friend? What shall be the love-gifts which alone can be acceptable to him?

II. OFFER AN IMPERFECT GIFT TO YOUR GOVERNOR. If a man wants to show his respect, or to indicate his gratitude for some favour received, he is always most particular in the selection of his present. He takes care that there is no flaw in it; he selects the best possible; he is most anxious about its being conveyed without injury. If the governor has any spirit, he will not look at or receive anything but the very best. Is God our supreme Governor? Then how can we fail to offer the very best possible to him?

III. OFFER AN IMPERFECT GIFT TO YOUR GOD. Has he not more claim than either friend or governor to the perfect offering? How should we respond to (1) his authority; (2) his holiness; (3) his redemption? Though out of our sight, he searchingly tests all our gifts, offerings, and sacrifices. Open out how we may be offering the imperfect in (1) our acts of worship; (2) our acts of benevolence; (3) our acts of ministry and service.—R. T.

Ver. 9.—*Regarding the person.* "Will he regard your persons?" The idea of the verse is somewhat difficult to trace; but it appears to be this: "You are expecting that God will accept you just because you are priests, on account of your official standing alone. You think that it does not matter to him what you are morally, so long as you go through the routine of his service according to the standards." It is intimated plainly enough that their intercessions on behalf of the people must be in vain so long as they are acting unworthily.

I. THE SENSE IN WHICH GOD DOES REGARD THE PERSON. 1. He deals with each individual, never loses the one in the many; each person stands out distinctly before him as if there were no other. This truth needs to be dwelt on, because men readily hide themselves from their own view, and think to hide themselves from God's view, in the class to which they belong. The sins of the priests may not deeply humble any particular priest. 2. He deals with a man's moral condition. That belongs exclusively to the man. It is his personality. It is the matter of supreme concern to God.

II. THE SENSE IN WHICH GOD DOES NOT REGARD THE PERSON. He is no "Respecter of persons." This enlarges the idea, and we may see: 1. That God takes no account of bodily peculiarities. "Man looketh on the outward appearance, but God looketh on the heart." 2. God takes no account of social rank. He pays no deference to the high-born and rich; he shows no indifference to the low-born and poor. His supreme interest is in men, not in the accidents of men. This is not meant to imply any failure in our estimating the value of social status and influence; it only emphasizes that these are not the matters of Divine consideration. They do not belong to the essence of manhood. 3. God takes no account of official position. No man stands in the special favour of God because he is a king, and no man has any special ground for pleading with God in the fact that he is a priest or clergyman. A man's power of intercession with God is dependent on his personal relations with God, but it is assumed that every priest and every minister is what he ought to be—in accepted personal relations with God. No matter what our office may be, if there is not at the heart of it a right state of mind and heart, the acceptance of the ministry of that office cannot be assured.—R. T.

Ver. 10.—*Self-serving religion.* " One of the works on which Nehemiah looked back with most satisfaction was that he had secured to the Levites the payment of a sufficient remuneration for their work. It was a right thing in itself. It asserted what we have learnt to call the principle of an ' established' Church, and of a fair division of its income. But that spirit might easily pass, and had actually passed, into the temper which is always clamorous for rights and privileges, which will work only when those rights and privileges are secured. The spirit of the hireling takes the place of that of the worshipper. And so, amongst the foremost sins which the prophet is called on to condemn we find this, noted with special reference to the functions of those Levites over whose interests Nehemiah had been so watchful. ' Who is there even among you,' he asks,' ' that would shut the doors for naught ? ' And the hireling spirit, once fostered, showed itself, as it always does, in neglect, evasion, dishonesty " (Plumptre).

I. THE WORKMAN IS WORTHY OF HIS HIRE. This sentence embodies a good working principle, which has its proper application in religious as well as in secular spheres. They who minister in spiritual things may reasonably claim to be ministered unto in carnal things. Clergymen share all common bodily and family wants ; and we have no sympathy with those who talk as if some wrong were done when spiritual men are concerned for their material interests. Priests and Levites deserved their pay.

II. THE WORKMAN IS WORTHY ONLY WHEN HE DOES NOT WORK FOR HIS HIRE. This is only true in a *higher sense* of the Levite ; it is really true of every workman. A man is on a low plane when he works just for his wage. He is but a time-server, a self-server. The best work never is done by such men ; and their work is never the best blessing to them. A man must work for the love of his work if he is to do it nobly. A religious man must work for God if his work is to be acceptable. To work for gain is to work for self. The " sons of Eli," and Simon Magus, illustrate the moral degradation when the servants of God make money-conditions.—R. T.

Ver. 11.—*The universal worship that is to be.* These words are usually taken as a prophetic announcement of the future rejection of Israel and calling of the Gentiles ; but it is difficult to trace the connection of thought, if this be regarded as the prophet's meaning. The LXX. rightly uses the present, not the future, tense throughout this verse. " My Name is great," etc. This gives an actual *present* comparison of the fear of God's Name among Gentiles and among Jews, to the manifest disadvantage of the Jew. God found a devoutness, earnestness, and sincerity outside his own people, which wholly put to shame their indifference, formality, and time-serving. This suggestion is in the line of Malachi's teaching, whereas a description of future religious conditions seems to introduce a new subject. Dean Plumptre says, " It was given to the last of the prophets to proclaim, with an entirely new distinctness, not only as Isaiah had done, the accession of Gentile proselytes to the worship and faith of Israel, but the acceptance of their worship wherever it might be offered." The Gentile religion in the mind of the prophet was probably that of Zoroaster, the purest form that Gentile religion has ever taken.

I. THE BASIS OF THE UNIVERSAL WORSHIP. The prophet must not be regarded as giving a complete account of the universal worship. He deals with it only in view of his immediate object, and to point his appeal to the unfaithful and time-serving priests. He brings out three points. 1. One characteristic of the universal worship is *reverence for the Divine Name.* " My Name is great among the Gentiles." No religion can ever fit to the needs of men which does not at least *seem* to honour the Divine Name. This is our first test of every religion. 2. Another is the *demand for prayer.* " Incense is offered." Every true religion provides communion with God, and gives man hope in prayer. " When we have learned by experience the unutterable value of prayer, then shall theism become a religion fit for humanity." 3. Another is sincerity shown in purity of offerings. Our Lord expressed the universal worship in a sentence, when he said, " The true worshippers shall worship the Father in spirit and in truth."

II. THE REPROACH OF THE UNIVERSAL WORSHIP. It reproaches all who fail to meet these primal conditions, whatever their historical standing might be. It reproached the Jewish priests of Malachi's time, for they were dishonouring the Name, putting routine for prayer, and making unworthy and impure offerings which revealed their insincerity.—R. T.

Ver. 13.—*Religion a weariness.* "Ye said also, Behold, what a weariness is it!" It is clearly a bad sign when the people find the worship of God to be a weariness; but it is a much worse sign when the ministers of religion both feel the worship to be a weariness, and show that they feel it to be such. I. IN THE NATURE OF THINGS RELIGIOUS WORSHIP SHOULD NOT BE A WEARINESS. 1. Take it as the proper and fitting expression of the creature's dependence on his Creator. It ought to be full of the joy of thankfulness. 2. Take it as the natural impulse of the sinner's love to his Saviour. Man fallen should feel a joy in worship even beyond that of man unfallen. The song of the redeemed is an altogether nobler song than the innocent can ever sing. And religious worship, kept within the lines of Divine claims, never need be a weariness. It is religion with the multiplied added demands of men that is in danger of proving a weariness. No reasonable man could say that Mosaism was a weariness, so far as it was a Divine institution. But every man could say that Rabbinism was a weariness; for it laded men with burdens too grievous to be borne. Spiritual religion is always simplifying worship. As spirituality fails, exacting demands are increased, and religion tends to become a weariness. II. THROUGH THE MOODS OF MEN RELIGIOUS WORSHIP BECOMES A WEARINESS. What the priests of earlier times had done gladly and joyfully, the priests of Malachi's time dragged through. The joy of Levites in their work is expressed in the Korahite psalms (xlii., lxxxiv., etc.), which are full of longings for restoration to the temple service. There was no difference in the worship. The difference was in the moods of the men. Their spiritual life was low. They had no personal joy in God, so they could have no joy in the routine of God's worship. The sadness of the restored Judaism of the exiles was that, to so large an extent, it was the restoration of the Jewish formalities, without the restoration of that spiritual life which would have vitalized the formalities. And still the weariness men feel at the length of Christian services, etc., is the revelation of their wrong mood; of their lost personal joy in God their Saviour.—R. T.

Ver. 14.—*The great and dreadful Name.* The idea in the word "dreadful" would be better conveyed by "awe-ful," if that were a word in familiar use. "Dreadful" we reserve for something that is unusually calamitous and destructive. Awe of God; reverence of his august majesty; fear which leads to the symbolic removal of the shoes;—these things are essential to right and acceptable worship, and these things are absolutely befitting to man the creature, and much more to man the sinner. A man may be tested by the measure of his reverent awe of the Divine Name (comp. Josh. vii. 9). "With a startling reiteration, after every specific denunciation of the sins of priests and people, they are represented as asking, as if in utter unconsciousness of their sin, 'Wherein have we polluted thee? Wherein have we despised thy Name?' They have fallen into the last stage of selfish formalism when conscience ceases to do its work as an accusing witness, into the hypocrisy which does not even know itself to be hypocritical; the hypocrisy, in other words, of the scribes and Pharisees." I. REVERENCE FOR THE DIVINE NAME IS A SIGN OF SPIRITUAL LIFE. It was necessary that God should demand reverence for his Divine Name in one of his ten great commandments, "Thou shalt not take the Name of the Lord thy God in vain; for the Lord will not hold him guiltless that taketh his Name in vain." But that law is never needed by any man who has and cherishes right thoughts of God; he simply *cannot* take his Name in vain. All worship is truly reverent according to the spiritual life that is at the heart of it. Therefore we train children in reverence for the Divine Name, because it is the basis of spiritual religion. II. FAILING REVERENCE FOR THE DIVINE NAME IS A SIGN OF FAILING SPIRITUAL LIFE. It is one of the first, and one of the surest, signs. A light tone of speech, in reference to the infinitely Holy One, at once tells of lost spiritual health. Loosen the sense of awe, and innumerable evils can creep in. Reverence for the great Name keeps the gate of the soul safe shut against intruders ; and it is our continual inspiration to pure and holy living.—R. T.

Vers. 1—5.—*The sovereignty of God in relation to man's secular condition of life.* " The burden of the word of the Lord," etc. Malachi—which means " Messenger "— the last of the Hebrew prophets, is a man whose personal history is wrapped in utter obscurity. He is supposed to have lived after Haggai and Zechariah, and to be contemporary with Nehemiah. It is likely that he occupied a relationship to Nehemiah somewhat analogous to that which Haggai and Zechariah sustained to Zerubbabel. The general opinion is that he prophesied about the year B.C. 430. This was that brilliant period in Greece in which flourished some of its greatest men—Cimon, son of Miltiades, distinguished as a commander; Pericles, the greatest of Athenian states- men, under whom Athens attained a splendour that made her the wonder and admira- tion of all Greece; Phidias, the celebrated sculptor, and a host of distinguished artists; Simonides and Pindar, eminent lyric poets; Æschylus, Sophocles, and Euripides, dis- tinguished dramatists; and Herodotus, who has received a title really due to Moses, " the Father of History." From this passage the following truths may be legitimately deduced.

I. That some men on this earth seem to be more favoured by Providence than others, and yet they are often unconscious of it. This is the communica- tion or " burden " of the Divine message which Malachi had to deliver to Israel : " I have loved you, saith the Lord. Yet ye say, Wherein hast thou loved us ? " Israel here stands for all the tribes, all the descendants of Jacob. The Israelitish nation was more favoured than any nation on the face of the earth. In relation to their privileges Paul says of the Israelites, " to whom pertaineth the adoption, and the glory, and the covenants, and the giving of the Law, and the service of God, and the promises : whose are the fathers, and of whom as concerning the flesh Christ came " (Rom. ix. 4, 5). As *individuals*, some men are more favoured than others. As Jacob was more favoured than Esau, so some men in all generations are more blessed than others—blessed with more vigorous frames, more intellectual resources, more emotional wealth, etc. There is amongst men immense variety in the degree of natural endowments. Read the parable of the talents. But it is *man nationally* that is here referred to. " I have loved you," that is, " I have regarded you more than other nations." Is not our England more favoured than most if not all of the other nations of the earth ? She is, in some respects, as far exalted above all existing states, as Israel of old was above all the heathen nations that surrounded it. But individually, as was said above, all men are not treated alike. Some are born of healthier parents than others, live in more salu- brious climes than others, are endowed with higher faculties than others, brought up under more wholesome laws and higher educational influences than others. The existence of these distinctions is too obvious to require either argument or illustration. But whilst this is such a patent fact, the favoured ones are too often *unconscious of the distinction.* " Wherein hast thou loved us ? " Israel did not realize its exalted privileges. How often is this the case ! The men most favoured of Providence are often most unconscious of the favours, and they say, " Wherein hast thou loved us ? " As a rule, perhaps the most favoured of Providence are the greatest complainers. What *ingratitude* is here !

II. That this difference in the privileges of men is to be ascribed to the sovereignty of God. " I loved Jacob, and I hated Esau." Some read it, " I favoured Jacob, but rejected Esau." Why was Jacob more favoured than Esau ? Not because he had a nobler moral character. In some respects he appears more despicable than Esau. It was simply because God chose to distinguish him. The reason of distinction was in the mind of God, and nowhere else. " He worketh all things according to the counsel of his will." His sovereignty does not imply either of two things. 1. *Par- tiality on his part.* The fact that the Jewish people, the descendants of Jacob, in their history endured, perhaps, calamities as great as those that befell the Edomites, the descendants of Esau, proved that it was no partiality on God's part. He is no Respecter of persons. Nor does it imply : 2. *Irresponsibility on man's part.* " They who have least," says Godwin, " and bear most, may become better and happier than they who have most and suffer least." The permanent value of all things depends on the use which is made of them : the first often becoming last, and the last first. But no argument can be drawn from differences in men's condition as to which will be the most morally advantageous or disadvantageous according to their conduct. Whilst the differences of one kind depend solely on the Divine will, the differences of the other kind are not irrespective of human choice.

III. THOSE WHOM THE SOVEREIGNTY OF GOD DOES NOT FAVOUR ARE LEFT IN A SECULARLY UNENVIABLE CONDITION. 1. The words teach us that they will *have possessions destroyed.* " I hated Esau, and laid his mountains and his heritage waste for the dragons [jackals] of the wilderness." These men, the men of Edom, struggled hard to build up their kingdom and to give it wealth and power, but the product of all their labours was utterly destroyed. Their great things, their "mountains," their wealthy things, their " heritage," the scenes of their power, gave place to the " dragons of the wilderness." Where is Edom now ? If Heaven has determined that the fortune you have built up after years of earnest and indefatigable labour shall be swept away, it will depart as a vision of the night. 2. *That their efforts were frustrated.* " If Edom saith, We are impoverished, but we will return and build the desolate places ; thus saith the Lord of hosts, They shall build, but I will throw down ; and they shall call them, The border of wickedness, and, The people against whom the Lord hath indignation for ever." They struggle to restore their position, labour hard to build the desolate places, but in every effort they are thwarted. It is in vain to strive against destiny. Mark that all that is here said concerns only the *secular* prosperity of men. Divine sovereignty is always in favour of *spiritual* prosperity, progress in intelligence, purity, and happiness. In all these matters men cannot labour in vain. 3. *Their enemies prosper.* " And your eyes shall see, and ye shall say, The Lord will be magnified from the border of Israel." Edom hated Israel from the beginning, fought hard against it for centuries, struggled continually to destroy it, but all in vain. The time came when it found itself in ruins and its enemy in prosperity. " The argument of these verses is this," says Dr. Dods, " if you would see the difference between hatred and love, look at the different condition and prospects of Edom and Israel. The desolation with which their territory is visited is irremediable : they have no glorious future beyond : whereas the wretched condition of which you complain is but the bleakness of seed-time that precedes the richest harvest."

CONCLUSION. Are we not here in this England of ours among the peoples whom Heaven has specially favoured ? Are not the words specially applicable to us, " I have loved you, saith the Lord " ? But what is our practical response ? Does not our daily life speak out the ingratitude and unbelief of Israel, " Wherein hast thou loved us ? " We do not see it ; we do not feel it ; " Wherein ? " What ought we to think of our civilization, our liberties, our fruitful land and salubrious air ? above all, what of our Christ ? " Herein is love."—D. T.

Vers. 6—9.—*The profession and the practice of religion.* " A son honoureth his father, and a servant his master : if then I be a Father, where is mine honour ? and if I be a Master, where is my fear ? saith the Lord of hosts unto you, O priests, that despise my Name. And ye say, Wherein have we despised thy Name ? " etc. The subject of these words is the profession and the practice of religion ; and they suggest two thoughts.

I. THE PROFESSION AND THE PRACTICE SHOULD ALWAYS BE IN ACCORD. " A son honoureth his father, and a servant his master." This is stated as a fact. The son here, of course, must be supposed to be worthy of the name *son.* There are some children who are destitute of natural affection. What Aristotle of old said will be endorsed by all thoughtful men. " A son must always be his father's debtor, because he can never repay him for those greatest of all benefits, birth and upbringing, and in these the fathers resemble God." This being so, and you Israel being " my son, my firstborn," a relationship which you profess, " where is mine honour ? " If the language is, as some suppose, specially addressed to the priests, the appeal gets new emphasis. The idea is—You profess to regard me as your Father and your Master, and you should, therefore, in your life treat me with honour, reverential fear, and loyal devotion. " Why call ye me, Lord, Lord, and do not the things that I say ? " Any discrepancy between our profession and our practice is morally unnatural.   Our conduct should accord with our creed, our deeds with our doctrines.

II. THE PROFESSION AND THE PRACTICE ARE OFTENTIMES AT VARIANCE. The priests to whom these words were addressed practically contradicted their profession. They called him Father and Master, and yet see how they treated him in their sacrifices in the temple.   Look at them in their offerings.   They showed : 1. *A lawless spirit.* " Ye offer polluted bread upon mine altar."   This is directly contrary to the Law as given in Deuteronomy : " If there be any blemish therein, as if it be lame, or blind, or have any ill blemish, thou shalt not sacrifice it unto the Lord thy God."   " The sin with which the priests are charged is that of polluting God's altar by offering beasts not ceremonially clean, unfit for sacrifice.   Any beast was passed as good enough for sacrifice, the lame or blind, that had become useless for work, sick or torn, the beast that was dying on its feet, and could not be used for meat, or that which had been stolen, and so marked that it would not sell—anything, in short, that could serve no other purpose, was good enough for God.   His courts had the appearance of a knacker's yard."   2. *A niggardly spirit.*   Not only were they polluted, which is contrary to ceremonial law, but they were worthless : blind, lame, wretched skeletons were the beasts offered, worth nothing in the field or the market, mere refuse.   " A cheap religion," says one, " costing little, is rejected by God, worth nothing : it costs more than it is worth, for it is worth nothing, and so proves really dear."   God despiseth not the widow's mite, but he disdains the miser's gold.   3. *A captious spirit.*   They say, " Wherein have we despised thy Name ? "   " Wherein have we polluted thee ? " So blind and so insensible were they to moral propriety that they insulted the Almighty even in their formal efforts to serve him.   4. *A thoughtless spirit.*   " Offer it now unto thy governor ; will he be pleased with thee, or accept thy person ? saith the Lord of hosts?   And now, I pray you, beseech God that he will be gracious unto us : this hath been by your means : will he regard your persons ? saith the Lord of hosts."   This sentence is ironical : Ye dare not go before your governor with such presents ; but come now, I pray you, enter God's presence, and use your stock phrase of supplication (Numb. vi. 25), that he " would be gracious unto us."   Will he regard your persons ? How many who profess God to be their Father and their Master act out, even in their religious services, this lawless, niggardly, captious, thoughtless spirit !   Herein there is the discrepancy between profession and practice.   But, alas ! how common is it !

> With lip we call him Master,
>   In life oppose his Word,
> We ev'ry day deny him,
>   And yet we call him Lord !
>
> No more is our religion
>   Like his in soul or deed
> Than painted grain on canvas
>   Is like the living seed.
>
> In the balance we are weigh'd
>   And wanting we are found,
> In all that's true and Christly
>   The universe around.

CONCLUSION.   A fact narrated to me by the late Rev. Dr. Leifchild some years ago affords a striking illustration of the discrepancy between profession and practice in religion.   He told me that there was an old lady in his Church, very wealthy, and very loud in her professions, and apparently very enthusiastic in her devotions, but whose contributions for religious purposes were of the most niggardly kind.   One Sunday, in singing a hymn with which they closed the service of the Lord's Supper, she being near to the table, he observed her as the deacons were going round, according to their custom, collecting subscriptions for the poor.   It so happened that the verse they were singing at the time the deacon came to her with the plate was—

> Were the whole realm of nature mine,
>   That were a present far too small :
> Love so amazing, so Divine,
>   Demands my heart, my life, my all."

No one in the whole congregation seemed more hearty in shouting out those words with his voice than she. Meanwhile the deacon held the plate right under her eye, but she let it pass without enriching it by even a copper.—D. T.

Vers. 10—14.—*Wrong worship.* "Who is there even among you that would shut the doors for naught?" etc. The subject of these words is wrong worship, and they suggest the following remarks.

I. THAT WRONG WORSHIP IS WORSE THAN NO WORSHIP AT ALL. "Who is there even among you that would shut the doors for naught? neither do ye kindle fire on mine altar for naught. I have no pleasure in you, saith the Lord of hosts, neither will I accept an offering at your hand." Keil gives a version more in accordance with the original, "Oh that there were one among you who would shut the doors, that ye might not light mine altar to no purpose! I have no pleasure in you, saith Jehovah of hosts, and sacrificial offering does not please me from your hand." "As if," says Dr. Dods, "God were to say it were far better that the temple were shut than that such profane and fruitless worship were carried on in it (Isa. i. 12). Better that you and your offensive beasts be together shut out of the temple, and that no smoke ascend from the altar, since all such offerings as you present are offered in vain. The Hebrew word translated 'for naught,' is the etymological equivalent of 'gratis;' but the meaning here is not 'without reward,' but the closely allied, secondary meaning 'without result;' it is not the mercenary but the fruitless character of the services which is pointed at." There is a deal of wrong worship in the world, not only in heathen regions but in Christendom, not only in Popery but in Protestantism, not only in the Church but in Dissent. Some of the hymns used are not only gross but blasphemous, and some prayers, too, are repugnant alike to reason and conscience. No worship is a thousand times better than wrong worship. Wrong worship insults the Infinite Father, and degrades the human soul.

II. THAT WRONG WORSHIP WILL ONE DAY BE PRACTICALLY REPUDIATED. "From the rising of the sun even unto the going down of the same my Name shall be great among the Gentiles." A modern expositor expresses the idea thus: "Since ye Jewish priests and people 'despise my Name,' I shall find others who will magnify it (Matt. viii. 11). Do not think I shall have no worshippers because I have not you, for from the east to the west my Name shall be great among the Gentiles (Isa. lix. 19; lxvi. 19, 20), those very peoples whom ye look down on as abominable. 'And a pure offering,' not the blind, the lame, and the sick, such as ye offer." "In every place" implies the catholicity of the Christian Church (John iv. 21—23; 1 Tim. ii. 8). The incense is figurative of prayer (Ps. cxli. 2; Rev. viii. 3). Sacrifice is used metaphorically of the offering of a "broken and contrite heart." 1. *This period, though far in the future, is certain to dawn on the world.* God hath promised it, and it is "impossible for him to lie." "And the Gentiles shall come to thy light, and kings to the brightness of thy rising. . . . Then thou shalt see, and flow together, and thine heart shall fear, and be enlarged; because the abundance of the sea shall be converted into thee" (Isa. lx. 3—5). 2. *This period will exclude all false worship.* It will be in "every place." No room for the knee in the temple of the false worshipper. Neither in this mountain nor in that mountain shall ye worship the Father. "God is a Spirit, and they that worship him must worship him in spirit and in truth." 3. *In this period all human souls will be blended in love and devotion.* No more divisions. "Thy Name shall be great among the heathen." He will be the great centre around which all souls will revolve, from which all will draw their heat, their light, their harmony.

III. THAT WRONG WORSHIP IS SOMETIMES RENDERED EVEN BY THE RELIGIOUS TEACHERS OF MANKIND. "But ye have profaned it, in that ye say, the Table of the Lord is polluted; and the fruit thereof, even his meat, is contemptible." From these words we learn that these priests made worship appear: 1. *Contemptible.* Perhaps these priests did not literally say the Lord's table was contemptible, but in their acts they declared it. Is the word "contemptible" here intended to express the feeling of the priests themselves? Some have considered it as referring to the revenue which the priests drew from their services at the altar. The beasts which were brought for offering were so lean, diseased, and wretched, that the flesh which fell to their share for food was so poor that they could not eat it, it filled them with disgust, it was contemptible.

As if they had said, "The reward which we have for our services at the altar is truly contemptible." But this view can scarcely be adopted, inasmuch as they themselves accepted those worthless animals for sacrifice. It rather means that they had made worship appear contemptible to others, that their services had brought worship into contempt. How often do the religious leaders of mankind, by the crudity of their thoughts, the narrowness of their creeds, the worldliness of their spirits, bring religion into popular contempt! 2. *Burdensome.* "Behold, what a weariness is it!" etc. This is not, alas! an uncommon occurrence. Religious leaders, perhaps the majority of them, have in all ages, by their hoary platitudes, their vain repetitions, their long, dull prayers, their monotonous tones, their prosy twaddlings, made their hearers often exclaim, "Behold, what a weariness is it!" In truth, religious service is a weariness to all who have not their hearts in it. Dr. Pusey well remarks, "The service of God is its own reward. If not, it becomes a greater toil, with less reward from this earth than the things of this earth. Our only choice is between love and weariness."

IV. THAT WRONG WORSHIP EVERMORE INCURS THE JUST DISPLEASURE OF HEAVEN. "But cursed be the deceiver," etc. He is here called the deceiver, who has the means of presenting a valuable sacrifice, and yet presents a worthless one. He "hath in his flock a male," something that is valuable. It is not the man who openly denies God, and who makes no pretence of serving him, that is here cursed, but the man who professes to serve him, and yet is destitute of the true spirit of devotion. He who offers to him the mere dregs of his time, his strength, his means, virtually presents that "polluted bread" upon the altar which is abhorrent to the Almighty.

CONCLUSION. Let all eschew vain worship, a worship that may be either the worship of a *wrong* god, some idol, or the worship of the *right* God in a *wrong* way. Let those of us who presume to be the religious leaders of our race take care that we do not bring public worship into contempt; and by our lack of spiritual vivacity and the exciting inspiration of true devotion, cause the people to exclaim, "Behold, what a weariness is it!"—D. T.

EXPOSITION.

CHAPTER II.

Vers. 1—4.—§ 4. *For these derelictions of duty the priests are threatened with punishment.*

Ver. 1.—**This commandment.** The threat or announcement is called a commandment, because God ordains it and imposes its execution on certain instruments. (For the expression, comp. Lev. xxv. 21.) The threat is contained in vers. 2, 3.

Ver. 2.—**I will even send a curse**; Revised Version, *then will I send the curse.* St. Jerome, regarding the temporal effect of the curse, translates, *egestatem,* "scarcity" (comp. Deut. xxvii. 15—26; xxviii. 15, etc.). **I will curse your blessings.** The blessings which as priests they had to pronounce upon the people (Lev. ix. 22, 23; Numb. vi. 23—27). These God would not ratify, but would turn them into curses, and thus punish the people who connived at and imitated the iniquities of the priests. Or the expression may refer to the material benefits promised by God to the Israelites on their obedience. But as the announcement is made specially to the priests, this explanation seems less probable. **I have cursed**

them already. The curse has already begun to work. Dr. S. Cox ('Bible Educator,' iii. 67, etc.) points out here an allusion to Neh. xiii. 1, 2, wherein it is recorded that they read from the Book of Moses how that the Moabites "hired Balaam against them that he should curse them; howbeit our God turned the curse into a blessing." Malachi, who, as he thinks, was present on this occasion, may have been deeply impressed by these words; and it is probable that we hear an echo of them in the threat of ver. 2. "That of old God had turned a curse into a blessing, may have suggested the menace that he would now turn a blessing into a curse."

Ver. 3.—**I will corrupt your seed.** Henderson, "I will rebuke the seed to your hurt." God would mar the promise of their crops; but, as the priests did not concern themselves with agriculture, such a threat would have had no particular application to them. It is best, therefore, to take the pointing of some of the versions, and to translate, *I will rebuke your arm;* i.e. I will take from you the power of performing, or, I will neutralize your official duties, the arm being the instrument of labour, offering, and blessing. Others consider the threat to be that they should be deprived of their allotted portion of the sacrifice—the breast and shoulder (Lev. vii. 31, 32), or the shoulder, the two cheeks, and the maw (Deut. xviii. 3). Septuagint, Ἀφορίζω ὑμῖν τὸν ὦμον, "I take from you the shoulder;" Vulgate, *Ego projiciam vobis brachium.* Orelli takes "seed" in the sense of posterity, seeing here a reversal of such promises as Jer. xxxiii. 18, 22. **Spread dung upon your faces.** God will deliver them over to shameful treatment, which shall cover them with contempt. The idea is derived from the filth left in the courts by the victims (see the following clause). **Your solemn feasts** (*chaggim*); *i.e.* the animals slain at the sacrificial feasts. God calls them "your," not "my," because they were not celebrated really in his honour, but after their own self-will and pleasure. The dung of the sacrificial animals was by the Law carried forth and burned without the camp (Exod. xxix. 14; Lev. iv. 12; xvi. 27). **One shall take you away with it.** They shall be treated as filth, and cast away in some foul spot (comp. 1 Kings xiv. 10).

Ver. 4.—**Ye shall know.** My threats are not vain; this ye shall experience and be forced to acknowledge. **This commandment** is the purpose and threat, as in ver. 1 (where see note). **That my covenant might be with Levi;** *i.e.* that my covenant with Levi might remain firm. The covenant with Levi was the election of that tribe to be the ministers of the sanctuary. There is here a special allusion to the blessing pronounced on Phinehas for his conduct in the matter of Zimri (Numb. xxv. 12, 13). This election is called "a covenant," because, while conferring certain privileges, it involved certain duties. The difficulty in this interpretation is that the verb used here (*hayah*) does not mean "to remain," "to continue," but only "to be," "to exist." Hence many critics take "the commandment" as the subject, translating, "That it (my purpose) may be my covenant with Levi;" *i.e.* that as God observed the covenant made with the tribe of Levi in old time, so for the future this commandment and threat will be as vigorously observed and take the place of the old covenant. This explanation is too involved and refined to be acceptable. It is easiest to translate, with Henderson and Reinke, "Because my covenant was with Levi," and to understand God as implying that he warned and punished the priests, because he willed that the covenant with Levi should hold good, and he thus desired to have a body of priests who would keep their vows and maintain the true priestly character. What that character is he proceeds to unfold.

Vers. 5—9.—§ 5. *In contrast with these evil ministers, the character of the true priest is sketched, and thus the faults of the former are shown in darker colours.*

Ver. 5.—**My covenant was with him of** life and peace; rather, *with him was life and peace.* This is one side of the covenant, that which God gave—the blessing of life, abundance, prosperity, and secure and undisturbed enjoyment of these, in the everlasting priesthood, in agreement with the promise to Phinehas (Numb. xxv. 12; comp. Deut. xxxiii. 8—11). **I gave them to him for the fear,** etc. I gave him life and peace. The pronominal suffix "them" is not expressed in the Greek and Latin Versions, and is absent from many Hebrew manuscripts, which read, "I gave him fear." So the Vulgate, *Dedi eis timorem et timuit me;* Septuagint, Ἔδωκα αὐτῷ ἐν φόβῳ φοβεῖσθαί με, "I gave him the fear of me." This expresses man's part in the covenant: God gave him certain blessings on condition that he feared, reverenced, worshipped, and obeyed the Lord. The last part of the verse as now read is more simply explained, "and (my covenant with him was, or, I gave him) fear, and he did fear me." God's gifts were life and peace. Levi's part was fear of God: this he performed. The ideal priest observed all the duties of piety and reverence, and therefore in his case the covenant stood firm and was duly carried out.

Ver. 6.—**The law** (*teaching*) **of truth was in his mouth.** All his teaching rested on those truths which were enshrined in the Divine Law (Deut. xxxi. 10—13; xxxiii. 10). **Iniquity;** *unfair decision.* Neither false doctrine nor perverse judgment was found in him (Deut. xvii. 8—10; xix. 17). **Walked with me.** Not only his teaching was true, but his life was pure and good; he was the friend of God, living as always in his presence, in peace and uprightness. So Enoch and Noah are said to have "walked with God" (Gen. v. 24; vi. 9). **Did turn many away from iniquity.** The faithful discharge of duties and the holy life and teaching of the good priest led many sinners to repentance and amendment

Ver. 7.—**For the priest's lips should keep knowledge.** It was the priest's duty to study the Law and to teach it faithfully, as it is said of Aaron, in Ecclus. xlv. 17, "He gave unto him his commandments, and authority in the statutes of judgments, that he should teach Jacob the testimonies, and inform Israel in his laws." **The law,** here and vers 6, 8, means system of teaching, or the *torah.* **At his mouth.** The priest was the appointed interpreter of the Law (see Lev. x. 11; Deut. xvii. 9—11; xxxiii. 10;

and the note on Hag. ii. 11). **He is the messenger of the Lord.** He announces God's will to men, explaining the Law to meet the varied circumstances which occur in daily life; he intervenes between God and man, offering man's worship to the Lord. So Haggai (i. 13) is called "the Lord's messenger," or angel. Some see here an allusion to Malachi's own name or office (see Introduction, § II.; comp. Deut. xxi. 5; 2 Chron. xvii. 9).

Ver. 8.—**But ye are departed out of the way.** The priests of this time had far declined from the high ideal set forth in vers. 6, 7, the "way" in which God would have had them to walk. **Ye have caused many to stumble at** (*in*) **the law.** By their example and teaching they had made the Law a stumbling-block, causing many to err, while they fancied they were not infringing God's commandments. Septuagint, Ἠσθενήσατε πολλοὺς ἐν νόμῳ, "Ye made many weak [equivalent to ἠσθενώσατε] in the Law." **Ye have corrupted the covenant of Levi** (see ver. 5). They broke their part of the covenant, therefore Jehovah held himself no longer bound by it. They did not pay him due reverence and obedience; he withdrew the blessings promised to Levi, as threatened (ver. 2).

Ver. 9.—**Contemptible.** The glory of the priesthood and the honour that belonged to it (Ecclus. xlv. 7, etc.) were now turned into disgrace and contempt, when men compared the actual with the ideal. "Them that honour me I will honour, and they that despise me shall be lightly esteemed" (1 Sam. ii. 30). **Have been partial in the law;** Revised Version, *have had respect of persons in the law;* or, *in your teaching,* as vers. 6, 8. The prophet names one special sin of the priests, and that the most flagrant—perversion of judgment, partiality in the administration of the Law. The same complaint is found in Micah iii. 11 (comp. 2 Chron. xix. 7).

Vers. 10—16.—Part II. CONDEMNATION OF PRIESTS AND PEOPLE FOR ALIEN MARRIAGES AND FOR DIVORCES.

Ver. 10.—**Have we not all one Father?** In proceeding to his new subject, the violations of the law of marriage, the prophet pursues his habitual method. He starts with a general principle, here assuming an interrogative form, and on it builds his rebuke. The priests were guilty, if not of profane marriages, at any rate of sinful neglect in not warning the people against them. Many take the "one-father" to be Abraham (Isa. li. 2), and it is no objection to this view that he was also the progenitor of Ishmaelites, Edomites, etc., because there

was at this time no question about marriage with these nations, but with Canaanites, Moabites, Egyptians, and so on. But the parallelism with the following clause shows that by the Father is meant Almighty God (comp. ch. i. 6; Deut. xxxii. 6; Isa. lxiii. 16). **Hath not one God created us?** Hath not God taken us as his peculiar people, so as to call us his sons and his firstborn (comp. Exod. iv. 22, 23; Deut. xxxii. 18; Isa. i. 2; Jer. iii. 19)? Of course, God created all men; but the Jews alone recognized him as Creator. The prophet's proposition is that all Israelites were spiritual brothers and sisters, equally loved and chosen by God. From this he argues that in sinning against one another, they offended their common Father, and broke the family compact. **Deal treacherously.** Act faithlessly against one another. He does not yet say in what this treachery consists, but adds, **by profaning the covenant of our fathers.** He unites himself with them, because he suffered in their sin. They violated the covenant by which God chose them to be his peculiar people and placed himself in mysterious relation to them, on condition that they should keep themselves aloof from the evil nations around them, and avoid all connection with them and their practices. By intermarriages with the heathen, they profaned this covenant. This evil was one which Ezra had done his best to eradicate, using most stringent measures for its suppression (Ezra ix., x.); Nehemiah, too, contended against those who had contracted these marriages, when he found on his return to Jerusalem many such transgressors (Neh. xiii. 23—28); and now the prophet lifts up his voice in the cause of purity and obedience. The warning against these mixed unions is found in Exod. xxxiv. 16; Deut. vii. 3; Josh. xxiii. 12, 13.

Ver. 11.—**Judah,** the whole nation, is guilty of this crime, has broken her promised faith. The special sin, mixed marriages, is named at the end of the verse. **In Israel and in Jerusalem.** The mention of Israel, the sacred covenant name, is meant to make the contrast between profession and practice more marked. But some critics would here cancel the word "Israel," as being a clerical error (see note, Zech. i. 19). Jerusalem is named as the centre of the theocracy, which gave its tone to the people. **For Judah hath profaned the holiness** (*sanctuary*) **of the Lord which he loved** (*loveth*); Septuagint, Ἐβεβήλωσεν Ἰούδας τὰ ἅγια Κυρίου, ἐν οἷς ἠγάπησε, "Judah profaned the holy things of the Lord in which he delighted." Many consider that by the "sanctuary" is meant the temple, into which these heathen wives had penetrated, either led by curiosity or introduced by their profane husbands. But we have no knowledge that this was the case. It is better to take "the sanctuary," or that which is holy unto the Lord, to be the chosen nation itself, the community beloved by God, which was holy by election and profession, even as Christians are commonly called saints in the Epistles. (For the term as applied to the Israelites, see Exod. xix. 6; xxii. 31; Lev. xi. 44; xix. 2; comp. Ezra ix. 2; Neh. xiii. 29.) **The daughter of a strange god.** A woman who is an idolatress, who adhered to a foreign deity (Jer. ii. 27), as the Israelites are called "sons of Jehovah," as joined to him in communion (Deut. xiv. 1; Prov. xiv. 26). The LXX. omits the point of the charge, rendering, καὶ ἐπετήδευσεν εἰς θεοὺς ἀλλοτρίους, "and followed after strange gods."

Ver. 12.—**Will cut off.** The Hebrew is an imprecation, "May the Lord cut off" (Deut. vii. 2, 3). It implies that the transgressor shall be deprived of his position as one of the covenant people, and shall leave no one to maintain his name and family. **The man.** Others render, "unto the man," making the following words the direct object of the verb. **The master and the scholar;** so the Vulgate, *magistrum et discipulum;* literally, *the watcher and the answerer,* i.e. the watchman and the inhabitants of the city; the LXX., reading somewhat differently, has, ἕως καὶ ταπεινωθῇ ἐκ σκηνωμάτων Ἰακώβ, "until he be brought low from the tents of Jacob," meaning, until he repent and return humbly to obedience. In this case the term "cut off" must be taken in some milder sense than "exterminate." The present text, however, seems to be a kind of alliterative proverbial saying to express totality, everybody; though whence it arose, and what is its exact signification, are matters of great uncertainty. Some take the phrase to mean, "every waking and speaking person," *i.e.* every living soul. The English and Latin Versions proceed on the assumption (which Pusey denies) that the first verb can be taken actively, "he that awakeneth," the teacher being so called as stimulating the scholar, who is named "the answerer." The Targum and Syriac explain it by "son and son's son." Of the various suggestions offered, the most probable is that it is a military phrase derived from the challenge of the sentinels and the answer thereto, which in time came to denote the whole inhabitants of a camp or city. **The tabernacles.** The dwellings. Or the word, as Dr. Cox supposes, may belong to the original saying, and have come down from the remote period when the Israelites lived in tents. **And him that offereth an offering** (*minchah*) **unto the Lord of hosts.**

The same punishment shall fall on one who offers even an oblation of meal for men who are guilty of this sin. This sin would appertain specially to the priests. Or we may take the clause in a general sense. God will cut off every such transgressor, even if he try to propitiate the Lord by making an offering before him (Ecclus. xxxv. [xxxii.] 12), "Do not think to corrupt with gifts; for such he will not receive: and trust not to unrighteous sacrifices; for the Lord is Judge, and with him is no respect of persons."

Ver. 13.—Not only did they marry heathen females, but they divorced their own legitimate wives to facilitate such unholy alliances. **This have ye done again;** *this again ye do.* Here is another and a further offence. Others take "again" in the sense of "a second time," referring to the fact that Ezra had effected a reform in this matter, but the people had relapsed into the same sin. But the first explanation is preferable. Septuagint, καὶ ταῦτα, ἃ ἐμίσουν, ἐποιεῖτε, "and this which I hated ye did." **Covering** (*ye cover*) **the altar of the Lord with tears.** The prophet, as before (ver. 10), does not at once declare what this fresh outrage is, but intimates its nature. The picture he exhibits is that of a multitude of repudiated wives coming to the temple with weeping and lamentation, and laying their cause before the Lord. **Insomuch that he regardeth not the offering any more.** This cruel and wicked conduct raised a barrier between them and God, so that he regarded with favour no offering of theirs.

Ver. 14.—**Yet ye say, Wherefore?** Here is the usual sceptical objection, as in ch. i. 6, 7. The people will not acknowledge their guiltiness, and ask, "Why is God displeased with us? why are our offerings not acceptable?" The prophet replies, **Because the Lord hath been witness,** etc. The sin is now disclosed. Their marriages had been made before God; he who first instituted matrimony (Gen. ii. 24) was a witness of the contract and gave it his sanction (comp. Gen. xxxi. 50). **The wife of thy youth.** Whom thou didst marry when thine affections were pure and fresh, and for whom thy love was strong and simple (Prov. v. 18). **Against whom thou hast dealt treacherously;** Septuagint, "whom thou hast deserted." This wife of thine thou hast betrayed, breaking faith with her by repudiating her. **The wife of thy covenant.** With whom thou didst make a solemn vow and covenant, to violate which is a monstrous crime. We have very little information respecting the religious ceremonies connected with a Jewish wedding. The previous espousal was a formal proceeding, conducted by friends and parents, and confirmed by oaths. The actual marriage seems to have been accompanied by certain solemn promises and blessings (see Prov. ii. 17; Ezek. xvi. 8; Gen. xxiv. 60; Ruth iv. 11, 12; Tobit vii. 13; Smith, 'Dict. of Bible').

Ver. 15.—**And did not he make one? Yet had he the residue of the spirit.** The passage has always been a *crux*, and has received many interpretations. The Anglican rendering (which, however, is probably not correct) is thus explained: God made at first one man and one woman, to show the oneness of marriage, and God gave man the breath of life and the residue to the woman; he made them both equally living souls; therefore divorce was never contemplated in the first institution of marriage. Others take "one" to mean Abraham, and explain: Abraham did not do so, *i.e.* did not repudiate his legitimate wife, though barren; and he had a share of the spirit of right, or he had excellence of spirit. But these are very forced interpretations, and do not occur naturally from a consideration of the words. The Hebrew may be translated more satisfactorily, "Not any one has done so who has a remnant of the spirit (*ruach*)." No one acts as you have done who has in him any of that Divine life which God at first breathed into man; in other words, no man of conscience and virtue has ever thus divorced his wife. The reading of the Septuagint varies here, the Vatican manuscript giving, Οὐ καλὸν ἐποίησε; "Did he not well?" and the Alexandrian, οὐκ ἄλλος ἐποίησε: but both seem to imply an interpretation such as we have just given. **And wherefore one? That he might seek a godly seed.** Why did one act in this way? was it that he might have godly children? Surely not. No one would divorce his lawful Hebrew wife, and marry an idolatress, who wished to leave a holy posterity behind him. Many commentators, thinking that Abraham is here meant, and that the prophet is meeting an objection which might be founded upon his action with regard to Hagar, translate, "And what did the one? He was seeking a godly seed." Abraham at Sarah's request took Hagar to wife, in order to have the promised seed; he dismissed her in order to carry out the purpose of God in confining the promise to Isaac. Therefore his conduct is no support for those who repudiate their own wives and marry strange women, not to raise up children for God, but to satisfy their carnal lusts. It is difficult, however, to see how the prophet's hearers could have understood the allusion without further explanation. As Ribera pithily observes (quoted by Knabenbauer), "Neque ita clare ex re allata designatur (Abraham), ut non potius divi-

natione quam explicatione opus sit ad eum eruendum." It may also be remarked that the reference to the patriarch would not have been altogether successful, if the auditors remembered the Keturahites, who, though sprung from Abraham, were not "a godly seed." The LXX. has, Καὶ εἴπατε, τί ἄλλο ἢ σπέρμα ζητεῖ ὁ Θεός; "And ye said, What else than seed doth God seek?" as if the increase of population, from whatever source, was the only object required. This may have been one thought of the people, but it can hardly be got out of the present Hebrew text. **Take heed to your spirit.** Beware lest ye lose the spirit which God has given you. By acting thus contrary to conscience and the light vouchsafed to them, they ran the risk of being deprived altogether of this heavenly guide, and losing all distinction between right and wrong.

Ver. 16.—**He hateth putting away.** This is another reason against divorce: God hates it. It is contrary to his original institution, and was only allowed for the hardness of men's hearts (see Deut. xxiv. 1, etc.; Matt. xix. 3—9). Septuagint, "If thou hate her and dismiss her," etc.; Vulgate, "If thou hate her, put her away," which seems to encourage divorce, whereas in the context divorce is strongly condemned. Hence Jerome considers these words to be spoken by the Jews, quoting in their defence Moses' precept. Others think that they are ironical—Put her away, if you please; but you must bear the consequences. **For one covereth violence with his garment.** He who thus divorces his wife shows himself openly to all beholders as an iniquitous man. So the clause is better rendered, *And one (who does so) covereth his garment with violence,* or, *violence covereth his garment.* Iniquity attaches itself to him plainly, encircling and enfolding him; the clothing of iniquity is the mark of the foul soul within. The notion of "garment" being here used figuratively for wife (as Hitzig supposes) is without proof. Such a metaphor is certainly unknown to Hebrew literature, though there is something like it in Arabic, "Wives are your attire, and ye are theirs" (Koran). Bishop Wordsworth considers that the phrase in the text refers to the custom of the bridegroom in espousals casting the skirt of his garment over her who was betrothed to him (see Ruth iii. 9). So the idea would be, "Ye cast your skirt over iniquity, and betroth violence to yourselves for a bride." But this seems somewhat forced. **Take heed . . . treacherously.** A repetition of the warning in ver. 15.

Ver. 17—ch. iv. 6.—**Part III. THE DAY OF THE LORD.**

Ver. 17—ch. iii. 6. — § 1. *The faithless*

people, disheartened by present circumstances, doubted God's providence, and disbelieved his promises; but the prophet announces the coming of the Lord to judgment, preceded by his messenger. He shall refine his people and exterminate sinners.

Ver. 17.—**Ye have wearied the Lord with your words.** This is the introduction to the new section. The prophet makes his charge. The faithless multitude have, as it were, worn out God's patience by their murmuring and discontent. Because their expectations of prosperity and glory were not at once fulfilled, they called in question God's justice and holiness, and even the future judgment. The LXX. connects this verse with the preceding, Καὶ οὐ μὴ ἐγκαταλίπητε

οἱ παροξύναντες τὸν Θεὸν ἐν τοῖς λόγοις ὑμῶν, "And forsake them not, ye who provoked God with your words." But it is best to take this as the beginning of a new subject. **Yet ye say.** This is the usual sceptical objection. **Every one that doeth evil is good in the sight of the Lord.** They complain that, though they are God's peculiar people, they are left in low estate, while the heathen, men that "do evil," are happy and prosperous (comp. Ps. xxxvii., lxxiii.). **He delighteth in them.** They choose to consider that the worldly prosperity of the heathen is a sign of God's special favour, or else that he acts unjustly. **Where is the God of judgment?** (Isa. xxx. 18). Why does not God perform his promises to Israel, and execute vengeance on the enemy?

HOMILETICS.

Ver. 2.—*Our blessings cursed.* The cursing of blessings is a " strange work " to the blessed God, " the Father of mercies," who rather delights to turn curses into blessings. We may note—
I. THE CAUSES OF THIS CURSE. It may be traced to two things. 1. A disregard of the great end of life, " to glorify God." The motto of every creature, and especially of every redeemed sinner, should be that of Ignatius Loyola in its best sense, " Ad majorem gloriam Dei." No grander object can be sought. To fail in the endeavour to " give unto the Lord the glory due unto his Name " is to begin to lose " the promise " which godliness gives of both worlds. It empties our " blessings " of their true blessedness, and begins to corrupt them with a curse like—

" The little pitted speck in garnered fruit,
That rotting inward slowly moulders all."

2. Neglect of God's appeals and warnings. He remonstrates, as he did again and again with the Jews, by his prophets. But if we neither hear nor heed, and will not lay these warnings to heart, the corrupting process goes on, the curse is ripening, " the rod hath blossomed; pride hath budded" (cf. Jer. vi. 16—20; Zech. i. 3—6; vii. 11—14). The remedies being cast aside, the disease holds on its course till " the whole head is sick," etc. (Isa. i. 5, 6). It is natural to God to sweeten the bitter waters of life and to neutralize its poisons (2 Kings ii. 19—22; iv. 38—41). But sin reverses these miracles of mercy, and constrains God to turn our water into blood, our food into poison, to curse our blessings.
II. THE SIGNS OF THIS CURSE. It may manifest itself in various ways; *e.g.*: 1. Withholding the gifts which God delights to bestow (Amos iv. 6—9; Hag. i. 9; ch. iii. 10, scarcity implied). 2. Withholding the power to enjoy the gifts which God does bestow. It may be the food of a wealthy invalid (Eccles. vi. 1, 2) or the money of a miser haunted by fear of the workhouse (Job xx. 22). The loss may be in the spiritual sphere—the power of receiving impressions of truth and duty may have been " taken away" (Matt. xiii. 12—15), because sinned away. The talents of an ungodly minister may be rather a curse than a blessing to him and to his flock, just as the blessings pronounced in words by these ungodly priests (Numb. vi. 22—26) may have become practically curses to the people. 3. Blessings themselves may be turned into curses. Illust.: The high wages of the working classes in recent years, and the general prosperity of the country, leading to a great increase of extravagance, self-indulgence, and intemperance. The blessing of enjoying free-will and the power of self-guidance and control may become a most terrible curse when we "lean on our own understanding " and pursue " a way which seemeth right " in our eyes, but the end whereof is death (Prov. xiv. 12; Ps. lxxxi. 11, 12). Our highest privileges may

thus become curses to us, as were the Christian profession of Ananias and the apostleship of Judas. Even Christ may become "a stone of stumbling and a rock of offence" (1 Pet. ii. 6—8; John ix. 40), and his ministers "a savour from death unto death" (2 Cor. ii. 16). As John Howe says, "When the gospel becomes deadly to a man, that is a most terrible sort of death; to die by a gospel plague is a most terrible way of dying."

Vers. 6, 7.—*The qualifications and objects of Christian ministers.* Aaron and the original priests of the house of Levi are here held up as a pattern to their degenerate descendants. Reference is made to the higher departments of the priest's work, for teaching is a nobler work than sacrificing, even according to a divinely appointed and typical ritual. Allusions to this work of teaching by priests or Levites may be found in Lev. x. 11; Deut. xxxiii. 10; 2 Chron. xv. 3; xvii. 8, 9; Neh. viii. 9; Micah iii. 11, etc. This work, being common to Jewish priests and Christian ministers, makes the application we have given to the words quite legitimate. We are reminded of the following qualifications and aims essential for a minister of Christ.

I. A MESSAGE FROM GOD. "He is the messenger of the Lord of hosts." We are sent to the world by our Divine Master with definite instructions. There is a "glorious gospel of the blessed God committed to our trust." That gospel embodies the doc'rines of "the faith which was once for all delivered unto the saints." If we have no definite gospel to preach, for which we are willing to contend, to suffer, and if needs be to die, we had better hold our peace, for we are not "messengers of the Lord of hosts." "Wherefore wilt thou run, my son, seeing thou hast no tidings ready?" (2 Sam. xviii. 22); "I have not sent these prophets, yet they ran: I have not spoken to them, yet they prophesied" (Jer. xxiii. 21). A self-styled ambassador, with no instructions from his monarch, would be an object hardly less pitiable and contemptible than a speaker arrogating the position of Christ's minister, but quite uncertain as to what to speak in Christ's Name. The burden of our message is not, "Thus *I think;*" but, "Thus *saith the Lord;*" "Hear what the Spirit saith to the Churches." Christ bids us to teach men "to observe all things whatsoever I have commanded you." When men gather around us they should be able to say, "Now therefore are we all here present before God, to hear all things that are commanded thee of God." We are thus reminded of the need of: 1. Careful study of the Law of God, like Ezra (vii. 6, 10), Daniel (ix. 2), Timothy (1 Tim. iv. 13). We must be scribes "instructed unto the kingdom of heaven," lest we should misread and misunderstand our message. 2. Of close communion with God; for errors that arise from sources that are spiritual may be more dangerous than those that are merely intellectual (see John iii. 20; v. 44; vii. 17; viii. 43; xii. 42, 43; Heb. iii. 12).

II. FIDELITY IN DELIVERING IT. We learn this from: 1. The unalterable claims of truth (ver. 6). All truth has the authority of a law. We must be prepared to teach others and to learn for ourselves that rather than deny God by a lie in business or any sphere of life, it would be better to be burned alive. A martyr's spirit is essential to a minister's character. If this is true of us, we may urge the same on our hearers, for there are no two standards of morality, one for the clergy the other for the laity. All are required to love the Lord their God with all their heart, and therefore never to "hold down the truth in unrighteousness" (Rom. i. 18). The urgent duty of fidelity on the part of Christ's ministers is seen further because of: 2. Our responsibility as "stewards of the mysteries of God." So far as those "mysteries," first revealed to the world by inspired apostles, are understood by us, we are stewards of them. And "it is required in stewards that a man be found faithful" (1 Cor. iv. 1, 2). We are to "keep knowledge" for those who at any time may "seek the law" at our mouths. If others teach "another gospel" which may be more popular and acceptable, we are to decline popularity, "not as pleasing men, but God which trieth the heart." "For if I pleased men I should not be the servant of Christ" (see Jer. xxiii. 28, 29; 2 Cor. ii. 17; iv. 1, 2; Gal. i. 10; 1 Thess. ii. 4). 3. Our relation to the souls of our hearers. Their object should be to seek God's law from our lips that they may do it, and ours to turn them from iniquity. Our one object should be to declare the whole counsel of God so clearly, faithfully, and affectionately, that, whether men will hear or forbear, we shall be free from the blood of all. Elihu's words are an excellent motto for a preacher

(Job xxxiii. 3). The words, "Death and life are in the power of the tongue," suggest solemn thoughts as to fidelity on the part of preachers. What need of care, both in public and private, in dealing with "seeking" souls, to point them direct to Christ, and not to any ceremonies or sacraments (Acts xx. 20, 21; 1 Cor. ii. 1—5), lest at some critical point in their spiritual history our lips should fail to impart the "knowledge," "the law," the message from the Lord of hosts which they need, and they should be directed along a wrong track rather than in "the way everlasting." The sin of unfaithfulness is exposed in vers. 8, 9. Ministers may be "partial in the Law," *e.g.* winking at follies and sins fashionable among the rich, while severely condemning the sins of the poor, etc. But fidelity needs to be combined with discrimination (Mark iv 33, 34; John xvi. 12; 1 Cor. iii. 1, 2; 2 Tim. ii. 15; Heb. v. 11, 12). "For as all men cannot dive and fetch precious stones from the deep, but he that is cunning and hath the art of it; so not all, but the wise can either teach or conceive the deep mysteries. First, children must be taught letters, then syllables, after words, then construction, and after all the matter."

III. A LIFE IN HARMONY WITH IT. "He walked with me in peace and equity." These words remind us of the essential elements of a truly consistent Christian life. There must be righteousness with God, bringing after it peace with God. This righteousness is twofold. 1. A justification, which makes us "*accepted in* the Beloved," and gives peace with God (Rom. v. 1; Eph. i. 6). 2. A right state of heart, a conscious integrity of purpose, which ensures our being "*accepted of* him," well pleasing to him, and which brings with it a still deeper and purer peace (Isa. xlviii. 18; Rom. xiv. 17, 18). God desires that we should live in his perfect peace and favour in order that we "might serve him without fear, in holiness and righteousness before him all the days of our life." Such peace and equity toward God will ensure the same blessings in relation to our fellow-men. This consistency of conduct is especially needed in the ministers of Christ. They must maintain this character in their homes (1 Tim. iii. 2—5), in the Church (1 Pet. v. 3), and in the world (1 Tim. iii. 7). The guilt and shame of inconsistent lives is exposed in vers. 8, 9, and is illustrated by the history of Eli's sons; 1 Sam. ii. 30 being fulfilled in them, and in these priests ("I have made you contemptible." They had said in their hearts, "The table of the Lord is contemptible;" so God would requite them "measure for measure"), and in all unfaithful ministers; who will be despised by the people they seek to conciliate and please.

IV. ZEAL FOR THE RECEPTION OF IT. By faithfully discharging the duties of his calling, Levi, *i.e.* the priesthood, "did turn many away from iniquity." In doing so he did nothing more than what the standing and vocation of the priest required. The knowledge communicated to the mind was to be imparted by the lips. Without zeal for the reception of the message, and love that seeks the salvation of souls by means of it, the knowledge and "the tongues" of preachers profit nothing. The charge given to Paul (Acts xxvi. 18) and to Timothy (2 Tim. iv. 5) applies to every "good minister of Jesus Christ." We are appointed as witnesses for God; as labourers together with God; as ambassadors to promote reconciliation with God. We are ministers of the good tidings of Christ; soldiers of Christ (to overcome men's "evil" by Christ's "good"). We are lights ("the lamp that burneth and shineth," John v. 35) to light men to Jesus Christ. We are fishers of men, that we may secure them for Christ; undershepherds of souls, that we may keep them; watchmen, that we may warn them. Mediately we may be said to be saviours of souls (Jas. v. 19, 20). So earnest should we be to secure this end, that our hearers should be able to say of us, as a plain woman did of Robert McCheyne of Dundee, "He seemed as though he were almost dyin' to have you converted." Such a ministry will secure its object (1 Tim. iv. 12—16). A painful contrast is suggested between this ideal of the ministry and our attainments in attempting to reach it. We should learn humility and be melted into penitence. For God holds us responsible for what we might have been and might have done after all that he has done for us—a truth we are reminded of by God's appeal in Isa. v. 4. But the lofty standard held out before us may also stimulate us to "forget the things that are behind," etc., and to make the aims of the Christ-like Apostle Paul our own (1 Cor. ix. 16—22; Col. i. 28, 29).

Vers. 10—16.— *The sin of conjugal unfaithfulness.* We here use the term "unfaithfulness" in its widest sense, extending far beyond the sin of unchastity. We note—

I. UNFAITHFULNESS TO GOD IS THE ROOT-SIN OF ALL OTHER FORMS OF INFIDELITY. The sins denounced in the earlier verses of this book are quite sufficient to account for the criminality here exposed. Those who profane the "covenant" and the "holiness" of God in their hearts, and who do not seek "to give glory" to his Name (ver. 2), are easily betrayed into glaring acts of wrong against the nearest and dearest on earth. "The backslider in heart shall be filled with his own ways," and those ways are all downward ways. The first sin of Adam and Eve led to mutual recrimination. Disobedience towards the heavenly Father paves the way for discord in the earthly home. "Therefore take heed *to your spirit*" (ver. 16).

II. THIS INFIDELITY SHOWED ITSELF IN TWO FORMS. 1. *In unlawful marriages.* (Ver. 11.) This was a proof of unfaithfulness both to the national covenant (Ezra ix. 10—12) and to God's purpose in marriage. Similar unfaithfulness shows itself under the Christian covenant when such precepts as 1 Cor. vii. 39 ("only in the Lord") and 2 Cor. vi. 14—18 are set at naught. For a Christian to marry an enemy of Christ, "a covetous person who is an idolater," or a slave of "the god of this world," is a breach of the sanctity of marriage. It tends to degrade it into a carnal union; it certainly grossly neglects its object as a spiritual bond, in which all material considerations are to be held as subordinate to that "great mystery," typical of the Divine union of Christ and his Church. By such sin a professed disciple of Christ virtually cuts himself off from the commonwealth of the saints, that he may join the congregation of the aliens. He thus exposes himself to the judgment of God, who will be impartial in his treatment of all classes, of those that lead into sin and those that are led (ver. 12; Job xii. 16), and who will accept no "offering," no outward service, that might be regarded as a blind to the eyes of the Judge, presented by a man who sought thus to compound for his sin (Prov. xxi. 27; xxviii. 9; Isa. i. 13—17; Amos v. 21—24). 2. *In ill treatment of their lawful wives.* This is the second form of unfaithfulness, and reminds us that "the way of sin is downhill, and one violation of the covenant is an inlet to another" (M. Henry). Unfaithfulness to the marriage vow in any form (unkindness or neglect, as well as adultery or divorce) is here condemned by the following considerations. (1) Religious services are marred by moral delinquencies (ver. 13). It is a terrible thing to send any soul weeping in its prayer to God, and really, if not intentionally, appealing to him for avengement. How much worse if that soul should be the partner of thy life! God seeks songs, not groans, in our services. He desires unity in the home, "that your prayers be not hindered" (1 Pet. iii. 7). How, then, must he regard the prayers of a wife deprecating the unkindness of her husband! (2) God was a witness of every word and vow at the marriage ceremony. Through the following years he notes how those promises are kept. He is still a witness of every act of wrong on the part of either husband or wife. And he is "the avenger of all such" (1 Thess. iv. 6). (3) The tender relations cruelly violated. Aggravations of this sin are suggested by each of the terms, "companion," "wife of thy youth," "wife of thy covenant." (4) God's design in marriage (ver. 15). Polygamy is fatal to godly family life and training, and discord most perilous to it. (5) The infectious influence of sins. If we deal treacherously against our "brother" (ver. 10), we tempt him to act in a similar way. This is applicable to the influence of an unfaithful husband on his wife, or on other husbands or on the unmarried whom by his example he may debauch and destroy. The master and the scholar, the blind leader of the blind,—all shall fall into the ditch. (6) The Divine hatred which such sins incur (ver. 16). There are several things which we are expressly told in Scripture God hates (cf. Deut. xii. 31; xvi. 22; Prov. vi. 16—19; viii. 13; Isa. lxi. 8; Jer. xliv. 4). Among these things divorce and every other form of conjugal treachery and unfaithfulness are included. Men may make light of many of these sins, may patronize the criminals, and deride their censors. But see Luke xvi. 14, 15, and the lesson it suggests. What God hates may we dread, and seek never to be unjust in the least, lest we be unjust also in much!

Ver. 10.—*The brotherhood of men.* "Liberty, equality, fraternity," are Divine ideas, though men have sometimes striven to embody them in crude or even repulsive and brutal forms. Men are equals, inasmuch as they are all the creatures of the one

God who created them. The revelation of that Creator as "the Father of spirits" constitutes those created spirits into a brotherhood. From this fraternal relation the claim to liberty and more than liberty follows.

I. SOUND ETHICS MUST BE BASED ON A TRUE THEOLOGY. Our relations to men depend on our relation to God. Our treatment of them will vary with our conceptions of those relations. False views of God are fatal to consistent conduct towards our brethren. And though our ethics may be partially true, they will be practically powerless unless supported by "the knowledge of the truth which is according to godliness." Hence the practical impotence of heathen ethics, whether those of Socrates or of Confucius. We must recognize such truths as these: that we are creatures of the one God, "in whose hand our breath is, and whose are all our ways;" that we are pensioners on his bounty; that we are sinners dependent on his mercy; and that, nevertheless, we are children entitled to claim our place in his family. We shall then recognize that we are bound to treat all our fellow-creatures as members of the same family, sharing with us in the same bounty and mercy of the Father of all, "who willeth that all men should be saved." Jesus Christ, in whom that will is revealed, is the bond of unity, for "the Head of every man is Christ."

II. THERE IS A "COVENANT OF OUR FATHERS" MORE EXTENSIVE THAN THAT WHICH GOD MADE WITH THE JEWS. We can trace it back beyond Moses or Abraham to "our first father;" "for God hath made of one blood all nations of men;" "for we are also his offspring." The terms of this covenant are found in "the law written in our hearts." Hence moral law and Divine retribution are found beyond the limits of an inspired revelation. We see in the Bible illustrations of God's judgments denounced on: 1. The sins of the Hebrews against their own brethren; *e.g.* the re-enslavement of the freedmen (Jer. xxxiv.). 2. The crimes of Hebrews towards strangers, though they were heathens; *e.g.* Saul's massacre of the Gibeonites (2 Sam. xxi.), Zedekiah's perjury against Nebuchadnezzar (2 Chron. xxxvi. 13). 3. The outrages of heathens upon their brother heathens, as when the King of Moab "burned the bones of the King of Edom into lime" (Amos ii. 1).

III. A SIN AGAINST A BROTHER IS A SIN AGAINST GOD, WHO MADE HIM A BROTHER. The warning of 1 Cor. viii. 12 is applicable beyond the limits of the Christian Church. It was a fearful prediction that "the brother shall betray the brother to death." Give to the term "brother" its Divine significance, and every act of treachery or unfaithfulness is seen to be odious to the Father of all. Hence the claims of truth towards our "neighbour, for we are members one of another;" of "all good fidelity" on the part of servants towards masters, "that they may adorn the doctrine of God;" of standing to our word, though it may be to our own hurt, that we may stand in the holy place of the Lord; of loving our enemies, that we may be children of our Father who is in heaven.

IV. THE FATHERHOOD OF GOD IS ONE GREAT MOTIVE FOR THE RIGHT TREATMENT OF HIS CHILDREN. Cruelty, tyranny, slavery, and every form of social wrong would then be banished from the family of God, the brotherhood of men. War would be as intolerable as fighting in the family circle. Punishment of offending brothers would only be inflicted under a grave sense of our responsibility towards their Father and ours. Practical benevolence would be inspired by God's love to us (1 John iii. 17). And as Abraham interceded for the preservation of the heathen Sodomites, so should we, by prayers and labours, seek the salvation of the whole nature ("spirit and soul and body," 1 Thess. v. 23) of those children of God who are still lost to the Father's home.

Notice, in conclusion, how the fuller revelation of the Fatherhood of God in Jesus Christ, and our adoption in him, gives power and pathos to all the truths we have mentioned and the motives to brotherly kindness we have enforced (1 John iv. 9—11). The knowledge of such a Father should inspire our hearts with the most tender compassion towards our brethren who know him not.

HOMILIES BY VARIOUS AUTHORS.

Ver. 2.—*The cursing of our blessings.* The direct address of this verse is to the priestly class, whose irreverence and indifference were so clearly shown in their offering the people's unworthy sacrifices, without attempting to reprove them, or endeavouring to awaken them to worthier and more spiritual views of sacrifice. When the ministry has become a fountain and a support of religious negligence and formality, the nation is placed in extreme peril, and severe providential dealings for the national and the priestly humiliation may be expected. The Divine threatening here is, "I will curse your blessings." This may mean either of three things; it may, quite possibly, include all three. It may mean, "I will turn the gifts of the people into curses." Or, "I will make the harvest of your work in the fields a failure and a curse instead of a blessing." Or, "I will make the blessing which you priests pronounce upon the people prove a curse to them." It should, however, be noticed that we now use the term "curse" with a connotation which is much more severe than that of Malachi. Our word "denunciation" would better fit the prophet's meaning.

I. TURNING THE PEOPLE'S GIFTS INTO CURSES. The priests received tithes, portions of the sacrifices, and offerings. God's judgment on the irreverent priests would come in limitation of tithes, disease from eating of the sick beasts offered as sacrifices, and the worthlessness of the offerings; for he who could give a mean thing to God would be sure to give mean things to his servants. Let God withdraw his added blessing, and our very "good things" fail to do us good. The psalmist recognizes this by praying that God would curse the blessings of his enemies (see Ps. lxix. 22). This is the permanent truth for all the ages, "The blessing of the Lord, it maketh rich, and he addeth no sorrow with it." Illustrate by the "little book" of Revelation, which was sweet to the taste, but bitter to the soul.

II. TURNING THE HARVEST OF TOIL INTO A CURSE. (Ver. 3.) What a blessing the harvest of the fields is, let the Harvest Home testify. These priests and Levites were compelled to go to their homes, and try and gain a living by the tillage of their land. But the judgment of God on irreverence and indifference would follow them there, and make their harvest a "heap." They would find that, whatever they touched, there was no Divine blessing on their work.

III. TURNING THE PRIESTLY BLESSING OF THE PEOPLE INTO A CURSE. The words of the priestly blessing are given in Numb. vi. 23—27. It is the deepest view of this Divine threatening to see it to mean this—The blessings which you, negligent and irreverent priests, pronounce in your formal way shall break in curses upon the heads of the people.—R. T.

Ver. 4.—*Judgments recalling covenant obligations.* Ver. 3 gives the great feature of God's judgment, first as a fact, and then by a figure. The Levites might shirk their temple duties, and go off to their fields; but God's hand would be upon them there; he would "corrupt" the seed they sowed, so that their harvest would be a failure. And so they would stand before the people impoverished, disgraced, and contemptible; with the stamp of failure on everything they touched. A recent account of the ceremony connected with the recovery of a Brahmin who had broken his caste explains the Eastern custom indicated in this verse. One part of the ceremony was the plastering of his entire body, except his eyes, with filth; he was then plunged into the river, and when the filth was washed away, the man was restored. The idea of ver. 4 is that this Divine judgment on unfaithful Levi must take the place of the covenant of life and peace which God had made with Levi, and would gladly have kept with his descendants. "I gave to Levi (that is, to you, the priestly tribe) a pledge of favour; but you have forfeited it, and it is now therefore turned into a threat of reprobation for your sins. No longer a covenant of peace, but of woe."

I. JUDGMENT IS GOD'S STRANGE WORK. It has not been sufficiently noticed, that God never threatens without indication of deep feeling of regret that he should be compelled to threaten. This may be illustrated from every part of Scripture, and especially in Divine dealings with the antediluvians, the Sodomites, the Israelites, and the Ninevites. The key-note is given in this exclamation, "Have I any pleasure at all in the death of the wicked?" God is most unworthily misrepresented when he is thought of as punishing in a spirit of coldness and indifference. To judge and afflict is holiest pain to him.

II. JUDGMENT IS GOD'S NECESSARY WORK. Punishment belongs to moral discipline.

It is an essential feature of it. It is part of all paternity. It is involved in the trust of childhood. God could not be his own Divine self if he did not punish. To let sin go would be unworthy of God. Father or King, he must be severe on wrong-doers.

III. THREATENING OF JUDGMENT IS GOD'S HUMBLING WORK. God always threatens before punishing. Threatening recalls obligations. Recalling obligations sets conduct in contrast with duty, and humbles us in the dust. Nothing bows us into penitence like seeing before us what we pledged ourselves to be, and being forced to place beside it what we are.—R. T.

Vers. 5, 6.—*The double feature of a Jehovah-covenant.* The covenant was made with the tribe of Levi; and the precise terms here referred to occur in the renewal of covenant with Phinehas, "Behold, I give unto him my covenant of peace: and he shall have it, and his seed after him, even the covenant of an everlasting priesthood" (Numb. xxv. 12, 13). A covenant is a mutual engagement entered into by two parties. Each party takes pledges; and each is exonorated from keeping his pledge if the other party breaks his. Too often the Divine covenant is treated as if it only involved God's putting himself under pledge of service to us. The truth needs to be emphasized that the covenant includes our pledge of faithful service to him. And this is true of the new covenant, sealed with the blood of Jesus Christ.

I. JEHOVAH'S PLEDGE TO LEVI. "My covenant was with him of life and peace." There is some reason for thinking that, before the Sinaitic revelation was made, the tribe of Levi provided the moral and religious teachers of the Israelites. They were designated for the special work of the priesthood, but the Divine covenant took a special shape in consequence of the loyalty and zeal of the Levites in the matter of the golden calf; and of Phinehas in vindicating the Divine claim to moral purity. God pledged two things: (1) "life," or permanence; and (2) "peace," or prosperity. Security that the honour and usefulness of the position should be quietly maintained. There is a Divine side to every covenant. God condescends to pledge himself to men. He promises his providings, preservings, guidings, redeemings, sanctifyings. In the new covenant, in the hands of the Mediator, the Lord Jesus Christ, all the old terms of covenant are renewed, and the special pledge of salvation from sin is added. He who has begun a good work in us is pledged to perfect it unto the day of Jesus Christ.

II. LEVI'S PLEDGE TO JEHOVAH. This side of covenant seldom receives sufficient attention. The Levites gave themselves to Jehovah's service; they pledged themselves to devote their lives to the services of his sanctuary, the teaching of his truth, and the upholding of his honour. So far as the early Levites were typified in Phinehas, they kept their pledge. Their personal characters honoured the covenant (ver. 6). Their steadfastness in duty, their cherished sense of right, and their active ministry against all iniquity, maintained the pledge of the covenant. Then how striking is the contrast suggested between the Levites of the early times and the Levites of Malachi's days! Their broken pledge meant that God was relieved of all obligation to keep his pledge to them.—R. T.

Ver. 6.—*The active influence of the steadfast man.* Levi is taken as the type of such a man. The man who walks with God in peace and equity cannot fail to exert a strong personal influence. He will "turn many from iniquity." The point of this sentence is that active influence for good is exerted by passive goodness. Men are powers by being established characters. Steadfastness is ministry. If it be so, then there are more workers for God than come into usual calculation. Priests and clergy have their power in what they *are*—in cultured, sanctified character—quite as truly as in Divine endowments and in trained efficiencies.

I. THE STEADFAST MAN EXERTS ACTIVE POWER OF REPROACH. He need utter no word; his steadfast goodness speaks loudly enough. There is no reproach comes to the evil liver like the simple presence of the good liver. Nothing shamed into silence the foulness of old prison scenes like the simple presence of the saintly Mrs. Fry. And in sublimer ways the truth is illustrated in the case of our Lord. The devils that possessed men felt the reproach of his simple presence, and cried out in their alarm. Every one of us who stands firm to righteousness and equity is actively reproving the unsteadiness and evil that are daily around us.

II. THE STEADFAST MAN EXERTS THE ACTIVE POWER OF EXAMPLE. The imitative faculty of man is more influential than we are wont to think. Everybody is disposed to make models. And all persons are materially helped by having high models of virtue in their spheres. Every individual has a sphere of influence. Within that sphere his example is an active power. We are all *ideals* to some one. Then " what manner of persons ought we to be ? "

III. THE STEADFAST MAN EXERTS A POSITIVE POWER ON MEN'S WILLS. To see a man who can stand fast to righteousness actually strengthens the decision and resolve of others. In it is the mastery of the tempter's lie that we cannot hope to be good. Our wills are weakened by the fear that goodness is unattainable, and it is of no use to try to be good. Every steadfast man proves that man can will the good and do it, and that God stands by such a man in his resolve.

IV. THE STEADFAST MAN EXERTS A POSITIVE SAVING INFLUENCE. He " turns men from iniquity." He cannot leave wrong-doers alone. If the priests of Malachi's time had been steadfast men, they would soon have turned the worshippers from the iniquity of bringing the lame and sick for sacrifice.—R. T.

Ver. 7.—*Reasonable expectations of God's ministers.* "The priest's lips should keep knowledge." The ideal priest is here characterized, not by ceremonial exactitude, but by moral integrity. Sacrificing is not so essential as religious knowledge, sound learning, and wholesome teaching. The proper expectation of God's ministers is that they will tell God's will to the people, not only because they *know* it, but even more because they *keep* it. In our religious teachers we look for adequacy of knowledge, and adequacy of experience.

I. ADEQUACY OF KNOWLEDGE. In some countries, and in some ages, the sacred ministry has been the chief source of secular knowledge for the people. That is not the case now, and in civilized countries. But still God's ministers need to be abreast, and to keep abreast, of all that is thought and known in their day, because to them is entrusted the work of conserving the Divine element in all knowledge, and the Divine relation to everything discovered. Unless ministers have adequate knowledge, they occupy a lower plane than the secular teachers, and fail to influence the higher range of students with Divine claims, truths, and principles. To put it in another way—The ministry must be on the level of the people if it is to sympathize with them ; but the ministry must be in intelligence and knowledge above the people, if it is to lift the people to higher things. Two points may be illustrated. 1. The ministers should gain knowledge *as men can gain it.* 2. The ministers should gain knowledge as *spiritual men only can gain it.* It is that spiritually acquired knowledge that is the minister's true efficiency ; and more especially that spiritual knowledge as it relates to the mysteries of the sacred Word.

II. ADEQUACY OF EXPERIENCE. There is book-knowledge, and there is experimental knowledge. It may be argued that for the common, everyday relations and duties of life, experience is a more valuable and practical teacher than books can be. It is certainly true that, for the ministry, experience is the essential thing. A man can only speak with power when " he has tasted and handled and felt the good word of life." The people have confidence in the teacher who has been taught of God in the discipline of life. What needs to be pointed out is that these two adequacies are not antagonistic. In their harmonious culture lies the true power.—R. T.

Ver. 10.—*Unfaithfulness to God involves injury to our brethren.* This verse begins a new subject, and it might have headed a new chapter. Answering to the indifference shown in regard to Divine worship was an indifference in regard to moral and family relations. Loose worship and loose social morality usually go together. Let men become careless about God's claims, and they will be found careless about marriage relations, and will lightly do wrong by the wives of their youth, in the mastery of their self-indulgence. Ezra and Nehemiah had to deal very sternly with the social evils arising from the ready divorce of Jewish wives for the sake of heathen wives. Malachi begins his expostulations on this matter by putting the people in mind that they owned one God and Father, in opposition to the idols of the heathen, and therefore should deal with one another as brethren. By the marriages with strangers they were dealing falsely and injuriously with their brethren and countrymen, by ill treating their daughters whom they had taken in marriage.

I. BREAKING GOD'S COVENANT BREAKS IT FOR OTHERS. Illustrate by the case of the golden calf. Those who took no part in the sin had to take part in the penalty. It is the bitterness of all wrong-doing that we can never keep its consequences to ourselves. "The fathers have eaten sour grapes, and the children's teeth are set on edge."

II. UNFAITHFULNESS TO GOD MAKES INJURY TO OUR BROTHER BY BEING A BAD EXAMPLE. Every man is bound to help his brother to be good. It is often shown that every man is bound to aid his brother in distress. It is not so often shown that every man has a claim on his brother, that he should help him to goodness. If a man does wrong, is unfaithful to God, he actually injures his brother by depriving him of his rights in his good example. Constantly we find wrong-doing excused by examples of wrong-doing. Sinners defraud their neighbours of their rights.

III. UNFAITHFULNESS TO GOD MAY LEAD TO POSITIVE ACTS OF INJURY TO OUR BRETHREN. The man who is strong enough to oppose God is usually masterful enough to injure his fellow. He who does not regard God is not likely to regard man. The love of God carries the love of man; the revolt against God is sure to involve the loosening of humanities.—R. T.

Ver. 11.—*Worship spoiled by the tears of the injured.* The divorced and abandoned wives went to the courts of the temple "with tears, with weeping, and with crying." "Their wail of lamentation mingled with the prayers and hymns of the sacrificing priests. How could the Lord 'regard the offering any more, or accept it at their hands,' when attended by such accompaniments?" The point forced on attention is this: Here were men bringing their sacrifices, and offering their prayers for God's blessing. And at the same time, here were the injured women praying against their prayers, and pleading that their worship should not be accepted. The tears were spoiling the worship. There is scarcely a thought more solemn and searching than the thought that few, if any, of our prayers go up to God unqualified and unchecked. We pray for, something prays against, and God withholds the blessing because the balance is in favour of the "against."

I. WE MAY PRAY AGAINST OUR OWN PRAYERS. It is said of St. Augustine that for some time he prayed, "Lord, convert me, but not yet." That was himself praying against himself. When duty prays one way and heart another; when we are not quite sure whether we want what we ask for; and when we are careless about receiving the answer,—we really pray against our own prayers. God may see our real prayer to be something quite other than our words.

II. OTHERS MAY BE PRAYING AGAINST OUR PRAYERS. This may be done unreasonably, and then God makes the prayer against strengthen the prayer for. Or it may be done reasonably, as when the cry of the widow, the fatherless, the divorced wife, the sweated workman, or the neglected sufferer, goes up to God against us. It would be well sometimes to ask ourselves whether there can be anything praying against our prayers.—R. T.

Ver. 15.—*God served by our meeting family obligations.* This verse is difficult to paraphrase. 'Speaker's Commentary' renders thus: "And hath no one acted thus (in putting away his wife) who yet had a remnant of sense in him?" The prophet makes the people say this in excuse of their conduct, and in allusion to the Patriarch Abraham, who put away his wife Hagar. Wordsworth puts the sentence interrogatively, "And did not one (Abraham) do it (*i.e.* put away his wife Hagar), and yet he had a remnant of the spirit?" The answer to the question is that Abraham was justified because he acted upon the special direction of God in seeking a seed within the covenant. But the people of Malachi's days were acting on pure self-willedness, and with no possible excuse of having received Divine directions. They were not serving God. God is served by the fulfilling of family obligations. He cannot be served by the shirking of ordinary obligations at the instance of unbridled passion.

I. FAMILY OBLIGATIONS SHOULD BE ENTERED UPON SERIOUSLY. And seriously means with (1) due self-control; (2) quietly; (3) thoughtfully; (4) prayerfully.

Early marriages are natural, and may be prudent; but when they are the result of impulse, of wrong-doing, or of lightness and inconsiderateness, they are a most fruitful source of trouble. No marriage should be consummated unless upon it the Divine blessing can be honestly, sincerely, heartily, and hopefully asked.

II. FAMILY OBLIGATIONS SHOULD BE MAINTAINED WITH PATIENT PERSISTENCY. Much occurs in married life to knit hearts together; but much must necessarily occur which, if permitted, would drive hearts asunder. Bearing and forbearing have to be resolute work until they become easy work. And every triumph over self makes every new triumph easier. If each lives for the other, all goes well. If either lives for self, all goes ill. "Let none deal unfaithfully by the wife of his youth."

III. FAMILY RELATIONS SHOULD BE BROKEN ONLY WITH EXTREME PAIN. Cases do occur. But every one who is anxious for the moral well-being of the nation looks with extreme anxiety on the increasing readiness with which divorces are sought and granted.—R. T.

Ver. 17.—*The sin of confusing moral distinctions.* "Ye say, Every one that doeth evil is good in the sight of the Lord, and he delighteth in them." Isaiah pleads in a similar way, "Woe unto them that call evil good, and good evil; that put darkness for light, and light for darkness; that put bitter for sweet, and sweet for bitter!" (Isa. v. 20). It seems that some, in the days of Malachi, answered his pleadings with insolent defiance, even daring to deny moral obligations altogether.

I. CALLING EVIL GOOD IS THE WAY TO EXCUSE OUR SINS. Daring men who are determined to "follow the devices and desires of their own hearts," will bravely say, "Evil, be thou my good." But the process of deterioration is usually slower and more subtle. We want to do wrong, and we begin to wish that it were not wrong. Then comes the doubt whether it is wrong. Then we begin to imagine that it is wrong only under particular circumstances. Then we find that our case does not come into the bad list. And the way is open to do the wrong under the shadow of our self-delusion that it really is good. There are family delusions that lead us to call evil good; society delusions; sectarian delusions; and personal delusions. These last are the most serious. A man can easily persuade himself that the pleasant is the right; and he may only mean the pleasant to the body. The pleasant to the soul, the pleasant because of God's benediction, helps to truer judgments.

II. CALLING GOOD EVIL IS THE WAY TO RUIN OUR SOULS. There is no hope for a man when he loses his sensitiveness to good, for with it goes his sensitiveness to God. A man is never lost while he can believe in goodness. There is anchorage in that. He is indeed driven with the wind and tossed hopelessly on the sea of life, if he ever comes to say, "All is evil;" "All is vanity and vexation of spirit;" "All men are liars;" "There is no good: there is neither good nor God." There is good, for there is God. He is God, and much that his creatures do bears the stamp of his goodness. Evil and good are contraries. Hope for humanity lies in their never getting confused.—R. T.

Vers. 1—3.—*Spiritual reformation.* "And now, O ye priests, this commandment is for you," etc. The grand subject we gather from these words is *spiritual reformation.* "Now, O ye priests." The priests are specially addressed and reproved, for they, whose mission it was to raise the people to true worship and to holiness, led them into sin. Notice—

I. THE NATURE OF THE SPIRITUAL REFORMATION REQUIRED. "If ye will not hear, and if ye will not lay it to heart, to give glory unto my Name, saith the Lord of hosts." From this language it would appear that true spiritual reformation involves two things. 1. *A practical application of the Word of God.* There should be right attention to it. That Word is not only to be heard, earnestly listened to, but to be laid to heart, which means practical attention. It is to be applied to correct the wrong that is in us, and to generate and develop the true. 2. *An entire dedication to the glory of God.* "To give glory unto my Name." All genuine spiritual reformation is implied in this—right attention to the Divine Word, right application of the Divine Word, and an entire dedication to the glory of God. This is a reformation not of parchment but of principle, not of systems but of souls. It is in truth the only reformation worth having.

II. THE URGENCY OF THE SPIRITUAL REFORMATION REQUIRED. The neglect thereof incurs: 1. *A curse.* "I will even send a curse upon you, and I will curse your blessings." "'I will curse your benedictions.' Not the personal advantages and perquisites enjoyed by the priests, but the blessings they pronounced upon the people. The service had been merely formal without any sort of reverence in it; the blessings they uttered should retributively be evacuated of all efficacy and should be a mere formula" (Dr. Dods). What an awful thing to have blessings turned into curses! and yet if we are unregenerate and unrenewed this takes place by the very laws of our moral constitution. As hemlock turns even the sunbeam into poison, corrupt souls turn God's blessings into maledictions. 2. *A rebuke.* According to Keil, Ewald, and others, the expression, "Behold, I will corrupt your seed," should be, "Behold, I will rebuke your arms." Perhaps the idea is—I will wither your power, I will check the growth of your posterity. There is no true prosperity without spiritual reformation. 3. *Contempt.* "I will spread dung upon your faces, even the dung of your solemn feasts." "The dung in the maw of the victims sacrificed on the feast-days. The maw was the perquisite of the priests (Deut. xviii. 3), which gives peculiar point to the threat here. You shall get the dung of the maw as your perquisite instead of the maw. And one shall take you away with it, *i.e.* you shall be taken away with it, it shall cleave to you wherever you go" (Moore). "Dung shall be thrown in your faces, and ye shall be taken away, *i.e.* removed out of the way, as dung would be, dung-begrimed as ye shall be (1 Kings xiv. 10; Jer. xvi. 4; xxii. 19)" (Fausset).

CONCLUSION. Are we the subjects of this spiritual reformation? Have we been renewed in the spirit of our minds? "Marvel not that I said unto thee, Ye must be born again."—D. T.

Vers. 4—9.—*The minister of Divine truth.* "My covenant was with him of life and peace," etc. We have here the minister of Divine truth as he always should be, and as he often is—

I. THE MINISTER OF DIVINE TRUTH AS HE ALWAYS SHOULD BE. We learn: 1. *That he should be a man divinely called.* "Ye shall know that I have sent this commandment unto you, that my covenant might be with Levi, saith the Lord of hosts." What was the Divine commission to the priesthood? Here it is: "Phinehas, the son of Eleazar, the son of Aaron the priest, hath turned my wrath away from the children of Israel, while he was zealous for my sake among them, that I consumed not the children of Israel in my jealousy. Wherefore say, Behold, I give unto him my covenant of peace: and he shall have it, and his seed after him" (Numb. xxv. 11—13). The Aaronic priests were called of God to be the ministers of life and peace to the people. Two of the greatest blessings of being. What is existence without life—intellectual and spiritual life? and what is life without peace—peace with self, the universe, and with God? 2. *That he should be a man of profound reverence.* "I gave them to him for the fear wherewith he feared me, and was afraid before my Name." The priest was not only to be entirely free from a volatile and frivolous spirit, but to be profoundly reverential, pervaded by a holy awe. He was to be impressed with the solemnity of the commission with which he was entrusted. 3. *That he should be a man of moral truthfulness.* "The law of truth was in his mouth, and iniquity was not found in his lips." The moral laws which he has to inculcate and administer are to be regal forces in his own soul, and embodied in his life. He is to be free from the control of all shams and theories, a man of stern, moral realities. 4. *That he should be a man of practical devotion.* "He walked with me in peace and equity." His life should be a walk; there should be progress in it; he should walk with God, and walk with God in "peace and equity." 5. *That he should be a man of the highest usefulness.* "And did turn many away from iniquity." Iniquity is man's curse and ruin; to turn him from that is to save him, and that is the work of the true minister. The commission given to Paul was to "turn men from darkness to light, and from the power of Satan unto God" (Acts xxvi. 18). 6. *That he should be a man of the highest intelligence.* "For the priest's lips should keep knowledge, and they should seek the Law at his mouth: for he is the messenger of the Lord of hosts." Being a "messenger of the Lord of hosts," he is to understand

and appreciate the wonderful message, and give it from his own mouth to the people. Such is what Levi, as an ideal priest was and did, and every minister of Divine truth must be and do the same. What a high standard to aim at! How its light condemns and abashes most of us!

II. THE MINISTER OF DIVINE TRUTH AS HE OFTEN IS. The false minister is here represented: 1. *As swerving from the right.* "But ye are departed out of the way." Ye are very different in your conduct from the ideal priest and even from your actual predecessors in office; your careless teaching, your superficial dealing, your contentment with formulas and external rites, and your personal laxity, have given men a prejudice against religion altogether. Instead of helping men to accept the truth and live godly lives, you have caused even those who wished to do so to take offence and turn away. A sceptical age is necessarily the result of externality and heartlessness in the religious teachers of previous generations. 2. *As leading the people astray.* "Ye have caused many to stumble at the Law." Not only by their speech, but by their conduct, do many who profess to be ministers of God's Word lead the people to stumble. Their inconsistent life, their theological jargon, their exclusive spirit, lead the people to "stumble" at Divine things. 3. *As perverting the truth.* "Ye have corrupted the covenant of Levi." How many there are who tamper with the Word of God, who employ it to support some favourite prejudice, or to buttress their little sect! How far, for example, is our conventional theology from being like the theology of Christ! 4. *As becoming contemptible.* "Therefore have I also made you contemptible and base before all the people." Ministers who hunt after honour, popularity, gain, become contemptible in the estimation of intelligent and unsophisticated souls. The pulpit of England is certainly sinking into contempt with the English people. This is a sad calamity. The decrease in the number of those who attend churches, compared with the increase of population; the growth of a literature in thorough antagonism to the spirit and aims of Christianity; and the fact that the great bulk of the reading and thinking men of England stand aloof from all Churches, plainly show that the pulpit of England is sinking into popular contempt. Primates and prelates and preachers are treated with ridicule in nearly all popular literature and scientific discussion. A more terrible sign of the times I know not than this. The "salt" of the pulpit has lost its "savour," and it is being trodden underfoot with disdain and contempt. Trodden underfoot by our authors, scientists, artisans, tradesmen, and merchants. Gracious Heaven, raise up men for our pulpits, so high in culture, so gifted in faculty, so Christly in love, so invincible in duty, so independent in action, that they shall not only counteract the downward tendency to ruin, but shall attract to it with reverence the intellect of the age!—D. T.

Vers. 10—12.—" *One Father.*" "Have we not all one Father," etc.? "This section," says Keil, "does not stand in any close connection with the preceding one. It does not furnish an example of the stumbling upon the Law mentioned in ver. 8; nor of the violation of the covenant of the fathers (ver. 10); or of the marriage covenant (ver. 14), appended to the neutralizing of the covenant of Levi on the part of the priests (vers. 8 and 4). For there is no indication in vers. 10—16 that the priests gave any impulse through their bad teaching to the breaches of the Law which are here condemned; and the violation of the covenant of the fathers and of the marriage covenant forms no more a thought by which the whole is ruled, than the violation of the covenant with Levi, in the previous section. The prophet rather passes over with ver. 10 to a perfectly new subject, viz. the condemnation of marriages with heathen women." From this passage the three following truths are deducible.

I. THAT THE GREAT GOD IS NOT ONLY THE CREATOR BUT THE COMMON FATHER OF MANKIND. "Have we not all one Father? hath not one God created us?" It is clear that the one Father does not mean either Adam the progenitor of the race, or Abraham the Father of the Israelitish nation, but Jehovah himself. He is the Creator of all things, but not the Father of all things. We could not regard him as the Father of the mountains, the valleys, the rivers, the oceans, the stars, though he is the Creator of all these. All things are created by him; but he is the Father of human souls. "We are all his offspring." This relationship implies two things. 1. *A resemblance in nature.* Children resemble their parents in nature and attributes. All intelligent moral beings bear a resemblance to the Infinite. They are spiritual in essence, moral in sentiment, free in action; they are formed in his image. 2. *The existence of parental sympathy.* While a human father has the ordinary sensibilities of a man, he has the peculiar affections of a parent, a tender interest in his offspring, which he feels for no other object in the world. So God is a Father. Whilst he has an interest in all the works of his hands, he has a special interest in a human soul. 3. *The obligation of filial devotion.* Filial love and loyalty raise and bind the souls of children to their parents. Such is the feeling that human spirits should cherish and develop in relation to God. Man is the only creature on this round earth that has the capacity, and consequently the obligation, to feel, entertain, or develop this filial affection. He then who is the Creator of all things in the world is the Father of man; all are his *creatures,* but men are his *children.* Sublime distinction this!

II. THAT THE FACT OF THIS UNIQUE RELATIONSHIP IS A MIGHTY ARGUMENT WHY MAN SHOULD DO NO WRONG AGAINST EITHER HIS FELLOW-CREATURE OR HIS GOD. "Why do we deal treacherously every man against his brother, by profaning the covenant of our fathers?" Two remarks are suggested concerning the wrong with which the Israelites are here charged. 1. *It was a wrong committed against mankind.* The special wrong referred to is the contraction of marriage with a heathen woman, and the putting away the Israelitish wife. This is the treachery and the "abomination" referred to. The repudiation of Jewish wives and the adoption of heathen. 2. *This wrong against mankind was a wrong against God himself.* "Judah hath profaned the holiness of the Lord which he loved, and hath married the daughter of a strange god." God's law with the Jewish people was that they were to be a separate people, separate from all the other people of the earth, and they were to sustain their distinction by not inter-marrying with other peoples. But now, at the period when the prophet wrote, they were doing so, and that to a great extent (see Neh. xiii. 23—29; Ezra ix. 1—4). It is a universal truth that a wrong against man is a wrong against God; to sin against our fellow-creatures is to sin against God himself; and this is an outrage against the relationship which we all sustain to him, not only as our common Creator, but our common Father. We are all children of the same Father, and therefore we should be fair in our dealings one with another. We should love one another, and co-operate with one another for our mutual advantage in all that is virtuous and noble. "Have we not all one Father?" Wherefore, then, should we cheat, hate, deceive, oppress, murder one another? How monstrous!

III. THAT THE PERPETRATION OF WRONG EXPOSES THE DOER TO THE MOST LAMENTABLE RESULTS. "The Lord will cut off the man that doeth this, the master and the scholar, out of the tabernacles of Jacob, and him that offereth an offering unto the Lord of hosts. And this have ye done," etc. This, perhaps, means utter extermi-nation. "The master and the scholar," some translate, "him that watcheth and him that answereth." In "master" the special reference is to the priest who ought to have taught the people piety, but who led them into evil; in "scholar," to the people themselves, who were the pupils of the priests. The idea is that both the priests and the people will suffer on account of the wrong they were committing. Great distress had come upon them already. "This have ye done" (see Ezra x.; Neh. xiii. 10—13). *Again,* this is only a shadowy picture of the evils that ever flow from wrong. "Sin brought death into our world, and all our woe." It is sin that kindles and feeds the flames of retribution.

CONCLUSION. Haste the time when men shall realize the fact that they are all children of one Father, so that all wrongs against one another shall cease, and the spirit of universal brotherhood prevail!

> "A happy bit hame this auld world would be,
>   If men when they're here could make shift to agree,
>   An' ilk said to his neighbour, in cottage an' ha',
> 'Come, gi'e me your hand—we are brethren a'.

> "I ken na why ane wi' anither should fight,
>   When to 'gree would make a' body cosie an' right;
>   When man meets wi' man, 'tis the best way ava,
>   To say, 'Gi'e me your hand—we are brethren a'.'

> " My coat is a coarse ane an' yours may be fine,
> And I maun drink water while you maun drink wine;
> But we both ha'e a leal heart, unspotted to shaw,
> 'Sae gi'e me your hand—we're brethren a'.'
>
> " Ye would scorn to do fausely by woman or man;
> I haud by the right, aye, as well as I can.
> We are ane in our joys, our affections an a',
> 'Come, gi'e me your hand—we are brethren a'.' "

(R. Nicol.)

D. T.

Vers. 14—16.—*The Divine institution of marriage.* " Yet ye say, Wherefore ? " etc. The subject of these verses is *the Divine institution of marriage.* In relation to this institution we observe—

I. THAT IT IMPLIES A LOVING UNION OF TWO, AND ONLY TWO, SOULS UNTIL DEATH. " Because the Lord hath been witness between thee and the wife of thy youth, against whom thou hast dealt treacherously : yet is she thy companion, and the wife of thy covenant. And did not he make one ? " " Wife of thy youth." The Jews had ever been accustomed to marry very young, the husband often being not more than thirteen years of age, and the wife younger. " Thy companion ; " not a slave, nor an inferior, but an equal and a friend. Love-companionship is the highest ideal of matrimony. " Wife of thy covenant." A relationship established by mutual agreement. Marriage (Prov. ii. 17) is called the covenant of God; it is so because he has ordained it. " Did not he make one ? " Thine exclusively. " Yet had he the residue of the spirit," etc. Maurier and Hengstenberg explain this verse thus : " The Jews had defended their conduct by the precedent of Abraham, who had taken Hagar to the injury of Sarah his lawful wife. To this Malachi says, ' Now no one [ever] did so in whom there was a residue of intelligence [discriminating between good and evil], and what did the one [Abraham, to whom you appeal for support] do, seeking a godly seed ? His object [viz. not to gratify passion, but to obtain the seed promised by God] makes the case wholly inapplicable to defend your position.' It is asked, ' And wherefore one ?' Wherefore only Eve for Adam, Sarah for Abraham ? " " Instead," says Dr. Henderson, " of forming two into one, the Creator might have given to Adam many wives. There was no lack of spiritual existence from which to furnish them with intelligent souls. When he gave to Eve such an existence he did not exhaust the universal fountain of being. There remained all with which the human race had been furnished throughout its generations. What, then, the prophet asks, was the design of the restriction? To this he replies—The securing of a pious offspring. Divorces and polygamy have ever been unfavourable to the education of children. It is only by the harmonious and loving attention bestowed by parents upon their children that they can be expected to be brought up in the fear of God. The reply bore hard upon the priests who had married idolatrous wives."

II. THAT IT HAS BEEN SADLY OUTRAGED IN ALL AGES. The Jews outraged it. The command here, " Take heed to your spirit, and let none deal treacherously against the wife of his youth," implies this. They dealt " treacherously " against the wife of their youth by marrying others. " Ye have transgressed, and have taken strange wives " (Ezra x. 10). They do so also by putting them away—by divorce. " For the Lord, the God of Israel, saith that he hateth putting away : for one covereth violence with his garment, saith the Lord of hosts." This has been done in all ages. 1. Polygamy is an outrage on it. 2. Cruelty is an outrage on it. 3. Mutual unfaithfulness is an outrage on it. The Divine idea of marriage is that the two souls shall be one, so united in love, sympathy, aim, that the two would think, feel, and act as one. But how few amongst the million matrimonial alliances reach this ideal !

III. THAT OUTRAGE OF THIS INSTITUTION IS FRAUGHT WITH CALAMITOUS RESULTS. 1. *It is abhorrent to God.* " The Lord, the God of Israel, saith that he hateth putting away." A separation of man and wife, a divorce, is abhorrent to the Almighty, although by the Law of Moses it was allowed because of the hardness of their hearts. 2. *It involves violence.* " For one covereth violence with his garment." Some suppose the garment here means the wife, and that the idea is that violence was done to her.

Others suppose it means the pretext they employed for doing so by the permission of Moses (Deut. xxiv. 1). Others suppose the garment means man's reputation, and that he would damage his influence by it. Whatever the particular meaning of the passage is, it is certain that the outrage of the institution of marriage is fraught with great evils.

CONCLUSION. An extract from my Marriage Service in the 'Biblical Liturgy' may not be out of place here. "Marriage is an institution of God: it accords with the dictates of nature and the laws of inspiration. It is coeval with human society; it was an essential ingredient in the happiness of Eden. It heightened, it perfected, the pure, fresh, and serene joys of that garden, the scene of every beauty and the temple of God. In mercy it has been perpetuated to the present hour as a social blessing to soothe and sustain our nature amidst the depressing circumstances of our fallen state. Jesus threw around this relationship a peculiar grandeur. He clothed it with sublimity: to his holy eye it was a holy thing; he ratified its contract, he guarded its obligations, he expounded its laws, he graced its celebration with his presence; the first miracle his sacred hands performed was at a bridal feast. The apostles caught the idea of their Master, and invested it with a mystic solemnity by representing it as a type of the substantial, invisible, and everlasting union existing between Christ and his Church. It involves the most tender, close, and lasting ties that can unite human beings together in this life. 'Therefore shall a man leave father and mother, and cleave unto his wife; and they both shall become one flesh.' It combines the earthly interest, fortunes, and happiness of two; it may influence the destinies of many. The interests of the parties united, the triumphs of truth, and the upward progress of humanity are all dependent on the nuptial bond."—D. T.

Ver. 17.—*The words of scepticism.* "Ye have wearied the Lord with your words. Yet ye say, Wherein have we wearied him? When ye say, Every one that doeth evil is good in the sight of the Lord, and he delighteth in them; or, Where is the God of judgment?" These words are directed against the spirit of scepticism and discontent which prevailed amongst the Israelites in the time of the prophets, and they lead us to offer two remarks on the words of scepticism.

I. THEY ARE WORDS OF COMPLAINT AGAINST GOD. "Ye say, Every one that doeth evil is good in the sight of the Lord." This is what they said; this was perhaps their current talk. A very old topic of complaint was theirs. It means this: "Wherefore doth the wicked prosper?" Wherefore are the righteous afflicted? This was the chief problem of the Book of Job; this was the burden of Ps. lxxiii. Since vice is here triumphant and virtue oppressed, "Where is the God of judgment?" If there is a God who governs the world, his righteousness is not seen; on the contrary, he shows more favour to the evil than to the good. "Where is the God of judgment?" We want him to put an end to this state of things.

II. THEY ARE WORDS UNGRATEFUL TO THE EAR OF GOD. "Ye have wearied the Lord with your words." Observe: 1. *God hears the words of men.* Every syllable enters his ears; he understands our thoughts afar off. 2. *Sceptical words are offensive to him.* "Ye have wearied the Lord with your words." Wearied him with their ignorance, their falseness, their impiety. The creating and the supporting of a universe does not weary God, for he "fainteth not, neither is weary." But the endless chatterings of sceptical and discontented souls weary him. 3. *The authors of sceptical words are indifferent to this terrible fact.* "Yet ye say, Wherein have we wearied him?" They go on talking against God in their families, their clubs, in their public halls, in their workshops and their warehouses, and are utterly indifferent to the fact that their words are offensive to the ears of the All-hearing One.

CONCLUSION. "I say unto you, That every idle word that men shall speak, they shall give account thereof in the day of judgment." Every idle word. Not merely the profane and impious language of the scoffer and blasphemer, but every idle word— words that have little or no meaning, the most airy words of wit and humour spoken in jest, not to delude or pain, but simply to please.—D. T.

process took effect especially among the religious people of that day (ver. 3). Judgment began at the house of God. Some priests believed in him; few, if any, confessed him. Of most he had to say Matt. xxi. 31; and see vers. 44, 45.

II. To THE MANIFESTATION OF CHRIST TO THE SOUL OF A MAN. It was not the mere fact of Christ having come to the world and being seen that made him like a refiner's fire; it was when he *came home* to men's hearts and was *manifested* to their consciences that the real testing began. In this sense Christ still comes to our homes and appears to our hearts. Of this manifestation we remark: 1. *We naturally dread it.* John i. 26 is too often true. Many shun that manifestation. They put up the shutters and close every chink, "lest the light," etc. (2 Cor. iv. 4). Thus they can tolerate secret sins of which they would be ashamed "in the light of his countenance." Imagine that we were living in the same house as Jesus Christ, that he noticed every act and word, and that we knew he was acquainted with our thoughts as well. How could we bear it? Should we not at times be constrained to cry out, in distress, if not in defiance, " Depart from me; for I am a sinful man, O Lord "? But alas! we often do not realize " the real presence " of the invisible Christ. When we do, our feelings will be those of guilty Adam or at least of righteous Job. 2. *Yet we ought to desire it.* For everything depends on our knowing ourselves as sinners, and Christ as our Saviour. This should make us very anxious that when Christ reveals himself it may be not simply as the light of God, but as the fire of God. Light merely reveals. Illust.: morning light dawning on the horrors of yesterday's battle-field. But fire may purify, and Christ is like a refiner's fire. The two figures of the text are suggestive. "Two sorts of material for cleansing are mentioned: the one severe, where the baser materials are inworked with the rich ore; the other mild, where the defilement is easily separable." (1) He is like a refiner's fire. Illust.: Zacchæus " purged from his old sins " by Christ, who not only *came* to his home, but *appeared*, manifested himself in his heart. Like the flame of the fiery furnace, the fire of the Lord's holy love consumed the bonds of sin, but the man himself stood upright and walked at liberty. This refining process may be a very severe one to us. But the refining fire is himself the Refiner. He knows the ore he has to deal with. We can calmly leave him to select every step in the process. We know that he is working towards an end which is, or ought to be, very dear to us—our own sanctification (Ps. lxxix. 9). (2) He is like fuller's soap. This is a milder process. Yet even this may imply some rough treatment like treading, beating, hammering with mallets. Linen after cleansing may show how much dirt there was in it before. So Christ's purifying power may show us how many secret sins there were ingrained in the very essence of our hearts. The discovery may prompt to confession and to prayer (Ps. li. 1—10), which will be met by the promise, Isa. i. 18. Christ is no mere reformer or disciplinarian. He himself is the fire; his blood is the cleansing fountain; his Spirit is the source of our sanctification. Our supreme desire should be that Christ should be manifested to our souls *now* as the purifying fire of that holy God who, because he changeth not, doth not consume us (ver. 6). For otherwise he will for the same reason (vers. 5, 6, "*For* I change not") consume us at last.

III. To THE SECOND COMING OF CHRIST. In this prophecy, as Augustine says, " the first and second advents of Christ are brought together." Malachi sees the great white throne in the background (ch. iv. 1). The result of that coming to us will depend on his treatment of us and our treatment of him now (2 Tim. i. 18).

Ver. 6.—*The twofold aspect of the unchangeableness of God.* Three truths are taught here.

I. THAT GOD IS UNCHANGEABLE. 1. His nature is a pledge of it. Being absolutely perfect, any change of nature must be for the worse. The "light" (1 John i. 5) would be dimmed; any "variation" would cause "a shadow that is cast by turning" (Jas. i. 17, Revised Version). He is " Alpha and Omega," and not an intervening letter can be displaced; not a "jot or tittle" can pass away. 2. His Name declares it. Whether we interpret the Divine Name, "I am that I am," or "I will be that I will be," unchangeableness is implied. He "is, and was, and is to come, the Almighty." He has emotions, but these are not the capricious feelings of a changeable creature; *e.g.* contrast the wrath of God and that of King Nebuchadnezzar in Dan. ii. and iii. He revokes promises or reverses threats; but he "cannot lie" (Titus i. 2; cf. Numb.

xxiii. 19). The strongest assurance of this truth is found in the revelation of the Divine Name in Jesus Christ, who through successive ages is *proving himself* to be " the same yesterday, to-day, and for ever."

II. THAT THIS UNCHANGEABLENESS OF GOD IS THE GROUND OF HOPE FOR THE GUILTY. For God hath an " eternal purpose, which he hath purposed in Christ Jesus our Lord." And he says, " My counsel shall stand, and I will do all my pleasure." That eternal purpose included his dealings with the elect race of the old covenant. In spite of their many sins, he wrought out his gracious purposes respecting them (cf. Lev. xxvi. 42—45; Deut. vii. 7, 8). And still God remembers the land and the people (Zech. xiv. 10, 11; Rom. xi. 25—29). The same unchangeableness brings hope to all of us who have been invited and have been led to trust in our Saviour-God, " who hath saved us," etc. (2 Tim. i. 9). Those unalterable purposes include our purification (cf. vers. 3, 4). For that end Christ gave himself for us (Eph. v. 26; Titus ii. 14), and towards that end God is ever working. Well may we marvel at the everlasting mercy and the unchanging faithfulness of God (Lam. iii. 22, 23). The immutability of God is the sheet-anchor of our souls when the storm of guilt and fear threatens our destruction. It was a high eulogy on a Roman commander in a time of national peril that he had not despaired of the republic. It is to the glory of God that he does not despair of us sinners, in spite of our inherited and inveterate sinfulness (ver. 7), but " waits, that he may be gracious," etc. (Isa. xxx. 18), and seeks to overcome our evil by his unchangeable good.

III. THAT THIS HOPE FOR THE GUILTY IS A PLEDGE OF THE DESTRUCTION OF THE IMPENITENT. This is seen by the connection of vers. 5 and 6. The unchangeableness of God requires that " the transgressors shall be destroyed together " (Ps. xxxvii. 38—40). " There needs no *scire facias—a writ calling one to show cause*, to revive God's judgment; for it is never antiquated or out of date; but against those that go on in their trespasses, the curse of his Law still remains in full force, power, and virtue " (M. Henry); cf. Eccles. viii. 11. But judgment deferred is not forgotten (2 Pet. iii. 8, 9). If judgment is to be escaped, men must change, for God cannot (see the argument in Ezek. xviii. 1—30; and cf. John iii. 7).

Learn: 1. The blessedness of being in unalterable unity with the unchangeable God. For this a reconciliation and a regeneration are provided by God himself (2 Cor. v. 17—21; Jas. i. 18). And then " if God be for us, who can be against us?" Changes in our circumstances need little affect us. Eden was no Paradise to Adam without God; the fiery furnace was no terror to Shadrach with God. 2. " It is a fearful thing to fall into the hands of the living God." For the unchangeable holiness of God is a consuming fire, which must destroy us in our sins if it does not separate us from them.

Vers. 7—10.—*The sin of robbing God.* The special form of sin which is here denounced (robbing God of tithes and offerings) is only one manifestation of a sin which is older than the law of tithes, and which survives in all nations to the present day. Observe—

I. THE NATURE OF THIS SIN. It is an ancient and an inveterate sin. The secret of it is alienation of heart from God (ver. 7). It is *due* to God, our Creator, Benefactor, Redeemer, that we make his will the law of our life, and therefore that we present ourselves a living sacrifice, according to the good and acceptable and perfect will of God. If we fail to do so, it must be either because we do not acknowledge the claims which God makes on us, or, acknowledging them, we yet deliberately withhold them. In the first case, we give the lie to God; in the second, we rob God. (Terrible alternative for every neglecter of God and Christ.) If it is robbery to withhold our hearts, ourselves, from God, it must be also to withhold anything from him. For what is there of which we can say, " This is not God's property; it is no part of his estate; we can do what we like with this "? It required no law of tithes to assert God's proprietorship and our stewardship. Cain robbed God when he withheld the offering which God would have accepted, or the spirit of dependence and faith without which even the right offering could not have been received. The withholding of a right spirit from God paves the way for other acts of robbery. The principle of tithes precedes and survives the law of tithes (Prov. iii. 9, 10; xi. 24, 25; 2 Cor. viii. 12; ix. 6—8, etc.). The precept, " Render unto God the things that are God's," applies to things as spiritual as souls

and as material as silver. If we are not proprietors but stewards, our one duty in regard to every talent we are entrusted with should be, "How will the Divine Proprietor wish me to use it?" If through selfishness or criminal carelessness we use it in a way which does not bring to God the honour that he has a right to expect, we are guilty of robbing God. "Give unto the Lord the glory *due* unto his Name."

II. IT IS A SIN WHICH MEN ARE HARD TO BE CONVICTED OF. 1. In ver. 7 we find a reproof and an appeal which should awaken great searchings of heart: "Lord, is it I?" (Lam. iii. 40, 41). But we may be so self-righteous or ignorant as to evade such general appeals as quite irrelevant. So the net must be drawn tighter; the indictment must be made more definite. 2. So the charge of robbing God is suggested. "Will a man rob God?" The very aversion we feel at the thought of being robbed (for we would rather give away or throw away our property than be cheated of it) should prompt the inquiry, "Is it possible that I may be robbing God?" *e.g.* of the reverence and godly fear due to the Almighty, as though we could disregard him and dare him to do his worst. Or of the gratitude and dependence he deserves as our Father, our Redeemer, as though we could to a considerable extent dispense with him during life, and then "make it up" at the last. Whose conscience could not convince him that in these or other ways he had been often guilty of robbing God? Yet so hard are men to be convinced of the sin, that to God's question and his direct charge there comes the glib reply, "Wherein have we robbed thee?" 3. Thus God is compelled to lay his finger on one most glaring act of robbery: "In tithes and offerings." Some of the offerings were less rigidly regulated by law than tithes, as is the case with the offerings of Christians for the kingdom of Christ and the claims of benevolence. But we may be guilty of robbing God "in offerings." (1) By grudging giving. If we do not "freely give," we withhold from God the right spirit, without which gifts cannot be acceptable. We act as if, though God had a right to demand our money, he had no right to expect the cheerful acknowledgment, "Of thine own have we given thee" (1 Chron. xxix. 14; Matt. x. 8; 2 Cor. ix. 7). (2) By scanty giving. For there is an amount, some proportion of all we are entrusted with, which it is "meet" to give. To "withhold more than is meet" is to rob God. If a man gives *not* "according to that he hath," but as though God had entrusted him with much less, his offerings are not accepted by God. A steward of God (as every one is) is bound conscientiously to consider what proportion of all he receives he should set apart for giving to religious and benevolent objects, so that he may honour the Lord "with the firstfruits of all his increase." The Jewish laws of tithes and offerings may aid him in the estimate. No rule can be laid down for one another, but the Christian steward may fairly start with the presumption that the scale of liberality has not been lowered in the kingdom of Christ, with all its privileges and motives so far in advance of the Jewish theocracy. Lest we should be guilty of robbing God, we should purpose in our heart to devote *so much and no less*, as God may prosper us. The cheerful, systematic dedication of a liberal proportion of our property to the service of God will preserve us from robbing God. We shall give not as small a proportion as we dare to offer, but as large a proportion as love and conscience in council will justify. Special circumstances may call for special sacrifices; but we shall form, as a first charge on our income, a sacred fund set apart for offerings to God. The experience of those who act on these Divine principles of giving may assure all that they will thus realize, as probably they may never have done before, the truth of our Lord's words, "It is more blessed to give than to receive."

III. IT IS A SIN WHICH SHUTS THE WINDOWS OF HEAVEN. The excuse which is generally urged for that parsimonious giving which is a robbery of God is, "I can't afford it." This may arise from a criminal ignorance of the claims of God and our relations to him, or from a feeble faith on the part of those who yet acknowledge themselves to be his stewards. The guilt of the former has been exposed; the fear of the latter is here met by God's own challenge, "Prove me now herewith;" "Have faith in God;" "Honour the Lord with thy substance;" "Seek first the kingdom of God;" and then see if God is not faithful to all his promises in regard to both temporal and spiritual blessings. Men may complain of hard times, and may want prosperity to precede liberality. "No," says God to these suffering Jews and to scanty Christian givers who may be in adversity, "honour me first by obedience and cheerful trust, and see if prosperous times will not come then." Illust.: widow (1 Kings xvii. 13);

poor Macedonians (2 Cor. viii. 1—4). Bad times may be the result of past unfaithfulness on the part of God's servants. You may be reaping sparingly because you have sown sparingly. Try the opposite plan. Now the windows of heaven are closed against ourselves by our own sins. God will open those windows as soon as we honour, obey, and trust. He can surpass our hopes and thoughts (Eph. iii. 20). His spiritual blessings will only be limited by our capacity for receiving them. Illust. : 2 Kings iv. 6; xiii. 18, 19. And with these best of blessings all temporal blessings that will be good for us will be added (ver. 11; Matt. vi. 33), and showers of blessing on our hearts and homes will descend through the windows of heaven once closed on God's dishonest servants, now opened to his faithful stewards.

Vers. 13—18.—*Hard speeches against God.* Once more God has to bring a charge against his people (ver. 13). Their words were "stout," bold, loud, defiant. Reverence and reticence were both wanting. Once more the plea is entered, "Not guilty." They will not admit that God is justified when he speaketh and clear when he judgeth. So once more God has to unfold the evidence, that their mouths may be stopped and they may be found guilty before God.

I. HARD SPEECHES AGAINST GOD. 1. God's service is unprofitable. They charge God with being an ungenerous Master, who allows them to work hard in order to keep his ordinances and to deny themselves (" walk mournfully "), and yet suffers them to enjoy little or no advantage therefrom. Even the service of God is "vanity and vexation of spirit." This is an old complaint (Job xxii. 15—17) often repeated (Ps. lxxiii.; Isa. lviii. 3, etc.). It reflects on God's equity as well as generosity. This is seen more clearly in the second charge. 2. The wicked are better off than we are. They seem to be " happy ; " they are evidently " set up," established by God's providence in much prosperity. And though, instead of " proving " God (ver. 10), they " tempt God," they go unpunished, and are delivered from trials which still oppress us. The facts noted form part of the world-wide and perplexing problem which has often caused atheists openly to blaspheme and Christians to weep in secret. But if ever the problem tries us, let us learn a lesson from the contrast between the conduct of the ungodly professors here and the godly Asaph. These speak openly to others against God, and thus encourage one another in unbelief. But Asaph (Ps. lxxiii. 15—17) speaks in secret to God about the question, and God guides him into truth and peace.

II. CONCLUSIVE REPLIES TO THEM. Answers to all these stout speeches may be found : 1. In the hollowness of the pretences of these stout speakers against God. They did not really " serve God " or " keep his ordinances." If they walked "mournfully," it was a sign that love, gratitude, gladness, were absent, or the joy of the Lord would have been their strength. Since their heart was far from God, so that he says, " In vain do they worship me " (Matt. xv. 8, 9), no wonder they have to confess, " It is vain to serve God." And whenever we find Christian worship or work bringing little profit to our souls, we may well institute great searchings of heart lest the radical difficulty should be found altogether in our own spiritual state in regard to God. If, however, our hearts condemn us not on this charge, we may see a further answer. 2. In the opposite experiences of those " who worship God in the spirit, and rejoice in Christ Jesus, and have no confidence in the flesh." While the murmurers have been talking to one another against God, another company has conversed together" (ver. 16). (Contrast the two gatherings—their spirit, their subjects, their tones.) They can tell a very different tale. They can speak words which God delights to hear and to record. Their experience of the faithfulness of God and the profitableness of his service even in dark days should neutralize the influence of distrustful complainers. Their characters attest their testimony. The confession of a Paul (2 Tim. i. 12) more than compensates for the desertion of a Demas. 3. In the fact that we have not yet " seen the end of the Lord." God speaks of a future, and bids us wait for that (vers. 17, 18). We have seen the end of the Lord in the case of Job (Jas. v. 11) and other tried but triumphant servants of God. We have not yet seen the end of the Lord in that drama of life (sometimes tragical) in which we are taking part. " Therefore judge nothing before the time " (1 Cor. iv. 5). In our present state of education and probation, " all thing are ours " by possession or by promise. In vers. 16 and 17 we are reminded of a few of our privileges. We have the ear of God, a record with God,

communion with God, protection by God, and a high estimate in his sight. The ultimate issue (ver. 18) will vindicate the confidence of his servants and silence the murmurs of his foes (Rom. viii. 31—39; Jude 14, 15).

Ver. 16.—*Christian converse.* "Then," etc. When? When ungodliness was rampant (vers. 13—15). As an excess of carbonic acid in the air makes the lamps in a mine burn dimly, so the atmosphere of prevailing ungodliness makes it hard to maintain a brightly burning piety. Christian converse is one means of sustaining a bright and vigorous godliness " in this present evil world," especially when the evil is more than usually " present" and pressing upon us. (1) *The servants of God conversing;* (2) *God listening and approving.*

I. THE SERVANTS OF GOD CONVERSING. The description of them, "They that feared the Lord," reminds us of the godly jealousy they cherished for the honour of God, like Noah, Nehemiah, and other servants of God in a corrupt age. Such fear is a source of purity (Ps. xix. 9; Prov. xiv. 27), and a safeguard in the most ungodly days (Isa. viii. 13, 14). Fearing God, they think much on his Name so deeply dishonoured in their midst; and they do so because (as the term implies) " they highly esteemed his Name." They feel the danger of spiritual contagion and disease (Matt. xxiv. 12). Lest their love should cool or their faith should fail, they conversed one with another. While the ungodly were uttering " stout" words against God (ver. 13), they were speaking warm words on his behalf. Learn : 1. Changing circumstances may call for new means of grace. *E.g.* the meetings of the sons of the prophets and traces of public religious services (2 Kings iv. 23) in the dark days of Elijah and Elisha. The institution of synagogue-worship in the Captivity. The secret services of the catacombs. The gatherings in woods or on moors of Covenanters, Nonconformists, and the martyr-Church of Madagascar. " The word of the Lord was precious in those days." 2. Private Christian communion may do much to supplement or to supply more public means of grace. From public Church-fellowship the godly could gain little in the days of Malachi. There was neither purity nor unity (ch. ii. 10, 11). In such circumstances all the more need for godly converse. " When the fire burns low, the coals that are alive should be brought together, that they may be blown into a flame." Illust.: Jonathan and David (1 Sam. xxiii. 16—18); Jeremiah and Baruch (Jer. xlv. 1—5); Paul in prison and his friends " which have been a comfort unto me " (Col. iv. 11; cf. Heb. iii. 13; x. 24, 25). Such converse is enjoined in the family (Deut. vi. 6—8) and among believers (Eph. v. 19). But to be a means of grace, it needs to be natural and spontaneous.

> " But conversation, choose what theme we may,
> And chiefly when religion leads the way,
> Should flow, like water after summer showers,
> Not as if raised by mere mechanic powers."

The spirit of it may be seen in Ps. xxxiv. 1—3, 11; lxvi. 16.

II. GOD LISTENING AND APPROVING. 1. " The Lord hearkened, and heard." It is a solemn truth that God listens to everything we say (Numb. xii. 2; Jer. viii. 6; Ps. cxxxix. 4). Here this truth wears a cheerful face. As illustrations: Two Christians encouraging one another in God; Christ in their midst (Matt. xviii. 20; Luke xxiv. 13—31). A Christian man on a lonely walk, courteously conversing with a stranger, and seeking to commend Christ to him. The stranger may go away to pray or to scoff. But that is not all. God hearkened and heard and noted the good deed done in his name. God listens with pleasure to all we say for him as well as to him. 2. " And a book of remembrance," etc. Older than the chronicles of the kings of Persia (Esth. vi. 1) or of Israel is the book of remembrance of the Divine King (Ps. lvi. 8). " Never was any good word spoken of God or for God from an honest heart, but it was registered, that it might be recompensed in the resurrection of the just, and in no wise lose its reward." That reward is referred to in ver. 17.

LESSON. (Col. iv. 6.) Supposing a Christian's talk for one day were taken down verbatim, what proportion of it could be entered in God's book of remembrance as " good to the use of edifying" (Eph. iv. 29), and of any service in the great day of account (Matt. xii. 37)?

Ver. **17.**—*The Divine Proprietor and his peculiar treasure.* We adopt, as a more accurate translation, the rendering, "And they shall be to me, saith Jehovah, in the day that I am preparing, a peculiar treasure," etc., and thus learn—

I. THAT THE SERVANTS OF GOD ARE HIS PECULIAR TREASURE. It is a joy to know that in such a world as this there is anything which God can regard as his own peculiar treasure. For sin is here. The serpent's trail is found in every earthly paradise. "The works of the devil" have done much to dim the glory and mar the beauty of the works of God. True, his material works are as attractive as ever (Ps. civ. 31). But a moral Being cannot find his peculiar treasure in material works. Of what value are the precious metals and the rare gems of earth to God? If they cannot satisfy the hunger of the created spirit, how can they be a special treasure to the Spirit that created all (Job xxxvi. 19)? It was a man who was first called "the friend of God" (Jas. ii. 23). It was to a nation that the promise was first given, "Ye shall be a peculiar treasure unto me above all people; for all the earth is mine" (Exod. xix. 5). Though the heavens are not pure in his sight, and he charges the angels with folly, yet he can find a peculiar treasure in sinful souls that fear and love him, that think upon his Name, and nurture in one another's hearts the elements of a Divine life. While the whole Church of God is his treasure, every individual is an object of special regard and value. God says, "I know thee *by name,* and *thou* hast found grace in my sight." Every believer may appropriate the love and sacrifice of Christ, "who loved *me,* and gave himself for me." So that each individual in the universal Church may be regarded as a jewel in the Divine treasury. They are God's "hidden ones," but not overlooked; scattered, but not lost; the world knoweth them not, but "the Lord knoweth them that are his." Apply to different classes; *e.g.* godly children; the obscure poor; uneducated saints ("rough diamonds"); the donors of widow's mites to the Master's service; an Abijah in the house of Jeroboam;—all are jewels in God's treasury of redeemed souls.

II. THAT THEY SHALL BE TREATED WITH PECULIAR CARE. "The day" which Jehovah was preparing may represent all the various troubles and dangers which may await both the righteous and the ungodly. We may apply the term: 1. To days of trial in this life. We do not expect exemption from all trials. But we may expect two things. (1) Spiritual safety in spite of our trials (1 Cor. x. 13). Nay, more, our trials will work for us "experience" (δοκιμήν, "probation," a state in which we have stood the test, and are the stronger and therefore the safer for having done so). We shall still be God's; "mine, saith the Lord." The great robber of God and murderer of souls shall fail to pluck us out of the mightier Shepherd's hands (John x. 27, 28). (2) Providential discrimination (ver. 18) and alleviation. God will "spare them as a man," etc. (see next sketch). Illust.: Ebed-melech (Jer. xxxix. 16—18); Baruch (Jer. xlv. 5); the Christians escaping to Pella before the destruction of Jerusalem (Matt. xxiv. 15—20; Ps. xxxiv. 19). 2. To the day of death. But "death is yours," and cannot "separate us from the love of God which is in Christ Jesus our Lord." The day of death is the day of promotion, when, in an especial sense, we become a peculiar treasure because redeemed from all iniquity and purified for all eternity unto all good works (Titus ii. 14). 3. The day of judgment. (Matt. xiii. 41—43; xxv. 34.) Who will not claim his offered place among the peculiar treasures of God? Who can bear the thought of hearing from the Judge in that day, "I never knew you; that is no part of my treasure; *take it away*"?

Ver. **17.**—*God's dealings with his servants and with his own beloved Son.* "I will spare them," etc. These words suggest a comparison and a contrast, and lessons therefrom.

I. GOD'S PROMISE TO HIS SERVANTS. These words are one of the "exceeding great and precious promises" on which we, the children of the kingdom, may rest. Loving protection is promised us by the great Father on the ground of our filial relationship ("his own son"), and as a reward of filial duty ("that serveth him"). Such is the assurance given to the adopted children of God. But now notice—

II. GOD'S DEALINGS WITH HIS OWN BELOVED SON. Contrast ver. 17 with Rom. viii. 32. There is one in the universe who is God's Son, not by adoption, but by nature and likeness. He is "his own Son;" his "only begotten Son" (where we lay the emphasis on " only " not on " begotten "). He stands in a relation to God which none other could occupy. None other is " the Brightness of his glory," etc. The universe knows only one incarnate God. And he was a Son " who served him." (John vi. 38; viii. 29). How well-beloved he was a voice from heaven twice declared (see John iii. 35, etc.). The love of Mordecai to his adopted Esther, of David to his worthless Absalom, and of Jacob to his dutiful Joseph, are conspicuous examples of earthly paternal love. But who can measure or imagine the love of God to his own sinless Son Jesus Christ? Surely such a Father will not permit such a Son to suffer. Surely he shall be anointed with the oil of gladness above his fellows. A cloud shall never sit on his brow; sorrow and sighing shall flee away. But no. He " spared not his own Son, but delivered him up for us all." His love to his sinful children made him willing to sacrifice his sinless Son (Heb. ii. 10). The Father's sacrifice in allowing Christ to suffer and die must be remembered if we would interpret the words, " God *so* loved the world," etc. (John iii. 16). In reading the parable of the wicked husbandmen (Mark xii. 1—9), we may have felt some surprise that the father should expose his beloved son to the treachery and cruelty of such wicked men. The reason is explained: " They will reverence my son." But the Divine Father knew what treatment his Son would receive among " his own; " yet " he spared him not." He knew what " travail of soul" would come on him when " the Lord laid on him the iniquity of us all; " yet " he spared him not." This contrast between what we might have expected and what we have seen in the experience of Jesus Christ, God's sinless Son, teaches us: 1. The reality of the atonement (Rom. iii. 25, 26; 2 Cor. v. 21). 2. The intensity of God's love to sinners (1 John iv. 9, 10). 3. The fuller blessings of salvation which God will give to reconciled sinners (Rom. v. 10; viii. 32). 4. The discipline and self-sacrifice which the saved children of God may be called to pass through if, like their Master, they seek " by all means " to " save some." The promise of protection (ver. 17) will not debar us from the privilege of self-denial (Matt. x. 24, 25).

HOMILIES BY VARIOUS AUTHORS.

Ver. 1.—*Preparation-work.* " Behold, I will send my messenger, and he shall prepare the way before me." It is fully recognized that the allusion here is to the ministry of John the Baptist. In him was realized the fulfilment of the promise that Elijah should come again. Our Lord declared that Elijah had come, in his time, and had not been recognized. And the disciples understood him to speak of John the Baptist. The more familiar figure of a " preparer of ways" is that given in Isa. xl. 3, 4. In vision the prophet sees the march of a triumphant king and army. The heralds pass on before, ordering the removal of every obstacle, making level and safe the road-way, and proclaiming with sound of trumpet the speedy coming of the great king. If John was the Lord's herald or messenger, he certainly was a very strange one. There was nothing whatever about him that suggested the herald; no gay clothing, no bannered trumpet. He did not hurry through the land, proclaiming his message in every market-place. He tarried by the banks of the Jordan, a quiet man, dressed only in cheap camel's hair garments, and satisfied with a leather thong for a girdle. The mission entrusted to him was distinctly and only a mission of *preparation*. But that work was complete in itself, and of the utmost importance in relation to the after-work of the Redeemer. The subject suggested is the mission of those who effect no results, but only prepare the way for those who achieve results.

I. PREPARATION-WORK IS ESSENTIAL. The secret of the failure of many enterprises that looked hopeful is found in the fact that they were not efficiently prepared for. The Reformers before the Reformation were preparers of the Reformation. A building depends upon the skill with which the lines for its walls are dug, and the concrete foundations laid. David did an invaluable work when he gathered the material for the temple which he might not build. Two things may be opened out. 1. The man prepared for can never do the preparer's work. He is not fitted for it. And yet he is wholly dependent on that preparer's faithfulness. With reverence we may say that our Lord could not do John's work, yet John's work must come before his. 2. Material preparations often precede spiritual missions. There is a removing of obstructions, a mastering of difficulties, and a smoothing of roads, which must precede the free exertion of moral and spiritual influences.

II. PREPARATION-WORK IS REALLY COMPLETE WORK. It always is relative to the man who does the preparations. It does not seem to be when we are judging the whole work. A man does his life-work well who just completes the preparations entrusted to him. But there is no encouragement of manifest results; and men entrusted with preparation-work have to be men of faith.—R. T.

Ver. 1.—*The unexpectedness of the advent.* " Shall suddenly come." Two messengers are spoken of in this verse. John, the messenger, prepares the way for Jesus; and Jesus, the Messenger, prepares the way for God. Each was a sent and commissioned one. The coming to the temple is a figure of speech, and means coming to the people, not our Lord's actually entering into the temple. The people of Israel were the temple of the Lord, and of that true temple the material building was a sign. The point indicated in the expression of the text is that Messiah came with surprising suddenness upon the preparing work of John the Baptist. Only some six months of heralding when the King came. The suddenness may be illustrated along three lines.

I. THERE WAS GENERAL EXPECTATION OF MESSIAH. But it was general and vague, and in no way definite and precise. It anticipated the coming of some great One, but when he was coming, or for what he was coming, none seemed quite to know. So when he did come everybody was surprised. They did not think of his coming then, or in that particular way. Stapfer says that " the expectation of Messiah was visionary indeed. It was confused, capricious, fantastic, and at the same time precise and minute in detail, just like a dream. The very name he was to bear was doubtful."

II. THERE WAS GENERAL DELUSION RESPECTING MESSIAH. We are familiar with the idea of his delivering Israel from the Roman yoke, and restoring the kingdom of David, but this was quite the most sober form of the delusion of the age. Extravagant ideas so occupied men's minds that they could give no room to the idea of a spiritual Saviour from sin. Misconceiving the images under which Christ's coming had been foreshadowed, the people were expecting an earthly deliverer, a champion who would free them from foreign bondage, and they would gladly have spread their garments, waved their palm branches, and shouted their hosannas, if he had come to them as a conquering King. John broke into their delusions by his demand of repentance. Jesus broke into them still further by his ministry to sufferers and sinners. Suddenness and surprise characterized his going to and fro among the people, healing the sufferers and preaching the gospel of the kingdom. Suddenness was needed to awaken them out of their delusions. The world had to be startled into thought.

III. THERE WAS GENERAL UNPREPAREDNESS FOR MESSIAH. The servants had not put the house ready for the Master. The priests had not. The scribes had not. Those who had prepared themselves were private persons who had very little influence on society. The unpreparedness is typified in this, " There was no room for him in the inn." His coming was not sudden to Simeon and Anna, because they were prepared through the revealed Word.—R. T.

Ver. 2.—*The severe side of Messiah's mission.* " Like a refiner's fire, and like fuller's soap." It is usually shown that the triumphant side of Messiah's mission wholly occupied the mind of the Jews, and that consequently the stern, judgment side needed to be presented vigorously. But some recent accounts of the actual condition of Jewish thought in the first century suggest that the *fears* of Messiah's time were so extravagant that they needed to be corrected and qualified. The stern things of the Gospels are mild and reasonable when compared with the extravagant fears of the people. " The people looked forward with dread to the coming of the Messianic era. They were afraid of seeing the war of Gog and Magog, which the scribes predicted as its precursor. They looked for fearful calamities. Rabbi Eliezar ben Abena said, ' When ye shall see nations rising up one against the other, then look for Messiah to follow. In the weeks of years in which the Son of David shall come, there will be in the first year abundance of rain upon one city, and drought upon another. In the second year the arrows of famine will go abroad. In the third there will be a great famine, and men, women, and children will die, as well as the saints and the rich ; and there will be a judgment of forgetfulness upon those that study the Law. In the fourth there will be abundance for some and barrenness for others. In the fifth a great abundance ; and they shall eat, drink, and rejoice, and the Law shall be again held in honour, among those who teach it. In the sixth year voices will be heard. In the seventh wars will break out, and at the end of the seventh the Son of David will appear.'" It was as necessary to correct these delusions as those which pictured a triumphant earthly conqueror. The severity must be fully recognized as a moral, not material, severity.

I. MESSIAH WORKS TO REVEAL EVIL. This his very presence does. Put a foul thing beside a pure thing, and the pure thing shows and intensifies the foulness. Let God show, in a man's human life among men, what he requires and what he can accept, and wherever that man goes he is sure to bring evil to light. Christ is doing that work still.

II. MESSIAH WORKS TO PUNISH EVIL. "All judgment is committed unto the Son." But the sphere of the punishment is moral and spiritual. Christ never asked the secular arm to carry out his condemnations.

III. MESSIAH WORKS TO DELIVER FROM EVIL. This is indicated in his work as *Refiner*. He is getting the metal freed from the dross. Much of our evil is not us, only attached to us, blended with us, a bondage of us.

IV. MESSIAH WORKS TO CLEANSE FROM EVIL. This is indicated in the soap figure. The evil is conceived of as *in* us, and as having to be got out by the severe processes of the fuller, or washer, by pounding.—R. T.

Ver. 3.—*Messiah as a Refiner.* Moses gives Messiah the Leader, who should permanently take his place. Isaiah gives us Messiah the Sufferer, Conqueror, and Comforter, matching the condition of Israel as suffering and exiled. Daniel gives us Messiah the Prince, matching the condition of the people as anticipating the restoration of their kingdom. Malachi gives Messiah the Refiner, matching the condition of the people as in a state of moral and religious degradation. It is important to note the many-sidedness of Christ's adaptation to human needs. This aspect of Christ as the Refiner is one that is suited to every age. Men make grave objections to the doctrine of human depravity, and yet all history declares, as with one united voice, that man has never yet been able to keep anything clean. Let him touch anything, and he brings in the stain. 1. Take the sphere of man's thinking. It is constantly observed that the followers of all great philosophers and teachers and thought-leaders always complicate and deteriorate their systems. They bring in the dirt and the dross. 2. Take the sphere of man's religion. All the world over, and all the ages through, you may see man recalled to pure principles, and soon losing them again under the accumulating and debasing dross of ceremonies and superstitions. 3. Take the sphere of man's social relations. Self-interest has always proved to be the dross that gathers on and spoils the most perfect social schemes man has ever devised. 4. Take the sphere of man's personal life. The noblest ideals are unattained, for the dross of self-indulgence soon gathers, and in middle life men are content with low attainments. Getting the dross away is the great Refiner's work in every age and sphere.

I. GOOD SILVER MIXED WITH DROSS. There is a compliment in speaking of God's people as "silver," for silver is worth refining. It is a genuine and valuable metal. For mixture with dross see how lead, silver, and gold are found in the ore, surrounded with that which is comparatively worthless. Humanity is thus represented. It is not as God made it ; it has become mixed. There is dross of heresy, vice, crime, etc.

II. GOOD SILVER FREED FROM DROSS. The result of renewed processes ; always involving suffering for the refined, and anxiety for the Refiner. Silver has to go through the process seven times. The issue is the purity of the metal, by getting the dross perfectly away. Nothing can be usefully done with the metal while the dross still clings to it. Conclude by showing that Messiah did (1) the work of his age ; (2) and does the work of *this* age. He did his own work as Refiner then ; he does God's refining work now.—R. T.

Ver. 4.—*The pleasantness of religious offerings.* The idea of offerings being *pleasant* to God reminds one of Noah's sacrifice on the cleansed and restored earth : "And

Noah builded an altar unto the Lord; and took of every clean beast, and of every clean fowl, and offered burnt offerings on the altar. And the Lord smelled a sweet savour." The opposite sentiment, God finding man's offerings unpleasant, and even offensive, reminds of Isaiah's opening reproaches, uttered in God's name: "Incense is an abomination unto me. . . . Your new moons and your appointed feasts my soul hateth : they are a trouble unto me; I am weary to bear them." The carelessness of the Levites in the time of Malachi had been making the offerings an offence to God. It was evident enough that they were routine and formality. One sign, and the first sign, of spiritual purification would be that the public sacrifices and services would take a new and acceptable tone.

I. THE GRACE OF GOD WHICH FINDS PLEASURE IN MAN'S OFFERINGS. It might have been that God only *required* offerings, and felt no personal concern in the offerings, as expressing the feelings of the offerers. It is the marvel of God's grace that he puts personal feeling into men's acts and relations; and by his personal feeling calls upon us to put our personal feeling into those acts. Then the value of an offering lies not in what it *is*, but in the pleasure which it gives to God; and that pleasure depends not on its mere value, but on the feeling of the offerer which it carries. The test of every offering is this—Can God be pleased with it ? Of the supreme offering of the obedient Son, God said, "This is my beloved Son, in whom I am well pleased." Of some offerings the apostle could say, "With such sacrifices God is well pleased."

II. THE DUTY OF MAN TO FIND GOD PLEASURE THROUGH HIS OFFERINGS. A duty resting on (1) obligation; (2) gratitude; (3) personal affection. If we realize what God claims, we must seek to please him. If we realize what he has done for us, we must seek to please him. And the impulses of love will surely lead us to seek to please him. What man asks by his gifts and sacrifices is, "Make thy face to shine upon thy servant." "The essence of all sacrifice is the same in every age. No sacrifice is pleasing to God, if not accompanied with the sacrifice of the heart and will, and of all the faculties, intellectual, spiritual, bodily, of the offerer; and no sacrifice is pleasing to God, except by virtue of its reference to the one sacrifice of the dearly beloved Son, in whom he is well pleased" (Bishop Wordsworth). Still, to God, formality is an offence; routine a weariness; hypocrisy the supreme offence; and still, to God, humility, thankfulness, trust, and love are a holy joy.—R. T.

Ver. 5.—*Messiah's relation to society sins.* It is important to see that God both considers and deals with society sins as well as individual sins. Not sufficiently is it pressed on attention, that he deals with the evils which are characteristic of aggregates of men—with sins of classes and of nations. It is in the necessary judgment of classes and nations as such that the innocent are wont to suffer with the guilty; and then the interest of the class must be seen to override the interests of the single individual. Society sins are much the same in every age. They are classed in this verse. They run riot when the religious restraint is weakened. 1. Religious deceptions. 2. Immoralities specially bearing on family life. 3. Untrustfulness in everyday relations. "False swearers." 4. Sweating the workman, and forcing down the wage of the labourer. 5. Taking advantage of the distressed to secure selfish advantage; the "widow, fatherless, and stranger." How these sins corrupt society to-day may be unfolded according to the skill of the preacher. The prophets teach that whenever God manifests himself, he puts forth his power against society sins, and Malachi declares this to be one of the most marked characteristics of Messiah.

I. MESSIAH CUTS DOWN SOCIETY SINS AS BEING FALSE GROWTHS. The farmer will go into his meadows and cut down the coarse grass, which the cattle would not eat, and whose rank growth is crushing out the useful white clover. When a field is left uncultivated, and the good plants are left unnourished, there soon springs up a plentiful crop of weeds, groundsel, rag-wort, and thistles, and if there is to be any reviving of profitable vegetation in that field, these rank growths must be cut down. Illustrate from our Lord's dealing with the society sentiment concerning rabbinism. With some society sins the same must be done now.

II. MESSIAH SEEKS TO CLEAR THE ROOTS OF SOCIETY SINS OUT OF THE SOIL. Cutting off is only a preliminary to rooting out. Presently the farmer ploughs up and harrows the soil, carefully gathering the roots for the burning. Malachi, in God's name, tried to get at the roots of the society evils of his day. He found them in the self-indulgence of the priesthood, and the self-seeking of the people. He prophesied that Messiah would do the same work.

III. MESSIAH ENRICHES THE SOIL TO BEAR GOOD GROWTHS. We should never see Christ's work only on the negative side. It has two sides. To remove society sins is to give a chance for the nourishment of Christly-toned society virtues.—R. T.

Ver. 6.—*Man's hope lies in God's unchangeableness.* "I am the Lord, I change not." Man had changed toward God, not in mere relations, but in spirit and purpose. God had been therefore compelled to alter his relations towards men; and his ways of dealing with them; but this must never be assumed to involve any change on the part of God's feeling towards them. Those whom he loves he loves with an ever-lasting love. In the motive of his dealings he is "the same yesterday, to-day, and for ever." Reference here is directly to the purpose to save Israel. No matter what the appearances of things might be, that purpose had never been changed, and never would be. "Because it is the Eternal's unchangeable will that the sons of Jacob, his chosen ones, should not perish as a nation, he will purify them by the eradication of the wicked among them, that the remnant may return to their allegiance."

I. MAN'S HOPE IN THE CHANGEABLENESS OF GOD'S ADAPTATIONS. Changeableness is not altogether the appropriate term, but it is required for the sake of contrast. If God's ways with us were ordered by fast and unvariable rules, we should lose all sense of personal feeling, personal relations, and personal adaptations. Adjustment to individuals upon exact knowledge of individuals, and adjustment to circumstances upon exact knowledge of circumstances, are the very glory of God. It is because of this Divine characteristic that we would rather fall into the hands of God than into the hands of men. If set rules had been worked without qualification or exception, then many a time Israel must have been abandoned or destroyed. Men make so much of being under the "reign of law;" but that is precisely what we had better not be. It is a truly awful *régime.* There is no considerateness, no pity, no adaptation, in it. Far better that we are in the personal rule of a Divine and infinitely loving Lawgiver.

II. MAN'S HOPE IN THE UNCHANGEABLENESS OF GOD'S PRINCIPLES. The Divine adaptations are always within the limitations of the Divine principles. We can never be sure that our fellow-man does not change through weakness, and risk principles in making change. We may have perfect confidence that God never does. "Hath he said, and shall he not do it? Hath he spoken, and shall he not make it good?" True to his word; but only speaking words that express eternal principles. The point of the text is, that God's unchangeableness guarantees Israel's security, and God's changeable-ness guarantees Israel's disciplining and refining.—R. T.

Ver. 7.—*A twofold return.* "Return unto me, and I will return unto you, saith the Lord of hosts." And Zechariah has a similar expression (i. 3), "Turn ye unto me, saith the Lord of hosts, and I will turn unto you, saith the Lord of hosts." The direction to *turn* from the evil way is very familiar in the books of the prophets, and should be read in the light of their work as social and moral reformers. Some evil custom is indicated, which the people were *turned to,* and this the prophets anxiously endeavoured to get them *turned from.* This turning is the root-idea of the term "conversion," which should always be associated with conviction, or the sense of sin, and contrition, or sorrow for sin. Then properly comes conversion, or turning from sin. This is met by the remission of sin, and acceptance as free from sin. The word "conversion" is generally used for the whole process, but this use is apt to produce confusion of ideas. Special significance may properly attach to the turning from sin, because it is the recognized sign and expression of sincerity and earnestness. If a man gives up things he loves that are evil, there is good evidence that he is sincere. Reference in this passage is to the national loyalty to the Mosaic ordinances. By it the national piety could be tested. But they were manifestly turned from anything like a loving, hearty, spiritual obedience of those ordinances, such as God could approve and accept. Consequently his favour and blessing were manifestly turned from them.

I. MAN CANNOT RETURN TO GOD UNTIL GOD RETURNS TO HIM. While God holds aloof from the sinner, that sinner may feel remorse and misery. "His bones may wax old through his roaring all the day long;" but he will feel no penitence, no element of *hope* can enter into his distress. The first move always comes from God. Zacchæus does not know that he is really seeking Jesus, until he discovers that Jesus is seeking him. Our Lord put this truth into his familiar expression, "No man can come unto me except the Father which hath sent me draw him." It is the testimony of universal experience that God is always beforehand with us. And, rightly viewed, this shows us to be without excuse if we keep on in sin.

II. GOD CANNOT RETURN TO MAN UNTIL MAN RETURNS TO HIM. This puts the truth in paradoxical form; and yet it is precisely the statement of the text. God speaks. But he says he will not turn till man does. God is first in opening negotiation, and yet he says he must come second. Explain that God cannot do his gracious work in the man until the man is in that right *moral state* represented by penitence and turning to God.—R. T

Ver. 8.—*Defrauding God.* The people of Malachi's days met his reproof in a quibbling and self-justifying spirit. Men who are self-satisfied can resist all appeal. Religious formalities have this as their supreme peril—they satisfy men, and prevent them from feeling moral and spiritual anxieties, and from responding to moral and spiritual demands. These men could not see that there was any sense in which they were depriving God of his rights. The prophet puts his finger on one thing. That suffices to prove his accusation. They were withholding and limiting the tithes and offerings due to God's house. How could citizens be loyal who neglected to pay in those taxes of the king which were the very sign of loyalty? "One might reasonably think such a presumption could not enter into any man's thoughts, as to rob God of those things which are dedicated to his service; when he considers that he hath received all things from him, and therefore ought in gratitude to set apart some share of his substance for the maintaining of his worship and the public exercises of religion" (Louth). Consider—

I. WHAT GOD'S CLAIMS ON MEN ARE. 1. His natural claims, as the Author, Designer, Creator, practical Arranger of man's body, life, relations, and associations. See the rights of a man in the house he builds, the garden he lays out, the machine he makes, the child he rears. Of everything that a man does he expects some appropriate form of return. 2. His revelational claims. Israel was under special obligation because it had received special revelation. 3. His experimental claims. He had gained rights, and reasonably formed expectations, out of his pitiful and gracious dealings through long years.

II. ON WHAT BASIS DO GOD'S CLAIMS REST. Not merely the supreme rights of Deity; but here especially man's own acceptance of his claims. Claims are sterner things when they are both made and *accepted.*

III. HOW GOD'S CLAIMS MAY BE NEGLECTED OR REFUSED. 1. By the delusion that those claims have been relaxed. 2. By the hope that something can be put in place of obedience to them. 3. By sheer listlessness. 4. By persistent wilfulness. 5. But it is more subtle and searching to say—God's claims are now chiefly missed through man's over-occupation. The world and self fill men up.

IV. HOW IS SUCH NEGLECT OF GOD'S CLAIMS TO BE DEALT WITH? 1. Call it by its right name—robbing God. 2. Bring discipline to bear upon the neglecters, etc.—R. T.

Ver. 10.—*Recognition of practical penitence.* "Bring ye all the tithes into the storehouse." *All* must include those which *ought* to have been brought and had not. It was the paying up of old debts which would show the practical and sincere character of the penitence. Sin brings its own punishment. God will treat us relatively to our treatment of him. He recompensed this restored nation of Israel according to their doings. He blighted their fields and blemished their flocks, so that the land groaned beneath the curse. The only way to remove the evil was for the people to turn from the evil of their way. The sign of such return would be an earnest effort to fulfil their religious obligations. Of such fulfilment the offering of tithes might be a representative instance.

I. THE MORAL HELPLESSNESS OF SENTIMENTAL PENITENCE. Remorse is the caricature of penitence on the one side, and sentimentality on the other. And sentimentality may be the more subtle evil. A man may be distressed about the consequences of sin, who has no estimate of the evil of the sin. A man may be carried away by a surrounding excitement of penitence without having any real humiliation of heart. This may be illustrated from the excitement produced by Savonarola's preaching at Florence, and by the bad sides of modern revivals and missions. Convictions which reach no further than a man's sentiments are not merely helpless to influence conduct, but they are morally mischievous, because they delude, persuading the man that he is right, when his motive and heart are untouched. Some men who persist in living in sin nevertheless have seasons of gushing penitence; but it is only surface feeling, they have no root in themselves. The test of repentance is found in this question—What does it make the man *do*?

II. THE MORAL VALUE OF PRACTICAL PENITENCE. The Apostle Paul calls it "godly sorrow," and reminds of its practical working. "Ye sorrowed after a godly sort, what carefulness it wrought in you, yea, what clearing of yourselves, yea, what indignation, yea, what fear, yea, what vehement desire, yea, what zeal, yea, what revenge!" If a man steals from another, all his protestations of sorrow are without moral value unless he restores what he has stolen. God looks for moral value in everything relating to his people; and finds it only when they bring in the tithes which they had been withholding. Restoring, dealing resolutely with cherished sins, "cutting off right hands, and plucking out right eyes," are the revelation of sincerity, depth, and moral value, in all professions of penitence. It is only when God can approve of and accept the penitence thus revealed that he can respond by opening the windows of heaven to pour out blessing.—R. T.

Vers. 14, 15.—*Doubt of profit in serving God.* "It is vain to serve God." The Prophet Zephaniah is more severe. "It shall come to pass at that time, that I will search Jerusalem with candles, and punish the men that are settled on their lees: that say in their heart, The Lord will not do good, neither will he do evil" (Zeph. i. 12). "The prophet condescends to identify himself with those whom he reproves. 'We call the proud happy; yea, we say, they that work wickedness are set up. Therefore it is vain to serve God.' But he suddenly quits the seat of the scorners. He retires aside from the crowd, who proudly rely on their own popular verdicts, vaunting their own intelligence, and setting at naught the decrees of God; and, standing aloft from them, he joins the smaller company of the faithful few who wait and fear the Lord, and think upon his Name."

I. THE SIN OF SERVING GOD FOR THE SAKE OF PROFIT. This is seen in the case of Ananias and of Simon Magus. It is illustrated by Bunyan, in his character of Pliable, the man who was going on pilgrimage for the sake of what he could get. God asks for the service of *love*. Such service as alone can please him is the service rendered under the impulse of love. It is not possible to serve God acceptably in the spirit of the hireling. It is equally true that God cannot be rightly served under the expectation of pay or reward in the next life.

II. THE SIN OF DOUBTING WHETHER GOD REWARDS SERVICE. It is the sin of unbelief. "He who comes to God must believe that he is, and that he is the Rewarder of them that diligently seek him." But it really is a deeper and a more subtle sin than that; it is the sin of self-centredness. Only the man who thinks overmuch about himself questions whether his work will be fittingly recognized. This is a constant secret sin, even of good people. They never master it until they can learn of Christ to work for love, and let rewards come or not as they may. A man never conceives of Divine indifference, or hardness, or unreasonableness, until he gets into a bad frame of mind himself, and then he makes God the shadow of his own badness. It was thus with the persons whom Malachi reproves. Only because they wanted to serve themselves did they think it was vain to serve God. The man who loves God and wants to serve him is sure never to think that.

III. THE SIN OF THINKING THOSE ARE REWARDED WHO SERVE OTHERS AND NOT GOD. (Ver. 15.) The proud, who serve themselves. Good people, like the poet Asaph, are often tempted to think that the wicked have the best of it in this life. To think so is to "offend against the generation of the upright," and to dishonour God.—R. T.

Vers. 16, 17.—*The list of the loyal ones.* " A book of remembrance was written before him. . . . They shall be mine . . . in that day when I make up my jewels." Reference is to those persons who " by their pious discourse confirmed each other in goodness, and armed themselves against the impressions which wicked and doubting suggestions might make upon their minds." " God took special notice of what these pious persons did and said : it was as safely laid up in his memory as if it had been entered into a register, in order to be produced at the day of judgment, to their praise and honour." It is possible that the reference of these verses may be to " the growth of something like a brotherhood or order, not claiming or professing the inspiration of the older schools of the prophets, not entering, as they had done, on any vigorous effort at correcting the corruptions that were eating into the nation's life, but bearing a silent witness by lives of holiness and devotion, associated by the bonds of prayer and mutual love, handing down from generation to generation the tradition of higher truths and better hopes." Illustration may be taken from the Chasidim, or Brothers of Mercy, in the time of Judas Maccabæus, or the Essenes of the New Testament period.

I. GOD'S LOYAL ONES ARE THEY WHO KEEP HIS HONOUR IN IMPERILLED TIMES. Compare the seven thousand in Elijah's day who had not bowed the knee to Baal. 1. The loyal ones may have no public spheres. But the truest work for God is done in the private spheres of home and social intercourse. 2. The loyal ones may have no voice with which to testify. But the mightiest of all arguments is a godly life ; the strongest of all persuasions is the winsomeness of a sanctified character. Our witness may have to be rendered in our simply standing aloof, and that may be the very holiest reproach. It may be ours thus simply, but persistently, to keep the honour of God's (1) Name, (2) claims, (3) Word, as these are imperilled by the self-seeking of our times.

II. GOD'S PRESERVING HAND IS EVER UPON HIS LOYAL AND FAITHFUL ONES. He is even represented as keeping a list of them before him, so that by no possibility shall the interests of any one of them be forgotten. And his personal concern is intimated by his speaking of them as his " jewels." The term suggests : 1. Their value in his sight. 2. Their variety ; they are of different colours and qualities and tints. 3. Their safety. They are all there in that day. Jesus said of his disciples, " None of them is lost."—R. T.

Vers. 1—4.—*Christ as a spiritual Reformer.* " Behold, I will send my messenger," etc. This passage seems to be an answer to the question of the sceptic in the last verse of the preceding chapter, " Where is the God of judgment ? " It informs us that he will come, but that a preparatory work is necessary. It points to the advent of John the Baptist, the herald of that great Messiah predicted by ancient prophets, and who was the " Desire of all nations " (Hag. ii. 7, Authorized Version). The passage points to Christ as the great spiritual Reformer of the world, and teaches that as a Reformer—

I. HE IS GLORIOUS. This appears : 1. *From the fact that a Divine messenger was sent to prepare the way for him.* This messenger who did the preparatory work was John the Baptist, to whom Isaiah (xl. 3—5) referred when he spoke of a voice crying in the wilderness. This man was not only the greatest of all the prophets, but Christ tells us he was more than a prophet. He presented to his age, on the banks of the Jordan, in words of flame and a voice of thunder, an epitome of all the teaching of the previous prophets. He denounced sin, he urged repentance. But this man, great as he was, only prepared the way for the true Reformer. 2. *From the description that is here given of him.* He is here represented as the Proprietor of the temple, and as the " Messenger of the covenant." Christ is the world's spiritual Reformer. He revolutionizes the thoughts, the emotions, the aims, and habits of mankind. No one else has ever done this, and no one else ever can do it.

II. HE IS AWE-INSPIRING. " Who may abide the day of his coming, and who shall stand when he appeareth ? " In the presence of this Reformer, whose eye will penetrate into the depths of every soul, unrenewed men everywhere will stand aghast and tremble at their own moral enormities. When he appeared to them he would not flatter their theocratic nation's prejudice, but he would subject their principles to the fiery test of his heart-searching truth. Listen to what John the Baptist, his herald, said of him : " And now also the axe is laid unto the root of the trees, therefore every tree which bringeth not forth good fruit is hewn down and cast into the fire. I indeed baptize you with water unto repentance : but he that cometh after me is mightier than I, whose shoes I am not worthy to bear : he shall baptize you with the Holy Ghost, and with fire : whose fan is in his hand, and he will throughly purge his floor, and gather his wheat into the garner; but he will burn up the chaff with unquenchable fire." Even Peter, in his awe-inspiring presence said, " Depart from me ; for I am a sinful man ! "

III. HE IS THOROUGH. " He is like a refiner's fire, and like fuller's soap." Two figures are here employed to indicate how thorough his reformation is. The smelter's fire, which burns out the corrupt ingredients that are mixed with the gold and silver ; and the fuller's soap, whose alkaline salt cleanses all polluted garments from their dirt. In Christ's reformation, everything that is wrong, that is impure, is worked out of the human soul.

IV. HE IS PERSISTENT. " He shall sit as a Refiner and Purifier of silver." He is intent upon the work, and makes no slight or passing business of it. As a refiner of gold and silver sits over the burning crucible until he sees his own face reflected in the metal, so Christ will continue his work until it is fully accomplished.

V. HE IS SUCCESSFUL. " He shall purify the sons of Levi, and purge them as gold and silver, that they may offer unto the Lord an offering in righteousness. Then shall the offering of Judah and Jerusalem be pleasant unto the Lord, as in the days of old, and as in former years." He will constitute for men one day a " holy priesthood," a priesthood that will render to the Almighty offerings that are holy and acceptable to him.

CONCLUSION. Blessed be the Eternal Father for sending such a Reformer into this corrupt world, One in every way qualified for the work, One who has reformed millions now in Paradise, is still reforming thousands on this earth, and will one day work out the moral reformation of the race. " He will not fail nor be discouraged, until he hath set judgment [rectitude] in the earth " (Isa. xlii. 4).—D. T.

Vers. 5, 6.—*The world of sinners.* " And I will come near to you to judgment." From this passage we are reminded—

I. THAT SINNERS EXIST IN THIS WORLD IN GREAT VARIETY. Here are " sorcerers," " adulterers," " false swearers," and heartless oppressors. The first were very general in Judæa. " There was," says Lightfoot, " hardly any people in the whole world that more used or were more fond of amulets, charms, mutterings, exorcisms, and all kinds of enchantments. The elder who was chosen to sit in the Sanhedrin was obliged to be skilled in the arts of astrologers, jugglers, and sorcerers, that he might be able to judge those who were accused of practising such arts." Perhaps we have few, if any, professional sorcerers in England; but what is as bad, if not worse, practical deceivers abound. Adulterers, too, and liars, and ruthless oppressors, where are they not ? Sinners exist, alas ! in a great variety of type and in a great variety of degree. " There is not a just man on earth that doeth good and sinneth not."

II. THAT SINNERS OF EVERY VARIETY ARE EXPOSED TO A DIVINE JUDGMENT. " I will come near to you to judgment; and I will be a swift Witness." I " whom ye challenged, saying, ' Where is the God of judgment ? ' ' I will be a swift Witness.' I whom ye think far off, and to be slow in judgment, am near, and will come as a ' swift Witness,' not only as a Judge, but as an Eye-witness ; for mine eyes see every sin, though ye think I take no heed. Earthly judges need witnesses to enable them to decide aright. I alone need none. Sinners will be awfully undeceived who flatter themselves, ' God will never see it. How doth God know ? and is there knowledge in the Most High ? ' (Ps. x. 11 ; lxxiii. 11 ; xciv. 7) " (Fausset).

III. THAT SINNERS ARE PRESERVED ON ACCOUNT OF THE IMMUTABILITY OF GOD. " I am the Lord, I change not ; therefore ye sons of Jacob are not consumed." Ewald translates this verse, " For I, Jehovah, have not changed ; but ye sons of Jacob, have not ye altered ? " I have not altered towards you, but you have altered towards me. Because I have not changed you are preserved. I determined to continue you a distinct people on the earth, and therefore, notwithstanding all your murmurings and transgressions, you are not " consumed." God's immutability explains the continuation of sinners on the earth. He is essentially Love, and a change in him would be a change from love, and a change from love would be the ruin of sinners. When he says, " I change not," it means, " I am as full of love as ever." " As I live, saith the Lord God, I have no pleasure in the death of a sinner."—D. T.

Vers. 7—12.—*A Divine complaint and a Divine invitation.* " Even from the days of your fathers ye are gone away from mine ordinances," etc. In these words we have two things—a Divine complaint and a Divine invitation ; and both are addressed to sinners. Notice—

I. A DIVINE COMPLAINT AGAINST SINNERS. The complaint involves three charges. 1. *The charge of apostasy.* " Even from the days of your fathers ye are gone away from mine ordinances." Your fathers who brought on themselves the Babylonian captivity departed from my ordinances, and you are doing what they did. All sin is an apostasy, a departure from God's "ordinances" both moral and positive. " My people have committed two evils ; they have forsaken me the Fountain of living waters, and hewed them out cisterns, broken cisterns, that can hold no water " (Jer. ii. 13). Like the prodigal son, we have all gone away from our Father into the " far country " of practical atheism and sin. 2. *The charge of dishonesty.* " Will a man rob God ? Yet he have robbed me. But ye say, Wherein have we robbed thee ? In tithes and offerings." Their dishonesty consisted in withholding from him his claims. Thus they robbed or defrauded him. " Ye have robbed me." " Ye have done so to me in respect to the tithes due to me ; viz. the tenth of all the remainder after the first-fruits were paid, which tenth was paid to the Levites for their support (Lev. xxvii. 30—33), a tenth paid by the Levites to the priests (Numb. xviii. 26—28), a second tenth paid by the people for the entertainment of the Levites and their own families at the tabernacle (Deut. xii. 18); another tithe every third year for the poor, etc. (Deut. xiv. 28, 29). ' *Offerings.*' Not less than one-sixth part of corn, wine, and oil (Deut. xviii. 4). The priests had this perquisite ; also the tenth of the tithes which were the Levites' perquisite. But they appropriated all the tithes, robbing the Levites of their due nine-tenths ; as they did also, according to Josephus, before the destruction of Jerusalem by Titus. Thus doubtless was God defrauded—the priests not discharging aright their sacrificial duties, and robbing God of the services of the Levites who were driven away by destitution " (Fausset). Thus men rob God now ; they keep back what belongs to him. They cannot take anything from him, and thus make him poorer, as in the case of man robbing man, but they can rob him by appropriating to their own use that which he demands, by acting like Ananias and Sapphira. 3. *The charge of insensibility.* " Ye say, Wherein have we robbed thee ? " They had lost all sense of their obligation in relation to these tithes, and become utterly indifferent to the Divine claims. " Wherein have we robbed thee ? " As if they did not know their fraud on God. Thus men go on keeping from God what is his due without any sense of wrong. Sinful habits blind and deaden a man's conscience to his momentous duties.

II. A DIVINE INVITATION TO SINNERS. Here is an invitation to return : 1. *To Divine friendship.* " Return unto me, and I will return unto you, saith the Lord of hosts." Return to me by rendering to me my dues, and working lovingly and loyally in my service. " Return to me "—this has been God's voice to sinners in all ages ; this was the invitation of Christ : " Come unto me," etc. The return is in a sense mutual. God says, " I will return unto you." This does not, of course, mean that God compromises, changes ; but it expresses his readiness to receive them, as the father of the prodigal was ready to receive his lost son. He waits to be gracious. 2. *To honest service.* " Bring ye all the tithes into the storehouse, that there may be meat in mine house." Nehemiah calls the "storehouse" (xiii. 5) a great chamber where they laid the meat offerings, the frankincense, and the vessels. To put this to its proper use is what Jehovah would have them to do, and he promises, if they accede : (1) To give them good in *abundance.* " Prove me now herewith, saith the Lord of hosts, if I will not open you the windows of heaven, and pour you out a blessing, that there shall not be room enough to receive it." From heaven all good comes. Sometimes the windows seem so closed up that blessings descend not to some men. When God says, " I will open you the windows," it means good shall come pouring down in abundance. (2) To *give them good in connection with the produce of the earth.* " And I will rebuke the devourer [perhaps the locusts] for your sakes, and he shall not destroy the fruits of your ground; neither shall your vine cast her fruit before the time in the field." Their vines should produce fruit in the season. (3) To give them good in the *affections of men.* "And all nations shall call you blessed: for ye shall be a delightsome land, saith the Lord of hosts;" "Happy art thou, O Israel, who is like unto thee, O people, saved by the Lord, the Shield of thy help, and who is the Sword of thy excellency? And thine enemies shall be found liars unto thee, and thou shalt tread upon their high places" (Deut. xxxiii. 29).

CONCLUSION. Learn: 1. *That a man is a bad man who withholds from God his due.* What are God's dues? All we have and are. "All souls are his." And if we render not up to him our souls—our all—we are bad. 2. *A bad man becomes good by surrendering his all to God.* By bringing his all into the storehouse of God, devoting all to the Divine service. 3. *The more good a man has in himself, the more good he has from the universe.* If his whole soul is filled with supreme love and reverence for right and God, all the heavens outside of him will "open their windows" and rain blessings on him. Religious liberality is of all profitable investments the most profitable. And the converse. The niggard is "cursed with a curse." The man who robs and defrauds God robs and defrauds himself. As the fabled eagle who robbed the altar set fire to her nest with the burning coals that adhered to the stolen flesh she bore away, so the soul that defrauds God of his claims will set itself in flames.—D. T.

Vers. 13, 14.—*Religion delineated and depreciated.* "Your words have been stout against me, saith the Lord," etc. In these words we have religion *delineated* and *depreciated.*

I. PRACTICAL RELIGION DELINEATED. Three expressions are here used to represent it. 1. *To serve God.* "Ye have said, It is vain to serve God." There is a great difference between serving God and serving man. (1) In the one case the servant benefits the master, in the other the sole benefit is the servant's. (2) In the one the service is estimated by work actually done, in the other by work earnestly purposed. (3) In the one there is a surrender of freedom; in the other there is the attainment of it. He who engages to serve man must surrender some portion of his liberty; he who serves God alone secures the highest freedom. 2. *To keep God's ordinances.* "We have kept his ordinance." This is only a branch of the service, or perhaps the method of doing it. God has ordinances or institutes, some of which are moral, some are ceremonial; the latter may cease to bind, the former are everlastingly in force. 3. *To walk mournfully before the Lord.* "We have walked mournfully before the Lord." To "walk" before the Lord is religion in perfection, religion in heaven. It implies an abiding consciousness of the Divine presence, and continual progress in the Divine will. Walking "mournfully" characterizes the religion of earth; it is associated with penitence, contrition, etc. The walk of religion is only mournful here.

II. PRACTICAL RELIGION DEPRECIATED. "Your words have been stout against me, saith the Lord. Yet ye say, What have we spoken so much against thee? Ye have said, It is vain to serve God: and what profit is it that we have kept his ordinance?" Men say this: 1. *When religion does not answer their secular expectations.* Many take up with religion in these days because of the secular good they expect will accrue from their profession of it; if the good comes not, they think it vain. 2. *When they see the truly religious in poverty and affliction.* Asaph saw this, and he said, "I have cleansed my heart in vain" (Ps. lxxiii. 13). 3. *When they have taken up religion from selfish motives.* A man who takes up with religion for the sake of good will get no good out of it: he will get disappointment and damnation; for "he that seeketh his life shall lose it." No truly religious man has said religion is *vain;* he feels it to be its own reward—the highest reward. For in truth, it is the only service on earth that will not prove vain. Whatever other labour fails, the success of this is ensured— ensured by the Word of God, the constitution of mind, and the arrangements of the universe. "Therefore be ye steadfast, unmovable, always abounding," etc. (1 Cor. 15, 58).—D. T.

Vers. 16—18.—*Genuine religion.* Then they that feared the Lord spake often one to another," etc. We shall use these words to illustrate *genuine religion*, and three things are noteworthy—

I. THE ESSENCE OF GENUINE RELIGION. "They that feared the Lord." The men who fear God may be divided into two classes. 1. *Those who fear him with a slavish fear.* The unrenewed millions when they think of him at all dread him; their guilty consciences invest him with attributes of such horror that they shudder at the idea of him, they flee from his presence. "I heard thy voice in the garden, and I was afraid." All that is superstitious in the world, all that is barbaric in the religion of Christendom, spring from this dread of God. 2. *Those who fear him with a filial fear.* The fear which a loving child has for a worthy and noble sire. There is, perhaps, always a kind of fear in connection with true love. We fear, not that the object will harm us, but that we may harm or displease the object. Our fear is that we shall not please the object up to the measure of our intense desire. The fear of genuine religion is not the fear of suffering, but the fear of sin, not for the consequences of wrong, but for the fact of wrong. This filial fear with all is the beginning of wisdom.

II. THE SOCIALITY OF GENUINE RELIGION. "Spake often one to another." We are social beings, and what interests us most has the chief power in bringing us together. Nothing interests a religious man so much as religion. Hence the few good people living in this corrupt age of Malachi met and "spake often one to another." Spake, no doubt, in language of mutual instruction, mutual comfort, mutual exhortation. There is no force in the world so socializing as religion; it brings souls together, and centres them in a common object of love, in a common current of sympathy, in a common course of life.

III. THE WORTH OF GENUINE RELIGION. See what God does with the genuinely religious. 1. *He specially attends to them.* "The Lord hearkened, and heard it, and a book of remembrance was written before him for them." This does not, of course, mean literally that God keeps a book, or that he has any difficulty in remembering what takes place. It is an anthropomorphism, a symbolizing of the special interest of God. 2. *He claims them as his own.* "And they shall be mine, saith the Lord of hosts." My friends, my children, mine to love and serve me. 3. *He appreciates them as precious.* "In that day when I make up my jewels." The word here rendered "jewels" is in Exodus (xix. 5) rendered "peculiar treasure." "They are peculiarly precious to me." He knows the worth of their existence, the cost of their restoration, the greatness of their capabilities. 4. *He distinguishes them from all others.* Here they are so mixed with worldly and worthless men that they are mostly undiscerned and undistinguished. One day he will separate them, the sheep from the goats.

CONCLUSION. To attain religion should be the supreme aim of our life. It is not a means to an end; it is the grand end of being; it is the Paradise of soul.—D. T.

EXPOSITION.

CHAPTER IV.

Vers. 1—3.—§ 4. *The final separation of the evil and the good at the day of judgment.*

Ver. 1.—Burn as an oven (*a furnace*). Fire is often spoken of in connection with the day of judgment and the advent of the Judge. It is a symbol of the holiness of God, which consumes all impurity, and also represents the punishment inflicted on the ungodly (Ps. l. 3; Isa. x. 17; lxvi. 15, 16; Dan. vii. 9, 10; Joel ii. 30; 1 Cor. iii. 13; 2 Pet. iii. 7, etc.). The LXX. adds, "and it shall burn them." **Stubble** (see note on Obad. 18); or, perhaps, *chaff*, as Matt. iii. 11, 12. **Root nor branch.** The ungodly are regarded as a tree which is given up to be burned so that nothing of it is left. The

same metaphor is used by John the Baptist (Matt. iii. 10; comp. Amos ii. 9). The Hebrew text includes this chapter in ch. iii.

Ver. 2.—The Sun of Righteousness. The sun which is righteousness, in whose wings, that is, rays, are healing and salvation. This Divine righteousness shall beam upon them that fear the Name of God, flooding them with joy and light, healing all wounds, removing all miseries, making them incalculably blessed. The Fathers generally apply the title of "Sun of Righteousness" to Christ, who is the Source of all justification and enlightenment and happiness, and who is called (Jer. xxiii. 6), "The Lord our Righteousness." **Grow up**; rather, *gambol*; σκιρτήσετε (Septuagint); *salietis* (Vulgate). "Ye shall leap!" comp. Jer. l. 11). The word is used of a horse galloping (Hab. i.

8). The happiness of the righteous is illustrated by a homely image drawn from pastoral pursuits. They had been, as it were, hidden in the time of affliction and temptation; they **shall go forth** boldly now, free and exulting, like calves driven from the stall to pasture (comp. Ps. cxiv. 4, 6; Cant. ii. 8, 17).

Ver. 3.—Ye **shall tread down the wicked** (comp. Micah iv. 13). They who were once oppressed and overborne by the powers of wickedness shall now rise superior to all hindrances, and themselves tread down the wicked as the ashes under their feet, to which the fire of judgment shall reduce them. **In the day that I shall do this**; rather, as in ch. iii. 17, *in the day which I am preparing*.

Vers. 4—6.—§ 5. *Concluding admonition to remember the Law, lest they should be liable to the curse. In order to avert this, the Lord, before his coming, would send Elijah to promote a change of heart in the nation.*

Ver. 4.—**If the** people would meet the judgment with confidence and secure for themselves the promised blessings, they must remember and obey the Law of Moses. Thus the last of the prophets set his seal to the Pentateuch, on obedience to which depended, as of old (see Lev. xxvi.; Deut. xxviii.), so now, the most abundant blessings. **My servant.** Moses was only the agent and interpreter of God. The origin and authority of the Law were Divine. **Horeb.** The mention of the mountain would remind the people of the awful wonders that accompanied the promulgation of the Law (Exod. xix. 16, etc.; Deut. iv. 10—15). **For all Israel** Not merely for the people who heard the Law given, but for the nation unto all time. Nor could they be true Israelites unless they observed the terms of the covenant then made. With the (*even*) **statutes and judgments.** These terms, which explain the word "Law," include all the enactments, legal, moral, ceremonial. Malachi might well remind the people of their duty, and thus support Nehemiah in his struggle to win them to obedience (see Neh. ix. 38; x. 29). The LXX. places this verse at the end of the chapter, probably because the original conclusion (ver. 6) was thought too harsh to be left as the close of the Old Testament. The Jews had a feeling that books in the Bible should end with the name *Jehovah*. In the case of Isaiah and Ecclesiastes, they repeated, after the last verse, the last but one.

Ver. 5.—Elijah the prophet. This is not the same personage as the "messenger" in ch. iii. 1; for the latter comes before the

first advent of the Lord, the former appears before the day of judgment; one comes to prepare the way of the Lord, and is followed immediately by Messiah's coming to his temple; the other is sent to convert the chosen people, lest the land be smitten with a curse. There seems to be no valid reason for not holding the literal sense of the words, and seeing in them a promise that Elijah the prophet, who was taken alive from the earth, shall at the last day come again to carry out God's wise purposes. That this was the view adopted by the Jews in all ages we see by the version of the LXX., who have here, "Elijah the Tishbite;" by the allusion in Ecclus. xlviii. 10; and by the question of our Lord's disciples in Matt. xvii. 10, "Why then say the scribes that Elias must first come." Christ himself confirms this opinion by answering, "Elias truly shall first come, and restore all things." He cannot be referring here to John the Baptist, because he uses the future tense; and when he goes on to say that "Elias is come already," he is referring to what was past, and he himself explains that he means John, who was announced to come in the spirit and power of Elias (Luke i. 17), but of whom it could not be said that he "restored all things." The same opinion is found in the Revelation (xi. 3, 6), where one of the witnesses is very commonly supposed to be Elijah. It is argued by Keil, Reinke, and others, that, as the promise of King David in such passages as Jer. xxx. 9; Ezek. xxxiv. 23; xxxvii. 24; Hos. iii. 5, etc., cannot imply the resurrection of David and his return to earth, so we cannot think of an actual reappearance of Elijah himself, but only of the coming of some prophet with his spirit and power. But, as Knabenbauer points out, for the attribution of the name David to Messiah, long and careful preparation had been made; *e.g.* by his being called "the rod of Jesse," the occupant of David's throne, etc.; and all who heard the expression would at once understand the symbolical application, especially as David was known to have died and been buried. But when they found Malachi speaking of the reappearance of "Elijah *the prophet*," who, as they were well aware, had never died, of whose connection with the coming Messenger they had never heard, they could not avoid the conclusion to which they came, viz. that before the great day of judgment Elias should again visit the earth in person. This prophecy concerns the very last days, and intimates that before the final consummation, when iniquity shall abound, God will send this great and faithful preacher of repentance, whose **mission** shall have such effects that the **purpose of God** for the salvation of Israel shall be accomplished. We may therefore assume that in the gospel the appellation "Elias" stands both for John and for Elijah himself; for the messenger who prepared the way for Christ's first advent, and for the prophet who was to convert the Israelites before the judgment day; for him who came in spirit and power, and him who shall come in bodily presence. **The great and dreadful day.** The day of final judgment. No other crisis could be named in such terms (see Joel ii. 31, whence the words are taken).

Ver. 6.—**He shall turn,** etc.; *i.e.*, taking the preposition, rendered "to," in the sense of "with," he shall convert one and all, fathers and children, young and old, unto the Lord. Or, in agreement with the versions, he shall bring back the Jews then living to the faith of their ancestors, who rejoiced to see the day of Christ (John viii. 56); and then the patriarchs, who for their unbelief had disowned them, shall recognize them as true Israelites, true children of Abraham. Others explain—He shall unite the Jews who are our fathers in the faith to us Christians who are their children (see Luke i. 17, where the angel Gabriel quotes part of the passage, and applies it to John the Baptist). **The heart.** Here not the seat of the intellectual powers, but of love and confidence, which lead to union and concord. **Lest I come and smite the earth with a curse;** or, *smite the land with the ban.* This is an allusion to the ban threatened in the Law, which involved extermination (see Lev. xxvii. 29; Deut. xiii. 16, 17; xx. 16, 17). So Elijah shall come and preach repentance, as the Baptist did at Christ's first coming; and unless the Jews listen to him and turn to Christ, they shall be destroyed, shall share in that eternal anathema which shall fall on the ungodly at the day of judgment.

HOMILETICS.

Ver. 2.—"*The Sun of Righteousness.*" In vers. 1 and 2 we are once more presented with the twofold aspect of a Divine fact. (See homilies on ch. iii. 2 and iii. 6.) "Dies iræ, *dies illa.*" But "that day" need not be a "day of wrath." It may be memorable, admirable, as the day of full salvation. As the first coming of Christ was for the "rising again" of some, "that they which see not might see" (John ix. 39), so at his second coming, though "revealed from heaven in flaming fire," he shall be "admired in all them that believe;" for he shall bring "rest" and full redemption to them (2 Thess. i. 6—10). The great and terrible day of the Lord will have both a bright and a dark side, like the cloud that came between the Egyptians and the Israelites. To "the proud and all that do wickedly" it will be a day of utter destruction. It will "burn like an oven," fire burning more fiercely in a furnace than in the open air. The wicked, having made themselves like "the dry tree," "ready for the burning," will be consumed root and branch, with no hope of renewed life such as might survive the stroke of the feller's axe (Job xiv. 7—9). These threats are applicable to all times of judgment, when "the day of the Lord of hosts shall be upon every one that is proud . . . and upon all the cedars of Lebanon," etc. (Isa. ii. 12—17). We may see fulfilments of them in successive epochs of judgment, from the troublous times that followed the days of Malachi down to the destruction of Jerusalem and the judgment of the great day. Similar figures of destruction by fire justify this extended application (Ps. xxi. 9, 10; Isa. v. 24; x. 17, 18; Nah. i. 5; Zeph. i. 18; Matt. iii. 12; 2 Pet. iii. 7—10). But such times need be no terror to the faithful servants of God, for "unto you that fear my Name shall the Sun of Righteousness arise with healing in his wings." As we do not confine the prediction of "the day of the Lord" to any one day, so we do not limit the promise of "the Sun of Righteousness" to any one person. Whenever a signal manifestation of God's righteousness is displayed on behalf of his servants, it is like the rising of the sun on a dark, cold, and unhealthy land. But the manifestation of the righteousness of God in the Person and work of Christ so far excels all other manifestations that we may limit our further application of the words to our Lord Jesus Christ, "that in all things he may have the pre-eminence." What the sun is to the material world, the Messiah is to the moral world. The following blessings are suggested by the figure. 1. Light after darkness. Such is Christ to all men (John i. 4, 9), especially to his own countrymen (Luke i. 78, 79; Matt. iv. 12), but in a deeper sense to all that followed him (John viii. 12). He brought the light of truth (Isa. ix. 2), for he was himself "the Truth." Where he rises, like the dawn, upon the benighted and bewildered traveller, he guides into the way of peace and of salvation. The light of truth shows us "the paths of righteousness" (Ps. cxliii. 8, 10). 2. Warmth after cold (Ps. xix. 6). Christ not only gives light, but life. His presence causes that spiritual warmth which is a life-giving power. He is "a quickening Spirit" (John v. 21, 25; vi. 47, etc.). There is a spiritual as well as a solar chemistry. The beams of the Sun of Righteousness both enlighten, warm, and quicken (1 Cor. i. 30). 3. Health after sickness. The figure of "wings" may allude to the rays of the sun, or perhaps to the breeze which in many hot regions, especially in the zones of the trade winds, begins to blow over the land early in the morning, bringing freshness and health with it. (In the West Indies and elsewhere this morning breeze is popularly called "the doctor.") The Jews had a proverbial saying, "As the sun riseth, infirmities decrease." Christ, when in our midst, scattered around him blessings of healing, both physical and spiritual. At Jericho he brought sight to blind Bartimæus and life to dead Zacchæus. So is it wherever he rises, like the light of life, on the souls of men (Ps. cxlvii. 3; Isa. lvii. 19; Ezek. xlvii. 12; 1 John v. 11, 12). The terms "righteousness" and "healing," being very comprehensive, remind us of the blessings brought by Christ at both his first and second comings. At the first advent he diffused the rays of righteousness, whereby he both justifies and sanctifies those who turn to him, just as the sun imparts light, life, and joy to all who turn towards it. At the second, he will own the righteousness which he gave, and will exhibit it, cleared of all the misjudgments of the world, before men and angels. By his first advent he gave spiritual healing, justification, and all its allied blessings, summed up in the royal gift of "eternal life." At his second he will bring full salvation, when, as one has said, there shall be "understanding without error, memory without forgetfulness, thought without distraction, love without simulation, sensation without offence, satisfying without satiety, universal health without sickness" (Isa. lx. 20, 21; Rev. xxi. 23; xxii. 1—5).

Vers. 4—6.— *The sufficiency of God's successive revelations.* The introduction of the appeal in ver. 4 between the predictions and promises of vers. 2, 3 and 5, 6 has at first sight an appearance of abruptness. The promise of ver. 5 lay in the indefinite, and as we know the distant, future. Malachi proved to be the last of the prophets of the old covenant. In the long interval between Malachi and John the Baptist there were times when Israel looked and longed for a new prophet to arise (1 Macc. ix. 27; xiv. 41), though sometimes this was only for the purpose of settling very unimportant questions (*e.g.* 1 Macc. iv. 41—46). But all the while they had in their hands a revelation from God that was amply sufficient for their present guidance, and the right use of which would prepare them for further blessings and preserve them from wrath to come. We are thus reminded of the truth of *the sufficiency of God's revelations for those to whom they are granted.* We may apply this truth—

I. To GOD'S UNWRITTEN REVELATIONS. The declarations of God's truth and of his will to Adam and the patriarchs were less definite than when "the Law came in beside" (Rom. v. 14, 20). But though in one sense "exceeding broad" as compared with the multifarious laws of Moses, they were sufficient to produce a conviction of sin (*e.g.* Gen. iv. 7; xlii. 21, 22, etc.), and therefore of the need of forgiveness (Gen. iv. 13, margin), and to enable men to walk with God (Gen. v. 24; vi. 9). So is it with the heathen (Rom. i. 20; ii. 14, 15). The revelations through the worlds of matter and of mind are sufficient as a rule of life, though not as a means of full salvation (comp. Acts x. 35, "acceptable" ($\delta\epsilon\kappa\tau\grave{o}s$) and iv. 12).

II. To THE LAW OF MOSES. This answered all needful questions as to the character and the will of God. Moses, the first writer in the Bible, and his Law are honourably mentioned by the last writer, this fact supplying one out of many testimonies to the unity of the Bible. Similar witness to the value and the sufficiency of the Law of Moses "for the time then present" is borne by Christ (Matt. v. 17—19; Mark xii. 28—34; Luke x. 25—28; xvi. 29; John v. 39, etc.). The prophets came not to supersede but to expound the Law, to bring out the fulness of its morality, and to apply its fundamental teachings to the changing scenes of national life (Isa. viii. 20; Jer. xxxiv. 12—14, etc.). Moses and the prophets "received not the promise" (Heb. xi. 32, 39), yet Christ could say, "Salvation is of the Jews" (John iv. 22).

III. To THE CHRISTIAN REVELATION. Upon us "the ends of the ages are come"

(1 Cor. x. 12). Yet there is an eternity beyond. We cannot believe that God has spoken his last word to the sons of men. Now we know in part. There are treasures of wisdom and knowledge still hidden in Christ. At times we long to have fuller access to them. We should be thankful if some infallible living teacher could expound to us "the book," or guide us in the path of duty. But we find ourselves between two great epochs, the first advent and the second. We live in what a distinguished writer has called one of the great "pauses" of the world. "Miracles have ceased. Prophecy has ceased. The Son of God is ascended. Apostles are no longer here to apply infallible judgment to each new circumstance as it arises, as St. Paul did to the state of the Corinthian Church." The written Word must be our appeal, and the Divine Spirit, leading each believer into the truth, must be our Interpreter. He may show us fresh truths in the old familiar Word, just as Christians after the destruction of Jerusalem saw further and fuller meaning in our Lord's predictions of his second coming. But the revelations of doctrine and duty in that written Word are all we now need, and all we have a right to expect. If there are future revelations, they are among "the secret things" that "belong unto the Lord our God;" it is "*those things that are revealed*" which "belong unto us and to our children for ever, that we may do all the words" of God's Law (Deut. xxix. 29). Then we may expect to "see greater things than these" (Matt. xiii. 12). As the Old Testament closes with promises of larger blessings (vers. 5, 6), so does the New Testament (Rev. xxi. 1—7, 9—27; xxii. 1—5). We know that a glorious future awaits the sons of God (1 John iii. 1, 2). Yet in the midst of the most glowing promises occur awful threats. Here we read of "the great and dreadful day of the Lord" and "the curse." In the New Testament we find, embedded in its final chapters, such words as Rev. xxi. 8; xxii. 11, 15, 18, 19 (like traces of a past volcanic eruption and warnings of a future one amidst the flowers and foliage of some sun-lit mountain). These warnings emphatically bid us "remember the Law," take heed to that gospel of Christ which comes to us with all the authority of a law (Acts xvii. 30; 1 John iii. 23), and is all that we need for salvation. The Jews, who would be wiser than the prophet, insert the fifth verse again, and read it a second time, because Malachi ends so awfully. But the Creator of men's hearts knew best how to reach the hearts he had created. In a somewhat similar way some Christians would not end God's present revelation where he ends it. In Christ's description of "the last day" which is revealed to us, they would, as it were, after Matt. xxv. 46, read again Matt. xxv. 34, and apply it to all. They would interpolate their own speculations of *what God may do* among the revelations of *what God would have us to do*. Instead of pursuing such a perilous path, we bid men "remember." We point them back to the only and unchangeable Saviour and the unalterable gospel (John iii. 18, 36; Gal. i. 8, 9), which is all that we need for salvation, and "whereunto we do well that we take heed," etc. (2 Pet. i. 19).

HOMILIES BY VARIOUS AUTHORS.

Ver. 1.—*The Divine fire.* "The day cometh that shall burn as an oven." Fire is one of the most familiar figures of the Divine working. It is one of the forces which man most dreads when it gets beyond control. And it is the force on which man most relies for the purifying of the good and the destruction of the evil. The fire of the oven is fire at its intensest. A hole is dug in the ground, a fire of stubble is kindled in it; by this fire a large stone is heated, and on the stone the bread can be baked. Malachi has already dealt with the refining power of the fire of God. That which is good is freed and cleansed and improved by means of it. The prophet does not see the whole of the features of the day of God; only those which are directly related to the condition and needs of the people in his day. Every prophet is one-sided; and we must learn from all if we would apprehend the *whole* of truth, even concerning the Divine fire. Malachi had to adapt his teachings to some who were sincere but mistaken. To them the Divine fire is disciplinary. "He shall purify the sons of Levi, and purge them as gold and silver." But he had also to adapt his teachings to some who were wilfully and persistently wrong. To them the Divine fire is, in some sense, destructive, consuming. "The proud shall be stubble, and the day that cometh shall burn them up." There are two things characteristic of the Divine fire, which are suggested by the double figure of refining and consuming.

I. THE OPERATION OF THE DIVINE FIRE DEPENDS ON WHAT IT OPERATES ON. This is one of the most marked peculiarities of common fire. It scatters water; it melts wax; it destroys wood; it hardens clay; it purifies metal. It makes silver valuable; it makes dross worthless. And so with the Divine fire. The apostle dwells on its testing power (1 Cor. iii. 13); but here its actual moral effect on differing characters is indicated. Take classes of character in Malachi's time, and show the different effects which Divine dealings had upon them. Take types of character now, and show how Divine dealings soften or harden.

II. THE DIVINE FIRE IS DESTRUCTIVE OF THE FORMS OF THINGS, NOT OF THINGS. Science now explains that common fire destroys nothing; it only changes the forms and relations of things. When the state of the wicked is irremediable by any existing moral forces, then their form and relation must be changed. As in the time of the Flood, humanity had to be put in new conditions. God's fire-destructions always begin a new *régime.*—R. T.

Ver. 2.—*The healing sunrise.* "The Sun of Righteousness arise with healing in his wings." "As the rising sun diffuses light and heat, so that all that is healthy in nature revives and lifts up its head, while plants that have no depth of root are scorched up and wither away, so the advent of the reign of righteousness, which will reward the good and the wicked, each according to his deserts, will dissipate all darkness of doubt, and heal all the wounds which the apparent injustice of the conduct of affairs has inflicted on the hearts of the righteous" (W. H. Lowe). The figure of "healing in his wings" may be illustrated by the fact that, off Smyrna, every morning about sunrise a fresh gale of air blows from the sea across the land, which from its wholesomeness and utility in clearing the infected air is always called "the doctor."

I. THE WORLD UNDER THE DARKNESS OF REIGNING EVIL. Represented by those dark, depressing, unhealthy days when there is no light in the sky, and the damp mists lie low. Then the plants droop, the flowers do not care to open, and the leaves hang. The song-birds are silent, and the hours drag on wearily. To the good the darkness of prevailing evil sentiment, evil opinion, evil practice, is necessarily afflictive. These things make an unnourishing atmosphere and bad circumstances. When the darkness of evil prevails in (1) the intellectual world, or (2) the moral world, or (3) the social world, then there will surely be abounding error, moral mischiefs, spiritual depression, and vital disease. As Malachi saw the people in his day, they were in the gloom of triumphant self-will, and there was no sunlight of God in their sky. That sunshine was his hope for the future.

II. THE WORLD IN THE LIGHT OF REIGNING RIGHTEOUSNESS. And that time he saw dawning when Messiah should appear. The birth of the Babe of Bethlehem was the strong sunrise of righteousness. Picture the dawning of the sun in full, clear strength after weeks of dulness, damp, and disease. How the sunbeams dry up the mists, warm the chilled earth, waken the music of the birds, make the flowers smile, and gladden man's heart. "Notice these flowers all around us, how they turn smiling to the sun's ardent gaze, bend forward in seeming reverence, throw open their pretty cups, and cast around their sweetest perfume. So, when the Sun of Righteousness shines, all moral goodness joyously responds. Evil slinks away into the shadows. When that Sun shines on through the eternal day, man's answering goodness may flourish abundantly."—R. T.

Ver. 3.—*The secret of triumph over wickedness.* The figure of "treading ashes" is suggested by the previous figure of "burning." When the wicked are burned up in the fire of God, all their power to injure the good will be gone. They will but be as ashes of the oven, ashes spread abroad, ashes made a path to walk over. The tone of the prophet is not one of glorying over the fate of the wicked, but of rejoicing in the removal of the hindrance which the wicked ever put in the way of God's faithful servants.

I. THE ILL ESTATE OF THE GOOD WHEN THE WICKED, OR GODLESS, TRIUMPH. This may be illustrated in every sphere. 1. *The national.* Illustrate from the times of Jeremiah, when a godless party held power in the state, and tried to force an Egyptian alliance. Or from the times of Malachi, when formalist and careless Levites were corrupting the religious sentiments of the people. Or from the state of the Jewish nation in the time of our Lord, when the fountains of religious and secular authority were corrupt, and the crucifixion of ideal virtue was a possibility. Show in what an evil case good people, who feared the Lord, were placed at such times. See the sufferings of Jeremiah and of our Divine Lord. So there are national times now when evil sentiment prevails, and the servants of God have to "keep silence," because it is an "evil time." 2. *The intellectual.* The deistic age of our grandfathers was an evil time for devout believers. This critical age of ours is a time of sore strain for those who would preserve the simplicity of faith. The same truth may be illustrated in the smaller spheres of family, or school, or business. Whenever self-indulgence, bad sentiments, or evil characters have power, those who would live godly, sober, and righteous lives are sorely put to it. Though for them this need be but culturing discipline, the treading on the camomile plant that makes it yield freely its fragrance.

II. THE ILL ESTATE OF THE WICKED WHEN THE GOOD, OR GOD-FEARING, TRIUMPH. This can be treated without any unworthy glorying over the disabilities of others. The point may be illustrated in every sphere, national, political, social, intellectual, or in the smaller spheres of the family, the school, the business, the Church. The point to dwell on is the distress of the wicked, not from personal suffering, but from their inability to do mischief. We may rejoice that the wicked are made helpless by the triumph of goodness.—R. T.

Ver. 4.—*Loyalty to God's revealed will.* It was characteristic of the restored exiles that they endeavoured exactly to reproduce the old Mosaic system; but there was a grave danger involved in their effort. They could not precisely reproduce everything. There must be some adjustment to the very different social and religious sentiments and relations. But those who claimed the authority to make the adjustments would be almost sure to carry their authority too far, and claim to alter and amend the very laws and rules. Under the guise of translation, adaptation, and amplification, the new law of the rabbis became established; and the mischief that it had become in the time of our Lord is evident in its actually overlaying the revealed Law of God, and making the Jehovah-religion a burden beyond bearing. Malachi seems to foresee the mischievous growth of an evil which had already begun in his time, and in this closing passage of his work solemnly calls the people back to the unquestionable and unrivalled authority of the Horeb-revelation given to Moses. It is the great recall that has been again and again found necessary in the course of the ages. It is the recall needed to-day. "To the Law and to the testimony; if they speak not according to this word, it is because there is no light in them" (Isa. viii. 20).

I. THE SIGN OF GOODNESS IN GOD'S PEOPLE. Practical interest in God's revealed Word. The old Jew had none of the difficulties which modern infidelity and modern criticism have put in our fathers' way and in ours. Our fathers were troubled by being assured that a book-revelation was impossible. They might have confidently, yet meekly replied, "But here it is." We are troubled by being told that the Bible is not at all what we think it to be, and is not trustworthy. We may quietly reply, "Whatever it is, it is 'a lamp to our feet and a light unto our path.'" Treatment of the Word is the best test of the godly life.

II. GOD'S REVEALED WORD SHOULD BE KEPT IN MIND. It is designed to replenish our life at its fountains of thought, knowledge, and feeling. Therefore the prophet says, "*Remember* ye the Law of Moses." Keep it in mind; freshen the memory continually.

III. GOD'S REVEALED WORD IS BEST KEPT IN MIND BY KEEPING IT IN THE LIFE. "If any will *do* his will, he shall know of the doctrine." Practical obedience is (1) the best teacher; and (2) our best and constant revealer of the need of teaching.—R. T.

Ver. 5.—*The mission of the second Elijah.* There is no reason for doubting that John the Baptist is referred to. Our Lord's allusions to John as fulfilling this prophecy should suffice to settle the question (see Mark ix. 11—13, Revised Version). There need be no difficulty in admitting John to be the second Elijah, if we apprehend the figurative and poetical character of the prophetical Scriptures. One who would do for

EXPOSITION.

CHAPTER III.

Ver. 1.—Behold, I will send (*I send*) **my messenger.** God answers that he is coming to show himself the God of judgment and justice. Are they ready to meet him and to bear his sentence? Who this "messenger" is is disputed. That no angel or heavenly visitant is meant is clear from historical considerations, as no such event took place immediately before the Lord came to his temple. Nor can Malachi himself be intended, as his message was delivered nearly four hundred years before Messiah came. The announcement is doubtless founded upon Isa. xl. 3, and refers to the same person as the older prophet mentions, who is generally allowed to be John the Baptist, the herald of Christ's advent (Matt. xi. 10; John i. 6). **Prepare the way before me.** The expression is borrowed from Isaiah, *loc. cit.* (comp. also lvii. 14; lxii. 10). He prepares the way by preaching repentance, and thus removing the obstacle of sin which stood between God and his people. **Whom ye seek.** When ye ask, "Where is the God of judgment?" **Shall suddenly come to his temple.** The Lord (*ha-Adon*) is Jehovah, as in Exod. xxiii. 17; Isa. i. 24; iii. 1, etc. There is a change of persons here, as frequently. Jehovah shall unexpectedly come to his temple (τὸν ναὸν ἑαυτοῦ) as King and God of Israel (comp. Ezek. xliii. 7). There was a literal fulfilment of this prophecy when Christ was presented in the temple as an infant (Luke ii. 22, etc.). **Even the messenger of the covenant.** He is identified with the Lord; and he is the covenant angel who guided the Israelites to the promised land, and who is seen in the various theophanies of the Old Testament. The Divinity of Messiah is thus unequivocally asserted. In him are fulfilled all the promises made under the old covenant, and he is called (Heb. ix. 15) "the Mediator of the new covenant." Some render, "and the Messenger," etc., thus distinguishing the Angel of the covenant from the forerunner who prepares the way. But this is already done by the expressions, "My Messenger," and "the Lord." **Whom ye delight in.** Whose advent ye expect with eager desire.

Ver. 2.—Who may abide the day of his coming? They had expected him to come and judge the heathen; the prophet warns them that they themselves shall be first judged (comp. Amos v. 18). "Malachi, like John the Baptist, sees the future Judge in the present Saviour" (Wordsworth); Joel ii. 11. **Who shall stand?** Who can stand up under the burden of this judgment?

The Vulgate Version, *Quis stabit ad videndum eum?* points to the brightness of his presence, which eye of man cannot endure. **Like a refiner's fire,** which separates the precious metal from the refuse. So the Lord at his coming shall sever the good among men from the evil (Isa. i. 25; Jer. vi. 29; Zech. xiii. 9). **Like fullers' soap;** Septuagint, ὡς ποιὰ πλυνόντων, "as the grass of washers;" Vulgate, *quasi herba fullonum.* What is to be understood exactly by the "soap" (*borith*), washing-herb, is not known. Probably the ashes of some plant yielding a lye, like carbonate of soda, are meant. Such plants are met with on the shores of the Mediterranean and Dead Seas, and at this day large quantities of alkalies are extracted from them and exported in different directions (see Tristram, 'Nat. Hist. of the Bible,' p. 480, etc.; comp. Isa. iv. 4; Jer. ii. 22). The Lord shall wash away all that is filthy (comp. Matt. iii. 10, 12).

Ver. 3.—He shall sit. As a judge. The prophet confines himself to the first of the two images presented in the preceding verse. **The sons of Levi.** Especially the priests, who ought to set an example, and teach holiness and obedience. Thus judgment should begin at the house of God (Ezek. ix. 6; 1 Pet. iv. 17). The purifying consists not only in exterminating the evil, but also in correcting and improving all who are not wholly incorrigible. We may call to mind Christ's purging of the temple, and his denunciations of the teaching body among the Jews, and see herein his way of trying his ministers in all ages, that they may shine like lights in the world, and adorn the doctrine of God in all things. **That they may offer** (*and they shall be offering*) **unto the Lord an offering** (*minchah*) **in righteousness.** The pure sacrifice shall then be offered with a pure heart. As firstfruits of this improved condition, we read in Acts vi. 7, "A great company of the priests were obedient to the faith."

Ver. 4.—The offering of Judah and Jerusalem. When the purification has taken place, and the priests offer pure worship, then the sacrifices of the whole nation will be acceptable. Judah and Jerusalem represent the kingdom of the Messiah; for salvation is of the Jews, and the gospel was first preached at Jerusalem. **As in former** (*ancient*) **years.** As in the days of Moses, David, and Solomon, or still earlier in the case of Abel, Noah, Abraham, and the patriarchs. (See the account of the ideal priesthood, ch. ii. 5, etc.) The prophet does not necessarily expect that the Mosaic ritual is to last for ever and to be maintained throughout the world, but he employs the terms with which the Jewish people were conversant to express the worship of the new covenant (comp. ch. i. 11, and note there).

Ver. 5.—I will come near to you to judgment. They had asked, "Where is the God of judgment?" (ch. ii. 17). He tells them that his judgment shall extend beyond the Levites even unto all the people; they will then see whether, as they supposed, the evil went unpunished. The announcement applies especially to the circumstances of Malachi's time, though, of course, it has an extended reference. Swift witness. God's judgments fall swiftly and unexpectedly; and when they fall the sinner is at once convicted, and no concealment, excuse, or subterfuge is possible. "How terrible is that judgment," says St. Jerome, "where God is at once Witness and Judge!" Sorcerers; τὰς φαρμακούς (Septuagint); maleficis (Vulgate); see Exod. vii. 11; xxii. 18; Deut. xviii. 10. The Jews had grown familiar with magical arts during the Captivity; that they practised them later we learn from Acts viii. 9; xiii. 6. Adulterers. They who were ready to marry heathen wives would not be likely to be restrained by any law from gratifying their passions. False swearers; Septuagint, "those who swear falsely by my name," which is from Zech. v. 4 (comp. Lev. xix. 12; and see note on Zech. v. 3). Oppress the hireling. Defraud him of his just wages (see Deut. xxiv. 14, 15; Jas. v. 4). The widow, and the fatherless (Exod. xxii. 22; Deut. xxiv. 17). Turn aside (bow down) the stranger; Septuagint, "pervert the judgment of the stranger;" Vulgate, opprimunt peregrinum (Exod. xxii. 21; Deut. xxvii. 19; Amos v. 12). And fear not me. This was the root of all the evil.

Ver. 6.—For I am the Lord, I change not; or, Jehovah, I change not. This is to show that God performs his promises, and effectually disposes of the allegation in ch. ii. 17, that he put no difference between the evil and the good. The great principles of right and wrong never alter; they are as everlasting as he who gave them. God here speaks of himself by his covenant name, which expresses his eternal, independent being, "the Father of lights, with whom is no variableness, neither shadow of turning" (Jas. i. 17). Therefore ye sons of Jacob are not consumed. Because God's eternal purpose stands good, and his "gifts and calling are without repentance" (Rom. xi. 29), therefore the Israelites are indeed chastised and corrected, but not wholly consumed; they have a place and a nation, and the great promises made to their forefathers will all be fulfilled in due time (Jer. xxx. 11; Micah vii. 20). He calls them

"sons of Jacob," to remind them of the covenant made with their great ancestor, which was the portion of all true Israelites (comp. Jer. xxxiii. 20, 21). Orelli would read, "Ye have not made an end," i.e. of your sins; so virtually the Septuagint, which joins this clause to the following verse. But the present text is most probably correct.

Vers. 7—12.—§ 2. God indeed is faithful to his promises, but the people's own conduct has occasioned the withholding of favours; they have been shamefully negligent in the matter of tithes and offerings; let them amend their practice, and they shall be blessed.

Ver. 7.—Ye are gone away (have turned aside) from mine ordinances. Disobedience was no new offence; they had always from early days been persistent in wickedness; and if the performance of God's sure promise was delayed, this was because they had not fulfilled the conditions on which rested its accomplishment. Return unto me, and I will return unto you (Zech. i. 3, where see note). Man must co-operate with God's preventing grace, and then God gives him further grace unto repentance and amendment. Here, if the people followed the preaching of the prophets and obeyed the promptings of the Holy Spirit, God promises to bless and save them. Wherein shall we return? Here is the Pharisaical spirit, as in ch. i. 6, etc. They do not acknowledge their offence; they consider that they are righteous and need no repentance.

Ver. 8.—Will a man rob God? The prophet shows the people how they have departed from God, in not keeping even the outward observances of religion. The word translated "rob," defraud, found also in Prov. xxii. 23, etc., is rendered in the Septuagint, πτερνιεῖ, "trip up," "supplant;" Vulgate, si affliget homo Deum, or, as St. Jerome first translated, "si affiget homo Deum," and referred the words to the crucifixion of our Lord. In tithes and offerings. These were due to the Lord, and therefore in withholding them they were defrauding not man but God. (For tithe, see Lev. xxvii. 30, etc.; Numb. xviii. 21. See the complaint of Nehemiah, ch. xiii. 10—12.) The "offering" meant is the heave offering, the breast and shoulder of the peace offering, which were the priests' portion (Exod. xxix. 27; Lev. vii. 14, 32—34; comp. Neh. x. 37—39).

Ver. 9.—Ye are cursed with a (the) curse. The effect of the curse was scarcity and barrenness, as we see from vers. 10—12 (comp. ch. ii. 2; Hag. i. 6). The Vulgate assumes the result: In penuria vos maledicti estis. The next clause gives the reason of the curse. **This whole nation.** Not individuals only, but the whole nation (he does not any longer call them God's people) were implicated in this sin. The LXX., reading differently, has, "The year is ended, and ye have brought," etc.

Ver. 10.—**All the tithes;** *the whole tithe*—not merely a portion of it. God is not served with partial service. **The storehouse.** The tithes were brought to the temple, and laid up in the chambers built to receive them (see Neh. x. 38, 39; xiii 5, 12, 13; 2 Chron. xxxi. 11, 12). That there **may be meat in mine house.** That they who minister about holy things may live of the things of the temple (1 Cor. ix. 13; Numb. xviii. 21). **Prove me now herewith.** Do your part, perform your duties, and then see if I will not reward your obedience. **Open you the windows of heaven.** The expression implies not only the removal of drought by copious showers of rain, but the diffusion of heavenly blessing in large abundance. **That there shall not be room enough to receive it;** or, *unto superabundance;* Vulgate, *usque ad abundantiam;* Septuagint, ἕως τοῦ ἱκανωθῆναι, "until it suffice;" Syriac, "until ye say, It is enough." The Authorized Version retains the negation in the sentence, and perhaps comes nearest to the meaning of the original (comp. Luke xii. 17, 18).

Ver. 11.—**The devourer.** The locust (see Introduction to Joel, § I.). God would not only give a fruitful season, so that the crops sprang up well, but would guard them from everything that could injure them before they were gathered in. Septuagint, διαστελῶ ὑμῖν εἰς βρῶσιν, which perhaps means, as Schleusner thinks, "I will give a charge unto consumption for your good," though Jerome renders, "dividam vobis cibos."

Ver. 12.—**Shall call you blessed;** or, *happy,* as ver. 15 (comp. Deut. xxxiii. 29; Zech. viii. 13, 23). **A delightsome land;** γῆ θελητή (Septuagint); literally, *a land of good pleasure*—a land in which God is well pleased (comp. Isa. lxii. 4; Jer. iii. 19).

Vers. 13—18.—**§ 3.** *The impious murmuring of the people is contrasted with the conduct of those who fear God; and the reward of the pious is set forth.*

Ver. 13.—**Your words have been stout against me.** Ye have spoken hard words of me (comp. Jude 15, where we read of "the hard speeches (σκληρῶν) which ungodly sinners have spoken against" God). Some specimens of these speeches are given in answer to the usual sceptical inquiry. They are of the same character as those in ch. ii. 17, and imply that the course of this world is not directed by a moral Governor. **What have we spoken** so much (*together*) **against**

thee? What have we said against thee in our conversations with one another?

Ver. 14.—**It is vain.** It brings no acknowledgment or reward. The Latin and Greek Versions have, "He is vain who serveth God." **Have kept his ordinance** (*charge*). Have done what he ordered. They are either wilfully deceiving themselves and others by pretending an obedience which they never really paid; or they think that the outward observance of certain legal requirements is all that is required. Some think that an interval of time separates this from the last section, and that meanwhile they had made some efforts at improvement, expecting, however, immediate results in added blessings; and as these did not come as quickly as they hoped, they relapsed into their old distrust. **Have walked mournfully;** *i.e.* in mourning apparel, as if fasting and mourning for sin (Ps. xxxv. 13, 14; Job xxx. 28). Septuagint, "Why went we as suppliants (ἱκέται)?" **Before the Lord.** Out of reverence and awe of Jehovah. They attributed a certain virtue to voluntary fasts, without any consideration of the spirit in which they were observed (see the reproof of such formal observances in Isa. lviii. 4, etc.).

Ver. 15.—**We call the proud happy.** This is still the speech of the murmurers. We, they say, do not reckon the humble and meek blessed; we consider that the only blessed ones are the arrogant heathen, or free-thinkers, who meet with prosperity and happiness in this world. For the "proud," the LXX. has, ἀλλοτρίους, "strangers," which, doubtless, gives the meaning (comp. Isa. xiii. 11). **Are set up;** literally, *are built up*—have wealth and families, and leave a name behind them (Ps. xvii. 14; see in the original, Gen. xvi. 2; xxx. 3; and comp. Exod. i. 21; Jer. xii. 16, where the phrase, "being built," includes all temporal prosperity). **They that tempt God are even delivered;** *they tempt God, and are delivered* (ver. 10). They try and provoke God by their impiety, and yet escape punishment. Septuagint, Ἀντέστησαν τῷ Θεῷ, καὶ ἐσώθησαν, "They resist God, and yet are safe."

Ver. 16.—With these impious murmurers the prophet contrasts those who fear God, as above (ch. ii. 5—7) he set the picture of the true priest in opposition to his delineation of the evil ministers. **Then.** When the impious made the above infidel remarks, the pious **spake often,** conversed together. What they said is not repeated, but it was language well-pleasing unto God, who deigned to listen to their words, and to console them by announcing the future destiny of the good and the evil. They may have argued with these impious talkers, and warned others against them; or they may have expostulated as Jer. xii. 1, but yet with full faith that what God does is always good; and this sentiment was all the harder to cherish because they lived under a system of temporal rewards and punishments. The Septuagint and Syriac have, "These things spake they that feared the Lord," as if the two preceding verses reported the words of the pious. Some Fathers and commentators have taken the same view. But it is difficult to conceive such words coming from the mouth of those who fear God; unless they are so called ironically. But this is inadmissible, as we see that in the present verse they are represented in their true character, and such a sudden change from irony to actuality is unnatural and quite opposed to the prophet's usual manner. A book of remembrance was written before him. The book represents God's providence and omniscience, his ever-wakeful care, his unfailing knowledge. "Are not these things noted in thy book?" says the psalmist (Ps. lvi. 8); and when the dead were judged, Daniel saw that the books were opened (Dan. vii. 10). The idea is taken from the national records wherein were noted events of importance, such as we find in the cuneiform inscriptions (comp. 1 Kings xi. 41, etc.; Ezra iv. 15; vi. 1; Esth. vi. 1; Rev. xx. 12). This book was to lie, as it were, always before the eyes of the Lord, to remind him of the pious. Rosenmüller compares the proverbial saying, Ἐγράφη ἐν Διὸς δέλτοις, "It is written on the tablets of Zeus," on which Erasmus comments in his 'Adagia,' under the title "Fides et Gravitas." For them that feared the Lord. For their benefit, to preserve their name for ever. Thought upon his Name. Prized his Name, regarded it with awe. Septuagint, εὐλαβουμένοις τὸ ὄνομα αὐτοῦ, "who reverenced his Name."

Ver. 17.—They shall be mine, etc. This is better rendered, in accordance with the Septuagint and Vulgate, "They shall be to me, saith the Lord of hosts, in the day which I am preparing, a peculiar treasure." This day of the Lord is the day of judgment, which God is always preparing by his visitation of nations and individuals. Then shall the righteous be to God a peculiar treasure (segullah), that which he prizes as his special possession (see Exod. xix. 5, whence the expression is derived; and comp. Deut. vii. 6; xiv. 2; xxvi. 18; Ps. cxxxv 4). I will spare them; i.e. when I punish sinners. They are spared on two grounds, because they are his sons, and because they serve him like obedient children (Ps. ciii. 13). Septuagint, αἱρετιῶ αὐτούς, "I will choose them."

Ver. 18.—Then shall ye return, and discern; or, ye shall again discern. They had already had many opportunities, both in the history of the nation and the life of individuals, of observing the different treatment of the godly and of sinners; but in the day of the Lord they should have a more plain and convincing proof of God's moral government (comp. Exod. xi. 7; Wisd. v. 1—5); "So that men shall say, Verily there is a reward for the righteous; verily there is a God that judgeth in the earth" (Ps. lviii. 11).

HOMILETICS.

Ver. 2.—*The manifestation of Christ a testing-time to all.* We may apply this truth—

I. To CHRIST'S FIRST MANIFESTATION TO THE WORLD. This truth was foreseen by Simeon (Luke ii. 34, 35). And when Jesus entered on his public ministry, his preaching and his very presence served as a testing-time to all. 1. His teaching was a process of sifting (Matt. iii. 12). Socrates used to go about Athens testing and refining men's ideas, and in his own unrivalled method extracting the few grains of gold from the mass of rubbish in young men's minds. Our Lord did a more valuable service, testing men's hearts rather than their heads, their characters rather than their opinions. Illust.: Nicodemus, tested, convicted of ignorance, but ultimately refined. Others when convicted were offended and repelled; e.g. Matt. xv. 12—14; John vi. 25—66; viii. 33—59. So severe was this testing process that Christ pronounced a special blessing on all who stood it (Luke vii. 23). Yet Christ's teaching held out the door of mercy to all. He showed to the world that in the midst of the dross of some of the foulest lives there were grains of gold, gems of Divinity, which his purifying power could disengage. Sinful men and women "loved much," because through his words they learned that they had been much forgiven. 2. The purity of his life made his very presence like the flame of a refiner's fire. Men could not be much with him without being either attracted and purified or repelled and made worse; e.g. the Gadarenes, the chief priests, Judas. On the other hand we note Zacchæus, the Samaritan woman, the "sinner" (Luke vii. 37), the eleven apostles. This testing his age a similar work to that which was done by Elijah for his age would, in Scripture, be called an Elijah. There is no occasion whatever for imagining that any miraculous reappearance of Elijah was in the mind of Malachi, or a part of his prophetic message. The Jews overpressed a literal interpretation, and to this day they earnestly pray for the coming of Elias, which, they assume, will immediately precede the appearance of Messiah. Dean Stanley says, " Elijah was the prophet for whose return in later years his countrymen have looked with most eager hope. . . . It was a fixed belief of the Jews that he had appeared again and again, as an Arabian merchant, to wise and good rabbis, at their prayers or on their journeys. A seat is still placed for him to superintend the circumcision of the Jewish children. Passover after Passover the Jews of our own day place the paschal cup on the table, and set the door wide open, believing that that is the moment when Elijah will reappear. When goods are found, and no owner comes ; when difficulties arise, and no solution appears, the answer is, ' Put them by till Elijah comes.' "

> " Twice in her season of decay,
> The fallen Church hath felt Elijah's eye,
> Dart from the wild its piercing ray, . . .
> The herald star,
> Whose torch afar
> Shadows and boding night-birds fly."
>
> (Keble.)

Matthew Henry, in a few skilful sentences, suggests the likenesses and the contrasts of the two Elijahs. " Elijah was a man of great austerity and mortification, zealous for God, bold in reproving sin, and active to reduce an apostate people to God and their duty. John the Baptist was animated by the same spirit and power, and preached repentance and reformation, as Elias had done ; and all held him for a prophet, as they did Elijah in his day, and that his baptism was from heaven, and not of men." Rabbi Eliezer closes a curious chapter on repentance with these words : " And Israel will not make great repentance till Elijah—his memory for blessing !—come." For fair comparison of the two Elijahs, it is necessary to make careful comparison of the times to which they were sent, noticing the essential sameness underneath the manifest differences. Rabbinism had really driven the spiritual religion of Jehovah from the land in John's days, just as the Astarte form of Baalism had driven the Jehovah-worship from Israel in the days of Elijah. The two men may be compared in relation to—

I. THEIR PERSONS. In each case there was an arresting personal appearance, and an unusual power of personal impression. In each case we have a man markedly different from surrounding men. This is noticeable in the dress, but more in the men themselves. And their mission largely lay in their *personnel.* Men minister for God in what they are in figure, countenance, and impression.

II. THEIR HABITS. Both were wilderness men, whose very food was a reproach of prevailing luxury. Their indifference to personal pleasure declared their absorption in their work for God.

III. THEIR MISSIONS. Both were sent to be forerunners of a coming God, in grace, to his people. Both were sent to call the people to repentance. *Turning*—turning the people to God, was the work of both. Both had to make the same abrupt demand.

IV. THEIR SPIRIT. Both were absolutely loyal to Jehovah. Both were perfectly fearless of all consequences in doing their work. Both were stern in their tone, and saw the sterner side of truth. Both were humanly weak in times of unexpected strain.

V. THEIR INCOMPLETENESS. That characterizes the work of all who have preparing work to do. Neither Elijah nor John could count up results. To both life-work might seem a failure. To Elijah, in a mood of depression, it did. But no life is incomplete that is but a piece of a whole, if, *as a piece,* it is complete. That is a comforting truth for the two Elijahs, and for us who now may have but pieces of work given us to do.—R. T.

Vers. 5, 6.—*The day of Divine manifestation.* The margin of the Revised Version gives the rendering *with*, as preferable to *to*, in the clause, "And he shall turn the heart of the fathers to the children," etc. Then the reference is to the work and influence of the second Elijah on all classes of society, on the hearts of both fathers and children. Keil, however, suggests a more difficult, yet more likely, explanation of the verse, "The fathers are rather the ancestors of the Israelitish nation, the patriarchs, and generally the pious forefathers. . . . The sons, or children, are the degenerate descendants of Malachi's own time and the succeeding ages." The Messiah is designed to be the bond of union for them all. What arrests attention in these closing verses of the Old Testament canon is that the stern side of Messiah's mission gains exclusive prominence. That sterner side specially interested the judgment-prophets of Israel's degenerate days. And it was more particularly suitable for Malachi, because the very form of evil that was to ninder Messiah was beginning in his day. Malachi saw rabbinism taking root.

I. THE DREADFULNESS OF MESSIAH'S DAY FOR THE JEWISH NATION. All days of God, all Divine manifestations, are necessarily two-sided. They are dealings with moral beings, and their results must depend on the response of the moral beings. Every day of God must be a "'savour of life unto life, or of death unto death.'" What the coming of Christ was to Simeon and Anna, to the disciples, and to the Church of all the ages, we are constantly dwelling on. That is the bright and sunny side of Messiah's mission. But we may ask—What was Messiah's coming to the officials of the Mosaic religion, and for the Jewish nation that rejected him, under the leading of those officials? It was their last opportunity, their final testing. It proved them to be beyond moral recovery. It removed the last check, and their woe came. Their house was left unto them desolate."

II. THE DREADFULNESS OF CHRIST'S DAY FOR THE SELF-WILLED IN EVERY AGE. For Christ's test of the Jewish nation did but illustrate the test that he is, wherever and whenever he comes. Men reject him still at a peril which they seldom recognize. There is the stern side to a preached gospel. Christ proclaimed as Saviour makes for every man a new and overwhelming condition for the testing of the judgment-day.—R. T.

Vers. 1—3.—*The day of the world's retribution.* "For, behold, the day cometh that shall burn as an oven," etc. A graphic representation of these verses is given by Stanley: "The day spoken of was to be like the glorious but terrible uprising of the Eastern sun, which should wither to the roots the insolence and the injustice of mankind; but as its rays extended, like the wings of the Egyptian sun, God should, by its healing and invigorating influences, call forth the good from their obscurity, prancing and bounding like the young cattle in the burst of spring, and treading down under their feet the dust and ashes to which the same bright sun had burnt up the tangled thicket of iniquitous dealing." These words lead us to consider the day of the world's retribution.

I. IT WILL BE A TERRIBLE DAY TO THE WICKED. "Behold, the day cometh that shall burn as an oven; and all the proud, yea, and all that do wickedly, shall be stubble: and the day that cometh shall burn them up, saith the Lord of hosts, that it shall leave them neither root nor branch." Primarily this may refer to the destruction of Jerusalem, which was indeed a time of judgment, but it points on through the whole period of retribution. Mark two things. 1. *How this retributive period regards the wicked.* They are "stubble;" without life, beauty, or value; utterly worthless. They may be wealthy, learned, influential; yet they are nothing but "stubble," destitute even of one grain of moral wheat. 2. *How this retributive period will destroy the wicked.* (1) Painfully; by fire. They shall writhe in the scorching flames of moral remorse and awful forebodings. (2) Completely. "Shall leave them neither root nor branch." To destroy them root and branch may not mean the extinction of their existence, but the extinction of all that makes existence tolerable or worth having. This day of retribution is really going on now, but it is only in dawn; the full noon is in the centuries to come.

II. IT WILL BE A GLORIOUS PERIOD TO THE RIGHTEOUS. "But unto you that fear my Name shall the Sun of Righteousness arise with healing in his wings; and ye shall go forth, and grow up as calves of the stall." This language may be regarded as indicating the blessedness of the world to a good man. 1. *It is a world of solar brightness.* "The Sun of Righteousness" arises on the horizon of his soul. There are souls that are lighted by sparks of their own kindling, and by the gaseous blaze springing from the bogs of inner depravity. All such lights, whether in the forms of philosophic theories or religious creeds, are dim, partial, transitory. The soul of a good man is lighted by the sun. The sun: (1) Throws his beams over the whole heavens. (2) Reveals all objects in their true aspects and proportions. (3) Quickens all into life and beauty. (4) Is the centre, holding the whole system in order. The soul of the good man is lighted by something more than the brightest lights of human genius; something more, in fact, than moon and stars; lighted by the Sun himself, the Source of all light and warmth and life. Christ is the Light of the good. 2. *It is a world of Divine rectitude.* "Sun of Righteousness." "The kingdom of God is within you." Eternal right is enthroned. God's will is the supreme law. The meat and drink of godly souls are to do the will of their Father who is in heaven. Such a soul is right : (1) In relation to *itself*. All its powers, passions, and impulses are rightly adjusted. (2) In relation to the *universe*. It renders to others what it would have that others should render unto it. (3) In relation to *God*. The best Being it loves the most ; the greatest Being it reverences the most ; the kindest Being it thanks the most. 3. *It is a world of remedial influence.* "With healing in his wings." The sun's beams are in Scripture called his wings (Ps. cxxxix. 9). The soul through sin is diseased, its eyes are dim, its ears are heavy, its limbs are feeble, its blood is poisoned. The godly is under remedial influences. The beams of the "Sun of Righteousness" work off the disease, repair the constitution, and enable it to run without being weary, and to walk without being faint. There is a proverb among the Jews that "as the sun riseth, infirmities decrease." The flowers which droop and languish all night revive in the morning. The late Mr. Robinson, of Cambridge, called upon a friend just as he had received a letter from his son, who was surgeon on a vessel then lying off Smyrna. The son mentioned in his letter that every morning about sunrise a fresh gale of air blew from the sea across the land, and from its wholesomeness and utility in cleansing the infected air the wind was called "the doctor." Christ is the Physician of souls. 4. *It is a world of buoyant energy.* "Ye shall go forth, and grow up as calves of the stall." See the calf which from its birth has been shut up in the stall, let forth for the first time into the green fields of May, how full of buoyant energy ! it leaps, and frolics, and frisks. This is the figure employed here to represent the gladsomeness with which the godly soul employs its faculties under the genial beams of the "Sun of Righteousness."—D. T.

HOMILETICAL INDEX

TO

THE BOOK OF MALACHI

———◆◆◆———